NATIONAL ACCOUNTS STATISTICS: MAIN AGGREGATES AND DETAILED TABLES, 1989

PART I

UNITED NATIONS
NEW YORK, 1991

NOTE

Symbols of United Nations documents are composed of capital letters combined with figures. Mention of such a symbol indicates a reference to a United Nations document.

The first 14 editions of the *Yearbook* were issued without series symbols.

ST/ESA/STAT/SER.X/16

UNITED NATIONS PUBLICATION

Sales No. E.91.XVII.16, Part I

ISBN 92-1-161339-6

Inquiries should be directed to:

PUBLISHING DIVISION
UNITED NATIONS
NEW YORK, N.Y. 10017

Copyright © United Nations, 1991
All rights reserved
Manufactured in the United States of America

CONTENTS

Introduction v
   I. System of National Accounts (SNA) ix
   II. System of Material Product Balances (MPS) xxi
   III. Country tables 1

Country	Page	Country	Page
Afghanistan	3	Denmark	398
Algeria	4	Djibouti	426
Angola	8	Dominica	429
Anguilla	9	Dominican Republic	432
Antigua and Barbuda	12	Ecuador	438
Argentina	14	Egypt	488
Australia	21	El Salvador	494
Austria	56	Equatorial Guinea	505
Bahamas	89	Ethiopia	509
Bahrain	98	Fiji	511
Bangladesh	101	Finland	528
Barbados	108	France	587
Belgium	111	French Polynesia	635
Belize	162	Gabon	639
Benin	165	Gambia	642
Bermuda	174	Germany, Fed. Rep. of	649
Bhutan	176	Ghana	716
Bolivia	179	Greece	723
Botswana	188	Grenada	742
Brazil	198	Guadeloupe	744
British Virgin Islands	202	Guatemala	746
Brunei Darussalam	209	Guinea-Bissau	750
Bulgaria	212	Guyana	755
Burkina Faso	219	Haiti	758
Burundi	229	Honduras	762
Byelorussian SSR	232	Hong Kong	771
Cameroon	233	Hungary	777
Canada	244	Iceland	803
Cape Verde	286	India	829
Cayman Islands	289	Indonesia	855
Central African Rep	299	Iran (Islamic Rep. of)	859
Chad	301	Iraq	869
Chile	305	Ireland	876
China	314	Israel	892
Colombia	316	Italy	905
Congo	337	Jamaica	947
Cook Islands	341	Japan	967
Costa Rica	343	Jordan	1019
Cote d'Ivoire	358	Kenya	1029
Cuba	363	Kiribati	1038
Cyprus	368	Korea, Republic of	1039
Czechoslovakia	386	Kuwait	1061

INTRODUCTION

This is the thirty-third issue of *National Accounts Statistics: Main Aggregates and Detailed Tables*[1], showing detailed national accounts estimates for 170 countries and areas. Like the previous issues, it has been prepared by the Statistical Office of the Department of International Economic and Social Affairs of the United Nations Secretariat with the generous co-operation of national statistical services. It is issued in accordance with the request of the Statistical Commission[2] that the most recent available data on national accounts for as many countries and areas as possible be published regularly.

The present publication (Parts I and II) forms part of a National Accounts Statistics series. Another publication in the same series, issued separately is *National Accounts Statistics: Analysis of Main Aggregates*[3], presenting in the form of analytical tables a summary of main national accounts aggregates extracted from this publication and supplemented by estimates made by the Statistical Office where official data are not available.

SCOPE OF PUBLICATION

National accounts estimates for countries or areas whose data are in terms of the United Nations System of National Accounts (SNA) are shown, where available, for each of the following tables:

Part 1. Summary information

1.1 Expenditures on the gross domestic product (current prices)

1.2 Expenditures on the gross domestic product (constant prices)

1.3 Cost components of the gross domestic product

1.4 General government current receipts and expenditures, summary

1.5 Current income and outlay of corporate and quasi-corporate enterprises, summary

1.6 Current income and outlay of households and non-profit institutions, summary

1.7 External transactions on current account, summary

1.8 Capital transactions of the nation, summary

1.9 Gross domestic product by institutional sector of origin

1.10 Gross domestic product by kind of activity (current prices)

1.11 Gross domestic product by kind of activity (constant prices)

1.12 Relations among national accounting aggregates

Part 2. Final expenditures on gross domestic product: detailed breakdowns and supporting tables

2.1 General government final consumption expenditure by function (current prices)

2.2 General government final consumption expenditure by function (constant prices)

2.3 Total government outlays by function and type (current prices)

2.4 Composition of general government social security benefits and social assistance grants to households

2.5 Private final consumption expenditure by type (current prices)

2.6 Private final consumption expenditure by type (constant prices)

2.7 Gross capital formation by type of good and owner (current prices)

2.8 Gross capital formation by type of good and owner (constant prices)

2.9 Gross capital formation by kind of activity of owner, ISIC major divisions (current prices)

2.10 Gross capital formation by kind of activity of owner, ISIC major divisions (constant prices)

2.11 Gross fixed capital formation by kind of activity of owner, ISIC divisions (current prices)

2.12 Gross fixed capital formation by kind of activity of owner, ISIC divisions (constant prices)

2.13 Stocks of reproducible fixed assets, by type of good and owner (current prices)

2.14 Stocks of reproducible fixed assets, by type of good and owner (constant prices)

2.15 Stocks of reproducible fixed assets by kind of activity (current prices)

2.16 Stocks of reproducible fixed assets by kind of activity (constant prices)

2.17 Exports and imports of goods and services, detail

Part 3. Institutional sector accounts: detailed flow accounts[4/]

1. General government

   3.11 Production account
   3.12 Income and outlay account
   3.13 Capital accumulation account
   3.14 Capital finance account

2. Corporate and quasi-corporate enterprises

   3.21 Production account: total and subsectors
   3.22 Income and outlay account: total and subsectors
   3.23 Capital accumulation account: total and subsectors
   3.24 Capital finance account: total and subsectors

3. Households and private unincorporated enterprises

   3.31 Production account: total and subsectors
   3.32 Income and outlay account: total and subsectors
   3.33 Capital accumulation account: total and subsectors
   3.34 Capital finance account: total and subsectors

4. Private non-profit institutions serving households

   3.41 Production account
   3.42 Income and outlay account
   3.43 Capital accumulation account
   3.44 Capital finance account

5. External transactions

   3.51 Current account, detail
   3.52 Capital accumulation account
   3.53 Capital finance account

Part 4. Production by kind of activity: detailed breakdowns and supporting tables

   4.1 Derivation of value added by kind of activity (current prices)
   4.2 Derivation of value added by kind of activity (constant prices)
   4.3 Cost components of value added

For the countries or areas whose data are in terms of the System of Material Product Balances (MPS), the estimates are shown, where available, for each of the following tables:

1. Net material product by use
2. Net material product by kind of activity of the material sphere
3. Primary incomes by kinds of activity of the material sphere
4. Primary incomes from net material product
5. Supply and disposition of goods and material services
6. Capital formation by kind of activity of the material and non-material spheres
7. Final consumption
8. Personal consumption according to source of supply of goods and material services
9. Total consumption of the population by object, commodity and service, and mode of acquisition

Estimates for the matrix tables are shown for some or all of the years 1980 through 1989. For the other tables, estimates are shown for some or all of the years 1970, 1975, 1980 through 1989.

CONCEPTUAL REFERENCES

The form and concepts of the statistical tables in the present publication generally conform, for the countries or areas with SNA data, to the recommendations in *A System of National Accounts* [5/], Studies in Methods, Series F, No. 2, Rev. 3. For the countries or areas with MPS data, the form and concepts generally conform to the recommendations in *Basic Methodological Principles Governing the Compilation of the System of Statistical Balances of the National Economy: Vol. I and Vol. II* [6/], Series F, No.

17/Rev. 1, New York 1989. A summary of the conceptual framework of both systems, their classifications and definitions of transactions is provided in chapters I and II of the present publication.

COMPILATION OF DATA

To compile the large volume of national accounts data, the Statistical Office each year sends to countries or areas prefilled SNA questionnaire and/or MPS questionnaire. The recipients are requested to update the questionnaire with the latest available national accounts estimates and to indicate where the scope and coverage of the country estimates differ for conceptual or statistical reasons from the definitions and classifications recommended in SNA or in MPS. Data obtained from these replies are supplemented by information gathered from correspondence with the national statistical services and from national and international source publications.

In the present publication, the data for each country or area are presented in separate chapters, as far as possible, under uniform table headings and classifications of SNA or MPS, as the case may be. Important deviations from the two systems, where known, are described in the general note, while differences in definition and coverage of specific items are indicated in footnotes to the relevant tables.

Country data in chapter III are presented in alphabetical order. Unless otherwise stated, the data in the country tables relate to the calendar year against which they are shown.

COMPARABILITY OF THE NATIONAL ESTIMATES

Every effort has been made to present the estimates of the various countries or areas in a form designed to facilitate international comparability. To this end, important differences in concept, scope, coverage and classification have been described in the notes which precede and accompany the country tables. Such differences should be taken into account if misleading comparisons among countries or areas are to be avoided.

REVISIONS

The figures shown are the most recent estimates and revisions available at the time of compilation. In general, figures for the most recent year are to be regarded as provisional. For more up to date information, reference is made to selected issues of the United Nations *Monthly Bulletin of Statistics* [7]

NOMENCLATURE

The information for the countries and areas shown in this publication reflect what is available to the Statistical Office of the United Nations as of 30 August 1991.

On 19 September 1991, Bylorussian SSR officially changed its name to Republic of Belarus. In accordance with United Nations practice, the short form - Belarus - is used.

On 24 August 1991. Ukrainian SSR officially changed its name to Ukraine.

EXPLANATION OF SYMBOLS

The following symbols have been employed:

Data not available . . . .

Category not applicable . . . .

Magnitude nil or less than half of the unit employed . . . . -

Decimal figures are always preceded by a point (.)

When a series is not homogeneous, it is indicated by presenting the data in separate rows.

Decimals and percentages in tables do not necessarily add to totals shown because of rounding.

GENERAL DISCLAIMER

The designations employed and the presentation of material in this publication do not imply the expression of any opinion whatsoever on the part of the Secretariat of the United Nations concerning the legal status of any country, territory, city or area or of its authorities, or concerning the delimitation of its frontiers and boundaries.

Where the designation "country or area" appears in the headings of tables, it covers countries, territories, cities or areas. In prior issues of this publication, where the designation "country" appears in the headings of tables, it covers countries, territories, cities or areas.

In some tables, the designations "developed" and "developing" economies are intended for statistical convenience and do not, necessarily, express a judgement about the stage reached by a particular country or area in the development process.

1/United Nations publication. The first 25 editions of this publication were issued under the title Yearbook of National Accounts Statistics under the following sales number: 1957, 58. XVII3; 1958, 59. XVII.3; 1959, 60. XVII.3; 1960, 61. XVII.4; 1961, 62. XVII.2; 1962, 63. XVII.2; 1963, 64. XVII.4; 1964, 65. XVII.2; 1965, 66. XVII.2; 1966, 67. XVII.14; 1967, 69. XVII.6; 1968, vol. 1, 70. XVII.2, vol. II, 70. XVII.3; 1969, vol. 1, 71. XVII.2, vol. II, 71. XVII.3; 1970, 72. XVII.3, vol. 1, 72. XVII.3, vol. II; 1971, (3 volumes), E.73.XVII.3; 1972, (3 volumes), E.74.XVII.3; 1973, (3 volumes), E.75.XVII.2; 1975, (3 volumes), E.75.XVII.5, 1975, (3 volumes), 1976.XVII.2; 1976 (2 volumes), E.77.XVII.2; 1977, (2 volumes), E.78 XVII.2; 1978, (2 volumes) E.79.XVII.8; 1979, (2 volumes), E.80.XVII, 11; 1980, (2 volumes) E.82.XVII.6; 1981 (2 volumes), E.83.XVII.3. Beginning with the twenty-sixth edition, this publication replaced Volume 1, individual country data, of the Yearbook and it was issued under the following sales number: 1982, E.85.XVII.4; 1983, E.86.XVII.3; 1984, E.86.XVII.26; 1985, E.87.XVII.10; 1986, E.89.XVII.7 (Parts I and II), 1987, E.90.XVII.2 (Parts I and II), 1988, E.90.XVII.18 (Part I and II).

2/See Official Records of the Economic and Social Council, First Year, Second Session, (E/39), annex III, chap. IV.

3/United Nations publication, Sales No. E.90.XVII.8.

4/Institutional sector accounts are shown only for those countries which have tables for all the institutional sectors.

5/United Nations publication, Sales No. E.69.XVII.3. The first addition of the report, published in 1953, was prepared by an expert committee appointed by the Secretary-General of the United Nations.

6/United Nations publication, Sales No. E.89.XVII.5.

I. SYSTEM OF NATIONAL ACCOUNTS (SNA)

The revised System of National Accounts (SNA) was adopted by the Statistical Commission at its fifteenth session [1] for the use of national statistical authorities and in the international reporting of comparable national accounting data. The present System [2] is a revision and extension of the former SNA which was first formulated in 1952.

A. STRUCTURE OF SNA

SNA provides a comprehensive and detailed framework for the systematic and integrated recording of transaction flows in an economy. It brings together into an articulated and coherent system data ranging in degree of aggregation from consolidated accounts of the nation to detailed input-output and flow-of-funds tables. It includes production and goods and services and outlay and capital finance accounts for institutional sectors and subsectors.

The country tables are divided into four parts. These are listed in the above introduction. Part 1 contains summary but comprehensive information, at current and, where appropriate, constant prices. This part includes not only the basic gross domestic product (final expenditures and cost composition) but also summary information on government receipts and disbursements, enterprise and household income and outlay, and external transactions, a summary capital transactions account, information on gross product by institutional sector of origin and kind of activity and, finally, a table showing the relations among the aggregate concepts used in the revised SNA and also commonly in national statistical systems. Tables 1.1, 1.3, 1.4, 1.5, 1.6, 1.7 and 1.8 form a simple, closed and balancing set of flow accounts, drawn from the much more complex and elaborate standard accounts of SNA; these tables can therefore be used not only to provide an overview of the operation of the economic system but also as a guide to the more detailed data that follow and as a framework to enforce conceptual and statistical consistency.

Part 2 shows detailed breakdowns of the final expenditure components on gross domestic product (consumption, capital formation, imports and exports), in current and constant prices, together with supporting tables giving additional information on government outlays and capital stock. This part also shows tables relating to stocks of reproducible tangible assets at current and constant prices.

Part 3 shows detailed institutional sector accounts. For each sector and subsector, five accounts are given: a production account, an income and outlay account, a capital formation account, a capital finance account, and a balance sheet. The latter four are standard SNA accounts, as shown in annex 8.3 to *A System of National Accounts* [2] and in annex 8.2 to *Provisional Guidelines on National and Sector Balance Sheets and Reconciliation Accounts of the System of National Accounts.* [4]

The SNA standard accounts do not include institutional sector production accounts, but provision is made for this information in the supporting tables.

The sectors and subsectors distinguished in part 3 are: general government (central, state or provincial, local, social security funds), corporate and quasi-corporate enterprises (non-financial, financial), households and private unincorporated enterprises (farm entrepreneurial, other farm, non-farm entrepreneurial, non-farm wage earner, other) and non-profit institutions serving households.

Part 4 contains kind-of-activity breakdowns. Two levels of detail are employed. All of the information is asked for at the major division (1-digit) level of the *International Standard Industrial Classification of All Economic Activities* [5] (ISIC). In some cases, data are also asked for at the ISIC division (2-digit) level, with a very small amount of further breakdown to the 3-digit level. Where appropriate, both current and constant prices are specified. The tables show the derivation of value added (gross output less intermediate consumption), the cost components of value added, and employment.

B. STANDARD CLASSIFICATIONS OF THE SNA

Detailed discussions of definitions and classifications are to be found in *A System of National Accounts,* [2] and in the other publications on SNA cited above. SNA distinguishes between transactor and transaction classifications. Below is a short summary of the main characteristics of each of the classifications used by the system.

I. *Classifications of transactors*

1. *Kind of activity*

The kind-of-activity classification employed is the major division (1-digit) level or, in some tables the division (2-digit) level of ISIC.

In SNA, this classification is intended to be applied to establishment-type units, defined as the smallest units for which separate production accounts can be compiled. SNA also employs a much broader kind of activity classification which divides producers into "industries" and three categories of "other producers". Industries are, broadly, establishments whose activities are intended to be self-sustaining, whether through production for the market or for own use, and it is to this category that the ISIC breakdown is generally applied.

All establishments falling into ISIC major divisions 1-8 should be classed as industries. Producers of government services, private non-profit services to households, and domestic services are classed as "other producers"; all of these should fall into ISIC category 9 "Community, social and personal services". ISIC category 9 also may, of course, include some establishments classed as industries. Where countries consider, however, that some establishments classed as other producers should appear in ISIC categories other than 9, the nature of the exceptions would be specified in footnotes to tables 1.10 and 1.11.

2. *Institutional sectors*

The basic SNA institutional sectoring is given in *A System of National Accounts*, 3/ table 5.1.

Institutional sectoring, in SNA, is intended to be applied to enterprise-type units, that is, units for which complete accounts can be compiled, as opposed to the establishment-type units employed in the kind-of-activity classification. This distinction is applicable mainly to the corporate and quasi-corporate enterprise sector.

The sectoring and subsectoring employed in the institutional sector accounts in part 3 is as follows:

General government

    Central
    State or provincial
    Local
    Social security funds

Corporate and quasi-corporate enterprises

    Non-financial
    Financial

Households and private unincorporated enterprises

    Farm entrepreneurial
    Other farm
    Non-farm entrepreneurial
    Non-farm wage earner
    Other

Non-profit institutions serving households

Rest of the world

(a) *General government.* This sector includes (1) *producers of government services*, all bodies, departments and establishments of any level of government that engage in administration, defence, regulation of the public order and health, cultural, recreational and other social services and social security arrangements that are furnished but not normally sold to the public; and (2) *industries of government*, ancillary departments and establishments mainly engaged in supplying goods and services to other units of government, such as printing plants, central transport pools and arsenals, and agencies mainly selling goods and services to the public but operating on a small scale and financially integrated with general government, such as government restaurant facilities in public buildings.

Non-profit institutions which, while not an official part of any organ of government, are wholly or mainly financed and controlled by it should be included in producers of government services. Ancillary agencies may occur in any kind of activity. Producers of government services normally occur only in major division 9 (which of course may also include ancillary agencies). .

Provision is made for four subsectors of general government, all of which may include the two components noted above. However, it is not intended that artificial distinctions should be introduced where they do not exist in the institutions of a particular country. It will, for instance, usually be desirable to separate state or provincial government from local government only in countries in which state or provincial governments exercise a considerable degree of autonomy. Similarly, social security funds should in general be distinguished separately only where they are organized separately from the other activities of general government and exercise substantial autonomy in their operations.

(b) *Corporate and quasi-corporate enterprises.* SNA defines this sector to include enterprises which meet any one of the following criteria: (1) they are incorporated; (2) they are owned by a non-resident; (3) they are relatively large partnerships or proprietorships with complete income statements and balance sheets; (4) they are non-profit institutions mainly serving business and financed and controlled by business; or (5) they are engaged in financial activities. Because of the difficulty that may be encountered in compiling separate production account data for incorporated and unincorporated units, a combined production account for these two sectors has also been provided for.

(c) *Households and private unincorporated enterprises.* This sector includes all private unincorporated enterprises not classed as quasi-corporations. SNA also includes in this sector private non-profit institutions serving households that employ less than the equivalent of two full-time persons.

The criterion for classifying the subsectors of the household sector in these tables differs slightly from that tentatively proposed in SNA. There, the subsectoring is based on the occupational status of the person designated "head of household". Here, the classification is based on the most important source of household income, taking all household members into account. It is considered that this criterion more accurately reflects both changing social views and changing labour force participation practices; it also responds to recent directives relating to the elimination of sex-based stereotypes.

(d) *Private non-profit institutions serving households.* This sector includes institutions, not mainly financed and controlled by general governments and employing the equivalent of two or more persons, that furnish educational, health, cultural, recreational and other social and community services to households free of charge or at prices that do not fully cover their costs of production.

As in the case of general government, SNA includes two components in this sector: (1) *producers of private non-profit services to households*, which engage in the activities enumerated above, and (2) *commercial activities* of these institutions, such as owning and letting dwellings, operating eating and lodging facilities, and publishing and selling books, for which it is possible to compile separate production accounts but not complete separate financial accounts. (Where separate financial accounts can be compiled, such activities would be classed as ordinary quasi-corporations.) In SNA, these commercial activities are considered to be "industries" and should be classed in the appropriate ISIC categories, whereas the non-profit services proper will all fall into ISIC category 9.

II. Classifications of transactions

1. Classification of the functions of government

Table 5.3 of *A System of National Accounts* [3] contains a classification of the purposes of government, the l-digit level of which was used in previous publications for classifying general government outlays. This classification has now been superseded by the *Classification of the Functions of Government*. [6]

2. Household consumption expenditure

Table 6.1 of SNA provides a classification of household goods and services. The classification used in the present publication is a slightly condensed version of the second level of this classification, in which some second-level categories have been combined.

3. Purposes of private non-profit bodies serving households

This classification appears in table 5.4 of SNA. It is used for classifying the final consumption expenditures of private non-profit institutions serving households.

4. Gross capital formation

Table 6.2 of SNA classifies stocks according to type, and table 6.3 classifies gross fixed capital formation according to type. These classifications are used in the present publication in slightly modified form, calling for less detail in some areas and slightly more detail in others (specifically, transport equipment).

5. Exports and imports of goods and services

This classification is given in table 6.4 of SNA.

6. Transfers

Table 7.1 of SNA contains a classification of unrequired current transfers, including direct taxes. This classification is not employed directly in the present publication but it is the source of the definitions of a number of flows, and will be referred to in that connection.

7. Financial assets and liabilities

Table 7.2 of SNA gives a classification of items appearing in the capital finance account.

8. Balance sheet categories

Classifications of the various types of assets not included in the previous classification are given in tables 5.1 and 5.2 of *Provisional Guidelines on National and Sector Balance Sheets and Reconciliation Accounts of the System of National Accounts*, [4], which deal respectively, with stocks and fixed assets, and non-reproducible tangible assets. These classifications are used in the capital stock tables in part 2 and the balance sheet tables in part 3 of the present publication.

C. DEFINITIONS OF FLOWS

The following section briefly defines the content of the flows appearing in the SNA tables of chapter III of the present publication.

I. Total supply of goods and services

1. Gross output of goods and services

Gross output of goods and services covers both the value of goods and services produced for sale and the value of goods and services produced for own use. It includes (a) the domestic production of goods and services which are either for sale or for transfer to others, (b) net additions to work in progress valued at cost and to stocks of finished goods valued in producers' prices; (c) products made on own account for government or private consumption or for gross fixed capital formation; and (d) rents received on structures, machinery and equipment (but not on land) and imputed rent for owner-occupied dwellings.

Production for own consumption of households includes all own-account production of primary products (agricultural, fishing, forestry, mining and quarrying), own-account production of such items as butter, flour, wine, cloth or furniture made from primary products, and other goods and services that are also commonly sold. Gross output of the distributive trades is defined as the difference between sales and purchase values of goods sold. Gross output of banks and similar financial institutions is defined as the sum of actual service charges and imputed service charges; the latter is equal to the excess of property income received over interest paid out on deposits. For casualty insurance companies, gross output is defined as the excess of premiums received over claims paid, and for life insurance schemes it is the excess of premiums received over the sum of claims paid and net additions to actuarial reserves, excluding the accrued interest of the policy-holders in these reserves. Gross output of general government includes the market value of sales and goods and services produced for own use. The latter should be valued at cost, that is, the sum of net purchases of goods and services for intermediate consumption (at purchasers' prices), consumption of fixed capital, compensation of employees and any indirect taxes paid.

The concept of gross output appears in the tables in both part 3 and part 4. In part 3, each sector production account aggregates to its gross output. In part 4, gross output of various kind-of-activity sectors appears in tables 4.1 - 4.2 and 4.5 - 4.10. In the sector production accounts (tables 3.11, 3.21, 3.31 and 3.41) and the supply tables (4.5, 4.6, 4.9 and 4.10), gross output is divided into marketed and non-marketed components. The marketed component includes all output offered for sale (whether or not a buyer is actually found) or valued on the basis of a market transaction, even if it reaches the ultimate recipient through a transfer.

2. *Imports of goods and services*

Imports of goods and services include broadly the equivalent of general imports of merchandise as defined in external trade statistics, plus imports of services and direct purchases abroad made by resident households and by the government on current account. Transfer of migrants' household and personal effects and gifts between households are also included. The following additions and deductions are required, however, to move from the general trade concept to the national accounting concept. Additions required include (1) the value of purchases of bankers, stores and ballast for ships, aircraft, etc., (2) fish and salvage purchased from foreign vessels, and (3) purchases from abroad of gold ore and gold for industrial uses Deductions required include (4) goods imported solely for improvement or repair and subsequently re-exported; and (5) leased or rented machinery, equipment and other goods; the value of the repairs or leasing and rental services is included, however. The valuation of imports is c.i.f. In principle, transactions should be recorded at the moment the transfer of ownership takes place and not when goods physically enter the domestic territory, but in practice the time of recording used in the national accounts usually must follow that used in the external trade statistics.

Total imports of goods and services appear in tables 1.1, 1.2, 1.7 and 3.51. A detailed breakdown is given in table 2.17.

II. *Disposition of total supply: intermediate and final uses*

1. *Intermediate consumption*

Intermediate consumption covers non-durable goods and services used up in production, including repair and maintenance, research and development and exploration costs. It also includes indirect outlays on financing capital formation, such as flotation costs for loans and transfer costs involved in the purchase and sale of intangible assets and financial claims. Intermediate consumption is, as far as possible, valued in purchasers' prices at the moment of use.

For producers of government services and private non-profit services to households, intermediate consumption includes (1) purchases of goods and services on current account *less* sales of similar second-hand goods and scraps and wastes, (2) value of goods in kind received as transfers or gifts from foreign governments, except those received for distribution to households without renovation or alteration, (3) durable goods acquired primarily for military purposes, and (4) goods and services paid for by government but furnished by private suppliers to individuals (e.g., medical services), provided that the individuals have no choice of supplier. However, intermediate consumption of these producers does not include (1) goods and services acquired for use in constructing capital assets, such as roads or buildings, (2) goods and services paid for by government but furnished by private suppliers to individuals, when the individuals can choose the supplier and (3) purchases of strategic materials for government stockpiles.

Intermediate consumption appears in each institutional sector production account in part 3, and in tables 4.1-4.2 by kind of activity. In addition to the flow numbers assigned in SNA, flow numbers have been introduced for two categories of intermediate consumption not separately numbered in *A System of National Accounts*. [3] The first is imputed bank service charges. The imputed bank service charge is defined as the excess of property income accruing to banks and similar financial institutions from the investment of deposits over the interest accruing to their depositors. This imputation is made because of the view that banks perform services for depositors for which no explicit payment is made, in return for the use of the deposits as earning assets. It is not possible to allocate the imputation to specific recipients of the services, however, so that it cannot be included, as would be desirable, as part of the intermediate consumption of each reception. It is therefore deducted as a lump-sum adjustment. The adjustment appears in the tables showing kind-of-activity breakdowns of value added or intermediate consumption, including tables 1.10, 1.11 and 4.1-4.2. The second addition is intermediate consumption of industries of government, required for constructing a production account for general government (table 3.11).

2. *Government final consumption expenditure*

Government final consumption expenditure is equal to the service produced by general government for its own use. Since these services are not sold, they are valued in the gross domestic product at their cost to the government. This cost is defined as the sum of (1) intermediate consumption, (2) compensation of employees, (3) consumption of fixed capital and (4) payments of indirect taxes, *less* (5) the value of own-account production of fixed assets, and *less* (6) sales of goods and services.

The latter item, government sales, includes all payments made by individuals for services received (whether nominal or full cost) and it also includes the provision of second-hand goods from government stores as transfers in kind to foreign governments. Sales of such items as timber from forest preserves, seeds from agricultural experiment stations and government publications would also appear here. Compensation of employees, consumption of fixed capital and indirect taxes paid (if any) should preferably relate to all general government activity, with intra-governmental purchases and sales of goods and services eliminated in order to avoid double counting. With this treatment, there will be no operating surplus for any general government unit. Where countries consider that ancillary agencies and/or unincorporated government enterprises selling to the general public are operated on commercial principles and that the prices charged reflect market values, treatment of these entities on a net basis is an acceptable alternative. In this treatment, their sales to other government agencies will appear as intermediate consumption of the latter, and their operating surplus will appear as an item of general government income. This treatment has a number of disadvantages: the boundary between ancillary agencies and other government agencies is very difficult to specify precisely, and variations in treatment are likely to lead to incomparability among countries. Also, the net treatment makes it impossible to obtain figures for such flows as total compensation of general government employees. Finally, the level of gross domestic product will vary when the government's internal transfer prices are altered, a result that is somewhat incongruous.

Total government consumption expenditures appear in tables 1.1, 1.2, 4.7 and 4.8. A breakdown by government subsectors appears in table 3.12. Tables 2.1-2.2 show detailed breakdowns by function.

3. *Private final consumption expenditure*

Private consumption expenditure measures the final consumption expenditure of all resident non-governmental units. Thus, it is the sum of final consumption expenditure of households and that of private non-profit institutions serving households.

(a) *Private non-profit institutions serving households.* Final consumption expenditure of these units, as in the case of government, is equal to services they produce for their own use and is valued at cost. Cost includes purchases and the value (in purchasers' prices) of transfers of goods and services received in kind, compensation of employees, consumption of fixed capital, and indirect taxes paid by these institutions, *less* their sales of goods and services. The definitions of purchases and sales on current account are much the same as those for general government. Private non-profit institutions serving households are defined to include units employing the equivalent of two or more full-time persons and providing educational, health, cultural, recreational, and other social and community services to households free of charge or at prices that are not intended to cover the full costs of their production. Units mainly financed and controlled by general government, however, are included in general government rather than here. Units primarily serving business, such as trade associations, are included with corporate and quasi-corporate enterprises. In applying these definitions, some judgement is required, and it will often be necessary to examine intent, as well as outcome. A normally profit-making unit that sustains a loss does not thereby become a non-profit institution.

Final expenditures of private non-profit institutions serving households appear in tables 1.1, 1.2 and 3.42, and a breakdown by purpose appears in tables 2.5 and 2.6. Definitions of the purpose categories are given in SNA classification 5.4

(b) *Resident households*. What is wanted as a component of the final uses of gross domestic product is the final consumption expenditure of resident households. What is most commonly available in the statistics, however, is not expenditure of resident units but expenditure in the domestic market. To adjust expenditure in the domestic market to expenditure of resident units, purchases abroad and net gifts in kind received from abroad have been added, and subtracted are purchases in the domestic market of non-resident units. Corresponding adjustments are made to exports (to ensure that they include purchases of non-residents in the domestic market) and to imports (to ensure that they include purchases of residents abroad). These adjustments include expenditures by tourists, ships' crews, border and seasonal workers and diplomatic and military personnel on goods and services, including local transportation, but they exclude expenditures reimbursible as travel expenses (which are counted as intermediate consumption). These adjustments are shown in tables 2.5 and 2.6.

Household final consumption expenditure includes outlays on non-durable and durable goods and services, *less* sales of second-hand goods and of scraps and wastes. In addition to market purchases, household final consumption expenditure includes the imputed gross rent of owner-occupied dwellings, food and other items produced on own account and consumed, and items provided as wages and salaries in kind by an employer, such as food, shelter or clothing, and other fringe benefits included in compensation of employees, except those considered to add to household saving. The imputed gross rent of owner-occupied dwellings should, in principle, be valued at the rent of similar facilities on the market but has been approximated by costs, including operating maintenance and repair charges, depreciation, mortgage interest, and interest on the owner's equity. Other non-marketed output included in final consumption is valued at producers' prices.

Total resident final consumption expenditure appears in tables 1.1, 1.2, 1.6 and 1.12. It is broken down by institutional subsectors in tables 3.32, and in tables 4.7 and 4.8 it is broken down by industrial origin. A detailed breakdown by type of good is shown in tables 2.5 and 2.6. The type-of-good categories are defined in SNA classification 6.1.

4. *Gross capital formation*

Gross capital formation is the sum of the increase in stocks and gross fixed capital formation, defined below. It appears in tables 1.1, 1.2 and 1.8. Breakdowns of gross capital formation appear in tables 2.7-2.12, 4.7 and 4.8. Gross capital formation of individual institutional sectors appears in tables 3.13, 3.23, 3.33, and 3.43.

(a) *Increase in stocks*. This flow includes the value of the physical change in (a) stocks of raw materials, work in progress and finished goods held by private producers, and (b) stocks of strategic materials held by the government. Work put in place on buildings and other structures, roads and other construction projects is treated as gross fixed capital formation rather than increase in stocks but is distinguished separately there to facilitate analysis. Increases in livestock raised for slaughter should be included in the increase in stocks, but breeding and draft animals, dairy cattle, and animals raised for wool clips are treated as fixed capital. The physical change in stocks during a period of account should be valued at average purchasers' prices during the period. In some cases, the available data relate to the change in the value of stocks held rather than the value of the physical change.

A classification of the increase in stocks by type is given in tables 2.7 and 2.8, and defined in SNA classification 6.2. The increase in stocks by kind of activity of owner is shown in tables 2.9 and 2.10.

(b) *Gross capital formation*. This flow is defined to include purchases and own-account production of new producers' durable goods, reduced by net sales to the rest of the world of similar second-hand or scrapped goods. Outlays of producers of government services for military purposes (except on land and certain civilian-type items, such as schools, hospitals, family-type housing and, in some cases, roads when for civilian use) are, however, considered to be current expenditures. "Military purposes" are here construed in terms of final expenditures: they include the military airport, but not the bulldozer used in constructing the airport. Gross fixed capital formation includes outlays on reclamation and improvement of land and development and extension of timber tracts, mines, plantations, orchards, vineyards etc., and on breeding and dairy cattle, draft animals, and animals raised for wool. Outlays on alteration or extension of fixed assets, which significantly extend their life or increase their productivity, are included, but outlays on repair and maintenance to keep fixed assets in good working order are not. All costs are included that are directly connected with the acquisition and installation of the fixed assets, such as customs duties and other indirect taxes, transport, delivery and installation charges, site clearing, planning and designing costs, legal fees and other transfer costs with respect to transactions in land, mineral deposits, timber tracts etc. However, the costs of financing, such as flotation costs, underwriters' commissions and the cost of advertising bond issues, are excluded; these items are included in intermediate consumption. The acquisition of fixed assets is to be recorded at the moment that the ownership of the goods passes to the buyer. In the case of construction projects, this is taken to be the time that the work is put in place but, as noted above, uncompleted construction projects are shown separately from completed ones.

A classification of fixed assets by type is given in tables 2.7 and 2.8, and the categories are defined in SNA classification 6.3. A classification by kind of activity of purchaser is given in tables 2.9, 2.10, 2.11 and 2.12, and a classification by producing industry is given in tables 4.7 and 4.8. Breakdowns by institutional sector are given in tables 3.13, 3.23, 3.33 and 3.43.

5. *Exports of goods and services*

Exports of goods and services are defined to be parallel to the definition of imports given above, and they are shown in the same tables and classifications. Exports are, however, valued f.o.b., whereas imports are valued c.i.f.

III. *Cost components and income shares*

1. *Value added and gross domestic product*

The value added of industries at producers' prices is equal to the gross output of the industries at producers' prices *less* the value of their intermediate consumption at purchasers' prices. Value added for the total of all domestic producers (*plus* import duties and value added tax which are not included in the value added of any domestic producer, and *less* imputed bank service charges which are deducted in a single line) is equal to the gross domestic product is shown in tables 1.9-1.11, and 4.1 - 4.2. Gross domestic product may be defined alternatively as the sum of final expenditures in the domestic economy (tables 1.1 and 1.2) or as the sum of incomes received in the domestic economy (tables 1.3, 1.9 and 4.3). In principle, all three methods should yield the same result but in statistical practice there are likely to be small discrepancies. Such statistical discrepancies are shown where they exist.

2. Compensation of employees

Compensation of employees appears in SNA as a domestic concept and as a national concept. Table 1.3 employs the domestic concept, that is, compensation of employees paid by resident producers. This includes payments to non-resident employees working in the country but excludes payments to resident employees temporarily working abroad. In order to show the relation of this concept to compensation received by resident households (shown in tables 1.6 and 3.32) and compensation paid to the rest of the world (shown in tables 1.7 and 3.51), the two components are shown separately in table 1.3. Each component includes (a) wages and salaries, (b) employers' contributions to social security schemes and (c) employers' contributions to private pension, insurance and similar schemes. The national concept of compensation of employees is shown in the household sector income and outlay account (tables 1.6 and 3.31), where compensation received by resident households from domestic producers and that received from the rest of the world are gathered together. The portion paid by resident producers appears in table 1.3; that paid by the rest of the world appears in table 1.7.

Wages and salaries include all payments to employees for their labour, whether in cash or in kind, before deduction of employee contributions to social security schemes, withholding taxes and the like. They include commissions, bonuses and tips, and cost of living, vacation and sick leave allowances paid directly by the employers to the employee but exclude reimbursement for travel and other expenses incurred by employees for business purposes, which is included in intermediate consumption. The pay and allowances of members of the armed forces, the fees, salaries and bonuses of members of boards of directors, managing directors, executives and other employees of incorporated enterprises and the fees of ministers of religion are included. Wages and salaries in kind are valued at their cost to the employer, and include goods and services furnished to employees free of charge or at markedly reduced cost that are clearly and primarily of benefit to the employees as consumers.

Employers' contributions to social security schemes include all social security contributions that employers make on behalf of their employees, but not the employees' own share of such contributions. Social security contributions may be broader than payments to social security funds, since not all social security arrangements are funded.

Employers' contributions to pension, insurance and similar schemes include paid and imputed contributions by employers on behalf of their employees to private funds, reserves or other schemes for providing pensions, family allowances, lay-off and severance pay, maternity leave, workmen's compensation, health and other casualty insurance life insurance and the like. Where employers make payments to employees for such benefits without the establishment a formal fund for this purpose, the contributions that would be required to support such a fund are imputed both here and subsequently as an imputed transfer from households to their employers, since of course the employees do not control the use of the fund.

3. Operating surplus

Operating surplus is the balancing item in the SNA production account. For an individual establishment, it is defined as the excess of value added over the sum of compensation of employees, consumption of fixed capital, and net indirect taxes. The operating surplus of all types of establishments -- corporate, quasi-corporate, and unincorporated, public and private -- is included in the figure shown in table 1.3. Operating surplus for each of the institutional sectors individually is shown in tables 3.11, 3.21 and 3.31; its breakdown by kind of activity is shown in table 4.3. It is also included in the totals for property and entrepreneurial income shown in tables 1.4, 1.5 and 1.6.

4. Consumption of fixed capital

Consumption of fixed capital includes allowances for normal wear and tear, foreseen obsolescence and probable (normally expected) accidental damage to fixed capital not made good by repair, all valued at current replacement cost. Unforeseen obsolescence, damages due to calamities, and depletion of natural resources are not included, since these are capital losses and should appear as changes in the balance sheet. Also not included is the revaluation of past allowances for consumption of fixed capital due to changes in the current replacement cost of fixed assets; this also will appear as part of the change in accumulated allowances shown in the balance sheet. Total consumption of fixed capital appears in tables 1.3, 1.8 and 1.12, consumption of fixed capital of individual institutional sectors in tables 3.11, 3.21, 3.31 and 3.41, and consumption of fixed capital by kind of activity in table 4.3. The accumulated consumption of fixed capital for specific types of assets and kind-of-activity sectors appears as the difference between the gross and net capital stock in tables 2.13-2.16, and for individual institutional sectors it appears in tables 3.15, 3.25, 3.35 and 3.45.

5. Indirect taxes

Indirect taxes are defined as taxes chargeable to the cost of production or sale of goods and services. They include (a) import and export duties, (b) excise, sales, entertainment and turnover taxes, (c) real estate and land taxes, unless they are merely an administrative device for collecting income tax, (d) levies on value added and the employment of labour (but not social security contributions), (e) motor-vehicle, driving-test, licence, airport and passport fees, when paid by producers, and (f) the operating surplus of government fiscal monopolies on such items as alcoholic beverages and tobacco (in principle reduced by the normal profit margin of similar business units). In the present publication, indirect taxes paid and subsidies received from supranational organizations (e.g., the European Economic Community) are shown separately. Also, the net treatment of value added taxes recommended by the European Economic Community has been employed.

Unlike all other indirect taxes, SNA does not allocate import duties among producers in tables by kind of activity. Indirect taxes are only allocated to a particular kind of activity where they are levied directly on the output of that activity (e.g., excise duties) or on the process of producing that output (e.g., employment taxes). Import duties, however, are levied on the output of foreign rather than domestic producers, and are therefore shown separately in tables by kind of activity, including tables 1.10, 1.11, 4.1, 4.2, 4.3, 4.5 and 4.6.

Total indirect taxes appear in table 1.3. Indirect taxes paid by individual institutional sectors appear in tables 3.11, 3.21, 3.31, and 3.41. Indirect taxes paid to supranational organizations appear in tables 1.7 and 1.12. Indirect taxes retained by government are shown in table 3.12.

6. *Subsidies*

Subsidies are grants on current account by the government to (a) private enterprises and public corporations, or (b) unincorporated public enterprises when clearly intended to compensate for losses resulting from the price policies of government. Total subsidies, including those paid by supranational organizations, as well as by government, appear in table 1.3; subsidies paid by supranational organizations in tables 1.7 and 1.12; and those paid by government in tables 1.4 and 3.12. Subsidies received by individual institutional sectors appear in tables 3.21, 3.31 and 3.41.

7. *Withdrawals from quasi-corporations*

Withdrawals from the entrepreneurial income of quasi-corporations consist of the actual payments made to the proprietors of quasi-corporations from the entrepreneurial income of these units. Entrepreneurial income of quasi-corporations is equal to their income from production (net operating surplus) *plus* their net income (receipts *less* payments) from property. In some cases, the whole of the entrepreneurial income will be treated as if paid out to the proprietors; in other cases, some of it is retained as net saving within the quasi-corporation. Withdrawals from quasi-corporations also include withdrawals from foreign branches of domestic companies or from domestic branches of foreign companies, since both of these categories are treated as quasi-corporations. The withdrawals may be negative, since proprietors may provide funds to the enterprises to compensate for losses.

SNA assigns separate flow numbers to withdrawals as they appear in the paying sectors (flow 4.4) and in the receiving sectors (flow 4.5). As disbursements, they appear in table 3.22 and as part of a larger total in table 1.5. As receipts, they appear in tables 3.12, 3.22, 3.32 and 3.42, and as parts of the larger total in tables 1.4, 1.5 and 1.6

8. *Property income*

Property income consists of payments of interest, dividends and land rents and royalties, all of which are assigned separate SNA flow numbers, both as payments and as receipts. Interest is defined as income payable and receivable on financial claims, such as bank and other deposits, bills and bonds, including public debt, and the equity of households in life insurance actuarial reserves and pension funds. Dividends consist of income payable and receivable on corporate equity securities and other forms of participation in the equity of private incorporated enterprises, public corporations and co-operatives. Rent payments include, in addition to net land rent, royalty payments for concessions to exploit mineral deposits or for the use of patents, copyrights, trademarks and the like. They exclude rent payments on machinery and equipment or buildings, which are treated as the purchase of a service rather than property income and appear in gross output of the seller and intermediate consumption of the purchaser. Payments of land rent are always treated as a domestic flow since the foreign owners are, for national accounting purposes, dealt with as residents of the country in which the land is located. When it is not possible to separate rent of buildings and rent of the land on which the buildings stand, the whole flow is attributed to the buildings, that is, excluded from property income and included in intermediate consumption.

Property income paid and received by individual institutional sectors is shown in tables 3.12, 3.22, 3.32 and 3.42. As part of a larger total it appears in the summary tables 1.4, 1.5 and 1.6.

IV. *Taxes and unrequited transfers*

The categories of taxes and unrequited transfers are classified and defined in SNA classification 7.1. SNA does not provide the full articulation of the to-whom from-whom relationships of these flows, but assigns flow numbers to the various combinations of them used in specific standard tables and accounts. In order to define less ambiguously the flows used in the present publication, a somewhat fuller listing of individual flow components is used.

1. *Casualty insurance transactions*

Casualty insurance transactions refer to health, accident fire, theft, unemployment and similar insurance schemes. The total of net premiums for the economy as a whole is equal to the total premiums payable *less* an imputed service charge which in turn is defined to be equal to the difference between premiums and claims. As a consequence, for the economy as a whole, net premiums and claims are equal. However, the total service charge is distributed to sectors of receipt and disbursement in proportion to the total (not net) premiums paid, so that net premiums and claims are not necessarily equal for each sector. In the former SNA, these insurance transactions were considered to be in part capital items, and this practice continues in the accounts of a number of countries. In the revised SNA, however, all casualty insurance transactions, including compensation for capital losses, are considered to be current flows. They are shown in detail in tables 3.12, 3.22, 3.32 and 3.42.

2. *Taxes and other government receipts*

Taxes and other government receipts include direct taxes, compulsory fees, fines and penalties, social security contributions, and other current transfers received by general government.

Direct taxes include two components. Direct taxes on income cover levies by public authorities at regular intervals (except social security contributions) on income from employment, property, capital gains or any other source. Real estate and land taxes are included only if they are merely administrative procedures for the assessment and collection of income tax. Other direct taxes cover levies by public authorities at regular intervals on the financial assets and the net of total worth of enterprises, private non-profit institutions and households, and on the possession or use of goods by households. Direct taxes received are shown in tables 1.4 and 3.2; payments of other sectors are shown in tables 3.22, 3.32 and 3.42.

Compulsory fees are payments to public authorities by households for services that are obligatory and unavoidable in the only circumstances in which they are useful. Examples of such fees are payments by households for driving tests and licenses, airport and court fees and the like. Similar payments by business units are treated as indirect taxes. Fines and penalties, however, include not only those paid by households but also those paid by corporate and quasi-corporate enterprises and private non-profit institutions serving households. They appear in the same tables as direct taxes.

Social security contributions consist of contributions for the account of employees, whether made by employees or by employers on their behalf, to the social security arrangements that are imposed, controlled or financed by the government for the purpose of providing social security benefits for the community or large sections of the community. They appear as receipts in tables 1.4 and 3.12, and as payments in tables 1.6 and 3.32.

Current transfers n.e.c. received by general government consist primarily of transfers received from the rest of the world and imputed employee welfare contributions. Transfers from the rest of the world include grants between governments to finance military outlays, outlays for health and educational purposes, and similar transfers in kind of military equipment, food, clothing etc. Payments and assessments and other periodic contributions to international organizations are also included. In addition to actual transfers, this item also includes imputed transfers arising from the obligation of the government as an employer to pay directly to its employees pensions, family allowances, severance and lay-off pay and other welfare benefits when there is no special fund, reserve or insurance for these purposes. In these circumstances, SNA provides for the establishment of an imputed fund to which imputed contributions are made, of a magnitude sufficient to support the unfunded benefit payments. The imputed contributions are included in compensation of employees, as an addition to actual payments, and are then shown as an imputed payment by the employees back to the government as an employer. These transfers appear in table 1.4 as an aggregate, and in table 3.12 in more detail.

3. *Household transfer receipts*

Household transfer receipts include social security benefits, social assistance grants, and unfunded employee welfare benefits. These flows, in varying detail, are shown in tables 1.6, 2.4 and 3.32.

Social security benefits are payments to individuals under the social security arrangements described above. The payments are often made out of a special fund and may be related to the income of individuals from employment or to contributions to social security arrangements made on their behalf. Examples are unemployment insurance benefits, old-age, disability and survivors' pensions, family allowances and reimbursements for medical and hospital expenses. It may be difficult to distinguish social security benefits from social assistance grants, on the one hand, and insurance benefits, on the other. The main criterion is method of finance; the actual content will vary from country to country. Medical services, for instance, may be supplied as social assistance, as a part of social security, as a casualty insurance benefit, or as a free government service.

Social assistance grants are cash grants to individuals and households, except social security benefits and unfunded employee welfare benefits. They may be made by public authorities, private non-profit institutions, or corporate and quasi-corporate enterprises. Examples are relief payments;

widows', guardians' and family allowances and payments of medical and dental expenses which are not part of social insurance schemes; war bonuses, pensions and service grants; and scholarships, fellowships and maintenance allowances for educational, training and similar purposes. They include payments made by public authorities for services provided by business enterprises and private non-profit institutions directly and individually to persons, whether these payments are made to the individuals or directly to the providers of the services that the persons are considered to have purchased. They exclude, however, transfers to persons or households as indemnities for property losses during floods, wars and similar calamities; these are considered to be capital items.

Unfunded employee welfare benefits are pensions, family allowances, severance and lay-off pay, maternity leave pay, workmen's and disability compensation and reimbursements for medical expenses and other casualties which employers pay directly to their former or present employees when there is no special fund, reserve or insurance for these purposes.

4. *Transfers received by private non-profit institutions*

Transfers received by private non-profit institutions serving households include grants and gifts, in cash and in kind, to non-profit institutions serving households which are intended to cover partially the cost of the provision of services by these institutions. They also include membership dues paid to political organizations, fraternal bodies and the like. They appear as a receipt in table 3.42, and as payments sometimes as part of a larger total, in tables 3.12, 3.22 and 3.32.

5. *Other current transfers n.e.c.*

Other current transfers n.e.c. include transfers to and from resident sectors that are not specifically included in any other flows. They may include migrants' remittances, transfers of immigrants' personal and household goods, and transfers between resident and non-resident households, in cash and in kind. They include allowances for bad debts.

V. *Finance of gross accumulation*

1. *Net saving*

Net saving is the balancing item in the SNA income and outlay account. It is defined as the difference between current receipts and current disbursements. Net saving for the nation as a whole appears in tables 1.8 and 1.12. Net saving for individual institutional sectors appears in tables 3.12, 3.13, 3.22, 3.23, 3.32, 3.33, 3.42 and 3.43.

2. *Surplus of the nation on current transactions*

The surplus of the nation on current transactions is the balancing item in the external transactions current accounts (tables 1.7 and 3.51). It also appears in table 1.8, the capital transactions account, in table 1.12, the table showing relationships among the national accounting aggregates, and table 3.52, the external transactions capital accumulation account.

3. *Purchases of land, net*

Purchases of land, net, include purchases *less* sales of land, subsoil deposits, forests and inland waters, including any improvements that are an integral part of these assets except buildings and other structures. The purchases and sales are valued at the transaction (sales) price of the land, forests etc., not including the transfer costs involved; such transfer costs are included in gross capital formation. Purchases and sales are assumed to take place when the legal title to the land is passed. They are considered to take place between resident institutions only. Where the land is purchased by a non-resident, a nominal resident institution is considered to be the owner of the land. The foreign owner is assigned equity in the resident institution equivalent to the purchase price of the land. The value recorded in the flow is the same for both the buyer and the seller. For the country as a whole, therefore, purchases and sales will cancel out. If the sales value of the structures situated on the land cannot be separated from the sales value of the land itself, the entire transaction should be recorded as a purchase and sale of structures (i.e., of second-hand assets), unless the structures are intended for immediate demolition. Purchases of land appear in the capital accumulation accounts of the individual institutional sectors, (tables 3.13, 3.23, 3.33 and 3.43).

4. *Purchases of intangible assets, net*

Purchases of intangible assets, net, are defined as purchases, *less* sales, of exclusive rights to mineral, fishing and other concessions and of patents, copyrights etc. These transactions involve the once-and-for-all relinquishment and acquisition of the exclusive rights, although they may be paid for over a period of years; they do not include concessions, leases, licences to use patents and permission to publish copyrighted materials which involve the periodic payment of royalties or rents, with eventual reversion of the rights to the seller. The purchases and sales are valued at the transaction (sales) value of the mineral concession, lease, patent, etc., not including any transfer costs involved. (The transfer costs are included in gross capital formation.) Purchases of intangible assets appear in the individual institutional sector capital accumulation accounts (tables 3.13, 3.23, 3.33, and 3.43) as a part of gross accumulation. Purchases from the rest of the world appear in table 3.52.

5. *Capital transfers*

Capital transfers are defined as unrequited transfers, in cash or in kind, which are used for purposes of capital formation or other forms of capital accumulation, are made out of wealth, or are non-recurrent. Examples of capital transfers are grants from one government to another to finance deficits in external trade, investment grants, unilateral transfers of capital goods, legacies, death duties and inheritance taxes, migrants' transfers of financial assets and indemnities in respect of calamities. Mixed transfers, considered by one party to the transaction as capital and the other as current, are treated as capital. Capital transfers appear in tables 3.13, 3.23, 3.33, 3.43 and 3.52.

6. *Net lending*

Net lending is defined as the excess of the sources of finance of accumulation (i.e., net saving, consumption of fixed capital and capital transfers received) over the uses of these funds for gross capital formation, net purchases of land and intangibles, and capital transfers paid. It appears in the capital accumulation accounts of the individual institutional sectors (tables 3.13, 3.23, 3.33 and 3.43), and in the external transactions capital accumulation account (table 3.52). Net lending is also equal to the difference between a sector's net acquisition of financial assets and its net incurrence of financial liabilities. It thus also appears in the institutional sector capital finance accounts (tables 3.14, 3.24, 3.34, 3.44 and 3.53). Although not for all countries, net lending derived in these two different ways are statistically identical.

VI. *Financial assets and liabilities*

Net acquisition of financial assets is defined as the difference between, on the one hand, acquisitions or purchases and, on the other, relinquishment or sales by given transactors of financial claims on second parties. Net incurrence of liabilities is equal to the issue or sale *less* redemption or payment of financial claims of second parties. A classification and definitions of financial assets and liabilities is given in SNA classification 7.2. Changes in financial assets and liabilities for individual institutional sectors appear in the capital finance accounts (tables 3.14, 3.24, 3.34, 3.44 and 3.53). Their total amount is shown in the sector balance sheets (tables 3.15, 3.25, 3.35 and 3.45).

VII. *Other assets*

1. *Reproducible tangible assets*

Reproducible tangible assets are classified and defined in table 5.1 of the *Provisional Guidelines on National and Sector Balance Sheets and Reconciliation Accounts of the System of National Accounts*. [4] They appear, classified by type of asset and broad sector, in tables 2.13 and 2.14, by kind of activity in tables 2.15 and 2.16 and for individual institutional sectors, in the sector balance sheets in tables 3.15, 3.25, 3.35 and 3.45

2. *Non-reproducible tangible assets*

Non-reproducible tangible assets are classified and defined in table 5.2 of the *Provisional Guidelines* (see above). Only the total appears in the tables, in the sector balance sheets (tables 3.15, 3.25, and 3.45).

3. *Non-financial intangible assets*

Non-financial intangible assets include the mineral, fishing and other concessions, leases, patents, copyrights etc., the purchase and sale of which is recorded in the capital accumulation account. These intangible assets are created at the time of the purchase or sale, that is, when a once-and-for-all lump-sum payment has been made for the lease, concession, patent or copyright. They appear in the sector balance sheets (tables 3.15, 3.25, 3.35 and 3.45).

---

[1] *Official records of the Economic and Social Council, Forty-fourth Session, Supplement No. 10*, (E/4471), paras. 8-24.

[2] The present system is published in *A System of National Accounts*, Studies in Methods, Series F, No. 2, Rev. 3 (United Nations publication, Sales No. E.69.XVII.3).

[3] *Ibid*

[4] Statistical Papers, Series M, No. 60 United Nations publication, Sales No. 77.XVII.10.

[5] Statistical Papers, Series M, No. 4, Rev. 2, Add. 1 (United Nations publication, Sales No. E.71.XVII.8).

[6] Statistical Papers, Series M, No. 70 (United Nations publication, Sales No. 80.XVII.17).

II. SYSTEM OF MATERIAL PRODUCT BALANCES (MPS)

The System of Material Product Balances (MPS) furnishes the means for standardizing the national accounting data which the Statistical Office of the the Department of International Economic and Social Affairs of the United Nations Secretariat receives from countries with centrally planned economies. Data collection follows the principles found in the *Basic Methodological Rules for the Compilation of the Statistical Balance of the National Economy*. [1] This system is also described in the *Basic Principles of the System of Balances of the National Economy*. [2]

A. STRUCTURE OF MPS

MPS is based on a system of balances. It includes material and financial balances, the balance of manpower resources and the balance of fixed capital and indicators of national wealth. The material balance is a presentation of the volume of the supply of goods and material services originating in domestically produced global product and imports and their disposition to consumption, capital formation and exports, classified by different production activity categories. The financial balance is a presentation of income flows generated in production in the material sphere, their redistribution through transactions in the non-material sphere and through other transfers flows and, finally, their disbursement to consumption and capital formation. The income flows of the financial balance are classified by institutional (social) sectors. The presentation is therefore comparable to that of production, income and outlay and capital finance accounts by institutional sectors in the System of National Accounts (SNA). The third type of balance, that is, the manpower balance, presents the allocation of available manpower to production activities and institutional or social sectors. This balance is expressed in the number of persons employed. The last balance is the one of national wealth and capital assets. It is a presentation of the volume of the stocks of tangible fixed and other assets available at the beginning and the end of the year and the increase that has taken place during the year. The tangible assets are classified by type of asset and by form of ownership and production activities of the national economy.

The MPS tables that are presented in chapter III and are listed in the introduction provide further detail on the material balances. Table 1 on net material product by use is similar to the SNA table on gross domestic product by kind of economic activity. Data regarding the production and goods and services transactions are included in tables 2, 3, 4 and 5 which present, respectively, activity breakdowns of net material product and of primary incomes, of the population and of enterprises, a breakdown by socio-economic sectors of these two types of primary incomes, and a breakdown of supply and disposition of goods and material services by kind of activity of the producers. Tables 6, 7, 8 and 9 present further details on the expenditure categories, such as a breakdown of fixed capital formation by kind of economic activity and by socio-economic sector and of increases in material circulating assets and of stocks by kind of activity, and a classification of final consumption, personal consumption and of total consumption of the population by type of expenditure.

B. DIFFERENCES BETWEEN MPS AND SNA

Apart from the differences in structure of the two systems, there are considerable differences between the coverage of the concepts used in MPS and in SNA. Since these differences limit the use of MPS and SNA data in cross-country types of analyses, a summary of those that are relevant to the MPS data published in chapter III of the present publication is reproduced below. [3]

1. *The treatment of material and non-material services*

In MPS there is a distinction different to that made in SNA, between the production of material and non-material services. Only the production of material services, together with that of goods, is covered by the gross output (global product) concept of MPS. The production of non-material services is excluded. Material goods and services used as input in the production of non-material services are considered to be a part of final consumption expenditure, while income flows resulting from this type of production are treated as income transfers. The material services are those that are directly linked to the production of goods and cover the services related to the repair, transportation and distribution of goods. All other services are treated as non-material services. This important difference between MPS and the present SNA results in the following concrete differences between the two systems:

(a) Expenditures by enterprises on cultural, sports and similar facilities for their employees are excluded in MPS from intermediate consumption. Instead, a transfer between enterprises and households is included, while the material goods and services involved in the above expenditures are allocated to final consumption of the population. SNA treats these expenditures as intermediate consumption;

(b) Depreciation of dwellings and other material goods and services involved in the provision of housing are allocated in MPS to final consumption expenditure. Since these are non-material services, no value-added contribution is included in net material product. In SNA, this contribution is included in gross domestic product;

(c) Travel expenses in connection with business are not included in intermediate consumption in MPS as they are in the present SNA. Instead, they are treated as a part of compensation of employees and the material goods and services involved are allocated to private final consumption expenditure;

(d) In SNA and MPS a different distinction is drawn between uniforms to be treated as intermediate consumption and those to be included in compensation of employees and final consumption expenditure of households. In SNA, the distinction is drawn between civilian (intermediate consumption) and military uniforms and in MPS, between dress and working uniforms;

(e) Tips are treated in SNA as a part of compensation of employees, while in MPS they are treated as income transfers, when they exceed the normal service charge.

2. *Capital formation*

The MPS and SNA guidelines differ, on the one hand, with regard to the treatment of capital gains and losses and the coverage of depreciation and, on the other, in the coverage of fixed capital formation and increases in stocks. The main differences are the following:

(a) In MPS, depreciation, as well as the replacement for losses due to certain foreseeable and non-forseeable damages to fixed assets and stocks, including those caused by accidents and calamities, are deducted in order to arrive at net fixed capital formation. In SNA, generally uses the concept of gross fixed capital formation only is generally used. However, if net capital formation were to be estimated, only depreciation on fixed assets would have to be deducted in that system. Losses in stocks or fixed assets would never be considered for deduction. Losses on fixed assets would be treated as capital losses and dealt with outside the national accounts flows, while losses in stocks would be treated as a part of intermediate consumption or as capital losses, depending on whether they are due to normal events in production or to calamities. The dividing line between losses and depreciation of fixed assets also differs in the two systems. In SNA, depreciation is assumed to cover, among other things, the average amount of accidental damage to fixed assets that is not made good by repair or replacement of parts--for example, damage arising from fire and accidents. In MPS, such damages are not reflected in depreciation but covered under losses;

(b) Depreciation in MPS is based on the original cost of the assets. However, every eight to ten years, adjustments to replacement cost are made to this asset value and these adjustments are also reflected in a corrected value of depreciation. Furthermore, differences that arise between the actual value and the written-off book value at the moment the assets are scrapped or sold are included in the value of depreciation for the year in which the sale or scrapping occurs. In SNA, instead, the replacement value of the assets is used as a basis for depreciation. Any change in this value, whether it happens at the moment the asset is sold or during the time it is used, is considered to be a capital gain or loss and is not accounted for in the national accounting flows;

(c) In addition, in MPS, depreciation includes capital consumption allowances with respect to afforestation, land improvements, roads, bridges and similar structures. In SNA, no imputations for depreciation of this type of asset are included;

(d) Expenditures on fixed assets for military purposes are treated in MPS as a part of net fixed capital formation. In SNA, these outlays are allocated to government final consumption expenditure, except for outlays by government on the construction and alteration of family dwellings for personnel of the armed forces, which are included in gross fixed capital formation;

(e) Transfer cost with regard to purchases and sales of existing fixed assets are treated in MPS as transfers since these are non-material services. In SNA, these costs are included in gross fixed capital formation;

(f) Work put in place on structures, roads, dams, ports and other forms of construction is allocated in MPS to increases in material circulating assets and stocks. Only when the construction is finished is its total value transferrred to net fixed capital formation. In SNA, these outlays are immediately allocated to gross fixed capital formation.

3. *External transactions*

The third area in which MPS and SNA differ is in the coverage of exports and imports of goods and services, in the distinction between residents and non-residents and in the treatment of monetary, as opposed to non-monetary gold. The differences are the following:

(a) In MPS, embassies, consulates and international bodies are treated as residents of the country in which they are located, while in SNA they are treated as residents of the country they represent. This difference in the residence concept has consequences for the allocation between countries of capital formation and government final consumption expenditure and also for the allocation of the income flows. Wages and salaries paid to local employees of these extraterritorial bodies are not included in SNA concept of gross domestic product. They are dealt with, however, as factor income from abroad and therefore accounted for in the national income concept in SNA. In MPS, such wages and salaries, if earned in the sphere of material production, are included in primary incomes of the population, as well as in net material product;

(b) In MPS, the territorial concept of final consumption expenditure, which includes purchases by non-residents in the domestic market and excludes purchases abroad by residents, is used. As a result, such flows are not accounted for in exports or imports. On the other hand, it does include, in exports and imports, transactions that, though they take place in the domestic market, are conducted in foreign currency. These transactions are treated as if they were transactions with non-residents. In SNA, the national concept of final consumption expenditure is used; taken into account in exports and imports, respectively, are the direct purchases in the domestic market by non-residents and the direct purchases abroad by non-residents. Furthermore, no distinction is made in SNA between transactions that are conducted in local or in foreign currency;

(c) Purchases and sales by external trade organizations of goods that do not cross the border of the country in question and also imported goods that are re-exported without being processed are treated in MPS as part of respectively, imports and exports. In SNA, they are not accounted for in the export and import flows, except for the margins received by resident units as payments for services rendered;

(d) Gifts in kind by households to and from abroad are included in exports and imports in SNA. In MPS, they are excluded from these flows;

(e) Transactions in intangible assets (patents, copyrights, trade-marks, exclusive rights to exploit mineral deposits etc.) with the rest of the world are included in MPS in exports and imports. In SNA, they are treated as property income or as sales or purchases of intangible assets to or from abroad, depending on whether the payment is for the use of the rights or for the outright transfer of those rights;

(f) Transactions with the rest of the world in monetary and non-monetary gold are included in MPS in exports and imports. In SNA, included in exports and imports are actual transactions in non-monetary gold only. Exports in addition include newly mined gold (whether actually exported or not) in order to transform gold as a commodity into a financial asset.

C. STANDARD CLASSIFICATIONS OF MPS

Two classifications are used in the MPS standard tables presented, that is, the kind-of-activity classification and the classification by socio-economic group. Contrary to SNA usage with respect to the activity and institutional classifications for different groups of transactions, the two MPS classifications are parallel ones that are applied to the same transaction categories: net material product and its component primary incomes and capital formation. Each of these classifications is described briefly below.

1. Kind of activity

All forms of activity in production are classified according to groups or branches, depending on the nature and results of the application of labour. The two major categories constitute branches of the material sphere and branches of the non-material sphere. The first category covers the production of goods, and services that are related to the production of goods, such as repair services, transportation services and goods distribution services. The second category includes the remaining services-producing activities. Each of the two categories is further broken down by branches which are similar in character to the ISIC categories used in SNA. The unit of classification is not the organizational unit (i.e., enterprise) but a smaller unit that performs one type of activity (i.e., establishment). If an enterprise or institution or other organizational unit carries on more than one type of economic activity, it is considered to consist of two or more establishments that perform different activities.

For the subclassification of net material product by kind of activity, only the activity breakdown of the material sphere is used since net material product originates in this sphere only. For capital formation, however, the activity categories of the non-material sphere are also used, since capital formation relates not only to the material sphere but also to non-material branches.

A rough correspondence based on the names of the activity categories can be established between the activity categories presented in SNA and in the MPS branches. The user should be aware, however, of the limitations that such a linkage may entail, as indicated in the following points:

(a) Mining and quarrying, manufacturing, and electricity, gas and water are shown as three separate categories in the SNA presentation and as one category (industrial production), in the MPS presentation;

(b) Hunting and the collection of forestry products is treated as a part of agriculture in the SNA presentation and as a part of forestry and logging in MPS;

(c) The distribution of gas, electricity and water to households is treated in MPS as a non-material service (including in housing). This activity is therefore not reflected in net material product, while its capital formation is dealt with as capital formation of the non-material sphere. In SNA, these distribution activities are an integral part of the activity category for electricity, gas and water;

(d) Printing and publishing, which is treated as a material activity in MPS, is allocated to the MPS category known as "other activities of the material sphere". In SNA, this activity is included with manufacturing;

(e) Cleaning, dyeing and repair services are included with industrial activity (manufacturing) in the MPS presentation and with community, social and personal services in SNA;

(f) In comparing the activity breakdown of net material product and gross domestic product, the user should be aware that the coverage of the MPS category known as "other activities of the material sphere" falls far short of the combined coverage of the two SNA categories for finance, insurance, real estate and business services and for community, social and personal services. The SNA categories include all non-material activities that are excluded from the MPS coverage of net material product. In addition, the shifts between activity categories that were outlined in the previous points affect this group. Other activities in the presentation of net material product include telegraph, news-gathering and editorial agencies, industrial services other than architectural design services, printing and publishing services, the production of motion pictures, phonograph records and prerecorded tapes, data-processing and tabulating services, waterway-maintenance services and the operation of flood-control systems, and services related to the conservation of natural resources and the protection of the environment.

2. *Socio-economic sectors*

The rates of development of the national economy and the basic features of production that support this development are largely determined by the social structure of the community. In order to study the process, the various activities involved in the production of material goods and services are classified in MPS by socio-economic sector. This classification is based on the form of ownership of the fixed and circulating capital. The form of ownership of the means of production determines the forms of ownership of the product and of the incomes generated by its disposal.

The basic socio-economic sectors are the socialist sector and the private sector.

The socialist sector embraces the enterprises and institutions in public, socialist ownership. The fixed and circulating assets of these enterprises are public property. The socialist sector also includes the personal plots of employees and members of co-operatives.

Within the socialist sector, the following socio-economic subsectors are distinguished: the state subsector; the co-operative subsector, which includes agricultural producers' co-operatives; associations; personal plots of employees; personal plots of members of co-operatives.

The state subsector includes the enterprises and institutions in state ownership. The State furnishes them with the fixed and circulating assets required for their operation. These economic units are administratively subordinated to central or local organs of state authority. The production of the state subsector and the income generated in it belong to the people as a country.

The co-operative subsector embraces the enterprises and institutions in collective or group onwership. The fixed and circulating assets of these economic bodies are originally built up from the entrance fees (initiation fees) of their members and the proceeds of sales of shares to them; and are later supplemented from part of their operating surplus. The output and income of the enterprises and institutions of the co-operative subsector are the property of their members.

The association subsector includes the enterprises and institutions owned by voluntary or semi-voluntary associations. The fixed and circulating assets of the economic bodies of this subsector are built up from the voluntary contributions of their members and from part of the operating surplus of such bodies. The output and income of this subsector belong to the associations.

The personal plots of employees and members of co-operatives embrace agricultural output, construction and other forms of activity (gathering of wild fruits and berries, scrap collection etc.).

The private sector includes the enterprises and institutions, the fixed and circulating assets of which are privately owned. The classification of enterprises and institutions of the private sector is based on the specific economic conditions in the country concerned. Within this sector, the subsector of craftsmen, artisans and peasants who are not members of co-operatives may be distinguished.

Peasants, craftsmen and artisans who do not belong to co-operatives operate small private ventures in which the productive process is carried out by their owners in person, as a rule without recourse to hired labour. This group also includes the subsidiary activities of the population occupied in the private sector of the national economy.

D. DEFINITIONS OF FLOWS

Given below are the definitions of the flows that appear in the MPS standard tables of chapter III. To make possible a comparison between SNA and MPS data, a description of the differences between the MPS and the SNA coverage is added to each of the sections. The items needed in order to convert the MPS coverage into a coverage that conforms to the SNA definition are only summarily indicated. For more information on these items, the user is therefore referred to the description of the differences between the two systems in section B above. The items described below have been grouped together into categories similar to those used for the SNA flows (see chap. I above, sect. C).

I. *Total supply and disposition of goods and material services*

1. *Gross output*

Global product covers the value of goods and material services produced. Deliveries of goods and material services within the same enterprise are generally excluded. Included are, among other things, the value of own-account constructed capital goods and capital repairs to fixed assets, the value of work-in-progress and the value of finished goods added to stocks. Covered is, furthermore, the value of goods and material services provided free to employees (the material services are valued at the material cost involved). Included in the contribution to global product by agriculture are seeds and feed produced and consumed at the same farm and agricultural and other goods produced on personal plots for own consumption or for sale, including the cost of their processing. This concept of gross output appears in MPS table 5.

To derive gross output in producers' prices as defined in SNA, global product as described above needs to be increased by:

plus: the gross output value of non-material services (including those of government), including the transfer cost on purchases and sales of existing second-hand fixed assets and land.

2. *Trade margins and transport charges*

The gross output of material goods and services is valued at both producers' and purchasers' values. The difference between the two sets of values gives the distributive trade margins (including restaurants, cafés and other catering) and the transportation margins. The gross output of the distributive-trade units is equal to the value of their gross margins on internal and external trade.

The gross margins on external trade are equivalent to the sum in domestic currency of (a) the value of imports of goods and material services in the domestic market *less* the actual value at which these imports are purchased from abroad and (b) the actual value at which exports of goods and material services are sold to abroad *less* the value of these exports in the domestic market. Trade margins and transport charges appear in MPS table 5.

3. *Intermediate material consumption, including depreciation*

Intermediate material consumption consists of the value of the goods and material services used up in the process of production during a period of account by units of the material sphere, including the consumption of fixed assets during the period. Consistent with the scope of the gross output of goods and material services included in intermediate consumption are certain items, for example, seeds and animal feed, which are produced and used by the same unit. The intermediate output of raw materials etc., is valued net of the value of scraps and wastes originating in the process of production. Purchased items are valued at purchasers' values; items produced on own account are valued at cost in the case of state and co-operative enterprises and at average purchasers' prices in the case of personal plots of households. This concept of intermediate material consumption appears in MPS table 5.

Depreciation or consumption of fixed assets includes an allowance for normal wear and tear and foreseen obsolescence of fixed assets based on standard rates of depreciation and, furthermore, the difference between the book value of scrapped fixed assets and their scrap value. The allowances for depreciation are often based on the original cost of the assets which may be periodically adjusted to replacement cost.

To arrive from intermediate material consumption, including depreciation as defined above, at the SNA concept of intermediate consumption, the MPS coverage needs to be increased and decreased by the following items:

plus: (i) material cost of non-material services;

plus: (ii) material expenditures by enterprises on cultural, sports and similar facilities for their employees;

plus: (iii) reimbursable expenditures for material goods and services purchased during business trips;

minus: (iv) consumption of fixed capital in the material sphere.

4. *Personal consumption*

This consists of all consumer goods, irrespective of durability, and material services (repair, transport, communication and similar services) which are purchased by households, received in kind as payment for work in state and collective enterprises and in private plots, or produced on own account on personal plots. Excluded is the purchase by households of dwellings (which is dealt with as capital formation) but included is the maintenance and depreciation of dwellings. Also included are reimbursable expenditures for material goods and services purchased during business trips. This concept of personal consumption appears in MPS tables 1 and 7. It appears according to source of supply of goods and material services in MPS table 8. In MPS, the domestic concept of consumption is used, so that direct purchases by foreign tourists, diplomatic personnel and other non-residents in the domestic market are included, while similar purchases abroad by residents are excluded.

5. *Material consumption in the units of the non-material sphere serving individuals*

This flow covers expenditures on non-durable goods and material services by units of the non-material sphere serving individuals, reduced by the increases in their stocks of goods. Also included is consumption of fixed assets used by these units. It appears in MPS tables 1 and 7.

6. *Material consumption in the units of the non-material sphere serving the community as a whole*

This flow consists of non-durable goods and material services purchased during a period of account by units of the non-material sphere serving the community as a whole, reduced by the increases in their stocks of goods during the period of account. Also included is consumption of fixed assets of these units. It appears in MPS tables 1 and 7.

To arrive from this concept at government final consumption expenditure as defined in SNA, the following additions to and subtraction from the MPS concept have to be made:

plus: (i) the difference between the value of non-material services produced by government and their material cost and depreciation

plus: (ii) government expenditures on fixed assets that have military uses;

plus: (iii) the difference between consumption expenditures (i.e., material and non-material cost, depreciation and compensation of employees) of extraterritorial bodies that represent the country abroad *minus* consumption expenditures incurred by extraterritorial bodies of other countries and international organizations located in the country in question;

plus: (iv) material expenditures by government (units in the non-material sphere serving individuals) on education, health, culture and other services provided free to individuals.

7. *Final consumption*

This flow is equal to the sum of personal consumption and material consumption in the units of the non-material sphere serving individuals and of those serving the community as a whole. Each of these concepts has been defined above. They appear in MPS tables 5 and 7.

8. *Consumption of the population*

Consumption of the population is the sum of personal consumption and material consumption in the units of the non-material sphere serving individuals. This concept is comparable to private final consumption expenditure in SNA, which can be derived from this MPS concept by adding and subtracting the following items:

plus: (i) the difference between the value of non-material services purchased by households, including housing services and the material cost and depreciation included in the value of these services;

minus: (ii) material expenditures by government (units in the non-material sphere serving individuals) on education, health, culture and other services provided free to individuals;

plus: (iii) the difference between direct purchases abroad by resident households and direct purchases in the domestic market by non-resident households as well as the difference between gifts sent abroad by household *minus* gifts received from abroad;

minus: (iv) reimbursable expenditures for material goods and services purchased during business trips;

minus: (v) material expenditures by enterprises on cultural sports and similar facilities for their employees.

9. *Total consumption of the population*

Total consumption of the population covers the consumption by the population of goods and material services and of non-material services, whether purchased by households or furnished free of charge. It therefore exceeds the consumption of the population (i.e., the sume of personal consumption and material consumption in the units of the non-material sphere serving individuals) by the value of the services of the units of the non-material sphere serving individuals, reduced by the consumption of goods and material services by these units. The value of the services of the units is equivalent to their costs of production, including operating surplus in some instances. In the case of dwellings provided by these units, their depreciation is not included when evaluating costs of production, since charges in respect of depreciation of these dwellings are included in personal consumption. Total consumption of the population appears classified by object in MPS table 9.

10. *Net fixed capital formation*

Net fixed capital formation consists of the value of new fixed assets purchased or constructed on own account and of completed capital repairs to these assets reduced by consumption of fixed assets for renewal of assets and capital repairs, and capital losses due to fire, floods and other calamities and furthermore reduced by the remaining value of scrappled fixed assets. Thus, it measures the net increase in the value of fixed assets during a period of account. This flow appears in MPS tables 5 and 6.

Fixed assets include completed dwellings, buildings and other structures; machinery, equipment and other durable goods acquired by units of the material and non-material sphere; cattle, excluding young cattle and cattle raised for meat; perennial plants; and expenditures on the improvement of land, forests and other natural resources. New fixed assets put into use are generally valued inclusive of acquisition and installation cost.

Capital repairs cover outlays on repairs that make up at least in part for the physical depreciation of the fixed assets and/or significantly raise the capacity and productivity of the fixed assets.

In order to convert the MPS concept of net fixed capital formation into gross fixed capital formation as defined in SNA, the following additions to and substractions from the MPS concept have to be made:

plus: (i) consumption of fixed capital in the material and non-material sphere, including that on afforestation, roads, bridges and similar structures;

plus: (ii) losses due to foreseeable as well as non-foreseeable damages to fixed assets;

plus: (iii) transfer cost with regard to purchases and sales of existing second-hand fixed assets, including land;

plus: (iv) work in progress on the construction of structures, roads, dams and ports on other forms of construction;

plus: (v) the difference between outlays on fixed capital formation by extraterritorial bodies representing the country in question abroad, *less* similar outlays by extraterritorial bodies of other countries and international organizations located in the country in question;

minus: (vi) government expenditures on fixed assets that have military uses.

11. *Gross fixed capital formation*

Gross fixed capital formation is equal to net fixed capital formation as defined above *plus* depreciation. Depreciation is defined in section 3 above, together with intermediate material consumption. Gross fixed capital formation classified by kind of activity appears in MPS table 6.

12. *Increases in material circulating assets and stocks*

This item consists of increases during the period of account in the stocks of enterprises in the material sphere, including wholesale and retail trade units, reduced by losses. Also covered are increases in government stockpiles, including stocks of defense items and state reserves of precious metals and precious stones. The stocks in the material sphere consist of raw materials, fuels, supplies and other non-durable goods; young cattle and cattle raised for meat; work in progress, including uncompleted construction projects; and finished goods not yet sold. Increases in material circulating assets and stocks appear in MPS tables 1 and 6.

In order to convert the MPS concept of increases in material circulating assets and stocks into increases in stocks as defined in SNA, the following addition to and subtractions from the MPS concept are needed:

plus: (i) losses due to foreseeable and non-foreseeable damages to stocks;

minus: (ii) work in progress on the construction of structures, roads, dams and ports and on other forms of construction;

minus: (iii) net increases in the holdings of gold ingots and other monetary gold.

13. *Losses*

This item is the sum of the value of the losses in fixed assets and losses in material circulating assets and stocks. Included are losses (a) due to fires, floods and other calamities, (b) in adult productive and working cattle, (c) due to abandoned or interrupted construction works and (d) in agricultural products in storage at state and co-operative agricultural enterprises and at farms. This flow appears in MPS tables 1 and 5.

In SNA, this final demand category is not identified separately from gross capital formation.

14. *Exports and imports of goods and material services*

Exports are defined to include: (a) outward-bound goods thast cross the border of the country, including imported goods which are exported without being processed; (b) goods which are purchased outside the country by an external trade organization of the country in question and shipped directly to a third country; (c) outward-bound monetary and non-monetary gold and other precious metals; (d) unilateral transfers of goods by the government and public organizations of the country (uncompensated foreign aid); (e) material services, such as transport, forwarding and communication services, rental, including rental payments for time-charter of ships and other transport equipment and, furthermore, export contract services rendered to other countries. The imports cover the same categories of goods and material services which are inward bound. Exports are valued f.o.b. while imports are valued c.i.f. They appear in MPS tables 1 and 5.

To arrive at the SNA coverage of exports of goods and services, the following additions to and subtractions from the MPS concept are needed:

plus: (i) the difference between the export value of non-material services and the material cost and depreciation included in these services;

plus: (ii) consumption expenditure (material and non-material cost, depreciation and compensation of employees) and outlays on fixed capital formation by extraterritorial bodies of foreign governments and international organizations located in the country in question;

plus: (iii) direct purchases in the domestic market by non-resident households and gifts sent abroad by households;

minus: (iv) sales abroad by an external trade organization of the country of goods that have not crossed the border of the country in question; as well as of goods that have crossed the border but that are re-exported without being processed;

minus: (v) the difference between exported monetary gold and the value of sales of newly produced gold ingots and bars.

MPS imports have to be adjusted in a similar manner. To be added are the import value of non-material services *minus* material cost and depreciation, consumption expenditure and fixed capital formation of extraterritorial bodies that represent the country abroad and direct purchases abroad by residents. To be deducted are re-exports and purchases abroad by external trade organizations of goods that do not cross the border of the country, and also the value of imported monetary gold and gifts received households from abroad.

III. Cost components and income shares

1. Net material product

Net material product is defined in MPS and is used in countries with centrally planned economies. It can be estimated from the production income and expenditure side in the same manner, as is indicated in chapter I above, section C.III, in which the SNA coverage of gross domestic product is described. Following the production approach, net material product is the difference between global product (i.e., gross output) of goods and material services and intermediate material consumption, including consumption of fixed assets. Net material product defined from the income side is the sum of primary incomes of the population (comparable to compensation of employees in SNA) and primary incomes of enterprises (comparable to operating surplus in SNA). The expenditure approach finally defines net material product as the sum of the final uses of goods and material services, that is, personal consumption, and material consumption of units in the non-material sphere serving individuals and that of similar units serving the community as a whole, net capital formation (i.e., net of depreciation), replacement for losses and the balance between exports and imports of goods and material services. These three different methods for deriving net material product are shown in MPS tables 1, 2 and 4.

To arrive at the SNA concept of gross domestic product, net material product needs to be increased and reduced as follows:

plus: (i) the excess value of non-material services (i.e., the gross output value *minus* material cost and depreciation) consumed by households and by government *plus* the difference between these excess values of exported and imported non-material services;

minus: (ii) material expenditures by enterprises on cultural, sports and similar facilities for their employees;

minus: (iii) reimbursable expenditures for material goods and services purchased during business trips;

plus: (iv) consumption of fixed capital in the material and non-material sphere, including that on afforestation, roads, bridges and similar structures;

plus: (v) losses of fixed assets and stocks due to accidental damage, such as fire, accidents etc.;

plus: (vi) transfer cost with regard to purchases and sales of existing second-hand fixed assets, including land.

2. Primary income of the population

The primary income of the population consists of (a) wages and salaries, including receipts in kind, and related income, such as bonuses and reimbursements of expenses on business trips received from state, co-operative and private units of the material sphere; (b) the net material product (net value added) originating from the personal plots of households; and (c) the net material product of self-employed craftsmen, artisans and peasants. This flow appears in MPS tables 3 and 4.

Primary income of the population is roughly comparable to the SNA concept of compensation of employees. However, several differences remain and in order to arrive from the MPS concept at compensation of employees as defined in SNA, the following additions and subtractions are needed:

plus: (i) compensation of employees, including employers' contributions to social security funds, paid out in connection with non-material activities, inclusive of those that are paid out in connection with the provision of cultural, sports and similar facilities by industries in the material sphere;

plus: (ii) employers' contributions to social security funds paid out in connection with material activities;

minus: (iii) income from private enterprises;

minus: (iv) reimbursable expenditures for material goods and services purchased during business trips.

3. Primary income of enterprises

Primary income of enterprises consists of the sum of the net material product of the units of the material sphere which have employees *less* the wages and salaries and related incomes which they pay out. The primary incomes of these units are the source of such items as their net income, turnover taxes, contributions to social insurance, payments of taxes, fines and other compulsory items, finance of purchases of non-material services, insurance premiums, interest on bank loans and other business costs. This flow appears in MPS tables 3 and 4.

Although the coverage of primary income of enterprises is similar to that of operating surplus in SNA, the following additions to and subtractions from the MPS concept are needed in order to arrive at operating surplus as defined in SNA:

plus: (i) the remaining value of non-material services (i.e., the gross output value *minus* material cost, depreciation and compensation of employees) consumed by households and government, *plus* the difference between the remaining values of exported and imported non-material services;

minus: (ii) material expenditures by enterprises on cultural, sports and similar facilities for their employees;

plus: (iii) consumption of fixed capital in the material and non-material sphere, including that on afforestation, roads, bridges and similar structures;

plus: (iv) losses of fixed assets and stocks due to accidental damage, such as fire, accidents etc.;

plus: (v) transfer cost with regard to purchases and sales of existing fixed assets, including land;

minus: (vi) employers' contributions to social security funds, paid out in connection with material activities;

plus: (vii) income from private plots and private enterprises.

1/ Standing Statistical Commission, Council of Mutual Economic Assistance (Moscow, 1969).

2/ Studies in Methods, Series F, No. 17 (United Nations publication, Sales No. E.71.XVII.10).

3/ For a more exhaustive list of differences between MPS and SNA, the user should refer to *Comparisons of the System of National Accounts and the System of Balances of the National Economy*, part One, *Conceptual Relationships* (United Nations publication, Sales No. 77.XVII.6).

III. COUNTRY TABLES

Afghanistan

Source. Reply to the United Nations National Accounts Questionnaire from the Central Statistical Office, Kabul.

General note. The estimates shown in the following tables have been prepared in accordance with the System of Material Product Balances. Therefore, these estimates are not comparable in concept and coverage with those conforming to the United Nations System of National Accounts.

2b Net Material Product by Kind of Activity of the Material Sphere in Constant Market Prices

Thousand Million Afghanis — Fiscal year beginning 21 March

	1970	1975	1980	1981	1982	1983	1984	1985	1986	1987	1988	1989
					At constant prices of:1978							
1 Agriculture and forestry	...	62.5	63.1	64.3	64.7	65.8	65.4	65.2	67.0	51.9	49.1	47.9
2 Industrial activity	...	11.5	13.7	12.8	13.3	14.9	15.3	16.4	17.1	16.6	15.1	16.4
3 Construction	...	1.9	2.9	3.3	3.0	3.6	3.9	3.9	4.4	5.1	5.0	3.5
4 Wholesale and retail trade and restaurants and other eating and drinking places	...	9.6	8.2	8.4	9.1	9.2	10.1	10.0	10.5	10.0	8.9	8.3
5 Transport and communication	...	2.9	2.8	2.9	3.1	3.4	3.7	2.7	2.5	3.1	2.8	2.7
6 Other activities of the material sphere	...	1.6	1.4	1.5	1.6	1.7	1.8	1.7	1.7	1.6	1.5	1.5
Net material product	...	90.0	92.1	93.2	94.8	98.6	100.2	99.9	103.2	88.3	82.4	80.3

Algeria

Source. Direction des Statistiques et de la Comptabilite Nationale, Secretariat d'Etat au Plan, Alger. Official estimates are published in 'Comptes Economiques'.
General note. The estimates shown in the following tables have been prepared in accordance with the United Nations System of National Accounts so far as the existing data would permit.

1.1 Expenditure on the Gross Domestic Product, in Current Prices

Million Algerian dinars

		1970	1975	1980	1981	1982	1983	1984	1985	1986	1987	1988	1989
1	Government final consumption expenditure	3579	7971	22351	26354	30660	34693	40800	45500	53500	56300	60000	...
2	Private final consumption expenditure	13444	31452	70179	87176	95559	106183	118300	134800	152000	152800	158800	...
3	Gross capital formation	8752	27838	63512	70836	77343	87819	94700	97500	92800	93300	98300	...
	A Increase in stocks	591	3863	8631	7791	5855	7500	7300	4800	-2500	500	1000	...
	B Gross fixed capital formation	8160	23975	54881	63045	71488	80319	87400	92700	95300	92800	97300	...
	Residential buildings	...	...	...	...	...	...	...	...	...	...	...	...
	Non-residential buildings	...	...	...	...	...	...	...	...	...	...	...	...
	Other construction and land improvement etc.	4637	11503	30224	32790	38493	47325	56200	...	...	...	...	...
	Other	3523	12473	24657	30255	32994	32994	31200	...	...	...	...	...
4	Exports of goods and services	5305	20714	55802	66182	64223	65344	67700	69200	39100	45500	48900	...
5	Less: Imports of goods and services	7007	26400	49338	59079	60233	60286	61600	59500	50900	40000	46000	...
	Equals: Gross Domestic Product	24073	61574	162507	191469	207552	233752	259900	287400	286500	307900	320000	...

1.2 Expenditure on the Gross Domestic Product, in Constant Prices

Million Algerian dinars

		1970	1975	1980	1981	1982	1983	1984	1985	1986	1987	1988	1989
						At constant prices of: 1974							
1	Government final consumption expenditure	4364	6638	...	...	...	...	...	...	...	...	...	...
2	Private final consumption expenditure	15761	24142	...	...	...	...	...	...	...	...	...	...
3	Gross capital formation	13415	25247	...	...	...	...	...	...	...	...	...	...
	A Increase in stocks	657	3512	...	...	...	...	...	...	...	...	...	...
	B Gross fixed capital formation	12758	21735	...	...	...	...	...	...	...	...	...	...
	Residential buildings	...	...	...	...	...	...	...	...	...	...	...	...
	Non-residential buildings	...	...	...	...	...	...	...	...	...	...	...	...
	Other construction and land improvement etc.	7563	10237	...	...	...	...	...	...	...	...	...	...
	Other	5195	11498	...	...	...	...	...	...	...	...	...	...
4	Exports of goods and services	21880	22617	...	...	...	...	...	...	...	...	...	...
5	Less: Imports of goods and services	11005	23369	...	...	...	...	...	...	...	...	...	...
	Statistical discrepancy	-625	213	...	...	...	...	...	...	...	...	...	...
	Equals: Gross Domestic Product	43790	55488	...	...	...	...	...	...	...	...	...	...

1.3 Cost Components of the Gross Domestic Product

Million Algerian dinars

		1970	1975	1980	1981	1982	1983	1984	1985	1986	1987	1988	1989
1	Indirect taxes, net	5470	13372	31134	38581	40416	44469	...	...	...	...	...	...
2	Consumption of fixed capital	1962	4915	13692	15150	18171	21504	...	...	...	...	...	...
3	Compensation of employees paid by resident producers to:	8407	20553	57133	65780	76889	88642	...	...	...	...	...	...
	A Resident households	8245	...	...	...	...	...	...	...	...	...	...	...
	B Rest of the world	162	...	...	...	...	...	...	...	...	...	...	...
4	Operating surplus	8233	22734	60549	71957	72076	79138	...	...	...	...	...	...
	Equals: Gross Domestic Product	24072	61574	162507	191469	207552	233752	...	...	...	...	...	...

Algeria

1.4 General Government Current Receipts and Disbursements

Million Algerian dinars

	1970	1975	1980	1981	1982	1983	1984	1985	1986	1987	1988	1989
Receipts												
1 Operating surplus	...	...	...	...	...	...	...	...	...	...	...	...
2 Property and entrepreneurial income	971	4810	...	...	...	...	...	...	...	...	...	...
3 Taxes, fees and contributions	5185	19922	...	...	...	...	...	...	...	...	...	...
A Indirect taxes	3106	7611	...	...	...	...	...	...	...	...	...	...
B Direct taxes	1941	11906	...	...	...	...	...	...	...	...	...	...
C Social security contributions	96	263	...	...	...	...	...	...	...	...	...	...
D Compulsory fees, fines and penalties	42	142	...	...	...	...	...	...	...	...	...	...
4 Other current transfers	362	843	...	...	...	...	...	...	...	...	...	...
Total Current Receipts of General Government	6518	25575	...	...	...	...	...	...	...	...	...	...
Disbursements												
1 Government final consumption expenditure	3579	8421	...	...	...	...	...	...	...	...	...	...
A Compensation of employees	2731	6447	...	...	...	...	...	...	...	...	...	...
B Consumption of fixed capital	...	...	...	...	...	...	...	...	...	...	...	...
C Purchases of goods and services, net	781	1848	...	...	...	...	...	...	...	...	...	...
D Less: Own account fixed capital formation	...	...	...	...	...	...	...	...	...	...	...	...
E Indirect taxes paid, net	67	126	...	...	...	...	...	...	...	...	...	...
2 Property income	117	510	...	...	...	...	...	...	...	...	...	...
3 Subsidies	143	4148	...	...	...	...	...	...	...	...	...	...
4 Other current transfers	1236	2566	...	...	...	...	...	...	...	...	...	...
A Social security benefits	396	839	...	...	...	...	...	...	...	...	...	...
B Social assistance grants			...	...	...	...	...	...	...	...	...	...
C Other	840	1727	...	...	...	...	...	...	...	...	...	...
5 Net saving	1443	17510	...	...	...	...	...	...	...	...	...	...
Total Current Disbursements and Net Saving of General Government	6518	25575	...	...	...	...	...	...	...	...	...	...

1.7 External Transactions on Current Account, Summary

Million Algerian dinars

	1970	1975	1980	1981	1982	1983	1984	1985	1986	1987	1988	1989
Payments to the Rest of the World												
1 Imports of goods and services	7007	... 26400	49338	59079	60233	60286	61600	...	...	...	...	...
2 Factor income to the rest of the world	1445	... 1030	6232	7896	7603	6969	7789	...	...	...	...	...
A Compensation of employees	162	... ...						...	...	...	...	...
B Property and entrepreneurial income	1283	... ...						...	...	...	...	...
3 Current transfers to the rest of the world	83	... 356	876	917	935	853	868	...	...	...	...	...
4 Surplus of the nation on current transactions	-1606	... -5484	2627	2701	-910	28	124	...	...	...	...	...
Payments to the Rest of the World and Surplus of the Nation on Current Transactions	6929	... 22302	59073	70593	67861	68136	70381	...	...	...	...	...

Algeria

1.7 External Transactions on Current Account, Summary
(Continued)

Million Algerian dinars

		1970	1975	1980	1981	1982	1983	1984	1985	1986	1987	1988	1989
				Receipts From The Rest of the World									
1	Exports of goods and services	5305	20714	55802	66182	64223	65344	67700	...	...	...	...	...
2	Factor income from rest of the world	1293	328	1560	2266	1546	1064	1079	...	...	...	...	...
	A Compensation of employees	1174	...	...	...	...	...	...	...	...	...	...	...
	B Property and entrepreneurial income	119	...	...	...	...	...	...	...	...	...	...	...
3	Current transfers from rest of the world	330	1260	1711	2145	2092	1728	1602	...	...	...	...	...
	Receipts from the Rest of the World on Current Transactions	6929	22302	59073	70593	67861	68136	70381	...	...	...	...	...

1.10 Gross Domestic Product by Kind of Activity, in Current Prices

Million Algerian dinars

		1970	1975	1980	1981	1982	1983	1984	1985	1986	1987	1988	1989
1	Agriculture, hunting, forestry and fishing	2428	4967	...	...	...	...	...	...	...	...	...	...
2	Mining and quarrying	3345	15904	...	...	...	...	...	...	...	...	...	...
3	Manufacturing	3367	5735	...	...	...	...	...	...	...	...	...	...
4	Electricity, gas and water	329	675	...	...	...	...	...	...	...	...	...	...
5	Construction	2229	6634	...	...	...	...	...	...	...	...	...	...
6	Wholesale and retail trade, restaurants and hotels	4600	5933	...	...	...	...	...	...	...	...	...	...
7	Transport, storage and communication	1263	2820	...	...	...	...	...	...	...	...	...	...
8	Finance, insurance, real estate and business services	1951	3459	...	...	...	...	...	...	...	...	...	...
9	Community, social and personal services	430	836	...	...	...	...	...	...	...	...	...	...
	Total, Industries	19942	46960	...	...	...	...	...	...	...	...	...	...
	Producers of Government Services	2732	6457	...	...	...	...	...	...	...	...	...	...
	Other Producers	...	...	...	...	...	...	...	...	...	...	...	...
	Subtotal	22674	53417	...	...	...	...	...	...	...	...	...	...
	Less: Imputed bank service charge	243	877	...	...	...	...	...	...	...	...	...	...
	Plus: Import duties	1652	4424	...	...	...	...	...	...	...	...	...	...
	Plus: Value added tax	...	...	...	...	...	...	...	...	...	...	...	...
	Plus: Other adjustments	-10	-249	...	...	...	...	...	...	...	...	...	...
	Equals: Gross Domestic Product	24073	56715	...	...	...	...	...	...	...	...	...	...

1.11 Gross Domestic Product by Kind of Activity, in Constant Prices

Million Algerian dinars

		1970	1975	1980	1981	1982	1983	1984	1985	1986	1987	1988	1989
				At constant prices of: 1974									
1	Agriculture, hunting, forestry and fishing	3376	4032	...	...	...	...	...	...	...	...	...	...
2	Mining and quarrying	16996	17749	...	...	...	...	...	...	...	...	...	...
3	Manufacturing	3832	5537	...	...	...	...	...	...	...	...	...	...
4	Electricity, gas and water	336	740	...	...	...	...	...	...	...	...	...	...
5	Construction	4721	6109	...	...	...	...	...	...	...	...	...	...
6	Wholesale and retail trade, restaurants and hotels	5207	5697	...	...	...	...	...	...	...	...	...	...
7	Transport, storage and communication	1412	2819	...	...	...	...	...	...	...	...	...	...
8	Finance, insurance, real estate and business services [a]	1687	2012	...	...	...	...	...	...	...	...	...	...
9	Community, social and personal services	481	777	...	...	...	...	...	...	...	...	...	...

Algeria

1.11 Gross Domestic Product by Kind of Activity, in Constant Prices
(Continued)

Million Algerian dinars

	1970	1975	1980	1981	1982	1983	1984	1985	1986	1987	1988	1989
				At constant prices of:1974								
Total, Industries	38048	45472	...	...	...	...	...	...	...	...	...	...
Producers of Government Services	...	...	...	...	...	...	...	...	...	...	...	...
Other Producers	...	...	...	...	...	...	...	...	...	...	...	...
Subtotal	...	...	...	...	...	...	...	...	...	...	...	...
Less: Imputed bank service charge	...	...	...	...	...	...	...	...	...	...	...	...
Plus: Import duties	...	...	...	...	...	...	...	...	...	...	...	...
Plus: Value added tax	...	...	...	...	...	...	...	...	...	...	...	...
Equals: Gross Domestic Product	...	...	...	...	...	...	...	...	...	...	...	...

a) Item 'Finance, insurance, real estate and business services' refers to real estate and business services only.

1.12 Relations Among National Accounting Aggregates

Million Algerian dinars

	1970	1975	1980	1981	1982	1983	1984	1985	1986	1987	1988	1989
Gross Domestic Product	24073	61574	162507	191469	207552	233752	259900	...	...	...	...	...
Plus: Net factor income from the rest of the world	-150	-702	-4672	-5630	-6057	-5904	-6710	...	...	...	...	...
Factor income from the rest of the world	1294	328	1560	2266	1546	1064	1079	...	...	...	...	...
Less: Factor income to the rest of the world	1444	1030	6232	7896	7603	6969	7789	...	...	...	...	...
Equals: Gross National Product	23923	60872	157835	185839	201495	227848	253190	...	...	...	...	...
Less: Consumption of fixed capital	1962	4915	13692	15150	18171	21504	...	...	...	...	...	...
Equals: National Income	21959	55957	144143	170689	183324	206344	...	...	...	...	...	...
Plus: Net current transfers from the rest of the world	247	904	836	1228	1157	874	734	...	...	...	...	...
Current transfers from the rest of the world	330	1260	1711	2145	2092	1728	1602	...	...	...	...	...
Less: Current transfers to the rest of the world	83	356	876	917	935	853	868	...	...	...	...	...
Equals: National Disposable Income	22207	56861	144979	171917	184481	207218	...	...	...	...	...	...
Less: Final consumption	17023	39423	92530	113530	126219	140876	159100	...	...	...	...	...
Statistical discrepancy	8	...	...	...	...	...	...	...	...	...	...	...
Equals: Net Saving	5192	17438	52449	58387	58262	66342	...	...	...	...	...	...
Less: Surplus of the nation on current transactions	-1606	-5484	2627	2701	-910	28	124	...	...	...	...	...
Statistical discrepancy	-8	...	...	...	...	...	...	...	...	...	...	...
Equals: Net Capital Formation	6790	22922	49822	55686	59172	66314	...	...	...	...	...	...

Angola

Source. Ministere du Plan du Government Angolais.

General note. The estimates shown in the following tables have been prepared in accordance with the United Nations System of National Accounts so far as the existing data would permit.

1.10 Gross Domestic Product by Kind of Activity, in Current Prices

Million Angolan kwanza

	1970	1975	1980	1981	1982	1983	1984	1985	1986	1987	1988	1989
1 Agriculture, hunting, forestry and fishing	...	...	...	...	...	16877	16074	14311	...	...	...	...
2 Mining and quarrying [a]	...	...	...	...	...	32980	41418	44601	...	...	...	...
3 Manufacturing [b]	...	...	...	...	...	9495	11576	12616	...	...	...	...
4 Electricity, gas and water	...	...	...	...	...	751	726	1030	...	...	...	...
5 Construction	...	...	...	...	...	3135	3378	6131	...	...	...	...
6 Wholesale and retail trade, restaurants and hotels	...	...	...	...	...	15636	14000	14656	...	...	...	...
7 Transport, storage and communication	...	...	...	...	...	4765	7489	7914	...	...	...	...
8 Finance, insurance, real estate and business services	...	...	...	...	...	34008	34554	35949	...	...	...	...
9 Community, social and personal services	...	...	...	...	...				...	...	...	...
Total, Industries	...	...	...	...	...	117647	129215	137208	...	...	...	...
Producers of Government Services	...	...	...	...	...	...	...	...	...	...	...	...
Other Producers	...	...	...	...	...	...	...	...	...	...	...	...
Subtotal [c]	...	...	...	...	...	117647	129215	137208	...	...	...	...
Less: Imputed bank service charge	...	...	...	...	...	...	...	...	...	...	...	...
Plus: Import duties	...	...	...	...	...	...	...	...	...	...	...	...
Plus: Value added tax	...	...	...	...	...	...	...	...	...	...	...	...
Plus: Other adjustments [d]	...	...	...	...	...	8710	12356	7537	...	...	...	...
Equals: Gross Domestic Product	...	...	...	...	...	126357	141570	144747	...	...	...	...

a) Item 'Mining and quarrying' refers to the extraction and refining of petroleum.
b) Mining is included in item 'Manufacturing'.
c) Gross domestic product in factor values.
d) Item 'Other adjustments' refers to indirect taxes net of subsidies.

1.12 Relations Among National Accounting Aggregates

Million Angolan kwanza

	1970	1975	1980	1981	1982	1983	1984	1985	1986	1987	1988	1989
Gross Domestic Product	...	...	...	...	...	126357	141570	144747	...	...	...	...
Plus: Net factor income from the rest of the world	...	...	...	...	...	-1021	-1716	-6977	...	...	...	...
Equals: Gross National Product	...	...	...	...	...	125336	139854	137770	...	...	...	...
Less: Consumption of fixed capital	...	...	...	...	...	...	...	...	...	...	...	...
Equals: National Income	...	...	...	...	...	...	...	...	...	...	...	...
Plus: Net current transfers from the rest of the world	...	...	...	...	...	...	...	...	...	...	...	...
Equals: National Disposable Income	...	...	...	...	...	...	...	...	...	...	...	...
Less: Final consumption	...	...	...	...	...	...	...	...	...	...	...	...
Equals: Net Saving	...	...	...	...	...	...	...	...	...	...	...	...
Less: Surplus of the nation on current transactions	...	...	...	...	...	...	...	...	...	...	...	...
Equals: Net Capital Formation	...	...	...	...	...	...	...	...	...	...	...	...

Anguilla

Source. The official estimates of the National Accounts of Anguilla was published for the first time in 'Anguilla - National Accounts Statistics, 1984-1987' by the Ministry of Finance and Economic Development on May 1988.

General note. The estimates shown in the following tables have been prepared in accordance with the United Nations System of National Accounts so far as the existing data would permit.

1.1 Expenditure on the Gross Domestic Product, in Current Prices

Thousand East Caribbean dollars

	1970	1975	1980	1981	1982	1983	1984	1985	1986	1987	1988	1989
1 Government final consumption expenditure	...	...	...	...	...	...	7116	7843	9219	11984	...	...
2 Private final consumption expenditure	...	...	...	...	...	...	23705	24255	26943	28384	...	...
3 Gross capital formation	...	...	...	...	...	...	11528	13410	15733	19670	...	...
A Increase in stocks	...	...	...	...	...	...	-	-	-	-	...	...
B Gross fixed capital formation	...	...	...	...	...	...	11528	13410	15733	19670	...	...
4 Exports of goods and services	...	...	...	...	...	...	14242	22334	31438	38642	...	...
5 Less: Imports of goods and services	...	...	...	...	...	...	20992	22363	25905	29789	...	...
Equals: Gross Domestic Product [a]	...	...	...	...	...	...	35601	45479	57428	68891	...	...

a) Data for this table have not been revised, therefore, data for some years are not comparable with those of other tables.

1.4 General Government Current Receipts and Disbursements

Thousand East Caribbean dollars

	1970	1975	1980	1981	1982	1983	1984	1985	1986	1987	1988	1989
Receipts												
1 Operating surplus	...	...	...	...	...	...	...	...	...	...	...	...
2 Property and entrepreneurial income	...	...	...	...	...	...	883	350	1136	780	1778	1791
3 Taxes, fees and contributions	...	...	...	...	...	...	5887	7914	11276	14811	18346	24315
A Indirect taxes	...	...	...	...	...	...	4973	6941	9993	12846	15776	21169
B Direct taxes	...	...	...	...	...	...	93	56	64	109	132	44
C Social security contributions	...	...	...	...	...	...	821	917	1219	1856	2438	3102
D Compulsory fees, fines and penalties	...	...	...	...	...	...	...	...	...	...	...	...
4 Other current transfers	...	...	...	...	...	...	2309	1317	1872	1749	1754	1627
Total Current Receipts of General Government	...	...	...	...	...	...	9079	9581	14284	17340	21878	27733
Disbursements												
1 Government final consumption expenditure	...	...	...	...	...	...	7116	7843	9219	11984	14970	17875
A Compensation of employees	...	...	...	...	...	...	6004	6922	8386	9886	13102	14895
B Consumption of fixed capital	...	...	...	...	...	...	...	...	...	...	...	...
C Purchases of goods and services, net	...	...	...	...	...	...	2549	2579	3398	4323	4432	5886
D Less: Own account fixed capital formation	...	...	...	...	...	...	...	...	...	...	...	...
E Indirect taxes paid, net	...	...	...	...	...	...	...	...	...	...	...	...
2 Property income	...	...	...	...	...	...	-	-	-	61	135	397
3 Subsidies	...	...	...	...	...	...	292	182	15	15	15	23
4 Other current transfers	...	...	...	...	...	...	1075	1152	1334	1547	1829	2101
A Social security benefits	...	...	...	...	...	...	48	67	109	182	259	292
B Social assistance grants	...	...	...	...	...	...	...	...	...	...	...	...
C Other	...	...	...	...	...	...	1027	1085	1225	1365	1570	1809
5 Net saving	...	...	...	...	...	...	596	404	3716	3733	4929	7337
Total Current Disbursements and Net Saving of General Government	...	...	...	...	...	...	9079	9581	14284	17340	21878	27733

1.10 Gross Domestic Product by Kind of Activity, in Current Prices

Thousand East Caribbean dollars

	1970	1975	1980	1981	1982	1983	1984	1985	1986	1987	1988	1989
1 Agriculture, hunting, forestry and fishing	...	...	...	...	...	...	2480	2810	2990	3130	3290	4520
2 Mining and quarrying	...	...	...	...	...	...	680	540	770	890	800	750
3 Manufacturing	...	...	...	...	...	...	380	500	540	770	780	810
4 Electricity, gas and water	...	...	...	...	...	...	640	700	1530	1250	2290	2030
5 Construction	...	...	...	...	...	...	6070	7080	11690	15840	18780	20090

Anguilla

1.10 Gross Domestic Product by Kind of Activity, in Current Prices
(Continued)

Thousand East Caribbean dollars

	1970	1975	1980	1981	1982	1983	1984	1985	1986	1987	1988	1989
6 Wholesale and retail trade, restaurants and hotels	...	...	...	...	...	...	9500	13170	15650	17120	24140	30780
7 Transport, storage and communication	...	...	...	...	...	...	4910	6100	7390	9570	12120	12900
8 Finance, insurance, real estate and business services	...	...	...	...	...	...	5070	5340	6420	8220	10750	13720
9 Community, social and personal services [a]	...	...	...	...	...	...	690	780	940	1290	1380	1490
Total, Industries	...	...	...	...	...	...	30420	37020	47920	58080	74330	87090
Producers of Government Services	...	...	...	...	...	...	6010	6930	8400	9900	13120	14910
Other Producers [a]	...	...	...	...	...	...	...	...	...	...	...	...
Subtotal [b]	...	...	...	...	...	...	36430	43950	56320	67980	87450	102000
Less: Imputed bank service charge	...	...	...	...	...	...	1970	2420	3200	4280	6530	9580
Plus: Import duties	...	...	...	...	...	...	...	...	...	...	...	...
Plus: Value added tax	...	...	...	...	...	...	...	...	...	...	...	...
Plus: Other adjustments [c]	...	...	...	...	...	...	4681	6759	9978	12831	15761	21146
Equals: Gross Domestic Product	...	...	...	...	...	...	39141	48289	63098	76531	96681	113566

a) Item 'Other producers' is included in item 'Community, social and personal services'.
b) Gross domestic product in factor values.
c) Item 'Other adjustments' refers to incirect taxes net of subsidies.

1.11 Gross Domestic Product by Kind of Activity, in Constant Prices

Thousand East Caribbean dollars

	1970	1975	1980	1981	1982	1983	1984	1985	1986	1987	1988	1989
				At constant prices of:1984								
1 Agriculture, hunting, forestry and fishing	...	...	...	...	...	...	2480	2710	2850	2910	3040	3650
2 Mining and quarrying	...	...	...	...	...	...	680	580	740	840	760	660
3 Manufacturing	...	...	...	...	...	...	380	440	470	610	630	640
4 Electricity, gas and water	...	...	...	...	...	...	640	760	820	690	1350	1560
5 Construction	...	...	...	...	...	...	6070	5900	8190	9500	10430	11160
6 Wholesale and retail trade, restaurants and hotels	...	...	...	...	...	...	9500	11590	13210	14290	17890	19100
7 Transport, storage and communication	...	...	...	...	...	...	4910	5970	6680	8400	9180	9450
8 Finance, insurance, real estate and business services	...	...	...	...	...	...	5070	5240	5510	6040	7050	7710
9 Community, social and personal services [a]	...	...	...	...	...	...	690	770	900	1210	1250	1300
Total, Industries	...	...	...	...	...	...	30420	33960	39370	44490	51580	55230
Producers of Government Services	...	...	...	...	...	...	6010	6230	6650	7290	7570	7710
Other Producers [a]	...	...	...	...	...	...	...	...	...	...	...	...
Subtotal	...	...	...	...	...	...	36430	40190	46020	51780	59150	62940
Less: Imputed bank service charge	...	...	...	...	...	...	1970	2410	2830	3680	5240	6010
Plus: Import duties	...	...	...	...	...	...	...	...	...	...	...	...
Plus: Value added tax	...	...	...	...	...	...	...	...	...	...	...	...
Equals: Gross Domestic Product [b]	...	...	...	...	...	...	34460	37780	43190	48100	53910	56930

a) Item 'Other producers' is included in item 'Community, social and personal services'.
b) Gross domestic product in factor values.

2.1 Government Final Consumption Expenditure by Function, in Current Prices

Thousand East Caribbean dollars

	1970	1975	1980	1981	1982	1983	1984	1985	1986	1987	1988	1989
1 General public services	...	...	...	...	...	...	1665	1790	1691	3166	3772	4030
2 Defence	...	...	...	...	...	...	...	...	...	...	...	...
3 Public order and safety	...	...	...	...	...	...	771	969	1213	1394	1798	2162
4 Education	...	...	...	...	...	...	1658	1872	2149	2817	3314	4201
5 Health	...	...	...	...	...	...	1022	1158	1456	1531	2116	2945
6 Social security and welfare	...	...	...	...	...	...	122	140	343	359	362	370
7 Housing and community amenities	...	...	...	...	...	...	563	502	735	880	978	1288
8 Recreational, cultural and religious affairs	...	...	...	...	...	...	...	...	...	...	...	...
9 Economic services	...	...	...	...	...	...	559	695	506	1056	946	1918

Anguilla

2.1 Government Final Consumption Expenditure by Function, in Current Prices
(Continued)

Thousand East Caribbean dollars

	1970	1975	1980	1981	1982	1983	1984	1985	1986	1987	1988	1989
A Fuel and energy	...	...	...	...	...	...	...	...	...	...	...	...
B Agriculture, forestry, fishing and hunting	...	...	...	...	...	...	192	223	232	263	417	489
C Mining, manufacturing and construction, except fuel and energy	...	...	...	...	...	...	...	...	...	...	...	...
D Transportation and communication	...	...	...	...	...	...	307	323	227	700	434	767
E Other economic affairs	...	...	...	...	...	...	60	149	47	93	95	662
10 Other functions	...	...	...	...	...	...	756	717	1126	781	1684	961
Total Government Final Consumption Expenditure	...	...	...	...	...	...	7116	7843	9219	11984	14970	17875

Antigua and Barbuda

Source. 'Economic Survey and Projections', British Development Division in the Caribbean.

General note. The estimates shown in the following tables have been prepared in accordance with the United Nations System of National Accounts so far as the existing data would permit.

1.1 Expenditure on the Gross Domestic Product, in Current Prices

Million East Caribbean dollars

	1970	1975	1980	1981	1982	1983	1984	1985	1986	1987	1988	1989
1 Government final consumption expenditure	...	...	57.4	63.4	70.8	83.2	86.5	98.7	121.2	...	...	...
2 Private final consumption expenditure	...	...	204.0	217.1	202.2	225.0	327.0	386.5	447.6	...	...	...
3 Gross capital formation	...	...	93.5	145.9	146.9	84.6	110.6	151.6	231.9	...	...	...
A Increase in stocks	...	...	-	-	-	-	-	-	-	...	...	...
B Gross fixed capital formation	...	...	93.5	145.9	146.9	84.6	110.6	151.6	231.9	...	...	...
4 Exports of goods and services	...	...	200.0	230.7	219.3	270.3	345.3	409.5	482.7	...	...	...
5 Less: Imports of goods and services	...	...	257.6	321.2	266.8	249.2	401.0	505.6	641.5	...	...	...
Equals: Gross Domestic Product	...	...	297.3	335.9	372.4	413.9	468.4	540.7	641.9	...	...	...

1.10 Gross Domestic Product by Kind of Activity, in Current Prices

Million East Caribbean dollars

	1970	1975	1980	1981	1982	1983	1984	1985	1986	1987	1988	1989
1 Agriculture, hunting, forestry and fishing	...	9.6	18.3	19.6	19.7	21.8	19.3	23.2	24.6	29.3	32.1	...
2 Mining and quarrying	...	0.7	1.5	1.7	1.5	2.3	3.0	4.6	9.9	14.4	16.8	...
3 Manufacturing	...	11.1	13.7	14.6	16.8	17.6	19.3	20.3	21.5	23.0	24.1	...
4 Electricity, gas and water	...	1.4	8.2	9.4	7.6	10.3	12.5	17.2	19.9	22.4	31.3	...
5 Construction	...	9.0	23.2	27.7	20.4	20.5	27.3	35.7	50.6	73.1	98.9	...
6 Wholesale and retail trade, restaurants and hotels	...	26.5	66.4	70.7	77.2	84.2	101.8	121.7	133.6	156.3	183.9	...
7 Transport, storage and communication	...	20.1	41.6	48.2	56.9	63.5	70.9	81.4	88.4	101.0	110.8	...
8 Finance, insurance, real estate and business services	...	24.0	42.2	48.6	56.7	65.3	74.5	79.9	85.0	94.2	103.7	...
9 Community, social and personal services	...	6.7	16.7	19.9	23.4	28.1	33.2	39.2	43.9	46.6	49.5	...
Total, Industries	...	109.0	231.8	260.4	280.2	313.6	361.8	423.2	477.4	560.3	651.1	...
Producers of Government Services	...	15.3	35.6	42.1	53.8	59.5	63.4	67.9	89.7	88.5	125.3	...
Other Producers	...	...	...	...	...	...	...	...	...	...	...	...
Subtotal a	...	124.3	267.4	302.5	334.0	373.1	425.2	491.1	567.1	648.8	776.4	...
Less: Imputed bank service charge	...	3.7	10.3	13.1	16.9	17.0	21.9	26.1	30.0	32.7	35.8	...
Plus: Import duties	...	...	...	...	...	...	...	...	...	...	...	...
Plus: Value added tax	...	...	...	...	...	...	...	...	...	...	...	...
Plus: Other adjustments b	...	...	40.0	46.7	55.3	57.7	65.0	75.9	104.7	...	...	...
Equals: Gross Domestic Product	...	120.6	297.1	336.1	372.4	413.8	468.3	540.9	641.8	...	...	...

a) Beginning 1977, gross domestic product in factor values.
b) Item 'Other adjustments' refers to indirect taxes net of subsidies.

1.11 Gross Domestic Product by Kind of Activity, in Constant Prices

Million East Caribbean dollars

	1970	1975	1980	1981	1982	1983	1984	1985	1986	1987	1988	1989
		1975			At constant prices of:			1977				
1 Agriculture, hunting, forestry and fishing	...	9.6	13.9	12.4	11.7	11.6	9.3	9.5	10.1	11.3	11.9	...
2 Mining and quarrying	...	0.7	1.2	1.1	0.9	1.1	1.6	2.5	5.6	7.6	8.3	...
3 Manufacturing	...	11.1	11.4	13.9	13.9	14.2	14.8	15.2	15.8	16.5	16.8	...
4 Electricity, gas and water	...	1.4	6.1	6.9	7.4	8.1	8.0	9.0	9.9	10.6	12.6	...
5 Construction	...	9.0	17.2	18.9	11.7	10.8	13.0	16.8	22.7	31.0	35.4	...

Antigua and Barbuda

1.11 Gross Domestic Product by Kind of Activity, in Constant Prices
(Continued)

Million East Caribbean dollars

	1970	1975	1980	1981	1982	1983	1984	1985	1986	1987	1988	1989
		At constant prices of:										
		1975					1977					
6 Wholesale and retail trade, restaurants and hotels	...	26.5	... 46.5	46.5	47.7	52.7	62.1	67.2	71.7	76.7	83.7	...
7 Transport, storage and communication	...	20.1	... 35.5	37.8	43.4	48.8	52.4	55.6	58.6	61.9	66.8	...
8 Finance, insurance, real estate and business services	...	24.0	... 34.6	36.4	36.1	37.8	38.9	40.6	42.3	44.1	46.3	...
9 Community, social and personal services	...	6.7	... 13.0	14.8	14.9	16.3	17.3	18.7	18.9	19.3	19.7	...
Total, Industries	...	109.0	... 179.4	188.7	187.7	201.4	217.4	235.1	255.6	279.0	301.5	...
Producers of Government Services	...	15.3	... 23.7	24.5	24.9	26.1	26.9	27.8	29.2	30.4	31.1	...
Other Producers	...	...	...	...	...	...	...	...	...	...	...	...
Subtotal	...	124.3	... 203.1	213.2	212.6	227.5	244.3	262.9	284.8	309.4	332.6	...
Less: Imputed bank service charge	...	3.7	... 8.9	9.4	8.0	8.9	9.4	9.8	10.4	11.0	11.7	...
Plus: Import duties	...	...	...	...	...	...	...	...	...	...	...	...
Plus: Value added tax	...	...	...	...	...	...	...	...	...	...	...	...
Equals: Gross Domestic Product [a]	...	120.6	... 194.2	203.8	204.6	218.6	234.9	253.1	274.4	298.3	320.9	...

a) Gross domestic product in factor values.

2.1 Government Final Consumption Expenditure by Function, in Current Prices

Thousand East Caribbean dollars

	1970	1975	1980	1981	1982	1983	1984	1985	1986	1987	1988	1989
1 General public services	...	...	12625	13625	13018	13821	15232	20238	28170	...	...	...
2 Defence	...	...	505	884	1106	1445	1475	1757	2453	...	...	...
3 Public order and safety	...	...	4581	5363	6857	6732	7643	9203	12527	...	...	...
4 Education	...	...	7286	9242	10351	10871	10595	11267	15885	...	...	...
5 Health	...	...	3823	5147	6434	5831	6496	9252	10754	...	...	...
6 Social security and welfare	...	...	4234	4151	4456	5770	5634	5329	7815	...	...	...
7 Housing and community amenities	...	...	2846	3098	4447	4831	4468	6171	6858	...	...	...
8 Recreational, cultural and religious affairs	...	...	201	196	201	229	317	458	556	...	...	...
9 Economic services	...	...	13743	12487	12660	18541	15085	16855	22846	...	...	...
A Fuel and energy	...	...	-	-239	-	24	24	91	175	...	...	...
B Agriculture, forestry, fishing and hunting	...	...	2164	2196	2526	2637	2570	3414	4906	...	...	...
C Mining, manufacturing and construction, except fuel and energy	...	...	7823	7884	7713	11590	8901	8889	11095	...	...	...
D Transportation and communication										...	...	...
E Other economic affairs	...	...	3756	2646	2421	4290	3590	4461	6670	...	...	...
10 Other functions	...	...	7	-	-	38	-	-	40	...	...	...
Total Government Final Consumption Expenditure [a]	...	...	49851	54193	59530	68109	66945	80530	107904	...	...	...

a) Only central government data are included in the general government estimates.

Argentina

General note. The preparation of national accounts statistics in Argentina is undertaken by Banco Central de la Republica Argentina, Buenos Aires. The official estimates are published on a quarterly basis in the 'Economic Reports'. In 1975 the publication 'Sistema de Cuentas del Producto e Ingreso de la Argentina' was presented. Volume I 'Metodologia y Fuentes' contains a detailed description of the sources and methods used for the national accounts estimation. Volume II 'Cuadros Estadisticos' presents estimates for the period 1950-1973, in accordance with the United Nations System of National Accounts (SNA). On 15 June 1985, a new currency called the Austral was introduced. One Austral is equivalent to 1,000 Pesos Argentinos. The following tables have been prepared from successive replies to the United Nations national accounts questionnaire. When the scope and coverage of the estimates differ for conceptual or statistical reasons from the definitions and classifications recommended in SNA, a footnote is indicated to the relevant tables.

Sources and methods:

(a) Gross domestic product. The main approach used to estimate GDP is the production approach.

(b) Expenditure on the gross domestic product. The expenditure approach is used to estimate government final consumption expenditure, increase in stocks, investment in construction, and exports and imports of goods and services. The commodity-flow approach is used to estimate the current value of gross investment other than for construction. Private final consumption expenditure is taken as a residual. Government final consumption expenditure, consisting of compensation of employees and net purchases of goods and services, is obtained from government accounts. Investment in construction is estimated through the use of accounting data for the public sector, agricultural census data for the agricultural sector, and construction licenses and miscellaneous sources for the urban private construction. The estimation of domestically produced capital goods is done on the basis of the industrial censuses. For the years between censuses, the data are up-dated through a combination of indexes of physical output and price indexes. Data on exports and imports of goods and services are obtained from the balance of payments accounts. Constant values of government consumption expenditures are obtained through extrapolating wages and salaries by the number of persons employed and through deflating purchases of goods and services by the wholesale price index for non-agricultural goods. Private consumption expenditure at constant prices is obtained as a residual. The current values of construction are deflated by indexes of construction costs or extrapolated by input volumes. Domestic machinery and equipment products are deflated by index of producer prices or extrapolated by volume of production. Imported machinery and equipment are deflated by price indexes. Price deflation is used for exports and imports of goods and services.

(c) Cost-structure of the gross domestic product. The estimates of compensation of employees are based on employment data, remuneration data and collective wage agreement data. Intercensal estimates are rough, except for those activities for which accounting data are available. Operating surplus is, in general, obtained as a residual. Consumption of fixed capital is calculated on the basis of accounting data from public enterprises, capital stock data in the case of private construction, gross investment data and estimated depreciation rates in the case of durable production equipment. Information on indirect taxes is obtained by type of government authority.

(d) Gross domestic product by kind of economic activity. The table of gross domestic product by kind of economic activity is prepared in factor values. The production approach is used to estimate value added of most industries. The basic statistics on agricultural production are obtained from the Secretaria de Agricultura y Ganaderia de la Nacion. The production is valued at farmers' prices, which are obtained by subtracting transportation costs and commercial mark-ups from wholesale prices. Production estimates for beef, mutton and pork, are defined as the value of sales for slaughter, adjusted for changes in stocks and exports of live animal. Own account consumption of agricultural products and meat is included in the estimates. Since no annual information is available, indirect indicators are used to estimate the value of intermediate consumption. For mining, information on quantities and prices is obtained from the government authorities concerned. Input data are supplied by state companies and balance sheets of a representative sample of mining enterprises. The general method used in estimating industrial production is by interpolating prices and quantities between census years. After the latest industrial census of 1963, extrapolation is used, based on changes in the production volume. Information on prices is obtained from the wholesale price index and miscellaneous sources for products not included in that index. Data on the number of construction permits issued are used to estimate the value of construction in the private sector. The data are converted into value figures by using the cost of construction index. Intermediate consumption is estimated from analysis of budgets, surveys, etc. For the public sector, data are obtained from the accounts of official organizations and state enterprises. Intermediate consumption is estimated on the basis of coefficients obtained from a study of records in the field of public works. Gross output of the trade sector is estimated through applying gross percentage mark-up rates to the value of goods recorded as entering the various marketing channels. Input values are based on information from balance sheets of joint stock companies and other inquiries. Value added in the transport sector is estimated from financial statements and accounts data, direct information or from survey data. For financial intermediaries the data used is based on the financial statements of all credit institutions in the country. The data needed to calculate value added of insurance services is provided by the Super-intendencia de Seguros de la Nacion. The value of rents paid is calculated on the basis of the population censuses and the rent component of the consumer price index. In the case of owner-occupied dwellings, the average gross rent for rented dwellings is applied. The value added of the producers of government, provincial government and local government services is based on the accounts and budget data of the concerned authorities. Business services and other professional services are estimated through population census data and income data. The value of domestic services is obtained by multiplying the number of employees by their average compensation. For the estimates in constant prices, extrapolation of the base year value by indexes of production volume or output quantity and occasionally of employment data are used for all sectors except public construction, in which case the current values are deflated by an index of construction costs.

1.1 Expenditure on the Gross Domestic Product, in Current Prices

Thousand Australes

	1970	1975	1980	1981	1982	1983	1984	1985	1986	1987	1988	1989
1 Government final consumption expenditure	1	19	3740	7474	16454	89136	...	...	...	...	...	...
2 Private final consumption expenditure [a]	6	87	18773	37515	101391	441931	...	...	...	...	...	...
3 Gross capital formation [b]	2	38	6440	10001	25010	118315	...	...	...	...	...	...
A Increase in stocks [b]	-	1	157	-271	1612	449	...	...	...	...	...	...
B Gross fixed capital formation	2	37	6283	10271	23399	117866	...	...	...	...	...	...
Residential buildings							...	...	...	...	...	...
Non-residential buildings	1	26	4390	7440	16419	78734	...	...	...	...	...	...
Other construction and land improvement etc.							...	...	...	...	...	...
Other	1	11	1892	2831	6979	39132	...	...	...	...	...	...
4 Exports of goods and services	1	11	1944	5173	19865	100165	...	...	...	...	...	...
5 Less: Imports of goods and services	1	12	2560	5410	15107	66895	...	...	...	...	...	...
Equals: Gross Domestic Product [c]	9	143	28337	54752	147613	682652	5281	39593	74309	173109	784793	25580259

a) Item 'Private final consumption expenditure' has been obtained as a residual.
b) Item 'Gross capital formation' includes increases of stocks of principal agricultural products and an important group of raw materials and manufactured goods. Other increases of stocks are included in private final consumption expenditure.
c) For the years 1984-1989, the estimates are in million Australes.

Argentina

1.2 Expenditure on the Gross Domestic Product, in Constant Prices

Australes

		1970	1975	1980	1981	1982	1983	1984	1985	1986	1987	1988	1989
		\multicolumn{12}{c}{At constant prices of:1970}
1	Government final consumption expenditure	6894	8176	9395	9005	8049	8365	8875	8329	8994	9100	8490	8148
2	Private final consumption expenditure												
3	Gross capital formation a	1860	2045	2674	2049	1645	1470	1307	1046	1228	1437	1282	885
	A Increase in stocks a	-1	78	99	-73	107	12	-19	-126	-48	-18	59	-3
	B Gross fixed capital formation	1861	1967	2576	2122	1538	1458	1326	1172	1276	1454	1223	888
	Residential buildings												
	Non-residential buildings	1161	1226	1457	1279	999	885	738	669	718	817	700	488
	Other construction and land improvement etc.												
	Other	700	741	1119	843	540	573	588	502	558	637	523	400
4	Exports of goods and services	810	771	1291	1362	1410	1519	1508	1697	1578	1563	1900	1988
5	Less: Imports of goods and services	789	890	2068	1869	1077	1026	1089	931	1094	1161	1029	849
	Equals: Gross Domestic Product	8775	10103	11292	10547	10026	10328	10602	10141	10706	10939	10643	10171

a) Item 'Gross capital formation' includes increases of stocks of principal agricultural products and an important group of raw materials and manufactured goods. Other increases of stocks are included in private final consumption expenditure.

1.3 Cost Components of the Gross Domestic Product

Thousand Australes

		1970	1975	1980	1981	1982	1983	1984	1985	1986	1987	1988	1989
1	Indirect taxes, net	1	9	4671	7496	17293	56816	...	...	...	...	...	...
2	Consumption of fixed capital	...	...	...	...	...	...	...	...	...	...	...	...
3	Compensation of employees paid by resident producers to:	...	...	...	...	...	...	...	...	...	...	...	...
4	Operating surplus	...	...	...	...	...	...	...	...	...	...	...	...
	Equals: Gross Domestic Product	9	143	28337	54752	147613	682652	...	...	...	...	...	...

1.4 General Government Current Receipts and Disbursements

Thousand Australes

		1970	1975	1980	1981	1982	1983	1984	1985	1986	1987	1988	1989
		\multicolumn{12}{c}{Receipts}
1	Operating surplus	-	1	135	...	...	...	...	...	...	...	...	...
2	Property and entrepreneurial income	-	-	271	...	...	...	...	...	...	...	...	...
3	Taxes, fees and contributions	2	22	8403	...	...	...	...	...	...	...	...	...
	A Indirect taxes	1	12	4886	...	...	...	...	...	...	...	...	...
	B Direct taxes	-	2	684	...	...	...	...	...	...	...	...	...
	C Social security contributions	1	8	2739	...	...	...	...	...	...	...	...	...
	D Compulsory fees, fines and penalties	-	-	94	...	...	...	...	...	...	...	...	...
4	Other current transfers	-	-	7	...	...	...	...	...	...	...	...	...
	Total Current Receipts of General Government	2	23	8816	...	...	...	...	...	...	...	...	...
		\multicolumn{12}{c}{Disbursements}
1	Government final consumption expenditure	1	19	4083	...	...	...	...	...	...	...	...	...
	A Compensation of employees	1	16	3137	...	...	...	...	...	...	...	...	...
	B Consumption of fixed capital	...	...	...	...	...	...	...	...	...	...	...	...
	C Purchases of goods and services, net	-	2	946	...	...	...	...	...	...	...	...	...
	D Less: Own account fixed capital formation	...	...	...	...	...	...	...	...	...	...	...	...
	E Indirect taxes paid, net	...	...	...	...	...	...	...	...	...	...	...	...
2	Property income	-	1	599	...	...	...	...	...	...	...	...	...
	A Interest	-	1	599	...	...	...	...	...	...	...	...	...
	B Net land rent and royalties	...	...	...	...	...	...	...	...	...	...	...	...

Argentina

1.4 General Government Current Receipts and Disbursements
(Continued)

Thousand Australes

		1970	1975	1980	1981	1982	1983	1984	1985	1986	1987	1988	1989
3	Subsidies	-	5	444	...	...	...	...	...	...	...	...	...
4	Other current transfers	1	10	3219	...	...	...	...	...	...	...	...	...
	A Social security benefits	1	9	2925	...	...	...	...	...	...	...	...	...
	B Social assistance grants	...	...	...	...	...	...	...	...	...	...	...	...
	C Other	-	1	294	...	...	...	...	...	...	...	...	...
5	Net saving	-	-11	471	...	...	...	...	...	...	...	...	...
	Total Current Disbursements and Net Saving of General Government	2	23	8816	...	...	...	...	...	...	...	...	...

1.10 Gross Domestic Product by Kind of Activity, in Current Prices

Thousand Australes

		1970	1975	1980	1981	1982	1983	1984	1985	1986	1987	1988	1989
1	Agriculture, hunting, forestry and fishing	1	13	2436	4939	17383	86377	...	...	...	...	...	...
2	Mining and quarrying	-	3	670	1590	4514	26955	...	...	...	...	...	...
3	Manufacturing	3	46	7082	13147	41918	210154	...	...	...	...	...	...
4	Electricity, gas and water	-	3	718	1632	2513	17216	...	...	...	...	...	...
5	Construction	1	11	2000	3306	7206	42344	...	...	...	...	...	...
6	Wholesale and retail trade, restaurants and hotels	1	22	5106	9716	24499	112520	...	...	...	...	...	...
7	Transport, storage and communication	1	11	2171	4414	9244	38661	...	...	...	...	...	...
8	Finance, insurance, real estate and business services	1	12	3885	7583	21383	43522	...	...	...	...	...	...
9	Community, social and personal services	-	6	1299	2894	7269	32862	...	...	...	...	...	...
	Total, Industries	8	127	25367	49221	135929	610611	...	...	...	...	...	...
	Producers of Government Services	1	16	2971	5532	11683	72041	...	...	...	...	...	...
	Other Producers	...	...	...	...	...	...	...	...	...	...	...	...
	Subtotal	9	143	28338	54753	147612	682652	...	...	...	...	...	...
	Less: Imputed bank service charge	...	...	...	...	...	...	...	...	...	...	...	...
	Plus: Import duties	...	...	...	...	...	...	...	...	...	...	...	...
	Plus: Value added tax	...	...	...	...	...	...	...	...	...	...	...	...
	Equals: Gross Domestic Product	9	143	28338	54753	147612	682652	...	...	...	...	...	...

1.11 Gross Domestic Product by Kind of Activity, in Constant Prices

Australes

		1970	1975	1980	1981	1982	1983	1984	1985	1986	1987	1988	1989
		\multicolumn{12}{c}{At constant prices of:1970}
1	Agriculture, hunting, forestry and fishing	1023	1172	1256	1280	1370	1403	1446	1421	1375	1415	1409	1375
2	Mining and quarrying	178	193	246	248	249	250	248	242	232	233	255	263
3	Manufacturing	2099	2485	2464	2078	1973	2170	2257	2024	2284	2272	2118	1969
4	Electricity, gas and water	181	263	351	347	358	387	412	418	449	476	499	492
5	Construction	503	527	652	567	437	380	304	284	311	357	305	207
6	Wholesale and retail trade, restaurants and hotels	1183	1342	1619	1464	1261	1315	1374	1260	1371	1390	1302	1197
7	Transport, storage and communication	381	959	1061	1020	993	1034	1091	1049	1101	1130	1098	1065
8	Finance, insurance, real estate and business services	592	634	895	847	750	698	707	698	747	769	764	745
9	Community, social and personal services	377	447	526	545	535	550	564	572	582	586	590	595
	Total, Industries	7017	8022	9070	8396	7926	8187	8403	7968	8452	8628	8340	7908
	Producers of Government Services	759	929	934	948	956	965	991	1017	1034	1065	1088	1104
	Other Producers	...	...	...	...	...	...	...	...	...	...	...	...
	Subtotal a	7774	8951	10005	9345	8883	9150	9393	8984	9486	9692	9429	9012
	Less: Imputed bank service charge	...	...	...	...	...	...	...	...	...	...	...	...
	Plus: Import duties	...	...	...	...	...	...	...	...	...	...	...	...
	Plus: Value added tax	...	...	...	...	...	...	...	...	...	...	...	...
	Plus: Other adjustments b	1001	1152	1287	1202	1143	1178	1209	1157	1220	1247	1214	1159
	Equals: Gross Domestic Product	8775	10103	11292	10547	10026	10328	10602	10141	10706	10939	10643	10171

a) Gross domestic product in factor values.
b) Item 'Other adjustments' refers to indirect taxes net of subsidies.

Argentina

4.1 Derivation of Value Added by Kind of Activity, in Current Prices

Thousand Australes

		1980			1981			1982			1983		
		Gross Output	Intermediate Consumption	Value Added	Gross Output	Intermediate Consumption	Value Added	Gross Output	Intermediate Consumption	Value Added	Gross Output	Intermediate Consumption	Value Added
					All Producers								
1	Agriculture, hunting, forestry and fishing	3236	801	2436	6407	1468	4939	22813	5430	17383	112362	25985	86377
	A Agriculture and hunting	...	...	2360	...	...	4802	...	...	16979	...	...	84356
	B Forestry and logging	...	...	40	...	...	56	...	...	190	...	...	1043
	C Fishing	...	...	36	...	...	81	...	...	214	...	...	978
2	Mining and quarrying	1131	461	670	2652	1062	1590	7894	3379	4514	54261	27306	26955
	A Coal mining	...	...	...	...	...	...	...	...	...	...	...	...
	B Crude petroleum and natural gas production	...	...	585	...	...	1398	...	...	4145	...	...	23684
	C Metal ore mining	...	...	15	...	...	33	...	...	143	...	...	778
	D Other mining	...	...	70	...	...	159	...	...	226	...	...	2493
3	Manufacturing	17009	9927	7082	31817	18670	13147	103410	61492	41918	509347	299194	210153
	A Manufacture of food, beverages and tobacco	...	...	1634	...	...	3257	...	...	9052	...	...	40415
	B Textile, wearing apparel and leather industries	...	...	600	...	...	1010	...	...	3836	...	...	21137
	C Manufacture of wood and wood products, including furniture	...	...	157	...	...	306	...	...	840	...	...	4051
	D Manufacture of paper and paper products, printing and publishing	...	...	378	...	...	738	...	...	2123	...	...	10544
	E Manufacture of chemicals and chemical petroleum, coal, rubber and plastic products	...	...	1365	...	...	3062	...	...	10031	...	...	52345
	F Manufacture of non-metallic mineral products, except products of petroleum and coal	...	...	432	...	...	784	...	...	2199	...	...	10592
	G Basic metal industries	...	...	471	...	...	842	...	...	3948	...	...	18119
	H Manufacture of fabricated metal products, machinery and equipment	...	...	1662	...	...	2461	...	...	7696	...	...	41896
	I Other manufacturing industries	...	...	382	...	...	688	...	...	2192	...	...	11054
4	Electricity, gas and water	1206	487	718	2975	1344	1632	7295	4782	2513	54880	37664	17216
	A Electricity, gas and steam	...	...	629	...	...	1444	...	...	2135	...	...	15855
	B Water works and supply	...	...	90	...	...	187	...	...	378	...	...	1361
5	Construction	4284	2285	2000	7200	3894	3306	16574	9368	7206	79538	37193	42344
6	Wholesale and retail trade, restaurants and hotels	6099	993	5106	11549	1833	9716	29299	4800	24499	135081	22562	112520
	A Wholesale and retail trade	...	...	4719	...	...	9008	...	...	22750	...	...	104230
	B Restaurants and hotels	...	...	387	...	...	708	...	...	1749	...	...	8290
7	Transport, storage and communication	3940	1770	2171	8245	3831	4414	18354	9110	9244	80535	41874	38661
	A Transport and storage	...	...	1875	...	...	3705	...	...	7604	...	...	32483
	B Communication	...	...	295	...	...	709	...	...	1640	...	...	6178
8	Finance, insurance, real estate and business services	4704	819	3885	9233	1651	7583	26069	4686	21383	67598	24077	43522
	A Financial institutions	...	...	1703	...	...	3468	...	...	10048	...	...	...
	B Insurance	...	...	246	...	...	421	...	...	811	...	...	...
	C Real estate and business services	...	...	1935	...	...	3693	...	...	10523	...	...	...
9	Community, social and personal services	...	...	1299	...	...	2894	...	...	7269	...	...	32862
	Total, Industries	...	...	25367	...	...	49221	...	...	135929	...	...	610610
	Producers of Government Services	...	...	2971	...	...	5532	...	...	11683	...	...	72041
	Other Producers	...	...	...	...	...	...	...	...	...	...	...	...
	Total	...	...	28337	...	...	54752	...	...	147613	...	...	682652
	Less: Imputed bank service charge	...	...	...	...	...	...	...	...	...	...	...	...
	Import duties	...	...	...	...	...	...	...	...	...	...	...	...
	Value added tax	...	...	...	...	...	...	...	...	...	...	...	...
	Total	...	...	28337	...	...	54752	...	...	147613	...	...	682652

Argentina

Australes

4.2 Derivation of Value Added by Kind of Activity, in Constant Prices

At constant prices of: 1970

All Producers

	1980 Gross Output	1980 Intermediate Consumption	1980 Value Added	1981 Gross Output	1981 Intermediate Consumption	1981 Value Added	1982 Gross Output	1982 Intermediate Consumption	1982 Value Added	1983 Gross Output	1983 Intermediate Consumption	1983 Value Added
1 Agriculture, hunting, forestry and fishing	...	...	1256	...	...	1280	...	...	1370	...	...	1403
A Agriculture and hunting	...	...	1235	...	...	1260	...	...	1346	...	...	1378
B Forestry and logging	...	...	13	...	...	12	...	...	14	...	...	15
C Fishing	...	...	8	...	...	8	...	...	10	...	...	9
2 Mining and quarrying	...	...	246	...	...	248	...	...	249	...	...	250
A Coal mining	...	...	3	...	...	4	...	...	4	...	...	4
B Crude petroleum and natural gas production	...	...	206	...	...	210	...	...	215	...	...	220
C Metal ore mining	...	...	7	...	...	7	...	...	7	...	...	7
D Other mining	...	...	31	...	...	27	...	...	24	...	...	20
3 Manufacturing	...	...	2464	...	...	2078	...	...	1973	...	...	2170
A Manufacture of food, beverages and tobacco	...	...	535	...	...	515	...	...	480	...	...	491
B Textile, wearing apparel and leather industries	...	...	246	...	...	197	...	...	195	...	...	219
C Manufacture of wood and wood products, including furniture	...	...	45	...	...	39	...	...	33	...	...	32
D Manufacture of paper and paper products, printing and publishing	...	...	122	...	...	100	...	...	106	...	...	113
E Manufacture of chemicals and chemical petroleum, coal, rubber and plastic products	...	...	365	...	...	338	...	...	334	...	...	368
F Manufacture of non-metallic mineral products, except products of petroleum and coal	...	...	133	...	...	110	...	...	99	...	...	111
G Basic metal industries	...	...	137	...	...	120	...	...	134	...	...	143
H Manufacture of fabricated metal products, machinery and equipment	...	...	711	...	...	516	...	...	466	...	...	544
I Other manufacturing industries	...	...	170	...	...	144	...	...	136	...	...	150
4 Electricity, gas and water	...	...	351	...	...	347	...	...	358	...	...	387
A Electricity, gas and steam	...	...	334	...	...	330	...	...	340	...	...	368
B Water works and supply	...	...	18	...	...	18	...	...	18	...	...	19
5 Construction	...	...	652	...	...	567	...	...	437	...	...	380
6 Wholesale and retail trade, restaurants and hotels	...	...	1619	...	...	1464	...	...	1261	...	...	1315
A Wholesale and retail trade	...	...	1476	...	...	1329	...	...	1128	...	...	1176
B Restaurants and hotels	...	...	143	...	...	136	...	...	133	...	...	139
7 Transport, storage and communication	...	...	1061	...	...	1020	...	...	993	...	...	1034
A Transport and storage	...	...	946	...	...	900	...	...	868	...	...	902
B Communication	...	...	116	...	...	121	...	...	126	...	...	132
8 Finance, insurance, real estate and business services	...	...	895	...	...	847	...	...	750	...	...	698
A Financial institutions	...	...	373	...	...	334	...	...	242	...	...	170
B Insurance	...	...	73	...	...	69	...	...	62	...	...	67
C Real estate and business services	...	...	450	...	...	445	...	...	446	...	...	461
9 Community, social and personal services	...	...	526	...	...	545	...	...	535	...	...	550
Total, Industries	...	...	9070	...	...	8396	...	...	7926	...	...	8187
Producers of Government Services	...	...	934	...	...	948	...	...	956	...	...	965
Other Producers	...	...	...	...	...	...	...	...	...	...	...	...
Total [a]	...	...	10005	...	...	9345	...	...	8883	...	...	9150
Less: Imputed bank service charge	...	...	...	...	...	...	...	...	...	...	...	...
Import duties	...	...	...	...	...	...	...	...	...	...	...	...
Value added tax	...	...	...	...	...	...	...	...	...	...	...	...
Other adjustments [b]	...	...	1287	...	...	1202	...	...	1143	...	...	1178
Total	...	...	11292	...	...	10547	...	...	10026	...	...	10328

Argentina

4.2 Derivation of Value Added by Kind of Activity, in Constant Prices

Australes

	1984 Gross Output	1984 Intermediate Consumption	1984 Value Added	1985 Gross Output	1985 Intermediate Consumption	1985 Value Added	1986 Gross Output	1986 Intermediate Consumption	1986 Value Added	1987 Gross Output	1987 Intermediate Consumption	1987 Value Added
					At constant prices of: 1970							
					All Producers							
1 Agriculture, hunting, forestry and fishing	...	...	1446	...	...	1421	...	...	1375	...	...	1415
A Agriculture and hunting	...	...	1423	...	...	1397	...	...	1350	...	...	1388
B Forestry and logging	...	...	16	...	...	16	...	...	16	...	...	16
C Fishing	...	...	7	...	...	9	...	...	9	...	...	11
2 Mining and quarrying	...	...	248	...	...	242	...	...	232	...	...	233
A Coal mining	...	...	4	...	...	3	...	...	2	...	...	2
B Crude petroleum and natural gas production	...	...	221	...	...	216	...	...	205	...	...	205
C Metal ore mining	...	...	7	...	...	8	...	...	8	...	...	6
D Other mining	...	...	17	...	...	15	...	...	17	...	...	20
3 Manufacturing	...	...	2257	...	...	2024	...	...	2284	...	...	2272
A Manufacture of food, beverages and tobacco	...	...	528	...	...	528	...	...	576	...	...	553
B Textile, wearing apparel and leather industries	...	...	224	...	...	174	...	...	213	...	...	196
C Manufacture of wood and wood products, including furniture	...	...	29	...	...	25	...	...	30	...	...	29
D Manufacture of paper and paper products, printing and publishing	...	...	114	...	...	111	...	...	116	...	...	111
E Manufacture of chemicals and chemical petroleum, coal, rubber and plastic products	...	...	387	...	...	365	...	...	398	...	...	389
F Manufacture of non-metallic mineral products, except products of petroleum and coal	...	...	103	...	...	80	...	...	98	...	...	107
G Basic metal industries	...	...	142	...	...	133	...	...	149	...	...	168
H Manufacture of fabricated metal products, machinery and equipment	...	...	573	...	...	468	...	...	546	...	...	562
I Other manufacturing industries	...	...	156	...	...	140	...	...	158	...	...	157
4 Electricity, gas and water	...	...	412	...	...	418	...	...	449	...	...	476
A Electricity, gas and steam	...	...	392	...	...	397	...	...	428	...	...	455
B Water works and supply	...	...	20	...	...	21	...	...	21	...	...	21
5 Construction	...	...	304	...	...	284	...	...	311	...	...	357
6 Wholesale and retail trade, restaurants and hotels	...	...	1374	...	...	1260	...	...	1371	...	...	1390
A Wholesale and retail trade	...	...	1224	...	...	1129	...	...	1245	...	...	1262
B Restaurants and hotels	...	...	150	...	...	131	...	...	126	...	...	128
7 Transport, storage and communication	...	...	1091	...	...	1049	...	...	1101	...	...	1130
A Transport and storage	...	...	948	...	...	904	...	...	951	...	...	972
B Communication	...	...	143	...	...	145	...	...	151	...	...	158
8 Finance, insurance, real estate and business services	...	...	707	...	...	698	...	...	747	...	...	769
A Financial institutions	...	...	152	...	...	145	...	...	164	...	...	170
B Insurance	...	...	83	...	...	72	...	...	84	...	...	93
C Real estate and business services	...	...	472	...	...	481	...	...	499	...	...	507
9 Community, social and personal services	...	...	564	...	...	572	...	...	582	...	...	586
Total, Industries	...	...	8403	...	...	7968	...	...	8452	...	...	8628
Producers of Government Services	...	...	991	...	...	1017	...	...	1034	...	...	1065
Other Producers	...	...	...	...	...	...	...	...	...	...	...	...
Total [a]	...	...	9393	...	...	8984	...	...	9486	...	...	9692
Less: Imputed bank service charge	...	...	...	...	...	...	...	...	...	...	...	...
Import duties	...	...	...	...	...	...	...	...	...	...	...	...
Value added tax	...	...	...	...	...	...	...	...	...	...	...	...
Other adjustments [b]	...	...	1209	...	...	1157	...	...	1220	...	...	1247
Total	...	...	10602	...	...	10141	...	...	10706	...	...	10939

Argentina

Australes

4.2 Derivation of Value Added by Kind of Activity, in Constant Prices

At constant prices of: 1970

All Producers

	1988 Gross Output	1988 Intermediate Consumption	1988 Value Added	1989 Gross Output	1989 Intermediate Consumption	1989 Value Added
1 Agriculture, hunting, forestry and fishing	...	...	1409	...	...	1375
A Agriculture and hunting	...	...	1383	...	...	1349
B Forestry and logging	...	...	16	...	...	16
C Fishing	...	...	10	...	...	10
2 Mining and quarrying	...	...	255	...	...	263
A Coal mining	...	...	3	...	...	3
B Crude petroleum and natural gas production	...	...	227	...	...	239
C Metal ore mining	...	...	7	...	...	7
D Other mining	...	...	18	...	...	13
3 Manufacturing	...	...	2118	...	...	1969
A Manufacture of food, beverages and tobacco	...	...	502	...	...	505
B Textile, wearing apparel and leather industries	...	...	192	...	...	191
C Manufacture of wood and wood products, including furniture	...	...	24	...	...	24
D Manufacture of paper and paper products, printing and publishing	...	...	106	...	...	102
E Manufacture of chemicals and chemical petroleum, coal, rubber and plastic products	...	...	389	...	...	368
F Manufacture of non-metallic mineral products, except products of petroleum and coal	...	...	99	...	...	83
G Basic metal industries	...	...	172	...	...	183
H Manufacture of fabricated metal products, machinery and equipment	...	...	487	...	...	378
I Other manufacturing industries	...	...	147	...	...	136
4 Electricity, gas and water	...	...	499	...	...	492
A Electricity, gas and steam	...	...	477	...	...	470
B Water works and supply	...	...	22	...	...	22
5 Construction	...	...	305	...	...	207
6 Wholesale and retail trade, restaurants and hotels	...	...	1302	...	...	1197
A Wholesale and retail trade	...	...	1178	...	...	1082
B Restaurants and hotels	...	...	124	...	...	114
7 Transport, storage and communication	...	...	1098	...	...	1065
A Transport and storage	...	...	941	...	...	899
B Communication	...	...	158	...	...	166
8 Finance, insurance, real estate and business services	...	...	764	...	...	745
A Financial institutions	...	...	167	...	...	152
B Insurance	...	...	84	...	...	79
C Real estate and business services	...	...	513	...	...	514
9 Community, social and personal services	...	...	590	...	...	595
Total, Industries	...	...	8340	...	...	7908
Producers of Government Services	...	...	1088	...	...	1104
Other Producers	...	...	...	...	...	...
Total [a]	...	...	9429	...	...	9012
Less: Imputed bank service charge	...	...	...	...	...	...
Import duties	...	...	...	...	...	...
Value added tax	...	...	...	...	...	...
Other adjustments [b]	...	...	1214	...	...	1159
Total	...	...	10643	...	...	10171

a) Gross domestic product in factor values.
b) Item 'Other adjustments' refers to indirect taxes net of subsidies.

Australia

General note. The preparation of national accounts statistics in Australia is undertaken by the Australian Bureau of Statistics (ABS), Canberra. The Australian National Accounts System corresponds closely to the United Nations System of National Accounts (SNA). Detailed descriptions of the concepts, definitions, sources and methods used are published in 'Australian National Accounts, Concepts, Sources and Methods'. Preliminary annual estimates for the latest financial year are published about 6 to 7 weeks after the end of the financial year in the Commonwealth Budget Paper 'National Income and Expenditure' while quarterly estimates are released usually about 9 weeks after the end of the quarter in the quarterly publication 'Australian National Accounts, National Income and Expenditure '. The most comprehensive national accounts publication is 'Australian National Accounts, National Income and Expenditure' which is released annually. In addition to these National Income and Expenditure publications, input-output tables have been published for the years 1958-59, 1962-63, 1968-69, 1974-75 and 1986-87 and annually from 1977-78 to 1983-84 in 'Australian National Accounts, Input-Output Tables'. Annual estimates of gross product at current and constant prices and indexes of gross product at constant prices per person employed and per hour worked, by industry, are published in 'Australian National Accounts, Gross Product, Employment and Hours Worked', and quarterly estimates of gross product at constant prices, by industry, are published in a quarterly publication of the same namebut different catalogue number. The following tables have been prepared from successive replies to the United Nations national accounts questionnaire. When the scope and coverage of the estimates differ for conceptual or statistical reasons from the definitions and classifications recommended in SNA, a footnote is placed on the relevant tables. Estimates relate to the fiscal year beginning 1 July. All data at constant prices are at average 1984-85 prices. Data in all tables (except table 4.4) are expressed in million of dollars. In table 4.4, data on number of persons are in units of thousand persons, while hours worked data are shown in units of millions of hours. More detailedemployment data have become available from 1983-84 (see Table 4.4). This has resulted in come industry reclassifications which are explained in the footnotes to this table.

Sources and methods Sources and Methods

(a) Gross domestic product. Gross domestic product is estimated using both the income and expenditure approaches. The difference between the two approaches is shown as a statistical discrepancy and, by convention, recorded on the expenditure side of the account.

(b) Expenditure on the gross domestic product. Government final consumption expenditure and public gross fixed capital formation are estimated from the accounting records of the government sector. Private final consumption expenditure on goods is mainly derived from information collected in retail censuses (held every five years) as well as data on production, imports and exports, and motor vehicle registrations. The results of a quarterly survey of retail sales are used to interpolate between census benchmarks and to extrapolate for the period since the last retail census. Benchmarks for dwellings rent are derived from population census data collected every five years. The consumer price index is used in conjunction with a perpetual inventory model of the stock of dwellings to interpolate between census year estimates and extrapolate from the most recent census. Estimates of expenditure on other services are based mainly on revenue or earnings data. Increase in stocks is based on book value levels of stocks reported in ABS economic censuses, taxation statistics and quarterly ABS surveys of stocks (less the stock valuation adjustment). Estimates of private gross fixed capital expenditure are obtained from a quarterly collection of building and engineering construction statistics and from a quarterly survey of new capital expenditure by private businesses on plant and equipment. Exports and imports of goods are estimated from customs data while exports and imports of services are derived from transportation survey data and from data obtained as by-products of the administration of foreign exchange transactions. Constant price estimates are derived quarterly with annual estimates obtained by summing the quarterly series. Government consumption expenditures are deflated by composite wage rate and material price indexes. Substantial use is made of data from consumer price index in the revaluation of private final consumption expenditure. Estimates of gross fixed capital expenditure are revalued using (output) building price indexes for building; composite wage material price indexes for engineering construction; domestic and overseas producer price indexes (including the computer equipment price index produced by the United States Bureau of Economic Analysis) and import price indexes for equipment; and quantity revaluation for real estate transfer expenses. For exports and imports, considerable use is made of the quantity reval uation technique with the remainder deflated using price indexes. Increase in stocks estimates are derived using detailed price indexes to revalue book value levels.

(c) Cost-structure of the gross domestic product. The components of indirect taxes (net) are estimated from government accounting records. Estimates of gross operating surplus are mainly based on taxation statistics. Estimates of the consumption of fixed capital arederived at current replacement cost using the Perpetual Inventory Method. Since December quarter 1981 the compensation of employees data have been based on a quarterly survey of employers - prior to that quarter, estimates were mainly based on payroll tax data.

(d) Gross domestic product by kind of economic activity. The table of gross domestic product by kind of economic activity is prepared at market prices. Constant price estimates of gross product forAgriculture, Mining and Gas industries are deverived using double deflation.Estimates for Finance, property and business services, and Public administration and defence are derived by extrapolating the base year value of gross product using hours worked estimates. Estimates for the Community services are derived by extrapolating the base year value of gross product using the sum of the relevant components of government and private final consumption expenditure. Estimates for the remaining industries are derived using the grossoutput method.

1.1 Expenditure on the Gross Domestic Product, in Current Prices

Million Australian dollars — Fiscal year beginning 1 July

	1970	1975	1980	1981	1982	1983	1984	1985	1986	1987	1988	1989
1 Government final consumption expenditure	4904	13199	24993	28525	32438	35909	40218	44734	48713	52654	56750	61673
2 Private final consumption expenditure	20830	44753	82770	94355	105951	116800	128265	143828	157612	175746	194847	216530
3 Gross capital formation a	9572	18599	35719	43034	38679	45746	52175	60777	62570	70686	88509	93733
A Increase in stocks a	441	159	502	1555	-2442	1430	1094	1464	-1421	-410	3742	4766
B Gross fixed capital formation a	9131	18440	35217	41479	41121	44316	51081	59313	63991	71096	84767	88967
Residential buildings	1889	4522	8516	9396	8245	9473	11326	12319	11859	13421	18520	20018
Non-residential buildings	2933	5950	10662	13157	13997	13742	15765	18995	20839	23349	26069	29120
Other construction and land improvement etc.												
Other	4288	7999	16040	18926	18879	21101	23990	27999	31293	34326	40178	39829
4 Exports of goods and services	5066	11197	22505	23300	25156	28595	34755	38693	43148	50058	53802	58923
5 Less: Imports of goods and services	5083	10901	25071	28997	28967	31192	39505	46087	48017	52599	60862	66291
Statistical discrepancy	-173	-204	-750	-2090	-1622	-1242	152	-1838	1108	3237	7740	7604
Equals: Gross Domestic Product	35116	76643	140166	158127	171635	194616	216060	240107	265134	299782	340786	372172

a) Livestock is excluded from items 'Increase in Stocks' and 'Gross Fixed Capital Formation' and as a result, from 'Gross Capital Formation'.

1.2 Expenditure on the Gross Domestic Product, in Constant Prices

Million Australian dollars — Fiscal year beginning 1 July

	1970	1975	1980	1981	1982	1983	1984	1985	1986	1987	1988	1989
		1979			At constant prices of:		1984					
1 Government final consumption expenditure	13837	... 29694	35133	35441	36455	38038	40218	42062	43101	44317	45077	46627
2 Private final consumption expenditure	53068	... 99384	114359	119146	120683	123854	128265	132837	133877	139289	144305	150647
3 Gross capital formation a	25992	... 40549	48522	52695	42929	48492	52176	54866	52132	55686	65695	66053
A Increase in stocks a	1246	... 158	687	1774	-2577	1770	1094	1257	-1114	-198	2986	3135
B Gross fixed capital formation a	24746	... 40391	47835	50921	45506	46722	51082	53609	53246	55884	62709	62918

Australia

1.2 Expenditure on the Gross Domestic Product, in Constant Prices
(Continued)

Million Australian dollars — Fiscal year beginning 1 July

	1970	1975	1980	1981	1982	1983	1984	1985	1986	1987	1988	1989
		At constant prices of:										
		1979					1984					
Residential buildings	5046	9233	11810	11640	9279	10161	11326	11314	10228	10893	12944	12595
Non-residential buildings	8516	14255	15352	16717	15648	14497	15765	17258	17604	18426	19093	19876
Other construction and land improvement etc.												
Other	11184	16762	20672	22564	20579	22064	23990	25037	25414	26564	30672	30447
4 Exports of goods and services	14728	23472	27804	28135	28216	30606	34754	36810	40051	42722	43114	46265
5 Less: Imports of goods and services	15306	25398	31938	35539	32504	34189	39506	40083	38948	42760	52806	54980
Statistical discrepancy	-387	-379	-986	-2543	-1802	-1288	152	-1675	976	2635	5827	5410
Equals: Gross Domestic Product	91932	167322	192894	197335	193977	205513	216059	224817	231189	241889	251212	260022

a) Livestock is excluded from items 'Increase in Stocks' and 'Gross Fixed Capital Formation' and as a result, from 'Gross Capital Formation'.

1.3 Cost Components of the Gross Domestic Product

Million Australian dollars — Fiscal year beginning 1 July

	1970	1975	1980	1981	1982	1983	1984	1985	1986	1987	1988	1989
1 Indirect taxes, net	3233	8023	15010	17080	19432	22417	25803	28496	31712	36974	40865	44140
A Indirect taxes	3579	8873	17250	19652	22539	25775	29526	32508	35788	40903	44938	47770
B Less: Subsidies a	346	850	2240	2572	3107	3358	3723	4012	4076	3929	4073	3630
2 Consumption of fixed capital	4540	10774	21103	24193	27738	30110	32741	37665	42473	46324	50549	55061
3 Compensation of employees paid by resident producers to: b	18884	42830	74054	85566	94949	100402	110778	122277	133933	147300	165698	184806
A Resident households b	18867	42786	73944	85441	94814	100244	110600	122113	133754	147090	165419	184462
B Rest of the world	17	44	110	125	135	158	178	164	179	210	279	344
4 Operating surplus	8459	15016	29999	31288	29516	41687	46738	51669	57016	69184	83674	88165
A Corporate and quasi-corporate enterprises	3717	5007	9258	9224	8378	14643	18119	19704	21569	28448	35423	35703
B Private unincorporated enterprises	4777	10172	20741	22064	21138	27044	28619	31965	35447	40737	48251	52462
C General government	...	...	...	...	...	...	...	...	...	...	...	...
Equals: Gross Domestic Product	35116	76643	140166	158127	171635	194616	216060	240107	265134	299782	340786	372172

a) Subsidies on wheat and wool are recorded on an accrual basis.
b) Some government contributions to superannuation are only recorded in compensation when benefits are paid.

1.4 General Government Current Receipts and Disbursements

Million Australian dollars — Fiscal year beginning 1 July

	1970	1975	1980	1981	1982	1983	1984	1985	1986	1987	1988	1989
Receipts												
1 Operating surplus	-	-	-	-	-	-	-	-	-	-	-	-
2 Property and entrepreneurial income a	969	1177	2610	3149	3838	4639	5701	8190	9560	9651	11294	12131
3 Taxes, fees and contributions	8361	21063	40376	47009	51627	56570	66181	73363	82892	94209	105864	115287
A Indirect taxes	3578	8860	17250	19652	22539	25775	29526	32508	35788	40903	44938	47770
B Direct taxes	4602	11831	22399	26469	28062	29621	35335	39437	45434	51366	58548	64507
C Social security contributions	...	...	...	...	...	...	...	...	...	...	...	...
D Compulsory fees, fines and penalties	181	372	727	888	1026	1174	1320	1418	1670	1940	2378	3010
4 Other current transfers	-	-	-	-	-	-	-	-	-	-	-	-
Total Current Receipts of General Government	9330	22240	42986	50158	55465	61209	71882	81553	92452	103860	117158	127418
Disbursements												
1 Government final consumption expenditure	4907	13201	24993	28525	32438	35909	40218	44734	48713	52654	56750	61673
2 Property income	848	1125	3001	3407	4023	5160	7097	9310	11176	12005	14512	16467
A Interest	848	1125	3001	3407	4023	5160	7097	9310	11176	12005	14512	16467
B Net land rent and royalties	...	...	-	-	-	-	-	-	-	-	-	-

Australia

1.4 General Government Current Receipts and Disbursements
(Continued)

Million Australian dollars — Fiscal year beginning 1 July

	1970	1975	1980	1981	1982	1983	1984	1985	1986	1987	1988	1989
3 Subsidies [b]	345	837	2240	2572	3107	3358	3723	4012	4076	3929	4073	3630
4 Other current transfers [c]	2110	7136	13346	15540	18889	22082	24845	26837	29055	31982	33967	37542
A Social security benefits	...	...	...	...	...	...	...	...	...	...	...	...
B Social assistance grants	1836	6260	11431	13250	16167	18903	21229	22927	24861	27684	29217	32354
C Other	274	876	1915	2290	2722	3179	3616	3910	4194	4298	4750	5188
5 Net saving	1119	-59	-594	114	-2992	-5300	-4001	-3340	-568	3290	7856	8106
Total Current Disbursements and Net Saving of General Government	9329	22240	42986	50158	55465	61209	71882	81553	92452	103860	117158	127418

a) All public enterprises are treated as if they were quasi-corporate.
b) Subsidies on wheat and wool are recorded on an accrual basis.
c) The Australian accounts do not distinguish between current and capital transfers to the rest of the world. They have all been treated as current transfers.

1.5 Current Income and Outlay of Corporate and Quasi-Corporate Enterprises, Summary

Million Australian dollars — Fiscal year beginning 1 July

	1970	1975	1980	1981	1982	1983	1984	1985	1986	1987	1988	1989
Receipts												
1 Operating surplus	4289	5007	9258	9224	8378	14643	18119	19704	21569	28448	35423	35703
2 Property and entrepreneurial income received	1705	4507	9627	11962	14279	15637	17664	22723	27605	28312	35615	43481
3 Current transfers	-	-	-	-	80	75	-	-	-	-	-	150
Total Current Receipts	5994	9514	18885	21186	22737	30355	35783	42427	49174	56760	71038	79334
Disbursements												
1 Property and entrepreneurial income	3197	6719	13630	17975	21694	24698	28580	36606	43259	45056	53894	63913
2 Direct taxes and other current payments to general government	1379	2464	4590	4923	4718	4492	5512	6026	6586	8660	10114	13284
3 Other current transfers	39	158	369	434	719	720	951	941	1068	1061	1209	1608
4 Net saving	1379	173	296	-2146	-4394	445	740	-1146	-1739	1983	5821	529
Total Current Disbursements and Net Saving	5994	9514	18885	21186	22737	30355	35783	42427	49174	56760	71038	79334

1.6 Current Income and Outlay of Households and Non-Profit Institutions

Million Australian dollars — Fiscal year beginning 1 July

	1970	1975	1980	1981	1982	1983	1984	1985	1986	1987	1988	1989
Receipts												
1 Compensation of employees	18880	42805	74063	85580	94972	100419	110800	122290	133919	147266	165609	184674
A From resident producers [a]	18867	42746	73944	85441	94814	100244	110600	122113	133754	147090	165419	184462
B From rest of the world	13	59	119	139	158	175	200	177	165	176	190	212
2 Operating surplus of private unincorporated enterprises	4777	10172	20741	22064	21138	27044	28619	31965	35447	40737	48251	52462
3 Property and entrepreneurial income	1981	4536	9384	12441	14813	16177	18173	23878	28548	30249	35711	41842
4 Current transfers	2239	7251	13988	16260	19782	23682	26854	29155	31968	35303	38023	41709
A Social security benefits	...	...	...	...	...	...	...	...	...	...	...	...
B Social assistance grants	1855	6261	11431	13250	16167	18903	21229	22927	24861	27684	29217	32354
C Other	384	990	2557	3010	3615	4779	5625	6228	7107	7619	8806	9355
Total Current Receipts	27877	64764	118176	136345	150705	167322	184446	207288	229882	253555	287594	320687
Disbursements												
1 Private final consumption expenditure	20830	44741	82770	94355	105951	116800	128265	143828	157612	175746	194847	216530
2 Property income	1098	3406	7133	9140	10895	11326	12395	16561	19893	21307	27550	33260
3 Direct taxes and other current transfers n.e.c. to general government	3357	9585	18259	22094	23970	25865	30609	34132	39732	43827	49915	53125
A Social security contributions	...	...	...	...	...	...	...	...	...	...	...	...
B Direct taxes	3175	9213	17532	21206	22944	24691	29289	32714	38062	41887	47537	50115
C Fees, fines and penalties	182	372	727	888	1026	1174	1320	1418	1670	1940	2378	3010
4 Other current transfers	165	397	690	818	969	1203	1394	1365	1418	1415	1546	1621
5 Net saving	2427	6635	9324	9938	8920	12128	11783	11402	11227	11260	13736	16151
Total Current Disbursements and Net Saving	27877	64764	118176	136345	150705	167322	184446	207288	229882	253555	287594	320687

a) Some government contributions to superannuation are only recorded in compensation when benefits are paid.

Australia

1.7 External Transactions on Current Account, Summary

Million Australian dollars — Fiscal year beginning 1 July

	1970	1975	1980	1981	1982	1983	1984	1985	1986	1987	1988	1989
Payments to the Rest of the World												
1 Imports of goods and services	5070	10830	25071	28997	28967	31192	39505	46087	48017	52599	60862	66291
A Imports of merchandise c.i.f. [a]	4219	8742	20483	24336	23104	25678	32017	38343	39859	43293	50136	54598
B Other	851	2088	4588	4661	5863	5514	7488	7744	8158	9306	10726	11693
2 Factor income to the rest of the world	627	1171	2816	3717	4754	6147	8067	9293	10534	12023	15507	19251
A Compensation of employees	17	44	110	125	135	158	178	164	179	210	279	344
B Property and entrepreneurial income	610	1127	2706	3592	4619	5989	7889	9129	10355	11813	15228	18907
By general government	88	86	374	373	541	671	931	1428	2227	2977	3191	3731
By corporate and quasi-corporate enterprises	522	1041	2332	3219	4078	5318	6958	7701	8128	8836	12037	15176
By other	...	...	...	...	...	...	...	...	...	...	...	...
3 Current transfers to the rest of the world [b]	322	701	1126	1330	1515	1643	1754	1808	1804	1881	2012	2172
A Indirect taxes to supranational organizations	...	...	...	...	...	...	...	...	...	...	...	...
B Other current transfers	322	701	1126	1330	1515	1643	1754	1808	1804	1881	2012	2172
4 Surplus of the nation on current transactions	-508	-848	-4840	-8845	-7585	-7121	-11064	-14358	-12285	-11067	-18287	-21190
Payments to the Rest of the World and Surplus of the Nation on Current Transactions	5511	11854	24173	25199	27651	31861	38262	42830	48070	55436	60094	66524
Receipts From The Rest of the World												
1 Exports of goods and services	5065	11101	22505	23300	25156	28595	34755	38693	43148	50058	53802	58923
A Exports of merchandise f.o.b.	4244	9432	18689	19140	20857	23576	29365	32307	35426	40555	43105	48665
B Other	821	1669	3816	4160	4299	5019	5390	6386	7722	9503	10697	10258
2 Factor income from rest of the world	152	343	682	761	1175	1508	1555	1620	1905	1833	2082	3083
A Compensation of employees	13	59	119	139	158	175	200	177	165	176	190	212
B Property and entrepreneurial income	139	284	563	622	1017	1333	1355	1443	1740	1657	1892	2871
By general government	-	-	3	31	21	20	24	37	43	47	74	118
By corporate and quasi-corporate enterprises	139	284	560	591	996	1313	1331	1406	1697	1610	1818	2753
By other	...	...	-	-	-	-	-	-	-	-	-	-
3 Current transfers from rest of the world [b]	294	410	986	1138	1320	1758	1952	2517	3017	3545	4210	4518
A Subsidies from supranational organisations	...	...	...	...	...	...	...	...	...	...	...	...
B Other current transfers	294	410	986	1138	1320	1758	1952	2517	3017	3545	4210	4518
Receipts from the Rest of the World on Current Transactions	5511	11854	24173	25199	27651	31861	38262	42830	48070	55436	60094	66524

a) Item 'Imports of merchandise C.I.F.' excludes freight on imports paid to resident carriers.
b) The Australian accounts do not distinguish between current and capital transfers to the rest of the world. They have all been treated as current transfers.

1.8 Capital Transactions of The Nation, Summary

Million Australian dollars — Fiscal year beginning 1 July

	1970	1975	1980	1981	1982	1983	1984	1985	1986	1987	1988	1989
Finance of Gross Capital Formation												
Gross saving	8869	17520	30129	32099	29472	37383	41263	44581	51393	62856	77962	80147
1 Consumption of fixed capital	4540	10774	21103	24193	27738	30110	32741	37665	42473	46324	50549	55061
A General government	687	1750	3175	3580	4072	4357	4600	5032	5455	5809	6183	6608
B Corporate and quasi-corporate enterprises	2298	5379	10510	12070	14106	15461	16738	19416	22152	24148	25756	28114
Public	752	1730	3259	3776	4470	4939	5478	6177	6965	7727	8426	9202
Private	1546	3649	7251	8294	9636	10522	11260	13239	15187	16421	17330	18912
C Other	1548	3592	7418	8543	9560	10292	11403	13217	14866	16367	18610	20339
2 Net saving	4329	6746	9026	7906	1734	7273	8522	6916	8920	16532	27413	25086
A General government	1119	-59	-594	114	-2992	-5300	-4001	-3340	-568	3290	7856	8106
B Corporate and quasi-corporate enterprises	802	173	296	-2146	-4394	445	740	-1146	-1739	1983	5821	529
C Other [a]	2427	6635	9324	9938	9120	12128	11783	11402	11227	11260	13736	16451
Less: Surplus of the nation on current transactions	-530	-875	-4840	-8845	-7585	-7121	-11064	-14358	-12285	-11067	-18287	-21190

Australia

1.8 Capital Transactions of The Nation, Summary
(Continued)

Million Australian dollars — Fiscal year beginning 1 July

	1970	1975	1980	1981	1982	1983	1984	1985	1986	1987	1988	1989
Statistical discrepancy	173	204	750	2090	1622	1242	-152	1838	-1108	-3237	-7740	-7604
Finance of Gross Capital Formation	9572	18599	35719	43034	38679	45746	52175	60777	62570	70686	88509	93733
Gross Capital Formation												
Increase in stocks [b]	441	159	502	1555	-2442	1430	1094	1464	-1421	-410	3742	4766
Gross fixed capital formation [b]	9131	18440	35217	41479	41121	44316	51081	59313	63991	71096	84767	88967
1 General government	1334	3373	3753	4124	4624	5306	6205	7267	7888	7496	7608	8832
2 Corporate and quasi-corporate enterprises	4834	7831	16893	21521	23005	22820	25327	31432	34901	38108	43380	46706
A Public	1401	3043	5611	7185	8512	8837	8963	10791	11263	9829	10607	12977
B Private	3433	4788	11282	14336	14493	13983	16364	20641	23638	28279	32773	33729
3 Other	2943	7267	14572	15834	13492	16190	19549	20614	21202	25492	33779	33429
Gross Capital Formation	9572	18599	35719	43034	38679	45746	52175	60777	62570	70686	88509	93733

a) Item 'Other' of net saving includes extraordinary insurance claimpaid.
b) Livestock is excluded from items 'Increase in Stocks' and 'Gross Fixed Capital Formation' and as a result, from 'Gross Capital Formation'.

1.10 Gross Domestic Product by Kind of Activity, in Current Prices

Million Australian dollars — Fiscal year beginning 1 July

	1970	1975	1980	1981	1982	1983	1984	1985	1986	1987	1988	1989
1 Agriculture, hunting, forestry and fishing	2033	3845	7415	7733	6056	9416	9486	9426	10262	12350	14740	15193
2 Mining and quarrying	1061	3366	8855	9845	11124	13226	14625	15649	13942	14125	13498	17030
3 Manufacturing	8528	15786	27069	30175	31105	34976	38351	41426	44123	49057	55426	59352
4 Electricity, gas and water [a]	1089	2172	4059	4740	6021	6956	7615	8430	9406	10030	11053	11264
5 Construction	3025	6799	11121	12013	12612	13449	15331	17201	19453	21398	25137	27603
6 Wholesale and retail trade, restaurants and hotels [b]	6214	13514	21793	24224	26425	30229	35093	40811	46595	52528	62759	67680
7 Transport, storage and communication	2640	5487	9931	11513	12208	14027	15805	17499	19319	22912	25203	27502
8 Finance, insurance, real estate and business services	5279	11739	24235	27106	31573	36221	39825	44308	51882	62972	72973	79905
9 Community, social and personal services [b]	4139	11162	20741	25101	28795	30725	33899	37416	41989	46548	52369	58042
Total, Industries	34008	73870	135219	152450	165919	189225	210030	232166	256971	291920	333158	363571
Producers of Government Services	1478	3731	6471	7209	8037	8301	8985	9994	10858	11885	12616	13248
Other Producers	...	...	...	...	...	...	...	...	...	...	...	...
Subtotal	35486	77601	141690	159659	173956	197526	219015	242160	267829	303805	345774	376819
Less: Imputed bank service charge	833	1890	3324	3592	4357	5239	5882	5335	5932	7654	8693	8548
Plus: Import duties	463	932	1800	2060	2036	2329	2927	3282	3237	3632	3705	3901
Plus: Value added tax	...	...	...	...	...	...	...	...	...	...	...	...
Equals: Gross Domestic Product	35116	76643	140166	158127	171635	194616	216060	240107	265134	299783	340786	372172

a) Item 'Electricity, gas and water' includes sewage services.
b) Restaurants and hotels are included in item 'Community, social and personal services'.

1.11 Gross Domestic Product by Kind of Activity, in Constant Prices

Million Australian dollars — Fiscal year beginning 1 July

At constant prices of: 1979 / 1984

	1970	1975	1980	1981	1982	1983	1984	1985	1986	1987	1988	1989
1 Agriculture, hunting, forestry and fishing	5971	7814	7264	8449	6602	9460	9486	9218	9511	9053	8951	9710
2 Mining and quarrying	4856	10733	11651	11292	11830	12947	14625	16863	16055	17603	17543	19688
3 Manufacturing	19391	33791	38226	39162	35951	36487	38351	39281	39806	42306	44819	46252
4 Electricity, gas and water [a]	2082	4978	6356	6695	6885	7173	7615	7951	8160	8573	8974	9514
5 Construction	8129	13306	15243	15865	14219	14055	15331	16171	15841	16559	18044	18216
6 Wholesale and retail trade, restaurants and hotels [b]	15794	29000	32288	33506	31938	33190	35093	35760	35391	37805	40130	40978
7 Transport, storage and communication	5285	9943	13655	14109	13894	14634	15805	16874	17497	18838	19941	20301
8 Finance, insurance, real estate and business services	15213	28162	35096	36686	37069	37848	39825	42164	44439	46948	49133	51477
9 Community, social and personal services [b]	11202	24584	29049	30083	30954	32804	33899	35406	36382	37731	39329	40784

Australia

1.11 Gross Domestic Product by Kind of Activity, in Constant Prices
(Continued)

Million Australian dollars — Fiscal year beginning 1 July

	1970	1975	1980	1981	1982	1983	1984	1985	1986	1987	1988	1989
		At constant prices of:										
		1979					1984					
Total, Industries	87923	162311	188828	195847	189342	198598	210030	219688	223082	235416	246864	256920
Producers of Government Services	4712	7330	7904	8072	8008	8683	8985	9045	9275	9476	9423	9285
Other Producers	...	...	...	...	...	...	...	...	...	...	...	...
Subtotal	92635	169641	196732	203919	197350	207281	219015	228733	232357	244892	256287	266205
Less: Imputed bank service charge	2430	5040	5502	5393	5426	5967	5882	5308	5523	6099	6576	5895
Plus: Import duties	1018	1736	2352	2647	2284	2438	2927	3040	2774	2955	3840	4029
Plus: Value added tax	...	...	...	...	...	...	...	...	...	...	...	...
Equals: Gross Domestic Product	91223	166337	193582	201173	194208	203752	216060	226465	229608	241748	253551	264339

a) Item 'Electricity, gas and water' includes sewage services.
b) Restaurants and hotels are included in item 'Community, social and personal services'.

1.12 Relations Among National Accounting Aggregates

Million Australian dollars — Fiscal year beginning 1 July

	1970	1975	1980	1981	1982	1983	1984	1985	1986	1987	1988	1989
Gross Domestic Product	35116	76643	140166	158127	171635	194616	216060	240107	265134	299782	340786	372172
Plus: Net factor income from the rest of the world	-485	-845	-2134	-2956	-3579	-4639	-6512	-7673	-8629	-10190	-13425	-16168
Factor income from the rest of the world	152	343	682	761	1175	1508	1555	1620	1905	1833	2082	3083
Less: Factor income to the rest of the world	637	1188	2816	3717	4754	6147	8067	9293	10534	12023	15507	19251
Equals: Gross National Product	34631	75798	138032	155171	168056	189977	209548	232434	256505	289592	327361	356004
Less: Consumption of fixed capital	4540	10774	21103	24193	27738	30110	32741	37665	42473	46324	50549	55061
Equals: National Income	30091	65024	116929	130978	140318	159867	176807	194769	214032	243268	276812	300943
Plus: Net current transfers from the rest of the world [a]	-28	-326	-140	-192	-195	115	198	709	1213	1664	2198	2346
Current transfers from the rest of the world	294	410	986	1138	1320	1758	1952	2517	3017	3545	4210	4518
Less: Current transfers to the rest of the world	322	736	1126	1330	1515	1643	1754	1808	1804	1881	2012	2172
Equals: National Disposable Income	30063	64698	116789	130786	140123	159982	177005	195478	215245	244932	279010	303289
Less: Final consumption [b]	25734	57952	107763	122880	138389	152709	168483	188562	206325	228400	251597	278203
Equals: Net Saving	4329	6746	9026	7906	1734	7273	8522	6916	8920	16532	27413	25086
Less: Surplus of the nation on current transactions	-530	-875	-4840	-8845	-7585	-7121	-11064	-14358	-12285	-11067	-18287	-21190
Statistical discrepancy	173	204	750	2090	1622	1242	-152	1838	-1108	-3237	-7740	-7604
Equals: Net Capital Formation	5032	7825	14616	18841	10941	15636	19434	23112	20097	24362	37960	38672

a) The Australian accounts do not distinguish between current and capital transfers to the rest of the world. They have all been treated as current transfers.
b) Item 'Final consumption expenditure' includes some expenditure of non-profit organisations.

2.1 Government Final Consumption Expenditure by Function, in Current Prices

Million Australian dollars — Fiscal year beginning 1 July

	1970	1975	1980	1981	1982	1983	1984	1985	1986	1987	1988	1989
1 General public services	...	1700	3157	3606	4187	4650	5120	5775	6591	7710	7563	7809
2 Defence	...	1618	3388	3835	4381	4528	5398	6221	6444	6779	6942	7617
3 Public order and safety	...	783	1646	1910	2214	2399	2627	2930	3223	3505	4046	4474
4 Education	...	3369	6265	7165	8026	8801	9474	10376	11135	11764	13027	14309
5 Health	...	2336	4319	4832	5215	6041	7072	7742	8717	9541	10649	11284
6 Social security and welfare	...	283	652	778	958	1173	1344	1602	1896	2111	2367	2666
7 Housing and community amenities	...	193	357	389	538	565	624	719	775	852	901	...
8 Recreational, cultural and religious affairs	...	503	909	1123	1256	1442	1728	1960	2110	2240	2362	...
9 Economic services	...	2408	4255	4860	5560	6289	6873	7450	7880	8263	8830	9634

Australia

2.1 Government Final Consumption Expenditure by Function, in Current Prices
(Continued)

Million Australian dollars — Fiscal year beginning 1 July

	1970	1975	1980	1981	1982	1983	1984	1985	1986	1987	1988	1989
A Fuel and energy	...	50	92	114	126	132	146	207	155	168	144	...
B Agriculture, forestry, fishing and hunting	...	541	931	1067	1261	1360	1449	1559	1721	1820	1907	...
C Mining, manufacturing and construction, except fuel and energy	...	82	254	264	335	343	362	448	390	432	510	...
D Transportation and communication	...	1412	2239	2577	2925	3331	3531	3783	3993	4220	4527	...
E Other economic affairs	...	323	739	838	913	1123	1385	1453	1621	1623	1742	...
10 Other functions	...	8	45	27	103	21	-42	-41	-58	-111	63	...
Total Government Final Consumption Expenditure	4907	13201	24993	28525	32438	35909	40218	44734	48713	52654	56750	61673

2.2 Government Final Consumption Expenditure by Function, in Constant Prices

Million Australian dollars — Fiscal year beginning 1 July

At constant prices of: 1979 (1970–1980), 1984 (1981–1989)

	1970	1975	1980	1981	1982	1983	1984	1985	1986	1987	1988	1989
1 General public services	...	...	...	...	...	...	...	...	...	...	...	...
2 Defence	2899	2357	4994	4807	5069	4977	5398	5734	5613	5688	5684	5740
3 Public order and safety	786	1135	...	...	...	...	...	...	...	...	...	...
4 Education	3002	4667	8743	8854	8974	9332	9474	9793	9957	10077	10360	11028
5 Health	2014	3692	6924	6998	6947	7648	8416	8808	9213	9574	10143	10209
6 Social security and welfare												
7 Housing and community amenities	...	...	...									
8 Recreational, cultural and religious affairs	...	...	...									
9 Economic services	...	...	...									
10 Other functions	...	...	...									
Total Government Final Consumption Expenditure	13837	18743	35133	35441	36455	38038	40218	42062	43101	44317	45077	46627

2.3 Total Government Outlays by Function and Type

Million Australian dollars — Fiscal year beginning 1 July

	Final Consumption Expenditures Total	Compensation of Employees	Other	Subsidies	Other Current Transfers & Property Income	Total Current Disbursements	Gross Capital Formation	Other Capital Outlays	Total Outlays
					1980				
1 General public services	3157	...	...	26	616	3799	385	-5	4179
2 Defence	3388	...	...	-	41	3429	-	-	3429
3 Public order and safety	1646	...	...	-	18	1664	155	1	1820
4 Education	6265	...	...	5	1096	7366	625	41	8032
5 Health	4319	...	...	80	1668	6067	283	4	6354
6 Social security and welfare	652	...	...	12	9726	10390	32	69	10491
7 Housing and community amenities	357	...	...	61	19	437	216	127	780
8 Recreation, culture and religion	909	...	...	12	77	998	339	30	1367
9 Economic services	4255	...	...	2027	60	6342	1758	18	8118
A Fuel and energy	92	...	...	82	4	178	27	-122	83
B Agriculture, forestry, fishing and hunting	931	...	...	325	1	1257	203	-	1460
C Mining (except fuels), manufacturing and construction	254	...	...	430	3	687	9	14	710
D Transportation and communication	2239	...	...	908	3	3150	1462	125	4737
E Other economic affairs	739	...	...	282	49	1070	57	1	1128
10 Other functions	45	...	...	17	3020	3082	27	-11	3098
Total	24993	...	...	2240	16341	43574	3820	274	47668

Australia

2.3 Total Government Outlays by Function and Type
(Continued)

Million Australian dollars — Fiscal year beginning 1 July

		Final Consumption Expenditures — Total	Compensation of Employees	Other	Subsidies	Other Current Transfers & Property Income	Total Current Disbursements	Gross Capital Formation	Other Capital Outlays	Total Outlays
	1981									
1	General public services	3606	...	...	34	713	4353	474	-5	4822
2	Defence	3835	...	...	-	43	3878	-	-	3878
3	Public order and safety	1910	...	...	-	17	1927	149	-	2076
4	Education	7165	...	...	5	1259	8429	619	49	9097
5	Health	4832	...	...	93	2052	6977	258	6	7241
6	Social security and welfare	778	...	...	15	11252	12045	39	103	12187
7	Housing and community amenities	389	...	...	58	20	467	261	167	895
8	Recreation, culture and religion	1123	...	...	15	87	1225	342	39	1606
9	Economic services	4860	...	...	2344	74	7278	1975	154	9407
	A Fuel and energy	114	...	...	98	4	216	93	2	311
	B Agriculture, forestry, fishing and hunting	1067	...	...	282	1	1350	224	-	1574
	C Mining (except fuels), manufacturing and construction	264	...	...	468	3	735	14	10	759
	D Transportation and communication	2577	...	...	1144	4	3725	1580	141	5446
	E Other economic affairs	838	...	...	352	62	1252	64	1	1317
10	Other functions	27	...	...	8	3426	3461	36	-3	3494
	Total	28525	...	...	2572	18943	50040	4153	510	54703
	1982									
1	General public services	4187	...	...	17	792	4996	465	-3	5458
2	Defence	4381	...	...	-	49	4430	-	-	4430
3	Public order and safety	2214	...	...	4	21	2239	182	1	2422
4	Education	8026	...	...	5	1525	9556	655	46	10257
5	Health	5215	...	...	97	2424	7736	267	4	8007
6	Social security and welfare	958	...	...	17	13757	14732	39	118	14889
7	Housing and community amenities	538	...	...	104	34	676	280	414	1370
8	Recreation, culture and religion	1256	...	...	13	102	1371	378	45	1794
9	Economic services	5560	...	...	2772	139	8471	2407	184	11062
	A Fuel and energy	126	...	...	111	4	241	181	4	426
	B Agriculture, forestry, fishing and hunting	1261	...	...	296	44	1601	279	11	1891
	C Mining (except fuels), manufacturing and construction	335	...	...	523	5	863	11	15	889
	D Transportation and communication	2925	...	...	1487	4	4416	1851	156	6423
	E Other economic affairs	913	...	...	355	82	1350	85	-2	1433
10	Other functions	103	...	...	78	4062	4243	5	8	4256
	Total	32438	...	...	3107	22905	58450	4678	817	63945
	1983									
1	General public services	4650	...	...	16	844	5510	481	-4	5987
2	Defence	4528	...	...	-	48	4576	-	-	4576
3	Public order and safety	2399	...	...	2	25	2426	219	2	2647
4	Education	8801	...	...	7	1768	10576	739	41	11356
5	Health	6041	...	...	114	2997	9152	370	8	9530
6	Social security and welfare	1173	...	...	30	15918	17121	91	113	17325
7	Housing and community amenities	565	...	...	85	46	696	321	593	1610
8	Recreation, culture and religion	1442	...	...	20	126	1588	418	36	2042
9	Economic services	6289	...	...	3032	274	9595	2653	208	12456
	A Fuel and energy	132	...	...	172	3	307	81	31	419
	B Agriculture, forestry, fishing and hunting	1360	...	...	347	20	1727	273	20	2020
	C Mining (except fuels), manufacturing and construction	343	...	...	526	7	876	11	13	900
	D Transportation and communication	3331	...	...	1528	7	4866	2210	131	7207
	E Other economic affairs	1123	...	...	459	237	1819	78	13	1910
10	Other functions	21	...	...	52	5194	5267	22	-1	5288
	Total	35909	...	...	3358	27240	66507	5314	996	72817

Australia

2.3 Total Government Outlays by Function and Type
(Continued)

Million Australian dollars — Fiscal year beginning 1 July

		Final Consumption Expenditures Total	Compensation of Employees	Other	Subsidies	Other Current Transfers & Property Income	Total Current Disbursements	Gross Capital Formation	Other Capital Outlays	Total Outlays
	1984									
1	General public services	5120	...	...	19	922	6061	594	-4	6651
2	Defence	5398	...	...	-	54	5452	-	-	5452
3	Public order and safety	2627	...	...	-	35	2662	244	2	2908
4	Education	9474	...	...	8	1940	11422	877	65	12364
5	Health	7072	...	...	144	4076	11292	435	13	11740
6	Social security and welfare	1344	...	...	68	17302	18714	119	118	18951
7	Housing and community amenities	624	...	...	168	54	846	447	719	2012
8	Recreation, culture and religion	1728	...	...	24	157	1909	538	75	2522
9	Economic services	6873	...	...	3270	274	10417	2997	285	13699
	A Fuel and energy	146	...	...	160	3	309	37	53	399
	B Agriculture, forestry, fishing and hunting	1449	...	...	503	2	1954	276	60	2290
	C Mining (except fuels), manufacturing and construction	362	...	...	575	8	945	18	8	971
	D Transportation and communication	3531	...	...	1561	6	5098	2557	157	7812
	E Other economic affairs	1385	...	...	471	255	2111	109	7	2227
10	Other functions	-42	...	...	22	7128	7108	-13	5	7100
	Total	40218	...	...	3723	31942	75883	6238	1278	83399
	1985									
1	General public services	5775	...	...	29	935	6739	736	-5	7470
2	Defence	6221	...	...	-	54	6275	-	-	6275
3	Public order and safety	2930	...	...	-	44	2974	348	1	3323
4	Education	10376	...	...	8	2172	12556	1030	90	13676
5	Health	7742	...	...	151	4523	12416	541	7	12964
6	Social security and welfare	1602	...	...	72	18572	20246	147	112	20505
7	Housing and community amenities	719	...	...	285	63	1067	473	638	2178
8	Recreation, culture and religion	1960	...	...	21	171	2152	697	107	2956
9	Economic services	7450	...	...	3429	268	11147	3274	155	14576
	A Fuel and energy	207	...	...	288	2	497	23	50	570
	B Agriculture, forestry, fishing and hunting	1559	...	...	482	6	2047	333	2	2382
	C Mining (except fuels), manufacturing and construction	448	...	...	444	7	899	30	34	963
	D Transportation and communication	3783	...	...	1714	8	5505	2830	58	8393
	E Other economic affairs	1453	...	...	501	245	2199	58	11	2268
10	Other functions	-41	...	...	17	9345	9321	29	-32	9318
	Total	44734	...	...	4012	36147	84893	7275	1073	93241
	1986									
1	General public services	6591	...	...	39	913	7543	820	-5	8358
2	Defence	6444	...	...	-	60	6504	-	-	6504
3	Public order and safety	3223	...	...	-	50	3273	388	1	3662
4	Education	11135	...	...	10	2416	13561	1156	51	14768
5	Health	8717	...	...	63	5075	13855	615	7	14477
6	Social security and welfare	1896	...	...	77	19889	21862	105	124	22091
7	Housing and community amenities	775	...	...	285	77	1137	467	709	2313
8	Recreation, culture and religion	2110	...	...	21	183	2314	870	109	3293
9	Economic services	7880	...	...	3567	370	11817	3400	142	15359
	A Fuel and energy	155	...	...	137	2	294	-39	78	333
	B Agriculture, forestry, fishing and hunting	1721	...	...	632	6	2359	388	-7	2740
	C Mining (except fuels), manufacturing and construction	390	...	...	390	8	788	29	14	831
	D Transportation and communication	3993	...	...	2043	9	6045	2864	48	8957
	E Other economic affairs	1621	...	...	365	345	2331	158	9	2498
10	Other functions	-58	...	...	14	11198	11154	13	-30	11137
	Total	48713	...	...	4076	40231	93020	7834	1108	101962

Australia

2.3 Total Government Outlays by Function and Type
(Continued)

Million Australian dollars — Fiscal year beginning 1 July

	Final Consumption Expenditures Total	Compensation of Employees	Other	Subsidies	Other Current Transfers & Property Income	Total Current Disbursements	Gross Capital Formation	Other Capital Outlays	Total Outlays
1987									
1 General public services	7710	...	...	29	922	8661	704	-250	9115
2 Defence	6779	...	...	-	61	6840	58	5	6903
3 Public order and safety	3505	...	...	-	51	3556	425	6	3987
4 Education	11764	...	...	10	2754	14528	1016	52	15596
5 Health	9541	...	...	21	5654	15216	620	32	15868
6 Social security and welfare	2111	...	...	83	21825	24019	128	138	24285
7 Housing and community amenities	852	...	...	204	88	1144	428	684	2256
8 Recreation, culture and religion	2240	...	...	28	252	2520	1046	34	3600
9 Economic services	8263	...	...	3537	346	12146	3112	149	15407
A Fuel and energy	168	...	...	194	3	365	29	35	429
B Agriculture, forestry, fishing and hunting	1820	...	...	446	6	2272	292	-6	2558
C Mining (except fuels), manufacturing and construction	432	...	...	370	8	810	33	-	843
D Transportation and communication	4220	...	...	2057	10	6287	2614	99	9000
E Other economic affairs	1623	...	...	470	319	2412	144	21	2577
10 Other functions	-111	...	...	17	12034	11940	-40	-37	11863
Total	52654	...	...	3929	43987	100570	7497	813	108880
1988									
1 General public services	7563	...	...	45	1165	8773	743	131	9647
2 Defence	6942	...	...	30	71	7043	-14	53	7082
3 Public order and safety	4046	...	...	-	79	4125	482	2	4609
4 Education	13027	...	...	18	3053	16098	1095	34	17227
5 Health	10649	...	...	3	6168	16820	664	38	17522
6 Social security and welfare	2367	...	...	70	22837	25274	122	116	25512
7 Housing and community amenities	901	...	...	253	122	1276	440	554	2270
8 Recreation, culture and religion	2362	...	...	30	257	2649	693	-115	3227
9 Economic services	8830	...	...	3577	176	12583	3240	255	16078
A Fuel and energy	144	...	...	124	3	271	20	58	349
B Agriculture, forestry, fishing and hunting	1907	...	...	318	7	2232	326	-	2558
C Mining (except fuels), manufacturing and construction	510	...	...	386	4	900	8	3	911
D Transportation and communication	4527	...	...	2147	5	6679	2699	129	9507
E Other economic affairs	1742	...	...	602	157	2501	187	65	2753
10 Other functions	63	...	...	47	14551	14661	104	-51	14714
Total	56750	...	...	4073	48479	109302	7569	1017	117888

2.4 Composition of General Government Social Security Benefits and Social Assistance Grants to Households

Million Australian dollars — Fiscal year beginning 1 July

	1980 SSB	1980 SAG	1981 SSB	1981 SAG	1982 SSB	1982 SAG	1983 SSB	1983 SAG	1984 SSB	1984 SAG	1985 SSB	1985 SAG
1 Education benefits	...	455	...	478	...	549	...	662	...	734	...	825
A Pre-primary and primary	...	-	...	1	...	1	...	1	...	3	...	4
B Secondary	...	36	...	40	...	58	...	83	...	100	...	141
C Tertiary	...	215	...	214	...	233	...	281	...	316	...	359
D Other	...	204	...	223	...	257	...	297	...	315	...	321
2 Health benefits	...	1454	...	1761	...	2060	...	2579	...	3597	...	4045
A Hospital	...	393	...	513	...	617	...	618	...	677	...	708
B Clinics and practitioners	...	747	...	851	...	1004	...	1459	...	2347	...	2704
C Public health	...	5	...	6	...	9	...	12	...	13	...	17
D Medicaments, etc.	...	309	...	391	...	430	...	489	...	560	...	616
3 Social security and welfare benefits	...	9481	...	10966	...	13429	...	15533	...	16783	...	17928
A Social security	...	9424	...	10891	...	13341	...	15436	...	16673	...	17807
Temporary sickness	...	174	...	225	...	271	...	336	...	365	...	392
Old age and permanent disability	...	4864	...	5540	...	5986	...	6625	...	7174	...	7644

Australia

2.4 Composition of General Government Social Security Benefits and Social Assistance Grants to Households
(Continued)

Million Australian dollars — Fiscal year beginning 1 July

	1980 SSB	1980 SAG	1981 SSB	1981 SAG	1982 SSB	1982 SAG	1983 SSB	1983 SAG	1984 SSB	1984 SAG	1985 SSB	1985 SAG
Unemployment	...	996	...	1224	...	2249	...	2912	...	2984	...	3122
Family assistance	...	1365	...	1648	...	2104	...	2432	...	2613	...	2825
Other	...	2025	...	2254	...	2731	...	3131	...	3537	...	3824
B Welfare	...	57	...	75	...	88	...	97	...	110	...	121
4 Housing and community amenities	...	5	...	9	...	20	...	30	...	40	...	45
5 Recreation and cultural benefits	...	3	...	3	...	3	...	5	...	2	...	2
6 Other	...	33	...	33	...	106	...	94	...	73	...	82
Total	...	11431	...	13250	...	16167	...	18903	...	21229	...	22927

	1986 SSB	1986 SAG	1987 SSB	1987 SAG	1988 SSB	1988 SAG	1989 SSB	1989 SAG
1 Education benefits	...	953	...	1208	...	1352	...	...
A Pre-primary and primary	...	4	...	15	...	16	...	...
B Secondary	...	157	...	290	...	309	...	...
C Tertiary	...	436	...	507	...	566	...	...
D Other	...	356	...	396	...	461	...	...
2 Health benefits	...	4526	...	5355	...	5812	...	...
A Hospital	...	775	...	1176	...	1326	...	...
B Clinics and practitioners	...	2990	...	3229	...	3377	...	...
C Public health	...	14	...	1	...	1	...	...
D Medicaments, etc.	...	747	...	949	...	1108	...	...
3 Social security and welfare benefits	...	19132	...	20859	...	21853	...	...
A Social security	...	19007	...	20712	...	21731	...	...
Temporary sickness	...	429	...	511	...	553	...	...
Old age and permanent disability	...	8244	...	9230	...	9892	...	...
Unemployment	...	3454	...	3375	...	3135	...	3068
Family assistance	...	2808	...	3094	...	3899	...	...
Other	...	4072	...	4502	...	4252	...	...
B Welfare	...	125	...	147	...	122	...	...
4 Housing and community amenities	...	60	...	59	...	77	...	...
5 Recreation and cultural benefits	...	3	...	3	...	3	...	...
6 Other	...	187	...	200	...	120	...	...
Total	...	24861	...	27684	...	29217	...	32354

2.5 Private Final Consumption Expenditure by Type and Purpose, in Current Prices

Million Australian dollars — Fiscal year beginning 1 July

Final Consumption Expenditure of Resident Households

	1970	1975	1980	1981	1982	1983	1984	1985	1986	1987	1988	1989
1 Food, beverages and tobacco [a]	5699	10812	19939	22341	24705	26788	28758	32254	35007	37744	41010	45273
A Food	3819	7104	13841	15542	17279	18728	20101	22740	24693	26482	29102	32130
B Non-alcoholic beverages												
C Alcoholic beverages	1321	2639	4517	5059	5540	5860	6268	6857	7314	8015	8353	9129
D Tobacco	559	1069	1581	1740	1886	2200	2389	2657	3000	3247	3555	4014
2 Clothing and footwear [b]	1830	3549	5794	6499	7198	7839	8539	9635	10522	11542	12198	12482
3 Gross rent, fuel and power	3166	7170	15460	17954	20650	22690	24928	27970	31275	34998	39356	43428
A Fuel and power	486	917	1756	2116	2581	2867	3074	3377	3681	3919	4199	4618
B Other	2680	6253	13704	15838	18069	19823	21854	24593	27594	31079	35157	38810
4 Furniture, furnishings and household equipment and operation [b]	1591	4244	6418	7314	7948	8816	9609	10716	11417	12835	13980	14845
5 Medical care and health expenses	1240	2915	5084	6065	7102	7898	8328	9250	10631	12065	13558	15099
6 Transport and communication	3174	6652	12785	14224	15909	17293	19295	21478	22635	25668	28656	32540
A Personal transport equipment	1045	1898	3545	3843	3927	4298	5112	5729	5625	6621	8021	9376
B Other	2129	4754	9240	10381	11982	12995	14183	15749	17010	19047	20635	23164
7 Recreational, entertainment, education and cultural services	1503	3555	6567	7648	8704	9952	11308	12746	14298	16000	17859	19906
A Education	231	488	887	1074	1304	1557	1770	1977	2193	2422	2694	2940

Australia

2.5 Private Final Consumption Expenditure by Type and Purpose, in Current Prices
(Continued)

Million Australian dollars — Fiscal year beginning 1 July

	1970	1975	1980	1981	1982	1983	1984	1985	1986	1987	1988	1989
B Other	1272	3067	5680	6574	7400	8395	9538	10769	12105	13578	15165	16966
8 Miscellaneous goods and services	2359	5419	10423	11981	13360	15135	16852	19413	21836	25472	29165	33216
Total Final Consumption Expenditure in the Domestic Market by Households, of which	20562	44316	82470	94026	105576	116411	127617	143462	157621	176324	195782	216789
Plus: Direct purchases abroad by resident households	207	779	1388	1592	1771	1945	2347	2455	2720	3204	3707	4323
Less: Direct purchases in the domestic market by non-resident households	151	326	1088	1263	1396	1556	1699	2089	2729	3782	4642	4582
Equals: Final Consumption Expenditure of Resident Households c	20618	44769	82770	94355	105951	116800	128265	143828	157612	175746	194847	216530

Final Consumption Expenditure of Private Non-profit Institutions Serving Households

	1970	1975	1980	1981	1982	1983	1984	1985	1986	1987	1988	1989
Equals: Final Consumption Expenditure of Private Non-profit Organisations Serving Households	...	...	...	...	...	...	...	...	...	...	...	...
Private Final Consumption Expenditure	20618	44769	82770	94355	105951	116800	128265	143828	157612	175746	194847	216530

a) Item 'Food, beverages and tobacco' includes food, beverages and tobacco consumed in institutions except hospitals and nursing homes.
b) Drapery is included in item 'Clothing and footwear'.
c) Item 'Final consumption expenditure of resident households' includes consumption expenditure of private non-profit institutions serving households.

2.6 Private Final Consumption Expenditure by Type and Purpose, in Constant Prices

Million Australian dollars — Fiscal year beginning 1 July

At constant prices of: 1979 (1970–1975), 1984 (1980–1989)

Final Consumption Expenditure of Resident Households

	1970	1975	1980	1981	1982	1983	1984	1985	1986	1987	1988	1989
1 Food, beverages and tobacco a	13992	16381	27734	28648	28579	28437	28758	29767	29628	30098	30069	30926
A Food	9326	11098	18635	19316	19615	19731	20101	21028	21047	21461	21460	22147
B Non-alcoholic beverages												
C Alcoholic beverages	3239	3786	6460	6610	6444	6282	6268	6357	6179	6233	6228	6403
D Tobacco	1427	1497	2639	2722	2520	2424	2389	2382	2402	2404	2381	2376
2 Clothing and footwear b	4824	5224	7400	7778	8102	8290	8539	8859	8818	8991	8908	8682
3 Gross rent, fuel and power	8778	11094	22544	23464	23895	24413	24928	25584	26199	26658	27247	28044
A Fuel and power	1168	1432	2898	3002	2971	3052	3074	3186	3311	3319	3393	3593
B Other	7610	9662	19646	20462	20924	21361	21854	22398	22888	23339	23854	24451
4 Furniture, furnishings and household equipment and operation b	3281	5536	7870	8405	8461	8945	9609	10067	9813	10449	10982	11419
5 Medical care and health expenses	3198	4157	7033	7593	8069	8457	8328	8666	9104	9566	9959	10364
6 Transport and communication	8176	9463	17852	18223	18333	18366	19295	19947	19598	20737	22117	23327
A Personal transport equipment	2384	2582	4828	4750	4475	4569	5112	5123	4261	4475	5020	5617
B Other	5792	6881	13024	13473	13858	13797	14183	14824	15337	16262	17097	17710
7 Recreational, entertainment, education and cultural services	3894	5150	9338	9704	9844	10497	11308	11776	12181	12641	13071	13716
A Education	632	675	1233	1327	1456	1649	1770	1870	1978	2092	2190	2284

Australia

2.6 Private Final Consumption Expenditure by Type and Purpose, in Constant Prices
(Continued)

Million Australian dollars — Fiscal year beginning 1 July

	1970	1975	1980	1981	1982	1983	1984	1985	1986	1987	1988	1989
		1979			At constant prices of:		1984					
B Other	3262	4475	8105	8377	8388	8848	9538	9906	10203	10549	10881	11432
8 Miscellaneous goods and services	6925	7612	14330	14927	15041	15954	16852	18138	18992	20998	22671	24426
Total Final Consumption Expenditure in the Domestic Market by Households, of which	53068	64618	114101	118742	120324	123359	127617	132804	134333	140138	145024	150904
Plus: Direct purchases abroad by resident households	...	1524	1802	2017	1954	2141	2347	1966	1874	2149	2712	2862
Less: Direct purchases in the domestic market by non-resident households	...	477	1544	1613	1595	1646	1699	1933	2330	2998	3431	3119
Equals: Final Consumption Expenditure of Resident Households c	53068	65665	114359	119146	120683	123854	128265	132837	133877	139289	144305	150647

Final Consumption Expenditure of Private Non-profit Institutions Serving Households

Equals: Final Consumption Expenditure of Private Non-profit Organisations Serving Households			...	...	...	...	...	...	...	...	...	...
Private Final Consumption Expenditure	53068	65665	114359	119146	120683	123854	128265	132837	133877	139289	144305	150647

a) Item 'Food, beverages and tobacco' includes food, beverages and tobacco consumed in institutions except hospitals and nursing homes.
b) Drapery is included in item 'Clothing and footwear'.
c) Item 'Final consumption expenditure of resident households' includes consumption expenditure of private non-profit institutions serving households.

2.7 Gross Capital Formation by Type of Good and Owner, in Current Prices

Million Australian dollars — Fiscal year beginning 1 July

	1980				1981				1982			
	TOTAL	Total Private	Public Enterprises	General Government	TOTAL	Total Private	Public Enterprises	General Government	TOTAL	Total Private	Public Enterprises	General Government
Increase in stocks, total a	502	771	-336	67	1555	797	729	29	-2442	-2476	-20	54
1 Goods producing industries a	1220	1220	...	...	1198	1198	...	...	-607	-607	...	...
2 Wholesale and retail trade	965	1519	-554	...	2314	1948	366	...	134	540	-406	...
3 Other, except government stocks	404	404	...	...	262	262	...	...	198	198	...	...
4 Government stocks	239	...	172	67	404	...	375	29	455	...	401	54
Statistical discrepancy b	-2326	-2372	46	...	-2623	-2611	-12	...	-2622	-2607	-15	...
Gross Fixed Capital Formation, Total acd	35218	25854	5611	3753	41479	30170	7185	4124	41121	27985	8512	4624
1 Residential buildings	8516	8199	290	27	9396	9041	322	33	8245	7717	467	61
2 Non-residential buildings												
3 Other construction	10662	4556	2951	3155	13157	5590	4044	3523	13997	5586	4555	3856
4 Land improvement and plantation and orchard development												
5 Producers' durable goods	14359	11418	2370	571	17265	13878	2819	568	17407	13210	3490	707
6 Breeding stock, dairy cattle, etc.	...	...	...	...	...	...	...	...	...	...	...	...
Statistical discrepancy	1681	1681	...	...	1661	1661	...	...	1472	1472	...	...
Total Gross Capital Formation ae	35720	26625	5275	3820	43034	30967	7914	4153	38679	25509	8492	4678

	1983				1984				1985			
	TOTAL	Total Private	Public Enterprises	General Government	TOTAL	Total Private	Public Enterprises	General Government	TOTAL	Total Private	Public Enterprises	General Government
Increase in stocks, total a	1430	201	1221	8	1094	967	94	33	1464	1806	-350	8
1 Goods producing industries a	976	976	...	...	1109	1109	...	...	1443	1443	...	...
2 Wholesale and retail trade	1821	792	1029	...	2409	2341	68	...	1440	2277	-837	...
3 Other, except government stocks	36	36	...	...	-17	-17	...	...	110	110	...	...
4 Government stocks	340	...	332	8	6	...	-27	33	153	...	145	8
Statistical discrepancy b	-1743	-1603	-140	...	-2413	-2466	53	...	-1682	-2024	342	...
Gross Fixed Capital Formation, Total acd	44316	30173	8837	5306	51081	35913	8963	6205	59313	41255	10791	7267

Australia

2.7 Gross Capital Formation by Type of Good and Owner, in Current Prices
(Continued)

Million Australian dollars — Fiscal year beginning 1 July

	1983 TOTAL	Total Private	Public Enterprises	General Government	1984 TOTAL	Total Private	Public Enterprises	General Government	1985 TOTAL	Total Private	Public Enterprises	General Government
1 Residential buildings	9473	8707	707	59	11326	10413	826	87	12319	11239	955	125
2 Non-residential buildings												
3 Other construction	13742	5247	4159	4336	15765	6174	4494	5097	18995	8400	4740	5855
4 Land improvement and plantation and orchard development												
5 Producers' durable goods	19067	14185	3971	911	21418	16754	3643	1021	25182	18799	5096	1287
6 Breeding stock, dairy cattle, etc.	...	...	...	...	...	...	...	...	...	...	...	...
Statistical discrepancy	2034	2034	...	...	2572	2572	...	...	2817	2817	...	...
Total Gross Capital Formation ae	45746	30374	10058	5314	52175	36880	9057	6238	60777	43061	10441	7275

	1986 TOTAL	Total Private	Public Enterprises	General Government	1987 TOTAL	Total Private	Public Enterprises	General Government	1988 TOTAL	Total Private	Public Enterprises	General Government
Increase in stocks, total a	-1421	-1071	-296	-54	-410	301	-712	1	3742	3692	89	-39
1 Goods producing industries a	1007	1007	...	...	1791	1791	...	...	2191	2191	...	...
2 Wholesale and retail trade	923	1185	-262	...	1709	1916	-207	...	3288	3087	201	...
3 Other, except government stocks	476	476	...	...	273	273	...	...	144	144	...	...
4 Government stocks	-84	...	-30	-54	-84	...	-85	1	110	...	149	-39
Statistical discrepancy b	-3743	-3739	-4	...	-4099	-3679	-420	...	-1991	-1730	-261	...
Gross Fixed Capital Formation, Total acd	63991	44840	11263	7888	71096	53771	9829	7496	84767	66552	10607	7608
1 Residential buildings	11859	10734	1011	114	13421	12468	801	152	18520	17515	847	158
2 Non-residential buildings												
3 Other construction	20839	9508	4943	6388	23349	12676	4833	5840	26069	14838	5407	5824
4 Land improvement and plantation and orchard development												
5 Producers' durable goods	28106	21411	5309	1386	29388	23689	4195	1504	33072	27093	4353	1626
6 Breeding stock, dairy cattle, etc.	...	...	...	...	...	...	...	...	...	...	...	...
Statistical discrepancy	3187	3187	...	...	4938	4938	...	...	7106	7106	...	...
Total Gross Capital Formation ae	62570	43769	10967	7834	70686	54072	9117	7497	88509	70244	10696	7569

	1989 TOTAL	Total Private	Public Enterprises	General Government
Increase in stocks, total a	4766	1600	3167	-1
1 Goods producing industries a	1646	1646	...	...
2 Wholesale and retail trade	1775	1794	-19	...
3 Other, except government stocks	686	686	...	...
4 Government stocks	2499	...	2500	-1
Statistical discrepancy b	-1840	-2526	686	...
Gross Fixed Capital Formation, Total acd	88967	67158	12977	8832
1 Residential buildings	20018	18410	1428	180
2 Non-residential buildings				
3 Other construction	29120	16660	5777	6683
4 Land improvement and plantation and orchard development				
5 Producers' durable goods	34628	26887	5772	1969
6 Breeding stock, dairy cattle, etc.	...	...	...	...
Statistical discrepancy	5201	5201	...	...
Total Gross Capital Formation ae	93733	68758	16144	8831

a) Livestock is excluded from items 'Increase in Stocks' and 'Gross Fixed Capital Formation' and as a result, from 'Gross Capital Formation'.
b) Item 'Statistical discrepancy' refers to stock valuation adjustment. The detailed data on changes in stock are based on book values.
c) All government expenditure on roads is treated as gross fixed capital formation.
d) All government expenditure on defence is treated as final consumption expenditure.
e) The estimates of 'Gross capital formation by type of good and owner' are based on enterprise data and are on an ownership basis throughout.

Australia

2.8 Gross Capital Formation by Type of Good and Owner, in Constant Prices

Million Australian dollars — Fiscal year beginning 1 July

	1980 TOTAL	1980 Total Private	1980 Public Enterprises	1980 General Government	1981 TOTAL	1981 Total Private	1981 Public Enterprises	1981 General Government	1982 TOTAL	1982 Total Private	1982 Public Enterprises	1982 General Government
				At constant prices of: 1984								
Increase in stocks, total [a]	687	1006	-408	89	1774	847	892	35	-2577	-2589	-48	60
1 Goods producing industries [a]	201	201	...	...	23	23	...	...	-1764	-1764	...	...
2 Wholesale and retail trade	-171	479	-650	...	1328	740	588	...	-1124	-819	-305	...
3 Other, except government stocks	568	326	242	...	388	84	304	...	251	-6	257	...
4 Government stocks	89	...	...	89	35	...	...	35	60	...	...	60
Gross Fixed Capital Formation, Total [abc]	47834	34432	8037	5365	50921	36491	9201	5229	45506	30792	9570	5144
1 Residential buildings	11810	11370	402	38	11640	11200	399	41	9279	8684	526	69
2 Non-residential buildings												
3 Other construction	15352	6560	4210	4582	16717	7114	5098	4505	15647	6252	5091	4304
4 Land improvement and plantation and orchard development												
5 Producers' durable goods	18340	14170	3425	745	20508	16121	3704	683	18733	14009	3953	771
6 Breeding stock, dairy cattle, etc.	...	...	...	...	...	...	...	...	...	...	...	...
Statistical discrepancy	2332	2332	...	...	2056	2056	...	...	1847	1847	...	...
Total Gross Capital Formation [ad]	48521	35438	7629	5454	52695	37338	10093	5264	42929	28203	9522	5204

	1983 TOTAL	1983 Total Private	1983 Public Enterprises	1983 General Government	1984 TOTAL	1984 Total Private	1984 Public Enterprises	1984 General Government	1985 TOTAL	1985 Total Private	1985 Public Enterprises	1985 General Government
				At constant prices of: 1984								
Increase in stocks, total [a]	1770	153	1609	8	1094	967	94	33	1257	1657	-407	7
1 Goods producing industries [a]	171	171	...	...	85	85	...	...	733	733	...	...
2 Wholesale and retail trade	1563	56	1507	...	1180	1154	26	...	369	893	-524	...
3 Other, except government stocks	28	-74	102	...	-204	-272	68	...	148	31	117	...
4 Government stocks	8	...	...	8	33	...	...	33	7	...	...	7
Gross Fixed Capital Formation, Total [abc]	46722	31753	9416	5553	51081	35913	8965	6203	53609	36949	9920	6740
1 Residential buildings	10161	9339	759	63	11326	10413	826	87	11314	10322	877	115
2 Non-residential buildings												
3 Other construction	14497	5544	4413	4540	15764	6174	4495	5095	17258	7569	4316	5373
4 Land improvement and plantation and orchard development												
5 Producers' durable goods	19596	14402	4244	950	21419	16754	3644	1021	22617	16638	4727	1252
6 Breeding stock, dairy cattle, etc.	...	...	...	...	...	...	...	...	...	...	...	...
Statistical discrepancy	2468	2468	...	...	2572	2572	...	...	2420	2420	...	...
Total Gross Capital Formation [ad]	48492	31906	11025	5561	52175	36880	9059	6236	54866	38606	9513	6747

	1986 TOTAL	1986 Total Private	1986 Public Enterprises	1986 General Government	1987 TOTAL	1987 Total Private	1987 Public Enterprises	1987 General Government	1988 TOTAL	1988 Total Private	1988 Public Enterprises	1988 General Government
				At constant prices of: 1984								
Increase in stocks, total [a]	-1114	-798	-268	-48	-198	442	-641	1	2986	2853	163	-30
1 Goods producing industries [a]	-453	-453	...	...	166	166	...	...	738	738	...	...
2 Wholesale and retail trade	-1092	-579	-513	...	-490	273	-763	...	2341	2158	183	...
3 Other, except government stocks	479	234	245	...	125	3	122	...	-63	-43	-20	...
4 Government stocks	-48	...	...	-48	1	...	...	1	-30	...	...	-30
Gross Fixed Capital Formation, Total [abc]	53246	36814	9565	6867	55883	41882	7730	6271	62709	48849	7765	6095
1 Residential buildings	10228	9257	872	99	10893	10119	650	124	12944	12241	592	111
2 Non-residential buildings												
3 Other construction	17604	7953	4172	5479	18426	9936	3759	4731	19093	10840	3806	4447
4 Land improvement and plantation and orchard development												
5 Producers' durable goods	23051	17241	4521	1289	23628	18891	3321	1416	27293	22389	3367	1537
6 Breeding stock, dairy cattle, etc.	...	...	...	...	...	...	...	...	...	...	...	...
Statistical discrepancy	2363	2363	...	...	2936	2936	...	...	3379	3379	...	...
Total Gross Capital Formation [ad]	52132	36016	9297	6819	55685	42324	7089	6272	65695	51702	7928	6065

Australia

2.8 Gross Capital Formation by Type of Good and Owner, in Constant Prices

Million Australian dollars — Fiscal year beginning 1 July

At constant prices of: 1984

	1989 TOTAL	Total Private	Public Enterprises	General Government
Increase in stocks, total [a]	3135	1172	1964	-1
1 Goods producing industries [a]	619	619	...	...
2 Wholesale and retail trade	2005	120	1885	...
3 Other, except government stocks	512	433	79	...
4 Government stocks	-1	...	...	-1
Gross Fixed Capital Formation, Total [abc]	62918	47236	8940	6742
1 Residential buildings	12595	11583	899	113
2 Non-residential buildings				
3 Other construction	19877	11283	3783	4811
4 Land improvement and plantation and orchard development				
5 Producers' durable goods	27986	21910	4258	1818
6 Breeding stock, dairy cattle, etc.	...	...	...	...
Statistical discrepancy	2460	2460	...	...
Total Gross Capital Formation [ad]	66053	48408	10904	6741

a) Livestock is excluded from items 'Increase in Stocks' and 'Gross Fixed Capital Formation' and as a result, from 'Gross Capital Formation'.
b) All government expenditure on roads is treated as gross fixed capital formation.
c) All government expenditure on defence is treated as final consumption expenditure.
d) The estimates of 'Gross capital formation by type of good and owner' are based on enterprise data and are on an ownership basis throughout.

2.17 Exports and Imports of Goods and Services, Detail

Million Australian dollars — Fiscal year beginning 1 July

Exports of Goods and Services

	1970	1975	1980	1981	1982	1983	1984	1985	1986	1987	1988	1989
1 Exports of merchandise, f.o.b. [ab]	4244	9432	18689	19140	20857	23576	29365	32307	35426	40555	43105	48665
2 Transport and communication	477	985	1895	1965	2041	2102	2480	2853	3219	3670	3752	3960
3 Insurance service charges	1	3	10	10	18	10	13	7	24	38	33	36
4 Other commodities [b]	181	287	755	931	988	1178	1275	1451	1679	1943	2215	2433
5 Adjustments of merchandise exports to change-of-ownership basis	-	44	29	-60	-201	106	-153	-99	-3	-14	-32	-850
6 Direct purchases in the domestic market by non-residential households	151	326	1088	1263	1396	1556	1699	2089	2729	3782	4642	4582
7 Direct purchases in the domestic market by extraterritorial bodies	11	24	39	51	57	67	76	85	74	84	87	97
Total Exports of Goods and Services	5065	11101	22505	23300	25156	28595	34755	38693	43148	50058	53802	58923

Imports of Goods and Services

	1970	1975	1980	1981	1982	1983	1984	1985	1986	1987	1988	1989
1 Imports of merchandise, c.i.f. [c]	4219	8742	20483	24336	23104	25678	32017	38343	39859	43293	50136	54598
A Imports of merchandise, f.o.b. [d]	3806	7932	18755	22365	21298	23648	29478	35516	37103	40437	46960	51329
B Transport of services on merchandise imports	411	803	1717	1962	1795	2018	2523	2803	2732	2832	3152	3245
By residents	...	...	...	...	...	...	...	...	...	...	...	...
By non-residents	411	803	1717	1962	1795	2018	2523	2803	2732	2832	3152	3245
C Insurance service charges on merchandise imports	2	7	11	9	11	12	16	24	24	24	24	24
By residents	...	...	...	...	...	...	...	...	...	...	...	...

Australia

2.17 Exports and Imports of Goods and Services, Detail
(Continued)

Million Australian dollars — Fiscal year beginning 1 July

	1970	1975	1980	1981	1982	1983	1984	1985	1986	1987	1988	1989
By non-residents	2	7	11	9	11	12	16	24	24	24	24	24
2 Adjustments of merchandise imports to change-of-ownership basis	-	-2	422	3	407	-151	615	160	56	-51	72	-338
3 Other transport and communication [e]	382	736	1494	1618	1676	1699	2092	2197	2114	2510	2912	3413
4 Other insurance service charges	12	-	48	44	118	197	184	312	283	288	357	360
5 Other commodities	189	483	1081	1227	1685	1601	1982	2304	2644	3087	3334	3565
6 Direct purchases abroad by government	61	92	155	177	206	223	268	316	341	311	307	385
7 Direct purchases abroad by resident households	207	779	1388	1592	1771	1945	2347	2455	2720	3161	3744	4308
Total Imports of Goods and Services	5070	10830	25071	28997	28967	31192	39505	46087	48017	52599	60862	66291
Balance of Goods and Services	-5	271	-2566	-5697	-3811	-2597	-4750	-7394	-4869	-2541	-7060	-7368
Total Imports and Balance of Goods and Services	5065	11101	22505	23300	25156	28595	34755	38693	43148	50058	53802	58923

a) Item 'Exports of merchandise, f.o.b.' refers to exports recorded at the time the goods cross the customs frontier. Sales of ships and aircraft stores, bunkers and ballasts are excluded.
b) Prior to January 1976, exports of gold are included in item 'Other commodities'. Since January 1976, they are included in item 'Export of merchandise, f.o.b.'.
c) Valuation basis is essentially Free Along Side (F.A.S.).
d) Item 'Imports of merchandise f.o.b.' is adjusted in respect to coverage and valuation. It is recorded at the time the goods cross the customs frontiers. It excludes purchase of ships and aircraft stores etc. which are included in net acquisition of foreign financial assets.
e) Item 'Other transport and communication' includes purchases of ships' stores etc. and crews' expenditure in foreign ports.

3.12 General Government Income and Outlay Account: Total and Subsectors

Million Australian dollars — Fiscal year beginning 1 July

	1980					1981				
	Total General Government	Central Government	State or Provincial Government	Local Government	Social Security Funds	Total General Government	Central Government	State or Provincial Government	Local Government	Social Security Funds

Receipts

1 Operating surplus	-	-	...	-	...	-	-	...	-	...
2 Property and entrepreneurial income [a]	2610	2507	...	1678	...	3149	2953	...	1945	...
A Withdrawals from public quasi-corporations [a]	365	272	...	93	...	553	430	...	123	...
B Interest	1617	2132	...	1060	...	1974	2418	...	1305	...
C Dividends	4	4	...	-	...	10	9	...	1	...
D Net land rent and royalties	624	99	...	525	...	612	96	...	516	...
3 Taxes, fees and contributions	40376	32770	...	7606	...	47009	38071	...	8938	...
A Indirect taxes	17250	10335	...	6915	...	19652	11543	...	8109	...
B Direct taxes	22399	22399	...	...	...	26469	26469	...	...	...
Income	22399	22399	...	...	...	26469	26469	...	...	...
Other [b]	...	...	...	...	...	...	...	...	...	...
C Social security contributions	...	...	...	...	...	...	...	...	...	...
D Fees, fines and penalties [b]	727	36	...	691	...	888	59	...	829	...
4 Other current transfers	-	-	...	10310	...	-	-	...	11403	...
A Casualty insurance claims	...	...	...	...	...	...	...	...	...	...
B Transfers from other government subsectors	...	-	...	10310	...	...	-	...	11403	...
C Transfers from the rest of the world	...	...	...	...	...	...	...	...	...	...
D Other transfers, except imputed	-	...	...	-	...	-	...	...	-	...
E Imputed unfunded employee pension and welfare contributions	...	...	...	...	...	...	...	...	...	...
Total Current Receipts	42986	35277	...	19594	...	50158	41024	...	22286	...

Disbursements

1 Government final consumption expenditure	24993	7742	...	17251	...	28525	8942	...	19583	...
2 Property income	3001	2575	...	2001	...	3407	2886	...	2270	...
A Interest	3001	2575	...	2001	...	3407	2886	...	2270	...
B Net land rent and royalties	-	...	...	...	...	-	...	...	...	...
3 Subsidies [c]	2240	1138	...	1102	...	2572	1232	...	1340	...

Australia

3.12 General Government Income and Outlay Account: Total and Subsectors
(Continued)

Million Australian dollars — Fiscal year beginning 1 July

	1980 Total General Government	1980 Central Government	1980 State or Provincial Government	1980 Local Government	1980 Social Security Funds	1981 Total General Government	1981 Central Government	1981 State or Provincial Government	1981 Local Government	1981 Social Security Funds
4 Other current transfers [d]	13346	22409	...	1247	...	15540	25503	...	1440	...
A Casualty insurance premiums, net	...	...	...	...	...	...	...	...	...	...
B Transfers to other government subsectors	...	10310	...	-	...	...	11403	...	-	...
C Social security benefits	...	...	...	...	...	...	...	...	...	...
D Social assistance grants	11431	11031	...	400	...	13250	12814	...	436	...
E Unfunded employee pension and welfare benefits	...	...	...	...	...	...	...	...	...	...
F Transfers to private non-profit institutions serving households	1228	381	...	847	...	1484	480	...	1004	...
G Other transfers n.e.c.	...	...	...	...	...	...	...	...	...	...
H Transfers to the rest of the world [d]	687	687	...	-	...	806	806	...	-	...
Net saving	-594	1413	...	-2007	...	114	2461	...	-2347	...
Total Current Disbursements and Net Saving	42986	35277	...	19594	...	50158	41024	...	22286	...

	1982 Total General Government	1982 Central Government	1982 State or Provincial Government	1982 Local Government	1982 Social Security Funds	1983 Total General Government	1983 Central Government	1983 State or Provincial Government	1983 Local Government	1983 Social Security Funds

Receipts

	1982 Total	1982 Central	1982 State/Prov	1982 Local	1982 SSF	1983 Total	1983 Central	1983 State/Prov	1983 Local	1983 SSF
1 Operating surplus	-	-	...	-	...	-	-	...	-	...
2 Property and entrepreneurial income [a]	3838	3591	...	2192	...	4639	4068	...	2659	...
A Withdrawals from public quasi-corporations [a]	816	737	...	79	...	1155	828	...	327	...
B Interest	2312	2729	...	1528	...	2488	2993	...	1583	...
C Dividends	5	5	...	-	...	7	6	...	1	...
D Net land rent and royalties	705	120	...	585	...	989	241	...	748	...
3 Taxes, fees and contributions	51627	41179	...	10448	...	56570	44917	...	11653	...
A Indirect taxes	22539	13052	...	9487	...	25775	15220	...	10555	...
B Direct taxes	28062	28062	...	...	...	29621	29621	...	...	...
Income	28062	28062	...	...	...	29621	29621	...	...	...
Other [b]	...	...	...	...	...	...	...	...	...	...
C Social security contributions	...	...	...	...	...	...	...	...	...	...
D Fees, fines and penalties [b]	1026	65	...	961	...	1174	76	...	1098	...
4 Other current transfers	-	-	...	13132	...	-	-	...	14996	...
A Casualty insurance claims	...	...	...	...	...	...	...	...	...	...
B Transfers from other government subsectors	...	-	...	13132	...	...	-	...	14996	...
C Transfers from the rest of the world	...	...	...	...	...	...	...	...	...	...
D Other transfers, except imputed	-	-	...	-	...	-	-	...	-	...
E Imputed unfunded employee pension and welfare contributions	...	...	...	...	...	...	...	...	...	...
Total Current Receipts	55465	44770	...	25772	...	61209	48985	...	29308	...

Disbursements

	1982 Total	1982 Central	1982 State/Prov	1982 Local	1982 SSF	1983 Total	1983 Central	1983 State/Prov	1983 Local	1983 SSF
1 Government final consumption expenditure	32438	10263	...	22175	...	35909	11374	...	24535	...
2 Property income	4023	3384	...	2584	...	5160	4331	...	2917	...
A Interest	4023	3384	...	2584	...	5160	4331	...	2917	...
B Net land rent and royalties	-	...	...	...	...	-	...	...	...	...
3 Subsidies [c]	3107	1337	...	1770	...	3358	1483	...	1875	...

Australia

3.12 General Government Income and Outlay Account: Total and Subsectors
(Continued)

Million Australian dollars — Fiscal year beginning 1 July

	1982					1983				
	Total General Government	Central Government	State or Provincial Government	Local Government	Social Security Funds	Total General Government	Central Government	State or Provincial Government	Local Government	Social Security Funds
4 Other current transfers [d]	18889	30233	...	1788	...	22082	34971	...	2107	...
A Casualty insurance premiums, net	...	...	...	...	...	...	...	...	...	...
B Transfers to other government subsectors	...	13132	...	-	...	...	14996	...	-	...
C Social security benefits	...	...	...	...	...	...	...	...	...	...
D Social assistance grants	16167	15598	...	569	...	18903	18300	...	603	...
E Unfunded employee pension and welfare benefits	...	...	...	...	...	...	...	...	...	...
F Transfers to private non-profit institutions serving households	1829	610	...	1219	...	2228	724	...	1504	...
G Other transfers n.e.c.	...	...	...	...	...	...	...	...	...	...
H Transfers to the rest of the world [d]	893	893	...	-	...	951	951	...	-	...
Net saving	-2992	-447	...	-2545	...	-5300	-3174	...	-2126	...
Total Current Disbursements and Net Saving	55465	44770	...	25772	...	61209	48985	...	29308	...

	1984					1985				
	Total General Government	Central Government	State or Provincial Government	Local Government	Social Security Funds	Total General Government	Central Government	State or Provincial Government	Local Government	Social Security Funds

Receipts

1 Operating surplus	-	-	...	-	...	-	-	...	-	...
2 Property and entrepreneurial income [a]	5701	4576	...	3357	...	8190	5789	...	4739	...
A Withdrawals from public quasi-corporations [a]	1416	1083	...	333	...	2538	2108	...	430	...
B Interest	3177	3205	...	2204	...	4454	3459	...	3333	...
C Dividends	12	3	...	9	...	10	3	...	7	...
D Net land rent and royalties	1096	285	...	811	...	1188	219	...	969	...
3 Taxes, fees and contributions	66181	53109	...	13072	...	73363	58966	...	14397	...
A Indirect taxes	29526	17687	...	11839	...	32508	19434	...	13074	...
B Direct taxes	35335	35335	...	...	...	39437	39437	...	...	...
Income	35335	35335	...	...	...	39437	39437	...	...	...
Other [b]	...	...	...	...	...	...	...	...	...	...
C Social security contributions	...	...	...	...	...	...	...	...	...	...
D Fees, fines and penalties [b]	1320	87	...	1233	...	1418	95	...	1323	...
4 Other current transfers	-	-	...	16479	...	-	-	...	17757	...
A Casualty insurance claims	...	...	...	...	...	...	...	...	...	...
B Transfers from other government subsectors	...	-	...	16479	...	...	-	...	17757	...
C Transfers from the rest of the world	...	...	...	...	...	...	...	...	...	...
D Other transfers, except imputed	-	-	...	-	...	-	-	...	-	...
E Imputed unfunded employee pension and welfare contributions	...	...	...	...	...	...	...	...	...	...
Total Current Receipts	71882	57685	...	32908	...	81553	64755	...	36893	...

Disbursements

1 Government final consumption expenditure	40218	13182	...	27036	...	44734	15001	...	29733	...
2 Property income	7097	5774	...	3555	...	9310	7070	...	4578	...
A Interest	7097	5774	...	3555	...	9310	7070	...	4578	...
B Net land rent and royalties	-	...	...	...	...	-	...	...	...	...
3 Subsidies [c]	3723	1731	...	1992	...	4012	1692	...	2320	...

39

Australia

3.12 General Government Income and Outlay Account: Total and Subsectors
(Continued)

Million Australian dollars — Fiscal year beginning 1 July

	1984					1985				
	Total General Government	Central Government	State or Provincial Government	Local Government	Social Security Funds	Total General Government	Central Government	State or Provincial Government	Local Government	Social Security Funds
4 Other current transfers [d]	24845	38979	...	2345	...	26837	42034	...	2560	...
A Casualty insurance premiums, net	...	...	...	...	...	...	...	...	...	...
B Transfers to other government subsectors	...	16479	...	-	...	...	17757	...	-	...
C Social security benefits	...	...	...	...	...	...	...	...	...	...
D Social assistance grants	21229	20568	...	661	...	22927	22218	...	709	...
E Unfunded employee pension and welfare benefits	...	...	...	...	...	...	...	...	...	...
F Transfers to private non-profit institutions serving households	2566	882	...	1684	...	2822	971	...	1851	...
G Other transfers n.e.c.	...	...	...	...	...	...	...	...	...	...
H Transfers to the rest of the world [d]	1050	1050	...	-	...	1088	1088	...	-	...
Net saving	-4001	-1981	...	-2020	...	-3340	-1042	...	-2298	...
Total Current Disbursements and Net Saving	71882	57685	...	32908	...	81553	64755	...	36893	...

	1986					1987				
	Total General Government	Central Government	State or Provincial Government	Local Government	Social Security Funds	Total General Government	Central Government	State or Provincial Government	Local Government	Social Security Funds

Receipts

1 Operating surplus	-	-	...	-	...	-	-	...	-	...
2 Property and entrepreneurial income [a]	9560	6538	...	5456	...	9651	5988	...	6145	...
A Withdrawals from public quasi-corporations [a]	3277	2821	...	456	...	2624	2104	...	520	...
B Interest	5259	3590	...	4103	...	5880	3665	...	4697	...
C Dividends	1	1	...	-	...	7	5	...	2	...
D Net land rent and royalties	1023	126	...	897	...	1140	214	...	926	...
3 Taxes, fees and contributions	82892	66644	...	16248	...	94209	75094	...	19115	...
A Indirect taxes	35788	21055	...	14733	...	40903	23508	...	17395	...
B Direct taxes	45434	45434	...	...	...	51366	51366	...	...	...
Income	45434	45434	...	...	...	51366	51366	...	...	...
Other [b]	...	...	...	...	...	...	...	...	...	...
C Social security contributions	...	...	...	...	...	...	...	...	...	...
D Fees, fines and penalties [b]	1670	155	...	1515	...	1940	220	...	1720	...
4 Other current transfers	-	24	...	19330	...	-	38	...	20766	...
A Casualty insurance claims	...	...	...	...	...	...	...	...	...	...
B Transfers from other government subsectors	...	24	...	19330	...	...	38	...	20766	...
C Transfers from the rest of the world	...	...	...	...	...	...	...	...	...	...
D Other transfers, except imputed	-	...	...	-	...	-	...	...	-	...
E Imputed unfunded employee pension and welfare contributions	...	...	...	...	...	...	...	...	...	...
Total Current Receipts	92452	73206	...	41034	...	103860	81120	...	46026	...

Disbursements

1 Government final consumption expenditure	48713	16219	...	32494	...	52654	17284	...	35370	...
2 Property income	11176	7963	...	5647	...	12005	7651	...	6836	...
A Interest	11176	7963	...	5647	...	12005	7651	...	6836	...
B Net land rent and royalties	-	...	...	...	...	-	...	...	...	...
3 Subsidies [c]	4076	1462	...	2614	...	3929	1295	...	2634	...

Australia

3.12 General Government Income and Outlay Account: Total and Subsectors
(Continued)

Million Australian dollars — Fiscal year beginning 1 July

	1986 Total General Government	1986 Central Government	1986 State or Provincial Government	1986 Local Government	1986 Social Security Funds	1987 Total General Government	1987 Central Government	1987 State or Provincial Government	1987 Local Government	1987 Social Security Funds
4 Other current transfers [d]	29055	45547	...	2862	...	31982	49654	...	3132	...
A Casualty insurance premiums, net	...	...	...	...	...	...	...	...	...	...
B Transfers to other government subsectors	...	19330	...	24	...	...	20766	...	38	...
C Social security benefits	...	...	...	...	...	...	...	...	...	...
D Social assistance grants	24861	24056	...	805	...	27684	26778	...	906	...
E Unfunded employee pension and welfare benefits	...	...	...	...	...	...	...	...	...	...
F Transfers to private non-profit institutions serving households	3136	1103	...	2033	...	3200	1012	...	2188	...
G Other transfers n.e.c.	...	...	...	...	...	...	...	...	...	...
H Transfers to the rest of the world [d]	1058	1058	...	-	...	1098	1098	...	-	...
Net saving	-568	2015	...	-2583	...	3290	5236	...	-1946	...
Total Current Disbursements and Net Saving	92452	73206	...	41034	...	103860	81120	...	46026	...

	1988 Total General Government	1988 Central Government	1988 State or Provincial Government	1988 Local Government	1988 Social Security Funds	1989 Total General Government	1989 Central Government	1989 State or Provincial Government	1989 Local Government	1989 Social Security Funds
Receipts										
1 Operating surplus	-	-	...	-	...	-	-	...	-	...
2 Property and entrepreneurial income [a]	11294	4733	...	9028	...	12131	4493	...	10171	...
A Withdrawals from public quasi-corporations [a]	1473	703	...	770	...	1705	844	...	861	...
B Interest	8551	3699	...	7318	...	9079	3293	...	8319	...
C Dividends	50	5	...	45	...	53	6	...	47	...
D Net land rent and royalties	1220	326	...	895	...	1294	350	...	944	...
3 Taxes, fees and contributions	105864	83650	...	22214	...	115287	91159	...	24128	...
A Indirect taxes	44938	24781	...	20157	...	47770	26205	...	21565	...
B Direct taxes	58548	58548	...	...	...	64507	64507	...	...	...
Income	58548	58548	...	...	...	64507	64507	...	...	...
Other [b]	...	...	...	...	...	...	...	...	...	...
C Social security contributions	...	...	...	...	...	...	...	...	...	...
D Fees, fines and penalties [b]	2378	321	...	2057	...	3010	447	...	2563	...
4 Other current transfers	-	5	...	21129	...	-	20	...	22786	...
A Casualty insurance claims	...	...	...	...	...	...	...	...	...	...
B Transfers from other government subsectors	...	5	...	21129	...	...	20	...	22786	...
C Transfers from the rest of the world	...	...	...	...	...	...	...	...	...	...
D Other transfers, except imputed	-	...	...	...	...	-	...	...	...	...
E Imputed unfunded employee pension and welfare contributions	...	...	...	...	...	...	...	...	...	...
Total Current Receipts	117158	88388	...	52371	...	127418	95672	...	57085	...
Disbursements										
1 Government final consumption expenditure	56750	18256	...	38494	...	61673	19338	...	42335	...
2 Property income	14512	7453	...	9526	...	16467	7343	...	11657	...
A Interest	14512	7453	...	9526	...	16467	7343	...	11657	...
B Net land rent and royalties	-	...	...	...	...	-	...	...	...	...
3 Subsidies [c]	4073	1296	...	2777	...	3630	1308	...	2322	...

Australia

3.12 General Government Income and Outlay Account: Total and Subsectors
(Continued)

Million Australian dollars — Fiscal year beginning 1 July

	1988 Total General Government	1988 Central Government	1988 State or Provincial Government	1988 Local Government	1988 Social Security Funds	1989 Total General Government	1989 Central Government	1989 State or Provincial Government	1989 Local Government	1989 Social Security Funds
4 Other current transfers [d]	33967	51662	...	3439	...	37542	56471	...	3877	...
A Casualty insurance premiums, net	...	...	...	...	...	...	...	...	...	...
B Transfers to other government subsectors	...	21129	...	5	...	...	22786	...	20	...
C Social security benefits	...	...	...	...	...	...	...	...	...	...
D Social assistance grants	29217	28208	...	1009	...	32354	31193	...	1161	...
E Unfunded employee pension and welfare benefits	...	...	...	...	...	...	...	...	...	...
F Transfers to private non-profit institutions serving households	3593	1168	...	2425	...	3910	1214	...	2696	...
G Other transfers n.e.c.	...	...	...	...	...	...	...	...	...	...
H Transfers to the rest of the world [d]	1157	1157	...	-	...	1278	1278	...	-	...
Net saving	7856	9721	...	-1865	...	8106	11212	...	-3106	...
Total Current Disbursements and Net Saving	117158	88388	...	52371	...	127418	95672	...	57085	...

a) All public enterprises are treated as if they were quasi-corporate.
b) Other direct taxes are included in item 'Taxes, fees and penalties'.
c) Subsidies on wheat and wool are recorded on an accrual basis.
d) The Australian accounts do not distinguish between current and capital transfers to the rest of the world. They have all been treated as current transfers.

3.13 General Government Capital Accumulation Account: Total and Subsectors

Million Australian dollars — Fiscal year beginning 1 July

	1980 Total General Government	1980 Central Government	1980 State or Provincial Government	1980 Local Government	1980 Social Security Funds	1981 Total General Government	1981 Central Government	1981 State or Provincial Government	1981 Local Government	1981 Social Security Funds
Finance of Gross Accumulation										
1 Gross saving	2581	1723	...	858	...	3694	2815	...	879	...
A Consumption of fixed capital	3175	310	...	2865	...	3580	354	...	3226	...
B Net saving	-594	1413	...	-2007	...	114	2461	...	-2347	...
2 Capital transfers	292	18	...	1947	...	313	6	...	2085	...
A From other government subsectors	23	...	...	1696	...	67	...	...	1845	...
B From other resident sectors	269	18	...	251	...	246	6	...	240	...
C From rest of the world	...	...	...	...	...	...	...	...	...	...
Finance of Gross Accumulation	2873	1741	...	2805	...	4007	2821	...	2964	...
Gross Accumulation										
1 Gross capital formation [a]	3820	390	...	3430	...	4153	482	...	3671	...
A Increase in stocks [a]	67	64	...	3	...	29	25	...	4	...
B Gross fixed capital formation [a]	3753	326	...	3427	...	4124	457	...	3667	...
2 Purchases of land, net [b]	-129	-154	...	25	...	13	-23	...	36	...
3 Purchases of intangible assets, net	...	...	...	...	...	...	...	...	...	...
4 Capital transfers [c]	403	1811	...	265	...	497	2005	...	270	...
A To other government subsectors	198	1673	...	198	...	177	1778	...	177	...
B To other resident sectors	205	138	...	67	...	320	227	...	93	...
C To rest of the world [c]	...	...	...	...	...	...	...	...	...	...
Net lending	-1221	-306	...	-915	...	-656	357	...	-1013	...
Gross Accumulation	2873	1741	...	2805	...	4007	2821	...	2964	...

	1982 Total General Government	1982 Central Government	1982 State or Provincial Government	1982 Local Government	1982 Social Security Funds	1983 Total General Government	1983 Central Government	1983 State or Provincial Government	1983 Local Government	1983 Social Security Funds
Finance of Gross Accumulation										
1 Gross saving	1080	-39	...	1119	...	-943	-2728	...	1785	...
A Consumption of fixed capital	4072	408	...	3664	...	4357	446	...	3911	...
B Net saving	-2992	-447	...	-2545	...	-5300	-3174	...	-2126	...
2 Capital transfers	386	2	...	2615	...	256	3	...	3046	...
A From other government subsectors	221	...	...	2452	...	99	...	...	2892	...
B From other resident sectors	165	2	...	163	...	157	3	...	154	...
C From rest of the world	...	...	...	...	...	...	...	...	...	...
Finance of Gross Accumulation	1466	-37	...	3734	...	-687	-2725	...	4831	...

Australia

3.13 General Government Capital Accumulation Account: Total and Subsectors
(Continued)

Million Australian dollars — Fiscal year beginning 1 July

	1982 Total General Government	1982 Central Government	1982 State or Provincial Government	1982 Local Government	1982 Social Security Funds	1983 Total General Government	1983 Central Government	1983 State or Provincial Government	1983 Local Government	1983 Social Security Funds
Gross Accumulation										
1 Gross capital formation [a]	4678	710	...	3968	...	5314	711	...	4603	...
A Increase in stocks [a]	54	50	...	4	...	8	3	...	5	...
B Gross fixed capital formation [a]	4624	660	...	3964	...	5306	708	...	4598	...
2 Purchases of land, net [b]	38	-29	...	67	...	-5	-42	...	37	...
3 Purchases of intangible assets, net	...	...	...	...	...	...	...	...	...	...
4 Capital transfers [c]	779	2505	...	505	...	1001	3160	...	634	...
A To other government subsectors	406	2231	...	406	...	539	2793	...	539	...
B To other resident sectors	373	274	...	99	...	462	367	...	95	...
C To rest of the world [c]	...	...	...	...	...	...	...	...	...	...
Net lending	-4029	-3223	...	-806	...	-6997	-6554	...	-443	...
Gross Accumulation	1466	-37	...	3734	...	-687	-2725	...	4831	...

	1984 Total General Government	1984 Central Government	1984 State or Provincial Government	1984 Local Government	1984 Social Security Funds	1985 Total General Government	1985 Central Government	1985 State or Provincial Government	1985 Local Government	1985 Social Security Funds
Finance of Gross Accumulation										
1 Gross saving	599	-1487	...	2086	...	1692	-481	...	2173	...
A Consumption of fixed capital	4600	494	...	4106	...	5032	561	...	4471	...
B Net saving	-4001	-1981	...	-2020	...	-3340	-1042	...	-2298	...
2 Capital transfers	187	2	...	3351	...	245	1	...	3490	...
A From other government subsectors	44	...	...	3210	...	72	...	...	3318	...
B From other resident sectors	143	2	...	141	...	173	1	...	172	...
C From rest of the world	...	...	...	...	...	...	...	...	...	...
Finance of Gross Accumulation	786	-1485	...	5437	...	1937	-480	...	5663	...
Gross Accumulation										
1 Gross capital formation [a]	6238	901	...	5337	...	7275	1060	...	6215	...
A Increase in stocks [a]	33	2	...	31	...	8	13	...	-5	...
B Gross fixed capital formation [a]	6205	899	...	5306	...	7267	1047	...	6220	...
2 Purchases of land, net [b]	-35	-91	...	56	...	-146	-90	...	-56	...
3 Purchases of intangible assets, net	...	...	...	...	...	...	...	...	...	...
4 Capital transfers [c]	1313	3604	...	875	...	1219	3612	...	853	...
A To other government subsectors	761	3169	...	758	...	708	3246	...	708	...
B To other resident sectors	552	435	...	117	...	511	366	...	145	...
C To rest of the world [c]	...	...	...	...	...	...	...	...	...	...
Net lending	-6730	-5899	...	-831	...	-6411	-5062	...	-1349	...
Gross Accumulation	786	-1485	...	5437	...	1937	-480	...	5663	...

	1986 Total General Government	1986 Central Government	1986 State or Provincial Government	1986 Local Government	1986 Social Security Funds	1987 Total General Government	1987 Central Government	1987 State or Provincial Government	1987 Local Government	1987 Social Security Funds
Finance of Gross Accumulation										
1 Gross saving	4887	2648	...	2239	...	9099	5929	...	3170	...
A Consumption of fixed capital	5455	633	...	4822	...	5809	693	...	5116	...
B Net saving	-568	2015	...	-2583	...	3290	5236	...	-1946	...
2 Capital transfers	299	-	...	3548	...	301	1	...	3338	...
A From other government subsectors	125	...	...	3374	...	89	...	...	3127	...
B From other resident sectors	174	-	...	174	...	212	1	...	211	...
C From rest of the world	...	...	...	...	...	...	...	...	...	...
Finance of Gross Accumulation	5186	2648	...	5787	...	9400	5930	...	6508	...
Gross Accumulation										
1 Gross capital formation [a]	7834	1166	...	6668	...	7497	1173	...	6324	...
A Increase in stocks [a]	-54	-35	...	-19	...	1	1	...	-	...
B Gross fixed capital formation [a]	7888	1201	...	6687	...	7496	1172	...	6324	...

Australia

3.13 General Government Capital Accumulation Account: Total and Subsectors
(Continued)

Million Australian dollars — Fiscal year beginning 1 July

	1986 Total General Government	1986 Central Government	1986 State or Provincial Government	1986 Local Government	1986 Social Security Funds	1987 Total General Government	1987 Central Government	1987 State or Provincial Government	1987 Local Government	1987 Social Security Funds
2 Purchases of land, net [b]	-144	-85	...	-59	...	-558	-393	...	-165	...
3 Purchases of intangible assets, net	...	...	...	...	...	...	...	...	...	...
4 Capital transfers [c]	1252	3601	...	900	...	1371	3431	...	978	...
A To other government subsectors	771	3250	...	770	...	756	3039	...	755	...
B To other resident sectors	481	351	...	130	...	615	392	...	223	...
C To rest of the world [c]	...	...	...	...	...	...	...	...	...	...
Net lending	-3756	-2034	...	-1722	...	1090	1719	...	-629	...
Gross Accumulation	5186	2648	...	5787	...	9400	5930	...	6508	...

	1988 Total General Government	1988 Central Government	1988 State or Provincial Government	1988 Local Government	1988 Social Security Funds	1989 Total General Government	1989 Central Government	1989 State or Provincial Government	1989 Local Government	1989 Social Security Funds
Finance of Gross Accumulation										
1 Gross saving	14039	10466	...	3573	...	14714	12028	...	2686	...
A Consumption of fixed capital	6183	745	...	5438	...	6608	816	...	5792	...
B Net saving	7856	9721	...	-1865	...	8106	11212	...	-3106	...
2 Capital transfers	306	1	...	3347	...	301	-	...	3805	...
A From other government subsectors	105	...	...	3147	...	87	...	...	3591	...
B From other resident sectors	201	1	...	200	...	214	-	...	214	...
C From rest of the world	...	...	...	...	...	...	...	...	...	...
Finance of Gross Accumulation	14345	10467	...	6920	...	15015	12028	...	6491	...
Gross Accumulation										
1 Gross capital formation [a]	7569	940	...	6629	...	8831	1205	...	7626	...
A Increase in stocks [a]	-39	-19	...	-20	...	-1	9	...	-10	...
B Gross fixed capital formation [a]	7608	959	...	6649	...	8832	1196	...	7636	...
2 Purchases of land, net [b]	-507	-79	...	-428	...	-118	74	...	-192	...
3 Purchases of intangible assets, net	...	...	...	...	...	...	...	...	...	...
4 Capital transfers [c]	1524	3477	...	1089	...	1680	3866	...	1318	...
A To other government subsectors	773	3063	...	752	...	1014	3513	...	1005	...
B To other resident sectors	751	414	...	337	...	666	353	...	313	...
C To rest of the world [c]	...	...	...	...	...	...	...	...	...	...
Net lending	5759	6129	...	-370	...	4622	6883	...	-2261	...
Gross Accumulation	14345	10467	...	6920	...	15015	12028	...	6491	...

a) Livestock is excluded from items 'Increase in Stocks' and 'Gross Fixed Capital Formation' and as a result, from 'Gross Capital Formation'.
b) Item 'Purchases of land, net' refers mainly to purchases less sales of land and existing building, other than dwellings, from and to other sectors.
c) The Australian accounts do not distinguish between current and capital transfers to the rest of the world. They have all been treated as current transfers.

3.22 Corporate and Quasi-Corporate Enterprise Income and Outlay Account: Total and Sectors

Million Australian dollars — Fiscal year beginning 1 July

	1980 TOTAL	1980 Non-Financial	1980 Financial	1981 TOTAL	1981 Non-Financial	1981 Financial	1982 TOTAL	1982 Non-Financial	1982 Financial	1983 TOTAL	1983 Non-Financial	1983 Financial
Receipts												
1 Operating surplus	9258	12184	-2926	9224	12917	-3693	8378	12389	-4011	14643	19299	-4656
2 Property and entrepreneurial income [a]	9627	2532	13776	11962	3330	18078	14279	3800	21693	15637	3728	23184
A Withdrawals from quasi-corporate enterprises	...	...	...	...	...	...	...	...	...	...	...	...
B Interest	9340	2157	13187	11681	2940	17373	13968	3369	20803	15287	3263	22126
C Dividends	218	277	589	204	282	705	214	303	890	241	323	1058
D Net land rent and royalties	69	98	-	77	108	-	97	128	-	109	142	-

Australia

3.22 Corporate and Quasi-Corporate Enterprise Income and Outlay Account: Total and Sectors
(Continued)

Million Australian dollars — Fiscal year beginning 1 July

	1980 TOTAL	1980 Non-Financial	1980 Financial	1981 TOTAL	1981 Non-Financial	1981 Financial	1982 TOTAL	1982 Non-Financial	1982 Financial	1983 TOTAL	1983 Non-Financial	1983 Financial
3 Current transfers	-	-	-	-	-	-	80	-	80	75	75	-
A Casualty insurance claims	-	-	-	-	-	-	80	-	80	75	75	-
B Casualty insurance premiums, net, due to be received by insurance companies	...	...	...	...	...	...	...	...	...	...	...	...
C Current transfers from the rest of the world	...	...	...	...	...	...	...	...	...	...	...	...
D Other transfers except imputed	...	...	...	...	...	...	...	...	...	...	...	...
E Imputed unfunded employee pension and welfare contributions	...	...	...	...	...	...	...	...	...	...	...	...
Total Current Receipts	18885	14716	10850	21186	16247	14385	22737	16189	17762	30355	23102	18528

Disbursements

	1980 TOTAL	1980 Non-Financial	1980 Financial	1981 TOTAL	1981 Non-Financial	1981 Financial	1982 TOTAL	1982 Non-Financial	1982 Financial	1983 TOTAL	1983 Non-Financial	1983 Financial
1 Property and entrepreneurial income	13630	10247	10064	17975	13442	13979	21694	15893	17015	24698	18257	17716
A Withdrawals from quasi-corporations	365	43	322	553	52	501	816	47	769	1155	245	910
Public	365	43	322	553	52	501	816	47	769	1155	245	910
Private	...	...	...	...	...	...	...	...	...	...	...	...
B Interest	10239	6798	9411	14147	9716	13028	17521	11972	15709	19433	13159	16244
C Dividends	2136	2487	297	2269	2637	415	2269	2738	510	2633	3343	430
D Net land rent and royalties	890	919	34	1006	1037	35	1088	1136	27	1477	1510	132
2 Direct taxes and other current transfers n.e.c. to general government	4590	4018	572	4923	4340	583	4718	4098	620	4492	3734	758
A Direct taxes	4590	4018	572	4923	4340	583	4718	4098	620	4492	3734	758
On income	4590	4018	572	4923	4340	583	4718	4098	620	4492	3734	758
Other	...	...	...	...	...	...	...	...	...	...	...	...
B Fines, fees, penalties and other current transfers n.e.c.	-	-	...	-	-	...	-	-	...	-	-	...
3 Other current transfers	369	369	-	434	434	-	719	519	200	720	720	-
A Casualty insurance premiums, net	304	304	...	361	361	...	634	434	...	617	617	...
B Casualty insurance claims liability of insurance companies	-	...	-	-	...	-	-	...	200	-	...	-
C Transfers to private non-profit institutions	65	65	...	73	73	...	85	85	...	103	103	...
D Unfunded employee pension and welfare benefits	...	...	...	...	...	...	...	...	...	...	...	...
E Social assistance grants	...	...	...	...	...	...	...	...	...	...	...	...
F Other transfers n.e.c.	...	...	...	...	...	...	...	...	...	...	...	...
G Transfers to the rest of the world	...	...	...	...	...	...	...	...	...	...	...	...
Net saving	296	82	214	-2146	-1969	-177	-4394	-4321	-73	445	391	54
Total Current Disbursements and Net Saving	18885	14716	10850	21186	16247	14385	22737	16189	17762	30355	23102	18528

	1984 TOTAL	1984 Non-Financial	1984 Financial	1985 TOTAL	1985 Non-Financial	1985 Financial	1986 TOTAL	1986 Non-Financial	1986 Financial	1987 TOTAL	1987 Non-Financial	1987 Financial

Receipts

	1984 TOTAL	1984 Non-Financial	1984 Financial	1985 TOTAL	1985 Non-Financial	1985 Financial	1986 TOTAL	1986 Non-Financial	1986 Financial	1987 TOTAL	1987 Non-Financial	1987 Financial
1 Operating surplus	18119	24274	-6155	19704	26677	-6973	21569	28948	-7379	28448	35653	-7205
2 Property and entrepreneurial income [a]	17664	4590	26613	22723	6978	34892	27605	7768	42762	28312	7527	45203
A Withdrawals from quasi-corporate enterprises	...	...	...	...	...	...	...	...	...	...	...	...
B Interest	17314	4106	25433	22100	6210	33588	26736	6725	41150	27815	6783	43503
C Dividends	194	293	1180	453	560	1304	608	742	1612	289	496	1700
D Net land rent and royalties	156	191	-	170	208	-	261	301	-	208	248	-

45

Australia

3.22 Corporate and Quasi-Corporate Enterprise Income and Outlay Account: Total and Sectors
(Continued)

Million Australian dollars — Fiscal year beginning 1 July

	1984 TOTAL	1984 Non-Financial	1984 Financial	1985 TOTAL	1985 Non-Financial	1985 Financial	1986 TOTAL	1986 Non-Financial	1986 Financial	1987 TOTAL	1987 Non-Financial	1987 Financial
3 Current transfers	-	-	-	-	-	-	-	-	-	-	-	-
A Casualty insurance claims	-	-	-	-	-	-	-	-	-	-	-	-
B Casualty insurance premiums, net, due to be received by insurance companies	...	...	...	...	...	...	...	...	...	...	...	...
C Current transfers from the rest of the world	...	...	...	...	...	...	...	...	...	...	...	...
D Other transfers except imputed	...	...	...	...	...	...	...	...	...	...	...	...
E Imputed unfunded employee pension and welfare contributions	...	...	...	...	...	...	...	...	...	...	...	...
Total Current Receipts	35783	28864	20458	42427	33655	27919	49174	36716	35383	56760	43180	37998

Disbursements

	1984 TOTAL	1984 Non-Financial	1984 Financial	1985 TOTAL	1985 Non-Financial	1985 Financial	1986 TOTAL	1986 Non-Financial	1986 Financial	1987 TOTAL	1987 Non-Financial	1987 Financial
1 Property and entrepreneurial income	28580	21672	20447	36606	26601	29152	43259	30579	35605	45056	33339	36135
A Withdrawals from quasi-corporations	1416	200	1216	2538	292	2246	3277	307	2970	2624	375	2249
Public	1416	200	1216	2538	292	2246	3277	307	2970	2624	375	2249
Private	...	...	...	...	...	...	...	...	...	...	...	...
B Interest	22551	16134	18478	29164	20707	26129	35099	24425	31815	36813	26490	32732
C Dividends	2882	3572	589	2850	3510	751	3058	3982	822	3528	4341	1094
D Net land rent and royalties	1731	1766	164	2054	2092	26	1825	1865	-2	2091	2133	60
2 Direct taxes and other current transfers n.e.c. to general government	5512	4405	1107	6026	4861	1165	6586	5345	1241	8660	6831	1829
A Direct taxes	5512	4405	1107	6026	4861	1165	6586	5345	1241	8660	6831	1829
On income	5512	4405	1107	6026	4861	1165	6586	5345	1241	8660	6831	1829
Other	...	...	...	...	...	...	...	...	...	...	...	...
B Fines, fees, penalties and other current transfers n.e.c.	-	-	...	-	-	...	-	-	...	-	-	...
3 Other current transfers	951	951	-	941	941	-	1068	1068	-	1061	1061	-
A Casualty insurance premiums, net	827	827	...	798	798	...	882	882	...	861	861	...
B Casualty insurance claims liability of insurance companies	-	-	...	-	-	...	-	-	...	-	-	...
C Transfers to private non-profit institutions	124	124	...	143	143	...	186	186	...	200	200	...
D Unfunded employee pension and welfare benefits	...	...	...	...	...	...	...	...	...	...	...	...
E Social assistance grants	...	...	...	...	...	...	...	...	...	...	...	...
F Other transfers n.e.c.	...	...	...	...	...	...	...	...	...	...	...	...
G Transfers to the rest of the world	...	...	...	...	...	...	...	...	...	...	...	...
Net saving	740	1836	-1096	-1146	1252	-2398	-1739	-276	-1463	1983	1949	34
Total Current Disbursements and Net Saving	35783	28864	20458	42427	33655	27919	49174	36716	35383	56760	43180	37998

	1988 TOTAL	1988 Non-Financial	1988 Financial	1989 TOTAL	1989 Non-Financial	1989 Financial

Receipts

	1988 TOTAL	1988 Non-Financial	1988 Financial	1989 TOTAL	1989 Non-Financial	1989 Financial
1 Operating surplus	35423	43299	-7876	35703	44713	-9010
2 Property and entrepreneurial income [a]	35615	8995	56693	43481	11801	67637
A Withdrawals from quasi-corporate enterprises	...	...	...	...	...	...
B Interest	35101	8013	54105	42876	10845	64411
C Dividends	324	751	2588	414	723	3226
D Net land rent and royalties	190	231	-	191	233	-

Australia

3.22 Corporate and Quasi-Corporate Enterprise Income and Outlay Account: Total and Sectors
(Continued)

Million Australian dollars — Fiscal year beginning 1 July

	1988 TOTAL	1988 Non-Financial	1988 Financial	1989 TOTAL	1989 Non-Financial	1989 Financial
3 Current transfers	-	-	-	150	-	150
A Casualty insurance claims	-	-	-	150	-	150
B Casualty insurance premiums, net, due to be received by insurance companies	...	...	...	...	...	...
C Current transfers from the rest of the world	...	...	...	...	...	...
D Other transfers except imputed	...	...	...	...	...	...
E Imputed unfunded employee pension and welfare contributions	...	...	...	...	...	...
Total Current Receipts	71038	52294	48817	79334	56514	58777

Disbursements

1 Property and entrepreneurial income	53894	40283	43684	63913	46264	53606
A Withdrawals from quasi-corporations	1473	426	1047	1705	744	961
Public	1473	426	1047	1705	744	961
Private	...	...	...	...	...	...
B Interest	45412	31625	40567	54250	35847	50532
C Dividends	5057	6236	1836	5867	7537	1865
D Net land rent and royalties	1952	1996	234	2091	2136	248
2 Direct taxes and other current transfers n.e.c. to general government	10114	7724	2390	13284	9946	3338
A Direct taxes	10114	7724	2390	13284	9946	3338
On income	10114	7724	2390	13284	9946	3338
Other	...	...	...	...	...	...
B Fines, fees, penalties and other current transfers n.e.c.	-	-	...	-	-	...
3 Other current transfers	1209	1209	-	1608	1308	300
A Casualty insurance premiums, net	951	951	...	1301	1001	...
B Casualty insurance claims liability of insurance companies	-	...	-	-	...	300
C Transfers to private non-profit institutions	258	258	...	307	307	...
D Unfunded employee pension and welfare benefits	...	...	...	...	...	...
E Social assistance grants	...	...	...	...	...	...
F Other transfers n.e.c.	...	...	...	...	...	...
G Transfers to the rest of the world	...	...	...	...	...	...
Net saving	5821	3078	2743	529	-1004	1533
Total Current Disbursements and Net Saving	71038	52294	48817	79334	56514	58777

a) Item 'Property and entrepreneurial income' excludes interest paid to/received by public non-financial enterprises.

3.23 Corporate and Quasi-Corporate Enterprise Capital Accumulation Account: Total and Sectors

Million Australian dollars — Fiscal year beginning 1 July

	1980 TOTAL	1980 Non-Fin	1980 Fin	1981 TOTAL	1981 Non-Fin	1981 Fin	1982 TOTAL	1982 Non-Fin	1982 Fin	1983 TOTAL	1983 Non-Fin	1983 Fin
Finance of Gross Accumulation												
1 Gross saving	10806	9877	929	9924	9256	668	9712	8789	923	15906	14756	1150
A Consumption of fixed capital	10510	9795	715	12070	11225	845	14106	13110	996	15461	14365	1096
B Net saving	296	82	214	-2146	-1969	-177	-4394	-4321	-73	445	391	54
2 Capital transfers	231	231	-	250	250	-	510	504	6	547	547	-
A From resident sectors	231	231	-	250	250	-	510	504	6	547	547	-
B From the rest of the world	...	...	...	...	...	...	...	...	...	...	...	...
Finance of Gross Accumulation	11037	10108	929	10174	9506	668	10222	9293	929	16453	15303	1150
Gross Accumulation												
1 Gross capital formation a	17083	15646	1437	22759	21124	1635	20781	18839	1942	23580	21761	1819

Australia

3.23 Corporate and Quasi-Corporate Enterprise Capital Accumulation Account: Total and Sectors
(Continued)

Million Australian dollars — Fiscal year beginning 1 July

	1980 TOTAL	1980 Non-Financial	1980 Financial	1981 TOTAL	1981 Non-Financial	1981 Financial	1982 TOTAL	1982 Non-Financial	1982 Financial	1983 TOTAL	1983 Non-Financial	1983 Financial
A Increase in stocks [a]	190	190	-	1238	1238	-	-2224	-2224	-	760	760	-
B Gross fixed capital formation [a]	16893	15456	1437	21521	19886	1635	23005	21063	1942	22820	21001	1819
2 Purchases of land, net [b]	129	118	11	-13	-48	35	-38	-88	50	5	-69	74
3 Purchases of intangible assets, net	...	...	...	...	...	...	...	...	...	...	...	...
4 Capital transfers	23	23	...	67	67	...	221	221	...	99	99	...
A To resident sectors	23	23	...	67	67	...	221	221	...	99	99	...
B To the rest of the world	...	...	...	...	...	...	...	...	...	...	...	...
Net lending	-6198	-5679	-519	-12639	-11637	-1002	-10742	-9679	-1063	-7231	-6488	-743
Gross Accumulation	11037	10108	929	10174	9506	668	10222	9293	929	16453	15303	1150

	1984 TOTAL	1984 Non-Financial	1984 Financial	1985 TOTAL	1985 Non-Financial	1985 Financial	1986 TOTAL	1986 Non-Financial	1986 Financial	1987 TOTAL	1987 Non-Financial	1987 Financial
Finance of Gross Accumulation												
1 Gross saving	17478	17363	115	18270	19205	-935	20413	20166	247	26131	24198	1933
A Consumption of fixed capital	16738	15527	1211	19416	17953	1463	22152	20442	1710	24148	22249	1899
B Net saving	740	1836	-1096	-1146	1252	-2398	-1739	-276	-1463	1983	1949	34
2 Capital transfers	771	771	-	804	799	5	866	866	-	941	937	4
A From resident sectors	771	771	-	804	799	5	866	866	-	941	937	4
B From the rest of the world	...	...	...	...	...	...	...	...	...	...	...	...
Finance of Gross Accumulation	18249	18134	115	19074	20004	-930	21279	21032	247	27072	25135	1937
Gross Accumulation												
1 Gross capital formation [a]	26373	23806	2567	32619	29711	2908	33687	30574	3113	37540	33874	3666
A Increase in stocks [a]	1046	1046	-	1187	1187	-	-1214	-1214	-	-568	-568	-
B Gross fixed capital formation [a]	25327	22760	2567	31432	28524	2908	34901	31788	3113	38108	34442	3666
2 Purchases of land, net [b]	35	28	7	146	114	32	144	54	90	558	522	36
3 Purchases of intangible assets, net	...	...	...	...	...	...	...	...	...	...	...	...
4 Capital transfers	44	44	...	72	72	...	125	125	...	89	89	...
A To resident sectors	44	44	...	72	72	...	125	125	...	89	89	...
B To the rest of the world	...	...	...	...	...	...	...	...	...	...	...	...
Net lending	-8203	-5744	-2459	-13763	-9893	-3870	-12677	-9721	-2956	-11115	-9350	-1765
Gross Accumulation	18249	18134	115	19074	20004	-930	21279	21032	247	27072	25135	1937

	1988 TOTAL	1988 Non-Financial	1988 Financial	1989 TOTAL	1989 Non-Financial	1989 Financial
Finance of Gross Accumulation						
1 Gross saving	31577	26736	4841	28643	24744	3899
A Consumption of fixed capital	25756	23658	2098	28114	25748	2366
B Net saving	5821	3078	2743	529	-1004	1533
2 Capital transfers	1161	1154	7	1338	1338	-
A From resident sectors	1161	1154	7	1338	1338	-
B From the rest of the world	...	...	...	...	...	...
Finance of Gross Accumulation	32738	27890	4848	29981	26082	3899
Gross Accumulation						
1 Gross capital formation [a]	46498	39987	6511	51417	44521	6896
A Increase in stocks [a]	3118	3118	-	4711	4711	-
B Gross fixed capital formation [a]	43380	36869	6511	46706	39810	6896
2 Purchases of land, net [b]	507	465	42	118	181	-63
3 Purchases of intangible assets, net	...	...	...	...	...	...
4 Capital transfers	105	105	...	87	87	...
A To resident sectors	105	105	...	87	87	...
B To the rest of the world	...	...	...	...	...	...
Net lending	-14372	-12667	-1705	-21641	-18707	-2934
Gross Accumulation	32738	27890	4848	29981	26082	3899

a) Livestock is excluded from items 'Increase in Stocks' and 'Gross Fixed Capital Formation' and, as a result, from 'Gross Capital Formation'.
b) Item 'Purchases of land, net' refers mainly to purchases less sales of land and existing building, other than dwellings, from and to other sectors.

Australia

3.32 Household and Private Unincorporated Enterprise Income and Outlay Account

Million Australian dollars — Fiscal year beginning 1 July

		1970	1975	1980	1981	1982	1983	1984	1985	1986	1987	1988	1989
						Receipts							
1	Compensation of employees [a]	18880	42805	74063	85580	94972	100419	110800	122290	133919	147266	165609	184674
2	Operating surplus of private unincorporated enterprises	4777	10172	20741	22064	21138	27044	28619	31965	35447	40737	48251	52462
3	Property and entrepreneurial income	1981	4536	9384	12441	14813	16177	18173	23878	28548	30249	35711	41842
	A Withdrawals from private quasi-corporations	...	...	...	...	...	...	...	...	...	...	...	...
	B Interest	1423	3870	8318	11336	13718	14966	16863	22350	26850	28412	33672	39647
	C Dividends	536	744	1015	1045	1035	1140	1235	1450	1614	1754	1947	2102
	D Net land rent and royalties	39	52	51	60	60	71	75	78	84	83	92	93
3	Current transfers	2239	7251	13988	16260	19782	23682	26854	29155	31968	35303	38023	41709
	A Casualty insurance claims	70	191	555	655	781	1128	1517	1443	1554	1493	1642	1728
	B Social security benefits	...	...	...	...	...	...	...	...	...	...	...	...
	C Social assistance grants	1855	6261	11431	13250	16167	18903	21229	22927	24861	27684	29217	32354
	D Unfunded employee pension and welfare benefits	...	...	...	...	...	...	...	...	...	...	...	...
	E Transfers from general government	105	543	1293	1557	1914	2331	2690	2965	3322	3400	3851	4217
	F Transfers from the rest of the world	209	256	709	798	920	1320	1418	1820	2231	2726	3313	3410
	G Other transfers n.e.c.	...	...	...	...	...	...	...	...	...	...	...	...
	Total Current Receipts	27877	64764	118176	136345	150705	167322	184446	207288	229882	253555	287594	320687
						Disbursements							
1	Final consumption expenditures	20830	44741	82770	94355	105951	116800	128265	143828	157612	175746	194847	216530
	A Market purchases	...	...	...	...	...	...	...	...	...	...	...	...
	B Gross rents of owner-occupied housing	1854	4442	10165	11817	13527	14864	16431	18537	20853	23548	26706	...
	C Consumption from own-account production	...	...	...	...	...	...	...	...	...	...	...	...
2	Property income	1098	3406	7133	9140	10895	11326	12395	16561	19893	21307	27550	33260
	A Interest	136	452	7007	8999	10745	11156	12213	16356	19689	21090	27324	33029
	Consumer debt	195	538	1233	1686	2185	2339	2619	3557	4427	4521	6352	8312
	Mortgage	518	1775	3630	4482	5157	5196	5385	6737	8053	8467	10374	12364
	Other	...	...	2144	2831	3403	3621	4209	6062	7209	8102	10598	12353
	B Net land rent and royalties	59	86	126	141	150	170	182	205	204	217	226	231
3	Direct taxes and other current transfers n.e.c. to government	3357	9585	18259	22094	23970	25865	30609	34132	39732	43827	49915	53125
	A Social security contributions	...	...	...	...	...	...	...	...	...	...	...	...
	B Direct taxes	3175	9213	17532	21206	22944	24691	29289	32714	38062	41887	47537	50115
	Income taxes	3175	9213	17532	21206	22944	24691	29289	32714	38062	41887	47537	50115
	Other [b]	...	...	...	...	...	...	...	...	...	...	...	...
	C Fees, fines and penalties [b]	182	372	727	888	1026	1174	1320	1418	1670	1940	2378	3010
4	Other current transfers	165	397	690	818	969	1203	1394	1365	1418	1415	1546	1621
	A Net casualty insurance premiums	31	84	251	294	347	511	690	645	672	632	691	727
	B Transfers to private non-profit institutions serving households	...	...	...	...	...	...	...	...	...	...	...	...
	C Transfers to the rest of the world	134	313	439	524	622	692	704	720	746	783	855	894
	D Other current transfers, except imputed	...	...	...	...	...	...	...	...	...	...	...	...
	E Imputed employee pension and welfare contributions	...	...	...	...	...	...	...	...	...	...	...	...
	Net saving	2427	6635	9324	9938	8920	12128	11783	11402	11227	11260	13736	16151
	Total Current Disbursements and Net Saving	27877	64764	118176	136345	150705	167322	184446	207288	229882	253555	287594	320687

a) Some government contributions to superannuation are only recorded in compensation when benefits are paid.
b) Other direct taxes are included in item 'Taxes, fees and penalties'.

Australia

3.33 Household and Private Unincorporated Enterprise Capital Accumulation Account

Million Australian dollars — Fiscal year beginning 1 July

	1970	1975	1980	1981	1982	1983	1984	1985	1986	1987	1988	1989
Finance of Gross Accumulation												
1 Gross saving	3962	10361	16742	18481	18480	22420	23186	24619	26093	27627	32346	36490
A Consumption of fixed capital	1548	3592	7418	8543	9560	10292	11403	13217	14866	16367	18610	20339
Owner-occupied housing	...	...	3610	4217	4663	5028	5750	6592	7396	8458	10380	11560
Other unincorporated enterprises	...	...	3808	4326	4897	5264	5653	6625	7470	7909	8230	8779
B Net saving	2414	6769	9324	9938	8920	12128	11783	11402	11227	11260	13736	16151
2 Capital transfers	-192	-157	78	140	375	341	412	248	216	221	164	429
A From resident sectors	-192	-157	78	140	375	341	412	204	216	221	164	429
B From the rest of the world	...	...	...	...	...	...	...	44	...	...	...	...
Total Finance of Gross Accumulation	3770	10204	16820	18621	18855	22761	23598	24867	26309	27848	32510	36919
Gross Accumulation												
1 Gross Capital Formation a	3036	7394	14817	16122	13220	16852	19564	20883	21049	25649	34442	33485
A Increase in stocks a	93	127	245	288	-272	662	15	269	-153	157	663	56
B Gross fixed capital formation a	2943	7267	14572	15834	13492	16190	19549	20614	21202	25492	33779	33429
2 Purchases of land, net	...	...	...	...	...	...	...	...	...	...	...	...
3 Purchases of intangibles, net	...	...	...	...	...	...	...	...	...	...	...	...
4 Capital transfers	227	314	175	139	71	44	13	6	4	3	2	1
A To resident sectors	227	314	175	139	71	44	13	6	4	3	2	1
B To the rest of the world	...	...	...	...	...	...	...	...	...	...	...	...
Net lending	507	2496	1828	2360	5564	5865	4021	3978	5256	2196	-1934	3433
Total Gross Accumulation	3770	10204	16820	18621	18855	22761	23598	24867	26309	27848	32510	36919

a) Livestock is excluded from items 'Increase in Stocks' and 'Gross Fixed Capital Formation' and as a result, from 'Gross Capital Formation'.

3.51 External Transactions: Current Account: Detail

Million Australian dollars — Fiscal year beginning 1 July

	1970	1975	1980	1981	1982	1983	1984	1985	1986	1987	1988	1989
Payments to the Rest of the World												
1 Imports of goods and services	5070	10830	25071	28997	28967	31192	39505	46087	48017	52599	60862	66291
A Imports of merchandise c.i.f. a	4219	8742	20483	24336	23104	25678	32017	38343	39859	43293	50136	54598
B Other	851	2088	4588	4661	5863	5514	7488	7744	8158	9306	10726	11693
2 Factor income to the rest of the world	627	1171	2816	3717	4754	6147	8067	9293	10534	12023	15507	19251
A Compensation of employees	17	44	110	125	135	158	178	164	179	210	279	344
B Property and entrepreneurial income	610	1127	2706	3592	4619	5989	7889	9129	10355	11813	15228	18907
By general government	88	86	374	373	541	671	931	1428	2227	2977	3191	3731
By corporate and quasi-corporate enterprises	522	1041	2332	3219	4078	5318	6958	7701	8128	8836	12037	15176
By other	...	...	...	...	...	...	...	...	...	...	...	...
3 Current transfers to the rest of the world b	322	701	1126	1330	1515	1643	1754	1808	1804	1881	2012	2172
A Indirect taxes by general government to supranational organizations	...	...	...	...	...	...	...	...	...	...	...	...
B Other current transfers	322	701	1126	1330	1515	1643	1754	1808	1804	1881	2012	2172
By general government	188	388	687	806	893	951	1050	1088	1058	1098	1157	1278
By other resident sectors	134	313	439	524	622	692	704	720	746	783	855	894
4 Surplus of the nation on current transactions	-508	-848	-4840	-8845	-7585	-7121	-11064	-14358	-12285	-11067	-18287	-21190
Payments to the Rest of the World, and Surplus of the Nation on Current Transfers	5511	11854	24173	25199	27651	31861	38262	42830	48070	55436	60094	66524
Receipts From The Rest of the World												
1 Exports of goods and services	5065	11101	22505	23300	25156	28595	34755	38693	43148	50058	53802	58923
A Exports of merchandise f.o.b.	4244	9432	18689	19140	20857	23576	29365	32307	35426	40555	43105	48665

Australia

3.51 External Transactions: Current Account: Detail
(Continued)

Million Australian dollars — Fiscal year beginning 1 July

	1970	1975	1980	1981	1982	1983	1984	1985	1986	1987	1988	1989
B Other	821	1669	3816	4160	4299	5019	5390	6386	7722	9503	10697	10258
2 Factor income from the rest of the world	152	343	682	761	1175	1508	1555	1620	1905	1833	2082	3083
A Compensation of employees	13	59	119	139	158	175	200	177	165	176	190	212
B Property and entrepreneurial income	139	284	563	622	1017	1333	1355	1443	1740	1657	1892	2871
By general government	-	-	3	31	21	20	24	37	43	47	74	118
By corporate and quasi-corporate enterprises	139	284	560	591	996	1313	1331	1406	1697	1610	1818	2753
By other	...	...	...	...	...	...	...	...	...	...	...	...
3 Current transfers from the rest of the world b	294	410	986	1138	1320	1758	1952	2517	3017	3545	4210	4518
A Subsidies to general government from supranational organizations	...	...	...	...	...	...	...	...	...	...	...	...
B Other current transfers	294	410	986	1138	1320	1758	1952	2517	3017	3545	4210	4518
To general government	85	154	277	340	400	438	534	697	786	819	897	1108
To other resident sectors	209	256	709	798	920	1320	1418	1820	2231	2726	3313	3410
Receipts from the Rest of the World on Current Transfers	5511	11854	24173	25199	27651	31861	38262	42830	48070	55436	60094	66524

a) Item 'Imports of merchandise C.I.F.' excludes freight on imports paid to resident carriers.
b) The Australian accounts do not distinguish between current and capital transfers to the rest of the world. They have all been treated as current transfers.

3.52 External Transactions: Capital Accumulation Account

Million Australian dollars — Fiscal year beginning 1 July

	1970	1975	1980	1981	1982	1983	1984	1985	1986	1987	1988	1989
Finance of Gross Accumulation												
1 Surplus of the nation on current transactions	-508	-848	-4840	-8845	-7585	-7121	-11064	-14358	-12285	-11067	-18287	-21190
2 Capital transfers from the rest of the world a	...	...	...	...	...	...	...	...	...	...	...	...
Total Finance of Gross Accumulation	-508	-848	-4840	-8845	-7585	-7121	-11064	-14358	-12285	-11067	-18287	-21190
Gross Accumulation												
1 Capital transfers to the rest of the world a	...	...	...	...	...	...	...	...	...	...	...	...
2 Purchases of intangible assets, n.e.c., net, from the rest of the world	...	...	...	...	...	...	...	...	...	...	...	...
Net lending to the rest of the world	-508	-848	-4840	-8845	-7585	-7121	-11064	-14358	-12285	-11067	-18287	-21190
Total Gross Accumulation	-508	-848	-4840	-8845	-7585	-7121	-11064	-14358	-12285	-11067	-18287	-21190

a) The Australian accounts do not distinguish between current and capital transfers to the rest of the world. They have all been treated as current transfers.

3.53 External Transactions: Capital Finance Account

Million Australian dollars — Fiscal year beginning 1 July

	1970	1975	1980	1981	1982	1983	1984	1985	1986	1987	1988	1989
Acquisitions of Foreign Financial Assets												
1 Gold and SDR's	679	-1052	1016	1364	2461	1853	-1520	-2140	3394	3924	873	2156
2 Currency and transferable deposits	...	...	...	...	...	...	...	...	...	...	...	...
3 Other deposits	...	...	...	...	...	...	...	...	...	...	...	...
4 Bills and bonds, short term	...	...	...	...	...	...	...	...	...	...	...	...
5 Bonds, long term	...	...	...	...	...	...	...	...	...	...	...	...
6 Corporate equity securities	-3	-2	189	218	1043	1174	2538	4777	6588	7184	6177	1733
A Subsidiaries abroad	...	...	168	204	377	1073	1841	2153	3355	7629	3247	3157
B Other	-3	-2	21	14	666	101	697	2624	3233	-445	2930	-1424
7 Short-term loans, n.e.c.	...	...	...	...	...	...	...	...	...	...	...	...
8 Long-term loans	45	130	-8	385	170	169	358	1007	273	2835	1643	1254
A Subsidiaries abroad	39	92	145	274	-27	-179	-532	-330	-552	760	893	-984
B Other	6	38	-153	111	197	348	890	1337	825	2075	750	2238
9 Prproietors' net additions to accumulation of quasi-corporate, non-resident enterprises	14	11	18	99	11	57	113	281	428	143	261	-40
10 Trade credit and advances	63	59	41	-50	94	873	1292	145	585	471	948	482
11 Other	-58	27	107	148	139	9	61	111	216	-494	33	-218
Total Acquisitions of Foreign Financial Assets	740	-827	1363	2164	3918	4135	2842	4181	11484	14063	9935	5367

Australia

3.53 External Transactions: Capital Finance Account
(Continued)

Million Australian dollars — Fiscal year beginning 1 July

	1970	1975	1980	1981	1982	1983	1984	1985	1986	1987	1988	1989
Incurrence of Foreign Liabilities												
1 Currency and transferable deposits	...	...	...	...	...	...	...	...	...	...	...	...
2 Other deposits	6	-18	-132	4	38	-15	-10	-16	18	-8	-	24
3 Bills and bonds, short term	...	...	...	...	...	...	...	...	...	...	...	...
4 Bonds, long term	...	...	...	...	...	...	...	...	...	...	...	...
5 Corporate equity securities	695	148	1887	563	1249	1184	804	2021	5994	3186	4982	3912
A Subsidiaries of non-resident incorporated units	...	129	579	-100	391	583	340	2143	1948	1024	3539	2421
B Other	695	19	1308	663	858	601	464	-122	4046	2162	1443	1491
6 Short-term loans, n.e.c.	...	...	...	...	...	...	...	...	...	...	...	...
7 Long-term loans	323	59	2776	8221	9038	8146	12684	16474	14568	17992	16801	13969
A Subsidiaries of non-residents	395	-166	522	1079	623	1032	1152	497	1470	2059	2425	1872
B Other	-72	225	2254	7142	8415	7114	11532	15977	13098	15933	14376	12097
8 Non-resident proprietors' net additions to accumulation of resident quasi-corporate enterprises	150	7	188	608	574	-769	99	-575	381	1440	2307	725
9 Trade credit and advances	...	53	111	240	12	556	233	-30	193	34	300	-310
10 Other	125	-2	354	502	124	511	384	335	-301	-12	-101	154
Total Incurrence of Liabilities	1299	247	5184	10138	11035	9613	14194	18209	20853	22632	24289	18474
Statistical discrepancy	-51	-226	1020	870	469	1643	-288	330	2916	2498	3934	8082
Net Lending	-508	-848	-4840	-8845	-7585	-7121	-11064	-14358	-12285	-11067	-18287	-21190
Total Incurrence of Liabilities and Net Lending	740	-827	1364	2163	3919	4135	2842	4181	11484	14063	9936	5366

4.3 Cost Components of Value Added

Million Australian dollars — Fiscal year beginning 1 July

	1980						1981					
	Compensation of Employees	Capital Consumption	Net Operating Surplus	Indirect Taxes	Less: Subsidies Received	Value Added	Compensation of Employees	Capital Consumption	Net Operating Surplus	Indirect Taxes	Less: Subsidies Received	Value Added
All Producers												
1 Agriculture, hunting, forestry and fishing	1325	1886	3806	495	97	7415	1518	2086	3704	511	86	7733
2 Mining and quarrying	1975	1187	2383	3330	20	8855	2405	1416	2598	3444	18	9845
3 Manufacturing	17324	3056	4430	2755	496	27069	19817	3422	4325	3168	557	30175
4 Electricity, gas and water [a]	1972	1546	471	197	127	4059	2268	1810	506	281	125	4740
5 Construction	6018	1789	3088	279	53	11121	6375	2036	3334	336	68	12013
6 Wholesale and retail trade, restaurants and hotels [b]	10643	1605	5476	4402	333	21793	11985	1853	5422	5278	314	24224
7 Transport, storage and communication	6360	2308	1760	476	973	9931	7426	2607	2145	557	1222	11513
8 Finance, insurance, real estate and business services	6799	5241	9720	2491	16	24235	7788	6148	10417	2776	23	27106
9 Community, social and personal services [b]	15855	1815	2189	1007	125	20741	19528	2082	2429	1221	159	25101
Total, Industries	68271	20433	33323	15432	2240	135219	79110	23460	34880	17572	2572	152450
Producers of Government Services	5783	670	-	18	-	6471	6456	733	-	20	-	7209
Other Producers	...	...	...	...	...	...	...	...	...	...	...	...
Total	74054	21103	33323	15450	2240	141690	85566	24193	34880	17592	2572	159659
Less: Imputed bank service charge	...	...	3324	...	...	3324	...	...	3592	...	...	3592
Import duties	...	...	...	1800	...	1800	...	...	...	2060	...	2060
Value added tax	...	...	...	...	...	...	...	...	...	...	...	...
Total	74054	21103	29999	17250	2240	140166	85566	24193	31288	19652	2572	158127
of which General Government:												
1 Agriculture, hunting, forestry and fishing	134	61	...	...	...	195	141	67	...	...	...	208
2 Mining and quarrying	10	9	...	...	...	19	12	10	...	...	...	22
3 Manufacturing	348	29	...	...	...	377	383	32	...	...	...	415
4 Electricity, gas and water	97	12	...	...	...	109	112	13	...	...	...	125

Australia

4.3 Cost Components of Value Added
(Continued)

Million Australian dollars — Fiscal year beginning 1 July

1980 / 1981

	Compensation of Employees	Capital Consumption	Net Operating Surplus	Indirect Taxes	Less: Subsidies Received	Value Added	Compensation of Employees	Capital Consumption	Net Operating Surplus	Indirect Taxes	Less: Subsidies Received	Value Added
5 Construction	1651	1231	...	...	...	2882	1724	1403	...	...	...	3127
6 Wholesale and retail trade, restaurants and hotels	11	3	...	...	...	14	12	3	...	...	...	15
7 Transport and communication	85	103	...	...	...	188	94	113	...	...	...	207
8 Finance, insurance, real estate & business services	187	34	...	...	...	221	206	38	...	...	...	244
9 Community, social and personal services	10076	1023	...	...	...	11099	11785	1168	...	...	...	12953
Total, Industries of General Government	12599	2505	...	...	...	15104	14469	2847	...	...	...	17316
Producers of Government Services	5783	670	...	18	-	6471	6456	733	...	20	-	7209
Total, General Government	18382	3175	...	18	-	21575	20925	3580	...	20	-	24525

1982 / 1983

	Compensation of Employees	Capital Consumption	Net Operating Surplus	Indirect Taxes	Less: Subsidies Received	Value Added	Compensation of Employees	Capital Consumption	Net Operating Surplus	Indirect Taxes	Less: Subsidies Received	Value Added

All Producers

1 Agriculture, hunting, forestry and fishing	1575	2314	1759	561	153	6056	1695	2453	4734	645	111	9416
2 Mining and quarrying	2769	1730	2880	3768	23	11124	3048	1972	4283	3953	30	13226
3 Manufacturing	20662	3896	3659	3522	634	31105	21539	4187	6216	3804	770	34976
4 Electricity, gas and water [a]	2740	2134	875	427	155	6021	3121	2349	1251	380	145	6956
5 Construction	6742	2334	3244	368	76	12612	6911	2538	3723	389	112	13449
6 Wholesale and retail trade, restaurants and hotels [b]	13121	2156	4983	6449	284	26425	14151	2339	6025	7983	269	30229
7 Transport, storage and communication	8331	3041	1769	620	1553	12208	8834	3333	2825	666	1631	14027
8 Finance, insurance, real estate and business services	9061	6932	12249	3362	31	31573	9687	7522	14926	4122	36	36221
9 Community, social and personal services [b]	22746	2384	2455	1407	197	28795	23984	2563	2943	1484	249	30725
Total, Industries	87747	26921	33873	20484	3106	165919	92970	29256	46926	23426	3353	189225
Producers of Government Services	7202	817	-	19	1	8037	7432	854	-	20	5	8301
Other Producers	...	...	...	...	...	...	...	...	...	...	...	...
Total	94949	27738	33873	20503	3107	173956	100402	30110	46926	23446	3358	197526
Less: Imputed bank service charge	...	...	4357	...	...	4357	...	...	5239	...	...	5239
Import duties	...	...	...	2036	...	2036	...	...	...	2329	...	2329
Value added tax	...	...	...	...	...	...	...	...	...	...	...	...
Total	94949	27738	29516	22539	3107	171635	100402	30110	41687	25775	3358	194616

of which General Government:

1 Agriculture, hunting, forestry and fishing	167	75	...	...	...	242	168	79	...	...	...	247
2 Mining and quarrying	15	11	...	...	...	26	13	11	...	...	...	24
3 Manufacturing	426	35	...	...	...	461	404	37	...	...	...	441
4 Electricity, gas and water	133	15	...	...	...	148	152	16	...	...	...	168
5 Construction	1931	1610	...	...	...	3541	2187	1754	...	...	...	3941
6 Wholesale and retail trade, restaurants and hotels	13	3	...	...	...	16	13	4	...	...	...	17
7 Transport and communication	108	126	...	...	...	234	68	131	...	...	...	199
8 Finance, insurance, real estate & business services	240	43	...	...	...	283	267	46	...	...	...	313
9 Community, social and personal services	13768	1337	...	...	...	15105	14778	1425	...	...	...	16203
Total, Industries of General Government	16801	3255	...	...	...	20056	18050	3503	...	...	...	21553
Producers of Government Services	7202	817	...	19	1	8037	7432	854	...	20	5	8301
Total, General Government	24003	4072	...	19	1	28093	25482	4357	...	20	5	29854

1984 / 1985

	Compensation of Employees	Capital Consumption	Net Operating Surplus	Indirect Taxes	Less: Subsidies Received	Value Added	Compensation of Employees	Capital Consumption	Net Operating Surplus	Indirect Taxes	Less: Subsidies Received	Value Added

All Producers

1 Agriculture, hunting, forestry and fishing	1784	2578	4433	774	83	9486	2062	2924	3817	693	70	9426
2 Mining and quarrying	3177	2137	4814	4550	53	14625	3778	2483	5022	4402	36	15649
3 Manufacturing	23149	4367	7465	4174	804	38351	24638	4980	8197	4576	965	41426
4 Electricity, gas and water [a]	3326	2581	1453	436	181	7615	3554	2895	1693	486	198	8430

Australia

4.3 Cost Components of Value Added
(Continued)

Million Australian dollars
Fiscal year beginning 1 July

1984 / 1985

	Compensation of Employees	Capital Consumption	Net Operating Surplus	Indirect Taxes	Less: Subsidies Received	Value Added	Compensation of Employees	Capital Consumption	Net Operating Surplus	Indirect Taxes	Less: Subsidies Received	Value Added
5 Construction	8042	2653	4312	431	107	15331	8761	2962	5097	467	86	17201
6 Wholesale and retail trade, restaurants and hotels b	16006	2513	7807	9136	369	35093	18096	2956	9228	10752	221	40811
7 Transport, storage and communication	9413	3669	3734	745	1756	15805	10195	4210	4231	800	1937	17499
8 Finance, insurance, real estate and business services	11185	8538	15445	4685	28	39825	12925	10007	16294	5202	120	44308
9 Community, social and personal services b	26638	2802	3157	1643	341	33899	29279	3265	3425	1816	369	37416
Total, Industries	102720	31838	52620	26574	3722	210030	113288	36682	57004	29194	4002	232166
Producers of Government Services	8058	903	-	25	1	8985	8989	983	-	32	10	9994
Other Producers	...	...	...	...	...	...	...	...	...	...	...	...
Total	110778	32741	52620	26599	3723	219015	122277	37665	57004	29226	4012	242160
Less: Imputed bank service charge	...	...	5882	...	...	5882	...	...	5335	...	...	5335
Import duties	...	...	...	2927	...	2927	...	...	...	3282	...	3282
Value added tax	...	...	...	...	...	...	...	...	...	...	...	...
Total	110778	32741	46738	29526	3723	216060	122277	37665	51669	32508	4012	240107

of which General Government:

1 Agriculture, hunting, forestry and fishing	172	83	...	...	...	255	162	89	...	...	...	251
2 Mining and quarrying	16	12	...	...	...	28	15	13	...	...	...	28
3 Manufacturing	455	39	...	...	...	494	482	42	...	...	...	524
4 Electricity, gas and water	161	17	...	...	...	178	167	18	...	...	...	185
5 Construction	2457	1809	...	...	...	4266	2531	1944	...	...	...	4475
6 Wholesale and retail trade, restaurants and hotels	14	4	...	...	...	18	18	4	...	...	...	22
7 Transport and communication	75	138	...	...	...	213	79	150	...	...	...	229
8 Finance, insurance, real estate & business services	300	50	...	...	...	350	326	57	...	...	...	383
9 Community, social and personal services	16094	1545	...	...	...	17639	17620	1732	...	...	...	19352
Total, Industries of General Government	19744	3697	...	...	...	23441	21400	4049	...	...	...	25449
Producers of Government Services	8058	903	...	25	1	8985	8989	983	...	32	10	9994
Total, General Government	27802	4600	...	25	1	32426	30389	5032	...	32	10	35443

1986 / 1987

	Compensation of Employees	Capital Consumption	Net Operating Surplus	Indirect Taxes	Less: Subsidies Received	Value Added	Compensation of Employees	Capital Consumption	Net Operating Surplus	Indirect Taxes	Less: Subsidies Received	Value Added

All Producers

1 Agriculture, hunting, forestry and fishing	2163	3165	4381	806	253	10262	2420	3178	5771	1056	75	12350
2 Mining and quarrying	3907	2830	4718	2527	40	13942	4018	3095	4581	2500	69	14125
3 Manufacturing	26181	5552	8060	5138	808	44123	28557	5816	9767	5670	753	49057
4 Electricity, gas and water a	3668	3216	2096	564	138	9406	3722	3566	2392	581	231	10030
5 Construction	9676	3257	6014	539	33	19453	10563	3455	6793	620	33	21398
6 Wholesale and retail trade, restaurants and hotels b	20037	3372	9720	13573	107	46595	22303	3613	11730	15125	243	52528
7 Transport, storage and communication	11239	4849	4581	929	2279	19319	11885	5329	6851	1039	2192	22912
8 Finance, insurance, real estate and business services	14531	11455	19721	6307	132	51882	17405	13075	24430	8105	43	62972
9 Community, social and personal services b	32816	3710	3657	2080	274	41989	35816	4068	4524	2427	287	46548
Total, Industries	124218	41406	62948	32463	4064	256971	136689	45195	76839	37123	3926	291920
Producers of Government Services	9715	1067	-	88	12	10858	10611	1129	-	148	3	11885
Other Producers	...	...	...	...	...	...	...	...	...	...	...	...
Total	133933	42473	62948	32551	4076	267829	147300	46324	76839	37271	3929	303805
Less: Imputed bank service charge	...	...	5932	...	...	5932	...	...	7654	...	...	7654
Import duties	...	...	...	3237	...	3237	...	...	...	3632	...	3632
Value added tax	...	...	...	...	...	...	...	...	...	...	...	...
Total	133933	42473	57016	35788	4076	265134	147300	46324	69185	40903	3929	299783

of which General Government:

1 Agriculture, hunting, forestry and fishing	167	96	...	...	...	263	174	100	...	...	...	274

Australia

4.3 Cost Components of Value Added
(Continued)

Million Australian dollars — Fiscal year beginning 1 July

1986 / 1987

	Compensation of Employees	Capital Consumption	Net Operating Surplus	Indirect Taxes	Less: Subsidies Received	Value Added	Compensation of Employees	Capital Consumption	Net Operating Surplus	Indirect Taxes	Less: Subsidies Received	Value Added
2 Mining and quarrying	24	14	...	...	...	38	24	15	...	...	...	39
3 Manufacturing	494	46	...	...	...	540	485	49	...	...	...	534
4 Electricity, gas and water	146	19	...	...	...	165	145	20	...	...	...	165
5 Construction	2616	2071	...	...	...	4687	2660	2182	...	...	...	4842
6 Wholesale and retail trade, restaurants and hotels	12	4	...	...	...	16	13	5	...	...	...	18
7 Transport and communication	91	161	...	...	...	252	94	169	...	...	...	263
8 Finance, insurance, real estate & business services	321	63	...	...	...	384	357	70	...	...	...	427
9 Community, social and personal services	19298	1914	...	...	...	21212	20536	2070	...	...	...	22606
Total, Industries of General Government	23169	4388	...	...	...	27557	24488	4680	...	...	...	29168
Producers of Government Services	9715	1067	...	88	12	10858	10611	1129	...	148	3	11885
Total, General Government	32884	5455	...	88	12	38415	35099	5809	...	148	3	41053

1988 / 1989

	Compensation of Employees	Capital Consumption	Net Operating Surplus	Indirect Taxes	Less: Subsidies Received	Value Added	Compensation of Employees	Capital Consumption	Net Operating Surplus	Indirect Taxes	Less: Subsidies Received	Value Added

All Producers

1 Agriculture, hunting, forestry and fishing	2912	3159	7699	1089	119	14740	3188	3278	7644	1148	65	15193
2 Mining and quarrying	4230	3304	4369	1652	57	13498	5077	3590	6599	1779	15	17030
3 Manufacturing	31693	5886	12564	6040	757	55426	34008	6237	13346	6560	799	59352
4 Electricity, gas and water [a]	3912	3873	2848	639	219	11053	3942	4200	2634	664	176	11264
5 Construction	12363	3623	8506	748	103	25137	14154	3815	8919	828	113	27603
6 Wholesale and retail trade, restaurants and hotels [b]	25825	3758	16042	17324	190	62759	29290	4034	15635	18899	178	67680
7 Transport, storage and communication	12942	5705	7367	1459	2270	25203	13906	6232	7531	1625	1792	27502
8 Finance, insurance, real estate and business services	20303	15601	27592	9507	31	72973	24539	17518	28622	9263	37	79905
9 Community, social and personal services [b]	40215	4441	5380	2655	322	52369	44825	4860	.5783	2984	410	58042
Total, Industries	154395	49350	92367	41113	4068	333158	172929	53764	96713	43750	3585	363571
Producers of Government Services	11303	1199	-	120	5	12616	11877	1297	-	119	45	13248
Other Producers	...	...	...	...	...	...	...	...	...	...	...	...
Total	165698	50549	92367	41233	4073	345774	184806	55061	96713	43869	3630	376819
Less: Imputed bank service charge	...	...	8693	...	...	8693	...	...	8548	...	...	8548
Import duties	...	...	...	3705	...	3705	...	...	...	3901	...	3901
Value added tax	...	...	...	...	...	...	...	...	...	...	...	...
Total	165698	50549	83674	44938	4073	340786	184806	55061	88165	47770	3630	372172

of which General Government:

1 Agriculture, hunting, forestry and fishing	186	106	...	...	...	292	200	114	...	...	...	314
2 Mining and quarrying	15	15	...	...	...	30	13	17	...	...	...	30
3 Manufacturing	586	52	...	...	...	638	458	56	...	...	...	514
4 Electricity, gas and water	295	21	...	...	...	316	390	23	...	...	...	413
5 Construction	2906	2297	...	...	...	5203	3176	2394	...	...	...	5570
6 Wholesale and retail trade, restaurants and hotels	10	5	...	...	...	15	11	5	...	...	...	16
7 Transport and communication	260	178	...	...	...	438	406	192	...	...	...	598
8 Finance, insurance, real estate & business services	518	81	...	...	...	599	653	94	...	...	...	747
9 Community, social and personal services	22299	2229	...	...	...	24528	23969	2416	...	...	...	26385
Total, Industries of General Government	27075	4984	...	...	...	32059	29276	5311	...	...	...	34587
Producers of Government Services	11303	1199	...	120	5	12617	11877	1297	...	119	45	13248
Total, General Government	38378	6183	...	120	5	44676	41153	6608	...	119	45	47835

a) Item 'Electricity, gas and water' includes sewage services.
b) Restaurants and hotels are included in item 'Community, social and personal services'.

Austria

General note. The preparation of annual national accounts statistics in Austria is undertaken by the Austrian Central Statistical Office, Vienna. The official estimates are published annually in 'Oesterreichs Volkseinkommen', (Austrian Central Statistcal Office, Beitrage zur Osterreichischen Statistik). The concepts, definitions, sources of basic statistics and methods of estima tion are described in the 1964-1977 and 1970-1980 issue of the above mentioned publication. The estimates are generally in accordance with the classifications and definitions recommended in the United Nations System of National Accounts (SNA). Input-output tables have been published for the years 1961, 1964 and 1976. The following tables have been prepared from successive replies to the United Nations national accounts questionnaire. When the scope and coverage of The estimates differ for conceptual or statistical reasons fromthe definitions and classifications recommended in SNA, a footnote is indic ated to the relevant tables.

Sources and methods:

(a) Gross domestic product. Gross domestic product is estimated mainly through the production approach.

(b) Expenditure on the gross domestic product. The estimates of government final consumption expenditure are derived from production accounts compiled on the basis of the accounting records of the various authorities. The values of private expenditure on goods are mostly obtained by means of the commodity flow method, either by multiplying the quantity data by average consumer prices or by adding distributive margins and turnover tax and indirect taxes to the value of goods produced domestically or imported. The sources of data include statistics on agricultural produce, industrial output data by commodities, data on energy and foreign trade by commodities, motor vehicle registration statistics, closed accounts for public transportation enterprises, communication, insurance and others. For price data the consumer price index is largely referred to. In addition, decennial household surveys provide bench-mark information on average prices. Own account consumption is valued at producers' prices, for use of owner occupied dwellings the corresponding market rents are imputed. For private expenditure on services, the estimates are mostly based on value added tax statistics. The data on increase in stocks are based on regular stock surveys covering almost all branches, those that are not covered are included in statistical discrepancy. For gross fixed capital formation in machinery and electrical equipment, the value of domestic production plus imports minus exports is adjusted to include transport costs, trade margins, customs duties, etc. The estimates of transport equipment are based on registration statistics and are obtained by multiplying the quantity by the current prices. For construction, the gross value is derived from data on characteristic gross output, with additions for material supplied, non-characteristic construction (including own account-construction, e.g. residential buildings). The estimates of exports and imports of goods and services are based on foreign trade statistics and the balance of payments. Constant price estimates of government final consumption expenditure are based on deflation for intermediate consumption and non-commodity sales. Compensation of employees is in certain activities also deflated, for others quantum indicators are used. For private consumption expenditure, direct revaluation at base-year prices is used where information is available on quantities of commodities consumed. Otherwise, the current estimates are deflated by appropriate price indexes. This same method is used for increase in stocks, exports and imports of goods and services and for gross fixed capital formation.

(c) Cost-structure of the gross domestic product. Estimates of compensation of employees are based on contributions paid by employers to government funds and wage statistics. Direct information is available on compensation of government employees. Operating surplus is basically derived as a residual item. Further breakdown is based on income tax statistics for unincorporated enterprises, independent professions and property. Corporate balance sheets and tax statistics are used for undistributed profits of corporations: for agriculture and forestry income is derived from the production account. In the case of the public sector, data are obtained from the accounting records of public bodies. Depreciation estimates of stocks are obtained either by using the perpetual inventory concept or, in some instances, are extrapolated by net output at constant prices and inflated by national accounts' price index for fixed capital formation. Indirect taxes and subsidies are obtained directly from the records of the various governments.

(d) Gross domestic product by kind of economic activity. The table of GDP by kind of economic activity is prepared at market prices, i.e. producers' values. The production approach is used to estimate value added of nearly all industries. The income approach is used to est imate value added of public administration and defense. The value added of agriculture is obtained by deducting the cost of all non-factor inputs from the gross value of production, which include an imputation for produce consumed on the farms. The calculations are based on production statistics for quantities, and on agricultural price surveys. Mining and quarrying, electricity, gas and water as well as large-scale manufacturing are surveyed by annual over-all censuses while small-scale manufacturing is surveyed annually by samples. Bench-mark estimates have been prepared for 1964, 1971, 1976 and 1983. When necessary extrapolation is based on output statistics, sample survey and turnover statistics. For construction, census type data on gross output and input have been available annually since 1968, own account construction is imputed for housing and agriculture. The estimates of turnover in retail and wholesale trade are based on the 1964, 1976 and 1983 census of non-agricultural establishments, the 1971 census of turnover and, since 1973, an annual sample survey. Estimates of restaurants and hotels are based on the 1964 industrial census and on a special survey in 1972, and 1976 and 1983 Censuses. For the intermediate years, value added tax and turnover tax statistics as well as other suitable indicators (private accommodation) are used. For railways and air transportation and communication, value added is derived from the accounts of concerned enterprises. For the other activities of the transport sector, bench-mark data have been provided by the 1964, 1976 and 1983 industrial censuses, extrapolated by various indicators. From 1973 onward, value added tax statistics provide the output indicators for most transportation other than large enterprises mentioned before. For the financial institutions, value added is derived from accounting records for banking, and other financial institutions from statistics of the supervisory board for insurance. Data on real estate are obtained from decennial housing censuses and micro-census data on housing and rents. In the case of owner-occupied dwellings, rents paid for comparable dwellings are applied. The value added of government services is estimated by adding the cost items obtained from accounting records. The estimates of other services are based on annual turnover statistics, value added tax statistics and various net to gross ratios obtained from the 1964 and 1976 census of non-agricultural establishments. The value of domestic and health services is calculated by means of VAT, social security and wage statistics. For the constant price estimates, double deflation is used, but not invariably, for agriculture, electricity, gas and water, construction, transportation and ownership of dwellings. In manufacturing, a combination of double deflation and fixed net ratios is applied. The turnover of wholesale and retail trade is deflated by appropriate price indexes. For the producers of government services, partly quantum indicators, partly suitable price (wage) indexes are used. For most of the remaining activities, value added is mostly calculated by deflation.

1.1 Expenditure on the Gross Domestic Product, in Current Prices

Thousand Million Austrian schillings

	1970	1975	1980	1981	1982	1983	1984	1985	1986	1987	1988	1989
1 Government final consumption expenditure	55.22	113.05	178.70	195.24	214.30	226.89	237.76	255.00	270.66	280.44	288.35	302.09
2 Private final consumption expenditure	205.29	368.26	552.53	596.50	640.19	694.84	733.18	775.53	804.41	835.46	875.30	927.93
3 Gross capital formation	111.69	170.59	282.89	278.18	260.23	263.74	303.90	315.58	327.74	350.65	394.33	434.73
A Increase in stocks [a]	14.51	-4.33	27.43	10.24	-2.65	-5.81	20.98	11.17	3.73	8.90	23.65	32.55
B Gross fixed capital formation [b]	97.18	174.92	255.46	267.94	262.88	269.55	282.92	304.41	324.01	341.75	370.68	402.19
Residential buildings	18.58	35.88	52.56	58.27	60.64	61.58	62.34	62.49	65.04	68.87	76.94	79.17
Non-residential buildings	34.90	63.62	82.42	83.75	79.18	83.41	86.26	90.85	98.19	107.36	115.44	128.70
Other construction and land improvement etc.												
Other	43.70	62.85	106.00	110.55	107.35	107.98	116.07	131.81	140.06	144.42	155.36	170.21
4 Exports of goods and services [c]	116.75	209.02	366.24	404.51	431.24	449.69	497.64	549.13	522.97	527.19	590.32	669.30
5 Less: Imports of goods and services [c]	113.07	204.81	385.66	418.47	412.44	433.93	495.71	546.81	509.80	519.83	583.62	660.62
Statistical discrepancy	-	-	-	0.01	-	-	-	-0.01	-	-	-	-
Equals: Gross Domestic Product	375.88	656.11	994.70	1055.97	1133.53	1201.23	1276.77	1348.60	1415.97	1473.90	1564.68	1673.43

a) Item 'Increase in stocks' includes breeding stock, draught animals and a statistical discrepancy. These estimates are shown separately as 'Statistical discrepancy' in tables 2.7, 2.8, 2.9, 2.10 and 2.11.
b) Item 'Gross fixed capital formation' includes value added tax on investments of investors not entitled to deduct invoiced value added tax. This component is not included in the sub-items. For years 1973-1975, 1977 and 1978 of the current prices table, special investment tax is included. c) The estimates on transit trade are on a net basis.

Austria

1.2 Expenditure on the Gross Domestic Product, in Constant Prices

Thousand Million Austrian schillings

	1970	1975	1980	1981	1982	1983	1984	1985	1986	1987	1988	1989
			1976		At constant prices of:	1983						
1 Government final consumption expenditure	100.71	122.57	... 212.27	216.99	221.97	226.89	227.38	231.80	235.65	236.59	237.37	238.74
2 Private final consumption expenditure	309.31	392.35	... 651.89	653.97	661.87	694.84	694.31	710.86	723.43	744.34	767.57	792.11
3 Gross capital formation	160.37	176.00	... 328.51	295.33	269.26	263.74	295.71	301.29	307.36	321.99	353.32	376.72
A Increase in stocks [a]	16.72	-5.77	... 29.18	0.13	-1.84	-5.81	20.47	12.28	7.71	13.79	26.73	32.27
B Gross fixed capital formation	143.65	181.77	... 299.33[b]	295.20[b]	271.10[b]	269.55[b]	275.24[b]	289.01[b]	299.65[b]	308.19[b]	326.59[b]	344.44[b]
Residential buildings	30.76	37.06	62.99	64.23	62.72	61.58	61.11	60.09	61.47	62.89	68.15	67.84
Non-residential buildings	47.40	67.47	98.19	94.81	81.29	83.41	85.03	87.93	91.48	97.54	102.31	110.18
Other construction and land improvement etc.												
Other	57.28	66.16	121.24	119.48	110.94	107.98	112.83	124.21	129.00	130.22	137.56	147.52
4 Exports of goods and services	159.33	212.76	... 404.61[c]	424.34[c]	435.79[c]	449.69[c]	477.07[c]	509.96[c]	496.14[c]	508.01[c]	556.09[c]	614.53[c]
5 Less: Imports of goods and services	158.25	210.65	... 428.60[c]	425.35[c]	411.15[c]	433.93[c]	476.90[c]	506.37[c]	500.45[c]	523.83[c]	577.52[c]	632.06[c]
Statistical discrepancy	-	-	-0.02	0.01	0.01	-	-	-	-	-	-	-
Equals: Gross Domestic Product	571.47	693.03	1168.66	1165.29	1177.75	1201.23	1217.57	1247.54	1262.12	1287.10	1336.82	1390.03

a) Item 'Increase in stocks' includes breeding stock, draught animals and a statistical discrepancy. These estimates are shown separately as 'Statistical discrepancy' in tables 2.7, 2.8, 2.9, 2.10 and 2.11.
b) Item 'Gross fixed capital formation' includes value added tax on investments of investors not entitled to deduct invoiced value added tax. This component is not included in the sub-items. For years 1973-1975, 1977 and 1978 of the current prices table, special investment tax is included.
c) The estimates on transit trade are on a net basis.

1.3 Cost Components of the Gross Domestic Product

Thousand Million Austrian schillings

	1970	1975	1980	1981	1982	1983	1984	1985	1986	1987	1988	1989
1 Indirect taxes, net	55.16	92.55	132.78	142.31	150.70	161.69	180.16	186.73	188.00	197.77	209.81	226.21
A Indirect taxes	61.68	111.53	162.83	174.40	184.98	197.08	216.09	225.93	234.04	245.15	254.89	271.64
B Less: Subsidies	6.52	18.98	30.05	32.09	34.28	35.39	35.93	39.20	46.05	47.38	45.08	45.44
2 Consumption of fixed capital	43.85	77.42	116.10	128.51	140.76	149.24	158.19	167.53	176.20	183.87	194.11	205.63
3 Compensation of employees paid by resident producers to:	175.82	353.60	545.63	589.01	616.85	642.44	676.33	717.09	761.25	792.73	822.36	876.23
4 Operating surplus	101.05	132.55	200.20	196.14	225.22	247.87	262.10	277.07	290.53	299.52	338.40	365.36
Statistical discrepancy	-	-0.01	-0.01	-	-	-0.01	-0.01	-	-	-	-	-
Equals: Gross Domestic Product	375.88	656.11	994.70	1055.97	1133.53	1201.23	1276.77	1348.42	1415.97	1473.90	1564.68	1673.43

1.4 General Government Current Receipts and Disbursements

Thousand Million Austrian schillings

	1970	1975	1980	1981	1982	1983	1984	1985	1986	1987	1988	1989
					Receipts							
1 Operating surplus	...	...	...	...	...	...	...	...	...	...	...	...
2 Property and entrepreneurial income	4.45	8.65	18.49	22.42	22.67	22.40	23.06	26.15	25.91	29.44	30.72	32.82
3 Taxes, fees and contributions	136.41	256.73	418.68	455.32	477.61	502.93	549.42	591.18	617.66	635.78	665.26	694.28
A Indirect taxes	61.68	111.53	162.83	174.40	184.98	197.08	216.09	225.93	234.04	245.15	254.89	271.64
B Direct taxes	41.11	76.24	128.39	144.21	149.48	156.64	173.77	193.63	203.77	203.36	214.46	214.22
C Social security contributions	32.91	67.65	124.58	133.36	139.76	145.46	155.46	167.80	175.99	183.34	191.82	204.08
D Compulsory fees, fines and penalties	0.71	1.31	2.89	3.36	3.39	3.75	4.10	3.82	3.86	3.93	4.10	4.35
4 Other current transfers	8.34	15.88	24.44	26.62	29.59	31.74	33.67	36.19	38.51	40.49	42.02	44.30
Total Current Receipts of General Government	149.20	281.25	461.62	504.36	529.87	557.06	606.14	653.53	682.08	705.71	738.00	771.40
					Disbursements							
1 Government final consumption expenditure	55.22	113.05	178.70	195.25	214.30	226.89	237.76	255.00	270.66	280.44	288.35	302.09

Austria

1.4 General Government Current Receipts and Disbursements
(Continued)

Thousand Million Austrian schillings

	1970	1975	1980	1981	1982	1983	1984	1985	1986	1987	1988	1989
A Compensation of employees	38.24	75.55	119.66	131.55	143.49	152.70	160.93	171.73	182.91	191.44	195.81	205.31
B Consumption of fixed capital	2.60	4.95	7.48	8.37	9.13	9.60	10.10	10.69	11.31	11.56	11.80	12.22
C Purchases of goods and services, net	13.61	30.93	49.62	53.35	59.54	62.27	64.27	69.93	73.57	74.53	77.82	81.22
D Less: Own account fixed capital formation	...	...	...	...	...	...	...	...	...	...	...	...
E Indirect taxes paid, net	0.77	1.61	1.94	1.98	2.15	2.34	2.47	2.65	2.87	2.91	2.91	3.34
2 Property income	4.05	8.56	24.74	29.29	35.21	36.62	43.09	47.85	51.88	58.36	61.79	66.85
A Interest	4.05	8.56	24.74	29.29	35.21	36.62	43.09	47.85	51.88	58.36	61.79	66.85
B Net land rent and royalties	...	...	...	...	...	...	...	...	...	...	...	...
3 Subsidies	6.52	18.99	30.05	32.09	34.28	35.39	35.93	39.20	46.05	47.38	45.08	45.44
4 Other current transfers	58.44	112.43	191.98	208.66	228.95	243.98	259.04	278.62	295.52	316.04	323.60	337.41
A Social security benefits	29.83	56.37	94.50	103.39	112.60	121.48	130.79	142.34	151.08	161.47	167.76	177.18
B Social assistance grants	14.48	30.16	56.16	60.08	67.03	69.91	72.29	76.27	80.44	87.04	85.22	85.20
C Other	14.13	25.90	41.32	45.18	49.32	52.59	55.96	60.00	64.00	67.53	70.61	75.04
5 Net saving	24.97	28.22	36.15	39.08	17.13	14.18	30.33	32.86	17.98	3.50	19.19	19.61
Total Current Disbursements and Net Saving of General Government	149.20	281.25	461.62	504.36	529.87	557.06	606.14	653.53	682.08	705.71	738.00	771.40

1.5 Current Income and Outlay of Corporate and Quasi-Corporate Enterprises, Summary

Thousand Million Austrian schillings

	1970	1975	1980	1981	1982	1983	1984	1985	1986	1987	1988	1989
Receipts												
1 Operating surplus	...	...	...	...	...	...	...	...	...	...	...	...
2 Property and entrepreneurial income received	...	...	...	...	...	...	...	...	...	...	...	...
3 Current transfers	...	...	...	...	...	...	...	...	...	...	...	...
Total Current Receipts	...	...	...	...	...	...	...	...	...	...	...	...
Disbursements												
1 Property and entrepreneurial income	...	...	...	...	...	...	...	...	...	...	...	...
2 Direct taxes and other current payments to general government	7.41	13.37	17.65	19.91	18.80	19.79	22.33	25.77	26.47	26.12	27.30	33.19
3 Other current transfers	...	...	...	...	...	...	...	...	...	...	...	...
4 Net saving	17.29	24.03	39.86	36.62	41.37	45.80	45.84	42.92	45.46	46.11	55.76	57.52
Total Current Disbursements and Net Saving	...	...	...	...	...	...	...	...	...	...	...	...

1.6 Current Income and Outlay of Households and Non-Profit Institutions

Thousand Million Austrian schillings

	1970	1975	1980	1981	1982	1983	1984	1985	1986	1987	1988	1989
Receipts												
1 Compensation of employees	175.82	353.60	545.63	589.01	616.85	642.44	676.33	717.09	761.25	792.73	822.36	876.23
2 Operating surplus of private unincorporated enterprises	...	...	...	...	...	...	...	...	...	...	...	...
3 Property and entrepreneurial income	75.97	97.13	152.20	150.93	183.06	201.69	219.35	237.24	248.33	260.59	291.89	318.33
4 Current transfers	64.94	125.24	215.29	235.09	258.53	274.14	292.49	314.50	333.59	360.48	371.31	388.56
A Social security benefits	29.83	56.37	94.50	103.39	112.60	121.48	130.79	142.34	151.08	161.47	167.76	177.18
B Social assistance grants	14.48	30.16	56.16	60.08	67.03	69.91	72.29	76.27	80.44	87.04	85.22	85.20
C Other	20.63	38.71	64.62	71.62	78.90	82.75	89.41	95.89	102.06	111.97	118.33	126.19
Total Current Receipts	316.73	575.97	913.12	975.03	1058.44	1118.27	1188.17	1268.83	1343.17	1413.80	1485.55	1583.12
Disbursements												
1 Private final consumption expenditure	205.29	368.26	552.53	596.50	640.19	694.84	733.18	775.53	804.41	835.46	875.30	927.93

Austria

1.6 Current Income and Outlay of Households and Non-Profit Institutions
(Continued)

Thousand Million Austrian schillings

	1970	1975	1980	1981	1982	1983	1984	1985	1986	1987	1988	1989
2 Property income	1.98	5.67	11.62	13.21	13.89	14.01	13.93	14.23	15.73	17.27	19.17	22.74
3 Direct taxes and other current transfers n.e.c. to general government	67.33	131.83	238.20	261.01	273.83	286.06	311.00	339.48	357.15	364.51	383.08	389.45
A Social security contributions	32.91	67.65	124.58	133.36	139.76	145.46	155.46	167.80	175.99	183.34	191.82	204.08
B Direct taxes	33.70	62.87	110.74	124.29	130.68	136.85	151.44	167.86	177.30	177.24	187.17	181.03
C Fees, fines and penalties	0.71	1.31	2.88	3.36	3.39	3.75	4.10	3.82	3.86	3.93	4.10	4.35
4 Other current transfers	14.29	29.65	46.41	51.75	57.37	60.53	64.45	69.82	74.03	82.12	86.63	90.87
5 Net saving	27.85	40.55	64.35	52.56	73.16	62.83	65.61	69.78	91.85	114.44	121.36	152.14
Total Current Disbursements and Net Saving	316.74	575.96	913.11	975.03	1058.44	1118.27	1188.17	1268.84	1343.17	1413.80	1485.55	1583.12

1.7 External Transactions on Current Account, Summary

Thousand Million Austrian schillings

	1970	1975	1980	1981	1982	1983	1984	1985	1986	1987	1988	1989
Payments to the Rest of the World												
1 Imports of goods and services [a]	113.07	204.81	385.66	418.47	412.44	433.93	495.71	546.81	509.80	519.83	583.62	660.62
A Imports of merchandise c.i.f. [a]	92.65	164.29	313.26	332.28	329.53	345.31	389.18	427.12	404.38	408.41	444.80	509.16
B Other	20.42	40.51	72.39	86.19	82.91	88.62	106.53	119.68	105.41	111.42	138.82	151.45
2 Factor income to the rest of the world	5.51	14.23	41.20	59.70	62.67	56.01	66.92	73.56	70.41	70.27	80.33	104.33
A Compensation of employees [b]	-	-	-	-	-	-	-	-	-	-	-	-
B Property and entrepreneurial income	5.51	14.23	41.20	59.70	62.67	56.01	66.92	73.56	70.41	70.27	80.33	104.33
By general government [c]	0.96	1.24	4.38	5.27	6.72	6.91	7.76	7.44	7.35	7.42	6.90	8.49
By corporate and quasi-corporate enterprises	...	...	...	...	...	...	...	...	...	...	...	...
By other	...	...	...	...	...	...	...	...	...	...	...	...
3 Current transfers to the rest of the world [b]	3.19	8.16	11.61	12.81	12.88	13.10	13.81	13.90	14.13	14.74	16.02	15.83
A Indirect taxes to supranational organizations	...	...	...	...	...	...	...	...	...	...	...	...
B Other current transfers	3.19	8.16	11.61	12.81	12.88	13.10	13.81	13.90	14.13	14.74	16.02	15.83
4 Surplus of the nation on current transactions	2.26	-0.37	-26.43	-21.41	12.19	8.31	-3.94	-2.49	3.75	-2.73	-3.91	0.17
Payments to the Rest of the World and Surplus of the Nation on Current Transactions	124.03	226.83	412.04	469.57	500.18	511.35	572.50	631.78	598.09	602.10	676.06	780.94
Receipts From The Rest of the World												
1 Exports of goods and services [a]	116.75	209.02	366.24	404.51	431.24	449.69	497.64	549.13	522.97	527.19	590.32	669.30
A Exports of merchandise f.o.b. [a]	74.23	133.66	225.78	255.15	266.92	274.55	312.40	359.45	342.15	342.71	374.43	423.21
B Other	42.53	75.36	140.46	149.36	164.32	175.14	185.24	189.68	180.82	184.47	215.88	246.08
2 Factor income from rest of the world	3.53	10.62	32.85	50.94	54.25	47.20	58.37	66.49	58.45	57.36	66.63	91.23
A Compensation of employees [b]	-	-	-	-	-	-	-	-	-	-	-	-
B Property and entrepreneurial income	3.53	10.62	32.85	50.94	54.25	47.20	58.37	66.49	58.45	57.36	66.63	91.23
3 Current transfers from rest of the world [b]	3.73	7.19	12.95	14.12	14.68	14.46	16.50	16.15	16.67	17.55	19.11	20.42
A Subsidies from supranational organisations	...	...	...	...	...	...	...	...	...	...	...	...
B Other current transfers	3.73	7.19	12.95	14.12	14.68	14.46	16.50	16.15	16.67	17.55	19.11	20.42
Receipts from the Rest of the World on Current Transactions	124.01	226.83	412.04	469.57	500.17	511.35	572.51	631.77	598.09	602.10	676.06	780.94

a) The estimates on transit trade are on a net basis.
b) Item 'Compensation of employees' is included in current transfers to/from the rest of the world.
c) Only central government data are included in the general government estimates.

Austria

1.8 Capital Transactions of The Nation, Summary

Thousand Million Austrian schillings

	1970	1975	1980	1981	1982	1983	1984	1985	1986	1987	1988	1989
Finance of Gross Capital Formation												
Gross saving	113.96	170.22	256.46	256.77	272.42	272.05	299.97	313.09	331.49	347.92	390.42	434.90
1 Consumption of fixed capital	43.85	77.42	116.10	128.51	140.76	149.24	158.19	167.53	176.20	183.87	194.11	205.63
A General government	2.60	4.95	7.48	8.37	9.13	9.60	10.10	10.69	11.31	11.56	11.80	12.22
B Corporate and quasi-corporate enterprises	41.25	72.47	108.62	120.14	131.64	139.64	148.10	156.84	164.89	172.31	182.31	193.41
C Other	-	-	-	-	-	-	-	-	-	-	-	-
2 Net saving	70.11	92.80	140.36	128.26	131.66	122.81	141.78	145.56	155.29	164.05	196.31	229.27
A General government	24.97	28.22	36.15	39.08	17.13	14.18	30.33	32.86	17.98	3.50	19.19	19.61
B Corporate and quasi-corporate enterprises	17.29	24.03	39.86	36.62	41.37	45.80	45.84	42.92	45.46	46.11	55.76	57.52
C Other	27.85	40.55	64.35	52.56	73.16	62.83	65.61	69.78	91.85	114.44	121.36	152.14
Less: Surplus of the nation on current transactions	2.26	-0.37	-26.43	-21.41	12.19	8.31	-3.94	-2.49	3.75	-2.73	-3.91	0.17
Finance of Gross Capital Formation	111.70	170.59	282.89	278.18	260.23	263.74	303.91	315.58	327.74	350.65	394.33	434.73
Gross Capital Formation												
Increase in stocks a	14.51	-4.33	27.43	10.24	-2.65	-5.81	20.98	11.16	3.73	8.90	23.65	32.55
Gross fixed capital formation b	97.18	174.92	255.46	267.94	262.88	269.55	282.92	304.41	324.01	341.75	370.68	402.19
1 General government	17.53	34.23	41.57	43.84	42.94	45.19	46.29	48.00	52.09	50.55	50.32	54.28
2 Corporate and quasi-corporate enterprises	...	...	...	...	...	...	...	...	...	...	...	...
3 Other	...	...	...	...	...	...	...	...	...	...	...	...
Gross Capital Formation	111.69	170.59	282.89	278.18	260.23	263.74	303.90	315.57	327.74	350.65	394.33	434.73

a) Item 'Increase in stocks' includes breeding stock, draught animals and a statistical discrepancy.
b) Item 'Gross fixed capital formation' includes value added tax on investments of investors not entitled to deduct invoiced value added tax. This component is not included in the sub-items. For years 1973-1975, 1977 and 1978 of the current prices table, special investment tax is included. These estimates are shown separately as 'Statistical discrepancy' in tables 2.7, 2.8, 2.9, 2.10 and 2.11.

1.9 Gross Domestic Product by Institutional Sectors of Origin

Thousand Million Austrian schillings

	1970	1975	1980	1981	1982	1983	1984	1985	1986	1987	1988	1989
Domestic Factor Incomes Originating												
1 General government	38.24	75.55	119.66	131.54	143.49	152.70	160.93	171.73	182.91	191.44	195.81	205.31
2 Corporate and quasi-corporate enterprises	...	...	...	...	...	...	...	...	...	...	...	...
3 Households and private unincorporated enterprises	...	...	...	...	...	...	...	...	...	...	...	...
4 Non-profit institutions serving households	2.12	3.71	5.81	6.36	6.82	7.86	8.26	8.77	9.25	9.72	9.77	10.10
Subtotal: Domestic Factor Incomes	276.87	486.16	745.83	785.15	842.07	890.30	938.43	994.16	1051.78	1092.26	1160.76	1241.59
Indirect taxes, net	55.16	92.54	132.78	142.31	150.70	161.69	180.16	186.73	188.00	197.77	209.81	226.21
A Indirect taxes	61.68	111.52	162.83	174.40	184.98	197.08	216.09	225.93	234.04	245.15	254.89	271.64
B Less: Subsidies	6.52	18.98	30.05	32.09	34.28	35.39	35.93	39.20	46.05	47.38	45.08	45.44
Consumption of fixed capital	43.85	77.42	116.10	128.51	140.76	149.24	158.19	167.53	176.20	183.87	194.11	205.63
Statistical discrepancy	-	-0.01	-0.01	-	-	-	-0.01	-	-	-	-	-
Gross Domestic Product	375.88	656.11	994.70	1055.97	1133.53	1201.23	1276.77	1348.42	1415.97	1473.90	1564.68	1673.43

1.10 Gross Domestic Product by Kind of Activity, in Current Prices

Thousand Million Austrian schillings

	1970	1975	1980	1981	1982	1983	1984	1985	1986	1987	1988	1989
1 Agriculture, hunting, forestry and fishing	25.78	33.07	44.29	43.43	43.73	44.14	48.70	44.99	47.11	48.47	49.07	51.80
2 Mining and quarrying	2.75	4.02	4.87	4.77	5.40	5.32	5.54	5.87	5.65	5.85	5.49	5.34
3 Manufacturing	126.70	187.72	276.67	288.91	308.08	322.82	340.06	362.80	375.65	381.53	414.53	446.51
4 Electricity, gas and water	10.39	18.68	30.67	31.96	38.00	39.09	38.61	39.85	43.92	47.21	47.26	48.68
5 Construction	30.65	57.95	81.21	84.79	85.10	87.45	87.06	89.06	93.50	99.63	106.08	114.45
6 Wholesale and retail trade, restaurants and hotels	68.07	109.81	166.75	175.32	188.30	201.83	206.86	215.06	223.83	232.36	248.70	268.61
7 Transport, storage and communication	22.31	35.17	57.83	62.63	64.96	68.11	74.76	78.42	81.53	86.15	93.53	99.51
8 Finance, insurance, real estate and business services	31.58	66.68	119.06	135.64	155.22	166.22	183.14	204.39	223.01	237.05	256.45	276.00
9 Community, social and personal services	11.56	19.52	32.23	34.36	36.74	40.54	43.54	46.78	51.24	55.17	59.25	63.73
Total, Industries	329.79	532.63	813.58	861.80	925.52	975.51	1028.26	1087.24	1145.45	1193.42	1280.35	1374.63
Producers of Government Services	41.60	82.12	129.08	141.90	154.76	164.63	173.49	185.07	197.09	205.91	210.53	220.86

Austria

1.10 Gross Domestic Product by Kind of Activity, in Current Prices
(Continued)

Thousand Million Austrian schillings

	1970	1975	1980	1981	1982	1983	1984	1985	1986	1987	1988	1989
Other Producers	2.99	4.80	7.17	7.90	8.36	9.23	9.70	10.23	10.82	11.26	11.35	11.71
Subtotal	374.38	619.55	949.83	1011.59	1088.64	1149.37	1211.44	1282.54	1353.35	1410.59	1502.23	1607.20
Less: Imputed bank service charge	11.74	26.49	45.12	53.36	60.23	61.06	63.30	68.56	75.03	80.51	85.81	92.36
Plus: Import duties	13.23	6.67	5.75	6.77	7.43	7.71	8.62	9.08	9.00	9.86	10.63	11.51
Plus: Value added tax	-	56.38	84.25	90.97	97.69	105.22	120.00	125.36	128.66	133.96	137.63	147.08
Plus: Other adjustments	0.01	-	-0.01	-0.01	-	-0.01	-	-	-	-	-	-
Equals: Gross Domestic Product	375.88	656.11	994.70	1055.97	1133.53	1201.23	1276.77	1348.42	1415.97	1473.90	1564.68	1673.43

1.11 Gross Domestic Product by Kind of Activity, in Constant Prices

Thousand Million Austrian schillings

	1970	1975	1980	1981	1982	1983	1984	1985	1986	1987	1988	1989
		1976			At constant prices of:	1983						
1 Agriculture, hunting, forestry and fishing	32.62	35.21	41.96	40.50	46.04	44.14	46.41	44.20	44.64	44.66	46.53	45.86
2 Mining and quarrying	3.99	4.03	5.65	5.69	5.69	5.32	5.25	5.02	4.45	5.13	4.63	4.57
3 Manufacturing	168.53	196.37	320.58	316.41	317.66	322.82	332.10	344.82	346.60	348.86	368.44	390.26
4 Electricity, gas and water	16.03	20.94	38.66	38.22	38.24	39.09	39.69	41.43	43.09	46.41	47.18	48.54
5 Construction	46.10	59.02	98.14	94.19	88.38	87.45	86.33	86.80	87.92	89.36	92.61	95.85
6 Wholesale and retail trade, restaurants and hotels	92.75	116.83	189.41	191.12	193.22	201.83	200.87	206.95	209.59	213.71	225.80	237.60
7 Transport, storage and communication	27.86	37.33	65.08	65.48	66.24	68.11	71.89	74.78	75.28	78.70	81.80	85.78
8 Finance, insurance, real estate and business services	53.18	70.79	151.65	154.77	161.57	166.22	172.02	175.95	180.99	185.29	191.27	197.55
9 Community, social and personal services	18.61	22.22	38.59	39.59	39.62	40.54	41.11	42.69	44.23	45.98	48.05	49.75
Total, Industries	459.67	562.74	949.72	945.98	956.65	975.51	995.66	1022.62	1036.77	1058.09	1106.29	1155.76
Producers of Government Services	75.42	88.00	154.67	158.74	162.11	164.63	166.61	169.12	171.38	173.22	174.51	175.75
Other Producers	5.20	5.35	9.06	9.25	9.21	9.23	9.28	9.31	9.41	9.43	9.43	9.46
Subtotal	540.28	656.09	1113.45	1113.97	1127.97	1149.37	1171.55	1201.05	1217.56	1240.74	1290.22	1340.97
Less: Imputed bank service charge	17.43	25.70	51.80	54.91	58.17	61.06	63.07	63.98	67.50	70.14	71.77	74.57
Plus: Import duties	3.46	4.98	7.88	7.44	7.33	7.71	8.19	8.41	8.99	9.57	10.21	11.02
Plus: Value added tax	45.16	57.65	99.14	98.79	100.64	105.22	100.90	102.07	103.07	106.92	108.16	112.62
Plus: Other adjustments	-0.01	0.01	-0.01	-	-0.02	-0.01	-	-0.01	-	-	-	-
Equals: Gross Domestic Product	571.47	693.03	1168.66	1165.29	1177.75	1201.23	1217.57	1247.54	1262.12	1287.10	1336.82	1390.03

1.12 Relations Among National Accounting Aggregates

Thousand Million Austrian schillings

	1970	1975	1980	1981	1982	1983	1984	1985	1986	1987	1988	1989
Gross Domestic Product	375.88	656.11	994.70	1055.97	1133.53	1201.23	1276.77	1348.42	1415.97	1473.90	1564.68	1673.43
Plus: Net factor income from the rest of the world	-1.97	-3.62	-8.35	-8.76	-8.42	-8.81	-8.55	-7.07	-11.97	-12.91	-13.70	-13.10
Factor income from the rest of the world	3.53	10.62	32.85	50.94	54.25	47.20	58.37	66.49	58.45	57.36	66.63	91.23
Less: Factor income to the rest of the world	5.51	14.23	41.20	59.70	62.67	56.01	66.92	73.56	70.41	70.27	80.33	104.33
Equals: Gross National Product	373.91	652.50	986.35	1047.21	1125.11	1192.42	1268.22	1341.35	1404.01	1461.00	1550.98	1660.33
Less: Consumption of fixed capital	43.85	77.42	116.10	128.51	140.76	149.24	158.19	167.53	176.20	183.87	194.11	205.63

Austria

1.12 Relations Among National Accounting Aggregates
(Continued)

Thousand Million Austrian schillings

	1970	1975	1980	1981	1982	1983	1984	1985	1986	1987	1988	1989
Equals: National Income	330.06	575.07	870.25	918.70	984.35	1043.18	1110.03	1173.83	1227.81	1277.13	1356.87	1454.70
Plus: Net current transfers from the rest of the world	0.55	-0.97	1.34	1.31	1.80	1.36	2.69	2.26	2.54	2.82	3.10	4.59
Current transfers from the rest of the world	3.73	7.19	12.95	14.12	14.68	14.46	16.50	16.15	16.67	17.55	19.11	20.42
Less: Current transfers to the rest of the world	3.18	8.16	11.61	12.81	12.88	13.10	13.81	13.90	14.13	14.74	16.02	15.83
Equals: National Disposable Income	330.61	574.10	871.59	920.01	986.16	1044.54	1112.72	1176.09	1230.35	1279.94	1359.96	1459.28
Less: Final consumption	260.51	481.31	731.23	791.75	854.49	921.73	970.94	1030.53	1075.06	1115.89	1163.66	1230.01
Equals: Net Saving	70.11	92.80	140.36	128.26	131.66	122.81	141.78	145.56	155.29	164.05	196.31	229.27
Less: Surplus of the nation on current transactions	2.26	-0.37	-26.43	-21.41	12.19	8.31	-3.94	-2.49	3.75	-2.73	-3.91	0.17
Equals: Net Capital Formation	67.85	93.18	166.79	149.67	119.47	114.50	145.72	148.05	151.54	166.78	200.21	229.10

2.1 Government Final Consumption Expenditure by Function, in Current Prices

Thousand Million Austrian schillings

		1970	1975	1980	1981	1982	1983	1984	1985	1986	1987	1988	1989
1	General public services	10.09	20.48	30.44	32.65	36.04	36.15	37.87	42.06	44.07	45.24	46.00	...
2	Defence	4.04	7.45	11.39	12.01	13.18	15.50	15.67	16.77	18.09	16.95	16.52	18.15
3	Public order and safety	3.16	5.79	8.88	9.70	10.54	11.26	11.90	12.33	13.09	13.36	13.25	...
4	Education	10.94	23.71	38.55	42.45	46.43	49.47	52.36	56.05	59.87	62.68	64.06	...
5	Health	11.88	25.47	43.67	47.75	50.85	52.99	55.37	59.90	64.08	69.75	72.72	...
6	Social security and welfare	9.71	20.58	32.38	36.12	40.64	42.34	43.94	46.89	49.39	50.00	53.04	...
7	Housing and community amenities	0.14	0.20	0.40	0.31	0.49	0.26	0.17	0.41	0.56	0.58	0.45	...
8	Recreational, cultural and religious affairs	0.79	1.92	3.10	3.47	3.87	4.06	4.44	4.83	5.12	5.35	5.51	...
9	Economic services	4.47	7.45	9.88	10.80	12.26	14.87	16.04	15.76	16.40	16.52	16.82	...
	A Fuel and energy	-	-	-	-	-	-	-	-	-	-	-	...
	B Agriculture, forestry, fishing and hunting	0.64	0.98	1.86	1.54	1.61	2.84	2.94	1.72	1.77	1.85	1.94	...
	C Mining, manufacturing and construction, except fuel and energy	1.89	3.51	4.97	5.42	5.82	6.00	6.29	6.95	7.50	7.92	8.37	...
	D Transportation and communication	1.92	2.91	2.93	3.73	4.70	5.72	6.45	6.70	6.71	6.34	6.08	...
	E Other economic affairs	0.02	0.05	0.12	0.11	0.13	0.31	0.36	0.39	0.42	0.41	0.42	...
10	Other functions	-	-	-	-	-	-	-	-	-	-	-	...
	Total Government Final Consumption Expenditure	55.22	113.05	178.70	195.25	214.30	226.89	237.76	255.00	270.66	280.44	288.35	302.09

2.2 Government Final Consumption Expenditure by Function, in Constant Prices

Thousand Million Austrian schillings

		1970	1975	1980	1981	1982	1983	1984	1985	1986	1987	1988	1989
				At constant prices of:									
			1976				1983						
1	General public services	17.59	22.54	... / 35.21	35.68	36.44	36.15	36.12	38.20	38.43	38.62	38.52	...
2	Defence	7.81	7.89	... / 13.83	13.57	13.75	15.50	14.76	14.95	15.54	14.12	13.37	14.49
3	Public order and safety	5.43	6.39	... / 10.49	10.70	10.87	11.26	11.53	11.37	11.54	11.52	11.26	...
4	Education	21.58	25.05	... / 45.25	46.53	48.25	49.47	50.47	51.76	52.57	53.15	53.72	...
5	Health	21.56	27.65	... / 52.41	53.02	52.79	52.99	52.82	53.79	55.40	57.69	58.01	...
6	Social security and welfare	17.32	22.52	... / 39.36	41.06	42.61	42.34	42.13	42.74	42.98	42.26	43.45	...
7	Housing and community amenities	0.25	0.22	... / 0.48	0.34	0.51	0.26	0.16	0.38	0.49	0.49	0.37	...
8	Recreational, cultural and religious affairs	1.35	2.11	... / 3.81	4.17	4.32	4.06	4.23	4.40	4.49	4.60	4.63	...
9	Economic services	7.81	8.20	... / 11.45	11.91	12.43	14.87	15.14	14.22	14.23	14.16	14.05	...

Austria

2.2 Government Final Consumption Expenditure by Function, in Constant Prices
(Continued)

Thousand Million Austrian schillings

	1970	1975	1980	1981	1982	1983	1984	1985	1986	1987	1988	1989
		1976			At constant prices of:	1983						
A Fuel and energy	0.01	-	...	-	-	-	-	-	-	-	-	...
B Agriculture, forestry, fishing and hunting	1.13	1.09	... 2.15	1.72	1.65	2.84	2.77	1.55	1.53	1.58	1.62	...
C Mining, manufacturing and construction, except fuel and energy	3.30	3.86	... 5.71	5.91	5.87	6.00	5.94	6.27	6.51	6.80	6.99	...
D Transportation and communication	3.34	3.20	... 3.45	4.16	4.78	5.72	6.09	6.04	5.81	5.43	5.08	...
E Other economic affairs	0.03	0.05	... 0.14	0.12	0.13	0.31	0.34	0.36	0.37	0.36	0.35	...
10 Other functions	-	-	... -	-	-	-	-	-	-	-	-	...
Total Government Final Consumption Expenditure	100.71	122.57	... 212.27	216.99	221.97	226.89	227.38	231.80	235.65	236.59	237.37	238.74

2.3 Total Government Outlays by Function and Type

Thousand Million Austrian schillings

	Final Consumption Expenditures Total	Compensation of Employees	Other	Subsidies	Other Current Transfers & Property Income	Total Current Disbursements	Gross Capital Formation	Other Capital Outlays	Total Outlays
					1980				
1 General public services	30.44	21.07	9.38	...	...	...	...	...	...
2 Defence	11.39	6.15	5.24	...	...	...	...	...	...
3 Public order and safety	8.88	8.85	0.03	...	...	...	...	...	...
4 Education	38.55	30.77	7.78	...	...	...	...	...	...
5 Health	43.67	15.43	28.24	...	...	...	...	...	...
6 Social security and welfare	32.38	28.24	4.14	...	...	...	...	...	...
7 Housing and community amenities	0.40	1.51	-1.11	...	...	...	...	...	...
8 Recreation, culture and religion	3.10	1.69	1.41	...	...	...	...	...	...
9 Economic services	9.88	5.95	3.93	...	...	...	...	...	...
A Fuel and energy	-	-	-	...	...	...	...	...	...
B Agriculture, forestry, fishing and hunting	1.86	1.45	0.41	...	...	...	...	...	...
C Mining (except fuels), manufacturing and construction	4.97	2.46	2.51	...	...	...	...	...	...
D Transportation and communication	2.93	2.03	0.90	...	...	...	...	...	...
E Other economic affairs	0.12	0.01	0.11	...	...	...	...	...	...
10 Other functions	...	...	...	...	...	...	...	...	...
Total	178.70	119.66	59.04	30.05	216.72	425.47	41.57	19.02	486.06
					1981				
1 General public services	32.65	23.03	9.62	-0.05	2.29	34.89	...	...	...
2 Defence	12.01	6.54	5.47	-	0.10	12.11	...	...	...
3 Public order and safety	9.70	9.63	0.07	-	0.15	9.85	...	...	...
4 Education	42.45	33.93	8.52	0.37	2.61	45.43	...	...	...
5 Health	47.75	17.19	30.56	5.95	1.03	54.73	...	...	...
6 Social security and welfare	36.12	31.02	5.10	0.83	195.97	232.92	...	...	...
7 Housing and community amenities	0.31	1.69	-1.38	1.09	2.30	3.70	...	...	...
8 Recreation, culture and religion	3.47	1.88	1.58	1.55	1.27	6.29	...	...	...
9 Economic services	10.80	6.64	4.16	22.35	2.92	36.07	...	...	...
A Fuel and energy	-	-	-	0.01	-	0.01	...	...	...
B Agriculture, forestry, fishing and hunting	1.54	1.19	0.35	7.95	1.15	10.64	...	...	...
C Mining (except fuels), manufacturing and construction	5.42	2.73	2.69	3.99	0.92	10.33	...	...	...
D Transportation and communication	3.73	2.71	1.02	10.08	0.35	14.16	...	...	...
E Other economic affairs	0.11	0.01	0.10	0.31	0.51	0.93	...	...	...
10 Other functions	...	...	...	-	29.29	29.29	...	...	...
Total	195.25	131.55	63.70	32.09	237.94	465.28	43.84	22.24	531.36

Austria

2.3 Total Government Outlays by Function and Type
(Continued)

Thousand Million Austrian schillings

	Final Consumption Expenditures — Total	Compensation of Employees	Other	Subsidies	Other Current Transfers & Property Income	Total Current Disbursements	Gross Capital Formation	Other Capital Outlays	Total Outlays
1982									
1 General public services	36.04	24.98	11.06	-0.08	2.37	38.33	...	...	...
2 Defence	13.18	7.34	5.84	-	0.10	13.28	...	...	...
3 Public order and safety	10.54	10.32	0.22	-	0.09	10.63	...	...	...
4 Education	46.43	36.80	9.63	0.36	2.73	49.52	...	...	...
5 Health	50.85	18.55	32.30	4.64	1.08	56.57	...	...	...
6 Social security and welfare	40.64	34.39	6.25	0.94	215.11	256.69	...	...	...
7 Housing and community amenities	0.49	1.83	-1.34	1.27	2.78	4.54	...	...	...
8 Recreation, culture and religion	3.87	2.08	1.79	1.57	1.34	6.78	...	...	...
9 Economic services	12.26	7.20	5.06	25.58	3.35	41.19	...	...	...
A Fuel and energy	-	-	-	-	-	-	...	...	...
B Agriculture, forestry, fishing and hunting	1.61	1.25	0.36	8.35	1.19	11.15	...	...	...
C Mining (except fuels), manufacturing and construction	5.82	2.97	2.85	5.14	1.26	12.22	...	...	...
D Transportation and communication	4.70	2.96	1.74	11.64	0.38	16.72	...	...	...
E Other economic affairs	0.13	0.02	0.11	0.45	0.52	1.10	...	...	...
10 Other functions	...	...	...	-	35.21	35.21	...	...	...
Total	214.30	143.49	70.81	34.28	264.16	512.74	42.94	21.77	577.45
1983									
1 General public services	36.15	26.37	9.78	-0.03	2.28	38.40	...	...	...
2 Defence	15.50	8.02	7.48	-	0.10	15.60	...	...	...
3 Public order and safety	11.26	10.91	0.35	-	0.10	11.36	...	...	...
4 Education	49.47	39.12	10.35	0.38	2.81	52.66	...	...	...
5 Health	52.99	19.73	33.26	4.73	1.22	58.94	...	...	...
6 Social security and welfare	42.34	36.89	5.45	1.77	230.92	275.03	...	...	...
7 Housing and community amenities	0.26	1.90	-1.64	0.64	3.16	4.06	...	...	...
8 Recreation, culture and religion	4.06	2.22	1.84	1.83	1.35	7.24	...	...	...
9 Economic services	14.87	7.54	7.33	26.07	2.03	42.97	...	...	...
A Fuel and energy	-	-	-	-	-	-	...	...	...
B Agriculture, forestry, fishing and hunting	2.84	1.34	1.50	9.86	0.31	13.01	...	...	...
C Mining (except fuels), manufacturing and construction	6.00	3.10	2.90	3.72	0.87	10.59	...	...	...
D Transportation and communication	5.72	3.08	2.64	11.85	0.41	17.98	...	...	...
E Other economic affairs	0.31	0.02	0.29	0.64	0.44	1.39	...	...	...
10 Other functions	...	...	...	-	36.62	36.62	...	...	...
Total	226.89	152.70	74.19	35.39	280.60	542.88	45.19	26.50	614.57
1984									
1 General public services	37.87	27.83	10.04	-0.03	2.34	40.18	...	...	...
2 Defence	15.67	7.99	7.68	-	0.11	15.78	...	...	...
3 Public order and safety	11.90	11.42	0.48	-	0.09	11.99	...	...	...
4 Education	52.36	41.74	10.62	0.41	2.83	55.60	...	...	...
5 Health	55.37	21.13	34.24	4.76	1.55	61.68	...	...	...
6 Social security and welfare	43.94	38.44	5.50	1.54	244.98	290.46	...	...	...
7 Housing and community amenities	0.17	2.01	-1.84	0.62	3.34	4.13	...	...	...
8 Recreation, culture and religion	4.44	2.39	2.05	1.87	1.37	7.68	...	...	...
9 Economic services	16.04	7.98	8.06	26.76	2.43	45.23	...	...	...
A Fuel and energy	-	-	-	-	0.01	0.01	...	...	...
B Agriculture, forestry, fishing and hunting	2.94	1.41	1.53	10.72	0.43	14.09	...	...	...
C Mining (except fuels), manufacturing and construction	6.29	3.24	3.05	3.22	1.06	10.57	...	...	...
D Transportation and communication	6.45	3.31	3.14	12.11	0.47	19.03	...	...	...
E Other economic affairs	0.36	0.02	0.34	0.71	0.46	1.53	...	...	...
10 Other functions	...	...	...	-	43.09	43.09	...	...	...
Total	237.76	160.93	76.83	35.93	302.13	575.82	46.29	26.90	649.01

Austria

2.3 Total Government Outlays by Function and Type
(Continued)

Thousand Million Austrian schillings

		Final Consumption Expenditures			Subsidies	Other Current Transfers & Property Income	Total Current Disbursements	Gross Capital Formation	Other Capital Outlays	Total Outlays
		Total	Compensation of Employees	Other						

1985

		Total	Comp. Emp.	Other	Subsidies	Other Curr. Trans.	Total Curr. Disb.	GCF	Other Cap.	Total Outlays
1	General public services	42.06	29.41	12.65	0.01	2.54	44.62	...	...	...
2	Defence	16.77	8.57	8.20	-	0.11	16.88	...	...	...
3	Public order and safety	12.33	12.16	0.17	-	0.10	12.43	...	...	...
4	Education	56.05	44.55	11.50	0.46	3.21	59.72	...	...	...
5	Health	59.90	22.92	36.98	5.41	2.11	67.42	...	...	...
6	Social security and welfare	46.89	40.97	5.92	2.05	263.68	312.62	...	...	...
7	Housing and community amenities	0.41	2.08	-1.67	0.76	2.35	3.52	...	...	...
8	Recreation, culture and religion	4.83	2.60	2.23	1.95	1.53	8.31	...	...	...
9	Economic services	15.76	8.48	7.28	28.55	2.99	47.30	...	...	...
	A Fuel and energy	-	-	-	-	0.01	0.01	...	...	...
	B Agriculture, forestry, fishing and hunting	1.72	1.46	0.26	11.50	0.48	13.70	...	...	...
	C Mining (except fuels), manufacturing and construction	6.95	3.46	3.49	3.21	1.50	11.65	...	...	...
	D Transportation and communication	6.70	3.54	3.16	13.09	0.52	20.31	...	...	...
	E Other economic affairs	0.39	0.02	0.37	0.76	0.48	1.63	...	...	...
10	Other functions	...	...	...	-	47.85	47.85	...	...	...
	Total	255.00	171.73	83.27	39.20	326.47	620.67	48.01	28.90	697.58

1986

		Total	Comp. Emp.	Other	Subsidies	Other Curr. Trans.	Total Curr. Disb.	GCF	Other Cap.	Total Outlays
1	General public services	44.07	30.85	13.22	0.31	2.59	46.97	...	...	...
2	Defence	18.09	9.06	9.04	-	0.12	18.21	...	...	...
3	Public order and safety	13.09	12.86	0.22	-	0.10	13.19	...	...	...
4	Education	59.87	47.94	11.93	0.41	3.34	63.62	...	...	...
5	Health	64.08	24.63	39.45	5.72	2.43	72.23	...	...	...
6	Social security and welfare	49.39	43.48	5.90	2.56	279.72	331.67	...	...	...
7	Housing and community amenities	0.56	2.25	-1.69	0.80	2.45	3.81	...	...	...
8	Recreation, culture and religion	5.12	2.80	2.32	2.13	1.56	8.80	...	...	...
9	Economic services	16.40	9.03	7.37	34.12	3.22	53.74	...	...	...
	A Fuel and energy	-	-	-	0.02	0.01	0.04	...	...	...
	B Agriculture, forestry, fishing and hunting	1.77	1.54	0.23	13.86	0.44	16.06	...	...	...
	C Mining (except fuels), manufacturing and construction	7.50	3.69	3.81	3.09	1.73	12.31	...	...	...
	D Transportation and communication	6.71	3.78	2.93	15.70	0.52	22.92	...	...	...
	E Other economic affairs	0.42	0.02	0.41	1.46	0.53	2.41	...	...	...
10	Other functions	...	...	...	-	51.88	51.88	...	...	...
	Total	270.66	182.91	87.75	46.05	347.40	664.10	52.09	29.73	745.93

1987

		Total	Comp. Emp.	Other	Subsidies	Other Curr. Trans.	Total Curr. Disb.	GCF	Other Cap.	Total Outlays
1	General public services	45.24	32.07	13.16	0.30	2.70	48.24	...	...	...
2	Defence	16.95	9.10	7.85	-	0.04	16.99	...	...	...
3	Public order and safety	13.36	13.12	0.24	-	0.11	13.47	...	...	...
4	Education	62.68	50.57	12.11	0.50	3.87	67.04	...	...	...
5	Health	69.75	27.38	42.37	5.55	2.63	77.93	...	...	...
6	Social security and welfare	50.00	44.57	5.43	1.97	299.27	351.25	...	...	...
7	Housing and community amenities	0.58	2.36	-1.78	0.88	2.65	4.11	...	...	...
8	Recreation, culture and religion	5.35	2.98	2.38	2.15	1.75	9.25	...	...	...
9	Economic services	16.52	9.29	7.24	36.02	3.02	55.57	...	...	...
	A Fuel and energy	-	-	-	0.04	0.01	0.05	...	...	...
	B Agriculture, forestry, fishing and hunting	1.85	1.58	0.27	16.54	0.50	18.89	...	...	...
	C Mining (except fuels), manufacturing and construction	7.92	3.81	4.11	2.55	1.39	11.86	...	...	...
	D Transportation and communication	6.34	3.89	2.46	15.62	0.53	22.49	...	...	...
	E Other economic affairs	0.41	0.02	0.40	1.27	0.59	2.28	...	...	...
10	Other functions	...	...	...	-	58.36	58.36	...	...	...
	Total	280.44	191.44	89.00	47.38	374.39	702.21	50.55	27.58	780.34

Austria

2.3 Total Government Outlays by Function and Type
(Continued)

Thousand Million Austrian schillings

	Final Consumption Expenditures Total	Compensation of Employees	Other	Subsidies	Other Current Transfers & Property Income	Total Current Disbursements	Gross Capital Formation	Other Capital Outlays	Total Outlays
1988									
1 General public services	46.00	32.54	13.46	-0.12	2.89	48.76	...	...	...
2 Defence	16.52	9.25	7.26	-	0.04	16.55	...	...	...
3 Public order and safety	13.25	13.19	0.06	-	0.11	13.36	...	...	...
4 Education	64.06	51.54	12.52	0.43	3.83	68.31	...	...	...
5 Health	72.72	27.94	44.78	5.72	2.54	80.98	...	...	...
6 Social security and welfare	53.04	46.51	6.53	1.33	306.22	360.60	...	...	...
7 Housing and community amenities	0.45	2.35	-1.90	1.03	2.93	4.40	...	...	...
8 Recreation, culture and religion	5.51	3.11	2.40	2.50	1.80	9.81	...	...	...
9 Economic services	16.82	9.39	7.43	34.19	3.25	54.26	...	...	...
A Fuel and energy	-	-	-	0.06	0.02	0.07	...	...	...
B Agriculture, forestry, fishing and hunting	1.94	1.66	0.28	15.51	0.57	18.02	...	...	...
C Mining (except fuels), manufacturing and construction	8.37	3.88	4.49	2.81	1.53	12.72	...	...	...
D Transportation and communication	6.08	3.83	2.26	14.66	0.50	21.24	...	...	...
E Other economic affairs	0.42	0.02	0.41	1.15	0.63	2.21	...	...	...
10 Other functions	...	...	...	-	61.34	61.34	...	...	...
Total	288.35	195.81	92.54	45.08	385.39	718.82	50.32	27.99	797.13
1989									
1 General public services	...	...	...	...	...	...	...	...	...
2 Defence	18.15	...	18.15	...	...	18.15	...	...	...
3 Public order and safety	...	...	...	...	...	...	...	...	...
4 Education	...	...	...	...	...	...	...	...	...
5 Health	...	...	...	...	...	...	...	...	...
6 Social security and welfare	...	...	...	...	...	...	...	...	...
7 Housing and community amenities	...	...	...	...	...	...	...	...	...
8 Recreation, culture and religion	...	...	...	...	...	...	...	...	...
9 Economic services	...	...	...	...	...	...	...	...	...
A Fuel and energy	...	...	...	...	...	...	...	...	...
B Agriculture, forestry, fishing and hunting	...	...	...	...	...	...	...	...	...
C Mining (except fuels), manufacturing and construction	...	...	...	...	...	...	...	...	...
D Transportation and communication	...	...	...	...	...	...	...	...	...
E Other economic affairs	...	...	...	...	...	...	...	...	...
10 Other functions	...	...	...	...	...	...	...	...	...
Total	302.09	205.31	96.78	45.44	404.26	751.79	54.28	23.27	829.34

2.4 Composition of General Government Social Security Benefits and Social Assistance Grants to Households

Thousand Million Austrian schillings

	1980 Social Security Benefits	1980 Social Assistance Grants	1981 Social Security Benefits	1981 Social Assistance Grants	1982 Social Security Benefits	1982 Social Assistance Grants	1983 Social Security Benefits	1983 Social Assistance Grants	1984 Social Security Benefits	1984 Social Assistance Grants	1985 Social Security Benefits	1985 Social Assistance Grants
1 Education benefits	...	...	...	2.53	...	2.63	...	2.69	...	2.70	...	3.09
2 Health benefits	0.01	...	0.01	1.02	0.01	1.06	0.01	1.20	0.01	1.52	0.26	1.67
3 Social security and welfare benefits	94.24	...	102.58	49.10	111.45	55.39	120.75	58.69	129.94	60.24	140.99	64.05
4 Housing and community amenities	...	...	...	2.30	...	2.78	...	3.16	...	3.35	...	2.34
5 Recreation and cultural benefits	...	...	...	1.27	...	1.34	...	1.34	...	1.36	...	1.51
6 Other	0.25	...	0.80	3.87	1.14	3.83	0.72	2.84	0.84	3.11	1.09	3.61
Total	94.50	56.16	103.39	60.08	112.60	67.03	121.48	69.91	130.79	72.29	142.34	76.27

Austria

2.4 Composition of General Government Social Security Benefits and Social Assistance Grants to Households
Thousand Million Austrian schillings

	1986 Social Security Benefits	1986 Social Assistance Grants	1987 Social Security Benefits	1987 Social Assistance Grants	1988 Social Security Benefits	1988 Social Assistance Grants	1989 Social Security Benefits	1989 Social Assistance Grants
1 Education benefits	...	3.19	...	3.71	...	3.66	...	...
2 Health benefits	0.35	1.86	0.38	2.05	0.38	1.99	...	...
3 Social security and welfare benefits	149.46	67.68	160.24	72.94	166.37	70.75	...	...
4 Housing and community amenities	...	2.45	...	2.65	...	2.92	...	...
5 Recreation and cultural benefits	...	1.55	...	1.74	...	1.79	...	...
6 Other	1.26	3.72	0.85	3.95	1.00	4.09	...	...
Total	151.08	80.44	161.47	87.04	167.76	85.22	177.18	85.20

2.5 Private Final Consumption Expenditure by Type and Purpose, in Current Prices
Thousand Million Austrian schillings

	1970	1975	1980	1981	1982	1983	1984	1985	1986	1987	1988	1989
Final Consumption Expenditure of Resident Households												
1 Food, beverages and tobacco	70.92	104.50	141.87	150.94	158.38	167.09	176.59	181.98	187.19	187.72	191.81	196.78
A Food	53.62	80.34	110.14	116.56	122.23	128.64	136.57	139.90	141.45	142.23	145.52	150.94
B Non-alcoholic beverages	1.46	2.28	3.86	4.15	4.20	4.39	4.62	4.96	5.49	5.84	5.98	5.98
C Alcoholic beverages	9.60	12.78	14.68	16.09	16.11	17.00	17.08	17.79	20.21	19.61	20.36	19.74
D Tobacco	6.24	9.09	13.19	14.15	15.84	17.05	18.31	19.34	20.05	20.03	19.96	20.12
2 Clothing and footwear	25.83	45.71	63.53	67.32	73.44	79.95	83.18	85.19	86.68	89.23	89.74	94.64
3 Gross rent, fuel and power	23.83	51.84	93.08	104.86	116.84	124.21	138.91	152.19	159.53	163.30	165.53	173.54
A Fuel and power	8.87	15.69	29.56	34.16	37.06	36.42	40.57	44.85	43.20	42.56	39.79	40.15
B Other	14.96	36.15	63.52	70.71	79.78	87.79	98.34	107.34	116.33	120.74	125.74	133.40
4 Furniture, furnishings and household equipment and operation	20.56	36.89	43.45	46.22	49.22	53.93	53.06	55.36	57.30	60.15	68.88	72.96
A Household operation	3.87	5.99	7.58	8.02	8.55	9.45	10.12	10.63	10.76	11.30	12.09	13.18
B Other	16.69	30.90	35.87	38.20	40.67	44.48	42.94	44.73	46.55	48.85	56.79	59.78
5 Medical care and health expenses	7.55	15.25	25.52	27.63	30.58	33.51	35.80	38.64	40.67	43.89	46.08	49.36
6 Transport and communication	26.83	56.13	98.07	105.20	110.92	122.96	125.23	133.01	130.11	132.39	141.08	162.00
A Personal transport equipment	6.07	11.91	23.37	20.88	22.56	30.78	26.38	30.87	33.16	32.26	37.50	48.13
B Other	20.78	44.22	74.70	84.32	88.36	92.18	98.85	102.14	96.95	100.13	103.58	113.88
7 Recreational, entertainment, education and cultural services	13.36	23.96	34.73	37.23	38.90	42.70	44.68	47.06	50.19	53.01	62.35	63.81
A Education	0.80	0.99	1.91	1.71	1.85	1.74	2.05	2.10	2.33	2.63	2.79	3.42
B Other	12.56	22.97	32.82	35.52	37.05	40.96	42.63	44.96	47.85	50.39	59.56	60.39
8 Miscellaneous goods and services	34.47	62.50	93.58	101.56	108.84	115.14	121.25	127.62	135.32	144.34	154.22	167.31
A Personal care	7.18	12.11	16.06	16.62	17.68	19.40	19.87	20.76	21.66	22.52	23.74	24.78
B Expenditures in restaurants, cafes and hotels	23.40	42.56	63.72	69.79	75.15	77.61	81.87	85.81	91.49	98.12	105.34	116.12
C Other	3.89	7.84	13.81	15.15	16.02	18.13	19.51	21.05	22.17	23.69	25.14	26.41
Total Final Consumption Expenditure in the Domestic Market by Households, of which	223.35	396.77	593.83	640.96	687.12	739.49	778.70	821.04	846.99	874.02	919.69	980.39
A Durable goods	25.65	48.86	67.76	67.84	71.96	85.08	79.33	86.63	91.50	93.77	112.32	122.61
B Semi-durable goods	32.54	56.54	77.39	82.02	88.78	96.39	99.48	101.96	104.34	107.30	108.83	115.06
C Non-durable goods	93.99	148.57	212.87	232.22	244.89	255.10	271.59	282.82	279.90	280.13	283.57	292.93
D Services	71.17	142.80	235.81	258.88	281.49	302.93	328.31	349.63	371.26	392.83	414.97	449.79
Plus: Direct purchases abroad by resident households	11.72	23.77	39.98	43.99	45.33	47.04	53.03	56.78	59.03	69.32	78.05	86.21
Less: Direct purchases in the domestic market by non-resident households	29.78	52.28	81.28	88.45	92.26	91.70	98.55	102.29	101.61	107.89	122.44	138.67
Equals: Final Consumption Expenditure of Resident Households [a]	205.29	368.26	552.53	596.50	640.20	694.84	733.18	775.53	804.41	835.46	875.30	927.93
Final Consumption Expenditure of Private Non-profit Institutions Serving Households												
Equals: Final Consumption Expenditure of Private Non-profit Organisations Serving Households	...	...	...	...	...	...	...	...	...	...	...	...
Private Final Consumption Expenditure	205.29	368.26	552.53	596.50	640.20	694.84	733.18	775.53	804.41	835.46	875.30	927.93

a) Item 'Final consumption expenditure of resident households' includes consumption expenditure of private non-profit institutions serving households.

Austria

2.6 Private Final Consumption Expenditure by Type and Purpose, in Constant Prices

Thousand Million Austrian schillings

	1970	1975	1980	1981	1982	1983	1984	1985	1986	1987	1988	1989
		1976	*At constant prices of:*			*1983*						

Final Consumption Expenditure of Resident Households

	1970	1975	1980	1981	1982	1983	1984	1985	1986	1987	1988	1989
1 Food, beverages and tobacco	99.87	110.58	162.04	162.35	162.25	167.09	166.30	168.70	170.22	169.79	172.62	175.70
A Food	75.24	85.02	124.43	123.77	125.03	128.64	128.29	130.32	130.36	130.68	133.93	137.40
B Non-alcoholic beverages	2.08	2.38	4.45	4.54	4.34	4.39	4.44	4.72	5.13	5.46	5.59	5.57
C Alcoholic beverages	13.57	13.08	16.55	17.21	16.20	17.00	16.74	16.59	17.61	16.79	16.90	16.73
D Tobacco	8.97	10.10	16.62	16.83	16.68	17.05	16.82	17.07	17.13	16.86	16.21	16.00
2 Clothing and footwear	36.35	47.70	70.29	72.05	75.67	79.95	80.07	79.00	77.88	78.64	76.76	78.21
3 Gross rent, fuel and power	44.08	57.85	119.94	121.56	122.76	124.21	129.24	134.21	137.38	140.21	140.24	143.86
A Fuel and power	14.67	17.07	38.18	37.37	36.69	36.42	38.13	41.06	41.90	44.21	42.60	43.09
B Other	29.41	40.78	81.76	84.19	86.07	87.79	91.12	93.15	95.48	96.00	97.64	100.77
4 Furniture, furnishings and household equipment and operation	27.55	38.59	48.93	49.55	50.54	53.93	51.02	51.76	51.98	54.07	61.01	63.09
A Household operation	5.73	6.41	8.81	8.78	8.89	9.45	9.67	9.92	9.79	10.13	10.69	11.42
B Other	21.82	32.18	40.13	40.76	41.65	44.48	41.35	41.84	42.19	43.93	50.32	51.67
5 Medical care and health expenses	14.78	17.09	31.28	31.67	32.29	33.51	33.74	34.70	34.70	35.69	36.18	37.05
6 Transport and communication	42.89	60.25	116.34	112.18	113.11	122.96	118.15	121.92	122.22	123.43	129.09	143.23
A Personal transport equipment	8.78	12.74	26.31	22.55	23.40	30.78	25.05	28.39	29.37	27.78	31.47	39.43
B Other	34.11	47.51	90.04	89.63	89.71	92.18	93.10	93.53	92.85	95.66	97.62	103.80
7 Recreational, entertainment, education and cultural services	18.47	25.19	41.28	41.90	40.89	42.70	42.82	43.91	45.51	47.53	55.24	53.79
A Education	1.08	1.15	2.23	1.92	1.96	1.74	1.98	1.97	2.06	2.17	2.21	2.24
B Other	17.39	24.04	39.05	39.98	38.94	40.96	40.84	41.94	43.45	45.36	53.03	51.55
8 Miscellaneous goods and services	57.91	66.41	109.50	112.00	113.98	115.14	114.75	116.31	118.47	123.81	128.20	135.40
A Personal care	11.17	12.84	17.89	17.94	18.56	19.40	18.81	19.31	19.79	20.85	21.88	22.67
B Expenditures in restaurants, cafes and hotels	40.24	45.49	74.70	76.91	78.28	77.61	77.17	77.45	78.56	82.10	84.79	90.69
C Other	6.50	8.08	16.91	17.15	17.14	18.13	18.77	19.55	20.12	20.86	21.53	22.04
Total Final Consumption Expenditure in the Domestic Market by Households, of which	341.89	423.66	699.61	703.24	711.50	739.49	736.08	750.50	758.37	773.16	799.34	830.32
A Durable goods	34.72	51.26	74.64	72.13	74.18	85.08	75.91	80.62	83.05	85.28	100.85	107.41
B Semi-durable goods	45.46	59.00	86.04	87.93	91.58	96.39	95.78	94.74	94.02	94.92	93.86	96.18
C Non-durable goods	138.11	158.33	249.71	249.00	248.30	255.10	256.36	261.93	263.70	266.77	270.63	276.45

Austria

2.6 Private Final Consumption Expenditure by Type and Purpose, in Constant Prices
(Continued)

Thousand Million Austrian schillings

	1970	1975	1980	1981	1982	1983	1984	1985	1986	1987	1988	1989
		1976	\multicolumn{10}{c}{At constant prices of:}					**1983**					
D Services	123.61	155.08	289.22	294.19	297.44	302.93	308.02	313.21	317.60	326.20	334.00	350.29
Plus: Direct purchases abroad by resident households	15.39	24.37	47.26	46.95	45.73	47.04	51.48	53.71	55.29	65.60	72.74	77.25
Less: Direct purchases in the domestic market by non-resident households	47.98	55.68	94.97	96.22	95.36	91.70	93.25	93.34	90.23	94.43	104.51	115.47
Equals: Final Consumption Expenditure of Resident Households [a]	309.31	392.35	651.89	653.97	661.87	694.84	694.31	710.86	723.43	744.34	767.57	792.11

Final Consumption Expenditure of Private Non-profit Institutions Serving Households

Equals: Final Consumption Expenditure of Private Non-profit Organisations Serving Households	...	...	...	...	...	...	...	...	...	...	...	...
Private Final Consumption Expenditure	309.31	392.35	651.89	653.97	661.87	694.84	694.31	710.86	723.43	744.34	767.57	792.11

a) Item 'Final consumption expenditure of resident households' includes consumption expenditure of private non-profit institutions serving households.

2.7 Gross Capital Formation by Type of Good and Owner, in Current Prices

Thousand Million Austrian schillings

	\multicolumn{4}{c	}{1980}	\multicolumn{4}{c	}{1981}	\multicolumn{4}{c}{1982}
	TOTAL	Total Private	Public Enterprises	General Government	TOTAL	Total Private	Public Enterprises	General Government	TOTAL	Total Private	Public Enterprises	General Government
Increase in stocks, total [a]	27.43	...	...	...	10.24	...	...	...	-2.65	...	...	...
1 Goods producing industries	6.09	...	...	...	-0.02	...	...	...	-5.48	...	...	...
A Materials and supplies	2.58	...	...	...	-2.14	...	...	...	-2.52	...	...	...
B Work in progress	-1.45	...	...	...	-0.08	...	...	...	-1.47	...	...	...
C Livestock, except breeding stocks, dairy cattle, etc.	-0.79	...	...	...	0.59	...	...	...	0.08	...	...	...
D Finished goods	5.75	...	...	...	1.61	...	...	...	-1.57	...	...	...
2 Wholesale and retail trade	11.92	...	...	...	4.36	...	...	...	0.46	...	...	...
3 Other, except government stocks [b]	0.04	...	...	...	0.09	...	...	...	0.27	...	...	...
4 Government stocks	...	...	...	...	...	...	...	...	...	...	...	...
Statistical discrepancy [c]	9.39	...	...	...	5.81	...	...	...	2.10	...	...	...
Gross Fixed Capital Formation, Total	255.46	...	...	41.57	267.94	...	...	43.84	262.88	...	...	42.14
1 Residential buildings	52.56	...	...	2.24	58.27	...	...	2.72	60.64	...	...	2.99
2 Non-residential buildings	82.42	...	...	12.21	83.75	...	...	13.37	79.18	...	...	14.29
3 Other construction		...	...	18.43		...	...	18.76		...	...	16.60
4 Land improvement and plantation and orchard development	...	...	...	...	...	...	...	...	...	...	...	...
5 Producers' durable goods	106.00	...	...	4.74	110.55	...	...	5.02	107.35	...	...	4.58
A Transport equipment [d]	16.45	...	...	-	15.23	...	...	-	14.80	...	...	-
Passenger cars	5.68	...	...	...	5.29	...	...	...	5.14	...	...	...
Other	10.77	...	...	...	9.94	...	...	...	9.66	...	...	...
B Machinery and equipment	89.55	...	...	4.74	95.32	...	...	5.02	92.55	...	...	4.58
6 Breeding stock, dairy cattle, etc. [a]	...	...	...	...	...	...	...	...	...	...	...	...
Statistical discrepancy [e]	14.48	...	...	3.95	15.37	...	...	3.97	15.72	...	...	3.68
Total Gross Capital Formation	282.89	...	...	41.57	278.18	...	...	43.84	260.23	...	...	42.14

	\multicolumn{4}{c	}{1983}	\multicolumn{4}{c	}{1984}	\multicolumn{4}{c}{1985}
	TOTAL	Total Private	Public Enterprises	General Government	TOTAL	Total Private	Public Enterprises	General Government	TOTAL	Total Private	Public Enterprises	General Government
Increase in stocks, total [a]	-5.81	...	...	...	20.98	...	...	...	11.17	...	...	...
1 Goods producing industries	-6.58	...	...	...	9.01	...	...	...	3.22	...	...	...
A Materials and supplies	2.30	...	...	...	5.54	...	...	...	1.37	...	...	...
B Work in progress	-1.53	...	...	...	2.04	...	...	...	2.03	...	...	...
C Livestock, except breeding stocks, dairy cattle, etc.	0.75	...	...	...	0.63	...	...	...	-0.24	...	...	...

Austria

2.7 Gross Capital Formation by Type of Good and Owner, in Current Prices
(Continued)

Thousand Million Austrian schillings

	1983 TOTAL	1983 Total Private	1983 Public Enterprises	1983 General Government	1984 TOTAL	1984 Total Private	1984 Public Enterprises	1984 General Government	1985 TOTAL	1985 Total Private	1985 Public Enterprises	1985 General Government
D Finished goods	-8.10	...	...	...	0.81	...	...	...	0.06	...	...	...
2 Wholesale and retail trade	1.80	...	...	...	12.79	...	...	...	5.78	...	...	...
3 Other, except government stocks [b]	-0.06	...	...	...	0.09	...	...	...	0.07	...	...	...
4 Government stocks	...	...	...	...	...	...	...	...	...	...	...	...
Statistical discrepancy [c]	-0.96	...	...	...	-0.91	...	...	...	2.10	...	...	...
Gross Fixed Capital Formation, Total	269.55	...	...	40.76	282.92	...	...	41.25	304.41	...	...	42.19
1 Residential buildings	61.58	...	...	3.32	62.34	...	...	2.73	62.49	...	...	1.89
2 Non-residential buildings	83.41	...	...	12.80	86.26	...	...	13.48	90.85	...	...	13.56
3 Other construction		...	...	16.38		...	...	16.28		...	...	17.46
4 Land improvement and plantation and orchard development	...	...	...	...	...	...	...	...	...	...	...	...
5 Producers' durable goods	107.98	...	...	4.62	116.07	...	...	4.68	131.81	...	...	5.17
A Transport equipment [d]	17.66	...	...	-	18.29	...	...	-	20.09	...	...	-
Passenger cars	6.51	...	...	...	6.47	...	...	...	7.73	...	...	...
Other	11.14	...	...	...	11.82	...	...	...	12.36	...	...	...
B Machinery and equipment	90.32	...	...	4.62	97.78	...	...	4.68	111.72	...	...	5.17
6 Breeding stock, dairy cattle, etc. [a]	...	...	...	...	...	...	...	...	...	...	...	...
Statistical discrepancy [e]	16.58	...	...	3.65	18.25	...	...	4.07	19.26	...	...	4.09
Total Gross Capital Formation	263.74	...	...	40.76	303.90	...	...	41.25	315.58	...	...	42.19

	1986 TOTAL	1986 Total Private	1986 Public Enterprises	1986 General Government	1987 TOTAL	1987 Total Private	1987 Public Enterprises	1987 General Government	1988 TOTAL	1988 Total Private	1988 Public Enterprises	1988 General Government
Increase in stocks, total [a]	3.73	...	...	...	8.90	...	...	...	23.65	...	...	...
1 Goods producing industries	...	...	...	...	...	...	...	...	...	...	...	...
A Materials and supplies	...	...	...	...	...	...	...	...	...	...	...	...
B Work in progress	...	...	...	...	...	...	...	...	...	...	...	...
C Livestock, except breeding stocks, dairy cattle, etc.	-0.41	...	...	...	...	...	...	...	...	...	...	...
D Finished goods	0.41	...	...	...	...	...	...	...	...	...	...	...
2 Wholesale and retail trade	...	...	...	...	...	...	...	...	...	...	...	...
3 Other, except government stocks [b]	...	...	...	...	...	...	...	...	...	...	...	...
4 Government stocks	...	...	...	...	...	...	...	...	...	...	...	...
Statistical discrepancy [c]	...	...	...	...	...	...	...	...	...	...	...	...
Gross Fixed Capital Formation, Total	324.01	...	...	45.79	341.75	...	...	45.31	370.68	...	...	43.96
1 Residential buildings	65.04	...	...	1.61	68.87	...	...	1.94	76.94	...	...	...
2 Non-residential buildings	98.19	...	...	15.77	107.36	...	...	14.67	115.44	...	...	...
3 Other construction		...	...	18.31		...	...	18.97		...	...	...
4 Land improvement and plantation and orchard development	...	...	...	...	...	...	...	...	...	...	...	...
5 Producers' durable goods	140.06	...	...	5.84	144.42	...	...	5.58	155.36	...	...	...
A Transport equipment [d]	22.32	...	...	-	23.40	...	...	-	26.89	...	...	...
Passenger cars	9.44	...	...	...	9.40	...	...	...	10.89	...	...	...
Other	12.88	...	...	...	13.99	...	...	...	16.00	...	...	...
B Machinery and equipment	117.74	...	...	5.84	121.02	...	...	5.58	128.47	...	...	...
6 Breeding stock, dairy cattle, etc. [a]	...	...	...	...	...	...	...	...	...	...	...	...
Statistical discrepancy [e]	20.72	...	...	4.26	21.11	...	...	4.15	22.94	...	...	...
Total Gross Capital Formation	327.74	...	...	45.79	350.65	...	...	45.31	394.33	...	...	43.96

a) Item 'Increase in stocks' includes breeding stock, draught animals and a statistical discrepancy.
b) Item 'Other, except government stocks' refers to transport only.
c) Item 'Statistical discrepancy' relates to the difference between the estimate of GDP through industrial origin approach and that of expenditure approach.
d) Item 'Transport equipment' refers to registered motor vehicles.
e) Item 'Gross fixed capital formation' includes value added tax on investments of investors not entitled to deduct invoiced value added tax. This component is not included in the sub-items. For years 1973-1975, 1977 and 1978 of the current prices table, special investment tax is included. These estimates are shown separately as 'Statistical discrepancy' in tables 2.7, 2.8, 2.9, 2.10 and 2.11.

Austria

2.8 Gross Capital Formation by Type of Good and Owner, in Constant Prices

Thousand Million Austrian schillings

	1980 TOTAL	Total Private	Public Enterprises	General Government	1981 TOTAL	Total Private	Public Enterprises	General Government	1982 TOTAL	Total Private	Public Enterprises	General Government
	\multicolumn{12}{c}{At constant prices of: 1983}
Increase in stocks, total [a]	29.17	...	...	...	0.14	...	...	...	-1.84	...	...	...
1 Goods producing industries	6.83	...	...	...	0.05	...	...	...	-4.38	...	...	...
A Materials and supplies	3.10	...	...	...	-1.92	...	...	...	-2.55	...	...	...
B Work in progress	-1.70	...	...	...	-0.10	...	...	...	-1.47	...	...	...
C Livestock, except breeding stocks, dairy cattle, etc.	-1.12	...	...	...	0.77	...	...	...	0.07	...	...	...
D Finished goods	6.55	...	...	...	1.31	...	...	...	-0.43	...	...	...
2 Wholesale and retail trade	12.78	...	...	...	4.46	...	...	...	0.47	...	...	...
3 Other, except government stocks [b]	0.05	...	...	...	0.10	...	...	...	0.27	...	...	...
4 Government stocks	...	...	...	...	...	...	...	...	...	...	...	...
Statistical discrepancy [c]	9.52	...	...	...	-4.47	...	...	...	1.79	...	...	...
Gross Fixed Capital Formation, Total	299.33	...	...	48.15	295.20	...	...	47.14	271.10	...	...	43.12
1 Residential buildings	62.99	...	...	2.53	64.23	...	...	2.91	62.72	...	...	3.00
2 Non-residential buildings	98.19	...	...	14.39	94.81	...	...	14.62	81.29	...	...	14.77
3 Other construction		...	...	21.34		...	...	19.95		...	...	16.85
4 Land improvement and plantation and orchard development	...	...	...	...	...	...	...	...	...	...	...	...
5 Producers' durable goods	121.24	...	...	5.34	119.48	...	...	5.42	110.94	...	...	4.75
A Transport equipment [d]	18.89	...	...	-	16.70	...	...	-	15.37	...	...	-
Passenger cars	6.39	...	...	...	5.74	...	...	...	5.35	...	...	...
Other	12.50	...	...	...	10.96	...	...	...	10.02	...	...	...
B Machinery and equipment	102.35	...	...	5.34	102.78	...	...	5.42	95.57	...	...	4.75
6 Breeding stock, dairy cattle, etc. [a]	...	...	...	...	...	...	...	...	...	...	...	...
Statistical discrepancy [e]	16.91	...	...	4.56	16.69	...	...	4.25	16.16	...	...	3.74
Total Gross Capital Formation	328.50	...	...	48.15	295.34	...	...	47.14	269.26	...	...	43.12

	1983 TOTAL	Total Private	Public Enterprises	General Government	1984 TOTAL	Total Private	Public Enterprises	General Government	1985 TOTAL	Total Private	Public Enterprises	General Government
	\multicolumn{12}{c}{At constant prices of: 1983}
Increase in stocks, total [a]	-5.81	...	...	...	20.47	...	...	...	12.28	...	...	...
1 Goods producing industries	-6.58	...	...	...	8.05	...	...	...	3.37	...	...	...
A Materials and supplies	2.30	...	...	...	5.55	...	...	...	1.74	...	...	...
B Work in progress	-1.53	...	...	...	1.99	...	...	...	1.90	...	...	...
C Livestock, except breeding stocks, dairy cattle, etc.	0.75	...	...	...	0.65	...	...	...	-0.33	...	...	...
D Finished goods	-8.10	...	...	...	-0.14	...	...	...	0.06	...	...	...
2 Wholesale and retail trade	1.79	...	...	...	12.54	...	...	...	5.57	...	...	...
3 Other, except government stocks [b]	-0.06	...	...	...	0.08	...	...	...	0.06	...	...	...
4 Government stocks	...	...	...	...	...	...	...	...	...	...	...	...
Statistical discrepancy [c]	-0.96	...	...	...	-0.21	...	...	...	3.27	...	...	...
Gross Fixed Capital Formation, Total	269.55	...	...	40.76	275.24	...	...	40.69	289.01	...	...	40.81
1 Residential buildings	61.58	...	...	3.32	61.11	...	...	2.72	60.09	...	...	1.86
2 Non-residential buildings	83.41	...	...	12.80	85.03	...	...	13.28	87.93	...	...	13.11
3 Other construction		...	...	16.38		...	...	16.38		...	...	17.19
4 Land improvement and plantation and orchard development	...	...	...	...	...	...	...	...	...	...	...	...
5 Producers' durable goods	107.98	...	...	4.62	112.83	...	...	4.65	124.21	...	...	5.04
A Transport equipment [d]	17.66	...	...	-	17.56	...	...	-	18.63	...	...	-
Passenger cars	6.51	...	...	...	6.25	...	...	...	7.16	...	...	...
Other	11.14	...	...	...	11.31	...	...	...	11.47	...	...	...
B Machinery and equipment	90.32	...	...	4.62	95.27	...	...	4.65	105.57	...	...	5.04
6 Breeding stock, dairy cattle, etc. [a]	...	...	...	...	...	...	...	...	...	...	...	...
Statistical discrepancy [e]	16.58	...	...	3.65	16.27	...	...	3.67	16.78	...	...	3.61
Total Gross Capital Formation	263.74	...	...	40.76	295.71	...	...	40.69	301.29	...	...	40.81

Austria

2.8 Gross Capital Formation by Type of Good and Owner, in Constant Prices

Thousand Million Austrian schillings

	1986 TOTAL	1986 Total Private	1986 Public Enterprises	1986 General Government	1987 TOTAL	1987 Total Private	1987 Public Enterprises	1987 General Government	1988 TOTAL	1988 Total Private	1988 Public Enterprises	1988 General Government
				At constant prices of: 1983								
Increase in stocks, total [a]	7.71	...	...	...	13.79	...	...	...	26.73	...	...	...
1 Goods producing industries	...	...	...	...	...	...	...	...	...	...	...	...
A Materials and supplies	...	...	...	...	...	...	...	...	...	...	...	...
B Work in progress	...	...	...	...	...	...	...	...	...	...	...	...
C Livestock, except breeding stocks, dairy cattle, etc.	0.52	...	...	...	...	...	...	...	...	...	...	...
D Finished goods	-0.52	...	...	...	...	...	...	...	...	...	...	...
2 Wholesale and retail trade	...	...	...	...	...	...	...	...	...	...	...	...
3 Other, except government stocks [b]	...	...	...	...	...	...	...	...	...	...	...	...
4 Government stocks	...	...	...	...	...	...	...	...	...	...	...	...
Statistical discrepancy [c]	...	...	...	...	...	...	...	...	...	...	...	...
Gross Fixed Capital Formation, Total	299.65	...	...	43.14	308.19	...	...	41.75	326.59	...	...	...
1 Residential buildings	61.47	...	...	1.54	62.89	...	...	1.80	68.15	...	...	...
2 Non-residential buildings	91.48	...	...	14.87	97.54	...	...	13.58	102.31	...	...	...
3 Other construction		...	...	17.52		...	...	17.62		...	...	...
4 Land improvement and plantation and orchard development	...	...	...	...	...	...	...	...	...	...	...	...
5 Producers' durable goods	129.00	...	...	5.54	130.22	...	...	5.22	137.56	...	...	...
A Transport equipment [d]	20.06	...	...	-	20.38	...	...	-	22.80	...	...	...
Passenger cars	8.50	...	...	...	8.21	...	...	...	9.26	...	...	...
Other	11.56	...	...	...	12.16	...	...	...	13.54	...	...	...
B Machinery and equipment	108.94	...	...	5.54	109.84	...	...	5.22	114.76	...	...	...
6 Breeding stock, dairy cattle, etc. [a]	...	...	...	...	...	...	...	...	...	...	...	...
Statistical discrepancy [e]	17.70	...	...	3.67	17.53	...	...	3.52	18.57	...	...	...
Total Gross Capital Formation	307.36	...	...	43.14	321.99	...	...	41.75	353.32	...	...	...

a) Item 'Increase in stocks' includes breeding stock, draught animals and a statistical discrepancy.
b) Item 'Other, except government stocks' refers to transport only.
c) Item 'Statistical discrepancy' relates to the difference between the estimate of GDP through industrial origin approach and that of expenditure approach.
d) Item 'Transport equipment' refers to registered motor vehicles.
e) Item 'Gross fixed capital formation' includes value added tax on investments of investors not entitled to deduct invoiced value added tax. This component is not included in the sub-items. For years 1973-1975, 1977 and 1978 of the current prices table, special investment tax is included. These estimates are shown separately as 'Statistical discrepancy' in tables 2.7, 2.8, 2.9, 2.10 and 2.11.

2.9 Gross Capital Formation by Kind of Activity of Owner, ISIC Major Divisions, in Current Prices

Thousand Million Austrian schillings

	1980 Total Gross Capital Formation	1980 Increase in Stocks	1980 Gross Fixed Capital Formation	1981 Total Gross Capital Formation	1981 Increase in Stocks	1981 Gross Fixed Capital Formation	1982 Total Gross Capital Formation	1982 Increase in Stocks	1982 Gross Fixed Capital Formation	1983 Total Gross Capital Formation	1983 Increase in Stocks	1983 Gross Fixed Capital Formation
				All Producers								
1 Agriculture, hunting, fishing and forestry	12.99	-0.04	13.03	13.15	-0.09	13.24	14.58	1.74	12.84	14.04	-0.42	14.45
2 Mining and quarrying	0.93	0.17	0.76	0.43	-0.11	0.54	0.45	-0.21	0.66	0.64	-0.02	0.66
3 Manufacturing	44.96	3.32	41.64	44.40	-2.01	46.41	37.53	-4.25	41.78	33.24	-4.05	37.29
4 Electricity, gas and water	15.03	1.04	13.99	19.22	2.71	16.51	18.90	-1.55	20.45	16.77	-1.63	18.40
5 Construction	7.23	1.60	5.63	4.98	-0.52	5.50	3.53	-1.23	4.76	4.37	-0.46	4.83
6 Wholesale and retail trade, restaurants and hotels	...	11.92	...	...	4.36	...	...	0.46	...	...	1.80	...
7 Transport, storage and communication	...	0.04	...	...	0.09	...	...	0.27	...	...	-0.06	...
8 Finance, insurance, real estate and business services	...	...	...	...	...	...	...	...	...	...	...	...
9 Community, social and personal services	...	...	...	...	...	...	...	...	...	...	...	...
Total Industries	...	18.05	...	...	4.43	...	...	-4.75	...	...	-4.85	...
Producers of Government Services	37.62	...	37.62	39.87	...	39.87	38.46	...	38.46	37.11	...	37.11
Private Non-Profit Institutions Serving Households	...	...	...	...	...	...	...	...	...	...	...	...
Statistical discrepancy [ab]	...	9.38	...	...	5.81	...	...	2.10	...	...	-0.96	...
Total	282.89	27.43	255.46	278.18	10.24	267.94	260.23	-2.65	262.88	263.74	-5.81	269.55

Austria

2.9 Gross Capital Formation by Kind of Activity of Owner, ISIC Major Divisions, in Current Prices

Thousand Million Austrian schillings

	1984 Total Gross Capital Formation	1984 Increase in Stocks	1984 Gross Fixed Capital Formation	1985 Total Gross Capital Formation	1985 Increase in Stocks	1985 Gross Fixed Capital Formation
			All Producers			
1 Agriculture, hunting, fishing and forestry	15.12	0.43	14.69	13.95	-1.67	15.62
2 Mining and quarrying	0.51	-0.12	0.63	0.77	0.08	0.69
3 Manufacturing	46.54	4.93	41.61	51.95	5.13	46.82
4 Electricity, gas and water	22.60	1.98	20.62	21.45	0.23	21.22
5 Construction	6.80	1.79	5.01	4.72	-0.55	5.27
6 Wholesale and retail trade, restaurants and hotels	...	12.79	...	...	5.78	...
7 Transport, storage and communication	...	0.09	...	...	0.07	...
8 Finance, insurance, real estate and business services	...	...	...	...	...	...
9 Community, social and personal services	...	...	...	...	...	...
Total Industries	...	21.90	...	...	9.06	...
Producers of Government Services	37.18	...	37.18	38.10	...	38.10
Private Non-Profit Institutions Serving Households	...	...	...	...	...	...
Statistical discrepancy [a,b]	...	-0.92	...	...	2.11	...
Total	303.90	20.98	282.92	315.58	11.17	304.41

a) Item 'Statistical discrepancy' relates to the difference between the estimate of GDP through industrial origin approach and that of expenditure approach.
b) Item 'Gross fixed capital formation' includes value added tax on investments of investors not entitled to deduct invoiced value added tax. This component is not included in the sub-items. For years 1973-1975, 1977 and 1978 of the current prices table, special investment tax is included. These estimates are shown separately as 'Statistical discrepancy' in tables 2.7, 2.8, 2.9, 2.10 and 2.11.

2.10 Gross Capital Formation by Kind of Activity of Owner, ISIC Major Divisions, in Constant Prices

Thousand Million Austrian schillings

	1980 TGCF	1980 IS	1980 GFCF	1981 TGCF	1981 IS	1981 GFCF	1982 TGCF	1982 IS	1982 GFCF	1983 TGCF	1983 IS	1983 GFCF
				At constant prices of:1983								
				All Producers								
1 Agriculture, hunting, fishing and forestry	...	-0.67	...	...	-0.48	...	...	2.86	...	...	-0.42	...
2 Mining and quarrying	1.05	0.20	0.86	0.47	-0.12	0.59	0.46	-0.21	0.67	0.64	-0.02	0.66
3 Manufacturing	51.52	3.93	47.59	48.29	-1.83	50.12	38.72	-4.26	42.98	33.60	-4.05	37.65
4 Electricity, gas and water	18.04	1.58	16.46	21.05	3.03	18.02	19.67	-1.54	21.20	16.77	-1.63	18.41
5 Construction	8.20	1.80	6.40	5.43	-0.55	5.98	3.63	-1.24	4.87	4.37	-0.46	4.83
6 Wholesale and retail trade, restaurants and hotels	...	12.78	...	...	4.46	...	...	0.47	...	...	1.79	...
7 Transport, storage and communication	...	0.05	...	...	0.10	...	...	0.27	...	...	-0.06	...
8 Finance, insurance, real estate and business services	...	...	...	...	...	...	...	...	...	...	...	...
9 Community, social and personal services	...	...	...	...	...	...	...	...	...	...	...	...
Total Industries	...	19.66	...	...	4.61	...	...	-3.63	...	...	-4.85	...
Producers of Government Services	...	...	...	...	...	...	...	...	...	...	...	...
Private Non-Profit Institutions Serving Households	...	...	...	...	...	...	...	...	...	...	...	...
Statistical discrepancy [a,b]	...	9.52	...	...	-4.47	...	...	1.79	...	...	-0.96	...
Total	328.50	29.17	299.33	295.34	0.14	295.21	269.26	-1.84	271.10	263.74	-5.81	269.55

	1984 TGCF	1984 IS	1984 GFCF	1985 TGCF	1985 IS	1985 GFCF	1986 TGCF	1986 IS	1986 GFCF	1987 TGCF	1987 IS	1987 GFCF
				At constant prices of:1983								
				All Producers								
1 Agriculture, hunting, fishing and forestry	...	-0.46	...	...	-1.71	...	...	...	...	...	...	...
2 Mining and quarrying	0.51	-0.11	0.62	0.73	0.07	0.66	...	...	0.63	...	...	0.57
3 Manufacturing	45.37	4.79	40.58	49.65	5.16	44.48	...	...	52.36	...	...	52.15
4 Electricity, gas and water	22.41	2.06	20.36	20.93	0.37	20.56	...	...	18.35	...	...	14.28

Austria

2.10 Gross Capital Formation by Kind of Activity of Owner, ISIC Major Divisions, in Constant Prices
(Continued)

Thousand Million Austrian schillings

	1984 Total Gross Capital Formation	1984 Increase in Stocks	1984 Gross Fixed Capital Formation	1985 Total Gross Capital Formation	1985 Increase in Stocks	1985 Gross Fixed Capital Formation	1986 Total Gross Capital Formation	1986 Increase in Stocks	1986 Gross Fixed Capital Formation	1987 Total Gross Capital Formation	1987 Increase in Stocks	1987 Gross Fixed Capital Formation
				At constant prices of: 1983								
5 Construction	6.64	1.77	4.86	4.42	-0.53	4.95	...	...	4.89	...	...	5.36
6 Wholesale and retail trade, restaurants and hotels	...	12.54	...	...	5.57	...	...	...	...	...	...	...
7 Transport, storage and communication	...	0.08	...	...	0.06	...	...	...	...	...	...	...
8 Finance, insurance, real estate and business services	...	...	...	...	...	...	...	...	...	...	...	...
9 Community, social and personal services	...	...	...	...	...	...	...	...	...	...	...	...
Total Industries	...	20.68	...	...	9.00	...	...	...	...	...	...	...
Producers of Government Services	...	...	...	...	...	...	...	...	...	...	...	...
Private Non-Profit Institutions Serving Households	...	...	...	...	...	...	...	...	...	...	...	...
Statistical discrepancy [ab]	...	-0.21	...	...	3.27	...	...	...	...	...	...	...
Total	295.71	20.47	275.24	301.29	12.28	289.01	307.36	...	299.65	321.99	...	308.19

a) Item 'Statistical discrepancy' relates to the difference between the estimate of GDP through industrial origin approach and that of expenditure approach.
b) Item 'Gross fixed capital formation' includes value added tax on investments of investors not entitled to deduct invoiced value added tax. This component is not included in the sub-items. For years 1973-1975, 1977 and 1978 of the current prices table, special investment tax is included. These estimates are shown separately as 'Statistical discrepancy' in tables 2.7, 2.8, 2.9, 2.10 and 2.11.

2.11 Gross Fixed Capital Formation by Kind of Activity of Owner, ISIC Divisions, in Current Prices

Thousand Million Austrian schillings

	1970	1975	1980	1981	1982	1983	1984	1985	1986	1987	1988	1989
						All Producers						
1 Agriculture, hunting, forestry and fishing	8.20	9.54	13.03	13.24	12.84	14.45	14.69	15.62	14.25	14.45	14.64	...
2 Mining and quarrying	0.42	0.65	0.76	0.54	0.66	0.66	0.63	0.69	0.67	0.62	...	...
3 Manufacturing	19.26	25.93	41.64	46.41	41.78	37.29	41.61	46.82	56.99	58.06	...	...
A Manufacturing of food, beverages and tobacco	2.50	3.77	4.86	5.39	5.00	5.69	5.81	6.50	6.39	6.99	...	...
B Textile, wearing apparel and leather industries	1.86	1.65	2.62	2.64	2.43	2.33	2.38	2.96	3.20	2.90	...	...
C Manufacture of wood, and wood products, including furniture	1.83	1.91	3.43	3.34	2.82	3.11	3.49	3.56	3.50	3.90	...	...
D Manufacture of paper and paper products, printing and publishing	1.71	2.18	2.80	2.94	3.52	4.33	7.80	4.70	7.56	8.08	...	...
E Manufacture of chemicals and chemical petroleum, coal, rubber and plastic products	3.32	4.64	7.31	6.53	6.12	5.39	5.68	7.63	11.61	12.59	...	...
F Manufacture of non-metalic mineral products except products of petroleum and coal	1.70	2.04	3.38	3.58	3.14	2.83	3.19	3.82	3.86	4.05	...	...
G Basic metal industries	1.72	3.63	5.32	4.22	4.80	3.01	2.38	4.03	4.16	2.53	...	...
H Manufacture of fabricated metal products, machinery and equipment	4.61	6.12	11.92	17.76	13.95	10.60	10.88	13.61	16.70	17.03	...	...
I Other manufacturing industries	...	...	...	...	...	...	...	...	...	...	...	...
4 Electricity, gas and water	5.91	13.32	13.99	16.51	20.45	18.40	20.62	21.22	19.83	15.81	...	...
A Electricity, gas and steam	5.58	12.84	13.21	15.67	19.50	17.45	19.72	20.40	18.87	14.66	...	...
B Water works and supply	0.33	0.48	0.78	0.83	0.94	0.95	0.90	0.82	0.95	1.15	...	...
5 Construction	3.09	4.23	5.63	5.50	4.76	4.83	5.01	5.27	5.36	6.01	...	...
6 Wholesale and retail trade, restaurants and hotels	...	...	...	...	...	...	...	...	...	...	...	...
7 Transport, storage and communication	...	...	...	...	...	...	...	...	...	...	...	...
8 Finance, insurance, real estate and business services	...	...	...	...	...	...	...	...	...	...	...	...
9 Community, social and personal services	...	...	...	...	...	...	...	...	...	...	...	...
Total Industries [a]	79.65	131.05	203.36	212.70	208.70	215.86	227.49	247.05	262.07	279.73	309.54	...
Producers of Government Services	17.53	31.31	37.62	39.87	38.46	37.11	37.18	38.10	41.53	41.16	40.04	...
Private Non-Profit Institutions Serving Households [a]	...	...	...	...	...	...	...	...	...	...	...	...
Statistical discrepancy [b]	...	12.56	14.48	15.37	15.72	16.58	18.25	19.26	20.40	20.86	21.10	...
Total	97.18	174.92	255.46	267.94	262.88	269.55	282.92	304.41	324.01	341.75	370.68	...

a) Item 'Private non-profit institutions serving households' is included with various industries above.
b) Item 'Gross fixed capital formation' includes value added tax on investments of investors not entitled to deduct invoiced value added tax. This component is not included in the sub-items. For years 1973-1975, 1977 and 1978 of the current prices table, special investment tax is included. These estimates are shown separately as 'Statistical discrepancy' in tables 2.7, 2.8, 2.9, 2.10 and 2.11.

Austria

2.12 Gross Fixed Capital Formation by Kind of Activity of Owner, ISIC Divisions, in Constant Prices

Thousand Million Austrian schillings

	1970	1975	1980	1981	1982	1983	1984	1985	1986	1987	1988	1989
					At constant prices of:1983							
					All Producers							
1 Agriculture, hunting, forestry and fishing	...	...	...	...	...	...	...	...	...	...	...	...
2 Mining and quarrying	...	...	0.86	0.59	0.67	0.66	0.62	0.66	0.63	0.57	...	...
3 Manufacturing	...	...	47.59	50.12	42.98	37.65	40.58	44.48	52.36	52.15	...	...
4 Electricity, gas and water	...	...	16.46	18.02	21.20	18.41	20.36	20.56	18.35	14.28	...	...
5 Construction	...	...	6.40	5.98	4.87	4.83	4.86	4.95	4.89	5.36	...	...
6 Wholesale and retail trade, restaurants and hotels	...	...	...	...	...	...	...	...	...	...	...	...
7 Transport, storage and communication	...	...	...	...	...	...	...	...	...	...	...	...
8 Finance, insurance, real estate and business services	...	...	...	...	...	...	...	...	...	...	...	...
9 Community, social and personal services	...	...	...	...	...	...	...	...	...	...	...	...
Total Industries	...	...	238.83	235.62	215.57	215.86	221.95	235.04	242.48	252.43	...	...
Producers of Government Services	...	...	43.59	42.90	39.37	37.11	37.02	37.19	39.47	38.23	...	...
Private Non-Profit Institutions Serving Households	...	...	...	...	...	...	...	...	...	...	...	...
Statistical discrepancy	...	...	16.91	16.69	16.16	16.58	16.27	16.78	17.70	17.53	...	...
Total	...	...	299.33	295.21	271.10	269.55	275.24	289.01	299.65	308.19	...	...

2.17 Exports and Imports of Goods and Services, Detail

Thousand Million Austrian schillings

	1970	1975	1980	1981	1982	1983	1984	1985	1986	1987	1988	1989
					Exports of Goods and Services							
1 Exports of merchandise, f.o.b. [a]	74.23	133.66	225.78	255.15	266.92	274.55	312.40	359.45	342.15	342.71	374.43	423.21
2 Transport and communication												
3 Insurance service charges	8.69	15.27	34.44	35.24	37.99	40.81	44.62	46.74	47.12	49.36	53.47	59.25
4 Other commodities												
5 Adjustments of merchandise exports to change-of-ownership basis	...	...	...	...	...	...	...	...	...	...	...	...
6 Direct purchases in the domestic market by non-residential households	29.78	52.28	81.28	88.45	92.26	91.70	98.55	102.29	101.61	107.89	122.44	138.67
7 Direct purchases in the domestic market by extraterritorial bodies	...	...	...	...	...	...	...	...	...	...	...	...
Statistical discrepancy [b]	4.05	7.81	24.74	25.66	34.08	42.63	42.09	40.64	32.09	27.22	39.98	48.16
Total Exports of Goods and Services [a]	116.75	209.02	366.24	404.51	431.24	449.69	497.64	549.13	522.97	527.19	590.32	669.30
					Imports of Goods and Services							
1 Imports of merchandise, c.i.f. [a]	92.65	164.29	313.26	332.28	329.53	345.31	389.18	427.12	404.38	408.41	444.80	509.16
2 Adjustments of merchandise imports to change-of-ownership basis	...	...	...	...	...	...	...	...	...	...	...	...
3 Other transport and communication												
4 Other insurance service charges	7.11	13.56	26.87	31.49	32.65	33.90	36.16	39.44	38.03	37.45	41.43	45.66
5 Other commodities												
6 Direct purchases abroad by government	12.06	24.38	40.83	44.73	46.06	47.87	53.91	57.65	59.93	70.38	79.24	86.21
7 Direct purchases abroad by resident households												
Statistical discrepancy [b]	1.25	2.57	4.70	9.97	4.21	6.85	16.46	22.59	7.46	3.59	18.15	19.59
Total Imports of Goods and Services [a]	113.07	204.81	385.66	418.47	412.44	433.93	495.71	546.81	509.80	519.83	583.62	660.62
Balance of Goods and Services	3.68	4.21	-19.42	-13.96	18.80	15.76	1.93	2.32	13.17	7.36	6.70	8.68
Total Imports and Balance of Goods and Services [a]	116.75	209.02	366.24	404.51	431.24	449.69	497.64	549.13	522.97	527.19	590.32	669.30

a) The estimates on transit trade are on a net basis.
b) Item 'Statistical discrepancy' refers to exports/imports of commodities not yet identified as merchandise or services. Before 1979, also including item 'Adjustments of merchandise export/import to change of ownership basis'.

Austria

4.1 Derivation of Value Added by Kind of Activity, in Current Prices

Thousand Million Austrian schillings

		1980			1981			1982			1983	
	Gross Output	Intermediate Consumption	Value Added	Gross Output	Intermediate Consumption	Value Added	Gross Output	Intermediate Consumption	Value Added	Gross Output	Intermediate Consumption	Value Added

All Producers

	Gross Output	Intermediate Consumption	Value Added	Gross Output	Intermediate Consumption	Value Added	Gross Output	Intermediate Consumption	Value Added	Gross Output	Intermediate Consumption	Value Added
1 Agriculture, hunting, forestry and fishing	66.23	21.94	44.29	66.89	23.47	43.43	68.33	24.59	43.73	69.94	25.80	44.14
2 Mining and quarrying	10.75	5.88	4.87	11.10	6.33	4.77	12.16	6.77	5.40	11.78	6.46	5.32
3 Manufacturing	783.81	507.14	276.67	838.20	549.29	288.91	875.41	567.33	308.08	901.43	578.62	322.82
A Manufacture of food, beverages and tobacco	135.83	94.15	41.68	146.83	101.81	45.02	156.17	109.30	46.87	158.14	109.97	48.17
B Textile, wearing apparel and leather industries	60.79	37.19	23.60	64.57	39.31	25.27	66.19	40.22	25.97	66.74	40.57	26.17
C Manufacture of wood and wood products, including furniture	57.28	36.52	20.77	54.06	34.27	19.79	55.12	33.62	21.50	59.24	36.05	23.19
D Manufacture of paper and paper products, printing and publishing	45.77	27.22	18.55	49.27	29.97	19.30	51.35	31.66	19.69	52.51	31.96	20.55
E Manufacture of chemicals and chemical petroleum, coal, rubber and plastic products [a]	139.09	100.52	38.57	158.44	119.06	39.38	154.43	110.52	43.90	155.43	109.76	45.67
F Manufacture of non-metallic mineral products, except products of petroleum and coal	36.56	20.69	15.87	40.02	22.99	17.03	41.34	23.45	17.89	42.62	23.91	18.72
G Basic metal industries	64.37	42.59	21.77	66.18	46.21	19.97	68.20	46.47	21.74	69.21	47.30	21.92
H Manufacture of fabricated metal products, machinery and equipment	244.12	148.26	95.86	258.84	155.68	103.16	282.62	172.10	110.52	297.54	179.10	118.44
I Other manufacturing industries	...	...	...	...	...	...	...	...	...	...	...	...
4 Electricity, gas and water	68.62	37.95	30.67	76.60	44.64	31.96	88.36	50.36	38.00	87.35	48.27	39.09
A Electricity, gas and steam	66.42	37.21	29.21	74.12	43.83	30.28	85.68	49.54	36.14	84.49	47.41	37.08
B Water works and supply	2.21	0.74	1.47	2.49	0.80	1.68	2.68	0.83	1.85	2.86	0.85	2.01
5 Construction	149.22	68.01	81.21	155.79	71.00	84.79	156.21	71.11	85.10	161.29	73.84	87.45
6 Wholesale and retail trade, restaurants and hotels	247.26	80.51	166.75	262.40	87.08	175.32	279.88	91.58	188.30	299.97	98.14	201.83
A Wholesale and retail trade	184.08	50.15	133.93	193.41	54.65	138.76	206.46	57.04	149.41	223.95	62.68	161.26
B Restaurants and hotels	63.18	30.36	32.82	68.99	32.44	36.56	73.42	34.54	38.88	76.03	35.46	40.57
7 Transport, storage and communication	115.99	58.16	57.83	125.24	62.61	62.63	129.12	64.16	64.96	135.89	67.78	68.11
A Transport and storage	91.84	55.10	36.74	99.05	59.11	39.94	101.16	60.21	40.95	105.93	63.70	42.23
B Communication	24.15	3.06	21.09	26.19	3.50	22.69	27.96	3.95	24.01	29.96	4.08	25.88
8 Finance, insurance, real estate and business services	164.75	45.69	119.06	186.67	51.03	135.64	210.69	55.47	155.22	226.03	59.82	166.22
A Financial institutions	52.01	9.02	42.99	60.68	10.24	50.43	66.60	11.73	54.87	67.45	12.28	55.17
B Insurance	17.52	4.53	12.99	19.28	5.04	14.24	22.30	5.41	16.89	23.67	6.02	17.65
C Real estate and business services	95.22	32.14	63.08	106.71	35.75	70.97	121.79	38.33	83.46	134.91	41.50	93.41
Real estate, except dwellings	64.68	23.32	41.35	72.39	25.31	47.07	84.05	26.82	57.23	94.24	29.10	65.14
Dwellings												
9 Community, social and personal services	48.40	16.17	32.23	51.83	17.47	34.36	55.79	19.04	36.74	60.92	20.37	40.54
A Sanitary and similar services [bc]	...	...	...	...	...	...	...	...	...	...	...	...
B Social and related community services [c]	23.38	6.21	17.17	25.40	6.74	18.66	27.24	7.20	20.04	29.08	7.72	21.36
Educational services [d]	...	...	...	...	...	...	...	...	...	...	...	...
Medical, dental, other health and veterinary services [c]	23.38	6.21	17.17	25.40	6.74	18.66	27.24	7.20	20.04	29.08	7.72	21.36
C Recreational and cultural services [dc]	13.77	6.06	7.71	14.10	6.45	7.65	15.39	7.31	8.08	17.56	7.81	9.75
D Personal and household services [bc]	11.25	3.91	7.33	12.32	4.28	8.04	13.16	4.54	8.62	14.29	4.86	9.43
Total, Industries	1655.02	841.45	813.58	1774.72	912.92	861.80	1875.94	950.42	925.52	1954.61	979.10	975.51
Producers of Government Services	213.57	84.49	129.08	234.14	92.24	141.90	256.19	101.43	154.76	272.25	107.62	164.63
Other Producers [b]	8.28	1.11	7.17	9.09	1.20	7.90	9.64	1.29	8.36	11.16	1.93	9.23
Total	1876.87	927.05	949.83	2017.95	1006.36	1011.59	2141.77	1053.13	1088.64	2238.02	1088.65	1149.37
Less: Imputed bank service charge	...	-45.12	45.12	...	-53.36	53.36	...	-60.23	60.23	...	-61.06	61.06
Import duties	5.75	...	5.75	6.77	...	6.77	7.43	...	7.43	7.71	...	7.71
Value added tax	84.25	...	84.25	90.97	...	90.97	97.69	...	97.69	105.22	...	105.22
Other adjustments	...	...	-0.01	...	...	-0.01	...	...	-0.01	...	...	-0.01
Total	1966.87	972.17	994.70	2115.69	1059.72	1055.97	2246.89	1113.36	1133.53	2350.95	1149.71	1201.23

Austria

4.1 Derivation of Value Added by Kind of Activity, in Current Prices

Thousand Million Austrian schillings

	1984 Gross Output	1984 Intermediate Consumption	1984 Value Added	1985 Gross Output	1985 Intermediate Consumption	1985 Value Added	1986 Gross Output	1986 Intermediate Consumption	1986 Value Added	1987 Gross Output	1987 Intermediate Consumption	1987 Value Added
				All Producers								
1 Agriculture, hunting, forestry and fishing	73.91	25.21	48.70	70.82	25.82	44.99	71.50	24.38	47.11	72.27	23.80	48.47
2 Mining and quarrying	12.32	6.78	5.54	13.16	7.28	5.87	12.52	6.87	5.65	12.00	6.15	5.85
3 Manufacturing	958.37	618.31	340.06	1013.01	650.21	362.80	997.68	622.04	375.65	998.11	616.58	381.53
A Manufacture of food, beverages and tobacco	164.35	114.11	50.24	171.18	118.81	52.37	172.33	118.91	53.42	172.39	117.29	55.10
B Textile, wearing apparel and leather industries	70.66	43.63	27.02	72.73	45.60	27.13	72.07	44.59	27.48	69.63	42.71	26.92
C Manufacture of wood and wood products, including furniture	61.18	38.01	23.17	61.54	37.92	23.62	63.36	38.53	24.83	68.27	41.88	26.38
D Manufacture of paper and paper products, printing and publishing	59.09	36.08	23.01	64.86	40.94	23.92	66.33	41.13	25.20	68.37	42.44	25.93
E Manufacture of chemicals and chemical petroleum, coal, rubber and plastic products [a]	172.53	122.81	49.72	182.20	130.68	51.53	159.25	100.77	58.47	159.80	100.78	59.02
F Manufacture of non-metallic mineral products, except products of petroleum and coal	45.32	25.43	19.89	47.26	26.39	20.87	48.34	26.89	21.45	49.88	27.62	22.25
G Basic metal industries	76.20	52.52	23.68	81.44	53.57	27.87	71.75	46.62	25.13	65.60	42.78	22.82
H Manufacture of fabricated metal products, machinery and equipment	309.04	185.71	123.33	331.81	196.31	135.50	344.27	204.59	139.68	344.19	201.08	143.11
I Other manufacturing industries	...	...	...	...	...	...	...	...	...	...	...	...
4 Electricity, gas and water	91.70	53.10	38.61	99.04	59.19	39.85	98.66	54.73	43.92	100.49	53.28	47.21
A Electricity, gas and steam	88.77	52.21	36.56	96.12	58.26	37.86	95.65	53.79	41.86	97.30	52.30	45.00
B Water works and supply	2.93	0.89	2.05	2.92	0.93	1.99	3.01	0.95	2.07	3.19	0.99	2.20
5 Construction	165.04	77.98	87.06	169.63	80.57	89.06	178.92	85.42	93.50	188.57	88.94	99.63
6 Wholesale and retail trade, restaurants and hotels	315.62	108.76	206.86	334.12	119.05	215.06	340.83	117.01	223.83	355.00	122.63	232.36
A Wholesale and retail trade	236.67	72.14	164.53	251.21	81.22	170.00	252.45	78.10	174.35	260.48	81.74	178.75
B Restaurants and hotels	78.95	36.61	42.34	82.90	37.83	45.07	88.38	38.91	49.48	94.51	40.90	53.62
7 Transport, storage and communication	149.94	75.18	74.76	156.48	78.06	78.42	158.94	77.42	81.53	165.74	79.59	86.15
A Transport and storage	116.47	70.56	45.91	120.91	73.17	47.74	121.34	72.23	49.11	125.97	74.72	51.25
B Communication	33.47	4.62	28.85	35.57	4.89	30.68	37.61	5.19	32.42	39.77	4.87	34.89
8 Finance, insurance, real estate and business services	244.90	61.76	183.14	271.07	66.68	204.39	295.62	72.61	223.01	315.41	78.36	237.05
A Financial institutions	69.81	12.23	57.59	76.80	13.59	63.21	82.52	15.08	67.43	87.79	16.62	71.17
B Insurance	25.47	6.51	18.96	27.49	7.05	20.44	28.76	7.41	21.34	29.92	7.74	22.17
C Real estate and business services	149.62	43.03	106.59	166.78	46.04	120.74	184.35	50.11	134.24	197.70	53.99	143.71
Real estate, except dwellings	105.36	29.48	75.88	117.21	30.81	86.40	128.62	32.87	95.75	134.81	34.12	100.68
Dwellings												
9 Community, social and personal services	64.96	21.41	43.54	69.62	22.84	46.78	75.45	24.20	51.24	81.50	26.33	55.17
A Sanitary and similar services [bc]	...	...	...	...	...	...	...	...	...	...	...	...
B Social and related community services [c]	30.80	8.15	22.65	33.04	8.75	24.29	35.29	9.35	25.93	37.20	9.90	27.30
Educational services [d]	...	...	...	...	...	...	...	...	...	...	...	...
Medical, dental, other health and veterinary services [c]	30.80	8.15	22.65	33.04	8.75	24.29	35.29	9.35	25.93	37.20	9.90	27.30
C Recreational and cultural services [dc]	18.96	8.08	10.88	20.33	8.64	11.69	22.72	9.10	13.62	26.32	10.80	15.52
D Personal and household services [bc]	15.21	5.19	10.02	16.26	5.46	10.80	17.44	5.75	11.69	17.98	5.63	12.35
Total, Industries	2076.75	1048.50	1028.26	2196.94	1109.70	1087.24	2230.11	1084.67	1145.45	2289.09	1095.67	1193.42
Producers of Government Services	285.94	112.45	173.49	305.81	120.74	185.07	323.92	126.83	197.09	336.11	130.20	205.91
Other Producers [b]	11.77	2.07	9.70	12.43	2.19	10.23	13.10	2.28	10.82	13.57	2.32	11.26
Total	2374.46	1163.02	1211.44	2515.18	1232.63	1282.54	2567.13	1213.78	1353.35	2638.77	1228.18	1410.59
Less: Imputed bank service charge	...	-63.30	63.30	...	-68.56	68.56	...	-75.03	75.03	...	-80.51	80.51
Import duties	8.62	...	8.62	9.08	...	9.08	9.00	...	9.00	9.86	...	9.86
Value added tax	120.00	...	120.00	125.37	...	125.36	128.66	...	128.66	133.96	...	133.96
Other adjustments	...	...	0.01	...	...	-0.02	...	...	-0.01	...	...	-0.01
Total	2503.08	1226.32	1276.77	2649.63	1301.19	1348.42	2704.78	1288.81	1415.97	2782.60	1308.70	1473.90

Austria

4.1 Derivation of Value Added by Kind of Activity, in Current Prices

Thousand Million Austrian schillings

		1988			1989		
		Gross Output	Intermediate Consumption	Value Added	Gross Output	Intermediate Consumption	Value Added
		All Producers					
1	Agriculture, hunting, forestry and fishing	73.23	24.17	49.07	76.90	25.10	51.80
2	Mining and quarrying	11.27	5.79	5.49	10.99	5.65	5.34
3	Manufacturing	1076.40	661.87	414.53	1162.95	716.44	446.51
	A Manufacture of food, beverages and tobacco	176.11	120.26	55.85	182.52	124.82	57.70
	B Textile, wearing apparel and leather industries	69.11	42.41	26.69	71.92	44.22	27.70
	C Manufacture of wood and wood products, including furniture	74.91	46.17	28.74	82.63	51.75	30.88
	D Manufacture of paper and paper products, printing and publishing	76.76	47.46	29.30	85.98	53.21	32.78
	E Manufacture of chemicals and chemical petroleum, coal, rubber and plastic products [a]	172.05	105.06	67.00	182.55	112.12	70.43
	F Manufacture of non-metallic mineral products, except products of petroleum and coal	53.80	29.92	23.87	55.94	31.15	24.79
	G Basic metal industries	74.36	48.63	25.73	78.64	51.33	27.31
	H Manufacture of fabricated metal products, machinery and equipment	379.31	221.96	157.34	422.77	247.84	174.93
	I Other manufacturing industries	...	...	...	...	...	...
4	Electricity, gas and water	99.29	52.03	47.26	101.85	53.18	48.68
	A Electricity, gas and steam	96.01	51.00	45.01	98.29	52.06	46.24
	B Water works and supply	3.29	1.03	2.26	3.56	1.12	2.44
5	Construction	202.45	96.37	106.08	216.09	101.64	114.45
6	Wholesale and retail trade, restaurants and hotels	381.50	132.80	248.70	411.55	142.95	268.61
	A Wholesale and retail trade	280.03	89.69	190.34	299.74	96.10	203.65
	B Restaurants and hotels	101.47	43.11	58.36	111.81	46.85	64.96
7	Transport, storage and communication	177.41	83.88	93.53	191.80	92.29	99.51
	A Transport and storage	134.28	78.76	55.52	146.64	86.91	59.73
	B Communication	43.13	5.12	38.01	45.16	5.38	39.78
8	Finance, insurance, real estate and business services	341.34	84.90	256.45	370.20	94.21	276.00
	A Financial institutions	94.84	18.20	76.64	105.14	21.06	84.08
	B Insurance	35.10	8.78	26.32	36.85	9.25	27.60
	C Real estate and business services	211.41	57.92	153.49	228.21	63.89	164.32
	Real estate, except dwellings	141.30	35.22	106.08	150.00	39.37	110.63
	Dwellings				...	...	...
9	Community, social and personal services	87.78	28.53	59.25	94.17	30.44	63.73
	A Sanitary and similar services [bc]	...	...	...	...	...	...
	B Social and related community services [c]	40.32	10.69	29.64	42.48	11.27	31.21
	Educational services [d]	...	...	...	...	...	...
	Medical, dental, other health and veterinary services [c]	40.32	10.69	29.64	42.48	11.27	31.21
	C Recreational and cultural services [dc]	28.66	12.04	16.62	32.08	13.17	18.91
	D Personal and household services [bc]	18.80	5.81	13.00	19.61	6.00	13.61
	Total, Industries	2450.68	1170.33	1280.35	2636.51	1261.89	1374.63
	Producers of Government Services	348.50	137.97	210.53	365.21	144.35	220.86

Austria

4.1 Derivation of Value Added by Kind of Activity, in Current Prices
(Continued)

Thousand Million Austrian schillings

	1988 Gross Output	1988 Intermediate Consumption	1988 Value Added	1989 Gross Output	1989 Intermediate Consumption	1989 Value Added
Other Producers [b]	13.82	2.47	11.35	14.28	2.56	11.71
Total	2813.00	1310.77	1502.23	3016.00	1408.80	1607.20
Less: Imputed bank service charge	...	-85.81	85.81	...	-92.36	92.36
Import duties	10.63	...	10.63	11.51	...	11.51
Value added tax	137.63	...	137.63	147.08	...	147.08
Other adjustments	...	...	...	...	...	...
Total	2961.26	1396.58	1564.68	3174.59	1501.16	1673.43

a) Item 'Crude petroleum and natural gas production' is included in item 'Manufacture of chemicals and chemical petroleum, coal, rubber and plastic products.'
b) Item 'Sanitary and similar services' is included in item 'Personal and household services' which excludes domestic services and caretakers that are included in item 'Other producers'.
c) Non-governmental only.
d) Item 'Educational services' is included in item 'Recreational and cultural services'.

4.2 Derivation of Value Added by Kind of Activity, in Constant Prices

Thousand Million Austrian schillings

At constant prices of: 1983

All Producers

		1980 Gross Output	1980 Interm. Cons.	1980 Value Added	1981 Gross Output	1981 Interm. Cons.	1981 Value Added	1982 Gross Output	1982 Interm. Cons.	1982 Value Added	1983 Gross Output	1983 Interm. Cons.	1983 Value Added
1	Agriculture, hunting, forestry and fishing	68.00	26.04	41.96	65.66	25.15	40.50	71.24	25.20	46.04	69.94	25.80	44.14
2	Mining and quarrying	12.49	6.84	5.65	12.37	6.68	5.69	12.31	6.62	5.69	11.78	6.46	5.32
3	Manufacturing	899.39	578.81	320.58	887.37	570.96	316.41	891.46	573.80	317.66	901.43	578.62	322.82
A	Manufacture of food, beverages and tobacco	154.70	107.90	46.80	158.33	110.48	47.85	161.49	112.42	49.08	158.14	109.97	48.17
B	Textile, wearing apparel and leather industries	70.58	43.12	27.46	70.46	42.89	27.57	67.94	41.35	26.59	66.74	40.57	26.17
C	Manufacture of wood and wood products, including furniture	59.82	36.82	23.00	53.55	33.16	20.40	55.19	33.70	21.50	59.24	36.05	23.19
D	Manufacture of paper and paper products, printing and publishing	51.92	31.54	20.37	51.03	31.10	19.93	52.06	31.84	20.22	52.51	31.96	20.55
E	Manufacture of chemicals and chemical petroleum, coal, rubber and plastic products [a]	171.83	119.86	51.97	160.65	112.13	48.52	153.66	108.38	45.28	155.43	109.76	45.67
F	Manufacture of non-metallic mineral products, except products of petroleum and coal	42.23	24.26	17.97	42.63	24.33	18.30	41.95	23.81	18.14	42.62	23.91	18.72
G	Basic metal industries	71.14	48.19	22.96	71.07	48.62	22.45	68.18	46.47	21.71	69.21	47.30	21.92
H	Manufacture of fabricated metal products, machinery and equipment	277.18	167.11	110.07	279.65	168.25	111.40	290.98	175.84	115.14	297.54	179.10	118.44
I	Other manufacturing industries	...	...	...	...	...	...	...	...	...	...	...	...
4	Electricity, gas and water	86.87	48.20	38.66	86.95	48.73	38.22	87.58	49.34	38.24	87.35	48.27	39.09
A	Electricity, gas and steam	84.15	47.40	36.75	84.19	47.91	36.28	84.79	48.51	36.27	84.49	47.41	37.08
B	Water works and supply	2.72	0.81	1.91	2.77	0.82	1.95	2.79	0.83	1.96	2.86	0.85	2.01
5	Construction	177.38	79.23	98.14	171.26	77.07	94.19	161.22	72.84	88.38	161.29	73.84	87.45
6	Wholesale and retail trade, restaurants and hotels	281.56	92.15	189.41	284.67	93.56	191.12	288.05	94.83	193.22	299.97	98.14	201.83
A	Wholesale and retail trade	208.29	58.17	150.12	209.47	58.63	150.84	211.56	59.23	152.34	223.95	62.68	161.26
B	Restaurants and hotels	73.27	33.98	39.29	75.20	34.92	40.28	76.49	35.61	40.88	76.03	35.46	40.57
7	Transport, storage and communication	130.50	65.42	65.08	131.63	66.15	65.48	132.17	65.93	66.24	135.89	67.78	68.11
A	Transport and storage	103.82	62.00	41.82	104.85	62.52	42.33	103.82	61.96	41.86	105.93	63.70	42.23
B	Communication	26.68	3.42	23.26	26.78	3.63	23.15	28.35	3.97	24.38	29.96	4.08	25.88
8	Finance, insurance, real estate and business services	206.87	55.22	151.65	211.62	56.85	154.77	218.89	57.32	161.57	226.03	59.82	166.22
A	Financial institutions	59.76	10.88	48.88	62.12	11.31	50.81	63.81	11.62	52.19	67.45	12.28	55.17
B	Insurance	19.86	5.05	14.81	21.18	5.39	15.79	23.45	5.96	17.49	23.67	6.02	17.65
C	Real estate and business services	127.25	39.29	87.96	128.32	40.15	88.17	131.63	39.74	91.89	134.91	41.50	93.41
	Real estate, except dwellings	88.27	27.41	60.86	88.98	28.16	60.82	91.42	27.47	63.95	94.24	29.10	65.14
	Dwellings												
9	Community, social and personal services	58.63	20.04	38.59	60.03	20.43	39.59	59.73	20.10	39.62	60.92	20.37	40.54
A	Sanitary and similar services [bc]	...	...	...	...	...	...	...	...	...	...	...	...
B	Social and related community services [c]	27.84	7.60	20.24	28.58	7.71	20.87	28.59	7.61	20.98	29.08	7.72	21.36

Austria

4.2 Derivation of Value Added by Kind of Activity, in Constant Prices
(Continued)

Thousand Million Austrian schillings

	1980 Gross Output	1980 Intermediate Consumption	1980 Value Added	1981 Gross Output	1981 Intermediate Consumption	1981 Value Added	1982 Gross Output	1982 Intermediate Consumption	1982 Value Added	1983 Gross Output	1983 Intermediate Consumption	1983 Value Added
						At constant prices of:1983						
Educational services d	...	...	...	...	...	...	...	...	...	...	...	...
Medical, dental, other health and veterinary services c	27.84	7.60	20.24	28.58	7.71	20.87	28.59	7.61	20.98	29.08	7.72	21.36
C Recreational and cultural services dc	16.83	7.70	9.13	17.38	7.93	9.45	17.26	7.76	9.50	17.56	7.81	9.75
D Personal and household services bc	13.96	4.74	9.22	14.07	4.80	9.27	13.89	4.74	9.15	14.29	4.86	9.43
Total, Industries	1921.67	971.95	949.72	1911.56	965.58	945.98	1922.64	965.99	956.65	1954.61	979.10	975.51
Producers of Government Services	254.78	100.11	154.67	260.24	101.50	158.74	266.59	104.49	162.11	272.25	107.62	164.63
Other Producers b	10.93	1.87	9.06	11.15	1.90	9.25	11.13	1.92	9.21	11.16	1.93	9.23
Total	2187.38	1073.94	1113.45	2182.95	1068.98	1113.97	2200.36	1072.40	1127.97	2238.02	1088.65	1149.37
Less: Imputed bank service charge	...	-51.80	51.80	...	-54.91	54.91	...	-58.17	58.17	...	-61.06	61.06
Import duties	7.88	...	7.88	7.44	...	7.44	7.33	...	7.33	7.71	...	7.71
Value added tax	99.14	...	99.14	98.79	...	98.79	100.64	...	100.64	105.22	...	105.22
Other adjustments	...	...	-0.01	...	...	0.01	...	...	-0.02	...	...	-0.01
Total	2294.40	1125.74	1168.66	2289.18	1123.89	1165.29	2308.33	1130.57	1177.75	2350.95	1149.71	1201.23

	1984 Gross Output	1984 Intermediate Consumption	1984 Value Added	1985 Gross Output	1985 Intermediate Consumption	1985 Value Added	1986 Gross Output	1986 Intermediate Consumption	1986 Value Added	1987 Gross Output	1987 Intermediate Consumption	1987 Value Added
						At constant prices of:1983						
						All Producers						
1 Agriculture, hunting, forestry and fishing	71.18	24.78	46.41	69.35	25.15	44.20	69.04	24.40	44.64	69.26	24.60	44.66
2 Mining and quarrying	11.76	6.51	5.25	11.72	6.70	5.02	10.80	6.35	4.45	10.91	5.78	5.13
3 Manufacturing	927.83	595.73	332.10	956.95	612.14	344.82	956.77	610.17	346.60	964.75	615.88	348.86
A Manufacture of food, beverages and tobacco	158.44	109.16	49.28	162.31	111.73	50.58	161.98	110.59	51.39	163.00	109.15	53.85
B Textile, wearing apparel and leather industries	67.98	41.44	26.54	69.10	41.47	27.63	67.47	40.18	27.29	64.63	39.37	25.26
C Manufacture of wood and wood products, including furniture	59.16	36.87	22.29	59.93	35.81	24.12	60.19	36.66	23.52	64.51	39.01	25.50
D Manufacture of paper and paper products, printing and publishing	56.84	35.08	21.76	60.60	38.29	22.30	61.67	39.14	22.54	64.45	40.46	24.00
E Manufacture of chemicals and chemical petroleum, coal, rubber and plastic products a	167.87	118.62	49.25	174.27	124.12	50.15	173.56	121.92	51.65	181.55	128.86	52.69
F Manufacture of non-metallic mineral products, except products of petroleum and coal	43.70	24.46	19.24	44.05	24.64	19.41	44.68	25.27	19.41	46.08	26.31	19.77
G Basic metal industries	73.55	50.53	23.02	74.25	50.36	23.88	69.92	44.88	25.04	69.62	45.68	23.94
H Manufacture of fabricated metal products, machinery and equipment	300.29	179.57	120.73	312.44	185.71	126.74	317.31	191.54	125.76	310.91	187.06	123.85
I Other manufacturing industries	...	...	...	...	...	...	...	...	...	...	...	...
4 Electricity, gas and water	92.81	53.12	39.69	97.25	55.81	41.43	98.00	54.92	43.09	100.54	54.13	46.41
A Electricity, gas and steam	90.00	52.28	37.72	94.40	54.97	39.44	95.16	54.07	41.09	97.71	53.29	44.42
B Water works and supply	2.80	0.83	1.97	2.84	0.85	2.00	2.84	0.85	2.00	2.83	0.84	1.98
5 Construction	162.22	75.89	86.33	163.32	76.53	86.80	168.22	80.30	87.92	172.03	82.67	89.36
6 Wholesale and retail trade, restaurants and hotels	298.80	97.94	200.87	307.51	100.57	206.95	311.67	102.08	209.59	318.74	105.03	213.71
A Wholesale and retail trade	223.04	62.43	160.61	231.29	64.80	166.49	234.32	65.76	168.56	238.20	67.06	171.14
B Restaurants and hotels	75.76	35.50	40.26	76.23	35.77	40.46	77.35	36.32	41.03	80.54	37.97	42.56
7 Transport, storage and communication	143.45	71.56	71.89	147.62	72.84	74.78	148.89	73.61	75.28	155.02	76.32	78.70
A Transport and storage	112.07	67.11	44.96	114.29	68.25	46.04	114.14	68.46	45.69	118.98	71.37	47.61
B Communication	31.38	4.45	26.93	33.33	4.59	28.74	34.74	5.16	29.59	36.05	4.95	31.09
8 Finance, insurance, real estate and business services	233.21	61.19	172.02	240.59	64.64	175.95	247.65	66.66	180.99	252.93	67.65	185.29
A Financial institutions	69.88	12.72	57.16	71.97	13.10	58.87	74.67	13.59	61.08	76.96	14.10	62.86

Austria

4.2 Derivation of Value Added by Kind of Activity, in Constant Prices
(Continued)

Thousand Million Austrian schillings

	1984 Gross Output	1984 Intermediate Consumption	1984 Value Added	1985 Gross Output	1985 Intermediate Consumption	1985 Value Added	1986 Gross Output	1986 Intermediate Consumption	1986 Value Added	1987 Gross Output	1987 Intermediate Consumption	1987 Value Added
					At constant prices of:1983							
B Insurance	24.21	6.16	18.05	24.59	6.25	18.34	24.47	6.22	18.25	24.48	6.25	18.23
C Real estate and business services	139.12	42.31	96.81	144.03	45.29	98.74	148.51	46.84	101.67	151.49	47.29	104.20
Real estate, except dwellings	97.89	29.71	68.18	101.14	32.17	68.97	104.26	33.28	70.98	105.85	33.24	72.61
Dwellings												
9 Community, social and personal services	61.15	20.05	41.11	63.37	20.68	42.69	65.65	21.42	44.23	67.78	21.80	45.98
A Sanitary and similar services [bc]	...	...	...	...	...	...	...	...	...	...	...	...
B Social and related community services [c]	29.81	7.83	21.98	30.66	8.03	22.63	30.84	8.06	22.78	31.24	8.10	23.14
Educational services [d]	...	...	...	...	...	...	...	...	...	...	...	...
Medical, dental, other health and veterinary services	29.81	7.83	21.98	30.66	8.03	22.63	30.84	8.06	22.78	31.24	8.10	23.14
C Recreational and cultural services [dc]	17.48	7.56	9.92	18.21	7.79	10.42	20.00	8.46	11.54	21.66	8.81	12.85
D Personal and household services [bc]	13.86	4.66	9.20	14.50	4.86	9.64	14.81	4.91	9.90	14.89	4.90	9.99
Total, Industries	2002.42	1006.76	995.66	2057.68	1035.06	1022.62	2076.68	1039.91	1036.77	2111.95	1053.86	1058.09
Producers of Government Services	272.84	106.23	166.61	277.60	108.48	169.12	281.22	109.84	171.38	282.77	109.55	173.22
Other Producers [b]	11.22	1.94	9.28	11.27	1.96	9.31	11.39	1.98	9.41	11.43	1.99	9.43
Total	2286.48	1114.93	1171.55	2346.55	1145.50	1201.05	2369.29	1151.73	1217.56	2406.14	1165.40	1240.74
Less: Imputed bank service charge	...	-63.07	63.07	...	-63.98	63.98	...	-67.50	67.50	...	-70.14	70.14
Import duties	8.19	...	8.19	8.41	...	8.41	8.99	...	8.99	9.57	...	9.57
Value added tax	100.90	...	100.90	102.07	...	102.07	103.07	...	103.07	106.92	...	106.92
Other adjustments	...	...	-0.01	...	...	-0.01	...	...	...	...	...	...
Total	2395.57	1178.00	1217.57	2457.03	1209.48	1247.54	2481.35	1219.23	1262.12	2522.64	1235.54	1287.10

	1988 Gross Output	1988 Intermediate Consumption	1988 Value Added	1989 Gross Output	1989 Intermediate Consumption	1989 Value Added
		At constant prices of:1983				
		All Producers				
1 Agriculture, hunting, forestry and fishing	70.97	24.44	46.53	71.09	25.23	45.86
2 Mining and quarrying	9.87	5.24	4.63	9.76	5.19	4.57
3 Manufacturing	1022.33	653.90	368.44	1080.67	690.41	390.26
A Manufacture of food, beverages and tobacco	167.24	112.70	54.55	173.04	116.79	56.26
B Textile, wearing apparel and leather industries	62.94	38.40	24.54	64.49	39.44	25.05
C Manufacture of wood and wood products, including furniture	69.08	41.95	27.13	76.55	47.32	29.24
D Manufacture of paper and paper products, printing and publishing	70.34	44.50	25.84	74.60	47.16	27.43
E Manufacture of chemicals and chemical petroleum, coal, rubber and plastic products [a]	194.97	137.70	57.27	199.85	139.21	60.63
F Manufacture of non-metallic mineral products, except products of petroleum and coal	49.17	28.25	20.93	50.67	29.19	21.48
G Basic metal industries	78.50	51.53	26.98	81.13	53.04	28.09
H Manufacture of fabricated metal products, machinery and equipment	330.09	198.89	131.20	360.35	218.27	142.08
I Other manufacturing industries	...	...	...	...	...	...
4 Electricity, gas and water	100.44	53.27	47.18	104.22	55.69	48.54
A Electricity, gas and steam	97.58	52.41	45.17	101.43	54.85	46.58
B Water works and supply	2.86	0.85	2.01	2.79	0.84	1.96
5 Construction	179.47	86.86	92.61	184.81	88.96	95.85
6 Wholesale and retail trade, restaurants and hotels	337.94	112.15	225.80	355.89	118.29	237.60
A Wholesale and retail trade	254.72	72.80	181.92	267.90	76.97	190.93
B Restaurants and hotels	83.22	39.34	43.88	87.99	41.32	46.68
7 Transport, storage and communication	162.75	80.95	81.80	171.90	86.12	85.78

Austria

4.2 Derivation of Value Added by Kind of Activity, in Constant Prices
(Continued)

Thousand Million Austrian schillings

		1988 Gross Output	1988 Intermediate Consumption	1988 Value Added	1989 Gross Output	1989 Intermediate Consumption	1989 Value Added
		\multicolumn{6}{c}{At constant prices of:1983}
	A Transport and storage	125.75	75.74	50.01	133.03	80.74	52.29
	B Communication	37.00	5.21	31.79	38.87	5.38	33.49
8	Finance, insurance, real estate and business services	261.92	70.65	191.27	272.03	74.48	197.55
	A Financial institutions	80.12	15.33	64.79	85.73	17.11	68.62
	B Insurance	26.49	6.80	19.69	25.95	6.69	19.26
	C Real estate and business services	155.31	48.52	106.78	160.35	50.68	109.67
	Real estate, except dwellings	108.40	34.01	74.39	111.87	35.60	76.27
	Dwellings						
9	Community, social and personal services	70.43	22.38	48.05	72.77	23.02	49.75
	A Sanitary and similar services [bc]	...	...	...	...	...	...
	B Social and related community services [c]	33.00	8.49	24.51	33.93	8.69	25.24
	Educational services [d]	...	...	...	...	...	...
	Medical, dental, other health and veterinary services [c]	33.00	8.49	24.51	33.93	8.69	25.24
	C Recreational and cultural services [dc]	22.34	8.96	13.38	23.49	9.33	14.16
	D Personal and household services [bc]	15.10	4.94	10.16	15.35	5.00	10.35
Total, Industries		2216.13	1109.84	1106.29	2323.13	1167.38	1155.76
Producers of Government Services		286.06	111.56	174.51	288.56	112.80	175.75
Other Producers [b]		11.43	2.00	9.43	11.48	2.02	9.46
Total		2513.61	1223.40	1290.22	2623.16	1282.20	1340.97
Less: Imputed bank service charge		...	-71.77	71.77	...	-74.57	74.57
Import duties		10.21	...	10.21	11.02	...	11.02
Value added tax		108.16	...	108.16	112.62	...	112.62
Other adjustments		...	...	...	...	...	...
Total		2631.99	1295.16	1336.82	2746.80	1356.77	1390.03

a) Item 'Crude petroleum and natural gas production' is included in item 'Manufacture of chemicals and chemical petroleum, coal, rubber and plastic products.'
b) Item 'Sanitary and similar services' is included in item 'Personal and household services' which excludes domestic services and caretakers that are included in item 'Other producers'.
c) Non-governmental only.
d) Item 'Educational services' is included in item 'Recreational and cultural services'.

4.3 Cost Components of Value Added

Thousand Million Austrian schillings

		1980 Compensation of Employees	1980 Capital Consumption	1980 Net Operating Surplus	1980 Indirect Taxes	1980 Less: Subsidies Received	1980 Value Added	1981 Compensation of Employees	1981 Capital Consumption	1981 Net Operating Surplus	1981 Indirect Taxes	1981 Less: Subsidies Received	1981 Value Added
		\multicolumn{12}{c}{All Producers}
1	Agriculture, hunting, forestry and fishing	...	12.17	...	0.61	1.38	44.29	...	13.00	...	0.67	1.62	43.43
2	Mining and quarrying	...	0.50	...	0.40	0.34	4.87	...	0.55	...	0.42	0.33	4.77
3	Manufacturing	...	28.93	...	30.00	12.45	276.67	...	32.13	...	31.46	14.12	288.91
	A Manufacture of food, beverages and tobacco	...	...	...	...	...	41.68	...	...	...	...	...	45.02

Austria

4.3 Cost Components of Value Added
(Continued)

Thousand Million Austrian schillings

	1980 Compensation of Employees	1980 Capital Consumption	1980 Net Operating Surplus	1980 Indirect Taxes	1980 Less: Subsidies Received	1980 Value Added	1981 Compensation of Employees	1981 Capital Consumption	1981 Net Operating Surplus	1981 Indirect Taxes	1981 Less: Subsidies Received	1981 Value Added
B Textile, wearing apparel and leather industries	...	...	...	...	...	23.60	...	...	...	...	...	25.27
C Manufacture of wood and wood products, including furniture	...	...	...	...	...	20.77	...	...	...	...	...	19.79
D Manufacture of paper and paper products, printing and publishing	...	...	...	...	...	18.55	...	...	...	...	...	19.30
E Manufacture of chemicals and chemical petroleum, coal, rubber and plastic products [a]	...	...	...	...	...	38.57	...	...	...	...	...	39.38
F Manufacture of non-metallic mineral products, except products of petroleum and coal	...	...	...	...	...	15.87	...	...	...	...	...	17.03
G Basic metal industries	...	...	...	...	...	21.77	...	...	...	...	...	19.97
H Manufacture of fabricated metal products, machinery and equipment	...	...	...	...	...	95.86	...	...	...	...	...	103.16
I Other manufacturing industries	...	...	...	...	...	...	...	...	...	...	...	...
4 Electricity, gas and water	...	8.16	...	0.92	0.67	30.67	...	9.05	...	0.98	0.69	31.96
A Electricity, gas and steam	...	...	...	...	...	29.21	...	...	...	...	...	30.28
B Water works and supply	...	...	...	...	...	1.47	...	...	...	...	...	1.68
5 Construction	...	3.98	...	3.40	1.37	81.21	...	4.29	...	3.56	1.36	84.79
6 Wholesale and retail trade, restaurants and hotels	...	10.72	...	20.78	2.13	166.75	...	12.16	...	22.20	2.00	175.32
A Wholesale and retail trade	...	8.87	...	16.46	1.51	133.93	...	10.05	...	17.46	1.42	138.76
B Restaurants and hotels	...	1.85	...	4.31	0.63	32.82	...	2.11	...	4.74	0.58	36.56
7 Transport, storage and communication	...	11.75	...	3.31	9.81	57.83	...	13.13	...	2.53	9.93	62.63
A Transport and storage	...	...	...	...	...	36.74	...	...	...	...	...	39.94
B Communication	...	...	...	...	...	21.09	...	...	...	...	...	22.69
8 Finance, insurance, real estate and business services	...	30.58	...	8.53	0.58	119.06	...	33.81	...	9.30	0.57	135.64
A Financial institutions	...	...	...	...	...	42.99	...	...	...	...	...	50.43
B Insurance	...	...	...	...	...	12.99	...	...	...	...	...	14.24
C Real estate and business services	...	...	...	...	...	63.08	...	...	...	...	...	70.97
Real estate, except dwellings	...	...	...	...	...	41.35	...	...	...	...	...	47.07
Dwellings	...	...	...	...	...	...	...	...	...	...	...	...
9 Community, social and personal services	...	1.14	...	2.90	1.31	32.23	...	1.26	...	3.51	1.46	34.36
A Sanitary and similar services [bc]	...	...	...	...	...	...	...	...	...	...	...	...
B Social and related community services [c]	...	...	...	...	...	17.17	...	...	...	...	...	18.66
Educational services [d]	...	...	...	...	...	...	...	...	...	...	...	...
Medical, dental, other health and veterinary services [c]	...	...	...	...	...	17.17	...	...	...	...	...	18.66
C Recreational and cultural services [dc]	...	...	...	...	...	7.71	...	...	...	...	...	7.65
D Personal and household services [bc]	...	...	...	...	...	7.33	...	...	...	...	...	8.04
Total, Industries	...	107.93	...	70.85	30.05	813.58	...	119.39	...	74.64	32.08	861.80
Producers of Government Services	...	7.48	...	1.94	-	129.08	...	8.37	...	1.98	-	141.90
Other Producers [b]	...	0.68	...	0.04	0.01	7.17	...	0.75	...	0.04	0.01	7.90
Total [e]	545.63	116.10	245.32	72.83	30.05	949.83	589.01	128.51	249.50	76.65	32.09	1011.59
Less: Imputed bank service charge	...	...	45.12	...	...	45.12	...	...	53.36	...	...	53.36
Import duties	...	...	...	5.75	...	5.75	...	...	...	6.77	...	6.77
Value added tax	...	...	...	84.25	...	84.25	...	...	...	90.97	...	90.97
Other adjustments	...	...	...	...	...	-0.01	...	...	...	...	...	-0.01
Total	545.63	116.10	200.20	162.83	30.05	994.70	589.01	128.51	196.14	174.39	32.09	1055.97

Austria

4.3 Cost Components of Value Added

Thousand Million Austrian schillings

		1982						1983				
	Compensation of Employees	Capital Consumption	Net Operating Surplus	Indirect Taxes	Less: Subsidies Received	Value Added	Compensation of Employees	Capital Consumption	Net Operating Surplus	Indirect Taxes	Less: Subsidies Received	Value Added
				All Producers								
1 Agriculture, hunting, forestry and fishing	...	14.02	...	0.56	1.67	43.73	...	14.53	...	0.81	1.72	44.14
2 Mining and quarrying	...	0.61	...	0.43	0.29	5.40	...	0.62	...	0.40	0.29	5.32
3 Manufacturing	...	35.23	...	32.90	15.42	308.08	...	36.92	...	33.99	14.30	322.82
A Manufacture of food, beverages and tobacco	...	...	...	...	...	46.87	...	...	...	...	...	48.17
B Textile, wearing apparel and leather industries	...	...	...	...	...	25.97	...	...	...	...	...	26.17
C Manufacture of wood and wood products, including furniture	...	...	...	...	...	21.50	...	...	...	...	...	23.19
D Manufacture of paper and paper products, printing and publishing	...	...	...	...	...	19.69	...	...	...	...	...	20.55
E Manufacture of chemicals and chemical petroleum, coal, rubber and plastic products [a]	...	...	...	...	...	43.90	...	...	...	...	...	45.67
F Manufacture of non-metallic mineral products, except products of petroleum and coal	...	...	...	...	...	17.89	...	...	...	...	...	18.72
G Basic metal industries	...	...	...	...	...	21.74	...	...	...	...	...	21.92
H Manufacture of fabricated metal products, machinery and equipment	...	...	...	...	...	110.52	...	...	...	...	...	118.44
I Other manufacturing industries	...	...	...	...	...	...	...	...	...	...	...	...
4 Electricity, gas and water	...	9.88	...	1.04	0.73	38.00	...	10.65	...	0.99	0.81	39.09
A Electricity, gas and steam	...	...	...	...	...	36.14	...	...	...	...	...	37.08
B Water works and supply	...	...	...	...	...	1.85	...	...	...	...	...	2.01
5 Construction	...	4.54	...	3.52	1.10	85.10	...	4.69	...	3.23	0.99	87.45
6 Wholesale and retail trade, restaurants and hotels	...	13.62	...	22.84	2.02	188.30	...	15.11	...	24.03	2.05	201.83
A Wholesale and retail trade	...	11.26	...	17.51	1.29	149.41	...	12.42	...	18.18	1.40	161.26
B Restaurants and hotels	...	2.36	...	5.33	0.72	38.88	...	2.69	...	5.85	0.64	40.57
7 Transport, storage and communication	...	14.48	...	2.71	11.41	64.96	...	15.43	...	2.70	11.49	68.11
A Transport and storage	...	...	...	...	...	40.95	...	...	...	...	...	42.23
B Communication	...	...	...	...	...	24.01	...	...	...	...	...	25.88
8 Finance, insurance, real estate and business services	...	37.03	...	9.78	0.29	155.22	...	39.34	...	10.61	1.82	166.22
A Financial institutions	...	...	...	...	...	54.87	...	...	...	...	...	55.17
B Insurance	...	...	...	...	...	16.89	...	...	...	...	...	17.65
C Real estate and business services	...	...	...	...	...	83.46	...	...	...	...	...	93.41
Real estate, except dwellings	...	...	...	...	...	57.23	...	...	...	...	...	65.14
Dwellings	...	...	...	...	...	...	...	...	...	...	...	...
9 Community, social and personal services	...	1.38	...	3.90	1.36	36.74	...	1.47	...	5.00	1.71	40.54
A Sanitary and similar services [bc]	...	...	...	...	...	...	...	...	...	...	...	...
B Social and related community services [c]	...	...	...	...	...	20.04	...	...	...	...	...	21.36
Educational services [d]	...	...	...	...	...	...	...	...	...	...	...	...
Medical, dental, other health and veterinary services [c]	...	...	...	...	...	20.04	...	...	...	...	...	21.36
C Recreational and cultural services [dc]	...	...	...	...	...	8.08	...	...	...	...	...	9.75
D Personal and household services [bc]	...	...	...	...	...	8.62	...	...	...	...	...	9.43
Total, Industries	...	130.81	...	77.67	34.27	925.52	...	138.76	...	81.77	35.17	975.51
Producers of Government Services	...	9.12	...	2.15	-	154.76	...	9.60	...	2.34	-	164.63

Austria

4.3 Cost Components of Value Added
(Continued)

Thousand Million Austrian schillings

	1982						1983					
	Compensation of Employees	Capital Consumption	Net Operating Surplus	Indirect Taxes	Less: Subsidies Received	Value Added	Compensation of Employees	Capital Consumption	Net Operating Surplus	Indirect Taxes	Less: Subsidies Received	Value Added
Other Producers [b]	...	0.83	...	0.04	0.01	8.36	...	0.88	...	0.05	0.22	9.23
Total [e]	616.85	140.76	285.45	79.86	34.28	1088.64	642.44	149.24	308.93	84.15	35.39	1149.37
Less: Imputed bank service charge	...	...	60.23	...	...	60.23	...	...	61.06	...	...	61.06
Import duties	...	...	...	7.43	...	7.43	...	...	...	7.71	...	7.71
Value added tax	...	...	...	97.69	...	97.69	...	...	...	105.22	...	105.22
Other adjustments	...	...	...	...	...	-	...	...	...	...	...	-0.01
Total	616.85	140.76	225.22	184.98	34.28	1133.53	642.44	149.24	247.87	197.08	35.39	1201.23

	1984						1985					
	Compensation of Employees	Capital Consumption	Net Operating Surplus	Indirect Taxes	Less: Subsidies Received	Value Added	Compensation of Employees	Capital Consumption	Net Operating Surplus	Indirect Taxes	Less: Subsidies Received	Value Added

All Producers

1 Agriculture, hunting, forestry and fishing	...	14.89	...	-	1.77	48.70	...	15.05	...	0.56	1.95	44.99
2 Mining and quarrying	...	0.64	...	0.40	0.28	5.54	...	0.65	...	0.42	0.27	5.87
3 Manufacturing	...	39.27	...	36.02	13.77	340.06	...	41.84	...	37.26	15.23	362.80
A Manufacture of food, beverages and tobacco	...	...	...	...	...	50.24	...	...	...	...	...	52.37
B Textile, wearing apparel and leather industries	...	...	...	...	...	27.02	...	...	...	...	...	27.13
C Manufacture of wood and wood products, including furniture	...	...	...	...	...	23.17	...	...	...	...	...	23.62
D Manufacture of paper and paper products, printing and publishing	...	...	...	...	...	23.01	...	...	...	...	...	23.92
E Manufacture of chemicals and chemical petroleum, coal, rubber and plastic products [a]	...	...	...	...	...	49.72	...	...	...	...	...	51.53
F Manufacture of non-metallic mineral products, except products of petroleum and coal	...	...	...	...	...	19.89	...	...	...	...	...	20.87
G Basic metal industries	...	...	...	...	...	23.68	...	...	...	...	...	27.87
H Manufacture of fabricated metal products, machinery and equipment	...	...	...	...	...	123.33	...	...	...	...	...	135.50
I Other manufacturing industries	...	...	...	...	...	...	...	...	...	...	...	...
4 Electricity, gas and water	...	11.37	...	1.02	0.74	38.61	...	12.05	...	1.06	0.84	39.85
A Electricity, gas and steam	...	...	...	...	...	36.56	...	...	...	...	...	37.86
B Water works and supply	...	...	...	...	...	2.05	...	...	...	...	...	1.99
5 Construction	...	4.83	...	3.26	1.05	87.06	...	4.94	...	3.35	1.20	89.06
6 Wholesale and retail trade, restaurants and hotels	...	16.33	...	24.28	3.03	206.86	...	17.67	...	25.25	3.22	215.06
A Wholesale and retail trade	...	13.34	...	18.21	2.32	164.53	...	14.40	...	18.83	2.46	170.00
B Restaurants and hotels	...	2.99	...	6.07	0.71	42.34	...	3.27	...	6.42	0.76	45.07
7 Transport, storage and communication	...	16.45	...	3.11	11.64	74.76	...	17.55	...	3.27	12.59	78.42
A Transport and storage	...	...	...	...	...	45.91	...	...	...	...	...	47.74
B Communication	...	...	...	...	...	28.85	...	...	...	...	...	30.68
8 Finance, insurance, real estate and business services	...	41.82	...	11.71	1.66	183.14	...	44.42	...	12.43	1.79	204.39
A Financial institutions	...	...	...	...	...	57.59	...	...	...	...	...	63.21
B Insurance	...	...	...	...	...	18.96	...	...	...	...	...	20.44
C Real estate and business services	...	...	...	...	...	106.59	...	...	...	...	...	120.74
Real estate, except dwellings	...	...	...	...	...	75.88	...	...	...	...	...	86.40
Dwellings	...	...	...	...	...	...	...	...	...	...	...	...
9 Community, social and personal services	...	1.57	...	5.15	1.77	43.54	...	1.68	...	5.20	1.88	46.78
A Sanitary and similar services [bc]	...	...	...	...	...	...	...	...	...	...	...	...
B Social and related community services [c]	...	...	...	...	...	22.65	...	...	...	...	...	24.29

Austria

4.3 Cost Components of Value Added
(Continued)

Thousand Million Austrian schillings

	1984						1985					
	Compensation of Employees	Capital Consumption	Net Operating Surplus	Indirect Taxes	Less: Subsidies Received	Value Added	Compensation of Employees	Capital Consumption	Net Operating Surplus	Indirect Taxes	Less: Subsidies Received	Value Added
Educational services d	...	...	...	...	...	...	...	...	...	...	...	...
Medical, dental, other health and veterinary services c	...	...	...	...	...	22.65	...	...	...	...	...	24.29
C Recreational and cultural services dc	...	...	...	...	...	10.88	...	...	...	...	...	11.69
D Personal and household services bc	...	...	...	...	...	10.02	...	...	...	...	...	10.80
Total, Industries	...	147.16	...	84.95	35.72	1028.26	...	155.83	...	88.80	38.98	1087.24
Producers of Government Services	...	10.10	...	2.47	-	173.49	...	10.69	...	2.65	-	185.07
Other Producers b	...	0.94	...	0.04	0.22	9.70	...	1.00	...	0.05	0.22	10.23
Total e	676.33	158.19	325.40	87.47	35.93	1211.44	717.09	167.53	345.65	91.48	39.20	1282.54
Less: Imputed bank service charge	...	...	63.30	...	...	63.30	...	...	68.56	...	...	68.56
Import duties	...	...	...	8.62	...	8.62	...	...	...	9.08	...	9.08
Value added tax	...	...	...	120.00	...	120.00	...	...	...	125.37	...	125.36
Other adjustments	...	...	...	...	...	-	...	...	...	...	...	-
Total	676.33	158.19	262.10	216.09	35.93	1276.77	717.09	167.53	277.09	225.93	39.20	1348.42

	1986						1987					
	Compensation of Employees	Capital Consumption	Net Operating Surplus	Indirect Taxes	Less: Subsidies Received	Value Added	Compensation of Employees	Capital Consumption	Net Operating Surplus	Indirect Taxes	Less: Subsidies Received	Value Added
					All Producers							
1 Agriculture, hunting, forestry and fishing	...	15.33	...	0.27	2.55	47.11	...	15.66	...	0.81	3.28	48.47
2 Mining and quarrying	...	0.68	...	0.44	0.27	5.65	...	0.63	...	0.45	0.24	5.85
3 Manufacturing	...	44.33	...	38.98	16.41	375.65	...	46.87	...	41.12	15.36	381.53
A Manufacture of food, beverages and tobacco	...	...	...	...	...	53.42	...	...	...	...	...	55.10
B Textile, wearing apparel and leather industries	...	...	...	...	...	27.48	...	...	...	...	...	26.92
C Manufacture of wood and wood products, including furniture	...	...	...	...	...	24.83	...	...	...	...	...	26.38
D Manufacture of paper and paper products, printing and publishing	...	...	...	...	...	25.20	...	...	...	...	...	25.93
E Manufacture of chemicals and chemical petroleum, coal, rubber and plastic products a	...	...	...	...	...	58.47	...	...	...	...	...	59.02
F Manufacture of non-metallic mineral products, except products of petroleum and coal	...	...	...	...	...	21.45	...	...	...	...	...	22.25
G Basic metal industries	...	...	...	...	...	25.13	...	...	...	...	...	22.82
H Manufacture of fabricated metal products, machinery and equipment	...	...	...	...	...	139.68	...	...	...	...	...	143.11
I Other manufacturing industries	...	...	...	...	...	...	...	...	...	...	...	...
4 Electricity, gas and water	...	12.83	...	1.14	1.08	43.92	...	13.14	...	1.18	0.95	47.21
A Electricity, gas and steam	...	...	...	...	...	41.86	...	...	...	...	...	45.00
B Water works and supply	...	...	...	...	...	2.07	...	...	...	...	...	2.20
5 Construction	...	5.15	...	3.60	1.21	93.50	...	5.95	...	3.83	1.28	99.63
6 Wholesale and retail trade, restaurants and hotels	...	18.89	...	26.50	4.84	223.83	...	18.82	...	27.46	6.60	232.36
A Wholesale and retail trade	...	15.39	...	19.92	4.02	174.35	...	15.58	...	20.15	5.77	178.75
B Restaurants and hotels	...	3.50	...	6.58	0.82	49.48	...	3.24	...	7.31	0.83	53.62
7 Transport, storage and communication	...	18.70	...	3.35	14.89	81.53	...	19.37	...	3.37	15.04	86.15
A Transport and storage	...	...	...	...	...	49.11	...	...	...	...	...	51.25
B Communication	...	...	...	...	...	32.42	...	...	...	...	...	34.89
8 Finance, insurance, real estate and business services	...	46.15	...	13.72	2.53	223.01	...	49.07	...	14.38	2.40	237.05
A Financial institutions	...	...	...	...	...	67.43	...	...	...	...	...	71.17
B Insurance	...	...	...	...	...	21.34	...	...	...	...	...	22.17
C Real estate and business services	...	...	...	...	...	134.24	...	...	...	...	...	143.71
Real estate, except dwellings	...	...	...	...	...	95.70	...	...	...	...	...	100.34

Austria

4.3 Cost Components of Value Added
(Continued)

Thousand Million Austrian schillings

	1986						1987					
	Compensation of Employees	Capital Consumption	Net Operating Surplus	Indirect Taxes	Less: Subsidies Received	Value Added	Compensation of Employees	Capital Consumption	Net Operating Surplus	Indirect Taxes	Less: Subsidies Received	Value Added
Dwellings	...	...	...	...	...	...	...	...	...	...	...	...
9 Community, social and personal services	...	1.78	...	5.48	2.03	51.24	...	1.76	...	5.77	2.03	55.17
A Sanitary and similar services bc	...	...	...	...	...	...	...	...	...	...	...	...
B Social and related community services c	...	...	...	...	...	25.93	...	...	...	...	...	27.30
Educational services d	...	...	...	...	...	...	...	...	...	...	...	...
Medical, dental, other health and veterinary services c	...	...	...	...	...	25.93	...	...	...	...	...	27.30
C Recreational and cultural services dc	...	...	...	...	...	13.62	...	...	...	...	...	15.52
D Personal and household services bc	...	...	...	...	...	11.69	...	...	...	...	...	12.35
Total, Industries	...	163.82	...	93.48	45.82	1145.45	...	171.27	...	98.37	47.17	1193.42
Producers of Government Services	...	11.31	...	2.87	-	197.09	...	11.56	...	2.91	-	205.91
Other Producers b	...	1.06	...	0.05	0.23	10.82	...	1.04	...	0.05	0.21	11.26
Total e	761.25	176.20	365.55	96.39	46.05	1353.35	792.73	183.87	380.04	101.33	47.38	1410.59
Less: Imputed bank service charge	...	...	75.03	...	...	75.03	...	...	80.51	...	...	80.51
Import duties	...	...	...	9.00	...	9.00	...	...	...	9.86	...	9.86
Value added tax	...	...	...	128.66	...	128.66	...	...	...	133.96	...	133.96
Other adjustments	...	...	...	...	...	-	...	...	...	...	...	-
Total	761.25	176.20	290.53	234.05	46.05	1415.97	792.73	183.87	299.52	245.15	47.38	1473.90

	1988						1989					
	Compensation of Employees	Capital Consumption	Net Operating Surplus	Indirect Taxes	Less: Subsidies Received	Value Added	Compensation of Employees	Capital Consumption	Net Operating Surplus	Indirect Taxes	Less: Subsidies Received	Value Added
				All Producers								
1 Agriculture, hunting, forestry and fishing	...	16.00	...	0.89	3.68	49.07	...	16.40	...	1.20	4.00	51.80
2 Mining and quarrying	...	0.72	...	0.45	0.20	5.49	...	0.74	...	0.47	0.33	5.34
3 Manufacturing	...	48.76	...	43.75	13.49	414.53	...	51.52	...	45.56	12.17	446.51
A Manufacture of food, beverages and tobacco	...	...	...	...	...	55.85	...	...	...	...	...	57.70
B Textile, wearing apparel and leather industries	...	...	...	...	...	26.69	...	...	...	...	...	27.70
C Manufacture of wood and wood products, including furniture	...	...	...	...	...	28.74	...	...	...	...	...	30.88
D Manufacture of paper and paper products, printing and publishing	...	...	...	...	...	29.30	...	...	...	...	...	32.78
E Manufacture of chemicals and chemical petroleum, coal, rubber and plastic products a	...	...	...	...	...	67.00	...	...	...	...	...	70.43
F Manufacture of non-metallic mineral products, except products of petroleum and coal	...	...	...	...	...	23.87	...	...	...	...	...	24.79
G Basic metal industries	...	...	...	...	...	25.73	...	...	...	...	...	27.31
H Manufacture of fabricated metal products, machinery and equipment	...	...	...	...	...	157.34	...	...	...	...	...	174.93
I Other manufacturing industries	...	...	...	...	...	...	...	...	...	...	...	...
4 Electricity, gas and water	...	14.22	...	1.23	0.78	47.26	...	15.05	...	1.29	0.95	48.68
A Electricity, gas and steam	...	...	...	...	...	45.01	...	...	...	...	...	46.24
B Water works and supply	...	...	...	...	...	2.26	...	...	...	...	...	2.44
5 Construction	...	5.58	...	4.08	1.24	106.08	...	5.77	...	4.38	1.30	114.45
6 Wholesale and retail trade, restaurants and hotels	...	20.93	...	27.93	6.66	248.70	...	22.31	...	29.12	6.79	268.61
A Wholesale and retail trade	...	17.13	...	20.29	5.92	190.34	...	18.26	...	21.37	6.03	203.65
B Restaurants and hotels	...	3.79	...	7.64	0.74	58.36	...	4.05	...	7.75	0.76	64.96
7 Transport, storage and communication	...	20.89	...	3.65	14.31	93.53	...	22.19	...	3.84	14.89	99.51
A Transport and storage	...	...	...	...	...	55.52	...	...	...	...	...	59.73
B Communication	...	...	...	...	...	38.01	...	...	...	...	...	39.78
8 Finance, insurance, real estate and business services	...	52.20	...	15.83	2.47	256.45	...	56.24	...	17.63	2.67	276.00
A Financial institutions	...	...	...	...	...	76.64	...	...	...	...	...	84.08

Austria

4.3 Cost Components of Value Added
(Continued)

Thousand Million Austrian schillings

	1988						1989					
	Compensation of Employees	Capital Consumption	Net Operating Surplus	Indirect Taxes	Less: Subsidies Received	Value Added	Compensation of Employees	Capital Consumption	Net Operating Surplus	Indirect Taxes	Less: Subsidies Received	Value Added
B Insurance	...	...	...	...	...	26.32	...	...	...	...	...	27.60
C Real estate and business services	...	...	...	...	...	153.49	...	...	...	...	...	164.32
Real estate, except dwellings	...	...	...	...	...	105.25	...	...	...	...	...	110.63
Dwellings	...	...	...	...	...	...	...	...	...	...	...	...
9 Community, social and personal services	...	1.91	...	5.86	2.04	59.25	...	2.01	...	6.19	2.12	63.73
A Sanitary and similar services bc	...	...	...	...	...	...	...	...	...	...	...	...
B Social and related community services c	...	...	...	...	...	29.64	...	...	...	...	...	31.21
Educational services d	...	...	...	...	...	...	...	...	...	...	...	...
Medical, dental, other health and veterinary services c	...	...	...	...	...	29.64	...	...	...	...	...	31.21
C Recreational and cultural services dc	...	...	...	...	...	16.62	...	...	...	...	...	18.91
D Personal and household services bc	...	...	...	...	...	13.00	...	...	...	...	...	13.61
Total, Industries	...	181.18	...	103.66	44.87	1280.35	...	192.22	...	109.67	45.22	1374.63
Producers of Government Services	...	11.80	...	2.91	-	210.53	...	12.22	...	3.34	-	220.86
Other Producers b	...	1.13	...	0.05	0.21	11.35	...	1.19	...	0.05	0.22	11.71
Total e	822.36	194.11	424.21	106.63	45.08	1502.23	876.23	205.63	457.73	113.05	45.44	1607.20
Less: Imputed bank service charge	...	...	85.81	...	...	85.81	...	...	92.36	...	...	92.36
Import duties	...	...	...	10.63	...	10.63	...	...	...	11.51	...	11.51
Value added tax	...	...	...	137.63	...	137.63	...	...	...	147.08	...	147.08
Other adjustments	...	...	...	...	...	-	...	...	...	...	...	-
Total	822.36	194.11	338.40	254.89	45.08	1564.68	876.23	205.63	365.36	271.64	45.44	1673.43

a) Item 'Crude petroleum and natural gas production' is included in item 'Manufacture of chemicals and chemical petroleum, coal, rubber and plastic products.'
b) Item 'Sanitary and similar services' is included in item 'Personal and household services' which excludes domestic services and caretakers that are included in item 'Other producers'.
c) Non-governmental only.
d) Item 'Educational services' is included in item 'Recreational and cultural services'.
e) Column 'Operating Surplus' is reduced for imputed bank service charges.

Bahamas

Source. Reply to the United Nations national accounts questionnaire from the Department of Statistics, Nassau. Official estimates are published in a series of reports entitled 'Expenditure on Gross Domestic Product'.

General note. The estimates shown in the following tables have been prepared in accordance with the United Nations System of National Accounts so far as the existing data would permit.

1.1 Expenditure on the Gross Domestic Product, in Current Prices

Million Bahamian dollars

	1970	1975	1980	1981	1982	1983	1984	1985	1986	1987	1988	1989
1 Government final consumption expenditure	...	96.9	173.3	207.3	218.8	250.6	267.6	294.5	306.3	333.8	370.1	...
2 Private final consumption expenditure	...	451.1	597.6	653.9	727.9	782.3	856.1	910.4	1032.1	1150.0	1132.8	...
A Households	...	...	597.6	653.9	727.9	782.3	856.1	910.4	1032.1	1150.0	1132.8	...
B Private non-profit institutions serving households	...	...	-	-	-	-	-	-	-	-	-	...
3 Gross capital formation	...	75.4	181.1	306.2	315.2	261.6	304.6	390.9	435.7	519.1	538.1	...
A Increase in stocks	...	...	9.0	40.1	14.2	-49.7	3.7	9.6	16.6	6.5	27.4	...
B Gross fixed capital formation	...	75.4	172.1	266.2	301.1	311.3	300.8	381.3	419.1	512.7	510.7	...
Residential buildings	...		59.1	57.1	65.3	79.7	89.3	105.7	120.2	128.2	128.9	...
Non-residential buildings	...	23.5	41.6	70.8	94.4	79.7	60.8	55.9	60.1	97.4	106.9	...
Other construction and land improvement etc.	...		8.2	31.4	30.5	28.2	9.7	21.4	44.0	54.4	51.9	...
Other	...	51.9	63.2	106.9	110.9	123.7	141.1	198.3	194.8	232.7	223.0	...
4 Exports of goods and services	...	605.2	1156.6	1200.4	1189.8	1238.2	1293.2	1511.9	1605.1	1773.0	1763.8	...
5 Less: Imports of goods and services	...	474.8	788.7	860.4	935.7	1039.7	1106.3	1239.4	1281.2	1451.6	1346.9	...
Equals: Gross Domestic Product	...	753.8	1319.6	1507.4	1516.1	1493.1	1615.2	1868.2	2097.9	2324.2	2457.9	...

1.2 Expenditure on the Gross Domestic Product, in Constant Prices

Million Bahamian dollars

	1970	1975	1980	1981	1982	1983	1984	1985	1986	1987	1988	1989
			At constant prices of:1980									
1 Government final consumption expenditure	...	...	173.3	207.3	218.8	251.4	253.0	267.0	274.0	290.5	370.1	...
2 Private final consumption expenditure	...	...	597.6	606.0	631.6	639.2	670.2	704.3	708.0	740.6	1132.8	...
A Households	...	...	597.6	606.0	631.6	639.2	670.2	704.3	708.0	740.6	1132.8	...
B Private non-profit institutions serving households	...	...	-	-	-	-	-	-	-	-	-	...
3 Gross capital formation	...	...	181.1	277.0	269.7	215.0	240.4	297.6	316.8	361.5	538.1	...
A Increase in stocks	...	...	9.0	36.1	12.1	-40.5	2.9	7.2	11.8	4.4	27.4	...
B Gross fixed capital formation	...	...	172.1	240.9	257.6	255.6	237.5	290.5	305.1	357.1	510.7	...
Residential buildings	...	...	100.7	115.1	136.1	130.0	117.7	121.3	128.3	153.8	235.8	...
Non-residential buildings	...	...										...
Other construction and land improvement etc.	...	...	8.2	28.2	26.0	23.1	7.6	16.1	31.3	37.2	51.9	...
Other	...	...	63.2	97.6	95.6	102.5	112.2	153.1	145.4	166.2	223.0	...
4 Exports of goods and services	...	...	1156.6	1253.1	1259.4	1204.8	1210.3	1370.1	1384.0	1461.0	1763.9	...
5 Less: Imports of goods and services	...	...	788.7	774.2	797.3	847.8	868.1	929.8	911.5	989.9	1349.9	...
Equals: Gross Domestic Product	...	...	1319.8	1569.2	1582.2	1462.7	1505.8	1709.2	1771.3	1863.7	2458.0	...

Bahamas

1.3 Cost Components of the Gross Domestic Product

Million Bahamian dollars

	1970	1975	1980	1981	1982	1983	1984	1985	1986	1987	1988	1989
1 Indirect taxes, net	...	...	197.9	204.2	209.4	241.5	254.0	303.1	322.8	335.4	386.7	...
A Indirect taxes	...	...	200.5	208.1	215.7	249.0	260.3	307.5	327.9	340.9	392.6	...
B Less: Subsidies	...	...	2.6	3.9	6.3	7.5	6.3	4.4	5.1	5.5	5.9	...
2 Consumption of fixed capital	...	...	2.6	3.4	3.6	3.7	3.7	5.5	6.5	7.1	6.3	...
3 Compensation of employees paid by resident producers to:	...	...	124.3	145.7	159.1	182.0	203.4	219.5	226.8	250.9	275.9	...
A Resident households	...	...	124.3	145.7	159.1	182.0	203.4	219.5	226.8	250.9	275.9	...
B Rest of the world	...	...	...	...	...	...	...	...	...	...	...	...
4 Operating surplus	...	...	995.1	1154.1	1144.0	1065.9	1154.0	1340.1	1541.9	1730.8	1789.1	...
Equals: Gross Domestic Product	...	...	1319.8	1507.4	1516.1	1493.1	1615.2	1868.2	2097.9	2324.2	2457.9	...

1.4 General Government Current Receipts and Disbursements

Million Bahamian dollars

	1970	1975	1980	1981	1982	1983	1984	1985	1986	1987	1988	1989
Receipts												
1 Operating surplus	...	...	-	-	0.1	0.1	0.1	-	0.1	0.1	0.2	...
2 Property and entrepreneurial income	...	...	17.0	24.4	52.3	42.7	55.1	48.1	47.5	41.1	38.7	...
3 Taxes, fees and contributions	...	...	238.7	250.8	257.2	298.8	314.7	377.4	400.9	412.1	472.6	...
A Indirect taxes	...	...	200.5	208.1	215.7	249.0	260.3	307.5	327.9	340.9	392.6	...
B Direct taxes	...	...	3.9	4.1	4.2	5.9	6.6	6.8	7.9	7.8	7.2	...
C Social security contributions	...	...	23.1	24.1	23.2	29.6	34.3	47.7	49.6	49.7	55.1	...
D Compulsory fees, fines and penalties	...	...	11.3	14.6	14.1	14.2	13.5	15.4	15.6	13.7	17.7	...
4 Other current transfers	...	...	5.4	6.6	7.5	10.0	10.2	9.4	9.4	10.0	12.1	...
Total Current Receipts of General Government	...	...	261.1	281.9	317.2	351.6	380.1	434.8	458.0	463.4	523.6	...
Disbursements												
1 Government final consumption expenditure	...	...	173.3	207.3	218.8	250.6	267.6	294.5	306.3	333.8	370.1	...
A Compensation of employees	...	...	124.3	145.7	159.1	182.0	203.4	219.5	226.8	250.9	275.9	...
B Consumption of fixed capital	...	...	2.6	3.4	3.6	3.7	3.7	5.5	6.5	7.1	6.3	...
C Purchases of goods and services, net	...	...	46.3	58.1	56.1	64.8	60.4	69.4	72.9	75.6	87.9	...
D Less: Own account fixed capital formation	...	...	...	...	...	...	...	...	...	...	...	...
E Indirect taxes paid, net	...	...	0.1	0.1	0.1	0.1	0.1	0.1	0.1	0.1	0.1	...
2 Property income	...	...	21.5	23.0	36.6	40.2	43.4	49.6	46.9	40.3	46.1	...
A Interest	...	...	21.5	23.0	36.6	40.2	43.4	49.6	46.9	40.3	46.0	...
B Net land rent and royalties	...	...	...	...	...	...	...	...	...	...	...	...
3 Subsidies	...	...	2.6	3.9	6.3	7.5	6.3	4.4	5.1	5.5	5.9	...
4 Other current transfers	...	...	19.9	23.9	28.5	38.0	41.6	43.6	48.6	50.5	59.1	...
A Social security benefits	...	...	5.4	8.3	11.3	15.3	17.8	21.4	24.0	25.6	28.3	...
B Social assistance grants	...	...	3.0	3.5	4.9	7.6	8.6	7.7	7.4	8.0	7.9	...
C Other	...	...	11.5	12.0	12.3	15.1	15.1	14.4	17.2	16.8	22.8	...
5 Net saving	...	...	43.8	23.8	26.9	15.2	21.3	42.9	51.2	33.3	42.4	...
Total Current Disbursements and Net Saving of General Government	...	...	261.1	281.9	317.2	351.6	380.1	434.8	458.0	463.4	523.6	...

1.7 External Transactions on Current Account, Summary

Million Bahamian dollars

	1970	1975	1980	1981	1982	1983	1984	1985	1986	1987	1988	1989
Payments to the Rest of the World												
1 Imports of goods and services	...	...	788.7	860.4	935.7	1039.7	1106.3	1239.4	1281.2	1451.6	1346.9	...
A Imports of merchandise c.i.f.	...	...	581.9	612.8	646.7	744.4	818.7	904.0	919.5	1044.9	914.3	...
B Other	...	...	206.8	247.6	289.0	295.3	287.6	335.4	361.7	406.7	432.6	...
2 Factor income to the rest of the world	...	...	126.6	153.4	139.0	138.6	167.3	183.0	183.3	180.9	164.9	...

Bahamas

1.7 External Transactions on Current Account, Summary
(Continued)

Million Bahamian dollars

	1970	1975	1980	1981	1982	1983	1984	1985	1986	1987	1988	1989
A Compensation of employees	...	...	...	...	...	...	...	...	...	...	...	...
B Property and entrepreneurial income			126.6	153.4	139.0	138.6	167.3	183.0	183.3	180.9	164.9	...
By general government			1.9	1.4	10.3	9.5	14.0	11.9	12.7	8.5	13.1	
By corporate and quasi-corporate enterprises			35.0	43.8	36.5	39.1	32.9	40.5	39.4	42.9	49.4	
By other			89.7	108.2	92.2	90.0	120.4	130.6	131.2	129.5	102.4	
3 Current transfers to the rest of the world			21.4	16.1	19.8	12.5	16.7	16.8	16.6	20.3	31.9	
4 Surplus of the nation on current transactions			252.4	200.8	140.9	77.9	35.6	109.9	159.7	154.9	252.8	
Payments to the Rest of the World and Surplus of the Nation on Current Transactions			1189.1	1230.7	1235.2	1268.7	1325.8	1549.1	1640.9	1807.8	1796.5	

Receipts From The Rest of the World

	1970	1975	1980	1981	1982	1983	1984	1985	1986	1987	1988	1989
1 Exports of goods and services			1156.6	1200.4	1189.8	1238.2	1293.2	1511.9	1605.1	1773.0	1763.8	
A Exports of merchandise f.o.b.			138.9	156.3	186.3	215.3	244.8	291.3	310.8	401.7	436.9	
B Other			1017.7	1044.1	1003.6	1022.9	1048.4	1220.6	1294.3	1371.3	1326.9	
2 Factor income from rest of the world			13.0	17.0	23.8	15.3	18.8	20.4	19.5	18.1	15.3	
A Compensation of employees			...	...	...	...	...	...	...	...	...	
B Property and entrepreneurial income			13.0	17.0	23.8	15.3	18.8	20.4	19.5	18.1	15.3	
By general government			...	...	...	...	...	...	...	...	...	
By corporate and quasi-corporate enterprises			0.9	0.8	4.5	1.8	0.9	1.0	0.8	0.4	0.4	
By other			12.1	16.2	19.3	13.5	17.9	19.4	18.7	17.7	14.9	
3 Current transfers from rest of the world			19.5	13.3	21.6	15.2	13.8	16.8	16.3	16.7	17.4	
Receipts from the Rest of the World on Current Transactions			1189.1	1230.7	1235.2	1268.7	1325.8	1549.1	1640.9	1807.8	1796.5	

1.10 Gross Domestic Product by Kind of Activity, in Current Prices

Million Bahamian dollars

	1970	1975	1980	1981	1982	1983	1984	1985	1986	1987	1988	1989
1 Agriculture, hunting, forestry and fishing	...	23.6	...	...	...	...	...	...	...	...	...	...
2 Mining and quarrying	...											
3 Manufacturing	...	88.1										
4 Electricity, gas and water	...											
5 Construction	...	14.8										
6 Wholesale and retail trade, restaurants and hotels	...	166.5										
7 Transport, storage and communication	...	77.4										
8 Finance, insurance, real estate and business services	...	88.1										
9 Community, social and personal services	...	114.7										
Total, Industries	...	573.2										
Producers of Government Services	...	...										
Other Producers	...	...										
Subtotal	...	573.2										
Less: Imputed bank service charge	...	...										
Plus: Import duties	...	64.1										
Plus: Value added tax	...	...										
Plus: Other adjustments	...	116.5										
Equals: Gross Domestic Product	...	753.8										

Bahamas

1.12 Relations Among National Accounting Aggregates

Million Bahamian dollars

	1970	1975	1980	1981	1982	1983	1984	1985	1986	1987	1988	1989
Gross Domestic Product	...	...	1319.8	1507.5	1516.1	1493.1	1615.2	1868.2	2097.9	2324.2	2457.9	...
Plus: Net factor income from the rest of the world	...	...	-113.6	-136.4	-115.2	-123.3	-148.5	-162.6	-163.8	-162.8	-149.6	...
Factor income from the rest of the world	...	...	13.0	17.0	23.8	15.3	18.8	20.4	19.5	18.1	15.3	...
Less: Factor income to the rest of the world	...	...	126.6	153.4	139.1	138.6	167.3	183.0	183.3	180.9	164.9	...
Equals: Gross National Product	...	...	1206.2	1371.0	1400.8	1369.8	1466.7	1705.6	1934.1	2161.4	2308.3	...
Less: Consumption of fixed capital	...	...	2.6	3.4	3.6	3.7	3.7	5.5	6.5	7.1	6.3	...
Equals: National Income	...	...	1203.6	1367.6	1397.1	1366.1	1463.0	1700.1	1927.7	2154.3	2302.1	...
Plus: Net current transfers from the rest of the world	...	...	-1.9	-2.8	1.8	2.7	-2.9	-	-0.3	-3.6	-14.5	...
Current transfers from the rest of the world	...	...	19.5	13.3	21.6	15.2	13.8	16.8	16.3	16.7	17.4	...
Less: Current transfers to the rest of the world	...	...	21.4	16.1	19.8	12.5	16.7	16.8	16.6	20.3	31.9	...
Equals: National Disposable Income	...	...	1201.7	1364.8	1398.9	1368.8	1460.1	1700.1	1927.4	2150.7	2287.6	...
Less: Final consumption	...	...	770.8	861.2	946.7	1033.0	1123.7	1204.9	1338.4	1483.8	1502.9	...
Equals: Net Saving	...	...	430.9	503.7	452.2	335.5	336.5	495.2	589.0	666.9	784.7	...
Less: Surplus of the nation on current transactions	...	...	252.4	200.8	140.7	77.9	35.6	109.9	159.7	155.0	252.8	...
Equals: Net Capital Formation	...	...	178.5	302.9	311.6	257.9	300.9	385.4	429.2	512.0	531.9	...

2.1 Government Final Consumption Expenditure by Function, in Current Prices

Million Bahamian dollars

		1970	1975	1980	1981	1982	1983	1984	1985	1986	1987	1988	1989
1	General public services	...	...	21.2	24.8	27.5	29.4	32.5	35.7	37.2	40.5	36.5	...
2	Defence	...	...	4.8	7.5	9.4	8.5	9.4	10.4	10.8	11.7	16.7	...
3	Public order and safety	...	...	21.5	26.6	28.1	31.8	34.0	37.4	38.9	42.4	51.4	...
4	Education	...	...	47.6	56.6	59.2	70.0	73.4	80.8	84.0	91.5	91.5	...
5	Health	...	...	35.3	40.4	45.4	50.2	53.9	59.3	61.7	67.3	82.7	...
6	Social security and welfare	...	...	3.5	4.8	6.0	6.8	6.6	7.2	7.5	8.2	14.8	...
7	Housing and community amenities	...	...	0.2	0.2	0.3	0.4	0.3	0.4	0.4	0.4	0.6	...
8	Recreational, cultural and religious affairs	...	...	2.0	2.4	2.5	2.8	3.1	3.4	3.5	3.8	5.6	...
9	Economic services	...	...	17.4	19.5	21.2	21.9	25.0	27.5	28.7	31.2	32.4	...
	A Fuel and energy	...	...	...	...	...	...	...	...	...	...	...	...
	B Agriculture, forestry, fishing and hunting	...	...	3.9	4.5	4.8	5.5	5.9	6.5	6.8	7.4	7.5	...
	C Mining, manufacturing and construction, except fuel and energy	...	...	...	...	...	...	...	...	...	...	...	...
	D Transportation and communication	...	...	11.3	12.6	12.7	13.4	15.9	17.5	18.2	19.8	21.9	...
	E Other economic affairs	...	...	2.2	2.4	2.7	3.0	3.2	3.5	3.7	4.0	3.0	...
10	Other functions a	...	...	19.8	24.4	20.2	28.8	29.4	32.4	33.7	36.7	38.0	...
	Total Government Final Consumption Expenditure	...	...	173.3	207.3	218.8	250.6	267.6	294.5	306.3	333.8	370.1	...

a) Tourism is included in item 'Other functions' in table 2.1. It is included in 'Other economic affairs' in table 2.3.

2.3 Total Government Outlays by Function and Type

Million Bahamian dollars

		Final Consumption Expenditures Total	Compensation of Employees	Other	Subsidies	Other Current Transfers & Property Income	Total Current Disbursements	Gross Capital Formation	Other Capital Outlays	Total Outlays
						1980				
1	General public services	21.2	18.4	2.8	2.6	6.9	30.7	-11.7	2.7	21.7
2	Defence	4.8	2.1	2.7	...	-	4.8	-	...	4.8
3	Public order and safety	21.5	17.8	3.7	...	0.1	21.6	1.0	...	22.6
4	Education	47.6	42.4	5.2	...	5.7	53.3	3.6	...	56.9
5	Health	35.3	25.5	9.9	...	0.1	35.4	2.2	...	37.6
6	Social security and welfare	3.5	2.5	1.0	...	7.0	10.5	0.7	...	11.2
7	Housing and community amenities	0.2	0.1	-	...	-	0.2	-	...	0.2
8	Recreation, culture and religion	2.0	1.1	0.9	...	0.1	2.0	1.0	...	3.0
9	Economic services	37.2	14.6	22.6	-	0.1	37.3	8.1	3.5	48.9

Bahamas

2.3 Total Government Outlays by Function and Type
(Continued)

Million Bahamian dollars

	Final Consumption Expenditures Total	Compensation of Employees	Other	Subsidies	Other Current Transfers & Property Income	Total Current Disbursements	Gross Capital Formation	Other Capital Outlays	Total Outlays
A Fuel and energy	...	...	...	...	...	...	...	...	...
B Agriculture, forestry, fishing and hunting	3.9	2.8	1.1	...	0.1	4.0	2.3	...	6.3
C Mining (except fuels), manufacturing and construction	...	...	...	...	...	...	...	...	...
D Transportation and communication	11.3	5.3	5.9	...	-	11.3	5.4	3.5	20.2
E Other economic affairs [a]	22.0	6.4	15.5	...	-	22.0	0.4	...	22.4
10 Other functions	-	-	-	...	21.5	21.5	-	...	21.5
Total	173.3	124.3	49.0	2.6	41.4	217.3	4.9	6.2	228.4
1981									
1 General public services	24.8	20.1	4.7	3.9	7.9	36.6	-34.0	4.9	7.5
2 Defence	7.5	3.4	4.1	...	-	7.5	-	...	7.5
3 Public order and safety	26.6	21.1	5.5	...	0.1	26.7	1.8	...	28.5
4 Education	56.6	49.1	7.6	...	5.7	62.3	6.2	...	68.5
5 Health	40.4	29.8	10.6	...	0.2	40.6	2.1	0.2	42.8
6 Social security and welfare	4.8	3.0	1.8	...	9.7	14.5	0.6	...	15.2
7 Housing and community amenities	0.2	0.2	-	...	-	0.2	-	...	0.2
8 Recreation, culture and religion	2.4	1.6	0.8	...	0.1	2.5	0.5	...	3.0
9 Economic services	43.9	17.5	26.4	-	0.2	44.1	16.1	...	60.2
A Fuel and energy	...	...	...	...	...	...	...	...	...
B Agriculture, forestry, fishing and hunting	4.5	3.5	1.1	...	0.2	4.7	1.5	...	6.3
C Mining (except fuels), manufacturing and construction	...	...	...	...	...	...	...	...	...
D Transportation and communication	12.6	6.7	5.9	...	-	12.6	14.4	...	27.1
E Other economic affairs [a]	26.8	7.3	19.4	...	-	26.8	0.1	...	26.9
10 Other functions	-	-	-	...	23.0	23.0	-	...	23.0
Total	207.3	145.7	61.6	3.9	46.9	258.1	-6.8	5.1	256.4
1982									
1 General public services	27.5	21.0	6.5	6.1	8.3	42.0	-2.4	9.0	48.6
2 Defence	9.4	4.1	5.2	...	-	9.4	-	...	9.4
3 Public order and safety	28.1	22.2	5.9	...	0.1	28.2	1.0	...	29.3
4 Education	59.2	53.6	5.6	0.2	6.5	65.8	6.1	...	71.9
5 Health	45.4	33.6	11.8	...	0.1	45.5	1.6	...	47.1
6 Social security and welfare	6.0	3.7	2.4	...	13.3	19.3	1.3	...	20.6
7 Housing and community amenities	0.3	0.2	0.1	...	-	0.3	-	...	0.3
8 Recreation, culture and religion	2.5	1.8	0.7	...	0.1	2.6	0.3	...	2.9
9 Economic services	40.5	18.8	21.7	-	0.2	40.7	12.1	-0.2	52.6
A Fuel and energy	...	...	...	...	...	...	...	...	...
B Agriculture, forestry, fishing and hunting	4.8	3.8	1.0	...	0.1	5.0	1.3	...	6.3
C Mining (except fuels), manufacturing and construction	...	...	...	...	...	...	...	...	...
D Transportation and communication	12.7	7.1	5.6	...	-	12.8	10.8	...	23.5
E Other economic affairs [a]	22.9	7.8	15.1	...	-	22.9	0.1	-0.2	22.7
10 Other functions	-	-	-	...	36.6	36.6	-	...	36.6
Total	218.8	159.1	59.7	6.3	65.1	290.2	20.2	8.9	319.3
1983									
1 General public services	29.4	23.2	6.2	7.5	11.9	48.8	1.0	3.5	53.3
2 Defence	8.5	4.9	3.5	...	-	8.5	-	...	8.5
3 Public order and safety	31.8	26.8	5.0	...	0.1	31.9	0.4	...	32.2
4 Education	70.0	59.8	10.2	...	7.0	77.1	4.3	...	81.4
5 Health	50.2	39.5	10.7	...	0.1	50.3	0.5	...	50.7
6 Social security and welfare	6.8	4.6	2.2	...	18.7	25.5	2.0	...	27.5
7 Housing and community amenities	0.4	0.3	0.1	...	-	0.4	-	...	0.4
8 Recreation, culture and religion	2.8	2.2	0.7	...	0.1	2.9	0.2	...	3.1
9 Economic services	50.7	20.6	30.1	0.1	0.1	50.9	6.4	0.1	57.4

Bahamas

2.3 Total Government Outlays by Function and Type
(Continued)

Million Bahamian dollars

	Final Consumption Expenditures Total	Compensation of Employees	Other	Subsidies	Other Current Transfers & Property Income	Total Current Disbursements	Gross Capital Formation	Other Capital Outlays	Total Outlays
A Fuel and energy	...	...	...	...	...	...	...	...	...
B Agriculture, forestry, fishing and hunting	5.5	4.3	1.3	0.1	-	5.7	2.8	...	8.5
C Mining (except fuels), manufacturing and construction	...	...	...	...	...	...	...	...	...
D Transportation and communication	13.4	7.6	5.7	...	-	13.4	3.5	0.1	17.1
E Other economic affairs [a]	31.8	8.7	23.1	...	-	31.8	0.1	...	31.8
10 Other functions	-	-	-	...	40.2	40.2	-	...	40.2
Total	250.6	182.0	68.6	7.5	78.3	336.4	14.8	3.6	354.8
1984									
1 General public services	32.5	27.9	4.6	6.3	13.1	51.8	1.2	5.0	58.0
2 Defence	9.4	4.9	4.5	...	-	9.4	-	...	9.4
3 Public order and safety	34.0	29.3	4.7	...	0.2	34.1	0.6	...	34.7
4 Education	73.4	67.9	5.4	...	9.5	82.9	2.9	...	85.9
5 Health	53.9	42.3	11.6	...	0.2	54.1	0.9	...	55.0
6 Social security and welfare	6.6	4.7	1.9	...	17.4	24.0	0.8	...	24.8
7 Housing and community amenities	0.3	0.2	0.1	...	0.1	0.4	-	...	0.4
8 Recreation, culture and religion	3.1	2.2	0.8	...	0.3	3.3	0.3	...	3.6
9 Economic services	54.4	24.0	30.4	-	0.9	55.3	6.0	0.9	62.2
A Fuel and energy	...	...	...	...	...	...	...	...	...
B Agriculture, forestry, fishing and hunting	5.9	4.9	1.1	...	0.2	6.1	1.3	...	7.4
C Mining (except fuels), manufacturing and construction	...	...	...	...	...	...	...	...	...
D Transportation and communication	15.9	9.0	6.9	...	0.3	16.2	4.5	0.9	21.6
E Other economic affairs [a]	32.6	10.1	22.5	...	0.4	33.0	0.1	...	33.1
10 Other functions	-	-	-	...	43.4	43.4	-	-	43.4
Total	267.6	203.4	64.1	6.3	84.9	358.8	12.6	5.9	377.4
1985									
1 General public services	35.7	30.1	5.7	4.4	13.8	53.9	1.0	5.0	59.9
2 Defence	10.4	5.3	5.1	...	-	10.4	-	...	10.4
3 Public order and safety	37.4	31.6	5.8	...	0.2	37.6	0.5	...	38.0
4 Education	80.8	73.3	7.5	...	10.4	91.2	2.5	...	93.6
5 Health	59.3	45.6	13.7	...	0.2	59.5	0.7	...	60.3
6 Social security and welfare	7.2	5.0	2.2	...	18.5	25.7	0.7	...	26.4
7 Housing and community amenities	0.4	0.2	0.2	...	-	0.4	-	...	0.4
8 Recreation, culture and religion	3.4	2.4	1.0	...	0.3	3.7	0.3	...	3.9
9 Economic services	59.9	25.9	34.0	-	0.2	60.1	5.0	0.9	65.9
A Fuel and energy	...	...	...	...	...	...	...	...	...
B Agriculture, forestry, fishing and hunting	6.5	5.3	1.2	...	-	6.7	1.1	...	7.8
C Mining (except fuels), manufacturing and construction	...	...	...	...	...	...	...	...	...
D Transportation and communication	17.5	9.7	7.8	...	-	17.5	3.8	0.9	22.2
E Other economic affairs [a]	35.9	11.0	24.9	...	-	35.9	0.1	...	36.0
10 Other functions	-	-	-	...	49.6	49.6	-	...	49.6
Total	294.4	219.5	75.0	4.4	93.1	391.9	10.5	5.9	408.4
1986									
1 General public services	37.2	31.1	6.1	5.1	14.7	57.0	0.8	5.0	62.8
2 Defence	10.8	5.4	5.3	...	-	10.8	-	...	10.8
3 Public order and safety	38.9	32.7	6.2	...	0.2	39.0	0.4	...	39.4
4 Education	84.0	75.8	8.3	...	10.7	94.7	2.0	...	96.7
5 Health	61.7	47.2	14.5	...	0.2	61.9	0.6	...	62.5
6 Social security and welfare	7.5	5.2	2.3	...	19.6	27.1	0.5	...	27.6
7 Housing and community amenities	0.4	0.2	0.1	...	0.3	0.6	-	...	0.6
8 Recreation, culture and religion	3.5	2.5	1.0	...	0.3	3.8	0.2	...	4.0
9 Economic services	62.3	26.8	35.5	-	2.7	65.0	4.0	0.9	69.8

Bahamas

2.3 Total Government Outlays by Function and Type
(Continued)

Million Bahamian dollars

	Final Consumption Expenditures Total	Compensation of Employees	Other	Subsidies	Other Current Transfers & Property Income	Total Current Disbursements	Gross Capital Formation	Other Capital Outlays	Total Outlays
A Fuel and energy	...	...	...		...	...	...		...
B Agriculture, forestry, fishing and hunting	6.8	5.4	1.4		0.2	7.0	0.9	...	7.9
C Mining (except fuels), manufacturing and construction	...	...	...		...	...	...		...
D Transportation and communication	18.2	10.0	8.2		-	18.2	3.0	0.9	22.1
E Other economic affairs [a]	37.4	11.4	26.0		2.5	39.9	-	...	39.9
10 Other functions	-	-	-	...	46.9	46.9	-	...	46.9
Total	306.3	226.8	79.5	5.1	95.4	406.8	8.4	5.9	421.1
				1987					
1 General public services	40.5	34.4	6.1	5.5	14.0	60.0	0.6	5.0	65.6
2 Defence	11.7	6.0	5.7	...	-	11.7	-	...	11.7
3 Public order and safety	42.4	36.1	6.2	...	0.2	42.5	0.3	...	42.8
4 Education	91.5	83.8	7.7	...	10.2	101.7	1.5	...	103.2
5 Health	67.3	52.2	15.1	...	0.2	67.4	0.4	...	67.8
6 Social security and welfare	8.2	5.8	2.4	...	18.6	26.8	0.4	...	27.2
7 Housing and community amenities	0.4	0.3	0.1	...	0.7	1.1	-	...	1.1
8 Recreation, culture and religion	3.8	2.8	1.0	...	0.3	4.1	0.2	...	4.3
9 Economic services	67.9	29.6	38.3	-	6.4	74.3	2.9	0.9	78.1
A Fuel and energy	...	...	...		...	...	...		...
B Agriculture, forestry, fishing and hunting	7.4	6.0	1.4		0.2	7.5	0.7	...	8.2
C Mining (except fuels), manufacturing and construction									
D Transportation and communication	19.8	11.0	8.8		2.8	22.6	2.2	0.9	25.7
E Other economic affairs [a]	40.7	12.5	28.1	...	3.5	44.1	0.1	...	44.2
10 Other functions	-	-	-	...	40.3	40.3	-	...	40.3
Total	333.8	250.9	82.9	5.5	90.8	430.1	6.3	5.9	442.3
				1988					
1 General public services	36.5	35.7	0.8	5.9	15.3	57.6	2.5	5.7	65.8
2 Defence	16.7	11.6	5.1	...	0.5	17.1	...	...	17.1
3 Public order and safety	51.4	40.7	10.7	...	0.7	52.1	3.1	0.1	55.3
4 Education	91.5	80.4	11.1	...	9.4	100.9	7.4	1.1	109.3
5 Health	82.7	60.9	21.8	...	0.2	83.0	6.3	0.1	89.4
6 Social security and welfare	14.8	11.0	3.8	...	32.3	47.1	0.4	1.3	48.8
7 Housing and community amenities	0.6	0.6	-	...	0.1	0.7	-	...	0.7
8 Recreation, culture and religion	5.6	4.2	1.4	...	0.3	5.9	0.2	0.4	6.5
9 Economic services	70.4	30.8	39.6	-	0.2	70.6	14.7	2.6	87.9
A Fuel and energy	...	...	...		...	...	...		...
B Agriculture, forestry, fishing and hunting	7.5	6.1	1.4		0.1	7.6	0.9	...	8.5
C Mining (except fuels), manufacturing and construction	...	...	...		...	...	...		...
D Transportation and communication	21.9	11.9	10.0		0.1	22.0	13.6	0.1	35.7
E Other economic affairs [a]	41.0	12.7	28.2	...	-	41.0	0.2	2.5	43.7
10 Other functions	-	-	-	...	46.1	46.1	-	...	46.1
Total	370.1	275.9	94.3	5.9	105.2	481.2	34.4	11.2	526.8

a) Tourism is included in item 'Other functions' in table 2.1. It is included in 'Other economic affairs' in table 2.3.

2.5 Private Final Consumption Expenditure by Type and Purpose, in Current Prices

Million Bahamian dollars

	1970	1975	1980	1981	1982	1983	1984	1985	1986	1987	1988	1989
			Final Consumption Expenditure of Resident Households									
1 Food, beverages and tobacco	...	...	115.6	136.2	149.1	155.8	165.2	168.7	222.4	248.1	226.9	...
A Food	...	...	100.3	118.1	129.4	135.0	143.2	146.1	192.9	215.3	196.8	...
B Non-alcoholic beverages	...	...	10.6	12.5	13.7	14.3	15.2	15.5	20.5	22.8	20.9	...
C Alcoholic beverages	...	...	3.1	3.6	4.0	4.2	4.4	4.5	6.0	6.6	6.1	...
D Tobacco	...	...	1.7	1.9	2.1	2.3	2.4	2.6	3.1	3.4	3.2	...

Bahamas

2.5 Private Final Consumption Expenditure by Type and Purpose, in Current Prices
(Continued)

Million Bahamian dollars

	1970	1975	1980	1981	1982	1983	1984	1985	1986	1987	1988	1989
2 Clothing and footwear	...	...	42.1	46.9	56.5	56.4	62.1	63.8	71.6	82.6	81.7	...
3 Gross rent, fuel and power	...	...	154.5	160.8	174.0	192.9	210.6	225.8	238.7	251.8	266.1	...
A Fuel and power	...	...	43.7	42.7	42.7	52.1	53.2	52.8	51.4	49.2	48.7	...
B Other	...	...	110.8	118.1	131.2	140.7	157.4	173.0	187.3	202.5	217.4	...
4 Furniture, furnishings and household equipment and operation	...	...	59.1	67.4	81.3	80.8	88.0	92.4	109.2	120.2	115.2	...
A Household operation	...	...	59.1	67.4	81.3	80.8	88.0	92.4	109.2	120.2	115.2	...
B Other	...	...	...	...	...	...	...	...	...	...	...	...
5 Medical care and health expenses	...	...	20.4	23.5	25.7	27.7	31.7	32.5	38.4	41.9	38.9	...
6 Transport and communication	...	...	106.4	106.7	121.9	138.2	157.2	176.9	179.3	216.3	214.4	...
A Personal transport equipment	...	...	36.1	29.8	38.7	46.3	57.0	72.2	56.7	75.6	78.9	...
B Other	...	...	70.2	76.9	83.1	92.0	100.2	104.7	122.6	140.7	135.5	...
7 Recreational, entertainment, education and cultural services	...	...	83.1	93.8	99.1	108.5	117.5	125.0	142.1	156.3	148.0	...
A Education	...	...	49.7	55.5	58.4	63.8	69.4	74.2	83.8	94.0	87.9	...
B Other	...	...	33.4	38.3	40.8	44.7	48.1	50.7	58.3	62.3	60.2	...
8 Miscellaneous goods and services	...	...	16.4	18.7	20.3	22.2	23.8	25.5	30.5	32.9	41.5	...
A Personal care	...	...	10.8	12.3	13.4	14.6	15.6	16.8	20.1	21.6	20.8	...
B Expenditures in restaurants, cafes and hotels	...	...	...	...	...	...	...	...	...	...	...	...
C Other	...	...	5.6	6.4	6.9	7.6	8.1	8.7	10.4	11.2	20.7	...
Total Final Consumption Expenditure in the Domestic Market by Households, of which [a]	...	...	597.6	653.9	727.9	782.3	856.1	910.4	1032.1	1150.0	1132.8	...
Plus: Direct purchases abroad by resident households	...	...	70.7	91.2	104.3	95.5	105.7	124.4	132.1	152.7	171.6	...
Less: Direct purchases in the domestic market by non-resident households	...	...	666.6	715.8	732.2	766.4	796.9	990.3	1099.8	1170.3	1130.5	...
Equals: Final Consumption Expenditure of Resident Households	...	...	597.6	653.9	727.9	782.3	856.1	910.4	1032.1	1150.0	1132.8	...

Final Consumption Expenditure of Private Non-profit Institutions Serving Households

	1970	1975	1980	1981	1982	1983	1984	1985	1986	1987	1988	1989
Equals: Final Consumption Expenditure of Private Non-profit Organisations Serving Households	...	...	...	...	...	...	...	...	...	...	...	...
Private Final Consumption Expenditure	...	...	597.6	653.9	727.9	782.3	856.1	910.4	1032.1	1150.0	1132.8	...

a) The breakdowns of total final consumption expenditure in the domestic market by household include the purchase abroad by residents households and purchases in the domestic market by non-residential households.

2.17 Exports and Imports of Goods and Services, Detail

Million Bahamian dollars

	1970	1975	1980	1981	1982	1983	1984	1985	1986	1987	1988	1989
Exports of Goods and Services												
1 Exports of merchandise, f.o.b.	...	57.7	138.9	156.3	186.3	215.3	244.8	291.3	310.8	401.7	436.9	...
2 Transport and communication	...	91.6	207.8	186.5	132.4	139.6	125.2	113.3	84.9	90.5	76.9	...
3 Insurance service charges	...	...	...	...	...	...	...	...	...	...	...	...
4 Other commodities	...	...	...	...	...	...	...	...	...	...	...	...
5 Adjustments of merchandise exports to change-of-ownership basis												
6 Direct purchases in the domestic market by non-residential households	...	312.7	666.6	715.8	732.2	766.4	796.9	990.3	1099.8	1170.3	1130.5	...
7 Direct purchases in the domestic market by extraterritorial bodies	...	61.7	143.3	141.8	139.0	116.9	126.3	117.0	109.6	110.5	119.5	...
Total Exports of Goods and Services	...	523.7	1156.6	1200.4	1189.8	1238.2	1293.2	1511.9	1605.1	1773.0	1763.8	...
Imports of Goods and Services												
1 Imports of merchandise, c.i.f.	...	285.8	581.9	612.8	646.7	744.4	818.7	904.0	919.5	1044.9	914.3	...

Bahamas

2.17 Exports and Imports of Goods and Services, Detail
(Continued)

Million Bahamian dollars

	1970	1975	1980	1981	1982	1983	1984	1985	1986	1987	1988	1989
2 Adjustments of merchandise imports to change-of-ownership basis	...	...	...	...	...	...	...	...	...	...	...	...
3 Other transport and communication	...	22.8	37.0	41.6	46.1	42.9	44.3	54.8	60.4	66.7	69.6	...
4 Other insurance service charges	...	...	...	...	...	...	...	...	...	...	...	...
5 Other commodities	...	50.1	99.1	114.8	138.6	156.9	137.6	156.2	169.2	187.3	191.4	...
6 Direct purchases abroad by government	...	...	...	...	...	...	...	...	...	...	...	...
7 Direct purchases abroad by resident households	...	45.6	70.7	91.2	104.3	95.5	105.7	124.4	132.1	152.7	171.6	...
Total Imports of Goods and Services	...	404.3	788.7	860.4	935.7	1039.7	1106.3	1239.4	1281.3	1451.6	1346.9	...
Balance of Goods and Services	...	119.4	367.9	340.0	254.2	198.5	187.0	272.5	323.8	321.3	416.9	...
Total Imports and Balance of Goods and Services	...	523.7	1156.6	1200.4	1189.8	1238.2	1293.2	1511.9	1605.1	1773.0	1763.8	...

Bahrain

Source. The estimates are published by the Ministry of Finance and National Economy in the National Accounts of Bahrain.
General note. The estimates shown in the following tables have been prepared by the Statistics Department in accordance with the United Nations System of National Accounts so far as the existing data would permit.

1.1 Expenditure on the Gross Domestic Product, in Current Prices

Million Bahraini dinars

	1970	1975	1980	1981	1982	1983	1984	1985	1986	1987	1988	1989
1 Government final consumption expenditure	...	55.4	150.9	188.6	233.3	254.5	302.2	312.8	312.4	310.9	339.9	356.7
2 Private final consumption expenditure		152.5	370.3	427.7	472.9	481.6	502.2	450.5	408.3	453.5	514.2	540.6
3 Gross capital formation		85.4	520.6	540.7	508.9	618.5	590.4	465.8	280.6	304.0	231.3	368.2
A Increase in stocks		-8.9	163.7	160.2	57.0	42.4	-45.6	-22.0	-110.2	-55.2	-113.5	-2.0
B Gross fixed capital formation		94.3	356.9	380.5	451.9	576.1	636.0	487.8	390.8	359.2	344.8	370.2
4 Exports of goods and services		521.5	1421.1	1714.0	1621.0	1344.2	1455.0	1397.4	1133.8	1216.5	1228.6	1300.0
5 Less: Imports of goods and services		432.5	1304.8	1567.3	1465.5	1294.4	1381.3	1233.6	936.9	1093.1	1051.1	1218.0
Equals: Gross Domestic Product		382.3	1158.1	1303.9	1370.8	1404.4	1468.5	1392.9	1198.2	1191.8	1262.9	1347.5

1.2 Expenditure on the Gross Domestic Product, in Constant Prices

Million Bahraini dinars

	1970	1975	1980	1981	1982	1983	1984	1985	1986	1987	1988	1989
					At constant prices of: 1985							
1 Government final consumption expenditure	...	123.0	202.5	220.1	252.9	264.4	294.6	312.8	344.0	354.9	383.4	382.4
2 Private final consumption expenditure		331.6	451.0	451.1	478.2	476.4	486.6	450.5	414.5	467.5	530.7	549.1
3 Gross capital formation		163.2	761.9	687.2	488.6	613.1	579.3	465.8	366.9	377.1	384.4	517.2
A Increase in stocks		25.1	438.6	360.9	108.5	128.3	29.9	-22.0	-72.8	-37.2	-10.6	103.4
B Gross fixed capital formation		138.1	323.3	326.3	380.1	484.8	549.4	487.8	439.7	414.3	395.0	413.7
4 Exports of goods and services		1131.9	1330.1	1445.6	1375.0	1266.4	1415.9	1397.4	1639.9	1605.7	1651.3	1633.3
5 Less: Imports of goods and services		859.5	1301.8	1438.2	1334.1	1265.3	1356.2	1233.6	1356.6	1403.9	1455.5	1551.5
Equals: Gross Domestic Product		890.2	1443.7	1365.8	1260.6	1354.8	1420.2	1392.9	1408.7	1401.3	1494.3	1530.5

1.3 Cost Components of the Gross Domestic Product

Million Bahraini dinars

	1970	1975	1980	1981	1982	1983	1984	1985	1986	1987	1988	1989
1 Indirect taxes, net	...	11.8	39.9	49.8	60.0	62.1	57.6	44.1	26.3	27.7	32.6	34.2
2 Consumption of fixed capital		48.1	120.6	135.5	149.0	166.9	199.1	203.9	210.0	208.8	225.9	224.6
3 Compensation of employees paid by resident producers to:		106.8	355.6	405.4	474.0	527.6	591.2	594.5	597.4	593.5	612.5	641.0
4 Operating surplus		215.6	642.0	713.2	687.8	647.8	620.6	550.4	364.6	361.8	391.9	447.7
Equals: Gross Domestic Product		382.3	1158.1	1303.9	1370.8	1404.4	1468.5	1392.9	1198.2	1191.8	1262.9	1347.5

1.7 External Transactions on Current Account, Summary

Million Bahraini dinars

	1970	1975	1980	1981	1982	1983	1984	1985	1986	1987	1988	1989
			Payments to the Rest of the World									
1 Imports of goods and services	...	...	1304.8	1567.3	1465.5	1294.4	1381.3	1233.6	936.9	1093.1	1051.1	1218.0
A Imports of merchandise c.i.f.	...	...	1281.2	1484.1	1321.6	1237.4	1305.1	1167.6	904.8	1021.5	919.6	1120.0
B Other	...	...	23.6	83.2	143.9	57.0	76.2	66.0	32.1	71.6	131.5	98.0
2 Factor income to the rest of the world	...	...	252.1	305.4	381.9	330.4	406.4	408.9	353.3	312.3	381.6	347.9
A Compensation of employees	...	...	88.3	98.0	99.5	92.2	102.5	206.9	191.1	179.9	178.4	186.2
B Property and entrepreneurial income	...	...	163.8	207.4	282.4	238.2	303.9	202.0	162.2	132.4	203.2	161.7
By general government	...	...	11.6	27.5	24.1	11.9	21.5	5.8	3.0	3.5	6.2	4.7
By corporate and quasi-corporate enterprises	...	...	105.2	145.8	194.0	203.9	229.3	157.4	106.3	80.0	147.6	100.8
By other	...	...	46.0	34.1	64.3	22.4	53.1	38.8	52.9	48.9	49.4	56.2
3 Current transfers to the rest of the world	...	...	...	...	...	...	...	...	...	...	...	...
4 Surplus of the nation on current transactions	...	...	68.7	131.7	117.5	-49.4	-31.0	-34.2	-15.7	-75.9	-63.1	-91.4
Payments to the Rest of the World and Surplus of the Nation on Current Transactions [a]	...	...	...	...	...	...	...	...	...	...	...	...

Bahrain

1.7 External Transactions on Current Account, Summary
(Continued)

Million Bahraini dinars

	1970	1975	1980	1981	1982	1983	1984	1985	1986	1987	1988	1989
					Receipts From The Rest of the World							
1 Exports of goods and services	...	...	1421.1	1714.0	1621.0	1344.2	1455.0	1397.4	1133.8	1216.5	1228.6	1300.0
A Exports of merchandise f.o.b.	...	...	1310.5	1566.4	1399.3	1186.5	1166.6	1084.1	837.2	929.7	816.6	1022.8
B Other	...	...	110.6	147.6	221.7	157.7	288.4	313.3	296.6	286.8	412.0	277.2
2 Factor income from rest of the world	...	...	204.5	290.4	343.9	269.6	348.9	299.2	240.2	204.6	213.6	249.2
A Compensation of employees	...	...	-	-	-	-	-	-	-	-	-	-
B Property and entrepreneurial income	...	...	204.5	290.4	343.9	269.6	348.9	299.2	240.2	204.6	213.6	249.2
By general government	...	...	16.3	41.6	46.3	30.0	33.6	31.3	27.3	24.0	13.4	35.7
By corporate and quasi-corporate enterprises	...	...	38.2	53.8	97.6	5.7	34.8	23.3	14.2	26.7	35.4	73.8
By other	...	...	150.0	195.0	200.0	233.9	280.5	244.6	198.7	153.9	164.8	139.7
3 Current transfers from rest of the world [b]	...	...	-	-	-	-38.4	-47.2	-88.3	-99.5	-91.6	-72.6	-74.7
A Subsidies from supranational organisations	...	...	...	...	...	...	...	...	...	...	...	...
B Other current transfers	...	...	-	-	-	-38.4	-47.2	-88.3	-99.5	-91.6	-72.6	-74.7
Receipts from the Rest of the World on Current Transactions [a]	...	...	...	...	...	...	...	...	...	...	...	...

a) Estimates are derived from Balance of Payment Accounts, therefore are not strictly comparable to those in other tables.
b) Current transfers from the rest of the world is net of current transfers to the rest of the world.

1.10 Gross Domestic Product by Kind of Activity, in Current Prices

Million Bahraini dinars

	1970	1975	1980	1981	1982	1983	1984	1985	1986	1987	1988	1989
1 Agriculture, hunting, forestry and fishing	...	4.2	11.4	13.2	14.5	16.2	16.4	16.4	16.4	16.0	15.4	15.8
2 Mining and quarrying	...	123.0	403.4	430.8	402.5	350.4	355.7	398.6	231.7	225.0	196.0	236.4
3 Manufacturing	...	63.8	187.9	202.3	170.1	167.2	182.8	138.8	166.1	191.0	235.3	239.8
4 Electricity, gas and water	...	1.2	12.0	15.5	19.0	22.0	24.5	25.5	20.9	21.9	23.2	27.8
5 Construction	...	25.7	81.0	105.1	133.3	137.2	156.7	133.7	102.8	86.8	90.1	87.6
6 Wholesale and retail trade, restaurants and hotels	...	48.7	135.3	139.8	158.7	177.3	141.9	119.5	108.9	117.8	135.5	137.0
7 Transport, storage and communication	...	26.9	101.1	125.3	158.4	183.3	182.3	165.9	147.9	139.9	147.3	152.5
8 Finance, insurance, real estate and business services	...	33.5	164.8	252.7	350.3	356.2	378.9	318.2	275.3	214.0	238.6	213.5
9 Community, social and personal services	...	15.5	39.1	45.4	45.3	52.3	55.8	62.0	61.1	63.8	69.5	70.4
Total, Industries	...	342.5	1136.0	1330.1	1452.1	1462.1	1495.0	1378.6	1131.1	1076.2	1150.9	1180.8
Producers of Government Services	...	48.2	135.4	156.3	186.1	205.9	241.1	253.7	261.3	271.3	288.0	299.6
Other Producers	...	...	...	...	...	...	...	...	...	...	...	...
Subtotal	...	390.7	1271.4	1486.4	1638.2	1668.0	1736.1	1632.3	1392.4	1347.5	1438.9	1480.4
Less: Imputed bank service charge	...	8.4	113.8	182.5	267.4	263.6	267.6	239.4	194.2	155.7	176.0	132.9
Plus: Import duties	...	...	...	...	...	...	...	...	...	...	...	...
Plus: Value added tax	...	...	...	...	...	...	...	...	...	...	...	...
Equals: Gross Domestic Product	...	382.3	1158.1	1303.9	1370.8	1404.4	1468.5	1392.9	1198.2	1191.8	1262.9	1347.5

1.11 Gross Domestic Product by Kind of Activity, in Constant Prices

Million Bahraini dinars

	1970	1975	1980	1981	1982	1983	1984	1985	1986	1987	1988	1989
					At constant prices of: 1985							
1 Agriculture, hunting, forestry and fishing	...	12.5	14.5	15.8	17.0	16.4	16.0	16.4	17.4	17.4	15.7	16.4
2 Mining and quarrying	...	417.5	641.4	553.8	346.0	356.5	400.9	398.6	416.1	366.1	369.6	384.0
3 Manufacturing	...	117.6	126.5	135.1	139.0	139.9	155.1	138.8	139.3	155.8	166.6	166.7
4 Electricity, gas and water	...	3.5	15.3	16.8	19.0	21.3	23.6	25.5	21.4	21.9	24.1	30.5
5 Construction	...	32.3	79.7	70.6	90.3	119.4	118.0	133.7	108.0	105.1	119.4	112.1
6 Wholesale and retail trade, restaurants and hotels	...	71.9	139.0	143.6	165.2	186.5	152.1	119.5	112.9	128.3	147.1	149.9
7 Transport, storage and communication	...	45.7	148.8	139.5	164.2	171.4	179.9	165.9	145.3	143.3	159.9	158.6
8 Finance, insurance, real estate and business services	...	51.7	121.4	150.0	237.6	301.2	294.9	318.2	315.4	256.2	271.0	211.7
9 Community, social and personal services	...	27.7	42.1	49.3	49.7	55.5	58.9	62.0	67.4	73.0	78.8	81.7

Bahrain

1.11 Gross Domestic Product by Kind of Activity, in Constant Prices
(Continued)

Million Bahraini dinars

	1970	1975	1980	1981	1982	1983	1984	1985	1986	1987	1988	1989
					At constant prices of:1985							
Total, Industries	...	780.4	1328.7	1274.7	1228.2	1368.1	1399.1	1378.6	1343.4	1267.0	1352.2	1311.6
Producers of Government Services	...	119.1	188.1	186.9	209.1	220.0	238.3	253.7	291.0	313.1	328.3	337.7
Other Producers	...	...	...	...	...	...	...	...	...	...	...	...
Subtotal	...	899.5	1516.8	1461.6	1437.3	1588.1	1637.4	1632.3	1634.4	1580.1	1680.5	1649.3
Less: Imputed bank service charge	...	9.3	72.7	95.9	176.7	233.3	217.2	239.4	225.6	178.8	186.2	118.8
Plus: Import duties	...	...	...	...	...	...	...	...	...	...	...	...
Plus: Value added tax	...	...	...	...	...	...	...	...	...	...	...	...
Equals: Gross Domestic Product	...	890.2	1443.7	1365.7	1260.6	1354.8	1420.2	1392.9	1408.8	1401.3	1494.3	1530.5

1.12 Relations Among National Accounting Aggregates

Million Bahraini dinars

	1970	1975	1980	1981	1982	1983	1984	1985	1986	1987	1988	1989
Gross Domestic Product	...	382.3	1158.1	1303.9	1370.8	1404.4	1468.5	1392.9	1198.2	1191.8	1262.9	1347.5
Plus: Net factor income from the rest of the world	...	-189.4	-107.1	-62.0	-67.6	-125.7	-131.0	-111.3	-113.1	-210.2	-272.9	-98.7
Equals: Gross National Product	...	192.9	1051.0	1240.9	1303.2	1278.7	1337.5	1281.6	1085.1	981.6	990.0	1248.8
Less: Consumption of fixed capital	...	48.1	120.6	135.5	149.0	166.8	199.0	203.9	210.0	208.8	225.9	224.6
Equals: National Income	...	144.8	930.4	1105.4	1154.2	1111.9	1138.5	1077.7	875.1	772.8	764.1	1024.2
Plus: Net current transfers from the rest of the world	...	...	...	...	...	...	...	...	...	...	...	...
Equals: National Disposable Income	...	...	...	...	...	...	...	...	...	...	...	...
Less: Final consumption	...	...	...	...	...	...	...	...	...	...	...	...
Equals: Net Saving	...	...	...	...	...	...	...	...	...	...	...	...
Less: Surplus of the nation on current transactions	...	...	...	...	...	...	...	...	...	...	...	...
Equals: Net Capital Formation	...	...	...	...	...	...	...	...	...	...	...	...

Bangladesh

Source. Reply to the United Nations National Accounts Questionnaire from the Bureau of Statistics, Dhake.
General note. The estimates shown in the following tables have been prepared by the Bureau of Statistics in accordance with the United Nations System of National Acounts so far as the existing data would permit.

1.1 Expenditure on the Gross Domestic Product, in Current Prices

Million Bangladesh taka — Fiscal year beginning 1 July

		1970	1975	1980	1981	1982	1983	1984	1985	1986	1987	1988	1989
1	Government final consumption expenditure	...	4493	15640	15911	16768	24012	29793	38083	40143	48555	62430	...
2	Private final consumption expenditure	...	110839	221131	256732	288685	340573	404669	442204	514396	559334	614815	...
3	Gross capital formation	...	10947	37232	39837	39212	43081	52102	57267	67577	71857	80708	...
	A Increase in stocks	...	-1202	301	455	581	1529	914	-1089	2522	-465	1499	...
	B Gross fixed capital formation	...	12149	36931	39382	38631	41552	51188	58356	65055	72322	79209	...
4	Exports of goods and services [a]	...	5242	16977	18842	24081	26065	31189	33856	37587	45015	51185	...
5	Less: Imports of goods and services [b]	...	19479	46708	57661	61775	64952	74361	77314	88112	101583	118958	...
	Equals: Gross Domestic Product	...	112042	244272	273661	306971	368779	443392	494096	571602	623178	690180	...

a) Item 'Exports of goods and services' refers to exports of goods and non-factor services.
b) Item 'Imports of goods and services' refers to imports of goods and non-factor services.

1.2 Expenditure on the Gross Domestic Product, in Constant Prices

Million Bangladesh taka — Fiscal year beginning 1 July

At constant prices of: 1972

		1970	1975	1980	1981	1982	1983	1984	1985	1986	1987	1988	1989
1	Government final consumption expenditure	...	2488	4036	3573	3477	3624	3835	...	...	...	...	...
2	Private final consumption expenditure	...	57301	62847	63007	61990	64633	68374	...	...	...	...	...
3	Gross capital formation	...	3028	6501	6386	6705	8702	8790	...	...	...	...	...
	A Increase in stocks	...	111	664	-486	198	-382	-225	...	...	...	...	...
	B Gross fixed capital formation	...	2917	5837	6872	6507	9084	9015	...	...	...	...	...
4	Exports of goods and services	...	2651	5907	7708	9748	9070	8618	...	...	...	...	...
5	Less: Imports of goods and services	...	6782	7647	8447	7085	8026	9195	...	...	...	...	...
	Equals: Gross Domestic Product [a]	...	58686	71644	72227	74835	78003	80422	...	...	...	...	...

a) Data for this table have not been revised, therefore, data for some years are not comparable with those of other tables.

1.10 Gross Domestic Product by Kind of Activity, in Current Prices

Million Bangladesh taka — Fiscal year beginning 1 July

		1970	1975	1980	1981	1982	1983	1984	1985	1986	1987	1988	1989
1	Agriculture, hunting, forestry and fishing	...	57339	108953	121839	135871	169328	212494	222407	259930	268588	287999	336598
2	Mining and quarrying	...	2	3	6	3	4	4	8	6	3	4	4
3	Manufacturing	...	8173	22861	25702	28070	30945	34632	37335	40208	43420	47969	55624
4	Electricity, gas and water	...	189	744	959	1612	1939	2348	2713	3545	4597	6719	7970
5	Construction	...	5514	13088	15863	15028	18095	22518	26058	28829	34602	39262	43675
6	Wholesale and retail trade, restaurants and hotels [a]	...	11120	20808	22337	25731	32945	38816	41505	45883	50369	55051	61386
7	Transport, storage and communication	...	10300	28677	32040	39866	41797	45655	54605	61901	65945	71774	75301
8	Finance, insurance, real estate and business services	...	10355	24044	25620	26598	33710	39333	46001	51104	61417	72992	80623
9	Community, social and personal services [a]	...	6122	18481	22626	25459	31082	34357	46098	59329	69502	79207	92317

Bangladesh

1.10 Gross Domestic Product by Kind of Activity, in Current Prices
(Continued)

Million Bangladesh taka — Fiscal year beginning 1 July

	1970	1975	1980	1981	1982	1983	1984	1985	1986	1987	1988	1989
Total, Industries	...	109114	237659	266992	298238	359845	430157	476730	550735	598443	660977	753498
Producers of Government Services	...	2928	6613	6669	8734	8934	13235	17366	20867	24735	29203	34023
Other Producers	...	...	...	...	...	...	...	...	...	...	...	...
Subtotal	...	112042	244272	273661	306971	368779	443392	494096	571602	623178	690180	787521
Less: Imputed bank service charge	...	...	...	...	...	...	...	...	...	...	...	...
Plus: Import duties	...	...	...	...	...	...	...	...	...	...	...	...
Plus: Value added tax	...	...	...	...	...	...	...	...	...	...	...	...
Equals: Gross Domestic Product	...	112042	244272	273661	306971	368779	443392	494096	571602	623178	690180	787521

a) Restaurants and hotels are included in item 'Community, social and personal services'.

1.11 Gross Domestic Product by Kind of Activity, in Constant Prices

Million Bangladesh taka — Fiscal year beginning 1 July

	1970	1975	1980	1981	1982	1983	1984	1985	1986	1987	1988	1989
			At constant prices of: 1972									
1 Agriculture, hunting, forestry and fishing	...	31865	34908	35225	36851	37442	38622	40078	40025	39664	39529	43112
2 Mining and quarrying	...	1	1	2	1	1	1	2	1	1	3	3
3 Manufacturing	...	5877	7602	7722	7598	7875	8132	8282	8811	9051	9303	9977
4 Electricity, gas and water	...	135	250	296	453	485	526	592	721	839	1081	1136
5 Construction	...	1742	2845	3004	3038	3649	4095	4169	4449	4995	5239	5545
6 Wholesale and retail trade, restaurants and hotels [a]	...	5523	6866	6554	7024	7703	7935	8049	8256	8519	8929	9148
7 Transport, storage and communication	...	5907	7275	7546	8083	8417	8827	9133	10147	10492	10933	11483
8 Finance, insurance, real estate and business services	...	5695	7338	7433	7549	7812	8280	8891	9227	9487	9752	10023
9 Community, social and personal services [a]	...	3281	4910	5225	5565	5941	6339	6734	7149	7567	8040	8538
Total, Industries	...	60026	71995	73007	76162	79325	82757	85930	88786	90615	92809	98965
Producers of Government Services	...	1398	1911	1707	2091	1946	2580	3108	3352	3617	3869	4168
Other Producers	...	...	...	...	...	...	...	...	...	...	...	...
Subtotal	...	61424	73906	74714	78253	81271	85337	89038	92138	94232	96678	103133
Less: Imputed bank service charge	...	...	...	...	...	...	...	...	...	...	...	...
Plus: Import duties	...	...	...	...	...	...	...	...	...	...	...	...
Plus: Value added tax	...	...	...	...	...	...	...	...	...	...	...	...
Equals: Gross Domestic Product	...	61424	73906	74714	78253	81271	85337	89038	92138	94232	96678	103133

a) Restaurants and hotels are included in item 'Community, social and personal services'.

2.3 Total Government Outlays by Function and Type

Million Bangladesh taka — Fiscal year beginning 1 July

	Final Consumption Expenditures Total	Compensation of Employees	Other	Subsidies	Other Current Transfers & Property Income	Total Current Disbursements	Gross Capital Formation	Other Capital Outlays	Total Outlays
					1980				
1 General public services	1456	694	762	1728	1258	4442	186	1	4629
2 Defence	1636	852	784	-	1	1637	145	-	1782
3 Public order and safety	1144	674	470	81	-	1225	101	-	1326
4 Education	1252	1123	129	-	624	1876	323	20	2219
5 Health	954	506	448	-	11	965	451	14	1430

Bangladesh

2.3 Total Government Outlays by Function and Type
(Continued)

Million Bangladesh taka — Fiscal year beginning 1 July

		Final Consumption Expenditures Total	Compensation of Employees	Other	Subsidies	Other Current Transfers & Property Income	Total Current Disbursements	Gross Capital Formation	Other Capital Outlays	Total Outlays
6	Social security and welfare	165	65	100	2	49	216	143	-	359
7	Housing and community amenities	278	162	116	-	509	787	1183	56	2026
8	Recreation, culture and religion	3	2	1	-	-	3	-	-	3
9	Economic services	4187	726	3461	1452	917	6556	9573	85	16214
	A Fuel and energy	120	52	68	-	2	122	-	-	122
	B Agriculture, forestry, fishing and hunting	359	43	316	-	207	566	2739	44	3349
	C Mining (except fuels), manufacturing and construction	2760	345	2415	1446	66	4272	778	14	5064
	D Transportation and communication	508	120	388	6	564	1078	1616	17	2711
	E Other economic affairs	440	166	274	-	78	518	4440	10	4968
10	Other functions	1234	391	843	43	140	1417	2031	100	3548
	Total	12309	5195	7114	3306	3509	19124	14136	276	33536

1981

1	General public services	4675	1296	3379	1143	2026	7844	4049	129	12022
2	Defence	1949	1015	934	-	-	1949	169	-	2118
3	Public order and safety	1693	872	821	8	-	1701	19	-	1720
4	Education	1486	1224	262	-	846	2332	629	24	2985
5	Health	909	640	269	10	-	919	569	19	1507
6	Social security and welfare	226	87	139	-	21	247	121	4	372
7	Housing and community amenities	308	160	148	-	1067	1375	1226	15	2616
8	Recreation, culture and religion	38	3	35	-	37	75	-	-	75
9	Economic services	3905	999	2906	1467	693	6065	9019	141	15225
	A Fuel and energy	441	10	431	15	200	656	685	41	1382
	B Agriculture, forestry, fishing and hunting	2074	347	1727	1437	90	3601	1174	47	4822
	C Mining (except fuels), manufacturing and construction	665	218	447	15	324	1004	2132	37	3173
	D Transportation and communication	654	381	273	-	77	731	5028	16	5775
	E Other economic affairs	71	43	28	-	2	73	-	-	73
10	Other functions	...	...	...	...	...	...	...	...	...
	Total	15189	6296	8893	2628	4690	22507	15801	332	38640

1982

1	General public services	3416	1209	2207	1852	2734	8002	5789	143	13934
2	Defence	2524	1289	1235	-	-	2524	218	-	2742
3	Public order and safety	1581	868	713	166	1	1748	411	2	2161
4	Education	1718	1275	443	11	1029	2758	846	5	3609
5	Health	1295	576	720	-	16	1312	757	13	2082
6	Social security and welfare	215	71	144	-	27	242	127	2	371
7	Housing and community amenities	465	109	356	-	585	1050	510	-	1560
8	Recreation, culture and religion	46	15	31	-	39	85	-	-	85
9	Economic services	4208	945	3263	2314	1252	7774	8412	93	16279
	A Fuel and energy	673	153	520	-	36	709	1027	8	1744
	B Agriculture, forestry, fishing and hunting	2625	402	2223	2313	278	5216	1211	46	6473
	C Mining (except fuels), manufacturing and construction	303	128	175	1	298	602	1716	32	2350
	D Transportation and communication	532	211	321	-	633	1165	4458	7	5630
	E Other economic affairs	75	51	24	-	7	82	-	-	82
10	Other functions	...	...	...	...	...	...	...	...	...
	Total	15469	6357	9112	4343	5683	25495	17070	258	42823

1983

1	General public services	3966	1519	2447	2009	3306	9281	6128	159	15568
2	Defence	4222	2159	2063	4	1	4227	364	-	4591
3	Public order and safety	1887	1039	848	177	-	2064	346	-	2410
4	Education	2409	1794	615	5	1093	3507	1099	6	4612
5	Health	1436	643	793	-	17	1453	912	8	2373

Bangladesh

2.3 Total Government Outlays by Function and Type
(Continued)

Million Bangladesh taka
Fiscal year beginning 1 July

		Final Consumption Expenditures Total	Compensation of Employees	Other	Subsidies	Other Current Transfers & Property Income	Total Current Disbursements	Gross Capital Formation	Other Capital Outlays	Total Outlays
6	Social security and welfare	204	70	134	-	36	240	163	44	447
7	Housing and community amenities	429	135	294	-	505	934	409	-	1343
8	Recreation, culture and religion	103	24	79	-	70	173	-	-	173
9	Economic services	6682	1424	5258	1794	626	9102	10045	150	19297
	A Fuel and energy	745	450	295	-	4	749	1292	44	2085
	B Agriculture, forestry, fishing and hunting	4245	422	3823	1790	313	6348	1714	36	8098
	C Mining (except fuels), manufacturing and construction	919	213	706	4	272	1195	2324	24	3543
	D Transportation and communication	661	263	398	-	29	690	4715	46	5451
	E Other economic affairs	112	76	36	-	8	120	-	-	120
10	Other functions	...	...	...	...	...	...	...	...	...
	Total	21338	8807	12531	3989	5654	30981	19466	367	50814
	1984									
1	General public services	3761	1546	2216	2127	1131	7020	7381	337	14738
2	Defence	4270	2221	2049	-	2	4272	371	-	4643
3	Public order and safety	2176	976	1200	-	-	2176	420	2	2598
4	Education	1699	1262	437	1	506	2206	1033	1	3240
5	Health	2110	1041	1069	-	23	2133	721	1	2855
6	Social security and welfare	202	88	114	17	16	235	198	-	433
7	Housing and community amenities	603	112	491	-	1543	2146	1106	92	3344
8	Recreation, culture and religion	138	51	87	-	117	255	-	-	255
9	Economic services	8371	1242	7129	154	1324	9849	8148	71	18068
	A Fuel and energy	255	135	120	-	282	537	1384	22	1943
	B Agriculture, forestry, fishing and hunting	5801	638	5163	150	677	6628	1400	38	8066
	C Mining (except fuels), manufacturing and construction	689	116	573	3	365	1057	1899	2	2958
	D Transportation and communication	1264	267	997	1	-	1265	3465	9	4739
	E Other economic affairs	362	86	276	-	-	362	-	-	362
10	Other functions	...	...	...	...	...	...	...	...	...
	Total	23331	8539	14792	2299	4662	30292	19378	504	50174
	1985									
1	General public services	6261	5205	1056	2596	4987	13844	188	-	14032
2	Defence	897	897	-	-	2	899	239	-	1138
3	Public order and safety	432	432	-	-	-	432	405	-	837
4	Education	2771	2620	151	-	2020	4791	856	14	5661
5	Health	2575	1893	682	-	20	2595	1152	-	3747
6	Social security and welfare	248	175	73	-	26	274	93	8	375
7	Housing and community amenities	1026	399	627	-	-	1026	1208	17	2251
8	Recreation, culture and religion	135	135	-	-	-	135	332	3	470
9	Economic services	11811	11045	766	-	129	11940	18500	1343	31783
	A Fuel and energy	1034	1034	-	-	-	1034	8080	232	9346
	B Agriculture, forestry, fishing and hunting	7310	7107	203	-	57	7367	1117	851	9335
	C Mining (except fuels), manufacturing and construction	545	528	17	-	28	573	1426	204	2203
	D Transportation and communication	722	516	206	-	44	766	5035	22	5823
	E Other economic affairs	2200	1860	340	-	-	2200	2842	34	5076
10	Other functions	310	310	-	-	100	410	3	-	413
	Total	26466	23111	3355	2596	7284	36346	22976	1385	60707
	1986									
1	General public services	11160	2094	9066	1590	2856	15606	171	-	15777
2	Defence	5350	5349	1	-	-	5350	465	-	5815
3	Public order and safety	3093	1828	1265	-	1	3094	348	-	3442
4	Education	4163	3491	672	15	2437	6615	579	1	7195
5	Health	2503	1574	929	9	22	2534	1142	9	3685

Bangladesh

2.3 Total Government Outlays by Function and Type
(Continued)

Million Bangladesh taka
Fiscal year beginning 1 July

		Final Consumption Expenditures Total	Compensation of Employees	Other	Subsidies	Other Current Transfers & Property Income	Total Current Disbursements	Gross Capital Formation	Other Capital Outlays	Total Outlays
6	Social security and welfare	245	105	140	-	29	274	98	-	372
7	Housing and community amenities	1275	383	892	-	11	1286	1295	15	2596
8	Recreation, culture and religion	160	91	69	-	132	292	1	-	293
9	Economic services	7017	2625	4392	46	1401	8464	22759	335	31558
	A Fuel and energy	1308	187	1121	32	474	1814	10228	44	12086
	B Agriculture, forestry, fishing and hunting	3444	1599	1845	6	148	3598	3723	276	7597
	C Mining (except fuels), manufacturing and construction	1438	437	1001	8	209	1655	4682	10	6347
	D Transportation and communication	622	250	372	-	200	822	4126	5	4953
	E Other economic affairs	205	152	53	-	370	575	-	-	575
10	Other functions	50	25	25	-	7	57	98	-	155
	Total	35016	17565	17451	1660	6896	43572	26956	360	70888
	1987									
1	General public services	10481	2915	7566	697	2394	13572	133	-	13705
2	Defence	6677	3473	3204	-	2	6679	580	-	7259
3	Public order and safety	3517	2211	1306	-	1	3518	417	-	3935
4	Education	4698	3896	802	-	3386	8084	1164	33	9281
5	Health	2505	1672	833	12	34	2551	850	1	3402
6	Social security and welfare	382	187	195	-	36	418	151	21	590
7	Housing and community amenities	1078	290	788	-	19	1097	1433	7	2537
8	Recreation, culture and religion	179	109	70	-	205	384	1	-	385
9	Economic services	6150	2697	3453	53	1611	7814	28374	130	36318
	A Fuel and energy	1170	212	958	39	488	1697	13362	29	15088
	B Agriculture, forestry, fishing and hunting	2662	1585	1077	7	266	2935	2536	34	5505
	C Mining (except fuels), manufacturing and construction	1246	417	829	7	324	1577	6649	62	8288
	D Transportation and communication	852	331	521	-	73	925	5827	5	6757
	E Other economic affairs	220	152	68	-	460	680	-	-	680
10	Other functions	59	6	53	-	-	59	114	5	178
	Total	35726	17456	18270	762	7688	44176	33217	197	77590
	1988									
1	General public services	11855	3449	8406	824	3555	16234	241	4	16479
2	Defence	7510	3605	3905	-	-	7510	652	-	8162
3	Public order and safety	4287	2604	1683	-	-	4287	299	-	4586
4	Education	5533	5054	479	209	3746	9488	1433	2	10923
5	Health	3626	2664	962	-	3	3629	1066	2	4697
6	Social security and welfare	383	177	206	2	48	433	269	33	735
7	Housing and community amenities	1466	501	965	-	17	1483	2261	64	3808
8	Recreation, culture and religion	211	124	87	-	178	389	7	-	396
9	Economic services	7864	3611	4253	76	3387	11327	25989	359	37675
	A Fuel and energy	936	158	778	22	1709	2667	11378	93	14138
	B Agriculture, forestry, fishing and hunting	4345	2437	1908	50	399	4794	4177	175	9146
	C Mining (except fuels), manufacturing and construction	1444	400	1044	3	622	2069	3399	88	5556
	D Transportation and communication	897	433	464	1	224	1122	6993	3	8118
	E Other economic affairs	242	183	59	-	433	675	42	-	717
10	Other functions	17	2	15	-	6	23	54	-	77
	Total	42752	21791	20961	1111	10940	54803	32271	464	87538
	1989									
1	General public services	14114	4048	10066	7157	6099	27370	215	4	27589
2	Defence	9349	4489	4860	-	-	9349	812	-	10161
3	Public order and safety	4721	2769	1952	-	-	4721	367	-	5088
4	Education	5951	5491	460	208	3965	10124	1470	8	11602
5	Health	4015	2942	1073	19	6	4040	1629	13	5682

Bangladesh

2.3 Total Government Outlays by Function and Type
(Continued)

Million Bangladesh taka — Fiscal year beginning 1 July

		Final Consumption Expenditures Total	Compensation of Employees	Other	Subsidies	Other Current Transfers & Property Income	Total Current Disbursements	Gross Capital Formation	Other Capital Outlays	Total Outlays
6	Social security and welfare	471	225	246	16	75	562	365	36	963
7	Housing and community amenities	1592	565	1027	-	1	1593	2147	69	3809
8	Recreation, culture and religion	256	144	112	-	188	444	8	-	452
9	Economic services	10173	4188	5985	260	2422	12855	29339	795	42989
	A Fuel and energy	1166	197	969	37	481	1684	7606	420	9710
	B Agriculture, forestry, fishing and hunting	5483	2851	2632	215	763	6461	6823	256	13540
	C Mining (except fuels), manufacturing and construction	2319	493	1826	8	326	2653	4896	115	7664
	D Transportation and communication	935	439	496	-	114	1049	9972	4	11025
	E Other economic affairs	270	208	62	-	738	1008	42	-	1050
10	Other functions	14	5	9	-	3	17	57	2	76
	Total	50656	24866	25790	7660	12759	71075	36409	927	108411

4.1 Derivation of Value Added by Kind of Activity, in Current Prices

Million Bangladesh taka — Fiscal year beginning 1 July

	1980 Gross Output	1980 Intermediate Consumption	1980 Value Added	1981 Gross Output	1981 Intermediate Consumption	1981 Value Added	1982 Gross Output	1982 Intermediate Consumption	1982 Value Added	1983 Gross Output	1983 Intermediate Consumption	1983 Value Added
						All Producers						
1 Agriculture, hunting, forestry and fishing	114081	5128	108953	127193	5354	121839	143180	7309	135871	177756	8428	169328
A Agriculture and hunting	100813	4730	96083	112549	4914	107635	126033	6794	119239	154274	7724	146550
B Forestry and logging	6029	181	5848	6753	203	6550	8764	263	8501	12243	367	11876
C Fishing	7239	217	7022	7891	237	7654	8383	252	8131	11239	337	10902
2 Mining and quarrying	...	...	3	...	...	6	...	...	3	...	...	4
3 Manufacturing	74019	51158	22861	83218	57516	25702	90885	62815	28070	107661	76716	30945
4 Electricity, gas and water	...	...	744	...	...	959	...	...	1612	...	...	1939
5 Construction	32720	19632	13088	39658	23795	15863	37570	22542	15028	45237	27142	18095
6 Wholesale and retail trade, restaurants and hotels	21903	1095	20808	23512	1175	22337	27084	1353	25731	34678	1733	32945
A Wholesale and retail trade	21903	1095	20808	23512	1175	22337	27084	1353	25731	34678	1733	32945
B Restaurants and hotels [a]	...	...	...	...	...	...	...	...	...	...	...	...
7 Transport, storage and communication	...	...	28677	...	...	32040	...	...	39866	...	...	41797
8 Finance, insurance, real estate and business services	...	...	24044	...	...	25620	...	...	26598	...	...	33710
9 Community, social and personal services [a]	...	...	18481	...	...	22626	...	...	25459	...	...	31082
Total, Industries	348123	110464	237659	393413	126421	266992	436770	138532	298238	525698	165853	359845
Producers of Government Services	7947	1334	6613	8053	1384	6669	10419	1686	8733	10659	1725	8934
Other Producers	...	...	...	...	...	...	...	...	...	...	...	...
Total	356070	111798	244272	401466	127805	273661	447189	140218	306971	536357	167578	368779
Less: Imputed bank service charge	...	...	...	...	...	...	...	...	...	...	...	...
Import duties	...	...	...	...	...	...	...	...	...	...	...	...
Value added tax	...	...	...	...	...	...	...	...	...	...	...	...
Total	356070	111798	244272	401466	127805	273661	447189	140218	306971	536357	167578	368779

	1984 Gross Output	1984 Intermediate Consumption	1984 Value Added	1985 Gross Output	1985 Intermediate Consumption	1985 Value Added	1986 Gross Output	1986 Intermediate Consumption	1986 Value Added	1987 Gross Output	1987 Intermediate Consumption	1987 Value Added
						All Producers						
1 Agriculture, hunting, forestry and fishing	222829	10335	212494	232451	10044	222407	271718	11788	259930	281998	13410	268588
A Agriculture and hunting	195435	9514	185921	194004	8890	185114	225838	10412	215426	232181	11916	220265
B Forestry and logging	12301	369	11932	20922	628	20294	24316	729	23587	24578	737	23841
C Fishing	15093	452	14641	17525	526	16999	21564	647	20917	25239	757	24482
2 Mining and quarrying	...	...	4	...	...	8	...	...	6	...	...	3
3 Manufacturing	120488	85856	34632	129892	92557	37335	139887	99679	40208	151061	107641	43420
4 Electricity, gas and water	...	...	2348	...	...	2713	...	...	3545	...	...	4597

Bangladesh

4.1 Derivation of Value Added by Kind of Activity, in Current Prices
(Continued)

Million Bangladesh taka
Fiscal year beginning 1 July

	1984 Gross Output	1984 Intermediate Consumption	1984 Value Added	1985 Gross Output	1985 Intermediate Consumption	1985 Value Added	1986 Gross Output	1986 Intermediate Consumption	1986 Value Added	1987 Gross Output	1987 Intermediate Consumption	1987 Value Added
5 Construction	56295	33777	22518	65145	39087	26058	72098	43269	28829	86505	51903	34602
6 Wholesale and retail trade, restaurants and hotels	40858	2042	38816	43688	2183	41505	48296	2413	45883	53018	2649	50369
A Wholesale and retail trade	40858	2042	38816	43688	2183	41505	48296	2413	45883	53018	2649	50369
B Restaurants and hotels [a]	...	...	...	...	...	...	...	...	...	...	...	...
7 Transport, storage and communication	...	...	45655	...	...	54605	...	...	61901	...	...	65945
8 Finance, insurance, real estate and business services	...	...	39333	...	...	46001	...	...	51104	...	...	61417
9 Community, social and personal services [a]	...	...	34357	...	...	46098	...	...	59329	...	...	69502
Total, Industries	611640	181483	430157	687588	210858	476730	778849	228114	550735	863134	264691	598443
Producers of Government Services	15791	2556	13235	20719	3353	17366	24896	4029	20867	29511	4776	24735
Other Producers	...	...	...	...	...	...	...	...	...	...	...	...
Total	627431	184039	443392	708307	214211	494096	803745	232143	571602	892645	269467	623178
Less: Imputed bank service charge	...	...	...	...	...	...	...	...	...	...	...	...
Import duties	...	...	...	...	...	...	...	...	...	...	...	...
Value added tax	...	...	...	...	...	...	...	...	...	...	...	...
Total	627431	184039	443392	708307	214211	494096	803745	232143	571602	892645	269467	623178

	1988 Gross Output	1988 Intermediate Consumption	1988 Value Added	1989 Gross Output	1989 Intermediate Consumption	1989 Value Added
			All Producers			
1 Agriculture, hunting, forestry and fishing	302721	14722	287999	352577	15979	336598
A Agriculture and hunting	247197	13057	234140	291637	14152	277485
B Forestry and logging	27176	815	26361	29755	892	28863
C Fishing	28348	850	27498	31185	935	30250
2 Mining and quarrying	...	...	4	...	...	4
3 Manufacturing	166888	118919	47969	193521	137897	55624
4 Electricity, gas and water	...	...	6719	...	...	7970
5 Construction	98155	58893	39262	109188	65513	43675
6 Wholesale and retail trade, restaurants and hotels	57947	2896	55051	64615	3229	61386
A Wholesale and retail trade	57947	2896	55051	64615	3229	61386
B Restaurants and hotels [a]	...	...	...	...	...	...
7 Transport, storage and communication	...	...	71774	...	...	75301
8 Finance, insurance, real estate and business services	...	...	72992	...	...	80623
9 Community, social and personal services [a]	...	...	79207	...	...	92317
Total, Industries	959178	298201	660977	1093439	339941	753498
Producers of Government Services	34842	5639	29203	40593	6570	34023
Other Producers	...	...	...	...	...	...
Total	994020	303840	690180	1134032	346511	787521
Less: Imputed bank service charge	...	...	...	...	...	...
Import duties	...	...	...	...	...	...
Value added tax	...	...	...	...	...	...
Total	994020	303840	690180	1134032	346511	787521

a) Restaurants and hotels are included in item 'Community, social and personal services'.

Barbados

Source. Reply to the United Nations National Accounts Questionnaire from the Barbados Statistical Service, Garrison, St. Michael. Information on concepts, sources and methods of estimation utilized, are published by the same Service in 'National Income and Product, 1960-1962'.

General note. The estimates have been prepared in accordance with the United Nations System of National Accounts so far as the existing data would permit.

1.1 Expenditure on the Gross Domestic Product, in Current Prices

Million Barbados dollars

	1970	1975	1980	1981	1982	1983	1984	1985	1986	1987	1988	1989
1 Government final consumption expenditure	...	134.8	258.2	321.2	329.0	346.1	387.6	456.3	468.8	497.5	537.3	...
2 Private final consumption expenditure	...	602.9	1081.1	1235.3	1263.0	1321.2	1431.9	1396.7	1692.3	1934.0	1956.3	...
3 Gross capital formation	...	156.2	424.3	525.0	450.5	421.2	373.9	371.8	423.8	466.7	543.3	...
A Increase in stocks	...	4.7	29.0	7.1	-3.9	6.2	-5.7	7.5	-3.5	6.8	8.4	...
B Gross fixed capital formation	...	151.5	395.3	517.9	454.4	415.0	379.6	364.3	427.3	459.9	534.9	...
4 Exports of goods and services	...	409.3	1213.7	1137.9	1270.2	1489.8	1656.4	1632.7	1495.9	1340.1	1536.8	...
5 Less: Imports of goods and services	...	490.8	1246.8	1314.8	1322.7	1465.6	1547.1	1447.6	1434.7	1324.6	1475.5	...
Equals: Gross Domestic Product	...	812.4	1730.5	1904.6	1990.0	2112.7	2302.8	2409.9	2646.0	2913.7	3098.3	...

1.10 Gross Domestic Product by Kind of Activity, in Current Prices

Million Barbados dollars

	1970	1975	1980	1981	1982	1983	1984	1985	1986	1987	1988	1989
1 Agriculture, hunting, forestry and fishing	40.3	93.5	152.3	128.9	122.1	135.5	139.2	138.0	146.3	171.6	172.9	153.0
2 Mining and quarrying	31.4	1.6	11.5	13.1	16.1	16.3	31.1	27.9	16.9	18.4	17.1	17.5
3 Manufacturing		71.9	183.5	189.7	205.5	238.7	264.1	231.7	229.3	223.6	240.2	233.3
4 Electricity, gas and water [a]	20.9	10.3	33.1	38.6	44.7	52.9	68.0	72.7	72.2	80.7	84.8	91.6
5 Construction	27.5	46.3	118.2	138.3	122.1	132.5	130.0	117.9	131.4	144.3	170.3	196.7
6 Wholesale and retail trade, restaurants and hotels [b]	71.2	192.0	501.9	575.4	579.1	565.0	619.0	676.0	719.6	799.9	862.9	942.3
7 Transport, storage and communication [a]	...	50.4	86.9	113.0	134.8	154.1	171.0	185.0	197.5	225.4	226.6	227.8
8 Finance, insurance, real estate and business services [c]	11.0	98.3	172.6	210.2	250.1	258.9	270.9	297.8	311.0	313.0	358.5	424.8
9 Community, social and personal services [bc]	45.0	30.8	57.6	69.4	76.7	80.9	85.7	89.6	94.1	97.3	99.2	106.1
Total, Industries	247.3	595.1	1317.6	1476.6	1551.2	1634.8	1779.0	1836.6	1918.3	2074.2	2232.5	2393.1
Producers of Government Services	42.7	105.5	218.2	229.7	233.0	264.3	295.5	344.0	379.0	424.8	435.1	503.4
Other Producers	...	...	...	...	...	...	...	...	...	...	...	...
Subtotal [d]	290.0	700.6	1535.8	1706.2	1784.2	1898.9	2074.6	2180.7	2297.3	2498.9	2667.6	2896.5
Less: Imputed bank service charge	...	...	...	...	...	...	...	...	...	...	...	...
Plus: Import duties	...	...	...	...	...	...	...	...	...	...	...	...
Plus: Value added tax	...	...	...	...	...	...	...	...	...	...	...	...
Plus: Other adjustments [e]	...	111.8	194.7	198.4	205.8	213.7	228.2	229.3	348.7	414.8	431.6	...
Equals: Gross Domestic Product	...	812.4	1730.5	1904.6	1990.0	2112.7	2302.8	2409.9	2646.0	2913.7	3099.2	...

a) For the first series, item 'Transport, storage and communication' is included in item 'Electricity, gas and water'.
b) For the first series, restaurants and hotels are included in item 'Community, social and personal services'.
c) For the first series, finance, insurance, real estate (except owner-occupied dwellings) and business services are included in item 'Community social and personal services'.
d) Gross domestic product in factor values.
e) Item 'Other adjustments' refers to indirect taxes net of subsidies.

1.11 Gross Domestic Product by Kind of Activity, in Constant Prices

Million Barbados dollars

	1970	1975	1980	1981	1982	1983	1984	1985	1986	1987	1988	1989
		At constant prices of:1974										
1 Agriculture, hunting, forestry and fishing	...	66.2	82.6	68.5	66.8	69.3	75.8	75.4	78.8	70.0	65.2	60.1
2 Mining and quarrying	...	0.9	4.3	3.9	4.0	4.9	6.8	7.3	7.7	7.2	6.6	6.2
3 Manufacturing	...	69.3	94.8	91.4	86.5	88.7	90.4	81.8	86.0	80.3	85.8	90.3
4 Electricity, gas and water	...	10.1	16.8	16.5	16.8	19.5	20.4	21.4	22.8	23.7	25.6	26.1
5 Construction	...	44.1	56.4	58.7	51.7	51.2	50.7	49.9	53.5	56.8	61.9	66.9

Barbados

1.11 Gross Domestic Product by Kind of Activity, in Constant Prices
(Continued)

Million Barbados dollars

	1970	1975	1980	1981	1982	1983	1984	1985	1986	1987	1988	1989
					At constant prices of: 1974							
6 Wholesale and retail trade, restaurants and hotels	...	175.8	267.6	261.7	234.6	228.5	240.2	244.7	260.0	283.7	299.7	315.2
7 Transport, storage and communication	...	43.4	49.7	51.9	53.5	54.3	57.0	58.7	61.4	64.5	64.8	68.9
8 Finance, insurance, real estate and business services	...	217.2	128.1	130.3	133.5	134.1	135.4	140.8	145.0	145.7	150.1	155.5
9 Community, social and personal services	...											
Total, Industries	...	627.0	700.3	682.9	647.4	650.5	676.7	680.0	715.2	731.9	759.7	789.2
Producers of Government Services	...	...	102.0	104.0	100.8	101.3	101.8	106.9	111.8	116.2	117.4	118.6
Other Producers	...	...	...	...	...	...	...	...	...	...	...	...
Subtotal a	...	627.0	802.3	786.9	748.2	751.8	778.5	786.9	827.0	848.1	877.8	907.8
Less: Imputed bank service charge	...	...	...	...	...	...	...	...	...	...	...	...
Plus: Import duties	...	...	...	...	...	...	...	...	...	...	...	...
Plus: Value added tax	...	...	...	...	...	...	...	...	...	...	...	...
Equals: Gross Domestic Product	...	...	...	...	...	...	...	...	...	...	...	...

a) Gross domestic product in factor values.

4.1 Derivation of Value Added by Kind of Activity, in Current Prices

Million Barbados dollars

	1980			1981		
	Gross Output	Intermediate Consumption	Value Added	Gross Output	Intermediate Consumption	Value Added
			All Producers			
1 Agriculture, hunting, forestry and fishing	319.0	166.7	152.3	259.1	130.2	128.9
A Agriculture and hunting	304.3	160.2	144.1	242.1	122.9	119.2
B Forestry and logging	...	...	...	...	...	...
C Fishing	14.7	6.5	8.2	17.0	7.3	9.7
2 Mining and quarrying	22.7	11.2	11.5	27.8	14.7	13.1
3 Manufacturing	...	...	183.5	...	...	189.7
A Manufacture of food, beverages and tobacco	...	...	62.8	...	...	72.9
B Textile, wearing apparel and leather industries	...	...	31.5	...	...	34.3
C Manufacture of wood and wood products, including furniture	...	...	4.0	...	...	4.5
D Manufacture of paper and paper products, printing and publishing	...	...	13.7	...	...	16.0
E Manufacture of chemicals and chemical petroleum, coal, rubber and plastic products	...	...	30.0	...	...	30.6
F Manufacture of non-metallic mineral products, except products of petroleum and coal	...	...	...	...	...	...
G Basic metal industries	...	...	...	...	...	...
H Manufacture of fabricated metal products, machinery and equipment	...	...	31.5	...	...	35.8
I Other manufacturing industries	...	...	9.9	...	...	9.8
4 Electricity, gas and water	...	...	33.1	...	...	38.6
5 Construction	...	...	118.2	...	...	138.3
6 Wholesale and retail trade, restaurants and hotels	...	...	501.9	...	...	575.4
A Wholesale and retail trade	...	...	319.0	...	...	368.8
B Restaurants and hotels	...	...	182.9	...	...	206.5
7 Transport, storage and communication	...	...	86.9	...	...	113.0
8 Finance, insurance, real estate and business services	...	...	172.6	...	...	210.2
9 Community, social and personal services	...	...	57.6	...	...	69.4
Total, Industries	...	...	1317.6	...	...	1476.5
Producers of Government Services	...	...	218.2	...	...	229.7

Barbados

4.1 Derivation of Value Added by Kind of Activity, in Current Prices
(Continued)

Million Barbados dollars

	1980 Gross Output	1980 Intermediate Consumption	1980 Value Added	1981 Gross Output	1981 Intermediate Consumption	1981 Value Added
Other Producers	...	...	...	...	...	...
Total [a]	...	...	1535.8	...	...	1706.2
Less: Imputed bank service charge	...	...	...	...	...	...
Import duties	...	...	...	...	...	...
Value added tax	...	...	...	...	...	...
Other adjustments [b]	...	...	194.7	...	...	198.4
Total	...	...	1730.5	...	...	1904.6

a) Gross domestic product in factor values.
b) Item 'Other adjustments' refers to indirect taxes net of subsidies.

Belgium

Source. Reply to the United Nations National Accounts Questionnaire from the Institut National de Statistique, Brussels. The official estimates are published annually by the Institut National in the July-August issue of the 'Bulletin de Statistique'.

General note. The estimates shown in the following tables have been prepared in accordance with the United Nations System of National Accounts so far as the existing data would permit.

1.1 Expenditure on the Gross Domestic Product, in Current Prices

Million Belgian francs

	1970	1975	1980	1981	1982	1983	1984	1985	1986	1987	1988	1989
1 Government final consumption expenditure	175300	388398	643590 / 613889	663743	700567	721520	755052	808931	838225	846837	845589	869836
2 Private final consumption expenditure [a]	769013	1421150	2224920 / 2171910	2333840	2550090	2686920	2873670	3105280	3196050	3356700	3506360	3764770
3 Gross capital formation	307511	499486	755714 / 752953	637920	677636	639302	724416	705060	749387	846907	990625	1192400
A Increase in stocks [b]	20437	-12442	27348 / 24668	-4959	5517	-29706	15388	-36225	-33528	11502	22024	38741
B Gross fixed capital formation	287074	511928	728366 / 728285	642879	672119	669008	709028	741285	782915	835405	968601	1153660
Residential buildings	71778	144839	224725 / 203517	121686	115076	115639	118092	130896	138521	152661	195510	246233
Non-residential buildings	102598	187851	274408 / 285919	282943	291992	275007	265172	268102	274084	280082	307691	335255
Other construction and land improvement etc.												
Other	112698	179238	229233 / 238849	238250	265051	278362	325764	342287	370310	402662	465400	572172
4 Exports of goods and services [c]	561900	1065200	2026400 / 2170200	2439000	2794300	3078900	3505200	3644900	3525600	3614400	4029600	4621900
5 Less: Imports of goods and services [c]	532800	1061100	2124700 / 2257800	2497000	2833500	3004300	3429000	3525900	3325000	3450700	3823700	4421000
Equals: Gross Domestic Product	1280920	2313140	3525920 / 3451150	3577510	3889090	4122340	4429340	4738270	4984270	5214150	5548480	6027900

a) For the first series, item 'Private final consumption expenditure' includes a statistical discrepancy.
b) Item 'Increase in stocks' includes the statistical adjustment concerning gross capital formation.
c) Beginning 1977 for the first series, disbursements and receipts are not compensated in the balance of payments. Therefore these series are not comparable with previous years.

1.2 Expenditure on the Gross Domestic Product, in Constant Prices

Million Belgian francs

	1970	1975	1980	1981	1982	1983	1984	1985	1986	1987	1988	1989
			At constant prices of: 1980					1985				
1 Government final consumption expenditure	425056	545573	643590 / 796654	798746	787692	788429	790010	808931	821748	827654	818172	808240
2 Private final consumption expenditure	1528280[a]	1892110[a]	2224920[a] / 3054230	3020600	3061050	3009670	3044940	3105280	3179080	3273820	3366070	3490660
3 Gross capital formation	619805	647893	755714 / 956330	759653	760713	694774	760121	705060	747821	832830	954098	1092350
A Increase in stocks [b]	30390	-22550	27348 / 38674	-10224	4022	-28629	24107	-36225	-26226	14100	25202	37298
B Gross fixed capital formation	589415	670443	728366 / 917656	769877	756691	723403	736014	741285	774047	818730	928896	1055050
Residential buildings	182761	209270	224725 / 241185	136221	129798	127286	124268	130896	133719	140179	175110	208568
Non-residential buildings	...	...	379721	347133	326892	300226	277288	268102	277334	284478	305428	314754
Other construction and land improvement etc.	...	...										
Other	...	...	296750	286523	300001	295891	334458	342287	362994	394073	448358	531727
4 Exports of goods and services	1082400[c]	1407600[c]	2026400[c] / 3207200	3289600	3332300	3423400	3605600	3644900	3849200	4094600	4435300	4742500
5 Less: Imports of goods and services	1106900[c]	1462000[c]	2124700[c] / 3453700	3353000	3358100	3315200	3501200	3525900	3790600	4113500	4432500	4793500
Equals: Gross Domestic Product	2548640	3031170	3525920 / 4560710	4515600	4583660	4601080	4699470	4738270	4807250	4915400	5141140	5340240

a) For the first series, item 'Private final consumption expenditure' includes a statistical discrepancy.
b) Item 'Increase in stocks' includes the statistical adjustment concerning gross capital formation.
c) Beginning 1977 for the first series, disbursements and receipts are not compensated in the balance of payments. Therefore these series are not comparable with previous years.

Belgium

1.3 Cost Components of the Gross Domestic Product

Million Belgian francs

		1970	1975	1980	1981	1982	1983	1984	1985	1986	1987	1988	1989
1	Indirect taxes, net	148241	233551	361765 289515	301849	338125	351659	368648	391249	403807	465906	489442	554884
	A Indirect taxes	165224	261082	412085 428031	448921	495208	530053	554687	582009	594660	644246	674478	733377
	B Less: Subsidies	16983	27531	50320 138516	147072	157083	178394	186039	190760	190853	178340	185036	178493
2	Consumption of fixed capital	124569	212444	312145 312145	332069	362874	398437	423383	455398	471492	494191	518085	553833
3	Compensation of employees paid by resident producers to:	629040	1309930	2062100 2071030	2150010	2278550	2383210	2528340	2658250	2796790	2865180	2979280	3137420
	A Resident households	625940	1301630	2048100 2057030	2135010	2260150	2364610	2509340	2637750	2775490	2841480	2952980	3106420
	B Rest of the world	3100	8300	14000 14000	15000	18400	18600	19000	20500	21300	23700	26300	31000
4	Operating surplus	379074	557211	789912 778463	793579	909543	989038	1108960	1233380	1312170	1388870	1561670	1781770
	A Corporate and quasi-corporate enterprises	...	...	211668	187264	266131	311421	378070	466676	495811	529922	617922	...
	B Private unincorporated enterprises	...	...	563380	604219	640630	675349	728578	765136	814839	857575	942179	...
	C General government	...	...	3415	2096	2782	2268	2312	1568	1523	1377	1567	1549
	Equals: Gross Domestic Product	1280920	2313140	3525920 3451150	3577510	3889090	4122340	4429340	4738270	4984270	5214150	5548480	6027900

1.4 General Government Current Receipts and Disbursements

Million Belgian francs

		1970	1975	1980	1981	1982	1983	1984	1985	1986	1987	1988	1989
						Receipts							
1	Operating surplus	...	...	3415	2096	2782	2268	2312	1568	1523	1377	1567	1549
2	Property and entrepreneurial income	12053	6563	20376 58185	70315	88706	79257	84942	89527	78996	70442	67215	79153
3	Taxes, fees and contributions	438450	926334	1481390 1533970	1611010	1816160	1923000	2114820	2268530	2353000	2477060	2562930	2666010
	A Indirect taxes	165224	261082	412085 428031	448921	495208	530053	554687	582009	594660	644246	674478	733377
	B Direct taxes	141493	374372	631633 639589	665487	779296	795589	879256	939341	963965	989952	1012440	1020970
	C Social security contributions	131733	290880	437669 466352	496603	541656	597354	680876	747182	794371	842864	876006	911660
	D Compulsory fees, fines and penalties [a]	...	...	...	...	...	...	...	...	...	...	...	...
4	Other current transfers [a]	700	2300	3391 105537	117445	128860	137881	146869	161697	169424	182805	174718	175825
	Total Current Receipts of General Government	451203	935197	1505150 1701110	1800870	2036510	2142400	2348940	2521320	2602940	2731690	2806430	2922540
						Disbursements							
1	Government final consumption expenditure	175300	388398	643590 613889	663743	700567	721520	755052	808931	838225	846837	845589	869836
	A Compensation of employees	...	...	...	...	...	...	...	...	...	...	...	...
	B Consumption of fixed capital	2797	5634	10521	...	...	...	...	...	...	...	...	...
	C Purchases of goods and services, net	...	...	...	...	...	...	...	...	...	...	...	...
	D Less: Own account fixed capital formation	...	...	...	...	...	...	...	...	...	...	...	...
	E Indirect taxes paid, net	...	...	...	...	...	...	...	...	...	...	...	...
2	Property income	43120	82484	211522 215622	289760	366455	395599	447044	515805	574820	566583	575103	639774
	A Interest	...	...	215622	289760	366455	395599	447044	515805	574820	566583	575103	639774
	B Net land rent and royalties	...	...	...	-	-	-	-	-	-	-	-	-

Belgium

1.4 General Government Current Receipts and Disbursements (Continued)

Million Belgian francs

		1970	1975	1980	1981	1982	1983	1984	1985	1986	1987	1988	1989
3	Subsidies	16983	27531	50320 138516	147072	157083	178394	186039	190760	190853	178340	185036	178493
4	Other current transfers	187799	453645	760612 893843	1006880	1092710	1176550	1234530	1287920	1333400	1409650	1450820	1523500
	A Social security benefits	157667	384269	655706 817683 [b]	922223	996084	1079742	1134819	1183187	1225861	1283690	1318638	1393575
	B Social assistance grants	22632	49676	78932 ...									
	C Other	7500	19700	25974 76160	84656	96622	96811	99706	104735	107540	125960	132185	129927
5	Net saving	28001	-16861	-160890 -160761	-306587	-280303	-329664	-273718	-282094	-334360	-269724	-250126	-289070
	Total Current Disbursements and Net Saving of General Government	451203	935197	1505150 1701110	1800870	2036510	2142400	2348940	2521320	2602940	2731690	2806430	2922540

a) Item 'Other current transfers' includes item 'Fees, fines and penalties'.
b) Including item 'Social assistance grants'.

1.5 Current Income and Outlay of Corporate and Quasi-Corporate Enterprises, Summary

Million Belgian francs

		1970	1975	1980	1981	1982	1983	1984	1985	1986	1987	1988	1989
	Receipts												
1	Operating surplus	...	...	211668	187264	266131	311421	378070	466676	495811	529922	617922	...
2	Property and entrepreneurial income received	...	...	747074	1020280	1151500	1090520	1287770	1319280	1248800	1261100	1406140	...
3	Current transfers	...	...	166668	178705	193794	212667	229565	244216	238137	253408	269891	...
	Total Current Receipts	...	...	1125410	1386250	1611420	1614610	1895410	2030170	1982750	2044430	2293960	...
	Disbursements												
1	Property and entrepreneurial income	...	...	845154	1107060	1270390	1234770	1444670	1498390	1374970	1398670	1582980	...
2	Direct taxes and other current payments to general government	...	...	89749	87528	112932	115049	132744	148427	156626	164401	177736	...
3	Other current transfers	...	...	163963	175749	189513	208420	225725	238022	233081	246531	264754	...
4	Net saving	...	...	26544	15911	38586	56365	92270	145328	218072	234832	268484	...
	Total Current Disbursements and Net Saving	...	...	1125410	1386250	1611420	1614610	1895410	2030170	1982750	2044430	2293960	...

1.6 Current Income and Outlay of Households and Non-Profit Institutions

Million Belgian francs

		1970	1975	1980	1981	1982	1983	1984	1985	1986	1987	1988	1989
	Receipts												
1	Compensation of employees	635640	1322730	2079000 2087930	2168210	2298250	2406710	2554940	2685150	2827490	2894980	3010880	3169320
	A From resident producers	625940	1301630	2048100 2057030	2135010	2260150	2364610	2509340	2637750	2775490	2841480	2952980	3106420
	B From rest of the world	9700	21100	30900 30900	33200	38100	42100	45600	47400	52000	53500	57900	62900
2	Operating surplus of private unincorporated enterprises	210690	306143	397116 563380	604219	640630	675349	728578	765136	814839	857575	942179	...
3	Property and entrepreneurial income	141625	249120	434607 314020	375537	441284	488581	556616	629054	652720	677597	729096	...
4	Current transfers	190999	447545	755538 954278	1068920	1149560	1238010	1304850	1366710	1409750	1483470	1536560	...
	A Social security benefits	157667	384269	655706 874238	982241	1058091	1143162	1202098	1253334	1298892	1359137	1398281	...
	B Social assistance grants												...
	C Other	33332	63276	99832 80040	86675	91470	94847	102754	113376	110853	124333	128280	...
	Total Current Receipts	1178950	2325540	3666260 3919610	4216880	4529730	4808650	5144990	5446050	5704800	5913620	6218720	...
	Disbursements												
1	Private final consumption expenditure	769013	1421150	2224920 2171910	2333840	2550090	2686920	2873670	3105280	3196050	3356700	3506360	...

Belgium

1.6 Current Income and Outlay of Households and Non-Profit Institutions
(Continued)

Million Belgian francs

	1970	1975	1980	1981	1982	1983	1984	1985	1986	1987	1988	1989
2 Property income	...	...	101603	117511	122741	114285	123918	126961	126027	130490	142469	...
3 Direct taxes and other current transfers n.e.c. to general government	242308	595137	979553 1016190	1074560	1208020	1277890	1427390	1538100	1601710	1668420	1710710	...
A Social security contributions	131733	290880	437669 466352	496603	541656	597354	680876	747182	794371	842864	876006	...
B Direct taxes	110575	304257	541884 549840	577959	666364	680540	746512	790914	807339	825551	834705	...
C Fees, fines and penalties [a]	...	...	...	...	...	...	...	...	...	...	...	...
4 Other current transfers [a]	8800	16600	31800 203430	228650	236994	249718	262117	275351	283451	298523	322139	...
5 Net saving	158833	292649	429990 426472	462315	411881	479830	457900	400356	497556	459487	537036	...
Total Current Disbursements and Net Saving	1178950	2325540	3666260 3919610	4216880	4529730	4808650	5144990	5446050	5704800	5913620	6218720	...

a) Item 'Other current transfers' includes item 'Fees, fines and penalties'.

1.7 External Transactions on Current Account, Summary

Million Belgian francs

	1970	1975	1980	1981	1982	1983	1984	1985	1986	1987	1988	1989
Payments to the Rest of the World												
1 Imports of goods and services [a]	532800	1061100	2124700 2257800	2497000	2833500	3004300	3429000	3525900	3325000	3450700	3823700	4421000
A Imports of merchandise c.i.f.	424900	858300	1698800 2029900	2234500	2565400	2714800	3106400	3165600	2939100	3025500	3337900	3822800
B Other	107900	202800	425900 227900	262500	268100	289500	322600	360300	385900	425200	485800	598200
2 Factor income to the rest of the world	43200	78600	230200 243500	489700	596900	571000	668500	798500	712700	682700	803000	1157600
A Compensation of employees	3100	8300	14000 14000	15000	18400	18600	19000	20500	21300	23700	26300	31000
B Property and entrepreneurial income	40100	70300	216200 229500	474700	578500	552400	649500	778000	691400	659000	776700	1126600
3 Current transfers to the rest of the world	16300	36300	57774 95786	113135	129579	138695	147336	155729	152131	166608	183161	193769
A Indirect taxes to supranational organizations	...	...	41606	45310	56087	56573	57261	59412	64613	77013	77417	80809
B Other current transfers	16300	36300	57774 54180	67825	73492	82122	90075	96317	87518	89595	105744	112960
4 Surplus of the nation on current transactions	35100	-3600	-150083 -148553	-134212	-144598	-34334	-24581	13928	103373	71879	82854	64421
Payments to the Rest of the World and Surplus of the Nation on Current Transactions	627400	1172400	2262590 2448530	2965620	3415380	3679660	4220260	4494060	4293200	4371890	4892720	5836790
Receipts From The Rest of the World												
1 Exports of goods and services [a]	561900	1065200	2026400 2170200	2439000	2794300	3078900	3505200	3644900	3525600	3614400	4029600	4621900
A Exports of merchandise f.o.b.	452800	856800	1596400 1802200	1991600	2308100	2531000	2903700	3012800	2874100	2904300	3247200	3711900

Belgium

1.7 External Transactions on Current Account, Summary
(Continued)

Million Belgian francs

	1970	1975	1980	1981	1982	1983	1984	1985	1986	1987	1988	1989
B Other	109100	208400	430000 368000	447400	486200	547900	601500	632100	651500	710100	782400	910000
2 Factor income from rest of the world	54100	91300	211900 217300	459700	538500	508200	608800	722100	648100	625900	736500	1081800
A Compensation of employees	9700	21100	30900 30900	33200	38100	42100	45600	47400	52000	53500	57900	62900
B Property and entrepreneurial income	44400	70200	181000 186400	426500	500400	466100	563200	674700	596100	572400	678600	1018900
3 Current transfers from rest of the world	11400	15900	24291 61033	66923	82581	92561	106255	127057	119504	131587	126615	133090
A Subsidies from supranational organisations	...	...	23902	21682	27835	29726	33100	42281	44627	42804	32829	28068
B Other current transfers	11400	15900	24291 37131	45241	54746	62835	73155	84776	74877	88783	93786	105022
Receipts from the Rest of the World on Current Transactions	627400	1172400	2262590 2448530	2965620	3415380	3679660	4220260	4494060	4293200	4371890	4892720	5836790

a) Beginning 1977 for the first series, disbursements and receipts are not compensated in the balance of payments. Therefore these series are not comparable with previous years.

1.8 Capital Transactions of The Nation, Summary

Million Belgian francs

	1970	1975	1980	1981	1982	1983	1984	1985	1986	1987	1988	1989
Finance of Gross Capital Formation												
Gross saving	342611	495886	605631 604400	503708	533038	604968	699835	718988	852760	918786	1073480	1256820
1 Consumption of fixed capital	124569	212444	312145 312145	332069	362874	398437	423383	455398	471492	494191	518085	553833
A General government	2797	5634	10521 12234	12863	13213	13809	14711	15454	16606	18201	19616	21814
B Corporate and quasi-corporate enterprises	121772	206810	301624 212109	223405	247250	274255	291386	314248	326407	343628	360487	...
C Other	...	...	... 87802	95801	102411	110373	117286	125696	128479	132362	137982	...
2 Net saving	218042	283442	293486 292255	171639	170164	206531	276452	263590	381268	424595	555394	702989
A General government	28001	-16861	-160890 -160761	-306587	-280303	-329664	-273718	-282094	-334360	-269724	-250126	-289070
B Corporate and quasi-corporate enterprises	31208	7654	24386 26544	15911	38586	56365	92270	145328	218072	234832	268484	...
Public	3188	3164	4866 ...	...	...	...	...	...	...	...	...	...
Private	28020	4490	19520 ...	...	...	...	...	...	...	...	...	...
C Other	158833	292649	429990 426472	462315	411881	479830	457900	400356	497556	459487	537036	...
Less: Surplus of the nation on current transactions	35100	-3600	-150083 -148553	-134212	-144598	-34334	-24581	13928	103373	71879	82854	64421
Finance of Gross Capital Formation	307511	499486	755714 752953	637920	677636	639302	724416	705060	749387	846907	990625	1192400
Gross Capital Formation												
Increase in stocks [a]	20437	-12442	27348 24668	-4959	5517	-29706	15388	-36225	-33528	11502	22024	38741
Gross fixed capital formation	287074	511928	728366 728285	642879	672119	669008	709028	741285	782915	835405	968601	1153660
1 General government	39420	66040	101398 125662	127009	126933	124069	114146	106001	100175	94629	100111	90252
2 Corporate and quasi-corporate enterprises	...	...	... 344763	345102	369610	359831	401057	422296	450548	485373	558838	689861
3 Other	...	...	... 257860	170768	175576	185108	193825	212988	232192	255403	309652	373547
Gross Capital Formation	307511	499486	755714 752953	637920	677636	639302	724416	705060	749387	846907	990625	1192400

a) Item 'Increase in stocks' includes the statistical adjustment concerning gross capital formation.

Belgium

1.9 Gross Domestic Product by Institutional Sectors of Origin

Million Belgian francs

	1970	1975	1980	1981	1982	1983	1984	1985	1986	1987	1988	1989
			Domestic Factor Incomes Originating									
1 General government	...	...	474986	514560	546763	557514	585194	622066	644305	642913	649780	676808
2 Corporate and quasi-corporate enterprises [a]	...	...	2374500	2429030	2641330	2814730	3052110	3269560	3464660	3611140	3891170	4242380
A Non-financial	...	...	2354340	2396540	2600870	2786380	3013960	3227270	3413060	3539120	3796140	4128180
B Financial	...	...	20166	32492	40457	28354	38155	42291	51603	72023	95027	114200
3 Households and private unincorporated enterprises [a]			...	...	...	...	...	...	...	...	...	...
4 Non-profit institutions serving households [a]			...	...	...	...	...	...	...	...	...	...
Subtotal: Domestic Factor Incomes	1008110	1867140	2852010 / 2849490	2943590	3188090	3372250	3637300	3891630	4108970	4254050	4540950	4919190
Indirect taxes, net	148241	233551	361765 / 289515	301849	338125	351659	368648	391249	403807	465906	489442	554884
A Indirect taxes	165224	261082	412085 / 428031	448921	495208	530053	554687	582009	594660	644246	674478	733377
B Less: Subsidies	16983	27531	50320 / 138516	147072	157083	178394	186039	190760	190853	178340	185036	178493
Consumption of fixed capital	124569	212444	312145 / 312145	332069	362874	398437	423383	455398	471492	494191	518085	553833
Gross Domestic Product	1280920	2313140	3525920 / 3451150	3577510	3889090	4122340	4429340	4738270	4984270	5214150	5548480	6027900

a) The estimates of Households and private unincorporated enterprises and Non-profit institutions serving households are included in item 'Corporate and quasi-corporate enterprises'.

1.10 Gross Domestic Product by Kind of Activity, in Current Prices

Million Belgian francs

	1970	1975	1980	1981	1982	1983	1984	1985	1986	1987	1988	1989
1 Agriculture, hunting, forestry and fishing	45997	68208	79390 / 73108	81371	90957	102375	105006	105138	106443	100950	105556	123587
2 Mining and quarrying	12023	18866	18607 / 7399	9141	14486	14172	11432	10975	6542	4071	2658	2209
3 Manufacturing [a]	411290	634200	861287 / 833834	808538	912123	966017	1027030	1115170	1157120	1187450	1281730	1403240
4 Electricity, gas and water [b]	29594	71020	109950 / 75002	84378	84315	101410	106295	118997	123245	126731	131613	139140
5 Construction	88629	165702	276681 / 259389	224694	235105	232482	233717	245778	249214	251454	283851	321868
6 Wholesale and retail trade, restaurants and hotels [cde]	222923	422122	653999 / 546968	550903	600782	658759	685531	759819	864011	923296	958929	1018470
7 Transport, storage and communication	92632	179078	279627 / 268450	273135	289584	304106	344848	374536	369291	394992	431642	448651
8 Finance, insurance, real estate and business services	137379	254274	460046 / 149581	188052	211957	205727	247852	263512	297864	316597	336319	366062
9 Community, social and personal services [cf]	98423	197696	318299 / 532987	588463	651207	712896	794871	844553	915111	983952	1069510	1186710
Statistical discrepancy	...	...	96	21676	8513	3528	31983	5480	-3283	-10160	-24796	-7775
Total, Industries	1138890	2011170	3057890 / 2746810	2830350	3099030	3301470	3588560	3843950	4085560	4279330	4577010	5002160
Producers of Government Services	135035	304696	514381 / 482609	524345	556134	568041	596368	634993	658367	658701	666732	695925
Other Producers [g]	16516	25670	40830 / 40830	42191	43714	45501	47304	49496	50667	50564	50584	50742

Belgium

1.10 Gross Domestic Product by Kind of Activity, in Current Prices
(Continued)

Million Belgian francs

	1970	1975	1980	1981	1982	1983	1984	1985	1986	1987	1988	1989
Subtotal	1290440	2341530	3613100 3270250	3396890	3698880	3915010	4232240	4528440	4794590	4988600	5294330	5748830
Less: Imputed bank service charge [h]	11755	26178	45083 109122	131558	146437	150629	178145	186425	207845	204227	200495	208065
Plus: Import duties [d]	...	...	34508	33628	41291	44930	45289	47013	41998	51133	49389	52507
Plus: Value added tax	...	...	255511	278548	295362	313027	329955	349242	355521	378647	405255	434633
Plus: Other adjustments [i]	2238	-2218	-42090	...	...	...	...	...	...	...	...	...
Equals: Gross Domestic Product	1280920	2313140	3525920 3451150	3577510	3889090	4122340	4429340	4738270	4984270	5214150	5548480	6027900
Memorandum Item: Mineral fuels and power	...	...	162592	166160	179135	199000	205711	223544	221876	222081	224571	243794

a) For the first series, item 'Manufacturing' specifically the manufacture of fabricated metal products, machinery and equipment includes garages.
b) Item 'Electricity, gas and water' includes also other energy products.
c) For the first series, restaurants and hotels are included in item 'Community, social and personal services'.
d) For the first series, item 'Import duties' is included in item 'Wholesale and retail trade'.
e) For the second series, including repairs.
f) For the second series, item 'Community, social and personal services' refers to health services only. All other market services are included in item 'Finance, insurance, real estate and business services'.
g) For the second series, item 'Other producers' refers to domestic services only. All other non-marketed services are included in item 'Finance, insurance, real estate and business services'.
h) For the first series, in line with Former SNA, item 'Less: Imputed bank service charge' refers only to intermediate consumption of imputed bank service charge.
i) For the first series, item 'Other adjustments' includes in addition to statistical discrepancy, a correction for own-account formation and beginning 1971, the deductible value-added tax on capital formation.

1.11 Gross Domestic Product by Kind of Activity, in Constant Prices

Million Belgian francs

	1970	1975	1980	1981	1982	1983	1984	1985	1986	1987	1988	1989
		At constant prices of:										
		1980						1985				
1 Agriculture, hunting, forestry and fishing	72048	68077	79390 89589	93618	99379	97328	106362	105138	110261	101985	108449	108854
2 Mining and quarrying	26701	22426	18607 15799	14613	16343	14534	12509	10975	9193	8982	5754	4141
3 Manufacturing	628674[a]	744979[a]	861287[a] 983253	979849	1017840	1077020	1105910	1115170	1116240	1143280	1216970	1273320
4 Electricity, gas and water [b]	43024	77015	109950 114728	118958	112517	114253	114801	118997	116867	123827	127342	131693
5 Construction	207963	235968	276681 345984	282889	269253	254217	244723	245778	253890	260696	287000	308034
6 Wholesale and retail trade, restaurants and hotels	486155[c,d]	582026[c,d]	653999[c,d] 800753[e]	769271[e]	786830[e]	779154[e]	764784[e]	759819[e]	776383[e]	778280[e]	784900[e]	775933[e]
7 Transport, storage and communication	236599	243480	279627 350575	339770	335797	338021	364787	374536	353168	370069	391100	405723
8 Finance, insurance, real estate and business services	283475	349617	460046 214879	250477	257486	241805	260887	263512	286817	314514	347876	372393
9 Community, social and personal services	217895[c]	283856[c]	318299[c] 738636[f]	760789[f]	783670[f]	796792[f]	838020[f]	844553[f]	876193[f]	913921[f]	973838[f]	1050920[f]
Statistical discrepancy	...	...	-1266	23265	24006	21603	12557	5480	3235	-5600	-5355	-5555
Total, Industries	2202530	2607440	3057890 3652930	3633500	3703120	3734730	3825340	3843950	3902240	4009950	4237870	4425450
Producers of Government Services	342176	435283	514381 618394	621416	618050	619070	624603	634993	643084	642341	643379	644222
Other Producers	44324	41699	40830 523739[g]	512349[g]	507599[g]	499919[g]	495709[g]	494969[g]	487379[g]	476639[g]	469469[g]	458909[g]
Subtotal	2589030	3084430	3613100 4323700	4306150	4371930	4403790	4499510	4528440	4594060	4699960	4928200	5115560
Less: Imputed bank service charge	24746[h]	35500[h]	45083[h] 161892	180215	181349	186037	189883	186425	196660	208161	223910	234188
Plus: Import duties	...	...	47028	44862	42157	42674	46859	47013	50914	55831	60148	64243
Plus: Value added tax	...	...	351880	344801	350920	340653	342980	349242	358936	367772	376705	394624
Plus: Other adjustments	-15652[i]	-17752[i]	-42090[i]	...	...	...	...	...	...	...	...	...
Equals: Gross Domestic Product	2548640	3031170	3525920 4560710	4515600	4583660	4601080	4699470	4738270	4807250	4915400	5141140	5340240
Memorandum Item: Mineral fuels and power	...	...	217433	215141	213294	226577	225913	223544	219011	232776	234319	241950

a) For the first series, item 'Manufacturing' specifically the manufacture of fabricated metal products, machinery and equipment includes garages.
b) Item 'Electricity, gas and water' includes also other energy products.
c) For the first series, restaurants and hotels are included in item 'Community, social and personal services'.
d) For the first series, item 'Import duties' is included in item 'Wholesale and retail trade'.
e) For the second series, including repairs.
f) For the second series, item 'Community, social and personal services' refers to health services only. All other market services are included in item 'Finance, insurance, real estate and business services'.
g) For the second series, item 'Other producers' refers to domestic services only. All other non-marketed services are included in item 'Finance, insurance, real estate and business services'.
h) For the first series, in line with Former SNA, item 'Less: Imputed bank service charge' refers only to intermediate consumption of imputed bank service charge.
i) For the first series, item 'Other adjustments' includes in addition to statistical discrepancy, a correction for own-account formation and beginning 1971, the deductible value-added tax on capital formation.

Belgium

1.12 Relations Among National Accounting Aggregates

Million Belgian francs

	1970	1975	1980	1981	1982	1983	1984	1985	1986	1987	1988	1989
Gross Domestic Product	1280920	2313140	3525920 / 3451150	3577510	3889090	4122340	4429340	4738270	4984270	5214150	5548480	6027900
Plus: Net factor income from the rest of the world	10900	12700	-18300 / -26200	-30000	-58400	-62800	-59700	-76400	-64600	-56800	-66500	-75800
Factor income from the rest of the world	54100	91300	211900 / 217300	459700	538500	508200	608800	722100	648100	625900	736500	1081800
Less: Factor income to the rest of the world	43200	78600	230200 / 243500	489700	596900	571000	668500	798500	712700	682700	803000	1157600
Equals: Gross National Product	1291820	2325840	3507620 / 3424950	3547510	3830690	4059540	4369640	4661870	4919670	5157350	5481980	5952100
Less: Consumption of fixed capital	124569	212444	312145 / 312145	332069	362874	398437	423383	455398	471492	494191	518085	553833
Equals: National Income	1167260	2113390	3195480 / 3112810	3215440	3467820	3661110	3946250	4206480	4448170	4663160	4963890	5398270
Plus: Net current transfers from the rest of the world	-4900	-20400	-33483 / -34753	-46212	-46998	-46134	-41081	-28672	-32627	-35021	-56546	-60679
Current transfers from the rest of the world	11400	15900	24291 / 61033	66923	82581	92561	106255	127057	119504	131587	126615	133090
Less: Current transfers to the rest of the world	16300	36300	57774 / 95786	113135	129579	138695	147336	155729	152131	166608	183161	193769
Equals: National Disposable Income	1162360	2092990	3162000 / 3078050	3169220	3420820	3614970	3905170	4177800	4415550	4628140	4907350	5337590
Less: Final consumption [a]	944313	1809550	2868510 / 2785800	2997590	3250660	3408440	3628720	3914210	4034280	4203540	4351950	4634600
Equals: Net Saving	218042	283442	293486 / 292255	171639	170164	206531	276452	263590	381268	424595	555394	702989
Less: Surplus of the nation on current transactions	35100	-3600	-150083 / -148553	-134212	-144598	-34334	-24581	13928	103373	71879	82854	64421
Equals: Net Capital Formation	182942	287042	443569 / 440808	305851	314762	240865	301033	249662	277895	352716	472540	638568

a) For the first series, item 'Private final consumption expenditure' includes a statistical discrepancy.

2.1 Government Final Consumption Expenditure by Function, in Current Prices

Million Belgian francs

	1970	1975	1980	1981	1982	1983	1984	1985	1986	1987	1988	1989
1 General public services	...	...	...	...	97809	104229	109638	121300	125660	...	...	...
2 Defence	...	...	...	...	110389	112225	115659	123608	128934	...	...	...
3 Public order and safety	...	...	...	...	60390	60106	65017	69946	78841	...	...	...
4 Education	...	...	...	...	271380	278389	290001	305378	309231	...	...	...
5 Health	...	...	...	...	21697	20473	22044	23742	23930	...	...	...
6 Social security and welfare	...	...	...	...	40393	42101	45194	47943	49777	...	...	...
7 Housing and community amenities	...	...	...	...	9914	9594	10632	11231	11497	...	...	...
8 Recreational, cultural and religious affairs	...	...	...	...	16728	17287	18512	20094	21119	...	...	...
9 Economic services	...	...	...	...	55909	58364	58372	62941	66855	...	...	...
A Fuel and energy	...	...	...	...	2	505	640	609	704	...	...	...
B Agriculture, forestry, fishing and hunting	...	...	...	...	5983	5231	4545	5040	5226	...	...	...
C Mining, manufacturing and construction, except fuel and energy	...	...	...	...	5840	5959	4505	4690	4592	...	...	...
D Transportation and communication	...	...	...	...	39089	41814	43176	46699	50610	...	...	...
E Other economic affairs	...	...	...	...	4995	4855	5506	5903	5723	...	...	...
10 Other functions	...	...	...	...	15958	18752	19983	22748	22381	...	...	...
Total Government Final Consumption Expenditure	...	...	...	...	700567	721520	755052	808931	838225	...	...	...

Belgium

2.3 Total Government Outlays by Function and Type

Million Belgian francs

		Final Consumption Expenditures			Subsidies	Other Current Transfers & Property Income	Total Current Disbursements	Gross Capital Formation	Other Capital Outlays	Total Outlays
		Total	Compensation of Employees	Other						

1982

		Total	Comp.	Other	Subsidies	Other Curr. Transf.	Total Curr. Disb.	Gross Cap. Form.	Other Cap. Outlays	Total Outlays
1	General public services	97809	...	...	38	14966	112813	9088	6889	128790
2	Defence	110389	...	...	220	2747	113356	1678	26	115060
3	Public order and safety	60390	...	...	1	751	61142	3783	118	65043
4	Education	271380	...	...	1399	12939	285718	44789	316	330823
5	Health	21697	...	...	8697	212810	243204	309	3282	246795
6	Social security and welfare	40393	...	...	9057	796639	846089	785	391	847265
7	Housing and community amenities	9914	...	...	12823	9154	31891	13648	8952	54491
8	Recreation, culture and religion	16728	...	...	1116	13648	31492	9692	2821	44005
9	Economic services	55909	...	...	95896	60950	212755	43161	42363	298279
A	Fuel and energy	2	...	...	1078	1491	2571	1	-12	2560
B	Agriculture, forestry, fishing and hunting	5983	...	...	4745	436	11164	827	2295	14286
C	Mining (except fuels), manufacturing and construction	5840	...	...	6165	12478	24483	1444	11652	37579
D	Transportation and communication	39089	...	...	75200	44587	158876	38931	27764	225571
E	Other economic affairs	4995	...	...	8708	1958	15661	1958	664	18283
10	Other functions	15958	...	...	1	278470	294429	-	18	294447
	Total	700567	...	...	129248	1403070	2232890	126933	65176	2425000

1983

		Total	Comp.	Other	Subsidies	Other Curr. Transf.	Total Curr. Disb.	Gross Cap. Form.	Other Cap. Outlays	Total Outlays
1	General public services	104229	...	...	43	17342	121614	5848	7640	135102
2	Defence	112225	...	...	265	3891	116381	1818	79	118278
3	Public order and safety	60106	...	...	34	824	60964	3799	90	64853
4	Education	278389	...	...	1256	14137	293782	43651	1092	338525
5	Health	20473	...	...	9635	225825	255933	300	267	256500
6	Social security and welfare	42101	...	...	8186	859836	910123	745	394	911262
7	Housing and community amenities	9594	...	...	13555	10261	33410	11359	8711	53480
8	Recreation, culture and religion	17287	...	...	1279	16951	35517	8815	2109	46441
9	Economic services	58364	...	...	114414	65170	237948	46488	37822	322258
A	Fuel and energy	505	...	...	1193	1518	3216	1	-5	3212
B	Agriculture, forestry, fishing and hunting	5231	...	...	5000	476	10707	820	2367	13894
C	Mining (except fuels), manufacturing and construction	5959	...	...	13686	12834	32479	1183	12903	46565
D	Transportation and communication	41814	...	...	87740	48480	178034	42779	22293	243106
E	Other economic affairs	4855	...	...	6795	1862	13512	1705	264	15481
10	Other functions	18752	...	...	1	301342	320095	1246	1385	322726
	Total	721520	...	...	148668	1515580	2385770	124069	59589	2569430

1984

		Total	Comp.	Other	Subsidies	Other Curr. Transf.	Total Curr. Disb.	Gross Cap. Form.	Other Cap. Outlays	Total Outlays
1	General public services	109638	...	...	71	14629	124338	6765	8395	139498
2	Defence	115659	...	...	202	5555	121416	1469	6	122891
3	Public order and safety	65017	...	...	28	834	65879	3120	58	69057
4	Education	290001	...	...	1481	17677	309159	39494	869	349522
5	Health	22044	...	...	6329	244075	272448	348	251	273047
6	Social security and welfare	45194	...	...	8498	897838	951530	629	556	952715
7	Housing and community amenities	10632	...	...	21622	10480	42734	12653	10617	66004
8	Recreation, culture and religion	18512	...	...	1222	18133	37867	6447	1948	46262
9	Economic services	58372	...	...	113485	78422	250279	43216	35612	329107
A	Fuel and energy	640	...	...	1440	1960	4040	1	-9	4032
B	Agriculture, forestry, fishing and hunting	4545	...	...	6594	1095	12234	885	1196	14315
C	Mining (except fuels), manufacturing and construction	4505	...	...	10610	20815	35930	1141	12247	49318
D	Transportation and communication	43176	...	...	87492	52522	183190	39281	21818	244289
E	Other economic affairs	5506	...	...	7349	2030	14885	1908	360	17153
10	Other functions	19983	...	...	1	336665	356649	5	12	356666
	Total	755052	...	...	152939	1624310	2532300	114146	58324	2704770

Belgium

2.3 Total Government Outlays by Function and Type
(Continued)

Million Belgian francs

		Final Consumption Expenditures			Subsidies	Other Current Transfers & Property Income	Total Current Disbursements	Gross Capital Formation	Other Capital Outlays	Total Outlays
		Total	Compensation of Employees	Other						

1985

		Total	Comp.	Other	Subsidies	Other Current	Total Current	Gross Capital	Other Capital	Total Outlays
1	General public services	121300	...	...	141	14610	136051	5943	9065	151059
2	Defence	123608	...	...	195	4981	128784	1419	-114	130089
3	Public order and safety	69946	...	...	131	891	70968	3180	115	74263
4	Education	305378	...	...	1481	17644	324503	38075	1382	363960
5	Health	23742	...	...	4074	259305	287121	317	906	288344
6	Social security and welfare	47943	...	...	8558	933355	989856	593	865	991314
7	Housing and community amenities	11231	...	...	16913	10798	38942	10341	10236	59519
8	Recreation, culture and religion	20094	...	...	1348	18701	40143	6535	1609	48287
9	Economic services	62941	...	...	115638	91786	270365	39027	42371	351763
	A Fuel and energy	609	...	...	1312	565	2486	1	86	2573
	B Agriculture, forestry, fishing and hunting	5040	...	...	6456	1138	12634	770	1667	15071
	C Mining (except fuels), manufacturing and construction	4690	...	...	11142	29441	45273	1051	18592	64916
	D Transportation and communication	46699	...	...	87955	58802	193456	35282	21143	249881
	E Other economic affairs	5903	...	...	8773	1840	16516	1923	883	19322
10	Other functions	22748	...	...	-	392244	414992	571	41	415604
	Total	808931	...	...	148479	1744320	2701730	106001	66476	2874200

1986

1	General public services	125660	...	...	147	13807	139614	5496	8538	153648
2	Defence	128934	...	...	215	4859	134008	1865	32	135905
3	Public order and safety	78841	...	...	146	4854	83841	3358	136	87335
4	Education	309231	...	...	1516	18000	328747	32545	501	361793
5	Health	23930	...	...	1316	273063	298309	408	1496	300213
6	Social security and welfare	49777	...	...	7327	960268	1017370	654	674	1018700
7	Housing and community amenities	11497	...	...	14071	11504	37072	8945	9556	55573
8	Recreation, culture and religion	21119	...	...	1306	15798	38223	5729	1548	45500
9	Economic services	66855	...	...	120179	111028	298062	40285	34973	373320
	A Fuel and energy	704	...	...	3331	541	4576	20	16	4612
	B Agriculture, forestry, fishing and hunting	5226	...	...	5964	1212	12402	593	1838	14833
	C Mining (except fuels), manufacturing and construction	4592	...	...	11000	37889	53481	987	13978	68446
	D Transportation and communication	50610	...	...	89882	69776	210268	36913	18566	265747
	E Other economic affairs	5723	...	...	10002	1610	17335	1772	575	19682
10	Other functions	22381	...	...	3	430427	452811	890	105	453806
	Total	838225	...	...	146226	1843610	2828060	100175	57559	2985790

2.5 Private Final Consumption Expenditure by Type and Purpose, in Current Prices

Million Belgian francs

		1970	1975	1980	1981	1982	1983	1984	1985	1986	1987	1988	1989
	Final Consumption Expenditure of Resident Households												
1	Food, beverages and tobacco	241700	388813	536869 / 462494	475669	542027	593666	634290	668606	682396	689830	693959	715084
	A Food	185437	293039	403876 / 379518	389403	442269	486802	524868	555296	565395	569517	572895	590008
	B Non-alcoholic beverages	8543	16540	23885 / 9542	9742	10899	11952	11940	12874	15035	16360	17573	20380
	C Alcoholic beverages	32339	53543	73708 / 38034	38908	43712	45753	44041	46014	46331	49324	47782	47355
	D Tobacco	15381	25691	35400 / 35400	37616	45147	49159	53441	54422	55635	54629	55709	57341
2	Clothing and footwear	56670	99945	153943 / 175913	181903	206544	210197	218803	232751	243629	255272	258525	283646
3	Gross rent, fuel and power	117182	218152	364289 / 364289	420176	464577	498035	543835	593378	575567	582135	592475	625379
	A Fuel and power	...	...	... / 136239	161387	179338	184595	202886	228486	189071	171300	157545	163622

Belgium

2.5 Private Final Consumption Expenditure by Type and Purpose, in Current Prices
(Continued)

Million Belgian francs

		1970	1975	1980	1981	1982	1983	1984	1985	1986	1987	1988	1989
	B Other	...	...	228050	258789	285239	313440	340949	364892	386496	410835	434930	461757
4	Furniture, furnishings and household equipment and operation	107541	212832	310804 / 252577	258422	270199	280791	289362	304842	332616	351330	373467	408821
	A Household operation	35452	62199	92708 / 30013	32454	35120	37158	40075	40818	44931	47350	47544	51817
	B Other	72089	150633	218096 / 222564	225968	235079	243633	249287	264024	287685	303980	325923	357004
5	Medical care and health expenses	48151	114228	193992 / 209535	229376	253826	280988	300117	323514	342930	361191	384369	412938
6	Transport and communication	79785	162264	274752 / 268644	287188	314900	341510	366053	388467	391927	413258	442165	483767
	A Personal transport equipment	25520	51119	84498 / 84498	79008	88993	101254	116086	123455	140366	150519	169321	185698
	B Other	54265	111145	190254 / 184146	208180	225907	240256	249967	265012	251561	262739	272844	298069
7	Recreational, entertainment, education and cultural services	30693	61242	104374 / 128239	140760	153452	160215	176872	186452	203890	218074	233015	245478
	A Education	1669	3184	4457	...	...	...	...	...	...	...	...	...
	B Other	29024	58058	99917 / 128239	140760	153452	160215	176872	186452	203890	218074	233015	245478
8	Miscellaneous goods and services [a]	85591	154676	263197 / 290270	311963	343368	360520	392902	417556	449799	488364	531195	582508
	A Personal care	21363	39698	66552 / 38299	41898	45393	47835	49864	50792	54312	55206	56815	57718
	B Expenditures in restaurants, cafes and hotels	37006	61485	95759 / 160419	171315	186979	204238	220315	234923	247707	261534	280728	307794
	C Other	27222	53493	100886 / 91552	98750	110996	108447	122723	131841	147780	171624	193652	216996
Statistical discrepancy		...	...	-13353	-2215	-8303	-32702	-40067	-5884	-29000	-8950	-14308	-5556
Total Final Consumption Expenditure in the Domestic Market by Households, of which		767313	1412150	2202220 / 2138610	2303240	2540590	2693220	2882170	3109680	3193750	3350500	3494860	3752070
Plus: Direct purchases abroad by resident households		20500	43000	78500 / 78500	88200	82600	88500	93300	100700	107100	121000	138800	137700
Less: Direct purchases in the domestic market by non-resident households		18800	34000	55800 / 45200	57600	73100	94800	101800	105100	104800	114800	127300	125000
Equals: Final Consumption Expenditure of Resident Households [b]		769013	1421150	2224920 / 2171910	2333840	2550090	2686920	2873670	3105280	3196050	3356700	3506360	3764770

Final Consumption Expenditure of Private Non-profit Institutions Serving Households

	1970	1975	1980	1981	1982	1983	1984	1985	1986	1987	1988	1989
Equals: Final Consumption Expenditure of Private Non-profit Organisations Serving Households	...	...	...	...	...	...	...	...	...	...	...	...
Private Final Consumption Expenditure	769013	1421150	2224920 / 2171910	2333840	2550090	2686920	2873670	3105280	3196050	3356700	3506360	3764770

a) For the first series, item 'Miscellaneous goods and services' includes a statistical discrepancy.
b) Item 'Final consumption expenditure of resident households' includes consumption expenditure of private non-profit institutions serving households.

2.6 Private Final Consumption Expenditure by Type and Purpose, in Constant Prices

Million Belgian francs

		1970	1975	1980	1981	1982	1983	1984	1985	1986	1987	1988	1989
				At constant prices of: 1980					1985				

Final Consumption Expenditure of Resident Households

		1970	1975	1980	1981	1982	1983	1984	1985	1986	1987	1988	1989
1	Food, beverages and tobacco	444859	493062	536869 / 666372	644202	668643	666070	659963	668606	673369	681282	683833	684521
	A Food	340112	367988	403876 / 542362	527024	545709	546429	543567	555296	561556	569375	572139	575336
	B Non-alcoholic beverages	14878	20422	23885 / 13120	12114	12579	12804	12384	12874	14499	15252	16267	18688
	C Alcoholic beverages	52686	64801	73708 / 54806	50058	51053	49353	45840	46014	45104	47723	45847	43559
	D Tobacco	37183	39851	35400 / 56084	55006	59302	57484	58172	54422	52210	48932	49580	46938

Belgium

2.6 Private Final Consumption Expenditure by Type and Purpose, in Constant Prices
(Continued)

Million Belgian francs

	1970	1975	1980	1981	1982	1983	1984	1985	1986	1987	1988	1989
				At constant prices of:								
			1980					1985				
2 Clothing and footwear	100822	127462	153943									
			230446	230603	246033	237323	234238	232751	227865	227760	222847	237504
3 Gross rent, fuel and power	266000	325507	364289									
			547221	553319	554192	555455	568225	593378	602547	611912	609434	615963
A Fuel and power	...	...	...									
			222938	216901	211072	205743	211262	228486	229687	230985	219303	215928
B Other	...	...	...									
			324283	336418	343120	349712	356963	364892	372860	380927	390131	400035
4 Furniture, furnishings and household equipment and operation	199675	260631	310804									
			328314	322741	324110	311523	304107	304842	319165	329221	344998	371003
A Household operation	82287	88983	92708									
			43756	45259	46383	43856	43216	40818	42535	43810	44269	46940
B Other	117388	171648	218096									
			284558	277482	277727	267667	260891	264024	276630	285411	300729	324063
5 Medical care and health expenses	98925	154054	193992									
			286005	298573	305713	313911	315118	323514	326565	335381	351210	369271
6 Transport and communication	181111	233878	274752									
			384459	377216	377797	377341	383579	388467	402182	416507	436903	455508
A Personal transport equipment	49588	69073	84498									
			126145	111671	113618	115577	121577	123455	134144	139337	150477	157727
B Other	131523	164805	190254									
			258314	265545	264179	261764	262002	265012	268038	277170	286426	297781
7 Recreational, entertainment, education and cultural services	65510	80904	104374									
			166661	176342	183559	178780	185167	186452	198206	207685	219787	229813
A Education	3526	3992	4457									
			...	...	...	...	...	...	...	...	...	...
B Other	61984	76912	99917									
			166661	176342	183559	178780	185167	186452	198206	207685	219787	229813
8 Miscellaneous goods and services	167973[a]	204010[a]	263197[a]									
			399450	398593	409964	395392	414801	417556	431152	455309	483742	513089
A Personal care	52920	58099	66552									
			55096	55036	54505	52721	52117	50792	50808	49612	49732	49438
B Expenditures in restaurants, cafés and hotels	79068	92804	95759									
			214184	212695	220096	221078	233260	234923	235964	242902	254567	268146
C Other	35985	53107	100886									
			130170	130862	135363	121593	129424	131841	144380	162795	179443	195505
Statistical discrepancy	...	...	...									
			-299	-19991	-20557	-19122	-11362	-5884	-4167	3058	2918	2883
Total Final Consumption Expenditure in the Domestic Market by Households, of which	1524880	1879510	2202220									
			3008630	2981600	3049450	3016670	3053840	3109680	3176880	3268120	3355670	3479560
Plus: Direct purchases abroad by resident households	41100	60300	78500									
			107300	112200	100000	98600	99500	100700	102000	112300	125800	120200
Less: Direct purchases in the domestic market by non-resident households	37700	47700	55800									
			61700	73200	88400	105600	108400	105100	99800	106600	115400	109100
Equals: Final Consumption Expenditure of Resident Households [b]	1528280	1892110	2224920									
			3054230	3020600	3061050	3009670	3044940	3105280	3179080	3273820	3366070	3490660

Final Consumption Expenditure of Private Non-profit Institutions Serving Households

Equals: Final Consumption Expenditure of Private Non-profit Organisations Serving Households	...	...	...	...	...	...	...	...	...	...	...	...
Private Final Consumption Expenditure	1528280	1892110	2224920									
			3054230	3020600	3061050	3009670	3044940	3105280	3179080	3273820	3366070	3490660

a) For the first series, item 'Miscellaneous goods and services' includes a statistical discrepancy.
b) Item 'Final consumption expenditure of resident households' includes consumption expenditure of private non-profit institutions serving households.

Belgium

2.7 Gross Capital Formation by Type of Good and Owner, in Current Prices

Million Belgian francs

	1980 TOTAL	1980 Total Private	1980 Public Enterprises	1980 General Government	1981 TOTAL	1981 Total Private	1981 Public Enterprises	1981 General Government	1982 TOTAL	1982 Total Private	1982 Public Enterprises	1982 General Government
Increase in stocks, total [a]	24668	...	...	...	-4959	...	...	...	5517	...	...	...
1 Goods producing industries	24668	...	...	...	-4959	...	...	...	5517	...	...	...
A Materials and supplies	...	...	...	...	...	...	...	...	...	...	...	...
B Work in progress	12616	...	...	...	5155	...	...	...	4992	...	...	...
C Livestock, except breeding stocks, dairy cattle, etc.	-603	...	...	...	-154	...	...	...	523	...	...	...
D Finished goods [b]	12655	...	...	...	-9960	...	...	...	2	...	...	...
2 Wholesale and retail trade	...	...	...	...	...	...	...	...	...	...	...	...
3 Other, except government stocks	...	...	...	...	...	...	...	...	...	...	...	...
4 Government stocks	...	...	...	...	...	...	...	...	...	...	...	...
Gross Fixed Capital Formation, Total	728285	...	...	...	642879	...	...	...	672119	...	...	...
1 Residential buildings	203517	...	...	...	121686	...	...	...	115076	...	...	...
2 Non-residential buildings												
3 Other construction	286050	...	...	...	283072	...	...	...	292122	...	...	...
4 Land improvement and plantation and orchard development												
5 Producers' durable goods	218144	...	...	...	224219	...	...	...	251147	...	...	...
A Transport equipment	51617	...	...	...	51993	...	...	...	57438	...	...	...
B Machinery and equipment	166527	...	...	...	172226	...	...	...	193709	...	...	...
6 Breeding stock, dairy cattle, etc.	-81	...	...	...	-1952	...	...	...	-215	...	...	...
Statistical discrepancy [c]	20655	...	...	...	15854	...	...	...	13989	...	...	...
Total Gross Capital Formation	752953	...	...	...	637920	...	...	...	677636	...	...	...

	1983 TOTAL	1983 Total Private	1983 Public Enterprises	1983 General Government	1984 TOTAL	1984 Total Private	1984 Public Enterprises	1984 General Government	1985 TOTAL	1985 Total Private	1985 Public Enterprises	1985 General Government
Increase in stocks, total [a]	-29706	...	...	...	15388	...	...	...	-36225	...	...	...
1 Goods producing industries	-29706	...	...	...	15388	...	...	...	-36225	...	...	...
A Materials and supplies	...	...	...	...	...	...	...	...	...	...	...	...
B Work in progress	-8453	...	...	...	11898	...	...	...	-4123	...	...	...
C Livestock, except breeding stocks, dairy cattle, etc.	1175	...	...	...	889	...	...	...	-1189	...	...	...
D Finished goods [b]	-22428	...	...	...	2601	...	...	...	-30913	...	...	...
2 Wholesale and retail trade	...	...	...	...	...	...	...	...	...	...	...	...
3 Other, except government stocks	...	...	...	...	...	...	...	...	...	...	...	...
4 Government stocks	...	...	...	...	...	...	...	...	...	...	...	...
Gross Fixed Capital Formation, Total	669008	...	...	...	709028	...	...	...	741285	...	...	...
1 Residential buildings	115639	...	...	...	118092	...	...	...	130896	...	...	...
2 Non-residential buildings												
3 Other construction	275165	...	...	...	265351	...	...	...	268367	...	...	...
4 Land improvement and plantation and orchard development												
5 Producers' durable goods	261214	...	...	...	307193	...	...	...	322033	...	...	...
A Transport equipment	60056	...	...	...	77046	...	...	...	69792	...	...	...
B Machinery and equipment	201158	...	...	...	230147	...	...	...	252241	...	...	...
6 Breeding stock, dairy cattle, etc.	817	...	...	...	244	...	...	...	200	...	...	...
Statistical discrepancy [c]	16173	...	...	...	18148	...	...	...	19789	...	...	...
Total Gross Capital Formation	639302	...	...	...	724416	...	...	...	705060	...	...	...

Belgium

2.7 Gross Capital Formation by Type of Good and Owner, in Current Prices

Million Belgian francs

	1986 TOTAL	Total Private	Public Enterprises	General Government	1987 TOTAL	Total Private	Public Enterprises	General Government	1988 TOTAL	Total Private	Public Enterprises	General Government
Increase in stocks, total [a]	-33528	...	...	...	11502	...	...	...	22024	...	...	...
1 Goods producing industries	-33528	...	...	...	11502	...	...	...	22024	...	...	...
A Materials and supplies	...	...	...	...	...	...	...	...	...	...	...	...
B Work in progress	516	...	...	...	-2263	...	...	...	5611	...	...	...
C Livestock, except breeding stocks, dairy cattle, etc.	1372	...	...	...	-440	...	...	...	1466	...	...	...
D Finished goods [b]	-35416	...	...	...	14205	...	...	...	14947	...	...	...
2 Wholesale and retail trade	...	...	...	...	...	...	...	...	...	...	...	...
3 Other, except government stocks	...	...	...	...	...	...	...	...	...	...	...	...
4 Government stocks	...	...	...	...	...	...	...	...	...	...	...	...
Gross Fixed Capital Formation, Total	782915	...	...	...	835405	...	...	...	968601	...	...	...
1 Residential buildings	138521	...	...	...	152661	...	...	...	195510	...	...	...
2 Non-residential buildings												
3 Other construction	274435	...	...	...	280407	...	...	...	308082	...	...	...
4 Land improvement and plantation and orchard development												
5 Producers' durable goods	346919	...	...	...	372636	...	...	...	430489	...	...	...
A Transport equipment	76852	...	...	...	93554	...	...	...	100389	...	...	...
B Machinery and equipment	270067	...	...	...	279082	...	...	...	330100	...	...	...
6 Breeding stock, dairy cattle, etc.	-687	...	...	...	-945	...	...	...	-474	...	...	...
Statistical discrepancy [c]	23727	...	...	...	30646	...	...	...	34994	...	...	...
Total Gross Capital Formation	749387	...	...	...	846907	...	...	...	990625	...	...	...

	1989 TOTAL	Total Private	Public Enterprises	General Government
Increase in stocks, total [a]	38741	...	...	...
1 Goods producing industries	38741	...	...	...
A Materials and supplies	...	...	...	...
B Work in progress	10080	...	...	...
C Livestock, except breeding stocks, dairy cattle, etc.	1801	...	...	...
D Finished goods [b]	26860	...	...	...
2 Wholesale and retail trade	...	...	...	...
3 Other, except government stocks	...	...	...	...
4 Government stocks	...	...	...	...
Gross Fixed Capital Formation, Total	1153660	...	...	...
1 Residential buildings	246233	...	...	...
2 Non-residential buildings				
3 Other construction	335695	...	...	...
4 Land improvement and plantation and orchard development				
5 Producers' durable goods	526423	...	...	...
A Transport equipment	125298	...	...	...
B Machinery and equipment	401125	...	...	...
6 Breeding stock, dairy cattle, etc.	-478	...	...	...
Statistical discrepancy [c]	45787	...	...	...
Total Gross Capital Formation	1192400	...	...	...

a) Item 'Increase in stocks' includes the statistical adjustment concerning gross capital formation. 'Finished goods'.
b) Items 'Wholesale and retail trade' and 'Other, except government stocks' are included in item c) Item 'Statistical discrepancy' refers to other products.

Belgium

2.8 Gross Capital Formation by Type of Good and Owner, in Constant Prices

Million Belgian francs

	1980				1981				1982			
	TOTAL	Total Private	Public Enterprises	General Government	TOTAL	Total Private	Public Enterprises	General Government	TOTAL	Total Private	Public Enterprises	General Government
	At constant prices of: 1985											
Increase in stocks, total	38674	...	...	...	-10224	...	...	...	4022	...	...	...
1 Goods producing industries	38674	...	...	...	-10224	...	...	...	4022	...	...	...
A Materials and supplies	...	...	...	...	...	...	...	...	...	...	...	...
B Work in progress	16779	...	...	...	6524	...	...	...	5896	...	...	...
C Livestock, except breeding stocks, dairy cattle, etc.	-733	...	...	...	-196	...	...	...	631	...	...	...
D Finished goods [a]	22628	...	...	...	-16552	...	...	...	-2505	...	...	...
2 Wholesale and retail trade	...	...	...	...	...	...	...	...	...	...	...	...
3 Other, except government stocks	...	...	...	...	...	...	...	...	...	...	...	...
4 Government stocks	...	...	...	...	...	...	...	...	...	...	...	...
Gross Fixed Capital Formation, Total	917656	...	...	...	769877	...	...	...	756691	...	...	...
1 Residential buildings	241185	...	...	...	136221	...	...	...	129798	...	...	...
2 Non-residential buildings												
3 Other construction	379892	...	...	...	347291	...	...	...	327034	...	...	...
4 Land improvement and plantation and orchard development												
5 Producers' durable goods	268581	...	...	...	269356	...	...	...	284243	...	...	...
A Transport equipment	71366	...	...	...	69829	...	...	...	71560	...	...	...
B Machinery and equipment	197215	...	...	...	199527	...	...	...	212683	...	...	...
6 Breeding stock, dairy cattle, etc.	-85	...	...	...	-2399	...	...	...	-234	...	...	...
Statistical discrepancy [a]	28083	...	...	...	19408	...	...	...	15850	...	...	...
Total Gross Capital Formation	956330	...	...	...	759653	...	...	...	760713	...	...	...

	1983				1984				1985			
	TOTAL	Total Private	Public Enterprises	General Government	TOTAL	Total Private	Public Enterprises	General Government	TOTAL	Total Private	Public Enterprises	General Government
	At constant prices of: 1985											
Increase in stocks, total	-28629	...	...	...	24107	...	...	...	-36225	...	...	...
1 Goods producing industries	-28629	...	...	...	24107	...	...	...	-36225	...	...	...
A Materials and supplies	...	...	...	...	...	...	...	...	...	...	...	...
B Work in progress	-9435	...	...	...	12659	...	...	...	-4123	...	...	...
C Livestock, except breeding stocks, dairy cattle, etc.	1285	...	...	...	943	...	...	...	-1189	...	...	...
D Finished goods [a]	-20479	...	...	...	10505	...	...	...	-30913	...	...	...
2 Wholesale and retail trade	...	...	...	...	...	...	...	...	...	...	...	...
3 Other, except government stocks	...	...	...	...	...	...	...	...	...	...	...	...
4 Government stocks	...	...	...	...	...	...	...	...	...	...	...	...
Gross Fixed Capital Formation, Total	723403	...	...	...	736014	...	...	...	741285	...	...	...
1 Residential buildings	127286	...	...	...	124268	...	...	...	130896	...	...	...
2 Non-residential buildings												
3 Other construction	300396	...	...	...	277473	...	...	...	268367	...	...	...
4 Land improvement and plantation and orchard development												
5 Producers' durable goods	276941	...	...	...	314674	...	...	...	322033	...	...	...
A Transport equipment	66325	...	...	...	80061	...	...	...	69792	...	...	...
B Machinery and equipment	210616	...	...	...	234613	...	...	...	252241	...	...	...
6 Breeding stock, dairy cattle, etc.	756	...	...	...	278	...	...	...	200	...	...	...
Statistical discrepancy [a]	18024	...	...	...	19321	...	...	...	19789	...	...	...
Total Gross Capital Formation	694774	...	...	...	760121	...	...	...	705060	...	...	...

Belgium

2.8 Gross Capital Formation by Type of Good and Owner, in Constant Prices

Million Belgian francs

	1986 TOTAL	Total Private	Public Enterprises	General Government	1987 TOTAL	Total Private	Public Enterprises	General Government	1988 TOTAL	Total Private	Public Enterprises	General Government
	\multicolumn{12}{c}{At constant prices of:1985}											
Increase in stocks, total	-26226	...	...	...	14100	...	...	...	25202	...	...	...
1 Goods producing industries	-26226	...	...	...	14100	...	...	...	25202	...	...	...
A Materials and supplies	...	...	...	...	...	...	...	...	...	...	...	...
B Work in progress	498	...	...	...	-2137	...	...	...	5215	...	...	...
C Livestock, except breeding stocks, dairy cattle, etc.	1854	...	...	...	-278	...	...	...	1575	...	...	...
D Finished goods [a]	-28578	...	...	...	16515	...	...	...	18412	...	...	...
2 Wholesale and retail trade	...	...	...	...	...	...	...	...	...	...	...	...
3 Other, except government stocks	...	...	...	...	...	...	...	...	...	...	...	...
4 Government stocks	...	...	...	...	...	...	...	...	...	...	...	...
Gross Fixed Capital Formation, Total	774047	...	...	...	818730	...	...	...	928896	...	...	...
1 Residential buildings	133719	...	...	...	140179	...	...	...	175110	...	...	...
2 Non-residential buildings												
3 Other construction	277691	...	...	...	284811	...	...	...	305820	...	...	...
4 Land improvement and plantation and orchard development		...	...	...		...	...	...		...	...	...
5 Producers' durable goods	339145	...	...	...	363402	...	...	...	413478	...	...	...
A Transport equipment	74286	...	...	...	88988	...	...	...	92606	...	...	...
B Machinery and equipment	264859	...	...	...	274414	...	...	...	320872	...	...	...
6 Breeding stock, dairy cattle, etc.	-743	...	...	...	-1055	...	...	...	-513	...	...	...
Statistical discrepancy [a]	24235	...	...	...	31393	...	...	...	35001	...	...	...
Total Gross Capital Formation	747821	...	...	...	832830	...	...	...	954098	...	...	...

	1989 TOTAL	Total Private	Public Enterprises	General Government
	\multicolumn{4}{c}{At constant prices of:1985}				
Increase in stocks, total	37298	...	...	...
1 Goods producing industries	37298	...	...	...
A Materials and supplies	...	...	...	...
B Work in progress	8969	...	...	...
C Livestock, except breeding stocks, dairy cattle, etc.	1596	...	...	...
D Finished goods [a]	26733	...	...	...
2 Wholesale and retail trade	...	...	...	...
3 Other, except government stocks	...	...	...	...
4 Government stocks	...	...	...	...
Gross Fixed Capital Formation, Total	1055050	...	...	...
1 Residential buildings	208568	...	...	...
2 Non-residential buildings				
3 Other construction	315172	...	...	...
4 Land improvement and plantation and orchard development		...	...	...
5 Producers' durable goods	488812	...	...	...
A Transport equipment	110024	...	...	...
B Machinery and equipment	378788	...	...	...
6 Breeding stock, dairy cattle, etc.	-539	...	...	...
Statistical discrepancy [a]	43036	...	...	...
Total Gross Capital Formation	1092350	...	...	...

a) Items 'Wholesale and retail trade' and 'Other, except government stocks' are included in item 'Finished goods'.

Belgium

2.11 Gross Fixed Capital Formation by Kind of Activity of Owner, ISIC Divisions, in Current Prices

Million Belgian francs

		1970	1975	1980	1981	1982	1983	1984	1985	1986	1987	1988	1989
						All Producers							
1	Agriculture, hunting, forestry and fishing	7492	10909	15294 / 15213	12135	15095	16956	17662	18223	18871	20246	19803	21049
2	Mining and quarrying	2214	2088	2999	...	...	...	...	...	...	...	...	...
3	Manufacturing	73453	106409	109189 / 106540	98270	119406	125658	138873	155000	178004	190137	222554	286382
	A Manufacturing of food, beverages and tobacco	...	...	17078	14774	16364	20109	18710	19865	24164	25841	30391	39415
	B Textile, wearing apparel and leather industries	...	...	5913	5450	7849	11716	15529	12478	14521	18164	19534	22425
	C Manufacture of wood, and wood products, including furniture [a]	...	...	...	...	...	...	...	...	...	...	...	...
	D Manufacture of paper and paper products, printing and publishing	...	...	7985	7376	8704	8787	12302	11309	17825	18801	21179	26806
	E Manufacture of chemicals and chemical petroleum, coal, rubber and plastic products	...	...	20070	17382	22301	23809	25396	30430	37895	39662	55065	72285
	F Manufacture of non-metalic mineral products except products of petroleum and coal	...	...	7366	5486	5092	6433	8086	9020	11736	16473	17204	22947
	G Basic metal industries	...	...	14083	15373	20299	18635	13359	19452	14696	15524	20121	29922
	H Manufacture of fabricated metal products, machinery and equipment	...	...	28207	27887	33192	28936	37621	45220	47793	43566	45739	57047
	I Other manufacturing industries [a]	...	...	5838	4542	5605	7233	7870	7226	9374	12106	13321	15535
4	Electricity, gas and water [b]	15724	35692	39592 / 43982	43605	47581	45502	50496	52811	43207	38577	40257	44980
5	Construction	8463	7917	12226 / 12226	13807	11290	8806	11347	12614	15107	15200	22779	30115
6	Wholesale and retail trade, restaurants and hotels [cd]	26300	49500	77500 / 55411	51563	58388	65203	73456	82020	94179	110023	135256	152310
	A Wholesale and retail trade [e]	...	...	48021	45040	50922	57496	64762	72581	82062	94018	116005	132558
	B Restaurants and hotels	...	...	7390	6523	7466	7707	8694	9439	12117	16005	19251	19752
7	Transport, storage and communication [f]	27437	56693	86331 / 87544	102323	105135	89871	96311	88272	82367	88263	81855	100825
	A Transport and storage	...	...	69110	83325	84078	67465	71923	65101	60458	66648	59931	78453

Belgium

2.11 Gross Fixed Capital Formation by Kind of Activity of Owner, ISIC Divisions, in Current Prices
(Continued)

Million Belgian francs

	1970	1975	1980	1981	1982	1983	1984	1985	1986	1987	1988	1989
B Communication	...	...	18434	18998	21057	22406	24388	23171	21909	21615	21924	22372
8 Finance, insurance, real estate and business services g	71778	144839	224725 / 18796	16569	18824	19614	23659	26634	30628	30471	33074	34511
A Financial institutions			18796	16569	18824	19614	23659	26634	30628	30471	33074	34511
B Insurance	...	...										
C Real estate and business services g			...	...								
Real estate except dwellings			...	...								
Dwellings	...	...	224725	139026	131375	132666	138250	152207	163835	183567	230438	289762
9 Community, social and personal services d,g	14793	31841	59112 / 262911	177598	169467	173329	183078	199710	220377	247859	312912	393236
Total Industries	247654	445888	626968 / 602623	515870	545186	544939	594882	635284	682740	740776	868490	1063410
Producers of Government Services	39420	66040	101398 / 125662	127009	126933	124069	114146	106001	100175	94629	100111	90252
Private Non-Profit Institutions Serving Households	...	...	...									
Total	287074	511928	728366 / 728285	642879	672119	669008	709028	741285	782915	835405	968601	1153660

a) Item 'Manufacture of wood and wood products, including furniture' is included in item 'Other manufacturing industries'.
b) Item 'Electricity, gas and water' includes also other energy products.
c) For the first series, item 'Wholesale and retail trade, restaurants and hotels' includes banks and insurance but excludes hotels and restaurants.
d) For the first series, restaurants and hotels are included in item 'Community, social and personal services'.
e) For the second series, including repairs.
f) For the first series, item 'Tranport, storage and communication' includes state investments on rivers, canals and ports.
g) Business services and real estate except dwellings are included in item 'Community, social and personal services'.

2.12 Gross Fixed Capital Formation by Kind of Activity of Owner, ISIC Divisions, in Constant Prices

Million Belgian francs

	1970	1975	1980	1981	1982	1983	1984	1985	1986	1987	1988	1989
			At constant prices of:									
			1980					1985				
					All Producers							
1 Agriculture, hunting, forestry and fishing	13554	13392	15294 / 19488	14865	17424	18238	18325	18223	18553	19883	19109	19385
2 Mining and quarrying	3581	2410	2999	...	...	...	...	...	...	...	...	...
3 Manufacturing	124364	126971	109189 / 129766	115535	132478	133163	142407	155000	175392	187613	216485	269177
A Manufacturing of food, beverages and tobacco	...	...	21031	17476	18258	21359	19237	19865	23820	25484	29527	36939
B Textile, wearing apparel and leather industries	...	...	7193	6423	8733	12421	15943	12478	14300	17924	19014	21084
C Manufacture of wood, and wood products, including furniture	...	...	...									
D Manufacture of paper and paper products, printing and publishing	...	...	9696	8637	9647	9285	12596	11309	17576	18561	20615	25217
E Manufacture of chemicals and chemical petroleum, coal, rubber and plastic products			24277	20414	24742	25313	26039	30430	37341	39173	53649	68082
F Manufacture of non-metalic mineral products except products of petroleum and coal			9099	6435	5648	6799	8302	9020	11545	16219	16637	21489
G Basic metal industries	...	...	16933	17990	22416	19679	13673	19452	14444	15319	19598	28189
H Manufacture of fabricated metal products, machinery and equipment			34313	32752	36756	30613	38535	45220	47119	42989	44520	53654
I Other manufacturing industries			7224[a]	5408[a]	6278[a]	7694[a]	8082[a]	7226[a]	9247[a]	11944[a]	12925[a]	14523[a]
4 Electricity, gas and water	32088	45953	39592 / 56150[b]	52382[b]	53677[b]	49123[b]	52459[b]	52811[b]	43210[b]	38698[b]	39576[b]	42187[b]

Belgium

2.12 Gross Fixed Capital Formation by Kind of Activity of Owner, ISIC Divisions, in Constant Prices
(Continued)

Million Belgian francs

	1970	1975	1980	1981	1982	1983	1984	1985	1986	1987	1988	1989
			At constant prices of:									
		1980						**1985**				
5 Construction	13379	9366	12226									
			15291	16622	12845	9445	11692	12614	14812	14828	21894	27842
6 Wholesale and retail trade, restaurants and hotels	51165 cd	63633 cd	77500 cd									
			72146	64295	67873	71196	76579	82020	93297	108718	130746	140273
A Wholesale and retail trade	...	...	62630 e	56376 e	59417 e	62784 e	67475 e	72581 e	81136 e	92619 e	111777 e	121779 e
B Restaurants and hotels	...	...	9516	7919	8456	8412	9104	9439	12161	16099	18969	18494
7 Transport, storage and communication	45966 f	67050 f	86331 f									
			112127	125214	117526	96184	99018	88272	81755	87376	79436	93471
A Transport and storage	...	...	89992	103053	94388	72596	74116	65101	60215	66060	58077	72365
B Communication	...	...	22135	22161	23138	23588	24902	23171	21540	21316	21359	21106
8 Finance, insurance, real estate and business services g	182761	209270	224725									
			24156	19969	21055	21129	24558	26634	30445	30393	32420	32402
A Financial institutions	...	...	24156	19969	21055	21129	24558	26634	30445	30393	32420	32402
B Insurance	...	...										
C Real estate and business services			...									
Real estate except dwellings			...									
Dwellings			269641	157466	148364	146044	145509	152207	159276	171457	209672	249284
9 Community, social and personal services	32715 dg	43401 dg	59112 dg									
			319785 h	204984 h	192060 h	190268 h	192231 h	199710 h	215424 h	235290 h	289904 h	345308 h
Total Industries	499573	581446	626968									
			748909	613866	614938	588746	617269	635284	672888	722799	829570	970045
Producers of Government Services	89842	88997	101398									
			168747	156011	141753	134657	118745	106001	101159	95931	99326	85004
Private Non-Profit Institutions Serving Households	...	...	...									
Total	589415	670443	728366									
			917656	769877	756691	723403	736014	741285	774047	818730	928896	1055050

a) Item 'Manufacture of wood and wood products, including furniture' is included in item 'Other manufacturing industries'.
b) Item 'Electricity, gas and water' includes also other energy products.
c) For the first series, item 'Wholesale and retail trade, restaurants and hotels' includes banks and insurance but excludes hotels and restaurants.
d) For the first series, restaurants and hotels are included in item 'Community, social and personal services'.
e) For the second series, including repairs.
f) For the first series, item 'Tranport, storage and communication' includes state investments on rivers, canals and ports.
g) Business services and real estate except dwellings are included in item 'Community, social and personal services'.
h) Item 'Finance, insurance, real estate and business services' includes only rented and owner-occupied dwellings.

2.17 Exports and Imports of Goods and Services, Detail

Million Belgian francs

	1970	1975	1980	1981	1982	1983	1984	1985	1986	1987	1988	1989
			Exports of Goods and Services									
1 Exports of merchandise, f.o.b.	452800	856800	1596400									
			1802200	1991600	2308100	2531000	2903700	3012800	2874100	2904300	3247200	3711900
2 Transport and communication												
3 Insurance service charges	90300	174400	374200									
			322800	389800	413100	453100	499700	527000	546700	595300	655100	785000
4 Other commodities												
5 Adjustments of merchandise exports to change-of-ownership basis	...	...	...									
6 Direct purchases in the domestic market by non-residential households	18800	34000	55800									
			45200	57600	73100	94800	101800	105100	104800	114800	127300	125000
7 Direct purchases in the domestic market by extraterritorial bodies	...	...	...									
Total Exports of Goods and Services a	561900	1065200	2026400									
			2170200	2439000	2794300	3078900	3505200	3644900	3525600	3614400	4029600	4621900
			Imports of Goods and Services									
1 Imports of merchandise, c.i.f. b	424900	858300	1698800									
			2029900	2234500	2565400	2714800	3106400	3165600	2939100	3025500	3337900	3822800

Belgium

2.17 Exports and Imports of Goods and Services, Detail
(Continued)

Million Belgian francs

	1970	1975	1980	1981	1982	1983	1984	1985	1986	1987	1988	1989
A Imports of merchandise, f.o.b.	424900	858300	1698800	...	...	...	...	...	...	...	...	...
B Transport of services on merchandise imports	...	...	...	...	...	...	...	...	...	...	...	...
C Insurance service charges on merchandise imports	...	...	...	...	...	...	...	...	...	...	...	...
2 Adjustments of merchandise imports to change-of-ownership basis	...	...	...	...	...	...	...	...	...	...	...	...
3 Other transport and communication												
4 Other insurance service charges	87400	159800	347400									
			149400	174300	185500	201000	229300	259600	278800	304200	347000	460500
5 Other commodities												
6 Direct purchases abroad by government	...	...	...	...	...	...	...	...	...	...	...	...
7 Direct purchases abroad by resident households	20500	43000	78500									
			78500	88200	82600	88500	93300	100700	107100	121000	138800	137700
Total Imports of Goods and Services [a]	532800	1061100	2124700									
			2257800	2497000	2833500	3004300	3429000	3525900	3325000	3450700	3823700	4421000
Balance of Goods and Services	29100	4100	-98300									
			-87600	-58000	-39200	74600	76200	119000	200600	163700	205900	200900
Total Imports and Balance of Goods and Services [a]	561900	1065200	2026400									
			2170200	2439000	2794300	3078900	3505200	3644900	3525600	3614400	4029600	4621900

a) Beginning 1977 for the first series, disbursements and receipts are not compensated in the balance of payments. Therefore these series are not comparable with previous years. b) Beginning 1972 for the first series, item 'Imports of merchandise f.o.b.' includes imports of military goods previously included in 'Other commodities'.

3.11 General Government Production Account: Total and Subsectors

Million Belgian francs

	1980					1981				
	Total General Government	Central Government	State or Provincial Government	Local Government	Social Security Funds	Total General Government	Central Government	State or Provincial Government	Local Government	Social Security Funds
	Gross Output									
1 Sales	...	...	...	...	...	...	...	...	...	...
2 Services produced for own use	613889	412547	...	165843	35499	663743	449766	...	174295	39682
3 Own account fixed capital formation	...	...	...	...	...	...	...	...	...	...
Gross Output [a]	626968	421129	...	168642	37197	676922	460171	...	175314	41437
	Gross Input									
Intermediate Consumption	139748	110250	...	19702	9796	149499	117309	...	21309	10881
Subtotal: Value Added	487220	310879	...	148940	27401	527423	342862	...	154005	30556
1 Indirect taxes, net	-	-	...	-	-	-	-	...	-	-
2 Consumption of fixed capital	12234	7799	...	3948	487	12863	8452	...	3905	506
3 Compensation of employees	471571	303080	...	142753	25738	512464	334410	...	149341	28713
4 Net Operating surplus	3415	-	...	2239	1176	2096	-	...	759	1337
Gross Input [a]	626968	421129	...	168642	37197	676922	460171	...	175314	41437

	1982					1983				
	Total General Government	Central Government	State or Provincial Government	Local Government	Social Security Funds	Total General Government	Central Government	State or Provincial Government	Local Government	Social Security Funds
	Gross Output									
1 Sales	...	...	...	...	...	...	...	...	...	...
2 Services produced for own use	700567	472623	...	185291	42653	721520	484832	...	192035	44653
3 Own account fixed capital formation	...	...	...	...	...	...	...	...	...	...
Gross Output [a]	714388	483104	...	186344	44940	737128	497395	...	193219	46514

Belgium

3.11 General Government Production Account: Total and Subsectors
(Continued)

Million Belgian francs

	\multicolumn{5}{c	}{1982}	\multicolumn{5}{c	}{1983}
	Total General Government	Central Government	State or Provincial Government	Local Government	Social Security Funds	Total General Government	Central Government	State or Provincial Government	Local Government	Social Security Funds
\multicolumn{11}{c}{Gross Input}
Intermediate Consumption	154412	120610	...	22270	11532	165805	128538	...	23721	13546
Subtotal: Value Added	559976	362494	...	164074	33408	571323	368857	...	169498	32968
1 Indirect taxes, net	-	-	...	-	-	-	-	...	-	-
2 Consumption of fixed capital	13213	8771	...	3837	605	13809	9313	...	3976	520
3 Compensation of employees	543981	353723	...	159395	30863	555246	359544	...	164575	31127
4 Net Operating surplus	2782	-	...	842	1940	2268	-	...	947	1321
Gross Input [a]	714388	483104	...	186344	44940	737128	497395	...	193219	46514

	\multicolumn{5}{c	}{1984}	\multicolumn{5}{c	}{1985}
	Total General Government	Central Government	State or Provincial Government	Local Government	Social Security Funds	Total General Government	Central Government	State or Provincial Government	Local Government	Social Security Funds
\multicolumn{11}{c}{Gross Output}
1 Sales	...	...	...	...	...	...	...	...	...	...
2 Services produced for own use	755052	502918	...	203707	48427	808931	539227	...	218491	51213
3 Own account fixed capital formation	...	...	...	...	...	...	...	...	...	...
Gross Output [a]	770122	514732	...	204935	50455	823690	551706	...	219766	52218
\multicolumn{11}{c}{Gross Input}
Intermediate Consumption	170217	130365	...	25258	14594	186170	144119	...	26264	15787
Subtotal: Value Added	599905	384367	...	179677	35861	637520	407587	...	193502	36431
1 Indirect taxes, net	-	-	...	-	-	-	-	...	-	-
2 Consumption of fixed capital	14711	9926	...	4230	555	15454	10681	...	4413	360
3 Compensation of employees	582882	374441	...	174565	33876	620498	396906	...	188069	35523
4 Net Operating surplus	2312	-	...	882	1430	1568	-	...	1020	548
Gross Input [a]	770122	514732	...	204935	50455	823690	551706	...	219766	52218

	\multicolumn{5}{c	}{1986}	\multicolumn{5}{c	}{1987}
	Total General Government	Central Government	State or Provincial Government	Local Government	Social Security Funds	Total General Government	Central Government	State or Provincial Government	Local Government	Social Security Funds
\multicolumn{11}{c}{Gross Output}
1 Sales	...	...	...	...	...	...	...	...	...	...
2 Services produced for own use	838225	556600	...	229152	52473	846837	564003	...	229266	53568
3 Own account fixed capital formation	...	...	...	...	...	...	...	...	...	...
Gross Output [a]	854038	569988	...	230561	53489	862420	577170	...	230731	54519
\multicolumn{11}{c}{Gross Input}
Intermediate Consumption	193127	149415	...	27651	16061	201306	155589	...	28125	17592
Subtotal: Value Added	660911	420573	...	202910	37428	661114	421581	...	202606	36927
1 Indirect taxes, net	-	-	...	-	-	-	-	...	-	-
2 Consumption of fixed capital	16606	11447	...	4786	373	18201	12499	...	5326	376
3 Compensation of employees	642782	409126	...	196997	36659	641536	409082	...	196108	36346
4 Net Operating surplus	1523	-	...	1127	396	1377	-	...	1172	205
Gross Input [a]	854038	569988	...	230561	53489	862420	577170	...	230731	54519

	\multicolumn{5}{c	}{1988}	\multicolumn{5}{c	}{1989}
	Total General Government	Central Government	State or Provincial Government	Local Government	Social Security Funds	Total General Government	Central Government	State or Provincial Government	Local Government	Social Security Funds
\multicolumn{11}{c}{Gross Output}
1 Sales	...	...	...	...	...	...	...	...	...	...
2 Services produced for own use	845589	555585	...	234975	55029	869836	567750	...	243674	58412
3 Own account fixed capital formation	...	...	...	...	...	...	...	...	...	...
Gross Output [a]	865827	573314	...	236566	55947	888362	584192	...	245437	58733
\multicolumn{11}{c}{Gross Input}
Intermediate Consumption	196431	151120	...	28298	17013	189740	143510	...	28778	17452
Subtotal: Value Added	669396	422194	...	208268	38934	698622	440682	...	216659	41281
1 Indirect taxes, net	-	-	...	-	-	-	-	...	-	-
2 Consumption of fixed capital	19616	13207	...	6016	393	21814	14524	...	6868	422
3 Compensation of employees	648213	408987	...	200979	38247	675259	426158	...	208381	40720
4 Net Operating surplus	1567	-	...	1273	294	1549	-	...	1410	139
Gross Input [a]	865827	573314	...	236566	55947	888362	584192	...	245437	58733

a) State or Provincial government is included in Local government.

Belgium

3.12 General Government Income and Outlay Account: Total and Subsectors

Million Belgian francs

	1980					1981				
	Total General Government	Central Government	State or Provincial Government	Local Government	Social Security Funds	Total General Government	Central Government	State or Provincial Government	Local Government	Social Security Funds

Receipts

1 Operating surplus	3415	-	...	2239	1176	2096	-	...	759	1337
2 Property and entrepreneurial income	58185	27856	...	11423	19746	70315	35271	...	14283	21597
A Withdrawals from public quasi-corporations	4455	4190	...	265	-	5096	3074	...	2022	-
B Interest	26744	3629	...	4218	19737	27013	3750	...	2528	21571
C Dividends	24522	19495	...	5018	9	35709	27946	...	7737	26
D Net land rent and royalties	2464	542	...	1922	-	2497	501	...	1996	-
3 Taxes, fees and contributions	1533970	1025000	...	63648	445320	1611010	1066150	...	71661	473196
A Indirect taxes	428031	418016	...	10015	-	448921	436952	...	11969	-
B Direct taxes	639589	591346	...	48243	-	665487	611730	...	53757	-
C Social security contributions	466352	15642	...	5390	445320	496603	17472	...	5935	473196
D Fees, fines and penalties [a]	...	...	...	...	...	...	...	...	...	...
4 Other current transfers	105537	80458	...	152289	233319	117445	83740	...	171137	302800
A Casualty insurance claims	2978	1298	...	1665	15	4152	1810	...	2321	21
B Transfers from other government subsectors	-	1009	...	132295	227225	-	1008	...	146279	292945
C Transfers from the rest of the world	24188	24188	...	-	-	22466	22466	...	-	-
D Other transfers, except imputed [a]	16541	10680	...	817	5044	20771	11138	...	955	8678
E Imputed unfunded employee pension and welfare contributions	61830	43283	...	17512	1035	70056	47318	...	21582	1156
Total Current Receipts [b]	1701110	1133320	...	229599	699561	1800870	1185170	...	257840	798930

Disbursements

1 Government final consumption expenditure	613889	412547	...	165843	35499	663743	449766	...	174295	39682
2 Property income	215622	171553	...	39969	4940	289760	241220	...	43931	5445
A Interest	215622	171553	...	39969	4940	289760	241220	...	43931	5445
B Net land rent and royalties	...	...	...	...	...	...	...	...	...	...
3 Subsidies	138516	131505	...	7011	-	147072	138647	...	8425	-
4 Other current transfers	893843	543920	...	39513	670939	1006880	645641	...	47184	754286
A Casualty insurance premiums, net	3104	1354	...	1735	15	4398	1918	...	2458	22
B Transfers to other government subsectors	...	359520	...	1009	-	...	439224	...	1008	-
C Social security benefits	685886	15642	...	5390	664854	770239	17472	...	5935	746832
D Social assistance grants [c]	69967	59567	...	10400	-	81928	69620	...	12308	-
E Unfunded employee pension and welfare benefits	61830	43283	...	17512	1035	70056	47318	...	21582	1156
F Transfers to private non-profit institutions serving households [c]	...	...	...	...	...	...	...	...	...	...
G Other transfers n.e.c.	20250	11748	...	3467	5035	22673	12504	...	3893	6276
H Transfers to the rest of the world	52806	52806	...	-	-	57585	57585	...	-	-
Net saving	-160761	-126207	...	-22737	-11817	-306587	-290109	...	-15995	-483
Total Current Disbursements and Net Saving [b]	1701110	1133320	...	229599	699561	1800870	1185170	...	257840	798930

	1982					1983				
	Total General Government	Central Government	State or Provincial Government	Local Government	Social Security Funds	Total General Government	Central Government	State or Provincial Government	Local Government	Social Security Funds

Receipts

1 Operating surplus	2782	-	...	842	1940	2268	-	...	947	1321
2 Property and entrepreneurial income	88706	54420	...	15303	20279	79257	45465	...	15047	20331
A Withdrawals from public quasi-corporations	6651	4459	...	2192	-	7675	5093	...	2582	-
B Interest	33357	11784	...	2618	20251	34844	14239	...	1931	20260
C Dividends	46112	37609	...	8475	28	34099	25652	...	8376	71
D Net land rent and royalties	2586	568	...	2018	-	2639	481	...	2158	-
3 Taxes, fees and contributions	1816160	1211080	...	90976	514104	1923000	1260090	...	95639	567263
A Indirect taxes	495208	481330	...	13878	-	530053	513932	...	16121	

Belgium

3.12 General Government Income and Outlay Account: Total and Subsectors
(Continued)

Million Belgian francs

	1982 Total General Government	1982 Central Government	1982 State or Provincial Government	1982 Local Government	1982 Social Security Funds	1983 Total General Government	1983 Central Government	1983 State or Provincial Government	1983 Local Government	1983 Social Security Funds
B Direct taxes	779296	709557	...	69739	-	795589	724450	...	71139	-
C Social security contributions	541656	20193	...	7359	514104	597354	21712	...	8379	567263
D Fees, fines and penalties [a]	...	...	...	...	...	...	...	...	...	...
4 Other current transfers	128860	93881	...	180947	345332	137881	101394	...	190566	360725
A Casualty insurance claims	4474	1951	...	2501	22	5046	2200	...	2821	25
B Transfers from other government subsectors	-	1414	...	153709	336177	-	1250	...	161014	352540
C Transfers from the rest of the world	29152	29152	...	-	-	30798	30798	...	-	-
D Other transfers, except imputed [a]	21003	11972	...	1186	7845	22162	13845	...	1480	6837
E Imputed unfunded employee pension and welfare contributions	74231	49392	...	23551	1288	79875	53301	...	25251	1323
Total Current Receipts [b]	2036510	1359380	...	288068	881655	2142400	1406950	...	302199	949640

Disbursements

1 Government final consumption expenditure	700567	472623	...	185291	42653	721520	484832	...	192035	44653
2 Property income	366455	312779	...	49506	5466	395599	334746	...	56446	5993
A Interest	366455	312779	...	49506	5466	395599	334746	...	56446	5993
B Net land rent and royalties	...	...	...	...	...	...	...	...	...	...
3 Subsidies	157083	146258	...	10825	-	178394	166440	...	11954	-
4 Other current transfers	1092710	715205	...	51787	817014	1176550	750306	...	55169	885882
A Casualty insurance premiums, net	4739	2066	...	2649	24	5284	2304	...	2954	26
B Transfers to other government subsectors	...	489886	...	1414	-	...	513554	...	1250	-
C Social security benefits	838644	20193	...	7359	811092	909366	21712	...	8379	879275
D Social assistance grants [c]	83209	70459	...	12750	-	90501	76983	...	13518	-
E Unfunded employee pension and welfare benefits	74231	49392	...	23551	1288	79875	53301	...	25251	1323
F Transfers to private non-profit institutions serving households [c]	...	...	...	...	...	...	...	...	...	...
G Other transfers n.e.c.	21244	12570	...	4064	4610	16652	7577	...	3817	5258
H Transfers to the rest of the world	70639	70639	...	-	-	74875	74875	...	-	-
Net saving	-280303	-287484	...	-9341	16522	-329664	-329371	...	-13405	13112
Total Current Disbursements and Net Saving [b]	2036510	1359380	...	288068	881655	2142400	1406950	...	302199	949640

	1984 Total General Government	1984 Central Government	1984 State or Provincial Government	1984 Local Government	1984 Social Security Funds	1985 Total General Government	1985 Central Government	1985 State or Provincial Government	1985 Local Government	1985 Social Security Funds

Receipts

1 Operating surplus	2312	-	...	882	1430	1568	-	...	1020	548
2 Property and entrepreneurial income	84942	48032	...	15081	23432	89527	48977	...	17180	24841
A Withdrawals from public quasi-corporations	8763	6265	...	2498	-	9473	6415	...	3058	-
B Interest	38733	15392	...	1563	23381	44265	19246	...	1701	24789
C Dividends	34559	25791	...	8717	51	32062	22013	...	9997	52
D Net land rent and royalties	2887	584	...	2303	-	3727	1303	...	2424	-
3 Taxes, fees and contributions	2114820	1353680	...	114889	646248	2268530	1437150	...	118562	712818
A Indirect taxes	554687	535958	...	18729	-	582009	563510	...	18499	-
B Direct taxes	879256	791817	...	87439	-	939341	847490	...	91851	-
C Social security contributions	680876	25907	...	8721	646248	747182	26152	...	8212	712818
D Fees, fines and penalties [a]	...	...	...	...	...	...	...	...	...	...

Belgium

3.12 General Government Income and Outlay Account: Total and Subsectors
(Continued)

Million Belgian francs

		1984					1985				
		Total General Government	Central Government	State or Provincial Government	Local Government	Social Security Funds	Total General Government	Central Government	State or Provincial Government	Local Government	Social Security Funds
4	Other current transfers	146869	108369	...	210791	353966	161697	122072	...	221547	315742
	A Casualty insurance claims	5246	2287	...	2933	26	5435	2370	...	3038	27
	B Transfers from other government subsectors	-	1388	...	180979	343890	-	1825	...	190496	305343
	C Transfers from the rest of the world	33643	33643	...	-	-	43277	43277	...	-	-
	D Other transfers, except imputed [a]	26358	16401	...	1407	8550	26640	16277	...	1585	8778
	E Imputed unfunded employee pension and welfare contributions	81622	54650	...	25472	1500	86345	58323	...	26428	1594
	Total Current Receipts [b]	2348940	1510080	...	341643	1025080	2521320	1608200	...	358309	1053950

Disbursements

1	Government final consumption expenditure	755052	502918	...	203707	48427	808931	539227	...	218491	51213
2	Property income	447044	385379	...	56208	7060	515805	452875	...	57665	6736
	A Interest	447044	385379	...	56208	7060	515805	452875	...	57665	6736
	B Net land rent and royalties	...	...	...	...	...	...	...	...	...	...
3	Subsidies	186039	177140	...	8899	-	190760	184535	...	6225	-
4	Other current transfers	1234530	774052	...	56513	930217	1287920	757233	...	59374	968979
	A Casualty insurance premiums, net	5615	2448	...	3139	28	5855	2553	...	3273	29
	B Transfers to other government subsectors	...	524869	...	1388	-	...	495839	...	1825	-
	C Social security benefits	956493	25907	...	8721	921865	992491	26152	...	8212	958127
	D Social assistance grants [c]	96704	82821	...	13883	-	104351	88761	...	15590	-
	E Unfunded employee pension and welfare benefits	81622	54650	...	25472	1500	86345	58323	...	26428	1594
	F Transfers to private non-profit institutions serving households [c]	...	...	...	...	...	...	...	...	...	...
	G Other transfers n.e.c.	20705	9971	...	3910	6824	24361	11086	...	4046	9229
	H Transfers to the rest of the world	73386	73386	...	-	-	74519	74519	...	-	-
	Net saving	-273718	-329406	...	16316	39372	-282094	-325669	...	16554	27021
	Total Current Disbursements and Net Saving [b]	2348940	1510080	...	341643	1025080	2521320	1608200	...	358309	1053950

		1986					1987				
		Total General Government	Central Government	State or Provincial Government	Local Government	Social Security Funds	Total General Government	Central Government	State or Provincial Government	Local Government	Social Security Funds

Receipts

1	Operating surplus	1523	-	...	1127	396	1377	-	...	1172	205
2	Property and entrepreneurial income	78996	35241	...	19411	26355	70442	27221	...	21304	23969
	A Withdrawals from public quasi-corporations	10595	7089	...	3506	-	11441	7637	...	3804	-
	B Interest	41407	14959	...	2161	26298	32640	8019	...	2766	23907
	C Dividends	23711	12509	...	11145	57	22669	10517	...	12090	62
	D Net land rent and royalties	3283	684	...	2599	-	3692	1048	...	2644	-
3	Taxes, fees and contributions	2353000	1471920	...	122563	758510	2477060	1545340	...	123960	807758
	A Indirect taxes	594660	575709	...	18951	-	644246	625646	...	18600	-
	B Direct taxes	963965	869344	...	94621	-	989952	893257	...	96695	-
	C Social security contributions	794371	26870	...	8991	758510	842864	26441	...	8665	807758
	D Fees, fines and penalties [a]	...	...	...	...	...	...	...	...	...	...
4	Other current transfers	169424	127737	...	231575	317736	182805	137315	...	223540	278807
	A Casualty insurance claims	5520	2407	...	3086	27	6076	2649	...	3396	31
	B Transfers from other government subsectors	-	1620	...	199381	306623	-	1657	...	187364	267836
	C Transfers from the rest of the world	45317	45317	...	-	-	43821	43821	...	-	-
	D Other transfers, except imputed [a]	28494	17609	...	1525	9360	35476	24468	...	1845	9163
	E Imputed unfunded employee pension and welfare contributions	90093	60784	...	27583	1726	97432	64720	...	30935	1777
	Total Current Receipts [b]	2602940	1634900	...	374676	1103000	2731690	1709880	...	369976	1110740

Belgium

3.12 General Government Income and Outlay Account: Total and Subsectors
(Continued)

Million Belgian francs

		1986					1987			
		Total General Government	Central Government	State or Provincial Government	Local Government	Social Security Funds	Total General Government	Central Government	State or Provincial Government	Local Government	Social Security Funds

Disbursements

1	Government final consumption expenditure	838225	556600	...	229152	52473	846837	564003	...	229266	53568
2	Property income	574820	510159	...	59421	7251	566583	507384	...	55043	6208
	A Interest	574820	510159	...	59421	7251	566583	507384	...	55043	6208
	B Net land rent and royalties	...	...	...	...	...	...	...	...	...	...
3	Subsidies	190853	186500	...	4353	-	178340	174460	...	3880	-
4	Other current transfers	1333400	774182	...	62667	1004180	1409650	747086	...	68635	1050790
	A Casualty insurance premiums, net	5787	2523	...	3235	29	6140	2677	...	3432	31
	B Transfers to other government subsectors	...	506004	...	1620	-	...	455200	...	1657	-
	C Social security benefits	1030130	26870	...	8991	994270	1073260	26441	...	8665	1038160
	D Social assistance grants [c]	105637	88692	...	16945	-	112994	93241	...	19753	-
	E Unfunded employee pension and welfare benefits	90093	60784	...	27583	1726	97432	64720	...	30935	1777
	F Transfers to private non-profit institutions serving households [c]	...	...	...	...	...	...	...	...	...	...
	G Other transfers n.e.c.	22992	10548	...	4293	8151	25972	10959	...	4193	10820
	H Transfers to the rest of the world	78761	78761	...	-	-	93848	93848	...	-	-
	Net saving	-334360	-392540	...	19083	39097	-269724	-283053	...	13152	177
	Total Current Disbursements and Net Saving [b]	2602940	1634900	...	374676	1103000	2731690	1709880	...	369976	1110740

		1988					1989			
		Total General Government	Central Government	State or Provincial Government	Local Government	Social Security Funds	Total General Government	Central Government	State or Provincial Government	Local Government	Social Security Funds

Receipts

1	Operating surplus	1567	-	...	1273	294	1549	-	...	1410	139
2	Property and entrepreneurial income	67215	23408	...	23093	24389	79153	32616	...	25760	24853
	A Withdrawals from public quasi-corporations	13149	9158	...	3991	-	13429	9233	...	4196	-
	B Interest	30886	6495	...	3715	24351	32610	6311	...	5522	24853
	C Dividends	19878	7153	...	12687	38	29849	16531	...	13318	-
	D Net land rent and royalties	3302	602	...	2700	-	3265	541	...	2724	-
3	Taxes, fees and contributions	2562930	1595390	...	126354	841185	2666010	1665020	...	126125	874862
	A Indirect taxes	674478	655604	...	18874	-	733377	713494	...	19883	-
	B Direct taxes	1012440	913985	...	98456	-	1020970	924240	...	96731	-
	C Social security contributions	876006	25797	...	9024	841185	911660	27287	...	9511	874862
	D Fees, fines and penalties [a]	...	...	...	...	...	...	...	...	...	...
4	Other current transfers	174718	123593	...	218182	325079	175825	123112	...	224616	305334
	A Casualty insurance claims	6376	2780	...	3564	32	6684	2914	...	3736	34
	B Transfers from other government subsectors	-	1755	...	179906	310475	-	1597	...	181962	293678
	C Transfers from the rest of the world	33823	33823	...	-	-	29119	29119	...	-	-
	D Other transfers, except imputed [a]	31457	16835	...	1940	12682	28458	16896	...	1966	9596
	E Imputed unfunded employee pension and welfare contributions	103062	68400	...	32772	1890	111564	72586	...	36952	2026
	Total Current Receipts [b]	2806430	1742390	...	368902	1190950	2922540	1820750	...	377911	1205190

Disbursements

1	Government final consumption expenditure	845589	555585	...	234975	55029	869836	567750	...	243674	58412
2	Property income	575103	518972	...	53796	6010	639774	584342	...	54798	4710
	A Interest	575103	518972	...	53796	6010	639774	584342	...	54798	4710
	B Net land rent and royalties	...	...	...	...	...	...	...	...	...	...
3	Subsidies	185036	181653	...	3383	-	178493	174796	...	3697	-

Belgium

3.12 General Government Income and Outlay Account: Total and Subsectors
(Continued)

Million Belgian francs

	1988 Total General Government	1988 Central Government	1988 State or Provincial Government	1988 Local Government	1988 Social Security Funds	1989 Total General Government	1989 Central Government	1989 State or Provincial Government	1989 Local Government	1989 Social Security Funds
4 Other current transfers	1450820	798749	...	72874	1071340	1523500	800081	...	78448	1122210
A Casualty insurance premiums, net	6773	2953	...	3786	34	7129	3108	...	3985	36
B Transfers to other government subsectors	...	490381	...	1755	-	...	475640	...	1597	-
C Social security benefits	1096330	25797	...	9024	1061510	1151530	27287	...	9511	1114730
D Social assistance grants c	119249	97932	...	21317	-	130486	108770	...	21716	-
E Unfunded employee pension and welfare benefits	103062	68400	...	32772	1890	111564	72586	...	36952	2026
F Transfers to private non-profit institutions serving households c	...	...	...	...	...	...	...	...	...	...
G Other transfers n.e.c.	25461	13335	...	4220	7906	23629	13521	...	4687	5421
H Transfers to the rest of the world	99951	99951	...	-	-	99169	99169	...	-	-
Net saving	-250126	-312572	...	3874	58572	-289070	-306220	...	-2706	19856
Total Current Disbursements and Net Saving b	2806430	1742390	...	368902	1190950	2922540	1820750	...	377911	1205190

a) Item 'Other current transfers' includes item 'Fees, fines and penalties'.
b) State or Provincial government is included in Local government.
c) Item 'Transfers to private non-profit institutions serving households' is included in item 'Social assistance grants'.

3.13 General Government Capital Accumulation Account: Total and Subsectors

Million Belgian francs

	1980 Total General Government	1980 Central Government	1980 State or Provincial Government	1980 Local Government	1980 Social Security Funds	1981 Total General Government	1981 Central Government	1981 State or Provincial Government	1981 Local Government	1981 Social Security Funds
Finance of Gross Accumulation										
1 Gross saving	-148527	-118408	...	-18789	-11330	-293724	-281657	...	-12090	23
A Consumption of fixed capital	12234	7799	...	3948	487	12863	8452	...	3905	506
B Net saving	-160761	-126207	...	-22737	-11817	-306587	-290109	...	-15995	-483
2 Capital transfers	13274	13472	...	15639	490	14105	14296	...	18960	9352
A From other government subsectors	...	198	...	15639	490	...	191	...	18960	9352
B From other resident sectors	12765	12765	...	...	...	13596	13596	...	...	...
C From rest of the world	509	509	...	...	...	509	509	...	...	...
Finance of Gross Accumulation a	-135253	-104936	...	-3150	-10840	-279619	-267361	...	6870	9375
Gross Accumulation										
1 Gross capital formation	125662	74614	...	50761	287	127009	78329	...	47912	768
A Increase in stocks	...	...	...	...	...	...	...	...	...	...
B Gross fixed capital formation	125662	74614	...	50761	287	127009	78329	...	47912	768
2 Purchases of land, net	12985	6836	...	6149	-	12027	7204	...	4823	-
3 Purchases of intangible assets, net	...	...	...	...	...	...	...	...	...	...
4 Capital transfers	47656	63235	...	748	-	63665	90655	...	1513	-
A To other government subsectors	...	16129	...	198	-	...	28312	...	191	-
B To other resident sectors	43356	42806	...	550	-	58740	57418	...	1322	-
C To rest of the world	4300	4300	...	...	...	4925	4925	...	...	...
Net lending	-321556	-249621	...	-60808	-11127	-482320	-443549	...	-47378	8607
Gross Accumulation a	-135253	-104936	...	-3150	-10840	-279619	-267361	...	6870	9375

	1982 Total General Government	1982 Central Government	1982 State or Provincial Government	1982 Local Government	1982 Social Security Funds	1983 Total General Government	1983 Central Government	1983 State or Provincial Government	1983 Local Government	1983 Social Security Funds
Finance of Gross Accumulation										
1 Gross saving	-267090	-278713	...	-5504	17127	-315855	-320058	...	-9429	13632
A Consumption of fixed capital	13213	8771	...	3837	605	13809	9313	...	3976	520
B Net saving	-280303	-287484	...	-9341	16522	-329664	-329371	...	-13405	13112
2 Capital transfers	13177	13422	...	19781	5422	13145	13430	...	18024	4889
A From other government subsectors	...	245	...	19781	5422	...	285	...	18024	4889
B From other resident sectors	12893	12893	...	...	...	13080	13080	...	...	...
C From rest of the world	284	284	...	...	...	65	65	...	...	...
Finance of Gross Accumulation a	-253913	-265291	...	14277	22549	-302710	-306628	...	8595	18521
Gross Accumulation										
1 Gross capital formation	126933	77699	...	48462	772	124069	83394	...	40009	666

Belgium

3.13 General Government Capital Accumulation Account: Total and Subsectors
(Continued)

Million Belgian francs

	1982					1983				
	Total General Government	Central Government	State or Provincial Government	Local Government	Social Security Funds	Total General Government	Central Government	State or Provincial Government	Local Government	Social Security Funds
A Increase in stocks	...	...	...	...	...	...	...	...	...	...
B Gross fixed capital formation	126933	77699	...	48462	772	124069	83394	...	40009	666
2 Purchases of land, net	8175	4853	...	3322	-	6442	4297	...	2145	-
3 Purchases of intangible assets, net	...	...	...	...	...	...	...	...	...	...
4 Capital transfers	57001	81030	...	1419	-	53147	75039	...	1306	-
A To other government subsectors	...	25203	...	245	-	...	22913	...	285	-
B To other resident sectors	50963	49789	...	1174	-	46322	45301	...	1021	-
C To rest of the world	6038	6038	...	...	-	6825	6825	...	...	-
Net lending	-446022	-428873	...	-38926	21777	-486368	-469358	...	-34865	17855
Gross Accumulation [a]	-253913	-265291	...	14277	22549	-302710	-306628	...	8595	18521

	1984					1985				
	Total General Government	Central Government	State or Provincial Government	Local Government	Social Security Funds	Total General Government	Central Government	State or Provincial Government	Local Government	Social Security Funds

Finance of Gross Accumulation

1 Gross saving	-259007	-319480	...	20546	39927	-266640	-314988	...	20967	27381
A Consumption of fixed capital	14711	9926	...	4230	555	15454	10681	...	4413	360
B Net saving	-273718	-329406	...	16316	39372	-282094	-325669	...	16554	27021
2 Capital transfers	14300	14451	...	18916	4831	16931	17053	...	18002	4839
A From other government subsectors	...	151	...	18916	4831	...	122	...	18002	4839
B From other resident sectors	13995	13995	...	...	...	16907	16907	...	...	...
C From rest of the world	305	305	...	...	...	24	24	...	...	...
Finance of Gross Accumulation [a]	-244707	-305029	...	39462	44758	-249709	-297935	...	38969	32220

Gross Accumulation

1 Gross capital formation	114146	79737	...	33813	596	106001	73921	...	31531	549
A Increase in stocks	...	...	...	...	...	...	...	...	...	...
B Gross fixed capital formation	114146	79737	...	33813	596	106001	73921	...	31531	549
2 Purchases of land, net	4633	3331	...	1302	-	6514	4834	...	1680	-
3 Purchases of intangible assets, net	...	...	...	...	...	...	...	...	...	...
4 Capital transfers	53691	76366	...	1223	-	59962	81708	...	1217	-
A To other government subsectors	...	23747	...	151	-	...	22841	...	122	-
B To other resident sectors	45793	44721	...	1072	-	51050	49955	...	1095	-
C To rest of the world	7898	7898	...	...	...	8912	8912	...	...	...
Net lending	-417177	-464463	...	3124	44162	-422186	-458398	...	4541	31671
Gross Accumulation [a]	-244707	-305029	...	39462	44758	-249709	-297935	...	38969	32220

	1986					1987				
	Total General Government	Central Government	State or Provincial Government	Local Government	Social Security Funds	Total General Government	Central Government	State or Provincial Government	Local Government	Social Security Funds

Finance of Gross Accumulation

1 Gross saving	-317754	-381093	...	23869	39470	-251523	-270554	...	18478	553
A Consumption of fixed capital	16606	11447	...	4786	373	18201	12499	...	5326	376
B Net saving	-334360	-392540	...	19083	39097	-269724	-283053	...	13152	177
2 Capital transfers	14827	14897	...	16547	4932	23753	24172	...	18149	4944
A From other government subsectors	...	70	...	16547	4932	...	419	...	18149	4944
B From other resident sectors	14614	14614	...	...	...	23716	23716	...	...	...
C From rest of the world	213	213	...	...	...	37	37	...	...	...
Finance of Gross Accumulation [a]	-302927	-366196	...	40416	44402	-227770	-246382	...	36627	5497

Gross Accumulation

1 Gross capital formation	100175	68756	...	30865	554	94629	54143	...	39901	585
A Increase in stocks	...	...	...	...	...	...	...	...	...	...
B Gross fixed capital formation	100175	68756	...	30865	554	94629	54143	...	39901	585

Belgium

3.13 General Government Capital Accumulation Account: Total and Subsectors
(Continued)

Million Belgian francs

		1986					1987				
		Total General Government	Central Government	State or Provincial Government	Local Government	Social Security Funds	Total General Government	Central Government	State or Provincial Government	Local Government	Social Security Funds
2	Purchases of land, net	4850	3319	...	1531	-	5527	3401	...	2126	-
3	Purchases of intangible assets, net	...	...	...	...	...	...	...	...	...	...
4	Capital transfers	52709	73170	...	1088	-	50864	72878	...	1498	-
	A To other government subsectors	...	21479	...	70	-	...	23093	...	419	-
	B To other resident sectors	44011	42993	...	1018	-	40550	39471	...	1079	-
	C To rest of the world	8698	8698	...	...	...	10314	10314	...	...	...
	Net lending	-460661	-511441	...	6932	43848	-378790	-376804	...	-6898	4912
	Gross Accumulation a	-302927	-366196	...	40416	44402	-227770	-246382	...	36627	5497

		1988					1989				
		Total General Government	Central Government	State or Provincial Government	Local Government	Social Security Funds	Total General Government	Central Government	State or Provincial Government	Local Government	Social Security Funds
				Finance of Gross Accumulation							
1	Gross saving	-230510	-299365	...	9890	58965	-267256	-291696	...	4162	20278
	A Consumption of fixed capital	19616	13207	...	6016	393	21814	14524	...	6868	422
	B Net saving	-250126	-312572	...	3874	58572	-289070	-306220	...	-2706	19856
2	Capital transfers	16799	16930	...	19270	3668	17334	17450	...	18410	3668
	A From other government subsectors	...	131	...	19270	3668	...	116	...	18410	3668
	B From other resident sectors	16685	16685	...	...	...	17256	17256	...	...	...
	C From rest of the world	114	114	...	...	...	78	78	...	...	...
	Finance of Gross Accumulation a	-213711	-282435	...	29160	62633	-249922	-274246	...	22572	23946
				Gross Accumulation							
1	Gross capital formation	100111	55157	...	44274	680	90252	45803	...	43814	635
	A Increase in stocks	...	...	...	...	...	...	...	...	...	...
	B Gross fixed capital formation	100111	55157	...	44274	680	90252	45803	...	43814	635
2	Purchases of land, net	7612	4639	...	2973	-	5742	4550	...	1192	-
3	Purchases of intangible assets, net	...	...	...	...	...	...	...	...	...	...
4	Capital transfers	53206	74520	...	1755	-	56203	77144	...	1253	-
	A To other government subsectors	...	22938	...	131	-	...	22078	...	116	-
	B To other resident sectors	42231	40607	...	1624	-	45026	43889	...	1137	-
	C To rest of the world	10975	10975	...	...	...	11177	11177	...	...	...
	Net lending	-374640	-416751	...	-19842	61953	-402119	-401743	...	-23687	23311
	Gross Accumulation a	-213711	-282435	...	29160	62633	-249922	-274246	...	22572	23946

a) State or Provincial government is included in Local government.

3.21 Corporate and Quasi-Corporate Enterprise Production Account: Total and Sectors

Million Belgian francs

		1980				1981				1982			
		\multicolumn{3}{c}{Corporate and Quasi-Corporate Enterprises}	ADDENDUM: Total, including Unincorporated	\multicolumn{3}{c}{Corporate and Quasi-Corporate Enterprises}	ADDENDUM: Total, including Unincorporated	\multicolumn{3}{c}{Corporate and Quasi-Corporate Enterprises}	ADDENDUM: Total, including Unincorporated
		TOTAL	Non-Financial	Financial		TOTAL	Non-Financial	Financial		TOTAL	Non-Financial	Financial	
				Gross Output									
1	Output for sale	...	...	...	...	...	...	...	...	...	...	...	...
2	Imputed bank service charge	...	...	109121	109121	...	...	131558	131558	...	...	146437	146437
3	Own-account fixed capital formation	...	...	...	...	...	...	...	...	...	...	...	...
	Gross Output	...	...	216075	...	...	...	265660	...	...	...	298553	...
				Gross Input									
	Intermediate consumption	...	...	173772	...	...	...	208025	...	...	...	229566	...
	1 Imputed banking service charge	...	...	109121	109121	...	...	131558	131558	...	...	146437	146437
	2 Other intermediate consumption	...	...	64651	...	...	...	76467	...	...	...	83129	...
	Subtotal: Value Added	...	...	42303	2673910	...	...	57635	2737910	...	...	68987	2992460

Belgium

3.21 Corporate and Quasi-Corporate Enterprise Production Account: Total and Sectors
(Continued)

Million Belgian francs

	1980 TOTAL	1980 Non-Financial	1980 Financial	1980 ADDENDUM: Total, including Unincorporated	1981 TOTAL	1981 Non-Financial	1981 Financial	1981 ADDENDUM: Total, including Unincorporated	1982 TOTAL	1982 Non-Financial	1982 Financial	1982 ADDENDUM: Total, including Unincorporated
1 Indirect taxes, net	...	...	7617	-504	...	...	9293	-10327	...	...	11670	1472
A Indirect taxes	...	...	16855	138012	...	...	19020	136745	...	...	20556	155587
B Less: Subsidies	...	...	9238	138516	...	...	9727	147072	...	...	8886	154115
2 Consumption of fixed capital	...	...	14520	299911	...	...	15850	319206	...	...	16860	349661
3 Compensation of employees	...	...	115190	1599460	...	...	123558	1637540	...	...	140961	1734570
4 Net operating surplus	...	...	-95024	775048	...	...	-91066	791483	...	...	-100504	906761
Gross Input	...	...	216075	2673910	...	...	265660	2737910	...	...	298553	2992460

	1983 TOTAL	1983 Non-Financial	1983 Financial	1983 ADDENDUM: Total, including Unincorporated	1984 TOTAL	1984 Non-Financial	1984 Financial	1984 ADDENDUM: Total, including Unincorporated	1985 TOTAL	1985 Non-Financial	1985 Financial	1985 ADDENDUM: Total, including Unincorporated
Gross Output												
1 Output for sale	...	...	...	...	...	...	...	...	...	...	...	...
2 Imputed bank service charge	...	...	150628	150628	...	...	178145	178145	...	...	186425	186425
3 Own-account fixed capital formation	...	...	...	...	...	...	...	...	...	...	...	...
Gross Output	...	...	291906	...	...	...	346256	...	...	...	369125	...
Gross Input												
Intermediate consumption	...	...	232155	...	...	...	272281	...	...	...	286364	...
1 Imputed banking service charge	...	...	150628	150628	...	...	178145	178145	...	...	186425	186425
2 Other intermediate consumption	...	...	81527	...	...	...	94136	...	...	...	99939	...
Subtotal: Value Added	...	...	59751	3193060	...	...	73975	3454190	...	...	82761	3704500
1 Indirect taxes, net	...	...	13717	-6298	...	...	14510	-6596	...	...	16800	-5006
A Indirect taxes	...	...	22542	170124	...	...	23942	179352	...	...	26698	185692
B Less: Subsidies	...	...	8825	176422	...	...	9432	185948	...	...	9898	190698
2 Consumption of fixed capital	...	...	17680	384628	...	...	21310	408672	...	...	23670	439944
3 Compensation of employees	...	...	152755	1827960	...	...	165454	1945460	...	...	174336	2037750
4 Net operating surplus	...	...	-124401	986770	...	...	-127299	1106650	...	...	-132045	1231810
Gross Input	...	...	291906	3193060	...	...	346256	3454190	...	...	369125	3704500

	1986 TOTAL	1986 Non-Financial	1986 Financial	1986 ADDENDUM: Total, including Unincorporated	1987 TOTAL	1987 Non-Financial	1987 Financial	1987 ADDENDUM: Total, including Unincorporated	1988 TOTAL	1988 Non-Financial	1988 Financial	1988 ADDENDUM: Total, including Unincorporated
Gross Output												
1 Output for sale	...	...	...	...	...	...	...	...	...	...	...	...
2 Imputed bank service charge	...	...	207845	207845	...	...	204227	204227	...	...	200495	200495
3 Own-account fixed capital formation	...	...	...	...	...	...	...	...	...	...	...	...
Gross Output	...	...	418116	...	...	...	447490	...	...	...	474490	...
Gross Input												
Intermediate consumption	...	...	321270	...	...	...	325104	...	...	...	327927	...
1 Imputed banking service charge	...	...	207845	207845	...	...	204227	204227	...	...	200495	200495
2 Other intermediate consumption	...	...	113425	...	...	...	120877	...	...	...	127432	...
Subtotal: Value Added	...	...	96846	3925840	...	...	122386	4123250	...	...	146563	4424440
1 Indirect taxes, net	...	...	19203	6288	...	...	22763	36126	...	...	23486	34798
A Indirect taxes	...	...	28278	197135	...	...	30896	214466	...	...	32609	219834
B Less: Subsidies	...	...	9075	190847	...	...	8133	178340	...	...	9123	185036
2 Consumption of fixed capital	...	...	26040	454886	...	...	27600	475990	...	...	28050	498469
3 Compensation of employees	...	...	188055	2154010	...	...	194657	2223640	...	...	203955	2331070
4 Net operating surplus	...	...	-136452	1310650	...	...	-122634	1387500	...	...	-108928	1560100
Gross Input	...	...	418116	3925840	...	...	447490	4123250	...	...	474490	4424440

Belgium

3.21 Corporate and Quasi-Corporate Enterprise Production Account: Total and Sectors

Million Belgian francs

	1989 Corporate and Quasi-Corporate Enterprises TOTAL	Non-Financial	Financial	ADDENDUM: Total, Including Unincorporated
Gross Output				
1 Output for sale	...	...	...	...
2 Imputed bank service charge	...	...	208064	208064
3 Own-account fixed capital formation	...	...	...	...
Gross Output	...	...	519431	...
Gross Input				
Intermediate consumption	...	...	348082	...
1 Imputed banking service charge	...	...	208064	208064
2 Other intermediate consumption	...	...	140018	...
Subtotal: Value Added	...	...	171349	4842140
1 Indirect taxes, net	...	...	27569	67744
A Indirect taxes	...	...	36157	246237
B Less: Subsidies	...	...	8588	178493
2 Consumption of fixed capital	...	...	29580	...
3 Compensation of employees	...	...	214295	2462160
4 Net operating surplus	...	...	-100095	...
Gross Input	...	...	519431	...

3.22 Corporate and Quasi-Corporate Enterprise Income and Outlay Account: Total and Sectors

Million Belgian francs

	1980 TOTAL	Non-Financial	Financial	1981 TOTAL	Non-Financial	Financial	1982 TOTAL	Non-Financial	Financial	1983 TOTAL	Non-Financial	Financial
Receipts												
1 Operating surplus	211668	306692	-95024	187264	278330	-91066	266131	366635	-100504	311421	435822	-124401
2 Property and entrepreneurial income	747074	...	747074	1020280	...	1020280	1151500	...	1151500	1090520	...	1090520
A Withdrawals from quasi-corporate enterprises	...	...	...	...	...	...	...	...	...	...	...	...
B Interest	740561	...	740561	1012210	...	1012210	1141420	...	1141420	1076570	...	1076570
C Dividends	6498	...	6498	8059	...	8059	10062	...	10062	13922	...	13922
D Net land rent and royalties	15	...	15	15	...	15	20	...	20	25	...	25
3 Current transfers	166668	79275	87393	178705	82446	96259	193794	85991	107803	212667	90361	122306
A Casualty insurance claims	36140	26020	10120	38858	26018	12840	43584	27934	15650	48876	31341	17535
B Casualty insurance premiums, net, due to be received by insurance companies	73973	...	73973	79829	...	79829	88203	...	88203	100371	...	100371
C Current transfers from the rest of the world	...	...	...	...	...	...	...	...	...	...	...	...
D Other transfers except imputed	...	...	...	...	...	...	...	...	...	...	...	...
E Imputed unfunded employee pension and welfare contributions	56555	53255	3300	60018	56428	3590	62007	58057	3950	63420	59020	4400
Total Current Receipts	1125410	385967	739443	1386250	360776	1025470	1611420	452626	1158800	1614610	526183	1088420
Disbursements												
1 Property and entrepreneurial income [a]	845154	219024	626130	1107060	229264	877796	1270390	264622	1005770	1234770	298901	935872
A Withdrawals from quasi-corporations	160	...	160	154	...	154	150	...	150	151	...	151
B Interest	813205	208743	604462	1067840	218056	849779	1214280	251720	962555	1177660	286640	891015
C Dividends	21508	...	21508	27863	...	27863	43065	...	43065	44706	...	44706
D Net land rent and royalties	10281	10281	...	11208	11208	...	12902	12902	...	12261	12261	...
2 Direct taxes and other current transfers n.e.c. to general government	89749	76689	13060	87528	71883	15645	112932	94299	18633	115049	94706	20343
A Direct taxes	89749	76689	13060	87528	71883	15645	112932	94299	18633	115049	94706	20343
B Fines, fees, penalties and other current transfers n.e.c. [b]	...	...	...	...	...	...	...	...	...	...	...	...

Belgium

3.22 Corporate and Quasi-Corporate Enterprise Income and Outlay Account: Total and Sectors
(Continued)

Million Belgian francs

	1980 TOTAL	1980 Non-Financial	1980 Financial	1981 TOTAL	1981 Non-Financial	1981 Financial	1982 TOTAL	1982 Non-Financial	1982 Financial	1983 TOTAL	1983 Non-Financial	1983 Financial
3 Other current transfers	163963	80790	83173	175749	84897	90852	189513	88184	101329	208420	92403	116017
A Casualty insurance premiums, net	33140	27535	5605	35569	28469	7100	38932	30127	8805	44233	33383	10850
B Casualty insurance claims liability of insurance companies	73973	...	73973	79829	...	79829	88203	...	88203	100371	...	100371
C Transfers to private non-profit institutions	...	...	...	...	...	...	...	...	...	...	...	...
D Unfunded employee pension and welfare benefits	56555	53255	3300	60018	56428	3590	62007	58057	3950	63420	59020	4400
E Social assistance grants		...			...			...			...	
F Other transfers n.e.c. [b]	295	...	295	333	...	333	371	...	371	396	...	396
G Transfers to the rest of the world		...			...			...			...	
Net saving	26544	9464	17080	15911	-25268	41179	38586	5521	33065	56365	40173	16192
Total Current Disbursements and Net Saving	1125410	385967	739443	1386250	360776	1025470	1611420	452626	1158800	1614610	526183	1088420

	1984 TOTAL	1984 Non-Financial	1984 Financial	1985 TOTAL	1985 Non-Financial	1985 Financial	1986 TOTAL	1986 Non-Financial	1986 Financial	1987 TOTAL	1987 Non-Financial	1987 Financial
Receipts												
1 Operating surplus	378070	505369	-127299	466676	598721	-132045	495811	632263	-136452	529922	652556	-122634
2 Property and entrepreneurial income	1287770	...	1287770	1319280	...	1319280	1248800	...	1248800	1261100	...	1261100
A Withdrawals from quasi-corporate enterprises	...	...	...	...	...	...	...	...	...	...	...	...
B Interest	1271370	...	1271370	1300270	...	1300270	1225140	...	1225140	1238010	...	1238010
C Dividends	16380	...	16380	18983	...	18983	23639	...	23639	23062	...	23062
D Net land rent and royalties	25	...	25	25	...	25	25	...	25	25	...	25
3 Current transfers	229565	95342	134223	244216	99085	145131	238137	100814	137323	253408	107556	145852
A Casualty insurance claims	53527	32812	20715	58793	33973	24820	53633	33163	20470	59139	37694	21445
B Casualty insurance premiums, net, due to be received by insurance companies	108763	...	108763	115276	...	115276	111473	...	111473	118822	...	118822
C Current transfers from the rest of the world	...	...	...	...	...	...	...	...	...	...	...	...
D Other transfers except imputed	...	...	...	...	...	...	...	...	...	...	...	...
E Imputed unfunded employee pension and welfare contributions	67275	62530	4745	70147	65112	5035	73031	67651	5380	75447	69862	5585
Total Current Receipts	1895410	600711	1294700	2030170	697806	1332360	1982750	733077	1249670	2044430	760112	1284320
Disbursements												
1 Property and entrepreneurial income [a]	1444670	353237	1091430	1498390	377518	1120870	1374970	355335	1019640	1398670	370155	1028510
A Withdrawals from quasi-corporations	160	...	160	176	...	176	200	...	200	238	...	238
B Interest	1393880	339217	1054660	1436740	360454	1076280	1317240	336742	980494	1340390	349329	991057
C Dividends	36609	...	36609	44414	...	44414	38942	...	38942	37217	...	37217
D Net land rent and royalties	14020	14020	...	17064	17064	...	18593	18593	...	20826	20826	...
2 Direct taxes and other current transfers n.e.c. to general government	132744	108333	24411	148427	121027	27400	156626	123716	32910	164401	130664	33737
A Direct taxes	132744	108333	24411	148427	121027	27400	156626	123716	32910	164401	130664	33737
B Fines, fees, penalties and other current transfers n.e.c. [b]	...	...	...	...	...	...	...	...	...	...	...	...

Belgium

3.22 Corporate and Quasi-Corporate Enterprise Income and Outlay Account: Total and Sectors
(Continued)

Million Belgian francs

	1984 TOTAL	1984 Non-Financial	1984 Financial	1985 TOTAL	1985 Non-Financial	1985 Financial	1986 TOTAL	1986 Non-Financial	1986 Financial	1987 TOTAL	1987 Non-Financial	1987 Financial
3 Other current transfers	225725	98653	127072	238022	102649	135373	233081	102677	130404	246531	107955	138576
A Casualty insurance premiums, net	49234	36119	13115	52112	37537	14575	48086	35026	13060	51738	38093	13645
B Casualty insurance claims liability of insurance companies	108763	...	108763	115276	...	115276	111473	...	111473	118822	...	118822
C Transfers to private non-profit institutions	...	...	...	...	...	...	...	...	...	...	...	...
D Unfunded employee pension and welfare benefits	67279	62534	4745	70147	65112	5035	73031	67651	5380	75447	69862	5585
E Social assistance grants		...			...			...			...	
F Other transfers n.e.c. [b]	449	...	449	487	...	487	491	...	491	524	...	524
G Transfers to the rest of the world		...			...			...			...	
Net saving	92270	40488	51782	145328	96612	48716	218072	151349	66723	234832	151338	83494
Total Current Disbursements and Net Saving	1895410	600711	1294700	2030170	697806	1332360	1982750	733077	1249670	2044430	760112	1284320

	1988 TOTAL	1988 Non-Financial	1988 Financial

Receipts

	TOTAL	Non-Financial	Financial
1 Operating surplus	617922	726850	-108928
2 Property and entrepreneurial income	1406140	...	1406140
A Withdrawals from quasi-corporate enterprises	...	...	...
B Interest	1374980	...	1374980
C Dividends	31129	...	31129
D Net land rent and royalties	30	...	30
3 Current transfers	269891	113156	156735
A Casualty insurance claims	62563	39343	23220
B Casualty insurance premiums, net, due to be received by insurance companies	127685	...	127685
C Current transfers from the rest of the world	...	...	...
D Other transfers except imputed	...	...	...
E Imputed unfunded employee pension and welfare contributions	79643	73813	5830
Total Current Receipts	2293960	840006	1453950

Disbursements

	TOTAL	Non-Financial	Financial
1 Property and entrepreneurial income [a]	1582980	412593	1170390
A Withdrawals from quasi-corporations	268	...	268
B Interest	1523670	390094	1133570
C Dividends	36548	...	36548
D Net land rent and royalties	22499	22499	...
2 Direct taxes and other current transfers n.e.c. to general government	177736	139233	38503
A Direct taxes	177736	139233	38503
B Fines, fees, penalties and other current transfers n.e.c. [b]	...	...	...

Belgium

3.22 Corporate and Quasi-Corporate Enterprise Income and Outlay Account: Total and Sectors
(Continued)

Million Belgian francs

	1988 TOTAL	Non-Financial	Financial
3 Other current transfers	264754	115786	148968
A Casualty insurance premiums, net	56843	41973	14870
B Casualty insurance claims liability of insurance companies	127685	...	127685
C Transfers to private non-profit institutions	...	...	...
D Unfunded employee pension and welfare benefits	79643	73813	5830
E Social assistance grants		...	
F Other transfers n.e.c. b	583	...	583
G Transfers to the rest of the world		...	
Net saving	268484	172394	96090
Total Current Disbursements and Net Saving	2293960	840006	1453950

a) Property and entrepreneurial income paid by non-financial corporate and quasi-corporate enterprises is net of property income received.
b) Item 'Other current transfers' includes item 'Fees, fines and penalties'.

3.23 Corporate and Quasi-Corporate Enterprise Capital Accumulation Account: Total and Sectors

Million Belgian francs

	1980 TOTAL	Non-Financial	Financial	1981 TOTAL	Non-Financial	Financial	1982 TOTAL	Non-Financial	Financial	1983 TOTAL	Non-Financial	Financial
Finance of Gross Accumulation												
1 Gross saving	238653	207053	31600	239316	182287	57029	285836	235911	49925	330620	296748	33872
A Consumption of fixed capital	212109	197589	14520	223405	207555	15850	247250	230390	16860	274255	256575	17680
B Net saving	26544	9464	17080	15911	-25268	41179	38586	5521	33065	56365	40173	16192
2 Capital transfers	41005	41005	...	55345	55345	...	48203	48203	...	43041	43041	...
Finance of Gross Accumulation	279658	248058	31600	294661	237632	57029	334039	284114	49925	373661	339789	33872
Gross Accumulation												
1 Gross capital formation	370034	351238	18796	340297	323728	16569	374604	355780	18824	328950	309336	19614
A Increase in stocks	25271	25271	...	-4805	-4805	...	4994	4994	...	-30881	-30881	...
B Gross fixed capital formation	344763	325967	18796	345102	328533	16569	369610	350786	18824	359831	340217	19614
2 Purchases of land, net	2532	2265	267	2133	2106	27	2440	2370	70	1823	1815	8
3 Purchases of intangible assets, net	...	...	...	...	...	...	...	...	...	...	...	...
4 Capital transfers	182	182	...	268	268	...	495	495	...	353	353	...
Net lending	-93090	-105627	12537	-48037	-88470	40433	-43500	-74531	31031	42535	28285	14250
Gross Accumulation	279658	248058	31600	294661	237632	57029	334039	284114	49925	373661	339789	33872

	1984 TOTAL	Non-Financial	Financial	1985 TOTAL	Non-Financial	Financial	1986 TOTAL	Non-Financial	Financial	1987 TOTAL	Non-Financial	Financial
Finance of Gross Accumulation												
1 Gross saving	383656	310564	73092	459576	387190	72386	544479	451716	92763	578460	467366	111094
A Consumption of fixed capital	291386	270076	21310	314248	290578	23670	326407	300367	26040	343628	316028	27600
B Net saving	92270	40488	51782	145328	96612	48716	218072	151349	66723	234832	151338	83494
2 Capital transfers	41067	41067	...	46254	46254	...	38967	38967	...	35208	35208	...
Finance of Gross Accumulation	424723	351631	73092	505830	433444	72386	583446	490683	92763	613668	502574	111094
Gross Accumulation												
1 Gross capital formation	415556	391897	23659	387260	360626	26634	415648	385020	30628	497315	466844	30471
A Increase in stocks	14499	14499	...	-35036	-35036	...	-34900	-34900	...	11942	11942	...
B Gross fixed capital formation	401057	377398	23659	422296	395662	26634	450548	419920	30628	485373	454902	30471
2 Purchases of land, net	2110	1877	233	3557	3443	114	2322	2336	-14	2376	2498	-122
3 Purchases of intangible assets, net	...	...	...	...	...	...	...	...	...	...	...	...
4 Capital transfers	666	666	...	3652	3652	...	311	311	...	8022	8022	...
Net lending	6391	-42809	49200	111361	65723	45638	165165	103016	62149	105955	25210	80745
Gross Accumulation	424723	351631	73092	505830	433444	72386	583446	490683	92763	613668	502574	111094

Belgium

3.23 Corporate and Quasi-Corporate Enterprise Capital Accumulation Account: Total and Sectors

Million Belgian francs

	1988 TOTAL	1988 Non-Financial	1988 Financial	1989 TOTAL	1989 Non-Financial	1989 Financial
Finance of Gross Accumulation						
1 Gross saving	628971	504831	124140	...	...	...
A Consumption of fixed capital	360487	332437	28050	...	...	...
B Net saving	268484	172394	96090	...	...	...
2 Capital transfers	35950	35950	...	38194	38194	...
Finance of Gross Accumulation	664921	540781	124140	...	...	...
Gross Accumulation						
1 Gross capital formation	579396	546322	33074	726801	692290	34511
A Increase in stocks	20558	20558	...	36940	36940	...
B Gross fixed capital formation	558838	525764	33074	689861	655350	34511
2 Purchases of land, net	3888	3331	557	3419	3269	150
3 Purchases of intangible assets, net	...	...	...	...	...	...
4 Capital transfers	-1	-1	...	383	383	...
Net lending	81638	-8871	90509	...	...	...
Gross Accumulation	664921	540781	124140	...	...	...

3.32 Household and Private Unincorporated Enterprise Income and Outlay Account

Million Belgian francs

	1970	1975	1980	1981	1982	1983	1984	1985	1986	1987	1988	1989
Receipts												
1 Compensation of employees	635640	1322730	2087930	2168210	2298250	2406710	2554940	2685150	2827490	2894980	3010880	3169320
A Wages and salaries	...	...	1649710	1710290	1827420	1903110	1995930	2066570	2162560	2187820	2263310	2375120
B Employers' contributions for social security	88182	195943	297028	303079	308227	335958	387074	437635	472734	504707	527986	560903
C Employers' contributions for private pension & welfare plans	...	...	141185	154844	162608	167645	171937	180942	192204	202449	219585	233295
2 Operating surplus of private unincorporated enterprises	210690	306143	563380	604219	640630	675349	728578	765136	814839	857575	942179	...
3 Property and entrepreneurial income	141625	249120	314020	375537	441284	488581	556616	629054	652720	677597	729096	...
A Withdrawals from private quasi-corporations	...	...	160	154	150	151	160	176	200	238	268	...
B Interest	60891	130870	230614	261815	300034	330415	381366	413318	416784	413815	425952	...
C Dividends	36595	58211	79206	109375	136839	153760	170716	210766	230898	258636	297953	...
D Net land rent and royalties	44139	60039	4040	4193	4261	4255	4374	4794	4838	4908	4923	...
3 Current transfers	190999	447545	954278	1068920	1149560	1238010	1304850	1366710	1409750	1483470	1536560	...
A Casualty insurance claims	-	-	38595	39669	42855	48499	50200	52028	54170	58437	61536	...
B Social security benefits	157667	384269	685886	770239	838644	909366	956493	992491	1030130	1073260	1096330	1151530
C Social assistance grants	-	-	69967	81928	83209	90501	96708	104351	105637	112994	119249	...
D Unfunded employee pension and welfare benefits	-	-	118385	130074	136238	143295	148897	156492	163124	172879	182705	194315
E Transfers from general government	...	...	20250	22673	21244	16652	20705	24361	22992	25972	25461	23629
F Transfers from the rest of the world	10700	13600	20900	24000	27000	29300	31400	36500	33200	39400	50700	...
G Other transfers n.e.c.	22632	49676	295	333	371	396	449	487	491	524	583	...
Total Current Receipts	1178950	2325540	3919610	4216880	4529730	4808650	5144990	5446050	5704800	5913620	6218720	...
Disbursements												
1 Final consumption expenditures	769013	1421150	2171910	2333840	2550090	2686920	2873670	3105280	3196050	3356700	3506360	...

Belgium

3.32 Household and Private Unincorporated Enterprise Income and Outlay Account
(Continued)

Million Belgian francs

	1970	1975	1980	1981	1982	1983	1984	1985	1986	1987	1988	1989
2 Property income	...	...	101603	117511	122741	114285	123918	126961	126027	130490	142469	...
A Interest	...	...	97465	113214	118376	109927	119452	122079	121074	125491	137413	...
B Net land rent and royalties	...	...	4138	4297	4365	4358	4466	4882	4953	4999	5056	...
3 Direct taxes and other current transfers n.e.c. to government	242308	595137	1016190	1074560	1208020	1277890	1427390	1538100	1601710	1668420	1710710	...
A Social security contributions	131733	290880	466352	496603	541656	597354	680876	747182	794371	842864	876006	...
B Direct taxes	110575	304257	549840	577959	666364	680540	746512	790914	807339	825551	834705	...
Income taxes	...	...	...	...	...	...	...	...	...	...	...	...
Other	...	...	...	...	...	...	...	...	...	...	...	...
C Fees, fines and penalties [a]	...	...	...	...	...	...	...	...	...	...	...	...
4 Other current transfers	8800	16600	203430	228650	236994	249718	262117	275351	283451	298523	322139	...
A Net casualty insurance premiums	-	-	39809	41112	44852	50224	52714	55099	56530	60214	64569	...
B Transfers to private non-profit institutions serving households	...	...	...	...	...	...	...	...	...	...	...	...
C Transfers to the rest of the world	8800	16600	31800	39300	38100	38500	41400	43900	42800	43700	49200	...
D Other current transfers, except imputed [a]	...	...	13436	18164	17804	17699	19106	19860	20997	21730	25665	...
E Imputed employee pension and welfare contributions	-	-	118385	130074	136238	143295	148897	156492	163124	172879	182705	...
Net saving	158833	292649	426472	462315	411881	479830	457900	400356	497556	459487	537036	...
Total Current Disbursements and Net Saving	1178950	2325540	3919610	4216880	4529730	4808650	5144990	5446050	5704800	5913620	6218720	...

a) Item 'Other current transfers' includes item 'Fees, fines and penalties'.

3.33 Household and Private Unincorporated Enterprise Capital Accumulation Account

Million Belgian francs

	1970	1975	1980	1981	1982	1983	1984	1985	1986	1987	1988	1989
			\multicolumn{9}{c	}{**Finance of Gross Accumulation**}	
1 Gross saving	...	...	514274	558116	514292	590203	575186	526052	626035	591849	675018	...
A Consumption of fixed capital	...	...	87802	95801	102411	110373	117286	125696	128479	132362	137982	...
B Net saving	...	...	426472	462315	411881	479830	457900	400356	497556	459487	537036	...
2 Capital transfers	...	...	2727	3877	3218	3781	5426	5696	5644	6342	7181	...
Total Finance of Gross Accumulation	...	...	517001	561993	517510	593984	580612	531748	631679	598191	682199	...
			\multicolumn{9}{c	}{**Gross Accumulation**}	
1 Gross Capital Formation	...	...	257257	170614	176099	186283	194714	211799	233564	254963	311118	...
A Increase in stocks	...	...	-603	-154	523	1175	889	-1189	1372	-440	1466	...
B Gross fixed capital formation	...	...	257860	170768	175576	185108	193825	212988	232192	255403	309652	...
2 Purchases of land, net	...	...	-15517	-14160	-10615	-8265	-6743	-10071	-7172	-7903	-11500	...
3 Purchases of intangibles, net	...	...	-	-	-	-	-	-	-	-	-	...
4 Capital transfers	...	...	12583	13328	12398	12727	13329	13255	14303	15694	16686	...
Net lending	...	...	262678	392211	339628	403239	379312	316765	390984	335437	365895	...
Total Gross Accumulation	...	...	517001	561993	517510	593984	580612	531748	631679	598191	682199	...

Belgium

3.51 External Transactions: Current Account: Detail

Million Belgian francs

		1970	1975	1980	1981	1982	1983	1984	1985	1986	1987	1988	1989
				Payments to the Rest of the World									
1	Imports of goods and services	532800	1061100	2124700 / 2257800	2497000	2833500	3004300	3429000	3525900	3325000	3450700	3823700	4421000
	A Imports of merchandise c.i.f.	424900	858300	1698800 / 2029900	2234500	2565400	2714800	3106400	3165600	2939100	3025500	3337900	3822800
	B Other	107900	202800	425900 / 227900	262500	268100	289500	322600	360300	385900	425200	485800	598200
2	Factor income to the rest of the world	43200	78600	230200 / 243500	489700	596900	571000	668500	798500	712700	682700	803000	1157600
	A Compensation of employees	3100	8300	14000 / 14000	15000	18400	18600	19000	20500	21300	23700	26300	31000
	B Property and entrepreneurial income	40100	70300	216200 / 229500	474700	578500	552400	649500	778000	691400	659000	776700	1126600
3	Current transfers to the rest of the world	16300	36300	57774 / 95786	113135	129579	138695	147336	155729	152131	166608	183161	193769
	A Indirect taxes by general government to supranational organizations	...	...	... / 41606	45310	56087	56573	57261	59412	64613	77013	77417	80809
	B Other current transfers	16300	36300	57774 / 54180	67825	73492	82122	90075	96317	87518	89595	105744	112960
	By general government	7500	19700	25974 / 11200	12275	14552	18302	16125	15107	14148	16835	22534	18360
	By other resident sectors	8800	16600	31800 / 42980	55550	58940	63820	73950	81210	73370	72760	83210	94600
4	Surplus of the nation on current transactions	35100	-3600	-150083 / -148553	-134212	-144598	-34334	-24581	13928	103373	71879	82854	64421
	Payments to the Rest of the World, and Surplus of the Nation on Current Transfers	627400	1172400	2262590 / 2448530	2965620	3415380	3679660	4220260	4494060	4293200	4371890	4892720	5836790
				Receipts From The Rest of the World									
1	Exports of goods and services	561900	1065200	2026400 / 2170200	2439000	2794300	3078900	3505200	3644900	3525600	3614400	4029600	4621900
	A Exports of merchandise f.o.b.	452800	856800	1596400 / 1802200	1991600	2308100	2531000	2903700	3012800	2874100	2904300	3247200	3711900
	B Other	109100	208400	430000 / 368000	447400	486200	547900	601500	632100	651500	710100	782400	910000
2	Factor income from the rest of the world	54100	91300	211900 / 217300	459700	538500	508200	608800	722100	648100	625900	736500	1081800
	A Compensation of employees	9700	21100	30900 / 30900	33200	38100	42100	45600	47400	52000	53500	57900	62900
	B Property and entrepreneurial income	44400	70200	181000 / 186400	426500	500400	466100	563200	674700	596100	572400	678600	1018900
3	Current transfers from the rest of the world	11400	15900	24291 / 61033	66923	82581	92561	106255	127057	119504	131587	126615	133090
	A Subsidies to general government from supranational organizations	...	...	... / 23902	21682	27835	29726	33100	42281	44627	42804	32829	28068
	B Other current transfers	11400	15900	24291 / 37131	45241	54746	62835	73155	84776	74877	88783	93786	105022
	To general government	700	2300	3391 / 286	784	1317	1072	543	996	690	1017	994	1051
	To other resident sectors	10700	13600	20900 / 36845	44457	53429	61763	72612	83780	74187	87766	92792	103971
	Receipts from the Rest of the World on Current Transfers	627400	1172400	2262590 / 2448530	2965620	3415380	3679660	4220260	4494060	4293200	4371890	4892720	5836790

Belgium

3.52 External Transactions: Capital Accumulation Account

Million Belgian francs

	1970	1975	1980	1981	1982	1983	1984	1985	1986	1987	1988	1989
Finance of Gross Accumulation												
1 Surplus of the nation on current transactions	35100	-3600	-150083 / -148553	-134212	-144598	-34334	-24581	13928	103373	71879	82854	64421
2 Capital transfers from the rest of the world	-2000	-2300	-3400 / 885	991	742	565	1005	924	813	1037	1014	1278
A By general government	...	...	... / 509	509	284	65	305	24	213	37	114	78
B By other resident sectors	...	...	... / 376	482	458	500	700	900	600	1000	900	1200
Total Finance of Gross Accumulation	33100	-5900	-153483 / -147668	-133221	-143856	-33769	-23576	14852	104186	72916	83868	65699
Gross Accumulation												
1 Capital transfers to the rest of the world	...	...	4300	4925	6038	6825	7898	8912	8698	10314	10975	11177
A By general government	...	...	4300	4925	6038	6825	7898	8912	8698	10314	10975	11177
B By other resident sectors	...	...	...	...	...	...	...	...	...	...	...	...
2 Purchases of intangible assets, n.e.c., net, from the rest of the world	...	...	...	...	...	...	...	...	...	...	...	...
Net lending to the rest of the world	33100	-5900	-153483 / -151968	-138146	-149894	-40594	-31474	5940	95488	62602	72893	54522
Total Gross Accumulation	33100	-5900	-153483 / -147668	-133221	-143856	-33769	-23576	14852	104186	72916	83868	65699

4.1 Derivation of Value Added by Kind of Activity, in Current Prices

Million Belgian francs

	1980 Gross Output	1980 Intermediate Consumption	1980 Value Added	1981 Gross Output	1981 Intermediate Consumption	1981 Value Added	1982 Gross Output	1982 Intermediate Consumption	1982 Value Added	1983 Gross Output	1983 Intermediate Consumption	1983 Value Added
All Producers												
1 Agriculture, hunting, forestry and fishing	...	...	73108	...	...	81371	...	...	90957	...	...	102375
2 Mining and quarrying	...	...	7399	...	...	9141	...	...	14486	...	...	14172
A Coal mining [a]	...	...	7399	...	...	9141	...	...	14486	...	...	14172
B Crude petroleum and natural gas production	...	...	...	...	...	...	...	...	...	...	...	...
C Metal ore mining	...	...	...	...	...	...	...	...	...	...	...	...
D Other mining [b]	...	...	...	...	...	...	...	...	...	...	...	...
3 Manufacturing	...	...	833834	...	...	808538	...	...	912123	...	...	966017
A Manufacture of food, beverages and tobacco	...	...	119190	...	...	126009	...	...	146552	...	...	154795
B Textile, wearing apparel and leather industries	...	...	63655	...	...	63124	...	...	69554	...	...	72284
C Manufacture of wood and wood products, including furniture	...	...	37070	...	...	36628	...	...	38088	...	...	36569
D Manufacture of paper and paper products, printing and publishing	...	...	44448	...	...	44197	...	...	50265	...	...	52767
E Manufacture of chemicals and chemical petroleum, coal, rubber and plastic products [a]	...	...	189136	...	...	180204	...	...	208907	...	...	224033
F Manufacture of non-metallic mineral products, except products of petroleum and coal [b]	...	...	49986	...	...	44271	...	...	47040	...	...	48725
G Basic metal industries	...	...	70258	...	...	69310	...	...	76865	...	...	87228
H Manufacture of fabricated metal products, machinery and equipment	...	...	247649	...	...	234510	...	...	263319	...	...	276347
I Other manufacturing industries	...	...	12442	...	...	10285	...	...	11533	...	...	13269
4 Electricity, gas and water	...	...	75002	...	...	84378	...	...	84315	...	...	101410
5 Construction	...	...	259389	...	...	224694	...	...	235105	...	...	232482
6 Wholesale and retail trade, restaurants and hotels	...	...	546968	...	...	550903	...	...	600782	...	...	658759
A Wholesale and retail trade [c]	...	...	464159	...	...	462943	...	...	505132	...	...	554008
B Restaurants and hotels	...	...	82809	...	...	87960	...	...	95650	...	...	104751
7 Transport, storage and communication	...	...	268450	...	...	273135	...	...	289584	...	...	304106

Belgium

4.1 Derivation of Value Added by Kind of Activity, in Current Prices
(Continued)

Million Belgian francs

	1980 Gross Output	1980 Intermediate Consumption	1980 Value Added	1981 Gross Output	1981 Intermediate Consumption	1981 Value Added	1982 Gross Output	1982 Intermediate Consumption	1982 Value Added	1983 Gross Output	1983 Intermediate Consumption	1983 Value Added
A Transport and storage	...	...	216281	...	...	217375	...	...	231834	...	...	240466
B Communication	...	...	52169	...	...	55760	...	...	57750	...	...	63640
8 Finance, insurance, real estate and business services [d]	...	...	149581	...	...	188052	...	...	211957	...	...	205727
A Financial institutions	...	...	149581	...	...	188052	...	...	211957	...	...	205727
B Insurance	...	...		...	...		...	...		...	...	
C Real estate and business services [d]	...	...	...	...	...	...	...	...	...	...	...	...
Real estate, except dwellings	...	...	...	...	...	...	...	...	...	...	...	...
Dwellings	...	...	168448	...	...	193295	...	...	212462	...	...	234195
9 Community, social and personal services [d]	...	...	532987	...	...	588463	...	...	651207	...	...	712896
Educational services	...	...	...	...	...	...	...	...	...	...	...	...
Medical, dental, other health and veterinary services	...	...	122740	...	...	136544	...	...	152449	...	...	168593
Statistical discrepancy	...	...	96	...	...	21676	...	...	8513	...	...	3528
Total, Industries	...	...	2746810	...	...	2830350	...	...	3099030	...	...	3301470
Producers of Government Services	...	...	482609	...	...	524345	...	...	556134	...	...	568041
Other Producers [e]	...	...	40830	...	...	42191	...	...	43714	...	...	45501
Total	...	...	3270250	...	...	3396890	...	...	3698880	...	...	3915010
Less: Imputed bank service charge	...	...	109122	...	...	131558	...	...	146437	...	...	150629
Import duties	...	...	34508	...	...	33628	...	...	41291	...	...	44930
Value added tax	...	...	255511	...	...	278548	...	...	295362	...	...	313027
Total [f]	...	...	3451150	...	...	3577510	...	...	3889090	...	...	4122340
Memorandum Item: Mineral fuels and power	...	...	162592	...	...	166160	...	...	179135	...	...	199000

	1984 Gross Output	1984 Intermediate Consumption	1984 Value Added	1985 Gross Output	1985 Intermediate Consumption	1985 Value Added	1986 Gross Output	1986 Intermediate Consumption	1986 Value Added	1987 Gross Output	1987 Intermediate Consumption	1987 Value Added
All Producers												
1 Agriculture, hunting, forestry and fishing	...	...	105006	...	...	105138	...	...	106443	...	...	100950
2 Mining and quarrying	...	...	11432	...	...	10975	...	...	6542	...	...	4071
A Coal mining [a]	...	...	11432	...	...	10975	...	...	6542	...	...	4071
B Crude petroleum and natural gas production	...	...	...	...	...	...	...	...	...	...	...	...
C Metal ore mining	...	...	...	...	...	...	...	...	...	...	...	...
D Other mining [b]	...	...	...	...	...	...	...	...	...	...	...	...
3 Manufacturing	...	...	1027030	...	...	1115170	...	...	1157120	...	...	1187450
A Manufacture of food, beverages and tobacco	...	...	163492	...	...	173151	...	...	178655	...	...	179500
B Textile, wearing apparel and leather industries	...	...	75307	...	...	80801	...	...	89756	...	...	89982
C Manufacture of wood and wood products, including furniture	...	...	38837	...	...	42412	...	...	45617	...	...	48923
D Manufacture of paper and paper products, printing and publishing	...	...	56365	...	...	61110	...	...	65742	...	...	68813
E Manufacture of chemicals and chemical petroleum, coal, rubber and plastic products [a]	...	...	256450	...	...	268619	...	...	280453	...	...	288615
F Manufacture of non-metallic mineral products, except products of petroleum and coal [b]	...	...	52640	...	...	52085	...	...	57223	...	...	61686
G Basic metal industries	...	...	93960	...	...	101209	...	...	99301	...	...	95073
H Manufacture of fabricated metal products, machinery and equipment	...	...	277419	...	...	323071	...	...	326895	...	...	341118
I Other manufacturing industries	...	...	12559	...	...	12708	...	...	13478	...	...	13737
4 Electricity, gas and water	...	...	106295	...	...	118997	...	...	123245	...	...	126731
5 Construction	...	...	233717	...	...	245778	...	...	249214	...	...	251454
6 Wholesale and retail trade, restaurants and hotels	...	...	685531	...	...	759819	...	...	864011	...	...	923296
A Wholesale and retail trade [c]	...	...	571816	...	...	636841	...	...	733837	...	...	784736
B Restaurants and hotels	...	...	113715	...	...	122978	...	...	130174	...	...	138560
7 Transport, storage and communication	...	...	344848	...	...	374536	...	...	369291	...	...	394992

Belgium

4.1 Derivation of Value Added by Kind of Activity, in Current Prices
(Continued)

Million Belgian francs

	1984 Gross Output	1984 Intermediate Consumption	1984 Value Added	1985 Gross Output	1985 Intermediate Consumption	1985 Value Added	1986 Gross Output	1986 Intermediate Consumption	1986 Value Added	1987 Gross Output	1987 Intermediate Consumption	1987 Value Added
A Transport and storage	...	...	272023	...	...	294707	...	...	284357	...	...	302280
B Communication	...	...	72825	...	...	79829	...	...	84934	...	...	92712
8 Finance, insurance, real estate and business services [d]	...	...	247852	...	...	263512	...	...	297864	...	...	316597
A Financial institutions	...	...	[247852]	...	...	[263512]	...	...	[297864]	...	...	[316597]
B Insurance	...	...		...	...		...	...		...	...	
C Real estate and business services [d]	...	...	...	...	...	...	...	...	...	...	...	...
Real estate, except dwellings	...	...	...	...	...	...	...	...	...	...	...	...
Dwellings	...	...	257857	...	...	277822	...	...	294692	...	...	314856
9 Community, social and personal services [d]	...	...	794871	...	...	844553	...	...	915111	...	...	983952
Educational services	...	...	...	...	...	...	...	...	...	...	...	...
Medical, dental, other health and veterinary services	...	...	182591	...	...	194740	...	...	205891	...	...	217005
Statistical discrepancy	...	...	31983	...	...	5480	...	...	-3283	...	...	-10160
Total, Industries	...	...	3588560	...	...	3843950	...	...	4085560	...	...	4279330
Producers of Government Services	...	...	596368	...	...	634993	...	...	658367	...	...	658701
Other Producers [e]	...	...	47304	...	...	49496	...	...	50667	...	...	50564
Total	...	...	4232240	...	...	4528440	...	...	4794590	...	...	4988600
Less: Imputed bank service charge	...	...	178145	...	...	186425	...	...	207845	...	...	204227
Import duties	...	...	45289	...	...	47013	...	...	41998	...	...	51133
Value added tax	...	...	329955	...	...	349242	...	...	355521	...	...	378647
Total [f]	...	...	4429340	...	...	4738270	...	...	4984270	...	...	5214150
Memorandum Item: Mineral fuels and power	...	...	205711	...	...	223544	...	...	221876	...	...	222081

	1988 Gross Output	1988 Intermediate Consumption	1988 Value Added	1989 Gross Output	1989 Intermediate Consumption	1989 Value Added
All Producers						
1 Agriculture, hunting, forestry and fishing	...	...	105556	...	...	123587
2 Mining and quarrying	...	...	2658	...	...	2209
A Coal mining [a]	...	...	2658	...	...	2209
B Crude petroleum and natural gas production	...	...	...	...	...	...
C Metal ore mining	...	...	...	...	...	...
D Other mining [b]	...	...	...	...	...	...
3 Manufacturing	...	...	1281730	...	...	1403240
A Manufacture of food, beverages and tobacco	...	...	181532	...	...	187280
B Textile, wearing apparel and leather industries	...	...	90491	...	...	99692
C Manufacture of wood and wood products, including furniture	...	...	51957	...	...	59064
D Manufacture of paper and paper products, printing and publishing	...	...	76223	...	...	88945
E Manufacture of chemicals and chemical petroleum, coal, rubber and plastic products [a]	...	...	308966	...	...	336123
F Manufacture of non-metallic mineral products, except products of petroleum and coal [b]	...	...	72640	...	...	81996
G Basic metal industries	...	...	127859	...	...	149406
H Manufacture of fabricated metal products, machinery and equipment	...	...	357037	...	...	384042
I Other manufacturing industries	...	...	15021	...	...	16693
4 Electricity, gas and water	...	...	131613	...	...	139140
5 Construction	...	...	283851	...	...	321868
6 Wholesale and retail trade, restaurants and hotels	...	...	958929	...	...	1018470
A Wholesale and retail trade [c]	...	...	809746	...	...	853927
B Restaurants and hotels	...	...	149183	...	...	164542
7 Transport, storage and communication	...	...	431642	...	...	448651

Belgium

4.1 Derivation of Value Added by Kind of Activity, in Current Prices
(Continued)

Million Belgian francs

	1988 Gross Output	1988 Intermediate Consumption	1988 Value Added	1989 Gross Output	1989 Intermediate Consumption	1989 Value Added
A Transport and storage	...	...	333356	...	...	344056
B Communication	...	...	98286	...	...	104595
8 Finance, insurance, real estate and business services d	...	...	336319	...	...	366062
A Financial institutions	...	...	336319	...	...	366062
B Insurance	...	...		...	...	
C Real estate and business services d	...	...	...	...	...	...
Real estate, except dwellings	...	...	...	...	...	...
Dwellings	...	...	335628	...	...	357146
9 Community, social and personal services d	...	...	1069510	...	...	1186710
Educational services	...	...	...	...	...	...
Medical, dental, other health and veterinary services	...	...	229839	...	...	247106
Statistical discrepancy	...	...	-24796	...	...	-7775
Total, Industries	...	...	4577010	...	...	5002160
Producers of Government Services	...	...	666732	...	...	695925
Other Producers e	...	...	50584	...	...	50742
Total	...	...	5294330	...	...	5748830
Less: Imputed bank service charge	...	...	200495	...	...	208065
Import duties	...	...	49389	...	...	52507
Value added tax	...	...	405255	...	...	434633
Total f	...	...	5548480	...	...	6027900
Memorandum Item: Mineral fuels and power	...	...	224571	...	...	243794

a) Agglomeration and briquettes of coal are included in item 'Coal mining'.
b) Item 'Manufacture of non-metallic mineral products, etc.' includes 'Other mining'.
c) For the second series, including repairs.
d) Business services and real estate except dwellings are included in item 'Community, social and personal services'.
e) For the second series, item 'Other producers' refers to domestic services only. All other non-marketed services are included in item 'Finance, insurance, real estate and business services'.
f) The breakdown by kind of economic activity used in this table is according to the classification NACE/CLIO.

4.2 Derivation of Value Added by Kind of Activity, in Constant Prices

Million Belgian francs

	1980 Gross Output	1980 Interm. Cons.	1980 Value Added	1981 Gross Output	1981 Interm. Cons.	1981 Value Added	1982 Gross Output	1982 Interm. Cons.	1982 Value Added	1983 Gross Output	1983 Interm. Cons.	1983 Value Added
					At constant prices of: 1985							
					All Producers							
1 Agriculture, hunting, forestry and fishing	...	...	89589	...	...	93618	...	...	99379	...	...	97328
2 Mining and quarrying	...	...	15799	...	...	14613	...	...	16343	...	...	14534
A Coal mining a	...	...	15799	...	...	14613	...	...	16343	...	...	14534
B Crude petroleum and natural gas production	...	...	...	...	...	...	...	...	...	...	...	...
C Metal ore mining	...	...	...	...	...	...	...	...	...	...	...	...
D Other mining b	...	...	...	...	...	...	...	...	...	...	...	...
3 Manufacturing	...	...	983253	...	...	979849	...	...	1017840	...	...	1077020
A Manufacture of food, beverages and tobacco	...	...	163695	...	...	161463	...	...	170254	...	...	172928
B Textile, wearing apparel and leather industries	...	...	85222	...	...	84671	...	...	81033	...	...	85406
C Manufacture of wood and wood products, including furniture	...	...	41736	...	...	38578	...	...	39005	...	...	36180
D Manufacture of paper and paper products, printing and publishing	...	...	56899	...	...	56680	...	...	58330	...	...	62174
E Manufacture of chemicals and chemical petroleum, coal, rubber and plastic products a	...	...	196968	...	...	203142	...	...	224550	...	...	253394
F Manufacture of non-metallic mineral products, except products of petroleum and coal b	...	...	63141	...	...	56208	...	...	57116	...	...	58120
G Basic metal industries	...	...	81424	...	...	91400	...	...	79826	...	...	87816
H Manufacture of fabricated metal products, machinery and equipment	...	...	271955	...	...	269491	...	...	290372	...	...	302056
I Other manufacturing industries	...	...	22213	...	...	18216	...	...	17355	...	...	18944
4 Electricity, gas and water	...	...	114728	...	...	118958	...	...	112517	...	...	114253

Belgium

4.2 Derivation of Value Added by Kind of Activity, in Constant Prices
(Continued)

Million Belgian francs

	1980 Gross Output	1980 Intermediate Consumption	1980 Value Added	1981 Gross Output	1981 Intermediate Consumption	1981 Value Added	1982 Gross Output	1982 Intermediate Consumption	1982 Value Added	1983 Gross Output	1983 Intermediate Consumption	1983 Value Added
					At constant prices of:1985							
5 Construction	...	...	345984	...	...	282889	...	...	269253	...	...	254217
6 Wholesale and retail trade, restaurants and hotels	...	...	800753	...	...	769271	...	...	786830	...	...	779154
A Wholesale and retail trade c	...	...	685685	...	...	654969	...	...	668390	...	...	660020
B Restaurants and hotels	...	...	115068	...	...	114302	...	...	118440	...	...	119134
7 Transport, storage and communication	...	...	350575	...	...	339770	...	...	335797	...	...	338021
A Transport and storage	...	...	276887	...	...	264919	...	...	264866	...	...	263341
B Communication	...	...	73688	...	...	74851	...	...	70931	...	...	74680
8 Finance, insurance, real estate and business services d	...	...	214879	...	...	250477	...	...	257486	...	...	241805
A Financial institutions	...	...	214879	...	...	250477	...	...	257486	...	...	241805
B Insurance												
C Real estate and business services c	...	...	...	...	...	...	...	...	...	...	...	...
Real estate, except dwellings			...			...			...			...
Dwellings	...	...	246561	...	...	256077	...	...	261212	...	...	266319
9 Community, social and personal services d	...	...	738636	...	...	760789	...	...	783670	...	...	796792
Educational services	...	...	...	...	...	...	...	...	...	...	...	...
Medical, dental, other health and veterinary services	...	...	168642	...	...	177150	...	...	182835	...	...	188651
Statistical discrepancy	...	...	-1266	...	...	23265	...	...	24006	...	...	21603
Total, Industries	...	...	3652930	...	...	3633500	...	...	3703120	...	...	3734730
Producers of Government Services	...	...	618394	...	...	621416	...	...	618050	...	...	619070
Other Producers e	...	...	52373	...	...	51234	...	...	50759	...	...	49991
Total	...	...	4323700	...	...	4306150	...	...	4371930	...	...	4403790
Less: Imputed bank service charge	...	...	161892	...	...	180215	...	...	181349	...	...	186037
Import duties	...	...	47028	...	...	44862	...	...	42157	...	...	42674
Value added tax	...	...	351880	...	...	344801	...	...	350920	...	...	340653
Total f	...	...	4560710	...	...	4515600	...	...	4583660	...	...	4601080
Memorandum Item: Mineral fuels and power	...	...	217433	...	...	215141	...	...	213294	...	...	226577
				of which General Government:								
1 Agriculture, hunting, forestry and fishing	...	...	...	...	...	...	...	...	...	...	...	...
2 Mining and quarrying	...	...	...	...	...	...	...	...	...	...	...	...
3 Manufacturing	...	...	...	...	...	...	...	...	...	...	...	...
4 Electricity, gas and water	...	...	...	...	...	...	...	...	...	...	...	...
5 Construction	...	...	...	...	...	...	...	...	...	...	...	...
6 Wholesale and retail trade, restaurants and hotels	...	...	...	...	...	...	...	...	...	...	...	...
7 Transport and communication	...	...	...	...	...	...	...	...	...	...	...	...
8 Finance, insurance, real estate and business services	...	...	...	...	...	...	...	...	...	...	...	...
9 Community, social and personal services	...	...	...	...	...	...	...	...	...	...	...	...
Total, Industries of General Government	...	...	6606	...	...	3991	...	...	4625	...	...	3680
Producers of Government Services	...	...	618129	...	...	621416	...	...	618050	...	...	619070
Total, General Government	...	...	624735	...	...	625407	...	...	622675	...	...	622750

	1984 Gross Output	1984 Intermediate Consumption	1984 Value Added	1985 Gross Output	1985 Intermediate Consumption	1985 Value Added	1986 Gross Output	1986 Intermediate Consumption	1986 Value Added	1987 Gross Output	1987 Intermediate Consumption	1987 Value Added
				At constant prices of:1985								
				All Producers								
1 Agriculture, hunting, forestry and fishing	...	...	106362	...	...	105138	...	...	110261	...	...	101985
2 Mining and quarrying	...	...	12509	...	...	10975	...	...	9193	...	...	8982
A Coal mining a	...	...	12509	...	...	10975	...	...	9193	...	...	8982
B Crude petroleum and natural gas production	...	...	...	...	...	...	...	...	...	...	...	...
C Metal ore mining	...	...	...	...	...	...	...	...	...	...	...	...
D Other mining b	...	...	...	...	...	...	...	...	...	...	...	...

Belgium

4.2 Derivation of Value Added by Kind of Activity, in Constant Prices
(Continued)

Million Belgian francs

	1984 Gross Output	1984 Intermediate Consumption	1984 Value Added	1985 Gross Output	1985 Intermediate Consumption	1985 Value Added	1986 Gross Output	1986 Intermediate Consumption	1986 Value Added	1987 Gross Output	1987 Intermediate Consumption	1987 Value Added
					At constant prices of: 1985							
3 Manufacturing	...	...	1105910	...	...	1115170	...	...	1116240	...	...	1143280
A Manufacture of food, beverages and tobacco	...	...	175874	...	...	173151	...	...	177595	...	...	179117
B Textile, wearing apparel and leather industries	...	...	82346	...	...	80801	...	...	87408	...	...	89174
C Manufacture of wood and wood products, including furniture	...	...	40136	...	...	42412	...	...	39708	...	...	40304
D Manufacture of paper and paper products, printing and publishing	...	...	64151	...	...	61110	...	...	63072	...	...	68700
E Manufacture of chemicals and chemical petroleum, coal, rubber and plastic products [a]	...	...	270965	...	...	268619	...	...	267560	...	...	285288
F Manufacture of non-metallic mineral products, except products of petroleum and coal [b]	...	...	57628	...	...	52085	...	...	54538	...	...	58687
G Basic metal industries	...	...	92790	...	...	101209	...	...	97233	...	...	99020
H Manufacture of fabricated metal products, machinery and equipment	...	...	306800	...	...	323071	...	...	313857	...	...	307536
I Other manufacturing industries	...	...	15218	...	...	12708	...	...	15264	...	...	15453
4 Electricity, gas and water	...	...	114801	...	...	118997	...	...	116867	...	...	123827
5 Construction	...	...	244723	...	...	245778	...	...	253890	...	...	260696
6 Wholesale and retail trade, restaurants and hotels	...	...	764784	...	...	759819	...	...	776383	...	...	778280
A Wholesale and retail trade [c]	...	...	641917	...	...	636841	...	...	652854	...	...	651133
B Restaurants and hotels	...	...	122867	...	...	122978	...	...	123529	...	...	127147
7 Transport, storage and communication	...	...	364787	...	...	374536	...	...	353168	...	...	370069
A Transport and storage	...	...	287976	...	...	294707	...	...	271161	...	...	280605
B Communication	...	...	76811	...	...	79829	...	...	82007	...	...	89464
8 Finance, insurance, real estate and business services [d]	...	...	260887	...	...	263512	...	...	286817	...	...	314514
A Financial institutions	...	...	[260887]	...	...	[263512]	...	...	[286817]	...	...	[314514]
B Insurance	...	...		...	...		...	...		...	...	
C Real estate and business services [c]	...	...		...	...		...	...		...	...	
Real estate, except dwellings	...	...		...	...		...	...		...	...	
Dwellings	...	...	271981	...	...	277822	...	...	283849	...	...	290111
9 Community, social and personal services [d]	...	...	838020	...	...	844553	...	...	876193	...	...	913921
Educational services	...	...		...	...		...	...		...	...	
Medical, dental, other health and veterinary services	...	...	192343	...	...	194740	...	...	195249	...	...	201310
Statistical discrepancy	...	...	12557	...	...	5480	...	...	3235	...	...	-5600
Total, Industries	...	...	3825340	...	...	3843950	...	...	3902240	...	...	4009950
Producers of Government Services	...	...	624603	...	...	634993	...	...	643084	...	...	642341
Other Producers [e]	...	...	49570	...	...	49496	...	...	48737	...	...	47663
Total	...	...	4499510	...	...	4528440	...	...	4594060	...	...	4699960
Less: Imputed bank service charge	...	...	189883	...	...	186425	...	...	196660	...	...	208161
Import duties	...	...	46859	...	...	47013	...	...	50914	...	...	55831
Value added tax	...	...	342980	...	...	349242	...	...	358936	...	...	367772
Total [f]	...	...	4699470	...	...	4738270	...	...	4807250	...	...	4915400
Memorandum Item: Mineral fuels and power	...	...	225913	...	...	223544	...	...	219011	...	...	232776
				of which General Government:								
1 Agriculture, hunting, forestry and fishing	...	...	...	...	...	...	...	...	...	...	...	...
2 Mining and quarrying	...	...	...	...	...	...	...	...	...	...	...	...
3 Manufacturing	...	...	...	...	...	...	...	...	...	...	...	...
4 Electricity, gas and water	...	...	...	...	...	...	...	...	...	...	...	...

Belgium

4.2 Derivation of Value Added by Kind of Activity, in Constant Prices
(Continued)

Million Belgian francs

	1984			1985			1986			1987		
	Gross Output	Intermediate Consumption	Value Added	Gross Output	Intermediate Consumption	Value Added	Gross Output	Intermediate Consumption	Value Added	Gross Output	Intermediate Consumption	Value Added
	At constant prices of:1985											
5 Construction	...	...	...	...	...	...	...	...	...	...	...	...
6 Wholesale and retail trade, restaurants and hotels	...	...	...	...	...	...	...	...	...	...	...	...
7 Transport and communication	...	...	...	...	...	...	...	...	...	...	...	...
8 Finance, insurance, real estate and business services	...	...	...	...	...	...	...	...	...	...	...	...
9 Community, social and personal services	...	...	...	...	...	...	...	...	...	...	...	...
Total, Industries of General Government	...	...	3714	...	...	2527	...	...	2458	...	...	2259
Producers of Government Services	...	...	624603	...	...	634993	...	...	643084	...	...	642341
Total, General Government	...	...	628317	...	...	637520	...	...	645542	...	...	644600

	1988			1989		
	Gross Output	Intermediate Consumption	Value Added	Gross Output	Intermediate Consumption	Value Added
	At constant prices of:1985					
	All Producers					
1 Agriculture, hunting, forestry and fishing	...	...	108449	...	...	108854
2 Mining and quarrying	...	...	5754	...	...	4141
A Coal mining [a]	...	...	5754	...	...	4141
B Crude petroleum and natural gas production	...	...	...	...	...	...
C Metal ore mining	...	...	...	...	...	...
D Other mining [b]	...	...	...	...	...	...
3 Manufacturing	...	...	1216970	...	...	1273320
A Manufacture of food, beverages and tobacco	...	...	178609	...	...	177654
B Textile, wearing apparel and leather industries	...	...	88896	...	...	97197
C Manufacture of wood and wood products, including furniture	...	...	41957	...	...	47532
D Manufacture of paper and paper products, printing and publishing	...	...	75120	...	...	82906
E Manufacture of chemicals and chemical petroleum, coal, rubber and plastic products [a]	...	...	303397	...	...	315871
F Manufacture of non-metallic mineral products, except products of petroleum and coal [b]	...	...	67553	...	...	74394
G Basic metal industries	...	...	113001	...	...	111753
H Manufacture of fabricated metal products, machinery and equipment	...	...	332656	...	...	349227
I Other manufacturing industries	...	...	15781	...	...	16782
4 Electricity, gas and water	...	...	127342	...	...	131693
5 Construction	...	...	287000	...	...	308034
6 Wholesale and retail trade, restaurants and hotels	...	...	784900	...	...	775933
A Wholesale and retail trade [c]	...	...	651661	...	...	635474
B Restaurants and hotels	...	...	133239	...	...	140459
7 Transport, storage and communication	...	...	391100	...	...	405723
A Transport and storage	...	...	297665	...	...	307093
B Communication	...	...	93435	...	...	98630
8 Finance, insurance, real estate and business services [d]	...	...	347876	...	...	372393
A Financial institutions	...	...	⎤ 347876	...	...	⎤ 372393
B Insurance	...	...		...	...	
C Real estate and business services [c]	...	...	...	...	...	...
Real estate, except dwellings	...	...	...	...	...	...
Dwellings	...	...	297207	...	...	304605
9 Community, social and personal services [d]	...	...	973838	...	...	1050920

Belgium

4.2 Derivation of Value Added by Kind of Activity, in Constant Prices
(Continued)

Million Belgian francs

	1988			1989		
	Gross Output	Intermediate Consumption	Value Added	Gross Output	Intermediate Consumption	Value Added
			At constant prices of: 1985			
Educational services	...	...	...	...	...	...
Medical, dental, other health and veterinary services	...	...	212299	...	...	223882
Statistical discrepancy	...	...	-5355	...	...	-5555
Total, Industries	...	...	4237870	...	...	4425450
Producers of Government Services	...	...	643379	...	...	644222
Other Producers [e]	...	...	46946	...	...	45890
Total	...	...	4928200	...	...	5115560
Less: Imputed bank service charge	...	...	223910	...	...	234188
Import duties	...	...	60148	...	...	64243
Value added tax	...	...	376705	...	...	394624
Total [f]	...	...	5141140	...	...	5340240
Memorandum Item: Mineral fuels and power	...	...	234319	...	...	241950
			of which General Government:			
1 Agriculture, hunting, forestry and fishing	...	...	...	...	...	...
2 Mining and quarrying	...	...	...	...	...	...
3 Manufacturing	...	...	...	...	...	...
4 Electricity, gas and water	...	...	...	...	...	...
5 Construction	...	...	...	...	...	...
6 Wholesale and retail trade, restaurants and hotels	...	...	...	...	...	...
7 Transport and communication	...	...	...	...	...	...
8 Finance, insurance, real estate and business services	...	...	...	...	...	...
9 Community, social and personal services	...	...	...	...	...	...
Total, Industries of General Government	...	...	2420	...	...	2359
Producers of Government Services	...	...	643379	...	...	644222
Total, General Government	...	...	645799	...	...	646581

a) Agglomeration and briquettes of coal are included in item 'Coal mining'.
b) Item 'Manufacture of non-metallic mineral products, etc.' includes 'Other mining'.
c) For the second series, including repairs.
d) Business services and real estate except dwellings are included in item 'Community, social and personal services'.
e) For the second series, item 'Other producers' refers to domestic services only. All other non-marketed services are included in item 'Finance, insurance, real estate and business services'.
f) The breakdown by kind of economic activity used in this table is according to the classification NACE/CLIO.

4.3 Cost Components of Value Added

Million Belgian francs

	1980						1981					
	Compensation of Employees	Capital Consumption	Net Operating Surplus	Indirect Taxes	Less: Subsidies Received	Value Added	Compensation of Employees	Capital Consumption	Net Operating Surplus	Indirect Taxes	Less: Subsidies Received	Value Added
					All Producers							
1 Agriculture, hunting, forestry and fishing	4205	...	-4863	...	...	73108	4193	...	-5134	...	...	81371
2 Mining and quarrying	...	...	...	...	...	7399	...	...	...	...	...	9141
A Coal mining	...	...	...	...	...	7399	...	...	...	...	...	9141
B Crude petroleum and natural gas production	...	...	...	...	...	...	...	...	...	...	...	...
C Metal ore mining	...	...	...	...	...	...	...	...	...	...	...	...
D Other mining [a]	...	...	...	...	...	...	...	...	...	...	...	...

Belgium

4.3 Cost Components of Value Added
(Continued)

Million Belgian francs

	1980 Compensation of Employees	Capital Consumption	Net Operating Surplus	Indirect Taxes	Less: Subsidies Received	Value Added	1981 Compensation of Employees	Capital Consumption	Net Operating Surplus	Indirect Taxes	Less: Subsidies Received	Value Added
3 Manufacturing	573395	...	...	16548	...	833834	576034	...	...	12344	...	808538
A Manufacture of food, beverages and tobacco	66684	...	...	18927	...	119190	69124	...	...	20879	...	126009
B Textile, wearing apparel and leather industries	50780	...	...	-277	...	63655	49630	...	...	-1907	...	63124
C Manufacture of wood and wood products, including furniture [b]	...	...	...	...	...	37070	...	...	...	...	...	36628
D Manufacture of paper and paper products, printing and publishing	35955	...	...	-150	...	44448	36916	...	...	-207	...	44197
E Manufacture of chemicals and chemical petroleum, coal, rubber and plastic products [c]	77381	...	...	-1083	...	189136	80213	...	...	-1014	...	180204
F Manufacture of non-metallic mineral products, except products of petroleum and coal [a]	37872	...	...	137	...	49986	35146	...	...	-181	...	44271
G Basic metal industries	66481	...	...	545	...	70258	66289	...	...	-2722	...	69310
H Manufacture of fabricated metal products, machinery and equipment	210627	...	...	-1523	...	247649	211726	...	...	-2453	...	234510
I Other manufacturing industries [b]	27615	...	...	-28	...	12442	26990	...	...	-51	...	10285
4 Electricity, gas and water [c]	61661	...	...	36729	...	75002	66961	...	...	34386	...	84378
5 Construction	156797	...	...	716	...	259389	140864	...	...	978	...	224694
6 Wholesale and retail trade, restaurants and hotels	421149	...	...	-3086	...	546968	440402	...	...	-68	...	550903
A Wholesale and retail trade [d]	...	...	...	-3147	...	464159	...	...	...	-170	...	462943
B Restaurants and hotels	...	...	...	61	...	82809	...	...	...	102	...	87960
7 Transport, storage and communication	42083	...	...	-64914	...	268450	45285	...	...	-66825	...	273135
A Transport and storage	...	...	...	-55625	...	216281	...	...	...	-58498	...	217375
B Communication	42083	...	...	-9289	...	52169	45285	...	...	-8327	...	55760
8 Finance, insurance, real estate and business services [e]	114699	...	...	7618	...	149581	122980	...	...	9245	...	188052
A Financial institutions	114699	...	...	7618	...	149581	122980	...	...	9245	...	188052
B Insurance												
C Real estate and business services [e]												
Real estate, except dwellings	...	...	...	...	...	...	...	...	...	...	...	...
Dwellings	...	...	...	...	...	168448	...	...	...	...	...	193295
9 Community, social and personal services [e]	184936	...	...	10748	...	532987	199008	...	...	4747	...	588463
Educational services	...	...	...	...	...	...	...	...	...	...	...	...
Medical, dental, other health and veterinary services	...	...	...	...	...	122740	...	...	...	...	...	136544
Statistical discrepancy	...	...	...	...	...	96	...	...	...	...	...	21676
Total, Industries	1558930	...	...	-504	...	2746810	1595730	...	...	-10327	...	2830350
Producers of Government Services	471272	...	...	...	...	482609	512090	...	...	...	...	524345
Other Producers	40830	...	...	...	...	40830	42191	...	...	...	...	42191
Total	2071030	...	...	-504	...	3270250	2150010	...	...	-10327	...	3396890
Less: Imputed bank service charge	...	...	...	...	...	109122	...	...	...	...	...	131558
Import duties	...	...	...	34508	...	34508	...	...	...	33628	...	33628
Value added tax	...	...	...	255511	...	255511	...	...	...	278548	...	278548
Total [fg]	2071030	...	...	289515	...	3451150	2150010	...	...	301849	...	3577510

of which General Government:

1 Agriculture, hunting, forestry and fishing	...	...	...	...	...	...	...	...	...	...	...	...
2 Mining and quarrying	...	...	...	...	...	...	...	...	...	...	...	...
3 Manufacturing	...	...	...	...	...	...	...	...	...	...	...	...
4 Electricity, gas and water	...	...	...	...	...	...	...	...	...	...	...	...

Belgium

4.3 Cost Components of Value Added
(Continued)

Million Belgian francs

	1980						1981					
	Compensation of Employees	Capital Consumption	Net Operating Surplus	Indirect Taxes	Less: Subsidies Received	Value Added	Compensation of Employees	Capital Consumption	Net Operating Surplus	Indirect Taxes	Less: Subsidies Received	Value Added
5 Construction	...	...	...	...	...	...	...	...	...	...	...	...
6 Wholesale and retail trade, restaurants and hotels	...	...	...	...	...	...	...	...	...	...	...	...
7 Transport and communication	...	...	...	...	...	...	...	...	...	...	...	...
8 Finance, insurance, real estate & business services	...	...	...	...	...	...	...	...	...	...	...	...
9 Community, social and personal services	...	...	...	...	...	...	...	...	...	...	...	...
Total, Industries of General Government	299	...	...	...	...	4611	374	...	...	...	...	3078
Producers of Government Services	471272	...	...	...	...	482609	512090	...	...	...	...	524345
Total, General Government	471571	...	...	...	...	487220	512464	...	...	...	...	527423

	1982						1983					
	Compensation of Employees	Capital Consumption	Net Operating Surplus	Indirect Taxes	Less: Subsidies Received	Value Added	Compensation of Employees	Capital Consumption	Net Operating Surplus	Indirect Taxes	Less: Subsidies Received	Value Added

All Producers

1 Agriculture, hunting, forestry and fishing	4570	...	...	-4858	...	90957	4989	...	...	-6361	...	102375
2 Mining and quarrying	...	...	...	...	...	14486	...	...	...	...	...	14172
A Coal mining	...	...	...	...	...	14486	...	...	...	...	...	14172
B Crude petroleum and natural gas production	...	...	...	...	...	...	...	...	...	...	...	...
C Metal ore mining	...	...	...	...	...	...	...	...	...	...	...	...
D Other mining [a]	...	...	...	...	...	...	...	...	...	...	...	...
3 Manufacturing	602313	...	...	20961	...	912123	639234	...	...	19728	...	966017
A Manufacture of food, beverages and tobacco	72486	...	...	24867	...	146552	77061	...	...	25687	...	154795
B Textile, wearing apparel and leather industries	52132	...	...	-361	...	69554	56605	...	...	-467	...	72284
C Manufacture of wood and wood products, including furniture [b]	...	...	...	...	...	38088	...	...	...	...	...	36569
D Manufacture of paper and paper products, printing and publishing	39083	...	...	-255	...	50265	41918	...	...	-266	...	52767
E Manufacture of chemicals and chemical petroleum, coal, rubber and plastic products [c]	88074	...	...	-1143	...	208907	94170	...	...	-1127	...	224033
F Manufacture of non-metallic mineral products, except products of petroleum and coal [a]	35831	...	...	-304	...	47040	36407	...	...	-87	...	48725
G Basic metal industries	66243	...	...	374	...	76865	70704	...	...	-418	...	87228
H Manufacture of fabricated metal products, machinery and equipment	220948	...	...	-2114	...	263319	233281	...	...	-3470	...	276347
I Other manufacturing industries [b]	27516	...	...	-103	...	11533	29088	...	...	-124	...	13269
4 Electricity, gas and water [c]	72611	...	...	43625	...	84315	74409	...	...	47836	...	101410
5 Construction	134143	...	...	747	...	235105	128281	...	...	516	...	232482
6 Wholesale and retail trade, restaurants and hotels	470327	...	...	1565	...	600782	498107	...	...	-1885	...	658759
A Wholesale and retail trade [d]	...	...	...	1481	...	505132	...	...	...	-1831	...	554008
B Restaurants and hotels	...	...	...	84	...	95650	...	...	...	-54	...	104751
7 Transport, storage and communication	49193	...	...	-74042	...	289584	51214	...	...	-86577	...	304106
A Transport and storage	...	...	...	-66914	...	231834	...	...	...	-73110	...	240466
B Communication	49193	...	...	-7128	...	57750	51214	...	...	-13467	...	63640
8 Finance, insurance, real estate and business services [e]	140314	...	...	11620	...	211957	152115	...	...	13665	...	205727
A Financial institutions	[140314	...	...	11620	...	211957	152115	...	...	13665	...	205727]
B Insurance	[ ]			[ ]		[ ]	[ ]			[ ]		[ ]
C Real estate and business services [e]	...	...	...	...	...	...	...	...	...	...	...	...
Real estate, except dwellings	...	...	...	...	...	...	...	...	...	...	...	...
Dwellings	...	...	...	...	...	212462	...	...	...	...	...	234195
9 Community, social and personal services [e]	217780	...	...	1854	...	651207	234520	...	...	6780	...	712896

Belgium

4.3 Cost Components of Value Added
(Continued)

Million Belgian francs

	1982						1983					
	Compensation of Employees	Capital Consumption	Net Operating Surplus	Indirect Taxes	Less: Subsidies Received	Value Added	Compensation of Employees	Capital Consumption	Net Operating Surplus	Indirect Taxes	Less: Subsidies Received	Value Added
Educational services	...	...	...	...	...	...	...	...	...	...	...	...
Medical, dental, other health and veterinary services	...	...	...	...	...	152449	...	...	...	...	...	168593
Statistical discrepancy	...	...	...	...	...	8513	...	...	...	...	...	3528
Total, Industries	1691250	...	...	1472	...	3099030	1782870	...	...	-6298	...	3301470
Producers of Government Services	543586	...	...	...	...	556134	554838	...	...	...	...	568041
Other Producers	43714	...	...	...	...	43714	45501	...	...	...	...	45501
Total	2278550	...	...	1472	...	3698880	2383210	...	...	-6298	...	3915010
Less: Imputed bank service charge	...	...	...	...	...	146437	...	...	...	...	...	150629
Import duties	...	...	...	41291	...	41291	...	...	...	44930	...	44930
Value added tax	...	...	...	295362	...	295362	...	...	...	313027	...	313027
Total [fg]	2278550	...	...	338125	...	3889090	2383210	...	...	351659	...	4122340

of which General Government:

1 Agriculture, hunting, forestry and fishing	...	...	...	...	...	...	...	...	...	...	...	...
2 Mining and quarrying	...	...	...	...	...	...	...	...	...	...	...	...
3 Manufacturing	...	...	...	...	...	...	...	...	...	...	...	...
4 Electricity, gas and water	...	...	...	...	...	...	...	...	...	...	...	...
5 Construction	...	...	...	...	...	...	...	...	...	...	...	...
6 Wholesale and retail trade, restaurants and hotels	...	...	...	...	...	...	...	...	...	...	...	...
7 Transport and communication	...	...	...	...	...	...	...	...	...	...	...	...
8 Finance, insurance, real estate & business services	...	...	...	...	...	...	...	...	...	...	...	...
9 Community, social and personal services	...	...	...	...	...	...	...	...	...	...	...	...
Total, Industries of General Government	395	...	...	...	...	3842	408	...	...	...	...	3282
Producers of Government Services	543586	...	...	...	...	556134	554838	...	...	...	...	568041
Total, General Government	543981	...	...	...	...	559976	555246	...	...	...	...	571323

	1984						1985					
	Compensation of Employees	Capital Consumption	Net Operating Surplus	Indirect Taxes	Less: Subsidies Received	Value Added	Compensation of Employees	Capital Consumption	Net Operating Surplus	Indirect Taxes	Less: Subsidies Received	Value Added

All Producers

1 Agriculture, hunting, forestry and fishing	5420	...	...	-5826	...	105006	5862	...	...	-6058	...	105138
2 Mining and quarrying	...	...	...	...	...	11432	...	...	...	...	...	10975
A Coal mining	...	...	...	...	...	11432	...	...	...	...	...	10975
B Crude petroleum and natural gas production	...	...	...	...	...	...	...	...	...	...	...	...
C Metal ore mining	...	...	...	...	...	...	...	...	...	...	...	...
D Other mining [a]	...	...	...	...	...	...	...	...	...	...	...	...
3 Manufacturing	680535	...	...	22445	...	1027030	705984	...	...	21297	...	1115170
A Manufacture of food, beverages and tobacco	82514	...	...	28153	...	163492	85264	...	...	28012	...	173151
B Textile, wearing apparel and leather industries	60740	...	...	-596	...	75307	62800	...	...	-897	...	80801
C Manufacture of wood and wood products, including furniture [b]	...	...	...	...	...	38837	...	...	...	...	...	42412
D Manufacture of paper and paper products, printing and publishing	44490	...	...	-365	...	56365	46727	...	...	-363	...	61110
E Manufacture of chemicals and chemical petroleum, coal, rubber and plastic products [c]	101519	...	...	-1160	...	256450	107608	...	...	-953	...	268619
F Manufacture of non-metallic mineral products, except products of petroleum and coal [a]	38272	...	...	-101	...	52640	37311	...	...	-41	...	52085
G Basic metal industries	76093	...	...	195	...	93960	75947	...	...	-692	...	101209
H Manufacture of fabricated metal products, machinery and equipment	246723	...	...	-3550	...	277419	259648	...	...	-3655	...	323071
I Other manufacturing industries [b]	30184	...	...	-131	...	12559	30679	...	...	-114	...	12708
4 Electricity, gas and water [c]	77570	...	...	47135	...	106295	81427	...	...	47762	...	118997

Belgium

4.3 Cost Components of Value Added
(Continued)

Million Belgian francs

	1984						1985					
	Compensation of Employees	Capital Consumption	Net Operating Surplus	Indirect Taxes	Less: Subsidies Received	Value Added	Compensation of Employees	Capital Consumption	Net Operating Surplus	Indirect Taxes	Less: Subsidies Received	Value Added
5 Construction	127730	...	...	529	...	233717	129824	...	...	569	...	245778
6 Wholesale and retail trade, restaurants and hotels	530316	...	...	-3893	...	685531	553058	...	...	-10891	...	759819
A Wholesale and retail trade d	...	...	...	-3909	...	571816	...	...	...	-10887	...	636841
B Restaurants and hotels	...	...	...	16	...	113715	...	...	...	-4	...	122978
7 Transport, storage and communication	56847	...	...	-87058	...	344848	59984	...	...	-87851	...	374536
A Transport and storage	...	...	...	-74445	...	272023	...	...	...	-74263	...	294707
B Communication	56847	...	...	-12613	...	72825	59984	...	...	-13588	...	79829
8 Finance, insurance, real estate and business services e	164680	...	...	14450	...	247852	173510	...	...	16754	...	263512
A Financial institutions	164680	...	...	14450	...	247852	173510	...	...	16754	...	263512
B Insurance												
C Real estate and business services e	...	...	...	...	...	...	...	...	...	...	...	...
Real estate, except dwellings	...	...	...	...	...	...	...	...	...	...	...	...
Dwellings	...	...	...	...	...	257857	...	...	...	...	...	277822
9 Community, social and personal services e	255537	...	...	5622	...	794871	279108	...	...	13412	...	844553
Educational services	...	...	...	...	...	...	...	...	...	...	...	...
Medical, dental, other health and veterinary services	...	...	...	...	...	182591	...	...	...	...	...	194740
Statistical discrepancy	...	...	...	...	...	31983	...	...	...	...	...	5480
Total, Industries	1898640	...	...	-6596	...	3588560	1988760	...	...	-5006	...	3843950
Producers of Government Services	582405	...	...	...	...	596368	619993	...	...	...	...	634993
Other Producers	47304	...	...	...	...	47304	49496	...	...	...	...	49496
Total	2528340	...	...	-6596	...	4232240	2658250	...	...	-5006	...	4528440
Less: Imputed bank service charge	...	...	...	...	...	178145	...	...	...	...	...	186425
Import duties	...	...	...	45289	...	45289	...	...	...	47013	...	47013
Value added tax	...	...	...	329955	...	329955	...	...	...	349242	...	349242
Total fg	2528340	...	...	368648	...	4429340	2658250	...	...	391249	...	4738270

of which General Government:

	1984						1985					
1 Agriculture, hunting, forestry and fishing	...	...	...	...	...	...	...	...	...	...	...	...
2 Mining and quarrying	...	...	...	...	...	...	...	...	...	...	...	...
3 Manufacturing	...	...	...	...	...	...	...	...	...	...	...	...
4 Electricity, gas and water	...	...	...	...	...	...	...	...	...	...	...	...
5 Construction	...	...	...	...	...	...	...	...	...	...	...	...
6 Wholesale and retail trade, restaurants and hotels	...	...	...	...	...	...	...	...	...	...	...	...
7 Transport and communication	...	...	...	...	...	...	...	...	...	...	...	...
8 Finance, insurance, real estate & business services	...	...	...	...	...	...	...	...	...	...	...	...
9 Community, social and personal services	...	...	...	...	...	...	...	...	...	...	...	...
Total, Industries of General Government	477	...	...	...	...	3537	505	...	...	...	...	2527
Producers of Government Services	582405	...	...	...	...	596368	619993	...	...	...	...	634993
Total, General Government	582882	...	...	...	...	599905	620498	...	...	...	...	637520

	1986						1987					
	Compensation of Employees	Capital Consumption	Net Operating Surplus	Indirect Taxes	Less: Subsidies Received	Value Added	Compensation of Employees	Capital Consumption	Net Operating Surplus	Indirect Taxes	Less: Subsidies Received	Value Added

All Producers

1 Agriculture, hunting, forestry and fishing	6328	...	...	-5048	...	106443	6733	...	...	-5644	...	100950
2 Mining and quarrying	...	...	...	...	...	6542	...	...	...	...	...	4071
A Coal mining	...	...	...	...	...	6542	...	...	...	...	...	4071
B Crude petroleum and natural gas production	...	...	...	...	...	...	...	...	...	...	...	...
C Metal ore mining	...	...	...	...	...	...	...	...	...	...	...	...
D Other mining a	...	...	...	...	...	...	...	...	...	...	...	...

Belgium

4.3 Cost Components of Value Added
(Continued)

Million Belgian francs

		1986						1987				
	Compensation of Employees	Capital Consumption	Net Operating Surplus	Indirect Taxes	Less: Subsidies Received	Value Added	Compensation of Employees	Capital Consumption	Net Operating Surplus	Indirect Taxes	Less: Subsidies Received	Value Added
3 Manufacturing	735718	...	...	17286	...	1157120	750466	...	...	17997	...	1187450
A Manufacture of food, beverages and tobacco	88078	...	...	24960	...	178655	90928	...	...	24229	...	179500
B Textile, wearing apparel and leather industries	63773	...	...	-1377	...	89756	64521	...	...	-1057	...	89982
C Manufacture of wood and wood products, including furniture [b]	...	...	...	...	...	45617	...	...	...	...	...	48923
D Manufacture of paper and paper products, printing and publishing	49047	...	...	-284	...	65742	51998	...	...	-415	...	68813
E Manufacture of chemicals and chemical petroleum, coal, rubber and plastic products [c]	115612	...	...	-1196	...	280453	121203	...	...	-1172	...	288615
F Manufacture of non-metallic mineral products, except products of petroleum and coal [a]	37722	...	...	50	...	57223	38730	...	...	-62	...	61686
G Basic metal industries	73415	...	...	-303	...	99301	70049	...	...	-365	...	95073
H Manufacture of fabricated metal products, machinery and equipment	275483	...	...	-4329	...	326895	280232	...	...	-3065	...	341118
I Other manufacturing industries [b]	32588	...	...	-235	...	13478	32805	...	...	-96	...	13737
4 Electricity, gas and water [c]	81443	...	...	50451	...	123245	79620	...	...	54927	...	126731
5 Construction	139200	...	...	635	...	249214	140915	...	...	609	...	251454
6 Wholesale and retail trade, restaurants and hotels	591705	...	...	-11728	...	864011	620604	...	...	-12021	...	923296
A Wholesale and retail trade [d]	...	...	...	-11763	...	733837	...	...	...	-12169	...	784736
B Restaurants and hotels	...	...	...	35	...	130174	...	...	...	148	...	138560
7 Transport, storage and communication	61963	...	...	-88886	...	369291	58687	...	...	-79022	...	394992
A Transport and storage	...	...	...	-75575	...	284357	...	...	...	-66875	...	302280
B Communication	61963	...	...	-13311	...	84934	58687	...	...	-12147	...	92712
8 Finance, insurance, real estate and business services [e]	187196	...	...	19131	...	297864	193748	...	...	22707	...	316597
A Financial institutions	[187196	...	...	19131	...	297864]	[193748	...	...	22707	...	316597]
B Insurance	[					]	[					]
C Real estate and business services [e]	...	...	...	...	...	...	...	...	...	...	...	...
Real estate, except dwellings	...	...	...	...	...	...	...	...	...	...	...	...
Dwellings	...	...	...	...	...	294692	...	...	...	...	...	314856
9 Community, social and personal services [e]	300330	...	...	24447	...	915111	322859	...	...	36573	...	983952
Educational services	...	...	...	...	...	...	...	...	...	...	...	...
Medical, dental, other health and veterinary services	...	...	...	...	...	205891	...	...	...	...	...	217005
Statistical discrepancy	...	...	...	...	...	-3283	...	...	...	...	...	-10160
Total, Industries	2103880	...	...	6288	...	4085560	2173630	...	...	36126	...	4279330
Producers of Government Services	642244	...	...	...	...	658367	640981	...	...	...	...	658701
Other Producers	50667	...	...	...	...	50667	50564	...	...	...	...	50564
Total	2796790	...	...	6288	...	4794590	2865180	...	...	36126	...	4988600
Less: Imputed bank service charge	...	...	...	...	...	207845	...	...	...	...	...	204227
Import duties	...	...	...	41998	...	41998	...	...	...	51133	...	51133
Value added tax	...	...	...	355521	...	355521	...	...	...	378647	...	378647
Total [fg]	2796790	...	...	403807	...	4984270	2865180	...	...	465906	...	5214150

of which General Government:

1 Agriculture, hunting, forestry and fishing	...	...	...	...	...	...	...	...	...	...	...	...
2 Mining and quarrying	...	...	...	...	...	...	...	...	...	...	...	...
3 Manufacturing	...	...	...	...	...	...	...	...	...	...	...	...
4 Electricity, gas and water	...	...	...	...	...	...	...	...	...	...	...	...

Belgium

4.3 Cost Components of Value Added
(Continued)

Million Belgian francs

	1986						1987					
	Compensation of Employees	Capital Consumption	Net Operating Surplus	Indirect Taxes	Less: Subsidies Received	Value Added	Compensation of Employees	Capital Consumption	Net Operating Surplus	Indirect Taxes	Less: Subsidies Received	Value Added
5 Construction	...	...	...	...	...	...	...	...	...	...	...	...
6 Wholesale and retail trade, restaurants and hotels	...	...	...	...	...	...	...	...	...	...	...	...
7 Transport and communication	...	...	...	...	...	...	...	...	...	...	...	...
8 Finance, insurance, real estate & business services	...	...	...	...	...	...	...	...	...	...	...	...
9 Community, social and personal services	...	...	...	...	...	...	...	...	...	...	...	...
Total, Industries of General Government	538	...	...	...	...	2544	555	...	...	...	...	2413
Producers of Government Services	642244	...	...	...	...	658367	640981	...	...	...	...	658701
Total, General Government	642782	...	...	...	...	660911	641536	...	...	...	...	661114

	1988						1989					
	Compensation of Employees	Capital Consumption	Net Operating Surplus	Indirect Taxes	Less: Subsidies Received	Value Added	Compensation of Employees	Capital Consumption	Net Operating Surplus	Indirect Taxes	Less: Subsidies Received	Value Added
				All Producers								
1 Agriculture, hunting, forestry and fishing	7663	...	...	-6787	...	105556	8211	...	...	-6860	...	123587
2 Mining and quarrying	...	...	...	...	...	2658	...	...	...	...	...	2209
A Coal mining	...	...	...	...	...	2658	...	...	...	...	...	2209
B Crude petroleum and natural gas production	...	...	...	...	...	...	...	...	...	...	...	...
C Metal ore mining	...	...	...	...	...	...	...	...	...	...	...	...
D Other mining [a]	...	...	...	...	...	...	...	...	...	...	...	...
3 Manufacturing	773974	...	...	17436	...	1281730	814791	...	...	19963	...	1403240
A Manufacture of food, beverages and tobacco	93737	...	...	24029	...	181532	98849	...	...	24685	...	187280
B Textile, wearing apparel and leather industries	64508	...	...	-965	...	90491	66448	...	...	-1009	...	99692
C Manufacture of wood and wood products, including furniture [b]	...	...	...	...	...	51957	...	...	...	...	...	59064
D Manufacture of paper and paper products, printing and publishing	55035	...	...	-431	...	76223	58076	...	...	-460	...	88945
E Manufacture of chemicals and chemical petroleum, coal, rubber and plastic products [c]	129170	...	...	-1496	...	308966	137580	...	...	-1325	...	336123
F Manufacture of non-metallic mineral products, except products of petroleum and coal [a]	41012	...	...	55	...	72640	44525	...	...	182	...	81996
G Basic metal industries	70609	...	...	-1646	...	127859	72722	...	...	-1749	...	149406
H Manufacture of fabricated metal products, machinery and equipment	285973	...	...	-2047	...	357037	301584	...	...	-333	...	384042
I Other manufacturing industries [b]	33930	...	...	-63	...	15021	35007	...	...	-28	...	16693
4 Electricity, gas and water [c]	72552	...	...	56955	...	131613	70601	...	...	64070	...	139140
5 Construction	158368	...	...	730	...	283851	173119	...	...	1497	...	321868
6 Wholesale and retail trade, restaurants and hotels	654547	...	...	-12158	...	958929	687184	...	...	-5954	...	1018470
A Wholesale and retail trade [d]	...	...	...	-12314	...	809746	...	...	...	-6159	...	853927
B Restaurants and hotels	...	...	...	156	...	149183	...	...	...	205	...	164542
7 Transport, storage and communication	60471	...	...	-82134	...	431642	62812	...	...	-83774	...	448651
A Transport and storage	...	...	...	-71285	...	333356	...	...	...	-73107	...	344056
B Communication	60471	...	...	-10849	...	98286	62812	...	...	-10667	...	104595
8 Finance, insurance, real estate and business services [e]	203033	...	...	23431	...	336319	213408	...	...	27513	...	366062
A Financial institutions	[203033	...	...	[23431	...	[336319	[213408	...	...	[27513	...	[366062
B Insurance	]	...	...	]	...	]	]	...	...	]	...	]
C Real estate and business services [e]	...	...	...	...	...	...	...	...	...	...	...	...
Real estate, except dwellings	...	...	...	...	...	...	...	...	...	...	...	...
Dwellings	...	...	...	...	...	335628	...	...	...	...	...	357146
9 Community, social and personal services [e]	350471	...	...	37325	...	1069510	381904	...	...	51289	...	1186710

160

Belgium

4.3 Cost Components of Value Added
(Continued)

Million Belgian francs

	\multicolumn{6}{c	}{1988}	\multicolumn{6}{c}{1989}
	Compensation of Employees	Capital Consumption	Net Operating Surplus	Indirect Taxes	Less: Subsidies Received	Value Added	Compensation of Employees	Capital Consumption	Net Operating Surplus	Indirect Taxes	Less: Subsidies Received	Value Added
Educational services	...	...	...	...	...	...	...	...	...	...	...	...
Medical, dental, other health and veterinary services	...	...	...	...	...	229839	...	...	...	...	...	247106
Statistical discrepancy	...	...	...	...	...	-24796	...	...	...	...	...	-7775
Total, Industries	2281080	...	...	34798	...	4577010	2412030	...	...	67744	...	5002160
Producers of Government Services	647618	...	...	...	...	666732	674646	...	...	...	...	695925
Other Producers	50584	...	...	...	...	50584	50742	...	...	...	...	50742
Total	2979280	...	...	34798	...	5294330	3137420	...	...	67744	...	5748830
Less: Imputed bank service charge	...	...	...	...	...	200495	...	...	...	...	...	208065
Import duties	...	...	...	49389	...	49389	...	...	...	52507	...	52507
Value added tax	...	...	...	405255	...	405255	...	...	...	434633	...	434633
Total [g]	2979280	...	...	489442	...	5548480	3137420	...	...	554884	...	6027900
\multicolumn{13}{c}{*of which General Government:*}
1 Agriculture, hunting, forestry and fishing	...	...	...	...	...	...	...	...	...	...	...	...
2 Mining and quarrying	...	...	...	...	...	...	...	...	...	...	...	...
3 Manufacturing	...	...	...	...	...	...	...	...	...	...	...	...
4 Electricity, gas and water	...	...	...	...	...	...	...	...	...	...	...	...
5 Construction	...	...	...	...	...	...	...	...	...	...	...	...
6 Wholesale and retail trade, restaurants and hotels	...	...	...	...	...	...	...	...	...	...	...	...
7 Transport and communication	...	...	...	...	...	...	...	...	...	...	...	...
8 Finance, insurance, real estate & business services	...	...	...	...	...	...	...	...	...	...	...	...
9 Community, social and personal services	...	...	...	...	...	...	...	...	...	...	...	...
Total, Industries of General Government	595	...	...	...	...	2664	613	...	...	...	...	2697
Producers of Government Services	647618	...	...	...	...	666732	674646	...	...	...	...	695925
Total, General Government	648213	...	...	...	...	669396	675259	...	...	...	...	698622

a) Item 'Manufacture of non-metallic mineral products, etc.' includes 'Other mining'.
b) Item 'Other manufacturing industries' includes item 'Manufacture of wood and paper products'.
c) Item 'Manufacture of chemicals and chemical petroleum, etc.' excludes energy products which are included in item 'Electricity, gas and water'.
d) For the second series, including repairs.
e) Business services and real estate except dwellings are included in item 'Community, social and personal services'.
f) The breakdown by kind of economic activity used in this table is according to the classification NACE/CLIO.
g) Column 4 refers to indirect taxes less subsidies received.

Belize

Source. Central Planning Unit, Ministry of Finance and Economic Planning, Belize. Official estimates are published in 'National Accounts Statistics'. Information on sources and methods of estimation can be found in 'National Accounts Statistics - Sources and Methods' and in 'Economic Accounts of the Public Sector'.

General note. The estimates shown in the following tables have been prepared in accordance with the United Nations System of National Accounts so far as the existing data would permit.

1.1 Expenditure on the Gross Domestic Product, in Current Prices

Million Belize dollars

	1970	1975	1980	1981	1982	1983	1984	1985	1986	1987	1988	1989
1 Government final consumption expenditure	...	22.8	66.8	73.4	84.2	89.7	93.0	95.4	102.8	...	...	...
2 Private final consumption expenditure	...	116.6	246.9	241.3	250.4	232.6	261.7	263.2	269.5	...	...	...
3 Gross capital formation	...	61.0	109.2	88.4	66.3	70.5	82.7	86.4	83.6	...	...	...
A Increase in stocks	...	8.0	5.7	4.9	-6.4	4.9	13.6	17.7	13.3	...	...	...
B Gross fixed capital formation	...	53.0	103.5	83.5	72.7	65.6	69.1	68.7	70.3	...	...	...
4 Exports of goods and services	...	150.1	215.7	206.0	172.0	185.5	217.9	201.3	233.1	...	...	...
5 Less: Imports of goods and services	...	161.7	296.2	250.5	228.2	227.5	268.9	256.6	264.1	...	...	...
Equals: Gross Domestic Product [a]	...	188.8	342.4	358.5	344.8	350.9	386.4	389.7	425.0	...	...	...

a) Data in this table have been revised, therefore they are not strictly comparable with the unrevised data in the other tables.

1.2 Expenditure on the Gross Domestic Product, in Constant Prices

Million Belize dollars

	1970	1975	1980	1981	1982	1983	1984	1985	1986	1987	1988	1989
			At constant prices of:									
			1980					1984				
1 Government final consumption expenditure	...	...	66.8	74.8 / 85.8	92.1	93.2	93.0	92.4	98.8	...	...	...
2 Private final consumption expenditure	...	...	246.9	228.3 / 256.0	243.2	235.3	261.7	249.7	249.6	...	...	...
3 Gross capital formation	...	...	109.2	105.0 / 92.4	62.3	55.6	82.7	79.6	81.5	...	...	...
A Increase in stocks	...	...	5.7	11.3 / 2.5	-11.9	-8.2	13.6	14.1	15.2	...	...	...
B Gross fixed capital formation	...	...	103.5	93.7 / 89.9	74.3	63.8	69.1	65.5	66.2	...	...	...
4 Exports of goods and services	...	...	215.7	212.2 / 181.2	203.1	213.0	217.9	228.5	253.6	...	...	...
5 Less: Imports of goods and services	...	...	296.2	276.6 / 239.7	225.3	230.4	268.9	255.0	274.2	...	...	...
Equals: Gross Domestic Product	...	...	342.4	347.3 / 375.8	375.5	366.7	386.4	395.1	409.2	...	...	...

1.3 Cost Components of the Gross Domestic Product

Million Belize dollars

	1970	1975	1980	1981	1982	1983	1984	1985	1986	1987	1988	1989
1 Indirect taxes, net	...	22.6	47.2	53.1	36.5	43.4	42.4	...	...	...	...	...
A Indirect taxes	...	22.6	50.2	55.8	47.9	54.9	...	...	...	...	...	...
B Less: Subsidies	...	-	3.0	2.7	11.4	11.5	...	...	...	...	...	...
2 Consumption of fixed capital	...	15.3	29.6	32.3	31.2	32.6	33.4	...	...	...	...	...
3 Compensation of employees paid by resident producers to:	...	150.9	265.6	280.7	264.6	275.7	...	...	...	...	...	...
4 Operating surplus	...							...	...	...	...	...
Equals: Gross Domestic Product	...	188.8	342.4	366.1	332.3	351.7	364.7	...	...	...	...	...

1.4 General Government Current Receipts and Disbursements

Million Belize dollars

	1970	1975	1980	1981	1982	1983	1984	1985	1986	1987	1988	1989
					Receipts							
1 Operating surplus	...	0.9	...	...	...	...	...	...	...	...	...	...
2 Property and entrepreneurial income	...	2.2	3.9	7.8	8.3	...	...	...	...	...	...	...
3 Taxes, fees and contributions	...	34.5	74.5	71.4	68.0	...	...	...	...	...	...	...
A Indirect taxes	...	22.6	50.2	55.8	47.9	...	...	...	...	...	...	...
B Direct taxes	...	10.8	23.3	14.6	19.6	...	...	...	...	...	...	...
C Social security contributions	...	0.2	-	-	-	...	...	...	...	...	...	...
D Compulsory fees, fines and penalties	...	0.9	1.0	1.0	0.5	...	...	...	...	...	...	...

Belize

1.4 General Government Current Receipts and Disbursements
(Continued)

Million Belize dollars

	1970	1975	1980	1981	1982	1983	1984	1985	1986	1987	1988	1989
4 Other current transfers	...	0.9	2.2	3.5	4.0	...	...	...	...	...	...	...
Total Current Receipts of General Government	...	38.4	80.6	82.7	80.3	...	...	...	...	...	...	...

Disbursements

	1970	1975	1980	1981	1982	1983	1984	1985	1986	1987	1988	1989
1 Government final consumption expenditure	...	22.8	66.8	77.1	85.2	...	...	...	...	...	...	...
A Compensation of employees	...	12.8	27.8	38.8	41.4	...	...	...	...	...	...	...
B Consumption of fixed capital	...	...	...	...	...	...	...	...	...	...	...	...
C Purchases of goods and services, net	...	10.0	39.0	38.3	43.8	...	...	...	...	...	...	...
D Less: Own account fixed capital formation	...	...	...	...	...	...	...	...	...	...	...	...
E Indirect taxes paid, net	...	...	...	...	...	...	...	...	...	...	...	...
2 Property income	...	2.6	-	-	-	...	...	...	...	...	...	...
3 Subsidies	...	-	3.0	2.7	11.4	...	...	...	...	...	...	...
4 Other current transfers	...	5.1	6.6	8.6	9.4	...	...	...	...	...	...	...
A Social security benefits	...	-	-	1.3	1.5	...	...	...	...	...	...	...
B Social assistance grants	...	4.5	...	...	...	...	...	...	...	...	...	...
C Other	...	0.6	...	...	...	...	...	...	...	...	...	...
5 Net saving	...	7.9	4.2	-5.7	-25.4	...	...	...	...	...	...	...
Total Current Disbursements and Net Saving of General Government	...	38.4	80.6	82.7	80.3	...	...	...	...	...	...	...

1.10 Gross Domestic Product by Kind of Activity, in Current Prices

Million Belize dollars

	1970	1975	1980	1981	1982	1983	1984	1985	1986	1987	1988	1989
1 Agriculture, hunting, forestry and fishing	...	52.5	69.7 / 91.7	86.2	67.5	67.9	72.9	69.4	73.3	95.2	104.1	117.7
2 Mining and quarrying	...	0.4	0.8 / 0.8	0.8	0.8	0.8	0.8	0.8	0.8	0.8	0.8	0.8
3 Manufacturing	...	23.0	44.8 / 50.1	42.6	31.9	37.5	45.0	37.7	37.7	52.9	56.2	62.2
4 Electricity, gas and water	...	1.5	3.9 / 2.8	2.2	5.4	0.8	8.2	10.3	14.3	15.1	16.6	18.4
5 Construction	...	11.4	18.9 / 19.9	20.8	18.8	16.4	19.6	19.2	20.5	26.8	33.8	37.4
6 Wholesale and retail trade, restaurants and hotels	...	27.2	56.7 / 58.1	58.4	51.5	49.8	56.1	54.5	59.0	68.3	87.0	96.3
7 Transport, storage and communication	...	10.7	26.7 / 17.2	21.9	24.1	29.4	32.2	35.0	36.9	43.4	52.1	57.6
8 Finance, insurance, real estate and business services	...	16.1	25.7 / 32.3	38.0	35.4	36.3	38.5	40.5	39.3	39.6	49.2	54.5
9 Community, social and personal services	...	12.6	24.9 / 21.8	24.6	32.0	35.1	36.4	36.3	37.5	39.1	40.3	44.6
Total, Industries	...	155.3	272.2 / 294.6	295.6	267.4	274.0	309.7	303.8	319.5	381.2	440.3	489.5
Producers of Government Services	...	15.1	30.9 / 25.0	28.2	36.7	40.2	41.7	41.6	46.7	53.1	57.9	64.1
Other Producers	...	...	...	...	...	...	...	...	...	...	...	...
Subtotal a	...	170.4	303.1 / 319.7	323.8	304.0	314.2	351.4	345.4	366.1	434.3	498.2	553.5
Less: Imputed bank service charge	...	4.3	7.9 / 11.5	14.3	12.4	11.8	12.4	10.2	11.9	14.5	21.1	23.3
Plus: Import duties	...	...	...	...	...	...	...	...	...	...	...	...
Plus: Value added tax	...	...	...	...	...	...	...	...	...	...	...	...
Plus: Other adjustments b	...	22.6	47.2 / ...	...	...	...	...	...	...	...	...	...
Equals: Gross Domestic Product c	...	188.8	342.4 / 308.1	309.4	291.6	302.4	339.0	335.2	354.2	419.8	477.1	530.2

a) Gross domestic product in factor values.
b) Item 'Other adjustments' refers to indirect taxes net of subsidies.
c) Second series, gross domestic product in factor values.

Belize

1.11 Gross Domestic Product by Kind of Activity, in Constant Prices

Million Belize dollars

	1970	1975	1980	1981	1982	1983	1984	1985	1986	1987	1988	1989
			At constant prices of:									
			1973				1984					
1 Agriculture, hunting, forestry and fishing	20.5	24.3	28.6 / 72.6	72.3	75.6	71.2	72.9	72.0	68.9	84.8	82.7	89.7
2 Mining and quarrying	0.2	0.3	0.4 / 0.8	0.8	0.8	0.8	0.8	0.8	0.8	0.8	0.8	0.8
3 Manufacturing	7.1	10.9	13.1 / 48.4	50.3	49.7	49.1	45.0	45.4	46.5	50.3	50.1	52.2
4 Electricity, gas and water	0.7	1.2	1.7 / 6.7	7.0	7.9	8.1	8.2	8.8	9.2	10.0	12.6	13.2
5 Construction	6.3	7.6	12.9 / 20.5	20.9	18.1	16.1	19.6	18.7	20.2	26.6	33.2	34.7
6 Wholesale and retail trade, restaurants and hotels	16.1	19.9	21.9 / 64.1	65.9	54.6	52.3	56.1	60.7	64.9	74.8	96.1	100.3
7 Transport, storage and communication	6.2	8.9	12.7 / 21.7	24.2	28.6	30.2	32.2	33.9	37.0	38.0	42.5	44.4
8 Finance, insurance, real estate and business services	14.1	15.5	16.2 / 40.9	42.0	39.2	38.5	38.5	40.0	41.4	48.2	49.8	51.9
9 Community, social and personal services	9.6	10.9	12.7 / 32.6	33.5	34.4	35.4	36.4	37.3	38.2	39.3	40.4	42.2
Total, Industries	80.8	99.5	120.2 / 308.3	317.0	309.0	301.7	309.7	317.6	327.1	372.8	408.2	429.3
Producers of Government Services	7.2	11.2	13.7 / 30.4	31.4	38.6	40.6	41.7	43.0	43.1	46.4	45.5	47.4
Other Producers	...	...	...	...	...	...	...	...	...	...	...	...
Subtotal a	88.0	110.7	133.9 / 338.7	348.4	347.6	342.3	351.4	360.6	370.2	419.2	453.7	476.8
Less: Imputed bank service charge	...	4.1	5.0 / 14.0	14.4	13.3	12.6	12.4	13.4	13.3	15.5	21.0	21.9
Plus: Import duties	...	...	...	...	...	...	...	...	...	...	...	...
Plus: Value added tax	...	...	...	...	...	...	...	...	...	...	...	...
Equals: Gross Domestic Product a	...	106.5	128.9 / 324.7	334.1	334.2	329.7	339.0	347.3	357.0	404.0	432.7	454.9

a) Gross domestic product in factor values.

1.12 Relations Among National Accounting Aggregates

Million Belize dollars

	1970	1975	1980	1981	1982	1983	1984	1985	1986	1987	1988	1989
Gross Domestic Product	...	188.8	342.4	366.1	332.2	351.7	364.7	...	...	...	...	...
Plus: Net factor income from the rest of the world	...	-16.7	-7.2	-7.9	-7.5	-8.0	-18.5	...	...	...	...	...
Factor income from the rest of the world	...	2.3	...	...	...	...	...	...	...	...	...	...
Less: Factor income to the rest of the world	...	18.9	...	...	...	...	...	...	...	...	...	...
Equals: Gross National Product	...	172.1	335.2	358.2	324.7	343.7	346.2	...	...	...	...	...
Less: Consumption of fixed capital	...	15.3	29.6	32.3	31.2	32.6	33.4	...	...	...	...	...
Equals: National Income	...	156.8	305.6	325.9	293.5	311.1	312.8	...	...	...	...	...
Plus: Net current transfers from the rest of the world	...	6.2	29.6	23.6	26.4	25.0	...	...	...	...	...	...
Current transfers from the rest of the world	...	7.0	...	...	...	...	...	...	...	...	...	...
Less: Current transfers to the rest of the world	...	0.8	...	...	...	...	...	...	...	...	...	...
Equals: National Disposable Income	...	163.0	335.2	349.5	319.9	336.1	...	...	...	...	...	...
Less: Final consumption	...	139.4	313.7	344.4	334.4	365.7	...	...	...	...	...	...
Equals: Net Saving	...	23.6	21.5	5.1	-14.5	-29.6	...	...	...	...	...	...
Less: Surplus of the nation on current transactions	...	-22.1	-24.4	-44.4	-50.4	-50.0	...	...	...	...	...	...
Equals: Net Capital Formation	...	45.7	45.9	49.5	35.9	20.4	...	...	...	...	...	...

Benin

Source. Reply to the United Nations National Accounts Questionnaire from the Institut National de la Statistique et de l'Analyse Economique, Direction Generale, Cotonou. Official estimates are published in 'Comptes de la Nation 1974-1975 et les estimations des aggregats de comptes nationaux a prix courants et a prix constants de 1970 a 1977'.

General note. The estimates shown in the following tables have been prepared in accordance with the United Nations System of National Accounts so far as the existing data would permit.

1.1 Expenditure on the Gross Domestic Product, in Current Prices

Million CFA francs

	1970	1975	1980	1981	1982	1983	1984	1985	1986	1987	1988	1989
1 Government final consumption expenditure	8976	13411	21729	25238	27187 / 43731	60213	62561	58842	63782	68699	57244	58313
2 Private final consumption expenditure	54081	95990	220024	276076	387981 / 343844	354119	371999	374128	381144	384549	402584	409359
3 Gross capital formation	11854	28793	57860	65350	103108 / 115037	72332	58801	74217	68072	66562	72988	57622
A Increase in stocks	1620	5958	9700	13100	17795 / 2337	2923	1453	11246	-486	-348	1852	-12500
B Gross fixed capital formation	10234	22835	48160	52250	85313 / 112700	69409	57348	62971	68558	66910	71135	70123
4 Exports of goods and services	19270	30647	59460	65050	58739 / 107648	83546	130718	156544	129461	128730	142482	99738
5 Less: Imports of goods and services	24470	55727	113460	130690	165134 / 193621	152772	164741	193953	179924	178986	192864	137507
Equals: Gross Domestic Product	69711	113112	245613	301024	411881 / 416638	417438	459340	469778	462535	469554	482434	487525

1.2 Expenditure on the Gross Domestic Product, in Constant Prices

Million CFA francs

At constant prices of: 1970

	1970	1975	1980	1981	1982	1983	1984	1985	1986	1987	1988	1989
1 Government final consumption expenditure	8976	9313	...	...	...	...	...	...	...	...	...	...
2 Private final consumption expenditure	54081	66658	...	...	...	...	...	...	...	...	...	...
3 Gross capital formation	11854	16576	...	...	...	...	...	...	...	...	...	...
A Increase in stocks	1620	3430	...	...	...	...	...	...	...	...	...	...
B Gross fixed capital formation	10234	13146	...	...	...	...	...	...	...	...	...	...
4 Exports of goods and services	19270	23965	...	...	...	...	...	...	...	...	...	...
5 Less: Imports of goods and services	24470	32082	...	...	...	...	...	...	...	...	...	...
Equals: Gross Domestic Product	69711	84430	...	...	...	...	...	...	...	...	...	...

1.3 Cost Components of the Gross Domestic Product

Million CFA francs

	1970	1975	1980	1981	1982	1983	1984	1985	1986	1987	1988	1989
1 Indirect taxes, net	...	9604	22264	30400	33872 / 47158	35456	37232	38309	39930	38754	31354	21790
A Indirect taxes	...	10144	22364	30510	34067 / 49646	38425	40011	43706	43767	42150	38638	...
B Less: Subsidies	...	540	100	110	195 / 2488	2970	2779	5397	3837	3396	7285	...
2 Consumption of fixed capital	...	5526	19772	22978	34964	...	...	...	...	...	...	...
3 Compensation of employees paid by resident producers to:	...	28338	...	...	92849 / 72637	86607	90984	93240	98455	102136	93302	96333
A Resident households	...	28255	...	...	...	...	...	...	...	...	...	...
B Rest of the world	...	83	...	...	...	...	...	...	...	...	...	...
4 Operating surplus	...	69646	...	...	250186 / 296844	295376	331123	338229	324149	328663	357778	369402
Equals: Gross Domestic Product	69711	113114	...	...	411881 / 416638	417438	459340	469778	462535	469554	482434	487525

Benin

1.7 External Transactions on Current Account, Summary

Million CFA francs	1970	1975	1980	1981	1982	1983	1984	1985	1986	1987	1988	1989
Payments to the Rest of the World													
1 Imports of goods and services	24470	55727	...	...	193621	152772	164741	193953	179924	178986	192864	137507
A Imports of merchandise c.i.f.	20350	50366	...	...	...	...	...	...	...	...	...	...
B Other	4120	5361	...	...	...	...	...	...	...	...	...	...
2 Factor income to the rest of the world	...	1103	...	...	2760	11854	13033	11600	10000	9600	10000	12300
A Compensation of employees	...	83	...	...	...	...	...	...	...	...	...	...
B Property and entrepreneurial income	...	1020	...	...	...	...	...	...	...	...	...	...
3 Current transfers to the rest of the world	...	1761	...	...	1494	1824	1342	2000	2000	2000	2000	2000
4 Surplus of the nation on current transactions	...	-16422	...	...	-50213	-37879	-5858	-6009	-19863	-17856	-15482	2941
Payments to the Rest of the World and Surplus of the Nation on Current Transactions	...	42169	...	...	147662	128571	173258	201544	172061	172730	189382	154748
Receipts From The Rest of the World													
1 Exports of goods and services	19270	30647	...	...	107648	83546	130718	156544	129461	128730	142482	99738
A Exports of merchandise f.o.b.	16090	24882	...	...	...	...	...	...	...	...	...	...
B Other	3180	5765	...	...	...	...	...	...	...	...	...	...
2 Factor income from rest of the world	...	1029	...	...	3502	1885	1331	2000	1000	1000	-	-
A Compensation of employees	...	279	...	...	...	...	...	...	...	...	...	...
B Property and entrepreneurial income	...	750	...	...	...	...	...	...	...	...	...	...
3 Current transfers from rest of the world	...	10493	...	...	36512	43140	41209	43000	41600	43000	46900	55010
Receipts from the Rest of the World on Current Transactions	...	42169	...	...	147662	128571	173258	201544	172061	172730	189382	154748

1.10 Gross Domestic Product by Kind of Activity, in Current Prices

Million CFA francs	1970	1975	1980	1981	1982	1983	1984	1985	1986	1987	1988	1989
1 Agriculture, hunting, forestry and fishing	28709	39193	97451	116299	144323 / 135373	138578	153224	150147	155796	156270	167932	177129
2 Mining and quarrying	5932	227	18389	20044	20005[a] / 718	9292	22926	21237	3828	5252	4184	4406
3 Manufacturing		10707			36365	34725	35113	35456	33226	33676	40226	42882
4 Electricity, gas and water	395	767	1581	1848	3164 / 1823	1471	3211	3447	3854	4047	4316	4107
5 Construction	2310	4876	10815	19949	28557 / 21472	16103	14363	15218	15115	15141	14759	15225
6 Wholesale and retail trade, restaurants and hotels [b]	12210	28050	60205	70018	84278 / 70170	63655	67221	74521	72940	73416	84358	82110
7 Transport, storage and communication	3832	8082	28269	34404	39978 / 29020	27637	31346	37443	37205	36664	36497	36475
8 Finance, insurance, real estate and business services	11593	4020	28666	33272	33990 / 41286	41515	43168	44903	47490	49863	51747	54808
9 Community, social and personal services [b]		586										

Benin

1.10 Gross Domestic Product by Kind of Activity, in Current Prices
(Continued)

Million CFA francs

	1970	1975	1980	1981	1982	1983	1984	1985	1986	1987	1988	1989
Total, Industries	...	96508	245376	295834	354295 / 336227	332976	370572	382373	369455	374329	404019	417141
Producers of Government Services	...	10960	19380	22971	23714 / 33253	49007	51536	49096	53150	56471	47061	48594
Other Producers	...	425	...	...	...	...	...	...	...	...	...	...
Subtotal c	64981	107893	264756	318805	378009 / 369480	381982	422100	431469	422603	430800	451080	465735
Less: Imputed bank service charge	743	980	...	...	...	...	...	...	...	...	...	...
Plus: Import duties d	5473	6201	22264	30400	33872 / 47158	35456	37232	38309	39930	38754	31354	21790
Plus: Value added tax	...	...	...	...	...	...	...	...	...	...	...	...
Equals: Gross Domestic Product	69711	113114	287020	349205	411881 / 416638	417438	459340	469778	462533	469554	482434	487525

a) Including item 'Manufacturing'.
b) Restaurants and hotels are included in item 'Community, social and personal services'.
c) Gross domestic product in factor values.
d) Item 'Import duties' refers to indirect taxes net of subsidies.

1.11 Gross Domestic Product by Kind of Activity, in Constant Prices

Million CFA francs

	1970	1975	1980	1981	1982	1983	1984	1985	1986	1987	1988	1989
			1970		1978			1985				
1 Agriculture, hunting, forestry and fishing	28577	26978	75368	74455	87788 / 115331	115322	137262	150147	157699	148592	167661	177167
2 Mining and quarrying	5189	6646	15073	16087	14613a / 753	10680	21878	21237	13427	15082	13703	12725
3 Manufacturing					38082	33848	31701	35456	33981	35877	42620	44283
4 Electricity, gas and water	351	441	1297	1483	2311 / 4521	3858	3130	3447	2881	2996	3617	3617
5 Construction	2072	2944	8390	13452	17859 / 25659	18036	15337	15218	14785	14387	13051	13134
6 Wholesale and retail trade, restaurants and hotels	11062	18112	49348	50373	57176 / 75908b	65176b	66919b	74521b	80402b	81542b	84176b	79546b
7 Transport, storage and communication	3546	5508	23152	24751	27122 / 35991	32163	34781	37443	35215	33146	30937	30164
8 Finance, insurance, real estate and business services	10411	10580	23497	24050	23060 / 45708	44219	44352	44903	46475	47754	48588	50395
9 Community, social and personal services												

Benin

1.11 Gross Domestic Product by Kind of Activity, in Constant Prices
(Continued)

Million CFA francs

	1970	1975	1980	1981	1982	1983	1984	1985	1986	1987	1988	1989
			1970		**At constant prices of:** **1978**			**1985**				
Total, Industries	...	...	196125	204651	229929 341954	323303	355360	382373	384866	379376	404353	411033
Producers of Government Services	...	...	15872	16514	16088 34555	50306	52377	49096	50815	50612	50308	49903
Other Producers	...	...	...	...	... ...	...	...	...	...	...	...	...
Subtotal	61208c	71209c	211997c	221165c	246017c 376509	373609	407737	431469	435681	429988	454661	460936
Less: Imputed bank service charge	...	...	...	...	... ...	...	...	...	...	...	...	...
Plus: Import duties	...	...	18399d	22125d	23506d 46668	31177	29149	38309	44190	42685	32355	22634
Plus: Value added tax	...	...	...	...	... ...							
Equals: Gross Domestic Product	61208c	71209c	230336	243290	269523 423177	404786	436886	469778	479871	472673	487016	483570

a) Including item 'Manufacturing'.
b) Restaurants and hotels are included in item 'Community, social and personal services'.
c) Gross domestic product in factor values.
d) Item 'Import duties' refers to indirect taxes net of subsidies.

1.12 Relations Among National Accounting Aggregates

Million CFA francs

	1970	1975	1980	1981	1982	1983	1984	1985	1986	1987	1988	1989
Gross Domestic Product	69711	113114	...	...	416638	417438	459340	469778	462535	469554	482434	487525
Plus: Net factor income from the rest of the world	...	-74	...	...	742	-9969	-11702	-9600	-9000	-8600	-10000	-12300
Factor income from the rest of the world	...	1029	...	...	3502	1885	1331	2000	1000	1000	-	-
Less: Factor income to the rest of the world	...	1103	...	...	2760	11854	13033	11600	10000	9600	10000	12300
Equals: Gross National Product	...	113040	...	...	417380	407469	447638	460178	453535	460954	472434	475225
Less: Consumption of fixed capital	...	5526	...	...	...	...	...	...	...	...	...	...
Equals: National Income a	...	107514	...	...	417380	407469	447638	460178	453535	460954	472434	475225
Plus: Net current transfers from the rest of the world	...	8732	...	...	35018	41316	39862	41000	39600	41000	44900	53010
Current transfers from the rest of the world	...	10493	...	...	36512	43140	41209	43000	41600	43000	46900	55010
Less: Current transfers to the rest of the world	...	1761	...	...	1494	1824	1342	2000	2000	2000	2000	2000
Equals: National Disposable Income b	...	116246	...	...	452398	448785	487505	501178	493135	501954	517334	528235
Less: Final consumption	63057	109401	...	...	387575	414332	434560	432970	444926	453248	459828	467672
Equals: Net Saving c	...	6845	...	...	64823	34453	52945	68208	48209	48706	57506	60563
Less: Surplus of the nation on current transactions	...	-16422	...	...	-50213	-37879	-5858	-6009	-19863	-17856	-15482	2941
Equals: Net Capital Formation d	...	23267	...	...	115037	72332	58801	74217	68072	66562	72988	57622

a) Item 'National income' includes consumption of fixed capital.
b) Item 'National disposable income' includes consumption of fixed capital.
c) Item 'Net saving' includes consumption of fixed capital.
d) Item 'Net capital formation' includes consumption of fixed capital.

Benin

4.1 Derivation of Value Added by Kind of Activity, in Current Prices

Million CFA francs

	1982 Gross Output	1982 Intermediate Consumption	1982 Value Added	1983 Gross Output	1983 Intermediate Consumption	1983 Value Added	1984 Gross Output	1984 Intermediate Consumption	1984 Value Added	1985 Gross Output	1985 Intermediate Consumption	1985 Value Added
All Producers												
1 Agriculture, hunting, forestry and fishing	161496	17056	144440	173254	13219	160035	199012	21045	177967	200937	21196	179741
A Agriculture and hunting	148172	15895	132277	159560	12025	147535	184081	19741	164340	185323	19833	165490
B Forestry and logging	4904	445	4459	5281	479	4802	6092	552	5540	6207	563	5644
C Fishing	8420	716	7704	8413	715	7698	8839	752	8087	9407	800	8607
2 Mining and quarrying	2207	706	1501	19036	6091	12945	35218	11270	23948	40954	13105	27849
3 Manufacturing	66757	45644	21113	66504	45657	20849	64233	44310	19923	63125	43208	19917
A Manufacture of food, beverages and tobacco	39975	25466	14509	43045	28155	14890	41883	27256	14627	36750	24009	12741
B Textile, wearing apparel and leather industries	9712	7834	1878	5725	4646	1079	5517	4966	551	8150	7043	1107
C Manufacture of wood and wood products, including furniture	2502	1685	817	2373	1649	724	1805	1115	690	2030	1067	963
D Manufacture of paper and paper products, printing and publishing	1097	633	464	1504	836	668	1665	1010	655	1612	840	772
E Manufacture of chemicals and chemical petroleum, coal, rubber and plastic products	2869	1458	1411	3165	2023	1142	3678	2152	1527	3113	2201	912
F Manufacture of non-metallic mineral products, except products of petroleum and coal	6657	5890	767	6830	5498	1332	6609	5666	943	8179	5722	2457
G Basic metal industries	...	...	...	...	...	...	...	...	...	...	...	...
H Manufacture of fabricated metal products, machinery and equipment	3812	2619	1193	3595	2723	872	2762	1998	764	3026	2201	825
I Other manufacturing industries	133	59	74	269	127	149	314	148	166	265	125	140
4 Electricity, gas and water	6499	3230	3269	4145	2429	1716	7443	3778	3665	6292	2618	3674
5 Construction	71537	42128	29409	63490	41401	22089	51869	33824	18045	71389	46552	24837
6 Wholesale and retail trade, restaurants and hotels	102615	17866	84749	96002	14468	81534	102440	14676	87764	114022	16251	97771
A Wholesale and retail trade	100973	16865	84108	91458	12300	79158	97605	12369	85236	108878	13798	95080
B Restaurants and hotels	1642	1001	641	4544	2168	2376	4835	2307	2528	5144	2453	2691
7 Transport, storage and communication	74416	33969	40447	95427	41341	54086	99530	54064	45466	106030	56637	49393
A Transport and storage	70912	33082	37830	91563	39954	51609	94840	52732	42108	100945	55135	45810
B Communication	3504	887	2617	3864	1387	2477	4690	1332	3358	5085	1502	3583
8 Finance, insurance, real estate and business services	46408	5357	41051	50337	7043	43294	46620	7094	39526	50999	7950	43049
A Financial institutions	10215	1285	8930	12871	1514	11357	12399	1678	10721	9920	1743	8177
B Insurance	860	531	329	738	285	453	681	403	278	1215	245	970
C Real estate and business services	35333	3541	31792	36728	5244	31484	32480	4377	28103	39864	5962	33902
9 Community, social and personal services	4884	2482	2402	4352	1593	2759	4593	1681	2912	3808	1356	2452
Total, Industries [a]	536819	168438	368381	572549	173242	399307	610958	191742	419216	657556	208873	448683
Producers of Government Services	28143	4428	23715	35644	3992	31652	42731	4260	38471	43149	4307	38842
Other Producers	421	78	343	504	87	417	525	92	433	547	97	450
Total [a]	565383	172944	392439	608697	177321	431376	654214	196094	458120	701252	213277	487975
Less: Imputed bank service charge	-	-8557	8557	-	-10942	10942	-	-7256	7256	-	-6579	6579
Import duties	27999	-	27999	18951	-	18951	15337	-	15337	18452	-	18452
Value added tax	...	...	...	...	...	...	...	...	...	...	...	...
Total [a]	593382	181501	411881	627648	188263	439385	669551	203350	466201	719704	219856	499848

	1986 Gross Output	1986 Intermediate Consumption	1986 Value Added
All Producers			
1 Agriculture, hunting, forestry and fishing	219259	18784	200475
A Agriculture and hunting	204499	17474	187025
B Forestry and logging	6769	623	6146
C Fishing	7991	687	7304
2 Mining and quarrying	14619	4678	9941

Benin

4.1 Derivation of Value Added by Kind of Activity, in Current Prices
(Continued)

Million CFA francs

	1986 Gross Output	1986 Intermediate Consumption	1986 Value Added
3 Manufacturing	59065	39726	19339
A Manufacture of food, beverages and tobacco	35563	23477	12086
B Textile, wearing apparel and leather industries	6669	4974	1695
C Manufacture of wood and wood products, including furniture	1883	1222	661
D Manufacture of paper and paper products, printing and publishing	1327	547	780
E Manufacture of chemicals and chemical petroleum, coal, rubber and plastic products	3339	2285	1054
F Manufacture of non-metallic mineral products, except products of petroleum and coal	6488	4539	1949
G Basic metal industries	...	...	...
H Manufacture of fabricated metal products, machinery and equipment	3529	2556	973
I Other manufacturing industries	267	126	141
4 Electricity, gas and water	7532	3138	4394
5 Construction	74912	48856	26056
6 Wholesale and retail trade, restaurants and hotels	114227	16317	97910
A Wholesale and retail trade	108967	13809	95158
B Restaurants and hotels	5260	2508	2752
7 Transport, storage and communication	110767	59167	51600
A Transport and storage	105456	57599	47857
B Communication	5311	1568	3743
8 Finance, insurance, real estate and business services	47709	7416	40293
A Financial institutions	8998	1579	7419
B Insurance	1205	249	956
C Real estate and business services	35900	4838	31062
9 Community, social and personal services	3356	1195	2161
Total, Industries a	651446	199277	452169
Producers of Government Services	44517	5195	39322
Other Producers	570	150	420
Total a	696533	204622	491911
Less: Imputed bank service charge	-	-7370	7370
Import duties	18125	-	18125
Value added tax	...	...	...
Total a	714658	211992	502666

a) Data for this table have not been revised, therefore, data for some years are not comparable with those of other tables.

4.3 Cost Components of Value Added

Million CFA francs

	1982 Compensation of Employees	1982 Capital Consumption	1982 Net Operating Surplus	1982 Indirect Taxes	1982 Less: Subsidies Received	1982 Value Added	1983 Compensation of Employees	1983 Capital Consumption	1983 Net Operating Surplus	1983 Indirect Taxes	1983 Less: Subsidies Received	1983 Value Added
All Producers												
1 Agriculture, hunting, forestry and fishing	14072	5584	124667	117	...	144440	15296	6018	138581	140	...	160035
A Agriculture and hunting	11967	4727	115482	101	...	132277	13174	5152	129086	123	...	147535
B Forestry and logging	251	134	4060	14	...	4459	270	144	4373	15	...	4802
C Fishing	1854	723	5125	2	...	7704	1852	722	5122	2	...	7698
2 Mining and quarrying	414	40	1043	4	...	1501	3573	350	8918	104	...	12945

Benin

4.3 Cost Components of Value Added
(Continued)

Million CFA francs

	1982						1983					
	Compensation of Employees	Capital Consumption	Net Operating Surplus	Indirect Taxes	Less: Subsidies Received	Value Added	Compensation of Employees	Capital Consumption	Net Operating Surplus	Indirect Taxes	Less: Subsidies Received	Value Added
3 Manufacturing	5686	3232	9590	2605	...	21113	6189	3663	9934	1063	...	20849
A Manufacture of food, beverages and tobacco	3460	1930	7035	2084	...	14509	4215	2318	7769	588	...	14890
B Textile, wearing apparel and leather industries	951	525	95	307	...	1878	645	329	-80	185	...	1079
C Manufacture of wood and wood products, including furniture	189	83	525	20	...	817	101	38	507	78	...	724
D Manufacture of paper and paper products, printing and publishing	293	87	87	-3	...	464	293	87	274	14	...	668
E Manufacture of chemicals and chemical petroleum, coal, rubber and plastic products	315	79	890	127	...	1411	333	136	515	158	...	1142
F Manufacture of non-metallic mineral products, except products of petroleum and coal	195	296	219	57	...	767	361	506	445	20	...	1332
G Basic metal industries	...	...	...	...	...	...	...	...	...	...	...	...
H Manufacture of fabricated metal products, machinery and equipment	281	230	668	14	...	1193	218	241	398	15	...	872
I Other manufacturing industries	2	1	71	-	...	74	23	8	106	5	...	142
4 Electricity, gas and water	675	1694	795	105	...	3269	890	976	-192	42	...	1716
5 Construction	12618	3171	12768	852	...	29409	12754	2335	5743	1257	...	22089
6 Wholesale and retail trade, restaurants and hotels	19335	6114	58829	471	...	84749	9558	2029	68556	1391	...	81534
A Wholesale and retail trade	18992	5978	58679	459	...	84108	8824	1799	67169	1366	...	79158
B Restaurants and hotels	343	136	150	12	...	641	734	230	1387	25	...	2376
7 Transport, storage and communication	14427	10377	15174	469	...	40447	9624	23417	18096	2949	...	54086
A Transport and storage	12930	9821	14610	469	...	37830	7991	22744	17925	2949	...	51609
B Communication	1497	556	564	-	...	2617	1633	673	171	-	...	2477
8 Finance, insurance, real estate and business services	2420	3749	33651	1231	...	41051	3224	5274	33608	1188	...	43294
A Financial institutions	1950	390	6345	245	...	8930	2629	1117	7225	386	...	11357
B Insurance	233	60	-8	44	...	329	322	64	23	44	...	453
C Real estate and business services	237	3299	27314	942	...	31792	273	4093	26360	758	...	31484
9 Community, social and personal services	106	43	2237	16	...	2402	74	48	2608	29	...	2759
Total, Industries [ab]	69753	34005	258753	5870	...	368381	61182	44110	285852	8163	...	399307
Producers of Government Services	22764	950	-	1	...	23715	30383	1216	-	53	...	31652
Other Producers	332	9	-	2	...	343	401	10	-	6	...	417
Total [ab]	92849	34964	258753	5873	...	392439	91966	45336	285852	8222	...	431376
Less: Imputed bank service charge	-	-	8557	-	...	8557	-	-	10942	-	...	10942
Import duties	-	-	-	27999	...	27999	-	-	-	18951	...	18951
Value added tax	...	...	...	...	...	...	...	...	...	...	...	...
Total [ab]	92849	34964	250196	33872	...	411881	91966	45336	274910	27173	...	439385

	1984						1985					
	Compensation of Employees	Capital Consumption	Net Operating Surplus	Indirect Taxes	Less: Subsidies Received	Value Added	Compensation of Employees	Capital Consumption	Net Operating Surplus	Indirect Taxes	Less: Subsidies Received	Value Added

All Producers

1 Agriculture, hunting, forestry and fishing	17138	6766	153894	169	...	177967	19150	6862	153559	170	...	179741
A Agriculture and hunting	14870	5850	143470	150	...	164340	16078	5884	143378	150	...	165490
B Forestry and logging	311	166	5046	17	...	5540	317	169	5140	18	...	5644
C Fishing	1957	750	5378	2	...	8087	2755	809	5041	2	...	8607
2 Mining and quarrying	6621	634	16623	70	...	23940	7699	737	19331	82	...	27849

Benin

4.3 Cost Components of Value Added
(Continued)

Million CFA francs

	1984						1985					
	Compensation of Employees	Capital Consumption	Net Operating Surplus	Indirect Taxes	Less: Subsidies Received	Value Added	Compensation of Employees	Capital Consumption	Net Operating Surplus	Indirect Taxes	Less: Subsidies Received	Value Added
3 Manufacturing	6200	3926	8399	1398	...	19923	5883	3680	9369	985	...	19917
A Manufacture of food, beverages and tobacco	4075	2350	7414	788	...	14627	3818	2098	6410	415	...	12741
B Textile, wearing apparel and leather industries	821	342	-666	54	...	551	629	128	280	70	...	1107
C Manufacture of wood and wood products, including furniture	99	124	387	80	...	690	92	140	605	126	...	963
D Manufacture of paper and paper products, printing and publishing	365	167	86	37	...	655	361	321	66	24	...	772
E Manufacture of chemicals and chemical petroleum, coal, rubber and plastic products	328	240	646	313	...	1527	465	271	57	119	...	912
F Manufacture of non-metallic mineral products, except products of petroleum and coal	348	499	-8	104	...	943	389	479	1376	213	...	2457
G Basic metal industries	...	...	...	...	...	...	...	...	...	...	...	...
H Manufacture of fabricated metal products, machinery and equipment	137	195	416	16	...	764	106	235	471	13	...	825
I Other manufacturing industries	27	9	124	6	...	166	23	8	104	5	...	140
4 Electricity, gas and water	893	2676	15	81	...	3665	973	1766	817	118	...	3674
5 Construction	10419	1925	4691	1000	...	18045	14340	2626	6457	1414	...	24837
6 Wholesale and retail trade, restaurants and hotels	8995	3199	74438	1132	...	87764	9996	3556	82948	1271	...	97771
A Wholesale and retail trade	8216	2954	72961	1105	...	85236	9166	3295	81376	1243	...	95080
B Restaurants and hotels	779	245	1477	27	...	2528	830	261	1572	28	...	2691
7 Transport, storage and communication	8072	20877	14331	2186	...	45466	10505	25250	10259	3379	...	49393
A Transport and storage	6667	20065	13191	2185	...	42108	9086	24254	9093	3377	...	45810
B Communication	1405	812	1140	1	...	3358	1419	996	1166	2	...	3583
8 Finance, insurance, real estate and business services	3221	6927	28613	765	...	39526	3329	4976	33697	1047	...	43049
A Financial institutions	2494	3153	4840	234	...	10721	2466	718	4842	151	...	8177
B Insurance	315	72	-156	47	...	278	372	82	419	97	...	970
C Real estate and business services	412	3702	23929	484	...	28527	491	4176	28436	799	...	33902
9 Community, social and personal services	78	51	2752	31	...	2912	65	42	2318	26	...	2452
Total, Industries [a][b]	61637	46991	303756	6832	...	419216	71940	49495	318756	8492	...	448683
Producers of Government Services	36908	1563	-	-	...	38471	37246	1595	-	1	...	38842
Other Producers	416	11	-	6	...	433	432	12	-	6	...	450
Total [a][b]	98961	48665	303756	6838	...	458120	109618	51102	318756	8499	...	487975
Less: Imputed bank service charge	-	-	7256	-		7256	-	-	6579	-		6579
Import duties	-	-	-	15337		15337	-	-	-	18452		18452
Value added tax	...	...	...	...		...	...	...	...	...		...
Total [a][b]	98961	48565	296500	22175	...	466201	109618	51102	312177	26951	...	499848

	1986					
	Compensation of Employees	Capital Consumption	Net Operating Surplus	Indirect Taxes	Less: Subsidies Received	Value Added
	All Producers					
1 Agriculture, hunting, forestry and fishing	21215	8149	170819	292	...	200475
A Agriculture and hunting	19102	7288	160364	271	...	187025
B Forestry and logging	345	184	5598	19	...	6146
C Fishing	1768	677	4857	2	...	7304
2 Mining and quarrying	2749	263	6900	29	...	9941

Benin

4.3 Cost Components of Value Added
(Continued)

Million CFA francs

			1986			
	Compensation of Employees	Capital Consumption	Net Operating Surplus	Indirect Taxes	Less: Subsidies Received	Value Added
3 Manufacturing	5890	3526	9007	916	...	19339
A Manufacture of food, beverages and tobacco	4070	1990	5554	472	...	12086
B Textile, wearing apparel and leather industries	555	113	968	59	...	1695
C Manufacture of wood and wood products, including furniture	62	132	446	21	...	661
D Manufacture of paper and paper products, printing and publishing	266	392	99	23	...	780
E Manufacture of chemicals and chemical petroleum, coal, rubber and plastic products	512	289	119	134	...	1054
F Manufacture of non-metallic mineral products, except products of petroleum and coal	308	380	1078	183	...	1949
G Basic metal industries	...	...	...	...	...	...
H Manufacture of fabricated metal products, machinery and equipment	94	222	638	19	...	973
I Other manufacturing industries	23	8	105	5	...	141
4 Electricity, gas and water	939	2697	646	112	...	4394
5 Construction	15134	2771	6659	1492	...	26056
6 Wholesale and retail trade, restaurants and hotels	10023	3594	83020	1273	...	97910
A Wholesale and retail trade	9174	3298	81442	1244	...	95158
B Restaurants and hotels	849	296	1578	29	...	2752
7 Transport, storage and communication	10974	26378	10748	3500	...	51600
A Transport and storage	9492	25338	9545	3482	...	47857
B Communication	1482	1040	1203	18	...	3743
8 Finance, insurance, real estate and business services	3980	4653	30657	1003	...	40293
A Financial institutions	2792	705	3760	162	...	7419
B Insurance	1047	156	482	127	...	1812
C Real estate and business services	141	3792	26415	714	...	31062
9 Community, social and personal services	57	37	2044	23	...	2161
Total, Industries [ab]	72961	52068	318500	8640	...	452169
Producers of Government Services	37617	1704	-	1	...	39322
Other Producers	308	1	109	2	...	420
Total [ab]	110886	53773	318609	8643	...	491911
Less: Imputed bank service charge	-	-	7370	-	...	7370
Import duties	-	-	-	18125	...	18125
Value added tax	...	...	...	...	...	...
Total [ab]	110886	53773	311239	26768	...	502666

a) Column 4 refers to indirect taxes less subsidies received.
b) Data for this table have not been revised, therefore, data for some years are not comparable with those of other tables.

Bermuda

Source. Reply to the United Nations national accounts questionnaire from the Statistical Department of Bermuda, Hamilton.
General note. The estimates shown in the following tables have been prepared in accordance with the United Nations System of National Accounts so far as the existing data would permit.

1.1 Expenditure on the Gross Domestic Product, in Current Prices

Million Bermuda dollars — Fiscal year beginning 1 April

	1970	1975	1980	1981	1982	1983	1984	1985	1986	1987	1988	1989
1 Government final consumption expenditure	...	39.7	73.2	85.6	100.5	114.2	126.9	138.5	143.2	159.7	173.4	192.1
2 Private final consumption expenditure	...	273.8	518.3	566.0	605.8	663.4	718.9	770.2	828.6	923.8	1023.2	1091.2
A Households	...	...	...	...	595.6	652.7	707.3	757.3	814.7	909.3	1008.0	1075.1
B Private non-profit institutions serving households	...	...	...	...	10.2	10.7	11.6	12.9	13.9	14.5	15.2	16.1
3 Gross capital formation	...	42.7	119.7	112.5	164.6	169.9	206.6	203.1	183.1	225.2	289.4	252.5
A Increase in stocks	...	...	...	...	...	...	...	...	...	...	...	...
B Gross fixed capital formation	...	42.7	119.7	112.5	164.6	169.9	206.6	203.1	183.1	225.2	289.4	252.5
Residential buildings	...	...	17.7	20.5	38.0	41.3	...	...	...	...	...	...
Non-residential buildings	...	...	34.1	25.9	40.1	44.7	...	...	...	...	...	...
Other construction and land improvement etc.	...	...	8.6	7.6	5.2	5.8	...	...	...	...	...	...
Other	...	...	59.3	58.5	81.3	78.1	95.2	66.9	84.7	...	...	...
4 Exports of goods and services	...	261.5	495.2	513.6	560.9	616.1	644.9	701.9	821.6	872.0	901.6	952.2
5 Less: Imports of goods and services	...	224.5	454.1	478.1	526.5	560.2	631.0	634.7	695.3	780.8	887.7	916.0
Equals: Gross Domestic Product	...	393.2	752.3	799.6	905.3	1003.4	1066.3	1179.0	1281.1	1397.5	1499.9	1571.7

1.2 Expenditure on the Gross Domestic Product, in Constant Prices

Million Bermuda dollars — Fiscal year beginning 1 April

At constant prices of: 1975

	1970	1975	1980	1981	1982	1983	1984	1985	1986	1987	1988	1989
1 Government final consumption expenditure	...	39.7	48.3	50.4	52.6	53.6	55.1	56.6	55.2	57.8	58.9	...
2 Private final consumption expenditure	...	273.8	330.6	326.6	327.7	339.8	350.0	364.0	376.1	401.3	420.1	...
3 Gross capital formation	...	42.7	79.0	68.6	90.9	89.7	103.0	93.4	83.5	96.0	114.8	...
A Increase in stocks	...	...	...	...	...	...	...	...	...	...	...	...
B Gross fixed capital formation	...	42.7	79.0	68.6	90.9	89.7	103.0	93.4	83.5	96.0	114.8	...
Residential buildings	...	20.7	...	...	...	...	...	...	...	...	...	...
Non-residential buildings	...		...	...	...	...	...	...	...	...	...	...
Other construction and land improvement etc.	...	...	...	...	...	...	...	...	...	...	...	...
Other	...	22.0	...	...	...	...	...	...	...	...	...	...
4 Exports of goods and services	...	261.5	322.6	297.5	298.0	299.8	294.2	308.1	340.2	344.2	332.7	...
5 Less: Imports of goods and services	...	224.5	302.5	291.3	308.1	319.6	349.8	344.4	364.5	388.1	412.3	...
Equals: Gross Domestic Product	...	393.2	478.0	451.8	461.1	463.3	452.5	477.7	490.5	510.4	514.2	...

1.4 General Government Current Receipts and Disbursements

Thousand Bermuda dollars — Fiscal year beginning 1 April

	1970	1975	1980	1981	1982	1983	1984	1985	1986	1987	1988	1989
Receipts
1 Operating surplus	...	...	...	...	...	...	...	...	...	...	...	...
2 Property and entrepreneurial income	...	3885	7971	11121	12289	13428	...	...	...	...	...	...
3 Taxes, fees and contributions	...	53294	111720	128201	143329	154754	...	...	...	...	...	...
A Indirect taxes	...	20813	51142	64441	73341	77975	...	...	...	...	...	...
B Direct taxes	...	32481	60578	63760	69988	76779	...	...	...	...	...	...
C Social security contributions	...	...	...	...	...	...	...	...	...	...	...	...
D Compulsory fees, fines and penalties	...	...	...	...	...	...	...	...	...	...	...	...
4 Other current transfers	...	868	7647	16719	22046	27697	...	...	...	...	...	...
Total Current Receipts of General Government	...	58047	127338	156041	177664	195879	...	...	...	...	...	...
Disbursements
1 Government final consumption expenditure	...	39736	73216	85634	100459	114228	...	...	...	...	...	...

Bermuda

1.4 General Government Current Receipts and Disbursements
(Continued)

Thousand Bermuda dollars — Fiscal year beginning 1 April

	1970	1975	1980	1981	1982	1983	1984	1985	1986	1987	1988	1989
A Compensation of employees	...	...	...	...	...	...	...	...	...	...	...	...
B Consumption of fixed capital	...	...	...	...	...	...	...	...	...	...	...	...
C Purchases of goods and services, net	...	39736	73216	85634	100459	114228	...	...	...	...	...	...
D Less: Own account fixed capital formation	...	...	...	...	...	...	...	...	...	...	...	...
E Indirect taxes paid, net	...	...	...	...	...	...	...	...	...	...	...	...
2 Property income	...	2475	2056	2116	1806	1946	...	...	...	...	...	...
A Interest	...	2475	2056	2116	1806	1946	...	...	...	...	...	...
B Net land rent and royalties	...	...	...	...	...	...	...	...	...	...	...	...
3 Subsidies	...	...	...	...	...	...	...	...	...	...	...	...
4 Other current transfers	...	12147	24872	38293	43771	49883	...	...	...	...	...	...
5 Net saving	...	3689	27194	29998	31628	29822	...	...	...	...	...	...
Total Current Disbursements and Net Saving of General Government	...	58047	127338	156041	177664	195879	...	...	...	...	...	...

1.12 Relations Among National Accounting Aggregates

Million Bermuda dollars — Fiscal year beginning 1 April

	1970	1975	1980	1981	1982	1983	1984	1985	1986	1987	1988	1989
Gross Domestic Product	...	393.2	752.3	799.6	905.3	1003.4	1066.3	1179.0	1281.1	1397.5	1499.9	1571.7
Plus: Net factor income from the rest of the world	...	...	24.1	10.0	13.0	24.0	27.0	36.0	32.0	35.0	40.0	70.0
Factor income from the rest of the world	...	...	...	...	...	46.0	53.0	57.0	57.0	57.0	63.0	93.0
Less: Factor income to the rest of the world	...	...	...	...	...	22.0	26.0	21.0	25.0	22.0	23.0	23.0
Equals: Gross National Product	...	...	776.4	809.6	918.3	1027.4	1093.3	1215.0	1313.1	1432.5	1539.9	1641.7
Less: Consumption of fixed capital	...	...	...	...	...	...	...	...	...	...	...	...
Equals: National Income	...	...	...	...	...	...	...	...	...	...	...	...
Plus: Net current transfers from the rest of the world	...	...	...	...	...	...	...	...	...	...	...	...
Equals: National Disposable Income	...	...	...	...	...	...	...	...	...	...	...	...
Less: Final consumption	...	...	...	...	...	...	...	...	...	...	...	...
Equals: Net Saving	...	...	...	...	...	...	...	...	...	...	...	...
Less: Surplus of the nation on current transactions	...	...	...	...	...	...	...	...	...	...	...	...
Equals: Net Capital Formation	...	...	...	...	...	...	...	...	...	...	...	...

2.1 Government Final Consumption Expenditure by Function, in Current Prices

Thousand Bermuda dollars — Fiscal year beginning 1 April

	1970	1975	1980	1981	1982	1983	1984	1985	1986	1987	1988	1989
1 General public services	...	12909	27029	30833	35726	43898	48387	50924	48515	53434	...	...
2 Defence	...	542	1547	2079	2262	2435	2566	2805	2997	3556	...	...
3 Public order and safety	...	...	...	...	...	...	...	...	...	...	...	...
4 Education	...	10406	16531	19437	22691	25131	27350	29293	31343	33806	...	...
5 Health	...	1532	2588	2945	3365	4030	4657	5165	5452	6041	...	...
6 Social security and welfare	...	984	2304	2889	3859	3905	3716	4911	5370	5601	...	...
7 Housing and community amenities	...	3029	5653	6922	7599	7626	7670	8214	9087	9750	...	...
8 Recreational, cultural and religious affairs	...	1211	2097	2371	2873	3165	3483	3947	4152	4569	...	...
9 Economic services	...	10680	18340	21512	25615	28340	33527	37369	40020	47355	...	...
10 Other functions [a]	...	-1557	-2873	-3354	-3531	-4302	-4630	-4801	-5715	-7143	...	...
Total Government Final Consumption Expenditure	...	39736	73216	85634	100459	114228	126726	137827	141221	156969	...	...

a) Item 'Other functions' refers to fees, sales and recoveries.

Bhutan

Source. Reply to the United Nations National Accounts Questionnaire from the Central Statistical Office. The official estimates are published in 'Revised Series on Gross Domestic Product of Bhutan: 1980-1987' and 'National Accounts Statistics, 1980-1988'.

General note. The estimates shown in the following tables have been prepared in accordance with the United Nations System of National Accounts so far as the existing data would permit.

1.1 Expenditure on the Gross Domestic Product, in Current Prices

Million Ngultrum

	1970	1975	1980	1981	1982	1983	1984	1985	1986	1987	1988	1989
1 Government final consumption expenditure	...	...	275.9	287.3	326.7	442.9	513.2	560.9	576.3	633.6	568.7	...
2 Private final consumption expenditure	...	...	748.6	922.2	1053.8	1195.1	1435.8	1506.3	1837.5	2320.8	2636.7	...
3 Gross capital formation	...	...	345.1	500.5	615.5	712.0	765.3	1084.5	1135.1	1088.2	1518.4	...
A Increase in stocks	...	...	14.7	74.7	59.8	21.3	10.4	81.6	32.0	-161.5	10.4	...
B Gross fixed capital formation	...	...	330.4	425.8	555.7	690.7	754.9	1002.9	1103.1	1249.7	1508.0	...
Residential buildings	...	...										...
Non-residential buildings	...	...	229.6	308.3	422.1	541.3	594.6	631.8	644.8	743.8	723.5	...
Other construction and land improvement etc.	...	...										...
Other	...	...	100.8	117.5	133.6	149.4	160.3	371.1	458.3	505.9	784.5	...
4 Exports of goods and services	...	...	145.4	207.4	213.2	227.8	290.2	367.5	550.5	767.5	1200.8	...
5 Less: Imports of goods and services	...	...	402.1	616.2	687.6	789.0	898.9	1127.8	1297.8	1202.6	1983.7	...
Equals: Gross Domestic Product	...	...	1112.9	1301.2	1521.6	1788.8	2105.6	2391.4	2801.6	3607.5	3940.9	...

1.3 Cost Components of the Gross Domestic Product

Million Ngultrum

	1970	1975	1980	1981	1982	1983	1984	1985	1986	1987	1988	1989
1 Indirect taxes, net [a]	...	...	17.9	21.2	23.6	34.8	45.6	41.8	43.0	76.7	82.8	...
2 Consumption of fixed capital [b]	...	...	61.2	73.8	86.3	103.0	118.9	137.6	191.6	330.6	367.3	...
3 Compensation of employees paid by resident producers to:	...	...	1033.8	1206.2	1411.7	1651.0	1941.1	2212.0	2567.0	3200.2	3490.8	...
4 Operating surplus	...	...										...
Equals: Gross Domestic Product	...	...	1112.9	1301.2	1521.6	1788.8	2105.6	2391.4	2801.6	3607.5	3940.9	...

a) Item 'Net indirect taxes' excludes excise refunds from the government of India.
b) The sharp increase in 1987 for 'Consumption of fixed capital' is due to the operation of the Chukha Hydel Project.

1.7 External Transactions on Current Account, Summary

Million Ngultrum

	1970	1975	1980	1981	1982	1983	1984	1985	1986	1987	1988	1989
Payments to the Rest of the World												
1 Imports of goods and services	...	...	402.1	616.2	687.6	789.0	898.9	1127.7	1297.8	1202.6	1983.6	...
A Imports of merchandise c.i.f.	...	...	394.6	585.9	646.5	730.0	825.2	1041.6	1205.4	1124.2	1817.0	...
B Other	...	...	7.5	30.3	41.1	59.0	73.7	86.1	92.4	78.4	166.6	...
2 Factor income to the rest of the world	...	...	217.0	294.6	357.8	496.6	437.7	515.4	523.6	432.9	468.5	...
A Compensation of employees	...	...	217.0	294.6	357.8	495.8	436.3	511.6	517.9	425.2	445.1	...
B Property and entrepreneurial income	...	...	-	-	-	0.8	1.4	3.8	5.7	7.7	23.4	...
3 Current transfers to the rest of the world	...	...	-	-	-	-	-	-	-	-	-	...
4 Surplus of the nation on current transactions	...	...	-450.2	-636.4	-738.2	-928.6	-887.2	-1089.4	-1079.6	-635.3	-967.4	...
Payments to the Rest of the World and Surplus of the Nation on Current Transactions	...	...	168.9	274.4	307.2	357.0	449.4	553.7	741.8	1000.2	1484.7	...
Receipts From The Rest of the World												
1 Exports of goods and services	...	...	145.4	207.4	213.2	227.8	290.2	367.5	550.5	767.5	1200.8	...
A Exports of merchandise f.o.b.	...	...	131.5	171.7	159.4	160.7	206.4	272.0	427.1	711.9	1072.6	...
B Other	...	...	13.9	35.7	53.8	67.1	83.8	95.5	123.4	55.6	128.2	...
2 Factor income from rest of the world	...	...	17.0	24.9	36.2	40.6	49.9	65.6	56.6	83.4	124.2	...
A Compensation of employees	...	...	-	-	-	-	-	-	-	-	-	...
B Property and entrepreneurial income	...	...	17.0	24.9	36.2	40.6	49.9	65.6	56.6	83.4	124.2	...
3 Current transfers from rest of the world	...	...	6.5	42.1	57.8	88.6	109.3	120.6	134.7	149.3	159.7	...
Receipts from the Rest of the World on Current Transactions	...	...	168.9	274.4	307.2	357.0	449.4	553.7	741.8	1000.2	1484.7	...

Bhutan

1.10 Gross Domestic Product by Kind of Activity, in Current Prices

Million Ngultrum

	1970	1975	1980	1981	1982	1983	1984	1985	1986	1987	1988	1989
1 Agriculture, hunting, forestry and fishing	...	...	621.4	676.7	804.3	934.2	1117.6	1236.2	1399.2	1623.5	1746.3	...
2 Mining and quarrying	...	...	6.8	8.9	12.5	10.2	23.3	20.2	37.4	37.0	33.4	...
3 Manufacturing	...	...	35.8	63.5	70.1	96.5	109.5	128.3	137.1	204.7	226.5	...
4 Electricity, gas and water [a]	...	...	2.5	2.7	3.7	6.7	5.9	6.8	96.6	377.0	394.6	...
5 Construction	...	...	88.5	142.8	188.2	238.6	276.5	290.5	267.5	349.9	309.0	...
6 Wholesale and retail trade, restaurants and hotels	...	...	121.5	155.6	162.1	170.0	182.4	203.0	234.1	248.2	258.5	...
7 Transport, storage and communication	...	...	47.9	58.1	66.2	76.8	80.6	104.1	114.2	126.0	180.6	...
8 Finance, insurance, real estate and business services	...	...	70.2	80.3	84.2	100.5	129.6	149.3	170.7	210.5	295.1	...
9 Community, social and personal services [b]	...	...	120.4	121.5	139.8	155.0	178.5	262.2	350.8	416.0	507.8	...
Total, Industries	...	...	1115.0	1310.1	1531.1	1788.5	2103.9	2400.6	2807.6	3592.8	3951.8	...
Producers of Government Services [b]												
Other Producers	...	...	...	...	...	...	...	...	...	...	...	...
Subtotal [c]	...	...	1115.0	1310.1	1531.1	1788.5	2103.9	2400.6	2807.6	3592.8	3951.8	...
Less: Imputed bank service charge	...	...	20.0	30.0	33.0	35.0	44.0	51.0	49.0	62.0	93.7	...
Plus: Import duties	...	...	...	...	...	...	...	...	...	...	...	...
Plus: Value added tax	...	...	...	...	...	...	...	...	...	...	...	...
Plus: Other adjustments [d]	...	...	17.9	21.2	23.6	34.8	45.6	41.8	43.0	76.7	82.8	...
Equals: Gross Domestic Product	...	...	1112.9	1301.3	1521.7	1788.3	2105.5	2391.4	2801.6	3607.5	3940.9	...

a) The sharp increase beginning 1986 for item 'Electricity, gas and water' is the result of the completion of Chukha Hydel Project.
b) Item 'Producers of government services' is included in item 'Community, social and personal services'.
c) Gross domestic product in factor values.
d) Item 'Other adjustments' refers to indirect taxes net of subsidies.

1.11 Gross Domestic Product by Kind of Activity, in Constant Prices

Million Ngultrum

	1970	1975	1980	1981	1982	1983	1984	1985	1986	1987	1988	1989
			At constant prices of: 1980									
1 Agriculture, hunting, forestry and fishing	...	...	621.4	636.1	692.2	742.2	806.5	833.9	881.0	925.8	939.7	...
2 Mining and quarrying	...	...	6.8	8.9	12.1	8.9	15.8	12.6	22.2	21.6	19.0	...
3 Manufacturing	...	...	35.8	59.1	59.6	62.9	67.2	75.4	71.0	105.0	110.3	...
4 Electricity, gas and water [a]	...	...	2.5	2.7	3.1	6.0	5.2	6.0	60.4	229.0	248.3	...
5 Construction	...	...	88.5	131.0	157.7	185.2	173.5	169.0	141.8	152.3	129.0	...
6 Wholesale and retail trade, restaurants and hotels	...	...	121.5	140.3	132.0	122.0	123.4	132.4	143.4	142.4	129.2	...
7 Transport, storage and communication	...	...	47.9	54.9	57.4	64.8	66.4	79.4	83.9	91.3	122.1	...
8 Finance, insurance, real estate and business services	...	...	70.2	80.3	77.0	91.1	109.4	110.1	126.2	135.7	169.4	...
9 Community, social and personal services [b]	...	...	120.4	121.5	102.1	113.1	130.3	126.0	168.6	200.0	210.0	...
Total, Industries	...	...	1115.0	1234.8	1293.2	1396.2	1497.7	1544.8	1698.5	2003.1	2077.0	...
Producers of Government Services [b]												
Other Producers	...	...	...	...	...	...	...	...	...	...	...	...
Subtotal	...	...	1115.0	1234.8	1293.2	1396.2	1497.7	1544.8	1698.5	2003.1	2077.0	...
Less: Imputed bank service charge	...	...	20.0	30.0	24.0	26.0	32.0	25.0	24.0	30.0	38.7	...
Plus: Import duties	...	...	...	...	...	...	...	...	...	...	...	...
Plus: Value added tax	...	...	...	...	...	...	...	...	...	...	...	...
Equals: Gross Domestic Product [c]	...	...	1095.0	1204.8	1269.2	1370.2	1465.7	1519.8	1674.5	1973.1	2038.3	...

a) The sharp increase beginning 1986 for item 'Electricity, gas and water' is the result of the completion of Chukha Hydel Project.
b) Item 'Producers of government services' is included in item 'Community, social and personal services'.
c) Gross domestic product in factor values.

1.12 Relations Among National Accounting Aggregates

Million Ngultrum

	1970	1975	1980	1981	1982	1983	1984	1985	1986	1987	1988	1989
Gross Domestic Product	...	...	1112.9	1301.3	1521.7	1788.3	2105.5	2391.4	2801.6	3607.5	3940.9	...
Plus: Net factor income from the rest of the world	...	...	-200.0	-269.7	-321.6	-456.1	-387.8	-449.7	-467.0	-349.5	-344.3	...
Factor income from the rest of the world	...	...	17.0	24.9	36.2	40.6	49.9	65.7	56.6	83.4	124.2	...
Less: Factor income to the rest of the world	...	...	217.0	294.6	357.8	496.7	437.7	515.4	523.6	432.9	468.5	...
Equals: Gross National Product	...	...	912.9	1031.6	1200.1	1332.2	1717.7	1941.7	2334.6	3258.0	3596.6	...
Less: Consumption of fixed capital	...	...	61.2	73.8	86.3	103.0	118.9	137.6	191.6	330.6	367.3	...

Bhutan

1.12 Relations Among National Accounting Aggregates
(Continued)

Million Ngultrum

	1970	1975	1980	1981	1982	1983	1984	1985	1986	1987	1988	1989
Equals: National Income	...	...	851.7	957.8	1113.8	1229.2	1598.8	1804.1	2143.0	2927.4	3229.3	...
Plus: Net current transfers from the rest of the world	...	...	6.5	42.1	57.8	88.6	109.3	120.6	134.7	149.3	159.7	...
Current transfers from the rest of the world	...	...	6.5	42.1	57.8	88.6	109.3	120.6	134.7	149.3	159.7	...
Less: Current transfers to the rest of the world	...	...	-	-	-	-	-	-	-	-	-	...
Equals: National Disposable Income	...	...	858.2	999.9	1171.6	1317.8	1708.1	1924.7	2277.7	3076.7	3389.0	...
Less: Final consumption	...	...	1024.5	1209.5	1380.5	1638.0	1949.0	2067.2	2413.8	2954.4	3205.4	...
Equals: Net Saving	...	...	-166.3	-209.6	-208.9	-320.2	-240.9	-142.5	-136.1	122.3	183.6	...
Less: Surplus of the nation on current transactions	...	...	-450.2	-636.4	-738.2	-928.7	-887.2	-1089.4	-1079.6	-635.3	-967.5	...
Equals: Net Capital Formation	...	...	283.9	426.8	529.3	608.5	646.3	946.9	943.5	757.6	1151.1	...

2.17 Exports and Imports of Goods and Services, Detail

Million Ngultrum

	1970	1975	1980	1981	1982	1983	1984	1985	1986	1987	1988	1989
Exports of Goods and Services												
1 Exports of merchandise, f.o.b.	...	...	131.5	171.7	159.4	160.7	206.4	272.0	427.1	711.9	1072.6	...
2 Transport and communication	...	...	-	0.1	-	1.6	2.1	3.5	4.1	4.2	3.5	...
3 Insurance service charges	...	...	...	...	...	...	...	...	...	...	...	...
4 Other commodities	...	...	...	...	...	...	...	...	...	...	...	...
5 Adjustments of merchandise exports to change-of-ownership basis	...	...	...	...	...	...	...	...	...	...	...	...
6 Direct purchases in the domestic market by non-residential households	...	...	9.5	30.5	48.0	58.6	73.6	83.0	109.0	46.1	118.3	...
7 Direct purchases in the domestic market by extraterritorial bodies	...	...	4.4	5.1	5.8	6.9	8.1	9.0	10.3	5.3	6.4	...
Total Exports of Goods and Services	...	...	145.4	207.4	213.2	227.8	290.2	367.5	550.5	767.5	1200.8	...
Imports of Goods and Services												
1 Imports of merchandise, c.i.f.	...	...	394.6	585.9	646.5	730.0	825.2	1041.6	1205.4	1124.2	1817.0	...
2 Adjustments of merchandise imports to change-of-ownership basis	...	...	...	...	...	...	...	...	...	...	...	...
3 Other transport and communication	...	...	-	-	-	1.5	2.1	2.2	1.5	1.4	36.9	...
4 Other insurance service charges	...	...	...	...	...	...	...	...	...	...	...	...
5 Other commodities	...	...	...	...	...	...	...	...	...	...	...	...
6 Direct purchases abroad by government	...	...	4.5	10.3	11.1	17.5	21.6	24.0	20.9	27.0	39.8	...
7 Direct purchases abroad by resident households	...	...	3.0	20.0	30.0	40.0	50.0	60.0	70.0	50.0	90.0	...
Total Imports of Goods and Services	...	...	402.1	616.2	687.6	789.0	898.9	1127.8	1297.8	1202.6	1983.7	...
Balance of Goods and Services	...	...	-256.7	-408.8	-474.4	-561.2	-608.7	-760.3	-747.3	-435.1	-782.9	...
Total Imports and Balance of Goods and Services	...	...	145.4	207.4	213.2	227.8	290.2	367.5	550.5	767.5	1200.8	...

Bolivia

General note. The preparation of national accounts statistics in Bolivia is undertaken by the Banco Central de Bolivia, La Paz. The official estimates together with methodological notes are published in a series of publications entitled 'Cuentas Nacionales de Bolivia'. The most detailed description of the sources and methods used for the national accounts estimation is found in 'Cuentas Nacionales, 1958-1966, Planeamiento'. On 1 January 1987, the Bolivian pesos has been re-denominated from pesos to Bolivianos. One Boliviano is equivalent to one million pesos. The estimates are generally in accordance with the classifications and recommendations recommended in the United Nations System of National Accounts (SNA). Input-output table for 1958 has been published in 'La Matriz de Transacciones Intersectoriales de Bienes Nacionales e Importados'. The following tables have been prepared from successive replies to the United Nations national accounts questionnaire. When the scope and coverage of the estimates differ for conceptual or statistical reasons from the definitions and classifications recommended in SNA, a footnote is indicated to the relevant tables.

Sources and methods:

(a) Gross domestic product. Gross domestic product is estimated mainly through the production approach.

(b) Expenditure on the gross domestic product. All components of GDP by expenditure type are estimated through the expenditure approach except private final consumption expenditure which is obtained as a residual. The estimates of the government final consumption expenditure are based on the annual government accounts furnished by the respective government agencies. Increase in stocks estimates are based on information obtained from the enterprises. For public capital information, estimates are obtained from financial statements of the public institutions. The estimates are classified by type of goods and sub-divisions of the public sector. For the estimates of private capital formation, the Instituto Nacional de Estadistica requests detailed information from the enterprises. The estimates of imported machinery and equipment are based on c.i.f. import values classified by use or economic destination. Trade margins and transport expenses are then added. The estimation of domestically produced capital goods is done on the basis of annual industrial statistics. Data on exports of goods and services are obtained from the balance of payments accounts. The value of non-monetary gold export is added to the f.o.b. figures while imports are estimated by the Banco Central. For the constant price estimates, government expenditure on wages and salaries are revalued at base-year prices while purchases of goods and services are deflated by implicit price or cost-of-living indexes. The estimates of private consumption expenditure is obtained as a residual. For the remaining items, price deflation is used.

(c) Cost-structure of the gross domestic product. The cost structure of the gross domestic product has not been estimated since 1969.

(d) Gross domestic product by kind of economic activity. The table of gross domestic product by kind of economic activity is prepared at market prices, i.e. producers' values. The production approach is used to estimate value added of most industries, but due to lack of information on intermediate consumption, value added coefficients established from the input-output table of 1958 have been utilized. The income approach is used to estimate value added of public administration and defence and some private industries. For agriculture, information relating to production volume is used, estimated on the basis of information on areas sown and production yields prepared by the Ministerio de Asuntos Campensinos y Agropecuarios and by special institutions. The gross value of production is estimated by using data on physical volumes and producer prices. Estimates of livestock production is based on existing livestock, information on meat cutting for domestic consumption and export data. The mining sector consists of the Corporacion Minera de Bolivia (COMIBOL), and of medium and small mines. The basic statistics are obtained from the accounts of COMIBOL, from Ministerio de Minera, from financial statements of medium-sized mines and from export statistics for small mines. The estimates for the manufacturing sector are based on information obtained from the annual industrial statistics published by the Instituto Nacional de Estadistica supplemented by statistics from private and public institutions and other studies. Information on electricity is obtained from the Direccion Nacional de Electricidad which controls all the public and private enterprises. The sources used for the construction estimates are the accounts of public institutions permits issued by municipalities and financial statements submitted by the construction enterprises. The value of production of private construction, which is based on permits issued and classified by surface area, is adjusted by a percentage for planned unfulfilled work. Information on trade margins and trade volumes is furnished by various concerned institutions. The gross trade margins are estimated from the price differences between the wholesale and producers prices as well as the consumer and wholesale prices for all the agricultural products and a sample of manufactured and imported goods entering the distribution channels. Restaurants and hotels estimates are based on a sample survey of the principal establishments in La Paz, blown up to cover the whole country by using the number of establishments as indicators. The estimates of railway transport are based on the accounts of the public railway enterprise. The gross value of production for urban passenger transport is estimated on the basis of the number of buses in operation, mileage, passenger volumes and average tariffs. Air transport estimates are based on the accounting statements of the national airline as well as taxes charged on foreign airlines. The accounting statements of the financial institutions are used for the financial sector. For ownership of dwellings, census information on population and housing is used supplemented by statistics on real estate. For public administration and defense, the main source is the annual financial statement requested by the Banco Central de Bolivia. Estimates for private services are obtained from concerned entities and institutions. For constant price estimates, value added for agriculture, mining and quarrying, manufacturing and transport sectors is extrapolatd by quantity index for output. Value added of construction is estimated by multiplying the annual authorized construction volume by the base-year prices. For the remaining industries, value added is deflated by appropriate price indexes.

1.1 Expenditure on the Gross Domestic Product, in Current Prices

Thousand Bolivianos

	1970	1975	1980	1981	1982	1983	1984	1985	1986	1987	1988	1989
1 Government final consumption expenditure	1	5	16	20	42	113	2555	238275	705309	942203	1325512	1619906
2 Private final consumption expenditure	9	35	82	105	268	968	14157	1793045	6213741	7440123	8803111	10392024
3 Gross capital formation	2	11	18	26	50	165	3374	484282	1193776	1514075	1387762	1443670
A Increase in stocks	-	2	1	5	-2	2	542	148441	234110	368390	-25825	-251552
B Gross fixed capital formation	2	9	18	22	52	163	2832	335841	959666	1145685	1413587	1695222
Residential buildings	-	1	4	...	...	...	...	...	...	...	...	...
Non-residential buildings	-	1	1	...	...	...	...	...	...	...	...	...
Other construction and land improvement etc.	-	2	5	...	...	...	...	...	...	...	...	...
Other	1	5	7	...	...	...	...	...	...	...	...	...
4 Exports of goods and services	3	12	32	37	142	513	7896	830101	2586796	2494306	2995097	3953199
5 Less: Imports of goods and services	3	16	25	33	100	298	4758	478994	1775526	2210602	2208808	2665347
Equals: Gross Domestic Product [a][b]	12	48	123	155	402	1463	23224	2866709	8924094	10180105	12302674	14743452

a) Data in this table have been revised, therefore they are not strictly comparable with the unrevised data in the other tables.
b) The estimates for the years 1970-1982 were prepared by the Central Bank. Beginning 1983, they were prepared by the Instituto Nacional de Estadistica.

1.2 Expenditure on the Gross Domestic Product, in Constant Prices

Bolivianos

	1970	1975	1980	1981	1982	1983	1984	1985	1986	1987	1988	1989
					At constant prices of: 1980							
1 Government final consumption expenditure	7968	13036	15904	17236	16734	14768	15331	14196	12192	13676	13129	13620
2 Private final consumption expenditure	59740	72666	82258	82541	79095	72924	74324	77213	81503	85171	86874	89046
3 Gross capital formation	14545	25323	18058	20762	12162	11570	15786	20958	18239	20276	15344	13659
A Increase in stocks	1808	5211	544	3677	13	1210	4314	7154	3689	5022	-295	-2495
B Gross fixed capital formation	12737	20112	17514	17085	12149	10360	11472	13804	14550	15254	15639	16154
4 Exports of goods and services	23877	30961	31521	32534	31522	32238	30044	26660	29698	27935	29703	33312
5 Less: Imports of goods and services	22292	30903	24795	28990	20839	18122	22788	27419	32804	35399	30087	31541
Equals: Gross Domestic Product [a][b]	83838	111083	122946	124083	118674	113378	112696	111608	108828	111659	114963	118096

a) Data in this table have been revised, therefore they are not strictly comparable with the unrevised data in the other tables.
b) The estimates for the years 1970-1982 were prepared by the Central Bank. Beginning 1983, they were prepared by the Instituto Nacional de Estadistica.

Bolivia

1.3 Cost Components of the Gross Domestic Product

Bolivianos

	1970	1975	1980	1981	1982	1983	1984	1985	1986	1987	1988	1989
1 Indirect taxes, net	942	5791	8266	11310	...	...	...	...	...	...	...	...
2 Consumption of fixed capital	756	2893	3288	4291	...	...	...	...	...	...	...	...
3 Compensation of employees paid by resident producers to:	4209	16364	41864	49794	...	...	...	...	...	...	...	...
A Resident households	4198	16244	46573	...	...	...	...	...	...	...	...	...
B Rest of the world	11	120	28	...	...	...	...	...	...	...	...	...
4 Operating surplus	6463	24153	69528	89501	...	...	...	...	...	...	...	...
Equals: Gross Domestic Product	12370	49201	122946	154896	...	...	...	...	...	...	...	...

1.7 External Transactions on Current Account, Summary

Bolivianos

	1970	1975	1980	1981	1982	1983	1984	1985	1986	1987	1988	1989
Payments to the Rest of the World												
1 Imports of goods and services	2514	13242	25850	33593	89642	443104	...	...	...	...	...	...
A Imports of merchandise c.i.f.	2302	12066	22440	29522	74126	410964	...	...	...	...	...	...
B Other	212	1176	3410	4071	15516	32140	...	...	...	...	...	...
2 Factor income to the rest of the world	340	1020	7123	9456	51020	99348	...	...	...	...	...	...
A Compensation of employees	11	120	28	27	130	244	...	...	...	...	...	...
B Property and entrepreneurial income	329	900	7095	9429	50890	99104	...	...	...	...	...	...
3 Current transfers to the rest of the world	4	76	62	59	296	975	...	...	...	...	...	...
4 Surplus of the nation on current transactions	-262	-3374	-4742	-15819	-35498	-225130	...	...	...	...	...	...
Payments to the Rest of the World and Surplus of the Nation on Current Transactions	2596	10964	28293	27289	105460	318297	...	...	...	...	...	...
Receipts From The Rest of the World												
1 Exports of goods and services	2494	10474	26373	25788	99284	287862	...	...	...	...	...	...
A Exports of merchandise f.o.b.	2355	9386	24120	23581	91039	265674	...	...	...	...	...	...
B Other	139	1088	2253	2207	8245	22188	...	...	...	...	...	...
2 Factor income from rest of the world	56	228	478	471	1186	5919	...	...	...	...	...	...
A Compensation of employees	25	74	110	91	385	887	...	...	...	...	...	...
B Property and entrepreneurial income	31	154	368	380	801	5032	...	...	...	...	...	...
3 Current transfers from rest of the world	46	262	1442	1030	4990	24516	...	...	...	...	...	...
Receipts from the Rest of the World on Current Transactions	2596	10964	28293	27289	105460	318297	...	...	...	...	...	...

1.10 Gross Domestic Product by Kind of Activity, in Current Prices

Thousand Bolivianos

	1970	1975	1980	1981	1982	1983	1984	1985	1986	1987	1988	1989
1 Agriculture, hunting, forestry and fishing	2	10	23	29	78	370	7027	832528	2450257	...	...	...
2 Mining and quarrying	1	6	19	20	97	215	2753	337557	890331	...	...	...
3 Manufacturing	2	6	18	24	33	142	2052	343156	1184356	...	...	...
4 Electricity, gas and water	-	-	1	1	2	5	124	25665	96333	...	...	...
5 Construction	1	3	5	6	12	54	1181	121481	254744	...	...	...
6 Wholesale and retail trade, restaurants and hotels	2	6	13	20	49	255	3203	310571	970203	...	...	...
7 Transport, storage and communication	1	3	7	9	31	81	1289	304425	1056002	...	...	...
8 Finance, insurance, real estate and business services	2	6	17	22	46	142	2309	303562	777652	...	...	...
9 Community, social and personal services	1	2	5	6	21	105	1228	133835	635561	...	...	...

Bolivia

1.10 Gross Domestic Product by Kind of Activity, in Current Prices
(Continued)

Thousand Bolivianos

	1970	1975	1980	1981	1982	1983	1984	1985	1986	1987	1988	1989
Total, Industries	12	42	108	136	369	1369	21167	2712780	8315439	...	...	...
Producers of Government Services	1	4	13	14	31	95	2072	177666	484056	...	...	...
Other Producers	-	-	1	1	2	8	110	13153	49743	...	...	...
Subtotal	13	46	122	151	402	1472	23349	2903599	8849238	...	...	...
Less: Imputed bank service charge	-	1	2	2	5	17	272	61883	66211	...	...	...
Plus: Import duties	1	2	3	4	4	8	147	24993	141067	...	...	...
Plus: Value added tax	...	...	...	...	...	...	...	...	...	...	...	...
Equals: Gross Domestic Product [a,b]	12	48	123	155	402	1463	23224	2866709	8924094	...	...	...

a) Data in this table have been revised, therefore they are not strictly comparable with the unrevised data in the other tables.
b) The estimates for the years 1970-1982 were prepared by the Central Bank. Beginning 1983, they were prepared by the Instituto Nacional de Estadistica.

1.11 Gross Domestic Product by Kind of Activity, in Constant Prices

Bolivianos

	1970	1975	1980	1981	1982	1983	1984	1985	1986	1987	1988	1989
	\multicolumn{12}{c}{At constant prices of:1980}
1 Agriculture, hunting, forestry and fishing	15042	20600	22563	22354	23900	19788	23553	25372	24478	25337	25951	25572
2 Mining and quarrying	14498	20715	19407	20139	19526	18112	16902	14211	12166	12351	14806	17047
3 Manufacturing	11227	15587	17974	16581	14531	14558	14707	13483	13742	14087	14852	15374
4 Electricity, gas and water	395	560	806	907	930	951	1025	986	1059	996	1051	1105
5 Construction	4199	5580	4521	4058	3698	3714	3518	3389	2662	2637	3019	3214
6 Wholesale and retail trade, restaurants and hotels	9999	12069	13261	14418	13464	15983	13243	13316	14768	15974	15350	15395
7 Transport, storage and communication	2896	4638	7321	8174	7799	7840	8471	8873	9346	9825	9868	10098
8 Finance, insurance, real estate and business services	10002	13668	17248	16829	16308	15028	15103	15437	14711	14112	14269	14370
9 Community, social and personal services	3397	4474	4881	4857	4710	4256	4002	3886	3819	3704	3741	3768
Total, Industries	71655	97891	107982	108317	104866	100230	99524	98953	96751	99023	102907	105943
Producers of Government Services	6433	9702	12940	13193	13749	13312	12777	12041	10118	10365	10210	10333
Other Producers	934	667	668	687	702	717	717	724	728	713	721	724
Subtotal	79022	108260	121590	121197	119317	114259	113018	111718	107597	110101	113838	117000
Less: Imputed bank service charge	839	1474	1932	1867	1733	1453	1370	1416	750	718	702	716
Plus: Import duties	5655	4297	3288	3753	1090	572	1048	1306	1981	2276	1827	1812
Plus: Value added tax	...	...	...	...	...	...	...	...	...	...	...	...
Equals: Gross Domestic Product [a]	83838	111083	122946	124083	118674	113378	112696	111608	108828	111659	114963	118096

a) Data in this table have been revised, therefore they are not strictly comparable with the unrevised data in the other tables.

1.12 Relations Among National Accounting Aggregates

Bolivianos

	1970	1975	1980	1981	1982	1983	1984	1985	1986	1987	1988	1989
Gross Domestic Product	12370	49201	128614	162810	398459	1515785	...	...	...	...	...	...
Plus: Net factor income from the rest of the world	-284	-792	-6645	-8985	-49834	-93429	...	...	...	...	...	...
Factor income from the rest of the world	56	228	478	471	1186	5919	...	...	...	...	...	...
Less: Factor income to the rest of the world	340	1020	7123	9456	51020	99348	...	...	...	...	...	...
Equals: Gross National Product	12086	48409	121969	153825	348625	1422356	...	...	...	...	...	...
Less: Consumption of fixed capital	756	2893	8137	...	...	...	...	...	...	...	...	...
Equals: National Income	11330	45516	113832	...	...	...	...	...	...	...	...	...
Plus: Net current transfers from the rest of the world	42	186	1380	971	4694	23541	...	...	...	...	...	...
Current transfers from the rest of the world	46	262	1442	1030	4990	24516	...	...	...	...	...	...
Less: Current transfers to the rest of the world	4	76	62	59	296	975	...	...	...	...	...	...
Equals: National Disposable Income	11372	45702	115212	...	...	...	...	...	...	...	...	...
Less: Final consumption	10279	39943	111290	150756	354984	1566341	...	...	...	...	...	...
Equals: Net Saving	1093	5759	3922	...	...	...	...	...	...	...	...	...
Less: Surplus of the nation on current transactions	-262	-3374	-4742	...	...	...	...	...	...	...	...	...
Equals: Net Capital Formation	1355	9133	8664	...	...	...	...	...	...	...	...	...

Bolivia

2.1 Government Final Consumption Expenditure by Function, in Current Prices

Bolivianos

	1970	1975	1980	1981	1982	1983	1984	1985	1986	1987	1988	1989
1 General public services	190	765	2331	...	...	...	...	...	...	...	...	...
2 Defence	185	902	2942	...	...	...	...	...	...	...	...	...
3 Public order and safety	95	403	1120	...	...	...	...	...	...	...	...	...
4 Education	427	1606	4796	...	...	...	...	...	...	...	...	...
5 Health	53	198	708	...	...	...	...	...	...	...	...	...
6 Social security and welfare	124	448	1877	...	...	...	...	...	...	...	...	...
7 Housing and community amenities	59	143	150	...	...	...	...	...	...	...	...	...
8 Recreational, cultural and religious affairs	4	5	65	...	...	...	...	...	...	...	...	...
9 Economic services	187	1229	5009	...	...	...	...	...	...	...	...	...
A Fuel and energy	1	3	27	...	...	...	...	...	...	...	...	...
B Agriculture, forestry, fishing and hunting	42	196	638	...	...	...	...	...	...	...	...	...
C Mining, manufacturing and construction, except fuel and energy	20	120	368	...	...	...	...	...	...	...	...	...
D Transportation and communication	89	601	3216	...	...	...	...	...	...	...	...	...
E Other economic affairs	35	309	760	...	...	...	...	...	...	...	...	...
10 Other functions	...	...	...	...	...	...	...	...	...	...	...	...
Total Government Final Consumption Expenditure	1324	5699	18998	...	...	...	...	...	...	...	...	...

2.7 Gross Capital Formation by Type of Good and Owner, in Current Prices

Bolivianos

	\multicolumn{4}{c}{1980}	\multicolumn{4}{c}{1981}
	TOTAL	Total Private	Public Enterprises	General Government	TOTAL	Total Private	Public Enterprises	General Government
Increase in stocks, total	-527	-850	323	-	...	...	...	15
Gross Fixed Capital Formation, Total	17328	7361	6738	3229	...	...	...	4563
1 Residential buildings	4191	3880	255	56	...	...	...	46
2 Non-residential buildings	1035	60	450	525	...	...	...	953
3 Other construction	5077	203	2917	1957	...	...	...	2210
4 Land improvement and plantation and orchard development	346	346	-	-	...	...	...	-
5 Producers' durable goods	6652	2851	3116	685	...	...	...	1336
A Transport equipment	2194	1748	374	72	...	...	...	199
B Machinery and equipment	4458	1103	2742	613	...	...	...	1137
6 Breeding stock, dairy cattle, etc.	27	21	-	6	...	...	...	18
Total Gross Capital Formation	16801	6511	7061	3229	...	...	...	4578

2.8 Gross Capital Formation by Type of Good and Owner, in Constant Prices

Bolivianos

	\multicolumn{4}{c}{1980}
	TOTAL	Total Private	Public Enterprises	General Government
	\multicolumn{4}{c}{At constant prices of:1970}
Increase in stocks, total [a]	-61	-99	...	38
Gross Fixed Capital Formation, Total [a]	2419	1074	-	1345
1 Residential buildings	635	588	-	47
2 Non-residential buildings	148	9	-	139
3 Other construction	655	26	-	629
4 Land improvement and plantation and orchard development	45	45	-	-
5 Producers' durable goods	930	401	-	529
A Transport equipment	326	259	-	67
B Machinery and equipment	604	142	-	462
6 Breeding stock, dairy cattle, etc.	6	5	-	1
Total Gross Capital Formation [a]	2358	975	-	1383

a) Column 'Public Enterprises' is included in column 'General Government'.

Bolivia

2.17 Exports and Imports of Goods and Services, Detail

Bolivianos

	1970	1975	1980	1981	1982	1983	1984	1985	1986	1987	1988	1989
Exports of Goods and Services												
1 Exports of merchandise, f.o.b.	2355	9386	24120	23581	91039	265674	...	...	...	...	...	...
2 Transport and communication	17	82	688	712	2392	6982	...	...	...	...	...	...
A In respect of merchandise imports	-	-	430	454	1508	5320	...	...	...	...	...	...
B Other	17	82	258	258	884	1662	...	...	...	...	...	...
3 Insurance service charges	50	92	352	164	780	1773	...	...	...	...	...	...
A In respect of merchandise imports	-	-	-	-	-	-	...	...	...	...	...	...
B Other	50	92	352	164	780	1773	...	...	...	...	...	...
4 Other commodities	-	474	175	216	1019	2327	...	...	...	...	...	...
5 Adjustments of merchandise exports to change-of-ownership basis	...	...	...	...	...	...	...	...	...	...	...	...
6 Direct purchases in the domestic market by non-residential households	33	408	38	37	156	332	...	...	...	...	...	...
7 Direct purchases in the domestic market by extraterritorial bodies	39	32	1000	1078	3898	10774	...	...	...	...	...	...
Total Exports of Goods and Services	2494	10474	26373	25788	99284	287862	...	...	...	...	...	...
Imports of Goods and Services												
1 Imports of merchandise, c.i.f.	2302	12066	22440	29522	74126	410964	...	...	...	...	...	...
A Imports of merchandise, f.o.b.	2000	10652	19038	25899	64477	395087	...	...	...	...	...	...
B Transport of services on merchandise imports	264	1300	3117	3334	8876	14607	...	...	...	...	...	...
C Insurance service charges on merchandise imports	38	114	285	289	773	1270	...	...	...	...	...	...
2 Adjustments of merchandise imports to change-of-ownership basis	...	...	...	...	...	...	...	...	...	...	...	...
3 Other transport and communication	36	282	565	1276	4083	6977	...	...	...	...	...	...
4 Other insurance service charges	39	118	413	309	864	1995	...	...	...	...	...	...
5 Other commodities	36	86	527	662	3077	9864	...	...	...	...	...	...
6 Direct purchases abroad by government	35	160	405	331	1420	2483	...	...	...	...	...	...
7 Direct purchases abroad by resident households	66	530	1500	1493	6072	10821	...	...	...	...	...	...
Total Imports of Goods and Services	2514	13242	25850	33593	89642	443104	...	...	...	...	...	...
Balance of Goods and Services	-20	-2768	523	-7805	9642	-155242	...	...	...	...	...	...
Total Imports and Balance of Goods and Services	2494	10474	26373	25788	99284	287862	...	...	...	...	...	...

4.1 Derivation of Value Added by Kind of Activity, in Current Prices

Bolivianos

	1980			1981			1982		
	Gross Output	Intermediate Consumption	Value Added	Gross Output	Intermediate Consumption	Value Added	Gross Output	Intermediate Consumption	Value Added
All Producers									
1 Agriculture, hunting, forestry and fishing	26145	3582	22563	33103	4549	28554	92624	14350	78274
2 Mining and quarrying	22967	3560	19407	25133	4676	20457	111839	14595	97244
A Coal mining	...	...	...	...	...	...	...	...	...
B Crude petroleum and natural gas production	...	...	...	...	...	...	67075	5154	61921
C Metal ore mining	...	...	...	...	...	...	...	...	...
D Other mining	...	...	...	...	...	...	...	...	...

Bolivia

4.1 Derivation of Value Added by Kind of Activity, in Current Prices
(Continued)

Bolivianos

	1980 Gross Output	1980 Intermediate Consumption	1980 Value Added	1981 Gross Output	1981 Intermediate Consumption	1981 Value Added	1982 Gross Output	1982 Intermediate Consumption	1982 Value Added
3 Manufacturing	50946	32972	17974	64455	39979	24466	151035	117615	33420
A Manufacture of food, beverages and tobacco	22411	14421	7990	30569	18406	12163	65140	46409	18731
B Textile, wearing apparel and leather industries	6467	3697	2770	7433	4054	3379	14316	8821	5495
C Manufacture of wood and wood products, including furniture	2711	1607	1104	3006	1794	1212	6407	3329	3078
D Manufacture of paper and paper products, printing and publishing	926	526	400	1161	660	501	2996	2327	669
E Manufacture of chemicals and chemical petroleum, coal, rubber and plastic products	6921	4250	2671	9553	5437	4116	19962	24635	-4673
F Manufacture of non-metallic mineral products, except products of petroleum and coal	1920	950	970	2374	1145	1229	5719	2877	2842
G Basic metal industries	7476	6271	1205	8062	7190	872	30512	25527	4985
H Manufacture of fabricated metal products, machinery and equipment	1742	1092	650	1913	1143	770	4296	3160	1136
I Other manufacturing industries	372	158	214	374	150	224	1687	530	1157
4 Electricity, gas and water	1522	716	806	2501	1099	1402	5215	3576	1639
5 Construction	10018	5497	4521	12226	6311	5915	30131	18300	11831
6 Wholesale and retail trade, restaurants and hotels	19495	6234	13261	28296	8283	20013	74438	25269	49169
7 Transport, storage and communication	13591	6270	7327	17385	8646	8739	56062	24851	31211
A Transport and storage	12491	5910	6581	15953	8116	7837	52442	22884	29558
B Communication	1100	360	740	1432	530	902	3620	1967	1653
8 Finance, insurance, real estate and business services	19164	1916	17248	24628	2258	22370	52800	7005	45795
9 Community, social and personal services	9447	4566	4881	12299	6429	5870	34603	14003	20600
Total, Industries	173295	65313	107982	220016	82230	137786	608747	239564	369183
Producers of Government Services	17322	4382	12940	20688	6387	14301	44994	14017	30977
Other Producers	668	-	668	908	-	908	2072	-	2072
Total	191285	69695	121590	241612	88617	152995	655813	253581	402232
Less: Imputed bank service charge	...	-1932	1932	...	-2390	2390	...	-4958	4958
Import duties	3288	...	3288	4291	...	4291	4890	...	4890
Value added tax	...	...	...	...	...	...	...	...	...
Total	194573	71627	122946	245903	91007	154896	660703	258539	402164

4.2 Derivation of Value Added by Kind of Activity, in Constant Prices

Bolivianos

	1980 Gross Output	1980 Intermediate Consumption	1980 Value Added	1981 Gross Output	1981 Intermediate Consumption	1981 Value Added	1982 Gross Output	1982 Intermediate Consumption	1982 Value Added	1983 Gross Output	1983 Intermediate Consumption	1983 Value Added

At constant prices of: 1980

All Producers

	1980 VA	1981 VA	1982 VA	1983 VA
1 Agriculture, hunting, forestry and fishing	22563	22354	23900	19981
2 Mining and quarrying	19407	20139	19526	18614
3 Manufacturing	17974	16581	13531	13863
A Manufacture of food, beverages and tobacco	7990	7671	6912	7142

Bolivia

4.2 Derivation of Value Added by Kind of Activity, in Constant Prices
(Continued)

Bolivianos

	1980 Gross Output	1980 Intermediate Consumption	1980 Value Added	1981 Gross Output	1981 Intermediate Consumption	1981 Value Added	1982 Gross Output	1982 Intermediate Consumption	1982 Value Added	1983 Gross Output	1983 Intermediate Consumption	1983 Value Added
At constant prices of: 1980												
B Textile, wearing apparel and leather industries	...	...	2770	...	...	2471	...	...	833	...	...	1591
C Manufacture of wood and wood products, including furniture	...	...	1104	...	...	858	...	...	642	...	...	518
D Manufacture of paper and paper products, printing and publishing	...	...	400	...	...	402	...	...	359	...	...	284
E Manufacture of chemicals and chemical petroleum, coal, rubber and plastic products	...	...	2671	...	...	2142	...	...	2183	...	...	2121
F Manufacture of non-metallic mineral products, except products of petroleum and coal	...	...	970	...	...	912	...	...	785	...	...	894
G Basic metal industries	...	...	1205	...	...	1512	...	...	1312	...	...	977
H Manufacture of fabricated metal products, machinery and equipment	...	...	650	...	...	507	...	...	342	...	...	179
I Other manufacturing industries	...	...	214	...	...	160	...	...	163	...	...	157
4 Electricity, gas and water	...	...	806	...	...	907	...	...	930	...	...	938
5 Construction	...	...	4521	...	...	4058	...	...	3698	...	...	3639
6 Wholesale and retail trade, restaurants and hotels	...	...	13261	...	...	14418	...	...	13464	...	...	11796
7 Transport, storage and communication	...	...	7321	...	...	8174	...	...	7799	...	...	7059
A Transport and storage	...	...	6581	...	...	7309	...	...	6850	...	...	5924
B Communication	...	...	740	...	...	865	...	...	949	...	...	1135
8 Finance, insurance, real estate and business services	...	...	17248	...	...	16829	...	...	16308	...	...	15964
9 Community, social and personal services	...	...	4881	...	...	4857	...	...	4710	...	...	4710
Total, Industries	...	...	107982	...	...	108317	...	...	104866	...	...	96564
Producers of Government Services	...	...	12940	...	...	13193	...	...	13749	...	...	14836
Other Producers	...	...	668	...	...	687	...	...	702	...	...	709
Total	...	...	121590	...	...	122197	...	...	119317	...	...	112109
Less: Imputed bank service charge	...	...	1932	...	...	1867	...	...	1733	...	...	1593
Import duties	...	...	3288	...	...	3753	...	...	1090	...	...	427
Value added tax	...	...	...	...	...	...	...	...	...	...	...	...
Total	...	...	122946	...	...	124083	...	...	118674	...	...	110943

	1984 Gross Output	1984 Intermediate Consumption	1984 Value Added	1985 Gross Output	1985 Intermediate Consumption	1985 Value Added	1986 Gross Output	1986 Intermediate Consumption	1986 Value Added
At constant prices of: 1980									
All Producers									
1 Agriculture, hunting, forestry and fishing	...	...	24552	...	...	26789	...	...	25534
2 Mining and quarrying	...	...	16335	...	...	14284	...	...	12062
3 Manufacturing	...	...	11925	...	...	10815	...	...	11038
A Manufacture of food, beverages and tobacco	...	...	5628	...	...	5505	...	...	5994
B Textile, wearing apparel and leather industries	...	...	1351	...	...	1150	...	...	1242
C Manufacture of wood and wood products, including furniture	...	...	676	...	...	326	...	...	381
D Manufacture of paper and paper products, printing and publishing	...	...	224	...	...	182	...	...	155
E Manufacture of chemicals and chemical petroleum, coal, rubber and plastic products	...	...	1979	...	...	1890	...	...	1882
F Manufacture of non-metallic mineral products, except products of petroleum and coal	...	...	730	...	...	685	...	...	617
G Basic metal industries	...	...	1066	...	...	863	...	...	528
H Manufacture of fabricated metal products, machinery and equipment	...	...	140	...	...	94	...	...	115
I Other manufacturing industries	...	...	131	...	...	120	...	...	124
4 Electricity, gas and water	...	...	938	...	...	948	...	...	987

Bolivia

4.2 Derivation of Value Added by Kind of Activity, in Constant Prices
(Continued)

Bolivianos

	1984 Gross Output	1984 Intermediate Consumption	1984 Value Added	1985 Gross Output	1985 Intermediate Consumption	1985 Value Added	1986 Gross Output	1986 Intermediate Consumption	1986 Value Added
			At constant	prices of: 1980					
5 Construction	...	...	3555	...	...	3168	...	...	2918
6 Wholesale and retail trade, restaurants and hotels	...	...	11652	...	...	12110	...	...	12895
7 Transport, storage and communication	...	...	7204	...	...	7337	...	...	7557
A Transport and storage	...	...	5895	...	...	6043	...	...	6078
B Communication	...	...	1309	...	...	1294	...	...	1479
8 Finance, insurance, real estate and business services	...	...	15455	...	...	15102	...	...	14972
9 Community, social and personal services	...	...	4239	...	...	3942	...	...	3904
Total, Industries	...	...	95855	...	...	94495	...	...	91867
Producers of Government Services	...	...	15149	...	...	15643	...	...	14646
Other Producers	...	...	710	...	...	714	...	...	719
Total	...	...	111714	...	...	110852	...	...	107232
Less: Imputed bank service charge	...	...	1434	...	...	1334	...	...	1267
Import duties	...	...	332	...	...	927	...	...	1246
Value added tax	...	...	...	...	...	...	...	...	...
Total	...	...	110612	...	...	110445	...	...	107211

4.3 Cost Components of Value Added

Bolivianos

	1980 Compensation of Employees	1980 Capital Consumption	1980 Net Operating Surplus	1980 Indirect Taxes	1980 Less: Subsidies Received	1980 Value Added	1981 Compensation of Employees	1981 Capital Consumption	1981 Net Operating Surplus	1981 Indirect Taxes	1981 Less: Subsidies Received	1981 Value Added
					All Producers							
1 Agriculture, hunting, forestry and fishing	4463	...	17984	116	...	22563	5597	...	22581	106	...	28554
2 Mining and quarrying	4732	...	8883	5792	...	19407	5093	...	9155	6209	...	20457
A Coal mining	...	...	...	...	...	...	...	...	...	...	...	...
B Crude petroleum and natural gas production	508	...	1659	2633	...	4800	...	...	...	...	...	...
C Metal ore mining	...	...	...	...	...	...	...	...	...	...	...	...
D Other mining	...	...	...	...	...	...	...	...	...	...	...	...
3 Manufacturing	5774	...	11941	259	...	17974	7432	...	14204	2830	...	24466
A Manufacture of food, beverages and tobacco	1869	...	5882	239	...	7990	2671	...	8100	1392	...	12163
B Textile, wearing apparel and leather industries	1684	...	1050	36	...	2770	1802	...	1540	37	...	3379
C Manufacture of wood and wood products, including furniture	416	...	663	25	...	1104	431	...	751	30	...	1212
D Manufacture of paper and paper products, printing and publishing	166	...	227	7	...	400	205	...	280	16	...	501
E Manufacture of chemicals and chemical petroleum, coal, rubber and plastic products	710	...	2070	-109	...	2671	1035	...	1793	1288	...	4116
F Manufacture of non-metallic mineral products, except products of petroleum and coal	428	...	520	22	...	970	603	...	615	11	...	1229
G Basic metal industries	182	...	1020	3	...	1205	264	...	626	-18	...	872
H Manufacture of fabricated metal products, machinery and equipment	246	...	381	23	...	650	347	...	360	63	...	770
I Other manufacturing industries	73	...	128	13	...	214	74	...	139	11	...	224
4 Electricity, gas and water	389	...	309	108	...	806	458	...	881	63	...	1402
5 Construction	2068	...	2370	83	...	4521	2897	...	2929	89	...	5915
6 Wholesale and retail trade, restaurants and hotels	1841	...	10858	562	...	13261	2745	...	16723	545	...	20013
7 Transport, storage and communication	3912	...	3229	180	...	7321	4507	...	3957	275	...	8739
A Transport and storage	3388	...	3073	120	...	6581	3962	...	3691	184	...	7837
B Communication	524	...	156	60	...	740	545	...	266	91	...	902
8 Finance, insurance, real estate and business services	3353	...	12996	899	...	17248	3769	...	17685	916	...	22370
9 Community, social and personal services	1731	...	2890	260	...	4881	2100	...	3506	264	...	5870

Bolivia

4.3 Cost Components of Value Added
(Continued)

Bolivianos

	1980						1981					
	Compensation of Employees	Capital Consumption	Net Operating Surplus	Indirect Taxes	Less: Subsidies Received	Value Added	Compensation of Employees	Capital Consumption	Net Operating Surplus	Indirect Taxes	Less: Subsidies Received	Value Added
Total, Industries [ab]	28263	...	71460	8259	...	107982	34598	...	91891	11297	...	137786
Producers of Government Services	12933	...	-	7	...	12940	14288	...	-	13	...	14301
Other Producers	668	...	-	-	...	668	908	...	-	-	...	908
Total [ab]	41864	...	71460	8266	...	121590	49794	...	91891	11310	...	152995
Less: Imputed bank service charge	...	...	1932	...	...	1932	...	...	2390	...	...	2390
Import duties	...	...	...	3288	...	3288	...	...	...	4291	...	4291
Value added tax	...	...	...	...	...	...	...	...	...	...	...	...
Total [ab]	41864	...	69528	11554	...	122946	49794	...	89501	15601	...	154896

a) Column 4 refers to indirect taxes less subsidies received.
b) Column 'Consumption of fixed capital' is included in column 'Net operating surplus'.

Botswana

General note. The preparation of national accounts statistics in Botswana is undertaken by the Central Statistics Office of the Ministry of Finance and Development Planning, Gaborone. Official estimates together with methodological notes are published in a series of reports entitled 'National Accounts of Botswana'. The most detailed description of the sources and methods used for the national accounts estimation is found in the fifth edition of this report published in July 1976 for the fiscal year 1973/74. The estimates are generally in accordance with the classifications and definitions recommended in the United Nations System of National Accounts (SNA). The following tables have been prepared from successive replies to the United Nations national accounts questionnaire. The estimates relate to fiscal year beginning 1 July. When the scope and coverage of the estimates differ for conceptual or statistical reasons from the definitions and classifications recommended in SNA, a footnote is indicated to the relevant tables.

Sources and methods:

(a) Gross domestic product. Gross domestic product is estimated mainly through the production approach.

(b) Expenditure on the gross domestic product. All components of GDP by expenditure type are estimated through the expenditure approach except private final consumption expenditure which is obtained as a residual. The estimates of government final consumption expenditure are based on annual statements of the accounts of central and local governments. Change in stocks is estimated on the basis of the production census for all sectors. Gross fixed capital formation of the government sector is estimated from the government accounts and of the private sector from the production census figures for sectors covered by the census questionnaire. Included in the capital formation estimates are the cost of land clearings and imputed values of new huts. The estimates of exports and imports of goods and services are based on balance-of-payments data. Exports and imports of goods have to be adjusted for duty content, in accordance with the Southern African customs union agreement. GDP by expenditure type at constant price is not estimated.

(c) Cost-structure of the gross domestic product. Estimates of compensation of employees are obtained from the Census of Production and Distribution (CPD). Data on payment of wages and salaries are distinguished whether paid to residents or to non-residents and are also classified by type. The main source for estimating consumption of fixed capital formation in the private sector is the CPD. For government assets, straight line depreciation is applied, the constant percentage varying for different types of assets. Indirect taxes are extracted from the Accountant-General's annual statement of accounts, the CPD and the Customs Statistics Unit.

(d) Gross domestic product by kind of economic activity. The table of gross domestic product by kind of economic activity is prepared at market prices, i.e. producers' values. The production approach is used to estimate value added of almost all industries. The income approach is used for some sub-groups of private services and for producers of government services. For the traditional farming of the agricultural sector, the main source used for crops is the annual agricultural sample survey and for cattle, the sources used include Rural Income Distribution Survey 1974/75 and annual reports of Botswana Meat Commission and the Ministry of Agriculture. The method has been to obtain quantities of production from the above-mentioned sources and apply unit values. Data from the 1974/75 Rural Income Distribution Survey also provided information on milk production for own use and the value of meat consumed. From this survey, detailed input-output activity analysis of the traditional farming sector is being carried out. For the freehold agriculture, the main source has been an attempted census of the accounts of all freehold farmers. For the non-respondents, a scaling up is made by reference to other farms of the same type. The small firms of the mining sector fill in a questionnaire about their accounts, whereas the two large groups of mining companies are interviewed at length. Manufacturing is dominated by Botswana Meat Commission which contributes more than 40 per cent of the sector's product. The main source is the questionnaire for Census of Production and Distribution (CPD). The CPD is based on the income and outlay accounts and balance sheets of a stratified sample of establishments within Botswana, covering all ISIC sectors. The census gives information for estimating the cost of intermediate consumption. The Government Printer's services are included in manufacturing and valued at cost. For construction, the private contractors and the brigades are covered by the CPD. Estimates of construction outlays for sites and services of low-cost housing are supplied by city and town councils while rural hut construction estimates are derived from the Rural Income Distribution Survey 1974/75. Estimates of construction carried out by government departments are derived from the analysis of government accounts. The main source of information for the trade sector is the CPD. The data obtained from this census are inflated to allow for under-coverage. Gross margins are estimated as the difference between sales and purchases of goods for resale. Taxes levied on imported goods are treated as indirect taxes collected by the trade sector. For transport, the main contributor is the transport service rendered by the Rhodesia Railways. The source of information is a series of returns received from General Manager of the Accounting Branch of Rhodesia Railways. Adjustments are made to convert the data to national accounts framework and significant imputations have to be made on the expenditure side. For other private firms of the transport sector, the financial sector and other services, the main source of information is the CPD. Gross output of financial institutions is made up of the actual sale of services and an imputed service charge. Estimates for producers of government services are based on the Annual Statement of Accounts of the Central Government. For the constant price estimates, the CPD data are deflated by a cost-of-living index.

1.1 Expenditure on the Gross Domestic Product, in Current Prices

Million Botswana pula — Fiscal year beginning 1 July

	1970	1975	1980	1981	1982	1983	1984	1985	1986	1987	1988	1989
1 Government final consumption expenditure	...	58.2	203.2	242.6	301.9	362.8	443.1	531.8	...	...	...	...
2 Private final consumption expenditure	...	155.3	409.8	488.4	571.2	629.3	746.3	840.1	...	...	...	...
A Households	...	152.0	402.4	478.8	558.8	621.8	733.4	829.9	...	...	...	...
B Private non-profit institutions serving households	...	3.3	7.4	9.6	12.4	7.5	12.9	10.2	...	...	...	...
3 Gross capital formation	...	115.0	344.9	350.4	308.1	317.8	499.2	399.7	...	...	...	...
A Increase in stocks	...	35.9	38.3	45.8	-12.2	-19.8	15.2	-12.2	...	...	...	...
B Gross fixed capital formation	...	79.1	306.6	304.6	320.3	337.6	484.0	411.9	...	...	...	...
Residential buildings	...	13.4	37.4	29.8	35.1	31.7	37.8	38.5	...	...	...	...
Non-residential buildings	...	10.7	50.8	40.7	30.8	50.6	46.9	68.5	...	...	...	...
Other construction and land improvement etc.	...	28.6	90.7	59.5	92.5	114.8	137.3	111.5	...	...	...	...
Other	...	26.4	127.7	174.6	161.9	140.5	262.0	193.4	...	...	...	...
4 Exports of goods and services [a]	...	135.2	398.0	349.9	618.3	772.3	970.3	1591.6	...	...	...	...
5 Less: Imports of goods and services [b]	...	187.5	565.7	638.4	749.8	780.1	998.2	1127.9	...	...	...	...
Statistical discrepancy	...	1.2	-	-	-	-	-	-	...	...	...	...
Equals: Gross Domestic Product	...	277.4	790.2	792.9	1049.7	1302.1	1660.7	2235.3	2647.5	3397.9	4987.9	...

a) Item 'Exports of goods and services' includes exports of goods only.
b) Item 'Imports of goods and services' includes imports of goods plus net imports of services.

1.2 Expenditure on the Gross Domestic Product, in Constant Prices

Million Botswana pula — Fiscal year beginning 1 July

	1970	1975	1980	1981	1982	1983	1984	1985	1986	1987	1988	1989
					At constant prices of: 1979							
1 Government final consumption expenditure	...	101.4	173.1	194.0	216.4	240.0	280.5	304.7	...	...	...	...
2 Private final consumption expenditure	...	234.4	356.4	382.6	398.8	402.1	443.7	454.4	...	...	...	...
A Households	...	229.4	349.5	373.9	390.0	396.3	434.3	447.3	...	...	...	...
B Private non-profit institutions serving households	...	5.0	6.9	8.7	8.8	5.8	9.4	7.1	...	...	...	...
3 Gross capital formation	...	181.7	296.3	286.1	198.5	194.5	309.9	238.9	...	...	...	...

Botswana

1.2 Expenditure on the Gross Domestic Product, in Constant Prices
(Continued)

Million Botswana pula — Fiscal year beginning 1 July

	1970	1975	1980	1981	1982	1983	1984	1985	1986	1987	1988	1989
					At constant prices of:1979							
A Increase in stocks	...	53.4	31.6	38.7	-13.2	-15.6	10.3	12.3	...	...	...	...
B Gross fixed capital formation	...	128.3	264.7	247.4	211.7	210.1	299.6	226.6	...	...	...	...
Residential buildings	...	21.9	32.5	24.3	23.2	19.5	23.2	21.3	...	...	...	...
Non-residential buildings	...	17.7	44.8	33.2	20.3	31.2	28.8	38.0	...	...	...	...
Other construction and land improvement etc.	...	48.8	78.3	48.5	61.1	70.8	84.4	62.0	...	...	...	...
Other	...	39.9	109.1	141.4	107.1	88.6	163.2	105.3	...	...	...	...
4 Exports of goods and services a	...	261.0	432.6	388.0	639.5	790.0	766.4	921.4	...	...	...	...
5 Less: Imports of goods and services b	...	319.5	491.0	503.4	509.6	498.6	614.6	616.3	...	...	...	...
Statistical discrepancy	...	-	4.0	6.2	-9.6	-7.5	25.6	5.1	...	...	...	...
Equals: Gross Domestic Product	...	459.0	771.4	753.5	934.0	1120.5	1211.5	1308.2	1441.0	1570.4	1783.0	...

a) Item 'Exports of goods and services' includes exports of goods only.
b) Item 'Imports of goods and services' includes imports of goods plus net imports of services.

1.3 Cost Components of the Gross Domestic Product

Million Botswana pula — Fiscal year beginning 1 July

	1970	1975	1980	1981	1982	1983	1984	1985	1986	1987	1988	1989
1 Indirect taxes, net	...	22.9	120.6	118.8	131.9	165.4	155.0	153.4	...	...	...	...
A Indirect taxes	...	22.9	121.7	123.3	133.3	166.1	160.4	160.4	...	...	...	...
B Less: Subsidies	...	-	1.1	4.5	1.4	0.7	5.4	7.0	...	...	...	...
2 Consumption of fixed capital	...	47.1	135.5	161.0	214.3	243.7	278.4	349.8	...	...	...	...
3 Compensation of employees paid by resident producers to:	...	107.9	287.3	347.1	409.8	476.4	553.6	650.2	...	...	...	...
A Resident households	...	107.9	284.7	344.8	408.2	475.8	553.3	650.0	...	...	...	...
B Rest of the world	...	-	2.6	2.3	1.6	0.6	0.3	0.2	...	...	...	...
4 Operating surplus	...	99.5	246.8	166.0	293.7	416.6	673.7	1081.9	...	...	...	...
A Corporate and quasi-corporate enterprises	...	40.5	169.1	91.6	223.1	345.2	590.3	990.6	...	...	...	...
B Private unincorporated enterprises	...	57.7	77.7	74.4	70.6	71.4	80.8	89.7	...	...	...	...
C General government	...	1.3	-	-	-	-	2.6	1.6	...	...	...	...
Equals: Gross Domestic Product	...	277.4	790.2	792.9	1049.7	1302.1	1660.7	2235.3	...	...	...	...

1.4 General Government Current Receipts and Disbursements

Million Botswana pula — Fiscal year beginning 1 July

	1970	1975	1980	1981	1982	1983	1984	1985	1986	1987	1988	1989
					Receipts							
1 Operating surplus	...	1.3	-	-	-	-	2.6	1.6	...	...	...	...
2 Property and entrepreneurial income	...	17.8	61.5	58.8	90.5	111.3	192.1	524.4	...	...	...	...
3 Taxes, fees and contributions	...	49.3	222.4	227.4	245.2	321.4	440.8	427.3	...	...	...	...
A Indirect taxes	...	22.9	121.7	123.3	133.3	166.1	160.4	160.4	...	...	...	...
B Direct taxes	...	25.1	98.4	101.7	111.9	155.3	280.4	266.9	...	...	...	...
C Social security contributions	...	0.4	-	-	-	-	-	-	...	...	...	...
D Compulsory fees, fines and penalties	...	0.9	2.3	2.4	-	-	-	-	...	...	...	...
4 Other current transfers	...	25.6	13.0	22.6	51.4	37.2	40.6	321.8	...	...	...	...
Total Current Receipts of General Government	...	94.0	296.9	308.8	387.1	469.9	676.1	1275.1	...	...	...	...
					Disbursements							
1 Government final consumption expenditure	...	58.2	203.2	242.6	301.9	362.8	443.1	531.8	...	...	...	...
A Compensation of employees	...	34.0	103.9	118.2	138.2	161.6	200.9	232.5	...	...	...	...
B Consumption of fixed capital	...	9.7	31.0	37.9	53.1	63.0	73.8	93.2	...	...	...	...
C Purchases of goods and services, net	...	14.5	68.2	86.3	110.4	138.2	168.4	206.1	...	...	...	...
D Less: Own account fixed capital formation	...	...	...	...	...	...	...	...	...	...	...	...
E Indirect taxes paid, net	...	...	0.1	0.2	0.2	-	-	-	...	...	...	...
2 Property income	...	3.3	4.9	5.9	12.4	13.9	21.7	23.6	...	...	...	...
A Interest	...	3.3	4.9	5.9	12.4	13.9	21.7	23.6	...	...	...	...
B Net land rent and royalties												

Botswana

1.4 General Government Current Receipts and Disbursements
(Continued)

Million Botswana pula	1970	1975	1980	1981	1982	1983	1984	1985	1986	1987	1988	1989
3 Subsidies	...	-	1.1	4.5	1.4	0.7	5.4	7.0	...	...	...	...
4 Other current transfers	...	9.5	31.0	43.8	53.4	58.7	72.8	100.5	...	...	...	...
A Social security benefits	...	-	...	...	...	...	...	...	...	...	...	...
B Social assistance grants	...	4.5	20.4	31.0	26.4	40.6	40.1	100.0	...	...	...	...
C Other	...	5.0	10.6	12.8	27.0	18.1	32.7	0.5	...	...	...	...
5 Net saving	...	23.0	56.7	12.0	18.0	33.8	133.1	612.2	...	...	...	...
Total Current Disbursements and Net Saving of General Government	...	94.0	296.9	308.8	387.1	469.9	676.1	1275.1	...	...	...	...

1.5 Current Income and Outlay of Corporate and Quasi-Corporate Enterprises, Summary

Million Botswana pula	1970	1975	1980	1981	1982	1983	1984	1985	1986	1987	1988	1989
Receipts												
1 Operating surplus	...	40.5	169.1	91.6	223.1	345.2	590.3	990.6	...	...	...	...
2 Property and entrepreneurial income received	...	22.9	81.7	64.8	90.3	118.9	283.4	213.8	...	...	...	...
3 Current transfers [a]	...	8.9	77.3	42.0	26.7	48.4	80.4	155.2	...	...	...	...
Total Current Receipts	...	72.3	328.1	198.4	340.1	512.5	954.1	1359.6	...	...	...	...
Disbursements												
1 Property and entrepreneurial income	...	82.6	277.7	155.5	327.8	389.8	673.6	1074.6	...	...	...	...
2 Direct taxes and other current payments to general government	...	17.5	77.0	77.1	100.4	121.0	240.4	208.5	...	...	...	...
3 Other current transfers	...	5.6	88.4	62.1	40.8	90.6	142.3	328.8	...	...	...	...
4 Net saving	...	-33.4	-115.0	-96.3	-128.9	-88.9	-102.2	-252.3	...	...	...	...
Total Current Disbursements and Net Saving	...	72.3	328.1	198.4	340.1	512.5	954.1	1359.6	...	...	...	...

a) Item 'Current transfers' includes imputed intercompany transfers.

1.6 Current Income and Outlay of Households and Non-Profit Institutions

Million Botswana pula	1970	1975	1980	1981	1982	1983	1984	1985	1986	1987	1988	1989
Receipts												
1 Compensation of employees	...	117.4	307.8	367.0	434.0	501.4	582.2	681.2	...	...	...	...
A From resident producers	...	107.9	287.3	347.1	409.8	471.7	553.3	650.0	...	...	...	...
B From rest of the world	...	9.5	20.5	19.9	24.2	29.7	28.9	31.2	...	...	...	...
2 Operating surplus of private unincorporated enterprises	...	57.7	77.7	74.4	70.6	71.4	80.8	89.7	...	...	...	...
3 Property and entrepreneurial income	...	9.5	17.9	0.1	71.1	44.2	5.0	18.2	...	...	...	...
4 Current transfers	...	5.6	23.0	106.7	81.1	91.9	120.5	70.9	...	...	...	...
Total Current Receipts	...	190.3	426.4	548.2	656.8	708.9	788.5	860.0	...	...	...	...
Disbursements												
1 Private final consumption expenditure	...	155.3	409.8	488.4	571.2	629.3	746.3	840.1	...	...	...	...
2 Property income	...	-	3.4	34.3	61.0	6.2	7.0	-	...	...	...	...
3 Direct taxes and other current transfers n.e.c. to general government	...	8.0	21.4	24.6	11.5	34.3	40.0	69.4	...	...	...	...
A Social security contributions	...	0.4	-	-	-	-	-	-	...	...	...	...
B Direct taxes	...	7.6	21.4	24.6	11.5	34.3	40.0	69.4	...	...	...	...
C Fees, fines and penalties	...	...	...	...	...	...	...	...	...	...	...	...
4 Other current transfers	...	5.0	16.1	18.1	5.3	5.0	7.0	46.5	...	...	...	...
5 Net saving	...	21.9	-24.3	-17.2	7.8	34.1	-11.8	-96.0	...	...	...	...
Total Current Disbursements and Net Saving	...	190.3	426.4	548.2	656.8	708.9	788.5	860.0	...	...	...	...

1.7 External Transactions on Current Account, Summary

Million Botswana pula	1970	1975	1980	1981	1982	1983	1984	1985	1986	1987	1988	1989
Payments to the Rest of the World												
1 Imports of goods and services [a]	...	187.5	565.7	638.4	749.8	780.1	998.2	1127.9	...	...	...	...
A Imports of merchandise c.i.f.	...	152.4	495.1	564.0	637.1	682.1	870.9	991.0	...	...	...	...
B Other	...	35.1	70.6	74.4	112.7	98.0	127.3	136.9	...	...	...	...
2 Factor income to the rest of the world	...	35.4	157.4	118.4	193.5	196.5	313.2	495.8	...	...	...	...

Botswana

1.7 External Transactions on Current Account, Summary
(Continued)

Million Botswana pula — Fiscal year beginning 1 July

	1970	1975	1980	1981	1982	1983	1984	1985	1986	1987	1988	1989
A Compensation of employees [b]	...	...	2.6	2.3	1.6	0.6	0.3	0.2	...	...	...	...
B Property and entrepreneurial income [c]	...	35.4	154.8	116.1	191.9	195.9	312.9	495.6	...	...	...	...
3 Current transfers to the rest of the world	...	3.2	24.2	3.7	4.9	5.9	5.0	68.5	...	...	...	...
A Indirect taxes to supranational organizations	...	...	...	...	...	...	...	...	...	...	...	...
B Other current transfers	...	3.2	24.2	3.7	4.9	5.9	5.0	68.5	...	...	...	...
4 Surplus of the nation on current transactions	...	-52.0	-294.8	-292.3	-196.9	-89.2	-201.7	213.9	...	...	...	...
Payments to the Rest of the World and Surplus of the Nation on Current Transactions	...	174.1	452.5	468.2	751.3	893.3	1114.7	1906.1	...	...	...	...
Receipts From The Rest of the World												
1 Exports of goods and services [d]	...	135.2	398.0	349.9	618.3	772.3	970.3	1591.6	...	...	...	...
2 Factor income from rest of the world	...	9.5	46.4	53.5	68.4	91.6	118.0	173.0	...	...	...	...
A Compensation of employees [b]	...	9.5	20.5	19.9	24.2	29.7	28.9	31.2	...	...	...	...
B Property and entrepreneurial income [c]	...	...	25.9	33.6	44.2	61.9	89.1	141.8	...	...	...	...
3 Current transfers from rest of the world [e]	...	29.4	8.1	64.8	64.6	29.4	26.4	141.5	...	...	...	...
A Subsidies from supranational organisations	...	...	...	...	...	...	...	...	...	...	...	...
B Other current transfers	...	...	8.1	64.8	64.6	29.4	26.4	141.5	...	...	...	...
Receipts from the Rest of the World on Current Transactions	...	174.1	452.5	468.2	751.3	893.3	1114.7	1906.1	...	...	...	...

a) Item 'Imports of goods and services' includes imports of goods plus net imports of services.
b) For 1973-75, compensation of employees from the rest of the world is net of compensation of employees paid to the rest of the world.
c) For 1973-75, property and entrepreneurial income paid is net of property and entrepreneurial income received.
d) Item 'Exports of goods and services' includes exports of goods only.
e) For 1973-75, item 'Current transfers from the rest of the world' refers to current and capital transfers which are net. Beginning 1976, current and capital transfers are gross, excluding loan waivers and direct grants which are assumed to be capital transfers.

1.8 Capital Transactions of The Nation, Summary

Million Botswana pula — Fiscal year beginning 1 July

	1970	1975	1980	1981	1982	1983	1984	1985	1986	1987	1988	1989
Finance of Gross Capital Formation												
Gross saving	...	58.6	52.9	59.5	111.2	222.7	297.5	613.0	...	...	...	...
1 Consumption of fixed capital	...	47.1	135.5	161.0	214.3	243.7	278.4	349.8	...	...	...	...
A General government	...	9.7	31.0	37.9	53.1	63.0	73.8	93.2	...	...	...	...
B Corporate and quasi-corporate enterprises	...	34.1	96.2	114.0	149.8	168.1	191.5	241.5	...	...	...	...
Public	...	2.5	8.2	8.0	16.1	29.1	23.0	31.1	...	...	...	...
Private	...	31.6	88.0	106.0	133.7	139.0	168.5	210.4	...	...	...	...
C Other	...	3.3	8.3	9.1	11.4	12.6	13.1	15.1	...	...	...	...
2 Net saving	...	11.5	-82.6	-101.5	-103.1	-21.0	19.1	263.9	...	...	...	...
A General government	...	23.0	56.7	12.0	18.0	33.8	133.1	612.2	...	...	...	...
B Corporate and quasi-corporate enterprises	...	-33.4	-115.0	-96.3	-128.9	-88.9	-102.2	-252.3	...	...	...	...
Public	...	4.8	-1.0	10.7	13.3	2.6	13.1	3.2	...	...	...	...
Private	...	-38.2	-114.0	-107.0	-142.2	-91.5	-115.3	-255.5	...	...	...	...
C Other	...	21.9	-24.3	-17.2	7.8	34.1	-11.8	-96.0	...	...	...	...
Less: Surplus of the nation on current transactions	...	-52.0	-294.8	-292.3	-196.9	-89.2	-201.7	213.9	...	...	...	...
Statistical discrepancy	...	4.4	-2.8	-1.4	-	5.9	-	0.6	...	...	...	...
Finance of Gross Capital Formation	...	115.0	344.9	350.4	308.1	317.8	499.2	399.7	...	...	...	...
Gross Capital Formation												
Increase in stocks	...	35.9	38.3	45.8	-12.2	-19.8	15.2	-12.3	...	...	...	...
Gross fixed capital formation	...	79.1	306.6	304.6	320.3	337.6	484.0	411.9	...	...	...	...
1 General government	...	29.5	90.5	100.1	123.1	126.3	181.8	197.1	...	...	...	...
2 Corporate and quasi-corporate enterprises	...	42.9	207.2	196.7	187.2	200.0	285.0	179.6	...	...	...	...
A Public [a]	...	9.8	35.8	43.2	73.5	90.7	211.3	39.0	...	...	...	...
B Private	...	33.1	171.4	153.5	113.7	109.3	73.7	140.6	...	...	...	...
3 Other	...	6.7	8.9	7.8	10.0	11.3	17.2	35.2	...	...	...	...
Gross Capital Formation	...	115.0	344.9	350.4	308.1	317.8	499.2	399.7	...	...	...	...

a) Item 'Public' of Corporate and quasi-corporate enterprises refers to non-financial sector only.

Botswana

1.10 Gross Domestic Product by Kind of Activity, in Current Prices

Million Botswana pula — Fiscal year beginning 1 July

	1970	1975	1980	1981	1982	1983	1984	1985	1986	1987	1988	1989
1 Agriculture, hunting, forestry and fishing	...	65.7	90.5	87.8	77.2	76.1	82.9	94.0	...	...	...	...
2 Mining and quarrying	...	33.6	203.8	130.1	287.0	405.9	618.5	938.5	...	...	...	...
3 Manufacturing	...	20.9	49.3	71.2	78.7	82.0	88.0	125.9	...	...	...	...
4 Electricity, gas and water	...	11.1	19.3	21.8	29.7	32.3	42.9	57.7	...	...	...	...
5 Construction	...	18.8	38.3	47.6	45.0	70.5	64.8	61.2	...	...	...	...
6 Wholesale and retail trade, restaurants and hotels	...	23.1	71.3	77.7	97.8	119.6	159.6	261.1	...	...	...	...
7 Transport, storage and communication	...	12.5	16.6	19.8	30.6	32.7	39.3	54.3	...	...	...	...
8 Finance, insurance, real estate and business services	...	18.2	52.8	62.1	71.0	86.5	110.1	142.6	...	...	...	...
9 Community, social and personal services	...	4.3	7.7	8.8	14.7	10.3	16.8	21.5	...	...	...	...
Total, Industries	...	208.2	549.6	526.9	731.7	915.9	1222.9	1756.8	...	...	...	...
Producers of Government Services	...	43.7	135.0	156.3	191.5	224.6	274.7	325.7	...	...	...	...
Other Producers	...	8.8	19.5	23.9	22.8	33.2	38.5	45.2	...	...	...	...
Subtotal	...	260.7	704.1	707.1	946.0	1173.7	1536.1	2127.7	...	...	...	...
Less: Imputed bank service charge	...	2.7	17.6	18.9	23.8	28.9	30.6	47.6	...	...	...	...
Plus: Import duties	...	19.4	103.7	104.7	127.5	157.3	155.2	155.2	...	...	...	...
Plus: Value added tax	...	...	...	...	...	...	...	...	...	...	...	...
Equals: Gross Domestic Product	...	277.4	790.2	792.9	1049.7	1302.1	1660.7	2235.3	...	...	...	...

1.11 Gross Domestic Product by Kind of Activity, in Constant Prices

Million Botswana pula — Fiscal year beginning 1 July

At constant prices of: 1979

	1970	1975	1980	1981	1982	1983	1984	1985	1986	1987	1988	1989
1 Agriculture, hunting, forestry and fishing	...	88.9	75.0	71.8	60.1	50.9	46.8	53.2	...	...	...	...
2 Mining and quarrying	...	87.5	260.7	222.4	393.6	533.9	560.2	573.2	...	...	...	...
3 Manufacturing	...	31.4	37.0	45.8	42.4	44.0	35.8	45.4	...	...	...	...
4 Electricity, gas and water	...	13.3	15.3	15.9	15.7	19.5	23.5	31.4	...	...	...	...
5 Construction	...	34.5	32.0	37.2	26.2	38.7	35.6	30.3	...	...	...	...
6 Wholesale and retail trade, restaurants and hotels [a]	...	73.7	163.8	150.7	162.1	182.2	205.7	236.8	...	...	...	...
7 Transport, storage and communication	...	10.5	14.8	18.1	23.8	23.1	28.6	39.3	...	...	...	...
8 Finance, insurance, real estate and business services	...	26.2	49.7	55.6	58.9	65.2	82.2	96.6	...	...	...	...
9 Community, social and personal services [b]	...	19.9	25.6	29.2	35.0	34.9	42.9	48.8	...	...	...	...
Total, Industries	...	385.9	673.9	646.7	817.8	992.4	1061.3	1155.0	...	...	...	...
Producers of Government Services	...	77.3	114.2	123.8	136.1	150.5	172.5	186.2	...	...	...	...
Other Producers [b]	...	...	...	...	...	...	...	...	...	...	...	...
Subtotal	...	463.2	788.1	770.5	953.9	1142.9	1233.8	1341.2	...	...	...	...
Less: Imputed bank service charge	...	4.2	16.7	17.0	19.9	22.4	22.3	33.0	...	...	...	...
Plus: Import duties [a]	...	...	...	...	...	...	...	...	...	...	...	...
Plus: Value added tax	...	...	...	...	...	...	...	...	...	...	...	...
Equals: Gross Domestic Product	...	459.0	771.4	753.5	934.0	1120.5	1211.5	1308.2	...	...	...	...

a) Item 'Import duties' is included in item 'Wholesale and retail trade'.
b) Item 'Other producers' is included in item 'Community, social and personal services'.

1.12 Relations Among National Accounting Aggregates

Million Botswana pula — Fiscal year beginning 1 July

	1970	1975	1980	1981	1982	1983	1984	1985	1986	1987	1988	1989
Gross Domestic Product	...	277.4	790.2	792.9	1049.7	1302.1	1660.7	2235.3	...	...	...	...
Plus: Net factor income from the rest of the world	...	-25.9	-111.1	-64.9	-125.1	-104.9	-195.2	-322.8	...	...	...	...
Factor income from the rest of the world	...	9.5	46.3	53.5	68.4	91.6	118.0	173.0	...	...	...	...
Less: Factor income to the rest of the world	...	35.4	157.4	118.4	193.5	196.5	313.2	495.8	...	...	...	...
Equals: Gross National Product	...	251.5	679.1	728.0	924.6	1197.2	1465.5	1912.5	...	...	...	...
Less: Consumption of fixed capital	...	47.1	135.5	161.0	214.3	243.7	278.4	349.8	...	...	...	...

Botswana

1.12 Relations Among National Accounting Aggregates
(Continued)

Million Botswana pula — Fiscal year beginning 1 July

	1970	1975	1980	1981	1982	1983	1984	1985	1986	1987	1988	1989
Equals: National Income	...	204.4	543.6	567.0	710.3	953.5	1187.1	1562.7	...	...	...	...
Plus: Net current transfers from the rest of the world	...	26.2	-16.1	61.1	59.7	23.5	21.4	73.0	...	...	...	...
Current transfers from the rest of the world	...	29.4	8.1	64.8	64.6	29.4	26.4	141.5	...	...	...	...
Less: Current transfers to the rest of the world	...	3.2	24.2	3.7	4.9	5.9	5.0	68.5	...	...	...	...
Equals: National Disposable Income	...	230.6	527.5	628.1	770.0	977.0	1208.5	1635.7	...	...	...	...
Less: Final consumption	...	213.5	613.0	731.0	873.1	992.1	1189.4	1371.9	...	...	...	...
Statistical discrepancy a	...	-5.6	2.9	1.4	-	-5.9	-	-	...	...	...	...
Equals: Net Saving	...	11.5	-82.6	-101.5	-103.1	-21.0	19.1	263.9	...	...	...	...
Less: Surplus of the nation on current transactions	...	-52.0	-294.8	-292.3	-196.9	-89.2*	-201.7	213.9	...	...	...	...
Statistical discrepancy b	...	11.0	-2.9	-1.4	-	5.9	-	-	...	...	...	...
Equals: Net Capital Formation	...	162.1	209.3	189.4	93.8	74.1	220.8	49.9	...	...	...	...

a) Item 'Statistical discrepancy' refers to discrepancy in income and outlay account.
b) Item 'Statistical discrepancy' refers to discrepancy in capital finance account.

2.9 Gross Capital Formation by Kind of Activity of Owner, ISIC Major Divisions, in Current Prices

Million Botswana pula — Fiscal year beginning 1 July

	1980 TGCF	1980 Incr. Stocks	1980 GFCF	1981 TGCF	1981 Incr. Stocks	1981 GFCF	1982 TGCF	1982 Incr. Stocks	1982 GFCF	1983 TGCF	1983 Incr. Stocks	1983 GFCF
					All Producers							
1 Agriculture, hunting, fishing and forestry	13.5	10.7	2.8	6.1	2.0	4.1	-16.9	-25.2	8.3	-13.6	-20.4	6.8
2 Mining and quarrying	121.5	-1.0	122.5	107.8	17.8	90.0	57.8	4.1	53.7	36.0	2.5	33.5
3 Manufacturing	20.5	12.2	8.3	18.8	2.5	16.3	12.7	-2.0	14.7	16.9	3.3	13.6
4 Electricity, gas and water	17.6	0.2	17.4	22.2	0.5	21.7	53.8	1.5	52.3	73.2	0.3	72.9
5 Construction	12.7	4.3	8.4	1.4	-4.0	5.4	9.0	4.6	4.4	1.5	-0.7	2.2
6 Wholesale and retail trade, restaurants and hotels	20.1	11.1	9.0	42.3	21.6	20.7	25.3	4.2	21.1	24.7	-6.8	31.5
7 Transport, storage and communication	8.8	0.2	8.6	19.0	4.0	15.0	14.2	0.4	13.8	17.7	1.6	16.1
8 Finance, insurance, real estate and business services	34.1	0.3	33.8	28.9	0.5	28.4	26.0	-	26.0	30.3	0.1	30.2
9 Community, social and personal services	1.3	0.3	1.0	1.7	0.9	0.8	1.4	0.2	1.2	2.2	0.2	2.0
Total Industries	250.1	38.3	211.8	248.2	45.8	202.4	183.3	-12.2	195.5	188.3	-19.9	208.8
Producers of Government Services	90.1	-	90.1	101.3	-	101.3	123.4	-	123.4	126.3	-	126.3
Private Non-Profit Institutions Serving Households	4.7	-	4.7	0.9	-	0.9	1.4	-	1.4	2.6	0.1	2.5
Total	344.9	38.3	306.6	350.4	45.8	304.6	308.1	-12.2	320.3	317.8	-19.8	337.6

	1984 TGCF	1984 Incr. Stocks	1984 GFCF	1985 TGCF	1985 Incr. Stocks	1985 GFCF
			All Producers			
1 Agriculture, hunting, fishing and forestry	-29.0	-35.5	6.5	-11.0	-19.9	8.9
2 Mining and quarrying	41.7	18.8	22.9	53.7	17.1	36.6
3 Manufacturing	21.0	10.9	10.1	5.7	-9.8	15.5
4 Electricity, gas and water	182.7	0.4	182.3	17.1	0.2	16.9
5 Construction	6.0	2.2	3.8	6.2	1.4	4.8
6 Wholesale and retail trade, restaurants and hotels	25.0	10.8	14.2	23.0	-1.1	24.1
7 Transport, storage and communication	26.4	1.6	24.8	50.5	-0.8	51.3
8 Finance, insurance, real estate and business services	45.0	3.0	42.0	38.8	0.5	38.3
9 Community, social and personal services	3.6	2.7	0.9	2.8	-	2.8
Total Industries	322.4	14.9	307.5	186.8	-12.4	199.2
Producers of Government Services	173.3	0.2	173.1	197.1	-	197.1
Private Non-Profit Institutions Serving Households	3.5	0.1	3.4	15.8	0.2	15.6
Total	499.2	15.2	484.0	399.7	-12.2	411.9

Botswana

2.10 Gross Capital Formation by Kind of Activity of Owner, ISIC Major Divisions, in Constant Prices

Million Botswana pula — Fiscal year beginning 1 July

	1980 Total Gross Capital Formation	1980 Increase in Stocks	1980 Gross Fixed Capital Formation	1981 Total Gross Capital Formation	1981 Increase in Stocks	1981 Gross Fixed Capital Formation	1982 Total Gross Capital Formation	1982 Increase in Stocks	1982 Gross Fixed Capital Formation	1983 Total Gross Capital Formation	1983 Increase in Stocks	1983 Gross Fixed Capital Formation
				At constant prices of: 1979 — All Producers								
1 Agriculture, hunting, fishing and forestry	11.5	9.0	2.5	4.9	1.6	3.3	-14.5	-19.9	5.4	-12.0	-16.6	4.6
2 Mining and quarrying	103.9	-1.3	105.2	89.0	15.2	73.8	36.8	0.8	36.0	23.1	2.0	21.1
3 Manufacturing	16.8	9.6	7.2	15.3	2.1	13.2	8.3	-1.4	9.7	10.8	2.2	8.6
4 Electricity, gas and water	15.2	0.2	15.0	18.0	0.4	17.6	35.6	1.0	34.6	45.4	0.2	45.2
5 Construction	11.1	3.8	7.3	1.2	-3.3	4.5	6.0	3.0	3.0	1.0	-0.4	1.4
6 Wholesale and retail trade, restaurants and hotels	17.3	9.5	7.8	34.5	17.6	16.9	16.8	2.9	13.9	15.4	-4.4	19.8
7 Transport, storage and communication	7.6	0.2	7.4	15.5	3.3	12.2	9.4	0.3	9.1	10.8	1.0	9.8
8 Finance, insurance, real estate and business services	29.8	0.3	29.5	23.4	0.3	23.1	17.3	-	17.3	18.7	0.1	18.6
9 Community, social and personal services	1.1	0.3	0.8	1.4	0.7	0.7	1.8	0.1	1.7	1.5	0.2	1.3
Total Industries	214.3	31.6	182.7	203.2	37.9	165.3	117.5	-13.2	130.7	114.7	-15.7	130.4
Producers of Government Services	77.9	-	77.9	82.1	-	82.1	81.0	-	81.0	78.2	-	78.2
Private Non-Profit Institutions Serving Households	4.1	-	4.1	0.8	0.8	-	-	-	-	1.6	0.1	1.5
Total	296.3	31.6	264.7	286.1	38.7	247.4	198.5	-13.2	211.7	194.5	-15.6	210.1

	1984 Total Gross Capital Formation	1984 Increase in Stocks	1984 Gross Fixed Capital Formation	1985 Total Gross Capital Formation	1985 Increase in Stocks	1985 Gross Fixed Capital Formation
			At constant prices of: 1979 — All Producers			
1 Agriculture, hunting, fishing and forestry	-23.4	-27.5	4.1	-9.8	-14.8	5.0
2 Mining and quarrying	33.3	18.9	14.4	33.4	10.6	22.8
3 Manufacturing	12.2	6.0	6.2	22.2	16.3	5.9
4 Electricity, gas and water	113.9	0.2	113.7	9.4	0.1	9.3
5 Construction	3.6	1.3	2.3	3.3	0.7	2.6
6 Wholesale and retail trade, restaurants and hotels	15.3	6.6	8.7	12.5	-0.6	13.1
7 Transport, storage and communication	16.0	1.0	15.0	27.3	-0.4	27.7
8 Finance, insurance, real estate and business services	27.7	1.9	25.8	21.4	0.3	21.1
9 Community, social and personal services	2.3	1.7	0.6	1.3	-	1.3
Total Industries	200.9	10.1	190.8	121.0	12.2	108.8
Producers of Government Services	106.8	0.1	106.7	110.5	-	110.5
Private Non-Profit Institutions Serving Households	2.2	0.1	2.1	7.4	0.1	7.3
Total	309.9	10.3	299.6	238.9	12.3	226.6

4.1 Derivation of Value Added by Kind of Activity, in Current Prices

Million Botswana pula — Fiscal year beginning 1 July

	1980 Gross Output	1980 Intermediate Consumption	1980 Value Added	1981 Gross Output	1981 Intermediate Consumption	1981 Value Added	1982 Gross Output	1982 Intermediate Consumption	1982 Value Added	1983 Gross Output	1983 Intermediate Consumption	1983 Value Added
				All Producers								
1 Agriculture, hunting, forestry and fishing	129.4	38.9	90.5	128.8	41.0	87.8	136.1	58.9	77.2	116.9	40.8	76.1
2 Mining and quarrying	301.9	98.1	203.8	250.1	120.0	130.1	444.7	157.7	287.0	587.2	181.3	405.9
3 Manufacturing	165.2	115.9	49.3	210.9	139.7	71.2	265.5	186.8	78.7	260.6	178.6	82.0
4 Electricity, gas and water	45.4	26.1	19.3	53.9	32.1	21.8	88.3	58.6	29.7	67.3	35.0	32.3
5 Construction	129.1	90.8	38.3	151.9	104.3	47.6	159.8	114.8	45.0	190.5	120.0	70.5
6 Wholesale and retail trade, restaurants and hotels	113.3	42.0	71.3	109.2	31.5	77.7	148.0	50.2	97.8	199.9	80.3	119.6
7 Transport, storage and communication	82.9	66.3	16.6	107.0	87.2	19.8	133.0	102.4	30.6	121.3	88.6	32.7
8 Finance, insurance, real estate and business services	76.2	23.4	52.8	86.7	24.6	62.1	89.5	18.5	71.0	107.1	20.6	86.5
9 Community, social and personal services	17.0	9.3	7.7	29.6	20.8	8.8	35.5	20.8	14.7	28.4	18.1	10.3

Botswana

4.1 Derivation of Value Added by Kind of Activity, in Current Prices
(Continued)

Million Botswana pula — Fiscal year beginning 1 July

	1980 Gross Output	1980 Intermediate Consumption	1980 Value Added	1981 Gross Output	1981 Intermediate Consumption	1981 Value Added	1982 Gross Output	1982 Intermediate Consumption	1982 Value Added	1983 Gross Output	1983 Intermediate Consumption	1983 Value Added
Total, Industries	1060.4	510.8	549.6	1128.1	601.2	526.9	1500.4	768.7	731.7	1679.2	763.3	915.9
Producers of Government Services	211.0	76.0	135.0	251.2	94.9	156.3	310.8	119.3	191.5	374.1	149.5	224.6
Other Producers	28.9	9.4	19.5	32.2	8.3	23.9	31.7	8.9	22.8	41.2	8.0	33.2
Total	1300.3	596.2	704.1	1411.5	704.4	707.1	1842.9	896.9	946.0	2094.5	920.8	1173.7
Less: Imputed bank service charge	...	-17.6	17.6	...	-18.9	18.9	...	-23.9	23.9	...	-28.9	28.9
Import duties	103.7	...	103.7	104.7	...	104.7	127.5	...	127.5	157.3	...	157.3
Value added tax	...	...	...	...	...	...	...	...	...	...	...	...
Total	1404.0	613.8	790.2	1516.2	723.3	792.9	1970.4	920.8	1049.6	2251.8	949.7	1302.1

	1984 Gross Output	1984 Intermediate Consumption	1984 Value Added	1985 Gross Output	1985 Intermediate Consumption	1985 Value Added
All Producers						
1 Agriculture, hunting, forestry and fishing	134.4	51.5	82.9	160.8	66.8	94.0
2 Mining and quarrying	772.1	153.6	618.5	1142.3	203.8	938.5
3 Manufacturing	312.5	224.5	88.0	397.3	271.4	125.9
4 Electricity, gas and water	75.6	32.7	42.9	89.7	32.0	57.7
5 Construction	192.1	127.3	64.8	195.1	133.9	61.2
6 Wholesale and retail trade, restaurants and hotels	232.7	73.1	159.6	336.6	75.5	261.1
7 Transport, storage and communication	140.4	101.1	39.3	160.7	106.4	54.3
8 Finance, insurance, real estate and business services	163.4	53.3	110.1	198.8	56.2	142.6
9 Community, social and personal services	56.1	39.3	16.8	57.6	36.1	21.5
Total, Industries	2079.3	856.4	1222.9	2738.9	982.1	1756.8
Producers of Government Services	449.5	174.8	274.7	539.1	213.4	325.7
Other Producers	49.4	10.9	38.5	58.3	13.1	45.2
Total	2578.2	1042.1	1536.1	3336.3	1208.6	2127.7
Less: Imputed bank service charge	...	-30.6	30.6	...	-47.6	47.6
Import duties	155.2	...	155.2	155.2	...	155.2
Value added tax	...	...	...	...	...	...
Total	2733.4	1072.7	1660.7	3491.5	1256.2	2235.3

4.2 Derivation of Value Added by Kind of Activity, in Constant Prices

Million Botswana pula — Fiscal year beginning 1 July

At constant prices of: 1979

	1980 Gross Output	1980 Intermediate Consumption	1980 Value Added	1981 Gross Output	1981 Intermediate Consumption	1981 Value Added	1982 Gross Output	1982 Intermediate Consumption	1982 Value Added	1983 Gross Output	1983 Intermediate Consumption	1983 Value Added
All Producers												
1 Agriculture, hunting, forestry and fishing	108.5	33.5	75.0	104.7	32.9	71.8	102.0	41.9	60.1	80.4	29.5	50.9
2 Mining and quarrying	346.9	86.2	260.7	315.5	93.1	222.4	506.8	113.2	393.6	657.9	124.0	533.9
3 Manufacturing	136.1	99.1	37.0	159.3	113.5	45.8	176.2	133.8	42.4	164.2	120.2	44.0
4 Electricity, gas and water	39.4	24.1	15.3	52.3	36.4	15.9	59.1	43.4	15.7	45.0	25.5	19.5
5 Construction	112.5	80.5	32.0	110.1	72.9	37.2	104.6	78.4	26.2	118.3	79.6	38.7
6 Wholesale and retail trade, restaurants and hotels	111.6	38.8	72.8	94.4	26.4	68.0	112.2	38.8	73.4	139.4	57.4	82.0
7 Transport, storage and communication	74.7	59.9	14.8	91.3	73.2	18.1	87.9	64.1	23.8	90.2	67.1	23.1
8 Finance, insurance, real estate and business services	87.1	37.4	49.7	99.2	43.6	55.6	94.0	35.1	58.9	111.1	45.9	65.2
9 Community, social and personal services	15.5	8.2	7.3	25.9	17.1	8.8	29.5	14.9	14.6	20.9	12.4	8.5
Total, Industries	1032.3	467.7	564.6	1052.7	509.1	543.6	1272.3	563.6	708.7	1427.4	561.6	865.8
Producers of Government Services	179.8	65.6	114.2	200.8	77.0	123.8	222.8	86.7	136.1	247.3	96.8	150.5
Other Producers	26.4	8.1	18.3	27.3	6.9	20.4	26.4	6.0	20.4	31.7	5.3	26.4
Total	1238.5	541.4	697.1	1280.8	593.0	687.8	1521.5	656.3	865.2	1706.4	663.7	1042.7
Less: Imputed bank service charge	...	-16.7	16.7	...	-17.0	17.0	...	-19.9	19.9	...	-22.4	22.4
Import duties	91.0	...	91.0	82.7	...	82.7	88.7	...	88.7	100.2	...	100.2
Value added tax	...	...	...	...	...	...	...	...	...	...	...	...
Total	1329.5	558.1	771.4	1363.5	610.0	753.5	1610.2	676.2	934.0	1806.6	686.1	1120.5

Botswana

4.2 Derivation of Value Added by Kind of Activity, in Constant Prices

Million Botswana pula — Fiscal year beginning 1 July

		1984			1985	
	Gross Output	Intermediate Consumption	Value Added	Gross Output	Intermediate Consumption	Value Added

At constant prices of: 1979
All Producers

1	Agriculture, hunting, forestry and fishing	80.7	33.9	46.8	91.0	37.8	53.2
2	Mining and quarrying	560.2	-	560.2	697.7	124.5	573.2
3	Manufacturing	176.3	140.5	35.8	143.3	97.9	45.4
4	Electricity, gas and water	44.8	21.3	23.5	48.8	17.4	31.4
5	Construction	118.1	82.5	35.6	96.6	66.3	30.3
6	Wholesale and retail trade, restaurants and hotels	156.8	48.8	108.0	191.4	42.9	148.5
7	Transport, storage and communication	95.1	66.5	28.6	116.3	77.0	39.3
8	Finance, insurance, real estate and business services	116.9	34.7	82.2	134.7	38.1	96.6
9	Community, social and personal services	39.5	25.1	14.4	42.1	26.4	15.7
	Total, Industries	1388.4	453.3	935.1	1561.9	528.3	1033.6
	Producers of Government Services	284.4	111.9	172.5	308.2	122.0	186.2
	Other Producers	35.8	7.3	28.5	42.7	9.6	33.1
	Total	1708.6	572.5	1136.1	1912.8	659.9	1252.9
	Less: Imputed bank service charge	...	-22.3	22.3	...	-33.0	33.0
	Import duties	97.7	...	97.7	88.3	...	88.3
	Value added tax	...	...	...	...	...	...
	Total	1806.3	594.8	1211.5	2001.1	692.9	1308.2

4.3 Cost Components of Value Added

Million Botswana pula — Fiscal year beginning 1 July

		1980						1981				
		Compensation of Employees	Capital Consumption	Net Operating Surplus	Indirect Taxes	Less: Subsidies Received	Value Added	Compensation of Employees	Capital Consumption	Net Operating Surplus	Indirect Taxes	Less: Subsidies Received	Value Added

All Producers

1	Agriculture, hunting, forestry and fishing	19.1	3.4	68.1	-0.1	...	90.5	20.6	3.9	63.4	-0.1	...	87.8
2	Mining and quarrying	30.7	49.5	123.6	-	...	203.8	41.8	58.1	29.4	0.8	...	130.1
3	Manufacturing	21.0	4.9	19.3	4.1	...	49.3	26.6	6.3	32.7	5.6	...	71.2
4	Electricity, gas and water	9.5	13.2	-3.2	-0.2	...	19.3	9.1	14.6	-1.9	-	...	21.8
5	Construction	29.5	4.8	4.1	-0.1	...	38.3	37.3	5.3	5.0	-	...	47.6
6	Wholesale and retail trade, restaurants and hotels	18.2	4.3	36.7	12.1	...	71.3	23.6	6.1	41.0	7.0	...	77.7
7	Transport, storage and communication	13.6	6.1	-4.2	1.1	...	16.6	18.2	8.0	-7.0	0.6	...	19.8
8	Finance, insurance, real estate and business services	20.7	15.5	16.5	0.1	...	52.8	25.5	17.8	19.0	-0.2	...	62.1
9	Community, social and personal services	2.2	0.5	4.9	0.1	...	7.7	3.4	0.6	4.6	0.2	...	8.8
	Total, Industries [a]	164.5	102.2	266.2	16.7	...	549.6	206.1	120.7	186.2	13.9	...	526.9
	Producers of Government Services	103.9	31.0	-	0.1	...	135.0	118.2	37.9	-	0.2	...	156.3
	Other Producers	18.9	2.3	-1.8	0.1	...	19.5	22.8	2.4	-1.3	-	...	23.9
	Total [a]	287.3	135.5	264.4	16.9	...	704.1	347.1	161.0	184.9	14.1	...	707.1
	Less: Imputed bank service charge	...	...	17.6	...	...	17.6	...	...	18.9	...	...	18.9
	Import duties	...	...	...	103.7	...	103.7	...	...	...	104.7	...	104.7
	Value added tax	...	...	...	...	...	...	...	...	...	...	...	...
	Total [a]	287.3	135.5	246.8	120.6	...	790.2	347.1	161.0	166.0	118.8	...	792.9

		1982						1983					
		Compensation of Employees	Capital Consumption	Net Operating Surplus	Indirect Taxes	Less: Subsidies Received	Value Added	Compensation of Employees	Capital Consumption	Net Operating Surplus	Indirect Taxes	Less: Subsidies Received	Value Added

All Producers

1	Agriculture, hunting, forestry and fishing	25.5	5.2	46.4	0.1	...	77.2	25.2	5.7	45.1	0.1	...	76.1
2	Mining and quarrying	50.2	73.6	162.6	0.6	...	287.0	54.9	80.6	269.2	1.2	...	405.9
3	Manufacturing	31.7	8.8	37.7	0.5	...	78.7	33.7	10.5	32.0	5.8	...	82.0
4	Electricity, gas and water	13.1	21.7	-5.1	-	...	29.7	12.5	25.6	-5.8	-	...	32.3

Botswana

4.3 Cost Components of Value Added
(Continued)

Million Botswana pula — Fiscal year beginning 1 July

1982 / 1983

	Compensation of Employees	Capital Consumption	Net Operating Surplus	Indirect Taxes	Less: Subsidies Received	Value Added	Compensation of Employees	Capital Consumption	Net Operating Surplus	Indirect Taxes	Less: Subsidies Received	Value Added
5 Construction	30.5	6.1	8.4	-	...	45.0	43.0	4.9	22.7	-0.1	...	70.5
6 Wholesale and retail trade, restaurants and hotels	30.5	8.3	55.9	3.1	...	97.8	45.0	11.0	63.2	0.4	...	119.6
7 Transport, storage and communication	22.5	10.7	-2.8	0.2	...	30.6	26.0	12.6	-6.1	0.2	...	32.7
8 Finance, insurance, real estate and business services	37.0	23.0	11.5	-0.5	...	71.0	41.4	25.5	19.3	0.3	...	86.5
9 Community, social and personal services	8.7	0.8	5.0	0.2	...	14.7	3.3	1.0	5.8	0.2	...	10.3
Total, Industries [a]	249.7	158.2	319.5	4.2	...	731.7	285.0	177.4	445.4	8.1	...	915.9
Producers of Government Services	138.2	53.1	-	0.2	...	191.5	161.6	63.0	-	-	...	224.6
Other Producers	21.8	3.0	-2.0	-	...	22.8	29.8	3.3	0.1	-	...	33.2
Total [a]	409.8	214.3	317.5	4.4	...	946.0	476.4	243.7	445.5	8.1	...	1173.7
Less: Imputed bank service charge	...	...	23.8	...	...	23.8	...	...	28.9	...	...	28.9
Import duties	...	...	...	127.5	...	127.5	...	...	...	157.3	...	157.3
Value added tax	...	...	...	...	...	...	...	...	...	...	...	...
Total [a]	409.8	214.3	293.7	131.9	...	1049.7	476.4	243.7	416.6	165.4	...	1302.1

1984 / 1985

	Compensation of Employees	Capital Consumption	Net Operating Surplus	Indirect Taxes	Less: Subsidies Received	Value Added	Compensation of Employees	Capital Consumption	Net Operating Surplus	Indirect Taxes	Less: Subsidies Received	Value Added
All Producers												
1 Agriculture, hunting, forestry and fishing	30.7	5.8	46.3	0.1	...	82.9	33.1	6.9	54.1	-0.1	...	94.0
2 Mining and quarrying	53.5	82.0	481.7	1.3	...	618.5	71.9	91.7	773.3	1.6	...	938.5
3 Manufacturing	34.8	11.2	43.1	-1.1	...	88.0	45.4	12.1	70.4	-2.0	...	125.9
4 Electricity, gas and water	13.2	41.6	-11.9	-	...	42.9	16.9	65.8	-25.0	-	...	57.7
5 Construction	49.3	5.1	10.7	-0.3	...	64.8	45.3	5.5	10.6	-0.2	...	61.2
6 Wholesale and retail trade, restaurants and hotels	42.2	11.9	105.4	0.1	...	159.6	48.8	14.9	197.0	0.4	...	261.1
7 Transport, storage and communication	29.2	15.0	-3.5	-1.4	...	39.3	30.9	21.9	2.7	-1.2	...	54.3
8 Finance, insurance, real estate and business services	55.7	27.5	26.1	0.8	...	110.1	71.7	32.0	40.0	-1.1	...	142.6
9 Community, social and personal services	7.3	1.1	8.2	0.2	...	16.8	11.6	1.4	7.8	0.7	...	21.5
Total, Industries [a]	315.9	201.2	706.1	-0.3	...	1222.9	375.6	252.2	1130.8	-1.8	...	1756.8
Producers of Government Services	200.9	73.8	-	-	...	274.7	232.5	93.2	-	-	...	325.7
Other Producers	36.8	3.4	-1.8	0.1	...	38.5	42.1	4.4	-1.3	-	...	45.2
Total [a]	553.6	278.4	704.8	-0.2	...	1536.1	650.2	349.8	1129.5	-1.8	...	2127.7
Less: Imputed bank service charge	...	...	30.6	...	...	30.6	...	...	47.6	...	...	47.6
Import duties	...	...	...	155.2	...	155.2	...	...	...	155.2	...	155.2
Value added tax	...	...	...	...	...	...	...	...	...	...	...	...
Total [a]	553.6	278.4	673.7	155.0	...	1660.7	650.2	349.8	1081.9	153.4	...	2235.3

a) Column 4 refers to indirect taxes less subsidies received.

Brazil

Source. Reply to the United Nations National Accounts Questionnaire from the Instituto Brasiliero de Geografia e Estadistica, in the DECNA, Departamento de Contas Nacionais, Rio de Janeiro. The official estimates are shown in a series of publications entitled 'Conjuntura'. Effective 3 March 1986, a new currency called Cruzados was introduced. One Cruzado is equivalent to 1000 Cruzeiros. Beginning 1980, the estimates of the new series are in New Cruzados. One New Cruzado is equivalent to 1000 Cruzados.

General note. The estimates shown in the following tables have been prepared in accordance with the United Nations System of National Accounts so far as the existing data would permit.

1.1 Expenditure on the Gross Domestic Product, in Current Prices

Million Cruzados

	1970	1975	1980	1981	1982	1983	1984	1985	1986	1987	1988	1989
1 Government final consumption expenditure	22	107	11391	2	5	11	32	137	391	1403	10865	181356
2 Private final consumption expenditure	133	713	86499	17	35	84	272	909	2482	7183	51169	729530
3 Gross capital formation	40	269	28903	6	11	19	61	265	699	2573	19666	314869
A Increase in stocks	3	25	55	-	-	-2	-4	31	-	-	-	-
B Gross fixed capital formation	37	245	28353	6	11	21	65	234	699	2573	19666	314869
Residential buildings												
Non-residential buildings	21	141	17152	4	7	14	44	159	493	1848	13200	224153
Other construction and land improvement etc.												
Other	15	104	11211	2	4	7	21	75	206	725	6466	90716
4 Exports of goods and services	14	76	11211	2	4	13	52	169	323	1091	9425	104511
5 Less: Imports of goods and services	14	116	14001	2	4	11	31	98	233	714	4928	63918
Equals: Gross Domestic Product [a]	194	1050	1240012	25	51	117	386	1383	3662	11537	86197	1266348

a) Beginning 1980, the currency new cruzado was used, 1 new cruzado is equal to 1,000 cruzados.

1.2 Expenditure on the Gross Domestic Product, in Constant Prices

Million Cruzados

	1970	1975	1980	1981	1982	1983	1984	1985	1986	1987	1988	1989
				At constant prices of:1980								
1 Government final consumption expenditure	4457	6890	978810	9	10	9	9	10	11	11	11	11
2 Private final consumption expenditure												
3 Gross capital formation	1162	2469	28903	2	2	2	2	2	3	3	3	3
A Increase in stocks	48	213	55	-	-	-	-	-	-	-	-	-
B Gross fixed capital formation	1115	2256	28353	2	2	2	2	2	3	3	3	3
4 Exports of goods and services	435	744	11211	1	1	1	2	2	2	2	2	2
5 Less: Imports of goods and services	635	1347	14001	1	1	1	1	1	1	1	1	1
Equals: Gross Domestic Product [a]	5419	8756	-1240012	12	12	12	12	13	14	15	15	15

a) Beginning 1980, the currency new cruzado was used, 1 new cruzado is equal to 1,000 cruzados.

1.3 Cost Components of the Gross Domestic Product

Million Cruzados

	1970	1975	1980	1981	1982	1983	1984	1985	1986	1987	1988	1989
1 Indirect taxes, net	32	118	12132	2	5	12	34	124	403	1154	8328	111992
A Indirect taxes	33	146	16732	3	6	15	40	146	457	1337	9384	136407
B Less: Subsidies	1	28	460	1	1	3	6	22	54	183	1056	24415
2 Consumption of fixed capital [a]	...	...	...	...	...	...	...	...	...	...	...	...
3 Compensation of employees paid by resident producers to:	67	341	432611[b]	22	45	105	352	1258	3259	10383	77869	1154356
4 Operating surplus [a]	97	591	6860									
Equals: Gross Domestic Product [c]	194	1050	1240012	25	51	117	386	1383	3662	11537	86197	1266348

a) Item 'Operating surplus' includes consumption of fixed capital.
b) Including item 'Compensation of employees paid by resident producers to:' through 'Operating surplus'.
c) Beginning 1980, the currency new cruzado was used, 1 new cruzado is equal to 1,000 cruzados.

Brazil

1.4 General Government Current Receipts and Disbursements

Million Cruzados

	1970	1975	1980	1981	1982	1983	1984	1985	1986	1987	1988	1989
Receipts												
1 Operating surplus	...	...	...	...	...	...	...	...	...	...	...	...
2 Property and entrepreneurial income	...	...	...	...	...	...	...	...	...	...	...	...
3 Taxes, fees and contributions	50	265	30583	6	12	29	84	311	929	2693	18868	277873
A Indirect taxes	32	146	16742	3	6	15	40	146	457	1337	9384	136407
B Direct taxes	18	119	13841	3	6	14	44	165	472	1356	9484	141466
C Social security contributions	...	...	...	...	...	...	...	...	...	...	...	...
D Compulsory fees, fines and penalties	...	...	...	...	...	...	...	...	...	...	...	...
4 Other current transfers	2	-8	-120	-	-1	-2	-3	-12	-61	204	2351	52638
Total Current Receipts of General Government [a]	53	257	29383	6	12	28	81	299	868	2897	21220	330512
Disbursements												
1 Government final consumption expenditure	22	107	11391	2	5	11	32	137	391	1403	10865	181356
2 Property income	...	...	...	...	...	...	...	...	...	...	...	...
3 Subsidies	1	28	460	-	1	1	3	6	22	54	183	1056	24415
4 Other current transfers	18	83	12011	3	6	15	54	254	683	2018	20108	378778
5 Net saving	11	39	138	-	-	-	-2	-11	-113	-261	-707	-10810	-254037
Total Current Disbursements and Net Saving of General Government [a]	53	257	29383	6	12	28	81	299	868	2897	21220	330512

a) Beginning 1980, the currency new cruzado was used, 1 new cruzado is equal to 1,000 cruzados.

1.7 External Transactions on Current Account, Summary

Million Cruzados

	1970	1975	1980	1981	1982	1983	1984	1985	1986	1987	1988	1989
Payments to the Rest of the World												
1 Imports of goods and services	14	116	14001	2	4	11	31	98	233	714	4928	63918
2 Factor income to the rest of the world	2	20	5071	1	2	7	25	86	182	475	3729	43116
A Compensation of employees	-	-	1 -	-	-	-	-	-	-	4	33	351
B Property and entrepreneurial income	2	20	5061	1	3	7	25	86	182	471	3696	42765
3 Current transfers to the rest of the world	-	1	9	-	-	-	-	-	1	4	10	59
4 Surplus of the nation on current transactions	-3	-54	-674 -1	-1	-3	-4	-	-1	-72	-56	1103	2906
Payments to the Rest of the World and Surplus of the Nation on Current Transactions [a]	15	83	12421	3	4	14	56	183	343	1137	9769	109999

Brazil

1.7 External Transactions on Current Account, Summary
(Continued)

Million Cruzados

	1970	1975	1980	1981	1982	1983	1984	1985	1986	1987	1988	1989
				Receipts From The Rest of the World								
1 Exports of goods and services	14	76	1121 1	2	4	13	52	169	323	1091	9425	104511
2 Factor income from rest of the world	1	6	103 -	-	-	1	3	13	19	39	309	4744
A Compensation of employees	-	-	1 -	-	-	-	-	-	-	-	2	14
B Property and entrepreneurial income	1	6	102 -	-	-	1	3	13	18	39	307	4730
3 Current transfers from rest of the world	-	1	18 -	-	-	-	-	1	2	6	35	745
Receipts from the Rest of the World on Current Transactions [a]	15	83	1242 1	3	4	14	56	183	343	1137	9769	109999

a) Beginning 1980, the currency new cruzado was used, 1 new cruzado is equal to 1,000 cruzados.

1.10 Gross Domestic Product by Kind of Activity, in Current Prices

Million Cruzados

	1970	1975	1980	1981	1982	1983	1984	1985	1986	1987	1988	1989
1 Agriculture, hunting, forestry and fishing	20	107	1232 1	2	4	12	40	145	364	1039	7914	98799
2 Mining and quarrying	1	8	126 -	-	1	2	13	41	87	231	1500	18086
3 Manufacturing	48	314	3746 4	7	16	35	119	425	1074	3318	24218	342465
4 Electricity, gas and water	4	20	218 -	-	1	2	8	29	77	339	2173	28083
5 Construction	9	62	813 1	2	3	7	21	76	234	876	6257	106250
6 Wholesale and retail trade, restaurants and hotels	29	145	1328 1	3	5	11	34	114	283	838	6314	90176
7 Transport, storage and communication	7	40	572 1	1	3	6	19	67	165	543	4247	63983
8 Finance, insurance, real estate and business services	27	132	1781 2	4	9	24	76	277	573	2693	21093	416165
9 Community, social and personal services	13	96	1482 1	3	6	13	42	147	382	1194	9490	147752
Total, Industries	158	924	11298 11	22	48	112	372	1321	3239	11071	83206	1311759
Producers of Government Services	16	75	781 1	2	4	8	22	96	267	896	6830	123056
Other Producers	...	...	... ...	...	...	...	...	...	...	...	...	...
Subtotal [a]	174	999	12079 12	24	52	120	394	1417	3506	11967	90036	1434815
Less: Imputed bank service charge	11	67	893 1	2	5	14	42	159	247	1584	12165	280458
Plus: Import duties	...	...	... ...	...	...	...	...	...	...	...	...	...
Plus: Value added tax	...	...	... ...	...	...	...	...	...	...	...	...	...
Plus: Other adjustments [b]	32	118	1214 1	3	4	11	34	125	403	1154	8326	111991
Equals: Gross Domestic Product [c]	194	1050	12400 12	25	51	117	386	1383	3662	11537	86197	1266348

a) Gross domestic product in factor values.
b) Item 'Other adjustments' refers to indirect taxes net of subsidies.
c) Beginning 1980, the currency new cruzado was used, 1 new cruzado is equal to 1,000 cruzados.

Brazil

1.12 Relations Among National Accounting Aggregates

Million Cruzados

	1970	1975	1980	1981	1982	1983	1984	1985	1986	1987	1988	1989
Gross Domestic Product	194	1050	12400 12	25	51	117	386	1383	3662	11537	86197	1266348
Plus: Net factor income from the rest of the world	-2	-14	-404 -	-1	-3	-7	-22	-74	-163	-436	-3420	-38373
Factor income from the rest of the world	1	6	103 -	-	-	1	3	13	19	39	309	4744
Less: Factor income to the rest of the world	2	20	507 1	1	2	7	25	86	182	475	3729	43116
Equals: Gross National Product	193	1036	11996 12	24	48	110	364	1309	3499	11101	82777	1227975
Less: Consumption of fixed capital	...	...	...	...	...	...	...	...	...	...	...	...
Equals: National Income [a]	193	1036	11996 12	24	48	110	364	1309	3499	11101	82777	1227975
Plus: Net current transfers from the rest of the world	-	-	9 -	-	-	-	-	1	1	3	25	686
Current transfers from the rest of the world	-	1	18 -	-	-	-	-	1	2	6	35	745
Less: Current transfers to the rest of the world	-	1	9 -	-	-	-	-	-	1	4	10	59
Equals: National Disposable Income [b]	193	1036	12005 12	24	48	110	364	1310	3500	11103	82803	1228661
Less: Final consumption	155	820	9788 10	19	40	95	304	1046	2873	8586	62034	910887
Equals: Net Saving [c]	38	216	2217 2	5	8	16	61	264	627	2517	20768	317775
Less: Surplus of the nation on current transactions	-3	-54	-674 -1	-1	-3	-4	-	-1	-72	-56	1103	2906
Equals: Net Capital Formation [d,e]	40	269	2890 3	6	11	20	61	265	699	2573	19665	314869

a) Item 'National income' includes consumption of fixed capital.
b) Item 'National disposable income' includes consumption of fixed capital.
c) Item 'Net saving' includes consumption of fixed capital.
d) Item 'Net capital formation' includes consumption of fixed capital.
e) Beginning 1980, the currency new cruzado was used, 1 new cruzado is equal to 1,000 cruzados.

British Virgin Islands

Source. Statistics Office, Finance Department, Road Town, Tortola.
General note. The estimates shown in the following tables have been prepared in accordance with the United Nations System of National Accounts so far as the existing data would permit.

1.1 Expenditure on the Gross Domestic Product, in Current Prices

Thousand United States dollars	1970	1975	1980	1981	1982	1983	1984	1985	1986	1987	1988	1989
1 Government final consumption expenditure	2188	2570	... 7120	9750	11480	14290	16840	16910	18730	20230	26350	...
2 Private final consumption expenditure	9032	11367	... 40010	42370	51880	57210	63110	66990	71310	85930	90460	...
3 Gross capital formation	13754	9778	... 22320	25940	28880	33170	34960	35970	39810	45700	48580	...
A Increase in stocks [a]	403	209	2350	1920	2180	2000	2120	2260	2420	2680	3520	...
B Gross fixed capital formation	13351	9569	... 19970	24020	26700	31170	32840	33710	37390	43020	45060	...
4 Exports of goods and services	6239	14383	... 36850	45520	55020	68580	75910	87280	98370	111410	141300	...
5 Less: Imports of goods and services	13433	17408	... 52120	64350	77530	94670	104520	117260	130390	146610	175350	...
Statistical discrepancy	-1833	683	...	...	...	...	...	...	...	...	...	...
Equals: Gross Domestic Product	15947	21373	... 54170	59230	69720	78570	86300	89880	97820	116660	131340	...

a) Item 'Increase in stocks' includes also unrecorded increase in stocks.

1.3 Cost Components of the Gross Domestic Product

Thousand United States dollars	1970	1975	1980	1981	1982	1983	1984	1985	1986	1987	1988	1989
1 Indirect taxes, net	1804	2363	...	...	...	...	8400	9480	11240	... 15140	...	...
A Indirect taxes	1900	2538	...	...	...	...	9710	10580	12030	... 15970	...	...
B Less: Subsidies	96	175	...	...	...	...	1310	1100	790	... 830	...	...
2 Consumption of fixed capital [a]	...	...	...	...	...	...	11590	9580	9550	... 10510	...	...
3 Compensation of employees paid by resident producers to:	8860	11786	...	...	...	...	41380	41550	42960	... 53620	...	...
4 Operating surplus [a]	5283	7224	...	...	...	...	24930	29260	34070	... 33550	...	...
Equals: Gross Domestic Product	15947	21373	...	...	...	...	86300	89880	97820	... 112820	...	...

a) Item 'Operating surplus' includes consumption of fixed capital.

1.4 General Government Current Receipts and Disbursements

Thousand United States dollars	1970	1975	1980	1981	1982	1983	1984	1985	1986	1987	1988	1989
Receipts												
1 Operating surplus	...	...	...									
2 Property and entrepreneurial income	...	...	678	872	1097	1005	1496	1492	1684	...	...	...
3 Taxes, fees and contributions	2499	4233	... 10645	14174	16360	17873	19019	18667	20924	25634	...	...
A Indirect taxes	1900	2538	... 6389	8049	9289	9373	9713	10580	12030	15968	...	...
B Direct taxes	465	799	3447	3458	4871	5899	6551	5288	5851	6352	...	...
C Social security contributions	84	806	... 809	2667	2200	2601	2755	2799	3043	3314	...	...
D Compulsory fees, fines and penalties	50	90	...	...	...	...	...	...	...	...	...	...
4 Other current transfers	...	...	1369	1949	1758	1695	1903	1839	2033	...	...	...
Total Current Receipts of General Government	2499	4233	... 12692	16995	19215	20573	22418	21998	24641	...	...	...

British Virgin Islands

1.4 General Government Current Receipts and Disbursements
(Continued)

Thousand United States dollars

Disbursements

	1970	1975	1980	1981	1982	1983	1984	1985	1986	1987	1988	1989
1 Government final consumption expenditure	2188	2570	7120	9753	11475	14286	16836	16906	18734	...	...	...
A Compensation of employees	1733	2686	...	...	...	...	...	...	...	...	...	...
B Consumption of fixed capital			...	...	...	...	...	...	...	...	...	...
C Purchases of goods and services, net	455	-116	...	...	...	...	...	...	...	...	...	...
D Less: Own account fixed capital formation			...	...	...	...	...	...	...	...	...	...
E Indirect taxes paid, net			...	...	...	...	...	...	...	...	...	...
2 Property income	296	686	99	48	20	48	53	42	34	31	...	...
3 Subsidies	96	175	490	790	940	880	1310	1100	790	...	...	...
4 Other current transfers	162	463	810	1418	1309	1394	1971	1938	2731	...	...	...
A Social security benefits	114	188	-	103	168	214	213	282	295	...	...	...
B Social assistance grants	48	275	...	...	...	...	...	...	...	...	...	...
C Other	...	...	810	1315	1141	1180	1758	1656	2436	...	...	...
5 Net saving	-243	339	4173	4986	5471	3965	2248	2012	2352	...	...	...
Total Current Disbursements and Net Saving of General Government	2499	4233	12692	16995	19215	20573	22418	21998	24641	...	...	...

1.7 External Transactions on Current Account, Summary

Thousand United States dollars

Payments to the Rest of the World

	1970	1975	1980	1981	1982	1983	1984	1985	1986	1987	1988	1989
1 Imports of goods and services	13433	17408	52120	64350	77530	94670	104520	117260	130390	...	...	...
A Imports of merchandise c.i.f.	11658	14350	40490	49810	58550	70570	77360	86210	94240	...	...	...
B Other	1775	3058	11630	14540	18980	24100	27160	31050	36150	...	...	...
2 Factor income to the rest of the world	2970	3425	...	...	...	...	...	...	...	...	...	...
3 Current transfers to the rest of the world	23	68	...	...	...	...	...	...	...	...	...	...
4 Surplus of the nation on current transactions	-9575	-4944	...	...	...	...	...	...	...	...	...	...
Payments to the Rest of the World and Surplus of the Nation on Current Transactions	6851	15957	...	...	...	...	...	...	...	...	...	...

Receipts From The Rest of the World

	1970	1975	1980	1981	1982	1983	1984	1985	1986	1987	1988	1989
1 Exports of goods and services	6239	14383	36850	45520	55020	68580	75910	87280	98370	...	...	...
A Exports of merchandise f.o.b.	253	1137	510	740	1090	2250	2290	2340	2490	...	...	...
B Other	5986	13246	36340	44780	53930	66330	73620	84940	95880	...	...	...
2 Factor income from rest of the world	602	881	...	...	...	...	...	...	...	...	...	...
3 Current transfers from rest of the world	10	693	...	...	...	...	...	...	...	...	...	...
Receipts from the Rest of the World on Current Transactions	6851	15957	...	...	...	...	...	...	...	...	...	...

British Virgin Islands

1.10 Gross Domestic Product by Kind of Activity, in Current Prices

Thousand United States dollars

	1970	1975	1980	1981	1982	1983	1984	1985	1986	1987	1988	1989
1 Agriculture, hunting, forestry and fishing	1139	1959	2660	2920	3210	3390	3560 / 3558	3652	3723	4345	4392	...
2 Mining and quarrying	945	1258	40	50	50	60	110 / 112	162	106	159	240	...
3 Manufacturing			1380	1620	1950	2110	2270 / 1785	1783	2303	3185	3425	...
4 Electricity, gas and water	208	339	790	1050	1240	2260	2050 / 2683	2856	3602	3842	4776	...
5 Construction	4813	3434	2680	3090	4930	6330	6830 / 6833	5914	5429	6109	7344	...
6 Wholesale and retail trade, restaurants and hotels	2441	4912	17220	16950	19320	22300	23840 / 23241	24849	26106	31993	34197	...
7 Transport, storage and communication	1306	1729	5580	5930	6920	6970	7790 / 7383	8119	9539	11278	14430	...
8 Finance, insurance, real estate and business services	2413	4002	12560	15130	17760	19070	20590 / 20754	21615	22870	24665	28019	...
9 Community, social and personal services	179	261	2490	3170	3620	4010	4750 / 4608	4670	4823	5452	6286	...
Total, Industries	13444	17894	45400	49910	59000	66500	71790 / 70957	73620	78501	91028	103109	...
Producers of Government Services	1383	2270	5010	6460	7400	8280	11280 / 11281	10254	11823	12714	17790	...
Other Producers	...	...	...	...	...	...	...	...	...	...	...	...
Subtotal a	14827	20164	50410	56370	66400	74780	83070 / 82240	83874	90324	103742	120899	...
Less: Imputed bank service charge	684	1154	2140	4400	5020	4690	5160 / 5160	5211	5274	6057	7179	...
Plus: Import duties	...	...	...	...	...	...	...	...	...	...	...	...
Plus: Value added tax	...	...	...	...	...	...	...	...	...	...	...	...
Plus: Other adjustments b	1804	2363	5900	7270	8350	8480	8390	...	...	...	...	...
Equals: Gross Domestic Product c	15947	21373	54170	59230	69720	78570	86300 / 77078	78663	85050	97685	113720	...

a) Gross domestic product in factor values.
b) Item 'Other adjustments' refers to indirect taxes net of subsidies.
c) Beginning 1984, gross domestic products in factor values.

1.11 Gross Domestic Product by Kind of Activity, in Constant Prices

Thousand United States dollars

	1970	1975	1980	1981	1982	1983	1984	1985	1986	1987	1988	1989
		1976			At constant prices of: 1977				1984			
1 Agriculture, hunting, forestry and fishing	1940	2090	2150	2120	2170	2170	2190 / 3558	3558	3542	4051	4275	...
2 Mining and quarrying	1160	1310	40	40	40	50	80 / 112	163	106	161	243	...
3 Manufacturing			1040	1100	1210	1270	1360 / 1785	1762	2237	3070	3120	...
4 Electricity, gas and water	250	340	570	740	840	1450	1260 / 2683	2897	3497	4059	4391	...
5 Construction	6340	3980	2210	2330	3020	3730	4030 / 6833	5976	5497	6185	7454	...

British Virgin Islands

1.11 Gross Domestic Product by Kind of Activity, in Constant Prices
(Continued)

Thousand United States dollars

	1970	1975	1980	1981	1982	1983	1984	1985	1986	1987	1988	1989
		1976	At constant prices of: 1977					1984				
6 Wholesale and retail trade, restaurants and hotels	2840	5210	15070	13630	12940	13280	13280 / 23241	24489	26106	29248	30973	...
7 Transport, storage and communication	1440	1940	4580	4760	4790	5000	5040 / 7383	8113	8131	9472	11900	...
8 Finance, insurance, real estate and business services	4250	4530	8040	8650	9060	9260	9890 / 20754	23031	24745	28431	30938	...
9 Community, social and personal services	210	310	1880	2090	2220	2170	2300 / 4608	4598	4377	6708	7164	...
Total, Industries	18430	19710	35580	35460	36290	38380	39430 / 70957	74587	78238	91385	100458	...
Producers of Government Services	1760	2580	3600	4160	4370	4660	5890 / 11281	10126	11153	11168	12585	...
Other Producers	...	...	...	...	...	...	...	...	...	...	...	...
Subtotal	20190[a]	22290[a]	39240	39620	40660	43040	45320 / 82240	84713	89391	102553	113043	...
Less: Imputed bank service charge	910	1260	1280	1420	1590	1680	1660 / 5160	6097	7582	9543	11747	...
Plus: Import duties	...	...	...	...	...	...	...	...	...	...	...	...
Plus: Value added tax	...	...	...	...	...	...	...	...	...	...	...	...
Plus: Other adjustments	2150[b]	2350[b]	...	...	...	...	...	...	...	...	...	...
Equals: Gross Domestic Product	21430	23380	37960[a]	38200[a]	39070[a]	41360[a]	43660[a] / 77078[a]	78616[a]	81809[a]	93010[a]	101296[a]	...

a) Gross domestic product in factor values.
b) Item 'Other adjustments' refers to indirect taxes net of subsidies.

2.1 Government Final Consumption Expenditure by Function, in Current Prices

Thousand United States dollars

	1970	1975	1980	1981	1982	1983	1984	1985	1986	1987	1988	1989
1 General public services	909	832	1229	2041	2232	3115	3488	3891	4043	4869	...	...
2 Defence	...	...	...	...	...	...	...	...	...	...	...	...
3 Public order and safety	...	...	762	889	1217	1392	1810	1813	2103	2301	...	...
4 Education	597	802	1837	2217	2623	3111	3879	3943	4208	4417	...	...
5 Health	419	544	977	1602	1651	1862	2518	2498	2686	3302	...	...
6 Social security and welfare	-	-	145	51	298	305	345	300	438	535	...	...
7 Housing and community amenities	-	-	342	474	519	670	740	680	817	1146	...	...
8 Recreational, cultural and religious affairs	-	-	34	55	91	112	129	133	132	102	...	...
9 Economic services	263	392	1743	2338	2756	3572	3653	3467	4087	4221	...	...

British Virgin Islands

2.1 Government Final Consumption Expenditure by Function, in Current Prices
(Continued)

Thousand United States dollars

	1970	1975	1980	1981	1982	1983	1984	1985	1986	1987	1988	1989
A Fuel and energy	...	...	...	...	...	...	...	...	...	...	...	...
B Agriculture, forestry, fishing and hunting	...	...	238	398	446	555	537	499	612	706	...	...
C Mining, manufacturing and construction, except fuel and energy	...	...	1193	1364	1467	1912	1889	1656	2006	1838	...	...
D Transportation and communication	...	...	...	...	...	...	...	...	...	...	...	...
E Other economic affairs	...	...	312	576	843	1105	1227	1312	1469	1677	...	...
10 Other functions	-	-	...	...	...	...	...	...	...	...	...	...
Total Government Final Consumption Expenditure a	2188	2570	7069	9667	11387	14139	16562	16725	18514	20893	...	...

a) Only central government data are included in the general government estimates.

2.17 Exports and Imports of Goods and Services, Detail

Thousand United States dollars

	1970	1975	1980	1981	1982	1983	1984	1985	1986	1987	1988	1989
Exports of Goods and Services												
1 Exports of merchandise, f.o.b.	253	1137	...	...	...	...	...	...	...	...	...	...
2 Transport and communication	501	991	...	...	...	...	...	...	...	...	...	...
3 Insurance service charges	...	...	...	...	...	...	...	...	...	...	...	...
4 Other commodities	615	555	...	...	...	...	...	...	...	...	...	...
5 Adjustments of merchandise exports to change-of-ownership basis	...	...	...	...	...	...	...	...	...	...	...	...
6 Direct purchases in the domestic market by non-residential households	4870	11700	...	...	...	...	...	...	...	...	...	...
7 Direct purchases in the domestic market by extraterritorial bodies	...	...	...	...	...	...	...	...	...	...	...	...
Total Exports of Goods and Services	6239	14383	...	...	...	...	...	...	...	...	...	...
Imports of Goods and Services												
1 Imports of merchandise, c.i.f.	11658	14350	...	...	...	...	...	...	...	...	...	...
2 Adjustments of merchandise imports to change-of-ownership basis	...	...	...	...	...	...	...	...	...	...	...	...
3 Other transport and communication	350	645	...	...	...	...	...	...	...	...	...	...
4 Other insurance service charges	...	...	...	...	...	...	...	...	...	...	...	...
5 Other commodities	715	1333	...	...	...	...	...	...	...	...	...	...
6 Direct purchases abroad by government	710	1080	...	...	...	...	...	...	...	...	...	...
7 Direct purchases abroad by resident households			...	...	...	...	...	...	...	...	...	...
Total Imports of Goods and Services	13433	17408	...	...	...	...	...	...	...	...	...	...
Balance of Goods and Services	-7194	-3025	...	...	...	...	...	...	...	...	...	...
Total Imports and Balance of Goods and Services	6239	14383	...	...	...	...	...	...	...	...	...	...

4.3 Cost Components of Value Added

Thousand United States dollars

	\multicolumn{6}{c}{1984}	\multicolumn{6}{c}{1985}
	Compensation of Employees	Capital Consumption	Net Operating Surplus	Indirect Taxes	Less: Subsidies Received	Value Added	Compensation of Employees	Capital Consumption	Net Operating Surplus	Indirect Taxes	Less: Subsidies Received	Value Added
All Producers												
1 Agriculture, hunting, forestry and fishing	470	490	2600	...	...	3560	500	550	2600	...	...	3660
A Agriculture and hunting	-	80	1460	...	...	1540	-	130	1400	...	...	1540
B Forestry and logging	...	...	...	...	...	...	...	...	...	...	...	...
C Fishing	470	410	1140	...	...	2020	500	420	1200	...	...	2120
2 Mining and quarrying	90	20	-	...	...	110	130	30	-	...	...	160
3 Manufacturing	1260	330	680	...	...	2270	1280	300	730	...	...	2310
4 Electricity, gas and water	1200	370	480	...	...	2050	1590	30	640	...	...	2260

206

British Virgin Islands

4.3 Cost Components of Value Added
(Continued)

Thousand United States dollars

	1984						1985					
	Compensation of Employees	Capital Consumption	Net Operating Surplus	Indirect Taxes	Less: Subsidies Received	Value Added	Compensation of Employees	Capital Consumption	Net Operating Surplus	Indirect Taxes	Less: Subsidies Received	Value Added
5 Construction	4270	480	2080	...	...	6830	4350	430	1130	...	...	5910
6 Wholesale and retail trade, restaurants and hotels	13260	6930	3640	...	...	23830	13440	5610	6130	...	...	25180
A Wholesale and retail trade	2610	1300	2940	...	...	6850	3050	1080	3010	...	...	7140
B Restaurants and hotels	10650	5630	700	...	...	16980	10390	4530	3120	...	...	18040
7 Transport, storage and communication	4780	1830	1180	...	...	7790	5420	1700	1630	...	...	8750
A Transport and storage	2910	980	360	...	...	4250	2910	1160	260	...	...	4330
B Communication	1870	850	820	...	...	3540	2510	540	1370	...	...	4420
8 Finance, insurance, real estate and business services	3040	560	16990	...	...	20590	2720	470	19130	...	...	22320
A Financial institutions	2590	350	4290	...	...	7230	2270	310	5460	...	...	8040
B Insurance				...	...					...	...	
C Real estate and business services	450	210	12700	...	...	13360	450	160	13670	...	...	14280
9 Community, social and personal services	2120	190	2440	...	...	4750	2130	200	2480	...	...	4810
Total, Industries	30490	11200	30040	...	...	71780	31560	9320	33470	...	...	75360
Producers of Government Services	10890	390	-	...	...	11280	9990	260	-	...	...	10250
Other Producers	...	...	...	...	...	...	...	...	...	...	...	...
Total a	41380	11590	30090	...	...	83060	41550	9580	34470	...	...	85610
Less: Imputed bank service charge	...	...	5160	...	...	5160	...	...	5210	...	...	5210
Import duties	...	...	...	...	...	...	...	...	...	...	...	...
Value added tax	...	...	...	...	...	...	...	...	...	...	...	...
Other adjustments	...	...	...	9710	1310	8390	...	...	...	10580	1100	9480
Total	41380	11590	24930	9710	1310	86300	41550	9580	29260	10580	1100	89880

	1986					
	Compensation of Employees	Capital Consumption	Net Operating Surplus	Indirect Taxes	Less: Subsidies Received	Value Added

All Producers

1 Agriculture, hunting, forestry and fishing	510	1010	2200	...	...	3720
A Agriculture and hunting	-	580	970	...	...	1550
B Forestry and logging	...	...	...	...	...	...
C Fishing	510	430	1230	...	...	2170
2 Mining and quarrying	120	40	-	...	...	160
3 Manufacturing	1760	380	730	...	...	2870
4 Electricity, gas and water	1650	40	1170	...	...	2860
5 Construction	2880	540	2010	...	...	5430
6 Wholesale and retail trade, restaurants and hotels	14270	5090	8030	...	...	27390
A Wholesale and retail trade	3340	1180	3360	...	...	7880
B Restaurants and hotels	10930	3910	4670	...	...	19510
7 Transport, storage and communication	5270	1420	1710	...	...	8400
A Transport and storage	2820	520	370	...	...	3710
B Communication	2450	900	1340	...	...	4690
8 Finance, insurance, real estate and business services	2890	430	20900	...	...	24220
A Financial institutions	2500	290	6480	...	...	9270
B Insurance				...	...	
C Real estate and business services	390	140	14420	...	...	14950
9 Community, social and personal services	2200	190	2570	...	...	4960
Total, Industries	31550	9140	39320	...	...	80010
Producers of Government Services	11410	410	-	...	...	11820

British Virgin Islands

4.3 Cost Components of Value Added
(Continued)

Thousand United States dollars

	1986					
	Compensation of Employees	Capital Consumption	Net Operating Surplus	Indirect Taxes	Less: Subsidies Received	Value Added
Other Producers........................	...	...	...	...	...	...
Total [a]	42960	9550	39320	...	...	91830
Less: Imputed bank service charge	...	...	5250	...	...	5250
Import duties	...	...	...	...	...	...
Value added tax	...	...	...	...	...	...
Other adjustments	...	...	...	12030	790	11240
Total	42960	9550	34070	12030	790	97820

a) Gross domestic product in factor values.

Brunei Darussalam

Source. Reply to the United Nations National Accounts Questionnaire from the British High Commission, Bandar Seri Begawan.
General note. The estimates shown in the following tables have been prepared by the Government of Brunei in accordance with the United Nations System of National Accounts so far as the existing data would permit.

1.1 Expenditure on the Gross Domestic Product, in Current Prices

Million Brunei dollars

	1970	1975	1980	1981	1982	1983	1984	1985	1986	1987	1988	1989
1 Government final consumption expenditure	...	305.4	735.7	860.7	913.6	922.4	2512.1	...	...	...	...	...
2 Private final consumption expenditure	...	...	...	...	...	...	...	...	...	...	...	...
3 Gross capital formation [a]	...	140.3	320.0	632.4	1125.9	804.6	526.7	...	...	...	...	...
A Increase in stocks [b]	...	3.5	6.4	16.0	-1.8	-2.7	2.1	...	...	...	...	...
B Gross fixed capital formation	...	136.8	313.5	616.4	1127.7	807.4	524.5	...	...	...	...	...
Residential buildings	...	40.0	51.5	161.7	315.7	335.6	173.9	...	...	...	...	...
Non-residential buildings	...	19.0	107.7	193.8	351.1	172.0	109.3	...	...	...	...	...
Other construction and land improvement etc.	...	41.8	102.6	190.4	345.5	237.9	187.8	...	...	...	...	...
Other	...	36.0	51.7	70.5	115.4	61.9	53.5	...	...	...	...	...
4 Exports of goods and services	...	...	...	...	...	...	...	...	...	...	...	...
5 Less: Imports of goods and services	...	...	...	...	...	...	...	...	...	...	...	...
Equals: Gross Domestic Product	...	2770.4	10553.6	9224.4	9125.5	8163.3	8068.5	...	...	...	...	...

a) Item 'Gross capital formation' includes general government sector only.
b) Land improvement is not included in item 'Other construction and land improvement, etc.'.

1.4 General Government Current Receipts and Disbursements

Million Brunei dollars

	1970	1975	1980	1981	1982	1983	1984	1985	1986	1987	1988	1989
Receipts												
1 Operating surplus	...	4.1	-1.5	2.4	17.0	17.5	23.5	...	...	...	...	...
2 Property and entrepreneurial income	...	470.3	3315.5	4813.1	4406.3	4803.6	4748.8	...	...	...	...	...
3 Taxes, fees and contributions	...	1077.9	2899.9	3527.2	3385.4	2863.5	2494.9	...	...	...	...	...
A Indirect taxes	...	20.8	51.2	51.7	60.5	74.9	73.4	...	...	...	...	...
B Direct taxes	...	1055.7	2845.8	3472.2	3321.1	2784.6	2415.0	...	...	...	...	...
C Social security contributions	...	...	...	...	...	...	...	...	...	...	...	...
D Compulsory fees, fines and penalties	...	1.4	2.9	3.3	3.8	4.0	6.5	...	...	...	...	...
4 Other current transfers	...	1.7	2.6	17.3	3.8	3.1	7.8	...	...	...	...	...
Total Current Receipts of General Government	...	1554.0	6216.6	8360.1	7812.6	7687.7	7275.0	...	...	...	...	...
Disbursements												
1 Government final consumption expenditure	...	305.4	735.7	860.7	913.6	922.4	2512.1	...	...	...	...	...
A Compensation of employees	...	116.4	388.8	428.5	477.4	557.8	817.0	...	...	...	...	...
B Consumption of fixed capital	...	...	...	...	...	...	...	...	...	...	...	...
C Purchases of goods and services, net	...	189.0	346.9	432.1	436.2	364.6	1695.1	...	...	...	...	...
D Less: Own account fixed capital formation	...	...	...	...	...	...	...	...	...	...	...	...
E Indirect taxes paid, net	...	...	...	...	...	...	...	...	...	...	...	...
2 Property income	...	...	...	...	...	...	...	...	...	...	...	...
3 Subsidies	...	10.1	69.4	43.6	41.6	42.7	48.0	...	...	...	...	...
4 Other current transfers	...	20.1	25.3	31.1	23.1	24.3	42.5	...	...	...	...	...
A Social security benefits	...	...	...	...	...	...	...	...	...	...	...	...
B Social assistance grants	...	8.1	24.9	30.6	22.5	23.5	39.5	...	...	...	...	...
C Other	...	...	...	...	...	...	...	...	...	...	...	...
5 Net saving	...	1218.4	5386.1	7424.7	6834.3	6698.3	4672.3	...	...	...	...	...
Total Current Disbursements and Net Saving of General Government	...	1554.0	6216.6	8360.1	7812.6	7687.7	7275.0	...	...	...	...	...

Brunei Darussalam

1.10 Gross Domestic Product by Kind of Activity, in Current Prices

Million Brunei dollars

	1970	1975	1980	1981	1982	1983	1984	1985	1986	1987	1988	1989
1 Agriculture, hunting, forestry and fishing	...	37.4	67.3	64.3	77.2	79.6	85.7	94.3	105.7	119.2	135.2	...
2 Mining and quarrying	...	2093.8	7546.1	6407.5	6086.2	5183.2	4889.4	4592.7	2218.4	2533.0	2179.9	...
3 Manufacturing	...	324.1	1246.8	916.2	903.9	816.0	816.7	783.7	539.9	580.7	561.4	...
4 Electricity, gas and water	...	6.4	-9.1	10.7	16.5	15.8	15.3	31.2	42.9	59.0	81.1	...
5 Construction	...	55.8	168.1	216.5	264.6	265.5	207.0	159.2	157.6	156.1	154.5	...
6 Wholesale and retail trade, restaurants and hotels	...	70.0	955.1	933.6	975.3	880.1	909.8	821.5	649.4	687.3	746.8	...
7 Transport, storage and communication	...	22.5	58.0	61.7	133.2	143.8	116.6	136.1	175.8	227.0	293.1	...
8 Finance, insurance, real estate and business services	...	56.4	159.2	229.3	255.1	267.7	285.3	292.2	334.5	390.3	459.0	...
9 Community, social and personal services	...	127.9	421.4	467.1	532.0	612.7	855.7	918.7	1090.1	1293.3	1534.5	...
Total, Industries		2794.3	10612.9	9306.9	9244.0	8264.4	8181.5	7829.6	5314.3	6045.9	6145.5	
Producers of Government Services												
Other Producers												
Subtotal		2794.3	10612.9	9306.9	9244.0	8264.4	8181.5	7829.6	5314.3	6045.9	6145.5	
Less: Imputed bank service charge		23.9	59.3	82.4	118.5	101.1	113.1	77.2	87.1	98.3	111.0	
Plus: Import duties												
Plus: Value added tax												
Equals: Gross Domestic Product		2770.4	10553.6	9224.5	9125.5	8163.3	8068.5	7752.3	5227.2	5947.5	6034.5	

1.11 Gross Domestic Product by Kind of Activity, in Constant Prices

Million Brunei dollars

	1970	1975	1980	1981	1982	1983	1984	1985	1986	1987	1988	1989
					At constant prices of:1974							
1 Agriculture, hunting, forestry and fishing	...	35.3	42.0	35.8	39.9	40.6	41.7	43.1	44.5	46.2	46.6	...
2 Mining and quarrying	...	1992.7	2957.4	2287.6	2347.1	2333.7	2223.5	2193.3	2045.2	1894.1	1859.3	...
3 Manufacturing	...	299.3	404.1	254.1	243.4	245.6	252.7	239.0	217.6	277.5	252.7	...
4 Electricity, gas and water	...	6.2	-6.3	6.8	9.8	9.3	8.8	17.4	22.0	27.9	35.2	...
5 Construction	...	51.2	98.3	112.2	133.5	123.0	94.8	72.9	67.8	63.1	58.7	...
6 Wholesale and retail trade, restaurants and hotels	...	67.1	358.6	317.2	357.8	320.0	339.0	285.4	271.7	302.7	324.3	...
7 Transport, storage and communication	...	21.3	37.2	36.8	58.4	80.7	65.2	73.7	87.0	102.8	121.4	...
8 Finance, insurance, real estate and business services	...	52.5	146.0	149.4	158.2	175.6	184.0	172.2	180.9	191.2	203.7	...
9 Community, social and personal services	...	125.5	277.5	292.1	312.8	357.1	485.7	510.7	574.4	646.1	726.7	...
Total, Industries		2648.1	4314.8	3492.0	3660.9	3685.6	3695.4	3607.7	3511.1	3551.6	3628.6	
Producers of Government Services												
Other Producers												
Subtotal		2648.1	4314.8	3492.0	3660.9	3685.6	3695.4	3607.7	3511.1	3551.6	3628.6	
Less: Imputed bank service charge		22.5	55.8	77.4	111.4	95.1	106.3	72.6	73.9	75.3	76.7	
Plus: Import duties												
Plus: Value added tax												
Equals: Gross Domestic Product		2625.6	4259.0	3414.6	3549.5	3590.6	3588.8	3535.3	3437.1	3476.2	3551.9	

2.1 Government Final Consumption Expenditure by Function, in Current Prices

Million Brunei dollars

	1970	1975	1980	1981	1982	1983	1984	1985	1986	1987	1988	1989
1 General public services	...	106.3	137.4	178.0	209.4	227.1	1740.3	...	...	...	...	...
2 Defence	...	99.6	326.3	369.8	378.4	325.4	322.1	...	...	...	...	...
3 Public order and safety	...	15.5	42.5	48.2	50.2	55.0	67.9	...	...	...	...	...
4 Education	...	40.6	103.5	125.3	129.6	140.1	163.9	...	...	...	...	...
5 Health	...	13.2	34.3	42.6	45.6	52.7	65.5	...	...	...	...	...
6 Social security and welfare	...	0.3	1.5	1.7	1.8	2.0	3.3	...	...	...	...	...
7 Housing and community amenities	...	2.4	6.9	6.9	6.7	6.9	9.2	...	...	...	...	...
8 Recreational, cultural and religious affairs	...	10.9	35.4	38.7	44.3	52.5	58.2	...	...	...	...	...
9 Economic services	...	16.2	39.5	47.7	46.0	51.0	63.7	...	...	...	...	...

Brunei Darussalam

2.1 Government Final Consumption Expenditure by Function, in Current Prices
(Continued)

Million Brunei dollars

	1970	1975	1980	1981	1982	1983	1984	1985	1986	1987	1988	1989
A Fuel and energy	...	...	...	...	...	...	...	...	...	...	...	...
B Agriculture, forestry, fishing and hunting	...	5.0	11.6	13.4	14.3	15.3	19.0	...	...	...	...	...
C Mining, manufacturing and construction, except fuel and energy	...	0.1	-	-	-	-	-	...	...	...	...	...
D Transportation and communication	...	10.7	25.8	31.1	28.9	33.2	41.6	...	...	...	...	...
E Other economic affairs	...	0.4	2.1	3.2	2.8	2.4	3.1	...	...	...	...	...
10 Other functions	...	0.5	1.7	1.8	1.6	9.8	18.0	...	...	...	...	...
Total Government Final Consumption Expenditure	...	305.4	729.1	860.7	913.6	922.4	2512.1	...	...	...	...	...

Bulgaria

Source. Reply to the United Nations National Accounts Questionnaire from the Central Statistical Office to the Council of Ministers, Sofia. Official estimates and descriptions are published annually by the same Office in 'Statisticheski Godishnik' (Statistical Yearbook) and 'Expanded Socialist Reproduction'.

General note. The estimates shown in the following tables have been prepared in accordance with the System of Material Product Balances. Therefore, these estimates are not comparable in concept and coverage with those conforming to the United Nations System of National Accounts. It should be noted that beginning 1970, all activities relating to transport and communication are included in the sphere of material production. In addition, selected tables in accordance with the United Nations System of National Accounts (SNA) so far as the existing data would permit are also shown.

1.1 Expenditure on the Gross Domestic Product, in Current Prices

Million Bulgarian leva

	1970	1975	1980	1981	1982	1983	1984	1985	1986	1987	1988	1989
1 Government final consumption expenditure	...	...	1457.0	1729.0	2096.0	2356.0	2383.5	2756.5	2954.1	2712.8	2744.5	...
2 Private final consumption expenditure	...	...	16049.0	17217.0	17837.0	18309.5	19197.7	20031.4	21247.2	22659.6	23417.8	...
A Households a	...	...	13973.0	14847.0	15578.0	16045.4	16789.3	17385.1	18367.2	19208.5	19902.9	...
B Private non-profit institutions serving households	...	...	2076.0	2370.0	2259.0	2264.1	2408.4	2646.3	2880.0	3451.1	3514.9	...
3 Gross capital formation	...	...	8768.0	9872.0	9902.0	9806.9	10515.8	10494.8	12350.0	12020.2	13197.4	...
A Increase in stocks	...	...	1479.0	2182.0	1929.0	1832.0	2404.1	1882.0	3059.1	2202.9	2937.4	...
B Gross fixed capital formation	...	...	7289.0	7690.0	7973.0	7974.9	8111.7	8612.8	9290.9	9817.3	10260.0	...
4 Exports of goods and services b	...	...	-483.0	-1000.0	-822.0	-657.8	-426.1	-687.4	-2127.6	-861.3	-1014.6	...
5 Less: Imports of goods and services	...	...										...
Equals: Gross Domestic Product			25791.0	27818.0	29013.0	29814.6	31670.9	32595.3	34423.7	36531.3	38345.1	

a) Household consumption includes the consumption of goods and services of resident and non-resident units in the country, without adjustments with purchases abroad and net gifts in kind. received from abroad. The imputed rent of owner-occupied dwellings is estimated with the volume of the current costs. b) The estimates include net exports, losses and unbalanced sum.

1.3 Cost Components of the Gross Domestic Product

Million Bulgarian leva

	1970	1975	1980	1981	1982	1983	1984	1985	1986	1987	1988	1989
1 Indirect taxes, net a	...	...	...	...	...	...	...	...	...	...	...	...
2 Consumption of fixed capital	...	...	3559.0	3733.0	3799.0	4010.9	4360.5	4464.5	4761.1	5254.7	5891.9	...
3 Compensation of employees paid by resident producers to:	...	...	13094.0	14299.0	14908.0	15144.5	15775.7	16474.7	17524.6	18314.5	19247.8	...
4 Operating surplus a	...	...	9138.0	9786.0	10306.0	10659.2	11534.7	11656.1	12138.1	12962.1	13205.4	...
Equals: Gross Domestic Product	...	...	25791.0	27818.0	29013.0	29814.6	31670.9	32595.3	34423.8	36531.3	38345.1	...

a) Item 'Operating surplus' includes net indirect taxes.

1a Net Material Product by Use at Current Market Prices

Million Bulgarian leva

	1970	1975	1980	1981	1982	1983	1984	1985	1986	1987	1988	1989
1 Personal consumption a	6654.8	9074.5	13716.9	14574.5	15140.6	15768.4	16484.2	17054.4	18030.2	18823.2	19473.1	21024.0
2 Material consumption in the units of the non-material sphere serving individuals a	464.6	884.9	1212.9	1276.1	1464.6	1507.0	1607.8	1783.6	1929.4	2069.1	2036.8	2095.0
Consumption of the Population	7119.4	9959.4	14929.8	15850.6	16605.2	17275.4	18092.0	18838.0	19959.6	20892.3	21509.9	23119.0
3 Material consumption in the units of the non-material sphere serving the community as a whole	296.9	626.9	775.2	867.5	927.0	1023.4	1055.5	1224.6	1391.0	1508.6	1586.5	1689.5
4 Net fixed capital formation	1947.8	2799.1	3178.1	3143.1	3936.6	3633.0	3096.3	3011.4	2815.6	4946.4	2842.9	2524.6
5 Increase in material circulating assets and in stocks	1111.9	2295.3	2030.6	2996.3	2165.7	2163.0	3059.0	3018.9	4773.3	1819.1	4462.6	4990.5
6 Losses												
7 Exports of goods and material services	51.4	-1392.1	-405.1	-924.4	-785.0	-615.8	-395.8	-642.4	-2088.1	-828.4	-979.3	-1483.9
8 Less: Imports of goods and material services												
Net Material Product b	10527.4	14288.6	20508.6	21933.1	22849.5	23479.0	24907.0	25450.5	26851.4	28338.0	29422.6	30839.7

a) All activities relating to transport and communication are included in the sphere of material production. b) The volume of net material product at current prices is influenced by depreciations, beginning 1977 estimated by new norms and on the basis of replacing value of the fixed assets.

Bulgaria

1b Net Material Product by Use at Constant Market Prices

Index numbers 1980=100

	1970	1975	1980	1981	1982	1983	1984	1985	1986	1987	1988	1989
			\multicolumn{10}{c}{At constant prices of:1980}								
1 Personal consumption	...	...	100.0	105.0	108.8	111.5	116.6	118.9	122.0	126.9	129.9	133.5
2 Material consumption in the units of the non-material sphere serving individuals	...	...	100.0	104.7	111.3	113.9	123.4	133.8	141.8	151.7	148.8	151.5
Consumption of the Population	...	...	100.0	104.9	108.9	111.6	117.1	120.1	123.6	128.9	131.5	135.1
3 Material consumption in the units of the non-material sphere serving the community as a whole	...	...	100.0	111.4	113.7	125.2	130.0	149.5	168.5	182.3	191.1	201.4
4 Net fixed capital formation	...	...	...	...	...	...	...	...	...	...	...	...
5 Increase in material circulating assets and in stocks	...	...	...	...	...	...	...	...	...	...	...	...
6 Losses	...	...	...	...	...	...	...	...	...	...	...	...
7 Exports of goods and material services	...	...	...	...	...	...	...	...	...	...	...	...
8 Less: Imports of goods and material services	...	...	...	...	...	...	...	...	...	...	...	...
Net Material Product	...	...	100.0	105.0	109.4	112.7	117.9	120.0	126.4	132.8	136.0	135.6

2a Net Material Product by Kind of Activity of the Material Sphere in Current Market Prices

Million Bulgarian leva

	1970	1975	1980	1981	1982	1983	1984	1985	1986	1987	1988	1989
1 Agriculture and forestry [a]	2378.9	3141.3	3463.4	4267.0	4601.0	3945.2	4599.0	3512.2	4062.1	3820.0	3820.2	3888.5
A Agriculture and livestock	2309.9	3062.6	3384.0	4185.6	4519.8	3864.3	4511.8	3425.1	3957.2	3712.1	3712.0	3798.2
B Forestry	69.0	78.7	79.4	81.4	81.2	80.9	87.2	87.1	104.9	107.9	108.2	90.3
C Other	...	...	...	...	...	...	...	...	...	...	...	...
2 Industrial activity	5167.5	7291.1	9938.8	10441.2	12237.6	13265.4	14090.7	15169.9	16676.8	16649.7	17088.3	17624.5
3 Construction	917.2	1256.7	1904.5	2063.0	2207.7	2270.4	2366.8	2489.6	2564.3	2674.7	2780.3	2859.1
4 Wholesale and retail trade and restaurants and other eating and drinking places [b]	1040.3	1119.9	2820.5	2766.9	1383.6	1528.5	1328.0	1801.0	1227.0	2499.8	2471.2	2910.3
5 Transport and communication [c]	730.3	1172.3	1659.2	1808.5	1795.7	1845.1	1911.7	1807.4	1752.2	2058.2	2596.4	2795.1
A Transport [c]	644.6	1035.3	1462.4	1599.1	1574.6	1601.5	1644.5	1516.2	1309.8	1567.6	2069.1	2224.6
B Communication [c]	85.7	137.0	196.8	209.4	221.1	243.6	267.2	291.2	442.4	490.6	527.3	570.5
6 Other activities of the material sphere [d]	293.2	307.3	722.2	586.5	623.9	624.4	610.8	670.4	569.0	635.6	666.2	762.2
Net material product [e]	10527.4	14288.6	20508.6	21933.1	22849.5	23479.0	24907.0	25450.5	26851.4	28338.0	29422.6	30839.7

a) Item 'Agriculture and forestry' excludes hunting, fishing and logging. When organized, they are included in item 'Industrial activity', when non-organized, they are included in item 'Other activities of the material sphere'. Since 1986, non-organized hunting and fishing are included in forestry.
b) Item 'Wholesale and retail trade and restaurants and other eating and drinking places' includes material and technical supply.
c) All activities relating to transport and communication are included in the sphere of material production.
d) Item 'Other activities of the material sphere' includes such activities as canning of processed meat, preservation of fruits and vegetables (excluding pickles) etc. by the population. Also included are activities for collection and purchase of usable scraps.
e) The volume of net material product at current prices is influenced by depreciations, beginning 1977 estimated by new norms and on the basis of replacing value of the fixed assets.

2b Net Material Product by Kind of Activity of the Material Sphere in Constant Market Prices

Index numbers 1980=100

	1970	1975	1980	1981	1982	1983	1984	1985	1986	1987	1988	1989
			\multicolumn{10}{c}{At constant prices of:1957}								
1 Agriculture and forestry [a]	118.1	128.3	100.0	104.4	110.4	92.7	103.5	82.6	100.5	86.2	84.9	80.5
A Agriculture and livestock	119.7	129.6	100.0	104.5	110.6	92.6	103.4	82.1	100.5	85.8	84.3	80.3
B Forestry	86.8	99.1	100.0	102.5	102.3	101.9	109.8	109.7	109.7	113.0	117.5	97.4
C Other	...	...	...									...
2 Industrial activity	46.2	72.1	100.0	105.0	115.3	125.1	133.2	140.0	148.0	156.3	159.7	155.5

Bulgaria

2b Net Material Product by Kind of Activity of the Material Sphere in Constant Market Prices
(Continued)

Index numbers 1980=100

	1970	1975	1980	1981	1982	1983	1984	1985	1986	1987	1988	1989
			At constant prices of:1957									
3 Construction	58.6	80.0	100.0	108.3	115.9	119.1	124.1	130.1	132.7	138.9	144.5	144.4
4 Wholesale and retail trade and restaurants and other eating and drinking places [b]	17.8	36.3	100.0	101.0	68.0	81.0	63.7	85.1	70.0	109.0	108.8	128.6
5 Transport and communication [c]	45.2	76.8	100.0	109.8	115.1	118.3	122.6	122.2	126.8	132.8	147.5	157.4
A Transport [c]	44.9	76.9	100.0	110.3	115.5	117.5	120.7	119.1	122.6	128.9	144.1	153.2
B Communication [c]	47.0	75.3	100.0	106.4	112.4	123.9	135.9	144.1	157.2	161.3	173.4	189.7
6 Other activities of the material sphere [d]	49.9	55.5	100.0	100.1	104.3	99.5	94.2	95.7	86.2	98.6	99.4	103.7
Net material product	50.9	74.2	100.0	105.0	109.4	112.7	117.9	120.0	126.4	132.8	136.0	135.6

a) Item 'Agriculture and forestry' excludes hunting, fishing and logging. When organized, they are included in item 'Industrial activity', when non-organized, they are included in item 'Other activities of the material sphere'. Since 1986, non-organized hunting and fishing are included in forestry.
b) Item 'Wholesale and retail trade and restaurants and other eating and drinking places' includes material and technical supply.
c) All activities relating to transport and communication are included in the sphere of material production.
d) Item 'Other activities of the material sphere' includes such activities as canning of processed meat, preservation of fruits and vegetables (excluding pickles) etc. by the population. Also included are activities for collection and purchase of usable scraps.

3 Primary Incomes by Kind of Activity of the Material Sphere in Current Market Prices

Million Bulgarian leva

	1980		1981		1982		1983		1984		1985	
	Primary Income of the Population	Primary Income of Enterprises	Primary Income of the Population	Primary Income of Enterprises	Primary Income of the Population	Primary Income of Enterprises	Primary Income of the Population	Primary Income of Enterprises	Primary Income of the Population	Primary Income of Enterprises	Primary Income of the Population	Primary Income of Enterprises
1 Agriculture and forestry [a]	2911.1	552.3	3400.2	866.8	3567.6	1033.4	3525.1	420.1	3785.2	813.8	3644.4	-132.2
A Agriculture and livestock	2877.8	506.2	3366.8	818.8	3532.7	987.1	3488.9	375.4	3748.1	763.7	3607.3	-182.2
B Forestry	33.3	46.1	33.4	48.0	34.9	46.3	36.2	44.7	37.1	50.1	37.1	50.0
C Other	-	-	-	-	-	-	-	-	-	-	-	-
2 Industrial activity	3792.1	6146.7	4092.8	6348.4	4300.1	7937.5	4490.0	8775.4	4686.6	9404.1	4844.4	10325.5
3 Construction	1209.5	695.0	1235.2	827.8	1293.8	913.9	1341.4	929.0	1365.5	1001.3	1447.6	1042.0
4 Wholesale and retail trade and restaurants and other eating and drinking places [b]	696.1	2124.4	736.3	2030.6	762.9	620.7	775.1	753.4	792.8	535.2	816.9	984.1
5 Transport and communication [c]	814.8	844.4	885.0	923.5	911.9	883.8	938.4	906.7	956.6	955.1	954.8	852.6
A Transport [c]	736.2	726.2	802.9	796.2	824.4	750.2	844.7	756.8	855.4	789.1	848.4	667.8
B Communication [c]	78.6	118.2	82.1	127.3	87.5	133.6	93.7	149.9	101.2	166.0	106.4	184.8
6 Other activities of the material sphere [d]	628.3	93.9	480.3	106.2	473.6	150.3	490.5	133.9	497.3	113.5	546.8	123.6
Total	10051.9	10456.7	10829.8	11103.3	11309.9	11539.6	11560.5	11918.5	12084.0	12823.0	12254.9	13195.6

	1986		1987		1988		1989	
	Primary Income of the Population	Primary Income of Enterprises	Primary Income of the Population	Primary Income of Enterprises	Primary Income of the Population	Primary Income of Enterprises	Primary Income of the Population	Primary Income of Enterprises
1 Agriculture and forestry [a]	3889.9	172.2	3850.5	-30.5	3964.0	-143.8	4127.7	-239.2
A Agriculture and livestock	3830.8	126.4	3793.5	-81.4	3904.9	-192.9	4057.5	-259.3
B Forestry	59.1	45.8	57.0	50.9	59.1	49.1	70.2	20.1
C Other	-	-	-	-	-	-	-	-
2 Industrial activity	5148.4	11528.4	5507.9	11141.8	5850.6	11237.7	6070.8	11553.7
3 Construction	1519.1	1045.2	1613.9	1060.8	1635.7	1144.6	1777.0	1082.1
4 Wholesale and retail trade and restaurants and other eating and drinking places [b]	872.2	354.8	905.9	1593.9	989.8	1481.4	1047.8	1862.5
5 Transport and communication [c]	1010.2	742.0	1021.8	1036.4	1086.3	1510.1	1255.9	1539.2
A Transport [c]	898.9	410.9	902.5	665.1	959.4	1109.7	1108.9	1115.7
B Communication [c]	111.3	331.1	119.3	371.3	126.9	400.4	147.0	423.5
6 Other activities of the material sphere [d]	512.6	56.4	550.7	84.9	589.8	76.4	593.3	168.9
Total	12952.4	13899.0	13450.7	14887.3	14116.2	15306.4	14872.5	15967.2

a) Item 'Agriculture and forestry' excludes hunting, fishing and logging. When organized, they are included in item 'Industrial activity', when non-organized, they are included in item 'Other activities of the material sphere'. Since 1986, non-organized hunting and fishing are included in forestry.
b) Item 'Wholesale and retail trade and restaurants and other eating and drinking places' includes material and technical supply.
c) All activities relating to transport and communication are included in the sphere of material production.
d) Item 'Other activities of the material sphere' includes such activities as canning of processed meat, preservation of fruits and vegetables (excluding pickles) etc. by the population. Also included are activities for collection and purchase of usable scraps.

Bulgaria

5a Supply and Disposition of Goods and Material Services in Current Market Prices

Million Bulgarian leva

	Gross Output at Producers Prices	Trade Margins and Transport Charges	Gross Output at Market Prices	Imports	Total Supply and Disposition	Intermediate Material Consumption including Depreciation	Final Consumption	Net Capital Formation	Losses	Exports
1980										
1 Agriculture and forestry [a]	7261.6	309.0	7570.6	125.6	7696.2	6131.8	898.8	272.8	54.6	338.2
A Agriculture and livestock	7178.8	309.0	7487.8	125.6	7613.4	6094.2	898.8	227.6	54.9	337.9
B Forestry	82.8	...	82.8	...	82.8	37.6	...	45.2	-0.3	0.3
C Other	...	...	...	...	...	...	...	...	...	...
2 Industrial activity	38139.9	5104.2	43244.1	6416.0	49660.1	29918.2	13150.7	1447.6	-994.8	6138.4
3 Construction	5311.7	...	5311.7	...	5311.7	885.8	574.3	3697.3	154.3	...
4 Transport and communication [b]	1152.8	334.9	1487.7	239.8	1727.5	336.8	937.5	...	9.7	443.5
A Transport [b]	869.3	334.9	1204.2	235.7	1439.9	221.8	778.8	...	-2.4	441.7
B Communication [b]	283.5	...	283.5	4.1	287.6	115.0	158.7	...	12.1	1.8
5 Other activities of the material sphere [c]	286.3	1.6	287.9	1.9	289.8	120.8	143.7	17.7	-19.7	27.3
Total [d]	52152.3	5749.7	57902.0	6783.3	64685.3	37393.4	15705.0	5435.4	-795.9	6947.4
1981										
1 Agriculture and forestry [a]	8440.3	297.4	8737.7	210.3	8948.0	7141.0	1099.5	447.0	-40.6	301.1
A Agriculture and livestock	8354.5	297.4	8651.9	210.2	8862.1	7104.5	1099.5	397.7	-40.4	300.8
B Forestry	85.8	...	85.8	0.1	85.9	36.5	...	49.3	-0.2	0.3
C Other	...	...	...	...	...	...	...	...	...	...
2 Industrial activity	40827.5	5246.7	46074.2	7535.7	53667.9	31636.9	13833.3	2045.0	-385.8	6538.5
3 Construction	5624.3	...	5624.3	...	5624.3	1101.7	662.5	3638.2	221.9	-
4 Transport and communication [b]	1221.8	403.1	1624.9	296.2	1921.1	385.7	994.9	...	27.5	513.0
A Transport [b]	913.7	403.1	1316.8	291.9	1608.7	272.4	822.7	...	3.1	510.5
B Communication [b]	308.1	...	308.1	4.3	312.4	113.3	172.2	...	24.4	2.5
5 Other activities of the material sphere [c]	302.6	-2.6	300.0	6.1	306.1	162.7	127.9	9.2	-6.8	13.1
Total [d]	56416.5	5944.6	62361.1	8048.3	70467.4	40428.0	16718.1	6139.4	-183.8	7365.7
1982										
1 Agriculture and forestry [a]	9049.8	305.7	9355.5	93.6	9449.1	9449.3	1157.2	530.7	-0.2	406.2
A Agriculture and livestock	8963.7	305.7	9269.4	93.5	9362.9	9364.4	1157.2	485.5	-1.5	406.0
B Forestry	86.1	...	86.1	0.1	86.2	84.9	-	45.2	1.3	0.2
C Other	...	...	...	...	...	...	...	...	...	...
2 Industrial activity	45402.1	3157.2	48559.3	8161.4	56788.9	57265.4	14447.2	1759.1	-476.5	7332.1
3 Construction	5792.8	...	5792.8	...	5792.8	5705.9	717.1	3768.5	86.9	-
4 Transport and communication [b]	2443.9	...	2443.9	345.1	2789.0	2781.0	1090.8	43.8	8.0	513.6
A Transport [b]	2117.1	...	2117.1	342.1	2459.2	2464.8	903.2	43.8	-5.6	511.0
B Communication [b]	326.8	...	326.8	3.0	329.8	316.2	187.6	...	13.6	2.6
5 Other activities of the material sphere [c]	356.0	1.8	357.8	2.5	360.3	354.5	119.9	0.2	5.8	9.9
Total [d]	63044.6	3464.7	66509.3	8602.6	75180.1	75556.1	17532.2	6102.3	-376.0	8261.8
1983										
1 Agriculture and forestry [a]	8541.4	302.6	8844.0	69.1	8913.1	7389.8	1160.4	18.9	1.4	342.6
A Agriculture and livestock	8454.8	302.6	8757.4	69.0	8826.4	7352.1	1160.4	-27.8	-0.8	342.5
B Forestry	86.6	...	86.6	0.1	86.7	37.7	...	46.7	2.2	0.1
C Other	...	...	...	...	...	...	...	...	...	...
2 Industrial activity	47743.7	3391.0	51134.7	8740.0	59943.5	35302.6	15118.8	1925.4	-72.0	7668.7
3 Construction	5971.6	...	5971.6	...	5971.6	1255.1	768.4	3808.2	139.9	-
4 Transport and communication [b]	2470.3	...	2470.3	317.4	2787.7	1123.6	1129.0	40.0	41.6	453.5
A Transport [b]	2111.9	...	2111.9	313.6	2425.5	990.7	924.0	40.0	20.3	450.5
B Communication [b]	358.4	...	358.4	3.8	362.2	132.9	205.0	-	21.3	3.0
5 Other activities of the material sphere [c]	364.3	-2.8	361.5	3.6	365.1	232.0	122.2	3.5	-2.9	10.3
Total [d]	65091.3	3690.8	68782.1	9130.1	77981.0	45303.1	18298.8	5796.0	108.0	8475.1

Bulgaria

5a Supply and Disposition of Goods and Material Services in Current Market Prices
(Continued)

Million Bulgarian leva

		Supply				Disposition				
		Gross Output at Producers Prices	Trade Margins and Transport Charges	Gross Output at Market Prices	Imports	Total Supply and Disposition	Intermediate Material Consumption including Depreciation	Final Consumption	Net Capital Formation	Losses	Exports
						1984					
1	Agriculture and forestry [a]	9432.6	338.6	9771.2	66.3	9837.5	7838.8	1262.5	399.5	49.7	275.9
	A Agriculture and livestock	9341.9	338.5	9680.4	66.1	9746.5	7798.2	1262.5	350.5	48.5	275.7
	B Forestry	90.7	0.1	90.8	0.2	91.0	40.6	...	49.0	1.2	0.2
	C Other	...	...	...	...	...	...	...	...	...	...
2	Industrial activity	50135.3	3217.0	53352.3	9527.7	62944.8	36757.6	15001.4	1929.1	-377.6	8883.4
3	Construction	6256.9	-	6256.9	-	6256.9	1328.6	594.6	3786.7	326.5	-
4	Transport and communication [b]	2512.5	...	2512.5	320.8	2833.3	1181.9	1119.3	41.3	103.3	322.0
	A Transport [b]	2119.6	...	2119.6	318.3	2437.9	1027.5	941.2	41.3	83.0	318.5
	B Communication [b]	392.9	...	392.9	2.5	395.4	154.4	178.1	...	20.3	3.5
5	Other activities of the material sphere [c]	370.3	-2.6	367.7	4.8	372.5	246.7	114.2	-1.3	-3.7	9.1
	Total [d]	68707.6	3553.0	72260.6	9919.6	82245.0	47353.6	18092.0	6155.3	98.2	9490.4
						1985					
1	Agriculture and forestry [a]	8372.0	385.2	8757.2	202.3	8959.5	7522.6	1302.0	-201.5	91.1	245.3
	A Agriculture and livestock	8279.4	385.2	8664.6	202.2	8866.8	7481.4	1302.0	-254.2	92.6	245.0
	B Forestry	92.6	...	92.6	0.1	92.7	41.2	...	52.7	-1.5	0.3
	C Other	...	...	...	...	...	...	...	...	...	...
2	Industrial activity	53335.9	3706.7	57042.6	10025.0	67152.4	39095.9	16720.1	2358.8	-603.3	9580.9
3	Construction	6437.9	-	6437.9	-	6437.9	1420.2	855.7	3825.4	336.6	-
4	Transport and communication [b]	2549.5	...	2549.5	337.9	2887.4	1422.9	1050.8	52.5	66.6	294.6
	A Transport [b]	2126.1	...	2126.1	335.6	2461.7	1257.5	813.3	52.5	47.3	291.1
	B Communication [b]	423.4	...	423.4	2.3	425.7	165.4	237.5	-	19.3	3.5
5	Other activities of the material sphere [c]	372.7	0.1	372.8	5.6	378.4	247.9	134.0	-4.9	-5.7	7.1
	Total [d]	71068.0	4092.0	75160.0	10570.8	85815.6	49709.5	20062.6	6030.3	-114.7	10127.9
						1986					
1	Agriculture and forestry [a]	9365.8	415.9	9781.7	316.5	10098.2	7876.0	1338.8	367.4	290.1	225.9
	A Agriculture and livestock	9255.2	411.6	9666.8	316.4	9983.2	7833.3	1326.1	314.3	288.4	221.1
	B Forestry	110.6	4.3	114.9	0.1	115.0	42.7	12.7	53.1	1.7	4.8
	C Other	...	...	...	...	...	...	...	...	...	...
2	Industrial activity	57346.2	3225.0	60571.2	11466.2	72127.1	41992.7	17838.6	3214.0	-461.5	9543.3
3	Construction	6658.2	-	6658.2	...	6658.2	1533.0	903.9	4007.5	213.8	-
4	Transport and communication [b]	2860.1	...	2860.1	402.9	3263.0	1703.9	1169.0	...	136.1	254.0
	A Transport [b]	2268.7	...	2268.7	398.1	2666.8	1456.8	836.8	...	124.0	249.2
	B Communication [b]	591.4	...	591.4	4.8	596.2	247.1	332.2	...	12.1	4.8
5	Other activities of the material sphere [c]	315.7	1.3	317.0	2.4	319.4	231.2	100.3	...	-13.6	1.5
	Total [d]	76546.0	3642.2	80188.2	12188.0	92465.9	53336.8	21350.6	7588.9	164.9	10024.7
						1987					
1	Agriculture and forestry [a]	9208.3	391.7	9600.0	133.7	9733.7	7907.6	1467.5	-89.2	252.1	195.7
	A Agriculture and livestock	9094.4	389.7	9484.1	131.2	9615.3	7858.5	1455.8	-113.3	226.2	188.1
	B Forestry	113.9	2.0	115.9	2.5	118.4	49.1	11.7	24.1	25.9	7.6
	C Other	...	...	...	...	...	...	...	...	...	...
2	Industrial activity	60035.8	4735.9	64771.7	11443.4	76303.8	44802.8	18623.9	3062.8	75.0	9739.3
3	Construction	6942.4	-	6942.4	-	6942.4	1675.7	930.8	3791.9	544.0	-
4	Transport and communication [b]	2993.1	...	2993.1	380.2	3373.3	1694.6	1267.2	...	94.5	317.0
	A Transport [b]	2335.6	...	2335.6	376.8	2712.4	1419.8	904.7	...	76.8	311.1
	B Communication [b]	657.5	...	657.5	3.4	660.9	274.8	362.5	...	17.7	5.9
5	Other activities of the material sphere [c]	365.7	0.6	366.3	3.1	369.4	254.8	111.5	...	-0.2	3.3
	Total [d]	79545.3	5128.2	84673.5	11960.4	96722.6	56335.5	22400.9	6765.5	965.4	10255.3

a) Item 'Agriculture and forestry' excludes hunting, fishing and logging. When organized, they are included in item 'Industrial activity', when non-organized, they are included in item 'Other activities of the material sphere'. Since 1986, non-organized hunting and fishing are included in forestry.
b) All activities relating to transport and communication are included in the sphere of material production.
c) Item 'Other activities of the material sphere' includes such activities as canning of processed meat, preservation of fruits and vegetables (excluding pickles) etc. by the population. Also included are activities for collection and purchase of usable scraps.
d) Beginning 1980, total supply (column 5) includes productions taken out of the country.

Bulgaria

7b Final Consumption at Constant Market Prices

Index numbers 1980=100

	1970	1975	1980	1981	1982	1983	1984	1985	1986	1987	1988	1989
				At constant prices of:1980								
1 Personal consumption	...	...	100.0	105.0	108.8	111.5	116.6	118.9	122.0	126.9	129.9	133.5
			a) Material Consumption in the Units of the Non-Material Sphere Serving Individuals									
2 Total non-material sphere serving individuals	...	...	100.0	104.7	111.3	113.9	123.4	133.8	141.8	151.7	148.8	151.5
			b) Material Consumption in the Units of the Non-Material Sphere Serving the Community as a Whole									
3 Total non-material sphere serving the community as a whole	...	...	100.0	111.4	113.7	125.2	130.0	149.5	168.5	182.3	191.1	201.4
Final consumption	...	...	100.0	105.3	109.2	112.4	117.9	121.8	126.2	132.0	134.9	138.8

9a Total Consumption of the Population in Current Market Prices

Million Bulgarian leva

	1970	1975	1980	1981	1982	1983	1984	1985	1986	1987	1988	1989
					By Object							
1 Housing except owner-occupied, communal and miscellaneous personal services	...	...	...	...	...	...	...	...	...	...	...	...
2 Education, culture and art	...	...	...	...	...	...	...	...	...	...	...	...
3 Health and social welfare services and sport	...	...	...	...	...	...	...	...	...	...	...	...
Total consumption of non-material services	...	...	3243.7	3632.3	3895.0	4049.1	4313.3	4741.4	5014.4	5322.9	5210.3	...
4 Personal consumption of goods and material services excluding depreciation of dwellings [a]	1320.8	2186.8	13959.8	14737.8	15343.2	15951.1	16634.9	17174.3	18097.0	18895.0	19633.4	...
Statistical discrepancy	6879.4	9202.2	...	...	...	...	...	...	...	...	...	...
Total consumption of the population [a]	8200.2	11389.0	17203.5	18370.1	19238.2	20000.2	20948.2	21915.7	23111.4	24217.9	24843.7	...
					By Commodity and Service							
1 Food	3018.8	3651.9	5617.1	5985.6	6204.2	6478.6	6814.5	7111.7	7436.9	7697.0	7806.6	
2 Beverages, coffee and tea	631.3	892.8	1506.2	1601.8	1620.3	1681.8	1769.7	1783.4	1889.0	1834.2	1936.6	
3 Tobacco	183.2	275.0	395.3	467.8	481.5	542.5	572.0	601.2	627.3	633.8	625.8	
4 Clothing and footwear	1144.8	1564.4	1949.1	1990.4	2037.0	2140.1	2196.6	2315.9	2416.2	2471.9	2503.4	
5 Gross rent	83.7	76.1	145.4	153.4	156.7	157.8	166.0	165.2	179.2	183.1	212.0	
6 Fuel, electricity, water and gas	160.8	223.9	627.6	451.5	478.7	459.8	495.8	569.2	622.2	669.2	693.1	
7 Furniture and household equipment	512.2	734.7	943.7	1065.3	1132.2	1192.7	1209.4	1252.1	1318.1	1352.7	1451.5	
8 Health	350.5	544.3	808.5	1005.9	1063.9	1100.7	1197.3	1288.6	1368.7	1486.0	1523.8	
9 Transport and communication	526.2	987.3	1700.2	1816.3	1910.2	1931.8	2043.9	1945.0	2083.8	2199.3	2590.1	
10 Education, recreation, sport	...	...	...	...	...	...	...	...	...	...	...	
11 Other	1588.7	2438.6	3510.4	3832.1	4153.5	4314.4	4483.0	4883.4	5170.0	5690.7	5500.8	
Total consumption of the population [a]	8200.2	11389.0	17203.5	18370.1	19238.2	20000.2	20948.2	21915.7	23111.4	24217.9	24843.7	
					By Mode of Acquisition							
1 Purchased	6019.3	8247.6	12288.3	12831.4	13407.5	13957.7	14593.1	15120.5	16053.3	16867.4	18097.8	
2 Free of charge	1152.9	2057.9	3030.3	3459.3	3744.8	3917.5	4129.9	4455.1	4669.0	4943.8	4418.5	
3 From own production	1028.0	1083.5	1884.9	2079.4	2085.9	2125.0	2225.2	2340.1	2389.1	2406.7	2327.4	
Total consumption of the population [a]	8200.2	11389.0	17203.5	18370.1	19238.2	20000.2	20948.2	21915.7	23111.4	24217.9	24843.7	...

a) The estimates include the depreciation of dwellings.

9b Total Consumption of the Population in Constant Market Prices

Index numbers 1980=100

	1970	1975	1980	1981	1982	1983	1984	1985	1986	1987	1988	1989
				At constant prices of:1980								
					By Object							
1 Housing except owner-occupied, communal and miscellaneous personal services	...	...	...	...	...	...	...	...	...	...	...	...
2 Education, culture and art	...	...	...	...	...	...	...	...	...	...	...	...
3 Health and social welfare services and sport	...	...	...	...	...	...	...	...	...	...	...	...
Total consumption of non-material services	40.7	67.4	100.0	112.0	120.1	124.8	133.0	146.2	154.6	164.1	160.6	...

Bulgaria

9b Total Consumption of the Population in Constant Market Prices
(Continued)

Index numbers 1980=100

	1970	1975	1980	1981	1982	1983	1984	1985	1986	1987	1988	1989
				At constant prices of:1980								
4 Personal consumption of goods and material services excluding depreciation of dwellings	49.3	65.9	100.0	105.6	109.9	114.3	119.2	123.0	129.6	135.4	140.6	...
Total consumption of the population	47.7	66.2	100.0	106.8	111.8	116.3	121.7	127.4	134.3	140.8	144.4	...
				By Commodity and Service								
1 Food	53.7	65.0	100.0	106.6	110.5	115.3	121.3	126.6	132.4	137.0	139.0	...
2 Beverages, coffee and tea	41.9	59.3	100.0	106.3	107.6	111.7	117.5	118.4	125.4	121.8	128.6	...
3 Tobacco	46.3	69.6	100.0	118.3	121.8	137.2	144.7	152.1	158.7	160.3	158.3	...
4 Clothing and footwear	58.7	80.3	100.0	102.1	104.5	109.8	112.7	118.8	124.0	126.8	128.4	...
5 Gross rent	57.6	52.3	100.0	105.5	107.8	108.5	114.2	113.6	123.2	125.9	145.8	...
6 Fuel, electricity, water and gas	25.6	35.7	100.0	71.9	76.3	73.3	79.0	90.7	99.1	106.6	110.4	...
7 Furniture and household equipment	54.3	77.9	100.0	112.9	120.0	126.4	128.2	132.7	139.7	143.3	153.8	...
8 Health	43.4	67.3	100.0	124.4	131.6	136.1	148.1	159.4	169.3	183.8	188.5	...
9 Transport and communication	30.9	58.1	100.0	106.8	112.4	113.6	120.2	114.4	122.6	129.4	152.3	...
10 Education, recreation, sport	...	...	...	...	...	...	...	...	...	...	...	...
11 Other	45.3	69.5	100.0	109.2	118.3	122.9	127.7	139.1	147.3	162.1	156.7	...
Total consumption of the population	47.7	66.2	100.0	106.8	111.8	116.3	121.8	127.4	134.3	140.8	144.4	...
				By Mode of Acquisition								
1 Purchased	49.0	67.1	100.0	104.4	109.1	113.6	118.8	123.0	130.6	137.3	147.3	...
2 Free of charge	38.0	67.9	100.0	114.2	123.6	129.3	136.3	147.0	154.1	163.1	145.8	...
3 From own production	54.5	57.5	100.0	110.3	110.7	112.7	118.1	124.1	126.7	127.7	123.5	...
Total consumption of the population	...	66.2	100.0	106.8	111.8	116.3	121.8	127.4	134.3	140.8	144.4	...

Burkina Faso

Source. Reply to the United Nations National Accounts Questionnaire from the Institut National de la Statistique et de la Demographie, Ouagadougou. Official estimates are published by the Institut in 'Comptes Nationaux du Burkina Faso'.

General note. The estimates shown in the following tables have been prepared in accordance with the United Nations System of National Accounts so far as the existing data would permit.

1.1 Expenditure on the Gross Domestic Product, in Current Prices

Million CFA francs

	1970	1975	1980	1981	1982	1983	1984	1985	1986	1987	1988	1989
1 Government final consumption expenditure	7028	23228	47439	60900	72461	78795	76922	72602	...	...	...	...
2 Private final consumption expenditure	77102	113892	231272	278651	315135	327566	308282	411900	...	...	...	...
A Households	...	...	228324	274333	310223	322316	300014	...				
B Private non-profit institutions serving households	...	...	2948	4318	4912	5250	8268	...				
3 Gross capital formation	9750	23867	72444	77154	91815	92987	94105	128992	...	...	...	...
A Increase in stocks	2250	6168	6445	7205	7757	2633	3277	15501				
B Gross fixed capital formation	7500	17699	65999	69949	84058	90354	90828	113491				
4 Exports of goods and services	8615	18441	43571	53563	56185	55853	88094	79155				
5 Less: Imports of goods and services	19640	52460	122708	146061	175993	174188	176837	223336				
Equals: Gross Domestic Product	82854	126967	272018	324207	359604	381013	390565	469313	503500	...	...	...

1.2 Expenditure on the Gross Domestic Product, in Constant Prices

Million CFA francs

	1970	1975	1980	1981	1982	1983	1984	1985	1986	1987	1988	1989
		At constant prices of:										
		1970						1975				
1 Government final consumption expenditure	7028	16270 / 23228	24477	24395	27520	25676	24717	...	...	...	...	...
2 Private final consumption expenditure	77102	87678 / 113892	144195	156942	157835	148672	140072	...				
3 Gross capital formation	9750	19717 / 23867	39178	39363	41480	35267	33684	...				
A Increase in stocks	2250	3797 / 6168	4027	2365	2665	715	402					
B Gross fixed capital formation	7500	15920 / 17699	35151	36998	38815	34552	33282					
4 Exports of goods and services	8615	11383 / 18441	30279	34226	28798	25653	27056					
5 Less: Imports of goods and services	19640	31600 / 52460	89048	95527	93963	81346	74880					
Equals: Gross Domestic Product	82854	103448 / 126967	149080	159400	161671	153922	150650					

1.3 Cost Components of the Gross Domestic Product

Million CFA francs

	1970	1975	1980	1981	1982	1983	1984	1985	1986	1987	1988	1989
1 Indirect taxes, net	7284	11645	19443	22988	27007	24084	22530	28498	...	...	...	...
A Indirect taxes	7284	12011	...	...	...	...	...	...				
B Less: Subsidies	...	366	...	...	...	...	...	...				
2 Consumption of fixed capital	...	...	...	...	...	...	...	...				
3 Compensation of employees paid by resident producers to:	...	...	71443	84051	99093	110072	114251	115346				
4 Operating surplus	...	...	181132	217167	233504	246858	253784	312038				
Equals: Gross Domestic Product	82854	126967	272018	324207	359604	381013	390565	455882				

1.4 General Government Current Receipts and Disbursements

Million CFA francs

	1970	1975	1980	1981	1982	1983	1984	1985	1986	1987	1988	1989
					Receipts							
1 Operating surplus	...	...	...	...	...	...	...	...	...	...	...	...
2 Property and entrepreneurial income	...	...	...	...	...	...	...	...	...	...	...	...
3 Taxes, fees and contributions	...	...	...	...	...	...	56142	...	...	...	...	...
A Indirect taxes	...	...	...	...	...	...	33500	...				
B Direct taxes	...	...	...	...	...	...	12510	...				
C Social security contributions	...	...	...	...	...	...	7654	...				
D Compulsory fees, fines and penalties	...	...	...	...	...	...	2478	...				

Burkina Faso

1.4 General Government Current Receipts and Disbursements
(Continued)

Million CFA francs

	1970	1975	1980	1981	1982	1983	1984	1985	1986	1987	1988	1989
4 Other current transfers	...	...	...	...	...	...	23586	...	...	...	...	...
Total Current Receipts of General Government	...	...	...	...	...	...	79728	...	...	...	...	...

Disbursements

	1970	1975	1980	1981	1982	1983	1984	1985	1986	1987	1988	1989
1 Government final consumption expenditure	...	...	...	...	...	...	57689	...	...	...	...	...
2 Property income	...	...	...	...	...	...	3924	...	...	...	...	...
3 Subsidies	...	...	...	...	...	...	350	...	...	...	...	...
4 Other current transfers	...	...	...	...	...	...	8175	...	...	...	...	...
A Social security benefits	...	...	...	...	...	...	807	...	...	...	...	...
B Social assistance grants	...	...	...	...	...	...	3555	...	...	...	...	...
C Other	...	...	...	...	...	...	3813	...	...	...	...	...
5 Net saving	...	...	...	...	...	...	9590	...	...	...	...	...
Total Current Disbursements and Net Saving of General Government	...	...	...	...	...	...	79728	...	...	...	...	...

1.7 External Transactions on Current Account, Summary

Million CFA francs

	1970	1975	1980	1981	1982	1983	1984	1985	1986	1987	1988	1989

Payments to the Rest of the World

	1970	1975	1980	1981	1982	1983	1984	1985	1986	1987	1988	1989
1 Imports of goods and services	19640	52460	122708	146061	175993	174188	176837	223336	...	...	...	...
A Imports of merchandise c.i.f.	...	40199	77821	94681	118250	...	...	...	...	...	...	...
B Other	...	12261	44887	51380	57743	...	...	...	...	...	...	...
2 Factor income to the rest of the world	589	1560	3483	4336	5529	5636	5884	5996	...	...	...	...
A Compensation of employees	22	24	67	111	177	134	140	143	...	...	...	...
B Property and entrepreneurial income	567	1535	3415	4225	5352	5502	5744	5853	...	...	...	...
3 Current transfers to the rest of the world	778	5452	13680	14467	13983	17569	18195	18589	...	...	...	...
4 Surplus of the nation on current transactions	2309	-7263	-54135	-62191	-76978	-72122	-45358	-100760	...	...	...	...
Payments to the Rest of the World and Surplus of the Nation on Current Transactions	23316	52209	85735	102674	118526	125271	155559	147161	...	...	...	...

Receipts From The Rest of the World

	1970	1975	1980	1981	1982	1983	1984	1985	1986	1987	1988	1989
1 Exports of goods and services	8615	18441	43571	53563	56185	55853	88094	79155	...	...	...	...
A Exports of merchandise f.o.b.	...	15750	33929	43302	41544	...	...	...	...	...	...	...
B Other	...	2691	9642	10261	14641	...	...	...	...	...	...	...
2 Factor income from rest of the world	759	2191	4537	3867	4525	3986	4162	4241	...	...	...	...
A Compensation of employees	286	838	1285	1465	1573	1762	1840	1875	...	...	...	...
B Property and entrepreneurial income	473	1353	3252	2402	2952	2224	2322	2366	...	...	...	...
3 Current transfers from rest of the world	13942	31576	37627	45244	57815	65432	63304	63766	...	...	...	...
Receipts from the Rest of the World on Current Transactions	23316	52209	85735	102674	118526	125271	155559	147161	...	...	...	...

1.10 Gross Domestic Product by Kind of Activity, in Current Prices

Million CFA francs

	1970	1975	1980	1981	1982	1983	1984	1985	1986	1987	1988	1989
1 Agriculture, hunting, forestry and fishing	33479	56527	107982	133703	143288	152052	164205	213968	...	...	...	...
2 Mining and quarrying	55	88	386	43	161	77	304	294	...	...	...	...
3 Manufacturing	10363	17079	29856	35024	40923	48053	47457	50901	...	...	...	...
4 Electricity, gas and water	610	813	2841	2164	3234	4055	4246	3192	...	...	...	...
5 Construction	3600	4341	7801	6174	6935	7749	4934	5333	...	...	...	...
6 Wholesale and retail trade, restaurants and hotels	11800	11633	36698	44763	47543	46344	42187	45418	...	...	...	...
7 Transport, storage and communication	5956	6810	22654	26733	26702	24211	29011	30913	...	...	...	...
8 Finance, insurance, real estate and business services	5593	6606	11519	11838	12997	14009	14510	15488	...	...	...	...
9 Community, social and personal services	813	259	1324	1599	1927	1877	1771	2026	...	...	...	...

Burkina Faso

1.10 Gross Domestic Product by Kind of Activity, in Current Prices
(Continued)

Million CFA francs

	1970	1975	1980	1981	1982	1983	1984	1985	1986	1987	1988	1989
Total, Industries	72269	104155	221061	262041	283710	298427	308625	367533	...	...	...	...
Producers of Government Services	5823	14960	38452	47777	58776	67556	67455	67405	...	...	...	...
Other Producers	984	1345	2068	3023	3442	3675	5788	6552	...	...	...	...
Subtotal	79076	120460	261581	312841	345928	369658	381868	441490	...	...	...	...
Less: Imputed bank service charge	739	1112	5591	6307	6805	6778	7523	6758	...	...	...	...
Plus: Import duties	4517	7619	16028	17672	20482	18131	16219	21151	...	...	...	...
Plus: Value added tax	...	...	...	...	...	...	...	...	...	...	...	...
Equals: Gross Domestic Product	82854	126967	272018	324207	359604	381013	390565	455882	...	...	...	...

1.11 Gross Domestic Product by Kind of Activity, in Constant Prices

Million CFA francs

	1970	1975	1980	1981	1982	1983	1984	1985	1986	1987	1988	1989
			At constant prices of:1979									
1 Agriculture, hunting, forestry and fishing	...	...	96058	104885	102842	102766	102588	126027	...	...	...	...
2 Mining and quarrying	...	...	330	237	342	193	207	225	...	...	...	...
3 Manufacturing	...	...	31499	32211	33724	32345	32047	32140	...	...	...	...
4 Electricity, gas and water	...	...	1816	1918	2080	2181	2166	2201	...	...	...	...
5 Construction	...	...	7466	5749	7751	4992	5292	5681	...	...	...	...
6 Wholesale and retail trade, restaurants and hotels	...	...	33990	35804	34888	34156	33763	34775	...	...	...	...
7 Transport, storage and communication	...	...	19699	17061	18644	19480	15733	16497	...	...	...	...
8 Finance, insurance, real estate and business services	...	...	10125	10308	10298	10584	10540	10633	...	...	...	...
9 Community, social and personal services	...	...	1162	1211	1556	1182	1008	999	...	...	...	...
Total, Industries	...	...	202145	209384	212126	207879	203344	229178	...	...	...	...
Producers of Government Services	...	...	43186	46888	50795	55155	64573	72593	...	...	...	...
Other Producers	...	...	1877	2472	2295	2154	3170	3421	...	...	...	...
Subtotal	...	...	247208	258744	265216	265188	271087	305192	...	...	...	...
Less: Imputed bank service charge	...	...	5070	5109	4918	5061	4831	4744	...	...	...	...
Plus: Import duties	...	...	14571	14338	13654	10622	8878	10629	...	...	...	...
Plus: Value added tax	...	...	...	...	...	...	...	...	...	...	...	...
Equals: Gross Domestic Product	...	...	256709	267972	273950	270747	275134	311077	...	...	...	...

1.12 Relations Among National Accounting Aggregates

Million CFA francs

	1970	1975	1980	1981	1982	1983	1984	1985	1986	1987	1988	1989
Gross Domestic Product	82854	126967	272018	324207	359604	381013	390565	455882	...	...	...	...
Plus: Net factor income from the rest of the world	170	632	1055	-469	-1002	-1651	-1723	-1756	...	...	...	...
Factor income from the rest of the world	759	2191	4537	3867	4525	3986	4162	4241	...	...	...	...
Less: Factor income to the rest of the world	589	1560	3482	4336	5529	5636	5884	5996	...	...	...	...
Equals: Gross National Product	83024	127599	273073	323738	358602	379362	388845	454126	...	...	...	...
Less: Consumption of fixed capital	...	...	...	...	...	...	...	...	...	...	...	...
Equals: National Income	...	...	...	...	...	...	...	...	...	...	...	...
Plus: Net current transfers from the rest of the world	13164	26124	23947	30776	43832	47863	45108	45177	...	...	...	...
Current transfers from the rest of the world	13942	31576	37627	45244	57815	65432	63304	63766	...	...	...	...
Less: Current transfers to the rest of the world	778	5452	13680	14467	13983	17569	18195	18589	...	...	...	...
Equals: National Disposable Income	...	...	...	...	...	...	...	...	...	...	...	...
Less: Final consumption	84129	137119	278711	339551	387596	406361	385204	471071	...	...	...	...
Equals: Net Saving [a]	...	...	18309	14963	14838	20865	48746	28232	...	...	...	...
Less: Surplus of the nation on current transactions	2309	-7263	-54135	-62191	-76978	-72122	-45358	-100760	...	...	...	...
Equals: Net Capital Formation	...	...	...	...	...	...	...	...	...	...	...	...

a) Item 'Net saving' includes consumption of fixed capital.

Burkina Faso

2.1 Government Final Consumption Expenditure by Function, in Current Prices

Million CFA francs

	1970	1975	1980	1981	1982	1983	1984	1985	1986	1987	1988	1989
1 General public services	642	1051	3021	2770	3115	3138	2841	...	...	...	...	...
2 Defence	1164	3871	7470	9216	10800	11172	11784	...	...	...	...	...
3 Public order and safety	846	1121	2589	2879	3324	3546	3389	...	...	...	...	...
4 Education	1328	2113	4632	5321	6344	7112	7359	...	...	...	...	...
5 Health	786	1068	2873	3233	3828	4083	3988	...	...	...	...	...
6 Social security and welfare								...	...	...	...	...
7 Housing and community amenities	75	98	124	98	103	172	82	...	...	...	...	...
8 Recreational, cultural and religious affairs	208	164	650	733	919	988	969	...	...	...	...	...
9 Economic services	557	1087	2838	3131	3784	4080	4194	...	...	...	...	...
A Fuel and energy	...	...	...	...	...	...	...	...	...	...	...	...
B Agriculture, forestry, fishing and hunting	395	885	2206	2401	2953	3195	3181	...	...	...	...	...
C Mining, manufacturing and construction, except fuel and energy	-	79	342	389	427	489	506	...	...	...	...	...
D Transportation and communication	162	123	291	341	404	397	508	...	...	...	...	...
E Other economic affairs	...	...	...	...	...	...	...	...	...	...	...	...
10 Other functions	1230	1866	4052	3871	5982	4572	4155	...	...	...	...	...
Total Government Final Consumption Expenditure a	6835	12439	28249	31252	38198	38864	38760	...	...	...	...	...

a) Only central government data are included in the general government estimates.

2.11 Gross Fixed Capital Formation by Kind of Activity of Owner, ISIC Divisions, in Current Prices

Million CFA francs

	1970	1975	1980	1981	1982	1983	1984	1985	1986	1987	1988	1989
					All Producers							
1 Agriculture, hunting, forestry and fishing	...	...	-	103	145	74	32	365	...	...	...	...
2 Mining and quarrying	...	...	432	196	310	86	573	19	...	...	...	...
3 Manufacturing	...	...	2812	3183	4532	2421	3141	3040	...	...	...	...
A Manufacturing of food, beverages and tobacco	...	...	1871	2186	1859	1391	2174	1408	...	...	...	...
B Textile, wearing apparel and leather industries	...	...	165	534	454	751	852	1151	...	...	...	...
C Manufacture of wood, and wood products, including furniture	...	...	13	14	5	6	22	47	...	...	...	...
D Manufacture of paper and paper products, printing and publishing	...	...	73	102	77	125	43	36	...	...	...	...
E Manufacture of chemicals and chemical petroleum, coal, rubber and plastic products	...	...	479	126	1816	60	68	124	...	...	...	...
F Manufacture of non-metalic mineral products except products of petroleum and coal	...	...	8	7	11	8	4	3	...	...	...	...
G Basic metal industries	...	...	203	214	310	80	-22	271	...	...	...	...
H Manufacture of fabricated metal products, machinery and equipment	...	...	...	...	...	...	...	...	...	...	...	...
I Other manufacturing industries	...	...	...	...	...	...	...	...	...	...	...	...
4 Electricity, gas and water	...	...	1622	4404	3085	3571	2211	3609	...	...	...	...
5 Construction	...	...	324	229	284	65	-558	6611	...	...	...	...
6 Wholesale and retail trade, restaurants and hotels	...	...	1842	2453	932	2190	-284	1641	...	...	...	...
7 Transport, storage and communication	...	...	12436	5866	6540	4109	1780	6373	...	...	...	...
8 Finance, insurance, real estate and business services	...	...	1357	759	1026	1173	1185	918	...	...	...	...
9 Community, social and personal services	...	...	624	727	962	493	574	926	...	...	...	...
Total Industries			21449	17920	17816	14182	8654	23502	...	...	...	...
Producers of Government Services	...	...	29560	35030	48573	57894	60301	66567	...	...	...	...
Private Non-Profit Institutions Serving Households	...	...	14991	16998	17669	18281	21874	23376	...	...	...	...
Total	...	...	65999	69949	84058	90354	90828	113444	...	...	...	...

Burkina Faso

2.17 Exports and Imports of Goods and Services, Detail

Million CFA francs

		1970	1975	1980	1981	1982	1983	1984	1985	1986	1987	1988	1989
					Exports of Goods and Services								
1	Exports of merchandise, f.o.b.	...	15750	33929	43302	41544	49500	60200	...	...	...	...	...
2	Transport and communication	...	351	1800	1976	2164	2100	2200	...	...	...	...	...
	A In respect of merchandise imports	...	...	-	-	-	-	-	...	...	...	...	...
	B Other	...	351	1800	1976	2164	2100	2200	...	...	...	...	...
3	Insurance service charges	...	163	519	613	348	300	400	...	...	...	...	...
	A In respect of merchandise imports	...	...	-	-	-	-	-	...	...	...	...	...
	B Other	...	163	519	613	348	300	400	...	...	...	...	...
4	Other commodities	...	662	829	1215	1518	1300	1500	...	...	...	...	...
5	Adjustments of merchandise exports to change-of-ownership basis	...	...	...	...	...	...	...	...	...	...	...	...
6	Direct purchases in the domestic market by non-residential households	...	455	1058	1076	1329	1300	1300	...	...	...	...	...
7	Direct purchases in the domestic market by extraterritorial bodies	...	1060	5436	5381	9283	9300	9400	...	...	...	...	...
	Total Exports of Goods and Services [a]	...	18441	43571	53563	56185	63800	75000	...	...	...	...	...
					Imports of Goods and Services								
1	Imports of merchandise, c.i.f. [b]	...	40199	77821	94681	118250	118500	115000	...	...	...	...	...
2	Adjustments of merchandise imports to change-of-ownership basis	...	...	...	...	...	...	...	...	...	...	...	...
3	Other transport and communication	...	4077	27244	30560	36602	35200	35800	...	...	...	...	...
4	Other insurance service charges	...	468	1006	1291	1208	1200	1200	...	...	...	...	...
5	Other commodities	...	2710	6265	6809	8128	7800	7900	...	...	...	...	...
6	Direct purchases abroad by government	...	2151	3610	4572	4191	4000	4100	...	...	...	...	...
7	Direct purchases abroad by resident households	...	2855	6762	8147	7615	7300	7400	...	...	...	...	...
	Total Imports of Goods and Services	...	52460	122708	146061	175993	174000	171400	...	...	...	...	...
	Balance of Goods and Services	...	-34019	-79137	-92498	-119808	-110200	-96400	...	...	...	...	...
	Total Imports and Balance of Goods and Services [a]	...	18441	43571	53563	56185	63800	75000	...	...	...	...	...

a) Data for this table have not been revised, therefore, data for some years are not comparable with those of other tables.
b) Imports of merchandise, f.o.b. rather than c.i.f.

4.1 Derivation of Value Added by Kind of Activity, in Current Prices

Million CFA francs

		1980			1981			1982			1983		
		Gross Output	Intermediate Consumption	Value Added	Gross Output	Intermediate Consumption	Value Added	Gross Output	Intermediate Consumption	Value Added	Gross Output	Intermediate Consumption	Value Added
					All Producers								
1	Agriculture, hunting, forestry and fishing	111315	6650	104665	138783	8832	129951	148378	9664	138713	157308	10114	147194
	A Agriculture and hunting	100685	6403	94282	127787	8565	119222	137071	9383	127688	145699	9819	135880
	B Forestry and logging	9355	126	9229	9534	129	9405	9715	131	9584	9898	134	9765
	C Fishing	1274	120	1154	1462	138	1324	1591	150	1441	1711	162	1549
2	Mining and quarrying	588	202	386	227	184	43	441	260	181	244	167	77

Burkina Faso

4.1 Derivation of Value Added by Kind of Activity, in Current Prices
(Continued)

Million CFA francs

		1980 Gross Output	1980 Intermediate Consumption	1980 Value Added	1981 Gross Output	1981 Intermediate Consumption	1981 Value Added	1982 Gross Output	1982 Intermediate Consumption	1982 Value Added	1983 Gross Output	1983 Intermediate Consumption	1983 Value Added
3	Manufacturing	81469	52249	29220	99018	64691	34327	103720	64267	39453	121363	74948	46415
	A Manufacture of food, beverages and tobacco	45275	28402	16873	56370	37596	18774	64129	39972	24157	75112	46534	28578
	B Textile, wearing apparel and leather industries	16350	10619	5731	19602	12776	6826	16682	10326	6356	24158	14993	9165
	C Manufacture of wood and wood products, including furniture	1586	1197	389	2012	1532	480	2744	2127	617	2229	1610	619
	D Manufacture of paper and paper products, printing and publishing	811	475	336	967	444	523	1137	634	503	1108	642	466
	E Manufacture of chemicals and chemical petroleum, coal, rubber and plastic products	5699	3944	1755	5932	3828	2104	5368	2991	2377	4803	2940	1863
	F Manufacture of non-metallic mineral products, except products of petroleum and coal	282	132	150	150	65	85	170	90	80	184	88	96
	G Basic metal industries	7311	6190	1121	8587	6776	1811	7312	6212	1100	7033	6051	982
	H Manufacture of fabricated metal products, machinery and equipment												
	I Other manufacturing industries	4155	1289	2866	5398	1674	3724	6179	1917	4262	6737	2090	4647
4	Electricity, gas and water	6608	3767	2841	7457	5292	2165	9495	6245	3250	10903	6848	4055
5	Construction	17257	9456	7801	16825	10651	6174	19215	12280	6935	18765	11016	7749
6	Wholesale and retail trade, restaurants and hotels	64039	27341	36698	79618	34855	44763	82506	34962	47544	79203	32859	46344
	A Wholesale and retail trade	63258	26884	36374	78806	34360	44446	81681	34539	47142	77877	32007	45870
	B Restaurants and hotels	781	457	324	812	494	318	825	423	402	1326	852	474
7	Transport, storage and communication	36693	20099	16594	44770	23939	20831	45105	24031	21074	40541	21725	18816
	A Transport and storage	33685	18995	14690	41177	23300	17877	40988	23225	17763	36235	20762	15472
	B Communication	3008	1104	1904	3593	639	2954	4118	807	3311	4307	963	3344
8	Finance, insurance, real estate and business services	15963	4020	11943	16659	4370	12289	19292	5005	14287	21040	5696	15344
	A Financial institutions	5873	1293	4580	6234	1323	4911	7410	1510	5900	8296	1770	6526
	B Insurance	547	309	238	755	526	229	970	678	292	1237	970	267
	C Real estate and business services	9543	2418	7125	9671	2523	7148	10913	2818	8095	11508	2956	8552
9	Community, social and personal services	1017	595	422	1284	717	567	1572	933	639	1506	991	515
	Total, Industries [a]	334949	124379	210570	404641	153531	251110	429724	157647	272076	450873	164364	286509
	Producers of Government Services	40360	6621	33739	43816	7123	36693	55994	9176	46818	56926	7626	49300
	Other Producers	2275	116	2159	2403	122	2281	2574	131	2443	2746	140	2606
	Total	377584	131116	246468	450860	160776	290084	488292	166954	321337	510545	172130	338415
	Less: Imputed bank service charge	...	-5138	5138	...	-5561	5561	...	-6755	6755	...	-6720	6720
	Import duties	...	-16028	16028	...	-17672	17672	...	-20482	20482	...	-18131	18131
	Value added tax	...	...	...	...	...	...	...	...	...	...	...	...
	Total [a]	377584	120225	257358	450860	148666	302194	488292	153228	335064	510545	160718	349827

		1984 Gross Output	1984 Intermediate Consumption	1984 Value Added

All Producers

		Gross Output	Intermediate Consumption	Value Added
1	Agriculture, hunting, forestry and fishing	169535	11691	157844
	A Agriculture and hunting	157575	11378	146197
	B Forestry and logging	10084	136	9948
	C Fishing	1876	177	1699
2	Mining and quarrying	466	162	304

Burkina Faso

4.1 Derivation of Value Added by Kind of Activity, in Current Prices
(Continued)

Million CFA francs

		1984		
		Gross Output	Intermediate Consumption	Value Added
3	Manufacturing	133327	82466	50861
	A Manufacture of food, beverages and tobacco	77108	46527	30581
	B Textile, wearing apparel and leather industries	32437	21459	10978
	C Manufacture of wood and wood products, including furniture	1675	1214	461
	D Manufacture of paper and paper products, printing and publishing	1446	792	654
	E Manufacture of chemicals and chemical petroleum, coal, rubber and plastic products	4950	3263	1687
	F Manufacture of non-metallic mineral products, except products of petroleum and coal	88	34	54
	G Basic metal industries	8413	6941	1472
	H Manufacture of fabricated metal products, machinery and equipment			
	I Other manufacturing industries	7210	2236	4974
4	Electricity, gas and water	11252	7006	4246
5	Construction	11871	6937	4934
6	Wholesale and retail trade, restaurants and hotels	72646	30459	42187
	A Wholesale and retail trade	71039	29619	41420
	B Restaurants and hotels	1607	840	767
7	Transport, storage and communication	51531	27977	23554
	A Transport and storage	47096	27169	19927
	B Communication	4435	808	3627
8	Finance, insurance, real estate and business services	21752	5796	15956
	A Financial institutions	8313	1712	6601
	B Insurance	1380	999	381
	C Real estate and business services	12059	3085	8974
9	Community, social and personal services	945	595	350
Total, Industries [a]		473325	173089	300236
Producers of Government Services		57829	5779	52050
Other Producers		2918	149	2769
Total		534072	179017	355055
Less: Imputed bank service charge		...	-7472	7472
Import duties		...	-16219	16219
Value added tax		...	...	...
Total [a]		534070	170270	363800

a) Data for this table have not been revised, therefore, data for some years are not comparable with those of other tables.

4.3 Cost Components of Value Added

Million CFA francs

	1980						1981					
	Compensation of Employees	Capital Consumption	Net Operating Surplus	Indirect Taxes	Less: Subsidies Received	Value Added	Compensation of Employees	Capital Consumption	Net Operating Surplus	Indirect Taxes	Less: Subsidies Received	Value Added
					All Producers							
1 Agriculture, hunting, forestry and fishing	223	1466	102902	74	...	104665	306	1883	127654	109	...	129951
A Agriculture and hunting	31	1139	93044	68	...	94282	85	1545	117491	102	...	119222
B Forestry and logging	-	290	8933	6	...	9229	-	295	9103	7	...	9405
C Fishing	192	38	924	-	...	1154	221	43	1060	-	...	1324
2 Mining and quarrying	255	68	55	8	...	386	314	140	-421	10	...	43

Burkina Faso

4.3 Cost Components of Value Added
(Continued)

Million CFA francs

	1980						1981					
	Compensation of Employees	Capital Consumption	Net Operating Surplus	Indirect Taxes	Less: Subsidies Received	Value Added	Compensation of Employees	Capital Consumption	Net Operating Surplus	Indirect Taxes	Less: Subsidies Received	Value Added
3 Manufacturing	7682	3969	15158	2410	...	29220	8033	4277	19219	2798	...	34327
A Manufacture of food, beverages and tobacco	3587	2093	9471	1722	...	16873	3837	1796	11240	1901	...	18774
B Textile, wearing apparel and leather industries	2018	1280	2272	161	...	5731	1856	1556	3251	163	...	6826
C Manufacture of wood and wood products, including furniture	242	117	13	17	...	389	303	115	45	17	...	480
D Manufacture of paper and paper products, printing and publishing	199	60	13	64	...	336	242	71	127	83	...	523
E Manufacture of chemicals and chemical petroleum, coal, rubber and plastic products	795	235	451	274	...	1755	890	434	434	346	...	2104
F Manufacture of non-metallic mineral products, except products of petroleum and coal	66	22	51	11	...	150	49	20	5	11	...	85
G Basic metal industries	546	113	321	141	...	1121	557	220	784	250	...	1811
H Manufacture of fabricated metal products, machinery and equipment					...						...	
I Other manufacturing industries	230	50	2566	20	...	2866	299	65	3334	26	...	3724
4 Electricity, gas and water	832	935	1001	72	...	2841	777	1414	-98	72	...	2165
5 Construction	3267	1257	2750	527	...	7801	3001	1666	769	738	...	6174
6 Wholesale and retail trade, restaurants and hotels	3203	2047	29418	2030	...	36698	3377	2885	35741	2760	...	44763
A Wholesale and retail trade	3049	2014	29323	1988	...	36374	3254	2846	35619	2727	...	44446
B Restaurants and hotels	154	33	95	42	...	324	124	39	122	33	...	318
7 Transport, storage and communication	9524	5349	831	890	...	16594	11082	6629	2092	1028	...	20831
A Transport and storage	8168	4755	1028	739	...	14690	9820	5951	1147	959	...	17877
B Communication	1356	594	-196	150	...	1904	1262	678	945	69	...	2954
8 Finance, insurance, real estate and business services	2241	1585	7895	222	...	11943	2563	1989	7543	194	...	12289
A Financial institutions	1819	225	2424	112	...	4580	2110	542	2205	54	...	4911
B Insurance	66	5	149	18	...	238	69	39	96	25	...	230
C Real estate and business services	356	1355	5322	92	...	7125	384	1408	5242	114	...	7148
9 Community, social and personal services	161	56	74	131	...	422	187	73	163	144	...	567
Total, Industries [a]	27388	16732	160084	6364	...	210570	29640	20956	192662	7853	...	251110
Producers of Government Services	33603	136	...	...	...	33739	36520	163	...	10	...	36693
Other Producers	2124	35	...	...	...	2159	2244	37	...	...	...	2281
Total	63115	16903	160084	6364	...	246468	68404	21156	192662	7863	...	290084
Less: Imputed bank service charge	...	...	5138	...	...	5138	...	...	5561	...	...	5561
Import duties	...	...	...	16028	...	16028	...	...	...	17672	...	17672
Value added tax	...	...	...	...	...	...	...	...	...	...	...	...
Total [a]	63115	16903	154946	22392	...	257358	68405	21156	187100	25533	...	302194

	1982						1983					
	Compensation of Employees	Capital Consumption	Net Operating Surplus	Indirect Taxes	Less: Subsidies Received	Value Added	Compensation of Employees	Capital Consumption	Net Operating Surplus	Indirect Taxes	Less: Subsidies Received	Value Added

All Producers

1 Agriculture, hunting, forestry and fishing	374	2029	136234	76	...	138713	394	2159	144573	68	...	147194
A Agriculture and hunting	134	1681	125804	69	...	127688	174	1801	133844	61	...	135880
B Forestry and logging	-	301	9276	7	...	9584	-	307	9451	7	...	9765
C Fishing	240	47	1154	-	...	1441	221	50	1278	-	...	1549
2 Mining and quarrying	349	140	-316	8	...	181	281	129	-334	1	...	77

Burkina Faso

4.3 Cost Components of Value Added
(Continued)

Million CFA francs

1982

	Compensation of Employees	Capital Consumption	Net Operating Surplus	Indirect Taxes	Less: Subsidies Received	Value Added
3 Manufacturing	8984	4736	22514	3219	...	39453
A Manufacture of food, beverages and tobacco	4311	2282	15149	2415	...	24157
B Textile, wearing apparel and leather industries	1922	1442	2863	129	...	6356
C Manufacture of wood and wood products, including furniture	391	70	138	18	...	617
D Manufacture of paper and paper products, printing and publishing	284	63	110	46	...	503
E Manufacture of chemicals and chemical petroleum, coal, rubber and plastic products	973	593	491	320	...	2377
F Manufacture of non-metallic mineral products, except products of petroleum and coal	64	22	-14	8	...	80
G Basic metal industries	696	189	-38	253	...	1100
H Manufacture of fabricated metal products, machinery and equipment					...	
I Other manufacturing industries	342	74	3816	30	...	4262
4 Electricity, gas and water	1138	1277	756	79	...	3250
5 Construction	3439	916	1817	763	...	6935
6 Wholesale and retail trade, restaurants and hotels	4385	3047	37123	2989	...	47544
A Wholesale and retail trade	4178	3006	37107	2851	...	47142
B Restaurants and hotels	207	41	16	138	...	402
7 Transport, storage and communication	11917	6408	1726	1023	...	21074
A Transport and storage	9993	5712	1170	888	...	17763
B Communication	1924	696	556	135	...	3311
8 Finance, insurance, real estate and business services	3010	2074	8915	288	...	14287
A Financial institutions	2422	430	2890	158	...	5900
B Insurance	80	43	130	39	...	292
C Real estate and business services	508	1600	5896	91	...	8095
9 Community, social and personal services	211	70	199	159	...	639
Total, Industries [a]	33807	20697	208968	8604	...	272076
Producers of Government Services	46305	511	...	2	...	46818
Other Producers	2403	40	...	...	...	2443
Total	82515	21248	208968	8606	...	321337
Less: Imputed bank service charge	...	...	6755	...		6755
Import duties	...	...	...	20482		20482
Value added tax	...	...	...	...		...
Total [a]	82516	21248	202212	29088		335064

1983

	Compensation of Employees	Capital Consumption	Net Operating Surplus	Indirect Taxes	Less: Subsidies Received	Value Added
3 Manufacturing	9680	3965	28953	3817	...	46415
A Manufacture of food, beverages and tobacco	4900	2236	18420	3022	...	28578
B Textile, wearing apparel and leather industries	2079	998	5861	227	...	9165
C Manufacture of wood and wood products, including furniture	374	62	158	25	...	618
D Manufacture of paper and paper products, printing and publishing	287	58	59	62	...	466
E Manufacture of chemicals and chemical petroleum, coal, rubber and plastic products	815	309	421	318	...	1863
F Manufacture of non-metallic mineral products, except products of petroleum and coal	64	24	-2	10	...	96
G Basic metal industries	788	198	-125	121	...	982
H Manufacture of fabricated metal products, machinery and equipment					...	
I Other manufacturing industries	373	81	4161	32	...	4647
4 Electricity, gas and water	1330	1424	1224	77	...	4055
5 Construction	3777	1238	2114	620	...	7749
6 Wholesale and retail trade, restaurants and hotels	4768	3177	34703	3696	...	46344
A Wholesale and retail trade	4280	2979	35039	3572	...	45870
B Restaurants and hotels	488	199	-336	123	...	474
7 Transport, storage and communication	10860	5674	1328	954	...	18816
A Transport and storage	9033	5052	561	826	...	15472
B Communication	1827	623	767	127	...	3344
8 Finance, insurance, real estate and business services	3589	2251	9130	374	...	15344
A Financial institutions	2904	406	2990	226	...	6526
B Insurance	120	79	24	44	...	267
C Real estate and business services	565	1766	6116	105	...	8552
9 Community, social and personal services	259	138	-7	125	...	515
Total, Industries [a]	34938	20155	221684	9732	...	286509
Producers of Government Services	49093	207	...	...	...	49300
Other Producers	2564	42	...	...	...	2606
Total	86595	20404	221684	9732	...	338415
Less: Imputed bank service charge	...	...	6720	...		6720
Import duties	...	...	...	18131		18131
Value added tax	...	...	...	...		...
Total [a]	86595	20405	214964	27863		349827

1984

All Producers

	Compensation of Employees	Capital Consumption	Net Operating Surplus	Indirect Taxes	Less: Subsidies Received	Value Added
1 Agriculture, hunting, forestry and fishing	427	2438	154858	121	...	157844
A Agriculture and hunting	186	2070	143827	114	...	146197
B Forestry and logging	-	312	9629	7	...	9948
C Fishing	242	55	1402	-	...	1699
2 Mining and quarrying	364	177	-251	14	...	304

Burkina Faso

4.3 Cost Components of Value Added
(Continued)

Million CFA francs

		1984				
	Compensation of Employees	Capital Consumption	Net Operating Surplus	Indirect Taxes	Less: Subsidies Received	Value Added
3 Manufacturing	9817	3714	32698	4632	...	50861
A Manufacture of food, beverages and tobacco	4588	2089	21012	2892	...	30581
B Textile, wearing apparel and leather industries	2356	1022	6674	926	...	10978
C Manufacture of wood and wood products, including furniture	283	50	83	44	...	461
D Manufacture of paper and paper products, printing and publishing	304	74	172	104	...	654
E Manufacture of chemicals and chemical petroleum, coal, rubber and plastic products	858	271	266	292	...	1687
F Manufacture of non-metallic mineral products, except products of petroleum and coal	47	9	-30	28	...	54
G Basic metal industries	982	113	68	309	...	1472
H Manufacture of fabricated metal products, machinery and equipment					...	
I Other manufacturing industries	399	87	4453	35	...	4974
4 Electricity, gas and water	1481	1594	1094	77	...	4246
5 Construction	2382	1079	1018	455	...	4934
6 Wholesale and retail trade, restaurants and hotels	5407	3753	29452	3575	...	42187
A Wholesale and retail trade	4886	2965	30143	3426	...	41420
B Restaurants and hotels	521	788	-691	149	...	767
7 Transport, storage and communication	13246	7496	1585	1227	...	23554
A Transport and storage	11454	6866	540	1067	...	19927
B Communication	1792	630	1045	160	...	3627
8 Finance, insurance, real estate and business services	4031	2350	9116	459	...	15956
A Financial institutions	3068	515	2768	250	...	6601
B Insurance	176	86	66	53	...	381
C Real estate and business services	787	1749	6282	156	...	8974
9 Community, social and personal services	277	86	-146	133	...	350
Total, Industries [a]	37432	22687	229424	10693	...	300236
Producers of Government Services	51910	140	...	...	...	52050
Other Producers	2724	45	...	...	...	2769
Total	92066	22872	229424	10693	...	355055
Less: Imputed bank service charge	...	...	7472	...	...	7472
Import duties	...	...	...	16219	...	16219
Value added tax	...	...	...	...	...	
Total [a]	92066	22871	221950	26913	...	363800

a) Data for this table have not been revised, therefore, data for some years are not comparable with those of other tables.

Burundi

Source. Reply to the United Nations National Accounts Questionnaire from the Departement des Etudes et Statistiques, Bujumbura.
General note. The estimates shown in the following tables have been prepared in accordance with the United Nations System of National Accounts so far as the existing data would permit.

1.1 Expenditure on the Gross Domestic Product, in Current Prices

Million Burundi francs

	1970	1975	1980	1981	1982	1983	1984	1985	1986	1987	1988	1989
1 Government final consumption expenditure	2075	3828	13746	15762	18183	20414	21132	22793	24252	28570	31491	24501
2 Private final consumption expenditure	18636	29887	70133	70006	73894	77516	92484	109478	104340	107015	114298	141748
3 Gross capital formation	962	2513	11876	14477	16430	18458	21774	20187	22107	24876	21672	29097
A Increase in stocks	113	-556	921	2529	-741	-1083	1410	73	3247	3763	-4029	...
B Gross fixed capital formation	849	3069	10955	11948	17170	19542	20364	20113	18860	21114	25701	...
4 Exports of goods and services	2270	2744	7328	6835	8697	9683	11782	13937	15625	13015	17298	17225
5 Less: Imports of goods and services	2468	6300	17476	17696	23109	23179	26721	25047	25482	29886	31852	38713
Equals: Gross Domestic Product a	21476	32671	85607	89383	94094	102892	120451	141347	140842	143590	152907	173857

a) Data in this table have been revised, therefore they are not strictly comparable with the unrevised data in the other tables.

1.2 Expenditure on the Gross Domestic Product, in Constant Prices

Million Burundi francs

	1970	1975	1980	1981	1982	1983	1984	1985	1986	1987	1988	1989
					At constant prices of:1980							
1 Government final consumption expenditure	10723	12030	13746	15391	16711	18751	18338	19204	19895	20313	...	...
2 Private final consumption expenditure	52754	55022	70133	72276	72479	72000	72512	80168	83474	86066	...	...
3 Gross capital formation	3431	4732	11876	14460	14939	17204	18807	17051	17604	17528	...	...
A Increase in stocks	638	-1446	921	2697	-1028	-1149	1016	-21	2475	626		
B Gross fixed capital formation	2793	6178	10955	11764	15968	18353	17790	17072	15129	16902		
4 Exports of goods and services	8255	9899	7328	10003	11690	12360	10622	12819	11349	12192		
5 Less: Imports of goods and services	9338	13723	17476	17181	21279	22836	22897	20480	19406	18559		
Equals: Gross Domestic Product	65825	67960	85607	94949	94540	97479	97382	108762	112916	117539	...	...

1.3 Cost Components of the Gross Domestic Product

Million Burundi francs

	1970	1975	1980	1981	1982	1983	1984	1985	1986	1987	1988	1989
1 Indirect taxes, net	1594	2205	8646	6704	9789	8849	13009	15124	17724	14030	17834	...
A Indirect taxes	...	...	9331	7776	11068	9157	13370	15548	18096	14938	18515	...
B Less: Subsidies	...	...	685	1073	1282	309	361	424	372	908	681	...
2 Consumption of fixed capital	317	480	1541	1788	1976	2572	3132	3534	4110	4807	5898	...
3 Compensation of employees paid by resident producers to:	13309	5317	15837	17519	19948	21093	24211	26856	28319	30868	33255	...
A Resident households	12718	4704	...	...	...	...	...	...	...	...	...	...
B Rest of the world	591	613	...	...	...	...	...	...	...	...	...	...
4 Operating surplus	6256	24671	59582	63373	62385	70378	80100	95833	90689	90775	95921	...
A Corporate and quasi-corporate enterprises	...	...	...	3915	4000	5666	4407	5135	6328	7355	...	...
B Private unincorporated enterprises	...	...	...	59611	58373	64708	75659	90544	84201	83240	...	...
C General government	...	...	...	-153	12	5	35	154	160	180	...	...
Equals: Gross Domestic Product	21476	32672	85607	89383	94094	102891	120451	141347	140842	140480	152907	...

1.7 External Transactions on Current Account, Summary

Million Burundi francs

	1970	1975	1980	1981	1982	1983	1984	1985	1986	1987	1988	1989
					Payments to the Rest of the World							
1 Imports of goods and services	2468	6300	17476	17696	23109	23179	26721	25047	25482	28754	...	...
A Imports of merchandise c.i.f.	2024	5025	...	...	...	...	...	...	...	...	...	...
B Other	444	1274	...	...	...	...	...	...	...	...	...	...
2 Factor income to the rest of the world	701	765	163	381	431	558	1161	1614	1925	2512	...	...

Burundi

1.7 External Transactions on Current Account, Summary
(Continued)

Million Burundi francs

	1970	1975	1980	1981	1982	1983	1984	1985	1986	1987	1988	1989
A Compensation of employees	591	613	...	...	...	...	...	...	...	...	...	...
B Property and entrepreneurial income	110	152	163	381	431	558	1161	1614	1925	2512	...	...
3 Current transfers to the rest of the world	12	81	1981	4392	4441	4541	5431	6007	6331	7120	...	...
4 Surplus of the nation on current transactions	203	-2576	-4952	-6491	-11248	-11266	-13069	-10498	-9376	-15422	...	...
Payments to the Rest of the World and Surplus of the Nation on Current Transactions	3384	4570	14668	15978	16733	17012	20244	22169	24362	22964	...	...
Receipts From The Rest of the World												
1 Exports of goods and services	2270	2744	7328	6835	8697	9683	11782	13937	15625	13088	...	...
A Exports of merchandise f.o.b.	2149	2542	...	...	...	...	...	...	...	...	...	...
B Other	122	201	...	...	...	...	...	...	...	...	...	...
2 Factor income from rest of the world	49	84	986	837	499	176	182	178	228	361	...	...
A Compensation of employees	...	...	...	...	...	...	...	...	...	...	...	...
B Property and entrepreneurial income	49	84	986	837	499	176	182	178	228	361	...	...
3 Current transfers from rest of the world	1065	1742	6355	8306	7537	7153	8280	8054	8509	9515	...	...
Receipts from the Rest of the World on Current Transactions	3384	4570	14668	15978	16733	17012	20244	22169	24362	22964	...	...

1.10 Gross Domestic Product by Kind of Activity, in Current Prices

Million Burundi francs

	1970	1975	1980	1981	1982	1983	1984	1985	1986	1987	1988	1989
1 Agriculture, hunting, forestry and fishing	13568	19754	47875	50369	48081	53726	64535	77657	72058	71490	...	...
2 Mining and quarrying [a]	64	127	234	387	508	620	444	639	906	990	...	...
3 Manufacturing	1346	2228	6971	6767	7213	11652	10720	11860	12500	13827	...	...
4 Electricity, gas and water [a]	...	...	...	...	...	...	...	...	...	...	...	...
5 Construction	450	987	3762	4280	4953	3991	3557	3908	3234	3869	...	...
6 Wholesale and retail trade, restaurants and hotels	1582	2932	6714	6665	6981	7837	9926	10750	11072	11039	...	...
7 Transport, storage and communication	238	439	1677	1595	2029	2288	2568	2994	3540	3878	...	...
8 Finance, insurance, real estate and business services	736	1068	1427	1698	1482	1612	1613	1781	1851	1925	...	...
9 Community, social and personal services											...	...
Total, Industries	17983	27535	68659	71759	71246	81736	93363	109589	105161	106918	...	...
Producers of Government Services	1446	2304	8771	10623	11917	12173	14054	16604	17956	19532	...	...
Other Producers	453	628									...	...
Subtotal	19882	30467	77430	82382	83164	93909	107417	126193	123117	126450	...	...
Less: Imputed bank service charge	...	...	...	...	...	...	...	...	...	...	...	...
Plus: Import duties	...	...	2831	2169	2904	2334	2282	2557	3647	4031	...	...
Plus: Value added tax	...	...	...	...	...	...	...	...	...	...	...	...
Plus: Other adjustments	1594	2205	5346	4832	8026	6649	10752	12597	14078	9999	...	...
Equals: Gross Domestic Product	21476	32672	85607	89383	94094	102892	120451	141347	140842	140480	...	...

a) Item 'Electricity, gas and water' is included in item 'Mining and Quarrying'.

1.11 Gross Domestic Product by Kind of Activity, in Constant Prices

Million Burundi francs

	1970	1975	1980	1981	1982	1983	1984	1985	1986	1987	1988	1989
				At constant prices of:1970								
1 Agriculture, hunting, forestry and fishing	13568	14225	15628	...	...	...	...	...	...	...	...	...
2 Mining and quarrying [a]	64	69	131	...	...	...	...	...	...	...	...	...
3 Manufacturing	1346	1653	2519	...	...	...	...	...	...	...	...	...
4 Electricity, gas and water [a]	...	...	...	...	...	...	...	...	...	...	...	...
5 Construction	450	410	1371	...	...	...	...	...	...	...	...	...

Burundi

1.11 Gross Domestic Product by Kind of Activity, in Constant Prices
(Continued)

Million Burundi francs

		1970	1975	1980	1981	1982	1983	1984	1985	1986	1987	1988	1989
		\multicolumn{12}{c}{At constant prices of:1970}
6	Wholesale and retail trade, restaurants and hotels	1582	1560	1912	...	...	...	...	...	...	...	...	...
7	Transport, storage and communication	238	381	563	...	...	...	...	...	...	...	...	...
8	Finance, insurance, real estate and business services	736	607	801	...	...	...	...	...	...	...	...	...
9	Community, social and personal services				...	...	...	...	...	...	...	...	...
	Statistical discrepancy	...	4	...	...	...	...	...	...	...	...	...	...
	Total, Industries	17983	18909	...	...	...	...	...	...	...	...	...	...
	Producers of Government Services	1446	1372	2735	...	...	...	...	...	...	...	...	...
	Other Producers	453	469		...	...	...	...	...	...	...	...	...
	Subtotal	19882	20750	25659	...	...	...	...	...	...	...	...	...
	Less: Imputed bank service charge	...	...	...	...	...	...	...	...	...	...	...	...
	Plus: Import duties	...	...	...	...	...	...	...	...	...	...	...	...
	Plus: Value added tax	...	...	...	...	...	...	...	...	...	...	...	...
	Plus: Other adjustments	1594	1437	2502	...	...	...	...	...	...	...	...	...
	Equals: Gross Domestic Product	21476	22187	28161	...	...	...	...	...	...	...	...	...

a) Item 'Electricity, gas and water' is included in item 'Mining and Quarrying'.

1.12 Relations Among National Accounting Aggregates

Million Burundi francs

	1970	1975	1980	1981	1982	1983	1984	1985	1986	1987	1988	1989
Gross Domestic Product	21476	32672	85607	89383	94094	102892	120451	141347	140842	140480	152907	...
Plus: Net factor income from the rest of the world	-652	-681	822	455	68	-382	-980	-1436	-1697	-2151	-2457	...
Factor income from the rest of the world	49	84	986	837	499	176	182	178	228	361	...	...
Less: Factor income to the rest of the world	701	765	163	381	431	558	1161	1614	1925	2512	...	...
Equals: Gross National Product	20824	31991	86429	89838	94162	102510	119471	139912	139145	138329	150450	...
Less: Consumption of fixed capital	...	...	1541	1788	1976	2572	3132	3534	4110	4807	5898	...
Equals: National Income	...	...	84888	88050	92186	99938	116339	136377	135035	133522	144552	...
Plus: Net current transfers from the rest of the world	...	...	4374	3914	3097	2612	2850	2047	2178	2395	1529	...
Current transfers from the rest of the world	...	...	6355	8306	7537	7153	8280	8055	8509	9515	...	...
Less: Current transfers to the rest of the world	...	...	1981	4392	4441	4540	5431	6007	6331	7120	...	...
Equals: National Disposable Income	...	...	89262	91964	95283	102550	119189	138424	137213	135917	146081	...
Less: Final consumption	20711	33715	83879	85768	92077	97930	113616	132270	128592	131756	145789	...
Equals: Net Saving	...	...	5383	6196	3206	4620	5573	6154	8621	4161	292	...
Less: Surplus of the nation on current transactions	...	...	-4952	-6491	-11248	-11266	-13069	-10498	-9376	-15421	-15482	...
Equals: Net Capital Formation	...	...	10335	12687	14454	15886	18642	16652	17997	19582	15774	...

Byelorussian SSR

Source. The Central Statistical Administration, Minsk.
General note. The estimates shown in the following tables have been prepared in accordance with the System of Material Product Balances. Therefore, these estimates are not comparable in concept and coverage with those conforming to the United Nations System of National Accounts.

1a Net Material Product by Use at Current Market Prices

Thousand Million USSR roubles

	1970	1975	1980	1981	1982	1983	1984	1985	1986	1987	1988	1989
1 Personal consumption	...	...	...	...	...	...	...	...	...	...	...	...
2 Material consumption in the units of the non-material sphere serving individuals	...	...	...	...	...	...	...	...	...	...	...	...
Consumption of the Population	...	...	...	...	...	...	...	...	15.7	16.5	...	...
3 Material consumption in the units of the non-material sphere serving the community as a whole												
4 Net fixed capital formation	...	...	...	...	...	...	...	...	5.6	5.5	...	...
5 Increase in material circulating assets and in stocks	...	...	...	...	...	...	...	...	...	...	...	...
6 Losses	...	...	...	...	...	...	...	...	...	...	...	...
7 Exports of goods and material services	...	...	...	...	...	...	...	...	...	...	...	...
8 Less: Imports of goods and material services	...	...	...	...	...	...	...	...	...	...	...	...
Net Material Product	...	...	...	...	...	...	...	...	21.3	22.0	...	...

2a Net Material Product by Kind of Activity of the Material Sphere in Current Market Prices

Thousand Million USSR roubles

	1970	1975	1980	1981	1982	1983	1984	1985	1986	1987	1988	1989
1 Agriculture and forestry	...	...	...	...	...	...	...	...	6.8	6.8	7.3	...
2 Industrial activity [a]	...	...	...	...	...	...	...	...	10.1	11.1	11.2	...
3 Construction	...	...	...	...	...	...	...	...	2.4	2.6	2.7	...
4 Wholesale and retail trade and restaurants and other eating and drinking places [b]	...	...	...	...	...	...	...	...	4.0	4.0	3.9	...
5 Transport and communication [c]	...	...	...	...	...	...	...	...	1.0	1.0	1.1	...
6 Other activities of the material sphere [b]	...	...	...	...	...	...	...	...	...	...	...	...
Net material product	...	...	...	...	...	...	...	...	24.3	25.5	26.2	...

a) Mining, quarrying, manufacturing and production of electricity and gas are all included in item 'Industrial activity'.
b) Item 'Other activities of the material sphere' is included in item 'Wholesale and retail trade and restaurants and other eating and drinking places'.
c) Only goods transport and communication serving branches of material production are included in item 'Transport and Communication'.

2b Net Material Product by Kind of Activity of the Material Sphere in Constant Market Prices

Index numbers 1980=100

	1970	1975	1980	1981	1982	1983	1984	1985	1986	1987	1988	1989
					At constant prices of:1980							
1 Agriculture and forestry	...	...	...	...	...	...	...	...	...	...	...	...
2 Industrial activity	...	...	...	...	...	...	...	...	...	...	...	...
3 Construction	...	...	...	...	...	...	...	...	...	...	...	...
4 Wholesale and retail trade and restaurants and other eating and drinking places	...	...	...	...	...	...	...	...	...	...	...	...
5 Transport and communication	...	...	...	...	...	...	...	...	...	...	...	...
6 Other activities of the material sphere	...	...	...	...	...	...	...	...	...	...	...	...
Net material product	52	78	100	109	113	120	126	131	139	140	143	...

6b Capital Formation by Kind of Activity of the Material and Non-Material Spheres in Constant Market Prices

Million USSR roubles

	1970	1975	1980	1981	1982	1983	1984	1985	1986	1987	1988	1989
					At constant prices of:1980							
			Gross Fixed Capital Formation by Socio-economic Sector and Industrial Use									
1 State and co-operative (excluding collective farms)	3025	4131	4838	5115	5171	5476	6440	6090	6453	7723	...	...
A Industry	1089	1308	1497	1642	1663	1778	2593	2123	2158	2715	...	...
B Construction	83	110	173	157	175	165	156	200	159	155	...	...
C Agriculture and forestry	720	1192	1279	1318	1312	1352	1336	1385	1469	1731	...	...
D Transport and communication	218	309	456	460	477	512	576	481	486	555	...	...
E Residential building	518	644	748	809	832	917	1004	1069	1256	1310	...	...
F Trade and other	397	568	685	729	712	752	775	832	925	1257	...	...
2 Collective farms	...	...	...	...	...	...	...	...	...	...	...	...
3 Other	...	...	...	...	...	...	...	...	...	...	...	...
Gross Fixed Capital Formation	3025	4131	4838	5115	5171	5476	6440	6090	6453	7723	...	...

Cameroon

Source. Reply to the United Nations National Accounts Questionnaire from the Direction de la Statistique et de la Comptabilite Nationale, Ministere de L'economie et du Plan, Yaounde. The official estimates are published annually in 'Comptes de la Nation'.

General note. The estimates shown in the following tables have been prepared in accordance with the United Nations System of National Accounts so far as the existing data would permit.

1.1 Expenditure on the Gross Domestic Product, in Current Prices

Thousand Million CFA francs — Fiscal year beginning 1 July

	1970	1975	1980	1981	1982	1983	1984	1985	1986	1987	1988	1989
1 Government final consumption expenditure	41.5	74.5	159.1	192.0	248.7	306.4	345.3	465.5	...	...	...	...
2 Private final consumption expenditure	233.6	481.6	1222.5	1538.5	1716.5	2008.0	2466.3	2689.7	...	...	...	...
3 Gross capital formation	56.7	121.7	488.4	538.7	680.1	828.9	955.3	957.0	...	...	...	...
A Increase in stocks	6.2	3.0	47.0	31.5	25.6	19.4	16.3	29.4	...	...	...	...
B Gross fixed capital formation	50.5	118.7	441.4	507.2	654.5	809.5	939.0	927.6	...	...	...	...
Residential buildings	...	29.9	116.7	130.6	168.9	234.4	278.3	259.0	...	...	...	...
Non-residential buildings	...	8.0							...	...	...	...
Other construction and land improvement etc.	...	26.4	100.9	114.2	154.6	209.8	251.9	265.0	...	...	...	...
Other	...	54.6	223.8	262.4	331.0	365.3	408.8	403.5	...	...	...	...
4 Exports of goods and services	82.0	150.4	388.5	434.8	547.5	646.5	799.9	881.9	...	...	...	...
5 Less: Imports of goods and services	92.5	171.1	462.1	531.2	574.7	594.7	727.9	859.0	...	...	...	...
Equals: Gross Domestic Product	321.3	657.2	1796.4	2172.8	2618.1	3195.0	3838.9	4135.1	4004.9	3769.9	...	...

1.2 Expenditure on the Gross Domestic Product, in Constant Prices

Thousand Million CFA francs — Fiscal year beginning 1 July

	1970	1975	1980	1981	1982	1983	1984	1985	1986	1987	1988	1989
				At constant prices of:1969								
1 Government final consumption expenditure	39.0	38.5	151.8	163.3	185.4	199.7	214.5	...	...	...	...	...
2 Private final consumption expenditure	219.6	264.4	1141.3	1301.5	1290.7	1298.6	1374.7	...	...	...	...	...
3 Gross capital formation	49.6	54.4	431.3	413.9	450.7	489.5	546.4	...	...	...	...	...
A Increase in stocks	5.8	4.8	41.5	24.2	17.0	11.5	9.3	...	...	...	...	...
B Gross fixed capital formation	43.8	49.6	389.8	389.7	433.7	478.0	537.1	...	...	...	...	...
4 Exports of goods and services	79.5	100.3	...	...	...	...	...	...	...	...	...	...
5 Less: Imports of goods and services	78.3	91.0	...	...	...	...	...	...	...	...	...	...
Equals: Gross Domestic Product	309.4	366.6	1650.6	1775.5	1897.1	2038.7	2204.0	...	...	...	...	...

1.3 Cost Components of the Gross Domestic Product

Thousand Million CFA francs — Fiscal year beginning 1 July

	1970	1975	1980	1981	1982	1983	1984	1985	1986	1987	1988	1989
1 Indirect taxes, net	37.4	85.6	236.8	299.4	348.9	416.8	473.0	488.1	...	...	...	...
A Indirect taxes [a]	42.4	91.9	241.3	304.5	355.0	434.1	485.4	534.0	...	...	...	...
B Less: Subsidies [b]	5.0	6.3	4.5	5.1	6.1	17.4	12.4	45.9	...	...	...	...
2 Consumption of fixed capital	...	57.3	125.5	142.9	158.1	165.2	194.7	173.0	...	...	...	...
3 Compensation of employees paid by resident producers to:	...	181.0	504.6	623.8	747.4	875.5	989.5	1114.3	...	...	...	...
A Resident households	...	172.0	493.9	609.5	730.6	855.7	986.3	1110.4	...	...	...	...
B Rest of the world	...	9.0	10.7	14.3	16.8	19.8	3.2	3.9	...	...	...	...
4 Operating surplus	...	333.5	929.6	1106.7	1363.7	1737.5	2181.7	2359.7	...	...	...	...
A Corporate and quasi-corporate enterprises	...	333.3	...	...	...	...	...	...	...	...	...	...
B Private unincorporated enterprises	...			...	...	...	...	...	...	...	...	...
C General government	...	0.2	...	...	...	...	...	...	...	...	...	...
Statistical discrepancy	...	-0.2	...	...	...	...	...	...	...	...	...	...
Equals: Gross Domestic Product	321.3	657.2	1796.5	2172.8	2618.1	3195.0	3838.9	4135.1	...	...	...	...

a) For 1974, 1975 and 1977, the estimates of indirect taxes are entered on accrual payment basis.
b) For 1976 and 1977, the estimates include equipment subsidies.

1.4 General Government Current Receipts and Disbursements

Thousand Million CFA francs — Fiscal year beginning 1 July

	1970	1975	1980	1981	1982	1983	1984	1985	1986	1987	1988	1989
					Receipts							
1 Operating surplus	-	0.2	-	-	-	-	-	-	...	...	...	...
2 Property and entrepreneurial income	1.0	0.7	12.5	13.7	17.5	21.7	22.8	32.0	...	...	...	...
3 Taxes, fees and contributions	51.1	117.1	350.5	451.1	528.2	632.9	719.0	842.0	...	...	...	...
A Indirect taxes	42.4	91.2	241.3	304.5	355.0	434.1	485.4	534.0	...	...	...	...

Cameroon

1.4 General Government Current Receipts and Disbursements
(Continued)

Thousand Million CFA francs — Fiscal year beginning 1 July

	1970	1975	1980	1981	1982	1983	1984	1985	1986	1987	1988	1989
B Direct taxes	12.8	17.9	88.3	120.2	143.8	160.7	193.1	252.4	...	...	...	...
C Social security contributions	1.8	7.3	20.3	25.7	28.7	37.1	38.6	54.6	...	...	...	...
D Compulsory fees, fines and penalties	0.1	0.7	0.6	0.7	0.7	1.0	1.9	1.0	...	...	...	...
4 Other current transfers	10.3	12.0	18.3	13.5	16.7	17.9	18.1	21.5	...	...	...	...
Total Current Receipts of General Government	62.4	130.0	381.3	478.3	562.4	672.6	759.9	895.5	...	...	...	...

Disbursements

	1970	1975	1980	1981	1982	1983	1984	1985	1986	1987	1988	1989
1 Government final consumption expenditure	41.5	74.5	159.0	192.0	248.7	306.4	345.3	465.5	...	...	...	...
A Compensation of employees	30.2	44.9	107.9	132.4	168.8	209.2	239.2	286.9	...	...	...	...
B Consumption of fixed capital	...	0.2	2.4	3.0	3.0	3.6	9.6	7.9	...	...	...	...
C Purchases of goods and services, net	...	29.3	...	...	...	...	...	...	...	...	...	...
D Less: Own account fixed capital formation	...	...	...	...	...	...	...	...	...	...	...	...
E Indirect taxes paid, net	...	...	...	...	...	...	...	...	...	...	...	...
2 Property income	...	4.0	31.6	34.6	37.8	38.9	53.6	91.2	...	...	...	...
3 Subsidies	...	6.3	4.5	5.1	6.1	17.4	12.4	45.9	...	...	...	...
4 Other current transfers	...	21.2	50.2	71.5	81.3	90.9	117.7	131.9	...	...	...	...
A Social security benefits	...	2.3	8.2	9.4	10.0	12.6	13.9	19.9	...	...	...	...
B Social assistance grants	...	3.9	2.1	2.9	3.9	4.9	6.5	16.4	...	...	...	...
C Other	...	15.0	39.9	59.2	67.4	73.4	97.3	95.6	...	...	...	...
Statistical discrepancy	2.2	...	...	...	...	...	...	...	...	...	...	...
5 Net saving	18.7	24.1	136.0	174.8	188.1	218.9	231.0	161.0	...	...	...	...
Total Current Disbursements and Net Saving of General Government	62.4	130.0	381.3	478.0	562.0	672.6	759.9	895.5	...	...	...	...

1.5 Current Income and Outlay of Corporate and Quasi-Corporate Enterprises, Summary

Thousand Million CFA francs — Fiscal year beginning 1 July

	1970	1975	1980	1981	1982	1983	1984	1985	1986	1987	1988	1989

Receipts

	1970	1975	1980	1981	1982	1983	1984	1985	1986	1987	1988	1989
1 Operating surplus	...	...	...	...	...	526.6	694.1	716.0	...	...	...	...
2 Property and entrepreneurial income received	...	...	...	...	...	45.7	50.0	78.6	...	...	...	...
3 Current transfers	...	...	...	...	...	28.0	40.4	46.1	...	...	...	...
Total Current Receipts	...	...	...	...	...	600.3	784.4	840.7	...	...	...	...

Disbursements

	1970	1975	1980	1981	1982	1983	1984	1985	1986	1987	1988	1989
1 Property and entrepreneurial income	...	...	...	...	...	185.8	195.1	245.6	...	...	...	...
2 Direct taxes and other current payments to general government	...	...	...	...	...	123.6	145.5	194.3	...	...	...	...
3 Other current transfers	...	...	...	...	...	53.1	172.0	180.9	...	...	...	...
4 Net saving	...	...	...	...	...	237.8	271.8	219.9	...	...	...	...
Total Current Disbursements and Net Saving	...	...	...	...	...	600.3	784.4	840.7	...	...	...	...

1.6 Current Income and Outlay of Households and Non-Profit Institutions

Thousand Million CFA francs — Fiscal year beginning 1 July

Receipts

	1970	1975	1980	1981	1982	1983	1984	1985	1986	1987	1988	1989
1 Compensation of employees	...	...	...	...	...	864.4	990.3	1111.2	...	...	...	...
2 Operating surplus of private unincorporated enterprises	...	...	...	...	...	1210.9	1487.7	1643.7	...	...	...	...
3 Property and entrepreneurial income	...	...	...	...	...	99.5	79.6	117.4	...	...	...	...
4 Current transfers	...	...	...	...	...	243.5	324.7	332.5	...	...	...	...
A Social security benefits	...	...	...	...	...	12.6	13.9	19.9	...	...	...	...
B Social assistance grants	...	...	...	...	...	4.9	6.5	16.4	...	...	...	...
C Other	...	...	...	...	...	226.0	304.3	296.3	...	...	...	...
Total Current Receipts	...	...	...	...	...	2418.2	2882.1	3204.8	...	...	...	...

Disbursements

	1970	1975	1980	1981	1982	1983	1984	1985	1986	1987	1988	1989
1 Private final consumption expenditure	...	...	...	...	...	2008.0	2466.3	2689.7	...	...	...	...

Cameroon

1.6 Current Income and Outlay of Households and Non-Profit Institutions
(Continued)

Thousand Million CFA francs — Fiscal year beginning 1 July

	1970	1975	1980	1981	1982	1983	1984	1985	1986	1987	1988	1989
2 Property income	...	...	...	...	...	9.8	11.0	33.0	...	...	...	...
3 Direct taxes and other current transfers n.e.c. to general government	...	...	...	...	...	75.2	88.0	113.7	...	...	...	...
A Social security contributions	...	...	...	...	...	37.1	38.6	54.6	...	...	...	...
B Direct taxes	...	...	...	...	...	37.3	48.1	58.5	...	...	...	...
C Fees, fines and penalties	...	...	...	...	...	0.8	1.3	0.6	...	...	...	...
4 Other current transfers	...	...	...	...	...	134.1	84.3	89.9	...	...	...	...
5 Net saving	...	...	...	...	...	191.1	232.5	278.5	...	...	...	...
Total Current Disbursements and Net Saving	...	...	...	...	...	2418.2	2882.1	3204.8	...	...	...	...

1.7 External Transactions on Current Account, Summary

Thousand Million CFA francs — Fiscal year beginning 1 July

	1970	1975	1980	1981	1982	1983	1984	1985	1986	1987	1988	1989
Payments to the Rest of the World												
1 Imports of goods and services	...	171.1	462.1	531.2	574.7	594.7	727.9	859.0	742.5	...	...	...
A Imports of merchandise c.i.f.	...	126.6	364.1	401.8	429.5	462.9	482.3	588.8	558.3	...	...	...
B Other	...	44.5	98.0	129.4	145.2	131.8	245.6	270.2	184.2	...	...	...
2 Factor income to the rest of the world	...	21.3	61.9	78.0	71.5	76.2	121.8	151.7	78.7	...	...	...
A Compensation of employees	...	9.0	10.7	14.3	16.9	19.8	3.2	3.9	3.9	...	...	...
B Property and entrepreneurial income	...	12.3	51.2	63.7	54.6	56.4	118.6	147.8	74.8	...	...	...
3 Current transfers to the rest of the world	...	3.6	22.7	23.2	22.5	23.8	13.5	30.1	60.7	...	...	...
4 Surplus of the nation on current transactions	...	-31.7	-132.8	-169.8	-92.1	-15.8	-25.3	-124.6	-236.7	...	...	...
Payments to the Rest of the World and Surplus of the Nation on Current Transactions	...	164.3	413.9	462.6	576.6	678.9	837.9	916.2	645.2	...	...	...
Receipts From The Rest of the World												
1 Exports of goods and services	...	150.4	388.5	434.8	547.5	646.5	799.9	881.9	620.6	...	...	...
A Exports of merchandise f.o.b.	...	112.3	290.8	306.3	407.2	483.2	577.7	693.0	508.2	...	...	...
B Other	...	38.1	97.7	128.5	140.3	163.3	222.2	188.9	112.4	...	...	...
2 Factor income from rest of the world	...	4.5	10.7	13.7	11.7	14.1	23.6	15.6	9.2	...	...	...
A Compensation of employees	...	2.2	4.9	5.7	6.9	8.7	4.0	0.8	0.8	...	...	...
B Property and entrepreneurial income	...	2.3	5.8	8.0	4.8	5.4	19.6	14.8	8.4	...	...	...
3 Current transfers from rest of the world	...	9.3	14.7	14.1	17.4	18.4	14.5	18.7	15.4	...	...	...
Receipts from the Rest of the World on Current Transactions	...	164.2	413.9	462.6	576.6	678.9	838.0	916.2	645.2	...	...	...

1.8 Capital Transactions of The Nation, Summary

Thousand Million CFA francs — Fiscal year beginning 1 July

	1970	1975	1980	1981	1982	1983	1984	1985	1986	1987	1988	1989
Finance of Gross Capital Formation												
Gross saving	...	89.9	355.7	368.9	588.1	813.2	930.1	832.4	...	...	...	...
1 Consumption of fixed capital	...	57.2	125.5	142.9	158.1	165.2	194.7	173.0	...	...	...	...
A General government	...	0.2	...	2.9	3.0	3.6	9.6	7.9	...	...	...	...
B Corporate and quasi-corporate enterprises [a]	...	57.0	...	...	...	120.6	141.9	125.2	...	...	...	...
C Other [a]	...	...	...	...	...	41.0	43.2	39.9	...	...	...	...
2 Net saving	...	32.7	230.2	226.0	430.0	647.9	735.4	659.4	...	...	...	...
A General government	...	24.1	...	174.8	188.1	218.9	231.1	161.0	...	...	...	...
B Corporate and quasi-corporate enterprises [a]	...	8.6	...	...	...	237.8	271.8	219.9	...	...	...	...
C Other [a]	...	...	...	...	...	191.1	232.5	278.5	...	...	...	...
Less: Surplus of the nation on current transactions	...	-31.7	-132.7	-169.8	-92.0	-15.8	-25.3	-124.6	...	...	...	...
Finance of Gross Capital Formation	56.7	121.6	488.4	538.7	680.1	828.9	955.3	957.0	...	...	...	...

Cameroon

1.8 Capital Transactions of The Nation, Summary
(Continued)

Thousand Million CFA francs — Fiscal year beginning 1 July

	1970	1975	1980	1981	1982	1983	1984	1985	1986	1987	1988	1989
Gross Capital Formation												
Increase in stocks	6.2	2.9	47.0	31.5	25.6	19.4	16.3	29.4	...	...	...	...
Gross fixed capital formation	50.5	118.7	441.4	507.2	654.5	809.5	939.0	927.6	...	...	...	...
1 General government	...	25.3	...	91.3	127.4	209.7	295.4	346.2	...	...	...	...
2 Corporate and quasi-corporate enterprises [a]	...	93.4	...	3.7	4.5	9.2	6.7	4.2	...	...	...	...
3 Other [a]	...	...	...	412.2	522.6	590.6	636.9	577.2	...	...	...	...
Gross Capital Formation	56.7	121.6	488.4	538.7	680.1	828.9	955.3	957.0	...	...	...	...

a) Item 'Other' is included in item 'Corporate and quasi-corporate enterprises'.

1.9 Gross Domestic Product by Institutional Sectors of Origin

Thousand Million CFA francs — Fiscal year beginning 1 July

	1970	1975	1980	1981	1982	1983	1984	1985	1986	1987	1988	1989
Domestic Factor Incomes Originating												
1 General government	...	44.8	107.9	132.4	168.8	209.2	239.2	...	...	...	...	...
2 Corporate and quasi-corporate enterprises	...	459.6	1303.9	1571.0	1909.7	2364.4	2889.6	...	...	...	...	...
3 Households and private unincorporated enterprises	...	6.9	15.3	18.4	22.3	26.6	27.9	...	...	...	...	...
4 Non-profit institutions serving households	...	2.8	7.2	8.7	10.2	12.8	14.5	...	...	...	...	...
Subtotal: Domestic Factor Incomes	...	514.2	1434.3	1730.5	2111.0	2613.0	3171.2	...	...	...	...	...
Indirect taxes, net	...	85.6	236.7	299.4	348.9	416.8	473.0	...	...	...	...	...
Consumption of fixed capital	...	57.3	125.5	142.9	158.1	165.2	194.7	...	...	...	...	...
Gross Domestic Product	...	657.2	1796.5	2172.8	2618.0	3195.0	3838.9	...	...	...	...	...

1.10 Gross Domestic Product by Kind of Activity, in Current Prices

Thousand Million CFA francs — Fiscal year beginning 1 July

	1970	1975	1980	1981	1982	1983	1984	1985	1986	1987	1988	1989
1 Agriculture, hunting, forestry and fishing	97.7	220.8	488.2	586.8	607.2	702.0	790.4	907.9	976.0	954.0	...	...
2 Mining and quarrying	2.1	2.0	201.5	263.1	400.5	520.5	629.7	504.7	359.4	352.8	...	...
3 Manufacturing	35.2	67.5	173.7	247.0	291.0	358.5	422.4	514.8	535.2	519.1	...	...
4 Electricity, gas and water	4.8	6.7	17.5	22.2	30.1	35.2	37.7	45.1	47.9	52.5	...	...
5 Construction	12.0	28.6	103.3	125.0	145.8	192.6	227.6	278.6	221.4	174.9	...	...
6 Wholesale and retail trade, restaurants and hotels	70.0	107.2	232.3	249.3	310.7	414.9	564.6	658.4	...	...	...	...
7 Transport, storage and communication	21.2	55.1	103.6	119.3	128.8	147.3	230.7	248.8	...	...	...	...
8 Finance, insurance, real estate and business services	25.7	72.5	248.0	285.0	355.2	396.8	455.3	470.4	...	...	...	...
9 Community, social and personal services	3.2	8.8	22.9	28.0	34.4	39.2	46.3	54.0	...	...	...	...
Total, Industries	271.9	569.2	1591.0	1925.7	2303.7	2806.9	3404.7	3682.7	...	...	...	...
Producers of Government Services	32.5	45.1	110.3	135.3	171.9	212.8	248.8	295.1	...	...	...	...
Other Producers	4.5	10.1	23.0	27.6	33.3	40.2	43.3	48.5	...	...	...	...
Subtotal	308.9	624.4	1724.3	2088.6	2508.9	3059.9	3696.8	4026.3	...	...	...	...
Less: Imputed bank service charge	...	...	30.5	42.2	37.5	38.1	32.2	26.0	...	...	...	...
Plus: Import duties	12.4	32.8	102.6	126.4	146.8	173.0	174.4	134.8	131.0	118.4	...	...
Plus: Value added tax	...	...	...	...	...	...	...	...	...	...	...	...
Equals: Gross Domestic Product	321.3	657.2	1796.4	2172.8	2618.2	3194.8	3839.0	4135.1	4004.9	3769.9	...	...

1.12 Relations Among National Accounting Aggregates

Thousand Million CFA francs — Fiscal year beginning 1 July

	1970	1975	1980	1981	1982	1983	1984	1985	1986	1987	1988	1989
Gross Domestic Product	321.3	657.2	1796.5	2172.8	2618.1	3195.0	3838.9	4135.1	4004.9	...	...	...
Plus: Net factor income from the rest of the world	...	-16.8	-51.2	-64.3	-59.7	-62.1	-98.2	-136.1	-69.5	...	...	...
Factor income from the rest of the world	...	4.5	10.7	13.7	11.7	14.1	23.6	15.6	9.2	...	...	...
Less: Factor income to the rest of the world	...	21.3	61.9	78.0	71.5	76.2	121.8	151.7	78.7	...	...	...
Equals: Gross National Product	...	640.4	1745.3	2108.5	2558.4	3132.9	3740.7	3999.0	3935.4	...	...	...
Less: Consumption of fixed capital	...	57.3	125.5	142.9	158.1	165.2	194.7	173.0	...	...	...	...

Cameroon

1.12 Relations Among National Accounting Aggregates
(Continued)

Thousand Million CFA francs — Fiscal year beginning 1 July

	1970	1975	1980	1981	1982	1983	1984	1985	1986	1987	1988	1989
Equals: National Income	...	583.1	1619.8	1965.6	2400.3	2967.7	3546.0	3826.0	...	...	...	...
Plus: Net current transfers from the rest of the world	...	5.7	-8.0	-9.1	-5.1	-5.5	1.0	-11.4	-45.3	...	...	...
Current transfers from the rest of the world	...	9.3	14.7	14.1	17.4	18.4	14.5	18.7	15.4	...	...	...
Less: Current transfers to the rest of the world	...	3.6	22.7	23.2	22.5	23.8	13.5	30.1	60.7	...	...	...
Equals: National Disposable Income	311.5	588.8	1611.8	1956.5	2395.1	2962.2	3547.0	3814.6	...	...	...	...
Less: Final consumption	275.1	556.2	1381.6	1730.5	1965.2	2314.3	2811.6	3155.2	...	...	...	...
Equals: Net Saving	36.4	32.7	230.2	226.0	430.0	647.9	735.4	659.4	...	...	...	...
Less: Surplus of the nation on current transactions	...	-31.7	-132.8	-169.8	-92.1	-15.8	-25.3	-124.6	...	...	...	...
Equals: Net Capital Formation	...	64.4	363.0	395.8	522.1	663.7	760.7	784.0	...	...	...	...

2.1 Government Final Consumption Expenditure by Function, in Current Prices

Thousand Million CFA francs — Fiscal year beginning 1 July

		1970	1975	1980	1981	1982	1983	1984	1985	1986	1987	1988	1989
1	General public services	...	26.4	54.5	64.1	82.7	102.1	110.3	139.4	...	...	...	...
2	Defence	...	12.9	23.0	28.4	38.6	48.7	42.6	53.8	...	...	...	...
3	Public order and safety	...								...	...	...	...
4	Education	...	9.0	31.5	40.2	49.9	62.1	69.0	82.0	...	...	...	...
5	Health	...	6.0	10.6	13.2	19.5	24.3	23.4	26.2	...	...	...	...
6	Social security and welfare	...	1.1	0.7	1.2	1.9	2.2	2.9	2.9	...	...	...	...
7	Housing and community amenities	...	1.8	6.3	9.0	10.0	11.8	17.1	25.4	...	...	...	...
8	Recreational, cultural and religious affairs	...	1.6	2.7	3.3	4.8	5.6	7.2	8.4	...	...	...	...
9	Economic services	...	8.3	12.9	13.2	18.8	22.1	35.0	52.8	...	...	...	...
10	Other functions	...	7.5	16.9	19.4	22.5	27.4	37.8	74.6	...	...	...	...
	Total Government Final Consumption Expenditure	...	74.5	159.1	192.0	248.7	306.4	345.3	465.5	...	...	...	...

2.7 Gross Capital Formation by Type of Good and Owner, in Current Prices

Thousand Million CFA francs — Fiscal year beginning 1 July

	1980 TOTAL	1980 Total Private	1980 Public Enterprises	1980 General Government	1981 TOTAL	1981 Total Private	1981 Public Enterprises	1981 General Government	1982 TOTAL	1982 Total Private	1982 Public Enterprises	1982 General Government
Increase in stocks, total	47.0	...	...	...	31.5	...	...	...	25.6	...	...	...
Gross Fixed Capital Formation, Total	441.4	131.6	228.5	81.3	507.2	151.1	264.8	91.3	654.5	206.4	320.7	127.4
1 Residential buildings	116.7	51.5	44.0	21.2	130.6	59.1	51.2	20.3	168.9	82.7	59.5	26.7
2 Non-residential buildings	...	...	...	...	...	...	...	...	...	...	...	...
3 Other construction	100.9	10.5	37.3	53.1	114.2	12.1	41.6	60.5	154.6	16.5	50.2	87.9
4 Land improvement and plantation and orchard development	...	...	...	...	...	...	...	...	...	...	...	...
5 Producers' durable goods	223.8	69.6	147.2	7.0	262.4	79.9	172.0	10.5	331.0	107.2	211.0	12.8
A Transport equipment	84.6	29.6	53.0	2.0	100.6	34.0	63.4	3.2	117.8	38.6	73.8	5.4
B Machinery and equipment	139.2	40.0	94.2	5.0	161.8	45.9	108.6	7.3	213.2	68.6	137.2	7.4
6 Breeding stock, dairy cattle, etc.	...	...	...	...	...	...	...	...	...	...	...	...
Total Gross Capital Formation	488.4	...	...	...	538.7	...	...	...	680.1	...	...	...

	1983 TOTAL	1983 Total Private	1983 Public Enterprises	1983 General Government	1984 TOTAL	1984 Total Private	1984 Public Enterprises	1984 General Government
Increase in stocks, total	19.4	...	...	...	16.3	...	...	...
Gross Fixed Capital Formation, Total	809.5	251.5	348.3	209.7	939.0	285.7	357.4	295.9
1 Residential buildings	234.4	105.8	71.8	56.8	278.3	120.3	92.2	65.8
2 Non-residential buildings	...	...	...	...	...	...	...	...
3 Other construction	209.8	20.1	52.7	137.0	251.9	22.8	27.9	201.2
4 Land improvement and plantation and orchard development	...	...	...	...	...	...	...	...
5 Producers' durable goods	365.3	125.6	223.8	15.9	408.7	143.0	237.3	28.4
A Transport equipment	135.0	47.2	80.9	6.9	93.2	53.7	31.3	8.2
B Machinery and equipment	230.3	78.4	142.9	9.0	315.5	89.3	206.0	20.2
6 Breeding stock, dairy cattle, etc.	...	...	...	...	...	...	...	...
Total Gross Capital Formation	828.9	...	...	...	955.3	...	...	...

Cameroon

2.17 Exports and Imports of Goods and Services, Detail

Thousand Million CFA francs — Fiscal year beginning 1 July

	1970	1975	1980	1981	1982	1983	1984	1985	1986	1987	1988	1989
Exports of Goods and Services												
1 Exports of merchandise, f.o.b.	...	112.2	290.8	306.3	407.2	483.2	577.7	693.0	508.2	...	...	...
2 Transport and communication	...	38.2	47.7	56.2	73.2	87.1	84.3	104.1	46.7	...	...	...
3 Insurance service charges	...									...	...	...
4 Other commodities	...	...	26.1	39.2	34.1	37.1	107.4	55.2	41.5	...	...	...
5 Adjustments of merchandise exports to change-of-ownership basis	...	...	...	...	...	...	...	...	...	...	...	...
6 Direct purchases in the domestic market by non-residential households	...	...	14.2	18.6	22.0	25.3	26.6	14.9	13.3	...	...	...
7 Direct purchases in the domestic market by extraterritorial bodies	...	...	9.7	14.5	11.0	13.8	3.9	14.8	10.9	...	...	...
Total Exports of Goods and Services	...	150.4	388.5	434.8	547.5	646.5	799.9	881.9	620.6	...	...	...
Imports of Goods and Services												
1 Imports of merchandise, c.i.f.	...	126.5	364.2	401.8	429.5	462.9	482.3	588.8	558.3	...	...	...
A Imports of merchandise, f.o.b.	...	44.5	...	...	...	...	...	...	...	...	...	...
B Transport of services on merchandise imports												
C Insurance service charges on merchandise imports												
2 Adjustments of merchandise imports to change-of-ownership basis												
3 Other transport and communication	...	...	15.3	18.8	19.9	21.6	18.5	32.0	22.2	...	...	...
4 Other insurance service charges	...	...	3.5	5.2	6.1	7.1	7.4	13.6	12.8	...	...	...
5 Other commodities	...	...	70.3	96.3	108.7	89.6	155.9	140.1	66.6	...	...	...
6 Direct purchases abroad by government	...	...	3.3	4.6	3.0	3.8	13.1	20.3	6.1	...	...	...
7 Direct purchases abroad by resident households	...	...	5.5	4.4	7.6	9.7	50.6	64.2	76.5	...	...	...
Total Imports of Goods and Services	...	171.0	462.1	531.2	574.8	594.7	727.9	859.0	742.5	...	...	...
Balance of Goods and Services	...	-20.6	-73.6	-96.4	-27.3	51.8	72.0	22.9	-121.9	...	...	...
Total Imports and Balance of Goods and Services	...	150.4	388.5	434.8	547.5	646.5	799.9	881.9	620.6	...	...	...

4.1 Derivation of Value Added by Kind of Activity, in Current Prices

Thousand Million CFA francs — Fiscal year beginning 1 July

	1980 Gross Output	1980 Intermediate Consumption	1980 Value Added	1981 Gross Output	1981 Intermediate Consumption	1981 Value Added	1982 Gross Output	1982 Intermediate Consumption	1982 Value Added	1983 Gross Output	1983 Intermediate Consumption	1983 Value Added
All Producers												
1 Agriculture, hunting, forestry and fishing	647.8	159.6	488.2	778.9	192.1	586.8	816.0	208.8	607.2	943.3	241.3	702.0
A Agriculture and hunting	559.3	114.5	444.8	662.1	125.9	536.2	693.4	142.2	551.2	798.1	166.0	632.1
B Forestry and logging	73.6	36.1	37.5	100.4	56.2	44.2	105.4	56.9	48.5	127.6	64.7	62.9
C Fishing	14.9	9.1	5.8	16.4	10.0	6.4	17.2	9.7	7.5	17.6	10.6	7.0
2 Mining and quarrying	285.3	83.8	201.5	357.3	94.2	263.1	518.1	117.6	400.5	658.7	138.2	520.5

Cameroon

4.1 Derivation of Value Added by Kind of Activity, in Current Prices
(Continued)

Thousand Million CFA francs — Fiscal year beginning 1 July

	1980 Gross Output	1980 Intermediate Consumption	1980 Value Added	1981 Gross Output	1981 Intermediate Consumption	1981 Value Added	1982 Gross Output	1982 Intermediate Consumption	1982 Value Added	1983 Gross Output	1983 Intermediate Consumption	1983 Value Added
3 Manufacturing	540.0	366.2	173.8	838.0	591.0	247.0	941.3	650.3	291.0	1123.7	765.2	358.5
A Manufacture of food, beverages and tobacco	231.3	154.9	76.4	328.8	221.3	107.5	378.9	247.3	131.6	489.3	323.4	166.0
B Textile, wearing apparel and leather industries	94.6	61.8	32.8	142.0	95.9	46.1	152.4	101.4	51.0	161.9	106.4	55.5
C Manufacture of wood and wood products, including furniture	40.4	24.0	16.0	63.3	40.8	22.5	64.3	40.9	23.4	82.8	52.2	30.6
D Manufacture of paper and paper products, printing and publishing	6.9	2.9	4.0	12.5	6.9	5.6	10.8	5.6	5.2	6.2	2.7	3.5
E Manufacture of chemicals and chemical petroleum, coal, rubber and plastic products	54.1	35.5	18.6	147.2	118.8	28.4	176.0	139.1	36.9	202.6	151.7	50.9
F Manufacture of non-metallic mineral products, except products of petroleum and coal	13.5	9.7	3.8	16.0	10.6	5.4	21.8	14.2	7.6	26.8	16.2	10.6
G Basic metal industries	51.9	43.9	8.0	75.3	64.0	11.3	76.4	64.3	12.1	91.7	74.4	17.3
H Manufacture of fabricated metal products, machinery and equipment	37.7	27.3	10.4	40.0	25.5	14.5	45.0	28.4	16.6	47.7	29.2	18.5
I Other manufacturing industries	9.7	5.8	3.9	12.9	7.2	5.7	15.7	9.1	6.6	14.7	9.1	5.6
4 Electricity, gas and water	31.4	13.8	17.6	40.2	18.0	22.2	51.5	21.4	30.1	55.7	20.5	35.2
5 Construction	197.3	94.0	103.3	224.6	99.6	125.0	265.0	119.2	145.8	328.6	136.0	192.6
6 Wholesale and retail trade, restaurants and hotels	326.1	93.8	232.3	344.8	95.5	249.3	418.7	108.0	310.7	571.5	156.6	414.9
A Wholesale and retail trade	305.5	82.5	223.0	321.2	83.1	238.1	391.8	94.0	297.8	544.3	142.4	401.9
B Restaurants and hotels	20.6	11.3	9.3	23.6	12.4	11.2	26.9	14.0	12.9	27.2	14.2	13.0
7 Transport, storage and communication	230.2	126.6	103.6	271.1	151.8	119.3	286.3	157.5	128.8	315.2	167.9	147.3
8 Finance, insurance, real estate and business services	345.4	97.4	248.0	418.4	133.4	285.0	522.2	167.0	355.2	592.5	195.6	396.9
A Financial institutions	75.6	24.5	51.1	135.5	54.2	81.3	172.8	65.7	107.1	188.3	51.4	136.9
B Insurance	...	...	...	...	...	...	...	...	...	...	...	...
C Real estate and business services	269.8	72.9	196.9	282.9	79.2	203.7	349.4	101.3	248.1	404.2	144.2	260.0
9 Community, social and personal services	43.0	20.1	22.9	51.6	23.6	28.0	59.4	25.0	34.4	64.7	25.5	39.2
Total, Industries	2646.5	1055.0	1591.2	3324.9	1399.2	1925.7	3878.5	1574.8	2303.7	4653.9	1846.9	2807.1
Producers of Government Services	171.3	61.0	110.3	207.8	72.5	135.3	267.7	95.8	171.9	329.7	116.9	212.8
Other Producers	24.9	1.9	23.0	29.6	2.0	27.6	35.5	2.2	33.3	43.1	2.9	40.2
Total	2842.7	1117.9	1724.5	3562.3	1473.7	2088.6	4181.7	1672.8	2508.9	5026.6	1966.7	3060.1
Less: Imputed bank service charge	...	-30.5	30.5	...	-42.2	42.2	...	-37.5	37.5	...	-38.1	38.1
Import duties	102.6	...	102.6	126.4	...	126.4	146.8	...	146.8	173.0	...	173.0
Value added tax	...	...	...	...	...	...	...	...	...	...	...	...
Total	2945.2	1148.7	1796.5	3688.8	1516.0	2172.8	4328.6	1710.5	2618.0	5199.6	2004.6	3195.0

	1984 Gross Output	1984 Intermediate Consumption	1984 Value Added	1985 Gross Output	1985 Intermediate Consumption	1985 Value Added
All Producers						
1 Agriculture, hunting, forestry and fishing	1068.7	278.3	790.4	1191.1	283.3	907.9
A Agriculture and hunting	886.3	185.7	700.6	1001.9	189.2	812.6
B Forestry and logging	167.0	82.2	84.8	173.5	85.0	88.5
C Fishing	15.4	10.4	5.0	15.8	9.0	6.7
2 Mining and quarrying	745.1	115.4	629.7	648.2	143.5	504.7

Cameroon

4.1 Derivation of Value Added by Kind of Activity, in Current Prices
(Continued)

Thousand Million CFA francs
Fiscal year beginning 1 July

	1984 Gross Output	1984 Intermediate Consumption	1984 Value Added	1985 Gross Output	1985 Intermediate Consumption	1985 Value Added
3 Manufacturing	1272.3	849.8	422.5	1483.4	968.6	514.8
A Manufacture of food, beverages and tobacco	546.7	349.6	197.1	665.6	426.1	239.5
B Textile, wearing apparel and leather industries	191.5	121.5	70.0	213.0	132.7	80.3
C Manufacture of wood and wood products, including furniture	106.4	69.3	37.1	136.7	91.9	44.8
D Manufacture of paper and paper products, printing and publishing	7.5	3.8	3.7	7.8	3.7	4.1
E Manufacture of chemicals and chemical petroleum, coal, rubber and plastic products	220.9	164.6	56.3	243.4	170.0	73.4
F Manufacture of non-metallic mineral products, except products of petroleum and coal	31.5	18.5	13.0	40.7	22.3	18.4
G Basic metal industries	98.4	79.8	18.6	95.1	73.1	22.0
H Manufacture of fabricated metal products, machinery and equipment	56.1	34.7	21.4	64.6	39.4	25.2
I Other manufacturing industries	13.4	8.1	5.3	16.5	9.4	7.1
4 Electricity, gas and water	60.8	23.1	37.7	68.8	23.7	45.1
5 Construction	383.8	156.2	227.6	482.0	203.4	278.6
6 Wholesale and retail trade, restaurants and hotels	714.7	150.2	564.5	846.5	188.1	658.4
A Wholesale and retail trade	674.9	129.2	545.7	792.3	161.0	631.3
B Restaurants and hotels	39.9	21.0	18.9	54.2	27.1	27.1
7 Transport, storage and communication	498.6	267.9	230.7	538.9	290.1	248.8
8 Finance, insurance, real estate and business services	669.3	214.0	455.3	701.5	231.1	470.4
A Financial institutions	234.9	59.0	175.9	241.4	65.3	176.2
B Insurance	...	...	...	...	...	...
C Real estate and business services	434.4	155.0	279.4	460.1	165.9	294.2
9 Community, social and personal services	79.4	33.2	46.2	86.3	32.3	54.0
Total, Industries	5492.9	2088.2	3404.7	6046.7	2364.1	3682.7
Producers of Government Services	372.7	123.9	248.8	495.2	200.1	295.1
Other Producers	46.9	3.5	43.4	53.0	4.5	48.5
Total	5912.5	2215.6	3696.9	6594.9	2568.6	4026.3
Less: Imputed bank service charge	...	-32.4	32.4	...	-26.0	26.0
Import duties	174.4	...	174.4	134.8	...	134.8
Value added tax	...	...	...	...	...	...
Total	6086.9	2248.0	3838.9	6729.7	2594.6	4135.1

4.3 Cost Components of Value Added

Thousand Million CFA francs
Fiscal year beginning 1 July

	1980 Compensation of Employees	1980 Capital Consumption	1980 Net Operating Surplus	1980 Indirect Taxes	1980 Less: Subsidies Received	1980 Value Added	1981 Compensation of Employees	1981 Capital Consumption	1981 Net Operating Surplus	1981 Indirect Taxes	1981 Less: Subsidies Received	1981 Value Added
					All Producers							
1 Agriculture, hunting, forestry and fishing	73.2	26.6	372.3	16.0	...	488.2	90.0	30.0	447.3	19.2	...	586.5
A Agriculture and hunting	56.4	21.2	358.4	8.8	...	444.8	69.1	23.8	432.4	10.7	...	536.0
B Forestry and logging	14.7	4.4	11.8	6.6	...	37.5	18.1	5.0	13.0	8.0	...	44.1
C Fishing	2.1	1.0	2.1	0.6	...	5.8	2.8	1.2	1.9	0.5	...	6.4
2 Mining and quarrying	8.2	20.2	167.2	5.9	...	201.5	10.8	16.5	217.7	18.1	...	263.1

Cameroon

4.3 Cost Components of Value Added
(Continued)

Thousand Million CFA francs — Fiscal year beginning 1 July

1980 / 1981

		Compensation of Employees	Capital Consumption	Net Operating Surplus	Indirect Taxes	Less: Subsidies Received	Value Added	Compensation of Employees	Capital Consumption	Net Operating Surplus	Indirect Taxes	Less: Subsidies Received	Value Added
3	Manufacturing	64.2	16.8	50.0	42.8	...	173.8	101.1	26.6	71.5	47.9	...	247.1
	A Manufacture of food, beverages and tobacco	18.8	7.3	19.0	31.3	...	76.4	33.2	8.2	32.7	33.3	...	107.4
	B Textile, wearing apparel and leather industries	15.9	3.9	7.9	5.1	...	32.8	23.8	5.4	10.4	6.6	...	46.2
	C Manufacture of wood and wood products, including furniture	8.6	1.2	4.3	1.9	...	16.0	14.4	1.4	4.0	2.7	...	22.5
	D Manufacture of paper and paper products, printing and publishing	1.3	0.1	2.7	-0.1	...	4.0	2.9	0.5	3.1	-0.9	...	5.6
	E Manufacture of chemicals and chemical petroleum, coal, rubber and plastic products	5.4	1.2	10.2	1.8	...	18.6	8.6	6.6	11.3	1.9	...	28.4
	F Manufacture of non-metallic mineral products, except products of petroleum and coal	1.6	0.6	1.0	0.6	...	3.8	1.4	0.7	2.7	0.6	...	5.4
	G Basic metal industries	5.0	1.1	1.4	0.5	...	8.0	5.8	2.3	2.3	0.9	...	11.3
	H Manufacture of fabricated metal products, machinery and equipment	6.5	0.9	1.9	1.1	...	10.4	9.6	0.9	2.6	1.6	...	14.7
	I Other manufacturing industries	1.1	0.4	1.6	0.8	...	3.9	1.4	0.6	2.4	1.2	...	5.6
4	Electricity, gas and water	6.5	1.8	9.1	0.2	...	17.6	8.2	2.9	11.0	0.1	...	22.2
5	Construction	51.3	7.9	34.2	9.9	...	103.3	58.4	9.0	47.4	10.2	...	125.0
6	Wholesale and retail trade, restaurants and hotels	88.7	9.5	96.4	37.7	...	232.3	92.9	10.9	97.7	47.8	...	249.3
	A Wholesale and retail trade	84.6	8.9	93.9	35.6	...	223.0	87.9	10.3	94.9	45.0	...	238.1
	B Restaurants and hotels	4.1	0.6	2.5	2.1	...	9.3	4.9	0.7	2.8	2.8	...	11.2
7	Transport, storage and communication	34.5	18.4	46.0	4.6	...	103.6	40.8	20.4	51.3	6.8	...	119.3
8	Finance, insurance, real estate and business services	35.3	20.0	180.0	12.8	...	248.0	47.4	21.5	198.3	17.7	...	284.9
	A Financial institutions	14.4	2.7	29.0	5.0	...	51.1	24.8	3.1	46.0	7.4	...	81.3
	B Insurance	...	...	...	...	...	...	...	...	...	...	...	...
	C Real estate and business services	20.8	17.3	151.0	7.8	...	196.9	22.6	18.4	152.3	10.3	...	203.6
9	Community, social and personal services	12.4	1.6	4.8	4.1	...	22.9	15.0	1.8	6.5	4.7	...	28.0
	Total, Industries [a]	374.2	122.8	960.0	134.0	...	1591.2	464.6	139.6	1148.7	172.5	...	1925.4
	Producers of Government Services	107.9	2.4	...	...	...	110.3	132.4	2.9	...	...	...	135.3
	Other Producers	22.5	0.3	-	0.2	...	23.0	27.1	0.3	-	0.2	...	27.6
	Total [a]	504.6	125.5	960.0	134.3	...	1724.5	624.1	142.8	1148.7	172.7	...	2088.3
	Less: Imputed bank service charge	...	...	30.5	...	...	30.5	...	...	42.2	...	...	42.2
	Import duties	...	...	...	102.6	...	102.6	...	...	...	126.4	...	126.4
	Value added tax	...	...	...	...	...	...	...	...	...	...	...	...
	Total [a]	504.6	125.5	929.6	236.7	...	1796.5	623.8	142.9	1106.7	299.4	...	2172.8

1982 / 1983

		Compensation of Employees	Capital Consumption	Net Operating Surplus	Indirect Taxes	Less: Subsidies Received	Value Added	Compensation of Employees	Capital Consumption	Net Operating Surplus	Indirect Taxes	Less: Subsidies Received	Value Added
	All Producers												
1	Agriculture, hunting, forestry and fishing	96.6	32.8	455.0	22.8	...	607.2	113.7	27.9	539.7	20.7	...	702.0
	A Agriculture and hunting	73.1	25.1	440.3	12.7	...	551.2	86.4	21.1	514.9	9.8	...	632.2
	B Forestry and logging	20.0	6.3	12.6	9.5	...	48.4	23.7	6.0	22.7	10.4	...	62.8
	C Fishing	3.5	1.4	2.1	0.6	...	7.6	3.6	0.8	2.1	0.5	...	7.0
2	Mining and quarrying	17.1	22.3	348.1	13.0	...	400.5	22.6	29.3	452.8	15.8	...	520.5

Cameroon

4.3 Cost Components of Value Added
(Continued)

Thousand Million CFA francs — Fiscal year beginning 1 July

	1982 Compensation of Employees	Capital Consumption	Net Operating Surplus	Indirect Taxes	Less: Subsidies Received	Value Added	1983 Compensation of Employees	Capital Consumption	Net Operating Surplus	Indirect Taxes	Less: Subsidies Received	Value Added
3 Manufacturing	112.1	29.9	95.4	53.7	...	291.1	130.8	32.5	138.1	57.2	...	358.5
A Manufacture of food, beverages and tobacco	37.7	9.8	47.8	36.5	...	131.8	48.7	11.5	68.2	37.8	...	166.0
B Textile, wearing apparel and leather industries	26.2	5.6	11.8	7.4	...	51.0	27.8	5.8	14.1	7.8	...	55.5
C Manufacture of wood and wood products, including furniture	14.6	1.6	4.4	2.8	...	23.4	16.9	2.1	7.9	3.7	...	30.6
D Manufacture of paper and paper products, printing and publishing	3.0	0.4	1.4	0.3	...	5.1	2.3	0.4	0.5	0.3	...	3.5
E Manufacture of chemicals and chemical petroleum, coal, rubber and plastic products	9.7	6.9	18.1	2.2	...	36.9	11.9	7.3	28.9	2.8	...	50.9
F Manufacture of non-metallic mineral products, except products of petroleum and coal	2.2	1.0	3.3	1.0	...	7.5	2.7	1.0	5.6	1.3	...	10.6
G Basic metal industries	7.2	2.9	1.4	0.7	...	12.2	7.8	2.9	5.6	1.0	...	17.3
H Manufacture of fabricated metal products, machinery and equipment	9.9	0.9	4.0	1.8	...	16.6	10.8	0.8	4.9	2.0	...	18.5
I Other manufacturing industries	1.6	0.8	3.2	1.0	...	6.6	1.7	0.7	2.4	0.7	...	5.5
4 Electricity, gas and water	10.3	3.1	16.4	0.2	...	30.0	12.1	3.8	19.1	0.2	...	35.2
5 Construction	72.8	6.3	56.1	10.6	...	145.8	78.6	10.4	90.7	12.9	...	192.6
6 Wholesale and retail trade, restaurants and hotels	114.7	13.2	119.2	63.6	...	310.7	130.9	13.9	170.2	99.9	...	414.9
A Wholesale and retail trade	109.0	12.5	115.6	60.7	...	297.8	125.1	13.3	166.6	96.9	...	401.9
B Restaurants and hotels	5.7	0.7	3.6	2.9	...	12.9	5.8	0.6	3.6	3.0	...	13.0
7 Transport, storage and communication	47.3	21.8	52.8	7.1	...	129.0	53.6	15.0	72.9	5.8	...	147.3
8 Finance, insurance, real estate and business services	57.1	23.3	248.8	26.0	...	355.2	64.8	26.3	279.8	26.0	...	396.9
A Financial institutions	28.9	3.5	62.6	12.1	...	107.1	35.5	5.3	78.7	17.4	...	136.9
B Insurance	...	...	...	...	...	...	...	...	...	...	...	...
C Real estate and business services	28.2	19.8	186.2	13.9	...	248.1	29.3	21.0	201.1	8.6	...	260.0
9 Community, social and personal services	17.9	1.9	9.7	5.0	...	34.5	19.9	2.1	12.2	5.1	...	39.3
Total, Industries [a]	545.9	154.6	1401.5	202.0	...	2304.0	627.0	161.2	1775.5	243.6	...	2807.2
Producers of Government Services	168.8	3.0	...	...	...	171.8	209.2	3.6	...	...	...	212.8
Other Producers	32.6	0.4	-	0.2	...	33.2	39.4	0.5	-	0.3	...	40.2
Total [a]	747.3	158.0	1401.5	202.2	...	2509.0	875.6	165.3	1775.5	244.1	...	3060.2
Less: Imputed bank service charge	...	...	37.5	...	...	37.5	...	...	38.1	...	...	38.1
Import duties	...	...	...	146.8	...	146.8	...	...	...	173.0	...	173.0
Value added tax	...	...	...	...	...	...	...	...	...	...	...	...
Total [a]	747.4	158.1	1363.7	348.9	...	2618.0	875.5	165.2	1737.5	416.7	...	3195.0

	1984 Compensation of Employees	Capital Consumption	Net Operating Surplus	Indirect Taxes	Less: Subsidies Received	Value Added	1985 Compensation of Employees	Capital Consumption	Net Operating Surplus	Indirect Taxes	Less: Subsidies Received	Value Added
					All Producers							
1 Agriculture, hunting, forestry and fishing	128.7	32.3	603.4	26.0	...	790.4	138.5	22.1	723.5	23.8	...	907.9
A Agriculture and hunting	96.9	23.4	569.4	11.0	...	700.7	105.1	17.9	680.9	8.8	...	812.6
B Forestry and logging	28.6	8.3	33.4	14.5	...	84.8	30.2	3.7	40.0	14.6	...	88.5
C Fishing	3.1	0.7	0.7	0.5	...	5.0	3.2	0.5	2.7	0.4	...	6.7
2 Mining and quarrying	23.2	49.2	542.4	14.9	...	629.7	20.9	41.6	419.0	23.2	...	504.7

Cameroon

4.3 Cost Components of Value Added
(Continued)

Thousand Million CFA francs — Fiscal year beginning 1 July

	1984 Compensation of Employees	1984 Capital Consumption	1984 Net Operating Surplus	1984 Indirect Taxes	1984 Less: Subsidies Received	1984 Value Added	1985 Compensation of Employees	1985 Capital Consumption	1985 Net Operating Surplus	1985 Indirect Taxes	1985 Less: Subsidies Received	1985 Value Added
3 Manufacturing	141.9	36.6	171.4	72.5	...	422.4	170.0	39.7	225.3	79.8	...	514.8
A Manufacture of food, beverages and tobacco	53.7	14.7	82.3	46.4	...	197.1	67.2	16.1	105.4	50.9	...	239.6
B Textile, wearing apparel and leather industries	29.1	5.7	24.8	10.4	...	70.0	36.2	5.7	30.3	8.1	...	80.3
C Manufacture of wood and wood products, including furniture	19.5	2.6	9.6	5.4	...	37.1	22.6	2.2	12.2	7.8	...	44.8
D Manufacture of paper and paper products, printing and publishing	2.5	0.5	0.4	0.2	...	3.6	3.0	0.5	0.5	0.1	...	4.1
E Manufacture of chemicals and chemical petroleum, coal, rubber and plastic products	12.7	7.3	33.2	3.1	...	56.3	15.9	9.5	44.0	4.0	...	73.4
F Manufacture of non-metallic mineral products, except products of petroleum and coal	2.7	1.3	6.2	2.8	...	13.0	3.2	1.5	10.6	3.2	...	18.4
G Basic metal industries	8.8	2.8	5.8	1.2	...	18.6	9.2	3.0	8.4	1.4	...	22.0
H Manufacture of fabricated metal products, machinery and equipment	11.1	1.0	6.9	2.3	...	21.3	10.7	0.6	10.2	3.6	...	25.2
I Other manufacturing industries	1.7	0.7	2.3	0.6	...	5.3	2.0	0.6	3.9	0.6	...	7.1
4 Electricity, gas and water	16.0	6.7	14.8	0.2	...	37.7	19.0	7.8	18.1	0.3	...	45.1
5 Construction	92.5	9.3	110.5	15.3	...	227.6	87.6	10.1	156.1	24.8	...	278.6
6 Wholesale and retail trade, restaurants and hotels	126.1	18.5	306.1	113.8	...	564.5	143.7	15.2	343.5	155.9	...	658.4
A Wholesale and retail trade	118.2	17.5	299.6	110.3	...	545.6	132.7	13.5	333.2	151.9	...	631.3
B Restaurants and hotels	7.9	1.0	6.5	3.5	...	18.9	11.0	1.7	10.3	4.0	...	27.1
7 Transport, storage and communication	76.8	13.0	126.9	14.0	...	230.7	89.1	13.0	137.1	9.5	...	248.8
8 Finance, insurance, real estate and business services	77.4	16.2	325.3	36.3	...	455.2	82.2	11.3	346.5	30.4	...	470.4
A Financial institutions	46.4	14.2	89.6	25.7	...	175.9	51.5	9.2	99.7	15.7	...	176.2
B Insurance	...	...	...	...	...	...	...	...	...	...	...	...
C Real estate and business services	31.0	2.0	235.8	10.7	...	279.4	30.7	2.1	246.8	14.7	...	294.2
9 Community, social and personal services	25.1	2.6	13.4	5.2	...	46.3	28.7	3.3	16.5	5.6	...	54.0
Total, Industries [a]	707.7	184.4	2214.1	298.2	...	3404.5	779.7	164.1	2385.7	353.3	...	3682.7
Producers of Government Services	239.2	9.6	...	...	...	248.8	286.9	7.9	...	0.3	...	295.1
Other Producers	42.4	0.7	...	0.4	...	43.6	47.7	1.0	...	-0.2	...	48.5
Total [a]	989.5	194.7	2214.1	298.6	...	3696.9	1114.3	173.0	2385.7	353.4	...	4026.3
Less: Imputed bank service charge	...	...	32.4	...	...	32.4	...	...	26.0	...	...	26.0
Import duties	...	...	...	174.4	...	174.4	...	...	...	134.8	...	134.8
Value added tax	...	...	...	...	...	...	...	...	...	...	...	...
Total [a]	989.5	194.7	2181.7	473.0	...	3838.9	1114.3	173.0	2359.7	488.2	...	4135.1

a) Column 4 refers to indirect taxes less subsidies received.

Canada

General note. The preparation of national accounts statistics in Canada is undertaken by Statistics Canada, Ottawa. Official estimates are published quarterly and annually in 'National Income and Expenditure Accounts'. A detailed description of the sources and methods used for the national accounts estimation is found in volume 3 of the above-mentioned publication published in September 1975. The estimates are generally in accordance with the classifications and definitions recommended in the United Nations System of National Accounts (SNA). Annual input-output tables at constant and current prices are published in 'The Input-Output Structure of the Canadian Economy'. The following tables have been prepared from successive replies to the United Nations national accounts questionnaire. When the scope and coverage of the estimates differ for conceptual or statistical reasons from the definitions and classifications recommended in SNA, a footnote is indicated to the relevant tables.

Sources and methods:

(a) Gross domestic product. Gross domestic product is estimated mainly through the income approach.

(b) Expenditure on the gross domestic product. All components of GDP by expenditure type are estimated through the expenditure approach. Government final consumption expenditure is based on public accounts and financial records and statements of the government bodies. At the federal and provincial levels, the figures are derived by eliminating from total government budgetary expenditures all outlays that are not made directly to purchases new goods and services. At the local level, the estimates are built up directly on a gross basis from the data sources subtracting revenues from sales of goods and services. Bench-mark estimates of consumption expenditure are based on the censuses of merchandising and services held in 1951, 1961, and 1966. These estimates are first adjusted to include commodities purchased through non-retail trade outlets and then broken down into trade groupings. For the non-census years, the bench-mark estimates of each trade group are interpolated or projected by using the movement of sales of equivalent kind-of-business groupings. For non-retail trade groups, surveys of wholesale and service trade, surveys of direct selling and surveys of vending machine sales are used. Estimates of consumer expenditure on services such as transport, health care and education are based on annual surveys or published reports. Estimates for other services are based on decennial censuses of merchandising and services with projections to other years being made on directly related series. Comprehensive figures on the quantities of physical stocks held on farms and grains in commercial channels are available from the Agriculture Division of Statistics Canada. Inventories held by Government agencies are obtained from government records. Estimates of inventory book values of non-farm business are based on annual censuses or sample surveys. The estimates of gross fixed capital investment are based on the results of annual surveys which are published in the 'Private and Public Investment in Canada: Outlook' reports. Data are available separately for residential and non-residential construction and machinery and equipment. The estimates of exports and imports of goods and services are based on information available in the balance of payments. For merchandise, the import and export figures are obtained from the customs entries while for services, the estimates draw upon a number of sources such as surveys of business firms and Department of Manpower and Immigration. Constant values of government consumption expenditure are obtained through extrapolating base-year wages and salaries by employment data and through deflating other current expenditure by base-weighted price indexes. Price deflation is also used for private final consumption expenditure, non-farm stocks, non-residential construction and machinery and equipment and part of exports and imports of goods and services. The constant price series of farm inventories is derived by valuing the physical quantities of stocks in prices relevant to the base period chosen. For residential construction, the estimates are derived by multiplying the quantity of work put in place by the base-year average unit value. Exports and imports of merchandise are each revalued by specially constructed current-weighted indexes.

(c) Cost-structure of the gross domestic product. The general method used in the preparation of the labour income estimates consists in calculating the payments made on labour account by the various industrial groups and summing the results. The estimates are based on monthly and annual samples of full-coverage surveys conducted by Statistics Canada, decennial or quinquennial censuses and published statements of governments. Another source of information is the tabulation of total wages and salaries submitted by employers with respect to employees' earnings, undertaken by the Department of National Revenue in connexion with the administration of the Canada Pension Plan. The estimates of corporation profits are obtained from two publications: 'Corporation Financial Statistics' and 'Corporation Taxation Statistics'. Estimates of interest and miscellaneous investment income are based on information obtained from various sources such as Department of National Revenue, Bank of Canada, accounts and financial statements of governments and others. For unincorporated business, estimates are obtained either through direct inquiry, projections from bench-mark data, subtracting expenses from gross income or through applying the ratio of net of gross income based on survey or income-tax data. The estimates of depreciation are calculated on an original cost valuation basis with a close link to the figures of book depreciation reported in the accounting records of business firms. For the government sector, capital consumption allowances are imputed while for the agricultural and housing sectors, replacement cost estimates of capital consumption are prepared from estimates of fixed reproducible capital at market values. The estimates of indirect taxes are based on accounting records of the various levels of government. Subsidies consist of federal production and consumption subsidies.

(d) Gross domestic product by kind of economic activity. The table of GDP by kind of economic activity is prepared in factor values. The income approach is used to estimate the value added of the various industries, except in the case of agriculture, for which the income approach is combined with the production approach through the use of an operating account for agricultural activity. The components of GDP at factor cost are classified by industry on the basis of establishment data. Wages, salaries and supplementary labour income as well as net incomes of farms and non-farm unincorporated businesses, corporation profits and capital consumption allowances are essentially built up by assembling data on an industry-by-industry basis. Certain imputations are made to include non-market activities. They are allocated to their appropriate industry of origin. For the estimates in constant prices, double deflation is used for agriculture, manufacturing, electricity and railway and air transports. Price deflation is used for non-residential and other engineering construction, road transport and advertising services. For producers of government services and producers of private non-profit services to households, various indicators are used to extrapolate or deflate value added. For the remaining industries, value added is exprapolated by various quantity indicators or indexes.

1.1 Expenditure on the Gross Domestic Product, in Current Prices

Million Canadian dollars

	1970	1975	1980	1981	1982	1983	1984	1985	1986	1987	1988	1989
1 Government final consumption expenditure	16389	33147	59097	68604	78443	84314	88882	95274	99878	105833	112987	120885
2 Private final consumption expenditure	51258	96251	170408	193839	208099	228221	248428	271099	293489	318551	345754	375542
3 Gross capital formation [a]	19250	43213	72624	87305	71574	78329	89460	96479	104117	118896	134019	147106
A Increase in stocks [a]	239	1368	336	1186	-9753	-2898	4761	2281	2557	2719	2483	3754
B Gross fixed capital formation [b]	19011	41845	72288	86119	81327	81227	84699	94198	101560	116177	131536	143352
Residential buildings	4511	11062	17455	20631	17648	21423	22348	25238	30823	39192	43589	47995
Non-residential buildings	3470	6953	10921	13115	11885	11362	12009	14518	15507	18183	20545	23472
Other construction and land improvement etc.	4738	10112	18556	21959	23699	21470	21549	22709	20159	19537	22262	23638
Other [c]	6292	13718	25356	30414	28095	26972	28793	31733	35071	39265	45140	48247
4 Exports of goods and services [d]	20078	38954	87579	96880	96651	103444	126035	134919	138119	144755	158731	162852
5 Less: Imports of goods and services [d]	17830	41362	81933	93001	82598	89832	110632	123388	133369	139867	154299	162523
Statistical discrepancy	-683	-97	-45	-173	-349	-2247	-862	-44	-808	-1651	986	2032
Equals: Gross Domestic Product	88462	170106	307730	353454	371820	402229	441311	474339	501426	546517	598178	645894

a) Increase in stocks of gross capital formation includes stocks of breeding stocks, draught animals, dairy cattle. Stocks of commodities internally processed are valued at cost.
b) Outlays on embassies, consulates and military establishments abroad are included under government current expenditure and imports.
c) Producers durable goods of gross fixed capital formation includes work put in place on uncompleted heavy machinery and equipment.
d) Exports and imports of merchandise are recorded on the basis of the crossing of frontiers. No data are available on the basis of changes in the ownership of the goods.

1.2 Expenditure on the Gross Domestic Product, in Constant Prices

Million Canadian dollars

	1970	1975	1980	1981	1982	1983	1984	1985	1986	1987	1988	1989
	At constant prices of:1986											
1 Government final consumption expenditure	61775	78797	88447	90668	92825	94137	95349	98332	99878	101686	104522	107191
2 Private final consumption expenditure	153236	207675	247918	253661	246991	255588	267565	281348	293489	306594	320075	332076
3 Gross capital formation [a]	48399	67978	86871	97816	78241	83349	90750	97799	104117	114880	124833	132525
A Increase in stocks [a]	1242	2167	284	1026	-7912	-2187	3388	2175	2557	2845	1391	3477
B Gross fixed capital formation [bc]	47157	65811	86587	96790	86153	85536	87362	95624	101560	112035	123442	129048

Canada

1.2 Expenditure on the Gross Domestic Product, in Constant Prices
(Continued)

Million Canadian dollars

	1970	1975	1980	1981	1982	1983	1984	1985	1986	1987	1988	1989
At constant prices of: 1986												
Residential buildings	14851	20839	23739	25120	21118	24746	24744	27202	30823	35596	36949	37822
Non-residential buildings	10292	12449	14256	15321	12896	12263	12966	15203	15507	17144	18248	19488
Other construction and land improvement etc.	15698	19851	24018	25287	25508	23060	21957	22505	20159	19215	21020	21889
Other [d]	12567	16891	26472	31369	27122	26236	28251	31325	35071	40080	47225	49849
4 Exports of goods and services [e]	57661	66088	97564	101853	99637	106017	124785	132218	138119	142288	154950	156076
5 Less: Imports of goods and services [e]	46534	69921	97035	105313	89343	97395	114058	123935	133369	142286	160607	168838
Statistical discrepancy	-5267	-3480	-2883	-2275	-5957	-5851	-735	-153	-808	-1548	923	1815
Equals: Gross Domestic Product	269270	347137	420882	436410	422394	435845	463656	485609	501426	521614	544696	560845

a) Increase in stocks of gross capital formation includes stocks of breeding stocks, draught animals, dairy cattle, etc. Stocks of commodities internally processed are valued at cost.
b) Outlays on embassies, consulates and military establishments abroad are included under government current expenditure and imports.
c) Prior to 1986, the estimates of the total is greater than the sum of its sub-items. The difference refers to an adjusting entry which is not shown.
d) Producers durable goods of gross fixed capital formation includes work put in place on uncompleted heavy machinery and equipment.
e) Exports and imports of merchandise are recorded on the basis of the crossing of frontiers. No data are available on the basis of changes in the ownership of the goods.

1.3 Cost Components of the Gross Domestic Product

Million Canadian dollars

	1970	1975	1980	1981	1982	1983	1984	1985	1986	1987	1988	1989
1 Indirect taxes, net	11095	17087	27272	36457	38908	40135	42714	47212	53827	58432	65205	73133
A Indirect taxes	11925	21287	35505	45956	48248	50150	54957	58789	64338	70956	76729	84735
B Less: Subsidies	830	4200	8233	9499	9340	10015	12243	11577	10511	12524	11524	11602
2 Consumption of fixed capital	9948	18760	35527	40677	44356	47060	50884	55926	60595	64066	67813	72915
3 Compensation of employees paid by resident producers to:	48952	96623	171424	197910	211604	221800	238849	257518	274801	298850	328562	358355
A Resident households	48952	96623	171424	197910	211604	221800	238849	257518	274801	298850	328562	358355
B Rest of the world	-	-	-	-	-	-	-	-	-	-	-	-
4 Operating surplus	17783	37538	73462	78237	76602	90987	108001	113638	111394	123517	137585	143523
Statistical discrepancy	684	98	45	173	350	2247	863	45	809	1652	-987	-2032
Equals: Gross Domestic Product	88462	170106	307730	353454	371820	402229	441311	474339	501426	546517	598178	645894

1.4 General Government Current Receipts and Disbursements

Million Canadian dollars

	1970	1975	1980	1981	1982	1983	1984	1985	1986	1987	1988	1989
Receipts												
1 Operating surplus	...	...	...	...	...	...	...	...	...	...	...	...
2 Property and entrepreneurial income	2665	7057	17787	20746	22097	25010	27975	29411	28236	29650	32621	35536
3 Taxes, fees and contributions	27604	54347	93743	115341	123100	130487	142887	154218	169742	188717	207346	220145
A Indirect taxes	11925	21287	35505	45956	48248	50150	54957	58789	64338	70956	76729	84735
B Direct taxes	12309	26222	45923	53844	57641	60684	66687	71830	79731	89606	99081	103712
C Social security contributions	2470	5963	10591	13603	14954	17156	18582	20847	22785	25090	28196	28127
D Compulsory fees, fines and penalties	900	875	1724	1938	2257	2497	2661	2752	2888	3065	3340	3571
4 Other current transfers	...	...	...	...	...	...	...	...	...	...	...	...
Total Current Receipts of General Government	30269	61404	111530	136087	145197	155497	170862	183629	197978	218367	239967	255681
Disbursements												
1 Government final consumption expenditure	16389	33147	59097	68604	78443	84314	88882	95274	99878	105833	112987	120885
A Compensation of employees	11274	22571	39345	45596	51986	55885	58871	61215	64646	68750	72983	78238
B Consumption of fixed capital	1206	2491	4553	5311	5881	6297	6773	7092	7371	7636	8065	8583
C Purchases of goods and services, net	3909	8085	15199	17697	20576	22132	23238	26967	27861	29447	31939	34064
D Less: Own account fixed capital formation	...	...	...	...	...	...	...	...	...	...	...	...
E Indirect taxes paid, net	...	...	...	...	...	...	...	...	...	...	...	...
2 Property income	3252	6538	16790	22268	27072	29419	34752	40183	42754	45965	50847	57718
A Interest	3252	6538	16790	22268	27072	29419	34752	40183	42754	45965	50847	57718
B Net land rent and royalties	...	...	...	...	...	...	...	...	...	...	...	...

Canada

1.4 General Government Current Receipts and Disbursements
(Continued)

Million Canadian dollars

		1970	1975	1980	1981	1982	1983	1984	1985	1986	1987	1988	1989
3	Subsidies	830	4200	8233	9499	9340	10015	12243	11577	10511	12524	11524	11602
4	Other current transfers	7225	17646	31283	35833	44692	51141	55107	59638	63391	68426	73749	78241
	A Social security benefits	3182	8741	16655	19305	25482	29135	31151	33963	36904	40396	43563	46993
	B Social assistance grants	3799	8313	13811	15653	18147	20812	22385	24032	24692	25861	27742	28908
	C Other	244	592	817	875	1063	1194	1571	1643	1795	2169	2444	2340
5	Net saving	2573	-127	-3873	-117	-14350	-19392	-20122	-23043	-18556	-14381	-9140	-12765
	Total Current Disbursements and Net Saving of General Government	30269	61404	111530	136087	145197	155497	170862	183629	197978	218367	239967	255681

1.5 Current Income and Outlay of Corporate and Quasi-Corporate Enterprises, Summary

Million Canadian dollars

		1970	1975	1980	1981	1982	1983	1984	1985	1986	1987	1988	1989
	Receipts												
1	Operating surplus	...	...	...	...	...	...	...	...	...	...	...	...
2	Property and entrepreneurial income received	15364	37132	86236	96603	93340	104481	122927	131874	127207	141690	159468	166392
3	Current transfers	...	...	...	...	...	...	...	...	...	...	...	...
	Statistical discrepancy [a]	-160	-2728	-7336	-7217	-3276	-2659	-2625	-1760	-1812	-3036	-3254	-1688
	Total Current Receipts	15204	34404	78900	89386	90064	101822	120302	130114	125395	138654	156214	164704
	Disbursements												
1	Property and entrepreneurial income	9154	21293	54686	71575	81314	79769	90228	95787	96877	100152	114896	125761
2	Direct taxes and other current payments to general government	3070	7494	12078	12796	11755	12320	14984	15563	14573	16878	17337	16816
3	Other current transfers	180	326	647	814	769	735	744	697	734	782	833	826
	Statistical discrepancy [a]	-160	-2728	-7336	-7217	-3276	-2659	-2625	-1760	-1812	-3036	-3254	-1688
4	Net saving	2960	8019	18825	11418	-498	11657	16971	19827	15023	23878	26402	22997
	Total Current Disbursements and Net Saving	15204	34404	78900	89386	90064	101822	120302	130114	125395	138654	156214	164704

a) Item 'Statistical discrepancy' refers to inventory valuation adjustment.

1.6 Current Income and Outlay of Households and Non-Profit Institutions

Million Canadian dollars

		1970	1975	1980	1981	1982	1983	1984	1985	1986	1987	1988	1989
	Receipts												
1	Compensation of employees	48952	96623	171424	197910	211604	221800	238849	257518	274801	298850	328562	358355
	A From resident producers	48952	96623	171424	197910	211604	221800	238849	257518	274801	298850	328562	358355
	B From rest of the world	...	...	...	...	...	...	...	...	...	...	...	...
2	Operating surplus of private unincorporated enterprises	7021	12080	16598	17853	20315	23629	27307	29255	32802	34707	38453	39615
3	Property and entrepreneurial income	4486	10641	27539	38120	44974	41896	47702	50729	52686	55720	63235	72961
4	Current transfers	7256	17585	31503	36155	44863	51159	54741	59215	62966	67736	72829	77454
	A Social security benefits	3182	8741	16655	19305	25482	29135	31151	33963	36904	40396	43563	46993
	B Social assistance grants	3799	8313	13811	15653	18147	20812	22385	24032	24692	25861	27742	28908
	C Other	275	531	1037	1197	1234	1212	1205	1220	1370	1479	1524	1553
	Total Current Receipts	67715	136929	247064	290038	321756	338484	368599	396717	423255	457013	503079	548385
	Disbursements												
1	Private final consumption expenditure	51258	96251	170408	193839	208099	228221	248428	271099	293489	318551	345754	375542
2	Property income	538	1351	3713	5362	5132	3785	3791	4233	4496	5267	6077	7974
3	Direct taxes and other current transfers n.e.c. to general government	12340	25101	45165	55479	61919	66974	71846	78797	89156	99669	111610	117057
	A Social security contributions	2470	5963	10591	13603	14954	17156	18582	20847	22785	25090	28196	28127
	B Direct taxes	8970	18263	32850	39938	44708	47321	50603	55198	63483	71514	80074	85359
	C Fees, fines and penalties	900	875	1724	1938	2257	2497	2661	2752	2888	3065	3340	3571
4	Other current transfers	176	258	364	385	443	473	500	554	602	633	648	704
5	Net saving	3403	13968	27414	34973	46163	39031	44034	42034	35512	32893	38990	47108
	Total Current Disbursements and Net Saving	67715	136929	247064	290038	321756	338484	368599	396717	423255	457013	503079	548385

Canada

1.7 External Transactions on Current Account, Summary

Million Canadian dollars

	1970	1975	1980	1981	1982	1983	1984	1985	1986	1987	1988	1989
Payments to the Rest of the World												
1 Imports of goods and services	17830	41362	81933	93001	82598	89832	110632	123388	133369	139867	154299	162523
A Imports of merchandise c.i.f. [a]	14758	35764	70912	80496	69665	75961	95404	106680	114425	119546	132617	139151
B Other	3072	5598	11021	12505	12933	13871	15228	16708	18944	20321	21682	23372
2 Factor income to the rest of the world	2397	4271	11466	15330	18149	17197	19849	21906	24118	24226	30201	30651
A Compensation of employees	-	-	-	-	-	-	-	-	-	-	-	-
B Property and entrepreneurial income	2397	4271	11466	15330	18149	17197	19849	21906	24118	24226	30201	30651
By general government	238	426	1592	1867	2816	3245	3755	4743	6502	7407	8489	10135
By corporate and quasi-corporate enterprises	2159	3845	9874	13463	15333	13952	16094	17163	17616	16819	21712	20516
By other	...	...	...	...	...	...	...	...	...	...	...	...
3 Current transfers to the rest of the world	448	903	1310	1422	1641	1800	2239	2355	2538	2926	3243	3180
A Indirect taxes to supranational organizations	...	...	...	...	...	...	...	...	...	...	...	...
B Other current transfers	448	903	1310	1422	1641	1800	2239	2355	2538	2926	3243	3180
4 Surplus of the nation on current transactions	841	-5126	-1977	-7225	1520	1862	1407	-3406	-11738	-12173	-15181	-22603
Payments to the Rest of the World and Surplus of the Nation on Current Transactions	21516	41410	92732	102528	103908	110691	134127	144243	148287	154846	172562	173751
Receipts From The Rest of the World												
1 Exports of goods and services	20078	38954	87579	96880	96651	103444	126035	134919	138119	144755	158731	162852
A Exports of merchandise f.o.b. [a,b]	17498	34614	78946	86939	87004	93311	114849	122468	123719	129887	142434	145914
B Other	2580	4340	8633	9941	9647	10133	11186	12451	14400	14868	16297	16938
2 Factor income from rest of the world	1046	1733	3639	3993	5479	5594	6363	7574	7716	8056	11319	8499
A Compensation of employees	-	-	-	-	-	-	-	-	-	-	-	-
B Property and entrepreneurial income	1046	1733	3639	3993	5479	5594	6363	7574	7716	8056	11319	8499
By general government	38	57	80	72	41	35	60	48	243	472	1072	1374
By corporate and quasi-corporate enterprises	890	1483	3125	3239	4389	4505	4820	6058	6055	6019	8647	5247
By other	118	193	434	682	1049	1054	1483	1468	1418	1565	1600	1878
3 Current transfers from rest of the world	392	723	1514	1655	1778	1653	1729	1750	2452	2035	2512	2400
A Subsidies from supranational organisations	...	...	...	...	...	...	...	...	...	...	...	...
B Other current transfers	392	723	1514	1655	1778	1653	1729	1750	2452	2035	2512	2400
Receipts from the Rest of the World on Current Transactions	21516	41410	92732	102528	103908	110691	134127	144243	148287	154846	172562	173751

a) Exports and imports of merchandise are recorded on the basis of the crossing of frontiers. No data are available on the basis of changes in the ownership of the goods.
b) Exports of Canadian produce and re-exports of foreign produce which are valued f.o.b. point of shipment in Canada plus inland freight and gold.

1.8 Capital Transactions of The Nation, Summary

Million Canadian dollars

	1970	1975	1980	1981	1982	1983	1984	1985	1986	1987	1988	1989
Finance of Gross Capital Formation												
Gross saving	18724	37892	70557	79734	72395	75697	89142	92984	90762	103420	120811	128567
1 Consumption of fixed capital	9948	18760	35527	40677	44356	47060	50884	55926	60595	64066	67813	72915
A General government	1206	2491	4553	5311	5881	6297	6773	7092	7371	7636	8065	8583
B Corporate and quasi-corporate enterprises	5677	10365	20753	23841	25956	27659	29887	33521	36779	38331	40785	43725
Public	625	1058	2268	2442	2892	3329	3863	4268	4433	4661	4746	4799
Private	5052	9307	18485	21399	23064	24330	26024	29253	32346	33670	36039	38926
C Other	3065	5904	10221	11525	12519	13104	14224	15313	16445	18099	18963	20607
2 Net saving	8776	19132	35030	39057	28039	28637	38258	37058	30167	39354	52998	55652
A General government	2573	-127	-3873	-117	-14350	-19392	-20122	-23043	-18556	-14381	-9140	-12765
B Corporate and quasi-corporate enterprises	2960	8019	18825	11418	-498	11657	16971	19827	15023	23878	26402	22997
Public	251	41	1929	2037	617	1219	1486	1529	1377	1900	2072	1636
Private	2709	7978	16896	9381	-1115	10438	15485	18298	13646	21978	24330	21361

Canada

1.8 Capital Transactions of The Nation, Summary
(Continued)

Million Canadian dollars

	1970	1975	1980	1981	1982	1983	1984	1985	1986	1987	1988	1989
C Other [a]	3243	11240	20078	27756	42887	36372	41409	40274	33700	29857	35736	45420
Less: Surplus of the nation on current transactions	841	-5126	-1977	-7225	1520	1862	1407	-3406	-11738	-12173	-15181	-22603
Statistical discrepancy	1367	195	90	346	699	4494	1725	89	1617	3303	-1973	-4064
Finance of Gross Capital Formation	19250	43213	72624	87305	71574	78329	89460	96479	104117	118896	134019	147106
Gross Capital Formation												
Increase in stocks	239	1368	336	1186	-9753	-2898	4761	2281	2557	2719	2483	3754
Gross fixed capital formation	19011	41845	72288	86119	81327	81227	84699	94198	101560	116177	131536	143352
1 General government	3173	6243	8223	9447	10519	10395	11390	12886	12567	12910	13704	15283
2 Corporate and quasi-corporate enterprises	10880	22982	43689	53182	51129	47076	48287	54385	57210	64172	74460	80520
3 Other	4958	12620	20376	23490	19679	23756	25022	26927	31783	39095	43372	47549
Gross Capital Formation	19250	43213	72624	87305	71574	78329	89460	96479	104117	118896	134019	147106

a) Item 'Other' includes inventory valuation adjustment.

1.10 Gross Domestic Product by Kind of Activity, in Current Prices

Million Canadian dollars

	1970	1975	1980	1981	1982	1983	1984	1985	1986	1987	1988	1989
1 Agriculture, hunting, forestry and fishing	3378	7603	11698	13221	12625	12080	13604	13337	14728	15737	...	...
2 Mining and quarrying	3060	6974	18067	17454	18503	21610	25565	27115	17502	20401	...	...
3 Manufacturing	17507	31511	55043	61648	57837	65261	75504	81673	86789	94808	...	...
4 Electricity, gas and water	1891	3343	8172	9250	10417	11891	13371	14668	15533	16417	...	...
5 Construction [a]	5505	12922	20266	25094	25563	25061	24481	26141	28082	32586	...	...
6 Wholesale and retail trade, restaurants and hotels	11520	22771	38520	43348	44349	47682	52663	57872	63190	69046	...	...
7 Transport, storage and communication	6092	10544	19554	21860	23348	25460	28366	29845	31466	33215	...	...
8 Finance, insurance, real estate and business services	11216	23654	48005	54451	60486	67452	72871	78506	85820	94890	...	...
9 Community, social and personal services	3458	7167	13679	15845	17281	18874	21033	23348	26139	28215	...	...
Total, Industries	63627	126489	233004	262171	270409	295371	327458	352503	369249	405315	...	...
Producers of Government Services	12105	24584	43015	49851	56535	60801	64322	67184	70724	74862	...	...
Other Producers	1958	3777	6602	7516	8588	9409	10241	11090	11866	12727	...	...
Subtotal [b]	77690	154850	282621	319538	335532	365581	402021	430776	451839	492905	...	...
Less: Imputed bank service charge	654	1434	2161	2540	2622	3488	3424	3649	4240	4819	...	...
Plus: Import duties [c]	11095	17087	27272	36457	38908	40135	42714	47212	53827	58432	...	...
Plus: Value added tax	...	...	...	...	...	...	...	...	...	...	...	...
Plus: Other adjustments	331	-397	-	-	-	-	-	-	-	-	...	...
Equals: Gross Domestic Product	88462	170106	307732	353455	371818	402228	441311	474340	501426	546517	...	...

a) The construction industry is defined on an activity basis. It includes all contract and own-account construction put in place.
b) Gross domestic product in factor values.
c) Item 'Import duties' refers to indirect taxes net of subsidies.

1.11 Gross Domestic Product by Kind of Activity, in Constant Prices

Million Canadian dollars

	1970	1975	1980	1981	1982	1983	1984	1985	1986	1987	1988	1989
				At constant prices of: 1981						1986		
1 Agriculture, hunting, forestry and fishing	10685	11594	12388	13221	13596	13783	13657	13250	14992 / 14728	13856	11655	12966
2 Mining and quarrying	19544	19521	19660	17454	16959	18058	20556	21466	20339 / 17502	18723	20220	19774
3 Manufacturing	42172	51601	59461	61648	53702	57168	64542	68180	68969 / 86790	90262	94692	95118
4 Electricity, gas and water	4713	6799	9117	9250	8994	9595	10047	10783	11051 / 15533	16136	16410	16406
5 Construction [a]	15416	18863	22527	25094	25109	24667	23111	24904	25722 / 28082	29742	31624	32988
6 Wholesale and retail trade, restaurants and hotels	28355	36395	42024	43348	40694	42780	45299	48638	51129 / 63190	67023	71162	72827
7 Transport, storage and communication	12080	16112	21208	21860	21064	22290	24414	25263	26225 / 31466	33636	36057	37826
8 Finance, insurance, real estate and business services	27320	37867	51457	54451	53828	54378	58184	61529	65299 / 85820	90520	95441	100781
9 Community, social and personal services	7898	11972	15249	15845	15597	15841	16690	17587	18563 / 26140	27150	28216	29807
Statistical discrepancy	-6821	-4286	-1647	...	...	...	...	...	...	...	...	...

Canada

1.11 Gross Domestic Product by Kind of Activity, in Constant Prices
(Continued)

Million Canadian dollars

	1970	1975	1980	1981	1982	1983	1984	1985	1986	1987	1988	1989
					At constant prices of: 1981					1986		
Total, Industries [b]	161362	206438	251444	262171	249542	258562	276500	291600	302285 / 369250	387048	405476	418494
Producers of Government Services	37570	45418	48764	49851	50278	50837	51472	51945	52500 / 70724	71744	72984	74644
Other Producers	5193	6490	7308	7516	8044	8459	8970	9276	9482 / 11866	12157	12553	12955
Subtotal [cb]	203025	257532	307389	319538	307864	317858	336941	352821	364266 / 451840	470949	491014	506093
Less: Imputed bank service charge	...	...	...	...	...	...	...	...	...	...	...	...
Plus: Import duties									...	...	...	...
Plus: Value added tax									...	...	...	...
Plus: Other adjustments	15069	23660	33489	33916	34227	35161	38553	40460	41064 / 49586	50665	53682	54752
Equals: Gross Domestic Product	218094	281192	340878	353454	342091	353019	375495	393281	405331 / 501426	521614	544695	560845

a) The construction industry is defined on an activity basis. It includes all contract and own-account construction put in place.
b) The estimates prior to 1981 have been deflated in two time periods - 1961-1971 and 1971-1981 - with price indices based on 1961 and 1971 respectively. The GDP by industry series are aggregated to the above categories from the worksheet level and then re-scaled on a 1981 time base such that the growth rate based on the original base year series are protected.
c) Gross domestic product in factor values.

1.12 Relations Among National Accounting Aggregates

Million Canadian dollars

	1970	1975	1980	1981	1982	1983	1984	1985	1986	1987	1988	1989
Gross Domestic Product	88462	170106	307730	353454	371820	402229	441311	474339	501426	546517	598178	645894
Plus: Net factor income from the rest of the world	-1351	-2538	-7827	-11337	-12670	-11603	-13486	-14332	-16402	-16170	-18882	-22152
Factor income from the rest of the world	1046	1733	3639	3993	5479	5594	6363	7574	7716	8056	11319	8499
Less: Factor income to the rest of the world	2397	4271	11466	15330	18149	17197	19849	21906	24118	24226	30201	30651
Equals: Gross National Product	87111	167568	299903	342117	359150	390626	427825	460007	485024	530347	579296	623742
Less: Consumption of fixed capital	9948	18760	35527	40677	44356	47060	50884	55926	60595	64066	67813	72915
Equals: National Income [a]	76479	148710	264331	301267	314444	341319	376078	404036	423620	464629	512470	552859
Plus: Net current transfers from the rest of the world	-56	-180	204	233	137	-147	-510	-605	-86	-891	-731	-780
Current transfers from the rest of the world	392	723	1514	1655	1778	1653	1729	1750	2452	2035	2512	2400
Less: Current transfers to the rest of the world	448	903	1310	1422	1641	1800	2239	2355	2538	2926	3243	3180
Equals: National Disposable Income	76423	148530	264535	301500	314581	341172	375568	403431	423534	463738	511739	552079
Less: Final consumption	67647	129398	229505	262443	286542	312535	337310	366373	393367	424384	458741	496427
Equals: Net Saving	8776	19132	35030	39057	28039	28637	38258	37058	30167	39354	52998	55652
Less: Surplus of the nation on current transactions	841	-5126	-1977	-7225	1520	1862	1407	-3406	-11738	-12173	-15181	-22603
Statistical discrepancy	1367	195	90	346	699	4494	1725	89	1617	3303	-1973	-4064
Equals: Net Capital Formation [bc]	9302	24453	37097	46628	27218	31269	38576	40553	43522	54830	66206	74191

a) Item 'National income' includes a statistical discrepancy.
b) Increase in stocks of gross capital formation includes stocks of breeding stocks, draught animals, dairy cattle, etc. Stocks of commodities internally processed are valued at cost.
c) Outlays on embassies, consulates and military establishments abroad are included under government current expenditure and imports.

2.5 Private Final Consumption Expenditure by Type and Purpose, in Current Prices

Million Canadian dollars

	1970	1975	1980	1981	1982	1983	1984	1985	1986	1987	1988	1989
	Final Consumption Expenditure of Resident Households											
1 Food, beverages and tobacco	11246	20104	32058	36335	39291	41695	44478	47199	50469	53353	56830	60982
A Food	7942	14553	23316	26240	27928	29183	31324	32806	34942	37247	39491	42268
B Non-alcoholic beverages												
C Alcoholic beverages	1901	3512	5530	6363	7055	7627	7962	8471	9094	9431	10081	10327
D Tobacco	1403	2039	3212	3732	4308	4885	5192	5922	6433	6675	7258	8387

Canada

2.5 Private Final Consumption Expenditure by Type and Purpose, in Current Prices
(Continued)

Million Canadian dollars

	1970	1975	1980	1981	1982	1983	1984	1985	1986	1987	1988	1989
2 Clothing and footwear	4095	6967	11673	12837	12996	13984	15225	16592	18011	19221	20312	21564
3 Gross rent, fuel and power	10114	17556	34905	40651	47279	52247	56057	60299	64314	68554	75275	83180
4 Furniture, furnishings and household equipment and operation	4846	9940	16750	18794	18895	20878	22877	24796	27529	30348	33194	36130
5 Medical care and health expenses	1891	3197	6319	7155	7965	9132	10314	11314	12501	13726	15033	16354
6 Transport and communication	7009	14206	25446	29615	30469	33713	37757	43070	45690	49553	53978	57095
A Personal transport equipment	2468	5459	8364	9047	7799	9824	12050	15225	16597	17946	19458	19970
B Other	4541	8747	17082	20568	22670	23889	25707	27845	29093	31607	34520	37125
7 Recreational, entertainment, education and cultural services	4807	10051	17727	20137	21252	23439	26235	28589	32013	34907	38771	42350
A Education	1546	2819	5031	5770	6353	7011	7570	7982	8624	9175	9796	10405
B Other	3261	7232	12696	14367	14899	16428	18665	20607	23389	25732	28975	31945
8 Miscellaneous goods and services	7133	13734	24907	27898	29335	31686	34222	38121	42842	47565	51015	55844
A Personal care	1288	2386	4326	4810	5029	5396	5815	6648	7404	8018	8626	9338
B Expenditures in restaurants, cafes and hotels	3221	6669	12026	13377	13870	14616	15634	17068	18865	20238	22395	24510
C Other	2624	4679	8555	9711	10436	11674	12773	14405	16573	19309	19994	21996
Total Final Consumption Expenditure in the Domestic Market by Households, of which	51141	95755	169785	193422	207482	226774	247165	269980	293369	317227	344408	373499
A Durable goods	7025	15737	25466	28116	26021	30032	34699	40278	44628	49514	54566	58312
B Semi-durable goods	6334	11458	19706	21947	22359	24131	26082	28147	30604	33169	35522	37843
C Non-durable goods	16533	30039	51180	59423	65483	69688	74632	79959	83597	88232	94662	101807
D Services	21249	38521	73433	83936	93619	102923	111752	121596	134540	146312	159658	175537
Plus: Direct purchases abroad by resident households	1323	2311	3972	4177	4341	5288	5679	6125	6452	7620	8239	9273
Less: Direct purchases in the domestic market by non-resident households	1206	1815	3349	3760	3724	3841	4416	5006	6333	6299	6894	7232
Equals: Final Consumption Expenditure of Resident Households [a]	51258	96251	170408	193839	208099	228221	248428	271099	293489	318551	345754	375542

Final Consumption Expenditure of Private Non-profit Institutions Serving Households

Equals: Final Consumption Expenditure of Private Non-profit Organisations Serving Households	...	...	...	...	...	...	...	...	...	...	...	...
Private Final Consumption Expenditure	51258	96251	170408	193839	208099	228221	248428	271099	293489	318551	345754	375542

a) Item 'Final consumption expenditure of resident households' includes consumption expenditure of private non-profit institutions serving households.

2.6 Private Final Consumption Expenditure by Type and Purpose, in Constant Prices

Million Canadian dollars

	1970	1975	1980	1981	1982	1983	1984	1985	1986	1987	1988	1989
					At constant prices of: 1986							
					Final Consumption Expenditure of Resident Households							
1 Food, beverages and tobacco [a]	40501	47620	49333	49895	49250	49471	49616	50420	50469	50755	52120	53285
A Food	28919	32244	32625	32823	32680	33232	33699	34488	34942	35639	36978	38429
B Non-alcoholic beverages												
C Alcoholic beverages	6113	8860	9846	10057	9503	9298	9146	9236	9094	8964	8952	8788
D Tobacco	6443	7375	7667	7833	7820	7506	7147	6930	6433	6152	6190	6068
2 Clothing and footwear	8893	12381	15068	15458	14709	15178	16100	17006	18011	18389	18440	18820
3 Gross rent, fuel and power	32198	40918	52104	54121	56305	57852	59992	62013	64314	66512	70125	73605
4 Furniture, furnishings and household equipment and operation	13255	19565	23170	23570	21724	22837	24310	25708	27529	29241	30703	31963
5 Medical care and health expenses	6306	7801	9987	10111	9928	10613	11365	11866	12501	12861	13260	13686
6 Transport and communication [a]	20830	32243	38149	38198	34438	36421	39565	43690	45690	48251	51337	51866
A Personal transport equipment	6531	11844	11923	11572	9544	11555	13630	16461	16597	17661	18322	17766
B Other	14313	20397	26254	26656	24933	24889	25945	27220	29093	30590	33015	34100
7 Recreational, entertainment, education and cultural services [a]	11029	17797	23512	24922	24611	25823	28124	29775	32013	33452	35508	37180
A Education	4736	5863	6774	7116	7550	7951	8376	8411	8624	8810	9008	9084

Canada

2.6 Private Final Consumption Expenditure by Type and Purpose, in Constant Prices
(Continued)

Million Canadian dollars

	1970	1975	1980	1981	1982	1983	1984	1985	1986	1987	1988	1989
					At constant prices of:1986							
B Other	6285	11929	16736	17804	17057	17867	19744	21363	23389	24642	26500	28096
8 Miscellaneous goods and services [a]	23717	29800	36552	37203	35540	35859	37248	39970	42842	45491	46596	48671
A Personal care	3267	4516	5330	5576	5557	5764	6091	6870	7404	7622	7971	8334
B Expenditures in restaurants, cafes and hotels	12138	15323	18222	18272	17010	16871	17275	18043	18865	19393	20446	21279
C Other	8625	10254	13198	13492	13066	13292	13937	15058	16573	18476	18179	19058
Statistical discrepancy	5634	3220	654	-418	-596	-504	-310	-179	...	...	...	...
Total Final Consumption Expenditure in the Domestic Market by Households, of which [a]	162362	211344	248529	253060	245907	253549	266011	280269	293369	304952	318089	329076
A Durable goods	16052	28335	32612	33227	29046	32493	36814	41961	44628	48282	51411	52689
B Semi-durable goods	15772	22172	26469	27158	25726	26436	27793	29036	30604	31721	32371	33063
C Non-durable goods	62870	75113	80456	80596	79231	79238	80216	82329	83597	84351	87632	90093
D Services	69105	86372	109747	112814	113128	116280	121726	127075	134540	140598	146675	153231
Plus: Direct purchases abroad by resident households	5044	6659	6541	6120	5825	6747	6616	6464	6452	7618	8471	9415
Less: Direct purchases in the domestic market by non-resident households	4543	4555	5560	5398	4637	4511	4949	5312	6333	5978	6485	6415
Equals: Final Consumption Expenditure of Resident Households [b][a]	153213	207659	247924	253664	246989	255572	267529	281320	293484	306594	320074	332076

Final Consumption Expenditure of Private Non-profit Institutions Serving Households

Equals: Final Consumption Expenditure of Private Non-profit Organisations Serving Households	...	...	...	...	...	...	...	...	...	...	...	...
Statistical discrepancy	23	16	-6	-3	2	16	36	28	5	...	...	...
Private Final Consumption Expenditure	153236	207675	247918	253661	246991	255588	267565	281348	293489	306594	320074	332076

a) Prior to 1986, the estimates of the total is greater than the sum of its sub-items. The difference refers to an adjusting entry which is not shown.
b) Item 'Final consumption expenditure of resident households' includes consumption expenditure of private non-profit institutions serving households.

2.7 Gross Capital Formation by Type of Good and Owner, in Current Prices

Million Canadian dollars

	1980				1981				1982			
	TOTAL	Total Private	Public Enterprises	General Government	TOTAL	Total Private	Public Enterprises	General Government	TOTAL	Total Private	Public Enterprises	General Government
Increase in stocks, total [a][b]	336	267	...	69	1186	1391	...	-205	-9753	-9822	...	69
1 Goods producing industries	344	344	...	...	2161	2161	...	...	-4248	-4248	...	...
2 Wholesale and retail trade	-633	-633	...	...	-253	-253	...	...	-5578	-5578	...	...
3 Other, except government stocks	556	556	...	...	-517	-517	...	...	4	4	...	...
4 Government stocks	69	...	...	69	-205	...	...	-205	69	...	...	69
Gross Fixed Capital Formation, Total [c][b]	72288	64065	...	8223	86119	76672	...	9447	81327	70808	...	10519
1 Residential buildings	17455	17402	...	53	20631	20569	...	62	17648	17587	...	61
2 Non-residential buildings	10921	8790	...	2131	13115	10584	...	2531	11885	8748	...	3137
3 Other construction	18472	13639	...	4833	21855	16545	...	5310	23596	17834	...	5762
4 Land improvement and plantation and orchard development [d]	84	84	...	...	104	104	...	...	103	103	...	...
5 Producers' durable goods [e]	25356	24150	...	1206	30414	28870	...	1544	28095	26536	...	1559
A Transport equipment [f]	7483	...	...	...	7716	7263	...	453	5603	5166	...	437
Passenger cars	...	...	...	...	1870	1711	...	159	1372	1212	...	160
Other	...	...	...	...	5846	5552	...	294	4231	3954	...	277
B Machinery and equipment [e][f]	17873	...	...	...	22698	21607	...	1091	22492	21370	...	1122
6 Breeding stock, dairy cattle, etc. [a]	...	...	...	...	...	...	...	...	...	...	...	...
Total Gross Capital Formation [c][b]	72624	64332	...	8292	87305	78063	...	9242	71574	60986	...	10588

	1983				1984				1985			
	TOTAL	Total Private	Public Enterprises	General Government	TOTAL	Total Private	Public Enterprises	General Government	TOTAL	Total Private	Public Enterprises	General Government
Increase in stocks, total [a][b]	-2898	-2853	...	-45	4761	4741	...	20	2281	2345	...	-64
1 Goods producing industries	-2959	-2959	...	...	1813	1813	...	...	695	695	...	...
2 Wholesale and retail trade	-193	-193	...	...	2974	2974	...	...	1583	1583	...	...
3 Other, except government stocks	299	299	...	...	-46	-46	...	...	67	67	...	...
4 Government stocks	-45	...	...	-45	20	...	...	20	-64	...	...	-64

Canada

2.7 Gross Capital Formation by Type of Good and Owner, in Current Prices
(Continued)

Million Canadian dollars

	1983 TOTAL	1983 Total Private	1983 Public Enterprises	1983 General Government	1984 TOTAL	1984 Total Private	1984 Public Enterprises	1984 General Government	1985 TOTAL	1985 Total Private	1985 Public Enterprises	1985 General Government
Gross Fixed Capital Formation, Total [cb]	81227	70832	...	10395	84699	73309	...	11390	94198	81312	...	12886
1 Residential buildings	21423	21312	...	111	22348	22328	...	20	25238	25222	...	16
2 Non-residential buildings	11362	8447	...	2915	12009	9024	...	2985	14518	11133	...	3385
3 Other construction	21375	15729	...	5646	21452	15554	...	5898	22650	15555	...	7095
4 Land improvement and plantation and orchard development [d]	95	95	...	...	97	97	...	...	59	59	...	...
5 Producers' durable goods [e]	26972	25249	...	1723	28793	26306	...	2487	31733	29343	...	2390
A Transport equipment [f]	6140	5652	...	488	7220	6515	...	705	7985	7283	...	702
Passenger cars	1888	1706	...	182	2612	2366	...	246	3000	2855	...	145
Other	4252	3946	...	306	4608	4149	...	459	4985	4428	...	557
B Machinery and equipment [ef]	20832	19597	...	1235	21573	19791	...	1782	23748	22060	...	1688
6 Breeding stock, dairy cattle, etc. [a]	...	...	...	...	...	...	...	...	...	...	...	...
Total Gross Capital Formation [cb]	78329	67979	...	10350	89460	78050	...	11410	96479	83657	...	12822

	1986 TOTAL	1986 Total Private	1986 Public Enterprises	1986 General Government	1987 TOTAL	1987 Total Private	1987 Public Enterprises	1987 General Government	1988 TOTAL	1988 Total Private	1988 Public Enterprises	1988 General Government
Increase in stocks, total [ab]	2557	2592	...	-35	2719	2757	...	-38	2483	2419	...	64
1 Goods producing industries	-30	-30	...	...	-2	-2	...	...	1073	1073	...	...
2 Wholesale and retail trade	2828	2828	...	...	3062	3062	...	...	747	747	...	...
3 Other, except government stocks	-206	-206	...	...	-303	-303	...	...	599	599	...	...
4 Government stocks	-35	...	...	-35	-38	...	...	-38	64	...	...	64
Gross Fixed Capital Formation, Total [cb]	101560	88993	...	12567	116177	103267	...	12910	131536	117832	...	13704
1 Residential buildings	30823	30806	...	17	39192	39177	...	15	43589	43560	...	29
2 Non-residential buildings	15507	12219	...	3288	18183	14275	...	3908	20546	16492	...	4054
3 Other construction	20104	13352	...	6752	19464	13120	...	6344	22181	15429	...	6752
4 Land improvement and plantation and orchard development [d]	55	55	...	...	73	73	...	...	80	80	...	...
5 Producers' durable goods [e]	35071	32561	...	2510	39265	36622	...	2643	45140	42271	...	2869
A Transport equipment [f]	9064	8414	...	650	10899	10287	...	612	14953	14177	...	776
Passenger cars	4112	3951	...	161	4867	4698	...	169	5251	5121	...	130
Other	4952	4463	...	489	6032	5589	...	443	9702	9056	...	646
B Machinery and equipment [ef]	26007	24147	...	1860	28366	26335	...	2031	30187	28094	...	2093
6 Breeding stock, dairy cattle, etc. [a]	...	...	...	...	...	...	...	...	...	...	...	...
Total Gross Capital Formation [cb]	104117	91585	...	12532	118896	106024	...	12872	134019	120251	...	13768

	1989 TOTAL	1989 Total Private	1989 Public Enterprises	1989 General Government
Increase in stocks, total [ab]	3754	3757	...	-3
1 Goods producing industries	503	503	...	...
2 Wholesale and retail trade	3213	3213	...	...
3 Other, except government stocks	41	41	...	...
4 Government stocks	-3	...	...	-3
Gross Fixed Capital Formation, Total [cb]	143352	128069	...	15283
1 Residential buildings	47995	47966	...	29
2 Non-residential buildings	23472	18983	...	4489

Canada

2.7 Gross Capital Formation by Type of Good and Owner, in Current Prices
(Continued)

Million Canadian dollars

	1989 TOTAL	Total Private	Public Enterprises	General Government
3 Other construction	23558	15783	...	7775
4 Land improvement and plantation and orchard development [d]	80	80	...	...
5 Producers' durable goods [e]	48247	45257	...	2990
A Transport equipment [f]	14701	13944	...	757
Passenger cars	5540	5408	...	132
Other	9161	8536	...	625
B Machinery and equipment [ef]	33546	31313	...	2233
6 Breeding stock, dairy cattle, etc. [a]	...	...	...	...
Total Gross Capital Formation [cb]	147106	131826	...	15280

a) Increase in stocks of gross capital formation includes stocks of breeding stocks, draught animals, dairy cattle, etc. Stocks of commodities internally processed are valued at cost.
b) Column 'Public enterprises' is included in column 'Total private'.
c) Outlays on embassies, consulates and military establishments abroad are included under government current expenditure and imports.
d) Item 'Land improvement and plantation and orchard development' comprises construction outlays on dams and reservoirs along with irrigation and land reclamation projects for primary industries.
e) Producers durable goods of gross fixed capital formation includes work put in place on uncompleted heavy machinery and equipment.
f) From 1981, the methodology has been changed in order to derive the estimates in greater detail. There is, therefore, a statistical break in the detail of producers' durable goods between 1980 and 1981.

2.8 Gross Capital Formation by Type of Good and Owner, in Constant Prices

Million Canadian dollars

	1980 TOTAL	Total Private	Public Enterprises	General Government	1981 TOTAL	Total Private	Public Enterprises	General Government	1982 TOTAL	Total Private	Public Enterprises	General Government
					At constant prices of: 1986							
Increase in stocks, total [ab]	284	236	...	77	1026	1209	...	-276	-7912	-8008	...	89
1 Goods producing industries	648	648	...	...	1729	1729	...	...	-3186	-3186	...	...
2 Wholesale and retail trade	-1105	-1105	...	...	-396	-396	...	...	-6510	-6510	...	...
3 Other, except government stocks	599	599	...	...	-620	-620	...	...	79	79	...	...
4 Government stocks	77	...	...	77	-276	...	...	-276	89	...	...	89
Statistical discrepancy	65	94	...	...	589	496	...	...	1616	1609	...	...
Gross Fixed Capital Formation, Total [cb]	86587	76394	...	10286	96790	86006	...	10765	86153	74967	...	11195
1 Residential buildings	23739	23593	...	72	25120	25155	...	75	21118	21044	...	73
2 Non-residential buildings	14256	11570	...	2700	15321	12477	...	2860	12896	9576	...	3295
3 Other construction	24018	17317	...	6632	25287	18872	...	6311	25508	18969	...	6435
4 Land improvement and plantation and orchard development [d]	...	...	...	...	...	...	...	...	...	...	...	...
5 Producers' durable goods [e]	26472	24875	...	1235	31369	29369	...	1571	27122	25264	...	1500
6 Breeding stock, dairy cattle, etc. [a]	...	...	...	...	...	...	...	...	...	...	...	...
Statistical discrepancy	-1898	-961	...	-353	-307	133	...	-52	-491	114	...	-108
Statistical discrepancy	-429	-530	...	-17	-384	-331	...	38	-2899	-2827	...	-19
Total Gross Capital Formation [cb]	86442	76100	...	10346	97432	86884	...	10527	75342	64132	...	11265

	1983 TOTAL	Total Private	Public Enterprises	General Government	1984 TOTAL	Total Private	Public Enterprises	General Government	1985 TOTAL	Total Private	Public Enterprises	General Government
					At constant prices of: 1986							
Increase in stocks, total [ab]	-2187	-2165	...	-50	3388	3390	...	22	2175	2229	...	-67
1 Goods producing industries	-2197	-2197	...	...	970	970	...	...	906	906	...	...
2 Wholesale and retail trade	-153	-153	...	...	3465	3465	...	...	1866	1866	...	...
3 Other, except government stocks	446	446	...	...	-114	-114	...	...	42	42	...	...
4 Government stocks	-50	...	...	-50	22	...	...	22	-67	...	...	-67
Statistical discrepancy	-233	-261	...	...	-955	-931	...	...	-572	-585	...	...
Gross Fixed Capital Formation, Total [cb]	85536	74742	...	10797	87362	75869	...	10504	95624	82863	...	12776
1 Residential buildings	24746	24619	...	128	24744	24752	...	22	27202	27184	...	17
2 Non-residential buildings	12263	9190	...	3053	12966	9800	...	3149	15203	11690	...	3502

253

Canada

2.8 Gross Capital Formation by Type of Good and Owner, in Constant Prices
(Continued)

Million Canadian dollars

	1983 TOTAL	1983 Total Private	1983 Public Enterprises	1983 General Government	1984 TOTAL	1984 Total Private	1984 Public Enterprises	1984 General Government	1985 TOTAL	1985 Total Private	1985 Public Enterprises	1985 General Government
				At constant prices of: 1986								
3 Other construction	23060	16952	...	6025	21957	15890	...	6000	22505	15395	...	7087
4 Land improvement and plantation and orchard development [d]	...	...	...	...	...	...	...	...	...	...	...	...
5 Producers' durable goods [e]	26236	24223	...	1667	28251	25559	...	2320	31325	28694	...	2218
6 Breeding stock, dairy cattle, etc. [a]	...	...	...	...	...	...	...	...	...	...	...	...
Statistical discrepancy	-769	-242	...	-76	-556	-132	...	-987	-611	-100	...	-48
Statistical discrepancy	-1235	-1188	...	-97	366	358	...	990	-43	-21	...	3
Total Gross Capital Formation [cb]	82114	71389	...	10650	91116	79617	...	11516	97756	85071	...	12712

	1986 TOTAL	1986 Total Private	1986 Public Enterprises	1986 General Government	1987 TOTAL	1987 Total Private	1987 Public Enterprises	1987 General Government	1988 TOTAL	1988 Total Private	1988 Public Enterprises	1988 General Government
				At constant prices of: 1986								
Increase in stocks, total [ab]	2557	2592	...	-35	2845	2882	...	-37	1391	1329	...	62
1 Goods producing industries	-30	-30	...	...	-451	-451	...	...	6	6	...	...
2 Wholesale and retail trade	2828	2828	...	...	3085	3085	...	...	733	733	...	...
3 Other, except government stocks	-206	-206	...	...	248	248	...	...	590	590	...	...
4 Government stocks	-35	...	...	-35	-37	...	...	-37	62	...	...	62
Statistical discrepancy	...	...	...	...	...	...	...	...	...	...	...	...
Gross Fixed Capital Formation, Total [cb]	101560	88993	...	12567	112035	99180	...	12855	123442	110175	...	13267
1 Residential buildings	30823	30806	...	17	35596	35582	...	14	36949	36925	...	24
2 Non-residential buildings	15507	12219	...	3288	17144	13425	...	3719	18248	14582	...	3666
3 Other construction	20159	13407	...	6752	19215	12804	...	6411	21020	14432	...	6588
4 Land improvement and plantation and orchard development [d]	...	...	...	...	...	...	...	...	...	...	...	...
5 Producers' durable goods [e]	35071	32561	...	2510	40080	37369	...	2711	47225	44236	...	2989
6 Breeding stock, dairy cattle, etc. [a]	...	...	...	...	...	...	...	...	...	...	...	...
Statistical discrepancy	...	...	...	...	...	...	...	...	...	...	...	...
Statistical discrepancy	...	...	...	...	...	...	...	...	...	...	...	...
Total Gross Capital Formation [cb]	104117	91585	...	12532	114880	102062	...	12818	124833	111504	...	13329

	1989 TOTAL	1989 Total Private	1989 Public Enterprises	1989 General Government
		At constant prices of: 1986		
Increase in stocks, total [ab]	3477	3478	...	-1
1 Goods producing industries	807	807	...	...
2 Wholesale and retail trade	2647	2647	...	...
3 Other, except government stocks	24	24	...	...
4 Government stocks	-1	...	...	-1
Statistical discrepancy	...	...	...	...
Gross Fixed Capital Formation, Total [cb]	129048	114691	...	14357
1 Residential buildings	37822	37799	...	23
2 Non-residential buildings	19488	15700	...	3788
3 Other construction	21889	14457	...	7432
4 Land improvement and plantation and orchard development [d]	...	...	...	...
5 Producers' durable goods [e]	49849	46735	...	3114
6 Breeding stock, dairy cattle, etc. [a]	...	...	...	...
Statistical discrepancy	...	...	...	...
Statistical discrepancy	...	...	...	...
Total Gross Capital Formation [cb]	132525	118169	...	14356

a) Increase in stocks of gross capital formation includes stocks of breeding stocks, draught animals, dairy cattle, etc. Stocks of commodities internally processed are valued at cost.
b) Column 'Public enterprises' is included in column 'Total private'.
c) Outlays on embassies, consulates and military establishments abroad are included under government current expenditure and imports.
d) Item 'Land improvement and plantation and orchard development' comprises construction outlays on dams and reservoirs along with irrigation and land reclamation projects for primary industries.
e) Producers durable goods of gross fixed capital formation includes work put in place on uncompleted heavy machinery and equipment.

Canada

2.9 Gross Capital Formation by Kind of Activity of Owner, ISIC Major Divisions, in Current Prices

Million Canadian dollars

	1980 TGCF	1980 IS	1980 GFCF	1981 TGCF	1981 IS	1981 GFCF	1982 TGCF	1982 IS	1982 GFCF	1983 TGCF	1983 IS	1983 GFCF
					All Producers							
1 Agriculture, hunting, fishing and forestry	4541	-204	4745	5543	477	5066	4336	-82	4418	3289	-876	4165
2 Mining and quarrying	8576	196	8380	9667	262	9405	10035	-205	10240	9249	-273	9522
3 Manufacturing	9673	245	9428	13785	1400	12385	7180	-3967	11147	6990	-1504	8494
4 Electricity, gas and water	6663	117	6546	7795	-26	7821	9241	238	9003	8106	-234	8340
5 Construction	1098	-10	1108	1353	48	1305	1061	-232	1293	1213	-72	1285
6 Wholesale and retail trade, restaurants and hotels [a]	1067	-633	1700	1712	-253	1965	-4109	-5578	1469	1799	-193	1992
7 Transport, storage and communication	6030	18	6012	8074	-109	8183	8179	-96	8275	6685	-170	6855
8 Finance, insurance, real estate and business services [bc]	21983	538	21445	25035	-408	25443	21150	100	21050	26045	469	25576
9 Community, social and personal services [bca]	4701	...	4701	5099	...	5099	3913	...	3913	4603	...	4603
Total Industries	64332	267	64065	78063	1391	76672	60986	-9822	70808	67979	-2853	70832
Producers of Government Services	8292	69	8223	9242	-205	9447	10588	69	10519	10350	-45	10395
Private Non-Profit Institutions Serving Households	...	...	...	...	...	...	...	...	...	...	...	...
Total [de]	72624	336	72288	87305	1186	86119	71574	-9753	81327	78329	-2898	81227

	1984 TGCF	1984 IS	1984 GFCF	1985 TGCF	1985 IS	1985 GFCF	1986 TGCF	1986 IS	1986 GFCF	1987 TGCF	1987 IS	1987 GFCF
					All Producers							
1 Agriculture, hunting, fishing and forestry	3506	-802	4308	4079	561	3518	3916	515	3401	3004	-569	3573
2 Mining and quarrying	9680	-60	9740	10854	147	10707	7376	-73	7449	6392	-417	6809
3 Manufacturing	10840	2286	8554	11254	86	11168	12707	-680	13387	14836	244	14592
4 Electricity, gas and water	7290	303	6987	6268	-144	6412	6461	129	6332	6670	-40	6710
5 Construction	1385	86	1299	1396	45	1351	1524	80	1444	1788	205	1583
6 Wholesale and retail trade, restaurants and hotels [a]	5427	2974	2453	4017	1583	2434	5420	2828	2592	5923	3062	2861
7 Transport, storage and communication	7068	88	6980	6995	64	6931	6214	-42	6256	7216	24	7192
8 Finance, insurance, real estate and business services [bc]	26781	-134	26915	31332	3	31329	38199	-165	38364	48708	248	48460
9 Community, social and personal services [bca]	6073	...	6073	7462	...	7462	9768	...	9768	11487	...	11487
Total Industries	78050	4741	73309	83657	2345	81312	91585	2592	88993	106024	2757	103267
Producers of Government Services	11410	20	11390	12822	-64	12886	12532	-35	12567	12872	-38	12910
Private Non-Profit Institutions Serving Households	...	...	...	...	...	...	...	...	...	...	...	...
Total [de]	89460	4761	84699	96479	2281	94198	104117	2557	101560	118896	2719	116177

	1988 TGCF	1988 IS	1988 GFCF	1989 TGCF	1989 IS	1989 GFCF
			All Producers			
1 Agriculture, hunting, fishing and forestry	3484	-360	3844	4314	337	3977
2 Mining and quarrying	8370	-269	8639	7453	209	7244
3 Manufacturing	18004	1216	16788	19506	147	19359
4 Electricity, gas and water	8163	403	7760	9377	-265	9642

Canada

2.9 Gross Capital Formation by Kind of Activity of Owner, ISIC Major Divisions, in Current Prices
(Continued)

Million Canadian dollars

	1988 Total Gross Capital Formation	1988 Increase in Stocks	1988 Gross Fixed Capital Formation	1989 Total Gross Capital Formation	1989 Increase in Stocks	1989 Gross Fixed Capital Formation
5 Construction	1943	83	1860	2175	75	2100
6 Wholesale and retail trade, restaurants and hotels [a]	3838	747	3091	6481	3213	3268
7 Transport, storage and communication	9530	106	9424	10263	74	10189
8 Finance, insurance, real estate and business services [bc]	54655	493	54162	59610	-33	59643
9 Community, social and personal services [bca]	12264	...	12264	12647	...	12647
Total Industries	120251	2419	117832	131826	3757	128069
Producers of Government Services	13768	64	13704	15280	-3	15283
Private Non-Profit Institutions Serving Households	...	...	...	...	...	...
Total [de]	134019	2483	131536	147106	3754	143352

a) Restaurants and hotels are included in item 'Community, social and personal services'.
b) For column 'Increase in stocks', item 'Community, social and personal services' is included in item 'Finance, insurance, real estate and business services'.
c) Business services are included in item 'Community, social and personal services'.
d) Outlays on embassies, consulates and military establishments abroad are included under government current expenditure and imports.
e) Increase in stocks of gross capital formation includes stocks of breeding stocks, draught animals, dairy cattle, etc. Stocks of commodities internally processed are valued at cost.

2.17 Exports and Imports of Goods and Services, Detail

Million Canadian dollars

	1970	1975	1980	1981	1982	1983	1984	1985	1986	1987	1988	1989
Exports of Goods and Services												
1 Exports of merchandise, f.o.b. [ab]	17498	34614	78946	86939	87004	93311	114849	122468	123719	129887	142434	145914
2 Transport and communication [c]	447	716	1697	1786	1531	1347	1225	1197	1097	1105	1117	1151
3 Insurance service charges	...	...	...	...	...	...	...	...	...	...	...	...
4 Other commodities [c]	927	1809	3587	4395	4392	4945	5545	6248	6997	7489	8317	8510
5 Adjustments of merchandise exports to change-of-ownership basis	...	...	...	...	...	...	...	...	...	...	...	...
6 Direct purchases in the domestic market by non-residential households [c]	1206	1815	3349	3760	3724	3841	4416	5006	6333	6299	6894	7232
7 Direct purchases in the domestic market by extraterritorial bodies	...	...	...	...	...	...	...	...	...	...	...	...
Total Exports of Goods and Services	20078	38954	87579	96880	96651	103444	126035	134919	138119	144755	158731	162852
Imports of Goods and Services												
1 Imports of merchandise, c.i.f. [a]	14758	35764	70912	80496	69665	75961	95404	106680	114425	119546	132617	139151
A Imports of merchandise, f.o.b. [d]	14316	34879	69576	79065	68475	74836	94088	105274	113021	118094	131237	137781
B Transport of services on merchandise imports	442	885	1336	1431	1190	1125	1316	1406	1405	1452	1380	1369
C Insurance service charges on merchandise imports	...	...	...	...	...	...	...	...	...	...	...	...
2 Adjustments of merchandise imports to change-of-ownership basis	...	...	...	...	...	...	...	...	...	...	...	...
3 Other transport and communication	216	344	439	497	455	395	382	385	435	390	393	449
4 Other insurance service charges	1355	2617	5726	6981	7162	7212	8123	9137	11019	11220	12136	...
5 Other commodities												...
6 Direct purchases abroad by government	170	327	887	852	977	978	1045	1063	956	904	844	854
7 Direct purchases abroad by resident households	1331	2310	3969	4175	4339	5286	5678	6123	6452	7620	8239	9335
Total Imports of Goods and Services	17830	41362	81933	93001	82598	89832	110632	123388	133369	139867	154299	162523
Balance of Goods and Services	2248	-2408	5646	3879	14053	13612	15403	11531	4750	4888	4432	329
Total Imports and Balance of Goods and Services	20078	38954	87579	96880	96651	103444	126035	134919	138119	144755	158731	162852

a) Exports and imports of merchandise are recorded on the basis of the crossing of frontiers. No data are available on the basis of changes in the ownership of the goods.
b) Exports of Canadian produce and re-exports of foreign produce which are valued f.o.b. point of shipment in Canada plus inland freight and gold.
c) Item 'Direct purchases in the domestic market by non-residential households' excludes crew expenditures which are included in item 'Transport and communication'. Diplomatic and military personnel expenditure are included in item 'Other commodities'.
d) Imports are valued f.o.b. point of shipment in the foreign country plus inland freight payments.

Canada

3.12 General Government Income and Outlay Account: Total and Subsectors

Million Canadian dollars

	1980					1981				
	Total General Government	Central Government	State or Provincial Government	Local Government	Social Security Funds	Total General Government	Central Government	State or Provincial Government	Local Government	Social Security Funds

Receipts

1 Operating surplus	...	...	...	...	...	...	...	...	...	...
2 Property and entrepreneurial income	17787	4618	10236	804	2129	20746	5323	11705	1154	2564
A Withdrawals from public quasi-corporations	...	...	...	...	...	...	...	...	...	...
B Interest	10923	3749	4301	744	2129	13950	4489	5802	1095	2564
C Dividends [a]	1564	851	653	60	...	1543	818	666	59	...
D Net land rent and royalties [b]	5300	18	5282	...	...	5253	16	5237	...	...
3 Taxes, fees and contributions	93743	45127	34669	10406	3541	115341	58648	40867	11855	3971
A Indirect taxes	35505	12254	13015	10236	...	45956	18986	15311	11659	...
B Direct taxes	45923	28532	17391	...	...	53844	33409	20435	...	...
Income	45213	28532	16681	...	...	53096	33409	19687	...	...
Other	710	-	710	...	...	748		748	...	...
C Social security contributions	10591	4324	2726	...	3541	13603	6238	3394	...	3971
D Fees, fines and penalties	1724	17	1537	170	...	1938	15	1727	196	...
4 Other current transfers	...	...	12641	19811	...	...	...	13955	22813	...
A Casualty insurance claims	...	...	...	...	...	...	...	...	...	...
B Transfers from other government subsectors	...	...	12641	19811	...	...	...	13955	22813	...
C Transfers from the rest of the world	...	...	...	...	...	...	...	...	...	...
D Other transfers, except imputed	...	...	...	...	...	...	...	...	...	...
E Imputed unfunded employee pension and welfare contributions	...	...	...	...	...	...	...	...	...	...
Total Current Receipts [cd]	111530	49745	57546	31021	5670	136087	63971	66527	35822	6535

Disbursements

1 Government final consumption expenditure	59097	13804	18847	26359	87	68604	16374	21837	30273	120
2 Property income	16790	9897	4828	2065	...	22268	13739	6185	2344	...
A Interest	16790	9897	4828	2065	...	22268	13739	6185	2344	...
B Net land rent and royalties	...	...	...	...	...	...	...	...	...	...
3 Subsidies	8233	5646	2175	412	...	9499	6634	2452	413	...
4 Other current transfers	31283	30105	30462	588	2580	35833	33630	35092	714	3165
A Casualty insurance premiums, net	...	...	...	...	...	...	...	...	...	...
B Transfers to other government subsectors	...	12831	19512	109	...	...	14087	22496	185	...
C Social security benefits	16655	12448	1640	...	2567	19305	14213	1943	...	3149
D Social assistance grants	13811	4022	9310	479	...	15653	4471	10653	529	...
E Unfunded employee pension and welfare benefits	...	...	...	...	...	...	...	...	...	...
F Transfers to private non-profit institutions serving households	...	...	...	...	...	...	...	...	...	...
G Other transfers n.e.c.	...	...	...	...	...	...	...	...	...	...
H Transfers to the rest of the world	817	804	...	...	13	875	859	...	...	16
Net saving	-3873	-9707	1234	1597	3003	-117	-6406	961	2078	3250
Total Current Disbursements and Net Saving [cd]	111530	49745	57546	31021	5670	136087	63971	66527	35822	6535

	1982					1983				
	Total General Government	Central Government	State or Provincial Government	Local Government	Social Security Funds	Total General Government	Central Government	State or Provincial Government	Local Government	Social Security Funds

Receipts

1 Operating surplus	...	...	...	...	...	...	...	...	...	...
2 Property and entrepreneurial income	22097	4862	12974	1196	3065	25010	6071	14449	1034	3456
A Withdrawals from public quasi-corporations	...	...	...	...	...	...	...	...	...	...
B Interest	16118	4990	6906	1157	3065	17504	5388	7663	997	3456

257

Canada

3.12 General Government Income and Outlay Account: Total and Subsectors
(Continued)

Million Canadian dollars

	1982					1983				
	Total General Government	Central Government	State or Provincial Government	Local Government	Social Security Funds	Total General Government	Central Government	State or Provincial Government	Local Government	Social Security Funds
C Dividends a	561	-138	660	39	...	1462	676	749	37	...
D Net land rent and royalties b	5418	10	5408	...	...	6044	7	6037	...	...
3 Taxes, fees and contributions	123100	60134	45281	12942	4743	130487	62377	49701	13823	4586
A Indirect taxes	48248	17588	17940	12720	...	50150	16303	20258	13589	...
B Direct taxes	57641	36136	21505	...	...	60684	37388	23296	...	...
Income	56865	36136	20729	...	...	59747	37388	22359	...	...
Other	776	-	776	...	...	937	-	937	...	...
C Social security contributions	14954	6395	3816	...	4743	17156	8670	3900	...	4586
D Fees, fines and penalties	2257	15	2020	222	...	2497	16	2247	234	...
4 Other current transfers	...	...	15647	26914	...	...	...	17295	28914	...
A Casualty insurance claims	...	...	...	...	...	...	...	...	...	...
B Transfers from other government subsectors	...	...	15647	26914	...	...	...	17295	28914	...
C Transfers from the rest of the world	...	...	...	...	...	...	...	...	...	...
D Other transfers, except imputed	...	...	...	...	...	...	...	...	...	...
E Imputed unfunded employee pension and welfare contributions	...	...	...	...	...	...	...	...	...	...
Total Current Receipts cd	145197	64996	73902	41052	7808	155497	68448	81445	43771	8042

Disbursements

	1982					1983				
1 Government final consumption expenditure	78443	18729	24908	34683	123	84314	19425	27623	37136	130
2 Property income	27072	16675	7765	2632	...	29419	17412	9045	2962	...
A Interest	27072	16675	7765	2632	...	29419	17412	9045	2962	...
B Net land rent and royalties	...	...	...	...	...	...	...	...	...	...
3 Subsidies	9340	5777	3025	538	...	10015	5662	3817	536	...
4 Other current transfers	44692	41267	41330	757	3899	51141	46886	44836	897	4731
A Casualty insurance premiums, net	...	...	...	...	...	...	...	...	...	...
B Transfers to other government subsectors	...	15844	26581	136	...	...	17637	28427	145	...
C Social security benefits	25482	19205	2398	...	3879	29135	21801	2627	...	4707
D Social assistance grants	18147	5175	12351	621	...	20812	6278	13782	752	...
E Unfunded employee pension and welfare benefits	...	...	...	...	...	...	...	...	...	...
F Transfers to private non-profit institutions serving households	...	...	...	...	...	...	...	...	...	...
G Other transfers n.e.c.	...	...	...	...	...	...	...	...	...	...
H Transfers to the rest of the world	1063	1043	...	...	20	1194	1170	...	...	24
Net saving	-14350	-17452	-3126	2442	3786	-19392	-20937	-3876	2240	3181
Total Current Disbursements and Net Saving cd	145197	64996	73902	41052	7808	155497	68448	81445	43771	8042

	1984					1985				
	Total General Government	Central Government	State or Provincial Government	Local Government	Social Security Funds	Total General Government	Central Government	State or Provincial Government	Local Government	Social Security Funds

Receipts

1 Operating surplus	...	...	...	...	...	...	...	...	...	...
2 Property and entrepreneurial income	27975	7129	15740	1233	3873	29411	7594	16246	1375	4196
A Withdrawals from public quasi-corporations	...	...	...	...	...	...	...	...	...	...
B Interest	19005	5716	8240	1176	3873	20879	6158	9220	1305	4196
C Dividends a	2519	1407	1055	57	...	2445	1428	947	70	...
D Net land rent and royalties b	6451	6	6445	...	...	6087	8	6079	...	...
3 Taxes, fees and contributions	142887	68116	54900	14728	5143	154218	74271	58537	15714	5696
A Indirect taxes	54957	18124	22368	14465	...	58789	18897	24459	15433	...
B Direct taxes	66687	40608	26079	...	...	71830	44796	27034	...	...
Income	65678	40608	25070	...	...	70835	44796	26039	...	...

258

Canada

3.12 General Government Income and Outlay Account: Total and Subsectors
(Continued)

Million Canadian dollars

1984 / 1985

	Total General Government 1984	Central Government 1984	State or Provincial Government 1984	Local Government 1984	Social Security Funds 1984	Total General Government 1985	Central Government 1985	State or Provincial Government 1985	Local Government 1985	Social Security Funds 1985
Other	1009	-	1009	...	...	995	-	995	...	...
C Social security contributions	18582	9366	4073	...	5143	20847	10556	4595	...	5696
D Fees, fines and penalties	2661	18	2380	263	...	2752	22	2449	281	...
4 Other current transfers	...	...	19531	29952	...	...	...	21329	31891	...
A Casualty insurance claims	...	...	...	...	...	...	...	...	...	...
B Transfers from other government subsectors	...	...	19531	29952	...	...	...	21329	31891	...
C Transfers from the rest of the world	...	...	...	...	...	...	...	...	...	...
D Other transfers, except imputed	...	...	...	...	...	...	...	...	...	...
E Imputed unfunded employee pension and welfare contributions	...	...	...	...	...	...	...	...	...	...
Total Current Receipts [cd]	170862	75245	90171	45913	9016	183629	81865	96112	48980	9892

Disbursements

1 Government final consumption expenditure	88882	21026	28088	39619	149	95274	23262	30056	41790	166
2 Property income	34752	20897	10694	3161	...	40183	24620	12128	3435	...
A Interest	34752	20897	10694	3161	...	40183	24620	12128	3435	...
B Net land rent and royalties	...	...	...	...	...	...	...	...	...	...
3 Subsidies	12243	7473	4184	586	...	11577	6369	4610	598	...
4 Other current transfers	55107	51147	46875	941	5627	59638	55093	50259	955	6551
A Casualty insurance premiums, net	...	...	...	...	...	...	...	...	...	...
B Transfers to other government subsectors	...	19905	29449	129	...	...	21746	31385	89	...
C Social security benefits	31151	22627	2925	...	5599	33963	24229	3217	...	6517
D Social assistance grants	22385	7072	14501	812	...	24032	7509	15657	866	...
E Unfunded employee pension and welfare benefits	...	...	...	...	...	...	...	...	...	...
F Transfers to private non-profit institutions serving households	...	...	...	...	...	...	...	...	...	...
G Other transfers n.e.c.	...	...	...	...	...	...	...	...	...	...
H Transfers to the rest of the world	1571	1543	...	...	28	1643	1609	...	...	34
Net saving	-20122	-25298	330	1606	3240	-23043	-27479	-941	2202	3175
Total Current Disbursements and Net Saving [cd]	170862	75245	90171	45913	9016	183629	81865	96112	48980	9892

1986 / 1987

	Total General Government 1986	Central Government 1986	State or Provincial Government 1986	Local Government 1986	Social Security Funds 1986	Total General Government 1987	Central Government 1987	State or Provincial Government 1987	Local Government 1987	Social Security Funds 1987

Receipts

1 Operating surplus	...	...	...	...	...	...	...	...	...	...
2 Property and entrepreneurial income	28236	8067	14317	1369	4483	29650	8574	14969	1379	4728
A Withdrawals from public quasi-corporations	...	...	...	...	...	...	...	...	...	...
B Interest	21562	6506	9287	1286	4483	23025	6980	10031	1286	4728
C Dividends [a]	2913	1553	1277	83	...	3025	1586	1346	93	...
D Net land rent and royalties [b]	3761	8	3753	...	...	3600	8	3592	...	...
3 Taxes, fees and contributions	169742	82146	64247	17103	6246	188717	90540	72563	18504	7110
A Indirect taxes	64338	21159	26401	16778	...	70956	23676	29116	18164	...
B Direct taxes	79731	49480	30251	...	...	89606	54649	34957	...	...
Income	78626	49480	29146	...	...	88424	54649	33775	...	...
Other	1105	-	1105	...	...	1182	-	1182	...	...
C Social security contributions	22785	11484	5055	...	6246	25090	12190	5790	...	7110
D Fees, fines and penalties	2888	23	2540	325	...	3065	25	2700	340	...

Canada

3.12 General Government Income and Outlay Account: Total and Subsectors
(Continued)

Million Canadian dollars

	1986					1987				
	Total General Government	Central Government	State or Provincial Government	Local Government	Social Security Funds	Total General Government	Central Government	State or Provincial Government	Local Government	Social Security Funds
4 Other current transfers	...	...	20671	34212	...	...	...	22243	35995	...
A Casualty insurance claims	...	...	...	...	...	...	...	...	...	...
B Transfers from other government subsectors	...	...	20671	34212	...	...	...	22243	35995	...
C Transfers from the rest of the world	...	...	...	...	...	...	...	...	...	...
D Other transfers, except imputed	...	...	...	...	...	...	...	...	...	...
E Imputed unfunded employee pension and welfare contributions	...	...	...	...	...	...	...	...	...	...
Total Current Receipts [cd]	197978	90213	99235	52684	10729	218367	99114	109775	55878	11838

Disbursements

1 Government final consumption expenditure	99878	23704	32070	43954	150	105833	24269	34369	47031	164
2 Property income	42754	26107	13261	3386	...	45965	27801	14627	3537	...
A Interest	42754	26107	13261	3386	...	45965	27801	14627	3537	...
B Net land rent and royalties	...	...	...	...	...	...	...	...	...	...
3 Subsidies	10511	4874	4980	657	...	12524	7150	4687	687	...
4 Other current transfers	63391	56035	53706	1071	7462	68426	59098	57076	1165	9325
A Casualty insurance premiums, net	...	...	...	...	...	...	...	...	...	...
B Transfers to other government subsectors	...	21089	33687	107	...	...	22714	35417	107	...
C Social security benefits	36904	25710	3772	...	7422	40396	26775	4347	...	9274
D Social assistance grants	24692	7481	16247	964	...	25861	7491	17312	1058	...
E Unfunded employee pension and welfare benefits	...	...	...	...	...	...	...	...	...	...
F Transfers to private non-profit institutions serving households	...	...	...	...	...	...	...	...	...	...
G Other transfers n.e.c.	...	...	...	...	...	...	...	...	...	...
H Transfers to the rest of the world	1795	1755	...	...	40	2169	2118	...	...	51
Net saving	-18556	-20507	-4782	3616	3117	-14381	-19204	-984	3458	2349
Total Current Disbursements and Net Saving [cd]	197978	90213	99235	52684	10729	218367	99114	109775	55878	11838

	1988					1989				
	Total General Government	Central Government	State or Provincial Government	Local Government	Social Security Funds	Total General Government	Central Government	State or Provincial Government	Local Government	Social Security Funds

Receipts

1 Operating surplus	...	...	...	...	...	...	...	...	...	...
2 Property and entrepreneurial income	32621	10008	16174	1385	5054	35536	11100	17611	1448	5377
A Withdrawals from public quasi-corporations	...	...	...	...	...	...	...	...	...	...
B Interest	24457	7501	10620	1282	5054	26190	8070	11405	1338	5377
C Dividends [a]	4615	2499	2013	103	...	5732	3022	2600	110	...
D Net land rent and royalties [b]	3549	8	3541	...	...	3614	8	3606	...	...
3 Taxes, fees and contributions	207346	98164	81538	19705	7939	220145	104475	85489	21379	8802
A Indirect taxes	76729	25043	32374	19312	...	84735	28572	35209	20954	...
B Direct taxes	99081	59512	39569	...	...	103712	63599	40113	...	...
Income	97848	59512	38336	...	...	102377	63599	38778	...	...
Other	1233	-	1233	...	...	1335	-	1335	...	...
C Social security contributions	28196	13585	6672	...	7939	28127	12270	7055	...	8802
D Fees, fines and penalties	3340	24	2923	393	...	3571	34	3112	425	...
4 Other current transfers	...	...	24165	38871	...	...	...	25116	41369	...
A Casualty insurance claims	...	...	...	...	...	...	...	...	...	...
B Transfers from other government subsectors	...	...	24165	38871	...	...	...	25116	41369	...
C Transfers from the rest of the world	...	...	...	...	...	...	...	...	...	...
D Other transfers, except imputed	...	...	...	...	...	...	...	...	...	...
E Imputed unfunded employee pension and welfare contributions	...	...	...	...	...	...	...	...	...	...

Canada

3.12 General Government Income and Outlay Account: Total and Subsectors
(Continued)

Million Canadian dollars

	1988					1989				
	Total General Government	Central Government	State or Provincial Government	Local Government	Social Security Funds	Total General Government	Central Government	State or Provincial Government	Local Government	Social Security Funds
Total Current Receipts cd	239967	108172	121877	59961	12993	255681	115575	128216	64196	14179

Disbursements

1 Government final consumption expenditure	112987	25599	36412	50800	176	120885	27122	38903	54655	205
2 Property income	50847	31688	15614	3545	...	57718	37336	16715	3667	...
A Interest	50847	31688	15614	3545	...	57718	37336	16715	3667	...
B Net land rent and royalties	...	...	...	...	...	...	...	...	...	...
3 Subsidies	11524	6123	4667	734	...	11602	5803	5009	790	...
4 Other current transfers	73749	63282	61477	1252	10774	78241	66017	65267	1344	12098
A Casualty insurance premiums, net	...	...	...	...	...	...	...	...	...	...
B Transfers to other government subsectors	...	24718	38219	99	...	...	25796	40601	88	...
C Social security benefits	43563	28208	4641	...	10714	46993	29924	5042	...	12027
D Social assistance grants	27742	7972	18617	1153	...	28908	8028	19624	1256	...
E Unfunded employee pension and welfare benefits	...	...	...	...	...	...	...	...	...	...
F Transfers to private non-profit institutions serving households	...	...	...	...	...	...	...	...	...	...
G Other transfers n.e.c.	...	...	...	...	...	...	...	...	...	...
H Transfers to the rest of the world	2444	2384	...	...	60	2340	2269	...	...	71
Net saving	-9140	-18520	3707	3630	2043	-12765	-20703	2322	3740	1876
Total Current Disbursements and Net Saving cd	239967	108172	121877	59961	12993	255681	115575	128216	64196	14179

a) Item 'Dividends' refers to remitted profits of government business enterprises.
b) Item 'Net land rent and royalties' refers to royalties only.
c) Local government includes hospitals.
d) Social security funds refers to Canada and Quebec pension plans only.

3.13 General Government Capital Accumulation Account: Total and Subsectors

Million Canadian dollars

	1980					1981				
	Total General Government	Central Government	State or Provincial Government	Local Government	Social Security Funds	Total General Government	Central Government	State or Provincial Government	Local Government	Social Security Funds

Finance of Gross Accumulation

1 Gross saving	680	-8897	2841	3733	3003	5194	-5483	2878	4549	3250
A Consumption of fixed capital	4553	810	1607	2136	-	5311	923	1917	2471	-
B Net saving	-3873	-9707	1234	1597	3003	-117	-6406	961	2078	3250
2 Capital transfers	72	1	71	...	...	54	1	53	...	...
A From other government subsectors	...	...	...	...	...	...	...	...	...	...
B From other resident sectors	72	1	71	...	...	54	1	53	...	...
C From rest of the world	...	...	...	...	...	...	...	...	...	...
Finance of Gross Accumulation ab	752	-8896	2912	3733	3003	5248	-5482	2931	4549	3250

Gross Accumulation

1 Gross capital formation	8292	992	3162	4138	...	9242	933	3676	4633	...
A Increase in stocks	69	69	...	...	...	-205	-205	...	...	...
B Gross fixed capital formation	8223	923	3162	4138	...	9447	1138	3676	4633	...
2 Purchases of land, net	...	...	...	...	...	...	...	...	...	...
3 Purchases of intangible assets, net	...	...	...	...	...	...	...	...	...	...
4 Capital transfers	1077	775	302	...	...	1231	900	331	...	...
A To other government subsectors	...	...	...	...	...	...	...	...	...	...
B To other resident sectors	1077	775	302	...	...	1231	900	331	...	...
C To rest of the world	...	...	...	...	...	...	...	...	...	...
Net lending c	-8617	-10663	-552	-405	3003	-5225	-7315	-1076	-84	3250
Gross Accumulation ab	752	-8896	2912	3733	3003	5248	-5482	2931	4549	3250

Canada

3.13 General Government Capital Accumulation Account: Total and Subsectors

Million Canadian dollars

	1982					1983				
	Total General Government	Central Government	State or Provincial Government	Local Government	Social Security Funds	Total General Government	Central Government	State or Provincial Government	Local Government	Social Security Funds
Finance of Gross Accumulation											
1 Gross saving	-8469	-16459	-1020	5224	3786	-13095	-19881	-1608	5213	3181
A Consumption of fixed capital	5881	993	2106	2782	-	6297	1056	2268	2973	-
B Net saving	-14350	-17452	-3126	2442	3786	-19392	-20937	-3876	2240	3181
2 Capital transfers	57	1	56	...	...	65	-	65	...	...
A From other government subsectors	...	...	...	...	...	...	...	...	...	...
B From other resident sectors	57	1	56	...	...	65	-	65	...	...
C From rest of the world	...	...	...	...	...	...	...	...	...	...
Finance of Gross Accumulation ab	-8412	-16458	-964	5224	3786	-13030	-19881	-1543	5213	3181
Gross Accumulation											
1 Gross capital formation	10588	1270	4092	5226	...	10350	1513	3660	5177	...
A Increase in stocks	69	69	...	...	...	-45	-45	...	...	...
B Gross fixed capital formation	10519	1201	4092	5226	...	10395	1558	3660	5177	...
2 Purchases of land, net	...	...	...	...	...	...	...	...	...	...
3 Purchases of intangible assets, net	...	...	...	...	...	...	...	...	...	...
4 Capital transfers	3168	2553	615	...	...	4660	3599	1061	...	...
A To other government subsectors	...	...	...	...	...	...	...	...	...	...
B To other resident sectors	3168	2553	615	...	...	4660	3599	1061	...	...
C To rest of the world	...	...	...	...	...	...	...	...	...	...
Net lending c	-22168	-20281	-5671	-2	3786	-28040	-24993	-6264	36	3181
Gross Accumulation ab	-8412	-16458	-964	5224	3786	-13030	-19881	-1543	5213	3181

	1984					1985				
	Total General Government	Central Government	State or Provincial Government	Local Government	Social Security Funds	Total General Government	Central Government	State or Provincial Government	Local Government	Social Security Funds
Finance of Gross Accumulation											
1 Gross saving	-13349	-24144	2707	4848	3240	-15951	-26243	1490	5627	3175
A Consumption of fixed capital	6773	1154	2377	3242	-	7092	1236	2431	3425	-
B Net saving	-20122	-25298	330	1606	3240	-23043	-27479	-941	2202	3175
2 Capital transfers	47	-	47	...	...	65	-	65	...	...
A From other government subsectors	...	...	...	...	...	...	...	...	...	...
B From other resident sectors	47	-	47	...	...	65	-	65	...	...
C From rest of the world	...	...	...	...	...	...	...	...	...	...
Finance of Gross Accumulation ab	-13302	-24144	2754	4848	3240	-15886	-26243	1555	5627	3175
Gross Accumulation											
1 Gross capital formation	11410	2511	3762	5137	...	12822	2197	4720	5905	...
A Increase in stocks	20	20	...	...	...	-64	-64	...	...	...
B Gross fixed capital formation	11390	2491	3762	5137	...	12886	2261	4720	5905	...
2 Purchases of land, net	...	...	...	...	...	...	...	...	...	...
3 Purchases of intangible assets, net	...	...	...	...	...	...	...	...	...	...
4 Capital transfers	4129	3369	760	...	...	3828	2984	844	...	...
A To other government subsectors	...	...	...	...	...	...	...	...	...	...
B To other resident sectors	4129	3369	760	...	...	3828	2984	844	...	...
C To rest of the world	...	...	...	...	...	...	...	...	...	...
Net lending c	-28841	-30024	-1768	-289	3240	-32536	-31424	-4009	-278	3175
Gross Accumulation ab	-13302	-24144	2754	4848	3240	-15886	-26243	1555	5627	3175

	1986					1987				
	Total General Government	Central Government	State or Provincial Government	Local Government	Social Security Funds	Total General Government	Central Government	State or Provincial Government	Local Government	Social Security Funds
Finance of Gross Accumulation											
1 Gross saving	-11185	-19213	-2288	7199	3117	-6745	-17881	1563	7224	2349
A Consumption of fixed capital	7371	1294	2494	3583	-	7636	1323	2547	3766	-
B Net saving	-18556	-20507	-4782	3616	3117	-14381	-19204	-984	3458	2349
2 Capital transfers	13	-	13	...	...	8	-	8	...	...

Canada

3.13 General Government Capital Accumulation Account: Total and Subsectors
(Continued)

Million Canadian dollars

	1986					1987				
	Total General Government	Central Government	State or Provincial Government	Local Government	Social Security Funds	Total General Government	Central Government	State or Provincial Government	Local Government	Social Security Funds
A From other government subsectors	...	...	...	...	...	...	...	...	...	...
B From other resident sectors	13	-	13	...	...	8	-	8	...	...
C From rest of the world	...	...	...	...	...	...	...	...	...	...
Finance of Gross Accumulation ab	-11172	-19213	-2275	7199	3117	-6737	-17881	1571	7224	2349
Gross Accumulation											
1 Gross capital formation	12532	1956	4516	6060	...	12872	1832	4407	6633	...
A Increase in stocks	-35	-35	...	...	...	-38	-38	...	...	...
B Gross fixed capital formation	12567	1991	4516	6060	...	12910	1870	4407	6633	...
2 Purchases of land, net	...	...	...	...	...	...	...	...	...	...
3 Purchases of intangible assets, net	...	...	...	...	...	...	...	...	...	...
4 Capital transfers	3608	2448	1160	...	...	2655	1900	755	...	...
A To other government subsectors	...	...	...	...	...	...	...	...	...	...
B To other resident sectors	3608	2448	1160	...	...	2655	1900	755	...	...
C To rest of the world	...	...	...	...	...	...	...	...	...	...
Net lending c	-27312	-23617	-7951	1139	3117	-22264	-21613	-3591	591	2349
Gross Accumulation ab	-11172	-19213	-2275	7199	3117	-6737	-17881	1571	7224	2349

	1988					1989				
	Total General Government	Central Government	State or Provincial Government	Local Government	Social Security Funds	Total General Government	Central Government	State or Provincial Government	Local Government	Social Security Funds
Finance of Gross Accumulation											
1 Gross saving	-1075	-17132	6320	7694	2043	-4182	-19230	5059	8113	1876
A Consumption of fixed capital	8065	1388	2613	4064	-	8583	1473	2737	4373	-
B Net saving	-9140	-18520	3707	3630	2043	-12765	-20703	2322	3740	1876
2 Capital transfers	7	-	7	...	...	2	-	2	...	...
A From other government subsectors	...	...	...	...	...	...	...	...	...	...
B From other resident sectors	7	-	7	...	...	2	-	2	...	...
C From rest of the world	...	...	...	...	...	...	...	...	...	...
Finance of Gross Accumulation ab	-1068	-17132	6327	7694	2043	-4180	-19230	5061	8113	1876
Gross Accumulation											
1 Gross capital formation	13768	2140	4372	7256	...	15280	2195	5062	8023	...
A Increase in stocks	64	64	...	...	...	-3	-3	...	...	...
B Gross fixed capital formation	13704	2076	4372	7256	...	15283	2198	5062	8023	...
2 Purchases of land, net	...	...	...	...	...	...	...	...	...	...
3 Purchases of intangible assets, net	...	...	...	...	...	...	...	...	...	...
4 Capital transfers	2431	1590	841	...	...	2408	1657	751	...	...
A To other government subsectors	...	...	...	...	...	...	...	...	...	...
B To other resident sectors	2431	1590	841	...	...	2408	1657	751	...	...
C To rest of the world	...	...	...	...	...	...	...	...	...	...
Net lending c	-17267	-20862	1114	438	2043	-21868	-23082	-752	90	1876
Gross Accumulation ab	-1068	-17132	6327	7694	2043	-4180	-19230	5061	8113	1876

a) Local government includes hospitals.
b) Social security funds refers to Canada and Quebec pension plans only.
c) Net lending of the capital accumulation account and the capital finance account have not been reconciled and are different due to different statistical sources.

3.14 General Government Capital Finance Account, Total and Subsectors

Million Canadian dollars

	1980					1981				
	Total General Government	Central Government	State or Provincial Government	Local Government	Social Security Funds	Total General Government	Central Government	State or Provincial Government	Local Government	Social Security Funds
Acquisition of Financial Assets											
1 Gold and SDRs	...	...	...	...	...	...	...	...	...	...
2 Currency and transferable deposits	1983	1744	-74	313	...	2990	3313	99	-422	...
3 Other deposits					...					...
4 Bills and bonds, short term	309	5	300	4	...	54	3	43	8	...
5 Bonds, long term	5512	-148	3630	106	1924	6517	17	4284	5	2211

263

Canada

3.14 General Government Capital Finance Account, Total and Subsectors
(Continued)

Million Canadian dollars

	1980					1981				
	Total General Government	Central Government	State or Provincial Government	Local Government	Social Security Funds	Total General Government	Central Government	State or Provincial Government	Local Government	Social Security Funds
A Corporations	140	4	96	40	...	88	-2	115	-25	...
B Other government subsectors	5372	-152	3534	66	1924	6429	19	4169	30	2211
C Rest of the world	-	-	-	-	...	-	-	-	-	...
6 Corporate equity securities [a]	14	6	8	-	...	659	1	658	-	...
7 Short-term loans, n.e.c. [b]	771	458	315	-2	...	346	-60	395	11	...
8 Long-term loans, n.e.c. [b]	69	-39	108	-	...	249	-38	287	-	...
A Mortgages	69	-39	108	-	...	249	-38	287	-	...
B Other	...	...	...	...	...	...	...	...	...	...
9 Other receivables	173	38	16	119	...	148	-6	35	119	...
10 Other assets	5909	1655	3078	97	1079	9102	2830	3947	1286	1039
Total Acquisition of Financial Assets [c]	14740	3719	7381	637	3003	20065	6060	9748	1007	3250

Incurrence of Liabilities

	1980					1981				
1 Currency and transferable deposits	61	61	-	-	...	61	61	-	-	...
2 Other deposits	...	...	...	...	...	...	...	...	...	...
3 Bills and bonds, short term	5662	5298	366	-2	...	456	-178	643	-9	...
4 Bonds, long term	12366	6460	4912	994	...	21017	12504	7367	1146	...
5 Short-term loans, n.e.c. [b]	1405	737	813	-145	...	392	-929	738	583	...
6 Long-term loans, n.e.c. [b]	2	-	-	2	...	2	-	-	2	...
7 Other payables	135	14	31	90	...	760	9	661	90	...
8 Other liabilities	1881	1770	-117	228	...	3064	2318	518	228	...
Total Incurrence of Liabilities	21512	14340	6005	1167	...	25752	13785	9927	2040	...
Net Lending [d]	-6772	-10621	1376	-530	3003	-5687	-7725	-179	-1033	3250
Incurrence of Liabilities and Net Worth [c]	14740	3719	7381	637	3003	20065	6060	9748	1007	3250

	1982					1983				
	Total General Government	Central Government	State or Provincial Government	Local Government	Social Security Funds	Total General Government	Central Government	State or Provincial Government	Local Government	Social Security Funds

Acquisition of Financial Assets

	1982					1983				
1 Gold and SDRs	...	...	...	...	...	...	...	...	...	...
2 Currency and transferable deposits	-713	-740	101	-74	...	-1907	-209	-70	-1628	...
3 Other deposits					...					...
4 Bills and bonds, short term	-899	7	-1020	114	...	-107	1	-170	62	...
5 Bonds, long term	7756	8	4700	324	2724	3979	21	1321	346	2291
A Corporations	64	-3	-41	108	...	385	-2	214	173	...
B Other government subsectors	7692	11	4741	216	2724	3594	23	1107	173	2291
C Rest of the world	-	-	-	-	...	-	-	-	-	...
6 Corporate equity securities [a]	746	129	617	-	...	628	7	621	-	...
7 Short-term loans, n.e.c. [b]	408	308	97	3	...	805	527	279	-1	...
8 Long-term loans, n.e.c. [b]	404	-30	434	-	...	132	-23	155	-	...
A Mortgages	404	-30	434	-	...	132	-23	155	-	...
B Other	...	...	...	...	...	...	...	...	...	...
9 Other receivables	115	38	-42	119	...	261	5	9	247	...
10 Other assets	-831	-687	-1831	625	1062	7633	2787	1764	2192	890
Total Acquisition of Financial Assets [c]	6986	-967	3056	1111	3786	11424	3116	3909	1218	3181

Incurrence of Liabilities

	1982					1983				
1 Currency and transferable deposits	186	186	-	-	...	-74	-74	-	-	...
2 Other deposits	...	...	...	...	...	...	...	...	...	...
3 Bills and bonds, short term	7110	5088	2026	-4	...	14370	13104	1266	-	...
4 Bonds, long term	26411	14295	10011	2105	...	22681	12916	8483	1282	...
5 Short-term loans, n.e.c. [b]	-357	-377	437	-417	...	246	84	-138	300	...
6 Long-term loans, n.e.c. [b]	2	-	-	2	...	2	-	-	2	...
7 Other payables	428	-18	356	90	...	540	-5	179	366	...
8 Other liabilities	678	363	87	228	...	4548	3332	911	305	...
Total Incurrence of Liabilities	34458	19537	12917	2004	...	42313	29357	10701	2255	...
Net Lending [d]	-27472	-20504	-9861	-893	3786	-30889	-26241	-6792	-1037	3181
Incurrence of Liabilities and Net Worth [c]	6986	-967	3056	1111	3786	11424	3116	3909	1218	3181

Canada

3.14 General Government Capital Finance Account, Total and Subsectors

Million Canadian dollars

1984

	Total General Government	Central Government	State or Provincial Government	Local Government	Social Security Funds
Acquisition of Financial Assets					
1 Gold and SDRs	...	...	...	...	...
2 Currency and transferable deposits	-3182	-3800	182	436	...
3 Other deposits					...
4 Bills and bonds, short term	3485	1	2900	584	...
5 Bonds, long term	3657	187	989	18	2463
A Corporations	155	-	147	8	...
B Other government subsectors	3502	187	842	10	2463
C Rest of the world	-	-	-	-	...
6 Corporate equity securities [a]	685	294	391	-	...
7 Short-term loans, n.e.c. [b]	484	695	-220	9	...
8 Long-term loans, n.e.c. [b]	-	-36	36	-	...
A Mortgages	-	-36	36	-	...
B Other	...	...	...	...	...
9 Other receivables	-142	-69	20	-93	...
10 Other assets	6908	623	4739	769	777
Total Acquisition of Financial Assets [c]	11895	-2105	9037	1723	3240
Incurrence of Liabilities					
1 Currency and transferable deposits	68	68	-	-	...
2 Other deposits	...	...	...	...	...
3 Bills and bonds, short term	11709	10112	1598	-1	...
4 Bonds, long term	23720	14778	7773	1169	...
5 Short-term loans, n.e.c. [b]	1547	958	785	-196	...
6 Long-term loans, n.e.c. [b]	13	-	-	13	...
7 Other payables	620	4	362	254	...
8 Other liabilities	2601	2090	475	36	...
Total Incurrence of Liabilities	40278	28010	10993	1275	...
Net Lending [d]	-28383	-30115	-1956	448	3240
Incurrence of Liabilities and Net Worth [c]	11895	-2105	9037	1723	3240

1985

	Total General Government	Central Government	State or Provincial Government	Local Government	Social Security Funds
Acquisition of Financial Assets					
1 Gold and SDRs	...	...	...	...	...
2 Currency and transferable deposits	2043	2093	-428	378	...
3 Other deposits					...
4 Bills and bonds, short term	4145	4	3769	372	...
5 Bonds, long term	3437	-80	1219	187	2111
A Corporations	-72	-	107	-179	...
B Other government subsectors	3509	-80	1112	366	2111
C Rest of the world	-	-	-	-	...
6 Corporate equity securities [a]	389	119	270	-	...
7 Short-term loans, n.e.c. [b]	824	778	46	-	...
8 Long-term loans, n.e.c. [b]	-113	-33	-80	-	...
A Mortgages	-113	-33	-80	-	...
B Other	...	...	...	...	...
9 Other receivables	204	22	37	145	...
10 Other assets	1635	1002	-183	-248	1064
Total Acquisition of Financial Assets [c]	12564	3905	4650	834	3175
Incurrence of Liabilities					
1 Currency and transferable deposits	75	75	-	-	...
2 Other deposits	...	...	...	...	...
3 Bills and bonds, short term	10026	9892	109	25	...
4 Bonds, long term	29276	21654	7120	502	...
5 Short-term loans, n.e.c. [b]	3762	2367	1067	328	...
6 Long-term loans, n.e.c. [b]	9	-	-	9	...
7 Other payables	217	6	15	196	...
8 Other liabilities	3855	3035	700	120	...
Total Incurrence of Liabilities	47220	37029	9011	1180	...
Net Lending [d]	-34656	-33124	-4361	-346	3175
Incurrence of Liabilities and Net Worth [c]	12564	3905	4650	834	3175

1986

	Total General Government	Central Government	State or Provincial Government	Local Government	Social Security Funds
Acquisition of Financial Assets					
1 Gold and SDRs	...	...	...	...	...
2 Currency and transferable deposits	-1090	-1726	744	-108	...
3 Other deposits					...
4 Bills and bonds, short term	750	12	264	474	...
5 Bonds, long term	5130	-150	2598	202	2480
A Corporations	173	-2	217	-42	...
B Other government subsectors	4957	-148	2381	244	2480
C Rest of the world	-	-	-	-	...
6 Corporate equity securities [a]	459	-59	518	-	...
7 Short-term loans, n.e.c. [b]	3363	1970	1395	-2	...
8 Long-term loans, n.e.c. [b]	-155	-25	-130	-	...
A Mortgages	-155	-25	-130	-	...
B Other	...	...	...	...	...
9 Other receivables	-5	-23	13	5	...
10 Other assets	5444	-1736	5839	704	637
Total Acquisition of Financial Assets [c]	13896	-1737	11241	1275	3117
Incurrence of Liabilities					
1 Currency and transferable deposits	61	61	-	-	...
2 Other deposits	...	...	...	...	...
3 Bills and bonds, short term	16177	11425	4776	-24	...

1987

	Total General Government	Central Government	State or Provincial Government	Local Government	Social Security Funds
Acquisition of Financial Assets					
1 Gold and SDRs	...	...	...	...	...
2 Currency and transferable deposits	937	550	17	370	...
3 Other deposits					...
4 Bills and bonds, short term	3897	86	3768	43	...
5 Bonds, long term	2347	77	412	69	1789
A Corporations	416	-3	336	83	...
B Other government subsectors	1931	80	76	-14	1789
C Rest of the world	-	-	-	-	...
6 Corporate equity securities [a]	46	-404	450	-	...
7 Short-term loans, n.e.c. [b]	991	633	358	-	...
8 Long-term loans, n.e.c. [b]	-219	-39	-180	-	...
A Mortgages	-219	-39	-180	-	...
B Other	...	...	...	...	...
9 Other receivables	70	9	21	40	...
10 Other assets	6822	3706	1943	613	560
Total Acquisition of Financial Assets [c]	14891	4618	6789	1135	2349
Incurrence of Liabilities					
1 Currency and transferable deposits	164	164	-	-	...
2 Other deposits	...	...	...	...	...
3 Bills and bonds, short term	5633	4276	1283	74	...

Canada

3.14 General Government Capital Finance Account, Total and Subsectors
(Continued)

Million Canadian dollars

	1986 Total General Government	1986 Central Government	1986 State or Provincial Government	1986 Local Government	1986 Social Security Funds	1987 Total General Government	1987 Central Government	1987 State or Provincial Government	1987 Local Government	1987 Social Security Funds
4 Bonds, long term	19455	10419	8299	737	...	28050	20996	6738	316	...
5 Short-term loans, n.e.c. [b]	-996	-1456	481	-21	...	1690	150	1284	256	...
6 Long-term loans, n.e.c. [b]	-	-	-	-	...	-	-	-	-	...
7 Other payables	-170	43	-233	20	...	-465	-46	-563	144	...
8 Other liabilities	4880	2164	2506	210	...	4362	293	3437	632	...
Total Incurrence of Liabilities	39407	22656	15829	922	...	39434	25833	12179	1422	...
Net Lending [d]	-25511	-24393	-4588	353	3117	-24543	-21215	-5390	-287	2349
Incurrence of Liabilities and Net Worth [c]	13896	-1737	11241	1275	3117	14891	4618	6789	1135	2349

	1988 Total General Government	1988 Central Government	1988 State or Provincial Government	1988 Local Government	1988 Social Security Funds	1989 Total General Government	1989 Central Government	1989 State or Provincial Government	1989 Local Government	1989 Social Security Funds
Acquisition of Financial Assets										
1 Gold and SDRs	...	...	...	...	...	...	...	...	...	...
2 Currency and transferable deposits	839	1700	-391	-470	...	543	-615	405	753	...
3 Other deposits					...					...
4 Bills and bonds, short term	4903	-26	3839	1090	...	5351	-26	4467	910	...
5 Bonds, long term	2592	131	745	214	1502	4209	-112	2951	150	1220
A Corporations	228	3	202	23	...	24	9	81	-66	...
B Other government subsectors	2364	128	543	191	1502	4185	-121	2870	216	1220
C Rest of the world	-	-	-	-	...	-	-	-	-	...
6 Corporate equity securities [a]	761	-10	771	-	...	89	-463	552	-	...
7 Short-term loans, n.e.c. [b]	507	523	-33	17	...	-486	-685	162	37	...
8 Long-term loans, n.e.c. [b]	-6	-18	12	-	...	-16	-16	-	-	...
A Mortgages	-6	-18	12	-	...	-16	-16	-	-	...
B Other	...	...	...	...	...	...	...	...	...	...
9 Other receivables	15	-34	6	43	...	53	13		40	...
10 Other assets	15332	7722	7371	-302	541	-6028	-2555	-3651	-478	656
Total Acquisition of Financial Assets [c]	24943	9988	12320	592	2043	3715	-4459	4886	1412	876
Incurrence of Liabilities										
1 Currency and transferable deposits	113	113	-	-	...	350	350	...	...	...
2 Other deposits	...	...	...	...	...	...	...	...	...	...
3 Bills and bonds, short term	18917	20005	-1050	-38	...	26880	24079	2678	123	...
4 Bonds, long term	19540	10342	8036	1162	...	5733	-2822	7232	1323	...
5 Short-term loans, n.e.c. [b]	103	-1011	971	143	...	-875	-755	-259	139	...
6 Long-term loans, n.e.c. [b]	-	-	-	-	...	-	-	-	...	...
7 Other payables	-882	-9	-1033	160	...	255	12	93	150	...
8 Other liabilities	4629	2584	2304	-259	...	-1078	-1001	-138	61	...
Total Incurrence of Liabilities	42420	32024	9228	1168	...	31265	19863	9606	1796	...
Net Lending [d]	-17477	-22036	3092	-576	2043	-27550	-24322	-4720	-384	1876
Incurrence of Liabilities and Net Worth [c]	24943	9988	12320	592	2043	3715	-4459	4886	1412	1876

a) Investment in short-term papers, bonds and corporate equity securities of the rest of the world cannot be split between long-term and short-term by purchasers, the total investment has been allocated to the item 'Corporate equity securities'.
b) Loans other than mortgages are included in item 'Short-term loans, n.e.c.'.
c) Social security funds refers to Canada and Quebec pension plans only.
d) Net lending of the capital accumulation account and the capital finance account have not been reconciled and are different due to different statistical sources.

3.22 Corporate and Quasi-Corporate Enterprise Income and Outlay Account: Total and Sectors

Million Canadian dollars

	1980 TOTAL	1980 Non-Financial	1980 Financial	1981 TOTAL	1981 Non-Financial	1981 Financial	1982 TOTAL	1982 Non-Financial	1982 Financial	1983 TOTAL	1983 Non-Financial	1983 Financial
Receipts												
1 Operating surplus	...	...	...	...	...	...	...	...	...	...	...	...
2 Property and entrepreneurial income	86236	...	...	96603	...	...	93340	...	...	104481	...	...
3 Current transfers	...	...	...	...	...	...	...	...	...	...	...	...
Statistical discrepancy [a]	-7336	...	...	-7217	...	...	-3276	...	...	-2659	...	...
Total Current Receipts [b]	78900	...	...	89386	...	...	90064	...	...	101822	...	...
Disbursements												
1 Property and entrepreneurial income	54686	...	...	71575	...	...	81314	...	...	79769	...	...

Canada

3.22 Corporate and Quasi-Corporate Enterprise Income and Outlay Account: Total and Sectors
(Continued)

Million Canadian dollars

	1980			1981			1982			1983		
	TOTAL	Non-Financial	Financial	TOTAL	Non-Financial	Financial	TOTAL	Non-Financial	Financial	TOTAL	Non-Financial	Financial
2 Direct taxes and other current transfers n.e.c. to general government	12078	...	...	12796	...	...	11755	...	...	12320	...	...
A Direct taxes	12078	...	...	12796	...	...	11755	...	...	12320	...	...
On income	12078	...	...	12796	...	...	11755	...	...	12320	...	...
Other	...	...	...	...	...	...	...	...	...	...	...	...
B Fines, fees, penalties and other current transfers n.e.c.	...	...	...	...	...	...	...	...	...	...	...	...
3 Other current transfers	647	...	...	814	...	...	769	...	...	735	...	...
A Casualty insurance premiums, net	...	...	...	...	...	...	...	...	...	...	...	...
B Casualty insurance claims liability of insurance companies	...	...	...	...	...	...	...	...	...	...	...	...
C Transfers to private non-profit institutions	518	...	...	652	...	...	634	...	...	602	...	...
D Unfunded employee pension and welfare benefits	...	...	...	...	...	...	...	...	...	...	...	...
E Social assistance grants	...	...	...	...	...	...	...	...	...	...	...	...
F Other transfers n.e.c.	...	...	...	...	...	...	...	...	...	...	...	...
G Transfers to the rest of the world	129	...	...	162	...	...	135	...	...	133	...	...
Statistical discrepancy [a]	-7336	...	...	-7217	...	...	-3276	...	...	-2659	...	...
Net saving	18825	...	...	11418	...	...	-498	...	...	11657	...	...
Total Current Disbursements and Net Saving [b]	78900	...	...	89386	...	...	90064	...	...	101822	...	...

	1984			1985			1986			1987		
	TOTAL	Non-Financial	Financial	TOTAL	Non-Financial	Financial	TOTAL	Non-Financial	Financial	TOTAL	Non-Financial	Financial

Receipts

1 Operating surplus	...	...	...	...	...	...	...	...	...	...	...	...
2 Property and entrepreneurial income	122927	...	...	131874	...	...	127207	...	...	141690	...	...
3 Current transfers	...	...	...	...	...	...	...	...	...	...	...	...
Statistical discrepancy [a]	-2625	...	...	-1760	...	...	-1812	...	...	-3036	...	...
Total Current Receipts [b]	120302	...	...	130114	...	...	125395	...	...	138654	...	...

Disbursements

1 Property and entrepreneurial income	90228	...	...	95787	...	...	96877	...	...	100152	...	...
2 Direct taxes and other current transfers n.e.c. to general government	14984	...	...	15563	...	...	14573	...	...	16878	...	...
A Direct taxes	14984	...	...	15563	...	...	14573	...	...	16878	...	...
On income	14984	...	...	15563	...	...	14573	...	...	16878	...	...
Other	...	...	...	...	...	...	...	...	...	...	...	...
B Fines, fees, penalties and other current transfers n.e.c.	...	...	...	...	...	...	...	...	...	...	...	...
3 Other current transfers	744	...	...	697	...	...	734	...	...	782	...	...
A Casualty insurance premiums, net	...	...	...	...	...	...	...	...	...	...	...	...
B Casualty insurance claims liability of insurance companies	...	...	...	...	...	...	...	...	...	...	...	...
C Transfers to private non-profit institutions	576	...	...	539	...	...	593	...	...	658	...	...
D Unfunded employee pension and welfare benefits	...	...	...	...	...	...	...	...	...	...	...	...
E Social assistance grants	...	...	...	...	...	...	...	...	...	...	...	...
F Other transfers n.e.c.	...	...	...	...	...	...	...	...	...	...	...	...
G Transfers to the rest of the world	168	...	...	158	...	...	141	...	...	124	...	...
Statistical discrepancy [a]	-2625	...	...	-1760	...	...	-1812	...	...	-3036	...	...
Net saving	16971	...	...	19827	...	...	15023	...	...	23878	...	...
Total Current Disbursements and Net Saving [b]	120302	...	...	130114	...	...	125395	...	...	138654	...	...

Canada

3.22 Corporate and Quasi-Corporate Enterprise Income and Outlay Account: Total and Sectors

Million Canadian dollars

	1988 TOTAL	1988 Non-Financial	1988 Financial	1989 TOTAL	1989 Non-Financial	1989 Financial
Receipts						
1 Operating surplus	...	...	...	...	...	...
2 Property and entrepreneurial income	159468	...	...	166400	...	...
3 Current transfers	...	...	...	...	...	...
Statistical discrepancy a	-3254	...	...	-1688	...	...
Total Current Receipts b	156214	...	...	164712	...	...
Disbursements						
1 Property and entrepreneurial income	114896	...	...	125761	...	...
2 Direct taxes and other current transfers n.e.c. to general government	17337	...	...	16816	...	...
A Direct taxes	17337	...	...	16816	...	...
On income	17337	...	...	16816	...	...
Other	...	...	...	...	...	...
B Fines, fees, penalties and other current transfers n.e.c.	...	...	...	...	...	...
3 Other current transfers	833	...	...	826	...	...
A Casualty insurance premiums, net	...	...	...	...	...	...
B Casualty insurance claims liability of insurance companies	...	...	...	...	...	...
C Transfers to private non-profit institutions	682	...	...	690	...	...
D Unfunded employee pension and welfare benefits	...	...	...	...	...	...
E Social assistance grants	...	...	...	...	...	...
F Other transfers n.e.c.	...	...	...	...	...	...
G Transfers to the rest of the world	151	...	...	136	...	...
Statistical discrepancy a	-3254	...	...	-1688	...	...
Net saving	26402	...	...	22997	...	...
Total Current Disbursements and Net Saving b	156214	...	...	164712	...	...

a) Item 'Statistical discrepancy' refers to inventory valuation adjustment.
b) Tables 3.22 and 3.23 cover corporate and government business enterprises only.

3.23 Corporate and Quasi-Corporate Enterprise Capital Accumulation Account: Total and Sectors

Million Canadian dollars

	1980 TOTAL	1980 Non-Financial	1980 Financial	1981 TOTAL	1981 Non-Financial	1981 Financial	1982 TOTAL	1982 Non-Financial	1982 Financial	1983 TOTAL	1983 Non-Financial	1983 Financial
Finance of Gross Accumulation												
1 Gross saving	39578	...	...	35259	...	...	25458	...	...	39316	...	...
A Consumption of fixed capital	20753	...	...	23841	...	...	25956	...	...	27659	...	...
B Net saving	18825	...	...	11418	...	...	-498	...	...	11657	...	...
2 Capital transfers	679	...	...	882	...	...	2344	...	...	3354	...	...
A From resident sectors	679	...	...	882	...	...	2344	...	...	3354	...	...
B From the rest of the world	...	...	...	...	...	...	...	...	...	...	...	...
Statistical discrepancy	-7336	...	...	-7217	...	...	-3276	...	...	-2659	...	...
Finance of Gross Accumulation a	32921	...	...	28924	...	...	24526	...	...	40011	...	...
Gross Accumulation												
1 Gross capital formation	44429	...	...	53879	...	...	41244	...	...	44970	...	...
A Increase in stocks	740	...	...	697	...	...	-9885	...	...	-2106	...	...
B Gross fixed capital formation	43689	...	...	53182	...	...	51129	...	...	47076	...	...
2 Purchases of land, net	...	...	...	...	...	...	...	...	...	...	...	...
3 Purchases of intangible assets, net	...	...	...	...	...	...	...	...	...	...	...	...
4 Capital transfers	...	...	...	...	...	...	...	...	...	...	...	...
Net lending b	-11508	...	...	-24955	...	...	-16718	...	...	-4959	...	...
Gross Accumulation a	32921	...	...	28924	...	...	24526	...	...	40011	...	...

Canada

3.23 Corporate and Quasi-Corporate Enterprise Capital Accumulation Account: Total and Sectors

Million Canadian dollars

	1984 TOTAL	1984 Non-Financial	1984 Financial	1985 TOTAL	1985 Non-Financial	1985 Financial	1986 TOTAL	1986 Non-Financial	1986 Financial	1987 TOTAL	1987 Non-Financial	1987 Financial
Finance of Gross Accumulation												
1 Gross saving	46858	...	...	53348	...	...	51802	...	...	62209	...	...
A Consumption of fixed capital	29887	...	...	33521	...	...	36779	...	...	38331	...	...
B Net saving	16971	...	...	19827	...	...	15023	...	...	23878	...	...
2 Capital transfers	3485	...	...	3308	...	...	3361	...	...	2444	...	...
A From resident sectors	3485	...	...	3308	...	...	3361	...	...	2444	...	...
B From the rest of the world	...	...	...	...	...	...	...	...	...	...	...	...
Statistical discrepancy	-2625	...	...	-1760	...	...	-1812	...	...	-3036	...	...
Finance of Gross Accumulation [a]	47718	...	...	54896	...	...	53351	...	...	61617	...	...
Gross Accumulation												
1 Gross capital formation	54055	...	...	56382	...	...	58955	...	...	67366	...	...
A Increase in stocks	5768	...	...	1997	...	...	1745	...	...	3194	...	...
B Gross fixed capital formation	48287	...	...	54385	...	...	57210	...	...	64172	...	...
2 Purchases of land, net	...	...	...	...	...	...	...	...	...	...	...	...
3 Purchases of intangible assets, net	...	...	...	...	...	...	...	...	...	...	...	...
4 Capital transfers	...	...	...	...	...	...	...	...	...	...	...	...
Net lending [b]	-6337	...	...	-1486	...	...	-5604	...	...	-5749	...	...
Gross Accumulation [a]	47718	...	...	54896	...	...	53351	...	...	61617	...	...

	1988 TOTAL	1988 Non-Financial	1988 Financial	1989 TOTAL	1989 Non-Financial	1989 Financial
Finance of Gross Accumulation						
1 Gross saving	67187	...	...	66722	...	...
A Consumption of fixed capital	40785	...	...	43725	...	...
B Net saving	26402	...	...	22997	...	...
2 Capital transfers	2139	...	...	2129	...	...
A From resident sectors	2139	...	...	2129	...	...
B From the rest of the world	...	...	...	...	...	...
Statistical discrepancy	-3254	...	...	-1688	...	...
Finance of Gross Accumulation [a]	66072	...	...	67163	...	...
Gross Accumulation						
1 Gross capital formation	77443	...	...	83812	...	...
A Increase in stocks	2983	...	...	3292	...	...
B Gross fixed capital formation	74460	...	...	80520	...	...
2 Purchases of land, net	...	...	...	...	...	...
3 Purchases of intangible assets, net	...	...	...	...	...	...
4 Capital transfers	...	...	...	...	...	...
Net lending [b]	-11371	...	...	-16649	...	...
Gross Accumulation [a]	66072	...	...	67163	...	...

a) Tables 3.22 and 3.23 cover corporate and government business enterprises only.
b) Net lending of the capital accumulation account and the capital finance account have not been reconciled and are different due to different statistical sources.

3.24 Corporate and Quasi-Corporate Enterprise Capital Finance Account: Total and Sectors

Million Canadian dollars

	1980 TOTAL	1980 Non-Financial	1980 Financial	1981 TOTAL	1981 Non-Financial	1981 Financial	1982 TOTAL	1982 Non-Financial	1982 Financial	1983 TOTAL	1983 Non-Financial	1983 Financial
Acquisition of Financial Assets												
1 Gold and SDRs	-541	...	-541	383	...	383	-664	...	-664	550	...	550
2 Currency and transferable deposits	6534	1598	4936	4249	1793	2456	2149	389	1760	-3782	-2234	-1548
3 Other deposits	...	...	...	...	...	...	...	...	...	...	...	...
4 Bills and bonds, short term	4441	961	3480	3593	-590	4183	8364	1730	6634	9036	4883	4153
5 Bonds, long term	9035	-105	9140	8499	-64	8563	10455	15	10440	13927	359	13568
A Corporate, resident	1448	-159	1607	4365	-81	4446	1978	-96	2074	1952	116	1836
B Government	7587	54	7533	4134	17	4117	8477	111	8366	11975	243	11732

Canada

3.24 Corporate and Quasi-Corporate Enterprise Capital Finance Account: Total and Sectors
(Continued)

Million Canadian dollars

	1980 TOTAL	1980 Non-Financial	1980 Financial	1981 TOTAL	1981 Non-Financial	1981 Financial	1982 TOTAL	1982 Non-Financial	1982 Financial	1983 TOTAL	1983 Non-Financial	1983 Financial
C Rest of the world	...	...	...	...	...	...	...	...	...	...	...	...
6 Corporate equity securities [a]	3415	1012	2403	4379	560	3819	2882	232	2650	6374	-245	6619
7 Short term loans, n.e.c. [b]	21713	707	21006	38284	907	37377	-2727	2009	-4736	-9455	-1074	-8381
8 Long term loans, n.e.c. [b]	10730	79	10651	7894	977	6917	3681	393	3288	11957	174	11783
A Mortgages	10730	79	10651	7894	977	6917	3681	393	3288	11957	174	11783
B Other	...	...	...	...	...	...	...	...	...	...	...	...
9 Trade credits and advances	13675	8757	4918	11532	7031	4501	1155	1155	-	4968	3009	1959
A Consumer credit	4690	-92	4782	4442	231	4211	-180	-49	-131	2152	134	2018
B Other	8985	8849	136	7090	6800	290	1335	1204	131	2816	2875	-59
10 Other receivables	...	...	...	...	...	...	...	...	...	...	...	...
11 Other assets	24646	12384	12262	35359	21580	13779	15491	8321	7170	13538	4469	9069
Total Acquisition of Financial Assets	93648	25393	68255	114172	32194	81978	40786	14244	26542	47113	9341	37772

Incurrence of Liabilities

	1980 TOTAL	1980 Non-Financial	1980 Financial	1981 TOTAL	1981 Non-Financial	1981 Financial	1982 TOTAL	1982 Non-Financial	1982 Financial	1983 TOTAL	1983 Non-Financial	1983 Financial
1 Currency and transferable deposits	38762	-	38762	39656	-	39656	2866	-	2866	5302	-	5302
2 Other deposits	...	...	...	...	...	...	...	...	...	...	...	...
3 Bills and bonds, short term	5410	2532	2878	1811	610	1201	2752	668	2084	4102	1216	2886
4 Bonds, long term	7864	5711	2153	13763	10876	2887	10614	8269	2345	7106	6590	516
5 Corporate equity securities	7703	5528	2175	13343	6644	6699	6498	3767	2731	10938	5894	5044
6 Short-term loans, n.e.c. [b]	12412	11794	618	34630	29757	4873	827	-1107	1934	-8263	-8008	-255
7 Long-term loans, n.e.c. [b]	1887	1813	74	1577	1581	-4	1451	1363	88	1296	1350	-54
8 Net equity of households in life insurance and pension fund reserves	12252	-	12252	14092	-	14092	14904	-	14904	15541	-	15541
9 Proprietors' net additions to the accumulation of quasi-corporations [c]	8877	3789	5088	18732	7217	11515	6491	7429	-938	9260	2798	6462
10 Trade credit and advances	4913	4955	-42	7398	7326	72	-326	-373	47	3977	3961	16
11 Other accounts payable	...	...	...	...	...	...	...	...	...	...	...	...
12 Other liabilities	8031	4346	3685	1480	497	983	6703	4542	2161	2892	2223	669
Total Incurrence of Liabilities	108111	40468	67643	146482	64508	81974	52780	24558	28222	52151	16024	36127
Net Lending [d]	-14463	-15075	612	-32310	-32314	4	-11994	-10314	-1680	-5038	-6683	1645
Incurrence of Liabilities and Net Lending	93648	25393	68255	114172	32194	81978	40786	14244	26542	47113	9341	37772

	1984 TOTAL	1984 Non-Financial	1984 Financial	1985 TOTAL	1985 Non-Financial	1985 Financial	1986 TOTAL	1986 Non-Financial	1986 Financial	1987 TOTAL	1987 Non-Financial	1987 Financial

Acquisition of Financial Assets

	1984 TOTAL	1984 Non-Financial	1984 Financial	1985 TOTAL	1985 Non-Financial	1985 Financial	1986 TOTAL	1986 Non-Financial	1986 Financial	1987 TOTAL	1987 Non-Financial	1987 Financial
1 Gold and SDRs	-1094	...	-1094	-112	...	-112	662	...	662	4464	...	4464
2 Currency and transferable deposits	3588	1212	2376	-3064	-1860	-1204	8018	1913	6105	5187	5618	-431
3 Other deposits	...	...	...	...	...	...	...	...	...	...	...	...
4 Bills and bonds, short term	7669	3735	3934	6588	1132	5456	17794	2252	15542	6456	5545	911
5 Bonds, long term	10002	429	9573	12924	513	12411	11530	461	11069	13245	284	12961
A Corporate, resident	1205	3	1202	1822	209	1613	5625	-46	5671	1777	-56	1833
B Government	8797	426	8371	11102	304	10798	5905	507	5398	11468	340	11128
C Rest of the world	...	...	...	...	...	...	...	...	...	...	...	...
6 Corporate equity securities [a]	9908	1362	8546	10357	489	9868	10173	977	9196	3213	763	2450
7 Short term loans, n.e.c. [b]	10041	1487	8554	15272	1085	14187	-3540	585	-4125	14574	823	13751
8 Long term loans, n.e.c. [b]	8287	-230	8517	15545	226	15319	22802	-163	22965	29637	124	29513
A Mortgages	8287	-230	8517	15545	226	15319	22802	-163	22965	29637	124	29513
B Other	...	...	...	...	...	...	...	...	...	...	...	...
9 Trade credits and advances	9780	5100	4680	11745	4486	7259	7102	56	7046	16067	6075	9992
A Consumer credit	4906	214	4692	7013	120	6893	6730	-	6730	9710	-	9710
B Other	4874	4886	-12	4732	4366	366	372	56	316	6357	6075	282
10 Other receivables	...	...	...	...	...	...	...	...	...	...	...	...
11 Other assets	13668	8116	5552	20518	10818	9700	33130	16927	16203	27134	10263	16871
Total Acquisition of Financial Assets	71849	21211	50638	89773	16889	72884	107671	23008	84663	119977	29495	90482

Incurrence of Liabilities

	1984 TOTAL	1984 Non-Financial	1984 Financial	1985 TOTAL	1985 Non-Financial	1985 Financial	1986 TOTAL	1986 Non-Financial	1986 Financial	1987 TOTAL	1987 Non-Financial	1987 Financial
1 Currency and transferable deposits	17123	-	17123	24567	-	24567	28812	-	28812	29310	-	29310
2 Other deposits	...	...	...	...	...	...	...	...	...	...	...	...
3 Bills and bonds, short term	2364	-9	2373	3584	2277	1307	10753	7152	3601	9490	6907	2583

Canada

3.24 Corporate and Quasi-Corporate Enterprise Capital Finance Account: Total and Sectors
(Continued)

Million Canadian dollars

	1984 TOTAL	1984 Non-Financial	1984 Financial	1985 TOTAL	1985 Non-Financial	1985 Financial	1986 TOTAL	1986 Non-Financial	1986 Financial	1987 TOTAL	1987 Non-Financial	1987 Financial
4 Bonds, long term	5194	4446	748	5657	3503	2154	12971	7095	5876	7153	4327	2826
5 Corporate equity securities	15231	8920	6311	19197	10306	8891	31043	12852	18191	26154	10528	15626
6 Short-term loans, n.e.c. [b]	7856	6384	1472	11690	5674	6016	-832	-1019	187	8628	5535	3093
7 Long-term loans, n.e.c. [b]	584	629	-45	2538	2580	-42	3120	3255	-135	6007	5678	329
8 Net equity of households in life insurance and pension fund reserves	16240	-	16240	17665	-	17665	17738	-	17738	18225	-	18225
9 Proprietors' net additions to the accumulation of quasi-corporations [c]	3135	3281	-146	3006	-290	3296	8705	6721	1984	13879	3501	10378
10 Trade credit and advances	4812	4816	-4	2261	2295	-34	-255	-429	174	3930	3796	134
11 Other accounts payable	...	...	...	...	...	...	...	...	...	...	...	...
12 Other liabilities	3637	-28	3665	6394	260	6134	3803	581	3222	1026	-3730	4756
Total Incurrence of Liabilities	76176	28439	47737	96559	26605	69954	115858	36208	79650	123802	36542	87260
Net Lending [d]	-4327	-7228	2901	-6786	-9716	2930	-8187	-13200	5013	-3825	-7047	3222
Incurrence of Liabilities and Net Lending	71849	21211	50638	89773	16889	72884	107671	23008	84663	119977	29495	90482

	1988 TOTAL	1988 Non-Financial	1988 Financial	1989 TOTAL	1989 Non-Financial	1989 Financial
Acquisition of Financial Assets						
1 Gold and SDRs	9450	...	9450	344	...	344
2 Currency and transferable deposits	1123	4273	-3150	3700	4175	-475
3 Other deposits	...	...	...	...	...	...
4 Bills and bonds, short term	15455	2217	13238	13429	3717	9712
5 Bonds, long term	9249	1445	7804	11421	726	10695
A Corporate, resident	4641	924	3717	5536	215	5321
B Government	4608	521	4087	5885	511	5374
C Rest of the world	...	...	...	...	...	...
6 Corporate equity securities [a]	1642	56	1586	9576	896	8680
7 Short term loans, n.e.c. [b]	22001	1017	20984	19609	935	18674
8 Long term loans, n.e.c. [b]	32577	134	32443	35405	608	34797
A Mortgages	32577	134	32443	35405	608	34797
B Other	...	...	...	...	...	...
9 Trade credits and advances	13967	4103	9864	10982	2144	8838
A Consumer credit	9720	-	9720	8258	-	8258
B Other	4247	4103	144	2724	2144	580
10 Other receivables	...	...	...	...	...	...
11 Other assets	27554	13724	13830	42862	24863	17999
Total Acquisition of Financial Assets	133018	26969	106049	147328	38064	109264
Incurrence of Liabilities						
1 Currency and transferable deposits	46301	-	46301	52972	...	52972
2 Other deposits	...	...	...	...	...	...
3 Bills and bonds, short term	13724	11769	1955	8214	6510	1704
4 Bonds, long term	14320	6898	7422	11187	10251	936
5 Corporate equity securities	6089	3851	2238	22850	10631	12219
6 Short-term loans, n.e.c. [b]	14533	8266	6267	19888	14333	5555
7 Long-term loans, n.e.c. [b]	9427	9478	-51	11267	11037	230
8 Net equity of households in life insurance and pension fund reserves	21735	-	21735	23970	...	23970
9 Proprietors' net additions to the accumulation of quasi-corporations [c]	18621	4769	13852	9947	8077	1870
10 Trade credit and advances	867	936	-69	1826	1880	-54
11 Other accounts payable	...	...	...	...	...	...
12 Other liabilities	6254	1361	4893	4118	-2735	6853
Total Incurrence of Liabilities	151871	47328	104543	166239	59984	106255
Net Lending [d]	-18853	-20359	1506	-18911	-21920	3009
Incurrence of Liabilities and Net Lending	133018	26969	106049	147328	38064	109264

a) Investment in short-term papers, bonds and corporate equity securities of the rest of the world cannot be split between long-term and short-term by purchasers, the total investment has been allocated to the item 'Corporate equity securities'.
b) Loans other than mortgages are included in item 'Short-term loans, n.e.c.'.
c) Item 'Proprietors' net additions to the accumulation of quasi-corporations' consists of corporate and government claims on their associated enterprises.
d) Net lending of the capital accumulation account and the capital finance account have not been reconciled and are different due to different statistical sources.

Canada

3.32 Household and Private Unincorporated Enterprise Income and Outlay Account

Million Canadian dollars

	1970	1975	1980	1981	1982	1983	1984	1985	1986	1987	1988	1989
					Receipts							
1 Compensation of employees	48952	96623	171424	197910	211604	221800	238849	257518	274801	298850	328562	358355
A Wages and salaries	45816	89210	156819	179965	192017	200449	215698	232256	247943	269485	295923	323820
B Employers' contributions for social security	1475	3564	6357	8151	8638	10212	11269	12573	13857	15154	17186	18305
C Employers' contributions for private pension & welfare plans	1661	3849	8248	9794	10949	11139	11882	12689	13001	14211	15453	16230
2 Operating surplus of private unincorporated enterprises [a]	7021	12080	16598	17853	20315	23629	27307	29255	32802	34707	38453	39615
3 Property and entrepreneurial income	4486	10641	27539	38120	44974	41896	47702	50729	52686	55720	63235	72961
A Withdrawals from private quasi-corporations	...	...	...	...	...	...	...	...	...	...	...	...
B Interest	3638	8461	22432	31646	37577	34564	40374	43084	44100	46035	53366	65056
C Dividends	848	2180	5107	6474	7397	7332	7328	7645	8586	9685	9869	7905
D Net land rent and royalties	...	...	...	...	...	...	...	...	...	...	...	...
3 Current transfers	7256	17585	31503	36155	44863	51159	54741	59215	62966	67736	72829	77454
A Casualty insurance claims	...	...	...	...	...	...	...	...	...	...	...	...
B Social security benefits	3182	8741	16655	19305	25482	29135	31151	33963	36904	40396	43563	46993
C Social assistance grants	3799	8313	13811	15653	18147	20812	22385	24032	24692	25861	27742	28908
D Unfunded employee pension and welfare benefits	...	...	...	...	...	...	...	...	...	...	...	...
E Transfers from general government	...	...	...	...	...	...	...	...	...	...	...	...
F Transfers from the rest of the world	123	258	519	545	600	610	629	681	777	821	842	863
G Other transfers n.e.c.	152	273	518	652	634	602	576	539	593	658	682	690
Total Current Receipts	67715	136929	247064	290038	321756	338484	368599	396717	423255	457013	503079	548385
					Disbursements							
1 Final consumption expenditures	51258	96251	170408	193839	208099	228221	248428	271099	293489	318551	345754	375542
2 Property income	538	1351	3713	5362	5132	3785	3791	4233	4496	5267	6077	7974
A Interest	538	1351	3713	5362	5132	3785	3791	4233	4496	5267	6077	7974
Consumer debt	538	1351	3713	5362	5132	3785	3791	4233	4496	5267	6077	7974
Mortgage	...	...	...	...	...	...	...	...	...	...	...	...
Other	...	...	...	...	...	...	...	...	...	...	...	...
B Net land rent and royalties	...	...	...	...	...	...	...	...	...	...	...	...
3 Direct taxes and other current transfers n.e.c. to government	12340	25101	45165	55479	61919	66974	71846	78797	89156	99669	111610	117057
A Social security contributions	2470	5963	10591	13603	14954	17156	18582	20847	22785	25090	28196	28127
B Direct taxes	8970	18263	32850	39938	44708	47321	50603	55198	63483	71514	80074	85359
Income taxes	8811	18019	32140	39190	43932	46384	49594	54203	62378	70332	78841	84024
Other	159	244	710	748	776	937	1009	995	1105	1182	1233	1335
C Fees, fines and penalties	900	875	1724	1938	2257	2497	2661	2752	2888	3065	3340	3571
4 Other current transfers	176	258	364	385	443	473	500	554	602	633	648	704
A Net casualty insurance premiums	...	...	...	...	...	...	...	...	...	...	...	...
B Transfers to private non-profit institutions serving households	...	...	...	...	...	...	...	...	...	...	...	...
C Transfers to the rest of the world	176	258	364	385	443	473	500	554	602	633	648	704
D Other current transfers, except imputed	...	...	...	...	...	...	...	...	...	...	...	...
E Imputed employee pension and welfare contributions	...	...	...	...	...	...	...	...	...	...	...	...
Net saving	3403	13968	27414	34973	46163	39031	44034	42034	35512	32893	38990	47108
Total Current Disbursements and Net Saving	67715	136929	247064	290038	321756	338484	368599	396717	423255	457013	503079	548385

a) Item 'Operating surplus' refers to net income of unincorporated business including net rent.

Canada

3.33 Household and Private Unincorporated Enterprise Capital Accumulation Account

Million Canadian dollars

	1970	1975	1980	1981	1982	1983	1984	1985	1986	1987	1988	1989
Finance of Gross Accumulation												
1 Gross saving	6468	19872	37635	46498	58682	52135	58258	57347	51957	50992	57953	67715
A Consumption of fixed capital	3065	5904	10221	11525	12519	13104	14224	15313	16445	18099	18963	20607
B Net saving	3403	13968	27414	34973	46163	39031	44034	42034	35512	32893	38990	47108
2 Capital transfers	399	870	1559	1753	2474	2857	2280	2297	2204	3605	5714	6613
A From resident sectors	10	205	398	349	824	1306	644	520	247	211	292	279
B From the rest of the world	389	665	1161	1404	1650	1551	1636	1777	1957	3394	5422	6334
Total Finance of Gross Accumulation	6867	20742	39194	48251	61156	54992	60538	59644	54161	54597	63667	74328
Gross Accumulation												
1 Gross Capital Formation	4833	12900	19903	24184	19742	23009	23995	27275	32630	38658	42808	48014
A Increase in stocks	-125	280	-473	694	63	-747	-1027	348	847	-437	-564	465
B Gross fixed capital formation	4958	12620	20376	23490	19679	23756	25022	26927	31783	39095	43372	47549
2 Purchases of land, net	...	...	...	...	...	...	...	...	...	...	...	...
3 Purchases of intangibles, net	...	...	...	...	...	...	...	...	...	...	...	...
4 Capital transfers	465	326	389	363	404	414	393	426	388	396	409	418
A To resident sectors	266	156	72	54	57	65	47	65	13	8	7	2
B To the rest of the world	199	170	317	309	347	349	346	361	375	388	402	416
Net lending [a]	1569	7516	18902	23704	41010	31569	36150	31943	21143	15543	20450	25896
Total Gross Accumulation	6867	20742	39194	48251	61156	54992	60538	59644	54161	54597	63667	74328

a) Net lending of the capital accumulation account and the capital finance account have not been reconciled and are different due to different statistical sources.

3.34 Household and Private Unincorporated Enterprise Capital Finance Account

Million Canadian dollars

	1970	1975	1980	1981	1982	1983	1984	1985	1986	1987	1988	1989
Acquisition of Financial Assets												
1 Gold	...	...	...	...	...	...	...	...	...	...	...	...
2 Currency and transferable deposits	3556	9254	22708	26900	8003	7284	21848	15539	27697	17957	42559	47821
3 Other deposits	...	...	...	...	...	...	...	...	...	...	...	...
4 Bills and bonds, short term	-498	-322	5229	-2616	3272	7864	1331	3439	5998	2245	3087	15673
5 Bonds, long term	856	3050	2186	8266	7093	7158	7496	7628	-6714	11770	6119	-15895
A Corporate	374	75	216	-271	-927	288	125	-216	-2220	-1200	2401	-3077
B Government	482	2975	1970	8537	8020	6870	7371	7844	-4494	12970	3718	-12818
C Rest of the world	-	-	-	-	-	-	-	-	-	-	-	-
6 Corporate equity securities [a]	-561	9	-577	-4769	3407	1503	488	6161	7247	8028	-6107	-1978
7 Short term loans, n.e.c.	...	...	...	...	...	...	...	...	...	...	...	...
8 Long term loans, n.e.c.	926	1416	436	1056	248	-167	256	71	-423	456	456	456
A Mortgages	926	1416	436	1056	248	-167	256	71	-423	456	456	456
B Other	-	-	-	-	-	-	-	-	-	-	-	-
9 Trade credit and advances	...	...	...	...	...	...	...	...	...	...	...	...
10 Net equity of households in life insurance and pension fund reserves	1807	5089	12239	14074	14884	15517	16214	17632	17705	18191	21698	23931
11 Proprietors' net additions to the accumulation of quasi-corporations	...	...	...	...	...	...	...	...	...	...	...	...
12 Other	458	2824	-1563	-5209	7101	1693	-3185	7160	-344	-1962	-3048	-6969
Total Acquisition of Financial Assets	6544	21320	40658	37702	44008	40852	44448	57630	51166	56685	64764	63039
Incurrence of Liabilities												
1 Short term loans, n.e.c. [b]	198	4490	10040	7058	-817	2537	4999	8369	10112	14359	15667	12671
2 Long term loans, n.e.c. [b]	2646	9498	9342	7579	2864	10552	7838	12808	19005	23765	23588	24578
A Mortgages	2646	9498	9342	7579	2864	10552	7838	12808	19005	23765	23588	24578
B Other	-	-	-	-	-	-	-	-	-	-	-	-
3 Trade credit and advances	795	743	2313	-341	822	-3620	-636	3041	1001	2641	3388	1494
4 Other accounts payable	...	...	...	...	...	...	...	...	...	...	...	...
5 Other liabilities	72	85	37	-5	263	80	-34	136	80	-194	-10	-98
Total Incurrence of Liabilities	3711	14816	21732	14291	3132	9549	12167	24354	30198	40571	42633	38645
Net Lending [c]	2833	6504	18926	23411	40876	31303	32281	33276	20968	16114	22131	24394
Incurrence of Liabilities and Net Lending	6544	21320	40658	37702	44008	40852	44448	57630	51166	56685	64764	63039

a) Investment in short-term papers, bonds and corporate equity securities of the rest of the world cannot be split between long-term and short-term by purchasers, the total investment has been allocated to the item 'Corporate equity securities'. b) Loans other than mortgages are included in item 'Short-term loans, n.e.c.'. c) Net lending of the capital accumulation account and the capital finance account have not been reconciled and are different due to different statistical sources.

Canada

3.51 External Transactions: Current Account: Detail

Million Canadian dollars

	1970	1975	1980	1981	1982	1983	1984	1985	1986	1987	1988	1989
Payments to the Rest of the World											
1 Imports of goods and services	17830	41362	81933	93001	82598	89832	110632	123388	133369	139867	154299	162523
A Imports of merchandise c.i.f. [a]	14758	35764	70912	80496	69665	75961	95404	106680	114425	119546	132617	139151
B Other	3072	5598	11021	12505	12933	13871	15228	16708	18944	20321	21682	23372
2 Factor income to the rest of the world	2397	4271	11466	15330	18149	17197	19849	21906	24118	24226	30201	30651
A Compensation of employees	-	-	-	-	-	-	-	-	-	-	-	-
B Property and entrepreneurial income	2397	4271	11466	15330	18149	17197	19849	21906	24118	24226	30201	30651
By general government	238	426	1592	1867	2816	3245	3755	4743	6502	7407	8489	10135
By corporate and quasi-corporate enterprises	2159	3845	9874	13463	15333	13952	16094	17163	17616	16819	21712	20516
By other	...	...	...	...	...	...	...	...	...	...	...	...
3 Current transfers to the rest of the world	448	903	1310	1422	1641	1800	2239	2355	2538	2926	3243	3180
A Indirect taxes by general government to supranational organizations	...	...	...	...	...	...	...	...	...	...	...	...
B Other current transfers	448	903	1310	1422	1641	1800	2239	2355	2538	2926	3243	3180
By general government	244	592	817	875	1063	1194	1571	1643	1795	2169	2444	2340
By other resident sectors	204	311	493	547	578	606	668	712	743	757	799	840
4 Surplus of the nation on current transactions	841	-5126	-1977	-7225	1520	1862	1407	-3406	-11738	-12173	-15181	-22603
Payments to the Rest of the World, and Surplus of the Nation on Current Transfers	21516	41410	92732	102528	103908	110691	134127	144243	148287	154846	172562	173751
Receipts From The Rest of the World											
1 Exports of goods and services	20078	38954	87579	96880	96651	103444	126035	134919	138119	144755	158731	162852
A Exports of merchandise f.o.b. [a,b]	17498	34614	78946	86939	87004	93311	114849	122468	123719	129887	142434	145914
B Other	2580	4340	8633	9941	9647	10133	11186	12451	14400	14868	16297	16938
2 Factor income from the rest of the world	1046	1733	3639	3993	5479	5594	6363	7574	7716	8056	11319	8499
A Compensation of employees	-	-	-	-	-	-	-	-	-	-	-	-
B Property and entrepreneurial income	1046	1733	3639	3993	5479	5594	6363	7574	7716	8056	11319	8499
By general government	38	57	80	72	41	35	60	48	243	472	1072	1374
By corporate and quasi-corporate enterprises	890	1483	3125	3239	4389	4505	4820	6058	6055	6019	8647	5247
By other	118	193	434	682	1049	1054	1483	1468	1418	1565	1600	1878
3 Current transfers from the rest of the world	392	723	1514	1655	1778	1653	1729	1750	2452	2035	2512	2400
A Subsidies to general government from supranational organizations	...	...	...	...	...	...	...	...	...	...	...	...
B Other current transfers	392	723	1514	1655	1778	1653	1729	1750	2452	2035	2512	2400
To general government	269	465	995	1110	1178	1043	1100	1069	1675	1214	1670	1537
To other resident sectors	123	258	519	545	600	610	629	681	777	821	842	863
Receipts from the Rest of the World on Current Transfers	21516	41410	92732	102528	103908	110691	134127	144243	148287	154846	172562	173751

a) Exports and imports of merchandise are recorded on the basis of the crossing of frontiers. No data are available on the basis of changes in the ownership of the goods.
b) Exports of Canadian produce and re-exports of foreign produce which are valued f.o.b. point of shipment in Canada plus inland freight and gold.

3.52 External Transactions: Capital Accumulation Account

Million Canadian dollars

	1970	1975	1980	1981	1982	1983	1984	1985	1986	1987	1988	1989
Finance of Gross Accumulation											
1 Surplus of the nation on current transactions	841	-5126	-1977	-7225	1520	1862	1407	-3406	-11738	-12173	-15181	-22603
2 Capital transfers from the rest of the world	389	665	1161	1404	1650	1551	1636	1777	1957	3394	5422	6334
A By general government	-	-	-	-	-	-	-	-	-	-	-	-
B By other resident sectors	389	665	1161	1404	1650	1551	1636	1777	1957	3394	5422	6334
Total Finance of Gross Accumulation	1230	-4461	-816	-5821	3170	3413	3043	-1629	-9781	-8779	-9759	-16269

Canada

3.52 External Transactions: Capital Accumulation Account
(Continued)

Million Canadian dollars

	1970	1975	1980	1981	1982	1983	1984	1985	1986	1987	1988	1989
					Gross Accumulation							
1 Capital transfers to the rest of the world	199	170	317	309	347	349	346	361	375	388	402	416
A By general government	-	-	-	-	-	-	-	-	-	-	-	-
B By other resident sectors	199	170	317	309	347	349	346	361	375	388	402	416
2 Purchases of intangible assets, n.e.c., net, from the rest of the world	-	-	-	-	-	-	-	-	-	-	-	-
Net lending to the rest of the world	1031	-4631	-1133	-6130	2823	3064	2697	-1990	-10156	-9167	-10161	-16685
Total Gross Accumulation	1230	-4461	-816	-5821	3170	3413	3043	-1629	-9781	-8779	-9759	-16269

3.53 External Transactions: Capital Finance Account

Million Canadian dollars

	1970	1975	1980	1981	1982	1983	1984	1985	1986	1987	1988	1989
					Acquisitions of Foreign Financial Assets							
1 Gold and SDR's [a]	1662	-405	-541	383	-664	550	-1094	-112	662	4464	9450	344
2 Currency and transferable deposits	1300	-474	3416	5672	383	1190	3394	-6216	6149	-5029	-2307	268
3 Other deposits	...	...	...	...	...	...	...	...	...	...	...	...
4 Bills and bonds, short term	...	...	...	...	...	...	...	...	...	...	...	...
5 Bonds, long term	...	...	...	...	...	...	...	...	...	...	...	...
6 Corporate equity securities	...	...	...	...	...	...	...	...	...	...	...	...
7 Short-term loans, n.e.c.	337	1363	4386	4247	-571	97	2404	-6	-2400	3529	4508	2063
8 Long-term loans	-	-	4	-27	-	-	-	-	-	-	-	-
9 Proprietors' net additions to accumulation of quasi-corporate, non-resident enterprises [b]	351	726	9683	9422	7437	4488	4202	7271	12701	7861	1485	7701
10 Trade credit and advances	-	-	1869	-148	-281	3765	1384	44	-426	1392	923	-180
11 Other	-81	192	811	1838	-23	2038	1548	6534	3818	2302	2524	3863
Total Acquisitions of Foreign Financial Assets	3569	1402	19628	21387	6281	12128	11838	7515	20504	14519	16583	14059
					Incurrence of Foreign Liabilities							
1 Currency and transferable deposits	1266	847	11014	11250	-5311	2827	1642	3966	397	364	-414	1526
2 Other deposits	...	...	...	...	...	...	...	...	...	...	...	...
3 Bills and bonds, short term	219	395	1093	1236	-875	1679	1588	-562	2388	2525	9196	641
4 Bonds, long term	572	4408	3534	11493	11984	4803	7725	11080	22560	7647	15890	17087
5 Corporate equity securities	-79	86	1489	-629	-307	913	154	1552	1877	6640	-2379	3870
6 Short-term loans, n.e.c.	5	333	1077	3291	1603	1161	1392	706	-669	2931	2583	6366
7 Long-term loans	54	85	-	-68	-16	-72	-108	-148	-99	-102	-12	-
8 Non-resident proprietors' net additions to accumulation of resident quasi-corporate enterprises [c]	824	695	3091	7596	-780	1844	1168	-2248	5877	6138	4449	4781
9 Trade credit and advances	-	-	72	431	-807	1585	1448	627	-217	1071	34	618
10 Other	-7	510	567	1373	73	16	569	766	1120	-441	1435	1237
Total Incurrence of Liabilities	2854	7359	21937	35973	5564	14756	15578	15739	33234	26773	30782	36126
Statistical discrepancy	-316	-1326	-1176	-8456	-2106	-5692	-6437	-6234	-2574	-3087	-4038	-5382
Net Lending	1031	-4631	-1133	-6130	2823	3064	2697	-1990	-10156	-9167	-10161	-16685
Total Incurrence of Liabilities and Net Lending	3569	1402	19628	21387	6281	12128	11838	7515	20504	14519	16583	14059

a) Item 'Gold and SDRs' refers to official international reserves.
b) Item 'Proprietors net additions to accumulation of quasi-corporate, non-resident enterprises' relates to claims on associated enterprises aboard.
c) Item 'Non-resident proprietors net additions to accumulation of resident quasi-corporate enterprises' relates to liabilities to associated enterprises abroad.

4.1 Derivation of Value Added by Kind of Activity, in Current Prices

Million Canadian dollars

	1980			1981			1982			1983		
	Gross Output	Intermediate Consumption	Value Added	Gross Output	Intermediate Consumption	Value Added	Gross Output	Intermediate Consumption	Value Added	Gross Output	Intermediate Consumption	Value Added
						All Producers						
1 Agriculture, hunting, forestry and fishing	22023	10324	11698	28924	15703	13221	28541	15917	12625	29169	17090	12080
A Agriculture and hunting	16490	7373	9116	23407	12796	10611	23404	13137	10267	22905	13738	9168
B Forestry and logging	4689	2661	2028	4585	2540	2045	4182	2417	1765	5323	2994	2329
C Fishing	844	290	554	932	367	565	955	363	593	941	358	583
2 Mining and quarrying	31940	13873	18067	32677	15224	17454	34211	15709	18503	38766	17156	21610
A Coal mining	792	362	430	912	446	466	1077	482	595	1115	461	654
B Crude petroleum and natural gas production	17199	8022	9177	18199	8413	9787	21630	9528	12102	25859	11024	14835

275

Canada

4.1 Derivation of Value Added by Kind of Activity, in Current Prices
(Continued)

Million Canadian dollars

	1980 Gross Output	1980 Intermediate Consumption	1980 Value Added	1981 Gross Output	1981 Intermediate Consumption	1981 Value Added	1982 Gross Output	1982 Intermediate Consumption	1982 Value Added	1983 Gross Output	1983 Intermediate Consumption	1983 Value Added
C Metal ore mining	8182	2986	5195	7150	3327	3822	5691	2932	2760	5809	2734	3075
D Other mining	5767	2503	3264	6416	3038	3378	5813	2767	3046	5983	2937	3046
3 Manufacturing	178067	123026	55043	201618	139970	61648	193575	135741	57837	210721	145459	65261
A Manufacture of food, beverages and tobacco	30069	22798	7271	33826	25384	8442	35051	25727	9324	36211	26072	10139
B Textile, wearing apparel and leather industries	10059	6181	3878	11137	6786	4351	10077	6169	3908	11474	6868	4606
C Manufacture of wood and wood products, including furniture	10801	6824	3976	11200	7054	4146	9546	6364	3183	12274	7812	4462
D Manufacture of paper and paper products, printing and publishing	20262	11448	8815	22266	12828	9438	21675	13226	8450	22926	13873	9054
E Manufacture of chemicals and chemical petroleum, coal, rubber and plastic products	31745	25482	6264	40611	33687	6925	40818	33895	6923	44601	36106	8495
F Manufacture of non-metallic mineral products, except products of petroleum and coal	4349	2531	1818	4927	2911	2016	4473	2705	1768	4886	2854	2032
G Basic metal industries	17677	12815	4862	18007	12906	5101	14638	10654	3984	16356	11612	4744
H Manufacture of fabricated metal products, machinery and equipment	49136	32414	16723	55181	35738	19442	52939	34421	18518	57490	37544	19946
I Other manufacturing industries	3969	2533	1435	4463	2676	1788	4358	2580	1779	4503	2718	1784
4 Electricity, gas and water	9641	1916	8172	11281	2537	9250	12869	3030	10417	14315	3028	11891
A Electricity, gas and steam	9641	1916	7724	11281	2537	8745	12869	3030	9839	14315	3028	11286
B Water works and supply	...	...	447	...	...	505	...	...	577	...	...	604
5 Construction a	51043	30777	20266	60399	35305	25094	59228	33665	25563	60178	35116	25061
6 Wholesale and retail trade, restaurants and hotels	58534	20014	38520	65870	22522	43348	68400	24050	44349	73509	25827	47682
A Wholesale and retail trade	45654	14579	31075	51525	16450	35075	53547	17842	35705	57928	19324	38604
B Restaurants and hotels	12880	5435	7445	14345	6072	8273	14853	6208	8644	15581	6503	9078
7 Transport, storage and communication	33090	13535	19554	37682	15822	21860	39342	15993	23348	41517	16057	25460
A Transport and storage	24967	11837	13129	28238	13809	14429	28497	13836	14661	29699	13701	15999
B Communication	8123	1698	6425	9444	2013	7431	10845	2157	8688	11818	2356	9461
8 Finance, insurance, real estate and business services	69607	21601	48005	79870	25420	54451	90326	29840	60486	99821	32369	67452
A Financial institutions	5405	1777	3628	6276	2024	4252	7429	2292	5137	8774	2501	6273
B Insurance	4041	2676	1364	4528	3062	1467	5620	3667	1953	6431	3954	2476
C Real estate and business services	60161	17148	43013	69066	20334	48733	77277	23881	53396	84616	25914	58703
Real estate, except dwellings	...	...	...	...	...	...	...	...	...	...	...	...
Dwellings	19800	5063	14737	23189	6101	17088	26859	6623	20236	29882	7068	22814
9 Community, social and personal services	52682	39002	13679	58924	43080	15845	62943	45663	17281	68020	49147	18874
A Sanitary and similar services	312	145	167	408	203	205	416	200	215	471	225	246
B Social and related community services	7102	1863	5239	8183	2150	6033	9159	2358	6803	10422	2569	7853
Educational services	783	238	545	882	260	622	1012	313	700	1090	339	751
Medical, dental, other health and veterinary services	6319	1625	4694	7301	1890	5411	8147	2045	6103	9332	2230	7102
C Recreational and cultural services	4497	1671	2826	5029	1796	3233	5504	1975	3529	5971	2142	3829
D Personal and household services b	40771	35323	5448	45304	38931	6373	47864	41130	6735	51156	44211	6946
Total, Industries	506626	274070	233004	577248	315582	262171	589436	319604	270409	636017	341250	295371
Producers of Government Services	...	...	43015	...	...	49851	...	...	56535	...	...	60801
Other Producers	...	...	6602	...	...	7516	...	...	8588	...	...	9409
Total c	...	...	282621	...	...	319538	...	...	335532	...	...	365581
Less: Imputed bank service charge	...	...	2161	...	...	2540	...	...	2622	...	...	3488
Import duties d	...	...	27272	...	...	36457	...	...	38908	...	...	40135
Value added tax	...	...	...	...	...	...	...	...	...	...	...	...
Total	...	...	307732	...	...	353455	...	...	371818	...	...	402228

Canada

4.1 Derivation of Value Added by Kind of Activity, in Current Prices

Million Canadian dollars

		1984			1985			1986			1987		
		Gross Output	Intermediate Consumption	Value Added	Gross Output	Intermediate Consumption	Value Added	Gross Output	Intermediate Consumption	Value Added	Gross Output	Intermediate Consumption	Value Added

All Producers

		1984 GO	1984 IC	1984 VA	1985 GO	1985 IC	1985 VA	1986 GO	1986 IC	1986 VA	1987 GO	1987 IC	1987 VA
1	Agriculture, hunting, forestry and fishing	30782	17179	13604	30768	17432	13337	31407	16678	14728	31983	16246	15737
	A Agriculture and hunting	23782	13404	10378	23443	13413	10030	23566	12509	11057	22579	11247	11332
	B Forestry and logging	6050	3423	2627	6136	3594	2542	6426	3734	2691	7676	4517	3160
	C Fishing	950	352	599	1189	425	765	1415	435	980	1728	482	1246
2	Mining and quarrying	44223	18659	25565	45467	18352	27115	33432	15928	17502	35930	15530	20401
	A Coal mining	1577	591	986	1594	661	932	1398	642	755	1376	627	749
	B Crude petroleum and natural gas production	28661	11723	16938	29889	11203	18686	18734	8971	9763	19957	8685	11272
	C Metal ore mining	7037	3161	3876	6724	3130	3595	6958	3278	3680	8459	3379	5081
	D Other mining	6948	3184	3765	7260	3358	3902	6342	3037	3305	6138	2839	3299
3	Manufacturing	240900	165399	75504	257848	176177	81673	262071	175280	86789	282608	187799	94808
	A Manufacture of food, beverages and tobacco	39045	28199	10847	40461	28673	11788	42258	29777	12481	44414	30892	13522
	B Textile, wearing apparel and leather industries	12025	7226	4800	12409	7444	4965	13571	8188	5383	14567	8907	5661
	C Manufacture of wood and wood products, including furniture	13150	8392	4757	14644	9145	5499	16547	10186	6361	19227	11843	7383
	D Manufacture of paper and paper products, printing and publishing	26627	15793	10835	28141	16739	11403	30935	17925	13009	34675	19448	15227
	E Manufacture of chemicals and chemical petroleum, coal, rubber and plastic products	48102	38762	9340	49869	39973	9896	41908	31133	10775	45790	34770	11019
	F Manufacture of non-metallic mineral products, except products of petroleum and coal	5399	3137	2262	6023	3448	2575	6790	3819	2971	7702	4224	3478
	G Basic metal industries	19692	13831	5861	19980	13901	6080	19852	13724	6128	22749	15481	7268
	H Manufacture of fabricated metal products, machinery and equipment	71749	47040	24709	80797	53598	27199	84497	56939	27557	87516	58576	28940
	I Other manufacturing industries	5111	3019	2093	5524	3256	2268	5713	3589	2124	5968	3658	2310
4	Electricity, gas and water	15983	3252	13371	17345	3345	14668	17848	3030	15533	19244	3573	16417
	A Electricity, gas and steam	15983	3252	12730	17345	3345	14001	17848	3030	14819	19244	3573	15671
	B Water works and supply	...	...	641	...	...	667	...	...	714	...	...	746
5	Construction [a]	62045	37564	24481	68032	41891	26141	71444	43363	28082	82125	49538	32586
6	Wholesale and retail trade, restaurants and hotels	80736	28073	52663	88567	30695	57872	96979	33789	63190	105443	36397	69046
	A Wholesale and retail trade	64143	21091	43052	70477	23088	47389	77000	25418	51581	83985	27336	56649
	B Restaurants and hotels	16593	6982	9611	18090	7607	10483	19979	8371	11609	21458	9061	12397
7	Transport, storage and communication	46728	18363	28366	50605	20759	29845	52541	21077	31466	55627	22413	33215
	A Transport and storage	33889	15883	18006	36907	17929	18977	37996	17743	20254	40369	19011	21359
	B Communication	12839	2480	10360	13698	2830	10868	14545	3334	11212	15258	3402	11856
8	Finance, insurance, real estate and business services	106831	33960	72871	116549	38043	78506	129946	44127	85820	143968	49077	94890
	A Financial institutions	9031	2673	6358	9739	2882	6858	11551	3348	8203	13035	3645	9390
	B Insurance	6265	4335	1930	6591	4798	1793	8577	5641	2937	9470	6441	3029
	C Real estate and business services	91535	26952	64583	100219	30363	69855	109818	35138	74680	121463	38991	82471
	Real estate, except dwellings	...	...	...	...	...	...	...	...	...	...	...	...
	Dwellings	32232	7412	24820	34787	7816	26970	37692	8679	29013	40768	9645	31122
9	Community, social and personal services	74540	53507	21033	82805	59456	23348	89185	63046	26139	95846	67632	28215
	A Sanitary and similar services	576	271	305	674	323	350	728	349	379	846	420	427
	B Social and related community services	11593	2906	8687	12554	3106	9448	13686	3389	10297	14884	3737	11147
	Educational services	1223	439	784	1330	492	838	1442	537	905	1547	619	928
	Medical, dental, other health and veterinary services	10370	2467	7903	11224	2614	8610	12244	2852	9392	13337	3118	10219
	C Recreational and cultural services	6969	2463	4506	7904	2879	5025	9446	3282	6163	10034	3761	6273
	D Personal and household services [b]	55402	47867	7535	61673	53148	8525	65325	56026	9300	70082	59714	10368

Canada

4.1 Derivation of Value Added by Kind of Activity, in Current Prices
(Continued)

Million Canadian dollars

	1984			1985			1986			1987		
	Gross Output	Intermediate Consumption	Value Added	Gross Output	Intermediate Consumption	Value Added	Gross Output	Intermediate Consumption	Value Added	Gross Output	Intermediate Consumption	Value Added
Total, Industries	702771	375953	327458	757934	406149	352503	784852	416316	369249	852774	448205	405315
Producers of Government Services	...	...	64322	...	...	67184	...	...	70724	...	...	74862
Other Producers	...	...	10241	...	...	11090	...	...	11866	...	...	12727
Total c	...	...	402021	...	...	430776	...	...	451839	...	...	492905
Less: Imputed bank service charge	...	...	3424	...	...	3649	...	...	4240	...	...	4819
Import duties d	...	...	42714	...	...	47212	...	...	53827	...	...	58432
Value added tax	...	...	...	...	...	...	...	...	...	...	...	...
Total	...	...	441311	...	...	474340	...	...	501426	...	...	546517

a) The construction industry is defined on an activity basis. It includes all contract and own-account construction put in place.
b) Columns 'Gross output' and 'Intermediate consumption' of item 'Personal and household services' include dummy industries.
c) Gross domestic product in factor values.
d) Item 'Import duties' refers to indirect taxes net of subsidies.

4.2 Derivation of Value Added by Kind of Activity, in Constant Prices

Million Canadian dollars

		1980			1981			1982			1983		
		Gross Output	Intermediate Consumption	Value Added	Gross Output	Intermediate Consumption	Value Added	Gross Output	Intermediate Consumption	Value Added	Gross Output	Intermediate Consumption	Value Added

At constant prices of: 1981

All Producers

1	Agriculture, hunting, forestry and fishing	...	...	12388	28924	15703	13221	28895	15299	13596	29502	15718	13783
	A Agriculture and hunting	...	...	9736	23407	12796	10611	23959	12682	11277	23667	12716	10951
	B Forestry and logging	...	...	2094	4585	2540	2045	4006	2297	1709	4953	2698	2254
	C Fishing	...	...	493	932	367	565	930	320	610	882	304	578
2	Mining and quarrying	...	...	19660	32677	15224	17454	31143	14185	16959	32628	14569	18058
	A Coal mining	...	...	431	912	446	466	915	423	492	947	371	576
	B Crude petroleum and natural gas production	...	...	11557	18199	8413	9787	18481	8474	10008	19944	9062	10882
	C Metal ore mining	...	...	4709	7150	3327	3822	6254	2643	3611	6124	2426	3697
	D Other mining	...	...	3487	6416	3038	3378	5493	2645	2848	5613	2710	2903
3	Manufacturing	...	...	59461	201618	139970	61648	180967	127264	53702	190422	133251	57168
	A Manufacture of food, beverages and tobacco	...	...	8389	33826	25384	8442	33325	25050	8275	33305	25245	8060
	B Textile, wearing apparel and leather industries	...	...	4194	11137	6786	4351	9600	5942	3659	10674	6599	4074
	C Manufacture of wood and wood products, including furniture	...	...	4164	11200	7054	4146	9349	6048	3300	11121	7135	3985
	D Manufacture of paper and paper products, printing and publishing	...	...	9534	22266	12828	9438	20527	12232	8294	21841	12822	9019
	E Manufacture of chemicals and chemical petroleum, coal, rubber and plastic products	...	...	6530	40611	33687	6925	36083	29886	6197	37451	30340	7111
	F Manufacture of non-metallic mineral products, except products of petroleum and coal	...	...	2094	4927	2911	2016	3979	2435	1544	4176	2466	1710
	G Basic metal industries	...	...	4711	18007	12906	5101	14548	10716	3832	15886	11560	4325
	H Manufacture of fabricated metal products, machinery and equipment	...	...	18333	55181	35738	19442	49368	32430	16938	51863	34592	17270
	I Other manufacturing industries	...	...	1648	4463	2676	1788	4188	2525	1663	4105	2492	1613
4	Electricity, gas and water	...	...	9117	11281	2537	9250	11176	2710	8994	11744	2669	9595
	A Electricity, gas and steam	...	...	8617	11281	2537	8745	11176	2710	8466	11744	2669	9075
	B Water works and supply	...	...	503	...	...	505	...	...	528	...	...	520
5	Construction a	...	...	22527	60399	35305	25094	55842	30734	25109	55297	30631	24667
6	Wholesale and retail trade, restaurants and hotels	...	...	42024	65870	22522	43348	62363	21668	40694	64700	21920	42780
	A Wholesale and retail trade	...	...	33943	51525	16450	35075	49062	15954	33108	51544	16168	35376
	B Restaurants and hotels	...	...	8081	14345	6072	8273	13301	5714	7586	13156	5752	7404
7	Transport, storage and communication	...	...	21208	37682	15822	21860	35794	14730	21064	36715	14425	22290
	A Transport and storage	...	...	14600	28238	13809	14429	26251	12633	13617	26890	12258	14632
	B Communication	...	...	6825	9444	2013	7431	9543	2097	7447	9825	2167	7659
8	Finance, insurance, real estate and business services	...	...	51457	79870	25420	54451	80955	27128	53828	82270	27891	54378
	A Financial institutions	...	...	4174	6276	2024	4252	6460	2077	4383	6027	2170	3857

Canada

4.2 Derivation of Value Added by Kind of Activity, in Constant Prices
(Continued)

Million Canadian dollars

	1980 Gross Output	1980 Intermediate Consumption	1980 Value Added	1981 Gross Output	1981 Intermediate Consumption	1981 Value Added	1982 Gross Output	1982 Intermediate Consumption	1982 Value Added	1983 Gross Output	1983 Intermediate Consumption	1983 Value Added
					At constant prices of:1981							
B Insurance	...	...	1454	4528	3062	1467	4754	3169	1585	4938	3139	1799
C Real estate and business services	...	...	45790	69066	20334	48733	69741	21882	47861	71305	22582	48723
Real estate, except dwellings	...	...	...	...	...	...	...	...	...	...	...	...
Dwellings	...	...	16386	23189	6101	17088	24241	6390	17852	25174	6531	18643
9 Community, social and personal services	...	...	15249	58924	43080	15845	57586	41989	15597	59690	43849	15841
A Sanitary and similar services	...	...	175	408	203	205	371	170	201	389	180	209
B Social and related community services	...	...	5888	8183	2150	6033	8186	2118	6067	8607	2180	6426
Educational services	...	...	584	882	260	622	964	285	679	984	287	696
Medical, dental, other health and veterinary services	...	...	5304	7301	1890	5411	7222	1833	5388	7623	1893	5730
C Recreational and cultural services	...	...	3184	5029	1796	3233	4956	1846	3110	4923	1859	3065
D Personal and household services	...	...	5981	45304	38931	6373	44073	37855	6218	45771	39630	6141
Statistical discrepancy	...	...	-1647	...	...	...	...	...	...	...	...	...
Total, Industries	...	...	251444	577248	315582	262171	544723	295709	249542	562970	304928	258562
Producers of Government Services	...	...	48764	...	...	49851	...	...	50278	...	...	50837
Other Producers	...	...	7308	...	...	7516	...	...	8044	...	...	8459
Total bc	...	...	307389	...	...	319538	...	...	307864	...	...	317858
Less: Imputed bank service charge	...	...	...	...	...	...	...	...	...	...	...	...
Import duties	...	...	...	...	...	...	...	...	...	...	...	...
Value added tax	...	...	...	...	...	...	...	...	...	...	...	...
Other adjustments	...	...	33489	...	...	33916	...	...	34227	...	...	35161
Total	...	...	340878	...	...	353454	...	...	342091	...	...	353019

	1984 Gross Output	1984 Intermediate Consumption	1984 Value Added	1985 Gross Output	1985 Intermediate Consumption	1985 Value Added	1986 Gross Output	1986 Intermediate Consumption	1986 Value Added
			At constant prices of:1981						
			All Producers						
1 Agriculture, hunting, forestry and fishing	29390	15733	13657	29474	16223	13250	31711	16719	14992
A Agriculture and hunting	23023	12426	10597	23015	12860	10154	25011	13169	11842
B Forestry and logging	5535	3001	2534	5466	3011	2455	5646	3160	2486
C Fishing	832	306	526	993	352	641	1054	390	664
2 Mining and quarrying	36595	16039	20556	38261	16794	21466	36145	15807	20339
A Coal mining	1387	467	920	1454	514	940	1346	511	835
B Crude petroleum and natural gas production	21188	9952	11236	22742	10718	12024	21444	10036	11408
C Metal ore mining	7642	2706	4936	7556	2584	4972	7753	2731	5022
D Other mining	6378	2914	3464	6509	2978	3530	5602	2529	3074

Canada

4.2 Derivation of Value Added by Kind of Activity, in Constant Prices
(Continued)

Million Canadian dollars

	1984 Gross Output	1984 Intermediate Consumption	1984 Value Added	1985 Gross Output	1985 Intermediate Consumption	1985 Value Added	1986 Gross Output	1986 Intermediate Consumption	1986 Value Added
				At constant prices of:1981					
3 Manufacturing	210169	145630	64542	220030	151852	68180	224157	155189	68969
A Manufacture of food, beverages and tobacco	34110	25722	8388	34956	26185	8770	35169	26531	8639
B Textile, wearing apparel and leather industries	10864	6613	4252	11014	6732	4282	11854	7300	4554
C Manufacture of wood and wood products, including furniture	11923	7498	4425	12906	7904	5002	13684	8599	5085
D Manufacture of paper and paper products, printing and publishing	23247	13762	9486	23842	14265	9578	25239	15198	10041
E Manufacture of chemicals and chemical petroleum, coal, rubber and plastic products	39555	31649	7906	40038	31961	8078	39780	31755	8024
F Manufacture of non-metallic mineral products, except products of petroleum and coal	4504	2633	1872	4840	2798	2042	5219	3083	2136
G Basic metal industries	18512	13223	5289	18993	13397	5595	18576	13152	5425
H Manufacture of fabricated metal products, machinery and equipment	62894	41808	21086	68643	45749	22895	69803	46529	23274
I Other manufacturing industries	4560	2722	1838	4798	2861	1938	4833	3042	1791
4 Electricity, gas and water	12387	2877	10047	13000	2747	10783	13176	2664	11051
A Electricity, gas and steam	12387	2877	9510	13000	2747	10253	13176	2664	10512
B Water works and supply	...	...	537	...	...	530	...	...	539
5 Construction a	55031	31919	23111	58768	33864	24904	59804	34082	25722
6 Wholesale and retail trade, restaurants and hotels	68294	22994	45299	72959	24321	48638	77157	26030	51129
A Wholesale and retail trade	54900	17132	37768	59014	18045	40968	62420	19307	43114
B Restaurants and hotels	13394	5862	7531	13945	6276	7670	14737	6723	8015
7 Transport, storage and communication	40226	15813	24414	42059	16795	25263	43929	17703	26225
A Transport and storage	29841	13487	16355	31024	14325	16699	32224	15039	17184
B Communication	10385	2326	8059	11035	2470	8564	11705	2664	9041
8 Finance, insurance, real estate and business services	86651	28467	58184	92362	30834	61529	99236	33939	65299
A Financial institutions	6205	2271	3934	6586	2329	4257	7050	2592	4458
B Insurance	5247	3501	1746	5771	3713	2059	6500	3921	2580
C Real estate and business services	75199	22695	52504	80005	24792	55213	85686	27426	58261
Real estate, except dwellings	...	...	...	...	...	...	...	...	...
Dwellings	26398	6922	19476	27391	7134	20257	28624	7524	21101
9 Community, social and personal services	62470	45781	16690	66355	48768	17587	69354	50794	18563
A Sanitary and similar services	456	208	248	514	237	277	532	255	277
B Social and related community services	9095	2399	6697	9383	2483	6900	9755	2612	7145
Educational services	1068	356	713	1098	383	715	1116	403	714
Medical, dental, other health and veterinary services	8027	2043	5984	8285	2100	6185	8639	2209	6431
C Recreational and cultural services	5397	2073	3323	5822	2298	3524	6579	2626	3954
D Personal and household services	47522	41101	6422	50636	43750	6886	52488	45301	7187
Statistical discrepancy	...	...	...	...	...	...	...	...	...
Total, Industries	601214	325251	276500	633270	342200	291600	654669	352923	302285
Producers of Government Services	...	...	51472	...	...	51945	...	...	52500
Other Producers	...	...	8970	...	...	9276	...	...	9482
Total bc	...	...	336941	...	...	352821	...	...	364266
Less: Imputed bank service charge	...	...	...	...	...	...	...	...	...
Import duties	...	...	...	...	...	...	...	...	...
Value added tax	...	...	...	...	...	...	...	...	...
Other adjustments	...	...	38553	...	...	40460	...	...	41064
Total	...	...	375495	...	...	393281	...	...	405331

a) The construction industry is defined on an activity basis. It includes all contract and own-account construction put in place.
b) Gross domestic product in factor values.
c) The estimates prior to 1981 have been deflated in two time periods - 1961-1971 and 1971-1981 with price indices based on 1961 and 1971 respectively. The GDP by industry series are aggregated to the above categories from the worksheet level and then re-scaled on a 1981 time base such that the growth rate based on the original base year series are protected.

Canada

4.3 Cost Components of Value Added

Million Canadian dollars

		1980					1981				
	Compensation of Employees	Capital Consumption	Net Operating Surplus	Indirect Taxes	Less: Subsidies Received	Value Added	Compensation of Employees	Capital Consumption	Net Operating Surplus	Indirect Taxes	Less: Subsidies Received	Value Added

All Producers

	Compensation of Employees	Capital Consumption	Net Operating Surplus	Indirect Taxes	Less: Subsidies Received	Value Added	Compensation of Employees	Capital Consumption	Net Operating Surplus	Indirect Taxes	Less: Subsidies Received	Value Added
1 Agriculture, hunting, forestry and fishing	2745	...	8953	851	916	11698	2991	...	10231	1036	1294	13221
A Agriculture and hunting	1092	...	8024	723	898	9116	1300	...	9312	884	1263	10611
B Forestry and logging	1477	...	551	112	12	2028	1534	...	511	132	25	2045
C Fishing	176	...	378	16	6	554	157	...	408	20	6	565
2 Mining and quarrying	4395	...	13673	952	74	18067	5033	...	12420	965	76	17454
A Coal mining	186	...	245	24	2	430	237	...	229	29	2	466
B Crude petroleum and natural gas production	1151	...	8027	596	60	9177	1368	...	8419	580	68	9787
C Metal ore mining	1495	...	3700	208	4	5195	1771	...	2051	194	4	3822
D Other mining	1563	...	1701	124	8	3264	1657	...	1721	162	2	3378
3 Manufacturing	37545	...	17497	2855	4273	55043	42738	...	18909	7493	4888	61648
A Manufacture of food, beverages and tobacco	4558	...	2713	283	169	7271	5170	...	3272	347	213	8442
B Textile, wearing apparel and leather industries	2897	...	981	79	12	3878	3188	...	1162	96	14	4351
C Manufacture of wood and wood products, including furniture	3222	...	754	151	24	3976	3494	...	651	184	35	4146
D Manufacture of paper and paper products, printing and publishing	5199	...	3615	286	63	8815	5938	...	3501	365	84	9438
E Manufacture of chemicals and chemical petroleum, coal, rubber and plastic products	3725	...	2539	1190	3885	6264	4445	...	2480	5393	4398	6925
F Manufacture of non-metallic mineral products, except products of petroleum and coal	1214	...	605	112	3	1818	1366	...	650	161	5	2016
G Basic metal industries	3284	...	1579	216	18	4862	3694	...	1407	291	27	5101
H Manufacture of fabricated metal products, machinery and equipment	12353	...	4369	489	89	16723	14156	...	5286	597	96	19442
I Other manufacturing industries	1093	...	342	49	10	1435	1287	...	500	59	16	1788
4 Electricity, gas and water	2082	...	5642	297	332	8172	2500	...	6245	467	301	9250
A Electricity, gas and steam	2082	...	5642	297	332	7724	2500	...	6245	467	301	8745
B Water works and supply [a]	...	...	...	...	...	447	...	...	...	...	...	505
5 Construction [b]	14649	...	5617	2604	9	20266	17979	...	7115	3018	14	25094
6 Wholesale and retail trade, restaurants and hotels	27987	...	10531	1648	66	38520	31746	...	11602	1895	78	43348
A Wholesale and retail trade	22775	...	8299	1275	59	31075	25824	...	9251	1470	61	35075
B Restaurants and hotels	5212	...	2232	373	7	7445	5922	...	2351	425	17	8273
7 Transport, storage and communication	12745	...	6809	1474	1009	19554	14737	...	7123	1819	1145	21860
A Transport and storage	8819	...	4310	1121	1008	13129	10096	...	4333	1389	1144	14429
B Communication	3926	...	2499	353	1	6425	4641	...	2790	430	1	7431
8 Finance, insurance, real estate and business services	17166	...	30837	7324	916	48005	19926	...	34524	8521	938	54451
A Financial institutions	3396	...	231	212	2	3628	3881	...	371	246	5	4252
B Insurance	2035	...	-671	402	16	1364	2285	...	-819	456	36	1467
C Real estate and business services	11735	...	31277	6710	898	43013	13760	...	34972	7819	897	48733
Real estate, except dwellings	...	...	...	...	...	...	...	...	...	...	...	...
Dwellings	...	...	14737	3848	244	14737	...	...	17088	4526	167	17088
9 Community, social and personal services	7056	...	6622	468	638	13679	8217	...	7629	542	767	15845
A Sanitary and similar services	102	...	65	17	-	167	127	...	78	23	-	205
B Social and related community services	2051	...	3187	116	2	5239	2420	...	3614	137	4	6033
Educational services	445	...	99	19	-	545	511	...	112	21	1	622
Medical, dental, other health and veterinary services	1606	...	3088	97	2	4694	1909	...	3502	116	3	5411
C Recreational and cultural services	1500	...	1326	155	620	2826	1717	...	1516	175	742	3233
D Personal and household services	3403	...	2044	180	16	5448	3953	...	2421	307	21	6373

Canada

4.3 Cost Components of Value Added
(Continued)

Million Canadian dollars

	1980					1981				
	Compensation of Employees	Capital Consumption	Net Operating Surplus	Indirect Taxes	Less: Subsidies Received	Value Added	Compensation of Employees	Capital Consumption	Net Operating Surplus	Indirect Taxes	Less: Subsidies Received	Value Added
Total, Industries	126372	...	106184	18472	8232	233004	145867	...	115798	25758	9499	262171
Producers of Government Services [a]	38909	...	4554	1460	...	43015	45045	...	5311	1916	...	49851
Other Producers	6141	...	461	15553	...	6602	6998	...	518	18282	...	7516
Total [cd]	171423	...	111198	35504	8232	282621	197910	...	121628	45956	9499	319538
Less: Imputed bank service charge	...	...	2161	...	...	2161	...	...	2540	...	...	2540
Import duties	...	...	...	...	...	27272	...	...	...	...	...	36457
Value added tax	...	...	...	...	...	...	...	...	...	...	...	...
Other adjustments	...	...	-45	...	...	-	...	...	-173	...	...	-
Total	171423	...	108992	35504	8232	307732	197910	...	118915	45956	9499	353455

	1982					1983				
	Compensation of Employees	Capital Consumption	Net Operating Surplus	Indirect Taxes	Less: Subsidies Received	Value Added	Compensation of Employees	Capital Consumption	Net Operating Surplus	Indirect Taxes	Less: Subsidies Received	Value Added

All Producers

1 Agriculture, hunting, forestry and fishing	2961	...	9664	1155	1078	12625	3296	...	8784	1271	1099	12080
A Agriculture and hunting	1420	...	8847	983	1041	10267	1532	...	7636	1079	1044	9168
B Forestry and logging	1375	...	390	147	27	1765	1599	...	730	166	36	2329
C Fishing	166	...	427	25	10	593	165	...	418	26	19	583
2 Mining and quarrying	5389	...	13114	1044	172	18503	5399	...	16211	1124	276	21610
A Coal mining	280	...	316	38	4	595	247	...	407	41	2	654
B Crude petroleum and natural gas production	1580	...	10521	680	161	12102	1682	...	13153	745	162	14835
C Metal ore mining	1739	...	1021	148	3	2760	1637	...	1438	165	108	3075
D Other mining	1790	...	1256	178	4	3046	1833	...	1213	173	4	3046
3 Manufacturing	43131	...	14705	7132	3594	57837	45395	...	19867	5625	2971	65261
A Manufacture of food, beverages and tobacco	5527	...	3797	415	305	9324	5837	...	4302	426	362	10139
B Textile, wearing apparel and leather industries	3049	...	859	106	16	3908	3326	...	1280	111	50	4606
C Manufacture of wood and wood products, including furniture	3203	...	-20	190	23	3183	3628	...	833	210	13	4462
D Manufacture of paper and paper products, printing and publishing	6247	...	2203	444	68	8450	6673	...	2381	442	87	9054
E Manufacture of chemicals and chemical petroleum, coal, rubber and plastic products	4797	...	2126	4743	2958	6923	5000	...	3495	3192	2287	8495
F Manufacture of non-metallic mineral products, except products of petroleum and coal	1294	...	473	175	4	1768	1352	...	681	167	4	2032
G Basic metal industries	3823	...	161	321	22	3984	3865	...	879	306	25	4744
H Manufacture of fabricated metal products, machinery and equipment	13882	...	4636	673	187	18518	14309	...	5637	702	131	19946
I Other manufacturing industries	1309	...	470	65	11	1779	1405	...	379	69	12	1784
4 Electricity, gas and water	2819	...	7021	538	423	10417	2971	...	8315	582	501	11891
A Electricity, gas and steam	2819	...	7021	538	423	9839	2971	...	8315	582	501	11286
B Water works and supply [a]	...	...	...	...	...	577	...	...	...	...	...	604
5 Construction [b]	17458	...	8105	2990	9	25563	16962	...	8099	3513	9	25061
6 Wholesale and retail trade, restaurants and hotels	33379	...	10971	2150	66	44349	34958	...	12725	2339	68	47682
A Wholesale and retail trade	27084	...	8621	1668	51	35705	28350	...	10255	1809	53	38604
B Restaurants and hotels	6295	...	2350	482	15	8644	6608	...	2470	530	15	9078
7 Transport, storage and communication	15661	...	7687	2020	1646	23348	16038	...	9421	2083	2254	25460
A Transport and storage	10552	...	4108	1513	1479	14661	10688	...	5310	1517	2068	15999
B Communication	5109	...	3579	507	167	8688	5350	...	4111	566	186	9461
8 Finance, insurance, real estate and business services	22396	...	38090	9790	1472	60486	23105	...	44347	10438	1943	67452
A Financial institutions	4615	...	522	314	6	5137	4743	...	1530	339	7	6273
B Insurance	2684	...	-731	506	13	1953	2887	...	-410	533	7	2476
C Real estate and business services	15097	...	38299	8970	1453	53396	15475	...	43227	9566	1929	58703
Real estate, except dwellings	...	...	...	...	...	...	...	...	...	...	...	...

Canada

4.3 Cost Components of Value Added
(Continued)

Million Canadian dollars

	1982						1983					
	Compensation of Employees	Capital Consumption	Net Operating Surplus	Indirect Taxes	Less: Subsidies Received	Value Added	Compensation of Employees	Capital Consumption	Net Operating Surplus	Indirect Taxes	Less: Subsidies Received	Value Added
Dwellings	...	...	20236	4999	343	20236	...	...	22814	5360	418	22814
9 Community, social and personal services	9171	...	8111	624	881	17281	9784	...	9091	684	897	18874
A Sanitary and similar services	142	...	73	25	-	215	149	...	97	28	1	246
B Social and related community services	2843	...	3960	153	16	6803	3251	...	4603	166	19	7853
Educational services	566	...	134	27	8	700	618	...	133	29	8	751
Medical, dental, other health and veterinary services	2277	...	3826	126	8	6103	2633	...	4470	137	11	7102
C Recreational and cultural services	1924	...	1605	210	857	3529	2076	...	1753	229	870	3829
D Personal and household services	4262	...	2473	236	8	6735	4308	...	2638	261	7	6946
Total, Industries	152367	...	117465	27439	9340	270409	157909	...	136858	27659	10015	295371
Producers of Government Services [a]	51233	...	5880	1689	...	56535	55108	...	6297	1343	...	60801
Other Producers	8004	...	584	19120	...	8588	8783	...	626	21147	...	9409
Total [cd]	211604	...	123929	48248	9340	335532	221800	...	143781	50150	10015	365581
Less: Imputed bank service charge	...	...	2622	...	...	2622	...	...	3488	...	...	3488
Import duties	...	...	...	...	...	38908	...	...	...	...	...	40135
Value added tax	...	...	...	...	...	...	...	...	...	...	...	...
Other adjustments	...	...	-350	...	...	-	...	...	-2247	...	...	-
Total	211604	...	120957	48248	9340	371818	221800	...	138046	50150	10015	402228

	1984						1985					
	Compensation of Employees	Capital Consumption	Net Operating Surplus	Indirect Taxes	Less: Subsidies Received	Value Added	Compensation of Employees	Capital Consumption	Net Operating Surplus	Indirect Taxes	Less: Subsidies Received	Value Added
	All Producers												
1 Agriculture, hunting, forestry and fishing	3551	...	10054	1178	1845	13604	3850	...	9487	1389	2470	13337
A Agriculture and hunting	1634	...	8744	997	1768	10378	1913	...	8117	1203	2421	10030
B Forestry and logging	1748	...	880	159	49	2627	1732	...	810	161	20	2542
C Fishing	169	...	430	22	28	599	205	...	560	25	29	765
2 Mining and quarrying	6178	...	19387	1195	418	25565	6675	...	20439	1258	1184	27115
A Coal mining	370	...	615	49	2	986	398	...	534	79	2	932
B Crude petroleum and natural gas production	1890	...	15049	794	317	16938	2115	...	16570	811	1093	18686
C Metal ore mining	1822	...	2054	181	95	3876	1811	...	1784	186	78	3595
D Other mining	2096	...	1669	171	4	3765	2351	...	1551	182	11	3902
3 Manufacturing	49495	...	26009	6014	3760	75504	53435	...	28237	5051	1643	81673
A Manufacture of food, beverages and tobacco	6103	...	4744	437	308	10847	6465	...	5323	463	321	11788
B Textile, wearing apparel and leather industries	3503	...	1297	112	38	4800	3621	...	1344	115	15	4965
C Manufacture of wood and wood products, including furniture	3853	...	904	227	18	4757	4238	...	1261	222	16	5499
D Manufacture of paper and paper products, printing and publishing	7130	...	3705	454	72	10835	7724	...	3679	486	44	11403
E Manufacture of chemicals and chemical petroleum, coal, rubber and plastic products	5367	...	3973	3485	3019	9340	5654	...	4242	2376	885	9896
F Manufacture of non-metallic mineral products, except products of petroleum and coal	1448	...	813	159	10	2262	1595	...	978	166	5	2575
G Basic metal industries	4346	...	1515	300	24	5861	4499	...	1580	315	18	6080
H Manufacture of fabricated metal products, machinery and equipment	16241	...	8469	766	262	24709	18035	...	9164	830	331	27199
I Other manufacturing industries	1504	...	589	74	9	2093	1603	...	666	78	8	2268
4 Electricity, gas and water	2922	...	9809	743	695	13371	3219	...	10781	718	555	14668
A Electricity, gas and steam	2922	...	9809	743	695	12730	3219	...	10781	718	555	14001
B Water works and supply [a]	...	...	...	...	...	641	...	...	...	...	...	667

Canada

4.3 Cost Components of Value Added
(Continued)

Million Canadian dollars

		1984					1985				
	Compensation of Employees	Capital Consumption	Net Operating Surplus	Indirect Taxes	Less: Subsidies Received	Value Added	Compensation of Employees	Capital Consumption	Net Operating Surplus	Indirect Taxes	Less: Subsidies Received	Value Added
5 Construction [b]	16904	...	7577	3477	19	24481	18526	...	7615	4049	14	26141
6 Wholesale and retail trade, restaurants and hotels	38366	...	14297	2568	139	52663	41901	...	15972	2718	261	57872
A Wholesale and retail trade	31158	...	11894	1974	118	43052	34150	...	13240	2078	199	47389
B Restaurants and hotels	7208	...	2403	594	21	9611	7751	...	2732	640	62	10483
7 Transport, storage and communication	17340	...	11026	2478	2298	28366	18280	...	11565	2733	2075	29845
A Transport and storage	11658	...	6348	1835	1939	18006	12474	...	6503	2050	1798	18977
B Communication	5682	...	4678	643	359	10360	5806	...	5062	683	277	10868
8 Finance, insurance, real estate and business services	25460	...	47412	11182	2041	72871	28448	...	50058	12125	2253	78506
A Financial institutions	5021	...	1338	382	14	6358	5321	...	1537	409	13	6858
B Insurance	3012	...	-1081	591	7	1930	3176	...	-1383	829	30	1793
C Real estate and business services	17427	...	47155	10209	2020	64583	19951	...	49904	10887	2210	69855
Real estate, except dwellings	...	...	...	...	...	...	...	...	...	...	...	...
Dwellings	...	...	24820	5501	453	24820	...	...	26970	5728	374	26970
9 Community, social and personal services	10853	...	10180	804	1028	21033	12036	...	11313	911	1123	23348
A Sanitary and similar services	191	...	114	40	2	305	223	...	128	51	1	350
B Social and related community services	3653	...	5034	190	53	8687	3964	...	5484	218	81	9448
Educational services	662	...	122	31	6	784	705	...	133	34	7	838
Medical, dental, other health and veterinary services	2991	...	4912	159	47	7903	3259	...	5351	184	74	8610
C Recreational and cultural services	2319	...	2187	271	964	4506	2565	...	2460	298	1035	5025
D Personal and household services	4690	...	2845	303	9	7535	5284	...	3241	344	6	8525
Total, Industries	171071	...	155746	29639	12243	327458	186369	...	165467	30955	11577	352503
Producers of Government Services [a]	58189	...	6774	1741	...	64322	60761	...	7091	1624	...	67184
Other Producers	9589	...	652	23577	...	10241	10389	...	700	26209	...	11090
Total [cd]	238849	...	163172	54957	12243	402021	257518	...	173258	58789	11577	430776
Less: Imputed bank service charge	...	...	3424	...	...	3424	...	...	3649	...	...	3649
Import duties	...	...	...	...	...	42714	...	...	...	...	...	47212
Value added tax	...	...	...	...	...	...	...	...	...	...	...	...
Other adjustments	...	...	-863	...	...	-	...	...	-45	...	...	-
Total	238849	...	158885	54957	12243	441311	257518	...	169564	58789	11577	474340

		1986					1987				
	Compensation of Employees	Capital Consumption	Net Operating Surplus	Indirect Taxes	Less: Subsidies Received	Value Added	Compensation of Employees	Capital Consumption	Net Operating Surplus	Indirect Taxes	Less: Subsidies Received	Value Added

All Producers

1 Agriculture, hunting, forestry and fishing	4037	...	10691	1515	2845	14728	4474	...	11263	1673	4217	15737
A Agriculture and hunting	2014	...	9043	1292	2795	11057	2101	...	9230	1428	4174	11332
B Forestry and logging	1775	...	916	186	24	2691	2062	...	1098	202	22	3160
C Fishing	248	...	732	37	26	980	311	...	935	43	21	1246
2 Mining and quarrying	6481	...	11022	1218	88	17502	6379	...	14022	1343	75	20401
A Coal mining	402	...	354	79	10	755	372	...	377	75	6	749
B Crude petroleum and natural gas production	1919	...	7844	769	28	9763	2089	...	9183	906	14	11272
C Metal ore mining	1946	...	1734	192	40	3680	1884	...	3197	195	41	5081
D Other mining	2214	...	1090	178	10	3305	2034	...	1265	167	14	3299

Canada

4.3 Cost Components of Value Added
(Continued)

Million Canadian dollars

		1986					1987				
	Compensation of Employees	Capital Consumption	Net Operating Surplus	Indirect Taxes	Less: Subsidies Received	Value Added	Compensation of Employees	Capital Consumption	Net Operating Surplus	Indirect Taxes	Less: Subsidies Received	Value Added
3 Manufacturing	56803	...	29986	3786	699	86789	60888	...	33921	4030	749	94808
A Manufacture of food, beverages and tobacco	6874	...	5607	525	281	12481	7246	...	6276	567	271	13522
B Textile, wearing apparel and leather industries	3852	...	1531	127	25	5383	4077	...	1584	134	11	5661
C Manufacture of wood and wood products, including furniture	4556	...	1805	237	14	6361	5262	...	2121	258	8	7383
D Manufacture of paper and paper products, printing and publishing	8428	...	4581	546	31	13009	8970	...	6257	547	28	15227
E Manufacture of chemicals and chemical petroleum, coal, rubber and plastic products	5974	...	4801	826	177	10775	6325	...	4695	888	122	11019
F Manufacture of non-metallic mineral products, except products of petroleum and coal	1756	...	1215	169	4	2971	1930	...	1548	187	2	3478
G Basic metal industries	4548	...	1580	346	17	6128	4768	...	2500	371	20	7268
H Manufacture of fabricated metal products, machinery and equipment	19094	...	8464	921	142	27557	20562	...	8378	981	282	28940
I Other manufacturing industries	1721	...	402	89	8	2124	1748	...	562	97	5	2310
4 Electricity, gas and water	3383	...	11436	789	598	15533	3628	...	12042	824	467	16417
A Electricity, gas and steam	3383	...	11436	789	598	14819	3628	...	12042	824	467	15671
B Water works and supply [a]	...	...	...	...	...	714	...	...	...	...	...	746
5 Construction [b]	19890	...	8192	4851	7	28082	23180	...	9407	5714	6	32586
6 Wholesale and retail trade, restaurants and hotels	45358	...	17833	3125	206	63190	49951	...	19095	3495	152	69046
A Wholesale and retail trade	36822	...	14760	2410	174	51581	40647	...	16002	2692	127	56649
B Restaurants and hotels	8536	...	3073	715	32	11609	9304	...	3093	803	25	12397
7 Transport, storage and communication	18924	...	12542	3202	2338	31466	19800	...	13415	3560	2785	33215
A Transport and storage	12951	...	7303	2468	2179	20254	13590	...	7769	2808	2429	21359
B Communication	5973	...	5239	734	159	11212	6210	...	5646	752	356	11856
8 Finance, insurance, real estate and business services	31638	...	54182	13637	2397	85820	36166	...	58724	15026	3050	94890
A Financial institutions	5591	...	2612	575	55	8203	5981	...	3409	651	32	9390
B Insurance	3427	...	-490	1128	-	2937	3749	...	-720	1323	-	3029
C Real estate and business services	22620	...	52060	11934	2342	74680	26436	...	56035	13052	3018	82471
Real estate, except dwellings	...	...	...	...	...	...	...	...	...	...	...	...
Dwellings	...	...	29013	6270	368	29013	...	...	31122	7019	629	31122
9 Community, social and personal services	13121	...	13018	1080	1333	26139	14519	...	13695	1217	1024	28215
A Sanitary and similar services	246	...	133	67	2	379	261	...	166	82	2	427
B Social and related community services	4343	...	5955	256	80	10297	4747	...	6400	291	71	11147
Educational services	772	...	134	41	2	905	790	...	138	50	1	928
Medical, dental, other health and veterinary services	3571	...	5821	215	79	9392	3957	...	6262	241	70	10219
C Recreational and cultural services	2783	...	3380	339	1246	6163	3040	...	3232	375	947	6273
D Personal and household services	5749	...	3550	418	5	9300	6471	...	3897	469	4	10368
Total, Industries	199635	...	168901	33205	10511	369249	218985	...	185584	36879	12525	405315
Producers of Government Services [a]	64068	...	7371	1366	...	70724	67973	...	7636	1880	...	74862
Other Producers	11099	...	767	29768	...	11866	11893	...	834	32197	...	12727
Total [c,d]	274801	...	177038	64338	10511	451839	298850	...	194054	70956	12525	492905
Less: Imputed bank service charge	...	...	4240	...	...	4240	...	...	4819	...	...	4819
Import duties	...	...	...	...	...	53827	...	...	...	...	...	58432
Value added tax	...	...	...	...	...	...	...	...	...	...	...	...
Other adjustments	...	...	-809	...	...	-	...	...	-1652	...	...	-
Total	274801	...	171989	64338	10511	501426	298850	...	187583	70956	12525	546517

a) Columns 'Compensation of employees' and 'Operating surplus' of item 'Producers of government services' include item 'Water works and supply'.
b) The construction industry is defined on an activity basis. It includes all contract and own-account construction put in place.
c) Gross domestic product in factor values.
d) Column 'Consumption of fixed capital' is included in column 'Net operating surplus'.

Cape Verde

Source. Reply to the United Nations National Accounts Questionnaire from the Ministerio do Plano e da Cooperacao, Direccao Geral de Estatistica. The official estimates are published in 'Boletim Anual de Estatistica'.

General note. The official estimates have been adjusted by the Direccao Geral de Estatistica to conform to the United Nations System of National Accounts so far as the existing data would permit.

1.1 Expenditure on the Gross Domestic Product, in Current Prices

Million Cape Verde escudos

	1970	1975	1980	1981	1982	1983	1984	1985	1986	1987	1988	1989
1 Government final consumption expenditure	...	...	807	980	1495	1954	2438	2748	3380	3673	3968	...
2 Private final consumption expenditure	...	...	5386	6141	7113	8498	10193	11471	13407	15134	17848	...
3 Gross capital formation	...	...	2429	3097	4371	4860	4930	5712	6880	7381	7287	...
A Increase in stocks	...	...	214	-175	149	21	-37	-246	439	328	-434	...
B Gross fixed capital formation	...	...	2214	3271	4222	4840	4966	5957	6440	7053	7721	...
Residential buildings	...	...	491	562	648	782	806	1029	1139	1785	2249	...
Non-residential buildings	...	...	362	776	625	744	744	1038	1243	1095	1295	...
Other construction and land improvement etc.	...	...	533	935	1699	1618	1521	1971	1977	1303	1404	...
Other	...	...	829	999	1250	1696	1895	1919	2082	2870	2773	...
4 Exports of goods and services	...	...	1089	1588	1880	2451	2562	2887	2733	2984	3190	...
5 Less: Imports of goods and services	...	...	3793	4753	6420	7622	8575	9736	10841	11189	11653	...
Equals: Gross Domestic Product	...	...	5919	7053	8438	10140	11548	13081	15558	17984	20640	...

1.2 Expenditure on the Gross Domestic Product, in Constant Prices

Million Cape Verde escudos

	1970	1975	1980	1981	1982	1983	1984	1985	1986	1987	1988	1989
					At constant prices of:1980							
1 Government final consumption expenditure	...	...	807	888	1184	1386	1543	1684	1797	1947	2060	...
2 Private final consumption expenditure	...	...	5386	5361	5407	5855	6352	6760	7098	7491	8370	...
3 Gross capital formation	...	...	2429	2606	3140	3120	2987	3172	3715	3737	3318	...
A Increase in stocks	...	...	214	-142	67	17	-91	-123	321	217	-358	...
B Gross fixed capital formation	...	...	2214	2747	3073	3103	3078	3296	3394	3520	3675	...
Residential buildings	...	...	491	490	505	531	512	586	606	954	1138	...
Non-residential buildings	...	...	362	680	483	506	458	603	676	591	667	...
Other construction and land improvement etc.	...	...	533	836	1337	1143	1029	1198	1142	750	805	...
Other	...	...	829	741	748	923	1080	909	970	1226	1066	...
4 Exports of goods and services	...	...	1089	1204	1293	1570	1473	1571	1412	1666	1632	...
5 Less: Imports of goods and services	...	...	3793	3762	4504	4810	4974	5176	5792	5990	5851	...
Equals: Gross Domestic Product	...	...	5919	6296	6520	7121	7381	8011	8229	8852	9528	...

1.7 External Transactions on Current Account, Summary

Million Cape Verde escudos

	1970	1975	1980	1981	1982	1983	1984	1985	1986	1987	1988	1989
					Payments to the Rest of the World							
1 Imports of goods and services	...	...	...	...	...	...	...	9736	10841	11189	11653	...
A Imports of merchandise c.i.f.	...	...	...	...	...	...	...	7663	8601	8596	8626	...
B Other	...	...	...	...	...	...	...	2073	2240	2593	3027	...
2 Factor income to the rest of the world	...	...	...	...	...	...	...	485	365	400	215	...
3 Current transfers to the rest of the world	...	...	...	...	...	...	...	82	107	492	541	...
4 Surplus of the nation on current transactions	...	...	...	...	...	...	...	-299	105	-1062	-399	...
Payments to the Rest of the World and Surplus of the Nation on Current Transactions	...	...	...	...	...	...	...	10004	11418	11019	12010	...
					Receipts From The Rest of the World							
1 Exports of goods and services	...	...	...	...	...	...	...	2887	2733	2984	3190	...
A Exports of merchandise f.o.b.	...	...	...	...	...	...	...	524	355	561	241	...
B Other	...	...	...	...	...	...	...	2364	2378	2424	2950	...
2 Factor income from rest of the world	...	...	...	...	...	...	...	198	161	256	541	...
3 Current transfers from rest of the world	...	...	...	...	...	...	...	6919	8525	7778	8278	...
Receipts from the Rest of the World on Current Transactions	...	...	...	...	...	...	...	10004	11418	11019	12010	...

Cape Verde

1.10 Gross Domestic Product by Kind of Activity, in Current Prices

Million Cape Verde escudos

	1970	1975	1980	1981	1982	1983	1984	1985	1986	1987	1988	1989
1 Agriculture, hunting, forestry and fishing	...	...	1099	1164	1153	1379	1599	2043	2493	3615	4177	...
2 Mining and quarrying	...	...	37	37	37	88	85	119	124	103	127	...
3 Manufacturing	...	...	267	264	379	487	509	723	816	1033	1113	...
4 Electricity, gas and water	...	...	-20	-36	-34	-18	8	16	86	172	208	...
5 Construction	...	...	692	903	938	1150	1330	1398	1705	1881	2238	...
6 Wholesale and retail trade, restaurants and hotels	...	...	1850	2229	2841	3181	3375	3607	4029	4377	5123	...
7 Transport, storage and communication	...	...	513	700	1001	1357	1626	1834	2143	2303	2595	...
8 Finance, insurance, real estate and business services	...	...	516	621	781	932	1108	1247	1482	1608	1846	...
9 Community, social and personal services	...	...	59	79	95	113	134	159	205	236	277	...
Total, Industries	...	...	5013	5962	7190	8669	9773	11145	13081	15328	17703	...
Producers of Government Services	...	...	547	663	783	933	1153	1288	1653	1877	2026	...
Other Producers	...	...	...	...	...	...	...	...	...	...	...	...
Subtotal	...	...	5560	6625	7973	9602	10926	12433	14733	17204	19729	...
Less: Imputed bank service charge	...	...	109	124	151	177	212	236	285	348	367	...
Plus: Import duties	...	...	468	552	616	715	834	884	1111	1128	1279	...
Plus: Value added tax	...	...	...	...	...	...	...	...	...	...	...	...
Equals: Gross Domestic Product	...	...	5919	7053	8438	10140	11548	13081	15559	17984	20640	...

1.11 Gross Domestic Product by Kind of Activity, in Constant Prices

Million Cape Verde escudos

	1970	1975	1980	1981	1982	1983	1984	1985	1986	1987	1988	1989
					At constant prices of: 1980							
1 Agriculture, hunting, forestry and fishing	...	...	1099	1064	882	867	923	1177	1263	1672	1830	...
2 Mining and quarrying	...	...	37	31	28	59	54	68	68	68	77	...
3 Manufacturing	...	...	267	232	294	326	310	422	422	533	430	...
4 Electricity, gas and water	...	...	-20	-17	-17	16	22	53	57	26	10	...
5 Construction	...	...	692	838	785	880	881	927	967	1051	1224	...
6 Wholesale and retail trade, restaurants and hotels	...	...	1850	1939	2088	2170	2192	2224	2196	2160	2395	...
7 Transport, storage and communication	...	...	513	629	725	878	959	938	935	950	1002	...
8 Finance, insurance, real estate and business services	...	...	516	536	580	595	628	668	704	736	796	...
9 Community, social and personal services	...	...	59	69	75	78	82	86	101	110	120	...
Total, Industries	...	...	5013	5319	5440	5867	6051	6562	6713	7305	7882	...
Producers of Government Services	...	...	547	614	661	735	812	897	973	1104	1193	...
Other Producers	...	...	...	...	...	...	...	...	...	...	...	...
Subtotal	...	...	5560	5933	6101	6602	6863	7459	7686	8409	9075	...
Less: Imputed bank service charge	...	...	109	107	111	113	121	127	136	160	161	...
Plus: Import duties	...	...	468	470	530	632	639	679	679	603	615	...
Plus: Value added tax	...	...	...	...	...	...	...	...	...	...	...	...
Equals: Gross Domestic Product	...	...	5919	6296	6520	7121	7381	8011	8229	8852	9529	...

1.12 Relations Among National Accounting Aggregates

Million Cape Verde escudos

	1970	1975	1980	1981	1982	1983	1984	1985	1986	1987	1988	1989
Gross Domestic Product	...	...	5919	7053	8438	10140	11548	13081	15558	17984	20640	...
Plus: Net factor income from the rest of the world	...	...	33	-191	-163	-309	-334	-287	-204	-144	326	...
Factor income from the rest of the world	...	...	...	...	...	...	...	198	161	256	541	...
Less: Factor income to the rest of the world	...	...	...	...	...	...	...	485	365	400	215	...
Equals: Gross National Product	...	...	5952	6862	8275	9831	11214	12794	15354	17840	20966	...
Less: Consumption of fixed capital	...	...	...	...	...	...	...	...	...	...	...	...

Cape Verde

1.12 Relations Among National Accounting Aggregates
(Continued)

Million Cape Verde escudos

	1970	1975	1980	1981	1982	1983	1984	1985	1986	1987	1988	1989
Equals: National Income	...	...	...	...	...	...	...	...	...	...	...	...
Plus: Net current transfers from the rest of the world	...	...	2955	2876	4088	5100	6091	6837	8418	7286	7737	...
Current transfers from the rest of the world	...	...	...	...	...	...	...	6919	8525	7778	8278	...
Less: Current transfers to the rest of the world	...	...	...	...	...	...	...	82	107	492	541	...
Equals: National Disposable Income	...	...	...	...	...	...	...	...	...	...	...	...
Less: Final consumption	...	...	...	...	...	...	...	...	...	...	...	...
Equals: Net Saving	...	...	...	...	...	...	...	...	...	...	...	...
Less: Surplus of the nation on current transactions	...	...	...	...	...	...	...	...	...	...	...	...
Equals: Net Capital Formation	...	...	...	...	...	...	...	...	...	...	...	...

Cayman Islands

Source. Reply to the United Nations National Accounts Questionnaire from the Government Statistics Office, Grand Cayman. The official estimates are published in 'National Income Estimates of the Cayman Islands'.

General note. The estimates shown in the following tables have been prepared by the Statistical Office in accordance with the United Nations System of National Accounts so far as the existing data would permit.

1.1 Expenditure on the Gross Domestic Product, in Current Prices

Million Cayman Islands Dollars

	1970	1975	1980	1981	1982	1983	1984	1985	1986	1987	1988	1989
1 Government final consumption expenditure	...	...	...	...	...	34	41	43	44	53	60	69
2 Private final consumption expenditure	...	...	...	...	...	137	152	166	181	215	268	296
A Households	...	...	...	...	...	137	152	166	181	215	268	296
B Private non-profit institutions serving households	...	...	...	...	...	...	...	...	...	...	...	...
3 Gross capital formation	...	...	...	...	...	53	56	57	69	81	103	110
A Increase in stocks	...	...	...	...	...	...	...	...	...	...	...	...
B Gross fixed capital formation	...	...	...	...	...	53	56	57	69	81	103	110
Residential buildings	...	...	...	...	...							
Non-residential buildings	...	...	...	...	...	37	36	39	41	39	47	50
Other construction and land improvement etc.	...	...	...	...	...							
Other	...	...	...	...	...	16	20	18	28	42	56	60
4 Exports of goods and services	...	...	...	...	...	134	154	167	190	250	289	315
5 Less: Imports of goods and services	...	...	...	...	...	161	176	185	204	246	291	313
Statistical discrepancy	...	...	...	...	...	12	8	7	5	-4	-	-
Equals: Gross Domestic Product	...	...	...	...	...	209	235	255	285	349	429	477

1.2 Expenditure on the Gross Domestic Product, in Constant Prices

Million Cayman Islands Dollars

At constant prices of: 1986

	1970	1975	1980	1981	1982	1983	1984	1985	1986	1987	1988	1989
1 Government final consumption expenditure	...	...	...	...	...	38	44	44	44	50	53	57
2 Private final consumption expenditure	...	...	...	...	...	151	162	169	181	202	236	247
A Households	...	...	...	...	...	151	162	169	181	202	236	247
B Private non-profit institutions serving households	...	...	...	...	...	...	...	...	...	...	...	...
3 Gross capital formation	...	...	...	...	...	59	60	58	69	76	91	92
A Increase in stocks	...	...	...	...	...	...	...	...	...	...	...	...
B Gross fixed capital formation	...	...	...	...	...	59	60	58	69	76	91	92
Residential buildings	...	...	...	...	...							
Non-residential buildings	...	...	...	...	...	41	38	40	41	36	42	45
Other construction and land improvement etc.	...	...	...	...	...							
Other	...	...	...	...	...	18	22	18	28	40	49	47
4 Exports of goods and services	...	...	...	...	...	149	164	170	190	236	255	262
5 Less: Imports of goods and services	...	...	...	...	...	179	187	189	204	232	257	261
Statistical discrepancy	...	...	...	...	...	14	8	6	5	-3	1	-
Equals: Gross Domestic Product	...	...	...	...	...	232	251	260	285	329	379	398

1.3 Cost Components of the Gross Domestic Product

Million Cayman Islands Dollars

	1970	1975	1980	1981	1982	1983	1984	1985	1986	1987	1988	1989
1 Indirect taxes, net	...	...	...	...	...	38	40	43	48	57	69	75
A Indirect taxes	...	...	...	...	...	39	41	44	49	58	70	76
B Less: Subsidies	...	...	...	...	...	1	1	1	1	1	1	1
2 Consumption of fixed capital	...	...	...	...	...	13	17	20	23	28	34	37
3 Compensation of employees paid by resident producers to:	...	...	...	...	...	130	146	159	179	204	245	270
A Resident households	...	...	...	...	...	126	141	153	172	196	233	257
B Rest of the world	...	...	...	...	...	4	5	6	7	8	12	13
4 Operating surplus	...	...	...	...	...	40	41	43	40	59	81	95
Statistical discrepancy	...	...	...	...	...	-12	-10	-9	-6	-	-	-
Equals: Gross Domestic Product	...	...	...	...	...	209	235	255	285	349	429	477

Cayman Islands

1.4 General Government Current Receipts and Disbursements

Million Cayman Islands Dollars

	1970	1975	1980	1981	1982	1983	1984	1985	1986	1987	1988	1989
Receipts												
1 Operating surplus	...	...	...	...	...	...	...	...	...	...	...	...
2 Property and entrepreneurial income	...	...	...	...	...	4	3	4	5	3	4	6
3 Taxes, fees and contributions	...	...	...	...	...	41	45	47	54	64	76	83
A Indirect taxes	...	...	...	...	...	39	41	43	49	59	72	78
B Direct taxes	...	...	...	...	...	2	4	4	4	4	5	6
C Social security contributions	...	...	...	...	...	...	...	...	...	...	...	...
D Compulsory fees, fines and penalties	...	...	...	...	...	-	-	-	1	1	1	1
4 Other current transfers	...	...	...	...	...	...	...	...	...	...	...	...
Statistical discrepancy	...	...	...	...	...	1	1	1	2	2	1	-
Total Current Receipts of General Government	...	...	...	...	...	46	49	52	61	69	85	96
Disbursements												
1 Government final consumption expenditure	...	...	...	...	...	34	41	43	44	53	60	69
A Compensation of employees	...	...	...	...	...	20	26	28	29	33	39	43
B Consumption of fixed capital	...	...	...	...	...	1	2	2	2	2	4	4
C Purchases of goods and services, net	...	...	...	...	...	13	14	13	13	17	17	22
D Less: Own account fixed capital formation	...	...	...	...	...	...	...	...	...	...	...	...
E Indirect taxes paid, net	...	...	...	...	...	...	...	...	...	...	...	...
2 Property income	...	...	...	...	...	1	1	1	1	1	2	2
A Interest	...	...	...	...	...	1	1	1	1	1	2	2
B Net land rent and royalties	...	...	...	...	...	...	...	...	...	...	...	...
3 Subsidies	...	...	...	...	...	1	1	1	1	1	1	1
4 Other current transfers	...	...	...	...	...	1	1	1	4	3	5	5
A Social security benefits	...	...	...	...	...	...	...	...	...	...	...	...
B Social assistance grants	...	...	...	...	...	...	...	...	...	...	...	...
C Other	...	...	...	...	...	1	1	1	4	3	5	5
5 Net saving	...	...	...	...	...	9	5	6	11	11	14	15
Total Current Disbursements and Net Saving of General Government	...	...	...	...	...	46	49	52	61	69	82	92

1.7 External Transactions on Current Account, Summary

Million Cayman Islands Dollars

	1970	1975	1980	1981	1982	1983	1984	1985	1986	1987	1988	1989
Payments to the Rest of the World												
1 Imports of goods and services	...	...	...	...	...	161	176	185	204	246	291	313
A Imports of merchandise c.i.f.	...	...	...	...	...	110	118	122	133	162	188	215
B Other	...	...	...	...	...	51	58	63	71	84	103	98
2 Factor income to the rest of the world	...	...	...	...	...	30	25	27	27	37	51	54
A Compensation of employees	...	...	...	...	...	2	2	2	3	4	6	6
B Property and entrepreneurial income	...	...	...	...	...	28	23	25	24	33	45	48
By general government	...	...	...	...	...	-	-	1	1	1	1	1
By corporate and quasi-corporate enterprises	...	...	...	...	...	28	23	24	23	32	44	47
By other	...	...	...	...	...	...	...	...	...	...	...	...
3 Current transfers to the rest of the world	...	...	...	...	...	...	...	...	...	...	...	...
4 Surplus of the nation on current transactions	...	...	...	...	...	...	...	...	...	...	...	...
Payments to the Rest of the World and Surplus of the Nation on Current Transactions	...	...	...	...	...	...	...	...	...	...	...	...
Receipts From The Rest of the World												
1 Exports of goods and services	...	...	...	...	...	134	154	167	190	250	289	315
A Exports of merchandise f.o.b.	...	...	...	...	...	1	1	1	2	2	2	2

Cayman Islands

1.7 External Transactions on Current Account, Summary
(Continued)

Million Cayman Islands Dollars

	1970	1975	1980	1981	1982	1983	1984	1985	1986	1987	1988	1989
B Other	...	...	...	...	...	133	153	166	188	248	287	313
2 Factor income from rest of the world	...	...	...	...	...	3	4	5	5	4	5	6
A Compensation of employees	...	...	...	...	...	-	-	-	-	-	-	-
B Property and entrepreneurial income	...	...	...	...	...	2	3	3	4	3	3	4
By general government	...	...	...	...	...	1	1	1	1	2	2	2
By corporate and quasi-corporate enterprises	...	...	...	...	...	-	-	-	-	-	-	-
By other	...	...	...	...	...	...	...	...	...	...	...	...
3 Current transfers from rest of the world	...	...	...	...	...	...	...	...	...	...	...	...
Receipts from the Rest of the World on Current Transactions	...	...	...	...	...	...	...	...	...	...	...	...

1.9 Gross Domestic Product by Institutional Sectors of Origin

Million Cayman Islands Dollars

	1970	1975	1980	1981	1982	1983	1984	1985	1986	1987	1988	1989
					Domestic Factor Incomes Originating							
1 General government	...	...	...	...	...	19	25	27	28	32	37	41
2 Corporate and quasi-corporate enterprises [a]	...	...	...	...	...	126	141	153	172	196	233	257
3 Households and private unincorporated enterprises [b]	...	...	...	...	...	13	12	12	14	36	56	67
4 Non-profit institutions serving households	...	...	...	...	...	...	...	...	...	...	...	...
Subtotal: Domestic Factor Incomes	...	...	...	...	...	158	178	192	214	264	326	365
Indirect taxes, net	...	...	...	...	...	38	40	43	48	57	69	75
A Indirect taxes	...	...	...	...	...	39	41	43	49	59	72	78
B Less: Subsidies	...	...	...	...	...	1	1	-	1	2	3	3
Consumption of fixed capital	...	...	...	...	...	13	17	20	23	28	34	37
Gross Domestic Product	...	...	...	...	...	209	235	255	285	349	429	477

a) Item 'Corporate and quasi-corporate enterprises' includes private unincorporated enterprises.
b) Only domestic servants and rental of dwellings are included in item 'Households and private unincorporated enterprises'.

1.10 Gross Domestic Product by Kind of Activity, in Current Prices

Million Cayman Islands Dollars

	1970	1975	1980	1981	1982	1983	1984	1985	1986	1987	1988	1989
1 Agriculture, hunting, forestry and fishing	...	...	...	...	...	1	1	1	2	1	2	1
2 Mining and quarrying	...	...	...	...	...	1	1	1	1	2	3	3
3 Manufacturing	...	...	...	...	...	5	6	6	6	7	8	9
4 Electricity, gas and water	...	...	...	...	...	5	5	6	7	9	12	15
5 Construction	...	...	...	...	...	27	27	25	27	28	38	50
6 Wholesale and retail trade, restaurants and hotels	...	...	...	...	...	45	50	54	60	73	92	98
7 Transport, storage and communication	...	...	...	...	...	24	29	33	38	43	54	59
8 Finance, insurance, real estate and business services [a]	...	...	...	...	...	65	70	79	86	110	134	148
9 Community, social and personal services	...	...	...	...	...	15	17	19	20	22	25	27
Statistical discrepancy	...	...	...	...	...	-12	-9	-9	-4	3	2	1
Total, Industries	...	...	...	...	...	176	197	215	243	297	369	411
Producers of Government Services	...	...	...	...	...	21	26	29	30	34	40	46
Other Producers	...	...	...	...	...	...	...	...	...	...	...	...
Subtotal	...	...	...	...	...	197	223	244	273	331	409	457
Less: Imputed bank service charge	...	...	...	...	...	6	7	9	10	10	14	17
Plus: Import duties	...	...	...	...	...	18	19	20	22	28	34	37
Plus: Value added tax	...	...	...	...	...	...	...	...	...	...	...	...
Equals: Gross Domestic Product	...	...	...	...	...	209	235	255	285	349	429	477

a) Item 'Finance, insurance, real estate and business services' excludes banks and insurance companies registered in Cayman Islands but with no physical presence in the Islands.

Cayman Islands

1.11 Gross Domestic Product by Kind of Activity, in Constant Prices

Million Cayman Islands Dollars

	1970	1975	1980	1981	1982	1983	1984	1985	1986	1987	1988	1989
					At constant prices of:1986							
1 Agriculture, hunting, forestry and fishing	...	...	...	...	...	1	1	1	2	1	1	1
2 Mining and quarrying	...	...	...	...	...	1	1	1	1	2	3	3
3 Manufacturing	...	...	...	...	...	6	6	6	6	7	7	8
4 Electricity, gas and water	...	...	...	...	...	5	6	6	7	8	9	11
5 Construction	...	...	...	...	...	32	30	26	27	26	35	41
6 Wholesale and retail trade, restaurants and hotels	...	...	...	...	...	48	53	56	60	70	80	82
7 Transport, storage and communication	...	...	...	...	...	26	31	34	38	42	50	52
8 Finance, insurance, real estate and business services [a]	...	...	...	...	...	71	76	79	86	100	117	123
9 Community, social and personal services	...	...	...	...	...	16	18	19	20	21	22	23
Statistical discrepancy	...	...	...	...	...	-12	-9	-8	-4	3	3	-3
Total, Industries	...	...	...	...	...	194	213	220	243	281	327	341
Producers of Government Services	...	...	...	...	...	25	26	29	30	32	34	38
Other Producers	...	...	...	...	...	...	...	...	...	...	...	...
Subtotal	...	...	...	...	...	219	239	249	273	313	361	379
Less: Imputed bank service charge	...	...	...	...	...	7	8	9	10	10	12	14
Plus: Import duties	...	...	...	...	...	20	20	20	22	26	30	33
Plus: Value added tax	...	...	...	...	...	...	...	...	...	...	...	...
Equals: Gross Domestic Product	...	...	...	...	...	232	251	260	285	329	379	398

a) Item 'Finance, insurance, real estate and business services' excludes banks and insurance companies registered in Cayman Islands but with no physical presence in the Islands.

1.12 Relations Among National Accounting Aggregates

Million Cayman Islands Dollars

	1970	1975	1980	1981	1982	1983	1984	1985	1986	1987	1988	1989
Gross Domestic Product	...	...	...	...	...	209	235	255	285	349	429	477
Plus: Net factor income from the rest of the world	...	...	...	...	...	-26	-21	-22	-22	-33	-46	-48
Factor income from the rest of the world	...	...	...	...	...	3	4	5	5	4	5	6
Less: Factor income to the rest of the world	...	...	...	...	...	30	25	27	27	37	51	54
Equals: Gross National Product	...	...	...	...	...	182	214	233	263	316	384	428
Less: Consumption of fixed capital	...	...	...	...	...	13	17	20	23	28	34	37
Equals: National Income	...	...	...	...	...	169	197	213	240	288	350	391
Plus: Net current transfers from the rest of the world	...	...	...	...	...	...	...	...	...	...	...	...
Equals: National Disposable Income	...	...	...	...	...	...	...	...	...	...	...	...
Less: Final consumption	...	...	...	...	...	...	...	...	...	...	...	...
Equals: Net Saving	...	...	...	...	...	...	...	...	...	...	...	...
Less: Surplus of the nation on current transactions	...	...	...	...	...	...	...	...	...	...	...	...
Equals: Net Capital Formation	...	...	...	...	...	...	...	...	...	...	...	...

2.1 Government Final Consumption Expenditure by Function, in Current Prices

Million Cayman Islands Dollars

	1970	1975	1980	1981	1982	1983	1984	1985	1986	1987	1988	1989
1 General public services	...	...	...	...	...	11	13	14	16	14	21	23
2 Defence	...	...	...	...	...	...	...	...	...	...	...	...
3 Public order and safety	...	...	...	...	...	4	6	7	7	9	10	12
4 Education	...	...	...	...	...	5	6	7	7	8	9	10
5 Health	...	...	...	...	...	6	7	7	7	8	9	10
6 Social security and welfare	...	...	...	...	...	1	1	1	1	2	2	2
7 Housing and community amenities	...	...	...	...	...	-	-	-	1	1	1	1
8 Recreational, cultural and religious affairs	...	...	...	...	...	...	...	...	...	...	...	...
9 Economic services	...	...	...	...	...	6	7	8	9	11	14	15

Cayman Islands

2.1 Government Final Consumption Expenditure by Function, in Current Prices
(Continued)

Million Cayman Islands Dollars

	1970	1975	1980	1981	1982	1983	1984	1985	1986	1987	1988	1989
A Fuel and energy	...	...	...	...	...	...	...	...	...	...	...	...
B Agriculture, forestry, fishing and hunting	...	...	...	...	...	-	1	1	1	1	2	2
C Mining, manufacturing and construction, except fuel and energy	...	...	...	...	...	-	-	-	-	-	4	4
D Transportation and communication	...	...	...	...	...	3	3	3	4	4	1	1
E Other economic affairs	...	...	...	...	...	3	4	4	4	6	7	8
10 Other functions	...	...	...	...	...	-	1	1	2	3	2	2
Total Government Final Consumption Expenditure [a]	...	...	...	...	...	33	41	45	50	55	68	75

a) The estimates include only the total government current expenditure.

2.2 Government Final Consumption Expenditure by Function, in Constant Prices

Million Cayman Islands Dollars

	1970	1975	1980	1981	1982	1983	1984	1985	1986	1987	1988	1989
						At constant prices of:1986						
1 General public services	...	...	...	...	...	12	14	14	16	13	18	19
2 Defence	...	...	...	...	...	...	...	...	...	...	...	...
3 Public order and safety	...	...	...	...	...	4	6	7	7	8	9	10
4 Education	...	...	...	...	...	6	6	7	7	8	8	8
5 Health	...	...	...	...	...	7	7	7	7	7	8	8
6 Social security and welfare	...	...	...	...	...	1	1	1	1	2	2	2
7 Housing and community amenities	...	...	...	...	...	-	-	-	1	1	1	1
8 Recreational, cultural and religious affairs	...	...	...	...	...	...	...	...	...	...	...	...
9 Economic services	...	...	...	...	...	7	8	9	9	10	12	12
A Fuel and energy	...	...	...	...	...	...	...	...	...	...	...	...
B Agriculture, forestry, fishing and hunting	...	...	...	...	...	-	1	1	1	1	2	2
C Mining, manufacturing and construction, except fuel and energy	...	...	...	...	...	-	-	-	-	-	3	3
D Transportation and communication	...	...	...	...	...	3	3	3	4	4	1	1
E Other economic affairs	...	...	...	...	...	4	4	5	4	6	6	7
10 Other functions	...	...	...	...	...	-	1	2	2	3	2	2
Total Government Final Consumption Expenditure [a]	...	...	...	...	...	37	44	46	50	53	58	61

a) The estimates include only the total government current expenditure.

2.17 Exports and Imports of Goods and Services, Detail

Million Cayman Islands Dollars

	1970	1975	1980	1981	1982	1983	1984	1985	1986	1987	1988	1989
					Exports of Goods and Services							
1 Exports of merchandise, f.o.b.	...	...	...	...	...	1	1	2	2	2	2	2
2 Transport and communication	...	...	...	...	...	27	31	34	38	49	56	74
3 Insurance service charges	...	...	...	...	...	...	...	...	...	...	...	...
4 Other commodities [a]	...	...	...	...	...	49	54	61	67	82	88	95
5 Adjustments of merchandise exports to change-of-ownership basis	...	...	...	...	...	...	...	...	...	...	...	...
6 Direct purchases in the domestic market by non-residential households	...	...	...	...	...	56	67	71	82	117	143	144
7 Direct purchases in the domestic market by extraterritorial bodies	...	...	...	...	...	...	...	...	...	...	...	...
Total Exports of Goods and Services	...	...	...	...	...	134	154	167	190	250	289	315
					Imports of Goods and Services							
1 Imports of merchandise, c.i.f.	...	...	...	...	...	110	118	122	133	162	188	215

Cayman Islands

2.17 Exports and Imports of Goods and Services, Detail
(Continued)

Million Cayman Islands Dollars

	1970	1975	1980	1981	1982	1983	1984	1985	1986	1987	1988	1989
A Imports of merchandise, f.o.b.	...	...	...	...	...	98	105	109	119	145	168	192
B Transport of services on merchandise imports	...	...	...	...	...	11	11	12	13	16	18	21
C Insurance service charges on merchandise imports	...	...	...	...	...	1	1	1	1	2	2	2
2 Adjustments of merchandise imports to change-of-ownership basis	...	...	...	...	...	...	...	...	...	...	...	...
3 Other transport and communication	...	...	...	...	...	23	26	29	31	37	42	48
4 Other insurance service charges	...	...	...	...	...	...	...	...	...	...	...	...
5 Other commodities [a]	...	...	...	...	...	14	15	17	19	23	21	21
6 Direct purchases abroad by government	...	...	...	...	...	5	4	5	6	7	8	9
7 Direct purchases abroad by resident households	...	...	...	...	...	9	13	13	14	17	31	19
Total Imports of Goods and Services	...	...	...	...	...	161	176	185	204	246	291	313
Balance of Goods and Services	...	...	...	...	...	-28	-22	-18	-15	4	-2	2
Total Imports and Balance of Goods and Services	...	...	...	...	...	134	154	167	190	250	289	315

a) Item 'Other commodities' refers to services only.

4.1 Derivation of Value Added by Kind of Activity, in Current Prices

Million Cayman Islands Dollars

	1983 Gross Output	1983 Intermediate Consumption	1983 Value Added	1984 Gross Output	1984 Intermediate Consumption	1984 Value Added	1985 Gross Output	1985 Intermediate Consumption	1985 Value Added	1986 Gross Output	1986 Intermediate Consumption	1986 Value Added
					All Producers							
1 Agriculture, hunting, forestry and fishing	2	-	2	2	-	2	2	-	2	2	1	1
2 Mining and quarrying	2	1	1	2	1	1	2	1	1	2	1	1
3 Manufacturing	15	12	3	16	13	3	18	14	4	20	14	6
4 Electricity, gas and water	15	11	4	16	11	5	18	13	5	20	13	7
5 Construction	53	26	27	52	25	27	50	24	26	57	30	27
6 Wholesale and retail trade, restaurants and hotels	87	37	50	96	40	56	103	43	60	115	51	64
A Wholesale and retail trade	46	12	34	51	13	38	55	14	41	58	15	43
B Restaurants and hotels	41	25	16	45	27	18	48	29	19	57	36	21
7 Transport, storage and communication	39	20	19	45	22	23	51	24	27	56	26	30
8 Finance, insurance, real estate and business services [a]	101	37	64	111	40	71	123	44	79	138	48	90
A Financial institutions	...	...	...	...	...	...	...	...	...	...	...	...
B Insurance	...	...	...	...	...	...	...	...	...	...	...	...
C Real estate and business services	...	...	...	...	...	...	...	...	...	...	...	...
9 Community, social and personal services	25	11	14	29	13	16	30	14	16	33	15	18
A Sanitary and similar services	...	...	...	...	...	...	...	...	...	...	...	...
B Social and related community services	...	...	...	...	...	...	...	...	...	...	...	...
C Recreational and cultural services	...	...	...	...	...	...	...	...	...	...	...	...
D Personal and household services	...	...	...	...	...	...	...	...	...	...	...	...
Total, Industries	339	155	184	369	165	204	397	177	220	443	199	244
Producers of Government Services	33	14	19	41	17	24	44	18	26	48	20	28
Other Producers	...	...	...	...	...	...	...	...	...	...	...	...
Total	372	169	203	410	182	228	441	195	246	491	219	272
Less: Imputed bank service charge	...	-8	8	...	-9	9	...	-10	10	...	-12	12
Import duties	18	-	18	19	-	19	20	-	20	23	-	23
Value added tax	...	...	...	...	...	...	...	...	...	...	...	...
Other adjustments	-6	...	-6	-5	...	-5	-5	...	-5	-	...	-
Total	384	177	207	424	191	233	456	205	251	514	231	283

Cayman Islands

4.1 Derivation of Value Added by Kind of Activity, in Current Prices

Million Cayman Islands Dollars

	1987 Gross Output	1987 Intermediate Consumption	1987 Value Added	1988 Gross Output	1988 Intermediate Consumption	1988 Value Added	1989 Gross Output	1989 Intermediate Consumption	1989 Value Added
				All Producers					
1 Agriculture, hunting, forestry and fishing	2	1	1	3	1	2	2	1	1
2 Mining and quarrying	2	1	1	4	1	3	4	1	3
3 Manufacturing	20	16	4	15	7	8	17	8	9
4 Electricity, gas and water	20	13	7	27	15	12	30	16	15
5 Construction	57	30	27	78	40	38	102	52	50
6 Wholesale and retail trade, restaurants and hotels	137	61	76	170	78	92	178	80	98
A Wholesale and retail trade	66	17	49	74	22	52	81	24	57
B Restaurants and hotels	71	44	27	96	56	40	97	56	41
7 Transport, storage and communication	65	29	36	115	61	54	132	73	59
8 Finance, insurance, real estate and business services [a]	168	60	108	190	56	134	205	57	148
A Financial institutions	...	...	...	80	28	52	90	26	64
B Insurance	...	...	...						
C Real estate and business services	...	...	...	110	28	82	115	31	84
9 Community, social and personal services	39	18	21	43	18	25	47	20	27
A Sanitary and similar services	...	...	...	...	...	...	...	...	...
B Social and related community services	...	...	...	...	...	...	...	...	...
C Recreational and cultural services	...	...	...	...	...	...	...	...	...
D Personal and household services	...	...	...	7	-	7	8	-	8
Total, Industries	510	229	281	645	277	368	717	308	410
Producers of Government Services	55	23	32	56	15	40	64	18	46
Other Producers	...	...	...	...	...	...	...	...	...
Total	565	252	313	701	292	408	781	326	456
Less: Imputed bank service charge	...	-13	13	...	-14	14	...	-17	17
Import duties	28	-	28	34	-	34	37	-	37
Value added tax	...	...	...	...	...	...	...	...	...
Other adjustments	1	...	1	-	...	-	-	...	-
Total	594	265	329	735	306	428	818	343	477

a) Item 'Finance, insurance, real estate and business services' excludes banks and insurance companies registered in Cayman Islands but with no physical presence in the Islands.

4.3 Cost Components of Value Added

Million Cayman Islands Dollars

	1983 Compensation of Employees	1983 Capital Consumption	1983 Net Operating Surplus	1983 Indirect Taxes	1983 Less: Subsidies Received	1983 Value Added	1984 Compensation of Employees	1984 Capital Consumption	1984 Net Operating Surplus	1984 Indirect Taxes	1984 Less: Subsidies Received	1984 Value Added
						All Producers						
1 Agriculture, hunting, forestry and fishing	-	...	...	...	...	2	-	...	...	...	...	2
2 Mining and quarrying	1	...	...	...	...	1	1	...	...	...	...	1
3 Manufacturing	2	...	...	...	...	3	2	...	...	...	...	3
4 Electricity, gas and water	2	...	...	...	...	4	3	...	...	...	...	5
5 Construction	17	...	...	...	...	27	17	...	...	...	...	27
6 Wholesale and retail trade, restaurants and hotels	30	...	...	...	...	50	33	...	...	...	...	56
A Wholesale and retail trade	18	...	...	...	...	34	20	...	...	...	...	38
B Restaurants and hotels	12	...	...	...	...	16	13	...	...	...	...	18
7 Transport, storage and communication	11	...	...	...	...	19	12	...	...	...	...	23
8 Finance, insurance, real estate and business services [a]	34	...	...	...	...	64	37	...	...	...	...	71
A Financial institutions	...	...	...	...	...	...	...	...	...	...	...	...

Cayman Islands

4.3 Cost Components of Value Added
(Continued)

Million Cayman Islands Dollars

	1983						1984					
	Compensation of Employees	Capital Consumption	Net Operating Surplus	Indirect Taxes	Less: Subsidies Received	Value Added	Compensation of Employees	Capital Consumption	Net Operating Surplus	Indirect Taxes	Less: Subsidies Received	Value Added
B Insurance	...	...	...	..	...	...	...	...	...	...	...	...
C Real estate and business services	...	...	...	...	...	...	...	...	...	...	...	...
9 Community, social and personal services	10	...	...	...	...	14	12	...	...	...	...	16
A Sanitary and similar services	...	...	...	...	...	...	...	...	...	...	...	...
B Social and related community services	...	...	...	...	...	...	...	...	...	...	...	...
C Recreational and cultural services	...	...	...	...	...	...	...	...	...	...	...	...
D Personal and household services	...	...	...	...	...	...	...	...	...	...	...	...
Total, Industries	107	...	...	...	...	184	117	...	...	...	...	204
Producers of Government Services	19	...	...	...	...	19	25	...	...	...	...	24
Other Producers	...	...	...	...	...	...	...	...	...	...	...	...
Total	126	...	...	...	...	203	142	...	...	...	...	228
Less: Imputed bank service charge	...	...	8	..	...	8	...	...	9	...	...	9
Import duties	...	...	...	..	...	18	...	...	...	...	...	19
Value added tax	...	...	...	...	...	...	...	...	...	...	...	...
Other adjustments	...	...	...	..	...	-6	...	...	...	...	...	-5
Total	126	...	...	...	...	207	142	...	...	...	...	233

	1985						1986					
	Compensation of Employees	Capital Consumption	Net Operating Surplus	Indirect Taxes	Less: Subsidies Received	Value Added	Compensation of Employees	Capital Consumption	Net Operating Surplus	Indirect Taxes	Less: Subsidies Received	Value Added
				All Producers								
1 Agriculture, hunting, forestry and fishing	1	...	...	...	...	2	1	...	...	...	...	1
2 Mining and quarrying	1	...	...	...	...	1	1	...	...	...	...	1
3 Manufacturing	2	...	...	...	...	4	2	...	6	...	...	6
4 Electricity, gas and water	3	...	...	...	...	5	4	...	...	...	...	7
5 Construction	16	...	...	...	...	26	16	...	8	...	...	27
6 Wholesale and retail trade, restaurants and hotels	35	...	...	...	...	60	39	...	27	...	...	64
A Wholesale and retail trade	21	...	...	...	...	41	23	...	21	...	...	43
B Restaurants and hotels	14	...	...	...	...	19	16	...	6	...	...	21
7 Transport, storage and communication	14	...	...	...	...	27	15	...	14	...	...	30
8 Finance, insurance, real estate and business services [a]	42	...	...	...	...	79	49	...	45	...	...	90
A Financial institutions	...	...	...	...	...	...	...	...	...	...	...	...
B Insurance	...	...	...	...	...	...	...	...	...	...	...	...
C Real estate and business services	...	...	...	...	...	...	...	...	...	...	...	...
9 Community, social and personal services	12	...	...	...	...	16	13	...	4	...	...	18
A Sanitary and similar services	...	...	...	...	...	...	...	...	...	...	...	...
B Social and related community services	...	...	...	...	...	...	...	...	...	...	...	...
C Recreational and cultural services	...	...	...	...	...	...	...	...	...	...	...	...
D Personal and household services	...	...	...	...	...	...	...	...	...	...	...	...
Total, Industries	126	...	...	...	...	220	140	...	104	...	...	244
Producers of Government Services	27	...	...	...	...	26	28	...	...	...	...	28
Other Producers	...	...	...	...	...	...	...	...	...	...	...	...
Total	153	...	...	...	...	246	168	...	104	...	...	272
Less: Imputed bank service charge	...	...	10	...	...	10	...	...	12	...	...	12
Import duties	...	...	...	...	...	20	...	...	...	...	...	23
Value added tax	...	...	...	...	...	...	...	...	...	...	...	...
Other adjustments	...	...	...	...	...	-5	...	...	...	...	...	-
Total	153	...	...	...	...	251	168	...	92	...	...	283

Cayman Islands

4.3 Cost Components of Value Added

Million Cayman Islands Dollars

1987

		Compensation of Employees	Capital Consumption	Net Operating Surplus	Indirect Taxes	Less: Subsidies Received	Value Added	Compensation of Employees	Capital Consumption	Net Operating Surplus	Indirect Taxes	Less: Subsidies Received	Value Added
										1988			

All Producers

		1987						1988					
1	Agriculture, hunting, forestry and fishing	1	...	...	...	...	1	1	...	...	...	...	2
2	Mining and quarrying	1	...	...	...	...	1	1	...	...	...	...	3
3	Manufacturing	2	...	...	...	...	4	4	...	...	...	...	8
4	Electricity, gas and water	4	...	...	...	...	7	4	...	...	...	...	12
5	Construction	16	...	...	...	...	27	21	...	...	...	...	38
6	Wholesale and retail trade, restaurants and hotels	46	...	...	...	...	76	57	...	...	...	...	92
	A Wholesale and retail trade	26	...	...	...	...	49	29	...	...	...	...	52
	B Restaurants and hotels	20	...	...	...	...	27	28	...	...	...	...	40
7	Transport, storage and communication	17	...	...	...	...	36	25	...	...	...	...	54
8	Finance, insurance, real estate and business services [a]	57	...	...	...	...	108	67	...	...	...	...	134
	A Financial institutions	...	...	...	...	...	...	36	...	...	...	...	52
	B Insurance	...	...	...	...	...	...						
	C Real estate and business services	...	...	...	...	...	...	31	...	...	...	...	82
9	Community, social and personal services	16	...	...	...	...	21	43	...	...	...	...	25
	A Sanitary and similar services	...	...	...	...	...	...	...	...	...	...	...	...
	B Social and related community services	...	...	...	...	...	...	...	...	...	...	...	...
	C Recreational and cultural services	...	...	...	...	...	...	...	...	...	...	...	...
	D Personal and household services	...	...	...	...	...	...	7	...	...	...	...	7
	Total, Industries	160	...	...	...	...	281	223	...	...	...	...	368
	Producers of Government Services	32	...	...	...	...	32	37	...	...	...	...	40
	Other Producers	...	...	...	...	...	...	...	...	...	...	...	...
	Total	192	...	...	...	...	313	260	...	...	...	...	408
	Less: Imputed bank service charge	...	13	...	...	...	13	...	14	...	...	...	14
	Import duties	...	...	...	...	...	28	...	...	...	...	...	34
	Value added tax	...	...	...	...	...	...	...	...	...	...	...	...
	Other adjustments	...	...	...	...	...	1	...	...	...	...	...	-
	Total	192	...	...	...	...	329	260	...	...	...	...	429

1989

		Compensation of Employees	Capital Consumption	Net Operating Surplus	Indirect Taxes	Less: Subsidies Received	Value Added

All Producers

1	Agriculture, hunting, forestry and fishing	1	...	...	...	...	1
2	Mining and quarrying	-	...	...	...	...	3
3	Manufacturing	4	...	...	...	...	9
4	Electricity, gas and water	5	...	...	...	...	15

Cayman Islands

4.3 Cost Components of Value Added
(Continued)

Million Cayman Islands Dollars

	Compensation of Employees	Capital Consumption	Net Operating Surplus	Indirect Taxes	Less: Subsidies Received	Value Added
	\multicolumn{6}{c}{1989}					
5 Construction	28	...	...	...	...	50
6 Wholesale and retail trade, restaurants and hotels	62	...	...	...	...	98
A Wholesale and retail trade	32	...	...	...	...	57
B Restaurants and hotels	30	...	...	...	...	41
7 Transport, storage and communication	27	...	...	...	...	59
8 Finance, insurance, real estate and business services [a]	69	...	...	...	...	148
A Financial institutions	42	...	...	...	...	64
B Insurance		...	...	...	...	
C Real estate and business services	27	...	...	...	...	84
9 Community, social and personal services	24	...	...	...	...	27
A Sanitary and similar services	...	...	...	...	...	...
B Social and related community services	...	...	...	...	...	...
C Recreational and cultural services	...	...	...	...	...	...
D Personal and household services	8	...	...	...	...	8
Total, Industries	220	...	...	...	...	410
Producers of Government Services	42	...	...	...	...	46
Other Producers	...	...	...	...	...	...
Total	263	...	...	...	...	457
Less: Imputed bank service charge	...	...	17	...	...	17
Import duties	...	...	...	...	...	37
Value added tax	...	...	...	...	...	...
Other adjustments	...	...	...	...	...	-
Total	263	...	...	...	...	477

a) Item 'Finance, insurance, real estate and business services' excludes banks and insurance companies registered in Cayman Islands but with no physical presence in the Islands.

Central African Rep.

Source. Reply to the United Nations National Accounts Questionnaire from the Ministere du Plan, de la Cooperation International et des Statistiques, Bangui.
General note. The estimates shown in the following tables have been prepared and adjusted by the Ministere Francais de la Cooperation to conform to the United Nations System of National Accounts so far as the existing data would permit.

1.1 Expenditure on the Gross Domestic Product, in Current Prices

Million CFA francs

		1970	1975	1980	1981	1982	1983	1984	1985	1986	1987	1988	1989
1	Government final consumption expenditure	10892	...	...	...	...	...	...	...	...	...	...	...
2	Private final consumption expenditure	39632	...	...	...	...	...	...	...	...	...	...	...
3	Gross capital formation	10323	...	...	...	...	...	...	...	...	...	...	...
	A Increase in stocks	2137	...	...	...	...	...	...	...	...	...	...	...
	B Gross fixed capital formation	8186	...	...	...	...	...	...	...	...	...	...	...
4	Exports of goods and services	11069	...	...	...	...	...	...	...	...	...	...	...
5	Less: Imports of goods and services	14933	...	...	...	...	...	...	...	...	...	...	...
	Equals: Gross Domestic Product	56983	...	...	...	...	...	...	...	...	...	...	...

1.3 Cost Components of the Gross Domestic Product

Million CFA francs

		1970	1975	1980	1981	1982	1983	1984	1985	1986	1987	1988	1989
1	Indirect taxes, net	6674	...	...	...	...	...	...	...	...	...	...	...
	A Indirect taxes	6867	...	...	...	...	...	...	...	...	...	...	...
	B Less: Subsidies	193	...	...	...	...	...	...	...	...	...	...	...
2	Consumption of fixed capital [a]	...	...	...	...	...	...	...	...	...	...	...	...
3	Compensation of employees paid by resident producers to:	13586	...	...	...	...	...	...	...	...	...	...	...
4	Operating surplus [a]	36723	...	...	...	...	...	...	...	...	...	...	...
	Equals: Gross Domestic Product	56983	...	...	...	...	...	...	...	...	...	...	...

a) Item 'Operating surplus' includes consumption of fixed capital.

1.10 Gross Domestic Product by Kind of Activity, in Current Prices

Million CFA francs

		1970	1975	1980	1981	1982	1983	1984	1985	1986	1987	1988	1989
1	Agriculture, hunting, forestry and fishing	17676	...	72831	86218	102702	99372	109275	130927	...	...	...	...
2	Mining and quarrying [a]	2360	...	5275	5021	5717	6155	7622	7822	...	...	...	...
3	Manufacturing [a]	7687	...	15953	18597	18357	19065	21691	23149	...	...	...	...
4	Electricity, gas and water		...	863	1103	1302	1285	2399	2557	...	...	...	...
5	Construction	2200	...	3341	3442	3392	5074	7297	7946	...	...	...	...
6	Wholesale and retail trade, restaurants and hotels [b]	11352	...	41465	44606	49324	51581	58291	68015	...	...	...	...
7	Transport, storage and communication	1500	...	7966	8815	9702	10230	11497	12982	...	...	...	...
8	Finance, insurance, real estate and business services	3101	...	6307	8845	9861	8962	9756	10805	...	...	...	...
9	Community, social and personal services [b]		...	6644	7975	9904	11337	12454	13973	...	...	...	...
	Total, Industries	45876	...	160645	184622	210261	213061	240282	278177	...	...	...	...
	Producers of Government Services	7484	...	21334	25871	28831	30289	28443	30372	...	...	...	...
	Other Producers	...	...	...	...	...	...	...	...	...	...	...	...
	Subtotal	53360	...	181979	210493	239092	243350	268725	308549	...	...	...	...
	Less: Imputed bank service charge	...	...	3554	5713	6689	5515	5840	6582	...	...	...	...
	Plus: Import duties	3623	...	9834	11530	13563	13220	15842	16710	...	...	...	...
	Plus: Value added tax	...	...	...	...	...	...	...	...	...	...	...	...
	Equals: Gross Domestic Product [cd]	56983	...	188259	216310	245966	251055	275730	311430	334470	313210	326420	...

a) Diamond cutting is included in item 'Manufacturing'.
b) For the first series, restaurants and hotels are included in item 'Community, social and personal services'.
c) For the first series, Gross domestic production. This differs from domestic product, primarily in the exclusion of the product originating in general government agencies and in public establishments of administrative nature.
d) Data for this table have not been revised, therefore, data for some years are not comparable with those of other tables.

Central African Rep.

1.11 Gross Domestic Product by Kind of Activity, in Constant Prices

Million CFA francs

	1970	1975	1980	1981	1982	1983	1984	1985	1986	1987	1988	1989
		1967			At constant prices of: 1982				1984			
1 Agriculture, hunting, forestry and fishing	16461	18545	... 94497	97185	102702	93925	104696 104900	107330	116250	114250	119470	...
2 Mining and quarrying	2065	1417	... 5722	5730	5717	5766	5877 7620	7640	7910	9220	8930	...
3 Manufacturing	4504	4432	... 18000	18626	18357	19678	20268 21650	22380	22250	20380	22530	...
4 Electricity, gas and water	620	697	... 1549	1300	1302	923	1452 1300	1180	1290	1840	1240	...
5 Construction	2719	2118	... 4014	3738	3392	4447	5856 6200	5630	5600	7260	6960	...
6 Wholesale and retail trade, restaurants and hotels	13229	11344	... 51723	50088	49324	43774	47317 51930	56623	58508	57168	57880	...
7 Transport, storage and communication	1170	1045	... 9997	9813	9702	8703	9447 10070	10987	11352	11092	11230	...
8 Finance, insurance, real estate and business services	3635	3982	... 7846	9786	9861	8387	8446 10120[a]	10030	7960	5080	4580	...
9 Community, social and personal services			... 36421[b]	38706[b]	38735[b]	38284[b]	35619[b] ...					...
Total, Industries	...	...	229768	234972	239092	223887	238977 213790	221800	231120	226290	232820	...
Producers of Government Services	...	...	...	...	...	...	... 39360	39630	40760	40340	41570	...
Other Producers	...	...	...				...					...
Subtotal	...	...	229768	234972	239092	223887	238977 253150	261430	271880	266630	274390	...
Less: Imputed bank service charge	...	...	4627	6536	6689	5069	5069 ...					...
Plus: Import duties	...	...	12802	13190	13563	12151	13749 13930	13900	14900	12600	12360	...
Plus: Value added tax	...	...	...	...	...	...	8650	9600	10030	8800	9010	...
Equals: Gross Domestic Product	44403	43580	237943	241626	245966	230969	247657 275730	284930	296810	288030	295760	...

a) Including item 'Community, social and personal services'.
b) Item 'Producers of government services' is included in item 'Community, social and personal services'.

Chad

Source. Reply to the United Nations National Accounts Questionnaire from the Sous-Direction de la Statistique, Direction du Plan et du Developpement, Ministere des Finances, de L'Economie et du Plan, Ndjamena.

General note. The official estimates have been adjusted by the Sous-Direction de la Statistique to conform to the United Nations System of National Accounts so far as the existing data would permit.

1.1 Expenditure on the Gross Domestic Product, in Current Prices

Thousand Million CFA francs

	1970	1975	1980	1981	1982	1983	1984	1985	1986	1987	1988	1989
1 Government final consumption expenditure	10.25	12.97	...	...	...	...	...	...	...	...	...	...
2 Private final consumption expenditure	77.01	133.25	...	...	...	...	...	...	...	...	...	...
3 Gross capital formation	9.62	27.75	...	...	...	...	...	...	...	...	...	...
A Increase in stocks	0.52	2.17	...	...	...	...	...	...	...	...	...	...
B Gross fixed capital formation	9.10	25.58	...	...	...	...	...	...	...	...	...	...
4 Exports of goods and services	21.11	25.26	...	...	...	...	...	...	...	...	...	...
5 Less: Imports of goods and services	27.48	50.65	...	...	...	...	...	...	...	...	...	...
Equals: Gross Domestic Product	90.50	148.57	...	...	...	...	...	...	...	...	...	...

1.2 Expenditure on the Gross Domestic Product, in Constant Prices

Thousand Million CFA francs

	1970	1975	1980	1981	1982	1983	1984	1985	1986	1987	1988	1989
					At constant prices of: 1970							
1 Government final consumption expenditure	10.25	8.77	...	...	...	...	...	...	...	...	...	...
2 Private final consumption expenditure	77.01	90.09	...	...	...	...	...	...	...	...	...	...
3 Gross capital formation	9.62	20.37	...	...	...	...	...	...	...	...	...	...
4 Exports of goods and services	21.11	21.55	...	...	...	...	...	...	...	...	...	...
5 Less: Imports of goods and services	27.48	31.86	...	...	...	...	...	...	...	...	...	...
Equals: Gross Domestic Product	90.50	108.93	...	...	...	...	...	...	...	...	...	...

1.3 Cost Components of the Gross Domestic Product

Thousand Million CFA francs

	1970	1975	1980	1981	1982	1983	1984	1985	1986	1987	1988	1989
1 Indirect taxes, net	...	7.32	...	...	...	...	...	...	...	...	...	...
A Indirect taxes	...	7.46	...	...	...	...	...	...	...	...	...	...
B Less: Subsidies	...	0.14	...	...	...	...	...	...	...	...	...	...
2 Consumption of fixed capital	...	5.32	...	...	...	...	...	...	...	...	...	...
3 Compensation of employees paid by resident producers to:	...	19.41	...	...	...	...	...	...	...	...	...	...
A Resident households	...	19.21	...	...	...	...	...	...	...	...	...	...
B Rest of the world	0.29	0.20	...	...	...	...	...	...	...	...	...	...
4 Operating surplus	...	116.52	...	...	...	...	...	...	...	...	...	...
Equals: Gross Domestic Product	90.50	148.57	...	...	...	...	...	...	...	...	...	...

1.7 External Transactions on Current Account, Summary

Thousand Million CFA francs

	1970	1975	1980	1981	1982	1983	1984	1985	1986	1987	1988	1989
					Payments to the Rest of the World							
1 Imports of goods and services	27.48	50.65	...	...	...	...	...	...	...	...	...	...
A Imports of merchandise c.i.f.	19.38	38.64	...	...	...	...	...	...	...	...	...	...
B Other	8.11	12.02	...	...	...	...	...	...	...	...	...	...
2 Factor income to the rest of the world	0.92	0.82	...	...	...	...	...	...	...	...	...	...
A Compensation of employees	0.29	0.20	...	...	...	...	...	...	...	...	...	...
B Property and entrepreneurial income	0.63	0.62	...	...	...	...	...	...	...	...	...	...
3 Current transfers to the rest of the world	1.79	2.42	...	...	...	...	...	...	...	...	...	...
4 Surplus of the nation on current transactions	-4.10	-18.36	...	...	...	...	...	...	...	...	...	...
Payments to the Rest of the World and Surplus of the Nation on Current Transactions	26.09	35.54	...	...	...	...	...	...	...	...	...	...
					Receipts From The Rest of the World							
1 Exports of goods and services	21.11	25.26	...	...	...	...	...	...	...	...	...	...

Chad

1.7 External Transactions on Current Account, Summary
(Continued)

Thousand Million CFA francs

	1970	1975	1980	1981	1982	1983	1984	1985	1986	1987	1988	1989
A Exports of merchandise f.o.b.	12.24	12.42	...	...	...	...	...	...	...	...	...	...
B Other	8.87	12.84	...	...	...	...	...	...	...	...	...	...
2 Factor income from rest of the world	0.15	0.13	...	...	...	...	...	...	...	...	...	...
A Compensation of employees	0.05	-	...	...	...	...	...	...	...	...	...	...
B Property and entrepreneurial income	0.10	0.13	...	...	...	...	...	...	...	...	...	...
3 Current transfers from rest of the world	4.84	10.14	...	...	...	...	...	...	...	...	...	...
Receipts from the Rest of the World on Current Transactions	26.09	35.53	...	...	...	...	...	...	...	...	...	...

1.10 Gross Domestic Product by Kind of Activity, in Current Prices

Thousand Million CFA francs

	1970	1975	1980	1981	1982	1983	1984	1985	1986	1987	1988	1989
1 Agriculture, hunting, forestry and fishing	...	60.93	...	...	...	...	...	...	...	...	...	...
2 Mining and quarrying	...	1.21	...	...	...	...	...	...	...	...	...	...
3 Manufacturing	...	16.53	...	...	...	...	...	...	...	...	...	...
4 Electricity, gas and water	...	0.97	...	...	...	...	...	...	...	...	...	...
5 Construction	...	4.18	...	...	...	...	...	...	...	...	...	...
6 Wholesale and retail trade, restaurants and hotels	...	42.20	...	...	...	...	...	...	...	...	...	...
7 Transport, storage and communication	...	3.55	...	...	...	...	...	...	...	...	...	...
8 Finance, insurance, real estate and business services	...	7.66	...	...	...	...	...	...	...	...	...	...
9 Community, social and personal services [a]	...	9.97	...	...	...	...	...	...	...	...	...	...
Total, Industries	...	...	...	...	...	...	...	...	...	...	...	...
Producers of Government Services	...	...	...	...	...	...	...	...	...	...	...	...
Other Producers [a]	...	...	...	...	...	...	...	...	...	...	...	...
Subtotal	...	147.18	...	...	...	...	...	...	...	...	...	...
Less: Imputed bank service charge	...	1.25	...	...	...	...	...	...	...	...	...	...
Plus: Import duties	...	2.64	...	...	...	...	...	...	...	...	...	...
Plus: Value added tax	...	...	...	...	...	...	...	...	...	...	...	...
Equals: Gross Domestic Product	...	148.57	...	...	...	...	...	...	...	...	...	...

a) Item 'Producers of government services' is included in item 'Community, social and personal services'.

1.11 Gross Domestic Product by Kind of Activity, in Constant Prices

Thousand Million CFA francs

	1970	1975	1980	1981	1982	1983	1984	1985	1986	1987	1988	1989
			At constant prices of:1977									
1 Agriculture, hunting, forestry and fishing	...	...	63.38	56.40	59.25	61.06	51.37	74.35	70.31	67.42	83.07	79.24
2 Mining and quarrying	...	...	0.06	0.06	0.06	0.10	0.21	0.36	0.39	0.41	0.42	0.48
3 Manufacturing	...	...	13.30	18.09	19.94	22.16	27.22	25.41	24.14	21.56	24.81	30.25
4 Electricity, gas and water	...	...	0.41	0.44	0.59	0.68	0.87	0.87	1.02	1.07	1.15	1.24
5 Construction	...	...	0.28	0.27	0.30	0.50	1.00	1.72	1.89	1.97	2.02	2.31
6 Wholesale and retail trade, restaurants and hotels	...	...										
7 Transport, storage and communication	...	...	32.74	35.73	37.99	41.64	44.28	53.08	53.60	50.42	56.53	59.28
8 Finance, insurance, real estate and business services	...	...										
9 Community, social and personal services [a]	...	...										
Total, Industries	...	...	110.17	110.98	118.12	126.14	124.96	155.79	151.37	142.84	167.99	172.80
Producers of Government Services	...	...	8.28	8.53	7.79	16.91	18.10	19.33	16.44	19.18	19.85	21.62
Other Producers [a]	...	...	...	...	...	...	...	...	...	...	...	...
Subtotal [b]	...	...	118.45	119.51	125.91	143.05	143.06	175.12	167.81	162.02	187.84	194.42
Less: Imputed bank service charge	...	...	...	...	...	...	...	...	...	...	...	...
Plus: Import duties	...	...	...	...	...	...	...	...	...	...	...	...
Plus: Value added tax	...	...	...	...	...	...	...	...	...	...	...	...
Plus: Other adjustments [c]	...	...	0.38	0.52	0.57	3.24	6.29	6.94	6.79	8.37	8.59	10.60
Equals: Gross Domestic Product	...	...	118.83	120.03	126.48	146.29	149.35	182.06	174.60	170.39	196.43	205.02

a) Item 'Producers of government services' is included in item 'Community, social and personal services'.
b) Gross domestic product in factor values.
c) Item 'Other adjustments' refers to indirect taxes net of subsidies.

Chad

1.12 Relations Among National Accounting Aggregates

Thousand Million CFA francs

	1970	1975	1980	1981	1982	1983	1984	1985	1986	1987	1988	1989
Gross Domestic Product	90.50	148.57	...	...	...	...	...	...	...	...	...	...
Plus: Net factor income from the rest of the world	-0.77	-0.70	...	...	...	...	...	...	...	...	...	...
Factor income from the rest of the world	0.15	0.13	...	...	...	...	...	...	...	...	...	...
Less: Factor income to the rest of the world	0.92	0.82	...	...	...	...	...	...	...	...	...	...
Equals: Gross National Product	89.73	147.87	...	...	...	...	...	...	...	...	...	...
Less: Consumption of fixed capital	...	5.32	...	...	...	...	...	...	...	...	...	...
Equals: National Income	...	142.55	...	...	...	...	...	...	...	...	...	...
Plus: Net current transfers from the rest of the world	3.05	7.73	...	...	...	...	...	...	...	...	...	...
Current transfers from the rest of the world	4.84	10.14	...	...	...	...	...	...	...	...	...	...
Less: Current transfers to the rest of the world	1.79	2.42	...	...	...	...	...	...	...	...	...	...
Equals: National Disposable Income	...	150.28	...	...	...	...	...	...	...	...	...	...
Less: Final consumption	87.26	146.22	...	...	...	...	...	...	...	...	...	...
Equals: Net Saving	...	4.07	...	...	...	...	...	...	...	...	...	...
Less: Surplus of the nation on current transactions	-4.10	-18.36	...	...	...	...	...	...	...	...	...	...
Equals: Net Capital Formation	...	22.43	...	...	...	...	...	...	...	...	...	...

2.1 Government Final Consumption Expenditure by Function, in Current Prices

Thousand Million CFA francs

		1970	1975	1980	1981	1982	1983	1984	1985	1986	1987	1988	1989
1	General public services	...	5.18	...	...	...	...	...	...	...	...	...	...
2	Defence	...	...	...	...	...	...	...	...	...	...	...	...
3	Public order and safety	...	...	...	...	...	...	...	...	...	...	...	...
4	Education	...	1.81	...	...	...	...	...	...	...	...	...	...
5	Health	...	0.80	...	...	...	...	...	...	...	...	...	...
6	Social security and welfare	...	0.07	...	...	...	...	...	...	...	...	...	...
7	Housing and community amenities	...	-	...	...	...	...	...	...	...	...	...	...
8	Recreational, cultural and religious affairs	...	0.08	...	...	...	...	...	...	...	...	...	...
9	Economic services	...	5.77	...	...	...	...	...	...	...	...	...	...
10	Other functions	...	-0.74	...	...	...	...	...	...	...	...	...	...
	Total Government Final Consumption Expenditure	...	12.97	...	...	...	...	...	...	...	...	...	...

2.17 Exports and Imports of Goods and Services, Detail

Thousand Million CFA francs

		1970	1975	1980	1981	1982	1983	1984	1985	1986	1987	1988	1989
	Exports of Goods and Services												
1	Exports of merchandise, f.o.b.	12.24	12.42	...	...	...	...	...	...	...	...	...	...
2	Transport and communication	0.74	2.30	...	...	...	...	...	...	...	...	...	...
	A In respect of merchandise imports	0.27	2.00	...	...	...	...	...	...	...	...	...	...
	B Other	0.47	0.30	...	...	...	...	...	...	...	...	...	...
3	Insurance service charges	0.25	0.65	...	...	...	...	...	...	...	...	...	...
	A In respect of merchandise imports	-	-	...	...	...	...	...	...	...	...	...	...
	B Other	0.25	0.65	...	...	...	...	...	...	...	...	...	...
4	Other commodities	1.43	1.94	...	...	...	...	...	...	...	...	...	...
5	Adjustments of merchandise exports to change-of-ownership basis	-	-	...	...	...	...	...	...	...	...	...	...
6	Direct purchases in the domestic market by non-residential households	6.46	7.95	...	...	...	...	...	...	...	...	...	...
7	Direct purchases in the domestic market by extraterritorial bodies	...	...	...	...	...	...	...	...	...	...	...	...
	Total Exports of Goods and Services	21.11	25.26	...	...	...	...	...	...	...	...	...	...
	Imports of Goods and Services												
1	Imports of merchandise, c.i.f.	19.38	38.64	...	...	...	...	...	...	...	...	...	...

Chad

2.17 Exports and Imports of Goods and Services, Detail
(Continued)

Thousand Million CFA francs

	1970	1975	1980	1981	1982	1983	1984	1985	1986	1987	1988	1989
A Imports of merchandise, f.o.b.	14.07	25.66	...	...	...	...	...	...	...	...	...	...
B Transport of services on merchandise imports	5.31	12.98	...	...	...	...	...	...	...	...	...	...
C Insurance service charges on merchandise imports	...	...	...	...	...	...	...	...	...	...	...	...
2 Adjustments of merchandise imports to change-of-ownership basis	...	...	...	...	...	...	...	...	...	...	...	...
3 Other transport and communication	0.93	1.39	...	...	...	...	...	...	...	...	...	...
4 Other insurance service charges	0.41	0.80	...	...	...	...	...	...	...	...	...	...
5 Other commodities	2.09	2.36	...	...	...	...	...	...	...	...	...	...
6 Direct purchases abroad by government	4.68	7.47	...	...	...	...	...	...	...	...	...	...
7 Direct purchases abroad by resident households			...	...	...	...	...	...	...	...	...	...
Total Imports of Goods and Services	27.48	50.65	...	...	...	...	...	...	...	...	...	...
Balance of Goods and Services	-6.37	-25.39	...	...	...	...	...	...	...	...	...	...
Total Imports and Balance of Goods and Services	21.11	25.26	...	...	...	...	...	...	...	...	...	...

Chile

General note. The preparation of national accounts statistics in Chile is undertaken by Banco Central de Chile, Santiago. The official estimates are published in 'Cuentas Nacionales de Chile'. The following presentation of sources and methods is mainly based on a detailed description received by the United Nations from ODEPLAN. However, descriptions can also be found in 'Cuentas Nacionales de Chile, 1960-1975', published in 1976. The estimates are generally in accordance with the classifications and definitions recommended in the United Nations System of National Accounts (SNA). The following tables have been prepared from successive replies to the United Nations national accounts questionnaire. When the scope and coverage of the estimates differ for conceptual or statistical reasons from the definitions and classifications recommended in SNA, a footnote is indicated to the relevant tables.

Sources and methods:

(a) Gross domestic product. The main approach used to estimate GDP is the production approach.

(b) Expenditure on the gross domestic product. The expenditure approach is used to estimate government final consumption expenditure, increase in stocks, exports and imports of goods and services and capital formation in new construction. The commodity-flow approach is used to estimate other construction. Private final consumption expenditure is estimated as a residual. Data on government consumption expenditure is obtained i.a. through special inquiries and direct information from the concerned authorities. Values of locally produced and imported capital goods are adjusted by coefficients by type of capital goods to arrive at purchasers' values. Estimates of exports and imports of goods and services are obtained from the balance of payments statements prepared by the Central Bank. To arrive at constant prices, value added of government services is deflated by index of wages and salaries. Purchases of goods and services are deflated by the wholesale price index and the price index of intermediate imported goods. For private consumption expenditure most domestically produced items are deflated by appropriate components of the consumer price index. Imported goods are deflated by the price index of imported consumer goods. For gross fixed capital formation, buildings and other construction are devalued using double deflation. Base year estimates of transport equipment, machinery and equipment are extrapolated by a quantity index for each industrial group, except for imports which are deflated by price indexes of imported capital goods. Price deflation is used for exports and imports of goods and services.

(c) Cost-structure of the gross domestic product. Wages and salaries are in most cases estimated from company accounts and/or direct information from the enterprises. Employers' contributions to social security schemes as well as wages and salaries in kind are included in the estimates. Operating surplus is obtained as a residual. Depreciation data are obtained from accounting statements of enterprises or computed from data of fixed assets by type of capital and useful life time. For indirect taxes, published fiscal statements by type of tax, are used.

(d) Gross domestic product by kind of economic activity. This table is prepared at market prices, i.e. producers' values. The production approach is used to estimate value added of most industries. The income approach is however used for government services, business services and domestic services. The general method of estimating gross value of agricultural production involves the use of physical quantities of production together with the respective wholesale or producers' prices. Quantities of livestock production are obtained from published data and directly from Instituto Nacional de Estadistica (INE). The estimates include both marketed and non-marketed production. The inputs into agriculture and forestry are based on information from the suppliers of input products. The estimates for the mining and quarrying sector are mainly based on data on sales and change in stocks, but in some cases on physical production valued at average sales price or on expenditure data in the construction and industrial sectors. For manufacturing, the required statistics for companies with 1 to 49 employees are found in their annual industrial declarations. For units with 50 or more employees, the industrial yearbook of INE is used. The gross value of construction in the public sector is obtained from accounts of the respective institutions. For the private sector the construction expenditure on all buildings is calculated on the basis of the municipal building permits. In order to estimate intermediate consumption and the components of value added, cost-structure by type of construction are applied to the gross value of production. Estimates of private sector trade is made on the basis of a continuous survey. For public enterprises, information provided in their accounting statements and in their budget statements is used. For transport, information is based on accounts, sales data and on the stock of motor vehicles. The production and input estimates for financial institutions and corporations, real estate and insurance are made possible through data from the Superintendencia de Bancos. Bench-mark estimates for actual rents paid and imputed rent for owner-occupied dwellings have been made on the basis of the housing censuses in 1960 and 1970. These estimates are projected annually by a value index which combines the increase in physical stock with a price index for rent. For public administration and defense, budgets and accounts provide the required basic data. For the constant price estimates, double deflation is used in the agricultural sector, the output value is extrapolated by quantity indexes by product, whereas intermediate inputs are deflated by an index of input prices. Value added of fishing, mining and quarrying, manufacturing and electricity is extrapolated by quantity indexes of production. Double deflation is used for construction, current gross values are deflated by price indexes for each type of construction. For intermediate consumption, input-structures are used. For trade, value added of the base year is extrapolated by a quantity index. Double deflation is used for the transport and financing, insurance, real estate and business services sector. For transport, current output is deflated separately for different uses and types of transport. For financial institutions, output is deflated by an implicit price index for expenditure. Output of ownership of dwellings is extrapolated by an index based on the change in the housing stock, whereas inputs are deflated by the value index for repairs. For community, social and personal services, double deflation is used.

1.1 Expenditure on the Gross Domestic Product, in Current Prices

Million Chilean pesos

		1970	1975	1980	1981	1982	1983	1984	1985	1986	1987	1988	1989
1	Government final consumption expenditure	13	5560	133886	167433	189790	220367	256316	335221 / 367095	410698	475087	568466	667006
2	Private final consumption expenditure	69	25941	760325	969819	904159	1100366	1326590	1852947 / 1785245	2237323	2811039	3534776	4520375
	A Households	...	25333	...	...	...	...	...	...	...	...	...	...
	B Private non-profit institutions serving households	...	609	...	...	...	...	...	...	...	...	...	...
3	Gross capital formation	16	4645	226058	283964	132353	171151	336899	473289 / 353215	474128	703098	918719	1378318
	A Increase in stocks	1	-1626	47074	47073	-36201	-20390	70120	53780 / -13213	1387	36335	36062	128400
	B Gross fixed capital formation	15	6271	178984	236891	168554	191541	266779	419509 / 366428	472741	666763	882657	1249918
	Residential buildings	...	1606	44839	65687	45285	46005	51197	85156	...	...	...	...
	Non-residential buildings	...	399	16018	21892	20700	16287	19329	28095	...	...	...	...
	Other construction and land improvement etc.	...	1613	44162	55408	54451	69135	94378	137815	...	...	...	...
	Other	...	2653	73965	93905	48119	60114	101875	168442	...	...	...	...
4	Exports of goods and services	15	9026	245387	209021	239863	375860	440922	747886 / 749205	994168	1394265	2022033	2533794
5	Less: Imports of goods and services	14	9726	290099	340616	263355	332069	458024	667866 / 678122	870211	1223727	1632969	2320050
	Equals: Gross Domestic Product	98	35447	1075557	1289621	1202808	1535676	1902702	2741478 / 2576638	3246106	4159762	5411025	6779443

Chile

1.2 Expenditure on the Gross Domestic Product, in Constant Prices

Million Chilean pesos

	1970	1975	1980	1981	1982	1983	1984	1985	1986	1987	1988	1989
					At constant prices of: 1977							
1 Government final consumption expenditure	34014	40428	44916	43502	42700	42183	41844	42940	42309	41409	43351	43736
2 Private final consumption expenditure	218507	180139	256505	290848	247946	233733	235201	232893	252722	264872	290422	317279
A Households	...	175682	...	...	...	...	...	...	...	...	...	...
B Private non-profit institutions serving households	...	4457	...	...	...	...	...	...	...	...	...	...
3 Gross capital formation	66123	35479	86961	101702	44011	34512	59558	49287	56635	71232	77290	102383
A Increase in stocks	8337	-3513	22848	26843	-2175	-4729	12920	-2002	265	5703	4753	14735
B Gross fixed capital formation	57786	38992	64113	74857	46186	39241	46638	51289	56370	65529	72537	87648
Residential buildings	...	11645	15669	19711	12669	10363	10173	13633				...
Non-residential buildings	...	2650	5560	6297	5583	3780	3806	4219	36374	40747	43463	
Other construction and land improvement etc.	...	10329	13426	14592	13144	13086	15096	16296				...
Other	...	14368	29458	34259	14790	12012	17563	17140	19996	24782	29074	...
4 Exports of goods and services	32450	42645	86077	78373	82069	82151	84022	94342	103504	112612	119481	135922
5 Less: Imports of goods and services	67997	45648	110461	127812	82647	67863	76795	68866	78543	91895	103014	129077
Equals: Gross Domestic Product	283097	253043	363998	386611	334078	324717	343828	350596	376627	398230	427530	470243

1.3 Cost Components of the Gross Domestic Product

Million Chilean pesos

	1970	1975	1980	1981	1982	1983	1984	1985	1986	1987	1988	1989
1 Indirect taxes, net	11	4961	129758	181459	165331	181465	255970	351281	...	...	...	...
A Indirect taxes	13	5569	150701	201488	182747	217603	299842	421815	...	...	...	...
B Less: Subsidies	2	608	20943	20029	17416	36138	43872	70534	...	...	...	...
2 Consumption of fixed capital	8	5200	103400	120325	129554	180922	226130	327832	...	...	...	...
3 Compensation of employees paid by resident producers to:	42	13817	409816	516861	509522	588215	695075	904947	...	...	...	...
4 Operating surplus	38	11469	432582	470976	398401	585074	725528	1157418	...	...	...	...
Equals: Gross Domestic Product	98	35447	1075557	1289621	1202808	1535676	1902702	2741478	...	...	...	...

1.4 General Government Current Receipts and Disbursements

Million Chilean pesos

	1970	1975	1980	1981	1982	1983	1984	1985	1986	1987	1988	1989
					Receipts							
1 Operating surplus	...	...	...	...	...	...	...	...	...	...	...	...
2 Property and entrepreneurial income	4	228	...	...	...	...	...	...	...	...	...	...
3 Taxes, fees and contributions	27	11249	...	...	...	...	...	...	...	...	...	...
A Indirect taxes	13	5617	...	...	...	...	...	...	...	...	...	...
B Direct taxes	5	2547	...	...	...	...	...	...	...	...	...	...
C Social security contributions	9	3086	...	...	...	...	...	...	...	...	...	...
D Compulsory fees, fines and penalties	...	...	...	...	...	...	...	...	...	...	...	...
4 Other current transfers	1	377	...	...	...	...	...	...	...	...	...	...
Total Current Receipts of General Government	32	11855	...	...	...	...	...	...	...	...	...	...
					Disbursements							
1 Government final consumption expenditure	13	5529	...	...	...	...	...	...	...	...	...	...
2 Property income	1	1419	...	...	...	...	...	...	...	...	...	...
A Interest	1	1419	...	...	...	...	...	...	...	...	...	...
B Net land rent and royalties	...	...	...	...	...	...	...	...	...	...	...	...

Chile

1.4 General Government Current Receipts and Disbursements
(Continued)

Million Chilean pesos	1970	1975	1980	1981	1982	1983	1984	1985	1986	1987	1988	1989
3 Subsidies	2	948	...	...	...	...	...	...	...	...	...	...
4 Other current transfers	9	3049	...	...	...	...	...	...	...	...	...	...
A Social security benefits	...	...	...	...	...	...	...	...	...	...	...	...
B Social assistance grants	...	...	...	...	...	...	...	...	...	...	...	...
C Other	-	16	...	...	...	...	...	...	...	...	...	...
5 Net saving	8	909	...	...	...	...	...	...	...	...	...	...
Total Current Disbursements and Net Saving of General Government	32	11855	...	...	...	...	...	...	...	...	...	...

1.6 Current Income and Outlay of Households and Non-Profit Institutions

Million Chilean pesos	1970	1975	1980	1981	1982	1983	1984	1985	1986	1987	1988	1989
Receipts												
1 Compensation of employees	41	13994	...	...	...	...	...	...	...	...	...	...
2 Operating surplus of private unincorporated enterprises	...	...	...	...	...	...	...	...	...	...	...	...
3 Property and entrepreneurial income	27	18722	...	...	...	...	...	...	...	...	...	...
4 Current transfers	9	3080	...	...	...	...	...	...	...	...	...	...
A Social security benefits	...	...	...	...	...	...	...	...	...	...	...	...
B Social assistance grants	...	...	...	...	...	...	...	...	...	...	...	...
C Other	...	47	...	...	...	...	...	...	...	...	...	...
Total Current Receipts	77	35796	...	...	...	...	...	...	...	...	...	...
Disbursements												
1 Private final consumption expenditure	69	35360	...	...	...	...	...	...	...	...	...	...
2 Property income	...	...	...	...	...	...	...	...	...	...	...	...
3 Direct taxes and other current transfers n.e.c. to general government	11	4333	...	...	...	...	...	...	...	...	...	...
A Social security contributions	9	3086	...	...	...	...	...	...	...	...	...	...
B Direct taxes	2	1247	...	...	...	...	...	...	...	...	...	...
C Fees, fines and penalties	...	...	...	...	...	...	...	...	...	...	...	...
4 Other current transfers	1	241	...	...	...	...	...	...	...	...	...	...
5 Net saving	-4	-4138	...	...	...	...	...	...	...	...	...	...
Total Current Disbursements and Net Saving	77	35796	...	...	...	...	...	...	...	...	...	...

1.7 External Transactions on Current Account, Summary

Million Chilean pesos	1970	1975	1980	1981	1982	1983	1984	1985	1986	1987	1988	1989
Payments to the Rest of the World												
1 Imports of goods and services	14	9726	290099	340616	263355	332069	458024	667866	870211	1223727	1632969	2320050
2 Factor income to the rest of the world	2	1429	48274	80699	120993	153625	229517	337967	408105	412776	515648	584434
3 Current transfers to the rest of the world	-	63	3151	3292	3814	5090	5636	9056	9608	9479	6885	6807
4 Surplus of the nation on current transactions	-1	-1841	-76552	-184445	-113609	-86283	-204779	-214595	-223047	-176920	-37964	-242874
Payments to the Rest of the World and Surplus of the Nation on Current Transactions	16	9378	264973	240162	274554	404500	488399	800294	1064877	1469062	2117538	2668417
Receipts From The Rest of the World												
1 Exports of goods and services	15	9026	245387	209021	239863	375860	440922	747886	994168	1394265	2022033	2533794
2 Factor income from rest of the world	-	41	12008	23622	25452	15939	31390	32172	43988	39911	45327	63854
3 Current transfers from rest of the world	1	311	7578	7519	9240	12701	16087	20236	26721	34886	50178	70768
Receipts from the Rest of the World on Current Transactions	16	9378	264973	240162	274554	404500	488399	800294	1064877	1469062	2117538	2668416

Chile

1.10 Gross Domestic Product by Kind of Activity, in Current Prices

Million Chilean pesos

	1970	1975	1980	1981	1982	1983	1984	1985	1986	1987	1988	1989
1 Agriculture, hunting, forestry and fishing	7	2334	77706	83369	75633	90414	135976	204754	...	...	...	...
2 Mining and quarrying	9	3683	91985	71403	93379	158040	159713	281470	...	...	...	...
3 Manufacturing	25	7187	230511	284241	233469	320484	436825	601649	...	...	...	...
4 Electricity, gas and water	2	739	22888	28948	35511	44613	53710	80778	...	...	...	...
5 Construction	5	1907	55763	81836	69083	69161	79779	112932	...	...	...	...
6 Wholesale and retail trade, restaurants and hotels	19	6655	198002	226118	170583	234334	280773	441374	...	...	...	...
7 Transport, storage and communication	5	2023	54961	67612	68213	84508	107321	149061	...	...	...	...
8 Finance, insurance, real estate and business services [a]	10	5134	182079	237126	257486	244590	261058	418080	...	...	...	...
9 Community, social and personal services	5	1441	65695	94467	88769	99914	117083	153844	...	...	...	...
Total, Industries	87	31102	979590	1175120	1092126	1346058	1632238	2443942	...	...	...	...
Producers of Government Services	10	3656	92027	117453	134193	149007	171493	212875	...	...	...	...
Other Producers	-	433	...	...	...	...	...	...	...	...	...	...
Subtotal	97	35191	1071617	1292573	1226319	1495065	1803731	2656817	...	...	...	...
Less: Imputed bank service charge	2	1047	55852	81244	80778	47528	41901	119130	...	...	...	...
Plus: Import duties	3	1303	59789	78293	57268	88142	140871	203793	...	...	...	...
Plus: Value added tax									...	...	...	...
Equals: Gross Domestic Product	98	35447	1075557	1289621	1202808	1535676	1902702	2741478	...	...	...	...

a) Beginning 1980, the estimates of private non-profit institutions are included in item 'Finance, insurance, real estate and business services'.

1.11 Gross Domestic Product by Kind of Activity, in Constant Prices

Million Chilean pesos

	1970	1975	1980	1981	1982	1983	1984	1985	1986	1987	1988	1989
					At constant prices of: 1977							
1 Agriculture, hunting, forestry and fishing	24071	25993	30031	31186	30961	30312	33027	35354	37107	38308	40398	42320
2 Mining and quarrying	18595	20095	26077	28084	29916	29291	30894	31899	31523	31525	32853	35629
3 Manufacturing	69912	54405	78332	80336	63500	65466	71289	73204	78507	82804	89997	98983
4 Electricity, gas and water	4792	5786	7754	7913	7918	8246	8834	9171	9744	10117	11060	11575
5 Construction	21141	14147	19420	23518	17981	15398	15742	18510	20852	23056	24454	27559
6 Wholesale and retail trade, restaurants and hotels [a]	51635	38925	71896	76844	62597	62103	64520	61371	62919	67635	74235	84622
7 Transport, storage and communication	13765	13262	20313	20691	18351	17762	18590	19561	21571	23755	26485	30286
8 Finance, insurance, real estate and business services [b]	31287	34611	55855	61100	59914	44666	42845	51365	...	...	...	...
9 Community, social and personal services	14591	12886	20145	20820	18359	18668	20035	21479	...	...	...	...
Total, Industries	249789	220110	329823	350492	309497	291912	305776	321914	...	...	...	...
Producers of Government Services	23476	29261	29215	28656	28323	28749	28526	29065	...	...	...	...
Other Producers	-	3083	...	...	...	...	...	...	...	...	...	...
Subtotal	273265	252454	359038	379148	337820	320661	334302	350979	...	...	...	...
Less: Imputed bank service charge	5631	7530	18889	24496	22550	10116	7652	15489	...	...	...	...
Plus: Import duties	15463	8119	23850	31959	18809	14170	17179	15106	...	...	...	...
Plus: Value added tax									...	...	...	...
Equals: Gross Domestic Product	283097	253043	363998	386611	334078	324717	343828	350596	376627	398230	427530	470243

a) Beginning 1986, restaurants and hotels are not included in item 'Wholesale and retail trade, restaurants and hotels'. b) Beginning 1980, the estimates of private non-profit institutions are included in item 'Finance, insurance, real estate and business services'.

Chile

1.12 Relations Among National Accounting Aggregates

Million Chilean pesos

	1970	1975	1980	1981	1982	1983	1984	1985	1986	1987	1988	1989
Gross Domestic Product	98	35447	1075557	1289621	1202808	1535676	1902702	2741478	3246106	4159762	5411025	6779443
Plus: Net factor income from the rest of the world	-2	-1388	-36266	-57077	-95541	-137686	-198127	-305795	-364117	-372865	-470321	-520579
Factor income from the rest of the world	...	41	12008	23622	25452	15939	31390	32172	43988	39911	45327	63854
Less: Factor income to the rest of the world	2	1429	48274	80699	120993	153625	229517	337967	408105	412776	515648	584434
Equals: Gross National Product	96	34058	1039291	1232544	1107267	1397990	1704575	2435683	2881989	3786897	4940704	6258864
Less: Consumption of fixed capital	8	5200	103400	120325	129554	180922	226130	327832	...	...	...	...
Equals: National Income	88	28858	935891	1112219	977713	1217068	1478445	2107851	...	...	...	...
Plus: Net current transfers from the rest of the world	-	248	4427	4227	5426	7611	10451	11180	17113	25407	43293	63961
Current transfers from the rest of the world	1	311	7578	7519	9240	12701	16087	20236	26721	34886	50178	70768
Less: Current transfers to the rest of the world	-	63	3151	3292	3814	5090	5636	9056	9608	9479	6885	6807
Equals: National Disposable Income	89	29105	940317	1116446	983139	1224680	1488896	2119031	...	...	...	...
Less: Final consumption	81	31501	894211	1137252	1093949	1320733	1582906	2188168	2648021	3286126	4103242	5187381
Equals: Net Saving	7	-2395	46106	-20806	-110810	-96053	-94010	-69137	...	...	...	...
Less: Surplus of the nation on current transactions	-1	-1841	-76551	-184445	-113609	-86283	-204779	-214595	-223047	-176920	-37964	-242874
Equals: Net Capital Formation	9	-555	122659	163639	2799	-9771	110769	145458	...	...	...	...

4.1 Derivation of Value Added by Kind of Activity, in Current Prices

Million Chilean pesos

	1980 Gross Output	1980 Intermediate Consumption	1980 Value Added	1981 Gross Output	1981 Intermediate Consumption	1981 Value Added	1982 Gross Output	1982 Intermediate Consumption	1982 Value Added	1983 Gross Output	1983 Intermediate Consumption	1983 Value Added
All Producers												
1 Agriculture, hunting, forestry and fishing	126797	49091	77706	136877	53507	83369	130396	54764	75633	177753	87339	90414
2 Mining and quarrying	161730	69744	91985	147952	76549	71403	176675	83297	93379	284998	126958	158040
3 Manufacturing	630943	400433	230510	717856	433616	284241	616359	382890	233469	887439	566955	320484
4 Electricity, gas and water	41373	18490	22888	50579	21632	28948	60603	25092	35511	79661	35049	44613
5 Construction	111006	55243	55763	152925	71089	81836	130214	61131	69083	143397	74236	69161
6 Wholesale and retail trade, restaurants and hotels	288233	90230	198002	337511	111392	226118	273534	102951	170583	366240	131906	234334
A Wholesale and retail trade	...	...	...	...	...	...	...	...	148216	...	...	209335
B Restaurants and hotels	...	...	...	...	...	...	...	...	22367	...	...	24999
7 Transport, storage and communication	128000	73039	54961	153430	85819	67612	155302	87089	68213	202382	117875	84508
8 Finance, insurance, real estate and business services [a]	213543	31462	182079	279676	42553	237126	297996	40509	257486	292427	47837	244590
9 Community, social and personal services	92154	26457	65695	129062	34594	94467	122772	34001	88770	140687	40775	99912
Total, Industries	1793779	814189	979589	2105868	930751	1175120	1963851	871724	1092127	2574984	1228930	1346056
Producers of Government Services	138927	46900	92027	171818	54364	117453	194230	60037	134193	225680	76673	149007
Other Producers	...	...	...	...	...	...	...	...	...	...	...	...
Total	1932706	861089	1071617	2277688	985115	1292573	2158082	931761	1226319	2800666	1305603	1495065
Less: Imputed bank service charge	...	-55852	55852	...	-81244	81244	...	-80778	80778	...	-47528	47528
Import duties	59789	...	59789	78293	...	78293	57268	...	57268	88142	...	88142
Value added tax	...	...	...	...	...	...	...	...	...	...	...	...
Total	1992495	916938	1075557	2355981	1066359	1289621	2215350	1012539	1202808	2888808	1353131	1535676

Chile

4.1 Derivation of Value Added by Kind of Activity, in Current Prices

Million Chilean pesos

	1984 Gross Output	1984 Intermediate Consumption	1984 Value Added	1985 Gross Output	1985 Intermediate Consumption	1985 Value Added
			All Producers			
1 Agriculture, hunting, forestry and fishing	252039	116062	135976	372577	167823	204754
2 Mining and quarrying	331689	171975	159713	550966	269496	281470
3 Manufacturing	1201259	764433	436825	1710916	1109268	601649
4 Electricity, gas and water	96744	43034	53710	140513	59735	80778
5 Construction	176169	96389	79779	269402	156471	112932
6 Wholesale and retail trade, restaurants and hotels	448254	167481	280773	668218	226844	441374
A Wholesale and retail trade	...	...	245473	...	...	385501
B Restaurants and hotels	...	...	35300	...	...	55873
7 Transport, storage and communication	260517	153196	107321	386752	237691	149061
8 Finance, insurance, real estate and business services [a]	323351	62292	261058	506360	88780	418080
9 Community, social and personal services	169628	52545	117082	226516	72675	153844
Total, Industries	3259650	1627407	1632237	4832720	2388783	2443942
Producers of Government Services	260599	89105	171493	340541	127666	212876
Other Producers	...	...	...	...	...	...
Total	3520249	1716512	1803730	5173261	2516449	2656817
Less: Imputed bank service charge	...	-41901	41901	...	-119130	119130
Import duties	140871	...	140871	203793	...	203793
Value added tax	...	...	...	...	...	...
Total	3661115	1758413	1902702	5377054	2635579	2741478

a) Beginning 1980, the estimates of private non-profit institutions are included in item 'Finance, insurance, real estate and business services'.

4.2 Derivation of Value Added by Kind of Activity, in Constant Prices

Million Chilean pesos

	1980 Gross Output	1980 Interm. Cons.	1980 Value Added	1981 Gross Output	1981 Interm. Cons.	1981 Value Added	1982 Gross Output	1982 Interm. Cons.	1982 Value Added	1983 Gross Output	1983 Interm. Cons.	1983 Value Added
					At constant prices of: 1977							
					All Producers							
1 Agriculture, hunting, forestry and fishing	46987	16956	30031	48351	17165	31186	47548	16587	30961	47143	16832	30312
2 Mining and quarrying	48335	22258	26077	52256	24172	28084	54314	24398	29916	53595	24304	29291
3 Manufacturing	214668	136336	78332	219820	139484	80336	177227	113726	63500	184446	118979	65467
A Manufacture of food, beverages and tobacco	...	...	26631	...	...	27251	...	...	25564	...	...	25792
B Textile, wearing apparel and leather industries	...	...	6880	...	...	6172	...	...	4165	...	...	4636
C Manufacture of wood and wood products, including furniture	...	...	4224	...	...	5061	...	...	2991	...	...	3091
D Manufacture of paper and paper products, printing and publishing	...	...	6877	...	...	7538	...	...	6860	...	...	7190
E Manufacture of chemicals and chemical petroleum, coal, rubber and plastic products	...	...	11946	...	...	12655	...	...	10202	...	...	10467
F Manufacture of non-metallic mineral products, except products of petroleum and coal	...	...	2882	...	...	3003	...	...	1527	...	...	2624
G Basic metal industries	...	...	3036	...	...	2885	...	...	2484	...	...	2985
H Manufacture of fabricated metal products, machinery and equipment	...	...	15001	...	...	14512	...	...	8480	...	...	7419
I Other manufacturing industries	...	...	854	...	...	1259	...	...	1228	...	...	1264
4 Electricity, gas and water	13399	5645	7754	13678	5765	7913	13687	5769	7918	14243	5996	8246

Chile

4.2 Derivation of Value Added by Kind of Activity, in Constant Prices
(Continued)

Million Chilean pesos

	1980 Gross Output	1980 Intermediate Consumption	1980 Value Added	1981 Gross Output	1981 Intermediate Consumption	1981 Value Added	1982 Gross Output	1982 Intermediate Consumption	1982 Value Added	1983 Gross Output	1983 Intermediate Consumption	1983 Value Added
					At constant prices of:1977							
5 Construction	37243	17823	19420	43792	20275	23518	34273	16292	17981	30390	14992	15398
6 Wholesale and retail trade, restaurants and hotels	101896	29999	71896	108574	31730	76844	88500	25903	62597	88041	25937	62103
A Wholesale and retail trade	...	...	...	...	...	...	...	...	58642	...	...	57975
B Restaurants and hotels	...	...	...	...	...	...	...	...	3955	...	...	4128
7 Transport, storage and communication	46136	25823	20313	47051	26360	20691	40660	22309	18351	38811	21049	17762
8 Finance, insurance, real estate and business services [a]	68186	12331	55855	75103	14003	61100	71850	11935	59914	55946	11280	44666
9 Community, social and personal services	28456	8312	20145	29462	8643	20820	25784	7424	18359	26021	7354	18668
Total, Industries	605306	275483	329823	638087	287597	350492	553843	244343	309497	538636	246723	291913
Producers of Government Services	46379	17164	29215	45265	16608	28656	44289	15967	28323	43628	14879	28749
Other Producers	...	...	...	...	...	...	...	...	...	...	...	...
Total	651687	292647	359038	683353	304205	379148	598131	260310	337820	582264	261602	320662
Less: Imputed bank service charge	...	-18889	18889	...	-24496	24496	...	-22550	22550	...	-10116	10116
Import duties	23850	...	23850	31959	...	31959	18809	...	18809	14170	...	14170
Value added tax	...	...	...	...	...	...	...	...	...	...	...	...
Total	675536	311538	363998	715312	328701	386611	616939	282861	334078	596435	271718	324717

	1984 Gross Output	1984 Intermediate Consumption	1984 Value Added	1985 Gross Output	1985 Intermediate Consumption	1985 Value Added
	At constant prices of:1977					
	All Producers					
1 Agriculture, hunting, forestry and fishing	50712	17685	33027	53924	18571	35354
2 Mining and quarrying	57035	26142	30894	59210	27311	31899
3 Manufacturing	199419	128130	71289	204268	131064	73204
A Manufacture of food, beverages and tobacco	...	...	27154	...	...	28032
B Textile, wearing apparel and leather industries	...	...	5431	...	...	5668
C Manufacture of wood and wood products, including furniture	...	...	3737	...	...	3836
D Manufacture of paper and paper products, printing and publishing	...	...	7399	...	...	7139
E Manufacture of chemicals and chemical petroleum, coal, rubber and plastic products	...	...	11140	...	...	11224
F Manufacture of non-metallic mineral products, except products of petroleum and coal	...	...	3369	...	...	3693
G Basic metal industries	...	...	3627	...	...	3549
H Manufacture of fabricated metal products, machinery and equipment	...	...	8135	...	...	9052
I Other manufacturing industries	...	...	1297	...	...	1012
4 Electricity, gas and water	15249	6416	8834	15828	6657	9171
5 Construction	31581	15838	15742	36788	18277	18510
6 Wholesale and retail trade, restaurants and hotels	91919	27397	64518	88202	26829	61371
A Wholesale and retail trade	...	...	59844	...	...	56262
B Restaurants and hotels	...	...	4676	...	...	5109
7 Transport, storage and communication	40487	21898	18590	41618	22058	19561
8 Finance, insurance, real estate and business services [a]	54841	11995	42845	63261	11896	51365
9 Community, social and personal services	28051	8015	20035	30131	8650	21479

Chile

4.2 Derivation of Value Added by Kind of Activity, in Constant Prices
(Continued)

Million Chilean pesos

	1984 Gross Output	1984 Intermediate Consumption	1984 Value Added	1985 Gross Output	1985 Intermediate Consumption	1985 Value Added
			At constant prices of: 1977			
Total, Industries	569294	263516	305774	593230	271313	321914
Producers of Government Services	42747	14220	28526	43962	14897	29065
Other Producers	...	...	...	...	...	...
Total	612039	277736	334302	637191	286210	350979
Less: Imputed bank service charge	...	-7652	7652	...	-15489	15489
Import duties	17179	...	17179	15106	...	15106
Value added tax	...	...	...	...	...	...
Total	629218	285389	343828	652297	301701	350596

a) Beginning 1980, the estimates of private non-profit institutions are included in item 'Finance, insurance, real estate and business services'.

4.3 Cost Components of Value Added

Million Chilean pesos

	1980 Compensation of Employees	1980 Capital Consumption	1980 Net Operating Surplus	1980 Indirect Taxes	1980 Less: Subsidies Received	1980 Value Added	1981 Compensation of Employees	1981 Capital Consumption	1981 Net Operating Surplus	1981 Indirect Taxes	1981 Less: Subsidies Received	1981 Value Added
					All Producers							
1 Agriculture, hunting, forestry and fishing	20071	11118	39115	7401	...	77706	24417	12086	38493	8373	...	83369
2 Mining and quarrying	31396	9191	56449	-5051	...	91985	36213	10480	29422	-4712	...	71403
3 Manufacturing	91068	21188	89298	28956	...	230510	109232	24375	108906	41727	...	284241
4 Electricity, gas and water	6948	8309	3452	4179	...	22888	8442	9324	6874	4308	...	28948
5 Construction	25440	1718	30133	-1529	...	55763	36475	2188	43639	-467	...	81836
6 Wholesale and retail trade, restaurants and hotels	46792	11797	120562	18851	...	198002	61333	13887	120011	30887	...	226118
7 Transport, storage and communication	26150	11236	9714	7861	...	54961	29395	13199	15706	9311	...	67612
8 Finance, insurance, real estate and business services a	33250	26618	115596	6615	...	182079	45036	31650	151359	9082	...	237126
9 Community, social and personal services	36938	2072	24158	2530	...	65695	50111	2973	37758	3626	...	94467
Total, Industries b	318053	103247	488477	69813	...	979590	400654	120162	552168	102135	...	1175120
Producers of Government Services	91763	153	-42	156	...	92027	116207	161	54	1031	...	117453
Other Producers	...	...	...	...	...	...	...	...	...	...	...	...
Total b	409816	103400	488435	69969	...	1071617	516861	120325	552222	103166	...	1292573
Less: Imputed bank service charge	...	...	55852	...	...	55852	...	...	81244	...	...	81244
Import duties	...	...	...	59789	...	59789	...	...	...	78293	...	78293
Value added tax	...	...	...	...	...	...	...	...	...	...	...	...
Total b	409816	103400	432582	129758	...	1075557	516861	120325	470976	181459	...	1289621

	1982 Compensation of Employees	1982 Capital Consumption	1982 Net Operating Surplus	1982 Indirect Taxes	1982 Less: Subsidies Received	1982 Value Added	1983 Compensation of Employees	1983 Capital Consumption	1983 Net Operating Surplus	1983 Indirect Taxes	1983 Less: Subsidies Received	1983 Value Added
					All Producers							
1 Agriculture, hunting, forestry and fishing	25963	12791	28911	7967	...	75633	26768	18078	38091	7474	...	90411
2 Mining and quarrying	35698	15659	46382	-4361	...	93379	45154	27063	96047	-10223	...	158040
3 Manufacturing	88216	20515	80682	44058	...	233471	120365	32645	126387	41088	...	320484
4 Electricity, gas and water	8793	12794	7809	6116	...	35511	10444	15572	12954	5642	...	44613
5 Construction	33257	2293	32623	910	...	69083	32996	3399	32826	-60	...	69161
6 Wholesale and retail trade, restaurants and hotels	56887	11792	72135	29771	...	170584	62612	16006	131694	24022	...	234334
7 Transport, storage and communication	31631	15325	11717	9539	...	68213	34634	20476	20669	8730	...	84508
8 Finance, insurance, real estate and business services a	46600	33940	167695	9251	...	257486	49383	41978	141432	11797	...	244590
9 Community, social and personal services	50051	3586	31221	3902	...	88760	58753	4696	32572	3890	...	99912

Chile

4.3 Cost Components of Value Added
(Continued)

Million Chilean pesos

	1982						1983					
	Compensation of Employees	Capital Consumption	Net Operating Surplus	Indirect Taxes	Less: Subsidies Received	Value Added	Compensation of Employees	Capital Consumption	Net Operating Surplus	Indirect Taxes	Less: Subsidies Received	Value Added
Total, Industries [b]	377096	128695	479175	107153	...	1092120	441109	179913	632672	92360	...	1346051
Producers of Government Services	132416	861	5	911	...	134193	147106	1010	-72	962	...	149008
Other Producers	...	...	...	...	...	...	...	...	...	...	...	...
Total [b]	509522	129554	479180	108064	...	1226313	588215	180922	632600	93322	...	1495059
Less: Imputed bank service charge	...	...	80778	...	...	80778	...	...	47528	...	...	47528
Import duties	...	...	...	57268	...	57268	...	...	...	88142	...	88142
Value added tax	...	...	...	...	...	...	...	...	...	...	...	...
Total [b]	509522	129554	398401	165331	...	1202808	588215	180922	585074	181465	...	1535676

	1984						1985					
	Compensation of Employees	Capital Consumption	Net Operating Surplus	Indirect Taxes	Less: Subsidies Received	Value Added	Compensation of Employees	Capital Consumption	Net Operating Surplus	Indirect Taxes	Less: Subsidies Received	Value Added

All Producers

1 Agriculture, hunting, forestry and fishing	34757	25297	64233	11689	...	135976	45689	39281	101394	18391	...	204754
2 Mining and quarrying	52697	37008	84978	-14969	...	159713	74261	60205	172827	-25823	...	281470
3 Manufacturing	145779	40673	203870	46503	...	436825	192501	56670	297204	55274	...	601649
4 Electricity, gas and water	12494	19470	16982	4764	...	53710	17642	26585	28878	7673	...	80778
5 Construction	37976	4535	37229	40	...	79779	49363	9101	53337	1132	...	112932
6 Wholesale and retail trade, restaurants and hotels	75186	19296	156195	30096	...	280773	93802	28182	275314	44077	...	441374
7 Transport, storage and communication	35424	24636	37158	10102	...	107321	48233	36731	53259	10839	...	149061
8 Finance, insurance, real estate and business services [a]	60231	48667	131151	21012	...	261061	80624	61580	247374	28507	...	418085
9 Community, social and personal services	71236	5443	35686	4719	...	117082	92460	8161	47171	6050	...	153844
Total, Industries [b]	525780	225025	767482	113956	...	1632240	694575	326496	1276758	146120	...	2443942
Producers of Government Services	169296	1107	-53	1143	...	171494	210372	1341	-209	1371	...	212876
Other Producers	...	...	...	...	...	...	...	...	...	...	...	...
Total [b]	695076	226132	767429	115099	...	1803734	904947	327832	1276549	147491	...	2656817
Less: Imputed bank service charge	...	...	41901	...	...	41901	...	...	119130	...	...	119130
Import duties	...	...	...	140871	...	140871	...	...	...	203793	...	203793
Value added tax	...	...	...	...	...	...	...	...	...	...	...	...
Total [b]	695075	226130	725528	255970	...	1902702	904947	327832	1157418	351281	...	2741478

a) Beginning 1980, the estimates of private non-profit institutions are included in item 'Finance, insurance, real estate and business services'.
b) Column 4 refers to indirect taxes less subsidies received.

China

Source. Communication from the State Statistical Bureau of the People's Republic of China, Beijing.

General note. The estimates shown in the following tables have been prepared in accordance with the System of Material Product Balances. Therefore, these estimates are not comparable in concept and coverage with those conforming to the United Nations System of National Accounts. In addition, the table 'Relations Among National Accounting Aggregates' in accordance with the United Nations System of National Accounts (SNA) so far as the existing data would permit is also shown.

1.12 Relations Among National Accounting Aggregates

Thousand Million Yuan Renminbi

	1970	1975	1980	1981	1982	1983	1984	1985	1986	1987	1988	1989
Gross Domestic Product	...	...	447.0	477.5	518.2	578.7	692.8	852.7	968.8	1130.7	1399.0	1579.4
Plus: Net factor income from the rest of the world	...	...	...	-0.2	1.1	2.2	3.4	3.0	0.9	-0.6	-0.6	-0.5
Equals: Gross National Product	...	...	447.0	477.3	519.3	580.9	696.2	855.8	969.6	1130.1	1398.4	1578.8
Less: Consumption of fixed capital	...	...	47.7	51.1	56.4	62.4	71.1	83.8	102.0	115.7	133.7	151.1
Equals: National Income	...	...	399.3	426.2	462.9	518.5	625.1	771.9	867.6	1014.4	1264.7	1427.8
Plus: Net current transfers from the rest of the world	...	...	...	...	0.1	0.1	0.1	0.1	0.1	0.1	0.2	0.1
Equals: National Disposable Income	...	...	...	...	463.0	518.6	625.2	772.0	867.7	1014.5	1264.9	1427.9
Less: Final consumption	...	...	...	...	...	...	...	...	...	...	...	...
Equals: Net Saving	...	...	...	...	...	...	...	...	...	...	...	...
Less: Surplus of the nation on current transactions	...	...	...	...	...	...	...	...	...	...	...	...
Equals: Net Capital Formation	...	...	...	...	...	...	...	...	...	...	...	...

1a Net Material Product by Use at Current Market Prices

Thousand Million Yuan Renminbi

	1970	1975	1980	1981	1982	1983	1984	1985	1986	1987	1988	1989
1 Personal consumption	...	...	...	...	...	...	...	...	...	...	...	...
2 Material consumption in the units of the non-material sphere serving individuals	...	...	...	...	...	...	...	...	...	...	...	...
Consumption of the Population	114.5	145.0	222.3	247.3	268.8	295.7	339.5	424.0	477.3	550.2	699.5	773.0
3 Material consumption in the units of the non-material sphere serving the community as a whole	11.3	17.1	30.8	32.6	36.6	40.1	51.0	63.9	77.9	88.4	104.3	117.3
4 Net fixed capital formation	41.9	64.8	89.3	77.8	96.9	112.5	145.3	188.3	219.6	271.8	336.0	295.3
5 Increase in material circulating assets and in stocks	19.9	18.2	27.2	32.8	26.7	29.6	34.3	74.5	74.8	58.0	87.1	172.1
6 Losses	...	...	...	...	...	...	...	...	...	...	...	...
7 Exports of goods and material services	7.5	17.5	27.1	36.8	41.4	43.8	58.1	80.9	108.2	147.0	176.7	195.6
8 Less: Imports of goods and material services	5.6	14.7	29.9	36.8	35.8	42.2	62.1	125.8	149.8	161.4	205.5	213.0
Statistical discrepancy	3.1	2.4	2.0	3.6	-8.8	-5.9	-0.9	-3.8	-22.1	-22.7	-24.3	-27.8
Net Material Product	192.6	250.3	368.8	394.1	425.8	473.6	565.2	702.0	785.9	931.3	1173.8	1312.5

2a Net Material Product by Kind of Activity of the Material Sphere in Current Market Prices

Thousand Million Yuan Renminbi

	1970	1975	1980	1981	1982	1983	1984	1985	1986	1987	1988	1989
1 Agriculture and forestry [a]	77.8	94.6	132.6	150.9	172.3	192.1	225.1	249.2	272.0	315.4	381.8	420.9
2 Industrial activity [a]	78.9	115.2	180.4	184.0	194.8	213.6	251.6	316.3	357.3	426.2	541.6	624.1
3 Construction	8.0	11.3	18.5	19.3	20.9	25.9	30.3	40.9	51.4	63.7	78.3	77.4
4 Wholesale and retail trade and restaurants and other eating and drinking places	20.5	19.6	24.7	26.8	23.1	25.4	37.7	69.7	73.2	87.6	126.1	138.8
5 Transport and communication	7.4	9.6	12.6	13.1	14.7	16.6	20.5	25.9	32.0	38.4	46.0	51.3
6 Other activities of the material sphere	...	...	...	...	...	...	...	...	...	...	...	...
Net material product	192.6	250.3	368.8	394.1	425.8	473.6	565.2	702.0	785.9	931.3	1173.8	1312.5

a) Beginning 1970, the output value of village industries are taken from 'Agriculture' and put into 'Industrial activity'.

6a Capital Formation by Kind of Activity of the Material and Non-Material Spheres in Current Market Prices

Thousand Million Yuan Renminbi

	1970	1975	1980	1981	1982	1983	1984	1985	1986	1987	1988	1989
					Gross Fixed Capital Formation							
1 Agriculture and forestry	...	3.8	5.2	2.9	3.4	3.5	3.7	3.7	3.7	4.2	4.6	5.1
2 Industrial activity	...	23.1	27.6	21.6	26.1	28.2	34.2	44.6	53.1	68.3	79.6	82.2
3 Construction	...	0.7	1.1	0.9	1.1	1.1	1.1	2.2	1.9	1.6	1.5	1.4
4 Wholesale and retail trade and restaurants and other eating and drinking places	...	1.2	2.9	2.8	3.6	2.9	3.5	7.2	6.9	7.8	5.1	4.5

China

6a Capital Formation by Kind of Activity of the Material and Non-Material Spheres in Current Market Prices
(Continued)

Thousand Million Yuan Renminbi

	1970	1975	1980	1981	1982	1983	1984	1985	1986	1987	1988	1989
5 Transport and communciation	...	6.9	6.2	4.0	5.7	7.8	10.8	17.1	18.1	19.0	20.8	16.7
6 Other activities of the material sphere	...	...	...	...	...	...	...	...	...	...	...	...
Total Material Sphere	...	...	...	...	...	...	...	...	...	...	...	...
7 Housing except owner-occupied, communal and miscellaneous personal services	...	...	...	...	...	...	...	...	...	...	...	...
8 Education, culture and art [a]	...	1.5	4.4	4.4	5.1	5.9	7.9	12.1	14.0	15.7	15.4	15.0
9 Health and social welfare services and sports	...											
Total Non-Material Sphere Serving Individuals	...	...	...	...	...	...	...	...	...	...	...	...
10 Government	...	...	...	...	...	...	...	...	...	...	...	...
11 Finance, credit and insurance	...	...	...	...	...	...	...	...	...	...	...	...
12 Research, scientific and technological institutes [a]	...	...	...	...	...	...	...	...	...	...	...	...
13 Other activities of the non-material sphere [b]	...	...	8.5	7.7	10.6	10.0	13.0	20.5	19.9	18.3	20.7	22.8
Total Non-Material Sphere Serving the Community as a Whole	...	...	...	...	...	...	...	...	...	...	...	...
14 Owner-occupied dwellings	...	...	...	...	...	...	...	...	...	...	...	...
Total Gross Fixed Capital Formation [c,d]	...	40.9	55.9	44.3	55.6	59.4	74.3	107.4	117.6	134.3	152.6	155.2

a) Scientific researches are included in item 'Education, culture and art'.
b) Item 'Other activities of the non-material sphere' refers to geological prospecting, civil public utilities and others.
c) Breakdown of activities refer to the material and non-material spheres.
d) Estimates in this table (Gross Fixed Capital Formation) not strictly comparable to those shown in table 1a. Gross fixed capital formation refers to construction investment of state-owned units.

Colombia

General note. The preparation of national accounts statistics in Colombia is undertaken by the Departamento Administrativo Nacional de Estadística (DANE), Bogota. Official estimates together with some methodological notes are published in 'Cuentas Nacionales de Colombia' (Revision 3). The estimates are generally in accordance with the classifications and definitions recommended in the United Nations System of Nationsl Accounts (SNA). The following tables have been prepared from successive replies to the United Nations National Accounts Questionnaire. When the scope and coverage of the estimates differ for conceptual or statistical reasons from the definitions and classifications recommended in SNA, a footnote is indicated to the relevant tables.

Sources and methods:

(a) Gross domestic product. Gross domestic product is estimated mainly through the production approach.

(b) Expenditure on the gross domestic product. The expenditure approach is used to estimate government final consumption expenditure, exports and imports of goods and services, part of increase in stocks and gross fixed capital formation in construction. For other gross fixed capital formation, the commodity-flow approach is used. Private final consumption expenditure and part of increase in stocks are obtained as a residual. The estimates of government final consumption expenditures are based on official sources such as Informe Financiero de la Contraloria General de la Republica. The estimates of private consumption expenditure are obtained as a residual except for the bench-mark year 1970 which were based on results from the family budget survey conducted that year. The estimates for changes in stocks are based on information obtained from various sources such as manufacturing surveys, commercial census, and the Federacion Nacional de Cafeteros. For gross fixed capital formation, the c.i.f. values of imported capital goods in the foreign trade statistics are adjusted to include customs duties, other taxes and transport and insurance costs. Adjustments are also made for trade margins and installation costs on goods passing through trade channels. For domestic production, estimates are based on manufacturing surveys. Estimates of capital formation in construction are obtained as by-product in the calculation of the construction sector's contribution to GDP whereas investments in the government sector is obtained from the government accounts. The estimates of exports and imports of goods are derived from foreign trade statistics while that of services are derived from the balance of payments. For the constant price estimates, current values of government expenditure and gross fixed capital formation estimates are deflated by appropriate price indexes. Estimates of private consumption expenditure at constant prices are obtained as a residual. No specific information is available for the remaining expenditure items.

(c) Cost-structure of the gross domestic product. The estimates of compensation of employees are obtained in the process of estimating value added by industrial origin. The estimates are obtained from the statistical surveys held in 1970 and from accounting data. In the case of agriculture, hunting, forestry and fishing, the estimates are based on projections from census data on employment and statistics of average wages and salaries. Depreciation of assets owned by general government are not included in the estimates. Operating surplus is obtained as a residual and no information is available for the estimates of consumption of fixed capital and of net indirect taxes.

(d) Gross domestic product by kind of economic activity. The table of gross domestic product by kind of economic activity is prepared at market prices, i.e. producers' values. The production approach is used to estimate value added of almost all industries. The income approach is used to estimate the value added of producers of government services and some private services, while the expenditure approach is used for ownership of dwellings. Gross output of the trade sector is estimated by the commodity-flow approach. For agriculture, the gross value of production is obtained by multiplying the output of each commodity by the price paid to producers. The production and price data are derived from agricultural sample surveys and from various concerned institutions. The Federacion Nacional de Cafeteros supplies information on data for coffee. For livestock, the estimates are based on statistics of government controlled slaughterings and net exports with rough estimates made for uncontrolled slaughterings. Data for the petroleum industry are obtained directly from the oil companies. Information on the output and value of minerals is available from censuses of mines and concerned institutions. For manufacturing, results of surveys carried out by the Departamento Administrativo Nacional de Estadistica are used. The estimates are projected by applying volume and price indexes to both output and input. The basic data for electricity, gas and water are obtained from concerned enterprises and surveys. Coefficients calculated from these surveys are used to estimate value added of plants not covered. For urban construction, estimates are derived from building permits issued while rural construction estimates are based on an estimation of economic life of existing constructions and on demographic data. Estimates of public construction are obtained from the government records. For the trade sector, value added is based on estimates of the flow of goods through trade channels. The gross margins are based on data provided by the Banco de la Republica or recalculated from the Commercial Census 1967. The mark-ups are kept constant over the period of analysis. For transport, estimates are based on indormation provided by the Banco de la Republica. Data to measure the contribution of the communication sector are obtained by direct inquiries. Estimates for the financial institutions are obtained directly from the enterprises concerned through the Superintendencia Bancaria. The contribution of the government sector is measured by the wages and salaries paid to employees. Value added of other private services is estimated by the Banco de la Republica using the results of the Census of services in 1970. Constant input-output ratios have been assumed. For the constant price estimates, value added of the majority of industries is extrapolated by quantity index for output. For ownership of dwellings and producers of government services, value added is deflated by an index of rents and an index of wages and salaries, respectively.

1.1 Expenditure on the Gross Domestic Product, in Current Prices

Million Colombian pesos

		1970	1975	1980	1981	1982	1983	1984	1985	1986	1987	1988	1989
1	Government final consumption expenditure	12284	36176	159371	206874	272766	334565	425631	531264	665814	868383	1182370	1572541
2	Private final consumption expenditure	95973	293239	1104816	1430105	1810438	2208216	2734007	3445593	4479169	5919495	7713527	9931380
3	Gross capital formation	26862	68838	301117	408927	511625	607566	731400	945549	1221911	1764660	2579693	3106637
	A Increase in stocks	2943	6709	36223	58879	75534	82719	76941	75083	17797	227425	292008	213037
	B Gross fixed capital formation	23919	62129	264894	350048	436091	524847	654459	870466	1204114	1537235	2287685	2893598
	Residential buildings	4056	8876	35695	45556	57619	79970	97862	121966	167269	244850	309806	394069
	Non-residential buildings	757	2243	9146	9416	13002	14927	12803	20792	32869	64128	97654	122027
	Other construction and land improvement etc.	8700	22810	98223	140156	177276	210710	279827	426715	547195	507534	857660	1117566
	Other	10406	28200	121830	154920	188194	219240	263967	300993	456781	720723	1022565	1259936
4	Exports of goods and services	18644	68730	274637	257482	299444	339988	485649	717413	1365264	1588458	2058766	2883375
5	Less: Imports of goods and services	20995	61875	260811	320615	396975	436198	520103	673936	944202	1316588	1803008	2304341
	Equals: Gross Domestic Product	132768	405108	1579130	1982773	2497298	3054137	3856584	4965883	6787956	8824408	11731348	15189592

1.2 Expenditure on the Gross Domestic Product, in Constant Prices

Million Colombian pesos

		1970	1975	1980	1981	1982	1983	1984	1985	1986	1987	1988	1989
		\multicolumn{12}{c}{At constant prices of: 1975}
1	Government final consumption expenditure	27310	36176	54364	56387	59006	58652	61070	63818	64711	68330	75061	78083
2	Private final consumption expenditure [a]	224576	292779	384698	395910	401759	403572	415128	422917	436600	453079	470019	480221
3	Gross capital formation	63148	68838	103358	117037	123279	120628	113521	102574	107038	116901	126264	118670
	A Increase in stocks	9947	6709	15337	23498	26972	23184	14865	9069	6388	15430	13762	7191
	B Gross fixed capital formation	53201	62129	88021	93539	96307	97444	98656	93505	100650	101471	112502	111479

Colombia

1.2 Expenditure on the Gross Domestic Product, in Constant Prices
(Continued)

Million Colombian pesos

	1970	1975	1980	1981	1982	1983	1984	1985	1986	1987	1988	1989
	\multicolumn{12}{c}{At constant prices of:1975}
Residential buildings	9043	8876	10788	11479	11886	14224	14327	14848	15931	17247	16705	16613
Non-residential buildings	2122	2243	2414	2071	2340	2312	1632	2203	2723	3927	4579	4474
Other construction and land improvement etc.	18461	22810	29496	32472	33599	33478	36300	38214	39682	30753	37407	37655
Other	23575	28200	45323	47517	48482	47430	46397	38240	42314	49544	53811	52737
4 Exports of goods and services	46034	64077	84450	74457	73297	72643	80129	91629	110601	119215	119514	130410
5 Less: Imports of goods and services	53572	56762	101105	106055	114505	104115	99993	93377	97169	102361	109067	103561
Equals: Gross Domestic Product	307496	405108	525765	537736	542836	551380	569855	587561	621781	655164	681791	703823

a) Item 'Private final consumption expenditure' excludes direct purchases abroad by resident households and direct purchases in the domestic market by non-resident households.

1.3 Cost Components of the Gross Domestic Product

Million Colombian pesos

	1970	1975	1980	1981	1982	1983	1984	1985	1986	1987	1988	1989
1 Indirect taxes, net	9914	31683	158384	167417	214529	253669	360710	516778	798587	1033014	1254445	1610053
A Indirect taxes	11396	35676	172044	186704	236779	279363	394501	551948	837793	1076166	1313527	1673272
B Less: Subsidies	1482	3993	13660	19287	22250	25694	33791	35170	39206	43152	59082	63219
2 Consumption of fixed capital a	...	...	...	...	...	...	...	...	...	...	...	...
3 Compensation of employees paid by resident producers to:	51814	153222	656984	848495	1076969	1339956	1672852	2017258	2575310	3351499	4465880	5788432
A Resident households	51666	152891	656417	847242	1075390	1336148	1666480	2004593	2559536	3329421	4454930	5773206
B Rest of the world	148	331	567	1253	1579	3808	6372	12665	15774	22078	10950	15226
4 Operating surplus a	71040	220203	763762	966861	1205800	1460512	1823022	2431847	3414059	4439895	6011023	7791107
Equals: Gross Domestic Product	132768	405108	1579130	1982773	2497298	3054137	3856584	4965883	6787956	8824408	11731348	15189592

a) Item 'Operating surplus' includes consumption of fixed capital.

1.4 General Government Current Receipts and Disbursements

Million Colombian pesos

	1970	1975	1980	1981	1982	1983	1984	1985	1986	1987	1988	1989
	\multicolumn{12}{c}{Receipts}
1 Operating surplus	-1119	-3361	-14163	-15663	-20567	-26065	-18412	-17318	2781	-209224	-54327	...
2 Property and entrepreneurial income	924	2839	14943	18607	24027	30964	39633	56914	79543	128976	178495	...
3 Taxes, fees and contributions	20760	65260	265749	314868	392041	457044	623682	852669	1250379	1655777	2164498	...
A Indirect taxes	11396	35676	172044	186704	236779	279363	394501	551948	837793	1076166	1313527	...
B Direct taxes	6304	20341	50946	69646	82674	83889	106469	142593	203690	302782	496122	...
C Social security contributions	2516	8538	39361	54795	68116	88792	114331	145887	192759	256870	336218	...
D Compulsory fees, fines and penalties	544	705	3398	3723	4472	5000	8381	12241	16137	19959	18631	...
4 Other current transfers	3026	11104	57549	77744	101364	131704	170419	199539	281226	370135	498076	...
Total Current Receipts of General Government	23591	75842	324078	395556	496865	593647	815322	1091804	1613929	1945664	2786742	...
	\multicolumn{12}{c}{Disbursements}
1 Government final consumption expenditure	12284	36176	159371	206874	272766	334565	425631	531264	665814	868383	1182370	...
2 Property income	953	3361	13612	21837	31907	39175	54281	62636	96753	128972	192577	...
3 Subsidies	1482	3993	13660	19287	22250	25694	33791	35170	39206	43152	59082	...
4 Other current transfers	5119	17400	88006	122351	160727	214884	276678	331262	459873	607321	810301	...
A Social security benefits	984	2856	16696	24457	32860	44364	59930	79734	105084	140904	190698	...
B Social assistance grants a	970	3071	12244	18347	25418	35398	43868	48424	68248	86889	110999	...
C Other	3165	11473	59066	79547	102449	135122	172880	203104	286541	379528	508604	...
5 Net saving	3753	14912	49429	25207	9215	-20671	24941	131472	352283	297836	542412	...
Total Current Disbursements and Net Saving of General Government	23591	75842	324078	395556	496865	593647	815322	1091804	1613929	1945664	2786742	...

a) Item 'Social assistance grants' refers to health only.

Colombia

1.5 Current Income and Outlay of Corporate and Quasi-Corporate Enterprises, Summary

Million Colombian pesos

	1970	1975	1980	1981	1982	1983	1984	1985	1986	1987	1988	1989
Receipts												
1 Operating surplus	21217	65579	240597	305740	379951	457160	578952	837314	1278072	1859877	2436005	3256104
2 Property and entrepreneurial income received	7227	30284	158459	233278	284202	338596	426352	551801	692410	902188	1336476	1922807
3 Current transfers	1114	4661	21208	29900	40288	47815	63616	78718	101036	143002	237660	347474
Total Current Receipts	29558	100524	420264	568918	704441	843571	1068920	1467833	2071518	2905067	4010141	5526385
Disbursements												
1 Property and entrepreneurial income	16080	62423	247684	345511	449921	529713	675602	924108	1221183	1600255	2147630	3128710
2 Direct taxes and other current payments to general government	3382	10593	31712	39858	46970	55649	69630	90859	134379	202596	370018	472871
3 Other current transfers	1605	5520	23057	32964	43577	51588	70422	89779	119942	170438	292679	389050
4 Net saving	8491	21988	117811	150585	163973	206621	253266	363087	596014	931778	1199814	1535754
Total Current Disbursements and Net Saving	29558	100524	420264	568918	704441	843571	1068920	1467833	2071518	2905067	4010141	5526385

1.6 Current Income and Outlay of Households and Non-Profit Institutions

Million Colombian pesos

	1970	1975	1980	1981	1982	1983	1984	1985	1986	1987	1988	1989
Receipts												
1 Compensation of employees	51858	153365	657977	849257	1078009	1337317	1668850	2007439	2562683	3332987	4459926	5779633
2 Operating surplus of private unincorporated enterprises	50942	157985	537328	676784	846416	1029417	1262482	1611851	2133206	2789242	3629345	4601256
3 Property and entrepreneurial income	7304	30686	104895	135027	182657	204274	241200	309749	413354	516481	690366	953509
4 Current transfers	4381	13872	66652	97850	123360	159035	220957	304231	476641	682972	886035	1207070
A Social security benefits	2227	6888	31603	46616	63733	85507	110356	138744	186078	248231	330963	481832
B Social assistance grants												
C Other	2154	6984	35049	51234	59627	73528	110601	165487	290563	434741	555072	725238
Total Current Receipts	114485	355908	1366852	1758918	2230442	2730043	3393489	4233270	5585884	7321682	9665672	12541466
Disbursements												
1 Private final consumption expenditure	95973	293239	1104816	1430105	1810438	2208216	2734007	3445593	4479169	5919495	7713527	9931380
2 Property income	1901	6256	29294	42736	60867	78432	101683	127681	156547	229375	342994	489644
3 Direct taxes and other current transfers n.e.c. to general government	5982	18991	61993	88306	108292	122032	159551	209862	278207	377015	480953	660341
A Social security contributions	2516	8538	39361	54795	68116	88792	114331	145887	192759	256870	336218	471050
B Direct taxes	3118	10002	20450	31175	37555	30289	40330	56379	76234	108686	134144	172676
C Fees, fines and penalties	348	451	2182	2336	2621	2951	4890	7596	9214	11459	10591	16615
4 Other current transfers	1193	5181	28767	38288	47439	59150	78603	97412	127177	175522	230511	332406
5 Net saving	9436	32241	141982	159483	203406	262213	319645	352722	544784	620275	897687	1127695
Total Current Disbursements and Net Saving	114485	355908	1366852	1758918	2230442	2730043	3393489	4233270	5585884	7321682	9665672	12541466

1.7 External Transactions on Current Account, Summary

Million Colombian pesos

	1970	1975	1980	1981	1982	1983	1984	1985	1986	1987	1988	1989
Payments to the Rest of the World												
1 Imports of goods and services	20995	61875	260811	320615	396975	436198	520103	673936	944202	1316588	1803008	2304341
2 Factor income to the rest of the world	4056	10529	35696	59690	85202	99406	144656	225702	335779	481120	564654	849918
A Compensation of employees	148	331	567	1253	1579	3808	6372	12665	15774	22078	10950	15226
B Property and entrepreneurial income	3908	10198	35129	58437	83623	95598	138284	213037	320005	459042	553704	834692
3 Current transfers to the rest of the world	628	1183	2222	2097	5300	1770	2590	4127	3691	5071	9005	9947
4 Surplus of the nation on current transactions	-5182	303	8105	-73652	-135031	-159403	-133548	-98268	271170	85229	60220	227795
Payments to the Rest of the World and Surplus of the Nation on Current Transactions	20497	73890	306834	308750	352446	377971	533801	805497	1554842	1888008	2436887	3392001

Colombia

1.7 External Transactions on Current Account, Summary
(Continued)

Million Colombian pesos

	1970	1975	1980	1981	1982	1983	1984	1985	1986	1987	1988	1989
					Receipts From The Rest of the World							
1 Exports of goods and services	18644	68730	274637	257482	299444	339988	485649	717413	1365264	1588458	2058766	2883375
2 Factor income from rest of the world	621	2441	24396	37280	34433	23281	16273	19922	33976	51651	80836	115535
A. Compensation of employees	192	474	1560	2015	2619	1169	2370	2846	3147	3566	4996	6427
B Property and entrepreneurial income	429	1967	22836	35265	31814	22112	13903	17076	30829	48085	75840	109108
3 Current transfers from rest of the world	1232	2719	7801	13988	18569	14702	31879	68162	155602	247899	297285	393091
Receipts from the Rest of the World on Current Transactions	20497	73890	306834	308750	352446	377971	533801	805497	1554842	1888008	2436887	3392001

1.8 Capital Transactions of The Nation, Summary

Million Colombian pesos

	1970	1975	1980	1981	1982	1983	1984	1985	1986	1987	1988	1989
					Finance of Gross Capital Formation							
Gross saving	21680	69141	309222	335275	376594	448163	597852	847281	1493081	1849889	2639913	3334432
1 Consumption of fixed capital	...	...	...	...	...	...	...	...	...	...	...	...
2 Net saving [a]	21680	69141	309222	335275	376594	448163	597852	847281	1493081	1849889	2639913	3334432
A General government	3753	14912	49429	25207	9215	-20671	24941	131472	352283	297836	542412	670983
B Corporate and quasi-corporate enterprises	8491	21988	117811	150585	163973	206621	253266	363087	596014	931778	1199814	1535754
C Other	9436	32241	141982	159483	203406	262213	319645	352722	544784	620275	897687	1127695
Less: Surplus of the nation on current transactions	-5182	303	8105	-73652	-135031	-159403	-133548	-98268	271170	85229	60220	227795
Finance of Gross Capital Formation	26862	68838	301117	408927	511625	607566	731400	945549	1221911	1764660	2579693	3106637
					Gross Capital Formation							
Increase in stocks	2943	6709	36223	58879	75534	82719	76941	75083	17797	227425	292008	213039
Gross fixed capital formation	23919	62129	264894	350048	436091	524847	654459	870466	1204114	1537235	2287685	2893598
1 General government	4212	10499	59219	81395	94111	113263	132789	136813	202928	279582	420716	543018
2 Corporate and quasi-corporate enterprises	14294	34121	139389	185608	238685	280819	369700	563183	746501	875451	1360135	1719172
3 Other	5413	17509	66286	83045	103295	130765	151970	170470	254685	382202	506834	631408
Gross Capital Formation	26862	68838	301117	408927	511625	607566	731400	945549	1221911	1764660	2579693	3106637

a) Item 'Net saving' includes consumption of fixed capital.

1.10 Gross Domestic Product by Kind of Activity, in Current Prices

Million Colombian pesos

	1970	1975	1980	1981	1982	1983	1984	1985	1986	1987	1988	1989
1 Agriculture, hunting, forestry and fishing	33308	96766	305718	381639	468621	571548	671390	843738	1186326	1594018	1964918	2454427
2 Mining and quarrying	2595	6937	36127	48820	64538	88646	127337	207074	331834	577797	722193	1132478
3 Manufacturing	27433	94086	367460	422615	529922	640794	852716	1062045	1525714	1792906	2482111	3128373
4 Electricity, gas and water	1402	3807	20716	33235	48006	62932	82784	106839	151327	200970	270592	371223
5 Construction	5267	13535	74526	102130	128767	169700	219951	342422	446597	494644	775750	999889
6 Wholesale and retail trade, restaurants and hotels	16580	54663	209553	269371	340848	413726	534613	698236	921231	1240291	1683524	2161596
7 Transport, storage and communication	11532	34117	140533	169787	207926	254255	317870	404730	527112	712573	969475	1266421
8 Finance, insurance, real estate and business services	18319	56570	216566	286042	364013	439148	503912	608309	766339	985367	1322970	1722045
9 Community, social and personal services	7042	19238	82942	110180	141090	177804	216151	255986	331969	431003	554909	744200
Total, Industries	123478	379719	1454141	1823819	2293731	2818553	3526724	4529379	6188449	8029569	10746442	13980652
Producers of Government Services	9650	28300	121461	162127	212620	266749	349012	424076	547273	713742	932252	1241160
Other Producers	...	...	...	...	...	...	...	...	...	...	...	...
Subtotal	133128	408019	1575602	1985946	2506351	3085302	3875736	4953455	6735722	8743311	11678694	15221812
Less: Imputed bank service charge	3450	11240	40189	58607	78757	105404	103850	118728	155853	226720	368615	540685
Plus: Import duties	3090	8329	43717	55434	69704	74239	84698	131156	208087	307817	421269	508465
Plus: Value added tax	...	...	...	...	...	...	...	...	...	...	...	...
Equals: Gross Domestic Product	132768	405108	1579130	1982773	2497298	3054137	3856584	4965883	6787956	8824408	11731348	15189592

Colombia

1.11 Gross Domestic Product by Kind of Activity, in Constant Prices

Million Colombian pesos

	1970	1975	1980	1981	1982	1983	1984	1985	1986	1987	1988	1989
					At constant prices of:1975							
1 Agriculture, hunting, forestry and fishing	77893	96766	119314	123135	120803	124196	126375	128456	132792	141270	145182	151746
2 Mining and quarrying	8192	6937	6661	7020	7143	8156	9948	13730	22262	27624	28876	32602
3 Manufacturing	65783	94086	117672	114556	112906	114197	121035	124610	132021	140229	142887	147056
4 Electricity, gas and water	2253	3807	5210	5381	5554	5640	5930	6111	6478	7056	7429	7892
5 Construction	10647	13535	17632	18884	19648	22193	23606	25641	26890	24191	27382	27487
6 Wholesale and retail trade, restaurants and hotels	38321	53767	66681	67789	68886	68598	69984	71239	73800	77059	80928	81845
7 Transport, storage and communication	23853	34117	48944	50945	53586	53131	54486	55044	55569	57426	59396	61555
8 Finance, insurance, real estate and business services	43802	56570	73463	78191	80641	84284	81764	83299	86953	91560	98816	103869
9 Community, social and personal services	13920	20134	25811	26646	27326	27945	28214	28324	29410	30950	31518	32189
Total, Industries	284664	379719	481388	492547	496493	508340	521342	536454	566175	597365	622414	646241
Producers of Government Services	21243	28300	40840	43211	44249	43371	47242	49272	52290	55989	59905	62175
Other Producers	...	...	...	...	...	...	...	...	...	...	...	...
Subtotal	305907	408019	522228	535758	540742	551711	568584	585726	618461	653354	682319	708416
Less: Imputed bank service charge	8585	11240	14095	16643	18391	19071	15503	14409	14380	16708	20584	24042
Plus: Import duties	10174	8329	17632	18621	20485	18740	16774	16244	17696	18518	20056	19449
Plus: Value added tax	...	...	...	...	...	...	...	...	...	...	...	...
Equals: Gross Domestic Product	307496	405108	525765	537736	542836	551380	569855	587561	621781	655164	681791	703823

1.12 Relations Among National Accounting Aggregates

Million Colombian pesos

	1970	1975	1980	1981	1982	1983	1984	1985	1986	1987	1988	1989
Gross Domestic Product	132768	405108	1579130	1982773	2497298	3054137	3856584	4965883	6787956	8824408	11731348	15189592
Plus: Net factor income from the rest of the world	-3435	-8088	-11300	-22410	-50769	-76125	-128383	-205780	-301803	-429469	-483818	-734383
Factor income from the rest of the world	621	2441	24396	37280	34433	23281	16273	19922	33976	51651	80836	115535
Less: Factor income to the rest of the world	4056	10529	35696	59690	85202	99406	144656	225702	335779	481120	564654	849918
Equals: Gross National Product	129333	397020	1567830	1960363	2446529	2978012	3728201	4760103	6486153	8394939	11247530	14455209
Less: Consumption of fixed capital	...	...	...	...	...	...	...	...	...	...	...	...
Equals: National Income [a]	129333	397020	1567830	1960363	2446529	2978012	3728201	4760103	6486153	8394939	11247530	14455209
Plus: Net current transfers from the rest of the world	604	1536	5579	11891	13269	12932	29289	64035	151911	242828	288280	383144
Current transfers from the rest of the world	1232	2719	7801	13988	18569	14702	31879	68162	155602	247899	297285	393091
Less: Current transfers to the rest of the world	628	1183	2222	2097	5300	1770	2590	4127	3691	5071	9005	9947
Equals: National Disposable Income [b]	129937	398556	1573409	1972254	2459798	2990944	3757490	4824138	6638064	8637767	11535810	14838353
Less: Final consumption	108257	329415	1264187	1636979	2083204	2542781	3159638	3976857	5144983	6787878	8895897	11503921
Equals: Net Saving [c]	21680	69141	309222	335275	376594	448163	597852	847281	1493081	1849889	2639913	3334432
Less: Surplus of the nation on current transactions	-5182	303	8105	-73652	-135031	-159403	-133548	-98268	271170	85229	60220	227795
Equals: Net Capital Formation [d]	26862	68838	301117	408927	511625	607566	731400	945549	1221911	1764660	2579693	3106637

a) Item 'National income' includes consumption of fixed capital.
b) Item 'National disposable income' includes consumption of fixed capital.
c) Item 'Net saving' includes consumption of fixed capital.
d) Item 'Net capital formation' includes consumption of fixed capital.

2.1 Government Final Consumption Expenditure by Function, in Current Prices

Million Colombian pesos

	1970	1975	1980	1981	1982	1983	1984	1985	1986	1987	1988	1989
1 General public services	3681	10733	44344	60705	79788	104278	132433	166107	207161	267555	354711	...
2 Defence	1736	3854	16614	19060	24438	36105	43597	61574	73822	99066	150136	...
3 Public order and safety	...	...	...	...	...	...	...	...	...	...	...	...
4 Education	3099	11558	42555	56317	76273	91368	127906	151915	197219	256184	332570	...
5 Health	1016	2758	14103	18068	22638	31101	31086	51851	62259	83983	113203	...
6 Social security and welfare	468	2029	11694	16344	21717	21046	29359	33334	37157	48191	69336	...
7 Housing and community amenities	218	377	1212	1374	1969	1137	1534	2139	3798	5865	7415	...
8 Recreational, cultural and religious affairs	78	298	1216	1718	2170	2993	3770	5252	6707	6629	10418	...
9 Economic services	1965	4457	27471	33006	41848	44323	52205	57715	76928	98954	141675	...
10 Other functions	23	112	162	282	1925	2214	3741	1377	763	1956	2906	...
Total Government Final Consumption Expenditure	12284	36176	159371	206874	272766	334565	425631	531264	665814	868383	1182370	...

Colombia

2.3 Total Government Outlays by Function and Type

Million Colombian pesos

		Final Consumption Expenditures Total	Compensation of Employees	Other	Subsidies	Other Current Transfers & Property Income	Total Current Disbursements	Gross Capital Formation	Other Capital Outlays	Total Outlays
						1980				
1	General public services	44344	35678	8666	22	1209	45575	6134	243	51952
2	Defence	16614	9974	6640	...	12	16626	301	3	16930
3	Public order and safety	...	...	...	...	...	...	...	...	...
4	Education	42555	39789	2766	735	607	43897	5344	33	49274
5	Health	14103	9120	4983	192	448	14743	2162	20	16925
6	Social security and welfare	11694	16721	-5027	5	30597	42296	6943	110	49349
7	Housing and community amenities	1212	805	407	1545	183	2940	2575	61	5576
8	Recreation, culture and religion	1216	866	350	65	247	1528	1335	27	2890
9	Economic services	27471	21942	5529	11096	3843	42410	30451	3787	76648
10	Other functions	162	...	162	...	9673	9835	...	...	9835
	Total	159371	134895	24476	13660	46819	219850	55245	4284	279379
						1981				
1	General public services	60705	50550	10155	89	1588	62382	7861	70	70313
2	Defence	19060	13330	5730	40	9	19109	1149	...	20258
3	Public order and safety	...	...	...	...	...	...	...	...	...
4	Education	56317	52649	3668	991	823	58131	5330	33	63494
5	Health	18068	12094	5974	322	375	18765	3095	8	21868
6	Social security and welfare	16344	22576	-6232	...	45274	61618	8383	210	70211
7	Housing and community amenities	1374	984	390	1514	324	3212	2164	51	5427
8	Recreation, culture and religion	1718	1179	539	168	313	2199	839	9	3047
9	Economic services	33006	25834	7172	16163	5398	54567	61840	11992	128399
10	Other functions	282	...	282	...	14170	14452	...	...	14452
	Total	206874	179196	27678	19287	68274	294435	90661	12373	397469
						1982				
1	General public services	79788	66022	13766	32	3149	82969	8638	149	91756
2	Defence	24438	17153	7285	...	112	24550	11	...	24561
3	Public order and safety	...	...	...	...	...	...	...	...	...
4	Education	76273	71378	4895	1287	1292	78852	5597	284	84733
5	Health	22638	15512	7126	154	669	23461	5095	41	28597
6	Social security and welfare	21717	30792	-9075	2	35601	57320	7803	254	65377
7	Housing and community amenities	1969	1631	338	2166	900	5035	3574	205	8814
8	Recreation, culture and religion	2170	1718	452	208	228	2606	1255	109	3970
9	Economic services	41848	33885	7963	18401	7085	67334	70555	9317	147206
10	Other functions	1925	...	1925	...	20840	22765	...	1	22766
	Total	272766	238091	34675	22250	69876	364892	102528	10360	477780
						1983				
1	General public services	104278	90076	14202	446	4406	109130	10540	206	119876
2	Defence	36105	24116	11989	...	51	36156	82	...	36238
3	Public order and safety	...	...	...	...	...	...	...	...	...
4	Education	91368	83236	8132	1039	1905	94312	8541	177	103030
5	Health	31101	21457	9644	33	446	31580	6333	2	37915
6	Social security and welfare	21046	37364	-16318	12	48313	69371	7235	57	76663
7	Housing and community amenities	1137	924	213	3270	178	4585	4986	1511	11082
8	Recreation, culture and religion	2993	2433	560	160	525	3678	1834	147	5659
9	Economic services	44323	42210	2113	20734	12865	77922	91115	11417	180454
10	Other functions	2214	...	2214	...	20973	23187	23	...	23210
	Total	334565	301816	32749	25694	89662	449921	130689	13517	594127

Colombia

2.3 Total Government Outlays by Function and Type
(Continued)

Million Colombian pesos

		Final Consumption Expenditures Total	Compensation of Employees	Other	Subsidies	Other Current Transfers & Property Income	Total Current Disbursements	Gross Capital Formation	Other Capital Outlays	Total Outlays
					1984					
1	General public services	132433	115860	16573	528	5694	138655	10536	473	149664
2	Defence	43597	29296	14301	-	31	43628	418	4	44050
3	Public order and safety	...	...	...	...	...	...	...	...	...
4	Education	127906	120204	7702	1063	1354	130323	9402	328	140053
5	Health	31086	21333	9753	212	661	31959	6875	71	38905
6	Social security and welfare	29359	49966	-20607	2	64411	93772	9915	75	103762
7	Housing and community amenities	1534	1257	277	3722	158	5414	3473	1052	9939
8	Recreation, culture and religion	3770	3087	683	68	631	4469	2549	220	7238
9	Economic services	52205	52570	-365	28196	17683	98084	87668	16297	202049
10	Other functions	3741	-	3741	-	29894	33635	-	-	33635
	Total	425631	393573	32058	33791	120517	579939	130836	18520	729295
					1985					
1	General public services	166107	138820	27287	204	9976	176287	12225	417	188929
2	Defence	61574	34111	27463	-	15	61589	292	1100	62981
3	Public order and safety	...	...	...	...	...	...	...	...	...
4	Education	151915	141394	10521	3700	2253	157868	14384	43	172295
5	Health	51851	34663	17188	416	684	52951	8766	104	61821
6	Social security and welfare	33334	58839	-25505	8	80751	114093	8366	84	122543
7	Housing and community amenities	2139	1732	407	1242	1118	4499	4539	925	9963
8	Recreation, culture and religion	5252	3818	1434	49	996	6297	3253	64	9614
9	Economic services	57715	63018	-5303	29551	23766	111032	78523	73844	263399
10	Other functions	1377	-	1377	-	34440	35817	126	-	35943
	Total	531264	476395	54869	35170	153999	720433	130474	76581	927488
					1986					
1	General public services	207161	179530	27631	268	14553	221982	23972	789	246743
2	Defence	73822	48461	25361	-	10	73832	1018	27	74877
3	Public order and safety	...	...	...	...	...	...	...	...	...
4	Education	197219	182057	15162	3952	3659	204830	18137	100	223067
5	Health	62259	41756	20503	79	2186	64524	10440	88	75052
6	Social security and welfare	37157	75107	-37950	147	106880	144184	15730	1593	161507
7	Housing and community amenities	3798	2594	1204	1608	430	5836	10815	2996	19647
8	Recreation, culture and religion	6707	4534	2173	513	782	8002	5014	130	13146
9	Economic services	76928	79837	-2909	32639	28788	138355	67989	26969	233313
10	Other functions	763	1	762	-	67207	67970	-	-	67970
	Total	665814	613877	51937	39206	224495	929515	153115	32692	1115322
					1987					
1	General public services	267555	226938	40617	27	22649	290231	26836	3546	320613
2	Defence	99066	63891	35175	-	25	99091	93	-	99184
3	Public order and safety	...	...	...	...	...	...	...	...	...
4	Education	256184	240008	16176	994	4444	261622	21873	583	284078
5	Health	83983	56892	27091	63	4038	88084	14223	223	102530
6	Social security and welfare	48191	97612	-49421	-	144990	193181	23335	1242	217758
7	Housing and community amenities	5865	4230	1635	604	396	6865	14140	907	21912
8	Recreation, culture and religion	6629	5969	660	659	2279	9567	4568	317	14452
9	Economic services	98954	103554	-4600	40805	40120	179879	161814	36831	378524
10	Other functions	1956	2	1954	-	84010	85966	275	180	86421
	Total	868383	799096	69287	43152	302951	1214486	267157	43829	1525472

Colombia

2.3 Total Government Outlays by Function and Type
(Continued)

Million Colombian pesos

		Final Consumption Expenditures		Subsidies	Other Current Transfers & Property Income	Total Current Disbursements	Gross Capital Formation	Other Capital Outlays	Total Outlays
		Total	Compensation of Employees	Other						

		Total	Comp. of Employees	Other	Subsidies	Other Current Transfers & Property Income	Total Current Disbursements	Gross Capital Formation	Other Capital Outlays	Total Outlays
	1988									
1	General public services	354711	292765	61946	58	32953	387722	44662	4227	436611
2	Defence	150136	83562	66574	-	21	150157	37	-	150194
3	Public order and safety	...	...	...	...	...	...	...	...	...
4	Education	332570	310303	22267	631	7715	340916	32086	348	373350
5	Health	113203	75260	37943	318	3841	117362	18015	142	135519
6	Social security and welfare	69336	126569	-57233	-	196774	266110	38034	1254	305398
7	Housing and community amenities	7415	6163	1252	2896	1521	11832	17912	200	29944
8	Recreation, culture and religion	10418	8084	2334	771	2055	13244	12640	1243	27127
9	Economic services	141675	141081	594	54408	54289	250372	274648	51262	576282
10	Other functions	2906	4	2902	-	122432	125338	105	-	125443
	Total	1182370	1043791	138579	59082	421601	1663053	438139	58676	2159868

2.5 Private Final Consumption Expenditure by Type and Purpose, in Current Prices

Million Colombian pesos

	1970	1975	1980	1981	1982	1983	1984	1985	1986	1987	1988	1989

Final Consumption Expenditure of Resident Households

	1970	1975	1980	1981	1982	1983	1984	1985	1986	1987	1988	1989
1 Food, beverages and tobacco	37976	120530	420313	537345	682012	813594	990210	1277061	1649754	2102010	2701902	3411174
A Food	32044	103779	353089	452377	578524	684545	831702	1064966	1371057	1739148	2251116	2821269
B Non-alcoholic beverages	745	2388	12821	15542	19004	24166	27054	34885	46567	67864	84335	108257
C Alcoholic beverages	3288	9776	41435	52997	64978	79053	99537	134988	183107	238843	295675	383818
D Tobacco	1899	4587	12968	16429	19506	25830	31917	42222	49023	56155	70776	97830
2 Clothing and footwear	7968	24412	76332	97332	113933	132277	178408	219183	272447	364368	489015	595330
3 Gross rent, fuel and power	12583	35123	138709	183551	238329	289727	352586	425307	527949	653873	817352	1047234
A Fuel and power	1016	2993	15085	21216	30928	40475	54403	70603	98463	125732	166835	225172
B Other	11567	32130	123624	162335	207401	249252	298183	354704	429486	528141	650517	822062
4 Furniture, furnishings and household equipment and operation	6105	16801	62046	78602	97623	116217	149048	191057	253653	348805	489601	630160
A Household operation	2120	7025	28064	37254	46594	56660	74075	100156	135406	182684	253316	331957
B Other	3985	9776	33982	41348	51029	59557	74973	90901	118247	166121	236285	298203
5 Medical care and health expenses	5298	13581	60935	85156	105883	131931	163852	203686	280243	376744	485657	656777
6 Transport and communication	10444	34677	159617	204626	259932	312050	394037	483357	636561	883337	1210306	1552079
A Personal transport equipment	3344	10794	58824	75084	93805	103912	127497	153568	199568	281390	384135	477959
B Other	7100	23883	100793	129542	166127	208138	266540	329789	436993	601947	826171	1074120
7 Recreational, entertainment, education and cultural services	5259	15598	58208	76287	96577	122566	150309	190997	258113	351194	454024	615500
A Education	1500	4260	15994	21122	27624	36629	42633	56190	71510	93922	122345	170248
B Other	3759	11338	42214	55165	68953	85937	107676	134807	186603	257272	331679	445252
8 Miscellaneous goods and services	9694	32057	132676	174797	225455	278573	343439	434737	556953	755076	1036411	1354073
A Personal care	705	2743	10283	13508	16806	20287	25788	36878	47374	61328	86873	114499
B Expenditures in restaurants, cafes and hotels	7088	24034	100907	133140	172787	212528	259059	317088	404986	549367	735603	954812
C Other	1901	5280	21486	28149	35862	45758	58592	80771	104593	144381	213935	284762
Total Final Consumption Expenditure in the Domestic Market by Households, of which	95327	292779	1108836	1437696	1819744	2196935	2721889	3425385	4435673	5835407	7684268	9862327
Plus: Direct purchases abroad by resident households	1671	5113	14514	14908	17612	31821	39420	51943	130096	176838	177438	241057
Less: Direct purchases in the domestic market by non-resident households	1025	4653	18534	22499	26918	20540	27302	31735	86600	92750	148179	172004
Equals: Final Consumption Expenditure of Resident Households a)	95973	293239	1104816	1430105	1810438	2208216	2734007	3445593	4479169	5919495	7713527	9931380

Final Consumption Expenditure of Private Non-profit Institutions Serving Households

	1970	1975	1980	1981	1982	1983	1984	1985	1986	1987	1988	1989
Equals: Final Consumption Expenditure of Private Non-profit Organisations Serving Households	...	...	...	...	...	...	...	...	...	...	...	...
Private Final Consumption Expenditure	95973	293239	1104816	1430105	1810438	2208216	2734007	3445593	4479169	5919495	7713527	9931380

a) Item 'Final consumption expenditure of resident households' includes consumption expenditure of private non-profit institutions serving households.

Colombia

2.6 Private Final Consumption Expenditure by Type and Purpose, in Constant Prices

Million Colombian pesos

	1970	1975	1980	1981	1982	1983	1984	1985	1986	1987	1988	1989
	\multicolumn{12}{c}{At constant prices of:1975}

Final Consumption Expenditure of Resident Households

	1970	1975	1980	1981	1982	1983	1984	1985	1986	1987	1988	1989
1 Food, beverages and tobacco	97675	120530	156402	160268	161321	161241	164559	169747	174805	178345	186048	192269
A Food	83373	103779	134192	137884	139354	138878	142072	146134	150794	153633	162177	168691
B Non-alcoholic beverages	1702	2388	3820	3736	3755	3871	3534	3655	3908	4365	4382	4323
C Alcoholic beverages	7511	9776	13452	13684	13397	13575	13860	14585	15207	15808	15473	15263
D Tobacco	5089	4587	4938	4964	4815	4917	5093	5373	4896	4539	4016	3992
2 Clothing and footwear	18666	24412	27635	28365	26513	26512	27143	26376	26993	27727	28344	27276
3 Gross rent, fuel and power	28827	35123	43790	45320	47038	48835	50642	52452	54351	56858	58833	60823
A Fuel and power	2017	2993	4060	4181	4567	4755	5043	5298	5510	5843	6080	6402
B Other	26810	32130	39730	41139	42471	44080	45599	47154	48841	51015	52753	54421
4 Furniture, furnishings and household equipment and operation	12324	16801	22589	22410	22537	22827	23250	22871	23819	25219	26774	26696
A Household operation	4268	7025	10285	10545	10824	10972	11094	11225	11952	12349	13193	13215
B Other	8056	9776	12304	11865	11713	11855	12156	11646	11867	12870	13581	13481
5 Medical care and health expenses	11344	13581	19670	21087	21358	21164	21854	22729	23309	25421	25312	25865
6 Transport and communication	22486	34677	50594	52635	56061	54536	55613	55245	56257	58491	61012	62362
A Personal transport equipment	7530	10794	16046	15855	16752	15167	15424	14784	15074	16774	17821	17213
B Other	14956	23883	34548	36780	39309	39369	40189	40461	41183	41717	43191	45149
7 Recreational, entertainment, education and cultural services	11853	15598	20835	21367	21724	22233	25318	24851	26787	28947	29338	30446
A Education	3380	4260	6006	6156	6227	6456	6026	6268	6692	7119	7486	7729
B Other	8473	11338	14829	15211	15497	15777	19292	18583	20095	21828	21852	22717
8 Miscellaneous goods and services	21401	32057	43183	44458	45627	46224	46749	48646	50279	52071	54358	54484
A Personal care	1403	2743	4155	4155	4196	4326	4081	4705	5032	5137	5470	5470
B Expenditures in restaurants, cafes and hotels	15984	24034	31522	32468	33442	33442	33944	34623	35662	36732	37828	37828
C Other	4014	5280	7506	7835	7989	8456	8724	9318	9585	10202	11060	11060
Total Final Consumption Expenditure in the Domestic Market by Households, of which	224576	292779	384698	395910	402179	403572	415128	422917	436600	453079	470019	480221
Plus: Direct purchases abroad by resident households	4629	5113	5958	5171	5316	8193	8201	7798	15528	15882	11905	12093
Less: Direct purchases in the domestic market by non-resident households	2676	4653	6117	7129	7240	4670	4773	4241	7490	7393	9269	8273
Equals: Final Consumption Expenditure of Resident Households a	226529	293239	384539	393952	400255	407095	418556	426474	444638	461568	472655	484041

Final Consumption Expenditure of Private Non-profit Institutions Serving Households

	1970	1975	1980	1981	1982	1983	1984	1985	1986	1987	1988	1989
Equals: Final Consumption Expenditure of Private Non-profit Organisations Serving Households	...	...	...	...	...	...	...	...	...	...	...	...
Private Final Consumption Expenditure	226529	293239	384539	393952	400255	407095	418556	426474	444638	461568	472655	484041

a) Item 'Final consumption expenditure of resident households' includes consumption expenditure of private non-profit institutions serving households.

4.1 Derivation of Value Added by Kind of Activity, in Current Prices

Million Colombian pesos

	1980			1981			1982			1983		
	Gross Output	Intermediate Consumption	Value Added	Gross Output	Intermediate Consumption	Value Added	Gross Output	Intermediate Consumption	Value Added	Gross Output	Intermediate Consumption	Value Added
	\multicolumn{12}{c}{All Producers}
1 Agriculture, hunting, forestry and fishing	375552	69834	305718	470801	89162	381639	577738	109117	468621	701413	129865	571548
A Agriculture and hunting a	361411	68887	292524	452720	87960	364760	553008	107621	445387	670896	128072	542824
B Forestry and logging	7408	327	7081	9057	376	8681	12334	489	11845	14644	587	14057
C Fishing a	6733	620	6113	9024	826	8198	12396	1007	11389	15873	1206	14667
2 Mining and quarrying	49387	13260	36127	66515	17695	48820	87933	23395	64538	120016	31370	88646

Colombia

4.1 Derivation of Value Added by Kind of Activity, in Current Prices
(Continued)

Million Colombian pesos

	1980 Gross Output	1980 Intermediate Consumption	1980 Value Added	1981 Gross Output	1981 Intermediate Consumption	1981 Value Added	1982 Gross Output	1982 Intermediate Consumption	1982 Value Added	1983 Gross Output	1983 Intermediate Consumption	1983 Value Added
3 Manufacturing	959202	591742	367460	1140193	717578	422615	1401854	871932	529922	1680559	1039765	640794
A Manufacture of food, beverages and tobacco	459452	290670	168782	516261	347771	168490	652783	430912	221871	784486	514344	270142
B Textile, wearing apparel and leather industries	105392	60446	44946	122309	69044	53265	140920	77737	63183	156127	86777	69350
C Manufacture of wood and wood products, including furniture	12787	6533	6254	14749	7445	7304	20366	10304	10062	24039	12293	11746
D Manufacture of paper and paper products, printing and publishing	46011	28919	17092	56101	36010	20091	72861	45364	27497	88225	53886	34339
E Manufacture of chemicals and chemical petroleum, coal, rubber and plastic products	175617	111820	63797	239058	146537	92521	288743	180634	108109	355760	220869	134891
F Manufacture of non-metallic mineral products, except products of petroleum and coal	33882	16105	17777	43281	21015	22266	56617	27226	29391	67334	32821	34513
G Basic metal industries	...	...	...	...	...	...	...	...	...	...	...	...
H Manufacture of fabricated metal products, machinery and equipment	116595	72955	43640	136535	84572	51963	153086	92297	60789	184684	110139	74545
I Other manufacturing industries	9466	4294	5172	11899	5184	6715	16478	7458	9020	19904	8636	11268
4 Electricity, gas and water	33461	12745	20716	50342	17107	33235	69608	21602	48006	89065	26133	62932
5 Construction	134171	59645	74526	183026	80896	102130	234302	105535	128767	294610	124910	169700
6 Wholesale and retail trade, restaurants and hotels [b]	231121	78187	152934	289695	97113	192582	355749	115788	239961	420943	133508	287435
A Wholesale and retail trade	231121	78187	152934	289695	97113	192582	355749	115788	239961	420943	133508	287435
B Restaurants and hotels	...	...	...	...	...	...	...	...	...	...	...	...
7 Transport, storage and communication	222734	82201	140533	277936	108149	169787	342627	134701	207926	412897	158642	254255
A Transport and storage	201686	75477	126209	249710	98783	150927	304511	122034	182477	362940	143149	219791
B Communication	21048	6724	14324	28226	9366	18860	38116	12667	25449	49957	15493	34464
8 Finance, insurance, real estate and business services	252234	35668	216566	333932	47890	286042	426294	62281	364013	515426	76278	439148
A Financial institutions [c]	134912	28586	106326	181393	38609	142784	231691	50252	181439	282996	61871	221125
B Insurance												
C Real estate and business services [c]	117322	7082	110240	152539	9281	143258	194603	12029	182574	232430	14407	218023
Real estate, except dwellings	...	...	...	...	...	...	...	...	...	...	...	...
Dwellings	117322	7082	110240	152539	9281	143258	194603	12029	182574	232430	14407	218023
9 Community, social and personal services [b]	197706	58145	139561	261545	74576	186969	336717	94740	241977	419765	115670	304095
A Sanitary and similar services	...	...	...	...	...	...	...	...	...	...	...	...
B Social and related community services	...	...	...	...	...	...	...	...	...	...	...	...
C Recreational and cultural services	...	...	...	...	...	...	...	...	...	...	...	...
D Personal and household services	197706	58145	139561	261545	74576	186969	336717	94740	241977	419765	115670	304095
Total, Industries	2455568	1001427	1454141	3073985	1250166	1823819	3832822	1539091	2293731	4654694	1836141	2818553
Producers of Government Services	166254	44793	121461	216877	54750	162127	285086	72466	212620	349758	83009	266749
Other Producers	...	...	...	...	...	...	...	...	...	...	...	...
Total	2621822	1046220	1575602	3290862	1304916	1985946	4117908	1611557	2506351	5004452	1919150	3085302
Less: Imputed bank service charge	...	-40189	40189	...	-58607	58607	...	-78757	78757	...	-105404	105404
Import duties	43717	...	43717	55434	...	55434	69704	...	69704	74239	...	74239
Value added tax	...	...	...	...	...	...	...	...	...	...	...	...
Total	2665539	1086409	1579130	3346296	1363523	1982773	4187612	1690314	2497298	5078691	2024554	3054137

	1984 Gross Output	1984 Intermediate Consumption	1984 Value Added	1985 Gross Output	1985 Intermediate Consumption	1985 Value Added	1986 Gross Output	1986 Intermediate Consumption	1986 Value Added	1987 Gross Output	1987 Intermediate Consumption	1987 Value Added
						All Producers						
1 Agriculture, hunting, forestry and fishing	837743	166353	671390	1063476	219738	843738	1472924	286598	1186326	1982515	388497	1594018
A Agriculture and hunting [a]	797539	164053	633486	1013564	216748	796816	1410742	282678	1128064	1900026	383277	1516749
B Forestry and logging	19386	745	18641	23845	987	22858	28297	1195	27102	37337	1590	35747
C Fishing [a]	20818	1555	19263	26067	2003	24064	33885	2725	31160	45152	3630	41522
2 Mining and quarrying	170222	42885	127337	270304	63230	207074	408166	76332	331834	707295	129498	577797

Colombia

4.1 Derivation of Value Added by Kind of Activity, in Current Prices
(Continued)

Million Colombian pesos

	1984 Gross Output	1984 Intermediate Consumption	1984 Value Added	1985 Gross Output	1985 Intermediate Consumption	1985 Value Added	1986 Gross Output	1986 Intermediate Consumption	1986 Value Added	1987 Gross Output	1987 Intermediate Consumption	1987 Value Added
3 Manufacturing	2195717	1343001	852716	2834983	1772938	1062045	3991715	2466001	1525714	5061796	3268890	1792906
A Manufacture of food, beverages and tobacco	1002047	638878	363169	1319252	837994	481258	1962396	1214875	747521	2130052	1475067	654985
B Textile, wearing apparel and leather industries	209654	114491	95163	270220	148968	121252	359691	202526	157165	492117	277439	214678
C Manufacture of wood and wood products, including furniture	32850	16292	16558	41655	20877	20778	56703	28352	28351	80244	39956	40288
D Manufacture of paper and paper products, printing and publishing	115126	72187	42939	151882	95214	56668	205962	127847	78115	278769	172191	106578
E Manufacture of chemicals and chemical petroleum, coal, rubber and plastic products	468010	291544	176466	602977	416693	186284	772551	527049	245502	1137458	771026	366432
F Manufacture of non-metallic mineral products, except products of petroleum and coal	86089	41772	44317	105336	51402	53934	150448	75481	74967	213994	104492	109502
G Basic metal industries	...	...	...	...	...	...	...	...	...	...	...	...
H Manufacture of fabricated metal products, machinery and equipment	254111	155971	98140	304760	185283	119477	436787	269334	167453	667676	401519	266157
I Other manufacturing industries	27830	11866	15964	38901	16507	22394	47177	20537	26640	61486	27200	34286
4 Electricity, gas and water	116342	33558	82784	149472	42633	106839	209829	58502	151327	278937	77967	200970
5 Construction	384616	164665	219951	567257	224835	342422	743941	297344	446597	814854	320210	494644
6 Wholesale and retail trade, restaurants and hotels [b]	543595	161579	382016	722200	206804	515396	964585	269331	695254	1280420	346669	933751
A Wholesale and retail trade	543595	161579	382016	722200	206804	515396	964585	269331	695254	1280420	346669	933751
B Restaurants and hotels	...	...	...	...	...	...	...	...	...	...	...	...
7 Transport, storage and communication	513401	195531	317870	646251	241521	404730	838576	311464	527112	1126340	413767	712573
A Transport and storage	445139	174773	270366	557980	214912	343068	717922	275512	442410	977281	368695	608586
B Communication	68262	20758	47504	88271	26609	61662	120654	35952	84702	149059	45072	103987
8 Finance, insurance, real estate and business services	591503	87591	503912	717852	109543	608309	916377	150039	766339	1180842	195475	985367
A Financial institutions [c]	313479	69566	243913	388532	86690	301842	519594	120116	399478	696026	159076	536950
B Insurance												
C Real estate and business services [c]	278024	18025	259999	329320	22853	306467	396783	29922	366861	484816	36399	448417
Real estate, except dwellings	...	...	...	...	...	...	...	...	...	...	...	...
Dwellings	278024	18025	259999	329320	22853	306467	396783	29922	366861	484816	36399	448417
9 Community, social and personal services [b]	511262	142514	368748	615366	176540	438826	796302	238356	557946	1054121	316578	737543
A Sanitary and similar services	...	...	...	...	...	...	...	...	...	...	...	...
B Social and related community services	...	...	...	...	...	...	...	...	...	...	...	...
C Recreational and cultural services	...	...	...	...	...	...	...	...	...	...	...	...
D Personal and household services	511262	142514	368748	615366	176540	438826	796302	238356	557946	1054121	316578	737543
Total, Industries	5864401	2337677	3526724	7587161	3057782	4529379	342415	4153966	6188449	3487120	5457551	8029569
Producers of Government Services	444006	94994	349012	556630	132554	424076	699210	151937	547273	918278	204536	713742
Other Producers	...	...	...	...	...	...	...	...	...	...	...	...
Total	6308407	2432671	3875736	8143791	3190336	4953455	1041625	4305903	6735722	4405398	5662087	8743311
Less: Imputed bank service charge	...	-103850	103850	...	-118728	118728	...	-155853	155853	...	-226720	226720
Import duties	84698	...	84698	131156	...	131156	208087	...	208087	307817	...	307817
Value added tax												
Total	6393105	2536521	3856584	8274947	3309067	4965883	1249712	4461756	6787956	4713215	5888807	8824408

	1988 Gross Output	1988 Intermediate Consumption	1988 Value Added	1989 Gross Output	1989 Intermediate Consumption	1989 Value Added
All Producers							
1 Agriculture, hunting, forestry and fishing	2483752	518834	1964918	3116367	661940	2454427
A Agriculture and hunting [a]	2377999	512067	1865932	2980266	653117	2327149
B Forestry and logging	51108	2064	49044	66132	2734	63398
C Fishing [a]	54645	4703	49942	69969	6089	63880
2 Mining and quarrying	898370	176177	722193	1371617	239139	1132478

Colombia

4.1 Derivation of Value Added by Kind of Activity, in Current Prices
(Continued)

Million Colombian pesos

		1988			1989		
		Gross Output	Intermediate Consumption	Value Added	Gross Output	Intermediate Consumption	Value Added
3	Manufacturing	6808624	4326513	2482111	8756618	5628245	3128373
	A Manufacture of food, beverages and tobacco	2769030	1826598	942432	3544824	2404063	1140761
	B Textile, wearing apparel and leather industries	707568	385749	321819	952205	517261	434944
	C Manufacture of wood and wood products, including furniture	116077	56586	59491	148586	74045	74541
	D Manufacture of paper and paper products, printing and publishing	377324	240458	136866	493876	314496	179380
	E Manufacture of chemicals and chemical petroleum, coal, rubber and plastic products	1459690	1037380	422310	1899494	1352047	547447
	F Manufacture of non-metallic mineral products, except products of petroleum and coal	300804	147523	153281	396972	192371	204601
	G Basic metal industries	...	...	...	...	...	...
	H Manufacture of fabricated metal products, machinery and equipment	989280	593942	395338	1200322	723050	477272
	I Other manufacturing industries	88851	38277	50574	120339	50912	69427
4	Electricity, gas and water	375040	104448	270592	512866	141643	371223
5	Construction	1265403	489653	775750	1632062	632173	999889
6	Wholesale and retail trade, restaurants and hotels [b]	1741848	468889	1272959	2220707	598945	1621762
	A Wholesale and retail trade	1741848	468889	1272959	2220707	598945	1621762
	B Restaurants and hotels	...	...	...	...	...	...
7	Transport, storage and communication	1515619	546144	969475	1976797	710376	1266421
	A Transport and storage	1299455	481818	817637	1675053	621285	1053768
	B Communication	216164	64326	151838	301744	89091	212653
8	Finance, insurance, real estate and business services	1603266	280296	1322970	2095771	373726	1722045
	A Financial institutions [c]	1011773	231654	780119	1353499	312317	1041182
	B Insurance						
	C Real estate and business services [c]	591493	48642	542851	742272	61409	680863
	Real estate, except dwellings	...	...	...	...	...	...
	Dwellings	591493	48642	542851	742272	61409	680863
9	Community, social and personal services [b]	1380281	414807	965474	1824257	540223	1284034
	A Sanitary and similar services	...	...	...	...	...	...
	B Social and related community services	...	...	...	...	...	...
	C Recreational and cultural services	...	...	...	...	...	...
	D Personal and household services	1380281	414807	965474	1824257	540223	1284034
Total, Industries		18072203	7325761	10746442	23507062	9526410	13980652
Producers of Government Services		1248828	316576	932252	1660683	419523	1241160
Other Producers		...	...	...	...	...	...
Total		19321031	7642337	11678694	25167745	9945933	15221812
Less: Imputed bank service charge		...	-368615	368615	...	-540685	540685
Import duties		421269	...	421269	508465	...	508465
Value added tax		...	...	...	...	...	...
Total		19742300	8010952	11731348	25676210	10486618	15189592

a) Hunting is included in item 'Fishing'.
b) Restaurants and hotels are included in item 'Community, social and personal services'.
c) Business services are included in the financial institutions.

Colombia

4.2 Derivation of Value Added by Kind of Activity, in Constant Prices

Million Colombian pesos

	1980 Gross Output	1980 Intermediate Consumption	1980 Value Added	1981 Gross Output	1981 Intermediate Consumption	1981 Value Added	1982 Gross Output	1982 Intermediate Consumption	1982 Value Added	1983 Gross Output	1983 Intermediate Consumption	1983 Value Added
						At constant prices of:1975 — All Producers						
1 Agriculture, hunting, forestry and fishing	145051	25737	119314	149490	26355	123135	147402	26599	120803	151164	26968	124196
A Agriculture and hunting [a]	140256	25407	114849	144661	26016	118645	142401	26252	116149	146053	26615	119438
B Forestry and logging	2366	109	2257	2229	103	2126	2417	112	2305	2473	114	2359
C Fishing [a]	2429	221	2208	2600	236	2364	2584	235	2349	2638	239	2399
2 Mining and quarrying	10803	4142	6661	11359	4339	7020	11788	4645	7143	13454	5298	8156
3 Manufacturing	329176	211504	117672	322240	207684	114556	317113	204207	112906	316911	202714	114197
A Manufacture of food, beverages and tobacco	153624	104423	49201	150449	103254	47195	150962	103325	47637	151576	102842	48734
B Textile, wearing apparel and leather industries	39800	23488	16312	38748	22777	15971	35593	20670	14923	33534	19464	14070
C Manufacture of wood and wood products, including furniture	4371	2038	2333	3899	1812	2087	3924	1824	2100	4029	1863	2166
D Manufacture of paper and paper products, printing and publishing	18890	11221	7669	18972	11229	7743	18902	11213	7689	18652	11005	7647
E Manufacture of chemicals and chemical petroleum, coal, rubber and plastic products	55717	37135	18582	56368	37318	19050	55911	37210	18701	57588	38051	19537
F Manufacture of non-metallic mineral products, except products of petroleum and coal	10621	4597	6024	10305	4444	5861	10441	4503	5938	10797	4633	6164
G Basic metal industries	...	...	...	...	...	...	...	...	...	...	...	...
H Manufacture of fabricated metal products, machinery and equipment	42880	26934	15946	40324	25238	15086	37780	23634	14146	37254	23097	14157
I Other manufacturing industries	3273	1668	1605	3175	1612	1563	3600	1828	1772	3481	1759	1722
4 Electricity, gas and water	8672	3462	5210	8935	3554	5381	9223	3669	5554	9335	3695	5640
5 Construction	39964	22332	17632	42606	23722	18884	44703	25055	19648	47806	25613	22193
6 Wholesale and retail trade, restaurants and hotels [b]	76857	23866	52991	77672	24032	53640	78442	24270	54172	77637	23872	53765
A Wholesale and retail trade	76857	23866	52991	77672	24032	53640	78442	24270	54172	77637	23872	53765
B Restaurants and hotels	...	...	...	...	...	...	...	...	...	...	...	...
7 Transport, storage and communication	72307	23363	48944	75060	24115	50945	78760	25174	53586	78054	24923	53131
A Transport and storage	62957	20883	42074	64611	21354	43257	67115	22095	45020	66190	21802	44388
B Communication	9350	2480	6870	10449	2761	7688	11645	3079	8566	11864	3121	8743
8 Finance, insurance, real estate and business services	87075	13612	73463	92825	14634	78191	95804	15163	80641	100065	15781	84284
A Financial institutions [c]	48813	10902	37911	53186	11836	41350	54857	12228	42629	57521	12755	44766
B Insurance												
C Real estate and business services [c]	38262	2710	35552	39639	2798	36841	40947	2935	38012	42544	3026	39518
Real estate, except dwellings	...	...	...	...	...	...	...	...	...	...	...	...
Dwellings	38262	2710	35552	39639	2798	36841	40947	2935	38012	42544	3026	39518
9 Community, social and personal services [b]	62497	22996	39501	64414	23619	40795	66070	24030	42040	67041	24263	42778
A Sanitary and similar services	...	...	...	...	...	...	...	...	...	...	...	...
B Social and related community services	...	...	...	...	...	...	...	...	...	...	...	...
C Recreational and cultural services	...	...	...	...	...	...	...	...	...	...	...	...
D Personal and household services	62497	22996	39501	64414	23619	40795	66070	24030	42040	67041	24263	42778
Total, Industries	832402	351014	481388	844601	352054	492547	849305	352812	496493	861467	353127	508340
Producers of Government Services	56706	15866	40840	59098	15887	43211	61330	17081	44249	61021	17650	43371
Other Producers	...	...	...	...	...	...	...	...	...	...	...	...
Total	889108	366880	522228	903699	367941	535758	910635	369893	540742	922488	370777	551711
Less: Imputed bank service charge	...	-14095	14095	...	-16643	16643	...	-18391	18391	...	-19071	19071
Import duties	17632	...	17632	18621	...	18621	20485	...	20485	18740	...	18740
Value added tax	...	...	...	...	...	...	...	...	...	...	...	...
Total	906740	380975	525765	922320	384584	537736	931120	388284	542836	941228	389848	551380

Colombia

4.2 Derivation of Value Added by Kind of Activity, in Constant Prices

Million Colombian pesos

	1984 Gross Output	1984 Intermediate Consumption	1984 Value Added	1985 Gross Output	1985 Intermediate Consumption	1985 Value Added	1986 Gross Output	1986 Intermediate Consumption	1986 Value Added	1987 Gross Output	1987 Intermediate Consumption	1987 Value Added
	At constant prices of: 1975											
	All Producers											
1 Agriculture, hunting, forestry and fishing	153966	27591	126375	156113	27657	128456	161687	28895	132792	171895	30625	141270
A Agriculture and hunting [a]	148583	27209	121374	150616	27270	123346	155972	28488	127484	165808	30196	135612
B Forestry and logging	2597	126	2471	2662	128	2534	2651	127	2524	2916	139	2777
C Fishing [a]	2786	256	2530	2835	259	2576	3064	280	2784	3171	290	2881
2 Mining and quarrying	16432	6484	9948	22566	8836	13730	32380	10118	22262	40388	12764	27624
3 Manufacturing	336758	215723	121035	343770	219160	124610	363574	231553	132021	382239	242010	140229
A Manufacture of food, beverages and tobacco	157902	107167	50735	164180	110975	53205	170938	115453	55485	169259	114402	54857
B Textile, wearing apparel and leather industries	35970	20972	14998	35877	20708	15169	38403	22300	16103	40020	23161	16859
C Manufacture of wood and wood products, including furniture	4234	1966	2268	4420	2036	2384	4999	2331	2668	5497	2542	2955
D Manufacture of paper and paper products, printing and publishing	20377	12037	8340	21208	12470	8738	22435	13261	9174	24603	14440	10163
E Manufacture of chemicals and chemical petroleum, coal, rubber and plastic products	60887	40381	20506	65099	42866	22233	68961	45240	23721	77563	50320	27243
F Manufacture of non-metallic mineral products, except products of petroleum and coal	11149	4816	6333	11459	4912	6547	13057	5609	7448	14243	6124	8119
G Basic metal industries	...	...	...	...	...	...	...	...	...	...	...	...
H Manufacture of fabricated metal products, machinery and equipment	42463	26469	15994	37569	23201	14368	40835	25342	15493	46978	28955	18023
I Other manufacturing industries	3776	1915	1861	3958	1992	1966	3946	2017	1929	4076	2066	2010
4 Electricity, gas and water	9839	3909	5930	10056	3945	6111	10657	4179	6478	11544	4488	7056
5 Construction	51049	27443	23606	54813	29172	25641	57800	30910	26890	51546	27355	24191
6 Wholesale and retail trade, restaurants and hotels [b]	79555	24521	55034	80331	24521	55810	83875	25745	58130	87610	26691	60919
A Wholesale and retail trade	79555	24521	55034	80331	24521	55810	83875	25745	58130	87610	26691	60919
B Restaurants and hotels	...	...	...	...	...	...	...	...	...	...	...	...
7 Transport, storage and communication	80076	25590	54486	80449	25405	55044	81369	25800	55569	83850	26424	57426
A Transport and storage	66792	22081	44711	66805	21828	44977	67561	22168	45393	70300	22892	47408
B Communication	13284	3509	9775	13644	3577	10067	13808	3632	10176	13550	3532	10018
8 Finance, insurance, real estate and business services	96635	14871	81764	98163	14864	83299	102620	15667	86953	107822	16262	91560
A Financial institutions [c]	52602	11727	40875	52589	11635	40954	55438	12319	43119	58564	12776	45788
B Insurance												
C Real estate and business services [c]	44033	3144	40889	45574	3229	42345	47182	3348	43834	49258	3486	45772
Real estate, except dwellings	...	...	...	...	...	...	...	...	...	...	...	...
Dwellings	44033	3144	40889	45574	3229	42345	47182	3348	43834	49258	3486	45772
9 Community, social and personal services [b]	67807	26463	41344	68398	24645	43753	70910	25830	45080	73695	26605	47090
A Sanitary and similar services	...	...	...	...	...	...	...	...	...	...	...	...
B Social and related community services	...	...	...	...	...	...	...	...	...	...	...	...
C Recreational and cultural services	...	...	...	...	...	...	...	...	...	...	...	...
D Personal and household services	67807	26463	41344	68398	24645	43753	70910	25830	45080	73695	26605	47090
Total, Industries	892117	372595	519522	914659	378205	536454	964872	398697	566175	1010589	413224	597365
Producers of Government Services	63939	16697	47242	66687	17415	49272	67700	15410	52290	72299	16310	55989
Other Producers	...	...	...	...	...	...	...	...	...	...	...	...
Total	956056	389292	566764	981346	395620	585726	1032572	414107	618465	1082888	429534	653354
Less: Imputed bank service charge	...	-15503	15503	...	-14409	14409	...	-14380	14380	...	-16708	16708
Import duties	16774	...	16774	16244	...	16244	17696	...	17696	18518	...	18518
Value added tax	...	...	...	...	...	...	...	...	...	...	...	...
Total	972830	404795	568035	997590	410029	587561	1050268	428487	621781	1101406	446242	655164

Colombia

4.2 Derivation of Value Added by Kind of Activity, in Constant Prices

Million Colombian pesos

	1988 Gross Output	1988 Intermediate Consumption	1988 Value Added	1989 Gross Output	1989 Intermediate Consumption	1989 Value Added
			At constant prices of: 1975			
			All Producers			
1 Agriculture, hunting, forestry and fishing	176530	31348	145182	183732	31986	151746
A Agriculture and hunting a	170399	30917	139482	177394	31541	145853
B Forestry and logging	2931	139	2792	3042	144	2898
C Fishing a	3200	292	2908	3296	301	2995
2 Mining and quarrying	42203	13327	28876	46950	14348	32602
3 Manufacturing	392499	249612	142887	402237	255181	147056
A Manufacture of food, beverages and tobacco	168815	115422	53393	179199	122303	56896
B Textile, wearing apparel and leather industries	43575	25188	18387	45239	26016	19223
C Manufacture of wood and wood products, including furniture	5794	2681	3113	6011	2772	3239
D Manufacture of paper and paper products, printing and publishing	25304	14857	10447	25708	15019	10689
E Manufacture of chemicals and chemical petroleum, coal, rubber and plastic products	77834	50875	26959	77610	50385	27225
F Manufacture of non-metallic mineral products, except products of petroleum and coal	15370	6615	8755	15378	6595	8783
G Basic metal industries	...	...	...	...	...	...
H Manufacture of fabricated metal products, machinery and equipment	51532	31808	19724	48774	29916	18858
I Other manufacturing industries	4275	2165	2109	4318	2175	2143
4 Electricity, gas and water	12164	4735	7429	12890	4998	7892
5 Construction	58465	31083	27382	58423	30936	27487
6 Wholesale and retail trade, restaurants and hotels b	92531	28229	64302	93242	28258	64984
A Wholesale and retail trade	92531	28229	64302	93242	28258	64984
B Restaurants and hotels	...	...	...	...	...	...
7 Transport, storage and communication	86677	27281	59396	89507	27952	61555
A Transport and storage	71652	23370	48282	73451	23798	49653
B Communication	15025	3911	11114	16056	4154	11902
8 Finance, insurance, real estate and business services	116578	17762	98816	122587	18718	103869
A Financial institutions c	65645	14161	51484	70024	15033	54991
B Insurance						
C Real estate and business services c	50933	3601	47332	52563	3685	48878
Real estate, except dwellings	...	...	...	...	...	...
Dwellings	50933	3601	47332	52563	3685	48878
9 Community, social and personal services b	75316	27172	48144	76365	27315	49050
A Sanitary and similar services	...	...	...	...	...	...
B Social and related community services	...	...	...	...	...	...
C Recreational and cultural services	...	...	...	...	...	...
D Personal and household services	75316	27172	48144	76365	27315	49050
Total, Industries	1052963	430549	622414	1085933	439692	646241
Producers of Government Services	79201	19296	59905	82420	20245	62175
Other Producers	...	...	...	...	...	...
Total	1132164	449845	682319	1168353	459937	708416
Less: Imputed bank service charge	...	-20584	20584	...	-24042	24042
Import duties	20056	...	20056	19449	...	19449
Value added tax	...	...	...	...	...	...
Total	1152220	470429	681791	1187802	483979	703823

a) Hunting is included in item 'Fishing'.
b) Restaurants and hotels are included in item 'Community, social and personal services'.
c) Business services are included in the financial institutions.

Colombia

4.3 Cost Components of Value Added

Million Colombian pesos

	1980						1981					
	Compensation of Employees	Capital Consumption	Net Operating Surplus	Indirect Taxes	Less: Subsidies Received	Value Added	Compensation of Employees	Capital Consumption	Net Operating Surplus	Indirect Taxes	Less: Subsidies Received	Value Added
				All Producers								
1 Agriculture, hunting, forestry and fishing	132977	...	172309	432	...	305718	167331	...	213950	358	...	381639
A Agriculture and hunting [a]	131085	...	161006	433	...	292524	164961	...	199386	413	...	364760
B Forestry and logging	1450	...	5631	-	...	7081	1780	...	6901	-	...	8681
C Fishing [a]	442	...	5672	-1	...	6113	590	...	7663	-55	...	8198
2 Mining and quarrying	8619	...	27145	363	...	36127	11983	...	36287	550	...	48820
3 Manufacturing	122216	...	145694	99550	...	367460	153514	...	174254	94847	...	422615
A Manufacture of food, beverages and tobacco	28967	...	65337	74478	...	168782	37405	...	74612	56473	...	168490
B Textile, wearing apparel and leather industries	28615	...	14712	1619	...	44946	34338	...	16183	2744	...	53265
C Manufacture of wood and wood products, including furniture	3504	...	2386	364	...	6254	4075	...	2758	471	...	7304
D Manufacture of paper and paper products, printing and publishing	7316	...	8772	1004	...	17092	8962	...	9932	1197	...	20091
E Manufacture of chemicals and chemical petroleum, coal, rubber and plastic products	19067	...	30052	14678	...	63797	24982	...	43136	24403	...	92521
F Manufacture of non-metallic mineral products, except products of petroleum and coal	8209	...	8378	1190	...	17777	10261	...	10415	1590	...	22266
G Basic metal industries	...	...	...	...	...	...	...	...	...	...	...	...
H Manufacture of fabricated metal products, machinery and equipment	23788	...	13924	5928	...	43640	29861	...	14528	7574	...	51963
I Other manufacturing industries	2750	...	2133	289	...	5172	3630	...	2690	395	...	6715
4 Electricity, gas and water	9406	...	11396	-86	...	20716	13467	...	20573	-805	...	33235
A Electricity, gas and steam	...	...	...	...	...	...	...	...	...	...	...	...
B Water works and supply	...	...	...	...	...	...	...	...	...	...	...	...
5 Construction	42703	...	28444	3379	...	74526	58133	...	40241	3756	...	102130
6 Wholesale and retail trade, restaurants and hotels [b]	32110	...	115698	5126	...	152934	41439	...	144673	6470	...	192582
A Wholesale and retail trade	32110	...	115698	5126	...	152934	41439	...	144673	6470	...	192582
B Restaurants and hotels	...	...	...	...	...	...	...	...	...	...	...	...
7 Transport, storage and communication	58098	...	85618	-3183	...	140533	74246	...	102021	-6480	...	169787
A Transport and storage	49632	...	80729	-4152	...	126209	61986	...	96835	-7894	...	150927
B Communication	8466	...	4889	969	...	14324	12260	...	5186	1414	...	18860
8 Finance, insurance, real estate and business services	63278	...	147691	5597	...	216566	80821	...	196001	9220	...	286042
A Financial institutions [c]	63278	...	42619	429	...	106326	80821	...	59547	2416	...	142784
B Insurance	...	...	...	...	...	...	...	...	...	...	...	...
C Real estate and business services [c]	...	...	105072	5168	...	110240	...	...	136454	6804	...	143258
Real estate, except dwellings	...	...	...	...	...	...	...	...	...	...	...	...
Dwellings	...	...	105072	5168	...	110240	...	...	136454	6804	...	143258
9 Community, social and personal services [b]	67083	...	69956	2522	...	139561	86846	...	97468	2655	...	186969
A Sanitary and similar services	...	...	...	...	...	...	...	...	...	...	...	...
B Social and related community services	...	...	...	...	...	...	...	...	...	...	...	...
C Recreational and cultural services	...	...	...	...	...	...	...	...	...	...	...	...
D Personal and household services	67083	...	69956	2522	...	139561	86846	...	97468	2655	...	186969
Total, Industries [de]	536490	...	803951	113700	...	1454141	687780	...	1025468	110571	...	1823819
Producers of Government Services	120494	...	...	967	...	121461	160715	...	...	1412	...	162127
Other Producers	...	...	...	...	...	...	...	...	...	...	...	...
Total [de]	656984	...	803951	114667	...	1575602	848495	...	1025468	111983	...	1985946
Less: Imputed bank service charge	...	...	40189	...	...	40189	...	...	58607	...	...	58607
Import duties	...	...	...	43717	...	43717	...	...	...	55434	...	55434
Value added tax	...	...	...	...	...	...	...	...	...	...	...	...
Total [de]	656984	...	763762	158384	...	1579130	848495	...	966861	167417	...	1982773

Colombia

4.3 Cost Components of Value Added

Million Colombian pesos

	1982							1983					
	Compensation of Employees	Capital Consumption	Net Operating Surplus	Indirect Taxes	Less: Subsidies Received	Value Added	Compensation of Employees	Capital Consumption	Net Operating Surplus	Indirect Taxes	Less: Subsidies Received	Value Added
All Producers											
1 Agriculture, hunting, forestry and fishing	195257	...	273513	-149	...	468621	236448	...	334908	192	...	571548
A Agriculture and hunting [a]	192008	...	253495	-116	...	445387	232697	...	309935	192	...	542824
B Forestry and logging	2429	...	9416	-	...	11845	2883	...	11174	-	...	14057
C Fishing [a]	820	...	10602	-33	...	11389	868	...	13799	-	...	14667
2 Mining and quarrying	16148	...	47591	799	...	64538	21397	...	66004	1245	...	88646
3 Manufacturing	194906	...	211830	123186	...	529922	234324	...	261368	145102	...	640794
A Manufacture of food, beverages and tobacco	48086	...	96226	77559	...	221871	59839	...	121076	89227	...	270142
B Textile, wearing apparel and leather industries	41549	...	18195	3439	...	63183	46309	...	19025	4016	...	69350
C Manufacture of wood and wood products, including furniture	5420	...	4051	591	...	10062	6729	...	4274	743	...	11746
D Manufacture of paper and paper products, printing and publishing	12009	...	13793	1695	...	27497	14836	...	17356	2147	...	34339
E Manufacture of chemicals and chemical petroleum, coal, rubber and plastic products	32776	...	46943	28390	...	108109	39613	...	60950	34328	...	134891
F Manufacture of non-metallic mineral products, except products of petroleum and coal	13442	...	13744	2205	...	29391	16452	...	15219	2842	...	34513
G Basic metal industries	...	...	...	...	...	...	...	...	...	...	...	...
H Manufacture of fabricated metal products, machinery and equipment	36886	...	15139	8764	...	60789	44735	...	18805	11005	...	74545
I Other manufacturing industries	4738	...	3739	543	...	9020	5811	...	4663	794	...	11268
4 Electricity, gas and water	18496	...	30353	-843	...	48006	23681	...	40451	-1200	...	62932
A Electricity, gas and steam	...	...	...	...	...	...	...	...	...	...	...	...
B Water works and supply	...	...	...	...	...	...	...	...	...	...	...	...
5 Construction	76776	...	48053	3938	...	128767	99992	...	61456	8252	...	169700
6 Wholesale and retail trade, restaurants and hotels [b]	55166	...	177566	7229	...	239961	70529	...	207456	9450	...	287435
A Wholesale and retail trade	55166	...	177566	7229	...	239961	70529	...	207456	9450	...	287435
B Restaurants and hotels	...	...	...	...	...	...	...	...	...	...	...	...
7 Transport, storage and communication	93532	...	120303	-5909	...	207926	113503	...	146172	-5420	...	254255
A Transport and storage	76491	...	113805	-7819	...	182477	91168	...	136744	-8121	...	219791
B Communication	17041	...	6498	1910	...	25449	22335	...	9428	2701	...	34464
8 Finance, insurance, real estate and business services	104042	...	248430	11541	...	364013	131069	...	293392	14687	...	439148
A Financial institutions [c]	104042	...	74387	3010	...	181439	131069	...	85419	4637	...	221125
B Insurance	...	...	...	...	...	...	...	...	...	...	...	...
C Real estate and business services [c]	...	...	174043	8531	...	182574	...	...	207973	10050	...	218023
Real estate, except dwellings	...	...	...	...	...	...	...	...	...	...	...	...
Dwellings	...	...	174043	8531	...	182574	...	...	207973	10050	...	218023
9 Community, social and personal services [b]	111746	...	126918	3313	...	241977	143953	...	154709	5433	...	304095
A Sanitary and similar services	...	...	...	...	...	...	...	...	...	...	...	...
B Social and related community services	...	...	...	...	...	...	...	...	...	...	...	...
C Recreational and cultural services	...	...	...	...	...	...	...	...	...	...	...	...
D Personal and household services	111746	...	126918	3313	...	241977	143953	...	154709	5433	...	304095
Total, Industries [de]	866069	...	1284557	143105	...	2293731	1074896	...	1565916	177741	...	2818553
Producers of Government Services	210900	...	...	1720	...	212620	265060	...	...	1689	...	266749
Other Producers	...	...	...	...	...	...	...	...	...	...	...	...
Total [de]	1076969	...	1284557	144825	...	2506351	1339956	...	1565916	179430	...	3085302
Less: Imputed bank service charge	...	...	78757	...	...	78757	...	...	105404	...	...	105404
Import duties	...	...	...	69704	...	69704	...	...	...	74239	...	74239
Value added tax	...	...	...	...	...	...	...	...	...	...	...	...
Total [de]	1076969	...	1205800	214529	...	2497298	1339956	...	1460512	253669	...	3054137

Colombia

4.3 Cost Components of Value Added

Million Colombian pesos

	1984 Compensation of Employees	Capital Consumption	Net Operating Surplus	Indirect Taxes	Less: Subsidies Received	Value Added	1985 Compensation of Employees	Capital Consumption	Net Operating Surplus	Indirect Taxes	Less: Subsidies Received	Value Added
All Producers												
1 Agriculture, hunting, forestry and fishing	276486	...	397407	-2503	...	671390	326373	...	520392	-3027	...	843738
A Agriculture and hunting [a]	271523	...	364451	-2488	...	633486	320261	...	479571	-3016	...	796816
B Forestry and logging	3823	...	14818	-	...	18641	4688	...	18170	-	...	22858
C Fishing [a]	1140	...	18138	-15	...	19263	1424	...	22651	-11	...	24064
2 Mining and quarrying	29541	...	96520	1276	...	127337	38436	...	166661	1977	...	207074
3 Manufacturing	290542	...	356870	205304	...	852716	340196	...	451118	270731	...	1062045
A Manufacture of food, beverages and tobacco	77934	...	147589	137646	...	363169	91649	...	206742	182867	...	481258
B Textile, wearing apparel and leather industries	56340	...	34394	4429	...	95163	66008	...	48217	7027	...	121252
C Manufacture of wood and wood products, including furniture	8469	...	7081	1008	...	16558	10586	...	8991	1201	...	20778
D Manufacture of paper and paper products, printing and publishing	17617	...	22993	2329	...	42939	20522	...	32574	3572	...	56668
E Manufacture of chemicals and chemical petroleum, coal, rubber and plastic products	48623	...	88221	39622	...	176466	57805	...	79036	49443	...	186284
F Manufacture of non-metallic mineral products, except products of petroleum and coal	20656	...	20207	3454	...	44317	24167	...	25416	4351	...	53934
G Basic metal industries	...	...	...	...	...	...	...	...	...	...	...	...
H Manufacture of fabricated metal products, machinery and equipment	52916	...	29518	15706	...	98140	59734	...	39317	20426	...	119477
I Other manufacturing industries	7987	...	6867	1110	...	15964	9725	...	10825	1844	...	22394
4 Electricity, gas and water	30264	...	52915	-395	...	82784	37558	...	69301	-20	...	106839
A Electricity, gas and steam	...	...	...	...	...	...	...	...	...	...	...	...
B Water works and supply	...	...	...	...	...	...	37558	...	69301	-20	...	106839
5 Construction	130037	...	78504	11410	...	219951	160180	...	165613	16629	...	342422
6 Wholesale and retail trade, restaurants and hotels [b]	87938	...	258557	35521	...	382016	107636	...	354780	52980	...	515396
A Wholesale and retail trade	87938	...	258557	35521	...	382016	107636	...	354780	52980	...	515396
B Restaurants and hotels	...											
7 Transport, storage and communication	142335	...	177453	-1918	...	317870	179626	...	218644	6460	...	404730
A Transport and storage	111816	...	164641	-6091	...	270366	140161	...	201933	974	...	343068
B Communication	30519	...	12812	4173	...	47504	39465	...	16711	5486	...	61662
8 Finance, insurance, real estate and business services	132394	...	353883	17635	...	503912	193574	...	387138	27597	...	608309
A Financial institutions [c]	132394	...	107013	4506	...	243913	193574	...	97313	10955	...	301842
B Insurance	...	...	...	...	...	...	...	...	...	...	...	...
C Real estate and business services [c]		...	246870	13129	...	259999		...	289825	16642	...	306467
Real estate, except dwellings	...	...	...	...	...	...	...	...	...	...	...	...
Dwellings		...	246870	13129	...	259999		...	289825	16642	...	306467
9 Community, social and personal services [b]	176367	...	184763	7618	...	368748	212788	...	216928	9110	...	438826
A Sanitary and similar services												
B Social and related community services	...	...	...	...	...	...	...	...	...	...	...	...
C Recreational and cultural services	...											
D Personal and household services	176367	...	184763	7618	...	368748	212788	...	216928	9110	...	438826
Total, Industries [de]	1295904	...	1956872	273948	...	3526724	1596367	...	2550575	382437	...	4529379
Producers of Government Services	346948	...		2064	...	349012	420891	...		3185	...	424076
Other Producers	...	...	...	...	...	...	...	...	...	...	...	...
Total [de]	1642852	...	1956872	276012	...	3875736	2017258	...	2550575	385622	...	4953455
Less: Imputed bank service charge		...	103850		...	103850		...	118728		...	118728
Import duties	...	...	...	84698	...	84698	...	...	...	131156	...	131156
Value added tax	...	...	...	...	...	...	...	...	...			
Total [de]	1642852	...	1853022	360710	...	3856584	2017258	...	2431847	516778	...	4965883

Colombia

4.3 Cost Components of Value Added

Million Colombian pesos

	\multicolumn{6}{c	}{1986}	\multicolumn{6}{c	}{1987}
	Compensation of Employees	Capital Consumption	Net Operating Surplus	Indirect Taxes	Less: Subsidies Received	Value Added	Compensation of Employees	Capital Consumption	Net Operating Surplus	Indirect Taxes	Less: Subsidies Received	Value Added

All Producers

	1986 CoE	1986 CC	1986 NOS	1986 IT	1986 LSR	1986 VA	1987 CoE	1987 CC	1987 NOS	1987 IT	1987 LSR	1987 VA
1 Agriculture, hunting, forestry and fishing	418887	...	769067	-1628	...	1186326	583006	...	1011194	-182	...	1594018
A Agriculture and hunting [a]	411485	...	718168	-1589	...	1128064	573239	...	943663	-153	...	1516749
B Forestry and logging	5558	...	21545	-1	...	27102	7310	...	28438	-1	...	35747
C Fishing [a]	1844	...	29354	-38	...	31160	2457	...	39093	-28	...	41522
2 Mining and quarrying	52965	...	274086	4783	...	331834	71402	...	500073	6322	...	577797
3 Manufacturing	438464	...	655068	432182	...	1525714	584953	...	686618	521335	...	1792906
A Manufacture of food, beverages and tobacco	118771	...	307629	321121	...	747521	151364	...	137142	366479	...	654985
B Textile, wearing apparel and leather industries	90675	...	58553	7937	...	157165	115081	...	88643	10954	...	214678
C Manufacture of wood and wood products, including furniture	13538	...	13600	1213	...	28351	18471	...	19512	2305	...	40288
D Manufacture of paper and paper products, printing and publishing	26716	...	46684	4715	...	78115	35490	...	64824	6264	...	106578
E Manufacture of chemicals and chemical petroleum, coal, rubber and plastic products	70910	...	113811	60781	...	245502	99538	...	187485	79409	...	366432
F Manufacture of non-metallic mineral products, except products of petroleum and coal	32101	...	36662	6204	...	74967	42091	...	58682	8729	...	109502
G Basic metal industries	...	...	...	...	...	...	...	...	...	...	...	...
H Manufacture of fabricated metal products, machinery and equipment	73369	...	66077	28007	...	167453	107568	...	114164	44425	...	266157
I Other manufacturing industries	12384	...	12052	2204	...	26640	15350	...	16166	2770	...	34286
4 Electricity, gas and water	47617	...	103924	-214	...	151327	64278	...	136611	81	...	200970
A Electricity, gas and steam	...	...	...	...	...	...	...	...	...	...	...	...
B Water works and supply	47617	...	103924	-214	...	151327	64278	...	136611	81	...	200970
5 Construction	196016	...	228851	21730	...	446597	202469	...	267658	24517	...	494644
6 Wholesale and retail trade, restaurants and hotels [b]	137995	...	493191	64068	...	695254	175256	...	680353	78142	...	933751
A Wholesale and retail trade	137995	...	493191	64068	...	695254	175256	...	680353	78142	...	933751
B Restaurants and hotels	...	...	...	...	...	...	...	...	...	...	...	...
7 Transport, storage and communication	234286	...	282918	9908	...	527112	307957	...	387800	16816	...	712573
A Transport and storage	180342	...	260051	2017	...	442410	248872	...	352306	7408	...	608586
B Communication	53944	...	22867	7891	...	84702	59085	...	35494	9408	...	103987
8 Finance, insurance, real estate and business services	235001	...	487262	44076	...	766339	303079	...	625890	56398	...	985367
A Financial institutions [c]	235001	...	143574	20903	...	399478	303079	...	207714	26157	...	536950
B Insurance	...	...	...	...	...	...	...	...	...	...	...	...
C Real estate and business services [c]	...	...	343688	23173	...	366861	...	...	418176	30241	...	448417
Real estate, except dwellings	...	...	...	...	...	...	...	...	...	...	...	...
Dwellings	...	...	343688	23173	...	366861	...	...	418176	30241	...	448417
9 Community, social and personal services [b]	271254	...	275545	11147	...	557946	352606	...	370418	14519	...	737543
A Sanitary and similar services	...	...	...	...	...	...	...	...	...	...	...	...
B Social and related community services	...	...	...	...	...	...	...	...	...	...	...	...
C Recreational and cultural services	...	...	...	...	...	...	...	...	...	...	...	...
D Personal and household services	271254	...	275545	11147	...	557946	352606	...	370418	14519	...	737543
Total, Industries [de]	2032485	...	3569912	586052	...	6188449	2645006	...	4666615	717948	...	8029569
Producers of Government Services	542825	...	...	4448	...	547273	706493	...	...	7249	...	713742
Other Producers	...	...	...	...	...	...	...	...	...	...	...	...
Total [de]	2575310	...	3569912	590500	...	6735722	3351499	...	4666615	725197	...	8743311
Less: Imputed bank service charge	...	...	155853	...	...	155853	...	...	226720	...	...	226720
Import duties	...	...	...	208087	...	208087	...	...	...	307817	...	307817
Value added tax	...	...	...	...	...	...	...	...	...	...	...	...
Total [de]	2575310	...	3414059	798587	...	6787956	3351499	...	4439895	1033014	...	8824408

Colombia

4.3 Cost Components of Value Added

Million Colombian pesos

		1988						1989				
	Compensation of Employees	Capital Consumption	Net Operating Surplus	Indirect Taxes	Less: Subsidies Received	Value Added	Compensation of Employees	Capital Consumption	Net Operating Surplus	Indirect Taxes	Less: Subsidies Received	Value Added

All Producers

1 Agriculture, hunting, forestry and fishing	781786	...	1181738	1394	...	1964918	1007729	...	1439722	6976	...	2454427
A Agriculture and hunting [a]	768799	...	1095697	1436	...	1865932	990982	...	1329149	7018	...	2327149
B Forestry and logging	10029	...	39016	-1	...	49044	12965	...	50433	...	...	63398
C Fishing [a]	2958	...	47025	-41	...	49942	3782	...	60140	-42	...	63880
2 Mining and quarrying	99412	...	605299	17482	...	722193	131522	...	970235	30721	...	1132478
3 Manufacturing	753556	...	1203019	525536	...	2482111	964446	...	1488695	675232	...	3128373
A Manufacture of food, beverages and tobacco	192616	...	438854	310962	...	942432	244425	...	521500	374836	...	1140761
B Textile, wearing apparel and leather industries	152227	...	156387	13205	...	321819	205506	...	208397	21041	...	434944
C Manufacture of wood and wood products, including furniture	25918	...	29944	3629	...	59491	33176	...	36026	5339	...	74541
D Manufacture of paper and paper products, printing and publishing	44008	...	84432	8426	...	136866	56066	...	108852	14462	...	179380
E Manufacture of chemicals and chemical petroleum, coal, rubber and plastic products	119678	...	197867	104765	...	422310	151554	...	249023	146870	...	547447
F Manufacture of non-metallic mineral products, except products of petroleum and coal	56799	...	84050	12432	...	153281	70324	...	116370	17907	...	204601
G Basic metal industries	...	...	...	...	...	...	...	...	...	...	...	...
H Manufacture of fabricated metal products, machinery and equipment	140794	...	186353	68191	...	395338	174741	...	213545	88986	...	477272
I Other manufacturing industries	21516	...	25132	3926	...	50574	28654	...	34982	5791	...	69427
4 Electricity, gas and water	88216	...	187429	-5053	...	270592	117416	...	258479	-4672	...	371223
A Electricity, gas and steam	...	...	...	...	...	...	...	...	...	...	...	...
B Water works and supply	...	...	...	...	...	...	...	...	...	...	...	...
5 Construction	289101	...	452842	33807	...	775750	358490	...	590637	50762	...	999889
6 Wholesale and retail trade, restaurants and hotels [b]	231031	...	918358	123570	...	1272959	295258	...	1162969	163535	...	1621762
A Wholesale and retail trade	231031	...	918358	123570	...	1272959	295258	...	1162969	163535	...	1621762
B Restaurants and hotels	...	...	...	...	...	...	...	...	...	...	...	...
7 Transport, storage and communication	405892	...	534761	28822	...	969475	532504	...	691165	42752	...	1266421
A Transport and storage	325154	...	477030	15453	...	817637	422700	...	607527	23541	...	1053768
B Communication	80738	...	57731	13369	...	151838	109804	...	83638	19211	...	212653
8 Finance, insurance, real estate and business services	437077	...	804282	81611	...	1322970	563392	...	1053282	105371	...	1722045
A Financial institutions [c]	437077	...	301902	41140	...	780119	563392	...	428489	49301	...	1041182
B Insurance	...	...	...	...	...	...	...	...	...	...	...	...
C Real estate and business services [c]	...	...	502380	40471	...	542851	...	...	624793	56070	...	680863
Real estate, except dwellings	...	...	...	...	...	...	...	...	...	...	...	...
Dwellings	...	...	502380	40471	...	542851	...	...	624793	56070	...	680863
9 Community, social and personal services [b]	456022	...	491910	17542	...	965474	587756	...	676608	19670	...	1284034
A Sanitary and similar services	...	...	...	...	...	...	...	...	...	...	...	...
B Social and related community services	...	...	...	...	...	...	...	...	...	...	...	...
C Recreational and cultural services	...	...	...	...	...	...	...	...	...	...	...	...
D Personal and household services	456022	...	491910	17542	...	965474	587756	...	676608	19670	...	1284034

Colombia

4.3 Cost Components of Value Added
(Continued)

Million Colombian pesos

	1988						1989					
	Compensation of Employees	Capital Consumption	Net Operating Surplus	Indirect Taxes	Less: Subsidies Received	Value Added	Compensation of Employees	Capital Consumption	Net Operating Surplus	Indirect Taxes	Less: Subsidies Received	Value Added
Total, Industries de	3542093	...	6379638	824711	...	10746442	4558513	...	8331792	1090347	...	13980652
Producers of Government Services	923787	...	...	8465	...	932252	1229919	...	...	11241	...	1241160
Other Producers	...	...	...	...	...	...	...	...	...	...	...	...
Total de	4465880	...	6379638	833176	...	11678694	5788432	...	8331792	1101588	...	15221812
Less: Imputed bank service charge	...	...	368615	...	...	368615	...	...	540685	...	...	540685
Import duties	...	...	...	421269	...	421269	...	...	...	508465	...	508465
Value added tax	...	...	...	...	...	...	...	...	...	...	...	...
Total de	4465880	...	6011023	1254445	...	11731348	5788432	...	7791107	1610053	...	15189592

a) Hunting is included in item 'Fishing'.
b) Restaurants and hotels are included in item 'Community, social and personal services'.
c) Business services are included in the financial institutions.
d) Column 4 refers to indirect taxes less subsidies received.
e) Column 'Consumption of fixed capital' is included in column 'Net operating surplus'.

Congo

Source. Reply to the United Nations National Accounts Questionnaire from the Centre National de la Statistique et des Etudes Economique, Brazzaville.
General note. The estimates shown in the following tables have been prepared by the Centre National in accordance with the United Nations System of National Accounts so far as the existing data would permit.

1.1 Expenditure on the Gross Domestic Product, in Current Prices

Million CFA francs

	1970	1975	1980	1981	1982	1983	1984	1985	1986	1987	1988	1989
1 Government final consumption expenditure	15232	35137	63385	72839	95759	124245	141696	159693	159804	142115	138722	144600
2 Private final consumption expenditure	44791	84865	147924	220222	284086	318459	372192	403583	380534	390669	396328	408500
A Households	...	...	147324	219372	282936	317199	370712	401955	378934	389229	394828	...
B Private non-profit institutions serving households	...	...	600	850	1150	1260	1480	1628	1600	1440	1500	...
3 Gross capital formation	21437	40855	128901	260991	424146	307122	291239	293982	188598	136205	122640	122924
A Increase in stocks	2587	4476	10157	21057	19451	4268	13974	17080	5742	-7811	-6518	-3776
B Gross fixed capital formation	18850	36379	118744	239934	404695	302854	277265	276902	182856	144016	129158	126700
4 Exports of goods and services	21393	55730	203029	314518	392435	463133	590696	551863	255152	288254	267723	368100
5 Less: Imports of goods and services	30400	70129	182842	326864	486406	413714	437314	438271	343681	266720	266448	270600
Equals: Gross Domestic Product	72453	146458	360397	541706	710020	799245	958509	970850	640407	690523	658964	773524

1.2 Expenditure on the Gross Domestic Product, in Constant Prices

Million CFA francs

	1970	1975	1980	1981	1982	1983	1984	1985	1986	1987	1988	1989
					At constant prices of:1978							
1 Government final consumption expenditure	27793	41583	56869	59900	71927	83667	94077	100530	98384	84894	82080	83886
2 Private final consumption expenditure	83147	108000	128582	169487	198746	205073	220678	229054	213466	216324	217361	215622
A Households	...	...	128043	168788	197883	204104	219678	227969	212526	...	...	...
B Private non-profit institutions serving households	...	...	539	699	863	969	1000	1085	940	...	...	...
3 Gross capital formation	47928	56998	103238	185134	264067	181474	161402	153359	98947	68068	58080	49771
A Increase in stocks	11073	8968	9192	16533	7851	2392	10306	8412	3035	-3103	-2649	-5796
B Gross fixed capital formation	36855	48030	94046	168601	256216	179082	151096	144947	95912	71171	60729	55567
4 Exports of goods and services	42309	67773	104687	112870	131532	154170	169264	158300	152812	153452	173179	186514
5 Less: Imports of goods and services	54054	81596	144774	226040	293898	231121	223770	224452	175501	133895	134989	133099
Equals: Gross Domestic Product	147123	192758	248602	301351	372374	393263	421651	416791	388108	388843	395711	402694

1.3 Cost Components of the Gross Domestic Product

Million CFA francs

	1970	1975	1980	1981	1982	1983	1984	1985	1986	1987	1988	1989
1 Indirect taxes, net	12021	25931	57077	90159	106750	125075	153724	148591	86690	89122	80672	106175
A Indirect taxes	12021	25931	60164	96916	114788	134529	162290	154437	91444	90790	82358	...
B Less: Subsidies	...	...	3087	6757	8038	9454	8566	5846	4754	1668	1686	...
2 Consumption of fixed capital	7453	25551	41191	60391	89635	120807	176986	167228	156074	164360	144647	148975
3 Compensation of employees paid by resident producers to:	33590	61607	119568	158649	206212	226115	257713	264454	264296	253198	245033	247514
4 Operating surplus	19389	33367	142561	232507	307423	327248	370086	390577	133347	183843	188612	270860
A Corporate and quasi-corporate enterprises	...	...	94831	170178	201084	212395	237834	248081	-4228	41403	34329	...
B Private unincorporated enterprises	...	...	47730	62329	106339	114853	132252	142496	137575	142440	154283	...
C General government	...	...	...	...	...	...	...	...	...	...	...	...
Equals: Gross Domestic Product	72453	146458	360397	541706	710020	799245	958509	970850	640407	690523	658964	773524

1.4 General Government Current Receipts and Disbursements

Million CFA francs

	1970	1975	1980	1981	1982	1983	1984	1985	1986	1987	1988	1989
					Receipts							
1 Operating surplus	...	...	...	...	...	...	...	...	...	...	...	...
2 Property and entrepreneurial income	...	...	10	1162	1453	1453	5954	4427	-	10883	7798	...
3 Taxes, fees and contributions	...	...	126351	210593	250838	287767	342227	307933	179767	133749	130495	...
A Indirect taxes	...	...	60164	96916	114788	134529	162290	154437	91444	90331	81898	...

Congo

1.4 General Government Current Receipts and Disbursements
(Continued)

Million CFA francs

	1970	1975	1980	1981	1982	1983	1984	1985	1986	1987	1988	1989
B Direct taxes	...	...	59522	107004	122270	137629	165601	138070	72375	23697	25597	...
C Social security contributions	...	...	5656	5800	13192	15236	13365	15000	15600	19621	22890	...
D Compulsory fees, fines and penalties	...	...	1009	873	588	373	971	426	348	100	110	...
4 Other current transfers	...	...	3306	7053	12950	23222	5635	13169	13915	14712	23377	...
Total Current Receipts of General Government	...	...	129667	218808	265241	312442	353816	325529	193682	159344	161670	...

Disbursements

	1970	1975	1980	1981	1982	1983	1984	1985	1986	1987	1988	1989
1 Government final consumption expenditure	...	...	63385	72839	95759	124245	141696	159693	159804	142115	138722	...
2 Property income	...	...	9100	10100	20053	20053	30225	42268	21683	40125	43394	...
A Interest	...	...	9100	10100	20053	20053	30225	42268	21683	40125	43394	...
B Net land rent and royalties	...	...	...	...	...	...	...	...	...	...	...	...
3 Subsidies	...	...	3087	6757	8038	9454	8566	5846	4754	...	...	...
4 Other current transfers	...	...	11180	19062	27232	33805	23265	28821	25355	43327	44154	...
A Social security benefits	...	...	2911	3969	4097	4494	4981	5731	5800	12571	13850	...
B Social assistance grants	...	...			1038	1120		100	900	8287	8517	...
C Other	...	...	8269	15093	22097	28191	18284	22990	18655	22469	21787	...
5 Net saving	...	...	42915	110050	114159	124885	150064	88901	-17914	-66223	-66402	...
Total Current Disbursements and Net Saving of General Government	...	...	129667	218808	265241	312442	353816	325529	193682	159344	161670	...

1.7 External Transactions on Current Account, Summary

Million CFA francs

	1970	1975	1980	1981	1982	1983	1984	1985	1986	1987	1988	1989

Payments to the Rest of the World

	1970	1975	1980	1981	1982	1983	1984	1985	1986	1987	1988	1989
1 Imports of goods and services	30400	70129	182842	326864	486406	413714	437314	438271	343681	266720	266448	...
2 Factor income to the rest of the world	...	...	34877	37690	66037	68147	72723	106547	44717	86030	93328	...
A Compensation of employees	...	...	-	-	-	-	-	-	-	140	200	...
B Property and entrepreneurial income	...	...	34877	37690	66037	68147	72723	106547	44717	85890	93128	...
3 Current transfers to the rest of the world	...	...	19070	16289	18174	41346	43645	32167	25512	36255	36264	...
4 Surplus of the nation on current transactions	...	...	-27366	-48760	-167292	-41823	57152	-1934	-138507	-66015	-101106	...
Payments to the Rest of the World and Surplus of the Nation on Current Transactions	...	...	209423	332083	403325	481384	610834	575051	275403	322990	294934	...

Receipts From The Rest of the World

	1970	1975	1980	1981	1982	1983	1984	1985	1986	1987	1988	1989
1 Exports of goods and services	...	...	203029	314518	392435	463133	590696	551863	255152	288254	267722	...
2 Factor income from rest of the world	...	...	2201	4511	6452	5258	5077	4103	2781	9333	3112	...
A Compensation of employees	...	...	506	-	-	-	-	-	-	150	1320	...
B Property and entrepreneurial income	...	...	1695	4511	6452	5258	5077	4103	2781	9183	1792	...
3 Current transfers from rest of the world	...	...	4193	13054	4438	12993	15061	19085	17470	25403	24100	...
Receipts from the Rest of the World on Current Transactions	...	...	209423	332083	403325	481384	610834	575051	275403	322990	294934	...

1.8 Capital Transactions of The Nation, Summary

Million CFA francs

	1970	1975	1980	1981	1982	1983	1984	1985	1986	1987	1988	1989

Finance of Gross Capital Formation

	1970	1975	1980	1981	1982	1983	1984	1985	1986	1987	1988	1989
Gross saving	12307	28610	101535	212231	256854	265299	348391	292048	50091	70190	21534	...
1 Consumption of fixed capital	7453	25551	41191	60391	89635	120807	176986	167228	156074	164360	144647	...
A General government	...	...	...	...	...	...	...	...	...	...	...	...
B Corporate and quasi-corporate enterprises	...	...	31939	48198	73905	105083	161038	149632	138039	144657	124116	...
Public	...	...	8178	11478	12914	24146	29513	30798	35141	34277	35158	...
Private	...	...	23761	36720	60991	80937	131525	118834	102898	110380	88958	...
C Other	...	...	9252	12193	15730	15724	15948	17596	18035	19703	20531	...
2 Net saving	4854	3059	60344	151840	167219	144492	171405	124820	-105983	-94170	-123113	...

Congo

1.8 Capital Transactions of The Nation, Summary
(Continued)

Million CFA francs

	1970	1975	1980	1981	1982	1983	1984	1985	1986	1987	1988	1989
A General government	...	...	42915	110050	114159	124885	150064	88901	-17914	-66223	-64602	...
B Corporate and quasi-corporate enterprises	...	...	14460	36835	35522	12567	16965	33991	-90636	-17604	-47834	...
Public	...	...	-1229	5208	-5987	-9526	-1845	13040	4946	-3194	-10331	...
Private	...	...	15689	31627	41509	22093	18810	20951	-95582	-14410	-37503	...
C Other	...	...	2969	4955	17538	7040	4376	1928	2567	-10343	-10677	...
Less: Surplus of the nation on current transactions	-9130	-12245	-27366	-48760	-167292	-41823	57152	-1934	-138507	-66015	-101106	...
Finance of Gross Capital Formation	21437	40855	128901	260991	424146	307122	291239	293982	188598	136205	122640	...

Gross Capital Formation

	1970	1975	1980	1981	1982	1983	1984	1985	1986	1987	1988	1989
Increase in stocks	2587	4476	10157	21057	19451	4268	13974	17080	5742	-7811	-6518	...
Gross fixed capital formation	18850	36379	118744	239934	404695	302854	277265	276902	182856	144016	129158	...
1 General government	...	...	15256	59554	89367	76426	92300	70166	36502	18632	14178	...
2 Corporate and quasi-corporate enterprises	...	...	91838	163531	295585	205224	167605	188578	132824	111584	101980	...
A Public	...	...	22991	43579	93080	90145	78487	97539	49317	32424	25569	...
B Private	...	...	68847	119952	202505	115079	89118	91039	83507	79160	76411	...
3 Other	...	...	11650	16849	19743	21204	17360	18158	13530	13800	13000	...
Gross Capital Formation	21437	40855	128901	260991	424146	307122	291239	293982	188598	136205	122640	...

1.9 Gross Domestic Product by Institutional Sectors of Origin

Million CFA francs

	1970	1975	1980	1981	1982	1983	1984	1985	1986	1987	1988	1989
Domestic Factor Incomes Originating												
1 General government	...	...	45352	54860	62319	74616	88605	97680	101495	102716	102603	...
2 Corporate and quasi-corporate enterprises	...	...	154879	254633	325274	348387	390706	397555	142154	174067	157855	...
A Non-financial	...	...	154288	252218	325620	345602	386443	386274	140676	172984	155721	...
Public	...	...	21879	32837	34503	42939	57254	62835	70569	66485	65668	...
Private	...	...	132409	219381	291117	302663	329189	323439	70107	106499	90053	...
B Financial	...	...	591	2415	-346	2785	4263	11281	1478	1083	2134	...
Public	...	...	591	2415	-346	2785	4263	11281	1478	1083	2134	...
Private	...	...	...	...	...	...	...	...	...	...	...	...
3 Households and private unincorporated enterprises	...	...	61498	81113	125362	129600	147988	159246	153258	159763	172687	...
4 Non-profit institutions serving households	...	...	400	550	680	760	500	550	550	495	500	...
Subtotal: Domestic Factor Incomes	...	...	262129	391156	513635	553363	627799	655031	397643	437041	433645	...
Indirect taxes, net	...	...	57077	90159	106750	125075	153724	148591	86690	89122	80672	...
A Indirect taxes	...	...	60164	96916	114788	134529	162290	154437	91444	90331	81898	...
B Less: Subsidies	...	...	3087	6757	8038	9454	8566	5846	4754	1209	1226	...
Consumption of fixed capital	...	...	41191	60391	89635	120807	176986	167228	156074	164360	144647	...
Gross Domestic Product	...	...	360397	541706	710020	799245	958509	970850	640407	690523	658964	...

1.10 Gross Domestic Product by Kind of Activity, in Current Prices

Million CFA francs

	1970	1975	1980	1981	1982	1983	1984	1985	1986	1987	1988	1989
1 Agriculture, hunting, forestry and fishing	16072	22648	42128	42687	55756	60651	66348	72331	77424	82434	91384	100839
2 Mining and quarrying	912	24769	120980	212807	275270	324772	413699	398041	99444	155188	110399	216192
3 Manufacturing	9396	15211	27079	34344	33896	44114	46449	54587	61277	59757	56917	54483
4 Electricity, gas and water	1345	1972	2906	3545	5642	9351	10119	11906	9054	10614	12714	14014
5 Construction	4566	5240	17060	25076	58374	55866	72112	58895	38806	21580	17117	13955
6 Wholesale and retail trade, restaurants and hotels	8782	17294	35053	60087	93769	95787	104487	110463	104377	102153	107588	111321
7 Transport, storage and communication	7825	13232	32781	43865	55460	57701	68529	70799	71067	71294	72600	70075
8 Finance, insurance, real estate and business services	6669	10322	26042	51762	53473	60666	63122	76240	64402	70975	71108	70503
9 Community, social and personal services												

Congo

1.10 Gross Domestic Product by Kind of Activity, in Current Prices
(Continued)

Million CFA francs

	1970	1975	1980	1981	1982	1983	1984	1985	1986	1987	1988	1989
Total, Industries	55567	110688	304029	474173	631640	708908	844865	853262	525851	573995	539827	651382
Producers of Government Services	11143	25379	45352	54860	62319	74616	88605	97680	101495	102716	102603	104306
Other Producers			700	1000	1230	1380	1700	1750	1550	1395	1400	1400
Subtotal	66710	136067	350081	530033	695189	784904	935170	952692	628896	678106	643830	757088
Less: Imputed bank service charge	...	...	7178	10286	15501	14711	13730	16054	16466	13116	13054	12500
Plus: Import duties	5743	10391	17494	21959	30332	29052	37069	34212	27977	25533	28188	28936
Plus: Value added tax	...	...	...	...	...	...	...	...	...	...	...	...
Equals: Gross Domestic Product	72453	146458	360397	541706	710020	799245	958509	970850	640407	690523	658964	773524

1.11 Gross Domestic Product by Kind of Activity, in Constant Prices

Million CFA francs

	1970	1975	1980	1981	1982	1983	1984	1985	1986	1987	1988	1989
At constant prices of:1978												
1 Agriculture, hunting, forestry and fishing	29530	27329	39609	38078	39915	41766	40942	41325	43635	45722	48758	51711
2 Mining and quarrying	4644	27756	38362	39489	50496	61469	63228	61838	66930	77255	82145	95206
3 Manufacturing	17003	19292	21166	25948	27548	36309	38463	42213	39601	39883	42467	37562
4 Electricity, gas and water	2398	3317	3435	4501	6073	9743	9670	10719	8084	10108	10634	11336
5 Construction	5210	5721	13597	17500	38838	36970	45521	34617	21807	11344	7466	5237
6 Wholesale and retail trade, restaurants and hotels	19329	23210	28655	43196	63107	54100	54345	54088	52610	50597	49544	49818
7 Transport, storage and communication	16824	18714	26907	33038	37712	41043	42423	42921	39875	37254	37689	36017
8 Finance, insurance, real estate and business services	16272	15576	23604	39128	41422	42369	41259	45156	37637	41705	40044	37398
9 Community, social and personal services												
Total, Industries	111210	140915	195335	240878	305111	323769	335851	332877	310179	313868	318747	324285
Producers of Government Services	24737	38380	42455	47007	50195	53632	62735	65766	67304	66379	65980	66000
Other Producers			655	857	991	992	1204	1178	1046	1032	1026	1004
Subtotal	135947	179295	238445	288742	356297	378393	399790	399821	378529	381279	385753	391289
Less: Imputed bank service charge	...	...	6508	7775	11398	10817	10095	11804	11812	11254	10230	9796
Plus: Import duties	11176	13463	16665	20384	27475	25687	31956	28774	21391	18818	20188	21201
Plus: Value added tax	...	...	...	...	...	...	...	...	...	...	...	...
Equals: Gross Domestic Product	147123	192758	248602	301351	372374	393263	421651	416791	388108	388843	395711	402694

1.12 Relations Among National Accounting Aggregates

Million CFA francs

	1970	1975	1980	1981	1982	1983	1984	1985	1986	1987	1988	1989
Gross Domestic Product	72453	146458	360397	541706	710020	799245	958509	970850	640407	690523	658964	...
Plus: Net factor income from the rest of the world	363	-6493	-32676	-33179	-59585	-62889	-67646	-102444	-41936	-76697	-90216	...
Factor income from the rest of the world	...	...	2201	4511	6452	5258	5077	4103	2781	9333	3112	...
Less: Factor income to the rest of the world	...	...	34877	37690	66037	68147	72723	106547	44717	86030	93328	...
Equals: Gross National Product	72816	139965	327721	508527	650435	736356	890863	868406	598471	613826	568748	...
Less: Consumption of fixed capital	7453	25551	41191	60391	89635	120807	176986	167228	156074	164360	144647	...
Equals: National Income	65363	114414	286530	448136	560800	615549	713877	701178	442397	449466	424101	...
Plus: Net current transfers from the rest of the world	-486	8647	-14877	-3235	-13736	-28353	-28584	-13082	-8042	-10852	-12164	...
Current transfers from the rest of the world	...	...	4193	13054	4438	12993	15061	19085	17470	25403	24100	...
Less: Current transfers to the rest of the world	...	...	19070	16289	18174	41346	43645	32167	25512	36255	36264	...
Equals: National Disposable Income	64877	123061	271653	444901	547064	587196	685293	688096	434355	438614	411937	...
Less: Final consumption	60023	120002	211309	293061	379845	442704	513888	563276	540338	532784	535050	...
Equals: Net Saving	4854	3059	60344	151840	167219	144492	171405	124820	-105983	-94170	-123113	...
Less: Surplus of the nation on current transactions	-9130	-12245	-27366	-48760	-167292	-41823	57152	-1934	-138507	-66015	-101106	...
Equals: Net Capital Formation	13984	15304	87710	200600	334511	186315	114253	126754	32524	-28155	-22007	...

Cook Islands

Source. Reply to the United Nations National Accounts Questionnaire from the Statistical Office of the Cook Islands, Rarotonga. Official estimates are published by the same Office in 'Gross Domestic Product Estimates of the Cook Islands for 1976 and 1977.'

General note. The estimates shown in the following tables have been prepared by the Statistical Office in accordance with the United Nations System of National Accounts so far as the existing data would permit.

1.1 Expenditure on the Gross Domestic Product, in Current Prices

Thousand New Zealand dollars

	1970	1975	1980	1981	1982	1983	1984	1985	1986	1987	1988	1989
1 Government final consumption expenditure	2654.1	...	...	...	...	...	...	...	...	...	...	...
2 Private final consumption expenditure	6667.2	...	...	...	...	...	...	...	...	...	...	...
3 Gross capital formation	2170.7	...	...	...	...	...	...	...	...	...	...	...
A Increase in stocks	852.7	...	...	...	...	...	...	...	...	...	...	...
B Gross fixed capital formation	1318.0	...	...	...	...	...	...	...	...	...	...	...
4 Exports of goods and services [a]	2691.6	2394.1	4189.7	5014.8	4980.0	4890.0	6514.6	6072.3	9233.0	12039.3	6628.4	4665.4
5 Less: Imports of goods and services [b]	5863.6	10523.3	23609.7	28735.0	26853.0	35086.0	36167.0	49663.0	50309.0	56982.0	64526.0	73078.0
Statistical discrepancy	-20.0	...	...	...	...	...	...	...	...	...	...	...
Equals: Gross Domestic Product	8300.0	...	...	...	...	...	...	...	...	...	...	...

a) Item 'Exports of goods and services' refers to exports of goods, f.o.b. only.
b) Item 'Imports of goods and services' refers to imports of goods, c.i.f. only.

1.10 Gross Domestic Product by Kind of Activity, in Current Prices

Thousand New Zealand dollars

	1970	1975	1980	1981	1982	1983	1984	1985	1986	1987	1988	1989
1 Agriculture, hunting, forestry and fishing	2189.0	...	...	...	...	...	...	...	...	...	...	...
2 Mining and quarrying	16.6	...	...	...	...	...	...	...	...	...	...	...
3 Manufacturing	907.0	...	...	...	...	...	...	...	...	...	...	...
4 Electricity, gas and water	157.8	...	...	...	...	...	...	...	...	...	...	...
5 Construction	763.9	...	...	...	...	...	...	...	...	...	...	...
6 Wholesale and retail trade, restaurants and hotels	1135.6	...	...	...	...	...	...	...	...	...	...	...
7 Transport, storage and communication	599.4	...	...	...	...	...	...	...	...	...	...	...
8 Finance, insurance, real estate and business services	268.8	...	...	...	...	...	...	...	...	...	...	...
9 Community, social and personal services	2262.0	...	...	...	...	...	...	...	...	...	...	...
Total, Industries	8300.0	...	...	...	...	...	...	...	...	...	...	...
Producers of Government Services	...	...	...	...	...	...	...	...	...	...	...	...
Other Producers	...	...	...	...	...	...	...	...	...	...	...	...
Subtotal	8300.0	...	...	...	...	...	...	...	...	...	...	...
Less: Imputed bank service charge	...	...	...	...	...	...	...	...	...	...	...	...
Plus: Import duties	...	...	...	...	...	...	...	...	...	...	...	...
Plus: Value added tax	...	...	...	...	...	...	...	...	...	...	...	...
Equals: Gross Domestic Product	8300.0	...	...	...	...	...	...	...	...	...	...	...

1.11 Gross Domestic Product by Kind of Activity, in Constant Prices

Thousand New Zealand dollars

	1970	1975	1980	1981	1982	1983	1984	1985	1986	1987	1988	1989
					At constant prices of:1980							
1 Agriculture, hunting, forestry and fishing	8089.0	...	...	...	...	...	...	...	...	...	...	...
2 Mining and quarrying	...	...	...	...	...	...	...	...	...	...	...	...
3 Manufacturing	3377.0	...	...	...	...	...	...	...	...	...	...	...
4 Electricity, gas and water	621.0	...	...	...	...	...	...	...	...	...	...	...
5 Construction	2823.0	...	...	...	...	...	...	...	...	...	...	...
6 Wholesale and retail trade, restaurants and hotels	4198.0	...	...	...	...	...	...	...	...	...	...	...
7 Transport, storage and communication	2213.0	...	...	...	...	...	...	...	...	...	...	...
8 Finance, insurance, real estate and business services	994.0	...	...	...	...	...	...	...	...	...	...	...
9 Community, social and personal services	8358.0	...	...	...	...	...	...	...	...	...	...	...

Cook Islands

1.11 Gross Domestic Product by Kind of Activity, in Constant Prices
(Continued)

Thousand New Zealand dollars

	1970	1975	1980	1981	1982	1983	1984	1985	1986	1987	1988	1989
				At constant prices of:1980								
Total, Industries	30673.0	...	...	...	...	...	...	...	...	...	...	...
Producers of Government Services	...	...	...	...	...	...	...	...	...	...	...	...
Other Producers	...	...	...	...	...	...	...	...	...	...	...	...
Subtotal	30673.0	...	...	...	...	...	...	...	...	...	...	...
Less: Imputed bank service charge	...	...	...	...	...	...	...	...	...	...	...	...
Plus: Import duties	...	...	...	...	...	...	...	...	...	...	...	...
Plus: Value added tax	...	...	...	...	...	...	...	...	...	...	...	...
Equals: Gross Domestic Product	...	...	...	...	...	...	...	...	...	...	...	...

Costa Rica

Source. Reply to the United Nations National Accounts Questionnaire from the Banco Central de Costa Rica, Departamento de Estudios Economicos, Seccion Cuentas Nacionales, San Jose. Official estimates are published in 'Cifras de Cuentas Nacionales de Costa Rica'.

General note. The estimates shown in the tables below have been prepared in accordance with the United Nations System of National Accounts so far as the existing data would permit.

1.1 Expenditure on the Gross Domestic Product, in Current Prices

Million Costa Rican colones

	1970	1975	1980	1981	1982	1983	1984	1985	1986	1987	1988	1989
1 Government final consumption expenditure	820	2558	7544	8987	14192	19527	25503	31175	37951	42652	54630	72283
2 Private final consumption expenditure	4805	12036	27140	34344	56397	79481	99837	118974	144381	176475	215794	257936
3 Gross capital formation	1340	3637	11003	16575	24070	31270	37003	51240	62162	77107	86288	113344
A Increase in stocks	70	-58	1109	2838	4262	8001	4324	13000	16139	20794	20077	28357
B Gross fixed capital formation	1270	3695	9895	13738	19809	23270	32679	38240	46023	56313	66211	84987
4 Exports of goods and services	1816	5052	10963	24707	43959	46601	56046	60807	77280	90067	120650	148118
5 Less: Imports of goods and services	2256	6478	15245	27510	41113	47565	55377	64277	75195	101767	127700	163611
Equals: Gross Domestic Product	6525	16805	41406	57103	97505	129314	163011	197920	246579	284533	349661	428071

1.2 Expenditure on the Gross Domestic Product, in Constant Prices

Million Costa Rican colones

	1970	1975	1980	1981	1982	1983	1984	1985	1986	1987	1988	1989
					At constant prices of:1966							
1 Government final consumption expenditure	660	961	1276	1205	1174	1140	1184	1196	1225	1252	1290	1335
2 Private final consumption expenditure	4089	4837	6238	5706	5158	5447	5842	6093	6418	6663	6819	7197
3 Gross capital formation	1129	1523	2753	1715	1278	1701	1887	2033	2660	2742	2557	2726
A Increase in stocks	51	-21	329	-106	-36	278	92	141	544	408	308	193
B Gross fixed capital formation	1078	1544	2425	1821	1314	1423	1795	1892	2116	2334	2249	2533
4 Exports of goods and services	1878	2720	3367	3742	3537	3491	3885	3729	3865	4677	5088	5814
5 Less: Imports of goods and services	2182	2568	3987	2937	2405	2785	3082	3267	3841	4517	4564	5267
Equals: Gross Domestic Product	5574	7473	9648	9430	8743	8993	9715	9785	10326	10818	11190	11804

1.3 Cost Components of the Gross Domestic Product

Million Costa Rican colones

	1970	1975	1980	1981	1982	1983	1984	1985	1986	1987	1988	1989
1 Indirect taxes, net	725	2117	4862	6782	11315	18624	23914	26671	33642	39128	44584	54846
A Indirect taxes	751	2153	5245	7503	12353	19561	25180	28663	36271	41994	49156	61042
B Less: Subsidies	26	36	383	720	1039	937	1266	1992	2629	2867	4572	6196
2 Consumption of fixed capital	416	892	2181	2711	3887	4210	4862	5488	6130	7114	8919	10578
3 Compensation of employees paid by resident producers to:	3058	7693	20495	24784	38123	56432	73430	92373	112667	134065	166373	209185
4 Operating surplus	2326	6102	13867	22825	44181	50048	60806	73388	94140	104227	129785	153462
Equals: Gross Domestic Product	6525	16805	41406	57103	97505	129314	163011	197920	246579	284533	349661	428071

1.4 General Government Current Receipts and Disbursements

Million Costa Rican colones

	1970	1975	1980	1981	1982	1983	1984	1985	1986	1987	1988	1989
					Receipts							
1 Operating surplus	...	...	...	...	...	...	...	...	...	...	...	...
2 Property and entrepreneurial income	28	65	229	337	328	957	1757	2315	3273	4767	7426	9581
3 Taxes, fees and contributions	1151	3414	8607	11838	20098	32836	41557	49404	60573	71562	85309	105543
A Indirect taxes	751	2153	5245	7503	12353	19561	25180	28663	36271	41994	49156	61042
B Direct taxes	176	447	1014	1489	2913	4719	4756	5025	5696	6317	8236	9507
C Social security contributions	206	776	2274	2724	4646	8309	11172	15133	17896	21801	26432	32878
D Compulsory fees, fines and penalties	18	37	73	122	186	247	449	583	710	1450	1485	2116
4 Other current transfers	14	40	105	180	222	271	417	1056	8720	11848	15849	15051
Total Current Receipts of General Government	1192	3519	8941	12356	20648	34064	43730	52775	72565	88178	108584	130175
					Disbursements							
1 Government final consumption expenditure	820	2558	7544	8987	14192	19527	25503	31175	37951	42652	54630	72283

Costa Rica

1.4 General Government Current Receipts and Disbursements
(Continued)

Million Costa Rican colones

	1970	1975	1980	1981	1982	1983	1984	1985	1986	1987	1988	1989
A Compensation of employees	693	2084	6289	7625	11323	15799	20543	25778	31580	36260	...	...
B Consumption of fixed capital	...	...	...	...	...	...	...	...	...	...	...	...
C Purchases of goods and services, net	...	...	...	...	...	...	...	...	...	...	...	...
D Less: Own account fixed capital formation	...	...	...	...	...	...	...	...	...	...	...	...
E Indirect taxes paid, net	...	...	...	...	...	...	...	...	...	...	...	...
2 Property income	72	176	935	1584	2500	3738	3571	3866	5253	6716	11344	14971
A Interest	72	176	935	1584	2500	3738	3571	3866	5253	6716	11344	14971
B Net land rent and royalties	...	...	...	...	...	...	...	...	...	...	...	...
3 Subsidies	26	36	383	720	1039	937	1266	1992	2629	2867	4572	6196
4 Other current transfers	107	243	749	1133	1962	2531	3608	5941	12529	19983	23058	24164
A Social security benefits	20	106	358	482	811	1303	1611	2304	3590	3892	5113	6491
B Social assistance grants	13	41	56	252	407	47	64	104	165	182	206	283
C Other	74	96	335	399	743	1180	1933	3533	8774	15909	17739	17390
5 Net saving	169	506	-672	-68	956	7331	9783	9800	14204	15960	14981	12561
Total Current Disbursements and Net Saving of General Government	1192	3519	8941	12356	20648	34064	43730	52774	72565	88178	108584	130175

1.7 External Transactions on Current Account, Summary

Million Costa Rican colones

	1970	1975	1980	1981	1982	1983	1984	1985	1986	1987	1988	1989
Payments to the Rest of the World												
1 Imports of goods and services	2256	6478	15245	27510	41113	47565	55377	64277	75195	101768	127700	163611
A Imports of merchandise c.i.f.	2073	5907	13989	25244	35185	41120	48741	55834	64882	86626	106670	141508
B Other	183	571	1256	2266	5928	6446	6636	8443	10313	15142	21030	22103
2 Factor income to the rest of the world	115	617	2283	7131	17602	15810	16085	17408	18587	22264	30577	39259
A Compensation of employees	9	30	72	121	367	154	229	297	294	540	499	774
B Property and entrepreneurial income	106	587	2211	7011	17235	15656	15856	17110	18293	21724	30077	38484
3 Current transfers to the rest of the world	35	81	176	208	316	407	462	537	603	703	870	318
4 Surplus of the nation on current transactions	-506	-1865	-6134	-8664	-12009	-13765	-11623	-14847	-9453	-24067	-23844	-40359
Payments to the Rest of the World and Surplus of the Nation on Current Transactions	1900	5311	11570	26186	47022	50017	60301	67375	84932	100668	135303	162829
Receipts From The Rest of the World												
1 Exports of goods and services	1816	5052	10963	24707	43959	46601	56046	60807	77280	90067	120650	148118
A Exports of merchandise f.o.b.	1530	4225	9248	21235	34561	35430	44288	47388	60838	69505	89317	107800
B Other	286	827	1715	3473	9398	11171	11758	13419	16442	20562	31333	40318
2 Factor income from rest of the world	26	94	296	697	1516	2136	2281	3293	3488	3649	4486	7653
A Compensation of employees	20	52	104	194	457	490	627	802	966	1099	1558	1760
B Property and entrepreneurial income	7	42	191	503	1059	1646	1654	2491	2522	2550	2928	5893
3 Current transfers from rest of the world	58	164	311	781	1547	1280	1974	3275	4164	6952	10167	7058
Receipts from the Rest of the World on Current Transactions	1900	5311	11570	26186	47022	50017	60301	67375	84932	100668	135303	162829

1.8 Capital Transactions of The Nation, Summary

Million Costa Rican colones

	1970	1975	1980	1981	1982	1983	1984	1985	1986	1987	1988	1989
Finance of Gross Capital Formation												
Gross saving	834	1772	4869	7911	12061	17506	25380	36393	52709	53041	62444	72986
1 Consumption of fixed capital	416	892	2181	2711	3887	4210	4862	5488	6130	7114	8919	10578
2 Net saving	418	880	2688	5201	8174	13296	20518	30905	46579	45927	53525	62408
A General government	169	506	-672	-70	958	7331	9783	9800	14204	15960	14981	12561
B Corporate and quasi-corporate enterprises [a]	74	285	254	740	-1765	5537	3961	2607	3940	10987	7627	9072

Costa Rica

1.8 Capital Transactions of The Nation, Summary
(Continued)

Million Costa Rican colones

	1970	1975	1980	1981	1982	1983	1984	1985	1986	1987	1988	1989
Public	74	285	254	740	-1765	5537	3961	2607	3940	10987	7627	9072
Private [a]	...	...	...	...	...	...	...	...	...	...	...	...
C Other [a]	176	88	3106	4531	8981	428	6775	18498	28436	18980	30917	40775
Less: Surplus of the nation on current transactions	-506	-1865	-6134	-8664	-12009	-13765	-11623	-14847	-9453	-24067	-23844	-40357
Finance of Gross Capital Formation	1340	3637	11003	16575	24070	31270	37003	51240	62162	77107	86288	113344
					Gross Capital Formation							
Increase in stocks	70	-58	1109	2838	4262	8001	4324	13000	16139	20794	20077	28357
Gross fixed capital formation	1270	3695	9895	13738	19809	23270	32679	38240	46023	56313	66211	84987
1 General government	...	...	1987	2437	2427	3398	4920	6444	5997	4871	5351	7623
2 Corporate and quasi-corporate enterprises	...	...	1838	2635	4602	4817	5444	7496	8375	7698	9073	11623
A Public	...	...	1838	2635	4602	4817	5444	7496	8375	7698	9073	11623
B Private	...	...	...	...	...	...	...	...	...	...	...	...
3 Other	...	...	6069	8666	12780	15054	22315	24300	31651	43744	51787	65741
Gross Capital Formation	1340	3637	11003	16575	24070	31270	37003	51240	62162	77107	86288	113344

a) Private corporate and quasi-corporate enterprises are included in item 'Other'.

1.10 Gross Domestic Product by Kind of Activity, in Current Prices

Million Costa Rican colones

	1970	1975	1980	1981	1982	1983	1984	1985	1986	1987	1988	1989
1 Agriculture, hunting, forestry and fishing	1469	3418	7372	13145	23884	28446	34571	37341	51530	51417	62774	73030
2 Mining and quarrying	1192	3427	7701	10818	19828	28263	36667	43715	52573	60698	74315	86805
3 Manufacturing												
4 Electricity, gas and water	110	304	882	1424	2264	4950	5536	6348	7413	8598	10292	13301
5 Construction	277	869	2584	2960	3005	3789	5807	7072	8127	9160	10544	14449
6 Wholesale and retail trade, restaurants and hotels	1371	3204	8315	10500	21125	25498	31701	40507	47367	58505	70592	85429
7 Transport, storage and communication	274	789	1744	2555	4487	6283	7842	9774	11639	14069	17367	20923
8 Finance, insurance, real estate and business services	801	1940	4686	5791	8084	10884	13194	17796	24522	31071	39424	50637
9 Community, social and personal services [a]	336	771	1835	2286	3505	5401	7150	9589	11829	14756	18380	23496
Total, Industries	5830	14722	35119	49479	86182	113514	142468	172142	215000	248273	303687	368070
Producers of Government Services	693	2084	6289	7625	11324	15800	20543	25778	31580	36260	45974	60001
Other Producers [a]	...	...	...	...	...	...	...	...	...	...	...	...
Subtotal	6525	16805	41406	57103	97505	129314	163011	197920	246580	284533	349661	428071
Less: Imputed bank service charge	...	...	...	...	...	...	...	...	...	...	...	...
Plus: Import duties	...	...	...	...	...	...	...	...	...	...	...	...
Plus: Value added tax	...	...	...	...	...	...	...	...	...	...	...	...
Equals: Gross Domestic Product	6525	16805	41406	57103	97505	129314	163011	197920	246580	284533	349661	428071

a) Item 'Other producers' is included in item 'Community, social and personal services'.

1.11 Gross Domestic Product by Kind of Activity, in Constant Prices

Million Costa Rican colones

	1970	1975	1980	1981	1982	1983	1984	1985	1986	1987	1988	1989
					At constant prices of: 1966							
1 Agriculture, hunting, forestry and fishing	1344	1586	1736	1825	1739	1808	1990	1880	1971	2053	2148	2272
2 Mining and quarrying	1036	1587	2120	2109	1869	1902	2100	2142	2299	2425	2478	2573
3 Manufacturing												
4 Electricity, gas and water	106	156	225	242	253	304	313	290	308	332	340	357
5 Construction	229	385	603	472	321	337	416	439	453	458	458	515
6 Wholesale and retail trade, restaurants and hotels	1110	1288	1741	1556	1374	1418	1580	1653	1768	1839	1863	1969
7 Transport, storage and communication	248	432	676	672	666	676	701	717	770	838	909	990
8 Finance, insurance, real estate and business services	664	924	1165	1166	1176	1211	1252	1284	1344	1413	1494	1580
9 Community, social and personal services [a]	288	347	416	403	389	396	408	420	435	456	477	504

Costa Rica

1.11 Gross Domestic Product by Kind of Activity, in Constant Prices
(Continued)

Million Costa Rican colones

	1970	1975	1980	1981	1982	1983	1984	1985	1986	1987	1988	1989
					At constant prices of:1966							
Total, Industries	5024	6703	8681	8445	7787	8052	8760	8826	9347	9815	10167	10760
Producers of Government Services	549	770	967	984	956	941	955	959	979	1003	1023	1044
Other Producers [a]	...	...	...	...	...	...	...	...	...	...	...	...
Subtotal	5574	7473	9648	9430	8743	8993	9715	9785	10326	10818	11190	11804
Less: Imputed bank service charge	...	...	...	...	...	...	...	...	...	...	...	...
Plus: Import duties	...	...	...	...	...	...	...	...	...	...	...	...
Plus: Value added tax	...	...	...	...	...	...	...	...	...	...	...	...
Equals: Gross Domestic Product	5574	7473	9648	9430	8743	8993	9715	9785	10326	10818	11190	11804

a) Item 'Other producers' is included in item 'Community, social and personal services'.

1.12 Relations Among National Accounting Aggregates

Million Costa Rican colones

	1970	1975	1980	1981	1982	1983	1984	1985	1986	1987	1988	1989
Gross Domestic Product	6525	16805	41406	57103	97505	129314	163011	197920	246579	284533	349661	428071
Plus: Net factor income from the rest of the world	-89	-522	-1988	-6434	-16086	-13673	-13804	-14115	-15098	-18615	-26091	-31606
Factor income from the rest of the world	...	...	296	697	1516	2136	2281	3293	3489	3649	4486	7653
Less: Factor income to the rest of the world	...	...	2283	7131	17602	15809	16085	17408	18587	22264	30577	39259
Equals: Gross National Product	6435	16283	39418	50669	81419	115641	149207	183805	231481	265918	323570	396465
Less: Consumption of fixed capital	416	892	2181	2711	3887	4210	4862	5488	6130	7114	8919	10578
Equals: National Income	6020	15391	37237	47958	77532	111431	144345	178317	225351	258804	314651	385887
Plus: Net current transfers from the rest of the world	23	83	135	573	1231	873	1512	2738	3560	6249	9297	6740
Equals: National Disposable Income	6043	15474	37372	48531	78763	112304	145857	181055	228911	265053	323948	392627
Less: Final consumption	5625	14594	34684	43330	70589	99008	125339	150149	182332	219127	270424	330219
Equals: Net Saving	418	880	2688	5201	8174	13296	20518	30905	46579	45926	53524	62408
Less: Surplus of the nation on current transactions	-506	-1865	-6134	-8663	-12009	-13765	-11623	-14847	-9453	-24067	-23844	-40359
Equals: Net Capital Formation	924	2745	8822	13864	20184	27061	32141	45752	56032	69993	77368	102767

2.7 Gross Capital Formation by Type of Good and Owner, in Current Prices

Million Costa Rican colones

	\multicolumn{4}{c}{1980}	\multicolumn{4}{c}{1981}	\multicolumn{4}{c}{1982}
	TOTAL	Total Private	Public Enterprises	General Government	TOTAL	Total Private	Public Enterprises	General Government	TOTAL	Total Private	Public Enterprises	General Government
Increase in stocks, total [a]	1109	992	112	5	2838	1666	1077	95	4262	2103	2003	156
Gross Fixed Capital Formation, Total	9895	6069	1839	1987	13738	8666	2635	2437	19809	12780	4602	2427
1 Residential buildings	...	...	...	...	...	...	...	...	...	...	...	...
2 Non-residential buildings	...	...	...	...	...	...	...	...	...	...	...	...
3 Other construction	...	...	...	...	...	...	...	...	...	...	...	...
4 Land improvement and plantation and orchard development	...	...	...	...	...	...	...	...	...	...	...	...
5 Producers' durable goods	4219	3549	218	453	6626	5871	197	557	9154	8487	239	427
6 Breeding stock, dairy cattle, etc.	...	...	...	...	...	...	...	...	...	...	...	...
Total Gross Capital Formation	11003	7061	1951	1992	16575	10332	3712	2531	24070	14883	6604	2583

	\multicolumn{4}{c}{1983}	\multicolumn{4}{c}{1984}	\multicolumn{4}{c}{1985}
	TOTAL	Total Private	Public Enterprises	General Government	TOTAL	Total Private	Public Enterprises	General Government	TOTAL	Total Private	Public Enterprises	General Government
Increase in stocks, total [a]	8001	6708	995	299	4324	4396	-324	252	13000	11245	1350	405
Gross Fixed Capital Formation, Total	23270	15054	4817	3398	32679	22315	5444	4920	38240	24300	7496	6444
1 Residential buildings	...	...	...	...	...	...	...	...	...	...	...	...
2 Non-residential buildings	...	...	...	...	...	...	...	...	...	...	...	...
3 Other construction	...	...	...	...	...	...	...	...	...	...	...	...
4 Land improvement and plantation and orchard development	...	...	...	...	...	...	...	...	...	...	...	...
5 Producers' durable goods	11207	9753	878	576	16568	15272	539	757	19422	16649	1932	842
6 Breeding stock, dairy cattle, etc.	...	...	...	...	...	...	...	...	...	...	...	...
Total Gross Capital Formation	31270	21762	5812	3697	37003	26711	5120	5172	51240	35545	8846	6849

Costa Rica

2.7 Gross Capital Formation by Type of Good and Owner, in Current Prices

Million Costa Rican colones

	1986 TOTAL	Total Private	Public Enterprises	General Government	1987 TOTAL	Total Private	Public Enterprises	General Government	1988 TOTAL	Total Private	Public Enterprises	General Government
Increase in stocks, total [a]	16139	16501	-630	268	20794	18318	1233	1243	20077	18836	603	639
Gross Fixed Capital Formation, Total	46023	31651	8375	5997	56313	43744	7698	4871	66211	51787	9073	5351
1 Residential buildings	...	...	...	...	...	...	...	...	...	...	...	...
2 Non-residential buildings	...	...	...	...	...	...	...	...	...	...	...	...
3 Other construction	...	...	...	...	...	...	...	...	...	...	...	...
4 Land improvement and plantation and orchard development	...	...	...	...	...	...	...	...	...	...	...	...
5 Producers' durable goods	24379	21503	1311	1565	32385	29602	1338	1445	36691	33102	1909	1681
6 Breeding stock, dairy cattle, etc.	...	...	...	...	...	...	...	...	...	...	...	...
Total Gross Capital Formation	62162	48152	7745	6265	77107	62062	8931	6114	86288	70623	9676	5990

	1989 TOTAL	Total Private	Public Enterprises	General Government
Increase in stocks, total [a]	28357	27526	886	-55
Gross Fixed Capital Formation, Total	84987	65741	11623	7623
1 Residential buildings	...	...	...	...
2 Non-residential buildings	...	...	...	...
3 Other construction	...	...	...	...
4 Land improvement and plantation and orchard development	...	...	...	...
5 Producers' durable goods	46469	41817	2601	2052
6 Breeding stock, dairy cattle, etc.	...	...	...	...
Total Gross Capital Formation	113344	93267	12509	7568

a) Item 'Increase in stocks' represents cattle and pig stocks, coffee, basic grains in silos and materials in the public sector.

2.8 Gross Capital Formation by Type of Good and Owner, in Constant Prices

Million Costa Rican colones

	1980 TOTAL	Total Private	Public Enterprises	General Government	1981 TOTAL	Total Private	Public Enterprises	General Government	1982 TOTAL	Total Private	Public Enterprises	General Government
	At constant prices of: 1966											
Increase in stocks, total [a]	329	344	-	-15	-106	-132	41	-15	-36	5	-24	-17
Gross Fixed Capital Formation, Total	2425	1556	403	465	1821	1165	339	317	1314	842	310	163
1 Residential buildings	...	...	...	...	...	...	...	...	...	...	...	...
2 Non-residential buildings	...	...	...	...	...	...	...	...	...	...	...	...
3 Other construction	...	...	...	...	...	...	...	...	...	...	...	...
4 Land improvement and plantation and orchard development	...	...	...	...	...	...	...	...	...	...	...	...
5 Producers' durable goods	1212	1019	63	130	909	806	27	77	602	558	16	28
6 Breeding stock, dairy cattle, etc.	...	...	...	...	...	...	...	...	...	...	...	...
Total Gross Capital Formation	2753	1900	403	450	1715	1033	380	302	1278	847	286	146

	1983 TOTAL	Total Private	Public Enterprises	General Government	1984 TOTAL	Total Private	Public Enterprises	General Government	1985 TOTAL	Total Private	Public Enterprises	General Government
	At constant prices of: 1966											
Increase in stocks, total [a]	278	233	35	10	92	112	-29	9	141	95	35	11
Gross Fixed Capital Formation, Total	1423	889	313	221	1795	1222	301	272	1892	1196	374	322
1 Residential buildings	...	...	...	...	...	...	...	...	...	...	...	...
2 Non-residential buildings	...	...	...	...	...	...	...	...	...	...	...	...
3 Other construction	...	...	...	...	...	...	...	...	...	...	...	...
4 Land improvement and plantation and orchard development	...	...	...	...	...	...	...	...	...	...	...	...
5 Producers' durable goods	678	590	53	35	903	832	29	41	962	825	96	42
6 Breeding stock, dairy cattle, etc.	...	...	...	...	...	...	...	...	...	...	...	...
Total Gross Capital Formation	1701	1122	348	232	1887	1334	272	281	2033	1291	409	333

Costa Rica

2.8 Gross Capital Formation by Type of Good and Owner, in Constant Prices

Million Costa Rican colones

	1986 TOTAL	1986 Total Private	1986 Public Enterprises	1986 General Government	1987 TOTAL	1987 Total Private	1987 Public Enterprises	1987 General Government	1988 TOTAL	1988 Total Private	1988 Public Enterprises	1988 General Government
				At constant prices of: 1966								
Increase in stocks, total [a]	544	582	-42	5	408	351	23	35	308	320	-13	2
Gross Fixed Capital Formation, Total	2116	1456	385	275	2334	1808	323	204	2249	1753	312	184
1 Residential buildings	...	...	...	...	...	...	...	...	...	...	...	...
2 Non-residential buildings	...	...	...	...	...	...	...	...	...	...	...	...
3 Other construction	...	...	...	...	...	...	...	...	...	...	...	...
4 Land improvement and plantation and orchard development	...	...	...	...	...	...	...	...	...	...	...	...
5 Producers' durable goods	1152	1016	62	74	1387	1268	57	62	1275	1150	66	58
6 Breeding stock, dairy cattle, etc.	...	...	...	...	...	...	...	...	...	...	...	...
Total Gross Capital Formation	2660	2038	343	279	2742	2159	346	239	2557	2073	299	186

	1989 TOTAL	1989 Total Private	1989 Public Enterprises	1989 General Government
		At constant prices of: 1966		
Increase in stocks, total [a]	193	219	-8	-18
Gross Fixed Capital Formation, Total	2533	1967	341	224
1 Residential buildings	...	...	...	...
2 Non-residential buildings	...	...	...	...
3 Other construction	...	...	...	...
4 Land improvement and plantation and orchard development	...	...	...	...
5 Producers' durable goods	1461	1315	82	65
6 Breeding stock, dairy cattle, etc.	...	...	...	...
Total Gross Capital Formation	2726	2186	333	206

a) Item 'Increase in stocks' represents cattle and pig stocks, coffee, basic grains in silos and materials in the public sector.

2.9 Gross Capital Formation by Kind of Activity of Owner, ISIC Major Divisions, in Current Prices

Million Costa Rican colones

	1980 Total Gross Capital Formation	1980 Increase in Stocks	1980 Gross Fixed Capital Formation	1981 Total Gross Capital Formation	1981 Increase in Stocks	1981 Gross Fixed Capital Formation	1982 Total Gross Capital Formation	1982 Increase in Stocks	1982 Gross Fixed Capital Formation	1983 Total Gross Capital Formation	1983 Increase in Stocks	1983 Gross Fixed Capital Formation
					All Producers							
1 Agriculture, hunting, fishing and forestry	727	6	721	1074	-	1074	1680	-	1680	2270	-	2270
2 Mining and quarrying	2527	978	1548	3785	1136	2649	6363	2012	4351	8408	3643	4765
3 Manufacturing												
4 Electricity, gas and water	952	44	907	1730	237	1494	2823	237	2586	2637	141	2497
5 Construction	477	-	477	468	-	468	605	-	605	967	-	967
6 Wholesale and retail trade, restaurants and hotels	429	-	429	1795	1151	644	2590	1483	1107	4982	3894	1088
7 Transport, storage and communication	1641	62	1579	2553	199	2354	3783	342	3441	4233	-12	4245
8 Finance, insurance, real estate and business services	2054	13	2041	2297	21	2276	2956	31	2926	3393	38	3355
9 Community, social and personal services	205	-	205	343	-	343	687	-	687	684	-	684
Total Industries	9012	1104	7908	14044	2743	11301	21487	4105	17382	27574	7702	19871
Producers of Government Services	1992	5	1987	2531	95	2437	2584	157	2427	3697	299	3398
Private Non-Profit Institutions Serving Households	...	...	...	...	...	...	...	...	...	...	...	...
Total	11003	1109	9895	16575	2838	13737	24070	4262	19809	31270	8000	23270

	1984 Total Gross Capital Formation	1984 Increase in Stocks	1984 Gross Fixed Capital Formation	1985 Total Gross Capital Formation	1985 Increase in Stocks	1985 Gross Fixed Capital Formation	1986 Total Gross Capital Formation	1986 Increase in Stocks	1986 Gross Fixed Capital Formation	1987 Total Gross Capital Formation	1987 Increase in Stocks	1987 Gross Fixed Capital Formation
					All Producers							
1 Agriculture, hunting, fishing and forestry	2824	-	2824	2703	-	2703	3197	-792	3989	6098	-299	6397
2 Mining and quarrying	9804	2720	7084	14776	6693	8083	21398	12010	9388	23327	11310	12017
3 Manufacturing												
4 Electricity, gas and water	2912	-44	2956	3495	-120	3615	6029	517	5512	5072	383	4689

Costa Rica

2.9 Gross Capital Formation by Kind of Activity of Owner, ISIC Major Divisions, in Current Prices
(Continued)

Million Costa Rican colones

	1984 Total Gross Capital Formation	1984 Increase in Stocks	1984 Gross Fixed Capital Formation	1985 Total Gross Capital Formation	1985 Increase in Stocks	1985 Gross Fixed Capital Formation	1986 Total Gross Capital Formation	1986 Increase in Stocks	1986 Gross Fixed Capital Formation	1987 Total Gross Capital Formation	1987 Increase in Stocks	1987 Gross Fixed Capital Formation
5 Construction	1710	-	1710	1374	-	1374	1285	-	1285	3434	-	3434
6 Wholesale and retail trade, restaurants and hotels	2658	1535	1123	7379	6175	1204	5328	3751	1577	9741	7601	2140
7 Transport, storage and communication	5704	-177	5881	7083	-251	7334	8989	353	8636	10392	455	9937
8 Finance, insurance, real estate and business services	5588	39	5549	6748	67	6681	7917	34	7883	10859	102	10757
9 Community, social and personal services	632	-	632	803	-	803	1753	-	1753	2071	-	2071
Total Industries	31831	4072	27759	44359	12564	31795	55897	15871	40026	70993	19551	51442
Producers of Government Services	5172	252	4920	6880	436	6444	6265	268	5997	6114	1243	4871
Private Non-Profit Institutions Serving Households	...	...	...	...	...	...	...	...	...	...	...	...
Total	37003	4324	32679	51240	13000	38240	62162	16139	46023	77107	20794	56313

	1988 Total Gross Capital Formation	1988 Increase in Stocks	1988 Gross Fixed Capital Formation	1989 Total Gross Capital Formation	1989 Increase in Stocks	1989 Gross Fixed Capital Formation
	All Producers					
1 Agriculture, hunting, fishing and forestry	7642	-191	7834	10799	837	9962
2 Mining and quarrying	26806	13073	13733	35325	17401	17924
3 Manufacturing						
4 Electricity, gas and water	6225	556	5669	6112	-479	6591
5 Construction	1975	-	1975	3155	-	3155
6 Wholesale and retail trade, restaurants and hotels	8550	5729	2821	14684	10941	3743
7 Transport, storage and communication	12225	233	11992	13869	-417	14286
8 Finance, insurance, real estate and business services	14321	39	14282	18685	129	18556
9 Community, social and personal services	2554	-	2554	3146	-	3146
Total Industries	80298	19438	60860	105777	28412	77365
Producers of Government Services	5990	639	5351	7567	-55	7622
Private Non-Profit Institutions Serving Households	...	...	...	...	...	...
Total	86288	20077	66211	113344	28357	84987

2.17 Exports and Imports of Goods and Services, Detail

Million Costa Rican colones

	1970	1975	1980	1981	1982	1983	1984	1985	1986	1987	1988	1989
	Exports of Goods and Services											
1 Exports of merchandise, f.o.b.	1530	4225	9248	21235	34561	35430	44288	47388	60838	69505	89317	107800
2 Transport and communication	41	154	191	320	419	744	1006	1003	1232	1570	1732	2502
3 Insurance service charges	31	40	106	227	285	183	262	290	357	433	613	701
4 Other commodities	51	139	484	741	1853	3213	3708	4730	5658	7888	12436	16039
5 Adjustments of merchandise exports to change-of-ownership basis	...	...	...	...	...	...	...	...	...	...	...	...
6 Direct purchases in the domestic market by non-residential households	164	494	933	2185	6842	7032	6783	7396	9196	10670	16552	21076
7 Direct purchases in the domestic market by extraterritorial bodies	...	...	...	...	...	...	...	...	...	...	...	...
Total Exports of Goods and Services	1816	5052	10963	24707	43959	46601	56046	60807	77280	90067	120650	148118
	Imports of Goods and Services											
1 Imports of merchandise, c.i.f.	2073	5907	13989	25244	35185	41120	48741	55834	64882	86622	106671	141509

Costa Rica

2.17 Exports and Imports of Goods and Services, Detail
(Continued)

Million Costa Rican colones

	1970	1975	1980	1981	1982	1983	1984	1985	1986	1987	1988	1989
A Imports of merchandise, f.o.b.	1899	5376	12707	23099	32011	37313	44253	50707	58843	78200	96693	128200
B Transport of services on merchandise imports	174	531	1283	2146	3174	3807	4488	5127	6038	8422	9978	13309
C Insurance service charges on merchandise imports	...	...	...	...	...	...	...	...	...	...	...	...
2 Adjustments of merchandise imports to change-of-ownership basis	...	...	...	...	...	...	...	...	...	...	...	...
3 Other transport and communication	36	93	213	358	1675	1293	962	1038	1092	1357	2232	2429
4 Other insurance service charges	...	...	...	...	...	...	...	...	...	...	...	...
5 Other commodities a	43	104	348	664	2184	2568	2740	3349	4176	7537	12293	11736
6 Direct purchases abroad by government	105	375	695	1244	2069	2585	2935	4056	5046	6249	6506	7938
7 Direct purchases abroad by resident households												
Total Imports of Goods and Services	2256	6478	15245	27510	41113	47565	55377	64277	75195	101768	127700	163611
Balance of Goods and Services	-440	-1426	-4282	-2803	2846	-964	669	-3470	2085	-11701	-7050	-15493
Total Imports and Balance of Goods and Services	1816	5052	10963	24707	43959	46601	56046	60807	77280	90067	120650	148118

a) Item 'Other commodities' relates to non-factor services.

4.1 Derivation of Value Added by Kind of Activity, in Current Prices

Million Costa Rican colones

	1980 Gross Output	1980 Intermediate Consumption	1980 Value Added	1981 Gross Output	1981 Intermediate Consumption	1981 Value Added	1982 Gross Output	1982 Intermediate Consumption	1982 Value Added	1983 Gross Output	1983 Intermediate Consumption	1983 Value Added
All Producers												
1 Agriculture, hunting, forestry and fishing	10071	2698	7372	17665	4521	13145	31462	7578	23884	38968	10522	28446
A Agriculture and hunting	9458	2466	6992	16872	4355	12517	30173	7304	22869	37476	10252	27224
B Forestry and logging	449	155	294	558	62	496	790	102	688	1002	108	894
C Fishing	164	78	86	235	103	132	499	172	327	490	162	328
2 Mining and quarrying	24260	16559	7701	40019	29201	10818	71295	51467	19828	92081	63818	28263
3 Manufacturing												
A Manufacture of food, beverages and tobacco	11610	8511	3099	18855	14405	4450	33465	26313	7152	43668	32701	10967
B Textile, wearing apparel and leather industries	1850	1162	688	2908	1867	1041	6089	4340	1749	7801	5144	2657
C Manufacture of wood and wood products, including furniture	1180	700	480	1716	1118	598	2470	1703	767	3170	1949	1221
D Manufacture of paper and paper products, printing and publishing	1134	810	324	1832	1401	431	3411	2400	1011	4876	3527	1349
E Manufacture of chemicals and chemical petroleum, coal, rubber and plastic products	4405	3263	1142	8482	6684	1798	15647	12037	3610	19134	14073	5061
F Manufacture of non-metallic mineral products, except products of petroleum and coal	618	362	256	928	597	331	1634	1111	523	2122	1418	704
G Basic metal industries	226	193	33	340	258	82	715	471	244	759	583	176
H Manufacture of fabricated metal products, machinery and equipment	2377	1679	698	3651	2526	1125	5823	3640	2183	6476	4613	1863
I Other manufacturing industries	52	32	20	84	55	29	165	106	59	231	141	90
4 Electricity, gas and water	1048	166	882	1734	310	1424	...	...	2264	...	...	4950
5 Construction	5686	3103	2584	7089	4129	2960	...	...	3005	...	...	3789
6 Wholesale and retail trade, restaurants and hotels	...	...	8315	...	...	10500	...	...	21125	...	...	25498
7 Transport, storage and communication	...	...	1744	...	...	2555	...	...	4487	...	...	6283
8 Finance, insurance, real estate and business services	...	...	4686	...	...	5791	...	...	8084	...	...	10884
A Financial institutions	...	...	2192	...	...	2907	...	...	4825	...	...	7140
B Insurance	...	...	...	...	...	...	...	...	...	...	...	...
C Real estate and business services	...	...	2495	...	...	2883	...	...	3258	...	...	3744
9 Community, social and personal services a	...	...	1835	...	...	2286	...	...	3505	...	...	5401

Costa Rica

4.1 Derivation of Value Added by Kind of Activity, in Current Prices
(Continued)

Million Costa Rican colones

	1980 Gross Output	1980 Intermediate Consumption	1980 Value Added	1981 Gross Output	1981 Intermediate Consumption	1981 Value Added	1982 Gross Output	1982 Intermediate Consumption	1982 Value Added	1983 Gross Output	1983 Intermediate Consumption	1983 Value Added
Total, Industries	...	...	35119	...	...	49479	...	...	86182	...	...	113514
Producers of Government Services	...	...	6289	...	...	7625	...	...	11324	...	...	15800
Other Producers [a]	...	...	...	...	...	...	...	...	...	...	...	...
Total	...	...	41406	...	...	57103	...	...	97505	...	...	129314
Less: Imputed bank service charge	...	...	...	...	...	...	...	...	...	...	...	...
Import duties	...	...	...	...	...	...	...	...	...	...	...	...
Value added tax	...	...	...	...	...	...	...	...	...	...	...	...
Total [b]	...	...	41406	...	...	57103	...	...	97505	...	...	129314

	1984 Gross Output	1984 Intermediate Consumption	1984 Value Added	1985 Gross Output	1985 Intermediate Consumption	1985 Value Added	1986 Gross Output	1986 Intermediate Consumption	1986 Value Added	1987 Gross Output	1987 Intermediate Consumption	1987 Value Added
					All Producers							
1 Agriculture, hunting, forestry and fishing	47871	13300	34571	52050	14709	37341	68643	17113	51530	71742	20314	51428
A Agriculture and hunting	45805	12957	32848	48965	14284	34681	64656	16568	48087	67583	19731	47852
B Forestry and logging	1208	132	1076	1602	166	1436	2284	253	2031	1917	286	1631
C Fishing	858	211	647	1483	258	1225	1704	293	1411	2242	296	1946
2 Mining and quarrying	112637	75970	36667	129318	85603	43715	162846	110273	52573	...	...	59986
3 Manufacturing												
A Manufacture of food, beverages and tobacco	54456	39345	15111	62865	44258	18607	81838	58821	23017	86011	61210	24801
B Textile, wearing apparel and leather industries	8321	5335	2986	9421	5840	3581	9655	6042	3613	10264	6447	3817
C Manufacture of wood and wood products, including furniture	4179	2473	1706	5184	3210	1974	5691	3595	2096	9082	6466	2616
D Manufacture of paper and paper products, printing and publishing	5485	3906	1579	7092	4915	2177	9005	6287	2718	12403	8675	3728
E Manufacture of chemicals and chemical petroleum, coal, rubber and plastic products	24201	17577	6624	26477	18666	7811	34279	24388	9891	38802	27516	11286
F Manufacture of non-metallic mineral products, except products of petroleum and coal	3231	1988	1243	3785	2378	1407	4637	2893	1744	6171	3837	2334
G Basic metal industries	380	342	38	134	157	-23	151	177	-26	-	-	-
H Manufacture of fabricated metal products, machinery and equipment	7765	5115	2650	9073	6902	2171	11735	8203	3532	15628	11029	4599
I Other manufacturing industries	307	181	126	383	235	148	412	254	158	489	302	187
4 Electricity, gas and water	...	...	5536	...	...	6348	...	...	7413	...	...	8591
5 Construction	...	...	5807	...	...	7072	...	...	8127	...	...	9086
6 Wholesale and retail trade, restaurants and hotels	...	...	31701	...	...	40507	...	...	47367	...	...	58830
7 Transport, storage and communication	...	...	7842	...	...	9774	...	...	11639	...	...	13990
8 Finance, insurance, real estate and business services	...	...	13194	...	...	17797	...	...	24522	...	...	31033
A Financial institutions	...	...	8451	...	...	10989	...	...	15478	...	...	19939
B Insurance	...	...	...	...	...	...	...	...	...	...	...	...
C Real estate and business services	...	...	4743	...	...	6808	...	...	9044	...	...	11094
9 Community, social and personal services [a]	...	...	7150	...	...	9589	...	...	11829	...	...	15141
Total, Industries	...	...	142468	...	...	172142	...	...	215000	...	...	248085
Producers of Government Services	...	...	20543	...	...	25778	...	...	31580	...	...	36254
Other Producers [a]	...	...	...	...	...	...	...	...	...	...	...	...
Total	...	...	163011	...	...	197920	...	...	246580	...	...	284339
Less: Imputed bank service charge	...	...	...	...	...	...	...	...	...	...	...	...
Import duties	...	...	...	...	...	...	...	...	...	...	...	...
Value added tax	...	...	...	...	...	...	...	...	...	...	...	...
Total [b]	...	...	163011	...	...	197920	...	...	246579	...	...	284339

Costa Rica

4.1 Derivation of Value Added by Kind of Activity, in Current Prices

Million Costa Rican colones

		1988			1989		
		Gross Output	Intermediate Consumption	Value Added	Gross Output	Intermediate Consumption	Value Added
		All Producers					
1	Agriculture, hunting, forestry and fishing	...	...	64910	...	...	75555
	A Agriculture and hunting	...	...	...	...	...	...
	B Forestry and logging	...	...	...	...	...	...
	C Fishing	...	...	...	...	...	...
2	Mining and quarrying	...	...	⎱ 75222 ⎰	...	...	⎱ 89740 ⎰
3	Manufacturing	...	...		...	...	
	A Manufacture of food, beverages and tobacco	108392	77407	30988	121288	86335	34953
	B Textile, wearing apparel and leather industries	13481	8462	5019	15886	9960	5926
	C Manufacture of wood and wood products, including furniture	8701	5502	3199	9815	6298	3517
	D Manufacture of paper and paper products, printing and publishing	17438	12293	5145	20796	14704	6092
	E Manufacture of chemicals and chemical petroleum, coal, rubber and plastic products	45503	32223	13280	54223	38383	15840
	F Manufacture of non-metallic mineral products, except products of petroleum and coal	7695	4807	2888	6161	4000	2161
	G Basic metal industries	186	218	-32	-	-	-
	H Manufacture of fabricated metal products, machinery and equipment	16992	11915	5077	23166	16463	6703
	I Other manufacturing industries	546	337	209	675	420	255
4	Electricity, gas and water	...	...	10224	...	...	12637
5	Construction	...	...	10703	...	...	13368
6	Wholesale and retail trade, restaurants and hotels	...	...	72360	...	...	90740
7	Transport, storage and communication	...	...	17446	...	...	21039
8	Finance, insurance, real estate and business services	...	...	40131	...	...	48687
	A Financial institutions	...	...	...	...	...	...
	B Insurance	...	...	...	...	...	...
	C Real estate and business services	...	...	...	...	...	...
9	Community, social and personal services [a]	...	...	19002	...	...	22575
	Total, Industries	...	...	309998	...	...	374340
	Producers of Government Services	...	...	45970	...	...	58796
	Other Producers [a]	...	...	...	...	...	...
	Total	...	...	355968	...	...	433136
	Less: Imputed bank service charge	...	...	...	...	...	...
	Import duties	...	...	...	...	...	...
	Value added tax	...	...	...	...	...	...
	Total [b]	...	...	355968	...	...	433136

a) Item 'Other producers' is included in item 'Community, social and personal services'.
b) Data for this table have not been revised, therefore, data for some years are not comparable with those of other tables.

4.2 Derivation of Value Added by Kind of Activity, in Constant Prices

Million Costa Rican colones

		1980			1981			1982			1983		
		Gross Output	Intermediate Consumption	Value Added	Gross Output	Intermediate Consumption	Value Added	Gross Output	Intermediate Consumption	Value Added	Gross Output	Intermediate Consumption	Value Added
		At constant prices of: 1966											
		All Producers											
1	Agriculture, hunting, forestry and fishing	2492	756	1736	2572	748	1824	2425	686	1739	2488	680	1808
	A Agriculture and hunting	2338	697	1641	2433	715	1718	2311	658	1653	2395	655	1740
	B Forestry and logging	95	31	64	91	10	81	72	8	64	53	6	47
	C Fishing	59	28	31	48	23	25	42	20	22	40	19	21

Costa Rica

4.2 Derivation of Value Added by Kind of Activity, in Constant Prices
(Continued)

Million Costa Rican colones

	1980 Gross Output	1980 Intermediate Consumption	1980 Value Added	1981 Gross Output	1981 Intermediate Consumption	1981 Value Added	1982 Gross Output	1982 Intermediate Consumption	1982 Value Added	1983 Gross Output	1983 Intermediate Consumption	1983 Value Added
				At constant prices of: 1966								
2 Mining and quarrying	...	...	2120	...	...	2109	...	...	1869	...	...	1902
3 Manufacturing	...	...		...	...		...	...		...	...	
A Manufacture of food, beverages and tobacco	...	...	...	...	...	...	...	...	...	...	...	...
B Textile, wearing apparel and leather industries	...	...	...	...	...	...	...	...	...	...	...	...
C Manufacture of wood and wood products, including furniture	...	...	...	...	...	...	...	...	...	...	...	...
D Manufacture of paper and paper products, printing and publishing	...	...	...	...	...	...	...	...	...	...	...	...
E Manufacture of chemicals and chemical petroleum, coal, rubber and plastic products	...	...	...	...	...	...	...	...	...	...	...	...
F Manufacture of non-metallic mineral products, except products of petroleum and coal	...	...	...	...	...	...	...	...	...	...	...	...
G Basic metal industries	...	...	...	...	...	...	...	...	...	...	...	...
H Manufacture of fabricated metal products, machinery and equipment	...	...	...	...	...	...	...	...	...	...	...	...
I Other manufacturing industries	...	...	...	...	...	...	...	...	...	...	...	...
4 Electricity, gas and water	...	...	225	...	...	242	...	...	253	...	...	304
5 Construction	...	...	603	...	...	472	...	...	321	...	...	337
6 Wholesale and retail trade, restaurants and hotels	...	...	1741	...	...	1556	...	...	1374	...	...	1418
7 Transport, storage and communication	...	...	676	...	...	672	...	...	666	...	...	676
8 Finance, insurance, real estate and business services	...	...	1165	...	...	1166	...	...	1176	...	...	1211
9 Community, social and personal services	...	...	416	...	...	403	...	...	389	...	...	396
Total, Industries	...	...	8681	...	...	8446	...	...	7787	...	...	8052
Producers of Government Services	...	...	967	...	...	984	...	...	956	...	...	941
Other Producers	...	...	...	...	...	...	...	...	...	...	...	...
Total	...	...	9648	...	...	9430	...	...	8743	...	...	8993
Less: Imputed bank service charge	...	...	...	...	...	...	...	...	...	...	...	...
Import duties	...	...	...	...	...	...	...	...	...	...	...	...
Value added tax	...	...	...	...	...	...	...	...	...	...	...	...
Total [a]	...	...	9648	...	...	9430	...	...	8743	...	...	8993

	1984 Gross Output	1984 Intermediate Consumption	1984 Value Added	1985 Gross Output	1985 Intermediate Consumption	1985 Value Added	1986 Gross Output	1986 Intermediate Consumption	1986 Value Added	1987 Gross Output	1987 Intermediate Consumption	1987 Value Added
				At constant prices of: 1966								
				All Producers								
1 Agriculture, hunting, forestry and fishing	2725	735	1990	2577	697	1880	2711	740	1971	2841	791	2053
A Agriculture and hunting	2610	703	1907	2445	659	1786	2546	698	1848	2690	746	1944
B Forestry and logging	62	6	56	70	7	63	98	10	88	73	7	66
C Fishing	52	25	27	62	30	32	67	32	35	77	37	40

Costa Rica

4.2 Derivation of Value Added by Kind of Activity, in Constant Prices
(Continued)

Million Costa Rican colones

	1984 G.O.	1984 I.C.	1984 V.A.	1985 G.O.	1985 I.C.	1985 V.A.	1986 G.O.	1986 I.C.	1986 V.A.	1987 G.O.	1987 I.C.	1987 V.A.
At constant prices of: 1966												
2 Mining and quarrying	...	...	2100	...	...	2142	...	...	2299	...	...	2425
3 Manufacturing	...	...		...	...		...	...		...	...	
A Manufacture of food, beverages and tobacco	...	...	...	...	...	...	...	...	...	88409	63836	24573
B Textile, wearing apparel and leather industries	...	...	...	...	...	...	...	...	...	9052	5684	3368
C Manufacture of wood and wood products, including furniture	...	...	...	...	...	...	...	...	...	6211	3910	2301
D Manufacture of paper and paper products, printing and publishing	...	...	...	...	...	...	...	...	...	9589	6687	2902
E Manufacture of chemicals and chemical petroleum, coal, rubber and plastic products	...	...	...	...	...	...	...	...	...	34043	24153	9890
F Manufacture of non-metallic mineral products, except products of petroleum and coal	...	...	...	...	...	...	...	...	...	5396	3380	2016
G Basic metal industries	...	...	...	...	...	...	...	...	...	-	-	-
H Manufacture of fabricated metal products, machinery and equipment	...	...	...	...	...	...	...	...	...	12941	9145	3796
I Other manufacturing industries	...	...	...	...	...	...	...	...	...	448	277	171
4 Electricity, gas and water	...	...	313	...	...	290	...	...	308	...	...	332
5 Construction	...	...	416	...	...	439	...	...	453	...	...	453
6 Wholesale and retail trade, restaurants and hotels	...	...	1580	...	...	1653	...	...	1768	...	...	1857
7 Transport, storage and communication	...	...	701	...	...	717	...	...	770	...	...	834
8 Finance, insurance, real estate and business services	...	...	1252	...	...	1284	...	...	1344	...	...	1413
9 Community, social and personal services	...	...	408	...	...	420	...	...	435	...	...	449
Total, Industries	...	...	8760	...	...	8826	...	...	9347	...	...	9815
Producers of Government Services	...	...	955	...	...	959	...	...	979	...	...	1003
Other Producers	...	...	...	...	...	...	...	...	...	...	...	...
Total	...	...	9715	...	...	9785	...	...	10326	...	...	10818
Less: Imputed bank service charge	...	...	...	...	...	...	...	...	...	...	...	...
Import duties	...	...	...	...	...	...	...	...	...	...	...	...
Value added tax	...	...	...	...	...	...	...	...	...	...	...	...
Total [a]	...	...	9715	...	...	9785	...	...	10326	...	...	10818

	1988 G.O.	1988 I.C.	1988 V.A.	1989 G.O.	1989 I.C.	1989 V.A.
At constant prices of: 1966						
All Producers						
1 Agriculture, hunting, forestry and fishing	...	...	2148	...	...	2266
A Agriculture and hunting	...	...	...	...	...	...
B Forestry and logging	...	...	...	...	...	...
C Fishing	...	...	...	...	...	...

Costa Rica

4.2 Derivation of Value Added by Kind of Activity, in Constant Prices
(Continued)

Million Costa Rican colones

	1988 Gross Output	1988 Intermediate Consumption	1988 Value Added	1989 Gross Output	1989 Intermediate Consumption	1989 Value Added
			At constant prices of:1966			
2 Mining and quarrying	...	...	2478	...	...	2610
3 Manufacturing	...	...		...	...	
A Manufacture of food, beverages and tobacco	87583	62458	25125	110457	78733	31724
B Textile, wearing apparel and leather industries	10962	6877	4085	14307	8966	5341
C Manufacture of wood and wood products, including furniture	7371	4653	2718	8862	5703	3159
D Manufacture of paper and paper products, printing and publishing	13815	9699	4116	18628	13145	5483
E Manufacture of chemicals and chemical petroleum, coal, rubber and plastic products	38987	27688	11299	49911	35366	14545
F Manufacture of non-metallic mineral products, except products of petroleum and coal	6479	4038	2441	5376	3489	1887
G Basic metal industries	146	171	-25	-	-	-
H Manufacture of fabricated metal products, machinery and equipment	14827	10409	4418	19283	13638	5645
I Other manufacturing industries	446	276	170	612	381	231
4 Electricity, gas and water	...	...	340	...	...	357
5 Construction	...	...	460	...	...	492
6 Wholesale and retail trade, restaurants and hotels	...	...	1890	...	...	2034
7 Transport, storage and communication	...	...	898	...	...	978
8 Finance, insurance, real estate and business services	...	...	1494	...	...	1560
9 Community, social and personal services	...	...	458	...	...	476
Total, Industries	...	...	10165	...	...	10771
Producers of Government Services	...	...	1028	...	...	1054
Other Producers	...	...	...	...	...	...
Total	...	...	11193	...	...	11825
Less: Imputed bank service charge	...	...	...	...	...	...
Import duties	...	...	...	...	...	...
Value added tax	...	...	...	...	...	...
Total [a]	...	...	11193	...	...	11825

a) Data for this table have not been revised, therefore, data for some years are not comparable with those of other tables.

4.3 Cost Components of Value Added

Million Costa Rican colones

	1980 Compensation of Employees	1980 Capital Consumption	1980 Net Operating Surplus	1980 Indirect Taxes	1980 Less: Subsidies Received	1980 Value Added	1981 Compensation of Employees	1981 Capital Consumption	1981 Net Operating Surplus	1981 Indirect Taxes	1981 Less: Subsidies Received	1981 Value Added
					All Producers							
1 Agriculture, hunting, forestry and fishing	2694	271	3860	...	...	7372	3261	327	7874	...	...	13145
2 Mining and quarrying	2740	503	2552	...	...	7701	3369	626	4084	...	...	10818
3 Manufacturing				...						...		
4 Electricity, gas and water	268	148	463	...	...	882	361	236	829	...	...	1424
5 Construction	1868	184	482	...	...	2584	2104	204	577	...	...	2960
6 Wholesale and retail trade, restaurants and hotels	3299	172	2530	...	...	8315	3709	219	4145	...	...	10500
7 Transport, storage and communication	922	278	693	...	...	1744	1278	354	1233	...	...	2555
8 Finance, insurance, real estate and business services	1146	548	2919	...	...	4686	1538	651	3534	...	...	5791
9 Community, social and personal services [a]	1268	79	367	...	...	1835	1540	95	547	...	...	2286

Costa Rica

4.3 Cost Components of Value Added
(Continued)

Million Costa Rican colones

	1980 Compensation of Employees	1980 Capital Consumption	1980 Net Operating Surplus	1980 Indirect Taxes	1980 Less: Subsidies Received	1980 Value Added	1981 Compensation of Employees	1981 Capital Consumption	1981 Net Operating Surplus	1981 Indirect Taxes	1981 Less: Subsidies Received	1981 Value Added
Total, Industries	14205	2181	13867	...	...	35119	17160	2711	22824	...	...	49479
Producers of Government Services	6289	...	...	...	...	6289	7625	...	...	...	...	7625
Other Producers [a]	...	...	...	...	...	...	...	...	...	...	...	...
Total	20495	2181	13867	...	...	41406	24785	2711	22824	...	...	57103
Less: Imputed bank service charge	...	...	...	...	...	...	...	...	...	...	...	...
Import duties	...	...	...	...	...	...	...	...	...	...	...	...
Value added tax	...	...	...	...	...	...	...	...	...	...	...	...
Total	20495	2181	13867	5245	383	41406	24785	2711	22824	7503	720	57103

	1982 Compensation of Employees	1982 Capital Consumption	1982 Net Operating Surplus	1982 Indirect Taxes	1982 Less: Subsidies Received	1982 Value Added	1983 Compensation of Employees	1983 Capital Consumption	1983 Net Operating Surplus	1983 Indirect Taxes	1983 Less: Subsidies Received	1983 Value Added
All Producers												
1 Agriculture, hunting, forestry and fishing	5697	454	13891	...	...	23884	8576	487	15301	...	...	28446
2 Mining and quarrying	5348	879	9937	...	...	19828	8306	938	13180	...	...	28263
3 Manufacturing				...	...					...	...	
4 Electricity, gas and water	553	590	1118	...	...	2264	824	660	3395	...	...	4950
5 Construction	2764	249	86	...	...	3005	3947	251	-543	...	...	3789
6 Wholesale and retail trade, restaurants and hotels	5578	299	11513	...	...	21125	8566	311	8970	...	...	25498
7 Transport, storage and communication	1965	492	2391	...	...	4487	3021	545	2646	...	...	6283
8 Finance, insurance, real estate and business services	2228	791	4750	...	...	8084	3155	882	6503	...	...	10884
9 Community, social and personal services [a]	2675	132	495	...	...	3505	4240	136	255	...	...	5401
Total, Industries	26808	3887	44181	...	...	86182	40635	4210	50044	...	...	113514
Producers of Government Services	11324	...	...	...	...	11324	15799	...	...	...	...	15800
Other Producers [a]	...	...	...	...	...	...	...	...	...	...	...	...
Total	38123	3887	44181	...	...	97505	56434	4210	50044	...	...	129314
Less: Imputed bank service charge	...	...	...	...	...	...	...	...	...	...	...	...
Import duties	...	...	...	...	...	...	...	...	...	...	...	...
Value added tax	...	...	...	...	...	...	...	...	...	...	...	...
Total	38123	3887	44181	12353	1039	97505	56434	4210	50044	19561	937	129314

	1984 Compensation of Employees	1984 Capital Consumption	1984 Net Operating Surplus	1984 Indirect Taxes	1984 Less: Subsidies Received	1984 Value Added	1985 Compensation of Employees	1985 Capital Consumption	1985 Net Operating Surplus	1985 Indirect Taxes	1985 Less: Subsidies Received	1985 Value Added
All Producers												
1 Agriculture, hunting, forestry and fishing	11039	530	19838	...	...	34571	12490	581	...	...	...	37341
2 Mining and quarrying	10864	1108	17528	...	...	36667	13521	1261	...	...	...	43715
3 Manufacturing				...	...				...	...	...	
4 Electricity, gas and water	1046	760	3599	...	...	5536	1376	835	...	...	...	6348
5 Construction	5199	277	14	...	...	5807	5926	295	...	...	...	7072
6 Wholesale and retail trade, restaurants and hotels	10742	375	9402	...	...	31701	15853	420	10143	...	...	40507
7 Transport, storage and communication	3935	636	2509	...	...	7842	4828	727	...	...	...	9774
8 Finance, insurance, real estate and business services	4290	1023	7291	...	...	13194	5721	1196	...	...	...	17795
9 Community, social and personal services [a]	5773	154	624	...	...	7150	6880	175	...	...	...	9589
Total, Industries	52888	4862	60806	...	...	142468	66595	5488	73388	...	...	172142
Producers of Government Services	20543	...	...	...	...	20543	25778	...	...	...	...	25778
Other Producers [a]	...	...	...	...	...	...	...	...	...	...	...	...
Total	73431	4862	60806	...	...	163011	92373	5488	73388	...	...	197920
Less: Imputed bank service charge	...	...	...	...	...	...	...	...	...	...	...	...
Import duties	...	...	...	...	...	...	...	...	...	...	...	...
Value added tax	...	...	...	...	...	...	...	...	...	...	...	...
Total	73431	4862	60806	25180	1266	163011	92373	5488	73388	28663	1992	197920

Costa Rica

4.3 Cost Components of Value Added

Million Costa Rican colones

1986 / 1987

	Compensation of Employees	Capital Consumption	Net Operating Surplus	Indirect Taxes	Less: Subsidies Received	Value Added	Compensation of Employees	Capital Consumption	Net Operating Surplus	Indirect Taxes	Less: Subsidies Received	Value Added
						All Producers						
1 Agriculture, hunting, forestry and fishing	16230	650	...	...	...	51530	19533	727	...	...	...	51417
2 Mining and quarrying	16335	1383	...	...	...	52573	19101	1601	...	...	...	60698
3 Manufacturing			...	...	...				...	...	...	
4 Electricity, gas and water	1820	972	...	...	...	7413	2165	1135	...	...	...	8598
5 Construction	6914	284	...	...	...	8127	7742	317	...	...	...	9160
6 Wholesale and retail trade, restaurants and hotels	19015	454	...	...	...	47367	23778	527	...	...	...	58505
7 Transport, storage and communication	5837	797	...	...	...	11639	6743	914	...	...	...	14069
8 Finance, insurance, real estate and business services	7157	1386	...	...	...	24522	8687	1644	...	...	...	31071
9 Community, social and personal services [a]	7777	204	...	...	...	11829	10057	250	...	...	...	14756
Total, Industries	81088	6130	94140	...	...	214999	97806	7114	...	...	...	248273
Producers of Government Services	31580	...	...	...	...	31580	36260	...	...	...	...	36260
Other Producers [a]	...	...	...	...	...	...	...	...	...	...	...	...
Total	112668	6130	94140	...	...	246579	134065	7114	104227	...	...	284533
Less: Imputed bank service charge	...	...	...	...	...	...	...	...	...	...	...	...
Import duties	...	...	...	...	...	...	...	...	...	...	...	...
Value added tax	...	...	...	...	...	...	...	...	...	...	...	...
Total	112668	6130	94140	36271	2629	246579	134065	7114	104227	41994	2867	284533

1988 / 1989

	Compensation of Employees	Capital Consumption	Net Operating Surplus	Indirect Taxes	Less: Subsidies Received	Value Added	Compensation of Employees	Capital Consumption	Net Operating Surplus	Indirect Taxes	Less: Subsidies Received	Value Added
						All Producers						
1 Agriculture, hunting, forestry and fishing	24239	887	...	...	...	62774	30978	1044	...	...	...	73030
2 Mining and quarrying	23668	2017	...	...	...	74315	27773	2326	...	...	...	86805
3 Manufacturing			...	...	...				...	...	...	
4 Electricity, gas and water	2597	1422	...	...	...	10292	3322	1733	...	...	...	13301
5 Construction	8975	352	...	...	...	10544	11947	351	...	...	...	14449
6 Wholesale and retail trade, restaurants and hotels	28815	667	...	...	...	70592	35945	793	...	...	...	85429
7 Transport, storage and communication	8545	1152	...	...	...	17367	10672	1317	...	...	...	20923
8 Finance, insurance, real estate and business services	11346	2091	...	...	...	39424	14116	2613	...	...	...	50637
9 Community, social and personal services [a]	12215	331	...	...	...	18380	14430	402	...	...	...	23496
Total, Industries	120400	8919	...	...	...	303687	149183	10578	...	...	...	368070
Producers of Government Services	45974	...	...	...	...	45974	60001	...	...	...	...	60001
Other Producers [a]	...	...	...	...	...	...	...	...	...	...	...	...
Total	166373	8919	129785	...	...	349661	209185	10578	153462	...	...	428071
Less: Imputed bank service charge	...	...	...	...	...	...	...	...	...	...	...	...
Import duties	...	...	...	...	...	...	...	...	...	...	...	...
Value added tax	...	...	...	...	...	...	...	...	...	...	...	...
Total	166373	8919	129785	49156	4572	349661	209185	10578	153462	61042	6196	428071

a) Item 'Other producers' is included in item 'Community, social and personal services'.

Cote d'Ivoire

Source. Communication from the Direction des Etudes de Developpement, Ministere du Plan, Abidjan. The official estimates are published annually in 'Comptes de la Nation'.

General note. The official estimates of Cote d'Ivoire have been adjusted by the Direction des Etudes de Developpement to conform to the present United Nations System of National Accounts so far as the existing data would permit.

1.1 Expenditure on the Gross Domestic Product, in Current Prices

Million CFA francs

	1970	1975	1980	1981	1982	1983	1984	1985	1986	1987	1988	1989
1 Government final consumption expenditure	64935	140639	357603	397972	427752	...	453300	441600	491749	...	...	...
2 Private final consumption expenditure	246058	517272	1388110	1495383	1590491	...	1783700	1836400	2004785	...	...	...
3 Gross capital formation	91311	187392	570461	594363	576524	...	348200	406100	360461	...	...	...
A Increase in stocks	7430	3446	46856	35979	37863	...	-39300	37000	-25696	...	...	...
B Gross fixed capital formation	83881	183946	523605	558384	538661	...	387500	369100	386157	...	...	...
Residential buildings						...	...	...	...			
Non-residential buildings	50686	118410	346117	391352	383027	...	...	...	...			
Other construction and land improvement etc.						...	...	...	...			
Other	33195	65536	177488	167032	155634							
4 Exports of goods and services	153808	315235	773515	826632	928709	...	1354600	1466300	1262232	...	...	...
5 Less: Imports of goods and services	141250	325993	939803	1022949	1036932	...	950400	1015600	874808	...	...	...
Equals: Gross Domestic Product [a]	414862	834545	2149886	2291401	2486544	2605913	2989400	3134800	3244419	...	...	...

a) Data for this table have not been revised, therefore, data for some years are not comparable with those of other tables.

1.2 Expenditure on the Gross Domestic Product, in Constant Prices

Million CFA francs

	1970	1975	1980	1981	1982	1983	1984	1985	1986	1987	1988	1989
					At constant prices of:1975							
1 Government final consumption expenditure	...	140639	...	...	...	...	...	...	...	...	...	...
2 Private final consumption expenditure	...	517272	...	...	...	...	...	...	...	...	...	...
3 Gross capital formation	...	187392	...	...	...	...	...	...	...	...	...	...
A Increase in stocks	...	3446	...	...	...	...	...	...	...	...	...	...
B Gross fixed capital formation	...	183946	...	...	...	...	...	...	...	...	...	...
4 Exports of goods and services	...	315235	...	...	...	...	...	...	...	...	...	...
5 Less: Imports of goods and services	...	325993	...	...	...	...	...	...	...	...	...	...
Equals: Gross Domestic Product	...	834545	...	...	...	...	...	...	...	...	...	...

1.3 Cost Components of the Gross Domestic Product

Million CFA francs

	1970	1975	1980	1981	1982	1983	1984	1985	1986	1987	1988	1989
1 Indirect taxes, net [a]	83844	149748	429422	373604	450183	...	...	...	...	...	...	...
A Indirect taxes	75212	145167	407179	439439	478328	...	...	...	...	...	...	...
B Less: Subsidies [a]	-8632	-4581	-22243	65835	28145	...	...	...	...	...	...	...
2 Consumption of fixed capital	15000	40000	184000	211300	208500	...	...	...	...	...	...	...
3 Compensation of employees paid by resident producers to:	142328	285403	748243	796224	873719	...	...	...	...	...	...	...
A Resident households	142178	285078	747243	785741	863987	...	...	...	...	...	...	...
B Rest of the world	150	325	1000	10483	9732	...	...	...	...	...	...	...
4 Operating surplus	173690	359394	788221	910273	954142	...	...	...	...	...	...	...
A Corporate and quasi-corporate enterprises	53240	102905	...	...	...							
B Private unincorporated enterprises	120122	256078	...	...	...							
C General government	328	411	...	...	...							
Equals: Gross Domestic Product	414862	834545	2149886	2291401	2486544							

a) Item 'Subsidies' includes the profit or loss of the Marketing Board.

1.4 General Government Current Receipts and Disbursements

Million CFA francs

	1970	1975	1980	1981	1982	1983	1984	1985	1986	1987	1988	1989
					Receipts							
1 Operating surplus [a]	328	411	...	...	...	...	...	...	...	...	...	...
2 Property and entrepreneurial income [b]	2637	7600	...	...	...	...	...	...	...	...	...	...
3 Taxes, fees and contributions	105784	198143	...	...	...	...	...	...	...	...	...	...
A Indirect taxes	74339	143139										

Cote d'Ivoire

1.4 General Government Current Receipts and Disbursements
(Continued)

Million CFA francs

	1970	1975	1980	1981	1982	1983	1984	1985	1986	1987	1988	1989
B Direct taxes	10277	27156	...	...	...	...	...	...	...	...	...	...
C Social security contributions	3506	9796	...	...	...	...	...	...	...	...	...	...
D Compulsory fees, fines and penalties c	17662	18052	...	...	...	...	...	...	...	...	...	...
4 Other current transfers	15021	32360	...	...	...	...	...	...	...	...	...	...
Total Current Receipts of General Government	123770	238514	...	...	...	...	...	...	...	...	...	...
Disbursements												
1 Government final consumption expenditure	64935	140639	...	...	...	...	...	...	...	...	...	...
2 Property income	2534	7098	...	...	...	...	...	...	...	...	...	...
3 Subsidies	9030	13471	...	...	...	...	...	...	...	...	...	...
4 Other current transfers	15456	39884	...	...	...	...	...	...	...	...	...	...
A Social security benefits	3313	3470	...	...	...	...	...	...	...	...	...	...
B Social assistance grants	4496	15132	...	...	...	...	...	...	...	...	...	...
C Other	7647	21282	...	...	...	...	...	...	...	...	...	...
5 Net saving d	31815	37422	...	...	...	...	...	...	...	...	...	...
Total Current Disbursements and Net Saving of General Government	123770	238514	...	...	...	...	...	...	...	...	...	...

a) Item 'Operating surplus' includes consumption of fixed capital.
b) Item 'Property and entrepreneurial income' includes consumption of fixed capital.
c) Item 'Fees, fines and penalties' has been reduced by the deductions of the Marketing Board.
d) Item 'Net saving' includes consumption of fixed capital.

1.5 Current Income and Outlay of Corporate and Quasi-Corporate Enterprises, Summary

Million CFA francs

	1970	1975	1980	1981	1982	1983	1984	1985	1986	1987	1988	1989
Receipts												
1 Operating surplus a	50515	94894	...	...	...	...	...	...	...	...	...	...
2 Property and entrepreneurial income received	9895	38707	...	...	...	...	...	...	...	...	...	...
3 Current transfers	4600	9416	...	...	...	...	...	...	...	...	...	...
Total Current Receipts	65010	143017	...	...	...	...	...	...	...	...	...	...
Disbursements												
1 Property and entrepreneurial income	21518	72602	...	...	...	...	...	...	...	...	...	...
2 Direct taxes and other current payments to general government	4638	14628	...	...	...	...	...	...	...	...	...	...
3 Other current transfers	7718	14057	...	...	...	...	...	...	...	...	...	...
4 Net saving b	31136	41730	...	...	...	...	...	...	...	...	...	...
Total Current Disbursements and Net Saving	65010	143017	...	...	...	...	...	...	...	...	...	...

a) Item 'Operating surplus' includes consumption of fixed capital.
b) Item 'Net saving' includes consumption of fixed capital.

1.7 External Transactions on Current Account, Summary

Million CFA francs

	1970	1975	1980	1981	1982	1983	1984	1985	1986	1987	1988	1989
Payments to the Rest of the World												
1 Imports of goods and services	141250	325993	939803	1022949	1036932	...	...	...	...	...	...	...
A Imports of merchandise c.i.f.	...	260562	699055	714546	737692	...	...	...	...	...	...	...
B Other	...	65431	240748	308403	299240	...	...	...	...	...	...	...
2 Factor income to the rest of the world	14213	33241	117491	179881	225335	...	...	...	...	...	...	...
A Compensation of employees	150	325	1000	10483	9732	...	...	...	...	...	...	...
B Property and entrepreneurial income	14063	32916	116491	169398	215603	...	...	...	...	...	...	...
3 Current transfers to the rest of the world	19163	54668	138796	135683	160452	...	...	...	...	...	...	...
4 Surplus of the nation on current transactions	-6934	-69514	-370278	-448401	-428138	...	...	...	...	...	...	...
Payments to the Rest of the World and Surplus of the Nation on Current Transactions	167692	344388	825812	890112	994581	...	...	...	...	...	...	...
Receipts From The Rest of the World												
1 Exports of goods and services	153808	315235	773515	826632	928709	...	...	...	...	...	...	...

Cote d'Ivoire

1.7 External Transactions on Current Account, Summary
(Continued)

Million CFA francs

	1970	1975	1980	1981	1982	1983	1984	1985	1986	1987	1988	1989
A Exports of merchandise f.o.b.	...	275397	...	...	...	...	...	...	...	...	...	...
B Other	...	39838	...	...	...	...	...	...	...	...	...	...
2 Factor income from rest of the world	2733	6005	7286	8098	10110	...	...	...	...	...	...	...
A Compensation of employees	350	645	5340	6270	6880	...	...	...	...	...	...	...
B Property and entrepreneurial income	2383	5360	1946	1828	3230	...	...	...	...	...	...	...
3 Current transfers from rest of the world	11151	23148	45011	55382	55762	...	...	...	...	...	...	...
Receipts from the Rest of the World on Current Transactions	167692	344388	825812	890112	994581	...	...	...	...	...	...	...

1.9 Gross Domestic Product by Institutional Sectors of Origin

Million CFA francs

	1970	1975	1980	1981	1982	1983	1984	1985	1986	1987	1988	1989
			Domestic Factor Incomes Originating									
1 General government	40584	84969	...	...	...	...	...	...	...	...	...	...
2 Corporate and quasi-corporate enterprises	124902	252554	...	...	...	...	...	...	...	...	...	...
A Non-financial	119565	240903	...	...	...	...	...	...	...	...	...	...
B Financial	5337	11651	...	...	...	...	...	...	...	...	...	...
3 Households and private unincorporated enterprises	169347	359598	...	...	...	...	...	...	...	...	...	...
4 Non-profit institutions serving households	1310	2497	...	...	...	...	...	...	...	...	...	...
Subtotal: Domestic Factor Incomes [a]	336143	699618	...	...	...	...	...	...	...	...	...	...
Indirect taxes, net [b]	83844	149748	...	...	...	...	...	...	...	...	...	...
Consumption of fixed capital	...	...	...	...	...	...	...	...	...	...	...	...
Statistical discrepancy	-5125	-14821	...	...	...	...	...	...	...	...	...	...
Gross Domestic Product	414862	834545	...	...	...	...	...	...	...	...	...	...

a) Item 'Domestic factor incomes' includes consumption of fixed capital.
b) Item 'Subsidies' includes the profit or loss of the Marketing Board.

1.10 Gross Domestic Product by Kind of Activity, in Current Prices

Million CFA francs

	1970	1975	1980	1981	1982	1983	1984	1985	1986	1987	1988	1989
1 Agriculture, hunting, forestry and fishing	112636	240414	616278	657881	651106	...	791517	...	...	...	...	...
2 Mining and quarrying	941	1636	5718	27425	52245	...	84075	...	...	...	...	...
3 Manufacturing	55111	109151	241025	229057	300868	...	341556	...	...	...	...	...
4 Electricity, gas and water	4594	13439	34439	40980	52903	...	35884	...	...	...	...	...
5 Construction	27693	54980	148943	128588	126328	...	62014	...	...	...	...	...
6 Wholesale and retail trade, restaurants and hotels [a]	84943	149078	392139	383934	456700	...	...	...	...	...	...	...
7 Transport, storage and communication	31616	72210	159691	181413	177576	...	212759	...	...	...	...	...
8 Finance, insurance, real estate and business services	27991	56175	210517	273122	295976	...	...	...	...	...	...	...
9 Community, social and personal services	3327	6860	21967	24572	23204	...	...	...	...	...	...	...
Total, Industries	348852	703943	1830717	1946972	2136906	...	2358321	...	...	...	...	...
Producers of Government Services	40039	82238	213688	243304	272583	...	...	...	...	...	...	...
Other Producers	3310	5897	15553	16909	16369	...	...	...	...	...	...	...
Subtotal	392201	792078	2059958	2207185	2425858	...	...	...	...	...	...	...
Less: Imputed bank service charge	5125	14821	67651	81266	86772	...	...	...	...	...	...	...
Plus: Import duties	27786	57288	157579	165482	147458	...	170199	...	...	...	...	...
Plus: Value added tax	...	...	...	...	...	...	...	...	...	...	...	...
Equals: Gross Domestic Product	414862	834545	2149886	2291401	2486544	...	2855779	...	...	...	...	...

a) Item 'Wholesale and retail trade, restaurants and hotels' includes the profit or loss of the Marketing Board.

Cote d'Ivoire

1.11 Gross Domestic Product by Kind of Activity, in Constant Prices

Million CFA francs

	1970	1975	1980	1981	1982	1983	1984	1985	1986	1987	1988	1989
					At constant prices of:1975							
1 Agriculture, hunting, forestry and fishing	...	240414	...	...	...	...	...	...	...	...	...	...
2 Mining and quarrying	...	1636	...	...	...	...	...	...	...	...	...	...
3 Manufacturing	...	109151	...	...	...	...	...	...	...	...	...	...
4 Electricity, gas and water	...	13439	...	...	...	...	...	...	...	...	...	...
5 Construction	...	54980	...	...	...	...	...	...	...	...	...	...
6 Wholesale and retail trade, restaurants and hotels [a]	...	149078	...	...	...	...	...	...	...	...	...	...
7 Transport, storage and communication	...	72210	...	...	...	...	...	...	...	...	...	...
8 Finance, insurance, real estate and business services	...	56175	...	...	...	...	...	...	...	...	...	...
9 Community, social and personal services	...	6860	...	...	...	...	...	...	...	...	...	...
Total, Industries	...	703943	...	...	...	...	...	...	...	...	...	...
Producers of Government Services	...	82238	...	...	...	...	...	...	...	...	...	...
Other Producers	...	5897	...	...	...	...	...	...	...	...	...	...
Subtotal	...	792078	...	...	...	...	...	...	...	...	...	...
Less: Imputed bank service charge	...	14821	...	...	...	...	...	...	...	...	...	...
Plus: Import duties	...	57288	...	...	...	...	...	...	...	...	...	...
Plus: Value added tax	...	...	...	...	...	...	...	...	...	...	...	...
Equals: Gross Domestic Product	...	834545	...	...	...	...	...	...	...	...	...	...

a) Item 'Wholesale and retail trade, restaurants and hotels' includes the profit or loss of the Marketing Board.

1.12 Relations Among National Accounting Aggregates

Million CFA francs

	1970	1975	1980	1981	1982	1983	1984	1985	1986	1987	1988	1989
Gross Domestic Product	414862	834545	2149886	2291401	2486544	...	...	...	...	...	...	...
Plus: Net factor income from the rest of the world	-11480	-27236	-110205	-171783	-215225	...	...	...	...	...	...	...
Factor income from the rest of the world	2733	6005	7286	8098	10110	...	...	...	...	...	...	...
Less: Factor income to the rest of the world	14213	33241	117491	179881	225335	...	...	...	...	...	...	...
Equals: Gross National Product	403382	807309	2039681	2119618	2271319	...	...	...	...	...	...	...
Less: Consumption of fixed capital	15000	40000	184000	211300	208500	...	...	...	...	...	...	...
Equals: National Income	388382	767309	1855681	1908318	2062819	...	...	...	...	...	...	...
Plus: Net current transfers from the rest of the world	-8012	-31520	-93785	-80301	-104690	...	...	...	...	...	...	...
Current transfers from the rest of the world	11151	23148	45011	55382	55762	...	...	...	...	...	...	...
Less: Current transfers to the rest of the world	19163	54668	138796	135683	160452	...	...	...	...	...	...	...
Equals: National Disposable Income	380370	735789	1761896	1828017	1958129	...	...	...	...	...	...	...
Less: Final consumption	310993	657911	1745713	1893355	2018243	...	...	...	...	...	...	...
Equals: Net Saving	69377	77878	16183	-65338	-60114	...	...	...	...	...	...	...
Less: Surplus of the nation on current transactions	-6934	-69514	-370278	-448401	-428138	...	...	...	...	...	...	...
Equals: Net Capital Formation	76311	147392	386461	383063	368024	...	...	...	...	...	...	...

2.17 Exports and Imports of Goods and Services, Detail

Million CFA francs

	1970	1975	1980	1981	1982	1983	1984	1985	1986	1987	1988	1989
					Exports of Goods and Services							
1 Exports of merchandise, f.o.b.	...	275397	...	...	...	...	...	...	...	...	...	...
2 Transport and communication	...	27878	...	...	...	...	...	...	...	...	...	...
3 Insurance service charges	...	...	...	...	...	...	...	...	...	...	...	...
4 Other commodities	...	3182	...	...	...	...	...	...	...	...	...	...
5 Adjustments of merchandise exports to change-of-ownership basis	...	...	...	...	...	...	...	...	...	...	...	...
6 Direct purchases in the domestic market by non-residential households	...	8778	...	...	...	...	...	...	...	...	...	...
7 Direct purchases in the domestic market by extraterritorial bodies	...	...	...	...	...	...	...	...	...	...	...	...
Total Exports of Goods and Services	153808	315235	...	...	...	...	...	...	...	...	...	...

Cote d'Ivoire

2.17 Exports and Imports of Goods and Services, Detail
(Continued)

Million CFA francs

	1970	1975	1980	1981	1982	1983	1984	1985	1986	1987	1988	1989
				Imports of Goods and Services								
1 Imports of merchandise, c.i.f.	...	260562	...	...	...	...	...	...	...	...	...	...
2 Adjustments of merchandise imports to change-of-ownership basis	...	...	...	...	...	...	...	...	...	...	...	...
3 Other transport and communication	...	13177	...	...	...	...	...	...	...	...	...	...
4 Other insurance service charges	...	...	...	...	...	...	...	...	...	...	...	...
5 Other commodities	...	31474	...	...	...	...	...	...	...	...	...	...
6 Direct purchases abroad by government	...	...	...	...	...	...	...	...	...	...	...	...
7 Direct purchases abroad by resident households	...	20780	...	...	...	...	...	...	...	...	...	...
Total Imports of Goods and Services	141250	325993	...	...	...	...	...	...	...	...	...	...
Balance of Goods and Services	12558	-10758	...	...	...	...	...	...	...	...	...	...
Total Imports and Balance of Goods and Services	153808	315235	...	...	...	...	...	...	...	...	...	...

Cuba

Source. Correspondence from the Comite Estatal de Estadisticas, Habana. The official estimates are published in 'Anuario Estadistico de Cuba'.
General note. The estimates shown in the following tables have been prepared in accordance with the System of Material Product Balances. Therefore, these estimates are not comparable in concept and coverage with those conforming to the United Nations System of National Accounts.

1a Net Material Product by Use at Current Market Prices

Million Cuban pesos

	1970	1975	1980	1981	1982	1983	1984	1985	1986	1987	1988	1989
1 Personal consumption	3372.0	5408.5	6692.4	7406.1	8172.5	8666.6	9277.1	9683.3	10047.8	10133.4	10390.6	10658.8
2 Material consumption in the units of the non-material sphere serving individuals	263.1	503.3	980.1	1188.5	1238.4	1357.0	1460.2	1497.1	1553.5	1432.2	1472.8	1454.2
Consumption of the Population	3635.1	5911.8	7672.5	8594.6	9410.9	10023.6	10737.3	11180.4	11601.3	11565.6	11863.4	12113.0
3 Material consumption in the units of the non-material sphere serving the community as a whole	150.0	314.2	663.8	821.7	880.8	1016.3	1133.2	1186.2	1208.5	1122.8	1119.2	1113.6
4 Net fixed capital formation	668.5	1348.4	1529.3	2246.8	1812.0	2242.6	2894.9	3098.3	2728.9	1994.3	2054.1	2233.0
5 Increase in material circulating assets and in stocks	...	733.8	576.9	711.4	601.5	552.7	590.3	663.0	-246.9	-260.0	-78.3	137.1
6 Losses	...	12.9	20.0	48.6	40.3	38.4	41.4	81.8	86.1	73.9	82.4	82.2
7 Exports of goods and material services	1088.4	3032.4	4129.4	4473.9	5074.1	5674.4	5743.7	-2220.6	-2304.2	-2072.5	-2211.4	-2681.2
8 Less: Imports of goods and material services	1338.1	3211.1	4766.1	5268.3	5718.4	6445.7	7416.9					
Statistical discrepancy		-29.8	27.3	-125.2	74.3	-176.4	-28.9	-37.4	-216.1	-139.8	-65.5	-206.8
Net Material Product	4203.9	8112.6	9853.1	11503.5	12175.5	12925.9	13695.0	13951.7	12857.4	12284.3	12763.9	12790.9

1b Net Material Product by Use at Constant Market Prices

Million Cuban pesos

	1970	1975	1980	1981	1982	1983	1984	1985	1986	1987	1988	1989
				At constant prices of: 1981								
1 Personal consumption	...	6296.8	7131.5	7406.1	7630.1	7683.4	7961.1	8144.3	8333.6	8290.1	8470.8	8597.3
2 Material consumption in the units of the non-material sphere serving individuals		525.5	1015.3	1188.5	1187.9	1265.1	1360.2	1374.7	1413.2	1314.3	1347.0	1330.0
Consumption of the Population	...	6822.3	8146.8	8594.6	8818.0	8948.5	9321.3	9519.0	9746.8	9604.4	9817.8	9927.3
3 Material consumption in the units of the non-material sphere serving the community as a whole		328.0	669.7	821.7	871.2	1000.0	1115.8	1171.5	1205.5	1110.9	1106.4	1100.4
4 Net fixed capital formation	...	1439.4	1615.1	2246.8	1812.0	2242.6	2894.9	3098.3	2771.2	2119.2	2225.3	2417.1
5 Increase in material circulating assets and in stocks		791.0	621.9	711.4	572.8	536.2	560.0	615.7	-179.3	-187.2	-56.4	98.8
6 Losses		14.6	22.7	48.6	40.3	38.4	41.4	81.6	82.0	73.9	83.1	83.0
7 Exports of goods and material services		3762.5	3993.3	4473.9	5031.8	5612.5	5484.5	-267.2	383.4	383.5	209.8	-163.0
8 Less: Imports of goods and material services		4900.4	5518.1	5268.3	5208.0	5625.1	5869.1					
Statistical discrepancy		-53.6	-28.3	-125.2	149.3	-7.9	147.4	41.7	-65.8	168.5	179.0	31.9
Net Material Product		8203.8	9523.1	11503.5	12087.4	12745.2	13696.2	14260.6	13943.8	13273.2	13565.0	13495.5

2a Net Material Product by Kind of Activity of the Material Sphere in Current Market Prices

Million Cuban pesos

	1970	1975	1980	1981	1982	1983	1984	1985	1986	1987	1988	1989
1 Agriculture and forestry	...	545.7	616.9	1474.4	1396.6	1342.1	1369.6	1362.2	1428.7	1440.8	1532.9	1554.6
A Agriculture and livestock		509.2	578.9	1394.7	1315.4	1251.5	1260.3	1252.3	1318.1	1333.1	1442.9	1456.5
B Forestry		34.8	44.6	60.2	63.1	78.3	88.4	93.7	94.9	92.7	76.7	82.2
C Other		1.7	-6.6	19.5	18.1	12.3	20.9	16.2	15.7	15.0	13.3	15.9
2 Industrial activity		3551.3	3816.7	3567.6	3920.6	4134.9	4734.4	5071.8	4806.3	4498.5	4782.2	4656.2
3 Construction		611.9	784.8	933.9	942.1	1078.5	1321.0	1312.6	1198.5	997.6	1082.5	1171.8
4 Wholesale and retail trade and restaurants and other eating and drinking places	...	2835.4	3803.3	4575.9	4943.9	5336.4	5124.5	5080.9	4333.7	4205.1	4209.5	4294.5
5 Transport and communication		552.9	782.1	893.3	909.2	957.9	1051.2	1039.6	986.3	1053.9	1073.4	1037.8
A Transport		496.7	669.4	768.7	774.6	807.7	890.0	871.8	823.1	867.6	879.8	851.0
B Communication		56.2	112.7	124.6	134.6	150.2	161.2	167.8	163.2	186.3	193.6	186.8
6 Other activities of the material sphere	...	15.4	49.3	58.4	63.1	76.1	94.3	84.6	103.9	88.4	83.4	76.0
Net material product	...	8112.6	9853.1	11503.5	12175.5	12925.9	13695.0	13951.7	12857.4	12284.3	12763.9	12790.9

Cuba

2b Net Material Product by Kind of Activity of the Material Sphere in Constant Market Prices

Million Cuban pesos

		1970	1975	1980	1981	1982	1983	1984	1985	1986	1987	1988	1989
					At constant prices of:1981								
1	Agriculture and forestry	...	1207.6	1241.4	1474.4	1408.2	1305.9	1335.0	1268.7	1236.2	1290.5	1318.3	1332.6
	A Agriculture and livestock	...	1154.1	1178.8	1394.7	1327.0	1210.7	1225.7	1162.9	1129.6	1186.4	1215.6	1217.3
	B Forestry	...	43.5	50.3	60.2	63.1	78.3	88.4	87.3	88.5	86.7	87.1	96.9
	C Other	...	10.0	12.3	19.5	18.1	16.9	20.9	18.5	18.1	17.4	15.6	18.4
2	Industrial activity	...	2495.9	2748.2	3567.6	3789.8	4059.6	4586.9	5098.5	4803.5	4586.3	4797.5	4720.9
3	Construction	...	612.9	746.5	933.9	943.9	1078.0	1320.5	1279.5	1225.5	1079.9	1181.8	1296.6
4	Wholesale and retail trade and restaurants and other eating and drinking places	...	3426.6	4032.8	4575.9	4948.8	5275.4	5304.8	5472.7	5566.3	5177.1	5116.0	5031.9
5	Transport and communication	...	443.5	709.0	893.3	926.5	942.8	1044.6	1011.7	991.8	1010.8	1035.2	984.0
	A Transport	...	377.8	597.4	768.7	790.8	794.3	885.2	845.7	815.1	830.2	847.3	795.5
	B Communication	...	65.7	111.6	124.6	135.7	148.5	159.4	166.0	176.7	180.6	187.9	188.5
6	Other activities of the material sphere	...	17.3	45.2	58.4	70.2	83.5	104.4	129.5	120.5	128.6	116.2	129.5
	Net material product	...	8203.8	9523.1	11503.5	12087.4	12745.2	13696.2	14260.6	13943.8	13273.2	13565.0	13495.5

3 Primary Incomes by Kind of Activity of the Material Sphere in Current Market Prices

Million Cuban pesos

		1987 Primary Income of the Population	1987 Primary Income of Enterprises	1988 Primary Income of the Population	1988 Primary Income of Enterprises	1989 Primary Income of the Population	1989 Primary Income of Enterprises
1	Agriculture and forestry	1326.1	-365.4	1509.0	-479.4	1593.7	-542.6
	A Agriculture and livestock	1262.4	-409.4	1439.7	-500.1	1515.2	-562.2
	B Forestry	54.3	38.4	58.8	17.9	68.0	14.2
	C Other	9.4	5.6	10.5	2.8	10.5	5.4
2	Industrial activity	1665.5	2833.0	1761.0	3021.2	1773.9	2882.3
3	Construction	753.5	244.1	839.4	243.1	908.3	263.5
4	Wholesale and retail trade and restaurants and other eating and drinking places	760.2	3444.9	784.8	3424.7	784.9	3509.6
5	Transport and communication	581.9	460.9	597.4	463.6	614.2	409.4
	A Transport	518.0	339.1	528.0	340.4	544.6	292.9
	B Communication	63.9	121.8	69.4	123.2	69.6	116.5
6	Other activities of the material sphere	42.4	46.0	46.0	37.4	50.7	25.3
	Total	5129.6	6663.5	5537.6	6710.6	5725.7	6547.5

6a Capital Formation by Kind of Activity of the Material and Non-Material Spheres in Current Market Prices

Million Cuban pesos

		1970	1975	1980	1981	1982	1983	1984	1985	1986	1987	1988	1989
					Gross Fixed Capital Formation								
1	Agriculture and forestry	...	587.4	638.8	963.8	826.4	890.6	1011.1	1089.6	1152.6	1025.7	1013.1	1145.2
2	Industrial activity	...	657.7	1088.1	1252.7	1189.5	1386.7	1571.3	1850.4	1691.9	1449.6	1609.6	1655.2
3	Construction	...	150.8	139.0	151.9	156.8	255.5	312.4	278.4	273.6	237.0	268.1	304.2
4	Wholesale and retail trade and restaurants and other eating and drinking places	...	44.9	78.7	94.9	94.4	139.1	189.2	190.3	178.2	146.3	122.7	150.6
5	Transport and communciation	...	402.7	438.8	539.4	502.8	577.4	592.1	585.5	698.4	616.9	672.6	698.6
6	Other activities of the material sphere	...	4.1	8.9	15.9	11.2	13.3	16.7	16.6	34.0	27.8	24.5	33.6
	Total Material Sphere	...	1847.6	2392.3	3018.6	2781.1	3262.6	3692.8	4010.8	4028.7	3503.3	3710.4	3987.4
7	Housing except owner-occupied, communal and miscellaneous personal services	...	173.1	252.4	282.6	222.1	223.3	328.0	281.6	314.0	291.6	353.0	395.4
8	Education, culture and art	...	245.9	150.4	123.6	74.8	95.1	143.3	139.7	142.4	174.6	159.2	166.3
9	Health and social welfare services and sports	...	46.8	59.7	75.7	102.6	73.4	90.1	115.8	167.6	186.1	195.7	184.6
	Total Non-Material Sphere Serving Individuals	...	465.8	462.5	481.9	399.5	391.8	561.4	537.1	624.0	652.3	707.9	746.5

Cuba

6a Capital Formation by Kind of Activity of the Material and Non-Material Spheres in Current Market Prices
(Continued)

Million Cuban pesos

	1970	1975	1980	1981	1982	1983	1984	1985	1986	1987	1988	1989
10 Government	...	40.2	51.8	228.9	228.9	323.9	487.3	537.2	273.3	170.9	139.8	134.3
11 Finance, credit and insurance	...	-	1.6	6.0	4.3	4.0	3.2	1.9	2.4	4.6	1.8	2.5
12 Research, scientific and technological institutes	...	17.7	19.2	17.9	23.1	25.8	34.7	42.5	50.0	44.7	45.2	55.8
13 Other activities of the non-material sphere	...	2.3	1.4	4.7	2.8	12.8	8.4	2.3	4.3	1.8	0.7	2.6
Total Non-Material Sphere Serving the Community as a Whole	...	60.2	74.0	257.5	259.1	366.5	533.6	583.9	330.0	222.0	187.5	195.2
14 Owner-occupied dwellings	...	-	-	-	-	-	-	-	-	-	-	-
Total Gross Fixed Capital Formation	...	2373.6	2928.8	3758.0	3439.7	4020.9	4787.8	5131.8	4982.7	4377.6	4606.0	4929.1

Increases in Material Circulating Assets and Stocks

	1970	1975	1980	1981	1982	1983	1984	1985	1986	1987	1988	1989
1 Agriculture and forestry	...	...	...	...	...	...	...	...	...	-14.9	129.9	-42.9
2 Industrial activity	...	...	...	...	...	...	...	...	...	-187.3	-18.8	195.0
3 Construction	...	...	...	...	...	...	...	...	...	-87.1	82.3	-5.7
4 Wholesale and retail trade and restaurants and other eating and drinking places	...	...	...	...	...	...	...	...	...	0.1	-331.8	-50.0
5 Transport and communication	...	...	...	...	...	...	...	...	...	-43.9	9.4	-6.7
6 Other activities of the non-material sphere	...	...	...	...	...	...	...	...	...	6.4	11.5	26.5
Total increase in material circulating assets	...	...	...	...	...	...	...	...	...	-326.7	-117.5	116.2
Statistical discrepancy	...	...	...	...	...	...	...	...	...	...	...	...
Increase in stocks of the non-material sphere [a]	...	733.8	576.9	711.4	601.5	552.7	590.3	663.0	-246.9	66.7	39.2	20.9

a) Prior to 1987, estimates include the increase in stocks of both material and non-material sphere.

6b Capital Formation by Kind of Activity of the Material and Non-Material Spheres in Constant Market Prices

Million Cuban pesos

	1970	1975	1980	1981	1982	1983	1984	1985	1986	1987	1988	1989
				At constant prices of: 1981								
				Gross Fixed Capital Formation								
1 Agriculture and forestry	...	662.7	678.7	963.8	826.4	890.6	1011.1	1089.6	1136.9	1065.8	1072.8	1213.1
2 Industrial activity	...	687.2	1138.0	1252.7	1189.5	1386.7	1571.3	1850.4	1718.4	1510.1	1656.7	1686.3
3 Construction	...	149.5	140.0	151.9	156.8	255.5	312.4	278.4	274.4	238.7	273.6	283.9
4 Wholesale and retail trade and restaurants and other eating and drinking places	...	44.3	78.2	94.9	94.4	139.1	189.2	190.3	180.8	147.3	125.6	151.9
5 Transport and communciation	...	399.1	435.3	539.4	502.8	577.4	592.1	585.5	704.5	622.0	691.0	684.0
6 Other activities of the material sphere	...	4.3	9.1	15.9	11.2	13.3	16.7	16.6	34.2	28.4	25.1	35.4
Total Material Sphere	...	1947.1	2479.3	3018.6	2781.1	3262.6	3692.8	4010.8	4049.2	3612.3	3844.8	4054.6
7 Housing except owner-occupied, communal and miscellaneous personal services	...	170.4	251.3	282.6	222.1	223.3	328.0	281.6	318.1	295.1	367.2	450.1
8 Education, culture and art	...	241.9	149.2	123.6	74.8	95.1	143.3	139.7	144.7	177.7	164.8	112.7
9 Health and social welfare services and sports	...	46.3	59.2	75.7	102.6	73.4	90.1	115.8	171.4	187.4	205.3	272.6
Total Non-Material Sphere Serving Individuals	...	458.6	459.7	481.9	399.5	391.8	561.4	537.1	634.2	660.2	737.3	845.4
10 Government	...	38.8	52.7	228.9	228.9	323.9	487.3	537.2	282.6	173.8	143.2	146.1
11 Finance, credit and insurance	...	-	2.0	6.0	4.3	4.0	3.2	1.9	2.4	5.5	1.8	5.1
12 Research, scientific and technological institutes	...	17.8	19.1	17.9	23.1	25.8	34.7	42.5	52.2	45.1	47.9	61.2
13 Other activities of the non-material sphere	...	2.3	1.8	4.7	2.8	12.8	8.4	2.3	4.4	3.1	0.8	5.1
Total Non-Material Sphere Serving the Community as a Whole	...	58.9	75.6	257.5	259.1	366.5	533.6	583.9	341.6	227.5	193.7	217.5
14 Owner-occupied dwellings	...	-	-	-	-	-	-	-	-	-	-	-
Total Gross Fixed Capital Formation	...	2464.6	3014.6	3758.0	3439.7	4020.9	4787.8	5131.8	5025.0	4500.0	4775.8	5117.5

Increases in Material Circulating Assets and Stocks

	1970	1975	1980	1981	1982	1983	1984	1985	1986	1987	1988	1989
1 Agriculture and forestry	...	...	...	...	...	...	...	...	...	...	...	...
2 Industrial activity	...	...	...	...	...	...	...	...	...	...	...	...

Cuba

6b Capital Formation by Kind of Activity of the Material and Non-Material Spheres in Constant Market Prices
(Continued)

Million Cuban pesos

	1970	1975	1980	1981	1982	1983	1984	1985	1986	1987	1988	1989
				At constant prices of:1981								
3 Construction	...	...	...	...	...	...	...	...	...	...	...	...
4 Wholesale and retail trade and restaurants and other eating and drinking places	...	...	...	...	...	...	...	...	...	...	...	...
5 Transport and communication	...	...	...	...	...	...	...	...	...	...	...	...
6 Other activities of the non-material sphere	...	...	...	...	...	...	...	...	...	...	...	...
Total increase in material circulating assets	...	...	...	...	...	...	...	...	...	...	...	...
Statistical discrepancy	...	...	...	...	...	...	...	...	...	...	...	...
Increase in stocks of the non-material sphere [a]	...	791.0	621.9	711.4	572.8	536.2	560.0	615.7	-179.3	-187.2	-56.4	98.8

a) Estimates include the increase in stocks of both material and non-material sphere.

7a Final Consumption at Current Market Prices

Million Cuban pesos

	1970	1975	1980	1981	1982	1983	1984	1985	1986	1987	1988	1989
1 Personal consumption	...	5408.5	6692.4	7406.1	8172.5	8666.6	9277.1	9683.3	10047.8	10133.4	10390.6	10658.8
	a) Material Consumption in the Units of the Non-Material Sphere Serving Individuals
Housing except owner-occupied, communal and miscellaneous personal services	...	93.8	203.6	293.2	314.9	371.0	423.5	437.5	435.6	397.0	386.5	381.7
Education, culture and art	...	280.9	552.1	626.2	649.9	704.7	732.0	734.6	742.2	662.8	683.9	650.0
Health and social welfare services and sports	...	128.6	224.4	269.1	273.6	281.3	304.7	325.0	375.7	372.4	402.4	422.5
Other	...	-	-	-	-	-	-	-	-	-	-	-
2 Total non-material sphere serving individuals	...	503.3	980.1	1188.5	1238.4	1357.0	1460.2	1497.1	1553.5	1432.2	1472.8	1454.2
	b) Material Consumption in the Units of the Non-Material Sphere Serving the Community as a Whole
Government	...	234.2	588.1	716.3	759.6	886.5	994.2	1042.9	1049.4	958.8	961.6	945.8
Finance, credit and insurance	...	5.2	8.3	9.9	14.8	15.2	16.1	15.3	17.5	19.9	19.4	19.6
Research, scientific and technological institutes	...	12.5	19.4	35.3	35.3	43.2	50.9	54.4	66.4	72.5	68.6	78.5
Other activities of the non-material sphere	...	62.3	48.0	60.2	71.1	71.4	72.0	73.6	75.2	71.6	69.6	69.7
3 Total non-material sphere serving the community as a whole	...	314.2	663.8	821.7	880.8	1016.3	1133.2	1186.2	1208.5	1122.8	1119.2	1113.6
Final consumption	...	6226.0	8336.3	9416.3	10291.7	11039.9	11870.5	12366.6	12809.8	12688.4	12982.6	13226.6

7b Final Consumption at Constant Market Prices

Million Cuban pesos

	1970	1975	1980	1981	1982	1983	1984	1985	1986	1987	1988	1989
				At constant prices of:1981								
1 Personal consumption	...	6296.8	7131.5	7406.1	7630.1	7683.4	7961.1	8144.3	8333.6	8290.1	8470.8	8597.3
	a) Material Consumption in the Units of the Non-Material Sphere Serving Individuals
Housing except owner-occupied, communal and miscellaneous personal services	...	102.3	218.9	293.2	312.6	367.8	420.1	433.8	423.5	393.9	383.4	378.6
Education, culture and art	...	291.3	567.1	626.2	611.0	633.3	654.7	639.1	641.4	571.6	587.3	556.5
Health and social welfare services and sports	...	131.9	229.3	269.1	264.3	264.0	285.4	301.8	348.3	348.8	376.3	394.9
Other	...	-	-	-	-	-	-	-	-	-	-	-
2 Total non-material sphere serving individuals	...	525.5	1015.3	1188.5	1187.9	1265.1	1360.2	1374.7	1413.2	1314.3	1347.0	1330.0
	b) Material Consumption in the Units of the Non-Material Sphere Serving the Community as a Whole
Government	...	242.3	592.0	716.3	754.9	878.8	985.9	1034.9	1056.4	954.0	956.5	940.7
Finance, credit and insurance	...	5.3	8.3	9.9	14.7	15.2	16.0	15.3	17.4	19.8	19.3	19.5
Research, scientific and technological institutes	...	14.3	20.5	35.3	34.4	41.1	48.8	52.3	62.8	71.4	67.4	77.0
Other activities of the non-material sphere	...	66.1	48.9	60.2	67.2	64.9	65.1	69.0	68.9	65.7	63.2	63.2
3 Total non-material sphere serving the community as a whole	...	328.0	669.7	821.7	871.2	1000.0	1115.8	1171.5	1205.5	1110.9	1106.4	1100.4
Final consumption	...	7150.3	8816.5	9416.3	9689.2	9948.5	10437.1	10690.5	10952.3	10715.3	10924.2	11027.7

Cuba

8 Personal Consumption According to Source of Supply of Goods and Material Services in Current Market Prices

Million Cuban pesos

	1970	1975	1980	1981	1982	1983	1984	1985	1986	1987	1988	1989
1 Purchases of goods in state and co-operative retail trade	...	4780.9	5906.5	6513.3	7234.2	7719.6	8274.8	8612.2	8907.4	8850.3	9083.1	9295.5
2 Purchases of goods in the free market and from private retail trade	...	...	...	...	...	...	...	...	...	...	...	...
3 Goods produced on own account and received in kind	...	99.2	116.3	143.4	145.8	134.8	132.2	151.3	150.0	148.3	159.1	158.7
4 Payments for transport and communication services	...	335.4	385.5	418.0	439.1	448.1	489.4	518.0	562.0	638.6	622.5	640.4
5 Purchases of electricity, gas and water	...	65.6	95.1	134.5	145.3	154.5	164.8	176.5	186.8	247.4	262.9	285.0
6 Purchases directly from handicrafts, repair shops and the like	...	41.8	96.5	102.5	111.8	109.6	113.8	119.9	128.4	128.1	131.9	144.5
7 Consumption of fixed assets in respect of all dwellings	...	85.6	92.5	94.4	96.3	100.0	102.1	105.4	113.2	120.7	131.1	134.7
8 Other	...	-	-	-	-	-	-	-	-	-	-	-
Personal consumption	...	5408.5	6692.4	7406.1	8172.5	8666.6	9277.1	9683.3	10047.8	10133.4	10390.6	10658.8

Cyprus

General note. The preparation of national accounts statistics in Cyprus is undertaken by the Department of Statistics and Research, Ministry of Finance, Nicosia. The official estimates are published annually in the 'Economic Report' and the 'Statistical Abstract', issued by the same Department. Information on concepts, sources and methods of estimation used can be found in the 'History and Analysis of the Methodology of National Accounts in Cyprus', published in 1977 and covers the period 1960-1975 and the 'New National Accounts of Cyprus 1976-1983', published in 1985 and covers the years 1976 and after. The estimates are generally in accordance with the classifications and definitions of the United Nations System of National Accounts (SNA). For the years 1950-1975 the 1958 SNA was used and since 1976 the 1968 SNA. To compare national accounts estimates based on the 1968 SNA and those based on the 1958 SNA the following differences should be taken into consideration: (1) Under the 1968 SNA, rents are treated as intermediate inputs instead of value added, (2) operating surplus is not equal to profits as it includes property income paid to owners, and (3) GDP is at market prices (instead of the factor cost pricing), under the 1958 SNA. The following tables have been prepared from successive replies to the United Nations National Accounts Questionnaire. Where the scope and coverage of the estimates differ for conceptual or statistical reasons from the definitions and classifications recommended in the SNA, a footnote is indicated to the relevant tables.

Sources and methods:

(a) Gross domestic product. Prior to 1976 gross domestic product was estimated through a combination of the income and the production methods. Since 1976 GDP is solely estimated through the production method.

(b) Expenditure on the gross domestic product. The expenditure method is used to estimate all the components of the expenditure account (i.e. government and private final consumption expenditure, capital formation, stocks and imports and exports of goods and services). Sources of data are the Treasury Report for Government financial accounts, the publications of the Department of Statistics and Research on industrial, agriculture, services, imports and exports which provide annual data. The Central Bank of Cyprus provide detailed data on balance of payments and its components. For constant price estimates the total cost of living allowance index is used to deflate wages and salaries in government final consumption expenditure and partial price indices from the retail price index are used to deflate the private final consumption expenditure. For the other expenditure items, various price deflators are used.

(c) Cost-structure of the gross domestic product. Separate estimates for compensation of employees and operating surplus were not available prior to 1976. Since 1976 separate estimates for compensation of employees and operating surplus are compiled from annual production surveys and other secondary sources. These estimates are published in the Economic Report. The estimate of consumption of fixed capital is based on a fixed percentage (10.0%) of the gross national product. An effort is being made to calculate consumption of fixed capital based on the existing capital stock. Net indirect taxes are available in the Financial Report, issued by the Treasury Department.

(d) Gross domestic product by kind of economic activity. Agricultural estimates were based mainly on ad-hoc inquiries of the Ministry of Agriculture and Natural Resources for years prior to 1969. From 1969 to 1974, estimates were derived from area sample surveys conducted twice a year. From 1975, the area sample was replaced by an annual survey of crop and livestock holders. Data on fishing and forestry are supplied by the Fisheries and Forestry Departments respectively. Estimates for Mining and Quarrying, Manufacturing and Electricity, Gas and Water are derived from the annual industrial production surveys and the censuses of industrial production held every five years since 1956. Construction sector consists of public and private construction. Public construction estimates are compiled from the annual Financial Report of the Treasury Department and the Annual Reports of semi-government organizations and Local Government Authorities. For private construction the data are derived from the annual construction surveys conducted since 1978 and based on the building permits. In addition ad hoc inquiries are undertaken for collecting data on inputs, labour, materials, investments etc. supplementing the surveys data. Prior to 1978 the same surveys were conducted every three years. Prior to 1981 Wholesale and Retail Trade estimates were based on gross trade margins, calculated through the commodity flow method. Since the 1981 Census of Wholesale and Retail, estiamtes are derived from an annual survey. For transport, prior to 1980, estimates were based on extrapolation of value added by using indices of the number of buses in use and bus fares, rented cars and fares as well as the number of taxis and their revenues. For lorry transport, estimates were based on the transport margins derived from the commodity flow method. Estimates for Port Services and Civil Aviation were compiled from the annual Financial Report of the Treasury Department and for Cyprus Airways data were obtained regularly from their annual report. For Storage, data were compiled from ad hoc inquiries collected through the Agricultural Surveys and later by conducting Special Surveys. For Communication, estimates were obtained for Postal Services from the Financial Report and for the Cyprus Telecommunication Authority data were compiled from its annual report. Since 1980 estimates are based on annual surveys on all activities of the Transport Sector. Data on financial institutions are collected by the Central Bank of Cyprus. Data on insurance activities are extracted from the records of the Office of the Supervisor of Insurance Companies and ad hoc surveys conducted by the Department of Statistics and Research. Data on Real Estate are based on land and buildings transfer fees and ad hoc surveys. Data on Business Services are derived from annual surveys. The main source of information for public administration and defence and public services is the annual Financial Report of the Treasury Department and annual returns submitted by the local authorities. Estimates for the private services are derived from the annual Services Survey. For the constant price estimates, the double deflation method is used for all items of agricultural outputs and inputs to arrive at value added estimates. Special price deflators for each category and or product items are constructed for both the output and inputs. Prior to 1976, value added was deflated by using a combination of indices for the remaining industries. Quantity indices for mining and quarrying, manufacturing and construction, price indices for wholesale and retail trade, base-year average prices for electricity, gas and water, employment and wage rate indices for all the other services sectors. Since 1976, double deflation method of output and inputs is used. For producers of Government services, the cost of living allowance index is used to deflate their value added which comprises mainly of compensation of employees.

1.1 Expenditure on the Gross Domestic Product, in Current Prices

Million Cyprus pounds

	1970	1975	1980	1981	1982	1983	1984	1985	1986	1987	1988	1989
1 Government final consumption expenditure	21.6	44.9	103.4	127.5	151.5	171.9	188.7	208.5	225.9	246.5	275.0	294.2
2 Private final consumption expenditure	171.5	208.7	508.4	573.8	678.0	765.8	851.5	945.8	979.2	1059.8	1210.2	1373.7
A Households	...	...	504.4	569.2	671.7	758.0	841.6	933.5	966.6	1045.0	1193.8	1353.5
B Private non-profit institutions serving households	...	...	4.0	4.6	6.3	7.8	9.9	12.3	12.6	14.8	16.4	20.2
3 Gross capital formation	55.2	57.9	287.5	296.2	325.1	342.3	449.3	449.7	415.0	447.7	532.4	660.9
A Increase in stocks	1.9	7.4	27.5	20.3	20.4	26.3	36.8	46.7	31.0	36.6	57.2	54.8
B Gross fixed capital formation	53.3	50.5	260.0	275.9	304.7	316.0	412.5	403.0	384.0	411.1	475.2	606.1
Residential buildings	17.4	13.5	105.3	102.5	107.3	115.4	125.0	145.3	150.2	151.3	170.7	190.3
Non-residential buildings	6.2	8.3	47.2	50.5	58.4	56.9	66.3	66.4	68.5	79.4	97.1	113.1
Other construction and land improvement etc.	7.0	11.7	34.2	45.9	42.7	51.3	59.4	56.4	65.7	79.3	71.0	79.4
Other	22.7	17.0	73.3	77.0	96.3	92.4	161.8	134.9	99.6	101.1	136.4	223.3
4 Exports of goods and services	85.9	91.2	344.1	440.2	521.9	573.0	731.0	722.4	721.0	841.8	959.8	1151.6
5 Less: Imports of goods and services	107.6	145.7	479.5	554.7	658.4	727.2	897.4	872.0	775.2	845.7	1010.3	1287.2
Statistical discrepancy	...	...	-3.5	-6.5	6.8	10.9	13.9	25.8	33.0	29.0	25.0	25.5
Equals: Gross Domestic Product	226.6	257.0	760.4	876.0	1024.9	1136.7	1337.0	1480.2	1598.9	1779.1	1992.1	2218.7

Cyprus

1.2 Expenditure on the Gross Domestic Product, in Constant Prices

Million Cyprus pounds

	1970	1975	1980	1981	1982	1983	1984	1985	1986	1987	1988	1989
	1967	**1973**	\multicolumn{5}{c}{At constant prices of: **1980**}		\multicolumn{4}{c}{**1985**}	
1 Government final consumption expenditure	16.5	38.6	103.4	111.1	115.5	122.7	127.4	208.5	216.0	227.5	244.7	252.9
2 Private final consumption expenditure	158.1	162.8	508.4	517.1	576.5	618.4	646.3	945.8	962.2	1014.7	1121.2	1227.9
A Households	...	...	504.4	512.7	571.6	612.8	640.1	933.5	949.9	999.8	1105.5	1209.8
B Private non-profit institutions serving households	...	...	4.0	4.4	4.9	5.6	6.2	12.3	12.3	14.9	15.7	18.1
3 Gross capital formation	44.6	47.3	287.5	261.1	269.4	268.3	328.3	449.7	404.5	426.1	477.4	554.9
A Increase in stocks	1.6	5.7	27.5	17.9	17.0	21.4	28.2	46.7	30.0	37.4	54.8	48.6
B Gross fixed capital formation	43.0	41.6	260.0	243.2	252.4	246.9	300.1	403.0	374.5	388.7	422.6	506.3
Residential buildings	14.1	11.2	105.3	89.1	86.0	88.4	88.8	145.3	147.7	145.8	154.0	160.7
Non-residential buildings	5.0	6.9	47.2	43.9	46.8	43.5	47.1	66.4	67.3	76.3	87.4	95.3
Other construction and land improvement etc.	5.6	9.8	34.2	40.0	33.7	38.5	41.2	56.4	64.6	75.4	64.4	67.1
Other	18.3	13.7	73.3	70.2	85.9	76.5	123.0	134.9	94.9	91.2	116.8	183.2
4 Exports of goods and services	74.0	69.9	344.1	392.6	423.6	458.2	527.4	722.4	710.3	807.5	916.1	1065.2
5 Less: Imports of goods and services	91.9	98.4	479.5	491.5	554.4	585.0	680.7	872.0	776.5	817.9	951.7	1171.6
Statistical discrepancy	...	1.8	-3.5	-6.8	2.3	-5.4	5.9 / 6.2	0.5 / 26.4	21.0	-12.9	-23.7	-27.0
Equals: Gross Domestic Product	201.3	222.0	760.4	783.6	832.9	877.2	954.6	1480.8	1537.4	1645.0	1784.0	1902.3

Cyprus

1.3 Cost Components of the Gross Domestic Product

Million Cyprus pounds

	1970	1975	1980	1981	1982	1983	1984	1985	1986	1987	1988	1989
1 Indirect taxes, net	17.6	16.5	50.4	55.2	73.2	82.6	97.6	124.7	137.9	150.3	165.0	194.5
A Indirect taxes	19.4	20.3	71.9	78.9	96.3	114.8	136.9	153.0	155.2	171.9	199.3	232.5
B Less: Subsidies	1.8	3.8	21.5	23.7	23.1	32.2	39.3	28.3	17.3	21.6	34.3	38.0
2 Consumption of fixed capital	10.5	27.1	70.4	88.8	104.1	119.0	140.5	160.3	171.3	189.9	212.4	237.6
3 Compensation of employees paid by resident producers to:	198.5	213.4	639.6	732.0	847.6	935.1	1098.9	1195.2	1289.7	1438.9	1614.7	1786.6
4 Operating surplus												
Equals: Gross Domestic Product	226.6	257.0	760.4	876.0	1024.9	1136.7	1337.0	1480.2	1598.9	1779.1	1992.1	2218.7

1.7 External Transactions on Current Account, Summary

Million Cyprus pounds

	1970	1975	1980	1981	1982	1983	1984	1985	1986	1987	1988	1989
Payments to the Rest of the World												
1 Imports of goods and services	...	...	479.5	554.7	658.4	727.2	897.4	872.0	775.2	845.7	1010.3	1287.2
A Imports of merchandise c.i.f.	...	...	424.3	489.5	577.6	642.0	796.5	762.3	659.1	711.4	866.8	1130.3
B Other	...	...	55.2	65.2	80.8	85.2	100.9	109.7	116.1	134.3	143.5	156.9
2 Factor income to the rest of the world	...	...	20.4	30.2	41.1	50.7	59.6	62.9	61.8	65.6	71.3	78.7
A Compensation of employees	...	...	2.3	2.2	2.7	2.5	2.2	2.9	3.6	3.5	5.1	4.8
B Property and entrepreneurial income	...	...	18.1	28.0	38.4	48.2	57.4	60.0	58.2	62.1	66.2	73.9
3 Current transfers to the rest of the world	...	...	1.4	1.4	1.5	1.6	1.8	1.5	1.5	1.3	1.5	1.7
4 Surplus of the nation on current transactions	...	...	-82.9	-61.0	-72.1	-93.4	-116.7	-98.8	-4.9	44.2	3.7	-72.8
Payments to the Rest of the World and Surplus of the Nation on Current Transactions	...	...	418.4	525.3	628.9	686.1	842.1	837.6	833.6	956.8	1086.8	1294.8
Receipts From The Rest of the World												
1 Exports of goods and services	...	...	344.1	440.2	521.9	573.0	731.0	722.4	721.0	841.8	959.8	1151.6
A Exports of merchandise f.o.b.	...	...	185.0	230.6	261.6	257.9	334.2	287.3	257.8	295.6	328.1	389.5
B Other	...	...	159.1	209.6	260.3	315.1	396.8	435.1	463.2	546.2	631.7	762.1
2 Factor income from rest of the world	...	...	47.0	57.2	71.6	72.5	83.8	88.7	87.6	92.6	101.1	122.5
A Compensation of employees	...	...	34.0	37.6	42.6	46.8	49.5	51.3	51.0	54.2	58.6	62.7
B Property and entrepreneurial income	...	...	13.0	19.6	29.0	25.7	34.3	37.4	36.6	38.4	42.5	59.8
3 Current transfers from rest of the world	...	...	27.3	27.9	35.4	40.6	27.3	26.5	25.0	22.4	25.9	20.7
Receipts from the Rest of the World on Current Transactions	...	...	418.4	525.3	628.9	686.1	842.1	837.6	833.6	956.8	1086.8	1294.8

1.10 Gross Domestic Product by Kind of Activity, in Current Prices

Million Cyprus pounds

	1970	1975	1980	1981	1982	1983	1984	1985	1986	1987	1988	1989
1 Agriculture, hunting, forestry and fishing	36.0	40.4	72.9	81.1	95.0	89.8	119.6	111.0	117.3	132.3	143.2	155.6
2 Mining and quarrying	12.7	6.1	9.9	9.8	8.8	8.0	8.0	7.1	7.5	6.7	7.1	6.5
3 Manufacturing	25.5	36.8	133.4	154.2	174.5	187.9	215.2	231.9	240.5	273.9	309.1	334.0
4 Electricity, gas and water	4.3	4.0	10.0	14.7	17.5	22.2	28.0	33.3	35.2	37.0	41.6	43.6
5 Construction	16.9	19.8	102.5	105.2	115.5	123.9	137.0	148.6	156.5	170.0	189.2	213.7

Cyprus

1.10 Gross Domestic Product by Kind of Activity, in Current Prices
(Continued)

Million Cyprus pounds

	1970	1975	1980	1981	1982	1983	1984	1985	1986	1987	1988	1989
6 Wholesale and retail trade, restaurants and hotels	36.8	41.2	115.6	137.5	165.8	187.0	231.7	277.0	303.9	346.4	386.3	453.0
7 Transport, storage and communication	19.8	16.9	60.5	72.0	84.6	100.6	120.6	138.3	155.9	168.0	182.2	199.2
8 Finance, insurance, real estate and business services	29.9	29.5	108.9	134.1	153.5	161.4	189.2	208.3	230.6	254.1	286.8	318.9
9 Community, social and personal services	9.4	20.8	25.8	32.5	37.7	46.9	56.8	68.4	78.9	90.1	104.6	118.3
Total, Industries	191.3	215.5	639.5	741.1	852.9	927.7	1106.1	1223.9	1326.3	1478.5	1650.1	1842.8
Producers of Government Services [a]	17.7	25.0	89.5	108.7	133.8	150.9	166.6	183.7	201.2	219.0	240.9	257.0
Other Producers	...	...	3.1	3.7	4.2	5.9	7.7	8.1	9.1	9.8	11.4	12.3
Subtotal [b]	209.0	240.5	732.1	853.5	990.9	1084.5	1280.4	1415.7	1536.6	1707.3	1902.4	2112.1
Less: Imputed bank service charge	...	...	23.0	33.4	36.8	31.1	37.8	39.9	40.8	42.7	47.6	56.3
Plus: Import duties	...	...	51.3	55.9	70.8	83.3	94.8	105.0	103.1	114.5	137.3	162.9
Plus: Value added tax	...	...	...	...	...	...	...	...	...	...	...	...
Plus: Other adjustments [c]	17.6	16.5	...	...	...	...	...	...	...	...	...	...
Equals: Gross Domestic Product	226.6	257.0	760.4	876.0	1024.9	1136.7	1337.4	1480.8	1598.9	1779.1	1992.1	2218.7

a) For the first series, item 'Producers of Government Services' includes public administration and defence only. All other activities of government are included in the corresponding industries.   b) For the first series, gross domestic product in factor values.   c) Item 'Other adjustments' refers to indirect taxes net of subsidies.

1.11 Gross Domestic Product by Kind of Activity, in Constant Prices

Million Cyprus pounds

	1970	1975	1980	1981	1982	1983	1984	1985	1986	1987	1988	1989
	1967	1973	At constant prices of: 1980					1985				
1 Agriculture, hunting, forestry and fishing	33.8	37.0	72.9	72.4	72.7	71.9	78.6	78.4 / 111.0	110.4	114.2	126.7	128.7
2 Mining and quarrying	9.8	6.3	9.9	9.0	8.4	7.5	7.1	7.2 / 7.1	7.1	6.7	6.6	5.5
3 Manufacturing	22.9	28.9	133.4	141.9	150.4	153.3	163.1	166.8 / 231.9	232.6	251.3	268.5	276.6
4 Electricity, gas and water	4.4	3.9	10.0	10.1	10.5	12.8	14.3	15.5 / 33.3	38.1	44.2	50.2	55.1
5 Construction	13.5	16.5	102.5	88.5	86.4	86.2	87.8	86.6 / 148.6	149.1	153.7	159.8	168.8
6 Wholesale and retail trade, restaurants and hotels	33.2	32.8	115.6	122.7	138.1	151.2	169.3	186.2 / 277.0	287.9	316.9	350.2	394.3
7 Transport, storage and communication	17.3	15.0	60.5	64.4	68.8	76.9	88.8	93.8 / 138.3	143.6	151.3	165.8	182.6
8 Finance, insurance, real estate and business services	27.5	27.8	108.9	125.2	138.7	141.2	157.1	165.9 / 208.3	225.0	240.0	261.9	280.5
9 Community, social and personal services	7.5	19.2	25.8	28.4	28.0	30.3	35.0	37.4 / 68.4	73.2	78.8	87.3	94.0
Total, Industries	169.9	187.4	639.5	662.6	702.0	731.3	801.1	837.9 / 1223.9	1267.0	1357.1	1477.0	1586.1
Producers of Government Services	13.7[a]	21.9[a]	89.5	94.5	101.1	106.6	111.7	116.4 / 183.7	191.7	200.3	212.4	219.3

Cyprus

1.11 Gross Domestic Product by Kind of Activity, in Constant Prices
(Continued)

Million Cyprus pounds

	1970	1975	1980	1981	1982	1983	1984	1985	1986	1987	1988	1989
	1967	1973	At constant prices of: 1980					1985				
Other Producers	...	...	3.1	3.4	3.6	4.2	4.5	4.7 / 8.1	8.7	10.2	10.6	10.4
Subtotal	183.6[b]	209.3[b]	732.1	760.5	806.7	842.1	917.3	959.0 / 1415.7	1467.4	1567.6	1700.0	1815.8
Less: Imputed bank service charge			23.0	29.8	30.0	24.1	27.1	27.0 / 39.9	39.0	39.2	42.5	48.4
Plus: Import duties			51.3	52.9	56.2	59.2	64.4	67.4 / 105.0	109.0	116.6	126.5	134.9
Plus: Value added tax			...	...	...	...	...	...	...	...	...	...
Plus: Other adjustments	17.7[c]	12.7[c]	...	...	...	...	...	...	...	...	...	...
Equals: Gross Domestic Product	201.3	222.0	760.4	783.6	832.9	877.2	954.6	999.4 / 1480.8	1537.4	1645.0	1784.0	1902.3

a) Item 'Producers of Government Services' includes public administration and defence only. All other activities of government are included in the corresponding industries.
b) Gross domestic product in factor values.
c) Item 'Other adjustments' refers to indirect taxes net of subsidies.

1.12 Relations Among National Accounting Aggregates

Million Cyprus pounds

	1970	1975	1980	1981	1982	1983	1984	1985	1986	1987	1988	1989
Gross Domestic Product	226.6	257.0	760.4	876.0	1024.9	1136.7	1337.4	1480.8	1598.9	1779.1	1992.1	2218.7
Plus: Net factor income from the rest of the world	7.4	14.2	26.6	27.0	30.5	21.8	24.2	25.8	25.8	27.0	29.8	43.8
Factor income from the rest of the world	...	...	47.0	57.2	71.6	72.5	83.8	88.7	87.6	92.6	101.1	122.5
Less: Factor income to the rest of the world	...	...	20.4	30.2	41.1	50.7	59.6	62.9	61.8	65.6	71.3	78.7
Equals: Gross National Product	234.0	271.2	787.0	903.0	1055.4	1158.5	1361.6	1507.6	1624.7	1806.1	2021.9	2262.5
Less: Consumption of fixed capital	10.5	27.1	70.4	88.8	104.1	119.0	140.5	160.3	171.3	189.9	212.4	237.6
Equals: National Income	223.5	244.1	716.6	814.2	951.3	1039.5	1221.1	1346.3	1453.4	1616.2	1809.5	2024.9
Plus: Net current transfers from the rest of the world	7.1	26.6	25.9	26.5	33.9	39.0	25.5	25.0	23.5	21.1	24.5	19.0
Current transfers from the rest of the world	...	27.7	27.3	27.9	35.4	40.6	27.3	26.5	25.0	22.4	25.9	20.7
Less: Current transfers to the rest of the world	...	1.1	1.4	1.4	1.5	1.6	1.8	1.5	1.5	1.3	1.5	1.7
Equals: National Disposable Income	230.6	270.7	742.5	840.7	985.2	1078.5	1246.6	1371.3	1476.9	1637.3	1833.9	2043.9
Less: Final consumption	193.1	253.6	611.8	701.3	829.5	937.7	1040.2	1154.3	1205.1	1306.3	1485.2	1667.9
Statistical discrepancy	-	-	3.5	7.0	-6.8	-10.9	-14.3	-26.4	-33.0	-29.0	-25.0	-25.5
Equals: Net Saving	37.5	17.1	134.2	146.4	148.9	129.9	192.1	190.6	238.8	302.0	323.7	350.5
Less: Surplus of the nation on current transactions	-7.2	-13.7	-82.9	-61.0	-72.1	-93.4	-116.7	-98.8	-4.9	44.2	3.7	-72.8
Equals: Net Capital Formation	44.7	30.8	217.1	207.4	221.0	223.3	308.8	289.4	243.7	257.8	320.0	423.3

Cyprus

2.1 Government Final Consumption Expenditure by Function, in Current Prices

Million Cyprus pounds

	1970	1975	1980	1981	1982	1983	1984	1985	1986	1987	1988	1989
1 General public services [a]	9.4	19.3	15.5	19.3	21.4	24.3	26.3	29.1	31.5	35.2	38.1	...
2 Defence	3.0	7.1	9.8	9.4	10.5	11.4	11.1	12.6	13.0	15.5	19.2	...
3 Public order and safety [a]	...	...	15.3	18.2	22.1	24.9	27.7	29.9	32.1	34.6	36.9	...
4 Education	4.4	8.9	23.7	29.4	35.6	40.0	43.6	48.5	52.4	57.5	64.4	...
5 Health	2.1	5.1	11.2	14.3	17.2	19.6	21.7	24.6	26.9	29.8	32.2	...
6 Social security and welfare			10.9	16.8	20.0	23.4	26.5	29.4	32.5	35.7	41.4	...
7 Housing and community amenities			4.2	4.2	5.8	6.3	7.9	8.5	10.0	10.1	12.5	...
8 Recreational, cultural and religious affairs			0.7	0.9	1.0	1.2	1.3	1.6	1.7	1.9	2.1	...
9 Economic services			11.7	14.7	17.2	20.0	22.4	24.2	25.7	26.2	27.7	...
A Fuel and energy	2.7	4.5	...	-	-	-	-	-	-	-	-	...
B Agriculture, forestry, fishing and hunting			4.8	5.4	6.3	7.6	8.2	8.5	8.9	9.5	10.3	...
C Mining, manufacturing and construction, except fuel and energy			1.4	2.0	2.4	2.6	2.9	3.1	3.3	3.3	3.4	...
D Transportation and communication			0.3	0.4	0.5	0.6	0.6	0.7	0.8	0.8	0.8	...
E Other economic affairs			5.2	6.9	8.0	9.2	10.7	11.9	12.7	12.6	13.2	...
10 Other functions			0.4	0.3	0.7	0.8	0.2	0.1	0.1	-	-	...
Total Government Final Consumption Expenditure	21.6	44.9	103.4	127.5	151.5	171.9	188.7	208.5	225.9	246.5	275.0	...

a) For the first series, item 'Public order and safety' is included in 'General public services'.

2.5 Private Final Consumption Expenditure by Type and Purpose, in Current Prices

Million Cyprus pounds

	1970	1975	1980	1981	1982	1983	1984	1985	1986	1987	1988	1989
Final Consumption Expenditure of Resident Households												
1 Food, beverages and tobacco	...	90.9	174.5	196.2	226.4	252.8	317.7	346.4	357.2	401.7	452.7	...
A Food	...	70.4	141.5	154.7	183.0	205.8	258.7	281.3	291.4	323.4	359.7	...
B Non-alcoholic beverages	...	3.4	7.5	11.0	11.1	11.7	16.2	18.5	14.0	15.8	17.5	...
C Alcoholic beverages	...	8.9	13.1	14.0	15.5	17.1	21.9	24.9	27.3	31.3	38.2	...
D Tobacco	...	8.2	12.4	16.5	16.8	18.2	20.9	21.7	24.5	31.2	37.3	...
2 Clothing and footwear	...	21.0	55.9	75.5	94.4	107.2	116.3	125.2	130.8	135.8	144.9	...
3 Gross rent, fuel and power	...	24.4	49.5	72.2	80.7	88.4	96.7	107.0	109.7	116.2	124.1	...
A Fuel and power	...	...	11.9	13.3	15.2	17.6	21.3	23.7	18.0	18.3	19.1	...
B Other	...	...	37.6	58.9	65.5	70.8	75.4	83.3	91.7	97.9	105.0	...
4 Furniture, furnishings and household equipment and operation	...	17.3	66.3	84.5	103.1	116.2	126.8	136.1	136.0	155.6	171.9	...
A Household operation	...	5.9	19.5	24.2	27.4	29.8	34.0	37.6	40.5	45.0	48.2	...
B Other	...	11.4	46.8	60.3	75.7	86.4	92.8	98.5	95.5	110.6	123.7	...
5 Medical care and health expenses	...	3.9	10.2	14.3	19.6	23.8	28.6	34.4	36.2	44.1	51.4	...
6 Transport and communication	...	42.0	132.4	128.0	147.9	171.3	179.5	187.0	197.6	208.9	261.0	...
A Personal transport equipment	...	4.8	34.6	35.7	44.6	51.1	52.6	55.9	63.0	64.1	95.2	...

Cyprus

2.5 Private Final Consumption Expenditure by Type and Purpose, in Current Prices
(Continued)

Million Cyprus pounds

	1970	1975	1980	1981	1982	1983	1984	1985	1986	1987	1988	1989
B Other	...	37.2	97.8	92.3	103.3	120.3	126.9	131.1	134.6	144.8	165.8	...
7 Recreational, entertainment, education and cultural services	...	12.7	40.3	56.5	66.9	73.6	79.0	91.6	88.9	98.9	118.1	...
A Education	...	1.4	5.7	4.0	5.4	7.5	9.8	12.1	14.1	16.5	19.4	...
B Other	...	11.3	34.6	52.5	61.5	66.1	69.2	79.5	74.8	82.4	98.7	...
8 Miscellaneous goods and services	...	18.7	83.8	76.1	102.2	135.3	151.6	180.3	206.7	247.8	296.2	...
A Personal care	...	5.8	22.6	8.6	10.8	13.0	14.8	18.5	18.8	23.1	26.8	...
B Expenditures in restaurants, cafes and hotels	...	9.5	43.9	51.3	70.1	92.8	105.4	126.9	145.2	176.8	215.6	...
C Other	...	3.4	17.3	16.2	21.3	29.5	31.4	34.9	42.7	47.9	53.8	...
Statistical discrepancy [a]	...	-1.6	-7.3	1.6	-1.4	-	-	-	-	-	-	...
Total Final Consumption Expenditure in the Domestic Market by Households, of which	...	229.3	605.6	704.9	839.8	968.6	1096.2	1208.0	1263.1	1409.0	1620.2	...
A Durable goods	...	...	...	...	126.5	142.8	146.5	160.2	163.6	178.6	224.8	...
B Semi-durable goods	...	...	...	...	165.9	184.5	201.2	217.6	225.0	245.2	270.2	...
C Non-durable goods	...	...	...	...	329.4	374.4	445.2	478.0	477.1	532.9	599.3	...
D Services	...	...	...	...	218.4	266.9	303.2	352.2	397.4	452.3	525.9	...
Plus: Direct purchases abroad by resident households	...	8.4	16.4	19.9	26.5	28.8	34.4	39.1	41.8	46.0	52.0	...
Less: Direct purchases in the domestic market by non-resident households	...	29.0	110.7	148.5	187.9	231.5	277.5	299.2	326.5	392.4	464.5	...
Equals: Final Consumption Expenditure of Resident Households [bc]	171.5	208.7	504.3	568.9	671.7	758.0	841.6	933.5	966.6	1044.9	1193.8	...

Final Consumption Expenditure of Private Non-profit Institutions Serving Households

	1970	1975	1980	1981	1982	1983	1984	1985	1986	1987	1988	1989
1 Research and science	...	...	...	-	-	-	-	-	-	-	-	...
2 Education	...	...	...	-	-	-	-	-	-	-	-	...
3 Medical and other health services	...	...	...	-	-	-	-	-	-	-	-	...
4 Welfare services	...	...	...	0.3	0.3	0.4	0.4	0.6	0.7	0.7	0.7	...
5 Recreational and related cultural services	...	...	...	0.7	1.5	2.3	3.4	4.3	3.8	5.7	6.4	...
6 Religious organisations	...	...	...	2.2	2.5	2.8	3.4	4.1	4.3	4.5	4.8	...
7 Professional and labour organisations serving households	...	...	...	1.5	1.8	2.2	2.6	3.2	3.6	3.7	4.1	...
8 Miscellaneous	...	...	...	0.2	0.1	0.1	0.1	0.1	0.2	0.3	0.4	...
Equals: Final Consumption Expenditure of Private Non-profit Organisations Serving Households	...	...	4.1	4.9	6.3	7.8	9.9	12.3	12.6	14.9	16.4	...
Private Final Consumption Expenditure	171.5	208.7	508.4	573.8	678.0	765.8	851.5	945.8	979.2	1059.8	1210.2	...

a) Item 'Statistical discrepancy' represents unclassified estimates.
b) First series, item 'Final consumption expenditure of resident households' includes consumption expenditure of private non-profit institutions serving households.
c) Beginning 1976, the components do not add up to the total. The difference refers to changes in stocks.

Cyprus

2.6 Private Final Consumption Expenditure by Type and Purpose, in Constant Prices

Million Cyprus pounds

		1970	1975	1980	1981	1982	1983	1984	1985	1986	1987	1988	1989
		1967	1973	At constant prices of: 1980					1985				

Final Consumption Expenditure of Resident Households

		1970	1975	1980	1981	1982	1983	1984	1985	1986	1987	1988	1989
1	Food, beverages and tobacco	...	...	174.5	170.1	187.3	203.1	236.4	246.0 / 346.4	348.3	382.6	412.1	...
A	Food	...	...	141.5	133.6	141.2	163.1	190.2	197.3 / 281.3	283.7	306.8	327.7	...
B	Non-alcoholic beverages	...	...	7.5	9.5	9.6	10.1	12.1	13.7 / 18.5	13.6	15.0	16.0	...
C	Alcoholic beverages	...	...	13.1	12.9	13.8	15.1	17.6	19.1 / 24.9	26.8	30.1	31.6	...
D	Tobacco	...	...	12.4	14.1	13.7	14.8	16.5	15.9 / 21.7	24.2	30.7	36.8	...
2	Clothing and footwear	...	...	55.9	70.8	81.8	86.3	87.6	87.2 / 125.2	126.4	127.5	128.1	...
3	Gross rent, fuel and power	...	...	49.5	66.1	70.9	74.0	76.1	79.8 / 106.9	113.4	119.7	127.9	...
A	Fuel and power	...	...	11.9	10.0	10.8	11.8	12.2	12.9 / 23.6	26.2	29.8	35.1	...
B	Other	...	...	37.6	56.1	60.1	62.2	63.9	66.9 / 83.3	87.2	89.9	92.8	...
4	Furniture, furnishings and household equipment and operation	...	...	66.3	76.9	88.0	96.0	101.3	105.4 / 136.2	133.0	150.1	162.7	...
A	Household operation	...	...	19.5	21.7	22.8	24.3	26.5	28.2 / 37.7	39.4	43.0	45.0	...
B	Other	...	...	46.8	55.2	65.2	71.7	74.8	77.2 / 98.5	93.6	107.1	117.7	...
5	Medical care and health expenses	...	...	10.2	12.6	15.8	17.5	19.5	22.4 / 34.4	35.1	41.0	46.7	...
6	Transport and communication	...	...	132.4	110.4	124.6	140.1	141.1	143.0 / 187.0	198.6	204.9	248.9	...
A	Personal transport equipment	...	...	34.6	29.4	40.4	44.4	43.1	45.7 / 55.9	60.6	56.6	80.2	...
B	Other	...	...	97.8	81.0	84.2	95.7	98.0	97.3 / 131.1	138.0	148.3	168.7	...
7	Recreational, entertainment, education and cultural services	...	...	40.3	55.3	63.1	65.7	67.4	73.1 / 91.6	87.7	95.2	109.8	...
A	Education	...	...	5.7	3.7	4.9	6.6	9.1	10.7 / 12.1	15.0	16.7	18.3	...
B	Other	...	...	34.6	51.6	58.2	59.1	58.3	62.4 / 79.5	72.7	78.5	91.5	...
8	Miscellaneous goods and services	...	...	83.8	67.5	83.3	100.5	103.9	115.8 / 180.3	198.3	227.2	264.8	...

Cyprus

2.6 Private Final Consumption Expenditure by Type and Purpose, in Constant Prices
(Continued)

Million Cyprus pounds

	1970	1975	1980	1981	1982	1983	1984	1985	1986	1987	1988	1989
	1967	1973	At constant prices of: 1980					1985				
A Personal care	...	...	22.6	7.8	8.9	9.8	10.4	12.2 / 18.5	17.9	21.0	23.7	...
B Expenditures in restaurants, cafes and hotels	...	...	43.9	44.2	54.8	65.2	67.1	76.0 / 126.9	138.2	160.7	191.1	...
C Other	...	...	17.3	15.5	19.5	25.5	26.4	27.6 / 34.9	42.2	45.5	50.0	...
Statistical discrepancy	...	...	-7.3[a]	-[a]	-[a]	-[a]	-[a]	-[a]	-	-	-	...
Total Final Consumption Expenditure in the Domestic Market by Households, of which	...	...	605.6	629.7	714.8	783.2	832.3	872.7 / 1208.0	1240.9	1348.4	1500.9	...
A Durable goods	...	...	...	...	117.4	128.9	126.9	136.0 / 160.2	160.7	169.4	206.2	...
B Semi-durable goods	...	...	...	...	142.2	149.6	152.7	155.1 / 217.6	217.5	230.1	243.3	...
C Non-durable goods	...	...	...	...	269.2	295.5	328.7	336.6 / 478.0	481.2	530.6	579.7	...
D Services	...	...	...	...	180.1	209.2	225.0	245.0 / 352.2	381.5	418.3	471.7	...
Plus: Direct purchases abroad by resident households	...	...	16.4	18.1	22.6	23.3	26.3	28.4 / 39.1	41.4	44.3	48.4	...
Less: Direct purchases in the domestic market by non-resident households	...	...	110.7	133.8	158.8	187.2	211.0	216.5 / 299.2	320.8	375.4	430.3	...
Equals: Final Consumption Expenditure of Resident Households	158.1[b]	162.8[b]	504.3[c]	512.4[c]	571.2[c]	612.8[c]	640.0[c]	674.0[c] / 933.5[c]	949.9[c]	999.7[c]	1105.5[c]	...

Final Consumption Expenditure of Private Non-profit Institutions Serving Households

1 Research and science	...	...	...	-	-	-	-	-	-	-	-	...
2 Education	...	...	...	-	-	-	-	-	-	-	-	...
3 Medical and other health services	...	...	...	-	-	-	-	-	-	-	-	...

Cyprus

2.6 Private Final Consumption Expenditure by Type and Purpose, in Constant Prices
(Continued)

Million Cyprus pounds

	1970	1975	1980	1981	1982	1983	1984	1985	1986	1987	1988	1989
	1967	1973		At constant prices of: 1980						1985		
4 Welfare services	...	...	...	0.3	0.2	0.2	0.2	0.3				
								0.6	0.6	0.5	0.6	...
5 Recreational and related cultural services	...	...	...	0.7	1.2	1.3	1.6	2.4				
								4.3	3.9	6.4	6.8	...
6 Religious organisations	...	...	...	2.2	2.4	2.4	2.6	2.9				
								4.1	4.2	4.2	4.4	...
7 Professional and labour organisations serving households	...	...	...	1.4	1.5	1.6	1.8	2.0				
								3.2	3.4	3.5	3.6	...
8 Miscellaneous	...	...	...	0.1	-	0.1	0.1	0.1				
								0.1	0.2	0.3	0.3	...
Equals: Final Consumption Expenditure of Private Non-profit Organisations Serving Households	...	...	4.1	4.7	5.3	5.6	6.3	7.7				
								12.3	12.3	14.9	15.7	...
Private Final Consumption Expenditure	158.1	162.8	508.4	517.1	576.5	618.4	646.3	681.7				
								945.8	962.2	1014.6	1121.2	...

a) Item 'Statistical discrepancy' represents unclassified estimates.
b) Item 'Final consumption expenditure of resident households' includes consumption expenditure of private non-profit institutions serving households.
c) Beginning 1976, the components do not add up to the total. The difference refers to changes in stocks.

2.11 Gross Fixed Capital Formation by Kind of Activity of Owner, ISIC Divisions, in Current Prices

Million Cyprus pounds

	1970	1975	1980	1981	1982	1983	1984	1985	1986	1987	1988	1989
					All Producers							
1 Agriculture, hunting, forestry and fishing	4.2	5.5	16.7	17.6	22.8	27.4	35.8	35.1	43.1	49.8	34.7	30.8
A Agriculture and hunting	...	...	...	...	...	...	...	34.2	42.0	48.6	33.2	...
B Forestry and logging	...	...	...	...	...	...	...	0.4	0.4	0.6	0.6	...
C Fishing	...	...	...	...	...	...	...	0.5	0.7	0.6	0.9	...
2 Mining and quarrying	0.8	1.2	1.3	1.5	0.9	0.4	0.8	0.5	0.7	0.4	0.5	0.6
A Coal mining	...	...	...	...	...	...	...	...	...	...	...	...
B Crude petroleum and natural gas production	...	...	...	...	...	...	...	...	...	...	...	...
C Metal ore mining	...	...	...	...	...	...	...	-	0.2	0.2	-	...
D Other mining	...	...	...	...	...	...	...	0.5	0.5	0.2	0.5	...

Cyprus

2.11 Gross Fixed Capital Formation by Kind of Activity of Owner, ISIC Divisions, in Current Prices
(Continued)

Million Cyprus pounds

	1970	1975	1980	1981	1982	1983	1984	1985	1986	1987	1988	1989
3 Manufacturing	9.7	6.6	27.6	24.9	27.5	24.5	31.4	34.7	31.4	37.1	43.1	45.7
A Manufacturing of food, beverages and tobacco	...	...	...	...	...	...	...	9.8	10.5	10.4	15.5	...
B Textile, wearing apparel and leather industries	...	...	...	...	...	...	...	6.1	4.9	8.2	7.5	...
C Manufacture of wood, and wood products, including furniture	...	...	...	...	...	...	...	2.6	2.1	2.8	4.3	...
D Manufacture of paper and paper products, printing and publishing	...	...	...	...	...	...	...	1.3	1.9	3.1	3.2	...
E Manufacture of chemicals and chemical petroleum, coal, rubber and plastic products	...	...	...	...	...	...	...	4.8	2.7	3.9	5.1	...
F Manufacture of non-metalic mineral products except products of petroleum and coal	...	...	...	...	...	...	...	2.7	3.0	3.3	2.9	...
G Basic metal industries	...	...	...	...	...	...	...	...	...	...	...	...
H Manufacture of fabricated metal products, machinery and equipment	...	...	...	...	...	...	...	6.4	5.8	4.9	3.9	...
I Other manufacturing industries	...	...	...	...	...	...	...	1.0	0.5	0.5	0.7	...
4 Electricity, gas and water	2.5	2.5	10.9	18.1	20.4	11.5	7.5	8.6	9.0	14.0	28.5	16.8
A Electricity, gas and steam	...	...	...	...	...	...	...	6.3	6.8	10.5	25.4	...
B Water works and supply	...	...	...	...	...	...	...	2.3	2.2	3.5	3.1	...
5 Construction	1.6	1.5	7.5	5.2	9.7	13.3	15.2	10.2	9.9	7.3	15.0	10.1
6 Wholesale and retail trade, restaurants and hotels [a]	2.7	3.1	37.3	40.5	47.8	53.7	61.3	59.4	61.3	72.8	81.3	98.0
A Wholesale and retail trade	...	...	...	...	...	...	...	29.9	30.2	35.8	40.5	...
B Restaurants and hotels	...	...	...	...	...	...	...	29.5	31.1	37.0	40.8	...
7 Transport, storage and communication	10.3	9.6	28.6	38.9	35.7	44.9	107.1	75.2	46.8	46.6	53.4	163.1
A Transport and storage	...	...	...	...	...	...	...	55.4	28.8	33.1	39.7	...
B Communication	...	...	...	...	...	...	...	19.8	18.0	13.5	13.7	...
8 Finance, insurance, real estate and business services [b]	17.7	14.0	107.7	105.0	111.1	119.9	129.5	151.8	155.8	157.6	180.4	202.6
A Financial institutions	...	...	...	...	...	...	...	3.0	2.2	2.5	5.8	...
B Insurance	...	...	...	...	...	...	...	1.1	0.9	1.4	1.6	...
C Real estate and business services	...	...	...	...	...	...	...	147.7	152.7	153.7	173.0	...
Real estate except dwellings	...	...	...	...	...	...	...	0.2	0.2	-	-	...

Cyprus

2.11 Gross Fixed Capital Formation by Kind of Activity of Owner, ISIC Divisions, in Current Prices
(Continued)

Million Cyprus pounds

	1970	1975	1980	1981	1982	1983	1984	1985	1986	1987	1988	1989
Dwellings	...	...	...	...	...	...	...	145.3	150.2	151.3	170.7	...
9 Community, social and personal services [a,b]	3.3	5.6	2.5	2.2	4.4	4.0	5.7	6.5	7.7	10.7	10.7	14.9
Total Industries	52.8	49.6	240.1	253.9	280.3	299.6	394.3	382.0	365.7	396.3	447.6	582.6
Producers of Government Services	0.5	0.9	4.0	5.6	6.8	6.2	4.6	6.0	7.8	11.2	22.9	18.3
Private Non-Profit Institutions Serving Households	...	...	0.9	1.6	1.5	1.7	2.1	4.4	4.5	3.6	4.7	5.2
Statistical discrepancy	...	...	15.0	14.8	16.1	8.5	11.5	10.6	6.0	-	-	-
Total	53.3	50.5	260.0	275.9	304.7	316.0	412.5	403.0	384.0	411.1	475.2	606.1

a) For the first series, restaurants and hotels are included in item 'Community, social and personal services'.　　b) For the first series, business services are included in item 'Community, social and personal services'.

2.12 Gross Fixed Capital Formation by Kind of Activity of Owner, ISIC Divisions, in Constant Prices

Million Cyprus pounds

	1970	1975	1980	1981	1982	1983	1984	1985	1986	1987	1988	1989
	1967	1973	\multicolumn{6}{c}{At constant prices of: 1980}	1985				
			\multicolumn{10}{c}{All Producers}
1 Agriculture, hunting, forestry and fishing	3.5	4.6	16.7	15.6	18.8	21.3	25.9	23.5 / 35.1	41.9	46.9	31.2	26.4
2 Mining and quarrying	0.7	1.0	1.3	1.3	0.8	0.4	0.5	0.4 / 0.7	0.6	0.4	0.4	0.5
3 Manufacturing	7.7	5.3	27.6	22.6	24.2	20.3	24.4	25.8 / 34.7	30.3	34.3	36.2	37.1
4 Electricity, gas and water	2.0	2.0	10.9	16.2	17.3	9.2	5.4	5.8 / 8.6	8.6	12.9	25.2	14.3
5 Construction	1.3	1.2	7.5	4.6	8.6	11.0	12.3	7.5 / 10.2	9.3	6.6	13.0	8.3
6 Wholesale and retail trade, restaurants and hotels	2.1 [a]	2.5 [a]	37.3	35.6	39.1	42.0	44.8	40.9 / 59.4	59.8	69.1	72.0	82.3
7 Transport, storage and communication	8.2	8.0	28.6	34.2	29.8	34.8	76.2	53.0 / 75.2	45.2	43.3	46.4	131.5
8 Finance, insurance, real estate and business services	14.4 [b]	11.6 [b]	107.7	91.4	89.3	92.1	92.3	100.9 / 151.8	154.1	153.7	164.2	173.2
9 Community, social and personal services	2.7 [a,b]	4.6 [a,b]	2.5	1.9	3.8	3.2	4.2	4.8 / 6.5	7.4	8.0	9.3	12.6
Total Industries	42.6	40.8	240.1	223.4	231.7	234.3	286.0	262.6 / 382.0	357.2	375.2	397.9	486.2
Producers of Government Services	0.4	0.8	4.0	5.0	5.6	4.9	3.3	4.0 / 6.0	7.5	10.1	20.5	15.8
Private Non-Profit Institutions Serving Households	...	...	0.9	1.4	1.2	1.4	1.6	3.0 / 4.4	4.4	3.4	4.2	4.3
Statistical discrepancy	...	...	15.0	13.4	13.9	6.3	9.2	7.3 / 10.6	5.4	-	-	-
Total	43.0	41.6	260.0	243.2	252.4	246.9	300.1	276.9 / 403.0	374.5	388.7	422.6	506.3

a) Restaurants and hotels are included in item 'Community, social and personal services'.
b) Business services are included in item 'Community, social and personal services'.

Cyprus

2.17 Exports and Imports of Goods and Services, Detail

Million Cyprus pounds

	1970	1975	1980	1981	1982	1983	1984	1985	1986	1987	1988	1989
Exports of Goods and Services												
1 Exports of merchandise, f.o.b.	...	...	185.0	230.6	261.6	257.9	334.2	287.3	257.8	295.6	328.1	389.5
2 Transport and communication	...	...	31.5	38.2	45.4	50.0	66.6	80.8	81.0	92.0	94.9	95.9
3 Insurance service charges	...	...	0.6	0.7	0.7	0.8	1.0	1.0	0.7	0.7	0.7	0.7
4 Other commodities	...	...	55.3	68.3	75.5	89.5	117.2	121.3	124.9	132.8	150.1	175.5
5 Adjustments of merchandise exports to change-of-ownership basis	...	...	71.7	102.4	138.7	174.8	212.0	232.0	256.6	320.7	386.0	490.0
6 Direct purchases in the domestic market by non-residential households	...	...	...	...	...	...	...	...	...	...	...	...
7 Direct purchases in the domestic market by extraterritorial bodies	...	...	...	...	...	...	...	...	...	...	...	...
Total Exports of Goods and Services	...	...	344.1	440.2	521.9	573.0	731.0	722.4	721.0	841.8	959.8	1151.6
Imports of Goods and Services												
1 Imports of merchandise, c.i.f.	...	...	424.3	489.5	577.6	642.0	796.5	762.3	659.1	711.4	866.8	1130.3
A Imports of merchandise, f.o.b.	...	...	381.0	439.4	518.3	575.9	720.7	687.2	591.5	638.3	777.8	1022.6
B Transport of services on merchandise imports	...	...	39.1	45.2	53.5	59.7	68.5	67.8	61.0	66.0	80.4	97.2
C Insurance service charges on merchandise imports	...	...	4.2	4.9	5.8	6.4	7.3	7.3	6.6	7.1	8.6	10.5
2 Adjustments of merchandise imports to change-of-ownership basis	...	...	...	...	...	...	...	...	...	...	...	...
3 Other transport and communication	...	...	22.1	23.5	28.1	29.3	34.4	37.1	38.6	45.1	45.6	49.0
4 Other insurance service charges	...	...	...	...	...	...	...	...	...	...	...	...
5 Other commodities	...	...	13.3	17.6	20.4	21.0	24.7	25.1	26.5	33.0	35.2	41.6
6 Direct purchases abroad by government	...	...	...	...	...	...	...	...	...	...	...	...
7 Direct purchases abroad by resident households	...	...	19.8	24.1	32.3	34.9	41.8	47.5	51.0	56.2	62.7	66.3
Total Imports of Goods and Services	...	...	479.5	554.7	658.4	727.2	897.4	872.0	775.2	845.7	1010.3	1287.2
Balance of Goods and Services	...	...	-135.4	-114.5	-136.5	-154.2	-166.4	-149.6	-54.2	-3.9	-50.5	-135.6
Total Imports and Balance of Goods and Services	...	...	344.1	440.2	521.9	573.0	731.0	722.4	721.0	841.8	959.8	1151.6

4.1 Derivation of Value Added by Kind of Activity, in Current Prices

Million Cyprus pounds

	1980			1981			1982			1983		
	Gross Output	Intermediate Consumption	Value Added	Gross Output	Intermediate Consumption	Value Added	Gross Output	Intermediate Consumption	Value Added	Gross Output	Intermediate Consumption	Value Added
All Producers												
1 Agriculture, hunting, forestry and fishing	126.7	53.8	72.9	145.2	64.1	81.1	166.8	71.8	95.0	169.0	79.2	89.8
A Agriculture and hunting	123.3	53.1	70.2	141.4	63.4	78.0	162.5	71.0	91.5	164.1	78.5	85.6
B Forestry and logging	1.4	0.5	0.9	1.3	0.5	0.8	1.6	0.6	1.0	1.4	0.4	1.0
C Fishing	2.0	0.2	1.8	2.5	0.2	2.3	2.7	0.2	2.5	3.5	0.3	3.2
2 Mining and quarrying	18.9	9.0	9.9	18.7	8.9	9.8	17.3	8.5	8.8	15.7	7.7	8.0
A Coal mining	-	-	-	-	-	-	-	-	-	-	-	-
B Crude petroleum and natural gas production	-	-	-	-	-	-	-	-	-	-	-	-
C Metal ore mining	2.9	1.1	1.8	2.9	1.2	1.7	2.3	1.0	1.3	1.4	0.6	0.8
D Other mining	16.0	7.9	8.1	15.8	7.7	8.1	15.0	7.5	7.5	14.3	7.1	7.2

Cyprus

4.1 Derivation of Value Added by Kind of Activity, in Current Prices
(Continued)

Million Cyprus pounds

		1980			1981			1982			1983		
		Gross Output	Intermediate Consumption	Value Added	Gross Output	Intermediate Consumption	Value Added	Gross Output	Intermediate Consumption	Value Added	Gross Output	Intermediate Consumption	Value Added
3	Manufacturing	404.7	271.3	133.4	489.0	334.8	154.2	535.6	361.1	174.5	580.8	392.9	187.9
	A Manufacture of food, beverages and tobacco	102.0	65.0	37.0	120.1	77.7	42.4	132.9	84.5	48.4	144.0	91.2	52.8
	B Textile, wearing apparel and leather industries	83.7	52.5	31.2	103.9	66.8	37.1	107.1	65.3	41.8	120.8	74.6	46.2
	C Manufacture of wood and wood products, including furniture	27.5	15.5	12.0	33.7	18.7	15.0	42.0	22.7	19.3	49.5	27.3	22.2
	D Manufacture of paper and paper products, printing and publishing	23.1	14.5	8.6	29.5	19.5	10.0	30.8	20.7	10.1	29.3	18.8	10.5
	E Manufacture of chemicals and chemical petroleum, coal, rubber and plastic products	81.1	70.4	10.7	98.4	86.6	11.8	107.7	94.0	13.7	121.2	105.2	16.0
	F Manufacture of non-metallic mineral products, except products of petroleum and coal	39.7	24.2	15.5	45.4	29.1	16.3	46.0	30.3	15.7	43.4	29.7	13.7
	G Basic metal industries	-	-	-	-	-	-	-	-	-	-	-	-
	H Manufacture of fabricated metal products, machinery and equipment	40.1	24.9	15.2	50.5	31.7	18.8	60.4	38.1	22.3	61.9	39.2	22.7
	I Other manufacturing industries	7.5	4.3	3.2	7.5	4.7	2.8	8.7	5.5	3.2	10.7	6.9	3.8
4	Electricity, gas and water	30.6	20.6	10.0	43.4	28.7	14.7	50.5	33.0	17.5	57.8	35.6	22.2
	A Electricity, gas and steam	29.0	19.9	9.1	41.7	28.0	13.7	47.1	31.4	15.7	53.9	33.4	20.5
	B Water works and supply	1.6	0.7	0.9	1.7	0.7	1.0	4.4	2.6	1.8	3.9	2.2	1.7
5	Construction	197.1	94.6	102.5	211.4	106.2	105.2	222.0	106.5	115.5	237.7	113.8	123.9
6	Wholesale and retail trade, restaurants and hotels	169.1	53.5	115.6	210.2	72.7	137.5	257.4	91.6	165.8	302.9	115.9	187.0
	A Wholesale and retail trade	121.7	32.6	89.1	143.4	43.4	100.0	168.1	51.9	116.2	190.0	65.9	124.1
	B Restaurants and hotels	47.4	20.9	26.5	66.8	29.3	37.5	89.3	39.7	49.6	112.9	50.0	62.9
	Restaurants	22.8	10.1	12.7	29.4	13.0	16.4	38.9	17.2	21.7	50.5	22.3	28.2
	Hotels and other lodging places	24.6	10.8	13.8	37.4	16.3	21.1	50.4	22.5	27.9	62.4	27.7	34.7
7	Transport, storage and communication	106.5	46.0	60.5	120.7	48.7	72.0	137.1	52.5	84.6	162.2	61.6	100.6
	A Transport and storage	88.4	44.1	44.3	100.7	46.3	54.4	112.9	49.4	63.5	133.8	58.1	75.7
	B Communication	18.1	1.9	16.2	20.0	2.4	17.6	24.2	3.1	21.1	28.4	3.5	24.9
8	Finance, insurance, real estate and business services	128.1	19.2	108.9	157.8	23.7	134.1	183.2	29.7	153.5	195.5	34.1	161.4
	A Financial institutions	29.4	3.8	25.6	41.7	4.4	37.3	47.0	6.7	40.3	43.9	8.1	35.8
	B Insurance	6.8	1.5	5.3	7.0	1.6	5.4	9.1	2.0	7.1	6.8	2.3	4.5
	C Real estate and business services	91.9	13.9	78.0	109.1	17.7	91.4	127.1	21.0	106.1	144.8	23.7	121.1
	Real estate, except dwellings	28.3	2.9	25.4	35.1	3.3	31.8	44.3	4.3	40.0	52.1	5.3	46.8
	Dwellings	50.8	5.6	45.2	56.9	6.6	50.3	61.6	7.6	54.0	66.5	8.0	58.5
9	Community, social and personal services	36.4	10.6	25.8	45.3	12.8	32.5	51.8	14.1	37.7	65.1	18.2	46.9
	A Sanitary and similar services	0.7	0.2	0.5	0.7	0.1	0.6	0.8	0.2	0.6	0.9	0.2	0.7
	B Social and related community services [a]	9.0	2.1	6.9	10.4	2.6	7.8	13.4	3.2	10.2	18.0	4.5	13.5
	Educational services	3.4	0.6	2.8	4.2	0.9	3.3	5.6	1.0	4.6	7.9	1.7	6.2
	Medical, dental, other health and veterinary services	5.2	1.4	3.8	5.7	1.5	4.2	6.9	2.2	4.9	9.1	2.5	6.1
	C Recreational and cultural services	8.6	3.7	4.9	13.0	4.5	8.5	13.1	5.0	8.1	16.7	6.6	10.1
	D Personal and household services	18.1	4.6	13.5	21.2	5.6	15.6	24.5	5.7	18.8	29.5	6.9	22.6
	Total, Industries	1218.1	578.6	639.5	1441.7	700.6	741.1	1621.7	768.8	852.9	1786.7	859.0	927.7
	Producers of Government Services	109.0	19.5	89.5	127.8	19.1	108.7	158.4	24.6	133.8	179.0	28.1	150.9
	Other Producers	4.7	1.6	3.1	5.7	2.0	3.7	7.0	2.8	4.2	8.6	2.7	5.9
	Total	1331.8	599.7	732.1	1575.2	721.7	853.5	1787.1	796.2	990.9	1974.3	889.8	1084.5
	Less: Imputed bank service charge	...	-23.0	23.0	...	-33.4	33.4	...	-36.8	36.8	...	-31.1	31.1
	Import duties	51.3	...	51.3	55.9	...	55.9	70.8	...	70.8	83.3	...	83.3
	Value added tax	...	...	...	...	...	...	...	...	...	...	...	...
	Total	1383.1	622.7	760.4	1631.1	755.1	876.0	1857.9	833.0	1024.9	2057.6	920.9	1136.7

Cyprus

4.1 Derivation of Value Added by Kind of Activity, in Current Prices

Million Cyprus pounds

		1984			1985			1986			1987		
		Gross Output	Intermediate Consumption	Value Added	Gross Output	Intermediate Consumption	Value Added	Gross Output	Intermediate Consumption	Value Added	Gross Output	Intermediate Consumption	Value Added
						All Producers							
1	Agriculture, hunting, forestry and fishing	202.9	83.3	119.6	198.0	87.0	111.0	203.9	86.6	117.3	221.6	89.3	132.3
	A Agriculture and hunting	196.9	82.5	114.4	191.5	86.2	105.3	196.3	85.8	110.5	213.7	88.2	125.4
	B Forestry and logging	1.5	0.5	1.0	1.7	0.5	1.2	1.6	0.4	1.2	2.0	0.7	1.3
	C Fishing	4.5	0.3	4.2	4.8	0.3	4.5	6.0	0.4	5.6	5.9	0.4	5.6
2	Mining and quarrying	15.2	7.1	8.1	15.2	8.1	7.1	14.5	7.0	7.5	14.1	7.4	6.7
	A Coal mining	-	-	-	-	-	-	-	-	-	-	-	-
	B Crude petroleum and natural gas production	-	-	-	-	-	-	-	-	-	-	-	-
	C Metal ore mining	1.2	0.6	0.6	1.7	0.9	0.8	1.0	0.7	0.3	1.6	1.1	0.5
	D Other mining	14.0	6.5	7.5	13.5	7.2	6.3	13.5	6.3	7.2	12.5	6.3	6.2
3	Manufacturing	663.0	447.8	215.2	685.9	454.0	231.9	670.9	430.4	240.5	752.6	478.7	273.9
	A Manufacture of food, beverages and tobacco	168.9	108.5	60.4	181.7	118.2	63.5	192.3	122.8	69.5	206.4	129.7	76.7
	B Textile, wearing apparel and leather industries	150.2	93.7	56.5	145.9	89.1	56.8	140.5	86.5	54.0	174.7	107.3	67.4
	C Manufacture of wood and wood products, including furniture	54.6	29.8	24.8	61.8	34.5	27.3	62.1	34.6	27.5	63.4	34.7	28.7
	D Manufacture of paper and paper products, printing and publishing	35.0	21.8	13.2	40.8	25.3	15.5	37.2	22.8	14.4	41.8	25.6	16.2
	E Manufacture of chemicals and chemical petroleum, coal, rubber and plastic products	127.2	110.4	16.8	115.8	97.0	18.8	93.3	73.5	19.8	105.8	83.2	22.6
	F Manufacture of non-metallic mineral products, except products of petroleum and coal	45.2	31.9	13.3	42.4	27.1	15.3	46.9	27.3	19.6	52.8	29.8	23.0
	G Basic metal industries	-	-	-	-	-	-	...	-	-	-	-	-
	H Manufacture of fabricated metal products, machinery and equipment	68.9	43.0	25.9	81.3	52.1	29.2	81.4	51.7	29.7	87.6	55.4	32.2
	I Other manufacturing industries	13.0	8.7	4.3	16.2	10.7	5.5	17.2	11.2	6.0	20.1	13.0	7.1
4	Electricity, gas and water	70.0	42.0	28.0	77.0	43.7	33.3	60.4	25.2	35.2	63.6	26.6	37.0
	A Electricity, gas and steam	64.9	39.0	25.9	70.4	40.3	30.1	52.5	21.9	30.6	54.8	23.0	31.8
	B Water works and supply	5.1	3.0	2.1	6.6	3.4	3.2	7.9	3.3	4.6	8.8	3.6	5.2
5	Construction	266.5	129.5	137.0	286.6	138.0	148.6	305.5	149.0	156.5	333.1	163.1	170.0
6	Wholesale and retail trade, restaurants and hotels	366.1	134.4	231.7	427.5	150.5	277.0	461.4	157.5	303.9	523.2	176.8	346.4
	A Wholesale and retail trade	224.2	73.5	150.7	257.9	80.3	177.6	268.9	82.5	186.4	289.6	87.9	201.7
	B Restaurants and hotels	141.9	60.9	81.0	169.6	70.2	99.4	192.5	75.0	117.5	233.6	88.9	144.7
	Restaurants	66.0	29.2	36.8	80.9	35.8	45.1	90.1	38.4	51.7	107.8	45.6	62.2
	Hotels and other lodging places	75.9	31.7	44.2	88.7	34.4	54.3	102.4	36.6	65.8	125.8	43.3	82.5
7	Transport, storage and communication	189.3	68.7	120.6	216.9	78.6	138.3	232.9	77.0	155.9	252.0	84.1	168.0
	A Transport and storage	152.3	64.7	87.6	171.8	74.0	97.8	186.5	72.5	114.0	201.2	79.2	122.0
	B Communication	37.0	4.0	33.0	45.1	4.6	40.5	46.4	4.5	41.9	50.8	4.9	46.0
8	Finance, insurance, real estate and business services	227.7	38.5	189.2	254.9	46.6	208.3	281.4	50.8	230.6	306.3	52.2	254.1
	A Financial institutions	53.9	9.2	44.7	56.3	11.8	44.5	59.4	11.7	47.7	64.5	12.4	52.1
	B Insurance	11.2	2.8	8.4	13.0	3.3	9.7	13.2	4.0	9.2	16.9	4.5	12.4
	C Real estate and business services	162.6	26.9	135.7	185.6	32.1	153.5	208.8	35.1	173.7	224.9	35.3	189.6
	Real estate, except dwellings	59.2	5.9	53.3	68.1	7.1	61.0	76.6	7.6	69.0	82.2	8.1	74.2
	Dwellings	71.5	8.7	62.8	77.7	9.6	68.1	85.2	10.4	74.8	91.2	11.1	80.1
9	Community, social and personal services	79.6	22.8	56.8	94.5	26.1	68.4	105.6	26.7	78.9	119.0	28.9	90.1
	A Sanitary and similar services	1.1	0.3	0.8	1.2	0.3	0.9	1.4	0.3	1.1	1.8	0.5	1.3
	B Social and related community services [a]	23.7	6.1	17.6	29.9	7.3	22.6	35.0	7.9	27.1	41.3	9.9	31.4
	Educational services	10.4	2.4	8.0	13.4	2.8	10.6	15.4	3.1	12.3	17.7	3.7	14.0
	Medical, dental, other health and veterinary services	13.3	3.7	9.6	14.9	4.0	10.9	17.7	4.3	13.4	21.1	5.5	15.6
	C Recreational and cultural services	20.3	8.4	11.9	23.6	8.8	14.8	25.4	8.7	16.7	26.8	8.4	18.4
	D Personal and household services	34.5	8.0	26.5	39.8	9.7	30.1	43.8	9.8	34.0	49.1	10.1	39.0

Cyprus

4.1 Derivation of Value Added by Kind of Activity, in Current Prices
(Continued)

Million Cyprus pounds

	1984 Gross Output	1984 Intermediate Consumption	1984 Value Added	1985 Gross Output	1985 Intermediate Consumption	1985 Value Added	1986 Gross Output	1986 Intermediate Consumption	1986 Value Added	1987 Gross Output	1987 Intermediate Consumption	1987 Value Added
Total, Industries	2080.3	974.2	1106.1	2256.5	1033.5	1223.9	2336.5	1010.2	1326.3	2585.5	1107.0	1478.5
Producers of Government Services	198.4	31.8	166.6	218.1	34.4	183.7	237.4	36.2	201.2	264.7	45.5	219.2
Other Producers	10.9	3.2	7.7	13.3	5.2	8.1	13.7	4.6	9.1	15.7	5.9	9.8
Total	2289.6	1009.2	1280.4	2487.9	1072.2	1415.7	2587.6	1051.0	1536.6	2865.9	1158.6	1707.3
Less: Imputed bank service charge	...	-37.8	37.8	...	-39.9	39.9	...	-40.8	40.8	...	-42.7	42.7
Import duties	94.8	...	94.8	105.0	...	105.0	103.1	...	103.1	114.5	...	114.5
Value added tax	...	...	...	...	...	...	...	...	...	...	...	...
Total	2384.4	1047.0	1337.4	2592.9	1112.1	1480.8	2690.7	1091.8	1598.9	2980.4	1201.3	1779.1

		1988 Gross Output	1988 Intermediate Consumption	1988 Value Added	1989 Gross Output	1989 Intermediate Consumption	1989 Value Added
		\multicolumn{6}{c}{All Producers}
1	Agriculture, hunting, forestry and fishing	239.9	96.7	143.2	256.1	100.5	155.6
A	Agriculture and hunting	231.2	95.6	135.6	246.4	99.2	147.2
B	Forestry and logging	2.1	0.7	1.4	2.2	0.8	1.4
C	Fishing	6.6	0.4	6.2	7.5	0.5	7.0
2	Mining and quarrying	14.3	7.2	7.1	12.8	6.3	6.5
A	Coal mining	-	-	-	-	-	-
B	Crude petroleum and natural gas production	-	-	-	-	-	-
C	Metal ore mining	1.8	1.1	0.7	1.4	0.8	0.6
D	Other mining	12.5	6.1	6.4	11.4	5.5	5.9
3	Manufacturing	839.7	530.6	309.1	908.9	574.9	334.0
A	Manufacture of food, beverages and tobacco	222.4	139.1	83.3	245.1	153.0	92.1
B	Textile, wearing apparel and leather industries	200.1	122.8	77.3	202.7	124.4	78.3
C	Manufacture of wood and wood products, including furniture	67.0	36.7	30.3	76.3	41.8	34.5
D	Manufacture of paper and paper products, printing and publishing	50.4	31.7	18.7	54.6	34.2	20.4
E	Manufacture of chemicals and chemical petroleum, coal, rubber and plastic products	118.2	89.9	28.3	130.1	99.7	30.4
F	Manufacture of non-metallic mineral products, except products of petroleum and coal	59.3	32.9	26.4	66.2	36.8	29.4
G	Basic metal industries	-	-	-	-	-	-
H	Manufacture of fabricated metal products, machinery and equipment	100.0	63.0	37.0	110.0	69.5	40.5
I	Other manufacturing industries	22.3	14.5	7.8	23.9	15.5	8.4
4	Electricity, gas and water	65.4	23.8	41.6	72.6	29.0	43.6
A	Electricity, gas and steam	56.0	20.1	35.9	62.5	25.0	37.5
B	Water works and supply	9.4	3.7	5.7	10.1	4.0	6.1
5	Construction	369.3	180.1	189.2	416.5	202.8	213.7
6	Wholesale and retail trade, restaurants and hotels	587.6	201.3	386.3	689.7	236.7	453.0
A	Wholesale and retail trade	305.8	96.5	209.3	338.7	107.2	231.5
B	Restaurants and hotels	281.8	104.8	177.0	351.0	129.5	221.5
	Restaurants	130.9	54.8	76.1	161.9	67.5	94.4
	Hotels and other lodging places	150.9	50.0	100.9	189.1	62.0	127.1
7	Transport, storage and communication	269.0	86.8	182.2	294.4	95.2	199.2
A	Transport and storage	212.4	81.9	130.5	227.0	88.9	138.1
B	Communication	56.6	4.9	51.7	67.4	6.3	61.1
8	Finance, insurance, real estate and business services	347.3	60.5	286.8	387.6	68.7	318.9
A	Financial institutions	74.4	16.0	58.4	83.7	18.0	65.7
B	Insurance	20.1	4.8	15.3	22.7	5.2	17.5
C	Real estate and business services	252.8	39.7	213.1	281.2	45.5	235.7
	Real estate, except dwellings	94.1	9.3	84.8	105.5	11.2	94.3

Cyprus

4.1 Derivation of Value Added by Kind of Activity, in Current Prices
(Continued)

Million Cyprus pounds

	1988 Gross Output	1988 Intermediate Consumption	1988 Value Added	1989 Gross Output	1989 Intermediate Consumption	1989 Value Added
Dwellings	98.2	12.1	86.1	105.9	13.4	92.5
9 Community, social and personal services	137.3	32.7	104.6	155.3	37.0	118.3
A Sanitary and similar services	2.0	0.5	1.5	2.1	0.6	1.5
B Social and related community services [a]	49.4	11.7	37.7	57.5	13.7	43.8
Educational services	21.0	4.3	16.7	23.9	4.9	19.0
Medical, dental, other health and veterinary services	25.5	6.5	19.0	30.4	7.7	22.7
C Recreational and cultural services	30.5	9.3	21.2	33.6	10.2	23.4
D Personal and household services	55.4	11.2	44.2	62.1	12.5	49.6
Total, Industries	2869.8	1219.7	1650.1	3193.9	1351.1	1842.8
Producers of Government Services	289.1	48.2	240.9	309.0	52.0	257.0
Other Producers	18.3	6.9	11.4	20.1	7.8	12.3
Total	3177.2	1274.8	1902.4	3523.0	1410.9	2112.1
Less: Imputed bank service charge	...	-47.6	47.6	...	-56.3	56.3
Import duties	137.3	...	137.3	162.9	...	162.9
Value added tax	...	...	...	...	...	...
Total	3314.5	1322.4	1992.1	3685.9	1467.2	2218.7

[a] Social and related community services include in addition to educational and health services also the services of commercial and professional associations, welfare institutions and other social and related community services.

4.2 Derivation of Value Added by Kind of Activity, in Constant Prices

Million Cyprus pounds

At constant prices of: 1985

All Producers

	1986 GO	1986 IC	1986 VA	1987 GO	1987 IC	1987 VA	1988 GO	1988 IC	1988 VA	1989 GO	1989 IC	1989 VA
1 Agriculture, hunting, forestry and fishing	200.2	89.8	110.4	206.3	92.1	114.2	222.7	96.0	126.7	226.5	97.8	128.7
A Agriculture and hunting	193.3	88.9	104.4	199.6	91.1	108.5	215.8	94.9	120.9	219.6	96.8	122.8
B Forestry and logging	1.7	0.5	1.2	1.9	0.6	1.3	1.9	0.5	1.4	1.9	0.5	1.4
C Fishing	5.2	0.4	4.8	4.8	0.4	4.4	5.0	0.6	4.4	5.0	0.5	4.5
2 Mining and quarrying	14.7	7.6	7.1	14.8	8.1	6.7	14.5	7.9	6.6	12.4	6.9	5.5
A Coal mining	-	-	-	-	-	-	-	-	-	-	-	-
B Crude petroleum and natural gas production	-	-	-	-	-	-	-	-	-	-	-	-
C Metal ore mining	1.1	0.8	0.3	1.5	1.1	0.4	1.6	1.2	0.4	1.3	1.0	0.3
D Other mining	13.6	6.8	6.8	13.3	7.0	6.3	12.9	6.7	6.2	11.1	5.9	5.2
3 Manufacturing	710.2	477.6	232.6	781.8	530.5	251.3	841.7	573.2	268.5	866.9	590.3	276.6
A Manufacture of food, beverages and tobacco	189.0	124.7	64.3	202.4	133.1	69.3	212.0	139.1	72.9	223.6	148.0	75.6
B Textile, wearing apparel and leather industries	144.6	88.4	56.2	174.2	109.4	64.8	190.2	122.5	67.7	186.8	121.2	65.6
C Manufacture of wood and wood products, including furniture	60.9	34.1	26.8	59.6	32.7	26.9	60.4	32.8	27.6	65.8	35.6	30.2
D Manufacture of paper and paper products, printing and publishing	37.3	23.8	13.5	40.3	26.0	14.3	46.9	29.8	17.1	48.2	30.0	18.2
E Manufacture of chemicals and chemical petroleum, coal, rubber and plastic products	130.8	111.7	19.1	143.8	123.8	20.0	161.0	136.4	24.6	164.1	138.6	25.5
F Manufacture of non-metallic mineral products, except products of petroleum and coal	49.4	31.1	18.3	57.0	37.2	19.8	60.7	40.4	20.3	66.2	43.1	23.1
G Basic metal industries	-	-	-	-	-	-	-	-	-	-	-	-
H Manufacture of fabricated metal products, machinery and equipment	81.1	52.8	28.3	85.0	55.3	29.7	89.1	57.7	31.4	89.2	58.2	31.0
I Other manufacturing industries	17.1	11.0	6.1	19.5	13.0	6.5	21.4	14.5	6.9	23.0	15.6	7.4
4 Electricity, gas and water	84.0	45.9	38.1	93.6	49.4	44.2	104.0	53.8	50.2	112.4	57.3	55.1
A Electricity, gas and steam	76.3	42.3	34.0	85.5	45.5	40.0	95.8	49.9	45.9	103.6	53.2	50.4
B Water works and supply	7.7	3.6	4.1	8.1	3.9	4.2	8.2	3.9	4.3	8.8	4.1	4.7

Cyprus

4.2 Derivation of Value Added by Kind of Activity, in Constant Prices
(Continued)

Million Cyprus pounds

		1986			1987			1988			1989		
		Gross Output	Intermediate Consumption	Value Added	Gross Output	Intermediate Consumption	Value Added	Gross Output	Intermediate Consumption	Value Added	Gross Output	Intermediate Consumption	Value Added
					At constant prices of:1985								
5	Construction	300.3	151.2	149.1	319.7	166.0	153.7	331.9	172.1	159.8	351.0	182.2	168.8
6	Wholesale and retail trade, restaurants and hotels	446.6	158.7	287.9	490.1	173.2	316.9	541.8	191.6	350.2	609.0	214.7	394.3
	A Wholesale and retail trade	263.6	83.0	180.6	277.5	86.3	191.2	294.7	92.4	202.3	314.7	99.1	215.6
	B Restaurants and hotels	183.0	75.7	107.3	212.6	86.9	125.7	247.1	99.2	147.9	294.3	115.6	178.7
	Restaurants	85.3	38.1	47.2	98.9	44.0	54.9	117.4	51.0	66.4	140.2	60.8	79.4
	Hotels and other lodging places	97.7	37.6	60.1	113.7	42.9	70.8	129.7	48.2	81.5	154.1	54.8	99.3
7	Transport, storage and communication	226.8	83.2	143.6	242.8	91.5	151.3	257.4	91.6	165.8	279.1	96.5	182.6
	A Transport and storage	181.0	78.5	102.5	192.7	86.6	106.1	201.7	86.7	115.0	212.6	86.3	126.3
	B Communication	45.8	4.7	41.1	50.1	4.9	45.2	55.7	4.9	50.8	66.5	10.2	56.3
8	Finance, insurance, real estate and business services	273.9	48.9	225.0	289.0	49.0	240.0	316.4	54.5	261.9	339.7	59.2	280.5
	A Financial institutions	58.8	10.9	47.9	62.0	11.2	50.8	69.2	13.9	55.3	75.1	15.1	60.0
	B Insurance	13.0	3.6	9.4	16.3	4.1	12.2	18.7	4.2	14.5	20.3	4.3	16.0
	C Real estate and business services	202.1	34.4	167.7	210.7	33.7	177.0	228.5	36.4	192.1	244.3	39.8	204.5
	Real estate, except dwellings	74.7	7.1	67.6	77.2	7.4	69.8	85.2	8.2	77.0	91.2	9.4	81.8
	Dwellings	80.9	10.1	70.8	83.9	10.3	73.6	87.0	10.5	76.5	90.5	10.8	79.7
9	Community, social and personal services	101.0	27.8	73.2	108.3	29.5	78.8	120.3	33.0	87.3	129.6	35.6	94.0
	A Sanitary and similar services	1.4	0.2	1.2	1.5	0.4	1.1	1.6	0.4	1.2	1.7	0.6	1.1
	B Social and related community services	33.3	8.0	25.3	37.0	9.8	27.2	41.0	11.2	29.8	45.4	12.5	32.9
	Educational services	14.7	3.1	11.6	15.7	3.6	12.1	17.2	4.1	13.1	19.0	4.5	14.5
	Medical, dental, other health and veterinary services	17.2	4.3	12.9	19.1	5.4	13.7	21.8	6.2	15.6	24.6	7.2	17.4
	C Recreational and cultural services	25.3	9.6	15.7	26.3	9.2	17.1	30.3	10.2	20.1	31.7	10.6	21.1
	D Personal and household services	41.0	10.0	31.0	43.5	10.1	33.4	47.4	11.2	36.2	50.8	11.9	38.9
Total, Industries		2357.6	1090.6	1267.0	2546.4	1189.3	1357.1	2750.7	1273.7	1477.0	2926.6	1340.5	1586.1
Producers of Government Services		228.4	36.7	191.7	245.9	45.6	200.3	258.4	46.0	212.4	267.0	47.7	219.3
Other Producers		13.4	4.7	8.7	16.1	5.9	10.2	17.3	6.7	10.6	17.7	7.3	10.4
Total		2599.4	1132.0	1467.4	2808.4	1240.8	1567.6	3026.4	1326.4	1700.0	3211.3	1395.5	1815.8
Less: Imputed bank service charge		...	-39.0	39.0	...	-39.2	39.2	...	-42.5	42.5	...	-48.4	48.4
Import duties		109.0	...	109.0	116.6	...	116.6	126.5	...	126.5	134.9	...	134.9
Value added tax		...	...	...	...	...	...	...	...	...	...	...	...
Total		2708.4	1171.0	1537.4	2925.0	1280.0	1645.0	3152.9	1368.9	1784.0	3346.2	1443.9	1902.3

Czechoslovakia

Source. Reply to the United Nations Material Balances Questionnaire from the Federal Statistical Office, Prague. The official estimates and descriptions are published annually in 'Statisticka Rocenka' (Statistical Yearbook), issued by the same Office.

General note. The estimates shown in the following tables have been prepared in accordance with the System of Material Product Balances. Therefore, these estimates are not comparable in concept and coverage with those conforming to the United Nations System of National Accounts.

1a Net Material Product by Use at Current Market Prices

Million Czechoslovak koruny

	1970	1975	1980	1981	1982	1983	1984	1985	1986	1987	1988	1989
1 Personal consumption [a]	175815	223547	268771	274371	283126	292021	300323	311139	319511	329269	344931	357645
2 Material consumption in the units of the non-material sphere serving individuals	23477	34671	46175	49745	52146	53806	57342	60736	65958	69670	72546	77755
Consumption of the Population	199292	258218	314946	324116	335272	345827	357665	371875	385469	398939	417477	435400
3 Material consumption in the units of the non-material sphere serving the community as a whole	19521	26727	34955	36566	37813	40780	46312	46012	48634	51503	54641	53854
4 Net fixed capital formation	49854	80426	76279	84988	70088	68848	83618	91316	93963	76102	82327	64717
5 Increase in material circulating assets and in stocks	30969	37349	47908	6839	26493	25617	17927	11002	18636	30116	17588	33037
6 Losses	5300	7033	5116	5140	6487	5770	6536	6078	6181	7982	8262	8593
7 Exports of goods and material services	6204	-5755	3248	11918	15236	16475	21956	22440	9281	10015	18314	13458
8 Less: Imports of goods and material services												
Net Material Product	311140	403998	482452	469567	491389	503317	534014	548723	562164	574657	598609	609059

a) In personal consumption there is included wear and tear of the buildings in ownership of population only. That of residential buildings in ownership of enterprises, state and co-operative organizations is included in the material consumption of units of non-material sphere serving the population.

1b Net Material Product by Use at Constant Market Prices

Million Czechoslovak koruny

	1970	1975	1980	1981	1982	1983	1984	1985	1986	1987	1988	1989
		1967			1977					1984		
1 Personal consumption	165002	208184	245781	250086	244716	250045	254884	259752 / 302978	309548	318386	333920	339660
2 Material consumption in the units of the non-material sphere serving individuals	22967	32577	44846	48015	49217	50558	51759	55314 / 63347	68525	72035	74634	83039
Consumption of the Population	187969	240761	290627	298101	293933	300603	306643	315066 / 366325	378073	390421	408554	422699
3 Material consumption in the units of the non-material sphere serving the community as a whole	18523	23112	33596	34901	34919	37576	40204	40701 / 46898	49418	52188	55225	56229
4 Net fixed capital formation	41443	68519	71379	79274	61616	56164	66632	67896 / 83051	78534	58514	64587	49924
5 Increase in material circulating assets and in stocks	21661	26093	37805	6229	20846	19695	4202	6769 / 1093	15899	34882	19304	34698
6 Losses	4982	6009	4974	4899	5816	5163	5655	5205 / 6254	6257	7050	7129	7297
7 Exports of goods and material services	4774	574	9199	23749	30608	38896	49480	50773 / 21396	10470	6409	8717	-5157
8 Less: Imports of goods and material services												
Net Material Product [a]	279352	365068	447580	447153	447738	458097	472816	486410 / 525017	538651	549464	563516	565690

a) For this table, the first series are at constant prices of 1 January 1967, the second series are at constant prices of 1 January 1977, and the third series are at constant prices of 1 January 1984.

2a Net Material Product by Kind of Activity of the Material Sphere in Current Market Prices

Million Czechoslovak koruny

	1970	1975	1980	1981	1982	1983	1984	1985	1986	1987	1988	1989
1 Agriculture and forestry	35180	37848	40597	33683	42247	44056	45150	41790	44269	43217	42876	62184
A Agriculture and livestock	...	...	...	...	...	...	...	...	...	...	...	...
B Forestry	3641	4032	5795	5045	4871	4472	4308	4656	4790	4499	4184	5934
C Other	31539	33816	34802	28638	37376	39584	40842	37134	39479	38718	38692	56250
2 Industrial activity	190583	262922	309066	285058	300534	311051	318031	333363	341948	350015	362169	360034

Czechoslovakia

2a Net Material Product by Kind of Activity of the Material Sphere in Current Market Prices
(Continued)

Million Czechoslovak koruny

	1970	1975	1980	1981	1982	1983	1984	1985	1986	1987	1988	1989
3 Construction	35032	51486	50983	50470	51636	52644	59486	60537	61042	62385	65074	65368
4 Wholesale and retail trade and restaurants and other eating and drinking places	35135	36365	59379	76966	74200	72496	87535	90031	90985	96151	104169	100075
5 Transport and communication	12009	11614	20542	21405	20966	21063	21899	20903	21648	20394	21756	18648
A Transport	8841	7497	12286	12867	12169	11912	12447	11033	11238	9533	10474	7170
B Communication	3168	4117	8256	8538	8797	9151	9452	9870	10410	10861	11282	11478
6 Other activities of the material sphere	3201	3763	1885	1985	1806	2007	1913	2099	2272	2495	2565	2750
Net material product [a]	311140	403998	482452	469567	491389	503317	534014	548723	562164	574657	598609	609059

a) The secondary activities of the Uniform Agricultural Co-operatives are included in the agricultural activity sector for the years prior to 1979. From 1979 onward, the activities are included in the different branches of the economic activity.

2b Net Material Product by Kind of Activity of the Material Sphere in Constant Market Prices

Million Czechoslovak koruny

	1970	1975	1980	1981	1982	1983	1984	1985	1986	1987	1988	1989
At constant prices of:		1967			1977				1984			
1 Agriculture and forestry	30589	32859	... 38813	33398	37069	37136	40240	37675 39879	40782	39422	38796	40984
A Agriculture and livestock	...	...	... ...	...	...	...	...	... ...	...	...	...	...
B Forestry	3574	3770	... 4707	4581	4833	4736	4822	4658 4103	3890	3566	3171	3055
C Other	27015	29089	... 34106	28817	32236	32400	35418	33017 35776	36892	35856	35625	37929
2 Industrial activity	172918	232592	... 267799	267466	263297	267634	280572	290094 314628	324842	337485	348884	358809
3 Construction	30498	44257	... 51436	52542	50993	52327	50283	54043 60998	61343	63121	64169	63061
4 Wholesale and retail trade and restaurants and other eating and drinking places	33273	43128	... 72617	75480	79097	83582	84927	88756 89155	90353	88472	89465	84393
5 Transport and communication	8656	8109	... 15148	16625	16156	16082	15794	14863 18275	19072	18405	19567	15649
A Transport	6158	4870	... 10885	12200	11494	11230	10677	9496 8760	9023	7879	8593	4557
B Communication	2498	3239	... 4263	4425	4662	4852	5117	5367 9515	10049	10526	10974	11092
6 Other activities of the material sphere	3418	4123	... 1767	1642	1126	1336	1000	979 2082	2259	2559	2635	2794
Net material product [a]	279352	365068	... 447580	447153	447738	458097	472816	486410 525017	538651	549464	563516	565690

a) For this table, the first series are at constant prices of 1 January 1967, the second series are at constant prices of 1 January 1977, and the third series are at constant prices of 1 January 1984.

3 Primary Incomes by Kind of Activity of the Material Sphere in Current Market Prices

Million Czechoslovak koruny

	1980 Primary Income of the Population	1980 Primary Income of Enterprises	1981 Primary Income of the Population	1981 Primary Income of Enterprises	1982 Primary Income of the Population	1982 Primary Income of Enterprises	1983 Primary Income of the Population	1983 Primary Income of Enterprises	1984 Primary Income of the Population	1984 Primary Income of Enterprises	1985 Primary Income of the Population	1985 Primary Income of Enterprises
1 Agriculture and forestry	37473	3124	38319	-4636	41468	779	43725	331	44691	459	44410	-2620
A Agriculture and livestock	...	...	...	...	...	...	...	...	...	...	...	...
B Forestry	3309	2486	3163	1882	3402	1469	3435	1037	3558	750	3680	976
C Other	34164	638	35156	-6518	38066	-690	40290	-706	41133	-291	40730	-3596
2 Industrial activity	94664	214402	96980	188078	100214	200320	103277	207774	106243	211788	108768	224595

Czechoslovakia

3 Primary Incomes by Kind of Activity of the Material Sphere in Current Market Prices
(Continued)

Million Czechoslovak koruny

	1980 Pop.	1980 Ent.	1981 Pop.	1981 Ent.	1982 Pop.	1982 Ent.	1983 Pop.	1983 Ent.	1984 Pop.	1984 Ent.	1985 Pop.	1985 Ent.
3 Construction	31178	19805	30787	19683	31853	19783	32343	20301	33185	26301	33758	26779
4 Wholesale and retail trade and restaurants and other eating and drinking places	21140	38239	21572	55394	22121	52079	22784	49712	23263	64272	23686	66345
5 Transport and communication	17908	2634	18162	3243	18502	2464	18715	2348	18915	2984	19063	1840
A Transport	14824	-2538	14958	-2091	15140	-2971	15315	-3403	15501	-3054	15599	-4566
B Communication	3084	5172	3204	5334	3362	5435	3400	5751	3414	6038	3464	6406
6 Other activities of the material sphere	1156	729	1236	749	1252	554	1269	738	1319	594	1292	807
Total ab	203519	278933	207056	262511	215410	275979	222113	281204	227616	306398	230977	317746

	1986 Pop.	1986 Ent.	1987 Pop.	1987 Ent.	1988 Pop.	1988 Ent.	1989 Pop.	1989 Ent.
1 Agriculture and forestry	45511	-1242	46123	-2906	47350	-4474	51193	10991
A Agriculture and livestock	...	...	...	...	...	...	...	...
B Forestry	3681	1109	3788	711	3829	355	3906	2028
C Other	41830	-2351	42335	-3617	43521	-4829	47287	8963
2 Industrial activity	115200	226748	117960	232055	121075	241094	123642	236392
3 Construction	32554	28488	33001	29384	34122	30952	34632	30736
4 Wholesale and retail trade and restaurants and other eating and drinking places	23144	67841	23782	72369	25420	78749	25657	74418
5 Transport and communication	18707	2941	19319	1075	19984	1772	20448	-1800
A Transport	15753	-4515	16281	-6748	16882	-6408	17234	-10064
B Communication	2954	7456	3038	7823	3102	8180	3214	8264
6 Other activities of the material sphere	1433	839	1409	1086	1560	1005	1660	1090
Total ab	236549	325615	241594	333063	249511	349098	257232	351827

a) Reimbursement of the travelling and similar expenses for the state and co-operative organizations in the productive sphere is included in 'primary income of enterprises', and not in 'primary income of the population'.

b) The secondary activities of the Uniform Agricultural Co-operatives are included in the agricultural activity sector for the years prior to 1979. From 1979 onward, the activities are included in the different branches of the economic activity.

4 Primary Incomes From Net Material Product

Million Czechoslovak koruny

	1970	1975	1980	1981	1982	1983	1984	1985	1986	1987	1988	1989
a) Primary Incomes of the Population
1 Socialist sector	137955	169948	201040	204602	212077	218413	223702	227560	232640	237558	245215	251793
A State sector	107059	133829	160862	164011	168805	173182	177483	181190	183822	187570	192722	196036
B Co-operative sector	20718	25607	30101	30281	31013	32259	33580	34377	35131	36005	37765	38804
C Personal plots of households	10178	10512	10077	10310	12259	12972	12639	11993	13687	13983	14728	16953
2 Private sector	2437	2058	2479	2454	3333	3700	3914	3417	3909	4036	4296	5439
Sub-total	140392	172006	203519	207056	215410	222113	227616	230977	236549	241594	249511	257232
b) Primary incomes of the enterprises
1 Socialist sector	170748	231992	278933	262511	275979	281204	306398	317746	325615	333063	349098	351827
A State sector	161131	216840	260950	248684	257800	262212	284456	297898	303308	310611	324971	308329
B Co-operative sector	9617	15152	17983	13827	18179	18992	21942	19848	22307	22452	24127	43498
2 Private sector	-	-	-	-	-	-	-	-	-	-	-	-
Sub-total	170748	231992	278933	262511	275979	281204	306398	317746	325615	333063	349098	351827
Total net material product a	311140	403998	482452	469567	491389	503317	534014	548723	562164	574657	598609	609059

a) Reimbursement of the travelling and similar expenses for the state and co-operative organizations in the productive sphere is included in 'primary income of enterprises', and not in 'primary income of the population'.

Czechoslovakia

5a Supply and Disposition of Goods and Material Services in Current Market Prices

Million Czechoslovak koruny

		Supply					Disposition			
		Gross Output at Producers Prices	Trade Margins and Transport Charges	Gross Output at Market Prices	Imports	Total Supply and Disposition	Intermediate Material Consumption including Depreciation	Final Consumption	Net Capital Formation	Losses	Exports
					1980						
1	Agriculture and forestry	127074	14592	141666	9372	151038	118646	25117	5158	2117	...
2	Industrial activity	856436	110897	967333	-14368	952965	595570	300425	55114	1856	...
3	Construction	120417	321	120738	1716	122454	29917	27479	63915	1143	...
4	Transport and communication	15397	-	15397	-	15397	-	15397	-	-	...
	A Transport	9767	-	9767	-	9767	-	9767	-	-	...
	B Communication	5630	-	5630	-	5630	-	5630	-	-	...
5	Other activities of the material sphere	5029	293	5322	32	5354	4645	709	-	-	...
	Total [ab]	1124353	126103	1250456	-3248	1247208	748778	369127	124187	5116	...
					1981						
1	Agriculture and forestry	124448	14751	139199	5259	144458	117978	25072	-573	1981	...
2	Industrial activity	865299	130168	995467	-16419	979048	635553	311328	30308	1859	...
3	Construction	120760	404	121164	-780	120384	29698	27294	62092	1300	...
4	Transport and communication	15899	-	15899	-	15899	-	15899	-	-	...
	A Transport	10019	-	10019	-	10019	-	10019	-	-	...
	B Communication	5880	-	5880	-	5880	-	5880	-	-	...
5	Other activities of the material sphere	5272	309	5581	22	5603	4848	755	-	-	...
	Total [ab]	1131678	145632	1277310	-11918	1265392	788077	380348	91827	5140	...
					1982						
1	Agriculture and forestry	140576	15466	156042	4371	160413	124862	29816	3396	2339	...
2	Industrial activity	920030	129482	1049512	-18265	1031247	680024	318185	30064	2974	...
3	Construction	126220	392	126612	-1355	125257	31978	28984	63121	1174	...
4	Transport and communication	16127	-	16127	-	16127	-	16127	-	-	...
	A Transport	10125	-	10125	-	10125	-	10125	-	-	...
	B Communication	6002	-	6002	-	6002	-	6002	-	-	...
5	Other activities of the material sphere	5326	312	5638	13	5651	4906	745	-	-	...
	Total [ab]	1208279	145652	1353931	-15236	1338695	841770	393857	96581	6487	...
					1983						
1	Agriculture and forestry	148099	15538	163637	4491	168128	132848	29055	3982	2243	...
2	Industrial activity	939597	127862	1067459	-19153	1048306	686265	330407	29324	2310	...
3	Construction	129169	662	129831	-1813	128018	34697	30945	61159	1217	...
4	Transport and communication	16649	-	16649	-	16649	-	16649	-	-	...
	A Transport	10399	-	10399	-	10399	-	10399	-	-	...
	B Communication	6250	-	6250	-	6250	-	6250	-	-	...
5	Other activities of the material sphere	5354	325	5679	-	5679	4904	775	-	-	...
	Total [ab]	1238868	144387	1383256	-16475	1366780	858714	407831	94465	5770	...
					1984						
1	Agriculture and forestry	156917	14694	171611	5494	177105	137977	30545	6024	2559	...
2	Industrial activity	1018465	151489	1169954	-25423	1144531	770184	347502	24028	2817	...
3	Construction	142802	767	143569	-2025	141544	36678	32213	71493	1160	...
4	Transport and communication	17590	-	17590	-	17590	-	17590	-	-	...
	A Transport	11082	-	11082	-	11082	-	11082	-	-	...
	B Communication	6508	-	6508	-	6508	-	6508	-	-	...
5	Other activities of the material sphere	5488	334	5822	-	5822	5016	806	-	-	...
	Total [ab]	1341262	167284	1508546	-21954	1486592	949855	428656	101545	6536	...
					1985						
1	Agriculture and forestry	156370	15186	171556	5674	177230	141686	30163	2892	2489	...
2	Industrial activity	1054067	154906	1208973	-26804	1182169	790126	359617	30226	2200	...
3	Construction	146009	743	146752	-1351	145401	39912	34900	69200	1389	...
4	Transport and communication	18260	-	18260	-	18260	-	18260	-	-	...
	A Transport	11482	-	11482	-	11482	-	11482	-	-	...
	B Communication	6778	-	6778	-	6778	-	6778	-	-	...
5	Other activities of the material sphere	5794	343	6137	-	6137	5348	789	-	-	...
	Total [ab]	1380500	171178	1551678	-22481	1529197	977072	443729	102318	6078	...

Czechoslovakia

5a Supply and Disposition of Goods and Material Services in Current Market Prices
(Continued)

Million Czechoslovak koruny

	Gross Output at Producers Prices	Trade Margins and Transport Charges	Gross Output at Market Prices	Imports	Total Supply and Disposition	Intermediate Material Consumption including Depreciation	Final Consumption	Net Capital Formation	Losses	Exports
1986										
1 Agriculture and forestry	162628	14346	176974	6666	183640	153904	25658	1495	2583	...
2 Industrial activity	1090204	156766	1246970	-15471	1231499	813359	375612	40351	2177	...
3 Construction	145587	740	146327	-498	145829	39333	34322	70753	1421	...
4 Transport and communication	18225	-	18225	-	18225	-	18225	-	-	...
A Transport	11230	-	11230	-	11230	-	11230	-	-	...
B Communication	6995	-	6995	-	6995	-	6995	-	-	...
5 Other activities of the material sphere	5965	848	6813	22	6835	440	6395	-	-	...
Total ab	1422609	172700	1595309	-9281	1586028	1007036	460212	112599	6181	...
1987										
1 Agriculture and forestry	166012	15478	181490	3620	185110	153262	26282	2446	3120	...
2 Industrial activity	1115395	161469	1276864	-14209	1262655	829809	384561	45066	3219	...
3 Construction	149206	608	149814	552	150366	48502	41515	58706	1643	...
4 Transport and communication	18972	-	18972	-	18972	-	18972	-	-	...
A Transport	11659	-	11659	-	11659	-	11659	-	-	...
B Communication	7313	-	7313	-	7313	-	7313	-	-	...
5 Other activities of the material sphere	6239	895	7134	22	7156	472	6684	-	-	...
Total ab	1455824	178450	1634274	-10015	1624259	1032045	478014	106218	7982	...
1988										
1 Agriculture and forestry	169210	15809	185019	6596	191615	158989	26872	2654	3100	...
2 Industrial activity	1133033	174788	1307821	-21011	1286810	842472	405685	34914	3739	...
3 Construction	154267	458	154725	-3908	150817	46854	40193	62347	1423	...
4 Transport and communication	19868	-	19868	-	19868	-	19868	-	-	...
A Transport	12059	-	12059	-	12059	-	12059	-	-	...
B Communication	7809	-	7809	-	7809	-	7809	-	-	...
5 Other activities of the material sphere	6617	1012	7629	9	7638	499	7139	-	-	...
Total ab	1482995	192067	1675062	-18314	1656748	1048814	499757	99915	8262	...
1989										
1 Agriculture and forestry	201836	18228	220064	4960	225024	186629	30654	4285	3456	...
2 Industrial activity	1106582	168853	1275435	-16865	1258570	805163	419682	30068	3657	...
3 Construction	152055	337	152392	-1563	150829	46032	39916	63401	1480	...
4 Transport and communication	19891	-	19891	-	19891	-	19891	-	-	...
A Transport	11964	-	11964	-	11964	-	11964	-	-	...
B Communication	7927	-	7927	-	7927	-	7927	-	-	...
5 Other activities of the material sphere	7453	1128	8581	10	8591	583	8008	-	-	...
Total ab	1487817	188546	1676363	-13458	1662905	1038407	518151	97754	8593	...

a) Column 'Imports' is net of column 'Exports'.
b) The secondary activities of the Uniform Agricultural Co-operatives are included in the agricultural activity sector for the years prior to 1979. From 1979 onward, the activities are included in the different branches of the economic activity.

5b Supply and Disposition of Goods and Material Services in Constant Market Prices

Million Czechoslovak koruny

	Gross Output at Producers Prices	Trade Margins and Transport Charges	Gross Output at Market Prices	Imports	Total Supply and Disposition	Intermediate Material Consumption including Depreciation	Final Consumption	Net Capital Formation	Losses	Exports
At constant prices of:1984										
1985										
1 Agriculture and forestry	156681	13941	170622	5507	176129	145183	25174	3191	2581	...
2 Industrial activity	1033676	155303	1188979	-25552	1163427	786777	352024	22443	2183	...
3 Construction	146009	743	146752	-1351	145401	46607	38794	58510	1490	...
4 Transport and communication	18260	-	18260	-	18260	-	18260	-	-	...
A Transport	11482	-	11482	-	11482	-	11482	-	-	...
B Communication	6778	-	6778	-	6778	-	6778	-	-	...
5 Other activities of the material sphere	5794	818	6612	-	6612	427	6185	-	-	...
Total a	1360420	170805	1531225	-21396	1509829	978994	440437	84144	6254	...

Czechoslovakia

5b Supply and Disposition of Goods and Material Services in Constant Market Prices
(Continued)

Million Czechoslovak koruny

		Supply					Disposition			
		Gross Output at Producers Prices	Trade Margins and Transport Charges	Gross Output at Market Prices	Imports	Total Supply and Disposition	Intermediate Material Consumption including Depreciation	Final Consumption	Net Capital Formation	Losses	Exports

At constant prices of: 1984

1986

1	Agriculture and forestry	160729	14301	175030	6883	181913	152834	24984	1496	2599	...
2	Industrial activity	1071152	156698	1227850	-16877	1210973	809553	366410	32844	2166	...
3	Construction	145587	740	146327	-498	145829	45336	38908	60093	1492	...
4	Transport and communication	18225	-	18225	-	18225	-	18225	-	-	...
	A Transport	11230	-	11230	-	11230	-	11230	-	-	...
	B Communication	6995	-	6995	-	6995	-	6995	-	-	...
5	Other activities of the material sphere	5965	848	6813	22	6835	440	6395	-	-	...
	Total a	1401658	172587	1574245	-10470	1563775	1008163	454922	94433	6257	...

1987

1	Agriculture and forestry	161814	14666	176480	4843	181323	150724	25309	2398	2892	...
2	Industrial activity	1097305	155034	1252339	-11826	1240513	820982	374335	42785	2411	...
3	Construction	149364	608	149972	552	150524	54459	46105	48213	1747	...
4	Transport and communication	18972	-	18972	-	18972	-	18972	-	-	...
	A Transport	11659	-	11659	-	11659	-	11659	-	-	...
	B Communication	7313	-	7313	-	7313	-	7313	-	-	...
5	Other activities of the material sphere	6239	873	7112	22	7134	471	6663	-	-	...
	Total a	1433694	171181	1604875	-6409	1598466	1026636	471384	93396	7050	...

1988

1	Agriculture and forestry	163897	15848	179745	6914	186659	154855	26380	2625	2799	...
2	Industrial activity	1123031	158241	1281272	-11732	1269540	841429	394792	30475	2844	...
3	Construction	152755	458	153213	-3908	149305	52624	44404	50791	1486	...
4	Transport and communication	19868	-	19868	-	19868	-	19868	-	-	...
	A Transport	12059	-	12059	-	12059	-	12059	-	-	...
	B Communication	7809	-	7809	-	7809	-	7809	-	-	...
5	Other activities of the material sphere	6613	924	7537	9	7546	491	7055	-	-	...
	Total a	1466164	175471	1641635	-8717	1632918	1049399	492499	83891	7129	...

1989

1	Agriculture and forestry	164972	17773	182745	5699	188444	153800	27726	4167	2751	...
2	Industrial activity	1123618	152928	1276546	1031	1277577	837313	407445	29840	2979	...
3	Construction	152938	337	153275	-1563	151712	53069	46461	50615	1567	...
4	Transport and communication	19891	-	19891	-	19891	-	19891	-	-	...
	A Transport	11964	-	11964	-	11964	-	11964	-	-	...
	B Communication	7927	-	7927	-	7927	-	7927	-	-	...
5	Other activities of the material sphere	7453	1006	8459	-10	8449	574	7875	-	-	...
	Total a	1468872	172044	1640916	5157	1646073	1044756	509398	84622	7297	...

a) At constant prices of 1 January 1984.

6a Capital Formation by Kind of Activity of the Material and Non-Material Spheres in Current Market Prices

Million Czechoslovak koruny

		1970	1975	1980	1981	1982	1983	1984	1985	1986	1987	1988	1989

Net Fixed Capital Formation

1	Agriculture and forestry	3512	8263	9164	8728	8400	9326	9939	13725	12020	13445	11826	7821
2	Industrial activity	17675	26414	26748	34515	24269	21241	29421	38523	30036	25223	27562	19128
3	Construction	1559	3040	2836	1455	1657	1811	1080	1412	2338	1752	2981	791
4	Wholesale and retail trade, restaurants and other eating and drinking places	3325	5549	3390	3623	3150	3884	3713	2732	3363	2745	3151	2950
5	Transport and communication	5882	7276	9815	14452	7490	8229	10249	8179	16622	7184	6666	9072
6	Other activities of the material sphere	275	65	12	196	27	65	49	58	135	183	122	129

391

Czechoslovakia

6a Capital Formation by Kind of Activity of the Material and Non-Material Spheres in Current Market Prices
(Continued)

Million Czechoslovak koruny

	1970	1975	1980	1981	1982	1983	1984	1985	1986	1987	1988	1989
Total Material Sphere	32228	50607	51965	62969	44993	44556	54451	64629	64514	50532	52308	39891
7 Housing except owner-occupied, communal and miscellaneous personal services	10444	14712	11737	10257	11185	12155	13158	12921	14813	10675	13282	10186
8 Education, culture and art	1860	4053	2944	3491	5056	2986	6386	3432	3752	2842	2736	2447
9 Health and social welfare services and sports	935	2026	1843	1931	2028	2227	2383	2845	2140	1324	1712	1987
Total Non-Material Sphere Serving Individuals	13239	20791	16524	15679	18269	17368	21927	19198	20705	14841	17730	14620
10 Government	...	...	...	...	...	...	...	...	...	...	...	...
11 Finance, credit and insurance	...	...	...	...	...	...	...	...	...	...	...	...
12 Research, scientific and technological institutes	...	...	...	...	...	...	...	...	...	...	...	...
13 Other activities of the non-material sphere	...	...	...	...	...	...	...	...	...	...	...	...
Total Non-Material Sphere Serving the Community as a Whole	1499	3951	4123	3510	2890	3273	3446	4018	5420	6997	7805	5695
14 Owner-occupied dwellings	2888	5077	3667	2830	3936	3651	3794	3471	3324	3732	4484	4511
Total Net Fixed Capital Formation	49854	80426	76279	84988	70088	68848	83618	91316	93963	76102	82327	64717

Gross Fixed Capital Formation

	1970	1975	1980	1981	1982	1983	1984	1985	1986	1987	1988	1989
1 Agriculture and forestry	8192	14058	16462	17050	17468	19117	20456	24893	23878	26025	25344	22284
2 Industrial activity	34266	50454	57239	67597	58474	57732	67947	79008	72696	70308	76016	69711
3 Construction	2867	5640	6290	5270	5600	5810	5317	5724	6812	6374	7929	5661
4 Wholesale and retail trade and restaurants and other eating and drinking places	4709	7764	6273	6672	6300	7213	7156	6276	6955	6432	6946	6756
5 Transport and communication	11503	15211	20089	25247	18848	20356	22718	21479	30217	21383	21348	24186
6 Other activities of the material sphere	353	212	94	293	126	154	139	150	221	304	277	267
Total Material Sphere	61890	93339	106447	122129	106816	110382	123733	137530	140779	130826	137860	128865
7 Housing except owner-occupied, communal and miscellaneous personal services	13463	18262	16871	15589	16785	18089	19324	19413	21555	17812	20759	18067
8 Education, culture and art	2976	5568	5240	5767	7484	5587	9116	6366	6793	6066	6093	5956
9 Health and social welfare services and sports	1456	2780	2780	2956	3119	3432	3727	4248	3779	3066	3536	3944
Total Non-Material Sphere Serving Individuals	17895	26610	24891	24312	27388	27108	32167	30027	32127	26944	30388	27967
10 Government	...	...	...	...	...	...	...	...	...	...	...	...
11 Finance, credit and insurance	...	...	...	...	...	...	...	...	...	...	...	...
12 Research, scientific and technological institutes	...	...	...	...	...	...	...	...	...	...	...	...
13 Other activities of the non-material sphere	...	...	...	...	...	...	...	...	...	...	...	...
Total Non-Material Sphere Serving the Community as a Whole	3086	6366	7449	7537	7433	7808	8150	9272	10922	12553	13622	11786
14 Owner-occupied dwellings	4408	6889	5943	5208	6384	6166	6375	6121	6046	6528	7352	7453
Total Gross Fixed Capital Formation	87279	133204	144730	159186	148021	151464	170425	182950	189874	176851	189222	176071

Increases in Material Circulating Assets and Stocks

	1970	1975	1980	1981	1982	1983	1984	1985	1986	1987	1988	1989
1 Agriculture and forestry	2871	1728	3542	1815	4021	4419	6199	3736	3368	1232	1356	4311
2 Industrial activity	11165	13791	23092	1977	3608	11178	-953	1064	6510	13046	9895	9352
3 Construction	2030	5051	4926	-3648	11141	930	7440	-2789	4150	7002	-1986	7297
4 Wholesale and retail trade and restaurants and other eating and drinking places	8529	10071	10138	2531	7192	4938	6658	5921	3940	4276	4362	7325
5 Transport and communication	427	3130	73	-782	-539	325	452	1391	1884	5719	-2761	-141
6 Other activities of the non-material sphere	343	226	169	-63	-20	43	81	96	97	12	106	-75
Total increase in material circulating assets	25365	33997	41940	1830	25403	21833	19877	9419	19949	31287	10972	28069
Statistical discrepancy	...	...	...	...	...	...	...	...	...	...	...	...
Increase in stocks of the non-material sphere	5604	3352	5968	5009	1090	3784	-1950	1583	-1313	-1171	6616	4968

Gross Fixed Capital Formation by Socio-economic Sector and Industrial Use

	1970	1975	1980	1981	1982	1983	1984	1985	1986	1987	1988	1989
1 State and co-operative (excluding collective farms)	79349	118502	128619	143650	130540	132909	151236	161301	168588	154562	166001	154467
A Industry	34266	50454	57239	67597	58474	57732	67947	79008	72696	70308	76016	69711

Czechoslovakia

6a Capital Formation by Kind of Activity of the Material and Non-Material Spheres in Current Market Prices
(Continued)

Million Czechoslovak koruny

	1970	1975	1980	1981	1982	1983	1984	1985	1986	1987	1988	1989
B Construction	2867	5640	6290	5270	5600	5810	5317	5724	6812	6374	7929	5661
C Agriculture and forestry	4740	6245	6294	6722	6371	6728	7642	9365	8638	10264	9487	8144
D Transport and communication	11503	15211	20089	25247	18848	20356	22718	21479	30217	21383	21348	24186
E Residential building	25973	40952	38707	38814	41247	42283	47612	45725	50225	46233	51221	46765
F Trade and other												
2 Collective farms	3716	8223	10257	10301	11096	12356	12832	15559	15273	15606	15857	14140
A Agriculture	3646	8223	10257	10301	11096	12356	12832	15559	15273	15606	15857	14140
B Other	70	-	-	-	-	-	-	-	-	-	-	-
3 Other	4214	6479	5854	5235	6385	6199	6357	6090	6013	6683	7364	7464
Gross Fixed Capital Formation	87279	133204	144730	159186	148021	151464	170425	182950	189874	176851	189222	176071

6b Capital Formation by Kind of Activity of the Material and Non-Material Spheres in Constant Market Prices

Million Czechoslovak koruny

	1970	1975	1980	1981	1982	1983	1984	1985	1986	1987	1988	1989
		1967		At constant prices of: 1977				1984				

Net Fixed Capital Formation

	1970	1975	1980	1981	1982	1983	1984	1985	1986	1987	1988	1989
1 Agriculture and forestry	2860	7243	8435	7901	7228	7543	8378	10506 / 13483	10145	11290	9684	6113
2 Industrial activity	14252	21749	24551	31798	20527	15949	22311	28971 / 34600	23410	18126	20361	13404
3 Construction	1379	2698	2618	1213	1297	1263	579	821 / 1022	1787	1224	2436	443
4 Wholesale and retail trade, restaurants and other eating and drinking places	2944	5010	3195	3407	2830	3349	2986	1894 / 2364	2776	2073	2473	2383
5 Transport and communication	4595	5618	9124	13670	6290	6489	7860	5285 / 6411	14321	4478	3996	6774
6 Other activities of the material sphere	249	52	8	189	47	51	36	40 / 47	124	166	104	121
Total Material Sphere [a]	26279	42370	47931	58178	38219	34644	42150	47517 / 57927	52563	37357	39054	29238
7 Housing except owner-occupied, communal and miscellaneous personal services	9280	13341	11406	9921	10549	11060	11187	10076 / 12446	13491	8844	11389	8346
8 Education, culture and art	1547	3653	2788	3334	4772	2523	5490	2533 / 3155	3206	2161	2041	1803
9 Health and social welfare services and sports	796	1810	1769	1845	1882	1984	2005	2287 / 2791	1875	1009	1399	1723
Total Non-Material Sphere Serving Individuals [a]	11623	18804	15963	15100	17203	15567	18682	14896 / 18392	18572	12014	14829	11872
10 Government	...	...	...	...	...	...	...	...	...	...	...	...
11 Finance, credit and insurance	...	...	...	...	...	...	...	...	...	...	...	...
12 Research, scientific and technological institutes	...	...	...	...	...	...	...	...	...	...	...	...
13 Other activities of the non-material sphere	...	...	...	...	...	...	...	...	...	...	...	...
Total Non-Material Sphere Serving the Community as a Whole	1190	3059	3966	3316	2516	2701	2694	2962 / 3616	4717	6191	7019	5107
14 Owner-occupied dwellings	2351	4286	3519	2681	3678	3252	3106	2521 / 3116	2682	2952	3685	3707
Total Net Fixed Capital Formation [a]	41443	68519	71379	79275	61616	56164	66632	67896 / 83051	78534	58514	64587	49924

Czechoslovakia

6b Capital Formation by Kind of Activity of the Material and Non-Material Spheres in Constant Market Prices
(Continued)

Million Czechoslovak koruny

	1970	1975	1980	1981	1982	1983	1984	1985	1986	1987	1988	1989
			1967		At constant prices of: 1977				1984			

Gross Fixed Capital Formation

	1970	1975	1980	1981	1982	1983	1984	1985	1986	1987	1988	1989
1 Agriculture and forestry	7776	13073	16315	16812	16852	17830	19287	21948 / 26915	24226	26031	25344	22685
2 Industrial activity	32221	46970	56427	66197	55909	53454	61643	69955 / 82484	73407	70451	76070	71082
3 Construction	2705	5235	6189	5126	5326	5307	4814	5096 / 5940	6847	6390	7934	5800
4 Wholesale and retail trade and restaurants and other eating and drinking places	4431	7268	6223	6587	6098	6784	6514	5503 / 6624	7064	6438	6940	6827
5 Transport and communciation	10815	14054	19906	24948	18104	19039	20680	18917 / 22568	30700	21411	21351	24494
6 Other activities of the material sphere	331	201	92	289	149	142	127	133 / 156	223	304	278	274
Total Material Sphere [a]	58279	86801	105152	119959	102438	102556	113065	121552 / 144687	142467	131025	137917	131162
7 Housing except owner-occupied, communal and miscellaneous personal services	12707	17174	16860	15570	16467	17309	17651	16840 / 20743	22048	17816	20704	18061
8 Education, culture and art	2802	5274	5217	5731	7314	5237	8317	5546 / 6768	6924	6069	6083	5996
9 Health and social welfare services and sports	1374	2605	2762	2926	3026	3239	3393	3720 / 4491	3838	3069	3534	3993
Total Non-Material Sphere Serving Individuals [a]	16883	25053	24839	24227	26807	25785	29361	26106 / 32002	32810	26954	30321	28050
10 Government	...	...	...	...	...	...	...	...	...	...	...	...
11 Finance, credit and insurance	...	...	...	...	...	...	...	...	...	...	...	...
12 Research, scientific and technological institutes	...	...	...	...	...	...	...	...	...	...	...	...
13 Other activities of the non-material sphere	...	...	...	...	...	...	...	...	...	...	...	...
Total Non-Material Sphere Serving the Community as a Whole [a]	2898	5565	7365	7415	7116	7274	7403	8173 / 9730	11067	12569	13615	11949
14 Owner-occupied dwellings	4137	6335	5943	5208	6275	5913	5826	5301 / 6552	6191	6528	7330	7423
Total Gross Fixed Capital Formation [a]	82197	123754	143299	156809	142636	141528	155655	161132 / 192971	192535	177076	189183	178584

Increases in Material Circulating Assets and Stocks

	1970	1975	1980	1981	1982	1983	1984	1985	1986	1987	1988	1989
1 Agriculture and forestry	2215	1207	3599	1653	3164	3397	1453	2298 / 371	2874	1427	1488	4528
2 Industrial activity	7866	9635	17787	1801	2839	8595	-224	655 / 106	5554	15110	10860	9822

Czechoslovakia

6b Capital Formation by Kind of Activity of the Material and Non-Material Spheres in Constant Market Prices
(Continued)

Million Czechoslovak koruny

	1970	1975	1980	1981	1982	1983	1984	1985	1986	1987	1988	1989
		1967			At constant prices of: 1977					1984		
3 Construction	1494	3529	4161	-3323	8766	715	1744	-1716 / -277	3540	8110	-2180	7664
4 Wholesale and retail trade and restaurants and other eating and drinking places	5946	7036	6332	2305	5659	3796	1561	3643 / 588	3361	4953	4788	7693
5 Transport and communication	-24	2186	-167	-712	-424	250	106	856 / 138	1607	6624	-3030	-148
6 Other activities of the non-material sphere	230	158	420	-57	-16	33	19	59 / 10	83	14	116	-79
Total increase in material circulating assets	17727	23751	32132	1667	19988	16786	4659	5795 / 936	17019	36238	12042	29480
Statistical discrepancy	...	...	...					...				
Increase in stocks of the non-material sphere [a]	3934	2342	5673	4562	858	2909	-457	974 / 157	-1120	-1356	7262	5218

Gross Fixed Capital Formation by Socio-economic Sector and Industrial Use

	1970	1975	1980	1981	1982	1983	1984	1985	1986	1987	1988	1989
1 State and co-operative (excluding collective farms)	74663	110163	127084	141361	125501	124061	137701	142128 / 170013	170883	154789	165982	156741
A Industry	32221	46970	56427	66197	55909	53454	61643	69955 / 82484	73407	70451	76070	71082
B Construction	2705	5235	6189	5126	5326	5307	4814	5096 / 5940	6847	6390	7934	5800
C Agriculture and forestry	4445	5817	6043	6572	6135	6276	7159	8245 / 10509	8765	10272	9488	8291
D Transport and communication	10815	14054	19906	24948	18104	19039	20680	18917 / 22568	30700	21411	21351	24494
E Residential building	24477	38087	38519	38518	40027	39985	43405	39915 / 48512	51164	46265	51139	47074
F Trade and other												
2 Collective farms	3495	7488	10337	10209	10711	11522	12121	13712 / 16413	15484	15604	15856	14394
A Agriculture	3429	7488	10337	10209	10711	11522	12121	13712 / 16413	15484	15604	15856	14394
B Other	66	-	... / -	-	-	-	-	-	-	-	-	-
3 Other	4039	6103	5878	5239	6424	5945	5833	5292 / 6545	6168	6683	7345	7449
Gross Fixed Capital Formation [a]	82197	123754	143299	156809	142636	141528	155655	161132 / 192971	192535	177076	189183	178584

a) For this table, the first series are at constant prices of 1 January 1967, the second series are at constant prices of 1 January 1977, and the third series are at constant prices of 1 January 1984.

Czechoslovakia

7a Final Consumption at Current Market Prices

Million Czechoslovak koruny

	1970	1975	1980	1981	1982	1983	1984	1985	1986	1987	1988	1989
1 Personal consumption [a]	175815	223547	268771	274371	283126	292021	300323	311139	319511	329269	344931	357645

a) Material Consumption in the Units of the Non-Material Sphere Serving Individuals

	1970	1975	1980	1981	1982	1983	1984	1985	1986	1987	1988	1989
Housing except owner-occupied, communal and miscellaneous personal services [a]	8069	12137	17702	19581	19581	19678	21019	22447	24028	25149	25636	27819
Education, culture and art	8480	12289	16151	17020	18315	19129	20241	21195	22402	23833	24685	26090
Health and social welfare services and sports	6928	10245	12322	13144	14250	14999	16082	17094	19528	20688	22225	23846
Other	...	...	...	...	...	...	...	...	...	...	...	...
2 Total non-material sphere serving individuals [a]	23477	34671	46175	49745	52146	53806	57342	60736	65958	69670	72546	77755

b) Material Consumption in the Units of the Non-Material Sphere Serving the Community as a Whole

	1970	1975	1980	1981	1982	1983	1984	1985	1986	1987	1988	1989
3 Total non-material sphere serving the community as a whole	19521	26727	34955	36566	37813	40780	46312	46012	48634	51503	54641	53854
Final consumption	218813	284945	349901	360682	373085	386607	403977	417889	434103	450442	472118	489254

a) In personal consumption there is included wear and tear of the buildings in ownership of population only. That of residential buildings in ownership of enterprises, state and co-operative organizations is included in the material consumption of units of non-material sphere serving the population.

7b Final Consumption at Constant Market Prices

Million Czechoslovak koruny

	1970	1975	1980	1981	1982	1983	1984	1985	1986	1987	1988	1989
		1967			At constant prices of: 1977				1984			
1 Personal consumption [a]	165002	208184	245781	250086	244716	250045	254884	259752 / 302978	309548	318386	333920	339660

a) Material Consumption in the Units of the Non-Material Sphere Serving Individuals

	1970	1975	1980	1981	1982	1983	1984	1985	1986	1987	1988	1989
Housing except owner-occupied, communal and miscellaneous personal services [a]	7845	11269	17625	19400	19017	19061	19647	21073 / 24193	25769	26732	27032	29578
Education, culture and art	8262	11313	15224	15887	16738	17382	17618	18723 / 21800	22963	24379	25168	27651
Health and social welfare services and sports	6860	9995	11997	12728	13462	14115	14494	15518 / 17354	19793	20924	22434	25349
Other	...	...	...	...	...	...	...	...	...	...	...	...
2 Total non-material sphere serving individuals [ab]	22967	32577	44846	48015	49217	50558	51759	55314 / 63347	68525	72035	74634	82578

b) Material Consumption in the Units of the Non-Material Sphere Serving the Community as a Whole

	1970	1975	1980	1981	1982	1983	1984	1985	1986	1987	1988	1989
3 Total non-material sphere serving the community as a whole	18523	23112	33596	34901	34919	37576	40204	40701 / 46898	49418	52188	55225	56229
Final consumption [b]	206492	263873	324223	333002	328852	338179	346847	355767 / 413223	427491	442609	463779	478467

a) In personal consumption there is included wear and tear of the buildings in ownership of population only. That of residential buildings in ownership of enterprises, state and co-operative organizations is included in the material consumption of units of non-material sphere serving the population.
b) For this table, the first series are at constant prices of 1 January 1967, the second series are at constant prices of 1 January 1977, and the third series are at constant prices of 1 January 1984.

Czechoslovakia

8 Personal Consumption According to Source of Supply of Goods and Material Services in Current Market Prices

Million Czechoslovak koruny

		1970	1975	1980	1981	1982	1983	1984	1985	1986	1987	1988	1989
1	Purchases of goods in state and co-operative retail trade	151025	195798	235078	239917	246107	253039	259918	269863	276006	284113	298414	308170
2	Purchases of goods in the free market and from private retail trade	1556	1961	1745	1598	2046	2102	2121	1973	2488	2333	2008	2482
3	Goods produced on own account and received in kind	9145	7724	7455	7337	8891	10085	10188	10030	10988	11571	12180	14555
4	Payments for transport and communication services	8144	9720	11569	11866	12002	12367	13113	13584	13457	14009	14569	14632
5	Purchases of electricity, gas and water	2516	3805	6855	7202	7548	7635	7940	8225	8491	8899	9100	9122
6	Purchases directly from handicrafts, repair shops and the like	1909	2727	3793	4073	4084	4278	4462	4814	5359	5548	5792	5742
7	Consumption of fixed assets in respect of all dwellings	1520	1812	2276	2378	2448	2515	2581	2650	2722	2796	2868	2942
8	Other	...	...	...	...	...	...	...	...	...	...	...	...
	Personal consumption [a]	175815	223547	268771	274371	283126	292021	300323	311139	319511	329269	344931	357645

a) In personal consumption there is included wear and tear of the buildings in ownership of population only. That of residential buildings in ownership of enterprises, state and co-operative organizations is included in the material consumption of units of non-material sphere serving the population.

Denmark

General note. The preparation of national accounts statistics in Denmark is undertaken by the Danmarks Statistik, Copenhagen. The official estimates are published three times annually in 'Statistiske Efterretninger (Nationalregnskab. Offentlige Finanser, Betalingsbalance)' and in more detail in the annual publication 'Nationalregnskabsstatistik'. The following presentation of sources and methods is mainly based on a report prepared by the Statistical Office of the European Communities in 1976 entitled 'Base statistics needed for the ESA accounts and tables: present situation and prospects for improvements' and on 'Input-output tabeller for Danmark 1966' published by Danmarks Statistik in 1973. The estimates are generally in accordance with the classifications and definitions recommended in the United Nations System of National Accounts (SNA). The following tables have been prepared from successive replies to the United Nations national accounts questionnaire. When the scope and coverage of the estimates differ for conceptual or statistical reasons from the definitions and classifications recommended in SNA, a footnote is indicated to the relevant tables.

Sources and methods:

(a) Gross domestic product. Gross domestic product is estimated mainly through the production approach.

(b) Expenditure on the gross domestic product. The expenditure approach is used to estimate government final consumption expenditure, increase in stocks and exports and imports of goods and services. The commodity-flow approach is used for private final consumption expenditure and gross fixed capital formation. The estimates of government consumption expenditure are mainly based on the accounts of the central and local government and on social secutiry funds. The estimates of private consumption expenditure, using the commodity-flow method, have a time-lag of two years. Therefore, short-term estimates are made, using turnover statistics for the retail trade. This is supplemented by family budget surveys which are conducted every five years. Changes in stocks are estimated on the basis of inventory statistics. For gross fixed capital formation, information is classified by product and by ownership branch. The valuation is made net of deductible value added tax. Estimates of investments in buildings are based partly on data available on construction starts, work under construction and work completed and partly on information from accounting data. Estimates of investments in machinery and equipment are based on production and foreign trade statistics adjusted to include gross margins, duties etc. Exports and imports of goods and services are estimated mainly form the balance-of-payments and foreign trade statistics. Special surveys are available for shipping and for payments to and receipts from the rest of the world by Danish enterprises. For the constant price estimates, price indexes arrived at for the supply of goods and services, broken down into 4,000 groups, are used for all components of GDP by expenditure type except that of exports for which the indexes for domestic output are used.

(c) Cost-structure of the gross domestic product. Data on the compensation of employees are taken directly from the annual surveys on current transactions. For consumption of fixed capital, only rough estimates are made. Total indirect taxes and subsidies are obtained from government accounts. Operating surplus is estimated as a residual.

(d) Gross domestic product by kind of economic activity. The table of GDP by kind of economic activity is prepared in factor values. The production approach is used to estimate the value added of almost all industries. The income approach is used to estimate the value added of producers of government services, parts of business services and other private services. The gross output of the trade sector is primarily estimated by means of the commodity-flow approach. The estimates of agricultural production are based on product-by-product data in terms of volume and prices which are obtained from the annual agricultural statistics. The estimates of gross output are supplemented by survey data on total costs and cost structure. For forestry and fishing, the main sources used are the annual agricultural reports and the annual reports of the Ministry of Fisheries. For manufacturing, estimates are based on an annual survey covering all enterprises employing 20 or more persons and on a quarterly survey on the turnover of 4,000 products. Censuses taken in 1966 and 1975 provide a product-by-product breakdown of intermediate inputs. The value-added tax returns of enterprises are used to make estimates for small enterprises and services not covered by direct surveys. For electricity, gas and water, the estimates are based on annual electricity statistics, accunting statistics of the municipalities and on local government reports, respectively. For private construction, various sources are used such as an annual accounting survey and investment statistics. Construction in the public sector is estimated from government accounts. The estimates of gross trade and trasnport margins are based on data obtained from a sample survey of trade enterprises adjusted for under-coverage, mark-ups and other non-available margins. Another method used is to estimate the size of the gross margins of each commodity and its share in the distributive channel. These estimates are partly based on information from the Price Directorate. For restaurants and hotels, value-added tax statistics are used. For the transport sector, the information is taken from the accounts of the exterprises concerned except road transport which makes use of the vaue-added tax returns. For the finanacial sector, the balance-sheets and complete accounts of the companies' current transactions are used. A bench-mark survey of housing rents is carried out every five years. For intervening years, changes in the average rent and total stock of residential buildings are used. Rents of rented dwellings are used for the imputation of rents of owner-occupied dwellings. Value-added tax statistics, population census and accouting data of advertising services are used for the business services sector. The main sources for the producers of government services are the account of the central and local government and social secutiry funds. For other services, value-added tax statistics are used except for professions like doctors and dentists, for which social security data are used. For the constant price estimates, double deflation is used. The data are deflated by means of a price index related to each of the 4,000 groups of goods and services. The price indexes are applied to domestic output as well as imports.

1.1 Expenditure on the Gross Domestic Product, in Current Prices

Million Danish kroner

		1970	1975	1980	1981	1982	1983	1984	1985	1986	1987	1988	1989
1	Government final consumption expenditure	23675	53182	99734	113215	131098	140544	146176	155481	159359	176214	188550	194636
2	Private final consumption expenditure	68078	119942	208814	228566	255639	279963	307889	337215	366747	377878	393084	409713
	A Households	67800	119184	207048	226705	253620	277680	305198	334191	363338	374135	388764	405090
	B Private non-profit institutions serving households	278	758	1766	1861	2019	2283	2691	3024	3409	3743	4319	4623
3	Gross capital formation	30431	45164	69187	63017	75734	81862	104104	120290	143386	132958	131274	144322
	A Increase in stocks	1148	-424	-1125	-800	1120	-187	6852	5098	5016	-5075	-3500	3000
	B Gross fixed capital formation	29283	45588	70312	63817	74614	82049	97252	115192	138370	138033	134774	141322
	Residential buildings	9538	14462	19833	16496	16772	20264	25788	26532	33429	33846	32761	32520
	Non-residential buildings	6737	10247	15194	12884	11906	12186	14831	19529	23078	27211	27620	25628
	Other construction and land improvement etc.	3563	5635	9149	9379	13697	14350	13066	15260	17247	17235	18726	21288
	Other	9445	15244	26136	25058	32239	35249	43567	53870	64617	59742	55667	61885
4	Exports of goods and services	33103	65049	122256	149042	168924	186311	207523	225566	213559	220084	237709	266411
5	Less: Imports of goods and services	36661	67081	126205	146050	166928	176140	200408	223480	216555	207226	215097	239067
	Equals: Gross Domestic Product	118626	216256	373786	407790	464467	512540	565284	615072	666496	699908	735520	776015

1.2 Expenditure on the Gross Domestic Product, in Constant Prices

Million Danish kroner

		1970	1975	1980	1981	1982	1983	1984	1985	1986	1987	1988	1989
						At constant prices of:1980							
1	Government final consumption expenditure	64943	79532	99734	102359	105508	105465	105030	107682	108205	110873	111069	109654
2	Private final consumption expenditure	182751	194675	208814	203992	206947	212292	219469	230365	243583	239929	238013	236135
	A Households	181904	193485	207048	202320	205342	210541	217539	228287	241352	237660	235541	233593
	B Private non-profit institutions serving households	847	1191	1766	1673	1605	1751	1930	2077	2231	2269	2472	2542
3	Gross capital formation	78876	69588	69187	55912	62373	62364	75009	82870	94682	85932	80358	85060

Denmark

1.2 Expenditure on the Gross Domestic Product, in Constant Prices
(Continued)

Million Danish kroner

	1970	1975	1980	1981	1982	1983	1984	1985	1986	1987	1988	1989
					At constant prices of:1980							
A Increase in stocks	2869	-359	-1125	-887	1552	417	5079	4156	2506	-2771	-2500	2000
B Gross fixed capital formation	76007	69947	70312	56799	60821	61947	69930	78714	92176	88703	82858	83060
Residential buildings	25505	21979	19833	14728	13479	15023	18072	17697	21475	20780	19019	17952
Non-residential buildings	17468	15903	15194	11536	9659	9116	10567	13167	15226	17284	16522	14527
Other construction and land improvement etc.	11123	9470	9149	8323	11001	10656	9218	10376	11982	11178	11499	12405
Other	21911	22595	26136	22212	26681	27152	32073	37473	43493	39461	35818	38176
4 Exports of goods and services	80104	97852	122256	132282	135592	142176	147108	154406	154454	162295	174112	184503
5 Less: Imports of goods and services	107088	111411	126205	124085	128774	131040	138184	149373	159457	156265	158471	165145
Equals: Gross Domestic Product	299586	330236	373786	370460	381646	391257	408432	425950	441467	442764	445081	450207

1.3 Cost Components of the Gross Domestic Product

Million Danish kroner

	1970	1975	1980	1981	1982	1983	1984	1985	1986	1987	1988	1989
1 Indirect taxes, net	17295	27543	57797	62671	67054	74671	83607	94555	110820	113963	115258	115124
A Indirect taxes	20484	33560	69591	75077	82040	91426	102228	112913	130880	135974	139484	139478
B Less: Subsidies	3189	6017	11794	12406	14986	16755	18621	18358	20060	22011	24226	24354
2 Consumption of fixed capital	8161	17859	33670	38000	42600	46900	50200	54800	57600	61600	66100	70800
3 Compensation of employees paid by resident producers to:	63859	122742	212722	230056	259944	283353	306095	330841	356230	388891	404744	415845
A Resident households	63790	122593	212426	229695	259482	282782	305445	330180	355526	388244	404000	415014
B Rest of the world	69	149	296	361	462	571	650	661	704	647	744	831
4 Operating surplus	29312	48112	69597	77063	94869	107617	125382	134876	141847	135455	149416	174246
Equals: Gross Domestic Product	118627	216256	373786	407790	464467	512541	565284	615072	666497	699909	735518	776015

1.4 General Government Current Receipts and Disbursements

Million Danish kroner

	1970	1975	1980	1981	1982	1983	1984	1985	1986	1987	1988	1989
					Receipts							
1 Operating surplus	...	-	-	-	-	-	-	-	-	-	-	-
2 Property and entrepreneurial income	...	5430	15119	16810	18966	23041	28479	30240	32654	31369	34043	37421
3 Taxes, fees and contributions	...	89372	169531	184730	206609	237914	268802	301149	337759	359647	375241	386009
A Indirect taxes	...	33562	69591	75070	82040	91426	102228	112913	130879	135974	139484	139478
B Direct taxes	...	54299	96343	105058	118035	136551	155156	175661	195466	208943	225806	235835
C Social security contributions	...	1252	3168	4127	6017	9377	10688	11749	10619	13798	8756	9404
D Compulsory fees, fines and penalties	...	259	429	475	517	560	730	826	795	932	1195	1292
4 Other current transfers	...	4992	10327	10778	12307	13900	16351	16110	18189	20721	21688	21788
Total Current Receipts of General Government	...	99794	194977	212318	237882	274855	313632	347499	388602	411737	430972	445218
					Disbursements							
1 Government final consumption expenditure	...	53182	99734	113215	131098	140544	146176	155481	159359	176214	188550	194636
A Compensation of employees	...	37233	69515	79950	93853	101183	104850	110282	114398	125773	136399	141285
B Consumption of fixed capital	...	1450	2925	3261	3734	4027	4328	4948	5412	5997	6420	6620
C Purchases of goods and services, net	...	14269	26841	29543	32981	34798	36243	39391	38578	43243	44902	45897
D Less: Own account fixed capital formation	...	...	...	...	...	...	...	...	...	...	...	...
E Indirect taxes paid, net	...	230	453	461	530	536	755	860	971	1201	829	834
2 Property income	...	2631	14747	21541	27894	41306	54149	60639	58692	57746	58305	57421
A Interest	...	2631	14747	21541	27894	41306	54149	60639	58692	57746	58305	57421
B Net land rent and royalties	...	...	...	...	...	...	...	...	...	...	...	...

Denmark

1.4 General Government Current Receipts and Disbursements
(Continued)

Million Danish kroner

	1970	1975	1980	1981	1982	1983	1984	1985	1986	1987	1988	1989
3 Subsidies	...	6017	11794	12404	14985	16756	18621	18358	20060	22011	24226	24354
4 Other current transfers	...	32294	68819	79554	92764	100824	106973	112584	117881	128971	144240	158186
A Social security benefits	...	29804	62155	72480	84075	91183	96155	100396	103307	113716	126927	140273
B Social assistance grants	...											
C Other	...	2490	6664	7074	8689	9641	10818	12188	14574	15255	17313	17913
5 Net saving	...	5670	-117	-14396	-28859	-24575	-12287	437	32610	26795	15651	10621
Total Current Disbursements and Net Saving of General Government	...	99794	194977	212318	237882	274855	313632	347499	388602	411737	430972	445218

1.7 External Transactions on Current Account, Summary

Million Danish kroner

	1970	1975	1980	1981	1982	1983	1984	1985	1986	1987	1988	1989
Payments to the Rest of the World												
1 Imports of goods and services	36661	67081	126205	146050	166928	176140	200408	223480	216555	207226	215097	239067
A Imports of merchandise c.i.f.	33101	59805	109673	124688	139812	148896	171826	191282	184388	173651	176047	195786
B Other	3560	7275	16532	21362	27116	27244	28582	32198	32167	33575	39050	43281
2 Factor income to the rest of the world	1234	3781	16845	23799	28828	28842	38960	43905	46612	48430	54930	69125
A Compensation of employees	69	149	296	361	462	571	650	661	704	647	744	831
B Property and entrepreneurial income	1165	3632	16549	23438	28366	28271	38310	43244	45908	47783	54186	68294
3 Current transfers to the rest of the world	943	2303	6035	6740	7532	8894	9553	11612	15029	14807	16225	15247
A Indirect taxes to supranational organizations	-	492	1236	1374	1626	1810	2033	2150	2260	2201	2383	2639
B Other current transfers	943	1811	4799	5366	5906	7084	7520	9462	12769	12606	13842	12608
4 Surplus of the nation on current transactions	-4571	-3268	-13658	-12309	-19734	-13232	-18540	-28381	-36215	-20602	-8840	-9365
Payments to the Rest of the World and Surplus of the Nation on Current Transactions	34267	69897	135427	164280	183554	200644	230381	250616	241981	249861	277412	314074
Receipts From The Rest of the World												
1 Exports of goods and services	33103	65049	122256	149042	168924	186311	207523	225566	213559	220084	237709	266411
A Exports of merchandise f.o.b.	25254	50201	96161	115104	130545	147474	166117	180090	171723	175132	186314	208664
B Other	7849	14848	26095	33938	38378	38837	41406	45476	41836	44952	51395	57747
2 Factor income from rest of the world	1021	2117	7563	11114	11012	10412	15101	17735	19119	20863	27197	37535
A Compensation of employees	137	220	434	518	665	833	864	937	914	942	1005	1092
B Property and entrepreneurial income	884	1897	7129	10596	10347	9579	14237	16798	18205	19921	26192	36443
3 Current transfers from rest of the world	142	2730	5608	4124	3619	3921	7758	7315	9303	8913	12505	10128
A Subsidies from supranational organisations	-	2213	4915	4286	4754	5641	7089	6531	8424	9837	9363	8626
B Other current transfers	142	517	693	-162	-1135	-1720	669	784	879	-924	3142	1502
Receipts from the Rest of the World on Current Transactions	34266	69896	135427	164280	183555	200644	230382	250616	241981	249860	277411	314074

1.8 Capital Transactions of The Nation, Summary

Million Danish kroner

	1970	1975	1980	1981	1982	1983	1984	1985	1986	1987	1988	1989
Finance of Gross Capital Formation												
Gross saving	25860	41896	55528	50708	56000	68631	85564	91909	107171	112356	122432	134957
1 Consumption of fixed capital	8161	17859	33670	38000	42600	46900	50200	54800	57600	61600	66100	70800
A General government	...	1450	2925	3261	3734	4027	4328	4948	5412	5997	6420	6620
B Corporate and quasi-corporate enterprises	...	...	...	...	...	...	...	...	...	...	...	...
C Other	...	...	...	...	...	...	...	...	...	...	...	...
2 Net saving	17699	24037	21858	12708	13400	21731	35364	37109	49571	50756	56332	64157
A General government	...	5670	-117	-14396	-28859	-24575	-12287	437	32610	26795	15651	10621
B Corporate and quasi-corporate enterprises	...	...	...	...	...	...	...	...	...	...	...	...

Denmark

1.8 Capital Transactions of The Nation, Summary
(Continued)

Million Danish kroner

	1970	1975	1980	1981	1982	1983	1984	1985	1986	1987	1988	1989
C Other	...	...	...	...	...	...	...	...	...	...	...	...
Less: Surplus of the nation on current transactions	-4571	-3268	-13658	-12309	-19734	-13232	-18540	-28381	-36215	-20602	-8840	-9365
Finance of Gross Capital Formation	30431	45164	69186	63017	75734	81863	104104	120290	143386	132958	131272	144322
Gross Capital Formation												
Increase in stocks	1148	-424	-1125	-800	1120	-187	6852	5098	5016	-5075	-3500	3000
Gross fixed capital formation	29283	45588	70312	63817	74614	82049	97252	115192	138370	138033	134774	141322
1 General government	...	8106	12883	12150	12104	10905	11845	14064	13869	15581	16836	17688
2 Corporate and quasi-corporate enterprises	...	...	...	...	...	...	...	...	...	...	...	...
3 Other	...	...	...	...	...	...	...	...	...	...	...	...
Gross Capital Formation	30431	45164	69187	63017	75734	81862	104104	120290	143386	132958	131274	144322

1.10 Gross Domestic Product by Kind of Activity, in Current Prices

Million Danish kroner

	1970	1975	1980	1981	1982	1983	1984	1985	1986	1987	1988	1989
1 Agriculture, hunting, forestry and fishing	6612	10927	17818	20962	26269	24940	31002	30100	30005	27338	28126	31926
2 Mining and quarrying	152	163	373	1209	3207	3339	4156	6039	5327	5389	4681	6308
3 Manufacturing	21967	39046	64311	67149	76263	86043	97505	105073	111703	113869	118765	122382
4 Electricity, gas and water	1814	3110	4520	4685	6800	7289	5872	6796	8508	9228	9914	12021
5 Construction	11129	16669	24383	22541	24232	24921	28640	30958	37686	43331	44289	45055
6 Wholesale and retail trade, restaurants and hotels	17994	31169	45257	49102	56315	65893	70659	80892	88350	87952	91289	96992
7 Transport, storage and communication	9329	15814	25899	29190	32404	35216	40391	43220	44770	48016	51271	56033
8 Finance, insurance, real estate and business services	12908	28475	52303	56424	62109	71595	82796	89995	100890	107231	113472	127495
9 Community, social and personal services	5454	10040	16229	18084	19945	21682	23577	25317	27774	30342	32552	35864
Total, Industries	87359	155415	251094	269346	307543	340918	384597	418391	455014	472697	494358	534076
Producers of Government Services	16218	38683	72440	83211	97587	105210	109178	115230	119810	131770	142819	147905
Other Producers	659	1242	2285	2368	2536	2779	3122	3400	3702	4009	4299	4704
Subtotal [a]	104236	195340	325818	354925	407665	448907	496897	537021	578526	608476	641476	686685
Less: Imputed bank service charge	2904	6626	9830	9805	10253	11037	15220	16504	22850	22530	21215	25794
Plus: Import duties	...	...	...	...	...	...	...	...	...	...	...	...
Plus: Value added tax	...	...	...	...	...	...	...	...	...	...	...	...
Plus: Other adjustments [b]	17295	27543	57797	62671	67054	74671	83607	94555	110820	113963	115258	115124
Equals: Gross Domestic Product	118627	216257	373786	407791	464467	512541	565284	615072	666496	699909	735519	776015
Memorandum Item: Mineral fuels and power	1715	3107	5532	6316	10362	10726	9673	12297	13011	13569	13177	16893

a) Gross domestic product in factor values.
b) Item 'Other adjustments' refers to indirect taxes net of subsidies.

1.11 Gross Domestic Product by Kind of Activity, in Constant Prices

Million Danish kroner

	1970	1975	1980	1981	1982	1983	1984	1985	1986	1987	1988	1989
					At constant prices of:1980							
1 Agriculture, hunting, forestry and fishing	13198	16259	17818	19294	21228	19404	23289	23191	22368	21311	22603	23935
2 Mining and quarrying	224	264	373	948	2271	2508	3125	4991	7841	10074	10372	11564
3 Manufacturing	47880	55471	64311	62267	63257	67510	70673	72920	72920	69933	70212	71078
4 Electricity, gas and water	2665	3407	4520	4183	4970	5153	5244	6064	6528	6356	6335	6733
5 Construction	29094	24442	24383	20169	19073	18499	20124	21431	25486	26573	25304	24836
6 Wholesale and retail trade, restaurants and hotels	37428	41204	45257	44158	46721	49110	49828	53516	56545	57106	57805	59023
7 Transport, storage and communication	24498	22223	25899	26215	25842	25532	26726	26477	26816	30349	32672	33298
8 Finance, insurance, real estate and business services	35846	46214	52303	51790	51697	53771	58369	60030	64293	65132	64823	68700
9 Community, social and personal services	13599	14654	16229	16201	16212	16166	16357	16695	17695	17248	17576	18216
Total, Industries	204432	224138	251094	245226	251272	257652	273735	285316	300493	304083	307701	317384
Producers of Government Services	44225	56259	72440	76093	79659	80074	79874	81615	82950	83398	84068	83590
Other Producers	2506	2143	2285	2115	2010	2106	2218	2309	2401	2403	2477	2610

Denmark

1.11 Gross Domestic Product by Kind of Activity, in Constant Prices
(Continued)

Million Danish kroner

	1970	1975	1980	1981	1982	1983	1984	1985	1986	1987	1988	1989
					At constant prices of:1980							
Subtotal [a]	251163	282540	325818	323433	332940	339832	355827	369240	385844	389884	394247	403584
Less: Imputed bank service charge	7845	10209	9830	8838	8343	8410	11043	11312	15291	14359	13468	15579
Plus: Import duties	...	...	...	...	...	...	...	...	...	...	...	...
Plus: Value added tax	...	...	...	...	...	...	...	...	...	...	...	...
Plus: Other adjustments [b]	56267	57905	57797	55864	57049	59836	63649	68021	70916	67240	64302	62203
Equals: Gross Domestic Product	299585	330236	373786	370460	381647	391258	408433	425949	441469	442765	445080	450208
Memorandum Item: Mineral fuels and power	2609	3686	5532	5404	7573	8195	8654	11311	14319	16445	16517	18310

a) Gross domestic product in factor values.
b) Item 'Other adjustments' refers to indirect taxes net of subsidies.

1.12 Relations Among National Accounting Aggregates

Million Danish kroner

	1970	1975	1980	1981	1982	1983	1984	1985	1986	1987	1988	1989
Gross Domestic Product	118627	216256	373785	407790	464467	512541	565284	615072	666496	699908	735520	776015
Plus: Net factor income from the rest of the world	-213	-1664	-9282	-12685	-17816	-18430	-23860	-26171	-27492	-27567	-27733	-31590
Factor income from the rest of the world	1021	2117	7563	11114	11012	10412	15101	17735	19119	20863	27197	37535
Less: Factor income to the rest of the world	1234	3781	16845	23799	28828	28842	38960	43905	46612	48430	54930	69125
Equals: Gross National Product	118414	214592	364503	395105	446650	494111	541424	588901	639004	672343	707786	744425
Less: Consumption of fixed capital	8161	17859	33670	38000	42600	46900	50200	54800	57600	61600	66100	70800
Equals: National Income	110253	196733	330833	357105	404050	447211	491224	534101	581404	610743	641686	673625
Plus: Net current transfers from the rest of the world	-801	427	-427	-2616	-3913	-4973	-1795	-4296	-5727	-5895	-3720	-5119
Current transfers from the rest of the world	142	2730	5608	4124	3619	3921	7758	7315	9303	8913	12505	10128
Less: Current transfers to the rest of the world	943	2303	6035	6740	7532	8894	9553	11612	15029	14807	16225	15247
Equals: National Disposable Income	109452	197160	330406	354489	400137	442238	489429	529805	575677	604848	637966	668506
Less: Final consumption	91753	173124	308548	341781	386737	420507	454065	492696	526106	554092	581634	604349
Equals: Net Saving	17699	24037	21858	12708	13400	21731	35364	37109	49571	50756	56332	64157
Less: Surplus of the nation on current transactions	-4571	-3268	-13658	-12309	-19734	-13232	-18540	-28381	-36215	-20602	-8840	-9365
Equals: Net Capital Formation	22270	27305	35517	25017	33134	34963	53904	65490	85786	71358	65174	73522

2.5 Private Final Consumption Expenditure by Type and Purpose, in Current Prices

Million Danish kroner

	1970	1975	1980	1981	1982	1983	1984	1985	1986	1987	1988	1989
				Final Consumption Expenditure of Resident Households								
1 Food, beverages and tobacco	20530	32337	52239	57952	64190	69215	75428	78377	81641	81422	84317	86061
A Food	14001	21928	35894	40265	44526	47182	52049	53872	55594	55859	57690	59626
B Non-alcoholic beverages	463	778	1262	1313	1453	1628	1751	1872	2016	2067	2333	2480
C Alcoholic beverages	2820	5237	7953	8819	9785	11113	11458	12033	12851	12764	13319	13585
D Tobacco	3247	4394	7130	7554	8425	9292	10170	10600	11180	10731	10974	10371
2 Clothing and footwear	5266	7682	12236	12980	14738	16225	17832	19881	22117	22089	22067	21985
3 Gross rent, fuel and power	12432	27138	55832	62326	69220	73477	78716	84790	90374	98045	102699	110309
A Fuel and power	3125	6856	16473	18878	20459	19243	19655	21508	22875	25034	23576	25018
B Other	9307	20282	39359	43447	48761	54234	59061	63281	67498	73011	79123	85291
4 Furniture, furnishings and household equipment and operation	6576	10823	15333	16049	17563	19112	20808	23097	25010	24790	26601	26133
A Household operation	1827	2724	3739	4157	4654	4940	5344	5683	6178	6092	6603	6416
B Other	4749	8100	11594	11892	12909	14171	15464	17413	18831	18698	19998	19717
5 Medical care and health expenses	1382	2417	3760	4178	4632	5100	5572	6001	5788	6933	7454	7664
6 Transport and communication	10208	18318	30229	33514	37830	45246	51869	59137	64437	63875	64294	65908
A Personal transport equipment	3332	5613	6234	6881	8642	12935	16573	20776	23417	19539	16027	14743
B Other	6876	12705	23995	26633	29188	32311	35296	38361	41020	44336	48267	51165
7 Recreational, entertainment, education and cultural services	5610	11473	18992	21407	23936	26383	29608	32440	35629	36048	37545	40383
A Education	421	1126	2734	3351	3969	4397	4737	5108	5488	5919	6673	7237
B Other	5190	10347	16258	18056	19967	21986	24871	27332	30141	30129	30871	33146
8 Miscellaneous goods and services	6596	10542	18392	20073	23374	25967	28845	32308	36945	39103	41820	44712

Denmark

2.5 Private Final Consumption Expenditure by Type and Purpose, in Current Prices
(Continued)

Million Danish kroner

	1970	1975	1980	1981	1982	1983	1984	1985	1986	1987	1988	1989
A Personal care	1098	1636	2843	3208	3723	4003	4330	4792	5300	5731	6098	6437
B Expenditures in restaurants, cafes and hotels	3562	5619	9738	10788	12486	13721	15290	16978	19622	20638	22151	23490
C Other	1936	3287	5811	6077	7165	8242	9225	10538	12023	12734	13572	14785
Total Final Consumption Expenditure in the Domestic Market by Households, of which	68600	120729	207013	228477	255482	280725	308678	336030	361942	372306	386796	403155
A Durable goods	8159	14871	19153	20641	23822	29842	35657	42042	46492	41351	39037	37827
B Semi-durable goods	11520	18598	29986	32091	36604	40146	44295	49439	54865	57214	60195	62745
C Non-durable goods	28237	47633	83874	93247	102270	107003	114655	120894	126601	129103	131421	134346
D Services	20685	39628	74000	82498	92786	103734	114071	123654	133985	144638	156143	168238
Plus: Direct purchases abroad by resident households	2009	3661	8402	8792	10600	10589	12116	14444	17089	18810	20502	20787
Less: Direct purchases in the domestic market by non-resident households	2809	5207	8367	10563	12462	13634	15596	16282	15693	16981	18533	18852
Equals: Final Consumption Expenditure of Resident Households	67800	119183	207048	226706	253620	277680	305198	334191	363338	374135	388764	405090

Final Consumption Expenditure of Private Non-profit Institutions Serving Households

	1970	1975	1980	1981	1982	1983	1984	1985	1986	1987	1988	1989
Equals: Final Consumption Expenditure of Private Non-profit Organisations Serving Households	278	758	1766	1861	2019	2283	2691	3024	3409	3743	4319	4623
Private Final Consumption Expenditure	68078	119941	208814	228567	255639	279963	307889	337215	366747	377878	393083	409713

2.6 Private Final Consumption Expenditure by Type and Purpose, in Constant Prices

Million Danish kroner

	1970	1975	1980	1981	1982	1983	1984	1985	1986	1987	1988	1989

At constant prices of: 1980

Final Consumption Expenditure of Resident Households

	1970	1975	1980	1981	1982	1983	1984	1985	1986	1987	1988	1989
1 Food, beverages and tobacco	47221	48717	52239	53027	53770	54009	54276	54312	55561	54897	55323	54532
A Food	33667	32812	35894	36298	36078	36480	36836	36912	37916	37881	38168	37763
B Non-alcoholic beverages	1075	1179	1262	1144	1083	1124	999	1030	1093	1074	1134	1197
C Alcoholic beverages	5729	7581	7953	8327	8599	8824	8641	8751	8951	8756	8858	8832
D Tobacco	6750	7145	7130	7258	8009	7582	7800	7619	7601	7186	7163	6740
2 Clothing and footwear	11735	11138	12236	11543	12075	12486	12997	13852	14841	14350	13449	12627
3 Gross rent, fuel and power	43648	50699	55832	54838	54852	54454	55168	56869	57748	58311	57836	57883
A Fuel and power	17675	16405	16473	14891	14455	13790	14025	15284	15724	15764	14766	14438
B Other	25973	34294	39359	39947	40398	40663	41143	41585	42024	42548	43070	43445
4 Furniture, furnishings and household equipment and operation	17137	16516	15333	14198	13943	14206	14480	15191	15945	15214	15830	14988
A Household operation	5513	4367	3739	3688	3709	3761	3754	3777	3985	3714	3893	3566
B Other	11624	12149	11594	10510	10233	10444	10726	11414	11961	11500	11937	11422
5 Medical care and health expenses	3234	3328	3760	3742	3765	3839	3909	3998	3756	4234	4315	4250
6 Transport and communication	29259	30572	30229	29290	30183	34324	37735	41479	43827	40717	37987	36838
A Personal transport equipment	9737	8853	6234	6440	7667	11076	13523	16128	17263	13237	10271	9018
B Other	19522	21719	23995	22850	22516	23249	24212	25351	26564	27480	27716	27820
7 Recreational, entertainment, education and cultural services	12982	16507	18992	19566	19916	20450	21879	22998	24796	23978	24167	25619
A Education	1177	1675	2734	3018	3195	3329	3422	3525	3620	3545	3730	3818
B Other	11805	14832	16258	16548	16721	17120	18457	19472	21175	20434	20438	21801
8 Miscellaneous goods and services	18803	18078	18392	18152	19145	19715	20425	21654	23753	24096	24731	25578
A Personal care	2756	2560	2843	2842	2858	2863	2901	2990	3201	3283	3306	3343
B Expenditures in restaurants, cafes and hotels	9373	9471	9738	9746	10245	10428	10734	11311	12541	12758	13129	13570
C Other	6674	6047	5811	5565	6042	6424	6790	7353	8011	8056	8297	8666
Total Final Consumption Expenditure in the Domestic Market by Households, of which	184019	195556	207013	204357	207650	213483	220869	230353	240227	235797	233639	232315
A Durable goods	21838	22604	19153	19020	20438	24521	28093	31611	33775	28332	26092	24888
B Semi-durable goods	27471	27852	29986	28324	29123	29763	30889	32888	35492	35322	34945	34660
C Non-durable goods	78169	79879	83874	81896	81914	81501	82053	83935	85895	85199	84634	82890

Denmark

2.6 Private Final Consumption Expenditure by Type and Purpose, in Constant Prices
(Continued)

Million Danish kroner

	1970	1975	1980	1981	1982	1983	1984	1985	1986	1987	1988	1989
					At constant prices of: 1980							
D Services	56541	65221	74000	75118	76175	77697	79835	81918	85065	86944	87968	89877
Plus: Direct purchases abroad by resident households	4723	6112	8402	7518	7956	7501	7878	9084	11480	12711	13218	12313
Less: Direct purchases in the domestic market by non-resident households	6838	8184	8367	9555	10264	10442	11208	11149	10354	10848	11316	11035
Equals: Final Consumption Expenditure of Resident Households	181904	193485	207048	202320	205342	210541	217539	228287	241352	237660	235541	233593

Final Consumption Expenditure of Private Non-profit Institutions Serving Households

	1970	1975	1980	1981	1982	1983	1984	1985	1986	1987	1988	1989
Equals: Final Consumption Expenditure of Private Non-profit Organisations Serving Households	847	1191	1766	1673	1605	1751	1930	2077	2231	2269	2472	2542
Private Final Consumption Expenditure	182751	194676	208814	203993	206947	212292	219469	230364	243583	239929	238013	236135

2.7 Gross Capital Formation by Type of Good and Owner, in Current Prices

Million Danish kroner

	1980 TOTAL	Total Private	Public Enterprises	General Government	1981 TOTAL	Total Private	Public Enterprises	General Government	1982 TOTAL	Total Private	Public Enterprises	General Government
Increase in stocks, total	-1125	...	...	...	-800	...	...	...	1120	...	...	...
1 Goods producing industries	1173	...	...	...	-1211	...	...	...	-895	...	...	...
A Materials and supplies	-78	...	...	...	-1538	...	...	...	-512	...	...	...
B Work in progress a	...	...	...	...	...	...	...	...	...	...	...	...
C Livestock, except breeding stocks, dairy cattle, etc.	33	...	...	...	109	...	...	...	-211	...	...	...
D Finished goods a	1218	...	...	...	218	...	...	...	-172	...	...	...
2 Wholesale and retail trade	-2105	...	...	...	-1363	...	...	...	-1802	...	...	...
3 Other, except government stocks	-268	...	...	...	1675	...	...	...	2828	...	...	...
4 Government stocks	75	...	...	...	99	...	...	...	989	...	...	...
Gross Fixed Capital Formation, Total	70312	...	...	...	63817	...	...	...	74614	...	...	...
1 Residential buildings	19833	...	...	...	16496	...	...	...	16772	...	...	...
2 Non-residential buildings	15194	...	...	...	12884	...	...	...	11906	...	...	...
3 Other construction	9149	...	...	...	9379	...	...	...	13697	...	...	...
4 Land improvement and plantation and orchard development	...	...	...	...	...	...	...	...	...	...	...	...
5 Producers' durable goods	26396	...	...	...	25221	...	...	...	32391	...	...	...
A Transport equipment	5500	...	...	...	6106	...	...	...	7444	...	...	...
B Machinery and equipment	20896	...	...	...	19115	...	...	...	24947	...	...	...
6 Breeding stock, dairy cattle, etc.	-260	...	...	...	-164	...	...	...	-152	...	...	...
Total Gross Capital Formation	69187	...	...	...	63017	...	...	...	75734	...	...	...

	1983 TOTAL	Total Private	Public Enterprises	General Government	1984 TOTAL	Total Private	Public Enterprises	General Government	1985 TOTAL	Total Private	Public Enterprises	General Government
Increase in stocks, total	-187	...	...	...	6852	...	...	...	5098	...	...	...
1 Goods producing industries	-221	...	...	...	2077	...	...	...	2950	...	...	...
A Materials and supplies	477	...	...	...	780	...	...	...	1660	...	...	...
B Work in progress a	...	...	...	...	...	...	...	...	...	...	...	...
C Livestock, except breeding stocks, dairy cattle, etc.	103	...	...	...	-381	...	...	...	-90	...	...	...
D Finished goods a	-801	...	...	...	1678	...	...	...	1380	...	...	...
2 Wholesale and retail trade	1575	...	...	...	3359	...	...	...	3154	...	...	...
3 Other, except government stocks	-2722	...	...	...	1491	...	...	...	-1520	...	...	...
4 Government stocks	1182	...	...	...	-74	...	...	...	514	...	...	...
Gross Fixed Capital Formation, Total	82049	...	...	...	97252	...	...	...	115192	...	...	...
1 Residential buildings	20264	...	...	...	25788	...	...	...	26532	...	...	...
2 Non-residential buildings	12186	...	...	...	14831	...	...	...	19529	...	...	...

Denmark

2.7 Gross Capital Formation by Type of Good and Owner, in Current Prices
(Continued)

Million Danish kroner

	1983				1984				1985			
	TOTAL	Total Private	Public Enterprises	General Government	TOTAL	Total Private	Public Enterprises	General Government	TOTAL	Total Private	Public Enterprises	General Government
3 Other construction	14350	...	...	...	13066	...	...	...	15260	...	...	...
4 Land improvement and plantation and orchard development	...	...	...	...	...	...	...	...	...	...	...	...
5 Producers' durable goods	35570	...	...	...	43863	...	...	...	53961	...	...	...
A Transport equipment	6803	...	...	...	8586	...	...	...	12228	...	...	...
B Machinery and equipment	28767	...	...	...	35276	...	...	...	41733	...	...	...
6 Breeding stock, dairy cattle, etc.	-321	...	...	...	-296	...	...	...	-91	...	...	...
Total Gross Capital Formation	81862	...	...	...	104104	...	...	...	120290	...	...	...

	1986				1987				1988			
	TOTAL	Total Private	Public Enterprises	General Government	TOTAL	Total Private	Public Enterprises	General Government	TOTAL	Total Private	Public Enterprises	General Government
Increase in stocks, total	5016	...	...	...	-5075	...	...	...	-3500	...	...	...
1 Goods producing industries	-915	...	...	...	-2363	...	...	...	...	...	...	...
A Materials and supplies	178	...	...	...	-821	...	...	...	...	...	...	...
B Work in progress [a]	...	...	...	...	...	...	...	...	...	...	...	...
C Livestock, except breeding stocks, dairy cattle, etc.	-244	...	...	...	-343	...	...	...	-188	...	...	...
D Finished goods [a]	-849	...	...	...	-1199	...	...	...	...	...	...	...
2 Wholesale and retail trade	4314	...	...	...	-1116	...	...	...	...	...	...	...
3 Other, except government stocks	2357	...	...	...	-814	...	...	...	...	...	...	...
4 Government stocks	-740	...	...	...	-782	...	...	...	-843	...	...	...
Gross Fixed Capital Formation, Total	138370	...	...	...	138033	...	...	...	134774	...	...	...
1 Residential buildings	33429	...	...	...	33846	...	...	...	32761	...	...	...
2 Non-residential buildings	23078	...	...	...	27211	...	...	...	27620	...	...	...
3 Other construction	17247	...	...	...	17235	...	...	...	18726	...	...	...
4 Land improvement and plantation and orchard development	...	...	...	...	...	...	...	...	...	...	...	...
5 Producers' durable goods	64941	...	...	...	60190	...	...	...	55852	...	...	...
A Transport equipment	16438	...	...	...	12846	...	...	...	10314	...	...	...
B Machinery and equipment	48503	...	...	...	47344	...	...	...	45538	...	...	...
6 Breeding stock, dairy cattle, etc.	-324	...	...	...	-448	...	...	...	-185	...	...	...
Total Gross Capital Formation	143386	...	...	...	132958	...	...	...	131274	...	...	...

	1989			
	TOTAL	Total Private	Public Enterprises	General Government
Increase in stocks, total	3000	...	...	...
1 Goods producing industries	...	...	...	...
A Materials and supplies	...	...	...	...
B Work in progress [a]	...	...	...	...
C Livestock, except breeding stocks, dairy cattle, etc.	109	...	...	...
D Finished goods [a]	...	...	...	...
2 Wholesale and retail trade	...	...	...	...
3 Other, except government stocks	...	...	...	...
4 Government stocks	-533	...	...	...
Gross Fixed Capital Formation, Total	141322	...	...	...
1 Residential buildings	32520	...	...	...
2 Non-residential buildings	25628	...	...	...

Denmark

2.7 Gross Capital Formation by Type of Good and Owner, in Current Prices
(Continued)

Million Danish kroner

	1989 TOTAL	Total Private	Public Enterprises	General Government
3 Other construction	21288	...	...	...
4 Land improvement and plantation and orchard development	...	...	...	...
5 Producers' durable goods	61940	...	...	...
A Transport equipment	14564	...	...	...
B Machinery and equipment	47376	...	...	...
6 Breeding stock, dairy cattle, etc.	-55	...	...	...
Total Gross Capital Formation	144322	...	...	...

a) Item 'Work in progress' is included in item 'Finished goods'.

2.8 Gross Capital Formation by Type of Good and Owner, in Constant Prices

Million Danish kroner

	1980 TOTAL	Total Private	Public Enterprises	General Government	1981 TOTAL	Total Private	Public Enterprises	General Government	1982 TOTAL	Total Private	Public Enterprises	General Government
				At constant prices of:1980								
Increase in stocks, total	-1125	...	...	...	-887	...	...	...	1552	...	...	...
1 Goods producing industries	1173	...	...	...	-895	...	...	...	-635	...	...	...
A Materials and supplies	-78	...	...	...	-1278	...	...	...	-361	...	...	...
B Work in progress a	...	...	...	...	...	...	...	...	...	...	...	...
C Livestock, except breeding stocks, dairy cattle, etc.	33	...	...	...	94	...	...	...	-161	...	...	...
D Finished goods a	1218	...	...	...	289	...	...	...	-113	...	...	...
2 Wholesale and retail trade	-2105	...	...	...	-1324	...	...	...	-864	...	...	...
3 Other, except government stocks	-193	...	...	...	1332	...	...	...	3051	...	...	...
4 Government stocks												
Gross Fixed Capital Formation, Total	70312	...	...	...	56799	...	...	...	60821	...	...	...
1 Residential buildings	19833	...	...	...	14728	...	...	...	13479	...	...	...
2 Non-residential buildings	15194	...	...	...	11536	...	...	...	9659	...	...	...
3 Other construction	9149	...	...	...	8323	...	...	...	11001	...	...	...
4 Land improvement and plantation and orchard development	...	...	...	...	...	...	...	...	...	...	...	...
5 Producers' durable goods	26396	...	...	...	22354	...	...	...	26797	...	...	...
A Transport equipment	5500	...	...	...	5424	...	...	...	6466	...	...	...
B Machinery and equipment	20896	...	...	...	16930	...	...	...	20330	...	...	...
6 Breeding stock, dairy cattle, etc.	-260	...	...	...	-143	...	...	...	-115	...	...	...
Total Gross Capital Formation	69187	...	...	...	55912	...	...	...	62373	...	...	...

	1983 TOTAL	Total Private	Public Enterprises	General Government	1984 TOTAL	Total Private	Public Enterprises	General Government	1985 TOTAL	Total Private	Public Enterprises	General Government
				At constant prices of:1980								
Increase in stocks, total	417	...	...	...	5079	...	...	...	4156	...	...	...
1 Goods producing industries	-158	...	...	...	1260	...	...	...	2062	...	...	...
A Materials and supplies	363	...	...	...	637	...	...	...	1100	...	...	...
B Work in progress a	...	...	...	...	...	...	...	...	...	...	...	...
C Livestock, except breeding stocks, dairy cattle, etc.	70	...	...	...	-285	...	...	...	-68	...	...	...
D Finished goods a	-591	...	...	...	908	...	...	...	1030	...	...	...
2 Wholesale and retail trade	1268	...	...	...	2503	...	...	...	2743	...	...	...
3 Other, except government stocks	-692	...	...	...	1316	...	...	...	-649	...	...	...
4 Government stocks												
Gross Fixed Capital Formation, Total	61947	...	...	...	69930	...	...	...	78714	...	...	...
1 Residential buildings	15023	...	...	...	18072	...	...	...	17697	...	...	...
2 Non-residential buildings	9116	...	...	...	10567	...	...	...	13167	...	...	...

Denmark

2.8 Gross Capital Formation by Type of Good and Owner, in Constant Prices
(Continued)

Million Danish kroner

	1983				1984				1985			
	TOTAL	Total Private	Public Enterprises	General Government	TOTAL	Total Private	Public Enterprises	General Government	TOTAL	Total Private	Public Enterprises	General Government
					At constant prices of:1980							
3 Other construction	10656	...	...	...	9218	...	...	...	10376	...	...	...
4 Land improvement and plantation and orchard development	...	...	...	...	...	...	...	...	...	...	...	...
5 Producers' durable goods	27395	...	...	...	32296	...	...	...	37540	...	...	...
A Transport equipment	5333	...	...	...	6370	...	...	...	8111	...	...	...
B Machinery and equipment	22063	...	...	...	25926	...	...	...	29429	...	...	...
6 Breeding stock, dairy cattle, etc.	-244	...	...	...	-223	...	...	...	-67	...	...	...
Total Gross Capital Formation	62364	...	...	...	75009	...	...	...	82870	...	...	...

	1986				1987				1988			
	TOTAL	Total Private	Public Enterprises	General Government	TOTAL	Total Private	Public Enterprises	General Government	TOTAL	Total Private	Public Enterprises	General Government
					At constant prices of:1980							
Increase in stocks, total	2506	...	...	...	-2771	...	...	...	-2500	...	...	...
1 Goods producing industries	-468	...	...	...	-1603	...	...	...	...	...	...	...
A Materials and supplies	203	...	...	...	-572	...	...	...	...	...	...	...
B Work in progress [a]	...	...	...	...	...	...	...	...	...	...	...	...
C Livestock, except breeding stocks, dairy cattle, etc.	-204	...	...	...	-301	...	...	...	-154	...	...	...
D Finished goods [a]	-467	...	...	...	-730	...	...	...	...	...	...	...
2 Wholesale and retail trade	2972	...	...	...	-642	...	...	...	...	...	...	...
3 Other, except government stocks	2	...	...	...	-526	...	...	...	...	...	...	...
4 Government stocks		...	...	...		...	...	...	...	...	...	...
Gross Fixed Capital Formation, Total	92176	...	...	...	88703	...	...	...	82858	...	...	...
1 Residential buildings	21475	...	...	...	20780	...	...	...	19019	...	...	...
2 Non-residential buildings	15226	...	...	...	17284	...	...	...	16522	...	...	...
3 Other construction	11982	...	...	...	11178	...	...	...	11499	...	...	...
4 Land improvement and plantation and orchard development	...	...	...	...	...	...	...	...	...	...	...	...
5 Producers' durable goods	43763	...	...	...	39855	...	...	...	35968	...	...	...
A Transport equipment	10493	...	...	...	7614	...	...	...	5913	...	...	...
B Machinery and equipment	33270	...	...	...	32241	...	...	...	30055	...	...	...
6 Breeding stock, dairy cattle, etc.	-270	...	...	...	-394	...	...	...	-150	...	...	...
Total Gross Capital Formation	94682	...	...	...	85932	...	...	...	80358	...	...	...

	1989			
	TOTAL	Total Private	Public Enterprises	General Government
	At constant prices of:1980			
Increase in stocks, total	2000	...	...	...
1 Goods producing industries	...	...	...	...
A Materials and supplies	...	...	...	...
B Work in progress [a]	...	...	...	...
C Livestock, except breeding stocks, dairy cattle, etc.	86	...	...	...
D Finished goods [a]	...	...	...	...
2 Wholesale and retail trade	...	...	...	...
3 Other, except government stocks	...	...	...	...
4 Government stocks	...	...	...	...
Gross Fixed Capital Formation, Total	83060	...	...	...
1 Residential buildings	17952	...	...	...
2 Non-residential buildings	14527	...	...	...

Denmark

2.8 Gross Capital Formation by Type of Good and Owner, in Constant Prices
(Continued)

Million Danish kroner

	1989 TOTAL	Total Private	Public Enterprises	General Government
				At constant prices of:1980
3 Other construction	12405	...	...	...
4 Land improvement and plantation and orchard development	...	...	...	...
5 Producers' durable goods	38218	...	...	...
A Transport equipment	8068	...	...	...
B Machinery and equipment	30150	...	...	...
6 Breeding stock, dairy cattle, etc.	-42	...	...	...
Total Gross Capital Formation	85060	...	...	...

a) Item 'Work in progress' is included in item 'Finished goods'.

2.11 Gross Fixed Capital Formation by Kind of Activity of Owner, ISIC Divisions, in Current Prices

Million Danish kroner

	1970	1975	1980	1981	1982	1983	1984	1985	1986	1987	1988	1989
					All Producers							
1 Agriculture, hunting, forestry and fishing	1455	4004	5289	3864	4634	4698	6247	8108	7552	6504	5978	7095
A Agriculture and hunting	1277	3588	4895	3517	4217	4147	5457	6895	6657	5695	...	...
B Forestry and logging	21	46	99	103	157	109	102	164	156	143	...	...
C Fishing	157	370	295	244	260	442	688	1048	740	666	...	...
2 Mining and quarrying	34	197	838	1484	4972	4586	1724	2205	2002	1316	1090	1379
A Coal mining	...	...	...	...	...	...	...	...	...	...	...	...
B Crude petroleum and natural gas production	-	152	753	1397	4867	4526	1631	2094	1788	1166	...	...
C Metal ore mining	...	...	...	...	...	...	...	...	...	...	...	...
D Other mining	34	45	85	87	105	59	93	111	214	149	...	...
3 Manufacturing	3622	5492	9262	8761	9247	10094	13509	18032	20942	19737	18485	19937
A Manufacturing of food, beverages and tobacco	753	1453	2204	2038	2005	2180	3016	3253	3723	3859	...	...
B Textile, wearing apparel and leather industries	285	186	282	283	361	405	607	719	902	771	...	...
C Manufacture of wood, and wood products, including furniture	237	206	464	385	378	450	791	1265	1204	976	...	...
D Manufacture of paper and paper products, printing and publishing	333	392	604	771	828	1143	1239	1960	2673	2590	...	...
E Manufacture of chemicals and chemical petroleum, coal, rubber and plastic products	588	763	1669	1257	1598	1788	2341	2879	3276	3159	...	...
F Manufacture of non-metalic mineral products except products of petroleum and coal	461	366	901	1110	741	481	762	1407	1513	1686	...	...
G Basic metal industries	48	422	244	162	139	175	178	216	234	202	...	...
H Manufacture of fabricated metal products, machinery and equipment	891	1662	2774	2657	3115	3367	4423	6118	6951	5980	...	...
I Other manufacturing industries	26	42	120	98	81	106	152	216	465	515	...	...
4 Electricity, gas and water	1119	1623	2932	4090	6465	6421	5733	6859	7980	7650	8190	9193
5 Construction	1004	1098	1878	1609	1781	2110	2924	4659	4751	4091	2869	3011
6 Wholesale and retail trade, restaurants and hotels	1397	1712	3066	2377	2899	3770	5090	6062	8524	8327	...	...
A Wholesale and retail trade	1397	1712	3066	2377	2899	3770	5090	6062	8524	8327	...	...
B Restaurants and hotels	...	...	...	...	...	...	...	...	...	...	...	...
7 Transport, storage and communication	3104	5510	8256	9155	10734	9190	11279	13975	19605	17895	...	...
A Transport and storage	2302	4081	5918	6776	8220	6792	8572	10767	15642	13421	...	...
B Communication	802	1430	2339	2379	2514	2398	2707	3208	3963	4474	...	...
8 Finance, insurance, real estate and business services	10187	15631	21891	18428	17962	22130	28102	28981	36219	37509	...	...
A Financial institutions	641	1138	2006	1877	1131	1768	2185	2318	2632	3488	...	...
B Insurance											...	...
C Real estate and business services	9546	14493	19885	16551	16831	20362	25917	26663	33587	34021	...	...
Real estate except dwellings	...	...	...	...	...	...	...	...	...	...	...	...

Denmark

2.11 Gross Fixed Capital Formation by Kind of Activity of Owner, ISIC Divisions, in Current Prices
(Continued)

Million Danish kroner

	1970	1975	1980	1981	1982	1983	1984	1985	1986	1987	1988	1989
Dwellings	9546	14493	19885	16551	16831	20362	25917	26663	33587	34021	...	...
9 Community, social and personal services	234	225	456	429	570	522	697	770	1076	1114	...	...
A Sanitary and similar services	...	...	...	...	...	...	...	...	...	...	...	...
B Social and related community services	...	...	...	...	...	...	...	...	...	...	...	...
C Recreational and cultural services	234	225	456	429	570	522	697	770	1076	1114	...	...
D Personal and household services	...	...	...	...	...	...	...	...	...	...	...	...
Statistical discrepancy	1513	1927	3658	1578	3366	7541	10079	11453	15652	18175	...	...
Total Industries	23671	37420	57526	51776	62631	71062	85385	101106	124304	122318	117631	123599
Producers of Government Services	5612	8167	12785	12040	11983	10987	11867	14086	14066	15715	17143	17723
Private Non-Profit Institutions Serving Households	...	...	...	...	...	...	...	...	...	...	...	...
Total	29283	45587	70311	63816	74614	82049	97252	115192	138370	138033	134774	141322

2.12 Gross Fixed Capital Formation by Kind of Activity of Owner, ISIC Divisions, in Constant Prices

Million Danish kroner

	1970	1975	1980	1981	1982	1983	1984	1985	1986	1987	1988	1989
					At constant prices of:1980							
					All Producers							
1 Agriculture, hunting, forestry and fishing	3605	6027	5289	3494	3731	3433	4327	5461	4841	3995	3543	4050
A Agriculture and hunting	3180	5377	4895	3171	3386	3019	3762	4649	4251	3469	...	...
B Forestry and logging	52	70	99	93	126	80	69	105	96	86	...	...
C Fishing	374	580	295	231	219	334	496	707	494	440	...	...
2 Mining and quarrying	85	309	838	1201	3824	3393	1115	1400	1320	823	632	759
A Coal mining	...	...	...	...	...	...	...	...	...	...	...	...
B Crude petroleum and natural gas production	-	243	753	1124	3739	3347	1044	1319	1171	722	...	...
C Metal ore mining	...	...	...	...	...	...	...	...	...	...	...	...
D Other mining	85	66	85	77	85	46	70	82	149	100	...	...
3 Manufacturing	8528	8032	9262	7754	7461	7559	9607	12250	13664	12324	11188	11552
A Manufacturing of food, beverages and tobacco	1755	2085	2204	1807	1613	1609	2097	2167	2416	2367	...	...
B Textile, wearing apparel and leather industries	631	264	282	249	295	305	437	494	602	498	...	...
C Manufacture of wood, and wood products, including furniture	578	304	464	337	297	329	570	879	817	650	...	...
D Manufacture of paper and paper products, printing and publishing	839	603	604	693	649	857	822	1229	1559	1443	...	...
E Manufacture of chemicals and chemical petroleum, coal, rubber and plastic products	1389	1122	1669	1092	1292	1346	1673	1958	2150	1946	...	...
F Manufacture of non-metalic mineral products except products of petroleum and coal	1076	540	901	980	596	357	567	1001	1016	1069	...	...
G Basic metal industries	108	618	244	144	113	126	117	139	139	118	...	...
H Manufacture of fabricated metal products, machinery and equipment	2091	2436	2774	2366	2541	2551	3214	4239	4662	3913	...	...
I Other manufacturing industries	62	60	120	85	65	80	109	146	301	320	...	...
4 Electricity, gas and water	3024	2488	2932	3570	5139	4787	4038	4635	5446	4900	4958	5278
5 Construction	2431	1638	1878	1442	1473	1668	2182	3306	3202	2650	1810	1818
6 Wholesale and retail trade, restaurants and hotels	3123	2459	3066	2170	2446	2939	3760	4258	5720	5426	...	...
A Wholesale and retail trade	3123	2459	3066	2170	2446	2939	3760	4258	5720	5426	...	...
B Restaurants and hotels	...	...	...	...	...	...	...	...	...	...	...	...
7 Transport, storage and communication	8025	8806	8256	8186	9261	7022	8318	9343	13233	11768	...	...
A Transport and storage	5658	6499	5918	6021	7125	5207	6364	7098	10262	8579	...	...

Denmark

2.12 Gross Fixed Capital Formation by Kind of Activity of Owner, ISIC Divisions, in Constant Prices
(Continued)

Million Danish kroner

	1970	1975	1980	1981	1982	1983	1984	1985	1986	1987	1988	1989
				At constant prices of: 1980								
B Communication	2367	2307	2339	2165	2136	1815	1954	2245	2971	3189	...	...
8 Finance, insurance, real estate and business services	26963	23556	21891	16523	14539	16556	19865	19597	23442	23290	...	...
A Financial institutions	1447	1547	2006	1744	1010	1454	1694	1801	1870	2405	...	...
B Insurance											...	...
C Real estate and business services	25516	22009	19885	14779	13529	15102	18171	17796	21572	20885	...	...
Real estate except dwellings	...	...	...	...	...	...	...	...	...	...	...	...
Dwellings	25516	22009	19885	14779	13529	15102	18171	17796	21572	20885	...	...
9 Community, social and personal services	491	291	456	396	479	418	548	584	799	834	...	...
A Sanitary and similar services	...	...	...	...	...	...	...	...	...	...	...	...
B Social and related community services	...	...	...	...	...	...	...	...	...	...	...	...
C Recreational and cultural services	491	291	456	396	479	418	548	584	799	834	...	...
D Personal and household services	...	...	...	...	...	...	...	...	...	...	...	...
Statistical discrepancy	3088	2631	3658	1458	2854	5979	7787	8557	11257	12840	...	...
Total Industries	59364	56238	57526	46194	51207	53754	61545	69390	82924	78849	72685	73063
Producers of Government Services	16643	13709	12785	10604	9615	8193	8385	9324	9252	9854	10173	9997
Private Non-Profit Institutions Serving Households	...	...	...	...	...	...	...	...	...	...	...	...
Total	76007	69947	70311	56798	60822	61947	69930	78714	92176	88703	82858	83060

2.17 Exports and Imports of Goods and Services, Detail

Million Danish kroner

	1970	1975	1980	1981	1982	1983	1984	1985	1986	1987	1988	1989
				Exports of Goods and Services								
1 Exports of merchandise, f.o.b.	25254	50201	96161	115104	130545	147474	166117	180090	171723	175132	186314	208664
2 Transport and communication	4617	8681	16350	22030	24437	22868	25071	26339	22213	22076	27534	33737
A In respect of merchandise imports	185	120	160	200	200	200	230	270	255	260	322	285
B Other	4432	8561	16190	21830	24237	22668	24841	26069	21958	21816	27212	33452
3 Insurance service charges	19	17	-122	-115	-11	-490	-1001	-1032	-1008	-877	-900	-814
4 Other commodities	404	943	1500	1460	1490	2825	1740	3887	4938	6772	6228	5972
5 Adjustments of merchandise exports to change-of-ownership basis	...	...	...	...	...	...	...	...	...	...	...	...
6 Direct purchases in the domestic market by non-residential households	2809	5207	8367	10563	12462	13634	15596	16282	15693	16981	18533	18852
7 Direct purchases in the domestic market by extraterritorial bodies	...	...	...	...	...	...	...	...	...	...	...	...
Total Exports of Goods and Services	33103	65049	122256	149042	168924	186311	207523	225566	213559	220084	237709	266411
				Imports of Goods and Services								
1 Imports of merchandise, c.i.f.	33101	59805	109673	124688	139812	148896	171826	191282	184388	173651	176047	195786
A Imports of merchandise, f.o.b. [a]	31051	57335	105313	119888	134612	143396	165426	184232	177578	167205	169461	188487
B Transport of services on merchandise imports	2050	2470	4360	4800	5200	5500	6400	7050	6810	6446	6586	7299
By residents	185	120	160	200	200	200	230	270	255	260	322	285

Denmark

2.17 Exports and Imports of Goods and Services, Detail
(Continued)

Million Danish kroner

	1970	1975	1980	1981	1982	1983	1984	1985	1986	1987	1988	1989
By non-residents	1865	2350	4200	4600	5000	5300	6170	6780	6555	6185	6264	7014
C Insurance service charges on merchandise imports [a]	...	...	...	...	...	...	...	...	...	...	...	...
2 Adjustments of merchandise imports to change-of-ownership basis	...	...	...	...	...	...	...	...	...	...	...	...
3 Other transport and communication	1510	3360	7679	11850	13990	13864	14978	16064	13935	14012	17955	21697
4 Other insurance service charges	...	...	...	...	...	...	...	...	...	...	...	...
5 Other commodities	41	254	451	720	2526	2791	1488	1690	1143	753	593	797
6 Direct purchases abroad by government	...	...	...	...	...	...	...	...	...	...	...	...
7 Direct purchases abroad by resident households	2009	3661	8402	8792	10600	10589	12116	14444	17089	18810	20502	20787
Total Imports of Goods and Services	36661	67081	126205	146050	166928	176140	200408	223480	216555	207226	215097	239067
Balance of Goods and Services	-3558	-2032	-3949	2992	1996	10171	7115	2086	-2996	12858	22612	27344
Total Imports and Balance of Goods and Services	33103	65049	122256	149042	168924	186311	207523	225566	213559	220084	237709	266411

a) Item 'Insurance service charges in respect of merchandise imports' is included in item 'Import of merchandise, f.o.b.'.

4.1 Derivation of Value Added by Kind of Activity, in Current Prices

Million Danish kroner

	1980 Gross Output	1980 Intermediate Consumption	1980 Value Added	1981 Gross Output	1981 Intermediate Consumption	1981 Value Added	1982 Gross Output	1982 Intermediate Consumption	1982 Value Added	1983 Gross Output	1983 Intermediate Consumption	1983 Value Added
						All Producers						
1 Agriculture, hunting, forestry and fishing	39786	21967	17818	45619	24657	20962	53578	27309	26269	54245	29304	24940
A Agriculture and hunting	36252	20975	15276	41627	23529	18098	48908	25974	22935	49474	28040	21434
B Forestry and logging	699	5	694	782	17	765	1177	7	1170	1022	-20	1041
C Fishing	2835	987	1848	3210	1111	2099	3493	1328	2165	3749	1284	2464
2 Mining and quarrying	1119	746	373	2207	997	1209	4386	1180	3207	5350	2011	3339
A Coal mining	...	...	...	...	...	...	...	...	...	...	...	...
B Crude petroleum and natural gas production	419	388	31	1495	636	859	3572	768	2804	4442	1556	2886
C Metal ore mining	...	...	...	...	...	...	...	...	...	...	...	...
D Other mining	700	358	342	712	361	350	814	412	402	908	455	453
3 Manufacturing	198037	133727	64311	218025	150875	67149	241259	164996	76263	259679	173637	86043
A Manufacture of food, beverages and tobacco	70605	56238	14367	80162	64306	15856	86492	68737	17755	87498	67951	19547
B Textile, wearing apparel and leather industries	10279	6315	3964	11030	6768	4262	12591	7762	4829	13279	7998	5281
C Manufacture of wood and wood products, including furniture	8585	5536	3049	9713	6234	3479	10168	6533	3636	11934	7495	4439
D Manufacture of paper and paper products, printing and publishing	16383	9410	6974	17425	10541	6884	20159	12033	8126	22338	13458	8880
E Manufacture of chemicals and chemical petroleum, coal, rubber and plastic products	28907	21140	7768	33435	25268	8167	36289	27019	9270	40926	30130	10797
F Manufacture of non-metallic mineral products, except products of petroleum and coal	7679	4223	3456	7493	4247	3246	8278	4574	3704	8791	4870	3921
G Basic metal industries	3223	2283	940	3165	2340	825	3055	2172	883	3405	2331	1073
H Manufacture of fabricated metal products, machinery and equipment	50003	27402	22601	52849	29863	22985	61124	34711	26413	68207	37872	30335
I Other manufacturing industries	2373	1180	1193	2753	1308	1445	3103	1455	1647	3301	1532	1769
4 Electricity, gas and water	11932	7413	4520	13908	9224	4685	17104	10303	6800	16622	9333	7289
A Electricity, gas and steam	11258	7208	4050	13189	9017	4172	16264	10061	6203	15655	9094	6560
B Water works and supply	674	205	470	719	207	512	840	242	597	967	239	728
5 Construction	52148	27766	24383	49502	26961	22541	56178	31946	24232	60610	35690	24921
6 Wholesale and retail trade, restaurants and hotels	67559	22301	45257	73157	24055	49102	82733	26418	56315	93787	27894	65893
A Wholesale and retail trade	58003	16775	41228	62681	18039	44642	70825	19569	51256	80693	20417	60276
B Restaurants and hotels	9556	5526	4030	10476	6016	4460	11908	6849	5059	13094	7477	5617
7 Transport, storage and communication	48170	22271	25899	57872	28682	29190	66011	33607	32404	70583	35368	35216
A Transport and storage	41700	20258	21442	50695	26434	24260	57613	31020	26593	60593	32331	28263

Denmark

4.1 Derivation of Value Added by Kind of Activity, in Current Prices
(Continued)

Million Danish kroner

	1980 Gross Output	1980 Intermediate Consumption	1980 Value Added	1981 Gross Output	1981 Intermediate Consumption	1981 Value Added	1982 Gross Output	1982 Intermediate Consumption	1982 Value Added	1983 Gross Output	1983 Intermediate Consumption	1983 Value Added
B Communication	6470	2013	4457	7177	2248	4929	8398	2587	5811	9990	3037	6953
8 Finance, insurance, real estate and business services	73324	21020	52303	79436	23012	56424	89577	27469	62109	102645	31051	71595
A Financial institutions	12259	3508	8750	12199	3948	8251	13332	4364	8969	14624	5062	9562
B Insurance	2190	991	1200	2030	1165	865	2248	1311	937	2957	1574	1383
C Real estate and business services	58875	16521	42353	65207	17899	47308	73997	21794	52203	85064	24415	60650
Real estate, except dwellings	...	...	...	...	...	...	...	...	...	...	...	...
Dwellings	38956	10018	28938	43025	10809	32216	48219	13476	34743	53662	13901	39760
9 Community, social and personal services	23684	7454	16229	26459	8375	18084	29592	9648	19945	32473	10792	21682
A Sanitary and similar services	...	...	...	...	...	...	...	...	...	...	...	...
B Social and related community services	5356	852	4504	5888	962	4925	6486	1111	5376	6925	1216	5709
Educational services	434	119	315	462	129	333	501	145	356	543	154	389
Medical, dental, other health and veterinary services	4922	733	4189	5426	833	4592	5985	966	5020	6382	1062	5320
C Recreational and cultural services	3551	554	2996	4307	701	3606	4452	761	3690	5049	935	4114
D Personal and household services	14777	6048	8729	16264	6712	9553	18654	7776	10879	20499	8641	11859
Total, Industries	515757	264663	251094	566183	296838	269346	640420	332877	307543	695994	355077	340918
Producers of Government Services	105241	32801	72440	119965	36754	83211	139166	41579	97587	149265	44055	105210
Other Producers	2577	292	2285	2676	307	2368	2869	333	2536	3149	370	2779
Total [a]	623574	297756	325818	688824	333899	354925	782455	374789	407665	848409	399502	448907
Less: Imputed bank service charge	...	-9830	9830	...	-9805	9805	...	-10253	10253	...	-11037	11037
Import duties	...	...	...	...	...	...	...	...	...	...	...	...
Value added tax	...	...	...	...	...	...	...	...	...	...	...	...
Other adjustments [b]	57797	...	57797	62671	...	62671	67054	...	67054	74671	...	74671
Total	681371	307586	373786	751495	343704	407791	849509	385042	464467	923080	410539	512541
Memorandum Item: Mineral fuels and power	23218	17685	5532	28199	21882	6316	33871	23509	10362	35530	24804	10726

	1984 Gross Output	1984 Intermediate Consumption	1984 Value Added	1985 Gross Output	1985 Intermediate Consumption	1985 Value Added	1986 Gross Output	1986 Intermediate Consumption	1986 Value Added	1987 Gross Output	1987 Intermediate Consumption	1987 Value Added
					All Producers							
1 Agriculture, hunting, forestry and fishing	61510	30508	31002	60811	30710	30100	59056	29051	30005	56415	29077	27338
A Agriculture and hunting	56432	28868	27564	55780	28854	26925	53953	27176	26777	51403	27219	24184
B Forestry and logging	1022	40	982	993	47	945	1057	41	1016	993	16	977
C Fishing	4056	1600	2456	4038	1809	2230	4046	1834	2212	4019	1842	2178
2 Mining and quarrying	6328	2172	4156	9192	3153	6039	7057	1730	5327	7321	1932	5389
A Coal mining	...	...	...	...	...	...	...	...	...	...	...	...
B Crude petroleum and natural gas production	5264	1667	3597	7961	2548	5413	5531	1272	4259	5803	1448	4355
C Metal ore mining	...	...	...	...	...	...	...	...	...	...	...	...
D Other mining	1064	505	559	1231	605	626	1526	458	1069	1518	484	1034

Denmark

4.1 Derivation of Value Added by Kind of Activity, in Current Prices
(Continued)

Million Danish kroner

	1984 Gross Output	1984 Intermediate Consumption	1984 Value Added	1985 Gross Output	1985 Intermediate Consumption	1985 Value Added	1986 Gross Output	1986 Intermediate Consumption	1986 Value Added	1987 Gross Output	1987 Intermediate Consumption	1987 Value Added
3 Manufacturing	295662	198159	97505	318521	213448	105073	321215	209513	111703	316251	202381	113869
A Manufacture of food, beverages and tobacco	94315	72872	21443	98517	75483	23033	98267	74026	24241	95317	70847	24470
B Textile, wearing apparel and leather industries	15552	9796	5756	16869	10733	6136	17653	11291	6362	17269	10939	6330
C Manufacture of wood and wood products, including furniture	14919	9380	5539	15409	9673	5737	16637	10354	6283	16299	10075	6223
D Manufacture of paper and paper products, printing and publishing	25656	15412	10244	28130	17311	10819	30954	18892	12062	32577	19732	12845
E Manufacture of chemicals and chemical petroleum, coal, rubber and plastic products	46863	35581	11282	48694	36100	12594	41764	28153	13611	42369	28138	14232
F Manufacture of non-metallic mineral products, except products of petroleum and coal	9767	5297	4470	10839	5963	4877	12548	6700	5848	12372	6434	5938
G Basic metal industries	4382	3122	1260	4458	3119	1338	4136	2784	1353	3668	2340	1327
H Manufacture of fabricated metal products, machinery and equipment	80322	44745	35577	91044	52629	38415	94197	54609	39588	91319	51326	39994
I Other manufacturing industries	3886	1954	1933	4561	2437	2124	5059	2704	2355	5061	2550	2511
4 Electricity, gas and water	16070	10199	5872	19398	12602	6796	20354	11846	8508	20797	11569	9228
A Electricity, gas and steam	15062	9934	5128	18310	12292	6018	19203	11507	7696	19627	11191	8436
B Water works and supply	1008	265	744	1088	310	778	1151	339	813	1170	378	792
5 Construction	68515	39875	28640	76506	45548	30958	90535	52849	37686	97883	54552	43331
6 Wholesale and retail trade, restaurants and hotels	102722	32063	70659	116760	35868	80892	127436	39085	88350	128962	41009	87952
A Wholesale and retail trade	88237	23856	64381	100473	26679	73794	109342	28838	80504	110211	30378	79833
B Restaurants and hotels	14485	8207	6278	16287	9189	7098	18094	10247	7847	18751	10631	8119
7 Transport, storage and communication	79713	39322	40391	86753	43533	43220	84967	40197	44770	90879	42863	48016
A Transport and storage	67438	35747	31691	73159	39286	33873	70262	34945	35317	73642	36092	37550
B Communication	12275	3575	8700	13594	4247	9347	14705	5252	9453	17237	6771	10466
8 Finance, insurance, real estate and business services	118454	35659	82796	130331	40336	89995	149249	48359	100890	162043	54812	107231
A Financial institutions	19253	5700	13553	21383	6793	14590	28401	8132	20269	28437	10128	18310
B Insurance	3565	1788	1778	3601	2245	1356	4419	2644	1775	5460	2312	3148
C Real estate and business services	95636	28171	67465	105347	31298	74049	116429	37583	78846	128146	42372	85774
Real estate, except dwellings	...	...	...	...	...	...	...	...	...	...	...	...
Dwellings	58459	15019	43440	62636	15670	46966	66826	18378	48448	72336	21025	51311
9 Community, social and personal services	35635	12060	23577	39084	13767	25317	42616	14842	27774	47577	17236	30342
A Sanitary and similar services	...	...	...	...	...	...	...	...	...	...	...	...
B Social and related community services	7147	1263	5884	7584	1349	6234	8180	1467	6712	8597	1571	7026
Educational services	609	172	437	640	190	450	693	205	488	754	238	516
Medical, dental, other health and veterinary services	6538	1091	5447	6944	1159	5784	7487	1262	6224	7843	1333	6510
C Recreational and cultural services	5692	1062	4630	6188	1423	4765	6859	1638	5221	7456	1710	5746
D Personal and household services	22796	9735	13062	25312	10995	14317	27577	11737	15840	31524	13955	17569
Total, Industries	784611	400014	384597	857355	438964	418391	902483	447469	455014	928130	455434	472697
Producers of Government Services	158768	49590	109178	168887	53657	115230	174715	54905	119810	192846	61076	131770
Other Producers	3557	435	3122	3881	481	3400	4257	555	3702	4640	631	4009
Total [a]	946935	450038	496897	1030120	493103	537021	1081460	502930	578526	1125620	517141	608476
Less: Imputed bank service charge	...	-15220	15220	...	-16504	16504	...	-22850	22850	...	-22530	22530
Import duties	...	...	...	...	...	...	...	...	...	...	...	...
Value added tax	...	...	...	...	...	...	...	...	...	...	...	...
Other adjustments [b]	83607	...	83607	94555	...	94555	110820	...	110820	113963	...	113963
Total	1030540	465258	565284	1124680	509607	615072	1192280	525780	666496	1239580	539671	699909
Memorandum Item: Mineral fuels and power	38056	28384	9673	43323	31026	12297	34177	21165	13011	34032	20462	13569

Denmark

4.1 Derivation of Value Added by Kind of Activity, in Current Prices

Million Danish kroner

	1988 Gross Output	1988 Intermediate Consumption	1988 Value Added	1989 Gross Output	1989 Intermediate Consumption	1989 Value Added
			All Producers			
1 Agriculture, hunting, forestry and fishing	58493	30366	28126	63591	31665	31926
A Agriculture and hunting	53337	28457	24880	58311	29578	28733
B Forestry and logging	1064	29	1034	1113	26	1087
C Fishing	4092	1880	2211	4167	2061	2106
2 Mining and quarrying	6389	1708	4681	8274	1966	6308
A Coal mining	...	...	...	...	...	...
B Crude petroleum and natural gas production	4867	1248	3619	6658	1536	5122
C Metal ore mining	...	...	...	...	...	...
D Other mining	1522	460	1062	1616	430	1186
3 Manufacturing	328435	209671	118765	351088	228709	122382
A Manufacture of food, beverages and tobacco	97884	71448	26436	101972	77603	24369
B Textile, wearing apparel and leather industries	16389	10393	5997	16557	10387	6170
C Manufacture of wood and wood products, including furniture	16853	10243	6610	18470	11574	6896
D Manufacture of paper and paper products, printing and publishing	34276	20830	13446	35467	21400	14068
E Manufacture of chemicals and chemical petroleum, coal, rubber and plastic products	44139	28786	15353	47633	31271	16362
F Manufacture of non-metallic mineral products, except products of petroleum and coal	12094	6289	5805	12604	6635	5969
G Basic metal industries	3955	2650	1305	4561	3098	1464
H Manufacture of fabricated metal products, machinery and equipment	97299	56162	41137	107620	63649	43971
I Other manufacturing industries	5546	2870	2676	6204	3092	3112
4 Electricity, gas and water	21219	11304	9914	23734	11714	12021
A Electricity, gas and steam	19772	10902	8870	22058	11251	10807
B Water works and supply	1447	402	1044	1676	463	1213
5 Construction	100025	55736	44289	100569	55514	45055
6 Wholesale and retail trade, restaurants and hotels	134342	43052	91289	140301	43308	96992
A Wholesale and retail trade	114384	31425	82958	119434	31924	87509
B Restaurants and hotels	19958	11627	8331	20867	11384	9483
7 Transport, storage and communication	101147	49877	51271	111411	55377	56033
A Transport and storage	82664	42047	40618	91526	47917	43608
B Communication	18483	7830	10653	19885	7460	12425
8 Finance, insurance, real estate and business services	174077	60606	113472	191228	63732	127495
A Financial institutions	28129	10772	17358	34200	12526	21674
B Insurance	6102	2336	3766	6582	2508	4074
C Real estate and business services	139846	47498	92348	150446	48698	101748
Real estate, except dwellings	...	...	...	...	...	...
Dwellings	78213	23198	55014	84298	23409	60889
9 Community, social and personal services	51540	18988	32552	55788	19924	35864
A Sanitary and similar services	...	...	...	...	...	...
B Social and related community services	9219	1741	7478	9649	1827	7822
Educational services	822	251	571	859	275	584
Medical, dental, other health and veterinary services	8397	1490	6907	8790	1552	7238
C Recreational and cultural services	7761	1828	5933	9437	2354	7083
D Personal and household services	34560	15419	19141	36702	15743	20959
Total, Industries	975668	481309	494358	1045980	511907	534076
Producers of Government Services	206786	63967	142819	214946	67041	147905

Denmark

4.1 Derivation of Value Added by Kind of Activity, in Current Prices
(Continued)

Million Danish kroner

	1988 Gross Output	1988 Intermediate Consumption	1988 Value Added	1989 Gross Output	1989 Intermediate Consumption	1989 Value Added
Other Producers	5108	810	4299	5583	879	4704
Total [a]	1187560	546086	641476	1266510	579827	686685
Less: Imputed bank service charge	...	-21215	21215	...	-25794	25794
Import duties	...	...	...	...	...	...
Value added tax	...	...	...	...	...	...
Other adjustments [b]	115258	...	115258	115124	...	115124
Total	1302820	567301	735519	1381640	605621	776015
Memorandum Item: Mineral fuels and power	32026	18849	13177	38585	21692	16893

a) Gross domestic product in factor values.
b) Item 'Other adjustments' refers to indirect taxes net of subsidies.

4.2 Derivation of Value Added by Kind of Activity, in Constant Prices

Million Danish kroner

At constant prices of: 1980

All Producers

		1980 GO	1980 IC	1980 VA	1981 GO	1981 IC	1981 VA	1982 GO	1982 IC	1982 VA	1983 GO	1983 IC	1983 VA
1	Agriculture, hunting, forestry and fishing	39786	21967	17818	40664	21371	19294	43184	21955	21228	41922	22518	19404
	A Agriculture and hunting	36252	20975	15276	37107	20477	16630	39159	20960	18198	38059	21578	16481
	B Forestry and logging	699	5	694	737	4	734	1146	36	1110	932	12	920
	C Fishing	2835	987	1848	2820	890	1931	2879	959	1920	2931	928	2002
2	Mining and quarrying	1119	746	373	1761	814	948	3156	885	2271	3933	1425	2508
	A Coal mining	...	...	...	...	...	...	...	...	...	...	...	...
	B Crude petroleum and natural gas production	419	388	31	1137	506	632	2515	565	1950	3268	1110	2158
	C Metal ore mining	...	...	...	...	...	...	...	...	...	...	...	...
	D Other mining	700	358	342	624	308	316	641	320	321	665	315	350
3	Manufacturing	198037	133727	64311	193795	131528	62267	193818	130560	63257	198024	130511	67510
	A Manufacture of food, beverages and tobacco	70605	56238	14367	71225	56496	14729	69097	54402	14695	67765	52063	15701
	B Textile, wearing apparel and leather industries	10279	6315	3964	10112	6178	3933	10562	6603	3959	10511	6219	4291
	C Manufacture of wood and wood products, including furniture	8585	5536	3049	8682	5633	3049	8476	5483	2993	9318	5731	3586
	D Manufacture of paper and paper products, printing and publishing	16383	9410	6974	15578	9278	6301	16288	9700	6588	16816	10239	6577
	E Manufacture of chemicals and chemical petroleum, coal, rubber and plastic products	28907	21140	7768	27839	20352	7486	27586	20124	7462	30083	21559	8524
	F Manufacture of non-metallic mineral products, except products of petroleum and coal	7679	4223	3456	6518	3476	3042	6417	3408	3009	6363	3388	2974
	G Basic metal industries	3223	2283	940	2990	2168	821	2523	1868	655	2683	1844	839
	H Manufacture of fabricated metal products, machinery and equipment	50003	27402	22601	48324	26733	21591	50246	27727	22519	51937	28293	23644
	I Other manufacturing industries	2373	1180	1193	2527	1214	1313	2623	1245	1378	2548	1175	1373
4	Electricity, gas and water	11932	7413	4520	10402	6219	4183	11296	6327	4970	11070	5916	5153
	A Electricity, gas and steam	11258	7208	4050	9734	6048	3686	10601	6151	4451	10370	5752	4617
	B Water works and supply	674	205	470	668	171	497	695	176	520	700	164	535
5	Construction	52148	27766	24383	44016	23846	20169	44467	25394	19073	44761	26262	18499
6	Wholesale and retail trade, restaurants and hotels	67559	22301	45257	65563	21405	44158	68183	21462	46721	70650	21540	49110
	A Wholesale and retail trade	58003	16775	41228	55961	15957	40004	58298	15834	42464	60626	15733	44893
	B Restaurants and hotels	9556	5526	4030	9602	5448	4154	9885	5628	4257	10024	5807	4216
7	Transport, storage and communication	48170	22271	25899	50188	23973	26215	51599	25757	25842	50869	25337	25532
	A Transport and storage	41700	20258	21442	43695	22016	21679	44896	23739	21157	44060	23092	20968
	B Communication	6470	2013	4457	6493	1957	4535	6703	2018	4685	6809	2245	4564
8	Finance, insurance, real estate and business services	73324	21020	52303	72689	20900	51790	73830	22134	51697	77065	23295	53771
	A Financial institutions	12259	3508	8750	10996	3532	7464	10848	3518	7331	11143	3794	7349

Denmark

4.2 Derivation of Value Added by Kind of Activity, in Constant Prices
(Continued)

Million Danish kroner

	1980			1981			1982			1983		
	Gross Output	Intermediate Consumption	Value Added	Gross Output	Intermediate Consumption	Value Added	Gross Output	Intermediate Consumption	Value Added	Gross Output	Intermediate Consumption	Value Added
At constant prices of: 1980												
B Insurance	2190	991	1200	1866	1035	831	1896	1042	854	2256	1151	1105
C Real estate and business services	58875	16521	42353	59827	16333	43495	61086	17574	43512	63666	18350	45317
Real estate, except dwellings	...	...	...	...	...	...	...	...	...	...	...	...
Dwellings	38956	10018	28938	39560	9946	29614	39953	10829	29124	40253	10519	29734
9 Community, social and personal services	23684	7454	16229	23648	7446	16201	23906	7693	16212	24159	7993	16166
A Sanitary and similar services	...	...	...	...	...	...	...	...	...	...	...	...
B Social and related community services	5356	852	4504	5335	853	4481	5369	891	4477	5321	909	4412
Educational services	434	119	315	430	113	317	429	110	318	428	115	313
Medical, dental, other health and veterinary services	4922	733	4189	4905	740	4164	4940	781	4159	4893	794	4099
C Recreational and cultural services	3551	554	2996	3924	654	3270	3720	651	3069	3782	736	3045
D Personal and household services	14777	6048	8729	14389	5939	8450	14817	6151	8665	15056	6348	8709
Total, Industries	515757	264663	251094	502726	257500	245226	513439	262167	251272	522452	264799	257652
Producers of Government Services	105241	32801	72440	108448	32355	76093	112012	32354	79659	112057	31982	80074
Other Producers	2577	292	2285	2390	276	2115	2278	269	2010	2383	278	2106
Total [a]	623574	297756	325818	613564	290130	323433	627730	294790	332940	636891	297059	339832
Less: Imputed bank service charge	...	-9830	9830	...	-8838	8838	...	-8343	8343	...	-8410	8410
Import duties	...	...	...	...	...	...	...	...	...	...	...	...
Value added tax	...	...	...	...	...	...	...	...	...	...	...	...
Other adjustments [b]	57797	...	57797	55864	...	55864	57049	...	57049	59836	...	59836
Total	681371	307586	373786	669428	298968	370460	684779	303133	381647	696727	305469	391258
Memorandum Item: Mineral fuels and power	23218	17685	5532	20861	15458	5404	22909	15336	7573	24629	16434	8195

	1984			1985			1986			1987		
	Gross Output	Intermediate Consumption	Value Added	Gross Output	Intermediate Consumption	Value Added	Gross Output	Intermediate Consumption	Value Added	Gross Output	Intermediate Consumption	Value Added
At constant prices of: 1980												
All Producers												
1 Agriculture, hunting, forestry and fishing	45557	22268	23289	46105	22914	23191	45107	22739	22368	45144	23833	21311
A Agriculture and hunting	41775	21170	20606	42334	21741	20593	41509	21329	20180	41608	22413	19196
B Forestry and logging	818	7	811	722	1	722	709	6	703	677	-4	680
C Fishing	2964	1091	1873	3049	1172	1876	2889	1404	1485	2859	1424	1435
2 Mining and quarrying	4406	1281	3125	6745	1754	4991	8937	1096	7841	11273	1199	10074
A Coal mining	...	...	...	...	...	...	...	...	...	...	...	...
B Crude petroleum and natural gas production	3668	938	2730	5925	1347	4578	7959	778	7180	10340	866	9474
C Metal ore mining	...	...	...	...	...	...	...	...	...	...	...	...
D Other mining	738	343	395	820	407	413	978	318	661	933	333	601

Denmark

4.2 Derivation of Value Added by Kind of Activity, in Constant Prices
(Continued)

Million Danish kroner

		1984			1985			1986			1987		
		Gross Output	Intermediate Consumption	Value Added	Gross Output	Intermediate Consumption	Value Added	Gross Output	Intermediate Consumption	Value Added	Gross Output	Intermediate Consumption	Value Added
					At constant prices of: 1980								
3	Manufacturing	209998	139323	70673	219271	146352	72920	227611	154687	72920	221655	151721	69933
	A Manufacture of food, beverages and tobacco	67927	52312	15614	71017	54254	16763	74076	56290	17786	72836	55576	17260
	B Textile, wearing apparel and leather industries	11629	7083	4546	12003	7336	4668	12139	7728	4410	11650	7671	3978
	C Manufacture of wood and wood products, including furniture	10793	6635	4157	10537	6399	4138	10867	6830	4036	10332	6617	3715
	D Manufacture of paper and paper products, printing and publishing	17895	10798	7097	18338	11367	6971	19538	12278	7259	19512	12490	7022
	E Manufacture of chemicals and chemical petroleum, coal, rubber and plastic products	31694	23531	8163	32191	23708	8483	34352	25873	8479	35165	26345	8820
	F Manufacture of non-metallic mineral products, except products of petroleum and coal	6684	3574	3109	6988	3903	3085	7895	4535	3360	7622	4495	3127
	G Basic metal industries	3191	2233	958	3146	2155	991	3073	2205	868	2779	1926	853
	H Manufacture of fabricated metal products, machinery and equipment	57387	31732	25656	61961	35517	26444	62299	37014	25285	58554	34785	23769
	I Other manufacturing industries	2798	1425	1373	3090	1713	1377	3372	1934	1438	3205	1816	1389
4	Electricity, gas and water	11519	6275	5244	13977	7913	6064	15355	8826	6528	15714	9359	6356
	A Electricity, gas and steam	10827	6094	4733	13278	7707	5571	14643	8607	6035	15012	9079	5933
	B Water works and supply	692	181	510	699	206	493	712	219	493	702	280	422
5	Construction	47986	27863	20124	51313	29881	21431	59650	34164	25486	60816	34242	26573
6	Wholesale and retail trade, restaurants and hotels	73337	23509	49828	78536	25019	53516	83702	27156	56545	84299	27193	57106
	A Wholesale and retail trade	63059	17484	45575	67608	18476	49131	72086	19815	52270	72729	19711	53018
	B Restaurants and hotels	10278	6025	4253	10928	6543	4385	11616	7341	4275	11570	7482	4088
7	Transport, storage and communication	52641	25915	26726	54250	27774	26477	56178	29362	26816	60838	30490	30349
	A Transport and storage	44795	23411	21384	45850	24919	20932	47079	25818	21260	50030	26186	23845
	B Communication	7846	2504	5342	8400	2855	5546	9099	3544	5556	10808	4304	6504
8	Finance, insurance, real estate and business services	83643	25273	58369	87131	27101	60030	95386	31094	64293	97698	32566	65132
	A Financial institutions	13970	3997	9972	14656	4480	10176	19006	5171	13835	18125	6028	12096
	B Insurance	2556	1224	1331	2430	1417	1013	2786	1645	1142	3220	1360	1860
	C Real estate and business services	67117	20052	47065	70045	21204	48841	73594	24278	49316	76353	25178	51176
	Real estate, except dwellings	...	...	...	...	...	...	...	...	...	...	...	...
	Dwellings	40735	10821	29914	41175	10861	30314	41613	11994	29619	42147	12160	29986
9	Community, social and personal services	24946	8590	16357	26041	9346	16695	27580	9885	17695	28247	10998	17248
	A Sanitary and similar services	...	...	...	...	...	...	...	...	...	...	...	...
	B Social and related community services	5088	913	4176	5223	934	4289	5446	987	4460	5341	999	4342
	Educational services	451	128	323	445	136	309	452	144	308	447	151	296
	Medical, dental, other health and veterinary services	4637	785	3853	4778	798	3980	4994	843	4152	4894	848	4046
	C Recreational and cultural services	4108	810	3298	4279	986	3293	4667	1088	3579	4803	1155	3648
	D Personal and household services	15750	6867	8883	16539	7426	9113	17467	7810	9657	18103	8844	9258
Total, Industries		554033	280298	273735	583370	298054	285316	619504	319011	300493	625683	321601	304083
Producers of Government Services		114088	34214	79874	116911	35297	81615	118471	35521	82950	121219	37821	83398
Other Producers		2525	307	2218	2637	328	2309	2759	358	2401	2780	377	2403
Total [a]		670646	314819	355827	702918	333678	369240	740733	354889	385844	749682	359799	389884
Less: Imputed bank service charge		...	-11043	11043	...	-11312	11312	...	-15291	15291	...	-14359	14359
Import duties		...	...	...	...	...	...	...	...	...	...	...	...
Value added tax		...	...	...	...	...	...	...	...	...	...	...	...
Other adjustments [b]		63649	...	63649	68021	...	68021	70916	...	70916	67240	...	67240
Total		734295	325862	408433	770939	344990	425949	811649	370180	441469	816922	374158	442765
Memorandum Item: Mineral fuels and power		26064	17410	8654	30443	19133	11311	35104	20785	14319	37770	21324	16445

Denmark

4.2 Derivation of Value Added by Kind of Activity, in Constant Prices

Million Danish kroner

		1988			1989		
		Gross Output	Intermediate Consumption	Value Added	Gross Output	Intermediate Consumption	Value Added
		\multicolumn{6}{c}{At constant prices of: 1980}					
		\multicolumn{6}{c}{All Producers}					
1	Agriculture, hunting, forestry and fishing	46163	23560	22603	47534	23598	23935
	A Agriculture and hunting	42851	22280	20571	43939	22227	21711
	B Forestry and logging	720	6	714	676	-4	680
	C Fishing	2592	1274	1318	2919	1375	1544
2	Mining and quarrying	11433	1061	10372	12591	1028	11564
	A Coal mining	...	...	...	...	...	...
	B Crude petroleum and natural gas production	10527	772	9755	11703	771	10932
	C Metal ore mining	...	...	...	...	...	...
	D Other mining	906	289	617	888	257	632
3	Manufacturing	220301	150085	70212	222863	151785	71078
	A Manufacture of food, beverages and tobacco	71839	54833	17006	71250	54594	16657
	B Textile, wearing apparel and leather industries	10873	7075	3798	10575	6894	3681
	C Manufacture of wood and wood products, including furniture	10172	6377	3794	10432	6531	3902
	D Manufacture of paper and paper products, printing and publishing	19141	12158	6982	18595	11724	6870
	E Manufacture of chemicals and chemical petroleum, coal, rubber and plastic products	35306	25768	9537	35552	26129	9423
	F Manufacture of non-metallic mineral products, except products of petroleum and coal	7003	4056	2947	7019	4116	2902
	G Basic metal industries	2842	1900	942	2982	2049	933
	H Manufacture of fabricated metal products, machinery and equipment	59738	35919	23818	62821	37724	25097
	I Other manufacturing industries	3387	1999	1388	3637	2024	1614
4	Electricity, gas and water	15723	9388	6335	15393	8661	6733
	A Electricity, gas and steam	14996	9082	5914	14677	8379	6298
	B Water works and supply	727	306	421	716	282	435
5	Construction	58554	33250	25304	55978	31142	24836
6	Wholesale and retail trade, restaurants and hotels	85074	27270	57805	86357	27334	59023
	A Wholesale and retail trade	73264	19661	53603	74410	19608	54802
	B Restaurants and hotels	11810	7609	4202	11947	7726	4221
7	Transport, storage and communication	64609	31937	32672	67425	34126	33298
	A Transport and storage	53866	27600	26266	56735	29989	26746
	B Communication	10743	4337	6406	10690	4137	6552
8	Finance, insurance, real estate and business services	97907	33084	64823	101823	33123	68700
	A Financial institutions	17027	5667	11360	19633	6330	13303
	B Insurance	3357	1241	2116	3444	1255	2189
	C Real estate and business services	77523	26176	51347	78746	25538	53208
	Real estate, except dwellings	...	...	...	...	...	...
	Dwellings	42654	12785	29869	43022	12254	30768
9	Community, social and personal services	28649	11073	17576	29260	11044	18216
	A Sanitary and similar services	...	...	...	...	...	...
	B Social and related community services	5267	991	4276	5283	989	4294
	Educational services	452	144	308	447	151	296
	Medical, dental, other health and veterinary services	4815	847	3968	4836	838	3998
	C Recreational and cultural services	4823	1114	3709	5514	1281	4232
	D Personal and household services	18559	8968	9591	18463	8774	9689

Denmark

4.2 Derivation of Value Added by Kind of Activity, in Constant Prices
(Continued)

Million Danish kroner

	1988			1989		
	Gross Output	Intermediate Consumption	Value Added	Gross Output	Intermediate Consumption	Value Added
	At constant prices of: 1980					
Total, Industries	628411	320709	307701	639224	321840	317384
Producers of Government Services	121291	37222	84068	120580	36990	83590
Other Producers	2880	403	2477	3033	423	2610
Total a	752582	358334	394247	762836	359252	403584
Less: Imputed bank service charge	...	-13468	13468	...	-15579	15579
Import duties	...	...	...	...	...	...
Value added tax	...	...	...	...	...	...
Other adjustments b	64302	...	64302	62203	...	62203
Total	816884	371802	445080	825039	374831	450208
Memorandum Item: Mineral fuels and power	36691	20174	16517	38670	20359	18310

a) Gross domestic product in factor values.
b) Item 'Other adjustments' refers to indirect taxes net of subsidies.

4.3 Cost Components of Value Added

Million Danish kroner

	1980						1981					
	Compensation of Employees	Capital Consumption	Net Operating Surplus	Indirect Taxes	Less: Subsidies Received	Value Added	Compensation of Employees	Capital Consumption	Net Operating Surplus	Indirect Taxes	Less: Subsidies Received	Value Added
	All Producers											
1 Agriculture, hunting, forestry and fishing	3433	...	14386	...	...	17818	3700	...	17263	...	...	20962
A Agriculture and hunting	2272	...	13005	...	...	15276	2401	...	15698	...	...	18098
B Forestry and logging	433	...	262	...	...	694	497	...	269	...	...	765
C Fishing	728	...	1119	...	...	1848	802	...	1296	...	...	2099
2 Mining and quarrying	261	...	112	...	...	373	334	...	876	...	...	1209
A Coal mining	...	...	...	...	...	...	...	...	...	...	...	...
B Crude petroleum and natural gas production	101	...	-70	...	...	31	187	...	672	...	...	859
C Metal ore mining	...	...	...	...	...	...	...	...	...	...	...	...
D Other mining	160	...	182	...	...	342	147	...	204	...	...	350
3 Manufacturing	47647	...	16664	...	...	64311	49979	...	17172	...	...	67149
A Manufacture of food, beverages and tobacco	9201	...	5166	...	...	14367	10098	...	5758	...	...	15856
B Textile, wearing apparel and leather industries	2824	...	1140	...	...	3964	2945	...	1318	...	...	4262
C Manufacture of wood and wood products, including furniture	2474	...	575	...	...	3049	2682	...	798	...	...	3479
D Manufacture of paper and paper products, printing and publishing	5870	...	1103	...	...	6974	5869	...	1015	...	...	6884
E Manufacture of chemicals and chemical petroleum, coal, rubber and plastic products	4474	...	3294	...	...	7768	4782	...	3385	...	...	8167
F Manufacture of non-metallic mineral products, except products of petroleum and coal	2642	...	813	...	...	3456	2552	...	694	...	...	3246
G Basic metal industries	855	...	85	...	...	940	817	...	8	...	...	825
H Manufacture of fabricated metal products, machinery and equipment	18497	...	4105	...	...	22601	19387	...	3598	...	...	22985
I Other manufacturing industries	810	...	383	...	...	1193	847	...	598	...	...	1445
4 Electricity, gas and water	1847	...	2674	...	...	4520	2084	...	2601	...	...	4685
A Electricity, gas and steam	1588	...	2463	...	...	4050	1798	...	2375	...	...	4172
B Water works and supply	259	...	211	...	...	470	286	...	226	...	...	512
5 Construction	16902	...	7480	...	...	24383	15821	...	6720	...	...	22541
6 Wholesale and retail trade, restaurants and hotels	28985	...	16273	...	...	45257	29589	...	19513	...	...	49102
A Wholesale and retail trade	26197	...	15031	...	...	41228	26620	...	18022	...	...	44642
B Restaurants and hotels	2788	...	1242	...	...	4030	2969	...	1491	...	...	4460
7 Transport, storage and communication	15493	...	10406	...	...	25899	17219	...	11971	...	...	29190
A Transport and storage	11831	...	9611	...	...	21442	13177	...	11084	...	...	24260

Denmark

4.3 Cost Components of Value Added
(Continued)

Million Danish kroner

1980 / 1981

	Compensation of Employees	Capital Consumption	Net Operating Surplus	Indirect Taxes	Less: Subsidies Received	Value Added	Compensation of Employees	Capital Consumption	Net Operating Surplus	Indirect Taxes	Less: Subsidies Received	Value Added
B Communication	3662	...	795	...	...	4457	4042	...	887	...	...	4929
8 Finance, insurance, real estate and business services	18008	...	34296	...	...	52303	20175	...	36248	...	...	56424
A Financial institutions	6710	...	2041	...	...	8750	7584	...	667	...	...	8251
B Insurance	2281	...	-1082	...	...	1200	2624	...	-1760	...	...	865
C Real estate and business services	9017	...	33337	...	...	42353	9967	...	37341	...	...	47308
Real estate, except dwellings	...	...	...	...	...	...	...	...	...	...	...	...
Dwellings	1280	...	27658	...	...	28938	1325	...	30891	...	...	32216
9 Community, social and personal services	8417	...	7811	...	...	16229	8911	...	9172	...	...	18084
A Sanitary and similar services	...	...	...	...	...	...	...	...	...	...	...	...
B Social and related community services	1162	...	3341	...	...	4504	1272	...	3653	...	...	4925
Educational services	28	...	287	...	...	315	30	...	303	...	...	333
Medical, dental, other health and veterinary services	1134	...	3054	...	...	4189	1242	...	3350	...	...	4592
C Recreational and cultural services	1859	...	1137	...	...	2996	2064	...	1541	...	...	3606
D Personal and household services	5396	...	3333	...	...	8729	5575	...	3978	...	...	9553
Total, Industries a	140993	...	110101	...	...	251094	147812	...	121534	...	...	269346
Producers of Government Services	69515	...	2925	...	...	72440	79950	...	3261	...	...	83211
Other Producers	2214	...	70	...	...	2285	2294	...	74	...	...	2368
Total ba	212722	...	113096	...	...	325818	230056	...	124869	...	...	354925
Less: Imputed bank service charge	...	...	9830	...	...	9830	...	...	9805	...	...	9805
Import duties	...	...	...	...	...	...	...	...	...	...	...	...
Value added tax	...	...	...	...	...	...	...	...	...	...	...	...
Other adjustments	...	...	...	69591	11794	57797	...	...	...	75077	12406	62671
Total a	212722	...	103266	69591	11794	373786	230056	...	115064	75077	12406	407791

1982 / 1983

	Compensation of Employees	Capital Consumption	Net Operating Surplus	Indirect Taxes	Less: Subsidies Received	Value Added	Compensation of Employees	Capital Consumption	Net Operating Surplus	Indirect Taxes	Less: Subsidies Received	Value Added
					All Producers							
1 Agriculture, hunting, forestry and fishing	4050	...	22221	...	...	26269	4517	...	20423	...	...	24940
A Agriculture and hunting	2602	...	20333	...	...	22935	2922	...	18512	...	...	21434
B Forestry and logging	599	...	571	...	...	1170	618	...	423	...	...	1041
C Fishing	849	...	1317	...	...	2165	977	...	1488	...	...	2464
2 Mining and quarrying	378	...	2829	...	...	3207	376	...	2963	...	...	3339
A Coal mining	...	...	...	...	...	...	...	...	...	...	...	...
B Crude petroleum and natural gas production	211	...	2593	...	...	2804	188	...	2698	...	...	2886
C Metal ore mining	...	...	...	...	...	...	...	...	...	...	...	...
D Other mining	167	...	236	...	...	402	188	...	265	...	...	453

Denmark

4.3 Cost Components of Value Added
(Continued)

Million Danish kroner

	1982						1983					
	Compensation of Employees	Capital Consumption	Net Operating Surplus	Indirect Taxes	Less: Subsidies Received	Value Added	Compensation of Employees	Capital Consumption	Net Operating Surplus	Indirect Taxes	Less: Subsidies Received	Value Added
3 Manufacturing	55071	...	21191	...	...	76263	59887	...	26157	...	...	86043
A Manufacture of food, beverages and tobacco	11019	...	6736	...	...	17755	11959	...	7588	...	...	19547
B Textile, wearing apparel and leather industries	3383	...	1446	...	...	4829	3630	...	1651	...	...	5281
C Manufacture of wood and wood products, including furniture	2785	...	850	...	...	3636	3261	...	1178	...	...	4439
D Manufacture of paper and paper products, printing and publishing	6675	...	1451	...	...	8126	7134	...	1746	...	...	8880
E Manufacture of chemicals and chemical petroleum, coal, rubber and plastic products	5221	...	4049	...	...	9270	5655	...	5142	...	...	10797
F Manufacture of non-metallic mineral products, except products of petroleum and coal	2762	...	942	...	...	3704	2797	...	1124	...	...	3921
G Basic metal industries	805	...	78	...	...	883	837	...	237	...	...	1073
H Manufacture of fabricated metal products, machinery and equipment	21492	...	4921	...	...	26413	23598	...	6737	...	...	30335
I Other manufacturing industries	929	...	718	...	...	1647	1016	...	754	...	...	1769
4 Electricity, gas and water	2335	...	4465	...	...	6800	2580	...	4708	...	...	7289
A Electricity, gas and steam	2014	...	4189	...	...	6203	2245	...	4315	...	...	6560
B Water works and supply	321	...	276	...	...	597	335	...	393	...	...	728
5 Construction	16682	...	7550	...	...	24232	18273	...	6648	...	...	24921
6 Wholesale and retail trade, restaurants and hotels	32709	...	23606	...	...	56315	35726	...	30168	...	...	65893
A Wholesale and retail trade	29386	...	21870	...	...	51256	31812	...	28464	...	...	60276
B Restaurants and hotels	3323	...	1736	...	...	5059	3914	...	1704	...	...	5617
7 Transport, storage and communication	19671	...	12732	...	...	32404	21323	...	13892	...	...	35216
A Transport and storage	15061	...	11532	...	...	26593	16351	...	11911	...	...	28263
B Communication	4610	...	1200	...	...	5811	4972	...	1981	...	...	6953
8 Finance, insurance, real estate and business services	22726	...	39382	...	...	62109	25701	...	45894	...	...	71595
A Financial institutions	8603	...	366	...	...	8969	9587	...	-25	...	...	9562
B Insurance	2945	...	-2009	...	...	937	3266	...	-1883	...	...	1383
C Real estate and business services	11178	...	41025	...	...	52203	12848	...	47802	...	...	60650
Real estate, except dwellings	...	...	...	...	...	...	...	...	...	...	...	...
Dwellings	1537	...	33206	...	...	34743	1742	...	38018	...	...	39760
9 Community, social and personal services	10015	...	9930	...	...	19945	11106	...	10575	...	...	21682
A Sanitary and similar services	...	...	...	...	...	...	...	...	...	...	...	...
B Social and related community services	1392	...	3984	...	...	5376	1569	...	4140	...	...	5709
Educational services	32	...	324	...	...	356	35	...	354	...	...	389
Medical, dental, other health and veterinary services	1360	...	3660	...	...	5020	1534	...	3786	...	...	5320
C Recreational and cultural services	2355	...	1335	...	...	3690	2631	...	1483	...	...	4114
D Personal and household services	6268	...	4611	...	...	10879	6906	...	4952	...	...	11859
Total, Industries [a]	163636	...	143907	...	...	307543	179489	...	161429	...	...	340918
Producers of Government Services	93853	...	3734	...	...	97587	101183	...	4027	...	...	105210
Other Producers	2455	...	81	...	...	2536	2681	...	98	...	...	2779
Total [ba]	259944	...	147722	...	...	407665	283353	...	165554	...	...	448907
Less: Imputed bank service charge	...	...	10253	...	...	10253	...	...	11037	...	...	11037
Import duties	...	...	...	...	...	...	...	...	...	...	...	...
Value added tax	...	...	...	...	...	...	...	...	...	...	...	...
Other adjustments	...	...	...	82040	14986	67054	...	...	...	91426	16755	74671
Total [a]	259944	...	137469	82040	14986	464467	283353	...	154517	91426	16755	512541

Denmark

4.3 Cost Components of Value Added

Million Danish kroner

		1984					1985				
	Compensation of Employees	Capital Consumption	Net Operating Surplus	Indirect Taxes	Less: Subsidies Received	Value Added	Compensation of Employees	Capital Consumption	Net Operating Surplus	Indirect Taxes	Less: Subsidies Received	Value Added

All Producers

	Compensation of Employees	Capital Consumption	Net Operating Surplus	Indirect Taxes	Less: Subsidies Received	Value Added	Compensation of Employees	Capital Consumption	Net Operating Surplus	Indirect Taxes	Less: Subsidies Received	Value Added
1 Agriculture, hunting, forestry and fishing	5007	...	25995	...	...	31002	5220	...	24880	...	...	30100
A Agriculture and hunting	3372	...	24192	...	...	27564	3682	...	23244	...	...	26925
B Forestry and logging	606	...	376	...	...	982	555	...	390	...	...	945
C Fishing	1029	...	1427	...	...	2456	983	...	1246	...	...	2230
2 Mining and quarrying	464	...	3691	...	...	4156	487	...	5552	...	...	6039
A Coal mining	...	...	...	...	...	...	...	...	...	...	...	...
B Crude petroleum and natural gas production	263	...	3334	...	...	3597	263	...	5150	...	...	5413
C Metal ore mining	...	...	...	...	...	...	...	...	...	...	...	...
D Other mining	201	...	357	...	...	559	224	...	402	...	...	626
3 Manufacturing	66616	...	30888	...	...	97505	72922	...	32149	...	...	105073
A Manufacture of food, beverages and tobacco	12743	...	8700	...	...	21443	13337	...	9696	...	...	23033
B Textile, wearing apparel and leather industries	4106	...	1650	...	...	5756	4438	...	1698	...	...	6136
C Manufacture of wood and wood products, including furniture	4003	...	1536	...	...	5539	4237	...	1499	...	...	5737
D Manufacture of paper and paper products, printing and publishing	7806	...	2438	...	...	10244	8421	...	2398	...	...	10819
E Manufacture of chemicals and chemical petroleum, coal, rubber and plastic products	6505	...	4777	...	...	11282	7072	...	5522	...	...	12594
F Manufacture of non-metallic mineral products, except products of petroleum and coal	3078	...	1391	...	...	4470	3216	...	1660	...	...	4877
G Basic metal industries	928	...	332	...	...	1260	939	...	399	...	...	1338
H Manufacture of fabricated metal products, machinery and equipment	26369	...	9209	...	...	35577	30035	...	8380	...	...	38415
I Other manufacturing industries	1078	...	855	...	...	1933	1227	...	897	...	...	2124
4 Electricity, gas and water	2693	...	3179	...	...	5872	2863	...	3934	...	...	6796
A Electricity, gas and steam	2334	...	2794	...	...	5128	2481	...	3537	...	...	6018
B Water works and supply	359	...	385	...	...	744	382	...	397	...	...	778
5 Construction	20991	...	7650	...	...	28640	23694	...	7264	...	...	30958
6 Wholesale and retail trade, restaurants and hotels	39394	...	31266	...	...	70659	43807	...	37086	...	...	80892
A Wholesale and retail trade	35076	...	29305	...	...	64381	38840	...	34954	...	...	73794
B Restaurants and hotels	4318	...	1961	...	...	6278	4967	...	2132	...	...	7098
7 Transport, storage and communication	22981	...	17410	...	...	40391	24470	...	18750	...	...	43220
A Transport and storage	17701	...	13991	...	...	31691	18889	...	14984	...	...	33873
B Communication	5280	...	3419	...	...	8700	5581	...	3766	...	...	9347
8 Finance, insurance, real estate and business services	28268	...	54527	...	...	82796	31024	...	58970	...	...	89995
A Financial institutions	10324	...	3229	...	...	13553	11266	...	3324	...	...	14590
B Insurance	3570	...	-1793	...	...	1778	3973	...	-2618	...	...	1356
C Real estate and business services	14374	...	53091	...	...	67465	15785	...	58264	...	...	74049
Real estate, except dwellings	...	...	...	...	...	...	...	...	...	...	...	...
Dwellings	2062	...	41378	...	...	43440	2005	...	44961	...	...	46966
9 Community, social and personal services	11826	...	11751	...	...	23577	12807	...	12508	...	...	25317
A Sanitary and similar services	...	...	...	...	...	...	...	...	...	...	...	...
B Social and related community services	1689	...	4195	...	...	5884	1841	...	4393	...	...	6234
Educational services	39	...	398	...	...	437	44	...	406	...	...	450
Medical, dental, other health and veterinary services	1650	...	3797	...	...	5447	1797	...	3987	...	...	5784
C Recreational and cultural services	2794	...	1837	...	...	4630	3014	...	1751	...	...	4765
D Personal and household services	7343	...	5719	...	...	13062	7952	...	6364	...	...	14317

Denmark

4.3 Cost Components of Value Added
(Continued)

Million Danish kroner

	\multicolumn{6}{c	}{1984}	\multicolumn{6}{c}{1985}
	Compensation of Employees	Capital Consumption	Net Operating Surplus	Indirect Taxes	Less: Subsidies Received	Value Added	Compensation of Employees	Capital Consumption	Net Operating Surplus	Indirect Taxes	Less: Subsidies Received	Value Added
Total, Industries [a]	198241	...	186357	...	...	384597	217297	...	201094	...	...	418391
Producers of Government Services	104850	...	4328	...	...	109178	110282	...	4948	...	...	115230
Other Producers	3005	...	117	...	...	3122	3262	...	138	...	...	3400
Total [ba]	306095	...	190802	...	...	496897	330841	...	206180	...	...	537021
Less: Imputed bank service charge	...	...	15220	...	...	15220	...	...	16504	...	...	16504
Import duties	...	...	...	...	...	...	...	...	...	...	...	...
Value added tax	...	...	...	...	...	...	...	...	...	...	...	...
Other adjustments	...	...	...	102228	18621	83607	...	...	...	112913	18358	94555
Total [a]	306095	...	175582	102228	18621	565284	330841	...	189676	112913	18358	615072

	\multicolumn{6}{c	}{1986}	\multicolumn{6}{c}{1987}
	Compensation of Employees	Capital Consumption	Net Operating Surplus	Indirect Taxes	Less: Subsidies Received	Value Added	Compensation of Employees	Capital Consumption	Net Operating Surplus	Indirect Taxes	Less: Subsidies Received	Value Added

All Producers

	Comp. Emp.	Cap. Cons.	Net Op. Surplus	Ind. Taxes	Less Subs.	Value Added	Comp. Emp.	Cap. Cons.	Net Op. Surplus	Ind. Taxes	Less Subs.	Value Added
1 Agriculture, hunting, forestry and fishing	5511	...	24494	...	...	30005	5778	...	21560	...	...	27338
A Agriculture and hunting	3970	...	22807	...	...	26777	4205	...	19979	...	...	24184
B Forestry and logging	528	...	488	...	...	1016	554	...	423	...	...	977
C Fishing	1013	...	1199	...	...	2212	1019	...	1158	...	...	2178
2 Mining and quarrying	577	...	4750	...	...	5327	675	...	4714	...	...	5389
A Coal mining	...	...	...	...	...	...	...	...	...	...	...	...
B Crude petroleum and natural gas production	320	...	3938	...	...	4259	...	...	...	...	...	4355
C Metal ore mining	...	...	...	...	...	...	...	...	...	...	...	...
D Other mining	257	...	812	...	...	1069	...	...	...	...	...	1034
3 Manufacturing	79046	...	32656	...	...	111703	83313	...	30557	...	...	113869
A Manufacture of food, beverages and tobacco	14212	...	10030	...	...	24241	15112	...	9358	...	...	24470
B Textile, wearing apparel and leather industries	4686	...	1675	...	...	6362	4768	...	1562	...	...	6330
C Manufacture of wood and wood products, including furniture	4675	...	1608	...	...	6283	4831	...	1392	...	...	6223
D Manufacture of paper and paper products, printing and publishing	9214	...	2847	...	...	12062	10129	...	2716	...	...	12845
E Manufacture of chemicals and chemical petroleum, coal, rubber and plastic products	7710	...	5901	...	...	13611	8612	...	5620	...	...	14232
F Manufacture of non-metallic mineral products, except products of petroleum and coal	3618	...	2230	...	...	5848	3970	...	1968	...	...	5938
G Basic metal industries	1050	...	303	...	...	1353	1064	...	263	...	...	1327
H Manufacture of fabricated metal products, machinery and equipment	32489	...	7099	...	...	39588	33358	...	6636	...	...	39994
I Other manufacturing industries	1392	...	963	...	...	2355	1469	...	1042	...	...	2511
4 Electricity, gas and water	3024	...	5485	...	...	8508	3320	...	5908	...	...	9228
A Electricity, gas and steam	2627	...	5069	...	...	7696	...	...	...	...	...	8436
B Water works and supply	397	...	416	...	...	813	...	...	...	...	...	792
5 Construction	28243	...	9444	...	...	37686	31031	...	12300	...	...	43331
6 Wholesale and retail trade, restaurants and hotels	48105	...	40245	...	...	88350	52293	...	35659	...	...	87952
A Wholesale and retail trade	42860	...	37644	...	...	80504	46429	...	33404	...	...	79833
B Restaurants and hotels	5245	...	2601	...	...	7847	5864	...	2255	...	...	8119
7 Transport, storage and communication	25543	...	19227	...	...	44770	28059	...	19959	...	...	48016
A Transport and storage	19616	...	15701	...	...	35317	21337	...	16214	...	...	37550
B Communication	5927	...	3526	...	...	9453	6722	...	3745	...	...	10466
8 Finance, insurance, real estate and business services	34279	...	66611	...	...	100890	39497	...	67734	...	...	107231
A Financial institutions	12395	...	7874	...	...	20269	...	...	...	...	...	18310
B Insurance	4314	...	-2539	...	...	1775	...	...	...	...	...	3148
C Real estate and business services	17570	...	61276	...	...	78846	20060	...	65714	...	...	85774
Real estate, except dwellings	...	...	...	...	...	...	...	...	...	...	...	...

423

Denmark

4.3 Cost Components of Value Added
(Continued)

Million Danish kroner

	\multicolumn{6}{c	}{1986}	\multicolumn{6}{c}{1987}
	Compensation of Employees	Capital Consumption	Net Operating Surplus	Indirect Taxes	Less: Subsidies Received	Value Added	Compensation of Employees	Capital Consumption	Net Operating Surplus	Indirect Taxes	Less: Subsidies Received	Value Added
Dwellings	1929	...	46519	...	...	48448	2074	...	49237	...	...	51311
9 Community, social and personal services	13946	...	13827	...	...	27774	15280	...	15061	...	...	30342
A Sanitary and similar services	...	...	...	...	...	...	...	...	...	...	...	...
B Social and related community services	1949	...	4763	...	...	6712	2039	...	4988	...	...	7026
Educational services	49	...	439	...	...	488	...	...	...	...	...	516
Medical, dental, other health and veterinary services	1900	...	4324	...	...	6224	...	...	...	...	...	6510
C Recreational and cultural services	3198	...	2023	...	...	5221	3274	...	2472	...	...	5746
D Personal and household services	8799	...	7041	...	...	15840	9967	...	7601	...	...	17569
Total, Industries [a]	238273	...	216741	...	...	455014	259246	...	213451	...	...	472697
Producers of Government Services	114398	...	5412	...	...	119810	125773	...	5997	...	...	131770
Other Producers	3558	...	144	...	...	3702	3872	...	137	...	...	4009
Total [ba]	356230	...	222297	...	...	578526	388891	...	219585	...	...	608476
Less: Imputed bank service charge	...	...	22850	...	...	22850	...	...	22530	...	...	22530
Import duties	...	...	...	...	...	...	...	...	...	...	...	...
Value added tax	...	...	...	...	...	...	...	...	...	...	...	...
Other adjustments	...	...	...	130880	20060	110820	...	...	...	135974	22011	113963
Total [a]	356230	...	199447	130880	20060	666496	388891	...	197055	135974	22011	699909

	\multicolumn{6}{c	}{1988}	\multicolumn{6}{c}{1989}
	Compensation of Employees	Capital Consumption	Net Operating Surplus	Indirect Taxes	Less: Subsidies Received	Value Added	Compensation of Employees	Capital Consumption	Net Operating Surplus	Indirect Taxes	Less: Subsidies Received	Value Added

All Producers

1 Agriculture, hunting, forestry and fishing	5860	...	22265	...	...	28126	6098	...	25827	...	...	31926
A Agriculture and hunting	4283	...	20597	...	...	24880	4490	...	24243	...	...	28733
B Forestry and logging	572	...	462	...	...	1034	585	...	501	...	...	1087
C Fishing	1005	...	1206	...	...	2211	1023	...	1083	...	...	2106
2 Mining and quarrying	581	...	4100	...	...	4681	627	...	5681	...	...	6308
A Coal mining	...	...	...	...	...	...	...	...	...	...	...	...
B Crude petroleum and natural gas production	...	...	...	...	...	3619	...	...	...	...	...	5122
C Metal ore mining	...	...	...	...	...	...	...	...	...	...	...	...
D Other mining	...	...	...	...	...	1062	...	...	...	...	...	1186
3 Manufacturing	84043	...	34722	...	...	118765	86990	...	35391	...	...	122382
A Manufacture of food, beverages and tobacco	15268	...	11168	...	...	26436	15407	...	8962	...	...	24369
B Textile, wearing apparel and leather industries	4445	...	1551	...	...	5997	4445	...	1725	...	...	6170
C Manufacture of wood and wood products, including furniture	4817	...	1794	...	...	6610	5199	...	1698	...	...	6896
D Manufacture of paper and paper products, printing and publishing	10455	...	2991	...	...	13446	10657	...	3411	...	...	14068
E Manufacture of chemicals and chemical petroleum, coal, rubber and plastic products	8790	...	6563	...	...	15353	9357	...	7005	...	...	16362
F Manufacture of non-metallic mineral products, except products of petroleum and coal	3820	...	1985	...	...	5805	3863	...	2106	...	...	5969
G Basic metal industries	1073	...	232	...	...	1305	1176	...	287	...	...	1464
H Manufacture of fabricated metal products, machinery and equipment	33921	...	7216	...	...	41137	35328	...	8643	...	...	43971
I Other manufacturing industries	1454	...	1222	...	...	2676	1558	...	1554	...	...	3112
4 Electricity, gas and water	3980	...	5934	...	...	9914	4286	...	7734	...	...	12021
A Electricity, gas and steam	...	...	...	...	...	8870	...	...	...	...	...	10807
B Water works and supply	...	...	...	...	...	1044	...	...	...	...	...	1213

Denmark

4.3 Cost Components of Value Added
(Continued)

Million Danish kroner

	1988						1989					
	Compensation of Employees	Capital Consumption	Net Operating Surplus	Indirect Taxes	Less: Subsidies Received	Value Added	Compensation of Employees	Capital Consumption	Net Operating Surplus	Indirect Taxes	Less: Subsidies Received	Value Added
5 Construction	31122	...	13167	...	...	44289	31083	...	13972	...	...	45055
6 Wholesale and retail trade, restaurants and hotels	52627	...	38662	...	...	91289	53014	...	43978	...	...	96992
A Wholesale and retail trade	46608	...	36350	...	...	82958	46847	...	40662	...	...	87509
B Restaurants and hotels	6019	...	2312	...	...	8331	6167	...	3316	...	...	9483
7 Transport, storage and communication	28681	...	22590	...	...	51271	29106	...	26927	...	...	56033
A Transport and storage	21698	...	18920	...	...	40618	22102	...	21506	...	...	43608
B Communication	6983	...	3670	...	...	10653	7004	...	5421	...	...	12425
8 Finance, insurance, real estate and business services	41859	...	71612	...	...	113472	42748	...	84747	...	...	127495
A Financial institutions	...	...	...	...	...	17358	...	...	...	...	...	21674
B Insurance	...	...	...	...	...	3766	...	...	...	...	...	4074
C Real estate and business services	21409	...	70939	...	...	92348	22489	...	79258	...	...	101748
Real estate, except dwellings	...	...	...	...	...	...	...	...	...	...	...	...
Dwellings	2132	...	52882	...	...	55014	2230	...	58659	...	...	60889
9 Community, social and personal services	15463	...	17089	...	...	32552	16110	...	19754	...	...	35864
A Sanitary and similar services	...	...	...	...	...	...	...	...	...	...	...	...
B Social and related community services	2153	...	5325	...	...	7478	2246	...	5576	...	...	7822
Educational services	...	...	...	...	...	571	...	...	...	...	...	584
Medical, dental, other health and veterinary services	...	...	...	...	...	6907	...	...	...	...	...	7238
C Recreational and cultural services	3515	...	2418	...	...	5933	3651	...	3432	...	...	7083
D Personal and household services	9795	...	9346	...	...	19141	10213	...	10746	...	...	20959
Total, Industries [a]	264218	...	230140	...	...	494358	270063	...	264012	...	...	534076
Producers of Government Services	136399	...	6420	...	...	142819	141285	...	6620	...	...	147905
Other Producers	4128	...	171	...	...	4299	4497	...	207	...	...	4704
Total [b,a]	404744	...	236731	...	...	641476	415845	...	270839	...	...	686685
Less: Imputed bank service charge	...	...	21215	...	...	21215	...	...	25794	...	...	25794
Import duties	...	...	...	...	...	...	...	...	...	...	...	...
Value added tax	...	...	...	...	...	...	...	...	...	...	...	...
Other adjustments	...	...	...	139484	24226	115258	...	...	...	139478	24354	115124
Total [a]	404744	...	215516	139484	24226	735519	415845	...	245045	139478	24354	776015

a) Column 'Consumption of fixed capital' is included in column 'Net operating surplus'.
b) Gross domestic product in factor values.

Djibouti

Source. Reply to the United Nations National Accounts Questionnaire from Direction Nationale de la Statistique, Djibouti. The official estimates are published by the same office in 'Annuaire Statistique de Djibouti'.

General note. The estimates shown in the following tables have been prepared in accordance with the United Nations System of National Accounts so far as the existing data would permit.

1.1 Expenditure on the Gross Domestic Product, in Current Prices

Million Djibouti francs

	1970	1975	1980	1981	1982	1983	1984	1985	1986	1987	1988	1989
1 Government final consumption expenditure	...	...	20256	20698	...	...	...	...	...	...	...	...
2 Private final consumption expenditure	...	...	38694	44768	...	...	...	...	...	...	...	...
3 Gross capital formation	...	...	8708	8509	...	...	...	...	...	...	...	...
A Increase in stocks	...	...	900	-230	...	...	...	...	...	...	...	...
B Gross fixed capital formation	...	...	7808	8739	...	...	...	...	...	...	...	...
4 Exports of goods and services	...	...	23550	30034	...	...	...	...	...	...	...	...
5 Less: Imports of goods and services	...	...	30895	36816	...	...	...	...	...	...	...	...
Equals: Gross Domestic Product	15300	30100	60313	67193	...	...	...	...	...	...	...	...

1.2 Expenditure on the Gross Domestic Product, in Constant Prices

Million Djibouti francs

	1970	1975	1980	1981	1982	1983	1984	1985	1986	1987	1988	1989
	\multicolumn{12}{c}{At constant prices of:1970}
1 Government final consumption expenditure	...	...	...	...	...	...	...	...	...	...	...	...
2 Private final consumption expenditure	...	...	...	...	...	...	...	...	...	...	...	...
3 Gross capital formation	...	...	...	...	...	...	...	...	...	...	...	...
4 Exports of goods and services	...	...	...	...	...	...	...	...	...	...	...	...
5 Less: Imports of goods and services	...	...	...	...	...	...	...	...	...	...	...	...
Equals: Gross Domestic Product	15509	19195	18701	...	...	...	...	...	...	...	...	...

1.3 Cost Components of the Gross Domestic Product

Million Djibouti francs

	1970	1975	1980	1981	1982	1983	1984	1985	1986	1987	1988	1989
1 Indirect taxes, net	...	...	10566	11326	...	...	...	...	...	...	...	...
A Indirect taxes	...	...	10973	...	...	...	...	...	...	...	...	...
B Less: Subsidies	...	...	407	...	...	...	...	...	...	...	...	...
2 Consumption of fixed capital [a]	...	...	...	...	...	...	...	...	...	...	...	...
3 Compensation of employees paid by resident producers to:	...	...	21867	23546	...	...	...	...	...	...	...	...
4 Operating surplus [a]	...	...	27880	32321	...	...	...	...	...	...	...	...
Equals: Gross Domestic Product	...	...	60313	67193	...	...	...	...	...	...	...	...

a) Item 'Operating surplus' includes consumption of fixed capital.

1.4 General Government Current Receipts and Disbursements

Million Djibouti francs

	1970	1975	1980	1981	1982	1983	1984	1985	1986	1987	1988	1989
	\multicolumn{12}{c}{Receipts}
1 Operating surplus	...	...	...	...	...	...	...	...	...	...	...	...
2 Property and entrepreneurial income	...	...	1700	...	...	...	...	...	...	...	...	...
3 Taxes, fees and contributions	...	...	16486	...	...	...	...	...	...	...	...	...
A Indirect taxes	...	...	10973	...	...	...	...	...	...	...	...	...
B Direct taxes	...	...	3250	...	...	...	...	...	...	...	...	...
C Social security contributions	...	...	1876	...	...	...	...	...	...	...	...	...
D Compulsory fees, fines and penalties	...	...	387	...	...	...	...	...	...	...	...	...
4 Other current transfers	...	...	11799	...	...	...	...	...	...	...	...	...
Total Current Receipts of General Government	...	...	29985	...	...	...	...	...	...	...	...	...
	\multicolumn{12}{c}{Disbursements}
1 Government final consumption expenditure	...	...	20256	...	...	...	...	...	...	...	...	...

Djibouti

1.4 General Government Current Receipts and Disbursements
(Continued)

Million Djibouti francs

	1970	1975	1980	1981	1982	1983	1984	1985	1986	1987	1988	1989
A Compensation of employees	...	...	13745	...	...	...	...	...	...	...	...	...
B Consumption of fixed capital	...	...	...	...	...	...	...	...	...	...	...	...
C Purchases of goods and services, net	...	...	6511	...	...	...	...	...	...	...	...	...
D Less: Own account fixed capital formation	...	...	...	...	...	...	...	...	...	...	...	...
E Indirect taxes paid, net	...	...	...	...	...	...	...	...	...	...	...	...
2 Property income	...	...	46	...	...	...	...	...	...	...	...	...
A Interest	...	...	46	...	...	...	...	...	...	...	...	...
B Net land rent and royalties	...	...	...	...	...	...	...	...	...	...	...	...
3 Subsidies	...	...	407	...	...	...	...	...	...	...	...	...
4 Other current transfers	...	...	3554	...	...	...	...	...	...	...	...	...
5 Net saving [a]	...	...	5722	...	...	...	...	...	...	...	...	...
Total Current Disbursements and Net Saving of General Government	...	...	29985	...	...	...	...	...	...	...	...	...

a) Item 'Net saving' includes consumption of fixed capital.

1.7 External Transactions on Current Account, Summary

Million Djibouti francs

	1970	1975	1980	1981	1982	1983	1984	1985	1986	1987	1988	1989
Payments to the Rest of the World												
1 Imports of goods and services	...	...	30895	...	...	...	...	...	...	...	...	...
A Imports of merchandise c.i.f.	...	...	29566	...	...	...	...	...	...	...	...	...
B Other	...	...	1329	...	...	...	...	...	...	...	...	...
2 Factor income to the rest of the world	...	...	8759	...	...	...	...	...	...	...	...	...
3 Current transfers to the rest of the world	...	...	1765	...	...	...	...	...	...	...	...	...
4 Surplus of the nation on current transactions	...	...	-2453	...	...	...	...	...	...	...	...	...
Payments to the Rest of the World and Surplus of the Nation on Current Transactions	...	...	38966	...	...	...	...	...	...	...	...	...
Receipts From The Rest of the World												
1 Exports of goods and services	...	...	23550	...	...	...	...	...	...	...	...	...
A Exports of merchandise f.o.b.	...	...	4295	...	...	...	...	...	...	...	...	...
B Other	...	...	19255	...	...	...	...	...	...	...	...	...
2 Factor income from rest of the world	...	...	2581	...	...	...	...	...	...	...	...	...
A Compensation of employees	...	...	1254	...	...	...	...	...	...	...	...	...
B Property and entrepreneurial income	...	...	1327	...	...	...	...	...	...	...	...	...
3 Current transfers from rest of the world	...	...	12835	...	...	...	...	...	...	...	...	...
Receipts from the Rest of the World on Current Transactions	...	...	38966	...	...	...	...	...	...	...	...	...

1.9 Gross Domestic Product by Institutional Sectors of Origin

Million Djibouti francs

	1970	1975	1980	1981	1982	1983	1984	1985	1986	1987	1988	1989
Domestic Factor Incomes Originating												
1 General government	...	...	13745	...	...	...	...	...	...	...	...	...
2 Corporate and quasi-corporate enterprises	...	...	36002	...	...	...	...	...	...	...	...	...
3 Households and private unincorporated enterprises	...	...		...	...	...	...	...	...	...	...	...
4 Non-profit institutions serving households	...	...	...	...	...	...	...	...	...	...	...	...
Subtotal: Domestic Factor Incomes [a]	...	...	49747	...	...	...	...	...	...	...	...	...
Indirect taxes, net	...	...	10566	...	...	...	...	...	...	...	...	...
Consumption of fixed capital	...	...	...	...	...	...	...	...	...	...	...	...
Gross Domestic Product	...	...	60313	...	...	...	...	...	...	...	...	...

a) Item 'Domestic factor incomes' includes consumption of fixed capital.

Djibouti

1.10 Gross Domestic Product by Kind of Activity, in Current Prices

Million Djibouti francs

	1970	1975	1980	1981	1982	1983	1984	1985	1986	1987	1988	1989
1 Agriculture, hunting, forestry and fishing	...	...	1932	2123	2531	2580	...	...	...	...	...	...
2 Mining and quarrying	...	...	...	...	...	...	...	...	...	...	...	...
3 Manufacturing	...	...	4515	4738	4821	4910	...	...	...	...	...	...
4 Electricity, gas and water	...	...	1384	1123	1550	1914	...	...	...	...	...	...
5 Construction	...	...	2897	3973	4439	4550	...	...	...	...	...	...
6 Wholesale and retail trade, restaurants and hotels	...	...	10134	10579	9658	9410	...	...	...	...	...	...
7 Transport, storage and communication	...	...	5077	5634	5770	5900	...	...	...	...	...	...
8 Finance, insurance, real estate and business services	...	...	4412	5610	6422	6630	...	...	...	...	...	...
9 Community, social and personal services	...	...	852	879	862	920	...	...	...	...	...	...
Total, Industries	...	...	31203	34659	36053	36814	...	...	...	...	...	...
Producers of Government Services	...	...	15313	15827	16071	16200	...	...	...	...	...	...
Other Producers	...	...	...	...	...	...	...	...	...	...	...	...
Subtotal [a]	...	...	46516	50486	52124	53014	...	...	...	...	...	...
Less: Imputed bank service charge	...	...	1993	3488	3597	3730	...	...	...	...	...	...
Plus: Import duties	...	...	9004	9820	10856	10713	...	...	...	...	...	...
Plus: Value added tax	...	...	...	...	...	...	...	...	...	...	...	...
Equals: Gross Domestic Product	...	...	53527	56818	59383	59997	...	...	...	...	...	...

a) Gross domestic product in factor values.

1.12 Relations Among National Accounting Aggregates

Million Djibouti francs

	1970	1975	1980	1981	1982	1983	1984	1985	1986	1987	1988	1989
Gross Domestic Product	...	...	60313 / 53527	56818	59383	59997	60234	...	...	...	...	...
Plus: Net factor income from the rest of the world	...	...	-6178 / -5647	-5087	-5052	-5905	-6645	...	...	...	...	...
Factor income from the rest of the world	...	...	2581	...	...	...	...	...	...	...	...	...
Less: Factor income to the rest of the world	...	...	8759	...	...	...	...	...	...	...	...	...
Equals: Gross National Product	...	...	54135 / 47880	51731	54331	54092	53589	...	...	...	...	...
Less: Consumption of fixed capital	...	...	...	...	...	...	...	...	...	...	...	...
Equals: National Income [a]	...	...	54135	...	...	...	...	...	...	...	...	...
Plus: Net current transfers from the rest of the world	...	...	11070	...	...	...	...	...	...	...	...	...
Current transfers from the rest of the world	...	...	12835	...	...	...	...	...	...	...	...	...
Less: Current transfers to the rest of the world	...	...	1765	...	...	...	...	...	...	...	...	...
Equals: National Disposable Income [b]	...	...	65205	...	...	...	...	...	...	...	...	...
Less: Final consumption	...	...	58950	...	...	...	...	...	...	...	...	...
Equals: Net Saving [c]	...	...	6255	...	...	...	...	...	...	...	...	...
Less: Surplus of the nation on current transactions	...	...	-2453	...	...	...	...	...	...	...	...	...
Equals: Net Capital Formation [d]	...	...	8708	...	...	...	...	...	...	...	...	...

a) Item 'National income' includes consumption of fixed capital.
b) Item 'National disposable income' includes consumption of fixed capital.
c) Item 'Net saving' includes consumption of fixed capital.
d) Item 'Net capital formation' includes consumption of fixed capital.

Dominica

Source. Reply to the United Nations National Accounts Questionnaire from the Ministry of Finance, Trade and Industry, Roseau.
General note. The estimates shown in the following tables have been prepared in accordance with the United Nations System of National Accounts so far as the existing data would permit.

1.1 Expenditure on the Gross Domestic Product, in Current Prices

Thousand East Caribbean dollars

	1970	1975	1980	1981	1982	1983	1984	1985	1986	1987	1988	1989
1 Government final consumption expenditure	...	18147	43540	45470	47750	52270	60230	59890	62070	68150	75030	86710
2 Private final consumption expenditure	...	43153	147470	151550	141790	144860	172490	192780	184920	219990	267250	312770
3 Gross capital formation	...	16009	81160	60670	60100	60570	89370	75820	67510	79330	105860	148550
A Increase in stocks	...	-	7000	-	-	-	-	-	-	-	-	-
B Gross fixed capital formation	...	16009	74160	60670	60100	60570	89370	75820	67510	79330	105860	148550
Residential buildings	...	...										
Non-residential buildings	...	...	47520	37430	35200	32350	44150	38580	30380	37070	39410	52950
Other construction and land improvement etc.	...	...										
Other	...	...	26640	23240	24900	28220	45220	37240	37130	42260	66450	95600
4 Exports of goods and services	...	30800	35100	61800	80200	88800	86400	97270	144700	158400	187400	173410
5 Less: Imports of goods and services	...	45200	147700	140700	135300	130700	165900	159580	156600	186600	242300	298720
Statistical discrepancy	...	-	...	...	...	...	...	...	...	...	...	...
Equals: Gross Domestic Product	...	62909	159570	178790	194540	215800	242590	266180	302600	339270	393240	422720

1.2 Expenditure on the Gross Domestic Product, in Constant Prices

Thousand East Caribbean dollars

	1970	1975	1980	1981	1982	1983	1984	1985	1986	1987	1988	1989
			At constant prices of:1977									
1 Government final consumption expenditure	...	20060	...	...	...	...	...	...	...	...	...	...
2 Private final consumption expenditure	...	63150	...	...	...	...	...	...	...	...	...	...
3 Gross capital formation	...	19942	...	...	...	...	...	...	...	...	...	...
4 Exports of goods and services	...	35402	...	...	...	...	...	...	...	...	...	...
5 Less: Imports of goods and services	...	61081	...	...	...	...	...	...	...	...	...	...
Equals: Gross Domestic Product	...	77473	...	...	...	...	...	...	...	...	...	...

1.3 Cost Components of the Gross Domestic Product

Thousand East Caribbean dollars

	1970	1975	1980	1981	1982	1983	1984	1985	1986	1987	1988	1989
1 Indirect taxes, net	...	...	15830	25880	30940	35380	39900	42900	49330	57510	68950	76550
A Indirect taxes	...	...	23930	30780	33140	37180	42100	44560	51180	59280	70800	78490
B Less: Subsidies	...	...	8100	4900	2200	1800	2200	1660	1850	1770	1850	1940
2 Consumption of fixed capital	...	...	...	...	...	...	...	...	...	...	...	...
3 Compensation of employees paid by resident producers to:	...	...	...	...	...	...	...	...	...	...	...	...
4 Operating surplus	...	...	...	...	...	...	...	...	...	...	...	...
Equals: Gross Domestic Product	...	62909	159570	178790	194540	215800	242590	266180	302600	339270	393240	422720

Dominica

1.10 Gross Domestic Product by Kind of Activity, in Current Prices

Thousand East Caribbean dollars

	1970	1975	1980	1981	1982	1983	1984	1985	1986	1987	1988	1989
1 Agriculture, hunting, forestry and fishing	...	19876	44050	48480	49780	52500	56800	62390	76640	82590	95900	89560
2 Mining and quarrying	...	628	1170	1300	1400	1330	1500	1460	1380	1760	2570	2910
3 Manufacturing	...	2396	6930	10230	13390	14120	12360	14370	16880	18250	20990	24530
4 Electricity, gas and water	...	902	3470	4880	5000	5230	5920	6240	6680	7390	8970	10040
5 Construction	...	3842	18480	14560	13690	12580	17170	15000	11820	14420	21050	24970
6 Wholesale and retail trade, restaurants and hotels	...	5901	14380	14700	15350	15980	16890	23700	28850	34050	37980	43590
7 Transport, storage and communication	...	5359	10490	11370	14700	22260	26520	29340	34350	41760	49520	53780
8 Finance, insurance, real estate and business services	...	7190	16170	17270	18290	20860	26110	28040	30010	33050	40100	47270
9 Community, social and personal services	...	696	1620	1910	2180	2310	2400	2490	2660	2910	3080	3630
Total, Industries	...	46789	116760	124700	133780	147170	165670	183030	209270	236180	280160	300280
Producers of Government Services	...	16120	33740	35410	37050	40630	47050	50120	54360	57630	59520	66980
Other Producers	...	...	...	...	...	...	...	...	...	...	...	...
Subtotal [a]	...	62910	150500	160110	170830	187800	212720	233150	263630	293810	339680	367260
Less: Imputed bank service charge	...	...	6760	7200	7230	7380	10030	9870	10360	12050	15390	21110
Plus: Import duties	...	...	...	...	...	...	...	...	...	...	...	...
Plus: Value added tax	...	...	...	...	...	...	...	...	...	...	...	...
Plus: Other adjustments [b]	...	...	15830	25880	30940	35380	39900	42900	49330	57510	68950	76550
Equals: Gross Domestic Product	...	62909	159570	178790	194540	215800	242590	266180	302600	339270	393240	422720

a) Gross domestic product in factor values.
b) Item 'Other adjustments' refers to indirect taxes net of subsidies.

1.11 Gross Domestic Product by Kind of Activity, in Constant Prices

Thousand East Caribbean dollars

	1970	1975	1980	1981	1982	1983	1984	1985	1986	1987	1988	1989
					At constant prices of:1977							
1 Agriculture, hunting, forestry and fishing	...	29119	23660	28920	29590	29840	31470	30680	36500	38340	40650	34810
2 Mining and quarrying	...	739	720	740	800	790	1000	970	920	1120	1380	1460
3 Manufacturing	...	2957	6200	7300	8570	8740	7870	8900	9280	9830	10830	11480
4 Electricity, gas and water	...	947	1670	1810	1830	1980	2120	2270	2400	2570	2740	2920
5 Construction	...	4390	11900	10080	8750	8260	11040	10370	8750	9860	12880	13590
6 Wholesale and retail trade, restaurants and hotels	...	6872	12360	12950	13010	12920	13110	14150	15600	17350	18840	20540
7 Transport, storage and communication	...	5665	5860	5480	6240	7900	8290	9220	10210	11690	12800	13490
8 Finance, insurance, real estate and business services	...	8347	11160	11390	11510	11650	11830	12190	12450	12890	13650	14320
9 Community, social and personal services	...	763	1090	1100	1170	1190	1210	1230	1270	1310	1360	1440
Total, Industries	...	59798	74620	79770	81470	83270	88540	89980	97380	104960	115130	114050
Producers of Government Services	...	17675	21090	21930	22590	22930	23390	23970	24210	24820	25560	25870

Dominica

1.11 Gross Domestic Product by Kind of Activity, in Constant Prices
(Continued)

Thousand East Caribbean dollars

	1970	1975	1980	1981	1982	1983	1984	1985	1986	1987	1988	1989
				At constant prices of:1977								
Other Producers	...	...	...	...	...	...	...	...	...	...	...	...
Subtotal [a]	...	77474	95710	101700	104060	106200	111930	113950	121590	129780	140690	139920
Less: Imputed bank service charge	...	...	3500	3580	3610	3630	3780	3970	4090	4290	5260	6010
Plus: Import duties	...	...	...	...	...	...	...	...	...	...	...	...
Plus: Value added tax	...	...	...	...	...	...	...	...	...	...	...	...
Plus: Other adjustments [b]	...	...	10150	16610	19000	20120	21290	21130	22880	25610	28800	29610
Equals: Gross Domestic Product	...	77473	102360	114730	119450	122690	129440	131110	140380	151100	164230	163520

a) Gross domestic product in factor values.
b) Item 'Other adjustments' refers to indirect taxes net of subsidies.

1.12 Relations Among National Accounting Aggregates

Thousand East Caribbean dollars

	1970	1975	1980	1981	1982	1983	1984	1985	1986	1987	1988	1989
Gross Domestic Product	...	...	159570	178790	194540	215800	242590	266180	302600	339270	393240	422720
Plus: Net factor income from the rest of the world	...	...	810	1620	540	1080	-2700	-3400	-6100	-6000	-1600	4410
Equals: Gross National Product	...	...	160380	180410	195080	216880	239890	262780	296500	333270	391640	427130
Less: Consumption of fixed capital	...	...	...	...	...	...	...	...	...	...	...	...
Equals: National Income	...	...	...	...	...	...	...	...	...	...	...	...
Plus: Net current transfers from the rest of the world	...	...	...	...	...	...	...	...	...	...	...	...
Equals: National Disposable Income	...	...	...	...	...	...	...	...	...	...	...	...
Less: Final consumption	...	...	...	...	...	...	...	...	...	...	...	...
Equals: Net Saving	...	...	...	...	...	...	...	...	...	...	...	...
Less: Surplus of the nation on current transactions	...	...	...	...	...	...	...	...	...	...	...	...
Equals: Net Capital Formation	...	...	...	...	...	...	...	...	...	...	...	...

Dominican Republic

General note. The preparation of national accounts statistics in Dominican Republic is undertaken by Banco Central de la Republica Dominicana, Santo Domingo. The official estimates are published in the series 'Cuentas Nacionales, Producto Nacional Bruto', which also includes a detailed description of the sources and methods used for the national accounts estimation. The estimates are generally in accordance with the classifications and definitions recommended in the United Nations System of National Accounts (SNA). The following tables have been prepared from successive replies to the United Nations national accounts questionnaire. When the scope and coverage of the estimates differ for conceptual or statistical reasons from the definitions and classifications recommended in SNA a footnote is indicated to the relevant tables.

Sources and methods:

(a) Gross domestic product. The main approach used to estimate GDP is the production approach.

(b) Expenditure on the gross domestic product. The expenditure approach is used to estimate government final consumption expenditure, increase in stocks and exports and imports of goods and services. Gross fixed capital formation is mainly estimated by the commodity-flow method, whereas private final consumption expenditure is taken as a residual, which also includes changes in stocks which could not be computed directly. Government consumption expenditure data for the central government is obtained from the Ministry of Finance and the National Budget Office. For gross fixed capital formation, import statistics are utilized for capital goods such as machinery, equipment and transport and communication equipment, since no such products are produced locally. To the import values are added customs duties, surcharges, mark-ups, etc. The data on exports and imports of goods and services are taken from the publication on balance of payments, prepared by the Central Bank. For the calculation of constant prices, price deflation is used for government consumption expenditure. Compensation of employees is deflated by means of the cost of living index, whereas for government purchases and sales general price indexes are used. Constant value of private consumption expenditure is obtained as a residual. The value of construction is deflated by a construction costs index. In the case of rural dwellings base-year prices are multiplied by number of dwellings built. The import price index is used as a deflator for exports and imports of goods and services.

(c) Cost-structure of the gross domestic product. The data on indirect taxes and subsidies are based on the annual reports of the Ministry of Finance and on information from the Treasury and the National Budget Office.

(d) Gross domestic product by kind of economic activity. The production approach is the basic method of estimation used for most sectors. The income approach is used for trade, transport and communication, finance, general government and other services. In agriculture gross output is estimated by multiplying the quantities harvested by the average price paid to the producers. Quantity data are available from the agricultural censuses of 1950, 1960 and 1970 and from estimates by the Banco Agricola, the Ministry of Agriculture and others. Own account consumption is included in the production series. Data on the volume of livestock production is provided by the Ministry of Agriculture, which also estimates the quantity of unreported slaughter and herd changes in livestock. The basic information for calculating gross output of the mining and quarrying sector is obtained directly from the reports on production and sales of enterprises. For manufacturing the main source of information is the series of annual bulletins of industrial statistics. The value of construction for 1960, which is taken as a bench-mark, is extrapolated by means of a value index. This index is a combination of a price index of construction costs and an index of main materials used. Value added is obtained by applying to gross output a coefficient representing the ratio of gross factor income. Data for the trade sector are available from the first national trade census carried out in 1955, and from total wholesale and retail sales figures published periodically by the National Statistical Office. Wages and salaries are calculated by combining average remunerations series with sectoral employment series. The Dominican merchant marine and the Dominican airline provide the data needed to estimate incomes, inputs and value added for shipping and air transport. For land transport the information obtained include data from transport enterprises and surveys among owners of trucks and taxis. For financial institutions the estimates are based on complete accounting information which is available for all banks and finance companies and most insurance companies. Value added of ownership of dwellings is taken as the difference between gross rents paid or imputed based on census data and the inputs for maintenance, upkeep and management and property taxes. For public administration and defence, data are obtained from Government Authorities, publications and from independent institutions. For other private services, data on the number of persons employed and mean income are used. The bench-mark data are extrapolated according to a specially constructed income index. For the computation of constant prices, the value added for agriculture is estimated by a revaluation at base-year prices of the harvested quantities. In the case of livestock products, estimates of annual changes in average meat yield per animal are utilized. For mining and quarrying value added is estimated by revaluating the different minerals at their respective 1962 prices. Value added of manufacturing is extrapolated by a quantity index of output. Current values of public and private construction are deflated by means of an index of construction costs. Wholesale and retail sales of locally produced and imported goods are deflated using the respective price indexes. For transport, storage and communication, value added is extrapolated by quantity index of output. For financial institutions value added is extrapolated by quantity indicators of personnel employed. For ownership of dwellings the indicator used is the number of urban and rural dwellings. Value added for public administration, defence and other services is extrapolated by an indicator of the number of personnel employed.

1.1 Expenditure on the Gross Domestic Product, in Current Prices

Million Dominican pesos

	1970	1975	1980	1981	1982	1983	1984	1985	1986	1987	1988	1989
1 Government final consumption expenditure	172.0	222.1	504.0	693.0	779.4	786.3	870.8	1112.0	1297.3	1205.2	1783.1	...
2 Private final consumption expenditure	1137.8	2495.6	5108.8	5163.4	5985.8	6355.9	7001.7	10832.8	12074.7	15361.3	21807.8	...
3 Gross capital formation [a]	284.3	882.1	1665.3	1716.3	1590.5	1816.8	2202.5	2799.1	3108.6	4919.2	6455.3	...
A Increase in stocks [a]	38.4	79.4	81.8	61.2	99.4	62.4	33.4	52.2	85.2	117.5	87.5	...
B Gross fixed capital formation	245.9	802.7	1583.5	1655.1	1491.1	1754.4	2169.1	2746.9	3023.4	4801.7	6367.8	...
4 Exports of goods and services	255.9	1009.1	1271.3	1512.6	1141.8	1241.8	3780.1	4087.5	4041.2	5432.2	10067.0	...
5 Less: Imports of goods and services	364.5	1009.8	1918.7	1818.4	1533.1	1577.6	3499.8	4859.1	4741.7	7381.8	11760.5	...
Equals: Gross Domestic Product	1485.5	3599.1	6630.7	7266.9	7964.4	8623.2	10355.3	13972.4	15780.4	19536.1	28352.7	42393.3

a) Item 'Gross capital formation' includes only increase of stocks of mining, manufacturing, peanuts, raw tobacco and beans.

1.2 Expenditure on the Gross Domestic Product, in Constant Prices

Million Dominican pesos

	1970	1975	1980	1981	1982	1983	1984	1985	1986	1987	1988	1989
	\multicolumn{12}{c}{At constant prices of: 1970}											
1 Government final consumption expenditure	172.0	179.3	260.7	332.1	337.4	347.4	345.9	361.0	386.8	318.3	348.6	353.7
2 Private final consumption expenditure	1137.8	1699.5	2201.7	2198.4	2309.8	2386.0	2284.2	2272.6	2366.6	2477.9	2325.1	2405.2
3 Gross capital formation [a]	284.3	612.1	748.0	667.5	548.0	594.7	622.8	593.5	617.2	873.4	945.1	1024.8
A Increase in stocks [a]	38.4	40.4	52.3	30.7	51.3	35.2	14.5	22.1	26.0	39.9	24.8	...
B Gross fixed capital formation	245.9	571.7	695.7	636.8	496.7	559.5	608.3	571.4	591.2	833.5	920.3	...
Residential buildings			...	...	...	...	...	...	...	...	...	...
Non-residential buildings	147.0	308.7	...	...	...	...	...	...	...	...	...	...
Other construction and land improvement etc.			...	...	...	...	...	...	...	...	...	...
Other [b]	98.9	263.0	...	...	...	...	...	...	...	...	...	...
4 Exports of goods and services	255.9	430.3	560.0	598.3	518.9	544.4	572.0	564.3	572.0	646.4	702.6	838.4
5 Less: Imports of goods and services	364.5	632.3	866.6	774.4	644.5	663.1	606.8	656.5	708.5	827.4	808.7	962.1
Equals: Gross Domestic Product	1485.5	2288.9	2903.7	3021.9	3069.2	3209.4	3218.1	3134.9	3234.0	3488.6	3512.7	3656.8

a) Item 'Gross capital formation' includes only increase of stocks of mining, manufacturing, peanuts, raw tobacco and beans. b) Item 'Other' of gross capital formation refers to producers' durable goods of the agricultural sector only.

Dominican Republic

1.3 Cost Components of the Gross Domestic Product

Million Dominican pesos

	1970	1975	1980	1981	1982	1983	1984	1985	1986	1987	1988	1989
1 Indirect taxes, net	160.2	432.1	507.7	541.0	472.7	574.2	789.3	1173.1	1570.9	1985.8	2948.4	...
2 Consumption of fixed capital	89.1	216.0	394.5	432.4	473.9	513.1	616.1	831.4	933.9	1155.8	1682.1	...
3 Compensation of employees paid by resident producers to:	1236.2	2951.0	5729.0	6293.5	7017.8	7536.0	8949.8	11967.9	13275.6	16394.5	23722.2	...
4 Operating surplus												...
Equals: Gross Domestic Product	1485.5	3599.1	6630.7	7266.9	7964.5	8623.3	10355.3	13972.4	15780.4	19536.1	28352.7	42393.0

1.10 Gross Domestic Product by Kind of Activity, in Current Prices

Million Dominican pesos

	1970	1975	1980	1981	1982	1983	1984	1985	1986	1987	1988	1989
1 Agriculture, hunting, forestry and fishing	345.1	772.8	1336.3	1349.5	1411.9	1484.9	1915.7	...	...	...	...	...
2 Mining and quarrying	22.7	107.8	351.7	270.6	206.3	229.2	243.6	238.8	216.3	235.5	215.1	173.9
3 Manufacturing [a,b]	275.4	752.1	1015.4	1133.1	1454.9	1527.5	1707.6	...	...	...	...	...
4 Electricity, gas and water	17.6	30.1	30.0	66.8	82.4	77.5	94.1	...	...	...	...	...
5 Construction	72.7	248.5	479.4	537.1	535.1	669.0	881.6	972.7	1120.9	1746.5	2116.3	...
6 Wholesale and retail trade, restaurants and hotels [c]	237.6	586.0	1047.8	1197.6	1350.3	1450.6	1781.9	...	...	...	...	...
7 Transport, storage and communication	114.8	217.8	362.3	408.5	419.8	462.9	522.7	...	...	...	...	...
8 Finance, insurance, real estate and business services [d]	127.2	308.9	793.9	968.0	1029.2	1090.4	1242.1	...	...	...	...	...
9 Community, social and personal services [c,d]	120.3	346.5	662.0	727.8	810.9	927.1	1153.7	...	...	...	...	...
Total, Industries	1333.4	3370.5	6078.8	6659.0	7300.8	7919.1	9543.0	...	...	...	...	...
Producers of Government Services	152.1	228.6	551.9	607.9	663.7	704.2	812.3	...	...	...	...	...
Other Producers	...	...	...	...	...	...	...	...	...	...	...	...
Subtotal	1485.5	3599.1	6630.7	7266.9	7964.5	8623.3	10355.3	...	...	...	...	...
Less: Imputed bank service charge	...	...	...	...	...	...	...	...	...	...	...	...
Plus: Import duties	...	...	...	...	...	...	...	...	...	...	...	...
Plus: Value added tax	...	...	...	...	...	...	...	...	...	...	...	...
Equals: Gross Domestic Product	1485.5	3599.1	6630.7	7266.9	7964.5	8623.3	10355.3	...	...	...	...	...

a) Item 'Manufacturing' includes handicrafts.
b) Repair services are included in item 'Manufacturing'.
c) Restaurants and hotels are included in item 'Community, social and personal services'.
d) Business services are included in item 'Community, social and personal services'.

1.11 Gross Domestic Product by Kind of Activity, in Constant Prices

Million Dominican pesos

	1970	1975	1980	1981	1982	1983	1984	1985	1986	1987	1988	1989
					At constant prices of:1970							
1 Agriculture, hunting, forestry and fishing	345.1	399.9	484.2	510.8	534.3	550.8	550.9	531.3	528.5	543.8	536.5	548.7
2 Mining and quarrying	22.7	121.7	124.6	135.6	93.8	124.8	135.1	134.7	119.7	150.7	140.2	139.3
3 Manufacturing [a,b]	275.4	428.5	530.2	544.5	562.3	568.1	554.4	515.0	550.8	610.0	590.8	604.4
4 Electricity, gas and water	17.5	30.0	49.0	53.4	48.4	50.3	56.6	59.4	62.7	69.4	67.1	61.5
5 Construction	72.7	152.6	197.5	196.5	183.1	226.7	226.8	192.0	221.8	297.4	306.9	347.5
6 Wholesale and retail trade, restaurants and hotels [c]	237.6	385.9	473.6	494.9	520.2	522.8	514.4	489.1	504.3	539.1	526.7	538.8
7 Transport, storage and communication	114.8	182.6	230.5	242.6	256.6	259.5	257.0	241.7	249.2	272.2	274.4	288.4
8 Finance, insurance, real estate and business services [d]	127.2	197.7	268.6	272.1	277.7	285.6	291.9	332.2	351.2	370.1	398.1	...
9 Community, social and personal services [c,d]	120.3	206.9	265.4	271.4	280.9	300.3	300.4	305.9	313.9	321.4	332.4	...
Total, Industries	1333.4	2105.8	2623.6	2721.8	2757.3	2888.9	2887.5	2801.3	2902.1	3174.1	3173.2	...
Producers of Government Services	152.1	183.1	280.3	300.1	311.9	320.5	330.6	333.6	331.9	314.6	339.5	349.0
Other Producers	...	...	...	...	...	...	...	...	...	...	...	...
Subtotal	1485.4	2288.9	2903.9	3021.9	3069.2	3209.4	3218.1	3134.9	3234.0	3488.7	3512.7	...
Less: Imputed bank service charge	...	...	...	...	...	...	...	...	...	...	...	...
Plus: Import duties	...	...	...	...	...	...	...	...	...	...	...	...
Plus: Value added tax	...	...	...	...	...	...	...	...	...	...	...	...
Equals: Gross Domestic Product	1485.5	2288.9	2903.7	3021.9	3069.2	3209.4	3218.1	3134.9	3234.0	3488.7	3512.7	...

a) Item 'Manufacturing' includes handicrafts.
b) Repair services are included in item 'Manufacturing'.
c) Restaurants and hotels are included in item 'Community, social and personal services'.
d) Business services are included in item 'Community, social and personal services'.

Dominican Republic

1.12 Relations Among National Accounting Aggregates

Million Dominican pesos

	1970	1975	1980	1981	1982	1983	1984	1985	1986	1987	1988	1989
Gross Domestic Product [a]	1485.5	3599.1	6630.7	7266.9	7964.5	8623.3	10335.3	13972.4	15780.4	19425.7	28270.2	...
Plus: Net factor income from the rest of the world [b]	-25.9	-112.8	-211.5	-276.6	-254.8	-297.1	-241.4	-705.1	-716.8	-1176.9	-1953.0	...
Equals: Gross National Product	1459.6	3486.3	6419.2	6990.3	7709.7	8326.2	10093.9	13267.3	15063.6	18248.8	26317.2	...
Less: Consumption of fixed capital	89.1	216.0	394.5	432.4	473.9	513.1	616.1	831.4	933.9	1155.8	1682.1	...
Equals: National Income	1370.5	3270.3	6024.7	6557.9	7235.9	7813.1	9477.8	12435.9	14129.7	17093.0	24635.1	...
Plus: Net current transfers from the rest of the world [b]	...	...	187.8	193.0	205.0	215.0	265.0	1110.1	787.4	1366.4	2578.6	...
Equals: National Disposable Income	...	...	6212.5	6750.9	7440.9	8028.1	9742.8	13546.0	14917.1	18459.4	27213.7	...
Less: Final consumption	1309.8	2717.7	5612.8	5856.4	6765.2	7142.2	8319.8	11961.9	13398.8	16196.7	23477.6	...
Equals: Net Saving	86.7	665.5	599.7	894.5	675.7	885.9	1423.0	1584.1	1518.3	2262.7	3736.1	...
Less: Surplus of the nation on current transactions [b]	...	...	-669.8	-405.9	-442.6	-417.9	-163.4	-335.2	-600.3	-1330.7	-808.3	...
Statistical discrepancy	...	...	1.3	-16.5	-1.7	-	-	48.2	56.1	170.0	228.8	...
Equals: Net Capital Formation [ca]	195.2	666.1	1270.8	1283.9	1116.6	1303.8	1586.4	1967.5	2174.7	3763.4	4773.2	...

a) Data for this table have not been revised, therefore, data for some years are not comparable with those of other tables.
b) Item 'Net current transfers from the rest of the world' includes mainly net interest receipts.
c) Item 'Gross capital formation' includes only increase of stocks of mining, manufacturing, peanuts, raw tobacco and beans.

4.1 Derivation of Value Added by Kind of Activity, in Current Prices

Million Dominican pesos

	1980 Gross Output	1980 Intermediate Consumption	1980 Value Added	1981 Gross Output	1981 Intermediate Consumption	1981 Value Added	1982 Gross Output	1982 Intermediate Consumption	1982 Value Added	1983 Gross Output	1983 Intermediate Consumption	1983 Value Added
						All Producers						
1 Agriculture, hunting, forestry and fishing	1511.6	...	1336.3	1507.8	...	1349.5	...	...	1411.9	...	...	1484.9
A Agriculture and hunting	1466.5	...	1294.4	1459.5	...	1286.6	1537.3	...	1362.5	1631.1	...	1434.9
B Forestry and logging	15.7	...	...	17.3	...	...	...	...	...	...	...	...
C Fishing	29.4	...	...	31.0	...	...	...	...	...	...	...	...
2 Mining and quarrying	466.3	36.9	351.7	383.3	45.1	270.6	224.4	18.7	206.3	265.0	36.6	229.2
3 Manufacturing [ab]	2370.0	...	1015.4	2664.7	...	1133.1	3387.7	...	1454.9	3550.4	...	1527.5
A Manufacture of food, beverages and tobacco	1530.0	...	663.5	1765.9	...	763.1	1998.9	...	884.3	2052.0	...	910.7
B Textile, wearing apparel and leather industries	117.0	...	65.8	118.9	...	67.0	176.5	...	99.1	184.6	...	103.6
C Manufacture of wood and wood products, including furniture	19.8	...	13.3	10.3	...	13.7	36.6	...	23.6	38.3	...	24.7
D Manufacture of paper and paper products, printing and publishing	65.3	...	33.3	73.3	...	37.3	119.9	...	60.1	125.4	...	62.9
E Manufacture of chemicals and chemical petroleum, coal, rubber and plastic products	430.9	...	153.8	473.1	...	164.3	687.2	...	233.9	705.3	...	237.2
F Manufacture of non-metallic mineral products, except products of petroleum and coal	88.1	...	35.0	83.3	...	33.1	136.9	...	56.0	162.7	...	66.6
G Basic metal industries	32.3	...	11.5	32.0	...	11.4	57.9	...	20.7	77.3	...	27.7
H Manufacture of fabricated metal products, machinery and equipment	77.5	...	28.0	87.1	...	30.8	142.5	...	60.3	163.9	...	71.4
I Other manufacturing industries	1.5	...	0.3	1.7	...	0.3	11.5	...	2.4	13.2	...	2.7
4 Electricity, gas and water	167.5	...	30.0	233.4	...	66.8	...	...	82.4	...	...	77.5
A Electricity, gas and steam	...	...	30.0	...	...	66.8	...	...	82.4	...	...	77.5
B Water works and supply	...	...	...	...	...	...	...	...	...	...	...	...
5 Construction	970.0	...	479.4	1070.1	...	537.1	1082.7	...	535.1	1353.8	...	669.0
6 Wholesale and retail trade, restaurants and hotels [c]	...	...	1047.8	...	...	1197.6	...	...	1350.3	...	...	1450.6
7 Transport, storage and communication	...	...	362.3	...	...	408.5	...	...	419.7	...	...	462.9
8 Finance, insurance, real estate and business services [d]	1004.4	...	793.9	1232.4	...	968.0	...	...	1029.2	...	...	1090.4
A Financial institutions	166.3	...	122.2	209.8	...	148.1	...	...	162.4	...	...	176.9
B Insurance	127.3	...	115.6	152.7	...	138.7	...	...	173.3	...	...	190.7
C Real estate and business services	710.8	...	556.2	869.9	...	681.2	...	...	693.5	...	...	722.7
Real estate, except dwellings	...	...	...	...	...	...	...	...	...	...	...	...

Dominican Republic

4.1 Derivation of Value Added by Kind of Activity, in Current Prices
(Continued)

Million Dominican pesos

	1980 Gross Output	1980 Intermediate Consumption	1980 Value Added	1981 Gross Output	1981 Intermediate Consumption	1981 Value Added	1982 Gross Output	1982 Intermediate Consumption	1982 Value Added	1983 Gross Output	1983 Intermediate Consumption	1983 Value Added
Dwellings	710.8	...	556.2	869.9	...	681.2	...	...	693.5	...	...	722.7
9 Community, social and personal services [cd]	...	...	662.0	...	...	727.8	...	...	810.9	...	...	927.1
A Sanitary and similar services	...	...	...	...	...	...	...	...	...	...	...	...
B Social and related community services	...	...	...	...	...	...	...	...	...	...	...	...
C Recreational and cultural services	...	...	...	...	...	...	...	...	...	...	...	...
D Personal and household services	7.6	...	4.0	9.1	...	4.8	...	...	...	...	...	...
Total, Industries	...	...	6078.8	...	...	6659.0	...	...	7300.7	...	...	7919.1
Producers of Government Services	...	...	551.9	...	...	608.0	...	...	663.7	...	...	704.2
Other Producers	...	...	...	...	...	...	...	...	...	...	...	...
Total	...	...	6630.7	...	...	7266.9	...	...	7964.4	...	...	8623.3
Less: Imputed bank service charge	...	...	...	...	...	...	...	...	...	...	...	...
Import duties	...	...	...	...	...	...	...	...	...	...	...	...
Value added tax	...	...	...	...	...	...	...	...	...	...	...	...
Total	...	...	6630.7	...	...	7266.9	...	...	7964.4	...	...	8623.3

	1984 Gross Output	1984 Intermediate Consumption	1984 Value Added

All Producers

	Gross Output	Intermediate Consumption	Value Added
1 Agriculture, hunting, forestry and fishing	...	...	1915.7
A Agriculture and hunting	2113.2	...	1854.5
B Forestry and logging	...	...	...
C Fishing	...	...	...
2 Mining and quarrying	280.8	37.2	243.6
3 Manufacturing [ab]	4014.0	...	1707.6
A Manufacture of food, beverages and tobacco	2616.9	...	1143.6
B Textile, wearing apparel and leather industries	108.4	...	75.4
C Manufacture of wood and wood products, including furniture	27.6	...	17.8
D Manufacture of paper and paper products, printing and publishing	90.5	...	45.4
E Manufacture of chemicals and chemical petroleum, coal, rubber and plastic products	724.5	...	233.8
F Manufacture of non-metallic mineral products, except products of petroleum and coal	190.6	...	69.8
G Basic metal industries	69.8	...	25.5
H Manufacture of fabricated metal products, machinery and equipment	125.6	...	54.4
I Other manufacturing industries	5.9	...	1.2
4 Electricity, gas and water	...	...	94.1
A Electricity, gas and steam	...	...	94.1
B Water works and supply	...	...	...
5 Construction	1783.9	...	881.6
6 Wholesale and retail trade, restaurants and hotels [c]	...	...	1781.9
7 Transport, storage and communication	...	...	522.7
8 Finance, insurance, real estate and business services [d]	...	...	1242.1
A Financial institutions	...	...	190.4
B Insurance	...	...	252.1
C Real estate and business services	...	...	799.6
Real estate, except dwellings	...	...	...

Dominican Republic

4.1 Derivation of Value Added by Kind of Activity, in Current Prices
(Continued)

Million Dominican pesos

	1984 Gross Output	Intermediate Consumption	Value Added
Dwellings	...	...	799.6
9 Community, social and personal services cd	...	...	1153.7
A Sanitary and similar services	...	...	...
B Social and related community services	...	...	...
C Recreational and cultural services	...	...	...
D Personal and household services	...	...	...
Total, Industries	...	...	9543.0
Producers of Government Services	...	...	812.3
Other Producers	...	...	...
Total	...	...	10355.3
Less: Imputed bank service charge	...	...	...
Import duties	...	...	...
Value added tax	...	...	...
Total	...	...	10355.3

a) Item 'Manufacturing' includes handicrafts.
b) Repair services are included in item 'Manufacturing'.
c) Restaurants and hotels are included in item 'Community, social and personal services'.
d) Business services are included in item 'Community, social and personal services'.

4.2 Derivation of Value Added by Kind of Activity, in Constant Prices

Million Dominican pesos

At constant prices of: 1970 — All Producers

	1980 Gross Output	1980 Interm. Cons.	1980 Value Added	1981 Gross Output	1981 Interm. Cons.	1981 Value Added	1989 Gross Output	1989 Interm. Cons.	1989 Value Added
1 Agriculture, hunting, forestry and fishing	544.5	...	484.2	574.3	...	510.9	...	...	548.7
A Agriculture and hunting	524.9	...	465.7	553.6	...	491.3	...	...	...
B Forestry and logging	9.6	...	9.1	10.4	...	9.9	...	...	...
C Fishing	10.0	...	9.4	10.3	...	9.7	...	...	...
2 Mining and quarrying	131.7	...	124.6	143.2	...	135.6	147.1	...	139.3
3 Manufacturing ab	1218.6	...	530.2	1251.5	...	544.5	...	...	604.4
A Manufacture of food, beverages and tobacco	810.9	...	346.5	832.8	...	355.7	...	...	...
B Textile, wearing apparel and leather industries	52.1	...	27.7	53.5	...	28.6	...	...	...
C Manufacture of wood and wood products, including furniture	15.9	...	12.0	16.3	...	12.4	...	...	...
D Manufacture of paper and paper products, printing and publishing	38.9	...	18.8	40.0	...	19.4	...	...	...
E Manufacture of chemicals and chemical petroleum, coal, rubber and plastic products	179.9	...	63.6	184.8	...	65.2	...	...	...
F Manufacture of non-metallic mineral products, except products of petroleum and coal	44.6	...	28.2	45.8	...	29.1	...	...	...
G Basic metal industries	25.9	...	8.6	26.6	...	8.6	...	...	...
H Manufacture of fabricated metal products, machinery and equipment	46.8	...	18.3	48.1	...	18.9	...	...	...
I Other manufacturing industries	1.3	...	5.3	1.3	...	6.1	...	...	...
4 Electricity, gas and water	...	...	49.0	...	...	53.4	...	...	61.5
A Electricity, gas and steam	...	...	49.0	...	...	53.4	...	...	...
B Water works and supply	...	...	...	...	...	...	...	...	...
5 Construction	399.8	...	197.5	397.5	...	196.5	...	...	347.5
6 Wholesale and retail trade, restaurants and hotels c	...	...	473.6	...	...	494.9	...	...	538.8
7 Transport, storage and communication	...	...	230.5	...	...	242.6	...	...	288.4
A Transport and storage	...	...	199.6	...	...	210.0	...	...	220.7

Dominican Republic

4.2 Derivation of Value Added by Kind of Activity, in Constant Prices
(Continued)

Million Dominican pesos

	1980 Gross Output	1980 Intermediate Consumption	1980 Value Added	1981 Gross Output	1981 Intermediate Consumption	1981 Value Added	1989 Gross Output	1989 Intermediate Consumption	1989 Value Added
			At constant prices of:1970						
B Communication	...	...	30.9	...	...	32.6	...	...	68.7
8 Finance, insurance, real estate and business services d	...	...	268.6	...	...	272.1	...	...	...
9 Community, social and personal services cd	...	...	265.4	...	...	271.4	...	...	344.7
A Sanitary and similar services	...	...	...	...	...	...	...	...	...
B Social and related community services	...	...	...	...	...	...	...	...	...
C Recreational and cultural services	...	...	...	...	...	...	...	...	...
D Personal and household services	2.3	...	1.2	2.3	...	0.5	...	...	...
Total, Industries	...	...	2623.6	...	...	2721.8	...	...	...
Producers of Government Services	...	...	280.1	...	...	300.1	...	...	349.0
Other Producers	...	...	...	...	...	...	...	...	...
Total	...	...	2903.8	...	...	3021.9	...	...	...
Less: Imputed bank service charge	...	...	...	...	...	...	...	...	...
Import duties	...	...	...	...	...	...	...	...	...
Value added tax	...	...	...	...	...	...	...	...	...
Total	...	...	2903.9	...	...	3021.9	...	...	...

a) Item 'Manufacturing' includes handicrafts.
b) Repair services are included in item 'Manufacturing'.
c) Restaurants and hotels are included in item 'Community, social and personal services'.
d) Business services are included in item 'Community, social and personal services'.

Ecuador

Source. Reply to the United Nations National Accounts Questionnaire from the Subgerencia de Cuentas Nacionales, Banco Central del Ecuador, Quito. The official estimates are published annually in 'Memoria del Gerente General del Banco Central del Ecuador'.

General note. The estimates shown in the following tables have been prepared in accordance with the United Nations System of National Accounts so far as the existing data would permit.

1.1 Expenditure on the Gross Domestic Product, in Current Prices

Million Ecuadoran sucres

		1970	1975	1980	1981	1982	1983	1984	1985	1986	1987	1988	1989
1	Government final consumption expenditure	3864	15624	42562	49742	58150	70055	99628	127330	166731	230417	337003	499620
2	Private final consumption expenditure	26375	70298	174875	214665	262206	369330	520593	715659	925775	1269416	2140102	3896928
	A Households	26375	70298	174875	214665	262206	369330	520593	715659	925775	1269416	2140102	3896928
	B Private non-profit institutions serving households	...	...	...	...	...	...	...	...	...	...	...	...
3	Gross capital formation	6371	28797	76630	80790	104821	98442	139962	201697	288493	406832	682681	1177926
	A Increase in stocks	529	3890	7304	3162	10649	5411	14732	23442	28491	234	15824	52223
	B Gross fixed capital formation	5842	24907	69326	77628	94172	93031	125230	178255	260002	406598	666857	1125703
	Residential buildings	850	3921	8456	10068	14688	15198	21029	25126	30965	41037	76931	102572
	Non-residential buildings	958	3127	10864	12430	14862	17636	22263	27903	35235	42538	71419	115791
	Other construction and land improvement etc.	2018	5435	17613	23979	27727	29129	35635	50622	73168	125970	155460	295057
	Other	2016	12424	32393	31151	36895	31068	46303	74604	120634	197053	363047	612283
4	Exports of goods and services	4909	28242	73797	75906	87563	133061	209858	296922	314740	431538	865318	1482600
5	Less: Imports of goods and services	6500	35221	74527	72441	97025	110617	157412	231668	312507	543702	920765	1592461
	Equals: Gross Domestic Product	35019	107740	293337	348662	415715	560271	812629	1109940	1383232	1794501	3104339	5464613

1.2 Expenditure on the Gross Domestic Product, in Constant Prices

Million Ecuadoran sucres

		1970	1975	1980	1981	1982	1983	1984	1985	1986	1987	1988	1989
					At constant prices of:1975								
1	Government final consumption expenditure	7600	15624	23611	24185	24299	22828	21997	21076	20904	21245	20084	20306
2	Private final consumption expenditure	49468	70298	99686	104511	106383	103785	106597	110441	111397	114115	117230	118954
	A Households	49468	70298	99686	104511	106383	103785	106597	110441	111397	114115	117230	118954
	B Private non-profit institutions serving households	...	...	...	...	...	...	...	...	...	...	...	...
3	Gross capital formation	14549	28797	39216	33953	38236	26294	25914	27975	28816	27915	28039	28732
	A Increase in stocks	973	3890	4241	1511	5569	2167	2879	3357	3139	1115	1877	2700
	B Gross fixed capital formation	13576	24907	34975	32442	32667	24127	23035	24618	25677	26800	26162	26032
	Residential buildings												
	Non-residential buildings	8902	12483	16016	15874	15977	14696	14160	14399	14367	14982	13665	13489
	Other construction and land improvement etc.												
	Other	4674	12424	18959	16568	16690	9431	8875	10219	11310	11818	12497	12543
4	Exports of goods and services	8333	28242	30792	32247	30647	31396	35331	39562	42944	36027	47614	46952
5	Less: Imports of goods and services	17038	35221	45683	41453	44300	33418	32613	35000	34925	40286	36101	37800
	Equals: Gross Domestic Product	62912	107740	147622	153443	155265	150885	157226	164054	169136	159016	176866	177144

1.3 Cost Components of the Gross Domestic Product

Million Ecuadoran sucres

		1970	1975	1980	1981	1982	1983	1984	1985	1986	1987	1988	1989
1	Indirect taxes, net	3766	10740	24388	32632	35731	46663	67690	128379	156453	204535	350626	652558
	A Indirect taxes	3881	11681	26931	35746	39327	48693	72358	152141	190845	228830	378577	710992
	B Less: Subsidies	115	941	2543	3114	3596	2030	4668	23762	34392	24295	27951	58434
2	Consumption of fixed capital [a]	...	...	...	...	...	...	...	...	...	...	...	...
3	Compensation of employees paid by resident producers to:	10764	32047	93662	105275	120017	135761	179524	232075	301524	401081	546340	770999
	A Resident households	10755	31364	92879	104445	118609	133574	176149	229738	297763	393690	536594	757463
	B Rest of the world	9	683	783	830	1408	2187	3375	2337	3761	7391	9746	13536
4	Operating surplus [a]	20489	64953	175287	210755	259967	377847	565415	749486	925255	1188885	2207373	4041056
	A Corporate and quasi-corporate enterprises [b]	2029	15399	52003	57262	74646	102234	168068	214248	217661	214309	472686	767235
	B Private unincorporated enterprises [c]	18505	49536	122984	153574	184746	275140	395670	533522	705213	970732	1730144	3268344
	C General government	-45	18	300	-81	575	473	1677	1716	2381	3844	4543	5477
	Equals: Gross Domestic Product	35019	107740	293337	348662	415715	560271	812629	1109940	1383232	1794501	3104339	5464613

a) Item 'Operating surplus' includes consumption of fixed capital.
b) Beginning 1976, item 'Corporate and quasi-corporate enterprises' includes quasi-corporate enterprises that up to 1975 were included with households.
c) Item 'Private unincorporated enterprises' relates to households.

Ecuador

1.4 General Government Current Receipts and Disbursements

Million Ecuadoran sucres

	1970	1975	1980	1981	1982	1983	1984	1985	1986	1987	1988	1989
Receipts												
1 Operating surplus	-45	18	300	-81	575	473	1677	1716	2381	3844	4543	5477
2 Property and entrepreneurial income	579	3757	10954	13748	15871	25204	33566	31298	29120	30644	65288	116175
3 Taxes, fees and contributions	5771	21502	58631	68456	83708	106049	161792	273900	299440	339389	569840	1072999
A Indirect taxes	3881	11681	26931	35746	39327	48693	72358	152141	190845	228830	378577	710992
B Direct taxes	772	6895	22390	22888	32834	41137	69653	93216	70004	63400	129407	273310
C Social security contributions	1035	2584	8092	8787	10279	14786	17597	25042	33454	41297	53393	71133
D Compulsory fees, fines and penalties	83	342	1218	1035	1268	1433	2184	3501	5137	5862	8463	17564
4 Other current transfers	561	3269	10540	13842	15351	18031	22770	44256	62386	70527	92374	112905
Total Current Receipts of General Government	6866	28546	80425	95965	115505	149757	219805	351170	393327	444404	732045	1307556
Disbursements												
1 Government final consumption expenditure	3864	15624	42562	49742	58150	70055	99628	127330	166731	230417	337003	499620
2 Property income	600	983	7590	11044	20525	24536	31184	48591	57085	56821	76639	179785
A Interest	600	983	7588	11041	20524	24534	31184	48591	57085	56821	76639	179785
B Net land rent and royalties	-	-	2	3	1	2	-	-	-	-	-	-
3 Subsidies	115	941	2543	3114	3596	2030	4668	23762	34392	24295	27951	58434
4 Other current transfers	1227	5010	16916	19780	22514	28506	37051	49195	60872	88223	105729	171302
A Social security benefits	778	1818	6746	7726	8988	12639	15629	20673	22385	39535	41912	58906
B Social assistance grants	155	645	1353	1787	1463	1520	2090	2625	2875	4214	5597	9603
C Other	294	2547	8817	10267	12063	14347	19332	25897	35612	44474	58220	102793
5 Net saving [a]	1060	5988	10814	12285	10720	24630	47274	102292	74247	44648	184723	398415
Total Current Disbursements and Net Saving of General Government	6866	28546	80425	95965	115505	149757	219805	351170	393327	444404	732045	1307556

a) Item 'Net saving' includes consumption of fixed capital.

1.5 Current Income and Outlay of Corporate and Quasi-Corporate Enterprises, Summary

Million Ecuadoran sucres

	1970	1975	1980	1981	1982	1983	1984	1985	1986	1987	1988	1989
Receipts												
1 Operating surplus [a]	2029	15399	52003	57262	74646	102234	168068	214248	217661	214309	472686	767235
2 Property and entrepreneurial income received	1047	3654	15780	19161	26637	43860	77216	103952	144072	205295	306100	431466
3 Current transfers	215	884	1796	2220	3217	4027	4974	7910	11930	19597	29701	45791
Total Current Receipts	3291	19937	69579	78643	104500	150121	250258	326110	373663	439201	808487	1244492
Disbursements												
1 Property and entrepreneurial income	1732	8071	32576	39989	53617	87750	154293	186170	246288	321598	504283	781801
2 Direct taxes and other current payments to general government	256	5904	20187	19148	30006	37764	64648	86072	59537	49863	111050	237974
3 Other current transfers	277	1330	2876	4726	5552	6194	7506	25610	39392	47138	64995	59357
4 Net saving [b]	1026	4632	13940	14780	15325	18413	23811	28258	28446	20602	128159	165360
Total Current Disbursements and Net Saving	3291	19937	69579	78643	104500	150121	250258	326110	373663	439201	808487	1244492

a) Item 'Operating surplus' includes consumption of fixed capital.
b) Item 'Net saving' includes consumption of fixed capital.

1.6 Current Income and Outlay of Households and Non-Profit Institutions

Million Ecuadoran sucres

	1970	1975	1980	1981	1982	1983	1984	1985	1986	1987	1988	1989
Receipts												
1 Compensation of employees	10755	31369	92924	104495	118671	133731	176324	230005	298243	394423	537712	759455
A From resident producers	10755	31364	92879	104445	118609	133574	176149	229738	297763	393690	536594	757463
B From rest of the world	-	5	45	50	62	157	175	267	480	733	1118	1992
2 Operating surplus of private unincorporated enterprises	18505	49536	122984	153574	184746	275140	395670	533522	705213	970732	1730144	3268344
3 Property and entrepreneurial income	270	1098	4430	6060	9999	13306	18572	37226	51553	70445	97618	140264
4 Current transfers	1460	4312	12037	14580	16880	22550	29383	41914	51657	104257	124121	193549
A Social security benefits	778	1818	6746	7726	8988	12639	15629	20673	22385	39535	41912	58906
B Social assistance grants												
C Other	682	2494	5291	6854	7892	9911	13754	21241	29272	64722	82209	134643
Total Current Receipts	30990	86315	232375	278709	330296	444727	619949	842667	1106666	1539857	2489595	4361612

Ecuador

1.6 Current Income and Outlay of Households and Non-Profit Institutions
(Continued)

Million Ecuadoran sucres

	1970	1975	1980	1981	1982	1983	1984	1985	1986	1987	1988	1989
						Disbursements						
1 Private final consumption expenditure	26375	70298	174875	214665	262206	369330	520593	715659	925775	1269416	2140102	3896928
2 Property income	360	1895	6707	8003	10984	13884	18687	25640	40246	57628	92332	115735
3 Direct taxes and other current transfers n.e.c. to general government	1634	3917	11513	13562	14375	19592	24786	35687	49058	60696	80213	124033
A Social security contributions	1035	2584	8092	8787	10279	14786	17597	25042	33454	41297	53393	71133
B Direct taxes	541	1146	2711	4107	3295	3905	5814	8678	12669	16433	22776	44087
C Fees, fines and penalties	58	187	710	668	801	901	1375	1967	2935	2966	4044	8813
4 Other current transfers	231	967	1827	2310	3043	3923	5319	8912	13006	19756	30620	43350
5 Net saving [a]	2390	9238	37453	40169	39688	37998	50564	56769	78581	132361	146328	181566
Total Current Disbursements and Net Saving	30990	86315	232375	278709	330296	444727	619949	842667	1106666	1539857	2489595	4361612

a) Item 'Net saving' includes consumption of fixed capital.

1.7 External Transactions on Current Account, Summary

Million Ecuadoran sucres

	1970	1975	1980	1981	1982	1983	1984	1985	1986	1987	1988	1989
					Payments to the Rest of the World							
1 Imports of goods and services	6500	35221	74527	72441	97025	110617	157412	231668	312507	543702	920765	1592461
A Imports of merchandise c.i.f.	5507	32527	63512	59391	80583	85154	127264	177399	242639	448150	723661	1308256
B Other	993	2694	11015	13050	16442	25463	30148	54269	69868	95552	197104	284205
2 Factor income to the rest of the world	694	2898	16932	20242	31899	43696	76962	84409	115517	126115	200609	385681
A Compensation of employees	9	683	783	830	1408	2187	3375	2337	3761	7391	9746	13536
B Property and entrepreneurial income	685	2215	16149	19412	30491	41509	73587	82072	111756	118724	190863	372145
3 Current transfers to the rest of the world	71	313	1011	1497	2031	2026	2497	3366	3833	6368	9843	15500
4 Surplus of the nation on current transactions	-1895	-8939	-14423	-13556	-39088	-17401	-18313	-14378	-107219	-209221	-223471	-432585
Payments to the Rest of the World and Surplus of the Nation on Current Transactions	5370	29493	78047	80624	91867	138938	218558	305065	324638	466964	907746	1561057
					Receipts From The Rest of the World							
1 Exports of goods and services	4909	28242	73797	75906	87563	133061	209858	296922	314740	431538	865318	1482600
A Exports of merchandise f.o.b.	4533	26058	64389	66050	76742	110999	183425	255387	250181	348095	679360	1219947
B Other	376	2184	9408	9856	10821	22062	26433	41535	64559	83443	185958	262653
2 Factor income from rest of the world	22	430	2395	1935	1014	1904	4391	2654	3868	3821	5648	9873
A Compensation of employees	-	5	45	50	62	157	175	267	480	733	1118	1992
B Property and entrepreneurial income	22	425	2350	1885	952	1747	4216	2387	3388	3088	4530	7881
3 Current transfers from rest of the world	439	821	1855	2783	3290	3973	4309	5489	6030	31605	36780	68584
Receipts from the Rest of the World on Current Transactions	5370	29493	78047	80624	91867	138938	218558	305065	324638	466964	907746	1561057

1.8 Capital Transactions of The Nation, Summary

Million Ecuadoran sucres

	1970	1975	1980	1981	1982	1983	1984	1985	1986	1987	1988	1989
					Finance of Gross Capital Formation							
Gross saving	4476	19858	62207	67234	65733	81041	121649	187319	181274	197611	459210	745341
1 Consumption of fixed capital	1373	7588	27304	34554	45019	64368	99292	136137	165920	301424	507347	829372
2 Net saving	3103	12270	34903	32680	20714	16673	22357	51182	15354	-103813	-48137	-84031
Less: Surplus of the nation on current transactions	-1895	-8939	-14423	-13556	-39088	-17401	-18313	-14378	-107219	-209221	-223471	-432585
Finance of Gross Capital Formation	6371	28797	76630	80790	104821	98442	139962	201697	288493	406832	682681	1177926
					Gross Capital Formation							
Increase in stocks	529	3890	7304	3162	10649	5411	14732	23442	28491	234	15824	52223

Ecuador

1.8 Capital Transactions of The Nation, Summary
(Continued)

Million Ecuadoran sucres

	1970	1975	1980	1981	1982	1983	1984	1985	1986	1987	1988	1989
Gross fixed capital formation	5842	24907	69326	77628	94172	93031	125230	178255	260002	406598	666857	1125703
1 General government	1790	6308	18846	25521	27180	26723	35524	54113	82307	115500	152978	251753
2 Corporate and quasi-corporate enterprises	2465	10737	36206	36883	45524	47345	62612	88379	133081	225860	398328	701221
A Public	543	3030	9063	11327	12973	17902	16685	19187	44704	50981	120213	218497
B Private	1922	7707	27143	25556	32551	29443	45927	69192	88377	174879	278115	482724
3 Other	1587	7862	14274	15224	21468	18963	27094	35763	44614	65238	115551	172729
Gross Capital Formation	6371	28797	76630	80790	104821	98442	139962	201697	288493	406832	682681	1177926

1.9 Gross Domestic Product by Institutional Sectors of Origin

Million Ecuadoran sucres

	1970	1975	1980	1981	1982	1983	1984	1985	1986	1987	1988	1989
					Domestic Factor Incomes Originating							
1 General government	3254	10545	29436	34169	39559	47049	71245	96899	127831	169078	234536	330408
2 Corporate and quasi-corporate enterprises	6382	29919	104426	124020	154388	201829	287906	401036	440820	537817	991454	1585217
A Non-financial	5643	27348	93395	111884	140020	184075	271794	381181	414948	485375	891616	1503264
Public	680	5163	32420	39182	49650	67857	105669	172950	151788	160067	265211	593815
Private	4963	22185	60975	72702	90370	116218	166125	208231	263160	325308	626405	909449
B Financial	739	2571	11031	12136	14368	17754	16112	19855	25872	52442	99838	81953
Public	310	1082	5583	5404	7559	10087	4028	1897	5667	27372	59492	31692
Private	429	1489	5448	6732	6809	7667	12084	17958	20205	25070	40346	50261
3 Households and private unincorporated enterprises	24095	64419	156360	188035	222599	314877	443413	591567	778810	1063900	1856469	3445617
4 Non-profit institutions serving households	...	...	...	...	...	...	...	...	...	...	...	...
Subtotal: Domestic Factor Incomes [a,b]	33731	104883	290222	346224	416546	563755	802564	1089502	1347461	1770795	3082459	5361242
Indirect taxes, net [c]	1921	4920	12024	12383	12130	15716	26776	42034	64344	77419	120877	196200
A Indirect taxes	1921	5297	12746	13183	12934	15755	26776	42034	64344	77419	120877	196200
B Less: Subsidies	-	377	722	800	804	39	-	-	-	-	-	-
Consumption of fixed capital	...	...	...	...	...	...	...	...	...	...	...	...
Statistical discrepancy [d]	-633	-2063	-8909	-9945	-12961	-19200	-16711	-21596	-28573	-53713	-98997	-92829
Gross Domestic Product	35019	107740	293337	348662	415715	560271	812629	1109940	1383232	1794501	3104339	5464613

a) Item 'Domestic factor incomes' includes consumption of fixed capital.
b) Item 'Domestic factor incomes' includes net indirect taxes other than import duties.
c) Item 'Indirect taxes, net' refers to import duties only.
d) Item 'Statistical discrepancy' relates to imputed bank service charges.

1.10 Gross Domestic Product by Kind of Activity, in Current Prices

Million Ecuadoran sucres

	1970	1975	1980	1981	1982	1983	1984	1985	1986	1987	1988	1989
1 Agriculture, hunting, forestry and fishing	8386	19333	35570	41631	50356	73005	110003	147979	208743	274583	468080	803047
2 Mining and quarrying [a]	543	12482	35686	44015	52412	86115	126833	189516	137969	122567	347095	714160
3 Manufacturing [a]	6372	17209	51799	59951	73874	103642	168016	210259	274177	350257	650362	1203499
4 Electricity, gas and water	333	809	2434	2546	3693	3285	4002	3401	6487	7413	1639	1937
5 Construction	1377	5988	21749	30522	37576	34423	36743	48593	67267	98981	112631	194142
6 Wholesale and retail trade, restaurants and hotels	5099	16949	42751	46339	57552	76347	130164	173338	246833	363144	631216	1149894
7 Transport, storage and communication	2359	6169	23145	29861	36025	54301	57944	94931	125565	169713	297335	451315
8 Finance, insurance, real estate and business services	3799	11237	34240	39845	46256	58638	67804	83884	104957	151419	244844	332273
9 Community, social and personal services	2189	4509	14534	18772	22018	29792	34984	46826	56968	77268	114868	213017
Total, Industries	30457	94685	261908	313482	379762	519548	736493	998727	1228966	1615345	2868070	5063284
Producers of Government Services	3008	9640	26590	30985	34855	41872	63169	86470	112969	147890	204867	283484
Other Producers	266	558	1724	1757	1929	2335	2902	4305	5526	7560	9522	14474
Subtotal	33731	104883	290222	346224	416546	563755	802564	1089502	1347461	1770795	3082459	5361242
Less: Imputed bank service charge	633	2063	8909	9945	12961	19200	16711	21596	28573	53713	98997	92829
Plus: Import duties	1921	4920	12024	12383	12130	15716	26776	42034	64344	77419	120877	196200
Plus: Value added tax	...	...	...	...	...	...	...	...	...	...	...	...
Equals: Gross Domestic Product	35019	107740	293337	348662	415715	560271	812629	1109940	1383232	1794501	3104339	5464613

a) Petroleum refining is included in item 'Crude petroleum and natural gas production'.

Ecuador

1.11 Gross Domestic Product by Kind of Activity, in Constant Prices

Million Ecuadoran sucres

	1970	1975	1980	1981	1982	1983	1984	1985	1986	1987	1988	1989
	At constant prices of: 1975											
1 Agriculture, hunting, forestry and fishing	15710	19333	21198	22647	23101	19891	22007	24178	26656	27323	29678	30581
2 Mining and quarrying [a]	-2314	12482	15070	15992	15527	19893	21879	23875	24513	11107	25319	23501
3 Manufacturing [a]	10803	17209	26807	29159	29584	29183	28643	28710	28241	28729	29381	28272
4 Electricity, gas and water	477	809	1115	1117	1241	1426	1836	1833	2232	2616	2789	2871
5 Construction	3940	5988	6906	7239	7285	6728	6583	6742	6841	7011	6359	6282
6 Wholesale and retail trade, restaurants and hotels	10731	16949	24789	25032	25562	22537	23467	24268	24793	25397	26256	26392
7 Transport, storage and communication	3765	6169	10038	10517	10687	10511	10914	11506	12571	12829	13486	14175
8 Finance, insurance, real estate and business services	7536	11237	17694	18274	18590	18972	17679	18162	18579	21095	22978	19629
9 Community, social and personal services	3629	4509	7612	8240	8710	9098	9366	9529	9773	10067	10190	10478
Total, Industries	54277	94685	131229	138217	140287	138239	142374	148803	154199	146174	166436	162181
Producers of Government Services	6005	9640	13709	14000	14224	14493	14775	14842	14898	15002	14231	14501
Other Producers	458	558	675	688	696	705	714	723	735	756	778	800
Subtotal	60740	104883	145613	152905	155207	153437	157863	164368	169832	161932	181445	177482
Less: Imputed bank service charge	1258	2063	5006	5059	5315	6158	4485	4519	4934	7122	8683	5114
Plus: Import duties	3430	4920	7015	5597	5373	3606	3848	4205	4238	4206	4104	4776
Plus: Value added tax	...	...	...	...	...	...	...	...	...	...	...	...
Equals: Gross Domestic Product	62912	107740	147622	153443	155265	150885	157226	164054	169136	159016	176866	177144

a) Petroleum refining is included in item 'Crude petroleum and natural gas production'.

1.12 Relations Among National Accounting Aggregates

Million Ecuadoran sucres

	1970	1975	1980	1981	1982	1983	1984	1985	1986	1987	1988	1989
Gross Domestic Product	35019	107740	293337	348662	415715	560271	812629	1109940	1383232	1794501	3104339	5464613
Plus: Net factor income from the rest of the world	-672	-2468	-14537	-18307	-30885	-41792	-72571	-81755	-111649	-122294	-194961	-375808
Factor income from the rest of the world	22	430	2395	1935	1014	1904	4391	2654	3868	3821	5648	9873
Less: Factor income to the rest of the world	694	2898	16932	20242	31899	43696	76962	84409	115517	126115	200609	385681
Equals: Gross National Product	34347	105272	278800	330355	384830	518479	740058	1028185	1271583	1672207	2909378	5088805
Less: Consumption of fixed capital	1373	7588	27304	34554	45019	64368	99292	136137	165920	301424	507347	829372
Equals: National Income	32974	97684	251496	295801	339811	454111	640766	892048	1105663	1370783	2402031	4259433
Plus: Net current transfers from the rest of the world	368	508	844	1286	1259	1947	1812	2123	2197	25237	26937	53084
Current transfers from the rest of the world	439	821	1855	2783	3290	3973	4309	5489	6030	31605	36780	68584
Less: Current transfers to the rest of the world	71	313	1011	1497	2031	2026	2497	3366	3833	6368	9843	15500
Equals: National Disposable Income	33342	98192	252340	297087	341070	456058	642578	894171	1107860	1396020	2428968	4312517
Less: Final consumption	30239	85922	217437	264407	320356	439385	620221	842989	1092506	1499833	2477105	4396548
Equals: Net Saving	3103	12270	34903	32680	20714	16673	22357	51182	15354	-103813	-48137	-84031
Less: Surplus of the nation on current transactions	-1895	-8939	-14423	-13556	-39088	-17401	-18313	-14378	-107219	-209221	-223471	-432585
Equals: Net Capital Formation	4998	21209	49326	46236	59802	34074	40670	65560	122573	105408	175334	348554

2.1 Government Final Consumption Expenditure by Function, in Current Prices

Million Ecuadoran sucres

	1970	1975	1980	1981	1982	1983	1984	1985	1986	1987	1988	1989
1 General public services	...	1550	6181	7188	7768	7546	10270	14758	27376	38301	55045	...
2 Defence	...	2304	5136	5703	7178	9611	17391	25063	21386	29770	44664	...
3 Public order and safety	...	1027	2348	2484	2989	3697	5431	7601	10608	13939	20185	...
4 Education	...	4226	13136	15745	17532	20691	29911	42950	56854	85060	118605	...
5 Health	...	761	2309	3053	4256	6009	7817	8685	10757	13653	17846	...
6 Social security and welfare	...	637	1910	2654	3550	4175	5489	6946	9264	12376	16797	...
7 Housing and community amenities	...	585	1338	1600	1591	1861	3059	3885	5233	6678	11663	...
8 Recreational, cultural and religious affairs	...	50	131	169	159	188	329	379	472	647	801	...
9 Economic services	...	2175	5062	6025	6423	8997	11059	16083	27178	41061	57656	...

Ecuador

2.1 Government Final Consumption Expenditure by Function, in Current Prices
(Continued)

Million Ecuadoran sucres

	1970	1975	1980	1981	1982	1983	1984	1985	1986	1987	1988	1989
A Fuel and energy	...	164	1094	1536	1422	2463	2440	4335	4864	6348	7993	...
B Agriculture, forestry, fishing and hunting	...	751	1530	1646	2013	2388	3641	4920	6547	9647	13170	...
C Mining, manufacturing and construction, except fuel and energy	...	104	386	527	578	634	1034	1486	2877	5574	8196	...
D Transportation and communication	...	987	1700	1772	1838	2292	2813	3901	11190	17051	25191	...
E Other economic affairs	...	169	352	544	572	1220	1131	1441	1700	2441	3106	...
10 Other functions	...	3747	7791	9108	11331	12802	15774	10650	9133	3867	16656	...
Total Government Final Consumption Expenditure a	...	17062	45342	53729	62777	75577	106530	137000	178261	245352	359918	...

a) Government final consumption expenditure in this table includes compensation of employees and intermediate consumption of the following departmental enterprises: electricity, gas and steam, water works and supply and medical and other health services.

2.3 Total Government Outlays by Function and Type

Million Ecuadoran sucres

	Final Consumption Expenditures Total	Compensation of Employees	Other	Subsidies	Other Current Transfers & Property Income	Total Current Disbursements	Gross Capital Formation	Other Capital Outlays	Total Outlays
1980									
1 General public services	6181	2932	3249	...	94	6275	469	91	6835
2 Defence	5136	2668	2468	...	...	5136	36	...	5172
3 Public order and safety	2348	2020	328	...	60	2408	125	...	2533
4 Education	13136	11978	1158	...	797	13933	1660	48	15641
5 Health	2309	1885	424	...	2207	4516	802	...	5318
6 Social security and welfare	1910	1587	323	...	5761	7671	720	70	8461
7 Housing and community amenities	1338	947	391	...	2	1340	2071	493	3904
8 Recreation, culture and religion	131	74	57	...	16	147	31	...	178
9 Economic services	5062	2632	2430	2543	131	7736	13644	1394	22774
A Fuel and energy	1094	526	568	242	33	1369	5221	1008	7598
B Agriculture, forestry, fishing and hunting	1530	942	588	146	41	1717	979	318	3014
C Mining (except fuels), manufacturing and construction	386	265	121	1722	42	2150	98	3	2251
D Transportation and communication	1700	725	975	420	1	2121	6296	59	8476
E Other economic affairs	352	174	178	13	14	379	1050	6	1435
10 Other functions	7791	26	7765	...	6772	14563	...	127	14690
Total abc	45342	26749	18593	2543	15840	63725	19558	2223	85506
1981									
1 General public services	7188	3332	3856	...	245	7433	1351	10	8794
2 Defence	5703	2862	2841	...	1	5704	80	89	5873
3 Public order and safety	2484	2120	364	...	18	2502	308	...	2810
4 Education	15745	13981	1764	...	864	16609	2273	25	18907
5 Health	3053	2260	793	...	3035	6088	1330	...	7418
6 Social security and welfare	2654	2134	520	...	6474	9128	886	13	10027
7 Housing and community amenities	1600	1136	464	...	10	1610	3034	1282	5926
8 Recreation, culture and religion	169	98	71	...	14	183	90	...	273
9 Economic services	6025	3307	2718	3114	238	9377	16943	4646	30966
A Fuel and energy	1536	606	930	217	34	1787	6809	4266	12862
B Agriculture, forestry, fishing and hunting	1646	1083	563	105	87	1838	1124	93	3055
C Mining (except fuels), manufacturing and construction	527	374	153	2297	78	2902	56	...	2958
D Transportation and communication	1772	955	817	327	1	2100	7707	273	10080
E Other economic affairs	544	289	255	168	38	750	1247	14	2011
10 Other functions	9108	43	9065	...	9932	19040	...	86	19126
Total abc	53729	31273	22456	3114	20831	77674	26295	6151	110120
1982									
1 General public services	7768	...	...	...	302	8070	867	...	8937
2 Defence	7178	...	...	...	111	7289	72	...	7361
3 Public order and safety	2989	...	...	...	18	3007	381	...	3388
4 Education	17532	...	...	...	878	18410	2771	31	21212
5 Health	4256	...	...	...	3468	7724	1259	7	8990

Ecuador

2.3 Total Government Outlays by Function and Type
(Continued)

Million Ecuadoran sucres

	Final Consumption Expenditures Total	Compensation of Employees	Other	Subsidies	Other Current Transfers & Property Income	Total Current Disbursements	Gross Capital Formation	Other Capital Outlays	Total Outlays
6 Social security and welfare	3550	...	...	...	7973	11523	687	8	12218
7 Housing and community amenities	1591	...	...	...	10	1601	3803	831	6235
8 Recreation, culture and religion	159	...	...	...	28	187	147	...	334
9 Economic services	6423	...	...	3596	263	10282	17762	5380	33424
A Fuel and energy	1422	...	...	109	21	1552	5560	5034	12146
B Agriculture, forestry, fishing and hunting	2013	...	...	84	90	2187	1072	89	3348
C Mining (except fuels), manufacturing and construction	578	...	...	2978	99	3655	43	4	3702
D Transportation and communication	1838	...	...	327	5	2170	8800	172	11142
E Other economic affairs	572	...	...	98	48	718	2287	81	3086
10 Other functions	11331	...	...	...	18386	29717	42	28	29787
Total abc	62777	...	...	3596	31437	97810	27791	6285	131886
1983									
1 General public services	7546	...	...	...	578	8124	688	1	8813
2 Defence	9611	...	...	...	3	9614	39	...	9653
3 Public order and safety	3697	...	...	...	111	3808	526	...	4334
4 Education	20691	...	...	...	812	21503	3733	18	25254
5 Health	6009	...	...	...	3699	9708	1443	8	11159
6 Social security and welfare	4175	...	...	...	11862	16037	1051	13	17101
7 Housing and community amenities	1861	...	...	20	10	1891	4173	810	6874
8 Recreation, culture and religion	188	...	...	...	24	212	128	...	340
9 Economic services	8997	...	...	2010	286	11293	15660	1466	28419
A Fuel and energy	2463	...	...	617	15	3095	3211	1147	7453
B Agriculture, forestry, fishing and hunting	2388	...	...	111	23	2522	1238	90	3850
C Mining (except fuels), manufacturing and construction	634	...	...	512	89	1235	46	174	1455
D Transportation and communication	2292	...	...	511	122	2925	8792	3	11720
E Other economic affairs	1220	...	...	259	37	1516	2373	52	3941
10 Other functions	12802	...	...	...	21965	34767	46	30	34843
Total abc	75577	...	...	2030	39350	116957	27487	2346	146790
1984									
1 General public services	10270	...	...	...	730	11000	1032	2	12034
2 Defence	17391	...	...	...	1	17392	-15	...	17377
3 Public order and safety	5431	...	...	...	136	5567	618	...	6185
4 Education	29911	...	...	...	966	30877	4227	35	35139
5 Health	7817	...	...	...	5451	13268	1710	396	15374
6 Social security and welfare	5489	...	...	...	13142	18631	791	531	19953
7 Housing and community amenities	3059	...	...	14	22	3095	5421	1167	9683
8 Recreation, culture and religion	329	...	...	...	37	366	153	...	519
9 Economic services	11059	...	...	4654	433	16146	21484	566	38196
A Fuel and energy	2440	...	...	3773	27	6240	4046	13	10299
B Agriculture, forestry, fishing and hunting	3641	...	...	70	28	3739	1995	7	5741
C Mining (except fuels), manufacturing and construction	1034	...	...	327	114	1475	81	423	1979
D Transportation and communication	2813	...	...	325	148	3286	11164	4	14454
E Other economic affairs	1131	...	...	159	116	1406	4198	119	5723
10 Other functions	15774	...	...	...	28656	44430	103	...	44533
Total abc	106530	...	...	4668	49574	160772	35524	2697	198993
1985									
1 General public services	14758	...	...	...	950	15708	1593	3	17304
2 Defence	25063	...	...	...	1	25064	66	...	25130
3 Public order and safety	7601	...	...	...	159	7760	748	...	8508
4 Education	42950	...	...	...	1205	44155	6169	49	50373
5 Health	8685	...	...	...	6916	15601	3245	454	19300

Ecuador

2.3 Total Government Outlays by Function and Type
(Continued)

Million Ecuadoran sucres

		Final Consumption Expenditures			Subsidies	Other Current Transfers & Property Income	Total Current Disbursements	Gross Capital Formation	Other Capital Outlays	Total Outlays
		Total	Compensation of Employees	Other						
6	Social security and welfare	6946	...	...	...	18041	24987	1379	626	26992
7	Housing and community amenities	3885	...	...	36	18	3939	6102	1196	11237
8	Recreation, culture and religion	379	...	...	...	50	429	203	...	632
9	Economic services	16083	...	...	23726	461	40270	34228	559	75057
	A Fuel and energy	4335	...	...	21485	46	25866	7756	12	33634
	B Agriculture, forestry, fishing and hunting	4920	...	...	177	36	5133	3265	3	8401
	C Mining (except fuels), manufacturing and construction	1486	...	...	823	146	2455	117	411	2983
	D Transportation and communication	3901	...	...	840	189	4930	17673	6	22609
	E Other economic affairs	1441	...	...	401	44	1886	5417	127	7430
10	Other functions	10650	...	...	...	44763	55413	380	...	55793
	Total abc	137000	...	...	23762	72564	233326	54113	2887	290326

1986

1	General public services	27376	...	...	...	1024	28400	2692	7	31099
2	Defence	21386	...	...	...	417	21803	1	...	21804
3	Public order and safety	10608	...	...	...	168	10776	1070	...	11846
4	Education	56854	...	...	...	1318	58172	8269	80	66521
5	Health	10757	...	...	...	8792	19549	5312	456	25317
6	Social security and welfare	9264	...	...	...	18789	28053	2046	661	30760
7	Housing and community amenities	5233	...	...	83	17	5333	13858	2270	21461
8	Recreation, culture and religion	472	...	...	...	16	488	230	9	727
9	Economic services	27178	...	...	34309	517	62004	48265	3031	113300
	A Fuel and energy	4864	...	...	27620	97	32581	12265	14	44860
	B Agriculture, forestry, fishing and hunting	6547	...	...	5241	33	11821	4597	394	16812
	C Mining (except fuels), manufacturing and construction	2877	...	...	74	158	3109	291	12	3412
	D Transportation and communication	11190	...	...	976	204	12370	22797	2339	37506
	E Other economic affairs	1700	...	...	398	25	2123	8315	272	10710
10	Other functions	9133	...	...	...	52424	61557	564	...	62121
	Total abc	178261	...	...	34392	83482	296135	82307	6514	384956

1987

1	General public services	38301	...	...	...	401	38702	3788	213	42703
2	Defence	29770	...	...	...	73	29843	12	...	29855
3	Public order and safety	13939	...	...	...	150	14089	1084	...	15173
4	Education	85060	...	...	...	1988	87048	12498	109	99655
5	Health	13653	...	...	...	12463	26116	7966	600	34682
6	Social security and welfare	12376	...	...	...	30404	42780	2736	846	46362
7	Housing and community amenities	6678	...	...	30	45	6753	20985	3438	31176
8	Recreation, culture and religion	647	...	...	...	5	652	239	23	914
9	Economic services	41061	...	...	24265	705	66031	67678	1111	134820
	A Fuel and energy	6348	...	...	17022	83	23453	22087	3	45543
	B Agriculture, forestry, fishing and hunting	9647	...	...	4687	61	14395	5090	447	19932
	C Mining (except fuels), manufacturing and construction	5574	...	...	66	232	5872	379	20	6271
	D Transportation and communication	17051	...	...	1780	299	19130	28658	639	48427
	E Other economic affairs	2441	...	...	710	30	3181	11464	2	14647
10	Other functions	3867	...	...	...	55265	59132	350	...	59482
	Total abc	245352	...	...	24295	101499	371146	117336	6340	494822

1988

1	General public services	55045	...	...	...	529	55574	5190	261	61025
2	Defence	44664	...	...	...	81	44745	14	...	44759
3	Public order and safety	20185	...	...	...	204	20389	1560	...	21949
4	Education	118605	...	...	...	2644	121249	16430	134	137813
5	Health	17846	...	...	...	16800	34646	14057	2587	51290

Ecuador

2.3 Total Government Outlays by Function and Type
(Continued)

Million Ecuadoran sucres

		Final Consumption Expenditures		Subsidies	Other Current Transfers & Property Income	Total Current Disbursements	Gross Capital Formation	Other Capital Outlays	Total Outlays
		Total	Compensation of Employees	Other						
6	Social security and welfare	16797	...	...	...	29761	46558	5128	115	51801
7	Housing and community amenities	11663	...	...	...	58	11721	22992	13181	47894
8	Recreation, culture and religion	801	...	...	...	7	808	474	15	1297
9	Economic services	57656	...	...	27951	927	86534	87108	1148	174790
	A Fuel and energy	7993	...	...	23614	92	31699	26126	4	57829
	B Agriculture, forestry, fishing and hunting	13170	...	...	76	77	13323	6822	594	20739
	C Mining (except fuels), manufacturing and construction	8196	...	...	...	315	8511	551	27	9089
	D Transportation and communication	25191	...	...	2715	407	28313	40031	443	68787
	E Other economic affairs	3106	...	...	1546	36	4688	13578	80	18346
10	Other functions	16656	...	...	...	74522	91178	25	...	91203
	Total abc	359918	...	...	27951	125533	513402	152978	17441	683821

a) Government final consumption expenditure in this table includes compensation of employees and intermediate consumption of the following departmental enterprises: electricity, gas and steam, water works and supply and medical and other health services.
b) Column 5 (Other current transfers and property income) includes current transfers n.e.c. and social security benefits. Column 8 (Other capital outlays) includes purchases of land, net, capital transfers and increase in stocks.
c) Beginning 1984, the estimates of total gross fixed capital formation (column 9) shown in this table is different from the estimates shown in table 3.13. This is because some functions of the general government which are included in the detailed account of table 3.13 could not be allocated to the items included in this table.

2.4 Composition of General Government Social Security Benefits and Social Assistance Grants to Households

Million Ecuadoran sucres

		1980		1981		1982		1983		1984		1985	
		Social Security Benefits	Social Assistance Grants	Social Security Benefits	Social Assistance Grants	Social Security Benefits	Social Assistance Grants	Social Security Benefits	Social Assistance Grants	Social Security Benefits	Social Assistance Grants	Social Security Benefits	Social Assistance Grants
1	Education benefits	...	...	...	...	...	...	...	...	...	...	...	...
2	Health benefits	1890	...	2446	...	3067	...	3417	...	4929	...	6091	...
3	Social security and welfare benefits	4856	...	5280	...	5921	...	9222	...	10700	...	19964	...
4	Housing and community amenities	...	...	...	...	...	...	...	...	...	...	...	...
5	Recreation and cultural benefits	...	...	...	...	...	...	...	...	...	...	...	...
6	Other	...	...	...	...	...	...	...	...	...	...	...	...
	Total	6746	...	7726	...	8988	...	12639	...	15629	...	20673	...

2.5 Private Final Consumption Expenditure by Type and Purpose, in Current Prices

Million Ecuadoran sucres

	1970	1975	1980	1981	1982	1983	1984	1985	1986	1987	1988	1989
Final Consumption Expenditure of Resident Households												
1 Food, beverages and tobacco	11889	29421	60723	74394	90843	146358	211398	274797	348256	452712	768972	1467907
A Food	10035	24844	49387	61432	74940	123777	178328	232583	289847	373510	632546	1236221
B Non-alcoholic beverages	365	887	2348	2586	3275	5225	8312	11005	17135	22094	34438	48250
C Alcoholic beverages	1142	2838	6250	7257	8735	11458	16227	20926	25825	34398	56393	100054
D Tobacco	347	852	2738	3119	3893	5898	8531	10283	15449	22710	45595	83382
2 Clothing and footwear	2278	7142	18347	21208	26451	34896	57104	78064	105035	141534	253266	470282
3 Gross rent, fuel and power a	2390	7121	19563	23525	27848	33051	41800	51276	63034	81658	122056	198598
A Fuel and power a	216	684	2583	3675	5003	5825	7312	9373	12946	18110	26370	42484
B Other	2174	6437	16980	19850	22845	27226	34488	41903	50088	63548	95686	156114
4 Furniture, furnishings and household equipment and operation	1418	4695	12892	14248	17724	19534	30647	43214	67291	105805	193711	344350
5 Medical care and health expenses	1203	2771	6692	7986	9805	13867	20147	27390	37983	54353	89195	158287
6 Transport and communication a	2398	5567	17769	24921	31218	45213	54137	89399	113607	163486	259702	455930
7 Recreational, entertainment, education and cultural services	...	...	...	...	...	...	...	...	...	...	...	...
8 Miscellaneous goods and services	4866	13456	37297	45408	55219	75826	105116	143505	192281	271746	455590	815817
A Personal care	...	...	...	...	...	...	...	...	...	...	...	...
B Expenditures in restaurants, cafes and hotels	989	2978	7820	9170	11179	15829	21149	26485	33845	45267	68226	132435

Ecuador

2.5 Private Final Consumption Expenditure by Type and Purpose, in Current Prices
(Continued)

Million Ecuadoran sucres

	1970	1975	1980	1981	1982	1983	1984	1985	1986	1987	1988	1989
C Other	3877	10478	29477	36238	44040	59997	83967	117020	158436	226479	387364	683382
Total Final Consumption Expenditure in the Domestic Market by Households, of which	26442	70173	173283	211690	259108	368745	520349	707645	927487	1271294	2142492	3911171
Plus: Direct purchases abroad by resident households	-	125	1592	2975	3098	585	244	8014	-1712	-1878	-2390	-14243
Less: Direct purchases in the domestic market by non-resident households	67	-	-	-	-	-	-	-	-	-	-	-
Equals: Final Consumption Expenditure of Resident Households [b]	26375	70298	174875	214665	262206	369330	520593	715659	925775	1269416	2140102	3896928

Final Consumption Expenditure of Private Non-profit Institutions Serving Households

	1970	1975	1980	1981	1982	1983	1984	1985	1986	1987	1988	1989
Equals: Final Consumption Expenditure of Private Non-profit Organisations Serving Households	...	...	...	...	...	...	...	...	...	...	...	...
Private Final Consumption Expenditure	26375	70298	174875	214665	262206	369330	520593	715659	925775	1269416	2140102	3896928

a) Fuel is included in item 'Transport and communication'.
b) Item 'Final consumption expenditure of resident households' includes consumption expenditure of private non-profit institutions serving households.

2.6 Private Final Consumption Expenditure by Type and Purpose, in Constant Prices

Million Ecuadoran sucres

	1970	1975	1980	1981	1982	1983	1984	1985	1986	1987	1988	1989

At constant prices of: 1975

Final Consumption Expenditure of Resident Households

	1970	1975	1980	1981	1982	1983	1984	1985	1986	1987	1988	1989
1 Food, beverages and tobacco	23021	29421	35303	36757	37666	35320	36170	36647	37052	37693	38724	39571
A Food	20160	24844	29339	30714	31483	29741	30531	30876	31276	31869	32915	33795
B Non-alcoholic beverages	579	887	1328	1327	1372	1488	1522	1522	1518	1496	1497	1391
C Alcoholic beverages	1745	2838	3554	3634	3673	3216	3190	3291	3267	3337	3356	3396
D Tobacco	537	852	1082	1082	1138	875	927	958	991	991	956	989
2 Clothing and footwear	4205	7142	11167	11348	11594	11510	11711	11803	11653	11783	11969	12120
3 Gross rent, fuel and power [a]	4921	7121	9845	10273	10587	11005	11456	12285	12822	13395	14004	14462
A Fuel and power [a]	290	684	1593	1837	2044	2255	2457	2719	3004	3263	3518	3677
B Other	4631	6437	8252	8436	8543	8750	8999	9566	9818	10132	10486	10785
4 Furniture, furnishings and household equipment and operation	2951	4695	7365	7326	7417	5808	5482	5767	6330	6510	6781	6891
5 Medical care and health expenses	1939	2771	3655	3895	4112	4469	4436	4881	4866	5412	5381	5599
6 Transport and communication [a]	3342	5567	9998	10537	10942	11323	11521	12126	12585	12842	13600	14367
7 Recreational, entertainment, education and cultural services	...	...	...	...	...	...	...	...	...	...	...	...
8 Miscellaneous goods and services	9108	13456	20516	21941	22642	23021	24537	25076	26127	26581	27029	27725
A Personal care	...	...	...	...	...	...	...	...	...	...	...	...
B Expenditures in restaurants, cafes and hotels	2178	2978	4451	4631	4695	4905	4980	4995	5074	5263	5439	5680
C Other	6930	10478	16065	17310	17947	18116	19557	20081	21053	21318	21590	22045
Total Final Consumption Expenditure in the Domestic Market by Households, of which	49487	70173	97849	102077	104960	102456	105313	108585	111435	114216	117488	120735
Plus: Direct purchases abroad by resident households	...	125	1837	2434	1423	1329	1284	1856	-38	-101	-258	-1781
Less: Direct purchases in the domestic market by non-resident households	19	-	-	-	-	-	-	-	-	-	-	-
Equals: Final Consumption Expenditure of Resident Households [b]	49468	70298	99686	104511	106383	103785	106597	110441	111397	114115	117230	118954

Final Consumption Expenditure of Private Non-profit Institutions Serving Households

	1970	1975	1980	1981	1982	1983	1984	1985	1986	1987	1988	1989
Equals: Final Consumption Expenditure of Private Non-profit Organisations Serving Households	...	...	...	...	...	...	...	...	...	...	...	...
Private Final Consumption Expenditure	49468	70298	99686	104511	106383	103785	106597	110441	111397	114115	117230	118954

a) Fuel is included in item 'Transport and communication'.
b) Item 'Final consumption expenditure of resident households' includes consumption expenditure of private non-profit institutions serving households.

Ecuador

2.7 Gross Capital Formation by Type of Good and Owner, in Current Prices

Million Ecuadoran sucres

	1980 TOTAL	1980 Total Private	1980 Public Enterprises	1980 General Government	1981 TOTAL	1981 Total Private	1981 Public Enterprises	1981 General Government	1982 TOTAL	1982 Total Private	1982 Public Enterprises	1982 General Government
Increase in stocks, total	7304	5647	945	712	3162	3459	-1071	774	10649	8029	2009	611
Gross Fixed Capital Formation, Total	69326	42001	8479	18846	77628	41417	10690	25521	94172	54788	12204	27180
1 Residential buildings	8456	8447	...	9	10068	10061	...	7	14688	14677	...	11
2 Non-residential buildings	10864	6824	1087	2953	12430	7797	376	4257	14862	9142	586	5134
3 Other construction	17613	419	4256	12938	23979	560	4867	18552	27727	974	7720	19033
4 Land improvement and plantation and orchard development	...	...	...	...	...	...	...	...	...	...	...	...
5 Producers' durable goods	31739	25657	3136	2946	30289	22140	5447	2702	35739	28839	3898	3002
6 Breeding stock, dairy cattle, etc.	654	654	...	-	862	859	...	3	1156	1156	...	-
Total Gross Capital Formation	76630	47648	9424	19558	80790	44876	9619	26295	104821	62817	14213	27791

	1983 TOTAL	1983 Total Private	1983 Public Enterprises	1983 General Government	1984 TOTAL	1984 Total Private	1984 Public Enterprises	1984 General Government	1985 TOTAL	1985 Total Private	1985 Public Enterprises	1985 General Government
Increase in stocks, total	5411	4622	25	764	14732	12121	1722	889	23442	20440	1972	1030
Gross Fixed Capital Formation, Total	93031	49586	16722	26723	125230	73973	15733	35524	178255	106054	18088	54113
1 Residential buildings	15198	15192	...	6	21029	21021	...	8	25126	25111	...	15
2 Non-residential buildings	17636	11318	581	5737	22263	14235	533	7495	27903	18019	1286	8598
3 Other construction	29129	1971	8813	18345	35635	2255	8243	25137	50622	2016	10406	38200
4 Land improvement and plantation and orchard development	...	...	...	...	...	...	...	...	...	...	...	...
5 Producers' durable goods	29396	19434	7327	2635	43823	33985	6956	2882	70146	56458	6395	7293
6 Breeding stock, dairy cattle, etc.	1672	1671	1	-	2480	2477	1	2	4458	4450	1	7
Total Gross Capital Formation	98442	54208	16747	27487	139962	86094	17455	36413	201697	126494	20060	55143

	1986 TOTAL	1986 Total Private	1986 Public Enterprises	1986 General Government	1987 TOTAL	1987 Total Private	1987 Public Enterprises	1987 General Government	1988 TOTAL	1988 Total Private	1988 Public Enterprises	1988 General Government
Increase in stocks, total	28491	21495	5931	1065	234	-6862	5696	1400	15824	8163	5150	2511
Gross Fixed Capital Formation, Total	260002	135952	41743	82307	406598	244256	46842	115500	666857	399727	114152	152978
1 Residential buildings	30965	30965	...	-	41037	41037	...	-	76931	76931	...	-
2 Non-residential buildings	35235	21583	1297	12355	42538	21647	848	20043	71419	41471	835	29113
3 Other construction	73168	1547	12857	58764	125970	10474	30501	84995	155460	5160	41927	108373
4 Land improvement and plantation and orchard development	...	...	...	...	...	...	...	...	...	...	...	...
5 Producers' durable goods	114926	76150	27588	11188	189903	163959	15492	10452	353009	266141	71388	15480
6 Breeding stock, dairy cattle, etc.	5708	5707	1	-	7150	7139	1	10	10038	10024	2	12
Total Gross Capital Formation	288493	157447	47674	83372	406832	237394	52538	116900	682681	407890	119302	155489

	1989 TOTAL	1989 Total Private	1989 Public Enterprises	1989 General Government
Increase in stocks, total	52223	19536	25345	7342
Gross Fixed Capital Formation, Total	1125703	659516	214434	251753
1 Residential buildings	102572	102572	...	-
2 Non-residential buildings	115791	64145	3338	48308
3 Other construction	295057	6365	105362	183330
4 Land improvement and plantation and orchard development	...	...	...	...
5 Producers' durable goods	592553	466730	105728	20095
6 Breeding stock, dairy cattle, etc.	19730	19704	6	20
Total Gross Capital Formation	1177926	679052	239779	259095

Ecuador

2.8 Gross Capital Formation by Type of Good and Owner, in Constant Prices

Million Ecuadoran sucres

1980–1982

At constant prices of: 1975

	1980 TOTAL	Total Private	Public Enterprises	General Government	1981 TOTAL	Total Private	Public Enterprises	General Government	1982 TOTAL	Total Private	Public Enterprises	General Government
Increase in stocks, total	4241	...	...	...	1511	...	...	...	5569	...	...	...
Gross Fixed Capital Formation, Total	34975	22447	4096	8432	32442	18789	4665	8988	32667	20802	4036	7829
1 Residential buildings												
2 Non-residential buildings	16016	7041	2258	6717	15874	6566	1754	7554	15977	7245	2255	6477
3 Other construction												
4 Land improvement and plantation and orchard development												
5 Producers' durable goods	18576	15023	1838	1715	16134	11791	2911	1432	16237	13104	1781	1352
6 Breeding stock, dairy cattle, etc.	383	383	...	-	434	432	...	2	453	453	...	-
Total Gross Capital Formation	39216	...	...	...	33953	...	...	...	38236	...	...	...

1983–1985

At constant prices of: 1975

	1983 TOTAL	Total Private	Public Enterprises	General Government	1984 TOTAL	Total Private	Public Enterprises	General Government	1985 TOTAL	Total Private	Public Enterprises	General Government
Increase in stocks, total	2167	...	...	...	2879	...	...	...	3357	...	...	...
Gross Fixed Capital Formation, Total	24127	13396	4425	6306	23035	14094	2847	6094	24618	14818	2623	7177
1 Residential buildings												
2 Non-residential buildings	14696	7020	2179	5497	14160	7117	1512	5531	14399	6694	1547	6158
3 Other construction												
4 Land improvement and plantation and orchard development												
5 Producers' durable goods	8972	5918	2245	809	8390	6494	1334	562	9594	7501	1075	1018
6 Breeding stock, dairy cattle, etc.	459	458	1	-	485	483	1	1	625	623	1	1
Total Gross Capital Formation	26294	...	...	...	25914	...	...	...	27975	...	...	...

1986–1988

At constant prices of: 1975

	1986 TOTAL	Total Private	Public Enterprises	General Government	1987 TOTAL	Total Private	Public Enterprises	General Government	1988 TOTAL	Total Private	Public Enterprises	General Government
Increase in stocks, total	3139	...	...	...	1115	...	...	...	1877	...	...	...
Gross Fixed Capital Formation, Total	25677	13712	3924	8041	26800	15983	3030	7787	26162	15557	4194	6411
1 Residential buildings												
2 Non-residential buildings	14367	6001	1396	6970	14982	5710	2129	7143	13665	5945	1841	5879
3 Other construction												
4 Land improvement and plantation and orchard development												
5 Producers' durable goods	10677	7079	2527	1071	11121	9577	901	643	11827	8943	2353	531
6 Breeding stock, dairy cattle, etc.	633	632	1	-	697	696	...	1	670	669	...	1
Total Gross Capital Formation	28816	...	...	...	27915	...	...	...	28039	...	...	...

1989

At constant prices of: 1975

	1989 TOTAL	Total Private	Public Enterprises	General Government
Increase in stocks, total	2700	...	...	...
Gross Fixed Capital Formation, Total	26032	15004	4785	6243
1 Residential buildings				
2 Non-residential buildings	13489	4966	2699	5824
3 Other construction				
4 Land improvement and plantation and orchard development				
5 Producers' durable goods	11834	9330	2086	418
6 Breeding stock, dairy cattle, etc.	709	708	...	1
Total Gross Capital Formation	28732	...	...	...

Ecuador

2.17 Exports and Imports of Goods and Services, Detail

Million Ecuadoran sucres

	1970	1975	1980	1981	1982	1983	1984	1985	1986	1987	1988	1989
					Exports of Goods and Services							
1 Exports of merchandise, f.o.b.	4533	26058	64389	66050	76742	110999	183425	255387	250181	348095	679360	1219947
2 Transport and communication	95	1263	5116	5650	5941	9849	12580	23143	33623	44672	99865	139892
A In respect of merchandise imports	38	359	1939	2023	...	...	...	...	...	...	...	...
B Other	57	904	3177	3627	...	...	...	...	...	...	...	...
3 Insurance service charges	3	34	98	89	132	129	189	485	448	525	437	582
A In respect of merchandise imports	2	20	96	86	...	...	...	...	...	...	...	...
B Other	1	14	2	3	...	...	...	...	...	...	...	...
4 Other commodities	9	8	499	402	451	1440	1521	483	1141	656	1131	2148
5 Adjustments of merchandise exports to change-of-ownership basis	-	-	-	-	-	-	-	-	-	-	-	-
6 Direct purchases in the domestic market by non-residential households	206	871	3270	3275	3803	9960	11072	15790	26410	33114	77696	107718
7 Direct purchases in the domestic market by extraterritorial bodies	63	8	425	440	494	684	1071	1634	2937	4476	6829	12313
Total Exports of Goods and Services	4909	28242	73797	75906	87563	133061	209858	296922	314740	431538	865318	1482600
					Imports of Goods and Services							
1 Imports of merchandise, c.i.f.	5507	32527	63512	59391	80583	85154	127264	177399	242639	448150	723661	1308256
A Imports of merchandise, f.o.b.	4943	29189	56881	52717	...	...	...	...	...	...	...	...
B Transport of services on merchandise imports	562	3318	6591	6632	...	...	...	...	...	...	...	...
By residents	38	359	1378	1386	...	...	...	...	...	...	...	...
By non-residents	524	2959	5213	5246	...	...	...	...	...	...	...	...
C Insurance service charges on merchandise imports	2	20	40	42	...	...	...	...	...	...	...	...
By residents	2	20	40	42	...	...	...	...	...	...	...	...
By non-residents	...	...	...	...	...	...	...	...	...	...	...	...
2 Adjustments of merchandise imports to change-of-ownership basis	...	...	...	...	...	...	...	...	...	...	...	...
3 Other transport and communication	199	696	3128	3125	4279	6614	7690	18469	25080	31941	69728	95481
4 Other insurance service charges	50	118	392	234	139	2316	975	1677	4882	6432	8034	26278
5 Other commodities	486	836	1290	2419	3918	4846	8185	7855	11110	18811	32049	47876
6 Direct purchases abroad by government	56	40	500	582	711	458	911	830	1161	2656	5158	8782
7 Direct purchases abroad by resident households	202	1004	5705	6690	7395	11229	12387	25438	27635	35712	82135	105788
Total Imports of Goods and Services	6500	35221	74527	72441	97025	110617	157412	231668	312507	543702	920765	1592461
Balance of Goods and Services	-1591	-6979	-730	3465	-9462	22444	52446	65254	2233	-112164	-55447	-109861
Total Imports and Balance of Goods and Services	4909	28242	73797	75906	87563	133061	209858	296922	314740	431538	865318	1482600

3.11 General Government Production Account: Total and Subsectors

Million Ecuadoran sucres

	1980					1981				
	Total General Government	Central Government	State or Provincial Government	Local Government	Social Security Funds	Total General Government	Central Government	State or Provincial Government	Local Government	Social Security Funds
					Gross Output					
1 Sales	8027	3869	...	2189	1969	9781	4916	...	2337	2528
2 Services produced for own use	42562	36645	...	4727	1190	49742	42158	...	5923	1661
3 Own account fixed capital formation	...	...	...	...	...	...	...	...	...	...
Gross Output [a]	50589	40514	...	6916	3159	59523	47074	...	8260	4189

Ecuador

3.11 General Government Production Account: Total and Subsectors
(Continued)

Million Ecuadoran sucres

	1980 Total General Government	1980 Central Government	1980 State or Provincial Government	1980 Local Government	1980 Social Security Funds	1981 Total General Government	1981 Central Government	1981 State or Provincial Government	1981 Local Government	1981 Social Security Funds
					Gross Input					
Intermediate Consumption	21153	18156	...	2184	813	25354	21820	...	2604	930
Subtotal: Value Added	29436	22358	...	4732	2346	34169	25254	...	5656	3259
1 Indirect taxes, net	...	...	...	...	...	...	...	...	...	...
2 Consumption of fixed capital [b]	...	...	...	...	...	...	...	...	...	...
3 Compensation of employees	29136	21954	...	4836	2346	34250	25212	...	5779	3259
4 Net Operating surplus [b]	300	404	...	-104	...	-81	42	...	-123	...
Gross Input [a]	50589	40514	...	6916	3159	59523	47074	...	8260	4189

	1982 Total General Government	1982 Central Government	1982 State or Provincial Government	1982 Local Government	1982 Social Security Funds	1983 Total General Government	1983 Central Government	1983 State or Provincial Government	1983 Local Government	1983 Social Security Funds
					Gross Output					
1 Sales	12379	6277	...	2933	3169	13858	6955	...	3394	3509
2 Services produced for own use	58150	48689	...	7295	2166	70055	58699	...	9018	2338
3 Own account fixed capital formation	...	...	...	...	...	...	...	...	...	...
Gross Output [a]	70529	54966	...	10228	5335	83913	65654	...	12412	5847
					Gross Input					
Intermediate Consumption	30970	26459	...	3362	1149	36864	31465	...	4140	1259
Subtotal: Value Added	39559	28507	...	6866	4186	47049	34189	...	8272	4588
1 Indirect taxes, net	...	...	...	...	...	...	...	...	...	...
2 Consumption of fixed capital [b]	...	...	...	...	...	...	...	...	...	...
3 Compensation of employees	38984	27851	...	6947	4186	46576	33612	...	8376	4588
4 Net Operating surplus [b]	575	656	...	-81	...	473	577	...	-104	...
Gross Input [a]	70529	54966	...	10228	5335	83913	65654	...	12412	5847

	1984 Total General Government	1984 Central Government	1984 State or Provincial Government	1984 Local Government	1984 Social Security Funds	1985 Total General Government	1985 Central Government	1985 State or Provincial Government	1985 Local Government	1985 Social Security Funds
					Gross Output					
1 Sales	19679	10384	...	4281	5014	28627	17514	...	4883	6230
2 Services produced for own use	96125	80164	...	12795	3166	134132	114717	...	15369	4046
3 Own account fixed capital formation	...	...	...	...	...	...	...	...	...	...
Gross Output [a]	115804	90548	...	17076	8180	162759	132231	...	20252	10276
					Gross Input					
Intermediate Consumption	48906	41119	...	5296	2491	69304	58850	...	7037	3417
Subtotal: Value Added	66898	49429	...	11780	5689	93455	73381	...	13215	6859
1 Indirect taxes, net	...	...	...	...	...	...	...	...	...	...
2 Consumption of fixed capital [b]	...	...	...	...	...	...	...	...	...	...
3 Compensation of employees	65208	47615	...	11904	5689	90924	70716	...	13349	6859
4 Net Operating surplus [b]	1690	1814	...	-124	...	2531	2665	...	-134	...
Gross Input [a]	115804	90548	...	17076	8180	162759	132231	...	20252	10276

a) Data for this table have not been revised, therefore, data for some years are not comparable with those of other tables.
b) Item 'Operating surplus' includes consumption of fixed capital.

3.12 General Government Income and Outlay Account: Total and Subsectors

Million Ecuadoran sucres

	1980 Total General Government	1980 Central Government	1980 State or Provincial Government	1980 Local Government	1980 Social Security Funds	1981 Total General Government	1981 Central Government	1981 State or Provincial Government	1981 Local Government	1981 Social Security Funds
					Receipts					
1 Operating surplus	300	404	...	-104	-	-81	42	...	-123	-
2 Property and entrepreneurial income	10954	7656	...	342	2956	13748	9582	...	260	3906
A Withdrawals from public quasi-corporations	...	...	...	...	...	...	...	...	...	...
B Interest	2974	70	...	34	2870	3898	89	...	34	3775
C Dividends	104	-	...	18	86	139	-	...	8	131
D Net land rent and royalties	7876	7586	...	290	-	9711	9493	...	218	-
3 Taxes, fees and contributions	58631	46156	...	4349	8126	68456	53798	...	5830	8828

Ecuador

3.12 General Government Income and Outlay Account: Total and Subsectors
(Continued)

Million Ecuadoran sucres

	1980 Total General Government	1980 Central Government	1980 State or Provincial Government	1980 Local Government	1980 Social Security Funds	1981 Total General Government	1981 Central Government	1981 State or Provincial Government	1981 Local Government	1981 Social Security Funds
A Indirect taxes	26931	25393	...	1538	-	35746	33734	...	2012	-
B Direct taxes	22390	19906	...	2484	-	22888	19466	...	3422	-
Income	22025	19770	...	2255	-	22478	19318	...	3160	-
Other	365	136	...	229	-	410	148	...	262	-
C Social security contributions	8092	-	...	-	8092	8787	-	...	-	8787
D Fees, fines and penalties	1218	857	...	327	34	1035	598	...	396	41
4 Other current transfers	10540	2561	...	7896	83	13842	4601	...	9156	85
A Casualty insurance claims	...	...	...	...	...	...	...	...	...	...
B Transfers from other government subsectors	8072	270	...	7763	39	9257	239	...	8980	38
C Transfers from the rest of the world	931	931	...	-	-	1541	1541	...	-	-
D Other transfers, except imputed	943	922	...	21	-	2308	2262	...	44	2
E Imputed unfunded employee pension and welfare contributions	594	438	...	112	44	736	559	...	132	45
Total Current Receipts	80425	56777	...	12483	11165	95965	68023	...	15123	12819

Disbursements

	1980 Total General Government	1980 Central Government	1980 State or Provincial Government	1980 Local Government	1980 Social Security Funds	1981 Total General Government	1981 Central Government	1981 State or Provincial Government	1981 Local Government	1981 Social Security Funds
1 Government final consumption expenditure	42562	36645	...	4727	1190	49742	42158	...	5923	1661
2 Property income	7590	6515	...	219	856	11044	9413	...	487	1144
A Interest	7588	6513	...	219	856	11041	9410	...	487	1144
B Net land rent and royalties	2	2	...	-	-	3	3	...	-	-
3 Subsidies	2543	2543	...	-	-	3114	3114	...	-	-
4 Other current transfers	16916	9365	...	724	6827	19780	11021	...	921	7838
A Casualty insurance premiums, net	...	...	...	...	...	...	...	...	...	...
B Transfers to other government subsectors	8072	7802	...	257	13	9257	8992	...	220	45
C Social security benefits	6746	-	...	-	6746	7726	-	...	-	7726
D Social assistance grants	1353	974	...	355	24	1787	1196	...	569	22
E Unfunded employee pension and welfare benefits	594	438	...	112	44	736	559	...	132	45
F Transfers to private non-profit institutions serving households	...	...	...	...	...	...	...	...	...	...
G Other transfers n.e.c.	46	46	...	-	-	71	71	...	-	-
H Transfers to the rest of the world	105	105	...	-	-	203	203	...	-	-
Net saving [a]	10814	1709	...	6813	2292	12285	2317	...	7792	2176
Total Current Disbursements and Net Saving	80425	56777	...	12483	11165	95965	68023	...	15123	12819

	1982 Total General Government	1982 Central Government	1982 State or Provincial Government	1982 Local Government	1982 Social Security Funds	1983 Total General Government	1983 Central Government	1983 State or Provincial Government	1983 Local Government	1983 Social Security Funds

Receipts

	1982 Total General Government	1982 Central Government	1982 State or Provincial Government	1982 Local Government	1982 Social Security Funds	1983 Total General Government	1983 Central Government	1983 State or Provincial Government	1983 Local Government	1983 Social Security Funds
1 Operating surplus	575	656	...	-81	-	473	577	...	-104	-
2 Property and entrepreneurial income	15871	10583	...	480	4808	25204	19050	...	682	5472
A Withdrawals from public quasi-corporations	...	...	...	...	...	...	...	...	...	...
B Interest	4974	88	...	191	4695	5587	98	...	192	5297
C Dividends	114	-	...	1	113	534	357	...	2	175
D Net land rent and royalties	10783	10495	...	288	-	19083	18595	...	488	-
3 Taxes, fees and contributions	83708	66703	...	6661	10344	106049	84096	...	7108	14845
A Indirect taxes	39327	36829	...	2498	-	48693	45934	...	2759	-
B Direct taxes	32834	29143	...	3691	-	41137	37317	...	3820	-
Income	32364	28954	...	3410	-	40607	37085	...	3522	-
Other	470	189	...	281	-	530	232	...	298	-
C Social security contributions	10279	-	...	-	10279	14786	-	...	-	14786
D Fees, fines and penalties	1268	731	...	472	65	1433	845	...	529	59

Ecuador

3.12 General Government Income and Outlay Account: Total and Subsectors
(Continued)

Million Ecuadoran sucres

	1982					1983				
	Total General Government	Central Government	State or Provincial Government	Local Government	Social Security Funds	Total General Government	Central Government	State or Provincial Government	Local Government	Social Security Funds
4 Other current transfers	15351	4670	...	10439	242	18031	5837	...	12090	104
A Casualty insurance claims	...	...	...	...	...	...	...	...	...	...
B Transfers from other government subsectors	10549	172	...	10187	190	12243	442	...	11765	36
C Transfers from the rest of the world	1736	1731	...	5	-	2273	2273	...	-	-
D Other transfers, except imputed	2013	1935	...	77	1	2056	1905	...	150	1
E Imputed unfunded employee pension and welfare contributions	1053	832	...	170	51	1459	1217	...	175	67
Total Current Receipts	115505	82612	...	17499	15394	149757	109560	...	19776	20421

Disbursements

1 Government final consumption expenditure	58150	48689	...	7295	2166	70055	58699	...	9018	2338
2 Property income	20525	17504	...	861	2160	24536	20971	...	974	2591
A Interest	20524	17503	...	861	2160	24534	20969	...	974	2591
B Net land rent and royalties	1	1	...	-	-	2	2	...	-	-
3 Subsidies	3596	3596	...	-	-	2030	2030	...	-	-
4 Other current transfers	22514	12896	...	517	9101	28506	14822	...	930	12754
A Casualty insurance premiums, net	...	...	...	...	...	...	...	...	...	...
B Transfers to other government subsectors	10549	10377	...	141	31	12243	11801	...	411	31
C Social security benefits	8988	-	...	-	8988	12639	-	...	-	12639
D Social assistance grants	1463	1229	...	203	31	1520	1159	...	344	17
E Unfunded employee pension and welfare benefits	1053	832	...	170	51	1459	1217	...	175	67
F Transfers to private non-profit institutions serving households	...	...	...	...	...	...	...	...	...	...
G Other transfers n.e.c.	105	105	...	-	-	358	358	...	-	-
H Transfers to the rest of the world	356	353	...	3	-	287	287	...	-	-
Net saving [a]	10720	-73	...	8826	1967	24630	13038	...	8854	2738
Total Current Disbursements and Net Saving	115505	82612	...	17499	15394	149757	109560	...	19776	20421

	1984					1985				
	Total General Government	Central Government	State or Provincial Government	Local Government	Social Security Funds	Total General Government	Central Government	State or Provincial Government	Local Government	Social Security Funds

Receipts

1 Operating surplus	1677	1801	...	-124	-	1716	1849	...	-133	-
2 Property and entrepreneurial income	33566	26810	...	863	5893	31298	21581	...	854	8863
A Withdrawals from public quasi-corporations	...	...	...	...	...	...	...	...	...	...
B Interest	6437	309	...	341	5787	9345	582	...	168	8595
C Dividends	2135	2023	...	6	106	1768	1479	...	21	268
D Net land rent and royalties	24994	24478	...	516	-	20185	19520	...	665	-
3 Taxes, fees and contributions	161792	135515	...	8634	17643	273900	237713	...	11072	25115
A Indirect taxes	72358	68407	...	3951	-	152141	146672	...	5469	-
B Direct taxes	69653	65779	...	3874	-	93216	88541	...	4675	-
Income	68903	65597	...	3306	-	92169	88284	...	3885	-
Other	750	182	...	568	-	1047	257	...	790	-
C Social security contributions	17597	-	...	-	17597	25042	-	...	-	25042
D Fees, fines and penalties	2184	1329	...	809	46	3501	2500	...	928	73
4 Other current transfers	22770	6360	...	16239	171	44256	21138	...	22755	363
A Casualty insurance claims	...	...	...	...	...	...	...	...	...	...
B Transfers from other government subsectors	16336	463	...	15866	7	21748	306	...	21433	9
C Transfers from the rest of the world	2292	2292	...	-	-	2853	2853	...	-	-
D Other transfers, except imputed	1817	1671	...	146	-	16181	15245	...	936	-
E Imputed unfunded employee pension and welfare contributions	2325	1934	...	227	164	3474	2734	...	386	354

Ecuador

3.12 General Government Income and Outlay Account: Total and Subsectors
(Continued)

Million Ecuadoran sucres

	1984					1985				
	Total General Government	Central Government	State or Provincial Government	Local Government	Social Security Funds	Total General Government	Central Government	State or Provincial Government	Local Government	Social Security Funds
Total Current Receipts	219805	170486	...	25612	23707	351170	282281	...	34548	34341

Disbursements

1 Government final consumption expenditure	99628	83078	...	13384	3166	127330	107046	...	16204	4080
2 Property income	31184	27657	...	963	2564	48591	43042	...	1707	3842
A Interest	31184	27657	...	963	2564	48591	43042	...	1707	3842
B Net land rent and royalties	-	-	...	-	-	-	-	...	-	-
3 Subsidies	4668	4668	...	-	-	23762	23741	...	21	-
4 Other current transfers	37051	20123	...	1050	15878	49195	27044	...	1077	21074
A Casualty insurance premiums, net	...	...	...	...	...	...	...	...	...	...
B Transfers to other government subsectors	16336	15873	...	401	62	21748	21442	...	272	34
C Social security benefits	15629	-	...	-	15629	20673	-	...	-	20673
D Social assistance grants	2090	1645	...	422	23	2625	2193	...	419	13
E Unfunded employee pension and welfare benefits	2325	1934	...	227	164	3474	2734	...	386	354
F Transfers to private non-profit institutions serving households	...	...	...	...	...	...	...	...	...	...
G Other transfers n.e.c.	284	284	...	-	-	71	71	...	-	-
H Transfers to the rest of the world	387	387	...	-	-	604	604	...	-	-
Net saving [a]	47274	34960	...	10215	2099	102292	81408	...	15539	5345
Total Current Disbursements and Net Saving	219805	170486	...	25612	23707	351170	282281	...	34548	34341

	1986					1987				
	Total General Government	Central Government	State or Provincial Government	Local Government	Social Security Funds	Total General Government	Central Government	State or Provincial Government	Local Government	Social Security Funds

Receipts

1 Operating surplus	2381	2527	...	-146	-	3844	4008	...	-164	-
2 Property and entrepreneurial income	29120	17080	...	1398	10642	30644	15602	...	1133	13909
A Withdrawals from public quasi-corporations	...	...	...	...	...	...	...	...	...	...
B Interest	11898	634	...	901	10363	15164	702	...	903	13559
C Dividends	1139	837	...	23	279	2958	2581	...	27	350
D Net land rent and royalties	16083	15609	...	474	-	12522	12319	...	203	-
3 Taxes, fees and contributions	299440	253466	...	12420	33554	339389	286859	...	11093	41437
A Indirect taxes	190845	182086	...	8759	-	228830	220779	...	8051	-
B Direct taxes	70004	67370	...	2634	-	63400	61572	...	1828	-
Income	68773	67029	...	1744	-	62088	61273	...	815	-
Other	1231	341	...	890	-	1312	299	...	1013	-
C Social security contributions	33454	-	...	-	33454	41297	-	...	-	41297
D Fees, fines and penalties	5137	4010	...	1027	100	5862	4508	...	1214	140
4 Other current transfers	62386	30694	...	31141	551	70527	29219	...	40658	650
A Casualty insurance claims	...	...	...	...	...	...	...	...	...	...
B Transfers from other government subsectors	29848	305	...	29530	13	37624	385	...	37224	15
C Transfers from the rest of the world	2963	2963	...	-	-	3271	3271	...	-	-
D Other transfers, except imputed	24948	23853	...	1095	-	23717	21034	...	2683	-
E Imputed unfunded employee pension and welfare contributions	4627	3573	...	516	538	5915	4529	...	751	635
Total Current Receipts	393327	303767	...	44813	44747	444404	335688	...	52720	55996

Disbursements

1 Government final consumption expenditure	166731	141797	...	19443	5491	230417	198377	...	24949	7091
2 Property income	57085	50755	...	1655	4675	56821	53302	...	1919	1600
A Interest	57085	50755	...	1655	4675	56821	53302	...	1919	1600
B Net land rent and royalties	-	-	...	-	-	-	-	...	-	-
3 Subsidies	34392	34371	...	21	-	24295	24281	...	14	-

Ecuador

3.12 General Government Income and Outlay Account: Total and Subsectors
(Continued)

Million Ecuadoran sucres

	1986					1987				
	Total General Government	Central Government	State or Provincial Government	Local Government	Social Security Funds	Total General Government	Central Government	State or Provincial Government	Local Government	Social Security Funds
4 Other current transfers	60872	36654	...	1204	23014	88223	46245	...	1715	40263
A Casualty insurance premiums, net	...	...	...	...	...	...	...	...	...	...
B Transfers to other government subsectors	29848	29543	...	228	77	37624	37239	...	298	87
C Social security benefits	22385	-	...	-	22385	39535	-	...	-	39535
D Social assistance grants	2875	2401	...	460	14	4214	3542	...	666	6
E Unfunded employee pension and welfare benefits	4627	3573	...	516	538	5915	4529	...	751	635
F Transfers to private non-profit institutions serving households	...	...	...	...	...	...	...	...	...	...
G Other transfers n.e.c.	494	494	...	-	-	151	151	...	-	-
H Transfers to the rest of the world	643	643	...	-	-	784	784	...	-	-
Net saving [a]	74247	40190	...	22490	11567	44648	13483	...	24125	7042
Total Current Disbursements and Net Saving	393327	303767	...	44813	44747	444404	335688	...	52720	55996

	1988					1989				
	Total General Government	Central Government	State or Provincial Government	Local Government	Social Security Funds	Total General Government	Central Government	State or Provincial Government	Local Government	Social Security Funds

Receipts

1 Operating surplus	4543	4794	...	-251	-	5477	5777	...	-300	-
2 Property and entrepreneurial income	65288	40477	...	2393	22418	116175	84126	...	3344	28705
A Withdrawals from public quasi-corporations	...	...	...	...	...	...	...	...	...	...
B Interest	19241	659	...	1386	17196	22547	750	...	1592	20205
C Dividends	5839	587	...	218	5034	9276	762	...	255	8259
D Net land rent and royalties	40208	39231	...	789	188	84352	82614	...	1497	241
3 Taxes, fees and contributions	569840	498526	...	17721	53593	1072999	978723	...	22643	71633
A Indirect taxes	378577	365595	...	12982	-	710992	694795	...	16197	-
B Direct taxes	129407	126478	...	2929	-	273310	269276	...	4034	-
Income	127296	126055	...	1241	-	270792	268579	...	2213	-
Other	2111	423	...	1688	-	2518	697	...	1821	-
C Social security contributions	53393	-	...	-	53393	71133	-	...	-	71133
D Fees, fines and penalties	8463	6453	...	1810	200	17564	14652	...	2412	500
4 Other current transfers	92374	40838	...	50364	1172	112905	21711	...	89345	1849
A Casualty insurance claims	...	...	...	...	...	...	...	...	...	...
B Transfers from other government subsectors	47741	507	...	47206	28	88459	595	...	87827	37
C Transfers from the rest of the world	3222	3222	...	-	-	4177	4177	...	-	-
D Other transfers, except imputed	32317	30239	...	2078	-	8346	8234	...	112	-
E Imputed unfunded employee pension and welfare contributions	9094	6870	...	1080	1144	11923	8705	...	1406	1812
Total Current Receipts	732045	584635	...	70227	77183	1307556	1090337	...	115032	102187

Disbursements

1 Government final consumption expenditure	337003	293958	...	33477	9568	499620	438065	...	46060	15495
2 Property income	76639	72888	...	1623	2128	179785	174853	...	2071	2861
A Interest	76639	72888	...	1623	2128	179785	174853	...	2071	2861
B Net land rent and royalties	-	-	...	-	-	-	-	...	-	-
3 Subsidies	27951	27910	...	41	-	58434	58434	...	...	-

Ecuador

3.12 General Government Income and Outlay Account: Total and Subsectors
(Continued)

Million Ecuadoran sucres

	1988 Total General Government	1988 Central Government	1988 State or Provincial Government	1988 Local Government	1988 Social Security Funds	1989 Total General Government	1989 Central Government	1989 State or Provincial Government	1989 Local Government	1989 Social Security Funds
4 Other current transfers	105729	60091	...	2413	43225	171302	107369	...	3035	60898
A Casualty insurance premiums, net	...	...	...	...	...	...	...	...	...	...
B Transfers to other government subsectors	47741	47234	...	385	122	88459	87864	...	453	142
C Social security benefits	41912	-	...	-	41912	58906	-	...	-	58906
D Social assistance grants	5597	4609	...	948	40	9603	8395	...	1176	32
E Unfunded employee pension and welfare benefits	9094	6870	...	1080	1144	11923	8705	...	1406	1812
F Transfers to private non-profit institutions serving households	...	...	...	...	...	...	...	...	...	...
G Other transfers n.e.c.	218	218	...	-	-	344	344	...	-	-
H Transfers to the rest of the world	1167	1160	...	-	7	2067	2061	...	-	6
Net saving [a]	184723	129788	...	32673	22262	398415	311616	...	63866	22933
Total Current Disbursements and Net Saving	732045	584635	...	70227	77183	1307556	1090337	...	115032	102187

a) Item 'Net saving' includes consumption of fixed capital.

3.13 General Government Capital Accumulation Account: Total and Subsectors

Million Ecuadoran sucres

	1980 Total General Government	1980 Central Government	1980 State or Provincial Government	1980 Local Government	1980 Social Security Funds	1981 Total General Government	1981 Central Government	1981 State or Provincial Government	1981 Local Government	1981 Social Security Funds
Finance of Gross Accumulation										
1 Gross saving	10814	1709	...	6813	2292	12285	2317	...	7792	2176
2 Capital transfers	...	...	...	...	...	19	19	...	...	...
A From other government subsectors	...	...	...	...	...	19	19	...	...	...
B From other resident sectors	...	...	...	...	...	...	...	...	...	...
C From rest of the world	...	...	...	...	...	...	...	...	...	...
Finance of Gross Accumulation	10814	1709	...	6813	2292	12304	2336	...	7792	2176
Gross Accumulation										
1 Gross capital formation	19558	12810	...	5833	915	26295	16956	...	8313	1026
A Increase in stocks	712	...	...	...	712	774	...	...	...	774
B Gross fixed capital formation	18846	12810	...	5833	203	25521	16956	...	8313	252
2 Purchases of land, net	200	170	...	-40	70	96	158	...	-75	13
3 Purchases of intangible assets, net	...	...	...	...	...	...	...	...	...	...
4 Capital transfers	1820	1385	...	435	-	5859	5251	...	608	-
A To other government subsectors	...	...	...	...	...	...	...	...	...	...
B To other resident sectors	1820	1385	...	435	...	5859	5251	...	608	...
C To rest of the world	...	...	...	...	...	...	...	...	...	...
Net lending [a]	-10764	-12656	...	585	1307	-19946	-20029	...	-1054	1137
Gross Accumulation	10814	1709	...	6813	2292	12304	2336	...	7792	2176

	1982 Total General Government	1982 Central Government	1982 State or Provincial Government	1982 Local Government	1982 Social Security Funds	1983 Total General Government	1983 Central Government	1983 State or Provincial Government	1983 Local Government	1983 Social Security Funds
Finance of Gross Accumulation										
1 Gross saving	10720	-73	...	8826	1967	24630	13038	...	8854	2738
2 Capital transfers	...	...	...	...	...	...	...	...	...	...
A From other government subsectors	...	...	...	...	...	...	...	...	...	...
B From other resident sectors	...	...	...	...	...	...	...	...	...	...
C From rest of the world	...	...	...	...	...	...	...	...	...	...
Finance of Gross Accumulation	10720	-73	...	8826	1967	24630	13038	...	8854	2738
Gross Accumulation										
1 Gross capital formation	27791	17778	...	9152	861	27487	16218	...	10013	1256
A Increase in stocks	611	...	...	...	611	764	...	...	...	764
B Gross fixed capital formation	27180	17778	...	9152	250	26723	16218	...	10013	492

Ecuador

3.13 General Government Capital Accumulation Account: Total and Subsectors
(Continued)

Million Ecuadoran sucres

	1982 Total General Government	1982 Central Government	1982 State or Provincial Government	1982 Local Government	1982 Social Security Funds	1983 Total General Government	1983 Central Government	1983 State or Provincial Government	1983 Local Government	1983 Social Security Funds
2 Purchases of land, net	-48	43	...	-97	6	-123	-4	...	-129	10
3 Purchases of intangible assets, net	...	...	...	...	...	...	...	...	...	...
4 Capital transfers	6037	5521	...	516	-	2085	1527	...	558	-
A To other government subsectors	...	...	...	...	...	...	...	...	...	...
B To other resident sectors	6037	5521	...	516	...	2085	1527	...	558	...
C To rest of the world	...	...	...	...	...	...	...	...	...	...
Net lending [a]	-23060	-23415	...	-745	1100	-4819	-4703	...	-1588	1472
Gross Accumulation	10720	-73	...	8826	1967	24630	13038	...	8854	2738

	1984 Total General Government	1984 Central Government	1984 State or Provincial Government	1984 Local Government	1984 Social Security Funds	1985 Total General Government	1985 Central Government	1985 State or Provincial Government	1985 Local Government	1985 Social Security Funds
Finance of Gross Accumulation										
1 Gross saving	47274	34960	...	10215	2099	102292	81408	...	15539	5345
2 Capital transfers	...	...	...	...	...	...	...	...	...	...
A From other government subsectors	...	...	...	...	...	...	...	...	...	...
B From other resident sectors	...	...	...	...	...	...	...	...	...	...
C From rest of the world	...	...	...	...	...	...	...	...	...	...
Finance of Gross Accumulation	47274	34960	...	10215	2099	102292	81408	...	15539	5345
Gross Accumulation										
1 Gross capital formation	36413	23928	...	10987	1498	55143	36644	...	15684	2815
A Increase in stocks	889	...	...	...	889	1030	...	...	...	1030
B Gross fixed capital formation	35524	23928	...	10987	609	54113	36644	...	15684	1785
2 Purchases of land, net	-222	-54	...	-168	-	-280	-60	...	-220	-
3 Purchases of intangible assets, net	...	...	...	...	...	...	...	...	...	...
4 Capital transfers	1610	938	...	672	-	1603	913	...	690	-
A To other government subsectors	...	...	...	...	...	...	...	...	...	...
B To other resident sectors	1610	938	...	672	...	1603	913	...	690	...
C To rest of the world	...	...	...	...	...	...	...	...	...	...
Net lending [a]	9473	10148	...	-1276	601	45826	43911	...	-615	2530
Gross Accumulation	47274	34960	...	10215	2099	102292	81408	...	15539	5345

	1986 Total General Government	1986 Central Government	1986 State or Provincial Government	1986 Local Government	1986 Social Security Funds	1987 Total General Government	1987 Central Government	1987 State or Provincial Government	1987 Local Government	1987 Social Security Funds
Finance of Gross Accumulation										
1 Gross saving	74247	40190	...	22490	11567	44648	13483	...	24123	7042
2 Capital transfers	...	...	...	...	...	...	...	...	...	...
A From other government subsectors	...	...	...	...	...	...	...	...	...	...
B From other resident sectors	...	...	...	...	...	...	...	...	...	...
C From rest of the world	...	...	...	...	...	...	...	...	...	...
Finance of Gross Accumulation	74247	40190	...	22490	11567	44648	13483	...	24123	7042
Gross Accumulation										
1 Gross capital formation	83372	58454	...	21900	3018	116900	87541	...	24925	4434
A Increase in stocks	1065	...	...	...	1065	1400	...	...	...	1400
B Gross fixed capital formation	82307	58454	...	21900	1953	115500	87541	...	24925	3034
2 Purchases of land, net	-154	129	...	-283	-	81	266	...	-185	-
3 Purchases of intangible assets, net	...	...	...	...	...	...	...	...	...	...
4 Capital transfers	4767	3539	...	1228	-	3933	2284	...	1649	-
A To other government subsectors	...	...	...	...	...	...	...	...	...	...
B To other resident sectors	4767	3539	...	1228	...	3933	2284	...	1649	...
C To rest of the world	...	...	...	...	...	...	...	...	...	...
Net lending [a]	-13738	-21932	...	-355	8549	-76266	-76608	...	-2266	2608
Gross Accumulation	74247	40190	...	22490	11567	44648	13483	...	24123	7042

Ecuador

3.13 General Government Capital Accumulation Account: Total and Subsectors

Million Ecuadoran sucres

	1988					1989				
	Total General Government	Central Government	State or Provincial Government	Local Government	Social Security Funds	Total General Government	Central Government	State or Provincial Government	Local Government	Social Security Funds
Finance of Gross Accumulation											
1 Gross saving	184723	129788	...	32673	22262	398415	311616	...	63866	22933
2 Capital transfers	...	...	...	...	...	...	...	...	...	...
A From other government subsectors	...	...	...	...	...	...	...	...	...	...
B From other resident sectors	...	...	...	...	...	...	...	...	...	...
C From rest of the world	...	...	...	...	...	...	...	...	...	...
Finance of Gross Accumulation	184723	129788	...	32673	22262	398415	311616	...	63866	22933
Gross Accumulation											
1 Gross capital formation	155489	120197	...	26189	9103	259095	198140	...	49565	11390
A Increase in stocks	2511	...	...	...	2511	7342	3504	...	...	3838
B Gross fixed capital formation	152978	120197	...	26189	6592	251753	194636	...	49565	7552
2 Purchases of land, net	139	351	...	-343	131	246	505	...	-483	224
3 Purchases of intangible assets, net	...	...	...	...	...	...	...	...	...	...
4 Capital transfers	13450	11689	...	1761	-	60575	58555	...	2020	-
A To other government subsectors	...	...	...	...	...	...	...	...	...	...
B To other resident sectors	13450	11689	...	1761	...	60575	58555	...	2020	...
C To rest of the world	...	...	...	...	...	...	...	...	...	...
Net lending a	15645	-2449	...	5066	13028	78499	54416	...	12764	11319
Gross Accumulation	184723	129788	...	32673	22262	398415	311616	...	63866	22933

a) Net lending of the capital accumulation account and the capital finance account have not been reconciled and are different due to different statistical sources.

3.14 General Government Capital Finance Account, Total and Subsectors

Million Ecuadoran sucres

	1980					1981				
	Total General Government	Central Government	State or Provincial Government	Local Government	Social Security Funds	Total General Government	Central Government	State or Provincial Government	Local Government	Social Security Funds
Acquisition of Financial Assets											
1 Gold and SDRs	-	...	...	...	...	-	...	...	...	...
2 Currency and transferable deposits	2695	...	...	...	...	5392	...	...	...	...
3 Other deposits	3496	...	...	...	...	-1116	...	...	...	...
4 Bills and bonds, short term	-	...	...	...	...	-	...	...	...	...
5 Bonds, long term a	2187	...	...	...	...	4204	...	...	...	...
6 Corporate equity securities	4104	...	...	...	...	5803	...	...	...	...
7 Short-term loans, n.e.c.	146	...	...	...	...	68	...	...	...	...
8 Long-term loans, n.e.c.	3818	...	...	...	...	2843	...	...	...	...
9 Other receivables b	-88	...	...	...	...	1499	...	...	...	...
10 Other assets c	1715	...	...	...	...	-351	...	...	...	...
Total Acquisition of Financial Assets	18073	...	...	...	...	18342	...	...	...	...
Incurrence of Liabilities											
1 Currency and transferable deposits	-	...	...	...	...	-	...	...	...	...
2 Other deposits	49	...	...	...	...	191	...	...	...	...
3 Bills and bonds, short term	-	...	...	...	...	-	...	...	...	...
4 Bonds, long term a	-359	...	...	...	...	1689	...	...	...	...
5 Short-term loans, n.e.c.	1678	...	...	...	...	11652	...	...	...	...
6 Long-term loans, n.e.c.	15580	...	...	...	...	19846	...	...	...	...
7 Other payables b	983	...	...	...	...	2053	...	...	...	...
8 Other liabilities d	9245	...	...	...	...	3351	...	...	...	...
Total Incurrence of Liabilities	27176	...	...	...	...	38782	...	...	...	...
Net Lending e	-9103	...	...	...	...	-20440	...	...	...	...
Incurrence of Liabilities and Net Worth	18073	...	...	...	...	18342	...	...	...	...

Ecuador

3.14 General Government Capital Finance Account, Total and Subsectors

Million Ecuadoran sucres

	1982					1983				
	Total General Government	Central Government	State or Provincial Government	Local Government	Social Security Funds	Total General Government	Central Government	State or Provincial Government	Local Government	Social Security Funds

Acquisition of Financial Assets

1 Gold and SDRs	-	...	...	...	...	-	...	...	...	...
2 Currency and transferable deposits	-968	...	...	...	...	8135	...	...	...	...
3 Other deposits	-7094	...	...	...	...	5796	...	...	...	...
4 Bills and bonds, short term	-	...	...	...	...	-	...	...	...	...
5 Bonds, long term [a]	2240	...	...	...	...	2563	...	...	...	...
6 Corporate equity securities	7747	...	...	...	...	9457	...	...	...	...
7 Short-term loans, n.e.c.	385	...	...	...	...	36	...	...	...	...
8 Long-term loans, n.e.c.	3059	...	...	...	...	7366	...	...	...	...
9 Other receivables [b]	1571	...	...	...	...	2086	...	...	...	...
10 Other assets [c]	350	...	...	...	...	379	...	...	...	...
Total Acquisition of Financial Assets	7290	...	...	...	...	35818	...	...	...	...

Incurrence of Liabilities

1 Currency and transferable deposits	-	...	...	...	...	-	...	...	...	...
2 Other deposits	277	...	...	...	...	1234	...	...	...	...
3 Bills and bonds, short term	-	...	...	...	...	-	...	...	...	...
4 Bonds, long term [a]	3991	...	...	...	...	9570	...	...	...	...
5 Short-term loans, n.e.c.	19552	...	...	...	...	-17030	...	...	...	...
6 Long-term loans, n.e.c.	-4523	...	...	...	...	45803	...	...	...	...
7 Other payables [b]	213	...	...	...	...	2543	...	...	...	...
8 Other liabilities [d]	9145	...	...	...	...	-243	...	...	...	...
Total Incurrence of Liabilities	28655	...	...	...	...	41877	...	...	...	...
Net Lending [e]	-21365	...	...	...	...	-6059	...	...	...	...
Incurrence of Liabilities and Net Worth	7290	...	...	...	...	35818	...	...	...	...

	1984					1985				
	Total General Government	Central Government	State or Provincial Government	Local Government	Social Security Funds	Total General Government	Central Government	State or Provincial Government	Local Government	Social Security Funds

Acquisition of Financial Assets

1 Gold and SDRs	-	...	...	...	...	-	...	...	...	...
2 Currency and transferable deposits	2320	...	...	...	...	17519	...	...	...	...
3 Other deposits	10182	...	...	...	...	21972	...	...	...	...
4 Bills and bonds, short term	-	...	...	...	...	-	...	...	...	...
5 Bonds, long term [a]	3233	...	...	...	...	-4363	...	...	...	...
6 Corporate equity securities	14036	...	...	...	...	24731	...	...	...	...
7 Short-term loans, n.e.c.	287	...	...	...	...	-227	...	...	...	...
8 Long-term loans, n.e.c.	9072	...	...	...	...	23590	...	...	...	...
9 Other receivables [b]	2730	...	...	...	...	7034	...	...	...	...
10 Other assets [c]	189	...	...	...	...	70	...	...	...	...
Total Acquisition of Financial Assets	42049	...	...	...	...	90326	...	...	...	...

Incurrence of Liabilities

1 Currency and transferable deposits	-	...	...	...	...	-	...	...	...	...
2 Other deposits	1341	...	...	...	...	1136	...	...	...	...
3 Bills and bonds, short term	-	...	...	...	...	-	...	...	...	...
4 Bonds, long term [a]	648	...	...	...	...	-5171	...	...	...	...
5 Short-term loans, n.e.c.	-857	...	...	...	...	1089	...	...	...	...
6 Long-term loans, n.e.c.	5438	...	...	...	...	30163	...	...	...	...
7 Other payables [b]	2831	...	...	...	...	-5030	...	...	...	...
8 Other liabilities [d]	25297	...	...	...	...	22398	...	...	...	...
Total Incurrence of Liabilities	34698	...	...	...	...	44585	...	...	...	...
Net Lending [e]	7351	...	...	...	...	45741	...	...	...	...
Incurrence of Liabilities and Net Worth	42049	...	...	...	...	90326	...	...	...	...

Ecuador

3.14 General Government Capital Finance Account, Total and Subsectors

Million Ecuadoran sucres

	1986 Total General Government	1986 Central Government	1986 State or Provincial Government	1986 Local Government	1986 Social Security Funds	1987 Total General Government	1987 Central Government	1987 State or Provincial Government	1987 Local Government	1987 Social Security Funds
Acquisition of Financial Assets										
1 Gold and SDRs	-	...	...	...	...		...	...	...	...
2 Currency and transferable deposits	5507	...	...	...	...	22903	...	...	...	...
3 Other deposits	-7732	...	...	...	...	-38865	...	...	...	...
4 Bills and bonds, short term	-	...	...	...	...	-	...	...	...	...
5 Bonds, long term [a]	-593	...	...	...	...	788	...	...	...	...
6 Corporate equity securities	17163	...	...	...	...	13746	...	...	...	...
7 Short-term loans, n.e.c.	-	...	...	...	...		...	...	...	...
8 Long-term loans, n.e.c.	27107	...	...	...	...	19618	...	...	...	...
9 Other receivables [b]	19729	...	...	...	...	28896	...	...	...	...
10 Other assets [c]	-394	...	...	...	...	-3	...	...	...	...
Total Acquisition of Financial Assets	60787	...	...	...	...	47083	...	...	...	...
Incurrence of Liabilities										
1 Currency and transferable deposits	-	...	...	...	...	-	...	...	...	...
2 Other deposits	2916	...	...	...	...	-164	...	...	...	...
3 Bills and bonds, short term	-	...	...	...	...		...	...	...	...
4 Bonds, long term [a]	3887	...	...	...	...	13648	...	...	...	...
5 Short-term loans, n.e.c.	17483	...	...	...	...	4048	...	...	...	...
6 Long-term loans, n.e.c.	39687	...	...	...	...	73867	...	...	...	...
7 Other payables [b]	-6838	...	...	...	...	42275	...	...	...	...
8 Other liabilities [d]	24113	...	...	...	...	-18859	...	...	...	...
Total Incurrence of Liabilities	81248	...	...	...	...	114815	...	...	...	...
Net Lending [e]	-20461	...	...	...	...	-67732	...	...	...	...
Incurrence of Liabilities and Net Worth	60787	...	...	...	...	47083	...	...	...	...

	1988 Total General Government	1988 Central Government	1988 State or Provincial Government	1988 Local Government	1988 Social Security Funds	1989 Total General Government	1989 Central Government	1989 State or Provincial Government	1989 Local Government	1989 Social Security Funds
Acquisition of Financial Assets										
1 Gold and SDRs	-	...	...	...	...	...	...	...	...	...
2 Currency and transferable deposits	14726	...	...	...	...	71777	...	...	...	...
3 Other deposits	45990	...	...	...	...	15045	...	...	...	...
4 Bills and bonds, short term	-	...	...	...	...		...	...	...	...
5 Bonds, long term [a]	5320	...	...	...	...	19418	...	...	...	...
6 Corporate equity securities	11201	...	...	...	...	15541	...	...	...	...
7 Short-term loans, n.e.c.		...	...	...	...		...	...	...	...
8 Long-term loans, n.e.c.	15743	...	...	...	...	20931	...	...	...	...
9 Other receivables [b]	7546	...	...	...	...	435	...	...	...	...
10 Other assets [c]	255083	...	...	...	...		...	...	...	...
Total Acquisition of Financial Assets	355609	...	...	...	...	143147	...	...	...	...
Incurrence of Liabilities										
1 Currency and transferable deposits	-	...	...	...	...		...	...	...	...
2 Other deposits	1428	...	...	...	...	25	...	...	...	...
3 Bills and bonds, short term	-	...	...	...	...		...	...	...	...
4 Bonds, long term [a]	21466	...	...	...	...	26308	...	...	...	...
5 Short-term loans, n.e.c.	81007	...	...	...	...	13360	...	...	...	...
6 Long-term loans, n.e.c.	209508	...	...	...	...	95677	...	...	...	...
7 Other payables [b]	-4994	...	...	...	...	8773	...	...	...	...
8 Other liabilities [d]	32785	...	...	...	...	-49314	...	...	...	...
Total Incurrence of Liabilities	341200	...	...	...	...	94829	...	...	...	...
Net Lending [e]	14409	...	...	...	...	48318	...	...	...	...
Incurrence of Liabilities and Net Worth	355609	...	...	...	...	143147	...	...	...	...

a) Item 'Bonds, long-term' includes both short-term and long-term bonds.
b) Item 'Other receivables/payables' refers to trade credits.
c) Item 'Other assets' refers to other receivables and accounting discrepancies.
d) Item 'Other liabilities' includes net equity in life insurance and unemployment, other payables and accounting discrepancies.
e) Net lending of the capital accumulation account and the capital finance account have not been reconciled and are different due to different statistical sources.

Ecuador

3.21 Corporate and Quasi-Corporate Enterprise Production Account: Total and Sectors

Million Ecuadoran sucres

	1980 TOTAL	1980 Non-Financial	1980 Financial	ADDENDUM: Total, including Unincorporated	1981 TOTAL	1981 Non-Financial	1981 Financial	ADDENDUM: Total, including Unincorporated	1982 TOTAL	1982 Non-Financial	1982 Financial	ADDENDUM: Total, including Unincorporated
Gross Output												
1 Output for sale	206225	201464	4761	...	251645	245985	5660	...	321325	315332	5993	...
2 Imputed bank service charge	8909	-	8909	...	9945	-	9945	...	12961	-	12961	...
3 Own-account fixed capital formation	...	...	...	...	...	...	...	...	...	...	...	...
Gross Output [a]	215134	201464	13670	...	261590	245985	15605	...	334286	315332	18954	...
Gross Input												
Intermediate consumption	119617	108069	11548	...	147515	134101	13414	...	192859	175312	17547	...
1 Imputed banking service charge	8909	-	8909	...	9945	-	9945	...	12961	-	12961	...
2 Other intermediate consumption	110708	108069	2639	...	137570	134101	3469	...	179898	175312	4586	...
Subtotal: Value Added [a]	95517	93395	2122	...	114075	111884	2191	...	141427	140020	1407	...
1 Indirect taxes, net	9666	9271	395	...	17218	16816	402	...	20255	19357	898	...
A Indirect taxes	11487	11092	395	...	19532	19130	402	...	23047	22149	898	...
B Less: Subsidies	1821	1821	-	...	2314	2314	-	...	2792	2792	-	...
2 Consumption of fixed capital [b]	...	...	...	...	...	...	...	...	...	...	...	...
3 Compensation of employees	33848	29037	4811	...	39595	33336	6259	...	46526	38644	7882	...
4 Net operating surplus [b]	52003	55087	-3084	...	57262	61732	-4470	...	74646	82019	-7373	...
Gross Input [a]	215134	201464	13670	...	261590	245985	15605	...	334286	315332	18954	...

	1983 TOTAL	1983 Non-Financial	1983 Financial	ADDENDUM: Total, including Unincorporated	1984 TOTAL	1984 Non-Financial	1984 Financial	ADDENDUM: Total, including Unincorporated	1985 TOTAL	1985 Non-Financial	1985 Financial	ADDENDUM: Total, including Unincorporated
Gross Output												
1 Output for sale	429551	423085	6466	...	590806	580401	10405	...	803011	788314	14697	...
2 Imputed bank service charge	19200	-	19200	...	21388	-	21388	...	18695	-	18695	...
3 Own-account fixed capital formation	...	...	...	...	...	...	...	...	...	...	...	...
Gross Output [a]	448751	423085	25666	...	612194	580401	31793	...	821706	788314	33392	...
Gross Input												
Intermediate consumption	266122	239010	27112	...	347358	315603	31755	...	451648	420695	30953	...
1 Imputed banking service charge	19200	-	19200	...	21388	-	21388	...	18695	-	18695	...
2 Other intermediate consumption	246922	239010	7912	...	325970	315603	10367	...	432953	420695	12258	...
Subtotal: Value Added [a]	182629	184075	-1446	...	264836	264798	38	...	370058	367619	2439	...
1 Indirect taxes, net	26997	24303	2694	...	32655	27823	4832	...	91559	85667	5892	...
A Indirect taxes	28988	26294	2694	...	37280	32448	4832	...	93872	87980	5892	...
B Less: Subsidies	1991	1991	-	...	4625	4625	-	...	2313	2313	-	...
2 Consumption of fixed capital [b]	...	...	...	...	...	...	...	...	73694	57253	16441	...
3 Compensation of employees	53398	43735	9663	...	61723	48817	12906	...	204805	224699	-19894	...
4 Net operating surplus [b]	102234	116037	-13803	...	170458	188158	-17700	...				...
Gross Input [a]	448751	423085	25666	...	612194	580401	31793	...	821706	788314	33392	...

a) Data for this table have not been revised, therefore, data for some years are not comparable with those of other tables.
b) Item 'Operating surplus' includes consumption of fixed capital.

3.22 Corporate and Quasi-Corporate Enterprise Income and Outlay Account: Total and Sectors

Million Ecuadoran sucres

	1980 TOTAL	1980 Non-Financial	1980 Financial	1981 TOTAL	1981 Non-Financial	1981 Financial	1982 TOTAL	1982 Non-Financial	1982 Financial	1983 TOTAL	1983 Non-Financial	1983 Financial
Receipts												
1 Operating surplus [a]	52003	55087	-3084	57262	61732	-4470	74646	82019	-7373	102234	116037	-13803
2 Property and entrepreneurial income	15780	2948	12832	19161	3853	15308	26637	5109	21528	43860	8648	35212
A Withdrawals from quasi-corporate enterprises	...	...	...	...	...	...	...	...	...	...	...	...
B Interest	15283	2617	12666	18574	3500	15074	25892	4629	21263	42075	7634	34441
C Dividends	493	327	166	587	353	234	745	480	265	1785	1014	771
D Net land rent and royalties	4	4	-	-	-	-	-	-	-	-	-	-

Ecuador

3.22 Corporate and Quasi-Corporate Enterprise Income and Outlay Account: Total and Sectors
(Continued)

Million Ecuadoran sucres

	1980 TOTAL	1980 Non-Financial	1980 Financial	1981 TOTAL	1981 Non-Financial	1981 Financial	1982 TOTAL	1982 Non-Financial	1982 Financial	1983 TOTAL	1983 Non-Financial	1983 Financial
3 Current transfers	1796	1483	313	2220	1843	377	3217	2369	848	4027	2829	1198
A Casualty insurance claims	629	604	25	876	846	30	1226	1168	58	1376	1297	79
B Casualty insurance premiums, net, due to be received by insurance companies	197	-	197	225	-	225	482	-	482	538	-	538
C Current transfers from the rest of the world	...	...	...	...	...	...	...	...	...	...	...	...
D Other transfers except imputed	...	...	...	...	...	...	107	3	104	358	39	319
E Imputed unfunded employee pension and welfare contributions	970	879	91	1119	997	122	1402	1198	204	1755	1493	262
Total Current Receipts	69579	59518	10061	78643	67428	11215	104500	89497	15003	150121	127514	22607

Disbursements

	1980 TOTAL	1980 Non-Financial	1980 Financial	1981 TOTAL	1981 Non-Financial	1981 Financial	1982 TOTAL	1982 Non-Financial	1982 Financial	1983 TOTAL	1983 Non-Financial	1983 Financial
1 Property and entrepreneurial income	32576	27949	4627	39989	33611	6378	53617	44043	9574	87750	71074	16676
A Withdrawals from quasi-corporations	92	16	76	138	13	125	76	16	60	87	33	54
Public	...	...	...	...	...	...	...	...	...	...	...	...
Private	92	16	76	138	13	125	76	16	60	87	33	54
B Interest	17440	13626	3814	21800	16564	5236	32617	24202	8415	51691	35882	15809
C Dividends [b]	6156	5419	737	7148	6131	1017	8696	7597	1099	14854	14041	813
D Net land rent and royalties	8888	8888	...	10903	10903	...	12228	12228	-	21118	21118	-
2 Direct taxes and other current transfers n.e.c. to general government	20187	19893	294	19148	18748	400	30006	29550	456	37764	37331	433
A Direct taxes	19679	19385	294	18781	18381	400	29539	29083	456	37232	36799	433
On income	19585	19291	294	18669	18269	400	29408	28952	456	37079	36646	433
Other	94	94	...	112	112	-	131	131	-	153	153	-
B Fines, fees, penalties and other current transfers n.e.c.	508	508	...	367	367	-	467	467	-	532	532	-
3 Other current transfers	2876	1744	1132	4726	2693	2033	5552	2986	2566	6194	3371	2823
A Casualty insurance premiums, net	665	639	26	938	908	30	1398	1340	58	1493	1406	87
B Casualty insurance claims liability of insurance companies	197	...	197	225	-	225	482	-	482	538	-	538
C Transfers to private non-profit institutions	...	...	...	...	...	...	...	...	...	...	...	...
D Unfunded employee pension and welfare benefits	970	879	91	1119	997	122	1402	1198	204	1755	1493	262
E Social assistance grants	1035	223	812	2392	778	1614	194	64	130	473	120	353
F Other transfers n.e.c.	...	...	...	...	...	...	1953	357	1596	1896	333	1563
G Transfers to the rest of the world	9	3	6	52	10	42	123	27	96	39	19	20
Net saving [c]	13940	9932	4008	14780	12376	2404	15325	12918	2407	18413	15738	2675
Total Current Disbursements and Net Saving	69579	59518	10061	78643	67428	11215	104500	89497	15003	150121	127514	22607

	1984 TOTAL	1984 Non-Financial	1984 Financial	1985 TOTAL	1985 Non-Financial	1985 Financial	1986 TOTAL	1986 Non-Financial	1986 Financial	1987 TOTAL	1987 Non-Financial	1987 Financial

Receipts

	1984 TOTAL	1984 Non-Financial	1984 Financial	1985 TOTAL	1985 Non-Financial	1985 Financial	1986 TOTAL	1986 Non-Financial	1986 Financial	1987 TOTAL	1987 Non-Financial	1987 Financial
1 Operating surplus [a]	168068	185898	-17830	214248	236520	-22272	217661	246742	-29081	214309	254012	-39703
2 Property and entrepreneurial income	77216	13206	64010	103952	19890	84062	144072	25445	118627	205295	34221	171074
A Withdrawals from quasi-corporate enterprises	...	...	...	...	...	...	...	...	...	...	...	...
B Interest	75405	11671	63734	101161	17913	83248	140098	22685	117413	199513	30222	169291
C Dividends	1811	1535	276	2791	1977	814	3974	2760	1214	5782	3999	1783
D Net land rent and royalties	-	-	-	-	-	-	-	-	-	-	-	-

Ecuador

3.22 Corporate and Quasi-Corporate Enterprise Income and Outlay Account: Total and Sectors
(Continued)

Million Ecuadoran sucres

		1984			1985			1986			1987	
		TOTAL	Non-Financial	Financial	TOTAL	Non-Financial	Financial	TOTAL	Non-Financial	Financial	TOTAL	Non-Financial	Financial
3	Current transfers	4974	3566	1408	7910	5700	2210	11930	8680	3250	19597	14069	5528
	A Casualty insurance claims	1784	1682	102	2451	2351	100	2957	2836	121	5341	5124	217
	B Casualty insurance premiums, net, due to be received by insurance companies	677	-	677	1011	-	1011	1365	-	1365	2495		2495
	C Current transfers from the rest of the world	...	...	...	...	...	...	...	...	...	...	...	...
	D Other transfers except imputed	284	35	249	71	31	40	494	448	46	151	113	38
	E Imputed unfunded employee pension and welfare contributions	2229	1849	380	4377	3318	1059	7114	5396	1718	11610	8832	2778
Total Current Receipts		250258	202670	47588	326110	262110	64000	373663	280867	92796	439201	302302	136899

Disbursements

		TOTAL	Non-Financial	Financial	TOTAL	Non-Financial	Financial	TOTAL	Non-Financial	Financial	TOTAL	Non-Financial	Financial
1	Property and entrepreneurial income	154293	104197	50096	186170	120801	65369	246288	154157	92131	321598	199936	121662
	A Withdrawals from quasi-corporations	91	36	55	246	168	78	470	216	254	826	274	552
	Public	...	...	...	...	...	...	...	...	...	...	...	...
	Private	91	36	55	246	168	78	470	216	254	826	274	552
	B Interest	107490	60494	46996	129731	67727	62004	184268	94947	89321	247813	131666	116147
	C Dividends [b]	18606	15561	3045	29972	26685	3287	37131	34575	2556	50094	45131	4963
	D Net land rent and royalties	28106	28106	-	26221	26221	-	24419	24419	-	22865	22865	-
2	Direct taxes and other current transfers n.e.c. to general government	64648	64263	385	86072	85159	913	59537	58283	1254	49863	48464	1399
	A Direct taxes	63839	63454	385	84538	83760	778	57335	56304	1031	46967	46029	938
	On income	63583	63198	385	84133	83355	778	56863	55832	1031	46468	45530	938
	Other	256	256	-	405	405	-	472	472	-	499	499	-
	B Fines, fees, penalties and other current transfers n.e.c.	809	809	-	1534	1399	135	2202	1979	223	2896	2435	461
3	Other current transfers	7506	4171	3335	25610	20735	4875	39392	28033	11359	47138	28425	18713
	A Casualty insurance premiums, net	1799	1698	101	2484	2363	121	3099	2968	131	5258	5029	229
	B Casualty insurance claims liability of insurance companies	677	-	677	1011	-	1011	1365	-	1365	2495	-	2495
	C Transfers to private non-profit institutions	...	...	...	...	...	...	...	...	...	...	...	...
	D Unfunded employee pension and welfare benefits	2229	1849	380	4377	3318	1059	7114	5396	1718	11610	8832	2778
	E Social assistance grants	1009	272	737	1583	477	1106	2982	408	2574	3842	571	3271
	F Other transfers n.e.c.	1699	276	1423	16029	14467	1562	24709	19191	5518	23511	13618	9893
	G Transfers to the rest of the world	93	76	17	126	110	16	123	70	53	422	375	47
Net saving [c]		23811	30039	-6228	28258	35415	-7157	28446	40394	-11948	20602	25477	-4875
Total Current Disbursements and Net Saving		250258	202670	47588	326110	262110	64000	373663	280867	92796	439201	302302	136899

		1988			1989		
		TOTAL	Non-Financial	Financial	TOTAL	Non-Financial	Financial

Receipts

		TOTAL	Non-Financial	Financial	TOTAL	Non-Financial	Financial
1	Operating surplus [a]	472686	530048	-57362	767235	860888	-93653
2	Property and entrepreneurial income	306100	50859	255241	431466	77930	353536
	A Withdrawals from quasi-corporate enterprises	...	...	...	...	...	...
	B Interest	297163	44741	252422	414266	68751	345515
	C Dividends	8937	6118	2819	17200	9179	8021
	D Net land rent and royalties	-	-	-	-	-	-

Ecuador

3.22 Corporate and Quasi-Corporate Enterprise Income and Outlay Account: Total and Sectors
(Continued)

Million Ecuadoran sucres

	1988 TOTAL	1988 Non-Financial	1988 Financial	1989 TOTAL	1989 Non-Financial	1989 Financial
3 Current transfers	29701	20592	9109	45791	30853	14938
A Casualty insurance claims	8322	7981	341	13575	13050	525
B Casualty insurance premiums, net, due to be received by insurance companies	3710	-	3710	7138	-	7138
C Current transfers from the rest of the world	...	...	...	...	...	...
D Other transfers except imputed	218	158	60	344	248	96
E Imputed unfunded employee pension and welfare contributions	17451	12453	4998	24734	17555	7179
Total Current Receipts	808487	601499	206988	1244492	969671	274821

Disbursements

1 Property and entrepreneurial income	504283	346698	157585	781801	516555	265246
A Withdrawals from quasi-corporations	1416	640	776	2090	774	1316
Public	...	...	...	...	...	...
Private	1416	640	776	2090	774	1316
B Interest	358226	203914	154312	552937	295215	257722
C Dividends [b]	86491	83994	2497	115960	109752	6208
D Net land rent and royalties	58150	58150	-	110814	110814	-
2 Direct taxes and other current transfers n.e.c. to general government	111050	108671	2379	237974	234425	3549
A Direct taxes	106631	105678	953	229223	226624	2599
On income	105900	104947	953	228329	225730	2599
Other	731	731	-	894	894	-
B Fines, fees, penalties and other current transfers n.e.c.	4419	2993	1426	8751	7801	950
3 Other current transfers	64995	44898	20097	59357	40900	18457
A Casualty insurance premiums, net	7856	7374	482	12810	12142	668
B Casualty insurance claims liability of insurance companies	3710	-	3710	7138	-	7138
C Transfers to private non-profit institutions	...	...	...	...	...	...
D Unfunded employee pension and welfare benefits	17451	12453	4998	24734	17555	7179
E Social assistance grants	3380	743	2637	5478	2432	3046
F Other transfers n.e.c.	32149	23958	8191	8153	7813	340
G Transfers to the rest of the world	449	370	79	1044	958	86
Net saving [c]	128159	101232	26927	165360	177791	-12431
Total Current Disbursements and Net Saving	808487	601499	206988	1244492	969671	274821

a) Item 'Operating surplus' includes consumption of fixed capital.
b) Item 'Dividends' includes profit-sharing by employees.
c) Item 'Net saving' includes consumption of fixed capital.

3.23 Corporate and Quasi-Corporate Enterprise Capital Accumulation Account: Total and Sectors

Million Ecuadoran sucres

	1980 TOTAL	1980 Non-Financial	1980 Financial	1981 TOTAL	1981 Non-Financial	1981 Financial	1982 TOTAL	1982 Non-Financial	1982 Financial	1983 TOTAL	1983 Non-Financial	1983 Financial
	\multicolumn{12}{c}{**Finance of Gross Accumulation**}
1 Gross saving	13940	9932	4008	14780	12376	2404	15325	12918	2407	18413	15738	2675
2 Capital transfers	1965	1797	168	5908	5859	49	6179	6037	142	3532	2282	1250
A From resident sectors	1958	1797	161	5859	5859	-	6166	6037	129	3525	2282	1243
B From the rest of the world	7	...	7	49	...	49	13	...	13	7	...	7
Finance of Gross Accumulation	15905	11729	4176	20688	18235	2453	21504	18955	2549	21945	18020	3925
	\multicolumn{12}{c}{**Gross Accumulation**}
1 Gross capital formation	41606	38647	2959	39164	35638	3526	53757	49571	4186	50377	44340	6037
A Increase in stocks	5400	4085	1315	2281	732	1549	8233	6955	1278	3032	1795	1237
B Gross fixed capital formation	36206	34562	1644	36883	34906	1977	45524	42616	2908	47345	42545	4800

Ecuador

3.23 Corporate and Quasi-Corporate Enterprise Capital Accumulation Account: Total and Sectors
(Continued)

Million Ecuadoran sucres

	1980 TOTAL	1980 Non-Financial	1980 Financial	1981 TOTAL	1981 Non-Financial	1981 Financial	1982 TOTAL	1982 Non-Financial	1982 Financial	1983 TOTAL	1983 Non-Financial	1983 Financial
2 Purchases of land, net	1703	1742	-39	2597	2396	201	3817	3185	632	3878	3260	618
3 Purchases of intangible assets, net	79	79	-	156	156	-	179	179	-	735	735	-
4 Capital transfers	560	42	518	507	19	488	1069	6	1063	659	260	399
A To resident sectors	560	42	518	507	19	488	1069	6	1063	659	260	399
B To the rest of the world	...	...	...	...	...	...	...	...	...	...	...	...
Net lending a	-28043	-28781	738	-21736	-19974	-1762	-37318	-33986	-3332	-33704	-30575	-3129
Gross Accumulation	15905	11729	4176	20688	18235	2453	21504	18955	2549	21945	18020	3925

	1984 TOTAL	1984 Non-Financial	1984 Financial	1985 TOTAL	1985 Non-Financial	1985 Financial	1986 TOTAL	1986 Non-Financial	1986 Financial	1987 TOTAL	1987 Non-Financial	1987 Financial
Finance of Gross Accumulation
1 Gross saving	23811	30039	-6228	28258	35415	-7157	28446	40394	-11948	20602	25477	-4875
2 Capital transfers	1853	1410	443	1855	1503	352	6286	6053	233	6264	6199	65
A From resident sectors	1853	1410	443	1855	1503	352	6286	6053	233	6264	6199	65
B From the rest of the world	-	...	-	-	...	-	-	-	-	-	...	-
Finance of Gross Accumulation	25664	31449	-5785	30113	36918	-6805	34732	46447	-11715	26866	31676	-4810
Gross Accumulation
1 Gross capital formation	72803	63532	9271	105736	95741	9995	155340	135683	19657	226454	208040	18414
A Increase in stocks	10191	5875	4316	17357	11794	5563	22259	11948	10311	594	-6162	6756
B Gross fixed capital formation	62612	57657	4955	88379	83947	4432	133081	123735	9346	225860	214202	11658
2 Purchases of land, net	4974	4424	550	6489	5350	1139	9296	5966	3330	9672	7804	1868
3 Purchases of intangible assets, net	948	948	-	1124	1124	-	1388	1388	-	2321	2321	-
4 Capital transfers	819	813	6	1410	989	421	3288	1237	2051	4165	1777	2388
A To resident sectors	819	813	6	1410	989	421	3288	1237	2051	4165	1777	2388
B To the rest of the world	...	...	...	...	...	...	...	...	...	...	...	...
Net lending a	-53880	-38268	-15612	-84646	-66286	-18360	-134580	-97827	-36753	-215746	-188266	-27480
Gross Accumulation	25664	31449	-5785	30113	36918	-6805	34732	46447	-11715	26866	31676	-4810

	1988 TOTAL	1988 Non-Financial	1988 Financial	1989 TOTAL	1989 Non-Financial	1989 Financial
Finance of Gross Accumulation
1 Gross saving	128159	101232	26927	165360	177791	-12431
2 Capital transfers	19631	18481	1150	70522	70518	4
A From resident sectors	19631	18481	1150	70522	70518	4
B From the rest of the world	-	...	-	-	...	-
Finance of Gross Accumulation	147790	119713	28077	235882	248309	-12427
Gross Accumulation
1 Gross capital formation	413257	364006	49251	754069	707515	46554
A Increase in stocks	14929	-19514	34443	52848	24911	27937
B Gross fixed capital formation	398328	383520	14808	701221	682604	18617
2 Purchases of land, net	11211	8957	2254	13590	11925	1665
3 Purchases of intangible assets, net	5457	5457	-	7150	7150	-
4 Capital transfers	10412	3735	6677	16325	4632	11693
A To resident sectors	10412	3735	6677	16325	4632	11693
B To the rest of the world	...	...	...	...	...	...
Net lending a	-292547	-262442	-30105	-555252	-482913	-72339
Gross Accumulation	147790	119713	28077	235882	248309	-12427

a) Net lending of the capital accumulation account and the capital finance account have not been reconciled and are different due to different statistical sources.

Ecuador

3.24 Corporate and Quasi-Corporate Enterprise Capital Finance Account: Total and Sectors

Million Ecuadoran sucres

	1980 TOTAL	1980 Non-Financial	1980 Financial	1981 TOTAL	1981 Non-Financial	1981 Financial	1982 TOTAL	1982 Non-Financial	1982 Financial	1983 TOTAL	1983 Non-Financial	1983 Financial
Acquisition of Financial Assets												
1 Gold and SDRs	158	-	158	173	-	173	-1929	-1	-1929	-7949	-	-7949
2 Currency and transferable deposits	3655	2245	1410	3136	1408	1728	1010	2318	-1308	8833	6829	2004
3 Other deposits	9704	1620	8084	-4942	4031	-8973	5045	8739	-3694	26181	8104	18077
4 Bills and bonds, short term	...	...	...	...	...	...	...	...	...	...	...	...
5 Bonds, long term [a]	3236	904	2332	2987	752	2235	6370	2088	4282	15935	2495	13440
6 Corporate equity securities	3535	2463	1072	4459	3162	1297	6290	5136	1154	4668	3413	1255
7 Short term loans, n.e.c.	19602	562	19040	29216	-561	29777	36770	3136	33634	62049	6583	55466
8 Long term loans, n.e.c.	6059	610	5449	9134	-31	9165	10148	-98	10246	101205	-342	101547
9 Trade credits and advances	19260	15196	4064	36908	29514	7394	25856	13131	12725	48963	22281	26682
10 Other receivables	2598	2056	542	2665	2387	278	3314	2382	932	9286	7004	2282
11 Other assets	...	...	...	...	...	...	...	...	...	...	...	...
Total Acquisition of Financial Assets	67807	25656	42151	83736	40662	43074	92874	36832	56042	269171	56367	212804
Incurrence of Liabilities												
1 Currency and transferable deposits	13429	-	13429	12142	-	12142	4722	-	4722	22079	-	22079
2 Other deposits	14721	1408	13313	12721	3033	9688	11401	4052	7349	27578	5141	22437
3 Bills and bonds, short term	-	-	-	-	-	-	-	-	-	-	-	-
4 Bonds, long term [a]	2715	9	2706	3400	267	3133	5414	495	4919	6527	542	5985
5 Corporate equity securities	11312	5856	5456	16653	9552	7101	19064	10123	8941	17367	6688	10679
6 Short-term loans, n.e.c.	25215	21547	3668	16881	8905	7976	34481	20866	13615	39578	19580	19998
7 Long-term loans, n.e.c.	5551	4789	762	16262	14641	1621	14534	11878	2656	109879	-5433	115312
8 Net equity of households in life insurance and pension fund reserves	149	-	149	334	-	334	245	-	245	274		274
9 Proprietors' net additions to the accumulation of quasi-corporations	-	-	-	-	-	-	-	-	-	-	-	-
10 Trade credit and advances	14283	12726	1557	21255	21151	104	24832	15156	9676	53465	42497	10968
11 Other accounts payable	1773	1294	479	4588	1976	2612	17492	10047	7445	22677	15339	7338
12 Other liabilities	...	...	...	...	...	...	...	...	...	...	...	...
Total Incurrence of Liabilities	89148	47629	41519	104236	59525	44711	132185	72617	59568	299424	84354	215070
Net Lending [b]	-21341	-21973	632	-20500	-18861	-1637	-39311	-35785	-3526	-30253	-27987	-2266
Incurrence of Liabilities and Net Lending	67807	25656	42151	83736	40662	43074	92874	36832	56042	269171	56367	212804

	1984 TOTAL	1984 Non-Financial	1984 Financial	1985 TOTAL	1985 Non-Financial	1985 Financial	1986 TOTAL	1986 Non-Financial	1986 Financial	1987 TOTAL	1987 Non-Financial	1987 Financial
Acquisition of Financial Assets												
1 Gold and SDRs	-3202	-	-3202	-5239	-	-5239	-5484	...	-5484	262	...	262
2 Currency and transferable deposits	8081	8602	-521	14971	9576	5395	26847	9577	17270	6079	15131	-9052
3 Other deposits	24443	11474	12969	14157	-7912	22069	-11301	10085	-21386	58571	35544	23027
4 Bills and bonds, short term	...	...	...	...	...	...	...	...	...	...	...	...
5 Bonds, long term [a]	15461	4681	10780	11245	2755	8490	9290	575	8715	49718	22742	26976
6 Corporate equity securities	6329	4899	1430	9247	5294	3953	17384	7961	9423	4338	-1970	6308
7 Short term loans, n.e.c.	49760	7310	42450	55668	5931	49737	79475	9610	69865	78297	18691	59606
8 Long term loans, n.e.c.	109237	47	109190	64383	355	64028	46124	360	45764	65592	-245	65837
9 Trade credits and advances	37833	26697	11136	82729	65547	17182	99890	62623	37267	223668	147576	76092
10 Other receivables	17323	2691	14632	41881	18342	23539	12471	10480	1991	4795	922	3873
11 Other assets	...	...	...	...	...	...	...	...	...	...	...	...
Total Acquisition of Financial Assets	265265	66401	198864	289042	99888	189154	274696	111271	163425	491320	238391	252929
Incurrence of Liabilities												
1 Currency and transferable deposits	31405	-	31405	47433	-	47433	40475	...	40475	55626	...	55626
2 Other deposits	64011	6747	57264	91414	7649	83765	70612	2627	67985	99921	19767	80154
3 Bills and bonds, short term	-	-	-	-	-	-	...	...	...	...	...	...
4 Bonds, long term [a]	9589	497	9092	11974	2434	9540	6782	1337	5445	41167	-752	41919
5 Corporate equity securities	25651	10953	14698	47359	22868	24491	46885	25824	21061	44757	27109	17648
6 Short-term loans, n.e.c.	33658	38480	-4822	32247	32784	-537	18572	20724	-2152	49244	44134	5110

Ecuador

3.24 Corporate and Quasi-Corporate Enterprise Capital Finance Account: Total and Sectors
(Continued)

Million Ecuadoran sucres

	1984 TOTAL	1984 Non-Financial	1984 Financial	1985 TOTAL	1985 Non-Financial	1985 Financial	1986 TOTAL	1986 Non-Financial	1986 Financial	1987 TOTAL	1987 Non-Financial	1987 Financial
7 Long-term loans, n.e.c.	107611	5095	102516	52217	11612	40605	55638	9466	46172	93185	70958	22227
8 Net equity of households in life insurance and pension fund reserves	558	-	558	582	-	582	878	-	878	1406	-	1406
9 Proprietors' net additions to the accumulation of quasi-corporations	-	-	-	-	-	-	-	-	-	...	...	...
10 Trade credit and advances	32400	28277	4123	81787	71855	9932	135165	117750	17415	253870	214517	39353
11 Other accounts payable	18051	17069	982	12914	21033	-8119	46414	46671	-257	65148	51324	13824
12 Other liabilities	...	...	...	...	...	...	...	...	...	...	...	...
Total Incurrence of Liabilities	322934	107118	215816	377927	170235	207692	421421	224399	197022	704324	427057	277267
Net Lending b	-57669	-40717	-16952	-88885	-70347	-18538	-146725	-113128	-33597	-213004	-188666	-24338
Incurrence of Liabilities and Net Lending	265265	66401	198864	289042	99888	189154	274696	111271	163425	491320	238391	252929

	1988 TOTAL	1988 Non-Financial	1988 Financial	1989 TOTAL	1989 Non-Financial	1989 Financial

Acquisition of Financial Assets

	1988 TOTAL	1988 Non-Financial	1988 Financial	1989 TOTAL	1989 Non-Financial	1989 Financial
1 Gold and SDRs	...	...	17801	...	...	23169
2 Currency and transferable deposits	...	...	6665	...	...	14632
3 Other deposits	...	...	86630	...	...	154287
4 Bills and bonds, short term	...	...	...	...	...	...
5 Bonds, long term a	...	...	28930	...	...	39435
6 Corporate equity securities	...	...	11864	...	...	12707
7 Short term loans, n.e.c.	...	...	141136	...	...	226612
8 Long term loans, n.e.c.	...	...	49609	...	...	50862
9 Trade credits and advances	...	...	26899	...	...	67958
10 Other receivables	...	...	13912	...	...	6908
11 Other assets	...	...	...	...	...	...
Total Acquisition of Financial Assets	...	...	383446	...	...	596570

Incurrence of Liabilities

	1988 TOTAL	1988 Non-Financial	1988 Financial	1989 TOTAL	1989 Non-Financial	1989 Financial
1 Currency and transferable deposits	...	...	146320	...	...	231263
2 Other deposits	...	...	228889	...	...	278249
3 Bills and bonds, short term	...	...	...	...	...	...
4 Bonds, long term a	...	...	26766	...	...	27832
5 Corporate equity securities	...	...	25703	...	...	22436
6 Short-term loans, n.e.c.	...	...	12812	...	...	-16847
7 Long-term loans, n.e.c.	...	...	-86600	...	...	37842
8 Net equity of households in life insurance and pension fund reserves	...	...	1714	...	...	3069
9 Proprietors' net additions to the accumulation of quasi-corporations	...	...	-	...	...	-
10 Trade credit and advances	...	...	29609	...	...	72160
11 Other accounts payable	...	...	18781	...	...	19601
12 Other liabilities	...	...	...	...	...	...
Total Incurrence of Liabilities	...	...	403994	...	...	675605
Net Lending b	...	...	-20548	...	...	-79035
Incurrence of Liabilities and Net Lending	...	...	383446	...	...	596570

a) Item 'Bonds, long-term' includes both short-term and long-term bonds.
b) Net lending of the capital accumulation account and the capital finance account have not been reconciled and are different due to different statistical sources.

3.31 Household and Private Unincorporated Enterprise Production Account

Million Ecuadoran sucres

	1970	1975	1980	1981	1982	1983	1984	1985	1986	1987	1988	1989
Gross Output
1 Output for sale	...	...	...	...	...	...	...	...	...	...	...	...
2 Non-marketed output	...	...	...	...	...	...	...	...	...	...	...	...
Gross Output a	38019	110724	239625	270306	316159	440857	680258	990871	...	...	...	...
Gross Input
Intermediate consumption	13924	46305	83265	82271	93560	125980	230922	343854	...	...	...	...

Ecuador

3.31 Household and Private Unincorporated Enterprise Production Account
(Continued)

Million Ecuadoran sucres

	1970	1975	1980	1981	1982	1983	1984	1985	1986	1987	1988	1989
Subtotal: Value Added	24095	64419	156360	188035	222599	314877	449336	647017	...	...	...	...
1 Indirect taxes net liability of unincorporated enterprises	717	1726	2698	3031	3346	3950	6574	7575	...	...	...	...
A Indirect taxes	717	1726	2698	3031	3346	3950	6574	7575	...	...	...	...
B Less: Subsidies	...	...	...	...	...	...	...	...	...	...	...	...
2 Consumption of fixed capital [b]	...	...	...	...	...	...	...	...	...	...	...	...
3 Compensation of employees	4873	13157	30678	31430	34507	35787	39099	42070	...	...	...	...
4 Net operating surplus [b]	18505	49536	122984	153574	184746	275140	403663	597372	...	...	...	...
Gross Input [a]	38019	110724	239625	270306	316159	440857	680258	990871	...	...	...	...

a) Data for this table have not been revised, therefore, data for some years are not comparable with those of other tables.
b) Item 'Operating surplus' includes consumption of fixed capital.

3.32 Household and Private Unincorporated Enterprise Income and Outlay Account

Million Ecuadoran sucres

	1970	1975	1980	1981	1982	1983	1984	1985	1986	1987	1988	1989
Receipts												
1 Compensation of employees	10755	31369	92924	104495	118671	133731	176324	230005	298243	394423	537712	759455
A Wages and salaries	10010	29250	87563	98932	111803	123520	163915	210975	271782	358464	485004	687872
B Employers' contributions for social security	538	1256	3797	3708	4413	6997	7855	11179	14720	18434	26163	34926
C Employers' contributions for private pension & welfare plans	207	863	1564	1855	2455	3214	4554	7851	11741	17525	26545	36657
2 Operating surplus of private unincorporated enterprises [a]	18505	49536	122984	153574	184746	275140	395670	533522	705213	970732	1730144	3268344
3 Property and entrepreneurial income	403	1748	6340	8600	13079	17344	24011	45466	62059	84472	115533	165416
A Withdrawals from private quasi-corporations	...	...	...	...	...	...	...	...	...	...	...	...
B Interest	134	862	2797	4045	7737	10445	15301	33470	47120	64446	91329	132651
C Dividends [b]	267	864	3083	4060	4785	6292	7842	10885	13482	18039	21529	29164
D Net land rent and royalties	2	22	460	495	557	607	868	1111	1457	1987	2675	3601
3 Current transfers	1339	3662	10186	12099	13860	18672	24062	33826	41390	90436	106374	168590
A Casualty insurance claims	28	92	299	517	760	826	780	1094	1407	2148	3609	5928
B Social security benefits	778	1818	6746	7726	8988	12639	15629	20673	22385	39535	41912	58906
C Social assistance grants	...	...	...	...	...	...	...	...	...	...	...	...
D Unfunded employee pension and welfare benefits	207	863	1564	1855	2455	3214	4554	7851	11741	17525	26545	36657
E Transfers from general government	155	645	1353	1787	1463	1520	2090	2625	2875	4214	5597	9603
F Transfers from the rest of the world	166	208	65	-	-	-	-	-	-	-	-	-
G Other transfers n.e.c.	5	36	159	214	194	473	1009	1583	2982	27014	28711	57496
Total Current Receipts	31002	86315	232434	278768	330356	444887	620067	842819	1106905	1540063	2489763	4361805
Disbursements												
1 Final consumption expenditures	26375	70298	174875	214665	262206	369330	520593	715659	925775	1269416	2140102	3896928
2 Property income	360	1895	6707	8003	10984	13884	18687	25640	40246	57628	92332	115735
A Interest	360	1895	6707	8003	10984	13884	18687	25640	40246	57628	92332	115735
B Net land rent and royalties	...	...	...	...	...	...	...	...	...	...	...	...
3 Direct taxes and other current transfers n.e.c. to government	1634	3917	11513	13562	14375	19592	24786	35687	49058	60696	80213	124033
A Social security contributions	1035	2584	8092	8787	10279	14786	17597	25042	33454	41297	53393	71133
B Direct taxes	541	1146	2711	4107	3295	3905	5814	8678	12669	16433	22776	44087
Income taxes	523	1079	2440	3809	2956	3528	5320	8036	11910	15620	21396	42463
Other	18	67	271	298	339	377	494	642	759	813	1380	1624
C Fees, fines and penalties	58	187	710	668	801	901	1375	1967	2935	2966	4044	8813

Ecuador

3.32 Household and Private Unincorporated Enterprise Income and Outlay Account
(Continued)

Million Ecuadoran sucres

	1970	1975	1980	1981	1982	1983	1984	1985	1986	1987	1988	1989
4 Other current transfers	243	967	1886	2369	3103	4083	5437	9064	13245	19962	30788	43543
A Net casualty insurance premiums	24	104	263	455	588	709	765	1061	1265	2231	4075	6693
B Transfers to private non-profit institutions serving households	...	...	...	...	...	...	...	...	...	...	...	...
C Transfers to the rest of the world	...	-	38	-	-	-	-	-	-	-	-	-
D Other current transfers, except imputed	12	-	21	59	60	160	118	152	239	206	168	193
E Imputed employee pension and welfare contributions	207	863	1564	1855	2455	3214	4554	7851	11741	17525	26545	36657
Net saving c	2390	9238	37453	40169	39688	37998	50564	56769	78581	132361	146328	181566
Total Current Disbursements and Net Saving	31002	86315	232434	278768	330356	444887	620067	842819	1106905	1540063	2489763	4361805

a) Item 'Operating surplus' includes consumption of fixed capital.
b) Item 'Dividends' includes profit-sharing by employees.
c) Item 'Net saving' includes consumption of fixed capital.

3.33 Household and Private Unincorporated Enterprise Capital Accumulation Account

Million Ecuadoran sucres

	1970	1975	1980	1981	1982	1983	1984	1985	1986	1987	1988	1989
Finance of Gross Accumulation												
1 Gross saving	2390	9238	37453	40169	39688	37998	50564	56769	78581	132361	146328	181566
2 Capital transfers	32	103	551	488	1069	267	819	1410	1772	2118	4657	7127
A From resident sectors	32	103	551	488	1069	267	819	1410	1772	2118	4657	7127
B From the rest of the world	...	...	...	...	...	...	...	...	...	...	...	...
Total Finance of Gross Accumulation	2422	9341	38004	40657	40757	38265	51383	58179	80353	134479	150985	188693
Gross Accumulation												
1 Gross Capital Formation	1638	8428	15466	15331	23273	20578	30746	40818	49781	63478	113935	164762
A Increase in stocks	51	566	1192	107	1805	1615	3652	5055	5167	-1760	-1616	-7967
B Gross fixed capital formation	1587	7862	14274	15224	21468	18963	27094	35763	44614	65238	115551	172729
Owner-occupied housing	850	3921	8447	10061	14677	15192	21021	25111	30965	41037	76931	102572
Other gross fixed capital formation	737	3941	5827	5163	6791	3771	6073	10652	13649	24201	38620	70157
2 Purchases of land, net	-133	-207	-1903	-2693	-3769	-3755	-4752	-6209	-9142	-9753	-11350	-13836
3 Purchases of intangibles, net	...	47	...	...	...	...	...	...	...	...	...	...
4 Capital transfers	12	1	129	-	129	1048	243	252	3	284	426	749
A To resident sectors	12	1	129	-	129	1048	243	252	3	284	426	749
B To the rest of the world	...	...	...	...	...	...	...	...	...	...	...	...
Net lending a	905	1072	24312	28019	21124	20394	25146	23318	39711	80470	47974	37018
Total Gross Accumulation	2422	9341	38004	40657	40757	38265	51383	58179	80353	134479	150985	188693

a) Net lending of the capital accumulation account and the capital finance account have not been reconciled and are different due to different statistical sources.

3.34 Household and Private Unincorporated Enterprise Capital Finance Account

Million Ecuadoran sucres

	1970	1975	1980	1981	1982	1983	1984	1985	1986	1987	1988	1989
Acquisition of Financial Assets												
1 Gold	...	-	-	-	-	-	-	-	-	...	...	...
2 Currency and transferable deposits	...	1857	7756	4608	1875	6415	17648	16919	22616	16529	...	...
3 Other deposits	...	1140	5346	3758	11101	12633	27494	72448	50405	107404	...	...
4 Bills and bonds, short term	...	-	-	-	-	-	-	-	...	...	...	...
5 Bonds, long term a	...	490	-2726	-1356	-84	-2396	-6780	-793	1884	3834	...	...
6 Corporate equity securities	...	1519	2221	5225	4526	1529	2798	9980	6275	14296	...	...
7 Short term loans, n.e.c.	...	...	...	...	...	...	...	...	...	...	...	...
8 Long term loans, n.e.c.	...	...	...	...	...	...	...	...	...	...	...	...
9 Trade credit and advances	...	-84	-7222	-18856	-10657	14434	-10251	-	-	-	...	...
10 Net equity of households in life insurance and pension fund reserves	...	1058	3626	4331	5143	6442	9179	10452	13311	18705	...	...
11 Proprietors' net additions to the accumulation of quasi-corporations	...	...	...	...	...	...	...	...	...	...	...	...
12 Other	...	...	...	...	...	...	...	...	...	...	...	...
Total Acquisition of Financial Assets b	...	5980	9001	-2290	11904	39057	40088	109006	94491	160768	...	...

Ecuador

3.34 Household and Private Unincorporated Enterprise Capital Finance Account
(Continued)

Million Ecuadoran sucres

	1970	1975	1980	1981	1982	1983	1984	1985	1986	1987	1988	1989
Incurrence of Liabilities												
1 Short term loans, n.e.c.	...	2205	2440	1511	5420	7853	12483	21135	24636	32933	...	...
2 Long term loans, n.e.c.	...	1962	4704	5703	6383	13428	22340	20453	36415	31519	...	...
3 Trade credit and advances	...	...	...	...	...	...	...	...	...	...	...	...
4 Other accounts payable	...	1420	-9764	-20280	-15169	3291	-18412	42554	-33951	10852	...	...
5 Other liabilities	...	35	...	...	...	...	...	...	...	...	...	...
Total Incurrence of Liabilities	...	5622	-2620	-13066	-3366	24572	16411	84142	27100	75304	...	...
Net Lending c	...	358	11621	10776	15270	14485	23677	24864	67391	85464	...	...
Incurrence of Liabilities and Net Lending b	...	5980	9001	-2290	11904	39057	40088	109006	94491	160768	...	...

a) Item 'Bonds, long-term' includes both short-term and long-term bonds.
b) Data for this table have not been revised, therefore, data for some years are not comparable with those of other tables.
c) Net lending of the capital accumulation account and the capital finance account have not been reconciled and are different due to different statistical sources.

3.51 External Transactions: Current Account: Detail

Million Ecuadoran sucres

	1970	1975	1980	1981	1982	1983	1984	1985	1986	1987	1988	1989
Payments to the Rest of the World												
1 Imports of goods and services	6500	35221	74527	72441	97025	110617	157412	231668	312507	543702	920765	1592461
A Imports of merchandise c.i.f.	5507	32527	63512	59391	80583	85154	127264	177399	242639	448150	723661	1308256
B Other	993	2694	11015	13050	16442	25463	30148	54269	69868	95552	197104	284205
2 Factor income to the rest of the world	694	2898	16932	20242	31899	43696	76962	84409	115517	126115	200609	385681
A Compensation of employees	9	683	783	830	1408	2187	3375	2337	3761	7391	9746	13536
B Property and entrepreneurial income	685	2215	16149	19412	30491	41509	73587	82072	111756	118724	190863	372145
3 Current transfers to the rest of the world	71	313	1011	1497	2031	2026	2497	3366	3833	6368	9843	15500
A Indirect taxes by general government to supranational organizations	...	...	...	...	...	...	...	...	...	...	...	...
B Other current transfers	71	313	1011	1497	2031	2026	2497	3366	3833	6368	9843	15500
By general government	13	72	105	203	356	287	387	604	643	784	1167	2067
By other resident sectors	58	241	906	1294	1675	1739	2110	2762	3190	5274	8525	13433
4 Surplus of the nation on current transactions	-1895	-8939	-14423	-13556	-39088	-17401	-18313	-14378	-107219	-209221	-223471	-432585
Payments to the Rest of the World, and Surplus of the Nation on Current Transfers	5370	29493	78047	80624	91867	138938	218558	305065	324638	466964	907746	1561057
Receipts From The Rest of the World												
1 Exports of goods and services	4909	28242	73797	75906	87563	133061	209858	296922	314740	431538	865318	1482600
A Exports of merchandise f.o.b.	4533	26058	64389	66050	76742	110999	183425	255387	250181	348095	679360	1219947
B Other	376	2184	9408	9856	10821	22062	26433	41535	64559	83443	185958	262653
2 Factor income from the rest of the world	22	430	2395	1935	1014	1904	4391	2654	3868	3821	5648	9873
A Compensation of employees	-	5	45	50	62	157	175	267	480	733	1118	1992
B Property and entrepreneurial income	22	425	2350	1885	952	1747	4216	2387	3388	3088	4530	7881
3 Current transfers from the rest of the world	439	821	1855	2783	3290	3973	4309	5489	6030	31605	36780	68584
A Subsidies to general government from supranational organizations	...	...	...	...	...	...	...	...	...	...	...	...
B Other current transfers	439	821	1855	2783	3290	3973	4309	5489	6030	31605	36780	68584
To general government	213	372	931	1541	1736	2273	2292	2853	2963	3271	3222	4177
To other resident sectors	226	449	924	1242	1554	1700	2017	2636	3067	28334	33558	64407
Receipts from the Rest of the World on Current Transfers	5370	29493	78047	80624	91867	138938	218558	305065	324638	466964	907746	1561057

Ecuador

3.52 External Transactions: Capital Accumulation Account

Million Ecuadoran sucres

	1970	1975	1980	1981	1982	1983	1984	1985	1986	1987	1988	1989
Finance of Gross Accumulation												
1 Surplus of the nation on current transactions	-1895	-8939	-14423	-13556	-39088	-17401	-18313	-14378	-107219	-209221	-223471	-432585
2 Capital transfers from the rest of the world	...	...	7	49	13	7	-	-	-	-	-	-
A By general government	...	...	...	...	...	...	...	...	...	...	...	...
B By other resident sectors	...	...	7	49	13	7	-	-	-	-	-	-
Total Finance of Gross Accumulation	-1895	-8939	-14416	-13507	-39075	-17394	-18313	-14378	-107219	-209221	-223471	-432585
Gross Accumulation												
1 Capital transfers to the rest of the world	...	...	...	...	...	...	...	...	...	...	...	...
2 Purchases of intangible assets, n.e.c., net, from the rest of the world	17	8	79	156	179	735	948	1124	1388	2321	5457	7150
Net lending to the rest of the world [a]	-1912	-8947	-14495	-13663	-39254	-18129	-19261	-15502	-108607	-211542	-228928	-439735
Total Gross Accumulation	-1895	-8939	-14416	-13507	-39075	-17394	-18313	-14378	-107219	-209221	-223471	-432585

a) Net lending of the capital accumulation account and the capital finance account have not been reconciled and are different due to different statistical sources.

3.53 External Transactions: Capital Finance Account

Million Ecuadoran sucres

	1970	1975	1980	1981	1982	1983	1984	1985	1986	1987	1988	1989
Acquisitions of Foreign Financial Assets												
1 Gold and SDR's	...	-118	-158	-173	1929	7949	3202	5239	5484	-262	-17801	-23169
2 Currency and transferable deposits	...	-64	23	149	112	149	126	218	779	106	612	1615
3 Other deposits	...	109	2285	3308	-4196	-644	5564	-386	9913	-7124	33445	54188
4 Bills and bonds, short term	...	-	-	-	-	-	-	-	-	-	-	-
5 Bonds, long term [a]	...	-7	-350	-350	-448	-489	-779	-117	-7	-	-	-
6 Corporate equity securities	...	202	1750	1500	1212	2210	3115	4224	8362	13969	23634	40873
7 Short-term loans, n.e.c.	...	263	9707	589	22225	-31672	-4763	-2022	-19981	1562	16724	-54302
8 Long-term loans	...	4619	15958	29834	3187	60539	17080	14860	58509	113361	49196	136028
9 Prporietors' net additions to accumulation of quasi-corporate, non-resident enterprises	...	...	...	...	...	...	...	...	...	...	...	...
10 Trade credit and advances	...	3879	5711	9134	500	-1250	10498	23540	26446	94743	50057	66119
11 Other [b]	...	111	-529	...	...	...	...	...	...	...	112441	280248
Total Acquisitions of Foreign Financial Assets	...	8994	34397	43991	24521	36792	34043	45556	89505	216355	268308	501600
Incurrence of Foreign Liabilities												
1 Currency and transferable deposits	...	-70	700	1143	-2693	1453	-3230	2194	15274	-10009	9460	-1760
2 Other deposits	...	-1496	6061	-11904	-6822	15154	2331	15641	-32243	20229	45132	107430
3 Bills and bonds, short term	...	-	-	-	-	-	-	-	-	-	-	-
4 Bonds, long term [a]	...	140	-9	396	-1327	-484	898	-831	-95	-475	25	1170
5 Corporate equity securities	...	118	298	334	711	497	627	823	2299	1592	4854	8371
6 Short-term loans, n.e.c.	...	250	122	-171	-73	12	-	-1052	-1197	-6366	-93	140
7 Long-term loans	...	...	...	...	...	...	...	...	...	...	...	...
8 Non-resident proprietors' net additions to accumulation of resident quasi-corporate enterprises	...	...	...	...	...	...	...	...	...	...	...	...
9 Trade credit and advances	...	49	2395	5377	-7775	8225	5579	6459	11108	34225	15488	13723
10 Other [b]	...	...	6007	18652	-2906	-9892	1197	4042	-5436	-18113	-	-
Total Incurrence of Liabilities	...	-1009	15574	13827	-20885	14965	7402	27276	-10290	21083	74866	129074
Net Lending [c]	...	10003	18823	30164	45406	21827	26641	18280	99795	195272	193442	372526
Total Incurrence of Liabilities and Net Lending	...	8994	34397	43991	24521	36792	34043	45556	89505	216355	268308	501600

a) Item 'Bonds, long-term' includes both short-term and long-term bonds.
b) Item 'Other' refers to other receivables/payables and accounting discrepancies.
c) Net lending of the capital accumulation account and the capital finance account have not been reconciled and are different due to different statistical sources.

Ecuador

4.1 Derivation of Value Added by Kind of Activity, in Current Prices

Million Ecuadoran sucres

		1980 Gross Output	1980 Intermediate Consumption	1980 Value Added	1981 Gross Output	1981 Intermediate Consumption	1981 Value Added	1982 Gross Output	1982 Intermediate Consumption	1982 Value Added	1983 Gross Output	1983 Intermediate Consumption	1983 Value Added
							All Producers						
1	Agriculture, hunting, forestry and fishing	42146	6576	35570	49675	8044	41631	60216	9860	50356	86459	13454	73005
	A Agriculture and hunting	36036	5821	30215	42452	6942	35510	50544	8260	42284	72020	11195	60825
	B Forestry and logging	3003	359	2644	3412	491	2921	4565	680	3885	5931	968	4963
	C Fishing	3107	396	2711	3811	611	3200	5107	920	4187	8508	1291	7217
2	Mining and quarrying	76371	40685	35686	83710	39695	44015	102221	49809	52412	142321	56206	86115
	A Coal mining [a]	...	...	...	...	...	...	...	...	...	...	...	...
	B Crude petroleum and natural gas production [b]	75210	40422	34788	82295	39362	42933	100565	49392	51173	138062	54821	83241
	C Metal ore mining [a]	...	...	...	...	...	...	...	...	...	...	...	...
	D Other mining [a]	1161	263	898	1415	333	1082	1656	417	1239	4259	1385	2874
3	Manufacturing	130232	78433	51799	149365	89414	59951	184236	110362	73874	265408	161766	103642
	A Manufacture of food, beverages and tobacco	60791	36834	23957	68777	42293	26484	84342	51601	32741	130279	79233	51046
	B Textile, wearing apparel and leather industries	21867	12103	9764	25110	13018	12092	30779	15510	15269	39551	20076	19475
	C Manufacture of wood and wood products, including furniture	8190	5603	2587	9288	6401	2887	12459	8724	3735	17027	12436	4591
	D Manufacture of paper and paper products, printing and publishing	7677	4377	3300	8836	4871	3965	10957	6424	4533	14610	7944	6666
	E Manufacture of chemicals and chemical petroleum, coal, rubber and plastic products	10332	6730	3602	12035	7996	4039	14453	9655	4798	20468	14210	6258
	F Manufacture of non-metallic mineral products, except products of petroleum and coal	12860	6988	5872	14949	7994	6955	18609	10068	8541	26322	15605	10717
	G Basic metal industries												
	H Manufacture of fabricated metal products, machinery and equipment	6365	4986	1379	7445	5755	1690	8999	7096	1903	12505	9660	2845
	I Other manufacturing industries	2150	812	1338	2925	1086	1839	3638	1284	2354	4646	2602	2044
4	Electricity, gas and water	5302	2868	2434	7062	4516	2546	9675	5982	3693	10794	7509	3285
5	Construction	41864	20115	21749	52666	22144	30522	64639	27063	37576	69583	35160	34423
6	Wholesale and retail trade, restaurants and hotels	69205	26454	42751	78132	31793	46339	96933	39381	57552	129408	53061	76347
	A Wholesale and retail trade	58182	21429	36753	65315	25528	39787	81270	31757	49513	108049	41406	66643
	B Restaurants and hotels	11023	5025	5998	12817	6265	6552	15663	7624	8039	21359	11655	9704
7	Transport, storage and communication	34515	11370	23145	45213	15352	29861	55111	19086	36025	80521	26220	54301
	A Transport and storage	32274	10891	21383	42820	14799	28021	52260	18408	33852	77199	25133	52066
	B Communication	2241	479	1762	2393	553	1840	2851	678	2173	3322	1087	2235
8	Finance, insurance, real estate and business services	40851	6611	34240	48332	8487	39845	56749	10493	46256	74428	15790	58638
	A Financial institutions	13670	2639	11031	15605	3469	12136	18954	4586	14368	25666	7912	17754
	B Insurance												
	C Real estate and business services	27181	3972	23209	32727	5018	27709	37795	5907	31888	48762	7878	40884
9	Community, social and personal services	18161	3627	14534	22917	4145	18772	27463	5445	22018	38021	8229	29792
	A Sanitary and similar services												
	B Social and related community services	...	...	...	...	...	...	...	...	...	...	...	...
	C Recreational and cultural services												
	D Personal and household services	18161	3627	14534	22917	4145	18772	27463	5445	22018	38021	8229	29792
Total, Industries		458647	196739	261908	537072	223590	313482	657243	277481	379762	896943	377395	519548
Producers of Government Services		44977	18387	26590	52590	21605	30985	61802	26947	34855	74243	32371	41872
Other Producers		1724	...	1724	1757	...	1757	1929	...	1929	2335	...	2335
Total		505348	215126	290222	591419	245195	346224	720974	304428	416546	973521	409766	563755
Less: Imputed bank service charge		...	-8909	8909	...	-9945	9945	...	-12961	12961	...	-19200	19200
Import duties		12024	...	12024	12383	...	12383	12130	...	12130	15716	...	15716
Value added tax		...	...	...	...	...	...	...	...	...	...	...	...
Total		517372	224035	293337	603802	255140	348662	733104	317389	415715	989237	428966	560271

Ecuador

4.1 Derivation of Value Added by Kind of Activity, in Current Prices
(Continued)

Million Ecuadoran sucres

		1980 Gross Output	1980 Intermediate Consumption	1980 Value Added	1981 Gross Output	1981 Intermediate Consumption	1981 Value Added	1982 Gross Output	1982 Intermediate Consumption	1982 Value Added	1983 Gross Output	1983 Intermediate Consumption	1983 Value Added
					of which General Government:								
1	Agriculture, hunting, forestry and fishing	...	...	...	...	...	...	...	...	...	...	...	...
2	Mining and quarrying	...	...	...	...	...	...	...	...	...	...	...	...
3	Manufacturing	...	...	...	...	...	...	...	...	...	...	...	...
4	Electricity, gas and water	665	206	459	1058	851	207	1550	642	908	1807	881	926
5	Construction	3035	1912	1123	3414	2176	1238	4088	2505	1583	4419	2643	1776
6	Wholesale and retail trade, restaurants and hotels	...	...	...	...	...	...	...	...	...	...	...	...
7	Transport and communication	...	...	...	...	...	...	...	...	...	...	...	...
8	Finance, insurance, real estate and business services	...	...	...	...	...	...	...	...	...	...	...	...
9	Community, social and personal services	1912	648	1264	2461	722	1739	3089	876	2213	3444	969	2475
	Total, Industries of General Government	5612	2766	2846	6933	3749	3184	8727	4023	4704	9670	4493	5177
	Producers of Government Services	44977	18387	26590	52590	21605	30985	61802	26947	34855	74243	32371	41872
	Total, General Government	50589	21153	29436	59523	25354	34169	70529	30970	39559	83913	36864	47049

		1984 Gross Output	1984 Intermediate Consumption	1984 Value Added	1985 Gross Output	1985 Intermediate Consumption	1985 Value Added	1986 Gross Output	1986 Intermediate Consumption	1986 Value Added	1987 Gross Output	1987 Intermediate Consumption	1987 Value Added
					All Producers								
1	Agriculture, hunting, forestry and fishing	133285	23282	110003	182315	34336	147979	254690	45947	208743	338321	63738	274583
	A Agriculture and hunting	112124	19721	92403	153618	28465	125153	208692	37489	171203	254401	49109	205292
	B Forestry and logging	8043	1394	6649	10308	1997	8311	14700	2718	11982	25681	3987	21694
	C Fishing	13118	2167	10951	18389	3874	14515	31298	5740	25558	58239	10642	47597
2	Mining and quarrying	208630	81797	126833	298926	109410	189516	243868	105899	137969	292850	170283	122567
	A Coal mining [a]	...	...	...	...	...	...	...	...	...	...	...	...
	B Crude petroleum and natural gas production [b]	201813	79111	122702	289644	105736	183908	228394	100608	127786	270245	162348	107897
	C Metal ore mining [a]	...	...	...	...	...	...	...	...	...	...	...	...
	D Other mining [a]	6817	2686	4131	9282	3674	5608	15474	5291	10183	22605	7935	14670
3	Manufacturing	420801	252785	168016	561617	351358	210259	765242	491065	274177	1035072	684815	350257
	A Manufacture of food, beverages and tobacco	212556	124524	88032	282097	170674	111423	375678	232336	143342	496786	308441	188345
	B Textile, wearing apparel and leather industries	62690	32055	30635	84628	46228	38400	110753	64083	46670	146529	86818	59711
	C Manufacture of wood and wood products, including furniture	24796	17929	6867	31084	23542	7542	45860	34468	11392	71444	56936	14508
	D Manufacture of paper and paper products, printing and publishing	20708	12169	8539	28733	18012	10721	42291	25699	16592	63139	37092	26047
	E Manufacture of chemicals and chemical petroleum, coal, rubber and plastic products	28925	22253	6672	39782	32112	7670	55347	44395	10952	73759	62594	11165
	F Manufacture of non-metallic mineral products, except products of petroleum and coal	43844	24923	18921	57764	34513	23251	80682	50200	30482	103761	72474	31287
	G Basic metal industries												
	H Manufacture of fabricated metal products, machinery and equipment	20223	15402	4821	28315	21533	6782	40403	32185	8218	59948	50914	9034
	I Other manufacturing industries	7059	3530	3529	9214	4744	4470	14228	7699	6529	19706	9546	10160
4	Electricity, gas and water	13797	9795	4002	17571	14170	3401	24386	17899	6487	36738	29325	7413
5	Construction	91781	55038	36743	121438	72845	48593	162867	95600	67267	239033	140052	98981
6	Wholesale and retail trade, restaurants and hotels	203654	73490	130164	281664	108326	173338	392353	145520	246833	563763	200619	363144
	A Wholesale and retail trade	174866	54847	120019	245261	83304	161957	345574	111540	234034	501920	156335	345585
	B Restaurants and hotels	28788	18643	10145	36403	25022	11381	46779	33980	12799	61843	44284	17559
7	Transport, storage and communication	95963	38019	57944	151901	56970	94931	199623	74058	125565	279205	109492	169713
	A Transport and storage	90836	36294	54542	144562	54032	90530	187462	68484	118978	264962	101013	163949

Ecuador

4.1 Derivation of Value Added by Kind of Activity, in Current Prices
(Continued)

Million Ecuadoran sucres

	1984 Gross Output	1984 Intermediate Consumption	1984 Value Added	1985 Gross Output	1985 Intermediate Consumption	1985 Value Added	1986 Gross Output	1986 Intermediate Consumption	1986 Value Added	1987 Gross Output	1987 Intermediate Consumption	1987 Value Added
B Communication	5127	1725	3402	7339	2938	4401	12161	5574	6587	14243	8479	5764
8 Finance, insurance, real estate and business services	90452	22648	67804	113950	30066	83884	145283	40326	104957	205391	53972	151419
A Financial institutions	27556	11444	16112	34832	14977	19855	46112	20240	25872	77844	25402	52442
B Insurance												
C Real estate and business services	62896	11204	51692	79118	15089	64029	99171	20086	79085	127547	28570	98977
9 Community, social and personal services	47937	12953	34984	65117	18291	46826	81920	24952	56968	116481	39213	77268
A Sanitary and similar services	...	...	...	...	...	...	...	...	...	...	...	...
B Social and related community services	...	...	...	...	...	...	...	...	...	...	...	...
C Recreational and cultural services	...	...	...	...	...	...	...	...	...	...	...	...
D Personal and household services	47937	12953	34984	65117	18291	46826	81920	24952	56968	116481	39213	77268
Total, Industries	1306300	569807	736493	1794499	795772	998727	2270232	1041266	1228966	3106854	1491509	1615345
Producers of Government Services	105308	42139	63169	134379	47909	86470	175560	62591	112969	241910	94020	147890
Other Producers	2902	...	2902	4305	...	4305	5526	...	5526	7560	...	7560
Total	1414510	611946	802564	1933183	843681	1089502	2451318	1103857	1347461	3356324	1585529	1770795
Less: Imputed bank service charge	...	-16711	16711	...	-21596	21596	...	-28573	28573	...	-53713	53713
Import duties	26776	...	26776	42034	...	42034	64344	...	64344	77419	...	77419
Value added tax	...	...	...	...	...	...	...	...	...	...	...	...
Total	1441286	628657	812629	1975217	865277	1109940	2515662	1132430	1383232	3433743	1639242	1794501

of which General Government:

	1984 Gross Output	1984 Intermediate Consumption	1984 Value Added	1985 Gross Output	1985 Intermediate Consumption	1985 Value Added	1986 Gross Output	1986 Intermediate Consumption	1986 Value Added	1987 Gross Output	1987 Intermediate Consumption	1987 Value Added
1 Agriculture, hunting, forestry and fishing	...	...	...	...	...	...	...	...	...	...	...	...
2 Mining and quarrying	...	...	...	...	...	...	...	...	...	...	...	...
3 Manufacturing	...	...	...	...	...	...	...	...	...	...	...	...
4 Electricity, gas and water	2899	576	2323	4337	1754	2583	5082	1573	3509	7286	1915	5371
5 Construction	6661	3940	2721	9189	5416	3773	15154	8838	6316	22174	12942	9232
6 Wholesale and retail trade, restaurants and hotels	...	...	...	...	...	...	...	...	...	...	...	...
7 Transport and communication	...	...	...	...	...	...	...	...	...	...	...	...
8 Finance, insurance, real estate and business services	...	...	...	...	...	...	...	...	...	...	...	...
9 Community, social and personal services	4962	1930	3032	6585	2500	4085	8402	3365	5037	11040	4455	6585
Total, Industries of General Government	14522	6446	8076	20111	9670	10441	28638	13776	14862	40500	19312	21188
Producers of Government Services	105308	42139	63169	134379	47909	86470	175560	62591	112969	241910	94020	147890
Total, General Government	119830	48585	71245	154490	57579	96911	204198	76367	127831	282410	113332	169078

	1988 Gross Output	1988 Intermediate Consumption	1988 Value Added	1989 Gross Output	1989 Intermediate Consumption	1989 Value Added

All Producers

	1988 Gross Output	1988 Intermediate Consumption	1988 Value Added	1989 Gross Output	1989 Intermediate Consumption	1989 Value Added
1 Agriculture, hunting, forestry and fishing	584307	116227	468080	1007241	204194	803047
A Agriculture and hunting	432266	91059	341207	756825	161590	595235
B Forestry and logging	42843	6481	36362	76224	11190	65034
C Fishing	109198	18687	90511	174192	31414	142778
2 Mining and quarrying	612634	265539	347095	1220546	506386	714160
A Coal mining [a]	...	...	...	...	...	...
B Crude petroleum and natural gas production [b]	558070	248379	309691	1143448	475456	667992
C Metal ore mining [a]	...	...	...	...	...	...
D Other mining [a]	54564	17160	37404	77098	30930	46168

Ecuador

4.1 Derivation of Value Added by Kind of Activity, in Current Prices
(Continued)

Million Ecuadoran sucres

		1988 Gross Output	1988 Intermediate Consumption	1988 Value Added	1989 Gross Output	1989 Intermediate Consumption	1989 Value Added
3	Manufacturing	1881860	1231498	650362	3359575	2156076	1203499
	A Manufacture of food, beverages and tobacco	843717	511892	331825	1516196	897579	618617
	B Textile, wearing apparel and leather industries	259043	158581	100462	495090	288919	206171
	C Manufacture of wood and wood products, including furniture	126807	101008	25799	228044	182885	45159
	D Manufacture of paper and paper products, printing and publishing	113844	66966	46878	200314	117762	82552
	E Manufacture of chemicals and chemical petroleum, coal, rubber and plastic products	145553	117670	27883	245623	202239	43384
	F Manufacture of non-metallic mineral products, except products of petroleum and coal	237739	158054	79685	380944	258144	122800
	G Basic metal industries						
	H Manufacture of fabricated metal products, machinery and equipment	114182	95359	18823	216808	166444	50364
	I Other manufacturing industries	40975	21968	19007	76556	42104	34452
4	Electricity, gas and water	52029	50390	1639	94381	92444	1937
5	Construction	344070	231439	112631	593491	399349	194142
6	Wholesale and retail trade, restaurants and hotels	983271	352055	631216	1753701	603807	1149894
	A Wholesale and retail trade	890338	279351	610987	1573578	471822	1101756
	B Restaurants and hotels	92933	72704	20229	180123	131985	48138
7	Transport, storage and communication	484121	186786	297335	790121	338806	451315
	A Transport and storage	459072	169769	289303	729798	303511	426287
	B Communication	25049	17017	8032	60323	35295	25028
8	Finance, insurance, real estate and business services	342055	97211	244844	498248	165975	332273
	A Financial institutions	146759	46921	99838	157980	76027	81953
	B Insurance						
	C Real estate and business services	195296	50290	145006	340268	89948	250320
9	Community, social and personal services	183421	68553	114868	339052	126035	213017
	A Sanitary and similar services	...	...	...	...	...	...
	B Social and related community services	...	...	...	...	...	...
	C Recreational and cultural services	...	...	...	...	...	...
	D Personal and household services	183421	68553	114868	339052	126035	213017
	Total, Industries	5467768	2599698	2868070	9656356	4593072	5063284
	Producers of Government Services	355600	150733	204867	531580	248096	283484
	Other Producers	9522	...	9522	14474	...	14474
	Total	5832890	2750431	3082459	202410	4841168	5361242
	Less: Imputed bank service charge	...	-98997	98997	...	-92829	92829
	Import duties	120877	...	120877	196200	...	196200
	Value added tax	...	...	...	...	...	...
	Total	5953767	2849428	3104339	398610	4933997	5464613

of which General Government:

		1988 Gross Output	1988 Intermediate Consumption	1988 Value Added	1989 Gross Output	1989 Intermediate Consumption	1989 Value Added
1	Agriculture, hunting, forestry and fishing	...	...	...	...	...	...
2	Mining and quarrying	...	...	...	...	...	...
3	Manufacturing	...	...	...	...	...	...
4	Electricity, gas and water	8861	2324	6537	10673	2754	7919

Ecuador

4.1 Derivation of Value Added by Kind of Activity, in Current Prices
(Continued)

Million Ecuadoran sucres

		1988 Gross Output	1988 Intermediate Consumption	1988 Value Added	1989 Gross Output	1989 Intermediate Consumption	1989 Value Added
5	Construction	30543	17517	13026	52886	30202	22684
6	Wholesale and retail trade, restaurants and hotels	...	...	...	...	...	...
7	Transport and communication	...	...	...	...	...	...
8	Finance, insurance, real estate and business services	...	...	...	...	...	...
9	Community, social and personal services	15108	5002	10106	26759	10438	16321
	Total, Industries of General Government	54512	24843	29669	90318	43394	46924
	Producers of Government Services	355600	150733	204867	531580	248096	283484
	Total, General Government	410112	175576	234536	621898	291490	330408

a) Items 'Coal mining' and 'Metal ore mining' are included in item 'Other mining'.
b) Petroleum refining is included in item 'Crude petroleum and natural gas production'.

4.2 Derivation of Value Added by Kind of Activity, in Constant Prices

Million Ecuadoran sucres

At constant prices of: 1975 — All Producers

		1980 GO	1980 IC	1980 VA	1981 GO	1981 IC	1981 VA	1982 GO	1982 IC	1982 VA	1983 GO	1983 IC	1983 VA
1	Agriculture, hunting, forestry and fishing	25678	4480	21198	27189	4542	22647	27910	4809	23101	24327	4436	19891
	A Agriculture and hunting	21995	3948	18047	23260	3979	19281	23542	4179	19363	20036	3818	16218
	B Forestry and logging	1782	242	1540	1840	247	1593	2008	269	1739	1990	266	1724
	C Fishing	1901	290	1611	2089	316	1773	2360	361	1999	2301	352	1949
2	Mining and quarrying	30114	15044	15070	30634	14642	15992	30835	15308	15527	33274	13381	19893
	A Coal mining a	...	...	...	...	...	...	...	...	...	...	...	...
	B Crude petroleum and natural gas production b	29493	14876	14617	29965	14472	15493	30156	15137	15019	32218	13113	19105
	C Metal ore mining a	...	...	...	...	...	...	...	...	...	...	...	...
	D Other mining a	621	168	453	669	170	499	679	171	508	1056	268	788
3	Manufacturing	76120	49313	26807	79696	50537	29159	81163	51579	29584	79386	50203	29183
	A Manufacture of food, beverages and tobacco	35477	23885	11592	36955	24778	12177	37528	25213	12315	35207	23689	11518
	B Textile, wearing apparel and leather industries	13608	7927	5681	13964	7569	6395	13963	7427	6536	13757	7005	6752
	C Manufacture of wood and wood products, including furniture	4876	3398	1478	5056	3567	1489	5522	3942	1580	5743	4129	1614
	D Manufacture of paper and paper products, printing and publishing	4306	2649	1657	4601	2831	1770	4805	2928	1877	4651	2848	1803
	E Manufacture of chemicals and chemical petroleum, coal, rubber and plastic products	6131	4392	1739	6483	4582	1901	6437	4623	1814	6877	4907	1970
	F Manufacture of non-metallic mineral products, except products of petroleum and coal	6685	3712	2973	7206	3649	3557	7543	3872	3671	7625	4062	3563
	G Basic metal industries												
	H Manufacture of fabricated metal products, machinery and equipment	3878	2919	959	4040	3052	988	4005	3079	926	3848	2916	932
	I Other manufacturing industries	1159	431	728	1391	509	882	1360	495	865	1678	647	1031
4	Electricity, gas and water	3163	2048	1115	3420	2303	1117	3756	2515	1241	3921	2495	1426
5	Construction	18325	11419	6906	18280	11041	7239	18282	10997	7285	16734	10006	6728
6	Wholesale and retail trade, restaurants and hotels	39439	14650	24789	39703	14671	25032	40592	15030	25562	36026	13489	22537
	A Wholesale and retail trade	33169	11521	21648	33238	11326	21912	34024	11598	22426	29396	10193	19203
	B Restaurants and hotels	6270	3129	3141	6465	3345	3120	6568	3432	3136	6630	3296	3334
7	Transport, storage and communication	17223	7185	10038	18013	7496	10517	18238	7551	10687	18007	7496	10511
	A Transport and storage	15888	6871	9017	16615	7169	9446	16659	7182	9477	16328	7102	9226

Ecuador

4.2 Derivation of Value Added by Kind of Activity, in Constant Prices
(Continued)

Million Ecuadoran sucres

	1980 Gross Output	1980 Intermediate Consumption	1980 Value Added	1981 Gross Output	1981 Intermediate Consumption	1981 Value Added	1982 Gross Output	1982 Intermediate Consumption	1982 Value Added	1983 Gross Output	1983 Intermediate Consumption	1983 Value Added
				At constant prices of:1975								
B Communication	1335	314	1021	1398	327	1071	1579	369	1210	1679	394	1285
8 Finance, insurance, real estate and business services	21412	3718	17694	22306	4032	18274	22804	4214	18590	23547	4575	18972
A Financial institutions	7280	1555	5725	7449	1738	5711	7775	1920	5855	8377	2311	6066
B Insurance												
C Real estate and business services	14132	2163	11969	14857	2294	12563	15029	2294	12735	15170	2264	12906
9 Community, social and personal services	9819	2207	7612	10619	2379	8240	11226	2516	8710	11717	2619	9098
A Sanitary and similar services	...	...	...	...	...	...	...	...	...	...	...	...
B Social and related community services	...	...	...	...	...	...	...	...	...	...	...	...
C Recreational and cultural services	...	...	...	...	...	...	...	...	...	...	...	...
D Personal and household services	9819	2207	7612	10619	2379	8240	11226	2516	8710	11717	2619	9098
Total, Industries	241293	110064	131229	249860	111643	138217	254806	114519	140287	246939	108700	138239
Producers of Government Services	24882	11173	13709	25502	11502	14000	25771	11547	14224	23707	9214	14493
Other Producers	675	...	675	688	...	688	696	...	696	705	...	705
Total	266850	121237	145613	276050	123145	152905	281273	126066	155207	271351	117914	153437
Less: Imputed bank service charge	...	-5006	5006	...	-5059	5059	...	-5315	5315	...	-6158	6158
Import duties	7015	...	7015	5597	...	5597	5373	...	5373	3606	...	3606
Value added tax	...	...	...	...	...	...	...	...	...	...	...	...
Total	273865	126243	147622	281647	128204	153443	286646	131381	155265	274957	124072	150885

	1984 Gross Output	1984 Intermediate Consumption	1984 Value Added	1985 Gross Output	1985 Intermediate Consumption	1985 Value Added	1986 Gross Output	1986 Intermediate Consumption	1986 Value Added	1987 Gross Output	1987 Intermediate Consumption	1987 Value Added
				At constant prices of:1975								
				All Producers								
1 Agriculture, hunting, forestry and fishing	26978	4971	22007	29578	5400	24178	32462	5806	26656	33453	6130	27323
A Agriculture and hunting	22439	4308	18131	24333	4630	19703	26379	4794	21585	26033	5003	21030
B Forestry and logging	1923	261	1662	1980	268	1712	2172	293	1879	2235	300	1935
C Fishing	2616	402	2214	3265	502	2763	3911	719	3192	5185	827	4358
2 Mining and quarrying	36252	14373	21879	38378	14503	23875	40556	16043	24513	26737	15630	11107
A Coal mining [a]	...	...	...	...	...	...	...	...	...	...	...	...
B Crude petroleum and natural gas production [b]	34887	14023	20864	37011	14150	22861	38981	15633	23348	25130	15205	9925
C Metal ore mining [a]	...	...	...	...	...	...	...	...	...	...	...	...
D Other mining [a]	1365	350	1015	1367	353	1014	1575	410	1165	1607	425	1182
3 Manufacturing	82068	53425	28643	85216	56506	28710	88460	60219	28241	90609	61880	28729
A Manufacture of food, beverages and tobacco	37094	25759	11335	37991	27143	10848	39794	29024	10770	41582	30507	11075
B Textile, wearing apparel and leather industries	13810	7151	6659	14113	7533	6580	14031	8095	5936	14013	8069	5944
C Manufacture of wood and wood products, including furniture	5681	4106	1575	5829	4255	1574	6331	4653	1678	6348	4667	1681
D Manufacture of paper and paper products, printing and publishing	4653	2886	1767	5004	3122	1882	5037	3045	1992	5203	3121	2082
E Manufacture of chemicals and chemical petroleum, coal, rubber and plastic products	6744	5018	1726	7184	5365	1819	7451	5595	1856	7309	5519	1790
F Manufacture of non-metallic mineral products, except products of petroleum and coal	8197	4724	3473	8849	5076	3773	9130	5515	3615	8855	5521	3334
G Basic metal industries												
H Manufacture of fabricated metal products, machinery and equipment	3865	2979	886	4154	3183	971	4499	3397	1102	4914	3663	1251
I Other manufacturing industries	2024	802	1222	2092	829	1263	2187	895	1292	2385	813	1572
4 Electricity, gas and water	4163	2327	1836	4463	2630	1833	4843	2611	2232	5378	2762	2616

Ecuador

4.2 Derivation of Value Added by Kind of Activity, in Constant Prices
(Continued)

Million Ecuadoran sucres

	1984 Gross Output	1984 Intermediate Consumption	1984 Value Added	1985 Gross Output	1985 Intermediate Consumption	1985 Value Added	1986 Gross Output	1986 Intermediate Consumption	1986 Value Added	1987 Gross Output	1987 Intermediate Consumption	1987 Value Added
					At constant prices of:1975							
5 Construction	16793	10210	6583	17223	10481	6742	17142	10301	6841	17448	10437	7011
6 Wholesale and retail trade, restaurants and hotels	37911	14444	23467	40141	15873	24268	41450	16657	24793	42349	16952	25397
A Wholesale and retail trade	31107	10816	20291	33237	11964	21273	34360	12481	21879	35058	12794	22264
B Restaurants and hotels	6804	3628	3176	6904	3909	2995	7090	4176	2914	7291	4158	3133
7 Transport, storage and communication	18827	7913	10914	19856	8350	11506	21537	8966	12571	21966	9137	12829
A Transport and storage	16953	7463	9490	17542	7784	9758	18206	8127	10079	18488	8253	10235
B Communication	1874	450	1424	2314	566	1748	3331	839	2492	3478	884	2594
8 Finance, insurance, real estate and business services	22422	4743	17679	23039	4877	18162	23568	4989	18579	26252	5157	21095
A Financial institutions	6957	2400	4557	6886	2432	4454	7098	2479	4619	9284	2568	6716
B Insurance												
C Real estate and business services	15465	2343	13122	16153	2445	13708	16470	2510	13960	16968	2589	14379
9 Community, social and personal services	12085	2719	9366	12318	2789	9529	12648	2875	9773	13049	2982	10067
A Sanitary and similar services	...	...	...	...	...	...	...	...	...	...	...	...
B Social and related community services												
C Recreational and cultural services	...	...	...	...	...	...	...	...	...	...	...	...
D Personal and household services	12085	2719	9366	12318	2789	9529	12648	2875	9773	13049	2982	10067
Total, Industries	257499	115125	142374	270212	121409	148803	282666	128467	154199	277241	131067	146174
Producers of Government Services	22919	8144	14775	21946	7104	14842	21757	6859	14898	22015	7013	15002
Other Producers	714	...	714	723	...	723	735	...	735	756	...	756
Total	281132	123269	157863	292881	128513	164368	305158	135326	169832	300012	138080	161932
Less: Imputed bank service charge	...	-4485	4485	...	-4519	4519	...	-4934	4934	...	-7122	7122
Import duties	3848	...	3848	4205		4205	4238	...	4238	4206	...	4206
Value added tax	...	...	...	...	...	...						
Total	284980	127754	157226	297086	133032	164054	309396	140260	169136	304218	145202	159016

	1988 Gross Output	1988 Intermediate Consumption	1988 Value Added	1989 Gross Output	1989 Intermediate Consumption	1989 Value Added
		At constant prices of:1975				
		All Producers				
1 Agriculture, hunting, forestry and fishing	36212	6534	29678	37224	6643	30581
A Agriculture and hunting	28441	5341	23100	29897	5518	24379
B Forestry and logging	2111	284	1827	2094	281	1813
C Fishing	5660	909	4751	5233	844	4389
2 Mining and quarrying	42819	17500	25319	39739	16238	23501
A Coal mining [a]	...	...	...	...	...	...
B Crude petroleum and natural gas production [b]	40768	16957	23811	37679	15692	21987
C Metal ore mining [a]	...	...	...	...	...	...
D Other mining [a]	2051	543	1508	2060	546	1514

Ecuador

4.2 Derivation of Value Added by Kind of Activity, in Constant Prices
(Continued)

Million Ecuadoran sucres

		1988			1989	
	Gross Output	Intermediate Consumption	Value Added	Gross Output	Intermediate Consumption	Value Added
			At constant prices of:1975			
3 Manufacturing	94785	65404	29381	95145	66873	28272
A Manufacture of food, beverages and tobacco	43301	32276	11025	43044	33144	9900
B Textile, wearing apparel and leather industries	14161	8343	5818	14525	8604	5921
C Manufacture of wood and wood products, including furniture	6281	4617	1664	6208	4549	1659
D Manufacture of paper and paper products, printing and publishing	5387	3240	2147	5517	3321	2196
E Manufacture of chemicals and chemical petroleum, coal, rubber and plastic products	7662	5763	1899	7593	5784	1809
F Manufacture of non-metallic mineral products, except products of petroleum and coal	10074	6334	3740	10025	6441	3584
G Basic metal industries						
H Manufacture of fabricated metal products, machinery and equipment	5246	3863	1383	5560	3992	1568
I Other manufacturing industries	2673	968	1705	2673	1038	1635
4 Electricity, gas and water	5696	2907	2789	5879	3008	2871
5 Construction	15685	9326	6359	15879	9597	6282
6 Wholesale and retail trade, restaurants and hotels	43844	17588	26256	44479	18087	26392
A Wholesale and retail trade	36344	13227	23117	36755	13438	23317
B Restaurants and hotels	7500	4361	3139	7724	4649	3075
7 Transport, storage and communication	22933	9447	13486	23962	9787	14175
A Transport and storage	18826	8402	10424	19124	8552	10572
B Communication	4107	1045	3062	4838	1235	3603
8 Finance, insurance, real estate and business services	28490	5512	22978	25491	5862	19629
A Financial institutions	11135	2876	8259	7543	3104	4439
B Insurance						
C Real estate and business services	17355	2636	14719	17948	2758	15190
9 Community, social and personal services	13213	3023	10190	13594	3116	10478
A Sanitary and similar services	...	...	...	...	...	...
B Social and related community services	...	...	...	...	...	...
C Recreational and cultural services	...	...	...	...	...	...
D Personal and household services	13213	3023	10190	13594	3116	10478
Total, Industries	303677	137241	166436	301392	139211	162181
Producers of Government Services	20853	6622	14231	21081	6580	14501
Other Producers	778	...	778	800	...	800
Total	325308	143863	181445	323273	145791	177482
Less: Imputed bank service charge	...	-8683	8683	...	-5114	5114
Import duties	4104	...	4104	4776	...	4776
Value added tax	...	...	...	...	...	...
Total	329412	152546	176866	328049	150905	177144

a) Items 'Coal mining' and 'Metal ore mining' are included in item 'Other mining'.
b) Petroleum refining is included in item 'Crude petroleum and natural gas production'.

4.3 Cost Components of Value Added

Million Ecuadoran sucres

	1980						1981					
	Compensation of Employees	Capital Consumption	Net Operating Surplus	Indirect Taxes	Less: Subsidies Received	Value Added	Compensation of Employees	Capital Consumption	Net Operating Surplus	Indirect Taxes	Less: Subsidies Received	Value Added
					All Producers							
1 Agriculture, hunting, forestry and fishing	6855	...	28273	442	...	35570	7150	...	33994	487	...	41631
A Agriculture and hunting	6565	...	23228	422	...	30215	6848	...	28203	459	...	35510
B Forestry and logging	57	...	2573	14	...	2644	59	...	2842	20	...	2921
C Fishing	233	...	2472	6	...	2711	243	...	2949	8	...	3200

Ecuador

4.3 Cost Components of Value Added
(Continued)

Million Ecuadoran sucres

	1980						1981					
	Compensation of Employees	Capital Consumption	Net Operating Surplus	Indirect Taxes	Less: Subsidies Received	Value Added	Compensation of Employees	Capital Consumption	Net Operating Surplus	Indirect Taxes	Less: Subsidies Received	Value Added
2 Mining and quarrying	1633	...	29372	4681	...	35686	1952	...	29516	12547	...	44015
A Coal mining [a]	...	...	...	...	...	...	...	...	...	...	...	...
B Crude petroleum and natural gas production [b]	1364	...	28750	4674	...	34788	1628	...	28762	12543	...	42933
C Metal ore mining [a]	...	...	...	...	...	...	...	...	...	...	...	...
D Other mining [a]	269	...	622	7	...	898	324	...	754	4	...	1082
3 Manufacturing	14628	...	32455	4716	...	51799	16289	...	39552	4110	...	59951
A Manufacture of food, beverages and tobacco	4080	...	17139	2738	...	23957	4691	...	19620	2173	...	26484
B Textile, wearing apparel and leather industries	3131	...	6156	477	...	9764	3338	...	8236	518	...	12092
C Manufacture of wood and wood products, including furniture	1595	...	976	16	...	2587	1683	...	1198	6	...	2887
D Manufacture of paper and paper products, printing and publishing	1218	...	1975	107	...	3300	1364	...	2488	113	...	3965
E Manufacture of chemicals and chemical petroleum, coal, rubber and plastic products	1597	...	1496	509	...	3602	1853	...	1707	479	...	4039
F Manufacture of non-metallic mineral products, except products of petroleum and coal	1873	...	3523	476	...	5872	2027	...	4465	463	...	6955
G Basic metal industries		...			...			...			...	
H Manufacture of fabricated metal products, machinery and equipment	914	...	127	338	...	1379	1096	...	288	306	...	1690
I Other manufacturing industries	220	...	1063	55	...	1338	237	...	1550	52	...	1839
4 Electricity, gas and water	1611	...	637	186	...	2434	2172	...	74	300	...	2546
5 Construction	12279	...	9322	148	...	21749	12639	...	17600	283	...	30522
6 Wholesale and retail trade, restaurants and hotels	11699	...	30647	405	...	42751	13159	...	32849	331	...	46339
A Wholesale and retail trade	10507	...	26004	242	...	36753	11790	...	27826	171	...	39787
B Restaurants and hotels	1192	...	4643	163	...	5998	1369	...	5023	160	...	6552
7 Transport, storage and communication	5678	...	16956	511	...	23145	6106	...	23046	709	...	29861
A Transport and storage	4682	...	16347	354	...	21383	5037	...	22474	510	...	28021
B Communication	996	...	609	157	...	1762	1069	...	572	199	...	1840
8 Finance, insurance, real estate and business services	6618	...	26469	1153	...	34240	8277	...	30175	1393	...	39845
A Financial institutions	4811	...	5825	395	...	11031	6259	...	5475	402	...	12136
B Insurance		...			...			...			...	
C Real estate and business services	1807	...	20644	758	...	23209	2018	...	24700	991	...	27709
9 Community, social and personal services	4347	...	10065	122	...	14534	4789	...	13894	89	...	18772
A Sanitary and similar services	...	...	...	...	...	...	...	...	...	...	...	...
B Social and related community services	...	...	...	...	...	...	...	...	...	...	...	...
C Recreational and cultural services	...	...	...	...	...	...	...	...	...	...	...	...
D Personal and household services	4347	...	10065	122	...	14534	4789	...	13894	89	...	18772
Total, Industries [cd]	65348	...	184196	12364	...	261908	72533	...	220700	20249	...	313482
Producers of Government Services	26590	...	...	...	...	26590	30985	...	...	...	...	30985
Other Producers	1724	...	...	...	...	1724	1757	...	...	...	...	1757
Total [cd]	93662	...	184196	12364	...	290222	105275	...	220700	20249	...	346224
Less: Imputed bank service charge	...	...	8909	...	...	8909	...	...	9945	...	...	9945
Import duties	...	...	...	12024	...	12024	...	...	...	12383	...	12383
Value added tax	...	...	...	...	...	...	...	...	...	...	...	...
Total [cd]	93662	...	175287	24388	...	293337	105275	...	210755	32632	...	348662

of which General Government:

1 Agriculture, hunting, forestry and fishing	...	...	...	...	...	...	...	...	...	...	...	...
2 Mining and quarrying	...	...	...	...	...	...	...	...	...	...	...	...
3 Manufacturing	...	...	...	...	...	...	...	...	...	...	...	...
4 Electricity, gas and water	159	...	300	...	...	459	288	...	-81	...	...	207

Ecuador

4.3 Cost Components of Value Added
(Continued)

Million Ecuadoran sucres

	1980 Compensation of Employees	Capital Consumption	Net Operating Surplus	Indirect Taxes	Less: Subsidies Received	Value Added	1981 Compensation of Employees	Capital Consumption	Net Operating Surplus	Indirect Taxes	Less: Subsidies Received	Value Added
5 Construction	1123	...	...	...	...	1123	1238	...	...	...	...	1238
6 Wholesale and retail trade, restaurants and hotels	...	...	...	...	...	...	...	...	...	...	...	...
7 Transport and communication	...	...	...	...	...	...	...	...	...	...	...	...
8 Finance, insurance, real estate & business services	...	...	...	...	...	...	...	...	...	...	...	...
9 Community, social and personal services	1264	...	...	...	...	1264	1739	...	...	...	...	1739
Total, Industries of General Government	2546	...	300	...	...	2846	3265	...	-81	...	...	3184
Producers of Government Services	26590	...	...	...	...	26590	30985	...	...	...	...	30985
Total, General Government	29136	...	300	...	...	29436	34250	...	-81	...	...	34169

	1982 Compensation of Employees	Capital Consumption	Net Operating Surplus	Indirect Taxes	Less: Subsidies Received	Value Added	1983 Compensation of Employees	Capital Consumption	Net Operating Surplus	Indirect Taxes	Less: Subsidies Received	Value Added
					All Producers							
1 Agriculture, hunting, forestry and fishing	7354	...	42703	299	...	50356	7792	...	64852	361	...	73005
A Agriculture and hunting	7043	...	34971	270	...	42284	7444	...	53051	330	...	60825
B Forestry and logging	61	...	3803	21	...	3885	68	...	4873	22	...	4963
C Fishing	250	...	3929	8	...	4187	280	...	6928	9	...	7217
2 Mining and quarrying	2218	...	35603	14591	...	52412	4206	...	66528	15381	...	86115
A Coal mining [a]	...	...	...	...	...	...	...	...	...	...	...	...
B Crude petroleum and natural gas production [b]	1829	...	34756	14588	...	51173	2445	...	65418	15378	...	83241
C Metal ore mining [a]	...	...	...	...	...	...	...	...	...	...	...	...
D Other mining [a]	389	...	847	3	...	1239	1761	...	1110	3	...	2874
3 Manufacturing	18374	...	51062	4438	...	73874	19845	...	75184	8613	...	103642
A Manufacture of food, beverages and tobacco	5242	...	25529	1970	...	32741	5701	...	40139	5206	...	51046
B Textile, wearing apparel and leather industries	3698	...	10943	628	...	15269	3889	...	14768	818	...	19475
C Manufacture of wood and wood products, including furniture	1920	...	1844	-29	...	3735	2080	...	2440	71	...	4591
D Manufacture of paper and paper products, printing and publishing	1532	...	2865	136	...	4533	1617	...	4885	164	...	6666
E Manufacture of chemicals and chemical petroleum, coal, rubber and plastic products	2003	...	2189	606	...	4798	2102	...	3313	843	...	6258
F Manufacture of non-metallic mineral products, except products of petroleum and coal	[2413	...	[5445	683]	...	[8541	2817	...	[7065	835]	...	[10717
G Basic metal industries	]	...	]	]	...	]	]	...	]	]	...	]
H Manufacture of fabricated metal products, machinery and equipment	1298	...	222	383	...	1903	1353	...	922	570	...	2845
I Other manufacturing industries	268	...	2025	61	...	2354	286	...	1652	106	...	2044
4 Electricity, gas and water	2616	...	652	425	...	3693	3310	...	-497	472	...	3285
5 Construction	15206	...	22091	279	...	37576	15449	...	18607	367	...	34423
6 Wholesale and retail trade, restaurants and hotels	14810	...	42212	530	...	57552	15413	...	60380	554	...	76347
A Wholesale and retail trade	13195	...	35981	337	...	49513	13679	...	52638	326	...	66643
B Restaurants and hotels	1615	...	6231	193	...	8039	1734	...	7742	228	...	9704
7 Transport, storage and communication	7020	...	28156	849	...	36025	7603	...	45662	1036	...	54301
A Transport and storage	5810	...	27444	598	...	33852	6047	...	45289	730	...	52066

Ecuador

4.3 Cost Components of Value Added
(Continued)

Million Ecuadoran sucres

	1982						1983					
	Compensation of Employees	Capital Consumption	Net Operating Surplus	Indirect Taxes	Less: Subsidies Received	Value Added	Compensation of Employees	Capital Consumption	Net Operating Surplus	Indirect Taxes	Less: Subsidies Received	Value Added
B Communication	1210	...	712	251	...	2173	1556	...	373	306	...	2235
8 Finance, insurance, real estate and business services	10214	...	33963	2079	...	46256	12188	...	42451	3999	...	58638
A Financial institutions	[7882	...	[5588	898]	...	14368	9663	...	[5397	2694]	...	17754
B Insurance	]	...	]		...			...			...	
C Real estate and business services	2332	...	28375	1181	...	31888	2525	...	37054	1305	...	40884
9 Community, social and personal services	5421	...	16486	111	...	22018	5748	...	23880	164	...	29792
A Sanitary and similar services	...	...	...	...	...	...	...	...	...	...	...	...
B Social and related community services	...	...	...	...	...	...	...	...	...	...	...	...
C Recreational and cultural services	...	...	...	...	...	...	...	...	...	...	...	...
D Personal and household services	5421	...	16486	111	...	22018	5748	...	23880	164	...	29792
Total, Industries [cd]	83233	...	272928	23601	...	379762	91554	...	397047	30947	...	519548
Producers of Government Services	34855	...	...	...	...	34855	41872	...	...	...	...	41872
Other Producers	1929	...	...	...	...	1929	2335	...	...	...	...	2335
Total [cd]	120017	...	272928	23601	...	416546	135761	...	397047	30947	...	563755
Less: Imputed bank service charge	...	...	12961	...	...	12961	...	...	19200	...	...	19200
Import duties	...	...	...	12130	...	12130	...	...	...	15716	...	15716
Value added tax	...	...	...	...	...	...	...	...	...	...	...	...
Total [cd]	120017	...	259967	35731	...	415715	135761	...	377847	46663	...	560271

of which General Government:

	1982						1983					
1 Agriculture, hunting, forestry and fishing	...	...	...	...	...	...	...	...	...	...	...	...
2 Mining and quarrying	...	...	...	...	...	...	...	...	...	...	...	...
3 Manufacturing	...	...	...	...	...	...	...	...	...	...	...	...
4 Electricity, gas and water	333	...	575	...	...	908	453	...	473	...	...	926
5 Construction	1583	...	...	...	...	1583	1776	...	...	...	...	1776
6 Wholesale and retail trade, restaurants and hotels	...	...	...	...	...	...	...	...	...	...	...	...
7 Transport and communication	...	...	...	...	...	...	...	...	...	...	...	...
8 Finance, insurance, real estate & business services	...	...	...	...	...	...	...	...	...	...	...	...
9 Community, social and personal services	2213	...	...	...	...	2213	2475	...	...	...	...	2475
Total, Industries of General Government	4129	...	575	...	...	4704	4704	...	473	...	...	5177
Producers of Government Services	34855	...	...	...	...	34855	41872	...	...	...	...	41872
Total, General Government	38984	...	575	...	...	39559	46576	...	473	...	...	47049

	1984						1985					
	Compensation of Employees	Capital Consumption	Net Operating Surplus	Indirect Taxes	Less: Subsidies Received	Value Added	Compensation of Employees	Capital Consumption	Net Operating Surplus	Indirect Taxes	Less: Subsidies Received	Value Added

All Producers

1 Agriculture, hunting, forestry and fishing	10114	...	99343	546	...	110003	12637	...	134646	696	...	147979
A Agriculture and hunting	9660	...	82244	499	...	92403	12030	...	112491	632	...	125153
B Forestry and logging	87	...	6530	32	...	6649	107	...	8163	41	...	8311
C Fishing	367	...	10569	15	...	10951	500	...	13992	23	...	14515
2 Mining and quarrying	5533	...	107427	13873	...	126833	6620	...	131698	51198	...	189516
A Coal mining [a]	...	...	...	...	...	...	...	...	...	...	...	...
B Crude petroleum and natural gas production [b]	3588	...	105246	13868	...	122702	4033	...	128684	51191	...	183908
C Metal ore mining [a]	...	...	...	...	...	...	...	...	...	...	...	...
D Other mining [a]	1945	...	2181	5	...	4131	2587	...	3014	7	...	5608

Ecuador

4.3 Cost Components of Value Added
(Continued)

Million Ecuadoran sucres

		1984					1985					
	Compensation of Employees	Capital Consumption	Net Operating Surplus	Indirect Taxes	Less: Subsidies Received	Value Added	Compensation of Employees	Capital Consumption	Net Operating Surplus	Indirect Taxes	Less: Subsidies Received	Value Added
3 Manufacturing	23586	...	130028	14402	...	168016	28165	...	163416	18678	...	210259
A Manufacture of food, beverages and tobacco	6258	...	72320	9454	...	88032	7024	...	93648	10751	...	111423
B Textile, wearing apparel and leather industries	5103	...	24293	1239	...	30635	7061	...	29482	1857	...	38400
C Manufacture of wood and wood products, including furniture	2315	...	4382	170	...	6867	2479	...	4845	218	...	7542
D Manufacture of paper and paper products, printing and publishing	1700	...	6575	264	...	8539	1725	...	8620	376	...	10721
E Manufacture of chemicals and chemical petroleum, coal, rubber and plastic products	2525	...	2964	1183	...	6672	2894	...	2801	1975	...	7670
F Manufacture of non-metallic mineral products, except products of petroleum and coal	3431	...	14324	1166	...	18921	4072	...	17537	1642	...	23251
G Basic metal industries		...			...			...			...	
H Manufacture of fabricated metal products, machinery and equipment	1894	...	2122	805	...	4821	2475	...	2731	1576	...	6782
I Other manufacturing industries	360	...	3048	121	...	3529	435	...	3752	283	...	4470
4 Electricity, gas and water	4378	...	-845	469	...	4002	5602	...	-2833	632	...	3401
5 Construction	18421	...	17639	683	...	36743	22429	...	25223	941	...	48593
6 Wholesale and retail trade, restaurants and hotels	17691	...	110418	2055	...	130164	21036	...	146973	5329	...	173338
A Wholesale and retail trade	15488	...	102827	1704	...	120019	18156	...	139014	4787	...	161957
B Restaurants and hotels	2203	...	7591	351	...	10145	2880	...	7959	542	...	11381
7 Transport, storage and communication	10629	...	45313	2002	...	57944	13818	...	78635	2478	...	94931
A Transport and storage	8401	...	44586	1555	...	54542	11251	...	77427	1852	...	90530
B Communication	2228	...	727	447	...	3402	2567	...	1208	626	...	4401
8 Finance, insurance, real estate and business services	15869	...	45259	6676	...	67804	21901	...	55943	6040	...	83884
A Financial institutions	12603	...	-1119	4628	...	16112	17560	...	-676	2971	...	19855
B Insurance		...			...			...			...	
C Real estate and business services	3266	...	46378	2048	...	51692	4341	...	56619	3069	...	64029
9 Community, social and personal services	7232	...	27544	208	...	34984	9092	...	37381	353	...	46826
A Sanitary and similar services	...	...	...	...	...	...	...	...	...	...	...	...
B Social and related community services	...	...	...	...	...	...	...	...	...	...	...	...
C Recreational and cultural services	...	...	...	...	...	...	...	...	...	...	...	...
D Personal and household services	7232	...	27544	208	...	34984	9092	...	37381	353	...	46826
Total, Industries cd	113453	...	582126	40914	...	736493	141300	...	771082	86345	...	998727
Producers of Government Services	63169	...	...	...	...	63169	86470	...	...	...	...	86470
Other Producers	2902	...	...	...	...	2902	4305	...	...	...	...	4305
Total	179524	...	582126	40914	...	802564	232075	...	771082	86345	...	1089502
Less: Imputed bank service charge	...	...	16711	...	...	16711	...	...	21596	...	...	21596
Import duties	...	...	...	26776	...	26776	...	...	...	42034	...	42034
Value added tax	...	...	...	...	...	...	...	...	...	...	...	...
Total cd	179524	...	565415	67690	...	812629	232075	...	749486	128379	...	1109940

of which General Government:

1 Agriculture, hunting, forestry and fishing	...	...	...	...	...	...	...	...	...	...	...	...
2 Mining and quarrying	...	...	...	...	...	...	...	...	...	...	...	...
3 Manufacturing	...	...	...	...	...	...	...	...	...	...	...	...
4 Electricity, gas and water	646	...	1677	...	...	2323	867	...	1716	...	...	2583

Ecuador

4.3 Cost Components of Value Added
(Continued)

Million Ecuadoran sucres

	1984						1985					
	Compensation of Employees	Capital Consumption	Net Operating Surplus	Indirect Taxes	Less: Subsidies Received	Value Added	Compensation of Employees	Capital Consumption	Net Operating Surplus	Indirect Taxes	Less: Subsidies Received	Value Added
5 Construction	2721	...	...	...	...	2721	3773	...	...	...	...	3773
6 Wholesale and retail trade, restaurants and hotels	...	...	...	...	...	...	...	...	...	...	...	...
7 Transport and communication	...	...	...	...	...	...	...	...	...	...	...	...
8 Finance, insurance, real estate & business services	...	...	...	...	...	...	...	...	...	...	...	...
9 Community, social and personal services	3032	...	...	...	...	3032	4085	...	...	...	...	4085
Total, Industries of General Government	6399	...	1677	...	...	8076	8725	...	1716	...	...	10441
Producers of Government Services	63169	...	...	...	...	63169	86470	...	...	...	...	86470
Total, General Government	69568	...	1677	...	...	71245	95195	...	1716	...	...	96911

	1986						1987					
	Compensation of Employees	Capital Consumption	Net Operating Surplus	Indirect Taxes	Less: Subsidies Received	Value Added	Compensation of Employees	Capital Consumption	Net Operating Surplus	Indirect Taxes	Less: Subsidies Received	Value Added

All Producers

1 Agriculture, hunting, forestry and fishing	16715	...	191172	856	...	208743	24960	...	248463	1160	...	274583
A Agriculture and hunting	15912	...	154516	775	...	171203	23798	...	180450	1044	...	205292
B Forestry and logging	140	...	11789	53	...	11982	213	...	21410	71	...	21694
C Fishing	663	...	24867	28	...	25558	949	...	46603	45	...	47597
2 Mining and quarrying	11508	...	83152	43309	...	137969	14796	...	41915	65856	...	122567
A Coal mining [a]	...	...	...	...	...	...	...	...	...	...	...	...
B Crude petroleum and natural gas production [b]	8130	...	76356	43300	...	127786	9586	...	32469	65842	...	107897
C Metal ore mining [a]	...	...	...	...	...	...	...	...	...	...	...	...
D Other mining [a]	3378	...	6796	9	...	10183	5210	...	9446	14	...	14670
3 Manufacturing	37496	...	207756	28925	...	274177	48410	...	262252	39595	...	350257
A Manufacture of food, beverages and tobacco	9333	...	119727	14282	...	143342	12125	...	155045	21175	...	188345
B Textile, wearing apparel and leather industries	9188	...	34010	3472	...	46670	12589	...	42668	4454	...	59711
C Manufacture of wood and wood products, including furniture	3166	...	7972	254	...	11392	3915	...	10202	391	...	14508
D Manufacture of paper and paper products, printing and publishing	2300	...	13649	643	...	16592	2971	...	22252	824	...	26047
E Manufacture of chemicals and chemical petroleum, coal, rubber and plastic products	3875	...	3310	3767	...	10952	4983	...	1491	4691	...	11165
F Manufacture of non-metallic mineral products, except products of petroleum and coal	5713	...	21692	3077	...	30482	6886	...	20487	3914	...	31287
G Basic metal industries												
H Manufacture of fabricated metal products, machinery and equipment	3351	...	1884	2983	...	8218	4246	...	1143	3645	...	9034
I Other manufacturing industries	570	...	5512	447	...	6529	695	...	8964	501	...	10160
4 Electricity, gas and water	7469	...	-2155	1173	...	6487	9389	...	-3620	1644	...	7413
5 Construction	24865	...	41308	1094	...	67267	31538	...	66177	1266	...	98981
6 Wholesale and retail trade, restaurants and hotels	25986	...	214855	5992	...	246833	33516	...	324362	5266	...	363144
A Wholesale and retail trade	22211	...	206860	4963	...	234034	28932	...	312769	3884	...	345585
B Restaurants and hotels	3775	...	7995	1029	...	12799	4584	...	11593	1382	...	17559
7 Transport, storage and communication	17079	...	105126	3360	...	125565	23206	...	141791	4716	...	169713
A Transport and storage	13368	...	103538	2072	...	118978	17680	...	142671	3598	...	163949

484

Ecuador

4.3 Cost Components of Value Added
(Continued)

Million Ecuadoran sucres

	1986						1987					
	Compensation of Employees	Capital Consumption	Net Operating Surplus	Indirect Taxes	Less: Subsidies Received	Value Added	Compensation of Employees	Capital Consumption	Net Operating Surplus	Indirect Taxes	Less: Subsidies Received	Value Added
B Communication	3711	...	1588	1288	...	6587	5526	...	-880	1118	...	5764
8 Finance, insurance, real estate and business services	29731	...	68321	6905	...	104957	43335	...	101361	6723	...	151419
A Financial institutions	24520	...	-508	1860	...	25872	36551	...	14010	1881	...	52442
B Insurance		...			...			...			...	
C Real estate and business services	5211	...	68829	5045	...	79085	6784	...	87351	4842	...	98977
9 Community, social and personal services	12180	...	44293	495	...	56968	16481	...	59897	890	...	77268
A Sanitary and similar services	...	...	...	...	...	...	...	...	...	...	...	...
B Social and related community services	...	...	...	...	...	...	...	...	...	...	...	...
C Recreational and cultural services	...	...	...	...	...	...	...	...	...	...	...	...
D Personal and household services	12180	...	44293	495	...	56968	16481	...	59897	890	...	77268
Total, Industries [cd]	183029	...	953828	92109	...	1228966	245631	...	1242598	127116	...	1615345
Producers of Government Services	112969	...	...	...	...	112969	147890	...	...	...	...	147890
Other Producers	5526	...	...	...	...	5526	7560	...	...	...	...	7560
Total [cd]	301524	...	953828	92109	...	1347461	401081	...	1242598	127116	...	1770795
Less: Imputed bank service charge	...	...	28573	...	...	28573	...	...	53713	...	...	53713
Import duties	...	...	...	64344	...	64344	...	...	...	77419	...	77419
Value added tax	...	...	...	...	...	...	...	...	...	...	...	...
Total [cd]	301524	...	925255	156453	...	1383232	401081	...	1188885	204535	...	1794501

of which General Government:

	Compensation of Employees	Capital Consumption	Net Operating Surplus	Indirect Taxes	Less: Subsidies Received	Value Added	Compensation of Employees	Capital Consumption	Net Operating Surplus	Indirect Taxes	Less: Subsidies Received	Value Added
1 Agriculture, hunting, forestry and fishing	...	...	...	...	...	...	...	...	...	...	...	...
2 Mining and quarrying	...	...	...	...	...	...	...	...	...	...	...	...
3 Manufacturing	...	...	...	...	...	...	...	...	...	...	...	...
4 Electricity, gas and water	1128	...	2381	...	...	3509	1527	...	3844	...	...	5371
5 Construction	6316	...	...	...	...	6316	9232	...	...	...	...	9232
6 Wholesale and retail trade, restaurants and hotels	...	...	...	...	...	...	...	...	...	...	...	...
7 Transport and communication	...	...	...	...	...	...	...	...	...	...	...	...
8 Finance, insurance, real estate & business services	...	...	...	...	...	...	...	...	...	...	...	...
9 Community, social and personal services	5037	...	...	...	...	5037	6585	...	...	...	...	6585
Total, Industries of General Government	12481	...	2381	...	...	14862	17344	...	3844	...	...	21188
Producers of Government Services	112969	...	...	...	...	112969	147890	...	...	...	...	147890
Total, General Government	125450	...	2381	...	...	127831	165234	...	3844	...	...	169078

	1988						1989					
	Compensation of Employees	Capital Consumption	Net Operating Surplus	Indirect Taxes	Less: Subsidies Received	Value Added	Compensation of Employees	Capital Consumption	Net Operating Surplus	Indirect Taxes	Less: Subsidies Received	Value Added

All Producers

	Compensation of Employees	Capital Consumption	Net Operating Surplus	Indirect Taxes	Less: Subsidies Received	Value Added	Compensation of Employees	Capital Consumption	Net Operating Surplus	Indirect Taxes	Less: Subsidies Received	Value Added
1 Agriculture, hunting, forestry and fishing	35422	...	430152	2506	...	468080	50168	...	749245	3634	...	803047
A Agriculture and hunting	33738	...	305185	2284	...	341207	47798	...	544130	3307	...	595235
B Forestry and logging	301	...	35912	149	...	36362	427	...	64391	216	...	65034
C Fishing	1383	...	89055	73	...	90511	1943	...	140724	111	...	142778
2 Mining and quarrying	21692	...	201111	124292	...	347095	30412	...	400680	283068	...	714160
A Coal mining [a]	...	...	...	...	...	...	...	...	...	...	...	...
B Crude petroleum and natural gas production [b]	15071	...	170351	124269	...	309691	20577	...	364382	283033	...	667992
C Metal ore mining [a]	...	...	...	...	...	...	...	...	...	...	...	...
D Other mining [a]	6621	...	30760	23	...	37404	9835	...	36298	35	...	46168

Ecuador

4.3 Cost Components of Value Added
(Continued)

Million Ecuadoran sucres

		1988					1989					
	Compensation of Employees	Capital Consumption	Net Operating Surplus	Indirect Taxes	Less: Subsidies Received	Value Added	Compensation of Employees	Capital Consumption	Net Operating Surplus	Indirect Taxes	Less: Subsidies Received	Value Added
3 Manufacturing	63314	...	520263	66785	...	650362	89363	...	1005227	108909	...	1203499
A Manufacture of food, beverages and tobacco	15750	...	280919	35156	...	331825	22307	...	538655	57655	...	618617
B Textile, wearing apparel and leather industries	17038	...	75798	7626	...	100462	24160	...	169652	12359	...	206171
C Manufacture of wood and wood products, including furniture	5045	...	19915	839	...	25799	7137	...	36767	1255	...	45159
D Manufacture of paper and paper products, printing and publishing	3824	...	41640	1414	...	46878	5390	...	74950	2212	...	82552
E Manufacture of chemicals and chemical petroleum, coal, rubber and plastic products	6463	...	13341	8079	...	27883	9185	...	21037	13162	...	43384
F Manufacture of non-metallic mineral products, except products of petroleum and coal	8848	...	64330	6507	...	79685	12344	...	99690	10766	...	122800
G Basic metal industries												
H Manufacture of fabricated metal products, machinery and equipment	5431	...	7103	6289	...	18823	7595	...	32570	10199	...	50364
I Other manufacturing industries	915	...	17217	875	...	19007	1245	...	31906	1301	...	34452
4 Electricity, gas and water	11902	...	-12885	2622	...	1639	17054	...	-19575	4458	...	1937
5 Construction	39319	...	70426	2886	...	112631	56007	...	133750	4385	...	194142
6 Wholesale and retail trade, restaurants and hotels	42916	...	579806	8494	...	631216	59707	...	1070960	19227	...	1149894
A Wholesale and retail trade	36752	...	568052	6183	...	610987	50981	...	1035353	15422	...	1101756
B Restaurants and hotels	6164	...	11754	2311	...	20229	8726	...	35607	3805	...	48138
7 Transport, storage and communication	30538	...	257128	9669	...	297335	47325	...	387614	16376	...	451315
A Transport and storage	22340	...	259431	7582	...	289303	31457	...	381745	13085	...	426287
B Communication	8198	...	-2303	2137	...	8032	15868	...	5869	3291	...	25028
8 Finance, insurance, real estate and business services	64658	...	169019	11167	...	244844	91324	...	226628	14321	...	332273
A Financial institutions	55782	...	41635	2421	...	99838	78965	...	-824	3812	...	81953
B Insurance												
C Real estate and business services	8876	...	127384	8746	...	145006	12359	...	227452	10509	...	250320
9 Community, social and personal services	22190	...	91350	1328	...	114868	31681	...	179356	1980	...	213017
A Sanitary and similar services	...	...	...	...	...	...	...	...	...	...	...	...
B Social and related community services												
C Recreational and cultural services												
D Personal and household services	22190	...	91350	1328	...	114868	31681	...	179356	1980	...	213017
Total, Industries [cd]	331951	...	2306370	229749	...	2868070	473041	...	4133885	456358	...	5063284
Producers of Government Services	204867	...	...	...	...	204867	283484	...	...	...	...	283484
Other Producers	9522	...	...	...	...	9522	14474	...	...	...	...	14474
Total [cd]	546340	...	2306370	229749	...	3082459	770999	...	4133885	456358	...	5361242
Less: Imputed bank service charge	...	...	98997	...	...	98997	...	...	92829	...	...	92829
Import duties	...	...	...	120877	...	120877	...	...	...	196200	...	196200
Value added tax	...	...	...	...	...	...	...	...	...	...	...	...
Total [cd]	546340	...	2207373	350626	...	3104339	770999	...	4041056	652558	...	5464613

of which General Government:

1 Agriculture, hunting, forestry and fishing	...	...	...	...	...	...	...	...	...	...	...	...
2 Mining and quarrying	...	...	...	...	...	...	...	...	...	...	...	...
3 Manufacturing	...	...	...	...	...	...	...	...	...	...	...	...
4 Electricity, gas and water	1994	...	4543	...	...	6537	2442	...	5477	...	...	7919

Ecuador

4.3 Cost Components of Value Added
(Continued)

Million Ecuadoran sucres

	1988						1989					
	Compensation of Employees	Capital Consumption	Net Operating Surplus	Indirect Taxes	Less: Subsidies Received	Value Added	Compensation of Employees	Capital Consumption	Net Operating Surplus	Indirect Taxes	Less: Subsidies Received	Value Added
5 Construction	13026	...	...	...	...	13026	22684	...	...	...	...	22684
6 Wholesale and retail trade, restaurants and hotels	...	...	...	...	...	...	...	...	...	...	...	...
7 Transport and communication	...	...	...	...	...	...	...	...	...	...	...	...
8 Finance, insurance, real estate & business services	...	...	...	...	...	...	...	...	...	...	...	...
9 Community, social and personal services	10106	...	...	...	...	10106	16321	...	...	...	...	16321
Total, Industries of General Government	25126	...	4543	...	...	29669	41447	...	5477	...	...	46924
Producers of Government Services	204867	...	...	...	...	204867	283484	...	...	...	...	283484
Total, General Government	229993	...	4543	...	...	234536	324931	...	5477	...	...	330408

a) Items 'Coal mining' and 'Metal ore mining' are included in item 'Other mining'.
b) Petroleum refining is included in item 'Crude petroleum and natural gas production'.
c) Column 'Consumption of fixed capital' is included in column 'Net operating surplus'.
d) Column 4 refers to indirect taxes less subsidies received.

Egypt

General note. The preparation of national accounts statistics in Egypt is undertaken by the Ministry of Planning, Cairo. Official estimates are published in the annual 'Statistical Yearbook' published by the same agency. The estimates are generally in accordance with the classifications and definitions recommended in the United Nations System of National Accounts (SNA). An input-output table for the year 1966-67 has been completed by CAPMAS. The following tables have been prepared from successive replies to the United Nations national accounts questionnaire. When the scope and coverage of the estimates differ for conceptual or statistical reasons from the definitions and classifications recommended in SNA, a footnote is indicated to the relevant tables.

Sources and methods:

(a) Gross domestic product. Gross domestic product is estimated mainly through the production approach.

(b) Expenditure on the gross domestic product. All components of GDP by expenditure type are estimated through the expenditure approach. The estimates of government final consumption expenditure are based on government budgets and accounts. For private consumption expenditures, the estimates are based on family budgets and household expenditure surveys. The Department of Statistics prepares data on inventories of cotton, covering both commercial stocks and stocks of spinning industry. Other sources of information for changes in stocks include data collected regularly by the Ministry of Supply. For gross fixed capital formation, the government sector is estimated directly together with government consumption expenditure. The private sector estimate is obtained by deducting the government estimate from total capital formation. Capital formation in machinery and equipment is estimated through the commodity-flow approach using information on domestic production, imports and exports of capital goods. The estimates of exports and imports of merchandise are generally based on foreign trade statistics. The estimates of GDP by expenditure type in constant prices are prepared by the CAPMAS on the basis of official index numbers of prices and quantities.

(c) Cost-structure of the gross domestic product. The estimates of wages and salaries are based on government accounts and on various sectoral surveys. No specific information is available for operating surplus, which is computed as a gross estimate, i.e., including consumption of fixed capital. Indirect taxes and subsidies are seperately available for all economic units in the compulsory standard accounts for public enterprises and in the economic surveys for the private sector.

(d) Gross domestic product by kind of economic activity. The table of gross domestic product by kind of economic activity is prepared in factor values. The production approach is used to estimate value added of most industries. The income approach is used to estimate value added of community, social and personal services. The Ministry of Agriculture collects, through annual sample surveys, data on crop area, yield and crop-cutting. Livestock data are obtained through special censuses every two years and prices received by farmers are collected annually. The estimated acreage of each of the main crops is multiplied by average productivity of the basic area of measurement. The gross output is evaluated at farm-gate prices and estimates of intermediate consumption are based on data collected from the co-operative societies and from censuses. For the industrial activity sector, annual statistics on industrial production, capital formation, employment, wages and salaries are available for industrial establishments with ten workers or more which form the organized sector of the economy. For the non-organized sector, estimates are made by using data from industrial censuses and by studying the cost-structure of each industry, productivity and degree of mechanization. The output of construction is estimated indirectly from the input side by means of employment data and data on intermediate consumption. The value of gross output and components of value added are obtained by using the relationship between available data on intermediate consumption and primary inputs in organized enterprises and applying this relationship on the estimated intermediate consumption of this industry. For trade, annual basic statistics are available for establishments with five or more workers, while those with less than five workers are covered by sample surveys conducted every three years. Estimates for restaurants are made by using data on establishments, wages and salaries, working hours and data from sample surveys. Estimates for hotels are obtained through annual questionnaires. Data on input, output and other elements of large-scale transport are available through annual accounts. For unorganized transport, estimates are based on information on the number of establishments and workers, on wages and salaries and on other sources. Indicators such as input-ratios are used to estimate value added. Gross output and input of public financial institutions and insurance companies are based on data collected annually. The estimates of real estate, business services, and imputed rents of owner-occupied dwellings are based on family budget surveys. The government accounts provide information to estimate government services. Annual data are available for non-profit institutions serving households. For the service activities of unincorporated enterprises, gross output and inputs are estimated by using available censuses of establishments, wages and salaries statistics. The constant prices of GDP by kind of economic activity are estimated by CAPMAS on the basis of official index numbers of prices and quantities such as wholesale prices, consumer prices and quantities of imported and exported merchandise.

1.1 Expenditure on the Gross Domestic Product, in Current Prices

Million Egyptian pounds — Fiscal year beginning 1 July

	1970	1975	1980	1981	1982	1983	1984	1985	1986	1987	1988	1989
1 Government final consumption expenditure	821.4	1344.1	2840.3	3584.1	...	...	...	...	...	...	...	...
2 Private final consumption expenditure	2275.6	3100.9	11154.8	12932.1	...	...	...	...	...	...	...	...
3 Gross capital formation	415.5	1723.8	5208.0	6250.0	...	...	...	...	...	...	...	...
A Increase in stocks	60.0	458.5	100.0	100.0	...	...	...	...	...	...	...	...
B Gross fixed capital formation	355.5	1265.3	5108.0	6150.0	...	...	...	...	...	...	...	...
Residential buildings												
Non-residential buildings	162.2	539.0										
Other construction and land improvement etc.												
Other	193.3	726.3										
4 Exports of goods and services	447.2	964.1	5306.7	5618.4	...	...	...	...	...	...	...	...
5 Less: Imports of goods and services	600.3	1886.3	7360.8	8163.1	...	...	...	...	...	...	...	...
Equals: Gross Domestic Product [a]	3359.4	5246.6	17149.0	20221.5	25772.5	31246.5	36617.9	40819.7	47743.8	...	...	...

a) For years 1972-1979 estimates relate to calendar year.

Egypt

1.2 Expenditure on the Gross Domestic Product, in Constant Prices

Million Egyptian pounds — Fiscal year beginning 1 July

	1970	1975	1980	1981	1982	1983	1984	1985	1986	1987	1988	1989
	At constant prices of:											
	1969					1975						
1 Government final consumption expenditure	782.3	... 1344.1	...	...	...	...	...	...	...	...	...	...
2 Private final consumption expenditure	1999.4	... 3100.9	...	...	...	...	...	...	...	...	...	...
3 Gross capital formation	428.4	... 1723.8	...	...	...	...	...	...	...	...	...	...
A Increase in stocks	78.5	... 458.5	...	...	...	...	...	...	...	...	...	...
B Gross fixed capital formation	349.9	... 1265.3	...	...	...	...	...	...	...	...	...	...
4 Exports of goods and services	451.5	... 964.1	...	...	...	...	...	...	...	...	...	...
5 Less: Imports of goods and services	555.3	... 1886.3	...	...	...	...	...	...	...	...	...	...
Statistical discrepancy	9.3	... ...	...	...	...	...	...	...	...	...	...	...
Equals: Gross Domestic Product [a]	3115.6	... 5246.6	...	...	...	...	...	...	...	...	...	...

a) For years 1972-1979 estimates relate to calendar year.

1.3 Cost Components of the Gross Domestic Product

Million Egyptian pounds — Fiscal year beginning 1 July

	1970	1975	1980	1981	1982	1983	1984	1985	1986	1987	1988	1989
1 Indirect taxes, net	382.4	... 185.3	431.1	124.5	1404.7	2290.5	2485.8	1760.2	3377.2	...	...	...
A Indirect taxes	424.7	... 807.4	2597.6	...	...	...	...	...	...	...	...	...
B Less: Subsidies	42.3	... 622.1	2166.5	...	...	...	...	...	...	...	...	...
2 Consumption of fixed capital [a]	...	... ...	...	...	...	...	...	...	...	...	...	...
3 Compensation of employees paid by resident producers to:	1337.6	... 2401.2	16717.9	20097.0	24367.8	28956.0	34132.1	39059.5	44366.6	...	...	...
4 Operating surplus [a]	1639.4	... 2660.1								...	...	...
Equals: Gross Domestic Product [b]	3359.4	... 5246.6	17149.0	20221.5	25772.5	31246.5	36617.9	40819.7	47743.8	...	...	...

a) Item 'Operating surplus' includes consumption of fixed capital.
b) For years 1972-1979 estimates relate to calendar year.

1.7 External Transactions on Current Account, Summary

Million Egyptian pounds — Fiscal year beginning 1 July

	1970	1975	1980	1981	1982	1983	1984	1985	1986	1987	1988	1989
	Payments to the Rest of the World											
1 Imports of goods and services	600.3	... 1886.3	7360.8	8163.1	...	...	...	...	...	...	...	...
A Imports of merchandise c.i.f.	600.3	... 1886.3	7360.8	8163.1	...	...	...	...	...	...	...	...
B Other	...	... ...	...	...	...	...	...	...	...	...	...	...
2 Factor income to the rest of the world	69.2	... 161.9	1124.8	...	...	...	...	...	...	...	...	...
A Compensation of employees [a]	...	... ...	...	...	...	...	...	...	...	...	...	...
B Property and entrepreneurial income [a]	69.2	... 161.9	1124.8	...	...	...	...	...	...	...	...	...
3 Current transfers to the rest of the world	0.3	... 22.3	1.4	...	...	...	...	...	...	...	...	...
4 Surplus of the nation on current transactions	-94.1	... -524.4	-1057.5	...	...	...	...	...	...	...	...	...
Payments to the Rest of the World and Surplus of the Nation on Current Transactions [b]	575.7	... 1546.1	7429.5	...	...	...	...	...	...	...	...	...
	Receipts From The Rest of the World											
1 Exports of goods and services	447.2	... 964.1	5306.7	5618.4	...	...	...	...	...	...	...	...

Egypt

1.7 External Transactions on Current Account, Summary
(Continued)

Million Egyptian pounds — Fiscal year beginning 1 July

	1970	1975	1980	1981	1982	1983	1984	1985	1986	1987	1988	1989
A Exports of merchandise f.o.b.	447.2	964.1	5306.7	5618.4	...	...	...	...	...	...	...	...
B Other	...	...	...	...	...	...	...	...	...	...	...	...
2 Factor income from rest of the world	6.6	145.8	1867.1	...	...	...	...	...	...	...	...	...
A Compensation of employees [a]	...	...	...	...	...	...	...	...	...	...	...	...
B Property and entrepreneurial income [a]	6.6	145.8	1867.1	...	...	...	...	...	...	...	...	...
3 Current transfers from rest of the world	121.9	436.2	255.7	...	...	...	...	...	...	...	...	...
Receipts from the Rest of the World on Current Transactions [b]	575.7	1546.1	7429.5	...	...	...	...	...	...	...	...	...

a) Item 'Compensation of employees' is included in item 'Property and entrepreneurial income'.
b) For years 1972-1979 estimates relate to calendar year.

1.10 Gross Domestic Product by Kind of Activity, in Current Prices

Million Egyptian pounds — Fiscal year beginning 1 July

	1970	1975	1980	1981	1982	1983	1984	1985	1986	1987	1988	1989
1 Agriculture, hunting, forestry and fishing	774.1	1468.1	3391.6	3931.8	4954.1	5584.6	6201.0	7416.3	8663.3	...	...	...
2 Mining and quarrying [a]	71.7	149.0	2768.1	2668.0	2771.7	3156.1	3533.9	3063.4	2012.4			
3 Manufacturing	568.4	887.6	2253.8	2670.2	3181.1	3895.9	5128.9	6294.3	7883.6			
4 Electricity, gas and water [b]	40.0	69.2	107.8	127.7	161.0	228.8	315.5	465.1	527.5			
5 Construction	66.7	242.5	740.0	1055.0	1169.0	1334.5	1597.6	1971.0	2204.8			
6 Wholesale and retail trade, restaurants and hotels	374.3	720.1	2255.2	2658.1	3931.5	5140.5	6304.5	7450.0	9011.8			
7 Transport, storage and communication	144.8	258.4	1458.3	1999.3	2363.0	2780.9	3044.2	3441.9	3846.1			
8 Finance, insurance, real estate and business services	246.7	360.0	1284.4	1737.7	2071.1	2332.8	2654.4	3064.8	3523.8			
9 Community, social and personal services [c,b]	204.9	272.4	643.7	859.7	1070.5	1281.6	1530.1	1781.6	2144.4			
Total, Industries	...	...										
Producers of Government Services	485.4	634.0	1815.0	2389.5	2694.8	3220.3	3822.0	4111.1	4548.9			
Other Producers [c]	...	...										
Subtotal [d]	2977.0	5061.3	16717.9	20097.0	24367.8	28956.0	34132.1	39059.5	44366.6			
Less: Imputed bank service charge	...	...	...	...	...	...	...	...	...			
Plus: Import duties	...	...										
Plus: Value added tax	...	...										
Plus: Other adjustments [e]	382.4	185.3	431.1	124.5	1404.7	2290.5	2485.8	1760.2	3377.2			
Equals: Gross Domestic Product [f]	3359.4	5246.6	17149.0	20221.5	25772.5	31246.5	36617.9	40819.7	47743.8	...	...	...

a) Item 'Mining and quarrying' refers to oil and its products.
b) Item 'Electricity, gas and water' refers to electricity only. Gas and water are included in item 'Community, social and personal services'.
c) Item 'Other producers' is included in item 'Community, social and personal services'.
d) Gross domestic product in factor values.
e) Item 'Other adjustments' refers to indirect taxes net of subsidies.
f) For years 1972-1979 estimates relate to calendar year.

# Egypt

1.11 Gross Domestic Product by Kind of Activity, in Constant Prices

Million Egyptian pounds — Fiscal year beginning 1 July

	1970	1975	1980	1981	1982	1983	1984	1985	1986	1987	1988	1989
	1969	1975	1975	\multicolumn{4}{c}{At constant prices of:}	1981				
1 Agriculture, hunting, forestry and fishing	761.5	1468.1	...	3931.8	4090.0	4258.0	4394.0	4540.0	4670.0	...	...	...
2 Mining and quarrying [a]	75.3	149.0	...	2668.0	3091.6	3535.6	3910.6	3949.3	3866.5	...	...	...
3 Manufacturing	559.5	887.6	...	2670.2	2995.4	3260.3	3584.1	3849.1	4128.7	...	...	...
4 Electricity, gas and water [b]	40.0	69.2	...	127.7	141.2	163.0	178.5	219.3	240.8	...	...	...
5 Construction	64.4	242.5	...	1055.0	1108.0	1179.0	1224.0	1272.9	1241.7	...	...	...
6 Wholesale and retail trade, restaurants and hotels	368.8	720.1	...	2658.1	3029.8	3238.6	3477.4	3545.1	3727.9	...	...	...
7 Transport, storage and communication	147.2	258.4	...	1999.3	2257.0	2483.5	2541.3	2704.8	2839.5	...	...	...
8 Finance, insurance, real estate and business services	246.8	360.0	...	1737.7	1920.9	2007.4	2235.9	2347.7	2499.7	...	...	...
9 Community, social and personal services [c,b]	201.6	272.4	...	859.7	921.4	1007.7	1097.3	1201.1	1302.8	...	...	...
Total, Industries		...	...	...								
Producers of Government Services	475.5	634.0	...	2389.5	2535.8	2715.0	2967.1	3199.9	3439.4	...	...	...
Other Producers [c]	...	...	...	...								
Subtotal [d]	2940.6	5061.3	...	20097.0	22091.1	23848.1	25610.2	26829.2	27957.0	...	...	...
Less: Imputed bank service charge	...	...		...								
Plus: Import duties	...	...		...								
Plus: Value added tax	...	...		...								
Plus: Other adjustments	394.3[e]	185.3[e]	...	...								
Equals: Gross Domestic Product [f]	3334.9	5246.6	...	...								

a) Item 'Mining and quarrying' refers to oil and its products.
b) Item 'Electricity, gas and water' refers to electricity only. Gas and water are included in item 'Community, social and personal services'.
c) Item 'Other producers' is included in item 'Community, social and personal services'.
d) Gross domestic product in factor values.
e) Item 'Other adjustments' refers to indirect taxes net of subsidies.
f) For years 1972-1979 estimates relate to calendar year.

1.12 Relations Among National Accounting Aggregates

Million Egyptian pounds — Fiscal year beginning 1 July

	1970	1975	1980	1981	1982	1983	1984	1985	1986	1987	1988	1989
Gross Domestic Product [a]	3359.4	5246.6	17149.0	20221.5	25772.5	31246.5	36617.9	40819.7	47743.8	...	...	...
Plus: Net factor income from the rest of the world	-62.6	-16.1	742.3	...	...	...	...	...	...			
Factor income from the rest of the world	6.6	145.8	1867.1	...								
Less: Factor income to the rest of the world	69.2	161.9	1124.8	...								
Equals: Gross National Product [a]	3296.8	5230.5	17891.3	...								
Less: Consumption of fixed capital	...	...										

Egypt

1.12 Relations Among National Accounting Aggregates
(Continued)

Million Egyptian pounds — Fiscal year beginning 1 July

	1970	1975	1980	1981	1982	1983	1984	1985	1986	1987	1988	1989
Equals: National Income [ba]	3296.8	5230.5	17891.3	...	...	...	...	...	...	...	...	...
Plus: Net current transfers from the rest of the world	121.6	413.9	254.3	...	...	...	...	...	...	...	...	...
Current transfers from the rest of the world	121.9	436.2	255.7	...	...	...	...	...	...	...	...	...
Less: Current transfers to the rest of the world	0.3	22.3	1.4	...	...	...	...	...	...	...	...	...
Equals: National Disposable Income [ca]	3418.4	5644.4	18145.6	...	...	...	...	...	...	...	...	...
Less: Final consumption	3097.0	4445.0	13995.1	...	...	...	...	...	...	...	...	...
Equals: Net Saving [da]	321.4	1199.4	4150.5	...	...	...	...	...	...	...	...	...
Less: Surplus of the nation on current transactions	-94.1	-524.4	-1057.5	...	...	...	...	...	...	...	...	...
Equals: Net Capital Formation [ea]	415.5	1723.8	5208.0	...	...	...	...	...	...	...	...	...

a) For years 1972-1979 estimates relate to calendar year.
b) Item 'National income' includes consumption of fixed capital.
c) Item 'National disposable income' includes consumption of fixed capital.
d) Item 'Net saving' includes consumption of fixed capital.
e) Item 'Net capital formation' includes consumption of fixed capital.

2.11 Gross Fixed Capital Formation by Kind of Activity of Owner, ISIC Divisions, in Current Prices

Million Egyptian pounds — Fiscal year beginning 1 July

	1970	1975	1980	1981	1982	1983	1984	1985	1986	1987	1988	1989
				All Producers								
1 Agriculture, hunting, forestry and fishing	53.3	94.6	370.2	450.4	492.1	520.2	664.6	772.4	888.6	...	...	...
2 Mining and quarrying	33.0	121.9	606.4	1007.2	263.8	292.1	374.7	281.3	178.9	...	...	...
3 Manufacturing	89.7	286.8	1288.1	1277.1	1498.5	1541.0	1616.2	1524.3	1611.4	...	...	...
4 Electricity, gas and water	23.1	53.3	481.5	372.0	547.7	503.4	487.2	588.2	546.2	...	...	...
5 Construction	8.9	30.6	184.0	239.9	214.1	210.3	194.7	169.8	244.9	...	...	...
6 Wholesale and retail trade, restaurants and hotels [a]	10.0	15.7	181.3	243.2	125.9	133.3	141.3	97.0	86.8	...	...	...
7 Transport, storage and communication	81.2	383.5	986.1	1190.7	1587.8	1612.1	1744.7	1636.6	1396.5	...	...	...
8 Finance, insurance, real estate and business services [a]	26.5	176.8	677.6	683.2	884.4	830.7	942.8	1353.0	1551.4	...	...	...
9 Community, social and personal services	35.8	119.1	559.2	822.8	784.3	1066.4	1105.4	1329.4	1195.3	...	...	...
Total Industries	361.5	1282.3	5334.4	6286.5	6398.6	6709.5	7271.6	7752.0	7700.0	...	...	...
Producers of Government Services	...	...										
Private Non-Profit Institutions Serving Households	...	...										
Total [bc]	361.5	1282.3	5334.4	6286.5	6398.6	6709.5	7271.6	7752.0	7700.0	...	...	...

a) Prior to 1973, finance and insurance are included in item 'Wholesale and retail trade, restaurants and hotels'.
b) For years 1972-1979 estimates relate to calendar year.
c) Gross fixed capital formation includes the value of land for estimates prior to 1981/82.

4.3 Cost Components of Value Added

Million Egyptian pounds — Fiscal year beginning 1 July

1980

	Compensation of Employees	Capital Consumption	Net Operating Surplus	Indirect Taxes	Less: Subsidies Received	Value Added
			All Producers			
1 Agriculture, hunting, forestry and fishing	739.2	...	2687.8	...	...	3427.0
2 Mining and quarrying	75.3	...	3029.7	...	...	3105.0
3 Manufacturing	1023.5	...	1183.6	...	...	2207.1
4 Electricity, gas and water	52.3	...	59.4	...	...	111.7

Egypt

4.3 Cost Components of Value Added
(Continued)

Million Egyptian pounds — Fiscal year beginning 1 July

	Compensation of Employees	Capital Consumption	Net Operating Surplus	Indirect Taxes	Less: Subsidies Received	Value Added
	1980					
5 Construction	361.9	...	431.1	...	...	793.0
6 Wholesale and retail trade, restaurants and hotels [a]	1307.2	...	1009.8	...	...	2317.0
7 Transport, storage and communication	287.8	...	1023.2	...	...	1311.0
8 Finance, insurance, real estate and business services [a]	48.1	...	1284.2	...	...	1332.3
9 Community, social and personal services [b]	2205.5	...	205.5	...	...	2411.0
Total, Industries [c]	6100.8	...	10914.3	...	...	17015.1
Producers of Government Services [b]	...	...	...	...	...	...
Other Producers [b]	...	...	...	...	...	...
Total [d,c,e]	6100.8	...	10914.3	...	...	17015.1
Less: Imputed bank service charge	...	...	...	...	...	...
Import duties	...	...	...	...	...	...
Value added tax	...	...	...	...	...	...
Other adjustments [f]	...	...	...	...	...	1026.1
Total [c]	...	...	...	...	...	18041.2

a) Prior to 1973, finance and insurance are included in item 'Wholesale and retail trade, restaurants and hotels'.
b) Items 'Other producers' and 'Producers of government services' are included in item 'Community, social and personal services'.
c) For years 1972-1979 estimates relate to calendar year.
d) Gross domestic product in factor values.
e) Column 'Consumption of fixed capital' is included in column 'Net operating surplus'.
f) Item 'Other adjustments' refers to indirect taxes net of subsidies.

El Salvador

General note. The preparation of national accounts statistics in El Salvador is undertaken by the Departamento de Investigaciones Economicas del Banco Central, San Salvador. The official estimates are published monthly in 'Revista Mensual'. A detailed description of the sources and methods used for the national accounts estimation is contained in 'Metodologia de Cuentas Nacionales de los Paises Centroamericanos' published by the Consejo Monetario Centroamericano Secretaria Ejecutiva in October 1976. The estimates are generally in accordance with the classifications and definitions recommended in the United Nations System of National Accounts (SNA). The following tables have been prepared from successive replies to the United Nations national accounts questionnaire. When the scope and coverage of the estimates differ for conceptual or statistical reasons from the definitions and classifications recommended in SNA, a footnote is indicated to the relevant tables.

Sources and methods:

(a) Gross domestic product. Gross domestic product is estimated mainly through the production approach.

(b) Expenditure on the gross domestic product. The expenditure approach is used to estimate government final consumption expenditure, increase in stocks, and exports and imports of goods and services. The commodity-flow approach supplemented by the expenditure approach is used for private final consumption expenditure and gross fixed capital formation. The estimates of government consumption expenditure are obtained directly from government sources. For private consumption expenditure, the commodity-flow approach is used with adjustments made for distribution and other costs which are included in the retail value. The estimates of increase in stocks are based on information on stored agricultural products, the stocks of the manufacturing and trade industries and the stocks of public construction. Private capital formation is estimated on the basis of data on domestically produced and imported capital goods and on statistics of construction and repair work. The imports data are adjusted to include import duties, trade margins and installation costs. For public expenditure on capital formation, data are obtained from official sources. Data on exports and imports of goods and services are obtained from the balance of payments. Export data on coffee are obtained from the Compania Salvadorena de Cafe, while other merchandise data are furnished by the Direccion General de Estadistica y Censos. GDP by expenditure at constant prices is not estimated.

(c) Cost-structure of the gross domestic product. Compensation of employees, combined with operating surplus, is obtained as a residual. The estimates of net indirect taxes are derived from the government accounts. No specific information is available on how consumption of fixed capital is estimated.

(d) Gross domestic product by kind of economic activity. The table of gross domestic product by kind of economic activity is prepared at market prices, i.e. producers' values. The production approach is used to estimate value added of most industries. The income approach is used for domestic services and public administration and defence while an indirect method is used for the trade sector. The agricultural data, which are provided by Ministerio de Agricultura y Ganaderia, are obtained through various periodic surveys. Data on the coffee harvest are supplied by the Compania Salvadorena de Cafe while coffee prices are taken from the Compania de Cafe's export prices. Information on the production of cotton is provided by the Cooperative Algodonera Salvadorena Ltda. The gross value of production is calculated by applying producers' prices to the quantity of each commodity produced. For the livestock sector, information is obtained from the Direccion General de Estadistica y Censos, external trade data and through direct studies on prices. Value added of forestry and logging is estimated by means of indirect methods. For the mining and quarrying sector, the estimates are based on 1961 census figures combined with a volume index constructed from square-metre construction data and on price index. The gross value of production in manufacturing is based on the results of annual surveys and industrial censuses held every five years. Estimates for small-scale manufacturing is extrapolated from census data. The estimates for electricity are based on industrial census results and on information furnished by the concerned agencies. For private construction, the information is obtained from the Direccion General de Estadistica y Censos. The basic sources include permits issued for urban construction. Rural population figures are used to determine the number of new dwellings in rural areas. The estimates for public construction are obtained from concerned institutions. For both public and private constructions, intermediate consumption is determined by using a fixed percentage of gross value of production. Gross output of the trade sector is determined on the basis of the values of domestic and imported goods marketed. The gross value of production of domestic goods and the c.i.f. values of imported goods are adjusted for changes in stocks and trade margin are added. An estimate of inputs, which is made from survey based on percentages for electricity, transport, etc., is deducted from the total gross value of production to arrive at value added. Estimates of restaurants and hotels are inter-and extrapolated on the basis of census figures. The enterprises concerned with road transport are classified into international, interdepartamental, urban and interurban transport. A sample from each category is taken in order to obtain average figures for estimating receipts per ton, which are multiplied by quantity figures to arrive at gross value of production and value added. For railways, air transport and communication, information is obtained directly from concerned companies. The estimates of the financial sector are based on financial statements furnished by the banks and insurance companies. Imputation is made for service charges by deducting interest from investment income. The estimate of ownership of dwellings are based on the number of urban and rural dwellings obtained from the population censuses and rents data from surveys, and using the cost of living index as an inflator. Ten percent of the gross value of production are deducted for inputs. The estimates of government services are based on information published by the Ministerio de Hacienda. For other services such as education, hospitals, religion, the estimates are obtained from concerned institutions or from publications such as Indicadores Economicas and Boletin Estadistico. For domestic services, the annual average wages for four regional areas of the country are applied to an estimate of the number of persons engaged. The latter is based on the 1961 census figures and average growth rates while the wage is estimated annually, applying the cost of living index. For the constant price estimates, value added for the agricultural, electricity, trade, transport and financial sectors is estimated by using volume or quantity indexes. Double deflation is used for the manufacturing sector. Price deflation is used for mining and quarrying, construction, restaurants and hotels and government services. For domestic services, wages paid in the base-year are applied to the number employed in the current year.

1.1 Expenditure on the Gross Domestic Product, in Current Prices

Million Salvadoran colones

	1970	1975	1980	1981	1982	1983	1984	1985	1986	1987	1988	1989
1 Government final consumption expenditure	276	501	1247	1369	1415	1607	1869	2220	2803	3181	3484	3930
2 Private final consumption expenditure	1935	3283	6405	6644	6877	7871	9184	11640	15206	18744	22151	26429
3 Gross capital formation	341	991	1183	1231	1185	1224	1394	1554	2619	2861	3503	5246
A Increase in stocks	33	-40	-27	58	56	44	58	-169	26	-297	85	1026
B Gross fixed capital formation	308	1031	1210	1173	1130	1180	1336	1723	2594	3158	3417	4219
Residential buildings	51	83	182	165	238	315	326	488	537	637	644	841
Non-residential buildings	10	31	21	5	4	6	8	7	110	146	231	193
Other construction and land improvement etc.	71	294	436	408	358	386	387	404	425	633	748	898
Other	176	623	571	595	530	473	614	824	1522	1742	1794	2287
4 Exports of goods and services	639	1480	3046	2307	2042	2486	2536	3199	4875	4395	4327	4261
5 Less: Imports of goods and services	631	1711	2964	2904	2553	3036	3327	4283	5740	6040	6099	7636
Statistical discrepancy	11	-66	...	...	...	...	...	...	...	...	...	...
Equals: Gross Domestic Product	2571	4478	8917	8647	8966	10152	11657	14331	19763	23141	27366	32230

El Salvador

1.2 Expenditure on the Gross Domestic Product, in Constant Prices

Million Salvadoran colones

	1970	1975	1980	1981	1982	1983	1984	1985	1986	1987	1988	1989
	\multicolumn{12}{c}{At constant prices of:1962}
1 Government final consumption expenditure	251	324	422	437	436	440	461	492	511	526	539	533
2 Private final consumption expenditure	1904	2341	2496	2279	2085	2096	2175	2251	2245	2259	2284	2316
3 Gross capital formation	288	481	412	396	356	326	335	317	385	368	437	587
A Increase in stocks	29	-38	-10	19	17	12	14	-37	5	-46	12	129
B Gross fixed capital formation	259	519	422	377	339	314	321	354	380	415	425	458
4 Exports of goods and services	510	747	838	690	588	705	674	648	566	637	577	476
5 Less: Imports of goods and services	560	769	879	786	617	696	710	714	694	697	693	735
Equals: Gross Domestic Product	2393	3124	3289	3017	2848	2870	2936	2994	3013	3094	3144	3177

1.3 Cost Components of the Gross Domestic Product

Million Salvadoran colones

	1970	1975	1980	1981	1982	1983	1984	1985	1986	1987	1988	1989
1 Indirect taxes, net	197	353	642	661	616	751	982	1245	2014	1764	1678	1649
A Indirect taxes	200	386	677	693	658	774	1009	1275	2056	1806	1722	1699
B Less: Subsidies	3	33	35	32	42	23	27	30	42	42	44	50
2 Consumption of fixed capital	125	198	369	358	371	420	482	591	815	955	1129	1328
3 Compensation of employees paid by resident producers to: [a]	2249	3926	7904	7628	7979	8981	10193	12495	16934	20422	24559	29253
4 Operating surplus												
Equals: Gross Domestic Product	2571	4478	8916	8647	8966	10152	11657	14331	19763	23141	27366	32230

a) Items 'Compensation of employees paid by resident producers' and 'Operating surplus' have been obtained as a residual.

1.7 External Transactions on Current Account, Summary

Million Salvadoran colones

	1970	1975	1980	1981	1982	1983	1984	1985	1986	1987	1988	1989
	\multicolumn{12}{c}{Payments to the Rest of the World}
1 Imports of goods and services	631	1711	2964	2904	2553	3036	3327	4283	5740	6040	6099	7636
A Imports of merchandise c.i.f.	536	1495	2405	2462	2142	2463	2742	3413	4674	4972	5035	6503
B Other	95	216	559	442	411	573	585	870	1066	1068	1064	1133
2 Factor income to the rest of the world	34	88	258	267	356	495	511	521	675	721	710	798
A Compensation of employees	3	2	3	5	17	17	20	18	...	...	...	...
B Property and entrepreneurial income	31	86	255	262	339	478	491	503	...	...	...	...
3 Current transfers to the rest of the world	5	15	10	37	8	7	9	8	12	12	12	12
4 Surplus of the nation on current transactions	22	-229	77	-595	-312	-241	-365	-579	583	696	262	-1346
Payments to the Rest of the World and Surplus of the Nation on Current Transactions	692	1585	3309	2614	2605	3298	3482	4234	7011	7469	7082	7100
	\multicolumn{12}{c}{Receipts From The Rest of the World}
1 Exports of goods and services	639	1480	3046	2307	2042	2486	2536	3199	4876	4395	4327	4261
A Exports of merchandise f.o.b.	591	1332	2688	1995	1749	2025	1920	2339	3775	2955	3044	2780
B Other	48	148	358	312	293	461	616	860	1101	1440	1283	1481
2 Factor income from rest of the world	13	19	131	119	127	126	168	168	203	196	200	230
A Compensation of employees	4	6	85	76	86	83	111	...	...	...	...	...
B Property and entrepreneurial income	9	13	46	43	41	43	57	...	...	...	...	...
3 Current transfers from rest of the world	41	86	132	188	435	686	778	867	1932	2878	2555	2608
Receipts from the Rest of the World on Current Transactions	692	1585	3309	2614	2605	3298	3482	4234	7011	7469	7082	7099

El Salvador

1.10 Gross Domestic Product by Kind of Activity, in Current Prices

Million Salvadoran colones

	1970	1975	1980	1981	1982	1983	1984	1985	1986	1987	1988	1989
1 Agriculture, hunting, forestry and fishing	731	1028	2480	2106	2075	2161	2320	2611	3969	3199	3801	3767
2 Mining and quarrying	4	7	11	13	14	15	18	21	27	38	47	58
3 Manufacturing	485	831	1339	1359	1382	1572	1837	2346	3086	4045	4808	5836
4 Electricity, gas and water	39	57	189	192	200	244	281	335	418	497	535	606
5 Construction	72	219	306	284	301	343	355	437	547	711	815	969
6 Wholesale and retail trade, restaurants and hotels [a]	581	1178	2038	2028	2089	2510	2995	3898	5627	7275	8721	10831
7 Transport, storage and communication	128	188	314	328	347	412	481	613	816	1061	1206	1416
8 Finance, insurance, real estate and business services	152	300	686	707	802	896	1032	1189	1503	1822	2299	2703
9 Community, social and personal services [a]	109	166	637	687	708	823	982	1278	1794	2286	2749	3330
Total, Industries	2302	3973	8001	7703	7916	8976	10291	12728	17786	20934	24981	29516
Producers of Government Services	200	384	916	944	1050	1177	1366	1603	1977	2207	2385	2714
Other Producers	69	120	...	...	...	...	...	...	...	...	...	...
Subtotal	2571	4477	8917	8647	8966	10153	11657	14331	19763	23141	27366	32230
Less: Imputed bank service charge	...	...	...	...	...	...	...	...	...	...	...	...
Plus: Import duties	...	...	...	...	...	...	...	...	...	...	...	...
Plus: Value added tax	...	...	...	...	...	...	...	...	...	...	...	...
Equals: Gross Domestic Product	2571	4478	8917	8647	8966	10152	11657	14331	19763	23141	27366	32230

a) Restaurants and hotels are included in item 'Community, social and personal services'.

1.11 Gross Domestic Product by Kind of Activity, in Constant Prices

Million Salvadoran colones

	1970	1975	1980	1981	1982	1983	1984	1985	1986	1987	1988	1989
	\multicolumn{12}{c	}{At constant prices of:1962}
1 Agriculture, hunting, forestry and fishing	627	787	841	788	751	727	751	743	720	735	728	731
2 Mining and quarrying	4	5	4	4	4	4	4	4	4	5	5	5
3 Manufacturing	438	578	586	525	481	491	497	515	528	544	560	574
4 Electricity, gas and water	45	71	106	102	100	105	108	113	116	118	120	121
5 Construction	64	128	111	94	90	92	87	91	93	104	110	114
6 Wholesale and retail trade, restaurants and hotels [a]	600	776	625	532	468	478	487	490	491	498	500	517
7 Transport, storage and communication	128	173	194	173	161	171	176	179	180	183	187	189
8 Finance, insurance, real estate and business services	141	188	233	227	236	239	242	247	249	255	264	257
9 Community, social and personal services [a]	103	174	248	227	201	198	200	201	202	205	207	211
Total, Industries	2151	2880	2947	2671	2492	2505	2552	2583	2583	2647	2681	2719
Producers of Government Services	183	244	342	346	356	366	384	412	430	447	463	458
Other Producers	60	...	...	...	...	...	...	...	...	...	...	...
Subtotal	2393	3124	3289	3017	2848	2870	2936	2994	3013	3094	3144	3177
Less: Imputed bank service charge	...	...	...	...	...	...	...	...	...	...	...	...
Plus: Import duties	...	...	...	...	...	...	...	...	...	...	...	...
Plus: Value added tax	...	...	...	...	...	...	...	...	...	...	...	...
Equals: Gross Domestic Product	2393	3124	3289	3017	2848	2870	2936	2994	3013	3094	3144	3177

a) Restaurants and hotels are included in item 'Community, social and personal services'.

1.12 Relations Among National Accounting Aggregates

Million Salvadoran colones

	1970	1975	1980	1981	1982	1983	1984	1985	1986	1987	1988	1989
Gross Domestic Product	2571	4478	8917	8647	8966	10152	11657	14331	19763	23141	27366	32230
Plus: Net factor income from the rest of the world	-21	-70	-128	-148	-229	-370	-343	-353	-472	-525	-510	-568
Factor income from the rest of the world	13	19	131	119	127	126	168	168	203	196	200	230
Less: Factor income to the rest of the world	34	88	258	267	356	495	511	521	675	721	710	798
Equals: Gross National Product	2550	4408	8789	8499	8737	9782	11314	13978	19291	22616	26856	31662
Less: Consumption of fixed capital	125	198	369	358	371	420	482	591	815	955	1129	1328

El Salvador

1.12 Relations Among National Accounting Aggregates
(Continued)

Million Salvadoran colones

	1970	1975	1980	1981	1982	1983	1984	1985	1986	1987	1988	1989
Equals: National Income	2425	4210	8420	8141	8366	9362	10832	13387	18476	21661	25727	30334
Plus: Net current transfers from the rest of the world	36	71	122	151	427	679	769	859	1920	2866	2543	2596
Current transfers from the rest of the world	41	86	132	188	435	686	778	867	1932	2878	2555	2608
Less: Current transfers to the rest of the world	5	15	10	37	8	7	9	8	12	12	12	12
Equals: National Disposable Income	2461	4281	8542	8292	8793	10041	11601	14246	20396	24527	28270	32930
Less: Final consumption	2210	3784	7652	8013	8291	9478	11054	13860	18009	21926	25635	30359
Statistical discrepancy	-13	67	...	...	...	...	...	...	...	...	...	...
Equals: Net Saving	238	564	890	279	502	563	547	386	2387	2601	2635	2571
Less: Surplus of the nation on current transactions	22	-229	77	-595	-312	-241	-365	-579	583	696	262	-1346
Equals: Net Capital Formation	216	793	813	874	814	804	912	965	1804	1905	2373	3917

2.5 Private Final Consumption Expenditure by Type and Purpose, in Current Prices

Million Salvadoran colones

	1970	1975	1980	1981	1982	1983	1984	1985	1986	1987	1988	1989
Final Consumption Expenditure of Resident Households												
1 Food, beverages and tobacco	827	1331	...	...	...	...	...	...	...	...	...	...
A Food	696	1128	...	...	...	...	...	...	...	...	...	...
B Non-alcoholic beverages	18	33	...	...	...	...	...	...	...	...	...	...
C Alcoholic beverages	78	118	...	...	...	...	...	...	...	...	...	...
D Tobacco	35	51	...	...	...	...	...	...	...	...	...	...
2 Clothing and footwear	197	348	...	...	...	...	...	...	...	...	...	...
3 Gross rent, fuel and power	144	266	...	...	...	...	...	...	...	...	...	...
4 Furniture, furnishings and household equipment and operation	236	402	...	...	...	...	...	...	...	...	...	...
A Household operation	130	220	...	...	...	...	...	...	...	...	...	...
B Other	106	182	...	...	...	...	...	...	...	...	...	...
5 Medical care and health expenses	85	145	...	...	...	...	...	...	...	...	...	...
6 Transport and communication	160	341	...	...	...	...	...	...	...	...	...	...
A Personal transport equipment	33	37	...	...	...	...	...	...	...	...	...	...
B Other	127	304	...	...	...	...	...	...	...	...	...	...
7 Recreational, entertainment, education and cultural services	113	205	...	...	...	...	...	...	...	...	...	...
A Education	24	42	...	...	...	...	...	...	...	...	...	...
B Other	89	164	...	...	...	...	...	...	...	...	...	...
8 Miscellaneous goods and services	109	190	...	...	...	...	...	...	...	...	...	...
A Personal care	39	50	...	...	...	...	...	...	...	...	...	...
B Expenditures in restaurants, cafes and hotels	38	66	...	...	...	...	...	...	...	...	...	...
C Other	32	74	...	...	...	...	...	...	...	...	...	...
Total Final Consumption Expenditure in the Domestic Market by Households, of which	1871	3227	...	...	...	...	...	...	...	...	...	...
Plus: Direct purchases abroad by resident households	68	105	...	...	...	...	...	...	...	...	...	...
Less: Direct purchases in the domestic market by non-resident households	25	77	...	...	...	...	...	...	...	...	...	...
Equals: Final Consumption Expenditure of Resident Households	1914	3255	...	...	...	...	...	...	...	...	...	...
Final Consumption Expenditure of Private Non-profit Institutions Serving Households												
1 Research and science	...	...	...	...	...	...	...	...	...	...	...	...
2 Education	21	28	...	...	...	...	...	...	...	...	...	...
3 Medical and other health services	...	...	...	...	...	...	...	...	...	...	...	...

El Salvador

2.5 Private Final Consumption Expenditure by Type and Purpose, in Current Prices
(Continued)

Million Salvadoran colones

	1970	1975	1980	1981	1982	1983	1984	1985	1986	1987	1988	1989
4 Welfare services	...	...	...	...	...	...	...	...	...	...	...	...
5 Recreational and related cultural services	...	...	...	...	...	...	...	...	...	...	...	...
6 Religious organisations	...	...	...	...	...	...	...	...	...	...	...	...
7 Professional and labour organisations serving households	...	...	...	...	...	...	...	...	...	...	...	...
8 Miscellaneous	...	...	...	...	...	...	...	...	...	...	...	...
Equals: Final Consumption Expenditure of Private Non-profit Organisations Serving Households	21	28	...	...	...	...	...	...	...	...	...	...
Private Final Consumption Expenditure	1935	3283	...	...	...	...	...	...	...	...	...	...

2.11 Gross Fixed Capital Formation by Kind of Activity of Owner, ISIC Divisions, in Current Prices

Million Salvadoran colones

	1970	1975	1980	1981	1982	1983	1984	1985	1986	1987	1988	1989
					All Producers							
1 Agriculture, hunting, forestry and fishing	13	48	20	23	21	40	48	61	81	85	53	67
2 Mining and quarrying	...	...	...	...	...	...	...	...	...	...	...	...
3 Manufacturing	68	242	158	140	127	149	187	220	484	469	522	567
4 Electricity, gas and water	4	22	12	15	15	14	11	16	94	100	86	109
5 Construction	145	447	655	585	611	721	741	928	1126	1485	1696	2058
6 Wholesale and retail trade, restaurants and hotels [a]	7	13	11	8	10	20	35	39	77	72	82	102
7 Transport, storage and communication	57	148	120	139	123	123	208	333	600	803	804	1037
8 Finance, insurance, real estate and business services [b]	-	1	1	-	1	-	1	4	4	1	2	5
9 Community, social and personal services [a,b]	7	38	20	29	23	23	26	40	38	41	50	64
Total Industries	300	961	996	940	932	1091	1257	1640	2504	3055	3294	4009
Producers of Government Services	8	70	214	233	198	89	79	83	90	103	123	210
Private Non-Profit Institutions Serving Households	...	...	...	...	...	...	...	...	...	...	...	...
Total	308	1031	1210	1173	1130	1180	1336	1723	2594	3158	3417	4219

a) Restaurants and hotels are included in item 'Community, social and personal services'.
b) Business services are included in item 'Community, social and personal services'.

4.1 Derivation of Value Added by Kind of Activity, in Current Prices

Million Salvadoran colones

	1980 Gross Output	1980 Intermediate Consumption	1980 Value Added	1981 Gross Output	1981 Intermediate Consumption	1981 Value Added	1982 Gross Output	1982 Intermediate Consumption	1982 Value Added	1983 Gross Output	1983 Intermediate Consumption	1983 Value Added
						All Producers						
1 Agriculture, hunting, forestry and fishing	3075	595	2480	2675	569	2106	2580	505	2075	2678	517	2161
A Agriculture and hunting	2988	583	2405	2568	555	2013	2463	496	1967	2571	508	2063
B Forestry and logging	34	-	34	34	-	34	35	-	35	36	-	36
C Fishing	53	12	41	73	14	59	82	9	73	71	9	62
2 Mining and quarrying	17	6	11	19	6	13	20	6	14	23	8	15
A Coal mining	...	...	...	...	...	...	...	...	...	...	...	...
B Crude petroleum and natural gas production	...	...	...	...	...	...	...	...	...	...	...	...
C Metal ore mining	17	6	11	19	6	13	20	6	14	23	8	15
D Other mining	...	...	...	...	...	...	...	...	...	...	...	...

El Salvador

4.1 Derivation of Value Added by Kind of Activity, in Current Prices
(Continued)

Million Salvadoran colones

	1980 Gross Output	1980 Intermediate Consumption	1980 Value Added	1981 Gross Output	1981 Intermediate Consumption	1981 Value Added	1982 Gross Output	1982 Intermediate Consumption	1982 Value Added	1983 Gross Output	1983 Intermediate Consumption	1983 Value Added
3 Manufacturing	3397	2058	1339	3431	2072	1359	3466	2084	1382	3931	2359	1572
A Manufacture of food, beverages and tobacco	1531	870	661	1577	887	690	1674	940	734	1887	1063	824
B Textile, wearing apparel and leather industries	577	354	223	556	341	215	481	293	188	512	314	198
C Manufacture of wood and wood products, including furniture	58	25	33	62	26	36	60	25	35	94	39	55
D Manufacture of paper and paper products, printing and publishing	119	75	44	114	73	41	101	64	37	122	77	45
E Manufacture of chemicals and chemical petroleum, coal, rubber and plastic products	705	501	204	748	534	214	783	558	225	881	625	256
F Manufacture of non-metallic mineral products, except products of petroleum and coal	116	48	68	116	47	69	127	52	75	153	63	90
G Basic metal industries	74	53	21	60	43	17	52	37	15	67	48	19
H Manufacture of fabricated metal products, machinery and equipment	143	83	60	125	71	54	116	65	51	136	77	59
I Other manufacturing industries	76	51	25	73	50	23	71	49	22	80	54	26
4 Electricity, gas and water	246	57	189	249	57	192	259	59	200	317	73	244
A Electricity, gas and steam	...	...	164	...	...	167	...	...	174	...	...	213
B Water works and supply	...	...	25	...	...	25	...	...	26	...	...	31
5 Construction	649	343	306	588	304	284	609	308	301	715	372	343
6 Wholesale and retail trade, restaurants and hotels	2166	128	2038	2158	130	2028	2222	133	2089	2670	160	2510
A Wholesale and retail trade	...	...	2038	...	...	2028	...	...	2089	...	...	2510
B Restaurants and hotels [a]	...	...	...	...	...	...	...	...	...	...	...	...
Restaurants	...	...	...	...	...	...	...	...	...	...	...	...
Hotels and other lodging places	...	...	16	...	...	18	...	...	20	...	...	28
7 Transport, storage and communication	490	177	313	511	183	328	511	164	347	607	195	412
8 Finance, insurance, real estate and business services	780	94	686	804	97	707	911	109	802	1023	127	896
A Financial institutions	...	...	...	...	...	...	...	...	...	...	...	...
B Insurance	...	...	...	...	...	...	...	...	...	...	...	...
C Real estate and business services	...	...	...	...	...	...	...	...	...	...	...	...
9 Community, social and personal services [a]	1298	661	637	1279	592	687	1057	349	708	1229	406	823
Total, Industries	12118	4119	8001	11714	4010	7703	11635	3719	7916	13192	4217	8975
Producers of Government Services	1247	331	916	1368	424	944	1415	365	1050	1607	430	1177
Other Producers	...	...	...	...	...	...	...	...	...	...	...	...
Total	13365	4450	8917	13082	4434	8647	13050	4084	8966	14799	4647	10152
Less: Imputed bank service charge	...	...	...	...	...	...	...	...	...	...	...	...
Import duties	...	...	...	...	...	...	...	...	...	...	...	...
Value added tax	...	...	...	...	...	...	...	...	...	...	...	...
Total	...	...	...	...	...	...	...	...	...	...	...	...

	1984 Gross Output	1984 Intermediate Consumption	1984 Value Added	1985 Gross Output	1985 Intermediate Consumption	1985 Value Added	1986 Gross Output	1986 Intermediate Consumption	1986 Value Added	1987 Gross Output	1987 Intermediate Consumption	1987 Value Added
					All Producers							
1 Agriculture, hunting, forestry and fishing	2864	544	2320	3179	568	2611	4952	983	3969	4233	1035	3198
A Agriculture and hunting	2732	528	2204	3048	550	2498	4781	958	3823	4062	1015	3047
B Forestry and logging	37	-	37	43	-	43	56	-	56	62	-	62
C Fishing	95	16	79	88	18	70	115	25	90	109	20	89
2 Mining and quarrying	27	9	18	31	10	21	40	13	27	56	18	38
A Coal mining	...	...	...	...	...	...	...	...	...	...	...	...
B Crude petroleum and natural gas production	...	...	...	...	...	...	...	...	...	...	...	...
C Metal ore mining	27	9	18	31	10	21	40	13	27	56	18	38
D Other mining	...	...	...	...	...	...	...	...	...	...	...	...

El Salvador

4.1 Derivation of Value Added by Kind of Activity, in Current Prices
(Continued)

Million Salvadoran colones

	1984 Gross Output	1984 Intermediate Consumption	1984 Value Added	1985 Gross Output	1985 Intermediate Consumption	1985 Value Added	1986 Gross Output	1986 Intermediate Consumption	1986 Value Added	1987 Gross Output	1987 Intermediate Consumption	1987 Value Added
3 Manufacturing	4727	2890	1837	5950	3604	2346	7587	4501	3086	9180	5135	4045
A Manufacture of food, beverages and tobacco	2392	1390	1002	3116	1826	1290	3951	2226	1725	4844	2562	2282
B Textile, wearing apparel and leather industries	593	371	222	706	441	265	904	553	351	1111	657	454
C Manufacture of wood and wood products, including furniture	109	48	61	150	66	84	187	72	115	227	75	152
D Manufacture of paper and paper products, printing and publishing	146	95	51	191	124	67	241	154	87	295	173	122
E Manufacture of chemicals and chemical petroleum, coal, rubber and plastic products	954	677	277	1052	713	339	1362	938	424	1517	993	524
F Manufacture of non-metallic mineral products, except products of petroleum and coal	161	69	92	206	88	118	273	118	155	335	130	205
G Basic metal industries	110	79	31	183	132	51	230	162	68	282	183	99
H Manufacture of fabricated metal products, machinery and equipment	154	89	65	205	118	87	262	166	96	335	204	131
I Other manufacturing industries	109	74	35	141	96	45	176	111	65	233	156	77
4 Electricity, gas and water	365	84	281	436	101	335	543	125	418	637	140	497
A Electricity, gas and steam	...	...	246	...	...	295	...	...	370	...	...	440
B Water works and supply	...	...	35	...	...	40	...	...	48	...	...	57
5 Construction	740	385	355	918	481	437	1098	551	547	1447	736	711
6 Wholesale and retail trade, restaurants and hotels	3188	193	2995	4147	249	3898	5987	360	5627	7770	495	7275
A Wholesale and retail trade	...	...	2995	4147	249	3898	5987	360	5627	7770	495	7275
B Restaurants and hotels [a]	...	...	...	...	...	...	...	...	...	...	...	...
Restaurants	...	...	...	...	...	...	...	...	...	...	...	...
Hotels and other lodging places	...	...	35	...	...	...	...	...	...	...	...	...
7 Transport, storage and communication	709	228	481	905	292	613	1203	387	816	1554	493	1061
8 Finance, insurance, real estate and business services	1158	126	1032	1348	159	1189	1703	200	1503	2089	267	1822
A Financial institutions	...	...	...	521	79	...	665	101	...	784	144	...
B Insurance	...	...	...	...	...	...	...	...	...	...	...	...
C Real estate and business services	...	...	...	827	80	747	1039	100	939	1305	123	1182
9 Community, social and personal services [a]	1466	484	982	1908	630	1278	2678	884	1794	3391	1104	2287
Total, Industries	15245	4954	10291	18820	6092	12728	25792	8006	17786	30357	9423	20934
Producers of Government Services	1869	503	1366	2220	617	1603	2803	826	1977	3181	974	2207
Other Producers	...	...	...	...	...	...	...	...	...	...	...	...
Total	17114	5457	11657	21040	6709	14331	28595	8832	19763	33538	10397	23141
Less: Imputed bank service charge	...	...	...	...	...	...	...	...	...	...	...	...
Import duties	...	...	...	...	...	...	...	...	...	...	...	...
Value added tax	...	...	...	...	...	...	...	...	...	...	...	...
Total	...	...	...	...	...	...	...	...	...	...	...	...

	1988 Gross Output	1988 Intermediate Consumption	1988 Value Added	1989 Gross Output	1989 Intermediate Consumption	1989 Value Added
	\multicolumn{6}{c}{All Producers}
1 Agriculture, hunting, forestry and fishing	4924	1123	3801	5149	1382	3767
A Agriculture and hunting	4689	1105	3584	4907	1362	3545
B Forestry and logging	66	-	66	69	-	69
C Fishing	169	18	151	173	20	153
2 Mining and quarrying	68	21	47	85	27	58
A Coal mining	...	...	...	...	...	...
B Crude petroleum and natural gas production	...	...	...	...	...	...
C Metal ore mining	68	21	47	85	27	58
D Other mining	...	...	...	...	...	...

El Salvador

4.1 Derivation of Value Added by Kind of Activity, in Current Prices
(Continued)

Million Salvadoran colones

		1988			1989		
		Gross Output	Intermediate Consumption	Value Added	Gross Output	Intermediate Consumption	Value Added
3	Manufacturing	11321	6513	4808	14142	8306	5836
	A Manufacture of food, beverages and tobacco	5943	3200	2743	7622	4302	3320
	B Textile, wearing apparel and leather industries	1403	855	548	1746	1071	675
	C Manufacture of wood and wood products, including furniture	285	101	184	369	143	226
	D Manufacture of paper and paper products, printing and publishing	371	232	139	467	294	173
	E Manufacture of chemicals and chemical petroleum, coal, rubber and plastic products	1836	1262	574	2100	1426	674
	F Manufacture of non-metallic mineral products, except products of petroleum and coal	496	252	244	553	242	311
	G Basic metal industries	301	171	130	464	312	152
	H Manufacture of fabricated metal products, machinery and equipment	403	244	159	503	310	193
	I Other manufacturing industries	283	196	87	317	205	112
4	Electricity, gas and water	686	151	535	776	170	606
	A Electricity, gas and steam	...	...	473	...	...	536
	B Water works and supply	...	...	62	...	...	70
5	Construction	1658	843	815	1985	1016	969
6	Wholesale and retail trade, restaurants and hotels	9391	670	8721	11671	839	10832
	A Wholesale and retail trade	9391	670	8721	11671	839	10832
	B Restaurants and hotels [a]	...	...	...	...	...	...
	Restaurants	...	...	...	...	...	...
	Hotels and other lodging places	...	...	...	...	...	...
7	Transport, storage and communication	1763	557	1206	2082	666	1416
8	Finance, insurance, real estate and business services	2629	330	2299	3149	446	2703
	A Financial institutions	947	168	...	1050	255	795
	B Insurance						
	C Real estate and business services	1682	162	1520	2100	192	1908
9	Community, social and personal services [a]	4074	1325	2749	4900	1570	3330
	Total, Industries	36514	11533	24981	43939	14422	29516
	Producers of Government Services	3484	1099	2385	4001	1287	2714
	Other Producers	...	...	...	...	...	...
	Total	39998	12632	27366	47940	15709	32230
	Less: Imputed bank service charge	...	...	...	...	...	...
	Import duties	...	...	...	...	...	...
	Value added tax	...	...	...	...	...	...
	Total	...	...	...	...	...	...

a) Restaurants and hotels are included in item 'Community, social and personal services'.

4.2 Derivation of Value Added by Kind of Activity, in Constant Prices

Million Salvadoran colones

		1980			1981			1982			1983		
		Gross Output	Intermediate Consumption	Value Added	Gross Output	Intermediate Consumption	Value Added	Gross Output	Intermediate Consumption	Value Added	Gross Output	Intermediate Consumption	Value Added

At constant prices of: 1962

All Producers

1	Agriculture, hunting, forestry and fishing	...	...	841	...	...	788	...	...	751	...	...	727
	A Agriculture and hunting	...	...	801	...	...	749	...	...	712	...	...	688
	B Forestry and logging	...	...	27	...	...	28	...	...	27	...	...	28
	C Fishing	...	...	13	...	...	11	...	...	12	...	...	11
2	Mining and quarrying	...	...	4	...	...	4	...	...	4	...	...	4
	A Coal mining	...	...	...	...	...	...	...	...	...	...	...	...
	B Crude petroleum and natural gas production	...	...	...	...	...	...	...	...	...	...	...	...

501

El Salvador

4.2 Derivation of Value Added by Kind of Activity, in Constant Prices
(Continued)

Million Salvadoran colones

	1980 Gross Output	1980 Intermediate Consumption	1980 Value Added	1981 Gross Output	1981 Intermediate Consumption	1981 Value Added	1982 Gross Output	1982 Intermediate Consumption	1982 Value Added	1983 Gross Output	1983 Intermediate Consumption	1983 Value Added
				At constant prices of:1962								
C Metal ore mining	...	...	4	...	...	4	...	...	4	...	...	4
D Other mining	...	...	...	...	...	...	...	...	...	...	...	...
3 Manufacturing	...	...	586	...	...	525	...	...	481	...	...	491
A Manufacture of food, beverages and tobacco	...	...	360	...	...	333	...	...	316	...	...	315
B Textile, wearing apparel and leather industries	...	...	52	...	...	46	...	...	36	...	...	33
C Manufacture of wood and wood products, including furniture	...	...	18	...	...	18	...	...	17	...	...	22
D Manufacture of paper and paper products, printing and publishing	...	...	24	...	...	20	...	...	14	...	...	15
E Manufacture of chemicals and chemical petroleum, coal, rubber and plastic products	...	...	53	...	...	46	...	...	44	...	...	47
F Manufacture of non-metallic mineral products, except products of petroleum and coal	...	...	27	...	...	23	...	...	22	...	...	24
G Basic metal industries	...	...	9	...	...	7	...	...	5	...	...	6
H Manufacture of fabricated metal products, machinery and equipment	...	...	32	...	...	24	...	...	20	...	...	21
I Other manufacturing industries	...	...	12	...	...	9	...	...	7	...	...	7
4 Electricity, gas and water	...	...	106	...	...	102	...	...	100	...	...	105
A Electricity, gas and steam	...	...	98	...	...	94	...	...	91	...	...	96
B Water works and supply	...	...	8	...	...	8	...	...	9	...	...	9
5 Construction	...	...	111	...	...	94	...	...	90	...	...	92
6 Wholesale and retail trade, restaurants and hotels	...	...	625	...	...	532	...	...	468	...	...	478
A Wholesale and retail trade	...	...	625	...	...	532	...	...	468	...	...	478
B Restaurants and hotels [a]	...	...	...	...	...	...	...	...	...	...	...	...
Restaurants	...	...	...	...	...	...	...	...	...	...	...	...
Hotels and other lodging places	...	...	6	...	...	5	...	...	5	...	...	6
7 Transport, storage and communication	...	...	194	...	...	173	...	...	161	...	...	171
8 Finance, insurance, real estate and business services	...	...	233	...	...	227	...	...	236	...	...	239
A Financial institutions	...	...	...	...	...	...	...	...	...	...	...	...
B Insurance	...	...	...	...	...	...	...	...	...	...	...	...
C Real estate and business services	...	...	...	...	...	...	...	...	...	...	...	...
9 Community, social and personal services [a]	...	...	248	...	...	227	...	...	201	...	...	198
Total, Industries	...	...	2948	...	...	2672	...	...	2492	...	...	2504
Producers of Government Services	...	...	342	...	...	346	...	...	356	...	...	366
Other Producers	...	...	...	...	...	...	...	...	...	...	...	...
Total	...	...	3289	...	...	3017	...	...	2848	...	...	2870
Less: Imputed bank service charge	...	...	...	...	...	...	...	...	...	...	...	...
Import duties	...	...	...	...	...	...	...	...	...	...	...	...
Value added tax	...	...	...	...	...	...	...	...	...	...	...	...
Total	...	...	...	...	...	...	...	...	...	...	...	...

	1984 Gross Output	1984 Intermediate Consumption	1984 Value Added	1985 Gross Output	1985 Intermediate Consumption	1985 Value Added	1986 Gross Output	1986 Intermediate Consumption	1986 Value Added	1987 Gross Output	1987 Intermediate Consumption	1987 Value Added
				At constant prices of:1962								
				All Producers								
1 Agriculture, hunting, forestry and fishing	...	...	751	...	...	743	...	...	720	...	...	735
A Agriculture and hunting	...	...	705	...	...	699	...	...	674	...	...	690
B Forestry and logging	...	...	29	...	...	29	...	...	29	...	...	29
C Fishing	...	...	17	...	...	15	...	...	17	...	...	16
2 Mining and quarrying	...	...	4	...	...	4	...	...	4	...	...	4
A Coal mining	...	...	...	...	...	...	...	...	...	...	...	...
B Crude petroleum and natural gas production	...	...	...	...	...	...	...	...	...	...	...	...

El Salvador

4.2 Derivation of Value Added by Kind of Activity, in Constant Prices
(Continued)

Million Salvadoran colones

	1984 Gross Output	1984 Intermediate Consumption	1984 Value Added	1985 Gross Output	1985 Intermediate Consumption	1985 Value Added	1986 Gross Output	1986 Intermediate Consumption	1986 Value Added	1987 Gross Output	1987 Intermediate Consumption	1987 Value Added
					At constant prices of:1962							
C Metal ore mining	...	...	4	...	...	4	...	...	4	...	...	4
D Other mining	...	...	...	...	...	...	...	...	...	...	...	...
3 Manufacturing	...	...	497	...	...	515	...	...	528	...	...	544
A Manufacture of food, beverages and tobacco	...	...	326	...	...	347	...	...	353	...	...	361
B Textile, wearing apparel and leather industries	...	...	33	...	...	30	...	...	32	...	...	32
C Manufacture of wood and wood products, including furniture	...	...	20	...	...	21	...	...	22	...	...	23
D Manufacture of paper and paper products, printing and publishing	...	...	14	...	...	13	...	...	11	...	...	11
E Manufacture of chemicals and chemical petroleum, coal, rubber and plastic products	...	...	46	...	...	44	...	...	44	...	...	46
F Manufacture of non-metallic mineral products, except products of petroleum and coal	...	...	21	...	...	23	...	...	24	...	...	28
G Basic metal industries	...	...	8	...	...	9	...	...	11	...	...	11
H Manufacture of fabricated metal products, machinery and equipment	...	...	20	...	...	20	...	...	21	...	...	22
I Other manufacturing industries	...	...	8	...	...	8	...	...	10	...	...	10
4 Electricity, gas and water	...	...	108	...	...	113	...	...	116	...	...	118
A Electricity, gas and steam	...	...	99	...	...	102	...	...	104	...	...	106
B Water works and supply	...	...	9	...	...	11	...	...	12	...	...	12
5 Construction	...	...	87	...	...	91	...	...	93	...	...	104
6 Wholesale and retail trade, restaurants and hotels	...	...	487	...	...	490	...	...	491	...	...	498
A Wholesale and retail trade	...	...	487	...	...	490	...	...	491	...	...	498
B Restaurants and hotels [a]	...	...	...	...	...	...	...	...	...	...	...	...
Restaurants	...	...	...	...	...	...	...	...	...	...	...	...
Hotels and other lodging places	...	...	6	...	...	...	...	...	...	...	...	...
7 Transport, storage and communication	...	...	176	...	...	179	...	...	180	...	...	183
8 Finance, insurance, real estate and business services	...	...	242	...	...	247	...	...	249	...	...	255
A Financial institutions	...	...	...	...	...	103	...	...	104	...	...	107
B Insurance	...	...	...	...	...	...	...	...	...	...	...	...
C Real estate and business services	...	...	...	...	...	144	...	...	145	...	...	148
9 Community, social and personal services [a]	...	...	200	...	...	201	...	...	202	...	...	205
Total, Industries	...	...	2552	...	...	2583	...	...	2583	...	...	2647
Producers of Government Services	...	...	384	...	...	412	...	...	430	...	...	447
Other Producers	...	...	...	...	...	...	...	...	...	...	...	...
Total	...	...	2936	...	...	2994	...	...	3013	...	...	3094
Less: Imputed bank service charge	...	...	...	...	...	...	...	...	...	...	...	...
Import duties	...	...	...	...	...	...	...	...	...	...	...	...
Value added tax	...	...	...	...	...	...	...	...	...	...	...	...
Total	...	...	...	...	...	...	...	...	...	...	...	...

	1988 Gross Output	1988 Intermediate Consumption	1988 Value Added	1989 Gross Output	1989 Intermediate Consumption	1989 Value Added
	At constant prices of:1962					
	All Producers					
1 Agriculture, hunting, forestry and fishing	...	...	728	...	...	731
A Agriculture and hunting	...	...	683	...	...	688
B Forestry and logging	...	...	29	...	...	29
C Fishing	...	...	16	...	...	14
2 Mining and quarrying	...	...	5	...	...	5
A Coal mining	...	...	...	...	...	...
B Crude petroleum and natural gas production	...	...	...	...	...	...

El Salvador

4.2 Derivation of Value Added by Kind of Activity, in Constant Prices
(Continued)

Million Salvadoran colones

		1988			1989	
	Gross Output	Intermediate Consumption	Value Added	Gross Output	Intermediate Consumption	Value Added
			At constant prices of: 1962			
C Metal ore mining	...	...	5	...	...	5
D Other mining	...	...	...	...	...	...
3 Manufacturing	...	...	560	...	...	574
A Manufacture of food, beverages and tobacco	...	...	370	...	...	380
B Textile, wearing apparel and leather industries	...	...	33	...	...	35
C Manufacture of wood and wood products, including furniture	...	...	24	...	...	25
D Manufacture of paper and paper products, printing and publishing	...	...	12	...	...	12
E Manufacture of chemicals and chemical petroleum, coal, rubber and plastic products	...	...	48	...	...	49
F Manufacture of non-metallic mineral products, except products of petroleum and coal	...	...	28	...	...	29
G Basic metal industries	...	...	11	...	...	11
H Manufacture of fabricated metal products, machinery and equipment	...	...	23	...	...	23
I Other manufacturing industries	...	...	11	...	...	10
4 Electricity, gas and water	...	...	120	...	...	121
A Electricity, gas and steam	...	...	120	...	...	121
Water works and supply	...	...	...	...	...	...
5 Construction	...	...	110	...	...	114
6 Wholesale and retail trade, restaurants and hotels	...	...	500	...	...	517
A Wholesale and retail trade	...	...	500	...	...	517
B Restaurants and hotels [a]	...	...	...	...	...	...
Restaurants	...	...	...	...	...	...
Hotels and other lodging places	...	...	...	...	...	...
7 Transport, storage and communication	...	...	187	...	...	189
8 Finance, insurance, real estate and business services	...	...	264	...	...	257
A Financial institutions	...	...	109	...	...	99
B Insurance	...	...	...	...	...	...
C Real estate and business services	...	...	155	...	...	158
9 Community, social and personal services [a]	...	...	207	...	...	211
Total, Industries	...	...	2681	...	...	2719
Producers of Government Services	...	...	463	...	...	458
Other Producers	...	...	...	...	...	...
Total	...	...	3144	...	...	3177
Less: Imputed bank service charge	...	...	...	...	...	...
Import duties	...	...	...	...	...	...
Value added tax	...	...	...	...	...	...
Total	...	...	...	...	...	...

a) Restaurants and hotels are included in item 'Community, social and personal services'.

Equatorial Guinea

Source. Reply to the United Nations National Accounts Questionnaire from the Ministerio de Planificacion y Desarrollo Economico, Direccion General de Estadistica, Malabo. The official estimates and information on concepts, sources and methods of estimation can be found in 'Las Cuentas Nacionales de Guinea Ecuatorial' published in July 1987.

General note. The estimates shown in the following tables have been prepared in accordance with the United Nations System of National Accounts (SNA) so far as the existing data would permit. The monetary unit was ekwele. On 2 January 1985, the ekwele was replaced by CFA francs. 4 bipkwele is equivalent to 1 CFA franc.

1.1 Expenditure on the Gross Domestic Product, in Current Prices

Million CFA francs

	1970	1975	1980	1981	1982	1983	1984	1985	1986	1987	1988	1989
1 Government final consumption expenditure	...	...	...	...	...	7080	8505	... 5909	7241	5269	7804	9297
2 Private final consumption expenditure	...	...	...	...	...	16083	17511	... 30547	28910	29492	35373	27465
A Households	...	...	...	...	...	16083	17511	... ...				
B Private non-profit institutions serving households	...	...	...	...	...	-	-	... ...	...	...	...	...
3 Gross capital formation	...	...	...	...	...	2860	3642	... 3493	7150	9488	10274	8952
A Increase in stocks	...	...	...	...	...	-158	418	... -1721	-624	654	-685	-7
B Gross fixed capital formation	...	...	...	...	...	3018	3224	... 5214	7774	8834	10959	8959
Residential buildings	...	...	...	...	...	...	...					
Non-residential buildings	...	...	...	...	...	...	...	... 3596	3263	4537	5741	4789
Other construction and land improvement etc.	...	...	...	...	...	...	...					
Other	...	...	...	...	...	...	...	1618	4511	4297	5218	4170
4 Exports of goods and services	...	...	...	...	...	1477	1886	... 10432	9373	12815	9228	11267
5 Less: Imports of goods and services	...	...	...	...	...	1851	2012	... 11625	14938	16848	18767	14058
Equals: Gross Domestic Product	...	...	...	...	...	25649	29532	... 38756	37736	40216	43912	42923

1.2 Expenditure on the Gross Domestic Product, in Constant Prices

Million CFA francs

	1970	1975	1980	1981	1982	1983	1984	1985	1986	1987	1988	1989
					At constant prices of:1985							
1 Government final consumption expenditure	...	...	...	...	...	...	...	5909	5583	3202	4588	5612
2 Private final consumption expenditure	...	...	...	...	...	...	...	30547	29390	26158	29432	25845
3 Gross capital formation	...	...	...	...	...	...	...	3493	6224	7677	7236	6593
A Increase in stocks	...	...	...	...	...	...	...	-1721	-595	666	-1066	-143
B Gross fixed capital formation	...	...	...	...	...	...	...	5214	6819	7011	8302	6736
4 Exports of goods and services	...	...	...	...	...	...	...	10432	9194	16408	14637	13081
5 Less: Imports of goods and services	...	...	...	...	...	...	...	11625	13104	13371	13704	10106
Equals: Gross Domestic Product	...	...	...	...	...	...	...	38756	37286	40074	42189	41025

1.10 Gross Domestic Product by Kind of Activity, in Current Prices

Million CFA francs

	1970	1975	1980	1981	1982	1983	1984	1985	1986	1987	1988	1989
1 Agriculture, hunting, forestry and fishing	...	...	...	...	...	16404	18149	22777 / 21695	22108	23146	22361	22991
2 Mining and quarrying	...	...	...	...	...	...	...	...	...	...	...	...
3 Manufacturing	...	...	...	...	...	212	240	563 / 695	471	857	532	545
4 Electricity, gas and water	...	...	...	...	...	181	176	456 / 977	762	685	1119	1277
5 Construction	...	...	...	...	...	2703	2690	2071 / 1921	1783	2425	3070	2402

Equatorial Guinea

1.10 Gross Domestic Product by Kind of Activity, in Current Prices
(Continued)

Million CFA francs

	1970	1975	1980	1981	1982	1983	1984	1985	1986	1987	1988	1989
6 Wholesale and retail trade, restaurants and hotels	...	...	...	...	...	1291	1376	2648 / 3211	2922	3364	4735	3594
7 Transport, storage and communication	...	...	...	...	...	269	240	656 / 1098	878	632	760	823
8 Finance, insurance, real estate and business services	...	...	...	...	...	359	360	686 / 862	886	918	947	966
9 Community, social and personal services	...	...	...	...	...	...	...	... / 3257	2970	3070	3658	3924
Total, Industries	...	...	...	...	...	21420	23231	29857 / 33716	32780	35097	37182	36522
Producers of Government Services	...	...	...	...	...	3931	5700	5362 / 2712	2892	3241	5201	5093
Other Producers	...	...	...	...	...	42	38	476	...	...	...	...
Subtotal	...	...	...	...	...	25394	28970	35695 / 36428	35672	38338	42383	41615
Less: Imputed bank service charge	...	...	...	...	...	...	...	...	...	...	...	...
Plus: Import duties	...	...	...	...	...	255	562	2328 / 2328	2064	1878	1529	1309
Plus: Value added tax	...	...	...	...	...	...	...	...	...	...	...	...
Equals: Gross Domestic Product	...	...	...	...	...	25649	29532	38023 / 38756	37736	40216	43912	42923

1.11 Gross Domestic Product by Kind of Activity, in Constant Prices

Million CFA francs

	1970	1975	1980	1981	1982	1983	1984	1985	1986	1987	1988	1989
					At constant prices of:1985							
1 Agriculture, hunting, forestry and fishing	...	...	...	...	...	...	...	21695	22841	25193	24553	24963
2 Mining and quarrying	...	...	...	...	...	...	...	...	...	...	...	...
3 Manufacturing	...	...	...	...	...	...	...	695	413	680	403	410
4 Electricity, gas and water	...	...	...	...	...	...	...	977	762	685	1076	1228
5 Construction	...	...	...	...	...	...	...	1921	1564	1924	2326	1806
6 Wholesale and retail trade, restaurants and hotels	...	...	...	...	...	...	...	3211	2681	2925	3819	2830
7 Transport, storage and communication	...	...	...	...	...	...	...	1098	770	502	576	619
8 Finance, insurance, real estate and business services	...	...	...	...	...	...	...	862	812	799	764	761
9 Community, social and personal services	...	...	...	...	...	...	...	5969	5378	5487	7144	7100
Total, Industries	...	...	...	...	...	...	...	...	...	...	...	...
Producers of Government Services	...	...	...	...	...	...	...	...	...	...	...	...
Other Producers	...	...	...	...	...	...	...	...	...	...	...	...
Subtotal	...	...	...	...	...	...	...	36428	35222	38196	40660	39716
Less: Imputed bank service charge	...	...	...	...	...	...	...	...	...	...	...	...
Plus: Import duties	...	...	...	...	...	...	...	2328	2064	1878	1529	1309
Plus: Value added tax	...	...	...	...	...	...	...	...	...	...	...	...
Equals: Gross Domestic Product	...	...	...	...	...	...	...	38756	37286	40074	42189	41025

4.1 Derivation of Value Added by Kind of Activity, in Current Prices

Million CFA francs

	1985			1986			1987			1988		
	Gross Output	Intermediate Consumption	Value Added	Gross Output	Intermediate Consumption	Value Added	Gross Output	Intermediate Consumption	Value Added	Gross Output	Intermediate Consumption	Value Added
						All Producers							
1 Agriculture, hunting, forestry and fishing	...	...	21695	...	...	22108	...	...	23146	...	...	22361
A Agriculture and hunting	...	...	18082	...	...	17639	...	...	17706	...	...	17748
B Forestry and logging	...	...	2676	...	...	3551	...	...	4516	...	...	3661
C Fishing	...	...	937	...	...	917	...	...	924	...	...	952
2 Mining and quarrying	...	...	...	...	...	...	...	...	...	...	...	...

Equatorial Guinea

4.1 Derivation of Value Added by Kind of Activity, in Current Prices
(Continued)

Million CFA francs

	1985 Gross Output	1985 Intermediate Consumption	1985 Value Added	1986 Gross Output	1986 Intermediate Consumption	1986 Value Added	1987 Gross Output	1987 Intermediate Consumption	1987 Value Added	1988 Gross Output	1988 Intermediate Consumption	1988 Value Added
3 Manufacturing	...	...	695	...	...	471	...	...	857	...	...	532
A Manufacture of food, beverages and tobacco	...	...	361	...	...	110	...	...	134	...	...	127
B Textile, wearing apparel and leather industries	...	...	3	...	...	4	...	...	4	...	...	4
C Manufacture of wood and wood products, including furniture	...	...	219	...	...	247	...	...	265	...	...	276
D Manufacture of paper and paper products, printing and publishing	...	...	56	...	...	54	...	...	61	...	...	61
E Manufacture of chemicals and chemical petroleum, coal, rubber and plastic products	...	...	17	...	...	18	...	...	21	...	...	22
F Manufacture of non-metallic mineral products, except products of petroleum and coal	...	...	...	...	...	...	...	...	...	...	...	...
G Basic metal industries	...	...	7	...	...	7	...	...	8	...	...	8
H Manufacture of fabricated metal products, machinery and equipment	...	...	...	...	...	...	...	...	...	...	...	...
I Other manufacturing industries	...	...	32	...	...	33	...	...	365	...	...	34
4 Electricity, gas and water	...	...	977	...	...	762	...	...	685	...	...	1119
5 Construction	...	...	1921	...	...	1783	...	...	2425	...	...	3070
6 Wholesale and retail trade, restaurants and hotels	...	...	3211	...	...	2922	...	...	3364	...	...	4735
A Wholesale and retail trade	...	...	3001	...	...	2708	...	...	3146	...	...	4512
B Restaurants and hotels	...	...	210	...	...	214	...	...	218	...	...	224
Restaurants	...	...	107	...	...	109	...	...	111	...	...	115
Hotels and other lodging places	...	...	103	...	...	105	...	...	107	...	...	109
7 Transport, storage and communication	...	...	1098	...	...	878	...	...	632	...	...	760
A Transport and storage	...	...	858	...	...	633	...	...	390	...	...	519
B Communication	...	...	240	...	...	245	...	...	242	...	...	241
8 Finance, insurance, real estate and business services	...	...	862	...	...	886	...	...	918	...	...	947
A Financial institutions	...	...	236	...	...	242	...	...	246	...	...	251
B Insurance	...	...	578	...	...	590	...	...	602	...	...	617
C Real estate and business services	...	...	48	...	...	54	...	...	71	...	...	80
9 Community, social and personal services	...	...	3257	...	...	2970	...	...	3070	...	...	3658
A Sanitary and similar services	...	...	...	...	...	...	...	...	...	...	...	...
B Social and related community services	...	...	2617	...	...	2312	...	...	2379	...	...	2936
Educational services	...	...	1681	...	...	1397	...	...	1415	...	...	1844
Medical, dental, other health and veterinary services	...	...	936	...	...	915	...	...	964	...	...	1092
C Recreational and cultural services	...	...	18	...	...	18	...	...	19	...	...	19
D Personal and household services	...	...	624	...	...	639	...	...	673	...	...	703
Total, Industries	...	...	33716	...	...	32780	...	...	35097	...	...	37182
Producers of Government Services	...	...	2712	...	...	2892	...	...	3241	...	...	5201
Other Producers	...	...	...	...	...	...	...	...	...	...	...	...
Total	...	...	36428	...	...	35672	...	...	38338	...	...	42383
Less: Imputed bank service charge	...	...	...	...	...	...	...	...	...	...	...	...
Import duties	...	...	2328	...	...	2064	...	...	1878	...	...	1529
Value added tax	...	...	...	...	...	...	...	...	...	...	...	...
Total	...	...	38756	...	...	37736	...	...	40216	...	...	43912

Equatorial Guinea

4.1 Derivation of Value Added by Kind of Activity, in Current Prices

Million CFA francs

	1989 Gross Output	1989 Intermediate Consumption	1989 Value Added
All Producers			
1 Agriculture, hunting, forestry and fishing	...	...	22991
A Agriculture and hunting	...	...	18121
B Forestry and logging	...	...	3891
C Fishing	...	...	979
2 Mining and quarrying	...	...	...
3 Manufacturing	...	...	545
A Manufacture of food, beverages and tobacco	...	...	127
B Textile, wearing apparel and leather industries	...	...	4
C Manufacture of wood and wood products, including furniture	...	...	284
D Manufacture of paper and paper products, printing and publishing	...	...	62
E Manufacture of chemicals and chemical petroleum, coal, rubber and plastic products	...	...	23
F Manufacture of non-metallic mineral products, except products of petroleum and coal	...	...	...
G Basic metal industries	...	...	8
H Manufacture of fabricated metal products, machinery and equipment	...	...	...
I Other manufacturing industries	...	...	35
4 Electricity, gas and water	...	...	1277
5 Construction	...	...	2402
6 Wholesale and retail trade, restaurants and hotels	...	...	3594
A Wholesale and retail trade	...	...	3365
B Restaurants and hotels	...	...	230
Restaurants	...	...	118
Hotels and other lodging places	...	...	112
7 Transport, storage and communication	...	...	823
A Transport and storage	...	...	453
B Communication	...	...	370
8 Finance, insurance, real estate and business services	...	...	966
A Financial institutions	...	...	254
B Insurance	...	...	629
C Real estate and business services	...	...	83
9 Community, social and personal services	...	...	3924
A Sanitary and similar services	...	...	...
B Social and related community services	...	...	3196
Educational services	...	...	2091
Medical, dental, other health and veterinary services	...	...	1105
C Recreational and cultural services	...	...	20
D Personal and household services	...	...	708
Total, Industries	...	...	36522
Producers of Government Services	...	...	5093
Other Producers	...	...	...
Total	...	...	41615
Less: Imputed bank service charge	...	...	...
Import duties	...	...	1309
Value added tax	...	...	...
Total	...	...	42923

Ethiopia

General note. The preparation of national accounts statistics in Ethiopia is undertaken by the Central Statistical Office, Addis Ababa. The official estimates with methodological notes are published annually in the 'Statistical Abstract'. The estimates are generally in accordance with the classifications and definitions recommended in the United Nations Systems of National Accounts (SNA). The following tables have been prepared from successive replies to the United Nations national accounts questionnaire. The Ethiopian Fiscal year which is from June to July has been used for all estimates except the 'External Transactions' table. When the scope and coverage of the estimates differ for conceptual or statistical reasons from the definitions and classifications recommended in SNA, a footnote is indicated to the relevant tables.

Sources and methods:

(a) Gross domestic product. Gross domestic product is estimated mainly through the production approach.

(b) Expenditure on the gross domestic product. The expenditure approach is used to estimate government final consumption expenditure and exports and imports of goods and services. This approach, in combination with the commodity-flow approach, is also used for estimating gross fixed capital formation. Private consumption expenditure is obtained as a residual which also includes increase in stocks. Government final consumption expenditure, consisting of compensation of employees and net purchases of goods and services, is obtained from the annual Budgetary Revenue and Expenditure report, from the Ministry of Finance and from municipalities. These sources are also used for estimating the public sector's capital formation in building and construction. The estimates of private construction in urban areas are based on building permits which are adjusted for timing by taking the average of the last two years and adding 5 percent for underreporting. Other urban private construction is estimated by applying the ratio of per capita consumption expenditure in Addis Ababa to the per capita consumption expenditure in other urban areas. Construction in the rural areas is estimated by multiplying the assumed number of tukuls built in a given year by an assumed average cost per tukul. For capital formation in machinery and equipment, import statistics are used. To the import values are added import duties, transport costs, trade margins and installation costs. The data on exports and imports of goods and services are obtained from the external trade statistics. GDP by expenditure type at constant prices is not estimated.

(c) Cost-structure of the gross domestic product. The cost-structure of the gross domestic product is not estimated.

(d) Gross domestic product by kind of economic activity. The table of GDP by kind of economic activity is prepared in factor values. The production approach is used to estimate value added of most industries. The income approach is also used in measuring the output of the modern sectors of the economy such as the industrial activity and the services sectors. The estimates of the value added of agriculture for the bench-mark years 1961-1963 are based on various sources such as population figures, assumed per capita consumption of food grains and wholesale prices. Recent years' estimates are also based on qualitative crop surveys and surveys on cultivated area. The net output by type of plant product is multiplied by wholesale prices adjusted for trade and transport margins. The 1961-1963 bench-mark estimates of livestock production were based on the number of livestock by type, on gross output and on value added. For subsequent years, gross output and value added are derived by applying growth factors linked to the population growth rate. For forestry, the sources include the Forestry Dept., the survey of wood working industries, family budget studies in 1967/68 and the annual surveys of manufacturing industries. Value added is derived by deducting 10 percent from gross value of production of industrial wood and firewood. The Ministry of Mines and the annual budgetary reports provide data for the mining sector. The value of production is estimated by multiplying the quantity produced of each mineral product by its average price. The source of data for large-scale manufacturing is the annual surveys of manufacturing industries. Values added is obtained by deducting the cost of inputs of raw materials, fuel and energy from the gross value of production. For small scale manufacturing and handicraft, value added is derived by assuming that the growth rate is half of the one observed for output of large-scale manufacturing. Data for electricity are obtained from annual returns to questionnaires submitted to concerned enterprises. Data on the number of building permits issued, the 1968 household expenditure survey and population estimates are used to estimate the value of construction in the private sector. The total value of Addis Ababa building permits is adjusted for timing and underreporting. Work done in other towns is estimated by applying the ratio of per capita consumption expenditure in Addis Ababa to the per capita consumption expenditure in other towns. For the public sector, data are obtained from the Budgetary Revenue and Expenditure reports as well as from questionnaires sent to municipalities and public agencies. The gross trade margin of imported goods is estimated at 15 percent of the value of imports based on the 1963 trade inquiry. Similar assumptions are made for locally produced goods. Value added in the transport sector is based on the annual reports of concerned enterprises for the railway, water and air transports. For road transport, data on passenger or ton kilometres, registration statistics, and passenger fares and freight rates are used. For the financial institutions the profit and loss statement and the annual reports of concerned institutions are used. Bench-mark estimates for 1961-1963 are available for ownership of dwellings. The gross rental income of the urban areas is obtained by multiplying the total number of housing units by assumed actual and imputed average annual rental rates, while for the rural areas the total number of tukuls is multiplied by the assumed average value per tukul. Value added of public administration and defence is equal to total wages and salaries paid to government employees, including payment in kind. The sources of data include annual reports and questionnaires sent to different agencies. For other government services such as education and health, value added is based on government reports. Value added per student enrolled in non-governmental schools is estimated as two-thirds of the value added per student in government schools. The value of domestic services is obtained by multiplying the number of employees by assumed average pay rates. For the constant price estimates, the current net output of plant products in the agricultural sector is revalued at base-year producer prices. For livestock, water supply and construction, value added at current factor costs is assumed to be equal to the value added at constant factor costs. Price indexes are used to deflate the current value added of mining and quarrying, small-scale manufacturing, trade, finance and most of the services sectors. For large-scale manufacturing, electricity, transport and domestic services, value added is extrapolated by volume indexes.

1.1 Expenditure on the Gross Domestic Product, in Current Prices

Million Ethiopian birr — Fiscal year ending 7 July

	1970	1975	1980	1981	1982	1983	1984	1985	1986	1987	1988	1989
1 Government final consumption expenditure	443.4	730.1	1293.2	1399.5	1486.8	1732.5	1841.4	1924.0	2045.2	2141.9	2330.5	3162.5
2 Private final consumption expenditure	3519.1	4406.9	6794.6	7076.6	7346.7	8027.4	7919.9	7686.5	8545.8	8672.0	8920.9	8732.1
3 Gross capital formation	512.5	579.7	854.0	921.8	1081.7	1119.4	1283.7	1382.1	1378.4	1633.2	1804.8	1661.2
A Increase in stocks	...	...	...	...	...	...	...	...	...	...	...	...
B Gross fixed capital formation	512.5	579.7	854.0	921.8	1081.7	1119.4	1283.7	1382.1	1378.4	1633.2	1804.8	1661.2
Residential buildings	171.5	217.1	...	...	...	...	...	...	...	...	...	...
Non-residential buildings	31.7	79.2	...	...	...	...	...	...	...	...	...	...
Other construction and land improvement etc.	141.3	85.8	...	...	...	...	...	...	...	...	...	...
Other	168.0	197.6	...	...	...	...	...	...	...	...	...	...
4 Exports of goods and services	489.5	683.1	1209.5	1147.2	1076.2	1142.2	1266.6	1136.8	1371.0	1289.6	1302.5	1469.3
5 Less: Imports of goods and services	503.9	875.3	1652.4	1642.3	1824.2	1990.7	2310.6	2239.7	2507.9	2540.9	2591.7	2534.1
Equals: Gross Domestic Product	4460.6	5524.5	8498.9	8902.8	9167.2	10030.8	10001.0	9889.6	10832.5	11195.8	11767.0	12491.0

1.10 Gross Domestic Product by Kind of Activity, in Current Prices

Million Ethiopian birr — Fiscal year ending 7 July

	1970	1975	1980	1981	1982	1983	1984	1985	1986	1987	1988	1989
1 Agriculture, hunting, forestry and fishing	2327.2	2423.4	3906.9	4071.5	4061.8	4388.7	4070.2	3915.8	4354.5	4317.9	4326.7	4665.7
2 Mining and quarrying	9.4	12.6	8.1	8.1	9.6	9.7	12.3	15.1	15.3	12.3	13.5	14.3
3 Manufacturing	372.3	569.4	830.0	871.4	901.9	984.2	1009.2	1023.0	1072.9	1167.3	1199.5	1230.1
4 Electricity, gas and water	29.9	40.5	55.4	58.0	59.3	62.0	67.6	73.6	109.9	134.8	143.6	159.0
5 Construction	190.0	232.3	295.9	320.8	325.8	346.0	387.3	383.3	397.6	422.6	418.8	439.8

Ethiopia

1.10 Gross Domestic Product by Kind of Activity, in Current Prices
(Continued)

Million Ethiopian birr — Fiscal year ending 7 July

	1970	1975	1980	1981	1982	1983	1984	1985	1986	1987	1988	1989
6 Wholesale and retail trade, restaurants and hotels [a]	350.6	522.7	812.2	853.4	893.4	980.4	997.5	962.1	1036.3	1056.9	1068.0	1121.2
7 Transport, storage and communication	202.1	272.9	355.1	364.8	443.9	523.1	564.9	614.0	718.1	713.0	721.4	783.0
8 Finance, insurance, real estate and business services [b]	214.1	306.5	444.7	498.0	490.2	544.4	510.4	542.9	577.4	624.6	704.8	668.7
9 Community, social and personal services [ab]	198.3	310.1	377.9	398.1	424.6	461.2	503.1	539.9	582.4	626.9	676.5	704.6
Total, Industries	3893.9	4690.4	7086.2	7444.1	7610.5	8299.7	8122.5	8069.7	8864.4	9076.3	9272.8	9786.4
Producers of Government Services	219.5	348.7	535.3	584.5	617.4	713.6	750.9	770.0	781.6	850.6	1142.0	1339.1
Other Producers	59.6	64.1	67.3	68.0	68.7	69.4	70.1	70.8	71.6	72.4	73.1	73.9
Subtotal [c]	4173.0	5103.2	7688.8	8096.6	8296.6	9082.7	8943.5	8910.5	9717.6	9999.3	10487.9	11199.4
Less: Imputed bank service charge	...	...	...	...	...	...	...	...	...	...	...	...
Plus: Import duties	...	...	...	...	...	...	...	...	...	...	...	...
Plus: Value added tax	...	...	...	...	...	...	...	...	...	...	...	...
Plus: Other adjustments [d]	287.6	421.3	845.1	806.2	870.6	948.1	1057.5	979.1	1114.9	1196.5	1279.1	1291.6
Equals: Gross Domestic Product	4460.6	5524.5	8533.9	8902.8	9167.2	10030.8	10001.0	9889.6	10832.5	11195.8	11767.0	12491.0

a) Restaurants and hotels are included in item 'Community, social and personal services'.
b) Business services are included in item 'Community, social and personal services'.
c) Gross domestic product in factor values.
d) Item 'Other adjustments' refers to indirect taxes net of subsidies.

1.11 Gross Domestic Product by Kind of Activity, in Constant Prices

Million Ethiopian birr — Fiscal year ending 7 July

At constant prices of: 1961 (1970); 1981 (1975–1989)

	1970	1975	1980	1981	1982	1983	1984	1985	1986	1987	1988	1989
1 Agriculture, hunting, forestry and fishing	1833.3	3640.1	3969.8	4071.5	4019.3	4208.9	3792.5	3176.0	3468.1	3968.9	3938.3	4060.1
2 Mining and quarrying	9.2	10.8	8.1	8.1	9.4	9.1	11.6	14.1	14.2	11.4	12.5	13.2
3 Manufacturing	308.7	666.1	834.3	871.4	905.3	956.2	988.1	998.3	1042.2	1093.0	1117.9	1139.6
4 Electricity, gas and water	33.6	46.3	55.6	58.0	65.2	69.4	74.5	81.2	85.6	91.9	98.1	102.0
5 Construction	190.0	306.0	319.2	320.8	317.3	330.1	362.5	353.0	358.7	371.5	359.1	359.7
6 Wholesale and retail trade, restaurants and hotels [a]	296.6	807.6	828.5	853.4	878.9	934.3	938.4	887.4	938.6	1013.2	1014.6	1041.3
7 Transport, storage and communication	195.3	290.1	350.9	364.8	385.1	411.9	429.2	469.2	525.6	526.9	551.5	577.8
8 Finance, insurance, real estate and business services [b]	183.8	359.2	466.2	498.0	520.5	550.1	522.1	533.1	560.7	590.4	647.7	605.9
9 Community, social and personal services [ab]	159.1	331.0	390.0	398.1	420.4	441.5	466.8	488.1	516.6	543.2	574.2	588.1
Total, Industries	3209.6	6457.2	7222.6	7444.1	7521.4	7911.5	7585.7	7000.4	7510.3	8210.4	8313.9	8487.7
Producers of Government Services	182.2	406.4	564.7	584.5	602.7	648.9	659.3	665.8	672.5	710.6	930.7	1029.5
Other Producers	59.6	64.1	67.3	68.0	68.7	69.4	70.1	70.8	71.6	72.4	73.1	73.9
Subtotal [c]	3451.4	6927.7	7854.6	8096.6	8192.8	8629.8	8315.1	7737.0	8254.4	8993.4	9317.7	9591.1
Less: Imputed bank service charge	...	...	...	...	...	...	...	...	...	...	...	...
Plus: Import duties	...	...	...	...	...	...	...	...	...	...	...	...
Plus: Value added tax	...	...	...	...	...	...	...	...	...	...	...	...
Equals: Gross Domestic Product [c]	3451.4	6927.7	7854.6	8096.6	8192.8	8629.8	8315.1	7737.0	8254.4	8993.4	9317.7	9591.1

a) Restaurants and hotels are included in item 'Community, social and personal services'.
b) Business services are included in item 'Community, social and personal services'.
c) Gross domestic product in factor values.

Fiji

General note. The preparation of national accounts statistics in Fiji is undertaken by the Bureau of Statistics, Suva. The official estimates together with methodological notes are published in a series of reports entitled 'National Accounts Studies'. The third volume of this series, 'The National Accounts of Fiji 1968-1972', contains a detailed description of the sources and methods used for the national accounts estimation. The estimates are generally in accordance with the classifications and definitions recommended in the United Nations System of National Accounts (SNA). Input-output tables have been compiled for the years 1966 and 1967. The 1967 tables were published in 1970 in 'An Input-Output Table for Fiji 1967'. The following tables have been prepared from successive replies to the United Nations national accounts questionnaire. When the scope and coverage of the estimates differ for conceptual or statistical reasons from the definitions and classifications recommended in SNA, a footnote is indicated to the relevant tables.

Sources and methods:

(a) Gross domestic product. Gross domestic product is estimated mainly through the production approach.

(b) Expenditure on the gross domestic product. All components of GDP by expenditure type are estimated through the expenditure approach except private final consumption expenditure which is mostly based on the commodity-flow approach. The estimates of government final consumption expenditure are based on the annual report 'An Economic and Functional Classification of Government Accounts'. For private consumption expenditure estimates, all imported items valued at landed cost from foreign trade statistics and producers' values from industrial censuses are grossed up by margins established in the 1970 Census of Distribution and Services. Special estimates are made for those items after consumer expenditure, such as food, electricity, gas and water, medical services and recreations, which are not covered by the commodity-flow approach. For these estimates data from the household budget survey in 1972, income tax statistics and the 1970 census of distribution are used. Estimates of gross capital formation for private industry are based on surveys of capital investment, for government industry and producers of government services the estimates are derived from government account and for the producers of private non-profit services to households from the 1970/1971 survey of non-profit making institutions. Value of imports and exports of goods and services are obtained from the balance of payments and annual shipping and aircraft statistics. For the constant price estimates, the current values of expenditure items are deflated by various price indexes such as consumer price index, index of rural produce prices, implicit price index of value added of building and construction, trade index of exports, etc.

(c) Cost-structure of the gross domestic product. Estimates of the cost-structure of GDP are made from the various sectoral surveys and taxation data. Estimates of indirect taxes and subsidies are based on government accounts.

(d) Gross domestic product by kind of economic activity. The table of GDP by kind of economic activity is prepared at market price, i.e. producers' values. The production approach is used to estimate value added of most industries, such as agriculture, mining, manufacturing, electricity, gas and water, construction, and for the trade sector in combination with the commodity-flow approach. The income approach is used to estimate value added of restaurants and hotels and most of the sub-sectors of the service industries. For agricultural sector, the total output of sugar-cane and copra are estimated from material inputs revealed by annual industrial censuses. The bench-mark estimates of substance output is based on the 1968 Agricultural Census, the 1965 Rural-Urban Household Expenditure Survey and Bureau of Statistics Data. The annual increases are based on estimates of population growth and an index of rural produce prices. For other agricultural produce gross output is based on 1968 and 1972 household budget surveys and intermediate consumption is based on case studies. The gross output and intermediate consumption of the industrial activity sectors are based on annual industrial censuses carried out since 1970. Estimates of gross output, intermediate consumption and compensation of employees of private construction are obtained from annual censuses of building and construction conducted annually since 1970. Government bodies engaged in construction are covered through their annual reports and operating budgets. For the trade sector, the estimates are based on statistics from the Inland Revenue Departments and on the Census of Distribution 1970. The producers' values and c.i.f. import values are grossed up by the margin established in the 1970 Census of Distribution. Banking estimates are obtained from income tax statistics while insurance estimates are derived from annual surveys. Imputed rent per urban household is derived from the household budget survey in 1968, grossed up by the consumer price index for rent and the growth in urban population. For rural areas, an estimated rent has been assumed in 1968 and grossed up annually by a rural price factor and growth in rural population. Estimates for producers of government services are based on the operating budgets and government accounts and finance. Other services estimates are derived from income tax statistics, the 1970/71 survey of non-profit institutions and 1970 Census of Distribution and Services. For the constant price estimates, the general approach used for the major crops of agriculture, industrial activity, transport, insurance and private services is extrapolated. Value added is extrapolated by production indexes. Price deflation is used for construction, trade, restaurants and hotels, real estate, banking and producers of government services, the current value being deflated by various price indexes such as consumer price index, index of wage rates, etc.

1.1 Expenditure on the Gross Domestic Product, in Current Prices

Million Fiji dollars

	1970	1975	1980	1981	1982	1983	1984	1985	1986	1987	1988	1989
1 Government final consumption expenditure	27	67	157	173	204	232	245	252	253	253	225	...
2 Private final consumption expenditure	125	382	575	660	685	748	794	838	873	960	1093	...
3 Gross capital formation	43	116	313	362	285	241	241	251	266	215	200	...
A Increase in stocks	8	13	63	82	22	2	23	12	51	5	12	...
B Gross fixed capital formation	35	103	250	280	263	239	218	239	215	210	188	...
Residential buildings	15	...	...	...	...	...	...	...	...	...	...	...
Non-residential buildings	...	...	...	...	...	...	...	...	...	...	...	...
Other construction and land improvement etc.	4	...	...	...	...	...	...	...	...	...	...	...
Other	16	...	...	...	...	...	...	...	...	...	...	...
4 Exports of goods and services	93	242	477	454	481	498	546	584	609	658	849	...
5 Less: Imports of goods and services	99	245	511	606	553	560	560	589	577	618	812	...
Statistical discrepancy	4	-	-27	13	11	-17	9	-20	38	-22	-17	...
Equals: Gross Domestic Product	192	562	984	1056	1113	1142	1275	1316	1462	1446	1538	...

1.2 Expenditure on the Gross Domestic Product, in Constant Prices

Million Fiji dollars

	1970	1975	1980	1981	1982	1983	1984	1985	1986	1987	1988	1989
		At constant prices of:										
		1968					1977					
1 Government final consumption expenditure	25	35	... / 123	119	132	136	149	150	150	166	163	...
2 Private final consumption expenditure	113	185	... / 423	438	426	442	444	462	448	471	500	...
3 Gross capital formation	36	49	... / 239	254	187	153	146	145	149	105	99	...
A Increase in stocks	7	7	... / 48	56	14	1	15	7	27	2	6	...
B Gross fixed capital formation	29	42	... / 191	198	173	152	131	138	122	103	93	...

Fiji

1.2 Expenditure on the Gross Domestic Product, in Constant Prices
(Continued)

Million Fiji dollars

	1970	1975	1980	1981	1982	1983	1984	1985	1986	1987	1988	1989
		1968			At constant prices of:			1977				
Residential buildings	11	...	...	...	...	...	...	...	...	...	...	...
Non-residential buildings	...	...	...	...	...	...	...	...	...	...	...	...
Other construction and land improvement etc.	3	...	...	...	...	...	...	...	...	...	...	...
Other	15	...	...	...	...	...	...	...	...	...	...	...
4 Exports of goods and services	79	91	341	334	341	331	367	399	374	349	414	...
5 Less: Imports of goods and services	90	133	349	369	328	355	337	343	369	336	437	...
Statistical discrepancy	5	-	-35	14	14	43	43	-33	83	29	51	...
Equals: Gross Domestic Product	169	227	742	790	772	750	812	780	835	784	788	...

1.3 Cost Components of the Gross Domestic Product

Million Fiji dollars

	1970	1975	1980	1981	1982	1983	1984	1985	1986	1987	1988	1989
1 Indirect taxes, net	23	46	83	102	93	110	124	139	136	135	153	...
A Indirect taxes	23	47	85	104	94	111	125	140	137	136	...	...
B Less: Subsidies	-	1	2	2	1	1	1	1	1	-	...	...
2 Consumption of fixed capital	9	...	64	77	88	93	88	95	103	112	125	...
3 Compensation of employees paid by resident producers to:	73	...	426	483	531	559	608	596	641	583	645	...
4 Operating surplus	87	...	411	394	401	380	455	487	582	616	615	...
Equals: Gross Domestic Product	192	562	984	1056	1113	1142	1275	1317	1462	1446	1538	...

1.4 General Government Current Receipts and Disbursements

Million Fiji dollars

	1970	1975	1980	1981	1982	1983	1984	1985	1986	1987	1988	1989
					Receipts							
1 Operating surplus	...	...	...	...	...	...	...	...	...	...	...	...
2 Property and entrepreneurial income	...	...	19	20	20	20	18	23	25	32	...	...
3 Taxes, fees and contributions	...	...	200	229	227	257	298	304	297	286	...	...
A Indirect taxes	...	...	84	104	94	111	125	140	136	136	...	...
B Direct taxes	...	...	105	114	121	131	154	147	144	135	...	...
C Social security contributions	...	...	-	-	-	-	-	1	-	-	...	...
D Compulsory fees, fines and penalties	...	...	11	12	12	14	19	19	15	15	...	...
4 Other current transfers	...	...	30	29	35	38	31	40	31	32	...	...
Total Current Receipts of General Government	...	...	250	278	283	314	346	367	353	350	...	...
					Disbursements							
1 Government final consumption expenditure	...	...	157	173	204	232	246	252	253	253	...	...
2 Property income	...	...	17	24	30	35	41	45	51	59	...	...
A Interest	...	...	17	24	30	35	41	45	51	59	...	...
B Net land rent and royalties	...	...	-	-	-	-	-	-	-	-	...	...
3 Subsidies	...	...	1	1	1	1	1	1	1	-	...	...
4 Other current transfers	...	...	20	25	30	33	50	43	43	48	...	...
A Social security benefits	...	...	2	2	3	3	3	2	4	6	...	...
B Social assistance grants	...	...									...	...
C Other	...	...	18	22	27	30	46	40	39	42	...	...
5 Net saving	...	...	55	56	17	13	9	26	6	-10	...	...
Total Current Disbursements and Net Saving of General Government	...	...	250	278	283	314	346	367	353	350	...	...

Fiji

1.7 External Transactions on Current Account, Summary

Million Fiji dollars	1970	1975	1980	1981	1982	1983	1984	1985	1986	1987	1988	1989
Payments to the Rest of the World												
1 Imports of goods and services	...	...	511	606	553	560	560	589	577	618	812	...
2 Factor income to the rest of the world	...	...	33	36	55	49	53	53	56	62	68	...
A Compensation of employees	...	...	-	-	-	-	-	-	-	-	-	...
B Property and entrepreneurial income	...	...	33	36	55	49	53	53	56	62	68	...
3 Current transfers to the rest of the world	...	...	26	24	24	23	25	34	33	46	36	...
4 Surplus of the nation on current transactions	...	...	-41	-165	-107	-87	-45	-47	-7	-18	11	...
Payments to the Rest of the World and Surplus of the Nation on Current Transactions	...	...	529	501	525	545	593	629	659	708	927	...
Receipts From The Rest of the World												
1 Exports of goods and services	...	...	477	454	481	498	546	584	609	658	849	...
2 Factor income from rest of the world	...	...	18	27	21	21	23	16	22	26	41	...
A Compensation of employees	...	...	3	7	6	7	10	7	8	10	19	...
B Property and entrepreneurial income	...	...	15	20	15	14	13	9	14	16	22	...
3 Current transfers from rest of the world	...	...	34	20	23	26	24	29	28	24	37	...
Receipts from the Rest of the World on Current Transactions	...	...	529	501	525	545	593	629	659	708	927	...

1.10 Gross Domestic Product by Kind of Activity, in Current Prices

Million Fiji dollars	1970	1975	1980	1981	1982	1983	1984	1985	1986	1987	1988	1989
1 Agriculture, hunting, forestry and fishing	47	...	200	190	207	190	220	216	277	305	280	...
2 Mining and quarrying	3	...	-2	1	6	6	1	14	18	31	39	...
3 Manufacturing	24	...	108	100	109	94	110	111	137	157	137	...
4 Electricity, gas and water	2	...	15	20	22	27	41	41	48	44	57	...
5 Construction	11	...	73	82	81	75	66	64	64	61	50	...
6 Wholesale and retail trade, restaurants and hotels	32	...	162	188	181	183	204	210	223	208	273	...
7 Transport, storage and communication	10	...	80	86	90	98	108	122	132	139	152	...
8 Finance, insurance, real estate and business services	21	...	112	126	139	141	152	166	182	182	197	...
9 Community, social and personal services	3	...	107	121	134	153	166	160	170	144	164	...
Total, Industries	153	...	855	914	969	967	1068	1104	1251	1271	1349	...
Producers of Government Services	16	...	61	68	82	90	101	94	113	82	90	...
Other Producers	6	...	16	17	18	22	23	27	27	27	31	...
Subtotal a	175	...	932	999	1069	1079	1192	1225	1391	1380	1470	...
Less: Imputed bank service charge	2	...	31	45	49	47	41	47	65	70	85	...
Plus: Import duties	19	...	...	...	...	...	...	...	...	...	...	...
Plus: Value added tax	...	...	...	...	...	...	...	...	136	136	153	...
Plus: Other adjustments b	...	...	83	102	93	110	124	139	136	136	153	...
Equals: Gross Domestic Product	192	562	984	1056	1113	1142	1275	1316	1462	1446	1538	...

a) Gross domestic product in factor values.
b) Item 'Other adjustments' refers to indirect taxes net of subsidies.

1.11 Gross Domestic Product by Kind of Activity, in Constant Prices

Million Fiji dollars	1970	1975	1980	1981	1982	1983	1984	1985	1986	1987	1988	1989
	At constant prices of: 1968						1977					
1 Agriculture, hunting, forestry and fishing	40	40	153	172	175	144	181	156	186	173	169	190
2 Mining and quarrying	3	2	-	-	1	1	1	1	1	1	2	2
3 Manufacturing	19	20	81	89	86	78	91	79	95	84	83	93
4 Electricity, gas and water	2	3	7	7	7	7	8	8	9	9	9	10
5 Construction	8	9	60	60	53	51	40	38	40	34	26	35

Fiji

1.11 Gross Domestic Product by Kind of Activity, in Constant Prices
(Continued)

Million Fiji dollars

	1970	1975	1980	1981	1982	1983	1984	1985	1986	1987	1988	1989
		1968			At constant prices of:			1977				
6 Wholesale and retail trade, restaurants and hotels	30	43	... 117	126	113	122	122	125	136	117	130	168
7 Transport, storage and communication	10	17	... 67	71	78	78	88	90	90	88	95	104
8 Finance, insurance, real estate and business services	20	32	... 84	88	91	94	96	98	98	95	96	99
9 Community, social and personal services	2	2	... 128	127	128	131	136	132	131	136	135	137
Total, Industries	133	171	... 697	740	732	706	763	727	786	737	745	838
Producers of Government Services	15	25	...	...	...	...	...	...	...	...	...	...
Other Producers	5	8	...	...	...	...	...	...	...	...	...	...
Subtotal	153	204	... 697[a]	740[a]	732[a]	706[a]	763[a]	727[a]	786[a]	737[a]	745[a]	838[a]
Less: Imputed bank service charge	2	2	... 18	20	20	22	22	23	24	22	23	24
Plus: Import duties	17	25	...	...	...	...	...	...	...	...	...	...
Plus: Value added tax	...	...	...	...	...	...	...	...	...	...	...	...
Plus: Other adjustments	...	...	63[b]	70[b]	60[b]	66[b]	71[b]	76[b]	73[b]	69[b]	66[b]	83[b]
Equals: Gross Domestic Product	169	227	... 742	790	772	750	812	780	835	784	788	897

a) Gross domestic product in factor values.
b) Item 'Other adjustments' refers to indirect taxes net of subsidies.

1.12 Relations Among National Accounting Aggregates

Million Fiji dollars

	1970	1975	1980	1981	1982	1983	1984	1985	1986	1987	1988	1989
Gross Domestic Product	192	562	984	1056	1113	1142	1275	1316	1462	1446	1538	...
Plus: Net factor income from the rest of the world	-8	...	-15	-9	-34	-28	-30	-36	-34	-36	-27	...
Factor income from the rest of the world	...	...	18	27	21	21	23	16	22	26	41	...
Less: Factor income to the rest of the world	...	...	33	36	55	49	53	53	56	62	68	...
Equals: Gross National Product	184	...	969	1047	1079	1114	1245	1280	1427	1410	1512	...
Less: Consumption of fixed capital	9	...	65	78	88	80	88	95	103	112	125	...
Equals: National Income	175	...	904	969	991	1034	1157	1185	1324	1298	1387	...
Plus: Net current transfers from the rest of the world	2	-	8	-4	-1	3	-1	-6	-5	-22	1	...
Current transfers from the rest of the world	...	...	34	20	23	26	24	28	28	24	37	...
Less: Current transfers to the rest of the world	...	...	26	24	24	23	25	34	33	46	36	...
Equals: National Disposable Income	177	...	912	965	990	1037	1156	1179	1319	1276	1388	...
Less: Final consumption	152	449	732	833	888	980	1039	1091	1126	1212	1318	...
Equals: Net Saving	25	...	180	132	102	57	117	88	193	64	70	...
Less: Surplus of the nation on current transactions	-9	...	-41	-166	-107	-88	-45	-47	-8	-18	11	...
Statistical discrepancy	...	...	27	-13	-12	17	-9	20	-37	22	17	...
Equals: Net Capital Formation	34	...	248	285	197	162	153	155	164	104	76	...

2.1 Government Final Consumption Expenditure by Function, in Current Prices

Million Fiji dollars

	1970	1975	1980	1981	1982	1983	1984	1985	1986	1987	1988	1989
1 General public services	7	14	24	27	31	44	41	54	41	40	...	...
2 Defence	-	1	8	9	14	14	15	15	15	26	...	...
3 Public order and safety	...	...	12	13	14	16	18	18	20	20	...	...
4 Education	6	18	47	53	60	67	74	70	70	69	...	...
5 Health	4	8	19	22	26	30	33	31	32	32	...	...

Fiji

2.1 Government Final Consumption Expenditure by Function, in Current Prices
(Continued)

Million Fiji dollars

	1970	1975	1980	1981	1982	1983	1984	1985	1986	1987	1988	1989
6 Social security and welfare	-	-	1	1	1	1	1	1	1	1	...	...
7 Housing and community amenities	1	1	3	2	3	3	3	4	5	4	...	...
8 Recreational, cultural and religious affairs	1	1	1	1	1	2	1	2	2	2	...	...
9 Economic services	9	20	42	45	54	55	59	57	67	59	...	...
A Fuel and energy	...	...	-	-	-	-	-	-	-	-	...	...
B Agriculture, forestry, fishing and hunting	...	...	5	5	8	7	7	7	16	9	...	...
C Mining, manufacturing and construction, except fuel and energy	...	...	8	8	10	10	11	13	20	18	...	...
D Transportation and communication	...	...	14	15	14	17	18	17	16	15	...	...
E Other economic affairs	...	...	15	17	22	21	23	20	15	17	...	...
10 Other functions	...	...	...	...	...	...	...	...	...	...	...	...
Total Government Final Consumption Expenditure	28	63	157	173	204	232	245	252	253	253	...	...

2.5 Private Final Consumption Expenditure by Type and Purpose, in Current Prices

Million Fiji dollars

	1970	1975	1980	1981	1982	1983	1984	1985	1986	1987	1988	1989
			Final Consumption Expenditure of Resident Households									
1 Food, beverages and tobacco	39	133	177	213	225	246	262	273	281	289	342	...
A Food	30	92	135	165	174	191	200	210	216	225	263	...
B Non-alcoholic beverages	1	3	9	10	11	12	16	17	16	13	17	...
C Alcoholic beverages	4	24	20	24	24	26	28	28	29	31	38	...
D Tobacco	5	15	13	14	16	17	18	18	20	20	24	...
2 Clothing and footwear	8	20	34	38	35	37	38	40	50	49	111	...
3 Gross rent, fuel and power	16	39	77	85	95	103	112	114	125	127	130	...
4 Furniture, furnishings and household equipment and operation	13	39	51	59	55	63	65	70	74	83	85	...
A Household operation	6	19	...	...	...	...	...	...	...	...	...	...
B Other	7	20	...	...	...	...	...	...	...	...	...	...
5 Medical care and health expenses	1	3	12	12	13	14	15	15	16	16	23	...
6 Transport and communication	14	48	72	88	88	97	107	110	111	120	123	...
A Personal transport equipment	2	6	...	...	...	...	...	...	...	...	...	...
B Other	11	42	...	...	...	...	...	...	...	...	...	...
7 Recreational, entertainment, education and cultural services	17	45	24	28	28	31	35	36	37	36	44	...
A Education	4	10	...	...	...	...	...	...	...	...	...	...
B Other	13	35	...	...	...	...	...	...	...	...	...	...
8 Miscellaneous goods and services	21	59	35	44	46	46	50	48	49	60	69	...
A Personal care	7	23	...	...	...	...	...	...	...	...	...	...
B Expenditures in restaurants, cafes and hotels	13	34	...	...	...	...	...	...	...	...	...	...
C Other	...	...	2	4	4	1	1	-2	-3	6	7	...
Statistical discrepancy	19	52	64	69	75	85	81	102	92	102	104	...
Total Final Consumption Expenditure in the Domestic Market by Households, of which	146	438	546	636	660	722	765	808	835	882	1031	...
A Durable goods	18	...	30	41	37	39	43	41	35	47	43	...
B Semi-durable goods	16	...	57	64	58	65	68	70	78	75	145	...
C Non-durable goods	65	...	293	346	365	397	413	445	453	483	551	...

Fiji

2.5 Private Final Consumption Expenditure by Type and Purpose, in Current Prices
(Continued)

Million Fiji dollars

	1970	1975	1980	1981	1982	1983	1984	1985	1986	1987	1988	1989
D Services	47	...	166	185	200	221	241	252	269	277	292	...
Plus: Direct purchases abroad by resident households	2	8	14	16	17	17	19	20	27	66	50	...
Less: Direct purchases in the domestic market by non-resident households	23	70	-	-	-	-	-	-	-	-	-	...
Equals: Final Consumption Expenditure of Resident Households	125	376	560	652	677	739	784	828	862	948	1081	...

Final Consumption Expenditure of Private Non-profit Institutions Serving Households

	1970	1975	1980	1981	1982	1983	1984	1985	1986	1987	1988	1989
Equals: Final Consumption Expenditure of Private Non-profit Organisations Serving Households	...	6	15	8	8	9	10	10	11	12	12	...
Private Final Consumption Expenditure	125	382	575	660	685	748	794	838	873	960	1093	...

2.6 Private Final Consumption Expenditure by Type and Purpose, in Constant Prices

Million Fiji dollars

	1970	1975	1980	1981	1982	1983	1984	1985	1986	1987	1988	1989

At constant prices of: 1977

Final Consumption Expenditure of Resident Households

1 Food, beverages and tobacco	...	...	146	156	144	151	150	148	147	140	160	...
A Food	...	...	114	123	113	120	120	120	116	113	129	...
B Non-alcoholic beverages	...	...	8	8	8	9	9	9	9	7	7	...
C Alcoholic beverages	...	...	15	16	14	13	12	11	14	13	16	...
D Tobacco	...	...	9	9	9	9	9	8	8	7	8	...
2 Clothing and footwear	...	...	20	19	21	23	23	24	20	18	39	...
3 Gross rent, fuel and power	...	...	48	47	49	50	51	52	51	54	55	...
4 Furniture, furnishings and household equipment and operation	...	...	34	38	36	38	38	46	46	47	46	...
5 Medical care and health expenses	...	...	10	7	7	7	8	7	7	6	8	...
6 Transport and communication	...	...	51	57	55	58	61	62	63	68	67	...
7 Recreational, entertainment, education and cultural services	...	...	19	20	19	20	22	22	18	17	20	...
8 Miscellaneous goods and services	...	...	24	30	30	29	29	28	25	29	30	...
A Personal care	...	...	...	...	...	...	...	...	...	...	...	...
B Expenditures in restaurants, cafes and hotels	...	...	...	...	...	...	...	...	...	...	...	...
C Other	...	...	...	...	3	1	1	1	-1	3	3	...
Statistical discrepancy	...	...	49	48	48	51	46	56	50	52	47	...
Total Final Consumption Expenditure in the Domestic Market by Households, of which	...	...	401	422	409	427	428	445	427	431	472	...
A Durable goods	...	...	24	27	23	23	26	29	23	28	25	...
B Semi-durable goods	...	...	32	35	43	39	39	39	34	30	52	...
C Non-durable goods	...	...	229	243	223	240	233	243	240	234	254	...
D Services	...	...	116	117	120	125	130	134	130	139	141	...
Plus: Direct purchases abroad by resident households	...	...	11	11	11	10	11	11	15	34	22	...
Less: Direct purchases in the domestic market by non-resident households	...	...	...	...	...	...	...	...	...	...	...	...
Equals: Final Consumption Expenditure of Resident Households	...	...	412	433	420	437	439	456	442	465	494	...

Final Consumption Expenditure of Private Non-profit Institutions Serving Households

Equals: Final Consumption Expenditure of Private Non-profit Organisations Serving Households	...	...	11	5	5	5	5	6	6	6	6	...
Private Final Consumption Expenditure	...	...	423	438	425	442	444	462	448	471	500	...

Fiji

2.7 Gross Capital Formation by Type of Good and Owner, in Current Prices
Million Fiji dollars

	1980				1981				1982			
	TOTAL	Total Private	Public Enterprises	General Government	TOTAL	Total Private	Public Enterprises	General Government	TOTAL	Total Private	Public Enterprises	General Government
Increase in stocks, total	63	60	2	1	82	81	1	-1	22	22	1	-1
1 Goods producing industries	13	11	2	-	8	7	1	-	14	13	-	-
A Materials and supplies	10	8	2	-	5	5	1	-	3	3	-	-
B Work in progress	10	10	-	-	5	5	-	-	-	-	-	-
C Livestock, except breeding stocks, dairy cattle, etc.	-	-	-	-	1	1	-	-	1	-	-	-
D Finished goods	-7	-7	-	-	-3	-3	-	-	10	10	-	-
2 Wholesale and retail trade	46	46	-	-	64	64	-	-	10	10	-	-
3 Other, except government stocks	4	4	-	-	10	10	-	-	-	-1	1	-
4 Government stocks	1	-	-	1	-1	-	-	-1	-1	-	-	-1
Gross Fixed Capital Formation, Total	250	134	70	45	280	139	77	64	263	113	88	61
Total Gross Capital Formation	313	195	72	46	362	220	78	64	285	135	90	60

	1983				1984			
	TOTAL	Total Private	Public Enterprises	General Government	TOTAL	Total Private	Public Enterprises	General Government
Increase in stocks, total	2	3	-	-	23	23	-	-
1 Goods producing industries	-7	-7	-	-	12	12	-	-
A Materials and supplies	3	3	-	-	-	-	-	-
B Work in progress	-1	-1	-	-	-	-	-	-
C Livestock, except breeding stocks, dairy cattle, etc.	-	-	-	-	-	-	-	-
D Finished goods	-9	-9	-	-	12	12	-	-
2 Wholesale and retail trade	9	8	-	-	6	6	-	-
3 Other, except government stocks	2	2	-	-	5	5	-	-
4 Government stocks	-	-	-	-	-	-	-	-
Gross Fixed Capital Formation, Total	239	112	91	36	218	131	49	38
Total Gross Capital Formation	242	115	91	36	241	154	49	38

2.9 Gross Capital Formation by Kind of Activity of Owner, ISIC Major Divisions, in Current Prices
Million Fiji dollars

	1980			1981			1982			1983		
	Total Gross Capital Formation	Increase in Stocks	Gross Fixed Capital Formation	Total Gross Capital Formation	Increase in Stocks	Gross Fixed Capital Formation	Total Gross Capital Formation	Increase in Stocks	Gross Fixed Capital Formation	Total Gross Capital Formation	Increase in Stocks	Gross Fixed Capital Formation
						All Producers						
1 Agriculture, hunting, fishing and forestry	17	-	17	16	1	15	10	1	9	11	-	11
2 Mining and quarrying	2	1	1	1	-	1	2	1	1	4	1	3
3 Manufacturing	32	-3	35	27	7	20	46	13	33	15	-7	22
4 Electricity, gas and water	72	1	71	94	-	94	97	-1	98	57	-	57
5 Construction	27	13	14	21	8	13	-9	-3	-6	2	-	2
6 Wholesale and retail trade, restaurants and hotels	66	46	20	88	64	24	36	10	26	23	8	15
7 Transport, storage and communication	31	-	31	37	3	34	30	-	30	42	-	42
8 Finance, insurance, real estate and business services	35	4	31	38	-	38	44	2	42	54	-	54
9 Community, social and personal services	31	1	30	40	-1	41	29	-1	30	33	-	33
Total Industries	312	63	250	362	82	280	285	22	263	241	2	239
Producers of Government Services	...	...	...	...	...	...	...	...	...	...	...	...
Private Non-Profit Institutions Serving Households	...	...	...	...	...	...	...	...	...	...	...	...
Total	313	63	250	362	82	280	285	22	263	241	2	239

Fiji

2.9 Gross Capital Formation by Kind of Activity of Owner, ISIC Major Divisions, in Current Prices

Million Fiji dollars

	1984 Total Gross Capital Formation	1984 Increase in Stocks	1984 Gross Fixed Capital Formation	1985 Total Gross Capital Formation	1985 Increase in Stocks	1985 Gross Fixed Capital Formation	1986 Total Gross Capital Formation	1986 Increase in Stocks	1986 Gross Fixed Capital Formation
All Producers									
1 Agriculture, hunting, fishing and forestry	10	-	10	12	-	12	11	-	11
2 Mining and quarrying	7	-	7	17	-	17	27	10	17
3 Manufacturing	30	12	18	21	-6	27	57	38	19
4 Electricity, gas and water	30	-	30	21	-	21	19	-	19
5 Construction	5	2	3	5	3	2	3	2	1
6 Wholesale and retail trade, restaurants and hotels	41	8	33	53	13	40	22	1	21
7 Transport, storage and communication	30	-	30	31	-	31	23	-	23
8 Finance, insurance, real estate and business services	52	1	51	50	-	50	64	1	63
9 Community, social and personal services	36	-	36	41	2	39	40	-1	41
Total Industries	241	23	218	251	12	239	266	51	215
Producers of Government Services	...	...	...	...	...	...	...	...	...
Private Non-Profit Institutions Serving Households	...	...	...	...	...	...	...	...	...
Total	241	23	218	251	12	239	266	51	215

4.1 Derivation of Value Added by Kind of Activity, in Current Prices

Million Fiji dollars

	1980 Gross Output	1980 Intermediate Consumption	1980 Value Added	1981 Gross Output	1981 Intermediate Consumption	1981 Value Added	1982 Gross Output	1982 Intermediate Consumption	1982 Value Added	1983 Gross Output	1983 Intermediate Consumption	1983 Value Added
All Producers												
1 Agriculture, hunting, forestry and fishing	248	48	200	247	57	190	266	59	207	249	59	190
A Agriculture and hunting	228	41	187	219	47	172	237	49	188	212	46	166
B Forestry and logging	11	4	7	10	4	6	10	3	7	12	4	8
C Fishing	9	3	6	18	6	12	19	7	12	25	9	16
2 Mining and quarrying	15	17	-2	17	16	1	19	13	6	24	18	6
A Coal mining	...	...	...	...	...	...	...	...	...	...	...	...
B Crude petroleum and natural gas production	...	...	...	...	...	...	...	...	...	...	...	...
C Metal ore mining	...	...	...	...	...	...	...	...	...	...	...	...
D Other mining	...	...	...	...	...	...	...	...	...	...	...	...
3 Manufacturing	427	319	108	426	326	100	455	346	109	400	306	94
A Manufacture of food, beverages and tobacco	301	235	66	293	236	57	323	253	70	248	204	44
B Textile, wearing apparel and leather industries	5	3	2	8	5	3	9	6	3	11	7	4
C Manufacture of wood and wood products, including furniture	30	19	11	29	20	9	24	16	8	29	19	10
D Manufacture of paper and paper products, printing and publishing	17	11	6	17	10	7	18	11	7	20	12	8
E Manufacture of chemicals and chemical petroleum, coal, rubber and plastic products	20	15	5	24	18	6	25	19	6	31	22	9
F Manufacture of non-metallic mineral products, except products of petroleum and coal	12	7	5	14	9	5	16	11	5	23	15	8
G Basic metal industries	...	...	...	...	...	...	...	...	...	...	...	...
H Manufacture of fabricated metal products, machinery and equipment	37	28	9	35	26	9	37	28	9	35	25	10
I Other manufacturing industries	5	1	4	6	2	4	3	2	1	3	2	1
4 Electricity, gas and water	40	25	15	49	29	20	56	34	22	54	27	27
5 Construction	149	76	73	174	92	82	181	100	81	170	95	75
6 Wholesale and retail trade, restaurants and hotels	248	86	162	307	119	188	306	125	181	314	131	183
A Wholesale and retail trade	183	48	135	231	74	157	213	70	143	231	82	149
B Restaurants and hotels	65	38	27	76	45	31	93	55	38	83	49	34
7 Transport, storage and communication	171	91	80	183	97	86	196	106	90	219	121	98
A Transport and storage	152	88	64	161	94	67	171	103	68	191	117	74

Fiji

4.1 Derivation of Value Added by Kind of Activity, in Current Prices
(Continued)

Million Fiji dollars

	1980 Gross Output	1980 Intermediate Consumption	1980 Value Added	1981 Gross Output	1981 Intermediate Consumption	1981 Value Added	1982 Gross Output	1982 Intermediate Consumption	1982 Value Added	1983 Gross Output	1983 Intermediate Consumption	1983 Value Added
B Communication	19	3	16	22	3	19	25	3	22	28	4	24
8 Finance, insurance, real estate and business services	173	61	112	180	54	126	197	58	139	204	63	141
A Financial institutions	43	9	34	58	12	46	66	12	54	59	12	47
B Insurance	8	2	6	11	2	9	13	3	10	9	2	7
C Real estate and business services	122	50	72	111	40	71	118	43	75	136	49	87
Real estate, except dwellings	52	33	19	40	25	15	45	28	17	48	30	18
Dwellings	70	17	53	71	15	56	73	15	58	88	19	69
9 Community, social and personal services	149	42	107	173	52	121	191	57	134	215	62	153
A Sanitary and similar services	...	...	...	...	...	...	...	...	...	...	...	...
B Social and related community services	91	11	80	103	16	87	118	18	100	133	20	113
Educational services	66	8	58	74	11	63	84	12	72	94	13	81
Medical, dental, other health and veterinary services	25	3	22	29	5	24	34	6	28	39	7	32
C Recreational and cultural services	17	10	7	22	12	10	20	11	9	24	13	11
D Personal and household services	41	21	20	48	24	24	53	28	25	58	29	29
Total, Industries	1620	765	855	1756	842	914	1867	898	969	1849	882	967
Producers of Government Services	91	30	61	100	32	68	118	36	82	135	45	90
Other Producers	19	3	16	21	4	17	30	12	18	39	17	22
Total [a]	1730	798	932	1877	878	999	2015	946	1069	2023	944	1079
Less: Imputed bank service charge	...	-31	31	...	-45	45	...	-49	49	...	-47	47
Import duties	...	...	...	...	...	...	...	...	...	...	...	...
Value added tax	...	...	...	...	...	...	...	...	...	...	...	...
Other adjustments [b]	83	...	83	102	...	102	93	...	93	110	...	110
Total	1813	829	984	1979	923	1056	2108	995	1113	2133	991	1142

	1984 Gross Output	1984 Intermediate Consumption	1984 Value Added	1985 Gross Output	1985 Intermediate Consumption	1985 Value Added	1986 Gross Output	1986 Intermediate Consumption	1986 Value Added	1987 Gross Output	1987 Intermediate Consumption	1987 Value Added
						All Producers						
1 Agriculture, hunting, forestry and fishing	290	69	221	284	68	216	341	64	277	375	70	305
A Agriculture and hunting	255	57	198	252	57	195	310	53	257	336	57	279
B Forestry and logging	12	4	8	12	4	8	12	4	8	13	4	9
C Fishing	23	8	15	20	7	13	19	7	12	26	9	17
2 Mining and quarrying	22	21	1	32	18	14	52	34	18	105	74	31
A Coal mining	...	...	...	...	...	...	...	...	...	103	72	31
B Crude petroleum and natural gas production	...	...	...	...	...	...	...	...	...	1	1	-
C Metal ore mining	...	...	...	...	...	...	...	...	...	1	1	-
D Other mining	...	...	...	...	...	...	...	...	...	...	...	...
3 Manufacturing	485	373	112	481	370	111	570	433	137	675	518	157
A Manufacture of food, beverages and tobacco	318	255	63	297	239	58	389	299	90	...	...	...
B Textile, wearing apparel and leather industries	14	8	6	18	13	5	17	12	5	...	...	...
C Manufacture of wood and wood products, including furniture	31	21	10	35	23	12	33	23	10	...	...	...
D Manufacture of paper and paper products, printing and publishing	20	13	7	22	14	8	24	16	8	...	...	...
E Manufacture of chemicals and chemical petroleum, coal, rubber and plastic products	35	26	9	38	28	10	37	29	8	...	...	...
F Manufacture of non-metallic mineral products, except products of petroleum and coal	24	16	8	26	18	8	23	18	5	...	...	...
G Basic metal industries	...	...	...	...	...	...	...	...	...	...	...	...
H Manufacture of fabricated metal products, machinery and equipment	40	32	8	41	32	9	43	33	10	...	...	...
I Other manufacturing industries	3	2	1	4	3	1	4	3	1	...	...	...
4 Electricity, gas and water	52	10	42	54	13	41	61	13	48	57	13	44

Fiji

4.1 Derivation of Value Added by Kind of Activity, in Current Prices
(Continued)

Million Fiji dollars

	1984 Gross Output	1984 Intermediate Consumption	1984 Value Added	1985 Gross Output	1985 Intermediate Consumption	1985 Value Added	1986 Gross Output	1986 Intermediate Consumption	1986 Value Added	1987 Gross Output	1987 Intermediate Consumption	1987 Value Added
5 Construction	137	75	62	137	73	64	160	96	64	143	82	61
6 Wholesale and retail trade, restaurants and hotels	342	138	204	351	141	210	376	153	223	342	134	208
A Wholesale and retail trade	242	79	163	251	82	169	263	86	177	256	84	172
B Restaurants and hotels	100	59	41	100	59	41	113	67	46	86	50	36
7 Transport, storage and communication	246	138	108	260	138	122	273	141	132	305	166	139
A Transport and storage	215	134	81	217	125	92	224	126	98	246	145	101
B Communication	31	4	27	43	13	30	49	15	34	59	21	38
8 Finance, insurance, real estate and business services	221	67	154	243	77	166	269	87	182	265	83	182
A Financial institutions	63	13	50	75	18	57	87	23	64	95	25	70
B Insurance	10	2	8	10	3	7	11	3	8	12	3	9
C Real estate and business services	148	52	96	158	56	102	171	61	110	158	55	103
Real estate, except dwellings	53	32	21	56	35	21	62	39	23	52	32	20
Dwellings	95	20	75	102	21	81	109	22	87	106	23	83
9 Community, social and personal services	232	67	165	230	70	160	245	76	169	214	69	145
A Sanitary and similar services	...	...	...	...	...	...	...	...	...	...	...	...
B Social and related community services	147	22	125	138	21	117	147	23	124	118	18	100
Educational services	104	15	89	97	14	83	98	15	83	83	12	71
Medical, dental, other health and veterinary services	43	7	36	41	7	34	49	8	41	35	6	29
C Recreational and cultural services	26	15	11	27	16	11	24	15	9	28	17	11
D Personal and household services	59	30	29	65	33	32	74	38	36	68	34	34
Total, Industries	2027	958	1069	2072	968	1104	2347	1097	1250	2481	1209	1272
Producers of Government Services	139	38	101	146	52	94	165	52	113	125	43	82
Other Producers	39	16	23	46	19	27	47	20	27	47	20	27
Total [a]	2205	1012	1193	2264	1039	1225	2559	1169	1390	2653	1272	1381
Less: Imputed bank service charge	...	-41	41	...	-47	47	...	-64	64	...	-70	70
Import duties	...	...	...	...	...	...	...	...	...	...	...	...
Value added tax	...	...	...	...	...	...	...	...	...	...	...	...
Other adjustments [b]	124	...	124	139	...	139	136	...	136	135	...	135
Total	2329	1053	1276	2403	1086	1317	2695	1233	1462	2788	1342	1446

	1988 Gross Output	1988 Intermediate Consumption	1988 Value Added
All Producers			
1 Agriculture, hunting, forestry and fishing	367	87	280
A Agriculture and hunting	328	74	254
B Forestry and logging	13	4	9
C Fishing	26	9	17
2 Mining and quarrying	112	73	39
A Coal mining	...	...	...
B Crude petroleum and natural gas production	...	...	...
C Metal ore mining	...	...	...
D Other mining	...	...	...

Fiji

4.1 Derivation of Value Added by Kind of Activity, in Current Prices
(Continued)

Million Fiji dollars

		1988		
		Gross Output	Intermediate Consumption	Value Added
3	Manufacturing	592	455	137
	A Manufacture of food, beverages and tobacco	...	...	...
	B Textile, wearing apparel and leather industries	...	...	...
	C Manufacture of wood and wood products, including furniture	...	...	...
	D Manufacture of paper and paper products, printing and publishing	...	...	...
	E Manufacture of chemicals and chemical petroleum, coal, rubber and plastic products	...	...	...
	F Manufacture of non-metallic mineral products, except products of petroleum and coal	...	...	...
	G Basic metal industries	...	...	...
	H Manufacture of fabricated metal products, machinery and equipment	...	...	...
	I Other manufacturing industries	...	...	...
4	Electricity, gas and water	75	18	57
5	Construction	102	52	50
6	Wholesale and retail trade, restaurants and hotels	447	174	273
	A Wholesale and retail trade	341	111	230
	B Restaurants and hotels	106	63	43
7	Transport, storage and communication	330	178	152
	A Transport and storage	264	154	110
	B Communication	66	24	42
8	Finance, insurance, real estate and business services	286	89	197
	A Financial institutions	116	30	86
	B Insurance	10	3	7
	C Real estate and business services	160	56	104
	Real estate, except dwellings	52	32	20
	Dwellings	108	24	84
9	Community, social and personal services	243	78	165
	A Sanitary and similar services	...	...	...
	B Social and related community services	136	21	115
	Educational services	98	14	84
	Medical, dental, other health and veterinary services	38	7	31
	C Recreational and cultural services	31	19	12
	D Personal and household services	76	38	38
Total, Industries		2554	1204	1350
Producers of Government Services		137	47	90
Other Producers		53	23	30
Total [a]		2744	1274	1470
Less: Imputed bank service charge		...	-85	85
Import duties		...	...	...
Value added tax		...	...	...
Other adjustments [b]		153	...	153
Total		2897	1359	1538

a) Gross domestic product in factor values.
b) Item 'Other adjustments' refers to indirect taxes net of subsidies.

Fiji

4.3 Cost Components of Value Added

Million Fiji dollars

	1980						1981					
	Compensation of Employees	Capital Consumption	Net Operating Surplus	Indirect Taxes	Less: Subsidies Received	Value Added	Compensation of Employees	Capital Consumption	Net Operating Surplus	Indirect Taxes	Less: Subsidies Received	Value Added

All Producers

	CE80	CC80	NOS80	IT80	LSR80	VA80	CE81	CC81	NOS81	IT81	LSR81	VA81
1 Agriculture, hunting, forestry and fishing	28	8	164	...	...	200	34	9	147	...	...	190
A Agriculture and hunting	23	6	158	...	...	187	27	7	138	...	...	172
B Forestry and logging	3	1	3	...	...	7	2	1	3	...	...	6
C Fishing	2	1	3	...	...	6	5	1	6	...	...	12
2 Mining and quarrying	8	-	-10	...	...	-2	6	1	-6	...	...	1
3 Manufacturing	48	10	50	...	...	108	48	10	42	...	...	100
A Manufacture of food, beverages and tobacco	24	6	36	...	...	66	23	6	28	...	...	57
B Textile, wearing apparel and leather industries	1	-	1	...	...	2	1	-	2	...	...	3
C Manufacture of wood and wood products, including furniture	6	2	3	...	...	11	7	1	1	...	...	9
D Manufacture of paper and paper products, printing and publishing	4	1	1	...	...	6	5	-	2	...	...	7
E Manufacture of chemicals and chemical petroleum, coal, rubber and plastic products	2	-	3	...	...	5	3	1	2	...	...	6
F Manufacture of non-metallic mineral products, except products of petroleum and coal	2	-	3	...	...	5	2	1	2	...	...	5
G Basic metal industries	...	...	...	...	...	...	...	...	...	...	...	...
H Manufacture of fabricated metal products, machinery and equipment	8	1	-	...	...	9	7	1	1	...	...	9
I Other manufacturing industries	1	-	3	...	...	4	-	-	4	...	...	4
4 Electricity, gas and water	5	4	6	...	...	15	7	12	1	...	...	20
5 Construction	44	3	26	...	...	73	59	4	19	...	...	82
6 Wholesale and retail trade, restaurants and hotels	60	13	89	...	...	162	74	15	99	...	...	188
A Wholesale and retail trade	46	9	80	...	...	135	57	10	90	...	...	157
B Restaurants and hotels	14	4	9	...	...	27	17	5	9	...	...	31
7 Transport, storage and communication	46	16	18	...	...	80	48	17	21	...	...	86
A Transport and storage	38	14	12	...	...	64	39	14	14	...	...	67
B Communication	8	2	6	...	...	16	9	3	7	...	...	19
8 Finance, insurance, real estate and business services	25	5	82	...	...	112	25	5	96	...	...	126
A Financial institutions	12	1	21	...	...	34	12	2	32	...	...	46
B Insurance	3	-	3	...	...	6	4	-	5	...	...	9
C Real estate and business services	10	4	58	...	...	72	9	3	59	...	...	71
Real estate, except dwellings	4	3	12	...	...	19	2	3	10	...	...	15
Dwellings	6	1	46	...	...	53	7	-	49	...	...	56
9 Community, social and personal services	90	3	14	...	...	107	100	4	17	...	...	121
A Sanitary and similar services	...	...	...	...	...	...	...	...	...	...	...	...
B Social and related community services	74	1	5	...	...	80	80	1	6	...	...	87
Educational services	57	1	-	...	...	58	62	1	-	...	...	63
Medical, dental, other health and veterinary services	17	-	5	...	...	22	18	-	6	...	...	24
C Recreational and cultural services	5	1	1	...	...	7	7	1	2	...	...	10
D Personal and household services	11	1	8	...	...	20	13	2	9	...	...	24
Total, Industries	354	62	439	...	...	855	401	77	436	...	...	914
Producers of Government Services	61	-	-	...	...	61	68	-	-	...	...	68

Fiji

4.3 Cost Components of Value Added
(Continued)

Million Fiji dollars

	1980						1981					
	Compensation of Employees	Capital Consumption	Net Operating Surplus	Indirect Taxes	Less: Subsidies Received	Value Added	Compensation of Employees	Capital Consumption	Net Operating Surplus	Indirect Taxes	Less: Subsidies Received	Value Added
Other Producers	11	2	3	...	...	16	14	-	3	...	...	17
Total a	426	64	442	...	...	932	483	77	439	...	...	999
Less: Imputed bank service charge	...	...	31	...	...	31	...	...	45	...	...	45
Import duties	...	...	...	...	...	...	...	...	...	...	...	...
Value added tax	...	...	...	...	...	...	...	...	...	...	...	...
Other adjustments	...	...	...	85	2	83	...	...	...	104	2	102
Total	426	64	411	85	2	984	483	77	394	104	2	1056

	1982						1983					
	Compensation of Employees	Capital Consumption	Net Operating Surplus	Indirect Taxes	Less: Subsidies Received	Value Added	Compensation of Employees	Capital Consumption	Net Operating Surplus	Indirect Taxes	Less: Subsidies Received	Value Added
	All Producers											
1 Agriculture, hunting, forestry and fishing	38	10	159	...	...	207	31	10	149	...	...	190
A Agriculture and hunting	30	8	150	...	...	188	22	7	137	...	...	166
B Forestry and logging	3	1	3	...	...	7	3	1	4	...	...	8
C Fishing	5	1	6	...	...	12	6	2	8	...	...	16
2 Mining and quarrying	6	1	-1	...	...	6	6	1	-1	...	...	6
3 Manufacturing	54	12	43	...	...	109	50	13	31	...	...	94
A Manufacture of food, beverages and tobacco	30	7	33	...	...	70	21	7	16	...	...	44
B Textile, wearing apparel and leather industries	2	-	1	...	...	3	2	-	2	...	...	4
C Manufacture of wood and wood products, including furniture	6	1	1	...	...	8	7	2	1	...	...	10
D Manufacture of paper and paper products, printing and publishing	5	1	1	...	...	7	6	1	1	...	...	8
E Manufacture of chemicals and chemical petroleum, coal, rubber and plastic products	3	1	2	...	...	6	3	1	5	...	...	9
F Manufacture of non-metallic mineral products, except products of petroleum and coal	2	1	2	...	...	5	4	1	3	...	...	8
G Basic metal industries	...	...	...	...	...	...	...	...	...	...	...	...
H Manufacture of fabricated metal products, machinery and equipment	6	1	2	...	...	9	6	1	3	...	...	10
I Other manufacturing industries	-	-	1	...	...	1	1	-	-	...	...	1
4 Electricity, gas and water	8	15	-1	...	...	22	6	15	6	...	...	27
5 Construction	64	4	13	...	...	81	61	3	11	...	...	75
6 Wholesale and retail trade, restaurants and hotels	72	18	91	...	...	181	78	17	88	...	...	183
A Wholesale and retail trade	52	12	79	...	...	143	60	12	77	...	...	149
B Restaurants and hotels	20	6	12	...	...	38	18	5	11	...	...	34
7 Transport, storage and communication	50	19	21	...	...	90	57	21	20	...	...	98
A Transport and storage	40	15	13	...	...	68	45	16	13	...	...	74
B Communication	10	4	8	...	...	22	12	5	7	...	...	24
8 Finance, insurance, real estate and business services	30	5	104	...	...	139	34	7	100	...	...	141
A Financial institutions	15	2	37	...	...	54	17	1	29	...	...	47
B Insurance	5	-	5	...	...	10	5	-	2	...	...	7
C Real estate and business services	10	3	62	...	...	75	12	6	69	...	...	87
Real estate, except dwellings	4	3	10	...	...	17	5	5	8	...	...	18
Dwellings	5	1	52	...	...	58	7	1	61	...	...	69
9 Community, social and personal services	111	3	20	...	...	134	126	5	22	...	...	153
A Sanitary and similar services	...	...	...	...	...	...	...	...	...	...	...	...
B Social and related community services	91	1	8	...	...	100	103	1	9	...	...	113

Fiji

4.3 Cost Components of Value Added
(Continued)

Million Fiji dollars

	1982						1983					
	Compensation of Employees	Capital Consumption	Net Operating Surplus	Indirect Taxes	Less: Subsidies Received	Value Added	Compensation of Employees	Capital Consumption	Net Operating Surplus	Indirect Taxes	Less: Subsidies Received	Value Added
Educational services	70	1	1	...	...	72	79	1	1	...	...	81
Medical, dental, other health and veterinary services	21	-	7	...	...	28	24	-	8	...	...	32
C Recreational and cultural services	6	1	2	...	...	9	7	2	2	...	...	11
D Personal and household services	14	1	10	...	...	25	16	2	11	...	...	29
Total, Industries	433	87	449	...	...	969	449	92	426	...	...	967
Producers of Government Services	82	-	-	...	...	82	90	-	-	...	...	90
Other Producers	16	1	1	...	...	18	20	1	1	...	...	22
Total a	531	88	450	...	...	1069	559	93	427	...	...	1079
Less: Imputed bank service charge	...	...	49	...	...	49	...	...	47	...	...	47
Import duties	...	...	...	...	...	...	...	...	...	...	...	...
Value added tax	...	...	...	...	...	...	...	...	...	...	...	...
Other adjustments	...	...	...	94	1	93	...	...	...	111	1	110
Total	531	88	401	94	1	1113	559	93	380	111	1	1142

	1984						1985					
	Compensation of Employees	Capital Consumption	Net Operating Surplus	Indirect Taxes	Less: Subsidies Received	Value Added	Compensation of Employees	Capital Consumption	Net Operating Surplus	Indirect Taxes	Less: Subsidies Received	Value Added
All Producers												
1 Agriculture, hunting, forestry and fishing	45	12	163	...	...	220	39	11	166	...	...	216
A Agriculture and hunting	36	9	152	...	...	197	30	9	156	...	...	195
B Forestry and logging	3	1	4	...	...	8	4	1	3	...	...	8
C Fishing	6	2	7	...	...	15	5	1	7	...	...	13
2 Mining and quarrying	6	3	-8	...	...	1	7	6	1	...	...	14
3 Manufacturing	62	13	35	...	...	110	63	15	33	...	...	111
A Manufacture of food, beverages and tobacco	34	7	22	...	...	63	33	8	17	...	...	58
B Textile, wearing apparel and leather industries	2	-	2	...	...	4	3	1	1	...	...	5
C Manufacture of wood and wood products, including furniture	5	2	1	...	...	8	7	2	3	...	...	12
D Manufacture of paper and paper products, printing and publishing	6	1	2	...	...	9	5	1	2	...	...	8
E Manufacture of chemicals and chemical petroleum, coal, rubber and plastic products	5	1	4	...	...	10	5	1	4	...	...	10
F Manufacture of non-metallic mineral products, except products of petroleum and coal	3	1	3	...	...	7	3	1	4	...	...	8
G Basic metal industries	...	...	...	...	...	...	...	...	...	...	...	...
H Manufacture of fabricated metal products, machinery and equipment	7	1	-	...	...	8	7	1	1	...	...	9
I Other manufacturing industries	-	-	1	...	...	1	-	-	1	...	...	1
4 Electricity, gas and water	9	7	25	...	...	41	9	7	25	...	...	41
5 Construction	47	2	17	...	...	66	44	2	18	...	...	64
6 Wholesale and retail trade, restaurants and hotels	82	17	105	...	...	204	84	17	109	...	...	210
A Wholesale and retail trade	60	11	92	...	...	163	62	11	96	...	...	169
B Restaurants and hotels	22	6	13	...	...	41	22	6	13	...	...	41
7 Transport, storage and communication	61	23	24	...	...	108	61	25	36	...	...	122
A Transport and storage	48	18	15	...	...	81	47	19	26	...	...	92
B Communication	13	5	9	...	...	27	14	6	10	...	...	30
8 Finance, insurance, real estate and business services	37	6	109	...	...	152	39	7	120	...	...	166
A Financial institutions	20	2	28	...	...	50	21	3	33	...	...	57
B Insurance	4	-	4	...	...	8	5	-	2	...	...	7
C Real estate and business services	13	4	77	...	...	94	13	4	85	...	...	102
Real estate, except dwellings	6	3	11	...	...	20	6	3	12	...	...	21

Fiji

4.3 Cost Components of Value Added
(Continued)

Million Fiji dollars

	1984						1985					
	Compensation of Employees	Capital Consumption	Net Operating Surplus	Indirect Taxes	Less: Subsidies Received	Value Added	Compensation of Employees	Capital Consumption	Net Operating Surplus	Indirect Taxes	Less: Subsidies Received	Value Added
Dwellings	7	1	66	...	...	74	7	1	73	...	...	81
9 Community, social and personal services	137	4	25	...	...	166	132	4	24	...	...	160
A Sanitary and similar services	...	...	...	...	...	...	...	...	...	...	...	...
B Social and related community services	114	1	10	...	...	125	107	-	10	...	...	117
Educational services	87	1	1	...	...	89	82	-	1	...	...	83
Medical, dental, other health and veterinary services	27	-	9	...	...	36	25	-	9	...	...	34
C Recreational and cultural services	7	1	3	...	...	11	7	2	2	...	...	11
D Personal and household services	16	2	12	...	...	30	18	2	12	...	...	32
Total, Industries	486	87	495	...	...	1068	478	94	532	...	...	1104
Producers of Government Services	101	-	-	...	...	101	94	-	-	...	...	94
Other Producers	21	1	1	...	...	23	24	1	2	...	...	27
Total [a]	608	88	496	...	...	1192	596	95	534	...	...	1225
Less: Imputed bank service charge	...	...	41	...	...	41	...	...	47	...	...	47
Import duties	...	...	...	...	...	...	...	...	...	...	...	...
Value added tax	...	...	...	...	...	...	...	...	...	...	...	...
Other adjustments	...	...	...	125	1	124	...	...	...	140	1	139
Total	608	88	455	125	1	1275	596	95	487	140	1	1317

	1986						1987					
	Compensation of Employees	Capital Consumption	Net Operating Surplus	Indirect Taxes	Less: Subsidies Received	Value Added	Compensation of Employees	Capital Consumption	Net Operating Surplus	Indirect Taxes	Less: Subsidies Received	Value Added
						All Producers						
1 Agriculture, hunting, forestry and fishing	46	11	220	...	...	277	40	11	254	...	...	305
A Agriculture and hunting	37	9	211	...	...	257	30	8	241	...	...	279
B Forestry and logging	4	1	3	...	...	8	4	1	4	...	...	9
C Fishing	5	1	6	...	...	12	6	2	9	...	...	17
2 Mining and quarrying	2	8	8	...	...	18	10	8	13	...	...	31
3 Manufacturing	64	17	56	...	...	137	65	24	68	...	...	157
A Manufacture of food, beverages and tobacco	35	10	45	...	...	90	...	...	...	...	...	...
B Textile, wearing apparel and leather industries	3	1	1	...	...	5	...	...	...	...	...	...
C Manufacture of wood and wood products, including furniture	7	2	1	...	...	10	...	...	...	...	...	...
D Manufacture of paper and paper products, printing and publishing	5	1	2	...	...	8	...	...	...	...	...	...
E Manufacture of chemicals and chemical petroleum, coal, rubber and plastic products	4	1	3	...	...	8	...	...	...	...	...	...
F Manufacture of non-metallic mineral products, except products of petroleum and coal	3	1	1	...	...	5	...	...	...	...	...	...
G Basic metal industries	...	...	...	...	...	...	...	...	...	...	...	...
H Manufacture of fabricated metal products, machinery and equipment	7	1	2	...	...	10	...	...	...	...	...	...
I Other manufacturing industries	-	-	1	...	...	1	...	...	...	...	...	...
4 Electricity, gas and water	10	7	31	...	...	48	11	8	25	...	...	44
5 Construction	45	2	17	...	...	64	41	2	18	...	...	61
6 Wholesale and retail trade, restaurants and hotels	90	19	114	...	...	223	82	17	109	...	...	208
A Wholesale and retail trade	65	12	100	...	...	177	63	12	97	...	...	172
B Restaurants and hotels	25	7	14	...	...	46	19	5	12	...	...	36
7 Transport, storage and communication	65	24	43	...	...	132	68	27	44	...	...	139
A Transport and storage	49	19	30	...	...	98	53	21	27	...	...	101
B Communication	15	6	13	...	...	34	15	6	17	...	...	38
8 Finance, insurance, real estate and business services	44	10	128	...	...	182	43	10	129	...	...	182
A Financial institutions	25	4	35	...	...	64	26	5	39	...	...	70

Fiji

4.3 Cost Components of Value Added
(Continued)

Million Fiji dollars

	1986						1987					
	Compensation of Employees	Capital Consumption	Net Operating Surplus	Indirect Taxes	Less: Subsidies Received	Value Added	Compensation of Employees	Capital Consumption	Net Operating Surplus	Indirect Taxes	Less: Subsidies Received	Value Added
B Insurance	5	1	2	...	...	8	5	1	3	...	...	9
C Real estate and business services	14	5	91	...	...	110	12	4	87	...	...	103
Real estate, except dwellings	7	4	12	...	...	23	5	3	12	...	...	20
Dwellings	7	1	79	...	...	87	7	1	75	...	...	83
9 Community, social and personal services	138	4	27	...	...	169	116	4	25	...	...	145
A Sanitary and similar services	...	...	...	...	...	...	...	...	...	...	...	...
B Social and related community services	111	1	12	...	...	124	91	-	9	...	...	100
Educational services	81	1	1	...	...	83	70	-	1	...	...	71
Medical, dental, other health and veterinary services	30	-	11	...	...	41	21	-	8	...	...	29
C Recreational and cultural services	7	1	1	...	...	9	6	2	3	...	...	11
D Personal and household services	20	2	14	...	...	36	19	2	13	...	...	34
Total, Industries	504	102	644	...	...	1250	476	111	685	...	...	1272
Producers of Government Services	113	-	-	...	...	113	82	-	-	...	...	82
Other Producers	24	1	2	...	...	27	25	1	1	...	...	27
Total [a]	641	103	646	...	...	1390	583	112	686	...	...	1381
Less: Imputed bank service charge	...	...	64	...	...	64	...	...	70	...	...	70
Import duties	...	...	...	...	...	...	...	...	...	...	...	...
Value added tax	...	...	...	...	...	...	...	...	...	...	...	...
Other adjustments	...	...	...	137	1	136	...	...	...	136	-1	135
Total	641	103	582	137	1	1462	583	112	616	136	-1	1446

	1988						
	Compensation of Employees	Capital Consumption	Net Operating Surplus	Indirect Taxes	Less: Subsidies Received	Value Added

All Producers

	Comp.	Cap.	NOS	IT	Sub	VA
1 Agriculture, hunting, forestry and fishing	46	14	220	...	...	280
A Agriculture and hunting	36	11	207	...	...	254
B Forestry and logging	4	1	4	...	...	9
C Fishing	6	2	9	...	...	17
2 Mining and quarrying	6	18	15	...	...	39
3 Manufacturing	73	16	48	...	...	137
A Manufacture of food, beverages and tobacco	...	...	...	...	...	...
B Textile, wearing apparel and leather industries	...	...	...	...	...	...
C Manufacture of wood and wood products, including furniture	...	...	...	...	...	...
D Manufacture of paper and paper products, printing and publishing	...	...	...	...	...	...
E Manufacture of chemicals and chemical petroleum, coal, rubber and plastic products	...	...	...	...	...	...
F Manufacture of non-metallic mineral products, except products of petroleum and coal	...	...	...	...	...	...
G Basic metal industries	...	...	...	...	...	...
H Manufacture of fabricated metal products, machinery and equipment	...	...	...	...	...	...
I Other manufacturing industries	...	...	...	...	...	...
4 Electricity, gas and water	11	10	36	...	...	57
5 Construction	30	1	19	...	...	50
6 Wholesale and retail trade, restaurants and hotels	107	22	144	...	...	273
A Wholesale and retail trade	84	16	130	...	...	230
B Restaurants and hotels	23	6	14	...	...	43
7 Transport, storage and communication	72	29	51	...	...	152

Fiji

4.3 Cost Components of Value Added
(Continued)

Million Fiji dollars

	Compensation of Employees	Capital Consumption	Net Operating Surplus	Indirect Taxes	Less: Subsidies Received	Value Added
			1988			
A Transport and storage	56	22	32	...	...	110
B Communication	16	7	19	...	...	42
8 Finance, insurance, real estate and business services	49	10	138	...	...	197
A Financial institutions	31	6	49	...	...	86
B Insurance	5	-	2	...	...	7
C Real estate and business services	13	4	87	...	...	104
Real estate, except dwellings	5	3	12	...	...	20
Dwellings	8	1	75	...	...	84
9 Community, social and personal services	133	5	27	...	...	165
A Sanitary and similar services	...	...	...	...	...	...
B Social and related community services	105	1	9	...	...	115
Educational services	82	1	1	...	...	84
Medical, dental, other health and veterinary services	23	-	8	...	...	31
C Recreational and cultural services	7	2	3	...	...	12
D Personal and household services	21	2	15	...	...	38
Total, Industries	527	125	698	...	...	1350
Producers of Government Services	90	-	-	...	...	90
Other Producers	28	-	2	...	...	30
Total [a]	645	125	700	...	...	1470
Less: Imputed bank service charge	...	...	85	...	...	85
Import duties	...	...	...	...	...	...
Value added tax	...	...	...	...	...	...
Other adjustments	...	...	...	153	-	153
Total	645	125	615	153	-	1538

a) Gross domestic product in factor values.

Finland

Source. Reply to the United Nations National Accounts Questionnaire from the Central Statistical Office, Helsinki. Official estimates are published annually in 'Tilastotiedotus Kansantalouden Tilinpito' (Statistical Report, National Accounting) issued by the same office. Information on concepts, sources and methods of estimation utilized can be found in 'Heikki Sourama-Olli Saariaho, Kansantalouden tilinipito, Rakenne, Maaritelmat ja luokitukset, Central Statistical Office of Finland, Studies No. 63, Helsinki, 1980'.

General note. The estimates shown in the following tables have been prepared by the Central Statistical Office in accordance with the United Nations System of National Accounts so far as the existing data would permit.

1.1 Expenditure on the Gross Domestic Product, in Current Prices

Million Finnish markkaa

	1970	1975	1980	1981	1982	1983	1984	1985	1986	1987	1988	1989
1 Government final consumption expenditure	6613	17799	34890	40835	46657	53327	59741	68218	74001	81339	88731	98119
2 Private final consumption expenditure	25901	57236	104375	118165	135301	151003	166177	181664	195008	213984	234946	256019
A Households	24989	55309	100863	114070	130610	145726	160503	175330	188264	206748	226864	247208
B Private non-profit institutions serving households	912	1927	3512	4095	4691	5277	5674	6334	6744	7236	8082	8811
3 Gross capital formation	13604	34994	55818	57328	64343	69872	74937	79612	81301	92381	114054	143029
A Increase in stocks	1594	2327	6687	2001	2097	-174	1511	-440	-2211	-889	3006	6424
B Gross fixed capital formation	12010	32667	49131	55327	62246	70046	73426	80052	83512	93270	111048	136605
Residential buildings	3107	8411	13970	15030	17146	18906	19899	20650	19939	21697	28499	37992
Non-residential buildings	2678	7267	10895	11801	13907	17591	17600	18771	19802	22029	26041	31620
Other construction and land improvement etc.	1785	4732	6210	6926	7821	8003	8391	9393	10424	10696	10958	12770
Other	4440	12257	18056	21570	23372	25546	27536	31238	33347	38848	45550	54223
4 Exports of goods and services	11745	24757	63489	72357	75801	82735	94190	98173	95634	100030	108750	116702
5 Less: Imports of goods and services	12310	30923	65016	69250	73762	81361	86137	94893	89898	97775	109866	125996
Statistical discrepancy	190	428	-951	-958	-2624	-929	-551	2212	1520	1638	4924	7624
Equals: Gross Domestic Product	45743	104291	192605	218477	245716	274647	308357	334986	357566	391597	441539	495497

1.2 Expenditure on the Gross Domestic Product, in Constant Prices

Million Finnish markkaa

	1970	1975	1980	1981	1982	1983	1984	1985	1986	1987	1988	1989
			At constant prices of:									
		1980					1985					
1 Government final consumption expenditure	20916	28117	56344	58767	60849	63113	64872	68218	70325	73458	75190	77389
2 Private final consumption expenditure	76917	94280	157702	159615	167053	171330	176038	181664	189113	199981	209956	218243
A Households	74044	91131	152221	153907	161092	165152	169928	175330	182627	193386	203273	211436
B Private non-profit institutions serving households	2873	3149	5481	5708	5961	6178	6110	6334	6486	6595	6683	6807
3 Gross capital formation	46349	57468	81139	75546	78805	79344	79306	79612	78069	83408	95547	111591
A Increase in stocks	5690	3994	9571	2428	2443	-124	1520	-440	-1997	-1007	2262	6082
B Gross fixed capital formation	40659	53474	71568	73118	76362	79468	77786	80052	80066	84415	93285	105509
Residential buildings	10681	13914	21241	20706	21935	21868	21286	20650	18945	19076	22271	26244
Non-residential buildings	9282	11878	16450	15993	17391	20091	18753	18771	18862	19303	20762	23067
Other construction and land improvement etc.	5984	7462	9085	9100	9555	8941	8838	9393	9980	9837	9501	10346
Other	14712	20220	24792	27319	27481	28568	28909	31238	32280	36199	40751	45852
4 Exports of goods and services	36448	37783	86509	90781	89792	92001	96993	98173	99498	102127	105897	107551
5 Less: Imports of goods and services	43515	54656	87451	83372	85415	87959	88857	94893	97795	106568	118405	128834
Statistical discrepancy	-2301	1742	-3928	-6434	-5622	-3291	-4167	2212	2807	3253	6800	8612
Equals: Gross Domestic Product	134814	164734	290315	294903	305462	314538	324185	334986	342017	355659	374985	394552

Finland

1.3 Cost Components of the Gross Domestic Product

Million Finnish markkaa

		1970	1975	1980	1981	1982	1983	1984	1985	1986	1987	1988	1989
1	Indirect taxes, net	4741	8875	19487	22463	25445	28100	33741	37459	41194	45907	55654	62457
	A Indirect taxes	6020	12830	25714	29728	33208	36978	43532	47806	52502	57593	66925	76180
	B Less: Subsidies	1279	3955	6227	7265	7763	8878	9791	10347	11308	11686	11271	13723
2	Consumption of fixed capital	5511	14974	28958	32824	36598	40563	44749	49198	53169	58143	64956	73473
3	Compensation of employees paid by resident producers to:	22784	59247	104660	121124	134135	148610	165445	184061	197329	214672	237260	265221
	A Resident households	22780	59225	104612	121071	134078	148539	165369	183982	197261	214604	237185	265158
	B Rest of the world	4	22	48	53	57	71	76	79	68	68	75	63
4	Operating surplus	12707	21195	39500	42066	49538	57374	64422	64268	65874	72875	83669	94346
	A Corporate and quasi-corporate enterprises	4143	4508	11682	12566	13994	18505	22418	20331	20141	27797	34780	38099
	B Private unincorporated enterprises	8562	16642	27944	29946	35516	38736	42001	43967	45819	45171	48956	56344
	C General government	2	45	-126	-446	28	133	3	-30	-86	-93	-67	-97
	Equals: Gross Domestic Product	45743	104291	192605	218477	245716	274647	308357	334986	357566	391597	441539	495497

1.4 General Government Current Receipts and Disbursements

Million Finnish markkaa

		1970	1975	1980	1981	1982	1983	1984	1985	1986	1987	1988	1989
						Receipts							
1	Operating surplus	2	45	-126	-446	28	133	3	-30	-86	-93	-67	-97
2	Property and entrepreneurial income	714	1040	2241	2717	3311	3830	4576	5062	5181	6606	5781	7224
3	Taxes, fees and contributions	14156	36478	63209	75264	83270	93040	109287	123326	136343	140434	165805	184947
	A Indirect taxes	6020	12830	25714	29728	33208	36978	43532	47806	52502	57593	66925	76180
	B Direct taxes	6005	17037	27718	34624	38042	42866	49381	55741	63127	61308	74454	82179
	C Social security contributions	1977	6249	9034	10013	10944	11936	14839	18023	18708	19375	21081	22495
	D Compulsory fees, fines and penalties	154	362	743	899	1076	1260	1535	1756	2006	2158	3345	4093
4	Other current transfers	705	1812	3654	4346	5055	5796	6472	7408	7954	8595	5229	5665
	Total Current Receipts of General Government	15577	39375	68978	81881	91664	102799	120338	135766	149392	155542	176748	197739
						Disbursements							
1	Government final consumption expenditure	6613	17799	34890	40835	46657	53327	59741	68218	74001	81339	88731	98119
	A Compensation of employees	4696	12098	23345	27416	31667	36364	41040	46533	50519	55369	60568	67113
	B Consumption of fixed capital	344	898	1914	2202	2464	2834	3176	3546	3899	4390	4998	5622
	C Purchases of goods and services, net	1573	4799	9622	11213	12515	14116	15511	18122	19565	21560	23143	25360
	D Less: Own account fixed capital formation	...	...	...	...	...	...	...	...	...	...	...	...
	E Indirect taxes paid, net	-	4	9	4	11	13	14	17	18	20	22	24
2	Property income	467	676	1964	2387	3100	4128	5042	5940	6003	6384	6951	6891
	A Interest	466	675	1961	2382	3097	4122	5035	5931	5993	6372	6936	6874
	B Net land rent and royalties	1	1	3	5	3	6	7	9	10	12	15	17
3	Subsidies	1279	3955	6227	7265	7763	8878	9791	10347	11308	11686	11271	13723
4	Other current transfers	3816	10161	19728	23004	28104	33005	36931	42339	46437	50789	51030	55147
	A Social security benefits	2146	5642	9963	11356	14408	17292	19355	22326	24110	25561	26856	28672
	B Social assistance grants	520	1365	3406	4006	4893	5767	6326	7375	7913	8871	9273	9932
	C Other	1150	3154	6359	7642	8803	9946	11250	12638	14414	16357	14901	16543
5	Net saving	3402	6784	6169	8390	6040	3461	8833	8922	11643	5344	18765	23859
	Total Current Disbursements and Net Saving of General Government	15577	39375	68978	81881	91664	102799	120338	135766	149392	155542	176748	197739

Finland

1.5 Current Income and Outlay of Corporate and Quasi-Corporate Enterprises, Summary

Million Finnish markkaa

	1970	1975	1980	1981	1982	1983	1984	1985	1986	1987	1988	1989
					Receipts							
1 Operating surplus	4143	4508	11682	12566	13994	18505	22418	20331	20141	27797	34780	38099
2 Property and entrepreneurial income received	3083	9158	20077	24584	27797	33910	44221	51815	52560	60559	76257	103881
3 Current transfers	2283	6473	15560	18893	20634	22320	24735	28323	31569	34811	43359	50790
Total Current Receipts	9509	20139	47319	56043	62425	74735	91374	100469	104270	123167	154396	192770
					Disbursements							
1 Property and entrepreneurial income	3659	10993	23893	29632	33437	39435	50482	57202	58249	67129	81791	112095
2 Direct taxes and other current payments to general government	864	2003	2821	3978	4540	5277	5514	5874	6661	5700	7087	8223
3 Other current transfers	1909	4978	12100	14693	16894	19488	22649	25651	29003	31647	37909	42763
4 Net saving	3077	2165	8505	7740	7554	10535	12729	11742	10357	18691	27609	29689
Total Current Disbursements and Net Saving	9509	20139	47319	56043	62425	74735	91374	100469	104270	123167	154396	192770

1.6 Current Income and Outlay of Households and Non-Profit Institutions

Million Finnish markkaa

	1970	1975	1980	1981	1982	1983	1984	1985	1986	1987	1988	1989
					Receipts							
1 Compensation of employees	22811	59297	105025	121501	134617	149098	165683	184316	197681	214993	237680	265540
A From resident producers	22780	59224	104612	121072	134078	148539	165369	183982	197261	214604	237185	265158
B From rest of the world	31	73	413	430	539	559	314	334	420	389	495	382
2 Operating surplus of private unincorporated enterprises	8562	16642	27944	29946	35516	38736	42001	43967	45819	45171	48956	56344
3 Property and entrepreneurial income	860	2369	5207	6147	6700	7799	9544	10794	10529	11751	15609	18750
4 Current transfers	5406	14684	29847	34769	41834	48528	54604	62206	68764	75418	82630	90326
A Social security benefits	2769	7894	16365	18869	23216	27652	31365	36038	40048	43576	50543	55449
B Social assistance grants	553	1431	3515	4161	5076	6027	6625	7674	8275	9171	9594	10282
C Other	2084	5359	9967	11739	13542	14849	16614	18494	20441	22671	22493	24595
Total Current Receipts	37639	92992	168023	192363	218667	244161	271832	301283	322793	347333	384875	430960
					Disbursements							
1 Private final consumption expenditure	25901	57236	104375	118165	135301	151003	166177	181664	195008	213984	234946	256019
2 Property income	984	2472	5275	6211	7100	8258	10159	11493	11954	13737	17692	22284
3 Direct taxes and other current transfers n.e.c. to general government	8432	25765	45112	53839	58710	64610	74904	86961	96334	98804	121699	136378
A Social security contributions	3050	10145	18930	21615	23316	24813	28472	33991	36527	39690	49437	56594
B Direct taxes	5228	15258	25439	31325	34318	38537	44897	51214	57801	56956	68917	75691
C Fees, fines and penalties	154	362	743	899	1076	1260	1535	1756	2006	2158	3345	4093
4 Other current transfers	1521	3833	7189	8513	9969	11125	12566	13720	15673	16882	14498	16304
5 Net saving	801	3686	6072	5635	7587	9165	8026	7445	3824	3926	-3960	-25
Total Current Disbursements and Net Saving	37639	92992	168023	192363	218667	244161	271832	301283	322793	347333	384875	430960

1.7 External Transactions on Current Account, Summary

Million Finnish markkaa

	1970	1975	1980	1981	1982	1983	1984	1985	1986	1987	1988	1989
					Payments to the Rest of the World							
1 Imports of goods and services	12310	30923	65016	69250	73762	81361	86137	94893	89898	97775	109866	125996
A Imports of merchandise c.i.f.	11138	28089	58046	60713	64542	70731	73496	80764	76736	81867	91232	104400
B Other	1172	2834	6970	8537	9220	10630	12641	14129	13162	15908	18634	21596
2 Factor income to the rest of the world	600	2037	5249	7477	8891	9459	11987	12930	12560	13599	16864	22318

Finland

1.7 External Transactions on Current Account, Summary
(Continued)

Million Finnish markkaa

	1970	1975	1980	1981	1982	1983	1984	1985	1986	1987	1988	1989
A Compensation of employees	4	22	48	53	57	71	76	79	68	68	75	63
B Property and entrepreneurial income	596	2015	5201	7424	8834	9388	11911	12851	12492	13531	16789	22255
3 Current transfers to the rest of the world	260	611	1631	2282	2806	3512	4276	4504	5122	4877	5879	6343
A Indirect taxes to supranational organizations	...	...	...	...	...	...	...	...	...	...	...	...
B Other current transfers	260	611	1631	2282	2806	3512	4276	4504	5122	4877	5879	6343
4 Surplus of the nation on current transactions	-1003	-7813	-5163	-1781	-3940	-5219	-49	-4517	-3828	-7915	-11608	-23657
Payments to the Rest of the World and Surplus of the Nation on Current Transactions	12167	25758	66733	77228	81519	89113	102351	107810	103752	108336	121001	131000

Receipts From The Rest of the World

	1970	1975	1980	1981	1982	1983	1984	1985	1986	1987	1988	1989
1 Exports of goods and services	11745	24757	63489	72357	75801	82735	94190	98173	95634	100030	108750	116702
A Exports of merchandise f.o.b.	9640	20288	52594	58913	61914	67959	78961	82475	81066	83826	91313	98266
B Other	2105	4469	10895	13444	13887	14775	15229	15698	14568	16204	17437	18436
2 Factor income from rest of the world	174	512	2007	3072	3544	3665	4883	6221	4976	5586	8497	11222
A Compensation of employees	31	73	413	430	539	559	314	334	420	389	495	382
B Property and entrepreneurial income	143	439	1594	2642	3005	3106	4569	5887	4556	5197	8002	10840
3 Current transfers from rest of the world	248	489	1237	1799	2174	2713	3278	3416	3142	2720	3754	3076
A Subsidies from supranational organisations	...	...	...	...	...	...	...	...	...	...	...	...
B Other current transfers	248	489	1237	1799	2174	2713	3278	3416	3142	2720	3754	3076
Receipts from the Rest of the World on Current Transactions	12167	25758	66733	77228	81519	89113	102351	107810	103752	108336	121001	131000

1.8 Capital Transactions of The Nation, Summary

Million Finnish markkaa

	1970	1975	1980	1981	1982	1983	1984	1985	1986	1987	1988	1989

Finance of Gross Capital Formation

	1970	1975	1980	1981	1982	1983	1984	1985	1986	1987	1988	1989
Gross saving	12791	27609	49704	54589	57779	63724	74337	77307	78993	86104	107370	126996
1 Consumption of fixed capital	5511	14974	28958	32824	36598	40563	44749	49198	53169	58143	64956	73473
A General government	349	1022	2205	2534	2840	3289	3604	3994	4451	5009	5657	6245
B Corporate and quasi-corporate enterprises	3302	9153	17045	19273	21397	23349	25695	28376	30644	33382	37232	41935
C Other	1860	4799	9708	11017	12361	13925	15450	16828	18074	19752	22067	25293
2 Net saving	7280	12635	20746	21765	21181	23161	29588	28109	25824	27961	42414	53523
A General government	3402	6784	6169	8390	6040	3461	8833	8922	11643	5344	18765	23859
B Corporate and quasi-corporate enterprises	3077	2165	8505	7740	7554	10535	12729	11742	10357	18691	27609	29689
C Other	801	3686	6072	5635	7587	9165	8026	7445	3824	3926	-3960	-25
Less: Surplus of the nation on current transactions	-1003	-7813	-5163	-1781	-3940	-5219	-49	-4517	-3828	-7915	-11608	-23657
Statistical discrepancy	-190	-428	951	958	2624	929	551	-2212	-1520	-1638	-4924	-7624
Finance of Gross Capital Formation	13604	34994	55818	57328	64343	69872	74937	79612	81301	92381	114054	143029

Gross Capital Formation

	1970	1975	1980	1981	1982	1983	1984	1985	1986	1987	1988	1989
Increase in stocks	1594	2327	6687	2001	2097	-174	1511	-440	-2211	-889	3006	6424
Gross fixed capital formation	12010	32667	49131	55327	62246	70046	73426	80052	83512	93270	111048	136605
1 General government	1603	4086	6679	7633	8817	9990	10196	11153	11850	13738	14443	15140
2 Corporate and quasi-corporate enterprises	6235	17545	22805	26613	29343	33719	35849	40366	43834	49572	59172	72768
3 Other	4172	11036	19647	21081	24086	26337	27381	28533	27828	29960	37433	48697
Gross Capital Formation	13604	34994	55818	57328	64343	69872	74937	79612	81301	92381	114054	143029

Finland

1.10 Gross Domestic Product by Kind of Activity, in Current Prices

Million Finnish markkaa

	1970	1975	1980	1981	1982	1983	1984	1985	1986	1987	1988	1989
1 Agriculture, hunting, forestry and fishing	5060	10152	16737	17411	19414	21059	23301	24125	23743	22431	24462	27617
2 Mining and quarrying	365	365	859	798	918	983	1113	1193	1128	1026	1350	1715
3 Manufacturing	10870	25196	48481	53092	57235	63279	70653	74588	76644	85710	93801	100746
4 Electricity, gas and water	1091	2764	4941	6657	7474	7783	8003	8768	9344	10002	9937	10161
5 Construction	4014	10419	13692	15533	17803	20768	22541	22880	24714	27691	33401	42113
6 Wholesale and retail trade, restaurants and hotels	4514	11161	20268	23022	25946	28776	31703	35179	36944	40709	45168	50487
7 Transport, storage and communication	3235	6644	13644	15462	16944	18969	21420	23406	25426	27944	30799	34359
8 Finance, insurance, real estate and business services	5116	12836	24076	28464	33169	37473	42833	47393	53556	59564	68851	79633
9 Community, social and personal services	1430	3258	5950	6762	7636	8838	10115	11299	12733	14482	16451	19402
Total, Industries	35695	82795	148648	167201	186539	207928	231682	248831	264232	289559	324220	366233
Producers of Government Services	5040	13000	25268	29622	34142	39211	44230	50096	54436	59779	65588	72759
Other Producers	999	1898	3344	3845	4331	4852	5437	6048	6562	7047	7905	8554
Subtotal	41734	97693	177260	200668	225012	251991	281349	304975	325230	356385	397713	447546
Less: Imputed bank service charge	656	2335	4699	5360	5646	6247	7322	8141	9328	11458	13251	16373
Plus: Import duties [a]	4665	8933	20044	23169	26350	28903	34330	38152	41664	46670	57077	64324
Plus: Value added tax							...	...	...	...	...	...
Equals: Gross Domestic Product	45743	104291	192605	218477	245716	274647	308357	334986	357566	391597	441539	495497

a) Item 'Import duties' includes also commodity indirect taxes net of subsidies.

1.11 Gross Domestic Product by Kind of Activity, in Constant Prices

Million Finnish markkaa

	1970	1975	1980	1981	1982	1983	1984	1985	1986	1987	1988	1989
			At constant prices of:									
			1980					1985				
1 Agriculture, hunting, forestry and fishing	14975	13225	24561	22639	22857	24015	24321	24125	22726	20458	22194	23841
2 Mining and quarrying	632	631	964	992	1110	1107	1149	1193	1195	1203	1299	1405
3 Manufacturing	31784	37937	63846	65947	66867	68989	71768	74588	75578	79331	82415	84990
4 Electricity, gas and water	2801	3868	7034	7342	7245	7561	8066	8768	8812	9464	9664	9635
5 Construction	11494	14156	21714	21408	22561	23460	22741	22880	22954	23105	24646	27496
6 Wholesale and retail trade, restaurants and hotels	14409	19198	30152	30105	31534	32165	33562	35179	36477	38911	41107	43661
7 Transport, storage and communication	9198	11438	21186	21645	21701	22339	22915	23406	23830	25793	27556	29451
8 Finance, insurance, real estate and business services	13913	18963	36241	37606	40239	42291	45055	47393	50952	54392	58783	63715
9 Community, social and personal services	5346	5937	9432	9678	10045	10441	10796	11299	11831	12460	12982	13997
Total, Industries	104552	125353	215130	217362	224159	232368	240373	248831	254355	265117	280646	298191
Producers of Government Services	15302	20253	42539	44508	46194	47578	48697	50096	50890	52707	54086	55371
Other Producers	3547	3246	5497	5655	5721	5837	5925	6048	6168	6116	6190	6272
Subtotal	123401	148852	263166	267525	276074	285783	294995	304975	311413	323940	340922	359834
Less: Imputed bank service charge	2985	3760	6564	6486	6646	7012	7561	8141	9518	11073	12318	14069
Plus: Import duties [a]	14398	19642	33713	33864	36034	35767	36751	38152	40122	42792	46381	48787
Plus: Value added tax	...	...	...	...	...	...	...	...	...	...	...	...
Equals: Gross Domestic Product	134814	164734	290315	294903	305462	314538	324185	334986	342017	355659	374985	394552

a) Item 'Import duties' includes also commodity indirect taxes net of subsidies.

Finland

1.12 Relations Among National Accounting Aggregates

Million Finnish markkaa

	1970	1975	1980	1981	1982	1983	1984	1985	1986	1987	1988	1989
Gross Domestic Product	45743	104291	192605	218477	245716	274647	308357	334986	357566	391597	441539	495497
Plus: Net factor income from the rest of the world	-426	-1525	-3242	-4405	-5347	-5794	-7104	-6709	-7584	-8013	-8367	-11096
Factor income from the rest of the world	174	512	2007	3072	3544	3665	4883	6221	4976	5586	8497	11222
Less: Factor income to the rest of the world	600	2037	5249	7477	8891	9459	11987	12930	12560	13599	16864	22318
Equals: Gross National Product	45317	102766	189363	214072	240369	268853	301253	328277	349982	383584	433172	484401
Less: Consumption of fixed capital	5511	14974	28958	32824	36598	40563	44749	49198	53169	58143	64956	73473
Equals: National Income	39806	87792	160405	181248	203771	228290	256504	279079	296813	325441	368216	410928
Plus: Net current transfers from the rest of the world	-12	-122	-394	-483	-632	-799	-998	-1088	-1980	-2157	-2125	-3267
Current transfers from the rest of the world	248	489	1237	1799	2174	2713	3278	3416	3142	2720	3754	3076
Less: Current transfers to the rest of the world	260	611	1631	2282	2806	3512	4276	4504	5122	4877	5879	6343
Equals: National Disposable Income	39794	87670	160011	180765	203139	227491	255506	277991	294833	323284	366091	407661
Less: Final consumption	32514	75035	139265	159000	181958	204330	225918	249882	269009	295323	323677	354138
Equals: Net Saving	7280	12635	20746	21765	21181	23161	29588	28109	25824	27961	42414	53523
Less: Surplus of the nation on current transactions	-1003	-7813	-5163	-1781	-3940	-5219	-49	-4517	-3828	-7915	-11608	-23657
Statistical discrepancy	-190	-428	951	958	2624	929	551	-2212	-1520	-1638	-4924	-7624
Equals: Net Capital Formation	8093	20020	26860	24504	27745	29309	30188	30414	28132	34238	49098	69556

2.1 Government Final Consumption Expenditure by Function, in Current Prices

Million Finnish markkaa

		1970	1975	1980	1981	1982	1983	1984	1985	1986	1987	1988	1989
1	General public services	...	1782	3595	4291	4638	5200	5717	6411	6677	7534	8283	9081
2	Defence	...	1379	2717	2996	3641	4373	4303	5190	5831	6208	6581	6829
3	Public order and safety	...	1200	2129	2474	2816	3196	3516	3902	4158	4482	4917	5311
4	Education	...	4942	9386	10813	12159	13774	15004	16915	18581	20448	22507	24899
5	Health	...	3751	7457	8788	10082	11373	13304	15324	16659	18197	19456	21888
6	Social security and welfare	...	2022	4460	5355	6233	7181	8681	10457	11479	12696	14207	16088
7	Housing and community amenities	...	645	1206	1449	1810	2059	2324	2367	2428	2663	2848	3128
8	Recreational, cultural and religious affairs	...	439	1075	1253	1467	1741	2012	2366	2630	2922	3157	3473
9	Economic services	...	1604	2697	3222	3576	4132	4537	4943	5146	5695	6372	7027
A	Fuel and energy	...	...	...	...	...	...	...	...	...	...	...	...
B	Agriculture, forestry, fishing and hunting	...	...	...	...	...	...	...	...	...	...	...	...
C	Mining, manufacturing and construction, except fuel and energy	...	...	...	...	...	...	...	...	...	...	...	...
D	Transportation and communication	...	1163	1871	2261	2385	2765	3035	3266	3321	3573	3878	4214
E	Other economic affairs	...	...	...	...	...	...	...	...	...	...	...	...
10	Other functions	...	35	168	194	235	298	343	343	412	494	403	395
	Total Government Final Consumption Expenditure	...	17799	34890	40835	46657	53327	59741	68218	74001	81339	88731	98119

2.2 Government Final Consumption Expenditure by Function, in Constant Prices

Million Finnish markkaa

		1970	1975	1980	1981	1982	1983	1984	1985	1986	1987	1988	1989
			At constant prices of: 1980					1985					
1	General public services	...	2816	5697	6026	5890	6038	6160	6411	6414	6856	7019	7186
2	Defence	...	2192	4073	4058	4553	4981	4585	5190	5580	5668	5650	5610
3	Public order and safety	...	1863	3412	3522	3639	3757	3838	3902	3937	3966	4008	4045
4	Education	...	7791	15318	15737	15760	16116	16155	16915	17397	18137	18645	19183
5	Health	...	5866	12363	12957	13587	13898	14653	15324	16034	16812	17148	17718
6	Social security and welfare	...	3301	7388	7861	8319	8678	9474	10457	10865	11407	11939	12649
7	Housing and community amenities	...	1015	1987	2142	2435	2513	2588	2367	2310	2413	2435	2478
8	Recreational, cultural and religious affairs	...	691	1748	1835	1942	2100	2228	2366	2491	2618	2677	2710

Finland

2.2 Government Final Consumption Expenditure by Function, in Constant Prices
(Continued)

Million Finnish markkaa

	1970	1975	1980	1981	1982	1983	1984	1985	1986	1987	1988	1989
		1980			At constant prices of:			**1985**				
9 Economic services	...	2525	...									
			4107	4377	4443	4696	4826	4943	4889	5112	5311	5476
A Fuel and energy	...	...	...	...	...	...	...	...	...	...	...	...
B Agriculture, forestry, fishing and hunting	...	...	...	...	...	...	...	...	...	...	...	...
C Mining, manufacturing and construction, except fuel and energy			...	...	...	...	...	...	...	...	...	...
D Transportation and communication	...	1837	2809	3037	2948	3119	3211	3266	3142	3202	3233	3268
E Other economic affairs	...	...	...	...	...	...	...	...	...	...	...	...
10 Other functions	...	57	251	252	281	336	365	343	408	469	358	334
Total Government Final Consumption Expenditure	...	28117	56344	58767	60849	63113	64872	68218	70325	73458	75190	77389

2.3 Total Government Outlays by Function and Type

Million Finnish markkaa

	Final Consumption Expenditures			Subsidies	Other Current Transfers & Property Income	Total Current Disbursements	Gross Capital Formation	Other Capital Outlays	Total Outlays
	Total	Compensation of Employees	Other						

1980

	Total	Comp. of Employees	Other	Subsidies	Other Current Transfers & Property Income	Total Current Disbursements	Gross Capital Formation	Other Capital Outlays	Total Outlays
1 General public services	3595	2216	1379	...	...	...	...	...	...
2 Defence	2717	1238	1479	...	...	...	...	...	...
3 Public order and safety	2129	1748	381	...	...	...	...	...	...
4 Education	9386	6447	2939	...	...	...	...	...	...
5 Health	7*57	5574	1883	...	...	...	...	...	...
6 Social security and welfare	4460	3274	1186	...	...	...	...	...	...
7 Housing and community amenities	1206	981	225	...	...	...	...	...	...
8 Recreation, culture and religion	1075	664	411	...	...	...	...	...	...
9 Economic services	2697	1168	1529	...	...	...	...	...	...
A Fuel and energy	...	...	...						
B Agriculture, forestry, fishing and hunting	...	...	...						
C Mining (except fuels), manufacturing and construction	...	...	...						
D Transportation and communication	1871	510	1361						
E Other economic affairs	...	...	...						
10 Other functions	168	35	133						
Total	34890	23345	11545	6227	21692	62809	...	...	...

1981

	Total	Comp. of Employees	Other	Subsidies	Other Current Transfers & Property Income	Total Current Disbursements	Gross Capital Formation	Other Capital Outlays	Total Outlays
1 General public services	4291	2677	1614	...	...	...	...	...	...
2 Defence	2996	1489	1507	...	...	...	...	...	...
3 Public order and safety	2474	2035	439	...	...	...	...	...	...
4 Education	10813	7403	3410	...	...	...	...	...	...
5 Health	8788	6518	2270	...	...	...	...	...	...
6 Social security and welfare	5355	3880	1475	...	...	...	...	...	...
7 Housing and community amenities	1449	1239	210	...	...	...	...	...	...
8 Recreation, culture and religion	1253	772	481	...	...	...	...	...	...
9 Economic services	3222	1382	1840	...	...	...	...	...	...
A Fuel and energy	...	...	...						
B Agriculture, forestry, fishing and hunting	...	...	...						
C Mining (except fuels), manufacturing and construction	...	...	...						
D Transportation and communication	2261	594	1667						
E Other economic affairs	...	...	...						
10 Other functions	194	21	173						
Total	40835	27416	13419	7265	25391	73491	...	...	...

Finland

2.3 Total Government Outlays by Function and Type
(Continued)

Million Finnish markkaa

	Final Consumption Expenditures Total	Compensation of Employees	Other	Subsidies	Other Current Transfers & Property Income	Total Current Disbursements	Gross Capital Formation	Other Capital Outlays	Total Outlays
1982									
1 General public services	4638	2884	1754	...	...	...	...	...	...
2 Defence	3641	1758	1883	...	...	...	...	...	...
3 Public order and safety	2816	2314	502	...	...	...	...	...	...
4 Education	12159	8495	3664	...	...	...	...	...	...
5 Health	10082	7591	2491	...	...	...	...	...	...
6 Social security and welfare	6233	4505	1728	...	...	...	...	...	...
7 Housing and community amenities	1810	1574	236	...	...	...	...	...	...
8 Recreation, culture and religion	1467	913	554	...	...	...	...	...	...
9 Economic services	3576	1607	1969	...	...	...	...	...	...
A Fuel and energy	...	...	...	...	...	...	...	...	...
B Agriculture, forestry, fishing and hunting	...	...	...	...	...	...	...	...	...
C Mining (except fuels), manufacturing and construction	...	...	...	...	...	...	...	...	...
D Transportation and communication	2385	659	1726	...	...	...	...	...	...
E Other economic affairs	...	...	...	...	...	...	...	...	...
10 Other functions	235	26	209	...	...	...	...	...	...
Total	46657	31667	14990	7763	31204	85624	...	...	...
1983									
1 General public services	5200	3255	1945	...	...	...	...	...	...
2 Defence	4373	2063	2310	...	...	...	...	...	...
3 Public order and safety	3196	2631	565	...	...	...	...	...	...
4 Education	13774	9797	3977	...	...	...	...	...	...
5 Health	11373	8593	2780	...	...	...	...	...	...
6 Social security and welfare	7181	5271	1910	...	...	...	...	...	...
7 Housing and community amenities	2059	1808	251	...	...	...	...	...	...
8 Recreation, culture and religion	1741	1089	652	...	...	...	...	...	...
9 Economic services	4132	1805	2327	...	...	...	...	...	...
A Fuel and energy	...	...	...	...	...	...	...	...	...
B Agriculture, forestry, fishing and hunting	...	...	...	...	...	...	...	...	...
C Mining (except fuels), manufacturing and construction	...	...	...	...	...	...	...	...	...
D Transportation and communication	2765	726	2039	...	...	...	...	...	...
E Other economic affairs	...	...	...	...	...	...	...	...	...
10 Other functions	298	52	246	...	...	...	...	...	...
Total	53327	36364	16963	8878	37133	99338	...	...	...
1984									
1 General public services	5717	3562	2155	...	...	...	...	...	...
2 Defence	4303	2276	2027	...	...	...	...	...	...
3 Public order and safety	3516	2884	632	...	...	...	...	...	...
4 Education	15004	10694	4310	...	...	...	...	...	...
5 Health	13304	10071	3233	...	...	...	...	...	...
6 Social security and welfare	8681	6207	2474	...	...	...	...	...	...
7 Housing and community amenities	2324	2054	270	...	...	...	...	...	...
8 Recreation, culture and religion	2012	1265	747	...	...	...	...	...	...
9 Economic services	4537	1974	2563	...	...	...	...	...	...
A Fuel and energy	...	...	...	...	...	...	...	...	...
B Agriculture, forestry, fishing and hunting	...	...	...	...	...	...	...	...	...
C Mining (except fuels), manufacturing and construction	...	...	...	...	...	...	...	...	...
D Transportation and communication	3035	792	2243	...	...	...	...	...	...
E Other economic affairs	...	...	...	...	...	...	...	...	...
10 Other functions	343	53	290	...	...	...	...	...	...
Total	59741	41040	18701	9791	41973	111505	...	...	...

Finland

2.3 Total Government Outlays by Function and Type
(Continued)

Million Finnish markkaa

		Final Consumption Expenditures			Subsidies	Other Current Transfers & Property Income	Total Current Disbursements	Gross Capital Formation	Other Capital Outlays	Total Outlays
		Total	Compensation of Employees	Other						

1985

1	General public services	6411	3960	2451	...	...	...	...	...	...
2	Defence	5190	2492	2698	...	...	...	...	...	...
3	Public order and safety	3902	3188	714	...	...	...	...	...	...
4	Education	16915	12095	4820	...	...	...	...	...	...
5	Health	15324	11599	3725	...	...	...	...	...	...
6	Social security and welfare	10457	7318	3139	...	...	...	...	...	...
7	Housing and community amenities	2367	2124	243	...	...	...	...	...	...
8	Recreation, culture and religion	2366	1495	871	...	...	...	...	...	...
9	Economic services	4943	2197	2746	...	...	...	...	...	...
	A Fuel and energy	...	...	...	...	...	...	...	...	...
	B Agriculture, forestry, fishing and hunting	...	...	...	...	...	...	...	...	...
	C Mining (except fuels), manufacturing and construction	...	...	...	...	...	...	...	...	...
	D Transportation and communication	3266	876	2390	...	...	...	...	...	...
	E Other economic affairs	...	...	...	...	...	...	...	...	...
10	Other functions	343	65	278	...	...	...	...	...	...
	Total	68218	46533	21685	10347	48279	126844	...	...	...

1986

1	General public services	6677	4273	2404	...	...	...	...	...	...
2	Defence	5831	2647	3184	...	...	...	...	...	...
3	Public order and safety	4158	3421	737	...	...	...	...	...	...
4	Education	18581	13334	5247	...	...	...	...	...	...
5	Health	16659	12517	4142	...	...	...	...	...	...
6	Social security and welfare	11479	8119	3360	...	...	...	...	...	...
7	Housing and community amenities	2428	2133	295	...	...	...	...	...	...
8	Recreation, culture and religion	2630	1669	961	...	...	...	...	...	...
9	Economic services	5146	2332	2814	...	...	...	...	...	...
	A Fuel and energy	...	...	...	...	...	...	...	...	...
	B Agriculture, forestry, fishing and hunting	...	...	...	...	...	...	...	...	...
	C Mining (except fuels), manufacturing and construction	...	...	...	...	...	...	...	...	...
	D Transportation and communication	3321	892	2429	...	...	...	...	...	...
	E Other economic affairs	...	...	...	...	...	...	...	...	...
10	Other functions	412	74	338	...	...	...	...	...	...
	Total	74001	50519	23482	11308	52440	137749	...	...	...

1987

1	General public services	7534	4712	2822	...	...	...	...	...	...
2	Defence	6208	2784	3424	...	...	...	...	...	...
3	Public order and safety	4482	3768	714	...	...	...	...	...	...
4	Education	20448	14734	5714	...	...	...	...	...	...
5	Health	18197	13511	4686	...	...	...	...	...	...
6	Social security and welfare	12696	8971	3725	...	...	...	...	...	...
7	Housing and community amenities	2663	2314	349	...	...	...	...	...	...
8	Recreation, culture and religion	2922	1849	1073	...	...	...	...	...	...
9	Economic services	5695	2643	3052	...	...	...	...	...	...
	A Fuel and energy	...	...	...	...	...	...	...	...	...
	B Agriculture, forestry, fishing and hunting	...	...	...	...	...	...	...	...	...
	C Mining (except fuels), manufacturing and construction	...	...	...	...	...	...	...	...	...
	D Transportation and communication	3573	996	2577	...	...	...	...	...	...
	E Other economic affairs	...	...	...	...	...	...	...	...	...
10	Other functions	494	83	411	...	...	...	...	...	...
	Total	81339	55369	25970	11686	57173	150198	...	...	...

Finland

2.3 Total Government Outlays by Function and Type
(Continued)

Million Finnish markkaa

		Final Consumption Expenditures			Subsidies	Other Current Transfers & Property Income	Total Current Disbursements	Gross Capital Formation	Other Capital Outlays	Total Outlays
		Total	Compensation of Employees	Other						

1988

		Total	Comp.	Other	Subsidies	Other Curr.	Total Curr. Disb.	Gross Cap.	Other Cap.	Total Outlays
1	General public services	8283	5250	3033	...	...	...	...	...	...
2	Defence	6581	3071	3510	...	...	...	...	...	...
3	Public order and safety	4917	4162	755	...	...	...	...	...	...
4	Education	22507	16131	6376	...	...	...	...	...	...
5	Health	19456	14310	5146	...	...	...	...	...	...
6	Social security and welfare	14207	9988	4219	...	...	...	...	...	...
7	Housing and community amenities	2848	2489	359	...	...	...	...	...	...
8	Recreation, culture and religion	3157	1980	1177	...	...	...	...	...	...
9	Economic services	6372	3077	3295	...	...	...	...	...	...
	A Fuel and energy	...	...	...	...	...	...	...	...	...
	B Agriculture, forestry, fishing and hunting	...	...	...	...	...	...	...	...	...
	C Mining (except fuels), manufacturing and construction	...	...	...	...	...	...	...	...	...
	D Transportation and communication	3878	1141	2737	...	...	...	...	...	...
	E Other economic affairs	...	...	...	...	...	...	...	...	...
10	Other functions	403	110	293	...	...	...	...	...	...
	Total	88731	60568	28163	11271	57981	157983	...	...	...

1989

		Total	Comp.	Other	Subsidies	Other Curr.	Total Curr. Disb.	Gross Cap.	Other Cap.	Total Outlays
1	General public services	9081	5763	3318	...	...	...	...	...	...
2	Defence	6829	3204	3625	...	...	...	...	...	...
3	Public order and safety	5311	4516	795	...	...	...	...	...	...
4	Education	24899	17847	7052	...	...	...	...	...	...
5	Health	21888	16155	5733	...	...	...	...	...	...
6	Social security and welfare	16088	11300	4788	...	...	...	...	...	...
7	Housing and community amenities	3128	2766	362	...	...	...	...	...	...
8	Recreation, culture and religion	3473	2196	1277	...	...	...	...	...	...
9	Economic services	7027	3249	3778	...	...	...	...	...	...
	A Fuel and energy	...	...	...	...	...	...	...	...	...
	B Agriculture, forestry, fishing and hunting	...	...	...	...	...	...	...	...	...
	C Mining (except fuels), manufacturing and construction	...	...	...	...	...	...	...	...	...
	D Transportation and communication	4214	1063	3151	...	...	...	...	...	...
	E Other economic affairs	...	...	...	...	...	...	...	...	...
10	Other functions	395	117	278	...	...	...	...	...	...
	Total	98119	67113	31006	13723	62038	173880	...	...	...

2.5 Private Final Consumption Expenditure by Type and Purpose, in Current Prices

Million Finnish markkaa

Final Consumption Expenditure of Resident Households

		1970	1975	1980	1981	1982	1983	1984	1985	1986	1987	1988	1989
1	Food, beverages and tobacco	8011	16190	27826	31066	36052	39288	42661	44867	48606	51328	54538	57118
	A Food	6044	12261	21103	23548	27370	29406	31829	33776	36177	37612	39113	40082
	B Non-alcoholic beverages	156	301	539	577	688	771	864	917	1014	1097	1231	1361
	C Alcoholic beverages	1097	2468	4026	4622	5255	5922	6406	6712	7559	8278	9416	10409
	D Tobacco	714	1160	2158	2319	2739	3189	3562	3462	3856	4341	4778	5266
2	Clothing and footwear	2076	3431	6292	6404	6871	7482	8203	9435	9797	11738	12561	13195
3	Gross rent, fuel and power	4484	10395	18644	22072	25129	27449	29946	32829	34381	35981	38065	41571
	A Fuel and power	679	1823	5105	6094	6592	6803	7082	8031	7375	8050	7819	8011
	B Other	3805	8572	13539	15978	18537	20646	22864	24798	27006	27931	30246	33560
4	Furniture, furnishings and household equipment and operation	1718	4177	7726	8377	9228	10686	11690	12310	13260	14800	16474	17617
	A Household operation	238	316	1183	1319	1456	1611	1855	2038	2155	2290	2395	2560

Finland

2.5 Private Final Consumption Expenditure by Type and Purpose, in Current Prices
(Continued)

Million Finnish markkaa

	1970	1975	1980	1981	1982	1983	1984	1985	1986	1987	1988	1989
B Other	1480	3861	6543	7058	7772	9075	9835	10272	11105	12510	14079	15057
5 Medical care and health expenses	700	1448	3275	3615	4063	4832	5499	6087	6713	7526	8667	9479
6 Transport and communication	3811	8997	17285	19703	22916	24944	27354	30918	32081	36198	41965	46626
A Personal transport equipment	1253	2796	4886	5366	7046	7199	8095	9874	10951	12705	15950	17534
B Other	2558	6201	12399	14337	15870	17745	19259	21044	21130	23493	26015	29092
7 Recreational, entertainment, education and cultural services	1608	4271	9613	11126	12233	14453	15774	16908	18789	20659	22392	25182
8 Miscellaneous goods and services	2723	6499	10522	12112	13840	15844	18165	20203	22245	25443	28575	31946
A Personal care	361	800	1609	1840	2051	2348	2767	2882	3084	3610	3756	4031
B Expenditures in restaurants, cafes and hotels	1281	3391	6387	7337	8368	9579	10855	12279	13529	15195	17197	19728
C Other	1081	2308	2526	2935	3421	3917	4543	5042	5632	6638	7622	8187
Total Final Consumption Expenditure in the Domestic Market by Households, of which	25131	55408	101183	114475	130332	144978	159292	173557	185872	203673	223237	242734
A Durable goods	2436	6388	10765	11831	14132	16022	17668	19903	21534	24295	28900	31562
B Semi-durable goods	3851	7516	14148	15179	16717	18370	19774	21774	23567	27464	29798	31903
C Non-durable goods	10447	22351	42418	47954	53952	58791	63657	67614	70503	75446	79849	84627
D Services	8397	19153	33852	39511	45531	51795	58193	64266	70268	76468	84690	94642
Plus: Direct purchases abroad by resident households	418	1151	2294	2659	3147	3599	4250	5031	5587	6811	7907	8958
Less: Direct purchases in the domestic market by non-resident households	560	1250	2614	3064	2869	2851	3039	3258	3195	3736	4280	4484
Equals: Final Consumption Expenditure of Resident Households	24989	55309	100863	114070	130610	145726	160503	175330	188264	206748	226864	247208

Final Consumption Expenditure of Private Non-profit Institutions Serving Households

	1970	1975	1980	1981	1982	1983	1984	1985	1986	1987	1988	1989
1 Research and science	...	28	58	63	68	75	83	89	96	104	115	127
2 Education	...	545	708	791	906	976	1052	1186	1278	1305	1420	1506
3 Medical and other health services	62	155	210	254	316	373	424	516	570	690	784	847
4 Welfare services	48	122	258	298	320	353	302	346	362	382	476	507
5 Recreational and related cultural services	...	194	427	537	618	695	772	854	894	943	1086	1227
6 Religious organisations	...	508	1019	1193	1373	1582	1701	1882	2011	2201	2392	2632
7 Professional and labour organisations serving households	...	166	383	446	516	584	647	719	758	801	905	999
8 Miscellaneous	...	209	449	513	574	639	693	742	775	810	904	966
Equals: Final Consumption Expenditure of Private Non-profit Organisations Serving Households	912	1927	3512	4095	4691	5277	5674	6334	6744	7236	8082	8811
Private Final Consumption Expenditure	25901	57236	104375	118165	135301	151003	166177	181664	195008	213984	234946	256019

2.6 Private Final Consumption Expenditure by Type and Purpose, in Constant Prices

Million Finnish markkaa

	1970	1975	1980	1981	1982	1983	1984	1985	1986	1987	1988	1989
			At constant prices of:									
			1980					1985				

Final Consumption Expenditure of Resident Households

	1970	1975	1980	1981	1982	1983	1984	1985	1986	1987	1988	1989
1 Food, beverages and tobacco	23522	26953	... / 43429	43211	44617	45220	45369	44867	47044	47966	49336	50084
A Food	18004	19995	... / 32867	32682	33863	34205	34006	33776	35128	35566	36671	36734
B Non-alcoholic beverages	600	604	... / 890	840	926	931	955	917	974	986	1073	1119
C Alcoholic beverages	2801	3966	... / 6182	6370	6366	6479	6623	6712	7282	7525	7742	8214
D Tobacco	2117	2388	... / 3490	3319	3462	3605	3785	3462	3660	3889	3850	4017
2 Clothing and footwear	5473	5385	... / 8879	8139	8248	8392	8670	9435	9370	10901	11517	11665
3 Gross rent, fuel and power	11573	14999	... / 27573	28324	29326	30233	31427	32829	33786	35145	36043	37149
A Fuel and power	2420	2759	... / 6932	7014	6998	6964	7225	8031	7914	8472	8232	8154

Finland

2.6 Private Final Consumption Expenditure by Type and Purpose, in Constant Prices
(Continued)

Million Finnish markkaa	1970	1975	1980	1981	1982	1983	1984	1985	1986	1987	1988	1989
		1980	At constant prices of:					**1985**				
B Other	9153	12240	20641	21310	22328	23269	24202	24798	25872	26673	27811	28995
4 Furniture, furnishings and household equipment and operation	5067	6636	11078	11020	11369	12110	12312	12310	12801	13716	14670	15062
A Household operation	1175	702	2043	1990	1964	1975	2022	2038	2072	2042	2015	1995
B Other	3892	5934	9035	9030	9405	10135	10290	10272	10729	11674	12655	13067
5 Medical care and health expenses	2004	2314	5551	5533	5679	5929	5941	6087	6337	6716	7045	7090
6 Transport and communication	12911	17113	25245	25938	28279	27730	28806	30918	32134	34447	37412	39727
A Personal transport equipment	4212	5447	7108	7208	8963	7908	8593	9874	10109	10983	12808	13363
B Other	8699	11666	18137	18730	19316	19822	20213	21044	22025	23464	24604	26364
7 Recreational, entertainment, education and cultural services	4714	6739	14661	15283	15627	16595	16841	16908	17872	18557	19263	20523
8 Miscellaneous goods and services	9222	11105	16910	17468	17864	18279	19380	20203	20901	22848	24336	25636
A Personal care	1108	1255	2482	2521	2560	2692	2929	2882	2928	3334	3400	3465
B Expenditures in restaurants, cafes and hotels	4419	5949	10721	11037	11165	11353	11834	12279	12569	13406	14304	15197
C Other	3695	3901	3707	3910	4139	4234	4617	5042	5404	6108	6632	6974
Total Final Consumption Expenditure in the Domestic Market by Households, of which	74486	91244	153326	154916	161009	164488	168746	173557	180245	190296	199622	206936
A Durable goods	7188	10426	14551	14990	17270	17518	18451	19903	20410	21873	24641	25781
B Semi-durable goods	10476	11981	20517	20024	20675	20954	21143	21774	22569	25212	26595	27338
C Non-durable goods	32380	38467	64624	64430	65418	66385	67115	67614	70478	72981	74665	76233
D Services	24442	30370	53634	55472	57646	59631	62037	64266	66788	70230	73721	77584
Plus: Direct purchases abroad by resident households	1204	1969	3160	3395	3767	3963	4464	5031	5437	6505	7363	8148
Less: Direct purchases in the domestic market by non-resident households	1646	2082	4265	4404	3684	3299	3282	3258	3055	3415	3712	3648
Equals: Final Consumption Expenditure of Resident Households	74044	91131	152221	153907	161092	165152	169928	175330	182627	193386	203273	211436

Final Consumption Expenditure of Private Non-profit Institutions Serving Households

1 Research and science	...	45	88	86	86	85	87	89	92	93	95	100
2 Education	...	882	1105	1094	1139	1125	1131	1186	1227	1182	1179	1173
3 Medical and other health services	180	243	316	343	386	416	451	516	552	649	654	659

Finland

2.6 Private Final Consumption Expenditure by Type and Purpose, in Constant Prices
(Continued)

Million Finnish markkaa

	1970	1975	1980	1981	1982	1983	1984	1985	1986	1987	1988	1989
					At constant prices of:							
		1980						1985				
4 Welfare services	141	197	408	421	412	413	322	346	340	344	376	374
5 Recreational and related cultural services	...	329	653	729	769	801	826	854	862	868	916	971
6 Religious organisations	...	795	1641	1723	1800	1903	1868	1882	1938	2002	1963	2015
7 Professional and labour organisations serving households	...	296	598	630	672	715	692	719	728	718	748	760
8 Miscellaneous	...	362	672	682	697	720	733	742	747	739	752	755
Equals: Final Consumption Expenditure of Private Non-profit Organisations Serving Households	2873	3149	5481	5708	5961	6178	6110	6334	6486	6595	6683	6807
Private Final Consumption Expenditure	76917	94280	157702	159615	167053	171330	176038	181664	189113	199981	209956	218243

2.11 Gross Fixed Capital Formation by Kind of Activity of Owner, ISIC Divisions, in Current Prices

Million Finnish markkaa

	1970	1975	1980	1981	1982	1983	1984	1985	1986	1987	1988	1989
						All Producers						
1 Agriculture, hunting, forestry and fishing	918	2366	4564	4747	5625	6018	6093	6336	6171	5865	6344	7139
A Agriculture and hunting	...	...	3379	3434	4211	4577	4509	4689	4479	4133	4416	5061
B Forestry and logging	...	...	1085	1222	1320	1342	1481	1537	1578	1613	1801	1940
C Fishing	...	...	100	91	94	99	103	110	114	119	127	138
2 Mining and quarrying	49	181	181	223	352	221	137	312	260	204	175	306
A Coal mining	...	...	...	...	...	...	...	...	...	...	...	...
B Crude petroleum and natural gas production	...	...	...	...	...	...	...	...	...	...	...	...
C Metal ore mining	...	...	...	...	...	...	...	...	113	14	21	73
D Other mining	...	...	...	...	...	...	...	...	147	190	154	233
3 Manufacturing	2491	6471	8519	9981	10855	10524	11419	13030	13610	17207	14595	21078
A Manufacturing of food, beverages and tobacco	...	...	1117	1100	1474	1432	1217	1304	1407	1957	1481	1952
B Textile, wearing apparel and leather industries	...	...	397	392	506	375	357	270	391	486	-90	353
C Manufacture of wood, and wood products, including furniture	...	...	860	874	731	813	762	879	821	839	692	1592
D Manufacture of paper and paper products, printing and publishing	...	...	2463	3014	3318	3122	3708	4535	4536	5602	5878	8281
E Manufacture of chemicals and chemical petroleum, coal, rubber and plastic products	...	...	1051	1587	1456	1414	1647	1636	1841	2911	2303	2683
F Manufacture of non-metalic mineral products except products of petroleum and coal	...	...	347	413	510	478	542	473	583	684	607	845
G Basic metal industries	...	...	516	683	525	423	458	740	1125	1535	1101	1417
H Manufacture of fabricated metal products, machinery and equipment	...	...	1729	1880	2285	2418	2678	3131	2837	3133	2540	3885
I Other manufacturing industries	...	...	39	38	50	49	50	62	69	60	83	70
4 Electricity, gas and water	567	3187	2221	2635	3690	3553	3502	4119	4298	4383	4089	5336
A Electricity, gas and steam	...	...	...	...	...	...	...	...	3750	3818	3550	4820
B Water works and supply	...	...	...	...	...	...	...	...	548	565	539	516
5 Construction	302	645	994	1160	1209	1820	1666	1004	1160	1599	2334	2689
6 Wholesale and retail trade, restaurants and hotels	929	1882	2847	3235	3447	4825	4850	5439	5842	6996	6622	11282
A Wholesale and retail trade	...	...	2482	2867	3134	4415	4413	4995	5340	6462	6097	9676
B Restaurants and hotels	...	...	365	368	313	410	437	444	502	534	525	1606
7 Transport, storage and communication	1224	3621	4701	5191	4809	5757	5470	5720	6824	7166	8001	10891
A Transport and storage	...	...	3689	3932	3526	4242	4019	3940	4675	4712	5206	7782

Finland

2.11 Gross Fixed Capital Formation by Kind of Activity of Owner, ISIC Divisions, in Current Prices
(Continued)

Million Finnish markkaa

	1970	1975	1980	1981	1982	1983	1984	1985	1986	1987	1988	1989
B Communication	...	...	1012	1259	1283	1515	1451	1780	2149	2454	2795	3109
8 Finance, insurance, real estate and business services	3643	9582	17182	19321	22085	25622	27732	30481	30712	32791	50862	57682
A Financial institutions	...	...	504	607	573	843	1077	954	1853	1375	-1007	1642
B Insurance	...	...	662	615	663	513	757	587	490	364	1962	998
C Real estate and business services	...	...	16016	18099	20849	24266	25898	28940	28369	31052	49907	55042
Real estate except dwellings	...	...	694	815	786	2249	2429	4122	3846	3936	13905	8189
Dwellings	...	...	14208	15302	17555	19451	20493	21305	20627	22476	29479	39219
9 Community, social and personal services	261	733	1159	1214	1318	1696	2119	2243	2462	2769	2972	4288
A Sanitary and similar services	...	...	662	672	720	882	1104	1063	1137	1060	1276	1579
B Social and related community services	...	...	91	109	122	140	168	199	222	295	376	482
Educational services	...	...	53	58	63	71	81	86	98	135	166	217
Medical, dental, other health and veterinary services	...	...	29	37	42	48	64	82	87	114	131	169
C Recreational and cultural services	...	...	210	216	256	405	535	624	715	956	792	1562
D Personal and household services	...	...	196	217	220	269	312	357	388	458	528	665
Total Industries	10384	28668	42368	47707	53390	60036	62988	68684	71339	78980	95994	120691
Producers of Government Services	1486	3635	6102	6942	8109	9235	9605	10453	11176	12971	13614	14374
Private Non-Profit Institutions Serving Households	140	364	661	678	747	775	833	915	997	1319	1440	1540
Total	12010	32667	49131	55327	62246	70046	73426	80052	83512	93270	111048	136605

2.12 Gross Fixed Capital Formation by Kind of Activity of Owner, ISIC Divisions, in Constant Prices

Million Finnish markkaa

	1970	1975	1980	1981	1982	1983	1984	1985	1986	1987	1988	1989
			1980	\multicolumn{5}{c}{At constant prices of:}	1985				
				\multicolumn{6}{c}{All Producers}				
1 Agriculture, hunting, forestry and fishing	3300	4040	6470	6105	6793	6675	6362	6336	5888	5388	5573	5984
A Agriculture and hunting	...	...	4769	4418	5101	5074	4693	4689	4274	3784	3885	4218
B Forestry and logging	...	...	1561	1569	1577	1488	1557	1537	1504	1493	1573	1646
C Fishing	...	...	140	118	115	113	112	110	110	111	115	120
2 Mining and quarrying	156	287	254	288	427	246	147	312	253	189	156	261
A Coal mining	...	...	...	...	...	...	...	...	...	...	...	...
B Crude petroleum and natural gas production	...	...	...	...	...	...	...	...	...	...	...	...
C Metal ore mining	...	...	...	...	...	...	...	...	111	15	21	63
D Other mining	...	...	...	...	...	...	...	...	143	174	135	198

Finland

2.12 Gross Fixed Capital Formation by Kind of Activity of Owner, ISIC Divisions, in Constant Prices
(Continued)

Million Finnish markkaa

	1970	1975	1980	1981	1982	1983	1984	1985	1986	1987	1988	1989
		1980	At constant prices of:					1985				
3 Manufacturing	8329	10414	11535	12344	12463	11902	12098	13030	13199	16020	13072	17022
A Manufacturing of food, beverages and tobacco	...	...	1522	1368	1709	1617	1286	1304	1350	1784	1342	1581
B Textile, wearing apparel and leather industries	...	...	535	483	582	422	377	270	375	446	-22	298
C Manufacture of wood, and wood products, including furniture	...	...	1108	1049	821	920	813	879	811	802	703	1403
D Manufacture of paper and paper products, printing and publishing	...	...	3425	3843	3838	3569	3958	4535	4423	5209	5021	6226
E Manufacture of chemicals and chemical petroleum, coal, rubber and plastic products	...	...	1404	1919	1653	1591	1730	1636	1765	2685	2060	2198
F Manufacture of non-metalic mineral products except products of petroleum and coal	...	...	458	506	586	540	576	473	573	650	543	707
G Basic metal industries	...	...	687	824	590	476	484	740	1108	1488	1014	1272
H Manufacture of fabricated metal products, machinery and equipment	...	...	2343	2303	2626	2712	2821	3131	2728	2900	2338	3276
I Other manufacturing industries	...	...	53	49	58	55	53	62	66	56	73	61
4 Electricity, gas and water	1839	5032	3170	3441	4499	3964	3672	4119	4109	4017	3559	4286
A Electricity, gas and steam	...	...	...	...	...	...	...	...	3590	3504	3101	3881
B Water works and supply	...	...	...	...	...	...	...	...	519	513	458	405
5 Construction	1021	1093	1428	1506	1466	2029	1747	1004	1124	1509	2131	2358
6 Wholesale and retail trade, restaurants and hotels	3259	3213	4255	4316	4243	5535	5175	5439	5599	6299	5825	9047
A Wholesale and retail trade	...	...	3708	3796	3861	5064	4704	4995	5117	5815	5358	7812
B Restaurants and hotels	...	...	547	520	382	471	471	444	482	484	467	1235
7 Transport, storage and communication	3947	5963	6793	6991	5882	6571	5801	5720	6581	6670	7383	9194
A Transport and storage	...	...	5394	5379	4344	4891	4282	3940	4486	4366	4851	6455
B Communication	...	...	1399	1612	1538	1680	1519	1780	2095	2304	2532	2739
8 Finance, insurance, real estate and business services	12484	15852	25912	26315	27946	29287	29466	30481	29267	28996	40400	41503
A Financial institutions	...	...	708	777	690	939	1130	954	1785	1276	-669	1365
B Insurance	...	...	1001	836	836	584	809	587	469	326	1606	761
C Real estate and business services	...	...	24203	24702	26420	27764	27527	28940	27013	27394	39463	39377
Real estate except dwellings	...	...	1060	1072	958	2478	2523	4122	3664	3431	10687	5847
Dwellings	...	...	21606	21078	22456	22494	21923	21305	19597	19755	23055	27139
9 Community, social and personal services	893	1188	1705	1619	1617	1908	2233	2243	2353	2499	2544	3418
A Sanitary and similar services	...	...	982	899	895	1000	1166	1063	1084	962	1075	1239
B Social and related community services	...	...	131	145	148	154	177	199	210	262	315	385

Finland

2.12 Gross Fixed Capital Formation by Kind of Activity of Owner, ISIC Divisions, in Constant Prices
(Continued)

Million Finnish markkaa

	1970	1975	1980	1981	1982	1983	1984	1985	1986	1987	1988	1989
			1980		At constant prices of:			1985				
Educational services	...	...	76	77	77	79	85	86	92	118	133	168
Medical, dental, other health and veterinary services	...	...	42	50	51	53	69	82	84	104	115	140
C Recreational and cultural services	...	...	309	289	307	455	562	624	688	869	706	1257
D Personal and household services	...	...	283	286	267	299	328	357	371	406	448	537
Total Industries	35228	47082	61522	62925	65336	68117	66701	68684	68373	71587	80643	93073
Producers of Government Services	4967	5803	9067	9284	10093	10467	10202	10453	10738	11654	11446	11257
Private Non-Profit Institutions Serving Households	464	589	979	909	933	884	883	915	956	1174	1196	1179
Total	40659	53474	71568	73118	76362	79468	77786	80052	80067	84415	93285	105509

2.13 Stocks of Reproducible Fixed Assets, by Type of Good and Owner, in Current Prices

Million Finnish markkaa

	TOTAL Gross	TOTAL Net	Total Private Gross	Total Private Net	Public Enterprises Gross	Public Enterprises Net	General Government Gross	General Government Net
				1980				
1 Residential buildings	303000	215510	303000	215510	...	...	...	...
2 Non-residential buildings	250119	164836	176479	113489	...	...	73640	51347
3 Other construction a	188094	123069	115059	68006	...	...	73035	55063
4 Land improvement and plantation and orchard development a	...	...	...	...	...	...	...	...
5 Producers' durable goods	222800	119723	216256	116113	...	...	6544	3610
6 Breeding stock, dairy cattle, etc.	...	...	...	...	...	...	...	...
Total	964013	623138	810794	513118	...	...	153219	110020
				1981				
1 Residential buildings	347955	246645	347955	246645	...	...	...	...
2 Non-residential buildings	288107	189172	202829	130108	...	...	85278	59064
3 Other construction a	214838	139317	130602	76275	...	...	84236	63042
4 Land improvement and plantation and orchard development a	...	...	...	...	...	...	...	...
5 Producers' durable goods	250240	134426	242858	130355	...	...	7382	4071
6 Breeding stock, dairy cattle, etc.	...	...	...	...	...	...	...	...
Total	1101140	709560	924244	583383	...	...	176896	126177
				1982				
1 Residential buildings	390180	275761	390180	275761	...	...	...	...
2 Non-residential buildings	323677	211956	227677	145802	...	...	96000	66154
3 Other construction a	236852	152349	143302	82830	...	...	93550	69519
4 Land improvement and plantation and orchard development a	...	...	...	...	...	...	...	...
5 Producers' durable goods	277849	148981	269637	144423	...	...	8212	4558
6 Breeding stock, dairy cattle, etc.	...	...	...	...	...	...	...	...
Total	1228560	789047	1030800	648816	...	...	197760	140231
				1983				
1 Residential buildings	448560	315881	448560	315881	...	...	...	...
2 Non-residential buildings	368913	241639	258037	165612	...	...	110876	76027
3 Other construction a	264150	168357	158969	90757	...	...	105181	77600
4 Land improvement and plantation and orchard development a	...	...	...	...	...	...	...	...
5 Producers' durable goods	300817	161196	291447	155919	...	...	9370	5277
6 Breeding stock, dairy cattle, etc.	...	...	...	...	...	...	...	...
Total	1382440	887073	1157010	728169	...	...	225430	158904

Finland

2.13 Stocks of Reproducible Fixed Assets, by Type of Good and Owner, in Current Prices
(Continued)

Million Finnish markkaa

		TOTAL Gross	TOTAL Net	Total Private Gross	Total Private Net	Public Enterprises Gross	Public Enterprises Net	General Government Gross	General Government Net
	1984								
1	Residential buildings	502805	352460	502805	352460	...	...	...	...
2	Non-residential buildings	409707	267675	285668	183198	...	...	124039	84477
3	Other construction a	285503	180187	171491	96693	...	...	114012	83494
4	Land improvement and plantation and orchard development a	...	...	...	...	...	...	...	...
5	Producers' durable goods	329860	176543	319302	170502	...	...	10558	6041
6	Breeding stock, dairy cattle, etc.	...	...	...	...	...	...	...	...
	Total	1527880	976865	1279270	802853	...	...	248610	174012
	1985								
1	Residential buildings	556124	387672	556124	387672	...	...	...	...
2	Non-residential buildings	451894	294276	313831	200922	...	...	138063	93354
3	Other construction a	307061	192225	183511	102427	...	...	123550	89798
4	Land improvement and plantation and orchard development a	...	...	...	...	...	...	...	...
5	Producers' durable goods	358631	192230	346741	185301	...	...	11890	6929
6	Breeding stock, dairy cattle, etc.	...	...	...	...	...	...	...	...
	Total	1673710	1066400	1400210	876322	...	...	273500	190078
	1986								
1	Residential buildings	602725	417108	602725	417108	...	...	...	...
2	Non-residential buildings	490436	318139	340452	217579	...	...	149984	100560
3	Other construction a	328135	203528	197388	109126	...	...	130747	94402
4	Land improvement and plantation and orchard development a	...	...	...	...	...	...	...	...
5	Producers' durable goods	383382	205520	369869	197507	...	...	13513	8013
6	Breeding stock, dairy cattle, etc.	...	...	...	...	...	...	...	...
	Total	1804680	1144300	1510430	941320	...	...	294250	202980
	1987								
1	Residential buildings	670229	460357	670229	460357	...	...	...	...
2	Non-residential buildings	550865	355973	381093	242987	...	...	169772	112986
3	Other construction a	348642	214969	206644	113086	...	...	141998	101883
4	Land improvement and plantation and orchard development a	...	...	...	...	...	...	...	...
5	Producers' durable goods	415637	223839	400258	214538	...	...	15379	9301
6	Breeding stock, dairy cattle, etc.	...	...	...	...	...	...	...	...
	Total	1985370	1255140	1658220	1030970	...	...	327146	224170
	1988								
1	Residential buildings	779274	532357	779274	532357	...	...	...	...
2	Non-residential buildings	627320	404198	436110	278012	...	...	191210	126186
3	Other construction a	376637	230340	221794	120012	...	...	154843	110328
4	Land improvement and plantation and orchard development a	...	...	...	...	...	...	...	...
5	Producers' durable goods	453153	246752	435741	236080	...	...	17412	10672
6	Breeding stock, dairy cattle, etc.	...	...	...	...	...	...	...	...
	Total	2236384	1413647	1872919	1166461	...	...	363465	247186
	1989								
1	Residential buildings	915810	623743	915810	623743	...	...	...	...
2	Non-residential buildings	705119	453338	489205	312307	...	...	215914	141031
3	Other construction a	411464	250091	240283	128969	...	...	171181	121122
4	Land improvement and plantation and orchard development a	...	...	...	...	...	...	...	...
5	Producers' durable goods	508003	280278	488163	268021	...	...	19840	12257
6	Breeding stock, dairy cattle, etc.	...	...	...	...	...	...	...	...
	Total	2540396	1607450	2133461	1333040	...	...	406935	274410

a) Item 'Land improvement and plantation and orchard development' is included in item 'Other construction'.

Finland

2.14 Stocks of Reproducible Fixed Assets, by Type of Good and Owner, in Constant Prices

Million Finnish markkaa

		TOTAL Gross	TOTAL Net	Total Private Gross	Total Private Net	Public Enterprises Gross	Public Enterprises Net	General Government Gross	General Government Net
		\multicolumn{9}{c}{At constant prices of: 1985}
		\multicolumn{9}{c}{**1980**}
1	Residential buildings	460696	327672	460696	327672	...	...	...	...
2	Non-residential buildings	377338	248769	264739	170257	...	...	112599	78512
3	Other construction a	275559	180291	168463	99549	...	...	107096	80742
4	Land improvement and plantation and orchard development a	...	...	...	...	...	...	...	...
5	Producers' durable goods	305970	164256	297225	159443	...	...	8745	4813
6	Breeding stock, dairy cattle, etc.	...	...	...	...	...	...	...	...
	Total	1419560	920988	1191120	756921	...	...	228440	164067
		\multicolumn{9}{c}{**1981**}
1	Residential buildings	479342	339779	479342	339779	...	...	...	...
2	Non-residential buildings	390246	256340	272977	175119	...	...	117269	81221
3	Other construction a	282100	182893	171798	100340	...	...	110302	82553
4	Land improvement and plantation and orchard development a	...	...	...	...	...	...	...	...
5	Producers' durable goods	316648	169919	307465	164863	...	...	9183	5056
6	Breeding stock, dairy cattle, etc.	...	...	...	...	...	...	...	...
	Total	1468340	948931	1231580	780101	...	...	236754	168830
		\multicolumn{9}{c}{**1982**}
1	Residential buildings	499143	352770	499143	352770	...	...	...	...
2	Non-residential buildings	404453	264996	281941	180572	...	...	122512	84424
3	Other construction a	288936	185796	175307	101353	...	...	113629	84443
4	Land improvement and plantation and orchard development a	...	...	...	...	...	...	...	...
5	Producers' durable goods	326655	175015	316986	169656	...	...	9669	5359
6	Breeding stock, dairy cattle, etc.	...	...	...	...	...	...	...	...
	Total	1519190	978577	1273380	804351	...	...	245810	174226
		\multicolumn{9}{c}{**1983**}
1	Residential buildings	518806	365349	518806	365349	...	...	...	...
2	Non-residential buildings	421258	275995	293314	188264	...	...	127944	87731
3	Other construction a	295006	187943	178053	101657	...	...	116953	86286
4	Land improvement and plantation and orchard development a	...	...	...	...	...	...	...	...
5	Producers' durable goods	336933	180501	326655	174712	...	...	10278	5789
6	Breeding stock, dairy cattle, etc.	...	...	...	...	...	...	...	...
	Total	1572000	1009790	1316830	829982	...	...	255175	179806
		\multicolumn{9}{c}{**1984**}
1	Residential buildings	537816	377002	537816	377002	...	...	...	...
2	Non-residential buildings	436620	285293	303617	194711	...	...	133003	90582
3	Other construction a	300826	189868	180577	101808	...	...	120249	88060
4	Land improvement and plantation and orchard development a	...	...	...	...	...	...	...	...
5	Producers' durable goods	346868	185609	335889	179329	...	...	10979	6280
6	Breeding stock, dairy cattle, etc.	...	...	...	...	...	...	...	...
	Total	1622130	1037770	1357900	852850	...	...	264231	184922
		\multicolumn{9}{c}{**1985**}
1	Residential buildings	556124	387672	556124	387672	...	...	...	...
2	Non-residential buildings	451894	294276	313831	200922	...	...	138063	93354
3	Other construction a	307061	192225	183511	102427	...	...	123550	89798
4	Land improvement and plantation and orchard development a	...	...	...	...	...	...	...	...
5	Producers' durable goods	358631	192230	346741	185301	...	...	11890	6929
6	Breeding stock, dairy cattle, etc.	...	...	...	...	...	...	...	...
	Total	1673710	1066400	1400210	876322	...	...	273503	190081

Finland

2.14 Stocks of Reproducible Fixed Assets, by Type of Good and Owner, in Constant Prices
(Continued)

Million Finnish markkaa

	TOTAL Gross	TOTAL Net	Total Private Gross	Total Private Net	Public Enterprises Gross	Public Enterprises Net	General Government Gross	General Government Net
At constant prices of: 1985								
1986								
1 Residential buildings	572660	396302	572660	396302	...	...	...	...
2 Non-residential buildings	467140	303025	324298	207254	...	...	142842	95771
3 Other construction [a]	313746	195030	186560	103204	...	...	127186	91826
4 Land improvement and plantation and orchard development [a]	...	...	...	...	...	...	...	...
5 Producers' durable goods	371004	198955	358015	191252	...	...	12989	7703
6 Breeding stock, dairy cattle, etc.	...	...	...	...	...	...	...	...
Total	1724550	1093310	1441530	898012	...	...	283017	195300
1987								
1 Residential buildings	589264	404745	589264	404745	...	...	...	...
2 Non-residential buildings	482685	311887	334671	213381	...	...	148014	98506
3 Other construction [a]	320091	197481	189080	103484	...	...	131011	93997
4 Land improvement and plantation and orchard development [a]	...	...	...	...	...	...	...	...
5 Producers' durable goods	386700	208500	372337	199814	...	...	14363	8686
6 Breeding stock, dairy cattle, etc.	...	...	...	...	...	...	...	...
Total	1778740	1122610	1485350	921424	...	...	293388	201189
1988								
1 Residential buildings	608998	416034	608998	416034	...	...	...	...
2 Non-residential buildings	499537	321885	346569	220936	...	...	152968	100949
3 Other construction [a]	326119	199602	191464	103665	...	...	134655	95937
4 Land improvement and plantation and orchard development [a]	...	...	...	...	...	...	...	...
5 Producers' durable goods	406059	221255	390201	211537	...	...	15858	9718
6 Breeding stock, dairy cattle, etc.	...	...	...	...	...	...	...	...
Total	1840710	1158780	1537230	952172	...	...	303481	206604
1989								
1 Residential buildings	632640	430881	632640	430881	...	...	...	...
2 Non-residential buildings	517174	332483	359768	229668	...	...	157406	102815
3 Other construction [a]	332730	202288	194383	104406	...	...	138347	97882
4 Land improvement and plantation and orchard development [a]	...	...	...	...	...	...	...	...
5 Producers' durable goods	428867	236909	411401	226118	...	...	17466	10791
6 Breeding stock, dairy cattle, etc.	...	...	...	...	...	...	...	...
Total	1911410	1202560	1598190	991073	...	...	313219	211488

a) Item 'Land improvement and plantation and orchard development' is included in item 'Other construction'.

2.15 Stocks of Reproducible Fixed Assets by Kind of Activity, in Current Prices

Million Finnish markkaa

	1980 Gross	1980 Net	1981 Gross	1981 Net	1982 Gross	1982 Net	1983 Gross	1983 Net	1984 Gross	1984 Net	1985 Gross	1985 Net
1 Residential buildings	303000	215510	347955	246645	390180	275761	448560	315881	502805	352460	556124	387672
2 Non-residential buildings	250119	164836	288107	189172	323677	211956	368913	241639	409707	267675	451894	294276
A Industries	168685	108147	193702	123829	217333	138668	246090	157375	272206	173932	298883	190661
1 Agriculture	22234	11113	24395	12301	26659	13686	29647	15510	31925	16820	33945	18018
2 Mining and quarrying	897	505	982	535	1072	576	1165	602	1222	604	1320	645
3 Manufacturing	45598	29023	52368	33092	59919	37761	66387	41548	72989	45232	80005	48991
4 Electricity, gas and water	9979	6711	11316	7529	12450	8197	14135	9221	15402	9912	16841	10746
5 Construction	3319	2387	3865	2764	4436	3164	5391	3896	6177	4460	6354	4396
6 Wholesale and retail trade	33912	21075	39023	24155	43442	26764	48052	29699	52955	32741	58013	35853
7 Transport and communication	6423	4859	7500	5618	8566	6366	9858	7228	11028	7979	12084	8602

Finland

2.15 Stocks of Reproducible Fixed Assets by Kind of Activity, in Current Prices
(Continued)

Million Finnish markkaa

	1980 Gross	1980 Net	1981 Gross	1981 Net	1982 Gross	1982 Net	1983 Gross	1983 Net	1984 Gross	1984 Net	1985 Gross	1985 Net
8 Finance, etc.	38889	27301	45707	31926	50955	35404	60398	42097	68037	47630	76504	53979
9 Community, social and personal services	7434	5173	8546	5909	9834	6750	11057	7574	12471	8554	13817	9431
B Producers of government services	73640	51347	85278	59064	96000	66154	110876	76027	124039	84477	138063	93354
C Other producers	7794	5342	9127	6279	10344	7134	11947	8237	13462	9266	14948	10261
3 Other construction [a]	188094	123069	214838	139317	236852	152349	264150	168357	285503	180187	307061	192225
A Industries	114212	67451	129623	75634	142210	82114	157760	89966	170179	95837	182084	101493
1 Agriculture	37359	21204	42871	23942	46771	25772	51473	27967	55326	29627	59173	31237
2 Mining and quarrying	781	519	909	602	1065	708	1232	807	1292	820	1384	851
3 Manufacturing	9991	6383	11161	6994	12241	7537	13603	8208	14675	8720	15565	9084
4 Electricity, gas and water	27437	14699	31057	16669	34370	18549	38356	20690	41298	22250	43999	23778
5 Construction	5	5	6	6	10	9	11	10	18	16	23	21
6 Wholesale and retail trade	521	303	582	332	619	350	683	382	719	395	750	404
7 Transport and communication	28157	17518	31454	19280	34317	20681	37831	22385	40594	23544	43556	24925
8 Finance, etc.	-	-	-	-	-	-	-	-	-	-	-	-
9 Community, social and personal services	9961	6820	11583	7809	12817	8508	14571	9517	16257	10465	17634	11193
B Producers of government services	73035	55063	84236	63042	93550	69519	105181	77600	114012	83494	123550	89798
C Other producers	847	555	979	641	1092	716	1209	791	1312	856	1427	934
4 Land improvement and development and plantation and orchard development [a]	...	...	...	...	...	...	...	...	...	...	...	...
5 Producers' durable goods	222800	119723	250240	134426	277849	148981	300817	161196	329860	176543	358631	192230
A Industries	215341	115625	241826	129806	268509	143822	290201	155254	317931	169766	345244	184488
1 Agriculture	24975	12849	28262	14427	30822	15700	34282	17364	36902	18693	38727	19588
2 Mining and quarrying	2342	1326	2592	1443	2850	1590	3094	1680	3295	1725	3580	1856
3 Manufacturing	80749	42918	91003	48782	101300	54382	103418	55238	113518	60509	124457	66645
4 Electricity, gas and water	23106	14953	25412	15955	27475	17051	30829	18801	33567	20121	36003	21272
5 Construction	7634	3551	8512	4019	9033	4314	10006	4982	10585	5446	11031	5798
6 Wholesale and retail trade	21392	10705	24404	12188	26793	13383	29793	15094	32744	16756	35906	18667
7 Transport and communication	43478	23056	47392	24886	52846	27072	57383	29142	61887	30948	65305	32024
8 Finance, etc.	8326	4525	10533	6181	13253	8188	16610	10422	20013	12601	24030	15113
9 Community, social and personal services	3339	1742	3716	1925	4137	2142	4786	2531	5420	2967	6205	3525
B Producers of government services	6544	3610	7382	4071	8212	4558	9370	5277	10558	6041	11890	6929
C Other producers	915	488	1032	549	1128	601	1246	665	1371	736	1497	813
6 Breeding stock, dairy cattle, etc.	...	...	...	...	...	...	...	...	...	...	...	...
Total	964013	623138	1101140	709560	1228560	789047	1382440	887073	1527880	976865	1673710	1066400

	1986 Gross	1986 Net	1987 Gross	1987 Net	1988 Gross	1988 Net	1989 Gross	1989 Net
1 Residential buildings	602725	417108	670229	460357	779274	532357	915810	623743
2 Non-residential buildings	490436	318139	550865	355973	627320	404198	705119	453338
A Industries	324156	206431	362450	230225	414895	263504	464986	295785
1 Agriculture	35870	19190	37726	20276	40059	21585	43464	23562
2 Mining and quarrying	1390	668	1516	703	1584	696	1735	736
3 Manufacturing	86227	52176	95941	57514	106609	61728	115871	66505
4 Electricity, gas and water	18058	11421	20139	12617	22120	13635	24741	15072
5 Construction	6609	4417	7355	4826	8309	5384	9428	6043
6 Wholesale and retail trade	62401	38569	69896	43162	76663	46695	87623	53931
7 Transport and communication	12964	9058	14580	10033	15972	10806	18699	12571
8 Finance, etc.	85616	60734	98368	69690	124960	90653	142246	103426
9 Community, social and personal services	15021	10198	16929	11404	18619	12322	21179	13939
B Producers of government services	149984	100560	169772	112986	191210	126186	215914	141031
C Other producers	16296	11148	18643	12762	21215	14508	24219	16522
3 Other construction [a]	328135	203528	348642	214969	376637	230340	411464	250091

Finland

2.15 Stocks of Reproducible Fixed Assets by Kind of Activity, in Current Prices
(Continued)

Million Finnish markkaa

	1986 Gross	1986 Net	1987 Gross	1987 Net	1988 Gross	1988 Net	1989 Gross	1989 Net
A Industries	195857	108113	204957	111966	219932	118766	238201	127569
1 Agriculture	64746	33720	67158	34489	71335	36077	76491	38124
2 Mining and quarrying	1474	882	1566	914	1711	975	1842	1024
3 Manufacturing	16599	9549	17513	9942	18881	10493	20574	11225
4 Electricity, gas and water	46843	25357	49083	26606	53013	28628	58085	31461
5 Construction	19	15	21	17	23	18	27	20
6 Wholesale and retail trade	780	413	814	424	868	440	939	466
7 Transport and communication	46282	26207	48554	27089	51378	28272	54715	29802
8 Finance, etc.	-	-	-	-	50	49	54	52
9 Community, social and personal services	19114	11970	20248	12485	22673	13814	25474	15395
B Producers of government services	130747	94402	141998	101883	154843	110328	171181	121122
C Other producers	1531	1013	1687	1120	1862	1246	2082	1400
4 Land improvement and development and plantation and orchard development [a]	...	...	...	...	...	...	...	...
5 Producers' durable goods	383382	205520	415637	223839	453153	246752	508003	280278
A Industries	368226	196604	398396	213495	433627	234872	485728	266618
1 Agriculture	40066	19976	41522	20290	42639	20653	44170	21489
2 Mining and quarrying	3683	1864	3776	1841	3860	1808	4061	1889
3 Manufacturing	132055	70891	143108	78015	159982	88419	178341	99959
4 Electricity, gas and water	38402	22385	40662	23323	43146	24308	47400	26154
5 Construction	11532	6074	12119	6374	13372	7205	15041	8280
6 Wholesale and retail trade	38382	20233	42289	22841	46465	25871	52130	30079
7 Transport and communication	68165	33154	71417	34488	71728	34826	81569	40567
8 Finance, etc.	28801	17880	34896	21218	42223	25616	50786	30671
9 Community, social and personal services	7140	4147	8607	5105	10212	6166	12230	7530
B Producers of government services	13513	8013	15379	9301	17412	10672	19840	12257
C Other producers	1643	903	1862	1043	2114	1208	2435	1403
6 Breeding stock, dairy cattle, etc.	...	...	...	...	...	...	...	...
Total	1804680	1144300	1985370	1255140	2236380	1413650	2540400	1607450

a) Item 'Land improvement and plantation and orchard development' is included in item 'Other construction'.

2.16 Stocks of Reproducible Fixed Assets by Kind of Activity, in Constant Prices

Million Finnish markkaa

	1980 Gross	1980 Net	1981 Gross	1981 Net	1982 Gross	1982 Net	1983 Gross	1983 Net	1984 Gross	1984 Net	1985 Gross	1985 Net
At constant prices of: 1985												
1 Residential buildings	460696	327672	479342	339779	499143	352770	518806	365349	537816	377002	556124	387672
2 Non-residential buildings	377338	248769	390246	256340	404453	264996	421258	275995	436620	285293	451894	294276
A Industries	252825	162091	260423	166482	268744	171470	279520	178754	289242	184817	298883	190661
1 Agriculture	29804	14845	30441	15317	31400	16094	32507	17001	33219	17500	33945	18018
2 Mining and quarrying	1364	766	1348	733	1362	731	1338	691	1307	646	1320	645
3 Manufacturing	69452	44053	71577	45136	74227	46702	76546	47891	78409	48587	80005	48991
4 Electricity, gas and water	15211	10194	15549	10323	15871	10433	16254	10600	16474	10601	16841	10746
5 Construction	4978	3568	5248	3746	5559	3959	6164	4454	6595	4761	6354	4396
6 Wholesale and retail trade	51684	32009	52702	32553	53595	32966	55272	34150	56666	35034	58013	35853
7 Transport and communication	9655	7280	10198	7623	10800	8013	11272	8262	11723	8481	12084	8602
8 Finance, etc.	59342	41516	61605	42939	63801	44260	67486	47022	71519	50064	76504	53979
9 Community, social and personal services	11335	7860	11755	8112	12129	8312	12681	8683	13330	9143	13817	9431
B Producers of government services	112599	78512	117269	81221	122512	84424	127944	87731	133003	90582	138063	93354
C Other producers	11914	8166	12554	8637	13197	9102	13794	9510	14375	9894	14948	10261
3 Other construction [a]	275559	180291	282100	182893	288936	185796	295006	187943	300826	189868	307061	192225
A Industries	167222	98735	170526	99508	173992	100490	176706	100775	179197	100907	182084	101493

Finland

2.16 Stocks of Reproducible Fixed Assets by Kind of Activity, in Constant Prices
(Continued)

Million Finnish markkaa

	1980 Gross	1980 Net	1981 Gross	1981 Net	1982 Gross	1982 Net	1983 Gross	1983 Net	1984 Gross	1984 Net	1985 Gross	1985 Net
					At constant prices of:1985							
1 Agriculture	56282	31959	56908	31795	57669	31796	58282	31682	58765	31476	59173	31237
2 Mining and quarrying	1143	763	1211	804	1308	871	1367	896	1368	866	1384	851
3 Manufacturing	14745	9427	14893	9338	15078	9286	15190	9167	15412	9159	15565	9084
4 Electricity, gas and water	40505	21717	41358	22213	42313	22845	42900	23144	43377	23372	43999	23778
5 Construction	7	7	9	9	12	11	13	11	19	17	23	21
6 Wholesale and retail trade	765	445	759	434	760	430	759	424	754	415	750	404
7 Transport and communication	38888	24215	39961	24508	40887	24650	41711	24682	42445	24620	43556	24925
8 Finance, etc.	-	-	-	-	-	-	-	-	-	-	-	-
9 Community, social and personal services	14887	10202	15427	10407	15965	10601	16484	10769	17057	10982	17634	11193
B Producers of government services	107096	80742	110302	82553	113629	84443	116953	86286	120249	88060	123550	89798
C Other producers	1241	814	1272	832	1315	863	1347	882	1380	901	1427	934
4 Land improvement and development and plantation and orchard development [a]	...	...	...	...	...	...	...	...	...	...	...	...
5 Producers' durable goods	305970	164256	316648	169919	326655	175015	336933	180501	346868	185609	358631	192230
A Industries	296043	158812	306221	164201	315686	168964	325299	173989	334473	178569	345244	184488
1 Agriculture	35463	18273	36361	18581	37261	18984	37791	19153	38323	19417	38727	19588
2 Mining and quarrying	3173	1797	3253	1812	3411	1903	3461	1880	3469	1817	3580	1856
3 Manufacturing	104953	55809	109076	58485	112680	60455	116016	62009	119728	63843	124457	66645
4 Electricity, gas and water	30731	19906	31373	19709	32842	20381	33958	20720	34946	20953	36003	21272
5 Construction	10876	5065	10928	5164	10846	5180	10993	5474	11015	5668	11031	5798
6 Wholesale and retail trade	31543	15803	32289	16137	32941	16458	33963	17215	34811	17819	35906	18667
7 Transport and communication	63456	33631	64880	34020	65036	33305	65881	33466	65856	32935	65305	32024
8 Finance, etc.	11223	6110	13269	7805	15703	9721	18000	11302	20678	13025	24030	15113
9 Community, social and personal services	4625	2418	4792	2488	4966	2577	5236	2770	5647	3092	6205	3525
B Producers of government services	8745	4813	9183	5056	9669	5359	10278	5789	10979	6280	11890	6929
C Other producers	1182	631	1244	662	1300	692	1356	723	1416	760	1497	813
6 Breeding stock, dairy cattle, etc.	...	...	...	...	...	...	...	...	...	...	...	...
Total	1419560	920988	1468340	948931	1519190	978577	1572000	1009790	1622130	1037770	1673710	1066400

	1986 Gross	1986 Net	1987 Gross	1987 Net	1988 Gross	1988 Net	1989 Gross	1989 Net
			At constant prices of:1985					
1 Residential buildings	572660	396302	589264	404745	608998	416034	632640	430881
2 Non-residential buildings	467140	303025	482685	311887	499537	321885	517174	332483
A Industries	308779	196638	318414	202253	329596	209329	342102	217617
1 Agriculture	34671	18552	35235	18959	35614	19236	35942	19527
2 Mining and quarrying	1328	638	1316	611	1285	566	1270	540
3 Manufacturing	81633	49406	83687	50225	82651	47969	84455	48582
4 Electricity, gas and water	17199	10879	17564	11016	17733	10958	17984	10979
5 Construction	6268	4190	6409	4210	6631	4307	6861	4408
6 Wholesale and retail trade	59460	36757	60927	37664	61184	37356	63725	39310
7 Transport and communication	12371	8645	12774	8800	13127	8902	13739	9256
8 Finance, etc.	81540	57854	85745	60816	96451	70137	102724	74856
9 Community, social and personal services	14309	9717	14757	9952	14920	9898	15402	10159
B Producers of government services	142842	95771	148014	98506	152968	100949	157406	102815
C Other producers	15519	10616	16257	11128	16973	11607	17666	12051
3 Other construction [a]	313746	195030	320091	197481	326119	199602	332730	202288
A Industries	185070	102220	187527	102452	189847	102585	192702	103279
1 Agriculture	59546	31008	59713	30610	59933	30305	60033	29912
2 Mining and quarrying	1400	837	1424	832	1443	823	1457	809
3 Manufacturing	15787	9079	16024	9094	16104	8951	16229	8858
4 Electricity, gas and water	44505	24087	44982	24374	45217	24420	45856	24847

Finland

2.16 Stocks of Reproducible Fixed Assets by Kind of Activity, in Constant Prices
(Continued)

Million Finnish markkaa

	1986 Gross	1986 Net	1987 Gross	1987 Net	1988 Gross	1988 Net	1989 Gross	1989 Net
	\multicolumn{8}{c}{At constant prices of:1985}
5 Construction	18	14	18	14	19	15	20	15
6 Wholesale and retail trade	745	394	744	387	739	374	739	367
7 Transport and communication	44840	25386	45878	25587	46977	25852	48222	26275
8 Finance, etc.	-	-	-	-	42	42	42	41
9 Community, social and personal services	18229	11415	18744	11554	19373	11803	20104	12155
B Producers of government services	127186	91826	131011	93997	134655	95937	138347	97882
C Other producers	1490	984	1553	1032	1617	1080	1681	1127
4 Land improvement and development and plantation and orchard development [a]	...	...	...	...	...	...	...	...
5 Producers' durable goods	371004	198955	386700	208500	406059	221255	428867	236909
A Industries	356415	190373	370586	198833	388267	210431	409291	224903
1 Agriculture	38581	19236	38105	18622	37903	18365	38069	18527
2 Mining and quarrying	3630	1835	3614	1759	3571	1673	3602	1678
3 Manufacturing	128929	69220	135387	73833	141743	78368	148448	83243
4 Electricity, gas and water	37110	21634	38106	21858	39059	22005	39927	22031
5 Construction	11157	5877	11540	6070	12483	6729	13605	7492
6 Wholesale and retail trade	36990	19497	38674	20900	41043	22910	44331	25651
7 Transport and communication	65420	31852	65688	31826	66520	32394	68572	34214
8 Finance, etc.	27767	17248	31781	19375	37182	22656	42605	25801
9 Community, social and personal services	6831	3974	7691	4590	8763	5331	10132	6266
B Producers of government services	12989	7703	14363	8686	15858	9718	17466	10791
C Other producers	1600	879	1751	981	1934	1106	2110	1215
6 Breeding stock, dairy cattle, etc.	...	...	...	...	...	...	...	...
Total	1724550	1093310	1778740	1122610	1840710	1158780	1911410	1202560

a) Item 'Land improvement and plantation and orchard development' is included in item 'Other construction'.

2.17 Exports and Imports of Goods and Services, Detail

Million Finnish markkaa

	1970	1975	1980	1981	1982	1983	1984	1985	1986	1987	1988	1989
	\multicolumn{12}{c}{**Exports of Goods and Services**}
1 Exports of merchandise, f.o.b. [a]	9640	20288	52594	58913	61914	67959	78961	82475	81066	83826	91313	98266
2 Transport and communication	1115	1804	4515	5343	5287	5765	6580	6216	5757	6370	7026	7662
A In respect of merchandise imports [b]	249	459	834	945	917	842	952	967	861	870	963	616
B Other	867	1345	3681	4398	4370	4923	5628	5249	4896	5500	6063	7046
3 Insurance service charges	29	39	295	282	408	244	12	-335	-121	-313	-575	-603
A In respect of merchandise imports [b]	-	-	-	-	-	-	-	-	-	-	-	-
B Other	29	39	295	282	408	244	12	-335	-121	-313	-575	-603
4 Other commodities	380	1315	3349	4614	5200	5782	5426	6369	5628	6292	6535	6625
5 Adjustments of merchandise exports to change-of-ownership basis	...	...	...	...	...	...	...	...	...	...	...	...
6 Direct purchases in the domestic market by non-residential households	560	1250	2614	3064	2869	2851	3039	3258	3195	3736	4280	4498
7 Direct purchases in the domestic market by extraterritorial bodies	21	61	122	140	123	134	172	190	109	120	171	256
Total Exports of Goods and Services	11745	24757	63489	72357	75801	82735	94190	98173	95634	100030	108750	116702
	\multicolumn{12}{c}{**Imports of Goods and Services**}
1 Imports of merchandise, c.i.f. [a]	11138	28089	58046	60713	64542	70731	73496	80764	76736	81867	91232	104400

Finland

2.17 Exports and Imports of Goods and Services, Detail
(Continued)

Million Finnish markkaa

	1970	1975	1980	1981	1982	1983	1984	1985	1986	1987	1988	1989
2 Adjustments of merchandise imports to change-of-ownership basis	...	...	...	...	...	...	...	...	...	...	...	...
3 Other transport and communication	347	576	1692	2255	2431	2565	2572	2545	2160	2610	3338	3869
4 Other insurance service charges	26	69	201	113	209	180	182	179	294	274	94	172
5 Other commodities	367	1000	2652	3351	3292	3987	5349	6022	4857	5921	7120	8393
6 Direct purchases abroad by government	14	38	131	159	142	300	289	354	264	294	176	194
7 Direct purchases abroad by resident households	418	1151	2294	2659	3147	3599	4250	5031	5587	6811	7907	8969
Total Imports of Goods and Services	12310	30923	65016	69250	73762	81361	86137	94893	89898	97775	109866	125996
Balance of Goods and Services	-565	-6166	-1527	3107	2039	1374	8053	3280	5736	2255	-1116	-9294
Total Imports and Balance of Goods and Services	11745	24757	63489	72357	75801	82735	94190	98173	95634	100030	108750	116702

a) Exports and imports of merchandise are recorded on the basis of the crossing of frontiers. No data are available on the basis of changes in the ownership of the goods.
b) Insurance service charges in respect of merchandise imports are included in transport and communication in respect of merchandise imports.

3.12 General Government Income and Outlay Account: Total and Subsectors

Million Finnish markkaa

	1980					1981				
	Total General Government	Central Government	State or Provincial Government	Local Government	Social Security Funds	Total General Government	Central Government	State or Provincial Government	Local Government	Social Security Funds

Receipts

1 Operating surplus	-126	-133	...	7	...	-446	-445	...	-1	...
2 Property and entrepreneurial income	2241	991	...	960	290	2717	1380	...	950	387
A Withdrawals from public quasi-corporations	369	-24	...	393	...	343	52	...	291	...
B Interest	1608	948	...	379	281	1962	1134	...	455	373
C Dividends	80	66	...	5	9	210	193	...	3	14
D Net land rent and royalties	184	1	...	183	-	202	1	...	201	-
3 Taxes, fees and contributions	63209	38892	...	15411	8906	75264	46420	...	18889	9955
A Indirect taxes	25714	25677	...	37	-	29728	29694	...	34	-
B Direct taxes	27718	12387	...	15331	-	34624	15816	...	18808	-
Income	27718	12387	...	15331	...	34624	15816	...	18808	...
Other	-	-	...	-	...	-	-	...	-	...
C Social security contributions	9034	128	...	-	8906	10013	58	...	-	9955
D Fees, fines and penalties	743	700	...	43	-	899	852	...	47	-
4 Other current transfers	3654	1448	...	12655	2267	4346	1624	...	14869	2678
A Casualty insurance claims	6	-	...	6	-	8	-	...	8	-
B Transfers from other government subsectors	...	419	...	10608	1689	...	428	...	12451	1946
C Transfers from the rest of the world	-	-	...	-	-	-	-	...	-	-
D Other transfers, except imputed	582	38	...	-	544	732	42	...	-	690
E Imputed unfunded employee pension and welfare contributions	3066	991	...	2041	34	3606	1154	...	2410	42
Total Current Receipts	68978	41198	...	29033	11463	81881	48979	...	34707	13020

Disbursements

1 Government final consumption expenditure	34890	11366	...	22516	1008	40835	12936	...	26709	1190
2 Property income	1964	1222	...	739	3	2387	1577	...	808	2
A Interest	1961	1221	...	737	3	2382	1576	...	804	2
B Net land rent and royalties	3	1	...	2	-	5	1	...	4	-
3 Subsidies	6227	5956	...	271	...	7265	6919	...	346	...

551

Finland

3.12 General Government Income and Outlay Account: Total and Subsectors
(Continued)

Million Finnish markkaa

	1980					1981				
	Total General Government	Central Government	State or Provincial Government	Local Government	Social Security Funds	Total General Government	Central Government	State or Provincial Government	Local Government	Social Security Funds
4 Other current transfers	19728	19773	...	3108	9563	23004	23024	...	3660	11145
A Casualty insurance premiums, net	12	-	...	12	-	13	-	...	13	-
B Transfers to other government subsectors	...	11521	...	914	281	...	13398	...	1019	408
C Social security benefits	9963	1453	...	-	8510	11356	1673	...	-	9683
D Social assistance grants	3406	2386	...	488	532	4006	2713	...	605	688
E Unfunded employee pension and welfare benefits	3453	2147	...	1289	17	4001	2445	...	1537	19
F Transfers to private non-profit institutions serving households	1683	1265	...	405	13	2027	1526	...	486	15
G Other transfers n.e.c.	882	672	...	-	210	1147	815	...	-	332
H Transfers to the rest of the world	329	329	...	-	-	454	454	...	-	-
Net saving	6169	2881	...	2399	889	8390	4523	...	3184	683
Total Current Disbursements and Net Saving	68978	41198	...	29033	11463	81881	48979	...	34707	13020

	1982					1983				
	Total General Government	Central Government	State or Provincial Government	Local Government	Social Security Funds	Total General Government	Central Government	State or Provincial Government	Local Government	Social Security Funds

Receipts

1 Operating surplus	28	8	...	20	...	133	121	...	12	...
2 Property and entrepreneurial income	3311	1936	...	994	381	3830	2228	...	1319	283
A Withdrawals from public quasi-corporations	437	255	...	182	...	706	260	...	446	...
B Interest	2228	1299	...	561	368	2427	1553	...	595	279
C Dividends	398	381	...	4	13	423	414	...	5	4
D Net land rent and royalties	248	1	...	247	-	274	1	...	273	-
3 Taxes, fees and contributions	83270	51142	...	21185	10943	93040	57416	...	23689	11935
A Indirect taxes	33208	33206	...	2	-	36978	36975	...	3	-
B Direct taxes	38042	16953	...	21089	-	42866	19298	...	23568	-
Income	38042	16953	...	21089	...	42866	19298	...	23568	...
Other	-	-	...	-	...	-	-	...	-	...
C Social security contributions	10944	1	...	-	10943	11936	1	...	-	11935
D Fees, fines and penalties	1076	982	...	94	-	1260	1142	...	118	-
4 Other current transfers	5055	1831	...	16936	3514	5796	2037	...	19237	5596
A Casualty insurance claims	10	-	...	10	-	11	-	...	11	-
B Transfers from other government subsectors	...	452	...	14137	2637	...	453	...	16042	4579
C Transfers from the rest of the world	-	-	...	-	-	-	-	...	-	-
D Other transfers, except imputed	880	51	...	-	829	1024	59	...	-	965
E Imputed unfunded employee pension and welfare contributions	4165	1328	...	2789	48	4761	1525	...	3184	52
Total Current Receipts	91664	54917	...	39135	14838	102799	61802	...	44257	17814

Disbursements

1 Government final consumption expenditure	46657	15044	...	30202	1411	53327	17371	...	34334	1622
2 Property income	3100	2171	...	925	4	4128	3096	...	1031	1
A Interest	3097	2170	...	923	4	4122	3094	...	1027	1
B Net land rent and royalties	3	1	...	2	-	6	2	...	4	-
3 Subsidies	7763	7377	...	386	...	8878	8459	...	419	...

Finland

3.12 General Government Income and Outlay Account: Total and Subsectors
(Continued)

Million Finnish markkaa

	1982					1983				
	Total General Government	Central Government	State or Provincial Government	Local Government	Social Security Funds	Total General Government	Central Government	State or Provincial Government	Local Government	Social Security Funds
4 Other current transfers	28104	26703	...	4482	14145	33005	32409	...	4912	16758
A Casualty insurance premiums, net	16	-	...	16	-	19	-	...	19	-
B Transfers to other government subsectors	...	15763	...	1269	194	...	19542	...	1423	109
C Social security benefits	14408	1816	...	-	12592	17292	2235	...	-	15057
D Social assistance grants	4893	3225	...	809	859	5767	3883	...	908	976
E Unfunded employee pension and welfare benefits	4626	2765	...	1839	22	5098	3098	...	1974	26
F Transfers to private non-profit institutions serving households	2292	1724	...	549	19	2535	1925	...	588	22
G Other transfers n.e.c.	1357	898	...	-	459	1625	1057	...	-	568
H Transfers to the rest of the world	512	512	...	-	-	669	669	...	-	-
Net saving	6040	3622	...	3140	-722	3461	467	...	3561	-567
Total Current Disbursements and Net Saving	91664	54917	...	39135	14838	102799	61802	...	44257	17814

	1984					1985				
	Total General Government	Central Government	State or Provincial Government	Local Government	Social Security Funds	Total General Government	Central Government	State or Provincial Government	Local Government	Social Security Funds

Receipts

1 Operating surplus	3	-7	...	10	...	-30	-1	...	-29	...
2 Property and entrepreneurial income	4576	2649	...	1694	233	5062	2986	...	1893	183
A Withdrawals from public quasi-corporations	1032	455	...	577	...	1206	650	...	556	...
B Interest	2812	1803	...	789	220	3140	2013	...	966	161
C Dividends	409	390	...	6	13	348	321	...	5	22
D Net land rent and royalties	323	1	...	322	-	368	2	...	366	-
3 Taxes, fees and contributions	109287	67424	...	27302	14561	123326	75471	...	30503	17352
A Indirect taxes	43532	43530	...	2	-	47806	47803	...	3	-
B Direct taxes	49381	22225	...	27156	-	55741	25384	...	30357	-
Income	49381	22225	...	27156	...	55741	25384	...	30357	...
Other	-	-	...	-	...	-	-	...	-	...
C Social security contributions	14839	278	...	-	14561	18023	671	...	-	17352
D Fees, fines and penalties	1535	1391	...	144	-	1756	1613	...	143	-
4 Other current transfers	6472	2196	...	22189	5574	7408	2355	...	25277	7500
A Casualty insurance claims	8	-	...	8	-	17	-	...	17	-
B Transfers from other government subsectors	...	467	...	18552	4468	...	471	...	21202	6051
C Transfers from the rest of the world	-	-	...	-	-	-	-	...	-	-
D Other transfers, except imputed	1124	74	...	-	1050	1451	66	...	-	1385
E Imputed unfunded employee pension and welfare contributions	5340	1655	...	3629	56	5940	1818	...	4058	64
Total Current Receipts	120338	72262	...	51195	20368	135766	80811	...	57644	25035

Disbursements

1 Government final consumption expenditure	59741	18374	...	39582	1785	68218	20672	...	45317	2229
2 Property income	5042	3824	...	1213	5	5940	4575	...	1362	3
A Interest	5035	3822	...	1208	5	5931	4573	...	1355	3
B Net land rent and royalties	7	2	...	5	-	9	2	...	7	-
3 Subsidies	9791	9340	...	451	...	10347	9878	...	469	...

Finland

3.12 General Government Income and Outlay Account: Total and Subsectors
(Continued)

Million Finnish markkaa

	1984					1985				
	Total General Government	Central Government	State or Provincial Government	Local Government	Social Security Funds	Total General Government	Central Government	State or Provincial Government	Local Government	Social Security Funds
4 Other current transfers	36931	35984	...	5689	18745	42339	40471	...	6677	22915
A Casualty insurance premiums, net	24	-	...	24	-	23	-	...	23	-
B Transfers to other government subsectors	...	21796	...	1566	125	...	25997	...	1603	124
C Social security benefits	19355	2347	...	-	17008	22326	2480	...	-	19846
D Social assistance grants	6326	4177	...	1130	1019	7375	3545	...	1604	2226
E Unfunded employee pension and welfare benefits	5776	3451	...	2294	31	6496	3796	...	2664	36
F Transfers to private non-profit institutions serving households	2619	1921	...	675	23	2822	2013	...	783	26
G Other transfers n.e.c.	1960	1421	...	-	539	2237	1580	...	-	657
H Transfers to the rest of the world	871	871	...	-	-	1060	1060	...	-	-
Net saving	8833	4740	...	4260	-167	8922	5215	...	3819	-112
Total Current Disbursements and Net Saving	120338	72262	...	51195	20368	135766	80811	...	57644	25035

	1986					1987				
	Total General Government	Central Government	State or Provincial Government	Local Government	Social Security Funds	Total General Government	Central Government	State or Provincial Government	Local Government	Social Security Funds

Receipts

1 Operating surplus	-86	-65	...	-21	...	-93	-60	...	-33	...
2 Property and entrepreneurial income	5181	2977	...	2047	157	6606	4385	...	2061	160
A Withdrawals from public quasi-corporations	1004	390	...	614	...	2446	1780	...	666	...
B Interest	3425	2269	...	1028	128	3268	2202	...	930	136
C Dividends	351	316	...	6	29	430	400	...	6	24
D Net land rent and royalties	401	2	...	399	-	462	3	...	459	-
3 Taxes, fees and contributions	136343	84365	...	33275	18703	140434	86145	...	34914	19375
A Indirect taxes	52502	52498	...	4	-	57593	57589	...	4	-
B Direct taxes	63127	30015	...	33112	-	61308	26580	...	34728	-
Income	63127	30015	...	33112	...	60934	26580	...	34354	...
Other	-	-	...	-	...	374	-	...	374	...
C Social security contributions	18708	5	...	-	18703	19375	-	...	-	19375
D Fees, fines and penalties	2006	1847	...	159	-	2158	1976	...	182	-
4 Other current transfers	7954	2482	...	27807	7878	8595	2776	...	30619	9477
A Casualty insurance claims	15	-	...	15	-	15	-	...	15	-
B Transfers from other government subsectors	...	479	...	23299	6435	...	534	...	25752	7991
C Transfers from the rest of the world	-	-	...	-	-	-	-	...	-	-
D Other transfers, except imputed	1441	69	...	-	1372	1478	70	...	-	1408
E Imputed unfunded employee pension and welfare contributions	6498	1934	...	4493	71	7102	2172	...	4852	78
Total Current Receipts	149392	89759	...	63108	26738	155542	93246	...	67561	29012

Disbursements

1 Government final consumption expenditure	74001	21907	...	49767	2327	81339	24285	...	54568	2486
2 Property income	6003	4582	...	1419	2	6384	4771	...	1612	1
A Interest	5993	4580	...	1411	2	6372	4769	...	1602	1
B Net land rent and royalties	10	2	...	8	-	12	2	...	10	-
3 Subsidies	11308	10833	...	475	...	11686	11184	...	502	...

Finland

3.12 General Government Income and Outlay Account: Total and Subsectors
(Continued)

Million Finnish markkaa

	1986					1987				
	Total General Government	Central Government	State or Provincial Government	Local Government	Social Security Funds	Total General Government	Central Government	State or Provincial Government	Local Government	Social Security Funds
4 Other current transfers	46437	43704	...	7967	24979	50789	49291	...	9156	26619
A Casualty insurance premiums, net	24	-	...	24	-	25	-	...	25	-
B Transfers to other government subsectors	...	27915	...	2167	131	...	31855	...	2290	132
C Social security benefits	24110	2600	...	-	21510	25561	2795	...	-	22766
D Social assistance grants	7913	3618	...	1877	2418	8871	3830	...	2416	2625
E Unfunded employee pension and welfare benefits	7315	4200	...	3073	42	8108	4566	...	3494	48
F Transfers to private non-profit institutions serving households	3147	2287	...	826	34	3550	2577	...	931	42
G Other transfers n.e.c.	2739	1895	...	-	844	3227	2221	...	-	1006
H Transfers to the rest of the world	1189	1189	...	-	-	1447	1447	...	-	-
Net saving	11643	8733	...	3480	-570	5344	3715	...	1723	-94
Total Current Disbursements and Net Saving	149392	89759	...	63108	26738	155542	93246	...	67561	29012

	1988					1989				
	Total General Government	Central Government	State or Provincial Government	Local Government	Social Security Funds	Total General Government	Central Government	State or Provincial Government	Local Government	Social Security Funds
Receipts											

1 Operating surplus	-67	-86	...	19	...	-97	-90	...	-7	...
2 Property and entrepreneurial income	5781	3347	...	2278	156	7224	4351	...	2602	271
A Withdrawals from public quasi-corporations	1304	449	...	855	...	1374	481	...	893	...
B Interest	3485	2435	...	919	131	4627	3244	...	1160	223
C Dividends	494	460	...	9	25	682	623	...	11	48
D Net land rent and royalties	498	3	...	495	-	541	3	...	538	-
3 Taxes, fees and contributions	165805	104742	...	39982	21081	184947	118783	...	43740	22424
A Indirect taxes	66925	66920	...	5	-	76180	76175	...	5	-
B Direct taxes	74454	34691	...	39763	-	82179	38708	...	43471	-
Income	74073	34691	...	39382	...	81777	38708	...	43069	...
Other	381	-	...	381	...	402	-	...	402	...
C Social security contributions	21081	-	...	-	21081	22495	71	...	-	22424
D Fees, fines and penalties	3345	3131	...	214	-	4093	3829	...	264	-
4 Other current transfers	5229	3243	...	29546	9630	5665	3464	...	33036	9548
A Casualty insurance claims	16	-	...	16	-	17	-	...	17	-
B Transfers from other government subsectors	...	645	...	28617	7928	...	698	...	32003	7682
C Transfers from the rest of the world	-	-	...	-	-	-	-	...	-	-
D Other transfers, except imputed	1743	127	...	-	1616	1920	148	...	-	1772
E Imputed unfunded employee pension and welfare contributions	3470	2471	...	913	86	3728	2618	...	1016	94
Total Current Receipts	176748	111246	...	71825	30867	197739	126508	...	79371	32243
Disbursements											
1 Government final consumption expenditure	88731	26758	...	59186	2787	98119	28828	...	66216	3075
2 Property income	6951	5181	...	1769	1	6891	4917	...	1974	-
A Interest	6936	5179	...	1756	1	6874	4915	...	1959	-
B Net land rent and royalties	15	2	...	13	-	17	2	...	15	-
3 Subsidies	11271	10712	...	559	...	13723	13059	...	664	...

Finland

3.12 General Government Income and Outlay Account: Total and Subsectors
(Continued)

Million Finnish markkaa

	1988 Total General Government	1988 Central Government	1988 State or Provincial Government	1988 Local Government	1988 Social Security Funds	1989 Total General Government	1989 Central Government	1989 State or Provincial Government	1989 Local Government	1989 Social Security Funds
4 Other current transfers	51030	53960	...	6650	27610	55147	59282	...	7484	28764
A Casualty insurance premiums, net	27	-	...	27	-	29	-	...	29	-
B Transfers to other government subsectors	...	34588	...	2445	157	...	37630	...	2588	165
C Social security benefits	26856	3015	...	-	23841	28672	3518	...	-	25154
D Social assistance grants	9273	4206	...	2578	2489	9932	4511	...	3140	2281
E Unfunded employee pension and welfare benefits	5635	4971	...	610	54	6219	5505	...	650	64
F Transfers to private non-profit institutions serving households	3924	2875	...	990	59	4368	3227	...	1077	64
G Other transfers n.e.c.	3551	2541	...	-	1010	3757	2721	...	-	1036
H Transfers to the rest of the world	1764	1764	...	-	-	2170	2170	...	-	-
Net saving	18765	14635	...	3661	469	23859	20422	...	3033	404
Total Current Disbursements and Net Saving	176748	111246	...	71825	30867	197739	126508	...	79371	32243

3.13 General Government Capital Accumulation Account: Total and Subsectors

Million Finnish markkaa

	1980 Total General Government	1980 Central Government	1980 State or Provincial Government	1980 Local Government	1980 Social Security Funds	1981 Total General Government	1981 Central Government	1981 State or Provincial Government	1981 Local Government	1981 Social Security Funds
Finance of Gross Accumulation										
1 Gross saving	8374	3686	...	3783	905	10924	5459	...	4764	701
A Consumption of fixed capital	2205	805	...	1384	16	2534	936	...	1580	18
B Net saving	6169	2881	...	2399	889	8390	4523	...	3184	683
2 Capital transfers a	-485	-1213	...	728	-	-472	-1283	...	811	-
A From other government subsectors	...	-729	...	729	-	...	-812	...	812	-
B From other resident sectors	-435	-434	...	-1	-	-470	-469	...	-1	-
C From rest of the world	-50	-50	...	-	-	-2	-2	...	-	-
Finance of Gross Accumulation	7889	2473	...	4511	905	10452	4176	...	5575	701
Gross Accumulation										
1 Gross capital formation	6886	2797	...	4073	16	7431	2676	...	4739	16
A Increase in stocks	207	207	...	-	-	-202	-202	...	-	-
B Gross fixed capital formation	6679	2590	...	4073	16	7633	2878	...	4739	16
2 Purchases of land, net	382	144	...	238	-	455	203	...	252	-
3 Purchases of intangible assets, net	...	...	...	...	...	...	...	...	...	...
4 Capital transfers a	...	...	...	...	...	...	...	...	...	...
Net lending	621	-468	...	200	889	2566	1297	...	584	685
Gross Accumulation	7889	2473	...	4511	905	10452	4176	...	5575	701

	1982 Total General Government	1982 Central Government	1982 State or Provincial Government	1982 Local Government	1982 Social Security Funds	1983 Total General Government	1983 Central Government	1983 State or Provincial Government	1983 Local Government	1983 Social Security Funds
Finance of Gross Accumulation										
1 Gross saving	8880	4659	...	4923	-702	6750	1639	...	5655	-544
A Consumption of fixed capital	2840	1037	...	1783	20	3289	1172	...	2094	23
B Net saving	6040	3622	...	3140	-722	3461	467	...	3561	-567
2 Capital transfers a	-895	-1849	...	954	-	-503	-1625	...	1122	-
A From other government subsectors	...	-956	...	956	-	...	-1123	...	1123	-
B From other resident sectors	-892	-890	...	-2	-	-503	-502	...	-1	-
C From rest of the world	-3	-3	...	-	-	-	-	...	-	-
Finance of Gross Accumulation	7985	2810	...	5877	-702	6247	14	...	6777	-544
Gross Accumulation										
1 Gross capital formation	9071	3522	...	5512	37	10325	4157	...	6094	74

Finland

3.13 General Government Capital Accumulation Account: Total and Subsectors
(Continued)

Million Finnish markkaa

	1982 Total General Government	Central Government	State or Provincial Government	Local Government	Social Security Funds	1983 Total General Government	Central Government	State or Provincial Government	Local Government	Social Security Funds
A Increase in stocks	254	254	...	-	-	335	335	...	-	-
B Gross fixed capital formation	8817	3268	...	5512	37	9990	3822	...	6094	74
2 Purchases of land, net	373	170	...	203	-	476	216	...	260	-
3 Purchases of intangible assets, net	...	...	...	...	...	...	...	...	...	...
4 Capital transfers [a]	...	...	...	...	...	...	...	...	...	...
Net lending	-1459	-882	...	162	-739	-4554	-4359	...	423	-618
Gross Accumulation	7985	2810	...	5877	-702	6247	14	...	6777	-544

	1984 Total General Government	Central Government	State or Provincial Government	Local Government	Social Security Funds	1985 Total General Government	Central Government	State or Provincial Government	Local Government	Social Security Funds
Finance of Gross Accumulation										
1 Gross saving	12437	5963	...	6616	-142	12916	6568	...	6432	-84
A Consumption of fixed capital	3604	1223	...	2356	25	3994	1353	...	2613	28
B Net saving	8833	4740	...	4260	-167	8922	5215	...	3819	-112
2 Capital transfers [a]	-599	-1732	...	1133	-	-585	-1805	...	1220	-
A From other government subsectors	...	-1134	...	1134	-	...	-1224	...	1224	-
B From other resident sectors	-555	-554	...	-1	-	-585	-581	...	-4	-
C From rest of the world	-44	-44	...	-	-	-	-	...	-	-
Finance of Gross Accumulation	11838	4231	...	7749	-142	12331	4763	...	7652	-84
Gross Accumulation										
1 Gross capital formation	10428	3990	...	6385	53	11346	4217	...	7093	36
A Increase in stocks	232	232	...	-	-	193	193	...	-	-
B Gross fixed capital formation	10196	3758	...	6385	53	11153	4024	...	7093	36
2 Purchases of land, net	265	134	...	131	-	540	156	...	384	-
3 Purchases of intangible assets, net	...	...	...	...	...	...	...	...	...	...
4 Capital transfers [a]	...	...	...	...	...	...	...	...	...	...
Net lending	1145	107	...	1233	-195	445	390	...	175	-120
Gross Accumulation	11838	4231	...	7749	-142	12331	4763	...	7652	-84

	1986 Total General Government	Central Government	State or Provincial Government	Local Government	Social Security Funds	1987 Total General Government	Central Government	State or Provincial Government	Local Government	Social Security Funds
Finance of Gross Accumulation										
1 Gross saving	16094	10178	...	6456	-540	10353	5317	...	5098	-62
A Consumption of fixed capital	4451	1445	...	2976	30	5009	1602	...	3375	32
B Net saving	11643	8733	...	3480	-570	5344	3715	...	1723	-94
2 Capital transfers [a]	-539	-1971	...	1432	-	-588	-2221	...	1633	-
A From other government subsectors	...	-1436	...	1436	-	...	-1637	...	1637	-
B From other resident sectors	-539	-535	...	-4	-	-588	-584	...	-4	-
C From rest of the world	-	-	...	-	-	-	-	...	-	-
Finance of Gross Accumulation	15555	8207	...	7888	-540	9765	3096	...	6731	-62
Gross Accumulation										
1 Gross capital formation	12200	4670	...	7462	68	14016	5414	...	8578	24
A Increase in stocks	350	350	...	-	-	278	278	...	-	-
B Gross fixed capital formation	11850	4320	...	7462	68	13738	5136	...	8578	24
2 Purchases of land, net	572	225	...	347	-	386	130	...	256	-
3 Purchases of intangible assets, net	...	...	...	...	...	...	...	...	...	...
4 Capital transfers [a]	...	...	...	...	...	...	...	...	...	...
Net lending	2783	3312	...	79	-608	-4637	-2448	...	-2103	-86
Gross Accumulation	15555	8207	...	7888	-540	9765	3096	...	6731	-62

Finland

3.13 General Government Capital Accumulation Account: Total and Subsectors
Million Finnish markkaa

	\multicolumn{5}{c	}{1988}	\multicolumn{5}{c	}{1989}
	Total General Government	Central Government	State or Provincial Government	Local Government	Social Security Funds	Total General Government	Central Government	State or Provincial Government	Local Government	Social Security Funds

Finance of Gross Accumulation

1 Gross saving	24422	16447	...	7469	506	30104	22330	...	7331	443
A Consumption of fixed capital	5657	1812	...	3808	37	6245	1908	...	4298	39
B Net saving	18765	14635	...	3661	469	23859	20422	...	3033	404
2 Capital transfers a	-3277	-5052	...	1775	-	-865	-2861	...	1996	-
A From other government subsectors	...	-1780	...	1780	-	...	-2002	...	2002	-
B From other resident sectors	-3277	-3272	...	-5	-	-865	-859	...	-6	-
C From rest of the world	-	-	...	-	-	-	-	...	-	-
Finance of Gross Accumulation	21145	11395	...	9244	506	29239	19469	...	9327	443

Gross Accumulation

1 Gross capital formation	14726	5770	...	8925	31	15233	5682	...	9508	43
A Increase in stocks	283	283	...	-	-	93	93	...	-	-
B Gross fixed capital formation	14443	5487	...	8925	31	15140	5589	...	9508	43
2 Purchases of land, net	705	218	...	487	-	56	131	...	-75	-
3 Purchases of intangible assets, net	...	...	...	...	...	...	...	...	...	...
4 Capital transfers a	...	...	...	...	...	...	...	...	...	...
Net lending	5714	5407	...	-168	475	13950	13656	...	-106	400
Gross Accumulation	21145	11395	...	9244	506	29239	19469	...	9327	443

a) Capital transfers received are recorded net of capital transfers paid.

3.14 General Government Capital Finance Account, Total and Subsectors
Million Finnish markkaa

	\multicolumn{5}{c	}{1980}	\multicolumn{5}{c	}{1981}
	Total General Government	Central Government	State or Provincial Government	Local Government	Social Security Funds	Total General Government	Central Government	State or Provincial Government	Local Government	Social Security Funds

Acquisition of Financial Assets

1 Gold and SDRs	...	...	...	...	...	...	...	...	...	...
2 Currency and transferable deposits	-741	-206	...	-285	-250	1230	826	...	139	265
3 Other deposits	636	399	...	215	22	-367	-275	...	-154	62
4 Bills and bonds, short term	...	...	...	...	...	...	...	...	...	...
5 Bonds, long term	592	237	...	110	245	15	38	...	-15	-8
A Corporations	492	237	...	8	247	28	38	...	4	-14
B Other government subsectors	100	-	...	102	-2	-13	-	...	-19	6
C Rest of the world	-	-	...	-	-	-	-	...	-	-
6 Corporate equity securities	1412	312	...	1089	11	1518	344	...	1162	12
7 Short-term loans, n.e.c.	178	-32	...	198	12	335	114	...	216	5
8 Long-term loans, n.e.c.	4204	2413	...	1205	586	3598	2283	...	976	339
A Mortgages	1579	1579	...	-	-	1544	1544	...	-	-
B Other	2625	834	...	1205	586	2054	739	...	976	339
9 Other receivables	-68	117	...	-388	203	1453	1018	...	366	69
10 Other assets	1413	707	...	706	-	2223	1026	...	1197	-
Total Acquisition of Financial Assets	7626	3947	...	2850	829	10005	5374	...	3887	744

Incurrence of Liabilities

1 Currency and transferable deposits	...	...	...	...	...	...	...	...	...	...
2 Other deposits	...	...	...	...	...	...	...	...	...	...
3 Bills and bonds, short term	54	40	...	14	-	1	-40	...	37	4
4 Bonds, long term	2837	2878	...	-41	-	2585	2631	...	-46	-
5 Short-term loans, n.e.c.	101	18	...	85	-2	547	455	...	91	1
6 Long-term loans, n.e.c.	2070	402	...	1668	-	2324	674	...	1653	-3
7 Other payables	675	972	...	-240	-57	345	149	...	133	63
8 Other liabilities	815	-	...	815	-	841	-	...	841	-
Total Incurrence of Liabilities	6552	4310	...	2301	-59	6643	3869	...	2709	65
Statistical discrepancy a	453	105	...	349	-1	796	208	...	594	-6
Net Lending	621	-468	...	200	889	2566	1297	...	584	685
Incurrence of Liabilities and Net Worth	7626	3947	...	2850	829	10005	5374	...	3887	744

Finland

3.14 General Government Capital Finance Account, Total and Subsectors

Million Finnish markkaa

	1982					1983				
	Total General Government	Central Government	State or Provincial Government	Local Government	Social Security Funds	Total General Government	Central Government	State or Provincial Government	Local Government	Social Security Funds

Acquisition of Financial Assets

1 Gold and SDRs	...	...	...	...	...	...	...	...	...	...
2 Currency and transferable deposits	1239	837	...	512	-110	-204	-786	...	195	387
3 Other deposits	-316	-410	...	118	-24	1829	1238	...	561	30
4 Bills and bonds, short term	...	...	...	...	...	...	...	...	...	...
5 Bonds, long term	-436	-23	...	-137	-276	39	127	...	-77	-11
A Corporations	-299	-23	...	-1	-275	101	127	...	-13	-13
B Other government subsectors	-137	-	...	-136	-1	-62	-	...	-64	2
C Rest of the world	-	-	...	-	-	-	-	...	-	-
6 Corporate equity securities	1626	380	...	1241	5	1576	303	...	1263	10
7 Short-term loans, n.e.c.	866	501	...	360	5	211	-166	...	350	27
8 Long-term loans, n.e.c.	3576	2633	...	1200	-257	2913	2658	...	1333	-1078
A Mortgages	1661	1661	...	-	-	673	673	...	-	-
B Other	1915	972	...	1200	-257	2240	1985	...	1333	-1078
9 Other receivables	469	9	...	376	84	-168	-351	...	79	104
10 Other assets	1897	828	...	1069	-	1085	342	...	743	-
Total Acquisition of Financial Assets	8921	4755	...	4739	-573	7281	3365	...	4447	-531

Incurrence of Liabilities

1 Currency and transferable deposits	...	...	...	...	...	...	...	...	...	...
2 Other deposits	...	...	...	...	...	...	...	...	...	...
3 Bills and bonds, short term	-30	-	...	-26	-4	13	-	...	13	-
4 Bonds, long term	4470	4382	...	88	-	5613	5653	...	-40	-
5 Short-term loans, n.e.c.	706	366	...	341	-1	319	199	...	101	19
6 Long-term loans, n.e.c.	3501	1306	...	2205	-10	3593	1717	...	1876	-
7 Other payables	531	-128	...	493	166	919	300	...	550	69
8 Other liabilities	884	-	...	884	-	1006	-	...	1006	-
Total Incurrence of Liabilities	10062	5926	...	3985	151	11463	7869	...	3506	88
Statistical discrepancy [a]	318	-289	...	592	15	372	-145	...	518	-1
Net Lending	-1459	-882	...	162	-739	-4554	-4359	...	423	-618
Incurrence of Liabilities and Net Worth	8921	4755	...	4739	-573	7281	3365	...	4447	-531

	1984					1985				
	Total General Government	Central Government	State or Provincial Government	Local Government	Social Security Funds	Total General Government	Central Government	State or Provincial Government	Local Government	Social Security Funds

Acquisition of Financial Assets

1 Gold and SDRs	...	...	...	...	...	...	...	...	...	...
2 Currency and transferable deposits	861	272	...	225	364	597	167	...	22	408
3 Other deposits	2665	1246	...	1426	-7	485	-17	...	478	24
4 Bills and bonds, short term	...	...	...	...	...	...	...	...	...	...
5 Bonds, long term	403	153	...	-4	254	-149	82	...	160	-391
A Corporations	399	153	...	-	246	-303	82	...	-	-385
B Other government subsectors	4	-	...	-4	8	154	-	...	160	-6
C Rest of the world	-	-	...	-	-	-	-	...	-	-
6 Corporate equity securities	1787	430	...	1348	9	2807	922	...	1841	44
7 Short-term loans, n.e.c.	708	303	...	414	-9	1230	455	...	542	233
8 Long-term loans, n.e.c.	2543	2455	...	899	-811	2436	2145	...	428	-137
A Mortgages	1354	589	...	767	-2	1197	742	...	457	-2
B Other	1189	1866	...	132	-809	1239	1403	...	-29	-135
9 Other receivables	-511	-594	...	-23	106	-130	-580	...	559	-109
10 Other assets	1788	1087	...	701	-	1143	840	...	303	-
Total Acquisition of Financial Assets	10244	5352	...	4986	-94	8419	4014	...	4333	72

Incurrence of Liabilities

1 Currency and transferable deposits	...	...	...	...	...	...	...	...	...	...
2 Other deposits	...	...	...	...	...	...	...	...	...	...
3 Bills and bonds, short term	11	-	...	2	9	-19	-	...	-15	-4
4 Bonds, long term	4154	4086	...	68	-	5034	4644	...	390	-
5 Short-term loans, n.e.c.	697	393	...	309	-5	574	-15	...	602	-13

Finland

3.14 General Government Capital Finance Account, Total and Subsectors
(Continued)

Million Finnish markkaa

	1984					1985				
	Total General Government	Central Government	State or Provincial Government	Local Government	Social Security Funds	Total General Government	Central Government	State or Provincial Government	Local Government	Social Security Funds
6 Long-term loans, n.e.c.	2561	1190	...	1376	-5	320	-1009	...	1320	9
7 Other payables	730	-177	...	804	103	690	132	...	352	206
8 Other liabilities	959	-	...	959	-	1316	-	...	1316	-
Total Incurrence of Liabilities	9112	5492	...	3518	102	7915	3752	...	3965	198
Statistical discrepancy a	-13	-247	...	235	-1	59	-128	...	193	-6
Net Lending	1145	107	...	1233	-195	445	390	...	175	-120
Incurrence of Liabilities and Net Worth	10244	5352	...	4986	-94	8419	4014	...	4333	72

	1986					1987				
	Total General Government	Central Government	State or Provincial Government	Local Government	Social Security Funds	Total General Government	Central Government	State or Provincial Government	Local Government	Social Security Funds
Acquisition of Financial Assets										
1 Gold and SDRs	...	...	...	...	...	...	...	...	...	...
2 Currency and transferable deposits	6510	7775	...	-295	-970	2441	1929	...	188	324
3 Other deposits	-1859	-2249	...	-159	549	-2497	-1208	...	-750	-539
4 Bills and bonds, short term	...	...	...	...	...	...	...	...	...	...
5 Bonds, long term	37	121	...	-83	-1	-137	-53	...	-81	-3
A Corporations	121	121	...	-	-	-53	-53	...	-	-
B Other government subsectors	-84	-	...	-83	-1	-84	-	...	-81	-3
C Rest of the world	-	-	...	-	-	-	-	...	-	...
6 Corporate equity securities	2628	837	...	1773	18	2739	1017	...	1688	34
7 Short-term loans, n.e.c.	-48	-218	...	343	-173	-968	3	...	-1179	208
8 Long-term loans, n.e.c.	2994	1872	...	1107	15	2351	2078	...	723	-450
A Mortgages	1079	798	...	264	17	...	...	...	...	...
B Other	1915	1074	...	843	-2	...	...	...	...	...
9 Other receivables	1362	1259	...	79	24	1715	279	...	1000	436
10 Other assets	880	304	...	576	-	166	-394	...	560	-
Total Acquisition of Financial Assets	12504	9701	...	3341	-538	5810	3651	...	2149	10
Incurrence of Liabilities										
1 Currency and transferable deposits	...	...	...	...	...	...	...	...	...	...
2 Other deposits	...	...	...	...	...	...	...	...	...	...
3 Bills and bonds, short term	-20	-	...	-18	-2	-22	2	...	-25	1
4 Bonds, long term	4700	4345	...	355	-	7130	7094	...	36	-
5 Short-term loans, n.e.c.	-887	-762	...	-131	6	607	761	...	-148	-6
6 Long-term loans, n.e.c.	1505	84	...	1453	-32	1953	-772	...	2724	1
7 Other payables	3411	2713	...	682	16	-681	-1058	...	251	126
8 Other liabilities	1208	-	...	1208	-	1200	-	...	1200	-
Total Incurrence of Liabilities	9917	6380	...	3549	-12	10187	6027	...	4038	122
Statistical discrepancy a	-196	9	...	-287	82	260	72	...	214	-26
Net Lending	2783	3312	...	79	-608	-4637	-2448	...	-2103	-86
Incurrence of Liabilities and Net Worth	12504	9701	...	3341	-538	5810	3651	...	2149	10

	1988				
	Total General Government	Central Government	State or Provincial Government	Local Government	Social Security Funds
Acquisition of Financial Assets					
1 Gold and SDRs	...	...	...	...	...
2 Currency and transferable deposits	-387	-965	...	248	330
3 Other deposits	1262	1191	...	14	57
4 Bills and bonds, short term	...	...	...	...	...
5 Bonds, long term	-60	-58	...	-	-2
A Corporations	-58	-58	...	-	-
B Other government subsectors	-2	-	...	-	-2
C Rest of the world	-	-	...	-	-
6 Corporate equity securities	2560	1015	...	1469	76
7 Short-term loans, n.e.c.	7752	6158	...	860	734
8 Long-term loans, n.e.c.	1735	1069	...	589	77
A Mortgages	...	...	...	...	...
B Other	...	...	...	...	...

Finland

3.14 General Government Capital Finance Account, Total and Subsectors
(Continued)

Million Finnish markkaa

	1988 Total General Government	Central Government	State or Provincial Government	Local Government	Social Security Funds
9 Other receivables	418	209	...	464	-255
10 Other assets	466	74	...	392	-
Total Acquisition of Financial Assets	13746	8693	...	4036	1017

Incurrence of Liabilities

1 Currency and transferable deposits	...	...	...	...	...
2 Other deposits	...	...	...	...	...
3 Bills and bonds, short term	18	-	...	20	-2
4 Bonds, long term	2339	2128	...	211	-
5 Short-term loans, n.e.c.	1257	712	...	545	-
6 Long-term loans, n.e.c.	1324	-989	...	2311	2
7 Other payables	1114	748	...	114	252
8 Other liabilities	1151	-	...	1151	-
Total Incurrence of Liabilities	7203	2599	...	4352	252
Statistical discrepancy [a]	829	687	...	-148	290
Net Lending	5714	5407	...	-168	475
Incurrence of Liabilities and Net Worth	13746	8693	...	4036	1017

a) Statistical discrepancy refers to adjustment made in order to reconcile the net lending of the Capital Accumulation Account and the Capital Finance Account.

3.22 Corporate and Quasi-Corporate Enterprise Income and Outlay Account: Total and Sectors

Million Finnish markkaa

	1980 TOTAL	1980 Non-Financial	1980 Financial	1981 TOTAL	1981 Non-Financial	1981 Financial	1982 TOTAL	1982 Non-Financial	1982 Financial	1983 TOTAL	1983 Non-Financial	1983 Financial
Receipts												
1 Operating surplus	11682	13979	-2297	12566	14828	-2262	13994	16333	-2339	18505	20950	-2445
2 Property and entrepreneurial income	20077	3188	16889	24584	3837	20747	27797	4647	23150	33910	6011	27899
A Withdrawals from quasi-corporate enterprises	-	-	-	-	-	-	-	-	-	-	-	-
B Interest	19610	2902	16708	24008	3507	20501	27079	4240	22839	32983	5461	27522
C Dividends	409	230	179	511	267	244	637	328	309	817	443	374
D Net land rent and royalties	58	56	2	65	63	2	81	79	2	110	107	3
3 Current transfers	15560	1630	13930	18893	2061	16832	20634	2151	18483	22320	2458	19862
A Casualty insurance claims	1434	928	506	1977	1180	797	1899	1132	767	2049	1265	784
B Casualty insurance premiums, net, due to be received by insurance companies	2763	-	2763	3508	-	3508	4237	-	4237	4940	-	4940
C Current transfers from the rest of the world	-	-	-	-	-	-	-	-	-	-	-	-
D Other transfers except imputed	10672	65	10607	12619	151	12468	13604	189	13415	14348	283	14065
E Imputed unfunded employee pension and welfare contributions	691	637	54	789	730	59	894	830	64	983	910	73
Total Current Receipts	47319	18797	28522	56043	20726	35317	62425	23131	39294	74735	29419	45316
Disbursements												
1 Property and entrepreneurial income	23893	14590	9303	29632	17679	11953	33437	19852	13585	39435	22593	16842
A Withdrawals from quasi-corporations	1382	1382	-	1468	1468	-	1716	1716	-	2058	2058	-
Public	369	369	-	343	343	-	437	437	-	706	706	-
Private	1013	1013	-	1125	1125	-	1279	1279	-	1352	1352	-
B Interest	20841	11794	9047	26053	14512	11541	29012	16039	12973	34263	18148	16115
C Dividends	1119	863	256	1469	1059	410	1909	1300	609	2263	1540	723
D Net land rent and royalties	551	551	-	642	640	2	800	797	3	851	847	4
2 Direct taxes and other current transfers n.e.c. to general government	2821	2033	788	3978	2999	979	4540	3352	1188	5277	3834	1443
A Direct taxes	2279	2033	246	3290	2999	291	3713	3352	361	4316	3834	482
On income	...	...	...	3270	2981	289	3663	3308	355	4258	3782	476
Other	...	...	...	20	18	2	50	44	6	58	52	6
B Fines, fees, penalties and other current transfers n.e.c.	542	-	542	688	-	688	827	-	827	961	-	961

Finland

3.22 Corporate and Quasi-Corporate Enterprise Income and Outlay Account: Total and Sectors
(Continued)

Million Finnish markkaa

	1980 TOTAL	1980 Non-Financial	1980 Financial	1981 TOTAL	1981 Non-Financial	1981 Financial	1982 TOTAL	1982 Non-Financial	1982 Financial	1983 TOTAL	1983 Non-Financial	1983 Financial
3 Other current transfers	12100	2346	9754	14693	2784	11909	16894	2972	13922	19488	3282	16206
A Casualty insurance premiums, net	1418	913	505	1958	1161	797	1885	1118	767	2043	1259	784
B Casualty insurance claims liability of insurance companies	2763	-	2763	3508	-	3508	4237	-	4237	4940	-	4940
C Transfers to private non-profit institutions	271	220	51	327	273	54	374	305	69	419	344	75
D Unfunded employee pension and welfare benefits	1246	1213	33	1387	1350	37	1590	1549	41	1726	1679	47
E Social assistance grants	6402	-	6402	7513	-	7513	8808	-	8808	10360	-	10360
F Other transfers n.e.c. [a]	...	...	...	...	...	...	...	...	...	...	...	...
G Transfers to the rest of the world	-	-	-	-	-	-	-	-	-	-	-	-
Net saving	8505	-172	8677	7740	-2736	10476	7554	-3045	10599	10535	-290	10825
Total Current Disbursements and Net Saving	47319	18797	28522	56043	20726	35317	62425	23131	39294	74735	29419	45316

	1984 TOTAL	1984 Non-Financial	1984 Financial	1985 TOTAL	1985 Non-Financial	1985 Financial	1986 TOTAL	1986 Non-Financial	1986 Financial	1987 TOTAL	1987 Non-Financial	1987 Financial
Receipts												
1 Operating surplus	22418	25348	-2930	20331	23941	-3610	20141	24517	-4376	27797	32914	-5117
2 Property and entrepreneurial income	44221	7936	36285	51815	9568	42247	52560	9189	43371	60559	9893	50666
A Withdrawals from quasi-corporate enterprises	-	-	-	-	-	-	-	-	-	-	-	-
B Interest	42894	7123	35771	50120	8528	41592	50475	7861	42614	57860	8090	49770
C Dividends	1215	705	510	1556	906	650	1936	1187	749	2519	1633	886
D Net land rent and royalties	112	108	4	139	134	5	149	141	8	180	170	10
3 Current transfers	24735	2676	22059	28323	3103	25220	31569	3443	28126	34811	3709	31102
A Casualty insurance claims	2379	1491	888	2659	1810	849	3151	2007	1144	3191	2159	1032
B Casualty insurance premiums, net, due to be received by insurance companies	5921	-	5921	6711	-	6711	7132	-	7132	7406	-	7406
C Current transfers from the rest of the world	-	-	-	-	-	-	-	-	-	-	-	-
D Other transfers except imputed	15385	215	15170	17902	258	17644	20172	339	19833	23038	392	22646
E Imputed unfunded employee pension and welfare contributions	1050	970	80	1051	1035	16	1114	1097	17	1176	1158	18
Total Current Receipts	91374	35960	55414	100469	36612	63857	104270	37149	67121	123167	46516	76651
Disbursements												
1 Property and entrepreneurial income	50482	27315	23167	57202	30114	27088	58249	31225	27024	67129	35191	31938
A Withdrawals from quasi-corporations	2516	2516	-	2711	2711	-	2499	2499	-	3999	3999	-
Public	1032	1032	-	1206	1206	-	1004	1004	-	2446	2446	-
Private	1484	1484	-	1505	1505	-	1495	1495	-	1553	1553	-
B Interest	44021	21609	22412	49659	23381	26278	50376	24218	26158	56715	25843	30872
C Dividends	2939	2192	747	3654	2851	803	4097	3237	860	4976	3916	1060
D Net land rent and royalties	1006	998	8	1178	1171	7	1277	1271	6	1439	1433	6
2 Direct taxes and other current transfers n.e.c. to general government	5514	3955	1559	5874	3983	1891	6661	4660	2001	5700	3529	2171
A Direct taxes	4468	3955	513	4499	3983	516	5293	4660	633	4295	3529	766
On income	4403	3896	507	4425	3916	509	5205	4581	624	4207	3450	757
Other	65	59	6	74	67	7	88	79	9	88	79	9
B Fines, fees, penalties and other current transfers n.e.c.	1046	-	1046	1375	-	1375	1368	-	1368	1405	-	1405

Finland

3.22 Corporate and Quasi-Corporate Enterprise Income and Outlay Account: Total and Sectors
(Continued)

Million Finnish markkaa

	1984 TOTAL	1984 Non-Financial	1984 Financial	1985 TOTAL	1985 Non-Financial	1985 Financial	1986 TOTAL	1986 Non-Financial	1986 Financial	1987 TOTAL	1987 Non-Financial	1987 Financial
3 Other current transfers	22649	3704	18945	25651	4263	21388	29003	4654	24349	31647	5026	26621
A Casualty insurance premiums, net	2355	1467	888	2644	1795	849	3138	1994	1144	3177	2145	1032
B Casualty insurance claims liability of insurance companies	5921	-	5921	6711	-	6711	7132	-	7132	7406	-	7406
C Transfers to private non-profit institutions	460	386	74	505	420	85	553	452	101	613	481	132
D Unfunded employee pension and welfare benefits	1903	1851	52	2079	2048	31	2242	2208	34	2436	2400	36
E Social assistance grants	12010	-	12010	13712	-	13712	15938	-	15938	18015	-	18015
F Other transfers n.e.c. [a]	...	...	...	...	...	...	...	...	...	...	...	...
G Transfers to the rest of the world	-	-	-	-	-	-	-	-	-	-	-	-
Net saving	12729	986	11743	11742	-1748	13490	10357	-3390	13747	18691	2770	15921
Total Current Disbursements and Net Saving	91374	35960	55414	100469	36612	63857	104270	37149	67121	123167	46516	76651

	1988 TOTAL	1988 Non-Financial	1988 Financial	1989 TOTAL	1989 Non-Financial	1989 Financial
Receipts						
1 Operating surplus	34780	40769	-5989	38099	45908	-7809
2 Property and entrepreneurial income	76257	12566	63691	103881	16649	87232
A Withdrawals from quasi-corporate enterprises	-	-	-	-	-	-
B Interest	72103	9673	62430	98807	13263	85544
C Dividends	3941	2693	1248	4838	3156	1682
D Net land rent and royalties	213	200	13	236	230	6
3 Current transfers	43359	3795	39564	50790	4102	46688
A Casualty insurance claims	3421	2418	1003	3749	2575	1174
B Casualty insurance premiums, net, due to be received by insurance companies	7641	-	7641	8767	-	8767
C Current transfers from the rest of the world	-	-	-	-	-	-
D Other transfers except imputed	31294	394	30900	37149	424	36725
E Imputed unfunded employee pension and welfare contributions	1003	983	20	1125	1103	22
Total Current Receipts	154396	57130	97266	192770	66659	126111
Disbursements						
1 Property and entrepreneurial income	81791	39700	42091	112095	50518	61577
A Withdrawals from quasi-corporations	3292	3292	-	3561	3561	-
Public	1304	1304	-	1374	1374	-
Private	1988	1988	-	2187	2187	-
B Interest	70225	29346	40879	98270	38259	60011
C Dividends	6701	5495	1206	8503	6943	1560
D Net land rent and royalties	1573	1567	6	1761	1755	6
2 Direct taxes and other current transfers n.e.c. to general government	7087	4734	2353	8223	5510	2713
A Direct taxes	5474	4734	740	6458	5510	948
On income	5385	4655	730	6355	5417	938
Other	89	79	10	103	93	10
B Fines, fees, penalties and other current transfers n.e.c.	1613	-	1613	1765	-	1765

Finland

3.22 Corporate and Quasi-Corporate Enterprise Income and Outlay Account: Total and Sectors
(Continued)

Million Finnish markkaa

	1988 TOTAL	1988 Non-Financial	1988 Financial	1989 TOTAL	1989 Non-Financial	1989 Financial
3 Other current transfers	37909	5408	32501	42763	5844	36919
A Casualty insurance premiums, net	3404	2401	1003	3724	2550	1174
B Casualty insurance claims liability of insurance companies	7641	-	7641	8767	-	8767
C Transfers to private non-profit institutions	710	579	131	801	643	158
D Unfunded employee pension and welfare benefits	2467	2428	39	2694	2651	43
E Social assistance grants	23687	-	23687	26777	-	26777
F Other transfers n.e.c. [a]	...	...	...	...	...	...
G Transfers to the rest of the world	-	-	-	-	-	-
Net saving	27609	7288	20321	29689	4787	24902
Total Current Disbursements and Net Saving	154396	57130	97266	192770	66659	126111

a) Item 'Other transfers n.e.c.' refers to transfers to households.

3.23 Corporate and Quasi-Corporate Enterprise Capital Accumulation Account: Total and Sectors

Million Finnish markkaa

	1980 TOTAL	1980 Non-Fin	1980 Fin	1981 TOTAL	1981 Non-Fin	1981 Fin	1982 TOTAL	1982 Non-Fin	1982 Fin	1983 TOTAL	1983 Non-Fin	1983 Fin
Finance of Gross Accumulation												
1 Gross saving	25550	16237	9313	27013	15696	11317	28951	17287	11664	33884	21766	12118
A Consumption of fixed capital	17045	16409	636	19273	18432	841	21397	20332	1065	23349	22056	1293
B Net saving	8505	-172	8677	7740	-2736	10476	7554	-3045	10599	10535	-290	10825
2 Capital transfers [a]	90	90	-	141	141	-	97	97	-	106	106	-
Finance of Gross Accumulation	25640	16327	9313	27154	15837	11317	29048	17384	11664	33990	21872	12118
Gross Accumulation												
1 Gross capital formation	29144	27508	1636	29152	26456	2696	30557	27693	2864	33205	30620	2585
A Increase in stocks	6339	6339	-	2539	2539	-	1214	1214	-	-514	-514	-
B Gross fixed capital formation	22805	21169	1636	26613	23917	2696	29343	26479	2864	33719	31134	2585
2 Purchases of land, net	103	55	48	149	134	15	223	207	16	445	323	122
3 Purchases of intangible assets, net	-	-	-	-	-	-	-	-	-	-	-	-
4 Capital transfers [a]	...	...	...	...	...	...	...	...	...	...	...	...
Net lending	-3607	-11236	7629	-2147	-10753	8606	-1732	-10516	8784	340	-9071	9411
Gross Accumulation	25640	16327	9313	27154	15837	11317	29048	17384	11664	33990	21872	12118

	1984 TOTAL	1984 Non-Fin	1984 Fin	1985 TOTAL	1985 Non-Fin	1985 Fin	1986 TOTAL	1986 Non-Fin	1986 Fin	1987 TOTAL	1987 Non-Fin	1987 Fin
Finance of Gross Accumulation												
1 Gross saving	38424	25150	13274	40118	24816	15302	41001	24963	16038	52073	33617	18456
A Consumption of fixed capital	25695	24164	1531	28376	26564	1812	30644	28353	2291	33382	30847	2535
B Net saving	12729	986	11743	11742	-1748	13490	10357	-3390	13747	18691	2770	15921
2 Capital transfers [a]	174	174	-	186	186	-	205	205	-	11	906	-895
Finance of Gross Accumulation	38598	25324	13274	40304	25002	15302	41206	25168	16038	52084	34523	17561
Gross Accumulation												
1 Gross capital formation	37057	33832	3225	39980	37122	2858	41577	37814	3763	49333	45850	3483
A Increase in stocks	1208	1208	-	-386	-386	-	-2257	-2257	-	-239	-239	-
B Gross fixed capital formation	35849	32624	3225	40366	37508	2858	43834	40071	3763	49572	46089	3483
2 Purchases of land, net	530	411	119	630	415	215	370	200	170	409	401	8
3 Purchases of intangible assets, net	-	-	-	-	-	-	-	-	-	-	-	-
4 Capital transfers [a]	...	...	...	...	...	...	...	...	...	...	...	...
Net lending	1011	-8919	9930	-306	-12535	12229	-741	-12846	12105	2342	-11728	14070
Gross Accumulation	38598	25324	13274	40304	25002	15302	41206	25168	16038	52084	34523	17561

Finland

3.23 Corporate and Quasi-Corporate Enterprise Capital Accumulation Account: Total and Sectors
Million Finnish markkaa

	1988 TOTAL	1988 Non-Financial	1988 Financial	1989 TOTAL	1989 Non-Financial	1989 Financial
Finance of Gross Accumulation						
1 Gross saving	64841	41522	23319	71624	43331	28293
A Consumption of fixed capital	37232	34234	2998	41935	38544	3391
B Net saving	27609	7288	20321	29689	4787	24902
2 Capital transfers a	1088	1230	-142	155	1841	-1686
Finance of Gross Accumulation	65929	42752	23177	71779	45172	26607
Gross Accumulation						
1 Gross capital formation	62308	58519	3789	78428	73501	4927
A Increase in stocks	3136	3136	-	5660	5660	-
B Gross fixed capital formation	59172	55383	3789	72768	67841	4927
2 Purchases of land, net	1619	1609	10	1517	1500	17
3 Purchases of intangible assets, net	-	-714	714	-	-	-
4 Capital transfers a	...	...	...	...	...	...
Net lending	2002	-16662	18664	-8166	-29829	21663
Gross Accumulation	65929	42752	23177	71779	45172	26607

a) Capital transfers received are recorded net of capital transfers paid.

3.24 Corporate and Quasi-Corporate Enterprise Capital Finance Account: Total and Sectors
Million Finnish markkaa

	1980 TOTAL	1980 Non-Fin.	1980 Fin.	1981 TOTAL	1981 Non-Fin.	1981 Fin.	1982 TOTAL	1982 Non-Fin.	1982 Fin.	1983 TOTAL	1983 Non-Fin.	1983 Fin.
Acquisition of Financial Assets												
1 Gold and SDRs	-6	-	-6	387	-	387	-101	-	-101	-132	-	-132
2 Currency and transferable deposits	3923	1156	2767	6839	586	6253	9554	1090	8464	1816	540	1276
3 Other deposits	2748	460	2288	1610	1493	117	6411	2525	3886	5138	2315	2823
4 Bills and bonds, short term	3662	-	3662	1984	-	1984	2889	-	2889	4433	-	4433
A Corporate and quasi-corporate, resident	3600	-	3600	2049	-	2049	2875	-	2875	3705	-	3705
B Government	54	-	54	-3	-	-3	-21	-	-21	9	-	9
C Rest of the world	8	-	8	-62	-	-62	35	-	35	719	-	719
5 Bonds, long term	2505	147	2358	370	363	7	2558	-33	2591	6328	-616	6944
A Corporate, resident	850	147	703	1017	363	654	1907	-33	1940	4233	-616	4849
B Government	1176	-	1176	347	-	347	1266	-	1266	1940	-	1940
C Rest of the world	479	-	479	-994	-	-994	-615	-	-615	155	-	155
6 Corporate equity securities	2705	1444	1261	2769	1428	1341	4349	3104	1245	5699	3706	1993
7 Short term loans, n.e.c.	2184	13	2171	762	881	-119	6803	2754	4049	10611	2980	7631
8 Long term loans, n.e.c.	17885	131	17754	20878	685	20193	28635	2044	26591	25319	2294	23025
A Mortgages	4387	-	4387	6114	-	6114	6168	-	6168	7155	-	7155
B Other	13498	131	13367	14764	685	14079	22467	2044	20423	18164	2294	15870
9 Trade credits and advances	8740	8732	8	9324	9501	-177	13966	13661	305	8618	8510	108
10 Other receivables	2731	1277	1454	2215	948	1267	608	687	-79	2297	738	1559
11 Other assets	-	-	-	-	-	-	-	-	-	-	-	-
Total Acquisition of Financial Assets	47077	13360	33717	47138	15885	31253	75672	25832	49840	70127	20467	49660
Incurrence of Liabilities												
1 Currency and transferable deposits	5573	-	5573	6213	-	6213	10909	-	10909	7348	-	7348
2 Other deposits	11820	-27	11847	9958	-46	10004	11740	5	11735	17127	57	17070
3 Bills and bonds, short term	3618	2941	677	1460	1470	-10	2619	1569	1050	3158	1578	1580
4 Bonds, long term	791	-578	1369	1564	-57	1621	4221	1341	2880	6367	1999	4368
5 Corporate equity securities	1651	1133	518	1023	730	293	2241	1540	701	3329	2173	1156
6 Short-term loans, n.e.c.	2848	-67	2915	2491	848	1643	11625	4511	7114	10707	5020	5687

Finland

3.24 Corporate and Quasi-Corporate Enterprise Capital Finance Account: Total and Sectors
(Continued)

Million Finnish markkaa

	1980 TOTAL	1980 Non-Financial	1980 Financial	1981 TOTAL	1981 Non-Financial	1981 Financial	1982 TOTAL	1982 Non-Financial	1982 Financial	1983 TOTAL	1983 Non-Financial	1983 Financial
7 Long-term loans, n.e.c.	11744	10128	1616	15304	12637	2667	20606	14676	5930	12953	11888	1065
8 Net equity of households in life insurance and pension fund reserves	-	-	-	-	-	-	-	-	-	-	-	-
9 Proprietors' net additions to the accumulation of quasi-corporations	1413	1413	-	2223	2223	-	1897	1897	-	1085	1085	-
10 Trade credit and advances	9960	9852	108	8414	8548	-134	12161	11916	245	7812	7521	291
11 Other accounts payable	2068	821	1247	2698	2185	513	669	306	363	518	-1111	1629
12 Other liabilities	...	...	...	...	...	...	...	...	...	...	...	...
Total Incurrence of Liabilities	51486	25616	25870	51348	28538	22810	78688	37761	40927	70404	30210	40194
Statistical discrepancy [a]	-802	-1020	218	-2063	-1900	-163	-1284	-1413	129	-617	-672	55
Net Lending	-3607	-11236	7629	-2147	-10753	8606	-1732	-10516	8784	340	-9071	9411
Incurrence of Liabilities and Net Lending	47077	13360	33717	47138	15885	31253	75672	25832	49840	70127	20467	49660

	1984 TOTAL	1984 Non-Financial	1984 Financial	1985 TOTAL	1985 Non-Financial	1985 Financial	1986 TOTAL	1986 Non-Financial	1986 Financial	1987 TOTAL	1987 Non-Financial	1987 Financial
Acquisition of Financial Assets												
1 Gold and SDRs	1072	-	1072	397	-	397	92	-	92	46	-	46
2 Currency and transferable deposits	22735	814	21921	1311	2998	-1687	8066	1044	7022	19367	367	19000
3 Other deposits	6874	3092	3782	4834	1624	3210	780	-244	1024	8099	3775	4324
4 Bills and bonds, short term	2073	-	2073	4717	-	4717	-141	-	-141	754	-	754
A Corporate and quasi-corporate, resident	985	-	985	4027	-	4027	-1399	-	-1399	1683	-	1683
B Government	10	-	10	-19	-	-19	-20	-	-20	-22	-	-22
C Rest of the world	1078	-	1078	709	-	709	1278	-	1278	-908	-	-908
5 Bonds, long term	5181	1	5180	6745	32	6713	14482	795	13687	5569	1340	4229
A Corporate, resident	5097	1	5096	4843	32	4811	8909	795	8114	3233	1340	1893
B Government	273	-	273	-937	-	-937	1443	-	1443	239	-	239
C Rest of the world	-189	-	-189	2839	-	2839	4130	-	4130	2097	-	2097
6 Corporate equity securities	9583	5988	3595	15778	10234	5544	9800	3863	5937	18523	9317	9206
7 Short term loans, n.e.c.	13857	8506	5351	14531	5090	9441	30470	7371	23099	29739	14094	15645
8 Long term loans, n.e.c.	28491	63	28428	30992	-615	31607	37647	-222	37869	51084	-418	51502
A Mortgages	6997	-	6997	7555	-	7555	7905	-	7905	...	-	...
B Other	21494	63	21431	23437	-615	24052	29742	-222	29964	...	-418	...
9 Trade credits and advances	7356	7213	143	3018	2626	392	-1474	-1767	293	7671	7304	367
10 Other receivables	6559	3217	3342	4775	1193	3582	3063	1475	1588	2732	347	2385
11 Other assets	-	-	-	-	-	-	-	-	-	-	-	-
Total Acquisition of Financial Assets	103781	28894	74887	87098	23182	63916	102785	12315	90470	143584	36126	107458
Incurrence of Liabilities												
1 Currency and transferable deposits	17044	-	17044	6973	-	6973	19026	-	19026	36379	-	36379
2 Other deposits	22342	39	22303	15417	15	15402	9796	12	9784	18764	-4	18768
3 Bills and bonds, short term	1040	4	1036	3891	3363	528	-1659	-4239	2580	1800	682	1118
4 Bonds, long term	10861	2730	8131	13150	5271	7879	17473	5077	12396	12702	2936	9766
5 Corporate equity securities	6653	4570	2083	14500	13128	1372	9500	6974	2526	16194	12984	3210
6 Short-term loans, n.e.c.	17762	7362	10400	9553	-4665	14218	33954	8100	25854	16870	10749	6121
7 Long-term loans, n.e.c.	12094	11530	564	18335	14659	3676	20632	18592	2040	28513	15654	12859
8 Net equity of households in life insurance and pension fund reserves	-	-	-	-	-	-	-	-	-	-	-	-
9 Proprietors' net additions to the accumulation of quasi-corporations	1788	1788	-	1143	1143	-	880	880	-	166	166	-
10 Trade credit and advances	8394	8389	5	1698	1893	-195	-2344	-3144	800	9200	9223	-23
11 Other accounts payable	5465	2213	3252	3612	2265	1347	677	-2575	3252	6299	596	5703
12 Other liabilities	...	...	...	...	...	...	...	...	...	...	...	...
Total Incurrence of Liabilities	103443	38625	64818	88272	37072	51200	107935	29677	78258	146887	52986	93901
Statistical discrepancy [a]	-673	-812	139	-868	-1355	487	-4409	-4516	107	-5645	-5132	-513
Net Lending	1011	-8919	9930	-306	-12535	12229	-741	-12846	12105	2342	-11728	14070
Incurrence of Liabilities and Net Lending	103781	28894	74887	87098	23182	63916	102785	12315	90470	143584	36126	107458

Finland

3.24 Corporate and Quasi-Corporate Enterprise Capital Finance Account: Total and Sectors

Million Finnish markkaa

		1988 TOTAL	1988 Non-Financial	1988 Financial
Acquisition of Financial Assets				
1	Gold and SDRs	364	-	364
2	Currency and transferable deposits	6808	326	6482
3	Other deposits	21594	10414	11180
4	Bills and bonds, short term	8730	-	8730
	A Corporate and quasi-corporate, resident	7415	-	7415
	B Government	18	-	18
	C Rest of the world	1297	-	1297
5	Bonds, long term	7857	1789	6068
	A Corporate, resident	4676	1789	2887
	B Government	1457	-	1457
	C Rest of the world	1724	-	1724
6	Corporate equity securities	26661	10423	16238
7	Short term loans, n.e.c.	62484	20942	41542
8	Long term loans, n.e.c.	75964	2018	73946
	A Mortgages	...	-	...
	B Other	...	2018	...
9	Trade credits and advances	11998	11409	589
10	Other receivables	11571	4332	7239
11	Other assets	-	-	-
	Total Acquisition of Financial Assets	234031	61653	172378
Incurrence of Liabilities				
1	Currency and transferable deposits	15990	-	15990
2	Other deposits	51824	100	51724
3	Bills and bonds, short term	6455	-322	6777
4	Bonds, long term	21932	3526	18406
5	Corporate equity securities	22729	15718	7011
6	Short-term loans, n.e.c.	64781	20416	44365
7	Long-term loans, n.e.c.	30294	26333	3961
8	Net equity of households in life insurance and pension fund reserves	-	-	-
9	Proprietors' net additions to the accumulation of quasi-corporations	466	466	-
10	Trade credit and advances	9302	8616	686
11	Other accounts payable	8681	3014	5667
12	Other liabilities	...	...	...
	Total Incurrence of Liabilities	232454	77867	154587
	Statistical discrepancy [a]	-425	448	-873
	Net Lending	2002	-16662	18664
	Incurrence of Liabilities and Net Lending	234031	61653	172378

a) Statistical discrepancy refers to adjustment made in order to reconcile the net lending of the Capital Accumulation Account and the Capital Finance Account.

3.32 Household and Private Unincorporated Enterprise Income and Outlay Account

Million Finnish markkaa

		1970	1975	1980	1981	1982	1983	1984	1985	1986	1987	1988	1989
Receipts														
1	Compensation of employees	22811	59297	105025	121501	134617	149098	165683	184316	197681	214993	237680	265540
	A Wages and salaries	19647	49309	85587	99231	110288	122830	136563	150346	160973	175117	192875	214023
	B Employers' contributions for social security	3164	9988	19438	22270	24329	26268	29120	33970	36708	39876	44805	51517
	C Employers' contributions for private pension & welfare plans	...	...	...	...	...	...	...	...	...	...	...	...
2	Operating surplus of private unincorporated enterprises	8587	16767	28823	30840	36355	39896	43538	45794	47659	47624	52164	60612
3	Property and entrepreneurial income	822	2267	4995	5893	6397	7432	9079	10255	9918	11107	14873	17894
	A Withdrawals from private quasi-corporations	-	381	1013	1125	1279	1352	1484	1505	1495	1553	1988	2187
	B Interest	669	1578	3469	4158	4380	5290	6656	7576	7102	8107	11285	13806

Finland

3.32 Household and Private Unincorporated Enterprise Income and Outlay Account
(Continued)

Million Finnish markkaa

	1970	1975	1980	1981	1982	1983	1984	1985	1986	1987	1988	1989
C Dividends	107	223	344	414	464	550	671	865	975	1073	1194	1451
D Net land rent and royalties	46	85	169	196	274	240	268	309	346	374	406	450
3 Current transfers	4458	12358	25906	30076	36548	42643	48197	55224	61123	67098	73400	80134
A Casualty insurance claims	256	565	806	970	1294	1325	1584	1822	2149	2521	2841	3541
B Social security benefits	2769	7894	16365	18869	23216	27652	31365	36038	40048	43576	50543	55449
C Social assistance grants	553	1431	3515	4161	5076	6027	6625	7674	8275	9171	9594	10282
D Unfunded employee pension and welfare benefits	799	2267	4813	5517	6367	7000	7862	8782	9795	10806	8395	9232
E Transfers from general government	35	74	106	121	114	141	192	275	353	447	550	677
F Transfers from the rest of the world	36	102	250	386	417	432	500	554	412	474	1371	820
G Other transfers n.e.c.	10	25	51	52	64	66	69	79	91	103	106	133
Total Current Receipts	36678	90689	164749	188310	213917	239069	266497	295589	316381	340822	378117	424180

Disbursements

	1970	1975	1980	1981	1982	1983	1984	1985	1986	1987	1988	1989
1 Final consumption expenditures	24989	55309	100863	114070	130610	145726	160503	175330	188264	206748	226864	247208
2 Property income	672	1839	4235	5044	5838	6846	8515	9742	10269	11982	15575	19705
A Interest	633	1768	4121	4911	5692	6675	8321	9529	10033	11723	15302	19405
B Net land rent and royalties	39	71	114	133	146	171	194	213	236	259	273	300
3 Direct taxes and other current transfers n.e.c. to government	8385	25715	45044	53726	58552	64428	74704	86738	96084	98566	121447	136083
A Social security contributions	3050	10145	18930	21615	23316	24813	28472	33991	36527	39690	49437	56594
B Direct taxes	5181	15208	25371	31212	34160	38355	44697	50991	57551	56718	68665	75396
Income taxes	5181	15208	25371	31195	34117	38304	44639	50924	57471	56638	68586	75302
Other	-	-	-	17	43	51	58	67	80	80	79	94
C Fees, fines and penalties	154	362	743	899	1076	1260	1535	1756	2006	2158	3345	4093
4 Other current transfers	1451	3666	6807	8040	9413	10433	11788	12905	14766	15979	13432	15096
A Net casualty insurance premiums	256	578	806	970	1294	1325	1584	1822	2149	2521	2841	3541
B Transfers to private non-profit institutions serving households	320	927	1768	2076	2333	2602	2946	3233	3494	3697	4061	4450
C Transfers to the rest of the world	19	93	281	372	471	474	539	489	1109	1054	1569	1727
D Other current transfers, except imputed	...	...	...	...	...	...	...	...	...	...	...	...
E Imputed employee pension and welfare contributions	856	2068	3952	4622	5315	6032	6719	7361	8014	8707	4961	5378
Net saving	1181	4160	7800	7430	9504	11636	10987	10874	6998	7547	799	6088
Total Current Disbursements and Net Saving	36678	90689	164749	188310	213917	239069	266497	295589	316381	340822	378117	424180

3.33 Household and Private Unincorporated Enterprise Capital Accumulation Account

Million Finnish markkaa

	1970	1975	1980	1981	1982	1983	1984	1985	1986	1987	1988	1989
Finance of Gross Accumulation												
1 Gross saving	2697	7819	15161	15749	18850	22099	22557	23395	20336	22017	16556	23620
A Consumption of fixed capital	1516	3659	7361	8319	9346	10463	11570	12521	13338	14470	15757	17532
B Net saving	1181	4160	7800	7430	9504	11636	10987	10874	6998	7547	799	6088
2 Capital transfers [a]	30	306	163	160	588	152	121	131	47	189	1662	155
Total Finance of Gross Accumulation	2727	8125	15324	15909	19438	22251	22678	23526	20383	22206	18218	23775
Gross Accumulation												
1 Gross Capital Formation	2485	6951	13940	13966	17694	18400	18691	18838	18893	18698	23401	30529
A Increase in stocks	-40	224	141	-336	629	5	71	-247	-304	-928	-413	671
B Gross fixed capital formation	2525	6727	13799	14302	17065	18395	18620	19085	19197	19626	23814	29858
2 Purchases of land, net	-390	-850	-658	-797	-796	-1153	-1070	-1463	-1206	-1067	-2729	-2058
3 Purchases of intangibles, net	...	...	...	...	...	-	-	-	-	...	...	...
4 Capital transfers [a]	...	...	...	...	...	...	...	...	...	...	...	...
Net lending	632	2024	2042	2740	2540	5004	5057	6151	2696	4575	-2454	-4696
Total Gross Accumulation	2727	8125	15324	15909	19438	22251	22678	23526	20383	22206	18218	23775

a) Capital transfers received are recorded net of capital transfers paid.

Finland

3.34 Household and Private Unincorporated Enterprise Capital Finance Account

Million Finnish markkaa

	1970	1975	1980	1981	1982	1983	1984	1985	1986	1987	1988	1989
Acquisition of Financial Assets													
1 Gold	...	...	...	...	...	...	...	...	...	...	...	...
2 Currency and transferable deposits	106	474	486	494	1299	207	1496	-419	-227	372	499	...
3 Other deposits	1889	4448	8324	8556	7950	10002	10497	10653	10391	14603	28773	...
4 Bills and bonds, short term	...	...	...	...	...	...	...	...	...	...	...	...
5 Bonds, long term	120	225	616	1120	2716	3462	2913	5775	3077	8386	4351	...
6 Corporate equity securities	695	1863	2729	2692	2575	4105	4055	4798	4500	5096	7008	...
7 Short term loans, n.e.c.	-	-	-6	15	1	20	21	-24	-17	60	117	...
8 Long term loans, n.e.c.	-	-	-	-	-	-	-	-	-	-	-	...
A Mortgages	...	...	...	...	...	...	...	...	...	...	...	...
B Other	-	-	-	-	-	-	-	-	-	-	-	...
9 Trade credit and advances	-	-	2	21	-21	15	136	-39	20	256	-280	...
10 Net equity of households in life insurance and pension fund reserves	-	-	-	-	-	-	-	-	-	-	-	...
11 Proprietors' net additions to the accumulation of quasi-corporations	-	-	-	-	-	-	-	-	-	-	-	...
12 Other	-	-	28	297	297	72	316	256	212	94	94	...
Total Acquisition of Financial Assets	2810	7010	12179	13195	14817	17883	19434	21000	17956	28867	40562	...
Incurrence of Liabilities													
1 Short term loans, n.e.c.	128	187	1063	989	469	994	1277	1675	509	1741	2389	...
2 Long term loans, n.e.c.	1306	4015	7555	7739	10498	10454	11116	12198	13800	21532	38447	...
A Mortgages	662	1900	4670	5609	6408	7251	6833	8864	8764	...	...	...
B Other	644	2115	2885	2130	4090	3203	4283	3334	5036	...	...	...
3 Trade credit and advances	156	217	265	357	245	480	605	144	502	-98	891	...
4 Other accounts payable	154	316	385	395	363	416	325	405	-113	1529	378	...
5 Other liabilities	...	...	...	...	...	...	...	...	...	...	...	...
Total Incurrence of Liabilities	1744	4735	9268	9480	11575	12344	13323	14422	14698	24704	42105	...
Statistical discrepancy [a]	434	251	869	975	702	535	1054	427	562	-412	911	...
Net Lending	632	2024	2042	2740	2540	5004	5057	6151	2696	4575	-2454	...
Incurrence of Liabilities and Net Lending	2810	7010	12179	13195	14817	17883	19434	21000	17956	28867	40562	...

a) Statistical discrepancy refers to adjustment made in order to reconcile the net lending of the Capital Accumulation Account and the Capital Finance Account.

3.42 Private Non-Profit Institutions Serving Households: Income and Outlay Account

Million Finnish markkaa

	1970	1975	1980	1981	1982	1983	1984	1985	1986	1987	1988	1989
Receipts													
1 Operating surplus	-25	-125	-879	-894	-839	-1160	-1537	-1827	-1840	-2453	-3208	-4268
2 Property and entrepreneurial income	38	102	212	254	303	367	465	539	611	644	736	856
A Withdrawals from quasi-corporations	-	-	-	-	-	-	-	-	-	-	-	-
B Interest	24	67	136	162	196	227	255	299	269	298	323	376
C Dividends	9	27	59	72	86	117	183	211	311	312	372	436
D Net land rent and royalties	5	8	17	20	21	23	27	29	31	34	41	44
3 Current transfers	948	2326	3941	4693	5286	5885	6407	6982	7641	8320	9230	10192
A Casualty insurance claims	13	22	58	69	76	87	96	101	107	104	123	148
B Current transfers from general government	517	1206	1683	2027	2292	2535	2619	2822	3147	3550	3924	4368
C Other transfers from resident sectors	...	...	...	...	...	...	...	...	...	...	...	...
D Current transfers received from the rest of the world	347	983	2003	2367	2659	2972	3359	3685	3981	4232	4690	5145
E Imputed unfunded employee pension and welfare contributions	70	114	195	227	256	288	329	370	402	429	488	525
Total Current Receipts	961	2303	3274	4053	4750	5092	5335	5694	6412	6511	6758	6780
Disbursements													
1 Final consumption expenditures	912	1927	3512	4095	4691	5277	5674	6334	6744	7236	8082	8811

Finland

3.42 Private Non-Profit Institutions Serving Households: Income and Outlay Account
(Continued)

Million Finnish markkaa

	1970	1975	1980	1981	1982	1983	1984	1985	1986	1987	1988	1989
A Compensation of employees	...	...	...	...	...	...	...	...	...	...	...	...
B Consumption of fixed capital	...	...	...	...	...	...	...	...	...	...	...	...
C Purchases of goods and services, net	912	1927	3512	4095	4691	5277	5674	6334	6744	7236	8082	8811
Purchases	912	1927	3512	4095	4691	5277	5674	6334	6744	7236	8082	8811
Less: Sales	-	-	-	-	-	-	-	-	-	-	-	-
2 Property income	312	633	1040	1167	1262	1412	1644	1751	1685	1755	2117	2579
A Interest	291	600	967	1090	1178	1319	1540	1629	1555	1622	1966	2424
B Net land rent and royalties	21	33	73	77	84	93	104	122	130	133	151	155
3 Direct taxes and other transfers to general government	47	50	68	113	158	182	200	223	250	238	252	295
A Direct taxes	47	50	68	113	158	182	200	223	250	238	252	295
B Fees, fines and penalties	-	-	-	-	-	-	-	-	-	-	-	-
4 Other current transfers	70	167	382	473	556	692	778	815	907	903	1066	1208
A Net casualty insurance premiums	13	22	58	69	76	87	96	101	107	111	126	155
B Social assistance grants	33	66	109	155	183	260	299	299	362	300	321	350
C Unfunded employee pension and welfare benefits	13	42	114	129	151	176	183	207	238	262	293	319
D Current transfers to the rest of the world	5	19	46	60	77	89	100	106	102	132	171	202
E Other current transfers n.e.c.	6	18	55	60	69	80	100	102	98	98	155	182
Net saving	-380	-474	-1728	-1795	-1917	-2471	-2961	-3429	-3174	-3621	-4759	-6113
Total Current Disbursements	961	2303	3274	4053	4750	5092	5335	5694	6412	6511	6758	6780

3.43 Private Non-Profit Institutions Serving Households: Capital Accumulation Account

Million Finnish markkaa

	1970	1975	1980	1981	1982	1983	1984	1985	1986	1987	1988	1989
					Finance of Gross Accumulation							
1 Gross saving	-36	666	619	903	1098	991	919	878	1562	1661	1551	1648
A Consumption of fixed capital	344	1140	2347	2698	3015	3462	3880	4307	4736	5282	6310	7761
B Net saving	-380	-474	-1728	-1795	-1917	-2471	-2961	-3429	-3174	-3621	-4759	-6113
2 Capital transfers [a]	47	89	182	169	207	245	260	268	287	388	527	555
A From resident sectors	47	89	182	169	207	245	260	268	287	388	527	555
Private	-	-	-	-	-	-	-	-	-	-	-	-
Public	47	89	182	169	207	245	260	268	287	388	527	555
B From the rest of the world	-	-	-	-	-	-	-	-	-	-	-	-
Finance of Gross Accumulation	11	755	801	1072	1305	1236	1179	1146	1849	2049	2078	2203
					Gross Accumulation							
1 Gross capital formation	1647	4309	5848	6779	7021	7942	8761	9448	8631	10334	13619	18839
A Increase in stocks	-	-	-	-	-	-	-	-	-	-	-	-
B Gross fixed capital formation	1647	4309	5848	6779	7021	7942	8761	9448	8631	10334	13619	18839
2 Purchases of land, net	47	115	173	193	200	232	275	293	264	272	405	485
3 Purchases of intangible assets, net	...	...	...	...	...	...	...	...	...	...	...	...
4 Capital transfers [a]	...	...	...	...	...	...	...	...	...	...	...	...
Net lending	-1683	-3669	-5220	-5900	-5916	-6938	-7857	-8595	-7046	-8557	-11946	-17121
Gross Accumulation	11	755	801	1072	1305	1236	1179	1146	1849	2049	2078	2203

a) Capital transfers received are recorded net of capital transfers paid.

3.44 Private Non-Profit Institutions Serving Households: Capital Finance Account

Million Finnish markkaa

	1970	1975	1980	1981	1982	1983	1984	1985	1986	1987	1988	1989
					Acquisition of Financial Assets							
1 Gold	...	...	...	...	...	...	...	...	...	...	...	...
2 Currency and transferable deposits	16	36	69	93	138	100	76	-41	176	126	92	...
3 Other deposits	29	71	90	171	84	54	143	11	281	365	370	...
4 Bills and bonds, short term	...	...	...	...	...	...	...	...	...	...	...	...
5 Bonds, long term	4	9	23	29	18	36	64	-40	31	40	49	...
A Corporate, resident	4	9	23	29	18	36	64	-40	31	40	49	...
B Government	...	...	...	...	...	...	...	...	...	...	...	...

Finland

3.44 Private Non-Profit Institutions Serving Households: Capital Finance Account (Continued)

Million Finnish markkaa	1970	1975	1980	1981	1982	1983	1984	1985	1986	1987	1988	1989
C Rest of the world	-	-	-	-	-	-	-	-	-	-	-	-
6 Corporate equity securities	72	132	290	255	294	255	251	225	309	330	251	401
7 Short-term loans, n.e.c.	13	9	48	16	48	-48	18	38	-204	-32	205	173
8 Long-term loans, n.e.c.	43	52	149	101	161	107	84	134	64	127	178	...
9 Other receivables	-48	-32	-187	-178	42	123	337	-71	88	204	45	...
10 Proprietors' net additions to the accumulation of quasi-corporations	-	-	-	-	-	-	-	-	-	-	-	...
11 Other assets	-	-	-	-	-	-	-	-	-	-	-	-
Total Acquisition of Financial Assets	129	277	482	562	689	663	993	98	938	1318	1308	...

Incurrence of Liabilities

	1970	1975	1980	1981	1982	1983	1984	1985	1986	1987	1988	1989
1 Short-term loans	29	53	167	245	227	120	423	116	88	297	222	...
2 Long-term loans	690	439	1062	1207	1530	1679	1578	1976	1735	3076	4436	...
3 Other liabilities	1093	2454	4473	5010	4848	5802	6849	6601	6161	6502	8596	...
Total Incurrence of Liabilities	1812	3946	5702	6462	6605	7601	8850	8693	7984	9875	13254	...
Statistical discrepancy [a]	-	-	-	-	-	-	-	-	-	-	-	...
Net Lending	-1683	-3669	-5220	-5900	-5916	-6938	-7857	-8595	-7046	-8557	-11946	...
Incurrence of Liabilities and Net Lending	129	277	482	562	689	663	993	98	938	1318	1308	...

[a] Statistical discrepancy refers to adjustment made in order to reconcile the net lending of the Capital Accumulation Account and the Capital Finance Account.

3.51 External Transactions: Current Account: Detail

Million Finnish markkaa	1970	1975	1980	1981	1982	1983	1984	1985	1986	1987	1988	1989

Payments to the Rest of the World

	1970	1975	1980	1981	1982	1983	1984	1985	1986	1987	1988	1989
1 Imports of goods and services	12310	30923	65011	69250	73762	81361	86137	94893	89898	97775	109866	125996
A Imports of merchandise c.i.f.	11138	28089	58046	60713	64542	70731	73496	80764	76736	81867	91232	104400
B Other	1172	2834	6970	8537	9220	10630	12641	14129	13162	15908	18634	21596
2 Factor income to the rest of the world	600	2037	5249	7477	6891	9456	11987	12930	12560	13599	16864	22318
A Compensation of employees	4	22	48	53	57	71	76	79	68	68	75	63
B Property and entrepreneurial income	596	2015	5201	7424	8834	9388	11911	12851	12492	13531	16789	22255
3 Current transfers to the rest of the world	260	611	1631	2282	2806	3512	4276	4504	5122	4877	5879	6343
A Indirect taxes by general government to supranational organizations	...	...	...	...	...	...	...	...	...	...	...	...
B Other current transfers	260	611	1631	2282	2806	3512	4276	4504	5122	4877	5879	6343
By general government	30	118	329	454	512	699	871	900	1189	1447	1764	2170
By other resident sectors	230	493	1302	1828	2294	2843	3405	3444	3933	3430	4115	4173
4 Surplus of the nation on current transactions	-1003	-7813	-5163	-1781	-3940	-5219	-49	-4517	-3828	-7915	-11608	-23657
Payments to the Rest of the World, and Surplus of the Nation on Current Transfers	12167	25758	66733	77228	81519	89113	102351	107810	103752	108336	121001	131000

Receipts From The Rest of the World

	1970	1975	1980	1981	1982	1983	1984	1985	1986	1987	1988	1989
1 Exports of goods and services	11745	24757	63489	72357	75801	82735	94190	98173	95634	100030	108750	116702
A Exports of merchandise f.o.b.	9640	20288	52694	58913	61914	67959	78961	82475	81066	83826	91313	98266
B Other	2105	4469	10795	13444	13887	14775	15229	15698	14568	16204	17437	18436
2 Factor income from the rest of the world	174	512	2007	3072	3544	3665	4883	6221	4976	5586	8497	11222
A Compensation of employees	31	73	413	430	539	559	334	420	389	495	382	...
B Property and entrepreneurial income	143	439	1594	2642	3005	3106	4569	5887	4556	5197	8002	10840
3 Current transfers from the rest of the world	248	489	1237	1799	2174	2713	3278	3416	3142	2720	3754	3076
A Subsidies to general government from supranational organizations	...	...	...	...	...	...	...	...	...	...	...	...
B Other current transfers	248	489	1237	1799	2174	2713	3278	3416	3142	2720	3754	3076
To general government	-	-	-	-	-	-	-	-	-	-	-	-
To other resident sectors	248	489	1237	1799	2174	2713	3278	3416	3142	2720	3754	3076
Receipts from the Rest of the World on Current Transfers	12167	25758	66733	77228	81519	89113	102351	107810	103752	108336	121001	131000

Finland

3.52 External Transactions: Capital Accumulation Account

Million Finnish markkaa

Finance of Gross Accumulation

	1970	1975	1980	1981	1982	1983	1984	1985	1986	1987	1988	1989
1 Surplus of the nation on current transactions	-1003	-7813	-5213	-1781	-3940	-5219	-49	-4517	-3828	-7915	-11608	-23657
2 Capital transfers from the rest of the world a	-	-2	-	-2	-3	-	-44	-	-	-	-	-
Total Finance of Gross Accumulation	-1003	-7815	-5213	-1783	-3943	-5219	-93	-4517	-3828	-7915	-11608	-23657

Gross Accumulation

	1970	1975	1980	1981	1982	1983	1984	1985	1986	1987	1988	1989
1 Capital transfers to the rest of the world a	...	...	...	...	...	...	...	...	...	...	...	...
2 Purchases of intangible assets, n.e.c., net, from the rest of the world	...	...	...	...	...	...	...	...	...	...	...	...
Net lending to the rest of the world	-1003	-7815	-5213	-1783	-3943	-5219	-93	-4517	-3828	-7915	-11608	-23657
Total Gross Accumulation	-1003	-7815	-5213	-1783	-3943	-5219	-93	-4517	-3828	-7915	-11608	-23657

a) Capital transfers received are recorded net of capital transfers paid.

3.53 External Transactions: Capital Finance Account

Million Finnish markkaa

Acquisitions of Foreign Financial Assets

	1970	1975	1980	1981	1982	1983	1984	1985	1986	1987	1988	1989
1 Gold and SDR's	49	-276	-6	387	-101	-132	1072	397	92	46	364	
2 Currency and transferable deposits	776	276	3596	4374	8008	1703	18261	-3088	4697	18420	3700	
3 Other deposits	136	362	-22	12	2389	-104	-2163	566	999	1906	175	
4 Bills and bonds, short term	-9	121	8	-62	35	719	1078	709	1878	-1364	1787	
5 Bonds, long term	34	-169	197	781	-448	116	-416	3048	4124	2097	1878	
6 Corporate equity securities	47	528	742	1036	1620	2328	2059	3287	3265	5970		
A Subsidiaries abroad	37	170	423	600	837	1455	2124	1911	3021			
B Other	10	27	105	142	199	165	204	148	266			
7 Short-term loans, n.e.c.	24	37	-	122	956	-280	876	2587	3612	8085	3350	4264
A Subsidiaries abroad	-	-	-	-	-	-	-	-	-	-	-	-
B Other	24	37	122	956	-280	876	2587	3612	8085	3350	4264	
8 Long-term loans	182	-84	167	310	709	-34	3314	293	1232	1397	3552	
A Subsidiaries abroad	182	-68	64	12	288	-3	355	162	620			
B Other	-	-16	103	298	421	-31	2959	131	612			
9 Proprietors' net additions to accumulation of quasi-corporate, non-resident enterprises	-	-	-	-	-	-	-	-	-	-	-	-
10 Trade credit and advances	209	-561	2613	1792	257	1934	-1801	58	-441	-1339	1235	
11 Other	-	135	303	108	-81	559	617	-111	1042	126	2754	
Total Acquisitions of Foreign Financial Assets	1448	38	8089	6593	12760	7257	24877	7542	23003	27804	25189	

Incurrence of Foreign Liabilities

	1970	1975	1980	1981	1982	1983	1984	1985	1986	1987	1988	1989
1 Currency and transferable deposits	517	1348	5431	1931	6687	7132	10137	2436	9098	32493	12678	
2 Other deposits	-	-	-	-	-	-	-	-	-	-	-	-
3 Bills and bonds, short term	76	358	-59	159	105	1016	1024	-89	301	1128		
4 Bonds, long term	115	1543	673	1825	3387	2241	6070	6908	8791	8126	14010	
5 Corporate equity securities	60	165	145	150	41	88	982	578	2660	378	1615	
A Subsidiaries of non-resident incorporated units	60	162	145	150	-24	88	332	365	1623			
B Other	3	-	-	65	-	650	213	1037				
6 Short-term loans, n.e.c.	14	-1	1539	476	3529	447	6360	1353	13529	-4780	5171	
A Subsidiaries of non-residents												
B Other	14	-1	1539	476	3529	447	6360	1353	13529	-4780	5171	
7 Long-term loans	454	2778	360	2307	472	296	-487	-448	-1922	2854	118	
A Subsidiaries of non-residents	36	111	-41	-75	43	-	-8	25				

Finland

3.53 External Transactions: Capital Finance Account
(Continued)

Million Finnish markkaa

	1970	1975	1980	1981	1982	1983	1984	1985	1986	1987	1988	1989
B Other	418	2667	401	2382	4515	296	-479	-473	...	...	...	...
8 Non-resident proprietors' net additions to accumulation of resident quasi-corporate enterprises	-	-	-	-	-	-	-	-	-	-	-	...
9 Trade credit and advances	1177	2499	4038	1917	-1498	1725	-43	-1383	-1633	-558	-238	...
10 Other	-	42	238	121	190	152	567	-28	530	2702	1000	...
Total Incurrence of Liabilities	2337	8450	12782	8668	16967	12186	24602	12441	30964	41516	35482	...
Statistical discrepancy a	114	-597	520	-292	-264	290	368	-382	-4043	-5797	1315	...
Net Lending	-1003	-7815	-5213	-1783	-3943	-5219	-93	-4517	-3828	-7915	-11608	...
Total Incurrence of Liabilities and Net Lending b	1448	38	8089	6593	12760	7257	24877	7542	23093	27804	25189	...

a) Statistical discrepancy refers to adjustment made in order to reconcile the net lending of the Capital Accumulation Account and the Capital Finance Account.
b) Total incurrence of liabilities includes allocated Special Drawing Rights.

4.1 Derivation of Value Added by Kind of Activity, in Current Prices

Million Finnish markkaa

	1980			1981			1982			1983		
	Gross Output	Intermediate Consumption	Value Added	Gross Output	Intermediate Consumption	Value Added	Gross Output	Intermediate Consumption	Value Added	Gross Output	Intermediate Consumption	Value Added
All Producers												
1 Agriculture, hunting, forestry and fishing	24903	8166	16737	27015	9604	17411	30766	11352	19414	32970	11911	21059
A Agriculture and hunting a	15372	7432	7940	16547	8741	7806	19967	10360	9607	22274	10875	11399
B Forestry and logging	8838	599	8239	9706	714	8992	9976	834	9142	9841	853	8988
C Fishing a	693	135	558	762	149	613	823	158	665	855	183	672
2 Mining and quarrying	1492	633	859	1619	821	798	1888	970	918	1980	997	983
A Coal mining	...	...	...	...	...	...	...	...	...	...	...	...
B Crude petroleum and natural gas production	...	...	...	...	...	...	...	...	...	...	...	...
C Metal ore mining	835	330	505	886	431	455	842	459	383	924	450	474
D Other mining	657	303	354	733	390	343	1046	511	535	1056	547	509
3 Manufacturing	157259	108778	48481	175810	122718	53092	186229	128994	57235	203396	140117	63279
A Manufacture of food, beverages and tobacco	26667	21575	5092	31064	25052	6012	34224	27438	6786	37334	29888	7446
B Textile, wearing apparel and leather industries	9448	5398	4050	10341	5747	4594	10512	5869	4643	10468	5978	4490
C Manufacture of wood and wood products, including furniture	14022	8948	5074	13356	8956	4400	12909	8859	4050	15212	10043	5169
D Manufacture of paper and paper products, printing and publishing	33608	23191	10417	38780	27414	11366	38794	27916	10878	43009	30382	12627
E Manufacture of chemicals and chemical petroleum, coal, rubber and plastic products	25148	19382	5766	28600	22106	6494	28213	21753	6460	31695	24340	7355
F Manufacture of non-metallic mineral products, except products of petroleum and coal	4557	2542	2015	5199	2995	2204	6129	3359	2770	6882	3627	3255
G Basic metal industries	11134	8792	2342	10619	8693	1926	12074	9877	2197	13353	10753	2600
H Manufacture of fabricated metal products, machinery and equipment	31803	18489	13314	36944	21275	15669	42376	23422	18954	44354	24537	19817
I Other manufacturing industries	872	461	411	907	480	427	998	501	497	1089	569	520
4 Electricity, gas and water	18529	13588	4941	23350	16693	6657	23809	16335	7474	24627	16844	7783
A Electricity, gas and steam	17870	13388	4482	22669	16467	6202	23066	16097	6969	23784	16587	7197
B Water works and supply	659	200	459	681	226	455	743	238	505	843	257	586
5 Construction	35640	21948	13692	38854	23321	15533	44124	26321	17803	50556	29788	20768
6 Wholesale and retail trade, restaurants and hotels	35157	14889	20268	39633	16611	23022	44375	18429	25946	48931	20155	28776
A Wholesale and retail trade	27709	10413	17296	31081	11487	19594	34654	12605	22049	37935	13567	24368
B Restaurants and hotels	7448	4476	2972	8552	5124	3428	9721	5824	3897	10996	6588	4408
7 Transport, storage and communication	23662	10018	13644	27095	11633	15462	29295	12351	16944	32725	13756	18969
A Transport and storage	19269	9057	10212	22116	10502	11614	23497	11059	12438	26086	12358	13728
B Communication	4393	961	3432	4979	1131	3848	5798	1292	4506	6639	1398	5241
8 Finance, insurance, real estate and business services	37637	13561	24076	44249	15785	28464	51204	18035	33169	57923	20450	37473
A Financial institutions	6534	1721	4813	7725	2038	5687	8492	2454	6038	9465	2872	6593

573

Finland

4.1 Derivation of Value Added by Kind of Activity, in Current Prices (Continued)

Million Finnish markkaa

	1980 Gross Output	1980 Intermediate Consumption	1980 Value Added	1981 Gross Output	1981 Intermediate Consumption	1981 Value Added	1982 Gross Output	1982 Intermediate Consumption	1982 Value Added	1983 Gross Output	1983 Intermediate Consumption	1983 Value Added
B Insurance	2586	1620	966	2792	1870	922	3403	1216	2187	3994	1364	2630
C Real estate and business services	28517	10874	17643	33732	12825	20907	39309	14365	24944	44464	16214	28250
Real estate, except dwellings	5599	3084	2515	6585	3640	2945	7340	4034	3306	8207	4445	3762
Dwellings	15048	4596	10452	17806	5339	12467	20451	5878	14573	22651	6503	16158
9 Community, social and personal services	9122	3172	5950	10391	3629	6762	11799	4163	7636	13722	4884	8838
A Sanitary and similar services	1123	308	815	1283	330	953	1493	403	1090	1752	470	1282
B Social and related community services [b]	1178	217	961	1333	245	1088	1524	281	1243	1807	331	1476
Educational services	273	75	198	306	84	222	364	99	265	411	112	299
Medical, dental, other health and veterinary services	905	142	763	1027	161	866	1160	182	978	1396	219	1177
C Recreational and cultural services [b]	2901	1194	1707	3359	1392	1967	3882	1610	2272	4571	1920	2651
D Personal and household services	3920	1453	2467	4416	1662	2754	4900	1869	3031	5592	2163	3429
Total, Industries	343401	147753	148648	388916	167201	220815	423489	185639	466830	258902	207928	
Producers of Government Services	38611	13343	25268	45118	15494	29622	51810	17668	34142	59333	20122	39211
Other Producers	5199	1855	3344	6077	2232	3845	6969	2638	4331	7890	3038	4852
Total	387211	209951	177260	438209	238541	200998	482298	225012	257286	534053	282092	251991
Less: Imputed bank service charge	-4699		-4699	-5360		-5360	-5646		-5646	-6247		-6247
Import duties	20044		20044	23169		23169	26350		26350	28903		28903
Value added tax	407255	192605	214650	462378	243901	218477	508618	262902	245716	562956	288509	274647
Total												

	1984 Gross Output	1984 Intermediate Consumption	1984 Value Added	1985 Gross Output	1985 Intermediate Consumption	1985 Value Added	1986 Gross Output	1986 Intermediate Consumption	1986 Value Added	1987 Gross Output	1987 Intermediate Consumption	1987 Value Added
All Producers												
1 Agriculture, hunting, forestry and fishing	35558	12257	23301	37072	12947	24125	36794	13051	23743	36016	13585	22431
A Agriculture and hunting [a]	23587	11146	12441	24193	11768	12425	24947	11896	13051	23318	12388	10930
B Forestry and logging	11005	913	10092	11831	977	10854	10911	947	9964	11736	972	10764
C Fishing [a]	966	198	768	1048	202	846	936	208	728	962	225	737
2 Mining and quarrying	2142	1029	1113	2326	1193	1133	2057	929	1128	1995	969	1026
A Coal mining	...	...	...	...	...	...	...	...	...	...	...	...
B Crude petroleum and natural gas production	...	...	...	...	...	...	...	...	...	...	...	...
C Metal ore mining	1045	431	614	1043	457	586	770	307	463	591	287	304
D Other mining	1097	598	499	1283	676	607	1287	622	665	1404	682	722
3 Manufacturing	224375	153722	70653	237531	162943	74588	232523	155879	76644	248327	162617	85710
A Manufacture of food, beverages and tobacco	40074	31857	8217	42309	33694	8615	44208	34597	9611	44882	34743	10139
B Textile, wearing apparel and leather industries	11404	6572	4832	11923	6735	5188	12131	7071	5060	11644	6536	5108
C Manufacture of wood and wood products, including furniture	16369	10828	5541	15746	10924	4822	16286	11182	5104	17884	11681	6203
D Manufacture of paper and paper products, printing and publishing	51705	35886	15819	52962	37067	15895	53020	36834	16186	57222	38779	18443
E Manufacture of chemicals and chemical products, petroleum, coal, rubber and plastic products	33753	25993	7760	35511	27073	8438	27358	18361	8997	29257	20126	9131
F Manufacture of non-metallic mineral products, except products of petroleum and coal	6727	3623	3104	7109	3905	3204	7190	3883	3307	8345	4447	3898
G Basic metal industries	15256	12148	3108	16150	13105	3045	14610	11302	3308	15180	11571	3609
H Manufacture of fabricated metal products, machinery and equipment	47872	26264	21608	54451	29765	24686	56275	31940	24335	62582	34064	28518
I Other manufacturing industries	1215	618	597	1370	675	695	1445	709	736	1331	670	661
4 Electricity, gas and water	26274	18271	8003	30002	8768	21234	28620	9276	19372	19370	10002	
A Electricity, gas and steam	25359	17972	7387	28983	20938	8045	27487	19000	8487	28193	19071	9122
B Water works and supply	915	299	616	1019	296	723	1133	276	857	1179	299	880

Finland

4.1 Derivation of Value Added by Kind of Activity, in Current Prices
(Continued)

Million Finnish markkaa

	1984			1985			1986			1987		
	Gross Output	Intermediate Consumption	Value Added	Gross Output	Intermediate Consumption	Value Added	Gross Output	Intermediate Consumption	Value Added	Gross Output	Intermediate Consumption	Value Added
5 Construction	52599	30058	22541	56343	33463	22880	58003	33289	24714	62800	35109	27691
6 Wholesale and retail trade, restaurants and hotels	53622	21919	31703	58971	23792	35179	62210	25266	36944	68688	27979	40709
A Wholesale and retail trade	41352	14568	26784	45090	15476	29614	46926	16110	30816	51519	17694	33825
B Restaurants and hotels	12270	7351	4919	13881	8316	5565	15284	9156	6128	17169	10285	6884
7 Transport, storage and communication	36424	15004	21420	39208	15802	23406	40527	15101	25426	44710	16766	27944
A Transport and storage	29030	13497	15533	31067	14141	16926	31886	13276	18610	34982	14664	20318
B Communication	7394	1507	5887	8141	1661	6480	8641	1825	6816	9728	2102	7626
8 Finance, insurance, real estate and business services	66254	23421	42833	74141	26748	47393	81729	28173	53556	90522	30958	59564
A Financial institutions	11330	3594	7736	13234	4297	8937	14793	4846	9947	18005	5830	12175
B Insurance	4183	1532	2651	4105	1738	2367	4590	1948	2642	4993	1906	3087
C Real estate and business services	50741	18295	32446	56802	20713	36089	62346	21379	40967	67524	23222	44302
Real estate, except dwellings	9471	5050	4421	11139	5822	5317	12153	5878	6275	13751	6344	7407
Dwellings	24920	7062	17858	27244	7977	19267	28911	7862	21049	29827	8458	21369
9 Community, social and personal services	15704	5589	10115	17588	6289	11299	19693	6960	12733	22157	7675	14482
A Sanitary and similar services	2051	549	1502	2436	649	1787	2675	698	1977	3108	793	2315
B Social and related community services b	2092	379	1713	2334	419	1915	2594	447	2147	2896	483	2413
Educational services	441	120	321	476	128	348	521	136	385	564	140	424
Medical, dental, other health and veterinary services	1651	259	1392	1858	291	1567	2073	311	1762	2332	343	1989
C Recreational and cultural services b	5172	2178	2994	5713	2406	3307	6458	2708	3750	7198	2968	4230
D Personal and household services	6389	2483	3906	7105	2815	4290	7966	3107	4859	8955	3431	5524
Total, Industries	512952	281270	231682	553182	304351	248831	562156	297924	264232	604587	315028	289559
Producers of Government Services	66981	22751	44230	76372	26276	50096	83134	28698	54436	91403	31624	59779
Other Producers	8796	3359	5437	9735	3687	6048	10536	3974	6562	11302	4255	7047
Total	588729	307380	281349	639289	334314	304975	655826	330596	325230	707292	350907	356385
Less: Imputed bank service charge	...	-7322	7322	...	-8141	8141	...	-9328	9328	...	-11458	11458
Import duties	34330	...	34330	38152	...	38152	41664	...	41664	46670	...	46670
Value added tax	...	...	...	...	...	...	...	...	...	...	...	...
Total	623059	314702	308357	677441	342455	334986	697490	339924	357566	753962	362365	391597

	1988			1989		
	Gross Output	Intermediate Consumption	Value Added	Gross Output	Intermediate Consumption	Value Added
	All Producers					
1 Agriculture, hunting, forestry and fishing	37849	13387	24462	41753	14136	27617
A Agriculture and hunting a	23136	12123	11013	26290	12780	13510
B Forestry and logging	13590	999	12591	14246	1055	13191
C Fishing a	1123	265	858	1217	301	916
2 Mining and quarrying	2396	1046	1350	2879	1164	1715
A Coal mining	...	...	...	...	...	...
B Crude petroleum and natural gas production	...	...	...	...	...	...
C Metal ore mining	886	300	586	1160	340	820
D Other mining	1510	746	764	1719	824	895

Finland

4.1 Derivation of Value Added by Kind of Activity, in Current Prices (Continued)

Million Finnish markkaa

	1988 Gross Output	1988 Intermediate Consumption	1988 Value Added	1989 Gross Output	1989 Intermediate Consumption	1989 Value Added
3 Manufacturing	264640	170839	93801	287196	186450	100746
A Manufacture of food, beverages and tobacco	47495	36366	11129	49926	38441	11485
B Textile, wearing apparel and leather industries	10381	5880	4501	9395	5197	4198
C Manufacture of wood and wood products, including furniture	19438	12650	6788	21743	14233	7510
D Manufacture of paper and paper products, printing and publishing	60392	38600	21792	65089	42762	22327
E Manufacture of chemicals and chemical products, petroleum, coal, rubber and plastic products	29456	20009	9447	32592	21593	10999
F Manufacture of non-metallic mineral products, except products of petroleum and coal	9078	4613	4465	10131	5078	5053
G Basic metal industries	19379	14727	4652	22543	16661	5882
H Manufacture of fabricated metal products, machinery and equipment	67532	37283	30249	74197	41686	32511
I Other manufacturing industries	1489	711	778	1580	799	781
4 Electricity, gas and water	29305	9937	19368	29615	9454	19161
A Electricity, gas and steam	28016	19061	8955	28265	19106	9156
B Water works and supply	1289	307	982	1350	345	1005
5 Construction	74679	41278	33401	92991	50878	42113
6 Wholesale and retail trade, restaurants and hotels	76047	30879	45168	84366	33879	50487
A Wholesale and retail trade	56612	19237	37375	62696	20976	41720
B Restaurants and hotels	19435	11642	7793	21670	12903	8767
7 Transport, storage and communication	49589	18790	30799	55625	21266	34359
A Transport and storage	38705	16323	22382	43917	18447	25470
B Communication	10884	2467	8417	11708	2819	8889
8 Finance, insurance, real estate and business services	103399	34548	68851	118591	38958	79633
A Financial institutions	20518	6707	13811	24954	8020	16934
B Insurance	5835	2211	3624	5439	2314	3125
C Real estate and business services	77046	25630	51416	88196	28624	59574
Real estate, except dwellings	16856	6928	9928	19809	7535	12274
Dwellings	32022	9064	22958	35367	9872	25495
9 Community, social and personal services	24804	8353	16451	28731	9329	19402
A Sanitary and similar services	3472	866	2606	4163	1003	3160
B Social and related community services b	4853	1071	3782	5592	1198	4394
Educational services	444	153	491	730	170	560
Medical, dental, other health and veterinary services	2689	363	2326	3065	393	2672
C Recreational and cultural services b	6454	2669	3785	7575	3055	4520
D Personal and household services	10025	3747	6278	11401	4073	7328
Total, industries	662708	338488	324220	741747	375514	366233
Producers of Government Services	99883	34295	65588	110508	37749	72759
Other Producers	12553	4648	7905	13675	5121	8554
Total	775144	377431	397713	865930	418384	447546
Less: Imputed bank service charge	–13251		–13251	–16373		–16373
Import duties	57077		57077	64324		64324
Value added tax	832221		306982			
Total	832221	309682	441539	930254	434757	495497

a) Hunting is included in item 'Fishing'.
b) ISIC groups 935 and 939 are included in item 'Recreational and cultural services', for the years prior to 1987.

576

Finland

4.2 Derivation of Value Added by Kind of Activity, in Constant Prices

Million Finnish markkaa

At constant prices of 1985

All Producers

	1980 Gross Output	1980 Intermediate Consumption	1980 Value Added	1981 Gross Output	1981 Intermediate Consumption	1981 Value Added	1982 Gross Output	1982 Intermediate Consumption	1982 Value Added	1983 Gross Output	1983 Intermediate Consumption	1983 Value Added
1 Agriculture, hunting, forestry and fishing	37389	12828	24561	35593	12954	22639	36613	13756	22857	37486	13471	24015
A Agriculture and hunting a	23303	11742	11561	22272	11822	10450	24182	12552	11630	25380	12300	13080
B Forestry and logging	13214	922	12292	12443	966	11478	10649	610	10486	11169	974	10195
Fishing a	872	164	708	878	167	711	1155	185	741	937	197	740
2 Mining and quarrying	1847	883	964	1895	903	992	2150	1040	1110	2146	1039	1107
A Coal mining	...	...	...	...	...	...	...	...	...	...	...	...
B Crude petroleum and natural gas production												
C Metal ore mining	1014	445	569	1080	474	606	1044	458	586	1029	451	578
D Other mining	833	438	395	815	429	386	1106	582	524	1117	588	529
3 Manufacturing	207635	143789	63846	211686	145739	65947	212664	145797	66867	221436	152447	68989
A Manufacture of food, beverages and tobacco	37897	30148	7749	39472	31383	8089	40000	31846	8154	41079	32734	8345
B Textile, wearing apparel and leather industries	12091	6803	5288	12430	7003	5427	12082	6809	5273	11386	6415	4971
C Manufacture of wood and wood products, including furniture	17018	11875	5143	15663	10871	4792	14742	10190	4552	15987	11071	4916
D Manufacture of paper and paper products, printing and publishing	45441	31990	13451	46345	32537	13808	44575	31148	13427	48381	33857	14524
E Manufacture of chemical and chemical petroleum, coal, rubber and plastic products	32679	25201	7478	31989	24492	7497	31007	23695	7312	33330	25495	7835
F Manufacture of non-metallic mineral products, except products of petroleum and coal	6401	2885	3516	6495	2926	3569	7044	3871	3173	7359	4042	3317
G Basic metal industries	13433	10601	2532	13079	10613	2466	13672	11096	2576	14476	11747	2729
H Manufacture of fabricated metal products, machinery and equipment	41624	22839	18785	45117	24733	20384	48398	26680	21818	48292	26523	21769
I Other manufacturing industries	1051	516	535	1096	538	558	1144	562	582	1146	563	583
4 Electricity, gas and water	23876	16842	7034	25007	17665	7342	24657	17412	7245	25756	18195	7561
A Electricity, gas and steam	22912	16552	6360	24056	17378	6678	23705	17125	6580	24779	17901	6878
B Water works and supply	964	290	674	951	287	664	952	287	665	977	294	683
5 Construction	53512	31798	21714	52721	31313	21408	55594	33033	22561	57882	34422	23460
6 Wholesale and retail trade, restaurants and hotels	52583	22431	30152	52586	30105	22481	54589	23055	31534	55211	23046	32165
Wholesale and retail trade	40022	14882	25140	39924	14872	25052	41742	15358	26384	42290	15303	26987
B Restaurants and hotels	12561	7549	5012	12662	7609	5053	12847	7697	5150	12921	7743	5178
7 Transport, storage and communication	36436	15250	21186	37186	15541	21645	37002	15301	21701	37780	15441	22339
A Transport and storage	30810	14101	16709	31042	14286	16756	30366	13946	16420	30569	13968	16601
B Communication	5626	1149	4477	6144	1255	4889	6636	1355	5281	7211	1473	5738
8 Finance, insurance, real estate and business services	57016	20775	36241	59190	21584	37606	62683	22444	40239	65878	23587	42291
A Financial institutions	9584	2771	6813	9955	2890	7065	10440	3145	7295	10903	3405	7498
B Insurance	3441	1363	2078	3523	1356	2167	3804	1458	2346	4038	1540	2498
C Real estate and business services	43991	16641	27350	45712	17338	28374	48439	17841	30598	50937	18642	32295
Real estate, except dwellings	8680	4670	4010	10001	4839	4162	9335	5015	4320	9771	5227	4544
Dwellings	22671	9846	15825	23389	7030	16359	24317	7082	17235	25290	7244	18046
9 Community, social and personal services	14696	5264	9432	15058	5380	9678	15649	5604	10045	16267	5826	10441
A Sanitary and similar services	1796	510	1286	1862	505	1357	1962	530	1432	2063	554	1509
B Social and related community services b	2139	382	1757	2143	382	1761	2199	396	1803	2261	406	1855
Educational services	441	117	324	443	117	326	480	127	353	482	128	354
Medical, dental, other health and veterinary services	1698	265	1433	1700	267	1435	1719	269	1450	1779	278	1501
C Recreational and cultural services b	4597	1935	2662	4760	2005	2755	5053	2132	2921	5280	2230	3050
D Personal and household services	6164	2437	3727	6293	2488	3805	6435	2546	3889	6663	2636	4027

577

Finland

4.2 Derivation of Value Added by Kind of Activity, in Constant Prices
(Continued)

Million Finnish markkaa

	1980			1981			1982			1983		
	Gross Output	Intermediate Consumption	Value Added	Gross Output	Intermediate Consumption	Value Added	Gross Output	Intermediate Consumption	Value Added	Gross Output	Intermediate Consumption	Value Added
	At constant prices of:1985											
Total, Industries	484990	269860	215130	490922	273560	217362	501601	277442	224159	519842	287474	232368
Producers of Government Services	62363	19824	42539	64908	20400	44508	67586	21392	46194	70242	22664	47578
Other Producers	8242	2745	5497	8556	2901	5655	8880	3159	5721	9221	3384	5837
Total	555595	292429	263166	564386	296861	267525	578067	301993	276074	599305	313522	285783
Less: Imputed bank service charge	...	-6564	6564	...	-6486	6486	...	-6646	6646	...	-7012	7012
Import duties	33713	...	33713	33864	...	33864	36034	...	36034	35767	...	35767
Value added tax	...	...	...	...	...	...	...	...	...	...	...	...
Total	589308	298993	290315	598250	303347	294903	614101	308639	305462	635072	320534	314538

	1984			1985			1986			1987		
	Gross Output	Intermediate Consumption	Value Added	Gross Output	Intermediate Consumption	Value Added	Gross Output	Intermediate Consumption	Value Added	Gross Output	Intermediate Consumption	Value Added
	At constant prices of:1985											
	All Producers											
1 Agriculture, hunting, forestry and fishing	37210	12889	24321	37072	12947	24125	35989	13263	22726	34315	13857	20458
A Agriculture and hunting [a]	24812	11696	13116	24193	11768	12425	24299	12144	12155	22054	12758	9296
B Forestry and logging	11411	989	10422	11931	977	10954	10757	913	9844	11352	890	10462
C Fishing [a]	987	204	783	948	202	746	933	206	727	909	209	700
2 Mining and quarrying	2228	1079	1149	2326	1133	1193	2343	1148	1195	2391	1188	1203
A Coal mining	...	...	...	...	...	...	...	...	...	...	...	...
B Crude petroleum and natural gas production	...	...	...	...	...	...	...	...	...	...	...	...
C Metal ore mining	1070	469	601	1043	457	586	985	432	553	821	360	461
D Other mining	1158	610	548	1283	676	607	1358	716	642	1570	828	742
3 Manufacturing	230392	158624	71768	237531	162943	74588	241085	165507	75578	253182	173851	79331
A Manufacture of food, beverages and tobacco	41405	32966	8439	42309	33694	8615	43585	34667	8918	44672	35534	9138
B Textile, wearing apparel and leather industries	11521	6504	5017	11923	6735	5188	11474	6474	5000	10958	6194	4764
C Manufacture of wood and wood products, including furniture	16339	11336	5003	15746	10924	4822	15985	11084	4901	16971	11754	5217
D Manufacture of paper and paper products, printing and publishing	52945	37117	15828	52962	37067	15895	54153	37901	16252	56415	39480	16935
E Manufacture of chemicals and chemical petroleum, coal, rubber and plastic products	34306	26185	8121	35511	27073	8438	35579	27089	8490	39044	29897	9147
F Manufacture of non-metallic mineral products, except products of petroleum and coal	6940	3812	3128	7109	3905	3204	6977	3835	3142	7654	4214	3440
G Basic metal industries	15586	12648	2938	16150	13105	3045	16602	13536	3066	17083	13899	3184
H Manufacture of fabricated metal products, machinery and equipment	50146	27464	22682	54451	29765	24686	55278	30206	25072	59036	32214	26822
I Other manufacturing industries	1204	592	612	1370	675	695	1452	715	737	1349	665	684
4 Electricity, gas and water	27548	19482	8066	30002	21234	8768	30084	21272	8812	32385	22921	9464
A Electricity, gas and steam	26575	19199	7376	28983	20938	8045	29015	20961	8054	31287	22602	8685
B Water works and supply	973	283	690	1019	296	723	1069	311	758	1098	319	779
5 Construction	56064	33323	22741	56343	33463	22880	55230	32276	22954	55601	32496	23105
6 Wholesale and retail trade, restaurants and hotels	56928	23366	33562	58971	23792	35179	61160	24683	36477	65237	26326	38911
A Wholesale and retail trade	43550	15350	28200	45090	15476	29614	46764	16059	30705	49948	17167	32781
B Restaurants and hotels	13378	8016	5362	13881	8316	5565	14396	8624	5772	15289	9159	6130
7 Transport, storage and communication	38582	15667	22915	39208	15802	23406	39813	15983	23830	43086	17293	25793
A Transport and storage	30916	14102	16814	31067	14141	16926	31244	14234	17010	33534	15344	18190
B Communication	7666	1565	6101	8141	1661	6480	8569	1749	6820	9552	1949	7603
8 Finance, insurance, real estate and business services	70194	25139	45055	74141	26748	47393	78771	27819	50952	83864	29472	54392
A Financial institutions	11907	3833	8074	13234	4297	8937	14683	4692	9991	16932	5411	11521
B Insurance	4123	1668	2455	4105	1738	2367	4328	1859	2469	4212	1817	2395
C Real estate and business services	54164	19638	34526	56802	20713	36089	59760	21268	38492	62720	22244	40476
Real estate, except dwellings	10403	5524	4879	11139	5822	5317	11846	6116	5730	12649	6459	6190

Finland

4.2 Derivation of Value Added by Kind of Activity, in Constant Prices
(Continued)

Million Finnish markkaa

	1984			1985			1986			1987		
	Gross Output	Intermediate Consumption	Value Added	Gross Output	Intermediate Consumption	Value Added	Gross Output	Intermediate Consumption	Value Added	Gross Output	Intermediate Consumption	Value Added
Dwellings	26256	7457	18799	27244	7977	19267	28129	7909	20220	29038	8128	20910
9 Community, social and personal services	16810	6014	10796	17588	6289	11299	18434	6603	11831	19357	6897	12460
A Sanitary and similar services	2210	592	1618	2436	649	1787	2519	671	1848	2766	737	2029
B Social and related community services b	2300	411	1889	2334	419	1915	2401	432	1969	3653	915	2738
Educational services	476	126	350	476	128	348	495	133	362	504	134	370
Medical, dental, other health and veterinary services	1824	285	1539	1858	291	1567	1906	299	1607	1992	312	1680
C Recreational and cultural services b	5452	2300	3152	5713	2406	3307	6077	2555	3522	5183	2175	3008
D Personal and household services	6848	2711	4137	7105	2815	4290	7437	2945	4492	7755	3070	4685
Total, Industries	535956	295583	240373	553182	304351	248831	562909	308554	254355	589418	324301	265117
Producers of Government Services	72739	24042	48697	76372	26276	50096	79037	28147	50890	82581	29874	52707
Other Producers	9466	3541	5925	9735	3687	6048	10138	3970	6168	10268	4152	6116
Total	618161	323166	294995	639289	334314	304975	652084	340671	311413	682267	358327	323940
Less: Imputed bank service charge	-7561		-7561	-8141		-8141	-9518		-9518	-11073		-11073
Import duties	36751		36751	38152		38152	40122		40122	42792		42792
Value added tax												
Total	654912	330727	324185	677441	342455	334986	692206	350189	342017	725059	369400	355659

At constant prices of 1985

All Producers

	1984			1985			1986			1987		
1 Agriculture, hunting, forestry and fishing	35760	13566	22194	37606	13765	23841						
A Agriculture and hunting a	22311	12426	9885	23337	12578	11359						
B Forestry and logging	12362	886	11476	12428	890	11538						
C Fishing a	1087	254	833	1241	297	944						
2 Mining and quarrying	2578	1279	1299	2785	1380	1405						
A Coal mining	...	...	...	...	...	...						
B Crude petroleum and natural gas production												
C Metal ore mining	904	396	508	992	434	558						
D Other mining	1674	883	791	1793	946	847						
3 Manufacturing	262963	180548	82415	268587	183597	84990						
A Manufacture of food, beverages and tobacco	46334	36788	9546	46637	37038	9599						
B Textile, wearing apparel and leather industries	9772	5541	4231	8713	4943	3770						
C Manufacture of wood and wood products, including furniture	17890	12370	5520	19066	13202	5864						
D Manufacture of paper and paper products, printing and publishing	59941	42000	17941	60938	42638	18300						
E Manufacture of chemicals and chemical products, petroleum, coal, rubber and plastic products	40409	30835	9574	39716	29997	9719						
F Manufacture of non-metallic mineral products, except products of petroleum and coal	7884	4337	3547	8337	4587	3750						
G Basic metal industries	17936	14582	3354	18499	15068	3431						
H Manufacture of fabricated metal products, machinery and equipment	61364	33389	27975	65243	35415	29828						
I Other manufacturing industries	1433	706	727	1438	709	729						
4 Electricity, gas and water	33049	23385	9664	32940	23305	9635						
A Electricity, gas and steam	31916	23056	8860	31806	22976	8830						
B Water works and supply	1133	329	804	1134	329	805						

Finland

4.2 Derivation of Value Added by Kind of Activity, in Constant Prices (Continued)

Million Finnish markkaa

	1988			1989		
	Gross Output	Intermediate Consumption	Value Added	Gross Output	Intermediate Consumption	Value Added
At constant prices of 1985						
5 Construction	60401	35755	24646	67828	40332	27496
6 Wholesale and retail trade, restaurants and hotels	68715	27608	41107	72472	28811	43661
A Wholesale and retail trade	52677	18000	34677	55632	18787	36845
B Restaurants and hotels	16038	9608	6430	16840	10024	6816
7 Transport, storage and communication	46088	18532	27556	49407	19956	29451
A Transport and storage	35577	16387	19190	38002	17629	20373
B Communication	10511	2145	8366	11405	2327	9078
8 Finance, insurance, real estate and business services	90130	31347	58783	97075	33360	63715
A Financial institutions	18371	5905	12466	20624	6423	14201
B Insurance	4382	1939	2443	4556	2092	2464
C Real estate and business services	67377	23503	43874	71895	24845	47050
Real estate, except dwellings	14238	7074	7164	15515	7531	7984
Dwellings	30017	8079	21938	31188	8216	22972
9 Community, social and personal services	20182	7200	12982	21567	7570	13997
A Sanitary and similar services	2888	769	2119	3191	833	2358
B Social and related community services b	3739	937	2802	3903	981	2922
Educational services	521	140	381	530	143	387
Medical, dental, other health and veterinary services	2038	319	1719	2103	322	1781
C Recreational and cultural services b	5441	2283	3158	5956	2465	3491
D Personal and household services	8114	3211	4903	8517	3291	5226
Total, Industries	619866	339220	280646	650267	352076	298191
Producers of Government Services	84684	30598	54086	87187	31816	55371
Other Producers	10404	4214	6190	10607	4335	6272
Total	714954	374032	340922	748061	388227	359834
Less: Imputed bank service charge		-12318	12318		-14069	14069
Import duties	46381		46381	48787		48787
Value added tax						
Total	761335	386350	374985	796848	402296	394552

a) Hunting is included in item 'Fishing'.
b) ISIC groups 935 and 939 are included in item 'Recreational and cultural services' for the years prior to 1987.

4.3 Cost Components of Value Added

Million Finnish markkaa

	1980							1981						
	Compensation of Employees	Capital Consumption	Net Operating Surplus	Indirect Taxes	Less: Subsidies Received	Value Added		Compensation of Employees	Capital Consumption	Net Operating Surplus	Indirect Taxes	Less: Subsidies Received	Value Added	
1 Agriculture, hunting, forestry and fishing	3020	3506	10936	97	822	16737		3503	3980	10813	107	992	17411	
A Agriculture and hunting a	1026	2440	5215	44	785	7940		1231	2777	4698	51	951	7806
B Forestry and logging	1978	967	5303	13	4	8239		2254	1095	5653	5	15	8992
C Fishing a	16	66	418	49	24	558		18	108	462	51	26	613
2 Mining and quarrying	508	185	200	4	38	859		561	204	69	4	40	798
A Coal mining	...	...	...	...	...	...		...	...	...	...	...	...
B Crude petroleum and natural gas production													
C Metal ore mining	328	134	77	1	35	505		361	142	-13	1	36	455
D Other mining	180	51	123	3	3	354		200	62	82	3	4	343

Finland

4.3 Cost Components of Value Added (Continued)

Million Finnish markkaa

	1980						1981					
	Compensation of Employees	Net Operating Surplus	Capital Consumption	Indirect Taxes	Less: Subsidies Received	Value Added	Compensation of Employees	Net Operating Surplus	Capital Consumption	Indirect Taxes	Less: Subsidies Received	Value Added
3 Manufacturing	30208	6098	12285	5143	404	48481	34302	6847	12063	478	598	53092
A Manufacture of food, beverages and tobacco	3299	613	1167	54	41	5092	3820	678	1520	65	71	6012
B Textile, wearing apparel and leather industries	2804	284	978	26	42	4050	3079	321	1218	31	55	4594
C Manufacture of wood and wood products, including furniture	3001	580	1509	40	56	5074	3175	621	632	48	76	4400
D Manufacture of paper and paper products, printing and publishing	5708	1867	2876	87	121	10417	6495	2108	2803	103	143	11366
E Manufacture of chemicals and chemical products, petroleum, coal, rubber and plastic products	2389	764	2594	38	19	5766	2809	876	2800	45	36	6494
F Manufacture of non-metallic mineral products, except of petroleum and coal	1159	263	595	11	13	2015	1334	297	578	13	18	2204
G Basic metal industries	1353	535	462	27	35	2342	1522	588	-174	32	42	1926
H Manufacture of fabricated metal products, machinery and equipment	10233	1167	1973	116	175	13314	11803	1329	2545	135	143	15669
I Other manufacturing industries	262	25	131	5	12	411	265	29	141	6	14	427
4 Electricity, gas and water	1801	2091	1078	38	67	4941	2088	2329	2289	43	92	6657
A Electricity, gas and steam	1625	1806	1081	36	66	4482	1887	2007	2358	41	91	6202
B Water works and supply	176	285	-3	2	1	459	201	322	-69	2	1	455
5 Construction	10206	871	2589	32	9	13692	11493	968	3040	38	9	15533
6 Wholesale and retail trade, restaurants and hotels	15248	2270	2590	187	27	20268	17262	2589	2984	226	39	23022
A Wholesale and retail trade	12763	2038	2323	178	6	17296	14429	2313	2645	215	8	19594
B Restaurants and hotels	2485	232	267	9	21	2972	2833	276	339	11	31	3428
7 Transport, storage and communication	7704	4001	1795	153	9	13644	8802	4430	2042	203	15	15462
A Transport and storage	5487	3152	1431	151	9	10212	6263	3482	1684	200	15	11614
B Communication	2217	849	364	2	-	3432	2539	948	358	3	-	3848
8 Finance, insurance, real estate and business services	7266	7050	9738	66	44	24076	8421	8166	11855	77	55	28464
A Financial institutions	3806	411	1624	4	32	4813	3147	465	2111	41	5	5687
B Insurance	901	133	587	2	-	1620	1001	163	706	3	1	1870
C Real estate and business services	3559	6506	7527	60	9	17643	4273	7538	9038	69	11	20907
Real estate, except dwellings	1126	364	1016	9	-	2515	1284	438	1213	10	-	2945
Dwellings	-	5524	4884	44	-	10452	-	6350	6096	51	-	12467
9 Community, social and personal services	3404	725	1841	27	47	5950	3875	826	2110	39	88	6762
A Sanitary and similar services	347	386	80	2	-	815	416	448	86	3	-	953
B Social and related community services b	301	65	598	5	8	961	337	71	684	5	9	1088
Educational services	127	46	33	-	8	198	142	50	39	-	9	222
Medical, dental, other health and veterinary services	174	19	565	5	-	763	195	21	645	5	-	866
C Recreational and cultural services b	1127	111	489	16	36	1707	1292	128	597	26	76	1967
D Personal and household services	1629	163	674	4	3	2467	1830	179	743	5	3	2754
Total, Industries	79365	26797	43052	8001	1574	148648	90307	30339	47265	1215	1925	167201
Producers of Government Services	23345	1914	-	9	-	25268	27416	2202	-	4	-	29622
Other Producers	1950	247	1147	-	-	3344	3401	283	161	-	-	3845
Total	104660	28958	44199	1017	1574	177260	121124	32824	47426	1219	1925	200068
Less: Imputed bank service charge			4699			4699			5360			5360
Import duties						20044						23169
Value added tax			24697	4653					26509	5340		
Other adjustments	104660	28958	39500	25714	6227	192605	121124	32824	42066	29728	7265	218477
Total												

Finland

4.3 Cost Components of Value Added

Million Finnish markkaa

	1982						1983					
	Compensation of Employees	Capital Consumption	Net Operating Surplus	Indirect Taxes	Less: Subsidies Received	Value Added	Compensation of Employees	Capital Consumption	Net Operating Surplus	Indirect Taxes	Less: Subsidies Received	Value Added
	All Producers											
1 Agriculture, hunting, forestry and fishing	3747	4347	12540	125	1345	19414	3778	4832	13781	147	1479	21059
A Agriculture and hunting [a]	1368	3045	6421	70	1297	9607	1431	3424	7891	79	1426	11399
B Forestry and logging	2360	1190	5599	6	13	9142	2324	1292	5378	7	13	8988
C Fishing [a]	19	112	520	49	35	665	23	116	512	61	40	672
2 Mining and quarrying	616	224	107	5	34	918	642	251	118	7	35	983
A Coal mining	...	...	...	...	...	...	...	...	...	...	...	...
B Crude petroleum and natural gas production	...	...	...	...	...	...	...	...	...	...	...	...
C Metal ore mining	383	148	-119	2	31	383	394	157	-50	3	30	474
D Other mining	233	76	226	3	3	535	248	94	168	4	5	509
3 Manufacturing	37203	7668	12413	524	573	57235	39779	7980	15537	580	597	63279
A Manufacture of food, beverages and tobacco	4069	741	1974	72	70	6786	4412	756	2257	80	59	7446
B Textile, wearing apparel and leather industries	3285	354	1028	31	55	4643	3333	370	810	36	59	4490
C Manufacture of wood and wood products, including furniture	3171	686	197	54	58	4050	3401	696	1073	62	63	5169
D Manufacture of paper and paper products, printing and publishing	7002	2411	1465	114	114	10878	7572	2501	2570	123	139	12627
E Manufacture of chemicals and chemical petroleum, coal, rubber and plastic products	3070	999	2365	57	31	6460	3364	1052	2924	60	45	7355
F Manufacture of non-metallic mineral products, except products of petroleum and coal	1485	327	965	13	20	2770	1642	342	1272	15	16	3255
G Basic metal industries	1629	624	-57	38	37	2197	1751	632	198	53	34	2600
H Manufacture of fabricated metal products, machinery and equipment	13194	1493	4305	138	176	18954	13975	1595	4284	131	168	19817
I Other manufacturing industries	298	33	171	7	12	497	329	36	149	20	14	520
4 Electricity, gas and water	2326	2529	2628	56	65	7474	2516	2834	2426	53	46	7783
A Electricity, gas and steam	2117	2173	2689	53	63	6969	2290	2437	2465	50	45	7197
B Water works and supply	209	356	-61	3	2	505	226	397	-39	3	1	586
5 Construction	12745	1031	3989	46	8	17803	14440	1121	5154	63	10	20768
6 Wholesale and retail trade, restaurants and hotels	19082	2846	3818	261	61	25946	21067	3109	4304	367	71	28776
A Wholesale and retail trade	15913	2534	3366	247	11	22049	17562	2763	3712	347	16	24368
B Restaurants and hotels	3169	312	452	14	50	3897	3505	346	592	20	55	4408
7 Transport, storage and communication	9655	4964	2151	189	15	16944	10632	5372	2765	215	15	18969
A Transport and storage	6807	3920	1540	186	15	12438	7364	4213	1954	212	15	13728
B Communication	2848	1044	611	3	-	4506	3268	1159	811	3	-	5241
8 Finance, insurance, real estate and business services	9612	9280	14241	87	51	33169	10912	10820	15692	116	67	37473
A Financial institutions	3516	513	2038	5	34	6038	3911	581	2144	5	48	6593
B Insurance	1175	187	825	3	3	2187	1315	222	1093	3	3	2630
C Real estate and business services	4921	8580	11378	79	14	24944	5686	10017	12455	108	16	28250
Real estate, except dwellings	1462	488	1343	13	-	3306	1611	571	1559	21	-	3762
Dwellings	-	7112	7405	56	-	14573	-	8175	7914	71	2	16158
9 Community, social and personal services	4358	927	2408	45	102	7636	4858	1049	2975	56	100	8838
A Sanitary and similar services	501	503	85	1	-	1090	586	574	120	2	-	1282
B Social and related community services [b]	376	79	789	9	10	1243	416	89	969	14	12	1476
Educational services	161	55	59	-	10	265	174	62	75	-	12	299
Medical, dental, other health and veterinary services	215	24	730	9	-	978	242	27	894	14	-	1177
C Recreational and cultural services [b]	1463	149	713	29	82	2272	1639	170	883	32	73	2651
D Personal and household services	2018	196	821	6	10	3031	2217	216	1003	8	15	3429

Finland

4.3 Cost Components of Value Added (Continued)

Million Finnish markkaa

	1982						1983					
	Compensation of Employees	Consumption of Capital	Net Operating Surplus	Indirect Taxes	Less: Subsidies Received	Value Added	Compensation of Employees	Consumption of Capital	Net Operating Surplus	Indirect Taxes	Less: Subsidies Received	Value Added
Total, Industries	33816	54295	185639	2254	1338	207928	2420	62752	37368	1604		
Producers of Government Services	31467	2464		11		34142	2834	-	13	-	39211	
Other Producers	3124	318	689		4331	3622	361	899		4852		
Total	34135	36598	55184	1349	2254	225012	148610	63621	1617	2420	251991	
Less: Imputed bank service charge		5646			5446			6247				6247
Import duties			26350								28903	
Value added tax			5509	18859		35361				6458		
Other adjustments	36598			77637	245716	5737		40563	35361	8878		
Total	134135	36598	49638	33208	7763	245716	148610	40563	57374	36978	8878	274647

	1984						1985					
	Compensation of Employees	Consumption of Capital	Net Operating Surplus	Indirect Taxes	Less: Subsidies Received	Value Added	Compensation of Employees	Consumption of Capital	Net Operating Surplus	Indirect Taxes	Less: Subsidies Received	Value Added

All Producers

1 Agriculture, hunting, forestry and fishing	4166	5218	15457	166	1706	23301	4350	5532	16038	182	1977	24125
A Agriculture and hunting a	1572	3723	6699	89	1642	12441	1625	3927	8872	105	1904	12425
B Forestry and logging	2565	1376	6163	7	19	10092	2690	1477	6801	9	23	10954
C Fishing a	29	119	595	70	45	768	35	128	565	68	50	746
2 Mining and quarrying	299	269	199	9	23	1113	685	290	234	9	25	1193
A Coal mining												
B Crude petroleum and natural gas production	...	...	...	...	...	...	...	...	...	...	...	...
C Metal ore mining	406	162	63	20	614	395	172	5	22	586		
D Other mining	256	107	136	3	3	499	290	118	4	3	607	
3 Manufacturing	43126	8773	18652	765	563	70653	46439	9898	18017	911	677	74588
A Manufacture of food, beverages and tobacco	4742	811	2594	101	31	8217	5008	1174	2281	113	41	8615
B Textile, wearing apparel and leather industries	3494	400	956	48	66	4832	3662	425	1131	56	86	5188
C Manufacture of wood and wood products, including furniture	3648	753	1125	76	61	5541	3729	805	248	94	54	4822
D Manufacture of paper and paper products, printing and publishing	8426	2780	4640	168	128	15886	9086	3096	3651	204	142	15895
E Manufacture of chemicals and chemical products, petroleum, coal, rubber and plastic products	3630	1160	2941	76	47	7760	3876	1269	3260	86	53	8438
F Manufacture of non-metallic mineral products, except petroleum and coal	1763	374	971	20	24	3104	1892	407	902	24	21	3204
G Basic metal industries	1893	680	491	19	63	3108	2083	723	185	78	24	3045
H Manufacture of fabricated metal products, machinery and equipment	15175	1775	4641	190	173	21608	16632	1956	6112	227	241	24686
I Other manufacturing industries	355	40	193	23	14	597	391	43	247	29	15	695
4 Electricity, gas and water	2791	3059	2157	57	53	8003	3076	3251	2463	42	64	8768
A Electricity, gas and steam	2535	2631	2227	49	55	7387	2796	2796	2477	38	62	8045
B Water works and supply	256	428	-70	4	2	616	280	455	-14	4	2	723
5 Construction	15965	1183	5286	117	10	22541	17349	1231	4133	177	10	22880
6 Wholesale and retail trade, restaurants and hotels	23413	3403	4486	481	80	31703	25854	3677	5194	545	91	35179
A Wholesale and retail trade	19510	3020	3827	451	24	26784	21575	3266	4290	511	28	29614
B Restaurants and hotels	3903	383	659	30	56	4919	4279	411	904	34	63	5565
7 Transport, storage and communication	11531	5811	3827	269	18	21420	12613	6205	4312	299	23	23406
A Transport and storage	7993	4550	2744	264	18	15533	8771	4849	3036	293	23	16926
B Communication	3538	1261	1083	5	-	5887	3842	1356	1276	6	-	6480
8 Finance, insurance, real estate and business services	12499	12278	17989	149	82	42833	14410	13809	19082	190	98	47393
A Financial institutions	4542	652	2604	9	4	7736	5350	728	2932	7	80	8937
B Insurance	1437	254	960	4	4	2651	1575	288	505	3	4	2367
C Real estate and business services	6520	11372	14425	139	10	32446	7485	12793	15645	180	14	36089
Real estate, except dwellings	1767	654	1970	30	-	4421	1915	747	2617	38	-	5317

583

Finland

4.3 Cost Components of Value Added (Continued)

Million Finnish markkaa

	1984					1985				
	Compensation of Employees	Consumption of Capital	Net Operating Surplus	Indirect Taxes	Less: Subsidies Received	Value Added	Compensation of Employees	Consumption of Capital	Net Operating Surplus	Indirect Taxes	Less: Subsidies Received	Value Added
Dwellings	-	9170	8603	2	87	17858	10169	8989	112	3	19267
9 Community, social and personal services	5223	1176	3486	70	140	10115	6201	1312	3886	76	176	11299
A Sanitary and similar services	689	643	167	3	-	1502	822	705	275	4	19	1787
B Social and related community services [b]	474	97	1139	17	14	1713	534	108	1271	18	16	1915
Educational services	193	66	76	-	14	321	214	72	78	-	16	348
Medical, dental, other health and veterinary services	281	31	1063	17	-	1392	320	36	1193	18	-	1567
C Recreational and cultural services [b]	1840	204	1014	39	103	2994	2053	246	1104	42	138	3307
D Personal and household services	2520	232	1166	11	23	3906	2792	253	1236	12	3	4290
Total, Industries	119676	41170	71439	2076	2679	231682	45205	73359	2431	3141	248831
Producers of Government Services	41040	3176	-	14	-	44230	46533	3546	-	17	50096
Other Producers	4729	403	305	-	-	5437	6551	447	-950	-	6048
Total	165445	44749	71744	2090	2679	281349	184061	49198	72409	2448	3141	304975
Less: Imputed bank service charge				7322		7322				8141		8141
Import duties				34330		34330				38152		38152
Value added tax				7112		7112				45358	7206	
Other adjustments				44422	9791	308357	184061	49198	64268	47806	10347	334986
Total	165445	44749	64422	44532	9791	308357						

	1986					1987				
	Compensation of Employees	Consumption of Capital	Net Operating Surplus	Indirect Taxes	Less: Subsidies Received	Value Added	Compensation of Employees	Consumption of Capital	Net Operating Surplus	Indirect Taxes	Less: Subsidies Received	Value Added

All Producers

1 Agriculture, hunting, forestry and fishing	4292	5843	15455	2051	23743	4391	6101	13967	215	2243	22431
A Agriculture and hunting [a]	1699	4133	9053	127	1961	13051	1689	4306	6949	138	2152	10930
B Forestry and logging	2562	1580	5836	10	24	9964	2669	1662	6453	10	30	10764
C Fishing [a]	31	130	566	67	66	728	33	133	565	67	61	737
2 Mining and quarrying	617	306	231	11	37	1128	586	322	150	14	46	1026
A Coal mining	...	...	...	...	...	...	...	...	...	...	...	...
B Crude petroleum and natural gas production												
C Metal ore mining	321	177	-9	6	32	463	251	180	-105	8	30	304
D Other mining	296	129	240	5	5	665	335	142	255	6	16	722
3 Manufacturing	48305	10541	17415	1112	729	76644	51037	11379	23012	1185	903	85710
A Manufacture of food, beverages and tobacco	5511	1249	2755	134	48	9611	5893	1346	2817	143	60	10139
B Textile, wearing apparel and leather industries	3713	445	915	47	80	5060	3680	470	986	69	97	5108
C Manufacture of wood and wood products, including furniture	3867	829	358	64	114	5104	4081	862	1212	130	82	6203
D Manufacture of paper and paper products, printing and publishing	9570	3298	3247	247	176	16186	10260	3578	4543	267	205	18443
E Manufacture of chemicals and chemical petroleum, coal, rubber and plastic products	4059	1374	3507	104	47	8997	4328	1502	3248	114	61	9131
F Manufacture of non-metallic mineral products, except products of petroleum and coal	1917	427	949	16	30	3307	2084	462	1338	35	21	3898
G Basic metal industries	2137	744	353	95	21	3308	2180	805	553	94	23	3609
H Manufacture of fabricated metal products, machinery and equipment	17122	2127	5061	286	261	24335	18125	2302	8131	295	335	28518
I Other manufacturing industries	409	48	260	16	4	736	406	52	184	38	19	661
4 Electricity, gas and water	3325	3459	2576	50	66	9344	3480	3669	2878	53	78	10002
A Electricity, gas and steam	3026	2973	2506	46	64	8487	3182	3156	2788	47	51	9122
B Water works and supply	299	486	70	4	2	857	298	513	90	6	27	880

Finland

4.3 Cost Components of Value Added (Continued)

Million Finnish markkaa

	1986						1987					
	Compensation of Employees	Net Capital Consumption	Operating Surplus	Indirect Taxes	Less: Subsidies Received	Value Added	Compensation of Employees	Net Capital Consumption	Operating Surplus	Indirect Taxes	Less: Subsidies Received	Value Added
5 Construction	18663	1302	4553	213	17	24714	20753	1364	5416	176	18	27691
6 Wholesale and retail trade, restaurants and hotels	27772	4041	4558	659	96	36944	30203	4450	5428	747	119	40709
A Wholesale and retail trade	23011	3617	3601	618	31	30816	24974	4008	4189	698	44	33825
B Restaurants and hotels	4761	424	957	41	55	6128	5229	442	1239	49	75	6884
7 Transport, storage and communication	13581	6462	5128	311	56	25426	14886	6256	5945	338	51	27944
A Transport and storage	9507	5015	3841	303	56	18610	10364	5255	4420	330	51	20318
B Communication	4074	1447	1287	8	-	6816	4522	1571	1525	8	-	7626
8 Finance, insurance, real estate and business services	16096	15365	21998	231	134	53556	18304	17454	23736	216	146	59564
A Financial institutions	5867	825	3349	8	102	9947	6877	945	4441	8	96	12175
B Insurance	1729	319	593	4	3	2642	1869	350	867	5	4	3087
C Real estate and business services	8500	14221	18056	219	29	40967	9558	16159	18428	203	46	44302
Real estate, except dwellings	2024	866	3339	46	-	6275	2198	1019	4148	42	-	7407
Dwellings	-	11078	9847	136	12	21049	-	12331	8927	125	14	21369
9 Community, social and personal services	6802	1464	4570	84	187	12733	7475	1650	5480	106	229	14482
A Sanitary and similar services	894	770	331	4	22	1977	1045	835	443	9	14	2315
B Social and related community services [b]	585	120	1439	22	19	2147	639	140	1624	31	21	2413
Educational services	231	78	95	-	19	385	254	89	102	-	21	424
Medical, dental, other health and veterinary services	354	42	1344	22	-	1762	385	51	1522	31	-	1989
C Recreational and cultural services [b]	2276	296	1277	44	143	3750	2494	359	1521	48	192	4230
D Personal and household services	3047	278	1523	14	3	4859	3297	316	1892	21	2	5524
Total, Industries	139453	48783	76484	2875	3363	264232	151115	53215	86012	3050	3833	289559
Producers of Government Services	50519	3899	-	18	-	54436	55369	4390	-	20	-	59779
Other Producers	7357	487	-1282	-	-	6562	8188	538	-1679	-	-	7047
Total	197329	53169	75202	2893	3363	325230	214672	58143	84333	3070	3833	356385
Less: Imputed bank service charge	-	9328	-	-	-	9328	-	11458	-	-	-	11458
Import duties	-	-	-	41464	-	41464	-	-	-	46670	-	46670
Value added tax	-	-	-	-	-	-	-	-	-	-	-	-
Other adjustments	-	49609	-	-	7945	41664	-	-	-	-	54523	7853
Total	197329	53169	75202	52502	11308	357566	214672	58143	72875	57593	11686	391597

All Producers

	1988						1989					
	Compensation of Employees	Net Capital Consumption	Operating Surplus	Indirect Taxes	Less: Subsidies Received	Value Added	Compensation of Employees	Net Capital Consumption	Operating Surplus	Indirect Taxes	Less: Subsidies Received	Value Added
1 Agriculture, hunting, forestry and fishing	4840	6271	15872	203	22446	2724	4945	6622	19661	242	3853	27617
A Agriculture and hunting [a]	1977	4330	7208	120	11013	2522	2017	4623	10460	150	3740	13510
B Forestry and logging	2829	1807	7979	10	12591	34	2891	1863	8462	10	35	13191
C Fishing [a]	34	134	685	73	858	68	37	136	739	82	78	916
2 Mining and quarrying	562	337	473	14	36	1350	545	358	818	29	35	1715
A Coal mining	...	...	...	...	...	...	...	...	...	...	...	...
B Crude petroleum and natural gas production	...	...	...	...	...	...	...	...	...	...	...	...
C Metal ore mining	222	180	201	11	28	586	202	183	443	22	30	820
D Other mining	340	157	272	3	8	764	343	175	375	7	5	895

Finland

4.3 Cost Components of Value Added
(Continued)

Million Finnish markkaa

	1988 Compensation of Employees	1988 Capital Consumption	1988 Net Operating Surplus	1988 Indirect Taxes	1988 Less: Subsidies Received	1988 Value Added	1989 Compensation of Employees	1989 Capital Consumption	1989 Net Operating Surplus	1989 Indirect Taxes	1989 Less: Subsidies Received	1989 Value Added
3 Manufacturing	54157	12672	27237	831	1096	93801	58552	14014	27899	1301	1020	100746
A Manufacture of food, beverages and tobacco	6401	1493	3194	114	73	11129	6864	1582	2922	173	56	11485
B Textile, wearing apparel and leather industries	3388	497	707	36	127	4501	3145	511	565	64	87	4198
C Manufacture of wood and wood products, including furniture	4299	909	1585	102	107	6788	4776	977	1728	134	105	7510
D Manufacture of paper and paper products, printing and publishing	11050	4116	6713	147	234	21792	12114	4801	5343	262	193	22327
E Manufacture of chemicals and chemical petroleum, coal, rubber and plastic products	4720	1693	3019	87	72	9447	5129	1854	3993	115	92	10999
F Manufacture of non-metallic mineral products, except products of petroleum and coal	2250	506	1714	21	26	4465	2517	551	1987	36	38	5053
G Basic metal industries	2211	900	1486	81	26	4652	2407	962	2423	118	28	5882
H Manufacture of fabricated metal products, machinery and equipment	19415	2500	8546	195	407	30249	21162	2714	8705	345	415	32511
I Other manufacturing industries	423	58	273	48	24	778	438	62	233	54	6	781
4 Electricity, gas and water	3796	3958	2225	45	87	9937	4005	4355	1788	72	59	10161
A Electricity, gas and steam	3487	3402	2085	40	59	8955	3678	3750	1696	65	33	9156
B Water works and supply	309	556	140	5	28	982	327	605	92	7	26	1005
5 Construction	23784	1509	7972	165	29	33401	28151	1707	12056	273	74	42113
6 Wholesale and retail trade, restaurants and hotels	33767	4869	6088	606	162	45168	38097	5419	6262	983	274	50487
A Wholesale and retail trade	27857	4413	4586	564	45	37375	31318	4936	4671	909	114	41720
B Restaurants and hotels	5910	456	1502	42	117	7793	6779	483	1591	74	160	8767
7 Transport, storage and communication	16510	7262	6806	306	85	30799	18623	7842	7544	446	96	34359
A Transport and storage	11477	5560	5130	300	85	22382	13148	5987	5992	434	91	25470
B Communication	5033	1702	1676	6	-	8417	5475	1855	1552	12	5	8889
8 Finance, insurance, real estate and business services	21380	20552	26175	951	207	68851	23958	24453	30951	582	311	79633
A Financial institutions	7936	1056	4899	34	114	13811	8643	1175	7186	39	109	16934
B Insurance	2118	416	1059	36	5	3624	2354	640	95	42	6	3125
C Real estate and business services	11326	19080	20217	881	88	51416	12961	22638	23670	501	196	59574
Real estate, except dwellings	2521	1350	5389	668	-	9928	2697	1651	7619	309	2	12274
Dwellings	-	14334	8508	150	34	22958	-	16829	8577	140	51	25495
9 Community, social and personal services	8326	1898	6367	115	255	16451	9560	2361	7578	125	222	19402
A Sanitary and similar services	1174	940	491	6	5	2606	1414	1058	696	9	17	3160
B Social and related community services b	1534	191	2086	36	65	3782	1771	225	2465	33	100	4394
Educational services	286	102	126	-	23	491	327	115	152	-	34	560
Medical, dental, other health and veterinary services	437	62	1791	36	-	2326	504	76	2063	33	4	2672
C Recreational and cultural services b	1948	414	1549	57	183	3785	2193	670	1678	50	71	4520
D Personal and household services	3670	353	2241	16	2	6278	4182	408	2739	33	34	7328
Total, Industries	167122	59328	99215	3236	4681	324220	186436	67131	114557	4053	5944	366233
Producers of Government Services	60568	4998	-	22	-	65588	67113	5622	-	24	-	72759
Other Producers	9570	630	-2295	-	-	7905	11672	720	-3838	-	-	8554
Total	237260	64956	96920	3258	4681	397713	265221	73473	110719	4077	5944	447546
Less: Imputed bank service charge	...	...	13251	...	...	13251	...	...	16373	...	...	16373
Import duties	...	...	...	...	...	57077	...	...	...	...	...	64324
Value added tax	...	...	...	...	...	...	...	...	...	...	...	...
Other adjustments	...	...	...	63667	6590	...	...	...	...	72103	7779	...
Total	237260	64956	83669	66925	11271	441539	265221	73473	94346	76180	13723	495497

a) Hunting is included in item 'Fishing'.
b) ISIC groups 935 and 939 are included in item 'Recreational and cultural services' for the years prior to 1987.

France

General note. The preparation of national accounts statistics in France is undertaken by the Institut national de la statistique et des etudes economiques, Paris. The official estimates are published annually in 'Rapport sur les comptes de la nation'. The following presentation of sources and methods is mainly based on a report prepared by the Statistical Office of the European Communities in 1976 entitled 'Basic statistics needed for the ESA accounts and tables: present situation and prospects for improvements' and on information contained in 'Presentation de la comptabilite nationale francaise'. The estimates are generally in accordance with the classifications and definitions recommended in the United Nations System of national accounts (SNA). 'Le Systeme elargi de comptabilite nationale' which is an adaptation by France of the European System of Integrated Economic Accounts (ESA) and closely resembles the present SNA, was introduced in 1976, and its concepts were described in 'Le Systeme elargi de comptabilite nationale-methodes'. Input-output tables have been published by the Institut national de la statistique et des etudes economiques. The following tables have been prepared from successive replies to the United Nations national accounts questionnaire. When the scope and coverage of the estimates differ for conceptual or statistical reasons from the definitions and classifications recommended in SNA, a footnote is indicated to the relevant tables.

Sources and methods :

(a) Gross domestic product. Gross domestic product is estimated mainly through the production approach.

(b) Expenditure on the gross domestic product. The expenditure approach is used to estimate government final consumption expenditure, gross fixed capital formation and exports and imports of goods and services. This approach, in combination with the commodity-flow approach is used to estimated private final consumption expenditure and increase in stocks. Government final consumption expenditure estimates referring to central government are based on budgetary accounts and on an accounting plan for enterprises. For local government, the centralized accounting scheme is used while for social security funds, an accounting plan is adopted for the general scheme and various sets of accounts are used for special schemes. Private consumption estimates are based on the annual input-output tables, results of expenditure surveys, estimates of fiscal revenues and statistics of retail sales derived from periodic surveys of large retail stores. Increase in stocks is estimated for producers, users and trade. For petroleum products and products of the iron and steel industry, the changes in quantity and value are available from specific sources. For other products, changes are valued on the basis of tax returns excluding stock assessment. Data for gross fixed capital formation in enterprises are available from the accounts of the large national enterprises, annual surveys, surveys of business cycles and income tax returns. Exports and imports of goods and services are estimated from customs returns and balance-of-payments statements. The constant price estimates of government consumption expenditure are obtained by using the implicit price index for producers of government services. For private consumption expenditure, estimates are obtained by extrapolation, use of quantum indexes, and price deflation. Price deflation is also used for the remaining expenditure items, except dwellings, for which the value of construction is extrapolated.

(c) Cost-structure of the gross domestic product. Wages and salaries of the private sector are calculated from various sources such as income and revenue statements of enterprises, quarterly surveys and statistics based on wage declarations of employees. Compensation of government employees is estimated from government accounts. Estimates of the income of enterprises are based on fiscal statistics of industrial and commercial profits and other sources. The enterprises are required to follow an accounting plan for taxation. The data from the plan are merged with information obtained from the annual survey of enterprises. Statistical information on agriculture is obtained from the Ministere de l'agriculture and on general government from an accounting plan, budgetary accounts and other sources. The depreciation estimates are based on information on the value of capital stock derived from various sources such as financial statements, sample surveys and accounts. Indirect taxes and subsidies are estimated on the basis of government accounts.

(d) Gross domestic product by kind of economic activity. The table of GDP by kind of economic activity is prepared at market prices. The production approach is used to estimate the value added of almost all industries. This is done within the framework of annual input-output tables, using the commodity-flow approach. For the agricultural sector, the Ministere de l'agriculture provides all output figures for quantities and prices while figures on intermediate consumption are derived indirectly from the suppliers of products used. Bench-mark information is derived from censuses and surveys held in 1955, 1963/64, 1970 and 1975. Agricultural output estimated on the basis of the total area of land used and yield per hectare for the different crops. For livestock, a survey on the structure of bovine herds is undertaken every 12-18 months supplemented every 3 or 4 years by a detailed survey. For the industrial activity and construction sector, the main sources of information consist of the branch surveys carried out by the employers' associations and the annual surveys of enterprises. The branch surveys record annual or quarterly output or sales in values and/or quantities, producers' stocks in terms of physical quantity and productive capital and intermediate consumption. The annual survey of enterprises covers all large enterprises and a representative sample of small enterprises. Gross fixed capital formation is broken down into transport equipment, building and construction, tools, land and buildings, etc. For government construction, information is obtained by analysing tax records. For the trade sector, bench-mark information is provided by the 1967 census of distribution and services. Annual fiscal information on turnover is provided by the tax authorities. Trade margins and distribution channels are based on estimates provided by professional organizations. The estimates for restaurants and hotels are mainly based on tax statistics. For the transport sector, the transport surveys and the accounts of nationalized enterprises or the structural surveys are used for the estimation of gross output and intermediate consumption, respectively. For the financial sector and insurance, information is obtained from sources such as the Banque de France, the accounting plans, the Direction des assurances du Ministere de l'economie and annual surveys. The value added of real estate is estimated on the basis of fiscal statistics and special surveys. For government services an accounting plan and the budgetary accounts are the main sources. The value of services by non-profit institutions are based on a detailed study conducted by the Centre de recherche et de documentation sur la consommation for 1971 and extrapolated for other years by growth rates. For other community and social services, estimates are classified by type of producer. Remuneration of domestic services is obtained by multiplying the number of persons on the work force by the wage-rates and adding social assessments. Constant price estimates of all industrial sectors are obtained by using double deflation and the commodity-flow method based on annual input-output tables. The estimates are calculated at the previous year's prices, the current value series being deflated by price indexes or extrapolated by a volume index using the preceding year as a base. The constant price estimates are subsequently converted to the base year by a process of chaining.

1.1 Expenditure on the Gross Domestic Product, in Current Prices

Million French francs

	1970	1975	1980	1981	1982	1983	1984	1985	1986	1987	1988	1989
1 Government final consumption expenditure	116640	243436	509274	595028	701299	782134	854300	910315	959509	1002120	1056540	1119200
2 Private final consumption expenditure	459577	862260	1653310	1907220	2200820	2435550	2651310	2871100	3062810	3244960	3436890	3665460
A Households	457196	857794	1645070	1897910	2190340	2424140	2639170	2858390	3049520	3231110	3422340	3650030
B Private non-profit institutions serving households	2381	4466	8239	9311	10481	11404	12134	12704	13288	13846	14553	15433
3 Gross capital formation	213118	344643	680079	693029	793087	795547	827948	887420	994673	1065580	1195390	1311380
A Increase in stocks	20181	-9667	34326	-7501	18809	-14054	-12416	-17871	17156	19347	30977	39905
B Gross fixed capital formation	192937	354310	645753	700530	774278	809601	840364	905291	977517	1046230	1164410	1271480
Residential buildings	63712	123115	208861	223383	239238	250437	254374	257751	268128	279908	297947	310408
Non-residential buildings	57941	105532	185267	203800	226275	232603	244092	258826	283324	307623	350514	389701
Other construction and land improvement etc.												
Other	71284	125663	251625	273347	308765	326561	341898	388714	426065	458702	515951	571369
4 Exports of goods and services	125428	279799	604422	714282	790351	900658	1053330	1123930	1074100	1103190	1221940	1425130
5 Less: Imports of goods and services	121244	262254	638791	744754	859536	907388	1024970	1092620	1021790	1095010	1218040	1408060
Equals: Gross Domestic Product	793519	1467880	2808300	3164800	3626020	4006500	4361910	4700140	5069300	5320830	5692730	6113120

France

1.2 Expenditure on the Gross Domestic Product, in Constant Prices

Million French francs

	1970	1975	1980	1981	1982	1983	1984	1985	1986	1987	1988	1989
	At constant prices of:1980											
1 Government final consumption expenditure	365822	429932	509274	525248	545045	556461	563017	575863	585855	602406	619614	629771
2 Private final consumption expenditure	1175840	1419470	1653310	1687230	1745530	1761580	1780450	1823160	1894290	1945890	2007590	2071890
A Households	1169430	1412090	1645070	1678940	1737210	1753270	1772230	1814930	1886020	1937350	1998800	2062910
B Private non-profit institutions serving households	6410	7384	8239	8289	8322	8307	8218	8230	8272	8539	8788	8976
3 Gross capital formation	549535	579874	680079	627748	648715	601618	586790	603289	656419	690339	741738	783110
A Increase in stocks	45214	-9534	34326	-5808	23847	-972	-139	-2648	23251	31200	26170	24239
B Gross fixed capital formation	504321	589408	645753	633556	624868	602590	586929	605937	633168	659139	715568	758871
Residential buildings	175450	209228	208861	203784	194352	188817	180466	176519	177377	178785	184568	188246
Non-residential buildings	160069	179829	185267	184601	184440	176264	174061	176804	188960	199414	221494	239440
Other construction and land improvement etc.												
Other	168802	200351	251625	245171	246076	237509	232402	252614	266831	280940	309506	331185
4 Exports of goods and services	306955	445253	604422	626644	616069	638799	683480	696510	686413	707847	766651	848793
5 Less: Imports of goods and services	369241	467527	638791	625537	641697	624550	641275	670442	718342	773819	840742	912961
Equals: Gross Domestic Product	2028910	2407000	2808300	2841330	2913660	2933900	2972460	3028380	3104640	3172660	3294850	3420600

1.3 Cost Components of the Gross Domestic Product

Million French francs

	1970	1975	1980	1981	1982	1983	1984	1985	1986	1987	1988	1989
1 Indirect taxes, net	103027	177624	356953	390152	460823	506002	554910	599896	627563	667573	738821	787829
A Indirect taxes	119002	212990	428590	480076	559807	619647	688426	742648	785542	836077	887047	928662
B Less: Subsidies	15975	35366	71637	89924	98984	113645	133516	142752	157979	168504	148226	140833
2 Consumption of fixed capital	72363	163602	346185	397229	456655	508546	551642	589380	631975	669684	712389	765389
3 Compensation of employees paid by resident producers to:	391444	801764	1575780	1792600	2054560	2259280	2425770	2582450	2708114	2820070	2964860	3153680
A Resident households	390761	799935	1570220	1786070	2046270	2248490	2411190	2562760	2688800	2803100	2944620	3135350
B Rest of the world	683	1829	5560	6534	8295	10796	14584	19689	19310	16969	20241	18329
4 Operating surplus	226685	324894	529373	584821	653983	732668	829588	928421	1101644	1163510	1276660	1406220
A Corporate and quasi-corporate enterprises	68416	82953	124476	133668	132849	154920	207225	253615	368361	397953	448114	494896
B Private unincorporated enterprises [a]	159404	243037	406094	452805	524766	578741	624687	678238	732714	762615	828198	912352
C General government	-1135	-1096	-1197	-1652	-3632	-993	-2324	-3432	569	2939	344	-1031
Equals: Gross Domestic Product	793519	1467880	2808300	3164800	3626020	4006500	4361910	4700140	5069300	5320830	5692730	6113120

a) Private unincorporated enterprises includes households.

1.4 General Government Current Receipts and Disbursements

Million French francs

	1970	1975	1980	1981	1982	1983	1984	1985	1986	1987	1988	1989
	Receipts											
1 Operating surplus	-1135	-1096	-1197	-1652	-3632	-993	-2324	-3432	569	2939	344	-1031
2 Property and entrepreneurial income	9402	17397	25696	37063	47143	54382	53411	66917	73895	66249	61486	68879
3 Taxes, fees and contributions	277765	532055	1150940	1296940	1520530	1706930	1905880	2046960	2170220	2310110	2435170	2612040
A Indirect taxes	118972	204989	410607	457252	531081	586917	653822	705103	736494	781898	824756	867392
B Direct taxes	56331	104927	236244	273399	320175	358740	407431	429321	469768	499111	514948	554760
C Social security contributions	100991	219799	500068	562383	663943	755445	837392	905143	955257	1019600	1086830	1179060
D Compulsory fees, fines and penalties	1471	2340	4016	3908	5329	5832	7231	7390	8705	9504	8635	10821
4 Other current transfers	19400	34501	74852	95927	102096	105819	115214	125977	134054	142328	168342	160191
Total Current Receipts of General Government	305432	582857	1250290	1428280	1666140	1866140	2072180	2236420	2378740	2521630	2665340	2840080
	Disbursements											
1 Government final consumption expenditure	116640	243436	509274	595028	701299	782134	854300	910315	959509	1002120	1056540	1119200

France

1.4 General Government Current Receipts and Disbursements
(Continued)

Million French francs

	1970	1975	1980	1981	1982	1983	1984	1985	1986	1987	1988	1989
A Compensation of employees	82568	177752	376678	436659	514315	572947	626251	669198	712439	732251	759867	805465
B Consumption of fixed capital	5720	16032	37945	44449	52342	59123	65923	72304	77663	83340	89549	97196
C Purchases of goods and services, net	26641	45447	84712	101249	118837	131718	140435	153290	153324	169785	190162	197857
D Less: Own account fixed capital formation	...	...	...	...	...	...	...	...	...	...	...	...
E Indirect taxes paid, net	1711	4205	9939	12671	15805	18346	21691	15523	16083	16743	16964	18679
2 Property income	8593	17399	41312	62565	73772	102230	116539	135075	145927	149476	157910	176413
A Interest	8591	17390	41251	62534	73729	102176	116484	135010	145859	149403	157828	176324
B Net land rent and royalties	2	9	61	31	43	54	55	65	68	73	82	89
3 Subsidies	15975	28598	54407	70422	79520	87423	107248	109854	118625	117482	106108	105986
4 Other current transfers	130752	282453	584378	698524	837974	948589	1044980	1140100	1212160	1271930	1350240	1424110
A Social security benefits	90118	202980	439730	527268	633340	705473	762685	823173	880391	915324	980311	1043560
B Social assistance grants	13886	25871	45387	53221	65045	76992	97336	117926	129284	130674	142503	144040
C Other	26748	53602	99261	118035	139589	166124	184957	199002	202489	225928	227421	236505
5 Net saving	33472	10971	60915	1741	-26430	-54234	-50888	-58926	-57483	-19374	-5457	14370
Total Current Disbursements and Net Saving of General Government	305432	582857	1250290	1428280	1666140	1866140	2072180	2236420	2378740	2521630	2665340	2840080

1.5 Current Income and Outlay of Corporate and Quasi-Corporate Enterprises, Summary

Million French francs

	1970	1975	1980	1981	1982	1983	1984	1985	1986	1987	1988	1989
					Receipts							
1 Operating surplus	68416	82953	124476	133668	132849	154920	207225	253615	368361	397953	448114	494896
2 Property and entrepreneurial income received	64669	188321	510717	690427	806744	881268	994270	1111300	1155200	1165300	1258990	1429660
3 Current transfers	33716	67008	144908	167638	201817	234090	256632	270947	280272	303896	308383	323380
Total Current Receipts	166801	338282	780101	991733	1141410	1270280	1458130	1635860	1803830	1867150	2015490	2247930
					Disbursements							
1 Property and entrepreneurial income	82335	225342	558388	767492	887908	967417	1077180	1199620	1216140	1226370	1323470	1507330
2 Direct taxes and other current payments to general government	18827	30509	65902	75624	89861	88612	105134	115852	136134	150707	161301	180626
3 Other current transfers	36985	72831	151771	186229	212148	228551	252238	275294	294334	308123	341075	342828
4 Net saving	28654	9600	4040	-37612	-48507	-14302	23572	45093	157222	181945	189642	217152
Total Current Disbursements and Net Saving	166801	338282	780101	991733	1141410	1270280	1458130	1635860	1803830	1867150	2015490	2247930

1.6 Current Income and Outlay of Households and Non-Profit Institutions

Million French francs

	1970	1975	1980	1981	1982	1983	1984	1985	1986	1987	1988	1989
					Receipts							
1 Compensation of employees	391442	801596	1573880	1791190	2052960	2255620	2419230	2573110	2700560	2815530	2961020	3151920
A From resident producers	390761	799935	1570220	1786070	2046270	2248490	2411190	2562760	2688800	2803100	2944620	3135350
B From rest of the world	681	1661	3656	5120	6690	7129	8037	10350	11757	12427	16401	16563
2 Operating surplus of private unincorporated enterprises	159404	243037	406094	452805	524766	578741	624687	678238	732714	762615	828198	912352
3 Property and entrepreneurial income	34457	78626	167378	210403	231568	257749	274798	304443	306159	321953	356634	407590
4 Current transfers	156601	330354	683149	805059	963780	1073610	1184250	1295270	1386680	1444450	1553060	1646970
A Social security benefits	90971	204885	443334	531130	637501	711500	770207	834620	896206	932957	1000750	1067450
B Social assistance grants	14078	26519	46879	55010	66896	79021	99437	120179	131665	133175	145130	146884
C Other	51552	98950	192936	218919	259383	283084	314604	340474	358804	378316	407177	432637
Total Current Receipts	741904	1453610	2830500	3259460	3773070	4165710	4502960	4851060	5126110	5344540	5698910	6118830
					Disbursements							
1 Private final consumption expenditure	459577	862260	1653310	1907220	2200820	2435550	2651310	2871100	3062810	3244960	3436890	3665460

France

1.6 Current Income and Outlay of Households and Non-Profit Institutions
(Continued)

Million French francs

	1970	1975	1980	1981	1982	1983	1984	1985	1986	1987	1988	1989
2 Property income	14299	39064	89600	96145	120190	131812	145715	164302	182239	185577	203411	232589
3 Direct taxes and other current transfers n.e.c. to general government	141879	300795	683552	774373	911893	1045080	1161790	1241440	1317130	1402360	1476350	1596460
A Social security contributions	103447	225144	511363	575393	679347	772521	856208	924924	979420	1049340	1119280	1216840
B Direct taxes	37318	73944	169455	196032	228645	268116	300447	311356	331724	346551	350409	370745
C Fees, fines and penalties	1114	1707	2734	2948	3901	4445	5135	5161	5984	6464	6667	8872
4 Other current transfers	41246	78620	151799	175322	205757	229710	241012	259964	277099	286214	300754	318790
5 Net saving	84903	172874	252239	306396	334409	323559	303137	314257	286835	225440	281496	305528
Total Current Disbursements and Net Saving	741904	1453610	2830500	3259460	3773070	4165710	4502960	4851060	5126110	5344540	5698910	6118830

1.7 External Transactions on Current Account, Summary

Million French francs

	1970	1975	1980	1981	1982	1983	1984	1985	1986	1987	1988	1989
Payments to the Rest of the World												
1 Imports of goods and services	121244	262254	638791	744754	859536	907388	1024970	1092620	1021790	1095010	1218040	1408060
A Imports of merchandise c.i.f.	106296	232778	576505	663485	768258	808900	914542	970814	893847	952251	1063870	1229350
B Other	14948	29476	62286	81269	91278	98488	110426	121805	127942	142757	154172	178707
2 Factor income to the rest of the world	7930	22297	79595	136672	168370	170399	206772	226699	190134	184380	202855	249460
A Compensation of employees	683	1829	5560	6534	8295	10796	14584	19689	19310	16969	20241	18329
B Property and entrepreneurial income	7247	20468	74035	130138	160075	159603	192188	207010	170824	167411	182614	231131
3 Current transfers to the rest of the world	16218	33780	66436	80315	98756	112491	110528	122924	128709	137175	159229	157983
A Indirect taxes to supranational organizations	30	8001	17983	22824	28726	32730	34604	37545	49048	54179	62291	61270
B Other current transfers	16188	25779	48453	57491	70030	79761	75924	85379	79661	82996	96938	96713
4 Surplus of the nation on current transactions	6274	12404	-16700	-25275	-76960	-31978	-485	2384	23876	-7885	-17319	-8944
Payments to the Rest of the World and Surplus of the Nation on Current Transactions	151666	330735	768122	936466	1049700	1158300	1341780	1444630	1364510	1408680	1562810	1806560
Receipts From The Rest of the World												
1 Exports of goods and services	125428	279799	604422	714282	790351	900658	1053330	1123930	1074100	1103190	1221940	1425130
A Exports of merchandise f.o.b.	99401	226420	488877	576389	631842	720442	845218	901379	860303	886740	992606	1136360
B Other	26027	53379	115545	137893	158509	180216	208110	222551	213792	216447	229338	288773
2 Factor income from rest of the world	11229	24668	92182	146949	170350	158672	183267	201020	173526	171913	191335	237491
A Compensation of employees	681	1661	3656	5120	6690	7129	8037	10350	11757	12427	16401	16563
B Property and entrepreneurial income	10548	23007	88526	141829	163660	151543	175230	190670	161769	159486	174934	220928
3 Current transfers from rest of the world	15009	26268	71518	75235	89001	98970	105188	119676	116887	133578	149530	143932
A Subsidies from supranational organisations	-	6768	17230	19502	19464	26222	26268	32898	39354	51022	42118	34847
B Other current transfers	15009	19500	54288	55733	69537	72748	78920	86778	77533	82556	107412	109085
Receipts from the Rest of the World on Current Transactions	151666	330735	768122	936466	1049700	1158300	1341780	1444630	1364510	1408680	1562810	1806560

1.8 Capital Transactions of The Nation, Summary

Million French francs

	1970	1975	1980	1981	1982	1983	1984	1985	1986	1987	1988	1989
Finance of Gross Capital Formation												
Gross saving	219392	357047	663379	667754	716127	763569	827463	889804	1018550	1057700	1178070	1302440
1 Consumption of fixed capital	72363	163602	346185	397229	456655	508546	551642	589380	631975	669684	712389	765389
A General government	7469	19359	44431	51804	60695	68303	75808	82842	88614	94907	101657	109968
B Corporate and quasi-corporate enterprises	43315	97490	198981	230251	266237	297608	323047	346588	370246	388678	409864	439390
C Other	21579	46753	102773	115174	129723	142635	152787	159950	173115	186099	200868	216031
2 Net saving	147029	193445	317194	270525	259472	255023	275821	300424	386574	388011	465681	537050
A General government	33472	10971	60915	1741	-26430	-54234	-50888	-58926	-57483	-19374	-5457	14370
B Corporate and quasi-corporate enterprises	28654	9600	4040	-37612	-48507	-14302	23572	45093	157222	181945	189642	217152

France

1.8 Capital Transactions of The Nation, Summary
(Continued)

Million French francs

	1970	1975	1980	1981	1982	1983	1984	1985	1986	1987	1988	1989
C Other	84903	172874	252239	306396	334409	323559	303137	314257	286835	225440	281496	305528
Less: Surplus of the nation on current transactions	6274	12404	-16700	-25275	-76960	-31978	-485	2384	23876	-7885	-17319	-8944
Finance of Gross Capital Formation	213118	344643	680079	693029	793087	795547	827948	887420	994673	1065580	1195390	1311380

Gross Capital Formation

	1970	1975	1980	1981	1982	1983	1984	1985	1986	1987	1988	1989
Increase in stocks	20181	-9667	34326	-7501	18809	-14054	-12416	-17871	17156	19347	30977	39905
Gross fixed capital formation	192937	354310	645753	700530	774278	809601	840364	905291	977517	1046230	1164410	1271480
1 General government	28886	54419	86602	98729	114865	119346	126127	144277	152435	161115	177682	194922
2 Corporate and quasi-corporate enterprises	89542	154131	292619	319096	357379	373546	393575	433249	475315	517405	584542	648692
3 Other	74509	145760	266532	282705	302034	316709	320662	327765	349767	367713	402188	427864
Gross Capital Formation	213118	344643	680079	693029	793087	795547	827948	887420	994673	1065580	1195390	1311380

1.9 Gross Domestic Product by Institutional Sectors of Origin

Million French francs

	1970	1975	1980	1981	1982	1983	1984	1985	1986	1987	1988	1989
					Domestic Factor Incomes Originating							
1 General government	84294	182230	385982	447086	524523	587471	640678	684315	731510	753993	779538	824509
2 Corporate and quasi-corporate enterprises	330092	626613	1182120	1336230	1499750	1654790	1810360	1958150	2152300	2267990	2424050	2600960
A Non-financial	327343	622023	1173070	1325640	1493920	1650100	1799490	1944670	2125520	2246580	2420770	2597250
B Financial [a]	2749	4590	9051	10588	5823	4692	10876	13476	26778	21416	3282	3701
3 Households and private unincorporated enterprises	201486	313695	529672	585799	674951	739543	793562	857058	914116	949251	1024930	1120670
4 Non-profit institutions serving households	2257	4120	7384	8306	9323	10146	10759	11347	11832	12342	12999	13768
Subtotal: Domestic Factor Incomes	618129	1126660	2105160	2377420	2708540	2991950	3255360	3510870	3809760	3983580	4241520	4559900
Indirect taxes, net	103027	177624	356953	390152	460823	506002	554910	599896	627563	667573	738821	787829
A Indirect taxes	119002	212990	428590	480076	559807	619647	688426	742648	785542	836077	887047	928662
B Less: Subsidies	15975	35366	71637	89924	98984	113645	133516	142752	157979	168504	148226	140833
Consumption of fixed capital	72363	163602	346185	397229	456655	508546	551642	589380	631975	669684	712389	765389
Gross Domestic Product	793519	1467880	2808300	3164800	3626020	4006500	4361910	4700140	5069300	5320830	5692730	6113120

a) Financial of Corporate and quasi-corporate enterprises refers to net of imputed bank service charges.

1.10 Gross Domestic Product by Kind of Activity, in Current Prices

Million French francs

	1970	1975	1980	1981	1982	1983	1984	1985	1986	1987	1988	1989
1 Agriculture, hunting, forestry and fishing	...	...	119024	130943	166219	169591	175216	182310	189495	188735	188070	214360
2 Mining and quarrying	...	...	23821	29257	27897	33492	35563	40112	35657	35400	29388	30239
3 Manufacturing	...	...	679520	733461	821520	900970	956273	1033140	1120100	1143380	1224090	1304380
4 Electricity, gas and water	...	...	50308	59923	70774	87500	104907	116869	118093	122639	122917	124181
5 Construction	...	...	193609	207197	228182	234603	242001	243898	262953	279069	309245	321573
6 Wholesale and retail trade, restaurants and hotels	...	...	395042	454817	512809	579607	635917	685011	747077	798629	875391	943881
7 Transport, storage and communication	...	...	164194	184480	213208	235988	259504	289050	310759	320924	329025	346453
8 Finance, insurance, real estate and business services	...	...	472578	548366	627587	696287	782100	861137	977594	1074060	1180630	1315490
9 Community, social and personal services	...	...	121265	141147	162972	189704	211658	231374	256333	274686	305457	331047
Total, Industries	...	...	2219360	2489590	2831170	3127740	3403140	3682900	4018060	4237520	4564220	4931610
Producers of Government Services	...	...	448211	519968	613983	684995	750506	795561	845325	872398	909244	966490
Other Producers	...	...										
Subtotal	...	...	2667570	3009560	3445150	3812740	4153650	4478460	4863390	5109920	5473460	5898100
Less: Imputed bank service charge	...	...	107503	124807	147548	162385	175627	192340	223272	247379	270440	298483
Plus: Import duties [a]	...	...	6339	6778	7813	7938	8696	8904	8976	9667	10747	11231
Plus: Value added tax	...	...	242015	273274	320814	348956	375609	405281	420379	449074	479260	502452
Plus: Other adjustments	...	...	-128	-	-209	-748	-410	-163	-173	-447	-305	-178
Equals: Gross Domestic Product	...	...	2808300	3164800	3626020	4006500	4361910	4700140	5069300	5320830	5692730	6113120

a) Item 'Import duties' includes also value added tax (VAT) on products.

France

1.11 Gross Domestic Product by Kind of Activity, in Constant Prices

Million French francs

At constant prices of 1980

	1970	1975	1980	1981	1982	1983	1984	1985	1986	1987	1988	1989
1 Agriculture, hunting, forestry and fishing	119024	118226	138019	131217	137323	138441	139457	141139	140751	145242
2 Mining and quarrying	23821	22801	21913	21209	20407	21700	20745	21427	19662	19092
3 Manufacturing	679520	674873	680762	683532	671038	668425	667256	684587	709209	712818
4 Electricity, gas and water	50308	57846	56782	63797	70040	74085	77261	81346	82414	81415
5 Construction	193609	192832	192720	187519	183153	180406	186861	188115	200568	205228
6 Wholesale and retail trade, restaurants and hotels	395042	402744	412474	418314	425030	413301	443225	451443	470319	481958
7 Transport, storage and communication	164194	168903	174577	179314	184483	191249	198339	209218	229692	245335
8 Finance, insurance, real estate and business services	472578	484236	493065	490659	507082	527799	566336	594334	617672	657237
9 Community, social and personal services	121265	124590	131183	138083	146489	152209	160419	168282	172169	182407
Total, Industries	2219380	2245660	2299972	2313550	2345050	2388662	2455400	2520400	2620400	2730730
Producers of Government Services	448211	457139	472369	481600	489752	498414	505807	513000	521097	531131
Other Producers	—	—	—	—	—	—	—	—	—	—
Subtotal	2667570	2703130	2772340	2795150	2834800	2885030	2964710	3028400	3141500	3261860
Less: Imputed bank service charge	107503	110500	114653	114024	118696	131917	140611	147580	158763
Plus: Import duties [a]	6339	6388	7138	7049	7271	7626	8482	9266	10315	11142
Plus: Value added tax	242015	242405	248907	248888	254556	263514	275582	290764	306503
Plus: Other adjustments	–128	–91	–69	–158	–148	–136	–149	–136	–148	–143
Equals: Gross Domestic Product	2808300	2841330	2913660	2933900	2972460	3028380	3104640	3172660	3294850	3420600

a) Item 'Import duties' includes also value added tax (VAT) on products.

1.12 Relations Among National Accounting Aggregates

Million French francs

	1970	1975	1980	1981	1982	1983	1984	1985	1986	1987	1988	1989
Gross Domestic Product	…	1467880	2808300	3164800	3626020	4006500	4361910	4700140	5069300	5320830	5692730	6113120
Plus: Net factor income from the rest of the world	…	3299	2371	12587	10277	1980	–11727	–23505	–25679	–16608	–12467	–11520	–11969
Factor income from the rest of the world	…	11229	24668	92182	146949	170350	158672	183267	201020	175226	191913	191335	237491
Less: Factor income to the rest of the world	…	7930	22297	79656	136672	168370	170399	206772	226699	190134	184380	202855	249460
Equals: Gross National Product	…	1470260	2810880	3175690	3628000	4338410	4677460	5026920	5308370	5681210	6101150
Less: Consumption of fixed capital	…	72363	163602	341850	397229	455655	508546	551642	589380	631975	699684	712389	765389
Equals: National Income	…	724455	1306650	2477000	2777850	3171350	3486230	3787650	4085080	4420710	4638680	4968820	5335760
Plus: Net current transfers from the rest of the world	…	–1209	–7512	–5080	5082	–13521	–9755	–5340	–3248	–11822	–3597	–9699	–14051
Current transfers from the rest of the world	…	15009	68268	71518	75235	89001	98970	105188	119676	116887	133578	149530	143932
Less: Current transfers to the rest of the world	…	16218	33780	66436	80315	98756	112491	110528	122924	128709	137175	159229	157983
Equals: National Disposable Income	…	723246	1299318	2471580	2772780	3161590	3472700	3781430	4081840	4408890	4635090	4959120	5321710
Less: Final consumption	…	576217	1105670	2162590	2502250	2902250	3217650	3506610	3781410	4022320	4247080	4493440	4784660
Equals: Net Saving	…	147029	193445	317194	270525	259472	255023	275821	300424	386574	388011	466981	537050
Less: Surplus of the nation on current transactions	…	6274	12404	–16700	–25275	–76960	–31978	–485	2384	23876	–7885	–17319	–8944
Equals: Net Capital Formation	…	140755	181041	333894	295800	336432	287001	276306	298040	362698	395896	483000	545994

2.1 Government Final Consumption Expenditure by Function, in Current Prices

Million French francs

	1970	1975	1980	1981	1982	1983	1984	1985	1986	1987	1988	1989
1 General public services	…	…	…	…	…	92422	102254	118110	126831	133092	…	…
2 Defence	…	…	…	…	…	130039	139304	150224	153648	162878	…	…
3 Public order and safety	…	…	…	…	…	35186	38957	41122	43522	45821	…	…
4 Education	…	…	…	…	…	203236	222305	233901	243879	255110	…	…
5 Health	…	…	…	…	…	128282	141328	149970	156086	164467	…	…
6 Social security and welfare	…	…	…	…	…	65093	69620	73729	75293	77927	…	…
7 Housing and community amenities	…	…	…	…	…	44286	49497	54033	58538	62773	…	…
8 Recreational, cultural and religious affairs	…	…	…	…	…	22193	24232	26878	28944	30642	…	…
9 Economic services	…	…	…	…	…	56273	58912	60420	62597	67108	…	…

592

France

2.1 Government Final Consumption Expenditure by Function, in Current Prices (Continued)

Million French francs

	1970	1975	1980	1981	1982	1983	1984	1985	1986	1987	1988	1989
A Fuel and energy												
B Agriculture, forestry, fishing and hunting												
C Mining, manufacturing and construction, except fuel and energy												
D Transportation and communication						26541	27950	29158	28170	31721	...	...
E Other economic affairs						27732	30962	31262	34427	35387	...	...
10 Other functions						5124	7891	1828	1871	2301	...	...
Total Government Final Consumption Expenditure						782134	854300	910315	959509	1002120	...	...

2.3 Total Government Outlays by Function and Type

Million French francs

	Final Consumption Expenditures Total	Compensation of Employees	Other	Subsidies	Current Transfers & Property Income	Other Current Disbursements	Total Current Outlays	Gross Capital Formation	Other Capital Outlays	Total Outlays
1983										
1 General public services	92422	66787	25635	3466	38493	134381	128226	3728	150935	
2 Defence	130039	68600	61979	1978	1567	133584	1293	4544	139421	
3 Public order and safety	35186	28243	6943	420	35	35641	2302	381	38324	
4 Education	203236	175820	27416	1523	6337	211096	15348	2488	228932	
5 Health	128282	104719	23563	2730	212138	343150	10296	1644	355720	
6 Social security and welfare	65093	63167	1926	6318	665757	737168	3483	4470	745121	
7 Housing and community amenities	44286	22298	21988	22448	24223	90957	37697	14453	143107	
8 Recreation, culture and religion	22193	12123	10070	1919	5438	29550	11884	1206	42640	
9 Economic services	56273	30469	25804	46740	7851	110864	21667	13849	146380	
A Fuel and energy	...	...	...	...	...	...	...	...	...	
B Agriculture, forestry, fishing and hunting										
C Mining (except fuels), manufacturing and construction										
D Transportation and communication	26541	13056	13485	1245	14175	41141	14217	4225	59617	
E Other economic affairs	29732	17413	12319	33351	9099	68969	7450	9624	86763	
10 Other functions	5124	1261	3863	266	88855	93988	1920	5856	105360	
Total	782134	572247	209887	87423	1052024	1920380	119346	56248	2095970	
1984										
1 General public services	102254	74395	27859	4358	143277	180116	38996	3842	165135	
2 Defence	138304	72609	65695	2391	1303	142998	1484	3434	147916	
3 Public order and safety	38957	31028	7929	40	489	39486	2427	333	42246	
4 Education	222305	192449	29856	1113	6757	230175	16024	2144	248343	
5 Health	141328	114482	26846	4614	244526	390468	11260	1744	403472	
6 Social security and welfare	69920	68690	1916	714	725740	801466	3137	4133	808736	
7 Housing and community amenities	49497	24538	24959	25005	25292	99794	35470	14423	149687	
8 Recreation, culture and religion	24232	13169	11063	2510	6251	32993	13021	1261	47275	
9 Economic services	58912	33179	25733	60809	10645	130437	23222	13295	166954	
A Fuel and energy										
B Agriculture, forestry, fishing and hunting	...	...	...	...	...	...	...	...	...	
C Mining (except fuels), manufacturing and construction										
D Transportation and communication	27950	14053	13897	1245	18834	48029	14631	4325	66985	
E Other economic affairs	30962	19126	11836	4206	9400	82408	8591	8970	99969	
10 Other functions	7891	1296	6595	231	105263	113385	2066	14366	129817	
Total	854300	626251	228049	107248	1162930	2124480	125127	58975	2309580	
1985										
1 General public services	118110	82302	35808	2825	40915	161850	20327	4283	186460	
2 Defence	150324	76758	73566	2183	1393	153900	1346	5846	161092	
3 Public order and safety	41122	33035	8087	42	778	41942	2759	373	45074	
4 Education	233901	205241	28660	1601	8232	243734	17264	2176	263174	
5 Health	149270	121433	28537	4029	450534	296935	11528	2012	464074

593

France

2.3 Total Government Outlays by Function and Type (Continued)

Million French francs

		Expenditures								
		Final Consumption					Current Transfers & Disbursements	Gross Capital Formation	Other Capital Outlays	Total Outlays
		Total	Compensation of Employees	Other	Subsidies	Current Property Income	Total			

1985

6 Social security and welfare	73729	73301	428	4560	...	763282	841571	4439	3723	849733
7 Housing and community amenities	54033	27247	27882	26660	110475	42633	11004	164112		
8 Recreation, culture and religion	28678	14410	12468	2328	4154	33360	16154	925	50439	
9 Economic services	60420	34539	25881	63718	11130	135268	25250	12663	173181	
A Fuel and energy	...	...	...	...	...	...	...	...	...	
B Agriculture, forestry, fishing and hunting	...	...	...	...	...	...	...	...	...	
C Mining (except fuels), manufacturing and construction	...	...	...	...	...	...	...	...	...	
D Transportation and communication	29158	13946	15212	20258	1046	50462	16689	4574	71625	
E Other economic affairs	31262	20583	10669	43460	10084	84806	8861	8089	101556	
10 Other functions	1828	1393	435	989	120197	122711	2577	17066	142356	
Total	910315	699198	211117	241498	1098654	1275180	2295350	144277	60073	2499700

1986

1 General public services	129631	92731	36900	2729	40551	172911	21074	4151	198136	
2 Defence	153648	82287	71361	2489	1440	157577	1392	5468	164437	
3 Public order and safety	43522	43445	77	46	946	44514	3412	352	48278	
4 Education	243979	219699	24280	1995	8483	259697	20207	2624	282888	
5 Health	156086	127727	28359	3809	191321	351216	13063	1730	366009	
6 Social security and welfare	75293	76359	−1066	4922	943190	1023410	4163	4485	1032050	
7 Housing and community amenities	58538	28703	29835	28118	28471	115127	43294	15252	173673	
8 Recreation, culture and religion	28944	15453	13491	824	4702	34470	16561	1307	52338	
9 Economic services	62597	33405	29192	72938	10763	146298	26759	17613	190670	
A Fuel and energy	...	...	...	...	...	...	...	...	...	
B Agriculture, forestry, fishing and hunting	...	...	...	...	...	...	...	...	...	
C Mining (except fuels), manufacturing and construction	...	...	...	...	...	...	...	...	...	
D Transportation and communication	28170	12804	15366	20365	1127	49662	17302	4656	71620	
E Other economic affairs	34427	20601	13826	52573	9636	96636	9457	12957	119050	
10 Other functions	1871	1430	441	755	128224	130850	2510	15728	149088	
Total	959609	712439	247070	118625	1358090	2436230	2436230	152435	68710	2657370

1987

1 General public services	133092	89418	43674	2293	44688	180073	22274	9247	211994	
2 Defence	162878	83516	79362	2644	2436	167956	1690	−778	168870	
3 Public order and safety	48521	35604	10217	44	1161	47026	3839	382	51247	
4 Education	255110	225623	29487	2318	9844	267272	20135	3324	290731	
5 Health	164467	135140	29327	4430	328403	497300	13045	2006	512351	
6 Social security and welfare	77927	80118	−2191	4981	853946	936734	5204	4177	946115	
7 Housing and community amenities	62773	30339	32434	25512	129679	47073	17739	185491		
8 Recreation, culture and religion	30642	15853	14789	498	5332	36472	15158	3221	54851	
9 Economic services	67108	35062	32046	74087	11608	152803	29620	16969	199292	
A Fuel and energy	...	...	...	...	...	...	...	...	...	
B Agriculture, forestry, fishing and hunting	...	...	...	...	...	...	...	...	...	
C Mining (except fuels), manufacturing and construction	...	...	...	...	...	...	...	...	...	
D Transportation and communication	31721	14879	16842	20930	1210	53861	18984	4936	77781	
E Other economic affairs	35387	20183	15204	53157	10398	98942	10636	11933	121511	
10 Other functions	2301	1578	723	795	1294144	1322240	2677	16299	151216	
Total	1002120	732251	269868	117482	1418960	2538660	161115	72486	2772160	

France

2.5 Private Final Consumption Expenditure by Type and Purpose, in Current Prices

Million French francs

Final Consumption Expenditure of Resident Households

	1970	1975	1980	1981	1982	1983	1984	1985	1986	1987	1988	1989
1 Food, beverages and tobacco	118874	201667	351554	403442	467798	510629	558718	592432	625560	646936	673436	714708
A Food	95980	164303	288155	330669	377700	416615	458512	486534	509730	528684	548684	581848
B Non-alcoholic beverages	2326	4158	7225	8515	10317	11760	12874	14047	15430	16265	17099	19109
C Alcoholic beverages	13706	23411	36925	43865	49751	56389	59598	64017	65533	67963	71492	
D Tobacco	6889	9795	17549	20393	25030	28125	30943	32253	34683	36462	39696	42459
2 Clothing and footwear a	43722	72487	128714	138236	162714	185080	198281	218764	226518	232116	239456	
3 Gross rent, fuel and power	69599	135254	287562	333610	380208	436138	491281	546046	571375	604318	644320	695282
A Fuel and power	16669	35392	85641	99619	111361	128364	144445	161183	148789	142178	133240	137218
B Other	53317	99862	201921	233991	268847	307774	346836	384863	422586	462140	511080	558064
4 Furniture, furnishings and household equipment and operation	46712	89355	156976	177613	202667	216449	239196	254963	267567	283229	298165	
A Household operation	14438	26405	45594	51602	60241	71441	76968	80124	83836	88515	93358	
B Other	32274	62960	111382	125111	142426	150131	154586	174845	183731	194714	204807	
5 Medical care and health expenses	32627	67092	127284	148094	169808	195354	225606	246474	270716	285316	313027	340325
6 Transport and communication	61211	123889	273642	317648	378609	416585	444418	482204	501845	544600	575810	618337
A Personal transport equipment	13318	28144	66340	74231	94749	102777	99827	105787	124556	140071	149129	162900
B Other	47893	95745	207302	243417	283860	313808	344591	376417	377289	404529	426681	455437
7 Recreational, entertainment, education and cultural services	31618	61991	119956	137310	160177	173581	188423	201960	220494	236089	252968	270707
A Education	2211	3718	6115	7218	8131	9956	11402	12968	14467	15780	17518	18708
B Other	29407	58273	113841	130092	152046	163625	177021	188992	206027	220309	235468	251992
8 Miscellaneous goods and services	53404	107258	216562	252586	291971	325283	351141	375609	403879	439430	470835	511148
A Personal care a	6699	13286	24838	29343	34108	39006	43216	47960	53063	58217	63360	69358
B Expenditures in restaurants, cafes and hotels	28006	53015	105639	123443	143984	161007	172931	187816	200733	214623	230174	251045
C Other	18403	40957	86085	99800	113879	125270	134994	143833	155583	166690	176401	190745
Total Final Consumption Expenditure in the Domestic Market by Households, of which:	458154	859003	1654250	1905640	2202040	2445950	2667730	2888470	3071100	3250770	3445760	3688120
A Durable goods	33266	70846	147062	160014	201186	211432	209656	219514	250825	273301	289628	314922
B Semi-durable goods	68796	156064	275165	309696	354697	385612	411866	438835	472428	493622	513906	537949
C Non-durable goods	183323	331141	620929	717351	825359	916032	1008810	1092040	1113120	1148300	1188560	1266910
D Services	155769	300962	611032	717278	820008	932871	1037580	1138070	1234370	1334970	1449670	1568690
Plus: Direct purchases abroad by resident households	6009	13082	25360	31305	33961	32865	37482	41421	45113	51328	58000	61919
Less: Direct purchases in the domestic market by non-resident households	6965	14291	34538	39036	45664	54664	60045	71496	66995	70992	81418	104011
Equals: Final Consumption Expenditure of Resident Households	457196	857794	1645070	1897910	2190340	2424140	2639170	2858390	3049520	3231110	3422340	3650030
Plus: Final Consumption Expenditure of Private Non-profit Organisations Serving Households	2381	4466	8239	10311	11404	12134	12704	13288	13846	13846¹	14553	15433
Equals: Private Final Consumption Expenditure	459577	862260	1653310	1907220	2200820	2435550	2651870	2871100	3062810	3244960	3436890	3665460

a) Personal effects are included in item 'Clothing and footwear'.

2.6 Private Final Consumption Expenditure by Type and Purpose, in Constant Prices

Million French francs

At constant prices of 1980

	1970	1975	1980	1981	1982	1983	1984	1985	1986	1987	1988	1989
1 Food, beverages and tobacco	292399	322057	351554	354602	360305	363311	369402	374428	380978	388136	396029	403360
A Food	242416	262437	288155	290808	295324	297428	303066	306667	311833	318401	324771	329373
B Non-alcoholic beverages	5458	6916	7225	7468	8137	8442	8635	8893	9346	9549	10247	11896
C Alcoholic beverages	32199	37383	38625	38532	38659	38729	38316	38417	39328	39331	40460	40895
D Tobacco	12326	15321	17549	17794	18185	18712	19385	20451	20471	20655	20551	21106
2 Clothing and footwear a	106316	116432	127414	124798	130135	130524	127675	128712	130997	129280	128170	128608
3 Gross rent, fuel and power	191911	236698	287562	289260	294577	319267	306606	319267²	333269	355612	361080	371575
A Fuel and power	65441	72468	85641	80626	79310	82720	84669	90893	93341	94427	89408	90107

France

2.6 Private Final Consumption Expenditure by Type and Purpose, in Constant Prices (Continued)

Million French francs

	1970	1975	1980	1981	1982	1983	1984	1985	1986	1987	1988	1989
						At constant prices of 1980						
B Other	124670	164170	201921	208964	215267	223916	227798	242376	252225	261385	271681	281468
4 Furniture, furnishings and household equipment and operation	114341	138885	156976	157270	161390	157583	153303	153569	157412	160329	165532	170569
A Household operation	44184	44221	45594	44650	45547	45427	45455	45954	46091	46891	46849	48648
B Other	70157	94564	111382	112620	115843	112166	107848	107615	111351	113438	117883	120721
5 Medical care and health expenses	76154	103529	127284	134056	141635	148943	160906	171655	183496	193287	203021	219302
6 Transport and communication	167602	216504	273642	281996	299949	302188	294481	298476	308255	324671	337842	349955
A Personal transport equipment	36461	46769	66340	66997	73744	77366	77375	69330	68924	75784	82460	91522
B Other	131141	169735	207302	215252	225252	224583	224813	227151	229552	235041	242211	251413	258433
7 Recreational, entertainment, and cultural services	76111	94591	119956	124053	131036	131038	132696	135004	142217	148345	159198	169513
A Education	6212	6544	6115	6327	6167	6830	7247	7836	8310	8576	8993	9106
B Other	69899	88047	113841	117726	124869	124208	125449	127168	133907	139769	150205	160404
8 Miscellaneous goods and services	147008	185432	216652	219412	227460	228810	231990	239846	247843	253222	260499	271291
A Personal care a	16939	22315	24838	24678	25562	26548	27468	28897	30604	31778	33230	34951
B Expenditures in restaurants, cafes and hotels	78995	93144	105639	106599	109901	110082	110276	112651	114887	114991	117302	121117
C Other	51074	69973	86085	88135	92180	92244	86298	102352	106453	109967	115223	
Total Final Consumption Expenditure in the Domestic Market by Households, of which	1171840	1414070	1654250	1685780	1746490	1769040	1791420	1834000	1899330	1940800	2012380	2084170
A Durable goods	74664	106957	147062	151367	168169	164185	153475	154169	168722	179234	192432	203845
B Semi-durable goods	212458	250017	275165	279791	291627	288064	283856	282131	287767	288764	292296	297716
C Non-durable goods	477520	549185	620991	625535	630021	647975	663927	680927	698900	714060	730119	750658
D Services	407200	509909	611032	629084	650670	669799	690423	716940	743945	766518	797533	831954
Plus: Direct purchases abroad by resident households	15149	21454	25360	27704	26931	27779	25181	26277	27839	30633	33639	36797
Less: Direct purchases in the domestic mark't by non-resident households	17565	23437	34538	34545	36210	39553	44367	45352	41154	42365	47217	58057
Equals: Final Consumption Expenditure of Resident Households	1169430	1412090	1645070	1678940	1737210	1757270	1772230	1814930	1886020	1937350	1998800	2062910
Final Consumption Expenditure of Private Non-profit Institutions Serving Households												
Equals: Final Consumption Expenditure of Private Non-profit Organisations Serving Households	6410	7384	8239	8289	8322	8307	8218	8230	8272	8539	8788	8976
Private Final Consumption Expenditure	1175840	1419470	1653310	1687230	1745530	1765580	1780450	1823160	1894290	1945890	2007590	2071890

a) Personal effects are included in item 'Clothing and footwear'.

2.9 Gross Capital Formation by Kind of Activity of Owner, ISIC Major Divisions, in Current Prices

Million French francs

	1980			1981			1982			1983		
	Total Gross Capital Formation	Increase in Stocks	Gross Fixed Capital Formation	Total Gross Capital Formation	Increase in Stocks	Gross Fixed Capital Formation	Total Gross Capital Formation	Increase in Stocks	Gross Fixed Capital Formation	Total Gross Capital Formation	Increase in Stocks	Gross Fixed Capital Formation
					All Producers								
1 Agriculture, hunting, fishing and forestry	24933	1483	23450	27370	980	26390	36730	6232	30498	35348	3830	31518
2 Mining and quarrying	1663	487	1176	1916	815	1101	998	-468	1466	1200	-478	1678
3 Manufacturing	113129	13994	99135	88871	-14063	102934	106876	-2439	109315	97962	-17689	115651
4 Electricity, gas and water	44507	5681	38826	48739	7085	41654	53194	4957	48237	54548	4083	50465
5 Construction	21821	625	21196	18845	-2378	21223	20365	-2909	23274	20187	-3040	23227
6 Wholesale and retail trade, restaurants and hotels	55870	12693	43177	46181	-3723	49904	68670	12462	56208	66115	7180	58935
7 Transport, storage and communication	60394	-183	60577	65582	1800	63782	66995	-403	69398	68079	-1110	69189
8 Finance, insurance, real estate and business services	265769	-457	266226	290635	1453	289182	311852	1041	310811	319813	-6494	326307
9 Community, social and personal services	12860	-5	12865	13194	-249	13443	19224	-187	19411	22496	-70	22566
Total Industries	600946	4318	596628	601333	-8280	609613	686904	18286	668618	685748	-13788	699536
Producers of Government Services	77682	8	77674	90054	779	89275	104334	523	103811	107786	-266	108052
Private Non-Profit Institutions Serving Households	1451	-	1451	1642	-	1642	1849	-	1849	2013	-	2013
Total	680079	4326	645753	693029	-7501	700530	793087	18809	774278	795547	-14054	809601

France

2.9 Gross Capital Formation by Kind of Activity of Owner, ISIC Major Divisions, in Current Prices

Million French francs

	1984			1985			1986			1987
	Total Gross Capital Formation	Gross Fixed Capital Formation	Increase in Stocks	Total Gross Capital Formation	Gross Fixed Capital Formation	Increase in Stocks	Total Gross Capital Formation	Gross Fixed Capital Formation	Increase in Stocks	Total Gross Capital Formation
All Producers										
1 Agriculture, hunting, fishing and forestry	26951	30137	-3186	29756	30775	-1019	31698	29726	1972	29578
2 Mining and quarrying	1338	-447	1785	1351	1405	-54	1141	-	1141	974
3 Manufacturing	101960	-16135	125295	130890	-14860	125298	145344	150478	-8208	156686	173751
4 Electricity, gas and water	50790	1525	49265	49265	48338	916	51022	51766	2807	48959	47064
5 Construction	21608	-877	22485	22485	28834	492	23342	26427	2882	23545	24970
6 Wholesale and retail trade, restaurants and hotels	76431	11873	64558	74866	5616	69052	66985	14792	81893	82793
7 Transport, storage and communication	70988	97	70891	77733	-893	78626	78724	-46	78770	86291
8 Finance, insurance, real estate and business services	330741	-4232	334973	339546	-10023	349569	382690	-40	382730	408753
9 Community, social and personal services	24052	-150	24202	25190	9	25184	32040	898	31172	33583
Total Industries	712059	-11532	723591	754696	-19623	774319	851649	15027	836622	877757
Producers of Government Services	1137747	-884	114631	130483	1752	128731	140680	2129	138551		146032
Private Non-Profit Institutions Serving Households	2142	-	2142	2241	-	2241	2344	-	2344	2444
Total	827948	-12416	840364	887420	-17871	905291	994673	17156	977517	1046230

	1988			1989
	Total Gross Capital Formation	Gross Fixed Capital Formation	Increase in Stocks	Total Gross Capital Formation
All Producers				
1 Agriculture, hunting, fishing and forestry	34611			38945
2 Mining and quarrying	1064			1111
3 Manufacturing	198075			220540
4 Electricity, gas and water	47773			46968
5 Construction	28930			31919
6 Wholesale and retail trade, restaurants and hotels	103791			113000
7 Transport, storage and communication	97660			112192
8 Finance, insurance, real estate and business services	450570			480877
9 Community, social and personal services	38382			45498
Total Industries	1000860			1091070
Producers of Government Services	160988			177687
Private Non-Profit Institutions Serving Households	2568			2723
Total	1164410			1271480

2.11 Gross Fixed Capital Formation by Kind of Activity of Owner, ISIC Divisions, in Current Prices

Million French francs

	1970	1975	1980	1981	1982	1983	1984	1985	1986	1987	1988	1989
All Producers												
1 Agriculture, hunting, forestry and fishing	6784	14536	23450	26390	30498	31518	30137	30775	29726	29578	34611	38945
2 Mining and quarrying	247	295	1176	1101	1466	1678	1785	1405	1141	974	1064	1111
A Coal mining	247	295	1176	1101	1466	1678	1785	1405	1141	974	1064	1111
B Crude petroleum and natural gas production	...	...	...	...	...	...	...	...	...	...	...	...
C Metal ore mining	...	...	...	...	...	...	...	...	...	...	...	...
D Other mining	...	...	...	...	...	...	...	...	...	...	...	...

France

2.11 Gross Fixed Capital Formation by Kind of Activity of Owner, ISIC Divisions, in Current Prices
(Continued)

Million French francs

	1970	1975	1980	1981	1982	1983	1984	1985	1986	1987	1988	1989
3 Manufacturing	37880	50566	99135	102934	109315	115651	125295	145344	158686	173751	198075	225540
A Manufacturing of food, beverages and tobacco	5101	7274	12986	15075	16916	18108	20221	22389	21919	22952	25780	28052
B Textile, wearing apparel and leather industries	2407	2536	4237	3484	5053	5869	6363	7207	6893	7225	8235	9520
C Manufacture of wood, and wood products, including furniture	1081	1955	3977	3714	4049	4283	5145	5363	5812	5827	7202	7994
D Manufacture of paper and paper products, printing and publishing	1857	2488	5323	4871	5226	6131	6459	8455	12697	15832	19613	22735
E Manufacture of chemicals and chemical petroleum, coal, rubber and plastic products	9465	10631	21905	22250	22408	23048	23353	28965	30708	33504	37802	41545
F Manufacture of non-metallic mineral products except products of petroleum and coal	3019	3089	6669	6903	6663	6702	6718	6650	8145	8885	11970	12413
G Basic metal industries	3999	5840	8784	8991	7858	8990	11927	13307	14295	17580	15645	17442
H Manufacture of fabricated metal products, machinery and equipment	10951	16753	35254	37646	41242	42520	43309	53008	58217	61946	70628	80839
I Other manufacturing industries	...	...	...	...	...	...	...	...	...	...	...	...
4 Electricity, gas and water	7971	15729	38826	41654	48237	50465	51022	48959	47064	47773	49866	
5 Construction	7030	11195	21196	21223	23274	23227	22485	23342	23545	24970	28830	31919
6 Wholesale and retail trade, restaurants and hotels	12618	22468	43177	49900	56208	59835	64558	69052	81893	92793	103791	113000
A Wholesale and retail trade	10484	18480	34094	39198	44151	45943	48912	52339	60728	69455	77146	83506
B Restaurants and hotels	2134	3988	9083	10706	12057	13992	15646	16713	21165	23338	26645	29494
7 Transport, storage and communication	13567	33831	60577	63782	68198	70891	78526	78770	86291	97660	112192	
A Transport and storage	9410	27718	37859	41252	45250	44388	44923	49579	52211	60406	72474	80237
B Communication	4157	12113	22588	22530	24148	24801	26918	29047	25559	25885	31955	31955
8 Finance, insurance, real estate and business services	77560	151019	266226	289182	310811	326307	334973	349669	382730	408753	450570	480877
A Financial institutions	2376	4773	7660	8795	10022	12029	15512	16714	18546	21083	22849	26162
B Insurance	298	862	1390	1879	1844	1334	2343	3120	4484	4760	6262	9846
C Real estate and business services	74886	145384	257176	278508	298945	312944	317118	329735	359700	382910	421459	444699
Real estate except dwellings	5641	9814	18552	24238	26905	27831	27806	36130	45569	50261	57654	58099
Dwellings	69245	135570	238624	254270	272040	285113	289312	293605	314131	332649	363805	386770
9 Community, social and personal services	2924	5392	12865	13443	19411	22566	24202	25184	31172	33583	38382	45498
Total Industries	166681	305031	555982	609613	699639	723591	777319	836622	897757	980980	1091070	
Producers of Government Services	25972	48497	77674	89275	103811	108052	114631	127131	138551	145032	160988	177687
Private Non-Profit Institutions Serving Households	384	782	1451	1642	1849	2013	2142	2241	2344	2444	2568	2723
Total	192937	354310	645753	700530	777278	809601	840364	905291	977517	1044230	1144410	1271480

2.12 Gross Fixed Capital Formation by Kind of Activity of Owner, ISIC Divisions, in Constant Prices

Million French francs

At constant prices of 1980

	1970	1975	1980	1981	1982	1983	1984	1985	1986	1987	1988	1989
					All Producers							
1 Agriculture, hunting, forestry and fishing	17968	23878	23450	23406	24094	22814	20333	20195	18452	17272	20028	22416
2 Mining and quarrying	615	495	1176	999	1190	1257	1244	938	737	617	642	641
A Coal mining	615	495	1176	999	1190	1257	1244	938	737	617	642	641
B Crude petroleum and natural gas production	...	...	...	...	...	...	...	...	...	...	...	...
C Metal ore mining	...	...	...	...	...	...	...	...	...	...	...	...
D Other mining	...	...	...	...	...	...	...	...	...	...	...	...

France

2.12 Gross Fixed Capital Formation by Kind of Activity of Owner, ISIC Divisions, in Constant Prices
(Continued)

Million French francs	1970	1975	1980	1981	1982	1983	1984	1985	1986	1987	1988	1989
At constant prices of 1980												
3 Manufacturing	94815	82440	99135	92109	86710	84371	85433	94312	99177	106037	118019	126817
A Manufacturing of food, beverages and tobacco	13013	11898	12986	13471	13457	13256	13548	14693	13796	14096	15411	16216
B Textile, wearing apparel and leather industries	6024	4115	4237	3112	3992	4262	4306	4647	4282	4402	5482	5450
C Manufacture of wood, and wood products, including furniture	2789	3210	3977	3301	3187	3118	3520	3505	3624	3523	4242	4569
D Manufacture of paper and paper products, printing and publishing	4533	4017	5223	4355	4142	4455	4381	5472	7914	9647	11648	12999
E Manufacture of chemicals and chemical products, petroleum, coal, rubber and plastic products	23920	17480	21905	19967	17850	16932	16032	18900	19331	20578	22688	24101
F Manufacture of non-metallic mineral products except products of petroleum and coal	7331	5008	6669	6225	5271	4941	4664	4393	5141	5463	7168	7155
G Basic metal industries	9973	8447	8784	8008	6280	6007	8163	8663	8962	10690	9242	9933
H Manufacture of fabricated metal products, machinery and equipment	27232	27265	32554	33610	32551	30800	29219	34039	36127	37638	42138	46394
I Other manufacturing industries	...	...	...	...	...	...	...	...	...	...	...	...
4 Electricity, gas and water	21090	25988	38826	37570	36019	37657	34610	34194	31924	27778	26512	28215
5 Construction	18598	18613	21196	19212	18842	17269	15752	15641	15104	15587	17611	18645
6 Wholesale and retail trade, restaurants and hotels	33192	37576	44989	44177	45303	43728	45171	46019	52587	58040	63451	69918
A Wholesale and retail trade	27498	30863	34094	35336	35577	34041	34151	34784	38969	43391	47110	49402
B Restaurants and hotels	5694	6713	9008	6853	9726	9687	11020	11235	13618	14649	16341	17516
7 Transport, storage and communication	33838	55905	60577	57780	55962	51232	49945	52715	49964	53590	55884	65301
A Transport and storage	25151	37206	37289	37181	36317	32666	30870	33231	33466	34337	41188	46147
B Communication	8987	18699	23288	20599	19645	18566	19075	19484	16498	19253	14696	19154
8 Finance, insurance, real estate and business services	209188	254810	266226	262911	251968	244179	244482	252917	233045	235690	260287	290624
A Financial institutions	4718	6737	7660	7809	8054	8726	6949	10428	11437	12907	13676	15173
B Insurance	783	1398	1390	1698	1483	971	1610	2117	2977	3099	3946	4836
C Real estate and business services	203687	246675	257176	253404	242431	234482	235917	240387	218605	219684	242681	270615
Real estate except dwellings	12703	15322	18552	21592	21526	19866	17977	22356	28875	32154	36542	35416
9 Dwellings	190984	231353	238624	231812	221116	214916	204940	200689	207467	212127	225221	235199
Community, social and personal services	7578	9888	12865	12160	15565	16726	16748	16705	20244	21361	24319	28179
Total Industries	436882	508591	566629	551136	538653	519233	503702	516309	539045	562569	611651	647756
Producers of Government Services	66516	79582	77674	80923	84697	81702	81820	80880	92554	94976	102270	109407
Private Non-Profit Institutions Serving Households	923	1235	1451	1497	1518	1537	1525	1548	1569	1594	1647	1708
Total	504321	589408	645753	633556	624868	602590	586929	605937	633168	659139	715565	758871

2.17 Exports and Imports of Goods and Services, Detail

Million French francs	1970	1975	1980	1981	1982	1983	1984	1985	1986	1987	1988	1989
Exports of Goods and Services												
1 Exports of merchandise, f.o.b.	99401	226420	488877	576389	631842	720442	845218	901379	860303	867740	992606	1136360
2 Transport and communication	10218	17655	36946	42535	45247	48150	51029	55823	49486	49738	52807	57938
3 Insurance service charges	367	563	1001	1233	1205	1467	1524	1502	1946	2622	2505	2485
4 Other commodities	8477	20870	43060	55089	66393	75930	89512	93730	95665	93065	92608	124336
5 Adjustments of merchandise exports to change-of-ownership basis	...	...	...	...	...	...	...	...	...	...	...	...
6 Direct purchases in the domestic market by non-residential households	6965	14291	34538	39036	45664	54669	66045	71496	66995	70992	81418	104014
7 Direct purchases in the domestic market by extraterritorial bodies	...	...	...	...	...	...	...	...	...	...	...	...
Total Exports of Goods and Services	125428	279799	604422	714282	790351	900668	1053330	1123390	1074400	1103190	1221940	1425130
Imports of Goods and Services												
1 Imports of merchandise, c.i.f.	106296	232778	576505	663485	768258	808900	914542	970814	893847	952251	1063870	1229350

France

2.17 Exports and Imports of Goods and Services, Detail
(Continued)

Million French francs

	1970	1975	1980	1981	1982	1983	1984	1985	1986	1987	1988	1989
2 Adjustments of merchandise imports to change-of-ownership basis	...	...	...	...	...	...	...	...	...	...	...	...
3 Other transport and communication	3799	6116	13693	18347	20718	23034	24048	27398	26416	27358	29344	31268
4 Other insurance service charges	421	456	873	1246	1473	2307	2625	1744	2614	4570	6091	6272
5 Other commodities	4721	9822	22360	30371	35126	40282	46271	51242	53799	59501	60737	75248
6 Direct purchases abroad by government	...	...	...	...	...	...	...	...	...	...	...	...
7 Direct purchases abroad by resident households	6007	13082	25360	31305	33961	32865	37482	41421	45113	51328	58000	65919
Total Imports of Goods and Services	121244	262254	638791	744754	859536	907388	1024970	1092620	1021790	1095010	1218040	1408060
Balance of Goods and Services	4184	17545	-34369	-30472	-69185	-6730	28360	31311	52306	8179	3900	17076
Total Imports and Balance of Goods and Services	125428	279799	604422	714282	790351	900658	1053330	1123930	1074100	1103190	1221940	1425130

3.11 General Government Production Account: Total and Subsectors

Million French francs

	1980					1981				
	Total General Government	Central Government	State or Provincial Government	Local Government	Social Security Funds	Total General Government	Central Government	State or Provincial Government	Local Government	Social Security Funds
Gross Output										
1 Sales	...	...	...	...	...	...	...	...	...	...
2 Services produced for own use	509274	309358	...	99598	100318	595028	357959	...	119110	117959
3 Own account fixed capital formation	97928	39066	...	39250	19612	113795	45828	...	45360	22607
Gross Output	607202	348424	...	138848	119930	708823	403787	...	164470	140566
Gross Input										
Intermediate Consumption	169058	97068	...	41888	30102	200034	114776	...	49594	35664
Subtotal: Value Added	438144	251356	...	96960	89828	508789	289011	...	114876	104902
1 Indirect taxes, net	7731	4293	...	-689	4127	9899	5357	...	-589	5131
A Indirect taxes	10474	5744	...	603	4127	13281	7432	...	718	5131
B Less: Subsidies	2743	1451	...	1292	-	3382	2075	...	1307	-
2 Consumption of fixed capital	44431	12968	...	27418	4045	51804	14679	...	32278	4847
3 Compensation of employees	387179	234387	...	71136	81656	448738	269241	...	84573	94924
4 Net Operating surplus	-1197	-292	...	-905	-	-1652	-266	...	-1386	-
Gross Input	607202	348424	...	138848	119930	708823	403787	...	164470	140566

	1982					1983				
	Total General Government	Central Government	State or Provincial Government	Local Government	Social Security Funds	Total General Government	Central Government	State or Provincial Government	Local Government	Social Security Funds
Gross Output										
1 Sales	...	...	...	...	...	...	...	...	...	...
2 Services produced for own use	701299	417906	...	142874	140519	782134	460012	...	165091	157031
3 Own account fixed capital formation	132073	53130	...	52928	26015	150960	60214	...	59963	30783
Gross Output	833372	471036	...	195802	166534	933094	520226	...	225054	187814
Gross Input										
Intermediate Consumption	234612	133243	...	58569	42800	263411	146920	...	67212	49279
Subtotal: Value Added	598760	337793	...	137233	123734	669683	373306	...	157842	138535
1 Indirect taxes, net	13542	7907	...	-584	6219	13909	7286	...	-730	7353
A Indirect taxes	16468	9407	...	842	6219	19098	10761	...	984	7353
B Less: Subsidies	2926	1500	...	1426	-	5189	3475	...	1714	-
2 Consumption of fixed capital	60695	16637	...	38319	5739	68303	18080	...	43657	6566
3 Compensation of employees	528155	315233	...	101146	111776	588464	347381	...	116467	124616
4 Net Operating surplus	-3632	-1984	...	-1648	-	-993	559	...	-1552	-
Gross Input	833372	471036	...	195802	166534	933094	520226	...	225054	187814

France

3.11 General Government Production Account: Total and Subsectors

Million French francs

	1984					1985				
	Total General Government	Central Government	State or Provincial Government	Local Government	Social Security Funds	Total General Government	Central Government	State or Provincial Government	Local Government	Social Security Funds
Gross Output										
1 Sales	...	...	...	...	...	...	...	...	...	...
2 Services produced for own use	854300	498886	...	183409	172005	910315	527508	...	199878	182929
3 Own account fixed capital formation	169136	66396	...	67825	34915	178881	68932	...	73906	36043
Gross Output	1023440	565282	...	251234	206920	1089200	596440	...	273784	218972
Gross Input										
Intermediate Consumption	289571	161237	...	74790	53544	313564	173702	...	82114	57748
Subtotal: Value Added	733865	404045	...	176444	153376	775632	422738	...	191670	161224
1 Indirect taxes, net	17379	7962	...	-649	10066	8475	834	...	-1095	8736
A Indirect taxes	22607	11402	...	1139	10066	16438	6424	...	1278	8736
B Less: Subsidies	5228	3440	...	1788	-	7963	5590	...	2373	-
2 Consumption of fixed capital	75808	19659	...	48763	7386	82842	21035	...	53730	8077
3 Compensation of employees	643002	377338	...	129740	135924	687747	403261	...	140075	144411
4 Net Operating surplus	-2324	-914	...	-1410	-	-3432	-2392	...	-1040	-
Gross Input	1023440	565282	...	251234	206920	1089200	596440	...	273784	218972

	1986					1987				
	Total General Government	Central Government	State or Provincial Government	Local Government	Social Security Funds	Total General Government	Central Government	State or Provincial Government	Local Government	Social Security Funds
Gross Output										
1 Sales	...	...	...	...	...	...	...	...	...	...
2 Services produced for own use	959509	546752	...	222347	190410	1002120	568368	...	234144	199607
3 Own account fixed capital formation	188450	53732	...	95240	39478	205496	62372	...	101752	41372
Gross Output	1147960	600484	...	317587	229888	1207620	630740	...	335896	240979
Gross Input										
Intermediate Consumption	323592	159925	...	103667	60000	351247	178586	...	110560	62101
Subtotal: Value Added	824367	440559	...	213920	169888	856368	452154	...	225336	178878
1 Indirect taxes, net	4243	-3971	...	-1227	9441	7468	-1092	...	-1261	9821
A Indirect taxes	16896	5968	...	1487	9441	17705	6330	...	1554	9821
B Less: Subsidies	12653	9939	...	2714	-	10237	7422	...	2815	-
2 Consumption of fixed capital	88614	21050	...	59015	8549	94907	22115	...	63781	9011
3 Compensation of employees	730941	422429	...	156614	151898	751054	427176	...	163832	160046
4 Net Operating surplus	569	1051	...	-482	-	2939	3955	...	-1016	-
Gross Input	1147960	600484	...	317587	229888	1207620	630740	...	335896	240979

	1988					1989				
	Total General Government	Central Government	State or Provincial Government	Local Government	Social Security Funds	Total General Government	Central Government	State or Provincial Government	Local Government	Social Security Funds
Gross Output										
1 Sales	...	...	...	...	...	...	...	...	...	...
2 Services produced for own use	1056540	600955	...	246755	208832	1119200	629123	...	264217	225857
3 Own account fixed capital formation	221763	68191	...	110071	43501	234745	72765	...	116586	45394
Gross Output	1278310	669146	...	356826	252333	1353940	701888	...	380803	271251
Gross Input										
Intermediate Consumption	387375	202754	...	119164	65457	405670	209281	...	127012	69377
Subtotal: Value Added	890930	466392	...	237662	186876	948272	492607	...	253791	201874
1 Indirect taxes, net	9735	1224	...	-1509	10020	13795	4577	...	-1591	10809
A Indirect taxes	18113	6438	...	1655	10020	19841	7284	...	1748	10809
B Less: Subsidies	8378	5214	...	3164	-	6046	2707	...	3339	-
2 Consumption of fixed capital	101657	23276	...	68889	9492	109968	24819	...	75025	10124
3 Compensation of employees	779194	441086	...	170744	167364	825540	463739	...	180860	180941
4 Net Operating surplus	344	806	...	-462	-	-1031	-528	...	-503	-
Gross Input	1278310	669146	...	356826	252333	1353940	701888	...	380803	271251

France

3.12 General Government Income and Outlay Account: Total and Subsectors

Million French francs

	1980					1981				
	Total General Government	Central Government	State or Provincial Government	Local Government	Social Security Funds	Total General Government	Central Government	State or Provincial Government	Local Government	Social Security Funds
Receipts										
1 Operating surplus	-1197	-292	...	-905	-	-1652	-266	...	-1386	-
2 Property and entrepreneurial income	25696	10804	...	4127	10765	37063	17541	...	5044	14478
A Withdrawals from public quasi-corporations	817	817	...	-	-	1088	1088	...	-	-
B Interest	18164	6368	...	1792	10004	24384	8393	...	2367	13624
C Dividends	5372	3111	...	1500	761	9483	6869	...	1760	854
D Net land rent and royalties	1343	508	...	835	-	2108	1191	...	917	-
3 Taxes, fees and contributions	1150940	567368	...	83499	500068	1296940	638925	...	95697	562320
A Indirect taxes	410607	357006	...	47731	5870	457252	395345	...	54813	7094
B Direct taxes	236244	200951	...	35293	-	273399	233010	...	40389	-
Income	177031	177031	...	-	-	203187	203187	...	-	-
Other	59213	23920	...	35293	-	70212	29823	...	40389	-
C Social security contributions	500068	5870	...	-	494198	562383	7157	...	-	555226
D Fees, fines and penalties	4016	3541	...	475	-	3908	3413	...	495	-
4 Other current transfers	74852	7857	...	77588	68034	95927	17012	...	90764	82962
A Casualty insurance claims	266	-	...	204	62	283	-	...	217	66
B Transfers from other government subsectors	...	-52932	...	71103	60456	...	-62043	...	82574	74280
C Transfers from the rest of the world	4353	4038	...	-	315	4639	4321	...	-	318
D Other transfers, except imputed	19869	9957	...	4044	5868	32939	20889	...	5364	6686
E Imputed unfunded employee pension and welfare contributions	50364	46794	...	2237	1333	58066	53845	...	2609	1612
Total Current Receipts	1250290	585737	...	164309	578867	1428280	673212	...	190119	659760
Disbursements										
1 Government final consumption expenditure	509274	309358	...	99598	100318	595028	357959	...	119110	117959
2 Property income	41312	22144	...	17715	1453	62565	39610	...	21288	1667
A Interest	41251	22083	...	17715	1453	62534	39579	...	21288	1667
B Net land rent and royalties	61	61	...	-	-	31	31	...	-	-
3 Subsidies	54407	48741	...	4512	1154	70422	63363	...	5135	1924
4 Other current transfers	584378	184236	...	30916	447853	698524	219587	...	35717	538031
A Casualty insurance premiums, net	583	8	...	441	134	624	11	...	471	142
B Transfers to other government subsectors	...	71850	...	4553	2224	...	87257	...	4742	2812
C Social security benefits	439730	-	...	-	439730	527268	-	...	-	527268
D Social assistance grants	45387	31336	...	14051	-	53221	36886	...	16335	-
E Unfunded employee pension and welfare benefits	52794	49224	...	2237	1333	61395	57174	...	2609	1612
F Transfers to private non-profit institutions serving households	2829	927	...	1527	375	3912	1673	...	1755	484
G Other transfers n.e.c.	23160	12533	...	8107	2520	29639	16691	...	9805	3143
H Transfers to the rest of the world	19895	18358	...	-	1537	22465	19895	...	-	2570
Net saving	60915	21258	...	11568	28089	1741	-7307	...	8869	179
Total Current Disbursements and Net Saving	1250290	585737	...	164309	578867	1428280	673212	...	190119	659760

	1982					1983				
	Total General Government	Central Government	State or Provincial Government	Local Government	Social Security Funds	Total General Government	Central Government	State or Provincial Government	Local Government	Social Security Funds
Receipts										
1 Operating surplus	-3632	-1984	...	-1648	-	-993	559	...	-1552	-
2 Property and entrepreneurial income	47143	25590	...	5783	15770	54382	29937	...	6767	17678
A Withdrawals from public quasi-corporations	3020	3020	...	-	-	8139	8139	...	-	-
B Interest	30538	12917	...	2783	14838	32817	13082	...	3324	16411

602

3.12 General Government Income and Outlay Account: Total and Subsectors
(Continued)

Million French francs

	1982					1983				
	Total General Government	Central Government	State or Provincial Government	Local Government	Social Security Funds	Total General Government	Central Government	State or Provincial Government	Local Government	Social Security Funds
C Dividends	10474	7590	...	1952	932	9507	5969	...	2271	1267
D Net land rent and royalties	3111	2063	...	1048	-	3919	2747	...	1172	-
3 Taxes, fees and contributions	1520530	744481	...	110579	665468	1706930	813273	...	132033	761628
A Indirect taxes	531081	457428	...	64179	9474	586917	499392	...	75264	12261
B Direct taxes	320175	274126	...	45769	280	358740	300380	...	54926	3434
Income	238484	238484	...	-	-	261334	261334	...	-	-
Other	81691	35642	...	45769	280	97406	39046	...	54926	3434
C Social security contributions	663943	8229	...	-	655714	755445	9512	...	-	745933
D Fees, fines and penalties	5329	4698	...	631	-	5832	3989	...	1843	-
4 Other current transfers	102096	8276	...	109598	110785	105819	-5256	...	123388	131984
A Casualty insurance claims	405	1	...	310	94	432	-	...	332	100
B Transfers from other government subsectors	...	-73163	...	99874	99852	...	-87538	...	113336	118499
C Transfers from the rest of the world	6418	6072	...	-	346	7621	7170	...	-	451
D Other transfers, except imputed	27130	12233	...	6413	8484	23764	6811	...	6380	10573
E Imputed unfunded employee pension and welfare contributions	68143	63133	...	3001	2009	74002	68301	...	3340	2361
Total Current Receipts	1666140	776363	...	224312	792023	1866140	838513	...	260636	911290
Disbursements										
1 Government final consumption expenditure	701299	417906	...	142874	140519	782134	460012	...	165091	157031
2 Property income	73772	46032	...	24899	2841	102230	67454	...	30479	4297
A Interest	73729	45989	...	24899	2841	102176	67400	...	30479	4297
B Net land rent and royalties	43	43	...	-	-	54	54	...	-	-
3 Subsidies	79520	71036	...	5923	2561	87423	77860	...	6311	3252
4 Other current transfers	837974	276793	...	42044	645700	948589	322479	...	49123	721284
A Casualty insurance premiums, net	708	25	...	516	167	819	30	...	609	180
B Transfers to other government subsectors	...	116533	...	5704	4326	...	131727	...	6640	5930
C Social security benefits	633340	-	...	-	633340	705473	-	...	-	705473
D Social assistance grants	65045	46167	...	18878	-	76992	55201	...	21791	-
E Unfunded employee pension and welfare benefits	71494	66484	...	3001	2009	79797	74096	...	3340	2361
F Transfers to private non-profit institutions serving households	4734	2148	...	2087	499	5835	3090	...	2465	280
G Other transfers n.e.c.	33711	19343	...	11858	2510	47913	30051	...	14278	3584
H Transfers to the rest of the world	28942	26093	...	-	2849	31760	28284	...	-	3476
Net saving	-26430	-35404	...	8572	402	-54234	-89292	...	9632	25426
Total Current Disbursements and Net Saving	1666140	776363	...	224312	792023	1866140	838513	...	260636	911290

	1984					1985				
	Total General Government	Central Government	State or Provincial Government	Local Government	Social Security Funds	Total General Government	Central Government	State or Provincial Government	Local Government	Social Security Funds
Receipts										
1 Operating surplus	-2324	-914	...	-1410	-	-3432	-2392	...	-1040	-
2 Property and entrepreneurial income	53411	24720	...	7462	21229	66917	35302	...	7959	23656
A Withdrawals from public quasi-corporations	5718	5718	...	-	-	16808	16808	...	-	-
B Interest	35284	12473	...	3727	19084	38272	13080	...	3948	21244
C Dividends	9079	4515	...	2419	2145	8147	3123	...	2612	2412
D Net land rent and royalties	3330	2014	...	1316	-	3690	2291	...	1399	-
3 Taxes, fees and contributions	1905880	896467	...	167131	842278	2046960	954903	...	183597	908457
A Indirect taxes	653822	544236	...	93372	16214	705103	588099	...	100893	16111
B Direct taxes	407431	334871	...	71515	1045	429321	348345	...	80758	218
Income	286939	286939	...	-	-	292902	292902	...	-	-

France

3.12 General Government Income and Outlay Account: Total and Subsectors
(Continued)

Million French francs

	1984					1985				
	Total General Government	Central Government	State or Provincial Government	Local Government	Social Security Funds	Total General Government	Central Government	State or Provincial Government	Local Government	Social Security Funds
Other	120492	47932	...	71515	1045	136419	55443	...	80758	218
C Social security contributions	837392	12373	...	-	825019	905143	13015	...	-	892128
D Fees, fines and penalties	7231	4987	...	2244	-	7390	5444	...	1946	-
4 Other current transfers	115214	-5141	...	113588	124387	125977	2034	...	125544	126309
A Casualty insurance claims	468	-	...	351	117	503	17	...	365	121
B Transfers from other government subsectors	...	-95735	...	102732	110623	...	-95822	...	113033	110699
C Transfers from the rest of the world	8611	8022	...	-	589	9807	9438	...	-	369
D Other transfers, except imputed	25360	8141	...	7130	10089	27877	7547	...	8497	11833
E Imputed unfunded employee pension and welfare contributions	80775	74431	...	3375	2969	87790	80854	...	3649	3287
Total Current Receipts	2072180	915132	...	286771	987894	2236420	989847	...	316060	1058420
Disbursements										
1 Government final consumption expenditure	854300	498886	...	183409	172005	910315	527508	...	199878	182929
2 Property income	116539	76282	...	35998	4259	135075	88302	...	41569	5204
A Interest	116484	76227	...	35998	4259	135010	88237	...	41569	5204
B Net land rent and royalties	55	55	...	-	-	65	65	...	-	-
3 Subsidies	107248	97554	...	6303	3391	109854	98488	...	7317	4049
4 Other current transfers	1044980	335933	...	45048	781617	1140100	374141	...	48146	845724
A Casualty insurance premiums, net	960	79	...	672	209	1046	29	...	761	256
B Transfers to other government subsectors	...	105691	...	4124	7805	...	113912	...	4507	9491
C Social security benefits	762685	-	...	-	762685	823173	-	...	-	823173
D Social assistance grants	97336	78807	...	18529	-	117926	98549	...	19377	-
E Unfunded employee pension and welfare benefits	89540	83196	...	3375	2969	96280	89344	...	3649	3287
F Transfers to private non-profit institutions serving households	7288	3889	...	2608	791	8059	4511	...	2850	698
G Other transfers n.e.c.	55911	36797	...	15740	3374	55280	33647	...	17002	4631
H Transfers to the rest of the world	31258	27474	...	-	3784	38337	34149	...	-	4188
Net saving	-50888	-93523	...	16013	26622	-58926	-98592	...	19150	20516
Total Current Disbursements and Net Saving	2072180	915132	...	286771	987894	2236420	989847	...	316060	1058420

	1986					1987				
	Total General Government	Central Government	State or Provincial Government	Local Government	Social Security Funds	Total General Government	Central Government	State or Provincial Government	Local Government	Social Security Funds
Receipts										
1 Operating surplus	569	1051	...	-482	-	2939	3955	...	-1016	-
2 Property and entrepreneurial income	73895	43365	...	8505	22025	66249	39216	...	8849	18184
A Withdrawals from public quasi-corporations	21917	21917	...	-	-	20409	20409	...	-	-
B Interest	38076	14333	...	4215	19528	32214	12021	...	4293	15900
C Dividends	10727	5414	...	2816	2497	10760	5505	...	2971	2284
D Net land rent and royalties	3175	1701	...	1474	-	2866	1281	...	1585	-
3 Taxes, fees and contributions	2170220	1013600	...	197700	958920	2310110	1079760	...	208543	1021810
A Indirect taxes	736494	610075	...	108497	17922	781898	650116	...	113376	18406
B Direct taxes	469768	382490	...	87020	258	499111	406038	...	92876	197
Income	321469	321469	...	-	-	349285	349285	...	-	-
Other	148299	61021	...	87020	258	149826	56753	...	92876	197
C Social security contributions	955257	14517	...	-	940740	1019600	16397	...	-	1003200
D Fees, fines and penalties	8705	6522	...	2183	-	9504	7213	...	2291	-

France

3.12 General Government Income and Outlay Account: Total and Subsectors (Continued)

Million French francs

	1986					1987				
	Total General Government	Central Government	State or Provincial Government	Local Government	Social Security Funds	Total General Government	Central Government	State or Provincial Government	Local Government	Social Security Funds
4 Other current transfers	134054	3055	...	143103	114673	142328	-8534	...	153456	129309
A Casualty insurance claims	572	...	...	452	120	620	471	...	471	149
B Transfers from other government subsectors	-101900	...	...	130196	84481	-118095	...	...	139395	110603
C Transfers from the rest of the world	8052	7775	...	277	...	10337	10007	...	-	330
D Other transfers, except imputed	29583	8859	...	8435	12289	32654	8919	...	9384	14351
E Imputed unfunded employee pension and welfare contributions	95847	88321	...	4020	3506	98717	90635	...	4206	3876
Total Current Receipts	2378740	1061080	...	348826	1095620	2521630	1114400	...	369832	1169300

Disbursements

1 Government final consumption expenditure	959509	546752	...	222247	190410	1002120	583368	...	234144	199607
2 Property income	145927	95608	...	45063	5256	149476	95255	...	48890	5331
A Interest	145859	95540	...	45063	5256	149403	95182	...	48890	5331
B Net land and royalties	68	68	...	-	-	73	73	...	-	-
3 Subsidies	118625	106217	...	8035	4373	117482	104109	...	8465	4908
4 Other current transfers	1212160	383598	...	49692	905651	1271930	407788	...	51336	944705
A Casualty insurance premiums, net	1161	56	...	853	252	1205	18	...	913	274
B Transfers to other government subsectors	...	111684	...	3831	11262	...	115200	...	3460	13243
C Social security benefits	883391	...	...	880391	915324	915324	...	...	...	915324
D Social assistance grants	129284	109435	...	19849	-	130674	110130	...	20544	-
E Unfunded employee pension and welfare benefits	101205	93679	...	4020	3506	103733	99251	...	4206	3876
F Transfers to private non-profit institutions serving households	7493	3809	...	3061	623	7927	4155	...	3202	570
G Other transfers n.e.c.	57426	33648	...	18078	5700	71208	45007	...	19011	7190
H Transfers to the rest of the world	35204	31287	...	-	3917	38255	34027	...	-	4228
Net saving	-57483	-71100	...	23689	-10072	-19374	-61119	...	26927	14748
Total Current Disbursements and Net Saving	2378740	1061080	...	348826	1095620	2521630	1114400	...	369832	1169300

Receipts

	1988					1989				
	Total General Government	Central Government	State or Provincial Government	Local Government	Social Security Funds	Total General Government	Central Government	State or Provincial Government	Local Government	Social Security Funds
1 Operating surplus	344	806	...	-462	-1031	-528	-503	...	...	...
2 Property and entrepreneurial income	61486	34145	...	9491	17850	68879	40091	...	10033	18755
A Withdrawals from public quasi-corporations	15135	15135	...	-	-	18469	18469	...	-	-
B Interest	30619	10973	...	4529	15117	31076	10478	...	4801	15797
C Dividends	12634	6891	...	3220	2733	16351	9991	...	3402	2957
D Net land and royalties	3098	1356	...	1742	-	2983	1153	...	1830	-
3 Taxes, fees and contributions	2435170	1121670	...	225053	1088440	2612040	1193940	...	239481	1178620
A Indirect taxes	824756	683828	...	122912	91016	867392	716930	...	131281	19181
B Direct taxes	514948	415096	...	99716	136	554760	448962	...	105530	268
Income	360707	360707	...	...	...	391500	391500	...	...	...
Other	154241	54389	...	99716	136	163260	57462	...	105530	268
C Social security contributions	1088830	165542	...	1070290	1179650	1179650	...	...	...	1179650...
D Fees, fines and penalties	8635	6200	...	2435	10821	8151	...	2670	-
4 Other current transfers	1683342	...	8949	161445	1393614	1619191	-10085	...	176280	1387731
A Casualty insurance claims	609	-	...	463	143	634	-	...	485	149
B Transfers from other government subsectors	...	-124011	...	146841	118583	-134011	...	...	160448	118298
C Transfers from the rest of the world	13320	13312	...	1	7	12853	12853	...	-	-
D Other transfers, except imputed	51000	24962	...	9691	16347	38547	12269	...	10693	15639
E Imputed unfunded employee pension and welfare contributions	103416	94686	...	4449	4281	108157	98804	...	4708	4645

France

3.12 General Government Income and Outlay Account: Total and Subsectors (Continued)

Million French francs

	1988					1989				
	Total General Government	Central Government	State or Provincial Government	Local Government	Social Security Funds	Total General Government	Central Government	State or Provincial Government	Local Government	Social Security Funds
Total Current Receipts	2665340	1165570	...	2840080	1245650	395537	1223420	...	425291	1336100

Disbursements

1 Government final consumption expenditure	1055540	600955	...	208832	245755	1111200	629123	...	264217	225857
2 Property income	157910	98568	5410	17641	52365	112653	58513	5275
A Interest	157828	98486	54106	176324	112536	58513	5275
B Net land rent and royalties		82		68	68				
3 Subsidies	106108	18814	5156	105986	91465	9297	5224
4 Other current transfers	1350240	422947	58568	1011840	142411	432027	60595	1072220
A Casualty insurance premiums, net	1252	19	962	271	1315	25	1074	216
B Transfers to other government subsectors	...	123045	3695	14673	...	123767	4466	16502
C Social security benefits	980311				1043560			1043560
D Social assistance grants	142503	125006	21997	144040	129044	...	230996
E Unfunded employee pension and welfare benefits	111269	102539	4449	4281	119055	109702	4708	4645
F Transfers to private non-profit institutions serving households	9717	5634	3570	513	8668	4665	3784	549
G Other transfers n.e.c.	55768	25768	22185	7795	50122	31462	23467	6083
H Transfers to the rest of the world	49415	45416	3999	46125	41462	4663
Net saving	-5457	-48718	28680	14581	14370	-41825	32669	25526
Total Current Disbursements and Net Saving	2665340	1165570	...	2840080	1245650	395537	1223420	...	425291	1336100

3.13 General Government Capital Accumulation Account: Total and Subsectors

Million French francs

	1980					1981				
	Total General Government	Central Government	State or Provincial Government	Local Government	Social Security Funds	Total General Government	Central Government	State or Provincial Government	Local Government	Social Security Funds

Finance of Gross Accumulation

1 Gross saving	105346	34226	38698	53545	7372	32134	41147	5226
A Consumption of fixed capital	44431	12968	27418	4045	51804	14679	32278	4847
B Net saving	60915	21258	11568	28089	1741	-7307	6988	379
2 Capital transfers	24421	8453	13867	2101	30339	12675	15912	1752
A From other government subsectors	-	-	-	-	-	-	-	-
B From other resident sectors	8529	6755	1274	500	13111	10852	1735	524
C From rest of the world	15892	1698	12593	1601	17228	1823	14177	1228
Finance of Gross Accumulation	129767	42679	52853	34235	83884	20047	57059	6778

Gross Accumulation

1 Gross capital formation	91104	19328	61422	10354	99801	17988	71135	10678
A Increase in stocks	4502	4482	20	1072	1030	42	-
B Gross fixed capital formation	86602	14846	61402	10354	98729	16958	71093	10678
2 Purchases of land, net	2933	986	1798	147	2427	696	1670	61
3 Purchases of intangible assets, net	86	50	36	80	54	26	-
4 Capital transfers	36144	30495	5234	415	42352	-6077	35665	5889	818
Net lending	-500	-8182	-15837	52853	20047	-34356	-21641	-4779
Gross Accumulation	129767	42679	52853	34235	83884	20047	57059	6778

	1982					1983				
	Total General Government	Central Government	State or Provincial Government	Local Government	Social Security Funds	Total General Government	Central Government	State or Provincial Government	Local Government	Social Security Funds

Finance of Gross Accumulation

1 Gross saving	34265	-18767	46891	6141	14069	-71212	53289	31992
A Consumption of fixed capital	60695	16637	38319	5739	68303	18080	43657	6566
B Net saving	-26430	-35404	8572	402	-54234	-89292	9632	25426
2 Capital transfers	33175	14136	17035	2004	35171	14587	18223	2361

France

3.13 General Government Capital Accumulation Account: Total and Subsectors
(Continued)

Million French francs

	1982					1983				
	Total General Government	Central Government	State or Provincial Government	Local Government	Social Security Funds	Total General Government	Central Government	State or Provincial Government	Local Government	Social Security Funds
A From other government subsectors	-		...			-		...		
B From other resident sectors	11421	1716	...	14361	1987	13753	616	...	11411	963
C From rest of the world	19422	2715	...	15319	1388	20810	3176	...	16236	1398
Finance of Gross Accumulation	67440	-4631	...	63926	8145	49240	-56625	...	71512	34353

Gross Accumulation

	1982					1983				
1 Gross capital formation	121412	26433	...	84278	10701	127347	28397	...	87640	11310
A Increase in stocks	6547	6508	...	39	-	8001	7946	...	55	-
B Gross fixed capital formation	114865	19925	...	84239	10701	119346	20451	...	87585	11310
2 Purchases of land, net	2571	905	...	1666	-	1150	2871	...	1527	194
3 Purchases of intangible assets, net	130	96	...	34	1	103	70	...	32	1
4 Capital transfers	43723	36049	...	7073	601	45273	35749	...	8003	1521
Net lending	-100396	-68114	...	-29125	-3157	-123854	-121991	...	-25690	21327
Gross Accumulation	67440	-4631	...	63926	8145	49240	-56625	...	71512	34353

	1984					1985				
	Total General Government	Central Government	State or Provincial Government	Local Government	Social Security Funds	Total General Government	Central Government	State or Provincial Government	Local Government	Social Security Funds

Finance of Gross Accumulation

	1984					1985				
1 Gross saving	24920	-73864	...	64776	23916	34008	-77557	...	72880	28593
A Consumption of fixed capital	75808	19659	...	48763	7386	82842	21035	...	53730	8077
B Net saving	-50888	-93523	...	16013	26622	-58826	-98592	...	19150	20516
2 Capital transfers	40023	15958	...	21745	2320	45763	17354	...	25821	2588
A From other government subsectors	-		...			-		...		
B From other resident sectors	15293	12474	...	1984	835	19158	13202	...	4884	1072
C From rest of the world	24730	3484	...	19761	1485	26605	4152	...	20937	1516
Finance of Gross Accumulation	64943	-57906	...	86521	36328	69679	-60203	...	98701	31181

Gross Accumulation

	1984					1985				
1 Gross capital formation	130158	28661	...	90174	11323	149388	33127	...	103755	12496
A Increase in stocks	4031	3998	...	33	-	5111	5089	...	22	-
B Gross fixed capital formation	126127	24663	...	90141	11323	144277	28038	...	103743	12496
2 Purchases of land, net	2982	1097	...	1619	266	2155	838	...	1094	223
3 Purchases of intangible assets, net	-106	-154	...	48	-	71	1	...	70	1607
4 Capital transfers	52068	41662	...	8138	1268	52736	40711	...	16446	16855
Net lending	-120159	-129172	...	-14458	23471	-134880	-134671	...	98701	31181
Gross Accumulation	64943	-57906	...	86521	36328	69679	-60203	...		

	1986					1987				
	Total General Government	Central Government	State or Provincial Government	Local Government	Social Security Funds	Total General Government	Central Government	State or Provincial Government	Local Government	Social Security Funds

Finance of Gross Accumulation

	1986					1987				
1 Gross saving	31131	-50050	...	82704	-1523	75533	-39004	...	90778	27759
A Consumption of fixed capital	88614	21050	...	59015	8549	94907	22115	...	63781	9011
B Net saving	-57483	-71100	...	23689	-10072	-19374	-61119	...	29697	14748
2 Capital transfers	51614	23806	...	25000	2808	56145	26639	...	25810	2696
A From other government subsectors	-		...			-		...		
B From other resident sectors	23018	18771	...	2668	1579	26065	21723	...	2993	1349
C From rest of the world	28596	5035	...	22332	1229	30080	4916	...	23817	1347
Finance of Gross Accumulation	82745	-26244	...	107704	1285	131678	-12365	...	117588	26455

Gross Accumulation

	1986					1987				
1 Gross capital formation	159504	36833	...	109013	13658	159645	29094	...	116122	14429

France

3.13 General Government Capital Accumulation Account: Total and Subsectors
(Continued)

Million French francs

	1986 Total General Government	1986 Central Government	1986 State or Provincial Government	1986 Local Government	1986 Social Security Funds	1987 Total General Government	1987 Central Government	1987 State or Provincial Government	1987 Local Government	1987 Social Security Funds
A Increase in stocks	7069	7079	...	-10	-	-1470	-1459	...	-11	-
B Gross fixed capital formation	152435	29754	...	109023	13658	161115	30553	...	116133	14429
2 Purchases of land, net	2805	852	...	918	1035	1758	905	...	590	263
3 Purchases of intangible assets, net	78	17	...	61	-	84	21	...	63	-
4 Capital transfers	58758	46873	...	10416	1469	72114	60459	...	10628	1027
Net lending	-138400	-110819	...	-12704	-14877	-101923	-102844	...	-9815	10736
Gross Accumulation	82745	-26244	...	107704	1285	131678	-12365	...	117588	26455

	1988 Total General Government	1988 Central Government	1988 State or Provincial Government	1988 Local Government	1988 Social Security Funds	1989 Total General Government	1989 Central Government	1989 State or Provincial Government	1989 Local Government	1989 Social Security Funds
Finance of Gross Accumulation										
1 Gross saving	96200	-25442	...	97569	24073	124338	-17006	...	107694	33650
A Consumption of fixed capital	101657	23276	...	68889	9492	109968	24819	...	75025	10124
B Net saving	-5457	-48718	...	28680	14581	14370	-41825	...	32669	23526
2 Capital transfers	60535	27708	...	30132	2695	65081	30834	...	31718	2529
A From other government subsectors	-	-	...	-	-	-	-	...	-	-
B From other resident sectors	27004	22376	...	3203	1425	30545	26005	...	3246	1294
C From rest of the world	33531	5332	...	26929	1270	34536	4829	...	28472	1235
Finance of Gross Accumulation	156735	2266	...	127701	26768	189419	13828	...	139412	36179
Gross Accumulation										
1 Gross capital formation	178511	35458	...	128374	14679	198451	41596	...	141176	15679
A Increase in stocks	829	841	...	-12	-	3529	3517	...	12	-
B Gross fixed capital formation	177682	34617	...	128386	14679	194922	38079	...	141164	15679
2 Purchases of land, net	1785	1067	...	522	196	3801	1715	...	1895	191
3 Purchases of intangible assets, net	94	25	...	69	-	76	-	...	76	-
4 Capital transfers	77794	64942	...	11749	1103	73365	60592	...	11670	1103
Net lending	-101449	-99226	...	-13013	10790	-86274	-90075	...	-15405	19206
Gross Accumulation	156735	2266	...	127701	26768	189419	13828	...	139412	36179

3.14 General Government Capital Finance Account, Total and Subsectors

Million French francs

	1980 Total General Government	1980 Central Government	1980 State or Provincial Government	1980 Local Government	1980 Social Security Funds	1981 Total General Government	1981 Central Government	1981 State or Provincial Government	1981 Local Government	1981 Social Security Funds
Acquisition of Financial Assets										
1 Gold and SDRs	242	242	...	...	...	-17	-17	...	...	...
2 Currency and transferable deposits	23639	11116	...	1951	10572	-2000	3091	...	1285	-6376
3 Other deposits	1911	312	...	256	1343	10286	3707	...	-155	6734
4 Bills and bonds, short term	-	...	...	-	-	...	...	...	...	-
5 Bonds, long term	1465	110	...	371	984	2012	149	...	324	1539
6 Corporate equity securities	21794	17659	...	-	4135	21063	19465	...	-	1598
7 Short-term loans, n.e.c.	2261	-513	...	-896	3670	26802	16417	...	335	10050
8 Long-term loans, n.e.c.	-4669	-4669	...	-	...	2676	2676	...	-	...
9 Other receivables	86	...	...	86	...	91	...	...	91	...
10 Other assets	7418	6383	...	518	517	17327	8865	...	5428	3034
Total Acquisition of Financial Assets	54147	30640	...	2286	21221	78240	54353	...	7308	16579
Incurrence of Liabilities										
1 Currency and transferable deposits	10886	10886	...	...	745	22310	22310	...	...	1019
2 Other deposits	2547	1437	...	365	...	-679	-1309	...	-389	...
3 Bills and bonds, short term	-5949	-5949	...	...	...	56748	56748	...	...	...

France

3.14 General Government Capital Finance Account, Total and Subsectors
(Continued)

Million French francs

	1980					1981				
	Total General Government	Central Government	State or Provincial Government	Local Government	Social Security Funds	Total General Government	Central Government	State or Provincial Government	Local Government	Social Security Funds
4 Bonds, long term	28862	27645	...	1217	-	18088	16858	...	1230	-
5 Short-term loans, n.e.c.	-8074	-694	...	-689	-6691	9948	-7088	...	4341	12695
6 Long-term loans, n.e.c.	21199	364	...	18598	2237	27901	-242	...	26309	1834
7 Other payables	-	-	...	-	-	-	-	...	-	...
8 Other liabilities	5176	5133	...	-1568	1611	4700	1432	...	-2542	5810
Total Incurence of Liabilities	54647	38822	...	17923	-2098	139016	88709	...	28949	21358
Net Lending	-500	-8182	...	-15637	23319	-60776	-34356	...	-21641	-4779
Incurrence of Liabilities and Net Worth	54147	30640	...	2286	21221	78240	54353	...	7308	16579

	1982					1983				
	Total General Government	Central Government	State or Provincial Government	Local Government	Social Security Funds	Total General Government	Central Government	State or Provincial Government	Local Government	Social Security Funds
Acquisition of Financial Assets										
1 Gold and SDRs	492	492	...	...	...	-88	-88	...	...	...
2 Currency and transferable deposits	55433	54362	...	500	571	-19460	-30299	...	3951	6888
3 Other deposits	9045	211	...	203	8631	5617	-35	...	-118	5770
4 Bills and bonds, short term	-	...	...	...	-	-	...	...	...	-
5 Bonds, long term	2216	127	...	446	1643	4810	34	...	444	4332
6 Corporate equity securities	49986	46382	...	-	3604	22877	18866	...	-	4011
7 Short-term loans, n.e.c.	21681	10111	...	3103	8467	32417	25253	...	3893	3271
8 Long-term loans, n.e.c.	16509	16509	...	-	...	-5591	-5591	...	-	...
9 Other receivables	203	...	...	203	...	133	...	...	133	...
10 Other assets	17813	10463	...	7463	-113	26078	6573	...	12319	7186
Total Acquisition of Financial Assets	173378	138657	...	11918	22803	66793	14713	...	20622	31458
Incurrence of Liabilities										
1 Currency and transferable deposits	25066	25066	...	...	1046	22996	22996	...	...	571
2 Other deposits	-53	-1264	...	165	...	1774	727	...	476	...
3 Bills and bonds, short term	85683	85683	...	...	...	41233	41233	...	...	...
4 Bonds, long term	31474	28690	...	2784	-	46449	44380	...	2069	-
5 Short-term loans, n.e.c.	30833	17852	...	1024	11957	9986	6606	...	-1386	4766
6 Long-term loans, n.e.c.	80984	41976	...	37065	1943	42619	3861	...	36347	2411
7 Other payables	-	-	...	-	-	-	-	...	-	-
8 Other liabilities	19787	8768	...	5	11014	28090	16901	...	8806	2383
Total Incurence of Liabilities	273774	206771	...	41043	25960	193147	136704	...	46312	10131
Net Lending	-100396	-68114	...	-29125	-3157	-126354	-121991	...	-25690	21327
Incurrence of Liabilities and Net Worth	173378	138657	...	11918	22803	66793	14713	...	20622	31458

	1984					1985				
	Total General Government	Central Government	State or Provincial Government	Local Government	Social Security Funds	Total General Government	Central Government	State or Provincial Government	Local Government	Social Security Funds
Acquisition of Financial Assets										
1 Gold and SDRs	149	149	...	...	...	41	41	...	...	...
2 Currency and transferable deposits	59711	21441	...	12762	25508	47214	18950	...	13199	15065
3 Other deposits	1177	1067	...	3614	-3504	723	1073	...	1361	-1711
4 Bills and bonds, short term	-	...	...	...	-	-	...	...	...	-
5 Bonds, long term	2855	487	...	588	1780	8022	531	...	571	6920
6 Corporate equity securities	14294	13005	...	-	1289	20691	18889	...	-	1802
7 Short-term loans, n.e.c.	-9707	16728	...	1720	-28155	-8242	-15023	...	-795	7576
8 Long-term loans, n.e.c.	7929	7929	...	-	...	452	452	...	-	...
9 Other receivables	140	...	...	140	...	131	...	...	131	...
10 Other assets	27432	6625	...	7559	13248	14724	10767	...	6365	-2408
Total Acquisition of Financial Assets	103980	67431	...	26383	10166	83756	35680	...	20832	27244
Incurrence of Liabilities										
1 Currency and transferable deposits	20222	20222	...	...	501	44309	44309	...	...	489
2 Other deposits	9119	8749	...	-131	...	-1884	-2043	...	-330	...
3 Bills and bonds, short term	48761	48761	...	...	...	20162	20162	...	...	...

609

France

3.14 General Government Capital Finance Account, Total and Subsectors
(Continued)

Million French francs

	1984					1985				
	Total General Government	Central Government	State or Provincial Government	Local Government	Social Security Funds	Total General Government	Central Government	State or Provincial Government	Local Government	Social Security Funds
4 Bonds, long term	82294	80084	...	2210	-	93083	89807	...	3276	-
5 Short-term loans, n.e.c.	8873	33621	...	2121	-26869	24685	21890	...	258	2537
6 Long-term loans, n.e.c.	48303	-1575	...	36639	13239	25711	-7561	...	31746	1526
7 Other payables	10	-	...	10	...	5	-	...	5	...
8 Other liabilities	6557	6741	...	-8	-176	12356	3996	...	2523	5837
Total Incurrence of Liabilities	224139	196603	...	40841	-13305	218427	170560	...	37478	10389
Net Lending	-120159	-129172	...	-14458	23471	-134671	-134880	...	-16646	16855
Incurrence of Liabilities and Net Worth	103980	67431	...	26383	10166	83756	35680	...	20832	27244

	1986					1987				
	Total General Government	Central Government	State or Provincial Government	Local Government	Social Security Funds	Total General Government	Central Government	State or Provincial Government	Local Government	Social Security Funds
Acquisition of Financial Assets										
1 Gold and SDRs	-116	-116	...	...	...	-20	-20	...	...	...
2 Currency and transferable deposits	-17383	-13064	...	2770	-7089	75585	78909	...	8410	-11734
3 Other deposits	-7790	-558	...	-366	-6866	-2790	1706	...	-644	-3852
4 Bills and bonds, short term	-	...	...	...	-	2069	...	...	...	2069
5 Bonds, long term	6680	4769	...	845	1066	6764	2419	...	855	3490
6 Corporate equity securities	55928	50474	...	-	5454	-32380	-43576	...	-	11196
7 Short-term loans, n.e.c.	-2190	-6487	...	4587	-290	48005	22099	...	6394	19512
8 Long-term loans, n.e.c.	-23296	-23296	...	-	...	5239	5239	...	-	...
9 Other receivables	127	...	...	127	...	127	...	...	127	...
10 Other assets	33282	23110	...	5991	4181	33695	23755	...	2165	7775
Total Acquisition of Financial Assets	45242	34832	...	13954	-3544	136294	90531	...	17307	28456
Incurrence of Liabilities										
1 Currency and transferable deposits	-14542	-14542	...	...	1039	41392	41392	...	...	168
2 Other deposits	-7545	-8584	...	-	...	2936	2768	...	-	...
3 Bills and bonds, short term	38364	38364	...	...	...	60443	60443	...	...	...
4 Bonds, long term	112416	111649	...	767	-	16988	20564	...	-3576	-
5 Short-term loans, n.e.c.	20396	21184	...	-5295	4507	75845	71555	...	920	3370
6 Long-term loans, n.e.c.	29997	1344	...	27539	1114	35733	1090	...	33432	1211
7 Other payables	111	101	...	10	...	84	74	...	10	...
8 Other liabilities	4445	-3865	...	3637	4673	4796	-4511	...	-3664	12971
Total Incurrence of Liabilities	183642	145651	...	26658	11333	238217	193375	...	27122	17720
Net Lending	-138400	-110819	...	-12704	-14877	-101923	-102844	...	-9815	10736
Incurrence of Liabilities and Net Worth	45242	34832	...	13954	-3544	136294	90531	...	17307	28456

	1988					1989				
	Total General Government	Central Government	State or Provincial Government	Local Government	Social Security Funds	Total General Government	Central Government	State or Provincial Government	Local Government	Social Security Funds
Acquisition of Financial Assets										
1 Gold and SDRs	291	291	...	...	...	-	-	...	...	...
2 Currency and transferable deposits	-54524	-47713	...	-5178	-1633	49588	38556	...	4929	6103
3 Other deposits	-646	2007	...	944	-3597	2425	5222	...	-	-2797
4 Bills and bonds, short term	1663	...	...	...	1663	-1773	...	...	...	-1773
5 Bonds, long term	6052	73	...	222	5757	7411	-759	...	2403	5767
6 Corporate equity securities	7877	4421	...	-	3456	16701	3966	...	-	12735
7 Short-term loans, n.e.c.	38598	14379	...	4555	19664	-7288	-7289	...	1	-
8 Long-term loans, n.e.c.	9957	9957	...	-	...	15235	15235	...	-	...
9 Other receivables	116	...	...	116	...	90	...	...	90	...
10 Other assets	30220	18406	...	8898	2916	33524	24047	...	1777	7700
Total Acquisition of Financial Assets	39604	1821	...	9557	28226	115913	78978	...	9200	27735
Incurrence of Liabilities										
1 Currency and transferable deposits	-1777	-1777	...	...	137	19944	19944	...	...	24
2 Other deposits	4653	4516	...	-	...	-1756	-1780	...	-	...
3 Bills and bonds, short term	15541	15541	...	...	...	70000	70000	...	...	...

610

France

3.14 General Government Capital Finance Account, Total and Subsectors (Continued)

Million French francs

	1988					1989				
	Total General Government	Central Government	State or Provincial Government	Local Government	Social Security Funds	Total General Government	Central Government	State or Provincial Government	Local Government	Social Security Funds
4 Bonds, long term	60090	62167	....	76508	786	76435	....	73	-
5 Short-term loans, n.e.c.	2039	-6890	....	4743	4186	-5111	-7981	....	2700	170
6 Long-term loans, n.e.c.	2767	4172	....	25280	1315	14941	-3170	....	18961	-850
7 Other payables	....	....	....	-3100	43	....	43	....	....	....
8 Other liabilities	31230	23318	....	11012	27618	15605	2828	....	9185
Total Incurrence of Liabilities	101053	101047	....	25570	7436	202187	169053	....	24605	8529
Net Lending	-101449	-99226	....	-13013	10790	-86274	-90075	....	-15405	19206
Incurrence of Liabilities and Net Worth	39604	1821	....	9557	28226	115913	78978	....	9200	27735

3.21 Corporate and Quasi-Corporate Enterprise Production Account: Total and Sectors

Million French francs

	1980				1981				1982			
	TOTAL	Non-Financial	Financial	ADDENDUM: Total, including Unincorporated	TOTAL	Non-Financial	Financial	ADDENDUM: Total, including Unincorporated	TOTAL	Non-Financial	Financial	ADDENDUM: Total, including Unincorporated
		Corporate and Quasi-Corporate Enterprises				Corporate and Quasi-Corporate Enterprises				Corporate and Quasi-Corporate Enterprises		
Gross Output												
1 Output for sale	3207040	3207040	68930	4189160	3692880	3619280	81596	4700000	4164350	4074470	88984	5298720
2 Imputed bank service charge	107503	....	107503	124807	124807	....	124807	147548	147548	....	147548
3 Own-account fixed capital formation	3207040	....										
Gross Output	3207040	3207040		338437	4313590	4313590		177333	3820403	3820403		5460940
Gross Input	3384370	3207040	177333	4313590	3822680	3619280	206403	4843400	4311000	4074470	236532	5460940
Intermediate consumption	1913240	1754630	158609	2199770	2163360	1977770	185596	2476570	2435370	2218070	217302	2780470
1 Imputed banking service charge	107503	....	107503	124807	124807	....	124807	147548	147548	....	147548
2 Other intermediate consumption	1805740	1754630	51106	2029270	2038560	1977770	60789	2351760	2287820	2218070	69754	2632920
Subtotal: Value Added	1471130	1452410	18724	2113820	1659320	1638510	20807	2366830	1875630	1856400	19230	2688520
1 Indirect taxes, net	90081	86241	3790	100847	96834	96361	3175	100147	109849	104457	5192	118802
A Indirect taxes	147678	143254	14884	174714	163254	162254	2044	191221	169849	168684	4337	214651
B Less: Subsidies	59147	46113	13034	90766	52140	55271	16969	86542	81672	62527	19145	95849
2 Consumption of fixed capital	196891	193098	5883	301077	230251	223207	7044	344651	266237	258022	8215	395074
3 Compensation of employees	1057640	991844	65799	1180850	1120550	1112560	7700	1335130	1369600	1276670	92226	1515680
4 Net operating surplus	124476	181224	-56748	530943	211485	197280	-61128	589803	132849	217252	-84403	668114
Gross Input	3384370	3207040	177333	4313590	3822680	3619280	206403	4843400	4311000	4074470	236532	5460940

	1983				1984				1985			
	TOTAL	Non-Financial	Financial	ADDENDUM: Total, including Unincorporated	TOTAL	Non-Financial	Financial	ADDENDUM: Total, including Unincorporated	TOTAL	Non-Financial	Financial	ADDENDUM: Total, including Unincorporated
		Corporate and Quasi-Corporate Enterprises				Corporate and Quasi-Corporate Enterprises				Corporate and Quasi-Corporate Enterprises		
Gross Output												
1 Output for sale	4546750	4440040	105811	5776600	5006610	4870530	136082	6332440	5418690	5252340	164558	6799910
2 Imputed bank service charge	162385	....	162385	162385	162385	....	175627	175627	192340	....	192340	192340
3 Own-account fixed capital formation												
Gross Output	4709140	4440040	268196	5963960	5182240	4870530	311709	6534510	5609230	5252340	356898	7020110
Intermediate consumption	2630070	2382570	247499	2994490	2903190	2625340	277858	3302250	3134720	2818780	315936	3522170
1 Imputed banking service charge	162385	....	162385	162385	162385	....	175627	175627	192340	....	192340	192340
2 Other intermediate consumption	2467680	2382570	85114	2832110	2727570	2625340	102231	3126830	2942380	2818780	123596	3329830
Subtotal: Value Added	2079070	2058370	20697	2969670	2279040	2245190	33851	3232250	2474520	2433550	40962	3497930
1 Indirect taxes, net	126672	120137	6535	158880	145633	133946	11687	153564	169780	154588	15192	177323
A Indirect taxes	217850	189830	28020	243568	252967	216285	36682	281442	281369	241512	39857	311949
B Less: Subsidies	91178	69693	21485	107708	107334	82339	24995	127878	111589	86924	24665	134626
2 Consumption of fixed capital	297608	288138	9470	438259	323047	311759	11288	474765	346698	333294	12294	505406
3 Compensation of employees	1498270	1480070	14800	1660110	1603140	1494530	108610	1774390	1704650	1586650	117885	1882690
4 Net operating surplus	154920	249241	-94321	734223	520725	304952	-97727	832352	258615	358024	-104409	932515
Gross Input	4709140	4440040	268196	5963960	5182240	4870530	311709	6534510	5609230	5252340	356898	7020110

France

Million French francs

3.21 Corporate and Quasi-Corporate Enterprise Production Account: Total and Sectors

	1986				1987				1988			
	TOTAL	Non-Financial	Financial	ADDENDUM: Corporate and Quasi-Corporate Enterprises Total, including Unincorporated	TOTAL	Non-Financial	Financial	ADDENDUM: Corporate and Quasi-Corporate Enterprises Total, including Unincorporated	TOTAL	Non-Financial	Financial	ADDENDUM: Corporate and Quasi-Corporate Enterprises Total, including Unincorporated
Gross Output												
1 Output for sale	5648860	5432400	214460	7108690	6003880	5736300	267582	7473700	6465990	6162610	303381	8081470
2 Imputed bank service charge	222272	-	222272	222272	247379	-	247379	247379	270440	-	270440	270440
3 Own-account fixed capital formation	...	5432400	437732	7359820	...	5736300	514961	7749490	...	6162610	573821	8382510
Gross Output	5870130	5432400	437732	7359820	6251260	5736300	514961	7749490	6736430	6162610	573821	8382510
Intermediate consumption	3160090	2778130	382472	3557190	3401310	2943830	457488	3757380	3677380	3152540	524841	4084840
1 Imputed banking service charge	222272	-	222272	222272	247379	-	247379	247379	270440	-	270440	270440
2 Other intermediate consumption	2937330	2778130	159200	3333920	3153920	2943830	210109	3509960	3406920	3152540	254401	3814400
Subtotal: Value Added	2705630	2654270	55260	3802630	2849950	2792470	57473	3992480	3050940	3010090	49880	4274270
1 Indirect taxes, net	186986	171857	15129	194059	171629	177629	21648	201728	225130	195418	29712	232996
A Indirect taxes	301611	261819	44292	339212	323911	276770	47141	359648	339768	291060	48672	378839
B Less: Subsidies	119125	89962	29163	145153	130634	105141	25493	157820	114638	95678	18960	139543
2 Consumption of fixed capital	370246	345893	13353	542156	388678	374269	14409	573509	398864	393878	15986	609397
3 Compensation of employees	1739940	1660090	123039	1846430	1740010	1674100	101010	1870040	1879540	1840090	133336	2171870
4 Net operating surplus	368361	464622	-96261	1101790	505568	397953	-107615	1161320	448114	580168	-132054	1277110
Gross Input	5870130	5432400	437732	7359820	6251260	5736300	514961	7749490	6736430	6162610	573821	8382510

3.22 Corporate and Quasi-Corporate Enterprise Income and Outlay Account: Total and Sectors

Million French francs

	1980			1981			1982			1983		
	TOTAL	Non-Financial	Financial	TOTAL	Non-Financial	Financial	TOTAL	Non-Financial	Financial	TOTAL	Non-Financial	Financial
Receipts												
1 Operating surplus	124476	181224	-56748	133668	199780	-66112	132849	217252	-84403	154920	249241	-94321
2 Property and entrepreneurial income	510717	48885	461832	690427	63401	627026	807744	67999	738745	881268	76404	804864
A Withdrawals from quasi-corporate enterprises												
B Interest	473110	19956	453154	643458	27481	615977	756101	33290	722811	823652	33587	790065
C Dividends	33417	24749	8668	42423	31386	11037	46277	30359	15918	50929	36149	14780
D Net land rent and royalties	4190	4180	10	4546	4534	12	4366	4350	16	6987	6968	19

France

3.22 Corporate and Quasi-Corporate Enterprise Income and Outlay Account: Total and Sectors
(Continued)

Million French francs

	1980			1981			1982			1983		
	TOTAL	Non-Financial	Financial	TOTAL	Non-Financial	Financial	TOTAL	Non-Financial	Financial	TOTAL	Non-Financial	Financial
3 Current transfers	144908	81857	63051	167638	93560	74078	201817	110317	91500	234090	124875	109215
A Casualty insurance claims	11640	11362	278	13954	13643	311	17174	16765	409	19422	18987	435
B Casualty insurance premiums, net, due to be received by insurance companies	48264	-	48264	56125	-	56125	68283	-	68283	74105	-	74105
C Current transfers from the rest of the world	...	...	...	...	...	...	...	...	...	...	...	...
D Other transfers except imputed	55658	42329	13329	63866	47611	16255	77547	56337	21210	96343	63750	32593
E Imputed unfunded employee pension and welfare contributions	29346	28166	1180	33693	32306	1387	38813	37215	1598	44220	42138	2082
Total Current Receipts	780101	311966	468135	991733	356741	634992	1141410	395568	745842	1270280	450520	819758
Disbursements												
1 Property and entrepreneurial income	558388	206134	352254	767492	264813	502679	887908	295002	592906	967417	332609	634808
A Withdrawals from quasi-corporations	817	817	-	1088	1088	-	3020	3020	-	8139	8139	-
B Interest	474486	134499	339987	660357	175698	484659	772763	200243	572520	826184	218415	607769
C Dividends a	74964	62697	12267	96446	78426	18020	100605	80219	20386	119838	92799	27039
D Net land rent and royalties	8121	8121	-	9601	9601	-	11520	11520	-	13256	13256	-
2 Direct taxes and other current transfers n.e.c. to general government	65902	51891	14011	75624	57376	18248	89861	60131	29730	88612	62800	25812
A Direct taxes	64650	50639	14011	74718	56470	18248	88506	58776	29730	87231	61419	25812
On income	7825	4968	2857	11004	6512	4492	13983	7886	6097	16860	9591	7269
Other	56825	45671	11154	63714	49958	13756	74523	50890	23633	70371	51828	18543
B Fines, fees, penalties and other current transfers n.e.c.	1252	1252	-	906	906	-	1355	1355	-	1381	1381	-
3 Other current transfers	151771	73328	78443	186229	86393	99836	212148	101259	110889	228551	114608	113943
A Casualty insurance premiums, net	15321	15009	312	17875	17547	328	21587	21167	420	24143	23696	447
B Casualty insurance claims liability of insurance companies	56970	-	56970	66681	-	66681	80877	-	80877	88901	-	88901
C Transfers to private non-profit institutions	531	531	-	625	625	-	701	701	-	759	759	-
D Unfunded employee pension and welfare benefits	48687	39060	9627	56446	45039	11407	64894	51731	13163	72764	57191	15573
E Social assistance grants	...	...	...	...	...	...	...	...	...	...	...	...
F Other transfers n.e.c.	30262	18728	11534	44602	23182	21420	44089	27660	16429	41984	32962	9022
G Transfers to the rest of the world	...	...	...	...	...	...	...	...	...	...	...	...
Net saving	4040	-19387	23427	-37612	-51841	14229	-48507	-60824	12317	-14302	-59497	45195
Total Current Disbursements and Net Saving	780101	311966	468135	991733	356741	634992	1141410	395568	745842	1270280	450520	819758

	1984			1985			1986			1987		
	TOTAL	Non-Financial	Financial	TOTAL	Non-Financial	Financial	TOTAL	Non-Financial	Financial	TOTAL	Non-Financial	Financial
Receipts												
1 Operating surplus	207225	304952	-97727	253615	358024	-104409	368361	464622	-96261	397953	505568	-107615
2 Property and entrepreneurial income	994270	89603	904667	1111300	100203	1011100	1155200	110029	1045170	1165300	118708	1046590
A Withdrawals from quasi-corporate enterprises	...	...	...	...	...	...	...	...	...	...	...	...
B Interest	924539	37912	886627	1025510	41905	983606	1049880	38929	1010950	1054880	42457	1012420
C Dividends	63600	45570	18030	78862	51397	27465	97915	63707	34208	102171	68017	34154
D Net land rent and royalties	6131	6121	10	6926	6901	25	7404	7393	11	8246	8234	12

613

France

3.22 Corporate and Quasi-Corporate Enterprise Income and Outlay Account: Total and Sectors
(Continued)

Million French francs

	1984			1985			1986			1987		
	TOTAL	Non-Financial	Financial	TOTAL	Non-Financial	Financial	TOTAL	Non-Financial	Financial	TOTAL	Non-Financial	Financial
3 Current transfers	256632	134844	121788	270947	144583	126364	280272	148203	132069	303896	147915	155981
A Casualty insurance claims	21851	21363	488	24473	23928	545	25374	24804	570	25846	25231	615
B Casualty insurance premiums, net, due to be received by insurance companies	80700	-	80700	85940	-	85940	88758	-	88758	94949	-	94949
C Current transfers from the rest of the world	...	...	...	...	...	...	...	...	...	...	...	...
D Other transfers except imputed	106943	68487	38456	110777	73192	37585	114160	73787	40373	130222	72264	57958
E Imputed unfunded employee pension and welfare contributions	47138	44994	2144	49757	47463	2294	51980	49612	2368	52879	50420	2459
Total Current Receipts	1458130	529399	928728	1635860	602810	1033050	1803830	722854	1080980	1867150	772191	1094950
Disbursements												
1 Property and entrepreneurial income	1077180	369875	707308	1199620	413131	786491	1216140	421334	794809	1226370	445349	781021
A Withdrawals from quasi-corporations	5718	5718	-	16808	16808		21917	21917	-	20409	20409	-
B Interest	919547	245360	674187	1002780	267840	734936	978228	255103	723125	948844	256246	692598
C Dividends a	137860	104739	33121	164151	112596	51555	199731	128047	71684	239377	150954	88423
D Net land rent and royalties	14058	14058	-	15887	15887	-	16267	16267	-	17740	17740	
2 Direct taxes and other current transfers n.e.c. to general government	105134	69774	35360	115852	81941	33911	136134	95849	40285	150707	108697	42010
A Direct taxes	103137	67777	35360	113703	79792	33911	133526	93241	40285	147888	105878	42010
On income	28280	12445	15835	32463	15690	16773	36756	17003	19753	38372	18414	19958
Other	74857	55332	19525	81240	64102	17138	96770	76238	20532	109516	87464	22052
B Fines, fees, penalties and other current transfers n.e.c.	1997	1997	-	2149	2149	-	2608	2608	-	2819	2819	-
3 Other current transfers	252238	124257	127981	275294	131546	143748	294334	140946	153388	308123	141211	166912
A Casualty insurance premiums, net	26763	26279	484	27568	27057	511	28987	28461	526	28600	28013	587
B Casualty insurance claims liability of insurance companies	97448	-	97448	103779	-	103779	107332	-	107332	113902	-	113902
C Transfers to private non-profit institutions	1071	1071	-	1240	1240	-	1366	1366	-	1277	1277	-
D Unfunded employee pension and welfare benefits	80094	62422	17672	87286	65443	21843	93719	67443	26276	98790	69254	29536
E Social assistance grants	...	...	...	...	...	...	...	...	...	...	...	...
F Other transfers n.e.c.	46862	34485	12377	55421	37806	17615	62930	43676	19254	65554	42667	22887
G Transfers to the rest of the world	...	...	...	...	...	...	...	...	...	...	...	...
Net saving	23572	-34507	58079	45093	-23808	68901	157222	64725	92497	181945	76934	105011
Total Current Disbursements and Net Saving	1458130	529399	928728	1635860	602810	1033050	1803830	722854	1080980	1867150	772191	1094950

	1988			1989		
	TOTAL	Non-Financial	Financial	TOTAL	Non-Financial	Financial
Receipts						
1 Operating surplus	448114	580168	-132054	494896	632784	-137888
2 Property and entrepreneurial income	1258990	127778	1131210	1429660	142535	1287120
A Withdrawals from quasi-corporate enterprises	...	...	...	...	...	...
B Interest	1137000	44635	1092370	1290060	46214	1243840
C Dividends	112240	73396	38844	131070	87792	43278
D Net land rent and royalties	9747	9747	-	8529	8529	-

614

France

3.22 Corporate and Quasi-Corporate Enterprise Income and Outlay Account: Total and Sectors
(Continued)

Million French francs

	1988			1989		
	TOTAL	Non-Financial	Financial	TOTAL	Non-Financial	Financial
3 Current transfers	308383	159503	148880	323380	163082	160298
A Casualty insurance claims	32275	31666	609	30026	29389	637
B Casualty insurance premiums, net, due to be received by insurance companies	100095	-	100095	105141	-	105141
C Current transfers from the rest of the world	...	...	...	...	...	...
D Other transfers except imputed	119470	73880	45590	128439	76593	51846
E Imputed unfunded employee pension and welfare contributions	56543	53957	2586	59774	57100	2674
Total Current Receipts	2015490	867449	1148040	2247930	938401	1309530
			Disbursements			
1 Property and entrepreneurial income	1323470	472648	850819	1507330	534580	972745
A Withdrawals from quasi-corporations	15135	15135	-	18469	18469	-
B Interest	1013320	267536	745787	1142320	306179	836140
C Dividends [a]	274087	169055	105032	327684	191079	136605
D Net land rent and royalties	20922	20922	-	18853	18853	-
2 Direct taxes and other current transfers n.e.c. to general government	161301	117905	43396	180626	131777	48849
A Direct taxes	159582	116186	43396	178960	130111	48849
On income	38243	18469	19774	39775	19003	20772
Other	121339	97717	23622	139185	111108	28077
B Fines, fees, penalties and other current transfers n.e.c.	1719	1719	-	1666	1666	-
3 Other current transfers	341075	150735	190340	342828	158046	184782
A Casualty insurance premiums, net	31366	30773	593	32634	32011	623
B Casualty insurance claims liability of insurance companies	119958	-	119958	125520	-	125520
C Transfers to private non-profit institutions	1370	1370	-	1448	1448	-
D Unfunded employee pension and welfare benefits	106126	72672	33454	113864	76000	37864
E Social assistance grants	...	...	...	...	...	...
F Other transfers n.e.c.	82255	45920	36335	69362	48587	20775
G Transfers to the rest of the world	...	...	...	...	...	...
Net saving	189642	126161	63481	217152	113998	103154
Total Current Disbursements and Net Saving	2015490	867449	1148040	2247930	938401	1309530

a) Item 'Dividends' includes profit-sharing by employees.

3.23 Corporate and Quasi-Corporate Enterprise Capital Accumulation Account: Total and Sectors

Million French francs

	1980			1981			1982			1983		
	TOTAL	Non-Financial	Financial	TOTAL	Non-Financial	Financial	TOTAL	Non-Financial	Financial	TOTAL	Non-Financial	Financial
						Finance of Gross Accumulation						
1 Gross saving	203021	173711	29310	192639	171366	21273	217730	197198	20532	283306	228641	54665
A Consumption of fixed capital	198981	193098	5883	230251	223207	7044	266237	258022	8215	297608	288138	9470
B Net saving	4040	-19387	23427	-37612	-51841	14229	-48507	-60824	12317	-14302	-59497	45195
2 Capital transfers	13799	10998	2801	17007	13642	3365	21718	15563	6155	22856	18219	4637
Finance of Gross Accumulation	216820	184709	32111	209646	185008	24638	239448	212761	26687	306162	246860	59302
						Gross Accumulation						
1 Gross capital formation	321298	310236	11062	311128	297647	13481	366363	351296	15067	348812	332100	16712

France

3.23 Corporate and Quasi-Corporate Enterprise Capital Accumulation Account: Total and Sectors
(Continued)

Million French francs

	1980 TOTAL	1980 Non-Financial	1980 Financial	1981 TOTAL	1981 Non-Financial	1981 Financial	1982 TOTAL	1982 Non-Financial	1982 Financial	1983 TOTAL	1983 Non-Financial	1983 Financial
1 Gross capital formation	286679	285720	-41	-7968	-7987	19	8984	8924	60	-24745	11
B Gross fixed capital formation	296219	285716	11103	319096	305634	13462	357379	342372	15007	373546	16701
2 Purchases of land, net	4899	4324	575	6797	6113	684	4646	3953	693	6225	5573	652
3 Purchases of intangible assets, net	5460	5464	-4	4524	4516	8	5986	5979	7	7966	7953	13
4 Capital transfers	7479	5947	1532	11078	9143	1935	14167	5881	4586	14190	9238	4952
Net lending	-122316	-141253	18946	-123411	-124872	-18580	-151714	6334	-71031	-108004	36873
Gross Accumulation	216820	184709	32111	209694	185008	24686	239448	212761	26687	306162	246860	59302

	1984 TOTAL	1984 Non-Financial	1984 Financial	1985 TOTAL	1985 Non-Financial	1985 Financial	1986 TOTAL	1986 Non-Financial	1986 Financial	1987 TOTAL	1987 Non-Financial	1987 Financial
Finance of Gross Accumulation												
1 Gross saving	346619	277252	69367	391481	310468	81195	527468	421618	105850	570623	451203	119420
A Consumption of fixed capital	323047	311759	11288	346889	334294	12294	370246	358893	13353	388678	374269	14409
B Net saving	23572	-34507	58079	45093	-23808	68901	157222	64725	92497	181945	76934	105011
2 Capital transfers	27713	21462	6251	32538	26852	5686	39633	34274	5359	38702	32896	5806
Finance of Gross Accumulation	374332	298714	75618	424219	337338	86881	567101	455892	111209	609325	484099	125226
1 Gross capital formation	381534	360387	21147	413884	390024	23801	485224	456061	29163	532298	509757	29541
A Increase in stocks	-12041	-12029	-12	-19365	-20004	639	7209	7370	-161	21883	22107	-214
B Gross fixed capital formation	393575	372416	21159	433249	410087	23162	475315	448691	26624	517405	487650	29755
2 Purchases of land, net	7075	6245	830	5540	4785	755	8407	7501	906	8666	7673	993
3 Purchases of intangible assets, net	9860	9849	11	12046	12042	4	16395	16380	15	16948	16948	-
4 Capital transfers	17149	10559	6590	26077	17634	8443	29099	12046	17053	27970	14784	13186
Net lending	-41286	-88326	47040	-33328	-87206	53878	-30896	-96109	64772	-65063	-81506	16443
Gross Accumulation	374332	298714	75618	424219	337338	86881	567101	455892	111209	603925	484099	125226

	1988 TOTAL	1988 Non-Financial	1988 Financial	1989 TOTAL	1989 Non-Financial	1989 Financial
Finance of Gross Accumulation						
1 Gross saving	599506	520039	79467	656542	535511	121031
A Consumption of fixed capital	409864	398878	15986	433390	421513	17877
B Net saving	189642	126161	63481	217152	113998	103154
2 Capital transfers	38568	32310	6258	37907	31208	6699
Finance of Gross Accumulation	638074	552349	85725	694449	566719	127730
1 Gross capital formation	622575	589894	32681	677232	637954	39278
A Increase in stocks	39033	39051	-18	28540	28530	10
B Gross fixed capital formation	584542	550843	33699	648692	609424	39268
2 Purchases of land, net	7778	6658	1120	9184	7835	1349
3 Purchases of intangible assets, net	19194	19194	-	20159	20159	-
4 Capital transfers	26944	12203	14741	29982	15145	14837
Net lending	-39417	-75600	36183	-42108	-114374	72266
Gross Accumulation	638074	552349	85725	694449	566719	127730

3.24 Corporate and Quasi-Corporate Enterprise Capital Finance Account: Total and Sectors

Million French francs

	1980 TOTAL	1980 Non-Financial	1980 Financial	1981 TOTAL	1981 Non-Financial	1981 Financial	1982 TOTAL	1982 Non-Financial	1982 Financial	1983 TOTAL	1983 Non-Financial	1983 Financial
Acquisition of Financial Assets												
1 Gold and SDRs	13445	1220	12225	11883	1667	-2405	-13550	-570	-1835	18833	-63	18896
2 Currency and transferable deposits	67558	4997	62561	16280	-19020	35300	33993	17471	16522	76708	62392	14316
3 Other deposits	295263	19785	275478	110000	14625	95441	224309	20453	203856	261597	17318	244279
4 Bills and bonds, short term	-5619	-	-5619	60937	-2	60939	22227	-	22227	41029	-	41029

616

France

3.24 Corporate and Quasi-Corporate Enterprise Capital Finance Account: Total and Sectors (Continued)

Million French francs

	1980			1981			1982			1983		
	TOTAL	Non-Financial	Financial	TOTAL	Non-Financial	Financial	TOTAL	Non-Financial	Financial	TOTAL	Non-Financial	Financial

Acquisition of Financial Assets

5 Bonds, long term	45156	39924	5232	43383	37781	5602	81236	7828	73408	121838	5289	116549
6 Corporate equity securities	35824	25250	10574	62370	28194	34176	58870	31979	26891	123284	60995	62319
7 Short term loans, n.e.c.	137524	11243	126281	203660	170174	33486	350609	305840	45069	41930	31774	10156
8 Long term loans, n.e.c.	239151		239151	258692		258692	355858		355858	346256		346256
9 Trade credits and advances	122570	117942	4628	144765	136910	7855	137626	129693	7933	162940	157251	10818
10 Other receivables	2819	2740	79	3362	3291	71	7548	7337	211	4910	4805	105
11 Other assets	...	...	...	...	...	...	...	...	...	...	...	...
Total Acquisition of Financial Assets	953691	173733	779958	892522	259073	633849	1340260	257193	1083070	1204460	3397141	864723

Incurrence of Liabilities

1 Currency and transferable deposits	96278	96278	-	74261	74261	-	152073	152073	-	66136	66136	-
2 Other deposits	464912	11002	453910	321265	13311	307954	435764	10617	425147	447617	12794	434823
3 Bills and bonds, short term	330	-	330	4189	-	4189	6544	-	6544	-204	-	-204
4 Bonds, long term	69706	16844	52862	67359	7355	60004	167334	38849	128485	157623	34646	122977
5 Corporate equity securities	71401	55940	15461	198661	82501	54753	277453	43027	44805	171286	69937	101349
6 Short-term loans, n.e.c.	141040	57084	83956	193171	104232	87139	346479	118519	227960	49368	59990	-10622
7 Long-term loans, n.e.c.	86898	67356	19480	108690	84942	23748	134458	93557	49901	201698	143849	57849
8 Net equity in life insurance and pension fund reserves	13138	-	13138	16564	-	16564	18634	-	18634	25371	-	25371
9 Proprietors' net additions to the accumulation of quasi-corporations	...	...	...	...	...	...	...	...	...	...	...	...
10 Trade credit and advances	124531	121263	3268	139177	134446	4731	126160	121938	4222	147050	141842	5208
11 Other accounts payable	15944	-	15944	18539	-	18539	26168	-	26168	24026	-	24026
12 Other liabilities	1084120	325080	759027	1023920	399039	624877	1506850	425507	1080340	1289970	463058	826913
Total Incurrence of Liabilities	...	...	...	...	...	...	...	...	...	...	...	...
Statistical discrepancy a	-8109	1985	-7113	442	-7555	442	-14898	-11266	-3602	-14476	-15313	837
Net Lending	-123316	-141262	18946	-123881	-132411	8530	-151714	-158048	6334	-71031	-108004	36973
Incurrence of Liabilities and Net Lending	953691	173733	779958	892522	259073	633849	1340260	257193	1083070	1204460	3397141	864723

	1984			1985			1986			1987		
	TOTAL	Non-Financial	Financial	TOTAL	Non-Financial	Financial	TOTAL	Non-Financial	Financial	TOTAL	Non-Financial	Financial

Acquisition of Financial Assets

1 Gold and SDRs	45726	6053	39673	26390	-2021	28411	3613	-2753	6366	-801	5334	-6135
2 Currency and transferable deposits	85167	18256	66911	64990	-8784	73774	15293	88886	53356	36303
3 Other deposits	324492	8741	315751	290650	36729	253921	283586	16728	266858	404906	12460	392448
4 Bills and bonds, short term	47223	-	47223	51645	10258	41287	9696	1417	7929	212259	97092	115167
5 Bonds, long term	170885	3007	167878	237120	6722	230398	26321	2032	26118	134454	670	133784
6 Corporate equity securities	129088	8208	120311	57037	63274	213011	88162	124139	299830	117723	182207
7 Short term loans, n.e.c.	136420	73348	63072	167655	32805	134850	127261	69708	57553	463313	27427	435886
8 Long term loans, n.e.c.	305078		305078	220907		220907	214367		214367	340239		340239
9 Trade credits and advances	177673	10303	167373	47182	5097	52279	71865	7113	78978	110025	-328
10 Other receivables	2106	1981	125	4339	4237	102	4450	98	4923	4830	93
11 Other assets	...	...	...	...	...	...	...	...	...	...	...	...
Total Acquisition of Financial Assets	1419360	3589760	1060390	1236290	190502	1045780	1382740	279902	1102840	2022280	392614	1629660

Incurrence of Liabilities

1 Currency and transferable deposits	186080	-	186080	101128	-	101128	154888	-	154888	192070	-	192070
2 Other deposits	438466	11446	427020	422980	19227	403753	366990	11333	355276	545800	24622	521178
3 Bills and bonds, short term	-1538		-1538	31837	3300	28537	68647	22413	46234	169883	15688	154245
4 Bonds, long term	163617	27526	130091	183562	18585	164977	166899	44309	122590	155660	15115	140545
5 Corporate equity securities	228377	73158	155219	302750	99361	203389	458144	177091	281053	355401	163832	191569
6 Short-term loans, n.e.c.	85879	64853	23726	50889	4576	5413	-23203	-47388	24185	280937	48131	232806

France

3.24 Corporate and Quasi-Corporate Enterprise Capital Finance Account: Total and Sectors
(Continued)

Million French francs

	1984			1985			1986			1987		
	TOTAL	Non-Financial	Financial	TOTAL	Non-Financial	Financial	TOTAL	Non-Financial	Financial	TOTAL	Non-Financial	Financial
7 Long-term loans, n.e.c.	129838	110357	19481	35208	40062	-4854	-10758	31064	-41822	88563	90239	-1676
8 Net equity of households in life insurance and pension fund reserves	34346	-	34346	47350	-	47350	67527	-	67527	83039	-	83039
9 Proprietors' net additions to the accumulation of quasi-corporations	...	...	...	...	...	...	...	...	...	...	...	...
10 Trade credit and advances	163631	158524	5107	58085	41271	16814	78498	78071	427	115269	115756	-487
11 Other accounts payable	27083	-	27083	24242	-	24242	21725	-	21725	25485	-	25485
12 Other liabilities	...	...	...	...	...	...	...	...	...	...	...	...
Total Incurrence of Liabilities	1458480	445864	1012620	1258030	267282	990749	1348980	316893	1032080	2012110	473333	1538770
Statistical discrepancy a	2168	1438	730	11583	10426	1157	3088	-895	3983	-6272	-15656	9384
Net Lending	-41286	-88326	47040	-33328	-87206	53878	30676	-36096	66772	16443	-65063	81506
Incurrence of Liabilities and Net Lending	1419360	358976	1060390	1236290	190502	1045780	1382740	279902	1102840	2022280	392614	1629660

	1988			1989		
	TOTAL	Non-Financial	Financial	TOTAL	Non-Financial	Financial
	Acquisition of Financial Assets					
1 Gold and SDRs	-26474	1409	-27883	-1136	3490	-4626
2 Currency and transferable deposits	34811	14379	20432	100721	41099	59622
3 Other deposits	241895	17727	224168	244714	22483	222231
4 Bills and bonds, short term	158252	9421	148831	277942	82006	195936
5 Bonds, long term	245190	8638	236552	215838	32839	182999
6 Corporate equity securities	340785	255017	85768	441519	294680	146839
7 Short term loans, n.e.c.	243423	111451	131972	417982	57835	360147
8 Long term loans, n.e.c.	364606	-	364606	436291	-	436291
9 Trade credits and advances	158240	145521	12719	191329	184089	7240
10 Other receivables	5085	4996	89	4075	4000	75
11 Other assets	...	...	...	...	...	...
Total Acquisition of Financial Assets	1765810	568559	1197250	2329280	722521	1606750
	Incurrence of Liabilities					
1 Currency and transferable deposits	855	-	855	203605	...	203605
2 Other deposits	354787	19735	335052	403108	6113	396995
3 Bills and bonds, short term	191146	20700	170446	250146	64600	185546
4 Bonds, long term	215976	47047	168929	219956	41956	178000
5 Corporate equity securities	436356	168053	268303	516232	229193	287039
6 Short-term loans, n.e.c.	163390	113168	50222	238343	130564	107779
7 Long-term loans, n.e.c.	153978	146581	7397	258034	253054	4980
8 Net equity of households in life insurance and pension fund reserves	123360	-	123360	158775	-	158775
9 Proprietors' net additions to the accumulation of quasi-corporations	...	...	...	...	...	...
10 Trade credit and advances	147187	135237	11950	135317	128362	6955
11 Other accounts payable	15983	-	15983	14321	-	14321
12 Other liabilities	...	...	...	...	...	...
Total Incurrence of Liabilities	1803020	650521	1152500	2397840	853842	1544000
Statistical discrepancy a	2212	-6362	8574	-26454	-16947	-9507
Net Lending	-39417	-75600	36183	-42108	-114374	72266
Incurrence of Liabilities and Net Lending	1765810	568559	1197250	2329280	722521	1606750

a) Statistical discrepancy refers to adjustment made in order to reconcile the net lending of the Capital Accumulation Account and the Capital Finance Account.

3.31 Household and Private Unincorporated Enterprise Production Account

Million French francs

	1970	1975	1980	1981	1982	1983	1984	1985	1986	1987	1988	1989
	Gross Output											
1 Output for sale	308766	501986	912285	1002130	1135270	1229850	1325830	1383010	1461830	1469820	1615480	1750750
2 Non-marketed output	5981	10697	16929	18587	22776	24975	26438	27859	27858	28407	30603	32189
Gross Output	314747	512683	929214	1020720	1158050	1254830	1352270	1410870	1489690	1498230	1646090	1782940
	Gross Input											
Intermediate consumption	88531	150270	286529	313205	345104	364424	399061	387453	396588	355697	407459	434120

618

France

3.31 Household and Private Unincorporated Enterprise Production Account
(Continued)

Million French francs

	1970	1975	1980	1981	1982	1983	1984	1985	1986	1987	1988	1989
Subtotal: Value Added	226216	362413	642685	707510	812941	890402	953211	1023420	1093100	1142530	1238630	1348820
1 Indirect taxes net liability of unincorporated enterprises	3311	2304	10917	7311	9153	9208	7931	7543	7073	8451	14166	13526
A Indirect taxes	5025	9569	20536	21713	23330	25738	28475	30580	33101	35637	39071	38020
B Less: Subsidies	1714	7265	9619	14402	14177	16530	20544	23037	26028	27186	24905	24494
2 Consumption of fixed capital	21419	46414	102096	114400	128837	141651	151718	158818	171910	184831	199533	214624
3 Compensation of employees	42002	70482	123205	132564	149686	160240	168255	178158	180689	185881	195934	207481
4 Net operating surplus	159484	243213	406467	453235	525265	579303	625307	678900	733427	763370	828994	913187
Gross Input	314747	512683	929214	1020720	1158050	1254830	1352270	1410870	1489690	1498230	1646090	1782940

3.32 Household and Private Unincorporated Enterprise Income and Outlay Account

Million French francs

	1970	1975	1980	1981	1982	1983	1984	1985	1986	1987	1988	1989
Receipts												
1 Compensation of employees	391442	801596	1573880	1791190	2052960	2255620	2419230	2573110	2700560	2815530	2961020	3151920
A Wages and salaries	297699	603876	1162640	1324310	1508560	1644070	1755250	1855000	1945810	2024480	2125010	2261270
B Employers' contributions for social security	73799	158564	331529	375121	437439	493327	536059	580556	606927	639450	676046	722720
C Employers' contributions for private pension & welfare plans	19944	39156	79710	91759	106956	118222	127913	137547	147827	151596	159960	167931
2 Operating surplus of private unincorporated enterprises	159484	243213	406467	453235	525265	579303	625307	678900	733427	763370	828994	913187
3 Property and entrepreneurial income	34269	78291	166725	209664	230713	256819	273808	303406	305074	320822	355445	406329
A Withdrawals from private quasi-corporations	...	...	...	...	...	...	...	...	...	...	...	...
B Interest	14116	45046	111745	142540	165544	177554	185902	200298	186774	177745	192713	208324
C Dividends	14716	25501	44162	55876	53527	66428	72719	86311	101706	129155	148545	183167
D Net land rent and royalties	5437	7744	10818	11248	11642	12837	15187	16797	16594	13922	14187	14838
3 Current transfers	152826	323251	670050	789650	945636	1053410	1161370	1271040	1361870	1418550	1524580	1618110
A Casualty insurance claims	11363	23391	47377	54787	65634	72702	79524	84577	87659	92703	98717	102483
B Social security benefits	90971	204885	443334	531130	637501	711500	770207	834620	896206	932957	1000750	1067450
C Social assistance grants	14078	26519	46879	55010	66896	79021	99437	120179	131665	133175	145130	146884
D Unfunded employee pension and welfare benefits	24267	47568	92369	107050	123824	138013	152966	162704	169348	177696	184828	195954
E Transfers from general government	...	...	...	...	...	...	...	...	...	...	...	...
F Transfers from the rest of the world	1439	2746	5801	5656	5869	5947	6421	5807	6207	6628	6523	8557
G Other transfers n.e.c.	10708	18142	34290	36017	45912	46223	52813	63148	70787	75388	88630	96786
Total Current Receipts	738021	1446350	2817120	3243740	3754570	4145140	4479710	4826450	5100930	5318270	5670040	6089550
Disbursements												
1 Final consumption expenditures	457196	857794	1645070	1897910	2190340	2424140	2639170	2858390	3049520	3231110	3422340	3650030
2 Property income	14282	39030	89538	96075	120111	131726	145623	164206	182139	185473	203302	232473
A Interest	9266	31883	79257	85347	108912	118798	130985	148239	166994	173213	190598	219775
B Net land rent and royalties	5016	7147	10281	10728	11199	12928	14638	15967	15145	12260	12704	12698
3 Direct taxes and other current transfers n.e.c. to government	141879	300783	683517	774333	911843	1045030	1161710	1241350	1317030	1402250	1476230	1596330
A Social security contributions	103447	225144	511363	575393	679347	772521	856208	924924	979420	1049340	1119280	1216840
B Direct taxes	37318	73932	169420	195992	228595	268062	300368	311265	331624	346442	350289	370618
Income taxes	27722	51063	119822	138985	162926	189865	210857	210404	223547	238662	238199	251006
Other	9596	22869	49598	57007	65669	78197	89511	100861	108077	107780	112090	119612
C Fees, fines and penalties	1114	1707	2734	2948	3901	4445	5135	5161	5984	6464	6667	8872

France

3.32 Household and Private Unincorporated Enterprise Income and Outlay Account
(Continued)

Million French francs

	1970	1975	1980	1981	1982	1983	1984	1985	1986	1987	1988	1989
4 Other current transfers	40658	77481	149610	172900	202981	226704	237829	256625	273631	282558	296913	314774
A Net casualty insurance premiums	8371	16457	33549	39052	47560	52255	56785	60635	62662	67499	70969	74212
B Transfers to private non-profit institutions serving households	2861	5495	9673	10802	12617	13504	14416	14826	15825	16568	17264	18277
C Transfers to the rest of the world	4255	7170	12783	14832	15570	16674	15890	16728	15525	14736	14249	15071
D Other current transfers, except imputed	5321	9203	13895	16455	20278	26049	22825	26889	31792	32159	34472	39283
E Imputed employee pension and welfare contributions	19850	39156	79710	91759	106956	118222	127913	137547	147827	151596	159959	167931
Net saving	84006	171263	249385	302521	329295	317542	295375	305874	278616	216878	271247	295937
Total Current Disbursements and Net Saving	738021	1446350	2817120	3243740	3754570	4145140	4479710	4826450	5100930	5318270	5670040	6089550

3.33 Household and Private Unincorporated Enterprise Capital Accumulation Account

Million French francs

	1970	1975	1980	1981	1982	1983	1984	1985	1986	1987	1988	1989
					Finance of Gross Accumulation							
1 Gross saving	105425	217677	351481	416921	458132	459193	447093	464692	450526	401709	470780	510561
A Consumption of fixed capital	21419	46414	102096	114400	128837	141651	151718	158818	171910	184831	199533	214624
B Net saving	84006	171263	249385	302521	329295	317542	295375	305874	278616	216878	271247	295937
2 Capital transfers	1540	4540	11742	15802	12362	10763	10739	10777	10920	13162	30349	20705
Total Finance of Gross Accumulation	106965	222217	363223	432723	470494	469956	457832	475469	461446	414871	501129	531266
					Gross Accumulation							
1 Gross Capital Formation	77099	143303	265604	279754	302670	316513	313197	320945	349295	363146	389634	431809
A Increase in stocks	3138	-1340	1145	-605	3278	2679	-4406	-3617	2878	-1076	-8885	7836
B Gross fixed capital formation	73961	144643	264459	280359	299392	313834	317603	324562	346417	364222	398519	423973
2 Purchases of land, net	-3421	-6062	-7865	-9261	-7259	-9142	-10106	-7746	-11265	-10479	-9621	-13047
3 Purchases of intangibles, net	-1770	-2884	-5546	-4604	-6116	-8069	-9754	-12117	-16473	-17032	-19288	-20235
4 Capital transfers	2651	5078	8737	12708	13062	13237	13841	14722	18979	20881	24527	25998
Net lending	32406	82782	102293	154126	168137	157417	150654	159665	120910	58355	115877	106741
Total Gross Accumulation	106965	222217	363223	432723	470494	469956	457832	475469	461446	414871	501129	531266

3.34 Household and Private Unincorporated Enterprise Capital Finance Account

Million French francs

	1970	1975	1980	1981	1982	1983	1984	1985	1986	1987	1988	1989
					Acquisition of Financial Assets							
1 Gold	-238	-114	1000	8446	4558	-201	-161	51	-8241	-1008	6741	13954
2 Currency and transferable deposits	11588	31856	30660	66925	62638	41313	40948	31609	65500	48128	48330	52227
3 Other deposits	41334	106770	123348	121885	152813	161703	135080	134259	67021	150891	130803	61640
4 Bills and bonds, short term	-	-	-	-	-	-	-	-	-	7168	7163	-2514
5 Bonds, long term	964	6035	46561	33486	63477	35531	12448	6278	18111	13005	3385	4452
6 Corporate equity securities	2296	3063	16324	20087	-7241	29046	86487	132274	188604	107314	117823	94093
7 Short term loans, n.e.c.	3109	4152	24894	13128	38768	-21484	15888	-62283	6255	24352	-10175	-433
8 Long term loans, n.e.c.	...	...	...	...	...	...	...	...	...	...	...	...
9 Trade credit and advances	2105	6353	-52	7129	11007	20310	11409	-2060	-7930	1722	26022	25219
10 Net equity of households in life insurance and pension fund reserves	2691	5539	13138	16564	18634	25371	34346	47350	67527	83039	123360	158775
11 Proprietors' net additions to the accumulation of quasi-corporations	...	...	...	...	...	...	...	...	...	...	...	...
12 Other	3499	6515	13149	15264	18818	19166	24976	20327	17677	20854	11184	9936
Total Acquisition of Financial Assets	67348	170169	269022	302914	363472	310755	361421	307805	414524	455465	464636	417349
					Incurrence of Liabilities							
1 Short term loans, n.e.c.	11619	7873	25934	27219	38696	-5782	30774	11371	134150	162645	116017	98972

France

3.34 Household and Private Unincorporated Enterprise Capital Finance Account
(Continued)

Million French francs

	1970	1975	1980	1981	1982	1983	1984	1985	1986	1987	1988	1989
2　Long term loans, n.e.c.	13884	44558	112152	100374	119996	105293	114382	121441	136041	202497	197394	137200
3　Trade credit and advances	3676	10194	9202	23633	19971	32444	59999	12758	21006	20916	33668	70477
4　Other accounts payable	...	...	...	...	...	...	...	...	...	...	...	...
5　Other liabilities	-	...	-84	-52	225	135	-138	73	82	-5	797	106
Total Incurrence of Liabilities	29179	62625	147204	151174	178888	132090	205017	145643	291279	386053	347876	306755
Statistical discrepancy a	5763	24762	19525	-2386	16447	21248	5750	2497	2335	11057	883	3853
Net Lending	32406	82782	102293	154126	168137	157417	150654	159665	120910	58355	115877	106741
Incurrence of Liabilities and Net Lending	67348	170169	269022	302914	363472	310755	361421	307805	414524	455465	464636	417349

a) Statistical discrepancy refers to adjustment made in order to reconcile the net lending of the
Capital Accumulation Account and the Capital Finance Account.

3.41 Private Non-Profit Institutions Serving Households: Production Account

Million French francs

	1970	1975	1980	1981	1982	1983	1984	1985	1986	1987	1988	1989
Gross Output												
1　Sales	3056	5522	9774	10978	12329	13477	14300	15262	15918	16659	17595	18584
2　Non-marketed output	2381	4466	8239	9311	10481	11404	12134	12704	13288	13846	14553	15433
Gross Output	5437	9988	18013	20289	22810	24881	26434	27966	29206	30505	32148	34017
Gross Input												
Intermediate consumption	3010	5502	9904	11155	12540	13684	14534	15411	16090	16812	17726	18749
Subtotal: Value Added	2427	4486	8109	9134	10270	11197	11900	12555	13116	13693	14422	15268
1　Indirect taxes, net	10	27	48	54	61	67	72	76	79	83	88	93
2　Consumption of fixed capital	160	339	677	774	886	984	1069	1132	1205	1268	1335	1407
3　Compensation of employees	2337	4296	7757	8736	9822	10708	11379	12009	12545	13097	13795	14603
4　Net operating surplus	-80	-176	-373	-430	-499	-562	-620	-662	-713	-755	-796	-835
Gross Input	5437	9988	18013	20289	22810	24881	26434	27966	29206	30505	32148	34017

3.42 Private Non-Profit Institutions Serving Households: Income and Outlay Account

Million French francs

	1970	1975	1980	1981	1982	1983	1984	1985	1986	1987	1988	1989
Receipts												
1　Operating surplus	-80	-176	-373	-430	-499	-562	-620	-662	-713	-755	-796	-835
2　Property and entrepreneurial income	188	335	653	739	855	930	990	1037	1085	1131	1189	1261
A　Withdrawals from quasi-corporations	-	-	-	-	-	-	-	-	-	-	-	-
B　Interest	188	335	653	739	855	930	990	1037	1085	1131	1189	1261
C　Dividends	-	-	-	-	-	-	-	-	-	-	-	-
D　Net land rent and royalties	-	-	-	-	-	-	-	-	-	-	-	-
3　Current transfers	3775	7103	13099	15409	18144	20199	22880	24238	24803	25901	28479	28857
A　Casualty insurance claims	13	31	66	70	92	101	105	113	119	129	128	134
B　Current transfers from general government	787	1330	2829	3912	4734	5835	7288	8059	7493	7927	9717	8998
C　Other transfers from resident sectors	...	...	...	...	...	...	...	...	...	...	...	...
D　Current transfers received from the rest of the world	2975	5742	10204	11427	13318	14263	15487	16066	17191	17845	18634	19725
E　Imputed unfunded employee pension and welfare contributions	...	...	...	...	...	...	...	...	...	...	...	...
Total Current Receipts	3883	7262	13379	15718	18500	20567	23250	24613	25175	26277	28872	29283
Disbursements												
1　Final consumption expenditures	2381	4466	8239	9311	10481	11404	12134	12704	13288	13846	14553	15433
2　Property income	17	34	62	70	79	86	92	96	100	104	109	116
A　Interest	17	34	62	70	79	86	92	96	100	104	109	116
B　Net land rent and royalties	...	...	...	...	...	...	...	...	...	...	...	...
3　Direct taxes and other transfers to general government	-	12	35	40	50	54	79	91	100	109	120	127

France

3.42 Private Non-Profit Institutions Serving Households: Income and Outlay Account
(Continued)

Million French francs

	1970	1975	1980	1981	1982	1983	1984	1985	1986	1987	1988	1989
4 Other current transfers	588	1139	2189	2422	2776	3006	3183	3339	3468	3656	3841	4016
A Net casualty insurance premiums	13	22	46	54	79	85	83	87	89	106	108	113
B Social assistance grants	...	...	...	...	...	...	...	...	...	...	...	...
C Unfunded employee pension and welfare benefits	473	960	1682	2017	2271	2470	2628	2752	2879	3000	3153	3344
D Current transfers to the rest of the world	...	...	...	...	...	...	...	...	...	...	...	...
E Other current transfers n.e.c.	102	157	461	351	426	451	472	500	500	550	580	559
Net saving	897	1611	2854	3875	5114	6017	7762	8383	8219	8562	10249	9591
Total Current Disbursements	3883	7262	13379	15718	18500	20567	23250	24613	25175	26277	28872	29283

3.43 Private Non-Profit Institutions Serving Households: Capital Accumulation Account

Million French francs

	1970	1975	1980	1981	1982	1983	1984	1985	1986	1987	1988	1989
Finance of Gross Accumulation												
1 Gross saving	1057	1950	3531	4649	6000	7001	8831	9515	9424	9830	11584	10998
A Consumption of fixed capital	160	339	677	774	886	984	1069	1132	1205	1268	1335	1407
B Net saving	897	1611	2854	3875	5114	6017	7762	8383	8219	8562	10249	9591
2 Capital transfers	146	270	584	815	951	1139	1386	1415	1739	1755	1993	2041
Finance of Gross Accumulation	1203	2220	4115	5464	6951	8140	10217	10930	11163	11585	13577	13039
Gross Accumulation												
1 Gross capital formation	548	1117	2073	2346	2642	2875	3059	3203	3350	3491	3669	3891
A Increase in stocks	-	-	-	-	-	-	-	-	-	-	-	-
B Gross fixed capital formation	548	1117	2073	2346	2642	2875	3059	3203	3350	3491	3669	3891
2 Purchases of land, net	9	18	33	37	42	46	49	51	53	55	58	62
3 Purchases of intangible assets, net	-	-	-	-	-	-	-	-	-	-	-	-
4 Capital transfers	52	96	180	304	230	250	266	279	291	304	320	339
Net lending	594	989	1829	2777	4037	4969	6843	7397	7469	7735	9530	8747
Gross Accumulation	1203	2220	4115	5464	6951	8140	10217	10930	11163	11585	13577	13039

3.44 Private Non-Profit Institutions Serving Households: Capital Finance Account

Million French francs

	1970	1975	1980	1981	1982	1983	1984	1985	1986	1987	1988	1989
Acquisition of Financial Assets												
1 Gold	...	...	...	...	...	...	...	...	...	...	...	...
2 Currency and transferable deposits	-15	288	194	1255	1295	1857	1297	462	223	7680	-5281	6338
3 Other deposits	611	26	611	-67	92	844	871	640	1110	1083	-99	120
4 Bills and bonds, short term	...	...	...	...	...	...	...	...	...	...	...	...
5 Bonds, long term	6	-14	55	37	52	89	157	-	-	-	-	76
6 Corporate equity securities	...	...	...	...	...	...	...	...	...	...	...	...
7 Short-term loans, n.e.c.	50	-113	210	-70	228	155	551	563	-220	1128	9622	433
8 Long-term loans, n.e.c.	...	...	...	...	...	...	...	...	...	...	...	...
9 Other receivables	4	7	15	16	20	20	23	20	19	18	16	-
10 Proprietors' net additions to the accumulation of quasi-corporations	...	...	...	...	...	...	...	...	...	...	...	...
11 Other assets	30	790	259	1397	2232	2494	4890	7161	6463	1420	7833	2944
Total Acquisition of Financial Assets	686	984	1344	2568	3919	5459	7789	8846	7595	11329	12091	9911
Incurrence of Liabilities												
1 Short-term loans	-	-6	69	-12	22	278	599	272	-97	3514	1401	768
2 Long-term loans	94	-	-547	-200	-150	202	326	1144	155	-32	978	381
3 Other liabilities	-2	1	-7	3	10	10	21	33	68	112	182	15
Total Incurrence of Liabilities	92	-5	-485	-209	-118	490	946	1449	126	3594	2561	1164
Net Lending	594	989	1829	2777	4037	4969	6843	7397	7469	7735	9530	8747
Incurrence of Liabilities and Net Lending	686	984	1344	2568	3919	5459	7789	8846	7595	11329	12091	9911

France

3.51 External Transactions: Current Account: Detail

Million French francs

	1970	1975	1980	1981	1982	1983	1984	1985	1986	1987	1988	1989
Payments to the Rest of the World												
1 Imports of goods and services	121244	262254	638791	744754	859536	907388	1024970	1092620	1021790	1095010	1218040	1408060
A Imports of merchandise c.i.f.	106296	232778	576505	663485	768258	808900	914542	970814	893847	952251	1063870	1229350
B Other	14948	29476	62286	81269	91278	98488	110426	121805	127942	142757	154172	178707
2 Factor income to the rest of the world	7930	22297	79595	136672	168370	170399	206772	226699	190134	184380	202855	249460
A Compensation of employees	683	1829	5560	6534	8295	10796	14584	19689	19310	16969	20241	18329
B Property and entrepreneurial income	7247	20468	74035	130138	160075	159603	192188	207010	170824	167411	182614	231131
3 Current transfers to the rest of the world	16218	33780	66436	80315	98756	112491	110528	122924	128709	137175	159229	157983
A Indirect taxes by general government to supranational organizations	30	8001	17983	22824	28726	32730	34604	37545	49048	54179	62291	61270
B Other current transfers	16188	25779	48453	57491	70030	79761	75924	85379	79661	82996	96938	96713
4 Surplus of the nation on current transactions	6274	12404	-16700	-25275	-76960	-31978	-485	2384	23876	-7885	-17319	-8944
Payments to the Rest of the World, and Surplus of the Nation on Current Transfers	151666	330735	768122	936466	1049700	1158300	1341780	1444630	1364510	1408680	1562810	1806560
Receipts From The Rest of the World												
1 Exports of goods and services	125428	279799	604422	714282	790351	900658	1053330	1123930	1074100	1103190	1221940	1425130
A Exports of merchandise f.o.b.	99401	226420	488877	576389	631842	720442	845218	901379	860303	886740	992606	1136360
B Other	26027	53379	115545	137893	158509	180216	208110	222551	213792	216447	229338	288773
2 Factor income from the rest of the world	11229	24668	92182	146949	170350	158672	183267	201020	173526	171913	191335	237491
A Compensation of employees	681	1661	3656	5120	6690	7129	8037	10350	11757	12427	16401	16563
B Property and entrepreneurial income	10548	23007	88526	141829	163660	151543	175230	190670	161769	159486	174934	220928
3 Current transfers from the rest of the world	15009	26268	71518	75235	89001	98970	105188	119676	116887	133578	149530	143932
A Subsidies to general government from supranational organizations	-	6768	17230	19502	19464	26222	26268	32898	39354	51022	42118	34847
B Other current transfers	15009	19500	54288	55733	69537	72748	78920	86778	77533	82556	107412	109085
Receipts from the Rest of the World on Current Transfers	151666	330735	768122	936466	1049700	1158300	1341780	1444630	1364510	1408680	1562810	1806560

3.52 External Transactions: Capital Accumulation Account

Million French francs

	1970	1975	1980	1981	1982	1983	1984	1985	1986	1987	1988	1989
Finance of Gross Accumulation												
1 Surplus of the nation on current transactions	6274	12404	-16700	-25275	-76960	-31978	-485	2384	23876	-7885	-17319	-8944
2 Capital transfers from the rest of the world	-	224	669	471	829	1141	906	785	907	1268	6276	1324
Total Finance of Gross Accumulation	6274	12628	-16031	-24804	-76131	-30837	421	3169	24783	-6617	-11043	-7620
Gross Accumulation												
1 Capital transfers to the rest of the world	1050	1661	2663	2950	3805	4162	4369	4106	4128	12773	4416	5274
2 Purchases of intangible assets, n.e.c., net, from the rest of the world	...	...	...	...	...	...	...	...	...	...	...	...
Net lending to the rest of the world	5224	10967	-18694	-27754	-79936	-34999	-3948	-937	20655	-19390	-15459	-12894
Total Gross Accumulation	6274	12628	-16031	-24804	-76131	-30837	421	3169	24783	-6617	-11043	-7620

3.53 External Transactions: Capital Finance Account

Million French francs

	1970	1975	1980	1981	1982	1983	1984	1985	1986	1987	1988	1989
Acquisitions of Foreign Financial Assets												
1 Gold and SDR's	5662	16455	14953	-3314	1820	18010	46187	26617	-8176	-1421	-17570	12818
2 Currency and transferable deposits	33	1004	19665	-7775	-16976	11573	-7092	10021	19336	-22507	-6068	10598
3 Other deposits	5386	31751	79666	4260	19664	5425	65132	16932	46224	225527	150190	178907
4 Bills and bonds, short term	-	-	-	-	-	-	-	2473	-897	740	-81	576

France

3.53 External Transactions: Capital Finance Account (Continued)

Million French francs

	1970	1975	1980	1981	1982	1983	1984	1985	1986	1987	1988	1989
5 Bonds, long term	425	1543	5535	1893	165	10828	4874	27347	33441	7360	19934	19550
6 Corporate equity securities	2288	6801	17065	35848	20753	18234	21499	16743	66895	67123	81690	144394
7 Short-term loans, n.e.c.	6739	-2145	5678	16169	-4946	-585	16014	9036	3900	16113	-2439	77750
8 Long-term loans	1444	9180	27503	40396	58030	38370	26108	23272	-1477	9096	11775	45359
9 Proprietors' net additions to accumulation of quasi-corporate, non-resident enterprises												
10 Trade credit and advances	5843	5101	9243	9884	2924	14369	11579	-1743	5209	27410	32671	34954
11 Other	196	197	432	509	733	598	620	914	915	687	659	-
Total Acquisitions of Foreign Financial Assets	28016	69887	179740	97570	82167	116822	184921	131612	145370	330127	270677	524906

Incurrence of Foreign Liabilities

	1970	1975	1980	1981	1982	1983	1984	1985	1986	1987	1988	1989
1 Currency and transferable deposits	-3324	296	5044	6476	5979	12560	-247	11318	6731	26614	-28454	25273
2 Other deposits	10853	34463	125908	82624	69341	25190	50959	11829	61443	220166	134974	271466
3 Bills and bonds, short term	25				-	-	-	2827	12418	9570	39528	27067
4 Bonds, long term	1638	6692	10866	8422	48392	52632	64440	52572	24754	25785	41883	88237
5 Corporate equity securities	4254	9166	14524	13829	6970	14313	20017	46222	48317	47744	51477	108356
6 Short-term loans, n.e.c.	11	-489	-242	1175	-502	247	1687	-1440	4040	2256	-1060	28
7 Long-term loans	2913	3939	12661	15503	28951	47517	10450	-14583	-37113	-9622	18329	4389
8 Non-resident proprietors' net additions to accumulation of resident quasi-corporate enterprises												
9 Trade credit and advances	4615	-1598	17950	6479	181	5002	20380	9385	-1567	21969	22523	15365
10 Other	88	151	307	315	312	395	458	39	269	250	241	220
Total Incurrence of Liabilities	21073	48920	187018	134823	160524	180951	118469	118292	344732	283041	560401	
Statistical discrepancy [a]	1719	9100	9416	-9499	6772	1579	7918	14080	5423	4785	3056	-22601
Net Lending	5224	10967	-18694	-27754	-79336	-34999	-3948	-937	20655	-19390	-15459	-12894
Total Incurrence of Liabilities and Net Lending	28016	69887	179740	97570	82167	116822	184921	131612	145370	330127	270677	524906

[a] Statistical discrepancy refers to adjustment made in order to reconcile the net lending of the Capital Accumulation Account and the Capital Finance Account.

4.1 Derivation of Value Added by Kind of Activity, in Current Prices

Million French francs

	1980			1981			1982			1983		
	Gross Output	Intermediate Consumption	Value Added	Gross Output	Intermediate Consumption	Value Added	Gross Output	Intermediate Consumption	Value Added	Gross Output	Intermediate Consumption	Value Added

All Producers

1 Agriculture, hunting, forestry and fishing	251146	132122	119024	277084	148141	130943	333501	167282	166219	365526	195835	169691
A Agriculture, hunting	237356	129056	108260	264887	144565	120322	318094	163460	154634	343417	186653	156764
B Forestry and logging	9566	690	8875	9400	812	8588	9735	901	8834	10835	964	9871
C Fishing	4225	2336	1889	4797	2033	2764	5672	2921	2751	6274	3318	2956
2 Mining and quarrying	56095	32235	23821	73440	29257	44183	75875	47978	27897	83906	50414	33492
A Coal mining	14415	10169	4246	18371	12561	5810	18945	13358	5587	18253	12948	5305
B Crude petroleum and natural gas production	30228	16446	13782	43020	25667	17353	43808	28227	15581	51110	30581	20529
C Metal ore mining	3051	1460	1591	2811	1439	1372	3471	1524	1947	4085	1538	2547
D Other mining	8362	4160	4202	9238	4516	4722	9651	4869	4782	10458	5347	5111

France

4.1 Derivation of Value Added by Kind of Activity, in Current Prices (Continued)

Million French francs

	1980 Gross Output	1980 Intermediate Consumption	1980 Value Added	1981 Gross Output	1981 Intermediate Consumption	1981 Value Added	1982 Gross Output	1982 Intermediate Consumption	1982 Value Added	1983 Gross Output	1983 Intermediate Consumption	1983 Value Added
3 Manufacturing	1910470	1300950	609520	1737380	2088440	2484670	1526950	821520	2531320	1683050	9009970	
A Manufacture of food, beverages and tobacco	325694	237223	88471	370636	270881	99755	425490	301283	123307	455172	331429	123743
B Textile, wearing apparel and leather industries	131954	76844	55110	133922	82038	52884	158378	94036	64342	173149	102525	70624
C Manufacture of wood and wood products, including furniture	58950	34715	24235	62242	36926	25316	67155	39074	28081	70742	41431	29311
D Manufacture of paper and paper products, printing and publishing	107696	64371	43325	122077	77722	48305	139673	85229	54444	153710	93794	59916
E Manufacture of chemicals and chemical products, petroleum, coal, rubber and plastic products	407059	290151	119608	461957	335657	126300	496817	357695	139122	535023	370725	164298
F Manufacture of non-metallic mineral products, except products of petroleum and coal	67673	34611	33062	73380	37754	35626	77685	40482	37203	81744	42973	38771
G Basic metal industries	160232	121267	38965	162254	127291	38463	172979	128919	44060	178912	132476	46436
H Manufacture of fabricated metal products, machinery and equipment	622908	357877	265031	689444	399532	289912	777779	463702	316075	849199	498153	351046
I Other manufacturing industries	25604	13891	11713	27529	15029	12500	31420	14886	16534	33670	16845	16825
4 Electricity, gas and water	90370	40062	50308	104764	44841	59923	122962	52188	70774	141391	53891	87500
5 Construction	404451	210842	193609	442446	235249	207197	480959	252777	228182	492476	257873	234603
6 Wholesale and retail trade, restaurants and hotels	550830	155658	395042	625757	170940	454817	712376	199567	512809	795236	215629	579607
A Wholesale and retail trade	448462	110702	337760	506921	118856	387066	574388	141647	432741	640210	153176	487034
B Restaurants and hotels	102168	44886	57282	118838	51085	67751	137988	57920	80068	155026	62453	92573
7 Transport, storage and communication	250067	85873	164194	282243	97763	184480	326548	113340	213208	357879	121991	235888
A Transport and storage	186577	75548	111029	211181	86049	125132	241706	99527	142179	261274	106320	155854
B Communication	63490	10325	53165	71062	11714	59348	84842	13813	71029	96505	15671	80134
8 Finance, insurance, real estate and business services	651538	178960	472578	752787	204421	548366	841113	235626	627487	946469	268362	696287
9 Community, social and personal services	189704	78680	265524	162972	65997	228969	141147	55753	196800	121265	47176	...
Total, industries	4331770	2886270	594010	2831170	2662610	5493690	2486590	2377660	2298360	4866900	2138310	3127740
Producers of Government Services	605659	242934	927929	613983	217466	831449	519968	185280	705248	448211	157422	684995
Other Producers	...	...	3109200	3445150	2880080	2885230	3009600	2566750	2667250	2271250	3812740	4938800
Total	3107740	3107740	3445150	6252350	3000950	5572100	2667570	2271230	4938800			
Less: imputed bank service charge	-162385	...	147548	-147548	...	-124807	124807	...	-107503	107503		
Import duties [a]	7938	...	7938	7813	...	7813	6778	...	6778	6339	...	6339
Value added tax	349566	...	349566	320814	...	320814	273274	...	273274	242015	...	242015
Other adjustments	-748	...	-748	-209	...	-209	...	...	...	-128	...	-128
Total	4006500	3271590	3625020	3027620	3164800	2687760	5852560	2803000	5187030	2378730		

All Producers

	1984 Gross Output	1984 Intermediate Consumption	1984 Value Added	1985 Gross Output	1985 Intermediate Consumption	1985 Value Added	1986 Gross Output	1986 Intermediate Consumption	1986 Value Added	1987 Gross Output	1987 Intermediate Consumption	1987 Value Added
1 Agriculture, hunting, forestry and fishing	380791	205575	175216	393941	211631	182310	403678	214183	189495	401139	212404	188735
A Agriculture and hunting	362196	200948	161248	373454	206489	166965	381208	203572	177936	377255	207506	169519
B Forestry and logging	12030	1178	10852	13026	1244	11782	14119	1360	12759	15483	1417	14066
C Fishing	6565	3449	3116	7461	3898	3563	8351	4800	3551	8631	3481	5150
2 Mining and quarrying	91450	55887	35563	98736	58624	40112	83609	47952	35657	72589	37189	35400
A Coal mining	19391	13844	5547	18974	14023	4951	16452	11357	5095	13526	9071	4455
B Crude petroleum and natural gas production	56986	34718	22268	64637	37021	27616	51750	28981	22769	43634	20384	23250
C Metal ore mining	4281	1726	2555	3614	2058	1556	3803	2145	1658	3464	1648	1816
D Other mining	10792	5599	5193	11511	6024	5487	11604	5956	5648	11965	6086	5879

625

France

4.1 Derivation of Value Added by Kind of Activity, in Current Prices (Continued)

Million French francs

	1984			1985			1986			1987		
	Gross Output	Intermediate Consumption	Value Added	Gross Output	Intermediate Consumption	Value Added	Gross Output	Intermediate Consumption	Value Added	Gross Output	Intermediate Consumption	Value Added
3 Manufacturing	2764990	1808720	956273	2924120	1890860	1033140	2918800	1797700	1120100	2995860	1852480	1143380
A Manufacture of food, beverages and tobacco	495555	360715	134840	514442	370313	144129	527178	374539	147239	523313	376065	147248
B Textile, wearing apparel and leather industries	187381	114413	72968	201860	128210	79050	204402	123993	84409	204523	117333	87190
C Manufacture of wood and wood products, including furniture	71927	42746	29181	73638	43664	29974	78739	46315	32424	82477	48940	33537
D Manufacture of paper and paper products, printing and publishing	176147	111196	64951	189656	118802	70854	201135	127738	78397	216618	130921	85697
E Manufacture of petroleum, coal, rubber and plastic products	598515	425769	172746	631402	435971	195431	552698	326410	226288	558887	339521	219366
F Manufacture of non-metallic mineral products, except products of petroleum and coal	87795	44486	39309	88088	48490	40598	83515	48774	44741	100566	51336	49230
G Basic metal industries	200359	149953	50406	212152	157096	55056	202863	144495	58368	197993	138867	59126
H Manufacture of fabricated metal products, machinery and equipment	914801	541735	373066	927719	574242	398477	1021550	593328	428224	1072050	629721	443330
I Other manufacturing industries	36509	17703	18806	39160	19590	19570	40119	20109	20010	39434	19779	19655
4 Electricity, gas and water	162192	57285	104907	178932	62063	116869	181153	63060	118093	188257	65622	122635
5 Construction	512310	270309	242001	529694	285796	243898	573590	310637	262953	334984		270906
6 Wholesale and retail trade, restaurants and hotels	877989	242072	635917	954942	269931	685011	1030040	282961	747077	1092560	293930	798629
A Wholesale and retail trade	710812	174876	535936	733359	197852	575507	833802	209679	626823	884008	216744	667264
B Restaurants and hotels	167177	67196	99981	181583	72079	109504	196236	73982	120254	208551	77186	131365
7 Transport, storage and communication	392218	132714	259504	434641	145591	289050	453517	3107598	3107598	473281	152357	320924
A Transport and storage	282343	116180	161163	308827	125631	182296	318845	125562	195263	323239	131941	200198
B Communication	109875	16534	93341	125814	19060	106754	134672	19196	115476	141142	20416	120726
8 Finance, insurance, real estate and business services	1091890	309788	782100	1216030	355089	861137	1394460	416861	977594	1572280	498217	1074060
9 Community, social and personal services	294253	82855	211658	323175	91801	231374	355895	99562	256333	381716	107030	274686
Total, Industries	6668090	3169490	3404040	7054210	3371310	3682900	7394740	3376899	4018090	3554220	3554220	4237520
Producers of Government Services	1016300	265791	750506	1083060	287496	795661	1142250	296925	845325	1195870	323474	872398
Other Producers	...	...	...	...	...	...	...	...	...	...	...	...
Total	7584380	3430730	4153650	8137270	3658810	4478460	8536990	3673600	4863390	3877610	3877610	5109920
Less: Imputed bank service charge	-175627		-175627	-192340		-192340	-223272		-223272	247379		-247379
Import duties [a]	8698		8698	8904		8904	8976		8976	9667		9667
Value added tax	375609		375609	405281		405281	420279		420279	449074		449074
Other adjustments	-410		-410	-163		-163	-173		-173	-447		-447
Total	7968270	3606360	4361910	8551290	3851150	4700140	8961780	3898670	5069300	9445900	4125070	5320830

All Producers

	1988			1989		
	Gross Output	Intermediate Consumption	Value Added	Gross Output	Intermediate Consumption	Value Added
1 Agriculture, hunting, forestry and fishing	410571	222501	188070	435335	220975	214360
A Agriculture and hunting	384662	217247	167415	404079	214952	189127
B Forestry and logging	17211	1587	15624	18881	1796	18085
C Fishing	8698	3667	5031	11375	4227	7148
2 Mining and quarrying	66644	37256	29388	69716	39477	30239
A Coal mining	12085	9323	2762	12473	9601	2872
B Crude petroleum and natural gas production	38117	19541	18576	40519	21162	19357
C Metal ore mining	3605	1857	1748	3582	1905	1677
D Other mining	12837	6535	6302	13142	6809	6333

France

4.1 Derivation of Value Added by Kind of Activity, in Current Prices (Continued)

Million French francs

	1988 Gross Output	1988 Intermediate Consumption	1988 Value Added	1989 Gross Output	1989 Intermediate Consumption	1989 Value Added
3 Manufacturing	3222220	1999130	1224090	3498920	2194530	1304380
A Manufacture of food, beverages and tobacco	543797	390154	153643	575900	407811	168089
B Textile, wearing apparel and leather industries	205820	119976	85844	212735	125279	87456
C Manufacture of wood and wood products, including furniture	89070	53012	36058	94419	58317	36102
D Manufacture of paper and paper products, printing and publishing	235191	143732	91459	256875	158861	98014
E Manufacture of chemicals and chemical products, coal, rubber and plastic products	600095	358229	241866	650186	398687	251499
F Manufacture of non-metallic mineral products, except products of petroleum and coal	111057	56167	54890	117249	59845	57404
G Basic metal industries	228285	158855	69690	256054	179654	76400
H Manufacture of fabricated metal products, machinery and equipment	1169720	694614	475104	1293380	778866	514510
I Other manufacturing industries	40188	24549	15639	42123	27213	14910
4 Electricity, gas and water	190779	122917	67862	201699	127518	74181
5 Construction	680266	371021	309245	407301 (?) 730198	408625	321573
6 Wholesale and retail trade, restaurants and hotels	1189200	313810	875391	1277780	335894	943881
A Wholesale and retail trade	964351	233937	730414	1033570	250134	783433
B Restaurants and hotels	224850	79873	144977	246208	85760	160448
7 Transport, storage and communication	493384	164359	329025	528519	182066	346453
A Transport and storage	357540	143370	213970	382738	158291	224447
B Communication	135844	20789	115055	145781	23775	122006
8 Finance, insurance, real estate and business services	1754050	1180630	573413	2013320	697834 (?)	1315490
9 Community, social and personal services	420045	114588	305457	456936	125889	331047
Total, Industries	8428160	3863940	4564220	9214420	4282810	4931610
Producers of Government Services	1264810	355564	909244	1337740	371246	966490
Other Producers						
Total	9692970	4219500	5473460	5522000 (?)	4651060 (?)	5889100
Less: Imputed bank service charge	-270440		270440	-298483		298483
Import duties a	107477		107477	112311		112311
Value added tax	472960		472960	502452		502452
Other adjustments	-305		-305	-178		-178
Total	10182670	4489900	5692770	11065565	4952540	6113120

a) Item 'Import duties' includes also value added tax (VAT) on products.

4.2 Derivation of Value Added by Kind of Activity, in Constant Prices

Million French francs

At constant prices of: 1980

All Producers

	1980 Gross Output	1980 Intermediate Consumption	1980 Value Added	1981 Gross Output	1981 Intermediate Consumption	1981 Value Added	1982 Gross Output	1982 Intermediate Consumption	1982 Value Added	1983 Gross Output	1983 Intermediate Consumption	1983 Value Added
1 Agriculture, hunting, forestry and fishing	251146	132122	119024	249282	131056	118226	272213	131194	141019	264995	131378	133617(?)/131217
A Agriculture and hunting	237356	129096	108260	235959	127948	108011	258969	131272	127697	251445	130769	120676
B Forestry and logging	9655	690	8875	9138	712	8426	8985	696	8289	8271	656	8615
C Fishing	4225	2336	1889	4185	2396	1789	4259	2226	2033	4279	2353	1926
2 Mining and quarrying	56099	32235	23235 (?)	55624	32823	22801	49677	30264	19313	51057	29848	21209
A Coal mining	14415	10169	4246	14026	9641	4385	12591	9125	3466	11936	8714	3222
B Crude petroleum and natural gas production	30228	16446	13782	31127	18056	13071	27181	16233	10948	29312	16264	13048
C Metal ore mining	3051	1460	1591	2544	1261	1283	2455	1186	1269	2496	1105	1391
D Other mining	8362	4160	4202	7927	3865	4062	7350	3720	3630	7313	3765	3548

627

France

4.2 Derivation of Value Added by Kind of Activity, in Constant Prices
(Continued)

Million French francs

	1980			1981			1982			1983		
	Gross Output	Intermediate Consumption	Value Added	Gross Output	Intermediate Consumption	Value Added	Gross Output	Intermediate Consumption	Value Added	Gross Output	Intermediate Consumption	Value Added
	At constant prices of:1980											
3 Manufacturing	1910470	1230950	679520	1870540	1195670	674873	1861880	1181120	680762	1846230	1162700	683532
A Manufacture of food, beverages and tobacco	325694	237223	88471	328681	240744	87937	334754	239092	95662	331402	242778	88624
B Textile, wearing apparel and leather industries	131954	76844	55110	127813	73710	54103	130372	74511	55861	130066	74329	55737
C Manufacture of wood and wood products, including furniture	58950	34715	24235	56851	34185	22666	56104	33001	23103	54786	32394	22392
D Manufacture of paper and paper products, printing and publishing	107696	64371	43325	107513	65678	41835	110671	68424	42247	113176	70625	42551
E Manufacture of chemicals and chemical petroleum, coal, rubber and plastic products	409759	290151	119608	389347	264510	124837	376591	251305	125286	378912	245336	133576
F Manufacture of non-metallic mineral products, except products of petroleum and coal	67673	34611	33062	63538	32255	31283	60867	30646	30221	58935	29907	29028
G Basic metal industries	160232	121267	38965	151536	113526	38010	139163	103758	35405	129690	96401	33289
H Manufacture of fabricated metal products, machinery and equipment	622908	357877	265031	620386	357499	262887	626096	366036	260060	622622	358204	264418
I Other manufacturing industries	25604	13891	11713	24877	13562	11315	27259	14342	12917	26639	12722	13917
4 Electricity, gas and water	90370	40062	50308	92688	35906	56782	95120	37274	57846	100230	36433	63797
5 Construction	404451	210842	193609	402127	209295	192832	393850	201130	192720	375875	188356	187519
6 Wholesale and retail trade, restaurants and hotels	550630	155588	395042	553752	151008	402744	569400	156926	412474	573904	155590	418314
A Wholesale and retail trade	448462	110702	337760	451477	106312	345165	463622	111812	351810	466934	111190	355744
B Restaurants and hotels	102168	44886	57282	102275	44696	57579	105778	45114	60664	106970	44400	62570
7 Transport, storage and communication	250067	85873	164194	252319	83416	168903	259341	84764	174577	263368	84049	179319
A Transport and storage	186577	75548	111029	182640	72783	109857	184796	73633	111163	183731	72596	111135
B Communication	63490	10325	53165	69679	10633	59046	74545	11131	63414	79637	11453	68184
8 Finance, insurance, real estate and business services	651538	178960	472578	665501	181265	484236	679003	185938	493065	684405	193846	490559
9 Community, social and personal services	168441	47176	121265	174065	49475	124590	183427	52234	131193	193639	55556	138083
Total, Industries	4333170	2113810	2219360	4315900	2069910	2245990	4363810	2063840	2299970	4353700	2040150	2313550
Producers of Government Services	605633	157422	448211	622776	165637	457139	645537	173168	472369	658783	177183	481600
Other Producers	...	...	...	...	...	...	...	...	...	...	...	...
Total	4938800	2271230	2667570	4938680	2235550	2703130	5009350	2237010	2772340	5012480	2217340	2795150
Less: Imputed bank service charge	...	-107503	107503	...	-110500	110500	...	-114653	114653	...	-114024	114024
Import duties [a]	6339	...	6339	6388	...	6388	7138	...	7138	7049	...	7049
Value added tax	242015	...	242015	242405	...	242405	248907	...	248907	245888	...	245888
Other adjustments	-128	...	-128	-91	...	-91	-68	...	-68	-158	...	-158
Total	5187030	2378730	2808300	5187380	2346050	2841330	5265320	2351660	2913660	5265260	2331360	2933900

	1984			1985			1986			1987		
	Gross Output	Intermediate Consumption	Value Added	Gross Output	Intermediate Consumption	Value Added	Gross Output	Intermediate Consumption	Value Added	Gross Output	Intermediate Consumption	Value Added
	At constant prices of:1980											
	All Producers											
1 Agriculture, hunting, forestry and fishing	272934	135611	137323	272902	134461	138441	274698	135241	139457	280585	139446	141139
A Agriculture and hunting	259247	132726	126521	258679	131449	127230	259848	132149	127699	265306	136365	128941
B Forestry and logging	9565	687	8878	10059	678	9381	10617	719	9898	11081	751	10330
C Fishing	4122	2198	1924	4164	2334	1830	4233	2373	1860	4198	2330	1868
2 Mining and quarrying	50678	30271	20407	52800	31100	21700	52231	31486	20745	52321	30894	21427
A Coal mining	12094	8727	3367	11324	8357	2967	10687	7731	2956	9388	6654	2734
B Crude petroleum and natural gas production	29017	16756	12261	32175	18027	14148	31980	18940	13040	33359	19356	14003
C Metal ore mining	2408	1144	1264	2021	984	1037	2371	1071	1300	2292	1059	1233
D Other mining	7159	3644	3515	7280	3732	3548	7193	3744	3449	7282	3825	3457

628

France

4.2 Derivation of Value Added by Kind of Activity, in Constant Prices
(Continued)

Million French francs

	1984			1985			1986			1987		
	Gross Output	Intermediate Consumption	Value Added	Gross Output	Intermediate Consumption	Value Added	Gross Output	Intermediate Consumption	Value Added	Gross Output	Intermediate Consumption	Value Added

At constant prices of 1980

3 Manufacturing	1855620	1184580	671038	1865690	1197270	668425	1883630	1216370	667256	1909770	1244280	665487
A Manufacture of food, beverages and tobacco	336979	247855	89124	340489	248174	92315	345168	252998	92170	350252	258717	91535
B Textile, wearing apparel and leather industries	127121	74031	53090	127337	75584	51753	127509	76873	50636	124917	72999	51918
C Manufacture of wood and wood products, including furniture	52651	31050	21601	51131	30296	20835	52788	31798	20990	54337	33033	21304
D Manufacture of paper and paper products, printing and publishing	117031	74419	42612	119017	75894	43123	124462	79217	45245	126937	83231	43706
E Manufacture of chemicals and chemical products, coal, rubber and plastic products	387275	256799	130476	388139	261395	126744	385278	258889	125390	388689	266151	122538
F Manufacture of non-metallic mineral products, except products of petroleum and coal	57415	28480	28935	58189	29506	28683	59051	30149	28902	61515	31722	29793
G Basic metal industries	134529	100215	34314	133364	99728	33936	137555	100385	37170	139690	100056	38844
H Manufacture of fabricated metal products, machinery and equipment	615862	359283	256579	621725	363618	258107	629358	371522	257836	643361	385257	258104
I Other manufacturing industries	26754	12447	14307	26001	13072	12929	24457	13540	10917	22857	13112	9745
4 Electricity, gas and water	106376	36336	70040	112240	27085	85209	116825	39664	77261	122225	40079	82146
5 Construction	368242	185080	183153	366145	185739	180406	367787	185661	182126	392722	200207	188115
6 Wholesale and retail trade, restaurants and hotels	584286	159256	425030	601054	169753	431301	619490	176265	443225	633249	181806	451443
A Wholesale and retail trade	476673	115399	361274	491138	124650	366488	506309	129217	377092	520747	134685	386062
B Restaurants and hotels	107613	43857	63756	109916	45103	64813	113181	47048	66133	112502	47121	65381
7 Transport, storage and communication	292142	82659	184483	275999	84750	191274	288335	87996	198339	302094	92276	209218
A Transport and storage	183730	71458	112272	187724	72605	115119	195844	78421	117122	203745	80080	122665
B Communication	83412	11201	72211	88275	12145	76130	93369	12152	81217	98349	12796	85553
8 Finance, insurance, real estate and business services	712150	205068	507082	751116	223566	527699	820320	253984	566336	888149	293815	594334
9 Community, social and personal services	201108	54619	146489	210255	58046	152209	222734	62315	160419	228572	65680	162892
Total, industries	4418530	2073490	2345050	4509620	2128010	2398620	4660150	2201250	2458890	4814080	2298680	2515400
Producers of Government Services	668274	178522	489752	682634	184220	498414	694482	188875	505607	714631	201631	513000
Other Producers	2250010	...	2283400	2302620	...	2306230	2354630	...	2389820	2947610	...	2500310	3028400
Total	6508810	2252010	2834800	5197260	2300230	2885030	5354630	2389820	2947610	2500310	2803480	
Less: Imputed bank service charge	...	114264	-114264	...	118696	-118696	...	131917	-131917	...	140611	-140611
Import duties a	7271		7271	7626		7626	8482		8482	9426		9426
Value added tax	244808		244808	254556		254556	263514		263514	275582		275582
Other adjustments	-148		-148	-136		-136	-149		-149	-136		-136
Total	5387740	2366270	2972460	5453300	2424920	3028380	5626480	2521840	3104640	5813590	2640920	3172660

At constant prices of 1980

All Producers

1 Agriculture, hunting, forestry and fishing	283077	142326	140751	283967	138725	145242
A Agriculture and hunting	267009	139600	127961	267141	135183	131558
B Forestry and logging	11737	818	10919	12541	883	11658
C Fishing	4331	1871	2460	4285	2659	2026
2 Mining and quarrying	50535	30873	19662	50711	31619	19092
A Coal mining	9048	6720	2328	8591	6574	2017
B Crude petroleum and natural gas production	31257	18941	12316	32002	19843	12159
C Metal ore mining	2520	1159	1361	2433	1130	1303
D Other mining	7710	4053	3657	7685	4072	3613

France

4.2 Derivation of Value Added by Kind of Activity, in Constant Prices (Continued)

Million French francs

	1988			1989		
	Gross Output	Intermediate Consumption	Value Added	Gross Output	Intermediate Consumption	Value Added
	At constant prices of 1980					
3 Manufacturing	1996220	712818	1358600	2071420		687209	1309010
A Manufacture of food, beverages and tobacco	354301	95391	263035	358426	88671	265650
B Textile, wearing apparel and leather industries	122736	50545	72406	122951	50440	72296
C Manufacture of wood and wood products, including furniture	57273	22540	36076	58616	22638	34635
D Manufacture of paper and paper products, printing and publishing	134839	49458	92885	142343	46859	87980
E Manufacture of chemicals and chemical products, petroleum, coal, rubber and plastic products	409392	131531	289939	421470	129194	280198
F Manufacture of non-metallic mineral products, except products of petroleum and coal	66387	32726	35203	67929	34223	32164
G Basic metal industries	148183	40900	111773	151833	39785	108398
H Manufacture of fabricated metal products, machinery and equipment	679162	282552	440724	723276	269254	409908
I Other manufacturing industries	23944	8015	16660	24575	15740	8204
4 Electricity, gas and water	124083	81415	47007	128422	41669	82414
5 Construction	426943	205228	240600	445828	200568	226375
6 Wholesale and retail trade, restaurants and hotels	661757	481958	681177	199219	470319	191438
A Wholesale and retail trade	547305	414367	562762	143895	404159	143146
B Restaurants and hotels	114452	67591	50824	118415	66160	48292
7 Transport, storage and communication	330070	245335	352118	106783	226939	100431
A Transport and storage	219369	139888	231142	91254	132886	86483
B Communication	110701	105447	120976	15529	97253	13948
8 Finance, insurance, real estate and business services	947349	657237	1043860	386819	617672	326977
9 Community, social and personal services	240588	182407	254956	72549	172169	68419
Total, Industries	5090020	2730730	5312450	2581720	2620400	2440220
Producers of Government Services	736627	531131	747472	216541	521097	215530
Other Producers	5797250	3261860	6009100	2798260	3141500	2655750
Less: Imputed bank service charge	...	158763	...	-147580	-147580	...
Total	...	10315	11142	10315	11142	...
Import duties a	306503	...	306503	290764	...	290764
Value added tax	-148	-143	-148	-143	...	...
Other adjustments	6608180	3420600	6377830	2957030	3294850	2803330
Total						

a) Item "Import duties" includes also value added tax (VAT) on products.

4.3 Cost Components of Value Added

Million French francs

	1980						1981					
	Compensation of Employees	Capital Consumption	Net Operating Surplus	Indirect Taxes	Less: Subsidies Received	Value Added	Compensation of Employees	Capital Consumption	Net Operating Surplus	Indirect Taxes	Less: Subsidies Received	Value Added
	All Producers											
1 Agriculture, hunting, forestry and fishing	18856	...	102124	2670	4626	119024	20677	...	114633	3060	6763	130943
A Agriculture and hunting	14948	...	94880	2495	4063	108260	16414	...	107805	2866	6763	120322
B Forestry and logging	2565	...	6699	116	501	8875	2941	...	6112	123	588	8588
C Fishing	1343	...	549	59	62	1889	1322	...	716	71	76	2033
2 Mining and quarrying	16622	...	10357	905	4062	23821	18489	...	13331	1639	4202	29257
A Coal mining	7570	...	491	209	4024	4246	8485	...	1212	257	4144	5810
B Crude petroleum and natural gas production	4902	...	8410	501	31	13782	5981	...	10223	1187	38	17353
C Metal ore mining	1588	...	-64	68	1	1591	1052	...	279	46	5	1372
D Other mining	2562	...	1520	127	6	4202	2971	...	1617	149	15	4722

France

4.3 Cost Components of Value Added
(Continued)

Million French francs

	1980						1981					
	Compensation of Employees	Capital Consumption	Net Operating Surplus	Indirect Taxes	Less: Subsidies Received	Value Added	Compensation of Employees	Capital Consumption	Net Operating Surplus	Indirect Taxes	Less: Subsidies Received	Value Added
3 Manufacturing	464648	...	154219	75554	14902	679520	515155	...	158474	77106	17274	733461
A Manufacture of food, beverages and tobacco	47297	...	37049	12903	8778	88471	53703	...	41456	13882	9286	99755
B Textile, wearing apparel and leather industries	41536	...	11927	1879	232	55110	44078	...	11518	2056	368	57284
C Manufacture of wood and wood products, including furniture	15740	...	7555	1005	65	24235	17180	...	7184	1064	112	25316
D Manufacture of paper and paper products, printing and publishing	32074	...	10245	1448	442	43325	35785	...	11402	1698	580	48305
E Manufacture of chemicals and chemical petroleum, coal, rubber and plastic products	60684	...	13544	45667	287	119608	66825	...	16242	43731	498	126300
F Manufacture of non-metallic mineral products, except products of petroleum and coal	20571	...	11379	1170	59	33062	22567	...	11825	1339	105	35626
G Basic metal industries	28980	...	8554	1885	454	38965	31075	...	5612	2085	309	38463
H Manufacture of fabricated metal products, machinery and equipment	209494	...	50804	9224	4491	265031	234990	...	49956	10841	5875	289912
I Other manufacturing industries	8272	...	3162	373	94	11713	8952	...	3279	410	141	12500
4 Electricity, gas and water	19057	...	25902	6459	1110	50308	22425	...	31327	7520	1349	59923
5 Construction	126304	...	63476	5809	1980	193609	141679	...	61937	6281	2700	207197
6 Wholesale and retail trade, restaurants and hotels	213167	...	165132	26659	9916	395042	243595	...	191821	32300	12899	454817
A Wholesale and retail trade	184594	...	136746	25401	8981	337760	209539	...	158662	30797	11932	387066
B Restaurants and hotels	28573	...	28386	1258	935	57282	34056	...	33159	1503	967	67751
7 Transport, storage and communication	105842	...	66593	4193	12434	164194	120486	...	73803	5092	14901	184480
A Transport and storage	75531	...	44660	3221	12383	111029	85640	...	50383	3948	14839	125132
B Communication	30311	...	21933	972	51	53165	34846	...	23420	1144	62	59348
8 Finance, insurance, real estate and business services	167488	...	285953	39767	20630	472578	195715	...	333820	45001	26170	548366
9 Community, social and personal services	43905	...	71056	8153	1849	121265	52024	...	82918	9207	3002	141147
Total, Industries	1175890	...	944812	170169	71509	2219360	1330250	...	1062060	187206	89924	2489590
Producers of Government Services	399895	...	38249	10067	...	448211	462357	...	44793	12818	...	519968
Other Producers	...	...	...	...	...	...	...	...	...	...	...	...
Total	1575780	...	983061	180236	71509	2667570	1792600	...	1106860	200024	89924	3009560
Less: Imputed bank service charge	...	...	107503	...	...	107503	...	...	124807	...	...	124807
Import duties	...	...	...	6339	...	6339	...	...	...	6778	...	6778
Value added tax	...	...	...	242015	...	242015	...	...	...	273274	...	273274
Other adjustments	...	...	...	...	128	-128	...	...	...	...	-	-
Total a	1575780	...	875558	428590	71637	2808300	1792600	...	982050	480076	89924	3164800

	1982						1983					
	Compensation of Employees	Capital Consumption	Net Operating Surplus	Indirect Taxes	Less: Subsidies Received	Value Added	Compensation of Employees	Capital Consumption	Net Operating Surplus	Indirect Taxes	Less: Subsidies Received	Value Added
				All Producers								
1 Agriculture, hunting, forestry and fishing	23655	...	145193	3658	6287	166219	26073	...	146293	4091	6866	169591
A Agriculture and hunting	18597	...	137791	3445	5199	154634	20636	...	138053	3851	5776	156764
B Forestry and logging	3265	...	6293	139	863	8834	3469	...	7162	124	884	9871
C Fishing	1793	...	1109	74	225	2751	1968	...	1078	116	206	2956
2 Mining and quarrying	20294	...	11928	1507	5832	27897	22837	...	15524	1618	6487	33492
A Coal mining	9273	...	1851	258	5795	5587	10231	...	1337	183	6446	5305
B Crude petroleum and natural gas production	6387	...	8211	1010	27	15581	7491	...	11900	1168	30	20529
C Metal ore mining	1457	...	415	77	2	1947	1501	...	971	78	3	2547
D Other mining	3177	...	1451	162	8	4782	3614	...	1316	189	8	5111

France

4.3 Cost Components of Value Added
(Continued)

Million French francs

	1982						1983					
	Compensation of Employees	Capital Consumption	Net Operating Surplus	Indirect Taxes	Less: Subsidies Received	Value Added	Compensation of Employees	Capital Consumption	Net Operating Surplus	Indirect Taxes	Less: Subsidies Received	Value Added
3 Manufacturing	576077	...	179224	86788	20569	821520	618783	...	213165	92761	23739	900970
A Manufacture of food, beverages and tobacco	61319	...	55821	16327	10160	123307	66317	...	52795	16665	12034	123743
B Textile, wearing apparel and leather industries	48733	...	14467	2284	1142	64342	53992	...	16244	2418	2030	70624
C Manufacture of wood and wood products, including furniture	18824	...	8136	1200	79	28081	19839	...	8160	1403	91	29311
D Manufacture of paper and paper products, printing and publishing	39814	...	14403	1912	1685	54444	43561	...	16233	2072	1950	59916
E Manufacture of chemicals and chemical petroleum, coal, rubber and plastic products	75289	...	16010	48307	484	139122	80531	...	32364	51907	504	164298
F Manufacture of non-metallic mineral products, except products of petroleum and coal	24116	...	11665	1495	73	37203	25477	...	11743	1642	91	38771
G Basic metal industries	36198	...	5862	2421	421	44060	36810	...	7693	2486	553	46436
H Manufacture of fabricated metal products, machinery and equipment	261592	...	48362	12426	6305	316075	281208	...	62554	13613	6329	351046
I Other manufacturing industries	10192	...	4498	416	220	14886	11048	...	5379	555	157	16825
4 Electricity, gas and water	26593	...	37041	8565	1425	70774	31088	...	48110	9924	1622	87500
5 Construction	157540	...	65994	7376	2728	228182	161836	...	67297	8207	2737	234603
6 Wholesale and retail trade, restaurants and hotels	276761	...	208230	39196	11378	512809	310639	...	234731	49825	15588	579607
A Wholesale and retail trade	236012	...	169681	37409	10361	432741	262949	...	190435	47696	14046	487034
B Restaurants and hotels	40749	...	38549	1787	1017	80068	47690	...	44296	2129	1542	92573
7 Transport, storage and communication	140436	...	83128	6276	16632	213208	153777	...	92563	7067	17419	235988
A Transport and storage	99157	...	54713	4905	16596	142179	107214	...	60524	5484	17368	155854
B Communication	41279	...	28415	1371	36	71029	46563	...	32039	1583	51	80134
8 Finance, insurance, real estate and business services	225874	...	380273	51148	29708	627587	253497	...	418423	57888	33521	696287
9 Community, social and personal services	62110	...	94446	10632	4216	162972	73906	...	107948	12768	4918	189704
Total, Industries	1509340	...	1205460	215146	98775	2831170	1652440	...	1344050	244149	112897	3127740
Producers of Government Services	545220	...	52729	16034	...	613983	606846	...	59545	18604	...	684995
Other Producers	...	...	...	...	...	...	...	...	...	...	...	...
Total	2054560	...	1258190	231180	98775	3445150	2259280	...	1403600	262753	112897	3812740
Less: Imputed bank service charge	...	...	147548	...	...	147548	...	...	162385	...	...	162385
Import duties	...	...	...	7813	...	7813	...	...	...	7938	...	7938
Value added tax	...	...	...	320814	...	320814	...	...	...	348956	...	348956
Other adjustments	...	...	...	...	209	-209	...	...	...	...	748	-748
Total a	2054560	...	1110640	559807	98984	3626020	2259280	...	1241210	619647	113645	4006500

	1984						1985					
	Compensation of Employees	Capital Consumption	Net Operating Surplus	Indirect Taxes	Less: Subsidies Received	Value Added	Compensation of Employees	Capital Consumption	Net Operating Surplus	Indirect Taxes	Less: Subsidies Received	Value Added
					All Producers							
1 Agriculture, hunting, forestry and fishing	27910	...	150382	5316	8392	175216	29241	...	156238	5271	8440	182310
A Agriculture and hunting	22008	...	141269	5012	7041	161248	22734	...	146488	4990	7247	166965
B Forestry and logging	3663	...	8230	141	1182	10852	3682	...	8960	145	1005	11782
C Fishing	2239	...	883	163	169	3116	2825	...	790	136	188	3563
2 Mining and quarrying	23263	...	17275	1924	6899	35563	23689	...	22004	1568	7149	40112
A Coal mining	10049	...	1949	407	6858	5547	10011	...	1687	376	7123	4951
B Crude petroleum and natural gas production	8317	...	12754	1217	20	22268	8812	...	17901	915	12	27616
C Metal ore mining	1416	...	1057	86	4	2555	1259	...	732	66	-1	2058
D Other mining	3481	...	1515	214	17	5193	3607	...	1684	211	15	5487

France

4.3 Cost Components of Value Added
(Continued)

Million French francs

	1984						1985					
	Compensation of Employees	Capital Consumption	Net Operating Surplus	Indirect Taxes	Less: Subsidies Received	Value Added	Compensation of Employees	Capital Consumption	Net Operating Surplus	Indirect Taxes	Less: Subsidies Received	Value Added
3 Manufacturing	652928	...	228254	105568	30477	956273	685646	...	261592	118211	32310	1033140
A Manufacture of food, beverages and tobacco	70640	...	59592	18081	13473	134840	76781	...	64389	19831	16872	144129
B Textile, wearing apparel and leather industries	55903	...	15568	2899	1402	72968	57227	...	18591	3584	352	79050
C Manufacture of wood and wood products, including furniture	20158	...	7829	1410	216	29181	20302	...	8226	1444	-2	29974
D Manufacture of paper and paper products, printing and publishing	47301	...	17211	2572	2133	64951	50636	...	19612	2851	2245	70854
E Manufacture of chemicals and chemical petroleum, coal, rubber and plastic products	85295	...	30020	57908	477	172746	92567	...	35393	67980	509	195431
F Manufacture of non-metallic mineral products, except products of petroleum and coal	25928	...	11437	2022	78	39309	26673	...	12043	1977	95	40598
G Basic metal industries	38644	...	9410	2960	608	50406	39520	...	13408	2704	576	55056
H Manufacture of fabricated metal products, machinery and equipment	297446	...	70458	17175	12013	373066	309373	...	83222	17257	11375	398477
I Other manufacturing industries	11613	...	6729	541	77	18806	12567	...	6708	583	288	19570
4 Electricity, gas and water	34434	...	60449	11759	1735	104907	36483	...	69761	12429	1804	116869
5 Construction	167968	...	68176	9034	3177	242001	165140	...	72667	9101	3010	243898
6 Wholesale and retail trade, restaurants and hotels	334351	...	261589	56341	16364	635917	366315	...	271828	66528	19660	685011
A Wholesale and retail trade	281355	...	214740	53971	14130	535936	309257	...	220199	63034	16983	575507
B Restaurants and hotels	52996	...	46849	2370	2234	99981	57058	...	51629	3494	2677	109504
7 Transport, storage and communication	162932	...	109879	8209	21516	259504	176966	...	126682	8598	23196	289050
A Transport and storage	112643	...	68503	6515	21498	166163	123327	...	75358	6789	23178	182296
B Communication	50289	...	41376	1694	18	93341	53639	...	51324	1809	18	106754
8 Finance, insurance, real estate and business services	277280	...	474653	69464	39297	782100	301497	...	525999	74755	41114	861137
9 Community, social and personal services	82537	...	119828	14542	5249	211658	90490	...	130596	16194	5906	231374
Total, Industries	1763600	...	1490490	282157	133106	3403140	1875470	...	1637370	312655	142589	3682900
Producers of Government Services	662170	...	66372	21964	...	750506	706979	...	72774	15808	...	795561
Other Producers	...	...	...	...	...	...	...	...	...	...	...	...
Total	2425770	...	1556860	304121	133106	4153650	2582450	...	1710140	328463	142589	4478460
Less: Imputed bank service charge	...	...	175627	...	...	175627	...	...	192340	...	...	192340
Import duties	...	...	...	8696	...	8696	...	...	...	8904	...	8904
Value added tax	...	...	...	375609	...	375609	...	...	...	405281	...	405281
Other adjustments	...	...	...	...	410	-410	...	...	...	...	163	-163
Total a	2425770	...	1381230	688426	133516	4361910	2582450	...	1517800	742648	142752	4700140

	1986					
	Compensation of Employees	Capital Consumption	Net Operating Surplus	Indirect Taxes	Less: Subsidies Received	Value Added

All Producers

1 Agriculture, hunting, forestry and fishing	29685	...	164899	5524	10613	189495
A Agriculture and hunting	23445	...	152802	5196	9507	171936
B Forestry and logging	3674	...	9901	173	989	12759
C Fishing	2566	...	2196	155	117	4800
2 Mining and quarrying	22434	...	18740	1913	7429	35657
A Coal mining	10078	...	1966	433	7382	5095
B Crude petroleum and natural gas production	7629	...	13959	1197	16	22769
C Metal ore mining	1287	...	792	69	3	2145
D Other mining	3440	...	2023	214	28	5648

France

4.3 Cost Components of Value Added
(Continued)

Million French francs

	1986					
	Compensation of Employees	Capital Consumption	Net Operating Surplus	Indirect Taxes	Less: Subsidies Received	Value Added
3 Manufacturing	702594	...	325928	124843	33266	1120100
A Manufacture of food, beverages and tobacco	80326	...	65911	19173	18171	147239
B Textile, wearing apparel and leather industries	58594	...	23315	2991	491	84409
C Manufacture of wood and wood products, including furniture	20846	...	10349	1469	240	32424
D Manufacture of paper and paper products, printing and publishing	54033	...	21061	4083	780	78397
E Manufacture of chemicals and chemical petroleum, coal, rubber and plastic products	96644	...	56694	73778	828	226288
F Manufacture of non-metallic mineral products, except products of petroleum and coal	27148	...	15779	1949	136	44741
G Basic metal industries	36908	...	18992	2816	348	58368
H Manufacture of fabricated metal products, machinery and equipment	315589	...	106810	17985	12160	428224
I Other manufacturing industries	12506	...	7017	599	112	20010
4 Electricity, gas and water	36937	...	69437	13781	2062	118093
5 Construction	175239	...	81553	9593	3432	262953
6 Wholesale and retail trade, restaurants and hotels	383437	...	316669	72724	25753	747077
A Wholesale and retail trade	319973	...	260481	68930	22561	626823
B Restaurants and hotels	63464	...	56188	3794	3192	120254
7 Transport, storage and communication	184702	...	140984	9238	24165	310759
A Transport and storage	127197	...	84815	7416	24145	195283
B Communication	57505	...	56169	1822	20	115476
8 Finance, insurance, real estate and business services	327084	...	611345	84685	45520	977594
9 Community, social and personal services	95225	...	149181	17493	5566	256333
Total, Industries	1957340	...	1878740	339794	157806	4018060
Producers of Government Services	750777	...	78155	16393	...	845325
Other Producers	...	...	...	...	...	...
Total	2708110	...	1956890	356187	157806	4863390
Less: Imputed bank service charge	...	...	223272	...	...	223272
Import duties	...	...	...	8976	...	8976
Value added tax	...	...	...	420379	...	420379
Other adjustments	...	...	...	...	173	-173
Total [a]	2708110	...	1733620	785542	157979	5069300

a) Column 'Consumption of fixed capital' is included in column 'Net operating surplus'.

French Polynesia

Source. Reply to the United Nations National Accounts Questionnaire from the Institute National de la Statistique et des Etudes Economiques (INSEE), Paris. Official estimates and descriptions are published by the same Institute in 'Comptes Economiques de la Polynesie Francaise'.

General note. The estimates shown in the following tables have been adjusted by the INSEE to conform to the United Nations System of National Accounts so far as the existing data would permit.

1.1 Expenditure on the Gross Domestic Product, in Current Prices

Million CFP francs

	1970	1975	1980	1981	1982	1983	1984	1985	1986	1987	1988	1989
1 Government final consumption expenditure	10012	18738	48375	57870	68039	82176	92147	94951	104685	...	...	...
2 Private final consumption expenditure	17288	29963	59491	73129	87179	105464	121425	119842	143944	...	...	...
3 Gross capital formation	4948	13477	23597	31074	36746	42972	59108	80994	89389	...	...	...
A Increase in stocks	-	296	-700	-500	1100	-800	4000	945	1078	...	...	...
B Gross fixed capital formation	4948	13181	24297	31574	35646	43772	55108	80049	88311	...	...	...
4 Exports of goods and services	2800	5159	6811	9204	11830	14102	14597	19847	21575	...	...	...
5 Less: Imports of goods and services	13580	22317	41442	54797	62220	74225	85470	88862	92658	...	...	...
Equals: Gross Domestic Product [a]	21468	45020	96832	116480	141574	170489	201807	226772	266935	...	...	...

a) Data in this table have been revised, therefore they are not strictly comparable with the unrevised data in the other tables.

1.2 Expenditure on the Gross Domestic Product, in Constant Prices

Million CFP francs

	1970	1975	1980	1981	1982	1983	1984	1985	1986	1987	1988	1989
					At constant prices of:1976							
1 Government final consumption expenditure	...	...	21684	22278	25304	...	...	...	...	...	...	...
2 Private final consumption expenditure	...	...	43670	47449	50304	...	...	...	...	...	...	...
A Households	...	...	43670	47449	50304	...	...	...	...	...	...	...
B Private non-profit institutions serving households	...	...	-	-	-	...	...	...	...	...	...	...
3 Gross capital formation	...	...	19496	24446	23551	...	...	...	...	...	...	...
A Increase in stocks	...	...	...	...	...	...	...	...	...	...	...	...
B Gross fixed capital formation	...	...	19496	24446	23551	...	...	...	...	...	...	...
4 Exports of goods and services	...	...	7056	7666	8567	...	...	...	...	...	...	...
5 Less: Imports of goods and services	...	...	29529	34157	33295	...	...	...	...	...	...	...
Equals: Gross Domestic Product	...	...	62377	67682	74431	...	...	...	...	...	...	...

1.3 Cost Components of the Gross Domestic Product

Million CFP francs

	1970	1975	1980	1981	1982	1983	1984	1985	1986	1987	1988	1989
1 Indirect taxes, net	2209	2862	...	...	...	...	...	...	...	...	...	...
A Indirect taxes	2642	4029	...	...	...	...	...	...	...	...	...	...
B Less: Subsidies	433	1167	917	1386	2307	1115	1084	2374	2829	...	...	...
2 Consumption of fixed capital	3523	10771	...	...	...	...	...	...	...	...	...	...
3 Compensation of employees paid by resident producers to:	10938	22488	41992	47558	57110	70018	80327	89347	96924	...	...	...
4 Operating surplus	4798	8899	41960	53084	66286	75082	89342			...	...	...
Equals: Gross Domestic Product	21468	45020	96832	116480	141574	170489	201807	226772	266935	...	...	...

1.4 General Government Current Receipts and Disbursements

Million CFP francs

	1970	1975	1980	1981	1982	1983	1984	1985	1986	1987	1988	1989
					Receipts							
1 Operating surplus	...	...	...	...	...	...	...	...	...	...	...	...
2 Property and entrepreneurial income			355	454	828	867	1093	1344	1258	...	...	...
3 Taxes, fees and contributions	...	...	17503	21483	25575	32895	41640	50182	54423	...	...	...
A Indirect taxes	...	...	13481	16383	18881	25006	31258	37667	40921	...	...	...
B Direct taxes	...	...								...	...	...
C Social security contributions	...	...	4022	5100	6694	7889	10382	12515	13502	...	...	...
D Compulsory fees, fines and penalties	...	...								...	...	...
4 Other current transfers	...	...	57725	69465	81973	99719	110038	120524	144736	...	...	...
Total Current Receipts of General Government	...	...	75583	91402	108376	133481	152771	172050	200417	...	...	...

French Polynesia

1.4 General Government Current Receipts and Disbursements
(Continued)

Million CFP francs

	1970	1975	1980	1981	1982	1983	1984	1985	1986	1987	1988	1989
					Disbursements							
1 Government final consumption expenditure	...	...	48375	57870	68039	82176	92147	94951	104685	...	...	...
A Compensation of employees	...	...	27672	31350	37703	45014	50698	56636	60554	...	...	...
B Consumption of fixed capital	...	...	...	...	...	...	...	...	...	...	...	...
C Purchases of goods and services, net	...	...	...	...	...	...	...	...	...	...	...	...
D Less: Own account fixed capital formation	...	...	...	...	...	...	...	...	...	...	...	...
E Indirect taxes paid, net	...	...	...	...	...	...	...	...	...	...	...	...
2 Property income	...	...	869	1136	1348	1613	2124	2626	2852	...	...	...
A Interest	...	...	869	1136	1348	1613	2124	2626	2852	...	...	...
B Net land rent and royalties	...	...	...	...	...	...	...	...	...	...	...	...
3 Subsidies	...	...	917	1386	2307	1115	1084	2374	2829	...	...	...
4 Other current transfers	...	...	19299	23543	28474	37560	46010	54937	63726	...	...	...
5 Net saving a	...	...	6123	7467	8208	11017	11406	17162	26325	...	...	...
Total Current Disbursements and Net Saving of General Government	...	...	75583	91402	108376	133481	152771	172050	200417	...	...	...

a) Item 'Net saving' includes consumption of fixed capital.

1.5 Current Income and Outlay of Corporate and Quasi-Corporate Enterprises, Summary

Million CFP francs

	1970	1975	1980	1981	1982	1983	1984	1985	1986	1987	1988	1989
					Receipts							
1 Operating surplus	...	...	41765	52824	66039	74770	88995	99891	128832	...	...	...
2 Property and entrepreneurial income received	...	...	869	1136	1348	1613	2124	2626	2852	...	...	...
3 Current transfers	...	...	...	...	...	...	...	...	...	...	...	...
Total Current Receipts a	...	...	42634	53960	67387	76383	91119	102517	131684	...	...	...
					Disbursements							
1 Property and entrepreneurial income	...	...	18547	22497	27518	32613	37993	43086	50718	...	...	...
2 Direct taxes and other current payments to general government	...	...	3735	4276	5475	7207	9064	10683	10801	...	...	...
3 Other current transfers	...	...	1260	1350	1900	2232	2697	3108	3708	...	...	...
4 Net saving b	...	...	19092	25837	32494	34331	41365	45640	66457	...	...	...
Total Current Disbursements and Net Saving a	...	...	42634	53960	67387	76383	91119	102517	131684	...	...	...

a) Private unincorporated enterprises are included in corporate and quasi-corporate enterprises.
b) Item 'Net saving' includes consumption of fixed capital.

1.6 Current Income and Outlay of Households and Non-Profit Institutions

Million CFP francs

	1970	1975	1980	1981	1982	1983	1984	1985	1986	1987	1988	1989
					Receipts							
1 Compensation of employees	...	...	41992	47558	57110	70018	80327	89347	96924	...	...	...
2 Operating surplus of private unincorporated enterprises	...	...	...	...	...	...	...	...	...	...	...	...
3 Property and entrepreneurial income	...	...	18547	22497	27518	32613	37993	43086	50718	...	...	...
4 Current transfers	...	...	8918	11159	13801	17986	20531	26958	31116	...	...	...
Total Current Receipts	...	...	69457	81214	98429	120617	138851	159391	178758	...	...	...
					Disbursements							
1 Private final consumption expenditure	...	...	59491	73129	87179	105464	121425	119842	143944	...	...	...
2 Property income	...	...	...	...	...	...	...	...	...	...	...	...
3 Direct taxes and other current transfers n.e.c. to general government	...	...	688	753	914	1055	1358	2397	2350	...	...	...
4 Other current transfers	...	...	896	1019	1336	2151	3373	4017	5214	...	...	...
5 Net saving a	...	...	8382	6313	9000	11947	12695	33135	27250	...	...	...
Total Current Disbursements and Net Saving	...	...	69457	81214	98429	120617	138851	159391	178758	...	...	...

a) Item 'Net saving' includes consumption of fixed capital.

French Polynesia

1.7 External Transactions on Current Account, Summary

Million CFP francs

	1970	1975	1980	1981	1982	1983	1984	1985	1986	1987	1988	1989
Payments to the Rest of the World												
1 Imports of goods and services	...	...	41442	54797	62220	74225	85470	88862	92658	...	...	...
2 Factor income to the rest of the world	...	...	...	...	...	...	...	...	...	...	...	...
3 Current transfers to the rest of the world	...	...	317	313	393	493	555	-	-	...	...	...
4 Surplus of the nation on current transactions	...	...	10000	8543	12956	14323	6358	14943	30643	...	...	...
Payments to the Rest of the World and Surplus of the Nation on Current Transactions	...	...	51759	63653	75569	89041	92383	103805	123301	...	...	...
Receipts From The Rest of the World												
1 Exports of goods and services	...	...	6811	9204	11830	14102	14597	19847	21575	...	...	...
2 Factor income from rest of the world	...	...	...	...	...	...	...	...	...	...	...	...
3 Current transfers from rest of the world	...	...	44948	54449	63739	74939	77786	83958	101726	...	...	...
Receipts from the Rest of the World on Current Transactions	...	...	51759	63653	75569	89041	92383	103805	123301	...	...	...

1.8 Capital Transactions of The Nation, Summary

Million CFP francs

	1970	1975	1980	1981	1982	1983	1984	1985	1986	1987	1988	1989
Finance of Gross Capital Formation												
Gross saving	...	...	...	...	...	...	...	...	...	...	...	...
1 Consumption of fixed capital	...	...	...	...	...	...	...	...	...	...	...	...
2 Net saving a	...	...	33597	39617	49702	57295	65466	95937	120032	...	...	...
A General government	...	...	6123	7467	8208	11017	11406	17162	26325	...	...	...
B Corporate and quasi-corporate enterprises	...	...	19092	25837	32494	34331	41365	45640	66457	...	...	...
C Other	...	...	8382	6313	9000	11947	12695	33135	27250	...	...	...
Less: Surplus of the nation on current transactions	...	...	10000	8543	12956	14323	6358	14943	30643	...	...	...
Finance of Gross Capital Formation	...	...	23597	31074	36746	42972	59108	80994	89389	...	...	...
Gross Capital Formation												
Increase in stocks	...	...	-700	-500	1100	-800	4000	945	1078	...	...	...
Gross fixed capital formation	...	...	24297	31574	35646	43772	55108	80049	88311	...	...	...
1 General government	...	...	6484	9076	10857	12454	11109	18548	20588	...	...	...
2 Corporate and quasi-corporate enterprises	...	...	9707	13897	15059	20112	28931	42795	48373	...	...	...
3 Other	...	...	8106	8601	9730	11206	15068	18706	19350	...	...	...
Gross Capital Formation	...	...	23597	31074	36746	42972	59108	80994	89389	...	...	...

a) Item 'Net saving' includes consumption of fixed capital.

1.10 Gross Domestic Product by Kind of Activity, in Current Prices

Million CFP francs

	1970	1975	1980	1981	1982	1983	1984	1985	1986	1987	1988	1989
1 Agriculture, hunting, forestry and fishing	1488	2089	4533	4875	5982	6650	8142	8557	9249	...	...	...
2 Mining and quarrying	...	...	...	...	...	...	...	...	...	...	...	...
3 Manufacturing a	1340	2769	6393	7567	10185	12873	16779	19376	23490	...	...	...
4 Electricity, gas and water a	319	498	1164	1040	1143	1443	1544	1791	2525	...	...	...
5 Construction	1310	4442	9869	11957	14156	16793	20222	27251	30396	...	...	...
6 Wholesale and retail trade, restaurants and hotels	5106	11284	22502	28843	33815	41893	51117	...	...	...	...	...
7 Transport, storage and communication		2308	5448	7232	8810	10602	11857	13086	17391	...	...	...
8 Finance, insurance, real estate and business services	5287	7664	17562	21502	27038	31972	36404	...	...	...	...	...
9 Community, social and personal services								...	...	...	...	...

French Polynesia

1.10 Gross Domestic Product by Kind of Activity, in Current Prices
(Continued)

Million CFP francs

	1970	1975	1980	1981	1982	1983	1984	1985	1986	1987	1988	1989
Total, Industries	14850	31054	67471	83016	101129	122226	146065	164023	200222	...	...	...
Producers of Government Services	6548	13807	28994	33033	39913	47622	55033	61967	65901	...	...	...
Other Producers	70	159	367	431	532	641	709	782	812	...	...	...
Subtotal	21468	45020	96832	116480	141574	170489	201807	226772	266935	...	...	...
Less: Imputed bank service charge	...	...	...	...	...	...	...	...	...	...	...	...
Plus: Import duties	...	...	...	...	...	...	...	...	...	...	...	...
Plus: Value added tax	...	...	...	...	...	...	...	...	...	...	...	...
Equals: Gross Domestic Product	21468	45020	96832	116480	141574	170489	201807	226772	266935	...	...	...

a) Manufacturing of energy-generating products is included in item 'Electricity, gas and water'.

1.11 Gross Domestic Product by Kind of Activity, in Constant Prices

Million CFP francs

	1970	1975	1980	1981	1982	1983	1984	1985	1986	1987	1988	1989
				At constant prices of:1976								
1 Agriculture, hunting, forestry and fishing	...	...	3311	3450	3540	...	...	...	...	...	...	...
2 Mining and quarrying	...	...	...	...	...	...	...	...	...	...	...	...
3 Manufacturing a	...	...	4988	5288	6028	...	...	...	...	...	...	...
4 Electricity, gas and water a	...	...	835	689	723	...	...	...	...	...	...	...
5 Construction	...	...	6100	6476	6980	...	...	...	...	...	...	...
6 Wholesale and retail trade, restaurants and hotels	...	...	15616	17456	17951	...	...	...	...	...	...	...
7 Transport, storage and communication	...	...	3900	4533	4777	...	...	...	...	...	...	...
8 Finance, insurance, real estate and business services	...	...	12469	14335	16759	...	...	...	...	...	...	...
9 Community, social and personal services	...	...				...	...	...	...	...	...	...
Total, Industries	...	...	47219	52226	56757	...	...	...	...	...	...	...
Producers of Government Services	...	...	14890	15183	17386	...	...	...	...	...	...	...
Other Producers	...	...	268	273	288	...	...	...	...	...	...	...
Subtotal	...	...	62377	67682	74431	...	...	...	...	...	...	...
Less: Imputed bank service charge	...	...	...	...	...	...	...	...	...	...	...	...
Plus: Import duties	...	...	...	...	...	...	...	...	...	...	...	...
Plus: Value added tax	...	...	...	...	...	...	...	...	...	...	...	...
Equals: Gross Domestic Product	...	...	62377	67682	74431	...	...	...	...	...	...	...

a) Manufacturing of energy-generating products is included in item 'Electricity, gas and water'.

Gabon

Source. Reply to the United Nations National Accounts Questionnaire from the Direction de la Statistique et des Etudes Economiques, Libreville. The official estimates which conform to the present United Nations System of National Accounts are published annually by the same office in 'Comptes Economiques'.

General note. The estimates shown in the following tables have been prepared by the Direction de la Statistique et des Etudes Economiques to conform to the United Nations System of National Accounts so far as the existing data would permit.

1.1 Expenditure on the Gross Domestic Product, in Current Prices

Million CFA francs

	1970	1975	1980	1981	1982	1983	1984	1985	1986	1987	1988	1989
1 Government final consumption expenditure	17600	... 56531	119659	149500	186700	222300	284400	306300	303900	242200	220600	215387
2 Private final consumption expenditure	37400	... 108706	236670	280700	325100	385700	464700	501200	562100	496300	487900	565201
3 Gross capital formation	27600	... 289760	248967	381526	416318	454800	512900	613600	543482	272500	367300	271672
A Increase in stocks	1400	... 31614	...	...	...	...	...	...	...	...	...	...
B Gross fixed capital formation	26200	... 258146	...	...	...	...	...	...	...	...	...	...
Residential buildings	...	...	...	...	...	...	...	...	...	...	...	...
Non-residential buildings	...	...	...	...	...	...	...	...	...	...	...	...
Other construction and land improvement etc.	...	...	...	...	...	...	...	...	...	...	...	...
Other	...	... 72101	...	...	...	...	...	...	...	...	...	...
4 Exports of goods and services	44500	... 228955	585171	665000	732300	792500	919600	935700	475822	421200	377700	587000
5 Less: Imports of goods and services	34000	... 221511	285982	427100	471600	562700	625600	711000	684200	411600	439900	471200
Equals: Gross Domestic Product	93100	... 462441	904500	1049600	1188900	1292600	1556000	1645800	1201100	1020600	1013600	1168066

1.3 Cost Components of the Gross Domestic Product

Million CFA francs

	1970	1975	1980	1981	1982	1983	1984	1985	1986	1987	1988	1989
1 Indirect taxes, net	15400	... 90185	114046	119900	159000	163200	218200	232200	165400	124700	141100	128000
A Indirect taxes	16300	... 93013	...	...	...	...	...	...	...	...	...	...
B Less: Subsidies	900	... 2828	...	...	...	...	...	...	...	...	...	...
2 Consumption of fixed capital	21600	... 66536	84002	93566	119052	116200	176500	162700	230200	195600	121833	169337
3 Compensation of employees paid by resident producers to:	36800	... 113981	231514	275300	328100	374900	425600	478300	482100	408200	403500	409752
A Resident households	...	... 101794	...	...	...	...	...	...	...	...	...	...
B Rest of the world	...	... 12187	...	...	...	...	...	...	...	...	...	...
4 Operating surplus	19300	... 191739	419317	496834	508348	560000	649000	667700	231900	228900	271267	396421
A Corporate and quasi-corporate enterprises	...	...	...	...	...	...	...	...	...	...	...	...
B Private unincorporated enterprises	...	...	...	...	...	...	...	...	...	...	...	...
C General government	...	300	...	...	...	...	...	...	...	...	...	...
Statistical discrepancy	...	...	55606	64026	74318	78300	86700	104900	91500	63200	75900	64536
Equals: Gross Domestic Product	93100	... 462441	904500	1049600	1188900	1292600	1556000	1645800	1201100	1020600	1013600	1168066

1.7 External Transactions on Current Account, Summary

Million CFA francs

	1970	1975	1980	1981	1982	1983	1984	1985	1986	1987	1988	1989
Payments to the Rest of the World												
1 Imports of goods and services	...	221511	285982	427100	471600	562700	625600	711000	684200	411600	439900	471200
A Imports of merchandise c.i.f.	...	109434	192312	269256	294878	325700	390400	445000	437778	261600	284000	289200
B Other	...	74770	93670	157844	176722	237000	235200	266000	246422	150000	155900	182000
2 Factor income to the rest of the world	...	35198	55569	70877	68863	99000	104000	105000	70008	67666	79482	104900

Gabon

1.7 External Transactions on Current Account, Summary
(Continued)

Million CFA francs

	1970	1975	1980	1981	1982	1983	1984	1985	1986	1987	1988	1989
A Compensation of employees	...	12187	...	...	...	...	...	...	...	...	482	...
B Property and entrepreneurial income	...	23011	55569	70877	68863	99000	104000	105000	70008	67666	79000	104900
3 Current transfers to the rest of the world	...	11850	61655	61712	61840	75200	85000	99600	137326	87656	104376	98545
4 Surplus of the nation on current transactions a	...	-23008	210869	143543	184722	133400	169000	80300	-358552	-95733	-214172	-55945
Payments to the Rest of the World and Surplus of the Nation on Current Transactions a	...	245551	614075	703239	787016	870300	983600	995900	532982	471189	409586	618700

Receipts From The Rest of the World

	1970	1975	1980	1981	1982	1983	1984	1985	1986	1987	1988	1989
1 Exports of goods and services a	...	228955	585171	665000	732300	792500	919600	935700	475822	421200	377700	587000
A Exports of merchandise f.o.b.	...	204227	537101	596412	686230	738700	889400	887200	434129	389089	344273	517400
B Other	...	18219	48070	68588	46070	53800	30200	48500	41693	32111	33427	69600
2 Factor income from rest of the world	...	5586	5262	6852	6562	16500	20900	13100	6270	4800	4362	4200
A Compensation of employees	...	3919	...	...	...	...	...	...	...	...	...	...
B Property and entrepreneurial income	...	1667	5262	6852	6562	16500	20900	13100	6270	4800	4362	4200
3 Current transfers from rest of the world	...	11010	23642	31423	48147	61300	43100	47100	50890	45189	27524	27500
A Subsidies from supranational organisations	...	...	6481	4970	6098	7200	6800	8800	8167	9225	6087	7000
B Other current transfers	...	...	17160	26453	42049	54100	36300	38300	42723	35964	21437	20500
Receipts from the Rest of the World on Current Transactions	...	245551	614075	703239	787016	870300	983600	995900	532982	471189	409586	618700

a) Beginning 1976, estimates are not strictly comparable with those of other tables.

1.10 Gross Domestic Product by Kind of Activity, in Current Prices

Million CFA francs

	1970	1975	1980	1981	1982	1983	1984	1985	1986	1987	1988	1989
1 Agriculture, hunting, forestry and fishing	...	40772	66340	67162	72960	82200	96600	102200	109300	107400	108000	117200
2 Mining and quarrying	...	187163	404078	443258	526557	592000	766400	760100	267300	280400	217900	364100
3 Manufacturing a	...	22998	43813	45930	54577	68200	74100	87500	83800	70200	70100	64300
4 Electricity, gas and water	...	4909	13449	15069	17627	20100	23200	30000	26400	26400	28500	27700
5 Construction	...	79826	58971	72328	92825	78300	85500	103500	132600	70600	50300	62300
6 Wholesale and retail trade, restaurants and hotels	...	32152	67256	75097	71652	84800	93300	108600	117200	90400	139400	140000
7 Transport, storage and communication	...	18423	36476	46550	55755	63400	66700	78300	83600	79500	87600	92600
8 Finance, insurance, real estate and business services	...	26951	58119	95441	73916	42100	48500	57500	69200	54500	44400	49000
9 Community, social and personal services	...	1627	42095	53947	61014	79300	98500	87500	97100	65700	82500	77200
Total, Industries	...	414821	790592	914782	1026883	1110400	1352800	1415200	986600	845000	828600	994400
Producers of Government Services	...	23142	67511	83379	98844	118800	132100	148700	155800	141000	137100	134000
Other Producers	...	1648	...	...	...	...	...	...	...	...	...	...
Subtotal	...	439611	858108	998161	1125727	1229200	1484900	1563900	1142300	986000	965700	1128400
Less: Imputed bank service charge	...	9007	9574	12586	11156	14900	15600	23000	32800	28600	28030	24836
Plus: Import duties	...	31837	55606	64000	74300	78200	86700	104900	91500	63200	75900	64536
Plus: Value added tax	...	...	...	...	...	...	...	...	...	...	...	...
Equals: Gross Domestic Product	...	462441	904500	1049600	1188900	1292600	1556000	1645800	1201100	1020600	1013600	1168066

a) Repair services are included in item 'Manufacturing'.

1.12 Relations Among National Accounting Aggregates

Million CFA francs

	1970	1975	1980	1981	1982	1983	1984	1985	1986	1987	1988	1989
Gross Domestic Product	...	462441	904500	1049600	1188900	1292600	1556000	1645800	1201100	1020600	1013600	1168066
Plus: Net factor income from the rest of the world	...	-29612	-50307	-64025	-62301	-82500	-83100	-91900	-63730	-62866	-75120	-100700
Factor income from the rest of the world	...	5586	5262	6852	6562	16500	20900	13100	6270	4800	4362	4200
Less: Factor income to the rest of the world	...	35198	55569	70877	68863	99000	104000	105000	70008	67666	79482	104900
Equals: Gross National Product	...	432829	854193	985575	1126599	1210100	1472900	1553900	1137370	957734	938480	1067360
Less: Consumption of fixed capital	...	66536	84002	93566	119052	116200	176500	162700	230200	195600	121833	169337

Gabon

1.12 Relations Among National Accounting Aggregates
(Continued)

Million CFA francs

	1970	1975	1980	1981	1982	1983	1984	1985	1986	1987	1988	1989
Equals: National Income	...	366293	770191	892009	1007547	1093900	1296400	1391200	907170	762134	816642	898023
Plus: Net current transfers from the rest of the world	...	-840	-38013	-30289	-13693	-13900	-41900	-52500	-86436	-42467	-76852	-71045
Current transfers from the rest of the world	...	11010	23642	31423	48147	61300	43100	47100	50890	45189	27524	27500
Less: Current transfers to the rest of the world	...	11850	61655	61712	61840	75200	95000	99600	137326	87656	104376	98545
Equals: National Disposable Income	...	365453	732178	861720	993854	1080000	1254500	1338700	820730	719667	739795	826978
Less: Final consumption	...	165237	356328	430217	511866	608000	749100	807500	866000	738500	708500	780588
Equals: Net Saving	...	200216	375850	431503	481988	472000	505400	531200	-45270	-18833	31295	46390
Less: Surplus of the nation on current transactions [a]	...	-23008	210869	143543	184722	133400	169000	80300	-358552	-95733	-214172	-55945
Equals: Net Capital Formation	...	223224	164981	287960	297266	338600	336400	450900	313282	76900	245467	102335

a) Beginning 1976, estimates are not strictly comparable with those of other tables.

Gambia

Source. Reply to the United Nations National Accounts Questionnaire from the Central Statistics Department, Ministry of Economic Planning and Industrial Development, Banjul. The official estimates are published in 'Sources and Methods of Estimates of National Income at Current Prices in The Gambia' and 'Estimates of National Income at Constant Prices in The Gambia', published in1981.

General note. The estimates shown in the following tables have been prepared in accordance with the United Nations System of National Accounts so far as the existing data would permit.

1.1 Expenditure on the Gross Domestic Product, in Current Prices

Thousand Gambian dalasis
Fiscal year beginning 1 July

	1970	1975	1980	1981	1982	1983	1984	1985	1986	1987	1988	1989
1 Government final consumption expenditure	31112	37168	88461	103197	106711	118701	133462	161547	186569	239012	261521	292865
2 Private final consumption expenditure	...	...	...	...	...	...	...	...	...	...	...	...
3 Gross capital formation												
A Increase in stocks	...	...	...	...	...	...	...	...	...	...	...	...
B Gross fixed capital formation a	10995	14058	59518	64466	32517	58925	72816	77504	103542	125161	106560	128172
Residential buildings		5069	29550	18143	10159	8426	11241	24287	19771	21639	34211	14573
Non-residential buildings	5765											
Other construction and land improvement etc.		2533	21828	33710	16485	35556	43204	38064	57146	58919	38797	69616
Other	5230	6456	8141	12613	5873	14943	18371	15153	26625	46293	33552	43983
4 Exports of goods and services b	30911	77363	93280	110350	197630	313680	325250	470820	763944	790065	1010752	1122120
5 Less: Imports of goods and services c	42587	144367	290900	266060	286700	395050	388570	507400	839972	843460	1066492	1256040
Equals: Gross Domestic Product	96624	278326	411681	451230	605787	617837	781863	1094785	1526138	1707654	2062760	2534406

a) The estimates refer to central government capital formation only.
b) Item 'Exports of goods and services' includes net travel and tourism income.
c) Item 'Imports of goods and services' includes net freight and insurance.

1.3 Cost Components of the Gross Domestic Product

Thousand Gambian dalasis
Fiscal year beginning 1 July

	1970	1975	1980	1981	1982	1983	1984	1985	1986	1987	1988	1989
1 Indirect taxes, net	...	...	44140	45632	78892	98646	110802	158113	172246	225129	341420	394904
2 Consumption of fixed capital	...	...	50561	55689	65000	80000	100000	124698	169798	211256	227057	249656
3 Compensation of employees paid by resident producers to:	...	...	...	...	...	...	...	...	...	...	...	...
4 Operating surplus	...	...	...	...	...	...	...	...	...	...	...	...
Equals: Gross Domestic Product	...	...	411681	451230	605787	617837	781863	1094785	1526138	1707654	2062760	2534406

1.10 Gross Domestic Product by Kind of Activity, in Current Prices

Thousand Gambian dalasis
Fiscal year beginning 1 July

	1970	1975	1980	1981	1982	1983	1984	1985	1986	1987	1988	1989
1 Agriculture, hunting, forestry and fishing	48025	106074	115825	158016	173805	135776	192641	276989	490839	525514	500715	659367
2 Mining and quarrying	313	341	126	127	158	176	202	245	311	342	373	405
3 Manufacturing	1879	13838	28104	24797	59138	59663	61318	69150	51531	100000	125127	177046
4 Electricity, gas and water	258	1280	1850	1276	-92	2353	1505	6199	12494	14320	14994	17000
5 Construction	1902	13849	31215	24652	28887	32444	39510	40608	78917	53928	82898	127565
6 Wholesale and retail trade, restaurants and hotels	17422	64422	100703	94942	186821	223499	270336	370176	499633	541380	784445	934077
7 Transport, storage and communication	3632	17936	34706	38036	41947	50367	66392	111979	137449	187794	206705	236643
8 Finance, insurance, real estate and business services	2875	32346	49162	57291	53873	44413	57331	120618	168752	186887	235274	270931
9 Community, social and personal services	9922	5483	8600	10999	12418	14840	18639	26075	39375	45833	56000	64000
Total, Industries	...	255569	370291	410136	556955	563531	707874	1022039	1479301	1655998	2006531	2487034
Producers of Government Services		29165	55092	61338	71060	76417	86553	93064	95150	111656	146229	167372
Other Producers	...	...	...	...	...	...	...	...	...	...	...	...
Subtotal	86228	284734	425383	471474	628015	639948	794427	1115103	1574451	1767654	2152760	2654406
Less: Imputed bank service charge	...	6408	13702	20244	22228	22111	12564	20318	48313	60000	90000	120000
Plus: Import duties	10396	...	...	...	...	...	...	...	...	...	...	...
Plus: Value added tax	...	...	...	...	...	...	...	...	...	...	...	...
Equals: Gross Domestic Product	96624	278326	411681	451230	605787	617837	781863	1094785	1526138	1707654	2062760	2534406

Gambia

1.11 Gross Domestic Product by Kind of Activity, in Constant Prices

Thousand Gambian dalasis | Fiscal year beginning 1 July

At constant prices of 1976

	1970	1975	1980	1981	1982	1983	1984	1985	1986	1987	1988	1989
1 Agriculture, hunting, forestry and fishing	146468	104457	139157	131061	97169	107158	113602	121407	120317	115465	125405
2 Mining and quarrying	282	185	220	150	155	160	166	172	178	184	190
3 Manufacturing	18398	19103	26045	29070	28659	24929	27457	36310	42832	40497	40709
4 Electricity, gas and water	1303	1500	1465	1801	1736	1892	2088	2260	2486	2404	2517
5 Construction	16092	18509	14878	20552	22431	25463	23291	30004	19756	24739	29680
6 Wholesale and retail trade, restaurants and hotels	76836	95407	82547	152649	146383	135165	140789	143047	139250	152108	162111
7 Transport, storage and communication	17842	30323	32961	34157	40180	44514	56293	63127	76160	78287	87042
8 Finance, insurance, real estate and business services	35147	34872	39566	36201	29698	31274	41872	43952	46275	53315	57023
9 Community, social and personal services	6452	6738	7973	8244	8524	8814	9114	9423	9744	10075	10418
Total, Industries	318790	311094	344814	413885	374535	379369	414672	449792	456998	477074	515095
Producers of Government Services	33984	40857	41895	70780	69946	65426	60043	48500	50882	54900	54900
Other Producers											
Subtotal	352774	351951	386709	484665	444481	444795	474715	498292	507680	531974	569955
Less: Imputed bank service charge	7460	10187	13913	13980	12036	5629	6728	10950	12091	18182	26415
Plus: Import duties											
Plus: Value added tax											
Equals: Gross Domestic Product	345314	341764	372796	470685	432445	439166	467987	487342	495589	513792	543580

1.12 Relations Among National Accounting Aggregates

Thousand Gambian dalasis | Fiscal year beginning 1 July

	1970	1975	1980	1981	1982	1983	1984	1985	1986	1987	1988	1989
Gross Domestic Product	278326	411681	451230	605787	617837	781863	1094785	1526138	1707654	2062760	2534406
Plus: Net factor income from the rest of the world	3685	-6195	-3496	-12400	-23690	-10640	-74340	-136484	-94120	-80823	-109080
Equals: Gross National Product	282011	405486	447734	593387	594147	771223	1020445	1389654	1613534	1981937	2425326
Less: Consumption of fixed capital	22363	50561	55899	65000	80000	124698	169798	211256	227057	246656
Equals: National Income	259648	354925	392045	528387	514147	671223	895747	1219856	1402278	1754880	2175670
Plus: Net current transfers from the rest of the world [a]	102020	17850	33590	47980	69190	211220	351744	387340	372529	465480
Equals: National Disposable Income [b]	408015	409895	561977	466167	602033	1106967	1571600	1789618	2127409	2641150
Less: Final consumption											
Equals: Net Saving											
Less: Surplus of the nation on current transactions											
Equals: Net Capital Formation											

a) Item 'Net current transfers from the rest of the world' includes mainly net interest receipts.
b) Item 'National disposable income' includes unrequited private transfers and official transfers.

2.1 Government Final Consumption Expenditure by Function, in Current Prices

Thousand Gambian dalasis | Fiscal year beginning 1 July

	1970	1975	1980	1981	1982	1983	1984	1985	1986	1987	1988	1989
1 General public services							52515	59813	177283	256275	152961	168171
2 Defence												
3 Public order and safety												
4 Education [a]							25664	27775	29916	33131	49956	78871
5 Health							14136	14830	14198	56251	24379	42247
6 Social security and welfare							166	151	197	240	422	419
7 Housing and community amenities							11435	10240	18118	32654	23366	19645
8 Recreational, cultural and religious affairs [a]												
9 Economic services							104717	121272	152988	139468	144284	160028

Gambia

2.1 Government Final Consumption Expenditure by Function, in Current Prices (Continued)

Thousand Gambian dalasis — Fiscal year beginning 1 July

	1970	1975	1980	1981	1982	1983	1984	1985	1986	1987	1988	1989
A Fuel and energy												
B Agriculture, forestry, fishing and hunting						24840	53429	71411	60291	36608	44400	
C Mining, manufacturing and construction, except fuel and energy						16944	7595	14923	7231	7398	6346	
D Transportation and communication						57737	46762	47030	64159	75807	66195	
E Other economic affairs						5146	13486	19624	7787	24471	43087	
10 Other functions						14970	31314	73334	118879	165385	185309	
Total Government Final Consumption Expenditure b						223603	264795	466034	638898	560753	654690	

a) Item "Education" includes item "Recreational, cultural and religious affairs.
b) Only central government data are included in the general government estimates.

4.1 Derivation of Value Added by Kind of Activity, in Current Prices

Thousand Gambian dalasis — Fiscal year beginning 1 July

	1980 Gross Output	1980 Intermediate Consumption	1980 Value Added	1981 Gross Output	1981 Intermediate Consumption	1981 Value Added	1982 Gross Output	1982 Intermediate Consumption	1982 Value Added	1983 Gross Output	1983 Intermediate Consumption	1983 Value Added
All Producers												
1 Agriculture, hunting, forestry and fishing	131679	...	115854	177660	...	158016	192428	18623	173805	158135	22359	135776
A Agriculture and hunting	117756	...	105282	161193	...	145803	176162	15212	160950	137833	18014	119819
B Forestry and logging	2217	44	2173	2476	50	2426	2848	57	2791	3178	64	3114
C Fishing	11706	3336	8370	12932	163	12769	13418	3354	10064	17124	4281	12843
2 Mining and quarrying	142	16	126	163	18	145	18	...	158	196	20	176
3 Manufacturing	78352	50248	28104	100419	25817	74602	160140	56138	104002	...	...	...
4 Electricity, gas and water	10283	8433	1850	13312	12036	1276	15626	15718	-92	19301	16948	2353
A Electricity, gas and steam	7461	7172	289	10025	10042	-17	12043	12785	-742	15587	13879	1708
B Water works and supply	2822	1261	1561	3287	1994	1293	3583	2933	650	3714	3069	645
5 Construction	62333	31118	31215	48071	23419	24652	60358	31471	28887	65900	33456	32444
6 Wholesale and retail trade, restaurants and hotels	127764	100703	27061	118138	94942	23196	94942	46185	48815	188621	285695	223499
A Wholesale and retail trade	112641	76272	15390	102539	62879	18458	133938	18006	25349	170444	222777	193332
B Restaurants and hotels	15123	10299	4824	15599	10738	4861	40943	24566	16377	62918	37751	25167
7 Transport, storage and communication	60283	25577	34706	68211	38036	30175	48800	41947	107065	56698	50367	
A Transport and storage	55112	24189	30923	62469	34218	28251	47765	37362	39868	54379		
B Communication	5171	1388	3783	5742	1924	3818	5620	1035	4585	8718	2730	5988
8 Finance, insurance, real estate and business services	59105	9943	49162	68227	10936	57291	126485	53873	72301	44413		
A Financial institutions	16261	5526	10735	22575	6204	16371	81253	13108	68145	67357	1085	
Insurance	1919	578	1341	2885	710	2175	1328	476	852	1551	697	854
C Real estate and business services	40925	37086	3839	42767	4022	38745	43904	3991	39913	46721	4247	42474
9 Community, social and personal services	11266	2666	8600	14356	3357	10999	16208	3790	12418	19369	4529	14840
A Sanitary and similar services												
B Social and related community services	4567	1624	2943	6936	2343	4593						
C Recreational and cultural services												
D Personal and household services	6699	1042	5657	7420	1014	6406						
Total, industries	541207	170916	370291	607693	197557	410136	896242	339287	556955	932907	369376	563531
Producers of Government services	88461	33369	55092	98691	61338	37253	107703	36643	71060	119129	42712	76417
Other Producers	...	...	...	...	...	...	...	...	...	...	...	...
Total	629668	204285	425383	706284	234810	471474	1003945	375930	628015	1052036	412088	639948
Less: Imputed bank service charge	-13702		13702	-20244		20244	-22228		22228	-22111		22111
Import duties												
Value added tax												
Total	629668	217987	411681	706284	255054	451230	1003945	398158	605787	1052036	434199	617837

644

Gambia

4.1 Derivation of Value Added by Kind of Activity, in Current Prices

Thousand Gambian dalasis

Fiscal year beginning 1 July

	1984			1985			1986			1987		
	Gross Output	Intermediate Consumption	Value Added	Gross Output	Intermediate Consumption	Value Added	Gross Output	Intermediate Consumption	Value Added	Gross Output	Intermediate Consumption	Value Added
All Producers												
1 Agriculture, hunting, forestry and fishing	211491	18850	192641	304329	27340	276989	536657	45818	490839	566593	41079	525514
A Agriculture and hunting	186702	13409	173293	269114	19806	249308	467151	31608	435543	504897	29730	475167
B Forestry and logging	3287	65	3222	5517	110	5407	13766	275	13491	17716	354	17362
C Fishing	21502	5376	16126	29698	7424	22274	55740	13935	41805	43980	10995	32985
2 Mining and quarrying	224	22	202	272	27	245	346	35	311	380	38	342
3 Manufacturing	163613	102295	61318	201770	132620	69150	309545	258014	51531	410297	310297	100000
4 Electricity, gas and water	22658	21153	1505	29896	23697	6199	38848	26354	12494	48141	33821	14320
A Electricity, gas and steam	18471	17148	1323	23986	19459	4527	31575	21213	10362	39411	27475	11936
B Water works and supply	4187	4005	182	5910	4238	1672	7273	5141	2132	8730	6346	2384
5 Construction	81781	42271	39510	86531	45923	40608	178357	99440	78917	116590	62662	53928
6 Wholesale and retail trade, restaurants and hotels	354480	84144	270336	497306	127130	370176	677755	178122	499633	741338	199958	541380
A Wholesale and retail trade	264085	29907	234178	359141	44231	314910	487065	63708	423357	519243	66701	452542
B Restaurants and hotels	90395	54237	36158	138165	82899	55266	190690	114414	76276	222095	133257	88838
7 Transport, storage and communication	138936	72544	66392	227721	115742	111979	294442	156993	137449	394662	206868	187794
A Transport and storage	129109	70132	58977	211979	112194	99785	269251	149816	119435	357064	199207	157857
B Communication	9827	2412	7415	15742	3548	12194	25191	7177	18014	37598	7661	29937
8 Finance, insurance, real estate and business services	130402	73071	57331	141760	21142	120618	202966	34214	168752	224832	37945	186887
A Financial institutions	71721	66627	5094	47203	10709	36494	80270	20022	60248	98792	22378	76414
B Insurance	1970	1289	681	2410	1093	1317	2931	1850	1081	3358	2722	636
C Real estate and business services	56711	5155	51556	92147	9340	82807	119765	12342	107423	122682	12845	109837
9 Community, social and personal services	24327	5688	18639	34033	7958	26075	51391	12016	39375	59819	13986	45833
A Sanitary and similar services	...	...	...	...	...	...	...	...	...	...	...	...
B Social and related community services	...	...	...	...	...	...	...	...	...	...	...	...
C Recreational and cultural services	...	...	...	...	...	...	...	...	...	...	...	...
D Personal and household services	...	...	...	...	...	...	...	...	...	...	...	...
Total, Industries	1127912	420038	707874	1523618	501579	1022039	2290307	811006	1479301	2562652	906654	1655998
Producers of Government Services	136689	50136	86553	158686	65622	93064	186820	91670	95150	239012	127356	111656
Other Producers	...	...	...	...	...	...	...	...	...	...	...	...
Total	1264601	470174	794427	1682304	567201	1115103	2477127	902676	1574451	2801664	1034010	1767654
Less: Imputed bank service charge	...	-12564	12564		-20318	20318	...	-48313	48313	...	-60000	60000
Import duties	...	...	...	...	...	...	...	...	...	...	...	...
Value added tax	...	...	...	...	...	...	...	...	...	...	...	...
Total	1264601	482738	781863	1682304	587519	1094785	2477127	950989	1526138	2801664	1094010	1707654

4.2 Derivation of Value Added by Kind of Activity, in Constant Prices

Thousand Gambian dalasis

Fiscal year beginning 1 July

	1980			1981			1982			1983		
	Gross Output	Intermediate Consumption	Value Added	Gross Output	Intermediate Consumption	Value Added	Gross Output	Intermediate Consumption	Value Added	Gross Output	Intermediate Consumption	Value Added
At constant prices of:1976												
All Producers												
1 Agriculture, hunting, forestry and fishing	116135	11678	104457	151501	12344	139157	142338	11277	131061	111865	14696	97169
A Agriculture and hunting	104004	9463	94541	142179	11403	130776	133161	9479	123682	101824	12700	89124
B Forestry and logging	4466	90	4376	2087	42	2045	2158	43	2115	2231	44	2187
C Fishing	7665	2125	5540	7235	899	6336	7019	1755	5264	7810	1952	5858
2 Mining and quarrying	191	6	185	227	7	220	167	17	150	172	17	155
3 Manufacturing	69110	50007	19103	100070	74025	26045	98273	69203	29070	101175	72316	28859
4 Electricity, gas and water	6479	4979	1500	7658	6193	1465	8556	6755	1801	8569	6833	1736
A Electricity, gas and steam	4839	4231	608	5497	5309	188	6821	5964	857	7009	6122	887
B Water works and supply	1640	748	892	2161	884	1277	1735	791	944	1560	711	849

645

Gambia

4.2 Derivation of Value Added by Kind of Activity, in Constant Prices
(Continued)

Thousand Gambian dalasis

Fiscal year beginning 1 July

	1980			1981			1982			1983		
	Gross Output	Intermediate Consumption	Value Added	Gross Output	Intermediate Consumption	Value Added	Gross Output	Intermediate Consumption	Value Added	Gross Output	Intermediate Consumption	Value Added
	At constant prices of:1976											
5 Construction	40854	22345	18509	30476	15598	14878	41659	21107	20552	44652	22221	22431
6 Wholesale and retail trade, restaurants and hotels	120078	24671	95407	109292	26745	82547	185285	32636	152649	183945	37562	146383
A Wholesale and retail trade	111476	17889	93587	101041	16848	84193	159985	17636	142349	149695	17012	132683
B Restaurants and hotels	8602	6782	1820	8251	9897	-1646	25300	15000	10300	34250	20550	13700
7 Transport, storage and communication	44462	14139	30323	47392	14431	32961	50211	16054	34157	60494	20314	40180
A Transport and storage	40702	13192	27510	43650	13313	30337	45010	14500	30510	55091	18700	36391
B Communication	3760	947	2813	3742	1118	2624	5201	1554	3647	5403	1614	3789
8 Finance, insurance, real estate and business services	41423	6551	34872	46060	6492	39568	82052	45851	36201	68899	39801	29098
A Financial institutions	11750	3769	7981	14857	3605	11252	51938	43158	8780	38102	37046	1056
B Insurance	1391	394	997	1908	413	1495						
C Real estate and business services	28282	2388	25894	29295	2474	26821	30114	2693	27421	30797	2755	28042
9 Community, social and personal services	8377	1639	6738	9867	1894	7973	10202	1958	8244	10549	2025	8524
A Sanitary and similar services	...	...	...	...	...	...				...	...	...
B Social and related community services	3396	929	2467	4767	1305	3462						
C Recreational and cultural services	...	...	...	...	...	...						
D Personal and household services	4981	710	4271	5100	589	4511	...	...	...	...	...	...
Total, Industries	447109	136015	311094	502543	157729	344814	618743	204858	413885	590320	215785	374535
Producers of Government Services	64571	23714	40857	64408	22513	41895	140896	70116	70780	136707	67061	69646
Other Producers	...	...	...	...	...	...	...	...	...	...	...	...
Total	511680	159729	351951	566951	180242	386709	759639	274974	484665	727027	282846	444181
Less: Imputed bank service charge	...	-10187	10187	...	-13913	13913	...	-13980	13980	...	-12036	12036
Import duties	...	...	...	...	...	...	...	...	...	...	...	...
Value added tax	...	...	...	...	...	...	...	...	...	...	...	...
Total	511680	169916	341764	566951	194155	372796	759639	288954	470685	727027	294882	432145

	1984			1985			1986			1987		
	Gross Output	Intermediate Consumption	Value Added	Gross Output	Intermediate Consumption	Value Added	Gross Output	Intermediate Consumption	Value Added	Gross Output	Intermediate Consumption	Value Added
	At constant prices of:1976											
	All Producers											
1 Agriculture, hunting, forestry and fishing	117667	10509	107158	124266	10664	113602	132094	10687	121407	131339	11022	120317
A Agriculture and hunting	107066	8389	98677	110294	7720	102574	118060	7746	110314	118719	8453	110266
B Forestry and logging	2307	46	2261	2385	47	2338	2466	49	2417	2550	51	2499
C Fishing	8294	2074	6220	11587	2897	8690	11568	2892	8676	10070	2518	7552
2 Mining and quarrying	178	18	160	185	19	166	191	19	172	198	20	178
3 Manufacturing	74136	49207	24929	71827	44370	27457	94790	58480	36310	120328	77496	42832
4 Electricity, gas and water	9042	7150	1892	10152	8064	2088	11104	8844	2260	12481	9995	2486
A Electricity, gas and steam	7234	6325	909	8209	7178	1031	9036	7901	1135	10288	8995	1293
B Water works and supply	1808	825	983	1943	886	1057	2068	943	1125	2193	1000	1193
5 Construction	51621	26158	25463	47930	24639	23291	64703	34609	30094	40063	20307	19756
6 Wholesale and retail trade, restaurants and hotels	175709	40544	135165	177367	36578	140789	180877	37830	143047	176956	37706	139250
A Wholesale and retail trade	135209	16244	118965	140367	17878	122489	145377	19630	125747	140956	19606	121350
B Restaurants and hotels	40500	24300	16200	37000	18700	18300	35500	18200	17300	36000	18100	17900
7 Transport, storage and communication	71504	26990	44514	83848	27555	56293	97185	34058	63127	110379	34219	76160
A Transport and storage	65000	25047	39953	75295	25000	50295	83618	30005	53613	86236	27007	59229

Gambia

4.2 Derivation of Value Added by Kind of Activity, in Constant Prices
(Continued)

Thousand Gambian dalasis   Fiscal year beginning 1 July

	1984			1985			1986			1987		
	Gross Output	Intermediate Consumption	Value Added	Gross Output	Intermediate Consumption	Value Added	Gross Output	Intermediate Consumption	Value Added	Gross Output	Intermediate Consumption	Value Added
						At constant prices of:1976						
B Communication	6504	1943	4561	8553	2555	5998	13567	4053	9514	24143	7212	16931
8 Finance, insurance, real estate and business services	64521	33247	31274	48664	6792	41872	51874	7922	43952	54335	8060	46275
A Financial institutions	33016	30428	2588	16428	3907	12521	18871	4969	13902	20552	5037	15515
B Insurance												
C Real estate and business services	31505	2819	28686	32236	2885	29351	33003	2953	30050	33783	3023	30760
9 Community, social and personal services	10907	2093	8814	11278	2164	9114	11661	2238	9423	12058	2314	9744
A Sanitary and similar services	...	...	...	...	...	...	...	...	...	...	...	...
B Social and related community services	...	...	...	...	...	...	...	...	...	...	...	...
C Recreational and cultural services	...	...	...	...	...	...	...	...	...	...	...	...
D Personal and household services	...	...	...	...	...	...	...	...	...	...	...	...
Total, Industries	575285	195916	379369	575517	160845	414672	644479	194687	449792	658137	201139	456998
Producers of Government Services	128424	62998	65426	117858	57815	60043	95200	46700	48500	99484	48802	50682
Other Producers		...		...	...	...	...	...	...	...	...	...
Total	703709	258914	444795	693375	218660	474715	739679	241387	498292	757621	249941	507680
Less: Imputed bank service charge	...	-5629	5629	...	-6728	6728	...	-10950	10950	...	-12091	12091
Import duties	...	...	...	...	...	...	...	...	...	...	...	...
Value added tax	...	...	...	...	...	...	...	...	...	...	...	...
Total	703709	264543	439166	693375	225388	467987	739679	252337	487342	757621	262032	495589

Germany, Federal Republic of

On 3 October 1990, the Federal Republic of Germany and the German Democratic Republic united to form one sovereign State under the designation "Germany".

National Accounts estimates for Germany including the territory of the former German Democratic Republic are not available for the years 1970-1989. Therefore, the tables shown in the following country chapter are for the territoty of the former German Democratic Republic followed by tables for the territory of the Federal Republic of Germany before the unification .

German Democratic Rep.

Source: Reply to the United Nations Material Balances Questionnaire from the State Central Statistical Office of the former German Democratic Republic. The official estimates are published in the 'Statistisches Jahrbuch Der Deutschen Demokratischen Republik'(Statistical Yearbook) of the German Democratic Republic). The methodological explanations used in the compilation of the National Accounts can be found in 'Definitionen fur Planung, Rechnungsführung und Statistik', published by the Central Statistical Office as well as in the preliminary notes of Part IV of the Statistical Yearbook of the German Democratic Republic.

General note. The estimates shown in the following tables have been prepared in accordance with the System of Material Product Balances. These estimates are not comparable in concept and coverage with those conforming to the United Nations System of National Accounts(SNA). In addition, selected tables in accordance with the SNA are also available so far as the existing data would permit. When the scope and coverage of the estimates differ for conceptual or statistical reasons from the definitions and classifications recommended in SNA, a footnote is indicated to the relevant tables. The estimates include the relevant data relating to Berlin for which separate data have not been supplied. This is without prejudice to any question of status which may be involved.

1.1 Expenditure on the Gross Domestic Product, in Current Prices

Million Marks der DDR

	1970	1975	1980	1981	1982	1983	1984	1985	1986	1987	1988	1989
1 Government final consumption expenditure a	...	...	28132	28644	29088	30950	32377	34636	34616	39472	41385	
2 Private final consumption expenditure	...	...	150110	155353	159855	162211	174192	183397	192409	199818	207362	
3 Gross capital formation	...	...	64359	64435	66250	64723	69428	76299	83293	87770	100832	
A Increase in stocks	...	...	6328	5815	1026	2150	1961	8670	8030	4708	7795	
B Gross fixed capital formation	...	...	58307	61729	59224	62573	60477	67629	75263	83062	92837	
4 Exports of goods and services	...	...	80281	82531	104468	121967	127166	145060	143984	149400	147880	
5 Less: Imports of goods and services b	...	...	78459	91035	92085	103847	110634	129040	135108	144710	151590	
Statistical discrepancy	...	...	112	117	282	501	742	903	941	1060	460	
Equals: Gross Domestic Product	...	...	244811	253154	263858	276505	293271	311755	321935	332810	346129	

a) Item 'Government final consumption expenditure' includes private non-profit institutions serving households.
b) Item 'Exports/Imports of goods and services' excludes non-material services.

1.2 Expenditure on the Gross Domestic Product, in Constant Prices

Million Marks der DDR

At constant prices of 1985

	1970	1975	1980	1981	1982	1983	1984	1985	1986	1987	1988	1989
1 Government final consumption expenditure a	...	...	32920	32285	33193	33279	34636	34945	36684	37708		
2 Private final consumption expenditure	...	...	160388	164615	167423	170617	183897	192051	199398	206679		
3 Gross capital formation	...	...	78511	78099	66990	70533	72220	76299	82940	90707		
A Increase in stocks	...	...	8736	6786	1573	2620	7504	8670	7597	5525	7983	
B Gross fixed capital formation	...	...	69775	71313	68330	67913	64716	67629	71605	77415	82724	
4 Exports of goods and services	...	...	102952	112028	126830	140135	140439	145060	146283	149570	147637	
5 Less: Imports of goods and services b	...	...	123338	124836	123476	130531	125515	129040	129373	136130	139597	
Statistical discrepancy	...	...	1269	981	660	710	419	903	910	2320	2000	
Equals: Gross Domestic Product	...	...	252702	263172	270658	283024	296859	311755	324018	334782	345134	

a) Item 'Government final consumption expenditure' includes private non-profit institutions serving households.
b) Item 'Export/Imports of goods and services' excludes non-material services.

1.3 Cost Components of the Gross Domestic Product

Million Marks der DDR

	1970	1975	1980	1981	1982	1983	1984	1985	1986	1987	1988	1989
1 Indirect taxes, net												
2 Consumption of fixed capital	...	...	32480	33747	35063	36754	37729	39552	48437	49665	52373	
3 Compensation of employees paid by resident producers												
4 Operating surplus												
Equals: Gross Domestic Product	...	...	244811	253154	263858	276505	293271	311755	321935	332810	346129	

1.10 Gross Domestic Product by Kind of Activity, in Current Prices

Million Marks der DDR

	1970	1975	1980	1981	1982	1983	1984	1985	1986	1987	1988	1989
1 Agriculture, hunting, forestry and fishing a	...	...	19255	20267	18878	21444	32367	33288	34334	33877	32766	
2 Mining and quarrying	...	...	147635	152669	160230	165414	173827	180380	186278	194884		
3 Manufacturing a												
4 Electricity, gas and water												
5 Construction	...	...	12236	13328	12802	15523	16227	18132	19714	20227	20785	
6 Wholesale and retail trade, restaurants and hotels	...	...	19186	19969	19985	19833	21118	22295	22464	23522	25299	
7 Transport, storage and communication	...	...	10985	11460	15479	15607	16981	16902	17173	18644	19023	
8 Finance, insurance, real estate and business services	...	...	46760	48187	49998	52757	55860	58061	60227	63507	67153	
9 Community, social and personal services b												

650

German Democratic Rep.

1.10 Gross Domestic Product by Kind of Activity, in Current Prices
(Continued)

Million Marks der DDR	1970	1975	1980	1981	1982	1983	1984	1985	1986	1987	1988	1989
Total, Industries												
Producers of Government Services [b]												
Other Producers [b]	...	...	256027	265880	276672	290578	303342	325505	334292	346055	359910	...
Subtotal												
Less: imputed bank service charge [c]												
Plus: Import duties	...	...	...	...	...	...	...	...	...	...	...	...
Plus: Value added tax	...	...	-11216	-12726	-12814	-14073	-10071	-10750	-12357	-13245	-13781	
Plus: Other adjustments [d]												
Equals: Gross Domestic Product	...	...	244811	253154	263858	276505	293271	311755	321935	332810	346129	

a) Deep-sea fishing is excluded from item 'Agriculture, hunting, forestry and fishing' and is included in item 'Manufacturing'.
b) Items 'Other producers' and 'Producers of government services' are included in item 'Community, social and personal services'.
c) Imputed bank service charges are adjusted in the respective activity.
d) Item 'Statistical discrepancy or other adjustments' refers to price supports.

1.11 Gross Domestic Product by Kind of Activity, in Constant Prices

Million Marks der DDR	1970	1975	1980	1981	1982	1983	1984	1985	1986	1987	1988	1989
				At constant prices of 1985								
1 Agriculture, hunting, forestry and fishing [a]	...	...	27694	28063	29399	32095	33288	32992	32862	30902		
2 Mining and quarrying	...	...	135458	142851	148128	156295	164528	173827	182496	189193	196665	
3 Manufacturing [a]												
4 Electricity, gas and water												
5 Construction	...	...	14741	15493	15537	16242	17059	18132	19215	19888	20662	
6 Wholesale and retail trade, restaurants and hotels	...	...	19653	20384	20541	20791	21543	22255	23194	23954	25282	
7 Transport, storage and communication	...	...	14548	15062	15537	15976	16608	16902	17304	17672	18055	
8 Finance, insurance, real estate and business services	...	...	49432	50088	51657	54088	55785	58067	59599	62120	64498	
9 Community, social and personal services [b]												
Total, Industries												
Producers of Government Services [b]												
Other Producers [b]	...	...	261526	273396	279457	292791	307618	322505	334800	345689	359054	
Subtotal												
Less: imputed bank service charge [c]												
Plus: Import duties	...	...	...	...	...	...	...	...	...	...	...	
Plus: Value added tax	...	...	-8824	-8799	-9224	-8767	-9767	-10750	-10782	-10907	-10920	
Plus: Other adjustments [d]												
Equals: Gross Domestic Product	...	...	252702	263172	270658	283024	296859	311755	324018	334782	348134	

a) Deep-sea fishing is excluded from item 'Agriculture, hunting, forestry and fishing' and is included in item 'Manufacturing'.
b) Items 'Other producers' and 'Producers of government services' are included in item 'Community, social and personal services'.
c) Imputed bank service charges are adjusted in the respective activity.
d) Item 'Statistical discrepancy or other adjustments' refers to price supports.

1a Net Material Product by Use at Current Market Prices

Million Marks der DDR	1970	1975	1980	1981	1982	1983	1984	1985	1986	1987	1988	1989
1 Personal consumption	76512	94610	118261	121370	123977	125260	133695	140815	146515	152020	157811	163123
2 Material consumption in the non-material sphere serving individuals	6238	10026	14422	15653	16227	16951	18822	19517	21420	23465	24844	25764
Consumption of the Population	82750	104636	132683	137023	140204	142062	152517	160332	167935	175485	182655	188887
3 Material consumption in the units of the non-material sphere serving the community as a whole	6120	9056	12003	12606	12798	13133	13646	14473	15680	16693	16950	15451
4 Net fixed capital formation	23865	27742	35379	37688	33373	33417	36417	35962	38853	45565	53260	49967
5 Increase in material circulating assets and in stocks	4305	4198	6328	5815	1026	2150	8951	8670	8030	4708	7795	8210
6 Losses	...	...	...	...	...	...	...	...	...	...	...	...
7 Exports of goods and material services	29610	47472	80281	92531	106468	121967	127166	143060	145984	149400	147880	145007
8 Less: Imports of goods and material services	32890	48120	78459	91035	92085	103847	110634	129040	135108	144710	151590	153009
Statistical discrepancy	-960	112	553	117	282	501	742	903	941	1060	460	350
Net Material Product	112800	145537	188327	194745	202666	205666	212403	226864	241863	243360	249580	254863

651

German Democratic Rep.

1b Net Material Product by Use at Constant Market Prices

Million Marks der DDR

At constant prices of 1985

	1970	1975	1980	1981	1982	1983	1984	1985	1986	1987	1988	1989
1 Personal consumption	79925	101342	123401	125214	128215	129316	134636	140815	146820	152010	157890	163590
2 Material consumption in the units of the non-material sphere serving individuals	10355	15598	15881	18815	19592	19524	20345	21420	22794	24090	24864	25086
3 Consumption of the Population	90280	116940	142276	144029	147807	148840	154981	162235	169614	176100	182754	188676
4 Material consumption in the units of the non-material sphere serving the community as a whole	9019	13118	14788	14744	14630	14053	14091	14473	14766	15670	16058	14754
5 Net fixed capital formation	34424	41984	47021	47462	43303	42009	37998	42423	47585	50555	48977	...
6 Increase in material circulating assets and in stocks	6205	5874	8736	6786	1573	2620	7504	8670	7597	5525	7983	8463
7 Losses	...	...	...	...	...	...	...	...	...	...	...	...
8 Exports of goods and material services	48330	76972	102952	112228	126830	140135	140439	145060	146283	149570	147637	150696
Less: Imports of goods and material services	67876	97762	123338	124836	132476	130531	125515	129040	132873	138130	138917	140266
Statistical discrepancy	1811	1031	1269	981	660	710	419	903	910	2320	1990	2180
Net Material Product	121563	158157	193644	202971	208219	217836	229917	241863	252220	260640	268060	273480

2a Net Material Product by Kind of Activity of the Material Sphere in Current Market Prices

Million Marks der DDR

	1970	1975	1980	1981	1982	1983	1984	1985	1986	1987	1988	1989
1 Agriculture and forestry a	14420	16107	16191	17531	16046	18521	29305	30204	31314	30880	29614	30336
A Agriculture and livestock	13656	15237	15219	16498	15000	16330	27187	27955	29029	28560	27381	28052
B Forestry	764	870	1000	1045	1046	2191	2118	2249	2285	2320	2233	2284
C Other												
2 Industrial activity a	66155	87436	136644	141186	140018	152408	147762	159814	164955	172465	167972	
3 Construction	9493	10785	11740	12818	12282	15049	15915	17843	19225	19804	20377	20129
4 Wholesale and retail trade and restaurants and other eating and drinking places	13730	20197	18691	18440	18813	19487	20824	21984	21861	22955	24612	25116
5 Transport and communication	6962	8398	8386	8794	12596	12825	14141	14035	13314	14556	14780	15114
A Transport	5703	6930	6465	6813	10569	10775	11848	11668	10712	11955	12088	12332
B Communication	1259	1468	1921	1981	2029	2053	2293	2367	2602	2601	2692	2782
6 Other activities of the material sphere	4070	5126	7463	7702	7726	8183	8868	8733	9250	9635	10143	10306
Statistical discrepancy b	-2030	-2512	-11216	-12756	-12814	-14073	-10071	-10750	-12357	-13245	-13781	-14110
Net material product	112800	145537	188327	194745	202666	212403	226864	241863	242360	246980	258210	254863

a) Deep-sea fishery is included in item 'Industrial activity'.
b) Item 'Statistical discrepancy or other adjustments' refers to price supports.

2b Net Material Product by Kind of Activity of the Material Sphere in Constant Market Prices

Million Marks der DDR

	1970	1975	1980	1981	1982	1983	1984	1985	1986	1987	1988	1989
1 Agriculture and forestry a	22596	24965	25112	25813	25257	26603	29027	30204	29966	29861	27745	28682
A Agriculture and livestock	20800	23098	23020	23725	23163	24284	26887	27955	27682	27540	25501	26387
B Forestry	1796	1867	2092	2088	2094	2219	2140	2249	2284	2321	2244	2295
C Other												
2 Industrial activity a	73719	97668	124661	131571	136127	143355	151460	159814	167789	174125	180808	184501
3 Construction	9960	12465	14242	14883	15013	15766	16750	17843	18925	19966	20448	20491
4 Wholesale and retail trade and restaurants and other eating and drinking places	12183	16097	19126	19824	20038	20415	21221	21984	22822	23638	24847	25364
5 Transport and communication	8065	10434	11972	12420	12677	13223	13798	14035	14340	14585	14892	15148
A Transport	6809	8778	9978	10355	10544	11051	11522	11668	11987	11967	12185	12355
B Communication	1257	1543	1994	2055	2133	2172	2276	2367	2542	2618	2707	2793
6 Other activities of the material sphere	4123	5477	7355	7584	7906	8161	8420	8733	9160	8963	10240	10500
Statistical discrepancy b	-9043	-8949	-8824	-8799	-8224	-9767	-10759	-10750	-10782	-10907	-10920	-11206
Net material product	121563	158157	193644	202971	208219	217836	229917	241863	252220	260640	268060	273480

a) Deep-sea fishery is included in item 'Industrial activity'.
b) Item 'Statistical discrepancy or other adjustments' refers to price supports.

German Democratic Rep.

3 Primary Incomes by Kind of Activity of the Material Sphere in Current Market Prices

Million Marks der DDR

	1980		1981		1982		1983		1984		1985	
	Primary Income of the Population	Primary Income of Enterprises	Primary Income of the Population	Primary Income of Enterprises	Primary Income of the Population	Primary Income of Enterprises	Primary Income of the Population	Primary Income of Enterprises	Primary Income of the Population	Primary Income of Enterprises	Primary Income of the Population	Primary Income of Enterprises
1 Agriculture and forestry a	11385	5234	11745	5786	12287	3759	12552	5969	13867	15438	14365	15839
A Agriculture and livestock	10886	4733	11207	5279	11748	3252	11991	4339	13281	13906	13750	14205
B Forestry	499	501	538	507	539	507	561	1630	586	1532	615	1634
C Other	-	-	-	-	-	-	-	-	-	-	-	-
2 Industrial activity a	37332	99312	38645	102541	39691	108327	40730	111678	42021	105741	43346	116468
3 Construction	6774	4966	7092	5726	7243	5039	7415	7634	7591	8324	7813	10030
4 Wholesale and retail trade and restaurants and other eating and drinking places	7760	10931	8039	11401	8263	10550	8402	11085	8720	12104	9216	12768
5 Transport and communication	7100	1286	7230	1564	7510	5085	7637	5191	7842	6299	8100	5935
A Transport	5839	626	5928	885	6205	4361	6297	4478	6443	5405	6668	5000
B Communication	1261	660	1302	679	1305	724	1340	713	1399	894	1432	935
6 Other activities of the material sphere	3914	3549	4032	3670	4183	3543	4340	3843	4408	4580	4372	4361
Statistical discrepancy b	-	-11216	-	-12726	-	-12814	-	-14073	-	-10071	-	-10750
Total	74265	114062	76783	117962	79177	123489	81076	131327	84449	142415	87212	154651

	1986		1987		1988		1989	
	Primary Income of the Population	Primary Income of Enterprises	Primary Income of the Population	Primary Income of Enterprises	Primary Income of the Population	Primary Income of Enterprises	Primary Income of the Population	Primary Income of Enterprises
1 Agriculture and forestry a	14584	16730	14901	15979	15545	14069	16216	14120
A Agriculture and livestock	13951	15078	14258	14302	14848	12533	15499	12553
B Forestry	633	1652	643	1677	697	1536	717	1567
C Other	-	-	-	-	-	-	-	-
2 Industrial activity a	44602	115151	46519	118476	47798	124667	48743	119229
3 Construction	8009	11216	8292	11512	8441	11936	8454	11675
4 Wholesale and retail trade and restaurants and other eating and drinking places	9607	12254	9940	13015	10268	14344	10463	14653
5 Transport and communication	8439	4875	8970	5586	9186	5594	9355	5759
A Transport	6982	3730	7469	4486	7623	4465	7770	4562
B Communication	1457	1145	1501	1100	1563	1129	1585	1197
6 Other activities of the material sphere	4440	4810	4598	5037	4760	5383	4810	5496
Statistical discrepancy b	-	-12357	-	-13245	-	-13781	-	-14110
Total	89681	152679	93220	156360	95998	162212	98041	156822

a) Deep-sea fishery is included in item 'Industrial activity'.
b) Item 'Statistical discrepancy or other adjustments' refers to price supports.

4 Primary Incomes From Net Material Product

Million Marks der DDR

	1970	1975	1980	1981	1982	1983	1984	1985	1986	1987	1988	1989
a) Primary Incomes of the Population												
1 Socialist sector	43209	57703	68166	70521	72481	74286	76950	79256	81665	85008	87272	89154
A State sector	32024	46290	55792	57775	59391	60955	63078	65028	66953	69889	71723	72846
B Co-operative sector	11185	11413	12374	12746	13090	13331	13872	14228	14712	15119	15549	16308
C Personal plots of households	-	-	-	-	-	-	-	-	-	-	-	-
2 Private sector	9137	5613	6099	6262	6696	6790	7499	7956	8016	8212	8726	8887
Sub-total	52346	63316	74265	76783	79177	81076	84449	87212	89681	93220	95998	98041
b) Primary incomes of the enterprises												
1 Socialist sector	54401	83230	123359	128615	134201	143303	150196	162980	162371	166780	173071	167992
A State sector	46989	76203	116184	120900	128708	136536	138468	150990	152516	157236	165525	159811
B Co-operative sector	7412	7027	7175	7715	5493	6767	11728	11990	9855	9544	7546	8181
2 Private sector	8083	1503	1919	2073	2102	2097	2290	2421	2665	2825	2922	2940
Statistical discrepancy	-2030	-2512	-11216	-12726	-12814	-14073	-10071	-10750	-12357	-13245	-13781	-14110
Sub-total	60454	82221	114062	117962	123489	131327	142415	154651	152679	156360	162212	156822
Total net material product	112800	145537	188327	194745	202666	212403	226864	241863	242360	249580	258210	254863

German Democratic Rep.

5a Supply and Disposition of Goods and Material Services in Current Market Prices

Million Marks der DDR

	Supply					Disposition				
	Gross Output at Producers Prices	Trade Margins and Transport Charges	Gross Output at Market Prices	Imports	Total Supply and Disposition	Intermediate Material Consumption including Depreciation	Final Consumption	Net Capital Formation	Losses	Exports
1982										
1 Agriculture and forestry	44436	...	44436	4189	48625	39849	7477	118	...	1181
A Agriculture and livestock	43041	...	43041	3905	46946	38415	7444	-59	...	1146
B Forestry	1394	...	1394	284	1679	1433	33	177	...	35
C Other	-	...	-	-	-	-	-	-	...	-
2 Industrial activity	460706	...	460706	85410	546116	309918	105183	30732	...	100288
3 Construction	40303	...	40303	457	40761	8357	6633	25587	...	183
4 Transport and communication	25287	...	25287	2000	27287	16331	5712	478	...	4766
A Transport	22643	...	22643	2000	24642	15360	4039	478	...	4766
B Communication	2644	...	2644	-	2645	971	1673	-	...	-
5 Other activities of the material sphere	11247	...	11247	29	11276	4393	4768	2067	...	49
Statistical discrepancy a	30227	...	30227	-	30228	6963	22102	1162	...	1
Total	612207	...	612207	92085	704292	385809	151875	60143	...	106468
1987										
1 Agriculture and forestry	79801	...	79801	6519	86320	72199	10229	1049	...	2842
A Agriculture and livestock	77411	...	77411	5897	83308	69707	10180	704	...	2716
B Forestry	2389	...	2389	622	3011	2492	49	345	...	126
C Other	-	...	-	-	-	-	-	-	...	-
2 Industrial activity	609400	...	609400	132764	742164	419644	134784	50653	...	137082
3 Construction	48101	...	48101	564	48665	5910	12229	30040	...	485
4 Transport and communication	33102	...	33102	4828	37930	23837	5283	-	...	8811
A Transport	29808	...	29808	4828	34636	22147	3678	-	...	8811
B Communication	3295	...	3295	-	3295	1690	1605	-	...	-
5 Other activities of the material sphere	16031	...	16031	33	16065	8594	4860	2432	...	180
Statistical discrepancy a	36925	...	36925	2	36927	7159	26171	3596	...	-
Total	823361	...	823361	144710	968071	537344	193557	87770	...	149400

a) Item 'Statistical discrepancy' refers to wholesale and retail trade, restaurants and other eating and drinking places.

6a Capital Formation by Kind of Activity of the Material and Non-Material Spheres in Current Market Prices

Million Marks der DDR

	1970	1975	1980	1981	1982	1983	1984	1985	1986	1987	1988	1989
Net Fixed Capital Formation												
1 Agriculture and forestry	2756	2389	2015	2312	1738	1402	1098	1283	1926	2422	2869	2919
2 Industrial activity	9481	9203	14041	15011	13971	15072	12749	14695	12203	17912	24333	21594
3 Construction	335	422	107	-92	-301	-590	-431	-458	-558	-312	227	-37
4 Wholesale and retail trade, restaurants and other eating and drinking places	588	483	347	150	-114	-126	-58	236	126	133	296	634
5 Transport and communication	992	1755	1189	1584	383	676	730	1824	2178	1092	571	846
6 Other activities of the material sphere	645	421	476	303	244	309	290	596	673	741	987	719
Total Material Sphere	14797	14673	18175	19268	15921	16743	14378	18176	16548	21988	29283	26675
7 Housing except owner-occupied, communal and miscellaneous personal services	2555	4305	6889	7448	7146	8592	8660	9898	9989	10018	9958	9835
8 Education, culture and art	788	1153	1554	1663	1555	1571	1424	1441	1493	1680	1695	1646
9 Health and social welfare services and sports	471	821	990	1055	807	820	740	802	781	803	975	1041
Total Non-Material Sphere Serving Individuals	3814	6279	9433	10166	9508	10983	10824	12141	12263	12501	12628	12522
10 Government	...	...	...	...	...	...	...	...	...	...	...	...
11 Finance, credit and insurance	...	...	...	...	...	...	...	...	...	...	...	...
12 Research, scientific and technological institutes	...	...	...	...	...	...	...	...	...	...	...	...
13 Other activities of the non-material sphere	...	...	...	...	...	...	...	...	...	...	...	...
Total Non-Material Sphere Serving the Community as a Whole	5254	6790	7771	8254	8544	8691	8579	9245	10042	11076	11349	10770
14 Owner-occupied dwellings	...	...	...	...	...	...	...	...	...	...	...	...
Total Net Fixed Capital Formation	23865	27742	35379	37688	33973	36417	33781	39562	38853	45565	53260	49967

German Democratic Rep.

6a Capital Formation by Kind of Activity of the Material and Non-Material Spheres in Current Market Prices
(Continued)

Million Marks der DDR

	1970	1975	1980	1981	1982	1983	1984	1985	1986	1987	1988	1989
Gross Fixed Capital Formation												
1 Agriculture and forestry	4222	4730	4927	5372	4913	4681	4563	4779	5391	5863	6484	6789
2 Industrial activity	16568	19698	27770	29457	29258	31208	29207	32360	36643	43093	50924	50448
3 Construction	1025	1302	1273	1123	901	612	669	664	778	953	1521	1300
4 Wholesale and retail trade and restaurants and other eating and drinking places	1493	1445	1535	1392	1175	1182	1248	1596	1764	1770	2013	2421
5 Transport and communication	2832	4181	4315	4806	3815	4029	4192	5343	6798	6049	5805	6084
6 Other activities of the material sphere	1051	970	1283	1159	1110	1187	1195	1501	1584	1757	2113	1921
Total Material Sphere	27191	32326	41103	43309	41172	42899	41074	46243	52958	59485	68860	68963
7 Housing except owner-occupied, communal and miscellaneous personal services	2555	4305	6889	7448	7146	8592	8660	9898	9989	10018	9958	9835
8 Education, culture and art	788	1153	1554	1663	1555	1571	1424	1441	1493	1680	1695	1646
9 Health and social welfare services and sports	471	821	990	1055	807	820	740	802	781	803	975	1041
Total Non-Material Sphere Serving Individuals	3814	6279	9433	10166	9508	10983	10824	12141	12263	12501	12628	12522
10 Government	...	...	...	...	...	...	...	...	...	...	...	...
11 Finance, credit and insurance	...	...	...	...	...	...	...	...	...	...	...	...
12 Research, scientific and technological institutes	...	...	...	...	...	...	...	...	...	...	...	...
13 Other activities of the non-material sphere	...	...	...	...	...	...	...	...	...	...	...	...
Total Non-Material Sphere Serving the Community as a Whole	5254	6790	7771	8254	8544	8691	8579	9245	10042	11076	11349	10770
14 Owner-occupied dwellings	...	...	...	...	...	...	...	...	...	...	...	...
Total Gross Fixed Capital Formation	36259	45395	58307	61729	59224	62573	60477	67629	75263	83062	92837	92255
Increases in Material Circulating Assets and Stocks												
1 Agriculture and forestry	378	-362	85	326	-101	393	1222	1075	516	1167	136	1052
2 Industrial activity	2792	3101	3580	3289	3812	808	3619	4828	5107	2875	5741	4847
3 Construction	272	364	120	-30	-316	-80	183	301	444	272	161	143
4 Wholesale and retail trade and restaurants and other eating and drinking places	776	488	2100	1672	-1755	438	2304	1708	326	-834	1078	2234
5 Transport and communication	21	219	177	-49	-111	-209	-20	70	293	295	317	72
6 Other activities of the non-material sphere	26	-2	153	62	6	57	939	214	398	174	108	-122
Total increase in material circulating assets	4265	3808	6215	5270	1535	1407	8247	8196	7084	3949	7541	8226
Statistical discrepancy	...	...	...	...	...	...	...	...	...	...	...	...
Increase in stocks of the non-material sphere	40	390	113	545	-509	743	704	474	946	759	254	-16

6b Capital Formation by Kind of Activity of the Material and Non-Material Spheres in Constant Market Prices

Million Marks der DDR

	1970	1975	1980	1981	1982	1983	1984	1985	1986	1987	1988	1989
At constant prices of:1985												
Net Fixed Capital Formation												
1 Agriculture and forestry	4439	4346	3491	3669	2972	2146	1481	1283	1497	1951	2271	2329
2 Industrial activity	13647	14645	19237	19254	18109	18372	14932	14695	15822	19899	22029	20782
3 Construction	827	995	425	163	-98	-496	-331	-458	-382	-167	230	29
4 Wholesale and retail trade, restaurants and other eating and drinking places	1002	907	617	373	58	-74	59	236	276	278	394	633
5 Transport and communication	1898	3229	2246	2430	1020	1001	1227	1824	2527	1623	956	1327
6 Other activities of the material sphere	769	494	467	394	349	374	361	596	677	776	1032	750
Total Material Sphere	22582	24616	26483	26283	22410	21323	17729	18176	20417	24360	26912	25850
7 Housing except owner-occupied, communal and miscellaneous personal services	4003	6845	9073	9361	9014	9341	9297	9898	9855	9848	9867	9692
8 Education, culture and art	1120	1660	1946	2037	1968	1792	1576	1441	1434	1612	1567	1525
9 Health and social welfare services and sports	695	1180	1247	1329	1041	942	831	802	730	749	923	948
Total Non-Material Sphere Serving Individuals	5818	9685	12266	12727	12023	12075	11704	12141	12019	12209	12357	12165

655

German Democratic Rep.

6b Capital Formation by Kind of Activity of the Material and Non-Material Spheres in Constant Market Prices
(Continued)

Million Marks der DDR

	1970	1975	1980	1981	1982	1983	1984	1985	1986	1987	1988	1989
					At constant prices of:1985							
10 Government	...	...	...	...	...	...	...	...	...	...	...	...
11 Finance, credit and insurance	...	...	...	...	...	...	...	...	...	...	...	...
12 Research, scientific and technological institutes	...	...	...	...	...	...	...	...	...	...	...	...
13 Other activities of the non-material sphere	...	...	...	...	...	...	...	...	...	...	...	...
Total Non-Material Sphere Serving the Community as a Whole	6024	7683	8272	8452	8870	8611	8565	9245	9987	11016	11286	10962
14 Owner-occupied dwellings	...	...	...	...	...	...	...	...	...	...	...	...
Total Net Fixed Capital Formation	34424	41984	47021	47462	43303	42009	37998	39562	42423	47585	50555	48977
					Gross Fixed Capital Formation							
1 Agriculture and forestry	5905	6687	6403	6729	6147	5425	4946	4779	4962	5392	5886	6199
2 Industrial activity	20660	25000	32764	33490	33181	34272	31455	32360	34331	38864	42060	42535
3 Construction	1434	1876	1591	1378	1104	706	769	664	754	908	1330	1185
4 Wholesale and retail trade and restaurants and other eating and drinking places	1921	1878	1829	1640	1373	1260	1391	1596	1683	1665	1859	2162
5 Transport and communciation	3780	5640	5348	5628	4422	4323	4657	5343	6251	5576	5106	5513
6 Other activities of the material sphere	1213	1082	1302	1269	1210	1241	1229	1501	1618	1785	2170	1965
Total Material Sphere	34913	42163	49237	50134	47437	47227	44447	46243	49599	54190	58411	59559
7 Housing except owner-occupied, communal and miscellaneous personal services	4003	6845	9073	9361	9014	9341	9297	9898	9855	9848	9867	9692
8 Education, culture and art	1120	1660	1946	2037	1968	1792	1576	1441	1434	1612	1567	1525
9 Health and social welfare services and sports	695	1180	1247	1329	1041	942	831	802	730	749	923	948
Total Non-Material Sphere Serving Individuals	5818	9685	12266	12727	12023	12075	11704	12141	12019	12209	12357	12165
10 Government	...	...	...	...	...	...	...	...	...	...	...	...
11 Finance, credit and insurance	...	...	...	...	...	...	...	...	...	...	...	...
12 Research, scientific and technological institutes	...	...	...	...	...	...	...	...	...	...	...	...
13 Other activities of the non-material sphere	...	...	...	...	...	...	...	...	...	...	...	...
Total Non-Material Sphere Serving the Community as a Whole	6024	7683	8272	8452	8870	8611	8565	9245	9987	11016	11286	10962
14 Owner-occupied dwellings	...	...	...	...	...	...	...	...	...	...	...	...
Total Gross Fixed Capital Formation	46755	59531	69775	71313	68330	67913	64716	67629	71605	77415	82054	82686
					Increases in Material Circulating Assets and Stocks							
1 Agriculture and forestry	592	-567	133	511	-158	616	984	1075	417	1188	109	1090
2 Industrial activity	4084	4478	4709	3839	4627	972	3626	4828	5087	3378	5943	4974
3 Construction	368	497	149	-36	-379	-93	184	301	443	275	161	143
4 Wholesale and retail trade and restaurants and other eating and drinking places	882	537	2255	1782	-1824	545	2089	1708	321	-769	1080	2234
5 Transport and communication	41	379	291	-79	-171	-316	-48	70	282	305	318	72
6 Other activities of the non-material sphere	25	-40	199	43	-46	25	32	214	397	177	97	-110
Total increase in material circulating assets	5992	5284	7736	6060	2049	1749	6867	8196	6947	4554	7708	8403
Statistical discrepancy	...	...	...	...	...	...	...	...	...	...	...	...
Increase in stocks of the non-material sphere	213	590	1000	726	-476	871	637	474	650	971	275	60

German Democratic Rep.

7a Final Consumption at Current Market Prices

Million Marks der DDR

	1970	1975	1980	1981	1982	1983	1984	1985	1986	1987	1988	1989
1 Personal consumption	76512	94610	118261	121370	123977	125260	133695	140815	146515	152020	157811	163123
a) Material Consumption in the Units of the Non-Material Sphere Serving Individuals												
Housing except owner-occupied, communal and miscellaneous personal services	1775	2798	5068	5633	5928	6338	7999	8755	9830	10348	10649	10681
Education, culture and art	2019	3460	4262	4480	4540	4601	5135	5653	5986	6426	6644	6557
Health and social welfare services and sports	1819	3382	4402	4761	4963	5045	5513	6022	6469	6819	7043	7190
Other	625	386	690	779	796	838	870	990	1180	1251	1308	1336
2 Total non-material sphere serving individuals	6238	10026	14422	15653	16227	16822	19517	21420	23465	24844	25644	25764
b) Material Consumption in the Units of the Non-Material Sphere Serving the Community as a Whole												
3 Total non-material sphere serving the community as a whole	6120	9056	12003	12606	12798	13133	13646	14473	15680	16693	16950	15451
Final consumption	88870	113692	144686	149629	153002	155215	166858	176708	185660	193557	200405	204338

7b Final Consumption at Constant Market Prices

Million Marks der DDR

	1970	1975	1980	1981	1982	1983	1984	1985	1986	1987	1988	1989
At constant prices of:1985												
1 Personal consumption	79925	101342	123401	126214	128215	129316	134636	140815	146820	152010	157890	163590
a) Material Consumption in the Units of the Non-Material Sphere Serving Individuals												
Housing except owner-occupied, communal and miscellaneous personal services	3740	5025	7055	7507	7593	7956	8408	8755	9665	10159	10449	10540
Education, culture and art	2456	4607	5024	5136	5176	5090	5271	5653	5824	6246	6457	6406
Health and social welfare services and sports	2621	4826	5496	5688	5813	5510	5711	6022	6235	6556	6774	6950
Other	1538	1140	1240	1261	1102	968	955	990	1070	1129	1184	1190
2 Total non-material sphere serving individuals	10355	15598	18815	19592	19684	19524	20345	21420	22794	24090	24864	25086
b) Material Consumption in the Units of the Non-Material Sphere Serving the Community as a Whole												
3 Total non-material sphere serving the community as a whole	9019	13118	14788	14744	14630	14053	14091	14473	14766	15670	16058	14754
Final consumption	99299	130058	157004	160550	162529	162893	169072	176708	184380	191770	198812	203430

8 Personal Consumption According to Source of Supply of Goods and Material Services in Current Market Prices

Million Marks der DDR

	1970	1975	1980	1981	1982	1983	1984	1985	1986	1987	1988	1989
1 Purchases of goods in state and co-operative retail trade	64635	83073	101677	104201	105197	106049	110857	115697	120434	124650	129445	133721
2 Purchases of goods in the free market and from private retail trade												
3 Goods produced on own account and received in kind	2354	1776	1720	1623	1783	1829	1734	1781	1583	1489	1620	1574
4 Payments for transport and communication services	2425	2972	3226	3220	3292	3346	3502	3477	3506	3615	3598	3869
5 Purchases of electricity, gas and water	1040	1193	1420	1440	1523	1581	1667	1809	1831	1921	1946	1931
6 Purchases directly from handicrafts, repair shops and the like	1803	2283	3175	3378	3655	3806	3990	4157	4424	4727	4997	5210
7 Consumption of fixed assets in respect of all dwellings	-	-	-	-	-	-	-	-	-	-	-	-
8 Other	4255	3313	7043	7508	8527	8649	11945	13894	14737	15618	16205	16818
Personal consumption	76512	94610	118261	121370	123977	125260	133695	140815	146515	152020	157811	163123

9a Total Consumption of the Population in Current Market Prices

Million Marks der DDR

	1970	1975	1980	1981	1982	1983	1984	1985	1986	1987	1988	1989
By Object												
1 Housing except owner-occupied, communal and miscellaneous personal services	...	...	8941	9643	10092	10578	12463	13273	14500	15084	15572	...
2 Education, culture and art	...	...	12304	13019	13579	13755	14465	15424	15955	16651	17245	...
3 Health and social welfare services and sport	...	...	9914	10542	11411	11780	12699	13395	14259	14812	15426	...
Total consumption of non-material services	...	...	31159	33204	35082	36113	39627	42092	44714	46547	48243	...

657

German Democratic Rep.

9a Total Consumption of the Population in Current Market Prices
(Continued)

Million Marks der DDR

	1970	1975	1980	1981	1982	1983	1984	1985	1986	1987	1988	1989
4 Personal consumption of goods and material services excluding depreciation of dwellings	...	...	118261	121370	123977	125260	133695	140815	146515	152020	157811	...
Statistical discrepancy	...	...	690	779	796	838	870	990	1180	1251	1308	...
Total consumption of the population	...	...	150110	155353	159855	162211	174192	183897	192409	199818	207362	...
By Mode of Acquisition												
1 Purchased	...	...	113508	116455	118048	119351	124650	129788	135053	139849	145087	...
2 Free of charge	...	...	34882	37275	40024	41031	47808	52328	55773	58480	60655	...
3 From own production	...	...	1720	1623	1783	1829	1734	1781	1583	1489	1620	...
Total consumption of the population	...	...	150110	155353	159855	162211	174192	183897	192409	199818	207362	...

9b Total Consumption of the Population in Constant Market Prices

Million Marks der DDR

	1970	1975	1980	1981	1982	1983	1984	1985	1986	1987	1988	1989
At constant prices of:1985												
By Object												
1 Housing except owner-occupied, communal and miscellaneous personal services	...	...	...	...	...	...	...	13273	14355	14987	15480	...
2 Education, culture and art	...	...	...	...	...	...	...	15424	15873	16650	17067	...
3 Health and social welfare services and sport	...	...	...	...	...	...	...	13395	13933	14622	15058	...
Total consumption of non-material services	...	...	35747	37140	38106	38700	40426	42092	44161	46259	47605	...
4 Personal consumption of goods and material services excluding depreciation of dwellings	...	...	123401	126214	128215	129316	134636	140815	146820	152010	157890	...
Statistical discrepancy	...	...	1240	1261	1102	968	955	990	1070	1129	1184	...
Total consumption of the population	...	...	160388	164615	167423	168984	176017	183897	192051	199398	206679	...
By Mode of Acquisition												
1 Purchased	...	...	113748	116659	118308	119517	124554	129788	135056	139918	145174	...
2 Free of charge	...	...	44905	46319	47324	47629	49724	52328	55433	58023	59907	...
3 From own production	...	...	1735	1637	1791	1838	1739	1781	1562	1457	1598	...
Total consumption of the population	...	...	160388	164615	167423	168984	176017	183897	192051	199398	206679	...

Germany, Fed. Rep. of

General note. The preparation of national accounts statistics in the Federal Republic of Germany is undertaken by the Federal Statistical Office, Wiesbaden. The official estimates are published in the monthly bulletin 'Wirtschaft und Statistik'. Detailed data as well as description of the sources and methods used for the national accounts estimation are published annually in Fachserie 18 'Volkswirtschaftliche Gesamtrechnungen', Reihe 1 'Konten und Standardtabellen'. The estimates are in close accordance with the classifications and definitions recommended in the United Nations System of National Accounts (SNA). Input-output tables for 1978 and 1980 have been published in 1982 in Reihe 2 of Fachserie 18. The 1977 tables will be issued together with revised tables for 1978 and 1980 in 1987. The fo llowing tables have been prepared from successive replies to the United Nations national accounts questionnaire. Estimates shown include the relevant data relating to Berlin, for which separate data have not been supplied. This is without prejudice to any question of status which may be involved. When the scope and coverage of the estimates differ for conceptual or statistical reasons from the definitions and classifications recommended in SNA, a footnote is indicated to the relevant tables. As a general principle, the statistical units in the case of the data provided in the ISIC classification are institutional units (e.g. enterprises). Only the ownership of dwellings (including owner-occupied housing) is shown in a functional delimitation and fully allocated to the enterprise sector. The enterprise sector comprises all enterprises, i.e. also those which according to SNA should be shown in the sector of private households or general government, respectively.

Sources and methods :

(a) Gross domestic product. The main approach used to estimate GDP is the production approach.

(b) Expenditure on the gross domestic product. The expenditure approach is used to estimate all components of GDP by expenditure type except gross fixed capital formation which is calculated mainly by the commodity-flow approach. Government final consumption expenditure is based on records from all sectors of general government. Private final consumption expenditure is estimated mainly from data on retail sales. Data for certain base-years are derived mainly from censuses (trade census 1979, crafts census 1977, industrial production census 1979). Annual data are linked with these base-year data by means of current turnover and other supply statistics. The estimates of gross fixed capital formation are based on quarterly production reports, monthly construction reports, statistics on building activity and the previously mentioned censuses. Exports and imports of goods are based on foreign trade statistics, while exports and imports of services are obtained mainly from the Central Bank. For the calculation of constant prices, price deflation is used for all expenditure groups.

(c) Cost-structure of the gross domestic product. Compensation of employees is calculated from three sources - social security statistics, census data extrapolated by current data and taxation statistics. Capital consumption is calculated at constant prices and at current replacement costs according to the perpetual inventory method. Indirect taxes and subsidies are taken directly from the general government accounts. Operating surplus is then obtained as a residual.

(d) Gross domestic product by kind of economic activity. The table of GDP by kind of economic activity is prepared at market prices, i.e. producers' values. The production approach is used to estimate value added of most industries. The income approach is used to estimate value added of domestic services, private non-profit institutions and producers of government services. The value of agricultural production is defined as the difference between primary gross production and internally used quantities, times average prices, or, as the sum of sales, change in livestock and other stocks, own account consumption, investment and exports. The basic statistics used are mainly data on utilization of agricultural production. Inputs are derived from book-keeping records, foreign trade statistics and production and sales statistics from suppliers of agricultural input goods. The main sources for estimating mining and quarrying, manufacturing, electricity, gas and water and construction are the censuses of production industries, which provide bench-mark data, and annual data taken from several sources. Data on intermediate consumption for these sectors are taken from the censuses and cost-structure statistics. For trade, the bench-mark estimates are mainly based on the trade censuses 1979. Output is extrapolated by turnover data, while input is estimated from the trade censuses, cost-structure statistics and annual trade reports. For the transport sector, cost-structure statistics are used to estimate parts of output and intermediate consumption for most sub-sectors. Turnover tax statistics are utilized for preparing the current output estimates. Banking statistics, collected by Central Bank, and insurance statistics, collected by Federal Supervisory Board, provide the basis for estimating output of financial institutions including insurance. Input is estimated on the basis of bank company reports and insurance company reports. Rents are estimated separately for three different categories - old, medium and new buildings. The rents are based on data from censuses of buildings and dwellings, which include owner-occupied dwellings. The data are extrapolated by quantity and price indexes. The data used to estimate value added of government services, are mainly based on receipts and expenditure statistics of general government. For private non-profit institutions output is estimated as the sum of costs for wages and salaries, estimated capital consumption and indirect taxes. Double deflation is used in the calculations of constant prices, for all sectors except transport and real estate and business services. Output of most sectors is deflated by producer price indexes. However, for most agricultural products, current quantities are multiplied by base year prices, for some transport and communication services output is extrapolated by quantity indexes, and for insurance and business services extrapolation is used. Deflation by purchase price indexes or specially constructed input indexes is done for almost all sectors. For trade, and partly for transportation and communication, however, constant input-ouput ratios are assumed.

1.1 Expenditure on the Gross Domestic Product, in Current Prices

Million Deutsche marks

	1970	1975	1980	1981	1982	1983	1984	1985	1986	1987	1988	1989
1 Government final consumption expenditure	106470	210010	297790	318160	326190	336210	350230	365660	382720	397510	412650	418960
2 Private final consumption expenditure	368850	585330	840780	887850	918050	964160	1003570	1038340	1068610	1110300	1154280	1211300
A Households	363130	576950	829430	876110	905620	950650	989540	1023180	1051810	1092640	1135730	1191390
B Private non-profit institutions serving households	5720	8380	11350	11740	12430	13510	14030	15160	16800	17660	18550	19910
3 Gross capital formation	186250	204010	349600	323840	315390	342020	361230	360100	378890	394360	434110	487590
A Increase in stocks	14200	-5400	13800	-11400	-11500	-1800	6600	-700	1500	4390	18130	29180
B Gross fixed capital formation	172050	209410	335800	335240	326890	343820	354630	360800	377390	389970	415980	458410
Residential buildings	45440	59110	100570	101270	99170	106790	112430	102550	103070	103690	109530	119110
Non-residential buildings	60730	72250	107890	106320	102820	101430	104620	104400	112940	115790	121570	131680
Other construction and land improvement etc.												
Other	65880	78050	127340	127650	124900	135600	137580	153850	161380	170490	184880	207620
4 Exports of goods and services	143000	254700	391850	445680	479030	483780	540180	593490	580720	577320	620420	699240
5 Less: Imports of goods and services	129270	227150	401080	434600	440740	451330	499370	527100	479520	475740	510780	581510
Equals: Gross Domestic Product	675300	1026900	1478940	1540930	1597920	1674840	1755840	1830490	1931420	2003750	2110680	2235580

1.2 Expenditure on the Gross Domestic Product, in Constant Prices

Million Deutsche marks

	1970	1975	1980	1981	1982	1983	1984	1985	1986	1987	1988	1989
					At constant prices of:1980							
1 Government final consumption expenditure	211920	262810	297790	303290	300740	301440	308820	315310	323400	328420	335920	332870
2 Private final consumption expenditure	606810	713880	840780	836380	825230	839600	852290	863980	893390	922600	947480	963850
A Households	596510	703350	829430	825320	814160	828020	840610	851510	879840	908600	933100	948930
B Private non-profit institutions serving households	10300	10530	11350	11060	11070	11580	11680	12470	13550	14000	14380	14920
3 Gross capital formation	316310	263770	349600	308990	293280	310940	320400	314180	329320	337770	364870	396660

659

Germany, Fed. Rep. of

1.2 Expenditure on the Gross Domestic Product, in Constant Prices
(Continued)

Million Deutsche marks

	1970	1975	1980	1981	1982	1983	1984	1985	1986	1987	1988	1989
At constant prices of:1980												
A Increase in stocks	24400	-7500	13800	-10700	-9600	-1500	5500	-900	3920	5370	15520	22370
B Gross fixed capital formation	291910	271270	335800	319690	302880	312440	314900	315080	325400	332400	349350	374290
Residential buildings	85410	81770	100570	95990	91420	96450	98410	88530	87590	86260	89290	93860
Non-residential buildings	104520	97620	107890	101890	97870	96090	97130	96020	101960	102740	105860	111210
Other construction and land improvement etc.												
Other	101980	91880	127340	121810	113590	119900	119360	130530	135850	143400	154200	169220
4 Exports of goods and services	230660	303930	391850	422180	436370	432710	467400	500100	497510	499720	527140	579110
5 Less: Imports of goods and services	232880	289560	401080	389450	383790	390770	412920	427090	440410	458330	484920	526830
Equals: Gross Domestic Product	1132820	1254830	1478940	1481390	1471830	1493920	1535990	1566480	1603210	1630180	1690490	1745660

1.3 Cost Components of the Gross Domestic Product

Million Deutsche marks

	1970	1975	1980	1981	1982	1983	1984	1985	1986	1987	1988	1989
1 Indirect taxes, net	77270	109890	162860	169210	172470	182730	189990	192480	194990	200860	209550	232750
A Indirect taxes	89050	130280	193390	198340	201890	214510	226200	230290	236330	245640	257220	278160
B Less: Subsidies	11780	20390	30530	29130	29420	31780	36210	37810	41340	44780	47670	45410
2 Consumption of fixed capital	68030	115940	173740	188640	201110	211430	221980	231790	240750	249450	260410	276740
3 Compensation of employees paid by resident producers to:	359290	585930	842840	881200	900370	917570	950490	987180	1037210	1079050	1121600	1172040
A Resident households	358450	583980	840190	878370	897420	915410	948380	985090	1035120	1076930	1119420	1169770
B Rest of the world	840	1950	2650	2830	2950	2160	2110	2090	2090	2120	2180	2270
4 Operating surplus	170710	215140	299500	301880	323970	363110	393380	419040	458470	474390	519120	554050
A Corporate and quasi-corporate enterprises	170710	215140	299500	301880	323970	363110	393380	419040	458470	474390	519120	554050
B Private unincorporated enterprises	...	...	...	...	...	...	...	...	...	...	...	...
C General government	...	...	...	...	...	...	...	...	...	...	...	...
Equals: Gross Domestic Product	675300	1026900	1478940	1540930	1597920	1674840	1755840	1830490	1931420	2003750	2110680	2235580

1.4 General Government Current Receipts and Disbursements

Million Deutsche marks

	1970	1975	1980	1981	1982	1983	1984	1985	1986	1987	1988	1989
Receipts												
1 Operating surplus	...	...	...	...	...	...	...	...	...	...	...	...
2 Property and entrepreneurial income	7920	8650	15680	19790	29110	29710	30860	33650	32830	26040	18750	29940
3 Taxes, fees and contributions	242160	412580	618280	642820	667020	692880	731660	767020	796870	828130	865320	929510
A Indirect taxes	89050	130280	193390	198340	201890	214510	226200	230290	236330	245640	257220	278160
B Direct taxes	72840	123820	187750	188110	193180	200360	213020	229640	237040	245940	255440	281840
C Social security contributions	78210	154280	230200	248840	263950	269180	282760	297230	313390	325840	341220	357330
D Compulsory fees, fines and penalties	2060	4200	6940	7530	8000	8830	9680	9860	10110	10710	11440	12180
4 Other current transfers	8820	17400	27640	28380	28800	32230	33190	34010	36750	36230	39410	38500
Total Current Receipts of General Government	258900	438630	661600	690990	724930	754820	795710	834680	866450	890400	923480	997950
Disbursements												
1 Government final consumption expenditure	106470	210010	297790	318160	326190	336210	350230	365660	382720	397510	412650	418960
A Compensation of employees	59200	117020	162660	173000	178070	183590	187230	194110	203540	211740	217330	223180
B Consumption of fixed capital	3270	5700	9490	10480	11270	11950	12580	13090	13600	14190	14850	15690
C Purchases of goods and services, net	44000	87280	125680	134730	136920	140740	150510	158560	165710	171730	180620	180250
D Less: Own account fixed capital formation	90	170	280	290	310	320	350	360	380	400	400	410
E Indirect taxes paid, net	90	180	240	240	240	250	260	260	250	250	250	250
2 Property income	5710	12980	27480	34500	42940	49070	51570	54180	56130	56780	58990	59490
A Interest	5710	12980	27480	34500	42940	49070	51570	54180	56130	56780	58990	59490
B Net land rent and royalties	...	...	...	...	...	...	...	...	...	...	...	...

Germany, Fed. Rep. of

1.4 General Government Current Receipts and Disbursements (Continued)

Million Deutsche marks	1970	1975	1980	1981	1982	1983	1984	1985	1986	1987	1988	1989
3 Subsidies	11780	20390	30580	29420	31780	36210	37810	41340	44780	47670	45410	
4 Other current transfers	65530	201500	278670	302170	319750	325410	333900	341050	352730	369820	390360	405920
A Social security benefits	59970	125600	174390	184440	203430	208830	210200	215260	220980	232050	245500	254370
B Social assistance grants	14010	34940	43210	48420	48700	48400	48340	49070	52980	55500	56000	58130
C Other	21460	40960	63510	69310	67620	70180	75360	76720	77770	82270	89600	93420
5 Net saving	39410	-6250	27190	7030	6630	12350	28800	35980	33530	21510	13810	68170
Total Current Disbursements and Net Saving of General Government	258900	438650	661600	690990	724820	754830	795710	834680	866450	890400	923480	997950

1.5 Current Income and Outlay of Corporate and Quasi-Corporate Enterprises, Summary

Million Deutsche marks	1970	1975	1980	1981	1982	1983	1984	1985	1986	1987	1988	1989
Receipts												
1 Operating surplus	170710	215140	299500	301880	323970	363110	393380	419040	458470	473390	519120	554050
2 Property and entrepreneurial income received	70820	131540	225540	278460	297800	285530	309090	317430	319810	319330	329170	380510
3 Current transfers [a]	25560	43550	68990	73630	74920	78400	82290	87420	91540	90800	102480	106890
Total Current Receipts [a]	267140	390230	597600	653970	696690	727040	786640	823940	869820	891810	950770	1041450
Disbursements												
1 Property and entrepreneurial income	226000	325500	483300	527930	573160	585550	630730	661470	708060	718920	756230	...
2 Direct taxes and other current payments to general government	12720	15100	27820	27150	28730	31360	36390	41140	40860	36680	39820	45820
3 Current transfers [a]	23180	38510	52520	63310	65740	66680	72200	68540	82470	87900	93130	97620
4 Net saving [a]	5240	13120	28960	33780	27940	41590	47320	43620	38430	48410	61590	...
Total Current Disbursements and Net Saving	267140	390230	597600	653970	696690	727040	786640	823940	869820	891810	950770	1041450

[a] Selected items in this table (Current income and outlay of corporate and quasi-corporate enterprises) refers to corporate enterprises only.

1.6 Current Income and Outlay of Households and Non-Profit Institutions

Million Deutsche marks	1970	1975	1980	1981	1982	1983	1984	1985	1986	1987	1988	1989
Receipts												
1 Compensation of employees	360940	587200	844410	882950	902520	916010	954000	991000	1041350	1083440	1126040	1177640
A From resident producers	358450	582980	840190	878370	897420	915410	948380	985090	1035120	1076830	1119420	1169770
B From rest of the world	2190	4220	3250	4580	5100	5500	5620	5910	6230	6510	6620	6870
2 Operating surplus of private unincorporated enterprises	...	...	...	284100	285870	305660	339400	369670	392900	439410	460000	493950
3 Property and entrepreneurial income [a]	155310	204280	303570	329480	348250	355000	362680	374860	391240	432440	453710
4 Current transfers	108470	211110										
A Social security benefits	75370	162690	220670	240000	255700	259020	262420	269180	275520	293520	307160	319050
B Social assistance grants	33100	56420	82900	89400	92550	95570	100560	105690	111720	118790	125280	134660
C Other												
Total Current Receipts	624420	1010590	1432080	1498300	1556430	1615430	1688950	1758760	1872000	1951750	2052430	...
Disbursements												
1 Private final consumption expenditure	368850	585330	840780	878850	918050	964160	1003570	1038340	1068810	1111030	1154280	1211300
2 Property income	3340	6760	13850	17470	18040	17950	18340	18220	18210	18570	21100	
3 Direct taxes and other current transfers n.e.c. to general government	140120	265530	396160	416510	435650	445320	467960	494380	517080	543270	564470	602790
A Social security contributions	78030	153780	229480	248060	263120	268560	282150	296610	312750	325220	340560	356650
B Direct taxes	60440	103690	161180	162410	169680	176080	188280	196280	209420	214700	236500	
C Fees, fines and penalties	1650	3360	5500	6040	6410	7080	7750	7950	8050	8830	9210	9640
4 Other current transfers	34760	59910	88540	94540	95060	100040	107000	111540	114430	122610	128070	138830
5 Net saving	77350	92060	132080	118830	119830	88230	87990	90470	91600	151660	157360	187040
Total Current Disbursements and Net Saving	624420	1010590	1432080	1498300	1556430	1615430	1688950	1758760	1872000	1951750	2052430	...

[a] Item 'Property and entrepreneurial income' includes undistributed profits of unincorporated enterprises.

Germany, Fed. Rep. of

1.7 External Transactions on Current Account, Summary

Million Deutsche marks	1970	1975	1980	1981	1982	1983	1984	1985	1986	1987	1988	1989
Payments to the Rest of the World												
1 Imports of goods and services a	129270	227150	401080	434600	440740	451330	499370	527100	479520	475740	510780	581510
c.i.f. b	101120	172280	325090	349730	354280	363630	406690	435040	394410	382760	411880	474660
B Other	28150	47870	75990	84870	86460	87700	92680	92080	90110	92860	99800	106850
2 Factor income to the rest of the world	9530	14030	24190	32260	33930	35490	36540	40180	43730	50160	54920	62150
A Compensation of employees	840	1950	2650	2830	2950	2160	2110	2090	2090	2120	2180	2270
B Property and entrepreneurial income	8690	12080	21540	29430	31100	33330	34430	38090	41640	48040	52740	59880
By general government	60	390	1520	3180	5930	6450	6900	8190	9710	11590	11670	11340
By corporate and quasi-corporate enterprises	8630	11690	20020	26250	30450	26880	27530	29900	31930	36450	41070	48540
By other	...	...	...	...	...	...	...	...	...	...	...	...
3 Current transfers to the rest of the world c	12770	23920	34000	36890	38170	39590	45170	45600	45510	46250	52590	59180
A Indirect taxes to supranational organizations	12770	23920	34000	36890	38170	39590	45170	45600	45510	46250	52590	59180
B Other current transfers	...	...	...	...	...	...	...	...	...	...	...	...
4 Surplus of the nation on current transactions	3780	10860	-26960	-12460	8520	11340	22340	47450	85480	82370	88740	104920
Payments to the Rest of the World and Surplus of the Nation on Current Transactions	155350	275960	432310	491290	526760	537750	603420	660330	654240	645520	707030	807760
Receipts From The Rest of the World												
1 Exports of goods and services a	143000	254700	391850	445680	479030	483780	540180	593490	580720	577320	620420	669240
A Exports of merchandise f.o.b.	122800	219490	333920	384700	413320	416890	467320	517580	508110	506380	547390	615270
B Other	20200	35210	55230	60980	65710	66890	72860	75910	79150	70940	73030	83970
2 Factor income from rest of the world	9930	16590	30450	36430	38510	41050	50690	59060	67510	75710	67440	78780
A Compensation of employees	2190	3220	4220	4580	5100	5500	5620	5910	6230	6510	6620	6870
B Property and entrepreneurial income	7740	13310	26230	31850	33410	35550	44980	48080	51280	55600	60820	81000
By general government	140	130	80	120	130	110	120	120	120	90	120	140
By corporate and quasi-corporate enterprises	7040	12550	25180	30360	30260	31270	32070	40280	41270	43630	47740	65260
By other	560	630	970	1370	2010	3370	4580	4680	6690	7530	10640	15600
3 Current transfers from rest of the world c	2420	4730	10010	9180	8220	12920	12640	12850	16010	15190	19170	20650
A Subsidies from supranational organisations	2420	4730	10010	9180	8220	12920	12640	12850	16010	15190	19170	20650
B Other current transfers	...	...	...	...	...	...	...	...	...	...	...	...
Receipts from the Rest of the World on Current Transactions	155350	275960	432310	491290	526760	537750	603420	660330	654240	645520	707030	807760

a) Exports and imports of goods for purposes of repair and improvement are reduced to the value. c) Indirect taxes paid to and subsidies received from supranational organizations are included in 'Current transfers'.
b) Imports of merchandise, f.o.b. rather than c.i.f. of these services.

1.8 Capital Transactions of The Nation, Summary

Million Deutsche marks	1970	1975	1980	1981	1982	1983	1984	1985	1986	1987	1988	1989
Finance of Gross Capital Formation												
Gross saving	190030	214870	322640	311380	323910	335360	383570	407550	464370	477630	522850	592510
1 Consumption of fixed capital	66030	115940	173740	188640	201110	211430	221980	231790	240750	249450	260410	276740
A General government	3270	5700	9490	10480	11270	11950	12580	13090	13600	14190	14850	15690
B Corporate and quasi-corporate enterprises	62820	108600	161610	175340	188830	196380	206160	215350	223880	231660	243180	257110
C Other	940	1640	2580	2820	3010	3100	3240	3350	3470	3600	3730	3940
2 Net saving	122000	98930	148900	122740	122880	123930	141590	175760	223620	227280	262440	315770
A General government	39410	-6250	27190	7030	6630	12350	23800	35980	33530	21510	13810	6817 0
B Corporate and quasi-corporate enterprises	23470	1260	-1530	-22130	-18210	12160	8760	6510	41040	46330	79160	75070
C Other	59120	103920	123240	137840	134380	117420	129030	133270	149050	159440	169470	172530
Less: Surplus of the nation on current transactions	3780	10860	-26960	-12460	8520	11340	22340	47450	85480	82370	88740	104920
Finance of Gross Capital Formation	186250	204010	349600	323840	315390	342020	361230	360100	378890	394360	434110	487590

Germany, Fed. Rep. of

1.8 Capital Transactions of The Nation, Summary (Continued)

Gross Capital Formation

Million Deutsche marks	1970	1975	1980	1981	1982	1983	1984	1985	1986	1987	1988	1989
Increase in stocks	14200	-5400	13800	-11400	-11500	-1800	6600	-700	1500	4390	18130	29180
Gross fixed capital formation	172050	209410	335800	326890	343820	354630	360800	377390	389970	415980	458410	
1 General government	31060	39730	50090	48820	45260	41770	41740	42610	48700	48000	48860	52540
2 Corporate and quasi-corporate enterprises a	140960	169680	285710	281630	301890	312890	318190	342020	360100	377890	405870	
3 Other	...	...	...	...	...	...	...	...	...	...	...	...
Gross Capital Formation	186250	204010	349600	323840	315390	342020	361230	376890	394360	434110	487590	

a) Including gross fixed capital formation of private non-profit organizations.

1.9 Gross Domestic Product by Institutional Sectors of Origin

Domestic Factor Incomes Originating

Million Deutsche marks	1970	1975	1980	1981	1982	1983	1984	1985	1986	1987	1988	1989
1 General government	59200	117020	162660	173000	180170	183590	194110	203540	211740	217330	223180	
2 Corporate and quasi-corporate enterprises a	461760	629620	955080	983860	1018420	1075780	1115680	1177590	1257870	1301370	1383060	1460780
A Non-financial	460640	663430	950500	989840	1015800	1069940	1105800	1172220	1255600	1298180	1379190	
B Financial a	1120	3190	4580	3140	2620	1110	2460	3500	2780	3990	3900	...
3 Households and private unincorporated enterprises	1070	1290	1430	1430	1450	1480	1520	1540	1550	1540	1510	1500
4 Non-profit institutions serving households	7970	16140	23170	24670	26400	28030	29440	31500	34720	36690	38790	40630
Subtotal: Domestic Factor Incomes	530000	801070	1142300	1183080	1224340	1280680	1343870	1406220	1495680	1553440	1640720	1726090
Indirect taxes, net	77270	102210	162860	169210	172470	182730	192480	194990	208090	209550	232750	
A Indirect taxes	89050	102280	193330	198940	201890	214510	226200	230290	236330	245640	257220	278160
B Less: Subsidies	11780	20590	30530	29130	29420	31780	33720	35210	36210	43130	44780	45470
Consumption of fixed capital	68090	115940	173740	188660	211110	215640	221860	231790	240750	249450	260410	276750
Gross Domestic Product	675300	1029900	1478940	1540930	1597920	1678840	1755840	1830490	1931420	2003750	2110890	2235580

a) Financial of Corporate and quasi-corporate enterprises refers to net of imputed bank service charges.

1.10 Gross Domestic Product by Kind of Activity, in Current Prices

Million Deutsche marks	1970	1975	1980	1981	1982	1983	1984	1985	1986	1987	1988	1989
1 Agriculture, hunting, forestry and fishing	21780	28470	30370	31680	36340	32220	34650	33240	33660	30460	33110	36110
2 Mining and quarrying a	8220	11260	13870	14000	16490	17420	17560	17800	15110	13690	11910	...
3 Manufacturing abc	259450	354060	482840	487930	502850	524930	547240	583540	621020	627770	655560	695030
4 Electricity, gas and water	14500	26410	36330	38250	42280	45270	47790	50150	52500	55480	57670	...
5 Construction b	51550	63190	99160	98810	95360	97440	97960	94030	99350	100920	106460	116000
6 Wholesale and retail trade, restaurants and hotels	78310	110330	158880	167270	170970	179830	189690	192870	201560	211180	219700	199710
7 Transport, storage and communication	38070	59940	85670	86970	89630	93780	96770	102020	109160	111350	115460	129620
8 Finance, insurance, real estate and business services d	55590	106770	152900	163360	187930	205270	216880	225850	230890	250200	245020	260020
9 Community, social and personal services cd	50390	97800	163270	178140	187140	188740	203430	219380	235160	257460	284460	317330	370210
Total: Industries	573360	858190	1223330	1276670	1334740	1402580	1473170	1537800	1622900	1673440	1769680	1879280
Producers of Government Services	62560	122900	172390	183720	189580	195790	200070	207460	217390	226180	232430	239120
Other Producers	9990	19080	27200	28940	30880	32630	34220	36410	37770	42160	44060	46100
Subtotal	645910	996770	1422910	1489330	1555200	1631000	1707460	1781670	1878090	1947780	2045850	2164140
Less: Imputed bank service charge	17940	38850	53940	62360	73470	81720	84070	84240	83690	82270	85080	89190
Plus: Import duties	7420	10270	13480	14080	14810	15210	16480	16420	17010	16890	19710	23110
Plus: Value added tax	39910	57310	96490	100780	101380	103850	109350	115970	116660	118040	125250	130200	137520
Equals: Gross Domestic Product	675300	1029900	1478940	1540930	1597920	1678840	1755840	1830490	1931420	2003750	2110890	2235580

a) Quarrying is included in item 'Manufacturing'.
b) Structural steel erection is included in item 'Manufacturing'.
c) Publishing is included in item 'Community, social and personal services'.
d) Business services and real estate except dwellings are included in item 'Community, social and personal services'.

Germany, Fed. Rep. of

1.11 Gross Domestic Product by Kind of Activity, in Constant Prices

Million Deutsche marks

	1970	1975	1980	1981	1982	1983	1984	1985	1986	1987	1988	1989
					At constant prices of:1980							
1 Agriculture, hunting, forestry and fishing	28630	29170	30370	30550	36010	32840	35690	33800	36680	33890	36240	35930
2 Mining and quarrying a	19940	14550	13870	13720	13660	12690	12300	11840	9940	9100	7030	...
3 Manufacturing abc	392580	412350	482840	475520	464150	469360	482170	498450	498530	484160	498370	521560
4 Electricity, gas and water	20410	28220	36330	35520	34070	35850	35690	35650	38590	44440	47360	...
5 Construction b	89500	87950	99190	94400	90080	91530	91420	88220	89720	87180	90190	94420
6 Wholesale and retail trade, restaurants and hotels	125730	137660	158880	160680	156680	159880	166370	167790	173050	178280	183770	167090
7 Transport, storage and communication	58980	64500	85670	88120	88560	89700	93490	96890	98940	103160	107860	113510
8 Finance, insurance, real estate and business services d	96540	121290	152900	157500	162360	165870	169630	175350	182670	190350	196660	203380
9 Community, social and personal services cd	102400	126360	163270	168490	171240	178330	188560	198650	212630	229760	249220	278630
Total, Industries	934710	1022050	1223320	1224500	1216810	1236050	1275320	1306640	1340750	1360320	1416700	1470120
Producers of Government Services	124990	154390	172390	176370	177570	178640	180590	183250	185770	188100	190310	190940
Other Producers	20850	24140	27200	27640	28610	29370	30400	31650	33130	34060	35040	36040
Subtotal	1080550	1200580	1422910	1428510	1422990	1444060	1486310	1521540	1559650	1582480	1642050	1697100
Less: Imputed bank service charge	30120	38780	53940	55570	57150	59150	60560	63380	67260	70730	73830	76510
Plus: Import duties	8330	10380	13480	13440	13380	14590	15010	15680	16950	19380	20150	21090
Plus: Value added tax	74060	82650	96490	95010	92610	94420	95230	92640	93870	99050	102120	103980
Equals: Gross Domestic Product	1132820	1254830	1478940	1481390	1471830	1493920	1535990	1566480	1603210	1630180	1690490	1745660

a) Quarrying is included in item 'Manufacturing'.
b) Structural steel erection is included in item 'Manufacturing'.
c) Publishing is included in item 'Community, social and personal services'.

d) Business services and real estate except dwellings are included in item 'Community, social and personal services'.

1.12 Relations Among National Accounting Aggregates

Million Deutsche marks

	1970	1975	1980	1981	1982	1983	1984	1985	1986	1987	1988	1989
Gross Domestic Product	675300	1026900	1478940	1540930	1597920	1674840	1755840	1830490	1931420	2003750	2110680	2235580
Plus: Net factor income from the rest of the world	400	2500	6260	4170	-820	5560	14060	13810	13780	11850	12520	25720
Factor income from the rest of the world	9930	16530	30450	36430	38510	41050	50600	53990	57510	62010	67440	87870
Less: Factor income to the rest of the world	9530	14030	24190	32260	39330	35490	36540	40180	43730	50160	54920	62150
Equals: Gross National Product	675700	1029400	1485200	1545100	1597100	1680400	1769900	1844300	1945200	2015600	2123200	2261300
Less: Consumption of fixed capital	68030	115940	173740	188640	201110	211430	221980	231790	240750	249450	260410	276740
Equals: National Income	607670	913460	1311460	1356460	1395990	1468970	1547920	1612510	1704450	1766150	1862790	1984560
Plus: Net current transfers from the rest of the world a	-10350	-19190	-23990	-27710	-28950	-26670	-32530	-32750	-29500	-31060	-33420	-38530
Current transfers from the rest of the world	2420	4730	10010	9180	9220	12920	12640	12850	16010	15190	19170	20650
Less: Current transfers to the rest of the world	12770	23920	34000	36890	38170	39590	45170	45600	45510	46250	52590	59180
Equals: National Disposable Income	597320	894270	1287470	1328750	1367040	1442300	1515390	1579760	1674950	1735090	1829370	1946030
Less: Final consumption	475320	795340	1138570	1206010	1244240	1300370	1353800	1404000	1451330	1507810	1566930	1630260
Equals: Net Saving	122000	98930	148900	122740	122800	141930	161590	175760	223620	227280	262440	315770
Less: Surplus of the nation on current transactions	3780	10860	-26960	-12460	8520	11340	22340	47450	85480	82370	88740	104920
Equals: Net Capital Formation	118220	88070	175860	135200	114280	130590	139250	128310	138140	144910	173700	210850

a) Indirect taxes paid to and subsidies received from supranational organizations are included in 'Current transfers'.

2.1 Government Final Consumption Expenditure by Function, in Current Prices

Million Deutsche marks

	1970	1975	1980	1981	1982	1983	1984	1985	1986	1987	1988	1989
1 General public services	12630	22960	31400	32950	33720	34740	35760	37460	39510	42510	42700	...
2 Defence	19760	31900	40380	43670	45200	47800	48930	49900	51290	52300	52480	...
3 Public order and safety	8600	15930	23080	24840	25790	26660	27240	28280	29500	30790	31600	...
4 Education	19390	40680	60350	64370	66260	67980	69890	72380	74840	76160	77950	...
5 Health	25280	60100	86810	93870	94550	97260	104130	109940	115210	119940	129640	...
6 Social security and welfare	9270	19380	28240	29990	32380	33890	35560	37100	39710	41590	43500	...
7 Housing and community amenities	2380	4250	5750	5960	5540	5060	5070	5620	6160	6630	6820	...
8 Recreational, cultural and religious affairs	1940	4080	6920	7380	7450	7620	8040	8520	9130	9690	10230	...
9 Economic services	7220	10730	14860	15130	15300	15200	15610	16460	17370	17900	17730	...

664

Germany, Fed. Rep. of

2.1 Government Final Consumption Expenditure by Function, in Current Prices
(Continued)

Million Deutsche marks

	1970	1975	1980	1981	1982	1983	1984	1985	1986	1987	1988	1989
A Fuel and energy	60	210	80	80	60	80	80	120	120	100	110	...
B Agriculture, forestry, fishing and hunting	980	1490	1950	2000	2040	2050	2050	2100	2240	2270	2250	...
C Mining, manufacturing and construction, except fuel and energy	50	40	160	160	160	170	190	180	210	220	250	...
D Transportation and communication	5070	7380	10030	10170	10040	10040	9840	10600	10950	11220	11070	...
E Other economic affairs	1060	1610	2640	2720	2750	3000	3060	3250	3460	3850	4090	4050
10 Other functions	...	...	...	...	...	...	...	...	...	...	...	...
Total Government Final Consumption Expenditure	106470	210010	277790	318160	326190	336210	350230	365660	382720	397510	412650	...

2.3 Total Government Outlays by Function and Type

Million Deutsche marks

	Final Consumption Expenditures - Compensation of Employees	Final Consumption Expenditures - Other	Total	Subsidies	Other Current Transfers & Property Income	Total Current Disbursements	Gross Capital Formation	Other Capital Outlays	Total Outlays
1980									
1 General public services	31400	22020	9380	950	16640	48890	2220	6550	57760
2 Defence	40380	19840	20540	-	960	41340	210	210	41760
3 Public order and safety	23080	19300	3780	-	30	23110	2180	80	25370
4 Education	60350	47300	13050	40	6150	66540	8550	910	76000
5 Health	88810	18240	68570	160	530	87500	3990	1460	92950
6 Social security and welfare	28240	14240	14000	420	249140	277800	1220	8070	287090
7 Housing and community amenities	5750	8790	-3040	2090	20	7860	10480	3190	21530
8 Recreation, culture and religion	6920	4510	2410	400	1180	8500	3450	960	12910
9 Economic services	14860	8420	6440	26470	3960	45290	18530	14620	78440
A Fuel and energy	80	80	-	4290	-	4370	500	1420	6290
B Agriculture, forestry, fishing and hunting	1950	1230	720	9130	50	11130	390	1030	12550
C Mining (except fuels), manufacturing and construction	160	-	160	340	-	500	-	510	1010
D Transportation and communication	10030	5630	4400	7340	-	17370	16370	6740	40480
E Other economic affairs	2640	1560	1080	5370	3910	11920	1270	4920	18110
10 Other functions	-	-	-	-	27480	27480	-	-	27480
Total	297790	162660	135130	30530	308060	634410	50830	36090	721290
1981									
1 General public services	32350	23290	9660	1030	18300	52280	2290	5290	59860
2 Defence	43670	21100	22570	-	990	44660	200	170	45030
3 Public order and safety	24870	20680	4180	-	40	24880	2130	100	27110
4 Education	63710	50330	10400	40	6510	70250	8080	770	79750
5 Health	93870	19320	74550	210	520	94600	4130	1470	100200
6 Social security and welfare	29990	15180	14810	520	270010	300520	1540	7960	310020
7 Housing and community amenities	5960	9390	-3430	2250	30	8240	9710	3000	20950
8 Recreation, culture and religion	7380	4840	2540	450	1240	9070	3460	910	13440
9 Economic services	15130	8890	6240	24630	4530	44290	16150	13900	74340
A Fuel and energy	80	-	80	3390	-	3470	200	1590	5260
B Agriculture, forestry, fishing and hunting	2000	1300	700	7370	40	9410	310	760	10480
C Mining (except fuels), manufacturing and construction	160	-	160	370	-	530	-	630	1160
D Transportation and communication	10170	5920	4250	7870	10	18050	14570	5930	38550
E Other economic affairs	2720	1670	1050	5630	4480	12830	1070	4990	18890
10 Other functions	-	-	-	-	34500	34500	-	-	34500
Total	318160	173000	145160	29130	336670	683960	47670	33570	765200
1982									
1 General public services	33720	23880	9840	1250	19310	54280	2420	5630	62330
2 Defence	45200	21180	24020	-	1040	46240	210	190	46640
3 Public order and safety	25790	21310	4480	-	40	25830	1820	60	27710
4 Education	66260	51860	14400	70	6550	72880	6920	820	80620
5 Health	94550	20130	74420	230	570	95350	4610	1450	101410

665

Germany, Fed. Rep. of

2.3 Total Government Outlays by Function and Type (Continued)

Million Deutsche marks

	Total	Final Consumption of Employees Compensation	Other	Subsidies	Current Expenditures Other	Total Current Disbursements	Gross Capital Formation	Other Capital Outlays	Total Outlays
1983									
6 Social security and welfare	32380	16050	16330	620	266250	319250	1530	6970	327750
7 Housing and community amenities	5540	940	-4100	2340	50	7930	8450	2770	19150
8 Recreation, culture and religion	7450	4970	2480	520	1230	9200	2930	930	13060
9 Economic services	15300	9050	6250	24390	4710	44400	14330	14550	73280
A Fuel and energy	60	-	60	2990	-	3050	-	1650	4700
B Agriculture, forestry, fishing and hunting	2040	1320	720	7730	40	9810	230	740	10780
C Mining (except fuels), manufacturing and construction	160	-	160	540	-	700	-	870	1570
D Transportation and communication	10040	6000	4040	7940	4670	17980	12960	6650	37590
E Other economic affairs	3000	1730	1270	5190	-	12860	1140	4640	19460
10 Other functions	-	-	-	-	42940	42940	-	-	42940
Total	326190	178070	148120	29420	362690	718300	43220	33370	794890
1984									
1 General public services	35760	24990	10770	1330	23040	60130	2280	5490	67900
2 Defence	48830	22460	26370	-	1190	50120	220	240	50580
3 Public order and safety	27240	22420	4820	80	30	27270	1840	50	29160
4 Education	68960	54170	15720	80	74760	47790	5370	580	80710
5 Health	104130	21240	82890	150	600	104880	4470	1360	110710
6 Social security and welfare	35560	17140	18420	690	298120	334370	1420	5620	341410
7 Housing and community amenities	5070	10130	-5060	2740	70	7880	8120	2660	18660
8 Recreation, culture and religion	8040	5280	2760	580	1300	9920	2430	900	13250
9 Economic services	15610	9400	6210	30640	4760	51010	13980	18880	88370
A Fuel and energy	80	-	80	3920	-	4000	-	1030	5030
B Agriculture, forestry, fishing and hunting	2050	1320	730	11950	40	14040	190	810	15040
C Mining (except fuels), manufacturing and construction	190	-	190	1420	-	1610	-	500	2110
D Transportation and communication	10040	6180	3860	7690	-	17730	12790	6170	36690
E Other economic affairs	3250	1900	1350	5660	4720	13630	1000	10370	25000
10 Other functions	-	-	-	-	51570	51570	-	-	51570
Total	350230	187230	163000	36210	385470	771910	40130	35780	847820
1985									
1 General public services	37460	26000	11460	1490	23810	62760	2220	6230	71210
2 Defence	49900	26500	23400	-	1310	51210	220	270	51700
3 Public order and safety	28280	23230	5050	-	40	28320	1930	90	30340
4 Education	72380	56000	16380	90	4840	77310	5190	610	83110
5 Health	109940	22000	87940	140	590	110670	4580	1300	116550

999

Germany, Fed. Rep. of

2.3 Total Government Outlays by Function and Type (Continued)

Million Deutsche marks

	Total	Final Consumption Expenditures - Compensation of Employees	Final Consumption Expenditures - Other	Subsidies	Other Current Transfers & Disbursements	Total Current Disbursements	Gross Capital Formation	Other Capital Outlays	Total Outlays
1986									
1 General public services	39510	27380	12130	1670	24790	65970	2540	6130	74640
2 Defence	51290	24230	27060	-	1270	52560	250	230	53040
3 Public order and safety	29500	24340	5160	-	40	29540	2210	60	31810
4 Education	74840	58190	16650	100	5150	80090	5730	510	86330
5 Health	115210	23260	91950	140	270	115620	4460	1960	122040
6 Social security and welfare	397100	18940	20770	1070	313820	354600	1380	4880	360860
7 Housing and community amenities	6160	11120	-4960	90	9830	10360	3000	23190
8 Recreation, culture and religion	9130	5950	3180	690	1430	11250	2840	1180	15270
9 Economic services	17370	10130	7240	34090	5870	57330	15120	15480	87930
A. Fuel and energy	120	-	120	5100	-	5220	-	610	5830
B. Agriculture, forestry, fishing and hunting	2240	1430	810	14990	40	17270	230	930	18430
C. Mining (except fuels), manufacturing and construction	210	-	210	170	-	380	-	700	1080
D. Transportation and communication	10950	6560	4390	7180	-	18130	13770	6900	38800
E. Other economic affairs	3850	2140	1710	6650	5830	16330	1120	6340	23790
10 Other functions	56130	-	-	-	56130	56130	-	-	56130
Total	382720	203540	179180	41340	408860	832920	44890	33430	911240
1987									
1 General public services	42510	29160	13350	1850	25620	69980	2690	5590	78260
2 Defence	52300	24930	27370	-	1310	53680	250	200	54090
3 Public order and safety	30790	25380	5410	-	40	30830	2530	60	33420
4 Education	78160	59860	18360	90	5440	83690	5860	570	88110
5 Health	119940	24310	95630	160	290	120390	4430	2030	126850
6 Social security and welfare	415900	19800	21790	870	328600	371060	1250	4700	377010
7 Housing and community amenities	6830	11590	-4960	3210	90	9930	10990	2910	23830
8 Recreation, culture and religion	9690	6250	3440	770	1520	11980	3040	1210	16230
9 Economic services	17900	10520	7380	37830	690	62620	14980	16770	94330
A. Fuel and energy	100	-	100	8290	-	8390	-	1210	9600
B. Agriculture, forestry, fishing and hunting	2270	1480	790	15500	40	17810	220	990	19020
C. Mining (except fuels), manufacturing and construction	220	-	220	160	-	380	-	490	870
D. Transportation and communication	11220	6730	4490	7110	10	18340	13610	6990	38940
E. Other economic affairs	4090	2310	1780	6770	6980	17720	1150	7090	25960
10 Other functions	56780	-	-	-	56780	56780	-	-	56780
Total	397510	211740	185770	44780	426600	868890	46010	34040	948940
1988									
1 General public services	42700	30000	12700	1900	30830	75430	2740	5470	83640
2 Defence	52480	25410	27070	-	1300	53780	250	180	54210
3 Public order and safety	31600	26250	5350	-	40	31640	2500	110	34250
4 Education	77950	61250	16700	80	5650	83680	6180	400	90260
5 Health	129640	25110	104530	150	350	130140	4600	2120	136860

667

Germany, Fed. Rep. of

2.3 Total Government Outlays by Function and Type
(Continued)

Million Deutsche marks

	Final Consumption Expenditures			Subsidies	Other Current Transfers & Property Income	Total Current Disbursements	Gross Capital Formation	Other Capital Outlays	Total Outlays
	Total	Compensation of Employees	Other						
6 Social security and welfare	43500	20410	23090	1000	342200	386700	1380	4160	392240
7 Housing and community amenities	6820	11920	-5100	2650	90	9560	11440	2970	23970
8 Recreation, culture and religion	10230	6440	3790	800	1550	12580	3110	1180	16870
9 Economic services	17730	10540	7190	41090	8350	67170	14990	16830	98990
A Fuel and energy	110	-	110	8060	-	8170	-	760	8930
B Agriculture, forestry, fishing and hunting	2250	1470	780	17540	40	19830	220	1030	21080
C Mining (except fuels), manufacturing and construction	250	-	250	480	-	730	-	490	1220
D Transportation and communication	11070	6850	4220	7490	10	18570	13660	6700	38930
E Other economic affairs	4050	2220	1830	7520	8300	19870	1110	7850	28830
10 Other functions	-	-	-	-	58990	58990	-	-	58990
Total	412650	217330	195320	47670	449350	909670	47190	33420	990280

2.5 Private Final Consumption Expenditure by Type and Purpose, in Current Prices

Million Deutsche marks

	1970	1975	1980	1981	1982	1983	1984	1985	1986	1987	1988	1989
Final Consumption Expenditure of Resident Households												
1 Food, beverages and tobacco [a]	108300	151230	199980	212000	221910	227520	232150	234880	238470	243100	252020	264960
A Food												
B Non-alcoholic beverages	98470	138270	182810	194360	202780	206090	210930	213050	216260	220840	229210	241040
C Alcoholic beverages												
D Tobacco	9830	12960	17170	17640	19130	21430	21220	21830	22210	22260	22810	23920
2 Clothing and footwear	37170	56390	79150	81880	81700	84210	86570	89460	92860	96800	98500	100990
3 Gross rent, fuel and power [bc]	58860	100170	155900	170450	182820	195050	209830	223680	222140	224360	229060	241930
A Fuel and power [c]	13950	24970	44220	49860	52910	54490	59740	64340	55900	51020	47270	49690
B Other	44910	75200	111680	120590	129910	140560	150090	159340	166240	173340	181790	192240
4 Furniture, furnishings and household equipment and operation [b]	36580	57480	82090	84970	85150	88540	91200	92170	95640	101040	107280	113180
5 Medical care and health expenses	9610	15930	24130	26140	27410	29550	31370	32880	34160	35810	38980	39720
6 Transport and communication [c]	50700	81910	121750	128310	131900	144240	149520	156320	162780	173580	179200	193420
A Personal transport equipment	14020	20160	31320	31710	32980	39720	41100	43380	56970	62550	63410	66110
B Other [c]	36680	61750	90430	96600	98920	104520	108420	112940	105810	111030	115790	127310
7 Recreational, entertainment, education and cultural services	36910	63440	84090	87630	89000	92950	95810	98980	103930	108730	114150	118260
8 Miscellaneous goods and services [a]	22890	40000	62640	66210	68890	73080	79030	83610	87460	91880	97570	103960
A Personal care	6970	9420	13520	14380	14810	15420	16090	16430	16850	17880	18820	19130
B Expenditures in restaurants, cafes and hotels	...	...	...	...	...	...	...	...	...	...	...	...
C Other	...	...	...	...	...	...	...	...	...	...	...	...
Total Final Consumption Expenditure in the Domestic Market by Households, of which	361020	566550	809730	857590	888780	935140	975480	1011980	1037440	1075300	1116760	1176420
Plus: Direct purchases abroad by resident households	10850	22840	38070	40530	40680	40900	43130	41200	42380	45240	47970	49680
Less: Direct purchases in the domestic market by non-resident households	8740	12440	18370	22010	23840	25390	29070	30000	28010	27900	29000	34710
Equals: Final Consumption Expenditure of Resident Households	363130	576950	829430	876110	905620	950650	989540	1023180	1051810	1092640	1135730	1191390
Final Consumption Expenditure of Private Non-profit Institutions Serving Households												
Equals: Final Consumption Expenditure of Private Non-profit Organisations Serving Households	5720	8380	11350	11740	12430	13510	14030	15160	16800	17660	18550	19910
Private Final Consumption Expenditure	368850	585330	840780	887850	918050	964160	1003570	1038340	1068610	1110300	1154280	1211300

a) Expenditure in restaurants and cafes is included in item 'Food, beverages and tobacco', expenditure in hotels, etc., is included in item 'Miscellaneous goods and services'.
b) Indoor repairs and upkeep paid for by tenants are included in household equipment and operation.
c) Fuel for personal transport equipment is included in item 'Transport and communication'.

Germany, Fed. Rep. of

2.6 Private Final Consumption Expenditure by Type and Purpose, in Constant Prices

Million Deutsche marks

At constant prices of:1980

Final Consumption Expenditure of Resident Households

	1970	1975	1980	1981	1982	1983	1984	1985	1986	1987	1988	1989
1 Food, beverages and tobacco [a]	163590	177590	199980	202660	200060	199450	200560	201310	203140	208230	215660	221840
A Food												
B Non-alcoholic beverages	148720	161440	182810	185040	183730	182900	183920	184460	186520	191540	198770	205000
C Alcoholic beverages												
D Tobacco	14870	16150	17170	17620	16330	16550	16640	16850	16620	16690	16890	16840
2 Clothing and footwear	62280	69930	79150	77870	74570	74740	75020	75730	77230	79440	79860	80800
3 Gross rent, fuel and power [bc]	107230	128490	155900	158980	161370	166360	172440	178090	182240	184230	184630	186160
A Fuel and power [c]	35060	37570	44220	43320	42440	44100	46700	48760	49960	48900	46170	44130
B Other	72170	90920	111680	115660	118930	122260	125740	129330	132280	135330	138460	142030
4 Furniture, furnishings and household equipment and operation [b]	56960	68700	82090	80290	77120	77990	78810	78370	80350	83900	88030	91420
5 Medical care and health expenses	16900	19770	24130	24900	24400	24720	25840	26630	27110	28040	30070	28940
6 Transport and communication [c]	92710	101690	121750	117550	117270	124340	125970	128590	139330	146770	150200	154420
A Personal transport equipment	23160	24490	31320	30220	29510	33460	32910	33470	42650	45420	44680	45550
B Other [c]	69550	77200	90430	87330	87760	90880	93060	95120	96680	101350	105520	108870
7 Recreational, entertainment, education and cultural services	53600	74330	84090	84750	83310	84540	85370	86940	90530	93810	98040	100320
8 Miscellaneous goods and services [a]	39340	49370	62640	62470	62410	63700	67090	68860	70570	72630	74800	77570
A Personal care	11380	11430	13520	13610	13360	13490	13720	13740	13870	14560	15090	15050
B Expenditures in restaurants, cafes and hotels	...	...	...	...	...	...	...	...	...	...	...	...
C Other	...	...	...	...	...	...	...	...	...	...	...	...
Total Final Consumption Expenditure in the Domestic Market by Households, of which	592610	689870	809730	809470	800510	815840	831100	844520	870500	897050	921290	941470
Plus: Direct purchases abroad by resident households	17630	28620	38070	36720	34690	33750	33730	31450	31920	34050	34980	34470
Less: Direct purchases in the domestic market by non-resident households	13730	15140	18370	20870	21040	21570	24220	24460	22580	22500	23170	27010
Equals: Final Consumption Expenditure of Resident Households	596510	703350	829430	825320	814160	828020	840610	851510	879840	908600	933100	948930

Final Consumption Expenditure of Private Non-profit Institutions Serving Households

	1970	1975	1980	1981	1982	1983	1984	1985	1986	1987	1988	1989
Equals: Final Consumption Expenditure of Private Non-profit Organisations Serving Households	10300	10530	11350	11060	11070	11580	11680	12470	13550	14000	14380	14920
Private Final Consumption Expenditure	606810	713880	840780	836380	825230	839600	852290	863980	893390	922600	947480	963850

a) Expenditure in restaurants and cafes is included in item 'Food, beverages and tobacco', expenditure in hotels, etc., is included in item 'Miscellaneous goods and services'.
b) Indoor repairs and upkeep paid for by tenants are included in household equipment and operation.
c) Fuel for personal transport equipment is included in item 'Transport and communication'.

2.7 Gross Capital Formation by Type of Good and Owner, in Current Prices

Million Deutsche marks

	1980				1981				1982			
	TOTAL	Total Private	Public Enterprises	General Government	TOTAL	Total Private	Public Enterprises	General Government	TOTAL	Total Private	Public Enterprises	General Government
Increase in stocks, total [a]	13800	...	...	...	-11400	...	...	...	-11500	...	...	...
1 Goods producing industries	13510	...	...	...	-1930	...	...	...	-8100	...	...	...
A Materials and supplies	...	...	...	...	...	...	...	...	...	...	...	...
B Work in progress	...	...	...	...	...	...	...	...	...	...	...	...
C Livestock, except breeding stocks, dairy cattle, etc.	...	...	...	...	-100	...	...	...	400	...	...	...
D Finished goods	...	...	...	...	...	...	...	...	...	...	...	...
2 Wholesale and retail trade	-400	...	...	...	-9700	...	...	...	-3400	...	...	...
3 Other, except government stocks	190	...	...	...	30	...	...	...	...	...	...	...
4 Government stocks	500	...	...	...	200	...	...	...	...	...	...	...
Gross Fixed Capital Formation, Total	335800	...	...	...	335240	...	...	...	326890	...	...	...

Germany, Fed. Rep. of

2.7 Gross Capital Formation by Type of Good and Owner, in Current Prices
(Continued)

Million Deutsche marks

	1980				1981				1982			
	TOTAL	Total Private	Public Enterprises	General Government	TOTAL	Total Private	Public Enterprises	General Government	TOTAL	Total Private	Public Enterprises	General Government
1 Residential buildings	100570	...	...	...	101270	...	...	...	99170	...	...	...
2 Non-residential buildings		...	...	...		...	...	...		...	...	...
3 Other construction	107890	...	...	...	106320	...	...	...	102820	...	...	...
4 Land improvement and plantation and orchard development		...	...	...		...	...	...		...	...	...
5 Producers' durable goods	130950	...	...	...	132710	...	...	...	129580	...	...	...
A Transport equipment [b]	24860	...	...	...	26260	...	...	...	24980	...	...	...
B Machinery and equipment [b]	106090	...	...	...	106450	...	...	...	104600	...	...	...
6 Breeding stock, dairy cattle, etc. [a]	...	...	...	...	...	...	...	...	...	...	...	...
Statistical discrepancy [c]	-3610	...	...	...	-5060	...	...	...	-4680	...	...	...
Total Gross Capital Formation	349600	...	...	...	323840	...	...	...	315390	...	...	...

	1983				1984				1985			
	TOTAL	Total Private	Public Enterprises	General Government	TOTAL	Total Private	Public Enterprises	General Government	TOTAL	Total Private	Public Enterprises	General Government
Increase in stocks, total [a]	-1800	...	...	...	6600	...	...	...	-700	...	...	...
1 Goods producing industries	-4230	...	...	...	1240	...	...	...	-1490	...	...	...
A Materials and supplies	...	...	...	...	...	...	...	...	...	...	...	...
B Work in progress	...	...	...	...	...	...	...	...	...	...	...	...
C Livestock, except breeding stocks, dairy cattle, etc.	400	...	...	...	-400	...	...	...	-100	...	...	...
D Finished goods	...	...	...	...	...	...	...	...	...	...	...	...
2 Wholesale and retail trade	2500	...	...	...	5300	...	...	...	700	...	...	...
3 Other, except government stocks	-70	...	...	...	60	...	...	...	90	...	...	...
4 Government stocks	...	...	...	...	...	...	...	...	...	...	...	...
Gross Fixed Capital Formation, Total	343820	...	...	...	354630	...	...	...	360800	...	...	...
1 Residential buildings	106790	...	...	...	112430	...	...	...	102550	...	...	...
2 Non-residential buildings		...	...	...		...	...	...		...	...	...
3 Other construction	101430	...	...	...	104620	...	...	...	104400	...	...	...
4 Land improvement and plantation and orchard development		...	...	...		...	...	...		...	...	...
5 Producers' durable goods	140490	...	...	...	143000	...	...	...	159670	...	...	...
A Transport equipment [b]	29020	...	...	...	25020	...	...	...	29190	...	...	...
B Machinery and equipment [b]	111470	...	...	...	117980	...	...	...	130480	...	...	...
6 Breeding stock, dairy cattle, etc. [a]	...	...	...	...	...	...	...	...	...	...	...	...
Statistical discrepancy [c]	-4890	...	...	...	-5420	...	...	...	-5820	...	...	...
Total Gross Capital Formation	342020	...	...	...	361230	...	...	...	360100	...	...	...

	1986				1987				1988			
	TOTAL	Total Private	Public Enterprises	General Government	TOTAL	Total Private	Public Enterprises	General Government	TOTAL	Total Private	Public Enterprises	General Government
Increase in stocks, total [a]	1500	...	...	...	4390	...	...	...	18130	...	...	...
1 Goods producing industries	130	...	...	...	470	...	...	...	12270	...	...	...
A Materials and supplies	...	...	...	...	...	...	...	...	...	...	...	...
B Work in progress	...	...	...	...	...	...	...	...	...	...	...	...
C Livestock, except breeding stocks, dairy cattle, etc.	-100	...	...	...	-600	...	...	...	...	...	...	...
D Finished goods	...	...	...	...	...	...	...	...	...	...	...	...
2 Wholesale and retail trade	1570	...	...	...	4000	...	...	...	5900	...	...	...
3 Other, except government stocks	-200	...	...	...	-80	...	...	...	-40	...	...	...
4 Government stocks	...	...	...	...	...	...	...	...	...	...	...	...
Gross Fixed Capital Formation, Total	377390	...	...	...	389970	...	...	...	415980	...	...	...

Germany, Fed. Rep. of

2.7 Gross Capital Formation by Type of Good and Owner, in Current Prices
(Continued)

Million Deutsche marks

	1986				1987				1988			
	TOTAL	Total Private	Public Enterprises	General Government	TOTAL	Total Private	Public Enterprises	General Government	TOTAL	Total Private	Public Enterprises	General Government
1 Residential buildings	103070	...	...	...	103690	...	...	...	109530	...	...	...
2 Non-residential buildings		...	...	...		...	...	...		...	...	...
3 Other construction	112940	...	...	...	115790	...	...	...	121570	...	...	...
4 Land improvement and plantation and orchard development		...	...	...		...	...	...		...	...	...
5 Producers' durable goods	167830	...	...	...	177680	...	...	...	192990	...	...	...
A Transport equipment [b]	32340	...	...	...	33680	...	...	...	35370	...	...	...
B Machinery and equipment [b]	135490	...	...	...	144000	...	...	...	157620	...	...	...
6 Breeding stock, dairy cattle, etc. [a]	...	...	...	...	...	...	...	...	...	...	...	...
Statistical discrepancy [c]	-6450	...	...	...	-7190	...	...	...	-8110	...	...	...
Total Gross Capital Formation	378890	...	...	...	394360	...	...	...	434110	...	...	...

a) Item 'Breeding stocks, dairy cattle, etc.' is included in item 'Increase in stocks'.
b) Railroad equipment is included in item 'Machinery and equipment'.
c) Item 'Statistical discrepancy' relates to adjustment for net sales of used capital goods.

2.8 Gross Capital Formation by Type of Good and Owner, in Constant Prices

Million Deutsche marks

	1980				1981				1982			
	TOTAL	Total Private	Public Enterprises	General Government	TOTAL	Total Private	Public Enterprises	General Government	TOTAL	Total Private	Public Enterprises	General Government
	At constant prices of:1980											
Increase in stocks, total [a]	13800	...	...	...	-10700	...	...	...	-9600	...	...	...
A Materials and supplies	...	...	...	...	...	...	...	...	...	...	...	...
B Work in progress	...	...	...	...	...	...	...	...	...	...	...	...
C Livestock, except breeding stocks, dairy cattle, etc.	...	...	...	...	-100	...	...	...	300	...	...	...
D Finished goods	...	...	...	...	...	...	...	...	...	...	...	...
Gross Fixed Capital Formation, Total	335800	...	...	...	319690	...	...	...	302880	...	...	...
1 Residential buildings	100570	...	...	...	95990	...	...	...	91420	...	...	...
2 Non-residential buildings		...	...	...		...	...	...		...	...	...
3 Other construction	107890	...	...	...	101890	...	...	...	97870	...	...	...
4 Land improvement and plantation and orchard development		...	...	...		...	...	...		...	...	...
5 Producers' durable goods	130950	...	...	...	126660	...	...	...	117860	...	...	...
A Transport equipment [b]	24860	...	...	...	25150	...	...	...	22640	...	...	...
B Machinery and equipment [b]	106090	...	...	...	101510	...	...	...	95220	...	...	...
6 Breeding stock, dairy cattle, etc. [a]	...	...	...	...	...	...	...	...	...	...	...	...
Statistical discrepancy [c]	-3610	...	...	...	-4850	...	...	...	-4270	...	...	...
Total Gross Capital Formation	349600	...	...	...	308990	...	...	...	293280	...	...	...

	1983				1984				1985			
	TOTAL	Total Private	Public Enterprises	General Government	TOTAL	Total Private	Public Enterprises	General Government	TOTAL	Total Private	Public Enterprises	General Government
	At constant prices of:1980											
Increase in stocks, total [a]	-1500	...	...	...	5500	...	...	...	-900	...	...	...
A Materials and supplies	...	...	...	...	...	...	...	...	...	...	...	...
B Work in progress	...	...	...	...	...	...	...	...	...	...	...	...
C Livestock, except breeding stocks, dairy cattle, etc.	500	...	...	...	-300	...	...	...	-200	...	...	...
D Finished goods	...	...	...	...	...	...	...	...	...	...	...	...
Gross Fixed Capital Formation, Total	312440	...	...	...	314900	...	...	...	315080	...	...	...

Germany, Fed. Rep. of

2.8 Gross Capital Formation by Type of Good and Owner, in Constant Prices
(Continued)

Million Deutsche marks

	1983 TOTAL	Total Private	Public Enterprises	General Government	1984 TOTAL	Total Private	Public Enterprises	General Government	1985 TOTAL	Total Private	Public Enterprises	General Government
					At constant prices of:1980							
1 Residential buildings	96450	...	...	...	98410	...	...	...	88530	...	...	...
2 Non-residential buildings		...	...	...		...	...	...		...	...	...
3 Other construction	96090	...	...	...	97130	...	...	...	96020	...	...	...
4 Land improvement and plantation and orchard development		...	...	...		...	...	...		...	...	...
5 Producers' durable goods	124240	...	...	...	124030	...	...	...	135410	...	...	...
A Transport equipment b	25620	...	...	...	21340	...	...	...	24230	...	...	...
B Machinery and equipment b	98620	...	...	...	102690	...	...	...	111180	...	...	...
6 Breeding stock, dairy cattle, etc. a	...	...	...	...	...	...	...	...	...	...	...	...
Statistical discrepancy c	-4340	...	...	...	-4670	...	...	...	-4880	...	...	...
Total Gross Capital Formation	310940	...	...	...	320400	...	...	...	314180	...	...	...

	1986 TOTAL	Total Private	Public Enterprises	General Government	1987 TOTAL	Total Private	Public Enterprises	General Government	1988 TOTAL	Total Private	Public Enterprises	General Government
					At constant prices of:1980							
Increase in stocks, total a	3920	...	...	...	5370	...	...	...	15520	...	...	...
A Materials and supplies	...	...	...	'	...	...	...	...	...	...	...	...
B Work in progress	...	...	...	...	...	...	...	...	...	...	...	...
C Livestock, except breeding stocks, dairy cattle, etc.	-100	...	...	...	-700	...	...	...	...	...	...	...
D Finished goods	...	...	...	...	...	...	...	...	...	...	...	...
Gross Fixed Capital Formation, Total	325400	...	...	...	332400	...	...	...	349350	...	...	...
1 Residential buildings	87590	...	...	...	86260	...	...	...	89290	...	...	...
2 Non-residential buildings		...	...	...		...	...	...		...	...	...
3 Other construction	101960	...	...	...	102740	...	...	...	105860	...	...	...
4 Land improvement and plantation and orchard development		...	...	...		...	...	...		...	...	...
5 Producers' durable goods	141110	...	...	...	149120	...	...	...	160520	...	...	...
A Transport equipment b	26260	...	...	...	26880	...	...	...	27550	...	...	...
B Machinery and equipment b	114850	...	...	...	122240	...	...	...	132970	...	...	...
6 Breeding stock, dairy cattle, etc. a	...	...	...	...	...	...	...	...	...	...	...	...
Statistical discrepancy c	-5260	...	...	...	-5720	...	...	...	-6320	...	...	...
Total Gross Capital Formation	329320	...	...	...	337770	...	...	...	364870	...	...	...

a) Item 'Breeding stocks, dairy cattle, etc.' is included in item 'Increase in stocks'.
b) Railroad equipment is included in item 'Machinery and equipment'.
c) Item 'Statistical discrepancy' relates to adjustment for net sales of used capital goods.

2.11 Gross Fixed Capital Formation by Kind of Activity of Owner, ISIC Divisions, in Current Prices

Million Deutsche marks

	1970	1975	1980	1981	1982	1983	1984	1985	1986	1987	1988	1989
					All Producers							
1 Agriculture, hunting, forestry and fishing	5720	6880	9280	8710	9030	10430	9790	9870	9720	9560	9920	10950
A Agriculture and hunting a	5440	6540	8790	8230	8610	9860	9300	9400	9200	8990	9270	10290
B Forestry and logging a	280	340	490	480	420	570	490	470	520	570	650	660
C Fishing a	...	...	...	...	...	...	...	...	...	...	...	...
2 Mining and quarrying b	1010	2050	2420	3070	3730	3460	2710	2890	3040	2750	3150	...
A Coal mining	750	1580	1830	2390	2960	2870	2140	2230	2360	2260	2620	...
B Crude petroleum and natural gas production	...	...	...	...	...	...	...	...	...	...	...	...
C Metal ore mining	...	...	...	...	...	...	...	...	...	...	...	...
D Other mining	...	...	...	...	...	...	...	...	...	...	...	...

Germany, Fed. Rep. of

2.11 Gross Fixed Capital Formation by Kind of Activity of Owner, ISIC Divisions, in Current Prices
(Continued)

Million Deutsche marks

	1970	1975	1980	1981	1982	1983	1984	1985	1986	1987	1988	1989
3 Manufacturing	41100	37010	59680	59410	56190	58520	58870	68940	75030	79850	81960	...
A Manufacturing of food, beverages and tobacco	4360	4270	6250	6590	6160	6710	6410	6050	6320	7070	7620	...
B Textile, wearing apparel and leather industries	2180	1480	1990	1670	1630	2070	2100	2300	2400	2470	2570	...
C Manufacture of wood, and wood products, including furniture	1270	990	1700	1410	1190	1440	1520	1350	1380	1550	1950	...
D Manufacture of paper and paper products, printing and publishing c	2250	1610	3610	3230	2740	3130	2960	3770	4260	4490	5970	...
E Manufacture of chemicals and chemical petroleum, coal, rubber and plastic products	8890	8510	10760	11090	10650	10860	10730	12270	13830	15680	15740	...
F Manufacture of non-metallic mineral products except products of petroleum and coal b	2510	1710	3410	3240	2620	2970	3120	2930	2960	3170	3760	...
G Basic metal industries	4970	4670	5730	5640	4810	4340	4910	6780	5950	5710	5780	...
H Manufacture of fabricated metal products, machinery and equipment d	14500	13610	25950	26280	26130	26690	27280	32830	37560	39240	38070	...
I Other manufacturing industries	170	160	310	260	260	310	300	360	370	470	500	...
4 Electricity, gas and water	7220	14740	16570	16930	19110	19110	20720	20390	20810	20520	20110	...
A Electricity, gas and steam		13040	14330	14840	17280	17280	18890	18580	19060	18840	18200	...
B Water works and supply		1700	2240	2090	1830	1830	1830	1810	1750	1680	1910	...
5 Construction d	4320	3330	6250	4990	4250	4790	4500	4320	4730	5000	5310	...
6 Wholesale and retail trade, restaurants and hotels	9970	10840	16790	15750	15590	15750	16870	17460	19560	21670	25870	...
A Wholesale and retail trade	8840	9060	14500	13350	13170	14410	15000	14890	16910	18940	23030	...
B Restaurants and hotels	1330	1780	2290	2400	2420	2460	2460	2600	2650	2730	2840	...
7 Transport, storage and communication	15760	19160	26160	27610	27340	29050	30690	34760	36130	35980	36400	...
A Transport and storage	10630	12540	15700	16070	14890	17190	18450	18300	19220	18710	18410	...
B Communication	5130	6620	10460	11840	12450	12600	14500	14600	16910	17510	17990	...
8 Finance, insurance, real estate and business services	45850	60250	99310	101140	100310	102860	112840	103140	103550	103360	108940	...
A Financial institutions	1990	3390	3880	3860	4080	4520	5850	5850	5670	6130	5920	5340	5530
B Insurance	790	1120	1760	1860	2180	2320	2640	2980	2220	2910	2740	3370
C Real estate and business services e	43170	55740	93610	94880	99770	104190	94760	94720	95280	100040	108910	...
Real estate except dwellings												
Dwellings	43170	55740	93610	94880	99770	104190	94760	94720	95280	100040	108910	...
9 Community, social and personal services cc	10030	17350	47320	47320	49320	47200	52000	55610	58910	60730	66910	79080
Educational services												...
Medical, dental, other health and veterinary services	1810	3820	9040	8270	8400	8940	9720	9490	9720	10710	12490	...
Total Industries	14080	171610	283780	287230	282750	303230	314450	320410	333300	345300	370740	410630
Producers of Government Services	29780	37470	50450	47590	43350	40190	40290	40920	45060	46210	47440	51060
Private Non-Profit Institutions Serving Households	3230	3670	5180	5480	5290	5290	5310	5290	5480	5650	5910	6220
Statistical discrepancy f	-2040	-3340	-3610	-5060	-4680	-4890	-5420	-5420	-5820	-6450	-7190	-8110	-9560
Total	172050	209410	335800	335240	326890	343820	354680	360800	377390	389970	415980	458410

b) Quarrying is included in item 'Manufacture of non-metallic mineral products except products of petroleum and coal'.
c) Publishing is included in item 'Community, social and personal services'.
d) Structural steel erection is included in item 'Manufacture of fabricated metal products'.
e) Business services and real estate except dwellings are included in item 'Community, social and personal services'.
f) Item 'Statistical discrepancy' relates to adjustment for net purchases of used capital goods, machinery and equipment.

2.12 Gross Fixed Capital Formation by Kind of Activity of Owner, ISIC Divisions, in Constant Prices

Million Deutsche marks

At constant prices of 1980

	1970	1975	1980	1981	1982	1983	1984	1985	1986	1987	1988	1989
1 Agriculture, hunting, forestry and fishing	9760	8540	8280	8220	8110	9100	8320	8210	7980	7780	7970	8570
A Agriculture and hunting a	9320	8150	8790	7790	7770	8600	7900	7810	7530	7300	7430	8040
B Forestry and logging a	440	390	490	450	380	500	420	400	450	480	540	530
C Fishing a												
2 Mining and quarrying b	1810	2540	2420	2920	3370	3020	2300	2420	2520	2270	2570	...

673

Germany, Fed. Rep. of

2.12 Gross Fixed Capital Formation by Kind of Activity of Owner, ISIC Divisions, in Constant Prices (Continued)

Million Deutsche marks — At constant prices of 1980

	1970	1975	1980	1981	1982	1983	1984	1985	1986	1987	1988	1989
A Coal mining	1340	1950	1830	2270	2670	2500	1820	1860	1960	1870	2150	...
B Crude petroleum and natural gas production												
C Metal ore mining												
D Other mining												
3 Manufacturing	66120	44800	52580	52150	51960	51230	58120	62630	66020	66810		
A Manufacturing of food, beverages and tobacco	7230	5270	6260	5580	5910	5540	5050	5180	5700	5970		
B Textile, wearing apparel and leather industries	3660	1840	1990	1600	1490	1830	1810	1940	1990	2020	2080	
C Manufacturing of wood, and wood products, including furniture	2030	1210	1700	1350	1090	1280	1310	1130	1140	1280	1590	
D Manufacture of paper and paper products, printing and publishing c	3710	3610	3910	3060	2470	2760	2540	3150	3470	3620	4760	
E Manufacture of chemicals and chemical petroleum, coal, rubber and plastic products	14530	10340	10760	10550	9700	9620	8310	10270	11450	12880	12720	
F Manufacture of non-metallic mineral products except products of petroleum and coal b	3960	2060	3410	3100	2400	2660	2730	2490	2480	2630	3060	
G Basic metal industries	8010	5650	5730	5360	4370	3830	4230	5710	4970	4730	4730	
H Manufacture of fabricated metal products, machinery and equipment, d	22710	16290	25950	25080	23910	23790	23500	28080	31650	32780	31500	
I Other manufacturing industries	280	190	310	250	240	280	260	300	300	380	400	
4 Electricity, gas and water	11440	18170	16570	16330	18040	17940	18090	18410	18510	17990	17380	
A Electricity, gas and steam	16000	14330	14310	16290	16190	17350	17170	16900	16470	15690		
B Water works and supply	...	2170	2240	2020	1750	1750	1740	1700	1610	1520	1690	
5 Construction d	7040	4080	6250	4740	3830	4210	3880	3650	3890	4050	4230	
6 Wholesale and retail trade, restaurants and hotels	16150	13580	16790	14500	14250	15030	15220	14990	14460	18040	21210	
A Wholesale and retail trade	13980	11320	14500	12710	12020	12820	13060	12740	14210	18860		
B Restaurants and hotels	2170	2260	2290	2280	2230	2210	2160	2250	2250	2300	2350	
7 Transport, storage and communication	24830	28850	26120	26830	25720	27820	28520	31560	32490	32290	32180	
A Transport and storage	17000	16690	15700	15390	13900	15910	15030	15870	16950	16210	15790	
B Communication	7830	8160	10460	11440	11820	11910	13490	15190	15540	16080	16390	
8 Finance, insurance, real estate and business services	85650	82840	99310	95910	92490	97820	98820	87980	86090	88990		
A Financial institutions	3130	4270	3840	3890	4180	5310	4950	5260	5090	4590	4710	
B Insurance	1370	1460	1860	2070	2140	2390	2610	1910	2500	2330	2830	
C Real estate and business services e	81150	77110	93610	89560	90170	86170	91140	81750	80390	79170	81450	85710
Real estate except dwellings												
Dwellings	81150	77110	93610	89560	90170	86170	91140	81750	80390	79170	81450	85710
9 Community, social and personal services e	15220	21080	47320	46970	43400	46730	46990	51340	52670	57700	67880	
Educational services												
Medical, dental, other health and veterinary services	2790	4650	9040	8840	7750	8070	8600	8280	8460	9350	10850	
Total Industries	238020	219480	283780	273520	260460	273890	277250	285130	292230	309220	333100	
Producers of Government Services	51530	50820	50450	45830	41660	38230	37550	37630	40720	41020	41450	43320
Private Non-Profit Institutions Serving Households	5720	4980	5180	5190	5030	4860	4770	4710	4810	4870	5000	5080
Statistical discrepancy f	-3360	-4010	-3610	-4850	-4270	-4340	-4670	-4880	-5260	-5720	-6320	-7210
Total	291910	271270	335800	319690	302880	312440	314900	315080	325400	332400	349350	372290

a) Hunting and fishing are included in item "Forestry and logging".
b) Quarrying is included in item "Manufacture of non-metallic mineral products except of petroleum and coal."
c) Publishing is included in item "Community, social and personal services".
d) Structural steel erection is included in item "Manufacture of fabricated metal products".
e) Business services and real estate except dwellings are included in item "Community, social and personal services".
f) Item "Statistical discrepancy" relates to adjustment for net purchases of used capital goods.

Germany, Fed. Rep. of

2.13 Stocks of Reproducible Fixed Assets, by Type of Good and Owner, in Current Prices

Thousand Million Deutsche marks

	TOTAL Gross	TOTAL Net	Private Total Gross	Private Total Net	Public Enterprises Gross	Public Enterprises Net	General Government Gross	General Government Net
1980								
1 Residential buildings	2784.2	2035.1	2784.2	2035.1	...	...	...	...
2 Non-residential buildings	...	...	...	...	...	...	...	...
3 Other construction	2160.5	1490.3	1227.5	1175.3	...	...	433.1	315.0
4 Land improvement and plantation and orchard development	...	...	...	...	...	...	...	...
5 Producers' durable goods	1426.5	774.9	1360.7	737.1	...	...	65.8	37.8
6 Breeding stock, dairy cattle, etc. a	...	...	...	...	...	...	...	...
Total b	6371.2	4300.3	5872.4	3947.5	...	...	498.8	352.8
1981								
1 Residential buildings	3001.2	2184.8	3001.2	2184.8	...	...	...	...
2 Non-residential buildings	...	...	...	...	...	...	...	...
3 Other construction	2321.1	1593.5	1851.9	1253.3	...	...	469.2	340.2
4 Land improvement and plantation and orchard development	...	...	...	...	...	...	...	...
5 Producers' durable goods	1546.5	837.1	1475.3	797.0	...	...	71.2	40.1
6 Breeding stock, dairy cattle, etc. a	...	...	...	...	...	...	...	...
Total b	6868.7	4615.5	6328.4	4235.2	...	...	540.4	380.3
1982								
1 Residential buildings	3135.1	2271.2	3135.1	2271.2	...	...	...	...
2 Non-residential buildings	...	...	...	...	...	...	...	...
3 Other construction	2399.6	1637.8	1909.0	1283.6	...	...	490.6	354.2
4 Land improvement and plantation and orchard development	...	...	...	...	...	...	...	...
5 Producers' durable goods	1625.9	871.8	1550.7	830.6	...	...	75.2	41.2
6 Breeding stock, dairy cattle, etc. a	...	...	...	...	...	...	...	...
Total b	7160.5	4780.8	6594.8	4385.5	...	...	565.7	395.3
1983								
1 Residential buildings	3338.0	2407.2	3338.0	2407.2	...	...	...	...
2 Non-residential buildings	...	...	...	...	...	...	...	...
3 Other construction	2530.7	1718.5	2009.1	1344.0	...	...	521.6	374.5
4 Land improvement and plantation and orchard development	...	...	...	...	...	...	...	...
5 Producers' durable goods	1706.7	909.5	1627.5	867.4	...	...	79.2	42.1
6 Breeding stock, dairy cattle, etc. a	...	...	...	...	...	...	...	...
Total b	7575.4	5035.2	6974.6	4618.6	...	...	600.8	416.6
1984								
1 Residential buildings	3520.7	2527.0	3520.7	2527.0	...	...	...	...
2 Non-residential buildings	...	...	...	...	...	...	...	...
3 Other construction	2647.1	1789.1	2104.0	1401.5	...	...	543.1	387.6
4 Land improvement and plantation and orchard development	...	...	...	...	...	...	...	...
5 Producers' durable goods	1775.2	940.4	1692.2	897.3	...	...	82.9	43.1
6 Breeding stock, dairy cattle, etc. a	...	...	...	...	...	...	...	...
Total b	7942.9	5256.5	7316.9	4825.8	...	...	626.1	430.7
1985								
1 Residential buildings	3653.0	2605.9	3653.0	2605.9	...	...	...	...
2 Non-residential buildings	...	...	...	...	...	...	...	...
3 Other construction	2758.7	1853.3	2199.3	1456.5	...	...	559.5	396.7
4 Land improvement and plantation and orchard development	...	...	...	...	...	...	...	...
5 Producers' durable goods	1835.9	972.0	1749.7	927.9	...	...	86.2	44.2
6 Breeding stock, dairy cattle, etc. a	...	...	...	...	...	...	...	...
Total b	8247.7	5431.2	7602.0	4990.3	...	...	645.7	440.9

Germany, Fed. Rep. of

2.13 Stocks of Reproducible Fixed Assets, by Type of Good and Owner, in Current Prices
(Continued)

Thousand Million Deutsche marks

	TOTAL Gross	TOTAL Net	Total Private Gross	Total Private Net	Public Enterprises Gross	Public Enterprises Net	General Government Gross	General Government Net
1986								
1 Residential buildings	3811.2	2701.3	3811.2	2701.3	...	...	...	...
2 Non-residential buildings	...	...	...	...	...	...	...	...
3 Other construction	2891.9	1933.2	2309.2	1522.5	...	...	582.7	410.7
4 Land improvement and plantation and orchard development								
5 Producers' durable goods	1903.4	1008.4	1814.1	962.9	...	...	89.3	45.5
6 Breeding stock, dairy cattle, etc. [a]								
Total [b]	8606.5	5642.8	7934.5	5186.6	...	...	672.0	456.2
1987								
1 Residential buildings	3964.2	2790.9	3964.2	2790.9	...	...	...	...
2 Non-residential buildings	...	...	...	...	...	...	...	...
3 Other construction	3016.6	2006.6	2410.0	1581.6	...	...	606.6	425.1
4 Land improvement and plantation and orchard development								
5 Producers' durable goods	1964.9	1043.7	1871.5	996.1	...	...	93.3	47.6
6 Breeding stock, dairy cattle, etc. [a]								
Total [b]	8945.7	5841.2	8245.8	5368.6	...	...	699.9	472.7
1988								
1 Residential buildings	4159.4	2909.1	4159.4	2909.1	...	...	...	...
2 Non-residential buildings	...	...	...	...	...	...	...	...
3 Other construction	3190.1	2112.2	2551.1	1667.1	...	...	639.1	445.1
4 Land improvement and plantation and orchard development								
5 Producers' durable goods	2060.9	1100.7	1963.7	1051.1	...	...	97.2	49.6
6 Breeding stock, dairy cattle, etc. [a]								
Total [b]	9410.4	6122.1	8674.1	5627.4	...	...	736.3	494.7
1989								
1 Residential buildings	4435.8	3083.5	4435.8	3083.5	...	...	...	...
2 Non-residential buildings	...	...	...	...	...	...	...	...
3 Other construction	3419.3	2254.6	2737.3	1782.5	...	...	682.0	472.1
4 Land improvement and plantation and orchard development								
5 Producers' durable goods	2168.7	1168.8	2066.4	1116.3	...	...	102.4	52.5
6 Breeding stock, dairy cattle, etc. [a]								
Total [b]	10023.9	6506.9	9239.5	5982.3	...	...	784.4	524.6

[a] Item 'Breeding stocks, dairy cattle, etc.' is included in item 'Increase in stocks'.
[b] Column 'Public enterprises' is included in column 'Total private'.

2.14 Stocks of Reproducible Fixed Assets, by Type of Good and Owner, in Constant Prices

Thousand Million Deutsche marks

At constant prices of: 1980

	TOTAL Gross	TOTAL Net	Total Private Gross	Total Private Net	Public Enterprises Gross	Public Enterprises Net	General Government Gross	General Government Net
1980								
1 Residential buildings	2718.9	1987.4	2718.9	1987.4	...	...	...	...
2 Non-residential buildings	...	...	...	...	...	...	...	...
3 Other construction	2116.5	1459.6	1694.0	1152.3	...	...	422.5	307.4
4 Land improvement and plantation and orchard development								
5 Producers' durable goods	1402.7	762.0	1338.4	725.1	...	...	64.2	36.9
6 Breeding stock, dairy cattle, etc. [a]								
Total [b]	6238.1	4209.0	5751.3	3864.7	...	...	486.7	344.3

Germany, Fed. Rep. of

2.14 Stocks of Reproducible Fixed Assets, by Type of Good and Owner, in Constant Prices (Continued)

Thousand Million Deutsche marks

	TOTAL Gross	TOTAL Net	Total Private Gross	Total Private Net	Public Enterprises Gross	Public Enterprises Net	General Government Gross	General Government Net
At constant prices of 1980								
1981								
1 Residential buildings	2802.2	2040.0	2802.2	2040.0	...	...	...	...
2 Non-residential buildings	2186.7	1500.6	1751.0	1184.7	...	...	435.7	315.9
3 Other construction	1443.9	781.6	1377.2	744.0	...	...	66.8	37.6
4 Land improvement and plantation and orchard development	...	...	...	...	...	...	...	...
5 Producers' durable goods	6432.8	4322.2	5930.4	3968.7	...	...	502.4	353.5
6 Breeding stock, dairy cattle, etc. a								
Total b								
1982								
1 Residential buildings	2881.5	2087.5	2881.5	2087.5	...	...	...	...
2 Non-residential buildings	2254.0	1538.2	1806.0	1214.8	...	...	448.0	323.4
3 Other construction	1474.0	790.4	1405.5	752.9	...	...	68.5	37.5
4 Land improvement and plantation and orchard development	...	...	...	...	...	...	...	...
5 Producers' durable goods	6609.5	4416.1	6093.0	4055.2	...	...	516.5	361.0
6 Breeding stock, dairy cattle, etc. a								
Total b								
1983								
1 Residential buildings	2964.5	2137.8	2964.5	2137.8	...	...	...	...
2 Non-residential buildings	2321.4	1575.7	1862.2	1246.0	...	...	459.2	329.7
3 Other construction	1506.3	802.7	1436.5	765.6	...	...	69.9	37.2
4 Land improvement and plantation and orchard development	...	...	...	...	...	...	...	...
5 Producers' durable goods	6792.2	4516.2	6263.2	4149.4	...	...	529.0	366.9
6 Breeding stock, dairy cattle, etc. a								
Total b								
1984								
1 Residential buildings	3048.2	2187.9	3048.2	2187.9	...	...	...	...
2 Non-residential buildings	2389.5	1614.1	1919.6	1278.8	...	...	469.8	335.3
3 Other construction	1533.0	812.1	1461.8	775.1	...	...	71.2	37.0
4 Land improvement and plantation and orchard development	...	...	...	...	...	...	...	...
5 Producers' durable goods	6970.6	4614.0	6429.6	4241.8	...	...	541.0	372.3
6 Breeding stock, dairy cattle, etc. a								
Total b								
1985								
1 Residential buildings	3122.2	2227.3	3122.2	2227.3	...	...	...	...
2 Non-residential buildings	2456.3	1649.9	1976.1	1309.4	...	...	480.2	340.5
3 Other construction	1567.8	830.1	1495.1	792.8	...	...	72.7	37.3
4 Land improvement and plantation and orchard development	...	...	...	...	...	...	...	...
5 Producers' durable goods	7146.4	4707.3	6593.4	4329.5	...	...	553.0	377.8
6 Breeding stock, dairy cattle, etc. a								
Total b								
1986								
1 Residential buildings	3194.6	2264.3	3194.6	2264.3	...	...	...	...
2 Non-residential buildings	2526.9	1688.8	2035.7	1342.6	...	...	491.3	346.3
3 Other construction	1606.3	851.0	1531.9	813.1	...	...	74.4	37.9
4 Land improvement and plantation and orchard development	...	...	...	...	...	...	...	...
5 Producers' durable goods	7327.8	4804.1	6762.2	4419.9	...	...	565.6	384.2
6 Breeding stock, dairy cattle, etc. a								
Total b								

Germany, Fed. Rep. of

2.14 Stocks of Reproducible Fixed Assets, by Type of Good and Owner, in Constant Prices
(Continued)

Thousand Million Deutsche marks

	TOTAL		Total Private		Public Enterprises		General Government	
	Gross	Net	Gross	Net	Gross	Net	Gross	Net
At constant prices of:1980								
1987								
1 Residential buildings	3265.4	2298.9	3265.4	2298.9	...	...	...	...
2 Non-residential buildings	...	...	...	...	...	...	...	...
3 Other construction	2598.1	1727.7	2095.6	1375.5	...	...	502.6	352.2
4 Land improvement and plantation and orchard development	...	...	...	...	...	...	...	...
5 Producers' durable goods	1649.8	876.4	1573.8	837.6	...	...	76.0	38.8
6 Breeding stock, dairy cattle, etc. [a]	...	...	...	...	...	...	...	...
Total [b]	7513.3	4902.9	6934.8	4512.0	...	...	578.6	390.9
1988								
1 Residential buildings	3338.2	2334.8	3338.2	2334.8	...	...	...	...
2 Non-residential buildings	...	...	...	...	...	...	...	...
3 Other construction	2671.8	1768.4	2158.0	1410.6	...	...	513.7	357.8
4 Land improvement and plantation and orchard development	...	...	...	...	...	...	...	...
5 Producers' durable goods	1701.8	908.9	1624.6	869.6	...	...	77.2	39.4
6 Breeding stock, dairy cattle, etc. [a]	...	...	...	...	...	...	...	...
Total [b]	7711.8	5012.1	7120.8	4614.9	...	...	591.0	397.2
1989								
1 Residential buildings	3414.8	2373.7	3414.8	2373.7	...	...	...	...
2 Non-residential buildings	...	...	...	...	...	...	...	...
3 Other construction	2748.9	1812.2	2223.8	1448.7	...	...	525.0	363.5
4 Land improvement and plantation and orchard development	...	...	...	...	...	...	...	...
5 Producers' durable goods	1766.1	951.8	1687.3	911.4	...	...	78.8	40.4
6 Breeding stock, dairy cattle, etc. [a]	...	...	...	...	...	...	...	...
Total [b]	7929.7	5137.7	7325.9	4733.8	...	...	603.8	403.9

a) Item 'Breeding stocks, dairy cattle, etc.' is included in item 'Increase in stocks'.
b) Column 'Public enterprises' is included in column 'Total private'.

2.15 Stocks of Reproducible Fixed Assets by Kind of Activity, in Current Prices

Thousand Million Deutsche marks

	1980		1981		1982		1983		1984		1985	
	Gross	Net	Gross	Net	Gross	Net	Gross	Net	Gross	Net	Gross	Net
1 Residential buildings	2784.2	2035.1	3001.2	2184.8	3135.1	2271.2	3338.0	2407.2	3520.7	2527.0	3653.0	2605.9
2 Non-residential buildings [a]	...	...	...	...	...	...	...	...	...	...	...	...
3 Other construction [ab]	2160.5	1490.3	2321.1	1593.5	2399.6	1637.8	2530.7	1718.5	2647.1	1789.1	2758.7	1853.3
A Industries	1607.7	1085.1	1723.2	1156.8	1777.1	1185.1	1870.4	1241.1	1960.4	1295.7	2050.6	1347.7
1 Agriculture	152.0	83.6	157.7	86.2	164.2	89.3	166.4	90.0	167.9	90.3	175.3	93.8
2 Mining and quarrying [c]	19.6	11.0	20.5	11.5	21.1	11.8	21.6	12.0	22.1	12.1	22.5	12.2
3 Manufacturing [c]	389.7	221.2	412.1	230.3	417.2	229.2	428.7	231.2	438.1	232.6	447.4	233.7
4 Electricity, gas and water	192.5	145.9	204.4	154.2	211.4	158.4	218.7	162.6	230.8	170.5	242.9	178.1
5 Construction	25.9	18.3	28.1	19.6	28.6	19.6	30.6	20.6	31.8	21.1	32.6	21.2
6 Wholesale and retail trade	178.4	129.7	193.2	139.1	195.9	139.6	211.0	148.9	220.2	154.1	228.2	158.3
7 Transport and communication	261.5	173.7	275.4	181.2	281.4	183.7	289.2	187.0	305.5	196.2	321.5	205.1
8 Finance, etc.	93.5	72.4	101.5	78.2	108.9	83.5	116.0	88.7	123.3	94.0	128.7	97.4
9 Community, social and personal services	294.7	229.2	330.3	256.6	348.5	270.1	388.3	300.2	420.6	324.8	451.6	347.9
B Producers of government services [d]	433.1	315.0	469.2	340.2	490.6	354.2	521.6	374.5	543.1	387.6	559.5	396.7
C Other producers	119.8	90.2	128.7	96.5	131.9	98.4	138.7	102.9	143.6	105.8	148.7	108.8
4 Land improvement and development and plantation and orchard development [b]	...	...	...	...	...	...	...	...	...	...	...	...
5 Producers' durable goods	1426.5	774.9	1546.5	837.1	1625.9	871.8	1706.7	909.5	1775.2	940.4	1835.9	972.0
A Industries	1342.6	727.4	1455.7	786.7	1530.0	819.9	1606.2	856.5	1670.1	886.2	1727.2	916.7
1 Agriculture	116.0	58.9	122.7	61.6	127.4	63.1	131.6	65.0	134.6	66.1	135.6	66.1
2 Mining and quarrying [c]	26.5	13.7	28.9	15.1	31.1	16.6	33.3	18.0	34.2	18.3	34.8	18.5

678

Germany, Fed. Rep. of

2.15 Stocks of Reproducible Fixed Assets by Kind of Activity, in Current Prices
(Continued)

Thousand Million Deutsche marks

	1980		1981		1982		1983		1984		1985	
	Gross	Net	Gross	Net	Gross	Net	Gross	Net	Gross	Net	Gross	Net
3 Manufacturing c	565.1	294.5	606.1	317.0	627.7	327.4	650.5	339.2	669.1	348.8	688.8	361.7
4 Electricity, gas and water	115.0	62.7	123.4	66.3	131.7	70.8	139.5	75.0	147.9	79.8	154.3	83.2
5 Construction	46.0	23.0	47.6	23.4	47.2	22.5	46.8	21.9	45.7	20.9	44.2	19.9
6 Wholesale and retail trade	81.2	43.1	86.2	45.2	89.0	45.7	91.7	46.5	93.7	47.1	94.6	47.1
7 Transport and communication	197.0	103.7	211.0	110.1	220.0	113.4	230.0	118.0	236.1	120.3	243.1	124.4
8 Finance, etc.	18.2	10.5	19.8	11.3	22.0	12.6	24.6	14.2	26.6	15.3	29.0	16.8
9 Community, social and personal services	177.7	117.3	210.0	136.7	234.0	147.7	258.2	158.7	282.1	169.7	303.0	179.0
B Producers of government services	65.8	37.8	71.2	40.1	75.2	41.2	79.2	42.1	82.9	43.1	86.2	44.2
C Other producers	18.2	9.8	19.6	10.4	20.7	10.8	21.4	10.9	22.1	11.1	22.5	11.2
6 Breeding stock, dairy cattle, etc.	...	...	...	...	...	...	...	...	...	...	...	...
Total	6371.2	4300.3	6868.7	4615.5	7160.5	4780.8	7575.4	5035.2	7942.9	5256.5	8247.7	5431.2

	1986		1987		1988		1989	
	Gross	Net	Gross	Net	Gross	Net	Gross	Net
1 Residential buildings	3811.2	2701.3	3964.2	2790.9	4159.4	2909.1	4435.8	3083.5
2 Non-residential buildings a	...	...	...	...	...	...	...	...
3 Other construction ab	2891.9	1933.2	3016.6	2006.6	3190.1	2112.2	3419.3	2254.6
A Industries	2153.2	1409.1	2248.7	1465.1	2381.2	1545.3	2555.4	1652.9
1 Agriculture	177.6	94.3	178.9	94.3	184.5	96.6	195.1	101.4
2 Mining and quarrying c	23.1	12.4	23.5	12.4	24.2	12.6	...	...
3 Manufacturing c	462.0	238.6	474.6	242.9	492.8	249.8	...	...
4 Electricity, gas and water	256.2	186.7	268.2	193.8	285.4	204.6	...	...
5 Construction	33.6	21.4	34.4	21.6	35.8	22.0	...	...
6 Wholesale and retail trade	238.6	164.2	247.9	169.3	261.6	177.8	...	...
7 Transport and communication	340.3	216.1	358.8	227.0	382.1	240.3	...	...
8 Finance, etc.	135.4	102.0	142.6	106.6	151.1	112.2	...	...
9 Community, social and personal services	486.4	373.3	519.9	397.2	563.8	429.3	...	...
B Producers of government services d	582.7	410.7	606.6	425.1	639.1	445.1	682.0	472.1
C Other producers	156.1	113.4	161.4	116.5	169.9	121.8	181.9	129.6
4 Land improvement and development and plantation and orchard development b	...	...	...	...	...	...	...	...
5 Producers' durable goods	1903.4	1008.4	1964.9	1043.7	2060.9	1100.7	2168.7	1168.8
A Industries	1791.3	951.6	1848.1	984.6	1939.4	1039.1	2041.2	1103.9
1 Agriculture	135.5	65.9	135.4	65.7	136.2	66.2	138.7	68.0
2 Mining and quarrying c	35.6	18.8	35.8	18.8	36.7	19.2	...	...
3 Manufacturing c	717.0	379.3	739.9	394.3	775.3	415.2	...	...
4 Electricity, gas and water	161.2	86.5	166.3	89.1	171.8	91.2	...	...
5 Construction	44.0	19.9	42.9	19.6	42.7	19.9	...	...
6 Wholesale and retail trade	96.8	48.5	99.1	50.5	105.2	55.3	...	...
7 Transport and communication	249.4	127.5	252.9	128.3	259.5	131.0	...	...
8 Finance, etc.	30.6	17.9	32.2	18.7	34.4	19.9	...	...
9 Community, social and personal services	321.2	187.3	343.5	199.6	377.8	221.3	...	...
B Producers of government services	89.3	45.5	93.3	47.6	97.2	49.6	102.4	52.5
C Other producers	22.8	11.3	23.4	11.6	24.3	12.0	25.1	12.5
6 Breeding stock, dairy cattle, etc.	...	...	...	...	...	...	...	...
Total	8606.5	5642.8	8945.7	5841.2	9410.4	6122.1	10023.9	6506.9

a) Item 'Non-residential buildings' is included in item 'Other construction'.
b) Item 'Land improvement and plantation and orchard development' is included in item 'Other construction'.
c) Quarrying is included in item 'Manufacturing'.
d) Item 'Producers of government services' does not include government civil engineering works.

Germany, Fed. Rep. of

2.16 Stocks of Reproducible Fixed Assets by Kind of Activity, in Constant Prices

Thousand Million Deutsche marks

	1980		1981		1982		1983		1984		1985	
	Gross	Net	Gross	Net	Gross	Net	Gross	Net	Gross	Net	Gross	Net
At constant prices of:1980												
1 Residential buildings	2718.9	1987.4	2802.2	2040.0	2881.5	2087.5	2964.5	2137.8	3048.2	2187.9	3122.2	2227.3
2 Non-residential buildings a	...	...	...	...	...	...	...	...	...	...	...	...
3 Other construction ab	2116.5	1459.6	2186.7	1500.6	2254.0	1538.2	2321.4	1575.7	2389.5	1614.1	2456.3	1649.9
A Industries	1577.5	1064.5	1630.6	1094.4	1681.7	1122.1	1734.4	1151.2	1788.2	1182.0	1841.3	1210.7
1 Agriculture	150.3	82.6	150.9	82.5	151.5	82.3	152.2	82.3	152.8	82.2	153.4	82.0
2 Mining and quarrying c	19.3	10.8	19.5	10.9	19.9	11.1	20.3	11.3	20.4	11.2	20.5	11.1
3 Manufacturing c	382.0	216.9	387.8	216.8	391.9	215.4	394.5	212.9	395.9	210.4	398.1	208.2
4 Electricity, gas and water	190.1	144.1	199.1	150.2	207.5	155.6	215.7	160.6	224.4	166.0	232.5	170.8
5 Construction	25.3	17.8	26.0	18.1	26.6	18.2	27.2	18.4	27.8	18.5	28.2	18.4
6 Wholesale and retail trade	174.2	126.7	178.7	128.7	183.1	130.6	187.8	132.8	192.8	135.1	197.5	137.1
7 Transport and communication	257.6	171.2	266.8	175.6	276.0	180.0	285.6	184.7	296.0	190.0	306.8	195.6
8 Finance, etc.	90.8	70.3	94.5	72.8	98.1	75.3	102.4	78.4	107.0	81.6	110.6	83.8
9 Community, social and personal services	288.0	224.0	307.3	238.8	327.1	253.5	348.6	269.9	371.2	287.0	393.8	303.7
B Producers of government services d	422.5	307.4	435.7	315.9	448.0	323.4	459.2	329.7	469.8	335.3	480.2	340.5
C Other producers	116.5	87.8	120.4	90.3	124.2	92.7	127.9	94.8	131.4	96.8	134.8	98.7
4 Land improvement and development and plantation and orchard development b	...	...	...	...	...	...	...	...	...	...	...	...
5 Producers' durable goods	1402.7	762.0	1443.9	781.6	1474.0	790.4	1506.3	802.7	1533.0	812.1	1567.8	830.1
A Industries	1320.8	715.6	1359.3	734.5	1387.5	743.5	1418.3	756.3	1443.5	765.9	1476.7	783.7
1 Agriculture	112.7	57.2	112.4	56.4	111.8	55.4	111.9	55.3	111.2	54.6	110.3	53.8
2 Mining and quarrying c	26.1	13.4	26.8	14.0	27.8	14.9	28.4	15.3	28.6	15.3	28.9	15.3
3 Manufacturing c	556.0	289.8	565.0	295.3	568.6	296.5	572.9	298.5	574.4	299.1	582.8	305.7
4 Electricity, gas and water	113.4	61.9	115.9	62.2	120.4	64.7	124.5	66.8	129.0	69.5	132.8	71.5
5 Construction	45.2	22.6	44.1	21.7	42.4	20.2	41.0	19.1	39.3	17.9	37.6	16.9
6 Wholesale and retail trade	80.1	42.5	80.8	42.3	80.8	41.5	81.0	41.0	81.0	40.6	80.6	40.1
7 Transport and communication	194.3	102.2	198.1	103.3	201.0	103.6	204.7	105.0	207.2	105.6	211.8	108.5
8 Finance, etc.	17.9	10.3	18.9	10.8	20.2	11.5	22.0	12.7	23.4	13.4	25.2	14.6
9 Community, social and personal services	175.2	115.7	197.4	128.5	214.6	135.4	231.9	142.3	249.6	149.9	266.8	157.4
B Producers of government services	64.2	36.9	66.8	37.6	68.5	37.5	69.9	37.2	71.2	37.0	72.7	37.3
C Other producers	17.6	9.5	17.9	9.5	18.1	9.4	18.2	9.3	18.3	9.2	18.3	9.1
6 Breeding stock, dairy cattle, etc.	...	...	...	...	...	...	...	...	...	...	...	...
Total e	6238.1	4209.0	6432.8	4322.2	6609.5	4416.1	6792.2	4516.2	6970.6	4614.0	7146.4	4707.3

	1986		1987		1988		1989	
	Gross	Net	Gross	Net	Gross	Net	Gross	Net
At constant prices of:1980								
1 Residential buildings	3194.6	2264.3	3265.4	2298.9	3338.2	2334.8	3414.8	2373.7
2 Non-residential buildings a	...	...	...	...	...	...	...	...
3 Other construction ab	2526.9	1688.8	2598.1	1727.7	2671.8	1768.4	2748.9	1812.2
A Industries	1897.5	1242.1	1953.9	1273.2	2012.8	1306.5	2075.1	1342.8
1 Agriculture	153.8	81.7	154.1	81.3	154.4	80.8	154.6	80.4
2 Mining and quarrying c	20.6	11.1	20.6	10.9	20.7	10.8	...	...
3 Manufacturing c	401.9	207.8	406.5	208.3	410.5	208.4	...	...
4 Electricity, gas and water	241.1	175.8	248.8	179.9	256.9	184.3	...	...
5 Construction	28.5	18.2	28.8	18.1	29.2	17.9	...	...
6 Wholesale and retail trade	202.7	139.6	208.1	142.3	214.6	146.0	...	...
7 Transport and communication	318.7	202.4	331.3	209.5	342.7	215.5	...	...
8 Finance, etc.	114.4	86.2	117.7	88.1	121.3	90.2	...	...
9 Community, social and personal services	415.8	319.4	438.0	334.9	462.7	352.6	...	...
B Producers of government services d	491.3	346.3	502.6	352.2	513.7	357.8	525.0	363.5

680

Germany, Fed. Rep. of

2.16 Stocks of Reproducible Fixed Assets by Kind of Activity, in Constant Prices
(Continued)

Thousand Million Deutsche marks	1986		1987		1988		1989	
	Gross	Net	Gross	Net	Gross	Net	Gross	Net
At constant prices of:1980								
C Other producers	138.2	100.5	141.7	102.3	145.2	104.1	148.8	106.0
4 Land improvement and plantation and orchard development b	...	851.0	1649.8	876.4	1701.8	908.9	1766.1	951.8
5 Producers' durable goods	1606.3	803.9	1555.3	828.4	1606.0	860.4	1668.6	902.1
A Industries	1513.5							
1 Agriculture	109.2	53.1	107.9	52.3	106.8	51.9	106.3	52.1
2 Mining and quarrying c	29.2	15.4	29.4	15.3	29.8	15.5	...	...
3 Manufacturing c	595.5	314.5	610.6	324.8	627.2	335.2	...	...
4 Electricity, gas and water	136.1	73.0	139.4	74.6	141.4	74.9	...	...
5 Construction	36.1	16.3	34.9	15.9	33.9	15.8	...	...
6 Wholesale and retail trade	81.0	40.5	82.3	41.9	85.5	44.9	...	...
7 Transport and communication	215.4	110.2	218.1	110.8	220.8	111.7	...	...
8 Finance, etc.	27.1	15.8	28.7	16.6	30.4	17.6	...	...
9 Community, social and personal services	283.9	165.2	304.1	176.2	330.3	193.0	...	...
B Producers of government services	74.4	37.9	76.0	38.8	77.2	39.4	78.8	40.4
C Other producers	18.4	9.1	18.5	9.1	18.6	9.2	18.6	9.2
6 Breeding stock, dairy cattle, etc.								
Total e	7327.8	4804.1	7513.3	4902.9	7711.8	5012.1	7929.7	5137.7

a) Item 'Producers of government services' does not include government civil engineering works. b) Item 'Non-residential buildings' is included in item 'Other construction'. c) Quarrying is included in item 'Manufacturing'. d) Item 'Land improvement and plantation and orchard development' is included in the data of this table (Stocks of Reproducible Fixed Assets by kind of activity). e) Public underground construction is not contained in the data of this table (Stocks of construction).

2.17 Exports and Imports of Goods and Services, Detail

Million Deutsche marks	1970	1975	1980	1981	1982	1983	1984	1985	1986	1987	1988	1989
Exports of Goods and Services												
1 Exports of merchandise, f.o.b.	122800	219490	333320	384700	413320	416890	467320	517580	508110	506380	547390	615270
2 Transport and communication	11460	22770	34160	38970	41870	41500	45910	44600	43030	43030	44030	49260
3 Insurance service charges	...	...	...	...	...	...	...	...	...	...	...	...
4 Other commodities	...	...	...	...	...	...	...	...	...	...	...	...
5 Adjustments of merchandise exports to change-of-ownership basis	...	...	...	...	...	...	...	...	...	...	...	...
6 Direct purchases in the domestic market by non-residential households	8740	12440	18370	22010	23840	25390	28400	30000	28010	27910	29000	34710
7 Direct purchases in the domestic market by extraterritorial bodies	...	...	...	...	...	...	...	...	...	...	...	...
Total Exports of Goods and Services a	143000	254700	391850	445680	479030	483780	540180	593490	580720	577320	620420	699240
Imports of Goods and Services												
1 Imports of merchandise, c.i.f.	101120	179280	325090	349730	354280	363630	406990	435060	394310	382760	411880	474660

Germany, Fed. Rep. of

2.17 Exports and Imports of Goods and Services, Detail
(Continued)

Million Deutsche marks

	1970	1975	1980	1981	1982	1983	1984	1985	1986	1987	1988	1989
A Imports of merchandise, f.o.b.	101120	179280	325090	349730	354280	363630	406690	435040	389410	382760	411880	474660
B Transport of services on merchandise imports	...	...	...	...	...	...	...	...	...	...	...	...
C Insurance service charges on merchandise imports	...	...	...	...	...	...	...	...	...	...	...	...
2 Adjustments of merchandise imports to change-of-ownership basis	...	...	...	...	...	...	...	...	...	...	...	...
3 Other transport and communication	17300	25030	37920	44340	45780	46800	49550	50860	47730	47740	50930	57170
4 Other insurance service charges	...	...	...	...	...	...	...	...	...	...	...	...
5 Other commodities	...	...	...	...	...	...	...	...	...	...	...	...
6 Direct purchases abroad by government	...	...	...	...	...	...	...	...	...	...	...	...
7 Direct purchases abroad by resident households	10850	22840	38070	40530	40680	40900	43130	41200	42380	45240	47970	49680
Total Imports of Goods and Services [a]	129270	227150	401080	434600	440740	451330	499370	527100	479520	475740	510780	581510
Balance of Goods and Services	13730	27550	-9230	11080	38290	32450	40810	66390	101200	101580	109640	117730
Total Imports and Balance of Goods and Services	143000	254700	391850	445680	479030	483780	540180	593490	580720	577320	620420	699240

a) Exports and imports of goods for purposes of repair and improvement are reduced to the value of these services.

3.11 General Government Production Account: Total and Subsectors

Million Deutsche marks

	1980					1981				
	Total General Government	Central Government	State or Provincial Government	Local Government	Social Security Funds	Total General Government	Central Government	State or Provincial Government	Local Government	Social Security Funds
Gross Output										
1 Sales	40890	2150	9950	28760	30	44550	2470	10650	31350	80
2 Services produced for own use	297790	56620	95380	53960	91830	318160	60580	101060	57460	99060
3 Own account fixed capital formation	280	-	130	150	-	290	-	140	150	-
Gross Output	338960	58770	105460	82870	91860	363000	63050	111850	88960	99140
Gross Input										
Intermediate Consumption	166570	30310	18560	35420	82280	179280	32750	19470	38180	88880
Subtotal: Value Added	172390	28460	86900	47450	9580	183720	30300	92380	50780	10260
1 Indirect taxes, net	240	10	100	120	10	240	10	100	120	10
A Indirect taxes	240	10	100	120	10	240	10	100	120	10
B Less: Subsidies	...	...	...	...	...	...	...	...	...	...
2 Consumption of fixed capital	9490	600	2900	5660	330	10480	660	3200	6260	360
3 Compensation of employees	162660	27850	83900	41670	9240	173000	29630	89080	44400	9890
4 Net Operating surplus	...	...	...	...	...	...	...	...	...	...
Gross Input	338960	58770	105460	82870	91860	363000	63050	111850	88960	99140

	1982					1983				
	Total General Government	Central Government	State or Provincial Government	Local Government	Social Security Funds	Total General Government	Central Government	State or Provincial Government	Local Government	Social Security Funds
Gross Output										
1 Sales	48020	2810	11590	33530	90	50960	2700	12220	35950	90
2 Services produced for own use	326190	62630	104070	58810	100680	336210	65690	107580	58980	103960
3 Own account fixed capital formation	310	-	140	170	-	320	-	150	170	-
Gross Output	374520	65440	115800	92510	100770	387490	68390	119950	95100	104050
Gross Input										
Intermediate Consumption	184940	34800	20250	40010	89880	191700	36780	21240	41020	92660
Subtotal: Value Added	189580	30640	95550	52500	10890	195790	31610	98710	54080	11390
1 Indirect taxes, net	240	10	100	120	10	250	10	110	120	10
A Indirect taxes	240	10	100	120	10	250	10	110	120	10
B Less: Subsidies	...	...	...	...	...	...	...	...	...	...
2 Consumption of fixed capital	11270	720	3440	6710	400	11950	770	3640	7110	430
3 Compensation of employees	178070	29910	92010	45670	10480	183590	30830	94960	46850	10950
4 Net Operating surplus	...	...	...	...	...	...	...	...	...	...
Gross Input	374520	65440	115800	92510	100770	387490	68390	119950	95100	104050

Germany, Fed. Rep. of

3.11 General Government Production Account: Total and Subsectors

Million Deutsche marks

	1984					1985				
	Total General Government	Central Government	State or Provincial Government	Local Government	Social Security Funds	Total General Government	Central Government	State or Provincial Government	Local Government	Social Security Funds
Gross Output										
1 Sales	53190	2750	12990	37370	80	55150	2730	13560	38810	50
2 Services produced for own use	350230	67520	108970	61340	111500	365660	69250	113720	65100	117590
3 Own account fixed capital formation	350	...	160	190	...	360	-	170	190	...
Gross Output	403770	70270	123020	98900	111580	421170	71980	127450	104100	117640
Intermediate Consumption	203700	37960	22420	43380	99940	213710	38310	23660	46220	105520
Subtotal: Value Added	200070	32310	100600	55520	11640	207460	33670	103790	57880	12120
1 Indirect taxes, net	260	10	120	120	10	260	10	120	120	10
A Indirect taxes	260	10	120	120	10	260	10	120	120	10
B Less: Subsidies	...	...	...	...	...	...	...	...	...	...
2 Consumption of fixed capital	12580	820	3840	7450	470	13060	860	4020	7690	520
3 Compensation of employees	187230	31480	96640	47950	11160	194110	32800	99650	50070	11590
4 Net Operating surplus	...	...	...	...	...	...	...	...	...	...
Gross Input	403770	70270	123020	98900	111580	421170	71980	127450	104100	117640

	1986					1987				
	Total General Government	Central Government	State or Provincial Government	Local Government	Social Security Funds	Total General Government	Central Government	State or Provincial Government	Local Government	Social Security Funds
Gross Output										
1 Sales	57990	2640	14410	40880	60	60380	2510	14900	42900	70
2 Services produced for own use	382720	71380	118930	68480	123930	397510	73370	123340	71410	129390
3 Own account fixed capital formation	380	-	180	200	...	400	-	190	210	-
Gross Output	441090	74020	133520	109560	123990	458290	75880	138430	114520	129460
Intermediate Consumption	223700	39070	25200	48310	111120	232110	39740	26360	50050	115960
Subtotal: Value Added	217390	34950	108320	61250	12870	226180	36140	112070	64470	13500
1 Indirect taxes, net	250	-	120	120	10	250	-	120	120	10
A Indirect taxes	250	-	120	120	10	250	-	120	120	10
B Less: Subsidies	...	...	...	...	...	...	...	...	...	...
2 Consumption of fixed capital	13600	890	4190	7970	550	14190	940	4410	8260	580
3 Compensation of employees	203540	34060	104010	53160	12310	211740	35200	107540	56090	12910
4 Net Operating surplus	...	...	...	...	...	...	...	...	...	...
Gross Input	441090	74020	133520	109560	123990	458290	75880	138430	114520	129460

	1988					1989				
	Total General Government	Central Government	State or Provincial Government	Local Government	Social Security Funds	Total General Government	Central Government	State or Provincial Government	Local Government	Social Security Funds
Gross Output										
1 Sales	63730	3190	15490	44970	80	66040	3010	16070	46900	60
2 Services produced for own use	412650	73200	126710	72840	139900	418960	75670	130930	76010	136350
3 Own account fixed capital formation	400	-	190	210	...	410	-	190	220	-
Gross Output	476780	76390	142390	118020	139980	485410	78680	147190	123130	136410
Intermediate Consumption	244350	39380	27370	51600	126000	245290	40460	29200	54550	122080
Subtotal: Value Added	232430	37010	115020	66420	13960	239210	38220	117990	68580	14330
1 Indirect taxes, net	250	-	120	120	10	250	-	120	120	10
A Indirect taxes	250	-	120	120	10	250	-	120	120	10
B Less: Subsidies	...	...	...	...	...	...	...	...	...	...
2 Consumption of fixed capital	14850	990	4630	8530	600	15690	1060	4920	9090	620
3 Compensation of employees	217330	36020	110270	57670	13370	223180	37160	112950	59370	13700
4 Net Operating surplus	...	...	...	...	...	...	...	...	...	...
Gross Input	476780	76390	142390	118020	139980	485410	78680	147190	123130	136410

683

Germany, Fed. Rep. of

3.12 General Government Income and Outlay Account: Total and Subsectors

Million Deutsche marks

1980 | 1981

Receipts

	1980 Total General Government	1980 Central Government	1980 State or Provincial Government	1980 Local Government	1980 Social Security Funds	1981 Total General Government	1981 Central Government	1981 State or Provincial Government	1981 Local Government	1981 Social Security Funds
1 Operating surplus	...	...	...	...	...	...	...	...	...	...
2 Property and entrepreneurial income	15680	5720	1630	4050	5350	19790	8170	2140	4100	6350
3 Taxes, fees and contributions	618280	197140	138570	52040	230530	642820	202860	139780	51060	249120
A Indirect taxes	193330	118820	47060	27510	-	198340	124490	47720	26130	-
B Direct taxes	187750	78320	78970	21460	-	188110	78370	88190	21550	-
* Income	179340	...	...	...	...	179760	...	...	...	...
Other	8410	...	...	...	...	8350	...	...	...	...
C Social security contributions	230200	-	-	-	230200	248840	-	-	-	248840
D Fees, fines and penalties	6940	-	3540	3070	330	7530	-	3870	3380	280
4 Other current transfers	27640	12020	34570	31410	39130	28880	11360	37360	32860	44140
A Casualty insurance claims	1300	-	-	220	1080	1370	-	-	270	1100
B Transfers from other government subsectors	...	920	21830	29390	37250	...	920	23590	30630	42200
C Transfers from the rest of the world	7930	7820	110	...	...	7030	6900	130	...	...
D Other transfers, except imputed	...	...	...	...	...	...	...	...	...	...
E Imputed unfunded employee pension and welfare contributions	18410	3280	12530	1800	800	19980	3540	13640	1960	840
Total Current Receipts	661600	214880	174770	87500	275010	699090	222390	172980	88020	299610

Disbursements

	1980 Total	1980 Central	1980 State	1980 Local	1980 SS	1981 Total	1981 Central	1981 State	1981 Local	1981 SS
1 Government final consumption expenditure	277790	56620	95380	59360	66430	318160	60580	101060	57460	99060
2 Property income	27480	14000	8560	5970	20	34500	18020	10490	6880	80
A Interest	27480	14000	8560	5970	20	34500	18020	10490	6880	80
B Net land rent and royalties	-	-	-	-	-	-	-	-	-	-
3 Subsidies	30530	21130	7050	1390	960	29130	20010	6750	1470	900
4 Other current transfers	278610	116650	58990	14280	178180	302170	128620	62760	15760	192370
A Casualty insurance premiums, net	3780	3560	-	220	-	3750	3480	-	270	-
B Transfers to other government subsectors	-	58550	28620	2320	-	-	64690	30060	2590	-
C Social security benefits	174390	-	-	-	174390	188440	-	-	-	188440
D Social assistance grants	43210	28630	8870	5710	-	48420	32530	9160	6280	-
E Unfunded employee pension and welfare benefits	26930	7800	14670	3660	800	28660	8090	15800	3930	840
F Transfers to private non-profit institutions serving households	8400	1070	5090	2240	-	9060	1060	5440	2560	-
G Other transfers n.e.c.	...	...	...	...	...	...	...	...	...	...
H Transfers to the rest of the world	21900	17040	1740	2990	130	23840	18770	1850	3090	130
Net saving	27190	6480	4790	4020	7030	-4840	-1780	6450	7200	...
Total Current Disbursements and Net Saving	661600	214880	174770	87500	275010	699090	222390	172980	88020	299610

1982 | 1983

Receipts

	1982 Total	1982 Central	1982 State	1982 Local	1982 SS	1983 Total	1983 Central	1983 State	1983 Local	1983 SS
1 Operating surplus	...	...	...	...	...	...	...	...	...	...
2 Property and entrepreneurial income	29110	16930	2570	4390	6310	29710	17980	2560	4620	5570
3 Taxes, fees and contributions	667020	208380	144310	52090	265240	692880	215760	152430	55150	269540
A Indirect taxes	201890	125900	49450	26540	-	214510	132120	53690	28700	-
B Direct taxes	193180	84800	90700	22000	-	200360	83640	94120	22600	-
Income	184450	...	...	...	...	191440	...	...	...	...
Other	8730	...	...	...	...	8920	...	...	...	...
C Social security contributions	263950	-	-	-	263950	269180	-	-	-	269180
D Fees, fines and penalties	8000	-	4160	3550	290	8830	-	4620	3850	360

Germany, Fed. Rep. of

3.12 General Government Income and Outlay Account: Total and Subsectors (Continued)

Million Deutsche marks

	1982					1983				
	Total General Government	Central Government	State or Provincial Government	Local Government	Social Security Funds	Total General Government	Central Government	State or Provincial Government	Local Government	Social Security Funds

Receipts

	1982					1983				
1 Operating surplus	...	...	...	...	...	...	...	...	...	...
2 Property and entrepreneurial income	30860	18530	2850	5090	5540	33650	20090	2750	5350	5740
3 Taxes, fees and contributions	731660	227110	162490	58800	283260	767020	255570	171390	62340	277720
A Indirect taxes	226290	137500	57740	30960	-	230290	138470	59000	32820	-
B Direct taxes	213020	98610	99710	23700	-	229640	97100	107210	25330	-
Income	204430	8590	...	...	...	221220	...	...	...	...
Other	8590	...	...	...	8420	...	...	...	...	...
C Social security contributions	282760	-	-	-	282760	297230	-	-	-	297230
D Fees, fines and penalties	9860	-	5040	4140	500	9860	5180	4190	490	...
4 Other current transfers	33190	14470	38480	34060	4280	34010	14570	39680	36070	4430
A Casualty insurance claims	1450	...	270	1180	1420	-	260	1160	...	...
B Transfers from other government subsectors	...	880	23460	31650	40310	...	950	23940	33560	41990
C Transfers from the rest of the world	9910	9800	110	...	9730	9600	130	...	...	...
D Other transfers, except imputed	...	...	...	...	...	...	...	...	...	...
E Imputed unfunded employee pension and welfare contributions	21830	3790	14910	2140	990	22660	4020	15610	2250	980
Total Current Receipts	795170	260110	203820	97950	331280	834680	270040	213820	103760	347590

Disbursements

	1982					1983				
1 Government final consumption expenditure	350230	67520	109870	61340	111500	365660	69250	113720	65100	117590
2 Property income	51570	28140	17280	7280	20	54180	29570	18510	7170	20
A Interest	42940	22450	13550	8010	20	49070	26820	15720	7540	10
B Net land rent and royalties	...	...	...	...	460	31780	22320	7490	1570	400
3 Subsidies	29420	20710	6760	1490	460	...	...	...	...	...
4 Other current transfers	319750	133570	64030	17710	207670	325410	129980	63030	16990	211260
A Casualty insurance premiums, net	3800	3530	-	270	-	3830	3550	-	280	-
B Transfers to other government subsectors	68640	30630	2960	...	...	63210	29540	3100	...	...
C Social security benefits	203430	-	-	-	203430	208830	-	-	-	208830
D Social assistance grants	48700	32430	9470	6600	...	48400	32600	8950	6850	-
E Unfunded employee pension and welfare benefits	29670	8120	16400	4170	980	30250	8080	16800	4380	990
F Transfers to private non-profit institutions serving households	9270	1160	5520	2590	...	9560	1350	5950	2260	-
G Other transfers n.e.c.	...	...	...	...	...	...	...	...	...	...
H Transfers to the rest of the world	24880	19690	1810	3260	120	26540	21190	1790	120	3440
Net saving	6990	-4880	-3150	4910	9750	12350	2940	-100	2270	2240
Total Current Disbursements and Net Saving	724930	234480	185260	89930	318580	754820	247750	193720	92350	317870

	1984					1985				
	Total General Government	Central Government	State or Provincial Government	Local Government	Social Security Funds	Total General Government	Central Government	State or Provincial Government	Local Government	Social Security Funds

Receipts

	1984					1985				
1 Operating surplus	...	...	...	...	...	...	...	...	...	...
2 Property and entrepreneurial income	30860	18530	2850	5090	5540	33650	20090	2750	5350	5740
3 Taxes, fees and contributions	731660	227110	162490	58800	283260	767020	255570	171390	62340	277720
A Indirect taxes	226290	137500	57740	30960	-	230290	138470	59000	32820	-
B Direct taxes	213020	98610	99710	23700	-	229640	97100	107210	25330	-
Income	204430	...	...	...	...	221220	...	...	...	...
Other	8590	...	...	...	8420	...	...	...	...	...
C Social security contributions	282760	-	-	-	282760	297230	-	-	-	297230
D Fees, fines and penalties	9860	-	5040	4140	500	9860	5180	4190	490	-
4 Other current transfers	33190	14470	38480	34060	4280	34010	14570	39680	36070	4430
A Casualty insurance claims	1450	-	270	1180	1420	-	260	1160	...	...
B Transfers from other government subsectors	-	880	23460	31650	40310	-	950	23940	33560	41990
C Transfers from the rest of the world	9910	9800	110	...	9730	9600	130	...	...	...
D Other transfers, except imputed	...	...	...	...	...	...	...	...	...	...
E Imputed unfunded employee pension and welfare contributions	21830	3790	14910	2140	990	22660	4020	15610	2250	980
Total Current Receipts	795170	260110	203820	97950	331280	834680	270040	213820	103760	347590

Disbursements

	1984					1985				
1 Government final consumption expenditure	350230	67520	109870	61340	111500	365660	69250	113720	65100	117590
2 Property income	51570	28140	17280	7280	20	54180	29570	18510	7170	20

685

Germany, Fed. Rep. of

3.12 General Government Income and Outlay Account: Total and Subsectors
(Continued)

Million Deutsche marks

	1984					1985				
	Total General Government	Central Government	State or Provincial Government	Local Government	Social Security Funds	Total General Government	Central Government	State or Provincial Government	Local Government	Social Security Funds

Receipts

1 Operating surplus	...	...	...	...	...	...	...	...	...	...
2 Property and entrepreneurial income	32830	20660	2150	5510	5550	26040	15070	1010	5400	5560
3 Taxes, fees and contributions	796870	240280	178190	64420	313780	828130	250630	185160	66290	326080
A Indirect taxes	258330	140460	95960	34220	-	147830	64350	33660	-	-
B Direct taxes	237040	99820	111090	26130	-	245940	103000	114910	28030	-
Income	227440	...	...	...	...	235850	...	...	...	...
Other	9600	...	...	...	...	10090	...	...	...	...
C Social security contributions	313390	-	-	-	313390	325840	-	-	-	325840
D Fees, fines and penalties	10110	5450	4270	390	1070	-	5900	4570	240	
4 Other current transfers	36750	16240	41400	37410	44260	36230	15200	42940	39290	46490
A Casualty insurance claims	1450	-	280	1170	1490	-	-	280	1210	
B Transfers from other government subsectors	-	940	48460	34750	42030	...	890	26110	36650	44130
C Transfers from the rest of the world	11290	11080	210	...	...	10090	9980	110	...	...
D Other transfers, except imputed										
E Imputed unfunded employee pension and welfare contributions	24010	4220	16350	2380	1060	24650	4330	16720	2450	1150
Total Current Receipts	866450	277180	221740	107540	363600	890400	280600	229110	110950	378130

Disbursements

1 Government final consumption expenditure	382720	71380	118930	68480	123930	397510	73370	123340	71410	129390
2 Property income	56130	30680	19560	6920	20	56780	31310	19700	6740	30
A Interest	56130	30680	19560	6920	20	56780	31310	19700	6740	30
B Net land rent and royalties										
3 Subsidies	41340	28480	10220	1840	800	44780	31190	10600	1970	1020

	1986					1987				
	Total General Government	Central Government	State or Provincial Government	Local Government	Social Security Funds	Total General Government	Central Government	State or Provincial Government	Local Government	Social Security Funds

A Interest	51570	28140	17280	7280	20	54180	29570	18510	7170	20
B Net land rent and royalties										
3 Subsidies	36210	25310	8840	1610	450	37810	25350	10240	1710	510
4 Other current transfers	333900	132340	63380	17600	216880	341050	135060	66150	19060	221190
A Casualty insurance premiums, net	3960	3690	-	270	-	3840	3580	-	260	-
B Transfers to other government subsectors	-	62260	10100	3030	-	-	64420	32770	3250	-
C Social security benefits	210200	-	-	-	210200	215260	-	-	-	215260
D Social assistance grants	48340	33720	7280	7340	-	49070	33400	7240	8430	-
E Unfunded employee pension and welfare benefits	30420	7860	17170	4400	990	31440	7960	17950	4550	980
F Transfers to private non-profit institutions serving households	10020	1360	6250	2410	-	10230	1330	6500	2400	-
G Other transfers n.e.c.	...	...	...	...	...	...	...	...	...	...
H Transfers to the rest of the world	30960	23450	1670	150	5690	31210	24400	1690	170	4950
Net saving	23800	6800	4450	10120	2430	39980	11780	5200	10720	8280
Total Current Disbursements and Net Saving	795710	260110	203820	97500	331280	834680	271040	213820	103760	347590

989

Germany, Fed. Rep. of

3.12 General Government Income and Outlay Account: Total and Subsectors
(Continued)

Million Deutsche marks

	1986					1987				
	Total General Government	Central Government	State or Provincial Government	Local Government	Social Security Funds	Total General Government	Central Government	State or Provincial Government	Local Government	Social Security Funds
4　Other current transfers	352730	139160	69090	20900	226140	369820	144700	73230	22140	237440
A　Casualty insurance premiums, net	3910	3630	-	280	-	4070	3790	-	280	-
B　Transfers to other government subsectors	-	65210	33950	3400	-	-	68280	35810	3600	-
C　Social security benefits	220980	-	-	-	220980	232050	-	-	-	232050
D　Social assistance grants	52980	35220	8100	9660	-	55500	36400	8880	10220	-
E　Unfunded employee pension and welfare benefits	32830	8180	18820	4770	1060	34330	8360	19830	4990	1150
F　Transfers to private non-profit institutions serving households	10850	1640	6600	2610	-	11740	1820	7110	2810	-
G　Other transfers n.e.c.	...	...	...	...	...	...	...	...	...	...
H　Transfers to the rest of the world	31180	25280	1620	180	4100	32130	26050	1600	240	4240
Net saving	33530	7480	3940	9400	12710	21510	330	2240	8690	10250
Total Current Disbursements and Net Saving	866450	277180	221740	107540	363600	890400	280900	229110	110950	378130

	1988					1989				
	Total General Government	Central Government	State or Provincial Government	Local Government	Social Security Funds	Total General Government	Central Government	State or Provincial Government	Local Government	Social Security Funds
Receipts										
1　Operating surplus	...	...	...	...	...	...	...	...	...	...
2　Property and entrepreneurial income	18750	8360	240	5350	5670	29940	18650	480	5680	6030
3　Taxes, fees and contributions	865320	260910	192540	70430	341440	929510	287030	209390	75370	357720
A　Indirect taxes	257220	153610	66960	36650	-	278160	168290	71140	38730	-
B　Direct taxes	255440	107300	119220	28920	-	281840	118740	131600	31500	-
Income	245280	...	...	...	...	270850	...	...	...	...
Other	10160	...	...	...	...	10990	...	...	...	...
C　Social security contributions	341220	-	-	-	341220	357330	-	-	-	357330
D　Fees, fines and penalties	11440	-	6360	4860	220	12180	-	6650	5140	390
4　Other current transfers	39410	17660	44670	40510	50050	38500	16210	47210	42260	53680
A　Casualty insurance claims	1530	-	-	290	1240	1540	-	-	320	1220
B　Transfers from other government subsectors	...	910	27250	37690	47630	...	920	29340	39350	51250
C　Transfers from the rest of the world	12470	12300	170	...	...	10850	10680	170	...	...
D　Other transfers, except imputed	...	...	...	...	...	...	...	...	...	...
E　Imputed unfunded employee pension and welfare contributions	25410	4450	17250	2530	1180	26110	4610	17700	2590	1210
Total Current Receipts	923480	286930	237450	116290	397160	997950	321890	257080	123310	417430
Disbursements										
1　Government final consumption expenditure	412650	73200	126710	72840	139900	418960	75670	130930	76010	136350
2　Property income	58990	32740	20390	6700	30	59490	32460	21100	6800	30
A　Interest	58990	32740	20390	6700	30	59490	32460	21100	6800	30
B　Net land rent and royalties	...	...	...	...	...	...	...	...	...	...
3　Subsidies	47670	34010	10560	2060	1040	45410	30980	11440	2160	830
4　Other current transfers	390360	153890	75770	23500	250680	405920	160930	80050	25480	260320
A　Casualty insurance premiums, net	4050	3760	-	290	-	4110	3790	-	320	-
B　Transfers to other government subsectors	-	72810	36830	3840	-	-	78040	38610	4210	-
C　Social security benefits	245000	-	-	-	245000	254370	-	-	-	254370
D　Social assistance grants	56000	35740	9300	10960	-	58130	36670	9780	11680	-
E　Unfunded employee pension and welfare benefits	35480	8460	20700	5140	1180	36770	8630	21610	5320	1210
F　Transfers to private non-profit institutions serving households	12270	1890	7400	2980	-	13040	2110	7760	3170	-
G　Other transfers n.e.c.	...	...	...	...	...	...	...	...	...	...
H　Transfers to the rest of the world	37560	31230	1540	290	4500	39500	31690	2290	780	4740
Net saving	13810	-6910	4020	11190	5510	68170	21850	13560	12860	19900
Total Current Disbursements and Net Saving	923480	286930	237450	116290	397160	997950	321890	257080	123310	417430

Germany, Fed. Rep. of

3.13 General Government Capital Accumulation Account: Total and Subsectors

Million Deutsche marks

	1980 Total General Government	1980 Central Government	1980 State or Provincial Government	1980 Local Government	1980 Social Security Funds	1981 Total General Government	1981 Central Government	1981 State or Provincial Government	1981 Local Government	1981 Social Security Funds
Finance of Gross Accumulation										
1 Gross saving	36680	7080	7690	17560	4350	17510	-4180	1420	12710	7560
A Consumption of fixed capital	9490	600	2900	5660	330	10480	660	3200	6250	360
B Net saving	27190	6480	4790	11900	4020	7030	-4840	-1780	6450	7200
2 Capital transfers	7230	260	10830	19620	1560	7080	460	10320	18270	930
A From other government subsectors	170	-	9570	15290	10	140	-	8990	13520	50
B From other resident sectors	7090	20	1190	4330	1550	6990	280	1280	4550	880
C From rest of the world	140	70	70	-	-	90	40	50	-	-
Finance of Gross Accumulation	43910	7340	18520	37180	5910	24590	-3720	11740	30980	8490
Gross Accumulation										
1 Gross capital formation	50830	6930	8870	34290	740	5850	-	8370	32370	1080
A Increase in stocks	500	500	-	-	-	200	200	-	-	-
B Gross fixed capital formation	50330	6430	8870	34290	740	5650	-	8370	32370	1080
Own account	280	-	130	150	-	290	-	140	150	-
Other	50050	6430	8740	34140	740	5360	-	8230	32220	1080
2 Purchases of land, net	2760	420	450	1810	80	2350	400	370	1530	50
3 Purchases of intangible assets, net	...	...	...	...	...	...	...	...	...	...
4 Capital transfers	33290	25020	26830	5360	1120	31220	22860	24970	5230	1060
A To other government subsectors	-	9180	14860	900	100	-	8500	13380	940	80
B To other resident sectors	29840	12400	11960	4460	1020	28980	12130	11580	4290	980
C To rest of the world	3450	3440	10	-	-	2240	2230	10	-	-
Net lending	-42970	-25030	-17630	-4280	3970	-56650	-32830	-21970	-8150	6300
Gross Accumulation	43910	7340	18520	37180	5910	24590	-3720	11740	30980	8490

	1982 Total General Government	1982 Central Government	1982 State or Provincial Government	1982 Local Government	1982 Social Security Funds	1983 Total General Government	1983 Central Government	1983 State or Provincial Government	1983 Local Government	1983 Social Security Funds
Finance of Gross Accumulation										
1 Gross saving	17900	-4160	290	11620	10150	24300	3710	3540	14380	2670
A Consumption of fixed capital	11270	720	3440	6710	400	11950	770	3640	7110	430
B Net saving	6630	-4880	-3150	4910	9750	12350	2940	-100	7270	2240
2 Capital transfers	6210	220	10420	17370	50	6340	270	10500	17050	70
A From other government subsectors	150	-	8830	12820	50	160	-	8760	12560	70
B From other resident sectors	6100	20	1530	4550	-	6190	20	1680	4490	-
C From rest of the world	110	50	60	-	-	150	90	60	-	-
Finance of Gross Accumulation	24110	-3940	10710	28990	10200	30640	3980	14040	31430	2740
Gross Accumulation										
1 Gross capital formation	43220	5230	8280	28540	1170	40030	5460	8120	25150	1300
A Increase in stocks	-	-	-	-	-	-	-	-	-	-
B Gross fixed capital formation	43220	5230	8280	28540	1170	40030	5460	8120	25150	1300
Own account	310	-	140	170	-	320	-	150	170	-
Other	42910	5230	8140	28370	1170	39710	5460	7970	24980	1300
2 Purchases of land, net	2040	420	420	1160	40	1740	450	390	910	-10
3 Purchases of intangible assets, net	...	...	...	...	...	...	...	...	...	...
4 Capital transfers	31330	23920	23520	4600	1140	31180	24320	23250	3650	1510
A To other government subsectors	-	8190	12540	1040	80	-	8050	12380	1020	100
B To other resident sectors	29020	13430	10970	3560	1060	28930	14020	10870	2630	1410
C To rest of the world	2310	2300	10	-	-	2250	2250	-	-	-
Net lending	-52480	-33510	-21510	-5310	7850	-42310	-26250	-17720	1720	-60
Gross Accumulation	24110	-3940	10710	28990	10200	30640	3980	14040	31430	2740

Germany, Fed. Rep. of

3.13 General Government Capital Accumulation Account: Total and Subsectors

Million Deutsche marks

	1984					1985				
	Total General Government	Central Government	State or Provincial Government	Local Government	Social Security Funds	Total General Government	Central Government	State or Provincial Government	Local Government	Social Security Funds
Finance of Gross Accumulation											
1 Gross saving	36380	7620	8290	17570	2900	49070	12640	9220	18410	8800
A Consumption of fixed capital	12580	820	3840	7450	470	13090	860	4020	7690	520
B Net saving	23800	6800	4450	10120	2430	35980	11780	5200	10720	8280
2 Capital transfers	5810	210	10070	16480	30	5670	270	11360	16990	20
A From other government subsectors	13270	140	9150	12560	30	130	...	9550	13270	20
B From other resident sectors	5740	30	1790	3920	-	5490	30	1740	3720	-
C From rest of the world	70	40	30	-	-	180	110	70	-	-
Finance of Gross Accumulation	42190	7830	19260	34050	2930	54740	12910	20580	35400	8820
Gross Accumulation											
1 Gross capital formation	40130	5890	8410	24910	1130	40720	5680	8630	25080	1330
A Increase in stocks	-	-	-	-	-	-	-	-	-	-
B Gross fixed capital formation	40130	5890	8410	24910	1130	40720	5680	8630	25080	1330
Own account	350	-	160	190	-	360	-	170	190	-
Other	39780	5890	8250	24720	1130	40360	5680	8460	24890	1330
2 Purchases of land, net	1610	400	330	840	40	1890	430	360	1080	20
3 Purchases of intangible assets, net	...	...	...	...	...	...	...	...	...	...
4 Capital transfers	34170	24710	24870	4440	2030	33050	24210	24640	4790	2380
A To other government subsectors	8430	-	12320	1020	110	-	8440	12680	1090	560
B To other resident sectors	31820	18390	12550	3420	1920	30440	12980	11940	3700	1820
C To rest of the world	2350	2350	-	-	-	2610	2590	20	-	-
Net lending	-33720	-22960	-14350	3860	-270	-17410	-13050	-20920	4450	5090
Gross Accumulation	42190	7830	19260	34050	2930	54740	12910	20580	35400	8820

	1986					1987				
	Total General Government	Central Government	State or Provincial Government	Local Government	Social Security Funds	Total General Government	Central Government	State or Provincial Government	Local Government	Social Security Funds
Finance of Gross Accumulation											
1 Gross saving	47130	8370	8130	17370	13260	35700	1270	6650	16950	10830
A Consumption of fixed capital	13600	890	4190	7970	550	14190	940	4410	8260	580
B Net saving	33530	7480	3940	9400	12710	21510	330	2240	8690	10250
2 Capital transfers	5870	320	10860	17990	30	6350	240	11890	18710	30
A From other government subsectors	15020	210	8810	14400	-	140	-	9330	15020	30
B From other resident sectors	5710	20	2100	3590	-	6160	20	2450	3690	-
C From rest of the world	160	90	70	-	-	190	80	110	-	-
Finance of Gross Accumulation	53000	8690	19110	35360	13290	42050	1510	18540	35660	10860
Gross Accumulation											
1 Gross capital formation	44890	6000	8490	28300	1100	46010	6140	9690	29240	940
A Increase in stocks	-	-	-	-	-	-	-	-	-	-
B Gross fixed capital formation	44890	6000	8490	28300	1100	46010	6140	9660	29240	940
Own account	380	-	180	200	-	400	-	190	210	-
Other	44510	6000	8310	28100	1100	45610	6140	9500	29030	940
2 Purchases of land, net	1980	410	390	1180	-	1990	480	360	1130	20
3 Purchases of intangible assets, net	...	...	...	...	...	...	...	...	...	...
4 Capital transfers	31450	22740	24060	5140	2960	23050	23080	25120	5120	3250
A To other government subsectors	-	7930	13270	900	1350	-	8430	13680	890	1520
B To other resident sectors	29100	12490	10760	4240	1610	27790	12390	11440	4230	1730
C To rest of the world	2350	2320	30	-	-	2260	2260	-	-	-
Net lending	-25320	-20460	-14830	740	9230	-38000	-28190	-16830	170	6650
Gross Accumulation	53000	8690	19110	35360	13290	42050	1510	18540	35660	10860

Germany, Fed. Rep. of

3.13 General Government Capital Accumulation Account: Total and Subsectors

Million Deutsche marks

	1988					1989				
	Total General Government	Central Government	State or Provincial Government	Local Government	Social Security Funds	Total General Government	Central Government	State or Provincial Government	Local Government	Social Security Funds
Finance of Gross Accumulation										
1 Gross saving	28660	-5920	8650	19820	6110	83860	22910	18480	21950	20520
A Consumption of fixed capital	14850	990	4630	8630	600	15690	1060	4920	9090	620
B Net saving	13810	-6910	4020	11190	5510	68170	21850	13560	12860	19900
2 Capital transfers	6690	200	11850	18830	30	6470	300	14200	19370	30
A From other government subsectors	-	120	9160	14910	30	-	100	11850	15450	30
B From other resident sectors	6540	10	2610	3920	-	6210	20	2270	3920	-
C From rest of the world	150	70	80	-	-	260	180	80	-	-
Finance of Gross Accumulation	35350	-5720	20500	38650	6140	90330	23210	32680	41320	20550
Gross Accumulation										
1 Gross capital formation	47190	6170	9750	30240	1030	50810	6490	10540	32670	1110
A Increase in stocks	-	-	-	-	-	-	-	-	-	-
B Gross fixed capital formation	47190	6170	9750	30240	1030	50810	6490	10540	32670	1110
Own account	400	-	190	210	-	410	-	190	220	-
Other	46790	6170	9560	30030	1030	50400	6490	10350	32450	1110
2 Purchases of land, net	1670	190	430	990	60	1730	250	410	1060	10
3 Purchases of intangible assets, net	...	...	...	...	...	...	...	...	...	...
4 Capital transfers	31750	22360	25260	4850	3500	32330	25330	26410	4910	3110
A To other government subsectors	-	8240	13530	960	1490	-	10890	14030	980	1530
B To other resident sectors	29260	11630	11730	3890	2010	29430	11540	12380	3930	1580
C To rest of the world	2490	2490	-	-	-	2900	2900	-	-	-
Net lending	-45260	-34440	-14940	2570	1550	5460	-8860	-4680	2680	16320
Gross Accumulation	35350	-5720	20500	38650	6140	90330	23210	32680	41320	20550

3.14 General Government Capital Finance Account, Total and Subsectors

Million Deutsche marks

	1980					1981				
	Total General Government	Central Government	State or Provincial Government	Local Government	Social Security Funds	Total General Government	Central Government	State or Provincial Government	Local Government	Social Security Funds
Acquisition of Financial Assets										
1 Gold and SDRs	-	-	...	...	-	-	-	...	...	-
2 Currency and transferable deposits	-3230	-3090	...	...	-140	-220	-570	...	...	350
3 Other deposits	9730	6560	...	...	3170	10210	6800	...	...	3410
4 Bills and bonds, short term	10	10	...	...	-	-	-	...	...	-
5 Bonds, long term	-50	-300	...	...	250	20	270	...	...	-250
6 Corporate equity securities	910	910	...	...	-	860	860	...	...	-
7 Short-term loans, n.e.c.	400	-280	...	...	680	400	220	...	...	180
8 Long-term loans, n.e.c.	4880	4780	...	...	100	7500	4820	...	...	2680
9 Other receivables	...	...	...	...	...	...	...	...	...	...
10 Other assets	40	40	...	...	-	60	60	...	...	-
Total Acquisition of Financial Assets	12690	8630	...	...	4060	18830	12460	...	...	6370
Incurrence of Liabilities										
1 Currency and transferable deposits	-	-	...	...	-	-	-	...	...	-
2 Other deposits	-	-	...	...	-	-	-	...	...	-
3 Bills and bonds, short term	-2170	-2170	...	...	-	4720	4720	...	...	-
4 Bonds, long term	2140	2140	...	...	-	-4310	-4310	...	...	-
5 Short-term loans, n.e.c.	6150	6070	...	...	80	7580	7510	...	...	70
6 Long-term loans, n.e.c.	49470	49460	...	...	10	67440	67440	...	...	-
7 Other payables	...	...	...	...	...	...	...	...	...	...
8 Other liabilities	-	-	...	...	-	-	-	...	...	-
Total Incurrence of Liabilities	55590	55500	...	...	90	75430	75360	...	...	70
Net Lending	-42900	-46870	...	...	3970	-56600	-62900	...	...	6300
Incurrence of Liabilities and Net Worth	12690	8630	...	...	4060	18830	12460	...	...	6370

Germany, Fed. Rep. of

3.14 General Government Capital Finance Account, Total and Subsectors

Million Deutsche marks

1982 / 1983

	1982					1983				
	Total General Government	Central Government	State or Provincial Government	Local Government	Social Security Funds	Total General Government	Central Government	State or Provincial Government	Local Government	Social Security Funds

Acquisition of Financial Assets

1 Gold and SDRs	-	-				-	-			
2 Currency and transferable deposits	440	910			-470	2680	1800			880
3 Other deposits	3890	2360			1530	6850	9140			-2290
4 Bills and bonds, short term	10	10			-	-30	-30			-
5 Bonds, long term	1590	-450			2040	750	360			390
6 Corporate equity securities	200	200			-	730	730			-
7 Short-term loans, n.e.c.	30	-480			510	1010	190			820
8 Long-term loans, n.e.c.	4940	4940			4100	1380	1190			190
9 Other receivables	...	...			...	...	...			...
10 Other assets	110	110				80	80			-
Total Acquisition of Financial Assets	15310	7600			7710	13450	13460			-10

Incurrence of Liabilities

1 Currency and transferable deposits										
2 Other deposits	-	-			-	-	-			-
3 Bills and bonds, short term	8330	8330			-	-1290	-1290			-
4 Bonds, long term	24930	24930			-	33780	33780			-
5 Short-term loans, n.e.c.	-930	-770			-160	-3850	-3890			40
6 Long-term loans, n.e.c.	35410	35400			10	27130	27130			-
7 Other payables	...	...			...	...	...			...
8 Other liabilities	67740	67890			-150	55770	55730			40
Total Incurrence of Liabilities										
Net Lending	-52430	-60290			7860	-42320	-42270			-50
Incurrence of Liabilities and Net Worth	15310	7600			7710	13450	13460			-10

1984 / 1985

	1984					1985				
	Total General Government	Central Government	State or Provincial Government	Local Government	Social Security Funds	Total General Government	Central Government	State or Provincial Government	Local Government	Social Security Funds

Acquisition of Financial Assets

1 Gold and SDRs										
2 Currency and transferable deposits	530	260			270	2260	1700			560
3 Other deposits	6710	9160			-2450	13320	8930			4390
4 Bills and bonds, short term	70	70			-	20	20			-
5 Bonds, long term	130	780			-650	-860	-240			-620
6 Corporate equity securities	680	680			-	760	760			-
7 Short-term loans, n.e.c.	1050	-10			1060	740	330			410
8 Long-term loans, n.e.c.	4610	3250			1360	5480	5030			450
9 Other receivables	...	...			...	...	...			...
10 Other assets	50	50			-	90	90			-
Total Acquisition of Financial Assets	13830	14240			-410	21810	16620			5190

Incurrence of Liabilities

1 Currency and transferable deposits										
2 Other deposits	-	-			-	-	-			-
3 Bills and bonds, short term	-6260	-6260			-	-480	-480			-
4 Bonds, long term	34700	34700			-	38120	38120			-
5 Short-term loans, n.e.c.	-1330	-1370			40	-2190	-2200			10
6 Long-term loans, n.e.c.	20410	20590			-180	7280	7220			60
7 Other payables	...	...			...	...	...			...
8 Other liabilities	-	-			-	-	-			-
Total Incurrence of Liabilities	47520	47660			-140	42730	42660			70
Net Lending	-33690	-33420			-270	-20920	-26040			5120
Incurrence of Liabilities and Net Worth	13830	14240			-410	21810	16620			5190

Germany, Fed. Rep. of

3.14 General Government Capital Finance Account, Total and Subsectors

Million Deutsche marks

	1986				1987			
	Total General Government	Central Government	State or Provincial Government	Local Government	Total General Government	Central Government	State or Provincial Government	Local Government	Social Security Funds

Acquisition of Financial Assets

1 Gold and SDRs	...	...	...	...	...	...	...	...	...
2 Currency and transferable deposits	-2010	-910	...	-1100	3670	3590	...	80
3 Other deposits	12590	4700	...	7890	5300	5360	...	-60
4 Bills and bonds, short term	20	20	-	-	-40	-40	...	...
5 Bonds, long term	-730	-20	...	-710	-870	-200	...	-670
6 Corporate equity securities	160	160	-	-	-2160	-2160	...	...
7 Short-term loans, n.e.c.	1210	620	...	590	3320	3190	...	130
8 Long-term loans, n.e.c.	7620	4850	...	2770	7530	500	...	7030
9 Other receivables	...	...	...	...	...	...	...	...
10 Other assets	80	80	-	...	280	280	...	...
Total Acquisition of Financial Assets	18940	9500	...	9440	17030	10520	...	6510

Incurrence of Liabilities

1 Currency and transferable deposits	...	...	...	...	...	...	...	...
2 Other deposits	-	-	-	-	-	-	...	...
3 Bills and bonds, short term	-1820	-1820	-	-	-3200	-3200	...	...
4 Bonds, long term	51190	51190	-	-	49910	49910	...	...
5 Short-term loans, n.e.c.	2470	2450	...	20	-1650	-1590	...	-60
6 Long-term loans, n.e.c.	-7590	-7620	...	30	7600	7610	...	-10
7 Other payables	...	...	...	...	...	...	...	...
8 Other liabilities	...	...	...	...	...	...	...	...
Total Incurrence of Liabilities	44250	44200	...	50	52660	52730	...	-70
Net Lending	-25310	-34700	...	9390	-35620	-42210	...	6580
Incurrence of Liabilities and Net Worth	18940	9500	...	9440	17030	10520	...	6510

3.21 Corporate and Quasi-Corporate Enterprise Production Account: Total and Sectors

Million Deutsche marks

	1980				1981				1982			
	TOTAL	Non-Financial	Financial	ADDENDUM: Total, including Unincorporated Corporate and Quasi-Corporate Enterprises	TOTAL	Non-Financial	Financial	ADDENDUM: Total, including Unincorporated Corporate and Quasi-Corporate Enterprises	TOTAL	Non-Financial	Financial	ADDENDUM: Total, including Unincorporated Corporate and Quasi-Corporate Enterprises

Gross Output

1 Output for sale												
2 Imputed bank service charge												
3 Own-account fixed capital formation												
Gross Output	3446410	3346040	100370	...	3629710	3517560	112150	...	3733840	3607080	126560	...

Gross Input

Intermediate consumption
1 Imputed banking service charge	2277030	2189120	87910	...	2416300	2316270	100030	...	2472370	2359270	113100	...
2 Other intermediate consumption	59940	59940	-	...	63260	63260	-	...	73470	73470	-	...
	2223090	2189120	33970	...	2353040	2316270	36770	...	2398900	2359270	39630	...
Subtotal: Value Added	1169380	1156920	12460	...	1213410	1201290	12120	...	1261270	1247810	13460	...
1 Indirect taxes, net	5230	4750	5070	...	5490	4820	5870	...	56020	48570	7450	...
A Indirect taxes	8160	8090	5070	...	8220	7350	5870	...	85440	77990	7450	...
B Less: Subsidies	3050	3050	-	...	29130	29130	-	...	29420	29420	...	...
2 Consumption of fixed capital	161670	158860	2810	...	175340	172230	3110	...	188830	184440	3390	...
3 Compensation of employees	665580	621210	34370	...	682100	645790	36310	...	694450	655070	38830	...
4 Net operating surplus	299500	329290	-29790	...	301880	335050	-33170	...	359270	359730	-35760	...
Gross Input	3446410	3346040	100370	...	3629710	3517560	112150	...	3733840	3607080	126560	...

Gross Output

	1983				1984				1985			
1 Output for sale	3866590	3729390	137200	...	4110300	3965480	144820	...	4287510	4136500	151010	...
2 Imputed bank service charge												
3 Own-account fixed capital formation												
Gross Output												

692

Germany, Fed. Rep. of

3.21 Corporate and Quasi-Corporate Enterprise Production Account: Total and Sectors
(Continued)

Million Deutsche marks

	1983 TOTAL	1983 Non-Financial	1983 Financial	1983 ADDENDUM: Corporate and Quasi-Corporate Enterprises Total, including Unincorporated	1984 TOTAL	1984 Non-Financial	1984 Financial	1984 ADDENDUM: Total, including Unincorporated	1985 TOTAL	1985 Non-Financial	1985 Financial	1985 ADDENDUM: Total, including Unincorporated
Intermediate consumption	2545730	2421890	123840	...	2721200	2591700	129500	...	2833950	2700210	133740	...
1 Imputed banking service charge	8170	-	8170	...	8070	-	8070	...	8240	-	8240	...
2 Other intermediate consumption	2464010	2421890	42120	...	2591700	2549430	...	...	2749710	2700210	49500	...
Subtotal: Value Added	1320860	1307500	13360	...	1389100	1373780	15320	...	1453560	1436290	17270	...
1 Indirect taxes, net	56900	48370	8530	...	57260	48530	8730	...	59140	48260	8320	...
A Indirect taxes	88880	80150	8530	...	94270	84740	8730	...	99650	87830	8320	...
B Less: Subsidies	31780	31780	-	...	36210	36210	...	...	37810	37810	-	...
2 Consumption of fixed capital	196380	192660	3720	...	206160	202030	4130	...	215350	210900	4450	...
3 Compensation of employees	704470	663850	40620	...	732300	691060	...	...	760030	715560	...	...
4 Net operating surplus	363110	402920	-39810	...	411030	396480	...	...	418040	459980	-40940	...
Gross Input	3866590	3729390	137200	...	4110300	3965480	144820	...	4287510	4135500	151010	...

Gross Output

| | 1 Output for sale | 2 Imputed bank service charge | 3 Own-account fixed capital formation | Gross Output |

Gross Input

	1986 TOTAL	1986 Non-Financial	1986 Financial	1986 ADDENDUM	1987 TOTAL	1987 Non-Financial	1987 Financial	1987 ADDENDUM	1988 TOTAL	1988 Non-Financial	1988 Financial	1988 ADDENDUM
Intermediate consumption	2743490	2606700	136790	...	2736660	2602270	134390	...	2882880	2741990	140890	...
1 Imputed banking service charge	8360	-	8360	...	8270	-	8270	...	8080	-	8080	...
2 Other intermediate consumption	2685080	2606700	5310	...	2654390	2602270	52120	...	2797800	2741990	55810	...
Subtotal: Value Added	1539210	1522240	16970	...	1571170	1531110	18060	...	1684280	1665090	19190	...
1 Indirect taxes, net	59660	50150	9510	...	56340	47170	9170	...	59360	49230	10130	...
A Indirect taxes	101000	91490	9510	...	101120	91950	9170	...	107020	96900	10130	...
B Less: Subsidies	41340	41340	-	...	44780	44780	-	...	47670	47670	-	...
2 Consumption of fixed capital	226880	219000	4680	...	231660	226760	4900	...	248130	236670	5160	...
3 Compensation of employees	797400	749230	48170	...	828780	777300	51480	...	863970	808980	53990	...
4 Net operating surplus	458470	503860	-45390	...	474390	521880	-47490	...	519120	569210	-50090	...
Gross Input	4282700	4128940	153760	...	4327830	4175380	152450	...	4567160	4407080	160080	...

1989 Gross Output

| | 1 Output for sale | 2 Imputed bank service charge | 3 Own-account fixed capital formation | Gross Output | 4872920 | ... | ... | ... |

1989 Gross Input

Intermediate consumption	3083190	...	...	...
1 Imputed banking service charge	89190	-	89190	...
2 Other intermediate consumption	2994000	...	...	...
Subtotal: Value Added	1789730	1767770	21960	...
1 Indirect taxes, net	71840	...	...	...
A Indirect taxes	117250	...	...	...
B Less: Subsidies	45410	45410	...	...
2 Consumption of fixed capital	257110	...	...	...
3 Compensation of employees	906730	850630	56100	...
4 Net operating surplus	554050	...	...	...
Gross Input	4872920	...	...	...

Germany, Fed. Rep. of

3.22 Corporate and Quasi-Corporate Enterprise Income and Outlay Account: Total and Sectors

Million Deutsche marks

	1980 TOTAL	1980 Non-Financial	1980 Financial	1981 TOTAL	1981 Non-Financial	1981 Financial	1982 TOTAL	1982 Non-Financial	1982 Financial	1983 TOTAL	1983 Non-Financial	1983 Financial
Receipts												
1 Operating surplus	299500	329290	-29790	301880	331170	-29290	323970	335050	-33170	359730	395730	-35760	363110	402620	-39510
2 Property and entrepreneurial income	229540	227270	2270	278460	278460	...	247620	278400	...	297800	...	...	268150	285530	269000	258630
A Withdrawals from quasi-corporate enterprises	4640	4100	540	4750	4200	550	5140	4560	580	5260	4680	580
B Interest a	212360	198130	14230	260610	242440	18170	281170	262520	18650	269240	251630	25730
C Dividends	12540	8940	3600	13100	8470	4630	11490	6440	5050	11030	5710	5320
D Net land rent and royalties a	...	...	...	...	...	...	...	...	...	...	...	...
3 Current transfers	68590	28530	40030	73690	29410	44220	74920	27260	47660	78400	29810	48590
A Casualty insurance claims	4990	4800	190	5700	5440	260	6190	5910	280	6020	5740	280
B Casualty insurance premiums, net, due to be received by insurance companies	32860	-	32860	36700	-	36700	38900	-	38900	39920	-	39920
C Current transfers from the rest of the world	...	...	...	...	...	...	...	...	...	...	...	...
D Other transfers except imputed	8110	3560	4550	8410	3480	4930	9650	3530	6120	9220	3550	5670
E Imputed unfunded employee pension and welfare contributions	22600	20170	2430	22820	20490	2330	20180	17820	2360	23240	20520	2720
Total Current Receipts	597600	385090	212510	653970	395300	258670	696690	416640	280050	727040	459330	267710
Disbursements												
1 Property and entrepreneurial income	483300	336190	147110	529730	345730	183990	573160	371700	201460	585550	401280	184270
A Withdrawals from quasi-corporations	215030	215030	...	220880	220880	...	211790	211790	...	251480	251480	...
B Interest a	245740	101930	143810	305000	126820	178180	327660	140200	187460	298650	128680	169370
C Dividends	22530	19230	3300	22850	17040	5810	33710	19710	14000	35120	20220	14900
D Net land rent and royalties a	...	...	...	...	...	...	...	...	...	...	...	...
2 Direct taxes and other current transfers n.e.c. to general government	27820	22710	5110	27150	20710	6440	28730	20630	8100	31360	21770	9590
A Direct taxes	26380	21270	5110	25660	19220	6440	27140	19040	8100	29610	20020	9590
B Fines, fees, penalties and other current transfers n.e.c.	1440	1440	...	1490	1490	...	1590	1590	...	1750	1750	...
3 Other current transfers	57520	21250	36270	63310	22980	40330	66990	23930	42930	68540	24330	44210
A Casualty insurance premiums, net	5640	5450	190	6460	6200	260	6950	6670	280	6720	6440	280
B Casualty insurance claims liability of insurance companies	32860	-	32860	36700	-	36700	38900	-	38900	39920	-	39920
C Transfers to private non-profit institutions												
D Unfunded employee pension and welfare benefits	16740	15710	1030	17740	16680	1060	18300	17160	1140	18990	17770	1220
E Social assistance grants	2280	90	2190	2410	100	2310	2710	100	2610	2910	120	2790
F Other transfers n.e.c.	...	...	...	...	...	...	...	...	...	...	...	...
G Transfers to the rest of the world	...	...	...	...	...	...	...	...	...	...	...	...
Net saving	28960	4940	24020	33780	5870	27910	27940	380	27560	41590	11950	29640
Total Current Disbursements and Net Saving	597600	385090	212510	653970	395300	258670	696690	416640	280050	727040	459330	267710

	1984 TOTAL	1984 Non-Financial	1984 Financial	1985 TOTAL	1985 Non-Financial	1985 Financial	1986 TOTAL	1986 Non-Financial	1986 Financial	1987 TOTAL	1987 Non-Financial	1987 Financial
Receipts												
1 Operating surplus	393380	433120	-39740	419040	455980	-40940	458470	503860	-45390	474390	521880	-47490
2 Property and entrepreneurial income	309070	306630	2730040	317430	36380	281050	319810	40740	279070	319330	39260	280070
A Withdrawals from quasi-corporate enterprises	5810	5190	620	6350	5770	580	7240	6690	550	7320	6720	600
B Interest a	285820	266820	19000	292140	273440	18700	287990	269090	18930	288280	270190	18090
C Dividends	18340	12740	5600	18940	11910	7030	24580	15120	9460	23730	14450	9280
D Net land rent and royalties a	...	...	...	...	...	...	...	...	...	...	...	...

Germany, Fed. Rep. of

3.22 Corporate and Quasi-Corporate Enterprise Income and Outlay Account: Total and Sectors
(Continued)

Million Deutsche marks

	1984			1985			1986			1987		
	TOTAL	Non-Financial	Financial	TOTAL	Non-Financial	Financial	TOTAL	Non-Financial	Financial	TOTAL	Non-Financial	Financial
3 Current transfers	83290	32630	50660	87470	32880	54590	91540	34080	57460	98090	36680	61410
A Casualty insurance claims	6050	5810	240	6510	6220	290	6750	6450	300	7240	6920	320
B Casualty insurance premiums, net, due to be received by insurance companies	42530	-	42530	45260	-	45260	47300	-	47300	50360	-	50360
C Current transfers from the rest of the world	...	...	...	...	...	...	...	...	...	...	...	...
D Other transfers except imputed	9060	3690	5370	10110	3580	6530	10590	3630	6960	11420	3790	7630
E Imputed unfunded employee pension and welfare contributions	25650	23130	2520	25590	23080	2510	26900	24000	2900	29070	25970	3100
Total Current Receipts	786640	502680	283960	823940	529240	294700	869820	578680	291140	891810	597820	293990

Disbursements

	TOTAL	Non-Financial	Financial	TOTAL	Non-Financial	Financial	TOTAL	Non-Financial	Financial	TOTAL	Non-Financial	Financial
1 Property and entrepreneurial income	630730	433040	197690	661470	454900	206570	708060	503680	204380	718920	518080	200840
A Withdrawals from quasi-corporations	272610	272610	...	290910	290910	...	338290	338290	...	355240	355240	...
B Interest [a]	320190	137930	182260	327910	139420	188490	321290	135030	186260	318650	130890	187760
C Dividends	37930	22500	15430	42650	24570	18080	48480	30360	18120	45030	31950	13080
D Net land rent and royalties [a]	...	...	...	...	...	...	...	...	...	...	...	...
2 Direct taxes and other current transfers n.e.c. to general government	36390	26740	9650	41140	31150	9990	40860	30890	9970	36580	27520	9060
A Direct taxes	34460	24810	9650	39230	29240	9990	38800	28830	9970	34500	25440	9060
B Fines, fees, penalties and other current transfers n.e.c.	1930	1930	-	1910	1910	-	2060	2060	-	2080	2080	-
3 Other current transfers	72200	25300	46900	77710	27020	50690	82470	28960	53510	87900	30860	57040
A Casualty insurance premiums, net	6910	6670	240	7470	7180	290	7710	7410	300	8240	7920	320
B Casualty insurance claims liability of insurance companies	42530	-	42530	45260	-	45260	47300	-	47300	50360	-	50360
C Transfers to private non-profit institutions	...	...	...	...	...	...	...	...	...	...	...	...
D Unfunded employee pension and welfare benefits	19800	18500	1300	21070	19680	1390	22880	21410	1470	24390	22800	1590
E Social assistance grants	2960	130	2830	3910	160	3750	4580	140	4440	4910	140	4770
F Other transfers n.e.c.	...	...	...	...	...	...	...	...	...	...	...	...
G Transfers to the rest of the world	...	...	...	...	...	...	...	...	...	...	...	...
Net saving	47320	17600	29720	43620	16170	27450	38430	15150	23280	48410	21360	27050
Total Current Disbursements and Net Saving	786640	502680	283960	823940	529240	294700	869820	578680	291140	891810	597820	293990

	1988			1989		
	TOTAL	Non-Financial	Financial	TOTAL	Non-Financial	Financial

Receipts

	TOTAL	Non-Financial	Financial	TOTAL	Non-Financial	Financial
1 Operating surplus	519120	569210	-50090	554050	...	...
2 Property and entrepreneurial income	329170	37170	292000	380510	50760	329750
A Withdrawals from quasi-corporate enterprises	7820	7190	630	8250	7530	720
B Interest [a]	300500	20690	279810	343280	28290	314990
C Dividends	20850	9290	11560	28980	14940	14040
D Net land rent and royalties [a]	...	...	...	...	...	...
3 Current transfers	102480	37030	65450	106890	37770	69120
A Casualty insurance claims	7480	7120	360	7810	7450	360
B Casualty insurance premiums, net, due to be received by insurance companies	53890	-	53890	57140	-	57140
C Current transfers from the rest of the world	...	...	...	...	...	...
D Other transfers except imputed	11800	3760	8040	12210	3790	8420
E Imputed unfunded employee pension and welfare contributions	29310	26150	3160	29730	26530	3200
Total Current Receipts	950770	643410	307360	1041450	...	...

695

Germany, Fed. Rep. of

3.22 Corporate and Quasi-Corporate Enterprise Income and Outlay Account: Total and Sectors
(Continued)

Million Deutsche marks

		1988			1989	
	TOTAL	Non-Financial	Financial	TOTAL	Non-Financial	Financial
	Disbursements					
1 Property and entrepreneurial income	756230	554130	202100	...	...	244960
A Withdrawals from quasi-corporations	390440	390440	...	...	...	...
B Interest a	327010	130770	196240	372380	143350	229030
C Dividends	38780	32920	5860	54320	38390	15930
D Net land rent and royalties a	...	...	...	...	...	...
2 Direct taxes and other current transfers n.e.c. to general government	39820	29610	10210	45820	37310	8510
A Direct taxes	37590	27380	10210	43280	34770	8510
B Fines, fees, penalties and other current transfers n.e.c.	2230	2230	-	2540	2540	-
3 Other current transfers	93130	32240	60890	97620	33180	64440
A Casualty insurance premiums, net	8630	8270	360	9010	8650	360
B Casualty insurance claims liability of insurance companies	53890	-	53890	57140	-	57140
C Transfers to private non-profit institutions	...	...	...	...	...	...
D Unfunded employee pension and welfare benefits	25500	23820	1680	26100	24380	1720
E Social assistance grants	5110	150	4960	5370	150	5220
F Other transfers n.e.c.	...	...	...	...	...	...
G Transfers to the rest of the world	...	...	...	...	...	...
Net saving	61590	27430	34160	...	...	...
Total Current Disbursements and Net Saving	950770	643410	307360	...	...	...

a) Item 'Interest' includes item 'Net land rent and royalties'.

3.23 Corporate and Quasi-Corporate Enterprise Capital Accumulation Account: Total and Sectors

Million Deutsche marks

		1980			1981			1982			1983	
	TOTAL	Non-Financial	Financial	TOTAL	Non-Financial	Financial	TOTAL	Non-Financial	Financial	TOTAL	Non-Financial	Financial
					Finance of Gross Accumulation							
1 Gross saving	162720	135890	26830	156030	125010	31020	171630	140680	30950	211640	178280	33360
A Consumption of fixed capital	164250	161440	2810	178160	175050	3110	189840	186450	3390	199480	195760	3720
B Net saving	-1530	-25550	24020	-22130	-50040	27910	-18210	-45770	27560	12160	-17480	29640
2 Capital transfers	57230	57230	-	58380	58380	-	59360	59360	-	61090	61090	-
A From resident sectors	57230	57230	-	58380	58380	-	59360	59360	-	61090	61090	-
B From the rest of the world	...	...	...	...	...	...	...	...	...	...	...	...
Finance of Gross Accumulation a	219950	193120	26830	214410	183390	31020	230990	200040	30950	272730	239370	33360
					Gross Accumulation							
1 Gross capital formation	298770	292880	5890	276170	269880	6290	272170	265330	6840	301990	293570	8420
A Increase in stocks	13300	13110	190	-11600	-11630	30	-11500	-11500	-	-1800	-1730	-70
B Gross fixed capital formation	285470	279770	5700	287770	281510	6260	283670	276830	6840	303790	295300	8490
2 Purchases of land, net	-2760	-3090	330	-2350	-2660	310	-2040	-2930	890	-1740	-2580	840
3 Purchases of intangible assets, net	...	...	...	...	...	...	...	...	...	...	...	...
4 Capital transfers	19540	16240	3300	20590	16170	4420	19100	12330	6770	21990	14700	7290
A To resident sectors	19540	16240	3300	20590	16170	4420	19100	12330	6770	21990	14700	7290
B To the rest of the world	...	...	...	...	...	...	...	...	...	...	...	...
Net lending	-95600	-112910	17310	-80000	-100000	20000	-58240	-74690	16450	-49510	-66320	16810
Gross Accumulation a	219950	193120	26830	214410	183390	31020	230990	200040	30950	272730	239370	33360

Germany, Fed. Rep. of

3.23 Corporate and Quasi-Corporate Enterprise Capital Accumulation Account: Total and Sectors

Million Deutsche marks

	1984 TOTAL	1984 Non-Financial	1984 Financial	1985 TOTAL	1985 Non-Financial	1985 Financial	1986 TOTAL	1986 Non-Financial	1986 Financial	1987 TOTAL	1987 Non-Financial	1987 Financial
Finance of Gross Accumulation												
1 Gross saving	218160	184310	33850	225210	193310	31900	268190	240230	27960	281590	249640	31950
A Consumption of fixed capital	209400	205270	4130	218700	214250	4450	227150	222470	4680	252520	230360	4900
B Net saving	8760	-20960	29720	6510	-20940	27450	41040	17760	23280	46330	19280	27050
2 Capital transfers	67480	-	67480	67310	-	67310	66720	-	66720	70560	-	70560
A From resident sectors	67480	-	67480	67310	-	67310	66720	-	66720	70560	-	70560
B From the rest of the world	...	...	...	...	...	...	...	...	...	...	...	...
Finance of Gross Accumulation ª	285640	251790	33850	292520	260620	31900	334910	306950	27960	352150	320200	31950
Gross Accumulation												
1 Gross capital formation	321100	312390	8710	319380	310940	8440	334000	325370	8630	348350	340350	8000
A Increase in stocks	6600	6540	60	-700	-790	90	1500	1700	-200	4470	4550	-80
B Gross fixed capital formation	314500	305850	8650	320080	311730	8350	332500	323670	8830	343880	335800	8080
2 Purchases of land, net	-1610	-2090	480	-1890	-2410	520	-1980	-2220	240	-1990	-2440	450
3 Purchases of intangible assets, net	...	...	...	...	...	...	...	...	...	...	...	...
4 Capital transfers	23250	16110	7140	22850	14550	8300	21600	13680	7920	20440	14770	5670
A To resident sectors	23250	16110	7140	22850	14550	8300	21600	13680	7920	20440	14770	5670
B To the rest of the world	...	...	...	...	...	...	...	...	...	...	...	...
Net lending	-57100	-74620	17520	-47820	-62460	14640	-18710	-28880	11170	-14650	-32480	17830
Gross Accumulation ª	285640	251790	33850	292520	260620	31900	334910	306950	27960	352150	320200	31950

	1988 TOTAL	1988 Non-Financial	1988 Financial	1989 TOTAL	1989 Non-Financial	1989 Financial
Finance of Gross Accumulation						
1 Gross saving	327470	285400	39320	336120		
A Consumption of fixed capital	245560	240400	5160	261050		
B Net saving	79160	45000	34160	75070		
2 Capital transfers	65550	-	65550	68520	-	68520
A From resident sectors	65550	-	65550	68520	-	68520
B From the rest of the world	...	...	...	...	...	...
Finance of Gross Accumulation ª	394270	354950	39320	404640		
Gross Accumulation						
1 Gross capital formation	386920	377920	9000	436780		
A Increase in stocks	18130	18170	-40	29180		
B Gross fixed capital formation	368790	359750	9040	407600		
2 Purchases of land, net	-1670	-1320	-350	-1730		
3 Purchases of intangible assets, net	...	...	...	...	...	...
4 Capital transfers	20890	14980	5910	21820	14970	6850
A To resident sectors	20890	14980	5910	21820	14970	6850
B To the rest of the world	...	...	...	...	...	...
Net lending	-11870	-36630	24760	-52230		
Gross Accumulation ª	394270	354950	39320	404640		

a) Capital accumulation account of corporate and quasi-corporate enterprise includes private non-profit organizations.

3.24 Corporate and Quasi-Corporate Enterprise Capital Finance Account: Total and Sectors

Million Deutsche marks

	1980 TOTAL	1980 Non-Financial	1980 Financial	1981 TOTAL	1981 Non-Financial	1981 Financial	1982 TOTAL	1982 Non-Financial	1982 Financial	1983 TOTAL	1983 Non-Financial	1983 Financial
Acquisition of Financial Assets												
1 Gold and SDRs	11870	-	11870	7750	-	7750	6070	-	6070	-2050	-	-2050
2 Currency and transferable deposits	-2440	-8550	6110	-1880	-2880	1000	10090	3430	10140	11770	-1630	
3 Other deposits	18270	14320	3950	28490	10800	17690	3350	4520	-1170	16520	8170	8350
4 Bills and bonds, short term	-15980	-15940	-40	-7650	90	-7740	7690	70	7620	-1570	490	-2060
6 Bonds, long term	26950	410	26540	-1250	-25680	26880	63880	2720	61160	6310	8340	3630
6 Corporate equity securities	9420	2080	7340	8250	1110	7140	8040	2750	5310	2730	8340	4710
7 Short term loans, n.e.c.	71140	13880	57260	58790	22140	36650	35280	12520	22760	38120	10940	27180

Germany, Fed. Rep. of

3.24 Corporate and Quasi-Corporate Enterprise Capital Finance Account: Total and Sectors (Continued)

Million Deutsche marks

	1980 TOTAL	1980 Non-Financial	1980 Financial	1981 TOTAL	1981 Non-Financial	1981 Financial	1982 TOTAL	1982 Non-Financial	1982 Financial	1983 TOTAL	1983 Non-Financial	1983 Financial
Total Acquisition of Financial Assets	237380	45180	192200	272810	56930	215880	254750	46420	208330	282070	68470	213600
1 Currency and transferable deposits	5310	...	5310	-10430	...	-10430	26200	...	26200	25550	...	25550
2 Other deposits	75790	...	75790	79370	...	79370	68370	...	68370	62810	...	62810
3 Bills and bonds, short term	-1520	880	-2400	1090	70	1020	-110	690	-800	2050	500	2050
4 Bonds, long term	42510	820	41690	7120	70	7050	47810	3060	44750	51880	60	51820
5 Corporate equity securities	6960	5260	1700	5620	70	5550	1920	4500	1420	7280	5860	1420
6 Short-term loans, n.e.c.	68960	43000	25960	48430	4200	44230	38270	18840	17430	43680	15430	18250
7 Long-term loans, n.e.c.	8160	8660	510	8310	8880	470	8040	8120	-80	97740	9940	-20
8 Net equity of households in life insurance and pension fund reserves	37970	11710	26260	40980	11150	29830	40580	7500	33080	45370	9940	33830
9 Proprietors' net additions to the accumulation of quasi-corporations												
10 Trade credit and advances	3730	-	3730	8150	8150	-	2770	2770	-	1820	1820	-
11 Other accounts payable	...	...	...	...	...	...	...	...	...	...	...	...
12 Other liabilities	-440	...	-440	120	120	...	1790	1790	...	3390	3390	...
Total Incurrence of Liabilities	329150	154050	175100	350020	196370	153650	306940	117480	192160	325250	131350	196900
Net Lending	-91770	-108810	17040	-77210	-96720	19510	-54690	-71060	17470	-46180	-62880	16700
Lending	237380	45180	192200	272810	56930	215880	254750	46420	208330	282070	68470	213600

	1984 TOTAL	1984 Non-Financial	1984 Financial	1985 TOTAL	1985 Non-Financial	1985 Financial	1986 TOTAL	1986 Non-Financial	1986 Financial	1987 TOTAL	1987 Non-Financial	1987 Financial
Acquisition of Financial Assets												
1 Gold and SDRs	90	-	90	400	...	400	-2260	...	-2260	10660	-	10660
2 Currency and transferable deposits	16570	9480	7090	13960	5550	8420	24250	20480	3770	19720	15210	4510
3 Other deposits	41970	13550	28420	66000	9720	55880	114320	21230	93090	62420	18460	43960
4 Bills and bonds, short term	-7440	-70	-7370	7290	1060	6230	-9006	-450	-9456	25440	140	25300
5 Bonds, long term	46970	8860	38990	51920	8190	43310	34730	-5120	39850	52260	3210	49350
6 Corporate equity securities	6690	3010	3580	7040	1640	5400	15270	140	14130	15550	6080	9470
7 Short term loans, n.e.c.	3880	4430	3400	6950	17460	80	7410	-7330	80	-26930
8 Long term loans, n.e.c.	122390	8980	113410	114060	10170	103890	97500	9210	88290	122810	12840	109970
9 Trade credits and advances	11710	11710	-	3910	3910	...	520	520	...	-1210	-1210	-
10 Other receivables												
11 Other assets	3000	3000	-	3260	3260	...	4030	4030	...	4870	4870	-
Total Acquisition of Financial Assets	279680	64070	215610	293850	58950	234900	297440	58450	238990	285970	59680	226290
Incurrence of Liabilities												
1 Currency and transferable deposits	28440	-	28440	22960	...	22960	36800	...	36800	31950	...	31950
2 Other deposits	83650	...	83650	104240	...	104240	122050	...	122050	119730	-	119730
3 Bills and bonds, short term	-310	-630	320	1800	-	1800	-3560	-	-3560	-770	-500	-270
4 Bonds, long term	36120	1570	34550	38440	5390	33050	36240	6790	29450	39340	10820	28520
5 Corporate equity securities	6280	4550	1730	11000	4250	6750	16390	12450	3940	11890	8980	2910
6 Short-term loans, n.e.c.	47540	37060	10480	32940	21380	11110	-22730	-12220	-10510	-29540	-9360	-20180
7 Long-term loans, n.e.c.	80780	80890	90	76150	76190	-40	78840	78770	70	70900	290
8 Net equity of households in life insurance and pension fund reserves	47760	...	47760	35820	11940	50540	10560	39980	43340	52200	9870	43330
9 Proprietors' net additions to the accumulation of quasi-corporations												
10 Trade credit and advances	3000	3000	-	430	430	-	-4630	-4630	-	680	680	-
11 Other accounts payable	3180	...	3180	3570	...	3570	4290	...	4290	5340	...	5340
12 Other liabilities	336440	138180	198260	341620	120700	220920	316900	81030	228870	303010	91390	211620
Total Incurrence of Liabilities	-56760	-74110	17350	-47770	-61750	13980	-19460	-32580	13120	-17040	-31710	14670
Net Lending and Net Incurrence of Liabilities	279680	64070	215610	293850	58950	234900	297440	58450	238990	285970	59680	226290

869

Germany, Fed. Rep. of

3.32 Household and Private Unincorporated Enterprise Income and Outlay Account

Million Deutsche marks	1970	1975	1980	1981	1982	1983	1984	1985	1986	1987	1988	1989
Receipts												
1 Compensation of employees	360940	587200	827500	844410	882950	902520	954000	991000	1041350	1083440	1126040	1176640
A Wages and salaries	307900	485870	690150	719400	734790	745760	798380	838350	871630	906080	948200	
B Employers' contributions for social security	37000	72030	109840	117330	124010	127220	133190	140360	148170	153900	161040	168340
C Employers' contributions for private pensions & welfare plans	15740	29300	44420	46220	47910	43720	47930	51360	52260	54830	57910	60100
2 Operating surplus of private unincorporated enterprises	...	...	...	...	...	...	...	...	...	...	...	...
3 Property and entrepreneurial income	137080	216190	314590	347780	351810	369070	408530	430010	438800	458080	476380	514200
A Withdrawals from private quasi-corporations	113770	172270	240880	253040	252800	275650	305360	321670	328440	350000	365050	387990
B Interest [a]	21190	41170	70860	85890	91130	91630	100140	105190	104990	107520	121650	
C Dividends	2190	2700	2850	2850	2840	2290	3030	3150	3370	3500	3810	4560
D Net land and royalties [a]	...	...	...	...	...	...	...	...	...	...	...	...
3 Current transfers	108470	211110	303570	329750	348250	355000	362980	374860	391240	412310	432440	453710
A Casualty insurance claims	10320	16710	26160	29090	30700	31950	34520	36910	38620	41130	44320	46970
B Social security benefits	60910	127230	178270	191050	200370	209970	213410	219430	225830	227290	250410	260160
C Social assistance grants	14100	34960	43210	48420	48700	48400	48340	49070	52980	55500	56000	58130
D Unfunded employee pension and welfare benefits	19450	33440	45240	48080	48760	51150	52260	54690	58050	61180	63560	65510
E Transfers from general government	2400	4760	8400	9060	9270	9560	10020	10230	10850	11740	12270	13040
F Transfers from the rest of the world	140	110	280	360	440	460	550	820	990	1280	1680	5640
G Other transfers n.e.c.	1150	1920	3410	3420	3010	3510	3880	3810	3920	4190	4200	4260
Total Current Receipts [b]	609190	1022450	1462570	1554210	1602580	1644980	1725510	1795870	1869390	1953830	2034860	2144550
Disbursements												
1 Final consumption expenditures	368850	585330	840780	887850	918050	960190	1003570	1038340	1068610	1103000	1154280	1211300
A Market purchases	363130	576950	829430	876110	905620	956650	988540	1023180	1051810	1092640	1135730	1181390
B Gross rents of owner-occupied housing												
C Consumption from own-account production	5720	8380	11350	11740	12430	13510	14030	15160	16800	17660	18550	19910
2 Property income	3340	6760	13850	14470	19440	18040	17950	18340	18220	18210	18570	21100
A Interest	3340	6760	13850	14470	19440	18040	17950	18340	18220	18210	18570	21100
Mortgage	...	...	...	...	...	...	...	...	...	...	...	...
Consumer debt												
Other	...	...	...	...	...	...	...	...	...	...	...	...
B Net land rent and royalties	...	...	...	...	...	...	...	...	...	...	...	...
3 Direct taxes and other current transfers n.e.c. to government	140200	266660	396630	417700	435870	445600	462500	494690	517420	543650	549330	603310
A Social security contributions	78110	153910	225650	248250	253340	268840	282440	296920	313090	325600	341020	357170
B Direct taxes	60440	109360	161810	164210	166120	169680	178020	189620	192280	204420	209430	236500
Income taxes	58300	106460	157520	161180	162410	165750	173960	185680	191080	204750	210090	231280
Other	2140	2930	3660	3660	3750	3930	4100	4140	5200	4670	4610	5220
C Fees, fines and penalties	1650	3360	5500	6040	6410	7080	7750	7950	8050	8630	9210	9640
4 Other current transfers	34680	59780	88370	94350	96740	99766	107010	111230	116060	122230	127610	136310
A Net casualty insurance premiums	10440	17160	26810	29760	31390	32640	35190	37340	39080	41590	44690	47430
B Transfers to private non-profit institutions serving households	...	...	...	...	...	...	...	...	...	...	...	...
C Transfers to the rest of the world	6280	9380	11020	11760	11820	11610	12750	12920	12880	12640	13380	17720
D Other current transfers, except imputed	2220	3940	6120	6910	7910	7580	7410	8710	9300	10090	10620	11060
E Imputed employee pension and welfare contributions	15740	29300	44420	46220	47910	43720	47930	51360	52260	54830	57910	60100
Net saving	59120	103920	126240	137840	134380	117420	129060	133270	140650	159440	169470	172530
Total Current Disbursements and Net Saving [b]	609190	1022450	1462570	1554210	1602580	1644980	1725510	1795870	1869390	1953830	2034860	2144550

[a] Item "Interest" includes item "Net land rent and royalties".
[b] Private non-profit institutions serving households is included in household and private unincorporated enterprise.

Germany, Fed. Rep. of

3.33 Household and Private Unincorporated Enterprise Capital Accumulation Account

Million Deutsche marks

	1970	1975	1980	1981	1982	1983	1984	1985	1986	1987	1988	1989
Finance of Gross Accumulation												
1 Gross saving	59120	103920	123240	137840	134380	117420	129030	133270	149050	159440	169470	172530
A Consumption of fixed capital	...	...	...	...	...	...	...	...	...	...	...	...
B Net saving a	59120	103920	123240	137840	134380	117420	129030	133270	149050	159440	169470	172530
2 Capital transfers	8260	17660	21660	21910	19760	22260	23030	22160	21620	20100	21040	21160
A From resident sectors	8240	17640	21640	21880	19730	22230	22990	22110	21580	20070	21010	21110
B From the rest of the world	20	20	20	30	30	30	40	50	40	30	30	50
Total Finance of Gross Accumulation	67380	121580	144900	159750	154140	139680	152060	155430	170670	179540	190510	193690
Gross Accumulation												
1 Gross Capital Formation	...	...	...	...	...	...	...	...	...	...	...	...
2 Purchases of land, net	...	...	...	...	...	...	...	...	...	...	...	...
3 Purchases of intangibles, net	...	...	...	...	...	...	...	...	...	...	...	...
4 Capital transfers	12710	25360	36990	38080	37520	39120	41550	42040	43780	47070	47440	45020
A To resident sectors	12530	25110	36580	37680	37070	38590	41140	41620	43310	46560	46950	44590
B To the rest of the world	180	250	410	400	450	530	410	420	470	510	490	430
Net lending	54670	96220	107910	121670	116620	100560	110510	113390	126890	132470	143070	148670
Total Gross Accumulation	67380	121580	144900	159750	154140	139680	152060	155430	170670	179540	190510	193690

a) Item 'Net saving' excludes undistributed profits of unincorporated enterprises.

3.34 Household and Private Unincorporated Enterprise Capital Finance Account

Million Deutsche marks

	1970	1975	1980	1981	1982	1983	1984	1985	1986	1987	1988	1989
Acquisition of Financial Assets												
1 Gold	-	-	-	-	-	-	-	-	-	-	...	...
2 Currency and transferable deposits	3500	9810	3900	-1850	7910	9490	6140	5380	13290	13750	...	...
3 Other deposits	32670	62580	53730	44410	58320	40640	39850	46220	58320	42740	...	...
4 Bills and bonds, short term	-	-330	400	660	1880	-1370	-630	-410	-290	-1050	...	...
5 Bonds, long term	10030	8470	24790	47830	15980	15950	26600	21510	10020	27750	...	...
6 Corporate equity securities	1440	1590	-900	-2030	520	4060	700	3470	1640	4920	...	...
7 Short term loans, n.e.c.	-	-	-	-	-	-	-	-	-	-	...	...
8 Long term loans, n.e.c.	140	200	140	100	60	370	190	-540	320	200	...	...
9 Trade credit and advances	-	-	-	-	-	-	-	-	-	-	...	...
10 Net equity of households in life insurance and pension fund reserves	11340	21770	37970	40980	40580	43570	47760	50540	53210	53200	...	...
11 Proprietors' net additions to the accumulation of quasi-corporations	...	...	...	...	...	...	...	...	...	...	...	...
12 Other	-	-	-	-	-	-	-	-	-	-	...	...
Total Acquisition of Financial Assets	59120	104090	120030	130100	125250	112710	120610	126170	136510	141510	...	...
Incurrence of Liabilities												
1 Short term loans, n.e.c.	1150	1220	4770	2890	3200	2830	3510	3580	120	-740	...	...
2 Long term loans, n.e.c.	3300	6570	7890	4700	6270	9690	6970	9200	9880	12300	...	...
3 Trade credit and advances	-	-	-	-	-	-	-	-	-	-	...	...
4 Other accounts payable	...	...	...	...	...	...	...	...	...	...	...	...
5 Other liabilities	-	-	-	-	-	-	-	-	-	-	...	...
Total Incurrence of Liabilities	4450	7790	12660	7590	9470	12520	10480	12780	10000	11560	...	...
Net Lending	54670	96300	107370	122510	115780	100190	110130	113390	126510	129950	...	...
Incurrence of Liabilities and Net Lending	59120	104090	120030	130100	125250	112710	120610	126170	136510	141510	...	...

3.41 Private Non-Profit Institutions Serving Households: Production Account

Million Deutsche marks

	1970	1975	1980	1981	1982	1983	1984	1985	1986	1987	1988	1989
Gross Output												
1 Sales	7260	16810	25600	27760	29750	31140	32940	34780	37020	38980	40770	42290
2 Non-marketed output	5720	8380	11350	11740	12430	13510	14030	15160	16800	17660	18550	19910
A Services produced for own use	5720	8380	11350	11740	12430	13510	14030	15160	16800	17660	18550	19910
B Own account fixed capital formation	...	...	...	...	...	...	...	...	...	...	...	...
Gross Output	12980	25190	36950	39500	42180	44650	46970	49940	53820	56640	59320	62200
Gross Input												
Intermediate consumption	4060	7400	11180	11990	12750	13500	14270	15070	15600	16020	16770	17600

Germany, Fed. Rep. of

3.41 Private Non-Profit Institutions Serving Households: Production Account (Continued)

Million Deutsche marks	1970	1975	1980	1981	1982	1983	1984	1985	1986	1987	1988	1989
Subtotal: Value Added	8520	17790	25770	27510	29430	31150	32700	34870	38220	40650	42550	44600
1 Indirect taxes, net	10	10	50	20	20	10	20	20	30	30	30	30
2 Consumption of fixed capital	940	1640	2810	2820	3010	3100	3240	3350	3470	3600	3730	3940
3 Compensation of employees	7970	16140	23170	24670	26270	28030	29440	31500	34720	36990	38790	40630
A To residents	7970	16140	23170	24670	26270	28030	29440	31500	34720	36990	38790	40630
B To the rest of the world	...	...	...	...	...	...	...	...	...	...	...	...
4 Net operating surplus	12980	25190	36950	39500	42180	44650	46970	49960	52820	56640	59320	62200
Gross Input												

3.51 External Transactions: Current Account: Detail

Million Deutsche marks	1970	1975	1980	1981	1982	1983	1984	1985	1986	1987	1988	1989
Payments to the Rest of the World												
1 Imports of goods and services a	129270	227150	401080	434600	440740	451330	499370	527100	475520	475740	510780	581510
A Imports of merchandise c.i.f. b	101120	179280	325090	349730	354280	363630	406690	435040	389410	388760	411880	474660
B Other	28150	47870	75990	84870	86490	87700	92680	92060	86100	97580	98900	106850
2 Factor income to the rest of the world	9530	14030	24190	32260	33930	35490	36540	40180	43730	50160	54920	62150
A Compensation of employees	840	1950	2650	2830	2950	2160	2110	2090	2090	2120	2180	2270
B Property and entrepreneurial income	8690	12080	21540	29430	30380	33330	34430	38090	41640	48040	52740	59880
By general government	60	390	1520	3180	5930	6450	6900	8190	9710	11590	11670	11340
By corporate and quasi-corporate enterprises	8630	11690	20020	26250	30450	26880	27530	29900	31930	36450	41070	48540
By other												
3 Current transfers to the rest of the world	12770	23920	34000	36890	38170	39590	45170	45600	45510	46250	52590	59180
A Indirect taxes by general government to supranational organizations												
B Other current transfers	12770	23920	34000	36890	38170	39590	45170	45600	45510	46250	52590	59180
By general government	6990	13790	21900	23840	24880	26540	30960	31210	31180	37130	37560	39500
By other resident sectors	6780	10130	12100	13050	13290	13060	14210	14390	14330	14120	15030	19680
4 Surplus of the nation on current transactions	3780	10860	-26960	-12460	8520	11340	22340	47450	66330	82370	88740	104920
Payments to the Rest of the World, and Surplus of the Nation on Current Transfers	155350	275960	432310	491290	526760	537750	603420	660330	645240	654520	707030	807760
Receipts From The Rest of the World												
1 Exports of goods and services a	143000	254700	391850	445680	479030	483780	540180	593490	580720	577320	620420	699240
A Exports of merchandise f.o.b.	122800	219490	333920	384700	413320	416890	467320	517580	508110	506380	547390	615270
B Other	20200	35210	55230	60980	65710	66890	72860	75910	72610	70940	73030	83970
2 Factor income from the rest of the world	9930	16530	30450	36430	38510	40050	50600	53990	57510	62010	67440	87870
A Compensation of employees	2190	3220	4220	4580	5100	5500	5620	5910	6230	6510	6620	6870
B Property and entrepreneurial income	7740	13310	26230	31850	33410	35550	44980	48080	51280	55500	60820	81000
By general government	140	130	80	120	130	110	120	120	120	90	120	140
By corporate and quasi-corporate enterprises	7040	12550	25180	30360	31270	32070	40280	41270	43630	47740	50060	65260
By other	560	630	970	1370	2010	3370	4580	6990	7530	7670	10640	15600
3 Current transfers from the rest of the world	2420	4730	10010	8180	9220	12920	12640	12850	16010	15190	19170	20650
A Subsidies to general government from supranational organizations	...	...	...	10010	9180	12920	12640	12850	16010	15190	19170	20650
B Other current transfers	2420	4730	10010	8180	9220	12920	12640	12850	16010	15190	19170	20650
To general government	1920	4010	8840	7850	7620	11300	11040	10410	13890	12730	16280	13590
To other resident sectors	500	720	1170	1330	1600	1620	1620	1910	2120	2460	2890	7060
Receipts from the Rest of the World on Current Transfers	155350	275960	432310	491290	526760	537750	603420	660330	645240	654520	707030	807760

a) Exports and imports of goods for purposes of repair and improvement are reduced to the value of these services.
b) Imports of merchandise, f.o.b. rather than c.i.f.

701

Germany, Fed. Rep. of

3.52 External Transactions: Capital Accumulation Account

Million Deutsche marks	1970	1975	1980	1981	1982	1983	1984	1985	1986	1987	1988	1989
Finance of Gross Accumulation												
1 Surplus of the nation on current transactions	3780	10860	-26960	-12460	8520	11340	23240	47450	85480	82370	88740	104920
2 Capital transfers from the rest of the world	20	20	160	120	140	110	180	110	230	200	220	310
A By general government	-	-	140	90	110	150	150	70	180	160	190	260
B By other resident sectors	20	20	20	30	30	30	30	40	50	40	30	50
Total Finance of Gross Accumulation	3800	10880	-26800	-12340	8660	11520	22450	47680	85680	82590	88920	105230
Gross Accumulation												
1 Capital transfers to the rest of the world	660	820	3860	2640	2760	2780	2760	3030	2820	2770	2980	3330
A By general government	480	570	3450	2240	2310	2250	2350	2610	2350	2260	2490	2900
B By other resident sectors	180	250	410	400	450	530	410	420	470	510	490	430
2 Purchases of intangible assets, n.e.c., net, from the rest of the world	...	...	...	...	...	...	...	...	...	...	...	...
Net lending to the rest of the world	3140	10060	-30660	-14980	5900	8740	19690	44650	82860	79820	85940	101900
Total Gross Accumulation	3800	10880	-26800	-12340	8660	11520	22450	47680	85680	82690	88920	105230

3.53 External Transactions: Capital Finance Account

Million Deutsche marks	1970	1975	1980	1981	1982	1983	1984	1985	1986	1987	1988	1989
Acquisitions of Foreign Financial Assets												
1 Gold and SDR's	2090	1180	-11870	7750	6070	-2050	90	400	-2260	10660	...	...
2 Currency and transferable deposits	420	-550	1350	190	250	-1880	4010	2000	7780	890	...	...
3 Other deposits	1700	12590	9260	11990	-4760	-5560	15340	36440	82130	15630	...	...
4 Bills and bonds, short term	22900	-3980	-11080	-12780	2210	-3240	-2060	5720	13990	27860	...	...
5 Bonds, long term	850	1390	7340	6200	10980	5740	15710	27460	15510	25160	...	...
6 Corporate equity securities	2680	3440	3570	4650	3280	8320	5680	7460	15840	5040	...	...
7 Short-term loans, n.e.c.	-1900	1470	5280	5650	2020	5830	5220	7130	11200	12260	...	...
8 Long-term loans	6090	20350	16400	14590	13210	23280	25460	26720	22350	33980	...	...
9 Proprietors' net additions to accumulation of quasi-corporate, non-resident enterprises	...	...	...	...	...	...	...	...	...	...	...	...
10 Trade credit and advances	1200	2300	9400	11360	4630	7700	11710	3910	520	-1210	...	...
11 Other	-	-	-	-	-	-	-	-	-	-	...	...
Total Acquisitions of Foreign Financial Assets	36030	38190	29650	49600	37890	38140	81260	117240	167060	130270	...	...
Incurrence of Foreign Liabilities												
1 Currency and transferable deposits	1080	270	8420	-6300	4560	-660	9200	3360	9050	-4300	...	...
2 Other deposits	10420	13350	3360	-1930	8240	-6770	10480	15580	18960	24910	...	...
3 Bills and bonds, short term	1380	110	820	10	850	970	-620	140	-120	-490	...	...
4 Bonds, long term	770	-3440	290	-1450	2270	10800	13820	31460	58910	34960	...	...
5 Corporate equity securities	260	2030	1100	3080	460	2460	4000	7210	15170	-1360	...	...
6 Short-term loans, n.e.c.	8240	4180	14330	21740	5230	-630	15160	13870	-10240	3850	...	...
7 Long-term loans	5900	4570	24800	27270	15160	18320	6430	340	-1980	-5480	...	...
8 Non-resident proprietors' net additions to accumulation of resident quasi-corporate enterprises	...	...	...	...	...	...	...	...	...	...	...	...
9 Trade credit and advances	3200	6360	3730	8150	2770	1820	3000	430	-4630	680	...	...
10 Other	20	80	100	100	110	90	130	220	180	190	...	...
Total Incurrence of Liabilities	31270	27510	56950	60840	29480	26400	61900	44630	85300	52960	...	...
Net Lending	4760	10680	-27300	-11240	8410	11740	19660	44630	81760	77310	...	...
Total Incurrence of Liabilities and Net Lending	36030	38190	29650	49600	37890	38140	81260	117240	167060	130270	...	...

Germany, Fed. Rep. of

4.1 Derivation of Value Added by Kind of Activity, in Current Prices

Million Deutsche marks

	1980			1981			1982			1983		
	Gross Output	Intermediate Consumption	Value Added	Gross Output	Intermediate Consumption	Value Added	Gross Output	Intermediate Consumption	Value Added	Gross Output	Intermediate Consumption	Value Added
	All Producers											
1 Agriculture, hunting, forestry and fishing	63750	33380	30370	66990	35310	31680	72640	36300	36340	70030	37810	32220
A Agriculture and hunting [a]	56010	30310	25700	59460	32220	27240	65310	33120	32190	62790	34480	28310
B Forestry and logging [a]	7740	3070	4670	7530	3090	4440	7330	3180	4150	7240	3330	3910
C Fishing [a]	...	...	...	...	...	...	...	...	...	...	...	...
2 Mining and quarrying [b]	30610	16740	13870	33630	18830	14800	36060	19570	16490	33660	16240	17420
A Coal mining	27130	15140	11990	29660	17060	12600	32010	18140	13870	29390	14810	14580
B Crude petroleum and natural gas production	...	...	...	...	...	...	...	...	...	...	...	...
C Metal ore mining	...	...	...	...	...	...	...	...	...	...	...	...
D Other mining	3480	1600	1880	3970	1770	2200	4050	1430	2620	4270	1430	2840
3 Manufacturing	1319020	836180	482840	1369820	880090	489730	1389420	886570	502850	1425400	900470	524930
A Manufacture of food, beverages and tobacco	186240	128190	58050	193640	135790	57850	200200	138600	61600	203930	140020	63910
B Textile, wearing apparel and leather industries	68590	43070	25520	66860	42170	24690	65530	41230	24300	66420	41740	24680
C Manufacture of wood and wood products, including furniture	47560	29320	18240	44970	27330	17640	42190	25240	16950	43950	26390	17560
D Manufacture of paper and paper products, printing and publishing [c]	49490	29040	20450	52200	31360	20840	52370	31620	20750	54230	31980	22250
E Manufacture of chemicals and chemical petroleum, coal, rubber and plastic products	283500	198290	85210	308380	221440	86940	306490	217820	88670	317890	220050	97840
F Manufacture of non-metallic mineral products, except products of petroleum and coal [b]	50650	29320	21330	49730	29430	20300	49170	29260	19910	51280	30170	21110
G Basic metal industries	117730	78860	38870	115960	78110	37850	112260	75310	36950	110720	74210	36510
H Manufacture of fabricated metal products, machinery and equipment [d]	507650	295570	212080	530430	310360	220070	552950	323270	229680	569280	331890	237390
I Other manufacturing industries	7610	4520	3090	7650	4100	3550	8260	4220	4040	7700	4020	3680
4 Electricity, gas and water	105410	69080	36330	125830	87580	38250	140190	97910	42280	145910	100640	45270
A Electricity, gas and steam	100530	67100	33430	120570	85340	35230	134540	95370	39170	140080	98090	41990
B Water works and supply	4880	1980	2900	5260	2240	3020	5650	2540	3110	5830	2550	3280
5 Construction [d]	196710	97520	99190	195900	97090	98810	190550	95190	95360	197110	99670	97440
6 Wholesale and retail trade, restaurants and hotels	1112690	953810	158880	1166400	999130	167270	1187270	1016300	170970	1228700	1048870	179830
A Wholesale and retail trade	1065340	925360	139980	1115650	968770	146880	1135650	985700	149950	1175950	1017860	158090
B Restaurants and hotels	47350	28450	18900	50750	30360	20390	51620	30600	21020	52750	31010	21740
7 Transport, storage and communication	158430	72760	85670	167310	77680	89630	173450	79670	93780	178650	81880	96770
A Transport and storage	119820	67160	52660	126310	71150	55160	129370	72440	56930	133090	74810	58280
B Communication	38610	5600	33010	41000	6530	34470	44080	7230	36850	45560	7070	38490
8 Finance, insurance, real estate and business services	212050	59150	152900	232740	64380	168360	256470	68540	187930	277760	72490	205270
A Financial institutions	71260	19570	51690	80880	21070	59810	92530	22530	70000	101610	24630	76980
B Insurance	29110	14400	14710	31270	15700	15570	34030	17100	16930	35590	17490	18100
C Real estate and business services [e]	111680	25180	86500	120590	27610	92980	129910	28910	101000	140560	30370	110190
Real estate, except dwellings	...	...	...	...	...	...	...	...	...	...	...	...
Dwellings	111680	25180	86500	120590	27610	92980	129910	28910	101000	140560	30370	110190
9 Community, social and personal services [ce]	247740	84470	163270	271090	92950	178140	287590	98850	188740	309370	105940	203430
Educational services	...	...	...	...	...	...	...	...	...	...	...	...
Medical, dental, other health and veterinary services	46830	14250	32580	50450	15390	35060	50620	15310	35310	52070	15570	36500
Total, Industries	3446410	2223090	1223320	3629710	2353040	1276670	3733640	2398900	1334740	3866590	2464010	1402580
Producers of Government Services	338960	166570	172390	363000	179280	183720	374520	184940	189580	387490	191700	195790
Other Producers	38380	11180	27200	40930	11990	28940	43630	12750	30880	46130	13500	32630
Total	3823750	2400840	1422910	4033640	2544310	1489330	4151790	2596590	1555200	4300210	2669210	1631000
Less: Imputed bank service charge	...	-53940	53940	...	-63260	63260	...	-73470	73470	...	-81720	81720
Import duties	13480	...	13480	14080	...	14080	14810	...	14810	16210	...	16210
Value added tax	96490	...	96490	100780	...	100780	101380	...	101380	109350	...	109350
Total	3933720	2454780	1478940	4148500	2607570	1540930	4267980	2670060	1597920	4425770	2750930	1674840

Germany, Fed. Rep. of

4.1 Derivation of Value Added by Kind of Activity, in Current Prices

Million Deutsche marks

	1984			1985			1986			1987		
	Gross Output	Intermediate Consumption	Value Added	Gross Output	Intermediate Consumption	Value Added	Gross Output	Intermediate Consumption	Value Added	Gross Output	Intermediate Consumption	Value Added
All Producers												
1 Agriculture, hunting, forestry and fishing	72320	37670	34650	69370	37130	32240	67830	34170	33660	62560	32100	30460
A Agriculture and hunting [a]	65070	34310	30760	61560	33650	27910	60410	30820	29590	54990	28710	26280
B Forestry and logging [a]	7250	3360	3890	7810	3480	4330	7420	3350	4070	7570	3390	4180
C Fishing [a]	...	...	...	...	...	...	...	...	...	...	...	...
2 Mining and quarrying [b]	34890	17330	17560	36400	18600	17800	33180	18070	15110	30540	16850	13690
A Coal mining	30330	15800	14530	31690	17010	14680	28880	16290	12590	26690	14900	11790
B Crude petroleum and natural gas production	...	...	...	...	...	...	...	...	...	...	...	...
C Metal ore mining	...	...	...	...	...	...	...	...	...	...	...	...
D Other mining	4560	1530	3030	4710	1590	3120	4300	1780	2520	3850	1950	1900
3 Manufacturing	1516320	969080	547240	1607820	1024280	583540	1596400	975380	621020	1597300	970530	626770
A Manufacture of food, beverages and tobacco	209630	145100	64530	212140	145930	66210	211370	143550	67820	207010	139030	67980
B Textile, wearing apparel and leather industries	70660	45610	25050	73440	47470	25970	72780	45770	27010	72710	45430	27280
C Manufacture of wood and wood products, including furniture	44840	27280	17560	43160	26140	17020	44120	26530	17590	45890	27250	18640
D Manufacture of paper and paper products, printing and publishing [c]	59800	35500	24300	62630	37360	25270	63820	36500	27320	66110	37380	28730
E Manufacture of chemicals and chemical petroleum, coal, rubber and plastic products	345620	241400	104220	362050	252650	109400	319000	198920	120080	312840	199000	113840
F Manufacture of non-metallic mineral products, except products of petroleum and coal [b]	52630	31100	21530	50550	30060	20490	51930	29550	22380	52820	30360	22460
G Basic metal industries	123900	84640	39260	132170	88480	43690	124750	78610	46140	114500	70360	44140
H Manufacture of fabricated metal products, machinery and equipment [d]	601210	354130	247080	663230	391560	271670	699840	411330	288510	716240	416820	299420
I Other manufacturing industries	8030	4320	3710	8450	4630	3820	8790	4620	4170	9180	4900	4280
4 Electricity, gas and water	158970	111180	47790	171160	121010	50150	166000	113500	52500	155960	100480	55480
A Electricity, gas and steam	152760	108500	44260	164680	118020	46660	159750	110770	48980	150500	98340	52160
B Water works and supply	6210	2680	3530	6480	2990	3490	6250	2730	3520	5460	2140	3320
5 Construction [d]	202430	104470	97960	191710	97680	94030	200900	101550	99350	205260	104340	100920
6 Wholesale and retail trade, restaurants and hotels	1304740	1115050	189690	1342820	1149950	192870	1312730	1111170	201560	1319950	1108770	211180
A Wholesale and retail trade	1249230	1082690	166540	1285120	1116200	168920	1252710	1077490	175220	1256740	1074000	182740
B Restaurants and hotels	55510	32360	23150	57700	33750	23950	60020	33680	26340	63210	34770	28440
7 Transport, storage and communication	190300	88280	102020	198630	92470	106160	199890	88540	111350	206980	91520	115460
A Transport and storage	142700	80940	61760	148850	84310	64540	148270	80310	67960	152730	82460	70270
B Communication	47600	7340	40260	49780	8160	41620	51620	8230	43390	54250	9060	45190
8 Finance, insurance, real estate and business services	294910	78030	216880	310350	84500	225850	320000	89110	230890	325790	90770	235020
A Financial institutions	104910	26080	78830	106750	27810	78940	106890	28830	78060	104410	28490	75920
B Insurance	39910	19350	20560	44260	21690	22570	46870	24270	22600	48040	23630	24410
C Real estate and business services [e]	150090	32600	117490	159340	35000	124340	166240	36010	130230	173340	38650	134690
Real estate, except dwellings	...	...	...	...	...	...	...	...	...	...	...	...
Dwellings	150090	32600	117490	159340	35000	124340	166240	36010	130230	173340	38650	134690
9 Community, social and personal services [ce]	335420	116040	219380	359250	124090	235160	385770	128310	257460	423490	139030	284460
Educational services	...	...	...	...	...	...	...	...	...	...	...	...
Medical, dental, other health and veterinary services	55700	16830	38870	58120	17630	40490	59630	17730	41900	61870	18240	43630
Total, Industries	4110300	2637130	1473170	4287510	2749710	1537800	4282700	2659800	1622900	4327830	2654390	1673440
Producers of Government Services	403770	203700	200070	421170	213710	207460	441090	223700	217390	458290	232110	226180
Other Producers	48490	14270	34220	51480	15070	36410	55370	15600	39770	58180	16020	42160
Total	4562560	2855100	1707460	4760160	2978490	1781670	4779160	2899100	1880060	4844300	2902520	1941780
Less: Imputed bank service charge	...	-84070	84070	...	-84240	84240	...	-83690	83690	...	-82270	82270
Import duties	16480	...	16480	16420	...	16420	17010	...	17010	18990	...	18990
Value added tax	115970	...	115970	116640	...	116640	118040	...	118040	125250	...	125250
Total	4695010	2939170	1755840	4893220	3062730	1830490	4914210	2982790	1931420	4988540	2984790	2003750

Germany, Fed. Rep. of

4.1 Derivation of Value Added by Kind of Activity, in Current Prices

Million Deutsche marks

		1988			1989		
		Gross Output	Intermediate Consumption	Value Added	Gross Output	Intermediate Consumption	Value Added
				All Producers			
1	Agriculture, hunting, forestry and fishing	65530	32420	33110	69540	33430	36110
	A Agriculture and hunting [a]	57640	28870	28770	...	...	...
	B Forestry and logging [a]	7890	3550	4340	...	...	...
	C Fishing [a]	...	...	...	...	...	...
2	Mining and quarrying [b]	30010	18100	11910	...	...	...
	A Coal mining	25910	15680	10230	...	...	...
	B Crude petroleum and natural gas production	...	...	...	...	...	...
	C Metal ore mining	...	...	...	...	...	...
	D Other mining	4100	2420	1680	...	...	...
3	Manufacturing	1690330	1034770	655560	...	...	695030
	A Manufacture of food, beverages and tobacco	210270	142460	67810	...	...	...
	B Textile, wearing apparel and leather industries	73830	46780	27050	...	...	...
	C Manufacture of wood and wood products, including furniture	49220	29240	19980	...	...	...
	D Manufacture of paper and paper products, printing and publishing [c]	69690	40860	28830	...	...	...
	E Manufacture of chemicals and chemical petroleum, coal, rubber and plastic products	331760	207520	124240	...	...	...
	F Manufacture of non-metallic mineral products, except products of petroleum and coal [b]	56170	31700	24470	...	...	...
	G Basic metal industries	130850	83390	47460	...	...	...
	H Manufacture of fabricated metal products, machinery and equipment [d]	759080	447770	311310	...	...	...
	I Other manufacturing industries	9460	5050	4410	...	...	...
4	Electricity, gas and water	155930	98260	57670	...	...	...
	A Electricity, gas and steam	149060	95370	53690	...	...	...
	B Water works and supply	6870	2890	3980	...	...	...
5	Construction [d]	217290	110830	106460	...	...	116000
6	Wholesale and retail trade, restaurants and hotels	1375330	1155630	219700	...	...	...
	A Wholesale and retail trade	1308830	1119580	189250	...	...	199710
	B Restaurants and hotels	66500	36050	30450	...	...	...
7	Transport, storage and communication	218050	95450	122600	...	...	129620
	A Transport and storage	161150	86140	75010	...	...	...
	B Communication	56900	9310	47590	...	...	...
8	Finance, insurance, real estate and business services	341870	96850	245020	...	...	260020
	A Financial institutions	108840	29560	79280	...	...	...
	B Insurance	51240	26250	24990	...	...	...
	C Real estate and business services [e]	181790	41040	140750	...	...	148870
	Real estate, except dwellings	...	...	...	...	...	...
	Dwellings	181790	41040	140750	...	...	148870
9	Community, social and personal services [ce]	472820	155490	317330	...	...	370210
	Educational services	...	...	...	...	...	...
	Medical, dental, other health and veterinary services	69990	20630	49360	...	...	...

Germany, Fed. Rep. of

4.1 Derivation of Value Added by Kind of Activity, in Current Prices
(Continued)

Million Deutsche marks

	1988 Gross Output	1988 Intermediate Consumption	1988 Value Added	1989 Gross Output	1989 Intermediate Consumption	1989 Value Added
Total, Industries	4567160	2797800	1769360	4872920	2994000	1878920
Producers of Government Services	476780	244350	232430	485410	246290	239120
Other Producers	60830	16770	44060	63700	17600	46100
Total	5104770	3058920	2045850	5422030	3257890	2164140
Less: Imputed bank service charge	...	-85080	85080	...	-89190	89190
Import duties	19710	...	19710	23110	...	23110
Value added tax	130200	...	130200	137520	...	137520
Total	5254680	3144000	2110680	5582660	3347080	2235580

a) Hunting and fishing are included in item 'Forestry and logging'.
b) Quarrying is included in item 'Manufacture of non-metalic mineral products except products of petroleum and coal'.
c) Publishing is included in item 'Community, social and personal services'.
d) Structural steel erection is included in item 'Manufacture of fabricated metal products, machinery and equipment'.
e) Business services and real estate except dwellings are included in item 'Community, social and personal services'.

4.2 Derivation of Value Added by Kind of Activity, in Constant Prices

Million Deutsche marks

At constant prices of:1980
All Producers

	1980 Gross Output	1980 Intermediate Consumption	1980 Value Added	1981 Gross Output	1981 Intermediate Consumption	1981 Value Added	1982 Gross Output	1982 Intermediate Consumption	1982 Value Added	1983 Gross Output	1983 Intermediate Consumption	1983 Value Added
1 Agriculture, hunting, forestry and fishing	63750	33380	30370	63220	32670	30550	68110	32100	36010	65680	32840	32840
A Agriculture and hunting a	...	...	25700	...	...	26110	...	...	31510	...	...	28380
B Forestry and logging a	...	...	4670	...	...	4440	...	...	4500	...	...	4460
C Fishing a	...	...	...	...	...	...	...	...	...	...	...	...
2 Mining and quarrying bc	136020	85820	13870	136610	87370	13720	135720	87990	13660	136480	87940	12690
A Coal mining	...	...	11990	...	...	11980	...	...	11730	...	...	10570
B Crude petroleum and natural gas production	...	...	...	...	...	...	...	...	...	...	...	...
C Metal ore mining	...	...	...	...	...	...	...	...	...	...	...	...
D Other mining	...	...	1880	...	...	1740	...	...	1930	...	...	2120
3 Manufacturing	1319020	836180	482840	1291300	815780	475520	1253030	788880	464150	1266320	796960	469360
A Manufacture of food, beverages and tobacco	...	...	58050	...	...	58400	...	...	57000	...	...	57190
B Textile, wearing apparel and leather industries	...	...	25520	...	...	23830	...	...	22670	...	...	22460
C Manufacture of wood and wood products, including furniture	...	...	18240	...	...	16560	...	...	15110	...	...	15390
D Manufacture of paper and paper products, printing and publishing d	...	...	20450	...	...	20280	...	...	19690	...	...	20420
E Manufacture of chemicals and chemical petroleum, coal, rubber and plastic products	...	...	85210	...	...	82570	...	...	81470	...	...	85920
F Manufacture of non-metallic mineral products, except products of petroleum and coal b	...	...	21330	...	...	19730	...	...	18560	...	...	18970
G Basic metal industries	...	...	38870	...	...	37150	...	...	34040	...	...	33420
H Manufacture of fabricated metal products, machinery and equipment e	...	...	212080	...	...	213920	...	...	212350	...	...	212700
I Other manufacturing industries	...	...	3090	...	...	3080	...	...	3260	...	...	2890
4 Electricity, gas and water c	...	...	36330	...	...	35520	...	...	34070	...	...	35850
A Electricity, gas and steam	...	...	33430	...	...	32600	...	...	31170	...	...	32950
B Water works and supply	...	...	2900	...	...	2920	...	...	2900	...	...	2900
5 Construction e	196710	97520	99190	186940	92540	94400	179060	88980	90080	182960	91430	91530
6 Wholesale and retail trade, restaurants and hotels f	1065340	925360	158880	1046000	904360	160680	1013560	875230	156680	1048580	906850	159880
A Wholesale and retail trade	...	...	139980	...	...	141640	...	...	138330	...	...	141730
B Restaurants and hotels	...	...	18900	...	...	19040	...	...	18350	...	...	18150
7 Transport, storage and communication	158430	72760	85670	160930	72810	88120	161410	72850	88560	164030	74330	89700
A Transport and storage	...	...	52660	...	...	52330	...	...	51450	...	...	52270
B Communication	...	...	33010	...	...	35790	...	...	37110	...	...	37430
8 Finance, insurance, real estate and business services	212050	59150	152900	217420	59920	157500	224080	61720	162360	229980	64110	165870
A Financial institutions g	100370	33970	51690	101760	34410	51980	105150	35500	53700	107720	37130	54340

706

Germany, Fed. Rep. of

4.2 Derivation of Value Added by Kind of Activity, in Constant Prices
(Continued)

Million Deutsche marks

	1980			1981			1982			1983		
	Gross Output	Intermediate Consumption	Value Added	Gross Output	Intermediate Consumption	Value Added	Gross Output	Intermediate Consumption	Value Added	Gross Output	Intermediate Consumption	Value Added
						At constant prices of:1980						
B Insurance g	...	...	14710	...	...	15370	...	...	15950	...	...	16250
C Real estate and business services h	111680	25180	86500	115660	25510	90150	118930	26220	92710	122260	26980	95280
Real estate, except dwellings	...	...	...	...	...	...	...	...	...	...	...	...
Dwellings	111680	25180	86500	115660	25510	90150	118930	26220	92710	122260	26980	95280
9 Community, social and personal services dhf	295090	112920	163270	304090	116560	168490	308040	118450	171240	319270	122790	178330
Educational services	...	...	...	...	...	...	...	...	...	...	...	...
Medical, dental, other health and veterinary services	...	...	32580	...	...	33390	...	...	32410	...	...	32710
Total, Industries	3446410	2223090	1223320	3406510	2182010	1224500	3343010	2126200	1216810	3413300	2177250	1236050
Producers of Government Services i	377340	177750	172390	384350	180340	176370	384170	177990	177570	386010	178000	178640
Other Producers i	...	...	27200	...	...	27640	...	...	28610	...	...	29370
Total	3823750	2400840	1422910	3790860	2362350	1428510	3727180	2304190	1422990	3799310	2355250	1444060
Less: Imputed bank service charge	...	-53940	53940	...	-55570	55570	...	-57150	57150	...	-59150	59150
Import duties	13480	...	13480	13440	...	13440	13380	...	13380	14590	...	14590
Value added tax	96490	...	96490	95010	...	95010	92610	...	92610	94420	...	94420
Total	3933720	2454780	1478940	3899310	2417920	1481390	3833170	2361340	1471830	3908320	2414400	1493920

	1984			1985			1986			1987		
	Gross Output	Intermediate Consumption	Value Added	Gross Output	Intermediate Consumption	Value Added	Gross Output	Intermediate Consumption	Value Added	Gross Output	Intermediate Consumption	Value Added
						At constant prices of:1980						
						All Producers						
1 Agriculture, hunting, forestry and fishing	68100	32410	35690	66710	32910	33800	69390	32710	36680	66050	32160	33890
A Agriculture and hunting a	...	...	31380	...	...	28980	...	...	32080	...	...	29270
B Forestry and logging a	...	...	4310	...	...	4820	...	...	4600	...	...	4620
C Fishing a	...	...	...	...	...	...	...	...	...	...	...	...
2 Mining and quarrying bc	143890	95900	12300	148450	100960	11840	149600	101070	9940	154760	101220	9100
A Coal mining	...	...	10140	...	...	9880	...	...	7460	...	...	6670
B Crude petroleum and natural gas production	...	...	...	...	...	...	...	...	...	...	...	...
C Metal ore mining	...	...	...	...	...	...	...	...	...	...	...	...
D Other mining	...	...	2160	...	...	1960	...	...	2480	...	...	2430
3 Manufacturing	1310460	828290	482170	1359970	861520	498450	1394780	896250	498530	1403000	918840	484160
A Manufacture of food, beverages and tobacco	...	...	57190	...	...	56650	...	...	52860	...	...	49100
B Textile, wearing apparel and leather industries	...	...	22620	...	...	22830	...	...	22010	...	...	21590
C Manufacture of wood and wood products, including furniture	...	...	15400	...	...	14710	...	...	14120	...	...	14000
D Manufacture of paper and paper products, printing and publishing d	...	...	22160	...	...	21560	...	...	21870	...	...	22450
E Manufacture of chemicals and chemical petroleum, coal, rubber and plastic products	...	...	89650	...	...	91980	...	...	92980	...	...	84440
F Manufacture of non-metallic mineral products, except products of petroleum and coal b	...	...	19520	...	...	18380	...	...	18500	...	...	18060
G Basic metal industries	...	...	34520	...	...	37010	...	...	37990	...	...	36380
H Manufacture of fabricated metal products, machinery and equipment e	...	...	218240	...	...	232460	...	...	235200	...	...	235200
I Other manufacturing industries	...	...	2870	...	...	2870	...	...	3000	...	...	2940
4 Electricity, gas and water c	...	...	35690	...	...	35650	...	...	38590	...	...	44440
A Electricity, gas and steam	...	...	32680	...	...	32650	...	...	35640	...	...	41510
B Water works and supply	...	...	3010	...	...	3000	...	...	2950	...	...	2930
5 Construction e	184500	93080	91420	173480	85260	88220	178860	89140	89720	179210	92030	87180
6 Wholesale and retail trade, restaurants and hotels f	1078840	931350	166370	1100330	951460	167790	1124570	970810	173050	1147990	989670	178280
A Wholesale and retail trade	...	...	147490	...	...	148870	...	...	153760	...	...	158320
B Restaurants and hotels	...	...	18880	...	...	18920	...	...	19290	...	...	19960
7 Transport, storage and communication	171320	77830	93490	176810	79920	96890	180880	81940	98940	189780	86620	103160

Germany, Fed. Rep. of

4.2 Derivation of Value Added by Kind of Activity, in Constant Prices
(Continued)

Million Deutsche marks

	1984			1985			1986			1987		
	Gross Output	Intermediate Consumption	Value Added	Gross Output	Intermediate Consumption	Value Added	Gross Output	Intermediate Consumption	Value Added	Gross Output	Intermediate Consumption	Value Added
					At constant prices of:1980							
A Transport and storage	...	...	54060	...	...	55740	...	...	55870	...	...	58120
B Communication	...	...	39430	...	...	41150	...	...	43070	...	...	45040
8 Finance, insurance, real estate and business services	236150	66520	169630	245890	70540	175350	256920	74250	182670	264990	74640	190350
A Financial institutions g	110410	39250	55160	116560	41960	58050	124640	46120	61430	129660	45680	64060
B Insurance g	...	...	16000	...	...	16550	...	...	17090	...	...	19920
C Real estate and business services h	125740	27270	98470	129330	28580	100750	132280	28130	104150	135330	28960	106370
Real estate, except dwellings	...	...	...	...	...	...	...	...	...	...	...	...
Dwellings	125740	27270	98470	129330	28580	100750	132280	28130	104150	135330	28960	106370
9 Community, social and personal services dhf	335950	128510	188560	350270	132700	198650	367840	135920	212630	393580	143860	229760
Educational services	...	...	...	...	...	...	...	...	...	...	...	...
Medical, dental, other health and veterinary services	...	...	34840	...	...	36060	...	...	36510	...	...	37360
Total, Industries	3529210	2253890	1275320	3621910	2315270	1306640	3722840	2382090	1340750	3799360	2439040	1360320
Producers of Government Services i	395300	184310	180590	403890	188990	183250	414910	196010	185770	421590	199430	188100
Other Producers i	...	...	30400	...	...	31650	...	...	33130	...	...	34060
Total	3924510	2438200	1486310	4025800	2504260	1521540	4137750	2578100	1559650	4220950	2638470	1582480
Less: Imputed bank service charge	...	-60560	60560	...	-63380	63380	...	-67260	67260	...	-70730	70730
Import duties	15010	...	15010	15680	...	15680	16950	...	16950	19380	...	19380
Value added tax	95230	...	95230	92640	...	92640	93870	...	93870	99050	...	99050
Total	4034750	2498760	1535990	4134120	2567640	1566480	4248570	2645360	1603210	4339380	2709200	1630180

	1988			1989		
	Gross Output	Intermediate Consumption	Value Added	Gross Output	Intermediate Consumption	Value Added
		At constant prices of:1980				
		All Producers				
1 Agriculture, hunting, forestry and fishing	68460	32220	36240	67910	31980	35930
A Agriculture and hunting a	...	...	31470	...	...	...
B Forestry and logging a	...	...	4770	...	...	...
C Fishing a	...	...	...	...	...	...
2 Mining and quarrying bc	154640	100250	7030	...	...	...
A Coal mining	...	...	4800	...	...	...
B Crude petroleum and natural gas production	...	...	...	...	...	...
C Metal ore mining	...	...	...	...	...	...
D Other mining	...	...	2230	...	...	...
3 Manufacturing	1463320	964950	498370	...	...	521560
A Manufacture of food, beverages and tobacco	...	...	47310	...	...	...
B Textile, wearing apparel and leather industries	...	...	21340	...	...	...
C Manufacture of wood and wood products, including furniture	...	...	14150	...	...	...
D Manufacture of paper and paper products, printing and publishing d	...	...	21790	...	...	...
E Manufacture of chemicals and chemical petroleum, coal, rubber and plastic products	...	...	92250	...	...	...
F Manufacture of non-metallic mineral products, except products of petroleum and coal b	...	...	19330	...	...	...
G Basic metal industries	...	...	36410	...	...	...
H Manufacture of fabricated metal products, machinery and equipment e	...	...	242760	...	...	...
I Other manufacturing industries	...	...	3030	...	...	...
4 Electricity, gas and water c	...	...	47360	...	...	...
A Electricity, gas and steam	...	...	43810	...	...	...
B Water works and supply	...	...	3550	...	...	...

708

Germany, Fed. Rep. of

4.2 Derivation of Value Added by Kind of Activity, in Constant Prices
(Continued)

Million Deutsche marks

	1988 Gross Output	1988 Intermediate Consumption	1988 Value Added	1989 Gross Output	1989 Intermediate Consumption	1989 Value Added
			At constant prices of:1980			
5 Construction e	185920	95730	90190	...	...	94420
6 Wholesale and retail trade, restaurants and hotels f	1180490	1017330	183770	...	...	...
A Wholesale and retail trade	...	...	163160	...	...	167090
B Restaurants and hotels	...	...	20610	...	...	...
7 Transport, storage and communication	199010	91150	107860	...	...	113510
A Transport and storage	...	...	60280	...	...	...
B Communication	...	...	47580	...	...	...
8 Finance, insurance, real estate and business services	275280	78620	196660	...	...	203380
A Financial institutions g	136820	48430	67300	...	...	...
B Insurance g	...	...	21090	...	...	...
C Real estate and business services h	138460	30190	108270	...	...	110900
Real estate, except dwellings	...	...	...	...	...	...
Dwellings	138460	30190	108270	...	...	110900
9 Community, social and personal services dhf	426500	156670	249220	...	...	278630
Educational services	...	...	...	...	...	...
Medical, dental, other health and veterinary services	...	...	41910	...	...	...
Total, Industries	3953620	2536920	1416700	4079630	2609510	1470120
Producers of Government Services i	431680	206330	190310	430190	203210	190940
Other Producers i	...	...	35040	...	...	36040
Total	4385300	2743250	1642050	4509820	2812720	1697100
Less: Imputed bank service charge	...	-73830	73830	...	-76510	76510
Import duties	20150	...	20150	21090	...	21090
Value added tax	102120	...	102120	103980	...	103980
Total	4507570	2817080	1690490	4634890	2889230	1745660

a) Hunting and fishing are included in item 'Forestry and logging'.
b) Quarrying is included in item 'Manufacture of non-metalic mineral products except products of petroleum and coal'.
c) Gross output and intermediate consumption of electricity, gas and water are included in item 'Mining and quarrying'.
d) Publishing is included in item 'Community, social and personal services'.
e) Structural steel erection is included in item 'Manufacture of fabricated metal products, machinery and equipment'.

f) Gross output and intermediate consumption of restaurants and hotels are included in item 'Community, social and personal services'.
g) Gross output and intermediate consumption of insurance are included in item 'Financial institutions'.
h) Business services and real estate except dwellings are included in item 'Community, social and personal services'.
i) Gross output and intermediate consumption of 'Other producers' are included in item 'Producers of government services'.

4.3 Cost Components of Value Added

Million Deutsche marks

	1980 Compensation of Employees	1980 Capital Consumption	1980 Net Operating Surplus	1980 Indirect Taxes	1980 Less: Subsidies Received	1980 Value Added	1981 Compensation of Employees	1981 Capital Consumption	1981 Net Operating Surplus	1981 Indirect Taxes	1981 Less: Subsidies Received	1981 Value Added
						All Producers						
1 Agriculture, hunting, forestry and fishing	6930	9160	15050	-770	...	30370	7200	9720	15050	-290	...	31680
A Agriculture and hunting a	3330	8650	14420	-700	...	25700	3560	9200	14760	-280	...	27240
B Forestry and logging a	3600	510	630	-70	...	4670	3640	520	290	-10	...	4440
C Fishing a	...	...	...	...	...	...	...	...	...	...	...	...
2 Mining and quarrying b	11580	2220	2070	-2000	...	13870	12290	2360	1880	-1730	...	14800
A Coal mining	10810	1740	1490	-2050	...	11990	11460	1850	1090	-1800	...	12600
B Crude petroleum and natural gas production	...	...	...	...	...	...	...	...	...	...	...	...
C Metal ore mining	...	...	...	...	...	...	...	...	...	...	...	...
D Other mining	770	480	580	50	...	1880	830	510	790	70	...	2200

Germany, Fed. Rep. of

4.3 Cost Components of Value Added
(Continued)

Million Deutsche marks

	Compensation of Employees	Capital Consumption	Net Operating Surplus	Indirect Taxes	Less: Subsidies Received	Value Added	Compensation of Employees	Capital Consumption	Net Operating Surplus	Indirect Taxes	Less: Subsidies Received	Value Added
	1980						**1981**					
3 Manufacturing	328560	49190	63570	41520	...	482840	339090	52210	58070	40360	...	489730
A Manufacture of food, beverages and tobacco	24390	5800	13410	14450	...	58050	25530	6090	11940	14290	...	57850
B Textile, wearing apparel and leather industries	18950	2550	3570	450	...	25520	18590	2590	3110	400	...	24690
C Manufacture of wood and wood products, including furniture	12590	1650	3610	390	...	18240	12720	1750	2850	320	...	17640
D Manufacture of paper and paper products, printing and publishing c	14550	2380	3120	400	...	20450	15140	2560	2820	320	...	20840
E Manufacture of chemicals and chemical petroleum, coal, rubber and plastic products	44980	10170	8980	21080	...	85210	47190	10630	7990	21130	...	86940
F Manufacture of non-metallic mineral products, except products of petroleum and coal b	14260	3160	3240	670	...	21330	14380	3310	2080	530	...	20300
G Basic metal industries	30400	6040	1750	680	...	38870	30930	6230	200	490	...	37850
H Manufacture of fabricated metal products, machinery and equipment d	166140	17210	25440	3290	...	212080	172340	18810	26130	2790	...	220070
I Other manufacturing industries	2300	230	450	110	...	3090	2270	240	950	90	...	3550
4 Electricity, gas and water	14520	9530	8740	3540	...	36330	15460	10200	8110	4480	...	38250
A Electricity, gas and steam	13290	8610	8190	3340	...	33430	14170	9210	7610	4240	...	35230
B Water works and supply	1230	920	550	200	...	2900	1290	990	500	240	...	3020
5 Construction d	64430	5110	27640	2010	...	99190	65310	5360	26080	2060	...	98810
6 Wholesale and retail trade, restaurants and hotels	96490	11500	50060	830	...	158880	101010	12270	52180	1810	...	167270
A Wholesale and retail trade	86540	10000	43260	180	...	139980	89980	10670	45000	1230	...	146880
B Restaurants and hotels	9950	1500	6800	650	...	18900	11030	1600	7180	580	...	20390
7 Transport, storage and communication	54360	18840	17550	-5080	...	85670	57180	20210	18130	-5890	...	89630
A Transport and storage	35420	12820	9460	-5040	...	52660	36930	13490	10570	-5830	...	55160
B Communication	18940	6020	8090	-40	...	33010	20250	6720	7560	-60	...	34470
8 Finance, insurance, real estate and business services e	34370	38890	24150	6400	...	152900	36310	42530	30090	7030	...	168360
A Financial institutions	23950	2060	23360	2320	...	51690	25340	2270	29360	2840	...	59810
B Insurance	10420	750	790	2750	...	14710	10970	840	730	3030	...	15570
C Real estate and business services f	...	36080	...	1330	...	86500	...	39420	...	1160	...	92980
Real estate, except dwellings	...	...	...	...	...	...	...	...	...	...	...	...
Dwellings	...	36080	...	1330	...	86500	...	39420	...	1160	...	92980
9 Community, social and personal services cfe	44340	17230	144610	6180	...	163270	48250	20480	155550	6260	...	178140
Educational services	...	...	...	...	...	...	...	...	...	...	...	...
Medical, dental, other health and veterinary services	8420	3370	20810	-20	...	32580	9060	3920	22130	-50	...	35060
Total, Industries g	655580	161670	353440	52630	...	1223320	682100	175340	365140	54090	...	1276670
Producers of Government Services	162660	9490	-	240	...	172390	173000	10480	-	240	...	133720
Other Producers	24600	2580	-	20	...	27200	26100	2820	-	20	...	28940
Total g	842840	173740	353440	52890	...	1422910	881200	188640	365140	54350	...	1489330
Less: Imputed bank service charge	...	...	53940	...	...	53940	...	...	63260	...	...	63260
Import duties	...	...	...	13480	...	13480	...	...	...	14080	...	14080
Value added tax	...	...	...	96490	...	96490	...	...	...	100780	...	100780
Total g	842840	173740	299500	162860	...	1478940	881200	188640	301880	169210	...	1540930

	Compensation of Employees	Capital Consumption	Net Operating Surplus	Indirect Taxes	Less: Subsidies Received	Value Added	Compensation of Employees	Capital Consumption	Net Operating Surplus	Indirect Taxes	Less: Subsidies Received	Value Added
	1982						**1983**					
					All Producers							
1 Agriculture, hunting, forestry and fishing	7630	10220	19010	-520	...	36340	8020	10540	13700	-40	...	32220
A Agriculture and hunting a	3770	9670	19290	-540	...	32190	3980	9930	14510	-110	...	28310
B Forestry and logging a	3860	550	-280	20	...	4150	4040	610	-810	70	...	3910
C Fishing a	...	...	...	...	...	...	...	...	...	...	...	...
2 Mining and quarrying b	12750	2540	2200	-1000	...	16490	12490	2700	3380	-1150	...	17420

Germany, Fed. Rep. of

4.3 Cost Components of Value Added
(Continued)

Million Deutsche marks

	1982						1983					
	Compensation of Employees	Capital Consumption	Net Operating Surplus	Indirect Taxes	Less: Subsidies Received	Value Added	Compensation of Employees	Capital Consumption	Net Operating Surplus	Indirect Taxes	Less: Subsidies Received	Value Added
A Coal mining	11920	1990	1000	-1040	...	13870	11660	2130	1990	-1200	...	14580
B Crude petroleum and natural gas production	...	...	...	...	...	...	...	...	...	...	...	...
C Metal ore mining	...	...	...	...	...	...	...	...	...	...	...	...
D Other mining	830	550	1200	40	...	2620	830	570	1390	50	...	2840
3 Manufacturing	341880	54650	65840	40480	...	502850	343520	56900	83660	40850	...	524930
A Manufacture of food, beverages and tobacco	25920	6320	14840	14520	...	61600	25730	6500	16160	15520	...	63910
B Textile, wearing apparel and leather industries	18060	2610	3270	360	...	24300	17780	2590	3960	350	...	24680
C Manufacture of wood and wood products, including furniture	12310	1810	2550	280	...	16950	12430	1840	3040	250	...	17560
D Manufacture of paper and paper products, printing and publishing c	15150	2690	2590	320	...	20750	15300	2770	3840	340	...	22250
E Manufacture of chemicals and chemical petroleum, coal, rubber and plastic products	48990	10960	7440	21280	...	88670	50780	11310	14780	20970	...	97840
F Manufacture of non-metallic mineral products, except products of petroleum and coal b	14130	3390	1880	510	...	19910	14330	3420	2810	550	...	21110
G Basic metal industries	31090	6340	-720	240	...	36950	28620	6740	1320	-170	...	36510
H Manufacture of fabricated metal products, machinery and equipment d	173940	20270	32600	2870	...	229680	176260	21450	36720	2960	...	237390
I Other manufacturing industries	2290	260	1390	100	...	4040	2290	280	1030	80	...	3680
4 Electricity, gas and water	15760	10870	11270	4380	...	42280	16430	11440	12790	4610	...	45270
A Electricity, gas and steam	14450	9830	10740	4150	...	39170	15050	10390	12240	4310	...	41990
B Water works and supply	1310	1040	530	230	...	3110	1380	1050	550	300	...	3280
5 Construction d	65660	5490	22280	1930	...	95360	66410	5480	23780	1770	...	97440
6 Wholesale and retail trade, restaurants and hotels	102500	12910	53650	1910	...	170970	104630	13340	61570	290	...	179830
A Wholesale and retail trade	91140	11230	46250	1330	...	149950	92740	11580	54050	-280	...	158090
B Restaurants and hotels	11360	1680	7400	580	...	21020	11890	1760	7520	570	...	21740
7 Transport, storage and communication	58860	21360	19770	-6210	...	93780	59650	22160	21180	-6220	...	96770
A Transport and storage	37950	13970	11150	-6140	...	56930	38300	14210	11940	-6170	...	58280
B Communication	20910	7390	8620	-70	...	36850	21350	7950	9240	-50	...	38490
8 Finance, insurance, real estate and business services e	38380	45260	37710	8690	...	187930	40620	47810	42210	9740	...	205270
A Financial institutions	26810	2470	36630	4090	...	70000	28370	2700	41100	4810	...	76980
B Insurance	11570	920	1080	3360	...	16930	12250	1020	1110	3720	...	18100
C Real estate and business services f	...	41870	...	1240	...	101000	...	44090	...	1210	...	110190
Real estate, except dwellings	...	...	...	...	...	...	...	...	...	...	...	...
Dwellings	...	41870	...	1240	...	101000	...	44090	...	1210	...	110190
9 Community, social and personal services cde	51030	23530	165710	6360	...	188740	52700	26010	182560	7050	...	203430
Educational services	...	...	...	...	...	...	...	...	...	...	...	...
Medical, dental, other health and veterinary services	9900	4450	21010	-50	...	35310	10220	4890	21450	-60	...	36500
Total, Industries g	694450	186830	397440	56020	...	1334740	704470	196380	444830	56900	...	1402580
Producers of Government Services	178070	11270	-	240	...	189580	183590	11950	-	250	...	195790
Other Producers	27850	3010	-	20	...	30880	29510	3100	-	20	...	32630
Total g	900370	201110	397440	56280	...	1555200	917570	211430	444830	57170	...	1631000
Less: Imputed bank service charge	...	...	73470	...	...	73470	...	...	81720	...	...	81720
Import duties	...	...	...	14810	...	14810	...	...	...	16210	...	16210
Value added tax	...	...	...	101380	...	101380	...	...	...	109350	...	109350
Total g	900370	201110	323970	172470	...	1597920	917570	211430	363110	182730	...	1674840

Germany, Fed. Rep. of

4.3 Cost Components of Value Added

Million Deutsche marks

	1984						1985					
	Compensation of Employees	Capital Consumption	Net Operating Surplus	Indirect Taxes	Less: Subsidies Received	Value Added	Compensation of Employees	Capital Consumption	Net Operating Surplus	Indirect Taxes	Less: Subsidies Received	Value Added
1 Agriculture, hunting, forestry and fishing	8510	10820	16840	-1520	...	34650	8710	10980	15570	-3020	...	32240
A Agriculture and hunting a	4170	10180	17990	-1580	...	30760	4270	10330	16380	-3070	...	27910
B Forestry and logging a	4340	640	-1150	60	...	3890	4440	650	-810	50	...	4330
C Fishing a	...	...	...	...	...	...	...	...	...	...	...	...
2 Mining and quarrying b	12690	2810	3920	-1860	...	17560	12810	2870	4010	-1890	...	17800
A Coal mining	11810	2220	2420	-1920	...	14530	11880	2270	2430	-1900	...	14680
B Crude petroleum and natural gas production	...	...	...	...	...	...	...	...	...	...	...	...
C Metal ore mining	...	...	...	...	...	...	...	...	...	...	...	...
D Other mining	880	590	1500	60	...	3030	930	600	1580	10	...	3120
3 Manufacturing	356740	57770	82580	42450	...	547240	370010	60840	102450	44240	...	583540
A Manufacture of food, beverages and tobacco	25900	6600	15780	16250	...	64530	26910	6750	16220	16330	...	66210
B Textile, wearing apparel and leather industries	18020	2580	4090	360	...	25050	18290	2560	4750	370	...	25970
C Manufacture of wood and wood products, including furniture	12640	1840	2800	280	...	17560	12290	1860	2620	250	...	17020
D Manufacture of paper and paper products, printing and publishing c	15790	2870	5210	430	...	24300	16440	2980	5390	460	...	25270
E Manufacture of chemicals and chemical products, coal, rubber and plastic products	53210	11530	17440	22040	...	104220	56740	11880	18290	22490	...	109400
F Manufacture of non-metallic mineral products, except products of petroleum and coal b	14580	3450	2990	510	...	21530	14110	3470	2460	450	...	20490
G Basic metal industries	30470	7170	2420	-800	...	39260	31680	7200	5160	-350	...	43690
H Manufacture of fabricated metal products, machinery and equipment d	183740	22430	37620	3290	...	247080	197070	23820	46630	4150	...	271670
I Other manufacturing industries	2390	300	930	90	...	3710	2480	320	930	90	...	3820
4 Electricity, gas and water	16890	12140	14340	4630	...	47790	12850	14500	5170	...	50150
A Electricity, gas and steam	15290	11030	13560	4380	...	44260	16220	11710	13810	4920	...	46660
B Water works and supply	1390	1110	780	250	...	3530	1410	1140	690	250	...	3490
5 Construction d	68300	5390	22670	1600	...	97960	63380	5280	23780	1590	...	94030
6 Wholesale and retail trade, restaurants and hotels	110180	13680	65540	290	...	189690	114100	13980	64150	640	...	192870
A Wholesale and retail trade	97560	11860	57430	-310	...	166540	100630	12100	56240	-50	...	168920
B Restaurants and hotels	12620	1820	8110	600	...	23150	13470	1880	7910	690	...	23950
7 Transport, storage and communication	60800	23230	24050	-5940	...	102020	62710	24400	24710	-5660	...	106160
A Transport and storage	39160	14540	13990	-5930	...	61760	40300	14860	14910	-5650	...	64540
B Communication	21520	8690	10060	-10	...	40260	22410	9420	9800	-10	...	41620
8 Finance, insurance, real estate and business services e	42200	5120	44330	10020	...	216880	44440	53510	43300	10530	...	225850
A Financial institutions	29610	3000	41390	4830	...	78830	31390	3230	39420	4900	...	78940
B Insurance	12590	1130	2940	3900	...	20560	1220	3880	4420	...	22570
C Real estate and business services f	...	46990	...	1290	...	117490	...	49060	...	1210	...	124340
Real estate, except dwellings	...	...	...	...	...	...	...	...	...	...	...	...
Dwellings	...	46990	...	1290	...	117490	...	49060	...	1210	...	124340
9 Community, social and personal services de	56320	28200	196480	7590	...	219380	60240	30640	210810	7540	...	235160
Educational services	...	...	...	...	...	...	...	...	...	...	...	...
Medical, dental, other health and veterinary services	10890	5330	22680	-30	...	38870	12310	5730	22460	-10	...	40490

All Producers

712

Germany, Fed. Rep. of

4.3 Cost Components of Value Added
(Continued)

Million Deutsche marks

	1984						1985					
	Compensation of Employees	Capital Consumption	Net Operating Surplus	Indirect Taxes	Less: Subsidies Received	Value Added	Compensation of Employees	Capital Consumption	Net Operating Surplus	Indirect Taxes	Less: Subsidies Received	Value Added
Total, Industries 9	732300	206160	477450	57260	...	1473170	760030	215350	502280	59140	...	1537800
Producers of Government Services	187230	12580	-	260	...	200070	194110	13090	-	260	...	207460
Other Producers	30960	3240	-	20	...	34220	33040	3350	-	20	...	36410
Total 9	950490	221980	477450	57540	...	1707460	987180	231790	502280	59420	...	1781670
Less: Imputed bank service charge	...	...	...	8070	...	8070	...	...	...	8240	...	8240
Import duties	...	...	...	16480	...	16480	...	...	...	16420	...	16420
Value added tax	...	...	...	115970	...	115970	...	...	...	116440	...	116440
Total 9	950490	221980	393380	189900	...	1755840	987180	231790	419040	192480	...	1830490

	1986						1987					
	Compensation of Employees	Capital Consumption	Net Operating Surplus	Indirect Taxes	Less: Subsidies Received	Value Added	Compensation of Employees	Capital Consumption	Net Operating Surplus	Indirect Taxes	Less: Subsidies Received	Value Added

All Producers

1 Agriculture, hunting, forestry and fishing	8870	11020	17380	-3610	...	33660	8770	10990	13800	-3100	...	30460
A Agriculture and hunting [a]	4320	10360	18550	-3640	...	29590	4130	10320	14980	-3150	...	26280
B Forestry and logging [a]	4550	660	-1170	30	...	4070	4640	670	-1180	50	...	4180
C Fishing [a]	...	...	...	...	...	...	...	...	...	...	...	...
2 Mining and quarrying [b]	12930	2940	1740	-2500	...	15110	12980	2970	1690	-3350	...	13690
A Coal mining	12030	2320	780	-2540	...	12590	12080	2340	1350	-3980	...	11790
B Crude petroleum and natural gas production	...	...	...	...	...	...	...	...	...	...	...	...
C Metal ore mining	900	620	960	40	...	2520	900	630	340	30	...	1900
3 Manufacturing	394720	62360	118780	45160	...	621020	411390	63960	108220	43200	...	626770
A Manufacture of food, beverages and tobacco	27040	6890	17790	16120	...	67820	27820	6930	17170	16020	...	67980
B Textile, wearing apparel and leather industries	18520	2600	5440	450	...	27010	18630	2620	5560	470	...	27280
C Manufacture of wood and wood products, including furniture	12460	1840	3030	260	...	17590	12700	1820	3840	280	...	18640
D Manufacture of paper and paper products, printing and publishing [c]	17150	3120	6560	490	...	27320	17680	3260	7280	510	...	28730
E Manufacture of chemicals and chemical petroleum, coal, rubber and plastic products	58790	11690	27210	22390	...	120080	62230	11970	18660	20980	...	113840
F Manufacture of non-metallic mineral products, except products of petroleum and coal [b]	14370	3480	3970	560	...	22380	14900	3460	3550	550	...	22460
G Basic metal industries	23210	7030	6260	540	...	37040	32090	6640	5000	410	...	44140
H Manufacture of fabricated metal products, machinery and equipment [d]	211480	25390	47390	4250	...	288510	222570	26870	46000	3880	...	299420
I Other manufacturing industries	2600	340	1130	100	...	4170	2670	350	1160	100	...	4280
4 Electricity, gas and water	18340	13330	15650	4980	...	52500	19400	14040	17690	4350	...	55480
A Electricity, gas and steam	16910	12360	15010	4700	...	48980	18160	12850	17010	4140	...	52160
B Water works and supply	1430	1170	640	280	...	3520	1240	1190	680	210	...	3320
5 Construction [d]	65300	5210	27140	1700	...	99350	65350	5130	28850	1490	...	100920
6 Wholesale and retail trade, restaurants and hotels	118230	14320	69270	-260	...	201560	122750	14640	73690	100	...	211180
A Wholesale and retail trade	103770	12370	60090	-1010	...	175220	108110	12650	62650	-670	...	182740
B Restaurants and hotels	14460	1950	9180	750	...	26340	14640	1990	11040	770	...	28440
7 Transport, storage and communication	66010	25660	25070	-5390	...	111350	68820	26640	25340	-5140	...	115460
A Transport and storage	42530	15470	15340	-5380	...	67960	44240	15790	15370	-5130	...	70270
B Communication	23480	10190	9730	-10	...	43390	24380	10850	9970	-10	...	45190
8 Finance, insurance, real estate and business services [e]	48170	55850	38300	11000	...	230890	51480	58470	34780	10750	...	235020
A Financial institutions	34200	3390	35670	4800	...	78060	36510	3550	31510	4350	...	75920
B Insurance	13970	1290	2630	4710	...	22600	14970	1350	3270	4820	...	24410
C Real estate and business services [f]	...	51170	...	1490	...	130230	55370	...	1580	...	134690
Real estate, except dwellings	...	...	...	...	...	...	...	...	...	...	...	...

713

Germany, Fed. Rep. of

4.3 Cost Components of Value Added (Continued)

Million Deutsche marks

	1986						1987					
	Compensation of Employees	Capital Consumption	Net Operating Surplus	Indirect Taxes	Less: Subsidies Received	Value Added	Compensation of Employees	Capital Consumption	Net Operating Surplus	Indirect Taxes	Less: Subsidies Received	Value Added
Dwellings	5170	1490	...	130230	1580	134690						
9 Community, social and personal services d,e	64830	3270	8580	228830	86	257460	680	34820	25500	840	...	284460
Educational services	...	...	...	...	...	...	...	...	...	...	...	...
Medical, dental, other health and veterinary services	13390	6050	22500	-40	41900	13790	6350	23530	-40	43630		
Total, Industries 9	79740	22880	54260	59660	-40	162290	828780	231660	556660	56340	...	1673440
Producers of Government Services	203540	13600	-	250	-	217390	211740	14190	-	250	...	226180
Other Producers	36270	3470	-	30	-	39770	38530	3600	30	...	42160
Total 9	1037210	542160	240750	59940	18900	1900900	1070900	249450	556660	...	1941780
Less: Imputed bank service charge	8690	...	17010	...	8690	...	22770	82270				
Import duties	...	...	17010	...	17010	18990	18990					
Value added tax	...	...	118040	...	118040	125250	125250					
Total g	1037210	240750	458470	194660	1931420	1079050	249450	473390	200800	...	2003750

All Producers

	1988						1989					
	Compensation of Employees	Capital Consumption	Net Operating Surplus	Indirect Taxes	Less: Subsidies Received	Value Added	Compensation of Employees	Capital Consumption	Net Operating Surplus	Indirect Taxes	Less: Subsidies Received	Value Added
1 Agriculture, hunting, forestry and fishing	8900	11000	17330	-4120	9060	33110	...	...	...	...	...	36110
A Agriculture and hunting a	4150	10310	18470	-4160	...	28770						
B Forestry and logging a	4750	690	-1140	40	...	4340						
C Fishing a	...	...	...	...	...	...						
2 Mining and quarrying b	12580	3030	660	-4360	11910	...	...	...	...	...	...	...
A Coal mining	11660	2390	570	-4390	10230							
B Crude petroleum and natural gas production	...	...	...	...	...							
C Metal ore mining	...	...	...	...	...							
D Other mining	920	640	90	30	1680							
3 Manufacturing	425080	66040	118950	45490	655560	446230	...	...	...	...	695030	
A Manufacture of food, beverages and tobacco	27800	7150	16490	16370	67810							
B Textile, wearing apparel and leather industries	18810	2640	5120	480	27050							
C Manufacture of wood and wood products, including furniture	13580	1830	4230	340	19980							
D Manufacture of paper and paper products, printing and publishing c	18470	3450	6450	460	28830							
E Manufacture of chemicals and chemical products, petroleum, coal, rubber and plastic products	65530	12470	23480	22760	124240							
F Manufacture of non-metallic mineral products, except products of petroleum and coal b	15760	3500	4570	640	24470							
G Basic metal industries	32880	6250	7710	620	47460							
H Manufacture of fabricated metal products, machinery and equipment d	229520	28380	49700	3710	311310							
I Other manufacturing industries	2730	370	1200	110	4410							
4 Electricity, gas and water	20370	14620	17200	5480	57670	...	...	...	...	...	...	
A Electricity, gas and steam	18900	13400	16220	5170	53690							
B Water works and supply	1470	1220	980	310	3980							
5 Construction d	68900	5080	30840	1640	106460	72710	...	...	...	...	116000	
6 Wholesale and retail trade, restaurants and hotels	130250	15290	75410	-1250	219700							
A Wholesale and retail trade	114150	13230	63930	-2060	189250	121020	...	...	...	...	199710	
B Restaurants and hotels	16100	2060	11480	810	30450							
7 Transport, storage and communication	70880	27840	29420	-5540	122600	73130	...	...	...	...	129620	
A Transport and storage	46000	16230	18310	-5530	75010							
B Communication	24880	11610	11110	-10	47590							
8 Finance, insurance, real estate and business services e	53990	61170	34990	12520	245020	56100	...	...	...	...	260020	
A Financial institutions	37930	3730	32770	4850	...	79280						

Germany, Fed. Rep. of

4.3 Cost Components of Value Added
(Continued)

Million Deutsche marks

	1988						1989					
	Compensation of Employees	Capital Consumption	Net Operating Surplus	Indirect Taxes	Less: Subsidies Received	Value Added	Compensation of Employees	Capital Consumption	Net Operating Surplus	Indirect Taxes	Less: Subsidies Received	Value Added
B Insurance	16060	1430	2220	5280	...	24990	...	...	...	...	...	...
C Real estate and business services f	...	56010	...	2390	...	140750	...	...	...	...	...	148870
Real estate, except dwellings	...	...	...	...	...	...	...	...	...	...	...	...
Dwellings	...	56010	...	2390	...	140750	...	...	...	...	...	148870
9 Community, social and personal services cfe	73020	37760	279400	9500	...	317330	...	...	...	...	...	370210
Educational services	...	...	...	...	...	...	...	...	...	...	...	...
Medical, dental, other health and veterinary services	14190	6760	28520	-110	...	49360	...	...	...	...	...	...
Total, Industries g	863970	241830	604200	59360	...	1769360	906730	257110	643240	71840	...	1878920
Producers of Government Services	217330	14850	-	250	...	232430	223180	15690	-	250	...	239120
Other Producers	40300	3730	-	30	...	44060	42130	3940	-	30	...	46100
Total g	1121600	260410	604200	59640	...	2045850	1172040	276740	643240	72120	...	2164140
Less: Imputed bank service charge	...	...	85080	...	...	85080	...	...	89190	...	...	89190
Import duties	...	...	...	19710	...	19710	...	...	...	23110	...	23110
Value added tax	...	...	...	130200	...	130200	...	...	...	137520	...	137520
Total g	1121600	260410	519120	209550	...	2110680	1172040	276740	554050	232750	...	2235580

a) Hunting and fishing are included in item 'Forestry and logging'.
b) Quarrying is included in item 'Manufacture of non-metalic mineral products except products of petroleum and coal'.
c) Publishing is included in item 'Community, social and personal services'.
d) Structural steel erection is included in item 'Manufacture of fabricated metal products, machinery and equipment'.
e) Dwelling is excluded from columns 1 and 3 of item 'Finance, insurance, real estate and business services' and is included in columns 1 and 3 of item 'Community, social and personal services'.
f) Business services and real estate except dwellings are included in item 'Community, social and personal services'.
g) Column 4 refers to indirect taxes less subsidies received.

Ghana

General note. The preparation of national accounts statistics in Ghana is undertaken by the Central Bureau of Statistics, Accra. The official estimates are published by the bureau in the 'Economic Survey'. A detailed description of the sources and methods used for the national accounts estimations is contained in the publications 'Sources and Methods of Estimation of National Income at Current Prices in Ghana' and 'National Income of Ghana at Constant Prices'. The estimates are generally in accordance with the recommendations and definitions recommended in the United Nations System of National Accounts (SNA). Work relating to input-output analysis is being done at present. The following tables have been prepared from successive replies to the United Nations national accounts questionnaire. When the scope and coverage of the estimates differ for conceptual or statistical reasons from the definitions and classifications recommended in SNA, a footnote is indicated to the relevant tables.

Sources and methods:

(a) Gross domestic product. Gross domestic product is estimated mainly through the production approach.

A combination of the commodity-flow approach and the expenditure approach is used for the construction sector. For the agricultural sector, statistics of the Ghana Cocoa Marketing Board is the main source of information for the estimation of cocoa, which is the most important crop in Ghana. For other principal crops, information is collected through annual sample surveys. The production of crop is estimated as the product of area sown and yield per acre. For other crops output on the basis of movements in acreage and prices of the crops. Data on gross output of forestry and logging are obtained from the Forestry Department while for intermediate consumption, a small-scale survey has been carried out in a bench-mark year and a constant input ratio applied for subsequent years. Annual surveys are undertaken on a census basis for mining, large-scale manufacturing and electricity and water supply. In the case of manufacturing, the surveys provide detailed information on inputs and outputs for commodity-flow purposes. A sample survey was carried out in 1963 for small-scale and medium-scale manufacturing. The data collected formed the basis for the estimates in the subsequent years by using per worker input in the bench-mark year and projected employment data, extrapolated from population census. For the construction sector, data on works undertaken by the government are obtained by analysing the government accounts. Information on domestic production, imports and exports of construction materials, trade and transport margins and cost-composition of the total expenditure are available to prepare estimates of gross output. The gross margins of wholesale and retail trade estimates are based partly on spot-checks in a bench-mark year and partly on sample survey, while gross receipts and intermediate consumption estimates are based on income tax records and annual surveys. For the services sectors, information is generally obtained from the institutions concerned. The rental value of residential dwellings are imputed on the basis of cost components, estimated from the record of the Ministry of Local Government. For the constant price estimates, the general approach used for agriculture, industrial activity, gas and water and construction sectors is double deflation. The value added of the trade, transport and financial services is extrapolated by quantity indexes. Different kinds of price indexes are used to deflate the value added of restaurants and hotels as well as the education and recreational services.

(b) Expenditure on the gross domestic product. Gross fixed capital formation is estimated by using the commodity-flow approach. A combination of commodity-flow and expenditure approach is used for increase in stock. Private consumption expenditure is treated as a residual. Gross fixed capital formation is classified according to type of capital goods and not according to kind of economic activity. The estimates of increase in stocks are mainly based on special inquiries into the stocks held by selected kinds of producers and distributors. Adjustment is made to arrive at estimates on the equivalent of physical changes in the stocks, valued at average market prices during the period of account. Government consumption expenditure is estimated on a cash basis from government records. These records are reclassified according to governmental purposes. It is feasible to distinguish expenditure for military purposes and for civilian purposes which exclude durable goods. Sales of goods and services by government to the public are subtracted from total expenditure. Exports and imports of goods and services are mainly estimated from foreign trade statistics of merchandise trade supplemented by information from the Central Bank. For the constant price estimates, no specific information is available for government consumption expenditure, but wages and salaries paid by government are extrapolated by index numbers of employment. For gross capital formation, current values are deflated by appropriate price indexes. In the case of commodity trade, current values are deflated by Paasche indexes of prices specially prepared for this purpose. Private consumption expenditure is obtained as a residual.

(c) Cost-structure of the gross domestic product. In estimating the cost structure components of GDP, the perpetual inventory method is used for estimating consumption of fixed capital. Indirect taxes net of subsidies are obtained by analysing the taxes on production and expenditure in the revenue account of the government. The domestic factor income is obtained as a residual.

(d) Gross domestic product by kind of economic activity. The table of GDP by kind of economic activity is prepared at market prices i.e., producers values. The value added of the majority of industries is estimated through the production approach. A combination of the commodity-flow approach and the expenditure approach is used for the construction sector.

a) Cocoa is valued at cost to the Ghana Cocoa Marketing Board. Stocks of other export commodities, including minerals, are valued at export prices. b) Other construction includes expenditure on mining development but excludes minor engineering construction done by the private sector.

1.1 Expenditure on the Gross Domestic Product, in Current Prices

Million Ghanaian cedis

	1970	1975	1980	1981	1982	1983	1984	1985	1986	1987	1988	1989
1 Government final consumption expenditure	290	784	4784	6384	5603	10787	19641	32241	56596	74700	10480	
2 Private final consumption expenditure	1664	3873	35953	63333	77619	167147	233023	284621	413900	588300	805500	
3 Gross capital formation a	320	672	2410	3321	2920	-109	18607	32828	49428	100000	149400	
A Increase in stocks a	48	59	-203	-109	-133	-21	65	139	340	600	800	
B Gross fixed capital formation	271	614	2613	3430	3053	6922	18542	32689	49088	99400	148600	
Residential buildings	118	296	1627	2277	2121	4750	10494	17205	20730			
Non-residential buildings												
Other construction and land improvement b	37	100	234	351	352	381	1096	3291	4926			
Other	117	218	752	802	580	1791	6952	12192	12431			
4 Exports of goods and services	523	1023	3628	3454	2886	10225	20161	33185	81800	157800	217700	
5 Less: Imports of goods and services	539	974	3923	3866	2578	11022	20871	39826	90400	174700	220600	
Equals: Gross Domestic Product	2259	5283	42854	72626	86451	184038	270561	343048	511400	746000	1057900	

1.2 Expenditure on the Gross Domestic Product, in Constant Prices

Million Ghanaian cedis

At constant prices of: 1968 / 1975

	1970	1975	1980	1981	1982	1983	1984	1985	1986	1987	1988	1989
1 Government final consumption expenditure	260											
			982	689	1136	1010	990	862	835	850		
2 Private final consumption expenditure	1459											
			3873	4253	3892	3382	3443	3917	4181	4321		
3 Gross capital formation a	276											
			672	491	447	343	344	393	490	475		
A Increase in stocks a	45											
			59	-26	-9	-8	-1	1	1	2		
B Gross fixed capital formation	231											
			614	516	456	352	344	392	489	473		

Ghana

1.2 Expenditure on the Gross Domestic Product, in Constant Prices
(Continued)

Million Ghanaian cedis

	1970	1975	1980	1981	1982	1983	1984	1985	1986	1987	1988	1989
	1968				At constant prices of: 1975							
Residential buildings	138	296	288	235	188	175	202	189	167	...	...	...
Non-residential buildings												
Other construction and land improvement etc.		100b	42b	36b	31b	14b	21b	36b	40b	...	...	...
Other	93	218	186	184	133	155	169	264	266	...	...	...
4 Exports of goods and services	398	1023	655	597	688	373	409	435	616	...	...	...
5 Less: Imports of goods and services	472	974	842	727	449	402	423	522	560	...	...	...
Equals: Gross Domestic Product	1922	5283	5538	5344	4974	4747	5158	5420	5702	...	...	...

a) Cocoa is valued at cost to the Ghana Cocoa Marketing Board. Stocks of other export. b) Other construction includes expenditure on mining development but excludes minor commodities, including minerals, are valued at export prices. engineering construction done by the private sector.

1.3 Cost Components of the Gross Domestic Product

Million Ghanaian cedis

	1970	1975	1980	1981	1982	1983	1984	1985	1986	1987	1988	1989
1 Indirect taxes, net	308	631	2116	2849	2466	6704	13819	24137	46955	...	...	...
2 Consumption of fixed capital	134	323	1512	2218	2628	4197	11206	16339	29267	...	...	...
3 Compensation of employees paid by resident producers	1816	4329	2274	2301	2302	3743	5282	14964	27896	...	...	...
4 Operating surplus												
Equals: Gross Domestic Product	2259	5283	42854	72626	86451	184038	270561	343048	550515	...	...	...

1.7 External Transactions on Current Account, Summary

Million Ghanaian cedis

	1970	1975	1980	1981	1982	1983	1984	1985	1986	1987	1988	1989
Payments to the Rest of the World												
1 Imports of goods and services	539	974	3923	3866	2578	11022	20871.	39826	69881	...	...	...
A. Imports of merchandise c.i.f.	463	813	3343	3224	2055	11546	16495	32808	48833	...	...	...
B. Other	76	161	580	641	523	5482	4376	7018	21048	...	...	...
2 Factor income to the rest of the world	52	47	189	226	231	1644	3707	5867	12648	...	...	...
3 Current transfers to the rest of the world	18	14	27	28	21	320	385	511	1080	...	...	...
4 Surplus of the nation on current transactions	-67	59	-258	-406	310	-237	2961	-4989	14507	...	...	...
Payments to the Rest of the World and Surplus of the Nation on Current Transactions	542	1093	3880	3714	3141	12749	27924	41215	98116	...	...	...
Receipts From The Rest of the World												
1 Exports of goods and services	523	1023	3628	3454	2886	10225	20161	33185	76948	...	...	...
A. Exports of merchandise f.o.b.	488	921	3334	3125	2599	8782	18963	32070	73768	...	...	...
B. Other	36	102	294	329	288	1443	1198	1115	3180	...	...	...
2 Factor income from rest of the world	4	5	7	7	4	4	65	98	72	...	...	...
3 Current transfers from rest of the world	14	65	246	256	248	2520	7698	7933	21096	...	...	...
Receipts from the Rest of the World on Current Transactions	542	1093	3880	3714	3141	12749	27924	41216	98116	...	...	...

1.10 Gross Domestic Product by Kind of Activity, in Current Prices

Million Ghanaian cedis

	1970	1975	1980	1981	1982	1983	1984	1985	1986	1987	1988	1989
1 Agriculture, hunting, forestry and fishing	1060	2518	24821	38553	49572	109927	133232	154003	244417	...	...	...
2 Mining and quarrying	37	105	462	369	285	1944	3214	3822	8783	...	...	...
3 Manufacturing	248	736	3346	4338	3117	7101	17306	39562	61864	...	...	...
4 Electricity, gas and water	23	33	233	513	358	2166	4045	8957		...	...	...
5 Construction	94	236	1055	1491	1486	2796	5945	9780	12962	...	...	...

Ghana

1.10 Gross Domestic Product by Kind of Activity, in Current Prices
(Continued)

Million Ghanaian cedis

	1970	1975	1980	1981	1982	1983	1984	1985	1986	1987	1988	1989
6 Wholesale and retail trade, restaurants and hotels	281	642	7327	19074	22951	43120	76544	85031	125520	...	...	...
7 Transport, storage and communication	97	206	1130	2329	2568	7663	17451	18329	25333	...	...	...
8 Finance, insurance, real estate and business services	160	276	1314	1927	2621	3311	4676	7746	18381	...	...	...
9 Community, social and personal services	12	55	206	382	420	636	1051	2289	4420	...	...	...
Total, Industries	2012	4806	39884	68918	83532	176856	261584	324608	510537	...	...	...
Producers of Government Services	201	433	3136	4145	4052	7822	9141	18701	36831	...	...	...
Other Producers	11	25	88	136	128	212	206	277	489	...	...	...
Subtotal	2224	5264	43108	73199	87712	184890	270931	343586	547857	...	...	...
Less: Imputed bank service charge	27	77	651	1207	1802	2259	2865	5323	6903			
Plus: Import duties	61	96	397	634	541	1407	2494	4786	9561			
Plus: Value added tax	...	...	...	...	...	...	...	...	...			
Equals: Gross Domestic Product	2259	5283	42854	72626	86451	184038	270561	343048	550515	...	...	...

1.11 Gross Domestic Product by Kind of Activity, in Constant Prices

Million Ghanaian cedis

	1970	1975	1980	1981	1982	1983	1984	1985	1986	1987	1988	1989
	1968				At constant prices of:			1975				
1 Agriculture, hunting, forestry and fishing	817	... 2518	2957	2881	2724	2533	2780	2798	2890	...	...	...
2 Mining and quarrying	43	... 105	71	66	61	52	59	63	61			
3 Manufacturing	265	... 736	575	464	369	328	370	460	511	...	...	
4 Electricity, gas and water	20	33	43	48	44	41	39	46	55			
5 Construction	89	... 236	206	174	151	129	132	135	132	...		
6 Wholesale and retail trade, restaurants and hotels	233	642	556	545	489	463	510	580	632	...		
7 Transport, storage and communication	79	206	166	177	179	192	217	235	248			
8 Finance, insurance, real estate and business services	127	276	372	389	401	414	453	465	500			
9 Community, social and personal services	9	... 55	35	40	38	41	49	63	77	...	...	
Total, Industries	1681	... 4806	4980	4784	4455	4193	4608	4845	5106	...	...	
Producers of Government Services	179	... 433	609	650	623	660	663	693	710			
Other Producers	10	... 25	28	23	28	27	25	25	27	...	...	
Subtotal	1870	... 5264	5617	5457	5106	4880	5296	5563	5843	...		
Less: Imputed bank service charge	...	77	160	166	166	177	191	206	218			
Plus: Import duties	51	... 96	81	53	34	44	53	63	77			
Plus: Value added tax	...	...	...	...	...	...	...	...	...			
Equals: Gross Domestic Product	1922	... 5283	5538	5344	4974	4747	5158	5420	5702	...	...	...

1.12 Relations Among National Accounting Aggregates

Million Ghanaian cedis

	1970	1975	1980	1981	1982	1983	1984	1985	1986	1987	1988	1989
Gross Domestic Product	2259	5283	42854	72626	86451	184038	270561	343048	550515	746000	1057900	...
Plus: Net factor income from the rest of the world	-48	-42	-182	-222	-225	-1640	-3642	-5768	-12576	-21200	-26500	...
Factor income from the rest of the world	4	5	7	4	7	4	65	98	72	...	...	...
Less: Factor income to the rest of the world	52	47	189	226	231	1644	3707	5867	12648			
Equals: Gross National Product	2211	5241	42671	72404	86226	182398	266918	337280	537939	724800	1031400	...
Less: Consumption of fixed capital	134	323	1512	2218	2628	4197	11206	16339	29267	47600	68800	...

Ghana

1.12 Relations Among National Accounting Aggregates (Continued)

Million Ghanaian cedis

	1970	1975	1980	1981	1982	1983	1984	1985	1986	1987	1988	1989
Equals: National Income	2077	4918	41159	70186	83598	172201	255713	320941	508672	677200	962600
Plus: Net current transfers from the rest of the world	-4	51	219	228	227	2200	7313	7421	20016		
Current transfers from the rest of the world	14	65	246	256	248	2520	7698	7933	21096		
Less: Current transfers to the rest of the world	18	14	27	28	21	320	385	511	1080		
Equals: National Disposable Income	2073	4970	41379	70414	83824	180401	263026	328362	528688		
Less: Final consumption	1954	4562	40738	69717	83222	177934	255664	316862	494020		
Equals: Net Saving	118	408	641	697	602	2467	10363	11500	34668		
Less: Surplus of the nation on current transactions	-67	59	-258	-406	310	-237	2961	-4989	14507		
Equals: Net Capital Formation	185	349	899	1103	292	2704	7402	16489	20161		

2.17 Exports and Imports of Goods and Services, Detail

Million Ghanaian cedis

	1970	1975	1980	1981	1982	1983	1984	1985	1986	1987	1988	1989
Exports of Goods and Services												
1 Exports of merchandise, f.o.b.	488	921	3334	3125	2599	8782	18963	32070	73768		
2 Transport and communication	30	71	35	37	36	382	792	707	1716		
3 Insurance service charges	...	...	...	...	...	...	...	...	...		
4 Other commodities	6	30	259	292	252	1061	407	408	1464		
5 Adjustments of merchandise exports to change-of-ownership basis	...	...	...	...	...	...	...	...	...		
6 Direct purchases in the domestic market by non-residential households	...	...	...	...	...	...	...	...	...		
7 Direct purchases in the domestic market by extraterritorial bodies	...	...	...	...	...	...	...	...	...		
Total Exports of Goods and Services	523	1023	3628	3454	2886	10225	20161	33185	76948		
Imports of Goods and Services												
1 Imports of merchandise, c.i.f.	463	813	3343	3224	2055	11546	16495	32808	48833		
A Imports of merchandise, f.o.b.	409	748	3106	3041	1939	10222	14566	29649	40733		
B Transport of services on merchandise imports	54	65	237	183	116	924	1929	3159	8100		
C Insurance service charges on merchandise imports	...	...	...	...	...	...	...	...	...		
2 Adjustments of merchandise imports to change-of-ownership basis	...	...	...	...	...	...	...	...	...		
3 Other transport and communication	40	79	228	281	219	2442	1717	2719	6300		
4 Other insurance service charges	...	...	...	...	...	...	...	...	...		
5 Other commodities	35	81	352	361	303	3040	2660	4300	14748		
6 Direct purchases abroad by government	...	...	...	...	...	...	...	...	...		
7 Direct purchases abroad by resident households	...	...	...	...	...	...	...	...	...		
Total Imports of Goods and Services	539	974	3923	3866	2578	11022	20871	39826	69881		
Balance of Goods and Services	-15	49	-294	-412	308	-797	-710	-6641	7067		
Total Imports and Balance of Goods and Services	523	1023	3628	3454	2886	10225	20161	33185	76948		

4.1 Derivation of Value Added by Kind of Activity, in Current Prices

Million Ghanaian cedis

	1980			1981			1982			1983		
	Gross Output	Intermediate Consumption	Value Added	Gross Output	Intermediate Consumption	Value Added	Gross Output	Intermediate Consumption	Value Added	Gross Output	Intermediate Consumption	Value Added
All Producers												
1 Agriculture, hunting, forestry and fishing	26942	2121	24821	41907	1639	38553	54208	4636	49572	119168	9240	109927
A Agriculture and hunting	22674	7649	109324	44642	3358	48000	34755	2604	37359	22045	1639	22683
B Forestry and logging	1926	120	1806	2278	142	2135	3555	320	3235	6110	501	5609
C Fishing	1332	362	971	2271	607	1663	2653	958	1695	3134	1090	2044
2 Mining and quarrying	624	162	462	585	216	369	473	188	285	2350	406	1944

Ghana

4.1 Derivation of Value Added by Kind of Activity, in Current Prices (Continued)

Million Ghanaian cedis

	1980			1981			1982			1983		
	Gross Output	Intermediate Consumption	Value Added	Gross Output	Intermediate Consumption	Value Added	Gross Output	Intermediate Consumption	Value Added	Gross Output	Intermediate Consumption	Value Added
3 Manufacturing	6934	3588	3346	8764	4426	4338	6605	3488	3117	14973	7872	7101
4 Electricity, gas and water	352	128	223	610	155	456	762	249	513	671	313	358
A Electricity, gas and steam	220	39	180	431	69	363	486	72	414	596	128	468
B Water works and supply	132	89	43	179	86	93	276	177	99	75	185	-110
5 Construction	1996	942	1055	2848	1357	1491	2743	1257	1486	5680	2884	2796
6 Wholesale and retail trade, restaurants and hotels	10941	3613	7327	26540	7467	19074	33224	10273	22951	64544	21424	43120
A Wholesale and retail trade	10298	3121	7177	25599	6774	18825	31990	9365	22625	62409	19901	42508
B Restaurants and hotels	642	492	150	942	693	249	1234	908	326	2135	1523	612
7 Transport, storage and communication	2568	1438	1130	5202	2872	2329	5526	2958	2568	16940	9277	7663
A Transport and storage	2479	1403	1076	5094	2836	2258	5437	2918	2519	16746	9223	7523
B Communication	89	35	54	108	37	71	89	40	49	194	54	140
8 Finance, insurance, real estate and business services	1544	230	1314	2268	807	1547	1927	340	3121	2621	4100	3311
A Financial institutions	935	129	807	1547	200	1348	2212	295	1916	3095	557	2538
B Insurance	35	13	21	36	14	22	38	12	27	53	20	32
C Real estate and business services	574	88	486	684	126	558	871	194	677	952	212	740
9 Community, social and personal services	345	139	206	634	251	382	685	264	420	992	356	636
Total, Industries	52244	12361	39884	89356	20438	68918	107345	23813	83532	229419	52663	176856
Producers of Government Services	4926	1790	3136	6572	2427	4145	5789	1737	4052	11144	3322	7822
Other Producers	112	24	88	171	36	136	163	35	128	286	74	212
Total	57282	14175	43108	96099	22901	73199	113297	25585	87712	240849	55959	184890
Less: Imputed bank service charge		-651	651		-1207	1207		-1802	1802		-2259	2259
Import duties	397		397	634		634	541		541	1407		1407
Value added tax	...	...	...	...	...	...	...	...	...	...	...	...
Total	57679	14826	42854	96734	24107	72626	113838	27387	86451	242256	58218	184038

All Producers

	1984			1985			1986		
	Gross Output	Intermediate Consumption	Value Added	Gross Output	Intermediate Consumption	Value Added	Gross Output	Intermediate Consumption	Value Added
1 Agriculture, hunting, forestry and fishing	146442	13410	133232	170788	16785	154003	270686	26369	244317
A Agriculture and hunting	132513	10953	121560	145558	12147	137411	235007	18369	216638
B Forestry and logging	10342	1043	13075	1724	11351	21379	2509	18870	
C Fishing	3787	1415	2372	8155	2914	5241	14300	5491	8809
2 Mining and quarrying	4323	1109	3214	6409	2587	3822	14105	5322	8783
3 Manufacturing	36822	19517	17306	87916	48354	39562	131908	70044	61864
4 Electricity, gas and water	2980	814	2166	6080	2035	4045	11500	2543	8957
A Electricity, gas and steam	2525	379	2147						
B Water works and supply	454	435	19	11273	2053	9780	28490	15528	12962
5 Construction	12792	6847	5945	21053	11273	9780	28490	15528	12962
6 Wholesale and retail trade, restaurants and hotels	116223	19679	96544	126338	41307	85031	187460	61940	125520
A Wholesale and retail trade	113299	37410	75889						
B Restaurants and hotels	2924	2269	655						
7 Transport, storage and communication	39077	21627	17451	42490	24161	18329	58883	33550	25333
A Transport and storage	38709	21444	17265						
B Communication	368	182	186						
8 Finance, insurance, real estate and business services	6387	1711	4676	10636	2890	7746	22842	4461	18381
A Financial institutions	5112	1491	3621						
B Insurance	92	28	64						
C Real estate and business services	1182	192	991						
9 Community, social and personal services	1594	543	1051	3660	1371	2289	6596	2175	4420

Ghana

4.1 Derivation of Value Added by Kind of Activity, in Current Prices (Continued)

Million Ghanaian cedis

	1984 Gross Output	1984 Intermediate Consumption	1984 Value Added	1985 Gross Output	1985 Intermediate Consumption	1985 Value Added	1986 Gross Output	1986 Intermediate Consumption	1986 Value Added
Total, Industries	368840	105256	261584	475370	150763	324607	732469	221932	510537
Producers of Government Services	20497	11356	9141	34061	15360	18701	59191	22360	36831
Other Producers	580	374	206	706	429	277	822	333	489
Total	387917	116986	270931	510137	166552	343585	792482	244625	547857
Less: imputed bank service charge	...	2865	-2865	...	5323	-5323	...	6903	-6903
Import duties	2494	...	2494	4786	...	4786	9561	...	9561
Value added tax	...	...	...	...	...	...	...	...	...
Total	390411	119850	270561	514923	171875	343048	802043	251528	550515

4.2 Derivation of Value Added by Kind of Activity, in Constant Prices

Million Ghanaian cedis

	1980 Gross Output	1980 Intermediate Consumption	1980 Value Added	1981 Gross Output	1981 Intermediate Consumption	1981 Value Added	1982 Gross Output	1982 Intermediate Consumption	1982 Value Added	1983 Gross Output	1983 Intermediate Consumption	1983 Value Added
	At constant prices of 1975											
	All Producers											
1 Agriculture, hunting, forestry and fishing	3172	215	2957	3097	216	2881	2945	221	2724	2749	215	2534
A Agriculture and hunting	2739	177	2562	2696	174	2522	2521	174	2348	2289	156	2133
B Forestry and logging	324	20	304	284	18	266	306	19	287	338	29	309
C Fishing	110	18	92	117	24	93	118	29	89	122	30	92
2 Mining and quarrying	94	23	71	87	22	65	81	20	61	69	17	52
3 Manufacturing	1226	651	575	1032	568	464	820	451	369	679	351	328
4 Electricity, gas and water	73	30	43	85	37	48	77	33	44	48	21	27
A Electricity, gas and steam	55	20	35	65	30	35	52	19	33	31	11	19
B Water works and supply	18	10	8	29	16	13	26	14	11	17	10	8
5 Construction	354	148	206	294	120	174	243	92	151	210	81	129
6 Wholesale and retail trade, restaurants and hotels	874	318	556	837	291	545	783	294	489	727	264	463
A Wholesale and retail trade	786	250	537	775	245	530	705	234	471	655	208	447
B Restaurants and hotels	88	69	19	62	47	15	77	60	17	73	57	16
7 Transport, storage and communication	382	216	166	387	210	177	399	220	179	502	310	192
A Transport and storage	373	211	161	380	207	173	392	217	175	493	305	188
B Communication	9	5	5	7	4	4	7	4	4	9	5	4
8 Finance, insurance, real estate and business services	419	47	372	439	51	389	459	58	401	497	83	415
A Financial institutions	175	19	156	190	23	167	204	29	175	238	54	185
B Insurance	5	3	3	4	2	2	3	1	2	3	1	2
C Real estate and business services	239	25	213	246	27	220	253	28	224	256	28	228
9 Community, social and personal services	56	21	35	66	26	40	63	25	38	59	18	41
Total, Industries	6649	1669	4980	6324	1540	4784	5871	1415	4455	5539	1359	4180
Producers of Government Services	940	331	609	1003	353	650	961	338	623	1018	358	660
Other Producers	34	7	28	27	5	23	33	6	28	38	10	27
Total	7624	2006	5617	7355	1898	5457	6864	1758	5106	6595	1728	4867
Less: imputed bank service charge	...	161	-161	...	166	-166	...	166	-166	...	177	-177
Import duties	81	...	81	53	...	53	34	...	34	44	...	44
Value added tax	...	...	...	...	...	...	...	...	...	...	...	...
Total	7704	2167	5537	7408	2064	5344	5925	4974	6639	1905	4733	

At constant prices of 1975

All Producers

	1984 Gross Output	1984 Intermediate Consumption	1984 Value Added	1985 Gross Output	1985 Intermediate Consumption	1985 Value Added	1986 Gross Output	1986 Intermediate Consumption	1986 Value Added
1 Agriculture, hunting, forestry and fishing	3020	240	2780	3040	242	2798	3145	255	2890
A Agriculture and hunting	2548	173	2374	2553	172	2381	2632	177	2455
B Forestry and logging	350	37	313	350	37	313	357	40	317
C Fishing	122	30	93	137	33	104	156	38	118
2 Mining and quarrying	78	19	59	85	22	63	81	20	61

Ghana

4.2 Derivation of Value Added by Kind of Activity, in Constant Prices
(Continued)

Million Ghanaian cedis

At constant prices of 1975

	1984			1985			1986		
	Gross Output	Intermediate Consumption	Value Added	Gross Output	Intermediate Consumption	Value Added	Gross Output	Intermediate Consumption	Value Added
3 Manufacturing	780	410	370	919	459	460	1003	492	511
4 Electricity, gas and water	73	34	39	85	39	46	86	43	55
A Electricity, gas and steam	34	12	22	...	...	...	...	...	...
B Water works and supply	38	22	17	...	...	...	...	...	...
5 Construction	220	88	132	231	96	135	230	98	132
6 Wholesale and retail trade, restaurants and hotels	801	291	510	1131	551	580	1250	618	632
A Wholesale and retail trade	723	229	493	...	...	...	...	...	...
B Restaurants and hotels	78	61	17	...	...	...	...	...	...
7 Transport, storage and communication	479	263	217	514	279	235	548	300	248
A Transport and storage	470	258	212	...	...	...	...	...	...
B Communication	9	5	5	...	...	...	...	...	...
8 Finance, insurance, real estate and business services	607	154	453	621	156	465	651	151	500
A Financial institutions	341	126	215	...	...	...	...	...	...
B Insurance	3	1	2	...	...	...	...	...	...
C Real estate and business services	263	27	236	...	...	...	...	...	...
9 Community, social and personal services	66	17	49	83	20	63	102	25	77
Total, Industries	6123	1516	4608	6709	1864	4845	7108	2002	5106
Producers of Government Services	880	217	663	854	161	693	872	162	710
Other Producers	35	10	25	39	14	25	46	19	27
Total	7039	1743	5296	7602	2039	5563	8026	2183	5843
Less: imputed bank service charge	-191	...	-191	-206	...	-206	...	-218	218
Import duties	53	...	53	63	...	63	77	...	77
Value added tax	...	...	...	...	...	...	...	...	...
Total	7091	1934	5158	7665	2245	5420	8103	2401	5702

Greece

General note. The preparation of national accounts statistics in Greece is undertaken by the National Accounts Service, Ministry of National Economy, Athens. Official estimates are published in a series of reports entitled 'National Accounts of Greece'. The estimates are generally in accordance with the classifications and definitions recommended by the United Nations System of National Accounts (SNA). Input-output tables have been published for the years 1958 and 1970 in 'National Accounts of Greece 1970-1976'. The following tables have been prepared from successive replies to the United Nations national accounts questionnaire. When the scope and coverage of the estimates differ for conceptual or statistical reasons from the definitions and classifications recommended in SNA, a footnote is indicated to the relevant tables.

Sources and methods:

(a) Gross domestic product. Gross domestic product is estimated mainly through the production approach.

(b) Expenditure on the gross domestic product. The expenditure approach is used to estimate final consumption expenditure and exports and imports of goods and services. This approach, in combination with the commodity-flow approach, is also used to estimate gross capital formation. Private final consumption expenditure is estimated on the basis of the direct expenditure approach. The estimates of government final consumption expenditure are obtained from the accounts of the different government units. For private consumption expenditure, sources include the household budget surveys, tax statistics and other statistical information from the annual manufacturing and mining surveys as well as delayed information from the accounts of the public sector construction, estimates are derived from government budgetary accounts and replies from public enterprises and public funds that have been issued, while for the private construction, estimates are derived from information from the annual manufacturing and mining surveys as well as from government budgetary accounts and replies from public enterprises and public funds. Estimates of investments in private buildings are based on building permits method. Own-account construction is covered by information for machinery and equipment. Public enterprises and public funds are used for such construction works. For exports and imports of goods and services, foreign trade statistics based on the special trade principle are used. For the constant price estimates, price indices are used to deflate the wages and salaries of government employees. For the private expenditure, the annual quantities of food, fuel, light and water charges are multiplied by average base-year prices. Expenditure on other private goods and services are deflated by appropriate price indexes. Value added of residential and non-residential buildings is extrapolated by specially constructed indicators. For other components of gross capital formation, the base-year values of exports and imports of merchandise are extrapolated by volume indexes while other goods and services are deflated by mean value index of exports and imports.

(c) Cost-structure of the gross domestic product. Estimates of compensation of employees for various services such as finance, insurance and transport are estimated by using data derived from questionnaires sent to them by the National Accounts Service. For manufacturing and mining, data are derived from the annual industrial surveys. The employers' contributions are estimated by using data derived from statements of the social insurance funds. Capital consumption is estimated as a percentage of the corresponding capital stock figure for each industry and type of assets. The current-price estimates of capital stock and depreciation are calculated on a replacement cost basis. The estimates of indirect taxes and subsidies are obtained from government accounts. Operating surplus is calculated as a residual.

(d) Gross domestic product by kind of economic activity. The table of gross domestic product by kind of economic activity is prepared in factor values. The income approach is used for lignite mining, electricity, gas and water and parts of the service sectors such as transportation, communication, health and education, and miscellaneous services. For agricultural and animal breeding, the estimate of production is based on annual surveys conducted by the National Statistical Office of Greece. Intermediate consumption estimates are based on data taken from various sources such as Ministry of Agriculture and the Public Power Corporation. Agricultural product prices refer to prices obtained by farmers. The estimates of mining and quarrying and manufacturing are based on the annual survey of industrial establishments. The information from the survey is available within 2-3 years, meanwhile, value added is extrapolated by the index of industrial production and the wholesale price index. Value added of electricity, gas and water is estimated on the basis of annual questionnaires sent to the concerned enterprises. For construction, gross value is obtained from investment data of buildings and other construction to which values of military construction and repairs are added. The estimates of gross trade margins for agricultural products are based on traded quantities valued at the difference between consumers' and producers' prices. For industrial and imported products, percentages of gross trade margins are applied to the traded values at current prices. Intermediate consumption estimates are based on a survey conducted in 1970 for the compilation of the input-output table. Value added of transport and communication and finance and insurance services is based on data compiled through questionnaires sent to the concerned enterprises. For ownership of dwellings, the estimation of real or imputed rent is carried out at constant prices, based on the number of rooms existing and the average annual rent expenditure in a bench-mark year. These data are obtained from dwelling censuses and household budget surveys. Estimates concerning government services are obtained from general government accounts. For private health and educational services, only wages and salaries data are available. Value added of hotel is based on surveys conducted every three years by the National Accounts Service. For other services, employment data as well as data on average remuneration per person employed, double deflation is used for agriculture and electricity. For water, construction, transport and hotels, value added is extrapolated by quantity indicators. For the remaining sectors of the industries, price deflation is used.

1.1 Expenditure on the Gross Domestic Product, in Current Prices

Million Greek drachmas

	1970	1975	1980	1981	1982	1983	1984	1985	1986	1987	1988	1989
1 Government final consumption expenditure	37742	102007	280050	368550	471230	579370	742270	942050	1067240	1229420	1517470	1903860
2 Private final consumption expenditure	208613	454009	1104610	1383070	1734180	2053560	2461440	3025490	3718860	4323580	5116010	6096730
3 Gross capital formation	60009	181350	489373	520613	673207	543207	793235	983254	1061520	1071210	1411520	1716380
A Increase in stocks	14400	75688	64263	29807	49207	36335	102884	43418	25412	129179	8587	
B Gross fixed capital formation	70663	413865	456350	513500	624000	702900	880370	1018100	1045800	1282340	1630530	139867
Residential buildings	19740	37983	137517	126873	135292	163012	210780	152214	178072	248326	286869	325292	403477
Non-residential buildings	9679	18865	58564	68547	61358	73480	87741	96281	124848	140934	193431	216043
Other construction and land improvement etc.	16169	29380	79607	98632	98556	137392	235420	245608	207313	252138	304035
Other	25175	53722	146696	162498	218284	254659	288873	370597	394416	410681	507475	709073
4 Exports of goods and services a	29988	113349	357651	422380	470319	609449	824649	977623	1233100	1536780	1800880	2069540
5 Less: imports of goods and services	54996	180562	448881	556129	738303	925366	1133470	1515330	1703260	1993450	2290690	2839490
Statistical discrepancy	-4639	2005	-71898	-88430	9121	17697	88889	120219	202926	51691	-53224	-148627
Equals: Gross Domestic Product	298917	672158	1770930	2050060	2574650	3071980	3805690	4617820	5497680	6228030	7501970	8798390

a) Data on Exports of goods and services as well as transport, storage and communication exclude income from ocean-going cargo ships under Greek flag or ownership. However, remittances actually received by the bank of Greece from persons engaged in these enterprises are included in factor income from the rest of the world.

1.2 Expenditure on the Gross Domestic Product, in Constant Prices

Million Greek drachmas

	1970	1975	1980	1981	1982	1983	1984	1985	1986	1987	1988	1989
At constant prices of 1970												
1 Government final consumption expenditure	37742	56075	68940	73640	75330	77400	79760	82300	81626	82666	81108	82788
2 Private final consumption expenditure	208613	266884	319341	325851	328807	339425	345194	358671	361026	364018	372254	390828
3 Gross capital formation	60009	97760	111985	96655	86890	89148	82063	92509	83596	72596	88376	87853
A Increase in stocks	13346	21100	19280	10305	5790	3148	3763	10149	6362	2050	11599	4437
B Gross fixed capital formation	70663	74660	92705	85750	84100	83000	78300	82360	77234	70546	76777	83416

Greece

1.2 Expenditure on the Gross Domestic Product, in Constant Prices (Continued)

Million Greek drachmas

	1970	1975	1980	1981	1982	1983	1984	1985	1986	1987	1988	1989
At constant prices of 1970												
Residential buildings	19740	20476	27291	21452	20398	21124	17083	19397	20044	20991	21687	
Non-residential buildings	9579	10170	11622	11636	9252	9529	8648	9241	9752	9848	12154	11615
Other construction and land improvement etc.	16169	16010	15674	17269	14061	15396	17883	14737	10599	11012	11454	
Other	25175	28004	38118	35383	40389	36951	35407	38139	33346	30556	32920	38660
Exports of goods and services [a]	29988	56324	58865	83312	77321	83488	97628	88882	130770	142516	145464	
Less: Imports of goods and services	54996	80398	97373	100924	108017	115110	115350	130120	135070	157448	170066	188852
Statistical discrepancy	-4639	-12283	-17946	-4163	2610	3200	1401	3769	9072	17983	6207	16439
Equals: Gross Domestic Product	298917	382362	473510	473771	475641	477551	490966	500411	513020	510605	531395	546520

[a] Data on Exports of goods and services as well as transport, storage and communication exclude income from ocean-going cargo ships under Greek flag or ownership. However, remittances actually received by the bank of Greece from persons engaged in these enterprises are included in factor income from the rest of the world.

1.3 Cost Components of the Gross Domestic Product

Million Greek drachmas

	1970	1975	1980	1981	1982	1983	1984	1985	1986	1987	1988	1989
1 Indirect taxes, net	40917	78977	187210	190006	263964	345964	443098	480964	642036	794263	955296	943246
A Indirect taxes	43406	95961	227710	276520	385256	490394	607607	614851	1001150	1165010	1317490	1435810
B Less: Subsidies	2489	16984	41500	86434	121292	144460	164560	138387	359109	370749	362192	492568
2 Consumption of fixed capital	16860	47457	142082	175498	215399	329371	403045	505138	573017	573301	658783	792027
3 Compensation of employees to: [a]												
A Resident households [a]	93913	217793	647381	799618	1032790	1249430	1525010	1915920	2158930	2394950	2918560	3521760
B Rest of the world	462	1539	2529	3647	4283	6845	6435	6293	8298	10427	13538	19378
4 Operating surplus [a]	147227	327931	374261	884855	1062500	1212100	1500710	1817880	2191590	2463530	2969330	3541360
Equals: Gross Domestic Product	298917	672158	1170920	2050900	2574650	3079180	3805690	4617820	5497680	6228030	7501970	8798390

[a] Compensation of employees paid by resident producers to resident households excludes wages paid to agricultural workers which are included in item 'Operating surplus'.

1.4 General Government Current Receipts and Disbursements

Million Greek drachmas

	1970	1975	1980	1981	1982	1983	1984	1985	1986	1987	1988	1989
Receipts												
1 Operating surplus	...	...	...	...	...	...	...	...	...	...	...	...
2 Property and entrepreneurial income	5678	15851	39620	40740	43390	58850	74590	93681	90545	113314	96305	99966
3 Taxes, fees and contributions	75545	162283	477210	550108	780084	977660	1228490	1487650	1847600	2145290	2430260	2674480
A Indirect taxes	43406	95961	227710	267368	366694	465370	578870	705006	910625	1091850	1231360	1333080
B Direct taxes [a]	10484	25302	96020	151040	167990	226300	259040	378514	337540	448849	489317	
C Social security contributions	19655	45020	153890	187920	262350	334300	423320	523607	600938	672220	750050	852084
D Compulsory fees, fines and penalties [a]												
4 Other current transfers	975	1979	4417	6480	8461	12240	15290	17930	18283	23754	27083	
Total Current Receipts of General Government	80198	184113	521247	597328	831935	1033750	1324570	1596620	1956080	2274190	2550320	2801230
Disbursements												
1 Government final consumption expenditure	37742	102007	280050	368550	471230	579370	747270	942050	1067240	1229420	1517470	1903860
A Compensation of employees	27657	65545	195560	248200	326590	398030	505040	648022	730205	840285	1023710	
B Consumption of fixed capital												
C Purchases of goods and services, net												
D Less: Own account fixed capital formation												
E Indirect taxes paid, net												
2 Property income	2815	9261	41247	65250	66932	110020	173300	247030	316395	460876	611014	713452
3 Subsidies	2489	16984	41500	76300	66300	75650	76500	137610	153838	152091	121976	175000
4 Other current transfers	23950	51314	159608	226788	338243	417210	536930	689898	825625	935558	1146740	1400180
A Social security benefits	28816	49835	157520	224940	335105	411810	533070	685616	826568	931454	1141530	1339880
B Social assistance grants												
C Other	134	1379	1988	1848	3138	5400	3860	4280	5057	4104	5208	6300
5 Net saving	13202	4547	-1058	-13950	-119820	-142150	-204930	-419962	-407019	-503760	-846879	-1391270
Total Current Disbursements and Net Saving of General Government	80198	184113	521247	597328	831935	1033750	1324570	1596620	1956080	2274190	2550320	2801230

[a] Item 'Fees, fines and penalties' is included in item 'Direct taxes'.

Greece

1.6 Current Income and Outlay of Households and Non-Profit Institutions

Million Greek drachmas

	1970	1975	1980	1981	1982	1983	1984	1985	1986	1987	1988	1989
Receipts												
1 Compensation of employees [a]	95913	226740	671244	831388	1069310	1287290	1574530	1962740	2198080	2432780	2946990	3549550
A From resident producers [a]	93451	216254	644852	795971	1028510	1242590	1526070	1909630	2150620	2384520	2905020	3502380
B From rest of the world	2462	10486	26392	35417	40798	44702	48461	53107	47459	48263	41974	47176
2 Operating surplus of private unincorporated enterprises	...	...	...	...	...	...	...	...	...	...	...	...
3 Property and entrepreneurial income [b]	140318	324560	747656	915799	1074370	1233110	1516010	1839390	2227340	2609760	3297850	3961820
4 Current transfers	34153	74756	204199	285257	405258	494238	636960	795915	957808	1117840	1386480	1619680
A Social security benefits	23816	49935	158358	224940	335105	411810	533070	685616	820568	931454	1141530	1393880
B Social assistance grants	...	...	...	...	...	...	...	...	...	...	...	...
C Other	10337	24821	45841	60317	70153	82428	103890	110299	137240	186383	244950	225796
Total Current Receipts	270384	626056	1623100	2032440	2548940	3014640	3727500	4598040	5383230	6160380	7631330	9131050
Disbursements												
1 Private final consumption expenditure	206813	454009	1104610	1383070	1734180	2053580	2461440	3025490	3718860	4332380	5116010	6096730
2 Property income	...	...	...	...	...	...	...	...	...	...	...	...
3 Direct taxes and other current transfers n.e.c. to general government	28585	63281	227512	261940	380750	472470	606370	731399	853590	950567	1097810	1261100
A Social security contributions	19655	45020	153890	186720	262350	334300	423320	523607	600938	672220	750050	852084
B Direct taxes	8930	18261	73622	75220	118400	138170	183050	207792	252652	278347	347759	409017
C Fees, fines and penalties	...	...	...	...	...	...	...	...	...	...	...	...
4 Other current transfers	975	2079	5255	6480	8461	12240	21490	15290	17930	18283	23754	27083
Statistical discrepancy	-4639	2005	-71869	-88430	91217	88899	176697	202926	120219	51691	-53224	-148627
5 Net saving	38650	104682	357591	469381	334326	387458	461504	622932	672629	807452	1446980	1894760
Total Current Disbursements and Net Saving	270384	626056	1623100	2032440	2548940	3014640	3727500	4598040	5383230	6160380	7631330	9131050

a) Compensation of employees paid by resident producers to resident households excludes wages paid to agricultural workers which are included in item 'Operating surplus'.
b) Beginning 1975, item 'Property and entrepreneural income' includes savings of corporations.

1.7 External Transactions on Current Account, Summary

Million Greek drachmas

	1970	1975	1980	1981	1982	1983	1984	1985	1986	1987	1988	1989
Payments to the Rest of the World												
1 Imports of goods and services	54996	180562	448881	556129	738303	925366	1139110	1513530	1703260	1993450	2290690	2839490
A Imports of merchandise c.i.f.	49262	164227	404786	483648	658143	832678	1036040	1378310	1537950	1830340	2060660	2549480
B Other	5734	16335	44095	72481	80160	92688	103066	135222	165308	163106	230031	290008
2 Factor income to the rest of the world	2274	7554	23561	50593	57885	85245	131327	179570	199450	218174	254431	314824
A Compensation of employees	462	1539	2529	3647	4283	6845	6435	6293	8298	10427	13538	19378
B Property and entrepreneurial income	1812	6015	21032	46946	53602	78400	124892	173277	191152	207747	240893	295446
3 Current transfers to the rest of the world	134	1479	1988	11000	21700	30424	32648	44125	95277	77257	91335	111736
A Indirect taxes to supranational organizations	...	...	...	9152	18562	25024	28788	39845	90220	73153	86127	105436
B Other current transfers	134	1479	1988	1848	3138	5400	3860	4280	5057	4104	5208	6300
4 Surplus of the nation on current transactions	-9302	-24664	9242	-15294	-113402	-155301	-153290	-377239	-290768	-192216	-152634	-420855
Payments to the Rest of the World and Surplus of the Nation on Current Transactions	48102	164931	483672	602428	704486	885734	1149790	1359990	1707220	2096660	2483820	2845200
Receipts From The Rest of the World												
1 Exports of goods and services [a]	29988	113349	357651	422380	473019	609493	824649	977623	1233100	1536780	1800880	2069540
A Exports of merchandise f.o.b.	19276	74441	221109	237928	286281	392652	542666	629188	789995	954529	1083390	1281650

Greece

1.7 External Transactions on Current Account, Summary
(Continued)

Million Greek drachmas

	1970	1975	1980	1981	1982	1983	1984	1985	1986	1987	1988	1989
B Other	10712	38908	136542	184452	186738	216841	281983	348435	443109	582251	717494	787892
2 Factor income from rest of the world	7777	26761	80180	109597	115672	115653	133192	145786	131604	154842	197768	229590
A Compensation of employees	2462	10486	26392	35417	40798	44702	48461	53107	47459	48263	41974	47176
B Property and entrepreneurial income	5315	16275	53788	74180	74874	70951	84731	92679	84145	106579	155794	182414
3 Current transfers from rest of the world	10337	24821	45841	70451	115795	160588	191950	236576	342511	405041	485166	546064
A Subsidies from supranational organisations	...	...	...	10134	45642	78160	88060	126277	205271	218658	240216	320268
B Other current transfers	10337	24821	45841	60317	70153	82428	103890	110299	137240	186383	244950	225796
Receipts from the Rest of the World on Current Transactions	48102	164931	483672	602428	704486	885734	1149790	1359990	1707220	2096660	2483820	2845200

a) Data on Exports of goods and services as well as transport, storage and communication exclude income from ocean-going cargo ships under Greek flag or ownership. However, remittances actually received by the bank of Greece from persons engaged in these enterprises are included in factor income from the rest of the world.

1.8 Capital Transactions of The Nation, Summary

Million Greek drachmas

	1970	1975	1980	1981	1982	1983	1984	1985	1986	1987	1988	1989
Finance of Gross Capital Formation												
Gross saving	74707	156686	498615	505319	429905	517906	585945	606015	770748	878993	1258880	1295520
1 Consumption of fixed capital	16860	47457	142082	175498	215399	272598	329371	403045	505138	575301	658783	792027
2 Net saving	57847	109229	356533	329821	214506	245308	256574	202970	265610	303692	600098	503493
A General government	13202	4547	-1058	-139560	-119820	-142150	-204930	-419962	-407019	-503760	-846879	1391270
B Corporate and quasi-corporate enterprises a	5995	...	...	...	...	...	...	...	...	...	...	...
Public	...	...	...	...	...	...	...	...	...	...	...	...
Private	5995	...	...	...	...	...	...	...	...	...	...	...
C Other a	38650	104682	357591	469381	334326	387458	461504	622932	672629	807452	1446980	1894760
Less: Surplus of the nation on current transactions	-9302	-24664	9242	-15294	-113402	-155301	-153290	-377239	-290768	-192216	-152634	-420855
Finance of Gross Capital Formation	84009	181350	489373	520613	543307	673207	739235	983254	1061520	1071210	1411520	1716380
Gross Capital Formation												
Increase in stocks	13346	41400	75688	64263	29807	49207	36335	102884	43418	25412	129179	85847
Gross fixed capital formation	70663	139950	413685	456350	513500	624000	702900	880370	1018100	1045800	1282340	1630530
1 General government	13386	24599	43427	63500	72657	111050	162100	206973	227540	201733	243163	279804
2 Corporate and quasi-corporate enterprises b	6540	14221	52393	58000	80843	104250	123950	168097	156980	120998	131906	186136
A Public	6540	14221	52393	58000	80843	104250	123950	168097	156980	120998	131906	186136
B Private b	...	...	...	...	...	...	...	...	...	...	...	...
3 Other b	50737	101130	317865	334850	360000	408700	416850	505300	633578	723066	907267	1164590
Gross Capital Formation	84009	181350	489373	520613	543307	673207	739235	983254	1061520	1071210	1411520	1716380

a) Beginning 1975, item 'Corporate and quasi-corporate enterprises' is included in item 'Other'.
b) Private corporate and quasi-corporate enterprises are included in item 'Other'.

1.10 Gross Domestic Product by Kind of Activity, in Current Prices

Million Greek drachmas

	1970	1975	1980	1981	1982	1983	1984	1985	1986	1987	1988	1989
1 Agriculture, hunting, forestry and fishing	47058	110971	270058	329285	424415	462769	591395	713824	788062	851895	1079350	1337320
2 Mining and quarrying	3541	8460	23352	29914	44841	57083	77062	89776	79093	98866	104600	120918
3 Manufacturing	49266	118078	296955	361290	422602	503123	614818	752500	907415	971076	1148650	1346700
4 Electricity, gas and water	5152	9312	24045	36957	53625	64833	77281	105566	139875	155261	174513	194058
5 Construction	23017	43011	129934	142278	151669	187766	213678	262852	317525	328638	396995	468454
6 Wholesale and retail trade, restaurants and hotels a	31050	82221	196266	240033	295000	359605	438718	540367	656546	724827	851672	...
7 Transport, storage and communication b	19761	47955	118476	147213	188327	222670	264039	309287	372904	432113	519433	598839
8 Finance, insurance, real estate and business services c	27187	54875	132167	156015	191959	222975	264548	315510	383468	457568	567521	...
9 Community, social and personal services acd	29409	66008	185041	228536	290604	361080	441607	570846	674556	795106	956354	...
Total, Industries	235441	540891	1376290	1671520	2063040	2441900	2983150	3660530	4319440	4815350	5799090	...
Producers of Government Services	22559	52290	147430	188450	247646	291340	379442	476324	536200	618426	747582	...

726

Greece

1.10 Gross Domestic Product by Kind of Activity, in Current Prices (Continued)

Million Greek drachmas

	1970	1975	1980	1981	1982	1983	1984	1985	1986	1987	1988	1989
Other Producers d												
Subtotal e	258000	593181	1523720	1859670	2310690	2733240	3625900	4138650	4855640	5433780	6546670	7855140
Less: Imputed bank service charge												
Plus: Import duties												
Plus: Value added tax												
Plus: Other adjustments f	40917	78977	187210	190000	263996	345834	443890	480964	642036	794258	955296	
Equals: Gross Domestic Product	298917	672158	1710930	2050600	2574650	3079180	3805690	4617820	5497680	6228030	7501970	8798390

a) Restaurants and hotels are included in item 'Community, social and personal services'. b) Data on Exports of goods and services as well as transport, storage and communication exclude income from ocean-going cargo ships under Greek flag or ownership. However, remittances actually received by the bank of Greece from persons engaged in these enterprises are included in factor income from the rest of the world. c) Business services are included in item 'Community, social and personal services'. d) Item 'Other producers' is included in item 'Community, social and personal services'. e) Gross domestic product in factor values. f) Item 'Other adjustments' refers to indirect taxes net of subsidies.

1.11 Gross Domestic Product by Kind of Activity, in Constant Prices

Million Greek drachmas

	1970	1975	1980	1981	1982	1983	1984	1985	1986	1987	1988	1989
At constant prices of 1970												
1 Agriculture, hunting, forestry and fishing	47058	56733	60499	59516	60940	55518	59394	60523	62036	59493	63152	65267
2 Mining and quarrying	3541	4855	6245	6226	6537	6982	7827	7968	8000	8064	8790	8816
3 Manufacturing	49266	70944	89125	88888	89464	85436	84475	85429	89449	87306	91290	93203
4 Electricity, gas and water	5152	8596	13724	14149	14616	15172	16022	17032	17475	18419	19543	20461
5 Construction	23017	23147	26392	24201	22289	23055	21890	22525	22345	20937	22528	23024
6 Wholesale and retail trade, restaurants and hotels a	31050	42825	50380	50633	51388	52238	53238	55555	57096	57153	60296	
7 Transport, storage and communication b	19761	28616	39898	41277	41510	42971	45936	48733	49138	51054	53096	
8 Finance, insurance, real estate and business services c	27187	37892	49134	50159	51492	54158	55704	57198	59086	60380	62308	
9 Community, social and personal services	29409	36855	45152	45408	45813	45783	46220	47404	49323	50420	51750	
Total, Industries	235441	310491	380802	380181	382283	392706	406507	414224	411310	430627		
Producers of Government Services	22559	29342	36708	38090	39110	40068	41990	42912	42425	41796	42299	
Other Producers d												
Subtotal e	258000	339833	417510	418271	420641	422351	434696	449419	460520	453735	473926	488680
Less: Imputed bank service charge												
Plus: Import duties												
Plus: Value added tax												
Plus: Other adjustments f	40917	42529	55000	55500	55000	55200	55200	56000	56592	57000	56870	57469
Equals: Gross Domestic Product	298917	382362	472510	473771	475641	477551	496960	500611	513020	510609	531395	546520

a) Restaurants and hotels are included in item 'Community, social and personal services'. b) Data on Exports of goods and services as well as transport, storage and communication exclude income from ocean-going cargo ships under Greek flag or ownership. However, remittances actually received by the bank of Greece from persons engaged in these enterprises are included in factor income from the rest of the world. c) Business services are included in item 'Community, social and personal services'. d) Item 'Other producers' is included in item 'Community, social and personal services'. e) Gross domestic product in factor values. f) Item 'Other adjustments' refers to indirect taxes net of subsidies.

1.12 Relations Among National Accounting Aggregates

Million Greek drachmas

	1970	1975	1980	1981	1982	1983	1984	1985	1986	1987	1988	1989
Gross Domestic Product	298917	672158	1710930	2050600	2574650	3079180	3805690	4617820	5497680	6228030	7501970	8798390
Plus: Net factor income from the rest of the world	5503	19207	56119	57787	59004	30408	1865	-337840	-67846	-63332	-56663	-85234
Factor income from the rest of the world	7777	26761	80180	109597	115672	115653	133192	145786	131604	154842	177768	229690
Less: Factor income to the rest of the world	2274	7554	23561	50693	57885	85245	131327	179570	199450	218174	254431	314824
Equals: Gross National Product	304420	691385	1767550	2109060	2633560	3109690	3807550	4584030	5429860	6164700	7445310	8713160
Less: Consumption of fixed capital	16860	47457	142082	175498	215399	272598	329371	403205	505138	573001	688783	792027
Equals: National Income	287560	643908	1625470	1933560	2417040	2836990	3478180	4180900	4924700	5589400	6786520	7921130
Plus: Net current transfers from the rest of the world	10203	23342	43853	59451	90495	130104	159302	192451	247234	327784	393831	434328
Current transfers from the rest of the world	10337	24821	45841	70451	115795	160588	191950	236576	342511	405041	485166	546064
Less: Current transfers to the rest of the world	134	1479	1988	11000	21700	30424	32648	44125	95277	77257	91635	111736
Equals: National Disposable Income	297763	667250	1669320	1993010	2511140	2967150	3637480	4373440	5171930	5917190	7180360	8355460
Less: Final consumption	244555	550016	1388460	1751620	2205410	2632950	3204210	3967540	4781600	5581800	6633480	8000800
Statistical discrepancy	4639	-2005	71869	88430	91217	-88899	-176697	-202926	-120219	-51697	53224	148627
Equals: Net Saving	57847	109229	355633	329821	214506	245308	256574	202970	265610	303886	600800	503493
Less: Surplus of the nation on current transactions	-9302	-24664	9242	-1594	-11294	-15294	-153290	-153290	-307239	-290768	-192216	-426855
Equals: Net Capital Formation	67149	133893	347291	345115	327908	400609	409864	580209	556378	495902	752732	924348

727

Greece

2.1 Government Final Consumption Expenditure by Function, in Current Prices

Million Greek drachmas

	1970	1975	1980	1981	1982	1983	1984	1985	1986	1987	1988	1989
1 General public services	13990	33472	98102	128608	166885	208304	285430	367725	405939	477897	603840	...
2 Defence	13836	45422	100000	135082	164444	195700	245500	289840	319955	367575	445742	...
3 Public order and safety	...	...	...	...	...	...	...	...	...	...	...	...
4 Education	5648	12987	37224	47968	64348	98698	100144	137510	155682	175661	213987	...
5 Health	3030	7659	28358	36039	48490	57075	72703	83165	123302	136281	169900	...
6 Social security and welfare	495	1011	3811	5371	7190	9296	11387	15170	16738	18646	21839	...
7 Housing and community amenities	...	...	...	...	...	...	...	...	...	...	...	...
8 Recreational, cultural and religious affairs	...	...	...	...	...	...	...	...	...	...	...	...
9 Economic services [a]	743	1456	12515	15992	17873	22009	27606	36540	45623	54360	62163	...
10 Other functions [a]	...	...	...	...	...	...	...	...	...	...	...	...
Total Government Final Consumption Expenditure [b]	37742	102007	280050	368550	471230	579370	742770	942050	1067240	1229420	1517470	...

a) Item 'Other functions' is included in item 'Economic services'.
b) Data for this table have not been revised, therefore, data for some years are not comparable with those of other tables.

2.5 Private Final Consumption Expenditure by Type and Purpose, in Current Prices

Million Greek drachmas

Final Consumption Expenditure of Resident Households

	1970	1975	1980	1981	1982	1983	1984	1985	1986	1987	1988	1989
1 Food, beverages and tobacco	87322	190519	473996	607939	746444	873176	1049970	1244000	1514600	1746810	2024320	2383850
A Food	73420	164654	408398	528735	645280	745677	888551	1043820	1256050	1445070	1629470	1910780
B Non-alcoholic beverages	913	2696	11492	14790	18738	23803	28439	40655	49766	58995	72028
C Alcoholic beverages	5712	10243	32337	41008	49872	60438	80180	90166	117808	143633	183312
D Tobacco	7277	12926	27433	34817	46766	58889	77168	91557	115463	135667	188217	217727
2 Clothing and footwear	26212	52941	111569	130829	153618	170807	213660	273222	350191	418485	502440	584903
3 Gross rent, fuel and power	29503	57098	137792	174590	211270	240674	294310	346101	418143	515224	623737	721308
A Fuel and power	4948	11030	28976	41554	51789	66146	84318	119160	118905	145135	156275	163519
4 Furniture, furnishings and household equipment and operation	24555	46098	108716	133036	154481	177928	209662	249641	300548	370680	467462	557789
A Household operation	15597	40253	95648	119862	147310	183813	214993	267708	324428	380062	448822	529844
B Other	4961	13192	29444	36616	47398	61774	78001	101010	112748	143857	172164	204283
5 Medical care and health expenses	10636	27061	62204	82366	99662	122039	136962	166668	211680	244205	276758	325561
6 Transport and communication	8731	18345	42051	50320	60137	73049	87738	115559	144822	187618	211375	...
A Personal transport equipment	17604	50211	142412	181315	240139	279616	332139	440713	555650	597196	699496	844437
...	953	5414	16720	22450	45310	48401	64878	114922	139684	125129	144309	210668
7 Recreational, entertainment, education and cultural services	16651	44797	125692	158865	194829	228515	267261	325791	415966	472067	555187	633769
A Education	10143	22190	63459	83174	105365	126605	147357	185571	228957	277292	327439	377777
B Other	2652	6376	10607	11142	13051	13879	15743	18555	22860	25933	31601	37063
8 Miscellaneous goods and services	7491	15814	52852	72032	92314	108726	131614	167016	206097	251369	295838	340714
A Personal care	15849	38000	98504	122535	148239	178912	232782	294639	362674	454911	542639	634573
B Expenditures in restaurants, cafes and hotels	2213	7217	16413	19886	27632	33605	41117	55920	82082	85619	101173	115817
Other	9468	21138	61481	78437	92428	113415	152334	193387	231222	288965	344225	407707
Total Final Consumption Expenditure in the Domestic Market by Households, of which	4227	9645	20610	24412	28179	31892	39331	47132	62370	80327	97241	111049
A Durable goods	210961	469557	1165330	1469680	1812520	2125350	2572950	3169200	3901960	4562720	5356610	6288070
B Semi-durable goods	8342	26473	70042	95094	135062	151996	181575	253786	325420	339729	374306	479665
C Non-durable goods	32602	70820	152868	182973	219439	250415	310746	390419	325420	615774	740320	862538
	105691	235877	594445	760323	937750	1110940	1345000	1616380	1946000	2282420	2628880	3066150

Greece

2.5 Private Final Consumption Expenditure by Type and Purpose, in Current Prices (Continued)

Million Greek drachmas

	1970	1975	1980	1981	1982	1983	1984	1985	1986	1987	1988	1989
D Services	64326	136387	347556	431294	524271	619002	738124	905129	1104920	1324800	1613100	1879710
Plus: Direct purchases abroad by resident households	1659	4965	13349	20397	25292	32098	38342	51147	68911	104914	...	1333303
Less: Direct purchases in the domestic market by non-resident households	5807	20533	74070	107008	103632	138874	198850	194964	252261	299251	345511	324637
Equals: Final Consumption Expenditure of Resident Households a	206813	454009	1104610	1383070	1734180	2053580	2461440	3025490	3718860	4332380	5116010	6094730

Final Consumption Expenditure of Private Non-profit Serving Households

| Equals: Expenditure of Private Non-profit Organisations Serving Households | ... | ... | ... | ... | ... | ... | ... | ... | ... | ... | ... | ... |
| Private Final Consumption Expenditure | 206813 | 454009 | 1104610 | 1383070 | 1734180 | 2053580 | 2461440 | 3025490 | 3718860 | 4332380 | 5116010 | 6094730 |

a) Item 'Final consumption expenditure of resident households' includes consumption expenditure of private non-profit institutions serving households.

2.6 Private Final Consumption Expenditure by Type and Purpose, in Constant Prices

Million Greek drachmas

At constant prices of 1970
Final Consumption Expenditure of Resident Households

	1970	1975	1980	1981	1982	1983	1984	1985	1986	1987	1988	1989
1 Food, beverages and tobacco	87322	103980	121530	124842	128655	129949	131303	132492	134618	137900	141511	141651
A Food	73420	86113	95136	96816	96803	98851	98273	96964	97653	102919	102057	
B Non-alcoholic beverages	913	1549	2648	2818	2537	2802	2662	2832	2767	3023	3270	3564	3885
C Alcoholic beverages	5712	6172	8784	10292	10300	10800	11563	13221	13160	13599	14748	15485
D Tobacco	7277	10146	13792	15197	16950	17530	18635	19543	20782	21050	20280	20224
2 Clothing and footwear	26212	26212	33953	34484	33315	30639	27308	27200	28363	28924	28863	28636
3 Gross rent, fuel and power	29509	40573	52239	55410	55299	58394	60974	61928	65486	67467	69369
A Fuel and power	4948	6225	9292	9477	10351	11101	12081	12015	12895	13121	13463
B Other	24555	33848	42947	44225	45915	47343	48773	49847	51098	52551	54155	55906
4 Furniture, furnishings and household equipment and operation	15597	24072	28868	29335	28552	28299	27345	28527	27745	26809	30075
A Household operation	4961	7365	8173	8036	8089	8767	9263	9920	8827	9533	10269
B Other	10636	16707	20695	21299	20463	19532	18082	18607	18818	18218	18637	19806
5 Medical care and health expenses	8731	9866	11032	10797	10473	11274	11299	11857	11963	12350	12491	12799
6 Transport and communication	17604	28092	41074	42206	43956	46572	50704	57838	57111	55140	57613	62524
A Personal transport equipment	953	3398	3630	4212	4420	6381	7406	11417	10046	7717	8152	10948
B Other	16651	24694	37444	37994	38936	40291	43298	46421	47065	47423	49461	51576
7 Recreational, entertainment, education and cultural services	10143	12008	16546	19587	21008	19399	20160	20804	21567	21459	22023	22777
A Education	2652	3150	2257	2040	2039	1862	1803	1880	1907	1876	1972	2058
B Other	7491	8858	14289	17547	18969	17537	18357	18924	19660	19583	20051	20719
8 Miscellaneous goods and services	15849	21925	27283	27723	27597	26501	28027	29662	29863	30605	31559	32328
A Personal care	2213	4223	4366	4483	4919	4725	4778	5809	5702	5624	5964	6209
B Expenditures in restaurants, cafes and hotels	9409	12621	17564	17794	17743	17146	18509	19060	19011	19316	19533	19991
C Other	4227	5081	5353	4946	4935	4630	4740	4793	5150	5665	6062	6128
Total Final Consumption Expenditure in the Domestic Market by Households, of which:	210961	274589	333256	341415	349546	347796	357712	371471	374804	379054	389606	400159
A Durable goods	8342	16648	21398	24715	28569	25118	25576	29130	25830	25551	30673
B Semi-durable goods	32602	44234	46562	46672	44213	40282	40058	42155	43185	43317	44663	45460
C Non-durable goods	105691	130455	157072	160643	166055	170134	173889	178313	180452	187605	192135	194161

Greece

2.6 Private Final Consumption Expenditure by Type and Purpose, in Constant Prices (Continued)

Million Greek drachmas

	1970	1975	1980	1981	1982	1983	1984	1985	1986	1987	1988	1989
At constant prices of 1970
D Services	64326	83252	102824	108385	110709	112262	117189	121213	122037	123102	126560	129865
Plus: Direct purchases abroad by resident households	1659	2895	4076	5328	5681	5572	5456	5712	5696	4811	6333	7347
Less: Direct purchases in the domestic market by non-resident households	5807	10600	17991	20892	16720	13943	16974	18512	19847	19847	20188	16678
Equals: Final Consumption Expenditure of Resident Households [a]	208613	266884	319341	325851	338507	345425	345194	358671	361026	364018	375254	390828
Equals: Final Consumption Expenditure of Private Non-profit Organisations Serving Households	...	...	...	...	...	...	...	...	...	...	...	...
Private Final Consumption Expenditure	208613	266884	319341	325851	338507	345425	345194	358671	361026	364018	375254	390828

a) Item "Final consumption expenditure of resident households' includes consumption expenditure of private non-profit institutions serving households.

2.7 Gross Capital Formation by Type of Good and Owner, in Current Prices

Million Greek drachmas

	1980				1981				1982			
	TOTAL	Total Private	Public Enterprises	General Government	TOTAL	Total Private	Public Enterprises	General Government	TOTAL	Total Private	Public Enterprises	General Government
Increase in stocks, total	75888	66628	6625	2635	64263	40183	9132	14948	29807	26887	5178	-2258
1 Goods producing industries	63253	58720	4533	...	45960	39926	6034	...	33340	29720	3620	...
2 Wholesale and retail trade	4520	4398	122	...	4706	4626	80	...	-1341	-1377	36	...
3 Other, except government stocks	5480	3510	1970	...	-1351	-4369	3018	...	99	-1456	1522	...
4 Government stocks	2435	...	...	2435	14948	...	...	14948	-2258	...	...	-2258
Gross Fixed Capital Formation, Total	413685	317865	52393	43427	456350	334850	58000	63500	513500	360000	80843	72657
1 Residential buildings [a]	137517	135694	1676	147	126373	122627	3461	285	135292	130010	4162	1030
2 Non-residential buildings [a]	58664	48830	2529	7205	68547	51943	4552	12052	61368	42838	5748	12782
3 Other construction [a]	64646	20809	17164	26673	92902	31344	19279	42279	89575	16202	26642	46731
4 Land improvement and plantation and orchard development [ab]	6322	752	...	5570	6030	1020	...	5010	1968	1039	-	7942
5 Producers' durable goods [a]	146636	111780	31024	3832	162498	127916	30708	3874	218284	169821	44291	4172
A Transport equipment [a]	47136	38572	8340	224	49045	41892	6747	406	78217	69708	8971	338
B Machinery and equipment [a]	99500	73208	22684	3608	113453	86024	23961	3468	140067	101913	34320	3834
6 Breeding stock, dairy cattle, etc.	...	...	...	...	...	...	...	...	...	...	...	...
Total Gross Capital Formation	489373	384493	59018	45862	520613	375033	67132	78448	543307	386887	86021	70389

	1983				1984				1985			
	TOTAL	Total Private	Public Enterprises	General Government	TOTAL	Total Private	Public Enterprises	General Government	TOTAL	Total Private	Public Enterprises	General Government
Increase in stocks, total	49207	59246	4674	-14713	-3574	65089	7220	102884	107717	6100	...	-10933
1 Goods producing industries	61769	58620	3149	...	62012	66735	4723	96792	91687	5105	...	...
2 Wholesale and retail trade	231	380	-149	...	6330	6584	-254	11909	11909	-	...	...
3 Other, except government stocks	1920	246	1674	...	-756	-3507	2751	...	5116	4121	995	...
4 Government stocks	-14713	...	...	-14713	-3574	...	...	-3574	-10933	...	...	-10933
Gross Fixed Capital Formation, Total	624000	408700	104250	111050	702900	416850	123950	162100	880370	505300	168097	206973
1 Residential buildings [a]	163012	158332	3285	1395	152214	146753	4131	1330	178072	170630	5682	1760
2 Non-residential buildings [a]	73480	45344	4659	23477	87741	48275	6049	33417	96281	57419	9142	29720
3 Other construction [a]	122485	17008	35882	69595	162682	23165	36610	102907	220904	31496	42138	147270
4 Land improvement and plantation and orchard development [ab]	10364	1107	-	9257	11290	1220	-	10070	14516	1574	-	12942
5 Producers' durable goods [a]	254659	186909	60426	7324	288873	197437	77160	14376	370597	244181	111135	15281
A Transport equipment [a]	69942	62553	2463	926	64849	54735	9160	954	90364	73597	15345	1422
B Machinery and equipment [a]	188717	124356	57963	6398	224124	142702	68000	13422	280233	170584	95790	13859
6 Breeding stock, dairy cattle, etc.	...	...	...	...	...	...	...	...	...	...	...	...
Total Gross Capital Formation	673207	467946	108924	96337	739235	481939	131170	126126	983254	613017	174197	196040

Greece

2.7 Gross Capital Formation by Type of Good and Owner, in Current Prices

Million Greek drachmas

	1986				1987				1988			
	TOTAL	Total Private	Public Enterprises	General Government	TOTAL	Total Private	Public Enterprises	General Government	TOTAL	Total Private	Public Enterprises	General Government
Increase in stocks, total	43418	43012	8771	-8365	25412	19095	6697	-380	129179	116765	12425	-11
1 Goods producing industries	41649	37509	4140	...	27051	21037	6014	...	122294	116034	6260	...
2 Wholesale and retail trade	-7289	-7289	-	...	19472	19423	49	...	5058	5058	-	...
3 Other, except government stocks	17423	12792	4631	...	-20731	-21365	634	...	1838	-4327	6165	...
4 Government stocks	-8365	...	...	-8365	-380	...	...	-380	-11	...	...	-11
Gross Fixed Capital Formation, Total	1018100	633578	156980	227540	1045800	723066	120998	201733	1282340	907267	131906	243163
1 Residential buildings a	248326	240250	6512	1564	286869	277853	7754	1262	329292	317945	10626	721
2 Non-residential buildings a	124848	76794	10045	38009	140934	97453	8192	35289	193431	136362	10169	46900
3 Other construction a	228171	20362	52622	155187	190270	14601	42389	133280	232123	20240	52416	159467
4 Land improvement and plantation and orchard development ab	17337	2270	-	15067	17043	2526	-	14517	20015	3657	-	16358
5 Producers' durable goods a	399416	293902	87801	17713	410681	330633	62663	17385	507475	429063	58695	19717
A Transport equipment a	89966	81872	7230	864	89971	87884	1489	598	96232	94008	1459	765
B Machinery and equipment a	309450	212030	80571	16849	320710	242749	61174	16787	411243	335055	57236	18952
6 Breeding stock, dairy cattle, etc.	...	...	...	...	...	...	...	...	...	...	...	...
Total Gross Capital Formation	1061520	676590	165751	219175	1071210	742161	127695	201353	1411520	1024030	144331	243152

	1989			
	TOTAL	Total Private	Public Enterprises	General Government
Increase in stocks, total	85847	69290	16557	-
1 Goods producing industries	58822	52069	6753	...
2 Wholesale and retail trade	12621	12621	-	...
3 Other, except government stocks	14404	4600	9804	...
4 Government stocks	-	...	...	-
Gross Fixed Capital Formation, Total	1630530	1164590	186136	279804
1 Residential buildings a	403477	390989	11674	814
2 Non-residential buildings a	216043	154744	13301	47998
3 Other construction a	277863	22063	69213	186587
4 Land improvement and plantation and orchard development ab	26172	4855	-	21317
5 Producers' durable goods a	706973	591937	91948	23088
A Transport equipment a	127618	115935	11016	667
B Machinery and equipment a	579355	476002	80932	22421
6 Breeding stock, dairy cattle, etc.	...	...	...	...
Total Gross Capital Formation	1716380	1233880	202693	279804

a) For the years 1970-1978, items of column 'General government' are included in column 'Public enterprises'.   b) Item 'Land improvement and plantation and orchard development' includes outlays on land improvement and transfer costs on purchases and sales of agricultural land only.

2.8 Gross Capital Formation by Type of Good and Owner, in Constant Prices

Million Greek drachmas

	1980				1981				1982			
	TOTAL	Total Private	Public Enterprises	General Government	TOTAL	Total Private	Public Enterprises	General Government	TOTAL	Total Private	Public Enterprises	General Government
	At constant prices of:1970											
Increase in stocks, total	19280	16634	1538	1108	10305	5670	1700	2935	5790	4388	846	556
1 Goods producing industries	14636	13577	1059	...	8160	7041	1119	...	5146	4566	580	...
2 Wholesale and retail trade	1997	1978	19	...	845	824	21	...	-132	-155	23	...
3 Other, except government stocks	1539	1079	460	...	-1635	-2195	560	...	220	-23	243	...
4 Government stocks	1108	...	...	1108	2935	...	...	2935	556	...	...	556
Gross Fixed Capital Formation, Total	92705	70465	13231	9009	85750	63495	11693	10562	84100	60300	13776	10024
1 Residential buildings a	27291	26929	332	30	21452	20816	588	48	20398	19613	627	158
2 Non-residential buildings a	11622	9691	501	1430	11636	8818	772	2046	9252	6460	867	1925

Greece

2.8 Gross Capital Formation by Type of Good and Owner, in Constant Prices
(Continued)

Million Greek drachmas

	1980				1981				1982			
	TOTAL	Total Private	Public Enterprises	General Government	TOTAL	Total Private	Public Enterprises	General Government	TOTAL	Total Private	Public Enterprises	General Government
At constant prices of:1970												
3 Other construction [a]	14273	4493	4410	5370	16306	5449	3964	6893	12903	2217	4494	6192
4 Land improvement and plantation and orchard development [ab]	1401	150	-	1251	963	163	-	800	1158	133	-	1025
5 Producers' durable goods [a]	38118	29202	7988	928	35393	28249	6368	776	40389	31877	7787	725
A Transport equipment [a]	13987	11439	2482	66	12445	10623	1718	104	16427	14258	2098	71
B Machinery and equipment [a]	24131	17763	5506	862	22948	17626	4650	672	23962	17619	5689	654
6 Breeding stock, dairy cattle, etc.	...	...	...	...	...	...	...	...	...	...	...	...
Total Gross Capital Formation	111985	87099	14769	10117	96055	69165	13393	13497	89890	64688	14622	10580

	1983				1984				1985			
	TOTAL	Total Private	Public Enterprises	General Government	TOTAL	Total Private	Public Enterprises	General Government	TOTAL	Total Private	Public Enterprises	General Government
At constant prices of:1970												
Increase in stocks, total	6148	8164	619	-2635	3763	7882	822	-4941	10149	10599	557	-1007
1 Goods producing industries	8076	7656	420	...	7268	6749	519	...	9125	8659	466	...
2 Wholesale and retail trade	195	220	-25	...	1464	1464	-	...	894	894	-	...
3 Other, except government stocks	512	288	224	...	-28	-331	303	...	1137	1046	91	...
4 Government stocks	-2635	...	...	-2635	-4941	...	...	-4941	-1007	...	...	-1007
Gross Fixed Capital Formation, Total	83000	56000	14400	12600	78300	48570	14485	15245	82360	49670	16672	16018
1 Residential buildings [a]	21124	20524	425	175	17083	16471	463	149	17097	16382	546	169
2 Non-residential buildings [a]	9529	5882	603	3044	9848	5418	679	3751	9241	5511	877	2853
3 Other construction [a]	14249	1875	5041	7333	14957	2040	4154	8763	16780	2340	3939	10501
4 Land improvement and plantation and orchard development [ab]	1147	115	-	1032	1005	102	-	903	1103	113	-	990
5 Producers' durable goods [a]	36951	27604	8331	1016	35407	24539	9189	1679	38139	25324	11310	1505
A Transport equipment [a]	11207	10630	419	158	9081	7659	1288	134	10354	8429	1763	162
B Machinery and equipment [a]	25744	16974	7912	858	26326	16880	7901	1545	27785	16895	9547	1343
6 Breeding stock, dairy cattle, etc.	...	...	...	...	...	...	...	...	...	...	...	...
Total Gross Capital Formation	89148	64164	15019	9965	82063	56452	15307	10304	92509	60269	17229	15011

	1986				1987				1988			
	TOTAL	Total Private	Public Enterprises	General Government	TOTAL	Total Private	Public Enterprises	General Government	TOTAL	Total Private	Public Enterprises	General Government
At constant prices of:1970												
Increase in stocks, total	6362	6364	680	-682	2050	1617	473	-40	11599	10800	800	-1
1 Goods producing industries	3969	3648	321	...	2794	2369	425	...	11035	10632	403	...
2 Wholesale and retail trade	-436	-436	-	...	2814	2814	-	...	398	398	-	...
3 Other, except government stocks	3511	3152	359	...	-3518	-3566	48	...	167	-230	397	...
4 Government stocks	-682	...	...	-682	-40	...	...	-40	-1	...	...	-1
Gross Fixed Capital Formation, Total	77234	50525	12475	14234	70546	51585	7984	10977	76777	57515	7707	11555
1 Residential buildings [a]	19399	18768	508	123	20044	19414	542	88	20691	19978	668	45
2 Non-residential buildings [a]	9752	5999	785	2968	9848	6810	572	2466	12154	8569	639	2946
3 Other construction [a]	13684	1194	3695	8795	9702	744	2495	6463	10116	878	2646	6592
4 Land improvement and plantation and orchard development [ab]	1053	130	-	923	897	126	-	771	896	155	-	741
5 Producers' durable goods [a]	33346	24434	7487	1425	30055	24491	4375	1189	32920	27935	3754	1231
A Transport equipment [a]	8569	7794	692	83	7348	7176	123	49	6810	6650	106	54
B Machinery and equipment [a]	24777	16640	6795	1342	22707	17315	4252	1140	26110	21285	3648	1177
6 Breeding stock, dairy cattle, etc.	...	...	...	...	...	...	...	...	...	...	...	...
Total Gross Capital Formation	83596	56889	13155	13552	72596	53202	8457	10937	88376	68315	8507	11554

Greece

2.8 Gross Capital Formation by Type of Good and Owner, in Constant Prices

Million Greek drachmas

	1989 TOTAL	Total Private	Public Enterprises	General Government
		At constant prices of:1970		
Increase in stocks, total	4437	3450	987	-
1 Goods producing industries	1575	1144	431	...
2 Wholesale and retail trade	2010	2010	-	...
3 Other, except government stocks	852	296	556	...
4 Government stocks	...	...	...	-
Gross Fixed Capital Formation, Total	83416	62720	9429	11267
1 Residential buildings a	21687	21016	627	44
2 Non-residential buildings a	11615	8317	717	2581
3 Other construction a	10448	819	3013	6616
4 Land improvement and plantation and orchard development ab	1006	177	-	829
5 Producers' durable goods a	38660	32391	5072	1197
A Transport equipment a	7948	7214	693	41
B Machinery and equipment a	30712	25177	4379	1156
6 Breeding stock, dairy cattle, etc.	...	...	...	...
Total Gross Capital Formation	87853	66170	10416	11267

a) For the years 1970-1978, items of column 'General government' are included in column 'Public enterprises'.   b) Item 'Land improvement and plantation and orchard development' includes outlays on land improvement and transfer costs on purchases and sales of agricultural land only.

2.9 Gross Capital Formation by Kind of Activity of Owner, ISIC Major Divisions, in Current Prices

Million Greek drachmas

	1980 Total Gross Capital Formation	Increase in Stocks	Gross Fixed Capital Formation	1981 Total Gross Capital Formation	Increase in Stocks	Gross Fixed Capital Formation	1982 Total Gross Capital Formation	Increase in Stocks	Gross Fixed Capital Formation	1983 Total Gross Capital Formation	Increase in Stocks	Gross Fixed Capital Formation
						All Producers						
1 Agriculture, hunting, fishing and forestry	14048	-3881	17929	9438	-10634	20072	30085	7312	22773	33086	4743	28343
2 Mining and quarrying	22855	1243	21612	33918	1298	32620	22902	3400	19502	23618	-363	23981
3 Manufacturing	126597	61100	65497	120887	49263	71624	96543	19007	77536	143844	54241	89603
4 Electricity, gas and water	28644	4790	23854	30024	6034	23990	38154	3621	34533	56331	3148	53183
5 Construction	...	...	...	...	...	...	...	...	...	...	...	...
6 Wholesale and retail trade, restaurants and hotels a	4519	4519	...	4706	4706	...	-1341	-1341	...	231	231	...
7 Transport, storage and communication	65134	6285	58849	63659	-861	64520	98501	599	97902	95394	2346	93048
8 Finance, insurance, real estate and business services b	136567	-803	137370	125597	-491	126088	133730	-533	134263	161191	-426	161617
9 Community, social and personal services ab	45147	...	45147	53936	...	53936	54334	...	54334	63175	...	63175
Total Industries c	443511	73253	370258	442165	49315	392850	472908	32065	440843	576870	63920	512950
Producers of Government Services c	45862	2435	43427	78448	14948	63500	70399	-2258	72657	96337	-14713	111050
Private Non-Profit Institutions Serving Households	...	...	...	...	...	...	...	...	...	...	...	...
Total	489373	75688	413685	520613	64263	456350	543307	29807	513500	673207	49207	624000

	1984 Total Gross Capital Formation	Increase in Stocks	Gross Fixed Capital Formation	1985 Total Gross Capital Formation	Increase in Stocks	Gross Fixed Capital Formation	1986 Total Gross Capital Formation	Increase in Stocks	Gross Fixed Capital Formation	1987 Total Gross Capital Formation	Increase in Stocks	Gross Fixed Capital Formation
						All Producers						
1 Agriculture, hunting, fishing and forestry	58944	12507	46437	66077	9426	56651	56158	16160	39998	11125	-22086	33211
2 Mining and quarrying	31070	3523	27547	39838	2889	36949	28100	7192	20908	20967	-2589	23556
3 Manufacturing	148425	45982	102443	190742	79372	111370	181844	14157	167687	224920	45712	179208
4 Electricity, gas and water	63316	4723	58593	85648	5105	80543	63265	4140	59125	42833	6014	36819

733

Greece

2.9 Gross Capital Formation by Kind of Activity of Owner, ISIC Major Divisions, in Current Prices
(Continued)

Million Greek drachmas

	1984			1985			1986			1987		
	Total Gross Capital Formation	Increase in Stocks	Gross Fixed Capital Formation	Total Gross Capital Formation	Increase in Stocks	Gross Fixed Capital Formation	Total Gross Capital Formation	Increase in Stocks	Gross Fixed Capital Formation	Total Gross Capital Formation	Increase in Stocks	Gross Fixed Capital Formation
5 Construction	...	...	...	...	...	...	...	...	...	...	...	...
6 Wholesale and retail trade, restaurants and hotels [a]	6329	6329	...	11909	11909	...	-7289	-7289	...	19472	19472	...
7 Transport, storage and communication	91617	295	91322	125070	5472	119598	135366	17679	117687	104680	-19784	124464
8 Finance, insurance, real estate and business services [b]	149834	-1050	150884	175956	-356	176312	246506	-256	246762	284660	-947	285607
9 Community, social and personal services [ab]	63574	...	63574	91974	...	91974	138391	...	138391	161199	...	161199
Total Industries [c]	613109	72309	540800	787214	113817	673397	842341	51783	790558	869856	25792	844064
Producers of Government Services [c]	126126	-35974	162100	196040	-10933	206973	219175	-8365	227540	201353	-380	201733
Private Non-Profit Institutions Serving Households	...	...	...	...	...	...	...	...	...	...	...	...
Total	739235	36335	702900	983254	102884	880370	1061520	43418	1018100	1071210	25412	1045800

	1988			1989		
	Total Gross Capital Formation	Increase in Stocks	Gross Fixed Capital Formation	Total Gross Capital Formation	Increase in Stocks	Gross Fixed Capital Formation
			All Producers			
1 Agriculture, hunting, fishing and forestry	83795	36416	47379	48539	-8664	57203
2 Mining and quarrying	19028	-2589	21617	26244	-2589	28833
3 Manufacturing	307251	82207	225044	348860	63322	285538
4 Electricity, gas and water	53129	6260	46869	71527	6753	64774
5 Construction	...	...	...	...	...	...
6 Wholesale and retail trade, restaurants and hotels [a]	5058	5058	...	12621	12621	...
7 Transport, storage and communication	146567	3220	143347	207888	14077	193811
8 Finance, insurance, real estate and business services [b]	327189	-1382	328571	402990	327	402663
9 Community, social and personal services [ab]	226346	...	226346	317902	...	317902
Total Industries [c]	1168360	129190	1039170	1436570	85847	1350720
Producers of Government Services [c]	243152	-11	243163	279804	-	279804
Private Non-Profit Institutions Serving Households	...	...	...	...	...	...
Total	1411520	129179	1282340	1716380	85847	1630530

a) Gross fixed capital formation of item 'Wholesale and retail trade, restaurants and hotels' is included in item 'Community, social and personal services'.
b) Only ownership of dwellings is included in Gross fixed capital formation, all other activities are included in item 'Community, social and personal services'.
c) Beginning 1979, gross fixed capital formation and increase in stocks of public enterprises are included in item 'Total industries'.

2.10 Gross Capital Formation by Kind of Activity of Owner, ISIC Major Divisions, in Constant Prices

Million Greek drachmas

	1980			1981			1982			1983		
	Total Gross Capital Formation	Increase in Stocks	Gross Fixed Capital Formation	Total Gross Capital Formation	Increase in Stocks	Gross Fixed Capital Formation	Total Gross Capital Formation	Increase in Stocks	Gross Fixed Capital Formation	Total Gross Capital Formation	Increase in Stocks	Gross Fixed Capital Formation
					At constant prices of:1970							
					All Producers							
1 Agriculture, hunting, fishing and forestry	3069	-1052	4121	1406	-2340	3746	4548	979	3569	4053	461	3592
2 Mining and quarrying	5232	290	4942	6271	241	6030	3619	545	3074	3093	-49	3142
3 Manufacturing	29097	14278	14819	22949	9140	13809	16060	3040	13020	19356	7244	12112
4 Electricity, gas and water	7026	1119	5907	5797	1119	4678	6278	580	5698	7737	420	7317
5 Construction	...	...	...	...	...	...	...	...	...	...	...	...
6 Wholesale and retail trade, restaurants and hotels [a]	1997	1997	...	845	845	...	-132	-132	...	195	195	...
7 Transport, storage and communication	18376	1572	16804	13852	-1614	15466	19941	242	19699	15474	525	14949
8 Finance, insurance, real estate and business services [b]	27230	-32	27262	21382	-21	21403	20218	-22	20240	20936	-13	20949
9 Community, social and personal services [ab]	9841	...	9841	10056	...	10056	8776	...	8776	8339	...	8339
Total Industries [c]	101868	18172	83696	82558	7370	75188	79308	5232	74076	79183	8783	70400
Producers of Government Services [c]	10117	1108	9009	13497	2935	10562	10582	558	10024	9965	-2635	12600
Private Non-Profit Institutions Serving Households	...	...	...	...	...	...	...	...	...	...	...	...
Total	111985	19280	92705	96055	10305	85750	89890	5790	84100	89148	6148	83000

Greece

2.10 Gross Capital Formation by Kind of Activity of Owner, ISIC Major Divisions, in Constant Prices

Million Greek drachmas

	1984			1985			1986			1987		
	Total Gross Capital Formation	Increase in Stocks	Gross Fixed Capital Formation	Total Gross Capital Formation	Increase in Stocks	Gross Fixed Capital Formation	Total Gross Capital Formation	Increase in Stocks	Gross Fixed Capital Formation	Total Gross Capital Formation	Increase in Stocks	Gross Fixed Capital Formation

At constant prices of:1970

All Producers

1 Agriculture, hunting, fishing and forestry	6331	1305	5026	6243	1156	5087	4824	1997	2827	1503	-687	2190
2 Mining and quarrying	3429	387	3042	3700	264	3436	2106	556	1550	1429	-183	1612
3 Manufacturing	17015	5057	11958	18169	7239	10930	14091	1095	12996	15980	3239	12741
4 Electricity, gas and water	7205	519	6686	8340	466	7874	5187	321	4866	2751	425	2326
5 Construction	...	...	...	...	...	...	...	...	...	...	...	...
6 Wholesale and retail trade, restaurants and hotels [a]	1463	1463	...	894	894	...	-436	-436	...	2814	2814	...
7 Transport, storage and communication	12164	2	12162	14340	1145	13195	14157	3517	10640	5992	-3500	9492
8 Finance, insurance, real estate and business services [b]	16904	-30	16934	16920	-8	16928	19271	-6	19277	19938	-18	19956
9 Community, social and personal services [ab]	7247	...	7247	8892	...	8892	10844	...	10844	11252	...	11252
Total Industries [c]	71758	8703	63055	77498	11156	66342	70044	7044	63000	61659	2090	59569
Producers of Government Services [c]	10305	-4940	15245	15011	-1007	16018	13552	-682	14234	10937	-40	10977
Private Non-Profit Institutions Serving Households	...	...	...	...	...	...	...	...	...	...	...	...
Total	82063	3763	78300	92509	10149	82360	83596	6362	77234	72596	2050	70546

	1988			1989		
	Total Gross Capital Formation	Increase in Stocks	Gross Fixed Capital Formation	Total Gross Capital Formation	Increase in Stocks	Gross Fixed Capital Formation

At constant prices of:1970

All Producers

1 Agriculture, hunting, fishing and forestry	8252	5522	2730	513	-2268	2781
2 Mining and quarrying	1103	-183	1286	1258	-183	1441
3 Manufacturing	19559	5293	14266	18596	3595	15001
4 Electricity, gas and water	3101	403	2698	3667	431	3236
5 Construction	...	...	...	...	...	...
6 Wholesale and retail trade, restaurants and hotels [a]	398	398	...	2010	2010	...
7 Transport, storage and communication	9674	193	9481	12024	846	11178
8 Finance, insurance, real estate and business services [b]	20620	-26	20646	21649	6	21643
9 Community, social and personal services [ab]	14115	...	14115	16869	...	16869
Total Industries [c]	76822	11600	65222	76586	4437	72149
Producers of Government Services [c]	11554	-1	11555	11267	-	11267
Private Non-Profit Institutions Serving Households	...	...	...	...	...	...
Total	88376	11599	76777	87853	4437	83416

a) Gross fixed capital formation of item 'Wholesale and retail trade, restaurants and hotels' is included in item 'Community, social and personal services'.
b) Only ownership of dwellings is included in Gross fixed capital formation, all other activities are included in item 'Community, social and personal services'.
c) Beginning 1979, gross fixed capital formation and increase in stocks of public enterprises are included in item 'Total industries'.

2.17 Exports and Imports of Goods and Services, Detail

Million Greek drachmas

	1970	1975	1980	1981	1982	1983	1984	1985	1986	1987	1988	1989

Exports of Goods and Services

1 Exports of merchandise, f.o.b. [a]	19276	74441	221109	237928	286281	392652	542666	629188	789995	954529	1083390	1281650
2 Transport and communication												
3 Insurance service charges	3678	16785	58299	72974	79833	110014	127501	149374	187039	277936	368520	454152
4 Other commodities												
5 Adjustments of merchandise exports to change-of-ownership basis	...	...	...	...	...	...	...	...	...	...	...	...
6 Direct purchases in the domestic market by non-residential households	5807	20533	74070	107008	103632	103874	149850	194964	252261	299251	345511	324637
7 Direct purchases in the domestic market by extraterritorial bodies	1227	1590	4173	4470	3273	2953	4632	4097	3809	5064	3463	9103
Total Exports of Goods and Services	29988	113349	357651	422380	473019	609493	824649	977623	1233100	1536780	1800880	2069540

Imports of Goods and Services

1 Imports of merchandise, c.i.f.	49262	164227	404786	483648	658143	832678	1036040	1378310	1537950	1830340	2060660	2549480

Greece

2.17 Exports and Imports of Goods and Services, Detail
(Continued)

Million Greek drachmas

	1970	1975	1980	1981	1982	1983	1984	1985	1986	1987	1988	1989
A Imports of merchandise, f.o.b.	44828	149447	368355	440120	598910	757737	942796	1254260	1361090	1619850	1823680	2256290
B Transport of services on merchandise imports	4434	14780	36431	43528	59233	74941	93244	124048	176864	210489	236975	293191
C Insurance service charges on merchandise imports	...	...	...	...	...	...		...	...	...	...	...
2 Adjustments of merchandise imports to change-of-ownership basis	...	...		...		...		...	...	...	...	...
3 Other transport and communication												
4 Other insurance service charges												
5 Other commodities	2850	9650	24239	42672	44920	51209	51629	67554	77069	74721	99894	124343
6 Direct purchases abroad by government	1225	1700	6507	9412	9948	9381	13095	16521	19080	19474	25223	32362
7 Direct purchases abroad by resident households	1659	4985	13349	20397	25292	32098	38342	51147	69159	68911	104914	133303
Total Imports of Goods and Services	54996	180562	448881	556129	738303	925366	1139110	1513530	1703260	1993450	2290690	2839490
Balance of Goods and Services	-25008	-67213	-91230	-133749	-265284	-315873	-314457	-535906	-470156	-456668	-489802	-769949
Total Imports and Balance of Goods and Services	29988	113349	357651	422380	473019	609493	824649	977623	1233100	1536780	1800880	2069540

a) Data on Exports of goods and services as well as transport, storage and communication exclude income from ocean-going cargo ships under Greek flag or ownership. However, remittances actually received by the bank of Greece from persons engaged in these enterprises are included in factor income from the rest of the world.

4.1 Derivation of Value Added by Kind of Activity, in Current Prices

Million Greek drachmas

	1980			1981			1982			1983		
	Gross Output	Intermediate Consumption	Value Added	Gross Output	Intermediate Consumption	Value Added	Gross Output	Intermediate Consumption	Value Added	Gross Output	Intermediate Consumption	Value Added

All Producers

	Gross Output	Interm. Cons.	Value Added	Gross Output	Interm. Cons.	Value Added	Gross Output	Interm. Cons.	Value Added	Gross Output	Interm. Cons.	Value Added
1 Agriculture, hunting, forestry and fishing	...	...	270058	...	...	329285	...	...	424415	...	...	462769
A Agriculture and hunting	...	...	260503	...	...	317553	...	...	407420	...	...	442203
B Forestry and logging	...	...	4387	...	...	5163	...	...	5493	...	...	6911
C Fishing	...	...	5168	...	...	6569	...	...	11502	...	...	13655
2 Mining and quarrying	...	...	23352	...	...	29914	...	...	44841	...	...	57083
3 Manufacturing	...	...	296955	...	...	361290	...	...	422602	...	...	503123
A Manufacture of food, beverages and tobacco	...	...	54737	...	...	70074	...	...	84056	...	...	99256
B Textile, wearing apparel and leather industries	...	...	74785	...	...	86446	...	...	99180	...	...	118386
C Manufacture of wood and wood products, including furniture	...	...	16089	...	...	19423	...	...	22528	...	...	21398
D Manufacture of paper and paper products, printing and publishing	...	...	14688	...	...	18731	...	...	22389	...	...	29369
E Manufacture of chemicals and chemical petroleum, coal, rubber and plastic products	...	...	34927	...	...	40622	...	...	47977	...	...	61812
F Manufacture of non-metallic mineral products, except products of petroleum and coal	...	...	26398	...	...	32456	...	...	36016	...	...	40478
G Basic metal industries	...	...	16622	...	...	18983	...	...	20098	...	...	27778
H Manufacture of fabricated metal products, machinery and equipment	...	...	52947	...	...	67995	...	...	82003	...	...	93868
I Other manufacturing industries	...	...	5762	...	...	6560	...	...	8355	...	...	10778
4 Electricity, gas and water	...	...	24045	...	...	36957	...	...	53625	...	...	64833
A Electricity, gas and steam	...	...	24045	...	...	36957	...	...	53625	...	...	64833
B Water works and supply	...	...	...	...	...	...	...	...	...	...	...	...
5 Construction	...	...	129934	...	...	142278	...	...	151669	...	...	187766
6 Wholesale and retail trade, restaurants and hotels [a]	...	...	196266	...	...	240033	...	...	295000	...	...	359605
A Wholesale and retail trade	...	...	196266	...	...	240033	...	...	295000	...	...	359605
B Restaurants and hotels	...	...	...	...	...	...	...	...	...	...	...	...
7 Transport, storage and communication [b]	...	...	118476	...	...	147213	...	...	188327	...	...	222670
8 Finance, insurance, real estate and business services [c]	...	...	132167	...	...	156015	...	...	191959	...	...	222975
9 Community, social and personal services [acd]	...	...	185041	...	...	228536	...	...	290604	...	...	361080

Greece

4.1 Derivation of Value Added by Kind of Activity, in Current Prices
(Continued)

Million Greek drachmas

	1980			1981			1982			1983		
	Gross Output	Intermediate Consumption	Value Added	Gross Output	Intermediate Consumption	Value Added	Gross Output	Intermediate Consumption	Value Added	Gross Output	Intermediate Consumption	Value Added
Total, Industries	...	...	1376290	...	...	1671520	...	...	2063040	...	...	2441900
Producers of Government Services	...	...	147430	...	...	188450	...	...	247646	...	...	291340
Other Producers d	...	...	...	...	...	...	...	...	...	...	...	...
Total e	...	...	1523720	...	...	1859970	...	...	2310690	...	...	2733240
Less: Imputed bank service charge	...	...	...	...	...	...	...	...	...	...	...	...
Import duties	...	...	...	...	...	...	...	...	...	...	...	...
Value added tax	...	...	...	...	...	...	...	...	...	...	...	...
Other adjustments f	...	...	187210	...	...	190086	...	...	263964	...	...	345934
Total	...	...	1710930	...	...	2050060	...	...	2574650	...	...	3079180

	1984			1985			1986			1987		
	Gross Output	Intermediate Consumption	Value Added	Gross Output	Intermediate Consumption	Value Added	Gross Output	Intermediate Consumption	Value Added	Gross Output	Intermediate Consumption	Value Added

All Producers

	1984			1985			1986			1987		
	Gross Output	Intermediate Consumption	Value Added	Gross Output	Intermediate Consumption	Value Added	Gross Output	Intermediate Consumption	Value Added	Gross Output	Intermediate Consumption	Value Added
1 Agriculture, hunting, forestry and fishing	...	...	591395	...	...	713824	...	...	788062	...	...	851895
A Agriculture and hunting	...	...	567090	...	...	684531	...	...	749447	...	...	797373
B Forestry and logging	...	...	8293	...	...	10493	...	...	12609	...	...	18742
C Fishing	...	...	16012	...	...	18800	...	...	26006	...	...	35780
2 Mining and quarrying	...	...	77062	...	...	89776	...	...	79093	...	...	98866
3 Manufacturing	...	...	614818	...	...	752500	...	...	907415	...	...	971076
A Manufacture of food, beverages and tobacco	...	...	123649	...	...	159759	...	...	188111	...	...	190565
B Textile, wearing apparel and leather industries	...	...	149052	...	...	179169	...	...	224921	...	...	247972
C Manufacture of wood and wood products, including furniture	...	...	22703	...	...	26142	...	...	32775	...	...	35432
D Manufacture of paper and paper products, printing and publishing	...	...	37908	...	...	49085	...	...	59692	...	...	75391
E Manufacture of chemicals and chemical petroleum, coal, rubber and plastic products	...	...	75429	...	...	95449	...	...	110217	...	...	119494
F Manufacture of non-metallic mineral products, except products of petroleum and coal	...	...	47955	...	...	55187	...	...	69987	...	...	77899
G Basic metal industries	...	...	36792	...	...	44670	...	...	44899	...	...	42923
H Manufacture of fabricated metal products, machinery and equipment	...	...	106321	...	...	123782	...	...	156653	...	...	156028
I Other manufacturing industries	...	...	15009	...	...	19257	...	...	20160	...	...	25372
4 Electricity, gas and water	...	...	77281	...	...	105566	...	...	139875	...	...	155261
A Electricity, gas and steam	...	...	77281	...	...	105566	...	...	139875	...	...	155261
B Water works and supply	...	...	...	...	...	...	...	...	...	...	...	...
5 Construction	...	...	213678	...	...	262852	...	...	317525	...	...	328638
6 Wholesale and retail trade, restaurants and hotels a	...	...	438718	...	...	540367	...	...	656546	...	...	724827
A Wholesale and retail trade	...	...	438718	...	...	540367	...	...	656546	...	...	724827
B Restaurants and hotels	...	...	...	...	...	...	...	...	...	...	...	...
7 Transport, storage and communication b	...	...	264039	...	...	309287	...	...	372904	...	...	432113
8 Finance, insurance, real estate and business services c ..	...	...	264548	...	...	315510	...	...	383468	...	...	457568
9 Community, social and personal services acd	...	...	441607	...	...	570846	...	...	674556	...	...	795106
Total, Industries	...	...	2983150	...	...	3660530	...	...	4319440	...	...	4815350
Producers of Government Services	...	...	379442	...	...	476324	...	...	536200	...	...	618426
Other Producers d	...	...	...	...	...	...	...	...	...	...	...	...
Total e	...	...	3362590	...	...	4136850	...	...	4855640	...	...	5433780
Less: Imputed bank service charge	...	...	...	...	...	...	...	...	...	...	...	...
Import duties	...	...	...	...	...	...	...	...	...	...	...	...
Value added tax	...	...	...	...	...	...	...	...	...	...	...	...
Other adjustments f	...	...	443098	...	...	480964	...	...	642036	...	...	794258
Total	...	...	3805690	...	...	4617820	...	...	5497680	...	...	6228030

Greece

4.1 Derivation of Value Added by Kind of Activity, in Current Prices

Million Greek drachmas

	1988 Gross Output	1988 Intermediate Consumption	1988 Value Added	1989 Gross Output	1989 Intermediate Consumption	1989 Value Added
All Producers						
1 Agriculture, hunting, forestry and fishing	...	...	1079350	...	...	1337320
A Agriculture and hunting	...	...	1023230	...	...	...
B Forestry and logging	...	...	16190	...	...	...
C Fishing	...	...	39936	...	...	...
2 Mining and quarrying	...	...	104600	...	...	120918
3 Manufacturing	...	...	1148650	...	...	1346700
A Manufacture of food, beverages and tobacco	...	...	230995	...	...	283784
B Textile, wearing apparel and leather industries	...	...	268894	...	...	286363
C Manufacture of wood and wood products, including furniture	...	...	38198	...	...	46883
D Manufacture of paper and paper products, printing and publishing	...	...	82473	...	...	97181
E Manufacture of chemicals and chemical petroleum, coal, rubber and plastic products	...	...	158825	...	...	200106
F Manufacture of non-metallic mineral products, except products of petroleum and coal	...	...	92035	...	...	101292
G Basic metal industries	...	...	65458	...	...	81037
H Manufacture of fabricated metal products, machinery and equipment	...	...	190164	...	...	224437
I Other manufacturing industries	...	...	21611	...	...	25613
4 Electricity, gas and water	...	...	174513	...	...	194058
A Electricity, gas and steam	...	...	174513	...	...	194058
B Water works and supply	...	...	...	...	...	...
5 Construction	...	...	396995	...	...	468454
6 Wholesale and retail trade, restaurants and hotels a	...	...	851672	...	...	...
A Wholesale and retail trade	...	...	851672	...	...	...
B Restaurants and hotels	...	...	...	...	...	...
7 Transport, storage and communication b	...	...	519433	...	...	598839
8 Finance, insurance, real estate and business services c	...	...	567521	...	...	...
9 Community, social and personal services acd	...	...	956354	...	...	...
Total, Industries	...	...	5799090	...	...	...
Producers of Government Services	...	...	747582	...	...	...
Other Producers d	...	...	...	...	...	...
Total e	...	...	6546670	...	...	7855140
Less: Imputed bank service charge	...	...	...	...	...	...
Import duties	...	...	...	...	...	...
Value added tax	...	...	...	...	...	...
Other adjustments f	...	...	955296	...	...	...
Total	...	...	7501970	...	...	...

a) Restaurants and hotels are included in item 'Community, social and personal services'.
b) Data on Exports of goods and services as well as transport, storage and communication exclude income from ocean-going cargo ships under Greek flag or ownership. However, remittances actually received by the bank of Greece from persons engaged in these enterprises are included in factor income from the rest of the world.
c) Business services are included in item 'Community, social and personal services'.
d) Item 'Other producers' is included in item 'Community, social and personal services'.
e) Gross domestic product in factor values.
f) Item 'Other adjustments' refers to indirect taxes net of subsidies.

4.2 Derivation of Value Added by Kind of Activity, in Constant Prices

Million Greek drachmas

	1980 Gross Output	1980 Intermediate Consumption	1980 Value Added	1981 Gross Output	1981 Intermediate Consumption	1981 Value Added	1982 Gross Output	1982 Intermediate Consumption	1982 Value Added	1983 Gross Output	1983 Intermediate Consumption	1983 Value Added
At constant prices of:1970												
All Producers												
1 Agriculture, hunting, forestry and fishing	...	...	60499	...	...	59516	...	...	60940	...	...	55518
A Agriculture and hunting	...	...	58029	...	...	57217	...	...	58647	...	...	53180
B Forestry and logging	...	...	1202	...	...	1093	...	...	1129	...	...	1217
C Fishing	...	...	1268	...	...	1206	...	...	1164	...	...	1121

Greece

4.2 Derivation of Value Added by Kind of Activity, in Constant Prices
(Continued)

Million Greek drachmas

	1980			1981			1982			1983		
	Gross Output	Intermediate Consumption	Value Added	Gross Output	Intermediate Consumption	Value Added	Gross Output	Intermediate Consumption	Value Added	Gross Output	Intermediate Consumption	Value Added
At constant prices of:1970												
2 Mining and quarrying	...	...	6245	...	...	6226	...	...	6537	...	...	6982
3 Manufacturing	...	...	89125	...	...	88865	...	...	86946	...	...	85436
A Manufacture of food, beverages and tobacco	...	...	16977	...	...	17415	...	...	17740	...	...	17833
B Textile, wearing apparel and leather industries	...	...	23697	...	...	23024	...	...	21534	...	...	20669
C Manufacture of wood and wood products, including furniture	...	...	3583	...	...	3682	...	...	3730	...	...	2863
D Manufacture of paper and paper products, printing and publishing	...	...	3568	...	...	3512	...	...	3475	...	...	3652
E Manufacture of chemicals and chemical petroleum, coal, rubber and plastic products	...	...	11384	...	...	11596	...	...	11505	...	...	12090
F Manufacture of non-metallic mineral products, except products of petroleum and coal	...	...	7823	...	...	7466	...	...	7310	...	...	7059
G Basic metal industries	...	...	5396	...	...	4986	...	...	4477	...	...	4880
H Manufacture of fabricated metal products, machinery and equipment	...	...	14558	...	...	15149	...	...	15124	...	...	14295
I Other manufacturing industries	...	...	2139	...	...	2035	...	...	2051	...	...	2095
4 Electricity, gas and water	...	...	13724	.:.	...	14149	...	...	14616	...	...	15172
A Electricity, gas and steam	...	...	13724	...	...	14149	...	...	14616	...	...	15172
B Water works and supply	...	...	...	...	...	...	...	...	...	...	...	...
5 Construction	...	...	26392	...	...	24201	...	...	22289	...	...	23025
6 Wholesale and retail trade, restaurants and hotels [a]	...	...	50633	...	...	50380	...	...	51388	...	...	53238
A Wholesale and retail trade	...	...	50633	...	...	50380	...	...	51388	...	...	53238
B Restaurants and hotels	...	...	...	...	...	...	...	...	...	...	...	...
7 Transport, storage and communication [b]	...	...	39898	...	...	41277	...	...	41510	...	...	42971
8 Finance, insurance, real estate and business services [c]	...	...	49134	...	...	50159	...	...	51492	...	...	54158
9 Community, social and personal services [acd]	...	...	45152	...	...	45408	...	...	45813	...	...	45783
Total, Industries	...	...	380802	...	...	380181	...	...	381531	...	...	382283
Producers of Government Services	...	...	36708	...	...	38090	...	...	39110	...	...	40068
Other Producers [d]	...	...	...	...	...	...	...	...	...	...	...	...
Total [e]	...	...	417510	...	...	418271	...	...	420641	...	...	422351
Less: Imputed bank service charge	...	...	...	...	...	...	...	...	...	...	...	...
Import duties	...	...	...	...	...	...	...	...	...	...	...	...
Value added tax	...	...	...	...	...	...	...	...	...	...	...	...
Other adjustments [f]	...	...	56000	...	...	55500	...	...	55000	...	...	55200
Total	...	...	473510	...	...	473771	...	...	475641	...	...	477551

	1984			1985			1986			1987		
	Gross Output	Intermediate Consumption	Value Added	Gross Output	Intermediate Consumption	Value Added	Gross Output	Intermediate Consumption	Value Added	Gross Output	Intermediate Consumption	Value Added
At constant prices of:1970												
All Producers												
1 Agriculture, hunting, forestry and fishing	...	...	59394	...	...	60523	...	...	62036	...	...	59493
A Agriculture and hunting	...	...	57051	...	...	58223	...	...	59617	...	...	57090
B Forestry and logging	...	...	1159	...	...	1150	...	...	1240	...	...	1153
C Fishing	...	...	1184	...	...	1150	...	...	1179	...	...	1250
2 Mining and quarrying	...	...	7827	...	...	7968	...	...	8000	...	...	8064

739

Greece

4.2 Derivation of Value Added by Kind of Activity, in Constant Prices
(Continued)

Million Greek drachmas

	1984			1985			1986			1987		
	Gross Output	Intermediate Consumption	Value Added	Gross Output	Intermediate Consumption	Value Added	Gross Output	Intermediate Consumption	Value Added	Gross Output	Intermediate Consumption	Value Added
	At constant prices of:1970											
3 Manufacturing	...	...	86475	...	...	89529	...	...	89449	...	...	87306
A Manufacture of food, beverages and tobacco	...	...	18773	...	...	20041	...	...	18986	...	...	18055
B Textile, wearing apparel and leather industries	...	...	20543	...	...	21286	...	...	22304	...	...	21929
C Manufacture of wood and wood products, including furniture	...	...	2540	...	...	2551	...	...	2538	...	...	2351
D Manufacture of paper and paper products, printing and publishing	...	...	4008	...	...	4444	...	...	4666	...	...	5111
E Manufacture of chemicals and chemical petroleum, coal, rubber and plastic products	...	...	12579	...	...	13225	...	...	12737	...	...	12803
F Manufacture of non-metallic mineral products, except products of petroleum and coal	...	...	7120	...	...	6926	...	...	7196	...	...	7334
G Basic metal industries	...	...	4987	...	...	5067	...	...	4864	...	...	4718
H Manufacture of fabricated metal products, machinery and equipment	...	...	13614	...	...	13539	...	...	14052	...	...	12754
I Other manufacturing industries	...	...	2311	...	...	2450	...	...	2106	...	...	2251
4 Electricity, gas and water	...	...	16022	...	...	17032	...	...	17475	...	...	18419
A Electricity, gas and steam	...	...	16022	...	...	17032	...	...	17475	...	...	18419
B Water works and supply	...	...	...	...	...	...	...	...	...	...	...	...
5 Construction	...	...	21890	...	...	22525	...	...	22345	...	...	20937
6 Wholesale and retail trade, restaurants and hotels [a]	...	...	53238	...	...	55595	...	...	57096	...	...	57153
A Wholesale and retail trade	...	...	53238	...	...	55595	...	...	57096	...	...	57153
B Restaurants and hotels	...	...	...	...	...	...	...	...	...	...	...	...
7 Transport, storage and communication [b]	...	...	45936	...	...	48733	...	...	49414	...	...	49138
8 Finance, insurance, real estate and business services [c]	...	...	55704	...	...	57198	...	...	59086	...	...	60380
9 Community, social and personal services [acd]	...	...	46220	...	...	47404	...	...	49323	...	...	50420
Total, Industries	...	...	392706	...	...	406507	...	...	414224	...	...	411310
Producers of Government Services	...	...	41990	...	...	42912	...	...	41796	...	...	42425
Other Producers [d]	...	...	...	...	...	...	...	...	...	...	...	...
Total [e]	...	...	434696	...	...	449419	...	...	456020	...	...	453735
Less: Imputed bank service charge	...	...	...	...	...	...	...	...	...	...	...	...
Import duties	...	...	...	...	...	...	...	...	...	...	...	...
Value added tax	...	...	...	...	...	...	...	...	...	...	...	...
Other adjustments [f]	...	...	56000	...	...	56592	...	...	57000	...	...	56870
Total	...	...	490696	...	...	506011	...	...	513020	...	...	510605

	1988			1989		
	Gross Output	Intermediate Consumption	Value Added	Gross Output	Intermediate Consumption	Value Added
	At constant prices of:1970					
	All Producers					
1 Agriculture, hunting, forestry and fishing	...	...	63152	...	...	65267
A Agriculture and hunting	...	...	60814	...	...	...
B Forestry and logging	...	...	1011	...	...	...
C Fishing	...	...	1327	...	...	...
2 Mining and quarrying	...	...	8790	...	...	8816

740

Greece

4.2 Derivation of Value Added by Kind of Activity, in Constant Prices
(Continued)

Million Greek drachmas

	1988			1989		
	Gross Output	Intermediate Consumption	Value Added	Gross Output	Intermediate Consumption	Value Added
				At constant prices of:1970		
3 Manufacturing	...	...	91206	...	...	93203
A Manufacture of food, beverages and tobacco	...	...	19559	...	...	21086
B Textile, wearing apparel and leather industries	...	...	21768	...	...	20970
C Manufacture of wood and wood products, including furniture	...	...	2484	...	...	2638
D Manufacture of paper and paper products, printing and publishing	...	...	4821	...	...	4833
E Manufacture of chemicals and chemical petroleum, coal, rubber and plastic products	...	...	14543	...	...	15634
F Manufacture of non-metallic mineral products, except products of petroleum and coal	...	...	7654	...	...	7337
G Basic metal industries	...	...	5284	...	...	5273
H Manufacture of fabricated metal products, machinery and equipment	...	...	13222	...	...	13535
I Other manufacturing industries	...	...	1871	...	...	1897
4 Electricity, gas and water	...	...	19543	...	...	20461
A Electricity, gas and steam	...	...	19543	...	...	20461
B Water works and supply	...	...	...	...	...	...
5 Construction	...	...	22528	...	...	23024
6 Wholesale and retail trade, restaurants and hotels a	...	...	60296	...	...	...
A Wholesale and retail trade	...	...	60296	...	...	...
B Restaurants and hotels	...	...	...	...	...	...
7 Transport, storage and communication b	...	...	51054	...	...	53096
8 Finance, insurance, real estate and business services c ..	...	...	62308	...	...	...
9 Community, social and personal services acd	...	...	51750	...	...	...
Total, Industries	...	...	430627	...	...	...
Producers of Government Services	...	...	43299	...	...	...
Other Producers d	...	...	...	...	...	...
Total e	...	...	473926	...	...	488680
Less: Imputed bank service charge	...	...	...	...	...	...
Import duties	...	...	...	...	...	...
Value added tax	...	...	...	...	...	...
Other adjustments f	...	...	57469	...	...	...
Total	...	...	531395	...	...	...

a) Restaurants and hotels are included in item 'Community, social and personal services'.
b) Data on Exports of goods and services as well as transport, storage and communication exclude income from ocean-going cargo ships under Greek flag or ownership. However, remittances actually received by the bank of Greece from persons engaged in these enterprises are included in factor income from the rest of the world.
c) Business services are included in item 'Community, social and personal services'.
d) Item 'Other producers' is included in item 'Community, social and personal services'.
e) Gross domestic product in factor values.
f) Item 'Other adjustments' refers to indirect taxes net of subsidies.

Grenada

Source. 'National Income Estimates of Grenada', St. George's.
General note. The estimates shown in the following tables have been prepared in

accordance with the United Nations System of National Accounts so far as the existing data would permit.

1.1 Expenditure on the Gross Domestic Product, in Current Prices

Million E.C. dollars

	1970	1975	1980	1981	1982	1983	1984	1985	1986	1987	1988	1989
1 Government final consumption expenditure	...	...	41.7	45.0	47.2	55.9	59.3	68.1	80.7	77.3	...	...
2 Private final consumption expenditure	...	...	171.5	180.0	195.0	183.9	213.2	240.1	261.6	295.0	...	...
3 Gross capital formation	...	...	61.1	98.1	107.1	10¹.6	81.7	91.9	116.5	150.0	...	...
A Increase in stocks	...	...	8.4	7.0	-0.1	-5.2	1.7	-5.2	-0.6	8.4		
B Gross fixed capital formation	...	...	52.7	91.1	107.2	106.8	80.0	97.1	117.1	141.6		
4 Exports of goods and services	...	...	106.9	106.1	103.4	105.0	112.8	149.0	163.4	173.5	...	...
5 Less: Imports of goods and services	...	...	179.2	212.5	213.3	193.8	192.1	237.9	271.8	289.7	...	...
Equals: Gross Domestic Product	...	...	202.0	216.7	239.4	252.9	274.9	311.2	350.4	406.1	...	...

1.10 Gross Domestic Product by Kind of Activity, in Current Prices

Million E.C. dollars

	1970	1975	1980	1981	1982	1983	1984	1985	1986	1987	1988	1989
1 Agriculture, hunting, forestry and fishing	12.0	23.1	... 41.4	44.8	40.7	41.3	44.9	44.2	52.9	69.5	...	...
2 Mining and quarrying	0.1	0.1	... 0.5	0.6	0.6	0.6	0.5	0.8	1.1	1.2	...	...
3 Manufacturing	2.7	3.6	... 6.6	8.7	10.2	10.5	9.8	12.5	13.3	16.0	...	...
4 Electricity, gas and water	0.6	1.4	... 3.4	3.1	4.4	4.4	4.0	6.4	7.5	8.7	...	...
5 Construction	8.5	5.7	... 11.3	17.3	20.3	17.3	18.4	19.4	23.4	28.3	...	...
6 Wholesale and retail trade, restaurants and hotels	10.9	14.6	... 33.5	30.2	36.8	36.5	41.0	48.8	54.9	60.7	...	...
7 Transport, storage and communication	5.6	7.8	... 21.5	22.5	25.4	27.4	30.1	31.5	38.5	42.5	...	...
8 Finance, insurance, real estate and business services	7.3	9.0	... 19.8	21.8	23.3	23.3	27.5	31.4	33.7	36.1	...	...
9 Community, social and personal services	6.3	8.0	... 8.5	9.0	9.7	10.2	10.6	11.0	11.5	12.0	...	...
Total, Industries a	54.0	73.3	... 146.5	158.0	171.4	171.5	186.8	206.0	236.8	275.0	...	...
Producers of Government Services	6.0	7.2	... 27.1	30.7	33.9	41.9	46.6	51.5	58.6	60.2	...	...
Other Producers	...	...	... ...	...	...	...	...	...	...	...	...	...
Subtotal b	60.0	80.5	... 173.6	188.7	205.3	213.4	233.4	257.5	295.4	335.2	...	...
Less: Imputed bank service charge	...	...	... 6.0	7.8	8.7	8.9	10.0	11.3	13.3	14.7	...	...
Plus: Import duties	...	...	... ...	...	...	...	...	...	...	...	...	...
Plus: Value added tax	...	...	...									
Plus: Other adjustments	...	...	... 34.4	35.8	42.8	48.4	51.5	65.0	68.4	85.6	...	...
Equals: Gross Domestic Product c	60.0	80.5	... 202.0	216.7	239.4	252.9	274.9	311.2	350.4	406.1	...	...

a) Gross domestic product in factor values.
b) Item 'Other adjustments' refers to indirect taxes net of subsidies.
c) For the first series, gross domestic product in factor values.

1.11 Gross Domestic Product by Kind of Activity, in Constant Prices

Million E.C. dollars

	1970	1975	1980	1981	1982	1983	1984	1985	1986	1987	1988	1989
					At constant prices of:1984							
1 Agriculture, hunting, forestry and fishing	...	...	40.6	43.1	38.8	39.3	43.9	42.0	41.8	45.4	...	...
2 Mining and quarrying	...	...	0.5	0.7	0.7	0.6	0.5	0.7	0.9	1.0	...	...
3 Manufacturing	...	...	8.9	10.7	11.9	11.6	9.8	11.7	11.8	13.8	...	...
4 Electricity, gas and water	...	...	4.0	4.0	4.0	3.9	4.0	4.7	5.3	5.8	...	...
5 Construction	...	...	16.1	20.8	22.6	18.2	18.4	19.3	22.2	25.6	...	...

742

Grenada

1.11 Gross Domestic Product by Kind of Activity, in Constant Prices
(Continued)

Million E.C. dollars

	1970	1975	1980	1981	1982	1983	1984	1985	1986	1987	1988	1989
At constant prices of:1984												
6 Wholesale and retail trade, restaurants and hotels	...	...	...	39.6	34.7	39.9	37.8	41.0	45.3	49.2	51.4	...
7 Transport, storage and communication	...	...	...	27.3	25.1	27.5	28.0	30.1	30.4	33.4	35.9	...
8 Finance, insurance, real estate and business services	...	...	...	23.7	25.5	26.3	25.9	27.5	28.9	29.7	30.7	...
9 Community, social and personal services	...	...	...	9.5	9.7	10.2	10.5	10.6	10.7	11.0	11.3	...
Total, Industries a	...	...	...	170.2	174.3	181.9	175.8	185.8	193.7	205.3	220.9	...
Producers of Government Services	...	...	...	31.2	32.7	36.4	45.0	46.6	51.5	54.0	54.0	...
Other Producers	...	...	...	201.4	207.0	218.3	220.8	232.4	245.2	259.3	274.9	...
Subtotal b												
Less: Imputed bank service charge	...	...	...	6.9	8.5	9.2	9.2	10.0	10.8	12.0	12.8	...
Plus: Import duties	...	...	...	...	...	...	...	...	...	...	...	...
Plus: Value added tax	...	...	...	...	...	...	...	...	...	...	...	...
Plus: Other adjustments	...	...	...	39.9	45.5	50.1	51.5	61.9	60.6	...	...	...
Equals: Gross Domestic Product	...	...	...	234.4	237.8	254.6	261.7	273.9	296.3	307.9	...	...

a) Gross domestic product in factor values.
b) Item 'Other adjustments' refers to indirect taxes net of subsidies.

1.12 Relations Among National Accounting Aggregates

Million E.C. dollars

	1970	1975	1980	1981	1982	1983	1984	1985	1986	1987	1988	1989
Gross Domestic Product	...	...	...	...	239.4	252.9	273.9	311.2	347.6	...	...	...
Plus: Net factor income from the rest of the world	...	...	...	...	0.8	0.5	-3.0	-3.5	-2.8	...	...	...
Factor income from the rest of the world	...	...	...	...	4.0	4.6	3.8	3.3	2.8	...	...	...
Less: Factor income to the rest of the world	...	...	...	...	3.2	4.1	6.8	6.8	5.6	...	...	...
Equals: Gross National Product	...	...	...	...	240.2	253.4	270.9	307.7	344.8	...	...	...
Less: Consumption of fixed capital	...	...	...	...	...	...	...	...	...	...	...	...
Equals: National Income	...	...	...	...	...	...	...	...	...	...	...	...
Plus: Net current transfers from the rest of the world	...	...	...	...	...	...	...	...	...	...	...	...
Equals: National Disposable Income	...	...	...	...	...	...	...	...	...	...	...	...
Less: Final consumption	...	...	...	...	...	...	...	...	...	...	...	...
Equals: Net Saving	...	...	...	...	...	...	...	...	...	...	...	...
Less: Surplus of the nation on current transactions	...	...	...	...	...	...	...	...	...	...	...	...
Equals: Net Capital Formation	...	...	...	...	...	...	...	...	...	...	...	...

Guadeloupe

Source. Reply to the United Nations National Accounts Questionnaire from the Institute national de la statistique et des etudes economiques (INSEE), Paris. Official estimates and descriptions are published by the same Institute in 'Comptes Economiques de la Guadeloupe'.

General note. The estimates shown in the following tables have been adjusted by the INSEE to conform to the United Nations System of National Accounts so far as the existing data would permit.

1.1 Expenditure on the Gross Domestic Product, in Current Prices

Million French francs

	1970	1975	1980	1981	1982	1983	1984	1985	1986	1987	1988	1989
1 Government final consumption expenditure	355.2	804.3	1856.7	2150.2	2576.2	2920.2	3187.6	3413.5	3659.4	...	...	...
2 Private final consumption expenditure	1208.8	2458.9	5101.7	5953.1	6910.5	7890.8	8566.9	9444.2	9718.8	...	...	...
3 Gross capital formation	274.7	537.9	1547.9	1384.4	1672.0	2147.1	1813.6	1879.4	2246.7	...	...	...
A Increase in stocks	10.4	-5.9	82.8	-30.9	-4.8	232.1	-133.9	-292.1	-140.9	...	...	...
B Gross fixed capital formation	264.3	543.8	1465.1	1415.3	1676.8	1915.0	1947.5	2171.5	2387.6	...	...	...
4 Exports of goods and services	209.0	359.8	458.0	559.0	554.7	560.3	603.9	751.4	726.8	817.6	...	...
5 Less: Imports of goods and services	717.7	1335.1	3104.1	3573.3	4173.2	5091.6	5290.4	5813.6	5873.7	...	...	...
Equals: Gross Domestic Product	1330.0	2825.8	5860.2	6473.5	7540.2	8426.8	9049.1	9650.3	10568.8	...	...	...

1.3 Cost Components of the Gross Domestic Product

Million French francs

	1970	1975	1980	1981	1982	1983	1984	1985	1986	1987	1988	1989
1 Indirect taxes, net	183.1	522.6	619.8	701.1	731.0	...	...	...	...	...	...	...
A Indirect taxes	200.9	564.3	728.4	878.7	970.5	...	...	...	...	...	...	...
B Less: Subsidies	17.8	41.7	108.6	177.5	239.5	...	...	...	...	...	...	...
2 Consumption of fixed capital a	...	...	...	...	...	...	...	...	...	...	...	...
3 Compensation of employees paid by resident producers to:	737.8	1710.0	4108.2	4584.4	5188.3	...	...	...	...	...	...	...
4 Operating surplus a	409.1	823.1	1132.2	1187.9	1620.9	...	...	...	...	...	...	...
Equals: Gross Domestic Product	1330.0	2825.8	5860.2	6473.5	7540.2	8426.8	9049.1	9650.3	10568.8	...	...	...

a) Item 'Operating surplus' includes consumption of fixed capital.

1.4 General Government Current Receipts and Disbursements

Million French francs

	1970	1975	1980	1981	1982	1983	1984	1985	1986	1987	1988	1989
Receipts												
1 Operating surplus	-	-	-	-	-	...	...	...	...	...	...	...
2 Property and entrepreneurial income	4.3	11.1	39.3	53.3	51.0	...	...	...	...	...	...	...
3 Taxes, fees and contributions	469.7	1039.0	2088.7	2462.6	2876.8	...	...	...	...	...	...	...
4 Other current transfers	411.2	980.6	2071.3	2331.3	2797.8	...	...	...	...	...	...	...
Total Current Receipts of General Government	885.2	2030.7	4199.3	4847.2	5725.6	...	...	...	...	...	...	...
Disbursements												
1 Government final consumption expenditure	355.1	804.3	1856.6	2150.3	2576.2	...	...	...	...	...	...	...
2 Property income	6.4	19.4	68.1	88.8	100.1	...	...	...	...	...	...	...
3 Subsidies	14.6	33.7	21.2	34.5	60.4	...	...	...	...	...	...	...
4 Other current transfers	377.1	888.1	1793.4	2155.3	2646.6	...	...	...	...	...	...	...
5 Net saving	132.0	285.2	460.0	418.3	342.3	...	...	...	...	...	...	...
Total Current Disbursements and Net Saving of General Government	885.2	2030.7	4199.3	4847.2	5725.6	...	...	...	...	...	...	...

1.7 External Transactions on Current Account, Summary

Million French francs

	1970	1975	1980	1981	1982	1983	1984	1985	1986	1987	1988	1989
Payments to the Rest of the World												
1 Imports of goods and services	717.7	1335.1	3104.1	3573.3	4173.1	...	...	...	...	...	...	...
2 Factor income to the rest of the world	28.1	63.3	244.9	273.1	334.3	...	...	...	...	...	...	...
A Compensation of employees	-	-	-	...	...	...	...	...	...	...	...	...
B Property and entrepreneurial income	28.1	63.3	244.9	273.1	334.3	...	...	...	...	...	...	...
3 Current transfers to the rest of the world	26.6	14.3	80.3	98.0	110.3	...	...	...	...	...	...	...
4 Surplus of the nation on current transactions	-142.0	-51.8	-712.9	-768.4	-889.3	...	...	...	...	...	...	...
Payments to the Rest of the World and Surplus of the Nation on Current Transactions	630.4	1360.9	2716.4	3176.0	3728.4	...	...	...	...	...	...	...

744

Guadeloupe

1.7 External Transactions on Current Account, Summary
(Continued)

Million French francs

	1970	1975	1980	1981	1982	1983	1984	1985	1986	1987	1988	1989
				Receipts From The Rest of the World								
1 Exports of goods and services	209.0	359.8	458.1	559.0	554.7	...	...	...	...	...	...	...
2 Factor income from rest of the world	7.4	13.3	89.2	122.0	173.0	...	...	...	...	...	...	...
A Compensation of employees	-	-	-	...	...	...	...	...	...	...	...	...
B Property and entrepreneurial income	7.4	13.3	89.2	122.0	173.0	...	...	...	...	...	...	...
3 Current transfers from rest of the world	414.0	987.8	2169.1	2495.0	3000.7	...	...	...	...	...	...	...
Receipts from the Rest of the World on Current Transactions	630.4	1360.9	2716.4	3176.0	3728.4	...	...	...	...	...	...	...

1.10 Gross Domestic Product by Kind of Activity, in Current Prices

Million French francs

	1970	1975	1980	1981	1982	1983	1984	1985	1986	1987	1988	1989
1 Agriculture, hunting, forestry and fishing	...	372.5	428.9	595.2	741.5	...	...	...	...	...	...	...
2 Mining and quarrying	...	171.0	357.4	380.6	389.3	...	...	...	...	...	...	...
3 Manufacturing	...					...	...	...	...	...	...	...
4 Electricity, gas and water	...	43.7	11.2	-22.4	-50.1	...	...	...	...	...	...	...
5 Construction	...	133.0	246.2	321.1	345.0	...	...	...	...	...	...	...
6 Wholesale and retail trade, restaurants and hotels	...	501.8	1023.5	1128.7	1249.2	...	...	...	...	...	...	...
7 Transport, storage and communication	...	79.8	255.1	288.7	355.0	...	...	...	...	...	...	...
8 Finance, insurance, real estate and business services	...	274.0	645.9	615.4	728.1	...	...	...	...	...	...	...
9 Community, social and personal services	...	325.0	895.8	948.4	1104.6	...	...	...	...	...	...	...
Total, Industries	...	1900.8	3864.0	4255.7	4862.6	...	...	...	...	...	...	...
Producers of Government Services	...	747.4	1695.3	1938.5	2333.0	...	...	...	...	...	...	...
Other Producers	...	58.2	122.5	137.5	162.3	...	...	...	...	...	...	...
Subtotal	...	2706.4	5681.8	6332.0	7357.9	...	...	...	...	...	...	...
Less: Imputed bank service charge	32.7	93.8	305.9	418.5	486.9	...	...	...	...	...	...	...
Plus: Import duties	73.4	89.7	238.9	256.3	302.3	...	...	...	...	...	...	...
Plus: Value added tax	56.3	123.5	245.4	303.7	366.9	...	...	...	...	...	...	...
Equals: Gross Domestic Product	1330.0	2825.8	5860.2	6473.5	7540.2	...	...	...	...	...	...	...

1.12 Relations Among National Accounting Aggregates

Million French francs

	1970	1975	1980	1981	1982	1983	1984	1985	1986	1987	1988	1989
Gross Domestic Product	1330.0	2825.8	5860.2	6473.5	7540.2	...	...	...	...	...	...	...
Plus: Net factor income from the rest of the world	-20.7	-50.0	-155.7	-151.1	-161.3	...	...	...	...	...	...	...
Factor income from the rest of the world	7.4	13.3	89.2	122.0	173.0	...	...	...	...	...	...	...
Less: Factor income to the rest of the world	28.1	63.3	244.9	273.1	334.3	...	...	...	...	...	...	...
Equals: Gross National Product	1309.3	2775.8	5704.5	6322.4	7378.9	...	...	...	...	...	...	...
Less: Consumption of fixed capital	...	...	...	...	...	...	...	...	...	...	...	...
Equals: National Income	...	...	...	...	...	...	...	...	...	...	...	...
Plus: Net current transfers from the rest of the world	387.4	973.5	2088.9	2397.0	2890.3	...	...	...	...	...	...	...
Current transfers from the rest of the world	414.0	987.8	2169.2	2494.9	3000.6	...	...	...	...	...	...	...
Less: Current transfers to the rest of the world	26.6	14.3	80.3	97.9	110.3	...	...	...	...	...	...	...
Equals: National Disposable Income	...	...	...	...	...	...	...	...	...	...	...	...
Less: Final consumption	1564.0	3263.2	6958.4	8103.4	9486.6	...	...	...	...	...	...	...
Equals: Net Saving	...	...	...	...	...	...	...	...	...	...	...	...
Less: Surplus of the nation on current transactions	-142.0	-51.8	-712.9	-768.4	-889.3	...	...	...	...	...	...	...
Equals: Net Capital Formation	...	...	...	...	...	...	...	...	...	...	...	...

Guatemala

Source. Reply to the United Nations National Accounts Questionnaire from the Banco de Guatemala, Guatemala City. The official estimates are published in 'Boletin Estadistico del Banco de Guatemala'.

General note. The estimates shown in the following tables have been prepared in accordance with the United Nations System of National Accounts so far as the existing data would permit.

1.1 Expenditure on the Gross Domestic Product, in Current Prices

Million Guatemalan quetzales

	1970	1975	1980	1981	1982	1983	1984	1985	1986	1987	1988	1989
1 Government final consumption expenditure	151.4	250.3	626.5	680.3	675.5	687.9	725.9	777.4	1123.9	1399.6	1639.8	1843.4
2 Private final consumption expenditure	1493.3	2874.9	6216.8	7021.7	7149.0	7500.7	7855.9	9295.9	12846.7	14989.2	17289.0	19831.9
3 Gross capital formation	244.2	586.8	1251.8	1466.1	1233.5	1002.5	1095.9	1285.4	1636.5	2463.7	2814.5	3198.5
A Increase in stocks	5.6	16.0	-43.5	23.0	-76.1	52.3	183.5	60.5	43.3	275.4	67.3	-1.6
B Gross fixed capital formation	238.6	570.8	1295.3	1443.1	1309.5	950.2	912.4	1224.9	1593.2	2188.3	2747.2	3200.1
Residential buildings	28.1	54.7	151.5	99.8	107.7	120.5	104.9	144.7	189.8	226.8	305.9	381.4
Non-residential buildings												
Other construction and land improvement etc.	52.8	127.6	437.3	616.9	537.5	369.6	290.5	271.2	327.4	417.7	530.7	632.0
Other	157.7	388.5	706.5	726.4	664.3	460.1	517.0	809.0	1076.0	1543.8	1910.6	2186.7
4 Exports of goods and services [a]	353.6	792.0	1747.6	1471.0	1288.7	1175.8	1256.2	2068.0	2542.1	2807.0	3308.5	4125.0
5 Less: Imports of goods and services	338.5	858.0	1963.3	2031.5	1629.3	1317.0	1463.6	2246.9	2311.1	3948.5	4506.8	5363.0
Equals: Gross Domestic Product	1904.0	3646.0	7879.4	8607.6	8717.3	9049.9	9470.3	11180.0	15838.1	17711.0	20544.9	23635.8

a) For 1976, item 'Exports of goods and services' does not include 51.2 million quetzales for insurance service charges.

1.2 Expenditure on the Gross Domestic Product, in Constant Prices

Million Guatemalan quetzales

	1970	1975	1980	1981	1982	1983	1984	1985	1986	1987	1988	1989
					At constant prices of:1958							
1 Government final consumption expenditure	125.6	148.5	222.7	232.6	229.7	229.9	236.0	230.6	243.0	259.9	273.0	279.4
2 Private final consumption expenditure	1399.5	1777.9	2318.8	2350.8	2279.6	2247.7	2272.5	2265.6	2283.8	2372.9	2470.1	2543.5
3 Gross capital formation	214.9	280.9	355.4	409.8	331.4	275.2	292.0	236.1	236.5	313.4	310.2	316.4
A Increase in stocks	5.3	10.3	-17.2	8.3	-26.3	17.0	57.1	15.9	8.0	47.3	10.4	-0.2
B Gross fixed capital formation	209.6	270.6	372.6	401.5	357.7	258.2	234.9	220.2	228.5	266.1	299.8	316.6
Residential buildings	25.8	27.3	40.6	25.0	26.7	29.5	25.4	28.4	31.2	33.8	41.1	46.0
Non-residential buildings												
Other construction and land improvement etc.	46.2	69.0	147.1	191.5	163.6	112.5	85.2	70.6	70.3	80.4	90.6	99.4
Other	137.6	174.3	184.9	185.0	167.4	116.2	124.3	121.2	127.0	151.9	168.1	171.2
4 Exports of goods and services	346.0	497.5	651.1	557.4	510.2	454.7	440.2	454.0	390.5	414.0	437.3	497.1
5 Less: Imports of goods and services	293.3	352.1	441.2	423.1	334.3	267.9	287.2	250.3	213.6	315.8	327.7	348.3
Equals: Gross Domestic Product	1792.7	2352.7	3106.8	3127.5	3016.6	2939.6	2953.5	2936.1	2940.2	3044.4	3162.9	3288.1

1.7 External Transactions on Current Account, Summary

Million Guatemalan quetzales

	1970	1975	1980	1981	1982	1983	1984	1985	1986	1987	1988	1989
					Payments to the Rest of the World							
1 Imports of goods and services	338.5	858.0	1963.3	2031.5	1629.3	1317.1	1463.6	2246.9	2311.1	3948.5	4506.8	5363.0
A Imports of merchandise c.i.f.	293.9	734.9	1598.2	1673.5	1388.0	1135.0	1304.1	2091.2	2101.3	3574.5	4048.1	4717.0
B Other	44.6	123.1	365.1	358.0	241.3	182.1	159.5	155.7	209.8	374.0	458.7	646.0
2 Factor income to the rest of the world	46.5	83.5	147.4	158.0	144.7	142.5	237.0	383.4	508.7	548.8	545.7	587.9
A Compensation of employees	...	...	...	...	...	...	...	...	...	...	...	...
B Property and entrepreneurial income	46.5	83.5	147.4	158.0	144.7	142.5	237.0	383.4	508.7	548.8	545.7	587.9
By general government	8.1	10.7	39.4	49.0	73.4	83.3	124.8	335.6	414.5	430.3	431.9	396.0
By corporate and quasi-corporate enterprises	33.3	60.0	52.3	51.3	26.3	16.3	67.4	23.4	25.6	62.2	73.2	128.1
By other	5.1	12.8	55.7	57.7	45.0	42.9	44.8	24.4	68.6	56.3	40.6	63.8
3 Current transfers to the rest of the world	2.2	11.3	15.5	6.0	3.4	3.6	2.9	2.3	2.4	6.4	9.2	15.0
4 Surplus of the nation on current transactions	-11.1	-62.3	-176.4	-572.4	-399.1	-224.0	-384.9	-474.5	-40.1	-1136.4	-1086.8	-1009.5
Payments to the Rest of the World and Surplus of the Nation on Current Transactions	376.1	890.5	1949.8	1623.1	1378.3	1239.1	1318.6	2157.9	2782.1	3367.3	3974.9	4956.5

Guatemala

1.7 External Transactions on Current Account, Summary
(Continued)

Million Guatemalan quetzales

	1970	1975	1980	1981	1982	1983	1984	1985	1986	1987	1988	1989
Receipts From The Rest of the World												
1 Exports of goods and services a	353.6	792.0	1747.6	1471.0	1288.7	1175.8	1256.2	2068.0	2542.1	2807.0	3308.5	4125.0
A Exports of merchandise f.o.b.	297.1	640.9	1519.8	1291.3	1170.4	1091.7	1154.8	1886.2	2285.8	2415.5	2790.9	3266.1
B Other	56.5	151.1	227.8	179.7	118.3	84.1	101.4	181.8	256.3	391.5	517.6	858.9
2 Factor income from rest of the world	4.3	14.5	76.8	55.2	23.5	29.1	30.2	52.5	73.0	76.4	74.6	55.9
A Compensation of employees	...	...	...	...	...	...	...	...	...	...	...	...
B Property and entrepreneurial income	4.3	14.5	76.8	55.2	23.5	29.1	30.2	52.5	73.0	76.4	74.6	55.9
By general government	4.0	13.6	73.5	54.2	23.4	28.9	30.0	51.6	72.1	76.1	66.6	45.4
By corporate and quasi-corporate enterprises	0.1	0.5	2.0	0.3	-	-	0.1	0.7	0.4	-	4.1	8.3
By other	0.2	0.4	1.3	0.7	0.1	0.2	0.1	0.2	0.5	0.3	3.9	2.2
3 Current transfers from rest of the world b	18.2	84.0	125.3	96.9	66.1	34.2	32.2	37.4	167.0	483.9	591.8	775.6
Receipts from the Rest of the World on Current Transactions	376.1	890.5	1949.8	1623.1	1378.3	1239.1	1318.6	2157.9	2782.1	3367.3	3974.9	4956.5

a) For 1976, item 'Exports of goods and services' includes 51.2 million quetzales for insurance service charges.   b) For 1976, item 'Current transfers from the rest of the world' includes gifts in kind received after the earthquake.

1.11 Gross Domestic Product by Kind of Activity, in Constant Prices

Million Guatemalan quetzales

	1970	1975	1980	1981	1982	1983	1984	1985	1986	1987	1988	1989
At constant prices of:1958												
1 Agriculture, hunting, forestry and fishing	489.7	659.9	772.0	781.4	757.9	744.9	756.5	759.3	753.0	782.4	817.6	847.0
2 Mining and quarrying	1.7	2.1	14.8	9.5	10.7	9.4	7.6	6.5	8.4	8.4	8.7	9.1
3 Manufacturing	282.9	356.3	517.3	501.2	475.1	466.0	468.4	464.8	467.9	477.4	487.9	498.0
4 Electricity, gas and water	21.5	32.8	53.2	53.0	51.9	51.5	54.0	56.3	63.2	68.1	74.1	79.9
5 Construction	28.4	43.9	97.9	116.5	103.0	75.8	54.3	49.7	51.3	58.7	67.9	76.0
6 Wholesale and retail trade, restaurants and hotels	518.0	648.7	839.1	844.1	797.2	764.4	773.1	747.0	730.9	752.8	776.2	807.2
7 Transport, storage and communication	98.2	150.8	215.8	211.2	201.2	199.7	206.3	209.8	210.6	220.8	230.4	247.7
8 Finance, insurance, real estate and business services	167.1	200.0	244.8	250.5	255.1	256.5	257.6	263.1	269.3	276.1	285.6	294.8
9 Community, social and personal services	98.3	140.0	188.9	190.0	187.8	186.3	186.9	187.6	186.1	189.5	196.0	202.8
Total, Industries	1705.8	2234.5	2943.8	2957.4	2839.9	2754.5	2764.7	2744.1	2740.7	2834.2	2944.4	3062.5
Producers of Government Services	86.9	118.2	163.0	170.1	176.7	185.1	188.8	192.0	199.5	210.2	218.5	225.6
Other Producers	...	...	...	...	...	...	...	...	...	...	...	...
Subtotal	1792.7	2352.7	3106.8	3127.5	3016.6	2939.6	2953.5	2936.1	2940.2	3044.4	3162.9	3288.1
Less: Imputed bank service charge	...	...	...	...	...	...	...	...	...	...	...	...
Plus: Import duties	...	...	...	...	...	...	...	...	...	...	...	...
Plus: Value added tax	...	...	...	...	...	...	...	...	...	...	...	...
Equals: Gross Domestic Product	1792.7	2352.7	3106.8	3127.5	3016.6	2939.6	2953.5	2936.1	2940.2	3044.4	3162.9	3288.1

1.12 Relations Among National Accounting Aggregates

Million Guatemalan quetzales

	1970	1975	1980	1981	1982	1983	1984	1985	1986	1987	1988	1989
Gross Domestic Product	1904.0	3646.0	7879.4	8607.6	8717.3	9049.9	9470.3	11180.0	15838.1	17711.0	20544.9	23635.8
Plus: Net factor income from the rest of the world	-42.2	-69.0	-70.6	-102.8	-121.2	-113.4	-206.8	-330.8	-435.7	-472.4	-471.1	-532.0
Factor income from the rest of the world	4.3	14.5	76.8	55.2	23.5	29.1	30.2	52.5	73.0	76.5	74.6	55.9
Less: Factor income to the rest of the world	46.5	83.5	147.4	158.0	144.7	142.5	237.0	383.3	508.7	548.9	545.7	587.9
Equals: Gross National Product	1861.8	3577.0	7808.8	8504.8	8596.1	8936.5	9263.5	10849.2	15402.4	17238.6	20073.8	23103.8
Less: Consumption of fixed capital	...	...	...	...	...	...	...	...	...	...	...	...

Guatemala

1.12 Relations Among National Accounting Aggregates
(Continued)

Million Guatemalan quetzales

	1970	1975	1980	1981	1982	1983	1984	1985	1986	1987	1988	1989
Equals: National Income a	1861.8	3577.0	7808.8	8504.8	8596.1	8936.5	9263.5	10849.2	15402.4	17238.6	20073.8	23103.8
Plus: Net current transfers from the rest of the world	16.0	72.7	109.8	90.9	62.7	30.6	29.3	35.1	164.6	477.5	582.5	760.6
Current transfers from the rest of the world b	18.2	84.0	125.3	96.9	66.1	34.2	32.2	37.4	167.0	483.9	591.8	775.6
Less: Current transfers to the rest of the world	2.2	11.3	15.5	6.0	3.4	3.6	2.9	2.3	2.4	6.4	9.3	15.0
Equals: National Disposable Income c	1877.8	3649.9	7918.6	8595.7	8658.8	8967.1	9292.8	10884.3	15567.0	17716.1	20656.3	23864.4
Less: Final consumption	1644.7	3125.2	6843.3	7702.0	7824.5	8188.6	8581.8	10073.4	13970.6	16388.8	18928.7	21675.3
Equals: Net Saving d	233.1	524.5	1075.4	893.7	834.3	778.5	711.0	810.9	1596.4	1327.3	1727.6	2189.1
Less: Surplus of the nation on current transactions	-11.1	-62.3	-176.4	-572.4	-399.1	-224.0	-384.9	-474.5	-40.1	-1136.4	-1086.8	-1009.4
Equals: Net Capital Formation e	244.2	586.8	1251.8	1466.1	1233.5	1002.5	1095.9	1285.4	1636.5	2463.7	2814.4	3198.5

a) Item 'National income' includes consumption of fixed capital.
b) For 1976, item 'Current transfers from the rest of the world' includes gifts in kind received after the earthquake.
c) Item 'National disposable income' includes consumption of fixed capital.
d) Item 'Net saving' includes consumption of fixed capital.
e) Item 'Net capital formation' includes consumption of fixed capital.

2.11 Gross Fixed Capital Formation by Kind of Activity of Owner, ISIC Divisions, in Current Prices

Million Guatemalan quetzales

	1970	1975	1980	1981	1982	1983	1984	1985	1986	1987	1988	1989
					All Producers							
1 Agriculture, hunting, forestry and fishing	19.5	54.4	73.9	92.4	65.4	61.9	70.7	93.5	128.8	164.6	186.7	215.5
2 Mining and quarrying	...	...	...	...	...	...	...	...	...	...	...	...
3 Manufacturing	127.4	270.1	554.2	572.5	588.0	402.2	442.0	662.3	873.7	1191.1	1499.7	1714.8
4 Electricity, gas and water	...	...	...	...	...	...	...	...	...	...	...	...
5 Construction	28.1	54.7	151.6	99.8	107.8	120.5	104.9	144.7	189.8	226.8	305.9	381.4
6 Wholesale and retail trade, restaurants and hotels	...	...	...	...	...	...	...	...	...	...	...	...
7 Transport, storage and communication	20.9	86.5	121.7	109.1	57.1	41.5	53.0	113.0	151.9	280.5	326.6	375.1
8 Finance, insurance, real estate and business services	...	...	...	...	...	...	...	...	...	...	...	...
9 Community, social and personal services	...	...	...	...	...	...	...	...	...	...	...	...
Total Industries	195.9	465.7	901.4	873.8	818.3	626.1	670.6	1013.5	1344.2	1863.0	2318.9	2686.8
Producers of Government Services	42.7	105.1	393.9	569.4	491.3	324.1	241.8	211.4	249.0	325.3	428.3	513.3
Private Non-Profit Institutions Serving Households	...	...	...	...	...	...	...	...	...	...	...	...
Total	238.6	570.8	1295.3	1443.2	1309.6	950.2	912.4	1224.9	1593.2	2188.3	2747.2	3200.1

2.12 Gross Fixed Capital Formation by Kind of Activity of Owner, ISIC Divisions, in Constant Prices

Million Guatemalan quetzales

	1970	1975	1980	1981	1982	1983	1984	1985	1986	1987	1988	1989
					At constant prices of:1958							
					All Producers							
1 Agriculture, hunting, forestry and fishing	17.4	27.0	23.1	26.3	19.2	17.4	19.1	18.3	18.9	20.7	21.1	21.8
2 Mining and quarrying	...	...	...	...	...	...	...	...	...	...	...	...
3 Manufacturing	111.8	126.4	151.1	150.0	150.0	103.2	107.8	105.3	107.5	123.0	137.4	139.9
4 Electricity, gas and water	...	...	...	...	...	...	...	...	...	...	...	...
5 Construction	25.8	27.3	40.6	25.0	26.7	29.5	25.4	28.4	31.2	33.8	41.1	46.0
6 Wholesale and retail trade, restaurants and hotels	...	...	...	...	...	...	...	...	...	...	...	...
7 Transport, storage and communication	17.8	35.0	27.0	24.8	13.0	9.3	11.7	12.3	14.6	23.0	24.4	24.9
8 Finance, insurance, real estate and business services	...	...	...	...	...	...	...	...	...	...	...	...
9 Community, social and personal services	...	...	...	...	...	...	...	...	...	...	...	...
Total Industries	172.8	215.7	241.8	226.1	208.9	159.4	164.0	164.3	172.2	200.5	224.0	232.6
Producers of Government Services	36.8	54.9	130.8	175.4	148.8	98.8	71.0	55.9	56.3	65.6	75.8	84.0
Private Non-Profit Institutions Serving Households	...	...	...	...	...	...	...	...	...	...	...	...
Total	209.6	270.6	372.6	401.5	357.7	258.2	235.0	220.2	228.5	266.1	299.8	316.6

Guatemala

2.17 Exports and Imports of Goods and Services, Detail

Million Guatemalan quetzales

	1970	1975	1980	1981	1982	1983	1984	1985	1986	1987	1988	1989
Exports of Goods and Services												
1 Exports of merchandise, f.o.b.	297.1	640.9	1519.8	1291.3	1170.4	1091.7	1154.8	1886.2	2285.8	2415.5	2790.9	3266.0
2 Transport and communication	10.3	19.8	30.3	29.7	24.7	16.8	9.3	11.6	16.3	22.2	44.1	68.7
A In respect of merchandise imports	0.3	1.5	4.4	3.5	2.7	1.9	0.3	0.7	-	-	0.9	29.8
B Other	10.0	18.3	25.9	26.2	22.0	14.9	9.0	10.9	16.3	22.2	43.2	38.9
3 Insurance service charges	3.5	4.5	11.4	15.5	9.2	2.1	5.5	1.3	0.7	1.8	5.7	19.3
A In respect of merchandise imports	0.6	2.5	3.3	3.3	1.8	0.7	0.3	0.7	0.2	0.5	0.6	4.0
B Other	2.9	2.0	8.1	12.2	7.4	1.4	5.2	0.6	0.5	1.3	5.1	15.3
4 Other commodities	17.5	33.1	82.3	59.4	34.4	20.6	39.4	56.9	106.8	180.8	146.8	267.7
5 Adjustments of merchandise exports to change-of-ownership basis	...	...	...	...	...	...	.	...	.	...	...	...
6 Direct purchases in the domestic market by non-residential households	12.1	78.0	61.6	30.5	12.0	6.8	11.7	23.6	64.1	126.1	161.3	310.4
7 Direct purchases in the domestic market by extraterritorial bodies	13.1	15.7	42.2	44.6	38.0	37.9	35.5	88.4	68.4	60.6	159.7	192.9
Total Exports of Goods and Services ª	353.6	792.0	1747.6	1471.0	1288.7	1175.9	1256.2	2068.0	2542.1	2807.0	3308.5	4125.0
Imports of Goods and Services												
1 Imports of merchandise, c.i.f.	293.9	734.9	1598.2	1673.5	1388.0	1135.0	1304.1	2091.2	2101.3	3574.5	4048.1	4717.0
A Imports of merchandise, f.o.b.	269.9	672.4	1472.6	1540.0	1284.2	1056.0	1205.8	1916.6	1919.5	3292.9	3674.3	4268.9
B Transport of services on merchandise imports	21.8	56.8	119.0	126.4	98.2	74.8	93.1	165.3	172.2	266.7	354.0	425.7
By residents	...	...	...	...	...	...	...	...	...	...	...	...
By non-residents	21.8	56.8	119.0	126.4	98.2	74.8	93.1	165.3	172.2	266.7	354.0	425.7
C Insurance service charges on merchandise imports	2.2	5.7	6.6	7.1	5.5	4.2	5.2	9.3	9.6	14.9	19.8	22.4
By residents	...	...	...	...	...	...	...	...	...	...	...	...
By non-residents	2.2	5.7	6.6	7.1	5.5	4.2	5.2	9.3	9.6	14.9	19.8	22.4
2 Adjustments of merchandise imports to change-of-ownership basis	...	...	...	...	...	...	...	...	...	...	...	...
3 Other transport and communication	10.6	19.9	53.3	54.4	35.1	19.8	15.9	16.0	19.2	25.7	42.3	54.9
4 Other insurance service charges	1.3	3.5	9.6	11.7	11.2	12.8	21.4	10.8	12.2	8.9	17.2	26.4
5 Other commodities	14.8	36.9	114.5	140.7	82.0	45.8	46.2	63.9	107.7	222.9	102.4	150.8
6 Direct purchases abroad by government	3.4	8.0	23.7	18.1	12.7	14.3	13.3	23.2	37.2	35.2	49.2	60.0
7 Direct purchases abroad by resident households	14.4	54.8	164.0	133.1	100.3	89.4	62.7	41.9	33.6	81.2	247.6	353.9
Total Imports of Goods and Services	338.4	858.0	1963.3	2031.5	1629.3	1317.1	1463.6	2246.9	2311.2	3948.5	4506.8	5363.0
Balance of Goods and Services	15.2	-66.0	-215.7	-560.5	-340.6	-141.3	-207.4	-178.9	230.9	-1141.5	-1198.3	-1238.0
Total Imports and Balance of Goods and Services	353.6	792.0	1747.6	1471.0	1288.7	1175.8	1256.2	2068.0	2542.1	2807.0	3308.5	4125.0

a) For 1976, item 'Exports of goods and services' includes 51.2 million quetzales for insurance service charges.

Guinea-Bissau

Source. Reply to the United Nations National Accounts Questionnaire from the Ministerio do Plano, Bissau.

General note. The estimates shown in the following tables have been prepared in accordance with the United Nations System of National Accounts so far as the existing data would permit.

1.1 Expenditure on the Gross Domestic Product, in Current Prices

Million Guinea-Bissau pesos

	1970	1975	1980	1981	1982	1983	1984	1985	1986	1987	1988	1989
1 Government final consumption expenditure	...	...	...	...	...	...	...	...	6423	10776	20134	...
2 Private final consumption expenditure	...	...	...	...	...	...	...	...	41844	82375	160420	...
A Households	...	...	...	...	...	...	...	...	41844	82375	160420	...
B Private non-profit institutions serving households	...	...	...	...	...	...	...	...	...	...	...	...
3 Gross capital formation	...	...	...	...	...	...	...	...	9967	21785	49864	...
A Increase in stocks	...	...	...	...	...	...	...	...	582	879	192	...
B Gross fixed capital formation	...	...	...	...	...	...	...	...	9385	20906	49672	...
4 Exports of goods and services	...	...	...	...	...	...	...	...	2211	13788	22666	...
5 Less: Imports of goods and services	...	...	...	...	...	...	...	...	13472	36349	81134	...
Equals: Gross Domestic Product	...	...	...	...	...	...	...	...	46973	92375	171949	...

1.2 Expenditure on the Gross Domestic Product, in Constant Prices

Million Guinea-Bissau pesos

	1970	1975	1980	1981	1982	1983	1984	1985	1986	1987	1988	1989
					At constant prices of: 1986						1987	
1 Government final consumption expenditure	...	...	...	...	...	...	...	...	6423	6743 / 10776	13296	...
2 Private final consumption expenditure	...	...	...	...	...	...	...	...	41844	46288 / 82375	89410	...
A Households	...	...	...	...	...	...	...	...	41844	46288 / 82375	89410	...
B Private non-profit institutions serving households	...	...	...	...	...	...	...	...	...	...	...	...
3 Gross capital formation	...	...	...	...	...	...	...	...	9967	7215 / 21785	26216	...
A Increase in stocks	...	...	...	...	...	...	...	...	582	322 / 879	-292	...
B Gross fixed capital formation	...	...	...	...	...	...	...	...	9385	6893 / 20906	26507	...
4 Exports of goods and services	...	...	...	...	...	...	...	...	2211	4130 / 13788	11307	...
5 Less: Imports of goods and services	...	...	...	...	...	...	...	...	13472	14753 / 36349	41447	...
Equals: Gross Domestic Product	...	...	...	...	...	...	...	...	46973	49623 / 92375	98782	...

1.3 Cost Components of the Gross Domestic Product

Million Guinea-Bissau pesos

	1970	1975	1980	1981	1982	1983	1984	1985	1986	1987	1988	1989
1 Indirect taxes, net	...	...	...	...	...	...	...	...	2534	10489	...	...
A Indirect taxes [a]	...	...	...	...	...	...	...	...	2534	10489	...	...
B Less: Subsidies	...	...	...	...	...	...	...	...	-	-	...	...
2 Consumption of fixed capital	...	...	...	...	...	...	...	...	...	...	...	...
3 Compensation of employees paid by resident producers to:				...	...	...	...	...	14723	27362	...	...
A Resident households	...	...	...	...	...	...	...	...	12816	21621	...	...
B Rest of the world	...	...	...	...	...	...	...	...	1907	5741	...	...
4 Operating surplus	...	...	...	...	...	...	...	...	30692	61320	...	...
A Corporate and quasi-corporate enterprises	...	...	...	...	...	...	...	...	-200	4874	...	...
B Private unincorporated enterprises [b]	...	...	...	...	...	...	...	...	30892	56446	...	...
C General government	...	...	...	...	...	...	...	...	...	...	...	...
Statistical discrepancy	...	...	...	...	...	...	...	...	-976	-6796	...	...
Equals: Gross Domestic Product	...	...	...	...	...	...	...	...	46973	92375	...	...

a) Item 'Indirect taxes' includes also fishing licences.
b) Private unincorporated enterprises includes households.

Guinea-Bissau

1.4 General Government Current Receipts and Disbursements

Million Guinea-Bissau pesos

	1970	1975	1980	1981	1982	1983	1984	1985	1986	1987	1988	1989
Receipts												
1 Operating surplus	...	...	...	...	...	...	...	...	...	...	...	...
2 Property and entrepreneurial income	...	...	...	...	...	...	...	...	...	...	...	...
3 Taxes, fees and contributions	...	...	...	...	...	...	...	...	3992	12282	...	...
A Indirect taxes a	...	...	...	...	...	...	...	...	2534	10489	...	...
B Direct taxes	...	...	...	...	...	...	...	...	1229	1423	...	...
C Social security contributions	...	...	...	...	...	...	...	...	229	370	...	...
D Compulsory fees, fines and penalties	...	...	...	...	...	...	...	...	...	...	...	...
4 Other current transfers	...	...	...	...	...	...	...	...	1179	2303	...	...
Total Current Receipts of General Government	...	...	...	...	...	...	...	...	5171	14585	...	...
Disbursements												
1 Government final consumption expenditure	...	...	...	...	...	...	...	...	6423	10776	...	...
A Compensation of employees	...	...	...	...	...	...	...	...	5207	5644	...	...
B Consumption of fixed capital	...	...	...	...	...	...	...	...	...	...	...	...
C Purchases of goods and services, net	...	...	...	...	...	...	...	...	...	...	...	...
D Less: Own account fixed capital formation	...	...	...	...	...	...	...	...	...	...	...	...
E Indirect taxes paid, net	...	...	...	...	...	...	...	...	...	...	...	...
2 Property income	...	...	...	...	...	...	...	...	1428	4464	...	...
A Interest	...	...	...	...	...	...	...	...	1428	4464	...	...
B Net land rent and royalties	...	...	...	...	...	...	...	...	...	...	...	...
3 Subsidies	...	...	...	...	...	...	...	...	...	...	...	...
4 Other current transfers	...	...	...	...	...	...	...	...	919	1958	...	...
A Social security benefits	...	...	...	...	...	...	...	...	117	424	...	...
B Social assistance grants	...	...	...	...	...	...	...	...	...	...	...	...
C Other	...	...	...	...	...	...	...	...	802	1534	...	...
5 Net saving	...	...	...	...	...	...	...	...	-3599	-2613	...	...
Total Current Disbursements and Net Saving of General Government	...	...	...	...	...	...	...	...	5171	14585	...	...

a) Item 'Indirect taxes' includes also fishing licences.

1.7 External Transactions on Current Account, Summary

Million Guinea-Bissau pesos

	1970	1975	1980	1981	1982	1983	1984	1985	1986	1987	1988	1989
Payments to the Rest of the World												
1 Imports of goods and services	...	...	...	...	...	...	...	...	13472	36349	...	...
2 Factor income to the rest of the world	...	...	...	...	...	...	...	...	3575	9665	...	...
A Compensation of employees	...	...	...	...	...	...	...	...	1907	5741	...	...
B Property and entrepreneurial income	...	...	...	...	...	...	...	...	1668	3924	...	...
By general government	...	...	...	...	...	...	...	...	888	113	...	...
By corporate and quasi-corporate enterprises	...	...	...	...	...	...	...	...	780	3811	...	...
By other	...	...	...	...	...	...	...	...	...	...	...	...
3 Current transfers to the rest of the world	...	...	...	...	...	...	...	...	304	350	...	...
Statistical discrepancy	...	...	...	...	...	...	...	...	2710	2417	...	...
4 Surplus of the nation on current transactions	...	...	...	...	...	...	...	...	-11613	-21615	...	...
Payments to the Rest of the World and Surplus of the Nation on Current Transactions	...	...	...	...	...	...	...	...	8448	27166	...	...
Receipts From The Rest of the World												
1 Exports of goods and services	...	...	...	...	...	...	...	...	2211	13788	...	...
A Exports of merchandise f.o.b.	...	...	...	...	...	...	...	...	2211	13788	...	...

Guinea-Bissau

1.7 External Transactions on Current Account, Summary
(Continued)

Million Guinea-Bissau pesos

	1970	1975	1980	1981	1982	1983	1984	1985	1986	1987	1988	1989
B Other	...	...	...	...	...	...	...	...	...	...	...	...
2 Factor income from rest of the world	...	...	...	...	...	...	...	...	2796	9241	...	...
A Compensation of employees	...	...	...	...	...	...	...	...	1907	5741	...	...
B Property and entrepreneurial income	...	...	...	...	...	...	...	...	889	3500	...	...
By general government	...	...	...	...	...	...	...	...	889	3500	...	...
By corporate and quasi-corporate enterprises	...	...	...	...	...	...	...	...	...	...	...	...
By other	...	...	...	...	...	...	...	...	...	...	...	...
3 Current transfers from rest of the world	...	...	...	...	...	...	...	...	1686	4136	...	...
Statistical discrepancy	...	...	...	...	...	...	...	...	1755	1	...	...
Receipts from the Rest of the World on Current Transactions	...	...	...	...	...	...	...	...	8448	27166	...	...

1.8 Capital Transactions of The Nation, Summary

Million Guinea-Bissau pesos

	1970	1975	1980	1981	1982	1983	1984	1985	1986	1987	1988	1989
Finance of Gross Capital Formation												
Gross saving	...	...	...	...	...	...	...	...	-691	2586	...	...
Less: Surplus of the nation on current transactions	...	...	...	...	...	...	...	...	-11613	-21615	...	...
Statistical discrepancy	...	...	...	...	...	...	...	...	-954	-2416	...	...
Finance of Gross Capital Formation	...	...	...	...	...	...	...	...	9967	21785	...	...
Gross Capital Formation												
Increase in stocks	...	...	...	...	...	...	...	...	582	879	...	...
Gross fixed capital formation	...	...	...	...	...	...	...	...	9385	20906	...	...
1 General government	...	...	...	...	...	...	...	...	6072	15244	...	...
2 Corporate and quasi-corporate enterprises	...	...	...	...	...	...	...	...	2247	3476	...	...
A Public	...	...	...	...	...	...	...	...	1508	3316	...	...
B Private	...	...	...	...	...	...	...	...	739	160	...	...
3 Other	...	...	...	...	...	...	...	...	1066	2186	...	...
Gross Capital Formation	...	...	...	...	...	...	...	...	9967	21785	...	...

1.9 Gross Domestic Product by Institutional Sectors of Origin

Million Guinea-Bissau pesos

	1970	1975	1980	1981	1982	1983	1984	1985	1986	1987	1988	1989
Domestic Factor Incomes Originating												
1 General government	...	...	...	...	...	...	...	...	5207	5644	...	...
2 Corporate and quasi-corporate enterprises	...	...	...	...	...	...	...	...	5523	7913	...	...
A Non-financial	...	...	...	...	...	...	...	...	5008	6649	...	...
Public	...	...	...	...	...	...	...	...	-226	-2617	...	...
Private	...	...	...	...	...	...	...	...	5234	9266	...	...
B Financial	...	...	...	...	...	...	...	...	515	1264	...	...
Public	...	...	...	...	...	...	...	...	515	1264	...	...
Private	...	...	...	...	...	...	...	...	-	-	...	...
3 Households and private unincorporated enterprises	...	...	...	...	...	...	...	...	36243	78818	...	...
4 Non-profit institutions serving households	...	...	...	...	...	...	...	...	...	...	...	...
Subtotal: Domestic Factor Incomes	...	...	...	...	...	...	...	...	46973	92375	...	...
Indirect taxes, net [a]	...	...	...	...	...	...	...	...	...	...	...	...
Consumption of fixed capital	...	...	...	...	...	...	...	...	...	...	...	...
Gross Domestic Product	...	...	...	...	...	...	...	...	46973	92375	...	...

a) Item 'Net indirect taxes' is included in the above items.

Guinea-Bissau

1.10 Gross Domestic Product by Kind of Activity, in Current Prices

Million Guinea-Bissau pesos

	1970	1975	1980	1981	1982	1983	1984	1985	1986	1987	1988	1989
1 Agriculture, hunting, forestry and fishing	...	...	...	...	...	...	...	...	21997	47096	78470	...
2 Mining and quarrying	...	...	...	...	...	...	...	...	31	15	57	...
3 Manufacturing	...	...	...	...	...	...	...	...	6959	7026	11763	...
4 Electricity, gas and water	...	...	...	...	...	...	...	...	16	640	1809	...
5 Construction	...	...	...	...	...	...	...	...	2621	4266	10947	...
6 Wholesale and retail trade, restaurants and hotels	...	...	...	...	...	...	...	...	9267	22874	41075	...
7 Transport, storage and communication	...	...	...	...	...	...	...	...	1337	3550	6375	...
8 Finance, insurance, real estate and business services	...	...	...	...	...	...	...	...	515	1264	5264	...
9 Community, social and personal services	...	...	...	...	...	...	...	...	-710	-	-	...
Total, Industries	...	...	...	...	...	...	...	...	42033	86731	155758	...
Producers of Government Services	...	...	...	...	...	...	...	...	5207	5644	8923	...
Other Producers	...	...	...	...	...	...	...	...	...	...	...	...
Subtotal	...	...	...	...	...	...	...	...	47240	92375	171949	...
Less: Imputed bank service charge	...	...	...	...	...	...	...	...	267	-	-	...
Plus: Import duties	...	...	...	...	...	...	...	...	...	...	...	...
Plus: Value added tax	...	...	...	...	...	...	...	...	...	...	...	...
Equals: Gross Domestic Product	...	...	...	...	...	...	...	...	46973	92375	171949	...

1.11 Gross Domestic Product by Kind of Activity, in Constant Prices

Million Guinea-Bissau pesos

	1970	1975	1980	1981	1982	1983	1984	1985	1986	1987	1988	1989
					At constant prices of: 1986						1987	
1 Agriculture, hunting, forestry and fishing	...	...	...	...	...	...	...	...	21997	24313 / 47096	43939	...
2 Mining and quarrying	...	...	...	...	...	...	...	...	31	10 / 15	28	...
3 Manufacturing	...	...	...	...	...	...	...	...	6959	6077 / 7026	7388	...
4 Electricity, gas and water	...	...	...	...	...	...	...	...	16	577 / 640	704	...
5 Construction	...	...	...	...	...	...	...	...	2621	1348 / 4266	5807	...
6 Wholesale and retail trade, restaurants and hotels	...	...	...	...	...	...	...	...	9267	10091 / 22874	23931	...
7 Transport, storage and communication	...	...	...	...	...	...	...	...	1337	1413 / 3550	3497	...
8 Finance, insurance, real estate and business services	...	...	...	...	...	...	...	...	515	1054 / 1264	2604	...
9 Community, social and personal services	...	...	...	...	...	...	...	...	-710	- / -	-	...
Total, Industries	...	...	...	...	...	...	...	...	42033	44883 / 86731	87899	...
Producers of Government Services	...	...	...	...	...	...	...	...	5207	4740 / 5644	6163	...
Other Producers	...	...	...	...	...	...	...	...	...	...	...	...
Subtotal	...	...	...	...	...	...	...	...	47240	49623 / 92375	98782	...
Less: Imputed bank service charge	...	...	...	...	...	...	...	...	267	-	-	...
Plus: Import duties	...	...	...	...	...	...	...	...	...	...	...	...
Plus: Value added tax	...	...	...	...	...	...	...	...	...	...	...	...
Equals: Gross Domestic Product	...	...	...	...	...	...	...	...	46973	49623 / 92375	98782	...

Guinea-Bissau

1.12 Relations Among National Accounting Aggregates

Million Guinea-Bissau pesos

	1970	1975	1980	1981	1982	1983	1984	1985	1986	1987	1988	1989
Gross Domestic Product	...	...	...	...	...	...	...	...	46973	92375	...	...
Plus: Net factor income from the rest of the world	...	...	...	...	...	...	...	...	-779	-424	...	...
Factor income from the rest of the world	...	...	...	...	...	...	...	...	2796	9241	...	...
Less: Factor income to the rest of the world	...	...	...	...	...	...	...	...	3575	9665	...	...
Equals: Gross National Product	...	...	...	...	...	...	...	...	46194	91951	...	...
Less: Consumption of fixed capital	...	...	...	...	...	...	...	...	...	...	...	...
Equals: National Income	...	...	...	...	...	...	...	...	46194	91951	...	...
Plus: Net current transfers from the rest of the world	...	...	...	...	...	...	...	...	1382	3786	...	...
Current transfers from the rest of the world	...	...	...	...	...	...	...	...	1686	4136	...	...
Less: Current transfers to the rest of the world	...	...	...	...	...	...	...	...	304	350	...	...
Equals: National Disposable Income	...	...	...	...	...	...	...	...	47576	95737	...	...
Less: Final consumption	...	...	...	...	...	...	...	...	48267	93151	...	...
Equals: Net Saving	...	...	...	...	...	...	...	...	-691	2586	...	...
Less: Surplus of the nation on current transactions	...	...	...	...	...	...	...	...	-11613	-21615	...	...
Statistical discrepancy	...	...	...	...	...	...	...	...	-955	-2416	...	...
Equals: Net Capital Formation	...	...	...	...	...	...	...	...	9967	21785	...	...

2.1 Government Final Consumption Expenditure by Function, in Current Prices

Million Guinea-Bissau pesos

	1970	1975	1980	1981	1982	1983	1984	1985	1986	1987	1988	1989
1 General public services	...	...	...	...	...	...	...	...	2829	4746	...	...
2 Defence	...	...	...	...	...	...	...	...	...	...	...	...
3 Public order and safety	...	...	...	...	...	...	...	...	...	...	...	...
4 Education	...	...	...	...	...	...	...	...	1183	1985	...	...
5 Health	...	...	...	...	...	...	...	...	758	1272	...	...
6 Social security and welfare	...	...	...	...	...	...	...	...	57	130	...	...
7 Housing and community amenities	...	...	...	...	...	...	...	...	...	...	...	...
8 Recreational, cultural and religious affairs	...	...	...	...	...	...	...	...	...	...	...	...
9 Economic services	...	...	...	...	...	...	...	...	1456	2442	...	...
10 Other functions	...	...	...	...	...	...	...	...	140	201	...	...
Total Government Final Consumption Expenditure	...	...	...	...	...	...	...	...	6423	10776	...	...

2.2 Government Final Consumption Expenditure by Function, in Constant Prices

Million Guinea-Bissau pesos

	1970	1975	1980	1981	1982	1983	1984	1985	1986	1987	1988	1989
					At constant prices of:1986							
1 General public services	...	...	...	...	...	...	...	...	2829	2970	...	...
2 Defence	...	...	...	...	...	...	...	...	...	...	...	...
3 Public order and safety	...	...	...	...	...	...	...	...	...	...	...	...
4 Education	...	...	...	...	...	...	...	...	1183	1242	...	...
5 Health	...	...	...	...	...	...	...	...	758	796	...	...
6 Social security and welfare	...	...	...	...	...	...	...	...	57	59	...	...
7 Housing and community amenities	...	...	...	...	...	...	...	...	...	...	...	...
8 Recreational, cultural and religious affairs	...	...	...	...	...	...	...	...	...	...	...	...
9 Economic services	...	...	...	...	...	...	...	...	1456	1528	...	...
10 Other functions	...	...	...	...	...	...	...	...	140	148	...	...
Total Government Final Consumption Expenditure	...	...	...	...	...	...	...	...	6423	6743	...	...

Guyana

Source. Reply to the United Nations National Accounts Questionnaire from the Statistical Bureau, Georgetown. Official estimates have been published by the Statistical Bureau in 'Annual Statistical Abstract'.

General note. The estimates shown in the following tables have been prepared in accordance with the United Nations System of National Accounts so far as the existing data would permit.

1.1 Expenditure on the Gross Domestic Product, in Current Prices

Million Guyana dollars

	1970	1975	1980	1981	1982	1983	1984	1985	1986	1987	1988	1989
1 Government final consumption expenditure	90.9	232.9	436.0	470.0	435.0	465.0	550.0	720.0	876.0	952.0	1162.0	...
2 Private final consumption expenditure	322.0	562.5	796.2	922.0	876.0	893.0	1015.0	1035.0	1000.0	1715.0	2279.0	...
3 Gross capital formation	121.9	392.5	449.0	530.0	380.0	395.0	390.0	410.0	586.0	1123.0	890.0	...
A Increase in stocks	9.2	42.3	45.0	30.0	-	-	-	-	-	-	-	...
B Gross fixed capital formation	112.6	350.3	404.0	500.0	380.0	395.0	390.0	410.0	586.0	1123.0	890.0	...
4 Exports of goods and services	302.4	890.7	1042.0	1050.0	792.0	675.0	897.0	1042.0	1092.0	2827.0	2967.0	...
5 Less: Imports of goods and services	305.4	881.6	1215.0	1375.0	1037.0	973.0	1152.0	1243.0	1335.0	3518.0	3698.0	...
Statistical discrepancy	3.7	-9.1	-	-	-	-	-	-	-	-	-	...
Equals: Gross Domestic Product	535.6	1187.9	1508.2	1597.0	1446.0	1455.0	1700.0	1964.0	2219.0	3382.0	3600.0	...

1.2 Expenditure on the Gross Domestic Product, in Constant Prices

Million Guyana dollars

	1970	1975	1980	1981	1982	1983	1984	1985	1986	1987	1988	1989
					At constant prices of:1970							
1 Government final consumption expenditure	90.9	155.2	...	...	...	...	...	...	...	...	...	...
2 Private final consumption expenditure	322.0	378.3	...	...	...	...	...	...	...	...	...	...
3 Gross capital formation	121.9	204.2	...	...	...	...	...	...	...	...	...	...
A Increase in stocks	9.2	28.9	...	...	...	...	...	...	...	...	...	...
B Gross fixed capital formation	112.6	175.3	...	...	...	...	...	...	...	...	...	...
4 Exports of goods and services	302.4	269.4	...	...	...	...	...	...	...	...	...	...
5 Less: Imports of goods and services	305.4	352.2	...	...	...	...	...	...	...	...	...	...
Statistical discrepancy	3.7	-6.1	...	...	...	...	...	...	...	...	...	...
Equals: Gross Domestic Product	535.6	648.7	...	...	...	...	...	...	...	...	...	...

1.3 Cost Components of the Gross Domestic Product

Million Guyana dollars

	1970	1975	1980	1981	1982	1983	1984	1985	1986	1987	1988	1989
1 Indirect taxes, net	65.6	90.0	172.2	247.0	196.0	255.0	290.0	334.0	399.0	506.0	...	...
A Indirect taxes	...	...	...	...	...	...	...	...	...	...	...	...
B Less: Subsidies	4.2	32.9	...	...	...	...	...	...	...	...	...	...
2 Consumption of fixed capital	33.8	46.5	95.0	103.0	118.0	120.0	125.0	126.0	134.0	140.0	...	...
3 Compensation of employees paid by resident producers to:	262.2	491.8	1241.0	1247.0	1132.0	1080.0	1285.0	1504.0	1686.0	2711.0	...	...
4 Operating surplus	174.0	559.6									...	...
Equals: Gross Domestic Product	535.6	1187.9	1508.2	1597.0	1446.0	1455.0	1700.0	1964.0	2219.0	3357.0	...	...

1.10 Gross Domestic Product by Kind of Activity, in Current Prices

Million Guyana dollars

	1970	1975	1980	1981	1982	1983	1984	1985	1986	1987	1988	1989
1 Agriculture, hunting, forestry and fishing	90.2	341.5	312.0	300.0	292.0	291.0	347.0	439.0	465.0	910.0	936.0	1897.0
2 Mining and quarrying	95.5	141.0	221.0	101.0	88.0	17.0	65.0	50.0	116.0	339.0	360.0	109.0
3 Manufacturing	57.0	161.6	162.0	201.0	179.0	158.0	183.0	227.0	266.0	404.0	460.0	810.0
4 Electricity, gas and water												
5 Construction a	36.8	74.4	95.0	110.0	95.0	98.0	100.0	120.0	124.0	141.0	246.0	394.0
6 Wholesale and retail trade, restaurants and hotels b	53.5	94.2	115.0	145.0	123.0	120.0	125.0	133.0	134.0	152.0	290.0	370.0
7 Transport, storage and communication	27.7	49.9	75.0	90.0	85.0	98.0	100.0	128.0	139.0	184.0	299.0	346.0
8 Finance, insurance, real estate and business services c	27.1	49.7	72.0	87.0	105.0	115.0	125.0	132.0	134.0	169.0	250.0	313.0
9 Community, social and personal services bc	17.7	25.6	34.0	40.0	45.0	48.0	50.0	55.0	55.0	65.0	125.0	156.0
Total, Industries	405.5	938.0	1086.0	1074.0	1012.0	945.0	1095.0	1284.0	1433.0	2364.0	2966.0	4395.0
Producers of Government Services	64.5	159.8	250.0	276.0	238.0	255.0	315.0	346.0	387.0	554.0	634.0	772.0

Guyana

1.10 Gross Domestic Product by Kind of Activity, in Current Prices
(Continued)

Million Guyana dollars

	1970	1975	1980	1981	1982	1983	1984	1985	1986	1987	1988	1989
Other Producers	...	...	...	...	...	...	...	...	...	...	...	...
Subtotal d	470.0	1097.8	1336.0	1350.0	1250.0	1200.0	1410.0	1630.0	1820.0	2918.0	3600.0	5167.0
Less: Imputed bank service charge	...	...	...	...	...	...	...	...	...	...	...	...
Plus: Import duties	...	...	...	...	...	...	...	...	...	...	...	...
Plus: Value added tax	...	...	...	...	...	...	...	...	...	...	...	...
Plus: Other adjustments e	65.6	90.0	172.0	247.0	196.0	255.0	290.0	334.0	399.0	...	...	...
Equals: Gross Domestic Product	535.6	1187.9	1508.0	1597.0	1446.0	1455.0	1700.0	1964.0	2219.0	...	...	...

a) Item 'Construction' includes engineering and sewage services.
b) Restaurants and hotels are included in item 'Community, social and personal services'.
c) Business services are included in item 'Community, social and personal services'.

d) Gross domestic product in factor values.
e) Item 'Other adjustments' refers to indirect taxes net of subsidies.

1.11 Gross Domestic Product by Kind of Activity, in Constant Prices

Million Guyana dollars

	1970	1975	1980	1981	1982	1983	1984	1985	1986	1987	1988	1989
					At constant prices of:							
		1970					1977					
1 Agriculture, hunting, forestry and fishing	90.2	97.2	214.0	219.0	216.0	208.0	215.0	215.0	223.0	210.0	190.0	188.0
2 Mining and quarrying	95.5	85.1	140.0	124.0	85.0	51.0	62.0	74.0	68.0	75.0	74.0	54.0
3 Manufacturing	57.0	89.6	132.0	140.0	122.0	102.0	96.0	93.0	93.0	86.0	82.0	73.0
4 Electricity, gas and water												
5 Construction a	36.8	51.3	70.0	71.0	64.0	61.0	61.0	61.0	60.0	63.0	60.0	58.0
6 Wholesale and retail trade, restaurants and hotels b	53.5	73.0	89.0	85.0	68.0	55.0	58.0	58.0	58.0	61.0	62.0	59.0
7 Transport, storage and communication	27.7	33.8	64.0	64.0	63.0	63.0	65.0	62.0	63.0	71.0	64.0	60.0
8 Finance, insurance, real estate and business services c	27.1	35.2	57.0	58.0	56.0	56.0	57.0	59.0	59.0	63.0	63.0	65.0
9 Community, social and personal services bc	17.7	16.8	21.0	21.0	21.0	21.0	20.0	20.0	20.0	21.0	21.0	21.0
Total, Industries	405.5	482.1	787.0	782.0	695.0	617.0	634.0	642.0	644.0	650.0	617.0	578.0
Producers of Government Services	64.5	106.1	207.0	207.0	191.0	187.0	187.0	187.0	187.0	187.0	187.0	187.0
Other Producers	...	...	...	...	...	...	...	...	...	...	...	...
Subtotal d	470.0	588.1	994.0	989.0	886.0	804.0	821.0	829.0	831.0	837.0	804.0	765.0
Less: Imputed bank service charge	...	...	...	...	...	...	...	...	...	...	...	...
Plus: Import duties	...	...	...	...	...	...	...	...	...	...	...	...
Plus: Value added tax	...	...	...	...	...	...	...	...	...	...	...	...
Plus: Other adjustments	65.6e	60.6e	...	...	...	...	...	...	...	...	...	...
Equals: Gross Domestic Product	535.6	648.7	...	...	...	...	...	...	...	...	...	...

a) Item 'Construction' includes engineering and sewage services.
b) Restaurants and hotels are included in item 'Community, social and personal services'.
c) Business services are included in item 'Community, social and personal services'.

d) Gross domestic product in factor values.
e) Item 'Other adjustments' refers to indirect taxes net of subsidies.

1.12 Relations Among National Accounting Aggregates

Million Guyana dollars

	1970	1975	1980	1981	1982	1983	1984	1985	1986	1987	1988	1989
Gross Domestic Product	535.6	1187.9	1508.2	1597.0	1446.0	1455.0	1700.0	1964.0	2219.0	3357.0	...	...
Plus: Net factor income from the rest of the world	-42.5	-33.0	-83.0	-151.0	-156.0	-172.0	-182.0	-245.0	-283.0	-606.0	...	...
Equals: Gross National Product	493.1	1154.9	1425.2	1446.0	1290.0	1283.0	1518.0	1719.0	1936.0	2751.0	...	...
Less: Consumption of fixed capital	33.8	46.5	95.0	103.0	118.0	120.0	125.0	126.0	134.0	140.0	...	...
Equals: National Income	459.3	1108.4	1330.2	1343.0	1172.0	1163.0	1393.0	1593.0	1802.0	2611.0	...	...

Guyana

1.12 Relations Among National Accounting Aggregates
(Continued)

Million Guyana dollars	1970	1975	1980	1981	1982	1983	1984	1985	1986	1987	1988	1989
Plus: Net current transfers from the rest of the world	0.1	-9.0	-2.0	1.0	-25.0	2.0	18.0	20.0	29.0	45.0	...	...
Equals: National Disposable Income	459.4	1099.4	1328.2	1344.0	1147.0	1165.0	1411.0	1613.0	1831.0	2656.0	...	...
Less: Final consumption	413.0	795.4	1232.2	1392.0	1311.0	1358.0	1565.0	1755.0	1876.0	2206.0	...	...
Equals: Net Saving	46.4	304.0	96.0	-48.0	-164.0	-193.0	-154.0	-142.0	-45.0	450.0	...	...
Less: Surplus of the nation on current transactions	-45.4	-33.0	-258.0	-475.0	-426.0	-468.0	-418.0	-426.0	-497.0	-435.0	...	...
Statistical discrepancy	-3.7	9.1	...	...	...	...	...	...	...	...	...	...
Equals: Net Capital Formation	88.1	346.1	354.0	427.0	262.0	275.0	264.0	284.0	452.0	885.0	...	...

Haiti

Source: Reply to the United Nations National Accounts Questionnaire from the Institut Haitien de Statistique, Port-au-prince. The official estimates are published by the Institut in "Le Bulletin de Statistique Annuel Supplément de l'Institut".

General note: The estimates shown in the following tables have been prepared in accordance with the United Nations System of National Accounts so far as the existing data would permit.

1.1 Expenditure on the Gross Domestic Product, in Current Prices

Million Haitian gourdes — Fiscal year ending 30 September

	1970	1975	1980	1981	1982	1983	1984	1985	1986	1987	1988	1989
1 Government final consumption expenditure	1571	3165	6835	7188	7535	7866	8678	9471	10472	9366	9653	10036
2 Private final consumption expenditure												
3 Gross capital formation	167	540	1238	1252	1230	1331	1441	1673	1614	1546	1501	1791
4 Exports of goods and services	261	784	2148	2139	2015	2172	2328	2063	2086	1817	1825
5 Less: Imports of goods and services	343	1082	3038	3334	3132	3064	3209	3425	2972	3052	3176	2840
Equals: Gross Domestic Product	1656	3407	7183	7397	7425	8148	9082	10047	11177	9946	9795	10812

1.2 Expenditure on the Gross Domestic Product, in Constant Prices

Million Haitian gourdes — Fiscal year ending 30 September

At constant prices of: 1976

	1970	1975	1980	1981	1982	1983	1984	1985	1986	1987	1988	1989
1 Government final consumption expenditure												
2 Private final consumption expenditure	3108	3460	5161	5116	4555	4584	4684	4715	4807	4833	5007	4865
3 Gross capital formation	307	595	934	941	877	824	967	1078	987	997	955	901
4 Exports of goods and services	548	961	1436	1349	1546	1399	1352	1342	1110	1103	1024	1035
5 Less: Imports of goods and services	599	963	2182	2210	1960	1850	1832	2051	1769	1793	1799	1569
Equals: Gross Domestic Product	3364	4053	5349	5196	5018	5056	5071	5084	5135	5140	5187	5232

1.11 Gross Domestic Product by Kind of Activity, in Constant Prices

Million Haitian gourdes — Fiscal year ending 30 September

At constant prices of: 1976

	1970	1975	1980	1981	1982	1983	1984	1985	1986	1987	1988	1989
1 Agriculture, hunting, forestry and fishing	1482	1658	1723	1699	1627	1567	1621	1631	1670	1688	1722	1730
2 Mining and quarrying	72	62	67	57	70	5	5	5	5	8	8	7
3 Manufacturing	438	556	976	856	842	888	836	812	815	783	781	788
4 Electricity, gas and water	10	19	36	38	40	42	45	46	47	49	54	58
5 Construction	88	205	288	298	269	286	291	328	308	315	320	323
6 Wholesale and retail trade, restaurants and hotels	549	680	898	936	937	904	914	912	902	900	901	
7 Transport, storage and communication	59	80	99	103	97	106	92	85	88	99	105	108
8 Finance, insurance, real estate and business services	210	239	262	269	272	280	285	283	290	291	293	298
9 Community, social and personal services	94	104	149	167	143	161	188	195	202	177	176	177
Total, Industries	3002	3605	4598	4422	4256	4271	4267	4300	4338	4313	4362	4391
Producers of Government Services	159	302	515	539	549	540	575	580	596	605	605	609
Other Producers												
Subtotal	3161	3907	5114	4961	4805	4811	4842	4880	4934	4918	4967	5000
Less: Imputed bank service charge												
Plus: Import duties	204	147	234	235	210	245	230	204	201	222	220	232
Plus: Value added tax												
Equals: Gross Domestic Product	3365	4054	5348	5196	5015	5056	5072	5084	5135	5140	5187	5232

1.12 Relations Among National Accounting Aggregates

Million Haitian gourdes — Fiscal year ending 30 September

	1970	1975	1980	1981	1982	1983	1984	1985	1986	1987	1988	1989
Gross Domestic Product	1656	3407	7183	7397	7425	8148	9082	10047	11177	9946	9795	10812
Plus: Net factor income from the rest of the world	-14	-34	-72	-66	-72	-73	-92	-101	-100	-105	-126	-128
Equals: Gross National Product	1642	3374	7111	7331	7353	8075	8990	9946	11077	9841	9669	10684
Less: Consumption of fixed capital	48	89	197	200	197	212	229	266	257	240	239	253
Equals: National Income	1594	3285	6914	7131	7156	7863	8761	9680	10820	9601	9430	10431

Haiti

1.12 Relations Among National Accounting Aggregates
(Continued)

Million Haitian gourdes — Fiscal year ending 30 September

	1970	1975	1980	1981	1982	1983	1984	1985	1986	1987	1988	1989
Plus: Net current transfers from the rest of the world	109	197	444	697	559	552	615	725	759	855	964	830
Equals: National Disposable Income	1703	3482	7358	7828	7715	8415	9376	10405	11579	10456	10394	11261
Less: Final consumption	1571	3165	6835	7535	7187	7866	8678	9471	10472	9366	9653	10036
Equals: Net Saving	132	317	523	293	527	549	698	934	1107	1090	741	1225
Less: Surplus of the nation on current transactions	12	-135	-518	-759	-506	-570	-514	-473	-250	-216	-521	-313
Equals: Net Capital Formation	120	452	1041	1052	1033	1119	1212	1407	1357	1306	1262	1538

4.2 Derivation of Value Added by Kind of Activity, in Constant Prices

Million Haitian gourdes — Fiscal year ending 30 September

	1980			1981			1982			1983		
	Gross Output	Intermediate Consumption	Value Added	Gross Output	Intermediate Consumption	Value Added	Gross Output	Intermediate Consumption	Value Added	Gross Output	Intermediate Consumption	Value Added

At constant prices of:1976

All Producers

1 Agriculture, hunting, forestry and fishing	...	...	1723	...	...	1699	...	...	1627	...	...	1567
A Agriculture and hunting	...	...	1444	...	...	1415	...	...	1396	...	...	1331
B Forestry and logging	...	...	279	...	...	284	...	...	231	...	...	236
C Fishing	...	...		...	...		...	...		...	...	
2 Mining and quarrying	...	...	67	...	...	57	...	...	70	...	...	5
3 Manufacturing	...	...	976	...	...	856	...	...	842	...	...	887
A Manufacture of food, beverages and tobacco	...	...	348	...	...	344	...	...	303	...	...	369
B Textile, wearing apparel and leather industries	...	...	134	...	...	124	...	...	117	...	...	123
C Manufacture of wood and wood products, including furniture	...	...	...	...	...	...	...	...	...	...	...	...
D Manufacture of paper and paper products, printing and publishing	...	...	...	...	...	...	...	...	...	...	...	...
E Manufacture of chemicals and chemical petroleum, coal, rubber and plastic products	...	...	98	...	...	54	...	...	66	...	...	63
F Manufacture of non-metallic mineral products, except products of petroleum and coal	...	...	36	...	...	36	...	...	31	...	...	33
G Basic metal industries	...	...	...	...	...	...	...	...	...	...	...	...
H Manufacture of fabricated metal products, machinery and equipment	...	...	230	...	...	198	...	...	210	...	...	178
I Other manufacturing industries	...	...	130	...	...	99	...	...	114	...	...	121
4 Electricity, gas and water	...	...	36	...	...	38	...	...	41	...	...	42
5 Construction	...	...	288	...	...	298	...	...	269	...	...	286
6 Wholesale and retail trade, restaurants and hotels	...	...	998	...	...	936	...	...	894	...	...	937
A Wholesale and retail trade	...	...	963	...	...	904	...	...	863	...	...	906
B Restaurants and hotels	...	...	35	...	...	32	...	...	31	...	...	31
7 Transport, storage and communication	...	...	99	...	...	103	...	...	97	...	...	106
8 Finance, insurance, real estate and business services	...	...	263	...	...	268	...	...	274	...	...	280
A Financial institutions	...	...	13	...	...	15	...	...	15	...	...	16
B Insurance	...	...		...	...		...	...		...	...	
C Real estate and business services	...	...	250	...	...	253	...	...	259	...	...	264
9 Community, social and personal services	...	...	149	...	...	167	...	...	143	...	...	161
Total, Industries	...	...	4599	...	...	4422	...	...	4259	...	...	4271
Producers of Government Services	...	...	515	...	...	539	...	...	549	...	...	540
Other Producers	...	...	...	...	...	...	...	...	...	...	...	...
Total	...	...	5114	...	...	4961	...	...	4808	...	...	4811
Less: Imputed bank service charge	...	...	...	...	...	...	...	...	...	...	...	...
Import duties	...	...	234	...	...	235	...	...	211	...	...	245
Value added tax	...	...	...	...	...	...	...	...	...	...	...	...
Total	...	...	5348	...	...	5196	...	...	5019	...	...	5056

Haiti

4.2 Derivation of Value Added by Kind of Activity, in Constant Prices

Million Haitian gourdes — Fiscal year ending 30 September

At constant prices of 1976 — All Producers

	1984 Gross Output	1984 Intermediate Consumption	1984 Value Added	1985 Gross Output	1985 Intermediate Consumption	1985 Value Added	1986 Gross Output	1986 Intermediate Consumption	1986 Value Added	1987 Gross Output	1987 Intermediate Consumption	1987 Value Added
1 Agriculture, hunting, forestry and fishing	...	...	1621	...	...	1631	...	...	1670	...	...	1688
A Agriculture and hunting	...	...	1381	...	...	1387	...	...	1422	...	...	1432
B Forestry and logging	...	...	[240	...	...	[244	...	...	[248	...	...	[256
C Fishing	...	...	5	...	...	6	...	...	5	...	...	8
2 Mining and quarrying	...	...	5	...	...	6	...	...	5	...	...	8
3 Manufacturing	...	...	836	...	...	812	...	...	815	...	...	783
A Manufacture of food, beverages and tobacco	...	...	326	...	...	332	...	...	335	...	...	292
B Textile, wearing apparel and leather industries	...	...	120	...	...	118	...	...	119	...	...	113
C Manufacture of wood and wood products, including furniture	...	...	...	...	...	...	...	...	...	...	...	...
D Manufacture of paper and paper products, printing and publishing	...	...	...	...	...	...	...	...	...	...	...	...
E Manufacture of chemicals and chemical petroleum, coal, rubber and plastic products	...	...	51	...	...	27	...	...	34	...	...	44
F Manufacture of non-metallic mineral products, except products of petroleum and coal	...	...	35	...	...	41	...	...	37	...	...	37
G Basic metal industries	...	...	...	...	...	...	...	...	...	...	...	...
H Manufacture of fabricated metal products, machinery and equipment	...	...	173	...	...	183	...	...	191	...	...	191
I Other manufacturing industries	...	...	130	...	...	112	...	...	99	...	...	105
4 Electricity, gas and water	...	...	45	...	...	46	...	...	47	...	...	49
5 Construction	...	...	291	...	...	327	...	...	308	...	...	315
6 Wholesale and retail trade, restaurants and hotels	...	...	904	...	...	914	...	...	912	...	...	902
A Wholesale and retail trade	...	...	876	...	...	885	...	...	888	...	...	873
B Restaurants and hotels	...	...	28	...	...	29	...	...	23	...	...	29
7 Transport, storage and communication	...	...	92	...	...	86	...	...	88	...	...	99
8 Finance, insurance, real estate and business services	...	...	285	...	...	283	...	...	290	...	...	291
A Financial institutions	...	...	[16	...	...	[9	...	...	[10	...	...	[6
B Insurance												
C Real estate and business services	...	...	269	...	...	274	...	...	280	...	...	285
9 Community, social and personal services	...	...	189	...	...	195	...	...	202	...	...	177
Total, Industries	...	...	4267	...	...	4300	...	...	4337	...	...	4313
Producers of Government Services	...	...	575	...	...	580	...	...	596	...	...	605
Other Producers	...	...	...	...	...	...	...	...	...	...	...	...
Total	...	...	4842	...	...	4880	...	...	4934	...	...	4918
Less: imputed bank service charge	...	...	...	...	...	...	...	...	...	...	...	...
Import duties	...	...	230	...	...	204	...	...	201	...	...	222
Value added tax	...	...	...	...	...	...	...	...	...	...	...	...
Total	...	...	5072	...	...	5084	...	...	5135	...	...	5140

At constant prices of 1976 — All Producers

	1988 Gross Output	1988 Intermediate Consumption	1988 Value Added	1989 Gross Output	1989 Intermediate Consumption	1989 Value Added
1 Agriculture, hunting, forestry and fishing	...	...	1722	...	...	1730
A Agriculture and hunting	...	...	1455	...	...	1456
B Forestry and logging	...	...	[266	...	...	[272
C Fishing	...	...	...	...	...	7
2 Mining and quarrying	...	...	8	...	...	7

Haiti

4.2 Derivation of Value Added by Kind of Activity, in Constant Prices
(Continued)

Million Haitian gourdes   Fiscal year ending 30 September

	1988			1989		
	Gross Output	Intermediate Consumption	Value Added	Gross Output	Intermediate Consumption	Value Added
			At constant prices of:1976			
3 Manufacturing	...	...	781	...	...	788
A Manufacture of food, beverages and tobacco	...	...	294	...	...	323
B Textile, wearing apparel and leather industries	...	...	112	...	...	107
C Manufacture of wood and wood products, including furniture	...	...	...	...	...	...
D Manufacture of paper and paper products, printing and publishing	...	...	...	...	...	...
E Manufacture of chemicals and chemical petroleum, coal, rubber and plastic products	...	...	46	...	...	42
F Manufacture of non-metallic mineral products, except products of petroleum and coal	...	...	40	...	...	35
G Basic metal industries	...	...	...	...	...	...
H Manufacture of fabricated metal products, machinery and equipment	...	...	183	...	...	207
I Other manufacturing industries	...	...	105	...	...	76
4 Electricity, gas and water	...	...	54	...	...	58
5 Construction	...	...	320	...	...	323
6 Wholesale and retail trade, restaurants and hotels	...	...	900	...	...	901
A Wholesale and retail trade	...	...	876	...	...	880
B Restaurants and hotels	...	...	24	...	...	21
7 Transport, storage and communication	...	...	105	...	...	108
8 Finance, insurance, real estate and business services	...	...	293	...	...	298
A Financial institutions	...	...	[6	...	...	[5
B Insurance	...	...	[	...	...	[
C Real estate and business services	...	...	287	...	...	293
9 Community, social and personal services	...	...	176	...	...	177
Total, Industries	...	...	4362	...	...	4391
Producers of Government Services	...	...	605	...	...	609
Other Producers	...	...	...	...	...	...
Total	...	...	4967	...	...	5000
Less: Imputed bank service charge	...	...	...	...	...	...
Import duties	...	...	220	...	...	232
Value added tax	...	...	...	...	...	...
Total	...	...	5187	...	...	5232

Honduras

General note. The preparation of national accounts statistics in Honduras is undertaken by the Departamento de Estudios Economicos, Banco Central de Honduras, Tegucigalpa, D.C. The official estimates are published in "Cuentas Nacionales". A detailed description of sources and methods used for the national accounts estimation is found in "Metodologia de cuentas nacionales de los paises centroamericanos" issued by the Consejo Monetario Centroamericano in October 1976. The estimates are generally in accordance with the classifications and definitions recommended in the United Nations System of National Accounts (SNA). The following tables have been prepared from successive replies to the United Nations national accounts questionnaire. When the scope and coverage of the estimates differ from conceptual or statistical reasons from the definitions and classifications recommended in SNA, a footnote is indicated to the relevant tables.

Sources and methods:
(a) Gross domestic product. Gross domestic product is estimated mainly through the production approach.
(b) Expenditure on the gross domestic product. The expenditure approach is used to estimate government final consumption expenditure and exports and imports of goods and services. The commodity-flow approach is used for private final consumption expenditure and for gross capital formation. Government final consumption expenditure is estimated on the basis of government accounts. Changes in stocks is estimated on the basis of information obtained from various sectors such as the banana industry, the mines, the petroleum sector and the trade enterprises. Private investment consists of gross value of production in the construction sector, plus imports and domestic production of capital goods which are adjusted to purchasers' values. Public investment is estimated from public sector data on settlements by type of construction and classes of machinery and equipment. The estimates on exports and imports of goods and services are based on the balance of payment data. Private consumption expenditure is estimated as a residual. For the constant price estimates, private final consumption expenditure is derived as a residual while all other items of GDP by expenditure type are deflated by various price indexes.
(c) Cost-structure of the gross domestic product. Estimates of labour income are derived from sources such as censuses and surveys, supplemented by information on wages and salaries paid by various government agencies and other public bodies. Estimates of profits of enterprises and professional incomes are obtained from the Direccion General del impuesto sobre la Renta. Estimates of interest and dividend payments received by household and private non-profit institutions are derived as a residual. Indirect taxes and subsidies are estimated on the basis of government sources. For consumption of fixed capital, no specific information is available.
(d) Gross domestic product by kind of economic activity. The table of gross domestic product by kind of economic activity is prepared in factor values. The production approach is used to estimate value added of most industries. The income approach is, however, used to estimate value added of producers of government services, part of the transport sectors and other private services. For the agricultural crop production, information is obtained directly from the most important export enterprises while for other products, estimates are obtained from consumption per capita data adjusted for exports and imports. Surveys are conducted to obtain information on basic production of grains. Agricultural censuses were held in 1953, 1965 and 1974. The Instituto Hondureño del Café provides complete information for coffee production. The banana companies in the northern zone are visited annually while for the rest of the country, consumption per capita data are taken into account together with prices collected from native producers. Livestock production information is gathered from the most important producers with adjustments made for clandestine or uncontrolled transactions. Inputs are estimated as 30 percent of the gross value of production. The production in the forestry sector is calculated as a function of household and industrial consumption of firewood, and information from the Direccion General de Pesca, the foreign trade statistics per capita consumption data. For metal mining, the statistical information is obtained directly while estimates for non-metallic mineral are based on inputs used in the construction sector using certain coefficients derived from analysis of construction costs. The estimates of manufacturing are based on censuses, surveys and sample data provided by the Direccion General de Industrias and the Departamento de Estudios Industriales. Information on electricity, gas and water is obtained directly from concerned enterprises. The data available cover gross values of production, aggregated values, physical production, installed capacity and personal occupation. Information on public construction is taken directly from the municipalities. Based on the information obtained from them, a sample is taken which the growth of private construction can be measured. For the trade sector, the estimates are also taken into account of manufacturing census for dwellings, the housing censuses and the gross value of agricultural and industrial production by item. The value of imports and exports are estimated from foreign trade statistics and expenditure received from the Direccion de Tributacion Directa. In estimating road transport, information on registered vehicles for rental is used. Data on income and expenditure by type of vehicle, depreciation and profits are obtained. Information for financial institutions is obtained from the Superintendencia de Bancos, which provides financial statements for all banks in the system and insurance companies. The estimates of ownership of dwellings are based on census information for 1949, 1961 and 1974 covering the number of dwellings and the average rents paid from the Contaduria General de la Nacion and the Asesoria Tecnica Municipal. For private services, use is made of employment data, classified by type of service rendered and data on average wages and salaries from other information sources. For domestic services, data on employment and wages are basis for estimating the value added in kind. For the constant price estimates, value added of the agricultural sector is either extrapolated by quantity indexes for output or deflated by price indexes. For the industrial activity sector, trade, transport and storage, financial institutions and private services, current values are extrapolated by quantity index. For the remaining sectors, current values are deflated by various price indexes.

1.1 Expenditure on the Gross Domestic Product, in Current Prices

Million Honduran lempiras

	1970	1975	1980	1981	1982	1983	1984	1985	1986	1987	1988	1989
1 Government final consumption expenditure	166	278	678	758	800	877	952	1046	1297	1371	1468	1607
2 Private final consumption expenditure	1009	1754	3563	4035	4310	4504	4764	5064	5380	5869	6558	7190
3 Gross capital formation	302	426	1248	1151	776	897	1231	1264	1075	1196	1166	1201
A Increase in stocks	34	-50	13	100	-190	-176	-95	12	-13	161	25	-105
B Gross fixed capital formation	268	476	1235	1051	996	1073	1326	1252	1088	1035	1141	1306
Residential buildings	44	73	132	126	143	146	149	162	160	176	252	271
Non-residential buildings	23	45	94	71	92	91	109	129	125	106	110	116
Other construction and land improvement etc.	77	126	181	352	463	529	587	572	391	335	301	459
Other	124	232	628	502	268	307	481	389	412	418	478	460
4 Exports of goods and services	395	680	1860	1735	1505	1556	1641	1754	1971	1874	1980	2135
5 Less: Imports of goods and services	490	890	2261	2126	1629	1799	2126	2120	2127	2182	2242	2351
Equals: Gross Domestic Product	1382	2248	5088	5553	5762	6035	6462	7008	7596	8128	8937	9782

1.2 Expenditure on the Gross Domestic Product, in Constant Prices

Million Honduran lempiras

At constant prices of 1978

	1970	1975	1980	1981	1982	1983	1984	1985	1986	1987	1988	1989
1 Government final consumption expenditure	271	337	512	524	507	513	532	560	668	689	715	730
2 Private final consumption expenditure	1638	1905	2732	2705	2767	2692	2738	2812	2864	3053	3270	3336
3 Gross capital formation	543	573	1021	856	511	620	875	869	736	791	752	714
A Increase in stocks	58	-64	10	75	-134	-119	-64	8	-8	96	14	-56
B Gross fixed capital formation	485	637	1011	781	645	739	939	861	744	695	738	770

Honduras

1.2 Expenditure on the Gross Domestic Product, in Constant Prices
(Continued)

Million Honduran lempiras

	1970	1975	1980	1981	1982	1983	1984	1985	1986	1987	1988	1989
	At constant prices of:1978											
Residential buildings	77	94	101	84	92	91	92	100	...	...	...	...
Non-residential buildings	41	55	70	47	60	57	68	80	...	...	...	...
Other construction and land improvement etc.	133	163	302	247	309	342	386	361	...	...	...	...
Other	234	325	538	403	184	249	393	320	...	...	...	...
4 Exports of goods and services	961	1124	1534	1569	1372	1516	1524	1582	1651	1655	1715	1794
5 Less: Imports of goods and services	1010	1063	1709	1501	1085	1279	1494	1500	1475	1514	1537	1544
Equals: Gross Domestic Product	2403	2876	4090	4153	4072	4062	4175	4323	4444	4674	4915	5030

1.3 Cost Components of the Gross Domestic Product

Million Honduran lempiras

	1970	1975	1980	1981	1982	1983	1984	1985	1986	1987	1988	1989
1 Indirect taxes, net	139	221	539	597	577	616	705	842	829	945	1036	1095
A Indirect taxes	141	223	545	610	594	627	756	902	881	984	1053	1109
B Less: Subsidies	2	2	6	13	17	11	51	60	52	39	17	14
2 Consumption of fixed capital	53	95	261	285	216	251	288	307	270	275	282	306
3 Compensation of employees paid by resident producers to:	572	962	2230	2498	2639	2848	3023	3185	3463	3712	4009	4236
4 Operating surplus	618	970	2058	2173	2330	2320	2446	2674	3034	3196	3610	4145
Equals: Gross Domestic Product	1382	2248	5088	5553	5762	6035	6462	7008	7596	8128	8937	9782

1.4 General Government Current Receipts and Disbursements

Million Honduran lempiras

	1970	1975	1980	1981	1982	1983	1984	1985	1986	1987	1988	1989
	Receipts											
1 Operating surplus	...	...	...	...	...	...	...	...	...	...	...	...
2 Property and entrepreneurial income	7	42	55	60	69	89	100	114	...	...	...	...
3 Taxes, fees and contributions	174	290	795	789	819	816	980	1101	...	...	...	...
A Indirect taxes [a]	124	185	496	538	542	544	661	766	856	947	986	1043
B Direct taxes	46	86	254	203	235	228	273	285	...	...	...	...
C Social security contributions	4	19	45	48	42	44	46	50	...	...	...	...
D Compulsory fees, fines and penalties	...	...	...	...	...	...	...	...	...	...	...	...
4 Other current transfers	13	37	58	65	77	107	142	207	...	...	...	...
Total Current Receipts of General Government	194	369	908	914	965	1012	1222	1422	...	...	...	...
	Disbursements											
1 Government final consumption expenditure	166	278	678	758	800	877	952	1046	1297	1371	1468	1607
2 Property income	8	20	58	57	81	119	137	153	...	...	...	...
3 Subsidies [b]	-15	-36	-43	-59	-35	-72	-44	-75	-27	-2	-50	-52
4 Other current transfers	9	15	47	43	47	49	54	61	...	...	...	...
5 Net saving	26	92	168	115	72	39	123	237	...	...	...	...
Total Current Disbursements and Net Saving of General Government	194	369	908	914	965	1012	1222	1422	...	...	...	...

a) Item 'Indirect taxes' includes profits of government enterprises.
b) Item 'Subsidies' includes losses of government enterprises.

1.6 Current Income and Outlay of Households and Non-Profit Institutions

Million Honduran lempiras

	1970	1975	1980	1981	1982	1983	1984	1985	1986	1987	1988	1989
	Receipts											
1 Compensation of employees	582	962	2230	2498	2639	2848	3023	3185	3463	3712	4009	4236
2 Operating surplus of private unincorporated enterprises	...	...	...	...	...	...	...	...	...	...	...	...
3 Property and entrepreneurial income	492	827	1572	1747	1827	1933	2058	2177	...	...	...	...
4 Current transfers	18	27	62	65	75	80	86	98	...	...	...	...
Total Current Receipts	1092	1816	3864	4310	4541	4861	5167	5460	...	...	...	...
	Disbursements											
1 Private final consumption expenditure	1009	1754	3563	4035	4310	4504	4764	5064	5380	5869	6568	7190

Honduras

1.6 Current Income and Outlay of Households and Non-Profit Institutions
(Continued)

Million Honduran lempiras

	1970	1975	1980	1981	1982	1983	1984	1985	1986	1987	1988	1989
2 Property income	5	9	16	17	16	21	24	27	...	...	...	...
3 Direct taxes and other current transfers n.e.c. to general government	29	70	212	182	206	205	236	221	...	...	...	...
A Social security contributions	...	...	...	...	...	...	...	...	...	...	...	...
B Direct taxes	29	70	212	182	206	205	236	221	...	...	...	...
C Fees, fines and penalties	...	...	...	...	...	...	...	...	...	...	...	...
4 Other current transfers	9	15	30	32	45	49	64	68	...	...	...	...
5 Net saving	40	-32	43	44	-36	82	79	80	...	...	...	...
Total Current Disbursements and Net Saving	1092	1816	3864	4310	4541	4861	5167	5460	...	...	...	...

1.7 External Transactions on Current Account, Summary

Million Honduran lempiras

	1970	1975	1980	1981	1982	1983	1984	1985	1986	1987	1988	1989
Payments to the Rest of the World												
1 Imports of goods and services	490	890	2261	2126	1629	1799	2126	2120	2127	2182	2242	2351
A Imports of merchandise c.i.f.	479	857	2189	2056	1565	1728	2026	2018	2024	2067	2122	2229
B Other	11	33	72	69	70	71	100	102	103	115	120	122
2 Factor income to the rest of the world	53	71	350	341	447	358	393	416	528	494	544	547
3 Current transfers to the rest of the world	7	12	32	30	20	22	23	24	25	26	26	24
4 Surplus of the nation on current transactions	-122	-226	-633	-605	-449	-438	-633	-408	-294	-450	-459	-543
Payments to the Rest of the World and Surplus of the Nation on Current Transactions	428	747	2010	1892	1647	1741	1909	2152	2386	2252	2353	2379
Receipts From The Rest of the World												
1 Exports of goods and services	395	680	1860	1735	1505	1556	1641	1754	1971	1874	1980	2135
A Exports of merchandise f.o.b.	369	624	1720	1586	1370	1414	1493	1598	1801	1708	1805	1953
B Other	26	56	140	149	135	142	149	156	169	166	175	182
2 Factor income from rest of the world	13	21	75	72	62	74	85	85	74	90	78	76
3 Current transfers from rest of the world	20	46	75	85	80	111	183	315	342	289	296	168
Receipts from the Rest of the World on Current Transactions	428	747	2010	1892	1647	1741	1909	2152	2386	2252	2353	2379

1.8 Capital Transactions of The Nation, Summary

Million Honduran lempiras

	1970	1975	1980	1981	1982	1983	1984	1985	1986	1987	1988	1989
Finance of Gross Capital Formation												
Gross saving	181	202	614	545	327	459	598	855	781	747	708	658
1 Consumption of fixed capital	53	95	261	285	216	251	288	307	270	275	282	306
A General government	13	22	51	61	75	74	87	96	98	92	96	112
B Corporate and quasi-corporate enterprises	17	37	102	116	67	84	...	...	...	...	...	...
C Other	23	36	108	108	74	93	...	...	...	...	...	...
2 Net saving	128	107	353	260	111	208	310	548	511	472	426	352
A General government	26	92	168	115	72	39	123	237	...	...	...	...
B Corporate and quasi-corporate enterprises	61	45	143	102	75	87	...	...	...	...	...	...
C Other	41	-30	42	43	-36	82	79	80	...	...	...	...
Less: Surplus of the nation on current transactions	-121	-224	-634	-606	-449	-438	-633	-409	-294	-449	-458	-543
Finance of Gross Capital Formation	302	426	1248	1151	776	897	1231	1264	1075	1196	1166	1201
Gross Capital Formation												
Increase in stocks	34	-50	13	100	-190	-176	-95	12	-13	161	25	-105
Gross fixed capital formation	268	476	1235	1051	966	1073	1326	1252	1088	1035	1141	1306
Gross Capital Formation	302	426	1248	1151	776	897	1231	1264	1075	1196	1166	1201

Honduras

1.10 Gross Domestic Product by Kind of Activity, in Current Prices

Million Honduran lempiras

	1970	1975	1980	1981	1982	1983	1984	1985	1986	1987	1988	1989
1 Agriculture, hunting, forestry and fishing	383	554	1132	1166	1186	1226	1253	1328	1495	1518	1630	1779
2 Mining and quarrying	28	51	96	93	105	109	117	131	114	105	118	134
3 Manufacturing	179	319	687	726	766	832	913	926	962	1055	1232	1369
4 Electricity, gas and water	13	27	64	71	78	87	99	103	232	236	242	255
5 Construction	63	108	296	290	382	356	359	366	350	311	343	395
6 Wholesale and retail trade, restaurants and hotels a	173	305	725	837	813	800	802	843	905	952	1019	1093
7 Transport, storage and communication	77	132	313	359	365	373	388	424	479	509	567	599
8 Finance, insurance, real estate and business services	152	253	538	587	622	719	823	923	1001	1094	1216	1389
9 Community, social and personal services a	131	212	481	564	597	631	677	758	846	964	1062	1125
Total, Industries	1199	1961	4332	4693	4918	5141	5445	5816	6384	6744	7429	8138
Producers of Government Services	44	66	217	263	267	278	312	350	383	439	472	549
Other Producers	...	...	...	...	...	...	...	...	...	...	...	...
Subtotal b	1243	2027	4549	4956	5185	5419	5757	6166	6767	7183	7901	8687
Less: Imputed bank service charge	...	...	...	...	...	...	...	...	...	...	...	...
Plus: Import duties	...	...	...	...	...	...	...	...	...	...	...	...
Plus: Value added tax	...	...	...	...	...	...	...	...	...	...	...	...
Plus: Other adjustments c	139	221	539	597	577	616	705	842	829	945	1036	1095
Equals: Gross Domestic Product	1382	2248	5088	5553	5762	6035	6462	7008	7596	8128	8937	9782

a) Restaurants and hotels are included in item 'Community, social and personal services'.
b) Gross domestic product in factor values.
c) Item 'Other adjustments' refers to indirect taxes net of subsidies.

1.11 Gross Domestic Product by Kind of Activity, in Constant Prices

Million Honduran lempiras

At constant prices of 1978

	1970	1975	1980	1981	1982	1983	1984	1985	1986	1987	1988	1989
1 Agriculture, hunting, forestry and fishing	752	751	1014	1053	1047	1040	1053	1084	1110	1156	1177	1203
2 Mining and quarrying	52	54	66	60	72	78	87	83	69	69	78	78
3 Manufacturing	287	398	538	525	506	533	578	568	585	644	698	710
4 Electricity, gas and water	19	32	49	49	50	50	52	55	110	112	114	117
5 Construction	111	139	251	193	241	225	222	218	199	166	177	183
6 Wholesale and retail trade, restaurants and hotels a	306	383	556	581	513	475	456	457	484	512	527	516
7 Transport, storage and communication	169	195	243	267	284	295	303	311	319	333	356	366
8 Finance, insurance, real estate and business services	239	313	416	434	433	444	454	476	488	518	565	607
9 Community, social and personal services a	186	250	360	362	349	344	340	357	378	406	430	425
Total, Industries	2121	2515	3493	3524	3495	3484	3545	3615	3756	3916	4113	4205
Producers of Government Services	40	79	164	169	182	163	175	189	198	218	225	239
Other Producers	...	...	...	...	...	...	...	...	...	...	...	...
Subtotal b	2161	2594	3657	3706	3664	3647	3720	3804	3954	4134	4338	4444
Less: Imputed bank service charge	...	...	...	...	...	...	...	...	...	...	...	...
Plus: Import duties	...	...	...	...	...	...	...	...	...	...	...	...
Plus: Value added tax	...	...	...	...	...	...	...	...	...	...	...	...
Plus: Other adjustments c	242	282	433	447	408	415	455	519	490	540	577	586
Equals: Gross Domestic Product	2403	2876	4090	4153	4072	4062	4175	4323	4444	4674	4915	5030

a) Restaurants and hotels are included in item 'Community, social and personal services'.
b) Gross domestic product in factor values.
c) Item 'Other adjustments' refers to indirect taxes net of subsidies.

1.12 Relations Among National Accounting Aggregates

Million Honduran lempiras

	1970	1975	1980	1981	1982	1983	1984	1985	1986	1987	1988	1989
Gross Domestic Product	1382	2248	5088	5553	5762	6035	6462	7008	7596	8128	8937	9782
Plus: Net factor income from the rest of the world	-40	-50	-275	-269	-385	-284	-308	-334	-455	-404	-466	-471
Factor income from the rest of the world	13	21	75	72	62	74	85	82	74	90	78	76
Less: Factor income to the rest of the world	53	71	350	341	447	358	393	416	529	494	544	547
Equals: Gross National Product	1342	2198	4813	5284	5377	5751	6154	6674	7141	7724	8471	9311
Less: Consumption of fixed capital	53	95	261	285	216	251	288	307	270	275	282	306

Honduras

1.12 Relations Among National Accounting Aggregates
(Continued)

Million Honduran lempiras

	1970	1975	1980	1981	1982	1983	1984	1985	1986	1987	1988	1989
Equals: National Income	1289	2103	4552	4999	5161	5500	5866	6367	6870	7449	8189	9005
Plus: Net current transfers from the rest of the world	13	34	43	55	60	89	160	291	317	263	270	144
Current transfers from the rest of the world	20	46	75	85	80	111	183	315	342	289	296	168
Less: Current transfers to the rest of the world	7	12	32	30	20	22	23	24	25	26	26	24
Equals: National Disposable Income	1302	2137	4595	5054	5221	5589	6026	6658	7187	7712	8459	9149
Less: Final consumption	1175	2032	4241	4793	5110	5381	5716	6110	6677	7240	8033	8797
Equals: Net Saving	127	105	354	261	111	208	310	548	511	472	426	352
Less: Surplus of the nation on current transactions	-122	-226	-633	-605	-449	-438	-633	-408	-294	-450	-459	-543
Equals: Net Capital Formation	249	331	987	866	560	646	943	957	805	921	884	895

2.1 Government Final Consumption Expenditure by Function, in Current Prices

Million Honduran lempiras

	1970	1975	1980	1981	1982	1983	1984	1985	1986	1987	1988	1989
1 General public services	45	68	216	242	236	263	296	391	468	413	436	412
2 Defence	21	43	114	121	134	140	162	188	211	245	264	276
3 Public order and safety	...	...	...	...	...	...	...	...	...	...	...	...
4 Education	48	77	151	186	209	225	244	269	315	366	404	449
5 Health	28	46	63	71	76	83	92	96	120	141	175	191
6 Social security and welfare	...	...	...	...	...	...	...	...	...	...	...	...
7 Housing and community amenities	...	...	...	...	...	...	...	...	...	...	...	...
8 Recreational, cultural and religious affairs	...	...	...	...	...	...	...	...	...	...	...	...
9 Economic services	...	...	...	...	...	...	...	...	...	...	...	...
10 Other functions	24	44	134	138	145	166	158	142	183	206	189	279
Total Government Final Consumption Expenditure	166	278	678	758	800	877	952	1046	1297	1371	1468	1607

2.5 Private Final Consumption Expenditure by Type and Purpose, in Current Prices

Million Honduran lempiras

	1970	1975	1980	1981	1982	1983	1984	1985	1986	1987	1988	1989
1 Food, beverages and tobacco	449	789	1605	1828	1943	2037	2144	2274	2241	2082	2446	
A Food	411	722	1470	1674	1780	1866	1963	2082	2241			
B Non-alcoholic beverages	32	56	114	130	137	144	152	161	173			
C Alcoholic beverages												
D Tobacco	6	11	21	24	26	27	29	31	32			
2 Clothing and footwear	90	159	323	368	391	410	432	458	493			
3 Gross rent, fuel and power	224	393	799	910	968	1015	1066	1133	1218			
4 Furniture, furnishings and household equipment and operation	83	145	295	336	357	375	393	419	450	...	...	...
A Household operation	38	66	135	154	164	172	180	192	206	...	...	...

Honduras

2.5 Private Final Consumption Expenditure by Type and Purpose, in Current Prices (Continued)

Million Honduran lempiras	1970	1975	1980	1981	1982	1983	1984	1985	1986	1987	1988	1989
Final Consumption Expenditure of Resident Households												
5 Medical care and health expenses	45	79	160	182	193	203	213	227	244	...	...	...
B Other	70	122	249	283	301	316	332	352	379	...	...	...
6 Transport and communication	30	53	107	121	129	135	142	151	162	...	...	...
7 Recreational, entertainment, education and cultural services	24	42	84	97	103	108	114	121	130	...	...	...
8 Miscellaneous goods and services	29	51	103	117	125	131	138	146	157	...	...	...
Total Final Consumption Expenditure in the Domestic Market by Households, of which	999	1754	3565	4060	4317	4527	4761	5054	5435	...	...	...
Plus: Direct purchases abroad by resident households	24	31	62	54	46	41	49	53	60	...	...	...
Less: Direct purchases in the domestic market by non-resident households	14	31	64	79	68	64	68	74	74	...	...	...
Equals: Final Consumption Expenditure of Resident Households a	1009	1754	3563	4035	4295	4504	4742	5033	5421	...	...	...
Final Consumption Expenditure of Private Non-profit Institutions Serving Households												
Equals: Final Consumption Expenditure of Private Non-profit Organisations Serving Households												
Private Final Consumption Expenditure b	1009	1754	3563	4035	4295	4504	4742	5033	5421	...	...	...

a) Item 'Final consumption expenditure of resident households' includes consumption expenditure. b) Data for this table have not been revised, therefore, data for some years are not comparable with those of other tables. of private non-profit institutions serving households.

2.6 Private Final Consumption Expenditure by Type and Purpose, in Constant Prices

Million Honduran lempiras	1970	1975	1980	1981	1982	1983	1984	1985	1986	1987	1988	1989
At constant prices of 1966												
Final Consumption Expenditure of Resident Households												
1 Food, beverages and tobacco	429	509	669	684	655	...	...	...	...	...	...	...
A Food	393	468	640	626	600	...	...	...	...	...	...	...
B Non-alcoholic beverages	30	34	49	48	46	...	...	...	...	...	...	...
C Alcoholic beverages	9	7	10	10	9	...	...	...	...	...	...	...
D Tobacco												
2 Clothing and footwear	87	102	141	138	133	...	...	...	...	...	...	...
3 Gross rent, fuel and power	213	252	346	340	325	...	...	...	...	...	...	...
4 Furniture, furnishings and household equipment and operation	79	93	129	126	121	...	...	...	...	...	...	...
A Household operation	36	42	70	69	66	...	...	...	...	...	...	...
B Other	43	51	59	57	55	...	...	...	...	...	...	...
5 Medical care and health expenses	66	79	108	106	101	...	...	...	...	...	...	...
6 Transport and communication	29	35	47	46	44	...	...	...	...	...	...	...
7 Recreational, entertainment, education and cultural services	23	28	45	43	42	...	...	...	...	...	...	...
8 Miscellaneous goods and services	28	34	38	37	35	...	...	...	...	...	...	...
Total Final Consumption Expenditure in the Domestic Market by Households, of which	954	1132	1553	1520	1456	...	...	...	...	...	...	...
Plus: Direct purchases abroad by resident households	22	21	27	24	22	...	...	...	...	...	...	...
Less: Direct purchases in the domestic market by non-resident households	14	20	25	31	28	...	...	...	...	...	...	...
Equals: Final Consumption Expenditure of Resident Households a	962	1133	1555	1513	1450	...	...	...	...	...	...	...
Final Consumption Expenditure of Private Non-profit Institutions Serving Households												
Equals: Final Consumption Expenditure of Private Non-profit Organisations Serving Households												
Private Final Consumption Expenditure b	962	1133	1555	1513	1450	...	...	...	...	...	...	...

a) Item 'Final consumption expenditure of resident households' includes consumption expenditure. b) Data for this table have not been revised, therefore, data for some years are not comparable with those of other tables. of private non-profit institutions serving households.

Honduras

2.7 Gross Capital Formation by Type of Good and Owner, in Current Prices

Million Honduran lempiras

	1980				1981				1982			
	TOTAL	Total Private	Public Enterprises	General Government	TOTAL	Total Private	Public Enterprises	General Government	TOTAL	Total Private	Public Enterprises	General Government
Increase in stocks, total	13	-20	29	4	100	63	45	-8	-190	-195	9	-4
Gross Fixed Capital Formation, Total	1235	758	265	212	1051	597	283	171	996	435	365	196
1 Residential buildings	132	...	...	...	126	...	...	...	143	...	...	...
2 Non-residential buildings	94	...	...	...	71	...	...	...	92	...	...	...
3 Other construction	346	...	...	...	330	...	...	...	433	...	...	...
4 Land improvement and plantation and orchard development	35	...	...	...	22	...	...	...	30	...	...	...
5 Producers' durable goods	628	...	...	...	502	...	...	...	268	...	...	...
A Transport equipment	177	...	...	...	110	...	...	...	69	...	...	...
B Machinery and equipment	451	...	...	...	392	...	...	...	199	...	...	...
6 Breeding stock, dairy cattle, etc.	...	...	...	...	...	...	...	...	...	...	...	...
Total Gross Capital Formation	1248	738	294	216	1151	660	328	163	776	240	374	162

	1983				1984				1985			
	TOTAL	Total Private	Public Enterprises	General Government	TOTAL	Total Private	Public Enterprises	General Government	TOTAL	Total Private	Public Enterprises	General Government
Increase in stocks, total	-176	-197	18	3	-95	...	...	...	12	...	...	...
Gross Fixed Capital Formation, Total	1073	463	419	190	1326	...	...	...	1252	...	...	...
1 Residential buildings	146	...	...	...	149	...	...	...	162	...	...	...
2 Non-residential buildings	91	...	...	...	109	...	...	...	129	...	...	...
3 Other construction	487	...	...	...	546	...	...	...	540	...	...	...
4 Land improvement and plantation and orchard development	42	...	...	...	40	...	...	...	32	...	...	...
5 Producers' durable goods	307	...	...	...	489	...	...	...	389	...	...	...
A Transport equipment	51	...	...	...	85	...	...	...	90	...	...	...
B Machinery and equipment	256	...	...	...	404	...	...	...	299	...	...	...
6 Breeding stock, dairy cattle, etc.	...	...	...	...	...	...	...	...	...	...	...	...
Total Gross Capital Formation	897	266	437	193	1231	...	...	...	1264	...	...	...

	1986				1987				1988			
	TOTAL	Total Private	Public Enterprises	General Government	TOTAL	Total Private	Public Enterprises	General Government	TOTAL	Total Private	Public Enterprises	General Government
Increase in stocks, total	-13	...	...	...	161	...	...	...	25	...	...	...
Gross Fixed Capital Formation, Total	1088	...	...	...	1035	...	...	...	1141	...	...	...
1 Residential buildings	160	...	...	...	176	...	...	...	252	...	...	...
2 Non-residential buildings	125	...	...	...	106	...	...	...	110	...	...	...
3 Other construction	359	...	...	...	297	...	...	...	245	...	...	...
4 Land improvement and plantation and orchard development	32	...	...	...	38	...	...	...	56	...	...	...
5 Producers' durable goods	412	...	...	...	418	...	...	...	478	...	...	...
A Transport equipment	88	...	...	...	122	...	...	...	153	...	...	...
B Machinery and equipment	324	...	...	...	296	...	...	...	325	...	...	...
6 Breeding stock, dairy cattle, etc.	...	...	...	...	...	...	...	...	...	...	...	...
Total Gross Capital Formation	1075	...	...	...	1196	...	...	...	1166	...	...	...

Honduras

2.7 Gross Capital Formation by Type of Good and Owner, in Current Prices

Million Honduran lempiras

	1989			
	TOTAL	Total Private	Public Enterprises	General Government
Increase in stocks, total	-105	...	...	...
Gross Fixed Capital Formation, Total	1306	...	...	...
1　Residential buildings	271	...	...	...
2　Non-residential buildings	116	...	...	...
3　Other construction	386	...	...	...
4　Land improvement and plantation and orchard development	73	...	...	...
5　Producers' durable goods	460	...	...	...
A Transport equipment	108	...	...	...
B Machinery and equipment	352	...	...	...
6　Breeding stock, dairy cattle, etc.	...	...	...	...
Total Gross Capital Formation	1201	...	...	...

2.8 Gross Capital Formation by Type of Good and Owner, in Constant Prices

Million Honduran lempiras

	1980				1981			
	TOTAL	Total Private	Public Enterprises	General Government	TOTAL	Total Private	Public Enterprises	General Government
	At constant prices of:1966							
Increase in stocks, total	30	6	22	2	30	10	19	1
Gross Fixed Capital Formation, Total	416	290	70	56	314	201	63	50
1　Residential buildings	54	...	...	...	45	...	...	...
2　Non-residential buildings	39	...	...	...	25	...	...	...
3　Other construction	72	...	...	...	88	...	...	...
4　Land improvement and plantation and orchard development	10	...	...	...	10	...	...	...
5　Producers' durable goods	241	...	...	...	146	...	...	...
A Transport equipment	70	...	...	...	26	...	...	...
B Machinery and equipment	171	...	...	...	120	...	...	...
6　Breeding stock, dairy cattle, etc.	...	...	...	...	...	...	...	...
Total Gross Capital Formation	446	296	92	58	344	211	82	51

2.11 Gross Fixed Capital Formation by Kind of Activity of Owner, ISIC Divisions, in Current Prices

Million Honduran lempiras

	1970	1975	1980	1981	1982	1983	1984	1985	1986	1987	1988	1989
	All Producers											
1　Agriculture, hunting, forestry and fishing	52	80	292	218	...	...	...	...	...	...	...	...
2　Mining and quarrying	5	11	-8	32	...	...	...	...	...	...	...	...
3　Manufacturing	41	72	125	98	...	...	...	...	...	...	...	...
4　Electricity, gas and water	25	25	171	209	...	...	...	...	...	...	...	...
5　Construction	7	15	87	72	...	...	...	...	...	...	...	...
6　Wholesale and retail trade, restaurants and hotels	39	37	134	108	...	...	...	...	...	...	...	...
7　Transport, storage and communication	28	30	151	177	...	...	...	...	...	...	...	...
8　Finance, insurance, real estate and business services	51	55	75	65	...	...	...	...	...	...	...	...
9　Community, social and personal services	31	70	135	91	...	...	...	...	...	...	...	...
Total Industries	279	395	1162	1070	...	...	...	...	...	...	...	...
Producers of Government Services	23	31	86	81	...	...	...	...	...	...	...	...
Private Non-Profit Institutions Serving Households	...	...	...	...	...	...	...	...	...	...	...	...
Total	268	476	1235	1051	...	...	...	...	...	...	...	...

Honduras

2.17 Exports and Imports of Goods and Services, Detail

Million Honduran lempiras

	1970	1975	1980	1981	1982	1983	1984	1985	1986	1987	1988	1989
Exports of Goods and Services												
1 Exports of merchandise, f.o.b.	369	624	1720	1586	1385	1414	1514	1599	1801	...	...	...
2 Transport and communication	21	47	124	131	117	114	120	126	140	...	...	...
3 Insurance service charges												
4 Other commodities	5	9	16	18	18	28	29	29	30	...	...	...
5 Adjustments of merchandise exports to change-of-ownership basis												
6 Direct purchases in the domestic market by non-residential households												
7 Direct purchases in the domestic market by extraterritorial bodies	...	...	...	...	...	...	...	...	...	...	...	...
Total Exports of Goods and Services	395	680	1860	1735	1520	1556	1663	1754	1971	...	...	...
Imports of Goods and Services												
1 Imports of merchandise, c.i.f.	479	857	2189	2057	1565	1729	2026	2018	2014	...	...	...
A Imports of merchandise, f.o.b.	407	745	1908	1797	1361	1513	1769	1758	1741	...	...	...
B Transport of services on merchandise imports	72	112	281	260	204	216	257	260	273	...	...	...
C Insurance service charges on merchandise imports												
2 Adjustments of merchandise imports to change-of-ownership basis												
3 Other transport and communication												
4 Other insurance service charges												
5 Other commodities	11	33	72	69	64	70	100	102	105	...	...	...
6 Direct purchases abroad by government												
7 Direct purchases abroad by resident households												
Total Imports of Goods and Services	490	890	2261	2126	1629	1799	2126	2120	2119	...	...	...
Balance of Goods and Services	-95	-210	-401	-391	-109	-243	-463	-366	-148	...	...	...
Total Imports and Balance of Goods and Services a	395	680	1860	1735	1520	1556	1663	1754	1971	...	...	...

a) Data for this table have not been revised, therefore, data for some years are not comparable with those of other tables.

Hong Kong

General note. The preparation of national accounts statistics in Hong Kong is undertaken by the Census and Statistics Department, Hong Kong. The official estimates together with methodological notes of the estimates have been published annually since 1973. The estimates are generally in accordance with the definitions and classifications recommended in the United Nations System of National Accounts (SNA). The following tables have been prepared from successive replies to the United Nations national accounts questionnaire received from the Overseas Development Administration, Foreign and Commonwealth Office, London. When the scope and coverage of the estimates differ from the conceptual or statistical reasons from the definitions and classifications recommended in SNA, a footnote is indicated to the relevant tables.

Sources and methods:

(a) Gross domestic product. Gross domestic product is estimated mainly through the expenditure approach.

(b) Expenditure on the gross domestic product. The expenditure approach is used to estimate government final consumption expenditure and exports and imports of goods and services. The commodity-flow approach is used for private final consumption expenditure and gross capital formation supplemented by the expenditure approach. Government consumption expenditure data up to 1972 were obtained from the Annual Reports of the Accountant-General which provided data on the actual expenditure of each department by financial year ending 31 March. Since 1973, quarterly figures have been available from the Treasury and adjustment to a calendar year basis is no longer required. The estimates relate to current expenditure on goods and services by government departments not engaged in trading activities. For the large proportion of the commodities included in private consumption expenditure which is imported, adequate and detailed trade statistics are available. Trade statistics of retained imports are supported and complemented by data from the household expenditure surveys, censuses/surveys of manufacturing establishments, sample surveys on sales of business establishments, administrative statistics and other sources. Foodstuffs produced domestically for local consumption are compiled from the annual output estimates made by the Agriculture and Fisheries Department and other government departments concerned. Imported and domestically produced commodities are reported in importers' and producers' values, respectively, and the retail value is arrived at by adding transport expenses and distributors' profit margins. Estimates of change in stock of distributors and manufacturers have been compiled based on results of the censuses/surveys of manufacturing establishments and distributive trades from companies are obtained from the Industry Department. For gross fixed capital formation, investment in plant, machinery and equipment is based mainly on the value of retained imports of capital goods, with a percentage added to allow for profit, transport, assembly charges and installation expenses. Estimates of domestically manufactured plant, machinery and equipment purchased locally are calculated from results of the censuses/surveys of manufacturing establishments. Private sector investment in building and construction prior to 1979 is based on monthly statistical returns of the Building Ordinance Office. From 1979 it is based on the results of annual Survey of Building, Construction and Real Estate Sectors while investment in the government sector is obtained from an analysis of accounts of government departments. The estimates of exports and imports of merchandise are obtained from detailed external trade statistics. For port and airport charges and expenditure of non-residents in Hong Kong and that of Hong Kong residents abroad, the main sources of data are the surveys conducted by the Hong Kong Tourist Association, surveys on expenditure of Hong Kong residents abroad, and government accounts. The estimates of other items of imports and exports of services were not available prior to 1978. From 1978 onwards, an annual survey of imports and exports of services has been conducted to provide estimates in respect of the other items of services. Token estimates were made for years prior to 1978 based on benchmark information obtained from the annual survey. For the constant price estimates, price deflators are used for most of the expenditure items. The current values are deflated by various price indexes such as specially constructed salary rate index, consumer price indexes, tourist price index, cost index of building and construction, overall index of unit values of exports and imports, etc. For increase in stocks, unit value index of imports of appropriate commodity groups are used.

(c) Cost-structure of the gross domestic product. The main components of the table from economic censuses and operating surplus are compiled using the production approach. Data, available since 1980, are based on information collected from economic censuses/surveys conducted for the various major economic sectors.

(d) Gross domestic product by kind of economic activity. The estimates are compiled using the production approach. Data, available since 1980, are based on information collected from economic censuses/surveys conducted for the various major economic sectors.

1.1 Expenditure on the Gross Domestic Product, in Current Prices

Million Hong Kong dollars

	1970	1975	1980	1981	1982	1983	1984	1985	1986	1987	1988	1989
1 Government final consumption expenditure	1639	3526	8828	12402	14910	16724	18292	19916	22969	25779	30008	36334
2 Private final consumption expenditure	14779	31195	85262	102454	118928	138826	158805	168855	191677	221756	255745	284241
A Households	14066	29373	80898	96928	111928	130772	149826	158654	185537	207956	239301	264393
B Private non-profit institutions serving households	713	1822	4364	5526	7000	8054	9112	10301	12140	13800	16444	19848
3 Gross capital formation	4683	11259	59060	49293	54976	56197	61381	58684	72122	99016	126230	130090
A Increase in stocks	171	731	3745	3953	4403	4329	5803	1469	6183	6746	1479	2512
B Gross fixed capital formation	4512	10528	45548	55407	57858	51868	55578	57115	65939	89272	112051	128388
Residential buildings a	529	1477	6433	7206	8422	8210	8797	9816	11667	12868	17390	19050
Non-residential buildings	478	1037	5062	6957	8429	8545	7867	7479	6803	9922	12036	15638
Other construction and land improvement, etc. b	378	1668	6238	7737	9537	9616	9123	7739	8659	11755	14128	17855
Other	3127	6346	27815	33505	31470	25494	29791	30081	38810	54727	68497	75845
4 Exports of goods and services	20330	38507	149318	149318	157989	197624	265288	309817	330817	448866	578476	668929
5 Less: Imports of goods and services	19552	38023	126706	158561	164760	201809	254838	266158	316767	426144	556378	627754
Equals: Gross Domestic Product	21879	46464	130701	164973	186328	207562	247562	261195	300818	369275	434081	490550

a) Item 'Residential buildings' includes also combined residential and non-residential buildings.
b) Land improvement and plantation and orchard development refers to transfer costs of land and buildings.

1.2 Expenditure on the Gross Domestic Product, in Constant Prices

Million Hong Kong dollars

	1970	1975	1980	1981	1982	1983	1984	1985	1986	1987	1988	1989
At constant prices of: 1980												
1 Government final consumption expenditure	4125	5760	8828	10790	11391	11994	12323	12546	13328	13889	14600	15445
2 Private final consumption expenditure	33167	46002	85262	91723	96693	104658	115076	110620	125267	138489	150075	154645
A Households	31385	42996	80898	86953	91920	98828	104523	108599	118387	131372	142691	146860
B Private non-profit institutions serving households	1782	3006	4364	4770	5303	5730	6097	6477	6880	7117	7384	7785
3 Gross capital formation	14395	21870	49293	53387	51599	49414	50927	47562	54304	63496	69069	63972

Hong Kong

1.2 Expenditure on the Gross Domestic Product, in Constant Prices (Continued)

Million Hong Kong dollars

	1970	1975	1980	1981	1982	1983	1984	1985	1986	1987	1988	1989
			At constant prices of 1980									
A Increase in stocks	491	901	3745	3796	1185	3217	3999	1026	4394	6324	8195	2275
B Gross fixed capital formation	13904	20969	45548	45591	50414	46197	49728	46536	49910	57172	60874	61697
Residential buildings a	1818	3083	6433	6463	6339	6665	6912	7702	8616	8201	8937	8546
Non-residential buildings	1643	2165	5062	6240	6946	6938	8146	5650	4806	5939	5918	6990
Other construction and land improvement etc. b	1634	3854	6238	6745	8049	8203	7481	6328	6799	8142	7858	8213
Other	8809	11867	27815	30143	28480	24391	26389	26656	29689	34890	38161	38258
4 Exports of goods and services	49049	59244	120404	137072	134992	153658	183367	193821	223433	291523	362188	397502
5 Less: Imports of goods and services	44892	55115	126706	142985	140463	155174	177688	189059	214982	277976	348387	378428
Equals: Gross Domestic Product	55844	76761	137081	149987	154512	164550	180149	201350	229421	247545	253136	

a) Item 'Residential buildings' includes also combined residential and non-residential buildings.
b) Land improvement and plantation and orchard development refers to transfer costs of land and buildings.

1.3 Cost Components of the Gross Domestic Product

Million Hong Kong dollars

	1970	1975	1980	1981	1982	1983	1984	1985	1986	1987	1988	1989
1 Indirect taxes, net	...	...	5196	6117	6230	8103	9894	12333	14750	18649	21451	
2 Consumption of fixed capital a	...	...	...	...	...	...	...	...	...	...	...	
3 Compensation of employees paid by resident producers to:	...	...	63027	77248	90088	101558	119318	131708	148927	175953	205325	
4 Operating surplus a	...	...	65386	63472	58008	86112	92421	110174	132515	172364	208024	
Statistical discrepancy b	...	...	3472	770	3898	5480	8542	6439	4545	2309	-719	
Equals: Gross Domestic Product	...	...	137081	164973	183628	207562	247628	261195	300818	369275	434081	

a) Item 'Operating surplus' includes consumption of fixed capital.
b) The estimates shown refers to the difference between production estimate and expenditure estimate.

1.10 Gross Domestic Product by Kind of Activity, in Current Prices

Million Hong Kong dollars

	1970	1975	1980	1981	1982	1983	1984	1985	1986	1987	1988	1989
1 Agriculture, hunting, forestry and fishing	...	...	1109	1122	1229	1242	1273	1238	1332	1358	1437	
2 Mining and quarrying	...	...	213	253	306	308	316	299	385	346	257	229
3 Manufacturing	...	...	30549	36049	36390	44140	55355	53071	62779	75761	83182	
4 Electricity, gas and water	...	...	1703	2229	3243	4740	5687	6666	8385	9691	10200	
5 Construction	...	...	8570	11922	12904	12269	12218	12038	13556	16400	19900	
6 Wholesale and retail trade, restaurants and hotels	...	...	26169	30749	33647	37893	51117	52831	58960	80720	98518	
7 Transport, storage and communication	...	...	9645	11853	13632	15980	17958	19677	22855	30309	38029	
8 Finance, insurance, real estate and business services a	...	...	41589	51263	58869	57465	61381	62661	78641	99266	122941	
9 Community, social and personal services	...	...	7247	9866	13017	14694	16898	19512	20797	22777	26355	
Statistical discrepancy	...	...	3472	770	3898	5480	8542	6439	4545	2309	-719	
Total, Industries	...	...	130266	157979	176957	194219	230608	238117	273166	338848	400072	
Producers of Government Services	...	...	5665	7133	9646	11258	12973	14789	17062	19150	22019	
Other Producers	...	...	3154	4069	4900	5829	6758	7678	8919	10371	11821	
Subtotal b	...	...	139085	169181	191503	211306	250339	260584	299147	368369	433912	
Less: Imputed bank service charge	...	...	7200	10325	11405	11847	11725	11722	13079	17743	21282	
Plus: Import duties	...	...	...	...	...	...	...	...	...	...	...	
Plus: Value added tax	...	...	...	...	...	...	...	...	...	...	...	
Plus: Other adjustments c	...	...	5196	6117	6230	8103	9894	12333	14750	18649	21451	
Equals: Gross Domestic Product	...	...	137081	164973	186328	207562	248728	261195	300818	369275	434081	

a) Finance is included in item 'Wholesale and retail trade, restaurants and hotels'.
b) Gross domestic product in factor values.
c) Item 'Other adjustments' refers to indirect taxes net of subsidies.

2.5 Private Final Consumption Expenditure by Type and Purpose, in Current Prices

Million Hong Kong dollars

	1970	1975	1980	1981	1982	1983	1984	1985	1986	1987	1988	1989
			Final Consumption Expenditure of Resident Households									
1 Food, beverages and tobacco	5497	10211	19466	23266	26456	30313	32861	33377	35051	38860	43410	48430
A Food	4835	9154	17519	20889	23724	27327	29727	29922	31282	34611	38296	42551
B Non-alcoholic beverages												772
C Alcoholic beverages	358	591	1040	1319	1470	1580	1564	1693	2091	2652	3137	3287

Hong Kong

2.5 Private Final Consumption Expenditure by Type and Purpose, in Current Prices
(Continued)

Million Hong Kong dollars

	1970	1975	1980	1981	1982	1983	1984	1985	1986	1987	1988	1989
D Tobacco	304	466	907	1058	1262	1406	1570	1762	1658	1597	1977	2592
2 Clothing and footwear a	2718	4871	16776	18030	21247	25665	29330	31339	39214	48143	58126	61116
3 Gross rent, fuel and power	2165	4792	12053	14773	17704	20796	23502	25580	28543	32271	37597	43773
4 Furniture, furnishings and household equipment and operation	1430	2435	9329	12161	12777	15803	19566	19811	23947	28937	33526	34239
A Household operation	276	543	1502	1845	2170	2431	2753	3052	3423	3860	4499	5080
B Other	1154	1892	7827	10316	10607	13372	16813	16759	20524	25077	29027	29159
5 Medical care and health expenses	758	1703	4449	5272	6096	7937	8961	9720	10706	12352	13482	15119
6 Transport and communication	1232	2119	6554	7985	9598	10545	12228	13306	14480	17222	21106	23197
7 Recreational, entertainment, education and cultural services	1369	2422	6590	8303	9674	11271	13519	15425	17209	20716	24568	28371
A Education	285	504	885	1045	1208	1363	1568	1715	1937	2185	2460	2841
B Other	1084	1918	5705	7258	8466	9908	11951	13710	15272	18531	22108	25530
8 Miscellaneous goods and services	652	1931	5997	7834	8808	9771	11695	13161	14533	18620	20638	24240
Total Final Consumption Expenditure in the Domestic Market by Households, of which	15821	30484	81214	97624	112360	132101	151662	161719	183663	217121	252453	278485
Plus: Direct purchases abroad by resident households	670	2039	6483	7757	8681	10424	12268	13056	14424	17079	21259	24011
Less: Direct purchases in the domestic market by non-resident households	2425	3150	6799	8453	9113	11753	14437	15221	18550	26244	34411	38103
Equals: Final Consumption Expenditure of Resident Households	14066	29373	80898	96928	111928	130772	149493	159554	179537	207956	239301	264393

Final Consumption Expenditure of Private Non-profit Institutions Serving Households

	1970	1975	1980	1981	1982	1983	1984	1985	1986	1987	1988	1989
Equals: Final Consumption Expenditure of Private Non-profit Organisations Serving Households	713	1822	4364	5526	7000	8054	9112	10301	12140	13800	16444	19848
Private Final Consumption Expenditure	14779	31195	85262	102454	118928	138826	158605	169855	191677	221756	255745	284241

a) Personal effects are included in item 'Clothing and footwear'.

2.6 Private Final Consumption Expenditure by Type and Purpose, in Constant Prices

Million Hong Kong dollars

	1970	1975	1980	1981	1982	1983	1984	1985	1986	1987	1988	1989
At constant prices of:1980												
Final Consumption Expenditure of Resident Households												
1 Food, beverages and tobacco	12309	14696	19466	20433	21405	22023	22069	22655	23504	24472	25128	25377
A Food	10897	13160	17519	18291	19104	20188	20425	20978	21779	22609	22961	23100
B Non-alcoholic beverages	...	...	...	...	...	...	...	...	...	...	...	...
C Alcoholic beverages	681	756	1040	1190	1280	1117	962	985	1114	1309	1512	1474
D Tobacco	731	780	907	952	1021	718	682	692	611	554	655	803
2 Clothing and footwear a	6862	6665	16776	17129	18559	20339	21038	21848	25508	28772	32520	31996
3 Gross rent, fuel and power	4956	7668	12053	12995	14170	15403	16383	16947	18457	20239	22766	25013
4 Furniture, furnishings and household equipment and operation	2705	3438	9329	11152	11256	13122	14874	14953	17335	19921	21710	21139
A Household operation	810	1001	1502	1590	1618	1651	1693	1749	1859	1966	2067	2105
B Other	1895	2437	7827	9562	9638	11471	13181	13204	15476	17955	19643	19034
5 Medical care and health expenses	1766	2717	4449	4647	4797	5564	5485	5610	5973	6674	6736	6968
6 Transport and communication	2924	3530	6554	6946	7154	7116	7425	7665	7962	8948	10348	10643
7 Recreational, entertainment, education and cultural services	3044	3682	6590	7438	7790	8531	9385	10152	10774	12382	13696	15073
A Education	502	679	885	914	909	865	867	824	835	835	813	799

773

Hong Kong

2.6 Private Final Consumption Expenditure by Type and Purpose, in Constant Prices
(Continued)

Million Hong Kong dollars

	1970	1975	1980	1981	1982	1983	1984	1985	1986	1987	1988	1989
					At constant prices of:1980							
B Other	2542	3003	5705	6524	6881	7666	8518	9328	9939	11547	12883	14274
8 Miscellaneous goods and services	1817	3051	5997	6747	6647	6809	7582	8275	8939	11334	11241	11718
Total Final Consumption Expenditure in the Domestic Market by Households, of which	36383	45447	81214	87487	91778	98907	104241	108105	118452	132742	144145	147927
Plus: Direct purchases abroad by resident households	1535	2963	6483	7154	7585	8763	9832	10131	10956	12766	15352	16333
Less: Direct purchases in the domestic market by non-resident households	6533	5414	6799	7688	7673	8742	9550	9637	11021	14136	16806	17400
Equals: Final Consumption Expenditure of Resident Households	31385	42996	80898	86953	91690	98928	104523	108599	118387	131372	142691	146860

Final Consumption Expenditure of Private Non-profit Institutions Serving Households

	1970	1975	1980	1981	1982	1983	1984	1985	1986	1987	1988	1989
Equals: Final Consumption Expenditure of Private Non-profit Organisations Serving Households	1782	3006	4364	4770	5303	5730	6097	6477	6880	7117	7384	7785
Private Final Consumption Expenditure	33167	46002	85262	91723	96993	104658	110620	115076	125267	138489	150075	154645

a) Personal effects are included in item 'Clothing and footwear'.

2.7 Gross Capital Formation by Type of Good and Owner, in Current Prices

Million Hong Kong dollars

	1980				1981				1982			
	TOTAL	Total Private	Public Enterprises	General Government	TOTAL	Total Private	Public Enterprises	General Government	TOTAL	Total Private	Public Enterprises	General Government
Increase in stocks, total	3745	3745	...	...	3953	3953	...	...	1403	1403	...	...
Gross Fixed Capital Formation, Total	45548	38825	...	...	55407	47205	...	...	57858	46352	...	...
1 Residential buildings a	6433	4553	...	...	7208	5214	...	...	8422	5946	...	...
2 Non-residential buildings	5062	4533	...	...	6957	6090	...	...	8429	7113	...	...
3 Other construction	5128	1440	...	...	5772	1506	...	...	7936	1388	...	...
4 Land improvement and plantation and orchard development b	1110	1110	...	...	1965	1965	...	...	1601	1601	...	...
5 Producers' durable goods	14545	13919	...	...	17615	16540	...	...	16988	15822	...	...
A Transport equipment	3647	3178	...	...	3642	2846	...	...	3571	2748	...	...
B Machinery and equipment	10898	10741	...	...	13973	13694	...	...	13417	13074	...	...
6 Breeding stock, dairy cattle, etc.	...	...	...	...	...	...	...	...	...	...	...	...
Statistical discrepancy c	13270	13270	...	...	15890	15890	...	...	14482	14482	...	...
Total Gross Capital Formation	49293	42570	...	...	59360	51158	...	...	59261	47755	...	...

	1983				1984				1985			
	TOTAL	Total Private	Public Enterprises	General Government	TOTAL	Total Private	Public Enterprises	General Government	TOTAL	Total Private	Public Enterprises	General Government
Increase in stocks, total	4329	4329	...	...	5803	5803	...	...	1469	1469	...	...
Gross Fixed Capital Formation, Total	51868	39719	...	...	55578	44397	...	...	55115	46426	...	...
1 Residential buildings a	8210	5751	...	...	8797	6399	...	...	9816	7680	...	...
2 Non-residential buildings	8545	7106	...	...	7867	6379	...	...	7479	6013	...	...
3 Other construction	8357	1382	...	...	7750	1501	...	...	5675	1402	...	...
4 Land improvement and plantation and orchard development b	1262	1262	...	...	1373	1373	...	...	2064	2064	...	...
5 Producers' durable goods	18294	17018	...	...	23422	22376	...	...	23334	22520	...	...
A Transport equipment	3036	2230	...	...	2763	2470	...	...	3273	3036	...	...
B Machinery and equipment	15258	14788	...	...	20659	19906	...	...	20061	19484	...	...
6 Breeding stock, dairy cattle, etc.	...	...	...	...	...	...	...	...	...	...	...	...
Statistical discrepancy c	7200	7200	...	...	6369	6369	...	...	6747	6747	...	...
Total Gross Capital Formation	56197	44048	...	...	61381	50200	...	...	56584	47895	...	...

	1986				1987				1988			
	TOTAL	Total Private	Public Enterprises	General Government	TOTAL	Total Private	Public Enterprises	General Government	TOTAL	Total Private	Public Enterprises	General Government
Increase in stocks, total	6183	6183	...	...	9746	9746	...	...	14179	14179	...	...
Gross Fixed Capital Formation, Total	65939	57297	...	...	89272	78377	...	...	112051	98668	...	...
1 Residential buildings a	11667	9347	...	...	12868	9719	...	...	17390	13123	...	...
2 Non-residential buildings	6803	5177	...	...	9922	8133	...	...	12036	10130	...	...
3 Other construction	5933	1894	...	...	7472	2343	...	...	9076	3152	...	...

774

Hong Kong

2.7 Gross Capital Formation by Type of Good and Owner, in Current Prices
(Continued)

Million Hong Kong dollars

	1986				1987				1988			
	TOTAL	Total Private	Public Enterprises	General Government	TOTAL	Total Private	Public Enterprises	General Government	TOTAL	Total Private	Public Enterprises	General Government
4 Land improvement and plantation and orchard development b	2726	2726	...	...	4283	4283	...	...	5052	5052	...	...
5 Producers' durable goods	29273	28616	...	...	39834	39006	...	...	47691	46405	...	...
A Transport equipment	4301	4028	...	...	7234	6880	...	...	6016	5474	...	...
B Machinery and equipment	24972	24588	...	...	32600	32126	...	...	41675	40931	...	...
6 Breeding stock, dairy cattle, etc.	...	...	...	...	...	...	...	...	...	...	...	...
Statistical discrepancy c	9537	9537	...	...	14893	14893	...	...	20806	20806	...	...
Total Gross Capital Formation	72122	63480	9018	8823	126230	128847	...	...	...	...	...	...

	1989			
	TOTAL	Total Private	Public Enterprises	General Government
Increase in stocks, total	2512	2512	...	...
Gross Fixed Capital Formation, Total	128388	110986	...	...
1 Residential buildings a	19050	13824	...	...
2 Non-residential buildings	15838	12242	...	...
3 Other construction	12016	4773	...	...
4 Land improvement and plantation and orchard development b	5839	5839	...	...
5 Producers' durable goods	50403	48866	...	...
A Transport equipment	7408	6674	...	...
B Machinery and equipment	42995	42192	...	...
6 Breeding stock, dairy cattle, etc.	...	...	...	...
Statistical discrepancy c	25442	25442	...	...
Total Gross Capital Formation	130900	113498	...	...

a) Item 'Residential buildings' includes also combined residential and non-residential buildings.
b) Item 'Land improvement and plantation and orchard development' refers to transfer costs of land and buildings.
c) Item 'Statistical discrepancy' refers to real estate developers' margin.

2.8 Gross Capital Formation by Type of Good and Owner, in Constant Prices

Million Hong Kong dollars

	1980				1981				1982			
	TOTAL	Total Private	Public Enterprises	General Government	TOTAL	Total Private	Public Enterprises	General Government	TOTAL	Total Private	Public Enterprises	General Government

At constant prices of 1980

Increase in stocks, total	3745	3745	...	...	3796	3796	...	...	1185	1185	...	...
Gross Fixed Capital Formation, Total	45548	38825	...	...	49591	42254	...	...	50414	40975	...	...
1 Residential buildings a	6433	4553	...	...	6463	4675	...	...	6939	4901	...	...
2 Non-residential buildings	5062	4533	...	...	6240	5462	...	...	6946	5862	...	...
3 Other construction	5128	1440	...	...	5177	1351	...	...	6532	1143	...	...
4 Land improvement and plantation and orchard development b	1110	1110	...	...	1568	1568	...	...	1517	1517	...	...
5 Producers' durable goods	14545	13919	...	...	15730	14785	...	...	13522	12594	...	...
A Transport equipment	3647	3178	...	...	3262	2565	...	...	2845	2189	...	...
B Machinery and equipment	10898	10741	...	...	12468	12220	...	...	10677	10405	...	...
6 Breeding stock, dairy cattle, etc.	...	...	...	...	...	...	...	...	...	...	...	...
Statistical discrepancy c	13270	13270	...	...	14413	14413	...	...	14958	14958	...	...
Total Gross Capital Formation	49293	42570	...	...	53387	46050	...	...	51599	42160	...	...

	1983				1984				1985			
	TOTAL	Total Private	Public Enterprises	General Government	TOTAL	Total Private	Public Enterprises	General Government	TOTAL	Total Private	Public Enterprises	General Government

At constant prices of 1980

Increase in stocks, total	3217	3217	...	...	3999	3999	...	...	1026	1026	...	...
Gross Fixed Capital Formation, Total	46197	36468	...	...	49628	38271	...	...	46356	39737	...	...
1 Residential buildings a	6665	4669	...	...	6912	4994	...	...	7702	5786	...	...
2 Non-residential buildings	6938	5769	...	...	6146	4981	...	...	5650	4532	...	...
3 Other construction	6770	1120	...	...	6052	1172	...	...	4282	1057	...	...

Hong Kong

2.8 Gross Capital Formation by Type of Good and Owner, in Constant Prices
(Continued)

Million Hong Kong dollars

	1983				1984				1985			
	TOTAL	Private Total	Public Enterprises	General Government	TOTAL	Private Total	Public Enterprises	General Government	TOTAL	Private Total	Public Enterprises	General Government

At constant prices of 1980

4 Land improvement and plantation and orchard development b	1433	1433	...	...	1429	1429	...	...	2046	2046	...	...
5 Producers' durable goods	13006	12092	...	...	15489	14795	...	...	14917	15457	...	...
A Transport equipment	2168	1590	...	...	1824	1630	...	...	2166	2009	...	...
B Machinery and equipment	10838	10502	...	...	13665	13165	...	...	13291	12908	...	...
6 Breeding stock, dairy cattle, etc.	...	...	...	...	...	...	...	...	...	...	...	...
Statistical discrepancy c	11385	11385	...	...	10900	10900	...	...	11399	11399	...	...
Total Gross Capital Formation	49414	39685	...	...	50927	42270	...	...	47562	40763	...	...

	1986				1987				1988			
	TOTAL	Private Total	Public Enterprises	General Government	TOTAL	Private Total	Public Enterprises	General Government	TOTAL	Private Total	Public Enterprises	General Government

At constant prices of 1980

Increase in stocks, total	4394	4394	...	...	6324	6324	...	...	8195	8195	...	...
Gross Fixed Capital Formation, Total	49910	43489	...	...	57172	50176	...	...	60874	53848	...	...
1 Residential buildings a	8616	6581	...	...	8201	5826	...	...	8937	6426	...	...
2 Non-residential buildings	4806	3648	...	...	5939	4848	...	...	5918	4976	...	...
3 Other construction	4178	1327	...	...	4493	1408	...	...	4462	1545	...	...
4 Land improvement and plantation and orchard development b	2621	2621	...	...	3649	3649	...	...	3396	3396	...	...
5 Producers' durable goods	16796	16419	...	...	21372	20927	...	...	24282	23626	...	...
A Transport equipment	2478	2323	...	...	3886	3698	...	...	3068	2791	...	...
B Machinery and equipment	14318	14096	...	...	17486	17229	...	...	21214	20835	...	...
6 Breeding stock, dairy cattle, etc.	...	...	...	...	...	...	...	...	...	...	...	...
Statistical discrepancy c	12893	12893	...	...	13518	13518	...	...	13879	13879	...	...
Total Gross Capital Formation	54304	47883	...	...	63496	56500	...	...	69069	62043	...	...

	1989			
	TOTAL	Private Total	Public Enterprises	General Government

At constant prices of 1980

Increase in stocks, total	2275	2275	...	...
Gross Fixed Capital Formation, Total	61697	53742	...	...
1 Residential buildings a	8546	5880	...	...
2 Non-residential buildings	6680	5225	...	...
3 Other construction	5118	2036	...	...
4 Land improvement and plantation and orchard development b	3095	3095	...	...
5 Producers' durable goods	24828	24076	...	...
A Transport equipment	3650	3291	...	...
B Machinery and equipment	21178	20785	...	...
6 Breeding stock, dairy cattle, etc.	...	...	...	...
Statistical discrepancy c	13430	13430	...	...
Total Gross Capital Formation	63972	56017	...	...

a) Item 'Residential buildings' includes also combined residential and non-residential buildings.
b) Item Land improvement and plantation and orchard development refers to transfer costs of land and buildings.
c) Item 'Statistical discrepancy' refers to real estate developers' margin.

Hungary

General note. The preparation of statistics of national accounting in Hungary are undertaken by the Central Statistical Office, Budapest. The official estimates are published in the "Statisztikai Evkonyv" (Statistical Yearbook). Detailed data are published annually in the series of "Nepgazdasagi Merlegek" (National Balances) for the years 1960-1983 and in the series of "A nepgazdasag fejlodesenek fobb mutatoi" (Main indicators of the development of the national economy) since 1984. Detailed data for income and consumption of the households are published yearly in the series of "A lakossag jovedelme es fogyasztasa" (The income and consumption of the household). The method of national accounting is built so that it is possible to provide the main categories of both MPS and SNA. The present note relates to the set of data estimated according to the recommendations of SNA. When the scope and coverage of the estimates differ significantly for conceptual or statistical reasons from the definitions and classifications recommended in SNA, a footnote is indicated to the relevant tables. As a general principle, the statistical units in the case of ISIC classification are institutional units (e.g. enterprises) except producers of government services. The data relating to 1975 are shown in two forms because not only was the base year changed but a few methodological modifications have been introduced. Data for 1989 are preliminary.

Sources and methods:

(a) Gross domestic product. Gross domestic product is estimated from three approaches: production, expenditure and cost structure. Gross output of financial services, insurance and owner-occupied housing is estimated at cost level.

(b) Expenditure on the gross domestic product. The expenditure approach is used to estimate all components of GDP expenditure type. Private final consumption expenditure is estimated mainly from data on retail trade while subsistence consumption from data on agricultural production surveys. Data derived from households budget statistics are also used. Government final expenditure is based on records of general government; it also includes the following: (i) social, health and cultural expenditure of enterprises; (ii) final consumption expenditure of non-profit institutions; (iii) gross output of financial services and insurance, estimated at cost level. The estimates of gross capital formation are based on investment statistics. The estimates of increase in stocks are mainly based on accounts of enterprises and on records of government. Exports and imports of goods are based on foreign trade statistics, which data on exports and imports of services are obtained from the balance of payments. For calculation of

1.1 Expenditure on the Gross Domestic Product, in Current Prices

Million Hungarian forint

	1970	1975	1980	1981	1982	1983	1984	1985	1986	1987	1988	1989
1 Government final consumption expenditure a	57858	86312 98582	134875	147257	159995	171584	183274	201539	219335	230078	289928	362650
2 Private final consumption expenditure b	170660	248918 250601	380465	409643	439293	470481	512524	552294	592144	665723	721924	840050
3 Gross capital formation	111723	182016 181910	221256	231342	248106	257155	251775	258423	292739	327484	358947	445200
A. Increase in stocks c	11464	20966 21400	13569	24701	27880	17137	26415	26294	31561	23947	6375	100200
B Gross fixed capital formation	100259	160954 161000	207687	206441	213926	220018	225360	232129	261178	303337	295572	345000
4 Exports of goods and services d	100209	183390 200200	281871	308221	321809	360713	401961	436180	431585	464391	530395	621600
5 Less: Imports of goods and services e	107902	234053 238620	297436	316451	315032	343566	371078	414778	447003	470306	491738	565500
Equals: Gross Domestic Product	332548	481477 482209	721031	779912	847871	896367	978456	1033658	1088800	1226370	1409517	1706000

a) Item 'Government final consumption expenditure' includes health, social and cultural expenditure of enterprises and final consumption expenditure of non-profit institutions, and gross output of financial services and insurance valued at cost level.
b) Item 'Private consumption expenditure' covers total final consumption expenditure in domestic market of households. Consumption from subsistence production is evaluated at market prices.
c) Item 'Increase in stocks' includes gains or losses arising from fluctuations in prices other than official prices.
d) Item 'Exports of goods and services', excludes direct purchases in the domestic market by non-resident households.
e) Item 'Imports of goods and services', excludes direct purchases abroad by resident households. All payments to and from financial institutions and insurance companies are treated as current transfers. The wage-like part of the business travel cost (i.e. per diem) is treated as final

777

imports of services are obtained from the balance of payments. For calculation of constant prices, price deflation is used.

(c) Cost-structure of the gross domestic product. Wages and salaries of employees of enterprises and government are available from the accounts of enterprises and government, respectively. Indirect taxes and subsidies are based on the accounts of enterprises and taxation statistics. Estimates on income of enterprises are based on accounts of enterprises. Estimates on income of private unincorporated enterprises are based on production taxation statistics and special surveys (e.g. household accounts of enterprises). Estimates of consumption of fixed capital at current prices are based on charges made by enterprises and producers of government services, while in the case of private unincorporated enterprises estimates are based on taxation statistics or special surveys.

(d) Gross domestic product by kind of economic activity. In the table of GDP by kind of economic activity, value added of industries excludes net taxes on commodities which are included in indirect taxes and subsidies, respectively. The main sources of the estimations at current prices are: accounts of enterprises, agricultural statistics, foreign trade statistics, taxation statistics, building and investment statistics. Intermediate consumption includes all goods and services used for production. Excluded are: wage-like part of business travel cost, social, cultural expenditure of enterprises, cost of financial services. Intermediate consumption at current prices includes gains or losses on stocks, arising from fluctuations of prices other than official prices. (The counterpart of the effect appears in increase in stocks.) For estimation at constant prices mainly the double deflation method is used. Output of most sectors is deflated by producer price indices. However, for most agricultural products, current quantities are multiplied by base year prices, output of trade is extrapolated by volume indices of trade. Output of government services, intermediate consumption at constant prices is deflated by the help of input-output ratios and of relevant price indices. Capital consumption at constant prices is estimated according to the perpetual inventory method, with help of price deflation. In those cases, when the output is evaluated at cost level, output at constant prices is estimated by adding deflated each cost element. Net value added of these sectors are calculated by their base year net value added multiplied by indices on employees.

Hungary

1.2 Expenditure on the Gross Domestic Product, in Constant Prices

Million Hungarian forint

	1970	1975	1980	1981	1982	1983	1984	1985	1986	1987	1988	1989
		1976				**At constant prices of:**						
							1981					
1 Government final consumption expenditure a	68579	89177 113600	142741	148420	152338	153514	155631	160957	166519	168736	171802	165800
2 Private final consumption expenditure b	213822	266921 358307	401066	410829	413829	415426	420088	424796	433166	450521	430098	431900
3 Gross capital formation	123682	179715 216000	226071	221537	213711	197990	193229	186512	202581	208997	202201	204000
A Increase in stocks	3281	11515 22500	10317	14896	10290	1591	4040	3090	7246	-5560	7214	700
B Gross fixed capital formation	120401	168200 193500	215754	206641	203421	196399	189189	183422	195335	214557	194987	203300
4 Exports of goods and services c	119572	189106 209400	292570	308221	319133	340415	363001	381906	373406	391140	416375	420300
5 Less: Imports of goods and services d	151846	218558 257300	311422	316451	304506	307096	310429	334730	343653	353668	355315	358500
Equals: Gross Domestic Product	373809	506361 640000	751026	772556	794505	800249	821520	819441	832019	865726	865161	863500

a) Item 'Government final consumption expenditure' includes health, social and cultural expenditure of enterprises and final consumption expenditure of non-profit institutions, and gross output of financial services and insurance valued at cost level.
b) Item 'Private consumption expenditure' covers total final consumption expenditure in domestic market of households. Consumption from subsistence production is evaluated at market prices. All payments to and from financial institutions and insurance companies are treated as current transfers. The wage-like part of the business travel cost (i.e. per diem) is treated as final consumption expenditure of households.
c) Item 'Exports of goods and services' excludes direct purchases in the domestic market by non-resident households.
d) Item 'Imports of goods and services' excludes direct purchases abroad by resident households.

1.3 Cost Components of the Gross Domestic Product

Million Hungarian forint

	1970	1975	1980	1981	1982	1983	1984	1985	1986	1987	1988	1989
1 Indirect taxes, net	...	...	69555	75573	95769	89584	76395	67829	37765	61247	160767	...
A Indirect taxes			206412	225977	249214	257629	245169	255460	257378	300052	377938	...
B Less: Subsidies			136857	150404	153445	168045	168774	187631	219613	238805	217171	
2 Consumption of fixed capital a	...	...	89031	92754	97350	99496	105668	108277	116956	124776	132739	
3 Compensation of employees paid by resident producers to:	...	...	311270	331792	358479	381368	432534	467777	503221	548142	695106	
4 Operating surplus	...	...	242603	270617	285382	314516	349792	376561	418574	477000	402869	...
A Corporate and quasi-corporate enterprises			185963	208438	215648	230162	247175	259369	281317	330109	254668	
B Private unincorporated enterprises			55773	61545	69236	81619	99569	114229	134434	143200	144253	...
C General government			867	634	498	2735	3048	2963	2823	3691	3948	
Statistical discrepancy b	...	...	8572	9176	10891	11403	14067	13214	12284	15205	18036	
Equals: Gross Domestic Product			721031	779912	847871	896367	978456	1033658	1088800	1226370	1409517	

a) Item 'Consumption of fixed capital' is estimated on the basis of the charges actually made by producers.
b) Item 'Statistical discrepancy' refers to the difference between subsistence production valued at approximated basis values and final consumption of goods from subsistence production valued at consumer prices.

1.9 Gross Domestic Product by Institutional Sectors of Origin

Million Hungarian forint

	1970	1975	1980	1981	1982	1983	1984	1985	1986	1987	1988	1989
					Domestic Factor Incomes Originating							
1 General government	...	...	59633	63761	68600	75104	81229	90236	98694	109676	140530	...
2 Corporate and quasi-corporate enterprises	...	...	436049	473838	502658	535453	597395	635047	683281	765075	801568	...
A Non-financial	...	...	431781	467579	494845	528282	590053	627300	672356	754822	784667	
B Financial	...	...	4268	6259	7813	7171	7342	7747	10925	10253	16901	
3 Households and private unincorporated enterprises	...	...	58191	64810	72603	85327	103702	119055	139820	150391	155877	...
4 Non-profit institutions serving households	...	...	-	-	-	-	-	-	-	-	-	...
Subtotal: Domestic Factor Incomes			553873	602409	643861	695884	782326	844338	921795	1025142	1097975	
Indirect taxes, net	...	...	69555	75573	95769	89584	76395	67829	37765	61247	160767	...
A Indirect taxes	...	...	206412	225977	249214	257629	245169	255460	257378	300052	377938	...
B Less: Subsidies	...	...	136857	150404	153445	168045	168774	187631	219613	238805	217171	
Consumption of fixed capital	...	...	89031	92754	97350	99496	105668	108277	116956	124776	132739	...
Statistical discrepancy	...	...	8572	9176	10891	11403	14067	13214	12284	15205	18036	
Gross Domestic Product	...	...	721031	779912	847871	896367	978456	1033658	1088800	1226370	1409517	...

Hungary

1.10 Gross Domestic Product by Kind of Activity, in Current Prices

Million Hungarian forint

	1970	1975	1980	1981	1982	1983	1984	1985	1986	1987	1988	1989
1 Agriculture, hunting, forestry and fishing [a]	...	...	120652	134582	148494	152927	166144	166664	182569	189222	209454	...
2 Mining and quarrying	...	...	40106	47282	55984	58414	58670	59392	56512	56360	55446	...
3 Manufacturing [b]	...	...	190499	207527	218773	227879	254477	272452	275451	308902	327184	...
4 Electricity, gas and water [c]	...	...	22277	24080	25822	29511	30116	34443	44750	54293	64501	...
5 Construction	...	...	53467	55589	60073	65447	71120	73950	78966	92233	96775	...
6 Wholesale and retail trade, restaurants and hotels	...	...	64812	67147	69922	76763	86821	96741	107977	128107	125857	...
7 Transport, storage and communication	...	...	58513	64032	70430	71425	74176	77731	86250	94425	101170	...
8 Finance, insurance, real estate and business services [de]	...	...	30130	32349	34575	39967	46688	53500	59926	70275	86511	...
9 Community, social and personal services [e]	...	...	4754	5398	5732	5690	6357	7490	8280	9430	15220	...
Total, Industries [f]	...	...	585210	637986	689805	728023	794569	842363	900681	1003247	1082118	...
Producers of Government Services [g]	...	...	60324	65466	68656	74171	80605	89066	96538	107092	131957	...
Other Producers	...	...	...	...	...	...	...	...	...	...	...	...
Subtotal	...	...	645534	703452	758461	802194	875174	931429	997219	1110339	1214075	...
Less: Imputed bank service charge	...	...	...	...	...	...	...	...	...	...	...	...
Plus: Import duties [h]	...	...	66925	67284	78519	82770	89215	89015	79297	100826	177406	...
Plus: Value added tax	...	...	...	...	...	...	...	...	...	...	...	...
Plus: Other adjustments [i]	...	...	8572	9176	10891	11403	14067	13214	12284	15205	18036	...
Equals: Gross Domestic Product	...	...	721031	779912	847871	896367	978456	1033658	1088800	1226370	1409517	...

a) Item 'Agriculture, hunting, forestry and fishing' includes operation of irrigation systems and veterinary services.
b) Item 'Manufacturing' includes gas.
c) Item 'Electricity, gas and water' excludes gas and operation of irrigation systems.
d) Gross output of finance, insurance and that of owner-occupied housing are estimated at cost level.
e) Sanitary and similar services and personal and household services are included in item 'Finance, insurance, real estate and business services'

f) All types of repair services are included in the relevant industries.
g) Item 'Producers of government services' includes non-profit institutions.
h) Item 'Import duties' refers to all net taxes on commodities and are excluded from the value added of industries.
i) Item 'Statistical discrepancy' refers to the difference between subsistence production valued at approximated basis values and final consumption of goods from subsistence production valued at consumer prices.

1.11 Gross Domestic Product by Kind of Activity, in Constant Prices

Million Hungarian forint

	1970	1975	1980	1981	1982	1983	1984	1985	1986	1987	1988	1989
					At constant prices of:1981							
1 Agriculture, hunting, forestry and fishing [a]	...	...	131563	135951	151830	151948	158969	152521	157851	153117	165153	...
2 Mining and quarrying	...	...	50919	46682	47948	46551	45235	42383	40166	40020	39085	...
3 Manufacturing [b]	...	...	186775	201665	213549	218885	228014	226480	224478	233086	229450	...
4 Electricity, gas and water [c]	...	...	21373	23092	22411	23759	23192	21679	24996	25914	25968	...
5 Construction	...	...	53436	54060	53695	55202	52307	49885	49914	53815	50846	...
6 Wholesale and retail trade, restaurants and hotels	...	...	64992	66877	66183	67701	67475	69900	71279	75244	65483	...
7 Transport, storage and communication	...	...	61060	63938	64594	64819	66730	66117	68010	71045	71975	...
8 Finance, insurance, real estate and business services [de]	...	...	32765	34143	34531	36986	38718	41983	44663	50113	50674	...
9 Community, social and personal services [e]	...	...	4956	5398	5577	5273	5644	5870	6141	6998	7940	...
Total, Industries [f]	...	...	607839	631806	660318	671124	686284	676818	687498	709352	706574	...
Producers of Government Services [g]	...	...	62173	64290	65787	66433	69994	71753	73081	75367	75911	...
Other Producers	...	...	...	...	...	...	...	...	...	...	...	...
Subtotal	...	...	670012	696096	726105	737557	756278	748571	760579	784719	782485	...
Less: Imputed bank service charge	...	...	...	...	...	...	...	...	...	...	...	...
Plus: Import duties [h]	...	...	81014	76460	68400	62692	65242	70870	71440	81007	82676	...
Plus: Value added tax	...	...										...
Plus: Other adjustments [i]	...	...										...
Equals: Gross Domestic Product	...	...	751026	772556	794505	800249	821520	819441	832019	865726	865161	...

a) Item 'Agriculture, hunting, forestry and fishing' includes operation of irrigation systems and veterinary services.
b) Item 'Manufacturing' includes gas.
c) Item 'Electricity, gas and water' excludes gas and operation of irrigation systems.
d) Gross output of finance, insurance and that of owner-occupied housing are estimated at cost level.
e) Sanitary and similar services and personal and household services are included in item 'Finance, insurance, real estate and business services'

f) All types of repair services are included in the relevant industries.
g) Item 'Producers of government services' includes non-profit institutions.
h) Item 'Import duties' refers to all net taxes on commodities and are excluded from the value added of industries.
i) Item 'Statistical discrepancy' refers to the difference between subsistence production valued at approximated basis values and final consumption of goods from subsistence production valued at consumer prices.

Hungary

2.5 Private Final Consumption Expenditure by Type and Purpose, in Current Prices

Million Hungarian forint

Final Consumption Expenditure of Resident Households

	1970	1975	1980	1981	1982	1983	1984	1985	1986	1987	1988	1989
1 Food, beverages and tobacco [a]	90820	123784 / 123784	190053	199943	216519	228447	248817	262550	277533	307677	341257	...
A Food	66121	84779 / 84779	129997	137065	145032	154551	170298	179982	188589	212418	234455	...
B Non-alcoholic beverages	1006	2737 / 2737	4662	5165	5494	5998	6309	7059	7874	8592	9844	...
C Alcoholic beverages	19601	29988 / 29988	44961	46783	52903	54318	58113	61174	65565	67577	74055	...
D Tobacco	4092	6280 / 6280	10433	10930	13090	13580	14097	14335	15505	19090	22903	
2 Clothing and footwear	22817	30745 / 31167	39853	43224	44475	47486	49673	54868	57872	64586	63856	...
3 Gross rent, fuel and power [b]	11450	18178 / 18180	30673	32908	36854	39745	44688	52281	54594	61968	70974	...
A Fuel and power	6189	8826 / 8826	15972	16423	18713	19275	21262	27043	27195	31216	34075	...
B Other	5261	9352 / 9354	14701	16485	18141	20470	23426	25238	27399	30752	36899	
4 Furniture, furnishings and household equipment and operation [c]	15593	25010 / 25239	35468	39505	41511	43630	48230	50150	53771	62171	64301	...
A Household operation	2971	5574 / 5603	8164	8896	9594	9973	11008	11252	11815	12850	13821	...
B Other	12622	19436 / 19636	27304	30609	31917	33657	37222	38898	41956	49321	50480	
5 Medical care and health expenses	1022	1766 / 1766	2791	2945	3191	3391	3539	3856	4190	4528	5172	
6 Transport and communication	10877	20119 / 20480	33566	36924	40113	46116	49874	55065	61229	70012	77755	...
A Personal transport equipment	3660	7159 / 7159	11331	10316	10485	10778	12105	13291	15626	19174	19073	...
B Other [d]	7217	12960 / 13321	22235	26608	29628	35338	37769	41774	45603	50838	58682	
7 Recreational, entertainment, education and cultural services	10098	15507 / 15463	24442	27627	28855	30397	32946	36993	42419	48176	45385	...
A Education	1336	2502 / 2458	4525	5181	5332	5594	5750	5984	6337	6531	6600	
B Other	8762	13005 / 13005	19917	22446	23523	24803	27196	31009	36082	41645	38785	
8 Miscellaneous goods and services	7983	13809 / 14030	23619	26467	27775	31269	34757	36531	40536	46605	53224	...
A Personal care	2184	3427 / 3600	5703	6334	6430	7466	8047	8239	9112	10819	12601	...
B Expenditures in restaurants, cafes and hotels	667	1350 / 1350	2959	3508	3964	4570	5273	5710	6407	7801	10316	
C Other	5132	9032 / 9080	14957	16625	17381	19233	21437	22582	25017	27985	30307	...
Total Final Consumption Expenditure in the Domestic Market by Households, of which [e]	170660	248918 / 250109	380465	409543	439293	470481	512524	552294	592144	665723	721924	...
A Durable goods	14703	22591 / 22661	34077	36910	37355	38936	43677	48800	57212	69795	67894	...
B Semi-durable goods	32611	49728 / 50563	69096	75497	78210	83880	89579	95762	102118	114896	116152	...
C Non-durable goods	102908	145353 / 145353	229147	243968	265780	282482	307653	329299	347687	386309	428588	...

Hungary

2.5 Private Final Consumption Expenditure by Type and Purpose, in Current Prices
(Continued)

Million Hungarian forint

	1970	1975	1980	1981	1982	1983	1984	1985	1986	1987	1988	1989
D Services	20438	31246 31532	48145	53168	57948	65183	71615	78433	85127	94723	109290	...
Plus: Direct purchases abroad by resident households	...	... ...	...	...	...	...	...	...	...	...	...	...
Less: Direct purchases in the domestic market by non-resident households	...	... ...	...	...	...	...	...	...	...	...	...	...
Equals: Final Consumption Expenditure of Resident Households	170660	248918 250109	380465	409543	439293	470481	512524	552294	592144	665723	721924	...

Final Consumption Expenditure of Private Non-profit Institutions Serving Households

	1970	1975	1980	1981	1982	1983	1984	1985	1986	1987	1988	1989
Equals: Final Consumption Expenditure of Private Non-profit Organisations Serving Households	...	... ...	...	...	...	...	...	...	...	...	...	...
Private Final Consumption Expenditure	170660	248918 250109	380465	409543	439293	470481	512524	552294	592144	665723	721924	...

a) Item 'Food, beverages and tobacco' includes goods consumed in restaurants, cafes, hotels, hospitals, other medical institutions and schools.
b) Gross rent of owner-occupied housing is evaluated at cost level.
c) Service for insurance of household property is not taken into account.
d) Service charges on insurance of personal transport equipment is not taken into account.

e) Item 'Private consumption expenditure' covers total final consumption expenditure in domestic market of households. Consumption from subsistence production is evaluated at market prices. All payments to and from financial institutions and insurance companies are treated as current transfers. The wage-like part of the business travel cost (i.e. per diem) is treated as final consumption expenditure of households.

2.6 Private Final Consumption Expenditure by Type and Purpose, in Constant Prices

Million Hungarian forint

	1970	1975	1980	1981	1982	1983	1984	1985	1986	1987	1988	1989
		1976			At constant prices of:		1981					
					Final Consumption Expenditure of Resident Households							
1 Food, beverages and tobacco a	117920	137304 182365	197605	199943	201846	202741	202987	205563	209016	209637	204174	...
A Food	85963	97861 131471	135044	137065	137930	139149	138514	139138	141594	145469	141602	...
B Non-alcoholic beverages	1097	2771 3109	4790	5165	5442	5479	5323	5690	6189	6435	6180	...
C Alcoholic beverages	25745	30386 39361	47014	46783	47267	46537	47216	48610	48462	45263	43627	...
D Tobacco	5115	6286 8424	10757	10930	11207	11573	11934	12125	12771	12470	12765	...
2 Clothing and footwear	28650	32280 43974	42541	43224	42061	42248	39981	39842	38613	39459	32802	...
3 Gross rent, fuel and power b	14084	18582 23900	32528	34194	35813	36586	38345	39393	39553	42033	42709	...
A Fuel and power	6749	8754 11205	15967	16423	16994	16759	17995	18935	18619	20115	19778	...
B Other	7335	9828 12695	16561	17771	18819	19827	20350	20458	20934	21918	22931	...
4 Furniture, furnishings and household equipment and operation c	18818	25945 35322	36999	39505	40052	39923	41185	39717	40120	43765	39769	...
A Household operation	3375	5629 7492	8700	8896	9208	9067	9105	8770	8812	9125	8189	...
B Other	15443	20316 27830	28299	30609	30844	30856	32080	30947	31308	34640	31580	...
5 Medical care and health expenses	1127	1800 1993	2846	2945	3067	3221	3219	3395	3544	3750	3694	...
6 Transport and communication	11639	20617 30246	37795	36924	36569	35286	37285	38769	42193	47091	48754	...
A Personal transport equipment	3773	7208 8994	11390	10316	10214	9447	9907	10541	12073	14757	14661	...
B Other d	7866	13409 21252	26405	26608	26355	25839	27378	28228	30120	32334	34093	...
7 Recreational, entertainment, education and cultural services	11223	15822 20131	25478	27627	28478	28782	29967	31529	33334	37357	32593	...
A Education	1631	2564 3605	4626	5181	5192	5263	5130	5022	4855	5008	4842	...
B Other	9592	13258 16526	20852	22446	23286	23519	24837	26507	28479	32349	27751	...
8 Miscellaneous goods and services	10361	14571 20376	25274	26467	25943	26639	27119	26588	26793	27429	25603	...

Hungary

2.6 Private Final Consumption Expenditure by Type and Purpose, in Constant Prices
(Continued)

Million Hungarian forint

	1970	1975	1980	1981	1982	1983	1984	1985	1986	1987	1988	1989
		1976			At constant prices of:		**1981**					
A Personal care	2359	3480	6262	6334	6215	6498	6375	6283	6331	6678	6481	...
		4939										
B Expenditures in restaurants, cafes and hotels	986	1456	3307	3508	3623	3529	3657	3456	3173	3181	3168	...
		2248										
C Other	7016	9635	15705	16625	16105	16612	17087	16849	17289	17570	15954	...
		13189										
Total Final Consumption Expenditure in the Domestic Market by Households, of which e ..	213822	266921	401066	410829	413829	415426	420088	424796	433166	450521	430098	...
		358307										
A Durable goods	17237	23237	34512	36910	36589	35562	38183	40452	44898	53665	47531	...
		30937										
B Semi-durable goods	40470	52213	73151	75497	74440	74610	72429	70953	69866	72325	62842	...
		69438										
C Non-durable goods	131556	159238	240928	243968	247461	248343	250786	254443	259550	263594	258111	...
		215163										
D Services	24559	32233	52475	54454	55339	56911	58690	58948	58852	60937	61614	...
		42769										
Plus: Direct purchases abroad by resident households	...	...	...	...	...	...	...	...	...	...	...	...
		...										
Less: Direct purchases in the domestic market by non-resident households	...	...	...	...	...	...	...	...	...	...	...	...
		...										
Equals: Final Consumption Expenditure of Resident Households	213822	266921	401066	410829	413829	415426	420088	424796	433166	450521	430098	...
		358307										

Final Consumption Expenditure of Private Non-profit Institutions Serving Households

	1970	1975	1980	1981	1982	1983	1984	1985	1986	1987	1988	1989
Equals: Final Consumption Expenditure of Private Non-profit Organisations Serving Households	...	...	...	...	...	...	...	...	...	...	...	...
Private Final Consumption Expenditure	213822	266921	401066	410829	413829	415426	420088	424796	433166	450521	430098	...
		358307										

a) Item 'Food, beverages and tobacco' includes goods consumed in restaurants, cafes, hotels, hospitals, other medical institutions and schools.
b) Gross rent of owner-occupied housing is evaluated at cost level.
c) Service for insurance of household property is not taken into account.
d) Service charges on insurance of personal transport equipment is not taken into account.

e) Item 'Private consumption expenditure' covers total final consumption expenditure in domestic market of households. Consumption from subsistence production is evaluated at market prices. All payments to and from financial institutions and insurance companies are treated as current transfers. The wage-like part of the business travel cost (i.e. per diem) is treated as final consumption expenditure of households.

4.1 Derivation of Value Added by Kind of Activity, in Current Prices

Million Hungarian forint

	1980			1981			1982			1983		
	Gross Output	Intermediate Consumption	Value Added	Gross Output	Intermediate Consumption	Value Added	Gross Output	Intermediate Consumption	Value Added	Gross Output	Intermediate Consumption	Value Added
					All Producers							
1 Agriculture, hunting, forestry and fishing a	308884	188232	120652	348977	214395	134582	385226	236732	148494	403822	250895	152927
A Agriculture and hunting	295923	181074	114849	335457	206812	128645	369042	227023	142019	387016	240358	146658
B Forestry and logging	12961	7158	5803	13520	7583	5937	16184	9709	6475	16806	10537	6269
C Fishing	...	...	...	...	...	...	...	...	...	...	...	...
2 Mining and quarrying	58252	18146	40106	68156	20874	47282	79490	23506	55984	83885	25471	58414

Hungary

4.1 Derivation of Value Added by Kind of Activity, in Current Prices
(Continued)

Million Hungarian forint

	1980			1981			1982			1983		
	Gross Output	Intermediate Consumption	Value Added	Gross Output	Intermediate Consumption	Value Added	Gross Output	Intermediate Consumption	Value Added	Gross Output	Intermediate Consumption	Value Added
3 Manufacturing	838186	647687	190499	901200	693673	207527	951763	732990	218773	1009149	781270	227879
A Manufacture of food, beverages and tobacco	172541	152974	19567	185039	162359	22680	194875	173017	21858	205274	184647	20627
B Textile, wearing apparel and leather industries												
C Manufacture of wood and wood products, including furniture	128927	93110	35817	137607	97796	39811	136223	96211	40012	142081	100516	41565
D Manufacture of paper and paper products, printing and publishing												
E Manufacture of chemicals and chemical petroleum, coal, rubber and plastic products b	177561	147251	30310	201545	169610	31935	218162	185244	32918	236390	200427	35963
F Manufacture of non-metallic mineral products, except products of petroleum and coal	30603	19650	10953	33340	21378	11962	34838	22402	12436	36827	23922	12905
G Basic metal industries	95102	76982	18120	89725	75772	13953	92592	79144	13448	92504	82185	10319
H Manufacture of fabricated metal products, machinery and equipment	210564	146579	63985	227870	154693	73177	246849	164216	82633	266701	176556	90145
I Other manufacturing industries	22888	11141	11747	26074	12065	14009	28224	12756	15468	29372	13017	16355
4 Electricity, gas and water c	57184	34907	22277	66325	42245	24080	75237	49415	25822	86791	57280	29511
A Electricity, gas and steam	39865	26418	13447	46229	32039	14190	53194	37986	15208	60543	43011	17532
B Water works and supply	17319	8489	8830	20096	10206	9890	22043	11429	10614	26248	14269	11979
5 Construction	136843	83376	53467	141669	86080	55589	150817	90744	60073	162566	97119	65447
6 Wholesale and retail trade, restaurants and hotels	109878	45066	64812	118019	50872	67147	124585	54663	69922	138741	61978	76763
7 Transport, storage and communication	98491	39978	58513	109625	45593	64032	118979	48549	70430	127274	55849	71425
A Transport and storage	87682	37450	50232	96182	42541	53641	104305	45112	59193	112307	52109	60198
B Communication	10809	2528	8281	13443	3052	10391	14674	3437	11237	14967	3740	11227
8 Finance, insurance, real estate and business services de	60234	30104	30130	67889	35540	32349	76446	41871	34575	88599	48632	39967
A Financial institutions	5498	1420	4078	6402	1671	4731	6681	1863	4818	7513	2085	5428
B Insurance												
C Real estate and business services	54736	28684	26052	61487	33869	27618	69765	40008	29757	81086	46547	34539
9 Community, social and personal services e	11759	7005	4754	13108	7710	5398	13990	8258	5732	14282	8592	5690
Total, Industries f	1679711	1094501	585210	1834968	1196982	637986	1976533	1286728	689805	2115109	1387086	728023
Producers of Government Services g	124514	64190	60324	140705	75239	65466	148663	80007	68656	157998	83827	74171
Other Producers	...	...	...	...	...	...	...	...	...	...	...	...
Total	1804225	1158692	645534	1975673	1272221	703452	2125196	1366735	758461	2273107	1470913	802194
Less: Imputed bank service charge	...	...	...	...	...	...	...	...	...	...	...	...
Import duties h	66925	-	66925	67284	-	67284	78519	-	78519	82770	-	82770
Value added tax	...	...	...	...	...	...	...	...	...	...	...	...
Other adjustments i	8572	-	8572	9176	-	9176	10891	-	10891	11403	-	11403
Total	1879722	1158691	721031	2052133	1272221	779912	2214606	1366735	847871	2367280	1470913	896367

	1984			1985			1986			1987		
	Gross Output	Intermediate Consumption	Value Added	Gross Output	Intermediate Consumption	Value Added	Gross Output	Intermediate Consumption	Value Added	Gross Output	Intermediate Consumption	Value Added
					All Producers							
1 Agriculture, hunting, forestry and fishing a	435193	269049	166144	438795	272131	166664	470893	288324	182569	500916	311694	189222
A Agriculture and hunting	417033	257625	159408	419719	260277	159442	449036	274569	174467	477066	296896	180170
B Forestry and logging	18160	11424	6736	19076	11854	7222	21857	13755	8102	23850	14798	9052
C Fishing	...	...	...	...	...	...	...	...	...	...	...	...
2 Mining and quarrying	86576	27906	58670	94925	35533	59392	96011	39499	56512	97333	40973	56360

Hungary

4.1 Derivation of Value Added by Kind of Activity, in Current Prices
(Continued)

Million Hungarian forint

	1984			1985			1986			1987		
	Gross Output	Intermediate Consumption	Value Added	Gross Output	Intermediate Consumption	Value Added	Gross Output	Intermediate Consumption	Value Added	Gross Output	Intermediate Consumption	Value Added
3 Manufacturing	1095676	841199	254477	1151362	878910	272452	1196501	921050	275451	1284749	975847	308902
A Manufacture of food, beverages and tobacco	219932	199638	20294	217883	201065	16818	224816	213703	11113	242209	226898	15311
B Textile, wearing apparel and leather industries												
C Manufacture of wood and wood products, including furniture	156293	111373	44920	165814	116994	48820	174627	124856	49771	188390	135651	52739
D Manufacture of paper and paper products, printing and publishing												
E Manufacture of chemicals and chemical petroleum, coal, rubber and plastic products b	255556	210478	45078	268953	218419	50534	255761	211588	44173	267720	210565	57155
F Manufacture of non-metallic mineral products, except products of petroleum and coal	40287	25595	14692	40048	25615	14433	43185	27726	15459	47688	30328	17360
G Basic metal industries	101194	88341	12853	105985	94724	11261	111621	100482	11139	117326	104833	12493
H Manufacture of fabricated metal products, machinery and equipment	290077	191286	98791	317596	207239	110357	348097	226846	121251	378483	249616	128867
I Other manufacturing industries	32337	14488	17849	35083	14854	20229	38394	15849	22545	42933	17956	24977
4 Electricity, gas and water c	92570	62454	30116	103623	69180	34443	114723	69973	44750	128785	74492	54293
A Electricity, gas and steam	63904	47336	16568	73140	53129	20011	80958	51961	28997	91606	54632	36974
B Water works and supply	28666	15118	13548	30483	16051	14432	33765	18012	15753	37179	19860	17319
5 Construction	173500	102380	71120	175361	101411	73950	189115	110149	78966	210487	118254	92233
6 Wholesale and retail trade, restaurants and hotels	154947	68126	86821	169357	72616	96741	186321	78344	107977	220658	92551	128107
7 Transport, storage and communication	134399	60223	74176	139241	61510	77731	152323	66073	86250	167880	73455	94425
A Transport and storage	117731	55912	61819	120149	56577	63572	131237	60409	70828	143286	67045	76241
B Communication	16668	4311	12357	19092	4933	14159	21086	5664	15422	24594	6410	18184
8 Finance, insurance, real estate and business services de	100622	53934	46688	112447	58947	53500	126329	66403	59926	149561	79286	70275
A Financial institutions	8626	2393	6233	10774	3089	7685	13741	4668	9073	18977	6570	12407
B Insurance												
C Real estate and business services	91996	51541	40455	101673	55858	45815	112588	61735	50853	130584	72716	57868
9 Community, social and personal services e	16149	9792	6357	17966	10476	7490	20179	11899	8280	22565	13135	9430
Total, Industries f	2289632	1495063	794569	2403077	1560714	842363	2552395	1651714	900681	2782934	1779687	1003247
Producers of Government Services g	170713	90108	80605	189693	100627	89066	202267	105729	96538	220095	113003	107092
Other Producers	...	...	...	...	...	...	...	...	...	...	...	...
Total	2460345	1585171	875174	2592770	1661341	931429	2754662	1757443	997219	3003029	1892690	1110339
Less: Imputed bank service charge	...	...	...	...	...	...	...	...	...	...	...	...
Import duties h	89215	-	89215	89015	-	89015	79297	-	79297	100826	-	100826
Value added tax	...	...	...	...	...	...	...	...	...	...	...	...
Other adjustments i	14067	-	14067	13214	-	13214	12284	-	12284	15205	-	15205
Total	2563627	1585171	978456	2694999	1661341	1033658	2846243	1757443	1088800	3119060	1892690	1226370

	1988		
	Gross Output	Intermediate Consumption	Value Added

All Producers

	1988		
	Gross Output	Intermediate Consumption	Value Added
1 Agriculture, hunting, forestry and fishing a	533831	324377	209454
A Agriculture and hunting	508842	308953	199889
B Forestry and logging	24989	15424	9565
C Fishing	...	...	...
2 Mining and quarrying	95023	39577	55446

Hungary

4.1 Derivation of Value Added by Kind of Activity, in Current Prices
(Continued)

Million Hungarian forint

		1988	
	Gross Output	Intermediate Consumption	Value Added
3 Manufacturing	1347062	1019878	327184
A Manufacture of food, beverages and tobacco	253574	232729	20845
B Textile, wearing apparel and leather industries			
C Manufacture of wood and wood products, including furniture	195257	143009	52248
D Manufacture of paper and paper products, printing and publishing			
E Manufacture of chemicals and chemical petroleum, coal, rubber and plastic products b	286327	221724	64603
F Manufacture of non-metallic mineral products, except products of petroleum and coal	48679	31613	17066
G Basic metal industries	136603	114746	21857
H Manufacture of fabricated metal products, machinery and equipment	377015	253939	123076
I Other manufacturing industries	49607	22118	27489
4 Electricity, gas and water c	136433	71932	64501
A Electricity, gas and steam	101956	54419	47537
B Water works and supply	34477	17513	16964
5 Construction	226943	130168	96775
6 Wholesale and retail trade, restaurants and hotels	229567	103710	125857
7 Transport, storage and communication	183244	82074	101170
A Transport and storage	156529	74456	82073
B Communication	26715	7618	19097
8 Finance, insurance, real estate and business services de	188910	102399	86511
A Financial institutions	29025	10667	18358
B Insurance			
C Real estate and business services	159885	91732	68153
9 Community, social and personal services e	33415	18195	15220
Total, Industries f	2974428	1892310	1082118
Producers of Government Services g	253701	121744	131957
Other Producers	...	...	...
Total	3228129	2014054	1214075
Less: Imputed bank service charge	...	...	...
Import duties h	177406	-	177406
Value added tax	...	...	...
Other adjustments i	18036	-	18036
Total	3423571	2014054	1409517

a) Item 'Agriculture, hunting, forestry and fishing' includes operation of irrigation systems and veterinary services.
b) Item 'Manufacturing' includes gas.
c) Item 'Electricity, gas and water' excludes gas and operation of irrigation systems.
d) Gross output of finance, insurance and that of owner-occupied housing are estimated at cost level.
e) Sanitary and similar services and personal and household services are included in item 'Finance, insurance, real estate and business services'

f) All types of repair services are included in the relevant industries.
g) Item 'Producers of government services' includes non-profit institutions.
h) Item 'Import duties' refers to all net taxes on commodities and are excluded from the value added of industries.
i) Item 'Statistical discrepancy' refers to the difference between subsistence production valued at approximated basis values and final consumption of goods from subsistence production valued at consumer prices.

4.2 Derivation of Value Added by Kind of Activity, in Constant Prices

Million Hungarian forint

	1980			1981			1982			1983		
	Gross Output	Intermediate Consumption	Value Added	Gross Output	Intermediate Consumption	Value Added	Gross Output	Intermediate Consumption	Value Added	Gross Output	Intermediate Consumption	Value Added
	At constant prices of:1981											
	All Producers											
1 Agriculture, hunting, forestry and fishing a	332444	200881	131563	353745	217794	135951	381976	230146	151830	383744	231796	151948
A Agriculture and hunting	317074	192422	124652	338257	209016	129241	365637	220515	145122	366961	221633	145328
B Forestry and logging	15370	8459	6911	15488	8778	6710	16339	9631	6708	16783	10163	6620
C Fishing	...	...	...	...	...	...	...	...	...	...	...	...
2 Mining and quarrying	70397	19478	50919	68156	21474	46682	69951	22003	47948	68544	21993	46551

Hungary

4.2 Derivation of Value Added by Kind of Activity, in Constant Prices
(Continued)

Million Hungarian forint

	1980			1981			1982			1983		
	Gross Output	Intermediate Consumption	Value Added	Gross Output	Intermediate Consumption	Value Added	Gross Output	Intermediate Consumption	Value Added	Gross Output	Intermediate Consumption	Value Added
	At constant prices of:1981											
3 Manufacturing	876281	689506	186775	899886	698221	201665	922705	709156	213549	935702	716817	218885
A Manufacture of food, beverages and tobacco	180675	159512	21163	185014	162562	22452	193455	171222	22233	196483	178108	18375
B Textile, wearing apparel and leather industries												
C Manufacture of wood and wood products, including furniture	130187	94320	35867	135653	97210	38443	134037	94456	39581	136102	93458	42644
D Manufacture of paper and paper products, printing and publishing												
E Manufacture of chemicals and chemical petroleum, coal, rubber and plastic products [b]	197806	169191	28615	202401	172238	30163	205526	173139	32387	208720	173229	35491
F Manufacture of non-metallic mineral products, except products of petroleum and coal	33021	22148	10873	33336	22171	11165	33610	22106	11504	34139	22191	11948
G Basic metal industries	93968	81718	12250	88683	75831	12852	89067	76025	13042	87217	74782	12435
H Manufacture of fabricated metal products, machinery and equipment	217115	151011	66104	229697	156639	73058	240306	160007	80299	244783	161994	82789
I Other manufacturing industries	23509	11606	11903	25102	11570	13532	26704	12201	14503	28258	13055	15203
4 Electricity, gas and water [c]	62397	41024	21373	66337	43245	23092	67681	45270	22411	71287	47528	23759
A Electricity, gas and steam	43453	31835	11618	46229	32839	13390	47088	34457	12631	48654	35026	13628
B Water works and supply	18944	9189	9755	20108	10406	9702	20593	10813	9780	22633	12502	10131
5 Construction	143176	89740	53436	141351	87291	54060	140845	87150	53695	142169	86967	55202
6 Wholesale and retail trade, restaurants and hotels	113207	48215	64992	118181	51304	66877	119097	52914	66183	123243	55542	67701
7 Transport, storage and communication	104409	43349	61060	109731	45793	63938	110556	45962	64594	115734	50915	64819
A Transport and storage	92258	40601	51657	96288	42691	53597	96243	42627	53616	101154	47538	53616
B Communication	12151	2748	9403	13443	3102	10341	14313	3335	10978	14580	3377	11203
8 Finance, insurance, real estate and business services [de]	65133	32368	32765	70175	36032	34143	73765	39234	34531	79230	42244	36986
A Financial institutions	6078	1492	4586	6402	1671	4731	6550	1789	4761	7224	1959	5265
B Insurance												
C Real estate and business services	59055	30876	28179	63773	34361	29412	67215	37445	29770	72006	40285	31721
9 Community, social and personal services [e]	12663	7707	4956	13108	7710	5398	13377	7800	5577	13750	8477	5273
Total, Industries [f]	1780107	1172268	607839	1840670	1208864	631806	1899953	1239635	660318	1933403	1262279	671124
Producers of Government Services [g]	130753	68580	62173	137447	73157	64290	141869	76082	65787	140349	73916	66433
Other Producers	...	...	...	...	...	...	...	...	...	...	...	...
Total	1910860	1240848	670012	1978117	1282021	696096	2041822	1315717	726105	2073752	1336195	737557
Less: Imputed bank service charge	...	...	...	...	...	...	...	...	...	...	...	...
Import duties [h]												
Value added tax	81014	-	81014	76460	-	76460	68400	-	68400	62692	-	62692
Other adjustments [i]												
Total	1991874	1240848	751026	2054577	1282021	772556	2110222	1315717	794505	2136444	1336195	800249

	1984			1985			1986			1987		
	Gross Output	Intermediate Consumption	Value Added	Gross Output	Intermediate Consumption	Value Added	Gross Output	Intermediate Consumption	Value Added	Gross Output	Intermediate Consumption	Value Added
	At constant prices of:1981											
	All Producers											
1 Agriculture, hunting, forestry and fishing [a]	395205	236236	158969	386987	234466	152521	401389	243538	157851	406457	253340	153117
A Agriculture and hunting	377294	225655	151639	368738	223618	145120	382106	231422	150684	386566	240797	145769
B Forestry and logging	17911	10581	7330	18249	10848	7401	19283	12116	7167	19891	12543	7348
C Fishing	...	...	...	...	...	...	...	...	...	...	...	...
2 Mining and quarrying	68185	22950	45235	70027	27644	42383	70162	29996	40166	70057	30037	40020

Hungary

4.2 Derivation of Value Added by Kind of Activity, in Constant Prices
(Continued)

Million Hungarian forint

	1984			1985			1986			1987		
	Gross Output	Intermediate Consumption	Value Added	Gross Output	Intermediate Consumption	Value Added	Gross Output	Intermediate Consumption	Value Added	Gross Output	Intermediate Consumption	Value Added
	At constant prices of:1981											
3 Manufacturing	967876	739862	228014	972747	746267	226480	992550	768072	224478	1030136	797050	233086
A Manufacture of food, beverages and tobacco	203353	182470	20883	198919	177868	21051	201294	178742	22552	207337	183354	23983
B Textile, wearing apparel and leather industries												
C Manufacture of wood and wood products, including furniture	141685	97949	43736	140573	97295	43278	141994	101021	40973	145540	103924	41616
D Manufacture of paper and paper products, printing and publishing												
E Manufacture of chemicals and chemical petroleum, coal, rubber and plastic products b	217828	177038	40790	219643	180654	38989	222132	183935	38197	235052	194534	40518
F Manufacture of non-metallic mineral products, except products of petroleum and coal	35068	22730	12338	33696	21899	11797	34375	22750	11625	36704	24572	12132
G Basic metal industries	88895	77563	11332	88730	79284	9446	91241	81610	9631	92279	81721	10558
H Manufacture of fabricated metal products, machinery and equipment	251945	168336	83609	261419	175068	86351	270277	185246	85031	281231	193417	87814
I Other manufacturing industries	29102	13776	15326	29767	14199	15568	31237	14768	16469	31993	15528	16465
4 Electricity, gas and water c	73971	50779	23192	75053	53374	21679	77657	52661	24996	80277	54363	25914
A Electricity, gas and steam	51012	38107	12905	52132	40793	11339	53328	39105	14223	54940	40156	14784
B Water works and supply	22959	12672	10287	22921	12581	10340	24329	13556	10773	25337	14207	11130
5 Construction	140918	88611	52307	135563	85678	49885	138454	88540	49914	145288	91473	53815
6 Wholesale and retail trade, restaurants and hotels	127193	59718	67475	131037	61137	69900	135205	63926	71279	145295	70051	75244
7 Transport, storage and communication	120953	54223	66730	119667	53550	66117	123383	55373	68010	129523	58478	71045
A Transport and storage	105174	50482	54692	102452	49471	52981	109613	49147	60466	110232	53550	56682
B Communication	15779	3741	12038	17215	4079	13136	13770	6226	7544	19291	4928	14363
8 Finance, insurance, real estate and business services de	83888	45170	38718	88409	46426	41983	93792	49129	44663	105892	55779	50113
A Financial institutions	7904	2191	5713	9206	2674	6532	11105	3937	7168	14396	5298	9098
B Insurance												
C Real estate and business services	75984	42979	33005	79203	43752	35451	82687	45192	37495	91496	50481	41015
9 Community, social and personal services e	14895	9251	5644	15276	9406	5870	16020	9879	6141	17780	10782	6998
Total, Industries f	1993084	1306800	686284	1994766	1317948	676818	2048612	1361114	687498	2130705	1421353	709352
Producers of Government Services g	146517	76523	69994	152158	80405	71753	154085	81004	73081	158296	82929	75367
Other Producers	...	...	...	...	...	...	...	...	...	...	...	...
Total	2139601	1383323	756278	2146924	1398353	748571	2202697	1442118	760579	2289001	1504282	784719
Less: Imputed bank service charge	...	...	...	...	...	...	...	...	...	...	...	...
Import duties h												
Value added tax	65242	-	65242	70870	-	70870	71440	-	71440	81007	-	81007
Other adjustments i												
Total	2204843	1383323	821520	2217794	1398353	819441	2274137	1442118	832019	2370008	1504282	865726

	1988		
	Gross Output	Intermediate Consumption	Value Added
	At constant prices of:1981		
	All Producers		
1 Agriculture, hunting, forestry and fishing a	410555	245402	165153
A Agriculture and hunting	389819	232149	157670
B Forestry and logging	20736	13253	7483
C Fishing	...	...	...
2 Mining and quarrying	67525	28440	39085

Hungary

4.2 Derivation of Value Added by Kind of Activity, in Constant Prices
(Continued)

Million Hungarian forint

	1988 Gross Output	1988 Intermediate Consumption	1988 Value Added	
3 Manufacturing	1029247	799797	229450	**At constant prices of:1981**
A Manufacture of food, beverages and tobacco	203084	178908	24176	
B Textile, wearing apparel and leather industries				
C Manufacture of wood and wood products, including furniture	145112	105112	40000	
D Manufacture of paper and paper products, printing and publishing				
E Manufacture of chemicals and chemical petroleum, coal, rubber and plastic products b	238245	197275	40970	
F Manufacture of non-metallic mineral products, except products of petroleum and coal	36898	24817	12081	
G Basic metal industries	96603	84425	12178	
H Manufacture of fabricated metal products, machinery and equipment	277700	193523	84177	
I Other manufacturing industries	31605	15737	15868	
4 Electricity, gas and water c	80034	54066	25968	
A Electricity, gas and steam	54857	39895	14962	
B Water works and supply	25177	14171	11006	
5 Construction	142842	91996	50846	
6 Wholesale and retail trade, restaurants and hotels	137820	72337	65483	
7 Transport, storage and communication	133323	61348	71975	
A Transport and storage	112879	55813	57066	
B Communication	20444	5535	14909	
8 Finance, insurance, real estate and business services de	114971	64297	50674	
A Financial institutions	16940	5937	11003	
B Insurance				
C Real estate and business services	98031	58360	39671	
9 Community, social and personal services e	18742	10802	7940	
Total, Industries f	2135059	1428485	706574	
Producers of Government Services g	155697	79786	75911	
Other Producers	...	...	...	
Total	2290756	1508271	782485	
Less: Imputed bank service charge	...	...	...	
Import duties h				
Value added tax	82676	-	82676	
Other adjustments i				
Total	2373432	1508271	865161	

a) Item 'Agriculture, hunting, forestry and fishing' includes operation of irrigation systems and veterinary services.
b) Item 'Manufacturing' includes gas.
c) Item 'Electricity, gas and water' excludes gas and operation of irrigation systems.
d) Gross output of finance, insurance and that of owner-occupied housing are estimated at cost level.
e) Sanitary and similar services and personal and household services are included in item 'Finance, insurance, real estate and business services'

f) All types of repair services are included in the relevant industries.
g) Item 'Producers of government services' includes non-profit institutions.
h) Item 'Import duties' refers to all net taxes on commodities and are excluded from the value added of industries.
i) Item 'Statistical discrepancy' refers to the difference between subsistence production valued at approximated basis values and final consumption of goods from subsistence production valued at consumer prices.

4.3 Cost Components of Value Added

Million Hungarian forint

	1980 Compensation of Employees	1980 Capital Consumption	1980 Net Operating Surplus	1980 Indirect Taxes	1980 Less: Subsidies Received	1980 Value Added	1981 Compensation of Employees	1981 Capital Consumption	1981 Net Operating Surplus	1981 Indirect Taxes	1981 Less: Subsidies Received	1981 Value Added
					All Producers							
1 Agriculture, hunting, forestry and fishing a	49768	15403	60458	7039	12016	120652	54877	16135	67785	8250	12465	134582
A Agriculture and hunting	46823	14768	58722	5718	11182	114849	51758	15472	66367	6698	11650	128645
B Forestry and logging	2945	635	1736	1321	834	5803	3119	663	1418	1552	815	5937
C Fishing	...	...	...	...	...	...	...	...	...	...	...	...
2 Mining and quarrying	11166	3881	2456	23652	1049	40106	11721	3776	4957	28365	1537	47282

Hungary

4.3 Cost Components of Value Added
(Continued)

Million Hungarian forint

	1980 Compensation of Employees	Capital Consumption	Net Operating Surplus	Indirect Taxes	Less: Subsidies Received	Value Added	1981 Compensation of Employees	Capital Consumption	Net Operating Surplus	Indirect Taxes	Less: Subsidies Received	Value Added
3 Manufacturing	91058	27224	88426	23439	39648	190499	95316	28980	101884	20482	39135	207527
A Manufacture of food, beverages and tobacco	12295	3972	16669	1426	14795	19567	12949	4468	18450	1970	15157	22680
B Textile, wearing apparel and leather industries / C Manufacture of wood and wood products, including furniture / D Manufacture of paper and paper products, printing and publishing	21941	3825	14512	1532	5993	35817	22843	3832	17267	1525	5656	39811
E Manufacture of chemicals and chemical petroleum, coal, rubber and plastic products b	7672	7214	14808	6681	6065	30310	8174	7487	17531	5249	6506	31935
F Manufacture of non-metallic mineral products, except products of petroleum and coal	4998	2530	3302	358	235	10953	5158	2599	4170	341	306	11962
G Basic metal industries	7172	2786	9555	6095	7488	18120	7353	3203	5670	4510	6783	13953
H Manufacture of fabricated metal products, machinery and equipment	33274	6410	22149	7174	5022	63985	34834	6870	29355	6793	4675	73177
I Other manufacturing industries	3706	487	7431	173	50	11747	4005	521	9441	94	52	14009
4 Electricity, gas and water c	7437	6971	3487	5105	723	22277	7949	7319	3343	6313	844	24080
A Electricity, gas and steam	2468	4248	2480	4251	-	13447	2622	4357	2216	5021	26	14190
B Water works and supply	4969	2723	1007	854	723	8830	5327	2962	1127	1292	818	9890
5 Construction	27215	3405	20063	2948	164	53467	28129	3427	21273	2926	166	55589
6 Wholesale and retail trade, restaurants and hotels	28948	2943	37061	3034	7174	64812	31064	2915	34936	5900	7668	67147
7 Transport, storage and communication	27353	13517	19396	1066	2819	58513	28930	14189	23081	1139	3307	64032
A Transport and storage	23219	12128	16619	998	2732	50232	24468	12616	18590	1094	3127	53641
B Communication	4134	1389	2777	68	87	8281	4462	1573	4491	45	180	10391
8 Finance, insurance, real estate and business services de	12095	9562	8355	531	413	30130	13238	9949	10397	575	1810	32349
A Financial institutions	2407	155	1861	5	350	4078	2523	155	3736	4	1687	4731
B Insurance												
C Real estate and business services	9688	9407	6494	526	63	26052	10715	9794	6661	571	123	27618
9 Community, social and personal services e	2331	162	2653	350	742	4754	2525	164	2961	719	971	5398
Total, Industries f	257371	83068	242355	67164	64748	585210	273749	86854	270617	74669	67903	637986
Producers of Government Services g	53899	5963	248	460	246	60324	58043	5900	-	1523	-	65466
Other Producers	...	...	...	...	...	...	...	...	...	...	...	...
Total	311270	89031	242603	67624	64994	645534	331792	92754	270617	76192	67903	703452
Less: Imputed bank service charge	...	...					...	...	...			
Import duties h	...	...	...	138788	71863	66925	...	...	...	149785	82501	67284
Value added tax	...	...	...	...	...	...	...	...	...	...	...	...
Other adjustments i	...	...	...	...	...	8572	...	...	...	...	...	9176
Total	311270	89031	242603	206412	136857	721031	331792	92754	270617	225977	150404	779912

	1982 Compensation of Employees	Capital Consumption	Net Operating Surplus	Indirect Taxes	Less: Subsidies Received	Value Added	1983 Compensation of Employees	Capital Consumption	Net Operating Surplus	Indirect Taxes	Less: Subsidies Received	Value Added
All Producers												
1 Agriculture, hunting, forestry and fishing a	63190	17328	71386	9695	13105	148494	67708	17216	71170	10091	13258	152927
A Agriculture and hunting	59531	16488	69838	8404	12242	142019	63873	16400	69759	9095	12469	146658
B Forestry and logging	3659	840	1548	1291	863	6475	3835	816	1411	996	789	6269
C Fishing	...	...	...	...	...	...	...	...	...	...	...	...
2 Mining and quarrying	12699	4066	5679	35106	1566	55984	13529	4271	4823	37613	1822	58414

Hungary

4.3 Cost Components of Value Added (Continued)

Million Hungarian forint

1982 / 1983

	Compensation of Employees	Net Operating Surplus	Capital Consumption	Indirect Taxes	Less: Subsidies Received	Value Added	Compensation of Employees	Net Operating Surplus	Capital Consumption	Indirect Taxes	Less: Subsidies Received	Value Added
3 Manufacturing	100738	30005	20590	38517	218773	105047	29386	125064	16465	48083	227879	
A Manufacture of food, beverages and tobacco	13964	4860	1755	14646	21858	14917	4998	18239	2177	19704	20627	
B Textile, wearing apparel and leather industries												
C Manufacture of wood and wood products, including furniture	23573	3759	16420	1511	5251	40012	24271	3687	17531	1395	5319	41565
D Manufacture of paper and paper products, printing and publishing												
E Manufacture of chemicals and chemical products, coal, rubber and plastic products b	8738	7536	17342	5692	6390	32918	9483	7135	22828	3902	7385	35963
F Manufacture of non-metallic mineral products, except products of petroleum and coal	5423	2595	4273	408	263	12436	5493	2380	4883	353	204	12905
G Basic metal industries	7455	3509	5494	6294	13448	7475	3428	7288	613	8485	10319	
H Manufacture of fabricated metal products, machinery and equipment	37420	7211	35791	7828	5617	82633	39303	7290	42547	6923	9045	
I Other manufacturing industries	4165	535	10712	112	56	15468	4105	468	11748	97	63	16355
4 Electricity, gas and water c	8573	7827	3295	6937	810	25822	8458	8325	6056	6269	597	29511
A Electricity, gas and steam	2841	4537	2103	5729	2	15208	3375	4443	4879	7	17532	
B Water works and supply	5732	3290	1192	1208	808	10614	6083	3482	1614	1390	590	11979
5 Construction	29532	3396	24273	3102	230	60073	31197	3187	28262	3053	252	65447
6 Wholesale and retail trade, restaurants and hotels	33783	3230	38399	3229	8719	69822	36241	3268	42916	3492	9154	76763
7 Transport, storage and communication	31073	14781	21925	5328	2677	70430	32954	15339	20009	5494	2371	71425
A Transport and storage	25994	13094	17370	5200	2465	59193	27427	13527	16036	5390	2182	60196
B Communication	5079	1687	4555	128	212	11237	5527	1812	3973	104	189	11227
8 Finance, insurance, real estate and business services de	10724	14794	11583	871	3397	34575	17452	11858	11569	1285	2197	39967
A Financial institutions	2787	154	5026	5	3154	4818	3042	171	4129	7	1921	5428
B Insurance												
C Real estate and business services	12007	10570	6557	866	243	29757	14410	11687	7440	1278	276	34539
9 Community, social and personal services e	2712	180	2965	827	972	5732	3190	170	3932	803	1405	5690
Total, Industries f	297094	91537	285482	85685	66993	689809	315618	93020	313059	84558	72139	728023
Producers of Government Services 9	61385	5813	-100	1558	-	65886	6479	1457	1388	-	74171	
Other Producers												
Total	358479	97350	285382	87243	66993	758461	381368	94496	314516	85953	79139	802194
Less: Imputed bank service charge												
Import duties h			161971			78519	83452		76519			82770
Value added tax					10891						11403	
Other adjustments i												
Total	358479	97350	285382	249214	153445	847871	381368	94496	314516	257629	168045	896367

All Producers

1984 / 1985

	Compensation of Employees	Net Operating Surplus	Capital Consumption	Indirect Taxes	Less: Subsidies Received	Value Added	Compensation of Employees	Net Operating Surplus	Capital Consumption	Indirect Taxes	Less: Subsidies Received	Value Added
1 Agriculture, hunting, forestry and fishing a	75909	18496	75415	10618	14294	166144	77674	18701	73983	11322	15016	166664
A Agriculture and hunting	71582	17596	73968	9722	13460	73260	17797	72069	10296	13980	159442	
B Forestry and logging	4327	900	1447	896	834	6736	904	1914	1026	1036	7222	
C Fishing												
2 Mining and quarrying	15370	3609	36835	2780	5836	58670	17530	3591	38965	37025	2650	59392

Hungary

4.3 Cost Components of Value Added
(Continued)

Million Hungarian forint

	1984							1985						
	Compensation of Employees	Capital Consumption	Net Operating Surplus	Indirect Taxes	Less: Subsidies Received	Value Added		Compensation of Employees	Capital Consumption	Net Operating Surplus	Indirect Taxes	Less: Subsidies Received	Value Added

	1986						1987					
	Compensation of Employees	Capital Consumption	Net Operating Surplus	Indirect Taxes	Less: Subsidies Received	Value Added	Compensation of Employees	Capital Consumption	Net Operating Surplus	Indirect Taxes	Less: Subsidies Received	Value Added

All Producers

	1984						1985					
1 Agriculture, hunting, forestry and fishing a	82017	19583	88107	11723	18861	182569	87153	20085	89786	13399	21201	189222
2 Mining and quarrying	18720	4328	7989	2749	4274	55512	19142	5269	7060	28246	3357	56360
A Agriculture and hunting	77165	18647	85597	10590	17532	174467	81871	19056	86748	12137	19642	180170
B Forestry and logging	4852	936	2510	1133	1329	8102	5282	1029	3038	1262	1559	9052
C Fishing	...	...	...	...	...	...	...	...	...	...	...	...
3 Manufacturing	122702	30548	142843	15033	56649	254477	133190	30793	158625	18211	68367	272452
A Manufacture of food, beverages and tobacco	17714	5314	21832	1293	25859	20294	19179	5409	19794	2332	29896	16818
B Textile, wearing apparel and leather industries												
C Manufacture of wood and wood products, including furniture	27792	3876	18204	1476	6428	44920	29440	4013	21788	2043	8464	48820
D Manufacture of paper and paper products, printing and publishing												
E Manufacture of chemical and chemical products, petroleum, coal, rubber and plastic products b	11511	7447	29352	4424	7656	45078	13215	8134	33488	5432	9735	50534
F Manufacture of non-metallic mineral products, except products of petroleum and coal	6463	2440	5575	343	129	14692	6709	2445	5038	489	248	14433
G Basic metal industries	8874	3451	9437	579	8488	12853	9858	2760	9065	914	11677	11261
H Manufacture of fabricated metal products, machinery and equipment	45587	7529	45840	6814	6979	98791	49936	7509	54302	6867	8257	110357
I Other manufacturing industries	4761	491	12603	104	110	17849	4853	523	14809	134	90	20229
4 Electricity, gas and water c	11354	9596	7313	2419	566	30116	12813	10541	9448	2509	898	34443
A Electricity, gas and steam	4026	5626	5824	1094	2	16568	4656	6223	7689	1462	19	20011
B Water works and supply	7328	3970	1489	1325	564	13548	8157	4318	1759	1047	849	14432
5 Construction	35115	3059	30316	2829	199	71120	36058	2747	32728	2761	344	73950
6 Wholesale and retail trade, restaurants and hotels	41934	3324	49075	2729	10241	86821	45423	3421	55671	4518	12292	96741
7 Transport, storage and communication	36773	16717	19469	3390	2173	74176	39984	20144	3340	2597	77731	
A Transport and storage	30369	14568	15324	3284	1726	61819	32752	14679	15292	3202	2353	63572
B Communication	6404	2149	4145	106	447	12357	7186	2227	4852	138	244	14159
8 Finance, insurance, real estate and business services de	20145	12569	14227	1382	1635	46688	23046	13692	16700	1021	959	53500
A Financial institutions	3570	175	3772	4	1288	6233	4076	472	3986	39	588	7685
B Insurance												
C Real estate and business services	16575	12394	10455	1378	347	40455	18970	13014	13220	982	371	45815
9 Community, social and personal services e	3372	176	3712	741	1644	6357	3876	202	3834	1082	1504	7490
Total, Industries 1	362674	96089	348208	25777	94269	389548	375029	81789	104597	842363		
Producers of Government Services g	69980	7574	7586	1585	-	80805	78229	7683	1532	1622	-	96066
Total, Other Producers	432534	105668	349792	27361	90181	875174	467777	108277	377651	83411	104597	931429
Less: Imputed bank service charge	...	...	...	...	167808	78593	82215	...	...	...	...	172049	83034	89015
Import duties h												
Value added tax	...	...	...	...	14067	...	...	...	...	...	...	13214
Other adjustments i												
Total	432534	105668	349792	245169	187774	978456	467777	108277	377651	255460	187931	1033658

Hungary

4.3 Cost Components of Value Added
(Continued)

Million Hungarian forint

	1986						1987					
	Compensation of Employees	Capital Consumption	Net Operating Surplus	Indirect Taxes	Less: Subsidies Received	Value Added	Compensation of Employees	Capital Consumption	Net Operating Surplus	Indirect Taxes	Less: Subsidies Received	Value Added
3 Manufacturing	143069	32937	158517	20895	79967	275451	154578	35000	183859	25313	89848	308902
A Manufacture of food, beverages and tobacco	20763	5712	20461	1584	37407	11113	23233	6286	25330	3732	43270	15311
B Textile, wearing apparel and leather industries												
C Manufacture of wood and wood products, including furniture	30973	4169	22083	2172	9626	49771	32515	4486	24744	2934	11941	52738
D Manufacture of paper and paper products, printing and publishing												
E Manufacture of chemicals and chemical petroleum, coal, rubber and plastic products b	14329	8399	26308	6198	11061	44173	15956	9013	35799	6873	10481	57160
F Manufacture of non-metallic mineral products, except products of petroleum and coal	6951	2511	5744	563	310	15459	7492	2576	7095	633	436	17360
G Basic metal industries	10629	3719	9107	926	13242	11139	11025	4263	10225	1205	14226	12492
H Manufacture of fabricated metal products, machinery and equipment	54383	7877	57915	9305	8229	121251	58681	7806	61966	9781	9369	128865
I Other manufacturing industries	5041	550	16899	147	92	22545	5676	570	18700	155	125	24976
4 Electricity, gas and water c	14137	12737	11020	7568	712	44750	15317	13060	12261	14530	875	54293
A Electricity, gas and steam	5285	8056	9297	6363	4	28997	5760	7967	10036	13211	-	36974
B Water works and supply	8852	4681	1723	1205	708	15753	9557	5093	2225	1319	875	17319
5 Construction	38467	2787	37010	3112	2410	78966	43842	2840	45955	3807	4211	92233
6 Wholesale and retail trade, restaurants and hotels	48310	3705	63877	5969	13884	107977	52691	4021	77732	7167	13504	128107
7 Transport, storage and communication	42473	17820	25206	3399	2648	86250	45242	18511	31547	1782	2657	94425
A Transport and storage	34614	15335	20121	3116	2358	70828	36720	15838	24634	1345	2296	76241
B Communication	7859	2485	5085	283	290	15422	8522	2673	6913	437	361	18184
8 Finance, insurance, real estate and business services de	26074	14691	21155	922	2916	59926	30042	17120	22274	1148	309	70275
A Financial institutions	4827	768	6101	68	2691	9073	5996	2112	4257	137	113	12407
B Insurance												
C Real estate and business services	21247	13923	15054	854	225	50853	24046	15008	18017	1011	196	57868
9 Community, social and personal services e	4336	225	4375	953	1609	8280	4984	260	4994	885	1693	9430
Total, Industries f	417603	108813	417256	84290	127281	900681	452991	116166	475468	96277	137655	1003247
Producers of Government Services g	85618	8143	1318	1459	-	96538	95151	8610	1532	1799	-	107092
Other Producers	...	...	...	...	...	...	...	...	...	...	...	...
Total	503221	116956	418574	85749	127281	997219	548142	124776	477000	98076	137655	1110339
Less: Imputed bank service charge	...	...	...	...	...	...	...	...	...	...	...	...
Import duties h	...	...	...	171629	92332	79297	...	...	...	201976	101150	100826
Value added tax	...	...	...	...	...	...	...	...	...	...	...	...
Other adjustments i	...	...	...	...	...	12284	...	...	...	...	...	15205
Total	503221	116956	418574	257378	219613	1088800	548142	124776	477000	300052	238805	1226370

	1988					
	Compensation of Employees	Capital Consumption	Net Operating Surplus	Indirect Taxes	Less: Subsidies Received	Value Added
All Producers						
1 Agriculture, hunting, forestry and fishing a	106960	20450	96176	7547	21679	209454
A Agriculture and hunting	100551	19505	93588	6215	19970	199889
B Forestry and logging	6409	945	2588	1332	1709	9565
C Fishing	...	...	...	...	...	...
2 Mining and quarrying	27033	5809	588	30077	8061	55446

Hungary

4.3 Cost Components of Value Added
(Continued)

Million Hungarian forint

1988

	Compensation of Employees	Capital Consumption	Net Operating Surplus	Indirect Taxes	Less: Subsidies Received	Value Added
3 Manufacturing	193785	36080	139611	28913	71205	327184
A Manufacture of food, beverages and tobacco	30798	6445	25278	1768	43444	20845
B Textile, wearing apparel and leather industries						
C Manufacture of wood and wood products, including furniture	38598	4363	15073	1922	7708	52248
D Manufacture of paper and paper products, printing and publishing						
E Manufacture of chemicals and chemical petroleum, coal, rubber and plastic products b	21293	9012	31128	8404	5234	64603
F Manufacture of non-metallic mineral products, except products of petroleum and coal	9154	2518	4959	640	205	17066
G Basic metal industries	14426	5075	9674	2520	9838	21857
H Manufacture of fabricated metal products, machinery and equipment	71602	7900	35178	12909	4513	123076
I Other manufacturing industries	7914	767	18321	750	263	27489
4 Electricity, gas and water c	17488	13632	10908	23732	1259	64501
A Electricity, gas and steam	7516	8351	9276	22394	-	47537
B Water works and supply	9972	5281	1632	1338	1259	16964
5 Construction	59718	2934	36449	3757	6083	96775
6 Wholesale and retail trade, restaurants and hotels	63379	4542	62609	6710	10843	125857
7 Transport, storage and communication	54325	19281	26685	2229	1250	101170
A Transport and storage	43900	16145	21057	1938	967	82073
B Communication	10425	3136	5528	291	283	19097
8 Finance, insurance, real estate and business services d e	41983	20782	23210	1127	591	86511
A Financial institutions	10890	4269	3333	168	392	18358
B Insurance						
C Real estate and business services	31093	16513	19877	959	199	68153
9 Community, social and personal services e	8804	910	6662	560	1716	15220
Total, Industries f	-	573475	124420	402258	104652	122687	1082118
Producers of Government Services g	121631	8319	611	1396	-	131957
Other Producers						
Total	695106	132739	402869	106048	122687	1214075
Less: Imputed bank service charge						
Import duties h	...	...	...	271890	94484	177406
Value added tax	...	...	...	...	...	...
Other adjustments i	...	...	...	...	...	18036
Total	695106	132739	402869	377938	217171	1409517

a) Item 'Agriculture, hunting, forestry and fishing' includes operation of irrigation systems and veterinary services.
b) Item 'Manufacturing' includes gas.
c) Item 'Electricity, gas and water' excludes gas and operation of irrigation systems.
d) Gross output of finance, insurance and that of owner-occupied housing are estimated at cost level.
e) Sanitary and similar services and personal and household services are included in item 'Finance, insurance, real estate and business services'.
f) All types of repair services are included in the relevant industries.
g) Item 'Producers of government services' includes non-profit institutions.
h) Item 'Import duties' refers to all net taxes on commodities and are excluded from the value added of industries.
i) Item 'Statistical discrepancy' refers to the difference between subsistence production valued at approximated basis values and final consumption of goods from subsistence production valued at consumer prices.

793

Hungary

1a Net Material Product by Use at Current Market Prices

Thousand Million Hungarian forint

	1970	1975	1980	1981	1982	1983	1984	1985	1986	1987	1988	1989
1 Personal consumption	162.2	235.7										
2 Material consumption in the units of the non-material sphere serving individuals	16.0	25.9										
Consumption of the Population	178.2	261.6 / 263.3	406.5	439.4	474.8	507.6	549.0	585.9	626.8	669.6	756.2	898.0
3 Material consumption in the units of the non-material sphere serving the community as a whole	22.9 / 32.1	40.2	63.4	68.7	74.1	79.1	82.3	90.9	99.1	107.1	130.7	152.2
4 Net fixed capital formation	54.7	101.1 / 101.1	110.1	100.7	96.1	120.7	123.3	105.4	154.2	150.4	137.7	174.6
5 Increase in material circulating assets and in stocks a	22.6	30.1 / 26.4	18.5	34.3	44.6	13.6	18.6	38.7	16.6	48.4	89.4	131.2
6 Losses	4.2	6.9	-	-	-	-	-	-	-	-	-	-
7 Exports of goods and material services	100.2	198.4 / 200.2	281.8	308.2	321.8	360.7	402.0	436.2	431.6	464.4	530.4	621.6
8 Less: Imports of goods and material services	107.9	234.1 / 236.2	297.4	316.4	315.0	343.6	371.1	414.8	447.0	470.3	491.7	563.5
Net Material Product	274.9	395.0 / 396.1	582.9	634.9	696.4	738.1	804.1	842.3	881.3	999.6	1152.7	1414.1

a) Item 'Increase in material circulating assets and in stocks' includes changes in incompleted capital formation.

1b Net Material Product by Use at Constant Market Prices

Thousand Million Hungarian forint

At constant prices of: 1976 / 1981

	1970	1975	1980	1981	1982	1983	1984	1985	1986	1987	1988	1989
1 Personal consumption	200.8	253.6										
2 Material consumption in the units of the non-material sphere serving individuals	19.3	27.4										
Consumption of the Population	220.1	281.0 / 377.7	429.0	441.8	448.0	450.4	454.5	457.6	466.5	483.0	462.8	463.0
3 Material consumption in the units of the non-material sphere serving the community as a whole	26.0	33.5 / 50.4	67.1	69.1	70.0	70.5	71.3	74.6	76.5	76.7	80.8	75.0
4 Net fixed capital formation	66.2	102.1 / 115.4	105.5	89.2	75.2	98.6	78.7	49.6	82.2	66.5	41.2	43.8
5 Increase in material circulating assets and in stocks a	15.6	18.2 / 24.7	15.7	21.6	21.9	-9.4	-10.2	8.6	-11.5	6.2	20.5	15.7
6 Losses	5.4	7.3	-	-	-	-	-	-	-	-	...	...
7 Exports of goods and material services	119.5	189.1 / 209.4	292.5	308.2	319.1	340.4	363.0	381.9	373.4	391.1	416.4	420.3
8 Less: Imports of goods and material services	151.8	218.5 / 257.3	311.4	316.4	304.5	307.1	310.4	334.7	343.7	353.7	355.3	358.5
Net Material Product	301.0	412.7 / 520.3	598.4	613.5	629.7	631.4	646.9	637.6	643.4	669.8	666.4	659.3

a) Item 'Increase in material circulating assets and in stocks' includes changes in incompleted capital formation.

Hungary

2a Net Material Product by Kind of Activity of the Material Sphere in Current Market Prices

Thousand Million Hungarian forint

	1970	1975	1980	1981	1982	1983	1984	1985	1986	1987	1988	1989
1 Agriculture and forestry	48.9	65.1 65.6	85.3	93.7	97.2	97.8	105.6	100.3	110.6	112.5	126.5	...
2 Industrial activity	120.5	185.5 189.9	211.8	237.4	259.5	276.7	301.9	329.7	335.5	401.8	404.8	...
3 Construction	30.7	45.8 48.4	60.0	62.9	71.0	77.6	84.5	86.2	94.0	105.2	106.0	...
4 Wholesale and retail trade and restaurants and other eating and drinking places	54.6	69.8 60.3	69.2	73.1	75.6	81.3	93.0	101.1	114.4	114.6	135.3	...
5 Transport and communication	17.0	24.0 30.4	45.2	50.5	57.3	57.8	58.8	60.6	67.9	74.9	79.7	...
A Transport	13.7	19.5 25.9	38.8	42.2	48.3	48.9	49.2	49.4	55.7	60.4	65.4	...
B Communication	3.3	4.5 4.5	6.4	8.3	9.0	8.9	9.6	11.2	12.2	14.5	14.3	...
6 Other activities of the material sphere [a]	3.2	5.9 3.1	4.8	5.6	6.1	8.9	10.8	12.8	14.0	15.8	22.3	...
Statistical discrepancy [b]	...	... -2.7	106.6	111.7	129.7	138.0	149.5	151.6	144.9	174.8	278.1	...
Net material product	274.9	396.1 395.0	582.9	634.9	696.4	738.1	804.1	842.3	881.3	999.6	1152.7	...

a) For the second series, item 'Other activities of the material sphere' includes water, computer services etc.

b) Statistical discrepancy refers to taxes on commodities net and price difference which are not included in the above items, it also includes non-material services purchased by the material sphere.

2b Net Material Product by Kind of Activity of the Material Sphere in Constant Market Prices

Thousand Million Hungarian forint

	1970	1975	1980	1981	1982	1983	1984	1985	1986	1987	1988	1989
					At constant prices of:							
		1976					1981					
1 Agriculture and forestry	65.3	73.8 89.8	90.2	90.4	98.6	95.8	101.4	93.5	97.8	93.4	102.6	...
2 Industrial activity	132.7	190.5 175.9	214.0	224.2	236.4	245.6	249.8	246.7	243.8	252.7	245.7	...
3 Construction	34.6	45.8 48.7	60.0	61.7	62.8	62.7	59.2	54.1	54.6	55.5	48.1	...
4 Wholesale and retail trade and restaurants and other eating and drinking places	45.2	71.6 64.5	69.4	72.6	73.2	70.4	71.5	71.6	72.0	76.5	66.3	...
5 Transport and communication	18.1	24.0 40.5	45.3	47.7	48.0	47.5	48.9	47.3	48.9	51.3	52.2	...
A Transport	14.7	19.6 34.5	37.8	39.6	39.5	38.8	39.6	37.1	38.8	40.5	41.2	...
B Communication	3.4	4.4 6.0	7.5	8.1	8.5	8.7	9.3	10.2	10.1	10.8	11.0	...
6 Other activities of the material sphere	5.1	7.0 3.8[a]	5.2[a]	5.2[a]	4.9[a]	6.9[a]	7.6[a]	9.2[a]	10.4[a]	11.4[a]	15.4[a]	...
Statistical discrepancy	...	... 97.1[b]	114.3[b]	111.7[b]	105.8[b]	102.5[b]	108.5[b]	115.2[b]	115.9[b]	129.0[b]	136.4[b]	...
Net material product	301.0	412.7 520.3	598.4	613.5	629.7	631.4	646.9	637.6	643.4	669.8	666.4	...

a) For the second series, item 'Other activities of the material sphere' includes water, computer services etc.

b) Statistical discrepancy refers to taxes on commodities net and price difference which are not included in the above items, it also includes non-material services purchased by the material sphere.

4 Primary Incomes From Net Material Product

Thousand Million Hungarian forint

	1970	1975	1980	1981	1982	1983	1984	1985	1986	1987	1988	1989
			a) Primary Incomes of the Population									
1 Socialist sector	128.1	178.9	...	...	...	...	...	...	...	...	...	...
A State sector	74.7	110.1	...	...	...	...	...	...	...	...	...	...
B Co-operative sector	45.6	56.9	...	...	...	...	...	...	...	...	...	...
C Personal plots of households	7.8	11.9	...	...	...	...	...	...	...	...	...	...
2 Private sector	6.1	6.7	...	...	...	...	...	...	...	...	...	...
Sub-total	134.2	185.6	...	...	...	...	...	...	...	...	...	...
			b) Primary incomes of the enterprises									
1 Socialist sector	140.0	209.3	...	...	...	...	...	...	...	...	...	...
A State sector	121.8	175.7	...	...	...	...	...	...	...	...	...	...
B Co-operative sector	18.2	33.6	...	...	...	...	...	...	...	...	...	...
2 Private sector	0.7	1.2	...	...	...	...	...	...	...	...	...	...
Sub-total	140.7	210.5	...	...	...	...	...	...	...	...	...	...
Total net material product	274.9	396.1	...	...	...	...	...	...	...	...	...	...

Hungary

6a Capital Formation by Kind of Activity of the Material and Non-Material Spheres in Current Market Prices

Thousand Million Hungarian forint

	1970	1975	1980	1981	1982	1983	1984	1985	1986	1987	1988	1989
Net Fixed Capital Formation												
1 Agriculture and forestry	11.1	12.6	7.9 8.0	10.1	11.8	12.1	8.4	6.8	8.7	18.2	9.3	...
2 Industrial activity	16.5	37.7	26.8 26.0	21.6	17.8	32.7	35.8	13.1	45.1	35.6	28.0	...
3 Construction	0.6	1.0	-0.3 1.4	1.5	-0.4	0.1	0.4	-0.5	-0.1	0.9	0.5	...
4 Wholesale and retail trade, restaurants and other eating and drinking places	1.9	3.3	4.8 5.1	6.3	8.6	5.4	4.6	6.3	7.4	6.1	5.9	...
5 Transport and communication	7.6	9.5	15.1 15.3	8.7	6.2	9.9	11.4	9.5	11.2	11.1	10.3	...
6 Other activities of the material sphere	0.5	1.0	0.6 8.3	8.7	8.1	8.3	10.7	9.5	11.6	12.2	11.0	...
Total Material Sphere	38.2	65.1	54.9 64.1	56.9	52.1	68.5	71.3	44.7	83.9	84.1	65.0	...
7 Housing except owner-occupied, communal and miscellaneous personal services [a]	9.7	23.2	31.2 31.6	31.6	33.5	40.1	39.9	45.8	49.0	44.2	52.9	...
8 Education, culture and art	1.3	3.6	5.9 5.9	5.3	4.5	5.2	4.2	4.1	5.9	6.4	6.7	...
9 Health and social welfare services and sports	2.1	2.7	7.1 4.2	3.4	2.5	1.7	4.6	3.4	3.3	4.3	4.0	...
Total Non-Material Sphere Serving Individuals	13.1	29.5	44.2 41.7	40.3	40.5	48.0	48.7	53.3	58.2	54.9	63.6	...
10 Government	...	...	...	...	...	...	...	...	...	...	...	...
11 Finance, credit and insurance	...	...	...	...	...	...	...	...	...	...	...	...
12 Research, scientific and technological institutes	...	...	...	...	...	...	...	...	...	...	...	...
13 Other activities of the non-material sphere	...	...	...	...	...	...	...	...	...	...	...	...
Total Non-Material Sphere Serving the Community as a Whole	3.4	6.5	11.0 4.3	3.5	3.5	4.1	3.2	7.4	12.1	11.5	8.8	...
14 Owner-occupied dwellings [a]	...	...	...	...	...	...	...	...	...	...	...	...
Total Net Fixed Capital Formation	54.7	101.1	110.1 110.1	100.7	96.1	120.6	123.3	105.4	154.2	150.5	137.4	...
Gross Fixed Capital Formation												
1 Agriculture and forestry	16.3	22.0	23.6 26.1	28.9	31.4	31.1	28.5	26.6	29.1	38.9	30.8	...
2 Industrial activity	31.5	59.5	66.3 62.4	59.7	57.7	72.6	77.8	58.1	94.4	87.0	80.7	...
3 Construction	1.9	3.1	4.1 4.8	4.9	3.0	3.3	3.6	2.4	2.7	3.8	3.5	...
4 Wholesale and retail trade and restaurants and other eating and drinking places	2.8	4.9	7.7 8.0	9.2	11.8	8.7	8.0	9.8	11.1	10.1	10.4	...
5 Transport and communication	14.2	18.0	28.2 28.8	22.9	21.0	25.3	28.1	26.4	29.0	29.6	29.6	...
6 Other activities of the material sphere	0.9	1.8	1.7 12.1	12.7	12.5	13.2	16.2	15.5	18.0	19.0	18.3	...
Total Material Sphere	67.6	109.3	131.6 142.2	138.3	137.4	154.2	162.2	138.8	184.3	188.4	173.3	...
7 Housing except owner-occupied, communal and miscellaneous personal services [a]	13.9	29.1	39.7 40.1	40.5	42.9	50.2	50.5	57.1	60.8	56.9	63.6	...
8 Education, culture and art	2.6	5.5	8.9 8.3	7.6	7.0	8.9	7.3	7.2	9.2	9.9	10.4	...
9 Health and social welfare services and sports	2.7	3.5	8.4 5.5	4.7	3.9	3.1	6.3	5.2	5.3	6.5	6.4	...
Total Non-Material Sphere Serving Individuals	19.2	38.1	57.0 53.9	52.8	53.8	62.2	64.1	69.5	75.3	73.3	80.4	...

Hungary

6a Capital Formation by Kind of Activity of the Material and Non-Material Spheres in Current Market Prices
(Continued)

Thousand Million Hungarian forint

	1970	1975	1980	1981	1982	1983	1984	1985	1986	1987	1988	1989
10 Government	...	...	... ...	...	...	...	...	...	...	...	...	...
11 Finance, credit and insurance	...	...	... ...	...	...	...	...	...	...	...	...	...
12 Research, scientific and technological institutes	...	...	... ...	...	...	...	...	...	...	...	...	...
13 Other activities of the non-material sphere	...	...	... ...	...	...	...	...	...	...	...	...	...
Total Non-Material Sphere Serving the Community as a Whole	4.5	8.5	14.2 6.7	5.9	6.0	7.1	6.8	11.4	16.5	17.4	15.8	...
14 Owner-occupied dwellings a	...	...	... ...	...	...	...	...	...	...	...	...	...
Total Gross Fixed Capital Formation	91.3	155.9	202.8 202.8	197.0	197.2	223.5	233.1	219.7	276.1	279.1	269.5	...

Gross Fixed Capital Formation by Socio-economic Sector and Industrial Use

	1970	1975	1980	1981	1982	1983	1984	1985	1986	1987	1988	1989
1 State and co-operative (excluding collective farms)	55.5	92.2	115.4 162.8	152.1	146.2	165.2	169.0	150.0	202.2	201.9	192.0	...
A Industry	31.5	59.5	66.3 62.4	59.7	57.6	72.5	77.7	58.0	94.2	87.0	80.7	...
B Construction	1.9	3.1	4.1 4.8	4.8	3.0	3.2	3.6	2.3	2.6	3.7	3.5	...
C Agriculture and forestry	4.2	4.9	7.4 10.3	10.4	10.7	11.0	9.7	9.4	11.4	14.1	10.6	...
D Transport and communication	14.2	18.0	28.2 28.8	22.8	20.8	25.1	27.7	25.4	28.2	29.6	29.6	...
E Residential building b	...	...	... ...	...	...	...	...	...	...	...	...	...
F Trade and other	3.7	6.7	9.4 56.5	54.4	54.1	53.4	50.3	54.9	65.8	67.5	67.6	...
2 Collective farms	11.5	16.3	16.2 14.9	17.9	20.5	22.8	20.5	18.7	19.7	26.1	19.6	...
A Agriculture	11.5	16.3	16.2 14.9	17.9	20.5	22.8	20.5	18.7	19.7	26.1	...	...
B Other	-	-	... ...	...	...	...	...	...	...	...	...	...
3 Other b	24.3	47.4	71.2 25.1	27.0	30.5	35.5	43.6	51.0	54.2	51.1	57.9	...
Gross Fixed Capital Formation	91.3	155.9	202.8 202.8	197.0	197.2	223.5	233.1	219.7	276.1	279.1	269.5	...

a) Item 'Owner-occupied dwellings' is included in item 'Housing except owner-occupied, communal, and miscellaneous personal services'.
b) Item 'Residential buildings' is included in item 'Other'.

6b Capital Formation by Kind of Activity of the Material and Non-Material Spheres in Constant Market Prices

Thousand Million Hungarian forint

	1970	1975	1980	1981	1982	1983	1984	1985	1986	1987	1988	1989
			At constant prices of:									
		1976						1981				
			Net Fixed Capital Formation									
1 Agriculture and forestry	13.3	12.3	5.0 6.4	7.6	7.4	4.8	1.2	-1.7	-0.9	4.9	-2.1	...
2 Industrial activity	18.6	36.9	23.6 22.5	17.2	11.2	22.5	21.5	-1.7	25.0	12.6	2.2	...
3 Construction	0.7	0.8	-0.4 1.4	1.3	-0.8	-0.6	-0.5	-1.5	-1.2	-0.4	-0.9	...
4 Wholesale and retail trade, restaurants and other eating and drinking places	2.3	3.3	4.2 5.4	6.1	8.1	4.2	2.9	3.8	4.5	2.8	2.1	...
5 Transport and communication	9.8	9.5	13.0 13.8	6.6	3.1	6.2	7.1	3.9	4.0	3.2	2.3	...
6 Other activities of the material sphere	0.4	0.9	0.4 8.5	8.4	7.4	6.9	8.8	6.8	7.7	7.0	5.7	...

Hungary

6b Capital Formation by Kind of Activity of the Material and Non-Material Spheres in Constant Market Prices
(Continued)

Thousand Million Hungarian forint

	1970	1975	1980	1981	1982	1983	1984	1985	1986	1987	1988	1989
					At constant prices of:							
Total Material Sphere	45.1	**1976** 63.7	45.8 58.0	47.2	36.4	44.0	**1981** 41.0	9.6	39.1	30.1	9.3	...
7 Housing except owner-occupied, communal and miscellaneous personal services [a]	12.5	25.0	26.9 32.7	30.2	29.6	31.0	28.1	28.8	28.3	22.1	20.3	...
8 Education, culture and art	1.7	3.7	5.2 6.0	5.1	4.0	6.3	2.5	2.7	3.8	3.9	3.7	...
9 Health and social welfare services and sports	2.8	2.9	3.7 4.4	3.2	2.3	1.4	4.8	2.5	2.2	2.8	2.3	...
Total Non-Material Sphere Serving Individuals	17.0	31.6	35.8 43.1	38.5	35.9	38.7	35.4	34.0	34.3	28.8	26.3	...
10 Government	...	...	... ...	...	...	...	...	...	...	...	...	...
11 Finance, credit and insurance	...	...	... ...	...	...	...	...	...	...	...	...	...
12 Research, scientific and technological institutes	...	...	... ...	...	...	...	...	...	...	...	...	...
13 Other activities of the non-material sphere	...	...	... ...	...	...	...	...	...	...	...	...	...
Total Non-Material Sphere Serving the Community as a Whole	4.1	6.8	10.6 4.7	3.5	2.9	3.9	2.3	5.9	8.7	7.5	5.1	...
14 Owner-occupied dwellings [a]	...	...	...	...	...	...	...	...	...	...	...	...
Total Net Fixed Capital Formation	66.2	102.1	92.2 105.8	89.2	75.2	86.6	78.7	49.5	82.1	66.4	40.7	...
					Gross Fixed Capital Formation							
1 Agriculture and forestry	19.7	23.5	21.1 27.4	29.5	30.6	28.2	24.5	21.5	22.1	28.0	21.1	...
2 Industrial activity	37.4	62.5	60.7 63.5	60.5	56.7	69.7	70.8	49.3	77.7	66.9	58.2	...
3 Construction	2.2	3.2	3.7 4.9	5.0	2.9	3.1	3.2	2.1	2.3	2.9	2.5	...
4 Wholesale and retail trade and restaurants and other eating and drinking places	3.4	5.1	7.1 8.3	9.3	11.6	8.0	7.0	8.1	9.1	7.8	7.4	...
5 Transport and communciation	17.6	19.4	26.0 30.0	23.5	20.5	24.1	25.4	22.6	23.0	22.5	22.0	...
6 Other activities of the material sphere	1.0	1.9	1.6 12.6	12.8	12.4	12.3	14.5	12.8	14.1	13.8	12.8	...
Total Material Sphere	81.3	115.6	120.2 146.7	140.6	134.7	145.4	145.4	116.4	148.3	141.9	124.0	...
7 Housing except owner-occupied, communal and miscellaneous personal services [a]	17.4	31.3	35.2 42.7	40.7	40.7	42.5	40.2	41.3	41.3	35.5	34.1	...
8 Education, culture and art	3.3	5.9	8.5 8.6	7.8	6.8	9.4	5.6	6.0	7.3	7.6	7.6	...
9 Health and social welfare services and sports	3.4	3.8	5.1 5.8	4.7	3.9	3.1	6.5	4.4	4.2	5.0	4.6	...
Total Non-Material Sphere Serving Individuals	24.1	41.0	48.8 57.1	53.2	51.4	55.0	52.3	51.7	52.8	48.1	46.3	...

Hungary

6b Capital Formation by Kind of Activity of the Material and Non-Material Spheres in Constant Market Prices
(Continued)

Thousand Million Hungarian forint

	1970	1975	1980	1981	1982	1983	1984	1985	1986	1987	1988	1989
				At constant prices of:								
		1976					1981					
10 Government	...	...	...	...	...	...	...	...	...	...	...	...
			...									
11 Finance, credit and insurance	...	...	...	...	...	...	...	...	...	...	...	...
			...									
12 Research, scientific and technological institutes	...	...	...	...	...	...	...	...	...	...	...	...
			...									
13 Other activities of the non-material sphere	...	...	...	...	...	...	...	...	...	...	...	...
			...									
Total Non-Material Sphere Serving the Community as a Whole	5.6	9.0	14.1									
			6.9	6.1	5.7	7.0	5.7	9.7	12.9	12.8	11.4	...
14 Owner-occupied dwellings a	...	...	...	...	...	...	...	...	...	...	...	...
			...									
Total Gross Fixed Capital Formation	111.0	165.6	183.1									
			210.7	199.9	191.8	207.4	203.4	177.8	214.0	202.8	181.7	...

a) Item 'Owner-occupied dwellings' is included in item 'Housing except owner-occupied, communal, and miscellaneous personal services'.

7a Final Consumption at Current Market Prices

Thousand Million Hungarian forint

	1970	1975	1980	1981	1982	1983	1984	1985	1986	1987	1988	1989
1 Personal consumption	162.2	235.7	355.6	...	...	...	...	...	...	...	...	...
a) Material Consumption in the Units of the Non-Material Sphere Serving Individuals												
Housing except owner-occupied, communal and miscellaneous personal services	5.7	9.3	22.0	...	...	...	...	...	...	...	...	...
Education, culture and art	6.2	10.3	16.3	...	...	...	...	...	...	...	...	...
Health and social welfare services and sports	4.1	6.3	11.3	...	...	...	...	...	...	...	...	...
Other	...	...	...	...	...	...	...	...	...	...	...	...
2 Total non-material sphere serving individuals	16.0	25.9	49.6	...	...	...	...	...	...	...	...	...
b) Material Consumption in the Units of the Non-Material Sphere Serving the Community as a Whole												
3 Total non-material sphere serving the community as a whole	22.9	32.1	51.4	...	...	...	...	...	...	...	...	...
Final consumption	201.1	293.7	456.6	...	...	...	...	...	...	...	...	...

7b Final Consumption at Constant Market Prices

Thousand Million Hungarian forint

	1970	1975	1980	1981	1982	1983	1984	1985	1986	1987	1988	1989
				At constant prices of:1976								
1 Personal consumption	200.8	253.6	285.4	...	...	...	...	...	...	...	...	...
a) Material Consumption in the Units of the Non-Material Sphere Serving Individuals												
Housing except owner-occupied, communal and miscellaneous personal services	6.8	10.4	16.0	...	...	...	...	...	...	...	...	...
Education, culture and art	7.4	10.5	14.5	...	...	...	...	...	...	...	...	...
Health and social welfare services and sports	5.1	6.5	8.5	...	...	...	...	...	...	...	...	...
Other	...	...	...	...	...	...	...	...	...	...	...	...
2 Total non-material sphere serving individuals	19.3	27.4	39.0	...	...	...	...	...	...	...	...	...
b) Material Consumption in the Units of the Non-Material Sphere Serving the Community as a Whole												
3 Total non-material sphere serving the community as a whole	26.0	33.5	44.7	...	...	...	...	...	...	...	...	...
Final consumption	246.1	314.5	369.1	...	...	...	...	...	...	...	...	...

Hungary

8 Personal Consumption According to Source of Supply of Goods and Material Services in Current Market Prices

Thousand Million Hungarian forint

	1970	1975	1980	1981	1982	1983	1984	1985	1986	1987	1988	1989
1 Purchases of goods in state and co-operative retail trade [a]	112.4	175.3	267.9	...	...	...	...	...	...	...	...	...
2 Purchases of goods in the free market and from private retail trade [a]	7.2	8.3	11.5	...	...	...	...	...	...	...	...	...
3 Goods produced on own account and received in kind	17.2	16.3	21.7	...	...	...	...	...	...	...	...	...
4 Payments for transport and communication services	6.0	8.4	10.8	...	...	...	...	...	...	...	...	...
5 Purchases of electricity, gas and water	2.7	4.5	9.1	...	...	...	...	...	...	...	...	...
6 Purchases directly from handicrafts, repair shops and the like	16.7	22.9	34.6	...	...	...	...	...	...	...	...	...
7 Consumption of fixed assets in respect of all dwellings	...	...	...	...	...	...	...	...	...	...	...	...
8 Other	...	...	...	...	...	...	...	...	...	...	...	...
Personal consumption	162.2	235.7	355.6	...	...	...	...	...	...	...	...	...

a) Private retail trade is included in items 'Purchases of goods in state and co-operative retail trade'
and 'Purchases of goods in the free market and from private and retail trade'.

9a Total Consumption of the Population in Current Market Prices

Thousand Million Hungarian forint

	1970	1975	1980	1981	1982	1983	1984	1985	1986	1987	1988	1989
					By Object							
1 Housing except owner-occupied, communal and miscellaneous personal services	8.8	14.3	...	...	...	...	...	...	...	...	...	...
2 Education, culture and art	12.8	20.4	...	...	...	...	...	...	...	...	...	...
3 Health and social welfare services and sport	8.8	14.2	...	...	...	...	...	...	...	...	...	...
Total consumption of non-material services	30.4	48.9	...	...	...	...	...	...	...	...	...	...
4 Personal consumption of goods and material services excluding depreciation of dwellings	162.2	235.7	...	...	...	...	...	...	...	...	...	...
Total consumption of the population	192.6	284.6 / 286.1	441.2	477.7	515.1	551.2	600.5	649.3	695.5	778.5	854.5	...
					By Commodity and Service							
1 Food	64.2	81.8 / 85.1	128.6	136.4	143.6	152.3	169.5	180.2	188.2	212.6	235.6	...
2 Beverages, coffee and tea	21.4	34.6 / 37.5	59.2	61.4	69.5	72.5	76.3	79.9	86.0	89.4	97.0	...
3 Tobacco	4.1	6.3 / 6.3	10.4	10.9	13.1	13.6	14.1	14.3	15.5	19.1	22.9	...
4 Clothing and footwear	23.2	31.3 / 31.7	40.6	44.1	45.3	48.4	50.7	56.0	59.1	65.8	65.0	...
5 Gross rent	6.8	11.2 / 11.2	17.1	18.9	20.6	23.0	25.7	27.6	29.7	33.2	39.5	...
6 Fuel, electricity, water and gas	6.3	9.0 / 9.0	16.2	16.7	19.0	19.6	21.9	27.7	27.9	32.0	34.9	...
7 Furniture and household equipment	15.6	25.0 / 25.2	35.5	39.5	41.5	43.6	48.2	50.2	53.8	62.2	64.3	...
8 Health	11.4	18.4 / 15.7	26.2	29.9	32.7	34.8	37.2	40.3	44.2	49.2	56.5	...
9 Transport and communication	12.3	22.0 / 20.5	33.6	36.9	40.1	46.1	49.9	55.1	61.2	70.0	77.7	...
10 Education, recreation, sport	20.3	33.0 / 33.0	54.4	61.9	67.1	71.9	78.2	86.8	95.1	105.2	113.9	...

Hungary

9a Total Consumption of the Population in Current Market Prices
(Continued)

Thousand Million Hungarian forint

	1970	1975	1980	1981	1982	1983	1984	1985	1986	1987	1988	1989
11 Other	7.0	12.0 10.9	19.4	21.1	22.6	25.4	28.8	31.2	34.8	39.8	47.2	...
Total consumption of the population	192.6	284.6 286.1	441.2	477.7	515.1	551.2	600.5	649.3	695.5	778.5	854.5	...
By Mode of Acquisition												
1 Purchased	147.6	224.8 224.1	344.5	371.1	399.6	429.9	469.0	509.6	548.7	615.2	665.6	...
2 Free of charge	25.5	39.9 36.0	60.7	68.1	75.8	80.7	87.9	97.0	103.3	112.7	132.6	...
3 From own production a	19.5	19.9 26.0	36.0	38.5	39.7	40.6	43.6	42.7	43.5	50.6	56.3	...
Total consumption of the population	192.6	284.6 286.1	441.2	477.7	515.1	551.2	600.5	649.3	695.5	778.5	854.5	...

a) For the second series, consumption of the population from own production covers the consumption of agricultural products from own-production which is valued at consumer prices and the capital consumption of owner-occupied dwellings.

9b Total Consumption of the Population in Constant Market Prices

Thousand Million Hungarian forint

	1970	1975	1980	1981	1982	1983	1984	1985	1986	1987	1988	1989
					At constant prices of:							
	1976						1981					
By Object												
1 Housing except owner-occupied, communal and miscellaneous personal services	...	... ...	...	...	...	...	...	...	...	...	...	...
2 Education, culture and art	...	... ...	...	...	...	...	...	...	...	...	...	...
3 Health and social welfare services and sport	...	... ...	...	...	...	...	...	...	...	...	...	...
Total consumption of non-material services	37.4	50.5 ...										
4 Personal consumption of goods and material services excluding depreciation of dwellings	200.8	253.6 ...								...	...	...
Total consumption of the population	238.2	304.1 411.5	467.4	479.7	485.8	488.3	494.1	500.8	510.8	530.0	507.8	...
By Commodity and Service												
1 Food	82.0	94.7 131.7	134.4	136.4	137.6	139.4	139.0	140.0	141.9	146.9	142.6	...
2 Beverages, coffee and tea	28.0	35.8 50.1	60.9	61.4	62.2	60.8	61.1	62.6	63.6	59.6	57.2	...
3 Tobacco	5.1	6.3 8.4	10.8	10.9	11.2	11.6	11.9	12.1	12.8	12.5	12.8	...
4 Clothing and footwear	29.1	32.9 44.8	43.4	44.1	42.9	43.0	40.8	40.6	39.4	40.2	33.3	...
5 Gross rent	9.1	11.7 14.8	19.1	20.4	21.5	22.6	23.2	23.4	23.9	25.0	26.2	...
6 Fuel, electricity, water and gas	6.9	8.9 11.4	16.2	16.7	17.3	17.1	18.3	19.3	19.0	20.5	20.2	...
7 Furniture and household equipment	18.8	25.9 35.3	37.0	39.5	40.0	39.9	41.2	39.7	40.1	43.8	39.8	...
8 Health	13.6	18.8 22.3	28.4	30.0	31.2	31.3	31.3	31.8	32.8	34.2	32.9	...
9 Transport and communication	12.7	22.6 30.2	37.8	36.9	36.6	35.3	37.3	38.8	42.2	47.1	48.8	...
10 Education, recreation, sport	23.7	33.9 46.4	59.1	62.3	64.2	65.6	67.1	69.2	71.6	76.4	70.0	...

Hungary

9b Total Consumption of the Population in Constant Market Prices
(Continued)

Thousand Million Hungarian forint

	1970	1975	1980	1981	1982	1983	1984	1985	1986	1987	1988	1989
					At constant prices of:							
		1976					**1981**					
11 Other	9.2	12.6										
		16.1	20.3	21.1	21.1	21.7	22.9	23.3	23.5	23.8	24.0	...
Total consumption of the population	238.2	304.1										
		411.5	467.4	479.7	485.8	488.3	494.1	500.8	510.8	530.0	507.8	...
					By Mode of Acquisition							
1 Purchased	180.9	239.0										
		320.0	361.9	371.1	374.4	376.3	380.9	387.0	396.6	411.7	389.9	...
2 Free of charge	30.8	41.6										
		53.2	66.3	68.9	71.9	72.9	74.0	76.0	77.6	79.5	77.7	...
3 From own production	26.5	23.5										
		38.3	39.2	39.7	39.5	39.1	39.2	37.8	36.6	38.8	40.2	...
Total consumption of the population	238.2	304.1										
		411.5	467.4	479.7	485.8	488.3	494.1	500.8	510.8	530.0	507.8	...

Iceland

General note. The preparation of national accounts statistics in Iceland is undertaken by 'ÞJÓÐHAGSSTOFNUN' (National Economic Institute), Reykjavik. The official estimates are published once or twice a year in 'ÞJÓÐARBÚSKAPURINN' (The Icelandic Economy) and in more detail but irregularly in that serie on national accounts especially in no. 3 to 7. The estimates shown in Accounts Publications). A detailed description of the sources and methods is found in the following tables have been prepared in accordance with the United Nations System of National Accounts.

(a) **Gross domestic product.** Gross domestic product is estimated mainly through the expenditure approach. The production approach is used in estimating GDP by kind of economic activity as well as cost-structure of GDP as described below. The difference between the two methods of GDP is explicitly presented as a statistical discrepancy' on the cost components side of GDP.

(b) **Expenditure on the gross domestic product.** All components of GDP by expenditure type are estimated through the expenditure approach. Government final consumption expenditure is mainly based on government accounts. Estimates of private consumption expenditure are based on various sources. A vital source is the import of consumer goods plus import duties and trade and transport margin. The Agricultural Production Board is the source for the estimate of the consumption of domestically produced agricultural products. A considerable part of the consumption of services is derived from the Industrial Statistics and the Family Expenditure Survey which is used as a weight in consumer price index. Gross capital formation is based on import of investment goods, direct inquiries to the main constructors and domestical producers of investment goods and government accounts. Exports and imports of goods and services are estimated from foreign trade statistics and balance of payment statistics. Price deflation is used for most of

the expenditure items at constant prices. Various price indices are used.

(c) **Cost-structure of the gross domestic product.** (See 'Gross domestic product by kind of economic activity' below.)

(d) **Gross domestic product by kind of economic activity.** The production approach is used to estimate both cost-structure of domestic product and GDP by kind of activity. The main source are the annual accounts of enterprises. From the tax assessments data are a sample of establishments drawn from almost every single branch of industry. The sample is drawn from the tax records presenting the total value of wages and salaries of all employees and calculated income of self-employed. These amounts are classified by enterprises and establishments within each enterprise which enables breakdown by activity within enterprises. A sample of annual reports of enterprises, including operating accounts and balance sheets, are compiled from tax authorities. After processing these sources the samples are blown-up according to the total value of wages and salaries in each branch of industry in the above-mentioned tax records. The operating accounts as presented in operating accounts of the firms is not suitable for national accounting purposes. One of the reason is the price increases during the year and therefore adjustments are made for the effects of inflation on the valuation of stocks at the beginning and the end of the year. These adjustments, 'the stock appreciation' is in most cases estimated as the value of the stock at the beginning of the year multiplied by the percentage increase of the credit term index from the beginning to the end of the current year. The credit term index is a weighted average of the consumer price index and the building cost index. For the constant price estimates the general approach for almost all industries is the deflation of the gross output or extrapolation of base-year value of output. Double-deflation is not used except in the case of the fishing industry.

1.1 Expenditure on the Gross Domestic Product, in Current Prices

Million Icelandic krónur

	1970	1975	1980	1981	1982	1983	1984	1985	1986	1987	1988	1989
1 Government final consumption expenditure	57	335	2546	4039	6644	11559	14056	20136	27236	36791	47468	56369
2 Private final consumption expenditure	269	1188	8846	14327	22939	39418	53886	74705	96933	131712	158200	176254
3 Gross capital formation	101	673	4007	6182	10164	13057	19142	23482	27590	40926	49882	54855
A Increase in stocks a	-3	37	80	253	913	-1070	786	-978	-2094	-416	1850	-655
B Gross fixed capital formation	104	636	3927	5929	9251	14127	18356	24460	29684	41342	48032	55510
Residential buildings	21	135	964	1317	2251	3495	4714	5380	5770	7752	10106	12740
Non-residential buildings	26	126	683	1119	2035	3337	4391	6217	8283	12534	12590	15038
Other construction and land improvement etc.	29	211	1241	1895	2718	3900	4474	5288	6078	7663	10471	12271
Other	28	165	1039	1598	2247	3395	4777	7575	9553	13093	14865	15011
4 Exports of goods and services	208	718	5746	8724	12714	27078	34295	49819	63125	73466	84131	108968
5 Less: Imports of goods and services	197	883	5648	8936	14329	25275	33871	49061	56342	74496	85042	100366
Equals: Gross Domestic Product	439	2031	15487	24436	38132	65837	87508	119091	158597	208099	254639	296080

a) Item 'Increase in stocks' includes stocks of export products only.

1.2 Expenditure on the Gross Domestic Product, in Constant Prices

Million Icelandic krónur
At constant prices of 1980

	1970	1975	1980	1981	1982	1983	1984	1985	1986	1987	1988	1989
1 Government final consumption expenditure	1297	2057	2546	2733	2902	3038	3043	3232	3455	3665	3818	3910
2 Private final consumption expenditure	4863	6416	8846	8470	9272	9364	9660	10099	10904	12691	12183	11209
3 Gross capital formation	1816	3749	4007	4135	4302	3254	3900	3769	3607	4456	4601	4039
A Increase in stocks a	-66	484	80	170	357	-207	122	-85	-201	-75	130	-51
B Gross fixed capital formation	1882	3265	3927	3965	3945	3461	3778	3854	3808	4531	4471	4090
Residential buildings	434	713	964	870	952	865	955	825	711	812	898	919
Non-residential buildings	508	661	683	739	858	823	889	952	1019	1311	1118	1083
Other construction and land improvement etc.	576	1151	1240	1265	1153	943	927	842	812	842	953	935
Other	404	767	1040	1091	982	830	1007	1235	1266	1566	1502	1153
4 Exports of goods and services	3255	3713	5746	5819	5261	5202	5976	6631	7043	7328	7525	7215
5 Less: Imports of goods and services	3005	4445	5648	6024	5988	5649	6174	6775	6792	8345	8084	7282
Statistical discrepancy	60	-241										
Equals: Gross Domestic Product	8287	11249	15487	16133	16449	15809	16405	16956	18217	19795	19643	19091

a) Item 'Increase in stocks' includes stocks of export products only.

Iceland

1.3 Cost Components of the Gross Domestic Product

Million Icelandic krónur

	1970	1975	1980	1981	1982	1983	1984	1985	1986	1987	1988	1989
1 Indirect taxes, net	76	424	3030	5016	7810	12282	17673	22850	29736	41531	51067	59355
A Indirect taxes	90	516	3520	5778	9202	14486	20062	26341	33964	46314	58875	69133
B Less: Subsidies	13	93	490	762	1392	2204	2389	3491	4228	4783	7808	9808
2 Consumption of fixed capital	61	283	1810	2871	4742	8724	10691	14502	18423	22030	27067	33473
3 Compensation of employees paid by resident producers	226	1008	7746	12036	18839	29545	38430	56409	74583	110975	136958	151500
4 Operating surplus	76	246	1805	2735	3809	6659	15630	17368	23831	27945	34571	42277
Statistical discrepancy a	...	70	1107	1678	2933	5427	5084	7962	11924	5618	4976	7505
Equals: Gross Domestic Product	439	2031	15498	24336	38133	68837	87508	119091	158697	208099	254639	296080

a) The estimates shown refers to the difference between production estimate and expenditure estimate.

1.4 General Government Current Receipts and Disbursements

Million Icelandic krónur

	1970	1975	1980	1981	1982	1983	1984	1985	1986	1987	1988	1989

Receipts

1 Operating surplus	-	...	...	...	...	...	...	...	...	...	...	...
2 Property and entrepreneurial income	...	5	331	474	980	2365	2706	3883	4094	5077	6072	8523
3 Taxes, fees and contributions	130	677	4825	7774	12600	19662	27053	34796	46879	61708	83958	99845
A Indirect taxes	89	516	3520	5778	9202	14486	20062	26341	33964	46314	58875	69133
B Direct taxes	30	142	1082	1735	2965	4486	5892	7063	10803	12537	21777	26348
C Social security contributions	10	18	215	249	393	654	1056	1333	2039	2729	3137	4034
D Compulsory fees, fines and penalties	-	1	8	12	20	36	43	59	73	128	169	330
4 Other current transfers	-	...	...	...	...	...	...	...	...	-	-	-
Total Current Receipts of General Government	135	691	5156	8248	13580	22027	29759	38679	50973	66785	90030	108368

Disbursements

1 Government final consumption expenditure	42	335	2546	4039	6644	11559	14056	20136	27291	36792	47468	56369
A Compensation of employees	24	189	1614	2544	4112	6686	8036	11516	16010	22357	30472	35076
B Consumption of fixed capital	4	24	95	148	240	427	541	735	948	1151	1357	1680
C Purchases of goods and services, net	14	122	838	1347	2292	4446	5480	7885	10333	12383	15640	19613
D Less: Own account fixed capital formation	...	...	...	...	...	...	...	...	...	...	...	...
E Indirect taxes paid, net	...	...	...	...	...	...	...	...	...	...	...	...
2 Property income	3	24	255	458	797	2031	2544	3668	4434	5132	8289	11207
A Interest	3	24	255	458	797	2031	2544	3668	4434	5132	8289	11207
B Net land rent and royalties	...	...	...	...	...	...	...	...	...	...	...	...
3 Subsidies	15	93	490	762	1392	2204	2389	3491	4228	4783	7808	9808
4 Other current transfers	39	118	717	1162	1986	2995	4025	5777	7593	10591	14181	17640
A Social security benefits	39	116	705	1143	1831	2914	3882	5587	7297	10214	13664	16952
B Social assistance grants	...	...	...	...	...	...	...	...	...	...	...	...
C Other	...	2	12	19	35	81	144	192	296	376	517	688
5 Net saving	36	121	1146	1827	2882	3239	3744	6744	7427	9488	12286	13344
Total Current Disbursements and Net Saving of General Government	135	691	5154	8248	13581	22028	27758	38679	50973	66785	90032	108368

804

Iceland

1.7 External Transactions on Current Account, Summary

Million Icelandic krónur

	1970	1975	1980	1981	1982	1983	1984	1985	1986	1987	1988	1989
Payments to the Rest of the World												
1 Imports of goods and services	197	883	5648	8336	14329	25275	33871	49051	56342	74496	85042	100366
A Imports of merchandise c.i.f.	126	680	4802	7485	11647	20596	26744	37600	45910	61237	68723	80250
B Other	71	203	846	1451	2682	4679	7127	11451	10432	13259	16319	20116
2 Factor income to the rest of the world	8	52	478	874	1844	3444	5051	6255	7042	7281	9461	15087
A Compensation of employees	...	...	10	14	29	39	41	50	89	175	331	519
B Property and entrepreneurial income [a]	...	...	468	960	1815	3405	5010	6205	6953	7106	9130	14568
3 Current transfers to the rest of the world	-	2	5	12	18	32	43	47	72	66	80	228
A Indirect taxes to supranational organizations	...	...	...	...	...	...	...	...	...	...	...	...
B Other current transfers	-	2	5	12	18	32	43	47	72	66	80	228
4 Surplus of the nation on current transactions	6	-216	-318	-1035	-3128	-1295	-4173	-4863	482	-7299	-9324	-4843
Payments to the Rest of the World and Surplus of the Nation on Current Transactions	211	722	5813	8887	13063	27456	34792	50490	63938	74544	85259	110838
Receipts From The Rest of the World												
1 Exports of goods and services	208	718	5746	8724	12714	27078	34295	49819	63125	73466	84131	108968
A Exports of merchandise f.o.b.	128	474	4460	6536	8479	18623	23557	33750	44968	53053	61667	80072
B Other	80	244	1286	2188	4235	8455	10738	16069	18157	20413	22464	28896
2 Factor income from rest of the world	3	4	67	163	349	378	497	671	813	1078	1128	1870
A Compensation of employees	4	5	9	23	42	71	86	185	171	253
B Property and entrepreneurial income [a]	...	...	63	158	340	355	455	600	727	893	957	1617
3 Current transfers from rest of the world	...	...	-	-	-	-	-	-	-	-	-	-
A Subsidies from supranational organisations	...	...	-	-	-	-	-	-	-	-	-	-
B Other current transfers	...	...	-	-	-	-	-	-	-	-	-	-
Receipts from the Rest of the World on Current Transactions	211	722	5813	8887	13063	27456	34792	50490	63938	74544	85259	110838

a) Item 'Property and entrepreneurial income' paid/received refers to interest payments.

1.8 Capital Transactions of The Nation, Summary

Million Icelandic krónur

	1970	1975	1980	1981	1982	1983	1984	1985	1986	1987	1988	1989
Finance of Gross Capital Formation												
Gross saving	107	458	3689	5147	7036	11762	14969	18619	28072	33327	40558	50012
1 Consumption of fixed capital	61	283	1810	2871	4742	8724	10691	14502	18425	22030	27067	33473
A General government	...	24	95	147	240	427	541	735	948	1151	1357	1680
B Corporate and quasi-corporate enterprises	...	...	...	...	...	...	...	...	...	...	...	...
C Other	...	...	...	...	...	...	...	...	...	...	...	...
2 Net saving	47	175	1879	2276	2294	3038	4278	4117	9647	11297	13491	16539
A General government	...	121	1146	1827	2882	3239	6744	5607	7427	9488	12286	13344
B Corporate and quasi-corporate enterprises	...	...	...	...	...	...	...	...	...	...	...	...
C Other	...	...	...	...	...	...	...	...	...	...	...	...
Less: Surplus of the nation on current transactions	6	-216	-318	-1035	-3128	-1295	-4173	-4863	482	-7299	-9324	-4843
Finance of Gross Capital Formation	101	674	4007	6182	10164	13057	19142	23482	27590	40626	49882	54855
Gross Capital Formation												
Increase in stocks [a]	-3	37	80	253	913	-1070	766	-978	-2094	-416	1850	-655
Gross fixed capital formation	104	636	3927	5929	9251	14127	18356	24460	29684	41042	48032	55510
1 General government	110	578	838	1508	2443	2970	4401	4797	7283	10336	13049
2 Corporate and quasi-corporate enterprises	...	...	...	...	...	...	...	...	...	...	...	...
3 Other	...	...	...	...	...	...	...	...	...	...	...	...
Gross Capital Formation	101	674	4007	6182	10164	13057	19142	23482	27590	40626	49882	54855

a) Item 'Increase in stocks' includes stocks of export products only.

Iceland

1.10 Gross Domestic Product by Kind of Activity, in Current Prices

Million Icelandic krónur

	1970	1975	1980	1981	1982	1983	1984	1985	1986	1987	1988	1989
1 Agriculture, hunting, forestry and fishing	189	1570	2302	2930	5133	7215	11433	15836	21130	25203	...	...
2 Mining and quarrying	...	...	...	...	...	...	...	...	...	...	...	...
3 Manufacturing	281	2410	3695	5516	9061	13067	17224	24077	32736	37536	...	...
4 Electricity, gas and water	62	515	716	1282	3326	4694	6559	9016	8448	9142	...	...
5 Construction	177	1052	1679	3001	4270	6599	7319	10226	14489	16825	...	...
6 Wholesale and retail trade, restaurants and hotels	157	1233	2030	2869	6193	8288	10534	13924	20205	23948	...	...
7 Transport, storage and communication	180	932	1609	2539	4653	6152	7383	9543	12651	15544	...	...
8 Finance, insurance, real estate and business services	227	1854	2654	4806	9084	10878	15802	17491	26074	34735	...	...
9 Community, social and personal services	87	559	870	1581	2618	3214	5083	6598	10051	14134	...	...
Total, Industries	1360	10124	15556	24525	44272	59196	80374	103863	143784	177067	...	...
Producers of Government Services	208	1662	2620	4236	6924	8352	11929	16511	23760	30969	...	...
Other Producers	20	97	147	245	400	533	798	1056	1484	2097	...	...
Subtotal	1587	11883	18323	29006	51596	68081	93101	121430	169028	210153	...	...
Less: Imputed bank service charge	48	523	682	1617	3468	3330	4822	4493	8078	11557	...	...
Plus: Import duties	...	...	...	...	...	...	...	...	...	...	...	...
Plus: Value added tax	...	...	...	...	...	...	...	...	...	...	...	...
Plus: Other adjustments [a]	492	4137	6694	10743	17709	22757	30812	41660	47149	56043	...	...
Equals: Gross Domestic Product	2032	15497	24335	38132	65837	87508	119091	155697	208099	254639	...	...

[a] Item 'Other adjustments' includes import duties, other indirect taxes less subsidies as well as residual error between production and expenditure approaches.

1.11 Gross Domestic Product by Kind of Activity, in Constant Prices

Million Icelandic krónur

	1970	1975	1980	1981	1982	1983	1984	1985	1986	1987	1988	1989
At constant prices of 1980												
1 Agriculture, hunting, forestry and fishing	...	1233	1570	1594	1544	1388	1543	1806	1825	1866	1924	...
2 Mining and quarrying	...	...	...	...	...	...	...	...	...	...	...	...
3 Manufacturing	...	1626	2410	2491	2398	2248	2407	2429	2550	2752	2545	...
4 Electricity, gas and water	...	1011	1052	1047	1110	1075	1126	1086	1121	1276	1257	...
5 Construction	...	1028	1233	1352	1424	1324	1386	1454	1577	1826	1777	...
6 Wholesale and retail trade, restaurants and hotels	...	780	832	971	972	1015	1076	1151	1257	1376	1357	...
7 Transport, storage and communication	...	1356	1854	1939	2067	2181	2362	2534	2676	2857	2967	...
8 Finance, insurance, real estate and business services	...	470	559	584	627	655	672	721	770	845	879	...
9 Community, social and personal services	...	7864	10124	10523	10746	10955	11341	11974	12600	13632	13575	...
Total, Industries	...	1357	1662	1789	1842	1933	1992	2094	2219	2415	2565	...
Producers of Government Services	...	73	97	108	117	120	127	136	146	159	175	...
Other Producers	...	9293	11883	12420	12706	12647	13461	14205	14965	16206	16315	...
Subtotal	...	386	523	541	558	587	670	748	838	882	942	...
Less: Imputed bank service charge												
Plus: Import duties	...	...	...	...	...	...	...	...	...	...	...	...
Plus: Value added tax	...	...	...	...	...	...	...	...	...	...	...	...
Equals: Gross Domestic Product [a]	8908	11360	11879	12147	12061	12790	13456	14127	15324	15373	...	...

[a] Gross domestic product in factor values.

1.12 Relations Among National Accounting Aggregates

Million Icelandic krónur

	1970	1975	1980	1981	1982	1983	1984	1985	1986	1987	1988	1989
Gross Domestic Product	439	2031	15497	24336	38132	65837	87508	119091	155697	208099	254639	296080
Plus: Net factor income from the rest of the world	-5	-49	-411	-811	-1495	-3066	-4554	-5584	-6229	-6203	-8333	-13217
Factor income from the rest of the world	3	4	67	163	349	378	497	671	813	1078	1128	1870
Less: Factor income to the rest of the world	8	52	478	974	1844	3444	5051	6255	7042	7281	9461	15087
Equals: Gross National Product	434	1982	15086	23525	36637	62771	82954	113507	152368	201896	246306	282863
Less: Consumption of fixed capital	61	283	1810	2871	4742	8724	10691	14502	18425	22030	27067	33473

Iceland

1.12 Relations Among National Accounting Aggregates
(Continued)

Million Icelandic kronur

	1970	1975	1980	1981	1982	1983	1984	1985	1986	1987	1988	1989
Equals: National Income	373	1699	13276	20654	31895	54047	72263	99005	133943	179866	219239	249390
Plus: Net current transfers from the rest of the world	-	-2	-5	-12	-18	-32	-43	-47	-72	-66	-80	-228
Current transfers from the rest of the world	-	-	-	-	-	-	-	-	-	-	-	-
Less: Current transfers to the rest of the world	-	2	5	12	18	32	43	47	72	66	80	228
Equals: National Disposable Income	373	1697	13271	20642	31877	54015	72220	98958	133871	179800	219159	249162
Less: Final consumption	326	1523	11392	18366	29583	50977	67942	94841	124224	168503	205668	232623
Equals: Net Saving	47	175	1879	2276	2294	3038	4278	4117	9647	11297	13491	16539
Less: Surplus of the nation on current transactions	6	-216	-318	-1035	-3128	-1295	-4173	-4863	482	-7299	-9324	-4843
Equals: Net Capital Formation	41	390	2197	3311	5422	4333	8451	8980	9165	18596	22815	21382

2.1 Government Final Consumption Expenditure by Function, in Current Prices

Million Icelandic kronur

	1970	1975	1980	1981	1982	1983	1984	1985	1986	1987	1988	1989
1 General public services	...	...	186	291	476	789	1023	1417	1846	2714	3686	4339
2 Defence	...	...	-	-	-	-	-	-	-	-	-	-
3 Public order and safety	...	...	223	338	546	911	1072	1478	2026	2849	3632	3880
4 Education	...	...	563	868	1410	2305	2803	4199	5686	7817	10026	12006
5 Health	...	...	836	1335	2201	4209	5080	7363	10162	13668	17949	21145
6 Social security and welfare	...	...	124	214	359	592	656	976	1560	2249	3142	3542
7 Housing and community amenities	...	...	81	130	207	347	414	568	715	1007	1235	1549
8 Recreational, cultural and religious affairs	...	...	104	166	281	454	593	764	1093	1383	1828	2371
9 Economic services	...	...	314	511	826	1435	1822	2432	3025	3777	4329	5493
A Fuel and energy	...	...	21	37	55	99	103	145	179	279	274	298
B Agriculture, forestry, fishing and hunting	...	...	66	96	149	248	329	464	556	758	858	939
C Mining, manufacturing and construction, except fuel and energy	...	...	9	19	23	33	59	80	74	116	161	155
D Transportation and communication	...	...	194	325	543	968	1200	1542	1974	2331	2678	3632
E Other economic affairs	...	...	24	35	56	88	131	201	242	292	358	470
10 Other functions	...	...	116	188	339	519	593	939	1178	1329	1642	2043
Total Government Final Consumption Expenditure	...	...	2546	4039	6644	11559	14056	20136	27291	36791	47468	56368

2.2 Government Final Consumption Expenditure by Function, in Constant Prices

Million Icelandic kronur

	1970	1975	1980	1981	1982	1983	1984	1985	1986	1987	1988	1989
			At constant prices of:1980									
1 General public services	...	...	186	197	208	211	226	230	236	270	295	300
2 Defence	...	...	-	-	-	-	-	-	-	-	-	-
3 Public order and safety	...	...	223	230	238	245	240	245	262	285	293	273
4 Education	...	...	563	590	616	623	632	700	741	785	815	853
5 Health	...	...	835	902	963	1087	1074	1131	1260	1350	1426	1438
6 Social security and welfare	...	...	124	146	156	164	156	195	207	228	258	260
7 Housing and community amenities	...	...	81	88	90	91	89	90	90	100	98	106
8 Recreational, cultural and religious affairs	...	...	104	113	123	123	131	125	140	138	147	165
9 Economic services	...	...	313	344	361	367	376	375	373	372	344	371
A Fuel and energy	...	...	20	25	24	27	24	25	24	28	22	21
B Agriculture, forestry, fishing and hunting	...	...	66	65	65	66	72	76	71	76	69	66
C Mining, manufacturing and construction, except fuel and energy	...	...	9	13	10	9	13	13	10	12	13	12
D Transportation and communication	...	...	194	217	238	241	238	229	237	228	210	240
E Other economic affairs	...	...	24	24	24	24	29	32	31	29	29	32
10 Other functions	...	...	117	124	145	127	123	141	143	138	142	145
Total Government Final Consumption Expenditure	...	...	2546	2733	2901	3038	3047	3232	3455	3665	3818	3911

Iceland

2.3 Total Government Outlays by Function and Type

Million Icelandic krónur

	Total	Final Consumption Expenditures – Compensation of Employees	Final Consumption Expenditures – Other	Subsidies	Current Transfers & Property Income	Total Current Disbursements	Gross Capital Formation	Other Capital Outlays	Total Outlays
1980									
1 General public services	186	150	36	–	12	198	5	–	203
2 Defence	–	–	–	–	–	–	–	–	–
3 Public order and safety	223	172	51	2	–	225	12	2	239
4 Education	563	430	133	8	–	571	84	54	709
5 Health	836	481	354	4	–	840	43	2	884
6 Social security and welfare	124	111	13	–	648	772	29	14	815
7 Housing and community amenities	81	48	33	–	–	81	30	89	200
8 Recreation, culture and religion	104	77	27	24	40	168	48	6	221
9 Economic services	314	145	168	466	4	784	314	250	1348
A Fuel and energy	21	18	2	46	–	66	2	81	149
B Agriculture, forestry, fishing and hunting	66	43	23	368	1	435	24	63	522
C Mining (except fuels), manufacturing and construction	9	8	1	15	–	23	1	19	43
D Transportation and communication	194	135	59	38	–	232	286	43	561
E Other economic affairs	24	17	7	1	2	27	2	45	74
10 Other functions	116	1	115	–	255	372	14	–15	371
Total	2546	1615	931	490	972	4009	578	403	4989
1981									
1 General public services	291	203	88	–	24	314	8	–	322
2 Defence	–	–	–	–	–	–	–	–	–
3 Public order and safety	338	260	78	3	–	341	12	5	358
4 Education	898	689	187	13	–	888	126	83	1089
5 Health	1335	763	572	8	–	1343	86	5	1434
6 Social security and welfare	214	194	19	–	1041	1255	58	37	1349
7 Housing and community amenities	130	81	48	–	–	130	24	145	299
8 Recreation, culture and religion	166	130	36	36	38	270	100	4	374
9 Economic services	511	232	278	724	7	1242	502	371	2115
A Fuel and energy	37	29	7	77	–	114	1	108	223
B Agriculture, forestry, fishing and hunting	96	63	33	555	2	654	24	85	763
C Mining (except fuels), manufacturing and construction	19	17	1	39	1	58	3	27	87
D Transportation and communication	325	97	228	50	–	375	474	87	936
E Other economic affairs	35	26	9	4	4	41	–	64	106
10 Other functions	188	–	189	1	458	646	23	–4	665
Total	4039	2544	1495	762	1620	6421	938	647	8006
1982									
1 General public services	476	318	158	–	39	515	10	–	525
2 Defence	–	–	–	–	–	–	–	–	–
3 Public order and safety	546	409	137	5	–	551	23	23	596
4 Education	1410	1080	330	17	–	1427	254	153	1834
5 Health	2201	1237	964	12	–	2214	136	5	2355
6 Social security and welfare	359	330	29	–	1672	2030	86	52	2168
7 Housing and community amenities	207	132	74	–	–	207	5	184	396
8 Recreation, culture and religion	281	222	59	59	110	449	155	13	617
9 Economic services	826	384	442	1333	11	2170	799	467	3436
A Fuel and energy	55	47	8	128	–	184	4	93	280
B Agriculture, forestry, fishing and hunting	149	103	46	1012	5	1166	34	148	1348
C Mining (except fuels), manufacturing and construction	23	20	3	64	–	87	5	44	137
D Transportation and communication	543	171	372	127	–	670	756	96	1522
E Other economic affairs	56	43	13	2	6	63	–	86	149
10 Other functions	339	–	339	2	797	1136	41	–57	1120
Total	6644	4112	2532	1392	2662	10699	1508	840	13046

Iceland

2.3 Total Government Outlays by Function and Type
(Continued)

Million Icelandic kronur

		Final Consumption Expenditures			Subsidies	Other Current Transfers & Property Income	Total Current Disbursements	Gross Capital Formation	Other Capital Outlays	Total Outlays
		Total	Compensation of Employees	Other						
	1983									
1	General public services	789	538	251	-	89	878	16	44	937
2	Defence	-	-	-	-	-	-	-	-	-
3	Public order and safety	911	654	257	-	13	925	53	-	978
4	Education	2305	1731	573	-	31	2336	343	362	3041
5	Health	4209	2053	2156	-	28	4237	208	12	4457
6	Social security and welfare	592	534	58	-	2621	3213	156	49	3418
7	Housing and community amenities	347	207	140	-	-	347	72	358	777
8	Recreation, culture and religion	454	363	90	108	186	748	236	30	1014
9	Economic services	1435	603	832	2095	24	3554	1265	1547	6367
	A Fuel and energy	99	85	14	393	5	497	4	877	1378
	B Agriculture, forestry, fishing and hunting	248	159	89	1431	10	1688	52	238	1979
	C Mining (except fuels), manufacturing and construction	33	25	8	87	-	120	1	92	212
	D Transportation and communication	968	272	695	179	-	1147	1207	169	2522
	E Other economic affairs	88	62	26	5	9	102	2	171	275
10	Other functions	519	-	519	-	2033	2552	93	8	2653
	Total	11559	6683	4876	2204	5025	18788	2443	2411	23642
	1984									
1	General public services	1023	671	352	-	59	1082	62	-	1143
2	Defence	-	-	-	-	-	-	-	-	-
3	Public order and safety	1072	759	313	-	19	1091	47	9	1146
4	Education	2803	2053	750	-	40	2843	479	355	3677
5	Health	5080	2550	2530	-	36	5116	179	35	5329
6	Social security and welfare	656	610	46	-	3559	4215	229	81	4525
7	Housing and community amenities	414	233	181	-	-	414	52	439	905
8	Recreation, culture and religion	593	394	199	123	287	1003	251	63	1317
9	Economic services	1822	750	1072	2263	23	4107	1557	1111	6775
	A Fuel and energy	103	84	19	601	2	706	4	211	921
	B Agriculture, forestry, fishing and hunting	329	205	124	1320	14	1663	145	290	2098
	C Mining (except fuels), manufacturing and construction	59	39	20	105	3	166	1	125	292
	D Transportation and communication	1200	333	867	231	-	1431	1401	214	3046
	E Other economic affairs	131	89	42	5	4	141	6	271	418
10	Other functions	593	17	576	4	2547	3144	116	-25	3235
	Total	14056	8037	6019	2389	6569	23015	2970	2065	28049
	1985									
1	General public services	1417	904	513	-	110	1527	35	8	1569
2	Defence	-	-	-	-	-	-	-	-	-
3	Public order and safety	1478	1051	427	-	22	1500	209	4	1713
4	Education	4199	3121	1078	-	85	4283	563	837	5684
5	Health	7363	3629	3734	-	9	7372	334	64	7770
6	Social security and welfare	976	945	31	-	5078	6054	415	127	6596
7	Housing and community amenities	568	298	270	-	-	568	99	1337	2004
8	Recreation, culture and religion	764	505	259	171	405	1340	503	55	1899
9	Economic services	2432	1052	1380	3319	68	5820	2075	1177	9073
	A Fuel and energy	145	123	22	651	2	798	12	186	996
	B Agriculture, forestry, fishing and hunting	464	308	156	2275	34	2774	135	459	3368
	C Mining (except fuels), manufacturing and construction	80	62	18	152	10	242	8	87	337
	D Transportation and communication	1542	448	1094	233	-	1775	1920	233	3928
	E Other economic affairs	201	111	90	8	22	231	-	212	444
10	Other functions	939	11	928	-	3669	4607	169	-39	4737
	Total	20136	11516	8620	3491	9445	33071	4402	3571	41045

Iceland

2.3 Total Government Outlays by Function and Type (Continued)

Million Icelandic krónur

	Final Consumption Expenditures			Subsidies	Current Transfers & Property Income	Total Current Disbursements	Gross Capital Formation	Other Capital Outlays	Total Outlays
	Total	Compensation of Employees	Other						

1986

1 General public services	1846	1214	632	-	108	1953	67	11	2031
2 Defence	-	-	-	-	-	-	-	-	-
3 Public order and safety	2026	1486	540	-	27	2053	94	-	2147
4 Education	5686	4414	1272	-	114	5801	572	1226	7599
5 Health	10162	4917	5245	-	-	10162	457	110	10729
6 Social security and welfare	1560	1454	106	-	6615	8175	392	181	8748
7 Housing and community amenities	715	419	296	-	-	715	83	1649	2447
8 Recreation, culture and religion	1093	716	377	215	673	1981	878	82	2941
9 Economic services	3025	1374	1651	4013	54	7092	2315	6513	15920
A. Fuel and energy	179	160	19	522	9	708	19	5330	6056
B. Agriculture, forestry, fishing and hunting	555	386	170	2909	24	3489	302	446	4236
C. Mining (except fuels), manufacturing and construction	74	83	-9	231	1	306	21	95	422
D. Transportation and communication	1974	598	1376	316	-	2289	1962	277	4528
E. Other economic affairs	242	148	94	35	23	300	12	366	677
10 Other functions	1178	16	1162	-	4436	5614	-61	-83	5470
Total	27291	16010	11281	4228	12026	43546	4797	9690	58032

1987

1 General public services	2714	1782	932	-	139	2853	175	17	3045
2 Defence	-	-	-	-	-	-	-	-	-
3 Public order and safety	2849	2137	712	-	42	2890	163	-	3053
4 Education	7817	6315	1502	-	144	7961	840	928	9729
5 Health	13668	7429	6239	16	-	13683	618	112	14413
6 Social security and welfare	2249	2097	152	-	9282	11531	638	233	12402
7 Housing and community amenities	1007	569	438	-	-	1007	128	1390	2525
8 Recreation, culture and religion	1383	1019	364	363	884	2630	1048	104	3782
9 Economic services	3777	1886	1891	4419	78	8275	3166	1962	13402
A. Fuel and energy	279	218	61	398	5	683	12	484	1179
B. Agriculture, forestry, fishing and hunting	758	532	226	3266	41	4065	599	528	5191
C. Mining (except fuels), manufacturing and construction	116	127	-11	364	1	480	7	392	879
D. Transportation and communication	2331	815	1516	340	-	2671	2532	275	5477
E. Other economic affairs	292	194	98	53	32	377	16	283	676
10 Other functions	1329	23	1306	-	5139	6467	506	-168	6805
Total	36791	23257	13534	4783	15723	57297	7282	4578	69157

1988

1 General public services	3686	2307	1379	-	327	4013	459	21	4493
2 Defence	-	-	-	-	-	-	-	-	-
3 Public order and safety	3632	2709	923	-	41	3674	228	-	3902
4 Education	10026	8155	1871	-	221	10247	1449	1661	13357
5 Health	17949	9974	7975	184	-	18133	645	141	18919
6 Social security and welfare	3142	2911	231	-	12165	15306	983	254	16543
7 Housing and community amenities	1235	706	529	-	-	1235	106	1867	3208
8 Recreation, culture and religion	1828	1311	517	716	1160	3703	1605	130	5438
9 Economic services	4329	2368	1961	7092	66	11486	4269	2789	18544
A. Fuel and energy	274	236	38	252	1	528	9	267	803
B. Agriculture, forestry, fishing and hunting	858	620	238	5952	13	6823	607	1006	8436
C. Mining (except fuels), manufacturing and construction	161	168	-7	359	21	541	5	189	735
D. Transportation and communication	2678	1100	1578	418	-	3097	3610	351	7058
E. Other economic affairs	358	245	113	110	30	499	37	976	1512
10 Other functions	1642	32	1610	-	8305	9947	593	-200	10340
Total	47468	30472	16996	7808	22469	77745	10336	6663	94744

Iceland

2.3 Total Government Outlays by Function and Type
(Continued)

Million Icelandic kronur

		Final Consumption Expenditures			Subsidies	Other Current Transfers & Property Income	Total Current Disbursements	Gross Capital Formation	Other Capital Outlays	Total Outlays
		Total	Compensation of Employees	Other						
	1989									
1	General public services	4339	2718	1621	-	520	4859	717	10	5585
2	Defence	-	-	-	-	-	-	-	-	-
3	Public order and safety	3880	2855	1025	-	56	3936	241	-	4177
4	Education	12006	9517	2489	-	259	12265	1670	1851	15786
5	Health	21145	11311	9834	-	175	21321	594	159	22074
6	Social security and welfare	3542	3477	65	-	14692	18234	1172	326	19733
7	Housing and community amenities	1549	837	712	-	1	1550	118	1319	2987
8	Recreation, culture and religion	2371	1633	738	614	1761	4746	2226	136	7107
9	Economic services	5493	2691	2802	9194	172	14859	4523	6305	25687
	A Fuel and energy	298	251	47	371	3	672	12	3569	4253
	B Agriculture, forestry, fishing and hunting	939	662	277	7534	36	8509	284	1142	9934
	C Mining (except fuels), manufacturing and construction	155	185	-30	461	18	634	13	245	891
	D Transportation and communication	3632	1316	2316	552	-	4184	4175	421	8780
	E Other economic affairs	470	277	193	275	115	860	40	929	1829
10	Other functions	2043	38	2005	-	11212	13254	1788	-243	14800
	Total	56368	35076	21292	9808	28847	95023	13049	9864	117936

2.5 Private Final Consumption Expenditure by Type and Purpose, in Current Prices

Million Icelandic kronur

	1970	1975	1980	1981	1982	1983	1984	1985	1986	1987	1988	1989
Final Consumption Expenditure of Resident Households												
1 Food, beverages and tobacco	83	343	2302	3617	5439	10057	13508	19408	22865	29192	...	...
A Food	64	247	1683	2643	3863	7611	10055	14492	16520	20524	...	...
B Non-alcoholic beverages	4	23	186	290	521	793	1051	1533	2180	3221	...	...
C Alcoholic beverages	7	42	227	367	562	883	1227	1795	2257	2997	...	...
D Tobacco	8	31	207	317	493	770	1176	1588	1909	2451	...	...
2 Clothing and footwear	28	106	850	1299	2119	3561	4980	7085	9445	13158	...	...
3 Gross rent, fuel and power	46	219	1484	2311	3819	6913	9122	11852	14471	17406	...	...
A Fuel and power	12	57	299	450	799	1673	2238	2571	2709	3146	...	...
B Other	35	162	1184	1861	3019	5240	6884	9280	11762	14260	...	...
4 Furniture, furnishings and household equipment and operation	29	124	1177	1851	2788	4472	5579	7455	9764	14049	...	...
A Household operation	7	37	344	514	794	1530	1717	2672	3582	5023	...	...
B Other	21	87	833	1337	1994	2942	3862	4783	6182	9026	...	...
5 Medical care and health expenses	7	16	118	179	288	523	812	1142	1668	2103	...	...
6 Transport and communication	38	188	1390	2486	3923	6246	9013	11615	16147	23533	...	...
A Personal transport equipment	27	36	424	889	1251	1366	2471	2786	5893	10699	...	...
B Other	11	152	966	1597	2672	4880	6542	8829	10254	12834	...	...
7 Recreational, entertainment, education and cultural services	17	86	663	1046	1757	3201	4214	6184	8021	10798	...	...
A Education	1	5	30	45	66	123	191	258	350	420	...	...
B Other	16	81	633	1001	1692	3078	4023	5927	7672	10378	...	...
8 Miscellaneous goods and services	20	94	693	1164	2172	3390	4969	7669	11479	16413	...	...
A Personal care	4	16	126	229	346	597	740	1192	1719	2291	...	...
B Expenditures in restaurants, cafes and hotels	9	62	390	631	1363	2087	3186	4889	7529	10796	...	...

Iceland

2.5 Private Final Consumption Expenditure by Type and Purpose, in Current Prices
(Continued)

Million Icelandic krónur

	1970	1975	1980	1981	1982	1983	1984	1985	1986	1987	1988	1989
C Other	7	16	176	303	463	706	1043	1588	2231	3326		
Total Final Consumption Expenditure in the Domestic Market by Households, of which	268	1176	8676	13953	22304	38361	52196	72410	93860	126651		
Plus: Direct purchases abroad by resident households	7	33	293	545	983	1788	2852	4142	5622	8596		
Less: Direct purchases in the domestic market by non-resident households	6	21	123	171	348	732	1162	1848	2549	3536		
Equals: Final Consumption Expenditure of Resident Households a	269	1188	8846	14327	22939	39418	53886	74705	96933	131712		
Equals: Final Consumption Expenditure of Private Non-profit Organisations Serving Households	...	...	...	...	...	...	...	...	...	...		
Private Final Consumption Expenditure	269	1188	8846	14327	22939	39418	53886	74705	96933	131712		

a) Item 'Final consumption expenditure of resident households' includes consumption expenditure of private non-profit institutions serving households.

2.6 Private Final Consumption Expenditure by Type and Purpose, in Constant Prices

Million Icelandic krónur

At constant prices of: 1969 / 1980

Final Consumption Expenditure of Resident Households

	1970	1975	1980	1981	1982	1983	1984	1985	1986	1987	1988	1989
1 Food, beverages and tobacco	75	94	2302	2305	2340	2385	2391	2492	2456	2651		
A Food	55	69	1683	1671	1684	1741	1731	1829	1730	1833		
B Non-alcoholic beverages	4	7	186	173	193	159	169	193	219	270		
C Alcoholic beverages	7	9	227	241	240	251	252	253	285	316		
D Tobacco	8	9	207	220	223	234	240	217	223	231		
2 Clothing and footwear	25	33	850	878	977	861	903	990	977	1106		
3 Gross rent, fuel and power	45	55	1484	1520	1578	1624	1668	1686	1715	1757		
A Fuel and power	10	13	299	292	302	307	303	287	294	306		
B Other	35	42	1184	1228	1277	1317	1364	1399	1421	1451		
4 Furniture, furnishings and household equipment and operation	26	40	1177	1293	1341	1180	1184	1226	1285	1555		
A Household operation	6	12	344	353	365	382	350	420	426	481		
B Other	20	28	833	940	976	798	834	806	859	1074		
5 Medical care and health expenses	6	5	118	128	145	153	141	149	174	184		
6 Transport and communication	35	46	1390	1669	1726	1459	1647	1643	2238	2928		
A Personal transport equipment	13	11	424	622	624	349	467	409	923	1523		
B Other	22	35	966	1047	1102	1110	1180	1234	1315	1406		
7 Recreational, entertainment, education and cultural services	15	23	663	687	766	755	730	806	793	944		
A Education	1	1	31	31	31	32	32	32	33	35		
B Other	14	22	632	656	735	723	698	773	760	909		
8 Miscellaneous goods and services	16	24	693	749	890	799	797	925	1063	1217		
A Personal care	3	5	126	148	142	133	122	154	151	163		
B Expenditures in restaurants, cafés and hotels	7	14	390	395	535	471	462	531	643	727		

Iceland

2.6 Private Final Consumption Expenditure by Type and Purpose, in Constant Prices (Continued)

Million Icelandic krónur

	1970	1975	1980	1981	1982	1983	1984	1985	1986	1987	1988	1989
			At constant prices of:		1969				1980			
C Other	6	4		176	206	214	196	213	240	268	327	
Total Final Consumption Expenditure in the Domestic Market by Households, of which	241	316		8676	8229	9764	9216	9461	10700	9916	12341	
Plus: Direct purchases abroad by resident households	7	9		293	355	362	322	409	436	494	679	
Less: Direct purchases in the domestic market by non-resident households	6	9		123	114	153	173	211	253	289	330	
Equals: Final Consumption Expenditure of Resident Households a	242	320		8846	8470	9973	9364	9660	10900	10066	12691	
Final Consumption Expenditure of Private Non-profit Institutions Serving Households												
Equals: Final Consumption Expenditure of Private Non-profit Organisations Serving Households												
Statistical discrepancy	-1	...		...	...	...	...	...	...	...	...	
Private Final Consumption Expenditure	242	320		8846	8470	9973	9364	9660	10905	10066	12691	

a) Item 'Final consumption expenditure of resident households' includes consumption expenditure of private non-profit institutions serving households.

2.11 Gross Fixed Capital Formation by Kind of Activity of Owner, ISIC Divisions, in Current Prices

Million Icelandic krónur

	1970	1975	1980	1981	1982	1983	1984	1985	1986	1987	1988	1989
All Producers												
1 Agriculture, hunting, forestry and fishing	13	87	400	588	927	1402	1817	2519	4874	6559	8395	5808
A Agriculture and hunting	6	38	183	212	409	621	978	1609	2226	2367	2560	2448
B Forestry and logging	...	...	...	...	...	...	...	...	...	...	...	...
C Fishing	7	49	217	376	518	781	839	910	2648	4192	5835	3360
2 Mining and quarrying	16	71	555	790	1158	1785	2805	4160	4815	5701	6180	7130
3 Manufacturing												
4 Electricity, gas and water	14	127	774	1167	1489	1885	2120	1862	1739	2107	3532	5443
5 Construction a	3	20	103	156	325	375	580	603	764	1165	1305	1380
6 Wholesale and retail trade, restaurants and hotels bc	7	34	226	392	772	1494	1970	3214	4234	6949	6699	6532
7 Transport, storage and communication	6	76	414	661	933	1452	1695	2949	3123	4925	3311	6185
8 Finance, insurance, real estate and business services bd	21	135	964	1317	2251	3495	4714	5380	5720	7752	10106	12740
9 Community, social and personal services	...	...	...	...	...	...	...	...	...	...	...	...
Total Industries	83	550	3436	5071	7855	11888	15701	20687	25319	35158	39521	45218
Producers of Government Services	21	86	491	858	1396	2239	2655	3773	4365	5884	8511	10292
Private Non-Profit Institutions Serving Households												
Total	104	636	3927	5929	9251	14127	18356	24460	29684	41042	48032	55510

a) Item 'Construction' includes machinery only.
b) Computers in all economic activities are included in item 'Wholesale and retail trade'.
c) Item 'Wholesale and retail trade' includes computers.
d) Real estate refers to owner-occupied dwellings and rent only.

2.12 Gross Fixed Capital Formation by Kind of Activity of Owner, ISIC Divisions, in Constant Prices

Million Icelandic krónur

	1970	1975	1980	1981	1982	1983	1984	1985	1986	1987	1988	1989
			At constant prices of:		1969				1980			
All Producers												
1 Agriculture, hunting, forestry and fishing	12	24		400	398	345	400	380	413	635	744	797	434
A Agriculture and hunting	5	10		183	142	174	149	207	266	305	283	255	190
B Forestry and logging	...	...		...	...	...	...	...	...	...	...	...	...
C Fishing	7	14		217	256	226	196	173	147	330	461	542	244

813

Iceland

2.12 Gross Fixed Capital Formation by Kind of Activity of Owner, ISIC Divisions, in Constant Prices
(Continued)

Million Icelandic kronur

	1970	1975	1980	1981	1982	1983	1984	1985	1986	1987	1988	1989
						At constant prices of:						
		1969					**1980**					
2 Mining and quarrying	15	20	...									
3 Manufacturing			555	538	501	439	563	637	586	614	563	513
4 Electricity, gas and water	12	31	...									
			774	782	637	459	426	285	215	221	314	395
5 Construction a	3	6	...									
			103	107	139	87	109	87	87	122	140	115
6 Wholesale and retail trade, restaurants and hotels bc	6	8	...									
			226	262	333	381	451	578	604	835	681	512
7 Transport, storage and communication	9	21	...									
			414	440	399	357	360	458	419	570	334	467
8 Finance, insurance, real estate and business services bdc	18	30.	...									
			964	870	952	865	955	825	711	812	898	919
9 Community, social and personal services	...	...	...									
Total Industries	74	140	...									
			3436	3397	3361	2933	3244	3283	3257	3918	3727	3355
Producers of Government Services	18	19	...									
			491	568	584	528	534	571	551	613	744	735
Private Non-Profit Institutions Serving Households	...	...	...									
Total	92	159	...									
			3927	3965	3945	3461	3778	3854	3808	4531	4471	4090

a) Item 'Construction' includes machinery only.
b) Finance, insurance and business services are included in item 'Wholesale and retail trade, restaurants and hotels'.
c) Computers in all economic activities are included in item 'Wholesale and retail trade'.
d) Real estate refers to owner-occupied dwellings and rent only.

2.17 Exports and Imports of Goods and Services, Detail

Million Icelandic kronur

	1970	1975	1980	1981	1982	1983	1984	1985	1986	1987	1988	1989
					Exports of Goods and Services							
1 Exports of merchandise, f.o.b.	128	474	4460	6536	8479	18623	23557	33750	44968	53053	61667	80072
2 Transport and communication												
3 Insurance service charges	80	244	1286	2188	4235	8455	10738	16069	18157	20413	22464	28896
4 Other commodities												
5 Adjustments of merchandise exports to change-of-ownership basis	...	...	...	...	...	...	...	...	...	...	...	...
6 Direct purchases in the domestic market by non-residential households	...	...	...	...	...	...	...	...	...	...	...	...
7 Direct purchases in the domestic market by extraterritorial bodies	...	...	...	...	...	...	...	...	...	...	...	...
Total Exports of Goods and Services	208	718	5746	8724	12714	27078	34295	49819	63125	73466	84131	108968
					Imports of Goods and Services							
1 Imports of merchandise, c.i.f.	126	680	4802	7485	11647	20596	26744	37600	45910	61237	68723	80250

Iceland

2.17 Exports and Imports of Goods and Services, Detail
(Continued)

Million Icelandic kronur

	1970	1975	1980	1981	1982	1983	1984	1985	1986	1987	1988	1989
A Imports of merchandise, f.o.b.	126	680	4307	6732	10364	18156	23889	33760	40988	55020	61996	72603
B Transport of services on merchandise imports	...	...	495	753	1283	2440	2855	3840	4922	6217	6727	7647
C Insurance service charges on merchandise imports	...	...										
2 Adjustments of merchandise imports to change-of-ownership basis	...	...	...	...	...	...	...	...	...	...	...	...
3 Other transport and communication												
4 Other insurance service charges	63	203	846	1451	2682	4679	7127	11451	10432	13259	16319	20116
5 Other commodities												
6 Direct purchases abroad by government												
7 Direct purchases abroad by resident households	7	...	...	...	...	...	...	...	...	...	...	...
Total Imports of Goods and Services	197	883	5648	8936	14329	25275	33871	49051	56342	74496	85042	100366
Balance of Goods and Services	11	-165	98	-212	-1615	1803	424	768	6783	-1030	-911	8602
Total Imports and Balance of Goods and Services	208	718	5746	8724	12714	27078	34295	49819	63125	73466	84131	108968

4.1 Derivation of Value Added by Kind of Activity, in Current Prices

Million Icelandic kronur

	1980			1981			1982			1983		
	Gross Output	Intermediate Consumption	Value Added	Gross Output	Intermediate Consumption	Value Added	Gross Output	Intermediate Consumption	Value Added	Gross Output	Intermediate Consumption	Value Added
						All Producers						
1 Agriculture, hunting, forestry and fishing	2949	1382	1567	4521	2216	2305	6259	3261	2998	11151	5946	5205
A Agriculture and hunting	1083	497	586	1732	836	896	2555	1263	1292	4609	2331	2278
B Forestry and logging	-	-	-	-	-	-	-	-	-	-	-	-
C Fishing	1866	885	981	2789	1380	1409	3705	1999	1706	6542	3615	2927
2 Mining and quarrying	-	-	-	-	-	-	-	-	-	-	-	-
A Coal mining	...	...	...	...	...	...	...	...	...	...	...	...
B Crude petroleum and natural gas production	...	...	...	...	...	...	...	...	...	...	...	...
C Metal ore mining	...	...	...	...	...	...	...	...	...	...	...	...
D Other mining	...	...	-	...	...	-	...	...	-	...	...	-
3 Manufacturing	8041	5557	2484	12274	8486	3788	18654	13100	5554	32228	23070	9158
A Manufacture of food, beverages and tobacco	4549	3594	955	7097	5412	1685	10337	8201	2136	17457	14011	3446
B Textile, wearing apparel and leather industries	572	360	212	815	544	271	1195	774	421	2017	1287	730
C Manufacture of wood and wood products, including furniture	393	175	218	552	262	290	868	420	448	1379	688	691
D Manufacture of paper and paper products, printing and publishing	365	183	182	570	267	303	930	430	500	1900	1062	838
E Manufacture of chemicals and chemical petroleum, coal, rubber and plastic products	381	255	126	576	392	184	1033	634	399	1689	1192	497
F Manufacture of non-metallic mineral products, except products of petroleum and coal	330	200	130	506	301	205	1030	603	427	1464	871	593
G Basic metal industries	640	426	214	794	659	135	1233	1038	195	3166	2397	769
H Manufacture of fabricated metal products, machinery and equipment	719	322	397	1198	567	631	1687	776	911	2470	1121	1349
I Other manufacturing industries	92	42	50	166	82	84	340	223	117	687	442	245
4 Electricity, gas and water	872	300	572	1396	591	805	2518	1070	1448	5970	2359	3611
A Electricity, gas and steam	832	286	546	1334	568	766	2423	1032	1391	5795	2285	3510
B Water works and supply	40	15	25	62	23	39	95	38	57	175	74	101
5 Construction	3250	2069	1181	4843	3015	1828	9160	5777	3383	13517	8763	4754
6 Wholesale and retail trade, restaurants and hotels	3260	814	2446	5532	1528	4004	8765	2858	5907	16225	5183	11042
A Wholesale and retail trade	2882	599	2283	4903	1183	3720	7384	2021	5363	14140	4025	10115
B Restaurants and hotels	378	215	163	630	345	285	1381	836	545	2084	1157	927

Iceland

4.1 Derivation of Value Added by Kind of Activity, in Current Prices
(Continued)

Million Icelandic kronur

	1980			1981			1982			1983		
	Gross Output	Intermediate Consumption	Value Added	Gross Output	Intermediate Consumption	Value Added	Gross Output	Intermediate Consumption	Value Added	Gross Output	Intermediate Consumption	Value Added
Restaurants	216	130	86	397	227	170	976	628	348	1353	819	534
Hotels and other lodging places	162	85	77	233	118	115	405	209	196	731	338	393
7 Transport, storage and communication	2152	1133	1019	3745	2012	1733	5962	3200	2762	11334	6232	5102
A Transport and storage	1882	1080	802	3331	1927	1404	5272	3000	2272	9840	5857	3983
B Communication	269	53	216	413	84	329	690	200	490	1494	375	1119
8 Finance, insurance, real estate and business services	2730	735	1995	4036	1111	2925	7200	1920	5280	13650	3754	9896
A Financial institutions	676	104	572	915	175	740	2013	315	1698	4114	644	3470
B Insurance	217	82	135	271	77	194	392	110	282	637	206	431
C Real estate and business services	1837	549	1288	2850	860	1990	4795	1494	3301	8899	2903	5996
9 Community, social and personal services	1103	435	668	1617	602	1015	3119	1217	1902	5110	2013	3097
A Sanitary and similar services	...	...	...	...	...	...	...	...	...	...	...	...
B Social and related community services	141	37	104	190	51	139	398	94	304	710	207	503
C Recreational and cultural services	258	124	134	410	189	221	710	334	376	1494	684	810
D Personal and household services a	705	274	431	1016	362	654	2012	790	1222	2906	1122	1784
Total, Industries	24357	12425	11932	37965	19561	18404	61638	32403	29235	109186	57320	51866
Producers of Government Services	2764	1051	1713	4393	1695	2698	7235	2873	4362	12617	5486	7131
Other Producers	174	74	100	255	103	152	425	172	253	702	288	414
Total	27295	13550	13745	42613	21358	21255	69298	35447	33851	122505	63094	59411
Less: Imputed bank service charge	...	-523	523	...	-682	682	...	-1617	1617	...	-3468	3468
Import duties b	1168	...	1168	2085	...	2085	2965	...	2965	4467	...	4467
Value added tax	...	...	...	...	...	...	...	...	...	...	...	...
Other adjustments c	1107	...	1107	1678	...	1678	2933	...	2933	5427	...	5427
Total	29570	14073	15497	46376	22040	24336	75196	37064	38132	132399	66562	65837

	1984			1985			1986			1987		
	Gross Output	Intermediate Consumption	Value Added	Gross Output	Intermediate Consumption	Value Added	Gross Output	Intermediate Consumption	Value Added	Gross Output	Intermediate Consumption	Value Added
						All Producers						
1 Agriculture, hunting, forestry and fishing	15153	7791	7362	21557	10043	11514	28738	12715	16023	35219	13981	21238
A Agriculture and hunting	5480	2824	2656	7527	3329	4198	8849	3918	4931	10134	3946	6188
B Forestry and logging	-	-	-	-	-	-	-	-	-	-	-	-
C Fishing	9673	4967	4706	14030	6714	7316	19889	8797	11092	25085	10035	15050
2 Mining and quarrying	-	-	-	-	-	-	-	-	-	-	-	-
A Coal mining	...	...	...	...	...	...	...	...	...	...	...	...
B Crude petroleum and natural gas production	...	...	...	...	...	...	...	...	...	...	...	...
C Metal ore mining	...	...	...	...	...	...	...	...	...	...	...	...
D Other mining	...	...	-	...	...	-	...	...	...	...	...	...

Iceland

4.1 Derivation of Value Added by Kind of Activity, in Current Prices
(Continued)

Million Icelandic kronur

	1984			1985			1986			1987		
	Gross Output	Intermediate Consumption	Value Added	Gross Output	Intermediate Consumption	Value Added	Gross Output	Intermediate Consumption	Value Added	Gross Output	Intermediate Consumption	Value Added
3 Manufacturing	45770	31811	13959	61051	43230	17821	77452	52901	24551	100080	65694	34386
A Manufacture of food, beverages and tobacco	24866	19473	5393	35247	27568	7679	44786	33552	11234	55685	40642	15043
B Textile, wearing apparel and leather industries	2945	1870	1075	3982	2556	1426	4514	2844	1670	5927	3760	2167
C Manufacture of wood and wood products, including furniture	2032	1032	1000	2460	1242	1218	3188	1714	1474	4532	2018	2514
D Manufacture of paper and paper products, printing and publishing	2522	1303	1219	3507	1810	1697	5222	2844	2378	6350	3120	3230
E Manufacture of chemicals and chemical petroleum, coal, rubber and plastic products	2372	1566	806	3284	2230	1054	4138	2697	1441	5078	3253	1825
F Manufacture of non-metallic mineral products, except products of petroleum and coal	2074	1204	870	2365	1373	992	2960	1579	1381	3890	2031	1859
G Basic metal industries	4692	3186	1506	4699	3736	963	5269	4211	1058	6263	4659	1604
H Manufacture of fabricated metal products, machinery and equipment	3370	1587	1783	4142	1795	2347	5798	2419	3379	9240	3937	5303
I Other manufacturing industries	897	590	307	1365	923	442	1579	1041	538	3115	2274	841
4 Electricity, gas and water	8082	3072	5010	9670	3703	5967	10555	4151	6404	11809	4937	6872
A Electricity, gas and steam	7843	2973	4870	9316	3554	5762	10148	3985	6163	11246	4668	6578
B Water works and supply	239	99	140	354	149	205	407	166	241	563	269	294
5 Construction	17978	11600	6378	22682	14296	8386	31179	19932	11247	40523	24783	15740
6 Wholesale and retail trade, restaurants and hotels	22195	7046	15149	29817	9485	20332	39499	12902	26597	57229	17803	39426
A Wholesale and retail trade	18975	5205	13770	24850	6646	18204	31901	8169	23732	45911	12107	33804
B Restaurants and hotels	3220	1841	1379	4967	2839	2128	7598	4733	2865	11318	5696	5622
Restaurants	2075	1278	797	3317	2001	1316	5619	3741	1878	8348	4581	3767
Hotels and other lodging places	1145	563	582	1650	838	812	1979	992	987	2970	1114	1856
7 Transport, storage and communication	15335	8474	6861	19840	11576	8264	24547	14132	10415	29816	16134	13682
A Transport and storage	13296	7989	5307	17449	10862	6587	21520	13218	8302	25828	14887	10941
B Communication	2039	485	1554	2391	714	1677	3026	915	2111	3988	1246	2742
8 Finance, insurance, real estate and business services	17467	5395	12072	25567	8186	17381	29697	10154	19543	41955	13326	28629
A Financial institutions	4351	912	3439	6547	1388	5159	6416	2134	4282	11592	3101	8491
B Insurance	967	280	687	1384	394	990	1568	481	1087	2058	630	1428
C Real estate and business services	12149	4202	7947	17636	6404	11232	21713	7540	14173	28305	9595	18710
9 Community, social and personal services	6493	2725	3768	10648	4751	5897	13810	5979	7831	19839	8102	11737
A Sanitary and similar services	...	...	...	...	...	...	...	...	...	...	...	...
B Social and related community services	720	205	515	1343	372	971	1651	480	1171	2589	623	1966
C Recreational and cultural services	1907	933	974	3380	1983	1397	3579	1818	1761	5508	2805	2703
D Personal and household services [a]	3866	1587	2279	5925	2396	3529	8580	3680	4900	11741	4674	7067
Total, Industries	148474	77913	70561	200832	105271	95561	255476	132865	122611	336472	164760	171712
Producers of Government Services	15666	7066	8600	22404	10119	12285	30585	13579	17006	41680	17201	24479
Other Producers	929	377	552	1396	572	824	1867	775	1092	2613	1078	1535
Total	165068	85356	79712	224632	115962	108670	287928	147220	140708	380765	183040	197725
Less: Imputed bank service charge	...	-3330	3330	...	-4822	4822	...	-4493	4493	...	-8078	8078
Import duties [b]	6042	...	6042	7280	...	7280	10457	...	10457	12834	...	12834
Value added tax	...	...	...	...	...	...	...	...	...	...	...	...
Other adjustments [c]	5084	...	5084	7962	...	7962	11924	...	11924	5618	...	5618
Total	176194	88686	87508	239874	120784	119090	310309	151713	158596	399217	191118	208099

Iceland

4.1 Derivation of Value Added by Kind of Activity, in Current Prices

Million Icelandic kronur

	1988		
	Gross Output	Intermediate Consumption	Value Added
	All Producers		
1 Agriculture, hunting, forestry and fishing	43209	17822	25387
A Agriculture and hunting	11751	5475	6276
B Forestry and logging	-	-	-
C Fishing	31457	12347	19110
2 Mining and quarrying	-	-	-
A Coal mining	...	...	...
B Crude petroleum and natural gas production	...	...	...
C Metal ore mining	...	...	...
D Other mining	...	...	...
3 Manufacturing	112923	74763	38160
A Manufacture of food, beverages and tobacco	59392	45407	13985
B Textile, wearing apparel and leather industries	5669	3340	2329
C Manufacture of wood and wood products, including furniture	5430	2466	2964
D Manufacture of paper and paper products, printing and publishing	8098	4094	4004
E Manufacture of chemicals and chemical petroleum, coal, rubber and plastic products	6356	3779	2577
F Manufacture of non-metallic mineral products, except products of petroleum and coal	4730	2536	2194
G Basic metal industries	9350	6568	2782
H Manufacture of fabricated metal products, machinery and equipment	10148	3932	6216
I Other manufacturing industries	3750	2642	1108
4 Electricity, gas and water	15886	5905	9981
A Electricity, gas and steam	15103	5564	9539
B Water works and supply	783	341	442
5 Construction	49047	30575	18472
6 Wholesale and retail trade, restaurants and hotels	74781	24140	50641
A Wholesale and retail trade	60068	16738	43330
B Restaurants and hotels	14713	7402	7311
Restaurants	11097	6068	5029
Hotels and other lodging places	3616	1334	2282
7 Transport, storage and communication	35650	18395	17255
A Transport and storage	30254	16986	13268
B Communication	5396	1409	3987
8 Finance, insurance, real estate and business services	54872	17154	37718
A Financial institutions	16683	4505	12178
B Insurance	2542	856	1686
C Real estate and business services	35647	11794	23853
9 Community, social and personal services	26745	10652	16093
A Sanitary and similar services	...	...	...
B Social and related community services	3746	961	2785
C Recreational and cultural services	7520	3845	3675
D Personal and household services [a]	15479	5846	9633
Total, Industries	413113	199406	213707
Producers of Government Services	54497	22568	31929

Iceland

4.1 Derivation of Value Added by Kind of Activity, in Current Prices
(Continued)

Million Icelandic kronur

	1988		
	Gross Output	Intermediate Consumption	Value Added
Other Producers	3705	1536	2169
Total	471316	223510	247806
Less: Imputed bank service charge	...	-11557	11557
Import duties b	13414	...	13414
Value added tax	...	...	...
Other adjustments c	4976	...	4976
Total	489706	235067	254639

a) Item 'Personal and household services' includes also ISIC-code 96, residents directly employed at the NATO-base.
b) Item 'Import duties' includes all indirect taxes and subsidies not directly allocated to specified activities.
c) Item 'Other adjustments' includes residual error between production and expenditure approaches.

4.2 Derivation of Value Added by Kind of Activity, in Constant Prices

Million Icelandic kronur

	1980			1981			1982			1983		
	Gross Output	Intermediate Consumption	Value Added	Gross Output	Intermediate Consumption	Value Added	Gross Output	Intermediate Consumption	Value Added	Gross Output	Intermediate Consumption	Value Added
At constant prices of:1980												
All Producers												
1 Agriculture, hunting, forestry and fishing	...	...	1570	...	...	1594	...	...	1544	...	...	1388
A Agriculture and hunting	...	...	595	...	...	602	...	...	575	...	...	585
B Forestry and logging	...	...	...	...	...	...	...	...	...	...	...	...
C Fishing	...	...	975	...	...	992	...	...	969	...	...	803
2 Mining and quarrying	...	...	...	...	...	...	...	...	...	...	...	...
3 Manufacturing	...	...	2410	...	...	2491	...	...	2398	...	...	2248
A Manufacture of food, beverages and tobacco	...	...	1148	...	...	1212	...	...	1114	...	...	979
B Textile, wearing apparel and leather industries	...	...	201	...	...	193	...	...	192	...	...	183
C Manufacture of wood and wood products, including furniture	...	...	159	...	...	156	...	...	164	...	...	140
D Manufacture of paper and paper products, printing and publishing	...	...	158	...	...	161	...	...	165	...	...	182
E Manufacture of chemicals and chemical petroleum, coal, rubber and plastic products	...	...	98	...	...	95	...	...	98	...	...	107
F Manufacture of non-metallic mineral products, except products of petroleum and coal	...	...	85	...	...	74	...	...	78	...	...	80
G Basic metal industries	...	...	198	...	...	204	...	...	215	...	...	224
H Manufacture of fabricated metal products, machinery and equipment	...	...	320	...	...	346	...	...	327	...	...	298
I Other manufacturing industries	...	...	44	...	...	50	...	...	45	...	...	55
4 Electricity, gas and water	...	...	514	...	...	545	...	...	604	...	...	709
A Electricity, gas and steam	...	...	488	...	...	517	...	...	575	...	...	681
B Water works and supply	...	...	27	...	...	28	...	...	28	...	...	28
5 Construction	...	...	1052	...	...	1047	...	...	1110	...	...	1075
6 Wholesale and retail trade, restaurants and hotels	...	...	1233	...	...	1352	...	...	1424	...	...	1324
A Wholesale and retail trade	...	...	1118	...	...	1225	...	...	1285	...	...	1185
B Restaurants and hotels	...	...	115	...	...	127	...	...	139	...	...	139
Restaurants	...	...	56	...	...	68	...	...	78	...	...	88
Hotels and other lodging places	...	...	59	...	...	59	...	...	61	...	...	51
7 Transport, storage and communication	...	...	932	...	...	971	...	...	972	...	...	1015
A Transport and storage	...	...	753	...	...	776	...	...	750	...	...	765
B Communication	...	...	179	...	...	195	...	...	222	...	...	250
8 Finance, insurance, real estate and business services	...	...	1854	...	...	1939	...	...	2067	...	...	2181
A Financial institutions	...	...	574	...	...	593	...	...	612	...	...	644

Iceland

4.2 Derivation of Value Added by Kind of Activity, in Constant Prices
(Continued)

Million Icelandic kronur

	1980			1981			1982			1983		
	Gross Output	Intermediate Consumption	Value Added	Gross Output	Intermediate Consumption	Value Added	Gross Output	Intermediate Consumption	Value Added	Gross Output	Intermediate Consumption	Value Added
						At constant prices of:1980						
B Insurance	...	...	87	...	...	92	...	...	95	...	...	97
C Real estate and business services	...	...	1193	...	...	1253	...	...	1360	...	...	1440
9 Community, social and personal services	...	...	559	...	...	584	...	...	627	...	...	655
A Sanitary and similar services	...	...	...	...	...	...	...	...	...	...	...	...
B Social and related community services	...	...	100	...	...	110	...	...	117	...	...	127
C Recreational and cultural services	...	...	141	...	...	147	...	...	167	...	...	177
D Personal and household services [a]	...	...	318	...	...	328	...	...	344	...	...	352
Total, Industries	...	...	10124	...	...	10523	...	...	10746	...	...	10595
Producers of Government Services	...	...	1662	...	...	1789	...	...	1842	...	...	1933
Other Producers	...	...	97	...	...	108	...	...	117	...	...	120
Total	...	...	11883	...	...	12420	...	...	12706	...	...	12647
Less: Imputed bank service charge	...	...	523	...	...	541	...	...	558	...	...	587
Import duties	...	...	...	...	...	...	...	...	...	...	...	...
Value added tax	...	...	...	...	...	...	...	...	...	...	...	...
Total [b]	...	...	11360	...	...	11879	...	...	12147	...	...	12061

	1984			1985			1986			1987		
	Gross Output	Intermediate Consumption	Value Added	Gross Output	Intermediate Consumption	Value Added	Gross Output	Intermediate Consumption	Value Added	Gross Output	Intermediate Consumption	Value Added
						At constant prices of:1980						
						All Producers						
1 Agriculture, hunting, forestry and fishing	...	...	1543	...	...	1806	...	...	1825	...	...	1866
A Agriculture and hunting	...	...	662	...	...	744	...	...	749	...	...	796
B Forestry and logging	...	...	...	...	...	...	...	...	...	...	...	...
C Fishing	...	...	880	...	...	1062	...	...	1076	...	...	1070
2 Mining and quarrying	...	...	...	...	...	...	...	...	...	...	...	...
3 Manufacturing	...	...	2407	...	...	2429	...	...	2550	...	...	2752
A Manufacture of food, beverages and tobacco	...	...	1061	...	...	1046	...	...	1134	...	...	1198
B Textile, wearing apparel and leather industries	...	...	194	...	...	214	...	...	192	...	...	186
C Manufacture of wood and wood products, including furniture	...	...	151	...	...	153	...	...	147	...	...	178
D Manufacture of paper and paper products, printing and publishing	...	...	180	...	...	193	...	...	220	...	...	224
E Manufacture of chemicals and chemical petroleum, coal, rubber and plastic products	...	...	128	...	...	132	...	...	133	...	...	142
F Manufacture of non-metallic mineral products, except products of petroleum and coal	...	...	82	...	...	77	...	...	76	...	...	93
G Basic metal industries	...	...	242	...	...	228	...	...	239	...	...	251
H Manufacture of fabricated metal products, machinery and equipment	...	...	313	...	...	328	...	...	354	...	...	415
I Other manufacturing industries	...	...	56	...	...	59	...	...	56	...	...	65
4 Electricity, gas and water	...	...	768	...	...	793	...	...	824	...	...	834
A Electricity, gas and steam	...	...	738	...	...	761	...	...	791	...	...	799
B Water works and supply	...	...	30	...	...	32	...	...	33	...	...	36
5 Construction	...	...	1126	...	...	1086	...	...	1121	...	...	1276
6 Wholesale and retail trade, restaurants and hotels	...	...	1386	...	...	1454	...	...	1577	...	...	1826
A Wholesale and retail trade	...	...	1229	...	...	1278	...	...	1400	...	...	1631
B Restaurants and hotels	...	...	157	...	...	176	...	...	177	...	...	195
Restaurants	...	...	102	...	...	119	...	...	117	...	...	122
Hotels and other lodging places	...	...	55	...	...	57	...	...	60	...	...	73
7 Transport, storage and communication	...	...	1076	...	...	1151	...	...	1257	...	...	1376
A Transport and storage	...	...	801	...	...	842	...	...	891	...	...	942

820

Iceland

4.2 Derivation of Value Added by Kind of Activity, in Constant Prices
(Continued)

Million Icelandic kronur

	1984			1985			1986			1987		
	Gross Output	Intermediate Consumption	Value Added	Gross Output	Intermediate Consumption	Value Added	Gross Output	Intermediate Consumption	Value Added	Gross Output	Intermediate Consumption	Value Added
At constant prices of:1980												
B Communication	...	...	275	...	...	309	...	...	365	...	...	434
8 Finance, insurance, real estate and business services	...	...	2362	...	...	2534	...	...	2676	...	...	2857
A Financial institutions	...	...	735	...	...	820	...	...	920	...	...	968
B Insurance	...	...	103	...	...	113	...	...	118	...	...	124
C Real estate and business services	...	...	1523	...	...	1601	...	...	1638	...	...	1765
9 Community, social and personal services	...	...	672	...	...	721	...	...	770	...	...	845
A Sanitary and similar services	...	...	...	...	...	...	...	...	...	...	...	...
B Social and related community services	...	...	133	...	...	138	...	...	150	...	...	163
C Recreational and cultural services	...	...	169	...	...	192	...	...	205	...	...	230
D Personal and household services [a]	...	...	371	...	...	390	...	...	415	...	...	452
Total, Industries	...	...	11341	...	...	11974	...	...	12600	...	...	13632
Producers of Government Services	...	...	1992	...	...	2094	...	...	2219	...	...	2415
Other Producers	...	...	127	...	...	136	...	...	146	...	...	159
Total	...	...	13461	...	...	14205	...	...	14965	...	...	16206
Less: Imputed bank service charge	...	...	670	...	...	748	...	...	838	...	...	882
Import duties	...	...	...	...	...	...	...	...	...	...	...	...
Value added tax	...	...	...	...	...	...	...	...	...	...	...	...
Total [b]	...	...	12790	...	...	13456	...	...	14127	...	...	15324

	1988		
	Gross Output	Intermediate Consumption	Value Added
At constant prices of:1980			
All Producers			
1 Agriculture, hunting, forestry and fishing	...	...	1924
A Agriculture and hunting	...	...	706
B Forestry and logging	...	...	...
C Fishing	...	...	1218
2 Mining and quarrying	...	...	...
3 Manufacturing	...	...	2545
A Manufacture of food, beverages and tobacco	...	...	1078
B Textile, wearing apparel and leather industries	...	...	152
C Manufacture of wood and wood products, including furniture	...	...	174
D Manufacture of paper and paper products, printing and publishing	...	...	224
E Manufacture of chemicals and chemical petroleum, coal, rubber and plastic products	...	...	140
F Manufacture of non-metallic mineral products, except products of petroleum and coal	...	...	95
G Basic metal industries	...	...	256
H Manufacture of fabricated metal products, machinery and equipment	...	...	361
I Other manufacturing industries	...	...	66
4 Electricity, gas and water	...	...	869
A Electricity, gas and steam	...	...	834
B Water works and supply	...	...	35
5 Construction	...	...	1257
6 Wholesale and retail trade, restaurants and hotels	...	...	1777
A Wholesale and retail trade	...	...	1580
B Restaurants and hotels	...	...	197

Iceland

4.2 Derivation of Value Added by Kind of Activity, in Constant Prices
(Continued)

Million Icelandic kronur

	1988		
	Gross Output	Intermediate Consumption	Value Added
	At constant prices of:1980		
Restaurants	...	...	127
Hotels and other lodging places	...	...	70
7 Transport, storage and communication	...	...	1357
A Transport and storage	...	...	903
B Communication	...	...	454
8 Finance, insurance, real estate and business services	...	...	2967
A Financial institutions	...	...	1034
B Insurance	...	...	126
C Real estate and business services	...	...	1807
9 Community, social and personal services	...	...	879
A Sanitary and similar services	...	...	...
B Social and related community services	...	...	173
C Recreational and cultural services	...	...	237
D Personal and household services [a]	...	...	469
Total, Industries	...	...	13575
Producers of Government Services	...	...	2565
Other Producers	...	...	175
Total	...	...	16315
Less: Imputed bank service charge	...	...	942
Import duties	...	...	...
Value added tax	...	...	...
Total [b]	...	...	15373

a) Item 'Personal and household services' includes also ISIC-code 96, residents directly employed at the NATO-base.
b) Gross domestic product in factor values.

4.3 Cost Components of Value Added

Million Icelandic kronur

	1980						1981					
	Compensation of Employees	Capital Consumption	Net Operating Surplus	Indirect Taxes	Less: Subsidies Received	Value Added	Compensation of Employees	Capital Consumption	Net Operating Surplus	Indirect Taxes	Less: Subsidies Received	Value Added
	All Producers											
1 Agriculture, hunting, forestry and fishing	834	351	385	14	16	1568	1321	417	563	22	19	2304
A Agriculture and hunting	55	133	408	7	16	587	134	117	650	13	19	895
B Forestry and logging	-	-	-	-	-	-	-	-	-	-	-	-
C Fishing	779	218	-23	7	-	981	1187	300	-87	9	-	1409
2 Mining and quarrying	-	-	-	-	-	-	-	-	-	-	-	-

Iceland

4.3 Cost Components of Value Added (Continued)

Million Icelandic kronur

	1980							1981						
	Compensation of Employees	Capital Consumption	Net Operating Surplus	Indirect Taxes	Less: Subsidies Received	Value Added		Compensation of Employees	Capital Consumption	Net Operating Surplus	Indirect Taxes	Less: Subsidies Received	Value Added	
3 Manufacturing	1978	351	81	417	342	2485		2958	624	113	631	538	3788
A Manufacture of food, beverages and tobacco	959	138	51	137	329	956		1441	281	192	284	513	1685
B Textile, wearing apparel and leather industries	159	26	16	23	13	211		240	40	-19	35	25	271
C Manufacture of wood and wood products, including furniture	148	21	-10	59	...	218		182	27	-17	98	-	290
D Manufacture of paper and paper products, printing and publishing	137	17	4	25	...	183		209	30	21	44	-	304
E Manufacture of chemicals and chemical petroleum, coal, rubber and plastic products	70	24	4	28	-	126		106	43	1	34	-	184
F Manufacture of non-metallic mineral products, except products of petroleum and coal	68	17	-1	46	-	130		108	30	-	66	-	204
G Basic metal industries	103	78	17	17	-	215		155	121	-160	20	-	136
H Manufacture of fabricated metal products, machinery and equipment	297	28	-5	77	-	397		452	50	-5	134	-	631
I Other manufacturing industries	38	2	5	5	-	50		66	2	8	8	-	84
4 Electricity, gas and water	92	149	273	104	48	570		141	264	311	158	68	806
A Electricity, gas and steam	91	145	252	104	46	546		140	251	286	157	68	766
B Water works and supply	1	4	21	-	2	24		2	12	25	1	1	39
5 Construction	755	80	217	129	-	1181		1206	90	383	149	-	1828
6 Wholesale and retail trade, restaurants and hotels	935	135	163	1219	6	2446		1518	253	259	1996	22	4004
A Wholesale and retail trade	816	123	179	1171	6	2283		1329	242	244	1927	22	3720
B Restaurants and hotels	119	12	-16	48	-	163		189	11	15	69	-	284
Restaurants	63	7	-14	31	-	87		108	8	7	47	-	170
Hotels and other lodging places	56	5	-2	17	-	76		82	3	8	22	-	115
7 Transport, storage and communication	635	264	33	117	30	1019		1011	377	221	195	71	1733
A Transport and storage	500	198	55	80	30	803		811	293	233	138	71	1404
B Communication	135	66	-22	37	-	216		200	84	-12	57	-	329
8 Finance, insurance, real estate and business services	435	413	159	16	18	1005		639	673	354	273	3	2924
A Financial institutions	223	15	336	16	18	572		340	27	354	22	3	740
B Insurance	50	5	32	48	-	135		65	10	13	107	...	195
C Real estate and business services	163	393	637	95	...	1288		234	637	976	144	-	1991
9 Community, social and personal services	426	42	90	137	28	667		636	60	174	184	39	1015
A Sanitary and similar services	...	...	...	...	...	...		...	...	...	...	...	...
B Social and related community services	21	3	76	3	-	103		31	8	94	6	-	139
C Recreational and cultural services	105	21	15	20	28	133		155	29	39	37	39	221
D Personal and household services	300	18	-1	113	-	430		450	23	40	141	-	654
Total, industries	1609	1785	2248	2296	488	11932		9431	2759	3366	3609	761	18404
Producers of Government Services	1566	95	1	50	-	1712		2470	148	3	79	-	2700
Other Producers	69	10	-2	3	-	100		136	13	-2	5	-	152
Total	7746	1890	2248	2350	488	13746		12036	2920	3367	3693	761	21255
Less: Imputed bank service charge	...	...	523	...	...	523		...	...	682	...	...	682
Import duties [b]	...	...	...	1170	2	1168		...	...	...	2086	1	2085
Value added tax	...	...	...	...	...	...		...	...	...	...	...	...
Other adjustments [c]	...	...	...	...	...	1107		...	...	...	...	...	1678
Total [d]	7746	1890	1725	3520	490	15497		12036	2920	2685	5779	762	24336

Iceland

4.3 Cost Components of Value Added

Million Icelandic krónur

	1982						1983					
	Compensation of Employees	Capital Consumption	Net Operating Surplus	Indirect Taxes	Less: Subsidies Received	Value Added	Compensation of Employees	Capital Consumption	Net Operating Surplus	Indirect Taxes	Less: Subsidies Received	Value Added

All Producers

1 Agriculture, hunting, forestry and fishing	1705	976	249	95	26	2999	2624	1403	1105	136	63	5205
A Agriculture and hunting	187	316	794	21	26	1292	224	475	1611	31	63	2278
B Forestry and logging	-	-	-	-	-	-	-	-	-	-	-	-
C Fishing	1518	660	-544	74	-	1708	2400	928	-506	105	-	2927
2 Mining and quarrying	-	-	-	-	-	-	-	-	-	-	-	-
3 Manufacturing	4642	1062	-187	971	934	5554	7051	2202	-192	1411	1315	9157
A Manufacture of food, beverages and tobacco	2252	435	-187	298	901	2136	3399	882	-55	442	1221	3446
B Textile, wearing apparel and leather industries	363	64	-7	35	33	422	534	98	75	77	54	730
C Manufacture of wood and wood products, including furniture	285	22	22	118	-	447	425	58	-11	219	-	691
D Manufacture of paper and paper products, printing and publishing	323	41	73	63	-	500	555	103	85	95	-	838
E Manufacture of chemical and chemical petroleum, coal, rubber and plastic products	198	65	53	83	-	399	273	131	46	86	40	496
F Manufacture of non-metallic mineral products, except of petroleum and coal	178	51	75	123	-	427	296	155	-24	165	592
G Basic metal industries	243	308	-385	30	-	196	369	661	-316	54	-	768
H Manufacture of fabricated metal products, machinery and equipment	702	73	-71	207	-	911	1021	106	-19	241	-	1349
I Other manufacturing industries	98	3	-	15	-	116	179	8	27	31	-	245
4 Electricity, gas and water	213	603	466	291	125	1448	451	1156	1719	672	389	3609
A Electricity, gas and steam	210	579	436	290	124	1391	446	1101	1680	670	387	3510
B Water works and supply	3	24	30	1	1	57	5	55	39	2	2	99
5 Construction	2014	171	816	381	-	3382	2986	634	650	485	-	4755
6 Wholesale and retail trade, restaurants and hotels	2408	333	128	3078	40	5907	3816	779	1598	4893	43	11043
A Wholesale and retail trade	2082	290	128	2904	40	5364	3293	703	1527	4636	43	10116
B Restaurants and hotels	327	43	-	174	-	544	523	76	71	257	-	927
Restaurants	133	38	-17	134	-	348	294	58	-7	189	-	534
Hotels and other lodging places	133	5	18	40	-	196	229	18	78	68	-	393
7 Transport, storage and communication	1501	564	474	354	130	2763	2376	1107	1169	583	132	5103
A Transport and storage	1190	423	528	261	130	2272	1837	868	1024	387	132	3984
B Communication	311	141	-54	92	-	490	539	239	145	196	-	1119
8 Finance, insurance, real estate and business services	1081	1060	2665	503	29	5280	1804	2004	5211	893	15	9897
Financial institutions	555	19	1059	56	29	1699	914	98	2334	151	15	3470
B Insurance	95	13	-7	181	-	282	146	36	-85	334	-	431
C Real estate and business services	432	1028	1613	227	-	3300	744	1882	2962	408	-	5996
9 Community, social and personal services	1055	126	400	379	58	1902	1584	203	831	570	91	3097
A Sanitary and similar services	...	...	...	...	...	...	...	...	...	...	...	...
B Social and related community services	69	11	214	10	-	304	72	19	386	26	-	503
C Recreational and cultural services	252	58	60	63	58	375	392	98	270	141	91	810
D Personal and household services	734	57	125	306	-	1222	1120	86	174	403	-	1783
Total, industries	14620	4884	5011	6052	1342	29235	22693	9487	12092	9642	2047	51867
Producers of Government Services	3993	240	3	127	-	4363	6483	428	14	206	-	7131
Other Producers	226	22	-3	8	253	370	37	-8	14	156	413
Total	18839	5156	5011	6187	1342	33851	29545	9952	12098	9862	2047	59410
Less: imputed bank service charge	...	1617	...	...	...	1617	...	3468	...	...	...	3468
Import duties b	...	...	3015	50	...	2965	...	...	4624	156	4468
Value added tax	...	...	...	...	...	...	...	...	...	...	...	...
Other adjustments c	...	...	...	...	...	2933	...	...	...	...	...	5427
Total d	18839	5156	3394	9202	1392	38132	29545	9952	8630	14486	2203	65837

824

Iceland

4.3 Cost Components of Value Added

Million Icelandic kronur

	1984						1985					
	Compensation of Employees	Capital Consumption	Net Operating Surplus	Indirect Taxes	Less: Subsidies Received	Value Added	Compensation of Employees	Capital Consumption	Net Operating Surplus	Indirect Taxes	Less: Subsidies Received	Value Added
All Producers												
1 Agriculture, hunting, forestry and fishing	3850	2558	807	253	106	7362	5937	2745	2751	229	147	11515
A Agriculture and hunting	289	559	1798	109	99	2656	437	733	3006	166	143	4199
B Forestry and logging	-	-	-	-	-	-	-	-	-	-	-	-
C Fishing	3561	1999	-991	144	7	4706	5500	2012	-255	63	4	7316
2 Mining and quarrying	-	-	-	-	-	-	-	-	-	-	-	-
3 Manufacturing	9369	2828	900	2031	1169	13959	13563	3321	340	2683	2087	17820
A Manufacture of food, beverages and tobacco	4574	1224	181	517	1104	5392	6587	1512	690	768	1877	7680
B Textile, wearing apparel and leather industries	761	146	141	83	56	1075	1059	191	97	158	80	1425
C Manufacture of wood and wood products, including furniture	551	83	60	306	-	1000	750	84	-50	434	-	1218
D Manufacture of paper and paper products, printing and publishing	738	184	124	173	-	1219	1128	229	139	200	-	1696
E Manufacture of chemicals and chemical petroleum, coal, rubber and plastic products	375	174	128	139	10	806	639	254	62	230	130	1055
F Manufacture of non-metallic mineral products, except products of petroleum and coal	379	176	74	240	-	869	555	199	-67	305	-	992
G Basic metal industries	497	674	150	184	-	1505	704	650	-473	83	-	964
H Manufacture of fabricated metal products, machinery and equipment	1281	154	-1	349	-	1783	1830	185	-134	465	-	2346
I Other manufacturing industries	214	12	42	40	-	308	311	17	75	39	-	442
4 Electricity, gas and water	564	1521	2608	913	597	5009	877	2517	2200	1022	649	5967
A Electricity, gas and steam	556	1447	2552	909	595	4869	864	2435	2095	1014	648	5760
B Water works and supply	8	74	56	4	2	140	13	81	105	7	1	205
5 Construction	3516	1043	1100	720	-	6379	4585	1155	1579	1065	-	8384
6 Wholesale and retail trade, restaurants and hotels	5017	1039	2232	6882	21	15149	7613	1294	1627	9816	18	20332
A Wholesale and retail trade	4318	902	2092	6479	21	13770	6454	1132	1401	9235	18	18204
B Restaurants and hotels	699	137	140	403	-	1379	1159	162	225	581	-	2127
Restaurants	425	78	10	285	-	798	697	85	81	453	-	1316
Hotels and other lodging places	273	60	130	118	-	581	463	77	144	128	-	812
7 Transport, storage and communication	3152	1830	1170	872	163	6861	4636	1917	829	1082	200	8264
A Transport and storage	2513	1343	1037	577	163	5307	3705	1557	772	753	200	6587
B Communication	640	487	132	295	-	1554	931	360	57	329	-	1677
8 Finance, insurance, real estate and business services	2586	2659	5633	1258	64	12072	4004	3651	8147	1628	48	17382
A Financial institutions	1270	168	1853	212	64	3439	1946	247	2730	284	48	5159
B Insurance	189	34	27	436	-	686	295	67	138	490	-	990
C Real estate and business services	1127	2457	3753	610	-	7947	1764	3336	5279	854	-	11233
9 Community, social and personal services	2091	282	841	690	135	3769	3296	438	1350	1000	187	5897
A Sanitary and similar services	...	...	...	...	...	...	...	...	...	...	...	...
B Social and related community services	105	27	365	18	-	515	177	32	732	30	-	971
C Recreational and cultural services	503	118	345	144	135	975	811	199	406	167	187	1396
D Personal and household services [a]	1483	137	131	528	-	2279	2308	207	212	803	-	3530
Total, Industries	30144	13760	15292	13618	2254	70560	44511	17039	18824	18522	3334	95562
Producers of Government Services	7793	542	17	248	-	8600	11166	736	27	356	-	12285
Other Producers	493	48	-9	18	-	550	732	74	-9	27	-	824
Total	38430	14351	15300	13884	2254	79711	56409	17849	18842	18905	3334	108671
Less: Imputed bank service charge	...	...	3330	...	...	3330	...	...	4822	...	...	4822
Import duties [b]	...	...	...	6178	136	6042	...	...	...	7436	156	7280
Value added tax	...	...	...	...	...	...	...	...	...	...	...	...
Other adjustments [c]	...	...	...	...	...	5084	...	...	...	...	...	7962
Total [d]	38430	14351	11970	20062	2390	87508	56409	17849	14020	26341	3490	119091

Iceland

Million Icelandic kronur

4.3 Cost Components of Value Added

All Producers

	1986						1987					
	Compensation of Employees	Capital Consumption	Net Operating Surplus	Indirect Taxes	Less: Subsidies Received	Value Added	Compensation of Employees	Capital Consumption	Net Operating Surplus	Indirect Taxes	Less: Subsidies Received	Value Added
1 Agriculture, hunting, forestry and fishing	8468	3451	3918	306	120	16023	11850	4834	4447	300	192	21239
A Agriculture and hunting	590	1046	3180	235	120	4931	613	1219	4345	203	192	6188
B Forestry and logging	...	...	...	...	...	...	...	...	...	...	...	...
C Fishing	7878	2405	738	71	-	11092	11236	3614	102	97	-	15049
2 Mining and quarrying	...	...	...	...	...	...	...	...	...	...	...	...
3 Manufacturing	16941	4235	2901	2910	2435	24552	25574	4600	3981	2332	...	34384
A Manufacture of food, beverages and tobacco	8139	1960	2485	796	2145	11235	11508	2380	2075	1115	2036	15042
B Textile, wearing apparel and leather industries	1307	206	118	156	118	1669	2037	241	-206	255	159	2168
C Manufacture of wood and wood products, including furniture	835	118	36	485	-	1474	1563	239	-7	718	-	2513
D Manufacture of paper and paper products, printing and publishing	1488	316	314	261	-	2379	2214	296	353	368	-	3231
E Manufacture of chemicals and chemical products, petroleum, coal, rubber and plastic products	815	283	245	268	171	1440	1249	328	72	312	138	1823
F Manufacture of non-metallic mineral products, except products of petroleum and coal	666	273	107	335	-	1381	915	273	224	447	-	1859
G Basic metal industries	893	839	-757	82	-	1057	1137	554	-170	83	-	1604
H Manufacture of fabricated metal products, machinery and equipment	2430	205	275	469	-	3379	4326	248	131	596	-	5303
I Other manufacturing industries	367	35	77	60	-	539	623	40	69	88	-	840
4 Electricity, gas and water	914	2889	2304	879	582	6404	1360	3698	1400	831	406	6873
A Electricity, gas and steam	898	2794	2182	870	581	6163	1327	3562	1264	830	404	6579
B Water works and supply	16	95	122	8	1	240	33	126	136	1	2	294
5 Construction	6246	1047	2934	1021	-	11248	8814	874	4800	1252	-	15740
6 Wholesale and retail trade, restaurants and hotels	10045	1863	2017	12673	-	26598	16930	2455	1121	19222	2	39426
A Wholesale and retail trade	8439	1591	1923	11779	-	23732	13511	1456	1425	17414	2	33804
B Restaurants and hotels	1606	272	93	894	-	2865	3119	999	-305	1809	-	5622
Restaurants	1054	193	-116	747	-	1878	2243	408	-367	1482	-	3766
Hotels and other lodging places	551	79	209	147	-	986	877	590	62	326	-	1855
7 Transport, storage and communication	5372	2542	1629	1143	273	10413	8029	2623	1999	1384	353	13682
A Transport and storage	4109	2067	1621	779	273	8303	6230	2099	1984	981	353	10941
B Communication	1263	475	8	365	-	2111	1799	524	15	404	-	2742
8 Finance, insurance, real estate and business services	5756	4750	6865	2093	41	19543	8138	5835	12101	2930	374	28630
A Financial institutions	2937	444	608	334	41	4282	4134	549	3684	498	374	8491
B Insurance	406	79	76	-72	-	677	1087	82	-121	87	-	1428
C Real estate and business services	2413	4230	6449	1082	-	14174	3434	5204	8538	1534	-	18710
9 Community, social and personal services	4338	476	1844	1457	283	7832	6652	760	2639	2102	416	11737
A Sanitary and similar services	...	...	...	...	...	...	...	...	...	...	...	...
B Social and related community services	209	24	899	39	-	1171	278	49	1562	78	-	1967
C Recreational and cultural services	1140	229	425	250	283	1761	1730	277	609	503	415	2704
D Personal and household services [a]	2989	223	520	1168	-	4900	4644	434	469	1521	1	7067
Total, Industries	58079	21252	24532	22482	3734	122611	87047	25670	31067	32005	4076	171713
Producers of Government Services	15534	950	27	494	-	17005	22566	1154	40	718	-	24478
Other Producers	970	102	-15	36	-	1093	1362	143	-21	50	-	1534
Total	74583	22304	24543	23013	3734	140709	110975	26966	31086	32774	4076	197725
Less: Imputed bank service charge			4493			4493			8078			8078
Import duties [b]				10951	494	10457				13541	706	12835
Value added tax				...	...	...				...	...	...
Other adjustments [c]				11924						...		5618
Total [d]	74583	22304	20050	33964	4228	158897	110975	26966	23008	46315	4782	208099

Iceland

4.3 Cost Components of Value Added

Million Icelandic krónur

1988 — All Producers

	Compensation of Employees	Capital Consumption	Net Operating Surplus	Indirect Taxes	Less: Subsidies Received	Value Added
1 Agriculture, hunting, forestry and fishing	14331	5275	5597	359	175	25387
A Agriculture and hunting	765	1478	3968	241	175	6277
B Forestry and logging	...	...	...	...	...	...
C Fishing	13566	3797	1629	118	-	19110
2 Mining and quarrying	-	-	-	-	-	-
3 Manufacturing	29495	5167	2874	5377	4753	38160
A Manufacture of food, beverages and tobacco	13324	2692	693	1636	4360	13985
B Textile, wearing apparel and leather industries	2008	261	-82	305	163	2329
C Manufacture of wood and wood products, including furniture	1659	235	252	820	2	2964
D Manufacture of paper and paper products, printing and publishing	2587	335	561	554	33	4004
E Manufacture of chemicals and chemical petroleum, coal, rubber and plastic products	1628	454	137	407	49	2577
F Manufacture of non-metallic mineral products, except products of petroleum and coal	1198	333	140	530	7	2194
G Basic metal industries	1528	523	394	337	-	2782
H Manufacture of fabricated metal products, machinery and equipment	4820	290	541	691	126	6216
I Other manufacturing industries	742	45	237	97	13	1108
4 Electricity, gas and water	1806	4150	3186	1086	246	9982
A Electricity, gas and steam	1718	4012	2964	1083	238	9539
B Water works and supply	88	138	221	3	8	442
5 Construction	10514	979	5332	1647	-	18472
6 Wholesale and retail trade, restaurants and hotels	20137	3026	785	26739	46	50641
A Wholesale and retail trade	16497	1768	1129	23982	46	43330
B Restaurants and hotels	3641	1258	-344	2757	-	7312
Restaurants	2606	585	-475	2313	-	5029
Hotels and other lodging places	1035	673	131	444	-	2283
7 Transport, storage and communication	9713	3002	2829	2141	430	17255
A Transport and storage	7537	2389	2266	1505	430	13267
B Communication	2177	612	563	635	-	3987
8 Finance, insurance, real estate and business services	10927	7148	16660	4579	1596	37718
A Financial institutions	5339	794	6969	672	1596	12178
B Insurance	780	103	-573	1376	-	1686
C Real estate and business services	4807	6250	10265	2531	-	23853
9 Community, social and personal services	8541	960	4634	2536	578	16093
A Sanitary and similar services	...	...	...	...	...	...
B Social and related community services	463	62	2145	115	-	2785
C Recreational and cultural services	2181	324	1158	590	578	3675
D Personal and household services a	5897	573	1331	1831	-	9632
Total, Industries	105464	29706	41897	44464	7824	213707
Producers of Government Services	29567	1361	61	941	-	31930

827

Iceland

4.3 Cost Components of Value Added
(Continued)

Million Icelandic krónur

	1988						
	Compensation of Employees	Capital Consumption	Net Operating Surplus	Indirect Taxes	Less: Subsidies Received		Value Added
Other Producers	1927	203	-33	72	-		2169
Total	136958	31270	41925	45477	7824		247806
Less: Imputed bank service charge	...	...	11557	...	...		11557
Import duties b	...	...	13397	-16			13413
Value added tax	...	...	...	...	...		...
Other adjustments c	...	...	...	...	...		4976
Total d	136958	31270	30368	58874	7808		254639

a) Item 'Personal and household services' includes also ISIC-code 96, residents directly employed at the NATO-base.
b) Item 'Import duties' includes all indirect taxes and subsidies not directly allocated to specified activities.
c) Item 'Other adjustments' includes residual error between production and expenditure approaches.
d) The figures for column 'Capital consumption' are mainly derived from business accounting records and are not consistent with national accounting practices as presented in table 1.3.

India

General note. The preparation of national accounts statistics in India is undertaken by the National Accounts Division of the Central Statistical Organization (CSO), Department of Statistics, Ministry of Planning, New Delhi. Official estimates are published annually in the 'National Accounts Statistics'. The sources of data and methodology followed are given in 'National Accounts Statistics - Sources and Methods', 1989. The estimates are generally in accordance with the classifications and definitions recommended in the United Nations System of National Accounts (SNA). The estimates relate to fiscal year beginning 1 April. When the scope and coverage of the estimates differ for conceptual and statistical reasons from the definitions and classifications recommended in SNA, a footnote is indicated to the relevant tables.

Sources and methods :

(a) Gross domestic product. Gross domestic product is estimated mainly through the production approach for the commodity producing sectors and income approach for the services sectors.

(b) Expenditure on the gross domestic product. The expenditure approach is used to estimate government final consumption expenditure, increase in stocks and exports of goods and services. The commodity-flow approach is used to estimate private final consumption expenditure whereas the estimate of gross fixed capital formationis based on expenditure approaches. Estimates of government consumption expenditure are mainly obtained from budget documents and annual reports of the government bodies. Estimates of private expenditure on goods are obtained from commodity production data adjusted for stock changes and foreign trade and reduced by intermediate and government consumption and by quantities used for capital formation. Private expenditure on services is estimated as the value of the total output for each kind of service reduced by the estimated service expenditures by government and business. Estimates of increase in stocks for the public sector and organized (i.e. larger or modern) private industries are based on government budget documents and annual accounts and reports of industries respectively. Changes in stocks of unorganized private industries are based on sample survey data, data on bank advances and margins and on livestock censuses. For gross fixed capital formation, estimates of construction are compiled using data from a number of sources such as annual survey of industries, dispatches of cement for domestic consumption, sample surveys and government budget documents and the All-India debt and investment surveys. These estimates are extrapolated by the relevant indicators. For machinery and equipment, estimates are based on the annual survey of industries, foreign trade statistics, customs and excise revenue statements, data on trade, transport and other charges collected from leading manufacturing firms. The estimates of exports and imports of goods and services are based on balance of payment statistics supplemented by information supplied by government agencies. For the constant price estimates, private expenditure on goods is extrapolated by quantity indexes. Changes in stocks of livestock, mining and foodgrains are valued at 1980-81 prices. For government expenditure, private expenditure on services, increase in stock for other sectors and gross fixed capital formation, the current values are deflated by relevant price indexes. Import and export of goods and services are not estimated at constant prices.

(c) Cost-structure of the gross domestic product. Estimates of compensation of employees are based on budget documents, annual reports of enterprises, income and expenditure accounts of institutions and companies and sample surveys. Estimates of operating surplus are based on most of the sources used for compensation of employees. Consumption of fixed capital is estimated for each industry seperately. The sources include the All-India rural debt and investment surveys, livestock censuses, budget documents and annual accounts. Estimates of indirect taxes and subsidies are based on accounts and annual reports of government bodies.

(d) Gross domestic product by kind of economic activity. The table of GDP by kind of economic activity is prepared in factor values. The production approach is used to estimate value added for all commodity producing sectors and bench-mark estimates for small-scale manufacturing. Value added of construction is based on a combination of the commodity-flow and expenditure approaches. The income approach is used for all other sectors. The production estimates of principal agricultural crops are based on results of the random sample crop-cutting sueveys conducted by the respective state government agencies. The wholesale prices in the primary markets are used to evaluate the total production of each commodity. The annual estimates of livestock products are based on the livestock population by type and the corresponding average yield rates. Intermediate consumption is estimated by using a variety of sources such as the National SampleSurvey (NSS), the All-India rural debt and investment survey, and marketing reports. Estimates of the gross output of minerals are based on data available from the Indian Bureau of Mines. For large-scale manufacturing, estimates are prepared for 19 industry groups based on the Annual Surveys of Industries (ASI). Bench-mark estimates for the household and non-household small-scale manufacturing and other unorganised portions of trade, transport etc. have been prepared using data on value added per worker derived from the follow-up surveys of economic census of CSO and NSSO and estimated working force. Other years' estimates are extrapolated by means of indicators of physical output or input and prices. Estimates of pucca construction are compiled by the commodity flow approach using data on steel and cement production, foreign trade statistics, customs and excise revenue, etc. The estimates of kutcha construction are based on expenditure data from NSS, debt and investment surveys and other sources. For public sector trade, transport, administration, banks etc., estimates are based on the analysis of budget documents and annual accounts. The estimates of gross rents for urban and rural dwellings are based on the number of dwellings and estimated gross rental value per dwelling obtained from the NSSO surveys on consumer expenditure. For the constant price estimates, double deflation is used for the agriculture and mining sectors. Current values of large-scale manufacturing and construction are deflated by price indexes. For small-scale manufacturing, electricity, gas and water, trade, transport, ownership of dwellings and other services, value added is extrapolated by quantity indexes. Current price estimates of public administration are deflated with the consumer price index of industrial workers to obtain the constant price estimates.

1.1 Expenditure on the Gross Domestic Product, in Current Prices

Thousand Million Indian rupees — Fiscal year beginning 1 April

		1970	1975	1980	1981	1982	1983	1984	1985	1986	1987	1988	1989
1	Government final consumption expenditure	38.38	73.81	130.84	153.55	182.72	211.41	243.52	291.74	346.25	408.43	472.03	530.67
2	Private final consumption expenditure	325.45	578.22	981.28	1127.10	1241.12	1459.65	1614.55	1757.77	1963.41	2221.19	2600.29	2896.40
3	Gross capital formation	73.79	164.06	284.53	400.13	407.84	430.61	487.88	629.46	672.30	753.86	943.67	1043.96
	A Increase in stocks	10.74	30.76	21.77	85.58	50.15	30.70	32.20	86.91	59.70	45.48	111.62	95.59
	B Gross fixed capital formation [a]	63.05	133.30	262.76	314.55	357.69	399.91	455.68	542.55	612.60	708.38	832.05	948.37
	Residential buildings	8.26	21.71	31.32	38.95	46.78	48.55	59.77	68.76	80.80	90.27	99.93	...
	Non-residential buildings	15.50	23.15	29.32	38.37	39.64	42.92	49.37	55.94	58.65	64.98	80.28	...
	Other construction and land improvement etc.	15.83	28.54	75.85	86.68	96.85	105.02	118.05	145.06	157.25	172.66	204.99	...
	Other	23.46	59.90	126.27	150.55	174.42	203.42	227.03	265.92	323.52	346.60	416.78	...
4	Exports of goods and services	17.71	48.12	90.29	102.56	115.63	131.39	158.46	149.51	165.43	202.81	259.83	...
5	Less: Imports of goods and services	18.16	56.64	135.96	148.09	157.36	176.75	194.84	217.54	223.59	252.59	319.69	...
	Statistical discrepancy	-5.19	-17.51	9.15	-37.65	-8.63	19.58	4.30	8.26	-4.06	-7.54	-6.21	
	Equals: Gross Domestic Product [b]	431.63	787.61	1360.13	1597.60	1781.32	2075.89	2313.87	2619.20	2919.74	3326.16	3949.92	4427.69

a) Data for gross fixed capital formation are unadjusted for statistical discrepancy and therefore do not coincide with the data shown in the table 'Gross Capital Formation by Kind of Economic Activity of Owners'. b) Data in this table have been revised, therefore they are not strictly comparable with the unrevised data in the other tables.

1.2 Expenditure on the Gross Domestic Product, in Constant Prices

Thousand Million Indian rupees — Fiscal year beginning 1 April

		1970	1975	1980	1981	1982	1983	1984	1985	1986	1987	1988	1989
						At constant prices of:1980							
1	Government final consumption expenditure	84.92	97.99	130.84	136.63	150.75	157.50	169.83	189.24	208.49	226.74	239.28	...
2	Private final consumption expenditure [a]	715.22	800.63	992.92	1038.48	1070.71	1150.51	1194.64	1233.53	1290.58	1353.20	1463.06	1519.74
3	Gross capital formation	194.61	243.84	284.53	358.88	339.82	322.40	332.49	394.51	384.58	405.30	470.89	476.66
	A Increase in stocks	27.88	47.91	21.77	78.09	46.86	26.08	24.65	64.77	42.05	30.38	66.66	53.80
	B Gross fixed capital formation [b]	166.73	195.93	262.76	280.79	292.96	296.32	307.84	329.74	342.53	374.92	404.23	422.86

829

India

1.2 Expenditure on the Gross Domestic Product, in Constant Prices
(Continued)

Thousand Million Indian rupees   Fiscal year beginning 1 April

	1970	1975	1980	1981	1982	1983	1984	1985	1986	1987	1988	1989
					At constant prices of:1980							
Residential buildings	18.25	23.15	31.32	32.18	32.89	30.04	32.93	34.35	35.83	36.62	37.74	...
Non-residential buildings	40.36	34.76	29.32	32.41	27.73	23.91	23.68	25.88	22.61	25.35	28.44	...
Other construction and land improvement etc.	47.62	54.76	75.85	74.10	69.46	71.69	70.57	76.90	76.83	75.03	82.35	...
Other	60.50	83.26	126.27	142.10	162.88	170.68	179.58	188.68	212.44	220.15	237.37	...
4 Exports of goods and services	...	...	...	...	...	...	...	...	...	...	...	...
5 Less: Imports of goods and services	...	...	...	...	...	...	...	...	...	...	...	...
Equals: Gross Domestic Product c ..	1013.62	1166.75	1360.13	1449.00	1503.79	1615.47	1675.25	1766.82	1846.90	1938.04	2126.40	...

a) Item 'Private consumption expenditure' refers to expenditure in the domestic market only.   Activity of Owners'.
b) Data for gross fixed capital formation are unadjusted for statistical discrepancy and therefore   c) Data in this table have been revised, therefore they are not strictly comparable with the
do not coincide with the data shown in the table 'Gross Capital Formation by Kind of Economic   unrevised data in the other tables.

1.3 Cost Components of the Gross Domestic Product

Thousand Million Indian rupees   Fiscal year beginning 1 April

	1970	1975	1980	1981	1982	1983	1984	1985	1986	1987	1988	1989
1 Indirect taxes, net	34.55	75.60	135.86	165.44	187.37	208.66	228.10	284.44	329.19	383.50	432.68	...
A Indirect taxes	38.64	88.34	167.46	200.89	229.85	264.71	306.40	369.87	427.14	498.47	574.03	...
B Less: Subsidies	4.09	12.74	31.60	35.45	42.48	56.05	78.30	85.43	97.95	114.97	141.35	...
2 Consumption of fixed capital	30.62	64.15	120.87	144.59	168.86	192.29	220.91	262.39	298.23	336.86	390.90	...
3 Compensation of employees paid by resident producers to: a	...	...	...	...	...	...	...	...	...	...	...	...
A Resident households	...	...	...	...	...	...	...	...	...	...	...	...
B Rest of the world	...	...	0.35	0.27	0.72	0.72	1.13	1.12	1.78	3.80	3.90	...
4 Operating surplus	...	...	...	...	...	...	...	...	...	...	...	...
Equals: Gross Domestic Product b ..	431.63	787.61	1360.13	1597.60	1781.32	2075.89	2313.87	2619.20	2919.74	3326.16	3949.92	4427.69

a) Item 'Compensation of employees ' includes part of net operating surplus of unincorporated   b) Data in this table have been revised, therefore they are not strictly comparable with the
enterprises which cannot be separated from labour income of own-account.   unrevised data in the other tables.

1.4 General Government Current Receipts and Disbursements

Thousand Million Indian rupees   Fiscal year beginning 1 April

	1970	1975	1980	1981	1982	1983	1984	1985	1986	1987	1988	1989
					Receipts							
1 Operating surplus	1.58	1.77	3.18 -8.48	-10.49	-12.17	-14.93	-15.45	-12.35	-13.13	-13.92	-17.55	...
2 Property and entrepreneurial income	4.16	8.20	18.17 17.70	20.87	28.51	27.78	38.69	42.12	56.87	58.09	60.91	...
3 Taxes, fees and contributions	51.17	116.74	206.21 206.24	249.39	282.99	323.32	373.46	448.28	512.25	590.53	672.96	...
A Indirect taxes	38.64	88.34	167.44 167.46	200.89	229.85	264.71	306.40	369.87	427.14	499.62	565.25	...
B Direct taxes	10.91	26.43	35.74 35.75	44.61	48.35	53.55	58.06	65.74	73.28	78.67	93.86	...
C Social security contributions	...	...	...	...	...	...	...	...	...	...	...	...
D Compulsory fees, fines and penalties	1.62	1.97	3.03 3.03	3.89	4.79	5.06	9.00	12.67	11.83	12.24	13.85	...
4 Other current transfers	...	...	...	...	...	...	...	...	...	...	...	...
Total Current Receipts of General Government	56.91	126.71	227.56 215.46	259.77	299.33	336.17	396.70	478.05	555.99	634.70	716.32	...
					Disbursements							
1 Government final consumption expenditure	38.01	73.51	130.33 130.84	153.55	182.72	211.41	243.52	291.74	346.25	410.34	463.61	...
A Compensation of employees	23.69	46.81	81.56 80.37	92.34	110.46	129.02	149.26	172.03	200.55	242.58	273.37	...
B Consumption of fixed capital	...	...	7.64	9.25	11.32	13.23	15.78	19.40	22.64	26.27	30.74	...
C Purchases of goods and services, net	14.32	26.70	48.77 42.83	51.96	60.94	69.16	78.48	100.31	123.06	141.49	159.50	...
D Less: Own account fixed capital formation	...	...	...	...	...	...	...	...	...	...	...	...
E Indirect taxes paid, net	...	...	...	...	...	...	...	...	...	...	...	...
2 Property income	2.16	4.91	14.90 15.24	19.11	27.13	37.39	50.08	61.15	75.92	95.55	121.99	...

India

1.4 General Government Current Receipts and Disbursements (Continued)

Thousand Million Indian rupees	1970	1975	1980	1981	1982	1983	1984	1985	1986	1987	1988	1989
A Interest a	2.16	4.91	14.90 / 15.24	19.11	27.13	37.39	50.08	61.15	75.92	95.55	121.99	...
B Net land rent and royalties	-	-	-	-	-	-	-	-	-	-	-	...
3 Subsidies	3.37	11.20	28.39 / 31.60	35.45	42.48	56.05	78.30	85.43	97.95	118.17	142.63	...
4 Other current transfers	6.03	13.60	28.57 / 28.57	33.88	40.25	46.62	57.75	70.35	87.20	100.66	118.69	...
Statistical discrepancy b	0.78	-	-0.26 / 0.28	-0.15	1.28	0.85	1.43	5.87	8.44	7.90	4.71	...
5 Net saving	7.34	22.71	25.09 / 9.47	17.93	5.47	-16.15	-34.38	-36.49	-59.27	-97.92	-135.31	...
Total Current Disbursements and Net Saving of General Government	56.91	126.71	227.56 / 215.46	259.77	299.33	336.17	396.70	478.05	555.99	634.70	716.32	...

a) Item 'Interest' refers to interest on the public debt.
b) Item 'Statistical discrepancy' relates to inter-governmental accounting adjustments. For years prior to 1974, it is included in item 'Net saving'.

1.7 External Transactions on Current Account, Summary

Thousand Million Indian rupees	1970	1975	1980	1981	1982	1983	1984	1985	1986	1987	1988	1989
Payments to the Rest of the World												
1 Imports of goods and services	18.16	56.64	135.96	148.09	157.36	176.35	194.84	217.54	223.59	252.59	319.69	...
A Imports of merchandise c.i.f.	17.34	47.73	125.49	136.08	142.93	158.31	171.34	196.58	200.96	222.44	281.94	...
B Other	0.82	8.91	10.47	12.01	14.43	18.44	23.50	20.96	22.65	30.15	37.75	...
2 Factor income to the rest of the world	3.41	5.20	3.73	3.20	7.89	11.59	14.22	20.26	21.21	24.68	32.22	39.72
A Compensation of employees	0.11	0.11	0.35	0.27	0.72	0.72	1.13	1.12	1.78	3.80	3.90	...
B Property and entrepreneurial income	3.30	3.62	4.85	7.62	13.50	19.13	20.09	22.90	28.42	35.82	...	...
3 Current transfers to the rest of the world	0.13	0.13	0.12	0.16	0.14	0.11	0.15	0.14	0.15	0.34	0.24	...
A Indirect taxes to supranational organisations												
B Other current transfers	0.13	0.13	0.12	0.16	0.14	0.11	0.15	0.14	0.15	0.34	0.24	...
Statistical discrepancy a	0.86	-5.21	-0.06	0.06	2.78	6.20	2.08	15.46	15.06	25.73	24.49	60.08
4 Surplus of the nation on current transactions	-4.24	0.77	-20.94	-26.11	-25.66	-32.92	-62.34	-63.55	-68.25	-111.34	...	...
Payments to the Rest of the World and Surplus of the Nation on Current Transactions b	18.32	56.06	120.28	132.81	149.63	167.99	197.79	191.61	210.60	251.39	308.39	...
Receipts From The Rest of the World												
1 Exports of goods and services	17.71	48.12	90.29	102.56	115.63	131.39	158.46	149.51	165.43	202.81	259.83	...
A Exports of merchandise f.o.b.	14.03	41.78	67.11	78.06	88.03	97.71	117.44	108.95	124.52	156.74	203.02	...
B Other	3.68	6.34	23.18	24.50	27.60	33.68	41.02	40.56	40.91	46.07	56.81	...
2 Factor income from rest of the world	0.57	1.18	8.65	8.29	5.25	4.78	6.02	6.92	6.63	6.03	6.46	...
A Compensation of employees	0.08	0.02	0.06	0.09	0.10	0.09	0.12	0.14	0.09	0.17	0.33	...
B Property and entrepreneurial income	0.49	1.16	8.59	8.20	5.15	4.69	5.90	6.78	6.54	5.86	6.13	...
3 Current transfers from rest of the world	1.36	5.41	22.69	22.37	25.41	27.85	31.16	28.35	29.91	35.33	38.65	...
A Subsidies from supranational organisations												
B Other current transfers	1.36	5.41	22.69	22.37	25.41	27.85	31.16	28.35	29.91	35.33	38.65	...
Statistical discrepancy a	-1.32	1.35	-1.35	-0.41	3.34	3.97	2.15	6.83	8.63	7.22	3.45	...
Receipts from the Rest of the World on Current Transactions b	18.32	56.06	120.28	132.81	149.63	167.99	197.79	191.61	210.60	251.39	308.39	...

a) Item 'Statistical discrepancy' refers to difference of payment and ownership basis of imports and exports of merchandise.
b) Data in this table have been revised, therefore they are not strictly comparable with the unrevised data in the other tables.

India

1.8 Capital Transactions of The Nation, Summary

Thousand Million Indian rupees

Fiscal year beginning 1 April

	1970	1975	1980	1981	1982	1983	1984	1985	1986	1987	1988	1989
Finance of Gross Capital Formation												
Gross saving	67.83	149.28	287.86	334.78	340.68	389.71	421.58	516.64	537.38	675.61	832.98	...
1 Consumption of fixed capital	30.62	64.15	120.87	144.59	168.86	192.29	220.91	262.39	298.23	336.86	390.90	...
A General government	6.83	12.77	22.25	26.59	31.82	36.25	42.42	51.30	57.38	64.59	75.28	...
B Corporate and quasi-corporate enterprises	8.94	22.27	43.70	52.00	61.38	72.13	83.62	101.89	119.76	136.91	162.32	...
Public	4.37	11.88	26.70	31.99	37.98	44.31	51.66	62.58	73.57	84.70	99.97	...
Private a	4.57	10.39	17.00	20.01	23.40	27.82	31.96	39.31	46.19	52.21	62.35	...
C Other	14.85	29.11	54.92	66.00	75.66	83.91	94.87	109.18	121.06	135.36	153.30	...
2 Net saving	37.21	85.13	166.99	190.19	171.82	197.42	200.67	254.27	239.15	338.75	442.08	...
A General government	1.74	11.72	5.79	14.42	3.38	-17.46	-38.25	-41.85	-66.26	-97.81	-121.53	...
B Corporate and quasi-corporate enterprises	1.59	-2.82	-2.36	4.49	10.72	8.61	17.38	25.31	19.51	24.74	42.52	...
Public	-0.41	-2.98	-8.20	-0.46	5.04	4.71	9.43	12.54	15.30	21.01	23.71	...
Private a	2.00	0.16	5.84	4.95	5.68	3.90	7.95	12.77	4.21	3.73	18.81	...
C Other	33.88	76.23	163.56	171.28	157.72	206.27	221.54	270.81	285.90	411.82	521.09	...
Less: Surplus of the nation on current transactions	-4.24	0.77	-20.94	-26.11	-25.66	-25.17	-32.92	-62.34	-63.55	-68.25	-111.34	...
Statistical discrepancy	...	...	-24.27	39.24	41.50	15.73	33.38	50.48	71.37	10.00	-0.65	...
Finance of Gross Capital Formation b	71.77	148.11	284.53	400.13	407.84	430.61	487.88	629.46	672.30	753.86	943.67	...
Gross Capital Formation												
Increase in stocks	10.74	30.76	21.77	85.58	50.15	30.70	32.20	86.91	59.70	45.48	111.62	...
Gross fixed capital formation	63.05	133.30	262.76	314.55	357.69	399.91	455.68	542.55	612.60	708.38	832.05	...
1 General government	14.16	28.03	64.57	75.20	87.65	97.57	112.45	131.89	143.30	145.19	190.67	...
2 Corporate and quasi-corporate enterprises	15.98	45.60	87.77	129.06	172.15	174.25	203.42	243.54	311.18	302.65	326.85	...
A Public	9.78	27.97	52.36	70.78	98.21	106.93	121.51	143.12	189.24	200.42	204.75	...
B Private a	6.20	17.63	35.41	58.28	73.94	67.32	81.91	100.42	121.94	102.23	122.10	...
3 Other	32.91	59.67	110.42	110.29	97.89	128.09	139.81	167.11	158.12	260.54	314.53	...
Statistical discrepancy	-2.02	-15.95	...	...	...	...	...	...	...	...	...	...
Gross Capital Formation b	71.77	148.11	284.53	400.13	407.84	430.61	487.88	629.46	672.30	753.86	943.67	...

a) Estimates relate to private corporate sector enterprises only.
b) Data in this table have been revised, therefore they are not strictly comparable with the unrevised data in the other tables.

1.9 Gross Domestic Product by Institutional Sectors of Origin

Thousand Million Indian rupees

Fiscal year beginning 1 April

	1970	1975	1980	1981	1982	1983	1984	1985	1986	1987	1988	1989
Domestic Factor Incomes Originating												
1 General government	37.31	70.87	121.79 107.24	124.30	150.84	175.49	201.58	241.87	280.85	341.75	...	...
2 Corporate and quasi-corporate enterprises	57.52	119.97	229.43	...	...	...	...	...	...	...	...	...
A Non-financial	51.26	102.90	196.85	...	...	...	...	...	...	...	...	...
Public	8.63	29.80	65.42 57.19	78.54	99.92	118.31	138.97	160.21	199.59	218.81	...	...
Private	42.63	73.10	131.43	...	...	...	...	...	...	...	...	...
B Financial	6.26	17.07	32.58	...	...	...	...	...	...	...	...	...
Public	4.13	13.07	28.37 28.33	37.15	41.84	48.05	56.84	67.30	77.53	88.07	...	...

832

India

1.9 Gross Domestic Product by Institutional Sectors of Origin
(Continued)

Thousand Million Indian rupees	1970	1975	1980	1981	1982	1983	1984	1985	1986	1987	1988	1989
Private	2.13	4.00	4.21	...	...	...	...	...	...	...	...	...
3 Households and private unincorporated enterprises a	250.36	434.73	703.23	...	...	...	...	...	...	...	...	...
4 Non-profit institutions serving households a	...	...	...	...	...	...	...	...	...	...	...	...
Subtotal: Domestic Factor Incomes	345.19	625.57	1054.45 / 1101.39	1284.17	1419.65	1667.62	1857.78	2079.20	2305.13	2605.32	3094.41	
Indirect taxes, net	35.27	77.14	135.86 / 139.06	165.44	187.37	208.66	228.10	284.44	329.19	381.45	422.62	
A Indirect taxes	38.64	88.34	167.44 / 167.46	200.89	229.85	264.71	306.40	369.87	427.14	499.62	565.25	
B Less: Subsidies	3.37	11.20	28.39 / 31.60	35.45	42.48	56.05	78.30	85.43	97.95	118.17	142.63	
Consumption of fixed capital	22.17	40.73	81.03 / 120.87	144.59	168.86	192.91	220.91	262.39	293.29	338.76	394.55	
Gross Domestic Product	402.63	743.44	1274.53 / 1338.12	1594.20	1775.88	2068.57	2306.79	2626.03	2933.61	3325.53	3911.58	

a) Item "Non-profit institutions serving households" is included in item 'Households and private unincorporated enterprises'.

1.10 Gross Domestic Product by Kind of Activity, in Current Prices

Thousand Million Indian rupees	1970	1975	1980	1981	1982	1983	1984	1985	1986	1987	1988	1989
1 Agriculture, hunting, forestry and fishing	179.37	288.39	466.49	526.85	561.51	674.98	719.94	772.80	825.15	924.58	1147.58	1232.57
2 Mining and quarrying	3.78	8.84	18.87	35.40	43.95	49.09	54.58	58.19	67.96	70.80	80.68	86.55
3 Manufacturing	59.46	118.57	216.44	252.60	280.73	330.45	372.43	417.75	461.66	528.51	624.55	740.58
4 Electricity, gas and water	4.27	8.56	20.70	24.06	28.45	33.62	40.52	48.94	55.67	62.18	74.90	86.61
5 Construction	19.52	33.01	61.14	69.89	80.79	94.21	110.97	129.47	149.52	173.95	199.06	220.18
6 Wholesale and retail trade, restaurants and hotels	35.07	79.82	147.13	180.34	199.71	229.90	266.90	310.50	345.51	384.71	449.79	506.20
7 Transport, storage and communication	17.33	32.41	57.24	70.40	85.98	102.81	118.73	140.98	165.59	197.64	239.78	277.89
8 Finance, insurance, real estate and business services	39.81	67.88	107.91	125.35	141.55	155.91	175.95	198.82	223.60	251.24	295.78	341.12
9 Community, social and personal services	21.12	39.62	70.41	80.66	91.67	103.88	117.39	132.20	147.07	169.57	197.29	222.33
Total, Industries	379.73	677.73	1166.33	1365.55	1514.34	1774.85	1977.41	2209.65	2441.22	2763.18	3309.41	3714.03
Producers of Government Services	17.35	34.86	57.94	66.61	79.67	92.38	108.36	125.11	149.33	179.48	207.83	237.40
Subtotal a	397.08	712.01	1224.27	1432.16	1593.95	1867.23	2085.77	2334.76	2590.55	2942.66	3517.24	3951.43
Other Producers	...	...	...	...	...	...	...	...	...	...	...	...
Less: Imputed bank service charge b	...	...	...	...	...	...	...	...	...	...	...	...
Plus: Import duties	...	...	...	...	...	...	...	...	...	...	...	...
Plus: Value added tax	...	...	...	...	...	...	...	...	...	...	...	...
Plus: Other adjustments c	34.55	75.60	135.86	165.44	187.37	208.66	228.10	284.44	329.19	383.50	432.68	476.26
Equals: Gross Domestic Product d	431.63	787.61	1360.13	1597.60	1781.32	2075.89	2313.89	2619.20	2919.74	3326.16	3949.92	4427.69

a) Gross domestic product in factor values.
b) Imputed bank service charges are adjusted in the respective activity.
c) Item 'Other adjustments' refers to indirect taxes net of subsidies.
d) Data in this table have been revised, therefore they are not strictly comparable with the unrevised data in the other tables.

1.11 Gross Domestic Product by Kind of Activity, in Constant Prices

Thousand Million Indian rupees	1970	1975	1980	1981	1982	1983	1984	1985	1986	1987	1988	1989
			At constant prices of 1980									
1 Agriculture, hunting, forestry and fishing	402.14	446.66	466.49	494.06	488.03	540.80	540.97	542.52	533.35	535.49	617.89	
2 Mining and quarrying	11.71	15.17	18.87	21.41	23.87	24.51	24.86	26.23	29.78	30.78	33.39	
3 Manufacturing	145.98	171.95	216.44	233.82	249.08	273.77	291.53	303.20	324.45	348.01	377.10	
4 Electricity, gas and water	10.73	14.87	19.89	21.72	23.13	25.88	28.63	30.99	34.19	37.39	40.64	
5 Construction	45.38	48.25	61.14	64.25	61.48	65.76	68.28	71.83	74.07	76.81	80.68	
6 Wholesale and retail trade, restaurants and hotels	79.29	118.66	147.13	156.71	165.46	174.17	181.73	196.49	208.52	218.70	239.20	
7 Transport, storage and communication	31.55	43.55	57.24	60.13	62.80	66.92	73.02	79.51	84.93	92.32	96.94	
8 Finance, insurance, real estate and business services	72.56	86.51	108.41	113.54	122.15	128.59	137.14	147.08	157.08	167.06	179.25	
9 Community, social and personal services	52.61	60.82	70.41	73.56	77.66	80.50	84.57	90.85	96.43	102.33	106.87	
Total, Industries	869.95	1006.13	1166.02	1239.41	1273.66	1380.90	1430.73	1488.70	1543.63	1608.69	1773.96	
Producers of Government Services	34.31	43.55	57.94	59.26	65.26	67.48	74.46	77.75	80.16	88.07	96.93	103.56

India

1.11 Gross Domestic Product by Kind of Activity, in Constant Prices
(Continued)

Thousand Million Indian rupees — Fiscal year beginning 1 April

	1970	1975	1980	1981	1982	1983	1984	1985	1986	1987	1988	1989
Other Producers								At constant prices of 1980				
Subtotal [a]		904.26	1049.68	1223.96	1298.67	1339.67	1448.65	1505.19	1568.86	1631.70	1705.82	1877.52
Less: Imputed bank service charge [b]												
Plus: Import duties												
Plus: Value added tax												
Plus: Other adjustments [c]	109.36	117.07	136.17	150.33	164.65	166.82	170.06	197.96	215.20	232.22	248.48
Equals: Gross Domestic Product [d]	1013.62	1166.75	1360.13	1449.00	1503.79	1615.47	1675.25	1766.82	1846.90	1938.04	2126.40	2233.10

b) Imputed bank service charges are adjusted in the respective activity.
c) Item 'Other adjustments' refers to indirect taxes net of subsidies.
d) Data in this table have been revised, therefore they are not strictly comparable with the unrevised data in the other tables.

1.12 Relations Among National Accounting Aggregates

Thousand Million Indian rupees — Fiscal year beginning 1 April

	1970	1975	1980	1981	1982	1983	1984	1985	1986	1987	1988	1989
Gross Domestic Product	431.63	787.63	1360.13	1597.60	1781.32	2075.89	2313.87	2619.20	2919.74	3326.16	3949.92
Plus: Net factor income from the rest of the world	-2.84	-2.55	3.45	0.40	-6.34	-9.44	-14.24	-14.29	-18.05	-26.19	-33.26
Factor income from the rest of the world	0.57	1.18	8.65	8.29	5.25	4.78	6.02	6.92	6.63	6.03	6.46
Less: Factor income to the rest of the world	3.41	3.73	5.20	7.89	11.59	14.22	20.26	21.21	24.68	32.22	39.72
Equals: Gross National Product	428.79	785.06	1363.58	1598.00	1774.98	2066.45	2299.63	2604.91	2901.69	3299.97	3916.66
Less: Consumption of fixed capital	30.62	64.15	120.87	144.59	168.86	192.29	220.91	262.39	298.23	336.86	390.90
Equals: National Income	398.17	720.91	1242.71	1453.41	1606.12	1874.16	2078.72	2342.52	2603.46	2963.11	3525.76
Current transfers from the rest of the world	1.23	5.28	22.57	22.21	25.27	27.74	31.01	28.21	29.76	34.99	38.41
Current transfers to the rest of the world	1.36	5.41	22.69	22.37	25.41	27.85	31.16	28.35	29.91	35.33	38.65
Equals: National Disposable Income	399.17	726.19	1265.28	1475.62	1631.39	1901.90	2109.73	2370.73	2633.73	2998.10	3564.17
Less: Final consumption	363.48	649.58	1112.12	1280.65	1423.84	1671.06	1858.07	2049.51	2309.66	2629.62	3072.32
Statistical discrepancy	1.29	8.52	13.83	-4.78	-35.73	-33.42	-50.99	-66.97	-84.41	-29.23	-49.77
Equals: Net Saving	37.21	85.13	166.99	190.19	171.82	197.42	200.67	254.27	239.15	338.75	442.08
Less: Surplus of the nation on current transactions	-4.24	0.77	-20.94	-26.11	-25.66	-25.17	-32.92	-62.34	-63.55	-68.25	-111.34
Equals: Net Capital Formation [a]	41.15	83.96	187.93	216.30	197.48	222.59	233.59	316.61	302.70	407.00	553.42

a) Data in this table have been revised, therefore they are not strictly comparable with the unrevised data in the other tables.

2.1 Government Final Consumption Expenditure by Function, in Current Prices

Thousand Million Indian rupees — Fiscal year beginning 1 April

	1970	1975	1980	1981	1982	1983	1984	1985	1986	1987	1988	1989
1 General public services [a]	7.74	14.70	26.01	29.60	34.67	38.71	46.74	53.67	61.40	72.61
2 Defence	12.31	25.76	40.44	48.67	56.59	65.35	66.09	86.55	112.55	133.35
3 Public order and safety [a]	...	...	...	...	...	...	...	...	...	...
4 Education	3.14	6.54	14.35	17.30	21.17	25.13	28.47	35.54	39.75	48.99
5 Health	1.66	3.90	7.54	9.02	10.90	13.25	15.68	17.44	19.76	24.21
6 Social security and welfare	0.85	1.47	3.34	3.67	5.29	6.77	6.19	6.58	8.35	9.89
7 Housing and community amenities	0.48	1.13	2.17	2.68	3.39	3.23	4.28	5.32	6.21	7.39
8 Recreational, cultural and religious affairs	0.32	0.55	1.08	1.17	1.44	1.77	1.54	1.99	2.47	3.52
9 Economic services	4.33	7.91	16.76	20.34	23.16	26.17	29.18	32.99	39.10	46.37	...	...

India

2.1 Government Final Consumption Expenditure by Function, in Current Prices
(Continued)

Thousand Million Indian rupees — Fiscal year beginning 1 April

	1970	1975	1980	1981	1982	1983	1984	1985	1986	1987	1988	1989
A Fuel and energy	0.22	0.72	1.49	2.01	2.44	2.89	3.75	4.13	4.83	6.07	...	...
B Agriculture, forestry, fishing and hunting	1.57	2.91	6.70	7.61	9.21	6.98	11.37	11.66	14.22	17.08	...	...
C Mining, manufacturing and construction, except fuel	0.41	0.68	1.45	1.85	2.15	2.65	2.98	3.50	3.73	4.45	...	...
D Transportation and communication	1.35	2.01	4.54	5.49	5.80	6.43	6.61	8.05	8.88	10.17	...	...
E Other economic affairs	0.78	1.59	2.58	3.38	3.56	4.22	4.47	5.65	7.44	8.60	...	...
10 Other functions	0.88	1.62	1.61	1.87	1.73	2.24	1.15	1.79	1.17	1.33	...	...
Total Government Final Consumption Expenditure b-d	31.71	63.58	113.30	134.32	158.64	182.62	199.28	241.87	290.76	347.66	...	...

a) Item 'Public order and safety' is included in item 'General public services'.
b) Item 'Total government consumption expenditure' includes central and state government but excludes other local authorities. Consumption of fixed capital has also not been accounted for.
c) For series 1 (1970-1983), losses of departmental enterprises are treated as consumption expenditure of the government, whereas for series 2 (1984 onward), they are treated as losses of the government.
d) For series 1 (1970-1983), compensation of employees of the administrative departments includes pensions payable to the employees, whereas in series 2 (1984 onward), it has been allocated to departmental enterprises.

2.3 Total Government Outlays by Function and Type

Thousand Million Indian rupees — Fiscal year beginning 1 April

	Total	Final Consumption Expenditures — Compensation of Employees	Final Consumption Expenditures — Other	Subsidies	Total Current Transfers & Disbursements	Property Income	Gross Capital Formation	Other Capital Outlays	Total Outlays
1984									
1 General public services a	46.74	34.56	12.18	0.01	8.67	4.07	1.23		60.72
2 Defence	66.05	32.64	33.41	0.10	0.18	66.33	0.53	-	66.86
3 Public order and safety a									
4 Education	28.47	25.33	3.14	0.07	42.85	71.39	1.54	0.38	73.31
5 Health	15.68	11.09	4.59	-	1.99	17.67	1.62	-	19.29
6 Social security and welfare	6.19	3.81	2.38	2.61	7.50	16.30	2.05	0.23	18.58
7 Housing and community amenities	4.28	2.84	1.44	0.09	4.95	9.32	9.23	5.38	23.93
8 Recreation, culture and religion	1.54	0.94	0.60	0.01	0.83	2.38	0.26	0.03	2.67
9 Economic services	29.18	16.52	12.66	75.23	9.83	114.24	23.24	12.35	149.83
A Fuel and energy	3.75	2.07	1.68	2.33	1.78	7.86	5.42	3.41	16.69
B Agriculture, forestry, fishing and hunting	11.37	7.86	3.51	40.75	4.60	56.72	5.98	2.39	65.09
C Mining (except fuels), manufacturing and construction	2.98	2.34	0.64	21.27	1.50	25.75	0.51	3.39	29.65
D Transportation and communication	6.61	1.11	5.50	0.41	0.98	8.00	12.06	3.11	23.17
E Other economic affairs	4.47	3.53	0.94	10.47	0.97	15.91	-0.73	0.06	15.23
10 Other functions	1.15	0.24	0.91	0.01	1.02	2.18	0.45	0.18	2.81
Total b-d	199.28	127.97	71.31	78.13	77.82	355.23	42.99	19.78	418.00
1985									
1 General public services a	53.67	40.11	13.56	0.03	11.02	64.72	1.23	1.15	67.10
2 Defence	86.55	36.27	50.28	0.07	0.25	86.87	0.25	-	87.12
3 Public order and safety a									
4 Education	35.54	32.22	3.32	0.14	49.57	85.25	2.12	0.41	87.78
5 Health	17.44	12.38	5.06	-	2.63	20.07	2.11	0.04	22.22
6 Social security and welfare	6.58	4.40	2.18	2.65	7.91	17.14	0.64	0.36	18.14
7 Housing and community amenities	5.32	3.48	1.84	0.23	4.23	9.78	16.03	6.52	32.33
8 Recreation, culture and religion	1.99	1.08	0.91	-	1.14	3.13	0.45	0.03	3.61
9 Economic services	32.99	19.02	13.97	81.99	11.09	126.07	29.34	13.13	168.54
A Fuel and energy	4.13	1.87	2.26	1.26	1.60	6.99	7.78	3.99	18.76
B Agriculture, forestry, fishing and hunting	11.66	8.96	2.70	40.98	5.05	57.69	4.86	2.90	65.45
C Mining (except fuels), manufacturing and construction	3.50	2.77	0.73	27.33	1.86	32.69	0.86	2.98	36.53
D Transportation and communication	8.05	1.27	6.78	0.62	1.07	9.74	13.38	3.13	26.25
E Other economic affairs	5.65	4.15	1.50	11.80	1.51	18.96	2.46	0.13	21.55
10 Other functions	1.79	0.27	1.52	0.14	4.28	6.21	1.08	0.29	7.58
Total b-d	241.87	149.23	92.64	85.25	92.12	419.24	53.25	21.93	494.42

835

India

2.3 Total Government Outlays by Function and Type
(Continued)

Thousand Million Indian rupees — Fiscal year beginning 1 April

		Final Consumption Expenditures			Subsidies	Other Current Transfers & Property Income	Total Current Disbursements	Gross Capital Formation	Other Capital Outlays	Total Outlays
		Total	Compensation of Employees	Other						

1986

1	General public services [a]	61.40	46.81	14.59	0.42	13.05	74.87	7.52	1.61	84.00
2	Defence	112.55	45.29	67.26	0.08	0.46	113.09	0.56	-	113.65
3	Public order and safety [a]	...	...	...	...	...	...	...	...	...
4	Education	39.75	36.47	3.28	-	55.05	94.80	2.29	0.73	97.82
5	Health	19.76	14.30	5.46	-	2.84	22.60	2.30	0.16	25.06
6	Social security and welfare	8.35	5.05	3.30	1.61	11.16	21.12	2.44	1.08	24.64
7	Housing and community amenities	6.21	3.98	2.23	0.69	6.86	13.76	16.06	4.71	34.53
8	Recreation, culture and religion	2.47	1.28	1.19	0.01	1.88	4.36	0.63	0.06	5.05
9	Economic services	39.10	22.53	16.57	94.80	16.84	150.74	30.38	14.09	195.21
	A Fuel and energy	4.83	2.24	2.59	2.10	4.17	11.10	7.48	3.67	22.25
	B Agriculture, forestry, fishing and hunting	14.22	10.59	3.63	47.23	8.18	69.63	6.42	5.18	81.23
	C Mining (except fuels), manufacturing and construction	3.73	3.31	0.42	29.32	1.96	35.01	1.11	2.10	38.22
	D Transportation and communication	8.88	1.45	7.43	1.19	1.47	11.54	16.14	2.84	30.52
	E Other economic affairs	7.44	4.94	2.50	14.96	1.06	23.46	-0.77	0.30	22.99
10	Other functions	1.17	0.27	0.90	0.14	1.88	3.19	0.37	0.29	3.85
	Total [bcd]	290.76	175.98	114.78	97.75	110.02	498.53	62.55	22.73	583.81

1987

1	General public services [a]	72.61	55.66	16.95	0.52	13.44	86.57	8.17	2.11	96.85
2	Defence	133.35	57.06	76.29	0.12	1.01	134.48	0.62	-	135.10
3	Public order and safety [a]	...	...	...	...	...	...	...	...	...
4	Education	48.99	45.16	3.83	-	66.47	115.46	2.44	1.33	119.23
5	Health	24.21	17.61	6.60	-	3.25	27.46	2.64	0.24	30.34
6	Social security and welfare	9.89	6.14	3.75	1.18	13.60	24.67	3.74	1.28	29.69
7	Housing and community amenities	7.39	4.83	2.56	0.91	8.11	16.41	16.86	5.38	38.65
8	Recreation, culture and religion	3.52	1.56	1.96	0.01	2.15	5.68	0.69	0.06	6.43
9	Economic services	46.37	26.99	19.38	115.03	18.70	180.10	32.26	16.01	228.37
	A Fuel and energy	6.07	2.62	3.45	2.77	4.76	13.60	8.65	3.97	26.22
	B Agriculture, forestry, fishing and hunting	17.08	12.87	4.21	54.20	9.06	80.34	6.37	5.82	92.53
	C Mining (except fuels), manufacturing and construction	4.45	3.94	0.51	35.22	2.34	42.01	2.14	2.27	46.42
	D Transportation and communication	10.17	1.74	8.43	1.42	1.42	13.01	17.21	3.61	33.83
	E Other economic affairs	8.60	5.82	2.78	21.42	1.12	31.14	-2.11	0.34	29.37
10	Other functions	1.33	0.33	1.00	0.18	2.21	3.72	0.40	0.37	4.49
	Total [bcd]	347.66	215.34	132.32	117.95	128.94	594.55	67.82	26.78	689.15

a) Item 'Public order and safety' is included in item 'General public services'.
b) Item 'Total government consumption expenditure' includes central and state government but excludes other local authorities. Consumption of fixed capital has also not been accounted for.
c) For series 1 (1970-1983), losses of departmental enterprises are treated as consumption expenditure of the government, whereas for series 2 (1984 onward), they are treated as losses of the government.
d) For series 1 (1970-1983), compensation of employees of the administrative departments includes pension payable to the employees, whereas in series 2 (1984 onward), it has been allocated to departmental enterprises.

2.5 Private Final Consumption Expenditure by Type and Purpose, in Current Prices

Thousand Million Indian rupees — Fiscal year beginning 1 April

		1970	1975	1980	1981	1982	1983	1984	1985	1986	1987	1988	1989

Final Consumption Expenditure of Resident Households

1	Food, beverages and tobacco	204.18	352.03	574.73	658.90	705.20	842.43	921.03	975.13	1082.98	1207.86	1398.04	...
	A Food	188.70	329.85	536.58	614.85	659.49	789.53	864.87	918.54	1022.03	1140.39	1308.58	...
	B Non-alcoholic beverages	0.29	0.43	0.63	0.83	0.87	1.01	1.12	1.45	1.61	1.79	1.96	...
	C Alcoholic beverages	6.75	8.21	12.34	15.25	15.23	19.75	22.74	24.37	25.27	24.74	27.14	...
	D Tobacco	8.44	13.54	25.18	27.97	29.61	32.14	32.30	30.77	34.07	40.94	60.36	...
2	Clothing and footwear	27.98	57.01	111.41	120.59	136.00	157.67	174.87	205.56	228.35	259.38	312.30	...
3	Gross rent, fuel and power	46.52	74.63	122.91	138.22	154.53	167.38	186.55	205.92	229.75	252.76	278.71	...
	A Fuel and power	11.93	21.81	44.03	50.97	57.88	62.60	69.60	76.82	88.04	98.60	109.69	...
	B Other	34.59	52.82	78.88	87.25	96.65	104.78	116.95	129.10	141.71	154.16	169.02	...
4	Furniture, furnishings and household equipment and operation	10.31	20.82	37.60	44.45	50.67	59.46	63.15	71.89	81.11	94.07	112.55	...
	A Household operation	4.06	7.58	15.06	17.35	18.46	22.95	25.54	30.38	35.25	42.39	50.01	...

India

2.5 Private Final Consumption Expenditure by Type and Purpose, in Current Prices
(Continued)

Thousand Million Indian rupees

Fiscal year beginning 1 April

	1970	1975	1980	1981	1982	1983	1984	1985	1986	1987	1988	1989
B Other	6.25	13.24	22.54	27.10	32.21	36.51	37.61	41.51	45.86	51.68	62.54	...
5 Medical care and health expenses	6.18	13.86	29.70	34.53	40.14	46.66	48.29	50.88	53.55	59.23	63.90	...
6 Transport and communication	10.52	24.32	51.07	63.78	76.80	96.45	112.40	132.00	157.16	187.49	215.70	...
A Personal transport equipment	0.84	1.37	2.74	3.26	3.76	6.76	7.77	8.65	10.18	11.09	14.06	...
B Other	9.68	22.95	48.33	60.52	73.04	89.69	104.63	123.35	146.98	176.40	201.64	...
7 Recreational, entertainment, education and cultural services	9.67	17.04	29.85	33.78	38.46	42.69	48.45	53.20	67.05	72.76	79.78	...
A Education	4.54	8.71	17.25	19.16	21.09	23.54	25.48	26.13	38.03	40.32	43.20	...
B Other	5.13	8.33	12.60	14.62	17.37	19.15	22.97	27.07	29.02	32.44	36.58	...
8 Miscellaneous goods and services	10.09	18.51	33.56	40.31	45.11	48.10	55.67	65.94	78.48	91.72	103.97	...
A Personal care	2.93	5.77	10.49	13.40	14.68	12.62	15.06	17.83	24.81	28.58	33.14	...
B Expenditures in restaurants, cafes and hotels	2.10	4.71	8.72	10.63	11.97	13.70	15.27	17.30	19.05	20.84	24.61	...
C Other	5.06	8.03	14.35	16.28	18.46	21.78	25.34	30.81	34.62	42.30	46.22	...
Total Final Consumption Expenditure in the Domestic Market by Households, of which	325.45	578.22	990.83	1134.56	1246.91	1460.84	1610.41	1760.52	1978.43	2225.27	2564.95	...
A Durable goods	3.79	7.89	15.07	19.16	21.64	23.66	26.49	32.74	42.17	49.69	60.54	...
B Semi-durable goods	31.42	66.83	127.79	141.68	162.09	187.52	206.47	239.20	265.87	301.23	362.15	...
C Non-durable goods	227.56	397.40	671.69	772.25	834.02	989.17	1081.86	1155.14	1287.36	1442.63	1663.57	...
D Services	62.68	106.10	176.28	201.47	229.16	260.49	295.59	333.44	383.03	431.72	478.69	...
Plus: Direct purchases abroad by resident households	0.17	0.21	0.85	1.38	1.74	2.28	3.68	3.98	3.41	4.67	4.67	...
Less: Direct purchases in the domestic market by non-resident households	0.52	2.66	12.49	11.93	12.36	12.11	10.03	13.04	17.40	19.77	19.77	...
Equals: Final Consumption Expenditure of Resident Households a	325.10	575.77	979.19	1124.01	1236.29	1451.01	1604.06	1751.46	1964.44	2210.17	2549.85	...

Final Consumption Expenditure of Private Non-profit Institutions Serving Households

	1970	1975	1980	1981	1982	1983	1984	1985	1986	1987	1988	1989
Equals: Final Consumption Expenditure of Private Non-profit Organisations Serving Households	...	...	...	...	...	...	...	...	...	...	...	...
Private Final Consumption Expenditure	325.10	575.77	979.19	1124.01	1236.29	1451.01	1604.06	1751.46	1964.44	2210.17	2549.85	...

a) Item 'Final consumption expenditure of resident households' includes consumption expenditure of private non-profit institutions serving households.

2.6 Private Final Consumption Expenditure by Type and Purpose, in Constant Prices

Thousand Million Indian rupees

Fiscal year beginning 1 April

	1970	1975	1980	1981	1982	1983	1984	1985	1986	1987	1988	1989
At constant prices of:1980												
Final Consumption Expenditure of Resident Households												
1 Food, beverages and tobacco	442.27	475.20	574.73	598.99	602.09	649.79	675.23	684.35	698.31	718.31	782.37	...
A Food	411.42	446.71	536.58	557.92	560.79	605.79	630.50	644.01	657.84	678.96	734.77	...
B Non-alcoholic beverages	0.63	0.55	0.63	0.73	0.71	0.81	0.92	1.05	1.14	0.99	1.00	...
C Alcoholic beverages	11.14	10.72	12.34	14.00	13.71	17.37	19.20	19.38	19.42	15.84	15.99	...
D Tobacco	19.08	17.22	25.18	26.34	26.88	25.82	24.61	19.91	19.91	22.52	30.61	...
2 Clothing and footwear	62.88	82.47	111.41	114.67	125.79	136.68	138.76	150.93	161.72	171.32	191.13	...
3 Gross rent, fuel and pow	91.94	104.30	122.91	126.49	129.07	134.05	139.23	144.30	150.48	156.00	162.25	...
A Fuel and power	33.91	36.61	44.03	45.06	44.99	46.93	49.25	51.36	54.47	56.80	59.75	...
B Other	58.03	67.69	78.88	81.43	84.08	87.12	89.98	92.94	96.01	99.20	102.50	...
4 Furniture, furnishings and household equipment and operation	26.46	31.13	37.60	41.87	46.12	52.08	51.58	56.03	60.26	64.41	72.09	...
A Household operation	9.40	10.50	15.06	16.72	17.37	19.73	19.38	21.66	23.23	24.09	27.09	...
B Other	17.06	20.63	22.54	25.15	28.75	32.35	32.20	34.37	37.03	40.32	45.00	...
5 Medical care and health expenses	17.04	20.54	29.70	30.36	31.02	31.68	32.34	33.03	33.70	34.41	35.09	...
6 Transport and communication	26.35	34.47	51.07	56.20	60.61	69.72	76.01	81.56	89.08	98.97	109.32	...
A Personal transport equipment	2.02	2.04	2.74	2.91	3.21	5.72	6.23	6.53	6.80	7.04	7.96	...
B Other	24.33	32.43	48.33	53.29	57.40	64.00	69.78	75.03	82.28	91.93	101.36	...
7 Recreational, entertainment, education and cultural services	23.72	26.60	29.85	30.50	32.14	33.51	35.43	37.10	43.81	45.52	47.36	...
A Education	12.01	14.97	17.25	17.04	17.36	17.25	17.53	16.79	22.51	21.65	21.49	...

837

India

2.6 Private Final Consumption Expenditure by Type and Purpose, in Constant Prices (Continued)

Thousand Million Indian rupees | Fiscal year beginning 1 April

	1970	1975	1980	1981	1982	1983	1984	1985	1986	1987	1988	1989
At constant prices of 1980												
B Other	11.71	11.63	12.60	13.46	14.78	16.26	17.90	20.31	21.30	23.87	25.87	...
8 Miscellaneous goods and services	24.56	25.92	33.56	36.66	39.20	38.55	42.13	47.05	54.15	60.78	63.00	...
A Personal care	7.67	7.88	10.49	12.92	13.66	10.97	12.32	13.78	18.79	20.77	22.57	...
B Expenditures in restaurants, cafes and hotels	5.73	7.01	8.72	9.33	10.15	10.60	10.86	11.46	12.08	12.58	13.59	...
C Other	11.16	11.03	14.35	14.41	15.39	16.98	18.95	21.35	23.28	27.43	26.84	...
Total Final Consumption Expenditure in the Domestic Market by Households, of which	715.22	800.63	990.83	1035.74	1066.04	1146.06	1190.71	1234.35	1291.51	1349.72	1462.61	...
A Durable goods	9.63	11.14	15.07	18.25	20.12	21.10	22.44	25.89	32.00	37.21	41.69	...
B Semi-durable goods	73.22	97.44	127.79	134.05	149.01	163.33	166.52	180.16	193.56	205.36	228.88	...
C Non-durable goods	502.96	542.90	671.69	700.50	706.46	761.26	790.92	806.71	829.35	857.76	932.59	...
D Services	129.41	149.15	176.28	182.94	190.45	200.37	210.83	221.59	236.60	249.39	259.65	...
Plus: Direct purchases abroad by resident households												
Less: Direct purchases in the domestic market by non-resident households												
Equals: Final Consumption Expenditure of Resident Households												
Final Consumption Expenditure of Private Non-profit Institutions Serving Households												
Equals: Final Consumption Expenditure of Private Non-profit Organisations Serving Households												
Private Final Consumption Expenditure												

2.7 Gross Capital Formation by Type of Good and Owner, in Current Prices

Thousand Million Indian rupees | Fiscal year beginning 1 April

	1980				1981				1982			
	TOTAL	Total Private	Public Enterprises	General Government	TOTAL	Total Private	Public Enterprises	General Government	TOTAL	Total Private	Public Enterprises	General Government
Increase in stocks, total	47.40	20.98	2.09	24.33	95.81	64.44	2.24	29.13	59.35	40.72	17.98	0.65
1 Goods producing industries	37.83				48.13				38.52			
A Materials and supplies												
B Work in progress												
C Livestock, except breeding stocks, dairy cattle, etc.	1.20				1.39				1.61			
D Finished goods												
2 Wholesale and retail trade	6.24				44.06				18.82			
3 Other, except government stocks	3.01				3.27				1.58			
4 Government stocks	0.32				0.35				0.43			
Gross Fixed Capital Formation, Total abc	262.76	145.83	52.36	64.57	314.55	168.57	70.78	75.20	357.69	171.83	98.21	87.65
1 Residential buildings	31.32	38.95	1.70	36.94		2.01	46.78	44.64	-	2.14
2 Non-residential buildings d	29.32	16.66	5.40	7.26	20.73	38.37	9.47	8.17	39.64	19.48	10.23	9.93
3 Other construction	75.85	21.21	10.00	44.64	98.86	22.24	14.61	49.83	96.85	20.93	17.76	58.16
4 Land improvement and plantation and orchard development												
5 Producers' durable goods	124.94	77.01	36.96	10.97	148.98	87.09	46.70	15.19	172.58	84.94	70.22	17.42
A Transport equipment	30.41	21.46	4.95	4.00	35.48	25.34	4.34	5.80	43.01	28.37	7.75	6.89
B Machinery and equipment	94.53	55.55	32.01	6.97	113.50	61.75	42.36	9.39	129.57	56.57	62.47	10.53
6 Breeding stock, dairy cattle, etc.	1.33	-	-	1.33	1.57	1.57	-	-	1.84	1.84	...	-
Statistical discrepancy	-1.49				-49.68				-46.97			
Total Gross Capital Formation	308.67	170.16	73.34	66.99	360.68	233.01	99.91	77.44	370.07	212.55	116.19	88.30

	1983				1984				1985			
	TOTAL	Total Private	Public Enterprises	General Government	TOTAL	Total Private	Public Enterprises	General Government	TOTAL	Total Private	Public Enterprises	General Government
Increase in stocks, total	60.83	45.07	14.56	1.20	62.31	28.40	31.34	2.57	131.61	97.87	30.39	3.35
1 Goods producing industries	29.89				33.33				57.82			
A Materials and supplies												
B Work in progress												
C Livestock, except breeding stocks, dairy cattle, etc.	1.80				2.20				2.59			

838

India

2.7 Gross Capital Formation by Type of Good and Owner, in Current Prices
(Continued)

Thousand Million Indian rupees — Fiscal year beginning 1 April

	1983 TOTAL	1984 Total Private	1984 Public Enterprises	1984 General Government	1984 TOTAL	1985 Total Private	1985 Public Enterprises	1985 General Government
D Finished goods								
2 Wholesale and retail trade	30.35				26.54	70.67		
3 Other, except government stocks	0.26				1.90	2.23		
4 Government stocks	0.33				0.54	0.89		
Gross Fixed Capital Formation, Total abc	399.91	195.41	106.93	97.57	454.22	220.26	121.51	112.45	535.68	260.67	143.12	131.89
1 Residential buildings	48.55	44.95	—	3.60	59.77	55.99	—	3.78	68.76	63.68	—	5.08
2 Non-residential buildings d	42.92	19.12	13.33	10.47	49.37	22.59	15.28	11.50	55.94	26.59	15.55	13.80
3 Other construction	105.02	19.80	20.85	64.37	118.05	23.06	21.12	73.87	145.09	26.53	31.09	87.44
4 Land improvement and plantation and orchard development								
5 Producers' durable goods	201.06	109.18	72.75	19.13	224.33	115.92	85.11	23.30	262.86	140.81	96.48	25.57
A Transport equipment	45.40	33.73	4.45	7.22	51.95	36.63	7.97	7.35	63.76	48.59	7.55	7.62
B Machinery and equipment	155.66	75.45	68.30	11.91	172.38	79.29	77.14	15.95	199.10	92.22	88.93	17.95
6 Breeding stock, dairy cattle, etc	2.36	2.36	—		2.70	2.70	—		3.06	3.06	—	—
Statistical discrepancy	-31.19				-52.13				-68.12			
Total Gross Capital Formation	429.55	240.48	121.49	98.77	464.40	251.60	149.91	115.02	599.17	358.54	173.51	135.24

	1986 TOTAL	1986 Total Private	1986 Public Enterprises	1986 General Government	1987 TOTAL	1987 Total Private	1987 Public Enterprises	1987 General Government	1988 TOTAL	1988 Total Private	1988 Public Enterprises	1988 General Government
Increase in stocks, total	92.86	70.90	19.78	2.18	86.89	83.06	0.52	3.31	151.82	140.05	9.88	1.89
A Goods producing industries	49.12				54.21				63.20			
B Work in progress												
C Livestock, except breeding stocks, dairy cattle, etc	3.00				3.31				3.65			
D Finished goods												
2 Wholesale and retail trade	40.90				29.29				48.81			
3 Other, except government stocks	2.17				3.01				3.04			
4 Government stocks	0.67				0.38				0.77			
Gross Fixed Capital Formation, Total abc	620.22	287.96	189.24	143.02	674.51	324.30	200.42	149.79	402.50	204.75	194.73	
1 Residential buildings	66.55	58.65	—	8.08	90.27	83.69	—	6.58	86.93	79.62	—	7.31
2 Non-residential buildings d	58.66	20.95	20.42	17.28	64.98	25.84	20.90	18.24	80.28	36.49	21.50	22.29
3 Other construction	157.25	15.65	52.10	89.50	172.66	23.05	47.33	102.28	204.99	36.25	47.00	121.74
4 Land improvement and plantation and orchard development												
5 Producers' durable goods	319.98	173.53	116.72	29.73	342.25	187.37	132.19	22.69	411.92	232.28	136.25	43.39
A Transport equipment	78.09	50.60	15.46	12.03	88.84	65.15	14.56	9.13	110.43	78.48	20.53	11.42
B Machinery and equipment	241.89	122.93	101.26	17.70	256.41	122.22	117.63	16.56	301.49	153.80	115.72	31.97
6 Breeding stock, dairy cattle, etc	3.54	3.54	—	—	4.35	4.35	—	—	4.86	4.86	—	—
Statistical discrepancy	-76.62				-40.06				-18.36			
Total Gross Capital Formation	636.46	358.86	209.02	145.20	721.34	407.34	200.94	153.10	935.44	542.55	214.63	196.62

a) Gross fixed capital formation by kind of activity and by type of goods are prepared independently and therefore, do not always tally.
b) Data for gross fixed capital formation are unadjusted for statistical discrepancy and therefore, as such, differ from the total of the components.
c) For years 1970-1979, the estimates of gross fixed capital formation at the aggregate level in columns 2, 3 and 4 are only adjusted for the purchase and sale of second-hand physical assets and do not coincide with the data shown in the table 'Gross Capital Formation by Kind of Economic Activity of Owners'.
d) Item 'Non-residential buildings' includes residential house construction of public enterprises and the private corporate sector.

839

India

2.8 Gross Capital Formation by Type of Good and Owner, in Constant Prices

Thousand Million Indian rupees — Fiscal year beginning 1 April

At constant prices of 1980

	1980				1981				1982			
	TOTAL	Private	Public Enterprises	General Government	TOTAL	Private	Public Enterprises	General Government	TOTAL	Private	Public Enterprises	General Government
Increase in stocks, total	47.40	24.33	20.98	2.09	85.93	58.42	25.59	1.92	50.81	35.67	14.59	0.55
1 Goods producing industries	37.83	...	...	...	42.31	...	...	...	32.10	...	...	...
A Materials and supplies	...	...	...	...	...	...	...	...	...	...	...	...
B Work in progress	...	...	...	...	...	...	...	...	...	...	...	...
C Livestock, except breeding stocks, dairy cattle, etc.	1.20	...	...	...	1.28	...	...	...	1.37	...	...	...
D Finished goods	...	...	...	...	...	...	...	...	...	...	...	...
2 Wholesale and retail trade	6.24	...	...	...	40.30	...	...	...	16.92	...	...	...
3 Other, except government stocks	3.01	...	...	...	3.00	...	...	...	1.41	...	...	...
4 Government stocks	0.32	...	...	...	0.32	...	...	...	0.38	...	...	...
Gross Fixed Capital Formation, Total a b	262.76	145.83	52.36	64.57	280.79	149.27	63.83	67.69	292.96	140.49	82.33	70.14
1 Residential buildings	31.32	29.62	1.70	...	32.18	30.49	1.69	...	32.89	31.39	-	1.50
2 Non-residential buildings c	29.32	16.66	5.40	7.26	32.41	17.47	8.02	6.92	27.73	13.38	7.28	7.07
3 Other construction	75.85	21.21	10.00	44.64	74.10	15.51	13.39	45.20	69.46	8.65	14.36	46.45
4 Land improvement and plantation and orchard development												
5 Producers' durable goods	124.94	77.01	36.96	10.97	140.67	84.37	42.42	13.88	161.33	85.52	60.69	15.12
A Transport equipment	30.41	21.46	4.95	4.00	31.60	22.65	3.83	5.12	35.22	22.75	6.60	5.87
B Machinery and equipment	94.53	55.55	32.01	6.97	109.07	61.72	38.59	8.76	126.11	62.77	54.09	9.25
6 Breeding stock, dairy cattle, etc.	1.33	...	...	1.33	1.43	...	1.43	-	1.55	1.55	...	-
Statistical discrepancy	-1.49	...	...	...	-44.35	...	...	...	-38.47	...	...	...
Total Gross Capital Formation	308.67	170.16	73.34	66.66	322.37	207.69	89.42	69.61	305.30	176.16	96.92	70.69

At constant prices of 1980

	1983				1984				1985			
	TOTAL	Private	Public Enterprises	General Government	TOTAL	Private	Public Enterprises	General Government	TOTAL	Private	Public Enterprises	General Government
Increase in stocks, total	47.94	36.15	11.00	0.79	44.91	23.25	19.90	1.76	91.36	69.62	19.54	2.20
1 Goods producing industries	23.29	...	...	...	23.23	...	...	...	38.16	...	...	...
A Materials and supplies	...	...	...	...	...	...	...	...	...	...	...	...
B Work in progress	...	...	...	...	...	...	...	...	...	...	...	...
C Livestock, except breeding stocks, dairy cattle, etc.	1.38	...	...	...	1.49	...	...	...	1.61	...	...	...
D Finished goods	...	...	...	...	...	...	...	...	...	...	...	...
2 Wholesale and retail trade	24.17	...	...	...	19.81	...	...	...	50.95	...	...	...
3 Other, except government stocks	0.21	...	...	...	1.46	...	...	...	1.61	...	...	...
4 Government stocks	0.27	...	...	...	0.41	...	...	...	0.64	...	...	...
Gross Fixed Capital Formation, Total a b	296.32	140.81	83.43	72.08	306.76	142.43	89.19	75.14	325.81	155.01	94.24	76.56
1 Residential buildings	30.04	27.81	-	2.23	32.93	30.84	-	2.09	34.35	31.79	-	2.56
2 Non-residential buildings c	23.91	8.84	8.44	6.63	23.68	8.52	8.65	6.51	25.88	10.70	8.04	7.14
3 Other construction	71.69	9.15	15.43	47.11	70.57	8.69	13.89	47.99	76.90	10.68	17.79	48.43
4 Land improvement and plantation and orchard development												
5 Producers' durable goods	168.92	93.25	59.56	16.11	177.69	92.49	66.65	18.55	186.69	99.85	68.41	18.43
A Transport equipment	39.41	29.43	3.81	6.17	43.42	30.97	6.48	5.97	48.35	37.63	5.34	5.38
B Machinery and equipment	129.51	63.82	55.75	9.94	134.27	61.52	60.17	12.58	138.34	62.22	63.07	13.05
6 Breeding stock, dairy cattle, etc.	1.76	1.76	...	-	1.89	1.89	-	-	1.99	1.99	-	-
Statistical discrepancy	-23.11	...	...	...	-35.21	...	...	...	-41.43	...	...	...
Total Gross Capital Formation	321.15	176.96	94.43	72.87	316.46	165.68	109.09	76.90	375.74	224.63	113.78	78.76

India

2.8 Gross Capital Formation by Type of Good and Owner, in Constant Prices

Thousand Million Indian rupees
Fiscal year beginning 1 April

	1986				1987				1988			
	TOTAL	Private Enterprises	Public Enterprises	General Government	TOTAL	Private Enterprises	Public Enterprises	General Government	TOTAL	Private Enterprises	Public Enterprises	General Government
Increase in stocks, total	60.89	47.48	12.19	1.22	52.90	-1.13	2.05	86.69	80.47	5.22	1.00
1 Goods producing industries	31.19				32.28			35.06				
A Materials and supplies	...				...			...				
B Work in progress	...				...			...				
C Livestock, except cattle, etc.	1.75				1.92			2.10			2.10	
D Finished goods												
2 Wholesale and retail trade	27.76				18.47			49.38				
3 Other, except government stocks	1.48				1.91			1.79				
4 Government stocks	0.46				0.24			0.46				
Gross Fixed Capital Formation, Total [a,b]	347.71	155.51	115.26	76.94	357.15	168.04	116.40	72.71	385.90	189.78	107.88	88.24
1 Residential buildings	35.83	32.84	-	2.99	36.62	33.85	-	2.77	37.74	34.89	-	2.85
2 Non-residential buildings [c]	22.61	5.03	9.52	8.06	25.35	8.55	8.97	7.83	28.44	11.15	8.49	8.80
3 Other construction	78.83	3.75	27.17	45.91	75.03	7.62	19.99	47.42	82.35	11.80	19.91	51.36
4 Land improvement and plantation and orchard development												
5 Producers' durable goods	210.29	111.74	78.57	19.98	217.88	115.75	87.44	14.69	234.96	130.25	79.48	25.23
A Transport equipment	55.25	36.70	10.43	8.12	56.86	43.70	9.26	3.90	64.19	46.31	11.49	6.39
B Machinery and equipment	155.04	75.04	68.14	11.86	161.02	72.05	78.18	10.79	170.77	83.94	67.99	18.84
6 Breeding stock, dairy cattle, etc.	2.15	-	-	2.15	2.27	-	-	2.27	2.41	-	2.41	-
Statistical discrepancy	-42.96				-21.21			-8.83				
Total Gross Capital Formation	365.65	202.99	127.45	78.16	388.84	220.02	115.27	74.76	463.76	270.25	113.10	89.24

a) Gross fixed capital formation by kind of activity and by type of goods are prepared independently and therefore, do not always tally.
b) Data for gross fixed capital formation are unadjusted for statistical discrepancy and therefore do not coincide with the data shown in the table 'Gross Capital Formation by Kind of Economic and the private corporate sector.
c) Item 'Non-residential buildings' includes residential house construction of public enterprises

2.9 Gross Capital Formation by Kind of Activity of Owner, ISIC Major Divisions, in Current Prices

Thousand Million Indian rupees
Fiscal year beginning 1 April

	1980		1981		1982		1983	
	Total Gross Capital Formation	Increase in Stocks	Total Gross Capital Formation	Increase in Stocks	Total Gross Capital Formation	Increase in Stocks	Gross Fixed Capital Formation	Increase in Stocks

All Producers

1 Agriculture, hunting, fishing and forestry	49.03	1.38	47.65	2.30	54.47	2.13	58.68	61.18	2.53	58.65
2 Mining and quarrying	12.14	2.62	9.52	18.37	3.34	15.03	31.79	3.27	28.52	29.26	2.29	26.97
3 Manufacturing	78.46	28.69	49.77	100.78	32.99	67.79	101.15	27.36	73.79	117.59	23.43	94.16
4 Electricity, gas and water	32.12	3.18	28.94	42.78	3.32	39.46	48.93	2.47	46.46	51.35	2.16	49.19
5 Construction	7.03	1.95	5.08	13.85	6.18	7.67	12.19	3.28	8.91	7.68	-0.52	8.20
6 Wholesale and retail trade, restaurants and hotels	13.65	6.25	7.40	53.67	44.10	9.57	30.66	11.83	18.83	43.24	30.35	12.89
7 Transport, storage and communication	29.98	2.73	27.25	38.82	2.68	36.14	43.87	1.16	42.71	44.46	0.03	44.43
8 Finance, insurance, real estate and business services	33.12	0.08	33.04	41.34	0.18	41.16	49.94	0.13	49.81	52.26	0.18	52.08
9 Community, social and personal services	5.72	0.20	5.52	7.47	0.37	7.10	8.58	0.23	8.35	8.63	0.05	8.58
Total Industries [a]	261.25	47.08	214.17	371.55	95.46	276.09	387.92	58.92	329.00	415.65	60.50	355.15
Producers of Government Services	22.32	0.32	22.00	25.79	0.35	25.44	30.68	0.43	30.25	32.58	0.33	32.25
Private Non-Profit Institutions Serving Households												
Statistical discrepancy	25.10			-36.66			-48.53			-18.68		
Total [a,b]	308.67	47.40	236.17	360.98	95.81	301.53	370.07	59.35	359.35	429.55	60.83	387.40

	1984			1985			1986			1987		
	Total Gross Capital Formation	Increase in Stocks	Gross Fixed Capital Formation	Total Gross Capital Formation	Increase in Stocks	Gross Fixed Capital Formation	Total Gross Capital Formation	Increase in Stocks	Gross Fixed Capital Formation	Total Gross Capital Formation	Increase in Stocks	Gross Fixed Capital Formation

All Producers

1 Agriculture, hunting, fishing and forestry	70.11	4.08	66.03	75.37	3.60	71.77	82.94	4.96	77.98	92.73	4.77	87.96
2 Mining and quarrying	29.97	2.97	27.00	41.80	4.03	37.77	45.37	3.36	42.01	46.69	2.42	44.27
3 Manufacturing	124.08	20.41	103.67	161.89	40.31	121.58	172.79	35.63	137.16	192.78	40.72	152.06
4 Electricity, gas and water	56.63	3.52	53.11	72.53	4.93	67.60	96.41	3.85	92.56	105.22	4.26	100.96

841

India

2.9 Gross Capital Formation by Kind of Activity of Owner, ISIC Major Divisions, in Current Prices
(Continued)

Thousand Million Indian rupees   Fiscal year beginning 1 April

	1984			1985			1986			1987		
	Total Gross Capital Formation	Increase in Stocks	Gross Fixed Capital Formation	Total Gross Capital Formation	Increase in Stocks	Gross Fixed Capital Formation	Total Gross Capital Formation	Increase in Stocks	Gross Fixed Capital Formation	Total Gross Capital Formation	Increase in Stocks	Gross Fixed Capital Formation
5 Construction	11.17	2.35	8.82	12.79	4.95	7.84	10.62	1.32	9.30	10.83	2.04	8.79
6 Wholesale and retail trade, restaurants and hotels	41.62	26.54	15.08	88.03	70.67	17.36	60.97	40.90	20.07	50.12	29.29	20.83
7 Transport, storage and communication	58.07	1.99	56.08	63.58	1.69	61.89	80.86	0.33	80.53	82.52	2.44	80.08
8 Finance, insurance, real estate and business services	65.24	0.56	64.68	74.40	0.11	74.29	89.68	1.56	88.12	105.20	0.27	104.93
9 Community, social and personal services	10.04	-0.65	10.69	14.23	0.43	13.80	16.34	0.28	16.06	17.17	0.30	16.87
Total Industries [a]	466.93	61.77	405.16	604.62	130.72	473.90	655.98	92.19	563.79	703.26	86.51	616.75
Producers of Government Services	39.16	0.54	38.62	47.96	0.89	47.07	55.20	0.67	54.53	57.41	0.38	57.03
Private Non-Profit Institutions Serving Households	...	...	...	...	...	...	...	...	...	...	...	...
Statistical discrepancy	-41.69	...	...	-53.41	...	...	-74.72	...	...	-39.33	...	...
Total [ab]	464.40	62.31	443.78	599.17	131.61	520.97	636.46	92.86	618.32	721.34	86.89	673.78

	1988		
	Total Gross Capital Formation	Increase in Stocks	Gross Fixed Capital Formation
	All Producers		
1 Agriculture, hunting, fishing and forestry	108.75	4.58	104.17
2 Mining and quarrying	45.78	2.75	43.03
3 Manufacturing	225.40	48.11	177.29
4 Electricity, gas and water	119.26	5.47	113.79
5 Construction	12.41	2.29	10.12
6 Wholesale and retail trade, restaurants and hotels	109.75	84.81	24.94
7 Transport, storage and communication	104.32	2.38	101.94
8 Finance, insurance, real estate and business services	120.87	0.27	120.60
9 Community, social and personal services	19.83	0.39	19.44
Total Industries [a]	866.37	151.05	715.32
Producers of Government Services	66.47	0.77	65.70
Private Non-Profit Institutions Serving Households	...	...	...
Statistical discrepancy	2.60	...	...
Total [ab]	935.44	151.82	781.02

a) Gross fixed capital formation by kind of activity and by type of goods are prepared independently and therefore, do not always tally.
b) The estimates of 'Increase in stocks' and 'Gross fixed capital formation' (columns 2 and 3, respectively) are unadjusted for statistical discrepancy and therefore, do not add up to 'Gross capital formation' (column 1).

2.10 Gross Capital Formation by Kind of Activity of Owner, ISIC Major Divisions, in Constant Prices

Thousand Million Indian rupees   Fiscal year beginning 1 April

	1980			1981			1982			1983		
	Total Gross Capital Formation	Increase in Stocks	Gross Fixed Capital Formation	Total Gross Capital Formation	Increase in Stocks	Gross Fixed Capital Formation	Total Gross Capital Formation	Increase in Stocks	Gross Fixed Capital Formation	Total Gross Capital Formation	Increase in Stocks	Gross Fixed Capital Formation
	At constant prices of:1980											
	All Producers											
1 Agriculture, hunting, fishing and forestry	49.03	1.38	47.65	47.98	2.11	45.87	48.60	1.84	46.76	44.57	1.98	42.59
2 Mining and quarrying	12.14	2.62	9.52	15.70	2.14	13.56	26.37	1.85	24.52	22.41	1.21	21.20
3 Manufacturing	78.46	28.69	49.77	90.02	30.19	59.83	83.62	24.38	59.24	90.41	19.08	71.33
4 Electricity, gas and water	32.12	3.18	28.94	38.68	2.85	35.83	40.83	1.80	39.03	39.48	1.34	38.14

India

2.10 Gross Capital Formation by Kind of Activity of Owner, ISIC Major Divisions, in Constant Prices (Continued)

Thousand Million Indian rupees — Fiscal year beginning 1 April

At constant prices of 1980

	1980 Total Gross Capital Formation	1980 Increase in Stocks	1980 Gross Fixed Capital Formation	1981 Total Gross Capital Formation	1981 Increase in Stocks	1981 Gross Fixed Capital Formation	1982 Total Gross Capital Formation	1982 Increase in Stocks	1982 Gross Fixed Capital Formation	1983 Total Gross Capital Formation	1983 Increase in Stocks	1983 Gross Fixed Capital Formation
All Producers												
5 Construction	7.03	1.95	5.08	11.92	5.02	6.90	10.19	2.23	7.96	6.27	-0.32	6.59
6 Wholesale and retail trade, restaurants and hotels	13.65	6.25	7.40	48.76	8.42	40.34	26.55	16.98	9.57	33.81	24.17	9.64
7 Transport, storage and communication	29.98	2.73	27.25	32.72	2.45	30.27	33.94	1.03	32.91	35.37	0.03	35.34
8 Finance, insurance, real estate and business services	33.12	0.08	33.04	34.30	0.17	34.13	35.48	0.12	35.36	32.79	0.14	32.65
9 Community, social and personal services	5.72	0.20	5.52	6.47	0.34	6.13	6.58	0.20	6.38	6.04	0.04	6.00
Total Industries a	261.25	47.08	214.17	326.55	85.61	240.94	312.16	50.43	261.73	311.15	47.67	263.48
Producers of Government Services	22.32	0.32	22.00	23.46	0.32	23.14	24.72	0.38	24.34	23.87	0.27	23.60
Private Non-Profit Institutions Serving Households	...	...	...	...	...	...	...	...	...	...	...	...
Statistical discrepancy	25.10			-27.64			-31.58			-13.87		
Total ab	308.67	47.40	236.17	322.37	85.93	264.08	305.30	50.81	286.07	321.15	47.94	287.08

At constant prices of 1980

	1984 Total Gross Capital Formation	1984 Increase in Stocks	1984 Gross Fixed Capital Formation	1985 Total Gross Capital Formation	1985 Increase in Stocks	1985 Gross Fixed Capital Formation	1986 Total Gross Capital Formation	1986 Increase in Stocks	1986 Gross Fixed Capital Formation	1987 Total Gross Capital Formation	1987 Increase in Stocks	1987 Gross Fixed Capital Formation
All Producers												
1 Agriculture, hunting, fishing and forestry	47.90	2.93	44.97	46.07	2.33	43.74	47.24	3.08	44.16	48.46	2.85	45.61
2 Mining and quarrying	21.26	1.44	19.82	26.62	1.92	24.70	26.94	1.53	25.41	26.28	1.08	25.20
3 Manufacturing	89.19	15.59	73.67	106.96	28.98	77.98	106.41	24.34	82.07	111.78	25.84	85.94
4 Electricity, gas and water	40.00	2.04	37.96	45.64	2.43	43.21	56.98	1.64	55.34	58.19	1.64	56.55
5 Construction	8.03	1.30	6.73	7.87	2.50	5.37	6.62	0.60	6.02	6.26	0.87	5.39
6 Wholesale and retail trade, restaurants and hotels	30.32	19.81	10.51	50.95	10.91	39.59	27.76	11.83	30.07	18.47	11.60	
7 Transport, storage and communication	43.31	1.52	41.79	41.02	1.22	39.80	49.86	0.22	49.64	46.98	1.55	45.43
8 Finance, insurance, real estate and business services	36.74	0.43	36.31	37.88	0.08	37.80	41.19	1.07	40.12	45.39	0.17	45.22
9 Community, social and personal services	6.33	-0.49	6.82	8.21	0.31	7.90	8.76	0.19	8.57	8.60	0.19	8.41
Total Industries a	323.08	44.50	278.58	382.13	90.72	291.41	383.59	60.43	323.16	382.01	52.66	329.35
Producers of Government Services	26.43	0.41	26.02	28.15	0.64	27.51	29.96	0.46	29.50	28.63	0.24	28.39
Private Non-Profit Institutions Serving Households	...	...	...	...	...	...	...	...	...	...	...	...
Statistical discrepancy	-33.05			-34.54			-47.90			-21.80		
Total ab	316.46	44.91	304.60	375.74	91.36	318.92	365.65	60.89	352.66	388.84	52.90	357.74

At constant prices of 1980

	1988 Total Gross Capital Formation	1988 Increase in Stocks	1988 Gross Fixed Capital Formation
All Producers			
1 Agriculture, hunting, fishing and forestry	51.78	2.65	49.13
2 Mining and quarrying	23.29	1.07	22.22
3 Manufacturing	119.61	28.43	91.18
4 Electricity, gas and water	59.91	2.00	57.91
5 Construction	6.54	0.91	5.63
6 Wholesale and retail trade, restaurants and hotels	61.98	49.38	12.60
7 Transport, storage and communication	53.40	1.40	52.00
8 Finance, insurance, real estate and business services	48.84	0.16	48.68
9 Community, social and personal services	9.09	0.23	8.86
Total Industries a	434.44	86.23	348.21
Producers of Government Services	30.57	0.46	30.11
Private Non-Profit Institutions Serving Households	...	...	...
Statistical discrepancy	-1.25		...
Total ab	463.76	86.69	378.32

a) Gross fixed capital formation by kind of activity and by type of goods are prepared independently and therefore, do not always tally.
b) The estimates of 'Increase in stocks' and 'Gross fixed capital formation' (columns 2 and 3, respectively) are unadjusted for statistical discrepancy and therefore, do not add up to 'Gross capital formation' (column 1).

India

2.11 Gross Fixed Capital Formation by Kind of Activity of Owner, ISIC Divisions, in Current Prices

Thousand Million Indian rupees — Fiscal year beginning 1 April

	1970	1975	1980	1981	1982	1983	1984	1985	1986	1987	1988	1989
All Producers												
1 Agriculture, hunting, forestry and fishing	11.61	22.25	47.65	52.17	58.68	58.65	66.03	71.77	77.98	87.96	104.17	
A Agriculture and hunting	11.02	21.03	45.37	49.37	55.22	54.33	61.07	66.25	71.01	80.00	95.07	
B Forestry and logging	0.23	0.36	1.01	1.12	1.40	1.77	1.87	1.82	2.44	2.60	2.82	
C Fishing	0.36	0.86	1.27	1.68	2.06	2.55	3.09	3.70	4.53	5.36	6.28	
2 Mining and quarrying	0.88	4.25	9.52	15.03	28.52	26.97	27.00	37.77	42.01	44.27	43.03	
3 Manufacturing	12.04	36.28	49.77	67.79	73.79	91.94	103.67	121.58	137.16	152.06	177.29	
4 Electricity, gas and water	5.93	13.79	28.94	39.36	46.46	49.19	53.11	67.60	85.26	100.96	113.79	
A Electricity, gas and steam	5.55	12.80	25.57	35.48	41.97	43.67	47.58	60.89	85.00	91.46	103.99	
B Water works and supply	0.38	0.99	3.37	3.88	4.49	5.52	5.53	6.71	7.56	9.50	9.80	
5 Construction	1.11	2.08	5.08	7.67	8.91	8.20	8.82	7.84	9.30	8.79	10.12	
6 Wholesale and retail trade, restaurants and hotels	2.91	4.24	7.40	9.57	11.77	12.89	15.08	17.36	20.07	20.83	24.94	
A Wholesale and retail trade	1.94	3.91	5.12	6.24	8.59	8.58	10.34	11.65	13.33	13.69	16.58	
B Restaurants and hotels	0.97	0.33	2.28	3.33	4.51	4.30	4.74	5.51	6.74	7.14	8.36	
7 Transport, storage and communication	7.21	15.56	27.25	36.14	42.71	44.43	56.09	61.89	80.53	80.08	101.94	
A Transport and storage	6.66	13.69	24.24	31.23	37.04	37.54	48.40	52.85	69.94	65.70	82.10	
B Communication	0.55	1.87	3.01	4.91	5.67	6.89	7.68	9.04	10.59	14.38	19.84	
8 Finance, insurance, real estate and business services	8.56	22.41	33.04	41.16	49.81	52.08	64.68	74.29	88.12	104.93	120.60	
A Financial institutions	0.28	0.64	1.65	2.15	2.95	3.51	4.89	5.52	7.29	14.63	20.64	
B Insurance	...	...	...	...	...	...	...	...	...	...	...	
C Real estate and business services	8.28	21.77	31.39	39.01	46.86	48.57	59.79	68.77	80.83	90.30	99.96	
Real estate except dwellings	0.02	0.06	0.07	0.07	0.08	0.02	0.01	0.01	0.03	0.03	0.03	
Dwellings [a]	8.26	21.71	31.32	38.94	46.78	48.55	59.77	68.76	80.80	90.27	99.93	
9 Community, social and personal services	0.90	2.35	5.52	7.10	8.35	8.58	10.69	13.80	16.06	16.87	19.44	
Total Industries	51.15	123.21	214.17	276.09	329.00	355.15	405.16	473.90	563.79	616.75	715.32	
Producers of Government Services	4.87	8.05	22.00	25.44	30.25	32.25	38.62	47.07	54.53	57.03	65.70	
Private Non-Profit Institutions Serving Households	...	...	...	...	...	...	...	...	...	...	...	
Total	56.02	131.26	236.17	301.53	359.25	387.40	443.78	520.97	618.32	673.78	781.02	

a) Item 'Dwellings' includes residential house construction of general government.

2.12 Gross Fixed Capital Formation by Kind of Activity of Owner, ISIC Divisions, in Constant Prices

Thousand Million Indian rupees — Fiscal year beginning 1 April

At constant prices of 1980

	1970	1975	1980	1981	1982	1983	1984	1985	1986	1987	1988	1989
All Producers												
1 Agriculture, hunting, forestry and fishing	27.48	31.04	47.65	45.87	46.76	44.97	43.87	42.59	44.16	45.61	49.13	
A Agriculture and hunting	26.25	29.35	45.37	43.46	44.09	41.87	39.57	40.68	40.67	41.97	45.28	
B Forestry and logging	0.47	0.43	1.01	1.02	1.15	1.35	1.27	1.06	1.29	1.24	1.23	
C Fishing	0.76	1.26	1.27	1.39	1.52	1.67	1.83	2.00	2.20	2.40	2.62	
2 Mining and quarrying	2.12	5.92	9.52	13.56	24.52	21.20	19.82	24.70	25.41	25.20	22.22	
3 Manufacturing	30.90	52.54	49.77	59.83	59.24	71.33	73.67	77.98	82.07	85.94	91.18	
4 Electricity, gas and water	14.09	19.25	28.94	35.83	39.03	38.14	37.96	43.21	55.34	56.55	57.91	
5 Construction	2.73	2.92	5.08	6.90	7.96	6.59	6.73	5.37	6.02	5.39	5.63	
6 Wholesale and retail trade, restaurants and hotels	7.56	6.22	7.40	8.42	9.57	9.64	10.51	10.91	11.83	11.60	12.60	
A Wholesale and retail trade	...	...	5.12	5.51	5.89	6.48	7.27	7.50	7.90	7.71	8.46	
B Restaurants and hotels	...	...	2.28	2.91	3.68	3.16	3.24	3.41	3.93	3.89	4.14	
7 Transport, storage and communication	18.78	24.01	27.25	30.27	32.91	35.34	41.79	39.80	49.64	45.43	52.00	
A Transport and storage	...	...	24.24	25.83	28.25	30.04	36.33	34.14	43.53	37.48	42.09	
B Communication	1.35	2.64	3.01	4.44	4.66	5.30	5.46	5.66	6.11	7.95	9.91	
8 Finance, insurance, real estate and business services	19.05	24.08	33.04	34.13	35.36	32.65	36.31	37.80	40.12	45.22	48.68	
A Financial institutions	0.75	0.84	1.65	1.90	2.41	2.60	3.36	3.45	4.27	8.59	10.93	

India

2.12 Gross Fixed Capital Formation by Kind of Activity of Owner, ISIC Divisions, in Constant Prices
(Continued)

Thousand Million Indian rupees   Fiscal year beginning 1 April

	1970	1975	1980	1981	1982	1983	1984	1985	1986	1987	1988	1989
					At constant prices of:1980							
B Insurance	...	...	...	...	...	...	...	...	...	...	...	...
C Real estate and business services	18.30	23.24	31.39	32.23	32.95	30.05	32.95	34.35	35.85	36.63	37.75	...
Real estate except dwellings	0.05	0.09	0.07	0.06	0.06	0.01	0.01	-	-	-	-	...
Dwellings [a]	18.25	23.15	31.32	32.17	32.89	30.04	32.94	34.35	35.85	36.63	37.75	...
9 Community, social and personal services	2.54	3.48	5.52	6.13	6.38	6.00	6.82	7.90	8.57	8.41	8.86	...
Total Industries	125.25	169.46	214.17	240.94	261.73	263.48	278.58	291.41	323.16	329.35	348.21	...
Producers of Government Services	12.37	11.71	22.00	23.14	24.34	23.60	26.02	27.51	29.50	28.39	30.11	...
Private Non-Profit Institutions Serving Households	...	...	...	...	...	...	...	...	...	...	...	...
Total	137.62	181.17	236.17	264.08	286.07	287.08	304.60	318.92	352.66	357.74	378.32	...

a) Item 'Dwellings' includes residential house construction of general government.

2.17 Exports and Imports of Goods and Services, Detail

Thousand Million Indian rupees   Fiscal year beginning 1 April

	1970	1975	1980	1981	1982	1983	1984	1985	1986	1987	1988	1989
				Exports of Goods and Services								
1 Exports of merchandise, f.o.b.	14.03	41.78	65.76	77.65	91.37	101.68	119.59	115.78	133.15	163.96	...	...
2 Transport and communication	1.06	2.60	3.62	3.98	4.07	4.40	6.44	6.04	6.88	8.82	...	...
A In respect of merchandise imports	-	-	...	...	...	...	...	...	...	...	...	...
B Other	1.06	2.60	3.62	3.98	4.07	4.40	6.44	6.04	6.88	8.82	...	...
3 Insurance service charges	0.12	0.38	0.48	0.55	0.58	1.14	0.89	0.79	0.83	1.05	...	...
A In respect of merchandise imports	-	-	...	...	...	...	...	...	...	...	...	...
B Other	0.12	0.38	0.48	0.55	0.58	1.14	0.89	0.79	0.83	1.05	...	...
4 Other commodities	0.66	2.05	6.59	8.04	10.59	16.03	23.66	20.69	15.80	16.43	...	...
5 Adjustments of merchandise exports to change-of-ownership basis	1.32	-1.35	1.35	0.41	-3.34	-3.97	-2.15	-6.83	-8.63	-6.55	...	...
6 Direct purchases in the domestic market by non-residential households	0.51	2.60	12.38	11.75	12.24	11.93	9.92	13.04	17.13	19.38	...	...
7 Direct purchases in the domestic market by extraterritorial bodies	0.01	0.06	0.11	0.18	0.12	0.18	0.11	-	0.27	0.39	...	...
Total Exports of Goods and Services	17.71	48.12	90.29	102.56	115.63	131.39	158.46	149.51	165.43	203.48	...	...
				Imports of Goods and Services								
1 Imports of merchandise, c.i.f.	17.34	47.73	125.58	139.13	149.89	161.38	188.64	213.15	227.60	258.31	...	...
2 Adjustments of merchandise imports to change-of-ownership basis	-0.86	5.21	0.06	-2.78	-6.20	-2.08	-15.46	-15.06	-25.73	-32.94	...	...
3 Other transport and communication	0.65	1.67	3.40	4.55	6.23	6.17	7.33	6.65	6.57	9.89	...	...
4 Other insurance service charges	0.12	0.24	0.34	0.40	0.69	0.75	0.84	0.83	1.02	1.07	...	...
5 Other commodities	0.59	1.36	5.23	4.76	4.27	6.95	8.55	6.54	9.07	11.12	...	...
6 Direct purchases abroad by government	0.15	0.22	0.50	0.65	0.74	1.30	1.26	1.45	1.65	2.02	...	...
7 Direct purchases abroad by resident households	0.17	0.21	0.85	1.38	1.74	2.28	3.68	3.98	3.41	4.67	...	...
Total Imports of Goods and Services	18.16	56.64	135.96	148.09	157.36	176.75	194.84	217.54	223.59	254.14	...	...
Balance of Goods and Services	-0.45	-8.52	-45.67	-45.53	-41.73	-45.36	-36.38	-68.03	-58.16	-50.66	...	...
Total Imports and Balance of Goods and Services	17.71	48.12	90.29	102.56	115.63	131.39	158.46	149.51	165.43	203.48	...	...

4.1 Derivation of Value Added by Kind of Activity, in Current Prices

Thousand Million Indian rupees   Fiscal year beginning 1 April

	1980			1981			1982			1983		
	Gross Output	Intermediate Consumption	Value Added	Gross Output	Intermediate Consumption	Value Added	Gross Output	Intermediate Consumption	Value Added	Gross Output	Intermediate Consumption	Value Added
					All Producers							
1 Agriculture, hunting, forestry and fishing	613.02	156.65	464.79	688.01	173.75	523.69	725.56	180.30	556.22	860.19	204.97	667.66
A Agriculture and hunting	...	...	424.66	...	...	477.36	...	...	505.27	...	...	613.18
B Forestry and logging	...	...	30.92	...	...	36.25	...	...	39.21	...	...	40.00
C Fishing	...	...	9.21	...	...	10.08	...	...	11.74	...	...	14.48
2 Mining and quarrying [a]	24.82	5.95	18.87	44.84	9.44	35.40	56.25	12.30	43.95	65.79	16.70	49.09

845

India

4.1 Derivation of Value Added by Kind of Activity, in Current Prices (Continued)

Thousand Million Indian rupees

	1980 Gross Output	1980 Intermediate Consumption	1980 Value Added	1981 Gross Output	1981 Intermediate Consumption	1981 Value Added	1982 Gross Output	1982 Intermediate Consumption	1982 Value Added	Fiscal year beginning 1 April 1983 Gross Output	1983 Intermediate Consumption	1983 Value Added
A Coal mining	...	...	14.58	...	...	10.37	...	...	12.38	14.60	...	14.11
B Crude petroleum and natural gas production	...	...	4.03	...	...	3.48	...	...	1.54	29.61	3.31	26.30
C Metal ore mining	...	...	2.66	...	...	3.08	...	...	0.74	4.37	1.00	3.37
D Other mining	...	...	3.55	...	...	2.97	...	...	0.62	6.20	0.89	5.31
3 Manufacturing	...	...	216.44	...	...	252.60	...	...	280.73	...	...	330.45
A Manufacture of food, beverages and tobacco	...	...	18.99	...	...	22.44	...	...	24.54	...	...	34.77
B Textile, wearing apparel and leather industries	...	...	55.01	...	...	55.78	...	...	58.82	...	...	66.94
C Manufacture of wood and wood products, including furniture	...	...	9.73	...	...	11.33	...	...	10.78	...	...	12.98
D Manufacture of paper and paper products, printing and publishing	...	...	7.22	...	...	8.20	...	...	8.31	...	...	10.52
E Manufacture of chemicals and chemical products, petroleum, coal, rubber and plastic products	...	...	26.71	...	...	34.09	...	...	38.89	...	...	47.78
F Manufacture of non-metallic mineral products, except products of petroleum and coal	...	...	7.50	...	...	9.12	...	...	12.66	...	...	15.21
G Basic metal industries	...	...	16.41	...	...	21.14	...	...	22.18	...	...	25.67
H Manufacture of fabricated metal products, machinery and equipment	...	...	50.96	...	...	60.58	...	...	71.22	...	...	80.86
I Other manufacturing industries	...	...	23.91	...	...	29.92	...	...	33.33	...	...	35.72
4 Electricity, gas and water	...	...	19.89	...	...	23.06	...	...	27.20	...	...	33.62
A Electricity, gas and steam	...	...	17.93	...	...	20.68	...	...	24.39	...	...	30.29
B Water works and supply	...	...	1.96	...	...	2.38	...	...	2.81	...	...	3.33
5 Construction	160.38	99.24	61.14	193.48	123.59	69.89	218.01	137.22	80.79	249.56	155.35	94.21
6 Wholesale and retail trade, restaurants and hotels	...	...	147.13	...	...	180.34	...	...	193.71	...	...	229.90
A Wholesale and retail trade	...	...	138.39	...	...	169.73	...	...	187.73	...	...	216.44
B Restaurants and hotels	...	...	8.74	...	...	10.61	...	...	11.98	...	...	13.46
7 Transport, storage and communication	...	...	57.24	...	...	70.40	...	...	85.98	...	...	102.81
A Transport and storage	...	...	49.26	...	...	61.21	...	...	74.81	...	...	89.68
B Communication	...	...	7.98	...	...	9.19	...	...	11.17	...	...	13.13
8 Finance, insurance, real estate and business services	...	...	108.41	...	...	126.11	...	...	142.65	...	...	155.91
A Financial institutions	...	...	26.10	...	...	35.30	...	...	42.37	...	...	45.40
B Insurance	...	...	8.48	...	...	10.34	...	...	11.78	...	...	14.23
C Real estate and business services	...	...	73.83	...	...	80.47	...	...	88.50	...	...	96.28
Real estate, except dwellings [b]	...	...	2.00	...	...	2.25	...	...	2.53	...	...	4.02
Dwellings	...	...	71.83	...	...	78.22	...	...	85.97	...	...	92.26
9 Community, social and personal services	...	...	70.41	...	...	80.66	...	...	91.67	...	...	103.88
A Sanitary and similar services	...	...	2.89	...	...	3.26	...	...	3.77	...	...	4.39
B Social and related community services [c]	...	...	67.52	...	...	77.40	...	...	87.90	...	...	99.49
C Recreational and cultural services	...	...	...	...	...	...	...	...	...	...	...	...
D Personal and household services	...	...	...	...	...	...	...	...	...	...	...	...
Total, Industries	...	...	1164.32	...	...	1362.15	...	...	1508.90	...	...	1767.53
Producers of Government Services	...	...	57.94	...	...	66.61	...	...	79.61	...	...	92.38
Other Producers	...	...	1222.26	...	...	1428.76	...	...	1588.51	...	...	1859.91
Total [d]												
Less: Imputed bank service charge [e]	...	...	...	...	...	...	...	...	...	...	...	...
Import duties	...	...	...	...	...	...	...	...	...	...	...	...
Value added tax	...	...	...	...	...	...	...	...	...	...	...	...
Other adjustments [f]	...	...	135.86	...	...	165.44	...	...	187.37	...	...	208.66
Total	...	...	1358.12	...	...	1594.20	...	...	1775.88	...	...	2068.57
of which General Government:												
1 Agriculture, hunting, forestry and fishing	...	...	12.62	...	...	14.61	...	...	16.86	...	...	18.66

India

4.1 Derivation of Value Added by Kind of Activity, in Current Prices (Continued)

Thousand Million Indian rupees — Fiscal year beginning 1 April

	1980 Gross Output	1980 Intermediate Consumption	1980 Value Added	1981 Gross Output	1981 Intermediate Consumption	1981 Value Added	1982 Gross Output	1982 Intermediate Consumption	1982 Value Added	1983 Gross Output	1983 Intermediate Consumption	1983 Value Added
2 Mining and quarrying	...	...	...	...	...	...	...	...	...	...	...	...
3 Manufacturing	...	...	0.09	...	...	−0.22	...	...	1.54	...	...	1.81
4 Electricity, gas and water	...	...	2.31	...	...	2.50	...	...	2.60	...	...	2.29
5 Construction	...	...	8.66	...	...	9.03	...	...	10.38	...	...	12.05
6 Wholesale and retail trade, restaurants and hotels	...	...	0.15	...	...	0.20	...	...	0.11	...	...	0.27
7 Transport and communication	...	...	0.94	...	...	0.79	...	...	1.14	...	...	1.49
8 Finance, insurance, real estate and business services	...	...	0.55	...	...	0.82	...	...	0.97	...	...	1.14
9 Community, social and personal services	...	...	26.92	...	...	31.09	...	...	37.05	...	...	44.35
Statistical discrepancy	-	-	-	-	-	-	-	-	-	-	-	-
Total, Industries of General Government	...	...	52.34	...	...	58.82	...	...	70.65	...	...	82.06
Producers of Government Services	...	...	57.94	...	...	66.61	...	...	79.61	...	...	92.38
Total, General Government	...	...	110.28	...	...	125.43	...	...	150.26	...	...	174.44

	1984 Gross Output	1984 Intermediate Consumption	1984 Value Added	1985 Gross Output	1985 Intermediate Consumption	1985 Value Added	1986 Gross Output	1986 Intermediate Consumption	1986 Value Added	1987 Gross Output	1987 Intermediate Consumption	1987 Value Added
All Producers												
1 Agriculture, hunting, forestry and fishing	916.95	219.63	712.35	984.59	238.59	764.81	1054.30	237.84	815.74	1174.37	281.47	916.55
A Agriculture and hunting	...	...	651.81	...	...	699.64	...	...	744.05	...	...	837.27
B Forestry and logging	...	...	42.94	...	...	44.87	...	...	48.17	...	...	51.02
C Fishing	...	...	17.60	...	...	20.30	...	...	23.52	...	...	28.26
2 Mining and quarrying a	78.25	23.67	54.58	83.98	25.79	58.19	98.55	30.59	67.96	105.43	34.30	71.13
A Coal mining	31.58	17.54	14.04	34.46	19.15	15.31	39.52	22.00	17.52	43.13	24.03	19.10
B Crude petroleum and natural gas production	34.36	3.94	30.42	36.09	4.34	31.75	43.47	5.53	37.94	45.65	7.00	38.65
C Metal ore mining	5.42	1.20	4.22	6.09	1.31	4.78	6.89	1.44	5.45	7.46	1.56	5.90
D Other mining	6.89	0.99	5.90	7.34	0.99	6.35	8.67	1.62	7.05	9.19	1.71	7.48
3 Manufacturing	...	...	372.43	...	...	429.77	...	...	476.87	...	...	541.60
A Manufacture of food, beverages and tobacco	...	...	35.35	...	...	39.09	...	...	43.85	...	...	44.98
B Textile, wearing apparel and leather industries	...	...	76.78	...	...	82.95	...	...	87.34	...	...	104.12
C Manufacture of wood and wood products, including furniture	...	...	11.56	...	...	11.88	...	...	11.51	...	...	10.02
D Manufacture of paper and paper products, printing and publishing	...	...	13.63	...	...	14.22	...	...	16.87	...	...	17.87
E Manufacture of chemicals and chemical products, coal, rubber and plastic products	...	...	53.40	...	...	66.17	...	...	77.05	...	...	90.67
F Manufacture of non-metallic mineral products, except products of petroleum and coal	...	...	18.76	...	...	20.56	...	...	20.46	...	...	22.51
G Basic metal industries	...	...	27.64	...	...	34.27	...	...	34.49	...	...	39.67
H Manufacture of fabricated metal products, machinery and equipment	...	...	95.24	...	...	107.64	...	...	118.91	...	...	136.81
I Other manufacturing industries	...	...	40.07	...	...	52.99	...	...	66.39	...	...	74.95
4 Electricity, gas and water	...	...	40.52	...	...	48.94	...	...	55.60	...	...	62.68
A Electricity, gas and steam	...	...	36.53	...	...	44.08	...	...	50.07	...	...	56.06
B Water works and supply	...	...	3.99	...	...	4.86	...	...	5.53	...	...	6.62
5 Construction	289.25	178.28	110.97	338.27	210.32	127.95	380.32	231.22	149.10	421.31	250.99	170.32
6 Wholesale and retail trade, restaurants and hotels	...	...	266.90	...	...	310.47	...	...	343.22	...	...	372.25
A Wholesale and retail trade	...	...	251.58	...	...	293.11	...	...	324.10	...	...	351.34
B Restaurants and hotels	...	...	15.32	...	...	17.36	...	...	19.12	...	...	20.91
7 Transport, storage and communication	...	...	118.73	...	...	140.98	...	...	165.51	...	...	199.22
A Transport and storage	...	...	104.10	...	...	124.96	...	...	145.70	...	...	171.25
B Communication	...	...	14.63	...	...	16.02	...	...	19.81	...	...	27.97
8 Finance, insurance, real estate and business services	...	...	175.95	...	...	198.81	...	...	222.99	...	...	248.76
A Financial institutions	...	...	54.59	...	...	63.38	...	...	73.56	...	...	84.64

4.1 Derivation of Value Added by Kind of Activity, in Current Prices
(Continued)

Thousand Million Indian rupees | Fiscal year beginning 1 April

	1984			1985			1986			1987		
	Gross Output	Intermediate Consumption	Value Added	Gross Output	Intermediate Consumption	Value Added	Gross Output	Intermediate Consumption	Value Added	Gross Output	Intermediate Consumption	Value Added
B Insurance	...	...	16.22	...	...	19.27	...	...	22.99	...	...	26.77
C Real estate and business services	...	...	105.14	...	...	116.16	...	...	126.44	...	...	137.35
Real estate, except dwellings [b]	...	...	4.73	...	...	5.66	...	...	6.97	...	...	8.14
Dwellings	...	...	100.41	...	...	110.50	...	...	119.47	...	...	129.21
9 Community, social and personal services	...	...	117.90	...	...	136.56	...	...	158.10	...	...	182.28
A Sanitary and similar services	...	...	4.70	...	...	5.14	...	...	5.92	...	...	6.51
B Social and related community services [c]	...	...	113.20	...	...	131.42	...	...	152.18	...	...	175.77
C Recreational and cultural services	...	...	...	...	...	...	...	...	...	...	...	...
D Personal and household services	...	...	...	...	...	...	...	...	...	...	...	...
Total, Industries	...	...	1970.33	...	...	2216.48	...	...	2455.09	...	...	2764.79
Producers of Government Services	...	...	108.36	...	...	125.11	...	...	149.33	...	...	179.29
Other Producers	...	...	...	...	...	...	...	...	...	...	...	...
Total [d]	...	...	2078.69	...	...	2341.59	...	...	2604.42	...	...	2944.08
Less: Imputed bank service charge [e]	...	...	...	...	...	...	...	...	...	...	...	...
Import duties	...	...	...	...	...	...	...	...	...	...	...	...
Value added tax	...	...	...	...	...	...	...	...	...	...	...	...
Other adjustments [f]	...	...	228.10	...	...	284.44	...	...	329.19	...	...	381.45
Total	...	...	2306.79	...	...	2626.03	...	...	2933.61	...	...	3325.53
of which General Government:												
1 Agriculture, hunting, forestry and fishing	...	...	21.03	...	...	24.78	...	...	28.88	...	...	31.86
2 Mining and quarrying	...	...	-	...	...	-	...	...	-	...	...	-
3 Manufacturing	...	...	3.80	...	...	10.42	...	...	14.79	...	...	19.58
4 Electricity, gas and water	...	...	3.47	...	...	5.62	...	...	5.88	...	...	6.25
5 Construction	...	...	14.07	...	...	18.49	...	...	18.81	...	...	22.09
6 Wholesale and retail trade, restaurants and hotels	...	...	0.67	...	...	0.34	...	...	0.31	...	...	0.64
7 Transport and communication	...	...	1.73	...	...	1.29	...	...	1.27	...	...	1.32
8 Finance, insurance, real estate and business services	...	...	1.30	...	...	1.57	...	...	2.07	...	...	2.75
9 Community, social and personal services	...	...	50.20	...	...	58.17	...	...	65.01	...	...	78.44
Statistical discrepancy	...	...	-	...	...	-	...	...	-	...	...	-
Total, Industries of General Government	...	...	96.27	...	...	120.68	...	...	137.02	...	...	162.93
Producers of Government Services	...	...	108.36	...	...	125.11	...	...	149.33	...	...	179.29
Total, General Government	...	...	204.63	...	...	245.79	...	...	286.35	...	...	342.22

	1988		
	Gross Output	Intermediate Consumption	Value Added
All Producers			
1 Agriculture, hunting, forestry and fishing	...	...	1137.41
A Agriculture and hunting	...	...	1051.91
B Forestry and logging	...	...	54.41
C Fishing	...	...	31.09
2 Mining and quarrying [a]	120.33	40.51	79.82
A Coal mining	52.77	29.40	23.37
B Crude petroleum and natural gas production	48.81	7.41	41.40
C Metal ore mining	8.66	1.81	6.85
D Other mining	10.09	1.89	8.20

India

4.1 Derivation of Value Added by Kind of Activity, in Current Prices
(Continued)

Thousand Million Indian rupees   Fiscal year beginning 1 April

		1988		
		Gross Output	Intermediate Consumption	Value Added
3	Manufacturing	...	...	629.91
	A Manufacture of food, beverages and tobacco	...	...	52.37
	B Textile, wearing apparel and leather industries	...	...	120.85
	C Manufacture of wood and wood products, including furniture	...	...	11.58
	D Manufacture of paper and paper products, printing and publishing	...	...	20.80
	E Manufacture of chemicals and chemical petroleum, coal, rubber and plastic products	...	...	105.81
	F Manufacture of non-metallic mineral products, except products of petroleum and coal	...	...	26.20
	G Basic metal industries	...	...	46.28
	H Manufacture of fabricated metal products, machinery and equipment	...	...	159.17
	I Other manufacturing industries	...	...	86.85
4	Electricity, gas and water	...	...	71.75
	A Electricity, gas and steam	...	...	64.26
	B Water works and supply	...	...	7.49
5	Construction	489.51	290.95	198.56
6	Wholesale and retail trade, restaurants and hotels	...	...	437.14
	A Wholesale and retail trade	...	...	412.45
	B Restaurants and hotels	...	...	24.69
7	Transport, storage and communication	...	...	240.44
	A Transport and storage	...	...	202.75
	B Communication	...	...	37.69
8	Finance, insurance, real estate and business services	...	...	282.94
	A Financial institutions	...	...	...
	B Insurance	...	...	...
	C Real estate and business services	...	...	150.67
	Real estate, except dwellings [b]	...	...	...
	Dwellings	...	...	...
9	Community, social and personal services	...	...	205.88
	A Sanitary and similar services	...	...	...
	B Social and related community services [c]	...	...	...
	C Recreational and cultural services	...	...	...
	D Personal and household services	...	...	...
	Total, Industries	...	...	3283.85
	Producers of Government Services	...	...	205.11
	Other Producers	...	...	...
	Total [d]	...	...	3488.96
	Less: Imputed bank service charge [e]	...	...	...
	Import duties	...	...	...
	Value added tax	...	...	...
	Other adjustments [f]	...	...	422.62
	Total	...	...	3911.58

of which General Government:

1	Agriculture, hunting, forestry and fishing	...	...	36.15
2	Mining and quarrying	...	...	-
3	Manufacturing	...	...	20.97
4	Electricity, gas and water	...	...	8.69

849

India

4.1 Derivation of Value Added by Kind of Activity, in Current Prices
(Continued)

Thousand Million Indian rupees — Fiscal year beginning 1 April

	1988 Gross Output	Intermediate Consumption	Value Added
5 Construction	...	...	24.41
6 Wholesale and retail trade, restaurants and hotels	...	...	0.42
7 Transport and communication	...	...	1.55
8 Finance, insurance, real estate and business services	...	...	3.10
9 Community, social and personal services	...	...	86.31
Statistical discrepancy	...	...	-
Total, Industries of General Government	...	...	181.60
Producers of Government Services	...	...	205.11
Total, General Government	...	...	386.71

a) Estimates in columns 3 also include value added of the operation of irrigation system for which the gross output and intermediate consumption are not separately compiled.
b) Item 'Real estate, except dwellings' includes also business services other than legal services.
c) Item 'Social and related community services' includes legal services and the rest of the community, social and personal services other than sanitary services but excluding repair services which are included under manufacturing.
d) Gross domestic product in factor values.
e) Imputed bank service charges are adjusted in the respective activity.
f) Item 'Other adjustments' refers to indirect taxes net of subsidies.

4.2 Derivation of Value Added by Kind of Activity, in Constant Prices

Thousand Million Indian rupees — Fiscal year beginning 1 April

At constant prices of 1980

All Producers

	1980 Gross Output	1980 Intermediate Consumption	1980 Value Added	1981 Gross Output	1981 Intermediate Consumption	1981 Value Added	1982 Gross Output	1982 Intermediate Consumption	1982 Value Added	1983 Gross Output	1983 Intermediate Consumption	1983 Value Added
1 Agriculture, hunting, forestry and fishing	613.02	156.66	464.79	645.74	163.05	491.39	639.54	165.05	483.58	695.24	169.43	535.25
A Agriculture and hunting	...	...	424.66	...	...	451.45	...	...	445.70	...	...	497.53
B Forestry and logging	...	...	30.92	...	...	30.88	...	...	28.52	...	...	26.44
C Fishing	...	...	9.21	...	...	9.36	...	...	9.36	...	...	11.28
2 Mining and quarrying a	24.82	5.95	18.87	28.68	7.27	21.41	31.83	7.96	23.87	34.79	10.28	24.51
A Coal mining	14.58	4.21	10.37	16.02	5.54	10.48	...	...	10.95	17.64	7.91	9.73
B Crude petroleum and natural gas production	4.03	0.55	3.48	6.20	0.54	5.66	...	...	7.30	10.42	1.18	9.24
C Metal ore mining	2.66	0.61	2.05	2.68	0.63	2.05	...	...	2.20	2.71	0.61	2.10
D Other mining	3.55	0.58	2.97	3.78	0.56	3.22	...	...	3.42	4.02	0.58	3.44
3 Manufacturing	...	...	216.44	...	...	233.82	...	...	249.08	...	...	273.77
A Manufacture of food, beverages and tobacco	...	...	18.99	...	...	22.43	...	...	25.95	...	...	30.40
B Textile, wearing apparel and leather industries	...	...	55.01	...	...	54.69	...	...	55.29	...	...	58.63
C Manufacture of wood and wood products, including furniture	...	...	9.73	...	...	9.91	...	...	8.96	...	...	9.75
D Manufacture of paper and paper products, printing and publishing	...	...	7.22	...	...	7.61	...	...	7.25	...	...	8.46
E Manufacture of chemicals and chemical products, petroleum, coal, rubber and plastic products	...	...	26.71	...	...	30.27	...	...	33.77	...	...	39.77
F Manufacture of non-metallic mineral products, except products of petroleum and coal	...	...	7.50	...	...	8.16	...	...	9.44	...	...	10.48
G Basic metal industries	...	...	16.41	...	...	17.85	...	...	16.57	...	...	17.81
H Manufacture of fabricated metal products, machinery and equipment	...	...	50.96	...	...	54.76	...	...	61.36	...	...	67.01
I Other manufacturing industries	...	...	23.91	...	...	28.14	...	...	30.49	...	...	31.46
4 Electricity, gas and water	...	...	19.89	...	...	21.72	...	...	23.12	...	...	25.88
A Electricity, gas and steam	...	...	17.93	...	...	19.57	...	...	20.72	...	...	23.39
B Water works and supply	...	...	1.96	...	...	2.15	...	...	2.40	...	...	2.49
5 Construction	160.38	99.24	61.14	163.66	99.20	64.46	154.56	93.08	61.48	159.57	93.81	65.76
6 Wholesale and retail trade, restaurants and hotels	147.13	...	156.71	...	...	147.40	...	...	165.46	...	...	174.17
A Wholesale and retail trade	138.39	...	...	...	...	147.40	...	...	155.30	...	...	163.71
B Restaurants and hotels	8.74	...	...	9.31	...	...	10.16	...	...	10.46
7 Transport, storage and communication	57.24	...	...	60.13	...	...	62.80	...	...	66.92
A Transport and storage	49.26	...	...	51.55	...	...	53.77	...	...	57.31

850

India

4.2 Derivation of Value Added by Kind of Activity, in Constant Prices
(Continued)

Thousand Million Indian rupees

Fiscal year beginning 1 April

	1980			1981			1982			1983		
	Gross Output	Intermediate Consumption	Value Added	Gross Output	Intermediate Consumption	Value Added	Gross Output	Intermediate Consumption	Value Added	Gross Output	Intermediate Consumption	Value Added
At constant prices of:1980												
B Communication	...	...	7.98	...	...	8.58	...	...	9.03	...	...	9.61
8 Finance, insurance, real estate and business services	...	...	108.41	...	...	113.54	...	...	122.15	...	...	128.59
A Financial institutions	...	...	26.10	...	...	27.99	...	...	33.09	...	...	34.90
B Insurance	...	...	8.48	...	...	9.21	...	...	10.09	...	...	11.03
C Real estate and business services	...	...	73.83	...	...	76.34	...	...	78.97	...	...	82.66
Real estate, except dwellings	...	...	2.00	...	...	2.16	...	...	2.36	...	...	3.52
Dwellings	...	...	71.83	...	...	74.18	...	...	76.61	...	...	79.14
9 Community, social and personal services	...	...	70.41	...	...	73.56	...	...	77.66	...	...	80.50
A Sanitary and similar services	...	...	2.89	...	...	2.88	...	...	3.02	...	...	3.18
B Social and related community services [b]	...	...	67.52	...	...	70.68	...	...	74.64	...	...	77.32
C Recreational and cultural services	...	...	...	...	...	...	...	...	...	...	...	...
D Personal and household services	...	...	...	...	...	...	...	...	...	...	...	...
Total, Industries	...	...	1164.32	...	...	1236.74	...	...	1269.21	...	...	1375.35
Producers of Government Services	...	...	57.94	...	...	59.26	...	...	65.48	...	...	67.75
Other Producers	...	...	...	...	...	...	...	...	...	...	...	...
Total [c]	...	...	1222.26	...	...	1296.00	...	...	1334.69	...	...	1443.10
Less: Imputed bank service charge [d]	...	...	...	...	...	...	...	...	...	...	...	...
Import duties	...	...	...	...	...	...	...	...	...	...	...	...
Value added tax	...	...	...	...	...	...	...	...	...	...	...	...
Other adjustments [e]	...	...	135.86	...	...	150.11	...	...	164.64	...	...	166.82
Total	...	...	1358.12	...	...	1446.11	...	...	1499.33	...	...	1609.92
of which General Government:												
1 Agriculture, hunting, forestry and fishing	...	...	12.62	...	...	13.05	...	...	13.39	...	...	13.56
2 Mining and quarrying	...	...	-	...	...	-	...	...	-	...	...	-
3 Manufacturing	...	...	0.09	...	...	-0.18	...	...	1.18	...	...	1.26
4 Electricity, gas and water	...	...	2.31	...	...	2.31	...	...	2.15	...	...	1.72
5 Construction	...	...	8.66	...	...	8.03	...	...	8.58	...	...	8.89
6 Wholesale and retail trade, restaurants and hotels	...	...	0.15	...	...	0.16	...	...	0.08	...	...	0.21
7 Transport and communication	...	...	0.94	...	...	0.71	...	...	0.86	...	...	1.00
8 Finance, insurance, real estate and business services	...	...	0.65	...	...	0.67	...	...	0.68	...	...	0.72
9 Community, social and personal services	...	...	26.92	...	...	27.64	...	...	30.52	...	...	32.51
Statistical discrepancy	...	...	-	...	...	-	...	...	-	...	...	-
Total, Industries of General Government	...	...	52.34	...	...	52.39	...	...	57.44	...	...	59.87
Producers of Government Services	...	...	57.94	...	...	59.26	...	...	65.48	...	...	67.75
Total, General Government	...	...	110.28	...	...	111.65	...	...	122.92	...	...	127.62

	1984			1985			1986			1987		
	Gross Output	Intermediate Consumption	Value Added	Gross Output	Intermediate Consumption	Value Added	Gross Output	Intermediate Consumption	Value Added	Gross Output	Intermediate Consumption	Value Added
At constant prices of:1980												
All Producers												
1 Agriculture, hunting, forestry and fishing	701.37	175.55	535.44	706.57	179.37	536.98	702.08	184.17	527.82	700.47	180.01	530.53
A Agriculture and hunting	...	...	497.02	...	...	498.55	...	...	489.95	...	...	493.34
B Forestry and logging	...	...	26.27	...	...	26.27	...	...	25.37	...	...	24.28
C Fishing	...	...	12.15	...	...	12.16	...	...	12.50	...	...	12.91
2 Mining and quarrying [a]	37.91	13.05	24.86	39.96	13.73	26.23	44.93	15.15	29.78	48.15	17.04	31.11
A Coal mining	18.78	10.43	8.35	19.55	10.87	8.68	20.92	11.65	9.27	23.49	13.08	10.41
B Crude petroleum and natural gas production	11.97	1.39	10.58	12.82	1.55	11.27	14.48	1.86	12.62	15.11	2.32	12.79
C Metal ore mining	3.03	0.65	2.38	3.21	0.68	2.53	3.80	0.91	2.89	3.75	0.90	2.85
D Other mining	4.13	0.58	3.55	4.38	0.63	3.75	5.73	0.73	5.00	5.80	0.74	5.06

India

4.2 Derivation of Value Added by Kind of Activity, in Constant Prices (Continued)

Thousand Million Indian rupees

At constant prices of 1980

	1984 Gross Output	1984 Intermediate Consumption	1984 Value Added	1985 Gross Output	1985 Intermediate Consumption	1985 Value Added	1986 Gross Output	1986 Intermediate Consumption	1986 Value Added	1987 Gross Output	1987 Intermediate Consumption	1987 Value Added
3 Manufacturing	...	...	291.53	...	...	314.19	...	...	338.19	...	...	358.57
A Manufacture of food, beverages and tobacco	...	...	29.86	...	...	30.56	...	...	30.59	...	...	30.22
B Textile, wearing apparel and leather industries	...	...	61.43	...	...	66.99	...	...	73.03	...	...	72.55
C Manufacture of wood and wood products, including furniture	...	...	8.30	...	...	8.23	...	...	7.78	...	...	6.70
D Manufacture of paper and paper products, printing and publishing	...	...	9.80	...	...	9.84	...	...	11.15	...	...	11.49
E Manufacture of chemicals and chemical products, coal, rubber and plastic products	...	...	42.86	...	...	48.94	...	...	54.42	...	...	60.88
F Manufacture of non-metallic mineral products, except products of petroleum and coal	...	...	12.15	...	...	12.72	...	...	12.64	...	...	13.70
G Basic metal industries	...	...	18.14	...	...	19.79	...	...	19.80	...	...	21.30
H Manufacture of fabricated metal products, machinery and equipment	...	...	75.37	...	...	76.35	...	...	80.29	...	...	87.70
I Other manufacturing industries	...	...	33.62	...	...	40.77	...	...	48.49	...	...	54.03
4 Electricity, gas and water	...	...	28.63	...	...	30.99	...	...	34.19	...	...	37.39
A Electricity, gas and steam	...	...	25.92	...	...	28.06	...	...	31.10	...	...	34.00
B Water works and supply	...	...	2.71	...	...	2.93	...	...	3.09	...	...	3.39
5 Construction	...	...	68.28	...	...	71.01	...	...	73.87	...	...	75.25
	161.92	93.64		171.96	100.95		173.39	99.52		176.02	100.77	
6 Wholesale and retail trade, restaurants and hotels	...	...	181.73	...	...	196.48	...	...	208.05	...	...	215.67
A Wholesale and retail trade	...	...	170.83	...	...	184.98	...	...	195.93	...	...	203.05
B Restaurants and hotels	...	...	10.90	...	...	11.50	...	...	12.12	...	...	12.62
7 Transport, storage and communication	...	...	73.02	...	...	79.51	...	...	84.93	...	...	92.32
A Transport and storage	...	...	62.55	...	...	68.76	...	...	73.45	...	...	80.11
B Communication	...	...	10.47	...	...	10.75	...	...	11.48	...	...	12.21
8 Finance, insurance, real estate and business services	...	...	137.14	...	...	147.08	...	...	157.91	...	...	167.06
A Financial institutions	...	...	40.26	...	...	45.97	...	...	52.10	...	...	57.68
B Insurance	...	...	11.27	...	...	12.31	...	...	13.57	...	...	13.75
C Real estate and business services	...	...	85.61	...	...	88.80	...	...	92.24	...	...	95.63
Real estate, except dwellings	...	...	3.85	...	...	4.32	...	...	4.94	...	...	5.40
Dwellings	...	...	81.76	...	...	84.48	...	...	87.30	...	...	90.23
9 Community, social and personal services	...	...	84.57	...	...	90.85	...	...	96.44	...	...	102.33
A Sanitary and similar services	...	...	3.19	...	...	3.20	...	...	3.21	...	...	3.33
B Social and related community services b	...	...	81.38	...	...	87.65	...	...	93.23	...	...	99.00
C Recreational and cultural services	...	...	...	...	...	...	...	...	...	...	...	...
D Personal and household services	...	...	...	...	...	...	...	...	...	...	...	...
Total, Industries	...	...	1425.20	...	...	1493.32	...	...	1551.17	...	...	1610.23
Producers of Government Services	...	...	74.46	...	...	91.80	...	...	88.07	...	...	96.93
Other Producers	...	...	...	...	...	...	...	...	...	...	...	...
Total c	...	...	1499.66	...	...	1573.48	...	...	1639.24	...	...	1707.16
Less: Imputed bank service charge d	...	...	...	...	...	...	...	...	...	...	...	...
Import duties	...	...	...	...	...	...	...	...	...	...	...	...
Value added tax	...	...	...	...	...	...	...	...	...	...	...	...
Other adjustments e	...	...	170.56	...	...	200.82	...	...	219.83	...	...	236.37
Total	...	...	1670.22	...	...	1774.30	...	...	1859.07	...	...	1943.53

of which General Government:

1 Agriculture, hunting, forestry and fishing	...	...	13.28	...	...	13.69	...	...	13.83	...	...	13.98
2 Mining and quarrying	...	...	2.37	...	...	-	...	...	-	...	...	-
3 Manufacturing	...	...	2.37	...	...	5.80	...	...	8.08	...	...	9.82
4 Electricity, gas and water	...	...	-2.39	...	...	3.31	...	...	3.18	...	...	3.12

852

India

4.2 Derivation of Value Added by Kind of Activity, in Constant Prices
(Continued)

Thousand Million Indian rupees

Fiscal year beginning 1 April

	1984			1985			1986			1987		
	Gross Output	Intermediate Consumption	Value Added	Gross Output	Intermediate Consumption	Value Added	Gross Output	Intermediate Consumption	Value Added	Gross Output	Intermediate Consumption	Value Added
					At constant prices of:1980							
5 Construction	...	...	9.75	...	...	12.00	...	...	11.25	...	...	12.12
6 Wholesale and retail trade, restaurants and hotels	...	...	0.44	...	...	0.21	...	...	0.16	...	...	0.35
7 Transport and communication	...	...	1.11	...	...	0.77	...	...	0.69	...	...	0.65
8 Finance, insurance, real estate and business services	...	...	0.76	...	...	0.84	...	...	0.87	...	...	0.92
9 Community, social and personal services	...	...	34.54	...	...	37.47	...	...	38.52	...	...	42.60
Statistical discrepancy			-			-			-			-
Total, Industries of General Government	...	...	64.64	...	...	74.09	...	...	76.58	...	...	83.56
Producers of Government Services	...	...	74.46	...	...	80.16	...	...	88.07	...	...	96.93
Total, General Government	...	...	139.10	...	...	154.25	...	...	164.65	...	...	180.49

	1988		
	Gross Output	Intermediate Consumption	Value Added

At constant prices of:1980

All Producers

	Gross Output	Intermediate Consumption	Value Added
1 Agriculture, hunting, forestry and fishing	...	...	622.77
A Agriculture and hunting	...	...	584.93
B Forestry and logging	...	...	23.90
C Fishing	...	...	13.94
2 Mining and quarrying a	51.90	18.28	33.62
A Coal mining	25.16	14.01	11.15
B Crude petroleum and natural gas production	16.41	2.50	13.91
C Metal ore mining	4.00	0.96	3.04
D Other mining	6.33	0.81	5.52
3 Manufacturing	...	...	388.08
A Manufacture of food, beverages and tobacco	...	...	34.09
B Textile, wearing apparel and leather industries	...	...	78.42
C Manufacture of wood and wood products, including furniture	...	...	8.61
D Manufacture of paper and paper products, printing and publishing	...	...	12.51
E Manufacture of chemicals and chemical petroleum, coal, rubber and plastic products	...	...	65.59
F Manufacture of non-metallic mineral products, except products of petroleum and coal	...	...	13.82
G Basic metal industries	...	...	22.98
H Manufacture of fabricated metal products, machinery and equipment	...	...	95.33
I Other manufacturing industries	...	...	56.73
4 Electricity, gas and water	...	...	40.64
A Electricity, gas and steam	...	...	37.10
B Water works and supply	...	...	3.54
5 Construction	188.75	110.13	78.62
6 Wholesale and retail trade, restaurants and hotels	...	...	232.46
A Wholesale and retail trade	...	...	218.83
B Restaurants and hotels	...	...	13.63
7 Transport, storage and communication	...	...	98.94
A Transport and storage	...	...	86.06
B Communication	...	...	12.88
8 Finance, insurance, real estate and business services	...	...	179.25
A Financial institutions	...	...	...

853

India

4.2 Derivation of Value Added by Kind of Activity, in Constant Prices
(Continued)

Thousand Million Indian rupees

Fiscal year beginning 1 April

	1988		
	Gross Output	Intermediate Consumption	Value Added
	At constant prices of: 1980		
B Insurance	...	...	...
C Real estate and business services	...	...	...
Real estate, except dwellings	...	...	...
Dwellings	...	...	...
9 Community, social and personal services	...	...	106.87
A Sanitary and similar services	...	...	...
B Social and related community services [b]	...	...	...
C Recreational and cultural services	...	...	...
D Personal and household services	...	...	...
Total, Industries	...	...	1781.25
Producers of Government Services	...	...	103.56
Other Producers	...	...	1884.81
Total [c]	...	...	...
Less: Imputed bank service charge [d]	...	...	...
Import duties	...	...	...
Value added tax	...	...	...
Other adjustments [e]	...	...	246.00
Total	...	...	2130.81

of which General Government:

1 Agriculture, hunting, forestry and fishing	...	...	...
2 Mining and quarrying	...	...	...
3 Manufacturing	...	...	...
4 Electricity, gas and water	...	...	...
5 Construction	...	...	...
6 Wholesale and retail trade, restaurants and hotels	...	...	...
7 Transport and communication	...	...	...
8 Finance, insurance, real estate and business services	...	...	...
9 Community, social and personal services	...	...	...
Statistical discrepancy	...	...	...
Total, Industries of General Government	...	...	...
Producers of Government Services	...	...	...
Total, General Government	...	...	...

a) Estimates in columns 3 also include value added of the operation of irrigation system for which the gross output and intermediate consumption are not separately compiled.
b) Item 'Social and related community services' includes legal services and the rest of the which are included under manufacturing.
c) Gross domestic product in factor values.
d) Imputed bank service charges are adjusted in the respective activity.
e) Item 'Other adjustments' refers to indirect taxes net of subsidies, community, social and personal services other than sanitary services but excluding repair services.

Indonesia

General note. The preparation of national accounts statistics in Indonesia is undertaken by the Central Bureau of Statistics, Jakarta. The official estimates are generally in accordance with the United Nations System of National Accounts (SNA). The Indonesian input-output tables were published in 1976 and 1980 for the year 1971 and 1975 respectively, with the title 'Table Input-Output Indonesia 1971' and 'Table Input-Output Indonesia 1975'. The following tables are prepared for the United Nation's national accounts questionnaire. Whenever the scope and coverage of the estimates differ from those recommended in the SNA, a footnote is indicated to the relevant tables.

Sources and methods:

(a) **Gross domestic product.** Gross domestic product is estimated mainly through the production approach.
The most important mining commodity is crude petroleum for which production data are available for all enterprises concerned. Estimates of prices and input costs are compiled on the basis of returns furnished by the largest firm. For the base-year 1971, data on output and input structure of manufacturing have been compiled for each industry group from statistics maintained by the CBS and from surveys and other studies undertaken. For other years industrial production indexes and output of the trade sector is calculated by multiplying estimates of the producers' values of the marketed surplus of agricultural products, domestically produced manufactured goods, selected mining and quarrying products and the cost of imported goods by the percentage distribution mark-ups gathered from special surveys undertaken in 1971. Estimates for other years are extrapolated by a quantity index of marketed goods traded and an implicit price index. For railway transport, the annual reports of the State Railway Company constitute the main source of data for estimating gross output, intermediate input and value added. For road transport, gross output and input values are estimated by multiplying the average earning of each type of vehicle by the corresponding number of vehicles. For other transports, estimates are based on cost-structure surveys and data from concerned authorities supplemented by special inquiries for other industry intermediaries. Basic data relating to real estate and business services were limited and rough procedures are adopted by using information gathered from current budget expenditure and information furnished by local bodies. Estimates of other services are calculated for the year 1971 as the bench-mark year, and estimates of other years are extrapolated by using employment and price indicators. For the constant price estimates, revaluation is used for the agricultural sector, while value added of public administration and defence, is deflated by a moving average of the consumer price index. In all other sectors value added is extrapolated by various quantity indicators and indexes.

(b) **Expenditure on the gross domestic product.** The expenditure approach is used to estimate government final consumption expenditure, exports and imports of goods and services. Private final consumption expenditure is derived as residual. The commodity-flow approach is used for gross fixed capital formation. The main sources of data for the estimation of central government consumption expenditure are the budgetary accounts of the Department of Finance, while local governments provide data directly to the Central Bureau of Statistics (CBS). Bench-mark data for capital formation are based on statistics of imports and domestic production of machineries and equipments are obtained from import statistics, while domestic production is compiled by using production and implicit price indexes to extrapolate the bench-mark estimates. The input-output ratios for buildings and structures have been established for 1971 on the basis of special surveys on construction projects in that year. Other years' estimates are extrapolated by quantity and price indexes of domestic production and imports of construction materials. Estimates of exports and imports of goods and services are obtained from foreign trade and balance of payment statistics. For the constant price estimates, current values of government expenditure items are deflated by the consumer price index and by the wholesale price index. For gross fixed capital formation referring to buildings and structures, the bench-mark values are deflated by the corresponding unit value indexes. Values of exports and imports are deflated by the corresponding unit value indexes.

(c) **Cost-structure of the gross domestic product.** Consumption of fixed capital for manufacturing, electricity, gas and water, is estimated from information available at the CBS. For other sectors the estimates are based on the results of special surveys. The main source of data for net indirect taxes are the budgetary accounts of the central and local governments. Compensation of employees together with operating surplus is obtained as a residual.

(d) **Gross domestic product by kind of economic activity.** The table on gross domestic product by kind of economic activity is prepared at market prices, i.e. producers' values. The production approach is used to estimate value-added of most of the industries. The income approach is used for government and domestic services while gross output of trade and construction is estimated on the basis of the commodity-flow approach. For agriculture, main food crops production is compiled on the basis of information relating to area harvested and average yield for each crop obtained from the CBS. The prices used are based on farm-gate prices obtaining from annual surveys. The consumption of vegetables by households is based on per capita consumption estimates derived from the Household Survey 1969/79 and 1976, extrapolated by population and price changes and adding 1 per cent to cover consumption outside households. For main food crops, commercial and estate crops, livestock, forestry, and fishing are obtained from the departments concerned. For livestock, intermediate inputs are calculated as fixed percentages of gross output.

1.1 Expenditure on the Gross Domestic Product, in Current Prices

Thousand Million Indonesian rupiahs

	1970	1975	1980	1981	1982	1983	1984	1985	1986	1987	1988	1989
1 Government final consumption expenditure	293	1254	5148	6452	7229	8077	9122	10893	11329	11764	12756	15698
2 Private final consumption expenditure	2579	8731	25695	32294	37924	47063	54067	57201	63355	71989	81045	88752
3 Gross capital formation	455	2572	11894	17324	17406	22561	23543	27204	29205	39146	44725	57772
A Increase in stocks	...	...	1345	3189	1583	2794	3406	4837	4243	8166	7922	12123
B Gross fixed capital formation	455	2572	10550	14135	15822	19468	20136	22367	24782	30980	36803	45650
4 Exports of goods and services	434	2897	16162	16177	15103	19847	22999	21534	20010	29874	34666	42503
5 Less: imports of goods and services	523	2812	9886	14119	15186	19626	19845	19835	21036	27956	31171	38395
Equals: Gross Domestic Product	3238	12643	48914	58127	62476	77623	88985	96997	102683	124817	142020	166330

Indonesia

1.2 Expenditure on the Gross Domestic Product, in Constant Prices

Thousand Million Indonesian rupiahs

	1970	1975	1980	1981	1982	1983	1984	1985	1986	1987	1988	1989
			At constant prices of:									
		1973					1983					
1 Government final consumption expenditure	484	836	... 6801	7567	8291	8077	8353	8991	9241	9226	9924	10965
2 Private final consumption expenditure	3905	5699	... 36037	39699	42172	47063	48942	49448	50530	52200	54225	56476
3 Gross capital formation	715	1650	... 12569	23134	21979	22261	22749	26257	27755	27646	26275	29798
A Increase in stocks	...	...	-3077	5475	3239	2794	4452	6641	6333	5049	1075	1230
B Gross fixed capital formation	715	1650	15646	17659	18740	19468	18297	19616	21422	22597	25201	28568
4 Exports of goods and services	834	1410	... 26182	21163	19242	19847	21145	19495	22460	25745	26016	27851
5 Less: Imports of goods and services	756	1964	... 14866	20010	20323	19626	18151	19109	19906	20299	16504	17768
Equals: Gross Domestic Product	5182	7631	... 66723	71553	71361	77623	83037	85082	90081	94518	99936	107321

1.3 Cost Components of the Gross Domestic Product

Thousand Million Indonesian rupiahs

	1970	1975	1980	1981	1982	1983	1984	1985	1986	1987	1988	1989
1 Indirect taxes, net	188	519	1635	1752	2133	2281 2451	2723	3597	6529	7130	9033	12464
2 Consumption of fixed capital	219	821	2962	3512	3876	4629 3881	4494	4850	5134	6241	7101	8317
3 Compensation of employees paid by resident producers to:	2831	11302	40849	48763	53624	64305 71290	82667	88551	91020	111446	125887	145549
4 Operating surplus												
Equals: Gross Domestic Product	3238	12643	45446	54027	59633	71215 77623	89885	96997	102683	124817	142020	166330

1.10 Gross Domestic Product by Kind of Activity, in Current Prices

Thousand Million Indonesian rupiahs

	1970	1975	1980	1981	1982	1983	1984	1985	1986	1987	1988	1989
1 Agriculture, hunting, forestry and fishing	1575	4003	... 11726	13698	15062	17765	20420	22513	24871	29116	34193	38998
2 Mining and quarrying	173	2485	... 11238	13218	12153	16107	16938	13571	11503	17267	17162	21730
3 Manufacturing	293	1124	... 6353	7067	7482	9896	13113	15503	17185	21150	26252	30573
4 Electricity, gas and water	15	70	231	292	341	314	354	396	647	747	869	1008
5 Construction	100	590	... 2582	3500	3769	4597	4757	5302	5314	6087	7169	8884
6 Wholesale and retail trade, restaurants and hotels a	536	2104	... 7323	8781	9947	11419	13435	15417	17122	21048	24379	28314
7 Transport, storage and communication	96	521	... 2211	2370	3164	4098	5051	6100	6407	7443	8140	9085
8 Finance, insurance, real estate and business services b	98	409	... 2152	2900	3514	4714	5631	6271	7013	8144	9058	10706
9 Community, social and personal services cb	169	473	... 1872	2099	2339	3001	3718	3999	4315	4903	5351	5857

Indonesia

1.10 Gross Domestic Product by Kind of Activity, in Current Prices
(Continued)

Thousand Million Indonesian rupiahs

	1970	1975	1980	1981	1982	1983	1984	1985	1986	1987	1988	1989
Total, Industries	3055	11778	... 45688	53924	57770	71911	83415	89072	94376	115905	132574	155155
Producers of Government Services	183	864	... 3225	4203	4706	5712	6470	7925	8307	8912	9446	11174
Other Producers	...	...	...	...	...	...	...	...	...	...	...	...
Subtotal	3238	12643	... 48914	58127	62476	77623	89885	96997	102683	124817	142020	166330
Less: Imputed bank service charge	...	...	...	...	...	...	...	...	...	...	...	...
Plus: Import duties	...	...	...	...	...	...	...	...	...	...	...	...
Plus: Value added tax	...	...	...	...	...	...	...	...	...	...	...	...
Equals: Gross Domestic Product	3238	12643	... 48914	58127	62476	77623	89885	96997	102683	124817	142020	166330

a) Restaurants and hotels are included in item 'Community, social and personal services'.
b) Business services are included in item 'Community, social and personal services'.
c) For the first series, restaurants and hotels are included in item 'Community, social and personal services'.

1.11 Gross Domestic Product by Kind of Activity, in Constant Prices

Thousand Million Indonesian rupiahs

	1970	1975	1980	1981	1982	1983	1984	1985	1986	1987	1988	1989
		1973			At constant prices of:			1983				
1 Agriculture, hunting, forestry and fishing	2356	2811	... 16303	17270	17407	17765	18513	19300	19799	20224	21168	22086
2 Mining and quarrying	522	828	... 16078	16340	13876	16107	17120	15480	16309	16366	15893	16727
3 Manufacturing	435	848	... 7304	7878	7973	9896	12079	13431	14678	16235	18182	19836
4 Electricity, gas and water	23	41	... 312	361	422	314	324	361	430	495	549	616
5 Construction	143	365	... 3850	4368	4409	4597	4394	4508	4609	4803	5259	5878
6 Wholesale and retail trade, restaurants and hotels	847[a]	1294[a]	... 10303	10968	11603	11419	11811	12399	13399	14356	15657	17230
7 Transport, storage and communication	165	303	... 2911	3309	3540	4098	4443	4487	4668	4937	5212	5667
8 Finance, insurance, real estate and business services [b]	136	300	... 2946	3585	3952	4714	5241	5460	6010	6184	6514	7169
9 Community, social and personal services	244[ab]	277[ab]	... 2663[b]	2792[b]	2851[b]	3001[b]	3117[b]	3180[b]	3299[b]	3422[b]	3570[b]	3716[b]
Total, Industries	4870	7067	... 62670	66871	66032	71911	77040	78627	83219	87152	92004	98924
Producers of Government Services	312	564	... 4053	4682	5329	5712	5997	6455	6862	7366	7932	8397
Other Producers	...	...	...	...	...	...	...	...	...	...	...	...
Subtotal	5182	7631	... 66723	71553	71361	77623	83037	85082	90081	94518	99936	107321
Less: Imputed bank service charge	...	...	...	...	...	...	...	...	...	...	...	...
Plus: Import duties	...	...	...	...	...	...	...	...	...	...	...	...
Plus: Value added tax	...	...	...	...	...	...	...	...	...	...	...	...
Equals: Gross Domestic Product	5182	7631	... 66723	71553	71361	77623	83037	85082	90081	94518	99936	107321

a) Restaurants and hotels are included in item 'Community, social and personal services'.
b) Business services are included in item 'Community, social and personal services'.

Indonesia

1.12 Relations Among National Accounting Aggregates

Thousand Million Indonesian rupiahs

	1970	1975	1980	1981	1982	1983	1984	1985	1986	1987	1988	1989
Gross Domestic Product	3238	12643	45446	54027	59633	71215 77623	89885	96997	102683	124817	142020	166330
Plus: Net factor income from the rest of the world	-49	-557	-2011	-1925	-1958	-3036 -3283	-4183	-3941	-4193	-6022	-6922	-8159
Equals: Gross National Product	3190	12086	43435	52102	57675	68179 74340	85702	93056	98490	118795	135099	158171
Less: Consumption of fixed capital	219	821	2962	3512	3876	4629 3881	4494	4850	5134	6241	7101	8317
Equals: National Income	2971	11265	40473	48590	53799	63550 70459	81208	88206	93356	112554	127998	149854
Plus: Net current transfers from the rest of the world	...	...	...	...	...	... ...	...	...	...	...	...	...
Equals: National Disposable Income	...	...	...	...	...	... ...	...	...	...	...	...	...
Less: Final consumption	...	...	...	...	...	... ...	...	...	...	...	...	...
Equals: Net Saving	...	...	...	...	...	... ...	...	...	...	...	...	...
Less: Surplus of the nation on current transactions	...	...	...	...	...	... ...	...	...	...	...	...	...
Equals: Net Capital Formation	...	...	...	...	...	... ...	...	...	...	...	...	...

Iran(Islamic Repub.of)

General note. The preparation of national accounts statistics in Iran is undertaken by the National Accounts Department, Bank Markazi Jomhouri Islami Iran, Tehran. The official estimates are published in the annual bulletin 'Bank Markazi Jomhouri Islami Iran, Economic Report and Balance Sheet'. Detailed data as well as description of sources and methods used for national accounts estimation are published in the latest volume of the National Accounts of Iran, 1959-1977. The estimates are generally in accordance with the classifications and definitions recommended in the United Nations System of National Accounts (SNA). Input-output tables have been compiled for the years 1965, 1969, 1973 and 1974. The following tables have been prepared from successive replies to the United Nations national accounts questionnaire. When the scope and coverage of the estimates differ for conceptual or statistical reasons from the definitions and classifications recommended in SNA, a footnote is indicated to the relevant tables.

Sources and methods :

(a) Gross domestic product. Gross Domestic Product is estimated mainly through production approach.

(b) Expenditure on the gross domestic product. The expenditure approach is used to estimate all components of Gross Domestic Product by expenditure type except gross fixed capital formation in machinery which is calculated mainly by commodity-flow approach. Estimates for government final consumption expenditure are based on records from all sectors of general government. Private final consumption expenditure is estimated using data from family budget surveys. The estimates of gross fixed capital formation in private construction are derived from annual surveys on construction. The data on investment in construction by the public sector is obtained from the accounts of different government units. The capital formation in machinery and equipment is estimated through commodity-flow approach using information on domestic production, imports and exports of capital goods. The estimates of exports and imports of goods and services are obtained from the balance of payments accounts and foreign trade statistics. For the constant price estimates all items of Gross Domestic Product by expenditure type are deflated by appropriate price indices.

(c) Cost-structure of the gross domestic product. The estimates of compensation of employees are obtained in the process of estimating value added by industrial origin. Consumption of fixed capital is estimated according to useful life time of different type of capital goods. Operating surplus is obtained as a residual. Estimates of indirect taxes and subsidies are based on government accounts.

(d) Gross domestic product by kind of economic activity. The table of Gross Domestic Product by kind of economic activity is prepared in factor values. The production approach is used to estimate the value added of most industries. The income approach is used for producers of government services, communication and part of other services. The agricultural estimates are based on annual surveys of agriculture, carried out by ministry of agriculture. The estimates are checked using the results of the annual family budget surveys. Data on the production of red meat are based on information supplied by slaughter houses in urban areas and on the results of expenditure surveys in rural areas. The data are then converted to current-price estimates by using wholesale price index. Statistics concerning forestry and fishing are obtained from concerned agencies. Mining estimates are based on annual sample surveys and the 1973 Census of Mining. The value added of oil sector is derived from the reports of the Ministry of Oil. The manufacturing estimates for large establishments which employ 10 workers or more are based on the results of the annual surveys of manufacturing. For small establishments, estimates are derived using the sample surveys of 1974 and 1976 and information from other sources. The estimates of electricity, gas and water are based on information obtained from the government accounts. Estimates for private construction in the urban areas are obtained from the results of Bank Markazi's annual surveys with adjustments made to cover contractors' profits which are not included in the surveys. As for the rural areas, the results of 1973 survey of rural construction by the Statistical Center of Iran are extrapolated using information concerning construction in small towns. For trade sector the gross margin is calculated using the results of the 1973 survey of wholesale and retail trade in the urban areas. Estimates for transport sector are generally based on the sample surveys by Bank Markazi Jomhouri Islami Iran and financial statements of the government organizations involved. The value added of financial institutions and insurance is obtained directly from the financial statements of concerned institutions. The estimates for dwellings are based on data obtained from family budget surveys and imputations are made for owner-occupied dwellings. For producers of government services estimates are derived from government accounts. Estimates for social and personal services are based on information from various sources mainly the family budget surveys. For constant price estimates, the current values are deflated by an appropriate price index for each kind of economic activity.

1.1 Expenditure on the Gross Domestic Product, in Current Prices

Thousand Million Iranian rials

Fiscal year beginning 21 March

	1970	1975	1980	1981	1982	1983	1984	1985	1986	1987	1988	1989
1 Government final consumption expenditure	140.5	817.5	1377.1	1676.6	1844.2	2100.2	2143.0	2442.6	2370.6	2707.3	3140.2	...
2 Private final consumption expenditure	493.2	1429.9	3505.6	4735.4	5713.0	7232.7	8129.6	9627.1	10438.7	12225.5	14905.5	...
A Households	492.7	1428.7	3487.3	4716.0	5692.4	7209.4	8110.0	9515.8	10306.8	12086.2	14774.8	...
B Private non-profit institutions serving households	0.5	1.2	18.3	19.4	20.6	23.3	19.6	111.3	131.9	139.3	130.7	...
3 Gross capital formation	266.6	1012.7	2135.5	2873.2	3157.7	4936.2	4813.1	3017.6	4400.3	5015.3	4549.1	...
A Increase in stocks	81.8	13.8	743.1	1297.9	1270.7	1991.6	1929.0	176.7	1794.4	2357.6	1615.9	...
B Gross fixed capital formation	184.8	998.9	1392.4	1575.3	1887.0	2944.6	2884.1	2840.9	2605.9	2657.7	2933.2	...
Residential buildings	50.0	235.4	612.9	596.1	698.1	1186.8	1241.1	1346.2	1255.4	1314.0	1420.2	...
Non-residential buildings	7.6	21.9	84.1	63.9	70.5	65.8	80.4	63.9	66.0	897.8	1092.6	...
Other construction and land improvement etc.	61.9	286.2	437.1	486.9	587.6	748.1	633.8	686.7	784.7			...
Other	65.3	455.4	258.3	428.4	530.8	943.9	928.8	744.1	499.8	446.3	420.4	...
4 Exports of goods and services	153.7	1440.0	880.1	876.3	1864.0	1885.2	1520.1	1251.1	553.1	747.8	660.8	...
5 Less: Imports of goods and services	158.4	1127.1	1088.9	1300.1	1250.9	1850.6	1605.2	1266.2	935.0	887.6	691.0	...
Statistical discrepancy	-124.2	-60.9	116.6	-538.5	-571.7	-554.2	29.0	1483.6	1297.8	1462.1	1023.3	...
Equals: Gross Domestic Product	771.4	3512.1	6926.0	8322.9	10756.3	13749.5	15029.6	16555.8	18125.5	21270.4	23587.9	...

Iran(Islamic Repub.of)

1.2 Expenditure on the Gross Domestic Product, in Constant Prices

Thousand Million Iranian rials

Fiscal year beginning 21 March

	1970	1975	1980	1981	1982	1983	1984	1985	1986	1987	1988	1989
			At constant prices of:1974									
1 Government final consumption expenditure	215.0	728.4	... 580.4	606.9	583.6	572.1	547.8	593.8	474.4	449.7	463.9	...
2 Private final consumption expenditure	699.6	1327.4	... 1459.7	1548.3	1642.9	1805.5	1848.8	2127.6	1936.4	1868.2	1816.0	...
A Households	698.9	1326.3	... 1452.2	1541.8	1637.3	1800.1	1844.9	2108.6	1918.2	1854.2	1806.6	...
B Private non-profit institutions serving households	0.7	1.1	... 7.5	6.5	5.6	5.4	3.9	19.0	18.2	14.0	9.4	...
3 Gross capital formation	408.8	887.6	... 860.4	1000.7	982.7	1367.9	1220.1	750.8	901.4	811.5	588.5	...
A Increase in stocks	122.8	13.0	... 306.6	437.9	364.2	508.3	450.4	43.5	357.7	366.7	206.0	...
B Gross fixed capital formation	286.0	874.6	... 553.8	562.8	618.5	859.6	769.7	707.3	543.7	444.8	382.5	...
Residential buildings	84.4	202.4	220.6	178.4	197.8	271.9	251.1	259.0	217.9	200.3	176.3	...
Non-residential buildings	12.8	18.7	... 30.0	18.7	19.6	15.8	17.0	12.9	11.9	150.7	141.5	...
Other construction and land improvement etc.	104.6	251.6	175.2	171.3	185.4	197.8	148.8	151.2	154.3			...
Other	84.2	401.9	... 128.0	194.4	215.7	374.1	352.8	284.2	159.6	93.8	64.7	...
4 Exports of goods and services	1005.3	1327.3	... 251.2	225.8	531.7	546.4	435.4	401.7	350.9	446.5	425.4	...
5 Less: Imports of goods and services	278.4	1006.3	... 594.1	672.9	632.4	927.2	795.0	660.2	478.5	585.0	340.6	...
Statistical discrepancy	-49.5	-88.0	... 79.3	-32.1	-24.4	122.0	237.9	437.4	159.3	315.8	193.4	...
Equals: Gross Domestic Product	2000.8	3176.4	... 2636.9	2676.7	3084.1	3486.7	3495.0	3651.1	3343.9	3306.7	3146.6	...

1.3 Cost Components of the Gross Domestic Product

Thousand Million Iranian rials

Fiscal year beginning 21 March

	1970	1975	1980	1981	1982	1983	1984	1985	1986	1987	1988	1989
1 Indirect taxes, net	57.9	79.9	... 167.1	104.4	134.8	278.2	326.6	607.6	612.9	665.0	539.7	...
A Indirect taxes	59.8	156.1	281.1	280.7	315.0	416.8	481.6	782.4	798.9	815.7	679.8	...
B Less: Subsidies	1.9	76.2	114.0	176.3	180.2	138.6	155.0	174.8	186.0	150.7	140.1	...
2 Consumption of fixed capital	74.2	154.2	... 462.2	583.4	708.1	932.9	1062.0	1324.6	1405.7	1475.6	2035.6	...
3 Compensation of employees paid by resident producers to:	226.6	856.3										...
A Resident households	207.7	754.9	6296.7	7635.1	9913.4	12538.4	13641.0	14623.6	16106.9	19129.8	21012.6	...
B Rest of the world	18.9	101.4										...
4 Operating surplus	412.7	2421.7										...
Equals: Gross Domestic Product	771.4	3512.1	6926.0	8322.9	10756.3	13749.5	15029.6	16555.8	18125.5	21270.4	23587.9	...

1.4 General Government Current Receipts and Disbursements

Thousand Million Iranian rials

Fiscal year beginning 21 March

	1970	1975	1980	1981	1982	1983	1984	1985	1986	1987	1988	1989
			Receipts									
1 Operating surplus	...	...	...	...	...	...	...	...	...	...	...	...
2 Property and entrepreneurial income	8.6	30.8	... 25.6	67.6	61.5	35.8	34.3	35.4	22.4	15.6	11.5	...
3 Taxes, fees and contributions	88.2	330.8	... 504.2	759.9	877.6	997.8	1277.1	1646.2	1687.7	1678.2	1696.4	...
A Indirect taxes	59.8	156.1	... 281.1	280.7	315.0	416.8	481.6	782.4	798.9	815.7	679.8	...

860

Iran(Islamic Repub.of)

1.4 General Government Current Receipts and Disbursements
(Continued)

Thousand Million Iranian rials — Fiscal year beginning 21 March

	1970	1975	1980	1981	1982	1983	1984	1985	1986	1987	1988	1989
B Direct taxes	19.4	136.4	117.8	326.0	366.6	360.4	533.3	584.6	603.1	554.8	649.2	...
C Social security contributions	5.7	26.0	103.7	151.6	194.5	217.2	256.0	274.3	280.5	302.4	361.6	...
D Compulsory fees, fines and penalties	3.3	12.3	1.6	1.6	1.5	3.4	6.2	4.9	5.2	5.3	5.8	...
4 Other current transfers	101.2	1469.1	1004.3	1191.9	1864.4	2076.3	1837.4	1468.6	484.6	1030.2	1197.0	...
Total Current Receipts of General Government	198.0	1830.7	1534.1	2019.4	2803.5	3109.9	3148.8	3150.2	2194.7	2724.0	2904.9	...

Disbursements

	1970	1975	1980	1981	1982	1983	1984	1985	1986	1987	1988	1989
1 Government final consumption expenditure	140.5	817.5	1377.1	1676.6	1844.2	2100.2	2143.0	2442.6	2370.6	2707.3	3140.2	...
A Compensation of employees	90.6	354.5	1122.8	1261.8	1362.1	1552.0	1600.5	1883.1	1927.4	2181.8	2423.2	
B Consumption of fixed capital	...	...	...	...	...	...	...	...	...	...	...	...
C Purchases of goods and services, net	49.9	463.0	254.3	414.8	482.1	548.2	542.5	559.5	443.2	525.5	717.0	...
D Less: Own account fixed capital formation	...	...	...	...	...	...	...	...	...	...	...	...
E Indirect taxes paid, net	...	...	...	...	...	...	...	...	...	...	...	...
2 Property income	8.9	34.4	35.3	20.9	16.7	10.5	6.3	9.6	4.6	4.1	4.6	...
A Interest	8.9	34.4	35.3	20.9	16.7	10.5	6.3	9.6	4.6	4.1	4.6	...
B Net land rent and royalties	-	-	-	-	-	-	-	-	-	-	-	...
3 Subsidies	1.9	76.2	114.0	176.3	180.2	138.6	155.0	174.8	186.0	150.7	140.1	...
4 Other current transfers	12.6	102.3	389.7	376.8	367.3	432.2	426.3	...	...	...	...	...
A Social security benefits	4.0	18.3	93.7	143.5	186.4	209.2	245.9	...	...	...	...	...
B Social assistance grants								...	...	...	...	...
C Other	8.6	84.0	296.0	233.3	180.9	223.0	180.4	...	...	...	...	...
5 Net saving	34.1	800.3	-382.0	-231.2	395.1	428.4	418.2	...	...	...	...	...
Total Current Disbursements and Net Saving of General Government	198.0	1830.7	1534.1	2019.4	2803.5	3109.9	3148.8	3150.2	2194.7	2724.0	2904.9	...

1.7 External Transactions on Current Account, Summary

Thousand Million Iranian rials — Fiscal year beginning 21 March

	1970	1975	1980	1981	1982	1983	1984	1985	1986	1987	1988	1989
Payments to the Rest of the World												
1 Imports of goods and services	158.4	1127.1	1088.9	1300.1	1250.9	1850.6	1605.2	1266.2	935.0	887.6	691.0	...
A Imports of merchandise c.i.f.	146.6	1045.3	962.8	1242.1	1213.8	1801.3	1547.6	1211.2	911.1	868.1	...	...
B Other [a]	11.8	81.8	126.1	58.0	37.1	49.3	57.6	55.0	23.9	19.5	...	...
2 Factor income to the rest of the world	49.6	146.5	93.7	79.0	89.5	115.1	102.1	94.4	61.3	65.4	72.4	

Iran(Islamic Repub.of)

1.7 External Transactions on Current Account, Summary
(Continued)

Thousand Million Iranian rials

Fiscal year beginning 21 March

	1970	1975	1980	1981	1982	1983	1984	1985	1986	1987	1988	1989
A Compensation of employees	18.9	101.4	... 65.2	57.0	70.3	99.0	89.0	85.7	56.2	60.8	66.7	
B Property and entrepreneurial income	30.7	45.1	... 28.5	22.0	19.2	16.1	13.1	8.8	5.1	4.6	5.7	...
3 Current transfers to the rest of the world	-	1.3	...	-	-	-	-	-	-	-	-	...
4 Surplus of the nation on current transactions	-44.6	296.9	... -202.4	-390.9	612.9	27.9	-96.5	-48.7	-400.5	-179.1	-75.0	
Payments to the Rest of the World and Surplus of the Nation on Current Transactions	163.4	1571.8	980.2	988.2	1953.3	1993.6	1610.8	1311.9	595.7	773.9	688.4	...

Receipts From The Rest of the World

	1970	1975	1980	1981	1982	1983	1984	1985	1986	1987	1988	1989
1 Exports of goods and services	153.7	1440.0	... 880.1	876.3	1864.0	1885.2	1520.1	1251.1	553.2	747.8	660.8	...
A Exports of merchandise f.o.b.	21.8	41.3	... 45.9	27.1	23.9	31.1	33.0	40.7	70.1	81.1	...	...
B Other b	131.9	1398.7	834.2	849.2	1840.1	1854.1	1487.1	1210.4	483.1	666.7	...	
2 Factor income from rest of the world	9.7	131.8	... 100.1	111.9	89.3	108.4	90.7	60.8	42.6	26.1	27.6	...
A Compensation of employees	9.1	79.7	... 28.6	40.7	37.8	39.3	36.5	26.2	14.6	11.7	12.2	...
B Property and entrepreneurial income	0.6	52.1	... 71.5	71.2	51.5	69.1	54.2	34.5	28.0	14.4	15.4	...
3 Current transfers from rest of the world	...	...	...	...	...	...	...	...	...	...	...	
Receipts from the Rest of the World on Current Transactions	163.4	1571.8	980.2	988.2	1953.3	1993.6	1610.8	1311.9	595.7	773.9	688.4	...

a) Item 'Other' of Imports of goods and services refers to imports of services only.
b) Item 'Other' of exports of goods and services includes export of oil.

1.8 Capital Transactions of The Nation, Summary

Thousand Million Iranian rials

Fiscal year beginning 21 March

	1970	1975	1980	1981	1982	1983	1984	1985	1986	1987	1988	1989
Finance of Gross Capital Formation												
Gross saving	222.0	1309.6	... 1933.1	2482.3	3770.6	4964.1	4716.6	2968.9	3999.7	4836.2	4474.1	...
1 Consumption of fixed capital	74.2	154.2	... 462.2	583.4	708.1	932.9	1062.0	1324.6	1405.7	1475.6	2035.6	...
2 Net saving	147.8	1155.4	1470.9	1898.9	3062.5	4031.2	3654.6	1644.3	2594.0	3360.6	2438.5	...
Less: Surplus of the nation on current transactions	-44.6	296.9	-202.4	-390.9	612.9	27.9	-96.5	-48.7	-400.6	-179.1	-75.0	
Finance of Gross Capital Formation	266.6	1012.7	2135.5	2873.2	3157.7	4936.2	4813.1	3017.6	4400.3	5015.3	4549.1	...
Gross Capital Formation												
Increase in stocks	81.8	13.8	743.1	1297.9	1270.7	1991.6	1929.0	176.7	1794.4	2357.6	1615.9	...
Gross fixed capital formation	184.8	998.9	1392.4	1575.3	1887.0	2944.6	2884.1	2840.9	2605.9	2657.7	2933.2	
1 General government a	100.6	485.3	678.3	805.5	1084.9	1274.4	1067.9	1086.7	1057.2	1042.4	1230.9	...
2 Corporate and quasi-corporate enterprises ab	...	...	...	...	...	...	...	...	...	...	...	
3 Other b	84.2	513.6	714.1	769.8	802.1	1670.2	1816.2	1754.2	1548.7	1615.3	1702.3	...
Gross Capital Formation	266.6	1012.7	2135.5	2873.2	3157.7	4936.2	4813.1	3017.6	4400.3	5015.3	4549.1	...

a) Public corporate and quasi corporate enterprises are included in item 'General government'.
b) Private corporate and quasi-corporate enterprises are included in item 'Other'.

Iran(Islamic Repub.of)

1.10 Gross Domestic Product by Kind of Activity, in Current Prices

Thousand Million Iranian rials

Fiscal year beginning 21 March

	1970	1975	1980	1981	1982	1983	1984	1985	1986	1987	1988	1989
1 Agriculture, hunting, forestry and fishing	126.3	306.2	1083.3	1525.6	1912.1	2138.5	2493.9	2848.5	3733.8	4812.9	4776.5	...
2 Mining and quarrying a	147.4	1401.3	1080.1	1074.6	1927.8	1951.8	1696.4	1594.9	746.6	1002.1	963.4	...
3 Manufacturing	84.5	278.7	602.2	731.6	894.4	1072.9	1167.3	1365.2	1393.1	1542.2	1787.4	...
4 Electricity, gas and water	11.9	39.2	61.3	77.8	98.6	90.9	107.0	139.7	162.6	198.6	211.0	...
5 Construction	30.8	207.3	529.8	546.5	685.6	1088.6	1115.2	1174.3	1153.1	1174.9	1203.9	...
6 Wholesale and retail trade, restaurants and hotels	69.4	238.3	753.5	1295.0	1702.8	2842.8	3205.4	3170.9	4527.7	5154.1	6349.7	...
7 Transport, storage and communication	38.8	181.1	553.8	620.7	709.8	947.6	1138.4	1182.1	1132.7	1319.9	1482.1	...
8 Finance, insurance, real estate and business services	94.3	502.7	1083.4	1099.8	1253.0	1627.5	1867.2	2177.3	2321.6	2645.1	3137.8	...
9 Community, social and personal services b	43.0	137.2	554.1	641.8	607.8	782.0	975.1	402.4	378.5	453.9	559.7	...
Total, Industries	646.4	3292.0	6301.5	7613.4	9791.9	12542.6	13765.9	14055.3	15549.7	18303.7	20471.5	...
Producers of Government Services	89.7	293.1	751.2	833.9	1040.5	1175.7	1189.8	1979.3	2043.9	2330.0	2591.7	...
Other Producers b	...	...	...	...	...	...	...	...	...	...	...	...
Subtotal c	736.1	3585.1	7052.7	8447.3	10832.4	13718.3	14955.7	16034.6	17593.6	20633.7	23063.2	...
Less: Imputed bank service charge	22.6	152.9	293.8	228.8	210.9	247.0	252.7	86.4	81.0	28.3	15.0	...
Plus: Import duties	...	...	...	...	...	...	...	...	...	...	...	...
Plus: Value added tax	...	...	...	...	...	...	...	...	...	...	...	...
Plus: Other adjustments d	57.9	79.9	167.1	104.4	134.8	278.2	326.6	607.6	612.9	665.0	539.7	...
Equals: Gross Domestic Product	771.4	3512.1	6926.0	8322.9	10756.3	13749.5	15029.6	16555.8	18125.5	21270.4	23587.9	...

a) Oil production is included in item 'Mining and quarrying'.
b) Item 'Other producers' is included in item 'Community, social and personal services'.
c) Gross domestic product in factor values.
d) Item 'Other adjustments' refers to indirect taxes net of subsidies.

1.11 Gross Domestic Product by Kind of Activity, in Constant Prices

Thousand Million Iranian rials

Fiscal year beginning 21 March

	1970	1975	1980	1981	1982	1983	1984	1985	1986	1987	1988	1989
					At constant prices of:1974							
1 Agriculture, hunting, forestry and fishing	233.9	303.9	362.9	404.0	436.0	429.0	446.7	526.0	548.5	562.9	502.2	...
2 Mining and quarrying a	1037.1	1286.2	356.9	299.1	554.3	558.4	480.6	496.9	424.5	479.2	512.1	...
3 Manufacturing	114.5	258.9	324.9	346.4	387.8	463.8	491.6	441.2	409.7	370.0	355.6	...
4 Electricity, gas and water	11.8	38.9	48.3	56.6	64.7	59.0	66.7	81.4	89.2	101.6	102.7	...
5 Construction	56.9	150.5	120.7	106.0	110.7	133.0	118.7	124.3	110.1	105.6	100.1	...
6 Wholesale and retail trade, restaurants and hotels	103.3	222.6	310.5	436.5	487.3	725.3	747.4	647.1	598.1	594.6	537.9	...
7 Transport, storage and communication	53.4	170.6	174.3	158.3	168.1	185.4	203.0	234.1	201.1	173.6	174.3	...
8 Finance, insurance, real estate and business services	137.2	447.1	453.6	412.1	420.9	444.6	445.5	484.1	440.4	428.9	435.0	...
9 Community, social and personal services b	61.0	114.0	227.4	217.3	177.0	197.2	218.3	88.4	71.3	78.9	87.5	...
Total, Industries	1809.1	2992.7	2379.4	2436.3	2806.8	3195.7	3218.5	3123.5	2892.9	2895.3	2807.4	...
Producers of Government Services	134.7	251.4	309.8	279.9	292.9	281.2	257.6	411.6	351.9	311.8	269.1	...

Iran(Islamic Repub.of)

1.11 Gross Domestic Product by Kind of Activity, in Constant Prices
(Continued)

Thousand Million Iranian rials

Fiscal year beginning 21 March

	1970	1975	1980	1981	1982	1983	1984	1985	1986	1987	1988	1989
					At constant prices of:1974							
Other Producers b	...	...	...									
Subtotal c	1943.8	3244.1	... 2689.2	2716.2	3099.7	3476.9	3476.1	3535.1	3244.8	3207.1	3076.5	
Less: Imputed bank service charge	32.5	139.2	... 121.2	76.8	59.4	59.1	54.8	18.0	14.0	3.8	1.6	...
Plus: Import duties	...	...	...									
Plus: Value added tax	...	...	...									
Plus: Other adjustments d	89.5	71.5	... 68.9	37.3	43.8	68.9	73.7	134.0	113.1	103.4	71.7	
Equals: Gross Domestic Product	2000.8	3176.4	... 2636.9	2676.7	3084.1	3486.7	3495.0	3651.1	3343.9	3306.7	3146.6	...

a) Oil production is included in item 'Mining and quarrying'.
b) Item 'Other producers' is included in item 'Community, social and personal services'.
c) Gross domestic product in factor values.
d) Item 'Other adjustments' refers to indirect taxes net of subsidies.

1.12 Relations Among National Accounting Aggregates

Thousand Million Iranian rials

Fiscal year beginning 21 March

	1970	1975	1980	1981	1982	1983	1984	1985	1986	1987	1988	1989
Gross Domestic Product	771.4	3512.1	... 6926.0	8322.9	10756.3	13749.5	15029.6	16555.8	18125.5	21270.4	23587.9	...
Plus: Net factor income from the rest of the world	-39.9	-14.7	... 6.4	32.9	-0.2	-6.7	-11.4	-33.6	-18.7	-39.3	-44.8	...
Factor income from the rest of the world	9.7	131.8	... 100.1	111.9	89.3	108.4	90.7	60.8	42.6	26.1	27.6	...
Less: Factor income to the rest of the world	49.6	146.5	... 93.7	79.0	89.5	115.1	102.1	94.4	61.3	65.4	72.4	...
Equals: Gross National Product	731.5	3497.4	... 6932.4	8355.8	10756.1	13742.8	15018.2	16522.2	18106.8	21231.1	23543.1	...
Less: Consumption of fixed capital	74.2	154.2	... 462.2	583.4	708.1	932.9	1062.0	1324.6	1405.7	1475.6	2035.6	...
Equals: National Income	657.3	3343.2	... 6470.2	7772.4	10048.0	12809.9	13956.2	15197.6	16701.1	19755.5	21507.5	...
Plus: Net current transfers from the rest of the world	-	-1.3	... -	-	-	-	-	-	-	-	-	...
Equals: National Disposable Income	657.3	3341.9	6470.2	7772.4	10048.0	12809.9	13956.2	15197.6	16701.1	19755.5	21507.5	...
Less: Final consumption	633.7	2247.4	... 4882.7	6412.0	7557.2	9332.9	10272.6	12069.7	12809.3	14932.8	18045.7	...
Statistical discrepancy	124.2	60.9	-116.6	538.5	571.7	554.2	-29.0	-1483.6	-1297.8	-1462.1	-1023.3	...
Equals: Net Saving	147.8	1155.4	1470.9	1898.9	3062.5	4031.2	3654.6	1644.3	2594.0	3360.6	2438.5	...
Less: Surplus of the nation on current transactions	-44.6	296.9	-202.4	-390.9	612.9	27.9	-96.5	-48.7	-400.6	-179.1	-75.0	...
Equals: Net Capital Formation	192.4	858.5	1673.3	2289.8	2449.6	4003.3	3751.1	1693.0	2994.6	3539.7	2513.5	...

2.1 Government Final Consumption Expenditure by Function, in Current Prices

Thousand Million Iranian rials

Fiscal year beginning 21 March

	1970	1975	1980	1981	1982	1983	1984	1985	1986	1987	1988	1989
1 General public services	22.5	58.9	... 41.3	45.3	53.5	48.3	57.9	57.3	90.7	86.9	103.4	...
2 Defence	52.4	374.5	... 298.8	271.6	278.5	279.3	315.0	927.8	867.3	1099.3	1327.7	...
3 Public order and safety			... 147.4	149.2	212.1	220.5	250.7	166.4	145.1	135.5	163.5	...
4 Education	20.9	80.9	338.8	328.6	322.7	388.5	441.5	492.2	586.0	561.4	667.3	...
5 Health	6.7	36.8	... 101.9	105.6	132.8	136.5	150.0	162.2	161.9	151.7	183.5	...
6 Social security and welfare	9.6	39.2	35.8	83.8	90.4	157.5	167.2	183.2	198.1	213.6	240.2	...
7 Housing and community amenities	0.6	6.5	... 5.5	5.1	5.5	4.2	4.3	5.6	14.0	8.8	13.4	...
8 Recreational; cultural and religious affairs	4.2	13.9	17.9	25.2	31.4	33.7	34.3	37.8	40.5	36.8	45.0	...
9 Economic services	12.5	122.6	207.9	226.3	223.1	132.3	261.4	204.1	108.8	213.6	185.2	...

Iran(Islamic Repub.of)

2.1 Government Final Consumption Expenditure by Function, in Current Prices
(Continued)

Thousand Million Iranian rials — Fiscal year beginning 21 March

	1970	1975	1980	1981	1982	1983	1984	1985	1986	1987	1988	1989
A Fuel and energy	2.1	12.3	22.0	23.5	29.5	2.1	6.8	...	...	...	...	...
B Agriculture, forestry, fishing and hunting	4.4	71.9	38.6	33.5	35.0	37.8	34.8	...	...	...	...	...
C Mining, manufacturing and construction, except fuel and energy	0.4	11.4	19.3	21.8	27.7	8.4	7.1	...	...	...	...	...
D Transportation and communication	4.6	17.2	35.8	40.2	33.2	29.4	35.6	...	...	...	...	...
E Other economic affairs	1.0	9.8	92.2	107.3	97.7	54.6	177.1	...	...	...	...	...
10 Other functions [a]	11.1	84.2	181.8	435.9	494.2	699.4	460.7	206.0	158.2	199.7	211.0	...
Total Government Final Consumption Expenditure	140.5	817.5	1377.1	1676.6	1844.2	2100.2	2143.0	2442.6	2370.6	2707.3	3140.2	...

a) Beginning 1985, the estimates of 'Other functions' exclude municipalities and social security fund.

2.2 Government Final Consumption Expenditure by Function, in Constant Prices

Thousand Million Iranian rials — Fiscal year beginning 21 March

	1970	1975	1980	1981	1982	1983	1984	1985	1986	1987	1988	1989
					At constant prices of:1974							
1 General public services	34.4	52.4	17.4	16.4	16.9	13.2	14.8	12.0	15.7	11.9	...	...
2 Defence	80.2	333.6	125.9	98.3	88.1	76.1	80.5	275.5	213.9	230.8	...	...
3 Public order and safety			62.1	54.0	67.1	60.0	64.1	35.0	25.2	18.5	...	...
4 Education	32.0	72.1	142.8	119.0	102.1	105.8	112.8	103.5	101.6	76.4	...	...
5 Health	10.3	32.8	42.9	38.2	42.1	37.2	38.3	34.1	28.1	20.7	...	...
6 Social security and welfare	14.6	35.0	15.2	30.3	28.6	42.9	42.7	38.5	34.3	29.1	...	...
7 Housing and community amenities	0.9	5.8	2.4	1.8	1.8	1.2	1.2	1.2	2.4	1.2	...	...
8 Recreational, cultural and religious affairs	6.5	12.4	7.5	9.2	9.9	9.2	8.8	7.9	7.0	5.0	...	...
9 Economic services	19.1	109.3	87.6	81.9	70.6	36.0	66.8	42.9	18.9	29.1	...	...
A Fuel and energy	3.2	10.9	9.3	8.5	9.3	0.6	1.7	...	...	...	...	...
B Agriculture, forestry, fishing and hunting	6.7	64.1	16.3	12.1	11.2	10.3	8.9	...	...	...	...	...
C Mining, manufacturing and construction, except fuel and energy	0.6	10.2	8.1	7.9	8.7	2.3	1.8	...	...	...	...	...
D Transportation and communication	7.1	15.3	15.0	14.6	10.5	8.0	9.1	...	...	...	...	...
E Other economic affairs	1.5	8.8	38.9	38.8	30.9	14.8	45.3	...	...	...	...	...
10 Other functions [a]	17.0	75.0	76.6	157.8	156.4	190.5	117.8	43.2	27.3	27.0	...	...
Total Government Final Consumption Expenditure	215.0	728.4	580.4	606.9	583.6	572.1	547.8	593.8	474.4	449.7	...	...

a) Beginning 1985, the estimates of 'Other functions' exclude municipalities and social security fund.

2.5 Private Final Consumption Expenditure by Type and Purpose, in Current Prices

Thousand Million Iranian rials — Fiscal year beginning 21 March

	1970	1975	1980	1981	1982	1983	1984	1985	1986	1987	1988	1989
				Final Consumption Expenditure of Resident Households								
1 Food, beverages and tobacco [a]	...	639.7	1439.2	2086.6	2513.4	3092.9	3560.7	4156.0	4834.0	5735.7	7022.7	...
2 Clothing and footwear	...	140.4	254.5	452.6	545.5	761.8	789.6	891.1	850.7	1136.1	1658.4	...
3 Gross rent, fuel and power	...	243.3	831.3	1032.4	1253.8	1652.4	1903.0	2348.8	2640.8	2912.8	3529.0	...
4 Furniture, furnishings and household equipment and operation	...	146.5	224.2	363.1	440.0	523.6	519.7	586.0	551.6	677.8	694.7	...

865

Iran(Islamic Repub.of)

2.5 Private Final Consumption Expenditure by Type and Purpose, in Current Prices
(Continued)

Thousand Million Iranian rials

	1970	1975	1980	1981	1982	1983	1984	1985	1986	1987	1988	1989
5 Medical care and health expenses	...	48.2	... 144.8	188.6	226.5	317.7	358.8	410.2	380.3	488.3	580.0	...
6 Transport and communication	...	106.5	... 233.5	318.0	384.1	449.6	495.2	605.2	616.6	721.2	745.5	...
7 Recreational, entertainment, education and cultural services	...	33.9	... 48.8	65.8	79.2	105.2	118.7	149.7	155.3	175.0	202.4	...
8 Miscellaneous goods and services	...	81.9	... 311.5	208.9	249.9	306.2	364.3	368.8	277.5	239.3	342.1	...
Total Final Consumption Expenditure in the Domestic Market by Households, of which	...	1440.4	... 3487.3	4716.0	5692.4	7209.4	8110.0	9515.8	10306.8	12086.2	14774.8	...
Plus: Direct purchases abroad by resident households	...	...	...	...	...	...	...	...	...	...	...	...
Less: Direct purchases in the domestic market by non-resident households	...	...	...	...	...	...	...	...	...	...	...	...
Equals: Final Consumption Expenditure of Resident Households	492.7	1440.4	... 3487.3	4716.0	5692.4	7209.4	8110.0	9515.8	10306.8	12086.2	14774.8	...
Final Consumption Expenditure of Private Non-profit Institutions Serving Households												
Equals: Final Consumption Expenditure of Private Non-profit Organisations Serving Households	0.5	1.2	... 18.3	19.4	20.6	23.3	19.6	111.3	131.9	139.3	130.7	...
Private Final Consumption Expenditure	493.2	1441.6	... 3505.6	4735.4	5713.0	7232.7	8129.6	9627.1	10438.7	12225.5	14905.5	...

a) Item 'Food, beverages and tobacco' includes expenditure in restaurants, cafes and hotels.

2.6 Private Final Consumption Expenditure by Type and Purpose, in Constant Prices

Thousand Million Iranian rials

	1970	1975	1980	1981	1982	1983	1984	1985	1986	1987	1988	1989
At constant prices of:1974												
Final Consumption Expenditure of Resident Households												
1 Food, beverages and tobacco a	...	608.4	... 564.2	583.4	616.4	660.5	704.6	784.2	732.1	716.8	762.1	...
2 Clothing and footwear	...	129.0	... 126.8	148.0	156.5	172.2	161.6	197.6	177.7	179.5	175.8	...
3 Gross rent, fuel and power	...	214.2	... 393.1	414.9	448.8	509.0	527.1	616.8	618.7	596.9	528.0	...
4 Furniture, furnishings and household equipment and operation	...	128.0	... 94.0	102.9	110.0	114.3	108.3	130.7	97.7	77.8	56.7	...

Iran(Islamic Repub.of)

2.6 Private Final Consumption Expenditure by Type and Purpose, in Constant Prices
(Continued)

Thousand Million Iranian rials   Fiscal year beginning 21 March

	1970	1975	1980	1981	1982	1983	1984	1985	1986	1987	1988	1989
At constant prices of:1974												
5 Medical care and health expenses	...	43.1	... 87.9	105.0	112.7	143.7	148.1	154.7	127.1	156.6	174.9	...
6 Transport and communication	...	98.3	... 88.6	86.2	91.6	89.4	84.8	105.8	91.9	76.2	58.5	...
7 Recreational, entertainment, education and cultural services	...	38.0	... 34.2	40.4	44.6	50.8	48.4	57.1	34.5	26.1	22.3	...
8 Miscellaneous goods and services	...	76.5	... 63.4	61.0	56.7	60.2	62.0	61.7	38.5	24.3	28.3	...
Total Final Consumption Expenditure in the Domestic Market by Households, of which	...	1335.5	... 1452.2	1541.8	1637.3	1800.1	1844.9	2108.6	1918.2	1854.2	1806.6	...
Plus: Direct purchases abroad by resident households	...	...	...	...	...	...	...	...	...	...	...	...
Less: Direct purchases in the domestic market by non-resident households	...	...	...	...	...	...	...	...	...	...	...	...
Equals: Final Consumption Expenditure of Resident Households	698.9	1335.5	... 1452.2	1541.8	1637.3	1800.1	1844.9	2108.6	1918.2	1854.2	1806.6	...
Final Consumption Expenditure of Private Non-profit Institutions Serving Households												
Equals: Final Consumption Expenditure of Private Non-profit Organisations Serving Households	0.7	1.1	... 7.5	6.5	5.6	5.4	3.9	19.0	18.2	14.0	9.4	...
Private Final Consumption Expenditure	699.6	1336.6	... 1459.7	1548.3	1642.9	1805.5	1848.8	2127.6	1936.4	1868.2	1816.0	...

a) Item 'Food, beverages and tobacco' includes expenditure in restaurants, cafes and hotels.

2.11 Gross Fixed Capital Formation by Kind of Activity of Owner, ISIC Divisions, in Current Prices

Thousand Million Iranian rials   Fiscal year beginning 21 March

	1970	1975	1980	1981	1982	1983	1984	1985	1986	1987	1988	1989
All Producers												
1 Agriculture, hunting, forestry and fishing	11.8	67.6	... 56.7	86.4	96.7	188.5	167.7	149.6	174.4	217.8	196.0	...
2 Mining and quarrying ab	10.6	69.7	... 68.5	86.6	140.9	147.1	121.9	104.2	133.3	79.4	244.5	...
3 Manufacturing b	34.2	179.2	... 109.0	117.8	158.5	227.0	231.8	160.1	159.4	209.8	304.6	...
4 Electricity, gas and water c	9.0	61.7	... 73.9	91.2	129.4	162.3	140.7	177.2	197.9	154.1	104.4	...
5 Construction	57.6	257.3	... 697.0	660.0	768.6	1252.6	1321.5	1392.4	1274.9	1328.9	1434.3	...
6 Wholesale and retail trade, restaurants and hotels	...	...	...	...	...	...	...	...	...	...	...	...
7 Transport, storage and communication	42.4	230.8	... 190.7	296.1	394.4	652.3	637.8	456.6	291.9	272.8	280.0	...
8 Finance, insurance, real estate and business services	19.2	132.6	... 196.6	237.2	198.5	314.8	262.7	400.8	374.1	395.3	369.4	...
9 Community, social and personal services												...
Total Industries	184.8	998.9	... 1392.4	1575.3	1887.0	2944.6	2884.1	2840.9	2605.9	2658.1	2933.2	...
Producers of Government Services	...	...	...	...	...	...	...	...	...	...	...	...
Private Non-Profit Institutions Serving Households	...	...	...	...	...	...	...	...	...	...	...	...
Total	184.8	998.9	... 1392.4	1575.3	1887.0	2944.6	2884.1	2840.9	2605.9	2658.1	2933.2	...

a) Item 'Mining and quarrying' refers only to oil and gas production.
b) Mining is included in item 'Manufacturing'.
c) Item 'Electricity, gas and water' excludes gas.

Iran(Islamic Repub.of)

2.12 Gross Fixed Capital Formation by Kind of Activity of Owner, ISIC Divisions, in Constant Prices

Thousand Million Iranian rials
Fiscal year beginning 21 March

	1970	1975	1980	1981	1982	1983	1984	1985	1986	1987	1988	1989
					At constant prices of:1974							
					All Producers							
1 Agriculture, hunting, forestry and fishing	17.9	59.6	24.5	35.1	34.5	62.2	55.7	42.3	39.4	36.6	24.1	...
2 Mining and quarrying ab	17.7	61.2	27.4	30.6	44.7	39.3	28.8	23.6	26.8	13.8	32.1	...
3 Manufacturing b	49.9	158.0	48.7	48.5	57.4	79.6	77.8	47.6	41.2	38.7	41.2	...
4 Electricity, gas and water c	13.2	54.4	31.1	35.3	44.5	50.9	37.9	46.6	43.5	28.0	14.3	...
5 Construction	97.2	221.1	250.6	197.1	217.4	287.7	268.1	276.7	224.1	203.4	178.5	...
6 Wholesale and retail trade, restaurants and hotels	...	...	...	...	...	...	...	...	...	...	...	
7 Transport, storage and communication	61.6	203.5	86.2	123.5	148.5	236.7	217.2	153.7	77.6	52.4	40.4	...
8 Finance, insurance, real estate and business services	28.5	116.8	85.3	92.7	71.5	103.2	84.2	116.8	91.1	71.9	51.9	...
9 Community, social and personal services												...
Total Industries	286.0	874.6	553.8	562.8	618.5	859.6	769.7	707.3	543.7	444.8	382.5	...
Producers of Government Services	...	...	...	...	...	...	...	...	...	...	...	
Private Non-Profit Institutions Serving Households	...	...	...	...	...	...	...	...	...	...	...	...
Total	286.0	874.6	553.8	562.8	618.5	859.6	769.7	707.3	543.7	444.8	382.5	...

a) Item 'Mining and quarrying' refers only to oil and gas production.
b) Mining is included in item 'Manufacturing'.
c) Item 'Electricity, gas and water' excludes gas.

Iraq

General note. The preparaton of national accounts statistics in Iraq is undertaken by the Central Statistical Organization, Baghdad. The following presentation of sources and methods is mainly based on information contained in a handbook entitled 'Technical Note on the Estimation of National Income of the Republic of Iraq, 1962-1965'. The estimates are generally in accordance with the classifications and definitions recommended in the United Nations System of National Accounts (SNA). Input-output tables have been published in 'Input-Output and Social Accounts of Iraq 1960-1963'. The following tables have been prepared from successive replies to the United Nations national accounts questionnaire. When the scope and coverage of the estimates differ for conceptual or statistical reasons from the definitions and classifications recommended in SNA, a footnote is indicated to the relevant tables.

Sources and methods :

(a) Gross domestic product. GDP is estimated mainly through the production approach.

(b) Expenditure on the gross domestic product. The expenditure approach is used to estimate government final consumption expenditure, increase in stocks, and exports and imports of goods and services. This approach, in combination with the commodity-flow approach is used for gross fixed capital formation. The commodity-flow approach is used for private consumption expenditure. The estimates of government final consumption expenditure, consisting of wages, salaries and allowances and intermediate consumption of goods and services are obtained from the final accounts of the government. The estimates of private final consumption expenditure is obtained as a residual for some years, while family budget surveys are used for other years. The data used for the estimation of increase in stocks are obtained from the final accounts of the establishments of the trade, transport and communication sectors. The industrial surveys provide data for the manufacturing industries. The gross fixed capital formation is classified according to economic activities and kinds of assets. Data are obtained from various sources such as the ordinary budget, actual expenditure on the development planning budget, reports and surveys. Foreign trade statistics provide data on imports of capital goods in c.i.f. values. Exports and imports of goods and services are estimated from foreign trade statistics and balance-of-payments data. GDP by expenditure type at constant prices is not estimated.

(c) Cost-structure of the gross domestic product. The estimates of compensation of employees in the socialist sector are obtained from the final accounts of the government and companies. For the private sector, the data are obtained from service surveys and internal trade surveys. Operating surplus is obtained as a residual. The depreciation estimates are prepared according to kinds of fixed assets and are based on the estimates of fixed capital formation, taking into consideration the prices of fixed assets and the average age of each kind of asset. The data on indirect taxes and subsidies are obtained from the actual accounts of the government or from the final accounts of the establishments of the socialist sector.

(d) Gross domestic product by kind of economic activity. The table of GDP by kind of economic activity is prepared in factor values. The production approach is used to estimate the value added of most industries. The income approach is used for transport and storage, private services and producers of government services. The commodity-flow approach is used to estimate gross output of the trade sector. Data on areas cultivated, average yield, quantity and value of each crop are obtained from the Central Statistical Organization while prices are based on a production survey. The production of various types of vegetables is estimated from data of the Ministry of Agriculture, and the valuation is made by using farm prices collected by the Central Statistical Organization. The results of the 1971 Agricultural census are used for estimating the value of fruit production. Intermediate consumption of these agricultural crops are estimated individually. The estimation of livestock products is based on sample surveys. The quantity of meat is estimated by multiplying the number of animals slaughtered in the abbatoirs by the average weight of the animals. The number of animals slaughtered outside the abbatoirs is estimated on the basis of data on exports of skins and guts. The estimate of the output of crude oil, natural gas and sulphur is based on the final accounts of the producing companies, from which data on the quantity and value of production and other factors of the value added are obtained. The data on manufacturing are obtained from the annual and quarterly industrial surveys which collect data on the number of establishments and employees, wages and salaries, quantity and value of inputs, increase in stocks and capital formation. The data for electricity, gas and water are obtained from the balance sheets and final accounts of the concerned establishments and from the Industrial Department of the Central Statistical Organization. The value added in the construction sector is based on the reports of the Central Statistical Organization and data on fixed capital formation which are based on the national development planning budget. The data used to estimate value added in the trade sector are taken from government final accounts, the internal trade survey and the hotel survey. For restaurants and hotels, a survey of services and hotels comprising the number of employees and establishments, wages and salaries, revenue, purchases, etc. is used. The final accounts of public establishments and the reports issued by the Central Statistical Organization are the basis for estimating transport and communication. The gross value of output is obtained by adding intermediate consumption to value added. Data on banking, insurance and other financing establishments have been obtained directly from concerned establishments. The services survey is used for the value added of real-estate services. For ownership of dwellings, rents are imputed based on the rent survey conducted by the Ministry of Finance and the family budget surveys. For government services, estimates are based on final government accounts and balance-sheets and final accounts of semi-governmental institutions. The services survey and the family budget surveys are used for estimating private services. GDP by kind of economic activity at constant prices is estimated taking 1964, 1969 and 1974 as base year.

1.1 Expenditure on the Gross Domestic Product, in Current Prices

Million Iraqi dinars

	1970	1975	1980	1981	1982	1983	1984	1985	1986	1987	1988	1989
1 Government final consumption expenditure	275.7	843.0	2390.4	3282.0	4715.1	5471.2	4788.1	4609.5	...	...	...	...
2 Private final consumption expenditure	577.7	1440.2	3601.9	4156.2	6035.6	6848.9	7815.2	8098.7	...	...	...	...
3 Gross capital formation	202.8	1419.6	4797.7	7054.8	7393.5	1919.4	2777.5	3362.3	...	...	...	...
A Increase in stocks	17.7	357.2	1326.2	1955.8	1696.8	-2793.2	-1150.9	-337.1	...	...	...	...
B Gross fixed capital formation	185.1	1062.4	3471.5	5099.0	5696.7	4712.6	3928.4	3699.4	3371.7	3657.8	2899.2	...
Residential buildings	32.8	116.8	675.6	890.7	1113.3	1100.5	1063.1	781.8	661.1	671.3	848.1	...
Non-residential buildings	28.1	128.6	518.4	690.4	840.2	744.7	466.6	378.5	680.0	1141.3	529.5	...
Other construction and land improvement etc.	42.3	370.8	933.6	1670.9	2002.3	1850.3	1578.8	1220.0	1217.9	1044.0	800.1	...
Other	82.0	446.2	1343.9	1847.0	1741.0	1017.1	819.9	641.7	812.7	801.2	721.5	...
4 Exports of goods and services	437.5	2079.7	10012.4	3587.8	3350.5	3107.9	3734.3	3774.7	...	...	...	...
5 Less: Imports of goods and services	236.6	1692.0	4977.6	7068.3	8447.6	4156.3	4316.4	4476.0	...	...	...	...
Equals: Gross Domestic Product	1257.1	4090.5	15824.8	11012.5	13047.4	13191.1	14798.7	15369.4	14870.1	17900.6	17356.2	...

1.3 Cost Components of the Gross Domestic Product

Million Iraqi dinars

	1970	1975	1980	1981	1982	1983	1984	1985	1986	1987	1988	1989
1 Indirect taxes, net	85.2	116.2	177.7	-203.3	62.4	200.8	371.0	482.1	411.0	300.6	321.4	...
A Indirect taxes	86.8	218.4	504.7	537.7	779.5	701.9	678.0	837.5	783.3	708.2	650.9	...
B Less: Subsidies	1.6	102.2	327.0	741.0	717.1	501.1	307.0	355.4	372.3	407.6	329.5	...
2 Consumption of fixed capital	68.4	296.8	798.2	1150.5	1508.1	1252.2	1660.0	1488.8	1445.9	1584.0	1533.1	...
3 Compensation of employees paid by resident producers to:	389.0	947.3	2802.2	3636.9	4345.3	4394.9	4709.0	4841.1	5100.4	5697.0	5725.0	...
4 Operating surplus	714.5	2730.2	12046.7	6428.4	7172.6	6886.6	8051.1	8557.4	7912.8	10319.0	9776.6	...
Equals: Gross Domestic Product	1257.1	4090.5	15824.8	11012.5	13088.4	12734.5	14791.1	15369.4	14870.1	17900.6	17356.2	...

Iraq

1.10 Gross Domestic Product by Kind of Activity, in Current Prices

Million Iraqi dinars

	1970	1975	1980	1981	1982	1983	1984	1985	1986	1987	1988	1989
1 Agriculture, hunting, forestry and fishing a	194.6	311.6	741.9	955.5	1310.4	1413.6	1941.9	2160.3	2173.7	2518.7	2791.3	...
2 Mining and quarrying	370.5	2061.5	9647.5	3295.0	3166.5	2863.8	3565.5	3484.5	2181.2	3594.8	3390.0	...
3 Manufacturing abc	116.0	270.6	709.0	717.1	949.8	1060.9	1255.4	1425.1	1639.9	2071.1	2073.2	...
4 Electricity, gas and water c	12.7	17.2	49.5	92.4	107.6	124.3	163.3	200.3	219.9	298.5	343.2	...
5 Construction	40.6	356.1	1135.6	1721.6	2250.1	1839.1	1416.8	1343.9	1297.1	1430.8	1061.8	...
6 Wholesale and retail trade, restaurants and hotels bc	98.6	208.7	811.4	1127.3	1520.4	1565.0	1854.9	1931.1	1916.3	2182.7	1867.3	...
7 Transport, storage and communication	71.2	184.6	667.2	782.6	848.9	801.7	807.9	772.3	1104.3	1269.7	1290.9	...
8 Finance, insurance, real estate and business services d	80.9	198.0	651.0	811.2	899.1	1042.5	1534.9	1300.2	1647.5	1788.6	1653.8	...
9 Community, social and personal services d	26.5	43.0	72.4	97.2	94.5	117.4	136.6	153.0	198.4	200.4	273.6	...
Total, Industries	1011.6	3651.3	14485.5	9600.0	11147.3	10828.3	12677.2	12770.7	12378.3	15355.3	14745.1	...
Producers of Government Services	187.5	453.8	1309.1	1750.3	2047.9	2103.9	2434.6	2687.7	2847.8	3228.0	3152.6	...
Other Producers					48.6	35.3	29.2					...
Subtotal e	1199.1	4105.1	15794.6	11350.3	13243.8	12967.5	15141.0	15458.4	15226.1	18583.3	17897.7	...
Less: Imputed bank service charge	27.2	130.8	147.6	134.3	217.8	433.8	720.9	571.1	767.0	983.3	862.9	...
Plus: Import duties	...	...	...	...	...	...	...	...	...	...	...	...
Plus: Value added tax	...	...	...	...	...	...	...	...	...	...	...	...
Plus: Other adjustments f	85.2	116.2	177.7	-203.3	62.4	200.8	371.0	482.1	411.0	300.6	321.4	...
Equals: Gross Domestic Product	1257.1	4090.5	15824.8	11012.5	13088.4	12734.5	14791.1	15369.4	14870.1	17900.6	17356.1	...

a) Agricultural services and related activities such as cotton ginning and pressing are included in item 'Manufacturing'.
b) Distribution of petroleum products is included in item 'Wholesale and retail trade'.
c) Gas distribution is included in item 'Wholesale and retail trade'.
d) Business services are included in item 'Community, social and personal services'.
e) Gross domestic product in factor values.
f) Item 'Other adjustments' refers to indirect taxes net of subsidies.

1.11 Gross Domestic Product by Kind of Activity, in Constant Prices

Million Iraqi dinars

	1970	1975	1980	1981	1982	1983	1984	1985	1986	1987	1988	1989
					At constant prices of:1975							
1 Agriculture, hunting, forestry and fishing a	319.1	311.6	370.8	378.0	418.8	403.2	446.9	517.7	495.5	453.9	471.4	...
2 Mining and quarrying	1496.0	2061.5	3026.2	1088.7	1050.8	1130.2	1399.6	1406.1	1747.2	2793.1	2681.2	...
3 Manufacturing abc	155.9	270.6	544.7	513.9	511.7	516.6	503.9	561.8	538.8	786.7	579.9	...
4 Electricity, gas and water c	9.2	17.2	37.2	41.0	64.6	65.7	73.2	79.1	84.8	87.4	102.5	...
5 Construction	77.6	356.1	758.6	1107.1	1195.2	964.9	684.4	599.7	534.0	543.4	372.0	...
6 Wholesale and retail trade, restaurants and hotels bc	131.1	208.7	574.5	659.9	676.1	602.2	660.1	641.4	630.6	618.0	507.7	...
7 Transport, storage and communication	87.7	184.6	454.2	460.1	358.9	296.0	276.7	253.5	357.7	359.8	351.0	...
8 Finance, insurance, real estate and business services d	89.9	198.0	495.3	552.6	493.0	510.0	607.9	498.0	593.9	577.0	518.1	...
9 Community, social and personal services d	35.9	43.0	49.3	57.1	74.8	60.4	53.0	50.2	64.3	56.8	74.4	...
Total, Industries	2402.4	3651.3	6310.8	4858.4	4843.9	4549.2	4705.7	4607.5	5046.8	6276.1	5658.2	...
Producers of Government Services	254.1	453.8	891.2	1029.0	1021.3	897.5	837.5	882.1	922.5	914.7	857.2	...
Other Producers												...
Subtotal e	2656.5	4105.1	7202.0	5887.4	5865.2	5446.7	5543.2	5489.6	5969.3	7190.8	6515.4	...
Less: Imputed bank service charge	29.8	130.8	100.4	79.1	127.6	184.1	246.9	187.4	248.5	278.6	234.6	...
Plus: Import duties	...	...	...	...	...	...	...	...	...	...	...	...
Plus: Value added tax	...	...	...	...	...	...	...	...	...	...	...	...
Equals: Gross Domestic Product e	2626.7	3974.3	7101.6	5808.3	5737.6	5262.6	5296.3	5302.2	5720.8	6912.7	6280.8	...

a) Agricultural services and related activities such as cotton ginning and pressing are included in item 'Manufacturing'.
b) Distribution of petroleum products is included in item 'Wholesale and retail trade'.
c) Gas distribution is included in item 'Wholesale and retail trade'.
d) Business services are included in item 'Community, social and personal services'.
e) Gross domestic product in factor values.

1.12 Relations Among National Accounting Aggregates

Million Iraqi dinars

	1970	1975	1980	1981	1982	1983	1984	1985	1986	1987	1988	1989
Gross Domestic Product a	1251.2	4022.4	15824.8	11012.5	13088.4	...	...	...	...	...	...	...
Plus: Net factor income from the rest of the world	-166.0	-115.0	474.1	-401.0	-724.9	...	...	...	...	...	...	...
Factor income from the rest of the world	...	...	942.8	1002.8	418.2	...	...	...	...	...	...	...
Less: Factor income to the rest of the world	...	...	468.6	1403.8	1143.1	...	...	...	...	...	...	...
Equals: Gross National Product	1085.2	3907.4	16298.9	10611.5	12363.5	...	...	...	...	...	...	...
Less: Consumption of fixed capital	74.4	296.8	798.2	1150.5	1508.1	...	...	...	...	...	...	...

Iraq

1.12 Relations Among National Accounting Aggregates
(Continued)

Million Iraqi dinars

	1970	1975	1980	1981	1982	1983	1984	1985	1986	1987	1988	1989
Equals: National Income	1010.8	3610.6	15500.7	9461.0	10855.4	...	...	...	...	...	...	...
Plus: Net current transfers from the rest of the world	0.7	-135.0	-176.2	-63.9	-19.4							
Equals: National Disposable Income	1011.5	3475.6	15324.6	9397.1	10836.0	...	...	...	...	...	...	...
Less: Final consumption	847.5	2266.7	5992.3	7438.2	10180.1							
Equals: Net Saving	164.0	1208.9	9332.3	1958.9	655.9							
Less: Surplus of the nation on current transactions	35.6	287.0	5332.8	-3945.4	-5841.4	...	...	...	...	...	...	...
Equals: Net Capital Formation a	128.4	921.9	3999.5	5904.3	6497.3	...						

a) Data for this table have not been revised, therefore, data for some years are not comparable with those of other tables.

2.7 Gross Capital Formation by Type of Good and Owner, in Current Prices

Million Iraqi dinars

	1980				1981				1982			
	TOTAL	Total Private	Public Enterprises	General Government	TOTAL	Total Private	Public Enterprises	General Government	TOTAL	Total Private	Public Enterprises	General Government
Increase in stocks, total	1326.2	...	...	...	1955.8	...	...	...	1696.8	...	...	...
Gross Fixed Capital Formation, Total	3471.5	748.0	...	...	5099.0	1009.5	...	...	5696.8	1122.4	...	...
1 Residential buildings	675.6	486.5	...	...	890.7	672.6	...	...	1113.3	733.1	...	...
2 Non-residential buildings	518.4	14.4	...	...	690.4	41.2	...	...	840.2	30.8	...	...
3 Other construction	933.5	-	...	...	1670.9	0.2	...	...	2002.3	0.1	...	...
4 Land improvement and plantation and orchard development	...	...	...	...	...	...	...	...	...	...	...	...
5 Producers' durable goods	1344.0	247.1	...	...	1847.0	295.5	...	...	1741.0	358.4	...	...
A Transport equipment	467.0	161.0	...	...	642.8	164.8	...	...	517.2	243.8	...	...
B Machinery and equipment	877.0	86.1	...	...	1204.2	130.7	...	...	1223.8	114.6	...	...
6 Breeding stock, dairy cattle, etc.	...	...	...	...	...	...	...	...	...	...	...	...
Total Gross Capital Formation	4797.7	...	...	...	7054.8	...	...	...	7393.5	...	...	...

	1983				1984				1985			
	TOTAL	Total Private	Public Enterprises	General Government	TOTAL	Total Private	Public Enterprises	General Government	TOTAL	Total Private	Public Enterprises	General Government
Increase in stocks, total	-2793.2	...	...	...	-1150.9	...	...	...	-337.1	...	...	...
Gross Fixed Capital Formation, Total	4712.6	819.9	...	...	3928.4	865.0	...	...	3699.4	707.0	...	...
1 Residential buildings	1100.5	718.6	...	...	1063.1	733.2	...	...	781.8	576.5	...	...
2 Non-residential buildings	744.7	25.4	...	...	466.6	34.5	...	...	378.5	36.2	...	...
3 Other construction	1850.3	3.6	...	...	1578.8	0.7	...	...	1220.0	1.2	...	...
4 Land improvement and plantation and orchard development	...	...	...	...	...	...	...	...	...	...	...	...
5 Producers' durable goods	1017.1	72.3	...	...	819.9	96.6	...	...	641.7	93.1	...	...
A Transport equipment	159.2	13.9	...	...	153.8	52.8	...	...	110.9	31.8	...	...
B Machinery and equipment	857.9	58.4	...	...	666.1	43.8	...	...	530.8	61.3	...	...
6 Breeding stock, dairy cattle, etc.	...	...	...	...	...	...	...	...	...	...	...	...
Total Gross Capital Formation	1919.4	...	...	...	2777.5	...	...	...	3362.3	...	...	...

	1986				1987				1988			
	TOTAL	Total Private	Public Enterprises	General Government	TOTAL	Total Private	Public Enterprises	General Government	TOTAL	Total Private	Public Enterprises	General Government
Increase in stocks, total	...	...	...	...	...	...	...	...	...	...	...	...
Gross Fixed Capital Formation, Total	3371.7	680.4	...	...	3657.8	623.6	...	...	2899.2	805.4	...	...
1 Residential buildings	661.1	561.4	...	...	671.3	541.5	...	...	848.1	748.2	...	...
2 Non-residential buildings	680.0	54.0	...	...	1141.3	42.8	...	...	529.5	26.4	...	...
3 Other construction	1217.9	0.2	...	...	1044.0	0.9	...	...	800.1	0.6	...	...
4 Land improvement and plantation and orchard development	...	...	...	...	...	...	...	...	...	...	...	...
5 Producers' durable goods	812.7	64.8	...	...	801.2	38.4	...	...	721.5	30.2	...	...
A Transport equipment	64.5	13.2	...	...	231.5	7.3	...	...	269.6	8.2	...	...
B Machinery and equipment	748.2	51.6	...	...	569.7	31.1	...	...	451.9	22.0	...	...
6 Breeding stock, dairy cattle, etc.	...	...	...	...	...	...	...	...	...	...	...	...
Total Gross Capital Formation	...	...	...	...	...	...	...	...	...	...	...	...

Iraq

2.8 Gross Capital Formation by Type of Good and Owner, in Constant Prices

Million Iraqi dinars

	1980				1981				1982			
	TOTAL	Total Private	Public Enterprises	General Government	TOTAL	Total Private	Public Enterprises	General Government	TOTAL	Total Private	Public Enterprises	General Government
	At constant prices of:1975											
Increase in stocks, total	...	...	...	...					...	...	...	...
Gross Fixed Capital Formation, Total	2375.9	515.7	...	...	3231.1	641.7	...	...	3321.4	667.3	...	...
1 Residential buildings	451.3	325.0	...	...	549.1	414.7	...	...	632.9	416.8	...	...
2 Non-residential buildings	346.3	9.6	...	...	425.6	25.4	...	...	477.6	17.5	...	...
3 Other construction	623.6	-	...	...	1030.1	-	...	...	1138.3	-	...	...
4 Land improvement and plantation and orchard development	...	...	...	...	...	...	...	...	...	...	...	...
5 Producers' durable goods	954.7	181.1	...	...	1226.3	201.6	...	...	1072.6	233.0	...	...
A Transport equipment	345.8	121.5	...	...	457.2	117.6	...	...	348.3	164.4	...	...
B Machinery and equipment	608.9	59.6	...	...	769.1	84.0	...	...	724.3	68.6	...	...
6 Breeding stock, dairy cattle, etc.												
Total Gross Capital Formation	...	...	...	...	...	...	...	...	...	...	...	...

	1983				1984				1985			
	TOTAL	Total Private	Public Enterprises	General Government	TOTAL	Total Private	Public Enterprises	General Government	TOTAL	Total Private	Public Enterprises	General Government
	At constant prices of:1975											
Increase in stocks, total	...	...	...	...	...	...	...	...	...	...	...	...
Gross Fixed Capital Formation, Total	2517.2	433.6	...	...	1941.2	426.4	...	...	1684.9	378.8	...	...
1 Residential buildings	577.4	377.0	...	...	514.3	354.8	...	...	438.9	300.1	...	...
2 Non-residential buildings	390.7	13.3	...	...	225.7	16.7	...	...	217.4	22.0	...	...
3 Other construction	970.8	1.9	...	...	763.8	0.3	...	...	669.2	0.3	...	...
4 Land improvement and plantation and orchard development	...	...	...	...	...	...	...	...	...	...	...	...
5 Producers' durable goods	578.3	41.4	...	...	437.4	54.6	...	...	359.4	56.4	...	...
A Transport equipment	101.4	32.5	...	...	92.7	31.8	...	...	60.1	26.1	...	...
B Machinery and equipment	476.9	8.9	...	...	344.7	22.8	...	...	299.3	30.3	...	...
6 Breeding stock, dairy cattle, etc.	...	...	...	...	...	...	...	...	...	...	...	...
Total Gross Capital Formation	...	...	...	...	...	...	...	...	...	...	...	...

	1986				1987				1988			
	TOTAL	Total Private	Public Enterprises	General Government	TOTAL	Total Private	Public Enterprises	General Government	TOTAL	Total Private	Public Enterprises	General Government
	At constant prices of:1975											
Increase in stocks, total	...	...	...	...	...	...	...	...	...	...	...	...
Gross Fixed Capital Formation, Total	1422.2	283.7	...	...	1437.1	356.5	...	...	1067.2	284.1	...	...
1 Residential buildings	272.2	231.1	...	...	254.9	307.9	...	...	297.2	262.1	...	...
2 Non-residential buildings	280.0	22.2	...	...	429.7	24.4	...	...	185.5	9.2	...	...
3 Other construction	501.4	0.1	...	...	396.5	0.5	...	...	280.4	0.2	...	...
4 Land improvement and plantation and orchard development	...	...	...	...	...	...	...	...	...	...	...	...
5 Producers' durable goods	368.6	30.3	...	...	356.0	23.7	...	...	304.1	12.6	...	...
A Transport equipment	34.7	7.1	...	...	119.5	4.9	...	...	129.6	4.0	...	...
B Machinery and equipment	333.9	23.2	...	...	236.5	18.8	...	...	174.5	8.6	...	...
6 Breeding stock, dairy cattle, etc.	...	...	...	...	...	...	...	...	...	...	...	...
Total Gross Capital Formation	...	...	...	...	...	...	...	...	...	...	...	...

2.11 Gross Fixed Capital Formation by Kind of Activity of Owner, ISIC Divisions, in Current Prices

Million Iraqi dinars

	1970	1975	1980	1981	1982	1983	1984	1985	1986	1987	1988	1989
	All Producers											
1 Agriculture, hunting, forestry and fishing	23.0	76.0	452.0	549.5	607.2	507.6	505.7	483.3	416.3	335.0	345.8	...
2 Mining and quarrying	7.6	87.1	191.3	211.6	241.5	194.3	141.6	333.9	181.3	215.3	343.0	...
3 Manufacturing	42.5	242.0	468.4	661.0	736.4	563.8	286.1	270.3	282.6	152.8	162.5	...
4 Electricity, gas and water	12.1	70.1	271.3	398.0	630.6	607.3	454.5	366.8	492.7	357.0	285.5	...

Iraq

2.11 Gross Fixed Capital Formation by Kind of Activity of Owner, ISIC Divisions, in Current Prices
(Continued)

Million Iraqi dinars

	1970	1975	1980	1981	1982	1983	1984	1985	1986	1987	1988	1989
5 Construction	3.9	35.9	137.1	177.7	142.8	24.3	69.6	42.8	22.0	20.8	24.8	...
6 Wholesale and retail trade, restaurants and hotels a	7.9	33.7	149.1	242.3	194.7	91.7	93.4	95.9	103.2	45.7	63.2	...
7 Transport, storage and communication	26.8	320.7	662.0	1195.0	1208.1	803.1	801.5	744.8	727.0	263.0	182.1	...
8 Finance, insurance, real estate and business services b	34.3	82.9	449.7	670.3	725.0	712.4	725.4	660.7	546.1	521.5	737.6	...
9 Community, social and personal services ab	4.3	1.2	1.3	29.4	16.7	2.6	3.0	4.0	3.4	4.3	2.5	...
Total Industries	162.4	949.6	2782.2	4134.8	4503.0	3507.1	3080.8	3002.5	2774.6	1915.4	2147.0	...
Producers of Government Services	22.7	112.8	689.3	964.2	1193.7	1205.5	847.6	696.9	597.1	1742.4	752.1	...
Private Non-Profit Institutions Serving Households	...	...	...	...	...	...	...	...	...	...	...	...
Total	185.1	1062.4	3471.5	5099.0	5696.7	4712.6	3928.4	3699.4	3371.7	3657.8	2899.1	...

a) Restaurants and hotels are included in item 'Community, social and personal services'.
b) Business services are included in item 'Community, social and personal services'.

4.3 Cost Components of Value Added

Million Iraqi dinars

	1980						1981					
	Compensation of Employees	Capital Consumption	Net Operating Surplus	Indirect Taxes	Less: Subsidies Received	Value Added	Compensation of Employees	Capital Consumption	Net Operating Surplus	Indirect Taxes	Less: Subsidies Received	Value Added
All Producers												
1 Agriculture, hunting, forestry and fishing a	255.2	...	486.7	...	...	741.9	328.7	...	626.8	...	...	955.5
2 Mining and quarrying	81.3	...	9566.2	...	...	9647.5	83.9	...	3211.1	...	...	3295.0
3 Manufacturing abc	253.5	...	455.5	...	...	709.0	305.0	...	412.1	...	...	717.1
4 Electricity, gas and water c	44.7	...	4.8	...	...	49.5	45.0	...	47.4	...	...	92.4
5 Construction	450.4	...	685.2	...	...	1135.6	669.8	...	1051.8	...	...	1721.6
6 Wholesale and retail trade, restaurants and hotels bc	138.2	...	673.2	...	...	811.4	154.6	...	972.7	...	...	1127.3
7 Transport, storage and communication	335.3	...	331.9	...	...	667.2	381.0	...	401.6	...	...	782.6
8 Finance, insurance, real estate and business services d	24.4	...	626.6	...	...	651.0	30.7	...	780.6	...	...	811.3
9 Community, social and personal services d	24.2	...	48.2	...	...	72.4	32.3	...	64.9	...	...	97.2
Total, Industries	1607.2	...	12878.3	...	...	14485.5	2031.0	...	7569.0	...	...	9600.0
Producers of Government Services	1195.1	...	114.0	...	...	1309.1	1605.9	...	144.4	...	...	1750.3
Other Producers		...		...	...			...		...	...	
Total e	2802.3	...	12992.3	...	...	15794.6	3636.9	...	7713.4	...	...	11350.3
Less: Imputed bank service charge	...	...	147.5	...	...	147.5	...	...	134.5	...	...	134.5
Import duties	...	...	...	...	...	...	...	...	...	...	...	...
Value added tax	...	...	...	...	...	...	...	...	...	...	...	...
Other adjustments	...	...	...	504.7	327.0	177.7	...	...	...	537.7	741.0	-203.3
Total f	2802.3	...	12844.8	504.7	327.0	15824.8	3636.9	...	7578.9	537.7	741.0	11012.5

	1982						1983					
	Compensation of Employees	Capital Consumption	Net Operating Surplus	Indirect Taxes	Less: Subsidies Received	Value Added	Compensation of Employees	Capital Consumption	Net Operating Surplus	Indirect Taxes	Less: Subsidies Received	Value Added
All Producers												
1 Agriculture, hunting, forestry and fishing a	450.5	...	859.1	...	...	1309.6	486.3	...	927.3	...	...	1413.6
2 Mining and quarrying	83.0	...	2862.0	...	...	2945.0	84.8	...	2779.0	...	...	2863.8
3 Manufacturing abc	331.8	...	618.0	...	...	949.8	346.5	...	642.1	...	...	988.6
4 Electricity, gas and water c	85.0	...	21.0	...	...	106.0	79.3	...	45.0	...	...	124.3
5 Construction	842.6	...	1259.7	...	...	2102.3	778.5	...	1060.6	...	...	1839.1
6 Wholesale and retail trade, restaurants and hotels bc	183.4	...	1306.7	...	...	1490.1	221.0	...	1344.0	...	...	1565.0
7 Transport, storage and communication	365.3	...	442.6	...	...	807.9	367.3	...	434.4	...	...	801.7
8 Finance, insurance, real estate and business services d	32.6	...	807.3	...	...	839.9	32.1	...	1010.4	...	...	1042.5
9 Community, social and personal services d	45.4	...	82.2	...	...	127.6	51.1	...	91.1	...	...	142.2

Iraq

4.3 Cost Components of Value Added
(Continued)

Million Iraqi dinars

	1982						1983					
	Compensation of Employees	Capital Consumption	Net Operating Surplus	Indirect Taxes	Less: Subsidies Received	Value Added	Compensation of Employees	Capital Consumption	Net Operating Surplus	Indirect Taxes	Less: Subsidies Received	Value Added
Total, Industries	2419.6	...	8258.6	...	...	10678.2	2446.9	...	8333.9	...	...	10780.8
Producers of Government Services	1925.7	...	168.1	...	...	2093.8	1948.0	...	166.4	...	...	2114.4
Other Producers		...			...	...		...			...	...
Total e	4345.3	...	8426.7	...	...	12772.0	4394.9	...	8500.3	...	...	12895.2
Less: Imputed bank service charge	...	...	217.8	...	...	217.8	...	...	433.8	...	...	433.8
Import duties	...	...	...	...	...	...	...	...	...	...	...	...
Value added tax	...	...	...	...	...	...	...	...	...	...	...	...
Other adjustments	...	...	...	779.5	717.1	62.3	...	...	...	701.9	501.1	200.8
Total f	4345.3	...	8208.9	779.5	717.1	12616.6	4394.9	...	8066.5	701.9	501.1	12662.2

	1984						1985					
	Compensation of Employees	Capital Consumption	Net Operating Surplus	Indirect Taxes	Less: Subsidies Received	Value Added	Compensation of Employees	Capital Consumption	Net Operating Surplus	Indirect Taxes	Less: Subsidies Received	Value Added
All Producers												
1 Agriculture, hunting, forestry and fishing a	668.0	...	1273.9	...	...	1941.9	743.2	...	1417.1	...	...	2160.3
2 Mining and quarrying	67.1	...	3498.4	...	...	3565.5	67.6	...	3416.9	...	...	3484.5
3 Manufacturing abc	329.1	...	926.4	...	...	1255.5	361.5	...	1063.6	...	...	1425.1
4 Electricity, gas and water c	76.0	...	87.2	...	...	163.2	69.5	...	130.8	...	...	200.3
5 Construction	738.0	...	678.8	...	...	1416.8	616.6	...	727.3	...	...	1343.9
6 Wholesale and retail trade, restaurants and hotels bc	207.0	...	1647.9	...	...	1854.9	159.9	...	1771.2	...	...	1931.1
7 Transport, storage and communication	380.4	...	427.5	...	...	807.9	332.2	...	440.1	...	...	772.3
8 Finance, insurance, real estate and business services d	32.1	...	1502.8	...	...	1534.9	33.3	...	1266.9	...	...	1300.2
9 Community, social and personal services d	62.3	...	92.4	...	...	154.7	62.7	...	90.3	...	...	153.0
Total, Industries	2560.0	...	10135.3	...	...	12695.3	2446.5	...	10324.2	...	...	12770.7
Producers of Government Services	2149.4	...	296.3	...	...	2445.7	2394.6	...	293.1	...	...	2687.7
Other Producers		...			...			...			...	
Total e	4709.4	...	10431.6	...	...	15141.0	4841.1	...	10617.3	...	...	15458.4
Less: Imputed bank service charge	...	...	720.9	...	...	720.9	...	...	571.1	...	...	571.1
Import duties	...	...	...	...	...	...	...	...	...	...	...	...
Value added tax	...	...	...	...	...	...	...	...	...	...	...	...
Other adjustments	...	...	...	678.4	306.9	371.5	...	...	...	837.5	355.4	482.1
Total f	4709.4	...	9710.7	678.4	306.9	14791.6	4841.1	...	10046.2	837.5	355.4	15369.4

	1986						1987					
	Compensation of Employees	Capital Consumption	Net Operating Surplus	Indirect Taxes	Less: Subsidies Received	Value Added	Compensation of Employees	Capital Consumption	Net Operating Surplus	Indirect Taxes	Less: Subsidies Received	Value Added
All Producers												
1 Agriculture, hunting, forestry and fishing a	747.8	...	1425.9	...	...	2173.7	866.4	...	1652.3	...	...	2518.7
2 Mining and quarrying	78.8	...	2102.4	...	...	2181.2	77.6	...	3517.2	...	...	3594.8
3 Manufacturing abc	397.6	...	1247.3	...	...	1639.9	410.3	...	1660.8	...	...	2071.1
4 Electricity, gas and water c	76.5	...	143.4	...	...	219.9	67.3	...	231.2	...	...	298.5
5 Construction	512.1	...	785.0	...	...	1297.1	602.7	...	828.1	...	...	1430.8
6 Wholesale and retail trade, restaurants and hotels bc	207.2	...	1709.1	...	...	1916.3	196.6	...	1986.1	...	...	2182.7
7 Transport, storage and communication	423.2	...	681.1	...	...	1104.3	475.3	...	794.4	...	...	1269.7
8 Finance, insurance, real estate and business services d	34.4	...	1613.1	...	...	1647.5	35.9	...	1752.7	...	...	1788.6
9 Community, social and personal services d	72.1	...	126.3	...	...	198.4	35.2	...	165.2	...	...	200.4
Total, Industries	2549.7	...	9828.6	...	...	12378.3	2767.3	...	12588.0	...	...	15355.3
Producers of Government Services	2550.7	...	297.1	...	...	2847.8	2929.7	...	298.3	...	...	3228.0
Other Producers		...			...			...			...	
Total e	5100.4	...	10125.7	...	...	15226.1	5697.0	...	12886.3	...	...	18583.3
Less: Imputed bank service charge	...	...	767.0	...	...	767.0	...	...	983.3	...	...	983.3
Import duties	...	...	...	...	...	...	...	...	...	...	...	...
Value added tax	...	...	...	...	...	...	...	...	...	...	...	...
Other adjustments	...	...	...	783.3	372.3	411.0	...	...	...	708.2	407.6	300.6
Total f	5100.4	...	9358.7	783.3	372.3	14870.1	5697.0	...	11903.0	708.2	407.6	17900.6

874

Iraq

4.3 Cost Components of Value Added

Million Iraqi dinars

1988 — All Producers

	Compensation of Employees	Capital Consumption	Net Operating Surplus	Indirect Taxes	Less: Subsidies Received	Value Added
1 Agriculture, hunting, forestry and fishing a	960.2	...	1831.1	...	...	2791.3
2 Mining and quarrying	78.2	...	3311.8	...	...	3390.0
3 Manufacturing abc	341.4	...	1731.9	...	...	2073.3
4 Electricity, gas and water c	59.5	...	283.7	...	...	343.2
5 Construction	630.0	...	431.8	...	...	1061.8
6 Wholesale and retail trade, restaurants and hotels bc	184.8	...	1682.5	...	...	1867.3
7 Transport, storage and communication	479.5	...	811.4	...	...	1290.9
8 Finance, insurance, real estate and business services d	38.2	...	1615.6	...	...	1653.8
9 Community, social and personal services d	100.1	...	173.4	...	...	273.5
Total, Industries	2871.9	...	11873.2	...	...	14745.1
Producers of Government Services	2853.1	...	299.5	...	...	3152.6
Other Producers	...	...	...	...	...	...
Total e	5725.0	...	12172.7	...	...	17897.7
Less: Imputed bank service charge	...	...	862.9	...	...	862.9
Import duties	...	...	...	...	...	...
Value added tax	...	...	...	...	...	...
Other adjustments	...	...	...	650.9	329.5	321.4
Total f	5725.0	...	11309.8	650.9	329.5	17356.2

a) Agricultural services and related activities such as cotton ginning and pressing are included in item 'Manufacturing'.
b) Distribution of petroleum products is included in item 'Wholesale and retail trade'.
c) Gas distribution is included in item 'Wholesale and retail trade'.
d) Business services are included in item 'Community, social and personal services'.
e) Gross domestic product in factor values.
f) Column 'Consumption of fixed capital' is included in column 'Net operating surplus'.

Ireland

General note. The preparation of national accounts statistics in Ireland is undertaken by the Central Statistics Office, Dublin. The official estimates are published annually in "National Income and Expenditure". The following presentation of sources and methods is mainly based on a report entitled "Basic statistics needed for the ESA accounts and tables: present situation and prospects for improvements", prepared by the Statistical Office of the European Communities in 1976 and on information received from Ireland's Central Statistics Office. The estimates are generally in accordance with the classifications and definitions recommended in the United Nations System of National Accounts (SNA). Official Input-Output tables have been published in respect of the years 1964, 1969 and 1975. The following tables have been prepared from successive replies to the United Nations national accounts questionnaire. When the scope and coverage of the estimates differ for conceptual or statistical reasons from the definitions and classifications recommended in SNA, a footnote is indicated to the relevant tables.

Sources and methods :

(a) **Gross domestic product.** Gross domestic product is estimated mainly through the income approach.

The data on economic activity is prepared in factor values. The income approach is used to estimate the value added of all industries except agriculture, for which the production approach is used. Annual estimates of agricultural output are calculated on a commodity basis for crops, livestock and livestock products. The data on quantities and values are obtained from various sources such as Department of Agriculture and Central Statistics Office. The total quantities purchased and barley are available from various inquiries about important agricultural items such as wheat and transport costs. For live exports, f.o.b. export value less an allowance for marketing margins, is taken as the output value. For the remaining items market prices are used as the basis for evaluation. Input data are obtained through the Department of Agriculture for fertilizers. Data for seeds are compiled indirectly from acreages and seeding rates. Own-account consumption of food and fuel is valued at agricultural prices. Quarterly surveys of turnover and employment are conducted for manufacturing. For more than three persons, annual censuses of distribution provide employing enterprises. For mining, quarrying and manufacturing enterprises employing small-scale manufacturing, the number of persons engaged, which is derived as the difference between population census data and that from the production census, interpolated for intercensal years and projected forward, are multiplied by average income per person. The estimates of electricity, gas and water and of construction are based on annual inquiries. For trade, censuses of distribution provide bench-mark data for turnover, purchase of products, wages and salaries and intermediate inputs. For intervening years, monthly turnover figures from a sample of 2,500 establishments are used together with annual estimates of the number of employees and trends in earnings. For restaurants and hotels, annual surveys and revenue data are used. Transport is mainly provided by public enterprises and are obtained from published accounts. Data obtained from annual reports, direct surveys on wages and salaries and revenue statistics are used for the estimates of the financial sector. For real estate and business services, data from population census, imputed average income and revenue accounts are used. The imputed rent of owner-occupied dwellings is taken as the average rent paid for similar dwellings in similar locations. Estimates of other private services are based on the results of inquiries into wages and salaries and on trends in operating surplus taken from revenue data. Data on government services are obtained from the government accounts. For the constant price estimates, double deflation is used for agriculture. Value added of all other economic activity sectors of GDP is extrapolated by a quantity index.

(b) **Expenditure on the gross domestic product.** The expenditure approach is used to estimate government final consumption expenditure, increase in stocks, and exports and imports of goods and services. The commodity-flow approach is used to estimate private final consumption expenditure and gross fixed capital formation except in the case of building and construction and government capital formation. Government final consumption expenditure is estimated from the accounts of the various government bodies such as the ministries, the local authorities and Health Boards, extrabudgetary funds and the Industrial Development Authority. Data on private consumption expenditure are also estimated from Household Budget Inquiries. Largescale Household Budget Surveys were carried out in 1951-52, 1965-66, 1973 and 1980. The 1951-52 and 1965-66 surveys were restricted to urban areas. Smallscale annual Household Budget Surveys were undertaken in 1974-1979 and 1981. These were restricted to urban areas for 1974-1979 but covered urban and rural areas in 1981. Estimates of transactions in goods and services are obtained from the censuses of industrial production and the statistics of imports and exports of merchandise. The goods are valued at national average retail prices where volume data are available. Otherwise, they are aggregated at appropriate producers' or import prices and adjusted for distribution costs. In building up the stock figures, industrial stocks from stocks inquiries and censuses of industrial production, and stockpiles of strategic commodities from the Department of Agriculture. Investment in building and construction is estimated through the use of data from the production surveys. Estimates of locally produced goods are obtained from production census data minus exports plus distribution margins. The estimates of imports and exports of goods and services are obtained from balance-of-payments, special studies and surveys. For the constant price estimates, direct revaluation at base-year prices is used for items of private final consumption expenditure where quantity data are available. For all other components of GDP by expenditure type, price deflation is used.

(c) **Cost-structure of the gross domestic product.** Estimates of compensation of employees are based on wage rates and number of farm worker for the agricultural

1.1 Expenditure on the Gross Domestic Product, in Current Prices

Million Irish pounds

	1970	1975	1980	1981	1982	1983	1984	1985	1986	1987	1988	1989
1 Government final consumption expenditure	237.3	705.3	1860.2	2260.3	2646.2	2857.3	3066.6	3301.0	3542.1	3576.6	3595.0	3683.0
2 Private final consumption expenditure	1116.0	2431.9	6157.6	7489.9	8001.0	8813.8	9651.7	10490.6	11691.5	11690.6	12782.8	13523.0
3 Gross capital formation	396.5	884.8	2604.2	3222.4	3716.2	3520.7	3733.4	3557.6	3535.7	3384.5	3544.0	4410.0
A Increase in stocks	28.0	23.0	-73.0	-145.7	168.9	101.7	217.0	159.4	136.7	10.3	-185.0	5.0
B Gross fixed capital formation	368.5	861.8	2677.2	3368.1	3547.3	3419.0	3516.4	3398.2	3399.0	3354.2	3729.0	4405.0
Residential buildings	61.7	209.7	578.0	708.5	759.2	786.7	856.6	845.4	881.7	835.9	774.0	947.0
Non-residential buildings and construction and land improvement etc.	127.7	249.8	829.6	1045.7	1188.5	985.5	984.2	928.0	920.4	850.7	985.0	1097.0
Other	179.1	402.3	1269.6	1613.9	1599.7	1646.8	1675.6	1624.8	1596.9	1667.6	1970.0	2361.0
4 Exports of goods and services	598.9	1619.0	4638.6	5503.9	6433.1	7751.6	9770.0	10738.4	10351.5	11785.1	13533.9	15991.0
5 Less: Imports of goods and services	728.5	1849.0	5889.9	7117.2	7414.5	8164.3	9815.1	10396.6	9960.4	10467.6	11565.0	13889.0
Equals: Gross Domestic Product	1620.2	3792.0	9360.7	11359.9	13389.0	14779.2	16406.0	17691.0	18736.9	2004.4	21483.0	23919.0

1.2 Expenditure on the Gross Domestic Product, in Constant Prices

Million Irish pounds

At constant prices of 1985

	1970	1975	1980	1981	1982	1983	1984	1985	1986	1987	1988	1989
1 Government final consumption expenditure	1713.8	2498.9	3163.1	3173.6	3276.6	3264.6	3241.9	3301.0	3383.7	3218.9	3084.0	2976.0
2 Private final consumption expenditure	6955.6	8293.2	10419.8	10496.8	9932.8	9848.9	10132.4	10490.6	10705.6	10944.9	11213.0	11792.0
3 Gross capital formation	2389.9	2531.9	3770.0	4329.1	4120.5	3877.6	3864.8	3557.6	3470.9	3236.1	3175.0	3759.0
A Increase in stocks	170.3	-47.6	-149.4	-175.8	-175.5	100.5	208.0	159.4	151.2	0.0	-208.0	-7.0
B Gross fixed capital formation	2219.5	2579.5	3922.5	4296.2	4149.6	3764.3	3669.6	3398.2	3319.7	3235.3	3383.0	3766.0

Ireland

1.2 Expenditure on the Gross Domestic Product, in Constant Prices (Continued)

Million Irish pounds

	1970	1975	1980	1981	1982	1983	1984	1985	1986	1987	1988	1989
At constant prices of 1985												
Residential buildings						875.9	841.0	845.4	845.6	791.7	691.0	788.0
Non-residential buildings				1406.4	1106.4	1032.6	928.0	879.9	790.7	880.0	937.0
Other construction and land improvement etc.			1881.1	1816.9	1761.9	1624.8	1594.2	1652.9	1812.0	2041.0
Other												
4 Exports of goods and services	3579.3	4637.4	7271.4	7413.6	7824.0	8441.8	10075.5	10738.4	11048.3	12527.0	13615.0	14990.0
5 Less: Imports of goods and services	4735.9	5438.6	8887.8	9039.8	8758.0	9166.6	10069.9	10396.9	10981.7	11530.2	11980.0	13283.0
Statistical discrepancy	-26.2	30.9	-53.3	-56.8	57.3							-
Equals: Gross Domestic Product	9876.4	12553.7	15686.2	16207.8	16577.9	16537.4	17257.5	17691.0	17626.8	18396.7	19107.0	20234.0

1.3 Cost Components of the Gross Domestic Product

Million Irish pounds

	1970	1975	1980	1981	1982	1983	1984	1985	1986	1987	1988	1989
1 Indirect taxes, net	235.6	389.1	830.4	1224.8	1567.7	1773.2	1873.6	1816.9	1987.7	2107.9	2151.0	2996.0
A Indirect taxes	314.7	645.8	1586.9	1980.6	2423.2	2794.4	3113.5	3269.6	3475.2	3672.4	3956.0	4368.0
B Less: Subsidies	79.1	256.7	740.8	755.8	855.5	1021.2	1239.9	1452.7	1487.5	1564.5	1814.0	1372.0
2 Consumption of fixed capital	134.9	303.0	1034.2	1163.5	1366.3	1528.3	1596.8	1723.9	1846.4	1993.9	2128.0	2336.0
3 Compensation of employees paid by resident producers to:												
A Resident households	844.8	2157.6	5685.0	6618.0	7551.6	8253.7	8957.1	9504.6	10093.5	10637.8	11140.0	11870.0
B Rest of the world	-	-	-	-	-	-	-	-	-	-	-	-
4 Operating surplus	404.9	942.3	1911.1	2552.4	2896.8	3224.0	3979.1	4645.6	4809.2	5301.7	6063.0	6717.0
Equals: Gross Domestic Product	1620.2	3792.0	9360.7	11359.0	13382.4	14779.2	16406.6	17691.0	18736.8	20041.3	21482.0	23919.0

1.4 General Government Current Receipts and Disbursements

Million Irish pounds

	1970	1975	1980	1981	1982	1983	1984	1985	1986	1987	1988	1989
Receipts												
1 Operating surplus	12.1	12.7	39.0	61.7	80.6	114.0	127.3	174.5	177.1	166.7	...	217.0
2 Property and entrepreneurial income	27.7	64.7	184.1	217.1	315.3	367.3	396.4	434.0	331.8	372.0	...	319.7
3 Taxes, fees and contributions	530.3	1234.0	3310.4	4130.4	5054.0	5783.3	6540.1	6830.8	7448.9	8010.1	...	8918.8
A Indirect taxes [a]	314.7	618.2	1472.1	1852.3	2261.7	2581.1	2874.8	3032.4	3191.4	3343.7	...	3671.9
B Direct taxes	146.1	377.9	1181.5	1476.3	1779.2	2051.2	2414.6	2564.2	2880.4	3178.6	...	3640.9
C Social security contributions	6.9	237.9	656.8	801.8	1012.5	1151.0	1250.7	1334.2	1407.1	1487.8	...	1606.0
D Compulsory fees, fines and penalties [a]	...	...	...	...	...	...	...	...	...	...	...	...
4 Other current transfers	1.5	2.0	96.9	85.7	155.0	180.2	122.6	170.1	157.8	237.3	...	181.0
Total Current Receipts of General Government	571.6	1313.4	3630.4	4494.9	5604.9	6444.8	7186.4	7709.4	8145.6	8786.1	...	9636.5
Disbursements												
1 Government final consumption expenditure [a]	237.6	705.3	1860.2	2260.3	2646.3	2857.3	3066.7	3301.0	3542.1	3575.5	...	3595.2
A Compensation of employees	162.9	460.3	1181.2	1475.0	1725.9	1876.8	2047.1	2176.1	2334.8	2412.7	...	2402.1
B Consumption of fixed capital	11.4	30.6	87.5	81.7	96.0	107.0	119.1	129.9	140.8	149.6	...	158.7
C Purchases of goods and services, net	...	...	...	...	...	...	...	...	...	...	...	...
D Less: Own account fixed capital formation	...	...	...	...	...	...	...	...	...	...	...	...
E Indirect taxes paid, net	60.3	157.9	590.6	821.9	1177.0	1350.8	1503.6	1764.1	1758.1	1894.9	...	1938.9
2 Property income	79.1	137.6	356.4	440.3	500.4	558.1	563.2	585.5	569.2	765.6	...	909.8
3 Subsidies	176.8	563.0	1404.1	1809.4	2396.4	2745.5	3006.2	3325.3	3634.5	3794.5	...	3946.9
4 Other current transfers	58.4	195.3	502.4	673.2	903.0	1044.6	1128.6	1231.8	1303.0	1339.4	...	1322.6
A Social security benefits	91.7	287.8	677.3	875.3	1184.8	1362.2	1514.7	1702.1	1897.5	2002.7	...	2157.4
B Social assistance grants	26.6	79.9	224.4	263.7	308.6	338.7	362.9	391.4	434.1	452.4	...	466.9
C Other	18.1	-250.4	-580.9	-836.9	-1115.3	-1066.7	-953.3	-1270.0	-1358.3	-1245.4	...	-754.3
5 Net saving												
Total Current Disbursements and Net Saving of General Government	571.6	1313.4	3630.4	4495.0	5604.8	6445.0	7186.4	7709.4	8145.6	8786.1	...	9636.5

[a] Item 'Fees, fines and penalties' is included in item 'Indirect taxes', or is offset against item 'Final consumption expenditure'.

877

Ireland

1.7 External Transactions on Current Account, Summary

Million Irish pounds

	1970	1975	1980	1981	1982	1983	1984	1985	1986	1987	1988	1989
Payments to the Rest of the World												
1 Imports of goods and services	728.5	1849.0	5899.9	7117.2	7414.5	8164.2	9815.1	10396.6	9860.4	10467.6	11565.0	13688.0
A Imports of merchandise c.i.f.	667.0	1672.1	5346.1	6486.9	6712.3	7334.2	8892.6	9390.2	8745.5	9137.0	10048.0	12114.0
B Other	61.5	176.9	553.8	630.3	702.2	830.0	922.5	1006.4	1114.9	1330.6	1517.0	1574.0
2 Factor income to the rest of the world	40.9	178.4	832.1	1083.1	1522.9	1745.4	2342.9	2772.9	2705.1	2739.6	3478.0	4311.0
A Compensation of employees	-	-	-	-	-	-	-	-	-	-	-	-
B Property and entrepreneurial income	40.9	178.4	832.1	1083.1	1522.9	1745.4	2342.9	2772.9	2705.1	2739.6	3478.0	4311.0
3 Current transfers to the rest of the world	2.6	34.3	123.4	154.6	191.5	251.6	283.1	312.5	373.7	378.5	363.0	372.0
A Indirect taxes to supranational organizations	-	27.6	99.0	128.3	161.5	213.3	238.7	237.2	283.8	328.8	293.0	318.0
B Other current transfers	2.6	6.7	24.4	26.3	30.0	38.3	44.4	75.3	89.9	49.7	70.0	54.0
4 Surplus of the nation on current transactions	-65.3	-57.7	-1101.0	-1674.8	-1414.7	-1016.7	-952.5	-700.5	-540.2	252.2	375.0	299.0
Payments to the Rest of the World and Surplus of the Nation on Current Transactions	706.7	2004.0	5754.4	6680.1	7714.2	9144.5	11488.6	12781.5	12399.0	13837.9	15781.0	18670.0
Receipts From The Rest of the World												
1 Exports of goods and services	598.9	1619.0	4638.6	5503.6	6433.3	7751.7	9770.0	10738.4	10351.5	11785.1	13533.0	15991.0
A Exports of merchandise f.o.b.	455.0	1370.8	4004.4	4789.2	5591.9	6812.7	8696.0	9526.8	9180.7	10447.1	12073.0	14358.0
B Other	143.9	248.2	634.2	714.4	841.4	939.0	1074.0	1211.6	1170.8	1338.0	1460.0	1632.0
2 Factor income from rest of the world	69.2	182.7	474.0	578.5	595.2	561.5	704.1	807.2	748.1	782.4	936.0	1272.0
A Compensation of employees	1.8	4.7	9.4	11.3	10.6	12.4	12.0	13.4	16.0	16.0	16.0	16.0
B Property and entrepreneurial income	67.4	178.0	464.6	567.2	584.6	549.1	692.1	793.8	732.1	766.4	920.0	1256.0
3 Current transfers from rest of the world	38.6	202.3	641.8	598.0	685.7	831.3	1014.4	1235.9	1299.5	1270.3	1312.0	1408.0
A Subsidies from supranational organisations	-	119.1	384.4	315.5	355.2	463.1	676.8	864.2	918.3	798.9	905.0	1011.0
B Other current transfers	38.6	83.2	257.4	282.5	330.5	368.2	337.6	371.7	381.2	471.4	407.0	397.0
Receipts from the Rest of the World on Current Transactions	706.7	2004.0	5754.4	6680.1	7714.2	9144.5	11488.5	12781.5	12399.1	13837.8	15781.0	18671.0

1.8 Capital Transactions of The Nation, Summary

Million Irish pounds

	1970	1975	1980	1981	1982	1983	1984	1985	1986	1987	1988	1989
Finance of Gross Capital Formation												
Gross saving	331.2	827.1	1503.2	1547.6	2301.6	2503.9	2780.8	2857.0	2995.5	3616.6	3918.0	4709.0
1 Consumption of fixed capital	134.9	303.0	1034.2	1163.5	1366.3	1528.3	1596.8	1723.9	1846.4	1993.9	2128.0	2336.0
A General government	11.4	30.6	87.5	81.7	96.0	107.0	119.1	129.9	140.8	149.6	158.7	160.0
B Corporate and quasi-corporate enterprises	123.5	272.4	946.7	1081.8	1270.3	1421.3	1477.7	1594.0	1705.6	1844.3	1969.3	2176.0
C Other	...	...	...	...	...	...	...	...	...	...	...	...
2 Net saving	196.3	524.1	469.0	384.1	935.3	975.6	1184.0	1133.1	1149.1	1622.7	1790.0	2373.0
A General government	18.1	-250.4	-580.9	-836.9	-1115.3	-1066.9	-953.3	-1270.0	-1358.3	-1245.4	-754.3	...
B Corporate and quasi-corporate enterprises	178.2	774.5	1049.9	1221.0	2050.6	2042.5	2137.3	2403.1	2507.4	2868.1	2544.3	...
C Other	...	...	...	...	...	...	...	...	...	...	...	...
Less: Surplus of the nation on current transactions	-65.3	-57.7	-1101.0	-1674.8	-1414.7	-1016.7	-952.5	-700.5	-540.2	252.2	375.0	299.0
Finance of Gross Capital Formation	396.5	884.8	2604.2	3222.4	3716.3	3520.6	3733.3	3557.5	3535.7	3364.4	3543.0	4410.0
Gross Capital Formation												
Increase in stocks	28.0	23.0	-73.0	-145.7	168.9	101.6	217.0	159.4	136.7	10.3	-185.0	5.0
Gross fixed capital formation	368.5	861.8	2677.2	3368.1	3547.4	3419.0	3516.4	3398.2	3399.0	3354.2	3729.0	4405.0
1 General government	60.2	164.9	412.3	505.6	623.3	649.1	661.6	710.9	693.4	577.5	440.3	...
2 Corporate and quasi-corporate enterprises	308.3	696.9	2264.9	2862.5	2924.1	2769.9	2854.8	2687.3	2705.6	2776.7	3288.7	...
3 Other	...	...	...	...	...	...	...	...	...	...	...	...
Gross Capital Formation	396.5	884.8	2604.2	3222.4	3716.3	3520.6	3733.4	3557.6	3535.7	3364.5	3544.0	4410.0

Ireland

1.10 Gross Domestic Product by Kind of Activity, in Current Prices

Million Irish pounds

	1970	1975	1980	1981	1982	1983	1984	1985	1986	1987	1988	1989
1 Agriculture, hunting, forestry and fishing	232.9	589.2	999.4	1116.8	1328.7	1479.4	1688.7	1555.1	1529.5	1799.2	1998.0	...
2 Mining and quarrying	22.9	49.9										...
3 Manufacturing	327.3	773.4	2520.6	2978.9	3580.4	4096.6	4612.8	5269.3	5540.0	5840.8	6299.0	
4 Electricity, gas and water	36.5	89.9										...
5 Construction	121.8	301.1	862.6	956.6	1026.4	1023.7	1002.7	967.2	945.2	955.5	989.0	
6 Wholesale and retail trade, restaurants and hotels	183.5	397.6	985.0	1275.1	1488.4	1595.6	1671.3	1929.9	1902.5	2015.3	2047.0	
7 Transport, storage and communication	98.9	237.8	463.9	553.1	637.0	656.6	716.1	860.4	1024.4	1128.2	1240.0	
8 Finance, insurance, real estate and business services	61.2	129.4	461.6	534.4	607.5	715.3	870.4	991.6	1097.6	1184.2	1385.0	
9 Community, social and personal services	141.0	353.5	1084.7	1337.2	1519.5	1716.7	1942.4	2021.4	2223.3	2418.5	2614.0	...
Total, Industries	1226.0	2921.8	7377.8	8752.1	10188.1	11283.9	12504.4	13594.9	14262.5	15341.7	16572.0	...
Producers of Government Services	206.1	583.3	1541.2	1911.5	2212.7	2433.6	2672.2	2865.3	3114.7	3279.6	3322.0	...
Other Producers												...
Subtotal	1432.1	3505.1	8919.0	10663.6	12400.8	13717.7	15176.8	16460.2	17377.3	18621.6	19895.0	...
Less: Imputed bank service charge	35.0	102.2	388.0	460.6	555.3	675.4	735.1	817.2	869.6	884.3	968.0	...
Plus: Import duties	...	...	359.3	538.1	585.5	543.3	597.4	633.3	678.3	691.7	791.0	...
Plus: Value added tax	...	...	470.4	617.9	951.5	1193.6	1367.5	1414.6	1550.8	1612.3	1764.0	...
Plus: Other adjustments [a]	223.1	389.1	...	...	...	...	...	...	...	...	...	...
Equals: Gross Domestic Product	1620.2	3792.0	9360.7	11359.0	13382.3	14779.2	16406.6	17690.9	18736.8	20041.3	21482.0	...

a) Item 'Other adjustments' refers to indirect taxes net of subsidies.

1.12 Relations Among National Accounting Aggregates

Million Irish pounds

	1970	1975	1980	1981	1982	1983	1984	1985	1986	1987	1988	1989
Gross Domestic Product	1620.2	3792.0	9360.7	11359.0	13382.3	14779.2	16406.6	17690.9	18736.8	20041.3	21482.0	23919.0
Plus: Net factor income from the rest of the world	28.3	4.3	-358.1	-504.6	-927.7	-1183.9	-1638.8	-1965.7	-1957.0	-1957.2	-2542.0	-3039.0
Factor income from the rest of the world	69.2	182.7	474.0	578.5	595.2	561.5	704.1	807.2	748.1	782.4	936.0	1272.0
Less: Factor income to the rest of the world	40.9	178.4	832.1	1083.1	1522.9	1745.4	2342.9	2772.9	2705.1	2739.6	3478.0	4311.0
Equals: Gross National Product	1648.5	3796.3	9002.6	10854.4	12454.6	13595.3	14767.8	15725.3	16779.8	18084.2	18940.0	20879.0
Less: Consumption of fixed capital	134.9	303.0	1034.2	1163.5	1366.3	1528.3	1596.8	1723.9	1846.4	1993.9	2128.0	2336.0
Equals: National Income	1513.6	3493.3	7968.4	9690.9	11088.3	12067.0	13171.0	14001.4	14933.4	16090.3	16812.0	18543.0
Plus: Net current transfers from the rest of the world	36.0	168.0	518.4	443.4	494.2	579.7	731.3	923.4	925.8	891.7	949.0	1036.0
Current transfers from the rest of the world	38.6	202.3	641.8	598.0	685.7	831.3	1014.4	1235.9	1299.5	1270.3	1312.0	1408.0
Less: Current transfers to the rest of the world	2.6	34.3	123.4	154.6	191.5	251.6	283.1	312.5	373.7	378.5	363.0	372.0
Equals: National Disposable Income	1549.6	3661.3	8486.8	10134.3	11582.5	12646.7	13902.3	14924.7	15859.2	16982.1	17761.0	19579.0
Less: Final consumption	1353.3	3137.2	8017.8	9750.2	10647.2	11671.1	12718.3	13791.6	14710.1	15359.4	15971.0	17206.0
Equals: Net Saving	196.3	524.1	469.0	384.1	935.3	975.6	1184.0	1133.1	1149.1	1622.7	1790.0	2373.0
Less: Surplus of the nation on current transactions	-65.3	-57.7	-1101.0	-1674.8	-1414.7	-1016.7	-952.5	-700.5	-540.2	252.1	375.0	299.0
Equals: Net Capital Formation	261.6	581.8	1570.0	2058.9	2350.0	1992.3	2136.5	1833.6	1689.3	1370.6	1415.0	2075.0

2.5 Private Final Consumption Expenditure by Type and Purpose, in Current Prices

Million Irish pounds

	1970	1975	1980	1981	1982	1983	1984	1985	1986	1987	1988	1989
Final Consumption Expenditure of Resident Households												
1 Food, beverages and tobacco	512.5	1149.1	2562.3	3068.6	3510.7	3807.8	4127.6	4296.1	4507.8	4651.1	4837.0	...
A Food	296.5	687.9	1548.1	1819.0	2023.9	2216.6	2383.0	2408.9	2495.2	2580.8	2641.0	...
B Non-alcoholic beverages	9.6	29.0	79.1	107.1	109.5	128.8	134.4	154.2	155.8	176.1	194.0	...
C Alcoholic beverages	128.3	303.3	695.9	844.6	1009.6	1040.5	1155.1	1233.6	1338.3	1371.8	1468.0	...
D Tobacco	78.0	128.9	239.1	297.9	367.7	422.0	455.0	499.4	518.5	522.4	534.0	...
2 Clothing and footwear	110.4	182.3	453.3	564.6	514.0	582.8	668.4	768.8	796.6	839.6	855.0	...
3 Gross rent, fuel and power	131.3	268.6	678.1	830.3	964.6	1033.0	1117.7	1253.4	1313.0	1336.7	1348.0	...
A Fuel and power	48.8	124.7	350.3	442.4	502.7	528.2	561.7	628.3	643.8	638.7	604.0	...
B Other	82.5	143.9	327.8	387.9	461.9	504.8	556.0	625.1	669.2	698.1	744.0	...
4 Furniture, furnishings and household equipment and operation	85.9	187.6	449.5	515.7	498.4	589.0	609.5	720.8	798.8	839.9	867.0	...
A Household operation	26.1	48.3	123.9	165.4	166.2	196.6	220.0	240.7	295.6	313.9	329.0	...

879

Ireland

2.5 Private Final Consumption Expenditure by Type and Purpose, in Current Prices (Continued)

Million Irish pounds

	1970	1975	1980	1981	1982	1983	1984	1985	1986	1987	1988	1989
B Other	59.7	139.3	325.6	350.3	332.2	392.2	389.4	480.1	503.2	526.0	538.0	...
5 Medical care and health expenses	25.1	52.5	128.3	158.9	184.7	217.9	267.2	308.2	347.2	405.1	435.0	...
6 Transport and communication	115.3	276.2	824.4	1081.9	1076.9	1142.9	1281.1	1389.2	1375.2	1413.8	1558.0	...
A Personal transport equipment	37.2	81.0	277.7	357.5	292.0	267.1	311.3	358.0	373.4	372.0	475.0	...
B Other	78.1	195.4	546.7	724.4	784.9	875.8	969.8	1031.2	1001.8	1041.8	1083.0	...
7 Recreational, entertainment, education and cultural services	88.3	189.1	619.3	768.5	750.4	830.1	903.6	1008.0	1087.5	1225.8	1374.0	...
A Education	18.7	48.2	137.3	175.1	177.8	211.9	245.5	277.5	322.8	376.9	381.0	...
B Other	69.7	140.9	482.0	593.4	572.6	618.4	658.0	730.6	764.6	849.2	993.0	...
8 Miscellaneous goods and services	74.7	150.1	435.0	491.2	509.3	637.2	740.8	862.3	923.0	1078.6	1127.0	...
A Personal care a	8.8	22.9	78.2	99.9	96.1	130.4	141.3	203.0	224.5	244.3	220.0	...
B Expenditures in restaurants, cafes and hotels	17.5	31.9	89.2	109.8	114.8	144.3	154.2	174.5	179.9	210.6	242.0	...
C Other	48.2	95.3	266.9	281.5	298.5	362.5	445.3	484.8	518.5	623.7	665.0	...
Total Final Consumption Expenditure in the Domestic Market by Households, of which	1143.5	2455.7	6150.3	7477.7	8008.1	8840.8	9715.9	10606.8	11149.1	11790.6	12401.0	...
Plus: Direct purchases abroad by resident households	40.1	94.2	283.4	318.5	346.9	363.0	378.0	401.7	511.1	556.3	630.0	...
Less: Direct purchases in the domestic market by non-resident households	74.3	118.0	281.9	308.3	355.0	390.0	442.0	518.0	492.2	564.0	655.0	...
Equals: Final Consumption Expenditure of Resident Households b	1109.3	2431.9	6151.9	7489.9	8001.0	8813.8	9651.7	10490.6	11168.0	11782.8	12376.0	...

Final Consumption Expenditure of Private Non-profit Institutions Serving Households

Equals: Final Consumption Expenditure of Private Non-profit Organisations Serving Households	...	...	...	...	...	...	...	...	...	...	...	...
Private Final Consumption Expenditure	1109.3	2431.9	6151.9	7489.9	8001.0	8813.8	9651.7	10490.6	11168.0	11782.8	12376.0	...

a) Item 'Personal care' excludes services of barbers, beauty shops etc.
b) Item 'Final consumption expenditure of resident households' includes consumption expenditure of private non-profit institutions serving households.

2.6 Private Final Consumption Expenditure by Type and Purpose, in Constant Prices

Million Irish pounds

At constant prices of: 1975 1980 1985

	1970	1975	1980	1981	1982	1983	1984	1985	1986	1987	1988	1989
Final Consumption Expenditure of Resident Households												
1 Food, beverages and tobacco	946.5	1149.1	2222.7	2552.7	2562.3	2565.1	2552.8	2565.1	4289.3	4274.8	4296.1	4192.9	4176.9	4233.0
A Food	581.9	687.9	1314.6	1548.1	1565.1	1596.1	2499.2	2522.7	2443.0	2408.9	2368.7	2375.5	2383.0
B Non-alcoholic beverages	19.5	29.0 60.1	79.1	93.2	82.8	131.3	144.6	143.6	154.2	127.3	141.0	159.0
C Alcoholic beverages	227.7	303.3 620.0	695.9	672.6	656.8 1220.7	1110.3	1174.4	1233.6	1224.8	1209.8	1245.0
D Tobacco	117.4	128.9 228.0	239.1	234.2	216.5 521.3	511.7	513.7	499.4	472.1	450.6	447.0
2 Clothing and footwear	216.1	364.7 182.3	453.3	493.2	410.1 610.8	664.0	711.3	768.8	767.2	801.9	807.0
3 Gross rent, fuel and power	245.7	552.3 268.6	678.9	687.9	713.1 1114.4	1180.3	1215.0	1253.5	1312.8	1334.0	1336.0
A Fuel and power	112.1	124.7 266.6	350.3	346.9	361.0 603.9	604.9	608.9	628.3	677.6	689.9	678.0
B Other	133.6	143.9 265.7	327.8	341.0	352.1 514.7	575.4	606.4	625.1	635.1	645.1	658.0
4 Furniture, furnishings and household equipment and operation	162.3	187.6 367.7	449.5	436.3	378.7 594.7	642.5	624.4	720.8	783.2	815.5	812.0
A Household operation	50.1	48.3 105.8	123.9	137.0 119.8	200.9	212.1	219.6	240.7	287.2	299.6	294.0

Ireland

2.6 Private Final Consumption Expenditure by Type and Purpose, in Constant Prices (Continued)

Million Irish pounds

	1970	1975	1980	1981	1982	1983	1984	1985	1986	1987	1988	1989
							At constant prices of:					
		1975			1980			1985				
B Other	112.2	139.3	325.6	299.3	394.3	430.4	404.8	480.1	496.0	515.9	518.0	...
			261.4									
5 Medical care and health expenses	40.4	52.5	128.3	133.7	134.4	251.7	262.0	288.7	308.2	332.5	349.6	348.0	...
			113.3									
6 Transport and communication	229.5	276.4	599.8	824.4	872.7	716.6	1278.3	1347.5	1389.6	1398.5	1373.6	1482.0	...
						1387.6						
A Personal transport equipment	68.1	81.0	154.5	277.7	307.4	204.2	317.3	333.6	358.0	352.1	325.0	394.0	...
						401.0						
B Other	161.4	195.4	445.3	546.7	565.3	512.4	961.0	1013.9	1031.2	1046.4	1048.5	1088.0	...
						987.5						
7 Recreational, entertainment, education and cultural services	178.3	189.1	405.3	619.3	651.9	550.0	919.2	958.6	1008.0	1016.1	1097.9	1199.0	...
						920.7						
A Education	43.7	48.2	128.0	137.2	147.2	193.4	215.1	261.0	277.5	281.0	300.3	291.0	...
						131.7						
B Other	134.6	140.9	277.3	482.0	504.7	418.3	704.1	697.3	730.6	735.1	797.6	908.0	...
						725.4						
8 Miscellaneous goods and services	148.7	150.1	351.5	413.0	435.0	370.2	728.3	779.8	862.3	884.2	1002.8	1019.0	...
						649.1						
A Personal care	15.5a	22.9a	46.4a	78.9a	83.8a	70.4a	143.1	145.2	203.0	216.8	230.4	203.0	...
						116.1						
B Expenditures in restaurants, cafes and hotels	38.1	31.9	78.7	89.2	91.8	82.2	170.7	166.2	174.5	170.7	193.8	212.0	...
						152.1						
C Other	95.1	95.3	226.4	266.9	237.4	217.6	414.4	468.3	484.8	496.6	578.7	604.0	...
						381.2						
Statistical discrepancy	...	...	...	...	...	-29.9	...	...	...	...	...	...	...
Total Final Consumption Expenditure in the Domestic Market by Households, of which	2167.4	2445.7	4946.9b	6150.3b	6253.8b	5825.9b	9963.7	10199.2	10606.9	10687.4	10952.2	11236.0	...
Plus: Direct purchases abroad by resident households	74.7	94.2	182.0	283.4	264.5	245.9	415.8	398.7	401.7	492.4	519.6	576.0	...
						438.8						
Less: Direct purchases in the domestic market by non-resident households	138.4	118.0	228.0	281.9	256.1	251.6	446.7	466.1	518.0	474.2	526.8	599.0	...
						449.0						
Equals: Final Consumption Expenditure of Resident Households	2103.7c	2431.9c	4900.9c	6151.8c	6262.1c	5820.2c	9932.8	10132.4	10490.6	10705.6	10944.9	11213.0	...
						9848.9						

Final Consumption Expenditure of Private Non-profit Institutions Serving Households

Equals: Final Consumption Expenditure of Private Non-profit Organisations Serving Households	...	...	...	...	...	...	...	...	...	...	...	...
Private Final Consumption Expenditure	2103.7	2431.9	4900.9	6151.8	6262.1	5820.2	9932.8	10132.4	10490.6	10705.6	10944.9	11213.0	...
						9848.9						

a) Item 'Personal care' excludes services of barbers, beauty shops etc.
b) For the years 1975-1977, the estimates at 1980 prices are derived by linking the old and new.
c) Item 'Final consumption expenditure of resident households' includes consumption expenditure of private non-profit institutions serving households.

1975 prices. As a consequence, the sub-totals do not add up to the total. 1978 in order to maintain the pattern of year to year change established at weighting at

Ireland

2.7 Gross Capital Formation by Type of Good and Owner, in Current Prices

Million Irish pounds

	1980				1981				1982			
	TOTAL	Total Private	Public Enterprises	General Government	TOTAL	Total Private	Public Enterprises	General Government	TOTAL	Total Private	Public Enterprises	General Government
Increase in stocks, total	-73.0	...	...	...	-145.7	...	...	...	168.9	...	...	...
1 Goods producing industries	-54.0	...	...	...	-69.2	...	...	...	53.5	...	...	...
A Materials and supplies	36.2	...	...	...	-28.6	...	...	...	42.2	...	...	...
B Work in progress												
C Livestock, except breeding stocks, dairy cattle, etc.	-110.5	...	...	...	-22.7	...	...	...	13.4	...	...	...
D Finished goods	20.3	...	...	...	-17.9	...	...	...	-2.1	...	...	...
2 Wholesale and retail trade	-19.0	...	...	...	-76.5	...	...	...	115.4	...	...	...
3 Other, except government stocks												
4 Government stocks	...	...	...	...	...	...	...	...	...	...	...	...
Gross Fixed Capital Formation, Total	2677.2	...	...	...	3368.1	...	...	...	3547.4	...	...	...
1 Residential buildings	578.0	...	...	...	708.5	...	...	...	759.2	...	...	...
2 Non-residential buildings	789.4	...	...	...	999.4	...	...	...	1135.1	...	...	...
3 Other construction												
4 Land improvement and plantation and orchard development	40.2	...	...	...	46.3	...	...	...	53.4	...	...	...
5 Producers' durable goods	1310.8	...	...	...	1596.2	...	...	...	1583.3	...	...	...
A Transport equipment	311.4	...	...	...	404.0	...	...	...	356.0	...	...	...
Passenger cars	168.0	...	...	...	219.2	...	...	...	180.4	...	...	...
Other	143.4	...	...	...	184.8	...	...	...	175.6	...	...	...
B Machinery and equipment	999.4	...	...	...	1192.2	...	...	...	1227.3	...	...	...
6 Breeding stock, dairy cattle, etc.	-41.2	...	...	...	17.7	...	...	...	16.4	...	...	...
Total Gross Capital Formation	2604.2	...	...	...	3222.4	...	...	...	3716.3	...	...	...

	1983				1984				1985			
	TOTAL	Total Private	Public Enterprises	General Government	TOTAL	Total Private	Public Enterprises	General Government	TOTAL	Total Private	Public Enterprises	General Government
Increase in stocks, total	101.6	...	...	...	217.0	...	...	...	159.4	...	...	...
1 Goods producing industries	-50.6	...	...	...	66.0	...	...	...	41.8	...	...	...
A Materials and supplies	-57.8	...	...	...	88.4	...	...	...	104.4	...	...	...
B Work in progress												
C Livestock, except breeding stocks, dairy cattle, etc.	-0.1	...	...	...	28.8	...	...	...	-33.4	...	...	...
D Finished goods	7.3	...	...	...	-51.2	...	...	...	-29.2	...	...	...
2 Wholesale and retail trade	152.2	...	...	...	151.0	...	...	...	117.6	...	...	...
3 Other, except government stocks												
4 Government stocks	...	...	...	...	...	...	...	...	...	...	...	...
Gross Fixed Capital Formation, Total	3419.0	...	...	...	3516.4	...	...	...	3398.2	...	...	...
1 Residential buildings	786.6	...	...	...	856.6	...	...	...	845.4	...	...	...
2 Non-residential buildings	936.9	...	...	...	924.1	...	...	...	892.2	...	...	...
3 Other construction												
4 Land improvement and plantation and orchard development	48.6	...	...	...	60.1	...	...	...	35.8	...	...	...
5 Producers' durable goods	1642.3	...	...	...	1665.0	...	...	...	1615.3	...	...	...
A Transport equipment	374.8	...	...	...	404.7	...	...	...	433.9	...	...	...
Passenger cars	163.9	...	...	...	187.6	...	...	...	218.8	...	...	...
Other	210.9	...	...	...	217.1	...	...	...	215.1	...	...	...
B Machinery and equipment	1267.5	...	...	...	1260.3	...	...	...	1181.4	...	...	...
6 Breeding stock, dairy cattle, etc.	4.6	...	...	...	10.7	...	...	...	9.5	...	...	...
Total Gross Capital Formation	3520.6	...	...	...	3733.4	...	...	...	3557.6	...	...	...

Ireland

2.7 Gross Capital Formation by Type of Good and Owner, in Current Prices

Million Irish pounds

	1986				1987				1988			
	TOTAL	Total Private	Public Enterprises	General Government	TOTAL	Total Private	Public Enterprises	General Government	TOTAL	Total Private	Public Enterprises	General Government
Increase in stocks, total	136.8	...	...	...	10.3	...	...	...	-185.0	...	...	...
1 Goods producing industries	44.3	...	...	...	-37.2	...	...	...	61.0	...	...	...
A Materials and supplies	57.2	...	...	...	-13.9	...	...	...	50.0	...	...	...
B Work in progress		...	...	...		...	...	...		...	...	...
C Livestock, except breeding stocks, dairy cattle, etc.	-46.5	...	...	...	10.3	...	...	...	-22.0	...	...	...
D Finished goods	33.6	...	...	...	-33.5	...	...	...	34.0	...	...	...
2 Wholesale and retail trade	92.5	...	...	...	47.5	...	...	...	-247.0	...	...	...
3 Other, except government stocks	...	...	...	...	...	...	...	...	...	...	...	...
4 Government stocks	...	...	...	...	...	...	...	...	...	...	...	...
Gross Fixed Capital Formation, Total	3398.9	...	...	...	3354.2	...	...	...	3729.0	...	...	...
1 Residential buildings	881.7	...	...	...	835.9	...	...	...	774.0	...	...	...
2 Non-residential buildings	886.7	...	...	...	825.5	...	...	...	948.0	...	...	...
3 Other construction		...	...	...		...	...	...		...	...	...
4 Land improvement and plantation and orchard development	33.7	...	...	...	25.2	...	...	...	37.0	...	...	...
5 Producers' durable goods	1621.0	...	...	...	1651.2	...	...	...	1868.0	...	...	...
A Transport equipment	512.3	...	...	...	510.7	...	...	...	592.0	...	...	...
Passenger cars	231.0	...	...	...	224.9	...	...	...	286.0	...	...	...
Other	281.3	...	...	...	285.8	...	...	...	306.0	...	...	...
B Machinery and equipment	1108.7	...	...	...	1140.5	...	...	...	1276.0	...	...	...
6 Breeding stock, dairy cattle, etc.	-24.1	...	...	...	16.4	...	...	...	102.0	...	...	...
Total Gross Capital Formation	3535.7	...	...	...	3364.5	...	...	...	3544.0	...	...	...

	1989			
	TOTAL	Total Private	Public Enterprises	General Government
Increase in stocks, total	5.0	...	...	...
1 Goods producing industries	134.0	...	...	...
A Materials and supplies	12.0	...	...	...
B Work in progress		...	...	...
C Livestock, except breeding stocks, dairy cattle, etc.	100.0	...	...	...
D Finished goods	22.0	...	...	...
2 Wholesale and retail trade	-128.0	...	...	...
3 Other, except government stocks	...	...	...	...
4 Government stocks	...	...	...	...
Gross Fixed Capital Formation, Total	4405.0	...	...	...
1 Residential buildings	947.0	...	...	...
2 Non-residential buildings	1074.0	...	...	...
3 Other construction		...	...	...
4 Land improvement and plantation and orchard development	23.0	...	...	...
5 Producers' durable goods	2275.0	...	...	...
A Transport equipment	859.0	...	...	...
Passenger cars	368.0	...	...	...
Other	491.0	...	...	...
B Machinery and equipment	1416.0	...	...	...
6 Breeding stock, dairy cattle, etc.	85.0	...	...	...
Total Gross Capital Formation	4410.0	...	...	...

Ireland

2.8 Gross Capital Formation by Type of Good and Owner, in Constant Prices

Million Irish pounds

At constant prices of 1985

	1980				1981				1982			
	TOTAL	Private	Public Enterprises	General Government	TOTAL	Private	Public Enterprises	General Government	TOTAL	Private	Public Enterprises	General Government
Increase in stocks, total	-149.4	...	...	...	-175.8	...	...	...	179.4	...	...	...
1 Goods producing industries	-123.9	...	...	...	-71.4	...	...	...	42.7	...	...	...
A Materials and supplies	56.4 }	...	...	...	-11.7 }	...	...	...	36.1 }	...	...	...
B Work in progress												
C Livestock, except breeding stocks, dairy cattle, etc.	-202.0	...	...	...	-33.9	...	...	...	12.2	...	...	...
D Finished goods	21.8	...	...	...	-25.8	...	...	...	-5.6	...	...	...
2 Wholesale and retail trade	-25.5	...	...	...	-104.4	...	...	...	136.7	...	...	...
3 Other, except government stocks	...	...	...	...	...	...	...	...	...	...	...	...
4 Government stocks	...	...	...	...	...	...	...	...	...	...	...	...
Gross Fixed Capital Formation, Total	3922.4	...	...	...	4296.2	...	...	...	4149.6	...	...	...
1 Residential buildings									862.1			
2 Non-residential buildings									1348.2 }			
3 Other construction												
4 Land improvement and plantation and orchard development									63.4			
5 Producers' durable goods									1864.7			
A Transport equipment									440.2			
Passenger cars									225.2			
Other									214.9			
B Machinery and equipment									1424.8			
6 Breeding stock, dairy cattle, etc.									15.6			
Total Gross Capital Formation	3773.0	...	...	...	4120.4	...	...	...	4329.0	...	...	...

At constant prices of 1985

	1983				1984				1985			
	TOTAL	Private	Public Enterprises	General Government	TOTAL	Private	Public Enterprises	General Government	TOTAL	Private	Public Enterprises	General Government
Increase in stocks, total	100.6	...	...	...	208.0	...	...	...	159.4	...	...	...
1 Goods producing industries	-55.3	...	...	...	62.0	...	...	...	41.8	...	...	...
A Materials and supplies	-64.2 }	...	...	...	88.5 }	...	...	...	104.4 }	...	...	...
B Work in progress												
C Livestock, except breeding stocks, dairy cattle, etc.	1.9	...	...	...	27.5	...	...	...	-33.4	...	...	...
D Finished goods	7.0	...	...	...	-54.0	...	...	...	-29.2	...	...	...
2 Wholesale and retail trade	155.9	...	...	...	146.1	...	...	...	117.6	...	...	...
3 Other, except government stocks	...	...	...	...	...	...	...	...	...	...	...	...
4 Government stocks	...	...	...	...	...	...	...	...	...	...	...	...
Gross Fixed Capital Formation, Total	3764.3	...	...	...	3669.7	...	...	...	3398.2	...	...	...
1 Residential buildings	841.0	...	...	...	875.9	...	...	...	845.4	...	...	...
2 Non-residential buildings	1051.8 }	...	...	...	969.6 }	...	...	...	892.2 }	...	...	...
3 Other construction												
4 Land improvement and plantation and orchard development	54.6	...	...	...	63.1	...	...	...	35.8	...	...	...
5 Producers' durable goods	1813.3	...	...	...	1752.3	...	...	...	1615.3	...	...	...
A Transport equipment	423.4	...	...	...	457.5	...	...	...	433.9	...	...	...
Passenger cars	191.9	...	...	...	200.2	...	...	...	218.8	...	...	...
Other	231.5	...	...	...	257.3	...	...	...	215.1	...	...	...
B Machinery and equipment	1389.8	...	...	...	1294.8	...	...	...	1181.4	...	...	...
6 Breeding stock, dairy cattle, etc.	3.5	...	...	...	8.8	...	...	...	9.5	...	...	...
Total Gross Capital Formation	3864.9	...	...	...	3877.7	...	...	...	3557.6	...	...	...

Ireland

2.8 Gross Capital Formation by Type of Good and Owner, in Constant Prices

Million Irish pounds

	1986				1987				1988			
	TOTAL	Total Private	Public Enterprises	General Government	TOTAL	Total Private	Public Enterprises	General Government	TOTAL	Total Private	Public Enterprises	General Government
At constant prices of:1985												
Increase in stocks, total	151.2	...	...	...	0.8	...	...	...	-208.0	...	...	...
1 Goods producing industries	58.0	...	...	...	-41.4	...	...	...	63.0	...	...	...
A Materials and supplies	72.5	...	...	...	-13.7	...	...	...	45.0	...	...	...
B Work in progress		...	...	...		...	...	...		...	...	...
C Livestock, except breeding stocks, dairy cattle, etc.	-49.0	...	...	...	9.4	...	...	...	-18.0	...	...	...
D Finished goods	34.5	...	...	...	-37.0	...	...	...	36.0	...	...	...
2 Wholesale and retail trade	93.2	...	...	...	42.2	...	...	...	-271.0	...	...	...
3 Other, except government stocks	...	...	...	...	...	...	...	...	...	...	...	...
4 Government stocks	...	...	...	...	...	...	...	...	...	...	...	...
Gross Fixed Capital Formation, Total	3319.7	...	...	...	3235.3	...	...	...	3383.0	...	...	...
1 Residential buildings	845.6	...	...	...	791.7	...	...	...	691.0	...	...	...
2 Non-residential buildings	847.7	...	...	...	767.2	...	...	...	847.0	...	...	...
3 Other construction		...	...	...		...	...	...		...	...	...
4 Land improvement and plantation and orchard development	32.2	...	...	...	23.5	...	...	...	33.0	...	...	...
5 Producers' durable goods	1618.8	...	...	...	1637.5	...	...	...	1731.0	...	...	...
A Transport equipment	491.4	...	...	...	464.5	...	...	...	515.0	...	...	...
Passenger cars	220.3	...	...	...	200.6	...	...	...	243.0	...	...	...
Other	271.1	...	...	...	263.8	...	...	...	272.0	...	...	...
B Machinery and equipment	1127.5	...	...	...	1173.0	...	...	...	1215.0	...	...	...
6 Breeding stock, dairy cattle, etc.	-24.7	...	...	...	15.5	...	...	...	81.0	...	...	...
Total Gross Capital Formation	3470.9	...	...	...	3236.1	...	...	...	3175.0	...	...	...

	1989			
	TOTAL	Total Private	Public Enterprises	General Government
At constant prices of:1985				
Increase in stocks, total	-7.0	...	...	...
1 Goods producing industries	118.0	...	...	...
A Materials and supplies	10.0	...	...	...
B Work in progress		...	...	...
C Livestock, except breeding stocks, dairy cattle, etc.	85.0	...	...	...
D Finished goods	23.0	...	...	...
2 Wholesale and retail trade	-125.0	...	...	...
3 Other, except government stocks	...	...	...	...
4 Government stocks	...	...	...	...
Gross Fixed Capital Formation, Total	3766.0	...	...	...
1 Residential buildings	788.0	...	...	...
2 Non-residential buildings	917.0	...	...	...
3 Other construction		...	...	...
4 Land improvement and plantation and orchard development	20.0	...	...	...
5 Producers' durable goods	1973.0	...	...	...
A Transport equipment	716.0	...	...	...
Passenger cars	296.0	...	...	...
Other	420.0	...	...	...
B Machinery and equipment	1257.0	...	...	...
6 Breeding stock, dairy cattle, etc.	68.0	...	...	...
Total Gross Capital Formation	3759.0	...	...	...

Ireland

2.11 Gross Fixed Capital Formation by Kind of Activity of Owner, ISIC Divisions, in Current Prices

Million Irish pounds

		1970	1975	1980	1981	1982	1983	1984	1985	1986	1987	1988	1989
	All Producers												
1	Agriculture, hunting, forestry and fishing	54.0	78.9	260.0	373.1	350.6	308.1	296.1	300.9	246.8	284.2	432.0	538.0
	A Agriculture and hunting	50.0	72.8	236.2	346.4	319.1	271.6	280.6	270.4	221.8	248.5	407.0	509.0
	B Forestry and logging	2.6	0.9	2.0	2.7	2.8	3.0	2.8	2.8	2.7	2.6	2.0	
	C Fishing	1.4	5.2	21.8	24.0	27.8	21.5	24.7	27.3	22.3	33.1	23.0	29.0
2	Mining and quarrying	6.8	22.5	33.5	33.7	33.3	39.2	20.6	18.1	27.2	23.5	30.0	42.0
3	Manufacturing	71.3	195.0	582.4	592.1	578.5	599.2	650.7	609.3	660.4	652.8	780.0	869.0
	A Manufacturing of food, beverages and tobacco	20.6	71.0	183.9	166.8	173.7	198.9	190.6	202.1	225.7	214.6	...	...
	B Textile, wearing apparel and leather industries	7.6	12.8	30.3	23.6	15.6	24.5	20.8	38.2	31.2	30.3	...	...
	C Manufacture of wood, and wood products, including furniture	4.1	2.7	18.3	18.9	20.4	14.4	20.8	13.7	18.2	23.8	...	...
	D Manufacture of paper and paper products, printing and publishing	2.8	10.1	23.6	19.5	17.6	19.2	20.8	26.8	32.8	40.0	...	...
	E Manufacture of chemicals and chemical petroleum, coal, rubber and plastic products	8.7	32.4	58.3	79.7	65.8	77.3	137.3	112.9	113.9	117.2	...	...
	F Manufacture of non-metallic mineral products except products of petroleum and coal	13.4	24.2	125.9	131.5	123.5	93.5	57.9	59.6	49.5	48.5	...	...
	G Basic metal industries	2.4	10.1	7.6	3.4	74.6	6.0	9.1	10.8	10.7	10.0	...	...
	H Manufacture of fabricated metal products, machinery and equipment	11.7	31.7	134.5	148.7	187.3	165.4	193.2	196.2	178.5	168.6	...	...
	I Other manufacturing industries	...	...	...	...	...	...	...	...	...	...	...	...
4	Electricity, gas and water	24.6	28.3	193.4	285.9	350.9	318.1	338.3	256.3	198.0	161.3	179.0	149.0
5	Construction	6.3	21.4	133.4	134.5	123.2	88.7	82.1	75.4	88.6	59.3	73.0	117.0
6	Wholesale and retail trade, restaurants and hotels	22.9	51.8	149.3	160.0	134.1	117.5	143.7	153.3	180.3	171.2	224.0	294.0
	A Wholesale and retail trade	22.9	51.8	149.3	160.0	134.1	117.5	143.7	153.3	180.3	171.2	224.0	294.0
	B Restaurants and hotels a	...	...	...	...	...	...	...	...	...	...	...	...
7	Transport, storage and communication	57.9	108.2	287.0	456.6	473.5	530.5	506.4	432.2	440.4	457.3	464.0	610.0
	A Transport and storage	47.3	56.5	159.5	238.9	269.6	332.4	289.6	314.5	303.9	333.9	333.0	460.0
	B Communication	10.6	51.7	127.5	217.7	203.9	198.1	216.8	117.7	136.5	123.4	131.0	150.0
8	Finance, insurance, real estate and business services	67.4	228.3	705.2	853.3	895.3	923.4	999.1	987.2	1026.2	995.6	976.0	1174.0
	A Financial institutions	5.7	18.6	127.2	144.8	136.1	137.3	143.3	141.8	144.5	159.7	202.0	227.0
	B Insurance	...	...	...	...	...	...	...	...	...	...	...	...
	C Real estate and business services	61.7	209.7	578.0	708.5	759.2	786.1	856.6	845.4	881.7	835.9	774.0	947.0
	Real estate except dwellings												
	Dwellings	61.7	209.7	578.0	708.5	759.2	786.1	856.6	845.4	881.7	835.9	774.0	947.0
9	Community, social and personal services b	47.1	99.7	270.2	401.7	415.8	426.0	382.1	421.9	435.3	453.4	453.0	479.0
	A Sanitary and similar services	28.6	54.5	153.0	259.7	260.0	255.5	228.8	232.3	257.2	268.5	299.0	340.0
	B Social and related community services	18.5	45.2	117.2	142.0	155.8	170.5	153.2	189.6	178.1	184.9	153.0	139.0
	Educational services	12.5	23.6	64.6	73.5	94.0	94.7	84.1	99.5	93.0	87.3	62.0	48.0
	Medical, dental, other health and veterinary services	6.0	21.6	52.6	68.5	61.8	75.8	69.2	90.1	85.1	97.6	91.0	91.0
	C Recreational and cultural services a	...	...	...	...	...	...	...	...	...	...	...	...
	D Personal and household services a	...	...	...	...	...	...	...	...	...	...	...	...
	Statistical discrepancy											...	1.0
	Total Industries	360.4	834.1	2620.4	3290.9	3455.2	3338.7	3431.9	3305.6	3303.7	3258.6	3611.0	4273.0
	Producers of Government Services c	8.1	27.7	56.8	77.2	92.2	80.3	84.5	92.7	95.6	95.5	118.0	132.0
	Private Non-Profit Institutions Serving Households b												
	Total	368.5	861.8	2677.2	3368.1	3547.4	3419.0	3516.4	3398.3	3398.8	3354.1	3729.0	4405.0

a) Items 'Restaurants and hotels', 'Recreational and cultural services' and 'Personal and household services' are included in item 'Community, social and Personal services'.
b) Item 'Private non-profit institutions serving households' is included in item 'Community, social and personal services'.
c) Item 'Producers of Government Services' includes public administration and defence only. All other activities of government are included in the corresponding industries.

Ireland

2.12 Gross Fixed Capital Formation by Kind of Owner, ISIC Divisions, in Constant Prices

Million Irish pounds

All Producers

At constant prices of: 1975 | 1980 | 1985

	1970	1975	1980	1981	1982	1983	1984	1985	1986	1987	1988	1989
1 Agriculture, hunting, forestry and fishing	112.0	74.3 151.9a	260.0a	278.9a	328.9a	332.2	320.8	300.9	244.7	277.8	384.0	458.0
A Agriculture and hunting	104.1	68.1 149.1	236.2	253.0	305.5	381.1	305.0	291.0	274.1	235.4	353.0	437.0
B Forestry and logging	5.7	0.9 1.9	2.0	2.4	2.2 3.4	2.9	2.8	2.6	2.4	2.0	-
C Fishing	2.2	5.3 1.1	21.0	23.8 27.8	23.7	21.0	26.9	24.0	24.6	33.0	29.0	21.0
2 Mining and quarrying	17.4	22.4 47.7	30.0	33.5 27.6	43.7	21.7	18.1	26.9	23.0	28.0	37.0
3 Manufacturing	139.6	195.4 387.4a	582.4a	526.3a 557.5a	669.4	679.7	660.3	658.8	648.6	726.0	757.0
A Manufacturing of food, beverages and tobacco	40.7	71.2 142.1	183.9	148.3 142.2 204.6	222.2	199.3	202.1	225.1	213.3	...	...
B Textile, wearing apparel and leather industries	14.9	12.8 25.5	30.3	20.9 12.8 18.5	27.4	21.8	38.2	31.1	30.0	...	...
C Manufacture of wood, and wood products, including furniture	8.0	2.7 5.4	18.3	16.8 24.1 16.7	16.1	21.8	13.7	18.2	23.7	...	...
D Manufacture of paper and paper products, printing and publishing	5.4	10.1 20.1	23.6	17.4 20.9 14.5	21.4	21.8	26.8	32.8	39.7	...	...
E Manufacture of chemicals and chemical petroleum, coal, rubber and plastic products	17.0	32.5 64.5	58.3	70.7 54.1 77.8	86.3	143.4	112.9	113.6	116.3	...	...
F Manufacture of non-metallic mineral products except products of petroleum and coal	26.3	24.3 48.2	125.9	117.2 102.0 146.6	104.4	60.5	59.6	49.4	48.2	...	...
G Basic metal industries	4.7	10.1 19.9	7.6	3.1 61.3 89.2	6.7	9.5	10.8	10.7	9.9	...	...
H Manufacture of fabricated metal products, machinery and equipment	22.6	31.7 63.0	134.5	131.9 153.9 221.4	184.8	201.9	196.2	177.9	167.5	...	...
I Other manufacturing industries		... ...	...	... ...	...	...	...	...	...	...	...
4 Electricity, gas and water	48.1	28.3 57.0	193.4	249.3 284.2 409.2	354.4	353.1	256.3	194.7	159.4	162.0	129.0
5 Construction	12.5	21.1 45.5	133.4	118.7 101.9 142.8	98.1	84.9	75.4	88.8	58.8	67.0	102.0
6 Wholesale and retail trade, restaurants and hotels	44.7	51.5 102.4	149.3	142.0 105.3 166.5	134.4	152.0	153.3	173.2	156.6	197.0	245.0
A Wholesale and retail trade	44.7	51.5 102.4	149.3	142.0 105.3 166.5	134.4	152.0	153.3	173.2	156.6	197.0	245.0
B Restaurants and hotels		... ...	...	... ...	...	...	...	...	...	...	...
7 Transport, storage and communication	113.3	110.3 219.9a	287.0a	403.1a 383.0a 560.1	588.0	558.2	432.2	425.4	432.5	419.0	527.0
A Transport and storage	91.3	58.6 108.5	159.5	211.3 219.6 319.5	369.0	334.5	314.5	292.8	314.2	299.0	395.0

887

Ireland

2.12 Gross Fixed Capital Formation by Kind of Activity of Owner, ISIC Divisions, in Constant Prices
(Continued)

Million Irish pounds

	1970	1975	1980	1981	1982	1983	1984	1985	1986	1987	1988	1989
					At constant prices of:							
		1975	1980					1985				
B Communication	22.0	51.7 / 122.0	127.5	191.8	163.4 / 241.0	219.0	223.7	117.7	132.6	118.3	120.0	132.0
8 Finance, insurance, real estate and business services	136.9	228.2 / 493.7a	705.2a	713.8a	689.2a / 1007.4	978.8	1012.9	987.2	990.2	950.9	879.0	987.0
A Financial institutions	11.2	18.5 / 34.5	127.2	129.8	113.0 / 144.8	138.3	137.0	141.8	144.6	159.2	188.0	199.0
B Insurance	...	...	...	...	... / ...	...	...	...	...	...	...	...
C Real estate and business services	125.7	209.7 / 464.4	578.0	584.0	576.2 / 862.1	840.5	875.9	845.4	845.6	791.7	691.0	788.0
Real estate except dwellings	...	...	...	...	... / ...	...	...	...	...	...	...	...
Dwellings	125.7	209.7 / 464.4	578.0	584.0	576.2 / 862.1	840.5	875.9	845.4	845.6	791.7	691.0	788.0
9 Community, social and personal services	94.1c	98.6c / 198.8c	270.2c	352.1c	330.6c / 495.3	475.9	399.1	421.9	424.2	437.5	414.0	412.0
A Sanitary and similar services	56.0b	53.3b / 108.2b	153.0b	227.2b	207.1b / 294.1	286.9	238.7	232.3	251.7	260.9	274.0	293.0
B Social and related community services	38.1	45.3 / 90.7	117.2	124.9	123.5 / 181.9	189.0	160.4	189.6	172.6	176.6	140.0	119.0
Educational services	26.3	23.6 / 49.2	64.6	64.5	74.8 / 111.1	105.9	88.0	99.5	89.4	82.1	56.0	41.0
Medical, dental, other health and veterinary services	11.8	21.7 / 41.8	52.6	60.4	48.7 / 71.0	83.1	72.5	90.1	83.2	94.4	84.0	78.0
C Recreational and cultural services	...	...	...	...	... / ...	...	...	...	...	...	...	...
D Personal and household services	...	...	...	...	... / ...	...	...	...	...	...	...	...
Total Industries	718.6	830.1 / 1704.6a	2620.4a	2864.2a	2758.2a / 4041.0	3674.9	3582.4	3305.6	3226.9	3145.1	3276.0	3654.0
Producers of Government Services	15.9d	27.7d / 56.0d	56.8d	68.1d	74.0d / 108.6	89.4	87.1	92.7	92.6	90.1	106.0	113.0
Private Non-Profit Institutions Serving Households	...	...	...	...	... / ...	...	...	...	...	...	...	...
Statistical discrepancy	...	...	...	...	... / ...	...	...	...	...	...	1.0	-1.0
Total	734.5	857.8 / 1760.6	2677.2	2932.3	2832.2 / 4149.6	3764.3	3669.5	3398.3	3319.5	3235.2	3383.0	3766.0

a) For the years 1975-1977, the estimates at 1980 prices are derived by linking the old and new weighting at 1978 in order to maintain the pattern of year to year change established at constant 1975 prices. As a consequence, the sub-totals do not add up to the total.
b) Items 'Restaurants and hotels', 'Recreational and cultural services' and 'Personal and household services' are included in item 'Sanitary and similar services'.
c) Item 'Private non-profit institutions serving households' is included in item 'Community, social and personal services'.
d) Item 'Producers of Government Services' includes public administration and defence only. All other activities of government are included in the corresponding industries.

2.17 Exports and Imports of Goods and Services, Detail

Million Irish pounds

	1970	1975	1980	1981	1982	1983	1984	1985	1986	1987	1988	1989
				Exports of Goods and Services								
1 Exports of merchandise, f.o.b.	455.0	1370.8	4004.4	4789.2	5591.9	6812.7	8696.0	9526.8	9180.7	10447.1	12073.0	14358.0
2 Transport and communication a	69.6	130.2	352.3	406.1	486.4	549.0	632.0	693.6	678.6	774.0	805.0	881.0
A In respect of merchandise imports b	7.2	9.9	37.1	43.4	68.9	73.0	80.9	84.8	69.1	69.9	61.0	64.0
B Other	62.4	120.3	315.2	362.7	417.5	476.0	551.1	608.8	609.5	704.1	743.0	817.0
3 Insurance service charges	...	...	...	...	...	...	...	...	...	...	...	...

Ireland

2.17 Exports and Imports of Goods and Services, Detail
(Continued)

Million Irish pounds

		1970	1975	1980	1981	1982	1983	1984	1985	1986	1987	1988	1989
4	Other commodities	...	...	...	...	...	...	...	...	...	...	...	...
5	Adjustments of merchandise exports to change-of-ownership basis	...	...	...	...	...	...	...	...	...	...	...	...
6	Direct purchases in the domestic market by non-residential households	74.3	118.0	281.9	308.3	355.0	390.0	442.0	518.0	492.2	564.0	655.0	751.0
7	Direct purchases in the domestic market by extraterritorial bodies	...	...	...	...	...	...	...	...	...	...	...	...
	Total Exports of Goods and Services	598.9	1619.0	4638.6	5503.6	6433.3	7751.7	9770.0	10738.4	10351.5	11785.1	13533.0	15991.0

Imports of Goods and Services

		1970	1975	1980	1981	1982	1983	1984	1985	1986	1987	1988	1989
1	Imports of merchandise, c.i.f.	667.0	1672.1	5346.1	6486.9	6712.3	7334.2	8892.6	9390.2	8745.5	9137.0	10048.0	12114.0
2	Adjustments of merchandise imports to change-of-ownership basis	...	...	...	...	...	...	...	...	...	...	...	...
3	Other transport and communication [a]	21.4	82.7	270.4	311.8	355.3	467.0	544.5	604.7	603.8	774.3	887.0	876.0
4	Other insurance service charges	...	...	...	...	...	...	...	...	...	...	...	...
5	Other commodities	...	...	...	...	...	...	...	...	...	...	...	...
6	Direct purchases abroad by government	...	...	...	...	...	...	...	...	...	...	...	...
7	Direct purchases abroad by resident households	40.1	94.2	283.4	318.5	346.9	363.0	378.0	401.7	511.1	556.3	630.0	698.0
	Total Imports of Goods and Services	728.5	1849.0	5899.9	7117.2	7414.5	8164.2	9815.1	10396.6	9860.4	10467.6	11565.0	13688.0
	Balance of Goods and Services	-129.6	-230.0	-1261.3	-1613.6	-981.2	-412.5	-45.1	341.8	491.1	1317.5	1968.0	2303.0
	Total Imports and Balance of Goods and Services	598.9	1619.0	4638.6	5503.6	6433.3	7751.7	9770.0	10738.4	10351.5	11785.1	13533.0	15991.0

a) Item 'Transport and communication' includes all services.
b) Item 'Direct purchases in the domestic market by non-residential households' refers to governmental and other services.

4.3 Cost Components of Value Added

Million Irish pounds

	1980						1981					
	Compensation of Employees	Capital Consumption	Net Operating Surplus	Indirect Taxes	Less: Subsidies Received	Value Added	Compensation of Employees	Capital Consumption	Net Operating Surplus	Indirect Taxes	Less: Subsidies Received	Value Added
All Producers												
1 Agriculture, hunting, forestry and fishing	93.3	197.6	700.0	60.4	51.9	999.4	96.2	227.0	820.1	52.2	78.7	1116.8
2 Mining and quarrying												
3 Manufacturing	1620.3	265.6	433.7	545.1	344.1	2520.6	1870.6	244.6	591.1	600.7	330.1	2978.9
4 Electricity, gas and water												
5 Construction	661.7	25.8	174.7	0.5	0.1	862.6	743.3	16.1	198.1	0.5	1.4	956.6
6 Wholesale and retail trade, restaurants and hotels	675.7	82.6	317.1	34.9	125.3	985.0	849.8	106.9	381.2	39.7	102.5	1275.1
A Wholesale and retail trade	524.8	73.6	271.8	27.4	125.3	772.3	678.6	96.1	327.0	31.1	102.5	1030.3
B Restaurants and hotels	150.9	9.0	45.3	7.5	-	212.7	171.2	10.8	54.2	8.6	-	244.8
7 Transport, storage and communication	371.5	93.6	102.3	7.3	110.8	463.9	425.0	116.5	126.1	8.3	122.8	553.1
A Transport and storage	248.3	71.7	58.3	6.4	71.5	313.2	274.9	89.3	64.3	7.3	86.3	349.5
B Communication	123.2	21.9	44.0	0.9	39.3	150.7	150.1	27.2	61.8	1.0	36.5	203.6
8 Finance, insurance, real estate and business services	242.4	96.6	117.0	7.7	2.1	461.6	275.8	111.5	139.7	15.1	7.7	534.4
9 Community, social and personal services	458.0	202.0	454.3	76.9	106.5	1084.7	544.9	253.2	556.7	95.0	112.6	1337.2
Total, Industries	4122.9	963.8	2299.1	732.8	740.8	7377.8	4805.6	1077.8	2813.0	811.5	755.8	8752.1
Producers of Government Services	1462.1	70.4	-	8.7	-	1541.2	1812.7	85.7	-	13.1	-	1911.5
Other Producers												
Total	5585.0	1034.2	2299.1	741.5	740.8	8919.0	6618.3	1163.5	2813.0	824.6	755.8	10663.6
Less: Imputed bank service charge	...	...	388.0	...	...	388.0	...	...	460.6	...	...	460.6
Import duties	...	...	...	359.3	...	359.3	...	...	...	538.1	...	538.1
Value added tax	...	...	...	470.4	...	470.4	...	...	...	617.9	...	617.9
Total	5585.0	1034.2	1911.1	1571.2	740.8	9360.7	6618.3	1163.5	2352.4	1980.6	755.8	11359.0

Ireland

4.3 Cost Components of Value Added

Million Irish pounds

1982

	Compensation of Employees	Consumption of Capital	Net Operating Surplus	Indirect Taxes	Less: Subsidies Received	Value Added
1 Agriculture, hunting, forestry and fishing	104.8	257.3	1023.9	36.5	93.7	1328.7
2 Mining and quarrying						
3 Manufacturing	2101.4	293.8	228.4	642.2	385.0	3580.7
4 Electricity, gas and water	806.0	18.9	201.5	0.6	0.7	1026.4
5 Construction						
6 Wholesale and retail trade, restaurants and hotels	964.8	116.2	480.9	47.0	120.4	1488.4
A Wholesale and retail trade	762.4	104.8	418.7	37.0	120.4	1202.5
B Restaurants and hotels	202.4	11.4	62.2	10.0	-	286.0
7 Transport, storage and communication	461.2	122.4	160.9	10.6	118.0	637.0
A Transport and storage	305.2	88.6	87.4	9.4	96.9	393.7
B Communication	155.9	33.8	73.5	1.2	21.1	243.3
8 Finance, insurance, real estate and business services	369.1	135.1	70.6	35.8	3.1	607.5
9 Community, social and personal services	647.1	322.3	585.9	88.8	134.6	1519.5
Total, Industries	5454.4	1265.6	3452.1	871.5	855.5	10188.1
Producers of Government Services	2097.1	100.7	-	14.9	-	2212.7
Other Producers						
Total	7551.6	1366.3	3452.1	886.4	855.5	12400.8
Less: imputed bank service charge						555.3
Import duties						585.3
Value added tax						951.5
Total	7551.6	1366.3	2896.8	2423.2	855.5	13382.3

1983

	Compensation of Employees	Consumption of Capital	Net Operating Surplus	Indirect Taxes	Less: Subsidies Received	Value Added
1 Agriculture, hunting, forestry and fishing	114.8	278.3	1177.0	21.3	111.8	1479.4
2 Mining and quarrying						
3 Manufacturing	2282.6	322.1	1183.0	771.5	462.9	4096.6
4 Electricity, gas and water	818.9	25.0	179.2	0.8	0.2	1023.7
5 Construction						
6 Wholesale and retail trade, restaurants and hotels	1085.5	140.3	454.9	63.7	148.8	1595.6
A Wholesale and retail trade	854.3	128.1	397.1	49.2	148.8	1279.9
B Restaurants and hotels	231.2	12.2	57.8	14.5	-	315.7
7 Transport, storage and communication	483.9	154.1	121.7	18.3	121.4	656.6
A Transport and storage	318.6	85.2	79.0	16.7	93.4	406.1
B Communication	165.3	75.1	36.5	1.6	28.0	250.5
8 Finance, insurance, real estate and business services	437.8	155.7	69.8	52.1	0.1	715.3
9 Community, social and personal services	726.1	373.0	681.4	112.6	176.5	1716.7
Total, Industries	5949.6	1416.1	3899.4	1040.3	1021.2	11283.9
Producers of Government Services	2304.1	112.2	-	17.3	-	2433.6
Other Producers						
Total	8253.7	1528.3	3899.4	1057.5	1021.2	13717.7
Less: imputed bank service charge						675.4
Import duties						543.3
Value added tax						1193.6
Total	8253.7	1528.3	3224.0	2794.4	1021.2	14779.2

1984

	Compensation of Employees	Consumption of Capital	Net Operating Surplus	Indirect Taxes	Less: Subsidies Received	Value Added
1 Agriculture, hunting, forestry and fishing	124.4	294.1	1395.5	38.7	164.0	1688.7
2 Mining and quarrying						
3 Manufacturing	2486.2	324.2	1554.5	808.7	560.7	4612.8
4 Electricity, gas and water	807.7	20.7	169.1	0.9	0.5	1002.7
5 Construction						
6 Wholesale and retail trade, restaurants and hotels	1126.3	148.5	531.2	75.4	210.1	1671.3
A Wholesale and retail trade	894.9	135.5	456.3	59.7	210.1	1336.3
B Restaurants and hotels	231.4	13.0	74.9	15.8	-	335.1
7 Transport, storage and communication	537.5	132.5	142.5	22.6	118.9	716.1
A Transport and storage	349.0	82.6	97.7	20.7	113.9	436.1
B Communication	188.5	49.9	44.8	1.9	5.0	280.1
8 Finance, insurance, real estate and business services	570.2	149.8	87.4	63.7	0.6	870.4
9 Community, social and personal services	773.5	402.1	835.0	116.9	185.1	1942.4
Total, Industries	6431.6	1471.9	4714.1	1126.9	1239.9	12504.4
Producers of Government Services	2525.5	124.9	-	21.8	-	2672.2
Other Producers						
Total	8957.1	1596.8	4714.1	1148.7	1239.9	15176.8
Less: imputed bank service charge						735.1
Import duties						597.4
Value added tax						1367.5
Total	8957.1	1596.8	3979.0	3113.6	1239.9	16406.6

1985

	Compensation of Employees	Consumption of Capital	Net Operating Surplus	Indirect Taxes	Less: Subsidies Received	Value Added
1 Agriculture, hunting, forestry and fishing	1555.1	192.7	38.4	1268.8	304.3	1362.7
2 Mining and quarrying						
3 Manufacturing	5269.3	653.2	600.0	860.0	2072.3	348.9	2641.4
4 Electricity, gas and water	967.2	0.4	1.1	142.0	16.8	807.7	1002.7
5 Construction						
6 Wholesale and retail trade, restaurants and hotels	1929.9	259.8	87.5	749.7	168.0	1184.5	1671.3
A Wholesale and retail trade	1552.8	259.8	69.3	679.9	138.5	924.9	1336.3
B Restaurants and hotels	377.1	-	18.2	69.8	29.5	259.6	335.1
7 Transport, storage and communication	860.4	117.0	24.6	216.5	162.2	57.1	716.1
A Transport and storage	498.4	117.0	22.3	137.3	87.2	368.6	436.1
B Communication	362.0	-	2.3	79.2	75.0	205.5	280.1
8 Finance, insurance, real estate and business services	991.6	1.5	68.3	153.5	156.0	615.0	870.4
9 Community, social and personal services	2021.4	228.2	121.5	859.8	437.6	830.7	1942.4
Total, Industries	13594.9	1452.7	1201.4	5462.5	1594.1	6789.5	12504.4
Producers of Government Services	2865.3	-	20.3	-	129.9	2715.1	2672.2
Other Producers						
Total	16460.2	1452.7	1221.7	5462.5	1723.9	9504.6	15176.8
Less: imputed bank service charge	817.2			817.2		735.1
Import duties	633.3		633.3			597.4
Value added tax	1414.6		1414.6			1367.5
Total	17690.9	1452.7	3269.6	4645.3	1723.9	9504.6	16406.6

4.3 Cost Components of Value Added

Million Irish pounds

	1986						1987					
	Compensation of Employees	Capital Consumption	Net Operating Surplus	Indirect Taxes	Less: Subsidies Received	Value Added	Compensation of Employees	Capital Consumption	Net Operating Surplus	Indirect Taxes	Less: Subsidies Received	Value Added
	All Producers											
1 Agriculture, hunting, forestry and fishing	141.7	312.7	1193.8	39.0	157.7	1529.5	150.0	320.6	1454.4	46.1	172.0	1799.2
2 Mining and quarrying												
3 Manufacturing	2810.6	382.9	2111.5	859.8	624.8	5540.0	2918.0	428.0	2267.9	926.9	700.0	5840.8
4 Electricity, gas and water												
5 Construction	777.0	16.1	151.1	1.2	0.2	945.2	782.3	19.3	152.6	1.3	-	955.5
6 Wholesale and retail trade, restaurants and hotels	1247.1	188.2	744.9	95.2	372.9	1902.5	1304.7	218.2	732.8	109.0	349.4	2015.3
A Wholesale and retail trade	963.1	153.9	662.8	75.5	372.7	1482.6	1011.7	177.7	636.8	87.4	349.4	1564.2
B Restaurants and hotels	284.0	34.3	82.1	19.7	0.2	419.9	293.0	40.5	96.0	21.6	-	451.1
7 Transport, storage and communication	620.7	179.2	300.2	25.8	101.5	1024.4	642.8	193.9	370.2	29.2	107.9	1128.2
A Transport and storage	395.9	100.5	176.6	23.4	101.5	594.9	408.2	103.5	222.0	26.6	107.9	652.4
B Communication	224.8	78.7	123.6	2.4	-	429.5	234.6	90.4	148.2	2.6	-	475.8
8 Finance, insurance, real estate and business services	663.9	164.4	200.3	69.0	-	1097.6	759.2	161.6	185.2	78.3	0.1	1184.2
9 Community, social and personal services	881.9	462.1	975.8	133.9	230.4	2223.3	974.6	502.7	1021.7	154.9	235.4	2418.5
Total, Industries	7143.0	1705.6	5677.6	1223.9	1487.5	14262.5	7531.7	1844.2	6184.8	1345.5	1564.5	15341.7
Producers of Government Services	2950.5	140.8	1.1	22.3	-	3114.7	3106.1	149.5	1.1	22.9	-	3279.6
Other Producers												
Total	10093.5	1846.4	5678.7	1246.2	1487.5	17377.3	10637.8	1993.9	6185.9	1368.4	1564.5	18621.6
Less: Imputed bank service charge	...	...	869.6	...	...	869.6	...	...	884.0	...	...	884.3
Import duties	...	...	...	678.3	...	678.3	...	...	...	691.7	...	691.7
Value added tax	...	...	...	1550.8	...	1550.8	...	...	...	1612.3	...	1612.3
Total	10093.5	1846.4	4809.1	3475.3	1487.5	18736.8	10637.8	1993.9	5301.9	3672.4	1564.5	20041.3

	1988					
	Compensation of Employees	Capital Consumption	Net Operating Surplus	Indirect Taxes	Less: Subsidies Received	Value Added
	All Producers					
1 Agriculture, hunting, forestry and fishing	158.0	329.0	1720.0	49.0	259.0	1998.0
2 Mining and quarrying						
3 Manufacturing	3078.0	467.0	2419.0	937.0	600.0	6299.0
4 Electricity, gas and water						
5 Construction	798.0	22.0	168.0	1.0	-	989.0
6 Wholesale and retail trade, restaurants and hotels	1363.0	232.0	924.0	114.0	586.0	2047.0
A Wholesale and retail trade	1067.0	189.0	816.0	91.0	586.0	1577.0
B Restaurants and hotels	296.0	44.0	108.0	23.0	-	471.0
7 Transport, storage and communication	685.0	205.0	429.0	32.0	112.0	1240.0
A Transport and storage	441.0	103.0	260.0	29.0	112.0	721.0
B Communication	244.0	102.0	169.0	3.0	-	518.0
8 Finance, insurance, real estate and business services	853.0	187.0	250.0	96.0	1.0	1385.0
9 Community, social and personal services	1050.0	527.0	1122.0	174.0	258.0	2614.0
Total, Industries	7985.0	1969.0	7030.0	1403.0	1814.0	16572.0
Producers of Government Services	3155.0	159.0	1.0	8.0	-	3322.0
Other Producers						
Total	11140.0	2128.0	7031.0	1410.0	1814.0	19895.0
Less: Imputed bank service charge	...	...	968.0	...	...	968.0
Import duties	...	...	...	791.0	...	791.0
Value added tax	...	...	...	1764.0	...	1764.0
Total	11140.0	2128.0	6063.0	3965.0	1814.0	21482.0

Israel

General note. The preparation of national accounts statistics in Israel is undertaken by the Central Bureau of Statistics, Jerusalem. The official estimates are published annually by the Bureau in the Statistical Abstract of Israel and in the May supplement to the Monthly Bulletin of Statistics. A detailed description of the National Income and Expenditure for the years 1950-1968 is found in Israel's National Income and Expenditure 1950-1962, published in 1964. Another edition of this publication for the years 1950-1968 published in 1970 included a description of the principal changes made in the method of estimation. The estimates are generally in accordance with the classifications and definitions recommended in the United Nations Systems of National Accounts (SNA). The following tables have been published in Input-Output Tables 1982/83. The Input-output tables have been prepared from successive replies to the United Nations national accounts questionnaire. When the scope and coverage of the estimates differ for conceptual or statistical reasons from the definitions and classifications recommended in SNA, a footnote is indicated to the relevant tables.

Sources and methods:

(a) **Gross domestic product.** Gross domestic product is estimated mainly through the expenditure approach.

(b) **Expenditure on the gross domestic product.** The expenditure approach is used to estimate government final consumption expenditure and exports and imports of goods and services. This approach, in combination with the commodity-flow approach, is used for private final consumption expenditure and gross capital formation. General government consumption expenditure is estimated on the basis of activity reports of the Accountant-General and the Budget Provision authorities and national institutions on the basis of financial statements supplemented by data from the Ministry of Finance. Expenditure of the local authorities and budget proposals. Private expenditure estimates on food, beverages and tobacco are based on data concerning quantities produced and marketed and on prices to the consumer, while estimates of expenditure on housing and business services, consumption of industrial products and other food products are based on family expenditure surveys held every five or six years. For the intervening years, estimates are computed by extrapolating year-to-year changes by the Budget Provision approach. Estimates of increase in stocks in agriculture, fuel and government strategic stocks are prepared by multiplying inventory stocks by their average prices. Regular quarterly and annual surveys are used to estimate inventory changes for industry and wholesale trade. The data obtained are adjusted to approximate the value of the physical change in stocks. Building and construction works are estimated either from reports of large companies, institutions and financial reports of the government bodies or by multiplying data on the areas under construction by the average cost per square meter for each type of construction. The estimates of imported machinery and equipment are based on the description found in the customs tariff while estimates of locally produced goods are based on a monthly report of sales by product obtained from the principal producers. Quantitative data and prices for investment assets in agriculture are available separately. The estimates of exports and imports of goods and services are based on foreign trade statistics and balance-of-payments data. Data pertaining to trade with the Administered Territories are a gross evaluation based on a sample enumeration of movement of goods through the official transit points. For the constant price estimates, government wages and salaries are extrapolated by the number of employees.

(c) **Cost-structure of the gross domestic product.** The estimates of wages and salaries are based either on surveys of the industrial branch and construction branches, surveys of parts of the transportation branch and surveys of government and private non-profit institutions and on employers' reports to the National Insurance Institute and indirect tax and supplementary payments. Profits, interest payments and rents are estimated by industry using the income approach. The estimate of consumption of fixed capital was calculated at replacement cost. Estimates of indirect taxes are based on the financial reports of the government and the local authorities.

(d) **Gross domestic product by kind of economic activity.** The table of GDP by kind of economic activity is prepared in net factor values. Net indirect taxes are estimated as totals only and not by industry. The production approach is used to estimate value added of the agricultural sector, the mining, quarrying and manufacturing sectors and the construction industry. For other sectors, the income approach is used. Estimates for recent years have been extrapolated by using the production approach. For the agricultural sector, data on output and input are based on the agricultural statistics series prepared by the Central Bureau of Statistics. Separate estimates are made for wages, interest and rent while net profit is obtained after deducting these expenses from total income. For mining and quarrying and manufacturing, estimates are based on industrial surveys carried out annually. For intervening years, estimates are interpolated and extrapolated using current production indexes. The Israel Electric Corporation and the Water Authority Commission supply data for their respective utility. Construction estimates have been obtained as the total payments by principal components, have been extrapolated with changes in inputs and outputs are taken into account. A special survey of wage and salary payments in the construction industry is also used. Bench-mark estimates for wholesale and retail trade have been based on a survey held in 1976/77. Extrapolation for other years is based on changes in sales to final users. The value added of the hotel industry is estimated by changes in revenue and inputs using data obtained from special surveys. For transport and communication, estimates are based on annual reports of the concerned establishments and on surveys of the trucking industry. Estimates for the financing and insurance industries are based on consolidated reports prepared by the Supervisor of Banks and the Supervisor of Insurance. Bench-mark estimate for residential rent for 1986 has been based on the family expenditure survey, extrapolated by the change in the value of inventories of dwellings. Estimates of government services are based on reports of the Accountant-General Budget Provisions, and from the Ministry of Finance. For other services, estimates are derived from a sample of income tax files, indirect tax data, manpower data and Kibbutz personal services. GDP by kind of economic activity is not estimated at constant prices.

1.1 Expenditure on the Gross Domestic Product, in Current Prices

Million New Sheqel

	1970	1975	1980	1981	1982	1983	1984	1985	1986	1987	1988	1989
1 Government final consumption expenditure	1	3	45 37	110	229	547	2925	10475	13946	19755	22820	25953
2 Private final consumption expenditure	1	5	63 59	145	343	909	4158	16544	27732	36071	43284	51679
A Households	1	4	55 57	141	334	886	4040	16126	27062	35180	42194	50317
B Private non-profit institutions serving households			8 2	4	9	23	118	418	670	891	1090	1363
3 Gross capital formation	1	2	25 25	56	140	360	1656	5264	8629	10895	12141	13874
A Increase in stocks			1 1	-3	5	5	100	-10	758	-72	-326	18
B Gross fixed capital formation	1	2	24 24	58	135	355	1556	5275	7871	10967	12467	13856
Residential buildings		1	10 10	24	51	114	507	1457	2115	2926	3502	4393
Non-residential buildings			3	6	13	33	145	469	687	1010	1276	1553
Other construction and land improvement etc.			2 2	5	12	29	106	360	667	991	1248	1441
Other		1	9 9	23	60	180	798	2988	4403	6040	6442	6469
4 Exports of goods and services		2	46 47	106	213	508	2886	12123	17759	21383	23488	30238
5 Less: Imports of goods and services	1	4	59 59	140	289	686	3582	14145	19300	26992	28184	33531
Equals: Gross Domestic Product	2	8	112 117	277	636	1638	8043	30261	47766	61112	73549	88213

Israel

1.2 Expenditure on the Gross Domestic Product, in Constant Prices

Thousand New sheqel

	1970	1975	1980	1981	1982	1983	1984	1985	1986	1987	1988	1989
		1970	**1975**			At constant prices of: **1980**					**1986**	
1 Government final consumption expenditure	673	1104 3407	2875 44707	47610	44676	42880	45405	47228	42744 13946	16327	16027	14601
2 Private final consumption expenditure	1129	1532 4625	5736 58840	66500	71840	78107	72591	73034	83801 27732	30086	31223	30905
A Households	1012	1368 4151	5182 57279	64817	70175	76464	70944	71391	82110 27062	29386	30519	30184
B Private non-profit institutions serving households	117	164 474	554 1561	1683	1665	1643	1647	1643	1691 670	700	704	720
3 Gross capital formation	539	788 2496	2012 25177	23861	27382	30129	27985	25013	27506 8629	8877	8710	8476
A Increase in stocks	35	36 163	33 842	-1451	783	176	1413	506	3141 758	-60	-186	67
B Gross fixed capital formation	504	752 2333	1979 24337	25313	26599	29953	26572	24507	24365 7871	8937	8896	8409
Residential buildings	175	291 895	752 10166	10377	10047	9585	8979	7900	7433 2115	2290	2288	2430
Non-residential buildings	77	112 367	236 2721	2471	2442	2675	2489	2390	2253 687	806	851	875
Other construction and land improvement etc.	54	65 214	184 2171	2161	2115	2153	1738	1683	2060 667	798	851	834
Other	198	284 857	807 9279	10304	11995	15540	13366	12534	12618 4403	5043	4906	4270
4 Exports of goods and services	466	746 2248	3269 46177	48433	46976	48034	54613	59265	62376 16759	18570	18158	18964
5 Less: Imports of goods and services	849	1346 4307	4229 58858	64387	66650	70565	70847	70319	76385 19300	22999	22435	21053
Equals: Gross Domestic Product	1958	2824 8469	9663 116043	122017	124224	128585	129747	134221	140042 47766[a]	50861[a]	51683[a]	51893[a]

a) Base year 1986 for the years 1986-1989 are in million new sheqel.

893

Israel

1.3 Cost Components of the Gross Domestic Product

Million New sheqel

	1970	1975	1980	1981	1982	1983	1984	1985	1986	1987	1988	1989
1 Indirect taxes, net [a]	-	1	12 11	15	60	179	693	4090	8004	10693	11643	13179
A Indirect taxes	-	2	21 20	47	114	311	1378	5948	9960	13194	14731	16303
B Less: Subsidies [a]	-	1	9 9	32	54	132	685	1858	1956	2501	3088	3124
2 Consumption of fixed capital	-	1	15 17	40	91	230	1208	4745	7137	8811	10301	12938
3 Compensation of employees paid by resident producers to:	1	4	55 56	136	312	823	4034	13939	22292	29389	36175	43171
A Resident households	...	...	... 55	133	305	802	3943	13606	21670	28403	35165	41956
B Rest of the world	...	...	... 1	3	7	21	91	333	622	986	1010	1215
4 Operating surplus	1	3	32 32	79	163	363	2050	7684	8977	11356	13574	17328
Statistical discrepancy	-	-	-1 -	6	10	43	58	-197	1356	863	1856	1597
Equals: Gross Domestic Product	2	8	112 117	277	636	1638	8043	30261	47766	61112	73549	88213

a) Beginning 1975, item 'Subsidies' includes subsidy component in government loans to industries.
In 1975, subsidy was 0.2 million new sheqel.

1.4 General Government Current Receipts and Disbursements

Million New sheqel

	1970	1975	1980	1981	1982	1983	1984	1985	1986	1987	1988	1989
Receipts												
1 Operating surplus	...	...	...	...	...	...	...	...	...	...	...	...
2 Property and entrepreneurial income	-	-	7 7	16	39	72	288	482	1132	982	1159	1869
3 Taxes, fees and contributions	1	3	48 47	110	259	664	2766	12332	20196	25524	29663	32867
A Indirect taxes	-	2	21 20	47	115	310	1378	5948	9960	13194	14731	16303
B Direct taxes	-	1	17 19	44	103	254	955	4521	7335	8842	10795	11600
C Social security contributions	-	-	7 8	19	40	96	419	1777	2715	3188	3773	4494
D Compulsory fees, fines and penalties [a]	-	-	1 -	-	1	4	15	85	186	300	364	470
4 Other current transfers	...	...	... 12	24	44	155	1210	5832	6671	5861	5999	7002
Total Current Receipts of General Government [bc]	1	3	55 66	150	342	891	4265	18645	27999	32367	36821	41738
Disbursements												
1 Government final consumption expenditure	1	3	37 45	110	229	547	2925	10475	13946	19755	22820	25953

Israel

1.4 General Government Current Receipts and Disbursements
(Continued)

Million New sheqel

	1970	1975	1980	1981	1982	1983	1984	1985	1986	1987	1988	1989
A Compensation of employees	-	1	15 21	49	110	280	1435	4633	7078	9087	11842	14499
B Consumption of fixed capital	...	...	... 2	5	11	25	127	470	746	973	1134	1377
C Purchases of goods and services, net	-	2	22 22	56	108	242	1362	5372	6123	9696	9844	10078
D Less: Own account fixed capital formation	...	...	... ...	...	...	...	...	...	...	...	...	...
E Indirect taxes paid, net	...	...	... ...	...	...	...	...	...	...	...	...	...
2 Property income d	-	-	12 12	30	68	163	983	3752	5373	6036	6760	8350
3 Subsidies	-	1	9 9	32	55	131	685	1858	1956	2501	3088	3124
4 Other current transfers	-	1	15 9	21	51	126	597	2425	4072	5197	6557	8466
5 Net saving bc	-	-2	-18 -9	-43	-61	-76	-925	135	2652	-1122	-2404	-4153
Total Current Disbursements and Net Saving of General Government bc	1	3	55 66	150	342	891	4265	18645	27999	32367	36821	41738

a) For the first series, item 'Compulsory fees, fines and other penalties' includes also other current transfers from households and private non-profit institutions.
b) For the first series, table 1.4 includes data on current receipts and disbursements of central government, local authorities and national institutions. Since 1980 the table covers also non-profit institutions whose expenditures are mainly financed by general government. The receipts of general government until 1980 do not include transfers from the rest of the world.
c) For the first series, the account does not include an imputation of employees' contributions in respect of governments' employees pensions and consumption of fixed capital.
d) Item 'Property income' relates to interest on public debt.

1.7 External Transactions on Current Account, Summary

Million New sheqel

	1970	1975	1980	1981	1982	1983	1984	1985	1986	1987	1988	1989
Payments to the Rest of the World												
1 Imports of goods and services	1	4	59 59	140	289	686	3582	14145	19300	26992	28184	33531
A Imports of merchandise c.i.f.	1	4	49 48	114	227	534	2769	11357	15485	22064	22594	26267
B Other	-	1	10 11	26	62	152	813	2788	3815	4928	5590	7264
2 Factor income to the rest of the world	...	1	12 11	30	73	172	985	3580	4490	5045	5380	6505
A Compensation of employees	...	-	2 2	4	10	26	127	436	766	1155	1167	1424
B Property and entrepreneurial income	...	-	10 9	26	63	146	858	3144	3724	3890	4213	5081
By general government	...	-	3 3	9	23	60	388	1618	1986	2165	2394	2554
By corporate and quasi-corporate enterprises	...	-	7 7	17	40	86	470	1526	1738	1725	1819	2527
By other	...											
3 Current transfers to the rest of the world	...	...	... 1	2	6	14	58	131	164	202	214	232
4 Surplus of the nation on current transactions	...	...	-1	-11	-47	-82	-37	1859	2149	-1704	-1295	1944
Payments to the Rest of the World and Surplus of the Nation on Current Transactions	...	...	... 70	161	321	790	4588	19715	26103	30535	32483	42212
Receipts From The Rest of the World												
1 Exports of goods and services	-	2	46 47	106	213	508	2886	12123	16759	21383	23488	30238
A Exports of merchandise f.o.b.	-	1	30 31	69	137	324	1910	7934	11520	14566	16152	20933

895

Israel

1.7 External Transactions on Current Account, Summary
(Continued)

Million New sheqel

	1970	1975	1980	1981	1982	1983	1984	1985	1986	1987	1988	1989
B Other	-	1	16 16	37	76	184	976	4189	5239	6817	7336	9305
2 Factor income from rest of the world	...	-	6 7	20	49	102	369	1157	1413	1517	1755	2645
A Compensation of employees	...	-	1 1	2	4	6	34	103	144	169	157	209
B Property and entrepreneurial income	...	-	5 6	18	45	96	335	1054	1269	1348	1598	2436
By general government	...	-	2 2	5	12	25	105	324	431	454	570	884
By corporate and quasi-corporate enterprises	...	-	4 4	13	33	71	230	730	838	894	1028	1552
By other	...											
3 Current transfers from rest of the world	...	...	... 16	35	59	180	1333	6435	7931	7635	7240	9329
Receipts from the Rest of the World on Current Transactions	...	...	... 70	161	321	790	4588	19715	26103	30535	32483	42212

1.8 Capital Transactions of The Nation, Summary

Million New sheqel

	1970	1975	1980	1981	1982	1983	1984	1985	1986	1987	1988	1989
Finance of Gross Capital Formation												
Gross saving	...	...	24	45	92	278	1620	7124	10778	9191	10846	15818
1 Consumption of fixed capital	...	...	17	40	91	230	1208	4746	7137	8811	10301	12938
A General government	...	...	2	5	10	25	126	470	746	973	1134	1377
B Corporate and quasi-corporate enterprises	...	...	15	35	81	205	1082	4275	6391	7838	9167	11561
C Other	...	...	...	...	...	...	...	...	...	...	...	...
2 Net saving	...	...	7	5	1	48	412	2378	3641	380	545	2880
A General government	...	...	-8	-42	-61	-76	-925	136	2652	-1123	-2404	-4156
B Corporate and quasi-corporate enterprises	...	...	15	47	62	124	1337	2241	989	1503	2949	7036
C Other	...	...										
Less: Surplus of the nation on current transactions	...	...	-1	-11	-47	-82	-37	1859	2149	-1704	-1295	1944
Finance of Gross Capital Formation	...	...	25	56	139	360	1657	5265	8629	10895	12141	13874
Gross Capital Formation												
Increase in stocks	...	...	1	-2	5	5	100	-10	758	-72	-326	18
Gross fixed capital formation	...	...	24	58	134	355	1557	5275	7871	10967	12467	13856
Gross Capital Formation	...	...	25	56	139	360	1657	5265	8629	10895	12141	13874

1.10 Gross Domestic Product by Kind of Activity, in Current Prices

Million New sheqel

	1970	1975	1980	1981	1982	1983	1984	1985	1986	1987	1988	1989
1 Agriculture, hunting, forestry and fishing	-	-	5 5	12	20	45	250	1062	1509	1749	1790	1922
2 Mining and quarrying	-	1	15 15	42	98	260	1377	5037	7000	8893	10191	11937
3 Manufacturing												
4 Electricity, gas and water	-	-	2 2	5	10	25	122	425	666	953	1274	1649
5 Construction	-	1	7 7	17	38	86	354	924	1470	2127	2727	3319
6 Wholesale and retail trade, restaurants and hotels	-	1	11 11	25	59	147	735	2971	4151	5313	5919	7174
7 Transport, storage and communication	-	-	6 6	15	32	78	379	1613	2494	3315	4758	5582
8 Finance, insurance, real estate and business services	-	1	19 19	45	101	248	1258	5111	6534	9125	11378	14344
9 Community, social and personal services	-	-	2 2	5	13	36	156	580	1116	1644	2030	2545

Israel

1.10 Gross Domestic Product by Kind of Activity, in Current Prices
(Continued)

Million New sheqel

	1970	1975	1980	1981	1982	1983	1984	1985	1986	1987	1988	1989
Statistical discrepancy [a]	...	-	6 6	12	21	45	227	550	630	794	705	575
Total, Industries	1	6	74 74	178	392	970	4858	18273	25570	33913	40772	49047
Producers of Government Services	-	1	20 21	50	112	286	1472	4764	7298	9447	12266	15068
Other Producers	...	...	... ...	...	...	...	...	...	...	...	...	...
Subtotal	2	7	93 95	228	505	1256	6330	23037	32868	43360	53038	64115
Less: Imputed bank service charge	-	-	7 7	14	30	68	243	1414	1600	2614	3289	3615
Plus: Import duties	...	...	... ...	...	...	...	...	...	...	...	...	...
Plus: Value added tax	...	...	... ...	...	...	...	...	...	...	...	...	...
Plus: Other adjustments [b]	-	-	-1 -1	6	10	43	58	-197	1356	863	1856	1597
Equals: Gross Domestic Product [c]	2	7	86 87	220	485	1230	6144	21426	32624	41609	51605	62097

a) Item 'Statistical discrepancy' relates to subsidy component in government loans to the business b) Item 'Other adjustments' includes errors and omissions. sector (on domestic production and exports) which could not be classified by industry. It was not c) Net domestic product in factor values rather than gross domestic product. possible to estimate this item for the years preceeding 1975.

1.12 Relations Among National Accounting Aggregates

Million New sheqel

	1970	1975	1980	1981	1982	1983	1984	1985	1986	1987	1988	1989
Gross Domestic Product	2	8	112 117	277	636	1638	8043	30261	47766	61112	73549	88213
Plus: Net factor income from the rest of the world	...	-	-6 -4	-10	-24	-70	-616	-2423	-3077	-3528	-3625	-3860
Factor income from the rest of the world	...	-	6 7	20	49	102	369	1157	1413	1517	1755	2645
Less: Factor income to the rest of the world	...	1	12 11	30	73	172	985	3580	4490	5045	5380	6505
Equals: Gross National Product	...	8	106 113	267	612	1568	7427	27838	44689	57584	69924	84353
Less: Consumption of fixed capital	-	1	15 17	40	91	230	1208	4745	7137	8811	10301	12938
Equals: National Income	...	7	91 96	227	521	1338	6219	23093	37552	48773	59623	71415
Plus: Net current transfers from the rest of the world	...	...	... 15	33	53	166	1275	6304	7767	7433	7026	9097
Current transfers from the rest of the world	...	...	... 16	35	59	180	1333	6435	7931	7635	7240	9329
Less: Current transfers to the rest of the world	...	...	... 1	2	6	14	58	131	164	202	214	232
Equals: National Disposable Income	...	...	... 111	260	574	1504	7494	29397	45319	56206	66649	80512
Less: Final consumption	2	8	... 104	255	572	1456	7083	27019	41678	55826	66104	77632
Equals: Net Saving	...	...	... 7	5	2	48	411	2378	3641	380	545	2880
Less: Surplus of the nation on current transactions	...	...	... -1	-11	-47	-82	-37	1859	2149	-1704	-1295	1944
Equals: Net Capital Formation	-	2	... 8	16	49	130	448	519	1492	2084	1840	936

2.1 Government Final Consumption Expenditure by Function, in Current Prices

Million New sheqel   Fiscal year beginning 1 April

	1970	1975	1980	1981	1982	1983	1984	1985	1986	1987	1988	1989
1 General public services	-	-	... 3	6	16	43	239	684	997	1287	...	...
2 Defence	1	3	... 33	75	150	407	2589	6345	7696	10983	...	...
3 Public order and safety	-	-	... 2	4	10	24	133	413	605	795	...	...
4 Education	-	-	... 9	20	48	127	708	1857	2604	3307	...	...
5 Health	-	-	... 5	10	23	61	351	932	1308	1630	...	...

Israel

2.1 Government Final Consumption Expenditure by Function, in Current Prices
(Continued)

Million New sheqel | Fiscal year beginning 1 April

	1970	1975	1980	1981	1982	1983	1984	1985	1986	1987	1988	1989
6 Social security and welfare	1	...	1	2	4	10	57	158	222	305	...	...
7 Housing and community amenities	1	...	2	5	12	73	215	310	414	...	...
8 Recreational, cultural and religious affairs	1	...	3	7	18	91	239	323	412	...	...
9 Economic services	1	...	3	5	16	83	250	353	431	...	...
A Fuel and energy	-	...	-	-	-	2	9	9	11	...	...
B Agriculture, forestry, fishing and hunting	1	...	2	5	30	83	109	124	...	...
C Mining, manufacturing and construction, except fuel and energy	-	...	-	-	1	4	13	18	27	...	...
D Transportation and communication	1	...	1	2	6	26	81	118	163	...	...
E Other economic affairs	-	...	1	1	4	21	67	99	106	...	...
10 Other functions	2	...	9	13	35	186	569	802	1035	...	...
Total Government Final Consumption Expenditure	1	3	58	131	281	753	4510	11662	15220	20599	...	...

2.5 Private Final Consumption Expenditure by Type and Purpose, in Current Prices

Million New sheqel

	1970	1975	1980	1981	1982	1983	1984	1985	1986	1987	1988	1989
Final Consumption Expenditure of Resident Households												
1 Food, beverages and tobacco a	1	18	18	38	98	234	1118	4712	7544	9395	11575	14086
A Food	1	16	16	33	76	204	974	4140	6633	8157	9912	12057
B Non-alcoholic beverages	1	-	1	2	6	16	86	329	523	791	985	1223
C Alcoholic beverages	1	1	1	3	7	27	106	166	207	253	281
D Tobacco	1	1	2	3	12	57	227	390	429	589	724
2 Clothing and footwear	3	10	25	55	215	1011	1956	2757	2782	2636
3 Gross rent, fuel and power	1	13	13	32	75	197	953	3778	5407	6671	8210	11131
A Fuel and power	-	2	2	4	10	22	100	431	544	613	736	1094
B Other	1	11	11	28	65	175	853	3347	4863	6058	7474	10037
4 Furniture, furnishings and household equipment and operation	1	7	7	17	39	110	430	1579	3093	4155	4837	5412
A Household operation	2	2	4	10	28	135	489	843	1265	1651	1921
B Other	5	5	13	29	82	295	1090	2250	2890	3186	3491
5 Medical care and health expenses	2	3	3	8	19	50	260	903	1474	2039	2503	3197
6 Transport and communication	6	6	15	40	108	476	1918	3206	4284	4928	5182
A Personal transport equipment	1	1	4	13	38	123	377	889	1322	1655	1151
B Other	5	5	12	27	70	353	1541	2317	2962	3273	4031
7 Recreational, entertainment, education and cultural services	3	10	23	59	269	1165	1963	2709	3192	3777
A Education	1	2	4	9	24	115	452	765	1079	1293	1579
B Other	2	2	6	14	35	154	713	1198	1630	1899	2198
8 Miscellaneous goods and services	5	5	14	34	91	419	1703	2717	3698	4528	5319

Israel

2.5 Private Final Consumption Expenditure by Type and Purpose, in Current Prices
(Continued)

Million New sheqel

	1970	1975	1980	1981	1982	1983	1984	1985	1986	1987	1988	1989
A Personal care	-	2	2	5	11	29	127	512	837	1134	1354	1582
B Expenditures in restaurants, cafes and hotels	-	2	5	11	33	163	722	1094	1508	1808	2239
C Other	-	2	4	12	29	129	469	786	1056	1366	1498
Total Final Consumption Expenditure in the Domestic Market by Households, of which	1	4	58/60	145	341	904	4140	16769	27360	35708	42555	50740
Plus: Direct purchases abroad by resident households			3	8	17	47	239	794	1340	1869	2085	2746
Less: Direct purchases in the domestic market by non-resident households			5	12	24	65	340	1437	1638	2398	2447	3170
Equals: Final Consumption Expenditure of Resident Households	1	4	55/58	141	334	886	4039	16126	27062	35179	42193	50316

Final Consumption Expenditure of Private Non-profit Institutions Serving Households

	1970	1975	1980	1981	1982	1983	1984	1985	1986	1987	1988	1989
1 Research and science b	...		1	1	-	1	3	9	16	19	23	27
2 Education b	-	-	3	1	1	2	13	49	80	103	127	148
3 Medical and other health services	-	-	3	2	1	5	28	95	151	209	253	324
4 Welfare services c	-	-	1	1	1	5	24	83	134	179	220	274
5 Recreational and related cultural services b	-	-	-	-	2	4	20	75	122	161	190	242
6 Religious organisations c	...	...	...	...	...	...	...	...	...	...	...	...
7 Professional and labour organisations serving households	...	...	...	...	1	2	6	30	107	167	220	278	348
8 Miscellaneous	...	...	...	...	...	...	...	...	...	...	...	...
Equals: Final Consumption Expenditure of Private Non-profit Organisations Serving Households	-	-	2/8	4	9	23	118	418	670	891	1091	1363
Private Final Consumption Expenditure	1	5	59/63	145	343	909	4157	16544	27732	36070	43284	51679

a) The sum of the components of item 'Food, beverages and tobacco' is greater than the totals   b) For the years 1970 and 1971, items 'Research and science' and 'Recreational and related cultural services' are included in item 'Education', shown because the sum has been adjusted for the expenditure included in other items of the national accounts.   c) Item 'Religious organisations' is included in item 'Welfare services'.

2.6 Private Final Consumption Expenditure by Type and Purpose, in Constant Prices

Thousand New sheqel

	1970	1975	1980	1981	1982	1983	1984	1985	1986	1987	1988	1989
			At constant prices of:									
			1970	1975			1980			1986		

Final Consumption Expenditure of Resident Households

	1970	1975	1980	1981	1982	1983	1984	1985	1986	1987	1988	1989
1 Food, beverages and tobacco	334a	1286a	1470a/1144a	17915a	18946a	19849a	21087a	21619a	22705a			
A Food	288	1105/349	1273	16010	17068	17716	18739	18752	19122	19991	6633	7009	8088	8558	8600
										7203	7229	7544
B Non-alcoholic beverages	12	15/61	74	761	811	901	1071	1134	1298	1510	663	725	772
										523		
C Alcoholic beverages	14	16/50	99	558	556	565	594	532	538	593	160	165	158
										167		
D Tobacco	23	36/76	90	982	1019	1132	1147	1071	1080	1138	410	561	586
										390		

Israel

2.6 Private Final Consumption Expenditure by Type and Purpose, in Constant Prices (Continued)

Thousand New sheqel	1970	1975	1980	1981	1982	1983	1984	1985	1986	1987	1988	1989
			At constant prices of:									
		1970		1975			1980			1986		
2 Clothing and footwear	90	122 289	342 3039	3825	4198	4097	3460	3947	4860	1956 2407	2239	2036
3 Gross rent, fuel and power	195	1037 299	1355 12941	13299	13861	14402	14720	15156	15614 5407	5564	5733	5899
A Fuel and power	20	28 113	141 1896	1786	1848	1955	1819	1832	1938	543 587	650	704
B Other	175	924 271	1214 11045	11513	12013	12447	12901	13324	13676 4863	4977	5083	5195
4 Furniture, furnishings and household equipment and operation	135	194 549	860 7107	8748	9243	10741	8298	8950	12366 3093	3343	3402	3312
A Household operation	41	53 155	163 1741	1811	1918	2055	2059	2143	2228 843	911	941	908
B Other	95	141 394	697 5366	6937	7325	8686	6239	6807	10138 2250	2432	2461	2404
5 Medical care and health expenses	30	50 143	160 3121	3484	3684	4091	4108	4006	4356 1474	1604	1631	1699
6 Transport and communication	93	133 397	493 5883	7580	8845	10310	9226	8124	9591 3206	3690	3916	3554
A Personal transport equipment	16	21 75	71 885	2042	2850	3615	2145	1575	2411	889 1113	1257	802
B Other	77	112 322	422 4998	5538	5995	6699	6781	6549	7180	2317 2577	2659	2752
7 Recreational, entertainment, education and cultural services	61	77 213	249 3882	4269	4513	4672	4381	4876	5412 1963	2167	2162	2140
A Education	23	27 80	89 1644	1825	1840	1982	1915	2045	2212	765 833	811	814
B Other	38	50 133	160 2238	2444	2673	2690	2466	2831	3200 1198	1334	1351	1326
8 Miscellaneous goods and services	92	111 342	457 5673	6240	6778	6829	7078	7104	7734	2717 2945	2982	3066
A Personal care	38	42 132	175 1928	2188	2231	2257	2108	2354	2645	837 900	908	925
B Expenditures in restaurants, cafes and hotels	39	41 126	156 1878	1992	2004	2313	2461	2687	2807	1094 1220	1203	1259

900

Israel

2.6 Private Final Consumption Expenditure by Type and Purpose, in Constant Prices
(Continued)

Thousand New sheqel

	1970	1975	1980	1981	1982	1983	1984	1985	1986	1987	1988	1989
At constant prices of:	1970	1975				1980				1986		
C Other	15	28 84	126 1867	2060	2443	2508	2260	2063	2282 786	825	871	882
Total Final Consumption Expenditure in the Domestic Market by Households, of which	1030	1400 4256	5386 59561	66391	70871	76478	71789	73782	82638 27360	29808	30623	30306
Plus: Direct purchases abroad by resident households	24	42 116	216 2862	3658	3902	4749	4427	3302	3960 1340	1507	1598	1759
Less: Direct purchases in the domestic market by non-resident households	42	73 219	420 5144	5234	4597	4760	5270	5691	4486 1638	1929	1702	1880
Equals: Final Consumption Expenditure of Resident Households	1012	1369 4153	5182 57279	64815	70176	76467	70946	71393	82112 27062[b]	29386[b]	30519[b]	30185[b]

Final Consumption Expenditure of Private Non-profit Institutions Serving Households

	1970	1975	1980	1981	1982	1983	1984	1985	1986	1987	1988	1989
1 Research and science	...	12[c] 34	35 37	39	37	35	36	38	41 16	15	16	15
2 Education	47[c]	58[c] 184	220 127	130	135	139	139	143	170 80	82	82	80
3 Medical and other health services	41	58 149	177 360	363	372	371	377	389	412 151	161	154	162
4 Welfare services	15[d]	15[d] 46[d]	59[d] 282[d]	302[d]	316[d]	327[d]	334[d]	329[d]	345[d] 134	142	145	148
5 Recreational and related cultural services	...	7[c] 19	22 272	321	303	281	289	290	303 122	126	126	132
6 Religious organisations	...	... ...	... ...	...	...	...	...	...	... ...	...	...	...
7 Professional and labour organisations serving households	...	... 42	39 484	528	502	490	472	455	440 167	174	181	183
8 Miscellaneous	14	14 ...	... ...	...	...	...	...	...	... ...	...	...	...
Equals: Final Consumption Expenditure of Private Non-profit Organisations Serving Households	117	164 474	554 1561	1683	1665	1643	1647	1643	1691 670	700	704	720
Private Final Consumption Expenditure	1129	1533 4627	5736 58840	66498	71841	78110	72593	73036	83803 27732[b]	30086[b]	31223[b]	30905[b]

a) The sum of the components of item 'Food, beverages and tobacco' is greater than the totals shown because the sum has been adjusted for the expenditure included in other items of the national accounts.

b) Base year 1986 for the years 1986-1989 are in million new sheqel.

c) For the years 1970 and 1971, items 'Research and science' and 'Recreational and related cultural services' are included in item 'Education'.

d) Item 'Religious organisations' is included in item 'Welfare services'.

Israel

2.11 Gross Fixed Capital Formation by Kind of Activity of Owner, ISIC Divisions, in Current Prices

Million New sheqel

	1970	1975	1980	1981	1982	1983	1984	1985	1986	1987	1988	1989
					All Producers			›				
1 Agriculture, hunting, forestry and fishing	-	-	1 1	2	6	17	72	272	337	433	449	413
2 Mining and quarrying	-	-	4 4	8	23	62	313	1311	1765	2234	2006	2302
3 Manufacturing												
4 Electricity, gas and water a	-	-	2 2	4	6	17	87	255	405	537	729	878
5 Construction b	-	-	- -	1	2	5	14	41	61	117	144	144
6 Wholesale and retail trade, restaurants and hotels c	-	-	4 4	11	26	74	320	1145	1747	2315	2691	3136
7 Transport, storage and communication	-	-	3 3	9	21	65	242	794	1441	2405	2946	2590
8 Finance, insurance, real estate and business services	-	1	10 10	24	51	114	507	1457	2115	2926	3502	4393
9 Community, social and personal services c	...	...	...	...	...	...	...	...	...	...	...	...
Total Industries	1	2	24 24	58	135	355	1556	5275	7871	10967	12467	13856
Producers of Government Services	...	...	...	...	...	...	...	...	...	...	...	...
Private Non-Profit Institutions Serving Households	...	...	...	...	...	...	...	...	...	...	...	...
Total	1	2	24 24	58	135	355	1556	5275	7871	10967	12467	13856

a) Item 'Electricity, gas and water' includes water projects.
b) Item 'Construction' includes construction equipment only.
c) All services are included in item 'Wholesale and retail trade, restaurants and hotels'.

2.12 Gross Fixed Capital Formation by Kind of Activity of Owner, ISIC Divisions, in Constant Prices

Thousand New sheqel

	1970	1975	1980	1981	1982	1983	1984	1985	1986	1987	1988	1989
	1970		1975			At constant prices of: 1980				1986		
					All Producers							
1 Agriculture, hunting, forestry and fishing	24	36 105	88 942	980	1114	1320	1109	1128	940 337	359	327	254
2 Mining and quarrying	82	122 391	311 3558	3694	4546	5386	5405	5577	5152 1765	1884	1565	1520
3 Manufacturing												
4 Electricity, gas and water	20a	35a 100a	167a 1827a	1798a	1226a	1438a	1426a	1141a	1281a 405	424	517	523

Israel

2.12 Gross Fixed Capital Formation by Kind of Activity of Owner, ISIC Divisions, in Constant Prices
(Continued)

Thousand New sheqel

	1970	1975	1980	1981	1982	1983	1984	1985	1986	1987	1988	1989
	1970	**1975**	At constant prices of: **1980**						**1986**			
5 Construction	8b	14b 42b	35b 386b	274b	292b	416b	242b	155b	166b 61	101	114	99
6 Wholesale and retail trade, restaurants and hotels	100c	158c 484c	352c 4205c	4589c	4915c	6034c	5302c	5123c	5250c 1747	1901	1948	1942
7 Transport, storage and communication	94	96 315	275 3387	3714	4502	5982	4327	3638	4143 1441	1978	2137	1641
8 Finance, insurance, real estate and business services	175	291 895	752 10166	10377	10047	9585	8979	7900	7433 2115	2290	2288	2430
9 Community, social and personal services	...	... ...	... ...	...	...	...	...	...	... ...	...	...	...
Total Industries	504	752 2311	1980 24337	25313	26599	29953	26572	24507	24364 7871	8937	8896	8409
Producers of Government Services	...	... ...	... ...	...	...	...	...	...	... ...	...	...	...
Private Non-Profit Institutions Serving Households	...	... ...	... ...	...	...	...	...	...	... ...	...	...	...
Total	504	752 2331	1980 24337	25313	26599	29953	26572	24507	24364 7871	8937	8896	8409

a) Item 'Electricity, gas and water' includes water projects.
b) Item 'Construction' includes construction equipment only.
c) All services are included in item 'Wholesale and retail trade, restaurants and hotels'.

2.17 Exports and Imports of Goods and Services, Detail

Million New sheqel

	1970	1975	1980	1981	1982	1983	1984	1985	1986	1987	1988	1989
					Exports of Goods and Services							
1 Exports of merchandise, f.o.b.	...	1	30 31	69	137	324	1910	7934	11520	14566	16152	20933
2 Transport and communication	...	-	7 7	17	35	75	409	1488	1885	2394	2659	3261
A In respect of merchandise imports	...	-	2 1	4	8	18	90	360	533	675	713	844
B Other	...	-	5 6	3	27	57	319	1128	1352	1719	1946	2417
3 Insurance service charges	...	-	-	-	1	-1	-12	19	35	53	76	96
A In respect of merchandise imports	...	-	-	-	-	1	6	30	45	57	74	92
B Other	...	-	-	-	-	-2	-18	-11	-10	-4	2	4
4 Other commodities	...	-	4 4	8	16	44	238	1240	1665	1949	2117	2715
5 Adjustments of merchandise exports to change-of-ownership basis	...	...	-	-	-	-	-	-	-	-	-	-
6 Direct purchases in the domestic market by non-residential households	...	-	5 5	12	24	66	340	1437	1638	2398	2447	3170
7 Direct purchases in the domestic market by extraterritorial bodies	...	-	-	-	-	-	1	5	16	23	37	63
Total Exports of Goods and Services	...	2	46 47	106	213	508	2886	12123	16759	21383	23488	30238

Israel

2.17 Exports and Imports of Goods and Services, Detail
(Continued)

Million New sheqel

	1970	1975	1980	1981	1982	1983	1984	1985	1986	1987	1988	1989
Imports of Goods and Services												
1 Imports of merchandise, c.i.f.	...	4	49 48	114	227	534	2769	11357	15485	22064	22594	26267
A Imports of merchandise, f.o.b.	...	3	46 46	107	211	496	2582	10600	14338	20599	21031	24404
B Transport of services on merchandise imports	...	-	2 2	7	14	36	179	720	1089	1395	1475	1753
By residents	...	-	2 1	5	8	18	90	360	533	675	713	844
By non-residents	...	-	1 1	2	6	18	89	360	556	720	762	909
C Insurance service charges on merchandise imports	...	-	- -	-	2	2	8	37	58	70	88	110
By residents	...	-	-	-	-	1	6	30	45	57	74	92
By non-residents	...	-	-	-	-	1	2	7	13	13	14	18
2 Adjustments of merchandise imports to change-of-ownership basis	...	...	- -	-	-	-	-	-	-	-	-	-
3 Other transport and communication	...	-	5 6	14	27	57	319	1128	1352	1719	1946	2417
4 Other insurance service charges	...	-	-	-	-	1	13	157	134	178	138	168
5 Other commodities	...	-	2 2	4	16	45	237	721	1007	1202	1473	1962
6 Direct purchases abroad by government	...	-	-	-	2	4	22	100	108	139	139	185
7 Direct purchases abroad by resident households	...	-	3 3	8	17	45	222	682	1214	1690	1894	2532
Total Imports of Goods and Services	...	4	59 59	140	289	686	3582	14145	19300	26992	28184	33531
Balance of Goods and Services	...	-2	-13 -12	-34	-76	-178	-696	-2022	-2541	-5609	-4696	-3293
Total Imports and Balance of Goods and Services	...	2	46 47	106	213	508	2886	12123	16759	21383	23488	30238

Italy

General note. The preparation of national accounts statistics in Italy is undertaken by the instituto Central di Statistica, Rome. The official estimates are published in the 'Annuario Statistico Italiano' and in 'Compendio Statistico Italiano'. The latter publication is also published in English under the title 'Italian Statistical Abstract'. The following presentation on sources and method is based mainly on information prepared by the Statistical Office of the European Communities in 1976 in a report entitled 'Basic statistics needed for the ESA accounts and tables: present situation and prospects for improvements'. The estimates are generally in accordance with the definitions and classifications recommended in the United Nations System of National Accounts (SNA). Input-output tables have been published in 'Supplemento Straordinario al Bolletiono Mensile di Statistica'. The following tables have been prepared from successive replies to the United Nations national accounts questionnaire. When the scope and coverage of the estimates differ for conceptual or statistical reasons from the definitions and classifications recommended in SNA, a footnote is indicated to the relevant tables.

Sources and methods :

(a) Gross domestic product. GDP is estimated mainly through the production approach.

(b) Expenditure on the gross domestic product. The expenditure approach is used to estimate government final consumption expenditure, increase in stocks and exports and imports of goods and services. This aproach, in combination with the commodity-flow approach is used to estimate private final consumption expenditure and gross fixed capital formation. For central government, the estimates are based on data obtained from the Bilancio dello Stato. Complete accounts for tHe other bodies of the general government are available after 39 months and for social security funds, after 27 months, Household consumption expenditure is primarily based on the quarterly surveys of family budgets suplemented by estimates based on commodity-flows. The surveys cover 36,000 households by rotation with 9000 new families each quarter. Surveys carried out by the Banco d'Italia provide consumption data for non-resident households on the domestic market and for residents abroad. The main statistical source used for estimating changes in stocks is the value-added surveys conducted for all enterprises in the industrial construction, trade and transport sectors that employ more than 20 persons. The stocks relate to industrial products only. Data for estimating gross fixed capital formation are obtained through a questionnaire attached to the value-added survey. Government capital expenditure are obtained from government accounts. For construction and building, the Istituto Central di Statistico conducts specific surveys such as surveys on residential buildings and on public works. The estimates of exports and imports of goods and services are based mainly on the balance-of-payments and foreign trade statistics. For the constant price estimates, most of the items of GDP by expenditure type are deflated by appropriate price indexes. Government building depreciation is estimated as a certain percentage of the stock value at constant prices. Private consumption of own-produced food and stock increases of agricultural products are revalued at base-year prices. Gross rent is extrapolated by the number of dwelling units.

(c) Cost-structure of the gross domestic product. Compensation of employees is estimated through use of the value-added survey and a survey carried out by the Ministry of Labour and Social Security for the industrial sector, minimum contractual wages and survey of the compensation of permanent employees for the agricultural sector, surveys and inquiries carried out by other institutes for the service sector and other indirect evaluation for sectors not covered by surveys. Information on operating surplus is obtained from the value-added surveys and from actual interest received and paid by the various sectors. Depreciation is valued on the basis of time series of gross fixed capital formation at constant prices by product and by branch of economic activity. Constant prices of 1970 are estimated by using the perpetual inventory method, assuming that the devaluation of the product is constant during its economic life. Estimates of indirect taxes and subsidies are obtained from government sources. Taxes linked to production and imports are broken down by branch according to the type of tax. Data on subsidies are classified by branch on the basis of the recipients indicated in the government budgets.

(d) Gross domestic product by kind of economic activity. The table of GDP by kind of economic activity is prepared at market prices, i.e., producers' values. The production approach is used to estimate the value added of most of the industries. This is supplemented by the income aproach for industries to which the value-added surveys are applied. The income approach alone is used for the producers of government services. Statistics on agricultural production prices, etc. are derived from current agricultural surveys. A new survey was carried out in 1975, covering 6,000 farms with complete accounts which produce about 10 percent of the total output. Crop surveys of major products are conducted annually. Information on gross marketable livestock production is available separately for major items. For forestry, a quarterly survey supplies data on production and prices. Monthly surveys of products unloaded in Italian ports are used for estimating value added of fishing. For the industrial activity sector, the estimates are based on value-added surveys and the product surveys. In addition to these surveys, the rapid surveys of large enterprises are also used for manufacturing. The annual value-added survey, which covers all enterprises employing more than 20 persons and is available after 15 months, includes transactions in goods and services, distributive transactions and employment data. The survey does not allow product-by-product analysis. The product survey which covers all enterprises employing more than 50 persons and is available after 24 months, is used for compiling input-output tables and is linked with the European Community surveys on industrial activity. The annual rapid survey, covering all enterprises employing more than 250 persons is available within 3 months. This survey provides information similar to that obtained in the value-added surveys. The surveys used for the manufacturing sector are also used for construction. In addition construction estimates are based on the results of surveys on the number of residential buildings, surveys of public works and sample surveys of work in progress on bUilding sites. For the trade sector, the main source is the value-added survey. However, to cover enterprises employing less than 20 persons, an indirect method, which consists in constructing an index of traded consumer goods, capital goods and goods for export, is used for estimating gross output of the trade sector. The value-added surveys are also used for the transport sector. Additional information is supplied directly by the relevant firms and public agencies. For the financial institutions, annual surveys are carried out which covers 97 percent of the activity. Special calculations are made for institutions not covered. Estimates of government services are based on surveys conducted by the social security funds and on data compiled by the Ragioneria generale dello Stato and the Istituto Centrale de Statistic. For other services, the Istituto Central di Statistica carries out a single direct survey of public hospitals. Other market services are valued indirectly, mostly on the basis of the results of family budgets surveys. For the constant price estimates, price deflation is used for community, social and personal services. Double deflation is used for all the other sectors. Output is either deflated by apropriate indexes or is extrapolated by quantum indexes while input is deflated by price indexes.

1.1 Expenditure on the Gross Domestic Product, in Current Prices

Thousand Million Italian lire

	1970	1975	1980	1981	1982	1983	1984	1985	1986	1987	1988	1989
1 Government final consumption expenditure	8709	19563	57013	74156	87386	103568	118034	133265	145960	164188	184259	199649
2 Private final consumption expenditure	39992	85972	236603	284030	335448	387830	443965	499587	551844	605104	664904	732966
A Households	39818	85593	235561	282833	334026	386226	441986	497350	549448	602644	662219	730124
B Private non-profit institutions serving households	174	379	1042	1197	1422	1604	1979	2237	2396	2460	2685	2842
3 Gross capital formation	18415	33185	104522	114833	128187	137535	167266	183190	185778	203127	231761	256393
A Increase in stocks	1883	-1383	10460	4150	6453	2943	13909	14960	9016	9521	15134	16152
B Gross fixed capital formation	16532	34568	94062	110683	121734	134592	153357	168230	176762	193606	216627	240241
Residential buildings	5674	10798	25991	32032	35890	42675	46670	48888	49568	50230	53267	56975
Non-residential buildings	4748	9835	23620	28219	30426	33069	35627	40055	43618	46186	51351	57924
Other construction and land improvement etc.												
Other	6110	13935	44451	50432	55418	58848	71060	79287	83576	97190	112009	125342
4 Exports of goods and services	11041	28467	84953	108344	125125	140016	165197	185022	181961	191841	210046	244176
5 Less: Imports of goods and services	10979	28555	95422	117333	131022	135508	167237	188313	168262	185402	208044	245196
Equals: Gross Domestic Product	67178	138632	387669	464030	545124	633441	727225	812751	897281	978858	1082930	1187990

Italy

1.2 Expenditure on the Gross Domestic Product, in Constant Prices

Thousand Million Italian lire

	1970	1975	1980	1981	1982	1983	1984	1985	1986	1987	1988	1989
					At constant prices of:1980							
1 Government final consumption expenditure	41826	49766	57013	58567	60237	61985	63528	65757	67662	70194	72169	72552
2 Private final consumption expenditure	156490	185981	236603	240373	242836	243930	249528	257602	269302	281479	294139	306377
A Households	155743	185027	235561	239340	241754	242822	248373	256410	268075	280225	292864	305097
B Private non-profit institutions serving households	747	954	1042	1033	1082	1108	1155	1192	1227	1254	1275	1280
3 Gross capital formation	83907	76342	104522	93916	90461	88073	96968	98461	98238	104850	112982	117490
A Increase in stocks	7409	-3491	10460	2820	4095	2508	7591	7811	6170	7472	9036	8214
B Gross fixed capital formation	76498	79833	94062	91096	86366	85565	89377	90650	92068	97378	103946	109276
Residential buildings	28367	26288	25991	25960	24855	25884	25734	24841	24437	23831	23514	23748
Non-residential buildings	24857	25925	23620	22529	20855	20496	20199	20876	21768	21886	22772	24210
Other construction and land improvement etc. Other	23274	27620	44451	42607	40656	39185	43444	44933	45863	51661	57660	61318
4 Exports of goods and services	48377	63507	84953	90203	90170	92548	98623	102244	104746	108118	112699	123055
5 Less: Imports of goods and services	62806	68414	95422	91673	91044	89457	99604	104276	109486	121106	130022	142896
Equals: Gross Domestic Product	267794	307182	387669	391386	392660	397079	409043	419788	430462	443535	461967	476578

1.3 Cost Components of the Gross Domestic Product

Thousand Million Italian lire

	1970	1975	1980	1981	1982	1983	1984	1985	1986	1987	1988	1989
1 Indirect taxes, net	5830	6894	22496	25604	30150	39303	44520	49811	56778	69185	84250	95998
A Indirect taxes	6977	11286	35846	41369	50208	62084	72097	77636	89071	101203	117851	132323
B Less: Subsidies	1147	4392	13350	15765	20058	22781	27577	27825	32293	32018	33601	36325
2 Consumption of fixed capital	7085	17850	45134	57202	69012	79381	90133	101126	108800	117723	127815	138935
3 Compensation of employees paid by resident producers to:	30541	70854	184063	224032	260859	300156	334994	374051	404065	439608	485841	532823
A Resident households	30498	70752	183828	223697	260403	299659	334423	373323	403326	438691	484543	530420
B Rest of the world	43	102	235	335	456	497	571	728	739	917	1298	2403
4 Operating surplus	23722	43034	135976	157192	185103	214601	257578	287763	327638	352342	385020	420232
Equals: Gross Domestic Product	67178	138632	387669	464030	545124	633441	727225	812751	897281	978858	1082930	1187990

1.4 General Government Current Receipts and Disbursements

Thousand Million Italian lire

	1970	1975	1980	1981	1982	1983	1984	1985	1986	1987	1988	1989
					Receipts							
1 Operating surplus	22	110	486 / 401	563	747	1000	1168	1320	1585	1784	2275	2684
2 Property and entrepreneurial income	591	1002	3338 / 2761	3749	3723	4117	4762	6305	7626	7164	6919	7214
3 Taxes, fees and contributions	17181	35562	115671 / 115301	142343	178400	215515	245654	275241	308804	344901	387660	444125
A Indirect taxes	7028	10962	34128 / 33522	38297	46649	57987	67283	72661	81743	93302	109104	123726
B Direct taxes	3439	8367	37788 / 37291	50916	64534	78402	91416	105466	115683	130610	145202	170467
C Social security contributions	6714	16233	43755 / 44488	53130	67217	79126	86955	97114	111378	120989	133354	149932
D Compulsory fees, fines and penalties	-	-	-	-	-	-	-	-	-	-	-	-
4 Other current transfers	1315	2492	8535 / 9340	11684	12600	18276	20696	25941	31494	29689	32248	34797
Total Current Receipts of General Government	19109	39166	128030 / 127803	158339	195470	238908	272280	308807	349509	383538	429102	488820
					Disbursements							
1 Government final consumption expenditure	8664	19362	55636 / 57013	74156	87386	103568	118034	133265	145960	164188	184259	199649
2 Property income	1112	4989	21196 / 20565	28700	38996	47491	58296	65300	76593	78477	88952	107255
A Interest	1112	4984	21173 / 20479	28583	38857	47320	58113	65069	76370	78224	88680	106950
B Net land rent and royalties	-	5	23 / 86	117	139	171	183	231	223	253	272	305

Italy

1.4 General Government Current Receipts and Disbursements
(Continued)

Thousand Million Italian lire

	1970	1975	1980	1981	1982	1983	1984	1985	1986	1987	1988	1989
3 Subsidies	940	2791	7960 11068	13298	16898	18381	22446	22878	27693	26125	26840	29093
4 Other current transfers	8277	20886	55703 57354	75493	91830	113979	127036	145617	162554	178859	199362	223932
A Social security benefits	7775	19616	53465 54696	72805	88609	109355	121556	139055	154826	170486	189532	210803
B Social assistance grants												
C Other	502	1270	2238 2658	2688	3221	4624	5480	6562	7728	8373	9830	13129
5 Net saving	116	-8862	-12465 -18197	-33308	-39640	-44511	-53532	-58253	-63291	-64111	-70311	-71109
Total Current Disbursements and Net Saving of General Government	19109	39166	128030 127803	158339	195470	238908	272280	308807	349509	383538	429102	488820

1.5 Current Income and Outlay of Corporate and Quasi-Corporate Enterprises, Summary

Thousand Million Italian lire

	1970	1975	1980	1981	1982	1983	1984	1985	1986	1987	1988	1989
Receipts												
1 Operating surplus	1799	-1607	5665 14551	14654	13668	29672	33721	47928	64492	64048	57806	...
2 Property and entrepreneurial income received	6614	23209	71017 78944	100199	114701	128847	144957	157508	156129	153893	167816	...
3 Current transfers	3087	7362	15439 15966	18034	20463	23784	26587	30103	32318	35588	39694	...
Total Current Receipts	11500	28964	92121 109461	132887	148832	182303	205265	235539	252939	253529	265316	...
Disbursements												
1 Property and entrepreneurial income	6532	21905	67340 75910	102240	120319	135653	149926	158112	150219	151717	160047	...
2 Direct taxes and other current payments to general government	793	1709	5353 4933	6989	9648	12378	14395	18052	22168	29275	25112	...
3 Other current transfers	3266	7871	16604 10865	13682	15438	20249	21774	26514	28248	33087	36769	...
Statistical discrepancy	...	...	... 5325	5459	5821	5575	6860	7933	8029	6755	7845	...
4 Net saving	909	-2521	2824 12428	4517	-2394	8448	12310	24928	44275	32695	35543	...
Total Current Disbursements and Net Saving	11500	28964	92121 109461	132887	148832	182303	205265	235539	252939	253529	265316	...

1.6 Current Income and Outlay of Households and Non-Profit Institutions

Thousand Million Italian lire

	1970	1975	1980	1981	1982	1983	1984	1985	1986	1987	1988	1989
Receipts												
1 Compensation of employees	30714	71618	185642 185672	225804	262938	302452	337537	376681	406738	441764	487831	...
A From resident producers	30306	71102	183919 183828	223697	260403	299659	334423	373323	403326	438691	484543	...
B From rest of the world	408	516	1723 1844	2107	2535	2793	3114	3358	3412	3073	3288	...
2 Operating surplus of private unincorporated enterprises	19493	34760	89485 121024	141975	170688	183929	222689	238515	261561	286510	324939	...
3 Property and entrepreneurial income	2465	8275	28659 33522	46983	61709	71464	80889	86794	95347	98067	111761	...
4 Current transfers	10435	25358	67151 66731	87188	105964	130771	145457	166692	183705	204331	227296	...
A Social security benefits	6172	16951	44684 58583	77998	94616	117344	129798	148667	164033	182182	202641	...
B Social assistance grants	2803	5016	14350									
C Other	1460	3391	8117 8148	9190	11348	13427	15659	18025	19672	22149	24655	...
Statistical discrepancy	...	...	... 6979	7418	8087	7274	8515	9897	10090	9302	10349	...
Total Current Receipts	63107	140011	370937 413928	509368	609386	695890	795087	878579	957441	1039970	1162180	...
Disbursements												
1 Private final consumption expenditure	39371	80571	208232 236603	284030	335448	387830	443965	499587	551844	605104	664904	...

907

Italy

1.6 Current Income and Outlay of Households and Non-Profit Institutions
(Continued)

Thousand Million Italian lire

	1970	1975	1980	1981	1982	1983	1984	1985	1986	1987	1988	1989
2 Property income	2147	6548	15474 19604	24004	26616	27853	29727	35293	41910	37906	47086	...
3 Direct taxes and other current transfers n.e.c. to general government	9438	23099	76418 77122	97354	122403	145448	164306	184883	205293	222747	253908	...
A Social security contributions	6792	16441	43983 44764	53427	67517	79424	87285	97470	111778	121412	133818	...
B Direct taxes	2646	6658	32435 32358	43927	54886	66024	77021	87413	93515	101335	120090	...
C Fees, fines and penalties	...	...	...	...	...	...	...	...	...	...	...	...
4 Other current transfers	3064	6190	17484 22433	26000	30095	36813	41741	48922	56589	57017	63204	...
Statistical discrepancy	...	...	1654	1959	2266	1699	1655	1964	2061	2547	2504	...
5 Net saving	9087	23603	53329 56512	76021	92558	96247	113693	107930	99744	114653	130570	...
Total Current Disbursements and Net Saving	63107	140011	370937 413928	509368	609386	695890	795087	878579	957441	1039970	1162180	...

1.7 External Transactions on Current Account, Summary

Thousand Million Italian lire

	1970	1975	1980	1981	1982	1983	1984	1985	1986	1987	1988	1989 ·
Payments to the Rest of the World												
1 Imports of goods and services	10979	28555	95422	117333	131022	135508	167237	188313	168262	185402	208044	245196
A Imports of merchandise c.i.f.	9573	25574	87170	107794	119148	122469	150887	168791	149542	162936	181449	211414
B Other	1406	2981	8252	9539	11874	13039	16350	19522	18720	22466	26595	33782
2 Factor income to the rest of the world	688	2073	5662	10988	13907	13422	16445	18600	18594	18157	20568	28079
A Compensation of employees	43	102	235	335	456	497	571	728	739	917	1298	2403
B Property and entrepreneurial income	645	1971	5427	10653	13451	12925	15874	17872	17855	17240	19270	25676
3 Current transfers to the rest of the world	432	1127	4007	5084	6224	7007	8359	9636	12737	13540	15988	19435
A Indirect taxes to supranational organizations	...	...	...	...	...	...	...	...	...	...	...	...
B Other current transfers	432	1127	4007	5084	6224	7007	8359	9636	12737	13540	15988	19435
4 Surplus of the nation on current transactions	529	-228	-8645	-10401	-8651	2030	-4662	-7459	4290	-2167	-8144	-16838
Payments to the Rest of the World and Surplus of the Nation on Current Transactions	12628	31527	96446	123004	142502	157967	187379	209090	203883	214932	236456	275872
Receipts From The Rest of the World												
1 Exports of goods and services	11041	28467	84953	108344	125125	140016	165197	185022	181961	191841	210046	244176
A Exports of merchandise f.o.b.	8258	22915	66987	87875	99732	110747	131026	146059	144675	150697	166639	193266
B Other	2783	5552	17966	20469	25393	29269	34171	38963	37286	41144	43407	50910
2 Factor income from rest of the world	999	1654	6452	8802	10255	9226	11709	13222	11687	11435	13064	17506
A Compensation of employees	424	573	1844	2107	2535	2793	3114	3358	3412	3073	3288	3421
B Property and entrepreneurial income	575	1081	4608	6695	7720	6433	8595	9864	8275	8362	9776	14085
3 Current transfers from rest of the world	588	1406	5041	5858	7122	8725	10473	10846	10235	11656	13346	14190
A Subsidies from supranational organisations	...	...	...	...	...	...	...	...	...	...	...	...
B Other current transfers	588	1406	5041	5858	7122	8725	10473	10846	10235	11656	13346	14190
Receipts from the Rest of the World on Current Transactions	12628	31527	96446	123004	142502	157967	187379	209090	203883	214932	236456	275872

Italy

1.8 Capital Transactions of The Nation, Summary

Thousand Million Italian lire

	1970	1975	1980	1981	1982	1983	1984	1985	1986	1987	1988	1989
Finance of Gross Capital Formation												
Gross saving	18944	32957	96877	104432	119536	135565	162604	175731	190068	200960	223617	239555
1 Consumption of fixed capital	7085	17850	45134	57202	69012	79381	90133	101126	108800	117723	127815	138935
A General government	...	...	862	1051	1251	1437	1681	1988	2334	2735	3223	3799
B Corporate and quasi-corporate enterprises	...	...	18670	26583	28683	32877	37273	41778	44737	48134	52133	...
C Other	...	...	25602	32468	39178	45067	51179	57399	61729	66899	72459	...
2 Net saving	11859	15107	50743	47230	50524	56184	72471	74605	81268	83237	95802	100620
A General government	-18197	...	-33308	-39604	-44511	-53532	-58253	-63291	-64111	-10311	-71109	
B Corporate and quasi-corporate enterprises	...	...	12428	4517	-2394	8448	12310	24928	44275	32695	35543	
C Other	...	...	55612	76021	92558	96247	113693	107930	99744	114653	130570	
Less: Surplus of the nation on current transactions	529	-228	-8465	-10401	-8651	2030	-4662	-7459	4290	-2167	-8144	-16838
Finance of Gross Capital Formation	18415	33185	104522	114833	128187	137535	167266	183190	185778	203127	231761	256393
Gross Capital Formation												
Increase in stocks	1883	-1383	10460	4150	2943	13909	14960	9016	9521	15134	16152	
Gross fixed capital formation	16532	34568	94062	110689	121734	134592	153357	168230	176762	193606	216627	240241
1 General government	...	...	12278	16918	20335	23540	26198	31787	34500	37599	42082	
2 Corporate and quasi-corporate enterprises	...	30697	35286	41061	44334	50242	56300	63013	72829	83833		
3 Other	...	52684	62629	66699	74798	85198	91395	93183	98039	109971		
Gross Capital Formation	18415	33185	104522	114833	128187	137535	167266	183190	185778	203127	231761	256393

1.10 Gross Domestic Product by Kind of Activity, in Current Prices

Thousand Million Italian lire

	1970	1975	1980	1981	1982	1983	1984	1985	1986	1987	1988	1989
1 Agriculture, hunting, forestry and fishing	5242	10007	22305	24812	27944	33304	33915	35683	38691	40160	39432	41907
2 Mining and quarrying	18183	38425	107810	123878	141022	155351	176573	195761	210849	225864	253746	275703
3 Manufacturing												
4 Electricity, gas and water	3167	6246	15053	16163	21975	28957	33809	37097	44331	49544	53011	58455
5 Construction	6369	12784	28458	34617	37930	41367	45554	48640	51638	54268	58728	63413
6 Wholesale and retail trade, restaurants and hotels a	10537	23503	70274	85474	103696	121008	132930	157680	171709	180014	202898	219739
7 Transport, storage and communication	3715	6451	20026	24326	29055	33574	40104	45886	53308	58668	66579	74033
8 Finance, insurance, real estate and business services	11414	27171	74480	91686	107255	129469	154811	177713	205023	221389	248048	275035
9 Community, social and personal services												
Total, Industries	58627	124587	338406	400968	468877	543830	623996	699360	775549	837907	922492	1008290
Producers of Government Services	6514	14329	42791	56252	65436	76317	86698	96007	105652	118240	133017	147792
Other Producers	665	1209	2939	3346	4282	5175	5860	7102	7862	7872	8733	10095
Subtotal	65806	140125	384136	460569	538595	625322	716449	802469	889063	964019	1064240	1163170
Less: Imputed bank service charge	1799	6311	16471	21887	26510	30119	34373	39853	40215	45757	49144	
Plus: Import duties	3171	4818	20004	23555	28416	34829	40895	44655	48071	55054	64441	73960
Plus: Value added tax												
Equals: Gross Domestic Product b	67178	138632	387669	464030	545124	633441	727225	812751	897281	978858	1082930	1187990

a) Item "Wholesale and retail trade, restaurants and hotels" includes repair services.
b) The branch breakdown used in this table (GDP by kind of activity) is according to the classification NACE/CLIO.

1.11 Gross Domestic Product by Kind of Activity, in Constant Prices

Thousand Million Italian lire

	1970	1975	1980	1981	1982	1983	1984	1985	1986	1987	1988	1989
At constant prices of 1980												
1 Agriculture, hunting, forestry and fishing	20310	20847	22305	22433	21842	22663	22803	22904	23363	24126	23307	23923
2 Mining and quarrying	61713	74764	107810	105941	105161	100601	107747	114046	116656	121162	130213	134093
3 Manufacturing												
4 Electricity, gas and water	12175	12955	15053	14963	14636	13864	13900	14082	14676	15082	15402	15720
5 Construction	27128	26528	28253	28458	28264	27328	27658	25659	25487	25707	26091	27128

Italy

1.11 Gross Domestic Product by Kind of Activity, in Constant Prices (Continued)

Thousand Million Italian lire

	1970	1975	1980	1981	1982	1983	1984	1985	1986	1987	1988	1989
			At constant prices of 1980									
6 Wholesale and retail trade, restaurants and hotels a	46533	55552	70274	71877	71555	72376	75548	77022	78404	80416	82530	84568
7 Transport, storage and communication	12064	14400	20026	20380	21061	20937	21649	22455	23241	24305	25214	27798
8 Finance, insurance, real estate and business services	48615	58577	74480	77654	79103	80735	84450	89238	92884	96150	100532	105282
9 Community, social and personal services												
Total, Industries	230523	265348	338406	340512	340666	344386	354956	365234	374931	387332	404726	418512
Producers of Government services	32484	38343	42791	43647	44302	44745	45461	45929	46465	47138	47730	48102
Other Producers	2231	2634	2939	3082	3223	3423	3516	3725	3838	3641	3700	3717
Subtotal	265238	306325	384136	387241	388211	392554	403933	414888	425234	438111	456156	470331
Less: Imputed bank service charge	11526	15193	16471	16361	16367	16368	17534	18106	18957	19878	20688
Plus: Import duties	14082	16050	20004	20506	20891	20883	21628	22434	23334	24381	25689	26935
Plus: Value added tax												
Equals: Gross Domestic Product b	267794	307182	387669	391386	392660	397079	409043	419788	430462	443635	461967	476578

a) Item 'Wholesale and retail trade' includes repair services.
b) The branch breakdown used in this table (GDP by kind of activity) is according to the classification NACE/CLIO.

1.12 Relations Among National Accounting Aggregates

Thousand Million Italian lire

	1970	1975	1980	1981	1982	1983	1984	1985	1986	1987	1988	1989
Gross Domestic Product	67178	138682	387669	464030	545124	633441	727225	812751	897281	978858	1082930	1187990
Plus: Net factor income from the rest of the world	311	-419	790	-2186	-3652	-4196	-4736	-5378	-6907	-6722	-7504	-10573
Factor income from the rest of the world	999	1654	6452	8802	10255	9226	11709	13222	11687	11435	13064	17506
Less: Factor income to the rest of the world	688	2073	5662	10988	13907	13422	16445	18600	18594	18157	20568	28079
Equals: Gross National Product	67489	138213	388459	461844	541472	629245	722489	807373	890374	972136	1075420	1177420
Less: Consumption of fixed capital	7085	17850	45134	57202	69012	79381	90133	101126	108800	117723	138935
Equals: National income	60404	120363	343325	404642	472460	549846	632356	706247	781574	854413	947607	1038480
Plus: Net current transfers from the rest of the world a	156	279	1034	774	898	1718	2114	1210	-2502	-1884	-2642	-5245
Current transfers from the rest of the world	588	1406	5041	5658	7122	8725	10473	10846	10235	11655	13346	14190
Less: Current transfers to the rest of the world	432	1127	4007	5084	6224	7007	8359	9636	12737	13540	15988	19435
Equals: National Disposable Income	60560	120642	344359	405416	473358	551582	634470	707457	779072	852629	944965	1033240
Less: Final consumption	48701	105535	293616	358186	422834	491398	561999	632852	697804	769292	849163	932615
Equals: Net Saving	11859	15107	50743	47230	50524	60184	72471	74605	81268	83237	95802	100620
Less: Surplus of the nation on current transactions	529	-228	-8645	-10401	-8651	2030	-4662	-7459	4290	-2167	-8144	-16838
Equals: Net Capital Formation	11330	15335	59388	57631	59175	58154	77133	82064	76978	85404	103946	117458

a) Item 'Net current transfers from the rest of the world' excludes indirect taxes, net to EEC.

2.1 Government Final Consumption Expenditure by Function, in Current Prices

Thousand Million Italian lire

	1970	1975	1980	1981	1982	1983	1984	1985	1986	1987	1988	1989
1 General public services	8747	11110	12836	15297	17033	20279	22033	25304	28175	30302
2 Defence	6430	8002	9596	12421	14366	16748	17751	20121	22820	24450
3 Public order and safety	5208	6600	7725	9460	11278	12542	13890	15655	17715	18920
4 Education	16419	21826	25998	29888	33881	37505	41596	45872	51769	56112
5 Health	11522	15018	17336	20218	22657	24938	27132	31719	35573	39119
6 Social security and welfare	2518	3101	3820	4454	5111	5797	6435	6968	7470	8573
7 Housing and community amenities	1506	2266	2677	3322	3777	4244	4490	4896	5219	5625
8 Recreational, cultural and religious affairs	739	1065	1324	1534	1765	1905	2060	2332	2594	2841
9 Economic services	3747	4770	5723	6721	7871	8871	10018	10940	12373	13376

910

Italy

2.1 Government Final Consumption Expenditure by Function, in Current Prices
(Continued)

Thousand Million Italian lire

	1970	1975	1980	1981	1982	1983	1984	1985	1986	1987	1988	1989
A Fuel and energy	...	...	384	588	694	764	854	953	1020	1165	1289	1377
B Agriculture, forestry, fishing and hunting	...	...	753	891	1049	1392	1625	1798	2041	2171	2466	2832
C Mining, manufacturing and construction, except fuel and energy	...	...	251	299	399	515	706	759	895	951	1197	1000
D Transportation and communication	...	...	2022	2586	3040	3362	3855	4248	4735	5175	5695	6216
E Other economic affairs	...	...	337	406	541	688	831	1113	1327	1478	1726	1951
10 Other functions	...	...	177	398	351	153	295	436	555	281	551	331
Total Government Final Consumption Expenditure	...	...	57013	74156	87386	103568	118034	133265	145960	164188	184259	199649

2.2 Government Final Consumption Expenditure by Function, in Constant Prices

Thousand Million Italian lire

	1970	1975	1980	1981	1982	1983	1984	1985	1986	1987	1988	1989
						At constant prices of:1980						
1 General public services	...	...	13955	14222	14542	15056	15430	16071	16691	17539	17947	18215
2 Defence	...	...	6430	6579	6848	7126	7365	7698	7938	8346	8527	8531
3 Public order and safety	...	...	...	...	...	...	...	...	...	...	...	...
4 Education	...	...	16419	16908	17245	17533	17697	17983	18199	18640	19282	19421
5 Health	...	...	11522	11836	12151	12599	13010	13467	13847	14373	14674	14715
6 Social security and welfare	...	...	2518	2584	2713	2793	2854	2960	3036	3123	3181	3189
7 Housing and community amenities	...	...	1506	1538	1626	1729	1791	1900	1978	2079	2103	2106
8 Recreational, cultural and religious affairs	...	...	739	762	800	844	879	917	953	1009	1036	1043
9 Economic services	...	...	3747	3806	4057	4208	4332	4528	4728	4944	5156	5185
10 Other functions	...	...	177	332	255	97	170	233	292	141	263	147
Total Government Final Consumption Expenditure	...	...	57013	58567	60237	61985	63528	65757	67662	70194	72169	72552

2.3 Total Government Outlays by Function and Type

Thousand Million Italian lire

	Final Consumption Expenditures			Subsidies	Other Current Transfers & Property Income	Total Current Disbursements	Gross Capital Formation	Other Capital Outlays	Total Outlays
	Total	Compensation of Employees	Other						
					1980				
1 General public services	8747	6215	2532	-	3320	12067	963	139	13169
2 Defence	6430	3913	2517	-	-	6430	42	-	6472
3 Public order and safety	5208	4537	671	-	106	5314	82	-	5396
4 Education	16419	14685	1734	75	566	17060	1403	13	18476
5 Health	11522	8071	3451	-	8588	20110	788	724	21622
6 Social security and welfare	2518	1941	577	-	48404	50922	185	12	51119
7 Housing and community amenities	1506	920	586	-	477	1983	2557	864	5404
8 Recreation, culture and religion	739	480	259	29	486	1254	419	38	1711
9 Economic services	3747	1961	1786	10964	1961	16672	5410	2586	24668
A Fuel and energy	384	247	137	79	270	733	765	14	1512
B Agriculture, forestry, fishing and hunting	753	478	275	567	331	1651	976	688	3315
C Mining (except fuels), manufacturing and construction	251	121	130	1782	370	2403	755	643	3801
D Transportation and communication	2022	919	1103	7482	882	10386	2258	914	13558
E Other economic affairs	337	196	141	1054	108	1499	656	327	2482
10 Other functions	177	9	168	-	14011	14188	429	27	14644
Total	57013	42732	14281	11068	77919	146000	12278	4403	162681
					1981				
1 General public services	11110	8116	2994	-	3634	14744	1346	133	16223
2 Defence	8002	5037	2965	-	-	8002	47	-	8049
3 Public order and safety	6600	5848	752	-	122	6722	102	-	6824
4 Education	21826	19538	2288	81	648	22555	1906	19	24480
5 Health	15018	10616	4402	-	8970	23988	684	38	24710
6 Social security and welfare	3101	2320	781	-	65284	68385	84	9	68478
7 Housing and community amenities	2266	1330	936	-	695	2961	2972	1113	7046
8 Recreation, culture and religion	1065	698	367	31	541	1637	656	24	2317

Italy

2.3 Total Government Outlays by Function and Type (Continued)

Thousand Million Italian lire

	Final Consumption Expenditures Total	Compensation of Employees	Other	Subsidies	Other Current Transfers & Disbursements	Total Current Disbursements	Gross Capital Formation	Other Capital Outlays	Total Outlays
9 Economic services	4770	2485	2285	13186	1841	19797	6954	2978	29729
A Fuel and energy	588	379	209	168	255	1011	1156	8	2175
B Agriculture, forestry, fishing and hunting	891	564	327	723	287	1901	1050	865	3816
C Mining (except fuels), manufacturing and construction	299	152	147	1737	311	2347	923	856	4126
D Transportation and communication	2586	1153	1433	9611	826	13023	2947	910	16880
E Other economic affairs	406	237	169	947	162	1515	878	339	2732
10 Other functions	398	147	251	-	22458	22856	2167	1062	26085
Total	74156	56135	18021	13298	104193	191647	16918	5376	213941
1982									
1 General public services	12835	9131	3705	-	4266	17102	1639	169	18910
2 Defence	9596	6909	3527	-	-	9596	60	-	9656
3 Public order and safety	7725	6633	1092	-	139	7864	136	-	8000
4 Education	25998	23066	2899	78	589	26665	2070	34	28769
5 Health	17336	12234	5102	-	11717	29053	518	40	29611
6 Social security and welfare	3820	2768	1052	-	78380	82200	116	15	82331
7 Housing and community amenities	2677	1545	1132	-	709	3386	4321	1259	9006
8 Recreation, culture and religion	1324	838	486	111	556	1991	888	49	2928
9 Economic services	5723	2928	2795	16709	2323	24755	8746	5762	39193
A Fuel and energy	694	449	245	143	395	1232	1632	37	2901
B Agriculture, forestry, fishing and hunting	1049	653	396	876	402	2327	1240	1293	4860
C Mining (except fuels), manufacturing and construction	399	180	219	2555	496	3450	1002	1454	5906
D Transportation and communication	3040	1351	1689	12065	876	15981	3736	2546	22263
E Other economic affairs	541	295	246	1070	154	1765	1066	432	3263
10 Other functions	351	43	308	-	32147	32498	1911	143	34552
Total	87386	65288	22098	16898	130826	235110	20335	7571	263016
1983									
1 General public services	15297	10463	4834	-	4591	19888	1900	243	22031
2 Defence	12421	7348	5073	-	-	12421	70	-	12491
3 Public order and safety	9460	8111	1349	-	186	9646	209	-	9855
4 Education	29988	26529	3459	125	774	30887	2112	51	33050
5 Health	20218	14360	5858	-	14033	34251	725	38	35014
6 Social security and welfare	4454	3261	1193	-	97312	101766	123	10	101899
7 Housing and community amenities	3322	1599	1723	-	834	4156	5487	1139	10782
8 Recreation, culture and religion	1534	955	579	97	717	2348	989	45	3382
9 Economic services	6721	3551	3170	18159	2844	27724	10607	6532	44863
A Fuel and energy	764	466	298	136	452	1352	2343	30	3725
B Agriculture, forestry, fishing and hunting	1392	887	505	1174	509	3075	1673	1278	6026
C Mining (except fuels), manufacturing and construction	515	214	301	3141	596	4252	1035	2028	7315
D Transportation and communication	3362	1626	1736	12488	1093	16943	4398	2932	24273
E Other economic affairs	688	358	330	1220	194	2102	1158	264	3524
10 Other functions	153	51	102	-	40179	40332	1818	479	42629
Total	103568	76228	27340	18381	161470	283419	23540	8537	315496
1984									
1 General public services	17033	11890	5143	-	4879	21912	2265	262	24439
2 Defence	14366	8610	5756	-	-	14366	84	-	14450
3 Public order and safety	11278	9723	1555	-	211	11489	256	-	11745
4 Education	33881	29803	4078	141	911	34933	2013	231	37177
5 Health	22657	15733	6924	-	15078	37735	936	40	38711
6 Social security and welfare	5111	3747	1364	-	108431	113542	161	54	113757
7 Housing and community amenities	3777	2024	1753	-	1058	4835	5917	1234	11986
8 Recreation, culture and religion	1765	1094	671	174	831	2770	1048	72	3890

Italy

2.3 Total Government Outlays by Function and Type (Continued)

Thousand Million Italian lire

	Final Consumption Expenditures Compensation of Employees	Total	Other	Subsidies	Current Transfers & Other Disbursements	Total Current Disbursements	Property Income	Gross Capital Formation	Other Capital Outlays	Total Outlays
1985										
9 Economic services	7871	4008	3863	22131	2840	32842	11702	7382	51926	
A Fuel and energy	854	514	340	300	341	1495	2260	55	3810	
B Agriculture, forestry, fishing and hunting	1625	1030	595	1204	437	3266	1888	1541	6695	
C Mining (except fuels), manufacturing and construction	706	279	427	3267	503	4476	1162	1961	7599	
D Transportation and communication	3855	1791	2064	16120	1294	21269	4887	3417	29573	
E Other economic affairs	831	394	437	1240	265	2336	1505	408	4249	
10 Other functions	295	60	235	51093	51388	1816	796	54000		
Total	118034	86421	31613	224496	185332	325812	26198	10071	362081	
1985										
1 General public services	20279	13717	6562	8119	28398	2918	5339	36655		
2 Defence	16748	9654	7094	-	-	16748	68	-	16837	
3 Public order and safety	12542	10695	1847	245	12787	312	-	13099		
4 Education	37505	32718	4787	147	1149	38801	2170	191	41162	
5 Health	24938	17126	7812	-	17912	42850	1063	18	43931	
6 Social security and welfare	5797	4212	1585	-	123461	129258	223	71	129552	
7 Housing and community amenities	4244	1846	2398	-	1382	5626	8220	1368	15214	
8 Recreation, culture and religion	1905	1166	739	294	1065	3264	959	132	4355	
9 Economic services	8871	4430	4441	22437	3387	34695	11986	9599	56280	
A Fuel and energy	953	535	418	387	403	1743	1992	68	3803	
B Agriculture, forestry, fishing and hunting	1798	1177	621	1359	453	3610	1591	1957	7158	
C Mining (except fuels), manufacturing and construction	759	307	452	3783	569	5111	1143	3011	9265	
D Transportation and communication	4248	1952	2296	16055	1709	22012	5938	4074	32024	
E Other economic affairs	1113	459	654	853	253	2219	1322	489	4030	
10 Other functions	436	73	363	-	54197	54633	2354	951	57938	
Total	133265	96637	37628	22878	210917	367060	30294	17669	415023	
1986										
1 General public services	22033	15052	6981	-	10211	32244	2896	1046	36186	
2 Defence	17751	10361	7390	-	-	17751	97	-	17848	
3 Public order and safety	13890	11774	2116	291	14181	322	-	14503		
4 Education	41596	36606	4991	226	1470	43292	2193	234	45719	
5 Health	27132	18570	8562	-	18862	45994	1352	57	47403	
6 Social security and welfare	6435	4614	1821	-	138331	144766	416	87	145269	
7 Housing and community amenities	4490	1945	2545	-	1694	6184	6939	1241	14364	
8 Recreation, culture and religion	2060	1345	715	389	961	3410	1168	190	4768	
9 Economic services	10018	4846	5172	27078	3884	40980	13432	10248	64660	
A Fuel and energy	1020	590	430	327	381	1728	2018	153	3899	
B Agriculture, forestry, fishing and hunting	2041	1270	771	1553	474	4068	1647	2212	7927	
C Mining (except fuels), manufacturing and construction	895	330	565	4876	543	6314	1605	2542	10461	
D Transportation and communication	4735	2123	2612	18955	2062	25752	6737	4925	37414	
E Other economic affairs	1327	533	794	1367	424	3118	1425	416	4959	
10 Other functions	555	63	492	-	63443	63998	2972	1142	68112	
Total	145960	105175	40785	27693	239147	412800	31787	14245	458832	
1987										
1 General public services	25304	16865	8439	-	9927	35231	3137	550	38918	
2 Defence	20121	11384	8737	-	-	20121	113	-	20234	
3 Public order and safety	15655	13173	2482	-	300	15955	363	-	16318	
4 Education	45972	40244	5728	222	1580	47774	2463	285	50522	
5 Health	31719	21783	9936	-	22918	54637	1394	23	56054	
6 Social security and welfare	6968	5070	1898	-	149671	156639	506	95	157240	
7 Housing and community amenities	4896	2132	2764	-	1569	6465	7623	1198	15286	
8 Recreation, culture and religion	2332	1482	850	575	1385	4292	1273	190	5755	

913

Italy

2.3 Total Government Outlays by Function and Type
(Continued)

Thousand Million Italian lire

	Final Consumption Expenditures			Subsidies	Other Current Transfers & Property Income	Total Current Disbursements	Gross Capital Formation	Other Capital Outlays	Total Outlays
	Total	Compensation of Employees	Other						
9 Economic services	10940	5217	5723	25328	3577	39845	14379	11882	66106
A Fuel and energy	1165	668	497	330	353	1848	2009	319	4176
B Agriculture, forestry, fishing and hunting	2171	1326	845	2030	468	4669	1927	2901	9497
C Mining (except fuels), manufacturing and construction	951	345	606	4503	501	5955	1682	2729	10366
D Transportation and communication	5175	2298	2877	16640	1881	23696	7076	5493	36265
E Other economic affairs	1478	580	898	1825	374	3677	1685	440	5802
10 Other functions	281	92	189	-	66409	66690	3249	826	70765
Total	164188	117442	46746	26125	257336	447649	34500	15049	497198
1988									
1 General public services	28175	19210	8965	-	11644	39819	3285	557	43661
2 Defence	22820	12889	9931	-	-	22820	123	-	22943
3 Public order and safety	17715	14919	2796	-	298	18013	397	-	18410
4 Education	51769	45364	6405	202	1622	53593	2759	301	56653
5 Health	35573	24283	11290	-	26970	62543	1570	23	64136
6 Social security and welfare	7470	5347	2123	-	165156	172626	551	100	173277
7 Housing and community amenities	5219	2391	2828	-	1537	6756	7664	1335	15755
8 Recreation, culture and religion	2594	1621	973	594	1464	4652	1406	252	6310
9 Economic services	12373	5807	6566	26044	3236	41653	16332	12554	70539
A Fuel and energy	1289	751	538	358	324	1971	2331	256	4558
B Agriculture, forestry, fishing and hunting	2466	1489	977	2136	393	4995	2151	2910	10056
C Mining (except fuels), manufacturing and construction	1197	408	789	4652	436	6285	1836	2969	11090
D Transportation and communication	5695	2479	3216	17894	1722	25311	8097	5765	39173
E Other economic affairs	1726	680	1046	1004	361	3091	1917	654	5662
10 Other functions	551	119	432	-	76387	76938	3512	1345	81795
Total	184259	131950	52309	26840	288314	499413	37599	16467	553479
1989									
1 General public services	30302	20168	10134	-	15384	45686	3905	409	50000
2 Defence	24450	14492	9958	-	-	24450	130	-	24580
3 Public order and safety	18920	16001	2919	-	304	19224	429	1	19654
4 Education	56112	49188	6924	205	1660	57977	3157	323	61457
5 Health	39119	26438	12681	-	28796	67915	1824	25	69764
6 Social security and welfare	8573	6071	2502	-	184067	192640	606	103	193349
7 Housing and community amenities	5625	2529	3096	-	1624	7249	8453	1490	17192
8 Recreation, culture and religion	2841	1764	1077	696	1499	5036	1639	269	6944
9 Economic services	13376	6529	6847	28192	3429	44997	18154	12477	75628
A Fuel and energy	1377	798	579	422	332	2131	2538	595	5264
B Agriculture, forestry, fishing and hunting	2832	1779	1053	2597	423	5852	2376	2861	11089
C Mining (except fuels), manufacturing and construction	1000	440	560	5154	426	6580	1914	3326	11820
D Transportation and communication	6216	2724	3492	19175	1828	27219	9198	5029	41446
E Other economic affairs	1951	788	1163	844	420	3215	2128	666	6009
10 Other functions	331	171	160	-	94424	94755	3785	1233	99773
Total	199649	143351	56298	29093	331187	559929	42082	16330	618341

2.5 Private Final Consumption Expenditure by Type and Purpose, in Current Prices

Thousand Million Italian lire

	1970	1975	1980	1981	1982	1983	1984	1985	1986	1987	1988	1989
Final Consumption Expenditure of Resident Households												
1 Food, beverages and tobacco	15562	29328	67658	79105	93712	105850	116766	127531	135776	142678	149749	160023
A Food	13002	25004	59156	69016	81327	91335	100867	110065	116770	122794	128616	137385
B Non-alcoholic beverages	160	302	705	862	1027	1220	1363	1523	1813	2090	2383	2662
C Alcoholic beverages	1280	2186	3940	4464	5056	5826	6150	6624	7199	7545	7760	8132
D Tobacco	1120	1836	3857	4763	6302	7469	8386	9319	9994	10249	10990	11844

Italy

2.5 Private Final Consumption Expenditure by Type and Purpose, in Current Prices
(Continued)

Thousand Million Italian lire

	1970	1975	1980	1981	1982	1983	1984	1985	1986	1987	1988	1989
2 Clothing and footwear	3545	8393	26964	30787	35261	39004	43245	48747	52723	59738	64806	70641
3 Gross rent, fuel and power	4905	11446	31660	39881	47092	58626	71431	78589	83456	90039	97000	105255
A Fuel and power	1309	2676	8632	11225	13874	18361	20808	23732	22214	23332	24722	26886
B Other	3596	8770	23028	28656	33218	40265	50623	54857	61242	66707	72278	78369
4 Furniture, furnishings and household equipment and operation	2811	7232	22413	26363	30828	34819	38318	42868	48088	52438	58212	65270
5 Medical care and health expenses	1531	3820	10862	13253	17553	21017	23676	27900	31037	36343	41767	46500
6 Transport and communication	4092	8863	29478	36143	42063	47883	55216	63388	70027	77672	86071	94842
A Personal transport equipment	1069	2122	9321	11043	12755	13683	16012	19016	21515	25035	29003	32855
B Other	3023	6741	20157	25100	29308	34200	39204	44372	48512	52637	57068	61987
7 Recreational, entertainment, education and cultural services	3124	6620	19162	22648	26005	30260	36000	41433	47591	51299	58889	67087
A Education	209	386	1015	1292	1624	2044	2596	3374	4154	4802	5569	6293
B Other	2915	6234	18147	21356	24381	28216	33404	38059	43437	46497	53320	60794
8 Miscellaneous goods and services	4793	11373	33161	40957	49987	59339	68476	78889	90827	102028	113692	127268
A Personal care	1096	2006	5252	6565	8110	9360	11067	13076	15402	17955	20124	22440
B Expenditures in restaurants, cafes and hotels	2843	6906	19212	24191	30465	36140	41597	47707	54014	60329	66116	73337
C Other	854	2461	8697	10201	11412	13839	15812	18106	21411	23744	27452	31491
Total Final Consumption Expenditure in the Domestic Market by Households, of which	40363	87075	241358	289137	342501	396798	453128	509345	559525	612235	670186	736886
Plus: Direct purchases abroad by resident households	494	676	1901	2044	2458	2579	3363	4023	4694	6296	8261	9778
Less: Direct purchases in the domestic market by non-resident households	1039	2158	7698	8348	10933	13151	14505	16018	14771	15887	16228	16540
Equals: Final Consumption Expenditure of Resident Households	39818	85593	235561	282833	334026	386226	441986	497350	549448	602644	662219	730124

Final Consumption Expenditure of Private Non-profit Institutions Serving Households

	1970	1975	1980	1981	1982	1983	1984	1985	1986	1987	1988	1989
Equals: Final Consumption Expenditure of Private Non-profit Organisations Serving Households	174	379	1042	1197	1422	1604	1979	2237	2396	2460	2685	2842
Private Final Consumption Expenditure	39992	85972	236603	284030	335448	387830	443965	499587	551844	605104	664904	732966

2.6 Private Final Consumption Expenditure by Type and Purpose, in Constant Prices

Thousand Million Italian lire

At constant prices of: 1980

Final Consumption Expenditure of Resident Households

	1970	1975	1980	1981	1982	1983	1984	1985	1986	1987	1988	1989
1 Food, beverages and tobacco	56197	60822	67658	67646	68994	69967	70688	71126	71784	72449	73224	73752
A Food	49620	53207	59156	59120	60437	61288	61980	62294	62772	63649	64421	64882
B Non-alcoholic beverages	533	573	705	736	756	786	793	823	927	1032	1129	1215
C Alcoholic beverages	3830	3862	3940	3876	3855	3903	3794	3794	3791	3752	3680	3617
D Tobacco	2214	3180	3857	3914	3946	3990	4121	4215	4294	4016	3994	4038
2 Clothing and footwear	14199	18929	26964	26177	26052	25113	24891	25363	25461	27165	27886	28633
3 Gross rent, fuel and power	20067	25403	31660	33368	33341	34551	35301	36306	37126	38220	39273	40170
A Fuel and power	5626	6446	8632	8877	8992	9744	9859	10300	10457	10796	10961	11235
B Other	14441	18957	23028	24491	24349	24807	25442	26006	26669	27424	28312	28935
4 Furniture, furnishings and household equipment and operation	11539	15182	22413	22033	22047	22070	22057	22570	23843	24788	26116	27419
5 Medical care and health expenses	4624	7133	10862	11041	12052	12699	12838	13400	14419	15818	16455	17457
6 Transport and communication	18769	21716	29478	30753	30337	29370	30391	32366	34174	36382	38938	41072
A Personal transport equipment	5612	5263	9321	9842	9757	9174	9745	10869	11764	13041	14521	15726
B Other	13157	16453	20157	20911	20580	20196	20646	21497	22410	23341	24417	25346
7 Recreational, entertainment, education and cultural services	10441	12516	19162	19596	19628	19506	20878	21927	23372	24244	26075	28145
A Education	763	870	1015	1055	1062	1148	1295	1501	1695	1806	1938	2035
B Other	9678	11646	18147	18541	18566	18358	19583	20426	21677	22438	24137	26110
8 Miscellaneous goods and services	21742	26450	33161	34208	35627	36268	37774	39736	42696	45297	47982	50413

Italy

2.6 Private Final Consumption Expenditure by Type and Purpose, in Constant Prices
(Continued)

Thousand Million Italian lire

	1970	1975	1980	1981	1982	1983	1984	1985	1986	1987	1988	1989
				At constant prices of:1980								
A Personal care	4483	4545	5252	5311	5515	5496	5785	6202	6712	7280	7656	8023
B Expenditures in restaurants, cafes and hotels	12654	15879	19212	19790	20894	21269	21821	22433	23224	24432	24971	25670
C Other	4605	6026	8697	9107	9218	9503	10168	11101	12760	13585	15355	16720
Total Final Consumption Expenditure in the Domestic Market by Households, of which	157578	188151	241358	244822	248078	249544	254818	262794	272875	284363	295949	307061
Plus: Direct purchases abroad by resident households	1954	1475	1901	1605	1645	1639	1877	2033	2531	3391	4235	5056
Less: Direct purchases in the domestic market by non-resident households	3789	4599	7698	7087	7969	8361	8322	8417	7331	7529	7320	7020
Equals: Final Consumption Expenditure of Resident Households	155743	185027	235561	239340	241754	242822	248373	256410	268075	280225	292864	305097
Final Consumption Expenditure of Private Non-profit Institutions Serving Households												
Equals: Final Consumption Expenditure of Private Non-profit Organisations Serving Households	747	954	1042	1033	1082	1108	1155	1192	1227	1254	1275	1280
Private Final Consumption Expenditure	156490	185981	236603	240373	242836	243930	249528	257602	269302	281479	294139	306377

2.11 Gross Fixed Capital Formation by Kind of Activity of Owner, ISIC Divisions, in Current Prices

Thousand Million Italian lire

	1970	1975	1980	1981	1982	1983	1984	1985	1986	1987	1988	1989
				All Producers								
1 Agriculture, hunting, forestry and fishing	846	1870	4747 8466	9641	10853	12605	13638	13902	14230	...	...	...
2 Mining and quarrying	2708	5439	12839	...	...	...	...	...	...	...	...	...
3 Manufacturing			...	...	...	...	...	...	...	...	...	...
A Manufacturing of food, beverages and tobacco	225	417	1316 ...	...	...	...	...	...	...	...	...	...
B Textile, wearing apparel and leather industries	199	421	1154 ...	...	...	...	...	...	...	...	...	...
C Manufacture of wood, and wood products, including furniture	67	128	461 ...	...	...	...	...	...	...	...	...	...
D Manufacture of paper and paper products, printing and publishing	117	220	677 ...	...	...	...	...	...	...	...	...	...
E Manufacture of chemicals and chemical petroleum, coal, rubber and plastic products	704	1371	1804 ...	...	...	...	...	...	...	...	...	...
F Manufacture of non-metalic mineral products except products of petroleum and coal	266	434	1361 ...	...	...	...	...	...	...	...	...	...
G Basic metal industries	363	923	1464 ...	...	...	...	...	...	...	...	...	...
H Manufacture of fabricated metal products, machinery and equipment	767	1525	4603 ...	...	...	...	...	...	...	...	...	...
I Other manufacturing industries	...	...	...	...	...	...	...	...	...	...	...	...
4 Electricity, gas and water	1064	1963	5772 ...	...	...	...	...	...	...	...	...	...
5 Construction	160	278	810 ...	...	...	...	...	...	...	...	...	...
6 Wholesale and retail trade, restaurants and hotels a	879	1825	5135 ...	...	...	...	...	...	...	...	...	...
A Wholesale and retail trade	738	1453	4155	...	...	...	...	...	...	...	...	...
B Restaurants and hotels	141	372	979 ...	...	...	...	...	...	...	...	...	...
7 Transport, storage and communication	1151	2842	7776 9302	11390	12075	13160	15848	17925	18570	...	...	...
A Transport and storage	838	1754	5218 ...	...	...	...	...	...	...	...	...	...

Italy

2.11 Gross Fixed Capital Formation by Kind of Activity of Owner, ISIC Divisions, in Current Prices
(Continued)

Thousand Million Italian lire

	1970	1975	1980	1981	1982	1983	1984	1985	1986	1987	1988	1989
B Communication	312	1089	2558 ...	...	...	...	...	...	...	...	...	...
8 Finance, insurance, real estate and business services	5191	9041	23922 ...	...	...	...	...	...	...	...	...	...
9 Community, social and personal services				...	...	...	...	...	...	...	...	...
Total Industries	11999	23258	61001 87565	103189	113117	125597	142645	157294	166197	...	...	...
Producers of Government Services	1435	2518	6015 7215	8379	8613	8737	10234	13135	13707	...	...	...
Private Non-Profit Institutions Serving Households	...	...	...	...	...	...	...	...	...	...	...	...
Total b	13434	25776	67016 94780	111568	121730	134334	152879	170429	179904	...	...	...

a) Item 'Wholesale and retail trade, restaurants and hotels' includes repair services.
b) Data for this table have not been revised, therefore, data for some years are not comparable
with those of other tables.

2.12 Gross Fixed Capital Formation by Kind of Activity of Owner, ISIC Divisions, in Constant Prices

Thousand Million Italian lire

	1970	1975	1980	1981	1982	1983	1984	1985	1986	1987	1988	1989
					At constant prices of:							
			1970					**1980**				
					All Producers							
1 Agriculture, hunting, forestry and fishing	846	951	1076 8466	8012	7820	8123	8023	7494	7345	...	...	...
2 Mining and quarrying	2708	2469	2859 ...	...	...	...	...	...	...	...	...	...
3 Manufacturing				...	...	...	...	...	...	...	...	...
A Manufacturing of food, beverages and tobacco	225	198	293 ...	...	...	...	...	...	...	...	...	...
B Textile, wearing apparel and leather industries	199	192	255 ...	...	...	...	...	...	...	...	...	...
C Manufacture of wood, and wood products, including furniture	67	59	101 ...	...	...	...	...	...	...	...	...	...
D Manufacture of paper and paper products, printing and publishing	117	100	149 ...	...	...	...	...	...	...	...	...	...
E Manufacture of chemicals and chemical petroleum, coal, rubber and plastic products	704	619	424 ...	...	...	...	...	...	...	...	...	...
F Manufacture of non-metalic mineral products except products of petroleum and coal	266	199	300 ...	...	...	...	...	...	...	...	...	...
G Basic metal industries	363	413	331 ...	...	...	...	...	...	...	...	...	...
H Manufacture of fabricated metal products, machinery and equipment	767	688	1006 ...	...	...	...	...	...	...	...	...	...
I Other manufacturing industries	...	...	... ...	...	...	...	...	...	...	...	...	...
4 Electricity, gas and water	1064	951	1259 ...	...	...	...	...	...	...	...	...	...
5 Construction	160	130	181 ...	...	...	...	...	...	...	...	...	...
6 Wholesale and retail trade, restaurants and hotels a	879	921	1229 ...	...	...	...	...	...	...	...	...	...
A Wholesale and retail trade	738	732	988 ...	...	...	...	...	...	...	...	...	...
B Restaurants and hotels	141	190	241 ...	...	...	...	...	...	...	...	...	...
7 Transport, storage and communication	1151	1528	1894 9302	9707	8958	5708	9636	10022	9942	...	...	...
A Transport and storage	838	881	1165 ...	...	...	...	...	...	...	...	...	...

Italy

2.12 Gross Fixed Capital Formation by Kind of Activity of Owner, ISIC Divisions, in Constant Prices
(Continued)

Thousand Million Italian lire

	1970	1975	1980	1981	1982	1983	1984	1985	1986	1987	1988	1989
						At constant prices of:						
		1970						**1980**				
B Communication	312	647	729									
			...	...	...	...	...	...	...	...	...	...
8 Finance, insurance, real estate and business services	5191	4463	5187									
			...									
9 Community, social and personal services				...	...	...	...	...	...	...	...	...
Total Industries	11999	11413	13685									
			87565	85799	81253	80473	83755	85809	86885	...	...	...
Producers of Government Services	1435	1332	1348									
			7215	6802	6032	5454	5954	6858	6911	...	...	...
Private Non-Profit Institutions Serving Households	...	...	...									
Total b	13434	12745	15033						...	...	...	...
			94780	92601	87285	85927	89709	92667	93796			

a) Item 'Wholesale and retail trade, restaurants and hotels' includes repair services.
b) Data for this table have not been revised, therefore, data for some years are not comparable with those of other tables.

2.17 Exports and Imports of Goods and Services, Detail

Thousand Million Italian lire

	1970	1975	1980	1981	1982	1983	1984	1985	1986	1987	1988	1989
					Exports of Goods and Services							
1 Exports of merchandise, f.o.b.	8258	22915	66987	87875	99732	110747	131026	146059	144675	150697	166639	193266
2 Transport and communication	...	...	...	...	...	...	...	...	...	...	...	...
3 Insurance service charges	...	...	...	...	...	...	...	...	...	...	...	...
4 Other commodities	...	...	...	...	...	...	...	...	...	...	...	...
5 Adjustments of merchandise exports to change-of-ownership basis	...	...	...	...	...	...	...	...	...	...	...	...
6 Direct purchases in the domestic market by non-residential households	1039	2158	7698	8348	10933	13151	14505	16018	14771	15887	16228	16540
7 Direct purchases in the domestic market by extraterritorial bodies	...	...	...	...	...	...	...	...	...	...	...	...
Total Exports of Goods and Services	11041	28467	84953	108344	125125	140016	165197	185022	181961	191841	210046	244176
					Imports of Goods and Services							
1 Imports of merchandise, c.i.f.	9573	25574	87170	107794	119148	122469	150887	168791	149542	162936	181449	211414
2 Adjustments of merchandise imports to change-of-ownership basis	...	...	...	...	...	...	...	...	...	...	...	...
3 Other transport and communication	...	...	...	...	...	...	...	...	...	...	...	...
4 Other insurance service charges	...	...	...	...	...	...	...	...	...	...	...	...
5 Other commodities	...	...	...	...	...	...	...	...	...	...	...	...
6 Direct purchases abroad by government	...	...	...	...	...	...	...	...	...	...	...	...
7 Direct purchases abroad by resident households	494	676	1901	2044	2458	2579	3363	4023	4694	6296	8261	9778
Total Imports of Goods and Services	10979	28555	95422	117333	131022	135508	167237	188313	168262	185402	208044	245196
Balance of Goods and Services	62	-88	-10469	-8989	-5897	4508	-2040	-3291	13699	6439	2002	-1020
Total Imports and Balance of Goods and Services	11041	28467	84953	108344	125125	140016	165197	185022	181961	191841	210046	244176

3.11 General Government Production Account: Total and Subsectors

Thousand Million Italian lire

	1980					1981				
	Total General Government	Central Government	State or Provincial Government	Local Government	Social Security Funds	Total General Government	Central Government	State or Provincial Government	Local Government	Social Security Funds
					Gross Output					
1 Sales	2526	1114	...	1230	182	2914	1212	...	1450	252
2 Services produced for own use	57013	30785	...	23833	2395	74156	39410	...	32871	1875
3 Own account fixed capital formation	...	...	...	...	...	...	...	...	...	...
Gross Output	59539	31899	...	25063	2577	77070	40622	...	34321	2127

Italy

3.11 General Government Production Account: Total and Subsectors
(Continued)

Thousand Million Italian lire

	1980					1981				
	Total General Government	Central Government	State or Provincial Government	Local Government	Social Security Funds	Total General Government	Central Government	State or Provincial Government	Local Government	Social Security Funds
Gross Input										
Intermediate Consumption	15133	6072	...	8373	688	18875	6717	...	11509	649
Subtotal: Value Added	44406	25827	...	16690	1889	58195	33905	...	22812	1478
1 Indirect taxes, net	411	411	...	-	-	446	446	...	-	-
A Indirect taxes	411	411	...	-	-	446	446	...	-	-
B Less: Subsidies	-	-	...	-	-	-	-	...	-	-
2 Consumption of fixed capital	862	433	...	391	38	1051	508	...	497	46
3 Compensation of employees	42732	24831	...	16143	1758	56135	32725	...	22137	1273
4 Net Operating surplus	401	152	...	156	93	563	226	...	178	159
Gross Input	59539	31899	...	25063	2577	77070	40622	...	34321	2127

	1982					1983				
	Total General Government	Central Government	State or Provincial Government	Local Government	Social Security Funds	Total General Government	Central Government	State or Provincial Government	Local Government	Social Security Funds
Gross Output										
1 Sales	3863	1705	...	1832	326	4771	2006	...	2400	365
2 Services produced for own use	87386	46459	...	38617	2310	103568	56030	...	44972	2566
3 Own account fixed capital formation	...	...	...	...	...	...	...	...	...	...
Gross Output	91249	48164	...	40449	2636	108339	58036	...	47372	2931
Gross Input										
Intermediate Consumption	23182	8611	...	13697	874	28817	11343	...	16489	985
Subtotal: Value Added	68067	39553	...	26752	1762	79522	46693	...	30883	1946
1 Indirect taxes, net	781	781	...	-	-	857	857	...	-	-
A Indirect taxes	781	781	...	-	-	857	857	...	-	-
B Less: Subsidies	-	-	...	-	-	-	-	...	-	-
2 Consumption of fixed capital	1251	605	...	593	53	1437	694	...	683	60
3 Compensation of employees	65288	37885	...	25922	1481	76228	44700	...	29902	1626
4 Net Operating surplus	747	282	...	237	228	1000	442	...	298	260
Gross Input	91249	48164	...	40449	2636	108339	58036	...	47372	2931

	1984					1985				
	Total General Government	Central Government	State or Provincial Government	Local Government	Social Security Funds	Total General Government	Central Government	State or Provincial Government	Local Government	Social Security Funds
Gross Output										
1 Sales	5658	2373	...	2857	428	6329	2665	...	3091	573
2 Services produced for own use	118034	64371	...	50556	3107	133265	72450	...	57243	3572
3 Own account fixed capital formation	...	...	...	...	...	...	...	...	...	...
Gross Output	123692	66744	...	53413	3535	139594	75115	...	60334	4145
Gross Input										
Intermediate Consumption	33430	12997	...	19269	1164	39520	15780	...	22305	1435
Subtotal: Value Added	90262	53747	...	34144	2371	100074	59335	...	38029	2710
1 Indirect taxes, net	992	992	...	-	-	1129	1129	...	-	-
A Indirect taxes	992	992	...	-	-	1129	1129	...	-	-
B Less: Subsidies	-	-	...	-	-	-	-	...	-	-
2 Consumption of fixed capital	1681	808	...	804	69	1988	980	...	936	72
3 Compensation of employees	86421	51443	...	32983	1995	95637	56737	...	36673	2227
4 Net Operating surplus	1168	504	...	357	307	1320	489	...	420	411
Gross Input	123692	66744	...	53413	3535	139594	75115	...	60334	4145

	1986					1987				
	Total General Government	Central Government	State or Provincial Government	Local Government	Social Security Funds	Total General Government	Central Government	State or Provincial Government	Local Government	Social Security Funds
Gross Output										
1 Sales	7117	2858	...	3545	714	7893	3447	...	3637	809
2 Services produced for own use	145960	79930	...	62135	3895	164188	89346	...	70664	4178
3 Own account fixed capital formation	...	...	...	...	...	...	...	...	...	...
Gross Output	153077	82788	...	65680	4609	172081	92793	...	74301	4987
Gross Input										
Intermediate Consumption	42875	17203	...	24141	1531	48807	20090	...	27166	1551

Italy

3.11 General Government Production Account: Total and Subsectors
(Continued)

Thousand Million Italian lire

	1986					1987				
	Total General Government	Central Government	State or Provincial Government	Local Government	Social Security Funds	Total General Government	Central Government	State or Provincial Government	Local Government	Social Security Funds
Subtotal: Value Added	110202	65585	...	41539	3078	123274	72703	...	47135	3436
1 Indirect taxes, net	1108	1108	...	-	-	1313	1313	...	-	-
A Indirect taxes	1108	1108	...	-	-	1313	1313	...	-	-
B Less: Subsidies	-	-	...	-	-	-		...	-	-
2 Consumption of fixed capital	2334	1154	...	1095	85	2735	1352	...	1283	100
3 Compensation of employees	105175	62796	...	39940	2439	117442	69406	...	45330	2706
4 Net Operating surplus	1585	527	...	504	554	1784	632	...	522	630
Gross Input	153077	82788	...	65680	4609	172081	92793	...	74301	4987

	1988					1989				
	Total General Government	Central Government	State or Provincial Government	Local Government	Social Security Funds	Total General Government	Central Government	State or Provincial Government	Local Government	Social Security Funds
Gross Output										
1 Sales	9410	4268	...	4181	961	11436	5386	...	4917	1133
2 Services produced for own use	184259	101264	...	78549	4446	199649	108440	...	85821	5388
3 Own account fixed capital formation	...	...	...	...	...	...	...	...	...	...
Gross Output	193669	105532	...	82730	5407	211085	113826	...	90738	6521
Gross Input										
Intermediate Consumption	54505	22547	...	30225	1733	58705	23059	...	33541	2105
Subtotal: Value Added	139164	82985	...	52505	3674	152380	90767	...	57197	4416
1 Indirect taxes, net	1716	1716	...	-	-	2546	2546	...	-	-
A Indirect taxes	1716	1716	...	-	-	2546	2546	...	-	-
B Less: Subsidies	-	-	...	-	-	-	-	...	-	-
2 Consumption of fixed capital	3223	1593	...	1512	118	3799	1879	...	1781	139
3 Compensation of employees	131950	78778	...	50377	2795	143351	85299	...	54676	3376
4 Net Operating surplus	2275	898	...	616	761	2684	1043	...	740	901
Gross Input	193669	105532	...	82730	5407	211085	113826	...	90738	6521

3.12 General Government Income and Outlay Account: Total and Subsectors

Thousand Million Italian lire

	1980					1981				
	Total General Government	Central Government	State or Provincial Government	Local Government	Social Security Funds	Total General Government	Central Government	State or Provincial Government	Local Government	Social Security Funds
Receipts										
1 Operating surplus	401	152	...	156	93	563	226	...	178	159
2 Property and entrepreneurial income	2761	1730	...	1314	1010	3749	1681	...	1941	1255
A Withdrawals from public quasi-corporations	...	...	...	...	...	...	...	...	...	...
B Interest	2384	1614	...	1054	1009	3249	1512	...	1610	1255
C Dividends a	...	...	...	...	...	...	...	...	...	...
D Net land rent and royalties a	377	116	...	260	1	500	169	...	331	-
3 Taxes, fees and contributions	115301	68729	...	2940	43776	142343	86227	...	4057	52211
A Indirect taxes	33522	32367	...	1155	-	38297	36979	...	1318	-
B Direct taxes	37291	35672	...	1763	...	50916	48356	...	2712	...
Income	37291	35672	...	1763	...	50916	48356	...	2712	...
Other	-	-	...	-	...	-	-	...	-	...
C Social security contributions	44488	690	...	22	43776	53130	892	...	27	52211
D Fees, fines and penalties	-	-	...	-	-	-	-	...	-	...
4 Other current transfers	9340	19659	...	36312	16353	11684	22051	...	43056	15706
A Casualty insurance claims a	...	...	...	...	...	...	...	...	...	...
B Transfers from other government subsectors	...	13586	...	33649	15749	...	14502	...	39819	14808
C Transfers from the rest of the world	143	69	...	74	...	157	85	...	72	...
D Other transfers, except imputed	4192	1540	...	2193	459	5164	1744	...	2626	794
E Imputed unfunded employee pension and welfare contributions	5005	4464	...	396	145	6363	5720	...	539	104
Total Current Receipts	127803	90270	...	40722	61232	158339	110185	...	49232	69331

Italy

3.12 General Government Income and Outlay Account: Total and Subsectors
(Continued)

Thousand Million Italian lire

	1980					1981				
	Total General Government	Central Government	State or Provincial Government	Local Government	Social Security Funds	Total General Government	Central Government	State or Provincial Government	Local Government	Social Security Funds
Disbursements										
1 Government final consumption expenditure	57013	30785	...	23833	2395	74156	39410	...	32871	1875
2 Property income	20565	18430	...	2379	1049	28700	26563	...	2966	299
A Interest	20479	18410	...	2314	1048	28583	26540	...	2874	297
B Net land rent and royalties	86	20	...	65	1	117	23	...	92	2
3 Subsidies	11068	8128	...	2940	...	13298	9998	...	3300	...
4 Other current transfers	57354	52066	...	9654	58762	75493	64633	...	11420	68721
A Casualty insurance premiums, net	...	...	...	...	...	...	...	...	...	...
B Transfers to other government subsectors	...	44391	...	5486	13251	...	54627	...	572	14082
C Social security benefits			...					...		
D Social assistance grants	54696	6877	...	2471	45348	72805	8871	...	9414	54520
E Unfunded employee pension and welfare benefits			...					...		
F Transfers to private non-profit institutions serving households	706	170	...	428	108	578	254	...	218	106
G Other transfers n.e.c.	1585	261	...	1269	55	1538	309	...	1216	13
H Transfers to the rest of the world	367	367	...	-	-	572	572	...	-	-
Net saving	-18197	-19139	...	1916	-974	-33308	-30419	...	-1325	-1564
Total Current Disbursements and Net Saving	127803	90270	...	40722	61232	158339	110185	...	49232	69331

	1982					1983				
	Total General Government	Central Government	State or Provincial Government	Local Government	Social Security Funds	Total General Government	Central Government	State or Provincial Government	Local Government	Social Security Funds
Receipts										
1 Operating surplus	747	282	...	237	228	1000	442	...	298	260
2 Property and entrepreneurial income	3723	2457	...	1821	1552	4117	3246	...	1770	1714
A Withdrawals from public quasi-corporations	...	...	...	...	...	...	...	...	...	...
B Interest	3030	2148	...	1440	1549	3229	2830	...	1298	1714
C Dividends [a]	...	...	...	...	...	...	...	...	...	...
D Net land rent and royalties [a]	693	309	...	381	3	888	416	...	472	-
3 Taxes, fees and contributions	178400	107819	...	4906	65865	215515	129990	...	8185	77599
A Indirect taxes	46649	44801	...	1848	-	57987	55007	...	2980	-
B Direct taxes	64534	61699	...	3025	...	78402	73496	...	5165	...
Income	64534	61699	...	3025	...	78402	73496	...	5165	...
Other	-	-	...	-	...	-	-	...	-	...
C Social security contributions	67217	1319	...	33	65865	79126	1487	...	40	77599
D Fees, fines and penalties	-	-	...	-	-	-	-	...	-	...
4 Other current transfers	12600	40502	...	52373	35923	18276	38332	...	69403	36023
A Casualty insurance claims [a]	...		...					...		
B Transfers from other government subsectors	...	32270	...	48587	35341	...	27441	...	63524	34517
C Transfers from the rest of the world	205	50	...	155	...	227	46	...	181	...
D Other transfers, except imputed	5004	1518	...	3043	443	8337	2030	...	5015	1292
E Imputed unfunded employee pension and welfare contributions	7391	6664	...	588	139	9712	8815	...	683	214
Total Current Receipts	195470	151060	...	59337	103568	238908	172010	...	79656	115596
Disbursements										
1 Government final consumption expenditure	87386	46459	...	38617	2310	103568	56030	...	44972	2566
2 Property income	38996	37376	...	3212	515	47491	45294	...	4066	744
A Interest	38857	37351	...	3101	512	47320	45260	...	3932	741
B Net land rent and royalties	139	25	...	111	3	171	34	...	134	3
3 Subsidies	16898	12603	...	4295	...	18381	13116	...	5115	...

921

Italy

3.12 General Government Income and Outlay Account: Total and Subsectors
(Continued)

Thousand Million Italian lire

	1982					1983				
	Total General Government	Central Government	State or Provincial Government	Local Government	Social Security Funds	Total General Government	Central Government	State or Provincial Government	Local Government	Social Security Funds
4 Other current transfers	91830	96180	...	14201	97837	113979	114399	...	17209	108112
A Casualty insurance premiums, net	...	...	...	...	...	...	...	...	...	...
B Transfers to other government subsectors	...	83920	...	784	31684	...	98022	...	975	26744
C Social security benefits			...					...		
D Social assistance grants	88609	10707	...	11971	65931	109355	14156	...	14070	81129
E Unfunded employee pension and welfare benefits			...					...		
F Transfers to private non-profit institutions serving households	663	315	...	204	144	1488	912	...	417	159
G Other transfers n.e.c.	1702	382	...	1242	78	2185	358	...	1747	80
H Transfers to the rest of the world	856	856	...	-	-	951	951	...	-	-
Net saving	-39640	-41558	...	-988	2906	-44511	-56829	...	8294	4174
Total Current Disbursements and Net Saving	195470	151060	...	59337	103568	238908	172010	...	79656	115596

	1984					1985				
	Total General Government	Central Government	State or Provincial Government	Local Government	Social Security Funds	Total General Government	Central Government	State or Provincial Government	Local Government	Social Security Funds
Receipts										
1 Operating surplus	1168	504	...	357	307	1320	489	...	420	411
2 Property and entrepreneurial income	4762	3458	...	2031	1989	6305	4749	...	2231	2568
A Withdrawals from public quasi-corporations	...	...	...	...	...	...	...	...	...	...
B Interest	3765	3036	...	1460	1985	5192	4203	...	1668	2564
C Dividends [a]	...	...	...	...	...	...	...	...	...	...
D Net land rent and royalties [a]	997	422	...	571	4	1113	546	...	563	4
3 Taxes, fees and contributions	245654	152011	...	8934	84987	275241	170761	...	9969	94882
A Indirect taxes	67283	63813	...	3470	-	72661	68951	...	3710	-
B Direct taxes	91416	86278	...	5416	...	105466	99630	...	6207	...
Income	91416	86278	...	5416	...	105466	99630	...	6207	...
Other	-	-	...	-	...	-	-	...	-	...
C Social security contributions	86955	1920	...	48	84987	97114	2180	...	52	94882
D Fees, fines and penalties	-	-	...	-	-	-	-	...	-	-
4 Other current transfers	20696	46583	...	75055	39945	25941	54526	...	83805	48655
A Casualty insurance claims [a]	...	...	...	...	...	...	...	...	...	...
B Transfers from other government subsectors	...	33894	...	68279	38714	...	38533	...	76486	46026
C Transfers from the rest of the world	297	74	...	223	...	431	103	...	328	...
D Other transfers, except imputed	8832	2126	...	5746	960	12394	4013	...	6124	2257
E Imputed unfunded employee pension and welfare contributions	11567	10489	...	807	271	13116	11877	...	867	372
Total Current Receipts	272280	202556	...	86377	127228	308807	230525	...	96425	146516
Disbursements										
1 Government final consumption expenditure	118034	64371	...	50556	3107	133265	72450	...	57243	3572
2 Property income	58296	55121	...	5366	525	65300	61275	...	6379	889
A Interest	58113	55084	...	5222	523	65069	61231	...	6195	886
B Net land rent and royalties	183	37	...	144	2	231	44	...	184	3
3 Subsidies	22446	16631	...	5563	...	22878	16656	...	6222	...

Italy

3.12 General Government Income and Outlay Account: Total and Subsectors
(Continued)

Thousand Million Italian lire

	1984					1985				
	Total General Government	Central Government	State or Provincial Government	Local Government	Social Security Funds	Total General Government	Central Government	State or Provincial Government	Local Government	Social Security Funds
4 Other current transfers	127036	127248	...	18376	122577	145617	146333	...	22391	138309
A Casualty insurance premiums, net	...	...	...	...	...	...	...	...	...	...
B Transfers to other government subsectors	...	106963	...	717	33485	...	122492	...	1313	37611
C Social security benefits			...					...		
D Social assistance grants	121556	17200	...	15534	88822	139055	20667	...	18003	100385
E Unfunded employee pension and welfare benefits			...					...		
F Transfers to private non-profit institutions serving households	2097	1409	...	496	192	1729	888	...	658	183
G Other transfers n.e.c.	2160	453	...	1629	78	3098	551	...	2417	130
H Transfers to the rest of the world	1223	1223	...	-	-	1735	1735	...	-	-
Net saving	-53532	-60815	...	6516	1019	-58253	-66189	...	4190	3746
Total Current Disbursements and Net Saving	272280	202556	...	86377	127228	308807	230525	...	96425	146516

	1986					1987				
	Total General Government	Central Government	State or Provincial Government	Local Government	Social Security Funds	Total General Government	Central Government	State or Provincial Government	Local Government	Social Security Funds
Receipts										
1 Operating surplus	1585	527	...	504	554	1784	632	...	522	630
2 Property and entrepreneurial income	7626	5248	...	2858	2681	7164	5428	...	2606	2710
A Withdrawals from public quasi-corporations	...	...	...	...	...	...	...	...	...	...
B Interest	6351	4631	...	2200	2681	5979	4811	...	2038	2710
C Dividends [a]	...	...	...	...	...	...	...	...	...	...
D Net land rent and royalties [a]	1275	617	...	658	-	1185	617	...	568	-
3 Taxes, fees and contributions	308804	188998	...	11639	108684	344901	214732	...	12802	117939
A Indirect taxes	81743	77224	...	4519	-	93302	88058	...	5244	-
B Direct taxes	115683	109136	...	7064	...	130610	123693	...	7489	...
Income	115683	109136	...	7064	...	130610	123693	...	7489	...
Other	-	-	...	-	...	-	...	...	...	...
C Social security contributions	111378	2638	...	56	108684	120989	2981	...	69	117939
D Fees, fines and penalties	-	-	...	-	-	-	...	...	...	...
4 Other current transfers	31494	63076	...	91007	47667	29689	61199	...	102196	49418
A Casualty insurance claims [a]	...	...	...	...	...	...	...	...	...	...
B Transfers from other government subsectors	...	41666	...	83132	45458	...	42496	...	93507	47121
C Transfers from the rest of the world	220	72	...	148	...	305	111	...	194	...
D Other transfers, except imputed	17154	8470	...	6918	1766	14626	5202	...	7563	1861
E Imputed unfunded employee pension and welfare contributions	14120	12868	...	809	443	14758	13390	...	932	436
Total Current Receipts	349509	257849	...	106008	159586	383538	281991	...	118126	170697
Disbursements										
1 Government final consumption expenditure	145960	79930	...	62135	3895	164188	89346	...	70664	4178
2 Property income	76593	71918	...	6939	897	78477	74492	...	7360	205
A Interest	76370	71871	...	6765	895	78224	74439	...	7164	201
B Net land rent and royalties	223	47	...	174	2	253	53	...	196	4
3 Subsidies	27693	20684	...	7009	...	26125	18648	...	7477	...

Italy

3.12 General Government Income and Outlay Account: Total and Subsectors
(Continued)

Thousand Million Italian lire

	1986					1987				
	Total General Government	Central Government	State or Provincial Government	Local Government	Social Security Funds	Total General Government	Central Government	State or Provincial Government	Local Government	Social Security Funds
4 Other current transfers	162554	155117	...	23622	153588	178859	170740	...	28884	162931
A Casualty insurance premiums, net										
B Transfers to other government subsectors	128555	...	...	967	41251	140616	...	...	1146	41934
C Social security benefits										
D Social assistance grants	154826	23916	...	19020	111890	170486	26239	...	23630	120617
E Unfunded employee pension and welfare benefits										
F Transfers to private non-profit institutions serving households	1454	433	...	793	228	1997	810	...	935	252
G Other transfers n.e.c.	3774	713	...	2842	219	4057	756	...	3173	128
H Transfers to the rest of the world	2500	2500	...	-	-	2319	2319	...	-	-
Net saving	-63291	-70800	...	6303	1206	-71235	-64111	...	3741	3383
Total Current Disbursements	349509	257849	...	106008	159586	383538	281991	...	118126	170697

	1988					1989				
	Total General Government	Central Government	State or Provincial Government	Local Government	Social Security Funds	Total General Government	Central Government	State or Provincial Government	Local Government	Social Security Funds

Receipts

1 Operating surplus	2275	898	...	616	761	2684	1043	...	740	901
2 Property and entrepreneurial income	6919	6009	...	1923		3015	7214		2039	3280
A Withdrawals from public quasi-corporations										
B Interest	5634	5326	...	1321		3015	5827		5509	1359	3280
C Dividends a										
D Net land rent and royalties a	1285	683	...	602	-	1387	707	...	680	-
3 Taxes, fees and contributions	387660	243937	...	14430	129909	444125	279669	...	19031	146077
Indirect taxes	109104	102854	...	6250	-	123726	115496	...	8230	-
Direct taxes	145202	137718	...	8100		160405	170467		10714	
Income	145202	137718	...	8100		160405	170467		10714	
Other										
C Social security contributions	133354	3365	...	80	129909	149932	3768	...	87	146077
D Fees, fines and penalties		-	-		-		-	-		-
4 Other current transfers	32248	66150	...	111972	52017	34797	71258	...	120968	57386
A Casualty insurance claims a										
B Transfers from other government subsectors	...	46471	...	101579	49841	...	50293	...	109568	54974
C Transfers from the rest of the world	251	76	...	175		330	80		250	...
D Other transfers, except imputed	16095	5156	...	9165	1774	16882	4808	...	10075	1999
E Imputed unfunded employee pension and welfare contributions	15902	14447	...	1053	402	17585	16077	...	1095	413
Total Current Receipts	429102	319994	...	128941	185702	488820	358186	...	142798	207644

Disbursements

1 Government final consumption expenditure	184259	101264	...	78549	4446	199649	108440	...	85221	5388
2 Property income	88852	85227	...	7525	228	107255	103323	...	8055	228
A Interest	88080	85169	...	7312	227	106950	103261	...	7786	224
B Net land rent and royalties	272	58	...	213	1	305	62	...	239	4
3 Subsidies	26840	18964	...	7876	...	29093	20709	...	8384	...

Italy

3.12 General Government Income and Outlay Account: Total and Subsectors (Continued)

Thousand Million Italian lire

	1988						1989					
	Total General Government	Central Government	State or Provincial Government	Local Government	Social Security Funds		Total General Government	Central Government	State or Provincial Government	Local Government	Social Security Funds
4 Other current transfers	184683	32932	180254	223832	205109		36761	197549			
A Casualty insurance premiums, net	...	...	...	...	...		...	...			
B Transfers to other general government subsectors	151413	980	4114		164526		1634	49327			
C Social security benefits											
D Social assistance grants	189532	28288	27502	133742	210803	32872		30122	147809		
E Unfunded employee pension and welfare benefits											
F Transfers to private non-profit institutions serving households	2260	871	1093	296	2861	875		1684	302		
G Other transfers n.e.c.	4534	1075	3357	102	4497	1065		3321	111		
H Transfers to the rest of the world	3036	3036	-	-	5771	5771		-	-		
Net saving	-70311	-73144	2059	774	-71109	-79395		3807	4479		
Total Current Disbursements and Net Saving	429102	316994	128941	185702	488820	358186		142798	207644		

a) Items 'Dividends' and 'Casualty insurance claim' are included in item 'Net land rent and royalties'.

3.13 General Government Capital Accumulation Account: Total and Subsectors

Thousand Million Italian lire

	1980						1981					
	Total General Government	Central Government	State or Provincial Government	Local Government	Social Security Funds		Total General Government	Central Government	State or Provincial Government	Local Government	Social Security Funds
Finance of Gross Accumulation												
1 Gross saving	-17335	-18706	...	2307	-936	-32257	-29911	...	-828	-1518		
A Consumption of fixed capital	862	433	...	391	38	1051	508	...	497	46		
B Net saving	-18197	-19139	...	1916	-974	-33308	-30419	...	-1325	-1564		
2 Capital transfers	1002	745	...	4580	361	1539	751	...	6790	3776		
Finance of Gross Accumulation	-16333	-17961	...	6887	-575	-30718	-29160	...	5962	2258		
Gross Accumulation												
1 Gross capital formation	12278	4407	...	7496	375	16918	5644	...	10963	311		
A Increase in stocks												
B Gross fixed capital formation	12278	4407	...	7496	375	16918	5644	...	10963	311		
2 Purchases of land, net	31	2	...	29	-	44	3	...	41	-		
3 Purchases of intangible assets, net												
4 Capital transfers	4372	5355	...	3701	-	5332	10856	...	4254	-		
Net lending a	-33014	-27725	...	-4339	-950	-53012	-45663	...	-9276	1947		
Gross Accumulation	-16333	-17961	...	6887	-575	-30718	-29160	...	5962	2258		

	1982						1983					
	Total General Government	Central Government	State or Provincial Government	Local Government	Social Security Funds		Total General Government	Central Government	State or Provincial Government	Local Government	Social Security Funds
Finance of Gross Accumulation												
1 Gross saving	-38389	-40953	...	-395	2959	-56285	-43074	...	8977	4234		
A Consumption of fixed capital	1251	605	...	593	53	1437	694	...	683	60		
B Net saving	-39640	-41558	...	-988	2906	-57722	-43768	...	8294	4174		
2 Capital transfers	4729	3606	...	8687	30	7810	7748	...	8212	33		
Finance of Gross Accumulation	-33660	-37347	...	8292	2989	-48537	-35264	...	17189	4267		
Gross Accumulation												
1 Gross capital formation	20235	6667	...	13088	580	23540	8740	...	13773	1027		
A Increase in stocks	...	...	...	...	...	...	...	...	...	...		
B Gross fixed capital formation	20235	6667	...	13088	580	23540	8740	...	13773	1027		
2 Purchases of land, net	44	3	...	41	-	51	7	...	44	-		
3 Purchases of intangible assets, net	-	-	...	-	-	-	-	...	-	-		
4 Capital transfers	7527	10678	...	4443	-	8486	12298	...	4371	-		
Net lending a	-61566	-54655	...	-9280	2409	-67341	-69582	...	-999	3240		
Gross Accumulation	-33660	-37347	...	8292	2989	-35264	-48537	...	17189	4267		

Italy

3.13 General Government Capital Accumulation Account: Total and Subsectors

Thousand Million Italian lire

	1984					1985				
	Total General Government	Central Government	State or Provincial Government	Local Government	Social Security Funds	Total General Government	Central Government	State or Provincial Government	Local Government	Social Security Funds
Finance of Gross Accumulation										
1 Gross saving	-51851	-60259	...	7320	1088	-56265	-65209	...	5126	3818
A Consumption of fixed capital	1681	808	...	804	69	1988	980	...	936	72
B Net saving	-53532	-61067	...	6516	1019	-58253	-66189	...	4190	3746
2 Capital transfers	3735	3119	...	7506	36	2268	1801	...	18858	-
Finance of Gross Accumulation	-48116	-57140	...	14826	1124	-53997	-63408	...	23984	3818
Gross Accumulation										
1 Gross capital formation	26198	8890	...	16119	1189	30294	8811	...	18679	2804
A Increase in stocks	...	...	...	...	...	...	...	...	...	...
B Gross fixed capital formation	26198	8890	...	16119	1189	30294	8811	...	18679	2804
2 Purchases of land, net	70	28	...	42	-	58	8	...	50	-
3 Purchases of intangible assets, net	-	-	...	-	-	-	-	...	...	-
4 Capital transfers	10001	11890	...	4953	-	17611	30072	...	5930	-
Net lending [a]	-84385	-77948	...	-6288	-65	-101960	-102299	...	-675	1014
Gross Accumulation	-48116	-57140	...	14826	1124	-53997	-63408	...	23984	3818

	1986					1987				
	Total General Government	Central Government	State or Provincial Government	Local Government	Social Security Funds	Total General Government	Central Government	State or Provincial Government	Local Government	Social Security Funds
Finance of Gross Accumulation										
1 Gross saving	-60957	-69646	...	7398	1291	-61376	-69883	...	5024	3483
A Consumption of fixed capital	2334	1154	...	1095	85	2735	1352	...	1283	100
B Net saving	-63291	-70800	...	6303	1206	-64111	-71235	...	3741	3383
2 Capital transfers	2334	1866	...	15469	-	2485	2122	...	18008	-
Finance of Gross Accumulation	-58623	-67780	...	22867	1291	-58891	-67761	...	23032	3483
Gross Accumulation										
1 Gross capital formation	31787	9641	...	20480	1666	34500	9460	...	22819	2221
A Increase in stocks	...	...	...	...	...	...	...	...	...	...
B Gross fixed capital formation	31787	9641	...	20480	1666	34500	9460	...	22819	2221
2 Purchases of land, net	70	6	...	64	-	68	5	...	63	-
3 Purchases of intangible assets, net	-	-	...	-	-	-	-	...	...	-
4 Capital transfers	14175	23232	...	5944	-	14981	26612	...	6014	-
Net lending [a]	-104655	-100659	...	-3621	-375	-108440	-103838	...	-5864	1262
Gross Accumulation	-58623	-67780	...	22867	1291	-58891	-67761	...	23032	3483

	1988					1989				
	Total General Government	Central Government	State or Provincial Government	Local Government	Social Security Funds	Total General Government	Central Government	State or Provincial Government	Local Government	Social Security Funds
Finance of Gross Accumulation										
1 Gross saving	-67088	-71551	...	3571	892	-67310	-77516	...	5588	4618
A Consumption of fixed capital	3223	1593	...	1512	118	3799	1879	...	1781	139
B Net saving	-70311	-73144	...	2059	774	-71109	-79395	...	3807	4479
2 Capital transfers	3198	2722	...	15987	635	4580	4013	...	18062	-
Finance of Gross Accumulation	-63890	-68829	...	19558	1527	-62730	-73503	...	23650	4618
Gross Accumulation										
1 Gross capital formation	37599	10733	...	24887	1979	42082	12230	...	27352	2500
A Increase in stocks	...	...	...	...	...	...	...	...	...	...
B Gross fixed capital formation	37599	10733	...	24887	1979	42082	12230	...	27352	2500
2 Purchases of land, net	69	5	...	64	-	66	5	...	61	-
3 Purchases of intangible assets, net	-	-	...	-	-	-	-	...	...	-
4 Capital transfers	16398	25828	...	6716	-	16264	26105	...	7654	-
Net lending [a]	-117956	-105395	...	-12109	-452	-121142	-111843	...	-11417	2118
Gross Accumulation	-63890	-68829	...	19558	1527	-62730	-73503	...	23650	4618

a) Net lending of the capital accumulation account and the capital finance account have not been reconciled and are different due to different statistical sources.

Italy

3.14 General Government Capital Finance Account, Total and Subsectors

Thousand Million Italian lire

	1980					1981				
	Total General Government	Central Government	State or Provincial Government	Local Government	Social Security Funds	Total General Government	Central Government	State or Provincial Government	Local Government	Social Security Funds
Acquisition of Financial Assets										
1 Gold and SDRs	...	...	...	...	...	...	...	...	...	...
2 Currency and transferable deposits	540	239	...	1567	-56	-5246	115	...	-2733	-42
3 Other deposits	110	16	...	-15	108	-207	29	...	-150	-85
4 Bills and bonds, short term	741	...	...	-	741	-188	...	...	-	-188
5 Bonds, long term	1451	1175	...	-	276	670	381	...	25	264
6 Corporate equity securities	4563	4357	...	191	15	5205	4477	...	716	11
7 Short-term loans, n.e.c.	-809	-836	...	...	27	367	275	...	...	92
8 Long-term loans, n.e.c.	870	2342	...	110	345	1529	3808	...	51	602
9 Other receivables	13	3	...	9	-	17	4	...	13	-
10 Other assets	...	...	...	...	...	...	...	...	...	...
Total Acquisition of Financial Assets	7479	7297	...	1863	1456	2145	9088	...	-2078	654
Incurrence of Liabilities										
1 Currency and transferable deposits	-1803	-592	...	...	...	8501	11089	...	...	...
2 Other deposits	3719	3719	...	...	...	1940	1940	...	...	...
3 Bills and bonds, short term	25500	25500	...	...	...	33783	33783	...	...	...
4 Bonds, long term	-1149	-1118	...	-32	...	8663	8688	...	-25	...
5 Short-term loans, n.e.c.	9437	9429	...	91	-83	6986	6554	...	400	32
6 Long-term loans, n.e.c.	-75	-161	...	2004	8	2370	1191	...	4131	-21
7 Other payables	...	...	...	...	...	...	...	...	...	...
8 Other liabilities	-	-	...	-	...	-	-	...	-	...
Total Incurrence of Liabilities	35629	36778	...	2064	-75	62243	63245	...	4506	11
Statistical discrepancy	4864	-1755	...	4138	2481	-7086	-8494	...	2713	-1304
Net Lending [a]	-33014	-27725	...	-4339	-950	-53012	-45663	...	-9296	1947
Incurrence of Liabilities and Net Worth	7479	7297	...	1863	1456	2145	9088	...	-2078	654

	1982					1983				
	Total General Government	Central Government	State or Provincial Government	Local Government	Social Security Funds	Total General Government	Central Government	State or Provincial Government	Local Government	Social Security Funds
Acquisition of Financial Assets										
1 Gold and SDRs	...	...	...	...	...	...	...	...	...	...
2 Currency and transferable deposits	715	611	...	1007	245	5047	742	...	6610	595
3 Other deposits	42	63	...	-28	6	6	21	...	11	-26
4 Bills and bonds, short term	-97	...	...	-	-97	255	...	...	-	255
5 Bonds, long term	1455	-91	...	9	1537	1386	560	...	7	818
6 Corporate equity securities	8338	8118	...	207	13	11199	10332	...	844	23
7 Short-term loans, n.e.c.	-177	-169	...	...	-8	4	161	...	...	-157
8 Long-term loans, n.e.c.	2190	5327	...	164	832	2115	5712	...	65	658
9 Other receivables	16	2	...	13	1	18	3	...	15	-
10 Other assets	...	...	...	...	...	...	...	...	...	...
Total Acquisition of Financial Assets	12482	13861	...	1373	2529	20030	17530	...	7553	2168
Incurrence of Liabilities										
1 Currency and transferable deposits	-1138	9	...	...	...	3432	6333	...	...	...
2 Other deposits	2931	2931	...	...	...	3724	3724	...	...	...
3 Bills and bonds, short term	32604	32604	...	...	...	11071	11071	...	...	...
4 Bonds, long term	24836	24871	...	-35	...	69095	69138	...	-43	...
5 Short-term loans, n.e.c.	9196	8046	...	1120	31	-320	-1010	...	-165	855
6 Long-term loans, n.e.c.	2997	1199	...	5886	45	3560	-51	...	7971	-40
7 Other payables	...	...	...	...	...	...	...	...	...	...
8 Other liabilities	-	-	...	-	...	-	-	...	-	...
Total Incurrence of Liabilities	71425	69659	...	6970	75	90562	89205	...	7764	815
Statistical discrepancy	2623	-1104	...	3682	44	-3192	-2093	...	788	-1887
Net Lending [a]	-61566	-54695	...	-9280	2409	-67341	-69582	...	-999	3240
Incurrence of Liabilities and Net Worth	12482	13861	...	1373	2529	20030	17530	...	7553	2168

Italy

3.14 General Government Capital Finance Account, Total and Subsectors

Thousand Million Italian lire

	1984					1985				
	Total General Government	Central Government	State or Provincial Government	Local Government	Social Security Funds	Total General Government	Central Government	State or Provincial Government	Local Government	Social Security Funds
Acquisition of Financial Assets										
1 Gold and SDRs	...	...	...	...	...	...	...	...	...	...
2 Currency and transferable deposits	-451	-1042	...	1130	625	1871	79	...	3004	845
3 Other deposits	354	235	...	-18	136	129	230	...	-107	6
4 Bills and bonds, short term	313	...	...	7	306	94	...	...	-8	102
5 Bonds, long term	1034	254	...	24	756	2170	506	...	41	1623
6 Corporate equity securities	8216	7409	...	780	28	7908	6908	...	980	20
7 Short-term loans, n.e.c.	-220	-259	...	...	39	475	-306	...	...	781
8 Long-term loans, n.e.c.	2959	5625	...	497	924	3451	8691	...	-305	-137
9 Other receivables	26	5	...	21	1	29	5	...	23	1
10 Other assets	...	...	...	...	...	...	...	...	...	...
Total Acquisition of Financial Assets	12231	12227	...	2441	2814	16125	16112	...	3628	3241
Incurrence of Liabilities										
1 Currency and transferable deposits	-82	1082	...	...	...	911	2968	...	...	...
2 Other deposits	6006	6006	...	...	...	7820	7820	...	...	...
3 Bills and bonds, short term	9301	9301	...	...	...	13181	13181	...	...	...
4 Bonds, long term	63138	63183	...	-45	...	92873	92923	...	-50	...
5 Short-term loans, n.e.c.	15601	12863	...	2590	149	3619	5131	...	-2331	819
6 Long-term loans, n.e.c.	5007	823	...	8250	21	4694	1894	...	7462	137
7 Other payables	...	...	...	...	...	...	...	...	...	...
8 Other liabilities	-	-	...	-	...	-	-	...	...	...
Total Incurrence of Liabilities	98971	93258	...	10795	169	123097	123916	...	5081	957
Statistical discrepancy	-2355	-3083	...	-1982	2710	-5012	-5505	...	-778	1271
Net Lending [a]	-84385	-77948	...	-6372	-65	-101960	-102299	...	-675	1014
Incurrence of Liabilities and Net Worth	12231	12227	...	2441	2814	16125	16112	...	3628	3241

	1986					1987				
	Total General Government	Central Government	State or Provincial Government	Local Government	Social Security Funds	Total General Government	Central Government	State or Provincial Government	Local Government	Social Security Funds
Acquisition of Financial Assets										
1 Gold and SDRs	...	...	...	...	...	...	...	...	...	...
2 Currency and transferable deposits	-2052	823	...	-1046	-30	-249	310	...	1347	-114
3 Other deposits	-48	-205	...	-28	186	-139	119	...	-57	-201
4 Bills and bonds, short term	-53	...	...	21	-74	-212	...	...	30	-242
5 Bonds, long term	3207	830	...	54	2323	2740	482	...	41	2217
6 Corporate equity securities	4041	2711	...	1320	10	2551	1199	...	1350	3
7 Short-term loans, n.e.c.	-696	266	...	...	-962	-465	-225	...	...	-240
8 Long-term loans, n.e.c.	6402	11518	...	376	457	4290	10006	...	370	-858
9 Other receivables	37	5	...	32	-	31	6	...	26	-
10 Other assets	...	...	...	...	...	...	...	...	...	...
Total Acquisition of Financial Assets	10838	15947	...	729	1910	8547	11896	...	3107	564
Incurrence of Liabilities										
1 Currency and transferable deposits	-977	822	...	...	...	1527	3319	...	...	...
2 Other deposits	10607	10607	...	...	...	12244	12244	...	...	...
3 Bills and bonds, short term	9697	9697	...	...	...	27482	27482	...	...	...
4 Bonds, long term	87420	87456	...	-36	...	56035	56071	...	-36	...
5 Short-term loans, n.e.c.	2386	2408	...	27	-49	10854	10016	...	542	296
6 Long-term loans, n.e.c.	271	-316	...	6421	115	4126	3181	...	5998	175
7 Other payables	...	...	...	...	...	...	...	...	...	...
8 Other liabilities	-	-	...	-	...	-	-	...	...	...
Total Incurrence of Liabilities	109404	110674	...	6412	66	112267	112312	...	6504	471
Statistical discrepancy	6089	5933	...	-2062	2219	4720	3422	...	2466	-1169
Net Lending [a]	-104655	-100659	...	-3621	-375	-108440	-103838	...	-5864	1262
Incurrence of Liabilities and Net Worth	10838	15947	...	729	1910	8547	11896	...	3107	564

Italy

3.14 General Government Capital Finance Account, Total and Subsectors

Thousand Million Italian lire

	1988				
	Total General Government	Central Government	State or Provincial Government	Local Government	Social Security Funds
Acquisition of Financial Assets					
1 Gold and SDRs	...	...	...	...	...
2 Currency and transferable deposits	-306	-163	...	1567	912
3 Other deposits	448	471	...	-1	-22
4 Bills and bonds, short term	-651	...	...	34	-685
5 Bonds, long term	2750	246	...	65	2439
6 Corporate equity securities	2837	1467	...	1370	-1
7 Short-term loans, n.e.c.	-164	-164	...	...	-
8 Long-term loans, n.e.c.	4229	13074	...	-5	1429
9 Other receivables	35	6	...	28	-
10 Other assets	...	...	...	...	...
Total Acquisition of Financial Assets	9178	14937	...	3059	4073
Incurrence of Liabilities					
1 Currency and transferable deposits	-2469	153	...	...	...
2 Other deposits	13370	13370	...	...	...
3 Bills and bonds, short term	42013	42013	...	...	...
4 Bonds, long term	61203	61240	...	-37	...
5 Short-term loans, n.e.c.	4180	2946	...	684	550
6 Long-term loans, n.e.c.	1266	837	...	10704	-6
7 Other payables	...	...	...	...	...
8 Other liabilities	-	-	...	-	...
Total Incurrence of Liabilities	119562	120559	...	11351	544
Statistical discrepancy	7572	-226	...	3817	3981
Net Lending [a]	-117956	-105395	...	-12109	-452
Incurrence of Liabilities and Net Worth	9178	14938	...	3059	4073

a) Net lending of the capital accumulation account and the capital finance account have not been reconciled and are different due to different statistical sources.

3.21 Corporate and Quasi-Corporate Enterprise Production Account: Total and Sectors

Thousand Million Italian lire

	1980			ADDENDUM: Total, including Unincorporated	1981			ADDENDUM: Total, including Unincorporated	1982			ADDENDUM: Total, including Unincorporated
	Corporate and Quasi-Corporate Enterprises				Corporate and Quasi-Corporate Enterprises				Corporate and Quasi-Corporate Enterprises			
	TOTAL	Non-Financial	Financial		TOTAL	Non-Financial	Financial		TOTAL	Non-Financial	Financial	
Gross Output												
1 Output for sale	330856	322174	8682	...	390195	378633	11562	...	444725	430936	13789	...
2 Imputed bank service charge	16471	...	16471	...	20091	...	20091	...	21887	...	21887	...
3 Own-account fixed capital formation	...	...	...	...	...	...	...	...	...	...	...	...
Gross Output	347327	322174	25153	...	410286	378633	31653	...	466612	430936	35676	...
Gross Input												
Intermediate consumption	214136	192359	21777	...	255855	228458	27397	...	292426	261767	30659	...
1 Imputed banking service charge	16471	-	16471	...	20091	-	20091	...	21887	-	21887	...
2 Other intermediate consumption	197665	192359	5306	...	235764	228458	7306	...	270539	261767	8772	...
Subtotal: Value Added	133191	129815	3376	...	154431	150175	4256	...	174186	169169	5017	...
1 Indirect taxes, net	3139	1583	1556	...	2834	978	1856	...	2411	201	2210	...
A Indirect taxes	12522	10964	1558	...	13899	12041	1858	...	17003	14791	2212	...
B Less: Subsidies	9383	9381	2	...	11065	11063	2	...	14592	14590	2	...
2 Consumption of fixed capital	18670	17668	1002	...	23683	22413	1270	...	28583	27052	1531	...
3 Compensation of employees	96831	85465	11366	...	113260	100736	12524	...	129524	115523	14001	...
4 Net operating surplus	14551	25099	-10548	...	14654	26048	-11394	...	13668	26393	-12725	...
Gross Input	347327	322174	25153	...	410286	378633	31653	...	466612	430936	35676	...

Italy

3.21 Corporate and Quasi-Corporate Enterprise Production Account: Total and Sectors

Thousand Million Italian lire

	1983			1983 ADDENDUM	1984			1984 ADDENDUM	1985			1985 ADDENDUM
	Corporate and Quasi-Corporate Enterprises			Total, including Unincorporated	Corporate and Quasi-Corporate Enterprises			Total, including Unincorporated	Corporate and Quasi-Corporate Enterprises			Total, including Unincorporated
	TOTAL	Non-Financial	Financial		TOTAL	Non-Financial	Financial		TOTAL	Non-Financial	Financial	
Gross Output												
1 Output for sale	545337	529998	15339	...	626880	609004	17876	...	706788	686320	20468	...
2 Imputed bank service charge	26510	...	26510	...	30119	...	30119	...	34373	...	34373	...
3 Own-account fixed capital formation	...	...	...	...	...	...	...	...	...	...	...	...
Gross Output	571847	529998	41849	...	656999	609004	47995	...	741161	686320	54841	...
Gross Input												
Intermediate consumption	351790	315090	36700	...	410314	368396	41918	...	456291	408272	48019	...
1 Imputed banking service charge	26510	-	26510	...	30119	-	30119	...	34373	-	34373	...
2 Other intermediate consumption	325280	315090	10190	...	380195	368396	11799	...	421918	408272	13646	...
Subtotal: Value Added	220057	214908	5149	...	246685	240608	6077	...	284870	278048	6822	...
1 Indirect taxes, net	6159	3680	2479	...	5126	2165	2961	...	5424	2343	3081	...
A Indirect taxes	21574	19094	2480	...	24689	21677	3012	...	25700	22435	3265	...
B Less: Subsidies	15415	15414	1	...	19563	19512	51	...	20276	20092	184	...
2 Consumption of fixed capital	32877	31117	1760	...	37273	35290	1983	...	41739	39479	2260	...
3 Compensation of employees	151349	133319	18030	...	170565	150791	19774	...	189779	168032	21747	...
4 Net operating surplus	29672	46792	-17120	...	33721	52362	-18641	...	47928	68194	-20266	...
Gross Input	571847	529998	41849	...	656999	609004	47995	...	741161	686320	54841	...

	1986			1986 ADDENDUM	1987			1987 ADDENDUM	1988			1988 ADDENDUM
	Corporate and Quasi-Corporate Enterprises			Total, including Unincorporated	Corporate and Quasi-Corporate Enterprises			Total, including Unincorporated	Corporate and Quasi-Corporate Enterprises			Total, including Unincorporated
	TOTAL	Non-Financial	Financial		TOTAL	Non-Financial	Financial		TOTAL	Non-Financial	Financial	
Gross Output												
1 Output for sale	720738	696523	24215	...	749535	725142	24393	...	852469	825688	26781	...
2 Imputed bank service charge	39853	...	39853	...	40215	...	40215	...	45757	...	45757	...
3 Own-account fixed capital formation	...	...	...	...	...	...	...	...	...	...	...	...
Gross Output	760591	696523	64068	...	789750	725142	64608	...	898226	825688	72538	...
Gross Input												
Intermediate consumption	440128	384697	55431	...	447505	389586	57919	...	532481	466904	65577	...
1 Imputed banking service charge	39853	-	39853	...	40215	-	40215	...	45757	-	45757	...
2 Other intermediate consumption	400275	384697	15578	...	407290	389586	17704	...	486724	466904	19820	...
Subtotal: Value Added	320463	311826	8637	...	342245	335556	6689	...	365745	358784	6961	...
1 Indirect taxes, net	9867	6244	3623	...	12476	8368	4108	...	15953	10944	5009	...
A Indirect taxes	32659	28926	3733	...	36435	32285	4150	...	40554	35541	5013	...
B Less: Subsidies	22792	22682	110	...	23959	23917	42	...	24601	24597	4	...
2 Consumption of fixed capital	44737	42314	2423	...	48134	45558	2576	...	52133	49336	2797	...
3 Compensation of employees	201367	177185	24182	...	217587	191152	26435	...	239853	211114	28739	...
4 Net operating surplus	64492	86083	-21591	...	64048	90478	-26430	...	57806	87390	-29584	...
Gross Input	760591	696523	64068	...	789750	725142	64608	...	898226	825688	72538	...

3.22 Corporate and Quasi-Corporate Enterprise Income and Outlay Account: Total and Sectors

Thousand Million Italian lire

	1980			1981			1982			1983		
	TOTAL	Non-Financial	Financial	TOTAL	Non-Financial	Financial	TOTAL	Non-Financial	Financial	TOTAL	Non-Financial	Financial
Receipts												
1 Operating surplus	14551	25099	-10548	14654	26048	-11394	13668	26393	-12725	29672	46792	-17120
2 Property and entrepreneurial income	78944	11002	67942	100199	13047	87152	114701	15590	99111	128847	15415	113432
A Withdrawals from quasi-corporate enterprises	...	...	...	...	...	...	...	...	...	...	...	...
B Interest	77085	9360	67725	98368	11443	86925	112190	13379	98811	126088	12989	113099
C Dividends	1547	1331	216	1543	1316	227	2145	1845	300	2255	1922	333
D Net land rent and royalties	312	311	1	288	288	-	366	366	-	504	504	-

Italy

3.22 Corporate and Quasi-Corporate Enterprise Income and Outlay Account: Total and Sectors
(Continued)

Thousand Million Italian lire

	1980			1981			1982			1983		
	TOTAL	Non-Financial	Financial	TOTAL	Non-Financial	Financial	TOTAL	Non-Financial	Financial	TOTAL	Non-Financial	Financial
3 Current transfers	15966	7900	8066	18034	9555	8479	20463	10520	9943	23784	11993	11791
A Casualty insurance claims	2281	1361	920	2812	1785	1027	2965	1856	1109	3434	2205	1229
B Casualty insurance premiums, net, due to be received by insurance companies	4047	...	4047	4937	...	4937	6166	...	6166	7121	...	7121
C Current transfers from the rest of the world	...	...	...	...	...	...	...	...	...	...	...	...
D Other transfers except imputed	424	196	228	485	235	250	523	303	220	609	409	200
E Imputed unfunded employee pension and welfare contributions	9214	6343	2871	9800	7535	2265	10809	8361	2448	12620	9379	3241
Total Current Receipts	109461	44001	65460	132887	48650	84237	148832	52503	96329	182303	74200	108103

Disbursements

	1980			1981			1982			1983		
1 Property and entrepreneurial income	75910	26826	49084	102240	38208	64032	120319	46295	74024	135653	51942	83711
A Withdrawals from quasi-corporations	952	952	...	1091	1091	...	1219	1219	...	1702	1702	...
B Interest	68082	19569	48513	92539	29299	63240	108021	35054	72967	121177	38743	82434
C Dividends	6192	5624	568	7724	6935	789	9779	8725	1054	11169	9897	1272
D Net land rent and royalties	684	681	3	886	883	3	1300	1297	3	1605	1600	5
2 Direct taxes and other current transfers n.e.c. to general government	4933	3960	973	6989	5361	1628	9648	6759	2889	12378	8263	4115
A Direct taxes	4933	3960	973	6989	5361	1628	9648	6759	2889	12378	8263	4115
B Fines, fees, penalties and other current transfers n.e.c.	...	...	...	...	...	...	...	...	...	...	...	...
3 Other current transfers	10865	4868	5997	13682	6602	7080	15438	6794	8644	20249	10084	10165
A Casualty insurance premiums, net	2322	1368	954	2660	1568	1092	3124	1946	1178	3640	2315	1325
B Casualty insurance claims liability of insurance companies	4047	...	4047	4937	...	4937	6166	...	6166	7121	...	7121
C Transfers to private non-profit institutions	120	...	120	162	...	162	181	...	181	435	...	435
D Unfunded employee pension and welfare benefits	...	...	...	...	...	...	...	...	...	...	...	...
E Social assistance grants	3534	2658	876	4627	3738	889	5227	4108	1119	6728	5444	1284
F Other transfers n.e.c.	842	842	...	1296	1296	...	740	740	...	2325	2325	...
G Transfers to the rest of the world	...	...	...	...	...	...	...	...	...	...	...	...
Statistical discrepancy	5325	3733	1592	5459	3844	1615	5821	4333	1488	5575	4033	1542
Net saving	12428	4614	7814	4517	-5365	9882	-2394	-11678	9284	8448	-122	8570
Total Current Disbursements and Net Saving	109461	44001	65460	132887	48650	84237	148832	52503	96329	182303	74200	108103

	1984			1985			1986			1987		
	TOTAL	Non-Financial	Financial	TOTAL	Non-Financial	Financial	TOTAL	Non-Financial	Financial	TOTAL	Non-Financial	Financial

Receipts

	TOTAL	Non-Financial	Financial	TOTAL	Non-Financial	Financial	TOTAL	Non-Financial	Financial	TOTAL	Non-Financial	Financial
1 Operating surplus	33721	52362	-18641	47928	68194	-20266	64492	86083	-21591	64048	90478	-26430
2 Property and entrepreneurial income	144957	18704	126253	157508	20575	136933	156129	20776	135353	153893	22716	131177
A Withdrawals from quasi-corporate enterprises	...	...	...	...	...	...	...	...	...	...	...	...
B Interest	141114	15324	125790	152281	16009	136272	149859	15396	134463	145651	15804	129847
C Dividends	3350	2887	463	4598	3937	661	5691	4801	890	7606	6276	1330
D Net land rent and royalties	493	493	-	629	629	-	579	579	-	636	636	-
3 Current transfers	26587	13186	13401	30103	15402	14701	32318	15740	16578	35588	17288	18300
A Casualty insurance claims	3813	2378	1435	4119	2468	1651	4205	2678	1527	4542	3010	1532
B Casualty insurance premiums, net, due to be received by insurance companies	8386	...	8386	9717	...	9717	11174	...	11174	12829	...	12829
C Current transfers from the rest of the world	...	...	...	...	...	...	...	...	...	...	...	...
D Other transfers except imputed	686	466	220	934	724	210	1219	999	220	1275	1045	230
E Imputed unfunded employee pension and welfare contributions	13702	10342	3360	15333	12210	3123	15720	12063	3657	16942	13233	3709

Italy

3.22 Corporate and Quasi-Corporate Enterprise Income and Outlay Account: Total and Sectors
(Continued)

Thousand Million Italian lire

	1984			1985			1986			1987		
	TOTAL	Non-Financial	Financial	TOTAL	Non-Financial	Financial	TOTAL	Non-Financial	Financial	TOTAL	Non-Financial	Financial
Total Current Receipts	205265	84252	121013	235539	104171	131368	252939	122599	130340	253529	130482	123047
Disbursements												
1 Property and entrepreneurial income	149926	57941	91985	158112	60538	97574	150219	59371	90848	151717	65596	86121
A Withdrawals from quasi-corporations	2289	2289	...	2737	2737	...	3087	3087	...	3461	3461	...
B Interest	132363	42016	90347	136789	41301	95488	125018	36988	88030	122145	38854	83291
C Dividends	13391	11759	1632	16318	14241	2077	19927	17119	2808	23648	20830	2818
D Net land rent and royalties	1883	1877	6	2268	2259	9	2187	2177	10	2463	2451	12
2 Direct taxes and other current transfers n.e.c. to general government	14395	9768	4627	18052	13256	4796	22168	16753	5415	29275	22847	6428
A Direct taxes	14395	9768	4627	18052	13256	4796	22168	16753	5415	29275	22847	6428
B Fines, fees, penalties and other current transfers n.e.c.	...	...	...	...	...	...	...	...	...	...	...	...
3 Other current transfers	21774	10061	11713	26514	12977	13537	28248	12968	15280	33087	15862	17225
A Casualty insurance premiums, net	4089	2546	1543	4383	2601	1782	4575	2907	1668	5003	3306	1697
B Casualty insurance claims liability of insurance companies	8386	...	8386	9717	...	9717	11174	...	11174	12829	...	12829
C Transfers to private non-profit institutions	508	...	508	620	...	620	663	...	663	770		770
D Unfunded employee pension and welfare benefits	...	...	...	...	...	...	...	...	...	...	...	...
E Social assistance grants	6713	5437	1276	7972	6554	1418	8086	6311	1775	10472	8543	1929
F Other transfers n.e.c.	2078	2078	...	3822	3822	...	3750	3750	...	4013	4013	...
G Transfers to the rest of the world	...	...	...	...	...	...	...	...	...	...	...	...
Statistical discrepancy	6860	5015	1845	7933	5802	2131	8029	5932	2097	6755	4883	1872
Net saving	12310	1467	10843	24928	11598	13330	44275	27575	16700	32695	21294	11401
Total Current Disbursements and Net Saving	205265	84252	121013	235539	104171	131368	252939	122599	130340	253529	130482	123047

	1988		
	TOTAL	Non-Financial	Financial
Receipts			
1 Operating surplus	57806	87390	-29584
2 Property and entrepreneurial income	167816	24089	143727
A Withdrawals from quasi-corporate enterprises	...	...	...
B Interest	159475	17121	142354
C Dividends	7618	6245	1373
D Net land rent and royalties	723	723	-
3 Current transfers	39694	18806	20888
A Casualty insurance claims	4876	3089	1787
B Casualty insurance premiums, net, due to be received by insurance companies	14723	...	14723
C Current transfers from the rest of the world	...	...	...
D Other transfers except imputed	1481	1241	240
E Imputed unfunded employee pension and welfare contributions	18614	14476	4138
Total Current Receipts	265316	130285	135031
Disbursements			
1 Property and entrepreneurial income	160047	67418	92629
A Withdrawals from quasi-corporations	3355	3355	...
B Interest	129784	40206	89578

932

Italy

3.22 Corporate and Quasi-Corporate Enterprise Income and Outlay Account: Total and Sectors
(Continued)

Thousand Million Italian lire

	1988		
	TOTAL	Non-Financial	Financial
C Dividends	23934	20896	3038
D Net land rent and royalties	2974	2961	13
2 Direct taxes and other current transfers n.e.c. to general government	25112	19671	5441
A Direct taxes	25112	19671	5441
B Fines, fees, penalties and other current transfers n.e.c.			
3 Other current transfers	36769	17019	19750
A Casualty insurance premiums, net	5452	3471	1981
B Casualty insurance claims liability of insurance companies	14723	...	14723
C Transfers to private non-profit institutions	808	808	...
D Unfunded employee pension and welfare benefits			
E Social assistance grants	11408	9170	2238
F Other transfers n.e.c.	4378	4378	...
G Transfers to the rest of the world	...	...	...
Statistical discrepancy	7845	5532	2313
Net saving	35543	20645	14898
Total Current Disbursements and Net Saving	265316	130285	135031

3.23 Corporate and Quasi-Corporate Enterprise Capital Accumulation Account: Total and Sectors

Thousand Million Italian lire

	1980			1981			1982			1983		
	TOTAL	Non-Financial	Financial	TOTAL	Non-Financial	Financial	TOTAL	Non-Financial	Financial	TOTAL	Non-Financial	Financial
Finance of Gross Accumulation												
1 Gross saving	31098	22282	8816	17048	15374	1670	26189	25683	1270	28605	27052	1531	41325	30995	10330
A Consumption of fixed capital	18670	17668	1002	23883	22413	1270	...		
B Net saving	12428	4614	7814	4517	-5365	9882	-2394	-11678	9284	8448	-122	8570
2 Capital transfers	2013	2013	...	1494	1494	...	4430	4430	...	5187	5187	...
Finance of Gross Accumulation	33111	24295	8816	29694	18542	11152	30619	19804	10815	46512	36182	10330
Gross Accumulation												
1 Gross capital formation	33770	32332	1438	36607	34897	1710	42960	40773	2187	45208	42118	3090
A Increase in stocks	3073	3073	...	1321	1321	...	1899	1899	...	874	874	...
B Gross fixed capital formation	30697	29259	1438	35286	33576	1710	41061	38874	2187	44334	41244	3090
2 Purchases of land, net	10	24	-14	8	-8	16	88	59	29	86	65	21
3 Purchases of intangible assets, net	545	545	-	1008	1008	-	898	898	-	824	824	-
4 Capital transfers	361	288	73	631	584	47	2173	2092	81	3903	3903	110
Net lending a	-1575	-8894	7319	-8560	-17939	9379	-15500	-24018	8518	-3619	-10728	7109
Gross Accumulation	33111	24295	8816	29694	18542	11152	30619	19804	10815	46512	36182	10330

	1984			1985			1986			1987		
	TOTAL	Non-Financial	Financial	TOTAL	Non-Financial	Financial	TOTAL	Non-Financial	Financial	TOTAL	Non-Financial	Financial
Finance of Gross Accumulation												
1 Gross saving	49583	36757	12826	51077	49667	15590	89012	69898	19123	80829	66852	13977
A Consumption of fixed capital	37273	35290	1983	39479	2260		44737	42314	2423	48134	45558	2576
B Net saving	12310	1467	10843	24828	11598	13330	44275	27575	16700	32695	21294	11401
2 Capital transfers	5886	5886	-	12469	7628	4841	8509	8509	-	10211	10211	-
Finance of Gross Accumulation	55469	42643	12826	79136	58705	20431	97521	78398	19123	91040	77063	13977
Gross Accumulation												
1 Gross capital formation	56897	53738	3159	62034	58845	3189	65939	62449	3490	77159	73561	3598

Italy

3.23 Corporate and Quasi-Corporate Enterprise Capital Accumulation Account: Total and Sectors (Continued)

Thousand Million Italian lire

	1984			1985			1986			1987		
	TOTAL	Non-Financial	Financial	TOTAL	Non-Financial	Financial	TOTAL	Non-Financial	Financial	TOTAL	Non-Financial	Financial
A Increase in stocks	6655	6655	-	5734	5734	-	2926	2926	-	4330	4330	-
B Gross fixed capital formation	50242	47083	3159	56300	53111	3189	63013	59523	3490	72829	69231	3598
2 Purchases of land, net	131	129	2	172	127	45	82	80	-2	163	152	11
3 Purchases of intangible assets, net	1235	1235	-	956	956	-	840	840	-	1017	1017	-
4 Capital transfers	1520	1393	127	663	361	302	818	331	487	589	293	296
Net lending a	-4314	-13852	9538	15311	-1584	16895	29844	14696	15148	12112	2040	10072
Gross Accumulation	55469	42643	12826	79136	58705	20431	97521	78398	19123	91040	77063	13977

1988

	TOTAL	Non-Financial	Financial
Finance of Gross Accumulation			
1 Gross saving	87676	69981	17695
A Consumption of fixed capital	52133	49336	2797
B Net saving	35543	20645	14898
2 Capital transfers	11019	11019	-
Finance of Gross Accumulation	98695	81000	17695
Gross Accumulation			
1 Gross capital formation	92764	88092	4672
A Increase in stocks	8931	8931	-
B Gross fixed capital formation	83833	79161	4672
2 Purchases of land, net	412	428	-16
3 Purchases of intangible assets, net	1041	1041	-
4 Capital transfers	846	609	237
Net lending a	3832	-9170	12802
Gross Accumulation	98695	81000	17695

a) Net lending of the capital accumulation account and the capital finance account have not been reconciled and are different due to different statistical sources.

3.24 Corporate and Quasi-Corporate Enterprise Capital Finance Account: Total and Sectors

Thousand Million Italian lire

	1980			1981			1982			1983		
	TOTAL	Non-Financial	Financial	TOTAL	Non-Financial	Financial	TOTAL	Non-Financial	Financial	TOTAL	Non-Financial	Financial
Acquisition of Financial Assets												
1 Gold and SDRs	-163	...	-163	-114	...	-114	7	...	7	-367	...	-367
2 Currency and transferable deposits	5145	4501	644	8256	7514	741	7026	9409	-2383	11980	9120	2860
3 Other deposits	2272	2286	-13	6227	6253	-26	913	920	-7	4261	4260	1
4 Bills and bonds, short term	12024	2038	9986	11774	2631	9143	19247	1448	17799	962	-577	1539
5 Bonds, long term	4103	-1	4104	10392	195	10197	25093	1746	23293	44875	4496	40379
6 Corporate equity securities	3809	2757	1052	8550	1392	7157	7304	4745	2559	13147	11577	1570
7 Short term loans, n.e.c.	33486	192	33294	42022	1533	40489	26346	-533	26880	33489	-199	33688
8 Long term loans, n.e.c.	11430	-499	11929	13963	-371	15743	82	15661	17080	635	16445	
9 Trade credits and advances	2649	2368	281	4827	1377	3450	1230	551	679	2856	2464	392
10 Other receivables	669	650	19	850	836	14	850	834	16	868	853	15
11 Other assets	5786	...	5786	4672	...	4672	3047	...	3047	956	...	956
Total Acquisition of Financial Assets	81211	14291	66920	111047	29199	81849	107453	19204	87549	130107	32630	97477
Incurrence of Liabilities												
1 Currency and transferable deposits	21898	...	21898	16051	...	16051	30595	...	30595	27747	...	27747
2 Other deposits	11811	...	11811	17395	...	17395	26451	...	26451	23271	...	23271
3 Bills and bonds, short term	1095	1023	72	813	606	207	-430	-388	-42	-375	-321	-53
4 Bonds, long term	5148	43	5105	7374	615	6759	11702	4349	7353	10854	4135	6719
5 Corporate equity securities	7742	6627	1115	13611	2198	11413	14486	2468	12018	22540	20444	2096
6 Short-term loans, n.e.c.	28640	15513	13128	34655	14973	19682	12124	794	11330	37386	19524	17862

Italy

3.24 Corporate and Quasi-Corporate Enterprise Capital Finance Account: Total and Sectors
(Continued)

Thousand Million Italian lire

	1980			1981			1982			1983		
	TOTAL	Non-Financial	Financial	TOTAL	Non-Financial	Financial	TOTAL	Non-Financial	Financial	TOTAL	Non-Financial	Financial
7 Long-term loans, n.e.c.	14929	13575	1354	21766	18677	3089	18494	14252	4242	15870	10977	4892
8 Net equity of households in life insurance and pension fund reserves	4668	2743	1925	4683	2673	2010	5150	3085	2065	6363	4033	2330
9 Proprietors' net additions to the accumulation of quasi-corporations	...	...	...	...	...	...	...	...	...	...	...	...
10 Trade credit and advances	1775	1775	...	4735	4735	...	-1059	-1059	...	2322	2322	...
11 Other accounts payable	1021	...	1021	1386	...	1386	1731	...	1731	1618	...	1618
12 Other liabilities	1694	...	1694	1840	...	1840	1394	...	1394	3100	...	3100
Total Incurrence of Liabilities	100421	41299	59122	124309	53692	70617	120639	43587	77052	150695	61114	89581
Statistical discrepancy	2987	2509	478	13438	11585	1853	13912	11932	1980	3670	2882	787
Net Lending a	-22197	-29516	7319	-26699	-36078	9379	-27797	-36315	8518	-24258	-31367	7109
Incurrence of Liabilities and Net Lending	81211	14291	66920	111047	29199	81849	106753	19204	87549	130107	32630	97477

	1984			1985			1986			1987		
	TOTAL	Non-Financial	Financial	TOTAL	Non-Financial	Financial	TOTAL	Non-Financial	Financial	TOTAL	Non-Financial	Financial
				Acquisition of Financial Assets								
1 Gold and SDRs	25	...	25	-385	...	-385	442	...	442	165	...	165
2 Currency and transferable deposits	12692	10197	2495	644	7964	-7320	18698	13862	4837	13959	8323	5636
3 Other deposits	3712	3739	-27	3980	3997	-17	2033	2016	17	2924	2819	105
4 Bills and bonds, short term	-8085	1688	-9773	-10389	-28	-10361	3672	-753	4425	-1703	5715	-7418
5 Bonds, long term	31866	6102	25764	63268	7241	56027	57274	9352	47922	21414	6477	14937
6 Corporate equity securities	12453	9986	2467	13621	10673	2948	24701	19171	5530	15122	10267	4855
7 Short term loans, n.e.c.	63010	274	62737	47419	2180	45239	24172	2860	21311	31167	3452	27716
8 Long term loans, n.e.c.	19173	1840	17333	12838	2521	10317	19485	3615	15870	23293	-993	24286
9 Trade credits and advances	5302	4176	1126	893	-1159	2052	1414	155	1259	3251	196	3055
10 Other receivables	1326	1309	17	1229	1214	15	1262	1243	18	1919	1900	19
11 Other assets	3843	...	3843	7777	...	7777	12148	...	12148	11106	...	11106
Total Acquisition of Financial Assets	145317	39310	106007	140894	34603	106291	165301	51520	113781	122618	38156	84463
				Incurrence of Liabilities								
1 Currency and transferable deposits	30634	...	30634	27595	...	27595	32718	...	32718	23517	...	23517
2 Other deposits	23474	...	23474	21091	...	21091	12099	...	12099	16723	...	16723
3 Bills and bonds, short term	-559	-505	-54	-195	-137	-58	-47	1	-48	760	672	88
4 Bonds, long term	6770	3435	3336	8155	3903	4252	12385	6720	5665	15028	5215	9813
5 Corporate equity securities	18882	16892	1990	20316	18741	1575	23374	18893	4481	16720	9897	6823
6 Short-term loans, n.e.c.	50421	30449	19972	35032	28113	6919	25250	17926	7324	25245	19662	5583
7 Long-term loans, n.e.c.	14353	9401	4952	14291	10564	3727	22004	17743	4261	25003	18982	6021
8 Net equity of households in life insurance and pension fund reserves	7835	5015	2820	9605	5802	3803	10633	5934	4699	10855	5349	5506
9 Proprietors' net additions to the accumulation of quasi-corporations	...	...	...	...	...	...	...	...	...	...	...	...
10 Trade credit and advances	3544	3544	...	1945	1945	...	181	181	...	3970	3970	...
11 Other accounts payable	2234	...	2234	2478	...	2478	2858	...	2858	3132	...	3132
12 Other liabilities	6554	...	6554	25948	...	25948	37665	...	37665	4124	...	4124
Total Incurrence of Liabilities	164144	68232	95912	166261	68930	97331	179118	67398	111721	145076	63747	81329
Statistical discrepancy	815	259	557	-11389	-3454	-7934	-16780	-3691	-13088	-12888	-5951	-6938
Net Lending a	-19642	-29180	9538	-13978	-30873	16895	2962	-12186	15148	-9569	-19641	10072
Incurrence of Liabilities and Net Lending	145317	39310	106007	140894	34603	106291	165301	51520	113781	122618	38156	84463

	1988		
	TOTAL	Non-Financial	Financial
	Acquisition of Financial Assets		
1 Gold and SDRs	-137	...	-137
2 Currency and transferable deposits	14003	6608	7395
3 Other deposits	3362	3234	128
4 Bills and bonds, short term	-1061	4981	-6042
5 Bonds, long term	6849	9147	-2298
6 Corporate equity securities	7595	3730	3865
7 Short term loans, n.e.c.	66438	1382	65056

Italy

3.24 Corporate and Quasi-Corporate Enterprise Capital Finance Account: Total and Sectors
(Continued)

Thousand Million Italian lire

	1988		
	TOTAL	Non-Financial	Financial
8 Long term loans, n.e.c.	33309	2562	30747
9 Trade credits and advances	6561	3045	3516
10 Other receivables	1400	1380	21
11 Other assets	11452		11452
Total Acquisition of Financial Assets	149771	36068	113703

Incurrence of Liabilities

1 Currency and transferable deposits	29310	...	29310
2 Other deposits	30067	...	30067
3 Bills and bonds, short term	-289	-274	-15
4 Bonds, long term	7679	686	6993
5 Corporate equity securities	13154	9869	3285
6 Short-term loans, n.e.c.	68058	45264	22795
7 Long-term loans, n.e.c.	35674	26378	9296
8 Net equity of households in life insurance and pension fund reserves	13408	6341	7066
9 Proprietors' net additions to the accumulation of quasi-corporations	2597	2597	...
10 Trade credit and advances	3147	...	3147
11 Other accounts payable			
12 Other liabilities	-12520	...	-12520
Total Incurrence of Liabilities	190285	90862	99423
Statistical discrepancy	-16046	-17524	1479
Net Lending a	-24468	-37270	12802
Incurrence of Liabilities and Net Lending	149771	36068	113703

a) Net lending of the capital accumulation account and the capital finance account have not been reconciled and are different due to different statistical sources.

3.31 Household and Private Unincorporated Enterprise Production Account

Thousand Million Italian lire

	1970	1975	1980	1981	1982	1983	1984	1985	1986	1987	1988	1989
Gross Output												
1 Output for sale			317911	390178	460833	489142	568309	627627	695362	781820	853281	
2 Non-marketed output												
Gross Output			317911	390178	460833	489142	568309	627627	695362	781820	853281	
Gross Input												
Intermediate consumption			127843	162329	183678	190109	218926	244475	276817	323535	339705	
Subtotal: Value Added			190020	227849	274455	299033	349383	383152	418545	458285	513576	
1 Indirect taxes net liability of unincorporated enterprises		-1058	-1231	-1458	-2542	-2493	-1397	-2268	342	2140		
A Indirect taxes		2909	3469	4008	4824	5221	6152	7233	8401	11140		
B Less: Subsidies		3967	4700	5466	7366	8014	7549	9501	8059	9000		
2 Consumption of fixed capital		25602	32468	39178	45067	51779	57399	67729	68854	72459		
3 Compensation of employees		44500	54637	72579	78000	88835	97523	104579	114038			
4 Net operating surplus		121024	141975	170688	222689	238615	261561	285610	324939			
Gross Input			317911	390178	460833	489142	568309	627627	695362	781820	853281	

3.32 Household and Private Unincorporated Enterprise Income and Outlay Account

Thousand Million Italian lire

	1970	1975	1980	1981	1982	1983	1984	1985	1986	1987	1988	1989
Receipts												
1 Compensation of employees	30714	71618	185672	225804	262938	302452	337537	376681	406738	441764	487831	
A Wages and salaries	22177	51300	136307	167564	193631	220899	247959	275692	294576	321910	355394	
B Employers' contributions for social security	5325	13514	33324	39866	48441	56665	61718	69401	78978	84477	93396	
C Employers' contributions for private pension & welfare plans	3212	6804	16041	18374	20866	24888	27860	31588	33184	35377	38441	

Italy

3.32 Household and Private Unincorporated Enterprise Income and Outlay Account (Continued)

Thousand Million Italian lire	1970	1975	1980	1981	1982	1983	1984	1985	1986	1987	1988	1989
2 Operating surplus of private unincorporated enterprises	19493	34760	121024	141975	170688	183929	222689	238515	261561	285510	324939	...
3 Property and entrepreneurial income	2447	8221	33522	46983	61709	71464	80889	86794	95347	98067	111761	...
A Withdrawals from private quasi-corporations	85	186	902	1031	1142	1600	2156	2550	2853	3168	3006	...
B Interest	2100	7702	27699	39610	52678	60725	68157	71664	78213	78995	92569	...
C Dividends	200	223	4475	5927	7481	8821	10012	11768	13439	14744	14418	...
D Net land rent and royalties	62	110	446	415	408	318	564	812	842	1160	1768	...
3 Current transfers	10105	24658	66731	87188	105964	130771	145457	166692	183705	204331	227296	...
A Casualty insurance claims	411	1156	2603	3085	4234	4823	5883	7118	8305	9662	11451	...
B Social security benefits	6172	16951	58583	77998	94616	117344	127798	148667	164033	182182	202641	...
C Social assistance grants	2803	5016	...	...	...	...	...	...	...	...	...	...
D Unfunded employee pension and welfare benefits												
E Transfers from general government			828	368	...	...	...	...	...	...	...	...
F Transfers from the rest of the world	289	338	1059	1325	1607	1727	1963	2062	1796	1574	1602	...
G Other transfers n.e.c.	62	369	4486	4780	5507	6877	7813	8845	9571	10913	11602	...
Statistical discrepancy	...	...	6979	7418	8087	7274	7813	8515	9887	10090	9302	10349
Total Current Receipts	62759	132257	413928	509368	609386	695890	795087	878579	957441	1039970	1162180	...

Disbursements

	1970	1975	1980	1981	1982	1983	1984	1985	1986	1987	1988	1989
1 Final consumption expenditures	39057	79906	236603	284030	335448	387830	443965	499587	551844	605104	664904	...
2 Property income	2137	6517	19604	24004	26616	27853	29727	35293	41910	37906	47086	...
A Interest	1972	6285	19008	23490	26197	27435	29401	34943	41550	37551	46611	...
B Net land rent and royalties	165	232	596	514	419	418	326	350	360	355	475	...
3 Direct taxes and other current transfers n.e.c. to government	9438	23099	77122	97354	122403	145448	164306	184883	205293	222747	253908	...
A Social security contributions	6792	16441	44764	53427	67517	79424	87285	97470	111778	121412	133818	...
B Direct taxes	2646	6658	32358	43927	54886	66024	77021	87413	93515	101335	120090	...
Income taxes	...	...	...	...	...	...	...	...	...	...	...	...
Other	...	...	...	...	...	...	...	...	...	...	...	...
C Fees, fines and penalties	...	...	...	...	...	...	...	...	...	...	...	...

937

Italy

3.32 Household and Private Unincorporated Enterprise Income and Outlay Account
(Continued)

Thousand Million Italian lire

	1970	1975	1980	1981	1982	1983	1984	1985	1986	1987	1988	1989
4 Other current transfers	3048	6155	22433	26000	30095	36813	41741	48922	56589	57017	63204	...
A Net casualty insurance premiums	445	1127	2529	3182	4008	4540	5545	6765	7895	9103	10780	...
B Transfers to private non-profit institutions serving households	86	229	... 208	239	284	320	396	447	479	492	537	...
C Transfers to the rest of the world	-	-	... -	-	-	-	-	-	-	-	-	...
D Other current transfers, except imputed	419	815	... 3655	4205	4937	7065	7940	10122	15031	12045	13446	...
E Imputed employee pension and welfare contributions	2098	3984	16041	18374	20866	24888	27860	31588	33184	35377	38441	...
Statistical discrepancy	...	...	1654	1959	2266	1699	1655	1964	2061	2547	2504	...
Net saving	9079	23580	... 56512	76021	92558	96247	113693	107930	99744	114653	130570	...
Total Current Disbursements and Net Saving	62759	139257	... 413928	509368	609386	695890	795087	878579	957441	1039970	1162180	...

3.33 Household and Private Unincorporated Enterprise Capital Accumulation Account

Thousand Million Italian lire

	1970	1975	1980	1981	1982	1983	1984	1985	1986	1987	1988	1989
Finance of Gross Accumulation												
1 Gross saving	11345	28848	... 82114	108489	131736	141314	164872	165329	161473	181507	203029	...
A Consumption of fixed capital	2266	5268	... 25602	32468	39178	45067	51179	57399	61729	66854	72459	...
B Net saving	9079	23580	... 56512	76021	92558	96247	113693	107930	99744	114653	130570	...
2 Capital transfers	295	389	2341	3784	3106	3242	4101	5082	4949	4554	5184	...
Total Finance of Gross Accumulation	11640	29237	... 84455	112273	134842	144556	168973	170411	166422	186061	208213	...
Gross Accumulation												
1 Gross Capital Formation	5341	7411	60071	65498	71540	76867	92452	100621	99273	103230	116174	...
A Increase in stocks	-620	-2666	... 7387	2829	4554	2069	7254	9226	6090	5191	6203	...
B Gross fixed capital formation	5961	10077	52684	62669	66986	74798	85198	91395	93183	98039	109971	...
2 Purchases of land, net	19	-30	-41	-52	-132	-137	-201	-230	-150	-231	-481	...
3 Purchases of intangibles, net	-12	-133	... -444	-884	-713	-732	-954	-700	-422	-685	-555	...
4 Capital transfers	109	103	409	630	2161	3355	1572	932	869	1121	1346	...
Net lending [a]	6183	21886	24460	47081	61986	65203	76104	69788	66852	82626	91729	...
Total Gross Accumulation	11640	29237	... 84455	112273	134842	144556	168973	170411	166422	186061	208213	...

a) Net lending of the capital accumulation account and the capital finance account have not been reconciled and are different due to different statistical sources.

3.34 Household and Private Unincorporated Enterprise Capital Finance Account

Thousand Million Italian lire

	1970	1975	1980	1981	1982	1983	1984	1985	1986	1987	1988	1989
Acquisition of Financial Assets												
1 Gold	...	...	...	...	...	...	...	...	...	...	...	...
2 Currency and transferable deposits	4850	2296	15028	14395	20902	14413	18742	18490	22206	17625	20789	...
3 Other deposits	-34	14679	13266	13239	28427	22727	25414	24802	20721	26181	39626	...
4 Bills and bonds, short term	1	77	14337	22972	9919	15644	19279	15647	5156	29673	41022	...

Italy

3.34 Household and Private Unincorporated Enterprise Capital Finance Account
(Continued)

Thousand Million Italian lire	1970	1975	1980	1981	1982	1983	1984	1985	1986	1987	1988	1989
5 Bonds, long term	778	2100	-1460	5171	9599	33582	34828	36381	52908	66782	...
6 Corporate equity securities	370	377	757	950	356	237	1815	4088	2932	519	...
7 Short term loans, n.e.c.	-	-	21	389	164	40	-201	81	706	260	125	...
8 Long term loans, n.e.c.	826	388	647	36	27	119	478	42	-447	-23	351	...
9 Trade credit and advances	...	...	...	...	...	...	...	...	...	...	...	...
10 Net equity of households in life insurance and pension fund reserves	1231	3146	4668	4683	5150	6363	7835	9605	10633	10855	13408	...
11 Proprietors' net additions to the accumulation of quasi-corporations	...	...	...	...	...	...	...	...	...	...	...	...
12 Other	...	...	766	1100	945	2119	2689	17022	38888	991	-12442	...
Total Acquisition of Financial Assets	8022	23063	48029	62935	75488	94905	111186	122330	138332	141402	170179	...

Incurrence of Liabilities

	1970	1975	1980	1981	1982	1983	1984	1985	1986	1987	1988	1989
1 Short term loans, n.e.c.	149	366	2071	743	1338	1129	2057	3127	4469	244	4632	...
2 Long term loans, n.e.c.	535	704	2572	2479	3233	3226	4019	4712	6625	9911	10618	...
3 Trade credit and advances	...	...	77	714	424	532	727	1500	-114	1232	1647	...
4 Other accounts payable	...	...	...	...	...	...	...	...	...	...	...	...
5 Other liabilities	9	20	...	...	...	...	...	...	...	...	...	...
Total Incurrence of Liabilities	694	1089	4719	4689	4241	4887	6803	9338	10979	11387	16897	...
Statistical discrepancy	1146	67	-1772	-6975	-3036	4176	12951	13915	33619	25708	33453	...
Net Lending a	6183	21907	45082	65220	74283	85842	91432	99077	93734	104307	119829	...
Incurrence of Liabilities and Net Lending	8023	23063	48029	62935	75488	94905	111186	122330	138332	141402	170179	...

a) Net lending of the capital accumulation account and the capital finance account have not been reconciled and are different due to different statistical sources.

3.42 Private Non-Profit Institutions Serving Households: Income and Outlay Account

Thousand Million Italian lire	1970	1975	1980	1981	1982	1983	1984	1985	1986	1987	1988	1989

Receipts

	1970	1975	1980	1981	1982	1983	1984	1985	1986	1987	1988	1989
1 Operating surplus	-	-										
2 Property and entrepreneurial income	18	54	...									
A Withdrawals from quasi-corporations												
B Interest	15	48	...									
C Dividends												
D Net land rent and royalties	3	6	...									
3 Current transfers	330	700	...									
A Casualty insurance claims												
B Current transfers from general government												
C Other transfers from resident sectors												
D Current transfers received from the rest of the world												
E Imputed unfunded employee pension and welfare contributions	314	665	...									
Total Current Receipts	16	35	...									
	348	754	...									

Disbursements

	1970	1975	1980	1981	1982	1983	1984	1985	1986	1987	1988	1989
1 Final consumption expenditures	314	665	...									
2 Property income	10	31	...									

Italy

3.42 Private Non-Profit Institutions Serving Households: Income and Outlay Account
(Continued)

Thousand Million Italian lire

	1970	1975	1980	1981	1982	1983	1984	1985	1986	1987	1988	1989
A Interest	10	31	...	...	...	...	...	...	...	...	...	...
B Net land rent and royalties	...	...	...	...	...	...	...	...	...	...	...	...
3 Direct taxes and other transfers to general government	...	...	...	...	...	...	...	...	...	...	...	...
4 Other current transfers	16	35	...	...	...	...	...	...	...	...	...	...
A Net casualty insurance premiums	...	...	...	...	...	...	...	...	...	...	...	...
B Social assistance grants	7	15	...	...	...	...	...	...	...	...	...	...
C Unfunded employee pension and welfare benefits	9	20	...	...	...	...	...	...	...	...	...	...
D Current transfers to the rest of the world	...	...	...	...	...	...	...	...	...	...	...	...
E Other current transfers n.e.c.	...	...	...	...	...	...	...	...	...	...	...	...
Net saving	8	23	...	...	...	...	...	...	...	...	...	...
Total Current Disbursements	348	754	...	...	...	...	...	...	...	...	...	...

3.43 Private Non-Profit Institutions Serving Households: Capital Accumulation Account

Thousand Million Italian lire

	1970	1975	1980	1981	1982	1983	1984	1985	1986	1987	1988	1989
Finance of Gross Accumulation												
1 Gross saving	18	46	...	...	...	...	...	...	...	...	...	...
A Consumption of fixed capital	10	23	...	...	...	...	...	...	...	...	...	...
B Net saving	8	23	...	...	...	...	...	...	...	...	...	...
2 Capital transfers	-	-	...	...	...	...	...	...	...	...	...	...
Finance of Gross Accumulation	18	46	...	...	...	...	...	...	...	...	...	...
Gross Accumulation												
1 Gross capital formation	18	25	...	...	...	...	...	...	...	...	...	...
A Increase in stocks	...	...	...	...	...	...	...	...	...	...	...	...
B Gross fixed capital formation	18	25	...	...	...	...	...	...	...	...	...	...
2 Purchases of land, net	...	...	...	...	...	...	...	...	...	...	...	...
3 Purchases of intangible assets, net	...	...	...	...	...	...	...	...	...	...	...	...
4 Capital transfers	-	-	...	...	...	...	...	...	...	...	...	...
Net lending	-	21	...	...	...	...	...	...	...	...	...	...
Gross Accumulation	18	46	...	...	...	...	...	...	...	...	...	...

3.51 External Transactions: Current Account: Detail

Thousand Million Italian lire

	1970	1975	1980	1981	1982	1983	1984	1985	1986	1987	1988	1989
Payments to the Rest of the World												
1 Imports of goods and services	10979	28555	95422	117333	131022	135508	167237	188313	168262	185402	208044	245196
A Imports of merchandise c.i.f.	9573	25574	87170	107794	119148	122469	150887	168791	149542	162936	181449	211414
B Other	1406	2981	8252	9539	11874	13039	16350	19522	18720	22466	26595	33782
2 Factor income to the rest of the world	688	2073	5662	10988	13907	13422	16445	18600	18594	18157	20568	28079
A Compensation of employees	43	102	235	335	456	497	571	728	739	917	1298	2403
B Property and entrepreneurial income	645	1971	5427	10653	13451	12925	15874	17872	17855	17240	19270	25676
3 Current transfers to the rest of the world	432	1127	4007	5084	6224	7007	8359	9636	12737	13540	15988	19435
A Indirect taxes by general government to supranational organizations	...	...	...	...	...	...	...	...	...	...	...	...
B Other current transfers	432	1127	4007	5084	6224	7007	8359	9636	12737	13540	15988	19435
By general government	...	...	367	572	856	951	1223	1735	2500	2319	3036	5771
By other resident sectors	...	...	3640	4512	5368	6056	7136	7901	10237	11221	12952	13664
4 Surplus of the nation on current transactions	529	-228	-8645	-10401	-8651	2030	-4662	-7459	4290	-2167	-8144	-16838
Payments to the Rest of the World, and Surplus of the Nation on Current Transfers	12628	31527	96446	123004	142502	157967	187379	209090	203883	214932	236456	275872
Receipts From The Rest of the World												
1 Exports of goods and services	11041	28467	84953	108344	125125	140016	165197	185022	181961	191841	210046	244176

Italy

3.51 External Transactions: Current Account: Detail (Continued)

Thousand Million Italian lire	1970	1975	1980	1981	1982	1983	1984	1985	1986	1987	1988	1989
A Exports of merchandise f.o.b.	8258	22915	66987	87875	97732	110747	131026	146059	144675	150697	166639	193266
B Other	2783	5552	17966	20469	25393	29269	34171	38963	37286	41144	43407	50910
2 Factor income from the rest of the world	999	1654	6452	8802	10255	12256	13709	13222	11687	11435	13064	17506
A Compensation of employees	424	573	1844	2107	2535	2793	3114	3358	3412	3073	3288	3421
B Property and entrepreneurial income	575	1081	4608	6695	7720	9463	8595	9864	8275	8362	9776	14085
3 Current transfers from the rest of the world	588	1406	5041	5858	7122	8725	10473	10846	10235	11656	13346	14190
A Subsidies to general government from supranational organizations	...	...	...	...	...	...	...	...	...	...	...	...
B Other current transfers	588	1406	5041	5858	7122	8725	10473	10846	10235	11656	13346	14190
To general government	143	157	205	227	297	431	220	305	251	330
To other resident sectors	4898	5701	8617	8498	10176	10415	10015	11351	13095	13860
Receipts from the Rest of the World on Current Transfers	12628	31527	96446	123004	142502	157967	187379	209060	203883	214932	236456	275872

3.52 External Transactions: Capital Accumulation Account

Thousand Million Italian lire	1970	1975	1980	1981	1982	1983	1984	1985	1986	1987	1988	1989
Finance of Gross Accumulation
1 Surplus of the nation on current transactions	529	-228	-8645	-10401	-8651	2030	-4662	-7459	4290	-2167	-8144	-16838
2 Capital transfers from the rest of the world	35	9	348	350	561	620	658	917	988	1020	1196	1790
Total Finance of Gross Accumulation	564	-219	-8297	-10051	-8090	2650	-3804	-6542	5176	-1147	-6948	-15048
Gross Accumulation
1 Capital transfers to the rest of the world	29	87	134	126	157	235	229	304	956	461	385	151
2 Purchases of intangible assets, n.e.c, net, from the rest of the world	29	59	101	124	185	92	281	256	418	332	486	646
Net lending to the rest of the world a	506	-365	-8532	-10301	-8432	2323	-4314	-7102	3802	-1940	-7819	-15845
Total Gross Accumulation	564	-219	-8297	-10051	-8090	2650	-3804	-6542	5176	-1147	-6948	-15048

a) Net lending of the capital accumulation account and the capital finance account have not been reconciled and are different due to different statistical sources.

3.53 External Transactions: Capital Finance Account

Thousand Million Italian lire	1970	1975	1980	1981	1982	1983	1984	1985	1986	1987	1988	1989
Acquisitions of Foreign Financial Assets
1 Gold and SDR's	...	...	-13	56	7	-367	25	-385	442	165	-137
2 Currency and transferable deposits	...	...	446	74	-2906	2783	2055	-5595	4333	5214	7628
3 Other deposits	...	...	507	-38	-3204	6354	2633	-7282	-838	1238	2305
4 Bills and bonds, short term	...	...	141	-3	-380	-231	-93	667	2000	3848	7990
5 Bonds, long term	...	...	1383	4651	2254	1663	3894	4148	4583	5984	4613	8400
6 Corporate equity securities	...	...	821	573	14359	2267	11197	9390	15050	-777	-926	11268
7 Short-term loans, n.e.c	...	...	649	907	1639	1966	1894	1053	1363
8 Long-term loans	...	...	...	...	...	...	...	...	...	...	...	...
9 Proprietors' net additions to accumulation of quasi-corporate, non-resident enterprises	...	...	2368	3450	551	2464	4176	-1159	155	196	3045
10 Trade credit and advances	...	...	427	581	80	487	550	546	-179	-130	-1193
11 Other	...	...	10588	21451	-1273	27488	24522	8391	13013	15271	40668
Total Acquisitions of Foreign Financial Assets	...	...	...	...	...	...	...	...	...	...	...	...
Incurrence of Foreign Liabilities
1 Currency and transferable deposits	...	...	-196	-202	-71	-355	-338	-419	-143	754	-74
2 Other deposits	...	...	-2	1	1	1	-	-	36	1722	4719
3 Bills and bonds, short term	...	...	2	152	217	-99	190	-131	352	1330	389	-2113	513
4 Bonds, long term	...	...	60	144	2249	2544	2154	-3303	819	11200
5 Corporate equity securities	...	...	11893	14084	184	16577	19426	3353	3726	1468	19089
6 Short-term loans, n.e.c	...	...	...	...	...	...	...	...	...	...	...	...

Italy

3.53 External Transactions: Capital Finance Account (Continued)

Thousand Million Italian lire	1970	1975	1980	1981	1982	1983	1984	1985	1986	1987	1988	1989
7 Long-term loans	11272	...	5652	12146	8097	4071	3800	7130	5100	12414	...	...
8 Non-resident proprietors' net additions to accumulation of resident quasi-corporate enterprises												
9 Trade credit and advances	728	...	1571	4072	-1314	2462	3145	1393	-1193	2147	...	...
10 Other												
Total Incurrence of Liabilities	47447	17211	19120	31752	7159	25165	28836	15493	9211	...	...	...
Net Lending [a]	-6779	-1940	-8532	-10301	-8432	2323	-4314	-7102	3802	...	...	...
Total Incurrence of Liabilities and Net Lending	40668	15271	10588	21451	-1273	27488	24522	8391	13013	...	...	...

[a] Net lending of the capital accumulation account and the capital finance account have not been reconciled and are different due to different statistical sources.

4.3 Cost Components of Value Added

Thousand Million Italian lire	1980						1981					
	Compensation of Employees	Net Operating Surplus	Capital Consumption	Indirect Taxes	Less: Subsidies Received	Value Added	Compensation of Employees	Net Operating Surplus	Capital Consumption	Indirect Taxes	Less: Subsidies Received	Value Added
All Producers												
1 Agriculture, hunting, forestry and fishing	6470	17123	129	1417	22305	7131	19281	150	1750	24812		
A Agriculture and hunting						21426				23777		
B Forestry and logging						428				451		
C Fishing						451				584		
2 Mining and quarrying [a]												
3 Manufacturing [a]	61676	45429	2971	2268	107810	71394	51203	3469	2188	123878		
A Manufacture of food, beverages and tobacco	4419	4821	2487	1206	10521	5235	5698	2958	1287	12594		
B Textile, wearing apparel and leather industries	6696	7932	95	128	17599	11383	8864	105	93	20259		
C Manufacture of wood and wood products, including furniture	3025	3189	33	52	6196	3523	3519	38	53	7027		
D Manufacture of paper and paper products, printing and publishing	3475	2447	31	123	5830	4003	2483	34	52	6468		
E Manufacture of chemicals and chemical products, coal, rubber and plastic products	7307	4601	109	60	11958	8080	5110	111	46	13255		
F Manufacture of non-metallic mineral products, except products of petroleum and coal	4034	4223	41	55	8243	4848	4729	46	45	9578		
G Basic metal industries	3261	2265	28	17	5536	3875	1977	30	5	5877		
H Manufacture of fabricated metal products, machinery and equipment	25783	15278	140	617	40584	29658	17973	139	599	47171		
I Other manufacturing industries	673	673	7	10	1343	789	860	8	8	1649		
4 Electricity, gas and water	3669	4317	7146	79	15053	4649	4055	7627	168	16163		
A Electricity, gas and steam						15053				16163		
B Water works and supply												
5 Construction	12326	16422	253	542	28458	15852	19111	285	631	34617		
6 Wholesale and retail trade, restaurants and hotels	17466	53352	579	1122	70274	21499	64294	609	928	85474		
A Wholesale and retail trade	14413	45711	498	1098	59523	17717	54756	551	900	72124		
B Restaurants and hotels	3053	7641	81	24	10751	3782	9538	58	28	13350		
7 Transport, storage and communication	15940	11325	242	7482	20026	19302	14351	284	9611	24326		
A Transport and storage	11908	10717	200	6886	15940	14452	12612	237	8416	18885		
B Communication	4032	608	42	596	4086	4850	1739	47	1195	5441		
8 Finance, insurance, real estate and business services	21688	48711	4522	440	74480	25458	61339	5390	489	91698		
9 Community, social and personal services												

942

Italy

4.3 Cost Components of Value Added (Continued)

Thousand Million Italian lire

1980 / 1981

	Compensation of Employees	Capital Consumption	Net Operating Surplus	Indirect Taxes	Less: Subsidies Received	Value Added	Compensation of Employees	Capital Consumption	Net Operating Surplus	Indirect Taxes	Less: Subsidies Received	Value Added
Total, Industries	139235	...	196679	13350	15842	338406	165285	...	233634	17814	15765	400968
Producers of Government Services	42064	...	727	...	...	42791	55357	...	895	...	...	56252
Other Producers	2764	...	175	...	...	2939	3390	...	-44	...	...	3346
Total	184063	...	197581	13350	15842	384136	224032	...	234485	17814	15765	460566
Less: Imputed bank service charge	...	...	16471	...	...	16471	...	...	20091	...	...	20091
Import duties	...	...	20004	...	...	20004	...	...	...	...	23555	23555
Value added tax	184063	...	181110	13350	15842	358846	387669	...	214394	41369	15765	464030
Total bc												

1982 / 1983

	Compensation of Employees	Capital Consumption	Net Operating Surplus	Indirect Taxes	Less: Subsidies Received	Value Added	Compensation of Employees	Capital Consumption	Net Operating Surplus	Indirect Taxes	Less: Subsidies Received	Value Added
All Producers												
1 Agriculture, hunting, forestry and fishing	7892	...	21799	204	1951	27944	9443	...	26488	231	2858	33304
A Agriculture and hunting					26748							32012
B Forestry and logging					430							421
C Fishing					766							873
2 Mining and quarrying a	8375	...	58300	4736	3389	141022	92118	...	63176	5661	4104	155951
3 Manufacturing a												
A Manufacture of food, beverages and tobacco	6009	...	7171	4026	1771	15525	6663	...	7976	4685	2125	17199
B Textile, wearing apparel and leather industries	12811	...	10273	143	170	23057	14621	...	11183	174	178	25800
C Manufacture of wood and wood products, including furniture	4032	...	3705	51	80	7708	4370	...	4072	63	87	8418
D Manufacture of paper and paper products, printing and publishing	4704	...	2839	46	150	7439	5194	...	3318	56	148	8420
E Manufacture of chemicals and chemical products, coal, rubber and plastic products	9296	...	5793	131	65	15155	10663	...	6603	191	74	17383
F Manufacture of non-metallic mineral products, except products of petroleum and coal	5739	...	4863	62	78	10586	6165	...	5006	76	89	11158
G Basic metal industries	4298	...	2702	41	216	6825	4917	...	2407	50	294	7080
H Manufacture of fabricated metal products, machinery and equipment	33471	...	19989	226	842	52844	37631	...	21697	353	1095	58586
I Other manufacturing industries	925	...	966	10	17	1883	994	...	914	13	14	1907
4 Electricity, gas and water	5333	...	7589	9196	143	21975	6189	...	10141	127763	136	28957
A Electricity, gas and steam					21975							28957
B Water works and supply												
5 Construction	18098	...	20234	335	737	37930	19598	...	22279	418	928	41367
6 Wholesale and retail trade, restaurants and hotels	26153	...	77717	893	1067	103696	29667	...	92047	1012	1718	121008
A Wholesale and retail trade	21374	...	65245	796	1018	86397	24652	...	76511	909	1646	100426
B Restaurants and hotels	4779	...	12472	97	49	17299	5015	...	15536	103	72	20582
7 Transport, storage and communication	23344	...	17417	359	12065	29055	26342	...	19269	451	12488	33574
A Transport and storage	17541	...	15016	296	10202	22651	19606	...	16498	380	10647	25837
B Communication	5803	...	2401	63	1863	6404	6736	...	2771	71	1841	7737
8 Finance, insurance, real estate and business services	30044	...	17848	6069	706	107255	37441	...	85858	6719	549	129469
9 Community, social and personal services	192239	...	274904	21792	20058	468877	219898	...	319258	27255	22781	543830
Producers of Government Services	64367	...	1069	...	...	65436	75109	...	1208	...	...	76317
Other Producers	4253	...	29	...	...	4282	5149	...	26	...	...	5175
Total	260859	...	276002	21792	20058	538655	300156	...	320492	27255	22781	625122
Less: imputed bank service charge			21887			21887			26510			26510
Import duties					28416	28416					34829	34829
Value added tax												
Total bc	260859	...	254115		20058	545124	300156	...	293982	62084	22781	633441

943

Italy

4.3 Cost Components of Value Added

Thousand Million Italian lire

	1984						1985					
	Compensation of Employees	Capital Consumption	Net Operating Surplus	Indirect Taxes	Less: Subsidies Received	Value Added	Compensation of Employees	Capital Consumption	Net Operating Surplus	Indirect Taxes	Less: Subsidies Received	Value Added
All Producers												
1 Agriculture, hunting, forestry and fishing	9862	...	27005	245	3197	33915	10928	...	28565	332	3242	36583
A Agriculture and hunting	...	...	...	...	...	32298	...	...	...	...	...	34661
B Forestry and logging	...	...	...	...	...	498	...	...	...	...	...	530
C Fishing	...	...	...	...	...	1133	...	...	...	...	...	1392
2 Mining and quarrying a	...	...	...	...	...	...	...	...	...	...	...	...
3 Manufacturing a	99558	...	75552	6119	4656	176573	109314	...	84947	6662	5162	195761
A Manufacture of food, beverages and tobacco	7421	...	8909	5104	2656	18778	8220	...	9767	5387	2775	20599
B Textile, wearing apparel and leather industries	16221	...	13409	179	160	29649	17554	...	16376	231	183	33978
C Manufacture of wood and wood products, including furniture	4676	...	4232	64	69	8903	5319	...	4657	83	71	9988
D Manufacture of paper and paper products, printing and publishing	5696	...	4205	57	282	9676	6469	...	4869	74	295	11117
E Manufacture of chemicals and chemical petroleum, coal, rubber and plastic products	11837	...	8818	191	92	20754	13315	...	9786	226	128	23199
F Manufacture of non-metallic mineral products, except products of petroleum and coal	6721	...	5225	76	81	11941	7078	...	5419	102	107	12492
G Basic metal industries	5185	...	3876	50	389	8722	5594	...	3905	63	500	9062
H Manufacture of fabricated metal products, machinery and equipment	40765	...	25780	385	913	66017	44613	...	28984	479	1086	72990
I Other manufacturing industries	1036	...	1098	13	14	2133	1152	...	1184	17	17	2336
4 Electricity, gas and water	7062	...	12413	14634	300	33809	7959	...	14452	15074	388	37097
A Electricity, gas and steam	...	...	...	...	...	33809	...	...	...	...	...	37097
B Water works and supply	...	...	...	...	...	...	...	...	...	...	...	...
5 Construction	20342	...	25677	456	921	45554	22117	...	27063	520	1060	48640
6 Wholesale and retail trade, restaurants and hotels	34817	...	105114	1125	1826	139230	39872	...	117753	1427	1372	157680
A Wholesale and retail trade	28747	...	87379	998	1716	115408	33413	...	97327	1261	1208	130793
B Restaurants and hotels	6070	...	17735	127	110	23822	6459	...	20426	166	164	26887
7 Transport, storage and communication	28612	...	27133	479	16120	40104	31434	...	29920	587	16055	45886
A Transport and storage	21126	...	22363	408	13213	30684	23162	...	25652	495	14604	34705
B Communication	7486	...	4770	71	2907	9420	8272	...	4268	92	1451	11181
8 Finance, insurance, real estate and business services	43734	...	103490	8144	557	154811	51121	...	118759	8379	546	177713
9 Community, social and personal services		...						...				
Total, Industries	243987	...	376384	31202	27577	623996	272745	...	421459	32981	27825	699360
Producers of Government Services	85174	...	1419	...	...	86593	94311	...	1696	...	...	96007
Other Producers	5833	...	27	...	...	5860	6995	...	107	...	...	7102
Total	334994	...	377830	31202	27577	716449	374051	...	423262	32981	27825	802469
Less: Imputed bank service charge	...	...	30119	...	...	30119	...	...	34373	...	...	34373
Import duties	...	...	...	40895	...	40895	...	...	...	44655	...	44655
Value added tax	...	...	...	...	...	...	...	...	...	...	...	...
Total bc	334994	...	347711	72097	27577	727225	374051	...	388889	77636	27825	812751

	1986						1987					
	Compensation of Employees	Capital Consumption	Net Operating Surplus	Indirect Taxes	Less: Subsidies Received	Value Added	Compensation of Employees	Capital Consumption	Net Operating Surplus	Indirect Taxes	Less: Subsidies Received	Value Added
All Producers												
1 Agriculture, hunting, forestry and fishing	11175	...	29865	396	2745	38691	11381	...	32218	417	3856	40160
A Agriculture and hunting	...	...	...	...	...	36616	...	...	...	...	...	38009
B Forestry and logging	...	...	...	...	...	571	...	...	...	...	...	548
C Fishing	...	...	...	...	...	1504	...	...	...	...	...	1702
2 Mining and quarrying a	...	...	...	...	...	...	...	...	...	...	...	...

Italy

4.3 Cost Components of Value Added (Continued)

Thousand Million Italian lire

	1986						1987					
	Compensation of Employees	Capital Consumption	Net Operating Surplus	Indirect Taxes	Less: Subsidies Received	Value Added	Compensation of Employees	Capital Consumption	Net Operating Surplus	Indirect Taxes	Less: Subsidies Received	Value Added
3 Manufacturing [a]	115275	...	94106	7515	6047	210849	124050	...	100508	7764	6458	225864
A Manufacture of food, beverages and tobacco	8672	...	11465	6106	2885	23358	9383	...	12479	6305	3444	24723
B Textile, wearing apparel and leather industries	18410	...	17446	298	258	35816	19594	...	17803	279	291	37385
C Manufacture of wood and wood products, including furniture	5507	...	5270	95	167	10705	5770	...	5600	122	177	11315
D Manufacture of paper and paper products, printing and publishing	6925	...	5849	82	374	12482	7699	...	6319	94	339	13773
E Manufacture of chemicals and chemical products, petroleum, coal, rubber and plastic products	14523	...	11505	249	136	16309	12696	...	260	128	29137
F Manufacture of non-metallic mineral products, except products of petroleum and coal	7828	...	6987	158	118	14775	8561	...	8130	116	156	16651
G Basic metal industries	5757	...	4391	68	418	9798	5952	...	4088	59	354	9745
H Manufacture of fabricated metal products, machinery and equipment	46400	...	29936	520	1588	75268	49446	...	32252	510	1554	80854
I Other manufacturing industries	1253	...	1257	19	23	2506	1336	...	1141	19	15	2481
4 Electricity, gas and water	8749	...	15116	20793	327	44331	9530	...	16767	23577	330	49544
A Electricity, gas and steam	...	...	...	...	...	44331	...	...	...	...	...	49544
B Water works and supply												
5 Construction	23934	...	28217	593	1106	51638	24905	...	29865	583	905	54268
6 Wholesale and retail trade, restaurants and hotels	43281	...	129109	1613	2294	171709	47121	...	141923	1864	2894	188014
A Wholesale and retail trade	36214	...	105500	1431	2080	141065	39513	...	116439	1682	2713	154921
B Restaurants and hotels	7067	...	23609	182	214	30644	7608	...	25484	182	181	33093
7 Transport, storage and communication	33913	...	37675	675	18955	53308	36785	...	37805	718	16640	58868
A Transport and storage	25534	...	31726	573	17162	40671	27416	...	30762	625	14410	44393
B Communication	8379	...	5949	102	1793	12637	9369	...	7043	93	2230	14275
8 Finance, insurance, real estate and business services	56549	...	138978	9415	819	205023	62138	...	148960	11226	935	221389
9 Community, social and personal services	[					]	[					]
Total, Industries	292876	...	473966	41000	32293	775549	315910	...	507866	46149	32018	837907
Producers of Government Services	103656	...	1996	...	...	105652	115893	...	2347	...	...	118240
Other Producers	7533	...	329	...	...	7862	7805	...	67	...	...	7872
Total	404065	...	476291	41000	32293	890883	439608	...	510280	46149	32018	964019
Less: Imputed bank service charge	...	...	...	...	...	39853	...	...	...	...	...	40215
Import duties	...	...	...	48071	...	48071	...	...	...	55054	...	55054
Value added tax	...	...	...	...	...	...	...	...	...	...	...	...
Total [bc]	404065	...	436438	89071	32293	897281	439608	...	470900	101203	32018	978858

	1988						1989					
	Compensation of Employees	Capital Consumption	Net Operating Surplus	Indirect Taxes	Less: Subsidies Received	Value Added	Compensation of Employees	Capital Consumption	Net Operating Surplus	Indirect Taxes	Less: Subsidies Received	Value Added
1 Agriculture, hunting, forestry and fishing	11814	...	31643	4501	476	39432	12760	...	34045	526	5424	41907
A Agriculture and hunting						37343						
B Forestry and logging						570						
C Fishing						1746						
2 Mining and quarrying [a]	...	...	...	...	...	...	...	...	...	...	...	...

All Producers

Italy

4.3 Cost Components of Value Added (Continued)

Thousand Million Italian lire

	1988						1989					
	Compensation of Employees	Capital Consumption	Net Operating Surplus	Indirect Taxes	Less: Subsidies Received	Value Added	Compensation of Employees	Capital Consumption	Net Operating Surplus	Indirect Taxes	Less: Subsidies Received	Value Added
3 Manufacturing a	136717	...	114661	9014	6646	253746	151633	...	121249	9480	6659	275703
A Manufacture of food, beverages and tobacco	10274	...	13522	6942	3491	27247	11325	...	13815	7251	3255	29096
B Textile, wearing apparel and leather industries	21171	...	18955	426	246	40306	22710	...	20382	454	308	43238
C Manufacture of wood and wood products, including furniture	6155	...	6419	222	146	12650	6786	...	6619	228	182	13451
D Manufacture of paper and paper products, printing and publishing	8490	...	7346	142	373	15605	9353	...	7591	152	290	16806
E Manufacture of chemicals and chemical products, petroleum, coal, rubber and plastic products	18079	...	14801	306	167	33019	20355	...	15585	339	150	36129
F Manufacture of non-metallic mineral products, except of petroleum and coal	9826	...	9387	159	158	19212	11341	...	9501	172	169	20845
G Basic metal industries	6343	...	6701	67	283	12828	6982	...	7873	77	282	14650
H Manufacture of fabricated metal products, machinery and equipment	54944	...	36231	722	1764	90133	61217	...	38402	777	1965	98431
I Other manufacturing industries	1437	...	1299	28	18	2746	1564	...	1481	30	18	3057
4 Electricity, gas and water	10335	...	16423	26611	358	53011	11247	...	17886	29744	422	58455
A Electricity, gas and steam						53011						58455
B Water works and supply												
5 Construction	27424	...	31527	700	923	58728	29311	...	34599	743	1240	63413
6 Wholesale and retail trade, restaurants and hotels	50816	...	151788	2640	2346	202898	55603	...	163766	2739	2369	219739
A Wholesale and retail trade	42646	...	125331	2425	2134	168268	46804	...	134332	2530	2130	181536
B Restaurants and hotels	8170	...	26457	215	212	34630	8799	...	29434	209	239	38203
7 Transport, storage and communication	39779	...	43680	864	17894	66299	44012	...	48257	939	19175	74033
A Transport and storage	30010	...	35867	768	15332	51313	33044	...	40556	827	16913	57514
B Communication	9669	...	7813	96	2562	15316	10968	...	7701	112	2262	16519
8 Finance, insurance, real estate and business services	69860	...	166016	13105	933	248046	76746	...	185133	14192	1036	275035
9 Community, social and personal services	346945	...	555738	33410	33601	922492	381312	...	604935	58363	36325	1008290
Producers of Government Services	1302241	...	2776			1330217	1415081	...	3284			1447921
Other Producers	8655	...	78			8733	10003	...	92			10095
Total	485841	...	568592	53410	33601	1064240	528823	...	608311	58363	36325	1163170
Less: imputed bank service charge				...	45757			...	49144			49144
Import duties				6444		6441				73960		73960
Value added tax												
Total bc	485841	...	512835	117851	33601	1082930	528823	...	559167	132323	36325	1187990

a) Item 'Mining and quarrying' is included in item 'Manufacturing'.
b) The branch breakdown used in this table (GDP by kind of activity) is according to the c) Column 'Consumption of fixed capital' is included in column 'Net operating surplus'. classification NACE/CLIO.

946

Jamaica

Source. Reply to the United Nations National Accounts Questionnaire from the Department of Statistics, Kingston. Official estimates, together with information on concepts, sources and methods of estimation utilized are published annually by the Department in 'National Income and Product'.

General note. The estimates have been prepared in accordance with the United Nations System of National Accounts so far as the existing data would permit.

1.1 Expenditure on the Gross Domestic Product, in Current Prices

Million Jamaican dollars

	1970	1975	1980	1981	1982	1983	1984	1985	1986	1987	1988	1989
1 Government final consumption expenditure	137.3	477.1	966.2	1095.0	1288.0	1406.2	1541.5	1741.5	2125.2	2436.0	3015.6	3150.0
2 Private final consumption expenditure	709.3	1722.5	3146.8	3681.9	4033.7	4874.2	6277.1	7771.7	8497.2	9801.0	11767.1	13467.0
3 Gross capital formation	368.7	670.1	759.2	1077.2	1224.4	1556.6	2163.9	2837.3	2585.0	3704.8	4963.9	6550.2
A Increase in stocks	1.5	60.5	69.1	123.4	56.6	120.2	183.2	256.1	153.2	160.1	98.6	47.2
B Gross fixed capital formation	367.2	609.6	690.1	953.8	1167.8	1436.4	1980.7	2581.2	2431.8	3544.7	4865.3	6503.0
Residential buildings	...	277.7	333.5	423.7	555.4	690.2	941.9	1101.2	1146.2	1598.2	2329.7	3367.6
Non-residential buildings	...											
Other construction and land improvement etc.	...	23.2	28.0	32.8	33.5	56.4	59.2	53.9	87.3	83.3	274.0	124.0
Other	...	308.7	328.7	497.4	579.0	689.7	979.5	1426.1	1198.4	1863.2	2261.6	3011.4
4 Exports of goods and services	389.0	917.0	2425.8	2510.3	2239.9	2621.1	4955.5	6521.4	7294.0	8404.5	8849.4	10589.3
5 Less: Imports of goods and services	438.0	1186.1	2524.9	3057.6	2918.9	3465.0	5579.6	7669.3	7001.3	8344.2	9848.0	11441.7
Equals: Gross Domestic Product [a]	1166.2	2600.5	4773.1	5306.9	5867.1	6993.2	9358.4	11202.6	13500.1	16002.1	18748.0	22314.9

a) Data in this table have been revised, therefore they are not strictly comparable with the unrevised data in the other tables.

1.2 Expenditure on the Gross Domestic Product, in Constant Prices

Million Jamaican dollars

	1970	1975	1980	1981	1982	1983	1984	1985	1986	1987	1988	1989
					At constant prices of:1974							
1 Government final consumption expenditure	...	392.3	444.7	454.4	471.4	466.7	434.0	419.8	422.2	444.3	484.3	457.2
2 Private final consumption expenditure	...	1482.3	1155.9	1178.8	1215.2	1310.8	1353.4	1328.9	1294.5	1423.1	1552.0	1635.2
3 Gross capital formation	...	574.8	233.4	285.1	300.2	311.2	280.4	282.0	238.4	300.3	350.8	417.0
A Increase in stocks	...	50.0	26.5	43.6	18.3	33.4	37.7	42.0	21.2	19.8	15.2	17.8
B Gross fixed capital formation	...	524.8	206.9	241.5	281.9	277.8	242.7	240.0	217.2	280.5	335.6	399.2
4 Exports of goods and services	...	670.3	648.8	651.7	580.2	634.9	747.0	830.5	886.3	967.4	930.7	993.5
5 Less: Imports of goods and services	...	1022.3	695.2	735.8	704.5	747.6	884.7	1014.1	982.3	1103.9	1282.5	1363.1
Statistical discrepancy	...	54.6	41.4	41.1	36.1	-33.8	-4.4	-9.9	10.5	-47.8	-22.7	-35.3
Equals: Gross Domestic Product [a]	1972.7	2152.6	1828.8	1875.5	1898.7	1942.2	1925.6	1836.1	1869.8	1983.4	2012.6	2104.4

a) Data in this table have been revised, therefore they are not strictly comparable with the unrevised data in the other tables.

1.3 Cost Components of the Gross Domestic Product

Million Jamaican dollars

	1970	1975	1980	1981	1982	1983	1984	1985	1986	1987	1988	1989
1 Indirect taxes, net	97.8	238.7	387.1	517.4	642.6	591.8	934.1	1029.2	2020.9	2538.1	2787.6	3356.6
A Indirect taxes	105.5	270.0	493.8	588.0	699.5	802.3	1028.1	1079.5	2077.5	2669.7	2954.0	3556.8
B Less: Subsidies	7.7	31.3	106.7	70.6	56.9	210.5	94.0	50.3	56.6	131.6	166.4	200.2
2 Consumption of fixed capital	117.0	230.6	421.6	471.9	534.5	627.1	867.9	1082.3	1148.4	1312.6	1371.2	1748.4
3 Compensation of employees paid by resident producers to:	586.1	1450.2	2428.5	2728.7	3151.8	3554.9	4308.9	4891.2	5582.0	6703.2	8012.1	9822.7
4 Operating surplus	365.2	681.0	1535.8	1588.9	1538.1	2219.3	3247.6	4199.8	4748.8	5448.3	6577.1	7387.2
Equals: Gross Domestic Product [a]	1166.2	2600.5	4773.1	5306.9	5867.1	6993.2	9358.4	11202.6	13500.1	16002.1	18748.0	22314.9

a) Data in this table have been revised, therefore they are not strictly comparable with the unrevised data in the other tables.

1.4 General Government Current Receipts and Disbursements

Million Jamaican dollars

	1970	1975	1980	1981	1982	1983	1984	1985	1986	1987	1988	1989
					Receipts							
1 Operating surplus	...	...	...	...	...	...	...	...	...	...	...	...
2 Property and entrepreneurial income	24.6	43.6	63.4	68.1	74.9	98.1	174.4	197.7	243.6	308.2	389.1	...
3 Taxes, fees and contributions	197.9	623.1	1280.5	1434.0	1570.1	1773.8	2456.2	2509.8	4070.7	5010.6	5710.9	...
A Indirect taxes	105.5	269.9	493.8	588.0	699.5	802.8	1028.1	1079.5	2077.5	2613.6	3058.8	...
B Direct taxes	79.9	327.1	726.4	779.9	776.6	876.8	1314.7	1308.2	1858.1	2250.6	2478.4	...
C Social security contributions	9.2	19.5	48.0	53.1	73.4	73.4	73.6	79.1	81.2	85.2	99.8	...
D Compulsory fees, fines and penalties	3.3	6.6	12.3	13.0	20.6	20.9	39.8	43.0	53.9	61.2	73.8	...

Jamaica

1.4 General Government Current Receipts and Disbursements
(Continued)

Million Jamaican dollars

	1970	1975	1980	1981	1982	1983	1984	1985	1986	1987	1988	1989
4 Other current transfers	0.7	1.5	2.3	2.8	11.3	6.1	15.3	164.7	111.5	63.7	53.7	...
Total Current Receipts of General Government	223.2	668.2	1346.2	1504.9	1656.3	1878.0	2646.0	2872.2	4425.8	5382.4	6153.5	...
Disbursements												
1 Government final consumption expenditure	137.3	477.1	966.2	1095.0	1288.0	1406.2	1541.5	1741.5	2125.2	2406.0	3031.3	...
2 Property income	15.8	58.1	349.2	426.0	520.4	599.5	1118.7	1547.8	2065.9	2724.7	2618.0	...
3 Subsidies	7.7	31.3	106.7	70.6	56.9	210.5	94.0	50.3	56.6	58.7	86.4	...
4 Other current transfers	11.6	32.2	73.8	87.4	113.9	119.4	136.8	185.0	200.9	231.3	306.5	...
A Social security benefits	0.7	6.4	18.7	21.7	36.7	43.2	45.0	47.8	49.2	68.5	98.3	...
B Social assistance grants	4.4	13.9	26.9	30.5	39.3	38.5	39.1	77.6	80.3	85.4	123.3	...
C Other	6.5	11.9	28.2	35.2	37.9	37.7	52.7	59.6	71.4	77.4	84.9	...
5 Net saving	50.9	69.5	-149.7	-174.2	-322.9	-457.7	-245.0	-652.6	-22.9	-38.3	111.3	...
Total Current Disbursements and Net Saving of General Government	223.2	668.2	1346.2	1504.9	1656.3	1878.0	2646.0	2872.2	4425.8	5382.4	6153.5	...

1.5 Current Income and Outlay of Corporate and Quasi-Corporate Enterprises, Summary

Million Jamaican dollars

	1970	1975	1980	1981	1982	1983	1984	1985	1986	1987	1988	1989
Receipts												
1 Operating surplus	...	...	970.3	966.6	859.8	1393.1	2238.4	2903.0	3287.1	3750.8	4212.2	...
2 Property and entrepreneurial income received	...	...	550.4	768.7	1033.2	1315.8	1932.3	2500.8	2790.6	3362.6	3759.3	...
3 Current transfers	...	...	8.5	17.3	17.2	20.9	19.0	23.6	17.9	28.0	1658.1	...
Total Current Receipts	...	...	1529.2	1752.5	1910.2	2729.8	4189.6	5427.3	6095.6	7141.3	9629.4	...
Disbursements												
1 Property and entrepreneurial income	...	...	712.6	848.1	1041.6	1289.1	2276.4	3188.1	3165.3	3762.6	4221.7	...
2 Direct taxes and other current payments to general government	...	...	537.0	504.4	425.8	480.1	797.6	705.4	1111.7	1284.2	1302.8	...
3 Other current transfers	...	...	13.0	26.1	25.4	31.8	25.8	29.8	24.2	37.7	1626.4	...
4 Net saving	...	...	266.5	373.8	417.4	928.9	1090.0	1504.0	1794.4	2056.9	2478.5	...
Total Current Disbursements and Net Saving	...	...	1529.2	1752.5	1910.2	2729.8	4189.6	5427.3	6095.6	7141.3	9629.4	...

1.6 Current Income and Outlay of Households and Non-Profit Institutions

Million Jamaican dollars

	1970	1975	1980	1981	1982	1983	1984	1985	1986	1987	1988	1989
Receipts												
1 Compensation of employees	...	...	2498.7	2794.6	3202.8	3639.7	4446.4	5034.3	5724.5	6983.2	8395.7	...
A From resident producers	...	...	2428.5	2728.7	3151.8	3554.9	4308.9	4891.2	5582.0	6658.7	7943.6	...
B From rest of the world	...	...	70.2	65.9	51.0	84.8	137.4	143.1	142.5	324.5	452.1	...
2 Operating surplus of private unincorporated enterprises	...	...	565.5	622.3	678.3	826.2	1009.2	1296.9	1461.7	1659.3	1859.6	...
3 Property and entrepreneurial income	...	...	162.5	198.7	265.0	363.2	523.0	776.7	913.0	1052.5	1184.1	...
4 Current transfers	...	...	293.3	386.0	426.3	617.2	684.9	1257.5	1252.9	1077.7	2695.2	...
Total Current Receipts	...	...	3520.1	4001.7	4572.3	5446.3	6663.5	8365.3	9352.1	10772.7	14134.6	...
Disbursements												
1 Private final consumption expenditure	...	...	3146.8	3681.9	4033.7	4874.2	6277.1	7771.7	8497.2	9849.0	11388.3	...
2 Property income	...	...	94.1	118.1	150.9	203.1	266.5	347.2	378.2	425.2	484.5	...
3 Direct taxes and other current transfers n.e.c. to general government	...	...	329.9	416.4	531.3	627.1	769.4	1131.6	1273.5	1432.9	1615.3	...
4 Other current transfers	...	...	...	...	...	...	...	...	...	...	...	...
5 Net saving	...	...	-50.7	-214.7	-143.5	-258.1	-649.5	-885.1	-796.8	-934.4	646.4	...
Total Current Disbursements and Net Saving	...	...	3520.1	4001.7	4572.3	5446.3	6663.5	8365.3	9352.1	10772.7	14134.6	...

Jamaica

1.7 External Transactions on Current Account, Summary

Million Jamaican dollars	1970	1975	1980	1981	1982	1983	1984	1985	1986	1987	1988	1989
Payments to the Rest of the World												
1 Imports of goods and services	438.0	1186.1	2524.9	3057.6	2918.9	3465.0	5579.6	7669.3	7001.3	8344.2	9848.0	11441.7
2 Factor income to the rest of the world	80.1	120.4	424.4	466.3	530.3	484.8	1366.6	1956.9	1921.2	2460.8	2498.7	2941.3
A Compensation of employees	1.0	2.0	12.5	17.6	17.1	38.0	59.3	153.2	168.3	197.5	202.4	209.4
B Property and entrepreneurial income	79.1	118.4	411.9	448.7	513.2	446.8	1307.3	1803.7	1752.9	2263.3	2296.3	2731.9
3 Current transfers to the rest of the world	5.2	35.1	69.3	70.2	74.7	111.7	115.8	240.6	248.1	223.3	162.8	171.2
4 Surplus of the nation on current transactions	-77.6	-230.3	-271.4	-620.4	-620.3	-739.0	-717.0	-1100.0	-1788.6	-461.9	-1224.3	-515.2	-1400.2
Payments to the Rest of the World and Surplus of the Nation on Current Transactions	445.7	1111.3	2747.0	2973.9	2785.0	3344.5	5961.4	8078.2	8708.6	9803.9	11994.3	13154.0
Receipts From The Rest of the World												
1 Exports of goods and services	389.0	917.0	2425.8	2510.3	2239.9	2621.1	4955.5	6521.4	7294.0	8404.5	8849.4	10589.3
2 Factor income from rest of the world	29.1	140.1	106.2	173.7	241.1	236.5	464.5	490.7	369.1	562.9	614.4	641.2
A Compensation of employees	15.2	37.4	82.7	83.6	68.1	122.8	196.7	296.3	310.8	522.0	428.5	455.7
B Property and entrepreneurial income	13.9	102.7	23.5	90.1	173.0	113.7	267.8	194.4	58.3	40.9	185.9	185.5
3 Current transfers from rest of the world	27.5	54.2	215.0	289.8	304.0	486.9	541.3	1066.1	1045.6	836.9	2530.6	1923.5
Receipts from the Rest of the World on Current Transactions	445.7	1111.3	2747.0	2973.9	2785.0	3344.5	5961.4	8078.2	8708.6	9803.9	11994.3	13154.0

1.10 Gross Domestic Product by Kind of Activity, in Current Prices

Million Jamaican dollars	1970	1975	1980	1981	1982	1983	1984	1985	1986	1987	1988	1989
1 Agriculture, hunting, forestry and fishing	75.0	191.4	392.2	397.7	396.0	450.5	544.2	671.5	820.3	963.3	1065.7	1203.8
2 Mining and quarrying	147.8	220.8	678.0	543.5	338.0	283.7	664.2	569.3	901.8	1147.5	1727.7	2199.3
3 Manufacturing	184.1	444.1	794.1	888.9	1054.2	1398.5	1731.5	2240.9	3017.5	3426.0	3758.6	4497.5
4 Electricity, gas and water	11.8	38.9	75.2	91.4	109.1	169.6	287.7	357.6	569.1	612.1	600.8	682.3
5 Construction	155.7	252.4	279.1	365.9	475.8	597.3	841.5	1014.2	1081.6	1405.0	2021.1	2659.8
6 Wholesale and retail trade, restaurants and hotels	245.6	563.1	996.4	1195.9	1348.1	1543.0	2125.3	2682.9	3096.1	3471.1	3967.0	4787.6
7 Transport, storage and communication	64.5	158.3	244.3	266.1	324.5	417.7	693.5	931.3	1073.7	1316.8	1463.0	1669.8
8 Finance, insurance, real estate and business services	151.6	353.2	635.1	815.5	961.2	1216.1	1398.8	1642.3	2035.6	1117.9	1410.4	1731.3
9 Community, social and personal services	40.2	77.9	122.6	149.4	162.1	180.5	212.9	259.4	294.9	358.4	411.6	495.1
Total, Industries	1076.1	2300.0	4216.9	4711.3	5169.6	6257.4	8499.6	10369.4	12894.9	13815.1	16425.9	19923.5
Producers of Government	91.6	327.8	667.9	754.0	893.8	994.8	1108.8	1152.2	1281.5	1425.5	1660.7	1843.0
Other Producers	18.9	40.1	44.2	47.9	52.6	56.8	70.0	84.5	111.3	117.9	148.2	181.5
Subtotal	1186.6	2667.9	4928.9	5513.2	6116.0	7309.0	9678.6	11606.1	14287.7	15356.5	18234.8	21948.0
Less: Imputed bank service charge	20.4	67.9	155.8	206.3	248.9	315.8	320.2	403.5	787.6	926.3	1166.9	1536.8
Plus: Import duties	...	...	...	...	...	...	...	...	...	...	...	...
Plus: Value added tax												
Equals: Gross Domestic Product	1166.2	2600.0	4773.1	5306.9	5867.1	6993.2	9358.4	11202.6	13500.1	14430.2	17067.9	20411.2

1.11 Gross Domestic Product by Kind of Activity, in Constant Prices

Million Jamaican dollars	1970	1975	1980	1981	1982	1983	1984	1985	1986	1987	1988	1989
At constant prices of 1974												
1 Agriculture, hunting, forestry and fishing	139.7	156.6	152.7	156.1	143.8	154.2	163.7	160.3	168.6	159.5	152.7
2 Mining and quarrying	139.7	152.7	162.2	164.8	170.0	117.7	118.5	95.4	101.6	106.6	101.6	140.1
3 Manufacturing	347.9	396.0	281.4	283.6	304.9	310.8	297.8	299.0	308.3	325.3	331.8	355.2
4 Electricity, gas and water	16.4	23.1	23.6	23.8	24.6	26.8	26.8	27.5	31.3	33.5	33.3	36.2
5 Construction	261.7	210.7	98.6	99.0	147.7	122.4	113.7	104.3	107.4	122.3	140.3	167.4
6 Wholesale and retail trade, restaurants and hotels	457.5	464.5	310.5	328.4	353.6	342.6	341.0	314.9	335.1	313.2	316.3	327.3
7 Transport, storage and communication	109.4	143.8	124.3	126.3	126.9	133.7	137.8	140.5	154.0	165.0	164.4	173.3
8 Finance, insurance, real estate and business services	267.1	299.6	324.6	340.8	345.0	376.4	360.1	346.6	372.4	389.1	421.0	452.5
9 Community, social and personal services	67.3	63.1	54.4	55.9	57.0	56.2	58.0	58.5	62.2	62.4	65.2

949

Jamaica

1.11 Gross Domestic Product by Kind of Activity, in Constant Prices (Continued)

Million Jamaican dollars

	1970	1975	1980	1981	1982	1983	1984	1985	1986	1987	1988	1989
At constant prices of 1974												
Total, Industries	1806.8	1914.6	1532.8	1578.2	1587.6	1640.5	1621.6	1549.9	1629.1	1680.0	1696.6	1869.9
Producers of Government Services	180.1	265.1	351.5	359.4	368.3	370.0	354.4	333.8	322.0	323.7	335.1	323.2
Other Producers	30.1	31.2	18.1	18.5	19.8	19.9	20.4	20.9	22.4	23.4	24.2	23.0
Subtotal	2017.0	2210.9	1902.3	1956.5	1975.7	2030.4	1996.4	1904.6	1973.5	2033.1	2055.9	2216.1
Less: Imputed bank service charge	44.3	58.3	73.5	81.0	76.9	88.2	70.9	68.5	103.7	107.1	131.4	169.3
Plus: Import duties	...	...	...	...	...	...	...	...	...	...	...	...
Plus: Value added tax	...	...	...	...	...	...	...	...	...	...	...	...
Equals: Gross Domestic Product	1972.7	2152.6	1828.9	1875.5	1898.7	1942.2	1925.6	1836.1	1869.8	1926.0	1924.5	2046.8

1.12 Relations Among National Accounting Aggregates

Million Jamaican dollars

	1970	1975	1980	1981	1982	1983	1984	1985	1986	1987	1988	1989
Gross Domestic Product	1166.2	2600.5	4773.1	5306.9	5867.1	6993.2	9358.4	11202.6	13500.1	16002.1	18748.0	22314.9
Plus: Net factor income from the rest of the world	-51.0	19.7	-318.2	-292.6	-289.2	-248.3	-902.1	-1466.2	-1552.1	-1897.8	-1884.3	-2300.1
Factor income from the rest of the world	29.1	140.1	106.2	173.7	241.1	236.5	464.5	490.7	369.1	562.9	614.4	641.2
Less: Factor income to the rest of the world	80.1	120.4	424.4	466.3	530.3	484.8	1366.6	1956.9	1921.2	2460.8	2498.7	2941.3
Equals: Gross National Product	1115.2	2620.2	4454.9	5014.3	5577.9	6744.9	8456.3	9736.4	11948.0	14104.2	16863.7	20014.8
Less: Consumption of fixed capital	117.0	230.7	421.6	471.7	534.5	627.1	867.9	1082.3	1148.9	1312.6	1371.2	1748.4
Equals: National Income	998.2	2389.5	4033.3	4542.6	5043.4	6117.8	7588.4	8654.1	10799.6	12791.7	15492.5	18266.4
Plus: Net current transfers from the rest of the world	22.3	19.1	145.7	219.7	229.4	375.4	425.5	825.5	797.5	613.3	2367.8	1752.2
Current transfers from the rest of the world	27.5	54.2	215.0	289.8	304.0	486.9	541.3	1066.1	1045.6	836.6	2530.6	1923.5
Less: Current transfers to the rest of the world	5.2	35.1	69.3	70.2	74.7	111.7	115.8	240.6	256.0	223.3	162.8	171.2
Equals: National Disposable Income	1020.6	2408.7	4179.0	4762.1	5272.8	6493.0	8013.9	9479.6	11597.1	13405.0	17860.1	20018.6
Less: Final consumption	846.6	2199.6	4113.0	4775.6	5332.7	6280.4	7818.6	9513.2	10622.4	12237.0	14782.7	16617.0
Equals: Net Saving	174.1	209.1	66.0	-15.0	-49.0	212.6	195.3	-33.6	974.7	1168.0	3077.6	3401.6
Less: Surplus of the nation on current transactions	-77.6	-230.3	-271.5	-620.3	-738.2	-717.0	-1100.0	-1788.6	-491.9	-1224.3	-515.2	-1400.2
Equals: Net Capital Formation	251.7	439.5	337.5	605.3	689	929.6	1295.9	1755.0	1436.6	2392.3	3592.8	4801.8

2.5 Private Final Consumption Expenditure by Type and Purpose, in Current Prices

Million Jamaican dollars

	1970	1975	1980	1981	1982	1983	1984	1985	1986	1987	1988	1989
Final Consumption Expenditure of Resident Households												
1 Food, beverages and tobacco	753.1	...	1551.7	1828.5	1898.2	2264.4	3110.2	3922.5	4475.5	5127.3	...	5644.9
A Food	581.9	...	1222.0	1463.2	1441.3	1743.3	2388.3	2988.6	3448.4	3883.8	...	4334.1
B Non-alcoholic beverages	23.3	...	33.2	56.1	62.4	71.3	85.1	120.7	169.2	185.3	...	189.4
C Alcoholic beverages	66.2	...	132.9	128.2	183.1	195.9	283.2	354.6	402.1	481.9	...	509.0
D Tobacco	81.7	...	163.5	180.6	226.2	253.2	343.6	458.5	453.8	576.3	...	612.3
2 Clothing and footwear	75.5	...	107.4	130.3	140.1	192.6	248.2	349.6	459.9	586.5	...	655.3
3 Gross rent, fuel and power	204.2	...	425.5	505.6	575.9	664.1	950.6	1190.0	1289.7	1431.7	...	1486.2
A Fuel and power	48.6	...	154.6	178.3	233.4	286.0	420.6	648.4	629.6	706.6	...	689.0
B Other	155.9	...	270.9	327.2	379.6	430.7	541.9	660.0	677.5	728.0	...	797.2
4 Furniture, furnishings and household equipment and operation	112.9	...	189.1	237.6	280.7	371.9	464.7	540.2	579.0	679.3	...	774.1
A Household operation	59.5	...	94.8	120.5	141.3	192.5	238.1	292.6	333.0	388.4	...	445.4
B Other	53.5	...	94.2	117.1	139.4	179.5	226.6	247.6	246.0	290.8	...	328.7
5 Medical care and health expenses	37.1	...	67.7	86.1	109.4	125.1	167.2	225.8	269.6	330.0	...	400.5
6 Transport and communication	221.7	...	508.2	540.5	596.8	743.8	1023.5	1345.5	1419.1	1551.4	...	1746.3
A Personal transport equipment	126.5	...	298.8	325.2	356.4	441.8	597.8	769.8	786.0	830.8	...	932.5
B Other	95.2	...	209.4	215.3	240.4	302.0	425.7	575.7	633.1	720.6	...	813.9
7 Recreational, entertainment, education and cultural services	77.3	...	123.5	140.0	161.2	194.4	221.2	240.2	257.9	280.9	...	317.9
A Education	6.0	...	8.8	9.4	10.5	12.4	15.2	13.8	17.3	19.8	...	28.4
B Other	71.3	...	114.7	130.6	150.7	184.0	206.0	226.4	240.6	261.1	...	289.5
8 Miscellaneous goods and services	310.4	...	573.2	664.5	745.5	1061.9	1554.1	1956.2	2222.0	2647.8	...	2756.9

Jamaica

2.5 Private Final Consumption Expenditure by Type and Purpose, in Current Prices
(Continued)

Million Jamaican dollars

	1970	1975	1980	1981	1982	1983	1984	1985	1986	1987	1988	1989
A Personal care	...	81.4	115.9	137.0	153.5	196.8	249.2	347.7	389.0	455.7	504.9	...
B Expenditures in restaurants, cafes and hotels	...	134.8	267.5	283.1	329.5	516.4	863.3	1138.4	1371.6	1596.0	1553.6	...
C Other	...	94.2	189.8	244.4	258.5	348.7	441.6	470.1	461.4	596.1	698.4	...
Statistical discrepancy	...	...	4.1	27.3	70.3	93.4	100.1	145.9	193.3	235.9	326.0	...
Total Final Consumption Expenditure in the Domestic Market by Households, of which	...	1792.4	3558.8	4160.2	4574.2	5713.6	7840.1	9916.5	11164.1	12870.7	14108.0	...
Plus: Direct purchases abroad by resident households	...	49.1	26.4	38.1	69.1	88.3	109.4	210.0	228.3	294.3	362.0	...
Less: Direct purchases in the domestic market by non-resident households	...	119.1	438.4	516.4	609.6	927.7	1672.4	2354.8	2895.2	3316.0	3081.7	...
Equals: Final Consumption Expenditure of Resident Households [a]	...	1722.5	3146.8	3681.9	4033.7	4874.2	6277.1	7771.7	8497.2	9849.0	11388.3	...
Final Consumption Expenditure of Private Non-profit Institutions Serving Households												
Equals: Final Consumption Expenditure of Private Non-profit Organisations Serving Households	...	...	...	...	...	...	...	...	...	...	...	...
Private Final Consumption Expenditure	...	1722.5	3146.8	3681.9	4033.7	4874.2	6277.1	7771.7	8497.2	9849.0	11388.3	...

a) Item 'Final consumption expenditure of resident households' includes consumption expenditure of private non-profit institutions serving households.

2.6 Private Final Consumption Expenditure by Type and Purpose, in Constant Prices

Million Jamaican dollars

	1970	1975	1980	1981	1982	1983	1984	1985	1986	1987	1988	1989
At constant prices of:1974												
Final Consumption Expenditure of Resident Households												
1 Food, beverages and tobacco	...	664.0	519.5	541.2	536.7	560.0	607.3	616.7	583.5	638.3	649.7	...
A Food	...	525.1	401.6	448.0	431.7	451.8	490.7	501.7	481.7	522.0	537.1	...
B Non-alcoholic beverages	...	17.5	8.6	13.2	10.9	11.5	11.3	13.2	15.1	14.0	13.5	...
C Alcoholic beverages	...	50.3	46.9	35.2	40.7	42.8	48.0	44.8	41.1	46.3	46.8	...
D Tobacco	...	71.1	62.3	44.7	53.5	53.9	57.4	57.0	45.6	56.0	52.3	...
2 Clothing and footwear	...	64.4	34.7	35.8	36.7	46.2	52.8	63.2	69.0	78.4	81.3	...
3 Gross rent, fuel and power	...	169.0	184.2	183.4	190.1	199.6	217.1	216.9	216.6	229.5	234.1	...
A Fuel and power	...	40.0	43.0	44.5	44.3	43.9	47.9	48.3	50.2	56.6	54.2	...
B Other	...	129.0	141.2	138.9	145.8	155.7	169.2	168.7	166.4	173.0	179.9	...
4 Furniture, furnishings and household equipment and operation	...	85.5	65.0	71.6	77.6	95.4	89.2	82.4	82.7	91.3	96.8	...
A Household operation	...	44.5	42.4	49.3	52.8	66.7	60.4	56.6	58.6	65.9	70.5	...
B Other	...	40.9	22.6	22.3	24.8	28.7	28.8	25.9	24.1	25.4	26.3	...
5 Medical care and health expenses	...	36.2	41.6	39.7	40.9	38.6	39.7	39.7	42.8	46.1	50.4	...
6 Transport and communication	...	188.1	147.3	149.3	162.1	178.4	197.7	209.6	218.7	237.6	257.7	...
A Personal transport equipment	...	106.7	84.3	87.6	95.9	102.5	109.3	110.8	112.1	116.5	122.2	...
B Other	...	81.4	63.0	61.6	66.3	75.9	88.3	98.8	106.6	121.1	135.5	...
7 Recreational, entertainment, education and cultural services	...	76.6	59.7	65.4	72.7	86.6	93.6	96.7	98.3	102.1	110.3	...
A Education	...	5.9	4.9	4.5	4.4	5.8	3.9	2.1	2.6	2.9	4.2	...
B Other	...	70.7	54.8	60.9	68.3	80.8	89.7	94.6	95.7	99.2	106.1	...
8 Miscellaneous goods and services	...	259.6	227.0	223.6	227.3	279.1	314.0	290.8	306.1	341.6	326.5	...
A Personal care	...	66.7	39.6	38.0	39.5	43.5	42.7	45.9	43.4	47.1	47.2	...
B Expenditures in restaurants, cafes and hotels	...	106.4	90.9	83.4	90.5	132.0	163.8	149.2	170.1	194.1	175.8	...
C Other	...	86.5	96.6	102.2	97.2	103.6	107.5	95.7	92.6	100.4	103.5	...

951

Jamaica

2.6 Private Final Consumption Expenditure by Type and Purpose, in Constant Prices (Continued)

Million Jamaican dollars

	1970	1975	1980	1981	1982	1983	1984	1985	1986	1987	1988	1989
At constant prices of 1974												
Statistical discrepancy	...	1.3	...	22.0	18.4	21.3	24.6	28.1	35.9			
Total Final Consumption Expenditure in the Domestic Market by Households, of which:	1280.2	1543.4	1317.5	1362.6	1505.8	1629.9	1637.5	1642.2	1793.1	1842.7		
Plus: Direct purchases abroad by resident households	42.4	8.2	10.6	18.1	20.1	30.6	29.0	35.1	39.9			
Less: Direct purchases in the domestic market by non-resident households	102.9	132.5	149.3	165.4	215.8	296.6	339.2	376.7	398.1	340.0		
Equals: Final Consumption Expenditure of Resident Households a	1482.3	1155.9	1178.7	1215.2	1310.8	1353.4	1328.4	1294.5	1430.0	1542.5		
Equals: Final Consumption Expenditure of Private Non-profit Organisations Serving Households												
Private Final Consumption Expenditure	1482.3	1155.9	1178.7	1215.2	1310.8	1353.4	1328.4	1294.5	1430.0	1542.5		

a) Item: Final consumption expenditure of resident households; includes consumption expenditure of private non-profit institutions serving households.

4.1 Derivation of Value Added by Kind of Activity, in Current Prices

Million Jamaican dollars

	1980			1981			1982			1983		
	Gross Output	Intermediate Consumption	Value Added	Gross Output	Intermediate Consumption	Value Added	Gross Output	Intermediate Consumption	Value Added	Gross Output	Intermediate Consumption	Value Added
All Producers												
1 Agriculture, hunting, forestry and fishing	809.7	417.5	392.2	843.1	445.3	397.7	872.6	476.0	396.0	1022.3	571.7	450.5
A Agriculture and hunting	767.7	399.3	368.4	796.2	424.9	371.3	821.4	453.8	367.6	964.5	545.6	418.9
B Forestry and logging	4.8	1.2	3.6	4.9	1.2	3.7	5.1	1.3	3.8	7.2	1.9	5.3
C Fishing	37.2	17.0	20.2	42.0	19.2	22.8	46.1	21.5	24.6	50.6	24.2	26.4
2 Mining and quarrying	1365.4	687.4	678.0	1377.0	543.5	833.5	936.4	598.5	338.0	828.7	545.5	283.2
A Coal mining	...	...	...	...	...	...	...	...	...	...	...	...
B Crude petroleum and natural gas production	...	...	...	...	...	...	...	...	...	...	...	...
C Metal ore mining	1348.9	677.8	671.1	1358.7	535.9	822.8	917.2	587.3	329.9	804.7	531.3	273.4
D Other mining	16.5	9.6	6.9	18.3	10.8	7.5	19.2	11.2	8.0	24.5	14.2	10.3
3 Manufacturing	2968.4	2164.3	794.1	3212.5	2326.5	886.9	3814.3	2760.3	1054.2	4655.8	3256.6	1398.5
A Manufacture of food, beverages and tobacco	1177.6	803.9	373.7	1393.5	967.9	425.6	1590.2	1100.2	490.0	1885.2	1302.3	582.9
B Textile, wearing apparel and leather industries	153.3	96.6	56.6	162.8	101.9	60.9	177.9	113.4	64.5	188.1	123.0	65.1
C Manufacture of wood and wood products, including furniture	99.0	27.8	71.2	102.8	35.2	67.6	141.9	97.1	44.8	176.1	127.0	49.1
D Manufacture of paper and paper products, printing and publishing	125.8	84.0	41.8	134.7	90.1	44.6	149.9	104.7	45.2	207.6	126.8	80.8
E Manufacture of chemical and chemical products, petroleum, coal, rubber and plastic products	820.3	644.0	176.3	796.2	617.8	178.4	1012.5	778.9	233.6	1279.8	905.2	374.6
F Manufacture of non-metallic mineral products, except products of petroleum and coal	70.7	50.7	20.0	73.7	54.6	19.1	127.0	86.3	40.7	162.1	106.6	55.5
G Basic metal industries	496.1	404.9	91.2	532.5	417.5	115.0	595.4	468.6	126.8	730.7	551.8	178.9
H Manufacture of fabricated metal products, machinery and equipment												
I Other manufacturing industries	15.6	8.8	6.8	16.3	9.1	7.2	19.5	11.1	8.4	25.7	13.9	11.8
4 Electricity, gas and water	257.3	182.0	75.2	308.8	91.4	217.4	360.9	251.8	109.1	423.6	254.0	169.6
A Electricity, gas and steam	215.2	160.8	54.4	259.7	199.2	60.5	290.9	224.7	66.2	342.0	214.7	127.3
B Water works and supply	42.1	21.2	20.9	49.1	18.2	30.9	70.0	27.1	42.9	81.6	39.3	42.3
5 Construction	864.6	585.5	279.1	1174.0	365.9	808.1	1444.8	969.0	475.8	1764.8	1167.1	597.7
6 Wholesale and retail trade, restaurants and hotels	1621.3	624.9	996.4	1844.3	648.4	1195.9	2111.8	763.7	1348.1	2442.6	899.6	1543.0
A Wholesale and retail trade	1278.4	363.1	915.3	1460.4	355.4	1105.0	1634.3	393.3	1241.0	1830.2	421.2	1409.0
B Restaurants and hotels	342.9	261.8	81.1	383.9	293.0	90.9	477.5	370.4	107.1	612.4	478.4	134.0
7 Transport, storage and communication	840.1	595.9	244.3	870.4	604.2	266.1	967.9	643.4	324.5	1235.9	818.2	417.7
A Transport and storage	714.4	554.3	160.1	715.6	535.1	180.5	801.2	577.7	223.5	1047.4	744.3	303.1

Jamaica

4.1 Derivation of Value Added by Kind of Activity, in Current Prices (Continued)

Million Jamaican dollars

	1980 Gross Output	1980 Intermediate Consumption	1980 Value Added	1981 Gross Output	1981 Intermediate Consumption	1981 Value Added	1982 Gross Output	1982 Intermediate Consumption	1982 Value Added	1983 Gross Output	1983 Intermediate Consumption	1983 Value Added
B Communication	125.7	41.6	84.1	154.8	69.3	85.5	166.7	65.7	101.0	188.5	73.9	114.6
8 Finance, insurance, real estate and business services	939.7	304.6	635.1	1200.7	385.1	815.5	1422.8	461.6	961.2	1769.2	553.1	1216.1
A Financial institutions	221.2	68.4	152.8	281.3	76.2	205.1	344.7	95.1	249.6	507.1	121.8	385.3
B Insurance	155.5	80.3	75.2	214.7	109.5	105.2	238.1	123.0	115.1	287.7	145.6	142.1
C Real estate and business services	563.0	155.9	407.1	704.7	199.4	505.3	840.0	243.5	596.5	974.7	285.7	689.0
Real estate, except dwellings	127.7	53.1	74.6	161.0	69.5	91.4	219.7	95.7	124.0	276.7	119.7	157.0
Dwellings	435.3	102.8	332.5	543.7	129.9	413.8	620.2	147.7	472.5	697.7	165.9	531.8
9 Community, social and personal services	277.3	154.6	122.6	335.7	149.4	186.4	367.6	162.6	205.0	407.8	227.3	180.5
A Sanitary and similar services	...	...	...	...	...	...	...	...	...	...	...	...
B Social and related services	79.7	35.9	43.8	97.4	53.3	44.1	119.1	58.3	60.8	139.1	68.1	71.0
Educational services	38.4	13.1	25.3	48.3	16.9	31.4	56.2	22.0	34.2	70.0	28.2	41.8
Medical, dental, other health and veterinary services	41.3	22.8	18.5	49.0	22.0	27.0	62.8	26.6	36.2	69.1	39.9	29.2
C Recreational and cultural services	131.6	95.7	35.9	154.9	42.1	112.8	161.8	45.8	116.0	175.8	126.4	49.4
D Personal and household services	66.0	23.0	43.0	83.4	29.5	53.9	86.7	30.7	56.0	92.9	32.8	60.1
Total, Industries	9933.6	5716.7	4216.9	11166.5	6455.2	4711.3	12299.1	7129.2	5169.9	14550.7	8293.1	6257.4
Producers of Government Services	998.2	330.4	667.8	1132.9	378.9	754.0	1327.8	434.0	893.8	1453.7	458.9	994.8
Other Producers	48.8	4.6	44.2	53.0	5.1	47.9	58.5	5.9	52.6	64.2	7.4	56.8
Total	10981.0	6051.7	4928.9	12352.1	6839.2	5513.2	13685.4	7569.8	6116.0	16068.3	8759.4	7309.0
Less: imputed bank service charge	155.8	155.8	...	206.3	-206.3	...	248.9	-248.9	...	315.8	315.8	
Import duties	...	...	...	...	...	...	...	...	...	...	...	...
Value added tax	...	...	...	...	...	...	...	...	...	...	...	...
Total	10981.0	6207.9	4773.1	12352.1	7045.2	5306.9	13685.4	7818.3	5867.1	16068.3	9075.1	6993.2

All Producers

	1984 Gross Output	1984 Intermediate Consumption	1984 Value Added	1985 Gross Output	1985 Intermediate Consumption	1985 Value Added	1986 Gross Output	1986 Intermediate Consumption	1986 Value Added	1987 Gross Output	1987 Intermediate Consumption	1987 Value Added
1 Agriculture, hunting, forestry and fishing	1348.4	544.2	804.2	1649.0	977.5	671.5	2047.1	1226.8	820.3	2396.3	1435.8	960.5
A Agriculture and hunting	1282.2	774.8	507.4	1560.0	939.5	620.5	1920.5	1170.3	750.0	2246.3	1369.3	877.0
B Forestry and logging	10.9	2.9	8.0	22.4	6.0	16.4	20.8	5.5	15.3	27.2	7.3	19.9
C Fishing	55.3	26.5	28.8	66.6	32.0	34.6	106.0	51.0	55.0	122.8	59.2	63.6
2 Mining and quarrying	1758.5	1094.2	664.2	1562.5	993.2	569.2	1651.8	750.1	901.8	1939.6	794.2	1147.3
A Coal mining	...	...	...	...	...	...	...	...	...	...	...	...
B Crude petroleum and natural gas production	...	...	...	...	...	...	...	...	...	...	...	...
C Metal ore mining	1727.7	1076.6	651.1	1527.0	973.6	553.4	1614.9	728.1	886.8	1897.8	769.4	1128.4
D Other mining	30.8	17.6	13.2	35.5	19.6	15.9	36.9	22.0	14.9	41.8	24.8	17.0

Jamaica

4.1 Derivation of Value Added by Kind of Activity, in Current Prices
(Continued)

Million Jamaican dollars

	1984 Gross Output	1984 Intermediate Consumption	1984 Value Added	1985 Gross Output	1985 Intermediate Consumption	1985 Value Added	1986 Gross Output	1986 Intermediate Consumption	1986 Value Added	1987 Gross Output	1987 Intermediate Consumption	1987 Value Added
3 Manufacturing	6339.6	4608.0	1731.5	8140.4	5899.7	2240.9	9052.1	6034.7	3017.5	10817.3	7381.8	3435.5
A Manufacture of food, beverages and tobacco	2520.7	1749.7	771.0	3353.0	2302.0	1051.0	3932.9	2675.6	1257.3	4538.8	3075.7	1463.1
B Textile, wearing apparel and leather industries	274.5	180.8	93.7	386.3	252.9	133.4	527.9	343.3	184.6	845.9	578.8	267.1
C Manufacture of wood and wood products, including furniture	212.3	141.5	70.8	251.8	167.8	84.0	237.7	158.3	79.4	280.9	186.8	94.1
D Manufacture of paper and paper products, printing and publishing	262.5	161.8	100.7	312.7	192.6	120.1	346.7	212.5	134.2	444.5	272.6	171.9
E Manufacture of chemicals and chemical petroleum, coal, rubber and plastic products	1866.3	1529.5	336.8	2427.5	2017.8	409.7	2433.7	1570.2	863.5	2738.3	1910.5	827.8
F Manufacture of non-metallic mineral products, except products of petroleum and coal	240.8	155.2	85.6	266.3	163.6	102.7	309.5	175.8	133.7	367.0	215.1	151.9
G Basic metal industries	932.5	674.3	258.2	1096.0	778.4	317.6	1201.9	865.7	336.2	1527.5	1101.2	426.3
H Manufacture of fabricated metal products, machinery and equipment												
I Other manufacturing industries	30.0	15.2	14.8	46.8	24.6	22.2	61.8	33.3	28.5	74.4	41.1	33.3
4 Electricity, gas and water	761.9	474.2	287.7	960.3	602.8	357.6	1032.9	463.8	569.1	1206.8	572.8	634.0
A Electricity, gas and steam	625.9	421.3	204.6	793.8	535.1	258.7	799.1	374.3	424.8	913.6	464.2	449.4
B Water works and supply	136.0	52.9	83.1	166.5	67.7	98.8	233.8	89.5	144.3	293.2	108.6	184.6
5 Construction	2469.9	1628.4	841.5	3160.4	2146.2	1014.2	3088.4	2002.3	1086.1	4378.3	2974.0	1404.3
6 Wholesale and retail trade, restaurants and hotels	3544.6	1419.3	2125.3	4628.8	1945.8	2682.9	5408.7	2312.6	3096.1	6635.5	2807.3	3828.2
A Wholesale and retail trade	2566.3	615.8	1950.5	3300.7	860.3	2440.4	3751.7	957.5	2794.2	4774.9	1303.8	3471.1
B Restaurants and hotels	978.3	803.5	174.8	1328.0	1085.5	242.5	1657.0	1355.1	301.9	1860.6	1503.5	357.1
7 Transport, storage and communication	1810.3	1116.8	693.5	2405.9	1474.5	931.3	2744.9	1671.2	1073.7	3280.8	1964.0	1316.8
A Transport and storage	1520.0	1003.9	516.1	2004.2	1349.3	654.9	2282.2	1535.8	746.4	2682.9	1750.2	932.7
B Communication	290.3	112.9	177.4	401.7	125.2	276.5	462.7	135.4	327.3	597.9	213.8	384.1
8 Finance, insurance, real estate and business services	2110.7	711.9	1398.8	2511.6	869.3	1642.3	3070.5	1034.9	2035.6	3588.1	1251.0	2337.1
A Financial institutions	573.6	171.6	402.0	683.0	220.1	462.9	1072.0	320.3	751.7	1342.5	437.9	904.6
B Insurance	332.8	170.4	162.4	388.2	200.5	187.7	405.1	210.7	194.4	452.7	234.9	217.8
C Real estate and business services	1204.3	369.9	834.4	1440.4	448.7	991.7	1593.4	503.9	1089.5	1792.9	578.2	1214.7
Real estate, except dwellings	384.5	176.6	207.9	476.3	223.3	253.0	552.3	260.2	292.1	662.9	313.1	349.8
Dwellings	819.8	193.2	626.6	964.1	225.5	738.6	1041.0	243.7	797.3	1130.0	265.1	864.9
9 Community, social and personal services	485.6	272.7	212.9	577.4	318.0	259.4	645.8	350.9	294.8	789.2	433.8	355.4
A Sanitary and similar services	...	...	...	...	...	...	...	...	...	...	...	...
B Social and related community services	173.1	87.4	85.7	223.6	116.5	107.1	246.4	127.2	119.2	311.7	162.8	148.9
Educational services	81.5	32.5	49.0	88.3	35.3	53.0	101.1	40.0	61.1	119.8	47.6	72.2
Medical, dental, other health and veterinary services	91.6	54.9	36.7	135.3	81.2	54.1	145.3	87.2	58.1	191.9	115.1	76.8
C Recreational and cultural services	197.4	143.5	53.9	204.9	147.4	57.5	224.6	160.0	64.5	275.9	196.3	79.6
D Personal and household services	115.1	41.7	73.4	148.9	54.1	94.8	174.8	63.7	111.1	201.6	74.7	126.9
Total, Industries	20629.5	12129.7	8499.8	25596.3	15227.0	10369.4	28742.2	15847.3	12894.9	35031.9	19614.7	15419.0
Producers of Government Services	1621.9	513.1	1108.8	1824.9	672.7	1152.2	2188.4	906.9	1281.5	2465.8	1042.6	1423.2
Other Producers	79.7	9.7	70.0	96.4	11.9	84.5	126.4	15.1	111.3	135.3	17.4	117.9
Total	22331.0	12652.5	9678.6	27517.4	15911.6	11606.1	31057.2	16769.3	14287.7	37632.8	20674.7	16960.1
Less: Imputed bank service charge	...	-320.2	320.2	...	-403.5	403.5	...	-787.6	787.6	...	-943.4	943.4
Import duties	...	...	...	...	...	...	...	...	...	...	...	...
Value added tax	...	...	...	...	...	...	...	...	...	...	...	...
Total	22331.0	12972.6	9358.4	27517.4	16314.8	11202.6	31057.2	17557.1	13500.1	37632.8	21616.1	16016.7

Jamaica

4.1 Derivation of Value Added by Kind of Activity, in Current Prices

Million Jamaican dollars

All Producers

	Gross Output	Intermediate Consumption	Value Added
	1988		
1 Agriculture, hunting, forestry and fishing	2688.5	1613.2	1075.2
A Agriculture and hunting	2530.4	1544.2	986.2
B Forestry and logging	34.2	9.1	25.1
C Fishing	123.9	59.9	64.0
2 Mining and quarrying	2280.8	813.5	1467.3
A Coal mining	...	...	...
B Crude petroleum and natural gas production	...	...	...
C Metal ore mining	2239.2	789.1	1450.1
D Other mining	41.6	24.4	17.2
3 Manufacturing	11721.3	7971.7	3749.5
A Manufacture of food, beverages and tobacco	4903.0	3323.3	1579.7
B Textile, wearing apparel and leather industries	805.5	551.5	254.0
C Manufacture of wood and wood products, including furniture	318.7	212.1	106.6
D Manufacture of paper and paper products, printing and publishing	482.3	294.8	187.5
E Manufacture of chemicals and chemical petroleum, coal, rubber and plastic products	2769.5	1852.9	916.6
F Manufacture of non-metallic mineral products, except products of petroleum and coal	453.9	262.0	191.9
G Basic metal industries	1903.1	1428.1	475.0
H Manufacture of fabricated metal products, machinery and equipment			
I Other manufacturing industries	85.3	47.0	38.3
4 Electricity, gas and water	1192.4	558.9	633.4
A Electricity, gas and steam	851.8	432.8	419.0
B Water works and supply	340.6	126.1	214.5
5 Construction	5804.6	3785.0	2019.6
6 Wholesale and retail trade, restaurants and hotels	7129.0	2806.8	4322.2
A Wholesale and retail trade	5309.0	1342.0	3967.0
B Restaurants and hotels	1820.0	1464.8	355.2
7 Transport, storage and communication	3525.8	2118.3	1407.5
A Transport and storage	2859.4	1873.6	985.8
B Communication	666.4	244.7	421.7
8 Finance, insurance, real estate and business services	3941.2	1382.5	2558.7
A Financial institutions	1440.7	472.3	968.4
B Insurance	543.6	278.4	265.2
C Real estate and business services	1956.9	631.8	1325.1
Real estate, except dwellings	717.8	341.0	376.8
Dwellings	1239.1	290.9	948.2
9 Community, social and personal services	896.4	487.5	408.9
A Sanitary and similar services	...	...	...
B Social and related community services	364.6	187.4	177.2
Educational services	149.7	58.5	91.2
Medical, dental, other health and veterinary services	214.9	128.9	86.0
C Recreational and cultural services	296.9	212.0	84.9
D Personal and household services	234.9	88.1	146.8

955

Jamaica

4.1 Derivation of Value Added by Kind of Activity, in Current Prices
(Continued)

Million Jamaican dollars

	1988 Gross Output	1988 Intermediate Consumption	1988 Value Added
Total, Industries	39179.9	21537.7	17642.2
Producers of Government Services	3097.6	1443.8	1653.8
Other Producers	169.3	21.1	148.2
Total	42446.8	23002.6	19444.2
Less: imputed bank service charge	-1002.8	1002.8	
Import duties	...	...	...
Value added tax	...	...	...
Total	42446.8	24005.4	18441.4

4.2 Derivation of Value Added by Kind of Activity, in Constant Prices

Million Jamaican dollars

At constant prices of 1974

All Producers

	1980 Gross Output	1980 Intermediate Consumption	1980 Value Added	1981 Gross Output	1981 Intermediate Consumption	1981 Value Added	1982 Gross Output	1982 Intermediate Consumption	1982 Value Added	1983 Gross Output	1983 Intermediate Consumption	1983 Value Added
1 Agriculture, hunting, forestry and fishing	152.7	...	...	156.1	...	...	143.8	...	...	154.2	...	...
A Agriculture and hunting	143.9	...	...	147.6	...	...	134.9	...	...	145.0	...	...
B Forestry and logging	0.9	...	...	0.9	...	...	0.9	...	...	1.2	...	...
C Fishing	7.8	...	...	7.7	...	...	7.9	...	...	8.1	...	...
2 Mining and quarrying	162.7	...	...	164.8	...	...	117.0	...	...	117.7	...	...
A Coal mining	...	...	...	...	...	...	...	...	...	...	...	...
B Crude petroleum and natural gas production	...	...	...	...	...	...	...	...	...	...	...	...
C Metal ore mining	158.3	...	...	160.5	...	...	112.4	...	...	112.8	...	...
D Other mining	4.4	...	...	4.3	...	...	4.6	...	...	4.9	...	...
3 Manufacturing	281.4	...	...	283.6	...	...	304.9	...	...	310.8	...	...
A Manufacture of food, beverages and tobacco	156.6	...	...	152.0	...	...	162.5	...	...	159.8	...	...
B Textile, wearing apparel and leather industries	17.5	...	...	16.4	...	...	17.0	...	...	15.5	...	...
C Manufacture of wood and wood products, including furniture	8.8	...	...	8.6	...	...	9.8	...	...	9.5	...	...
D Manufacture of paper and paper products, printing and publishing	15.5	...	...	16.5	...	...	18.1	...	...	15.8	...	...
E Manufacture of chemicals and chemical products, petroleum, coal, rubber and plastic products	46.4	...	...	47.2	...	...	50.3	...	...	58.4	...	...
F Manufacture of non-metallic mineral products, except products of petroleum and coal	7.2	...	...	7.3	...	...	10.8	...	...	12.1	...	...
G Basic metal industries	27.0	...	...	33.4	...	...	33.9	...	...	37.0	...	...
H Manufacture of fabricated metal products, machinery and equipment												
I Other manufacturing industries	2.1	...	...	2.2	...	...	2.4	...	...	2.6	...	...
4 Electricity, gas and water	23.6	...	...	23.8	...	...	24.6	...	...	26.8	...	...
A Electricity, gas and steam	16.0	...	...	16.2	...	...	16.7	...	...	18.4	...	...
B Water works and supply	7.6	...	...	7.6	...	...	7.9	...	...	8.4	...	...
5 Construction	98.6	...	...	99.0	...	...	114.7	...	...	122.4	...	...
6 Wholesale and retail trade, restaurants and hotels	310.5	...	...	328.4	...	...	353.6	...	...	342.6	...	...
A Wholesale and retail trade	273.8	...	...	291.3	...	...	311.2	...	...	295.6	...	...
B Restaurants and hotels	36.7	...	...	37.1	...	...	42.4	...	...	47.0	...	...
7 Transport, storage and communication	124.3	...	...	126.3	...	...	126.9	...	...	133.7	...	...
A Transport and storage	98.9	...	...	98.9	...	...	99.5	...	...	105.5	...	...
B Communication	25.4	...	...	27.4	...	...	27.4	...	...	28.1	...	...
8 Finance, insurance, real estate and business services	324.6	...	...	340.8	...	...	345.0	...	...	376.4	...	...
A Financial institutions	70.4	...	...	79.1	...	...	75.8	...	...	98.3	...	...

Jamaica

4.2 Derivation of Value Added by Kind of Activity, in Constant Prices
(Continued)

Million Jamaican dollars

	1980			1981			1982			1983		
	Gross Output	Intermediate Consumption	Value Added	Gross Output	Intermediate Consumption	Value Added	Gross Output	Intermediate Consumption	Value Added	Gross Output	Intermediate Consumption	Value Added
							At constant prices of:1974					
B Insurance	...	...	37.3	...	...	38.1	...	...	39.6	...	...	41.8
C Real estate and business services	...	...	216.9	...	...	223.6	...	...	229.5	...	...	236.2
Real estate, except dwellings	...	...	43.6	...	...	48.0	...	...	47.3	...	...	51.4
Dwellings	...	...	173.3	...	...	175.6	...	...	182.2	...	...	184.8
9 Community, social and personal services	...	...	54.4	...	...	55.9	...	...	57.0	...	...	55.9
A Sanitary and similar services	...	...	...	...	...	...	...	...	...	...	...	...
B Social and related community services	...	...	23.6	...	...	23.7	...	...	24.8	...	...	23.9
Educational services	...	...	13.4	...	...	13.3	...	...	13.6	...	...	13.6
Medical, dental, other health and veterinary services	...	...	10.2	...	...	10.4	...	...	11.3	...	...	10.3
C Recreational and cultural services	...	...	14.9	...	...	16.4	...	...	16.5	...	...	17.4
D Personal and household services	...	...	16.0	...	...	15.7	...	...	15.6	...	...	14.7
Total, Industries	...	...	1532.7	...	...	1578.6	...	...	1587.5	...	...	1640.5
Producers of Government Services	...	...	351.5	...	...	359.4	...	...	368.3	...	...	370.0
Other Producers	...	...	18.1	...	...	18.5	...	...	19.8	...	...	19.9
Total	...	...	1902.3	...	...	1956.5	...	...	1975.6	...	...	2030.4
Less: Imputed bank service charge	...	...	73.5	...	...	81.0	...	...	76.9	...	...	88.2
Import duties	...	...	...	...	...	...	...	...	...	...	...	...
Value added tax	...	...	...	...	...	...	...	...	...	...	...	...
Total	...	...	1828.8	...	...	1875.5	...	...	1898.7	...	...	1942.2

	1984			1985			1986			1987		
	Gross Output	Intermediate Consumption	Value Added	Gross Output	Intermediate Consumption	Value Added	Gross Output	Intermediate Consumption	Value Added	Gross Output	Intermediate Consumption	Value Added
						At constant prices of:1974						
						All Producers						
1 Agriculture, hunting, forestry and fishing	...	...	169.7	...	...	163.7	...	...	160.3	...	...	168.6
A Agriculture and hunting	...	...	160.2	...	...	153.6	...	...	149.0	...	...	157.3
B Forestry and logging	...	...	1.5	...	...	2.0	...	...	1.8	...	...	2.3
C Fishing	...	...	8.1	...	...	8.1	...	...	9.4	...	...	9.0
2 Mining and quarrying	...	...	118.5	...	...	95.4	...	...	101.6	...	...	106.6
A Coal mining	...	...	...	...	...	...	...	...	...	...	...	...
B Crude petroleum and natural gas production	...	...	...	...	...	...	...	...	...	...	...	...
C Metal ore mining	...	...	113.8	...	...	91.8	...	...	97.9	...	...	102.6
D Other mining	...	...	4.7	...	...	3.6	...	...	3.7	...	...	4.0
3 Manufacturing	...	...	297.8	...	...	299.0	...	...	308.3	...	...	325.3
A Manufacture of food, beverages and tobacco	...	...	158.6	...	...	156.7	...	...	159.9	...	...	169.0
B Textile, wearing apparel and leather industries	...	...	17.3	...	...	20.0	...	...	23.6	...	...	29.3
C Manufacture of wood and wood products, including furniture	...	...	10.9	...	...	11.0	...	...	10.2	...	...	10.7
D Manufacture of paper and paper products, printing and publishing	...	...	17.0	...	...	15.3	...	...	16.4	...	...	17.0
E Manufacture of chemicals and chemical petroleum, coal, rubber and plastic products	...	...	47.4	...	...	51.9	...	...	55.0	...	...	53.6
F Manufacture of non-metallic mineral products, except products of petroleum and coal	...	...	11.7	...	...	11.5	...	...	12.2	...	...	12.6
G Basic metal industries	...	...	32.3	...	...	29.6	...	...	27.9	...	...	30.0
H Manufacture of fabricated metal products, machinery and equipment	...	...		...	...		...	...		...	...	
I Other manufacturing industries	...	...	2.5	...	...	3.0	...	...	3.0	...	...	3.1
4 Electricity, gas and water	...	...	26.8	...	...	27.5	...	...	31.3	...	...	33.5
A Electricity, gas and steam	...	...	18.1	...	...	18.1	...	...	19.1	...	...	20.9
B Water works and supply	...	...	8.7	...	...	9.4	...	...	12.2	...	...	12.6

Jamaica

4.2 Derivation of Value Added by Kind of Activity, in Constant Prices
(Continued)

Million Jamaican dollars

	1984			1985			1986			1987		
	Gross Output	Intermediate Consumption	Value Added	Gross Output	Intermediate Consumption	Value Added	Gross Output	Intermediate Consumption	Value Added	Gross Output	Intermediate Consumption	Value Added
					At constant prices of:1974							
5 Construction	...	...	113.7	...	...	104.3	...	...	107.4	...	...	122.3
6 Wholesale and retail trade, restaurants and hotels	...	...	341.0	...	...	314.9	...	...	335.1	...	...	370.6
A Wholesale and retail trade	...	...	293.5	...	...	266.8	...	...	282.2	...	...	313.2
B Restaurants and hotels	...	...	47.5	...	...	48.1	...	...	52.9	...	...	57.4
7 Transport, storage and communication	...	...	137.8	...	...	140.5	...	...	154.0	...	...	165.0
A Transport and storage	...	...	109.1	...	...	110.3	...	...	120.8	...	...	130.9
B Communication	...	...	28.7	...	...	30.2	...	...	33.2	...	...	34.1
8 Finance, insurance, real estate and business services	...	...	360.1	...	...	346.6	...	...	372.4	...	...	389.7
A Financial institutions	...	...	85.4	...	...	75.3	...	...	95.1	...	...	99.9
B Insurance	...	...	42.8	...	...	43.8	...	...	43.8	...	...	44.2
C Real estate and business services	...	...	232.0	...	...	227.5	...	...	233.5	...	...	245.6
Real estate, except dwellings	...	...	48.7	...	...	46.1	...	...	45.3	...	...	48.1
Dwellings	...	...	183.4	...	...	181.4	...	...	188.2	...	...	197.5
9 Community, social and personal services	...	...	56.2	...	...	58.0	...	...	58.5	...	...	62.4
A Sanitary and similar services	...	...	...	...	...	...	...	...	...	...	...	...
B Social and related community services	...	...	24.0	...	...	25.4	...	...	25.7	...	...	27.9
Educational services	...	...	13.9	...	...	14.1	...	...	13.9	...	...	13.8
Medical, dental, other health and veterinary services	...	...	10.1	...	...	11.2	...	...	11.8	...	...	14.1
C Recreational and cultural services	...	...	17.6	...	...	16.3	...	...	16.1	...	...	17.7
D Personal and household services	...	...	14.6	...	...	16.4	...	...	16.7	...	...	16.7
Total, Industries	...	...	1621.7	...	...	1549.9	...	...	1629.1	...	...	1744.2
Producers of Government Services	...	...	354.4	...	...	333.8	...	...	322.0	...	...	323.6
Other Producers	...	...	20.4	...	...	20.9	...	...	22.4	...	...	23.2
Total	...	...	1996.5	...	...	1904.6	...	...	1973.5	...	...	2091.0
Less: Imputed bank service charge	...	...	70.9	...	...	68.5	...	...	103.7	...	...	111.2
Import duties	...	...	...	...	...	...	...	...	...	...	...	...
Value added tax	...	...	...	...	...	...	...	...	...	...	...	...
Total	...	...	1925.6	...	...	1836.1	...	...	1869.8	...	...	1979.8

	1988		
	Gross Output	Intermediate Consumption	Value Added
		At constant prices of:1974	
		All Producers	
1 Agriculture, hunting, forestry and fishing	...	...	161.1
A Agriculture and hunting	...	...	150.7
B Forestry and logging	...	...	2.8
C Fishing	...	...	7.6
2 Mining and quarrying	...	...	101.6
A Coal mining	...	...	...
B Crude petroleum and natural gas production	...	...	...
C Metal ore mining	...	...	97.6
D Other mining	...	...	4.0

Jamaica

4.2 Derivation of Value Added by Kind of Activity, in Constant Prices
(Continued)

Million Jamaican dollars

	1988			
	Gross Output	Intermediate Consumption	Value Added	
				At constant prices of:1974
3 Manufacturing	...	...	328.5	
A Manufacture of food, beverages and tobacco	...	...	170.0	
B Textile, wearing apparel and leather industries	...	...	26.2	
C Manufacture of wood and wood products, including furniture	...	...	11.0	
D Manufacture of paper and paper products, printing and publishing	...	...	18.0	
E Manufacture of chemicals and chemical petroleum, coal, rubber and plastic products	...	...	53.9	
F Manufacture of non-metallic mineral products, except products of petroleum and coal	...	...	14.7	
G Basic metal industries	...	...	31.4	
H Manufacture of fabricated metal products, machinery and equipment	...	...		
I Other manufacturing industries	...	...	3.3	
4 Electricity, gas and water	...	...	33.3	
A Electricity, gas and steam	...	...	20.7	
B Water works and supply	...	...	12.7	
5 Construction	...	...	140.2	
6 Wholesale and retail trade, restaurants and hotels	...	...	368.9	
A Wholesale and retail trade	...	...	316.8	
B Restaurants and hotels	...	...	52.1	
7 Transport, storage and communication	...	...	167.6	
A Transport and storage	...	...	133.2	
B Communication	...	...	34.4	
8 Finance, insurance, real estate and business services	...	...	404.4	
A Financial institutions	...	...	104.1	
B Insurance	...	...	45.5	
C Real estate and business services	...	...	254.8	
Real estate, except dwellings	...	...	49.2	
Dwellings	...	...	205.6	
9 Community, social and personal services	...	...	62.4	
A Sanitary and similar services	...	...	...	
B Social and related community services	...	...	28.5	
Educational services	...	...	14.3	
Medical, dental, other health and veterinary services	...	...	14.2	
C Recreational and cultural services	...	...	17.4	
D Personal and household services	...	...	16.6	
Total, Industries	...	...	1768.1	
Producers of Government Services	...	...	333.7	
Other Producers	...	...	24.2	
Total	...	...	2126.0	
Less: Imputed bank service charge	...	...	114.2	
Import duties	...	...	...	
Value added tax	...	...	...	
Total	...	...	2011.8	

Jamaica

4.3 Cost Components of Value Added

Million Jamaican dollars

	1980						1981					
	Compensation of Employees	Capital Consumption	Net Operating Surplus	Indirect Taxes	Less: Subsidies Received	Value Added	Compensation of Employees	Capital Consumption	Net Operating Surplus	Indirect Taxes	Less: Subsidies Received	Value Added
All Producers												
1 Agriculture, hunting, forestry and fishing	155.3	14.9	218.9	10.4	7.4	392.2	165.1	15.1	216.5	10.4	9.3	397.7
A Agriculture and hunting	145.9	...	...	...	...	368.4	154.7	...	...	...	...	371.3
B Forestry and logging	1.4	...	...	...	...	3.6	1.5	...	...	...	...	3.7
C Fishing	8.0	...	...	...	...	20.2	9.0	...	...	...	...	22.8
2 Mining and quarrying	114.2	61.7	497.7	4.4	-	678.0	126.6	62.8	349.2	4.9	-	543.5
A Coal mining	...	...	...	...	...	...	...	...	...	...	...	...
B Crude petroleum and natural gas production	...	...	...	...	...	...	...	...	...	...	...	...
C Metal ore mining	108.3	...	...	...	...	671.1	120.4	...	...	...	...	535.9
D Other mining	5.8	...	...	...	...	6.9	6.2	...	...	...	...	7.5
3 Manufacturing	359.6	46.2	106.8	282.6	1.1	794.1	403.4	48.7	138.0	296.9	1.1	885.9
A Manufacture of food, beverages and tobacco	151.2	...	...	...	...	373.7	177.9	...	...	...	...	425.6
B Textile, wearing apparel and leather industries	30.9	...	...	...	...	56.6	33.7	...	...	...	...	60.9
C Manufacture of wood and wood products, including furniture	16.6	...	...	...	...	27.8	17.7	...	...	...	...	35.2
D Manufacture of paper and paper products, printing and publishing	31.3	...	...	...	...	41.8	33.5	...	...	...	...	44.6
E Manufacture of chemicals and chemical petroleum, coal, rubber and plastic products	32.2	...	...	...	...	176.3	36.9	...	...	...	...	178.4
F Manufacture of non-metallic mineral products, except products of petroleum and coal	18.2	...	...	...	...	20.0	18.8	...	...	...	...	19.1
G Basic metal industries	75.8	...	...	...	...	91.2	81.8	...	...	...	...	115.0
H Manufacture of fabricated metal products, machinery and equipment		...						...				
I Other manufacturing industries	3.3	...	...	...	...	6.8	3.3	...	...	...	...	7.2
4 Electricity, gas and water	41.1	43.3	-9.2	-	-	75.2	45.2	46.5	-0.5	-	-	91.4
A Electricity, gas and steam	18.7	...	...	...	...	54.4	21.3	...	...	...	...	60.5
B Water works and supply	22.4	...	...	...	...	20.9	23.9	...	...	...	...	30.9
5 Construction	230.1	21.2	27.7	-	-	279.1	297.6	27.0	41.3	-	-	365.9
6 Wholesale and retail trade, restaurants and hotels [a]	317.7	17.7	593.9	108.2	51.8	996.4	335.1	21.9	669.1	177.3	20.8	1195.9
A Wholesale and retail trade	247.3	...	...	...	...	915.3	257.5	...	...	...	...	1105.0
B Restaurants and hotels	70.4	...	...	...	...	81.1	77.6	...	...	...	...	90.9
7 Transport, storage and communication	204.3	78.6	-11.7	15.5	42.4	244.3	194.5	80.4	12.0	15.5	36.4	266.1
A Transport and storage	152.4	...	...	...	...	160.1	147.2	...	...	...	...	180.5
B Communication	51.9	...	...	...	...	84.1	47.3	...	...	...	...	85.5
8 Finance, insurance, real estate and business services	216.0	123.8	247.6	49.0	1.3	635.1	266.2	152.8	338.2	59.3	1.1	815.5
A Financial institutions	83.4	...	...	...	...	152.8	107.7	...	...	...	...	205.1
B Insurance	66.3	...	...	...	...	75.2	76.1	...	...	...	...	105.2
C Real estate and business services	66.3	...	...	...	...	407.1	82.5	...	...	...	...	505.3
Real estate, except dwellings	41.2	...	...	...	...	74.6	49.8	...	...	...	...	91.4
Dwellings	25.1	...	...	...	...	332.5	32.7	...	...	...	...	413.8
9 Community, social and personal services [a]	78.6	14.0	19.9	23.5	2.7	122.6	93.6	16.4	31.4	23.2	2.0	149.4
A Sanitary and similar services	...	...	...	...	...	...	...	...	...	...	...	...
B Social and related community services	46.5	...	...	...	...	43.8	57.2	...	...	...	...	53.3
Educational services	30.4	...	...	...	...	25.3	38.1	...	...	...	...	31.4
Medical, dental, other health and veterinary services	16.1	...	...	...	...	18.5	19.1	...	...	...	...	22.0
C Recreational and cultural services	16.7	...	...	...	...	35.9	19.0	...	...	...	...	42.1
D Personal and household services	15.4	...	...	...	...	43.0	17.4	...	...	...	...	53.9

Jamaica

4.3 Cost Components of Value Added (Continued)

Million Jamaican dollars

	1980						1981					
	Compensation of Employees	Capital Consumption	Net Operating Surplus	Indirect Taxes	Less: Subsidies Received	Value Added	Compensation of Employees	Capital Consumption	Net Operating Surplus	Indirect Taxes	Less: Subsidies Received	Value Added
Total, Industries	1716.9	421.6	1691.7	493.6	106.7	4216.9	1927.4	471.7	1795.2	587.6	70.6	4711.3
Producers of Government Services	667.7	-	0.1	-	-	667.8	753.8	-	-	0.2	-	754.0
Other Producers	43.9	0.2	0.1	0.1	-	44.2	47.6	0.2	-	0.1	-	47.9
Total	2428.5	421.6	1691.7	493.8	106.7	4928.9	2728.7	471.9	1795.2	588.0	70.6	5513.2
Less: Imputed bank service charge		155.8				155.8		206.3				206.3
Import duties	...	...	...	...	...	...	...	...	...	...	...	...
Value added tax	...	...	...	...	...	...	...	...	...	...	...	...
Total	2428.5	421.6	1535.8	493.8	106.7	4773.1	2728.7	471.9	1588.9	588.0	70.6	5306.9

	1982						1983					
	Compensation of Employees	Capital Consumption	Net Operating Surplus	Indirect Taxes	Less: Subsidies Received	Value Added	Compensation of Employees	Capital Consumption	Net Operating Surplus	Indirect Taxes	Less: Subsidies Received	Value Added

All Producers

1 Agriculture, hunting, forestry and fishing	183.2	17.8	194.5	12.0	11.4	396.0	214.8	21.9	205.8	14.2	6.0	450.5
A Agriculture and hunting	171.4	...	...	...	...	367.6	201.0	...	...	...	...	418.9
B Forestry and logging	1.7	...	...	...	...	3.8	2.4	...	...	...	...	5.3
C Fishing	10.0	...	...	...	...	24.6	11.3	...	...	...	...	26.4
2 Mining and quarrying	145.2	65.5	119.6	7.7	-	338.0	128.1	59.3	88.5	7.8	-	283.7
A Coal mining												
B Crude petroleum and natural gas production												
C Metal ore mining	138.7	...	...	...	...	329.9	119.8	...	...	...	...	273.4
D Other mining	6.5	...	...	...	...	8.0	8.3	...	...	...	...	10.3
3 Manufacturing	455.7	64.3	204.2	331.5	1.4	1054.2	526.3	77.2	503.4	389.7	98.2	1398.5
A Manufacture of food, beverages and tobacco	204.6	...	...	...	...	490.0	240.6	...	...	...	...	582.9
B Textile, wearing apparel and leather industries	33.9	...	...	...	...	64.5	38.0	...	...	...	...	65.1
C Manufacture of wood and wood products, including furniture	26.8	...	...	...	...	44.8	30.4	...	...	...	...	49.1
D Manufacture of paper and paper products, printing and publishing	37.5	...	...	...	...	45.2	40.8	...	...	...	...	80.8
E Manufacture of chemicals and chemical petroleum, coal, rubber and plastic products	43.4	...	...	...	...	233.6	50.3	...	...	...	...	374.6
F Manufacture of non-metallic mineral products, except of petroleum and coal	20.6	...	...	...	...	40.7	23.4	...	...	...	...	55.5
G Basic metal industries	85.1	...	...	...	...	126.8	97.8	...	...	...	...	178.9
H Manufacture of fabricated metal products, machinery and equipment												
I Other manufacturing industries	3.7	...	...	...	...	8.4	4.9	...	...	...	...	11.8
4 Electricity, gas and water	57.9	51.0	0.2	-	-	109.1	65.9	57.3	46.2	0.1	-	169.6
A Electricity, gas and steam	26.9	...	...	...	...	66.2	27.4	...	...	...	...	127.3
B Water works and supply	30.9	...	...	...	...	42.9	38.6	...	...	...	...	42.3
5 Construction	370.4	27.2	78.2	-	-	475.8	443.9	30.4	123.0	0.7	0.4	597.7
6 Wholesale and retail trade, restaurants and hotels a	353.9	23.9	742.3	220.7	15.9	1348.1	372.4	48.4	918.0	248.7	72.5	1543.0
A Wholesale and retail trade	270.0	...	...	...	...	1241.0	266.3	...	...	...	...	1409.0
B Restaurants and hotels	83.9	...	...	...	...	107.1	106.1	...	...	...	...	134.0
7 Transport, storage and communication	221.0	87.0	26.0	16.9	26.4	324.5	257.9	98.4	76.4	17.4	32.3	417.7
A Transport and storage	162.7	...	...	...	...	223.5	196.4	...	...	...	...	303.1
B Communication	58.2	...	...	...	...	101.0	61.4	...	...	...	...	114.6
8 Finance, insurance, real estate and business services	314.4	178.4	391.9	77.8	1.4	961.2	378.0	211.5	540.6	87.1	1.1	1216.1
A Financial institutions	117.8	...	...	...	...	249.6	142.7	...	...	...	...	385.3
B Insurance	96.1	...	...	...	...	115.1	120.4	...	...	...	...	142.1
C Real estate and business services	100.6	...	...	...	...	596.5	114.9	...	...	...	...	688.7
Real estate, except dwellings	63.4	...	...	...	...	124.0	73.1	...	...	...	...	157.0

Jamaica

4.3 Cost Components of Value Added (Continued)

Million Jamaican dollars

	1982						1983					
	Compensation of Employees	Capital Consumption	Net Operating Surplus	Indirect Taxes	Less: Subsidies Received	Value Added	Compensation of Employees	Capital Consumption	Net Operating Surplus	Indirect Taxes	Less: Subsidies Received	Value Added
Dwellings	...	...	...	...	...	472.5	41.8	...	...	...	...	531.8
9 Community, social and personal services a	104.5	19.1	30.2	32.4	0.4	162.6	116.6	22.5	33.0	36.3	-	180.5
A Sanitary and similar services	...	...	...	...	...	...	...	...	...	...	...	...
B Social and related community services	65.5	...	60.9	8.0	...	73.9	...	...	...	...	...	71.0
Educational services	42.1	...	34.2	48.2	...	48.2	...	...	...	...	...	41.8
Medical, dental, other health and veterinary services	23.4	...	...	...	...	26.6	25.7	...	...	...	...	29.2
C Recreational and cultural services	21.2	...	...	...	...	45.8	23.2	...	...	...	...	49.4
D Personal and household services	17.8	...	...	...	...	56.0	19.5	...	...	...	...	60.1
Total, Industries	2206.0	...	1787.0	699.1	56.9	5169.6	2503.9	626.8	2535.1	802.0	210.5	6257.4
Producers of Government Services	893.6	-	-	0.3	-	893.8	994.7	-	-	-	-	994.8
Other Producers	52.2	0.2	-	0.2	...	52.6	56.3	0.3	-	0.2	-	56.8
Total	3151.8	534.3	1787.0	699.5	56.9	6116.0	3554.9	627.1	2535.1	802.3	210.5	7309.0
Less: Imputed bank service charge						248.9						315.8
Import duties	...	...	...	...	...	...	...	...	...	...	...	...
Value added tax	...	...	...	...	...	...	...	...	...	...	...	...
Total	3151.8	534.5	1538.1	699.5	56.9	5867.1	3554.9	627.1	2219.3	802.3	210.5	6993.2

	1984						1985					
	Compensation of Employees	Capital Consumption	Net Operating Surplus	Indirect Taxes	Less: Subsidies Received	Value Added	Compensation of Employees	Capital Consumption	Net Operating Surplus	Indirect Taxes	Less: Subsidies Received	Value Added
1 Agriculture, hunting, forestry and fishing	262.6	32.1	231.9	19.1	1.5	544.2	362.9	40.6	244.4	23.8	0.2	671.5
A Agriculture and hunting	246.7	...	...	...	...	507.4	341.0	...	...	...	...	620.5
B Forestry and logging	3.7	...	...	...	...	8.0	7.5	...	...	...	...	16.4
C Fishing	12.2	...	...	...	...	28.8	14.4	...	...	...	...	34.6
2 Mining and quarrying	188.2	125.8	337.1	13.1	-	664.2	168.9	130.6	252.9	17.0	-	569.3
A Coal mining	...	...	...	...	...	...	...	...	...	...	...	...
B Crude petroleum and natural gas production	...	...	...	...	...	...	...	...	...	...	...	...
C Metal ore mining	179.2	...	...	...	...	651.1	157.9	...	...	...	...	553.4
D Other mining	9.0	...	...	...	...	13.2	11.0	...	...	...	...	15.9
3 Manufacturing	627.7	103.1	545.6	466.6	11.5	1731.5	791.9	119.1	807.8	530.2	8.0	2240.9
A Manufacture of food, beverages and tobacco	275.7	...	...	...	...	771.0	351.6	...	...	...	...	1051.0
B Textile, wearing apparel and leather industries	47.1	...	...	...	...	93.7	65.8	...	...	...	...	133.4
C Manufacture of wood and wood products, including furniture	34.8	...	...	...	...	70.8	42.0	...	...	...	...	84.0
D Manufacture of paper and paper products, printing and publishing	47.5	...	...	...	...	100.7	58.8	...	...	...	...	120.1
E Manufacture of chemicals and chemical petroleum, coal, rubber and plastic products	57.5	...	...	...	...	336.8	74.4	...	...	...	...	409.7
F Manufacture of non-metallic mineral products, except products of petroleum and coal	28.1	...	...	...	...	85.6	34.2	...	...	...	...	102.7
G Basic metal industries	131.2	...	...	...	...	258.2	156.4	...	...	...	...	317.6
H Manufacture of fabricated metal products, machinery and equipment												
I Other manufacturing industries	5.8	...	...	...	...	14.8	8.7	...	...	...	...	22.2
4 Electricity, gas and water	81.3	105.1	100.7	0.5	-	287.7	106.3	157.7	92.6	1.1	-	357.6
A Electricity, gas and steam	29.5	...	...	...	...	204.6	39.9	...	...	...	...	258.7
B Water works and supply	51.9	...	...	...	...	83.1	66.4	...	...	...	...	98.8

962

Jamaica

4.3 Cost Components of Value Added
(Continued)

Million Jamaican dollars

	1984						1985					
	Compensation of Employees	Capital Consumption	Net Operating Surplus	Indirect Taxes	Less: Subsidies Received	Value Added	Compensation of Employees	Capital Consumption	Net Operating Surplus	Indirect Taxes	Less: Subsidies Received	Value Added
5 Construction	564.3	33.1	240.2	3.9	-	841.5	516.4	22.2	470.2	5.4	-	1014.2
6 Wholesale and retail trade, restaurants and hotels [a]	488.1	41.8	1269.7	336.3	53.8	2125.3	594.1	60.7	1716.1	254.9	9.4	2682.9
A Wholesale and retail trade	356.5	...	...	...	...	1950.5	418.1	...	...	...	...	2440.4
B Restaurants and hotels	131.7	...	...	...	...	174.8	175.9	...	...	...	...	242.5
7 Transport, storage and communication	318.1	143.9	231.3	24.4	24.1	693.5	399.6	200.6	328.8	32.5	30.2	931.3
A Transport and storage	246.0	...	...	...	...	516.1	301.0	...	...	...	...	654.9
B Communication	72.1	...	...	...	...	177.4	98.6	...	...	...	...	276.5
8 Finance, insurance, real estate and business services	459.6	253.6	587.3	101.4	3.1	1398.8	543.6	312.3	669.0	120.0	2.5	1642.3
A Financial institutions	175.6	...	...	...	...	402.0	214.0	...	...	...	...	462.9
B Insurance	138.1	...	...	...	...	162.4	157.8	...	...	...	...	187.7
C Real estate and business services	145.9	...	...	...	...	834.4	171.8	...	...	...	...	991.7
Real estate, except dwellings	96.0	...	...	...	...	207.9	112.5	...	...	...	...	253.0
Dwellings	49.9	...	...	...	...	626.6	59.3	...	...	...	...	738.6
9 Community, social and personal services [a]	140.8	28.9	23.9	62.4	-	212.9	171.9	38.0	21.7	94.4	-	259.4
A Sanitary and similar services	...	...	...	...	...	...	...	...	...	...	...	...
B Social and related community services	90.0	...	...	...	...	85.7	110.9	...	...	...	...	107.1
Educational services	55.9	...	...	...	...	49.0	60.5	...	...	...	...	53.0
Medical, dental, other health and veterinary services	34.1	...	...	...	...	36.7	50.4	...	...	...	...	54.1
C Recreational and cultural services	25.8	...	...	...	...	53.9	28.4	...	...	...	...	57.5
D Personal and household services	25.0	...	...	...	...	73.4	32.6	...	...	...	...	94.8
Total, Industries	3130.9	867.5	3567.7	1027.7	94.0	8499.8	3655.5	1081.7	4603.3	1079.2	50.3	10369.4
Producers of Government Services	1108.8	-	-	-	-	1108.8	1152.2	-	-	-	-	1152.2
Other Producers	69.2	0.4	-	0.3	-	70.0	83.5	0.5	-	0.4	-	84.5
Total	4308.9	867.9	3567.7	1028.1	94.0	9678.6	4891.2	1082.3	4603.3	1079.5	50.3	11606.1
Less: Imputed bank service charge	...	...	320.2	...	...	320.2	...	...	403.5	...	...	403.5
Import duties	...	...	...	...	...	...	...	...	...	...	...	...
Value added tax	...	...	...	...	...	...	...	...	...	...	...	...
Total	4308.9	867.9	3247.6	1028.1	94.0	9358.4	4891.2	1082.3	4199.8	1079.5	50.3	11202.6

	1986						1987					
	Compensation of Employees	Capital Consumption	Net Operating Surplus	Indirect Taxes	Less: Subsidies Received	Value Added	Compensation of Employees	Capital Consumption	Net Operating Surplus	Indirect Taxes	Less: Subsidies Received	Value Added
	All Producers											
1 Agriculture, hunting, forestry and fishing	435.3	51.4	304.4	29.4	0.2	820.3	519.8	60.2	347.2	33.4	0.1	960.5
A Agriculture and hunting	405.9	...	...	...	...	750.0	485.4	...	...	...	...	877.0
B Forestry and logging	7.0	...	...	...	...	15.3	9.2	...	...	...	...	19.9
C Fishing	22.4	...	...	...	...	55.0	25.2	...	...	...	...	63.6
2 Mining and quarrying	158.4	71.0	662.7	9.7	-	901.8	177.2	89.9	866.3	13.8	-	1147.3
A Coal mining	...	...	...	...	...	...	...	...	...	...	...	...
B Crude petroleum and natural gas production	...	...	...	...	...	...	...	...	...	...	...	...
C Metal ore mining	146.7	...	...	...	...	886.8	163.6	...	...	...	...	1128.4
D Other mining	11.7	...	...	...	...	14.9	13.7	...	...	...	...	17.0

Jamaica

4.3 Cost Components of Value Added (Continued)

Million Jamaican dollars

	1986						1987					
	Compensation of Employees	Capital Consumption	Net Operating Surplus	Indirect Taxes	Less: Subsidies Received	Value Added	Compensation of Employees	Capital Consumption	Net Operating Surplus	Indirect Taxes	Less: Subsidies Received	Value Added
3 Manufacturing	996.0	139.4	1131.5	800.2	14.2	3017.5	1189.8	159.8	1087.8	1016.2	18.0	3435.5
A Manufacture of food, beverages and tobacco	436.6	...	...	...	...	1257.3	527.3	...	...	...	...	1463.1
B Textile, wearing apparel and leather industries	93.0	...	...	...	...	184.6	145.7	...	...	...	...	267.1
C Manufacture of wood and wood products, including furniture	40.0	...	...	...	...	79.4	48.1	...	...	...	...	94.1
D Manufacture of paper and paper products, printing and publishing	68.5	...	...	...	...	134.2	87.1	...	...	...	...	171.9
E Manufacture of chemicals and chemical products, coal, rubber and plastic products	90.3	...	...	...	...	863.5	108.6	...	...	...	...	827.8
F Manufacture of non-metallic mineral products, except products of petroleum and coal	44.4	...	...	...	...	133.7	51.8	...	...	...	...	151.9
G Basic metal industries	175.3	...	...	...	...	336.2	206.2	...	...	...	...	426.3
H Manufacture of fabricated metal products, machinery and equipment	...	...	...	...	...	...	...	...	...	...	...	...
I Other manufacturing industries	12.5	...	...	...	...	28.5	15.0	...	...	...	...	33.3
4 Electricity, gas and water	93.9	163.7	207.5	104.0	-	569.1	66.0	169.1	263.2	102.7	-	634.0
A Electricity, gas and steam	44.9	...	...	...	...	424.8	47.9	...	...	...	...	449.4
B Water works and supply	49.0	...	...	...	...	144.3	51.2	...	...	...	...	184.6
5 Construction	556.6	24.3	497.2	8.1	-	1086.1	769.7	32.0	584.4	18.3	-	1404.3
6 Wholesale and retail trade, restaurants and hotels [a]	697.8	69.4	1362.5	887.5	3.7	3096.1	844.3	97.5	1623.0	1156.1	3.7	3828.2
A Wholesale and retail trade	478.6	...	...	...	...	2794.2	598.2	...	...	...	...	3471.1
B Restaurants and hotels	219.2	...	...	...	...	301.9	246.1	...	...	...	...	357.1
7 Transport, storage and communication	455.9	235.8	337.6	80.7	36.4	1073.7	512.5	343.0	431.2	64.9	34.9	1316.8
A Transport and storage	337.8	...	...	...	...	746.4	374.1	...	...	...	...	932.7
B Communication	118.1	...	...	...	...	327.3	138.4	...	...	...	...	384.1
8 Finance, insurance, real estate and business services	637.2	347.0	1016.0	37.5	2.2	2035.6	765.7	387.3	1114.7	71.5	1.9	2337.1
A Financial institutions	282.1	...	...	...	...	751.7	362.2	...	...	...	...	904.6
B Insurance	162.4	...	...	...	...	194.4	182.3	...	...	...	...	217.8
C Real estate and business services	192.7	...	...	...	...	1089.5	221.2	...	...	...	...	1214.7
Real estate, except dwellings	128.7	...	...	...	...	292.1	151.7	...	...	...	...	349.8
Dwellings	64.0	...	...	...	...	797.3	69.5	...	...	...	...	864.9
9 Community, social and personal services [a]	194.6	45.8	30.1	107.0	-	294.8	240.9	53.7	50.0	121.9	-	355.4
A Sanitary and similar services	...	...	...	...	...	...	...	...	...	...	...	...
B Social and related community services	123.6	...	...	...	...	119.2	153.7	...	...	...	...	148.9
Educational services	69.5	...	...	...	...	81.1	82.3	...	...	...	...	72.2
Medical, dental, other health and veterinary services	54.1	...	...	...	...	58.1	71.4	...	...	...	...	76.8
C Recreational and cultural services	33.1	...	...	...	...	64.5	42.2	...	...	...	...	79.6
D Personal and household services	37.9	...	...	...	...	111.1	45.0	...	...	...	...	126.9
Total, Industries	4190.3	1147.7	5549.2	2064.2	56.6	12894.9	5119.0	1392.3	6367.7	2598.8	58.7	15419.0
Producers of Government Services	1281.5	-	-12.2	12.2	-	1281.5	1423.2	-	-13.7	13.7	-	1423.2
Other Producers	110.1	0.7	-0.6	1.1	-	111.3	115.5	0.8	0.6	1.1	-	117.9
Total	5582.0	1148.4	5536.4	2077.5	56.6	14287.7	6658.7	1393.2	6353.4	2613.6	58.7	16960.1
Less: Imputed bank service charge			787.6			787.6			943.4			943.4
Import duties	...	...	...	...	...	...	...	...	...	...	...	...
Value added tax	...	...	...	...	...	...	...	...	...	...	...	...
Total	5582.0	1148.4	4748.8	2077.5	56.6	13500.1	6658.7	1393.2	5410.0	2613.6	58.7	16016.7

Jamaica

4.3 Cost Components of Value Added

Million Jamaican dollars

		1988				
	Compensation of Employees	Capital Consumption	Net Operating Surplus	Indirect Taxes	Less: Subsidies Received	Value Added
		All Producers				
1 Agriculture, hunting, forestry and fishing	593.2	68.6	405.0	39.0	30.6	1075.2
A Agriculture and hunting	557.3	...	...	...	...	986.2
B Forestry and logging	11.5	...	...	...	...	25.1
C Fishing	24.4	...	...	...	...	64.0
2 Mining and quarrying	243.4	94.7	1119.1	10.1	-	1467.3
A Coal mining	...	...	...	...	...	...
B Crude petroleum and natural gas production						
C Metal ore mining	229.5	...	...	...	...	1450.1
D Other mining	13.9	...	...	...	...	17.2
3 Manufacturing	1326.6	177.7	1248.7	1006.7	10.2	3749.5
A Manufacture of food, beverages and tobacco	590.7	...	...	...	...	1579.7
B Textile, wearing apparel and leather industries	138.6	...	...	...	...	254.0
C Manufacture of wood and wood products, including furniture	54.7	...	...	...	...	106.6
D Manufacture of paper and paper products, printing and publishing	95.1	...	...	...	...	187.5
E Manufacture of chemicals and chemical products, coal, rubber and plastic products	116.7	...	...	...	...	916.6
F Manufacture of non-metallic mineral products, except products of petroleum and coal	58.1	...	...	...	...	191.9
G Basic metal industries	255.3	...	...	...	...	475.0
H Manufacture of fabricated metal products, machinery and equipment	[	...	...	...	...	]
I Other manufacturing industries	17.4	...	...	...	...	38.3
4 Electricity, gas and water	112.1	158.4	267.3	95.6	-	633.4
A Electricity, gas and steam	52.7	...	...	...	...	419.0
B Water works and supply	59.5	...	...	...	...	214.5
5 Construction	1083.7	45.7	866.9	23.3	-	2019.6
6 Wholesale and retail trade, restaurants and hotels [a]	1077.1	57.3	1788.6	1291.9	4.2	4322.2
A Wholesale and retail trade	832.5	...	...	...	...	3967.0
B Restaurants and hotels	244.6	...	...	...	...	355.2
7 Transport, storage and communication	555.7	364.3	435.5	87.3	39.4	1407.5
A Transport and storage	398.7	...	...	...	...	985.8
B Communication	157.0	...	...	...	...	421.7
8 Finance, insurance, real estate and business services	898.7	429.1	1184.6	78.4	2.0	2558.7
A Financial institutions	404.4	...	...	...	...	966.4
B Insurance	224.7	...	...	...	...	265.2
C Real estate and business services	239.5	...	...	...	...	1325.1
Real estate, except dwellings	163.4	...	...	...	...	376.8
Dwellings	76.1	...	...	...	...	948.2
9 Community, social and personal services [a]	282.9	56.9	-231.0	410.7	-	408.9
A Sanitary and similar services	...	...	...	...	...	...
B Social and related community services	183.3	...	...	...	...	177.2
Educational services	103.3	...	...	...	...	91.2
Medical, dental, other health and veterinary services	80.0	...	...	...	...	86.0
C Recreational and cultural services	45.7	...	...	...	...	84.9
D Personal and household services	53.9	...	...	...	...	146.8

Jamaica

4.3 Cost Components of Value Added
(Continued)

Million Jamaican dollars

	Compensation of Employees	Capital Consumption	Net Operating Surplus	Indirect Taxes	Less: Subsidies Received	Value Added
			1988			
Total, Industries	6143.3	1452.6	7089.9	3042.9	86.4	17642.2
Producers of Government Services	1653.8	-	-14.6	14.6	-	1653.8
Other Producers	146.6	1.0	-0.6	1.3	-	148.2
Total	7943.6	1453.5	7074.6	3058.8	86.4	19444.2
Less: Imputed bank service charge	...	1002.8	...	1002.8	...	1002.8
Import duties	...	...	...	...	...	...
Value added tax	...	...	...	...	...	...
Total	7943.6	1453.5	6071.8	3058.8	86.4	18441.4

a) For columns 2 to 5, hotels and restaurants are included in item 'Community, social and personal services'.

Japan

General note. The preparation of national accounts statistics in Japan is undertaken by the Economic Research Institute of the Economic Planning Agency, Tokyo. The official estimates are published in 'Annual Report on National Accounts'. The following presentation of sources and methods is mainly based on information from 'A System of National Accounts in Japan' published by the Economic Planning Agency. The estimates are generally in accordance with the classifications and definitions recommended in the United Nations System of National Accounts (SNA, 1968). Input-output tables have been published by the Management and Coordination Agency (former Administrative Management Agency). The following tables have been prepared from successive replies to the United Nations national accounts questionnaire. When the scope and coverage of the estimates differ for conceptual or statistical reasons from the definitions and classifications recommended in SNA, a footnote is indicated to the relevant tables.

Sources and methods :

(a) Gross domestic product. Gross domestic product is estimated mainly through the production approach.

(b) Expenditure on the gross domestic product. Using the commodity flow method, output, intermediate consumption by industry, household final consumption expenditure, gross capital formation, exports and imports are estimated for each of approximately 2,200 commodities. Shipments estimates are derived directly or indirectly from the statistics such as 'Crop Survey', 'Census of Manufactures', 'Current Production Statistics Survey', 'Establishment Census' and 'Census of Commerce'. The distribution channels and the constant coeficients such as the distribution ratios, the transportation fee rates and the trade margin rates are decided for each of the commodities based on the information of the 'Input-output Table'. Services produced and consumed by the producers of government services and private non-profit services to households are estimated separately based on the settlement of accounts of governments, 'Survey of Private Non-profit Institutions' and so on. Gross domestic expenditure is obtained by adding up final consumption expenditure, gross capital formation, increase in stocks and current external transactions. Exports and Imports are estimated by the estimation method for external transactions, which rearranges the 'Balance of Payments' in consideration of its consistency with the 'Balance of Payments'. For final consumption expenditure of households, calendar-year figure is estimated by the commodity flow method. Each commodity is classified into one of the elements of a 43-objects x 5-uses matrix. Each element of the matrix corresponds to one of the 4 types of expenditure. Quarterly figures are estimated by distributing the calendar-year figure through expenditure approach which uses 'Survey of Farm Household Economy', 'Family Income and Expenditure Survey' and 'National Survey of Family Income and Expenditure'. For gross capital formation, quarterly and sectorial figures are estimated by breaking down the calendar-year figure estimated by the commodity flow method, on the basis of the quarterly and sectorial figures estimated through expenditure approach which uses settlements of accounts of government, 'Financial Statements of Corporations by Industry' and so on for gross fixed capital formation. For increase in stocks, special accounts for food administration, 'Financial Statements of Corporations by Industry' are used. GDP at constant prices is estimated mainly using price indexes called basic unit deflators which correspond to the approximately 400 commodities aggregated from the approximately 2,200 commodities used for the commodity flow method. Series at constant prices are obtained by dividing the nominal values of the 400 commodities by the basic unit deflators for each demand item. In other words, constant value is estimated using Paasche-type deflator weighted by 400 commodities. Government services and

private non-profit services to households are estimated using deflators by activities which correspond respectively to 6 activities of government services and 3 activities of private non-profit services to households.

(c) Cost-structure of the gross domestic product. Wages and salaries are estimated separately for the three groups of agriculture, forestry and fisheries, government services, and other industries. Concerning the other industries, quarterly cash allowances to employees by industries are calculated by multiplying the per head wage by the number of employees. In this case, the number of employees is based on the 'Population Census' conducted every five years and is interpolated in the mid-year of a five-year period by trends observed from the 'Labor Force Survey', while the cash allowances per head is mainly based on the 'Monthly Labor Survey'. Cash allowances to officers are estimated by multiplying the number of officers by the difference between the per head allowances of both officers and regular employees, which are obtained from the 'Financial Statements of Corporations by Industry', and the per head allowances of regular employees. Employers' contributions to social security schemes are estimated on the basis of the operational reports of these schemes. Employers' contributions to others and payments in kind are estimated on the basis of settlements of accounts of the central government and local governments data on taxation, business and housing survey data on payments for housing. The operating surplus is estimated through production approach (value-added method), and is distributed to each institutional sector according to the ratios of operating profits to the total by kind of income-earning subject (after inventory valuation adjustment). The ratios are estimated on the basis of statistical data such as 'Financial Statements of Corporations by Industry'. Consumption of fixed capital consists of loss from wear and tear (depreciation) and estimated damage from fire, typhoons, floods and other accidents. Depreciation is estimated on the basis of 'Financial Statements of Corporations by Industry', 'Financial Statistics of Local Public Enterprises' and so on. Accidental damage is estimated making use of settlements of accounts of insurance companies and so on. Indirect taxes and subsidies are estimated on the basis of settlements of accounts of central and local governments.

(d) Gross domestic product by kind of economic activity. The gross domestic product by kind of economic activity is prepared at market prices, i.e. producers' values. The output of each of the 82 industry groups is estimated from the V table --- a make matrix for commodity by activity --- of which the control total is given as the output of the 2200 commodities estimated by the commodity flow method. The intermediate input of each industry group is estimated from the U table --- a use matrix for commodity by activity --- in the base year which is compiled from 'Input-output Table' and the V table, and from the U table in the mid year which is separately compiled from the information of the cost structure estimated for about 4 or 15 items every year. The value-added and its component items by industry are estimated by substracting the intermediate input from the output. The output, intermediate input, value-added and its component items by the producers of government services and by the producers of private non-profit services to households are separately estimated using the settlement of accounts of government, 'Survey of Private Non-profit Institutions' and so on. Gross domestic product by industry at constant prices is estimated by the double deflation technique. The output by industry is estimated from the V table at constant prices which is obtained by dividing the output of each commodity by its output deflator. The intermediate input by industry is estimated from the U table at constant prices which is obtained by dividing the intermediate input of each commodity by its input deflator.

1.1 Expenditure on the Gross Domestic Product, in Current Prices

Thousand Million Japanese yen

	1970	1975	1980	1981	1982	1983	1984	1985	1986	1987	1988	1989
1 Government final consumption expenditure	5455	14890	23568	25585	26796	27996	29449	30685	32388	32975	34184	36240
2 Private final consumption expenditure	38333	84763	141324	149997	160833	169687	178631	188760	195969	204585	215122	228445
A Households	37805	83920	139506	147988	158854	167509	176267	186235	193308	201973	212237	225476
B Private non-profit institutions serving households	528	843	1818	2008	1980	2179	2364	2525	2661	2612	2885	2969
3 Gross capital formation	28616	48612	77434	80332	80921	79067	84262	90198	92953	99850	113705	125576
A Increase in stocks	2573	476	1613	1423	1187	186	1011	2159	1643	690	2630	3058
B Gross fixed capital formation	26043	48136	75821	78908	79735	78881	83251	88040	91310	99160	111074	122518
Residential buildings	5102	11253	16205	15773	15919	15049	14983	15446	16568	20301	22927	23917
Non-residential buildings	4219	8036	13631	14243	14224	14112	14583	15170	15123	15210	16514	19266
Other construction and land improvement etc.	5444	12374	21257	22205	22107	21410	21845	22057	22967	24447	26903	28062
Other	11278	16473	24727	26687	27485	28309	31840	35366	36652	39202	44730	51273
4 Exports of goods and services	7926	18982	32886	37977	39391	39275	45066	46307	38090	36210	37483	42352
5 Less: Imports of goods and services	6985	18919	35036	35927	37341	34258	36865	35532	24791	25195	29065	36768
Equals: Gross Domestic Product	73345	148328	240177	257964	270602	281767	300542	320419	334609	348425	371428	395845

Japan

1.2 Expenditure on the Gross Domestic Product, in Constant Prices

Thousand Million Japanese yen

	1970	1975	1980	1981	1982	1983	1984	1985	1986	1987	1988	1989
						At constant prices of:1985						
1 Government final consumption expenditure	16626	21617	26628	27904	28468	29320	30107	30623	31986	32124	32815	33510
2 Private final consumption expenditure	101288	132897	161925	164476	171738	177661	182529	188703	195079	203336	213983	223297
A Households	99576	131617	159968	162365	169668	175466	180199	186243	192525	200837	211283	220622
B Private non-profit institutions serving households	1712	1281	1958	2111	2070	2196	2330	2459	2554	2499	2700	2675
3 Gross capital formation	60884	66099	80344	82168	81885	80049	84614	90239	94051	101970	116126	126814
A Increase in stocks	4637	799	1421	1357	1190	130	973	2160	1780	876	2979	3597
B Gross fixed capital formation	56247	65300	78923	80811	80695	79919	83641	88079	92271	101094	113147	123217
Residential buildings	13057	16600	16917	16535	16394	15512	15154	15446	16646	20137	22432	22436
Non-residential buildings	10488	11869	14638	14987	14724	14564	14773	15179	15176	15237	16169	17937
Other construction and land improvement etc.	15575	19165	23052	23305	22740	21972	22003	22070	23068	24510	26395	27323
Other	17127	17666	24316	25984	26837	27871	31711	35385	37381	41210	48151	55521
4 Exports of goods and services	13115	20330	32235	36276	36613	38358	44035	46426	44153	44191	47295	51594
5 Less: Imports of goods and services	20251	27835	34410	34556	33702	32687	36098	35594	36453	39305	46652	54860
Equals: Gross Domestic Product	171662	213108	266722	276268	285002	292701	305187	320397	328816	342316	363567	380355

1.3 Cost Components of the Gross Domestic Product

Thousand Million Japanese yen

	1970	1975	1980	1981	1982	1983	1984	1985	1986	1987	1988	1989
1 Indirect taxes, net	4397	7529	14095	15710	16505	16664	19137	21250	21535	24961	27469	29001
A Indirect taxes	5202	9736	17688	19455	20285	20631	22943	24900	25213	28379	30878	32162
B Less: Subsidies	805	2207	3593	3745	3780	3968	3806	3650	3678	3419	3409	3161
2 Consumption of fixed capital	9730	19025	30701	34059	36216	38426	40778	43615	46170	48861	52306	57530
3 Compensation of employees paid by resident producers to:	31894	81581	130398	141490	149559	157357	166120	173892	181959	189069	200111	214623
A Resident households	31871	81524	130154	141165	149148	156946	165718	173505	181703	188789	199880	214349
B Rest of the world	23	57	244	325	411	411	401	387	256	281	232	274
4 Operating surplus	27415	39602	64757	66332	68217	69233	74395	81501	84787	86625	93250	96382
A Corporate and quasi-corporate enterprises	13768	15524	31555	32540	33035	33521	37043	40610	42695	42723	47960	50637
B Private unincorporated enterprises	13647	24078	33202	33791	35182	35712	37352	40890	42092	43901	45290	45745
C General government	...	...	...	...	...	...	...	...	...	...	...	...
Statistical discrepancy	-91	590	225	372	104	88	114	161	159	-1091	-1708	-1692
Equals: Gross Domestic Product	73345	148327	240176	257963	270601	281767	300543	320419	334609	348425	371429	395844

1.4 General Government Current Receipts and Disbursements

Thousand Million Japanese yen

	1970	1975	1980	1981	1982	1983	1984	1985	1986	1987	1988	1989
						Receipts						
1 Operating surplus	...	...	...	...	...	...	...	...	...	...	...	...
2 Property and entrepreneurial income	667	2021	4626	5665	6213	6686	7464	8369	9346	10009	11112	11621
3 Taxes, fees and contributions	14416	33518	61338	68828	72890	76426	82823	89909	93970	103111	110997	119596
A Indirect taxes	5202	9736	17688	19455	20285	20631	22943	24900	25213	28379	30878	32162
B Direct taxes	5966	14092	25876	29029	30680	32605	35291	38485	40639	44615	48329	53901
C Social security contributions	3165	9503	17513	20072	21645	22896	24270	26184	27761	29694	31363	33109
D Compulsory fees, fines and penalties	83	188	261	272	280	294	319	338	357	423	426	424
4 Other current transfers	44	108	250	302	351	393	421	487	543	603	665	743
Total Current Receipts of General Government	15127	35647	66214	74795	79455	83505	90707	98764	103860	113723	122774	131961
						Disbursements						
1 Government final consumption expenditure	5455	14890	23568	25585	26796	27996	29449	30685	32388	32975	34184	36240

Japan

1.4 General Government Current Receipts and Disbursements
(Continued)

Thousand Million Japanese yen

	1970	1975	1980	1981	1982	1983	1984	1985	1986	1987	1988	1989
A Compensation of employees	4311	12446	19077	20403	21272	21973	23083	24172	...	...	...	...
B Consumption of fixed capital	327	668	1393	1599	1752	1892	2012	2078	...	...	...	...
C Purchases of goods and services, net	813	1762	3068	3551	3738	4096	4318	4399	...	...	...	...
D Less: Own account fixed capital formation	...	...	...	...	...	...	...	...	...	...	...	...
E Indirect taxes paid, net	5	15	30	32	34	35	36	36	...	...	...	...
2 Property income	449	1795	7569	9229	10390	11944	13337	14318	14912	15346	15671	16023
A Interest	435	1738	7500	9142	10299	11848	13229	14212	14797	15225	15537	15871
B Net land rent and royalties	14	58	69	86	91	96	108	106	115	121	134	151
3 Subsidies	805	2207	3593	3745	3780	3968	3806	3650	3678	3419	3409	3161
4 Other current transfers	3588	12057	25269	28367	30917	33081	34426	36456	39163	42136	44089	45839
A Social security benefits	2464	8788	18919	21453	23627	25883	27596	28960	31478	34235	35922	37410
B Social assistance grants	929	2697	5250	5711	6038	5764	5349	5957	6073	6185	6313	6377
C Other	195	572	1100	1203	1252	1434	1480	1539	1615	1716	1854	2052
5 Net saving	4831	4698	6214	7868	7571	6516	9690	13655	13718	19848	25420	30699
Total Current Disbursements and Net Saving of General Government	15127	35647	66214	74795	79454	83505	90707	98764	103860	113723	122774	131961

1.5 Current Income and Outlay of Corporate and Quasi-Corporate Enterprises, Summary

Thousand Million Japanese yen

	1970	1975	1980	1981	1982	1983	1984	1985	1986	1987	1988	1989
					Receipts							
1 Operating surplus	13768	15524	31555	32540	33035	33521	37043	40610	42695	42723	47960	50637
2 Property and entrepreneurial income received	11443	32422	59808	68956	74611	79574	87628	93248	95839	100099	108846	126531
3 Current transfers	722	1626	3074	3335	3564	3801	3972	4111	4030	3832	3926	4057
Total Current Receipts	25933	49572	94437	104831	111210	116896	128643	137969	142564	146654	160733	181225
					Disbursements							
1 Property and entrepreneurial income	15261	41939	72721	83148	87502	92399	100033	105751	109776	112061	120891	140628
2 Direct taxes and other current payments to general government	2978	6757	11082	12213	12745	13246	15095	17381	17790	19690	22247	25897
3 Other current transfers	899	1911	3793	4183	4488	4705	4946	5207	5220	5131	5397	5626
4 Net saving	6795	-1035	6840	5287	6475	6545	8568	9630	9778	9773	12198	9074
Total Current Disbursements and Net Saving	25933	49572	94437	104831	111210	116896	128643	137969	142564	146654	160733	181225

1.6 Current Income and Outlay of Households and Non-Profit Institutions

Thousand Million Japanese yen

	1970	1975	1980	1981	1982	1983	1984	1985	1986	1987	1988	1989
					Receipts							
1 Compensation of employees	31942	81678	130368	141397	149514	157299	166026	173815	182006	189125	200192	214730
A From resident producers	31871	81525	130154	141165	149148	156946	165718	173505	181703	188789	199880	214349
B From rest of the world	71	154	214	233	366	354	308	311	303	336	312	381
2 Operating surplus of private unincorporated enterprises	13647	24078	33202	33791	35182	35712	37352	40890	42090	43901	45290	45745
3 Property and entrepreneurial income	5002	13811	24880	27493	28174	30201	31356	32551	34108	33275	33358	36840
4 Current transfers	7361	21577	41593	45912	49819	52806	54611	57685	61363	65112	68937	71044
A Social security benefits	2464	8788	18919	21453	23627	25883	27596	28960	31476	34235	35922	37410
B Social assistance grants	1136	3108	6214	6762	7362	7274	6866	7691	7930	8228	8545	8677
C Other	3761	9681	16460	17697	18830	19649	20149	21034	21957	22649	24470	24958
Total Current Receipts	57952	141144	230043	248594	262688	276019	289346	304942	319568	331413	347777	368359
					Disbursements							
1 Private final consumption expenditure	38333	84763	141324	149997	160833	169687	178631	188760	195969	204585	215122	228445

Japan

1.6 Current Income and Outlay of Households and Non-Profit Institutions
(Continued)

Thousand Million Japanese yen

	1970	1975	1980	1981	1982	1983	1984	1985	1986	1987	1988	1989
2 Property income	1607	4774	9071	10192	10992	11750	12479	12886	13424	13977	14534	15599
3 Direct taxes and other current transfers n.e.c. to general government	6236	17025	32568	37160	39860	42549	44784	47627	50967	55042	57872	61537
A Social security contributions	3165	9503	17513	20072	21646	22896	24270	26184	27761	29694	31363	33109
B Direct taxes	3029	7422	14899	16923	18044	19470	20323	21248	22995	25098	26268	28193
C Fees, fines and penalties	42	100	156	165	170	183	192	194	211	251	240	234
4 Other current transfers	3681	9400	16108	17250	18562	19458	19871	20873	21775	22652	24397	24713
5 Net saving	8096	25182	30971	33996	32441	32575	33580	34796	37434	35156	35852	38065
Total Current Disbursements and Net Saving	57952	141144	230043	248594	262688	276019	289346	304942	319568	331413	347777	368359

1.7 External Transactions on Current Account, Summary

Thousand Million Japanese yen

	1970	1975	1980	1981	1982	1983	1984	1985	1986	1987	1988	1989
Payments to the Rest of the World												
1 Imports of goods and services	6985	18919	35036	35927	37341	34258	36865	35532	24791	25195	29065	36768
A Imports of merchandise c.i.f. [a]	5484	15158	29153	29500	30655	27902	30328	28856	19356	18708	21330	26906
B Other	1501	3761	5883	6427	6686	6356	6538	6676	5435	6487	7735	9863
2 Factor income to the rest of the world	503	1430	2898	4384	5019	3900	4448	4631	4108	5553	7822	11911
A Compensation of employees	23	57	244	325	411	411	401	387	256	281	232	274
B Property and entrepreneurial income	480	1373	2654	4058	4608	3489	4047	4244	3853	5272	7590	11637
3 Current transfers to the rest of the world	75	115	342	349	350	359	373	355	292	463	497	475
A Indirect taxes to supranational organizations	...	...	...	...	...	...	...	...	...	...	...	...
B Other current transfers	75	115	342	349	350	359	373	355	292	463	497	475
4 Surplus on the nation on current transactions	744	-152	-2481	1251	1885	5083	8467	11660	14306	12697	10364	8100
Payments to the Rest of the World and Surplus of the Nation on Current Transactions	8308	20313	35794	41911	44595	43600	50153	52177	43497	43908	47748	57254
Receipts From The Rest of the World												
1 Exports of goods and services	7926	18982	32886	37977	39391	39275	45066	46307	38090	36210	37483	42352
A Exports of merchandise f.o.b.	6873	16579	29022	33656	34748	34964	40381	41555	34575	32490	33398	37372
B Other	1053	2403	3865	4321	4643	4311	4685	4752	3515	3720	4085	4980
2 Factor income from rest of the world	347	1273	2820	3837	5088	4211	4953	5768	5337	7607	10124	14761
A Compensation of employees	71	154	214	233	366	354	308	311	303	336	312	381
B Property and entrepreneurial income	276	1119	2606	3605	4722	3858	4646	5458	5035	7271	9811	14380
3 Current transfers from rest of the world	35	58	87	97	117	114	134	102	70	92	141	142
A Subsidies from supranational organisations	...	...	...	...	...	...	...	...	...	...	...	...
B Other current transfers	35	58	87	97	117	114	134	102	70	92	141	142
Receipts from the Rest of the World on Current Transactions	8308	20313	35794	41911	44595	43600	50153	52177	43497	43908	47748	57254

a) Imports of merchandise c.i.f. is not estimated in the Balance of Payments in Japan. Therefore, valuation basis is f.o.b.

1.8 Capital Transactions of The Nation, Summary

Thousand Million Japanese yen

	1970	1975	1980	1981	1982	1983	1984	1985	1986	1987	1988	1989
Finance of Gross Capital Formation												
Gross saving	29452	47871	74727	81211	82702	84062	92616	101697	107100	113638	125777	135368
1 Consumption of fixed capital	9730	19025	30701	34059	36216	38426	40778	43615	46170	48861	52306	57530
A General government	327	667	1392	1599	1752	1892	2012	2077	2144	2245	2325	2456
B Corporate and quasi-corporate enterprises	7048	12586	18682	20970	22280	23745	25301	27467	29445	31385	33832	37709
Public	787	1508	...	...	...	...	...	...	...	...	...	...
Private	6260	11078	...	...	...	...	...	...	...	...	...	...
C Other	2355	5772	10626	11489	12184	12788	13464	14071	14581	15232	16150	17365
2 Net saving	19722	28845	44026	47152	46486	45636	51838	58082	60930	64777	73470	77838

Japan

1.8 Capital Transactions of The Nation, Summary
(Continued)

Thousand Million Japanese yen

	1970	1975	1980	1981	1982	1983	1984	1985	1986	1987	1988	1989
A General government	4831	4698	6214	7868	7571	6516	9690	13655	13718	19848	25420	30699
B Corporate and quasi-corporate enterprises	6795	-1035	6840	5287	6475	6545	8568	9630	9778	9773	12198	9074
Public	36	-1515	-176	-639	-914	-1737	-1947	-2024	-2161	-1414	-784	1990
Private	6759	481	7016	5926	7389	8283	10516	11654	11940	11187	12981	7084
C Other	8096	25182	30971	33996	32441	32575	33580	34796	37434	35156	35852	38065
Less: Surplus of the nation on current transactions	744	-152	-2481	1251	1885	5083	8467	11660	14306	12697	10364	8100
Statistical discrepancy	-91	590	225	372	104	88	114	161	159	-1091	-1708	-1692
Finance of Gross Capital Formation	28616	48612	77434	80332	80921	79067	84262	90198	92953	99850	113705	125576
Gross Capital Formation												
Increase in stocks	2573	476	1613	1423	1187	186	1011	2159	1643	690	2630	3058
Gross fixed capital formation	26043	48136	75821	78908	79735	78881	83251	88040	91310	99160	111074	122518
1 General government	3276	7841	14685	15646	15679	15475	15164	15168	16048	17536	18860	19802
2 Corporate and quasi-corporate enterprises	15694	24510	38003	40650	41580	41456	46109	50006	51537	54235	61842	70886
A Public	2614	5577	8203	8632	8442	8105	7942	6480	6223	6194	6187	6158
B Private	13080	18933	29800	32017	33137	33351	38167	43526	45314	48041	55656	64728
3 Other	7073	15786	23133	22612	22476	21950	21979	22865	23726	27389	30372	31831
Gross Capital Formation	28616	48612	77434	80332	80921	79067	84262	90198	92953	99850	113705	125576

1.9 Gross Domestic Product by Institutional Sectors of Origin

Thousand Million Japanese yen

	1970	1975	1980	1981	1982	1983	1984	1985	1986	1987	1988	1989
Domestic Factor Incomes Originating												
1 General government	4311	12446	19077	20404	21272	21973	23083	24172	25357	26061	26952	28346
2 Corporate and quasi-corporate enterprises	54343	106522	172131	183262	192038	199845	212283	225760	235527	243590	259904	275748
3 Households and private unincorporated enterprises												
4 Non-profit institutions serving households	656	2215	3947	4156	4466	4772	5150	5461	5864	6044	6506	6912
Subtotal: Domestic Factor Incomes	59309	121183	195155	207822	217776	226590	240515	255393	266746	275694	293361	311004
Indirect taxes, net	4397	7529	14095	15710	16505	16664	19137	21250	21535	24961	27469	29001
A Indirect taxes	5202	9736	17688	19455	20285	20631	22943	24900	25213	28379	30878	32162
B Less: Subsidies	805	2207	3593	3745	3780	3968	3806	3650	3678	3419	3409	3161
Consumption of fixed capital	9730	19025	30701	34059	36216	38426	40778	43615	46170	48861	52306	57530
Statistical discrepancy	-91	590	225	373	104	89	114	161	159	-1091	-1708	-1692
Gross Domestic Product	73345	148327	240176	257963	270601	281767	300543	320419	334609	348425	371429	395844

1.10 Gross Domestic Product by Kind of Activity, in Current Prices

Thousand Million Japanese yen

	1970	1975	1980	1981	1982	1983	1984	1985	1986	1987	1988	1989
1 Agriculture, hunting, forestry and fishing	4488	8141	8847	9075	9238	9516	9957	10214	9975	9768	9754	10221
2 Mining and quarrying	620	776	1363	1276	1188	1071	1008	958	992	976	1058	1057
3 Manufacturing	26402	44801	70232	74939	78468	81748	89245	94673	96262	99297	106649	114405
4 Electricity, gas and water	1558	3002	6580	7385	7720	8792	9542	10305	11332	11337	11387	11382
5 Construction	5650	14322	22506	24547	24767	23273	23993	25381	26886	30129	34009	37607
6 Wholesale and retail trade, restaurants and hotels [a]	10531	21934	36792	38494	40427	41556	41977	42836	43567	45540	48010	50377
7 Transport, storage and communication	5044	9546	14787	16129	17095	18238	19958	21087	21910	22871	24220	25948
8 Finance, insurance, real estate and business services	9019	19934	35095	36710	39666	42779	45646	49330	52443	56962	61668	66910
9 Community, social and personal services [a]	7074	16251	28063	31328	34362	37286	40622	46391	49787	51881	54993	60672
Total, Industries	70388	138708	224266	239883	252930	264260	281948	301175	313154	328761	351749	378578
Producers of Government Services	4642	13128	20499	22035	23058	23899	25131	26285	27535	28342	29314	30845

Japan

1.10 Gross Domestic Product by Kind of Activity, in Current Prices
(Continued)

Thousand Million Japanese yen

	1970	1975	1980	1981	1982	1983	1984	1985	1986	1987	1988	1989
Other Producers	730	2363	4285	4556	4947	5342	5824	6218	6653	6923	7425	7905
Subtotal	75760	154199	249051	266474	280934	293502	312903	333678	347342	364027	388488	417327
Less: Imputed bank service charge	2822	7008	10413	10150	11748	13010	13811	14773	13938	15677	16568	20235
Plus: Import duties	498	547	1313	1267	1310	1187	1337	1353	1046	1166	1217	1892
Plus: Value added tax	...	...	...	...	...	...	...	...	...	...	...	...
Plus: Other adjustments b	-91	590	225	372	104	88	114	161	159	-1091	-1708	-3140
Equals: Gross Domestic Product	73345	148327	240176	257963	270601	281767	300543	320419	334609	348425	371429	395844

a) Restaurants and hotels are included in item 'Community, social and personal services'.
b) Item 'Other adjustments' refers to inventory valuation adjustment.

1.11 Gross Domestic Product by Kind of Activity, in Constant Prices

Thousand Million Japanese yen

	1970	1975	1980	1981	1982	1983	1984	1985	1986	1987	1988	1989
	At constant prices of:1985											
1 Agriculture, hunting, forestry and fishing	9597	10767	9135	9239	9693	9863	10242	10214	10006	10325	9995	10439
2 Mining and quarrying	1066	971	1182	1136	1179	1103	1009	958	996	937	960	897
3 Manufacturing	43057	52419	71482	74793	78130	81521	88426	94673	92113	98860	107999	114965
4 Electricity, gas and water	5315	6619	8181	8326	8869	9433	9570	10305	10437	10684	11431	12068
5 Construction	19968	24733	26326	27364	26723	24750	24714	25381	26297	29124	32071	33293
6 Wholesale and retail trade, restaurants and hotels a	16745	24677	38069	39084	40597	41861	42020	42836	44251	46963	49685	51412
7 Transport, storage and communication	13691	16813	16999	17563	17758	18706	19976	21087	21368	21937	23274	24393
8 Finance, insurance, real estate and business services	19801	29455	39493	40478	40917	43136	46349	49330	52511	56306	60162	64218
9 Community, social and personal services a	23699	27192	34686	36709	38562	40812	42835	46391	47808	47992	49711	52841
Total, Industries	152939	193647	245552	254692	262427	271185	285140	301175	305787	323129	345287	364527
Producers of Government Services	15812	19416	23487	24420	24923	25360	25864	26285	26503	26779	27000	27231
Other Producers	2947	3956	5065	5148	5392	5679	5969	6218	6439	6626	6917	7126
Subtotal	171698	217020	274103	284259	292742	302224	316973	333678	338729	356534	379205	398884
Less: Imputed bank service charge	4922	8203	10414	10324	10542	11981	13706	14773	14833	17105	18127	21705
Plus: Import duties	1950	801	1274	1213	1171	1134	1317	1353	1583	1830	2044	2936
Plus: Value added tax	...	...	...	...	...	...	...	...	...	...	...	...
Plus: Other adjustments b	2935	3490	1758	1121	1631	1324	603	139	3337	1056	445	239
Equals: Gross Domestic Product	171661	213108	266722	276268	285002	292701	305187	320397	328816	342316	363567	380355

a) Restaurants and hotels are included in item 'Community, social and personal services'.
b) Item 'Other adjustments' refers to inventory valuation adjustment.

1.12 Relations Among National Accounting Aggregates

Thousand Million Japanese yen

	1970	1975	1980	1981	1982	1983	1984	1985	1986	1987	1988	1989
Gross Domestic Product	73345	148327	240176	257963	270601	281767	300543	320419	334609	348425	371429	395844
Plus: Net factor income from the rest of the world	-157	-157	-77	-546	69	311	505	1137	1229	2054	2302	2849
Factor income from the rest of the world	347	1273	2820	3837	5088	4211	4953	5768	5337	7607	10124	14761
Less: Factor income to the rest of the world	503	1430	2898	4384	5019	3900	4448	4631	4108	5553	7822	11911
Equals: Gross National Product	73188	148170	240098	257416	270669	282078	301048	321556	335838	350479	373731	398693
Less: Consumption of fixed capital	9730	19025	30701	34059	36216	38426	40778	43615	46170	48861	52306	57530
Equals: National Income a	63550	128555	209172	222985	234350	243564	260157	277780	289508	302708	323133	342855
Plus: Net current transfers from the rest of the world	-40	-57	-254	-252	-233	-245	-239	-253	-222	-372	-356	-333
Current transfers from the rest of the world	35	58	87	97	117	114	134	102	70	92	141	142
Less: Current transfers to the rest of the world	75	115	342	349	350	359	373	355	292	463	497	475
Equals: National Disposable Income	63510	128498	208918	222733	234116	243319	259918	277527	289287	302337	322777	342522
Less: Final consumption	43788	99653	164892	175581	187630	197684	208080	219445	228357	237560	249306	264684
Equals: Net Saving	19722	28845	44026	47152	46486	45636	51838	58082	60930	64777	73470	77838
Less: Surplus of the nation on current transactions	744	-152	-2481	1251	1885	5083	8467	11660	14306	12697	10364	8100
Statistical discrepancy	-91	590	225	372	104	88	114	161	159	-1091	-1708	-1692
Equals: Net Capital Formation	18887	29586	46733	46273	44705	40641	43485	46583	46783	50989	61398	68046

a) Item 'National income' includes a statistical discrepancy.

Japan

2.1 Government Final Consumption Expenditure by Function, in Current Prices

Thousand Million Japanese yen / Fiscal year beginning 1 April

	1970	1975	1980	1981	1982	1983	1984	1985	1986	1987	1988	1989
1 General public services a	1556	4143	6461	6924	7164	7496	7859	8137	8859	8934	9108	9774
2 Defence	560	1285	2066	2236	2361	2560	2744	2961	3093	3219	3415	3643
3 Public order and safety a	...	...	...	...	...	...	...	...	...	...	...	...
4 Education	2078	5745	8991	9692	9984	10367	10845	11262	11655	11961	12417	12733
5 Health	256	628	908	1016	1046	1154	1276	1212	1230	1267	1362	1495
6 Social security and welfare	219	724	1208	1335	1396	1457	1562	1726	1819	1888	1931	2114
7 Housing and community amenities	217	783	1397	1470	1551	1654	1697	1796	1857	1936	2036	2176
8 Recreational, cultural and religious affairs	74	242	472	536	583	624	670	718	758	800	860	958
9 Economic services	675	1672	2532	2697	2776	2890	3034	3108	3162	3116	3228	3651
10 Other functions	12	40	88	96	100	103	121	119	125	121	208	172
Total Government Final Consumption Expenditure	5647	15262	24122	26002	26961	28304	29808	31038	32560	33241	34565	36716

a) Item 'Public order and safety' is included in item 'General public services'.

2.2 Government Final Consumption Expenditure by Function, in Constant Prices

Thousand Million Japanese yen / Fiscal year beginning 1 April

	1970	1975	1980	1981	1982	1983	1984	1985	1986	1987	1988	1989
					At constant prices of:1985							
1 General public services a	4653	5992	7240	7523	7600	7813	7943	7990	8880	8614	8585	8815
2 Defence	1496	1841	2279	2374	2432	2602	2668	2821	3045	3161	3322	3387
3 Public order and safety a	...	...	...	...	...	...	...	...	...	...	...	...
4 Education	6632	8258	10104	10593	10706	10943	11172	11304	11412	11575	11763	11620
5 Health	721	908	1039	1140	1169	1285	1417	1346	1219	1248	1322	1395
6 Social security and welfare	624	1033	1349	1446	1479	1524	1588	1707	1778	1831	1834	1920
7 Housing and community amenities	637	1124	1528	1560	1607	1716	1725	1797	1871	1942	2028	2071
8 Recreational, cultural and religious affairs	196	344	517	567	600	636	666	699	755	796	847	904
9 Economic services	1850	2373	2764	2842	2853	2934	2999	3005	3097	3040	3111	3374
10 Other functions	37	58	99	105	106	108	123	117	121	117	211	165
Total Government Final Consumption Expenditure	16845	21930	26917	28149	28553	29559	30300	30786	32178	32323	33024	33652

a) Item 'Public order and safety' is included in item 'General public services'.

2.3 Total Government Outlays by Function and Type

Thousand Million Japanese yen / Fiscal year beginning 1 April

	Final Consumption Expenditures			Subsidies	Other Current Transfers & Property Income	Total Current Disbursements	Gross Capital Formation	Other Capital Outlays	Total Outlays
	Total	Compensation of Employees	Other						
					1980				
1 General public services a	6461	5248	1213	46	...	...	859	...	...
2 Defence	2066	1133	934	-	...	...	-	...	...
3 Public order and safety a	...	...	...	...	...	...	...	...	...
4 Education	8991	7397	1594	1	...	...	2005	...	...
5 Health	908	1636	-728	150	...	...	419	...	...
6 Social security and welfare	1208	1173	35	126	...	...	297	...	...
7 Housing and community amenities	1397	824	573	387	...	...	2746	...	...
8 Recreation, culture and religion	472	250	222	11	...	...	462	...	...
9 Economic services	2532	1647	885	2933	...	...	8134	...	...
10 Other functions	88	74	14	-	...	...	18	...	...
Total	24122	19380	4742	3654	34031	61807	14938	2514	79259
					1981				
1 General public services a	6924	5634	1291	44	...	...	899	...	...
2 Defence	2236	1192	1045	-	...	...	-	...	...
3 Public order and safety a	...	...	...	...	...	...	...	...	...
4 Education	9692	7948	1744	-	...	...	1836	...	...
5 Health	1016	1750	-734	138	...	...	461	...	...
6 Social security and welfare	1335	1259	75	158	...	...	280	...	...
7 Housing and community amenities	1470	887	583	422	...	...	2954	...	...
8 Recreation, culture and religion	536	279	257	13	...	...	533	...	...
9 Economic services	2697	1742	956	3035	...	...	8572	...	...
10 Other functions	96	80	16	-	...	...	19	...	...
Total	26002	20770	5233	3811	38540	68353	15554	2607	86514

Japan

2.3 Total Government Outlays by Function and Type
(Continued)

Thousand Million Japanese yen

Fiscal year beginning 1 April

	Final Consumption Expenditures			Subsidies	Other Current Transfers & Property Income	Total Current Disbursements	Gross Capital Formation	Other Capital Outlays	Total Outlays
	Total	Compensation of Employees	Other						
1982									
1 General public services ᵃ	7164	5790	1374	30	...	...	869	...	...
2 Defence	2361	1213	1149	-	...	...	-	...	...
3 Public order and safety ᵃ	...	...	...	...	...	...	...	...	...
4 Education	9984	8149	1836	-	...	...	1636	...	...
5 Health	1046	1820	-773	152	...	...	501	...	...
6 Social security and welfare	1396	1300	96	109	...	...	283	...	...
7 Housing and community amenities	1551	912	639	509	...	...	2898	...	...
8 Recreation, culture and religion	583	294	289	19	...	...	536	...	...
9 Economic services	2776	1775	1001	3132	...	...	8952	...	...
10 Other functions	100	82	17	-	...	...	16	...	...
Total	26961	21334	5627	3950	42144	73055	15692	2624	91371
1983									
1 General public services ᵃ	7496	5997	1499	36	...	...	797	...	...
2 Defence	2560	1263	1297	-	...	...	-	...	...
3 Public order and safety ᵃ	...	...	...	...	...	...	...	...	...
4 Education	10367	8443	1924	-	...	...	1608	...	...
5 Health	1154	1902	-748	159	...	...	414	...	...
6 Social security and welfare	1457	1351	106	97	...	...	289	...	...
7 Housing and community amenities	1654	957	698	517	...	...	2834	...	...
8 Recreation, culture and religion	624	313	311	13	...	...	508	...	...
9 Economic services	2890	1837	1053	3175	...	...	8870	...	...
10 Other functions	103	84	19	-	...	...	14	...	...
Total	28304	22145	6159	3996	45875	78175	15333	2652	96160
1984									
1 General public services ᵃ	7859	6293	1566	83	...	...	880	...	...
2 Defence	2744	1359	1385	-	...	...	-	...	...
3 Public order and safety ᵃ	...	...	...	...	...	...	...	...	...
4 Education	10845	8836	2008	-	...	...	1573	...	...
5 Health	1276	2056	-781	150	...	...	374	...	...
6 Social security and welfare	1562	1435	127	78	...	...	248	...	...
7 Housing and community amenities	1697	1003	694	543	...	...	2801	...	...
8 Recreation, culture and religion	670	335	336	15	...	...	480	...	...
9 Economic services	3034	1933	1102	2984	...	...	8690	...	...
10 Other functions	121	101	20	-	...	...	15	...	...
Total	29808	23351	6457	3854	48705	82366	15060	2631	100058
1985									
1 General public services ᵃ	8137	6507	1630	73	...	...	840	...	...
2 Defence	2961	1470	1491	-	...	...	-	...	...
3 Public order and safety ᵃ	...	...	...	...	...	...	...	...	...
4 Education	11262	9255	2007	5	...	...	1420	...	...
5 Health	1212	2222	-1010	164	...	...	353	...	...
6 Social security and welfare	1726	1525	202	96	...	...	265	...	...
7 Housing and community amenities	1796	1056	740	610	...	...	3048	...	...
8 Recreation, culture and religion	718	359	359	16	...	...	454	...	...
9 Economic services	3108	2019	1089	2733	...	...	8964	...	...
10 Other functions	119	98	20	-	...	...	13	...	...
Total	31038	24511	6528	3697	51939	86674	15358	2744	104776

Japan

2.3 Total Government Outlays by Function and Type
(Continued)

Thousand Million Japanese yen — Fiscal year beginning 1 April

	Final Consumption Expenditures			Subsidies	Other Current Transfers & Property Income	Total Current Disbursements	Gross Capital Formation	Other Capital Outlays	Total Outlays
	Total	Compensation of Employees	Other						
1986									
1 General public services a	8860	6761	2099	63	...	...	910	...	...
2 Defence	3094	1551	1543	-	...	...	-	...	...
3 Public order and safety a	...	...	...	...	...	...	...	...	...
4 Education	11656	9613	2043	11	...	...	1156	...	...
5 Health	1230	2287	-1057	167	...	...	365	...	...
6 Social security and welfare	1819	1597	222	101	...	...	245	...	...
7 Housing and community amenities	1857	1106	751	631	...	...	3373	...	...
8 Recreation, culture and religion	758	380	378	16	...	...	515	...	...
9 Economic services	3162	2100	1062	2481	...	...	9674	...	...
10 Other functions	125	103	22	-	...	...	14	...	...
Total	32561	25498	7063	3470	55549	91580	16252	2780	110612
1987									
1 General public services a	8934	7013	1921	67	...	...	1287	...	...
2 Defence	3219	1576	1643	-	...	...	-	...	...
3 Public order and safety a	...	...	...	...	...	...	...	...	...
4 Education	11961	9841	2120	13	...	...	1159	...	...
5 Health	1267	2374	-1107	172	...	...	435	...	...
6 Social security and welfare	1888	1650	238	141	...	...	275	...	...
7 Housing and community amenities	1936	1170	766	658	...	...	3834	...	...
8 Recreation, culture and religion	800	397	403	19	...	...	566	...	...
9 Economic services	3116	2101	1015	2406	...	...	10884	...	...
10 Other functions	121	100	21	-	...	...	11	...	...
Total	33242	26222	7020	3476	58096	94814	18451	3382	116647
1988									
1 General public services a	9108	7295	1813	129	...	...	1339	...	...
2 Defence	3415	1642	1773	-	...	...	-	...	...
3 Public order and safety a	...	...	...	...	...	...	...	...	...
4 Education	12417	10230	2187	14	...	...	1059	...	...
5 Health	1362	2492	-1130	185	...	...	419	...	...
6 Social security and welfare	1931	1725	206	260	...	...	284	...	...
7 Housing and community amenities	2036	1169	867	645	...	...	4325	...	...
8 Recreation, culture and religion	860	416	444	17	...	...	597	...	...
9 Economic services	3228	2167	1061	2140	...	...	10592	...	...
10 Other functions	208	72	136	-	...	...	87	...	...
Total	34565	27208	7357	3390	60323	98278	18702	3982	120962
1989									
1 General public services a	9774	7691	2083	115	...	...	1180	...	...
2 Defence	3643	1698	1945	-	...	...	-	...	...
3 Public order and safety a	...	...	...	...	...	...	...	...	...
4 Education	12733	10472	2261	16	...	...	1276	...	...
5 Health	1495	2641	-1146	189	...	...	401	...	...
6 Social security and welfare	2114	1850	264	327	...	...	322	...	...
7 Housing and community amenities	2176	1221	955	1249	...	...	4501	...	...
8 Recreation, culture and religion	958	454	504	33	...	...	799	...	...
9 Economic services	3651	2417	1234	2961	...	...	11655	...	...
10 Other functions	172	75	97	-	...	...	91	...	...
Total	36716	28519	8197	4890	63354	104960	20225	3918	129103

a) Item 'Public order and safety' is included in item 'General public services'.

Japan

2.5 Private Final Consumption Expenditure by Type and Purpose, in Current Prices

Thousand Million Japanese yen

	1970	1975	1980	1981	1982	1983	1984	1985	1986	1987	1988	1989
Final Consumption Expenditure of Resident Households												
1 Food, beverages and tobacco	11503	23763	34045	36043	37479	39037	40193	41537	42043	42825	43888	45549
2 Clothing and footwear	2924	6778	10126	10230	11134	11458	11925	12490	12873	13374	13549	14280
3 Gross rent, fuel and power	6134	13015	25033	27364	29149	30949	32994	35082	36113	37919	40036	42807
4 Furniture, furnishings and household equipment and operation	2891	5291	8112	8346	9252	9939	10675	11478	11819	12329	12939	13653
5 Medical care and health expenses	2979	7502	13778	14923	16523	17683	18438	19549	20737	22053	23126	24002
6 Transport and communication	2934	8062	14072	14961	16073	17049	17582	18120	18620	19351	20904	22699
7 Recreational, entertainment, education and cultural services	3484	7322	12221	13154	14643	15624	17031	18259	19303	20069	21115	22660
8 Miscellaneous goods and services	4937	11858	21198	22083	23742	24893	26546	28819	30818	32784	34628	37118
Total Final Consumption Expenditure in the Domestic Market by Households, of which	37784	83591	138585	147103	157994	166632	175383	185335	192327	200704	210185	222768
A Durable goods	2350	4937	8184	8519	9368	10106	10846	11443	12568	13551	15176	16288
B Semi-durable goods	5374	11804	18192	18333	19825	20650	21396	22562	23157	23804	24470	26058
C Non-durable goods	14055	30212	46194	49605	52188	54524	56466	58361	58006	58595	59849	62468
D Services	16006	36639	66015	70646	76613	81352	86675	92969	98595	104753	110691	117954
Plus: Direct purchases abroad by resident households	131	425	1089	1069	1072	1100	1144	1196	1247	1591	2439	3158
Less: Direct purchases in the domestic market by non-resident households	110	96	167	184	213	223	260	297	266	322	387	450
Equals: Final Consumption Expenditure of Resident Households	37805	83920	139506	147988	158854	167509	176267	186235	193308	201973	212237	225476
Final Consumption Expenditure of Private Non-profit Institutions Serving Households												
Equals: Final Consumption Expenditure of Private Non-profit Organisations Serving Households	528	843	1818	2008	1980	2179	2364	2525	2661	2612	2885	2969
Private Final Consumption Expenditure	38333	84763	141324	149997	160833	169687	178631	188760	195969	204585	215122	228445

2.6 Private Final Consumption Expenditure by Type and Purpose, in Constant Prices

Thousand Million Japanese yen

	1970	1975	1980	1981	1982	1983	1984	1985	1986	1987	1988	1989
At constant prices of:1985												
Final Consumption Expenditure of Resident Households												
1 Food, beverages and tobacco	29887	36124	39112	39527	40752	41158	40706	41537	41863	43023	43941	44893
2 Clothing and footwear	7640	9705	11582	11261	11970	12055	12256	12490	12632	12952	13024	13215
3 Gross rent, fuel and power	15997	22694	29668	30768	31550	32526	33796	35082	35703	36992	38471	40243
4 Furniture, furnishings and household equipment and operation	6597	6904	8603	8531	9383	10049	10721	11478	11835	12438	13087	13724
5 Medical care and health expenses	6863	11924	16024	17021	18333	19571	19923	19549	20216	21036	22007	22585
6 Transport and communication	8780	13732	15874	16130	16320	17366	17757	18120	18904	19626	21349	23181
7 Recreational, entertainment, education and cultural services	9034	11222	13916	14134	15454	16227	17353	18259	19193	20193	21631	22935
8 Miscellaneous goods and services	14787	18718	23852	23856	25012	25586	26773	28819	30697	32395	34042	35611
Total Final Consumption Expenditure in the Domestic Market by Households, of which	99586	131022	158630	161227	168772	174539	179286	185335	191041	198655	207553	216387
A Durable goods	3472	5423	8107	8258	9113	9947	10724	11443	12967	14496	16962	18882
B Semi-durable goods	13313	16584	20294	19756	20978	21451	21855	22562	22896	23362	23847	24755
C Non-durable goods	36602	46140	52248	53247	55098	56535	56910	58361	58502	60025	61457	63118

Japan

2.6 Private Final Consumption Expenditure by Type and Purpose, in Constant Prices
(Continued)

Thousand Million Japanese yen

	1970	1975	1980	1981	1982	1983	1984	1985	1986	1987	1988	1989
					At constant prices of:1985							
D Services	46198	62875	77980	79967	83583	86605	89796	92969	96676	100772	105287	109633
Plus: Direct purchases abroad by resident households	288	744	1528	1338	1121	1159	1178	1205	1749	2504	4114	4671
Less: Direct purchases in the domestic market by non-resident households	298	150	191	200	226	232	265	296	265	321	384	436
Equals: Final Consumption Expenditure of Resident Households	99576	131617	159968	162365	169668	175466	180199	186243	192525	200837	211283	220622
Final Consumption Expenditure of Private Non-profit Institutions Serving Households												
Equals: Final Consumption Expenditure of Private Non-profit Organisations Serving Households	1712	1281	1958	2111	2070	2196	2330	2459	2554	2499	2700	2675
Private Final Consumption Expenditure	101288	132897	161925	164476	171738	177661	182529	188703	195079	203336	213983	223297

2.7 Gross Capital Formation by Type of Good and Owner, in Current Prices

Thousand Million Japanese yen

	1980				1981				1982			
	TOTAL	Total Private	Public Enterprises	General Government	TOTAL	Total Private	Public Enterprises	General Government	TOTAL	Total Private	Public Enterprises	General Government
Increase in stocks, total	1613	1913	-300	-	1423	1649	-225	-	1187	1542	-355	-
1 Goods producing industries	2080	...	...	...	1028	...	...	...	330	...	...	...
A Materials and supplies	141	...	...	...	-250	...	...	...	-165	...	...	...
B Work in progress	1193	...	...	...	854	...	...	...	-46	...	...	...
C Livestock, except breeding stocks, dairy cattle, etc.	...	...	...	...	...	...	...	...	...	...	...	...
D Finished goods	746	...	...	...	424	...	...	...	541	...	...	...
2 Wholesale and retail trade	-467	...	...	...	396	...	...	...	856	...	...	...
3 Other, except government stocks	...	...	...	...	...	...	...	...	...	...	...	...
4 Government stocks	...	...	...	...	...	...	...	...	...	...	...	...
Gross Fixed Capital Formation, Total	75821	52933	8203	14685	78908	54629	8632	15646	79735	55613	8442	15679
1 Residential buildings	16205	15317	889	...	15773	14885	888	...	15919	15041	878	...
2 Non-residential buildings	13631	...	...	...	14243	...	...	...	14224	...	...	...
3 Other construction	17415	...	...	...	18140	...	...	...	18002	...	...	...
4 Land improvement and plantation and orchard development	3843	...	...	...	4065	...	...	...	4105	...	...	...
5 Producers' durable goods	24727	...	...	...	26687	...	...	...	27485	...	...	...
A Transport equipment	5906	...	...	...	6097	...	...	...	5693	...	...	...
B Machinery and equipment	18822	...	...	...	20590	...	...	...	21791	...	...	...
6 Breeding stock, dairy cattle, etc.	...	...	...	...	...	...	...	...	...	...	...	...
Total Gross Capital Formation	77434	54846	7903	14685	80332	56278	8407	15646	80921	57155	8087	15679

	1983				1984				1985			
	TOTAL	Total Private	Public Enterprises	General Government	TOTAL	Total Private	Public Enterprises	General Government	TOTAL	Total Private	Public Enterprises	General Government
Increase in stocks, total	186	532	-345	-	1011	865	146	-	2159	1810	349	-
1 Goods producing industries	-89	...	...	...	1533	...	...	...	820	...	...	...
A Materials and supplies	-102	...	...	...	152	...	...	...	-226	...	...	...
B Work in progress	47	...	...	...	528	...	...	...	347	...	...	...
C Livestock, except breeding stocks, dairy cattle, etc.	...	...	...	...	...	...	...	...	...	...	...	...
D Finished goods	-34	...	...	...	853	...	...	...	698	...	...	...
2 Wholesale and retail trade	276	...	...	...	-522	...	...	...	1339	...	...	...
3 Other, except government stocks	...	...	...	...	...	...	...	...	...	...	...	...
4 Government stocks	...	...	...	...	...	...	...	...	...	...	...	...
Gross Fixed Capital Formation, Total	78881	55301	8105	15475	83251	60146	7942	15164	88040	66391	6480	15168
1 Residential buildings	15049	14138	912	...	14983	14098	885	...	15446	14633	813	...
2 Non-residential buildings	14112	...	...	...	14583	...	...	...	15170	...	...	...

Japan

2.7 Gross Capital Formation by Type of Good and Owner, in Current Prices
(Continued)

Thousand Million Japanese yen

	1983				1984				1985			
	TOTAL	Total Private	Public Enterprises	General Government	TOTAL	Total Private	Public Enterprises	General Government	TOTAL	Total Private	Public Enterprises	General Government
3 Other construction	17385	...	...	...	17677	...	...	...	17751	...	...	...
4 Land improvement and plantation and orchard development	4024	...	...	...	4169	...	...	...	4307	...	...	...
5 Producers' durable goods	28309	...	...	...	31840	...	...	...	35366	...	...	...
A Transport equipment	5976	...	...	...	5877	...	...	...	6648	...	...	...
B Machinery and equipment	22334	...	...	...	25962	...	...	...	28718	...	...	...
6 Breeding stock, dairy cattle, etc.	...	...	...	...	...	...	...	...	...	...	...	...
Total Gross Capital Formation	79067	55833	7760	15475	84262	61011	8088	15164	90198	68201	6829	15168

	1986				1987				1988			
	TOTAL	Total Private	Public Enterprises	General Government	TOTAL	Total Private	Public Enterprises	General Government	TOTAL	Total Private	Public Enterprises	General Government
Increase in stocks, total	1643	1170	473	-	690	746	-56	-	2630	3016	-386	-
1 Goods producing industries	-358	...	...	...	153	...	...	...	1205	...	...	...
A Materials and supplies	86	...	...	...	91	...	...	...	225	...	...	...
B Work in progress	-362	...	...	...	71	...	...	...	693	...	...	...
C Livestock, except breeding stocks, dairy cattle, etc.	...	...	...	...	...	...	...	...	...	...	...	...
D Finished goods	-81	...	...	...	-9	...	...	...	287	...	...	...
2 Wholesale and retail trade	2001	...	...	...	537	...	...	...	1425	...	...	...
3 Other, except government stocks	...	...	...	...	...	...	...	...	...	...	...	...
4 Government stocks	...	...	...	...	...	...	...	...	...	...	...	...
Gross Fixed Capital Formation, Total	91310	69040	6223	16048	99160	75430	6194	17536	111074	86027	6187	18860
1 Residential buildings	16568	15703	865	...	20301	19513	788	...	22927	22126	801	...
2 Non-residential buildings	15123	...	...	...	15210	...	...	...	16514	...	...	...
3 Other construction	18493	...	...	...	19694	...	...	...	21684	...	...	...
4 Land improvement and plantation and orchard development	4474	...	...	...	4753	...	...	...	5219	...	...	...
5 Producers' durable goods	36652	...	...	...	39202	...	...	...	44730	...	...	...
A Transport equipment	7323	...	...	...	8667	...	...	...	9672	...	...	...
B Machinery and equipment	29329	...	...	...	30535	...	...	...	35058	...	...	...
6 Breeding stock, dairy cattle, etc.	...	...	...	...	...	...	...	...	...	...	...	...
Total Gross Capital Formation	92953	70210	6696	16048	99850	76177	6138	17536	113704	89044	5801	18860

	1989			
	TOTAL	Total Private	Public Enterprises	General Government
Increase in stocks, total	3058	3215	-157	-
1 Goods producing industries	1536	...	...	...
A Materials and supplies	455	...	...	...
B Work in progress	443	...	...	...
C Livestock, except breeding stocks, dairy cattle, etc.	...	...	...	...
D Finished goods	637	...	...	...
2 Wholesale and retail trade	1523	...	...	...
3 Other, except government stocks	...	...	...	...
4 Government stocks	...	...	...	...
Gross Fixed Capital Formation, Total	122518	96559	6158	19802
1 Residential buildings	23917	23088	829	...
2 Non-residential buildings	19266	...	...	...

Japan

2.7 Gross Capital Formation by Type of Good and Owner, in Current Prices
(Continued)

Thousand Million Japanese yen

	1989			
	TOTAL	Total Private	Public Enterprises	General Government
3 Other construction	22377	...	...	...
4 Land improvement and plantation and orchard development	5685	...	...	...
5 Producers' durable goods	51273	...	...	...
A Transport equipment	12053	...	...	...
B Machinery and equipment	39219	...	...	...
6 Breeding stock, dairy cattle, etc.	...	...	...	...
Total Gross Capital Formation	125576	99774	6001	19802

2.8 Gross Capital Formation by Type of Good and Owner, in Constant Prices

Thousand Million Japanese yen

	1980				1981				1982			
	TOTAL	Total Private	Public Enterprises	General Government	TOTAL	Total Private	Public Enterprises	General Government	TOTAL	Total Private	Public Enterprises	General Government
	At constant prices of:1985											
Increase in stocks, total	1421	1781	-361	-	1357	1706	-349	-	1190	1665	-475	-
1 Goods producing industries	1935	...	...	...	958	...	...	...	354	...	...	...
A Materials and supplies	138	...	...	...	-239	...	...	...	-130	...	...	...
B Work in progress	1128	...	...	...	822	...	...	...	-34	...	...	...
C Livestock, except breeding stocks, dairy cattle, etc.	...	...	...	...	...	...	...	...	...	...	...	...
D Finished goods	669	...	...	...	375	...	...	...	518	...	...	...
2 Wholesale and retail trade	-514	...	...	...	399	...	...	...	837	...	...	...
3 Other, except government stocks	...	...	...	...	...	...	...	...	...	...	...	...
4 Government stocks	...	...	...	...	...	...	...	...	...	...	...	...
Gross Fixed Capital Formation, Total	78923	54624	8770	15529	80811	55730	8972	16109	80695	56142	8633	15920
1 Residential buildings	16917	15969	948	...	16535	15601	935	...	16394	15486	908	...
2 Non-residential buildings	14638	...	...	...	14987	...	...	...	14724	...	...	...
3 Other construction	18876	...	...	...	19031	...	...	...	18513	...	...	...
4 Land improvement and plantation and orchard development	4177	...	...	...	4274	...	...	...	4227	...	...	...
5 Producers' durable goods	24316	...	...	...	25984	...	...	...	26837	...	...	...
A Transport equipment	5964	...	...	...	6115	...	...	...	5640	...	...	...
B Machinery and equipment	18353	...	...	...	19869	...	...	...	21198	...	...	...
6 Breeding stock, dairy cattle, etc.	...	...	...	...	...	...	...	...	...	...	...	...
Total Gross Capital Formation	80344	56406	8409	15529	82168	57436	8622	16109	81886	57807	8159	15920

	1983				1984				1985			
	TOTAL	Total Private	Public Enterprises	General Government	TOTAL	Total Private	Public Enterprises	General Government	TOTAL	Total Private	Public Enterprises	General Government
	At constant prices of:1985											
Increase in stocks, total	130	592	-462	-	973	801	172	-	2160	1822	338	-
1 Goods producing industries	-112	...	...	...	1497	...	...	...	820	...	...	...
A Materials and supplies	-99	...	...	...	146	...	...	...	-225	...	...	...
B Work in progress	28	...	...	...	511	...	...	...	347	...	...	...
C Livestock, except breeding stocks, dairy cattle, etc.	...	...	...	...	...	...	...	...	...	...	...	...
D Finished goods	-41	...	...	...	840	...	...	...	698	...	...	...
2 Wholesale and retail trade	242	...	...	...	-523	...	...	...	1340	...	...	...
3 Other, except government stocks	...	...	...	...	...	...	...	...	...	...	...	...
4 Government stocks	...	...	...	...	...	...	...	...	...	...	...	...
Gross Fixed Capital Formation, Total	79919	55915	8275	15729	83641	60451	7983	15207	88079	66419	6484	15176
1 Residential buildings	15512	14571	940	...	15153	14259	894	...	15446	14633	813	...
2 Non-residential buildings	14564	...	...	...	14773	...	...	...	15179	...	...	...

979

Japan

2.8 Gross Capital Formation by Type of Good and Owner, in Constant Prices
(Continued)

Thousand Million Japanese yen

	1983				1984				1985			
	TOTAL	Total Private	Public Enterprises	General Government	TOTAL	Total Private	Public Enterprises	General Government	TOTAL	Total Private	Public Enterprises	General Government
	At constant prices of:1985											
3 Other construction	17831	...	...	...	17791	...	...	...	17760	...	...	...
4 Land improvement and plantation and orchard development	4141				4212				4309			
5 Producers' durable goods	27871	...	...	...	31711	...	...	...	35385	...	...	...
A Transport equipment	5947	...	...	...	5860	...	...	...	6652	...	...	...
B Machinery and equipment	21924	...	...	...	25851	...	...	...	28734	...	...	...
6 Breeding stock, dairy cattle, etc.	...	...	...	...	...	...	...	...	...	...	...	...
Total Gross Capital Formation	80049	56507	7813	15729	84614	61252	8155	15207	90239	68241	6822	15176

	1986				1987				1988			
	TOTAL	Total Private	Public Enterprises	General Government	TOTAL	Total Private	Public Enterprises	General Government	TOTAL	Total Private	Public Enterprises	General Government
	At constant prices of:1985											
Increase in stocks, total	1780	1197	583	-	876	825	51	-	2979	3218	-240	-
1 Goods producing industries	-393	...	...	...	253	...	...	...	1326	...	...	...
A Materials and supplies	153	...	...	...	96	...	...	...	129	...	...	...
B Work in progress	-412	...	...	...	155	...	...	...	871	...	...	...
C Livestock, except breeding stocks, dairy cattle, etc.	...	...	...	...	...	...	...	...	...	...	...	...
D Finished goods	-133	...	...	...	1	...	...	...	327	...	...	...
2 Wholesale and retail trade	2173	...	...	...	623	...	...	...	1653	...	...	...
3 Other, except government stocks	...	...	...	...	...	...	...	...	...	...	...	...
4 Government stocks	...	...	...	...	...	...	...	...	...	...	...	...
Gross Fixed Capital Formation, Total	92271	69825	6260	16186	101094	77002	6276	17816	113147	87811	6216	19119
1 Residential buildings	16646	15778	868	...	20137	19349	789	...	22432	21644	788	...
2 Non-residential buildings	15176	...	...	...	15237	...	...	...	16169	...	...	...
3 Other construction	18567	...	...	...	19733	...	...	...	21261	...	...	...
4 Land improvement and plantation and orchard development	4501	...	...	...	4777	...	...	...	5134	...	...	...
5 Producers' durable goods	37381	...	...	...	41209	...	...	...	48151	...	...	...
A Transport equipment	7469	...	...	...	9049	...	...	...	10075	...	...	...
B Machinery and equipment	29911	...	...	...	32160	...	...	...	38076	...	...	...
6 Breeding stock, dairy cattle, etc.	...	...	...	...	...	...	...	...	...	...	...	...
Total Gross Capital Formation	94051	71022	6842	16186	101969	77827	6326	17816	116126	91029	5977	19119

	1989			
	TOTAL	Total Private	Public Enterprises	General Government
	At constant prices of:1985			
Increase in stocks, total	3597	3684	-88	...
1 Goods producing industries	1858	...	...	...
A Materials and supplies	618	...	...	...
B Work in progress	510	...	...	...
C Livestock, except breeding stocks, dairy cattle, etc.	...	...	...	...
D Finished goods	731	...	...	...
2 Wholesale and retail trade	1738	...	...	...
3 Other, except government stocks	...	...	...	...
4 Government stocks	...	...	...	...
Gross Fixed Capital Formation, Total	123217	98174	6022	19020
1 Residential buildings	22436	21661	774	...
2 Non-residential buildings	17937	...	...	...

Japan

2.8 Gross Capital Formation by Type of Good and Owner, in Constant Prices
(Continued)

Thousand Million Japanese yen

	TOTAL	Total Private	Public Enterprises	General Government
		1989		
		At constant prices of:1985		
3 Other construction	21987	...	...	...
4 Land improvement and plantation and orchard development	5336	...	...	...
5 Producers' durable goods	55521	...	...	...
A Transport equipment	12838	...	...	...
B Machinery and equipment	42683	...	...	...
6 Breeding stock, dairy cattle, etc.	...	...	...	...
Total Gross Capital Formation	126813	101859	5934	19020

2.13 Stocks of Reproducible Fixed Assets, by Type of Good and Owner, in Current Prices

Thousand Million Japanese yen

	TOTAL		Total Private		Public Enterprises		General Government	
	Gross	Net	Gross	Net	Gross	Net	Gross	Net
				1980				
1 Residential buildings	...	133622	...	...	...	...	...	...
2 Non-residential buildings	...	116240	...	...	...	...	...	...
3 Other construction	...	186076	...	...	...	...	...	...
4 Land improvement and plantation and orchard development a	...	...	...	...	...	...	...	...
5 Producers' durable goods	...	90726	...	...	...	...	...	...
A Transport equipment	...	17490	...	...	...	...	...	...
B Machinery and equipment	...	73236	...	...	...	...	...	...
6 Breeding stock, dairy cattle, etc.	...	...	...	...	...	...	...	...
Total	...	526664	...	325549	...	65376	...	135738
				1981				
1 Residential buildings	...	140277	...	...	...	...	...	...
2 Non-residential buildings	...	125539	...	...	...	...	...	...
3 Other construction	...	203205	...	...	...	...	...	...
4 Land improvement and plantation and orchard development a	...	...	...	...	...	...	...	...
5 Producers' durable goods	...	95532	...	...	...	...	...	...
A Transport equipment	...	18406	...	...	...	...	...	...
B Machinery and equipment	...	77126	...	...	...	...	...	...
6 Breeding stock, dairy cattle, etc.	...	...	...	...	...	...	...	...
Total	...	564553	...	345943	...	70097	...	148514
				1982				
1 Residential buildings	...	146527	...	...	...	...	...	...
2 Non-residential buildings	...	133740	...	...	...	...	...	...
3 Other construction	...	216156	...	...	...	...	...	...
4 Land improvement and plantation and orchard development a	...	...	...	...	...	...	...	...
5 Producers' durable goods	...	100646	...	...	...	...	...	...
A Transport equipment	...	18386	...	...	...	...	...	...
B Machinery and equipment	...	82260	...	...	...	...	...	...
6 Breeding stock, dairy cattle, etc.	...	...	...	...	...	...	...	...
Total	...	597069	...	364726	...	73696	...	158648

Japan

2.13 Stocks of Reproducible Fixed Assets, by Type of Good and Owner, in Current Prices
(Continued)

Thousand Million Japanese yen

	TOTAL		Total Private		Public Enterprises		General Government	
	Gross	Net	Gross	Net	Gross	Net	Gross	Net
1983								
1 Residential buildings	...	149221	...	...	...	...	...	...
2 Non-residential buildings	...	140386	...	...	...	...	...	...
3 Other construction	...	227241	...	...	...	...	...	...
4 Land improvement and plantation and orchard development a	...	...	...	...	...	...	...	...
5 Producers' durable goods	...	104537	...	...	...	...	...	...
A Transport equipment	...	18561	...	...	...	...	...	...
B Machinery and equipment	...	85976	...	...	...	...	...	...
6 Breeding stock, dairy cattle, etc.	...	...	...	...	...	...	...	...
Total	...	621385	...	377412	...	76191	...	167783
1984								
1 Residential buildings	...	154757	...	...	...	...	...	...
2 Non-residential buildings	...	149009	...	...	...	...	...	...
3 Other construction	...	241231	...	...	...	...	...	...
4 Land improvement and plantation and orchard development a	...	...	...	...	...	...	...	...
5 Producers' durable goods	...	111488	...	...	...	...	...	...
A Transport equipment	...	18694	...	...	...	...	...	...
B Machinery and equipment	...	92794	...	...	...	...	...	...
6 Breeding stock, dairy cattle, etc.	...	...	...	...	...	...	...	...
Total	...	656485	...	398915	...	79244	...	178326
1985								
1 Residential buildings	...	159174	...	...	...	...	...	...
2 Non-residential buildings	...	156335	...	...	...	...	...	...
3 Other construction	...	252748	...	...	...	...	...	...
4 Land improvement and plantation and orchard development a	...	...	...	...	...	...	...	...
5 Producers' durable goods	...	119124	...	...	...	...	...	...
A Transport equipment	...	19352	...	...	...	...	...	...
B Machinery and equipment	...	99772	...	...	...	...	...	...
6 Breeding stock, dairy cattle, etc.	...	...	...	...	...	...	...	...
Total	...	687381	...	434084	...	66147	...	187151
1986								
1 Residential buildings	...	160968	...	...	...	...	...	...
2 Non-residential buildings	...	160209	...	...	...	...	...	...
3 Other construction	...	265817	...	...	...	...	...	...
4 Land improvement and plantation and orchard development a	...	...	...	...	...	...	...	...
5 Producers' durable goods	...	124903	...	...	...	...	...	...
A Transport equipment	...	20330	...	...	...	...	...	...
B Machinery and equipment	...	104573	...	...	...	...	...	...
6 Breeding stock, dairy cattle, etc.	...	...	...	...	...	...	...	...
Total	...	711897	...	450102	...	66537	...	195260
1987								
1 Residential buildings	...	172598	...	...	...	...	...	...
2 Non-residential buildings	...	168881	...	...	...	...	...	...
3 Other construction	...	281967	...	...	...	...	...	...
4 Land improvement and plantation and orchard development a	...	...	...	...	...	...	...	...
5 Producers' durable goods	...	131937	...	...	...	...	...	...
A Transport equipment	...	22082	...	...	...	...	...	...
B Machinery and equipment	...	109855	...	...	...	...	...	...
6 Breeding stock, dairy cattle, etc.	...	...	...	...	...	...	...	...
Total	...	755383	...	486763	...	60996	...	207623

Japan

2.13 Stocks of Reproducible Fixed Assets, by Type of Good and Owner, in Current Prices
(Continued)

Thousand Million Japanese yen

	TOTAL		Total Private		Public Enterprises		General Government	
	Gross	Net	Gross	Net	Gross	Net	Gross	Net
1988								
1 Residential buildings	...	182462	...	...	...	...	...	...
2 Non-residential buildings	...	177794	...	...	...	...	...	...
3 Other construction	...	301813	...	...	...	...	...	...
4 Land improvement and plantation and orchard development a	...	...	...	...	...	...	...	...
5 Producers' durable goods	...	143868	...	...	...	...	...	...
A Transport equipment	...	24553	...	...	...	...	...	...
B Machinery and equipment	...	119315	...	...	...	...	...	...
6 Breeding stock, dairy cattle, etc.	...	...	...	...	...	...	...	...
Total	...	805937	...	521078	...	63490	...	221369
1989								
1 Residential buildings	...	201232	...	...	...	...	...	...
2 Non-residential buildings	...	194941	...	...	...	...	...	...
3 Other construction	...	329322	...	...	...	...	...	...
4 Land improvement and plantation and orchard development a	...	...	...	...	...	...	...	...
5 Producers' durable goods	...	164087	...	...	...	...	...	...
A Transport equipment	...	28490	...	...	...	...	...	...
B Machinery and equipment	...	135597	...	...	...	...	...	...
6 Breeding stock, dairy cattle, etc.	...	...	...	...	...	...	...	...
Total	...	889582	...	579227	...	67161	...	241839

a) Item 'Land improvement and plantation and orchard development' is excluded from this table.

2.14 Stocks of Reproducible Fixed Assets, by Type of Good and Owner, in Constant Prices

Thousand Million Japanese yen

	TOTAL		Total Private		Public Enterprises		General Government	
	Gross	Net	Gross	Net	Gross	Net	Gross	Net
At constant prices of:1985								
1980								
1 Residential buildings	...	142549	...	...	...	...	...	...
2 Non-residential buildings	...	124818	...	...	...	...	...	...
3 Other construction	...	201613	...	...	...	...	...	...
4 Land improvement and plantation and orchard development a	...	...	...	...	...	...	...	...
5 Producers' durable goods	...	85429	...	...	...	...	...	...
A Transport equipment	...	17144	...	...	...	...	...	...
B Machinery and equipment	...	68285	...	...	...	...	...	...
6 Breeding stock, dairy cattle, etc.	...	...	...	...	...	...	...	...
Total	...	554409	...	...	...	...	...	...
1981								
1 Residential buildings	...	147306	...	...	...	...	...	...
2 Non-residential buildings	...	132119	...	...	...	...	...	...
3 Other construction	...	213682	...	...	...	...	...	...
4 Land improvement and plantation and orchard development a	...	...	...	...	...	...	...	...
5 Producers' durable goods	...	91213	...	...	...	...	...	...
A Transport equipment	...	17796	...	...	...	...	...	...
B Machinery and equipment	...	73417	...	...	...	...	...	...
6 Breeding stock, dairy cattle, etc.	...	...	...	...	...	...	...	...
Total	...	584320	...	...	...	...	...	...

Japan

2.14 Stocks of Reproducible Fixed Assets, by Type of Good and Owner, in Constant Prices
(Continued)

Thousand Million Japanese yen

	TOTAL		Total Private		Public Enterprises		General Government	
	Gross	Net	Gross	Net	Gross	Net	Gross	Net

At constant prices of:1985

1982

1 Residential buildings	...	151497	...	...	...	...	...	...
2 Non-residential buildings	...	138713	...	...	...	...	...	...
3 Other construction	...	224644	...	...	...	...	...	...
4 Land improvement and plantation and orchard development [a]	...	...	...	...	...	...	...	...
5 Producers' durable goods	...	96678	...	...	...	...	...	...
A Transport equipment	...	17899	...	...	...	...	...	...
B Machinery and equipment	...	78779	...	...	...	...	...	...
6 Breeding stock, dairy cattle, etc.	...	...	...	...	...	...	...	...
Total	...	611532	...	...	...	...	...	...

1983

1 Residential buildings	...	154440	...	...	...	...	...	...
2 Non-residential buildings	...	144710	...	...	...	...	...	...
3 Other construction	...	234372	...	...	...	...	...	...
4 Land improvement and plantation and orchard development [a]	...	...	...	...	...	...	...	...
5 Producers' durable goods	...	101969	...	...	...	...	...	...
A Transport equipment	...	18266	...	...	...	...	...	...
B Machinery and equipment	...	83703	...	...	...	...	...	...
6 Breeding stock, dairy cattle, etc.	...	...	...	...	...	...	...	...
Total	...	635491	...	...	...	...	...	...

1984

1 Residential buildings	...	156783	...	...	...	...	...	...
2 Non-residential buildings	...	150508	...	...	...	...	...	...
3 Other construction	...	243752	...	...	...	...	...	...
4 Land improvement and plantation and orchard development [a]	...	...	...	...	...	...	...	...
5 Producers' durable goods	...	109403	...	...	...	...	...	...
A Transport equipment	...	18489	...	...	...	...	...	...
B Machinery and equipment	...	90914	...	...	...	...	...	...
6 Breeding stock, dairy cattle, etc.	...	...	...	...	...	...	...	...
Total	...	660446	...	...	...	...	...	...

1985

1 Residential buildings	...	159174	...	...	...	...	...	...
2 Non-residential buildings	...	156335	...	...	...	...	...	...
3 Other construction	...	252748	...	...	...	...	...	...
4 Land improvement and plantation and orchard development [a]	...	...	...	...	...	...	...	...
5 Producers' durable goods	...	119124	...	...	...	...	...	...
A Transport equipment	...	19352	...	...	...	...	...	...
B Machinery and equipment	...	99772	...	...	...	...	...	...
6 Breeding stock, dairy cattle, etc.	...	...	...	...	...	...	...	...
Total	...	687381	...	...	...	...	...	...

1986

1 Residential buildings	...	162585	...	...	...	...	...	...
2 Non-residential buildings	...	161821	...	...	...	...	...	...
3 Other construction	...	261913	...	...	...	...	...	...
4 Land improvement and plantation and orchard development [a]	...	...	...	...	...	...	...	...
5 Producers' durable goods	...	129159	...	...	...	...	...	...
A Transport equipment	...	20643	...	...	...	...	...	...
B Machinery and equipment	...	108516	...	...	...	...	...	...
6 Breeding stock, dairy cattle, etc.	...	...	...	...	...	...	...	...
Total	...	715478	...	...	...	...	...	...

Japan

2.14 Stocks of Reproducible Fixed Assets, by Type of Good and Owner, in Constant Prices
(Continued)

Thousand Million Japanese yen

	TOTAL		Total Private		Public Enterprises		General Government	
	Gross	Net	Gross	Net	Gross	Net	Gross	Net
At constant prices of:1985								
1987								
1 Residential buildings	...	169068	...	...	...	...	...	...
2 Non-residential buildings	...	167071	...	...	...	...	...	...
3 Other construction	...	272044	...	...	...	...	...	...
4 Land improvement and plantation and orchard development [a]	...	...	...	...	...	...	...	...
5 Producers' durable goods	...	140653	...	...	...	...	...	...
A Transport equipment	...	23010	...	...	...	...	...	...
B Machinery and equipment	...	117643	...	...	...	...	...	...
6 Breeding stock, dairy cattle, etc.	...	...	...	...	...	...	...	...
Total	...	748836	...	...	...	...	...	...
1988								
1 Residential buildings	...	177179	...	...	...	...	...	...
2 Non-residential buildings	...	172970	...	...	...	...	...	...
3 Other construction	...	283503	...	...	...	...	...	...
4 Land improvement and plantation and orchard development [a]	...	...	...	...	...	...	...	...
5 Producers' durable goods	...	156011	...	...	...	...	...	...
A Transport equipment	...	25721	...	...	...	...	...	...
B Machinery and equipment	...	130290	...	...	...	...	...	...
6 Breeding stock, dairy cattle, etc.	...	...	...	...	...	...	...	...
Total	...	789663	...	...	...	...	...	...
1989								
1 Residential buildings	...	184707	...	...	...	...	...	...
2 Non-residential buildings	...	180388	...	...	...	...	...	...
3 Other construction	...	295613	...	...	...	...	...	...
4 Land improvement and plantation and orchard development [a]	...	...	...	...	...	...	...	...
5 Producers' durable goods	...	174402	...	...	...	...	...	...
A Transport equipment	...	29941	...	...	...	...	...	...
B Machinery and equipment	...	144461	...	...	...	...	...	...
6 Breeding stock, dairy cattle, etc.	...	...	...	...	...	...	...	...
Total	...	835110	...	...	...	...	...	...

a) Item 'Land improvement and plantation and orchard development' is excluded from this table.

2.17 Exports and Imports of Goods and Services, Detail

Thousand Million Japanese yen

	1970	1975	1980	1981	1982	1983	1984	1985	1986	1987	1988	1989
Exports of Goods and Services												
1 Exports of merchandise, f.o.b. [a]	6873	16579	29022	33656	34748	34964	40381	41555	34575	32490	33398	37372
2 Transport and communication	544	1518	2447	2709	2778	2460	2635	2607	1732	1738	1860	2313
A In respect of merchandise imports	...	...	...	...	...	...	...	...	...	...	...	...
B Other	544	1518	2447	2709	2778	2460	2635	2607	1732	1738	1860	2313
3 Insurance service charges	85	233	71	66	48	1	22	2	27	42	31	28
A In respect of merchandise imports	...	...	...	...	...	...	...	...	...	...	...	...
B Other	85	233	71	66	48	1	22	2	27	42	31	28
4 Other commodities	148	433	938	1022	1125	1195	1293	1324	1107	1318	1537	1901
5 Adjustments of merchandise exports to change-of-ownership basis [a]	...	...	...	...	...	...	...	...	...	...	...	...
6 Direct purchases in the domestic market by non-residential households	110	96	167	184	213	223	260	297	266	322	387	450
7 Direct purchases in the domestic market by extraterritorial bodies	167	125	241	341	479	432	476	522	383	300	270	288
Total Exports of Goods and Services	7926	18982	32887	37977	39391	39275	45066	46307	38090	36210	37483	42352

985

Japan

2.17 Exports and Imports of Goods and Services, Detail
(Continued)

Thousand Million Japanese yen

	1970	1975	1980	1981	1982	1983	1984	1985	1986	1987	1988	1989
					Imports of Goods and Services							
1 Imports of merchandise, c.i.f. [b]	5484	15158	29153	29500	30655	27902	30328	28856	19356	18708	21330	26906
A Imports of merchandise, f.o.b. [a]	5484	15158	29153	29500	30655	27902	30328	28856	19356	18708	21330	42352
B Transport of services on merchandise imports	...	...	...	...	...	...	...	...	...	...	...	...
C Insurance service charges on merchandise imports	...	...	...	...	...	...	...	...	...	...	...	...
2 Adjustments of merchandise imports to change-of-ownership basis [a]	...	...	...	...	...	...	...	...	...	...	...	...
3 Other transport and communication	931	2065	2915	3025	3109	2777	2832	2773	2018	2414	2648	3215
4 Other insurance service charges	105	279	171	159	146	129	158	129	142	172	171	174
5 Other commodities	323	989	1698	2157	2331	2323	2376	2542	1996	2288	2452	3286
6 Direct purchases abroad by government	12	4	11	18	28	28	29	36	32	22	25	30
7 Direct purchases abroad by resident households	131	425	1089	1069	1073	1100	1144	1196	1247	1591	2439	3158
Total Imports of Goods and Services	6985	18919	35036	35927	37341	34258	36866	35532	24791	25195	29065	36768
Balance of Goods and Services	941	63	-2149	2050	2050	5017	8200	10775	13299	11015	8418	5584
Total Imports and Balance of Goods and Services	7926	18982	32887	37977	39391	39275	45066	46307	38090	36210	37483	42352

a) Item 'Adjustment of merchandise export/import to change-of-ownership basis' is included in item 'Exports/Imports of merchandise, f.o.b.'.   b) Imports of merchandise c.i.f. is not estimated in the Balance of Payments in Japan. Therefore, valuation basis is f.o.b.

3.11 General Government Production Account: Total and Subsectors

Thousand Million Japanese yen

	1980					1981				
	Total General Government	Central Government	State or Provincial Government	Local Government	Social Security Funds	Total General Government	Central Government	State or Provincial Government	Local Government	Social Security Funds
					Gross Output					
1 Sales	...	...	...	...	...	...	...	...	...	...
2 Services produced for own use	23568	5676	...	18107	339	25585	6029	...	19601	372
3 Own account fixed capital formation	...	...	...	...	...	...	...	...	...	...
Gross Output [a]	27712	...	...	...	...	29974	...	...	...	...
					Gross Input					
Intermediate Consumption	7213	...	...	...	...	7940	...	...	...	...
Subtotal: Value Added	20500	...	...	...	...	22035	...	...	...	...
1 Indirect taxes, net	30	...	...	...	...	32	...	...	...	...
A Indirect taxes	30	...	...	...	...	32	...	...	...	...
B Less: Subsidies	...	...	...	...	...	...	...	...	...	...
2 Consumption of fixed capital	1393	...	...	...	...	1599	...	...	...	...
3 Compensation of employees	19077	...	...	...	...	20404	...	...	...	...
4 Net Operating surplus	...	...	...	...	...	...	...	...	...	...
Gross Input [a]	27713	...	...	...	...	29975	...	...	...	...
	1982					1983				
	Total General Government	Central Government	State or Provincial Government	Local Government	Social Security Funds	Total General Government	Central Government	State or Provincial Government	Local Government	Social Security Funds
					Gross Output					
1 Sales	...	...	...	...	...	...	...	...	...	...
2 Services produced for own use	26796	6258	...	20299	405	27996	6636	...	21169	499
3 Own account fixed capital formation	...	...	...	...	...	...	...	...	...	...
Gross Output [a]	31449	...	...	...	...	32884	...	...	...	...
					Gross Input					
Intermediate Consumption	8391	...	...	...	...	8985	...	...	...	...
Subtotal: Value Added	23058	...	...	...	...	23899	...	...	...	...

Japan

3.11 General Government Production Account: Total and Subsectors
(Continued)

Thousand Million Japanese yen

	1982					1983				
	Total General Government	Central Government	State or Provincial Government	Local Government	Social Security Funds	Total General Government	Central Government	State or Provincial Government	Local Government	Social Security Funds
1 Indirect taxes, net	34	...	...	...	...	35	...	...	...	...
A Indirect taxes	34	...	...	...	...	35	...	...	...	...
B Less: Subsidies	...	...	...	...	...	...	...	...	...	...
2 Consumption of fixed capital	1752	...	...	...	...	1892	...	...	...	...
3 Compensation of employees	21272	...	...	...	...	21973	...	...	...	...
4 Net Operating surplus	...	...	...	...	...	...	...	...	...	...
Gross Input ᵃ	31449	...	...	...	...	32885	...	...	...	...

	1984					1985				
	Total General Government	Central Government	State or Provincial Government	Local Government	Social Security Funds	Total General Government	Central Government	State or Provincial Government	Local Government	Social Security Funds
	Gross Output									
1 Sales	...	...	...	...	...	...	...	...	...	...
2 Services produced for own use	29449	7146	...	22112	550	30685	7489	...	22953	597
3 Own account fixed capital formation	...	...	...	...	...	...	...	...	...	...
Gross Output ᵃ	34760	...	...	...		36454	...	...	...	
	Gross Input									
Intermediate Consumption	9629	...	...	...	...	10170	...	...	...	...
Subtotal: Value Added	25131	...	...	...	...	26285	...	...	...	...
1 Indirect taxes, net	36	...	...	...	...	36	...	...	...	...
A Indirect taxes	36	...	...	...	...	36	...	...	...	...
B Less: Subsidies	...	...	...	...	...	...	...	...	...	...
2 Consumption of fixed capital	2012	...	...	...	...	2078	...	...	...	...
3 Compensation of employees	23083	...	...	...	...	24172	...	...	...	...
4 Net Operating surplus	...	...	...	...	...	...	...	...	...	...
Gross Input ᵃ	34760	...	...	...	...	36454	...	...	...	...

	1986					1987				
	Total General Government	Central Government	State or Provincial Government	Local Government	Social Security Funds	Total General Government	Central Government	State or Provincial Government	Local Government	Social Security Funds
	Gross Output									
1 Sales	...	...	...	...	...	...	...	...	...	...
2 Services produced for own use	32388	8094	...	23834	632	32975	7996	...	24567	679
3 Own account fixed capital formation	...	...	...	...	...	...	...	...	...	...
Gross Output ᵃ	38583	...	...	...	...	39547	...	...	...	...
	Gross Input									
Intermediate Consumption	11048	...	...	...	...	11205	...	...	...	...
Subtotal: Value Added	27535	...	...	...	...	28343	...	...	...	...
1 Indirect taxes, net	36	...	...	...	...	37	...	...	...	...
A Indirect taxes	36	...	...	...	...	37	...	...	...	...
B Less: Subsidies	...	...	...	...	...	...	...	...	...	...
2 Consumption of fixed capital	2144	...	...	...	...	2245	...	...	...	...
3 Compensation of employees	25355	...	...	...	...	26061	...	...	...	...
4 Net Operating surplus	...	...	...	...	...	...	...	...	...	...
Gross Input ᵃ	38583	...	...	...	...	39547	...	...	...	...

	1988					1989				
	Total General Government	Central Government	State or Provincial Government	Local Government	Social Security Funds	Total General Government	Central Government	State or Provincial Government	Local Government	Social Security Funds
	Gross Output									
1 Sales	...	...	...	...	...	...	...	...	...	...
2 Services produced for own use	34184	8332	...	25570	663	36240	8853	...	27124	709
3 Own account fixed capital formation	...	...	...	...	...	...	...	...	...	...
Gross Output ᵃ	41015	...	...	...	...	43453	...	...	...	...
	Gross Input									
Intermediate Consumption	11702	...	...	...	...	12608	...	...	...	...
Subtotal: Value Added	29314	...	...	...	...	30845	...	...	...	...

Japan

3.11 General Government Production Account: Total and Subsectors
(Continued)

Thousand Million Japanese yen

	1988					1989				
	Total General Government	Central Government	State or Provincial Government	Local Government	Social Security Funds	Total General Government	Central Government	State or Provincial Government	Local Government	Social Security Funds
1 Indirect taxes, net	37	...	...	...	...	43	...	...	...	...
A Indirect taxes	37	...	...	...	...	43	...	...	...	...
B Less: Subsidies	...	...	...	...	...	...	...	...	...	...
2 Consumption of fixed capital	2325	...	...	...	...	2456	...	...	...	...
3 Compensation of employees	26952	...	...	...	...	28346	...	...	...	...
4 Net Operating surplus	...	...	...	...	...	...	...	...	...	...
Gross Input a	41015	...	...	...	...	43453	...	...	...	...

a) The subsectors of general government, central government, local government, and social
security funds refer to fiscal year beginning 1 April.

3.12 General Government Income and Outlay Account: Total and Subsectors

Thousand Million Japanese yen

	1980					1981				
	Total General Government	Central Government	State or Provincial Government	Local Government	Social Security Funds	Total General Government	Central Government	State or Provincial Government	Local Government	Social Security Funds
Receipts										
1 Operating surplus	...	...	...	...	...	...	...	...	...	...
2 Property and entrepreneurial income	4626	1310	...	664	2933	5665	1735	...	786	3404
3 Taxes, fees and contributions	61338	29118	...	16555	18184	68828	31429	...	17980	20492
A Indirect taxes	17688	8397	...	9714	...	19455	9337	...	10298	...
B Direct taxes	25876	20592	...	6712	...	29029	21959	...	7547	...
Income	24954	...	...	...	...	28053	...	...	...	...
Other	921	...	...	...	...	976	...	...	...	...
C Social security contributions	17513	-	...	-	18177	20072	-	...	-	20484
D Fees, fines and penalties	261	129	...	129	7	272	133	...	135	8
4 Other current transfers	250	413	...	13424	5779	302	460	...	14404	6220
A Casualty insurance claims	6	3	...	3	-	7	4	...	4	-
B Transfers from other government subsectors	...	198	...	13418	5733	...	212	...	14397	6167
C Transfers from the rest of the world	10	14	...	-	...	13	8	...	-	...
D Other transfers, except imputed	227	194	...	...	46	274	232	...	...	53
E Imputed unfunded employee pension and welfare contributions ...	6	4	...	3	...	8	4	...	3	...
Total Current Receipts a	66214	30840	...	30642	26896	74795	33626	...	33168	30115
Disbursements										
1 Government final consumption expenditure	23568	5676	...	18107	339	25585	6029	...	19601	372
2 Property income	7569	5853	...	2162	-	9229	7126	...	2469	-
A Interest	7500	...	...	...	...	9142	...	...	...	...
B Net land rent and royalties	69	...	...	...	...	86	...	...	...	...
3 Subsidies	3593	2846	...	809	...	3745	2968	...	843	...
4 Other current transfers	25269	21147	...	4337	19880	28367	22744	...	4688	22288
A Casualty insurance premiums, net	6	3	...	3	-	7	4	...	4	-
B Transfers to other government subsectors	...	18900	...	229	220	...	20312	...	232	232
C Social security benefits	18919	-	...	-	19571	21453	-	...	-	21959
D Social assistance grants	5250	1750	...	3580	...	5711	1881	...	3874	...
E Unfunded employee pension and welfare benefits	6	4	...	3	-	8	4	...	3	-
F Transfers to private non-profit institutions serving households	1003	416	...	521	90	1108	462	...	576	98
G Other transfers n.e.c.	...	...	...	...	...	...	...	...	...	...
H Transfers to the rest of the world	84	74	...	-	...	80	81	...	-	...
Net saving	6214	-4680	...	5227	6677	7868	-5241	...	5567	7454
Total Current Disbursements and Net Saving a	66214	30840	...	30642	26896	74795	33626	...	33168	30115

Japan

3.12 General Government Income and Outlay Account: Total and Subsectors

Thousand Million Japanese yen

	1982					1983				
	Total General Government	Central Government	State or Provincial Government	Local Government	Social Security Funds	Total General Government	Central Government	State or Provincial Government	Local Government	Social Security Funds

Receipts

1 Operating surplus	...	...	...	...	...	...	...	...	...	...
2 Property and entrepreneurial income	6213	1640	...	806	3836	6686	1471	...	839	4484
3 Taxes, fees and contributions	72890	33134	...	19249	21951	76426	35376	...	20450	23163
A Indirect taxes	20285	9568	...	10940	...	20631	10137	...	11520	
B Direct taxes	30680	23432	...	8170	...	32605	25095	...	8785	
Income	29680	...	...	...	...	31516	...	...	...	
Other	1000	...	...	...	...	1089	...	...	...	
C Social security contributions	21645	-	...	-	21942	22896	-	...	-	23154
D Fees, fines and penalties	280	134	...	139	9	294	144	...	145	9
4 Other current transfers	351	508	...	15166	6664	393	476	...	15289	7368
A Casualty insurance claims	8	4	...	4	-	9	5	...	5	-
B Transfers from other government subsectors	...	212	...	15159	6603	...	139	...	15281	7309
C Transfers from the rest of the world	12	12	...	-	...	12	14	...	-	...
D Other transfers, except imputed	324	276	...	...	61	363	313	...	...	59
E Imputed unfunded employee pension and welfare contributions	7	4	...	3	...	8	5	...	3	...
Total Current Receipts [a]	79455	35281	...	35221	32451	83505	37323	...	36578	35014

Disbursements

1 Government final consumption expenditure	26796	6258	...	20299	405	27996	6636	...	21169	499
2 Property income	10390	7898	...	2769	-	11944	9365	...	3025	-
A Interest	10299	...	...	...	...	11848	...	...	...	...
B Net land rent and royalties	91	...	...	...	...	96	...	...	...	...
3 Subsidies	3780	3082	...	868	...	3968	3127	...	870	...
4 Other current transfers	30917	24015	...	4985	24451	33081	24422	...	5186	26605
A Casualty insurance premiums, net	9	5	...	5	-	10	5	...	5	-
B Transfers to other government subsectors	...	21466	...	273	235	...	21857	...	719	152
C Social security benefits	23627	-	...	-	24102	25883	-	...	-	26318
D Social assistance grants	6038	1951	...	4120	...	5764	1936	...	3747	...
E Unfunded employee pension and welfare benefits	7	4	...	3	-	8	5	...	3	-
F Transfers to private non-profit institutions serving households	1145	494	...	584	114	1306	499	...	711	134
G Other transfers n.e.c.	...	...	...	...	...	...	...	...	...	...
H Transfers to the rest of the world	91	96	...	-	...	111	121	...	-	...
Net saving	7571	-5971	...	6300	7595	6516	-6228	...	6328	7910
Total Current Disbursements and Net Saving [a]	79455	35281	...	35221	32451	83505	37323	...	36578	35014

	1984					1985				
	Total General Government	Central Government	State or Provincial Government	Local Government	Social Security Funds	Total General Government	Central Government	State or Provincial Government	Local Government	Social Security Funds

Receipts

1 Operating surplus	...	...	...	...	...	...	...	...	...	...
2 Property and entrepreneurial income	7464	1624	...	908	5152	8369	1726	...	1029	5841
3 Taxes, fees and contributions	82823	37927	...	22100	24579	89908	40493	...	23947	27130
A Indirect taxes	22943	10695	...	12488	...	24900	10926	...	13455	...
B Direct taxes	35291	27070	...	9456	...	38485	29390	...	10329	...
Income	33993	...	...	...	...	37081	...	...	...	...
Other	1299	...	...	...	...	1404	...	...	...	...
C Social security contributions	24270	-	...	-	24570	26184	-	...	-	27121
D Fees, fines and penalties	319	162	...	156	9	338	177	...	163	9

989

Japan

3.12 General Government Income and Outlay Account: Total and Subsectors
(Continued)

Thousand Million Japanese yen

	1984					1985				
	Total General Government	Central Government	State or Provincial Government	Local Government	Social Security Funds	Total General Government	Central Government	State or Provincial Government	Local Government	Social Security Funds
4 Other current transfers	421	466	...	15208	7717	487	541	...	16078	8244
A Casualty insurance claims	10	5	...	5	-	10	5	...	5	-
B Transfers from other government subsectors	...	99	...	15200	7664	...	103	...	16070	8184
C Transfers from the rest of the world	12	12	...	-	...	12	11	...	-	...
D Other transfers, except imputed	391	345	...		53	457	417	...		60
E Imputed unfunded employee pension and welfare contributions	8	5	...	3	...	8	5	...	3	...
Total Current Receipts ª	90707	40017	...	38216	37447	98764	42759	...	41054	41215
Disbursements										
1 Government final consumption expenditure	29449	7146	...	22112	550	30685	7489	...	22953	597
2 Property income	13337	10314	...	3300	-	14318	11121	...	3509	-
A Interest	13229	...	...	...	...	14212	...	...	...	...
B Net land rent and royalties	108	...	...	...	...	106	...	...	...	...
3 Subsidies	3806	2986	...	868	...	3650	2830	...	867	...
4 Other current transfers	34426	24650	...	5348	28057	36456	25935	...	5665	30067
A Casualty insurance premiums, net	11	5	...	5	-	11	5	...	5	-
B Transfers to other government subsectors	...	22094	...	755	115	...	23360	...	875	123
C Social security benefits	27596	-	...	-	27792	28960	-	...	-	29760
D Social assistance grants	5349	1956	...	3875	...	5957	1975	...	4021	...
E Unfunded employee pension and welfare benefits	8	5	...	3	-	8	5	...	3	-
F Transfers to private non-profit institutions serving households	1355	490	...	710	150	1430	509	...	761	184
G Other transfers n.e.c.	...	...	...	...	...	...	...	...	...	...
H Transfers to the rest of the world	107	100	...	-	...	90	81	...	-	...
Net saving	9690	-5079	...	6588	8839	13655	-4615	...	8059	10552
Total Current Disbursements and Net Saving ª	90707	40017	...	38216	37447	98764	42759	...	41054	41215

	1986					1987				
	Total General Government	Central Government	State or Provincial Government	Local Government	Social Security Funds	Total General Government	Central Government	State or Provincial Government	Local Government	Social Security Funds
Receipts										
1 Operating surplus	...	...	...	...	...	...	...	...	...	...
2 Property and entrepreneurial income	9346	1726	...	1004	6872	10009	2249	...	1011	7186
3 Taxes, fees and contributions	93970	43232	...	25308	28709	103111	47271	...	27965	30034
A Indirect taxes	25213	11792	...	14264	...	28379	13057	...	15669	...
B Direct taxes	40639	31259	...	10875	...	44615	33971	...	12107	...
Income	39162	...	...	...	...	43064	...	...	...	...
Other	1477	...	...	...	...	1550	...	...	...	...
C Social security contributions	27761	-	...	-	28700	29694	-	...	-	30025
D Fees, fines and penalties	357	181	...	171	9	423	243	...	189	9
4 Other current transfers	543	598	...	16270	8757	603	677	...	17014	8787
A Casualty insurance claims	10	5	...	5	-	10	5	...	5	-
B Transfers from other government subsectors	...	108	...	16262	8693	...	134	...	17006	8723
C Transfers from the rest of the world	7	11	...	-	...	9	8	...	-	...
D Other transfers, except imputed	519	469	...	...	64	575	525	...	...	64
E Imputed unfunded employee pension and welfare contributions	8	5	...	3	...	8	5	...	3	...
Total Current Receipts ª	103860	45556	...	42585	44338	113723	50196	...	45989	46008
Disbursements										
1 Government final consumption expenditure	32388	8094	...	23834	632	32975	7996	...	24567	679
2 Property income	14912	11581	...	3593	-	15346	11790	...	3647	3

Japan

3.12 General Government Income and Outlay Account: Total and Subsectors
(Continued)

Thousand Million Japanese yen

	1986					1987				
	Total General Government	Central Government	State or Provincial Government	Local Government	Social Security Funds	Total General Government	Central Government	State or Provincial Government	Local Government	Social Security Funds
A Interest	14797	...	...	...	...	15225	...	...	...	...
B Net land rent and royalties	115	...	...	...	...	121	...	...	...	...
3 Subsidies	3678	2601	...	870	...	3419	2568	...	913	...
4 Other current transfers	39163	26493	...	5970	32974	42136	27354	...	6125	35041
A Casualty insurance premiums, net	11	5	...	5	-	11	5	...	5	-
B Transfers to other government subsectors	...	23921	...	1016	127	...	24650	...	1069	144
C Social security benefits	31476	-	...	-	32632	34235	-	...	-	34639
D Social assistance grants	6073	1966	...	4137	...	6185	2058	...	4202	...
E Unfunded employee pension and welfare benefits	8	5	...	3	-	8	5	...	3	-
F Transfers to private non-profit institutions serving households	1516	516	...	810	216	1609	547	...	846	258
G Other transfers n.e.c.	...	...	...	...	...	...	...	...	...	...
H Transfers to the rest of the world	80	80	...	-	...	88	89	...	-	...
Net saving	13718	-3214	...	8318	10732	19848	488	...	10738	10287
Total Current Disbursements and Net Saving a	103860	45556	...	42585	44338	113723	50196	...	45989	46008

	1988					1989				
	Total General Government	Central Government	State or Provincial Government	Local Government	Social Security Funds	Total General Government	Central Government	State or Provincial Government	Local Government	Social Security Funds
Receipts										
1 Operating surplus	...	...	...	...	...	...	...	...	...	...
2 Property and entrepreneurial income	11112	2685	...	1175	7409	11621	2917	...	1505	7705
3 Taxes, fees and contributions	110997	51684	...	30905	31914	119596	56359	...	32727	34388
A Indirect taxes	30878	14325	...	17314	...	32162	15193	...	17972	...
B Direct taxes	48329	37146	...	13393	...	53901	40946	...	14545	...
Income	46677	...	...	...	...	52142	...	...	...	...
Other	1653	...	...	...	...	1758	...	...	...	...
C Social security contributions	31363	-	...	-	31905	33109	4	...	-	34379
D Fees, fines and penalties	426	213	...	198	9	424	216	...	210	9
4 Other current transfers	665	750	...	17875	10599	743	840	...	21143	10708
A Casualty insurance claims	9	5	...	5	-	10	5	...	5	-
B Transfers from other government subsectors	...	148	...	17867	10528	...	153	...	21135	10638
C Transfers from the rest of the world	9	6	...	-	...	14	16	...	-	...
D Other transfers, except imputed	638	585	...	...	71	711	660	...	...	70
E Imputed unfunded employee pension and welfare contributions	9	6	...	3	...	9	6	...	3	...
Total Current Receipts a	122774	55117	...	49952	49922	131961	60115	...	55376	52800
Disbursements										
1 Government final consumption expenditure	34184	8332	...	25570	663	36240	8853	...	27124	709
2 Property income	15671	12101	...	3710	3	16023	12432	...	3752	3
A Interest	15537	...	...	...	...	15871	...	...	...	...
B Net land rent and royalties	134	...	...	...	...	151	...	...	...	...
3 Subsidies	3409	2411	...	982	...	3161	3662	...	1228	...

Japan

3.12 General Government Income and Outlay Account: Total and Subsectors
(Continued)

Thousand Million Japanese yen

	1988					1989				
	Total General Government	Central Government	State or Provincial Government	Local Government	Social Security Funds	Total General Government	Central Government	State or Provincial Government	Local Government	Social Security Funds
4 Other current transfers	44089	29812	...	6520	36722	45839	33273	...	6724	39099
A Casualty insurance premiums, net	10	5	...	5	-	11	6	...	6	-
B Transfers to other government subsectors	...	27027	...	1359	156	...	30402	...	1359	165
C Social security benefits	35922	-	...	-	36310	37410	-	...	-	38652
D Social assistance grants	6313	2045	...	4240	...	6377	2016	...	4375	...
E Unfunded employee pension and welfare benefits	9	6	...	3	-	9	6	...	3	-
F Transfers to private non-profit institutions serving households	1731	600	...	912	256	1884	684	...	981	282
G Other transfers n.e.c.	...	...	...	...	...	...	...	...	...	...
H Transfers to the rest of the world	104	129	...	-	...	148	159	...	-	...
Net saving	25420	2462	...	13171	12535	30699	1897	...	16549	12989
Total Current Disbursements and Net Saving a	122774	55117	...	49952	49922	131961	60115	...	55376	52800

a) The subsectors of general government, central government, local government, and social security funds refer to fiscal year beginning 1 April.

3.13 General Government Capital Accumulation Account: Total and Subsectors

Thousand Million Japanese yen

	1980					1981				
	Total General Government	Central Government	State or Provincial Government	Local Government	Social Security Funds	Total General Government	Central Government	State or Provincial Government	Local Government	Social Security Funds
Finance of Gross Accumulation										
1 Gross saving	7608	-4442	...	6426	6686	9468	-4966	...	6932	7464
A Consumption of fixed capital	1393	238	...	1199	9	1599	275	...	1365	10
B Net saving	6215	-4680	...	5227	6677	7868	-5241	...	5567	7454
2 Capital transfers a	-1125	-6148	...	5158	-147	-1114	-6087	...	5311	-160
A From other government subsectors	...	-5889	...	5895	-6	...	-6072	...	6078	-7
B From other resident sectors	-1029	-259	...	-737	-141	-1010	-15	...	-767	-153
C From rest of the world	-96	...	...	...	...	-103	...	...	...	...
Finance of Gross Accumulation b	6483	-10590	...	11584	6539	8353	-11053	...	12243	7304
Gross Accumulation										
1 Gross capital formation	14685	2276	...	12611	51	15647	2258	...	13239	57
A Increase in stocks	...	...	...	...	...	...	...	...	...	...
B Gross fixed capital formation	14685	2276	...	12611	51	15647	2258	...	13239	57
2 Purchases of land, net	2396	386	...	2121	8	2585	356	...	2242	10
3 Purchases of intangible assets, net	...	...	...	...	...	...	...	...	...	...
4 Capital transfers a	...	...	...	...	...	...	...	...	...	...
Net lending c	-10599	-13253	...	-3147	6480	-9875	-13667	...	-3237	7238
Gross Accumulation b	6482	-10591	...	11585	6539	8357	-11053	...	12244	7305

	1982					1983				
	Total General Government	Central Government	State or Provincial Government	Local Government	Social Security Funds	Total General Government	Central Government	State or Provincial Government	Local Government	Social Security Funds
Finance of Gross Accumulation										
1 Gross saving	9323	-5679	...	7783	7606	8408	-5922	...	7938	7922
A Consumption of fixed capital	1752	292	...	1483	11	1892	306	...	1610	12
B Net saving	7571	-5971	...	6300	7595	6516	-6228	...	6328	7910
2 Capital transfers a	-741	-5787	...	5240	-176	-573	-5224	...	5077	-193
A From other government subsectors	...	-5928	...	5934	-7	...	-5751	...	5757	-7
B From other resident sectors	-632	141	...	-694	-169	-451	527	...	-680	-187
C From rest of the world	-109	...	...	...	...	-123	...	...	...	...
Finance of Gross Accumulation b	8581	-11466	...	13024	7431	7834	-11145	...	13016	7729
Gross Accumulation										
1 Gross capital formation	15679	2324	...	13303	65	15475	2427	...	12833	73

992

Japan

3.13 General Government Capital Accumulation Account: Total and Subsectors
(Continued)

Thousand Million Japanese yen

	1982					1983				
	Total General Government	Central Government	State or Provincial Government	Local Government	Social Security Funds	Total General Government	Central Government	State or Provincial Government	Local Government	Social Security Funds
A Increase in stocks	...	...	...	...	...	...	...	...	...	...
B Gross fixed capital formation	15679	2324	...	13303	65	15475	2427	...	12833	73
2 Purchases of land, net	2626	327	...	2281	16	2616	284	...	2354	14
3 Purchases of intangible assets, net	...	...	...	...	...	...	...	...	...	...
4 Capital transfers a	...	...	...	...	...	...	...	...	...	...
Net lending c	-9723	-14117	...	-2560	7350	-10257	-13856	...	-2171	7642
Gross Accumulation b	8586	-11466	...	13024	7431	7834	-11145	...	13016	7729

	1984					1985				
	Total General Government	Central Government	State or Provincial Government	Local Government	Social Security Funds	Total General Government	Central Government	State or Provincial Government	Local Government	Social Security Funds
Finance of Gross Accumulation										
1 Gross saving	11702	-4771	...	8308	8851	15732	-4316	...	9835	10567
A Consumption of fixed capital	2012	308	...	1720	12	2077	299	...	1776	15
B Net saving	9690	-5079	...	6588	8839	13655	-4615	...	8059	10552
2 Capital transfers a	-111	-4856	...	4835	-258	-465	-4787	...	4583	-266
A From other government subsectors	...	-5410	...	5456	-46	...	-5129	...	5175	-46
B From other resident sectors	4	553	...	-621	-212	-322	342	...	-592	-220
C From rest of the world	-117	...	...	...	...	-141	...	...	...	...
Finance of Gross Accumulation b	11590	-9627	...	13143	8593	15267	-9104	...	14418	10301
Gross Accumulation										
1 Gross capital formation	15164	2399	...	12589	72	15168	2482	...	12808	68
A Increase in stocks	...	...	...	...	...	...	...	...	...	...
B Gross fixed capital formation	15164	2399	...	12589	72	15168	2482	...	12808	68
2 Purchases of land, net	2664	245	...	2372	14	2703	228	...	2497	19
3 Purchases of intangible assets, net	...	...	...	...	...	...	...	...	...	...
4 Capital transfers a	...	...	...	...	...	...	...	...	...	...
Net lending c	-6237	-12270	...	-1818	8506	-2603	-11813	...	-887	10214
Gross Accumulation b	11589	-9627	...	13143	8593	15267	-9104	...	14418	10301

	1986					1987				
	Total General Government	Central Government	State or Provincial Government	Local Government	Social Security Funds	Total General Government	Central Government	State or Provincial Government	Local Government	Social Security Funds
Finance of Gross Accumulation										
1 Gross saving	15862	-2907	...	10162	10744	22092	811	...	12675	10300
A Consumption of fixed capital	2144	307	...	1844	12	2245	323	...	1937	13
B Net saving	13718	-3214	...	8318	10732	19848	488	...	10738	10287
2 Capital transfers a	-164	-4363	...	4982	-655	271	-4001	...	5050	-607
A From other government subsectors	...	-5173	...	5225	-52	...	-5256	...	5305	-49
B From other resident sectors	-37	810	...	-243	-603	427	1255	...	-255	-558
C From rest of the world	-126	...	...	...	...	-155	...	...	...	...
Finance of Gross Accumulation b	15697	-7271	...	15143	10089	22364	-3191	...	17725	9692
Gross Accumulation										
1 Gross capital formation	16048	2690	...	13491	72	17536	3297	...	15074	80
A Increase in stocks	...	...	...	...	...	...	...	...	...	...
B Gross fixed capital formation	16048	2690	...	13491	72	17536	3296	...	15074	80
2 Purchases of land, net	2781	279	...	2485	16	3220	342	...	3024	16
3 Purchases of intangible assets, net	...	...	...	...	...	...	...	...	...	...
4 Capital transfers a	...	...	...	...	...	...	...	...	...	...
Net lending c	-3130	-10240	...	-832	10002	1607	-6830	...	-373	9596
Gross Accumulation b	15697	-7271	...	15143	10089	22364	-3191	...	17725	9692

Japan

3.13 General Government Capital Accumulation Account: Total and Subsectors

Thousand Million Japanese yen

	1988					1989				
	Total General Government	Central Government	State or Provincial Government	Local Government	Social Security Funds	Total General Government	Central Government	State or Provincial Government	Local Government	Social Security Funds
Finance of Gross Accumulation										
1 Gross saving	27745	2761	...	15201	12548	33154	2205	...	18721	13003
A Consumption of fixed capital	2325	299		2030	13	2456	308	...	2172	14
B Net saving	25420	2462		13171	12535	30699	1897	...	16549	12989
2 Capital transfers a	530	-3444	...	4138	-316	231	-3440	...	4212	-319
A From other government subsectors	...	-4702		4751	-49	...	-4836	...	4884	-49
B From other resident sectors	701	1258		-613	-267	478	1396	...	-672	-270
C From rest of the world	-171	...		...	...	-246	...	...	...	...
Finance of Gross Accumulation b	28275	-683	...	19339	12232	33386	-1236	...	22933	12684
Gross Accumulation										
1 Gross capital formation	18860	3090	...	15538	74	19802	3139	...	17010	77
A Increase in stocks	...	...		...	...	...	...	...	...	...
B Gross fixed capital formation	18860	3090		15538	74	19802	3139	...	17010	77
2 Purchases of land, net	3829	416		3540	17	3829	274	...	3624	20
3 Purchases of intangible assets, net	...	...		...	...	...	...	...	...	...
4 Capital transfers a	...	...		...	...	...	...	...	...	...
Net lending c	5586	-4189	...	261	12141	9755	-4649	...	2298	12588
Gross Accumulation b	28275	-683	...	19339	12232	33386	-1236	...	22933	12684

a) Capital transfers received are recorded net of capital transfers paid.
b) The subsectors of general government, central government, local government, and social security funds refer to fiscal year beginning 1 April.
c) Net lending of the capital accumulation account and the capital finance account have not been reconciled and are different due to different statistical sources.

3.14 General Government Capital Finance Account, Total and Subsectors

Thousand Million Japanese yen

	1980					1981				
	Total General Government	Central Government	State or Provincial Government	Local Government	Social Security Funds	Total General Government	Central Government	State or Provincial Government	Local Government	Social Security Funds
Acquisition of Financial Assets										
1 Gold and SDRs a	...	...	...	...	...	...	...	...	...	...
2 Currency and transferable deposits	-153	37	...	-744	-913	13	-19	...	378	39
3 Other deposits	1563	-10	...	716	781	1431	-5	...	392	1046
4 Bills and bonds, short term	-834	136	...	-	-	398	-768	...	-	-
5 Bonds, long term	2337	1152	...	-	857	844	-18	...	1	773
6 Corporate equity securities	-	-	...	-	-	-	-1	...	-	1
7 Short-term loans, n.e.c.	1207	500	...	242	497	1413	767	...	268	446
8 Long-term loans, n.e.c.			...					...		
9 Other receivables	...	...		...	...	...	...	...	...	...
10 Other assets a	7169	4392		62	5342	6421	1595	...	87	5261
Total Acquisition of Financial Assets b	11289	6207	...	276	6564	10519	1553	...	1128	7565
Incurrence of Liabilities										
1 Currency and transferable deposits	...	...	...	...	...	...	...	...	...	...
2 Other deposits	...	...	...	...	...	...	...	...	...	...
3 Bills and bonds, short term	1873	3460	...	...	...	2440	2465	...	...	...
4 Bonds, long term	14709	14275	...	1015	...	15017	11773	...	1143	...
5 Short-term loans, n.e.c.	3974	1039	...	2764	150	4172	881	...	3470	22
6 Long-term loans, n.e.c.			...					...		
7 Other payables	...	...	...	...	...	...	...	...	...	...
8 Other liabilities	143	636	...	4	...	148	676	...	-2	...
Total Incurrence of Liabilities	20699	19410	...	3783	150	21777	15795	...	4611	22
Net Lending c	-9409	-13203	...	-3507	6414	-11257	-14243	...	-3484	7543
Incurrence of Liabilities and Net Worth b	11290	6207	...	276	6564	10519	1553	...	1128	7565

994

Japan

3.14 General Government Capital Finance Account, Total and Subsectors

Thousand Million Japanese yen

1982

	Total General Government	Central Government	State or Provincial Government	Local Government	Social Security Funds
Acquisition of Financial Assets					
1 Gold and SDRs a	...	...	...	...	...
2 Currency and transferable deposits	353	-5	...	48	-92
3 Other deposits	1213	9	...	1038	192
4 Bills and bonds, short term	549	9	...	911	-
5 Bonds, long term	-601	-1522	...	-	911
6 Corporate equity securities	9	-	...	9	-
7 Short-term loans, n.e.c.	1663	984	...	281	427
8 Long-term loans, n.e.c.	[	[		[	
9 Other receivables	...	...	...	...	...
10 Other assets a	5763	818	...	5376	74
Total Acquisition of Financial Assets b	8945	292	...	7666	595
Incurrence of Liabilities					
1 Currency and transferable deposits					
2 Other deposits	...	...	...	...	...
3 Bills and bonds, short term	-639	...	...	-688	379
4 Bonds, long term	13412	14219	...	16805	844
5 Short-term loans, n.e.c.	5351	2527	...	2635	21
6 Long-term loans, n.e.c.	]	]		]	
7 Other payables	254	755	...	300	16
8 Other liabilities	18377	14527	...	16836	3595
Total Incurrence of Liabilities	-9432	-14235	...	-10782	-3100
Net Lending c	8945	292	...	7666	495
Incurrence of Liabilities and Net Worth b					

1983

	Total General Government	Central Government	State or Provincial Government	Local Government	Social Security Funds
Acquisition of Financial Assets					
1 Gold and SDRs a	...	...	...	...	...
2 Currency and transferable deposits	-313	-10	...	-66	-252
3 Other deposits	1462	36	...	276	1207
4 Bills and bonds, short term	1070	1188	...	-1	818
5 Bonds, long term	1950	887	...	1	27
6 Corporate equity securities	27	1	...	200	377
7 Short-term loans, n.e.c.	1295	748	...		
8 Long-term loans, n.e.c.					
9 Other receivables	...	...	...	...	...
10 Other assets a	6382	263	...	85	5122
Total Acquisition of Financial Assets b	11873	3113	...	494	7299
Incurrence of Liabilities					
1 Currency and transferable deposits					
2 Other deposits	...	...	...	...	...
3 Bills and bonds, short term	-2974	...	...	-2974	...
4 Bonds, long term	6239	...	...	13224	
5 Short-term loans, n.e.c.	2851		...	2635	21
6 Long-term loans, n.e.c.					
7 Other payables	599	11	...	599	...
8 Other liabilities	22655	3702	...	16836	21
Net Lending c	-10782	7631	...	-13723	7278
Incurrence of Liabilities and Net Worth b	11873	3113	...	495	7299

1984

	Total General Government	Central Government	State or Provincial Government	Local Government	Social Security Funds
Acquisition of Financial Assets					
1 Gold and SDRs a	...	...	...	...	...
2 Currency and transferable deposits	-106	-13	...	509	-6
3 Other deposits	2137	22	...	2243	37
4 Bills and bonds, short term	-2226	-1610	...	1193	457
5 Bonds, long term	1988	1472	...	-42	118
6 Corporate equity securities	9	-2	...	8	5
7 Short-term loans, n.e.c.	1078	732	...	181	906
8 Long-term loans, n.e.c.	[	[		[	
9 Other receivables	...	...	...	...	...
10 Other assets a	5705	1925	...	294	3554
Total Acquisition of Financial Assets b	8582	2525	...	1069	5651
Incurrence of Liabilities					
1 Currency and transferable deposits					
2 Other deposits	188	2642	...	...	-757
3 Bills and bonds, short term	12438	11927	...	493	12855
4 Bonds, long term	3200	558	...	3108	77
5 Short-term loans, n.e.c.	]	]		]	
6 Long-term loans, n.e.c.	388	-360	...	-3	197
7 Other payables	16214	14767	...	3598	77
8 Other liabilities	-7631	-12242	...	...	-2529
Net Lending c	8582	2525	...	1069	5651
Incurrence of Liabilities and Net Worth b					

1985

	Total General Government	Central Government	State or Provincial Government	Local Government	Social Security Funds
Acquisition of Financial Assets					
1 Gold and SDRs a	...	...	...	...	...
2 Currency and transferable deposits	56	80	...	2	-106
3 Other deposits	1689	474	...	37	1441
4 Bills and bonds, short term	4	-	...	457	1193
5 Bonds, long term	1049	-	...	-105	118
6 Corporate equity securities	9	5	...	-6	-
7 Short-term loans, n.e.c.	161	174	...	909	906
8 Long-term loans, n.e.c.	[				
9 Other receivables	...	...	...	...	...
10 Other assets a	8523	54	...	1460	7489
Total Acquisition of Financial Assets b	11490	783	...	2451	11846
Incurrence of Liabilities					
2 Other deposits	...	...	...	-1041	-757
3 Bills and bonds, short term	-159	...	...	12730	12855
4 Bonds, long term	32	3461	...	763	3922
5 Short-term loans, n.e.c.	]			]	
7 Other payables	...	2	...	1877	197
8 Other liabilities	32	3305	...	14329	16216
Total Incurrence of Liabilities	11458	-2522	...	-11878	-4369
Net Lending c	11490	783	...	2451	11846
Incurrence of Liabilities and Net Worth b					

Japan

3.14 General Government Capital Finance Account, Total and Subsectors

Thousand Million Japanese yen

	1986					1987				
	Total General Government	Central Government	State or Provincial Government	Local Government	Social Security Funds	Total General Government	Central Government	State or Provincial Government	Local Government	Social Security Funds

Acquisition of Financial Assets

	1986					1987				
1 Gold and SDRs a	...	...	...	...	...	...	...	...	...	...
2 Currency and transferable deposits	-236	-13	...	103	-198	473	313	...	-134	360
3 Other deposits	2616	45	...	227	2157	8002	2372	...	2882	2618
4 Bills and bonds, short term	-1179	2021	...	-1	-4	1822	...	...	...	1
5 Bonds, long term	1434	340	...	-1	1644	384	470	-	-	803
6 Corporate equity securities	-231	-2328	...	4	18	-7132	-5028	...	5	31
7 Short-term loans, n.e.c.	5828	5556	]	208	84	1112	554	]	459	315
8 Long-term loans, n.e.c.										
9 Other receivables	...	...	...	...	...	...	...	...	...	...
10 Other assets a	11286	5287	...	155	7605	15957	8261	...	334	6529
Total Acquisition of Financial Assets b	19514	10908	...	1396	11306	23897	7823	...	3546	10656

Incurrence of Liabilities

1 Currency and transferable deposits	...	...	...	...	...	...	...	...	...	...
2 Other deposits	...	...	...	...	...	...	...	...	...	...
3 Bills and bonds, short term	2811	3362	...	...	4201	4714	...	...	...	...
4 Bonds, long term	10751	9044	...	62	7401	6588	...	-243	...	...
5 Short-term loans, n.e.c.	9104	6706	]	2650	12	2236	3533	]	11	...
6 Long-term loans, n.e.c.										
7 Other payables	...	...	...	...	...	...	...	...	...	...
8 Other liabilities	1179	1549	...	-12	...	157	610	...	-13	...
Total Incurrence of Liabilities	22138	22367	...	2700	12	18656	14147	...	3278	11
Net Lending c	-2623	-11460	...	-1304	11294	5241	-6324	...	269	10645
Incurrence of Liabilities and Net Worth b	19514	10908	...	1396	11306	23897	7823	...	3546	10656

	1988					1989				
	Total General Government	Central Government	State or Provincial Government	Local Government	Social Security Funds	Total General Government	Central Government	State or Provincial Government	Local Government	Social Security Funds

Acquisition of Financial Assets

1 Gold and SDRs a	...	...	...	...	...	...	...	...	...	...
2 Currency and transferable deposits	-132	-314	...	860	159	371	3072	...	563	-61
3 Other deposits	7130	1571	...	3469	3715	10466	4347	...	4414	2316
4 Bills and bonds, short term	-1097	189	...	-	-	-2889	-3160	...	-	-1
5 Bonds, long term	2610	423	...	-1	232	-3596	351	...	-2	-273
6 Corporate equity securities	-2766	-2857	...	9	24	39	22	...	5	12
7 Short-term loans, n.e.c.	134	668	]	199	-445	839	765	]	345	-67
8 Long-term loans, n.e.c.										
9 Other receivables	...	...	...	...	...	...	...	...	...	...
10 Other assets a	11621	5858	...	14	7941	11859	1065	...	168	7461
Total Acquisition of Financial Assets b	17500	5539	...	4547	11624	17086	6462	...	5494	9386

Incurrence of Liabilities

1 Currency and transferable deposits	...	...	...	...	...	...	...	...	...	...
2 Other deposits	...	...	...	...	...	...	...	...	...	...
3 Bills and bonds, short term	1271	3317	...	...	...	1827	788	...	...	...
4 Bonds, long term	4733	4979	...	-277	...	887	5902	...	-189	...
5 Short-term loans, n.e.c.	3386	1328	]	3657	19	6297	3529	]	3132	18
6 Long-term loans, n.e.c.										
7 Other payables	...	...	...	...	...	...	...	...	...	...
8 Other liabilities	381	693	...	12	...	202	861	...	20	8
Total Incurrence of Liabilities	9770	10317	...	3392	19	9213	11078	...	2964	18
Net Lending c	7730	-4778	...	1155	11605	7873	-4617	...	2530	9368
Incurrence of Liabilities and Net Worth b	17500	5539	...	4547	11624	17086	6462	...	5494	9386

a) Item 'Gold and SDRs' is included in item 'Other assets'.
b) The subsectors of general government, central government, local government, and social security funds refer to fiscal year beginning 1 April.
c) Net lending of the capital accumulation account and the capital finance account have not been reconciled and are different due to different statistical sources.

Japan

3.21 Corporate and Quasi-Corporate Enterprise Production Account: Total and Sectors

Thousand Million Japanese yen

	1980				1981				1982			
	Corporate and Quasi-Corporate Enterprises			ADDENDUM: Total,	Corporate and Quasi-Corporate Enterprises			ADDENDUM: Total,	Corporate and Quasi-Corporate Enterprises			ADDENDUM: Total,
	TOTAL	Non-Financial	Financial	including Unincorporated	TOTAL	Non-Financial	Financial	including Unincorporated	TOTAL	Non-Financial	Financial	including Unincorporated
Gross Output												
1 Output for sale	...	...	...	...	...	...	...	...	...	...	...	...
2 Imputed bank service charge	10413	...	...	...	10150	...	...	...	11748	...	...	...
3 Own-account fixed capital formation	...	...	...	...	...	...	...	...	...	...	...	...
Gross Output	...	...	...	...	...	...	...	...	...	...	...	...
Gross Input												
Intermediate consumption	...	...	...	...	...	...	...	...	...	...	...	...
Subtotal: Value Added	...	...	...	...	...	...	...	...	...	...	...	...
1 Indirect taxes, net	...	...	...	...	...	...	...	...	...	...	...	...
2 Consumption of fixed capital	18682	18077	605	...	20970	20338	632	...	22280	21654	626	...
3 Compensation of employees	...	...	...	...	...	...	...	...	...	...	...	...
4 Net operating surplus	31555	37315	-5760	...	32540	39056	-6516	...	33036	40093	-7057	...
Gross Input	...	...	...	...	...	...	...	...	...	...	...	...

	1983				1984				1985			
	Corporate and Quasi-Corporate Enterprises			ADDENDUM: Total,	Corporate and Quasi-Corporate Enterprises			ADDENDUM: Total,	Corporate and Quasi-Corporate Enterprises			ADDENDUM: Total,
	TOTAL	Non-Financial	Financial	including Unincorporated	TOTAL	Non-Financial	Financial	including Unincorporated	TOTAL	Non-Financial	Financial	including Unincorporated
Gross Output												
1 Output for sale	...	...	...	...	...	...	...	...	...	...	...	...
2 Imputed bank service charge	13010	...	...	...	13811	...	...	...	14774	...	...	...
3 Own-account fixed capital formation	...	...	...	...	...	...	...	...	...	...	...	...
Gross Output	...	...	...	...	...	...	...	...	...	...	...	...
Gross Input												
Intermediate consumption	...	...	...	...	...	...	...	...	...	...	...	...
Subtotal: Value Added	...	...	...	...	...	...	...	...	...	...	...	...
1 Indirect taxes, net	...	...	...	...	...	...	...	...	...	...	...	...
2 Consumption of fixed capital	23745	23049	696	...	25301	24530	771	...	27467	26607	860	...
3 Compensation of employees	...	...	...	...	...	...	...	...	...	...	...	...
4 Net operating surplus	33521	41181	-7660	...	37043	45522	-8479	...	40611	49750	-9139	...
Gross Input	...	...	...	...	...	...	...	...	...	...	...	...

	1986				1987				1988			
	Corporate and Quasi-Corporate Enterprises			ADDENDUM: Total,	Corporate and Quasi-Corporate Enterprises			ADDENDUM: Total,	Corporate and Quasi-Corporate Enterprises			ADDENDUM: Total,
	TOTAL	Non-Financial	Financial	including Unincorporated	TOTAL	Non-Financial	Financial	including Unincorporated	TOTAL	Non-Financial	Financial	including Unincorporated
Gross Output												
1 Output for sale	...	...	...	...	...	...	...	...	...	...	...	...
2 Imputed bank service charge	13938	...	...	...	15677	...	...	...	16568	...	...	...
3 Own-account fixed capital formation	...	...	...	...	...	...	...	...	...	...	...	...
Gross Output	...	...	...	...	...	...	...	...	...	...	...	...
Gross Input												
Intermediate consumption	...	...	...	...	...	...	...	...	...	...	...	...
Subtotal: Value Added	...	...	...	...	...	...	...	...	...	...	...	...
1 Indirect taxes, net	...	...	...	...	...	...	...	...	...	...	...	...
2 Consumption of fixed capital	29445	28558	887	...	31386	30334	1052	...	33832	32668	1164	...
3 Compensation of employees	...	...	...	...	...	...	...	...	...	...	...	...
4 Net operating surplus	42695	51537	-8842	...	42723	53452	-10729	...	47961	59018	-11057	...
Gross Input	...	...	...	...	...	...	...	...	...	...	...	...

	1989			
	Corporate and Quasi-Corporate Enterprises			ADDENDUM: Total,
	TOTAL	Non-Financial	Financial	including Unincorporated
Gross Output				
1 Output for sale	...	...	...	...
2 Imputed bank service charge	20235	...	...	...
3 Own-account fixed capital formation	...	...	...	...
Gross Output	...	...	...	...

Japan

3.21 Corporate and Quasi-Corporate Enterprise Production Account: Total and Sectors (Continued)

Thousand Million Japanese yen

	1989 Corporate and Quasi-Corporate Enterprises			ADDENDUM: Total, Including Unincorporated
	TOTAL	Non-Financial	Financial	
Intermediate consumption				
Subtotal: Value Added				
1 Indirect taxes, net	...	...	...	
2 Consumption of fixed capital	37709	36345	1364	...
3 Compensation of employees	...	...	...	
4 Net operating surplus	50637	63571	-12934	...
Gross Input	...	...	...	

3.22 Corporate and Quasi-Corporate Enterprise Income and Outlay Account: Total and Sectors

Thousand Million Japanese yen

	1980			1981			1982			1983		
	TOTAL	Non-Financial	Financial	TOTAL	Non-Financial	Financial	TOTAL	Non-Financial	Financial	TOTAL	Non-Financial	Financial
Receipts												
1 Operating surplus	31555	37315	-5760	32540	39056	-6516	33035	40093	-7057	33521	41181	-7660
2 Property and entrepreneurial income	59808	7348	52461	68956	7763	61194	74611	7551	67060	79574	7763	71811
A Withdrawals from quasi-corporate enterprises a	...	...	...	...	...	...	...	...	...	...	...	...
B Interest	57143	5827	51317	65914	6073	59841	71492	5903	65590	76146	6109	70037
C Dividends	2318	1174	1144	2642	1353	1289	2680	1210	1470	2990	1216	1773
D Net land rent and royalties	347	347	-	401	401	-	438	438	-	437	437	-
3 Current transfers	3074	857	2217	3335	951	2384	3563	1019	2545	3801	1065	2736
A Casualty insurance claims	874	806	68	943	869	75	1035	960	75	1070	1000	70
B Casualty insurance premiums, net, due to be received by insurance companies	2148	...	2148	2308	...	2308	2469	...	2469	2665	-	2665
C Current transfers from the rest of the world b	...	...	...	...	...	...	...	...	...	...	...	...
D Other transfers except imputed b	...	...	...	...	...	...	...	...	...	...	...	...
E Imputed unfunded employee pension and welfare contributions	52	50	1	83	82	1	60	59	1	66	65	1
Total Current Receipts	94437	45519	48918	104831	47769	57062	111210	48663	62547	116896	50010	66886
Disbursements												
1 Property and entrepreneurial income	72721	29563	43159	83148	30616	52532	87502	30678	56824	92399	31905	60493
A Withdrawals from quasi-corporations a	...	...	...	...	...	...	...	...	...	...	...	...
B Interest	65439	24894	40545	74723	25416	49307	78885	25575	53309	83069	26708	56391
C Dividends	5725	3190	2535	6642	3141	3501	6717	3291	3426	7375	3378	3997
D Net land rent and royalties	1558	1479	79	1782	1698	84	1901	1811	89	1925	1820	104
2 Direct taxes and other current transfers n.e.c. to general government	11082	1819	9264	12213	1774	10439	12745	1774	10577	13246	3007	10239
A Direct taxes	10777	1802	9175	10348	1759	12636	10439	1759	12584	13051	2982	10153
On income	10930	1798	9132	12056	1755	10301	12584	1755	10439	13051	2971	10080
Other	47	4	42	51	4	47	51	4	46	85	12	73
B Fines, fees, penalties and other current transfers n.e.c.	106	17	89	107	15	92	110	19	91	111	86	25

Japan

3.22 Corporate and Quasi-Corporate Enterprise Income and Outlay Account: Total and Sectors
(Continued)

Thousand Million Japanese yen

	1980			1981			1982			1983		
	TOTAL	Non-Financial	Financial	TOTAL	Non-Financial	Financial	TOTAL	Non-Financial	Financial	TOTAL	Non-Financial	Financial
3 Other current transfers	3793	1326	2467	4183	1517	2666	4487	1640	2847	4704	1663	3041
A Casualty insurance premiums, net	856	787	68	937	862	76	1033	957	76	1067	996	71
B Casualty insurance claims liability of insurance companies	2148	-	2148	2308	-	2308	2469	-	2469	2665	-	2665
C Transfers to private non-profit institutions b	...	...	...	...	...	...	...	...	...	...	...	...
D Unfunded employee pension and welfare benefits	52	51	1	83	82	1	60	59	1	66	65	1
E Social assistance grants b	737	488	249	855	574	281	925	624	302	907	603	304
F Other transfers n.e.c. b	...	...	...	...	...	...	...	...	...	...	...	...
G Transfers to the rest of the world b	...	...	...	...	...	...	...	...	...	...	...	...
Net saving	6840	5367	1473	5287	5197	90	6475	5768	707	6545	6200	345
Total Current Disbursements and Net Saving	94437	45519	48917	104831	47769	57062	111210	48663	62547	116896	50010	66886

	1984			1985			1986			1987		
	TOTAL	Non-Financial	Financial	TOTAL	Non-Financial	Financial	TOTAL	Non-Financial	Financial	TOTAL	Non-Financial	Financial

Receipts

	TOTAL	Non-Financial	Financial	TOTAL	Non-Financial	Financial	TOTAL	Non-Financial	Financial	TOTAL	Non-Financial	Financial
1 Operating surplus	37043	45521	-8479	40610	49750	-9139	42695	51537	-8842	42723	53452	-10729
2 Property and entrepreneurial income	87628	7906	79722	93248	8524	84723	95839	9019	86820	100099	9718	90381
A Withdrawals from quasi-corporate enterprises a	...	...	...	...	...	...	...	...	...	...	...	...
B Interest	83908	6193	77715	88802	6436	82366	90750	6732	84018	93437	6185	87252
C Dividends	3256	1250	2006	3961	1603	2357	4597	1795	2802	6096	2967	3129
D Net land rent and royalties	464	464	-	485	485	-	492	492	-	565	565	-
3 Current transfers	3972	1101	2871	4111	1139	2972	4030	1072	2958	3832	979	2853
A Casualty insurance claims	1117	1050	67	1157	1092	65	1081	1019	62	971	922	49
B Casualty insurance premiums, net, due to be received by insurance companies	2803	-	2803	2906	-	2906	2894	-	2894	2801	-	2801
C Current transfers from the rest of the world b	...	...	...	...	...	...	...	...	...	...	...	...
D Other transfers except imputed b	...	...	...	...	...	...	...	...	...	...	...	...
E Imputed unfunded employee pension and welfare contributions	52	51	1	48	47	1	55	53	2	60	57	2
Total Current Receipts	128643	54529	74114	137969	59413	78556	142564	61628	80936	146654	64149	82505

Disbursements

	TOTAL	Non-Financial	Financial	TOTAL	Non-Financial	Financial	TOTAL	Non-Financial	Financial	TOTAL	Non-Financial	Financial
1 Property and entrepreneurial income	100033	32253	67780	105751	33628	72122	109776	33847	75929	112061	33219	78841
A Withdrawals from quasi-corporations a	...	...	...	...	...	...	...	...	...	...	...	...
B Interest	90161	26944	63217	94855	28006	66849	97703	28015	69687	98117	26831	71286
C Dividends	7895	3453	4442	8840	3698	5142	9951	3846	6105	11574	4177	7397
D Net land rent and royalties	1977	1857	121	2056	1924	132	2123	1986	137	2369	2211	158
2 Direct taxes and other current transfers n.e.c. to general government	15096	11881	3215	17381	13823	3558	17790	13667	4123	19690	15336	4353
A Direct taxes	14968	11779	3189	17237	13707	3530	17644	13554	4090	19517	15202	4315
On income	14771	11608	3163	16968	13473	3495	17355	13312	4044	19216	14959	4257
Other	198	172	26	269	234	35	288	242	46	301	243	58
B Fines, fees, penalties and other current transfers n.e.c.	127	101	26	144	116	28	146	114	33	173	134	38

Japan

3.22 Corporate and Quasi-Corporate Enterprise Income and Outlay Account: Total and Sectors (Continued)

Thousand Million Japanese yen

	1984 TOTAL	1984 Non-Financial	1984 Financial	1985 TOTAL	1985 Non-Financial	1985 Financial	1986 TOTAL	1986 Non-Financial	1986 Financial	1987 TOTAL	1987 Non-Financial	1987 Financial
3 Other current transfers	4945	3229	1716	5207	3361	1846	5220	1805	3415	5131	1852	3278
A Casualty insurance premiums, net	1114	1046	68	1149	1082	66	1064	1001	63	950	901	50
B Casualty insurance claims liability of insurance companies	2803	...	2803	2906	...	2906	2894	...	2894	2801	...	2801
C Transfers to private non-profit institutions b	...	...	...	...	...	...	...	...	...	...	...	...
D Unfunded employee pension and welfare benefits	52	51	1	48	47	1	55	53	2	60	57	2
F Other transfers n.e.c. b	976	619	357	1105	717	388	1206	751	456	1319	895	425
G Transfers to the rest of the world b	...	...	...	...	...	...	...	...	...	...	...	...
Net saving	8568	8677	-109	9630	10116	-485	9778	12309	-2530	9773	13741	-3968
Total Current Disbursements and Net Saving	128643	54529	74114	137969	59413	78556	142564	61628	80936	146654	64149	82505

Receipts

	1988 TOTAL	1988 Non-Financial	1988 Financial	1989 TOTAL	1989 Non-Financial	1989 Financial
1 Operating surplus	47960	59018	-11057	50637	63571	-12934
2 Property and entrepreneurial income	108846	10227	98620	126531	11399	115132
A Withdrawals from quasi-corporate enterprises a	...	...	...	...	...	...
B Interest	101621	5943	95678	116445	5489	110956
C Dividends	6581	3639	2942	9325	5148	4178
D Net land rent and royalties	645	645	-	762	762	-
3 Current transfers	3926	1004	2921	4057	1073	2984
A Casualty insurance claims	951	938	13	969	1001	-32
B Casualty insurance premiums, net, due to be received by insurance companies	2906	-	2906	3012	-	3012
C Current transfers from the rest of the world b	...	...	...	...	...	...
D Other transfers except imputed b	...	...	...	...	...	...
E Imputed unfunded employee pension and welfare contributions	70	67	3	76	72	3
Total Current Receipts	160733	70249	90484	181225	76043	105183

Disbursements

	1988 TOTAL	1988 Non-Financial	1988 Financial	1989 TOTAL	1989 Non-Financial	1989 Financial
1 Property and entrepreneurial income	120891	34713	86178	140628	38829	101799
A Withdrawals from quasi-corporations a	...	...	...	...	...	...
B Interest	106336	27761	78575	121130	29989	91141
C Dividends	11850	4420	7430	16511	6076	10436
D Net land rent and royalties	2705	2532	173	2987	2765	222
2 Direct taxes and other current transfers n.e.c. to general government	22247	17812	4434	25897	21172	4725
A Direct taxes	22061	17663	4398	25707	21016	4691
On income	21744	17405	4339	25375	20736	4639
Other	317	258	59	332	280	52
B Fines, fees, penalties and other current transfers n.e.c.	186	149	37	190	156	34

Japan

3.22 Corporate and Quasi-Corporate Enterprise Income and Outlay Account: Total and Sectors
(Continued)

Thousand Million Japanese yen

	1988			1989		
	TOTAL	Non-Financial	Financial	TOTAL	Non-Financial	Financial
3 Other current transfers	5397	2024	3373	5626	2198	3428
A Casualty insurance premiums, net	932	919	14	954	985	-31
B Casualty insurance claims liability of insurance companies	2906	-	2906	3012	-	3012
C Transfers to private non-profit institutions b	...	...	...	...	...	...
D Unfunded employee pension and welfare benefits	70	67	3	76	72	3
E Social assistance grants b ...	1490	1039	451	1584	1141	443
F Other transfers n.e.c. b	...	...	...	...	...	...
G Transfers to the rest of the world b	...	...	...	...	...	...
Net saving	12198	15699	-3501	9074	13843	-4770
Total Current Disbursements and Net Saving	160733	70249	90484	181225	76043	105183

a) Item 'Withdrawals from quasi-corporate enterprises' is not included in the income and outlay accounts of the corporate and quasi-corporate enterprise table and household and private unincorporated enterprise table.   b) Unrequited current transfers are recorded on a net basis, so that those net estimates are included in item 'Social assistance grants'.

3.23 Corporate and Quasi-Corporate Enterprise Capital Accumulation Account: Total and Sectors

Thousand Million Japanese yen

	1980			1981			1982			1983		
	TOTAL	Non-Financial	Financial	TOTAL	Non-Financial	Financial	TOTAL	Non-Financial	Financial	TOTAL	Non-Financial	Financial
Finance of Gross Accumulation												
1 Gross saving	25523	23444	2078	26258	25536	722	28755	27421	1333	30291	29249	1041
A Consumption of fixed capital	18682	18077	605	20970	20338	632	22280	21654	626	23745	23049	696
B Net saving	6840	5367	1473	5287	5197	90	6475	5768	707	6545	6200	345
2 Capital transfers a	1602	1602	-	1709	1709	-	1473	1473	-	1380	1380	-
Finance of Gross Accumulation	27125	25047	2078	27966	27244	722	30228	28895	1333	31671	30629	1041
Gross Accumulation												
1 Gross capital formation	39546	38665	881	41878	40950	928	42597	41711	885	41530	40586	944
A Increase in stocks	1543	1543	...	1228	1228	...	1017	1017	...	74	74	...
B Gross fixed capital formation	38003	37121	881	40650	39722	928	41580	40694	885	41456	40511	944
2 Purchases of land, net	1242	1126	117	1484	1361	123	776	681	95	874	741	133
3 Purchases of intangible assets, net	...	...	...	...	...	...	...	...	...	...	...	...
4 Capital transfers a	...	...	...	...	...	...	...	...	...	...	...	...
Net lending b	-13664	-14744	1080	-15396	-15067	-329	-13144	-13497	353	-10733	-10698	-36
Gross Accumulation	27125	25047	2078	27966	27244	722	30228	28895	1333	31671	30629	1041

	1984			1985			1986			1987		
	TOTAL	Non-Financial	Financial	TOTAL	Non-Financial	Financial	TOTAL	Non-Financial	Financial	TOTAL	Non-Financial	Financial
Finance of Gross Accumulation												
1 Gross saving	33870	33208	662	37097	36723	374	39223	40866	-1643	41158	44074	-2916
A Consumption of fixed capital	25301	24530	771	27467	26607	860	29445	28558	887	31385	30334	1051
B Net saving	8568	8677	-109	9630	10116	-485	9778	12309	-2530	9773	13741	-3968
2 Capital transfers a	1006	1006	-	1456	1456	-	1494	1494	-	1422	1422	-
Finance of Gross Accumulation	34876	34214	662	38553	38179	374	40718	42360	-1643	42580	45496	-2916
Gross Accumulation												
1 Gross capital formation	47093	46024	1068	52058	50989	1069	52975	51787	1188	54818	53354	1464
A Increase in stocks	984	984	...	2052	2052	...	1438	1438	...	583	583	...
B Gross fixed capital formation	46109	45041	1068	50006	48937	1069	51537	50349	1188	54235	52771	1464
2 Purchases of land, net	465	332	133	2795	2614	182	2963	2722	241	5354	5070	283
3 Purchases of intangible assets, net	...	...	...	...	...	...	...	...	...	...	...	...
4 Capital transfers a	...	...	...	...	...	...	...	...	...	...	...	...
Net lending b	-12683	-12143	-540	-16300	-15423	-876	-15220	-12149	-3071	-17592	-12928	-4664
Gross Accumulation	34876	34214	662	38553	38179	374	40718	42360	-1643	42580	45496	-2916

Japan

3.23 Corporate and Quasi-Corporate Enterprise Capital Accumulation Account: Total and Sectors
Thousand Million Japanese yen

	1988			1989		
	TOTAL	Non-Financial	Financial	TOTAL	Non-Financial	Financial
Finance of Gross Accumulation						
1 Gross saving	46030	48367	-2337	46783	50188	-3405
A Consumption of fixed capital	33832	32668	1164	37709	36345	1364
B Net saving	12198	15699	-3501	9074	13843	-4770
2 Capital transfers a	1447	1447	-	1525	1525	-
Finance of Gross Accumulation	47477	49814	-2337	48308	51714	-3405
Gross Accumulation						
1 Gross capital formation	64410	62446	1964	73862	71392	2470
A Increase in stocks	2568	2568	...	2976	2976	...
B Gross fixed capital formation	61842	59878	1964	70886	68416	2470
2 Purchases of land, net	8437	8062	375	10178	9668	510
3 Purchases of intangible assets, net	...	...	...	...	...	...
4 Capital transfers a	...	...	...	...	...	...
Net lending b	-25370	-20694	-4676	-35732	-29347	-6385
Gross Accumulation	47477	49814	-2337	48308	51714	-3405

a) Capital transfers received are recorded net of capital transfers paid.
b) Net lending of the capital accumulation account and the capital finance account have not been reconciled and are different due to different statistical sources.

3.24 Corporate and Quasi-Corporate Enterprise Capital Finance Account: Total and Sectors
Thousand Million Japanese yen

	1980			1981			1982			1983		
	TOTAL	Non-Financial	Financial	TOTAL	Non-Financial	Financial	TOTAL	Non-Financial	Financial	TOTAL	Non-Financial	Financial
Acquisition of Financial Assets												
1 Gold and SDRs a	...	...	...	...	...	...	...	...	...	...	...	...
2 Currency and transferable deposits	-417	-1473	1056	3972	4293	-321	1750	1602	148	-296	-450	154
3 Other deposits	4777	4777	-	4930	4930	-	5261	5261	-	7671	7671	-
4 Bills and bonds, short term	2393	-35	2429	2175	181	1994	-1464	66	-1530	-2103	131	-2234
5 Bonds, long term	13018	1677	11342	15841	1697	14144	17025	1167	15859	19302	1190	18112
6 Corporate equity securities	1584	481	1104	3118	816	2302	2122	544	1578	2315	-94	2410
7 Short term loans, n.e.c.	34220	-	34221	34932	-	34932	41408	-	41408	42867	-	42868
8 Long term loans, n.e.c.												
9 Trade credits and advances	9977	9977	...	9736	9736	...	4199	4199	...	7370	7370	...
10 Other receivables	...	...	...	...	...	...	...	...	...	...	...	...
11 Other assets a	-1197	-2769	1571	7611	-368	7980	8073	3171	4902	9369	558	8811
Total Acquisition of Financial Assets	64356	12634	51722	82314	21283	61031	78374	16009	62365	86496	16376	70120
Incurrence of Liabilities												
1 Currency and transferable deposits	-1241	-	-1241	7253	-	7253	5304	-	5304	-155	-	-155
2 Other deposits	33231	...	33231	31844	...	31844	30468	...	30468	35374	...	35374
3 Bills and bonds, short term	-303	-303	-	-319	-319	-	-286	-286	-	-315	-315	-
4 Bonds, long term	5537	2777	2761	8004	3684	4320	10258	4008	6250	13027	3501	9526
5 Corporate equity securities	1976	1858	118	3231	2845	386	2456	2342	115	1685	1564	121
6 Short-term loans, n.e.c.	19928	18855	1074	20649	21122	-474	26514	22024	4490	27059	21684	5375
7 Long-term loans, n.e.c.												
8 Net equity of households in life insurance and pension fund reserves	5622	-	5622	6237	-	6237	7104	-	7104	7957	-	7957
9 Proprietors' net additions to the accumulation of quasi-corporations	-	-	-	-	-	-	-	-	-	-	-	-
10 Trade credit and advances	6243	6243	-	8462	8463	-	2358	2359	-	4717	4717	-
11 Other accounts payable	...	...	...	...	...	...	...	...	...	...	...	...
12 Other liabilities	3570	-4446	8016	9111	-2981	12092	8220	1238	6981	6334	-2198	8532
Total Incurrence of Liabilities	74563	24984	49579	94472	32814	61658	92394	31684	60710	95681	28952	66729
Net Lending b	-10207	-12349	2142	-12158	-11531	-626	-14020	-15675	1655	-9185	-12577	3392
Incurrence of Liabilities and Net Lending	64356	12634	51722	82314	21283	61031	78374	16009	62365	86496	16376	70120

1002

Japan

3.24 Corporate and Quasi-Corporate Enterprise Capital Finance Account: Total and Sectors

Thousand Million Japanese yen

	1984 TOTAL	1984 Non-Financial	1984 Financial	1985 TOTAL	1985 Non-Financial	1985 Financial	1986 TOTAL	1986 Non-Financial	1986 Financial	1987 TOTAL	1987 Non-Financial	1987 Financial
Acquisition of Financial Assets												
1 Gold and SDRs a	...	...	...	...	...	...	...	...	...	...	...	...
2 Currency and transferable deposits	2423	2250	173	1009	1128	-119	5025	5089	-64	-1163	-1547	384
3 Other deposits	6635	6635	...	12347	12347	...	17262	17262	...	29520	29520	...
4 Bills and bonds, short term	2421	45	2376	-1788	2	-1790	4092	779	3313	-1085	-969	-116
5 Bonds, long term	16675	563	16112	18561	1145	17416	28310	469	27841	22566	877	21689
6 Corporate equity securities	4760	497	4263	5356	212	5144	12248	349	11899	24629	3504	21125
7 Short term loans, n.e.c.	37181	...	37181	67905	...	67905	52997	...	52997	63878	-	63878
8 Long term loans, n.e.c.	13123	...	13123	2977	...	2977	-10869	...	-10869	28267	28267	...
10 Other receivables	...	...	...	...	...	...	...	...	...	...	...	...
11 Other assets a	22025	4306	17720	21835	6425	15410	41624	4494	37130	40464	-52	40516
Total Acquisition of Financial Assets	105243	27419	77824	110976	24234	86741	151689	17573	134115	207077	59599	147477
Incurrence of Liabilities												
1 Currency and transferable deposits	6236	-	6236	2893	-	2893	10470	-	10470	5667	...	5667
2 Other deposits	31371	-	31371	43002	-	43002	40011	...	40011	60918	...	60918
3 Bills and bonds, short term	-64	-64	...	142	142	...	96	96	...	-213	-213	...
4 Bonds, long term	14521	4909	9612	11550	5628	5922	25230	6835	18396	25537	7023	18514
5 Corporate equity securities	2385	156	2230	2389	2018	371	2508	303	2205	6144	4125	2020
6 Short-term loans, n.e.c.	25131	1326	23805	39258	13120	26138	36656	8331	28325	31281	26620	4660
7 Long-term loans, n.e.c.	...	...	...	...	...	...	...	...	...	...	...	...
8 Net equity of households in life insurance and pension fund reserves	10239	-	10239	11460	-	11460	15021	-	15021	18350	-	18350
9 Proprietors' net additions to the accumulation of quasi-corporations	-	-	-	1399	1399	-	-12041	-12040	-	27649	27649	-
10 Trade credit and advances	9146	9146	...	...	...	...	...	...	...	...	...	...
11 Other accounts payable	...	1423	17660	11633	1167	10466	47058	3987	43072	56090	14570	41516
12 Other liabilities	19082	...	19082	...	...	...	...	...	...	...	...	...
Total Incurrence of Liabilities	118046	41448	76598	123725	36491	87234	165010	29408	135603	231118	79774	151344
Net Lending b	-12803	1226	-14029	-12750	-493	-12257	-13321	-11834	-1487	-24041	-20174	-3867
Incurrence of Liabilities and Net Lending	105243	27419	77824	110976	24234	86741	151689	17573	134115	207077	59599	147477

	1988 TOTAL	1988 Non-Financial	1988 Financial	1989 TOTAL	1989 Non-Financial	1989 Financial
Acquisition of Financial Assets						
1 Gold and SDRs a	...	...	...	...	...	...
2 Currency and transferable deposits	4874	3590	1284	-6135	-5994	-141
3 Other deposits	19811	19811	-	27844	27844	-
4 Bills and bonds, short term	1725	-66	1792	4513	-191	4705
5 Bonds, long term	21696	856	20840	11359	961	10397
6 Corporate equity securities	22910	2918	19992	28510	3349	25161
7 Short term loans, n.e.c.	61580	-	61580	89527	-	89527
8 Long term loans, n.e.c.	17948	17948	...	31447	31447	...
9 Trade credits and advances	...	...	...	...	...	...
10 Other receivables	...	...	...	...	...	...
11 Other assets a	45400	7256	38144	...	...	22748
Total Acquisition of Financial Assets	195944	52312	143632	...	...	152396
Incurrence of Liabilities						
1 Currency and transferable deposits	10705	-	10705	4487	-	4487
2 Other deposits	52963	-613	-	75073	-207	-
3 Bills and bonds, short term	-613	-	-207	-		

Japan

3.24 Corporate and Quasi-Corporate Enterprise Capital Finance Account: Total and Sectors (Continued)

Thousand Million Japanese yen

	1988			1989		
	TOTAL	Non-Financial	Financial	TOTAL	Non-Financial	Financial
4 Bonds, long term	22111	7214	14897	21583	12585	8998
5 Corporate equity securities	8444	5226	3218	15012	10124	4888
6 Short-term loans, n.e.c.	37256	32167	5089	51869	41897	9972
7 Long-term loans, n.e.c.						
8 Net equity of households in life insurance and pension fund reserves	22474	-	22474	24321	-	24321
9 Proprietors' net additions to the accumulation of quasi-corporations						
10 Trade credit and advances	15627	-	15627	23154	23154	-
11 Other accounts payable	...	...	...	...	...	...
12 Other liabilities	52111	9258	42852	37561	6295	31266
Total Incurrence of Liabilities	221079	68880	152199	252852	93848	159004
Net Lending b	-25135	-16567	-8567	...	...	-6008
Incurrence of Liabilities and Net Lending	195944	52312	143632	...	...	152396

a) Item 'Gold and SDRs' is included in item 'Other assets'.
b) Net lending of the capital accumulation account and the capital finance account have not been reconciled and are different due to different statistical sources.

3.32 Household and Private Unincorporated Enterprise Income and Outlay Account

Thousand Million Japanese yen

	1970	1975	1980	1981	1982	1983	1984	1985	1986	1987	1988	1989
Receipts												
1 Compensation of employees	31942	81678	130368	141397	149614	157299	166026	173815	182006	189125	200192	214730
A Wages and salaries	29303	74316	115990	124186	131216	137697	145380	151291	157803	162580	172235	184864
B Employers' contributions for social security	1638	4846	10220	11045	11615	12360	13437	14610	15376	16258	17643	
C Employers' contributions for private pension & welfare plans	1002	2516	5457	6995	7254	7987	8286	9087	9593	11169	11699	12223
2 Operating surplus of private unincorporated enterprises	13647	24078	33203	33791	35182	35712	37352	40890	42092	43901	45290	45745
3 Property and entrepreneurial income	4860	13377	23920	26465	29074	27141	29074	30141	31317	32837	32141	35842
A Withdrawals from private quasi-corporations a	...	...	...	...	...	...	...	...	...	...	...	...
B Interest	3537	10328	19424	21335	21929	23549	24378	24938	25843	28881	23409	23771
C Dividends	1065	2081	3166	3642	3665	3977	4207	4765	5292	6387	6199	6796
D Net land rent and royalties	258	969	1330	1488	1548	1548	1556	1614	1702	1873	2088	2271
3 Current transfers	6666	20033	38607	42566	46142	48952	50650	53365	56759	60238	63543	65108
A Casualty insurance claims	269	590	1261	1347	1415	1573	1663	1726	1790	1807	1932	2018
B Social security benefits	2464	8788	18919	21453	23627	25883	27596	28960	31478	34235	35922	37410
C Social assistance grants	1136	3108	6214	6762	7362	7274	6889	7691	7931	8228	8545	8877
D Unfunded employee pension and welfare benefits	11	38	60	70	76	62	58	65	70	81	87	
E Transfers from general government												
F Transfers from the rest of the world	...	...	...	...	...	...	...	...	...	...	...	...
G Other transfers n.e.c.	2784	7509	12153	12911	13668	14145	14463	14929	15498	15898	17063	16916
Total Current Receipts	57114	139166	226098	244221	257979	271037	284170	299387	313693	325405	341340	361424
Disbursements												
1 Final consumption expenditures	37805	83920	139506	147988	158854	167509	177267	185235	193308	201973	212237	225476
2 Property income	1493	4445	8465	9828	10286	10972	11599	11985	12499	13045	13612	14462
A Interest	1406	4273	8125	9167	9911	10591	11217	11587	12079	12651	13186	14211
Consumer debt	217	481	751	846	917	1005	1116	1219	1360	1420	1629	1855
Mortgage	1189	3791	7374	8321	8994	9586	10101	10367	10719	11230	11558	12356
Other												
B Net land rent and royalties	87	172	340	361	375	382	383	399	420	394	426	452
3 Direct taxes and other current transfers n.e.c. to government	6236	17025	32568	37160	39860	42549	44784	47627	50967	55042	57872	61537
A Social security contributions	3165	9503	17513	20072	21646	22896	24270	26185	27761	29694	31363	33109
B Direct taxes	3029	7422	14899	16923	18044	19470	20233	21248	22995	25098	26268	28193
Income taxes	2891	6967	14025	15997	17096	18466	19222	20113	21806	23848	24933	26797

1004

Japan

3.32 Household and Private Unincorporated Enterprise Income and Outlay Account (Continued)

Thousand Million Japanese yen	1970	1975	1980	1981	1982	1983	1984	1985	1986	1987	1988	1989
Other	138	455	875	926	948	1004	1101	1135	1189	1250	1335	1426
C Fees, fines and penalties	42	100	156	165	170	184	192	194	211	251	240	234
4 Other current transfers	3472	8963	15132	16183	17222	17929	18334	19119	19897	20689	22145	23392
A Net casualty insurance premiums	279	599	1275	1351	1413	1571	1661	1729	1801	1822	1946	2029
B Transfers to private non-profit institutions serving households	427	875	1701	1910	2169	2220	2291	2526	2694	2820	3129	3471
C Transfers to the rest of the world	...	...	...	...	...	...	...	...	...	...	...	...
Other current transfers, except imputed	2755	7471	12095	12829	13570	14062	14320	14806	15338	15876	16989	16805
E Imputed employee pension and welfare contributions	11	38	60	94	70	76	62	58	65	70	81	87
Net saving	8109	24793	30426	33361	31758	32079	33185	34421	37022	34755	35475	37357
Total Current Disbursements and Net Saving	57115	139166	226921	244221	257979	271037	284170	293387	313693	325405	341340	361424

a) Item 'Withdrawals from quasi-corporate enterprises' is not included in the income and outlay accounts of the corporate and quasi-corporate enterprise table and household and private unincorporated enterprise table.

3.33 Household and Private Unincorporated Enterprise Capital Accumulation Account

Thousand Million Japanese yen	1970	1975	1980	1981	1982	1983	1984	1985	1986	1987	1988	1989
Finance of Gross Accumulation												
1 Gross saving	10396	30430	40761	44490	43498	44346	46025	47782	50860	49159	50761	53790
A Consumption of fixed capital	2287	5637	10335	11129	11741	12267	12840	13361	13838	14403	15286	16433
B Net saving	8109	24793	30426	33361	31758	32079	33185	34421	37022	34755	35475	37357
2 Capital transfers a	-338	-821	-1152	-1143	-1282	-1497	-1623	-1730	-2066	-2474	-2788	-2652
Total Finance of Gross Accumulation b	10058	29609	39607	43347	42216	42848	44401	46051	48794	46685	47973	51138
Gross Accumulation												
1 Gross Capital Formation	6578	15066	22400	21995	21805	21033	20861	21860	22868	26312	29097	30426
A Increase in stocks	17	83	69	195	170	112	27	107	205	107	63	81
B Gross fixed capital formation	6561	14983	22330	21800	21636	20921	20833	21753	22663	26205	29034	30345
2 Purchases of land, net	-2119	-2449	-3808	-4175	-3560	-3610	-3178	-5649	-5902	-8766	-12543	-14249
3 Purchases of intangibles, net	...	...	...	...	...	...	...	...	...	...	...	...
4 Capital transfers a												
Net lending c	5598	16992	21016	25527	24370	25425	26719	29840	31827	29139	31418	34961
Total Gross Accumulation b	10057	29609	39607	43347	42216	42848	44401	46051	48794	46685	47973	51138

a) Capital transfers received are recorded net of capital transfers paid.
b) Private non-profit institutions serving households is included in household and private unincorporated enterprise.
c) Net lending of the capital accumulation account and the capital finance account have not been reconciled and are different due to different statistical sources.

3.34 Household and Private Unincorporated Enterprise Capital Finance Account

Thousand Million Japanese yen	1970	1975	1980	1981	1982	1983	1984	1985	1986	1987	1988	1989
Acquisition of Financial Assets												
1 Gold a	...	...	...	...	...	...	...	...	...	...	...	...
2 Currency and transferable deposits	1620	2252	-749	3158	3025	291	3836	2042	5729	6418	6056	10170
3 Other deposits	5506	16324	22546	22950	21232	22773	19850	22185	19285	21812	24853	35486
4 Bills and bonds, short term	831	2577	3451	3818	5185	6567	7094	1484	3281	6294	-656	3149
5 Bonds, long term	493	381	-76	-153	357	-619	596	-567	-1554	4607	-1575	-1257
6 Corporate equity securities												
7 Short term loans, n.e.c.	...	...	...	...	...	...	...	...	...	...	...	...
8 Long term loans, n.e.c.	...	...	...	...	...	...	...	...	...	...	...	...
9 Trade credit and advances	...	...	...	...	...	...	...	...	...	...	...	...
10 Net equity of households in life insurance and pension fund reserves	1373	2732	5358	5899	6659	7466	9672	10799	14489	17217	20890	22455
11 Proprietors' net additions to the accumulation of the quasi-corporations	...	...	...	...	...	...	...	...	...	...	...	...
12 Other a	316	390	678	678	800	892	1118	1156	2223	1680	430	2229
Total Acquisition of Financial Assets b	10139	24656	31209	36471	37350	37595	42204	38166	43458	58028	49998	72232
Incurrence of Liabilities												
1 Short term loans, n.e.c.	2960	7503	10975	10923	10744	10359	9319	7572	12070	25784	19915	30989

1005

Japan

3.34 Household and Private Unincorporated Enterprise Capital Finance Account (Continued)

Thousand Million Japanese yen

	1970	1975	1980	1981	1982	1983	1984	1985	1986	1987	1988	1989
2 Long term loans, n.e.c.	...	...	...	...	...	...	...	...	...	...	...	...
3 Trade credit and advances	1728	3332	3488	1285	1686	2484	4245	1385	1080	587	2076	8035
4 Other accounts payable	...	...	...	...	...	...	...	...	...	...	...	...
5 Other liabilities	...	...	...	...	...	...	...	...	...	...	...	...
Total incurrence of Liabilities b	4688	10835	14463	12209	12429	12843	13564	8957	13150	26371	21991	39023
Net Lending c	5451	13821	16745	24262	24920	24753	28639	29209	30308	31656	28007	33209
Incurrence of Liabilities and Net Lending	10139	24656	31209	36471	37350	37596	42204	38166	43458	58028	49998	72232

a) Item "Gold and SDR's" is included in item "Other assets".
b) Private non-profit institutions serving households is included in household and private unincorporated enterprise.
c) Net lending of the capital accumulation account and the capital finance account have not been reconciled and are different due to different statistical sources.

3.41 Private Non-Profit Institutions Serving Households: Production Account

Thousand Million Japanese yen

	1970	1975	1980	1981	1982	1983	1984	1985	1986	1987	1988	1989
Gross Output												
1 Sales	...	...	...	...	...	...	...	...	...	...	...	...
2 Non-marketed output												
A Services produced for own use	519	820	1832	2009	1969	2245	2435	2548	2638	2677	2845	2821
B Own account fixed capital formation	...	...	...	...	...	...	...	...	...	...	...	...
Gross Output												
Intermediate consumption	487	1004	2861	2817	2921	3179	3418	3595	3740	4037	4301	4560
Subtotal: Value Added												
1 Indirect taxes, net	...	...	...	...	...	...	...	...	...	...	...	...
2 Consumption of fixed capital	71	140	292	360	443	522	624	710	743	828	863	932
3 Compensation of employees	674	2312	3947	4156	4466	4772	5150	5461	5864	6044	6506	6912
4 Net operating surplus	...	...	...	...	...	...	...	...	...	...	...	...
Gross Input	...	...	...	...	...	...	...	...	...	...	...	...

3.42 Private Non-Profit Institutions Serving Households: Income and Outlay Account

Thousand Million Japanese yen

	1970	1975	1980	1981	1982	1983	1984	1985	1986	1987	1988	1989
Receipts												
1 Operating surplus	...	...	...	...	...	...	...	...	...	...	...	...
2 Property and entrepreneurial income	143	434	960	1028	1032	1127	1215	1235	1271	1134	1043	999
A Withdrawals from quasi-corporations	...	...	...	...	...	...	...	...	...	...	...	...
B Interest	122	402	915	971	976	1067	1148	1164	1178	1015	911	811
C Dividends	4	12	19	29	30	33	36	37	57	81	91	149
D Net land rent and royalties	16	20	26	26	27	28	31	34	36	38	40	39
3 Current transfers	666	1544	2986	3346	3677	3855	3961	4321	4604	4874	5394	5936
A Casualty insurance claims	2	4	7	10	12	12	13	13	13	14	14	15
B Current transfers from general government	126	444	838	904	918	1063	1089	1129	1193	1267	1341	1423
C Other transfers from resident sectors	...	...	...	...	...	...	...	...	...	...	...	...
D Current transfers received from the rest of the world	568	1095	2139	2429	2745	2776	2857	3177	3396	3590	4037	4495
E Imputed unfunded employee pension and welfare contributions	-	1	2	2	2	2	2	2	2	2	3	3
Total Current Receipts	839	1978	3947	4374	4709	4982	5176	5555	5875	6008	6437	6935
Disbursements												
1 Final consumption expenditures	528	843	1818	2008	1980	2179	2364	2525	2661	2612	2885	2969
A Compensation of employees												
B Consumption of fixed capital	69	134	292	360	443	522	624	710	743	828	863	932
C Purchases of goods and services, net												
2 Property income	114	329	606	664	706	778	879	901	925	932	922	937
3 Direct taxes and other transfers to general government	...	...	...	...	...	...	...	...	...	...	...	...

Japan

3.42 Private Non-Profit Institutions Serving Households: Income and Outlay Account (Continued)

Thousand Million Japanese yen	1970	1975	1980	1981	1982	1983	1984	1985	1986	1987	1988	1989
4 Other current transfers	210	717	977	1066	1341	1530	1537	1754	1877	2063	2252	2321
A Net casualty insurance premiums	2	6	11	13	15	17	18	19	18	18	17	19
B Social assistance grants	207	411	964	1050	1324	1511	1517	1734	1857	2043	2232	2300
C Unfunded employee pension and welfare benefits	-	1	2	3	2	2	2	2	2	2	3	3
D Current transfers to the rest of the world	...	...	...	...	...	...	...	...	...	...	...	...
E Other current transfers n.e.c.	...	...	...	...	...	...	...	...	...	...	...	...
Net saving	-12	389	546	635	683	495	396	376	412	401	378	708
Total Current Disbursements	840	1978	3947	4374	4709	4982	5176	5555	5875	6008	6437	6935

3.43 Private Non-Profit Institutions Serving Households: Capital Accumulation Account

Thousand Million Japanese yen	1970	1975	1980	1981	1982	1983	1984	1985	1986	1987	1988	1989
Finance of Gross Accumulation												
1 Gross saving	57	523	838	966	1126	1017	1020	1086	1155	1229	1241	1640
A Consumption of fixed capital	69	134	292	360	443	522	624	710	743	828	863	932
B Net saving	-12	389	546	635	683	495	396	376	412	401	378	708
2 Capital transfers	170	426	579	445	441	569	613	597	610	625	640	649
Finance of Gross Accumulation	227	949	1417	1440	1567	1586	1633	1683	1765	1854	1881	2289
Gross Accumulation												
1 Gross capital formation	232	489	803	813	840	1029	1145	1112	1062	1184	1337	1486
A Increase in stocks	...	...	...	...	...	...	...	...	...	...	...	...
B Gross fixed capital formation	232	489	803	813	840	1029	1145	1112	1062	1184	1337	1486
2 Purchases of land, net	61	68	170	105	158	119	49	150	159	192	277	242
3 Purchases of intangible assets, net	...	...	...	...	...	...	...	...	...	...	...	...
4 Capital transfers	...	...	...	...	...	...	...	...	...	...	...	...
Net lending [a]	-66	393	444	522	569	438	438	421	544	477	266	561
Gross Accumulation	227	950	1417	1440	1567	1586	1633	1683	1765	1854	1881	2289

3.44 Private Non-Profit Institutions Serving Households: Capital Finance Account

Thousand Million Japanese yen	1970	1975	1980	1981	1982	1983	1984	1985	1986	1987	1988	1989
Acquisition of Financial Assets												
1 Gold	...	...	...	...	...	...	...	...	...	...	...	...
2 Currency and transferable deposits	39	137	78	110	175	163	83	-52	-46	-62	-92	81
3 Other deposits	96	722	1150	952	907	857	488	984	1199	1289	1375	1376
4 Bills and bonds, short term	...	...	...	...	...	...	...	...	...	...	...	...
5 Bonds, long term	33	56	129	105	143	132	145	114	159	133	158	131
6 Corporate equity securities	2	5	5	9	11	12	15	11	11	11	32	17
7 Short-term loans, n.e.c.	159	509	487	441	455	372	92	152	184	31	-79	11
8 Long-term loans, n.e.c.	...	...	...	...	...	...	...	...	...	...	...	...
9 Other receivables	...	...	...	...	...	...	...	...	...	...	...	...
10 Proprietors' net additions to the accumulation of quasi-corporations	...	...	...	...	...	...	...	...	...	...	...	...
11 Other assets	17	44	40	99	49	46	35	92	102	94	136	80
Total Acquisition of Financial Assets	346	1473	1889	1720	1741	1581	858	1301	1609	1496	1529	1697
Incurrence of Liabilities												
1 Short-term loans	320	925	1036	1042	918	878	702	985	1178	1059	1080	1221
2 Long-term loans	86	277	268	63	164	169	-273	208	168	105	273	290
3 Other liabilities	406	1202	1304	1104	1083	1047	429	1192	1346	1164	1353	1511
Total Incurrence of Liabilities	406	1202	1304	1104	1083	1047	429	1192	1346	1164	1353	1511
Net Lending [a]	-62	270	585	616	658	534	429	109	263	332	177	185
Incurrence of Liabilities and Net Lending	344	1472	1889	1720	1741	1581	858	1301	1609	1496	1529	1697

a) Net lending of the capital accumulation account and the capital finance account have not been reconciled and are different due to different statistical sources.

Japan

3.51 External Transactions: Current Account: Detail

Thousand Million Japanese yen

	1970	1975	1980	1981	1982	1983	1984	1985	1986	1987	1988	1989
Payments to the Rest of the World												
1 Imports of goods and services	6985	18919	35036	35927	37341	34258	36866	35532	24791	25195	29065	36768
A Imports of merchandise c.i.f. [a]	5484	15158	29153	29500	30655	27902	30328	28856	19356	18708	21330	26906
B Other	1501	3761	5883	6428	6686	6356	6538	6676	5436	6487	7736	9863
2 Factor income to the rest of the world	503	1430	2898	4384	5019	3900	4448	4631	4108	5553	7822	11911
A Compensation of employees	23	57	244	326	411	411	401	387	256	281	232	274
B Property and entrepreneurial income	480	1373	2654	4058	4608	3489	4047	4244	3853	5273	7590	11637
3 Current transfers to the rest of the world	75	115	342	349	350	359	373	355	292	463	497	475
A Indirect taxes by general government to supranational organizations	...	...	...	...	...	...	...	...	...	...	...	...
B Other current transfers	75	115	342	349	350	359	373	355	292	463	497	475
By general government	29	34	84	80	91	111	107	90	80	88	104	148
By other resident sectors	46	81	257	269	259	248	266	265	212	375	393	327
4 Surplus of the nation on current transactions	744	-152	-2481	1251	1885	5083	8467	11660	14306	12697	10364	8100
Payments to the Rest of the World, and Surplus of the Nation on Current Transfers	8307	20312	35795	41911	44595	43600	50154	52178	43497	43908	47748	57254
Receipts From The Rest of the World												
1 Exports of goods and services	7926	18982	32887	37977	39391	39275	45066	46307	38090	36210	37483	42352
A Exports of merchandise f.o.b.	6873	16579	29022	33656	34748	34964	40381	41555	34575	32490	33398	37372
B Other	1053	2403	3865	4321	4643	4311	4685	4752	3515	3720	4085	4980
2 Factor income from the rest of the world	347	1273	2820	3837	5088	4211	4953	5768	5338	7607	10124	14761
A Compensation of employees	71	154	214	233	366	354	308	311	303	336	312	381
B Property and entrepreneurial income	276	1119	2606	3605	4722	3858	4646	5458	5035	7271	9812	14380
3 Current transfers from the rest of the world	35	59	87	97	117	114	134	102	70	92	141	142
A Subsidies to general government from supranational organizations	...	...	...	...	...	...	...	...	...	...	...	...
B Other current transfers	35	59	87	97	117	114	134	102	70	92	141	142
To general government	2	5	10	13	12	12	13	12	7	9	9	14
To other resident sectors	33	53	78	84	104	102	122	90	63	82	132	128
Receipts from the Rest of the World on Current Transfers	8308	20314	35794	41911	44596	43600	50153	52177	43498	43909	47748	57254

a) Imports of merchandise c.i.f. is not estimated in the Balance of Payments in Japan. Therefore, valuation basis is f.o.b.

3.52 External Transactions: Capital Accumulation Account

Thousand Million Japanese yen

	1970	1975	1980	1981	1982	1983	1984	1985	1986	1987	1988	1989
Finance of Gross Accumulation												
1 Surplus of the nation on current transactions	744	-152	-2481	1251	1885	5083	8467	11660	14306	12697	10364	8100
2 Capital transfers from the rest of the world [a]	-35	-49	-96	-104	-110	-123	-117	-142	-127	-156	-172	-247
A By general government	-35	-49	-96	-104	-110	-123	-117	-142	-127	-156	-172	-247
B By other resident sectors	-	-	-	-	-	-	-	-	-	-	-	-
Total Finance of Gross Accumulation	709	-201	-2577	1147	1775	4960	8350	11518	14179	12541	10192	7853
Gross Accumulation												
1 Capital transfers to the rest of the world [a]	...	...	...	...	...	...	...	...	...	...	...	...
2 Purchases of intangible assets, n.e.c., net, from the rest of the world	...	...	...	...	...	...	...	...	...	...	...	...
Net lending to the rest of the world	709	-200	-2577	1147	1775	4960	8351	11518	14179	12541	10192	7853
Total Gross Accumulation	709	-200	-2577	1147	1775	4960	8351	11518	14179	12541	10192	7853

a) Capital transfers received are recorded net of capital transfers paid.

Japan

3.53 External Transactions: Capital Finance Account

Thousand Million Japanese yen

	1970	1975	1980	1981	1982	1983	1984	1985	1986	1987	1988	1989
Acquisitions of Foreign Financial Assets												
1 Gold and SDR's a	95	-15	13	20	26	-47	-16	75	39	58	51	-66
2 Currency and transferable deposits	...	...	...	...	...	...	...	...	...	...	...	...
3 Other deposits	...	...	...	...	...	...	...	...	...	...	...	...
4 Bills and bonds, short term	...	...	...	...	...	...	...	...	...	...	...	...
5 Bonds, long term	...	...	...	...	...	...	...	...	...	...	...	...
6 Corporate equity securities	...	...	...	...	...	...	...	...	...	...	...	...
7 Short-term loans, n.e.c.	...	...	...	...	...	...	...	...	...	...	...	...
8 Long-term loans	...	...	...	...	...	...	...	...	...	...	...	...
9 Prporietors' net additions to accumulation of quasi-corporate, non-resident enterprises	...	...	...	...	...	...	...	...	...	...	...	...
10 Trade credit and advances	...	...	...	...	...	...	...	...	...	...	...	...
11 Other	961	804	3456	5713	5460	8046	14017	19287	24609	25039	21240	24954
Total Acquisitions of Foreign Financial Assets	1056	789	3469	5733	5486	7999	14001	19362	24648	25097	21291	24888
Incurrence of Foreign Liabilities												
1 Currency and transferable deposits	...	...	...	...	...	...	...	...	...	...	...	...
2 Other deposits	...	...	...	...	...	...	...	...	...	...	...	...
3 Bills and bonds, short term	...	...	...	...	...	...	...	...	...	...	...	...
4 Bonds, long term	...	...	...	...	...	...	...	...	...	...	...	...
5 Corporate equity securities	...	...	...	...	...	...	...	...	...	...	...	...
6 Short-term loans, n.e.c.	...	...	...	...	...	...	...	...	...	...	...	...
7 Long-term loans	...	...	...	...	...	...	...	...	...	...	...	...
8 Non-resident proprietors' net additions to accumulation of resident quasi-corporate enterprises	...	...	...	...	...	...	...	...	...	...	...	...
9 Trade credit and advances	...	...	...	...	...	...	...	...	...	...	...	...
10 Other	303	990	6047	4587	3711	3038	5651	7844	10469	12556	11099	17035
Total Incurrence of Liabilities	303	990	6047	4587	3711	3038	5651	7844	10469	12556	11099	17035
Net Lending	753	-200	-2577	1147	1775	4960	8351	11518	14179	12541	10192	7853
Total Incurrence of Liabilities and Net Lending	1056	790	3470	5734	5486	7998	14002	19362	24648	25097	21291	24888

a) Item 'Gold and SDRs' excludes initial allocations of SDRs by IMF.

4.1 Derivation of Value Added by Kind of Activity, in Current Prices

Thousand Million Japanese yen

	1980			1981			1982			1983		
	Gross Output	Intermediate Consumption	Value Added	Gross Output	Intermediate Consumption	Value Added	Gross Output	Intermediate Consumption	Value Added	Gross Output	Intermediate Consumption	Value Added
All Producers												
1 Agriculture, hunting, forestry and fishing	16411	7563	8847	16787	7712	9075	17026	7788	9238	17413	7896	9517
2 Mining and quarrying	2621	1258	1363	2530	1254	1276	2344	1156	1188	2119	1048	1071
3 Manufacturing	242496	172264	70232	250841	175902	74939	254091	175623	78468	259644	177897	81747
A Manufacture of food, beverages and tobacco a	24059	16146	7913	26498	17706	8792	28219	18531	9688	30025	19479	10546
B Textile, wearing apparel and leather industries b	8759	6224	2535	8766	6183	2583	8600	6022	2578	8286	5715	2571
C Manufacture of wood and wood products, including furniture	...	...	...	...	...	...	...	...	...	...	...	...
D Manufacture of paper and paper products, printing and publishing c	8041	6032	2009	7764	5628	2136	7845	5728	2117	8068	5841	2227
E Manufacture of chemicals and chemical petroleum, coal, rubber and plastic products d	37733	29770	7963	39883	31056	8827	40588	31002	9586	39776	29517	10259
F Manufacture of non-metallic mineral products, except products of petroleum and coal	8236	5501	2735	8451	5484	2967	8369	5383	2986	8364	5161	3203
G Basic metal industries	41407	32523	8885	36412	28936	7476	35254	28172	7082	33931	27974	5957
H Manufacture of fabricated metal products, machinery and equipment	84568	56729	27839	92602	61552	31050	93937	61334	32603	98307	63947	34362
I Other manufacturing industries	29693	19338	10355	30466	19358	11108	31280	19451	11829	32885	20264	12621
4 Electricity, gas and water	13452	6872	6580	15217	7832	7385	15804	8085	7719	16670	7878	8792

Japan

4.1 Derivation of Value Added by Kind of Activity, in Current Prices
(Continued)

Thousand Million Japanese yen

	1980			1981			1982			1983		
	Gross Output	Intermediate Consumption	Value Added	Gross Output	Intermediate Consumption	Value Added	Gross Output	Intermediate Consumption	Value Added	Gross Output	Intermediate Consumption	Value Added
5 Construction	55168	32662	22506	56527	31980	24547	56695	31928	24767	55085	31812	23273
6 Wholesale and retail trade, restaurants and hotels	55396	18604	36792	57797	19303	38494	60528	20101	40427	63000	21444	41556
7 Transport, storage and communication	25546	10760	14787	27332	11204	16128	28758	11662	17096	30337	12098	18239
8 Finance, insurance, real estate and business services	42343	7249	35095	44890	8181	36709	48867	9202	39665	52762	9983	42779
9 Community, social and personal services e	52796	24733	28063	57886	26558	31328	63831	29469	34362	68919	31633	37286
Total, Industries	506229	281963	224266	529806	289923	239883	547943	295013	252930	565948	301688	264260
Producers of Government Services	27712	7213	20499	29974	7940	22034	31449	8391	23058	32884	8985	23899
Other Producers	7147	2861	4286	7373	2817	4556	7868	2921	4947	8521	3179	5342
Total	541087	292037	249050	567153	300680	266473	587260	306326	280934	607353	313852	293501
Less: Imputed bank service charge	...	-10413	10413	...	-10150	10150	...	-11748	11748	...	-13010	13010
Import duties	1313	...	1313	1267	...	1267	1310	...	1310	1187	...	1187
Value added tax	...	...	...	...	...	...	...	...	...	...	...	...
Other adjustments f	225	...	225	373	...	373	104	...	104	89	...	89
Total	542625	302449	240176	568793	310830	257963	588674	318073	270601	608629	326862	281767

	1984			1985			1986			1987		
	Gross Output	Intermediate Consumption	Value Added	Gross Output	Intermediate Consumption	Value Added	Gross Output	Intermediate Consumption	Value Added	Gross Output	Intermediate Consumption	Value Added
						All Producers						
1 Agriculture, hunting, forestry and fishing	18213	8256	9957	18400	8186	10214	17822	7847	9975	16812	7044	9768
2 Mining and quarrying	2022	1015	1007	1936	978	958	1892	900	992	1853	877	976
3 Manufacturing	279496	190251	89245	287810	193138	94673	275271	179009	96262	274715	175418	99297
A Manufacture of food, beverages and tobacco a	31547	20801	10746	32419	21285	11134	32455	20655	11800	32486	20343	12143
B Textile, wearing apparel and leather industries b	8155	5625	2530	8023	5478	2545	7522	5043	2479	7218	4725	2493
C Manufacture of wood and wood products, including furniture	...	...	...	...	...	...	...	...	...	...	...	...
D Manufacture of paper and paper products, printing and publishing c	8461	6122	2339	8411	6021	2390	8069	5511	2558	8306	5570	2736
E Manufacture of chemicals and chemical petroleum, coal, rubber and plastic products d	40469	29646	10823	39663	28707	10956	33603	21598	12005	32107	19631	12476
F Manufacture of non-metallic mineral products, except products of petroleum and coal	8589	5275	3314	8572	5124	3448	8467	4910	3557	8535	4751	3784
G Basic metal industries	36414	28607	7807	35424	27559	7865	29727	22693	7034	29765	22212	7553
H Manufacture of fabricated metal products, machinery and equipment	111340	72777	38563	118861	76536	42325	118184	76447	41737	117952	75784	42168
I Other manufacturing industries	34523	21400	13123	36436	22428	14008	37244	22154	15090	38346	22403	15943
4 Electricity, gas and water	17653	8111	9542	18425	8119	10306	17787	6454	11333	17507	6170	11337
5 Construction	56147	32154	23993	57660	32279	25381	59801	32914	26887	65597	35468	30129
6 Wholesale and retail trade, restaurants and hotels	64698	22721	41977	65896	23060	42836	67189	23622	43567	70158	24618	45540
7 Transport, storage and communication	32579	12621	19958	34095	13009	21086	34021	12111	21910	35169	12298	22871
8 Finance, insurance, real estate and business services	56269	10622	45647	60782	11451	49331	64652	12208	52444	71121	14158	56963
9 Community, social and personal services e	74761	34139	40622	81696	35306	46390	87270	37483	49787	92216	40335	51881
Total, Industries	601837	319888	281949	626700	325525	301175	625704	312549	313155	645147	316386	328761
Producers of Government Services	34760	9629	25131	36454	10170	26284	38583	11048	27535	39547	11205	28342
Other Producers	9242	3418	5824	9814	3595	6219	10393	3740	6653	10961	4037	6924
Total	645838	332936	312902	672968	339290	333678	674679	327337	347342	695655	331628	364027
Less: Imputed bank service charge	...	-13811	13811	...	-14774	14774	...	-13938	13938	...	-15677	15677
Import duties	1337	...	1337	1353	...	1353	1046	...	1046	1166	...	1166
Value added tax	...	...	...	...	...	...	...	...	...	...	...	...
Other adjustments f	114	...	114	161	...	161	159	...	159	-1091	...	-1091
Total	647289	346746	300543	674482	354063	320419	675884	341275	334609	695730	347305	348425

1010

Japan

4.1 Derivation of Value Added by Kind of Activity, in Current Prices

Thousand Million Japanese yen

	1988			1989		
	Gross Output	Intermediate Consumption	Value Added	Gross Output	Intermediate Consumption	Value Added
All Producers						
1 Agriculture, hunting, forestry and fishing	16791	7037	9754	17473	7252	10221
2 Mining and quarrying	1975	917	1058	2094	1037	1057
3 Manufacturing	296560	189911	106649	322312	207908	114404
A Manufacture of food, beverages and tobacco a	33378	21091	12287	34438	21550	12888
B Textile, wearing apparel and leather industries b	7434	4876	2558	7563	4931	2632
C Manufacture of wood and wood products, including furniture	...	...	...	...	...	...
D Manufacture of paper and paper products, printing and publishing c	8842	5880	2962	9672	6343	3329
E Manufacture of chemicals and chemical petroleum, coal, rubber and plastic products d	33188	20263	12925	36023	21834	14189
F Manufacture of non-metallic mineral products, except products of petroleum and coal	9177	5038	4139	9727	5274	4453
G Basic metal industries	33161	24292	8869	35765	26450	9315
H Manufacture of fabricated metal products, machinery and equipment	130349	84023	46326	145041	95256	49785
I Other manufacturing industries	41031	24447	16584	44084	26269	17815
4 Electricity, gas and water	17717	6330	11387	18087	6704	11383
5 Construction	72583	38574	34009	79371	41764	37607
6 Wholesale and retail trade, restaurants and hotels	74306	26296	48010	78432	28055	50377
7 Transport, storage and communication	37428	13207	24221	39718	13770	25948
8 Finance, insurance, real estate and business services	76329	14661	61668	84772	17862	66910
9 Community, social and personal services e	98941	43948	54993	109248	48576	60672
Total, Industries	692629	340880	351749	751505	372927	378578
Producers of Government Services	41015	11702	29313	43453	12608	30845
Other Producers	11725	4301	7424	12465	4560	7905
Total	745370	356882	388488	807422	390095	417327
Less: Imputed bank service charge	...	-16568	16568	...	-20235	20235
Import duties	1217	...	1217	1892	...	1892
Value added tax	...	...	...	...	...	...
Other adjustments f	-1708	...	-1708	-3140	...	-3140
Total	744879	373450	371429	806174	410331	395844

a) Item 'Manufacture of food, beverages and tobacco' excludes tobacco.
b) Item 'Textile, wearing apparel and leather industries' refers to textile only.
c) Item 'Manufacture of paper and paper products, printing and publishing' excludes printing and publishing.
d) Item 'Manufacture of chemical and chemical petroleum, coal, rubber and plastic products' excludes rubber and plastic products.
e) Restaurants and hotels are included in item 'Community, social and personal services'.
f) Item 'Other adjustments' refers to inventory valuation adjustment.

4.2 Derivation of Value Added by Kind of Activity, in Constant Prices

Thousand Million Japanese yen

	1980			1981			1982			1983		
	Gross Output	Intermediate Consumption	Value Added	Gross Output	Intermediate Consumption	Value Added	Gross Output	Intermediate Consumption	Value Added	Gross Output	Intermediate Consumption	Value Added
At constant prices of:1985												
All Producers												
1 Agriculture, hunting, forestry and fishing	16771	7636	9135	16701	7462	9239	17326	7633	9693	17605	7742	9863
2 Mining and quarrying	2542	1361	1181	2416	1279	1137	2293	1114	1179	2128	1025	1103
3 Manufacturing	241707	170225	71482	247311	172518	74793	248841	170711	78130	257131	175610	81521
A Manufacture of food, beverages and tobacco a	26517	16226	10291	27958	17328	10630	29567	18467	11100	30761	19236	11525

1011

Japan

4.2 Derivation of Value Added by Kind of Activity, in Constant Prices
(Continued)

Thousand Million Japanese yen

	1980 Gross Output	1980 Intermediate Consumption	1980 Value Added	1981 Gross Output	1981 Intermediate Consumption	1981 Value Added	1982 Gross Output	1982 Intermediate Consumption	1982 Value Added	1983 Gross Output	1983 Intermediate Consumption	1983 Value Added
					At constant prices of:1985							
B Textile, wearing apparel and leather industries b	8906	6161	2745	8818	6070	2748	8507	5817	2690	8351	5597	2754
C Manufacture of wood and wood products, including furniture	...	...	...	...	...	...	...	...	...	...	...	...
D Manufacture of paper and paper products, printing and publishing c	7626	5720	1906	7703	5491	2212	7852	5593	2259	8247	5891	2356
E Manufacture of chemicals and chemical petroleum, coal, rubber and plastic products d	37041	29837	7204	37924	29558	8366	37534	28175	9359	37930	28694	9236
F Manufacture of non-metallic mineral products, except products of petroleum and coal	8347	5658	2689	8240	5400	2840	8089	5275	2814	8139	5137	3002
G Basic metal industries	39668	31402	8266	35399	28505	6894	34316	27588	6728	33422	27433	5989
H Manufacture of fabricated metal products, machinery and equipment	83582	56717	26865	90280	61000	29280	91407	60705	30702	96906	63354	33552
I Other manufacturing industries	30021	18505	11516	30989	19167	11822	31568	19093	12475	33376	20270	13106
4 Electricity, gas and water	15393	7212	8181	15819	7493	8326	16161	7291	8870	16985	7552	9433
5 Construction	58933	32607	26326	59315	31951	27364	58438	31715	26723	56617	31867	24750
6 Wholesale and retail trade, restaurants and hotels	58269	20200	38069	59274	20191	39083	61069	20472	40597	63615	21754	41861
7 Transport, storage and communication	28561	11562	16999	29118	11555	17563	29399	11642	17757	30778	12072	18706
8 Finance, insurance, real estate and business services	47300	7807	39493	49008	8529	40479	50272	9355	40917	53265	10128	43137
9 Community, social and personal services e	60864	26178	34686	63748	27039	36709	68108	29546	38562	72517	31705	40812
Total, Industries	530340	284788	245552	542709	288017	254692	551906	289479	262427	570639	299455	271184
Producers of Government Services	31217	7730	23487	32606	8187	24419	33312	8389	24923	34366	9006	25360
Other Producers	7921	2856	5065	7913	2765	5148	8228	2836	5392	8805	3125	5680
Total	569477	295374	274103	583228	298969	284259	593446	300704	292742	613809	311586	302223
Less: Imputed bank service charge	...	-10414	10414	...	-10324	10324	...	-10542	10542	...	-11981	11981
Import duties	1274	...	1274	1213	...	1213	1171	...	1171	1134	...	1134
Value added tax	...	...	...	...	...	...	...	...	...	...	...	...
Other adjustments f	1758	...	1758	1121	...	1121	1631	...	1631	1324	...	1324
Total	572509	305787	266722	585562	309293	276268	596248	311246	285002	616267	323567	292701

	1984 Gross Output	1984 Intermediate Consumption	1984 Value Added	1985 Gross Output	1985 Intermediate Consumption	1985 Value Added	1986 Gross Output	1986 Intermediate Consumption	1986 Value Added	1987 Gross Output	1987 Intermediate Consumption	1987 Value Added
					At constant prices of:1985							
					All Producers							
1 Agriculture, hunting, forestry and fishing	18253	8011	10242	18400	8186	10214	18475	8468	10007	18285	7960	10325
2 Mining and quarrying	2014	1005	1009	1936	978	958	1969	973	996	1927	990	937
3 Manufacturing	276505	188079	88426	287810	193138	94672	292388	200275	92113	300950	202090	98860
A Manufacture of food, beverages and tobacco a	31241	20240	11001	32419	21285	11134	32944	22147	10797	33560	23092	10468
B Textile, wearing apparel and leather industries b	8058	5446	2612	8023	5478	2545	8110	5702	2408	7830	5387	2443
C Manufacture of wood and wood products, including furniture	...	...	...	...	...	...	...	...	...	...	...	...
D Manufacture of paper and paper products, printing and publishing c	8375	5980	2395	8411	6021	2390	8400	6054	2346	8761	6262	2499
E Manufacture of chemicals and chemical petroleum, coal, rubber and plastic products d	39872	29625	10247	39663	28707	10956	39027	30910	8117	40096	29213	10883
F Manufacture of non-metallic mineral products, except products of petroleum and coal	8355	5268	3087	8572	5124	3448	8581	5261	3320	8787	5242	3545
G Basic metal industries	35853	28250	7603	35424	27559	7865	33454	26463	6991	34125	26431	7694
H Manufacture of fabricated metal products, machinery and equipment	110046	72039	38007	118861	76536	42325	124006	80211	43795	128449	82286	46163
I Other manufacturing industries	34705	21231	13474	36436	22428	14008	37867	23526	14341	39341	24178	15163
4 Electricity, gas and water	17758	8188	9570	18425	8119	10306	18521	8083	10438	19316	8632	10684

1012

Japan

4.2 Derivation of Value Added by Kind of Activity, in Constant Prices
(Continued)

Thousand Million Japanese yen

	1984			1985			1986			1987		
	Gross Output	Intermediate Consumption	Value Added	Gross Output	Intermediate Consumption	Value Added	Gross Output	Intermediate Consumption	Value Added	Gross Output	Intermediate Consumption	Value Added
	At constant prices of:1985											
5　Construction	56695	31981	24714	57660	32279	25381	59906	33609	26297	65504	36380	29124
6　Wholesale and retail trade, restaurants and hotels	64880	22860	42020	65896	23060	42836	68421	24170	44251	72537	25573	46964
7　Transport, storage and communication	32589	12613	19976	34095	13009	21086	34372	13003	21369	35676	13739	21937
8　Finance, insurance, real estate and business services	57055	10707	46348	60782	11451	49331	64877	12366	52511	70705	14400	56305
9　Community, social and personal services e	76958	34122	42836	81696	35306	46390	86501	38693	47808	90391	42399	47992
Total, Industries	602706	317565	285141	626700	325525	301175	645427	339640	305787	675290	352161	323129
Producers of Government Services	35524	9661	25863	36454	10170	26284	38182	11680	26502	38685	11906	26779
Other Producers	9363	3394	5969	9814	3595	6219	10294	3854	6440	10836	4210	6626
Total	647593	330620	316973	672968	339290	333678	693903	355174	338729	724811	368277	356534
Less: Imputed bank service charge	...	-13706	13706	...	-14774	14774	...	-14833	14833	...	-17105	17105
Import duties	1317	...	1317	1353	...	1353	1583	...	1583	1830	...	1830
Value added tax	...	...	...	...	...	...	...	...	...	...	...	...
Other adjustments f	603	...	603	139	...	139	3337	...	3337	1056	...	1056
Total	649513	344326	305187	674460	354063	320397	698823	370007	328816	727697	385383	342315

	1988			1989		
	Gross Output	Intermediate Consumption	Value Added	Gross Output	Intermediate Consumption	Value Added
	At constant prices of:1985					
	All Producers					
1　Agriculture, hunting, forestry and fishing	17911	7916	9995	18156	7717	10439
2　Mining and quarrying	2020	1061	959	2055	1158	897
3　Manufacturing	327460	219461	107999	347522	232557	114965
A　Manufacture of food, beverages and tobacco a	34413	23574	10839	34691	23355	11336
B　Textile, wearing apparel and leather industries b	7989	5620	2369	7834	5491	2343
C　Manufacture of wood and wood products, including furniture	...	...	...	...	...	...
D　Manufacture of paper and paper products, printing and publishing c	9226	6508	2718	9791	6706	3085
E　Manufacture of chemicals and chemical petroleum, coal, rubber and plastic products d	42381	31962	10419	44501	32573	11928
F　Manufacture of non-metallic mineral products, except products of petroleum and coal	9498	5595	3903	9857	5735	4122
G　Basic metal industries	36594	28099	8495	37405	28864	8541
H　Manufacture of fabricated metal products, machinery and equipment	145187	92022	53165	159478	102788	56690
I　Other manufacturing industries	42173	26081	16092	43968	27047	16921
4　Electricity, gas and water	20515	9084	11431	21503	9434	12069
5　Construction	71238	39167	32071	74082	40789	33293
6　Wholesale and retail trade, restaurants and hotels	76958	27274	49684	79734	28322	51412
7　Transport, storage and communication	38101	14827	23274	39169	14775	24394
8　Finance, insurance, real estate and business services	74965	14803	60162	81649	17431	64218
9　Community, social and personal services e	95980	46269	49711	102237	49395	52842
Total, Industries	725149	379861	345288	766106	401579	364527
Producers of Government Services	39588	12589	26999	40451	13220	27231

Japan

4.2 Derivation of Value Added by Kind of Activity, in Constant Prices
(Continued)

Thousand Million Japanese yen

	1988			1989		
	Gross Output	Intermediate Consumption	Value Added	Gross Output	Intermediate Consumption	Value Added
	At constant prices of:1985					
Other Producers	11462	4545	6917	11848	4722	7126
Total	776199	396995	379204	818406	419522	398884
Less: Imputed bank service charge	...	-18127	18127	...	-21705	21705
Import duties	2044	...	2044	2936	...	2936
Value added tax	...	...	...	...	...	...
Other adjustments f	445	...	445	240	...	240
Total	778688	415121	363567	821582	441227	380355

a) Item 'Manufacture of food, beverages and tobacco' excludes tobacco.
b) Item 'Textile, wearing apparel and leather industries' refers to textile only.
c) Item 'Manufacture of paper and paper products, printing and publishing' excludes printing and publishing.

d) Item 'Manufacture of chemical and chemical petroleum, coal, rubber and plastic products' excludes rubber and plastic products.
e) Restaurants and hotels are included in item 'Community, social and personal services'.
f) Item 'Other adjustments' refers to inventory valuation adjustment.

4.3 Cost Components of Value Added

Thousand Million Japanese yen

	1980						1981					
	Compensation of Employees	Capital Consumption	Net Operating Surplus	Indirect Taxes	Less: Subsidies Received	Value Added	Compensation of Employees	Capital Consumption	Net Operating Surplus	Indirect Taxes	Less: Subsidies Received	Value Added
	All Producers											
1 Agriculture, hunting, forestry and fishing	2103	1754	5152	-161	...	8847	2140	1878	5138	-79	...	9075
2 Mining and quarrying	403	297	654	9	...	1363	437	253	571	15	...	1276
3 Manufacturing	35561	9220	18339	7112	...	70232	38398	9709	18706	8126	...	74939
A Manufacture of food, beverages and tobacco a	2837	662	2133	2281	...	7913	3122	652	2175	2844	...	8792
B Textile, wearing apparel and leather industries b	1604	290	526	115	...	2535	1645	262	551	124	...	2583
C Manufacture of wood and wood products, including furniture	...	...	...	...	...	...	...	...	...	...	...	...
D Manufacture of paper and paper products, printing and publishing c	906	344	662	98	...	2009	950	378	702	107	...	2136
E Manufacture of chemicals and chemical petroleum, coal, rubber and plastic products d	2436	1419	1987	2122	...	7963	2461	1544	2570	2254	...	8827
F Manufacture of non-metallic mineral products, except products of petroleum and coal	1688	484	436	127	...	2735	1749	500	580	139	...	2967
G Basic metal industries	2443	1697	4375	369	...	8885	2616	1574	2920	367	...	7476
H Manufacture of fabricated metal products, machinery and equipment	16635	3174	6463	1567	...	27839	18426	3639	7174	1811	...	31050
I Other manufacturing industries	7012	1153	1758	432	...	10355	7431	1161	2034	482	...	11108
4 Electricity, gas and water	1776	1473	2580	751	...	6580	1925	1943	2647	871	...	7385
5 Construction	13340	2212	6390	562	...	22506	14168	2642	7069	669	...	24547
6 Wholesale and retail trade, restaurants and hotels	20080	2233	12920	1560	...	36792	21811	2432	12566	1685	...	38494
7 Transport, storage and communication	11121	2695	1174	-201	...	14787	12125	2933	1442	-370	...	16128
8 Finance, insurance, real estate and business services	8080	6938	18932	1146	...	35095	8952	7493	18808	1457	...	36709
9 Community, social and personal services e	14911	2195	9027	1931	...	28063	16975	2818	9536	1999	...	31328
Total, Industries f	107374	29017	75170	12706	...	224266	116930	32099	76482	14371	...	239883
Producers of Government Services	19077	1393	-	30	...	20499	20403	1599	-	32	...	22034
Other Producers	3947	292	-	46	...	4286	4156	360	-	39	...	4556
Total f	130398	30701	75170	12782	...	249050	141490	34059	76482	14443	...	266473
Less: Imputed bank service charge	...	...	10413	...	...	10413	...	...	10150	...	...	10150
Import duties	...	...	...	1313	...	1313	...	...	...	1267	...	1267
Value added tax	...	...	...	...	...	...	...	...	...	...	...	...
Other adjustments g	...	...	...	...	...	225	...	...	...	...	...	373
Total f	130398	30701	64757	14095	...	240176	141490	34059	66332	15710	...	257963

1014

Japan

4.3 Cost Components of Value Added

Thousand Million Japanese yen

	1982						1983					
	Compensation of Employees	Consumption of Capital	Net Operating Surplus	Indirect Taxes	Less: Subsidies Received	Value Added	Compensation of Employees	Consumption of Capital	Net Operating Surplus	Indirect Taxes	Less: Subsidies Received	Value Added

All Producers

1 Agriculture, hunting, forestry and fishing	2238	1846	5252	-96	...	9238	2321	1833	5433	-69	...	9517
2 Mining and quarrying	470	218	491	9	...	1188	467	198	395	11	...	1071
3 Manufacturing	40204	10217	19630	8417	...	78468	42284	10736	20033	8693	...	81747
A Manufacture of food, beverages and tobacco a	3357	642	2761	2927	...	9688	3677	660	3042	3166	...	10546
B Textile, wearing apparel and leather industries b	1646	258	543	131	...	2578	1689	267	482	133	...	2571
C Manufacture of wood and wood products, including furniture	...	...	...	...	...	...	...	...	...	...	...	...
D Manufacture of paper and paper products, printing and publishing c	1000	382	623	112	...	2117	1068	406	639	116	...	2227
E Manufacture of chemicals and chemical petroleum, coal, rubber and plastic products d	2673	1531	3108	2274	...	9586	2792	1569	3631	2267	...	10259
F Manufacture of non-metallic mineral products, except products of petroleum and coal	1789	499	550	147	...	2986	1761	493	795	154	...	3203
G Basic metal industries	2689	1591	2424	378	...	7082	2799	1515	1274	368	...	5957
H Manufacture of fabricated metal products, machinery and equipment	19334	4110	7217	1942	...	32603	20406	4524	7454	1979	...	34362
I Other manufacturing industries	7716	1204	2404	506	...	11829	8093	1302	2716	511	...	12621
4 Electricity, gas and water	2136	2175	2507	906	...	7719	2280	2524	3032	957	...	8792
5 Construction	14791	2716	6587	672	...	24767	14968	2204	5221	580	...	23273
6 Wholesale and retail trade, restaurants and hotels	23060	2521	12971	1745	...	40427	24440	2989	12475	1653	...	41556
7 Transport, storage and communication	12988	3168	1192	-252	...	17096	13607	3344	1586	-297	...	18239
8 Finance, insurance, real estate and business services	9671	7939	20529	1527	...	39665	10338	8424	22390	1629	...	42779
9 Community, social and personal services e	18234	3120	10806	2202	...	34362	19907	3760	11379	2240	...	37286
Total, Industries 1	123821	34021	79965	15124	...	252930	130612	36012	82243	15394	...	264260
Producers of Government Services	21272	1752	-	34	...	23058	21973	1892	-	35	...	23899
Other Producers	4466	443	-	37	...	4947	4772	522	-	48	...	5342
Total, 1	149559	36216	79965	15195	...	280934	157357	38426	82243	15477	...	293501
Less: imputed bank service charge	...	...	11747	...	...	11747	...	...	13009	...	...	13010
Import duties	...	...	...	1310	...	1310	...	...	...	1187	...	1187
Value added tax	...	...	...	...	...	...	...	...	...	...	...	...
Other adjustments g	...	...	...	104	...	104	...	...	...	...	...	89
Total 1	149559	36216	68217	16605	...	270601	157357	38426	69233	16664	...	281767

	1984						1985					
	Compensation of Employees	Consumption of Capital	Net Operating Surplus	Indirect Taxes	Less: Subsidies Received	Value Added	Compensation of Employees	Consumption of Capital	Net Operating Surplus	Indirect Taxes	Less: Subsidies Received	Value Added

All Producers

1 Agriculture, hunting, forestry and fishing	2284	1812	5858	3	...	9957	2379	1866	5835	134	...	10214
2 Mining and quarrying	448	185	349	27	...	1007	479	200	261	18	...	958
3 Manufacturing	45361	11292	23040	9552	...	89245	47925	12001	24561	10185	...	94672
A Manufacture of food, beverages and tobacco a	3863	637	2806	3439	...	10746	4112	647	2772	3603	...	11134

Japan

4.3 Cost Components of Value Added (Continued)

Thousand Million Japanese yen

1984 / 1985

	Compensation of Employees	Capital Consumption	Net Operating Surplus	Indirect Taxes	Less: Subsidies Received	Value Added	Compensation of Employees	Capital Consumption	Net Operating Surplus	Indirect Taxes	Less: Subsidies Received	Value Added
B Textile, wearing apparel and leather industries b	1726	265	400	139	...	2530	1799	272	334	140	...	2545
C Manufacture of wood and wood products, including furniture	...	...	...	...	...	...	...	...	...	...	...	...
D Manufacture of paper and paper products, printing and publishing c	1151	418	647	123	...	2339	1224	456	576	135	...	2390
E Manufacture of chemicals and chemical petroleum, coal, rubber and plastic products d	3042	1495	3890	2397	...	10823	3176	1527	3831	2422	...	10956
F Manufacture of non-metallic mineral products, except products of petroleum and coal	1818	485	848	163	...	3314	1845	475	943	184	...	3448
G Basic metal industries	2976	1439	2969	423	...	7807	3077	1275	3068	446	...	7865
H Manufacture of fabricated metal products, machinery and equipment	22395	5117	8732	2319	...	38563	29348	5782	9941	2656	...	42325
I Other manufacturing industries	8389	1437	2747	550	...	13123	8747	1565	3097	600	...	14008
4 Electricity, gas and water	2342	2917	3169	1114	...	9542	2234	3399	3380	1292	...	10306
5 Construction	14986	2280	6109	618	...	23993	15584	2054	7018	725	...	25381
6 Wholesale and retail trade, restaurants and hotels	26183	2667	10885	2043	...	41777	26910	2967	10322	2037	...	42836
7 Transport, storage and communication	13988	3491	2590	-109	...	19958	14529	3813	2672	73	...	21086
8 Finance, insurance, real estate and business services	10742	8927	24011	1966	...	45647	11410	9513	25933	2476	...	49331
9 Community, social and personal services	21554	4370	12196	2502	...	40622	22810	5016	15692	2873	...	46390
Total, Industries [1]	137884	38141	88206	17714	...	281949	144260	40828	96274	19814	...	301175
Producers of Government Services	23083	2012	-	36	...	25131	24172	2078	-	36	...	26284
Other Producers	5150	624	-	50	...	5824	5461	710	-	47	...	6219
Total [1]	166120	40778	88206	17800	...	312902	173892	43615	96274	19897	...	333678
Less: Imputed bank service charge	...	13810	...	...	...	13811	...	14773	...	...	...	14774
Import duties	...	...	...	1337	...	1337	...	...	...	1353	...	1353
Value added tax	...	...	...	...	...	...	...	...	...	...	...	...
Other adjustments [9]	...	...	...	...	...	114	...	...	...	...	...	161
Total [1]	161120	40778	74395	19137	...	305043	173892	43615	81501	21250	...	320419

1986 / 1987

All Producers

	Compensation of Employees	Capital Consumption	Net Operating Surplus	Indirect Taxes	Less: Subsidies Received	Value Added	Compensation of Employees	Capital Consumption	Net Operating Surplus	Indirect Taxes	Less: Subsidies Received	Value Added
1 Agriculture, hunting, forestry and fishing	2246	1903	5705	121	...	9975	2238	1800	5594	136	...	9768
2 Mining and quarrying	485	198	304	5	...	992	492	195	283	9	...	976
3 Manufacturing	49728	12836	23665	10132	...	96262	50453	13408	24302	11134	...	99297
A Manufacture of food, beverages and tobacco	4288	668	3121	3723	...	11800	4412	722	3005	4003	...	12143
B Textile, wearing apparel and leather industries b	1887	279	180	134	...	2479	1904	282	157	150	...	2493
C Manufacture of wood and wood products, including furniture	...	...	...	...	...	...	...	...	...	...	...	...
D Manufacture of paper and paper products, printing and publishing c	1298	488	639	134	...	2558	1348	550	687	152	...	2736
E Manufacture of chemicals and chemical petroleum, coal, rubber and plastic products d	3320	1627	4684	2373	...	12005	3454	1718	4786	2519	...	12476
F Manufacture of non-metallic mineral products, except products of petroleum and coal	1894	492	994	178	...	3557	1963	507	1111	203	...	3784
G Basic metal industries	3152	1303	2163	417	...	7034	3095	1385	2601	473	...	7553
H Manufacture of fabricated metal products, machinery and equipment	24766	6267	8133	2574	...	41737	25011	6401	7813	2945	...	42168
I Other manufacturing industries	9124	1714	3653	599	...	15090	9267	1841	4144	691	...	15943
4 Electricity, gas and water	2350	3608	4170	1205	...	11333	2531	3882	3649	1275	...	11337

Japan

4.3 Cost Components of Value Added (Continued)

Thousand Million Japanese yen

	1986						1987					
	Compensation of Employees	Capital Consumption	Net Operating Surplus	Indirect Taxes	Less: Subsidies Received	Value Added	Compensation of Employees	Capital Consumption	Net Operating Surplus	Indirect Taxes	Less: Subsidies Received	Value Added
5 Construction	16256	2218	7687	756	...	26887	16764	2391	10071	904	...	30129
6 Wholesale and retail trade, restaurants and hotels	28293	3148	8983	2143	...	43567	30094	3245	9827	2374	...	45540
7 Transport, storage and communication	15134	3883	2616	277	...	21910	15176	4021	2749	925	...	22871
8 Finance, insurance, real estate and business services	12243	9977	27342	2882	...	52444	13393	10842	29074	3654	...	56963
9 Community, social and personal services e	24036	5512	17353	2887	...	49787	25825	6005	16754	3298	...	51881
Total, Industries 1	150740	42283	97107	20407	...	313155	156965	45788	102302	23706	...	328761
Producers of Government Services	25355	2144	-	36	...	27535	26061	2245	-	37	...	28342
Other Producers	5864	743	-	46	...	6653	6044	828	-	52	...	6924
Total 1	181959	45170	98725	20489	...	347342	189069	48861	102302	23795	...	364027
Less: Imputed bank service charge	...	...	...	...	13837	13838	...	...	...	...	15676	15677
Import duties	...	...	...	1046	...	1046	...	...	...	1166	...	1166
Value added tax	...	...	...	...	...	...	...	...	...	...	...	...
Other adjustments 9	...	...	...	...	...	159	...	...	...	...	...	-1091
Total 1	181959	45170	98725	21535	...	334609	189069	48861	102302	24961	...	348425

	1988						1989					
	Compensation of Employees	Capital Consumption	Net Operating Surplus	Indirect Taxes	Less: Subsidies Received	Value Added	Compensation of Employees	Capital Consumption	Net Operating Surplus	Indirect Taxes	Less: Subsidies Received	Value Added

All Producers

1 Agriculture, hunting, forestry and fishing	2266	1836	5506	146	...	9754	2260	1891	5680	390	...	10221
2 Mining and quarrying	462	206	371	20	...	1058	453	232	336	36	...	1057
3 Manufacturing	52998	14095	27460	12096	...	106649	56864	14983	30208	12349	...	114404
A Manufacture of food, beverages and tobacco a	4619	755	2768	4143	...	12287	4930	768	3073	4118	...	12888
B Textile, wearing apparel and leather industries b	1922	302	170	164	...	2558	1934	309	177	212	...	2632
C Manufacture of wood and wood products, including furniture	...	...	...	...	...	...	...	...	...	...	...	...
D Manufacture of paper and paper products, printing and publishing c	1399	603	792	168	...	2962	1492	684	924	231	...	3329
E Manufacture of chemicals and chemical products, coal, rubber and plastic products d	3577	1840	4752	2755	...	12925	3837	2001	5241	3112	...	14189
F Manufacture of non-metallic mineral products, except products of petroleum and coal	2140	523	1245	231	...	4139	2269	520	1354	311	...	4453
G Basic metal industries	3142	1473	3711	544	...	6889	3412	1509	3678	716	...	9315
H Manufacture of fabricated metal products, machinery and equipment	26512	6603	9907	3308	...	46326	28644	7069	11339	2730	...	49785
I Other manufacturing industries	9687	1996	4117	784	...	16564	10348	2125	4422	920	...	17815
4 Electricity, gas and water	2665	4099	3384	1240	...	11387	2796	4427	3125	1034	...	11383
5 Construction	18456	2755	11792	1006	...	34009	20282	3135	12612	1578	...	37607
6 Wholesale and retail trade, restaurants and hotels	31311	3445	10588	2666	...	48010	33331	4027	9531	3287	...	50377
7 Transport, storage and communication	15981	4310	2901	1029	...	24221	17203	4682	2841	1222	...	25948
8 Finance, insurance, real estate and business services	14207	11671	31499	4292	...	61668	15256	12794	34455	4406	...	66910
9 Community, social and personal services e	28308	6702	16320	3664	...	54993	30221	7972	17829	4151	...	60072
Total, Industries 1	166654	49118	109818	26159	...	351749	179366	54142	116617	28453	...	378578
Producers of Government Services	26952	2325	-	37	...	29313	28346	2456	-	43	...	30845

Japan

4.3 Cost Components of Value Added
(Continued)

Thousand Million Japanese Yen

	1988							1989						
	Compensation of Employees	Capital Consumption	Net Operating Surplus	Indirect Taxes	Less: Subsidies Received	Value Added		Compensation of Employees	Capital Consumption	Net Operating Surplus	Indirect Taxes	Less: Subsidies Received	Value Added
Other Producers	6506	863	-	56	...	7424		6912	932	-	61	...	7905
Total 1	200111	52306	109818	26252	...	388488		214623	57530	116917	28657	...	417327
Less: Imputed bank service charge	...	...	16567	...	...	16568		...	...	20234	...	...	20235
Import duties	...	...	...	1217	...	1217		...	...	...	1892	...	1892
Value added tax	...	...	...	...	...	...		...	...	...	...	...	...
Other adjustments g	...	...	...	...	...	-1708		...	...	...	...	...	-3140
Total 1	200111	52306	93250	27469	...	371429		214623	57530	96382	29001	...	395844

a) Item 'Manufacture of food, beverages and tobacco' excludes tobacco.
b) Item 'Textile, wearing apparel and leather industries' refers to textile only.
c) Item 'Manufacture of paper and paper products, printing and publishing' excludes printing and publishing.
d) Item 'Manufacture of chemical and chemical petroleum, coal, rubber and plastic products' excludes rubber and plastic products.
e) Restaurants and hotels are included in item 'Community, social and personal services'.
f) Column 4 refers to indirect taxes less subsidies received.
g) Item Other adjustments' refers to inventory valuation adjustment.

Jordan

General note. The preparation of national accounts statistics in the Hashemite Kingdom of Jordan is undertaken by the Department of Statistics, Amman. The annual official estimates together with methodological notes are published in a series of publications entitled 'National Accounts'. A comprehensive description of the concepts and definitions underlying the various tables is contained in 'The National Accounts 1970-1974', published in 1976 by the Department of Statistics. The estimates are generally in accordance with the classifications and definitions recommended in the United Nations System of National Accounts (SNA), national accounts questionnaire. Tables of the period 1960-1966 cover both the West Bank and the East Bank of Jordan, while tables for the period 1967 and onward cover only the East Bank of Jordan. When the scope and coverage of the estimates differ conceptual reasons from the definitions and classifications recommended in SNA, a footnote is indicated to the relevant tables.

Sources and methods:

(a) **Gross domestic product.** Gross domestic product is estimated mainly through the production approach.

(b) **Expenditure on the gross domestic product.** All components of GDP by expenditure type are estimated through the expenditure approach except private consumption expenditure and investment in machinery and equipment which are estimated by using the commodity-flow approach. The estimates of government final consumption expenditure are obtained from the records of the Ministry of Finance, National Planning Council and municipalities. The estimates of private final consumption expenditure are built up from studies of the origin and use of the country's economic resources and from the input-output analysis made for the years 1960-1969. Estimates of gross fixed capital formation in the private sector are based on building licence statistics, a special survey and on imports of machinery and equipment, while that of the government sector are mainly obtained from records of the Ministry of Finance. Estimates of increase in stocks are approximate and in most cases based on inquiries in the manufacturing industry. Imports and exports of goods and services are mainly estimated from the external trade statistics. GDP by expenditure at constant prices is not estimated.

(c) **Cost-structure of the gross domestic product.** The sources and methods applied in estimating the cost-structure components of GDP are based on income estimates. Separate estimates are made for income of agricultural workers, income of skilled labourers, and for income from property and capital assets. Gross operating surplus (i.e. including consumption of fixed capital) is arrived at as a residual.

(d) **Gross domestic product by kind of economic activity.** The table of GDP by kind of economic activity is prepared at factor costs. The production approach is used to estimate the value added of most industries, such as agriculture, forestry and fishing, mining and manufacturing, wholesale and retail trade, while the income approach is used for a number of service sectors. Annual agricultural surveys are undertaken on a country-wide basis providing production estimates for crops. The quantities obtained from these surveys are valued at farm prices which are assumed to be a certain percentage of the relevant wholesale or retail prices. Livestock estimates are obtained from the municipalities and the Ministry of Reconstruction and Development, adjusted to arrive at a total number of slaughterings for the country. The estimates of industrial production are based on 1967 and 1974 Industrial Censuses, balance sheets and companies and industrial statements. In 1970, and on analysis of large industrial companies and expenditure sample survey for the remaining years. Value added of private building construction is calculated from cost estimates obtained from special inquiries, while value of public construction is obtained from the records of the Ministry of Finance, National Planning Council and municipalities. Special sample surveys of wholesale and retail trade were conducted in the years 1967-1971 and supplemented by a systematic study of the origin and use of all goods imported and produced in the economy for the year 1975. For passenger and freight transport, the source of information is mainly based on the records of the corporation concerned. As for other services, estimates are based on a survey undertaken in 1974 and on special inquiries. The estimates for banking are based on returns sent to the Department of Statistics by the various banks. Information on the operation of insurance companies has been collected by means of special surveys undertaken during 1970-1974, covering also information on the activities of foreign exchange dealers. The income arising from ownership of dwellings represents the net rental value of all dwellings based initially on the assessments of the Ministry of Finance. For other services, data are provided by the Ministry of Finance or by the institutions concerned. GDP by kind of economic activity at constant prices is not estimated.

1.1 Expenditure on the Gross Domestic Product, in Current Prices

Million Jordanian dinars

	1970	1975	1980	1981	1982	1983	1984	1985	1986	1987	1988	1989
1 Government final consumption expenditure [a]	58.7	110.1	243.8	285.9	326.1	348.3	461.3	522.8	515.2	546.5	566.3	578.8	556.8
2 Private final consumption expenditure	152.8	304.6	829.3	1053.2	1219.5	1347.1	1448.7	1521.4	1579.0	1573.4	1547.0	1620.5	1737.4
3 Gross capital formation	22.1	88.8	404.1	588.0	619.3	510.1	609.9	561.4	494.7	453.2	473.5	503.2	597.7
A Increase in stocks	-3.1	0.9	6.3	23.2	22.0	7.3	53.4	31.0	39.1	29.8	61.7	88.2	132.7
B Gross fixed capital formation [b]	25.2	87.9	397.8	564.8	597.3	502.8	548.5	530.4	455.6	423.4	411.8	415.0	465.0
Residential buildings	9.4	24.2	120.5	147.1	157.1	158.6 / 159.8	163.0	124.4	114.7	85.0		
Non-residential buildings	0.0	2.8	18.6	21.8	23.6	25.2 / 188.6b	177.8	151.1	143.2	150.9		
Other construction and land improvement etc.	8.1	35.3	108.4	118.6	144.4	121.1						
Other	6.8	25.6	150.3	277.3	271.7	197.9 / 201.3	189.6	180.1	165.5	175.9		
4 Exports of goods and services	17.6	118.9	468.8	629.8	667.9	638.2 / 637.2	743.2	778.1	630.3	753.5	812.5	1350.5
5 Less: Imports of goods and services	76.8	301.1	961.7	1392.7	1511.6	1421.0 / 1421.0	1481.2	1468.9	1163.8	1251.8	1413.6	1701.8
Equals: Gross Domestic Product c	174.4	321.3	984.3	1164.2	1321.2	1728.1 / 1422.7	1867.6	1898.1	2039.6	2088.5	2201.4	2540.6

a) Government final consumption expenditure includes pension payments less employees', pension'. b) Including item 'Other construction and land improvement etc.'. c) Data in this table have been revised, therefore they are not strictly comparable with the contributions. Some non-capital development expenditure of the central government is included in other construction of gross domestic fixed capital formation. unrevised data in the other tables.

1.2 Expenditure on the Gross Domestic Product, in Constant Prices

Million Jordanian dinars

At constant prices of 1972

	1970	1975	1980	1981	1982	1983	1984	1985	1986	1987	1988	1989
1 Government final consumption expenditure	...	...	...	...	...	...	...	...	...	...	...	...
2 Private final consumption expenditure	...	...	...	...	...	...	...	...	...	...	...	...
3 Gross capital formation	...	...	...	...	...	...	...	...	...	...	...	...
4 Exports of goods and services	...	...	...	...	...	...	...	...	...	...	...	...
5 Less: Imports of goods and services	...	...	...	...	...	...	...	...	...	...	...	...
Equals: Gross Domestic Product	194.2	191.9	...	...	...	...	...	...	...	...	...	...

Jordan

1.3 Cost Components of the Gross Domestic Product

Million Jordanian dinars

	1970	1975	1980	1981	1982	1983	1984	1985	1986	1987	1988	1989
1 Indirect taxes, net	19.7	9.0	91.1	123.1	151.6	180.4	222.6	213.6	233.7	338.3	327.2	...
A Indirect taxes	...	...	147.1	173.3	206.8	216.7	251.7	263.8	262.0	344.9	338.0	...
B Less: Subsidies	...	...	56.0	50.2	55.2	36.3	29.1	49.9	28.3	6.6	10.8	...
2 Consumption of fixed capital	7.7	12.5	47.7	65.7	90.8	104.6	144.2	162.1	166.6	155.7	159.9	...
3 Compensation of employees paid by resident producers to:	72.1	134.5	409.9	474.1	550.3	604.4	680.3	732.4	777.2	831.7	865.6	...
4 Operating surplus	74.9	165.3	435.6	501.3	528.5	533.3	681.0	710.3	705.5	698.9	720.5	...
Equals: Gross Domestic Product	174.4	321.3	984.3	1164.2	1321.2	1422.7	1728.1	1818.7	1880.0	2024.6	2073.2	...

1.4 General Government Current Receipts and Disbursements

Million Jordanian dinars

	1970	1975	1980	1981	1982	1983	1984	1985	1986	1987	1988	1989
Receipts												
1 Operating surplus	...	...	...	...	...	...	...	...	...	...	...	...
2 Property and entrepreneurial income	...	...	11.1	21.4	22.7	9.4	23.0	24.0	16.0	139.0	126.2	...
3 Taxes, fees and contributions	...	...	203.9	240.0	295.3	334.3	348.3	352.0	348.1	484.5	478.6	...
A Indirect taxes	...	...	147.1	173.3	206.8	234.6	242.5	234.9	221.6	344.9	338.0	...
B Direct taxes	...	...	28.3	41.1	48.3	52.9	64.1	69.5	79.0	47.9	45.4	...
C Social security contributions	...	...	3.6	5.2	5.3	5.8	6.5	7.0	7.5	45.0	43.5	...
D Compulsory fees, fines and penalties	...	...	24.9	44.4	34.9	41.0	43.5	33.0	40.0	46.7	51.7	...
4 Other current transfers	...	...	388.8	416.5	363.7	289.6	257.9	288.7	200.0	258.0	254.2	...
Total Current Receipts of General Government	...	...	603.8	701.9	681.7	633.3	629.2	664.7	564.1	881.5	859.0	...
Disbursements												
1 Government final consumption expenditure	...	...	243.8	285.9	326.1	348.3	376.9	410.5	461.0	546.5	566.3	...
A Compensation of employees	...	...	167.6	188.0	214.5	227.5	233.4	257.0	288.6			...
B Consumption of fixed capital	...	...	2.6	3.2	4.8	4.5	4.3	5.5	6.1			...
C Purchases of goods and services, net	...	...	73.6	94.7	107.6	116.3	139.2	148.0	166.3			...
D Less: Own account fixed capital formation	...	...	...	...	...	...	...	...	...			...
E Indirect taxes paid, net	...	...	...	...	...	...	...	...	...			...
2 Property income	...	...	...	...	...	...	...	...	59.8	77.2		...
A Interest	...	...	...	...	...	...	...	...	59.8	77.2		...
B Net land rent and royalties	...	...	...	...	...	...	...	...	-			...

Jordan

1.4 General Government Current Receipts and Disbursements (Continued)

Million Jordanian dinars	1970	1975	1980	1981	1982	1983	1984	1985	1986	1987	1988	1989
3 Subsidies	...	56.0	50.2	58.3	37.1	50.8	37.1	6.6	8.2	10.8	...	...
4 Other current transfers	...	45.2	113.7	68.8	149.2	168.7	178.6	102.6 / 190.7	112.8	...	...	
A Social security benefits								7.4	9.1			
B Social assistance grants								3.0	2.6			
C Other								92.2	101.1			
5 Net saving	...	...	258.8	252.1	228.8	98.7	32.8	38.5	-95.8 / 160.0	92.0	...	...
Total Current Disbursements and Net Saving of General Government	...	...	603.8	701.9	681.7	633.3	629.2	664.7	564.1 / 881.5	859.0	...	...

1.7 External Transactions on Current Account, Summary

Million Jordanian dinars	1970	1975	1980	1981	1982	1983	1984	1985	1986	1987	1988	1989
Payments to the Rest of the World												
1 Imports of goods and services [a]	89.9	301.1	961.7	1392.7	1511.6	1421.0 / 1481.2	1468.9	1163.8	1251.8			
A Imports of merchandise c.i.f.	65.5	232.9	714.8	1046.4	1141.1	1102.0						
B Other	24.4	68.2	246.9	346.3	370.5	319.0						
2 Factor income to the rest of the world	0.7	...	23.5	37.6	39.4	46.4 / 55.0	73.6	85.6	94.6	101.7		
A Compensation of employees	...	...	...			8.6	11.5	11.0	10.2	7.4		
B Property and entrepreneurial income	...	...	...			46.4	62.1	74.6	84.4	94.3		
3 Current transfers to the rest of the world [a]	...	...	48.0	52.5	64.4	74.7 / 66.1	89.8	84.4	78.7	62.0		
4 Surplus of the nation on current transactions [a]	-7.8	21.5	111.9	-12.4	-118.3	-141.3 / -161.6	-122.4	-120.3	-32.4	-131.9		
Payments to the Rest of the World and Surplus of the Nation on Current Transactions	82.8	322.6	1145.1	1470.4	1497.1	1400.8 / 1380.5	1522.2	1518.6	1304.7	1283.6		
Receipts From The Rest of the World												
1 Exports of goods and services [a]	32.3	118.9	468.8	629.8	667.0	637.3 / 637.2	743.2	778.1	630.3	753.6		
A Exports of merchandise f.o.b.	12.2	48.9	171.5	242.6	264.5	210.6						
B Other	20.1	70.0	297.3	387.2	403.4	427.6						
2 Factor income from rest of the world [a]	13.3	10.6	38.6	67.2	72.9	62.9 / 104.1	87.2	80.8	77.2	51.6		
A Compensation of employees						40.3	47.5	40.3	41.4	31.8		
B Property and entrepreneurial income						63.8	37.7	40.5	35.8	19.8		
3 Current transfers from rest of the world [a]	37.2	193.1	637.7	773.4	757.2	699.7 / 639.2	691.8	659.7	597.2	478.5		
Receipts from the Rest of the World on Current Transactions	82.8	322.6	1145.1	1470.4	1497.1	1400.8 / 1380.5	1522.2	1518.6	1304.7	1283.6		

[a] For 1970-1974, estimates are derived from Balance of Payment Accounts, therefore are not strictly comparable to those in other tables.

Jordan

1.9 Gross Domestic Product by Institutional Sectors of Origin

Million Jordanian dinars

Domestic Factor Incomes Originating

	1970	1975	1980	1981	1982	1983	1984	1985	1986	1987	1988	1989
1 General government	167.6	...	188.0	214.5	227.5	233.4	257.0	288.6	302.3			
2 Corporate and quasi-corporate enterprises	663.2	...	770.2	844.7	887.3	940.4	966.8	943.3	983.4			
A Non-financial	572.0	...	676.8	738.6	780.4	826.8	847.3	817.4	855.2			
B Financial	91.2	...	93.4	106.1	106.9	113.6	122.5	125.9	128.2			
3 Households and private unincorporated enterprises												
4 Non-profit institutions serving households	14.7	...	17.2	19.6	22.5	22.1	26.7	27.8	28.7			
Subtotal: Domestic Factor Incomes	845.5	...	975.4	1078.8	1137.7	1195.9	1253.5	1259.7	1314.4			
Indirect taxes, net	91.1	...	123.1	151.6	180.4	183.4	210.2	229.4	239.0			
A Indirect taxes	147.1	...	173.3	206.8	216.7	233.9	247.3	237.6	247.3			
B Less: Subsidies	56.0	...	50.2	55.2	36.3	50.5	37.1	8.2	8.3			
Consumption of fixed capital	47.7	...	65.7	90.8	104.6	120.1	138.7	142.3	132.9			
Gross Domestic Product	984.3	...	1164.2	1321.2	1422.7	1499.4	1602.4	1631.4	1686.3			

1.10 Gross Domestic Product by Kind of Activity, in Current Prices

Million Jordanian dinars

	1970	1975	1980	1981	1982	1983	1984	1985	1986	1987	1988	1989
1 Agriculture, hunting, forestry and fishing	15.6	26.0	75.1	81.8	69.4	75.1	97.2 / 110.0	79.6	87.4	100.1	125.0	
2 Mining and quarrying	3.7	16.3	40.0	43.3	45.5	38.0 / 40.6	60.8	62.7	63.1	62.6		
3 Manufacturing	19.0	34.0	108.3	165.3	182.8	200.2 / 197.6	233.7	192.9	180.0	199.6		
4 Electricity, gas and water	1.9	3.1	18.2	17.6	21.3	24.4 / 22.1	32.0	40.1	44.2	48.5		
5 Construction	7.8	19.2	97.5	110.0	121.9	126.8 / 188.0	177.6	144.4	131.4	124.3		
6 Wholesale and retail trade, restaurants and hotels	33.6	57.3	164.9	194.1	217.4	238.3 / 241.3	252.3	290.4	275.7	271.8		
7 Transport, storage and communication	15.6	26.8	93.8	121.0	142.1	156.4 / 190.5	191.1	220.6	229.8	230.7		
8 Finance, insurance, real estate and business services	19.3	42.1	105.9	111.2	129.2	135.6 / 245.3	268.4	273.0	285.7	291.4		
9 Community, social and personal services	3.0	6.1	14.9	19.1	24.7	27.2 / 30.9	35.8	35.2	39.7	39.5		
Total, Industries	119.5	230.9	712.9	857.3	966.3	1056.9 / 1253.5	1331.3	1346.7	1349.6	1393.4		
Producers of Government Services	42.5	65.9	170.2	191.2	218.5	232.0 / 266.1	289.5	316.9	356.7	372.6		
Other Producers	3.6	5.7	15.4	18.2	20.7	23.7 / 17.8	18.9	19.0	18.7	19.3		
Subtotal a	165.6	301.8	898.5	1066.7	1205.9	1312.6 / 1537.4	1639.7	1682.6	1725.1	1785.3		
Less: Imputed bank service charge	1.3	2.9	10.5	13.0	17.2	22.2 / 31.9	34.9	36.3	38.8	39.3		
Plus: Import duties	10.1	22.4	96.3	110.5	132.5	132.3						
Plus: Value added tax	...	...	...	...	...	...						
Plus: Other adjustments b	...	...	...	...	...	225.6	213.9	233.7	338.3	327.2		
Equals: Gross Domestic Product	174.4	321.3	984.3	1164.2	1321.2	1422.7 / 1728.1	1818.7	1880.0	2024.6	2073.2		

a) Second series, gross domestic product in factor values.
b) Item 'Other adjustments', refers to indirect taxes net of subsidies.

Jordan

1.11 Gross Domestic Product by Kind of Activity, in Constant Prices

Million Jordanian dinars

	1970	1975	1980	1981	1982	1983	1984	1985	1986	1987	1988	1989
			At constant prices of:									
			1975						1985			
1 Agriculture, hunting, forestry and fishing	...	68.0	61.4	62.5	59.1	64.9	71.4	87.4	90.3	116.4	...	...
2 Mining and quarrying	...	47.3	51.4	53.2	57.5	77.9	86.2 / 62.7	66.4	70.2	...	...
3 Manufacturing	...	79.8	96.2	94.9	95.0	110.9	109.1 / 192.9	185.0	192.4	...	...
4 Electricity, gas and water	...	8.2	9.6	10.6	12.6	14.5	15.0 / 40.1	60.9	64.7	...	...
5 Construction	...	54.2	68.6	86.6	83.5	81.7	72.4 / 144.4	159.5	147.5	...	...
6 Wholesale and retail trade, restaurants and hotels	...	109.7	116.1	120.7	125.8	131.0	140.2 / 290.4	271.8	279.9	...	...
7 Transport, storage and communication	...	44.9	50.9	58.3	62.6	68.8	70.0 / 220.6	232.4	241.6	...	...
8 Finance, insurance, real estate and business services	...	74.9	68.0	77.3	75.4	82.0	86.2 / 273.0	290.5	298.2	...	...
9 Community, social and personal services	...	7.6	8.9	10.3	13.2	10.6	16.8 / 35.2	38.8	38.0	...	...
Total, Industries	...	494.6	531.1	574.4	582.1	644.9	667.3 / 1346.7	1395.5	1448.9	...	...
Producers of Government Services	...	105.0	97.3	106.2	112.7	115.8	115.7 / 316.9	339.8	364.3	...	...
Other Producers	...	8.8	10.1	11.3	13.2	14.4	15.8 / 19.0	19.0	19.8	...	...
Subtotal a	...	608.4	638.5	691.9	708.0	775.1	798.8 / 1682.6	1754.3	1833.0	...	...
Less: Imputed bank service charge	...	7.3	8.2	10.5	13.0	15.4	20.6 / 36.3	39.4	40.3	...	...
Plus: Import duties	...	...	...	...	...	...	...	...	...	...	...	...
Plus: Value added tax	...	...	...	...	...	...	...	...	...	...	...	...
Plus: Other adjustments b	...	46.8	48.1	47.1	48.0	47.5	56.9 / 233.7	344.0	336.0	...	...
Equals: Gross Domestic Product	...	647.9	678.4	728.5	743.0	807.2	835.1 / 1880.0	2058.9	2128.7	...	...

a) Gross domestic product in factor values.
b) Item "Other adjustments" refers to indirect taxes net of subsidies.

1.12 Relations Among National Accounting Aggregates

Million Jordanian dinars

	1970	1975	1980	1981	1982	1983	1984	1985	1986	1987	1988	1989
Gross Domestic Product	174.4	321.3	984.3	1164.2	1321.2	1422.7 / 1728.1	1867.6	1898.1	2039.6	2088.5	2201.4	2540.6
Plus: Net factor income from the rest of the world	7.1	10.6	15.1	29.6	33.6	49.1 / 17.5	13.6	-4.8	-17.4	-50.2	-88.6	-192.2
Factor income from the rest of the world	10.6	38.6	67.2	72.1	67.2	104.1 / 62.9	87.2	80.8	77.2	51.6	...	...
Less: Factor income to the rest of the world	23.5	37.6	39.4	46.4 / 55.0	73.6	85.6	94.6	101.7	...	...
Equals: Gross National Product	181.5	331.9	999.4	1193.8	1354.8	1440.2 / 1777.2	1881.2	1893.3	2022.5	2038.5	2112.8	2348.4
Less: Consumption of fixed capital	7.7	12.5	47.7	65.7	90.8	104.6 / 144.2	211.0	184.7	170.7	175.3	180.0	76.6

1023

Jordan

1.12 Relations Among National Accounting Aggregates
(Continued)

Million Jordanian dinars

	1970	1975	1980	1981	1982	1983	1984	1985	1986	1987	1988	1989
Equals: National Income	173.8	319.4	951.7	1128.7	1264.0	1335.6 / 1633.6	1670.2	1708.6	1851.5	1863.2	1932.8	2271.8
Plus: Net current transfers from the rest of the world	46.2	193.1	589.7	720.9	692.8	625.0 / 573.1	602.0	575.3	518.5	416.5	...	...
Current transfers from the rest of the world	...	193.1	637.7	773.4	757.2	699.7 / 647.7	691.8	659.7	597.2	478.5	...	...
Less: Current transfers to the rest of the world	...	...	48.0	52.5	64.4	74.7 / 66.1	89.8	84.4	78.7	62.0	...	...
Equals: National Disposable Income	220.0	512.5	1541.4	1849.0	1956.8	1960.6 / 2206.1	2272.2	2283.9	2370.0	2279.7	...	...
Less: Final consumption [a]	211.5	414.7	1073.1	1339.1	1545.7	1695.4 / 1910.0	2044.2	2094.2	2119.9	2113.3	...	...
Equals: Net Saving	8.5	97.8	468.3	509.9	411.2	265.2 / 296.1	228.0	189.7	250.1	166.4	...	...
Less: Surplus of the nation on current transactions	-5.9	21.5	111.9	-12.4	-118.3	-141.3 / -161.9	-122.4	-120.3	-32.4	-131.9	...	...
Equals: Net Capital Formation [a]	14.4	76.3	356.4	522.3	529.5	406.5 / 457.7	350.4	310.0	282.5	298.3	...	...

a) Government final consumption expenditure includes pension payments less employees' pension contributions. Some non-capital development expenditure of the central government is included in other construction of gross domestic fixed capital formation.

2.1 Government Final Consumption Expenditure by Function, in Current Prices

Million Jordanian dinars

	1970	1975	1980	1981	1982	1983	1984	1985	1986	1987	1988	1989
1 General public services	...	...	...	...	...	...	...	...	...	...	...	...
2 Defence	39.9	60.5	171.9	201.6	214.2	224.6	228.6	261.1	302.1	292.1	...	...
3 Public order and safety	...	...	...	...	...	...	...	...	...	...	...	...
4 Education	6.5	14.2	39.1	42.6	49.5	57.7	59.6	65.4	72.4	77.6	...	...
5 Health	2.2	3.6	12.0	14.6	16.9	17.6	18.3	21.5	24.8	26.0	...	...
6 Social security and welfare	1.8	3.1	1.5	2.2	2.2	2.8	2.3	2.4	2.5	2.5	...	...
7 Housing and community amenities	...	...	...	...	...	...	...	...	...	...	...	...
8 Recreational, cultural and religious affairs	...	...	...	...	...	...	...	...	...	...	...	...
9 Economic services	8.3	28.7	8.4	10.3	11.9	13.5	24.2	19.0	21.5	23.6	...	...
A Fuel and energy	...	...	...	...	...	...	...	...	...	...	...	...
B Agriculture, forestry, fishing and hunting	...	...	...	...	...	...	...	...	...	...	...	...
C Mining, manufacturing and construction, except fuel and energy	...	...	...	...	...	...	...	...	...	...	...	...
D Transportation and communication	...	8.4	10.3	11.9	13.5	24.2	18.7	20.0	18.7	...	...	...
E Other economic affairs	...	...	10.3	...	14.6	18.6	19.4	19.7	22.3	17.7	19.3	...
10 Other functions	...	...	...	...	...	...	...	...	...	...	...	...
Total Government Final Consumption Expenditure	58.7	110.1	243.8	285.9	326.1	348.3	376.9	410.5	461.0	459.8	...	...

2.5 Private Final Consumption Expenditure by Type and Purpose, in Current Prices

Million Jordanian dinars

	1970	1975	1980	1981	1982	1983	1984	1985	1986	1987	1988	1989
Final Consumption Expenditure of Resident Households												
1 Food, beverages and tobacco	82.0	149.9	387.1	449.7	500.2	561.9	571.4	570.7	504.0	...	...	...
A Food	76.4	140.2	356.6	406.5	456.2	515.6	523.3	525.6	464.4	...	...	...
B Non-alcoholic beverages	1.3	2.9	13.9	17.9	18.2	20.0	20.7	18.7	16.1	...	...	...
C Alcoholic beverages	...	...	...	...	...	...	...	...	...	...	...	...
D Tobacco	4.3	6.8	16.6	25.3	25.8	26.3	27.4	26.4	23.5	...	...	...
2 Clothing and footwear	13.0	22.1	68.5	76.6	80.3	83.0	83.7	80.2	69.3	...	...	...
3 Gross rent, fuel and power	12.8	18.3	55.4	74.5	82.4	89.5	91.5	92.0	80.5	...	...	...
4 Furniture, furnishings and household equipment and operation	10.1	16.4	44.4	63.0	67.2	69.0	70.0	68.6	60.7	...	...	...
5 Medical care and health expenses [a]	6.9	10.2	32.8	47.6	50.1	55.2	57.2	58.0	50.7	...	...	...
6 Transport and communication	13.8	20.2	55.3	75.0	79.9	81.3	82.9	83.6	73.1	...	...	...
7 Recreational, entertainment, education and cultural services	4.9	11.6	53.1	79.1	81.5	86.0	87.7	89.9	79.2	...	...	...
A Education	2.8	6.9	25.0	42.7	44.4	46.8	47.2	48.3	42.1	...	...	...

Jordan

2.5 Private Final Consumption Expenditure by Type and Purpose, in Current Prices
(Continued)

Million Jordanian dinars

	1970	1975	1980	1981	1982	1983	1984	1985	1986	1987	1988	1989
B Other	2.1	4.7	28.1	36.4	37.1	39.2	40.5	41.6	37.1	...	...	...
8 Miscellaneous goods and services	17.6	30.7	179.8	247.6	325.4	355.2	362.6	409.5	352.0	...	...	...
A Personal care [a]	15.7	25.8	...	...	...	...	...	...	...	...	...	...
B Expenditures in restaurants, cafes and hotels	1.9	4.9	...	...	...	...	...	...	...	...	...	...
C Other	...	...	...	...	...	...	...	...	...	...	...	...
Statistical discrepancy	...	5.6	...	...	...	...	...	...	...	...	...	...
Total Final Consumption Expenditure in the Domestic Market by Households, of which	161.3	285.0	878.4	1112.1	1267.0	1381.1	1407.0	1452.5	1269.5	...	...	...
Plus: Direct purchases abroad by resident households	9.4	18.1	107.8	124.6	136.0	149.1	141.1	166.4	155.2	...	...	...
Less: Direct purchases in the domestic market by non-resident households	18.0	22.2	154.9	183.5	183.5	183.1	173.2	204.2	186.3	...	...	...
Equals: Final Consumption Expenditure of Resident Households [b]	152.7	280.9	829.3	1053.2	1219.5	1347.1	1374.9	1414.7	1238.4	...	...	...

Final Consumption Expenditure of Private Non-profit Institutions Serving Households

	1970	1975	1980	1981	1982	1983	1984	1985	1986	1987	1988	1989
Equals: Final Consumption Expenditure of Private Non-profit Organisations Serving Households	...	...	...	...	...	...	...	...	...	...	...	...
Statistical discrepancy	...	23.7	...	...	...	...	...	...	...	...	...	...
Private Final Consumption Expenditure	152.8	304.6	829.3	1053.2	1219.5	1347.1	1374.9	1414.7	1238.4	...	...	...

a) Personal care is included in 'Medical care and health expenses'.
b) Item 'Final consumption expenditure of resident households' includes consumption expenditure of private non-profit institutions serving households.

2.11 Gross Fixed Capital Formation by Kind of Activity of Owner, ISIC Divisions, in Current Prices

Million Jordanian dinars

	1970	1975	1980	1981	1982	1983	1984	1985	1986	1987	1988	1989
					All Producers							
1 Agriculture, hunting, forestry and fishing	...	...	...	...	...	...	...	8.6	10.6	11.3	...	...
2 Mining and quarrying	...	...	...	...	...	...	...	0.9	1.3	5.7	...	...
3 Manufacturing	...	...	...	...	...	...	...	16.4	9.1	41.6	...	...
4 Electricity, gas and water	...	...	...	...	...	...	...	62.4	91.5	55.1	...	...
5 Construction	...	...	...	...	...	...	...	11.9	11.3	10.5	...	...
6 Wholesale and retail trade, restaurants and hotels	...	...	...	...	...	...	...	13.3	8.8	6.7	...	...
7 Transport, storage and communication	...	...	...	...	...	...	...	88.0	64.8	70.1	...	...
8 Finance, insurance, real estate and business services	...	...	...	...	...	...	...	131.4	119.4	89.8	...	...
9 Community, social and personal services	...	...	...	...	...	...	...	16.2	10.6	14.9	...	...
Total Industries	...	...	...	...	...	...	...	349.1	327.4	305.7	...	...
Producers of Government Services	...	...	...	...	...	...	...	104.8	94.3	104.7	...	...
Private Non-Profit Institutions Serving Households	...	...	...	...	...	...	...	1.7	1.7	1.4	...	...
Total	...	...	...	...	...	...	...	455.6	423.4	411.8	...	...

2.17 Exports and Imports of Goods and Services, Detail

Million Jordanian dinars

	1970	1975	1980	1981	1982	1983	1984	1985	1986	1987	1988	1989
					Exports of Goods and Services							
1 Exports of merchandise, f.o.b.	12.2	48.9	171.5	242.6	264.5	210.6	290.7	310.9	256.0	315.7	...	...
2 Transport and communication	0.2	14.8	76.5	101.2	117.4	108.8	137.9	156.0	91.0	117.0	...	...
3 Insurance service charges				26.3	27.1	29.5	37.4	33.3	22.4	21.1	...	...
4 Other commodities	15.9	19.5	65.9	78.9	75.4	105.2	104.0	73.8	74.6	103.3	...	...
5 Adjustments of merchandise exports to change-of-ownership basis	...	...	...	...	...	...	...	...	...	...	...	...
6 Direct purchases in the domestic market by non-residential households	4.9	35.7	154.9	180.8	183.5	183.1	173.2	204.1	186.3	196.5	...	...
7 Direct purchases in the domestic market by extraterritorial bodies	...	...	...	...	...	...	...	...	...	...	...	...
Total Exports of Goods and Services [a]	32.3	118.9	468.8	629.8	667.9	638.2	743.2	778.1	630.3	753.6	...	...

Jordan

2.17 Exports and Imports of Goods and Services, Detail
(Continued)

Million Jordanian dinars

	1970	1975	1980	1981	1982	1983	1984	1985	1986	1987	1988	1989
Imports of Goods and Services												
1 Imports of merchandise, c.i.f.	65.5	232.9	714.8	1046.4	1141.1	1102.0	1069.2	1072.5	847.8	915.6	...	...
2 Adjustments of merchandise imports to change-of-ownership basis	...	...	...	...	...	...	...	...	...	...	...	...
3 Other transport and communication	0.6	14.2	42.2	63.2	95.3	78.3	116.6	121.6	69.6	86.5	...	...
4 Other insurance service charges	...	...	...	...	...	...	...	...	...	...	...	...
5 Other commodities	14.4	18.3	96.9	161.5	144.0	108.3	148.9	108.4	91.2	102.0	...	...
6 Direct purchases abroad by government	...	...	...	...	...	...	...	...	...	...	...	...
7 Direct purchases abroad by resident households	9.4	35.7	107.8	121.6	131.3	132.4	146.5	166.4	155.2	150.7	...	...
Total Imports of Goods and Services a	89.9	301.1	961.7	1392.7	1511.6	1421.0	1481.2	1468.9	1163.8	1254.8	...	...
Balance of Goods and Services	-57.6	-182.2	-492.9	-762.9	-843.8	-782.8	-738.0	-690.8	-533.4	-501.2	...	...
Total Imports and Balance of Goods and Services	32.3	118.9	468.8	629.8	667.9	638.2	743.2	778.1	630.3	753.6	...	...

a) For 1970-1974, estimates are derived from Balance of Payment Accounts, therefore are not strictly comparable to those in other tables.

4.1 Derivation of Value Added by Kind of Activity, in Current Prices

Million Jordanian dinars

	1983			1984			1985			1986		
	Gross Output	Intermediate Consumption	Value Added	Gross Output	Intermediate Consumption	Value Added	Gross Output	Intermediate Consumption	Value Added	Gross Output	Intermediate Consumption	Value Added
All Producers												
1 Agriculture, hunting, forestry and fishing	162.4	69.0	93.4	155.7	79.9	75.8	167.2	84.0	83.2	180.5	83.3	97.2
2 Mining and quarrying	84.6	43.9	40.7	104.0	42.5	61.5	119.0	56.2	62.8	113.0	52.2	60.8
3 Manufacturing	688.8	465.9	222.9	864.3	619.1	245.2	815.4	582.3	233.1	752.7	425.1	327.6
4 Electricity, gas and water	58.8	40.6	18.2	67.6	40.0	27.6	82.1	44.4	37.7	92.2	48.0	44.2
5 Construction	493.2	304.9	188.3	486.3	308.3	178.0	402.1	257.2	144.9	380.5	248.5	132.0
6 Wholesale and retail trade, restaurants and hotels	361.3	109.7	251.6	386.0	117.6	268.4	427.5	130.2	297.3	430.7	146.4	284.3
7 Transport, storage and communication	414.3	215.9	198.4	415.9	218.4	197.5	454.2	226.5	227.7	449.8	212.8	237.0
8 Finance, insurance, real estate and business services	312.5	57.0	255.5	342.1	62.6	279.5	356.6	72.3	284.3	373.8	76.4	297.4
9 Community, social and personal services	52.6	21.5	31.1	58.8	22.8	36.0	57.6	22.2	35.4	59.3	19.0	40.3
Total, Industries	2628.5	1328.4	1300.1	2880.7	1511.2	1369.5	2881.7	1475.3	1406.4	2832.5	1311.7	1520.8
Producers of Government Services	485.5	219.4	266.1	549.6	260.1	289.5	545.6	228.7	316.9	580.2	223.5	356.7
Other Producers	19.2	1.4	17.8	20.4	1.5	18.9	20.5	1.5	19.0	20.4	1.7	18.7
Total	3133.2	1549.2	1584.0	3450.7	1772.8	1677.9	3447.8	1705.5	1742.3	3433.1	1536.9	1896.2
Less: Imputed bank service charge	...	-31.9	31.9	...	-34.9	34.9	...	-36.3	36.3	...	-38.8	38.8
Import duties	176.0	...	176.0	175.7	...	175.7	174.0	...	174.0	167.2	...	167.2
Value added tax	...	...	...	...	...	...	...	...	...	...	...	...
Total	3309.2	1581.1	1728.1	3626.4	1807.7	1818.7	3621.8	1741.8	1880.0	3600.3	1575.7	2024.6

	1987		
	Gross Output	Intermediate Consumption	Value Added
All Producers			
1 Agriculture, hunting, forestry and fishing	207.8	86.0	121.8
2 Mining and quarrying	112.2	48.1	64.1
3 Manufacturing	832.5	492.3	340.2
4 Electricity, gas and water	93.1	44.5	48.6
5 Construction	353.0	227.7	125.3
6 Wholesale and retail trade, restaurants and hotels	419.8	142.4	277.4
7 Transport, storage and communication	458.4	220.4	238.0
8 Finance, insurance, real estate and business services	380.7	75.3	305.4
9 Community, social and personal services	59.2	19.2	40.0

Jordan

4.1 Derivation of Value Added by Kind of Activity, in Current Prices
(Continued)

Million Jordanian dinars

	1987		
	Gross Output	Intermediate Consumption	Value Added
Total, Industries	2916.7	1355.9	1560.8
Producers of Government Services	603.8	231.2	372.6
Other Producers	23.8	4.5	19.3
Total	3544.3	1591.6	1952.7
Less: Imputed bank service charge	...	-39.3	39.3
Import duties	159.8	...	159.8
Value added tax	...	...	...
Total	3704.1	1630.9	2073.2

4.3 Cost Components of Value Added

Million Jordanian dinars

	1983						1984					
	Compensation of Employees	Capital Consumption	Net Operating Surplus	Indirect Taxes	Less: Subsidies Received	Value Added	Compensation of Employees	Capital Consumption	Net Operating Surplus	Indirect Taxes	Less: Subsidies Received	Value Added
	All Producers											
1 Agriculture, hunting, forestry and fishing	25.1	2.0	70.1	-3.8	...	93.4	27.0	2.1	50.5	-3.8	...	75.8
2 Mining and quarrying	15.6	8.8	16.2	0.1	...	40.7	17.7	10.3	32.8	0.7	...	61.5
3 Manufacturing	59.2	32.4	106.0	25.3	...	222.9	65.5	46.4	121.8	11.5	...	245.2
4 Electricity, gas and water	14.0	10.5	-2.4	-3.9	...	18.2	15.5	11.0	5.5	-4.4	...	27.6
5 Construction	92.7	41.0	54.3	0.3	...	188.3	91.2	37.2	49.2	0.4	...	178.0
6 Wholesale and retail trade, restaurants and hotels	69.2	6.7	165.4	10.3	...	251.6	78.0	8.3	166.0	16.1	...	268.4
7 Transport, storage and communication	82.5	29.6	78.4	7.9	...	198.4	86.4	29.7	75.0	6.4	...	197.5
8 Finance, insurance, real estate and business services	30.8	3.9	210.6	10.2	...	255.5	34.7	6.4	227.3	11.1	...	279.5
9 Community, social and personal services	15.3	1.3	14.3	0.2	...	31.1	17.0	1.7	17.1	0.2	...	36.0
Total, Industries [a]	404.4	136.2	712.9	46.6	...	1300.1	433.0	153.1	745.2	38.2	...	1369.5
Producers of Government Services	258.3	7.8	...	...	...	266.1	280.8	8.7	...	...	...	289.5
Other Producers	17.6	0.2	...	...	...	17.8	18.6	0.3	...	...	...	18.9
Total [a]	680.3	144.2	712.9	46.6	...	1584.0	732.4	162.1	745.2	38.2	...	1677.9
Less: Imputed bank service charge	...	...	31.9	...	...	31.9	...	...	34.9	...	...	34.9
Import duties	...	...	...	176.0	...	176.0	...	...	...	175.7	...	175.7
Value added tax	...	...	...	...	...	...	...	...	...	...	...	...
Total [a]	680.3	144.2	681.0	222.6	...	1728.1	732.4	162.1	710.3	213.9	...	1818.7

	1985						1986					
	Compensation of Employees	Capital Consumption	Net Operating Surplus	Indirect Taxes	Less: Subsidies Received	Value Added	Compensation of Employees	Capital Consumption	Net Operating Surplus	Indirect Taxes	Less: Subsidies Received	Value Added
	All Producers											
1 Agriculture, hunting, forestry and fishing	27.7	2.3	57.4	-4.2	...	83.2	28.4	3.2	68.5	-2.9	...	97.2
2 Mining and quarrying	19.2	13.4	30.1	0.1	...	62.8	19.9	14.5	28.7	-2.3	...	60.8
3 Manufacturing	71.7	53.5	67.7	40.2	...	233.1	72.4	42.6	65.0	147.6	...	327.6
4 Electricity, gas and water	20.4	12.3	7.4	-2.4	...	37.7	23.1	15.1	6.0	...	...	44.2
5 Construction	88.2	24.2	32.0	0.5	...	144.9	79.6	22.2	29.6	0.6	...	132.0
6 Wholesale and retail trade, restaurants and hotels	73.8	14.6	202.0	6.9	...	297.3	81.0	15.2	179.5	8.6	...	284.3
7 Transport, storage and communication	90.6	29.6	100.4	7.1	...	227.7	95.6	26.0	108.2	7.2	...	237.0
8 Finance, insurance, real estate and business services	39.2	5.3	228.5	11.3	...	284.3	41.2	4.9	239.6	11.7	...	297.4
9 Community, social and personal services	20.4	1.5	13.3	0.2	...	35.4	25.3	1.8	12.6	0.6	...	40.3
Total, Industries [a]	451.2	156.7	738.8	59.7	...	1406.4	466.5	145.5	737.7	171.1	...	1520.8
Producers of Government Services	307.2	9.7	...	...	...	316.9	346.7	10.0	...	...	...	356.7
Other Producers	18.8	0.2	...	...	...	19.0	18.5	0.2	...	...	...	18.7
Total [a]	777.2	166.6	738.8	59.7	...	1742.3	831.7	155.7	737.7	171.1	...	1896.2
Less: Imputed bank service charge	...	...	36.3	...	...	36.3	...	...	38.8	...	...	38.8
Import duties	...	...	...	174.0	...	174.0	...	...	...	167.2	...	167.2
Value added tax	...	...	...	...	...	...	...	...	...	...	...	...
Total [a]	777.2	166.6	702.5	233.7	...	1880.0	831.7	155.7	698.9	338.3	...	2024.6

Jordan

4.3 Cost Components of Value Added

Million Jordanian dinars

	1987					
	Compensation of Employees	Capital Consumption	Net Operating Surplus	Indirect Taxes	Less: Subsidies Received	Value Added
All Producers						
1 Agriculture, hunting, forestry and fishing	28.6	3.2	93.2	-3.2	...	121.8
2 Mining and quarrying	21.1	13.5	28.1	1.5	...	64.1
3 Manufacturing	75.2	44.8	79.6	140.6	...	340.2
4 Electricity, gas and water	23.0	17.3	8.2	0.1	...	48.6
5 Construction	83.9	17.4	23.0	1.0	...	125.3
6 Wholesale and retail trade, restaurants and hotels	78.1	14.6	179.1	5.6	...	277.4
7 Transport, storage and communication	103.5	31.4	95.8	7.3	...	238.0
8 Finance, insurance, real estate and business services	46.5	4.4	240.5	14.0	...	305.4
9 Community, social and personal services	25.2	1.9	12.4	0.5	...	40.0
Total, Industries [a]	485.1	148.5	759.8	167.4	...	1560.8
Producers of Government Services	361.4	11.2	...	...	...	372.6
Other Producers	19.1	0.2	...	...	...	19.3
Total [a]	865.6	159.9	759.8	167.4	...	1952.7
Less: Imputed bank service charge	...	...	39.3	...	...	39.3
Import duties	...	...	...	159.8	...	159.8
Value added tax	...	...	...	...	...	...
Total [a]	865.6	159.9	720.5	327.2	...	2073.2

a) Column 4 refers to indirect taxes less subsidies received.

Kenya

General note. The preparation of national accounts statistics in Kenya is undertaken by the Central Bureau of Statistics, Nairobi. The official estimates are published annually in the 'Statistical Abstract'. The estimates are generally in accordance with the classifications and definitions recommended in the United Nations System of National Accounts (SNA). A full revision of previous estimates for the years 1972-1975 were published in 1976, implementing improved methods and sources respectively in 'Input-Output Tables for Kenya'. The official tables for 1967 and 1971 were published in 1972 and 1976 respectively in 'Input-Output Tables for Kenya'. The following tables have been prepared from successive replies to the United Nations national accounts questionnaire. When the scope and coverage of the estimates differ from conceptual or statistical reasons from the definitions and classifications recommended in SNA, a footnote is indicated to the relevant tables.

Sources and methods:

(a) **Gross domestic product.** Gross domestic product is estimated mainly through the production approach.

(b) **Expenditure on the gross domestic product.** The expenditure approach is used to estimate government final consumption expenditure and exports and imports of goods and services. A combination of the commodity-flow and expenditure approaches is used to estimate gross capital formation. The estimates of government final consumption expenditure are derived from the accounts of the central and local government, the East African Community, the relevant statutory boards and the National Security Fund. All accounts are prepared on a cash basis. Private final consumption expenditure is obtained as a residual. Changes in stocks are recorded for agriculture, industrial activity, building and construction and wholesale and retail trade sectors. The sources of information are the large-farm censuses, the integrated rural survey, annual surveys or reports from concerned sectors and the survey of Distribution. The estimate of capital formation in building and construction is derived from annual completions reported by municipalities and from expenditure on other construction undertaken by government and industry. Included in gross fixed capital formation is the value of development expenditure estimates on machinery and equipment are derived by using the commodity-flow method. For import items, import duties are added to the c.i.f. values. For domestic production, the annual surveys of manufacturing are the source of information. The figures derived are converted to purchasers' values by adding transport and distribution margins. Exports and imports of goods and services are based on foreign trade reports and balance of payments estimates. For the constant price estimates, government expenditure on wages and salaries are extrapolated by an index of employment, while purchases of goods and services are deflated by various price indexes. Private consumption expenditure is obtained as a residual. For the remaining expenditure items, price deflation is used.

(c) **Cost-structure of the gross domestic product.** Wages and salaries paid in most industries are obtained from the annual surveys of employees and self-employed persons. Other sources include the integrated rural survey for small farms, logger licences and wage rate for forestry, reports and special questionnaires for transport, government accounts for the government sector and annual questionnaires for the private services. Information on indirect taxes and subsidies is obtained from concerned enterprises and from government records. Operating surplus, including consumption of fixed capital, is obtained as a residual.

(d) **Gross domestic product by kind of economic activity.** The table of gross domestic product by kind of economic activity is prepared in factor values. The production approach is used to estimate value added of most industries. The expenditure approach is used for construction and capital formation in residential and non-residential buildings while the income approach is used for agriculture, real estate. The main sources of information are the agricultural sector, annual integrated rural surveys and purchases by boards, co-operatives and large factories. The Ministry of Agriculture provides supplementary information. The censuses and surveys provide information on quantity and value of sales and quantity consumed at the farms. The prices for agricultural products used for producers are those obtained from the integrated rural survey, while prices in the local markets. Estimates for forestry and fishing are obtained reflecting departments. Information on gross output and intermediate consumption of mining and quarrying and electricity is obtained from the companies concerned. A census of manufacturing industry was held in 1972 including all establishments. Annual surveys are taken for all firms employing 50 or more persons and a sample is taken for firms employing between 20 and 49 persons. For firms with less than 20 employees, estimates are derived by inflating the value of gross output and intermediate consumption obtained in the 1972 census. The bench-mark estimate for construction contractors is based on the 1972 census of industry and the rural employment survey. Information from small contractors are available annually while those with less than 4 employees are covered by the labour force survey. Their estimates are obtained by applying an increasing factor to the labour figures. The estimates of own-account construction are derived from the large-farm censuses. Certain percentages are added for maintenance and labour costs. The East African Power and Lighting co., Ministry of Works, Forests Department and other local authorities provide information on their own-account construction activities. In the non-monetary sector, the value of output is the number of huts built multiplied by its current cost and 15 percent added for maintenance. For trade, the Survey of Distribution 1967 provided bench-mark information on the value of output and intermediate consumption. Value added by each sub-division is then extrapolated by using various indicators. The rural enterprise survey in 1972 provided bench-mark estimates for the rural areas. The sources of information for railway, shipping and air transports are the annual reports of the concerned companies and special questionnaires. For buses, data are obtained from the Kenya Bus Services Co., only and their ratios are applied to other bus firms. For the financial sector, the Central Bank of Kenya provides the information needed. Value added of real estate is calculated as net trade receipts of companies and individuals and 50 per cent of the rentals of owner-occupied dwellings, a stratified multi-stage sample is taken annually. The estimates of producers of government services are obtained from the accounts of the government, East-African Community and National Security Fund. For private services, bench-mark estimates are derived from a survey conducted in 1972. Domestic services are calculated from the estimated number of servants and their wage rate. For the constant price estimates, double deflation is used for agriculture, with current year's quantities revalued at base-year prices. Double deflation is also used for mining and quarrying, manufacturing and construction. For electricity, gas and water, trade, transport and community services, value added is extrapolated by various quantity indicators and indexes. Current values of financial institutions, insurance and real estate are deflated by price indexes.

1.1 Expenditure on the Gross Domestic Product, in Current Prices

Million Kenyan pounds

	1970	1975	1980	1981	1982	1983	1984	1985	1986	1987	1988	1989
1 Government final consumption expenditure	93.10	219.30	533.77	576.42	647.44	733.11	775.60	880.10	1075.91	1214.46	1287.46	1636.11
2 Private final consumption expenditure	344.69	813.75	1605.93	1836.86	2232.06	2443.43	2808.43	2924.46	3509.46	4050.57	4679.07	5206.97
3 Gross capital formation	139.66	217.08	789.19	861.89	767.69	829.32	925.74	1286.33	1278.44	1592.44	1893.07	2172.54
A Increase in stocks	26.96	-24.81	166.99	133.40	99.49	111.85	118.59	405.94	125.22	305.81	370.87	460.43
B Gross fixed capital formation	112.70	241.89	622.53	728.49	668.20	717.47	807.15	880.39	1153.22	1286.74	1522.20	1712.11
Residential buildings	18.66	42.47	105.86	119.55	125.46	112.64	133.39	131.11	171.59	190.96	212.10	231.91
Non-residential buildings	14.09	31.42	89.34	101.81	88.00	87.04	76.45	114.25	118.39	134.17	236.63	248.97
Other construction and land improvement etc.	22.80	62.96	124.76	148.33	157.64	142.80	174.98	191.51	211.97	214.48	275.48	295.54
Other	57.15	105.04	302.57	358.80	296.90	374.99	422.33	443.51	651.27	747.13	797.99	935.69
4 Exports of goods and services	170.83	356.90	753.30	796.91	877.60	996.34	1170.51	1274.84	1516.68	1399.59	1664.85	1997.68
5 Less: Imports of goods and services	175.62	413.00	1052.70	1048.67	1009.39	1014.18	1231.96	1328.40	1506.43	1734.12	2054.30	2492.37
Equals: Gross Domestic Product	572.66	1194.03	2629.49	3023.41	3515.40	3988.02	4448.02	5037.33	5874.17	6523.41	7470.15	8520.93

1029

Kenya

1.2 Expenditure on the Gross Domestic Product, in Constant Prices

Million Kenyan pounds

	1970	1975	1980	1981	1982	1983	1984	1985	1986	1987	1988	1989
		At constant prices of:		1964				1982				
1 Government final consumption expenditure	84.58	472.79	694.74	657.26	647.44	699.49	662.37	642.25	689.28	698.15	763.52	805.51
2 Private final consumption expenditure	320.85	1732.20	2177.83	2053.46	2232.46	2193.06	2371.22	2268.99	2894.13	2894.12	3067.39	3128.96
3 Gross capital formation	122.48	532.33	1031.00	868.91	767.69	665.41	969.20	847.16	745.97	870.55	951.64	1014.01
A Increase in stocks	26.96	-72.89	223.72	151.12	99.49	89.44	102.64	250.00	77.89	162.60	182.35	232.67
B Gross fixed capital formation	95.52	605.22	807.28	847.79	668.20	575.97	593.56	597.16	668.08	707.95	769.29	781.34
Residential buildings	13.40	104.61	131.99	136.94	125.46	100.65	111.54	96.33	118.74	118.32	96.13	114.33
Non-residential buildings	10.11	71.41	106.49	113.88	88.00	79.21	64.35	86.81	83.49	83.28	131.90	126.16
Other construction and land improvement etc.	16.64	127.76	148.28	167.31	157.84	128.46	127.75	129.86	136.86	126.27	146.41	145.16
Other	55.37	301.42	420.52	429.66	296.90	267.15	289.91	284.15	328.99	380.08	391.85	395.79
4 Exports of goods and services	159.65	822.47	887.72	874.76	877.60	857.55	865.04	823.16	1013.36	1022.44	1069.05	1176.98
5 Less: Imports of goods and services	164.13	1150.98	1524.08	1194.57	1009.39	823.70	970.87	901.73	1053.62	1193.61	1301.36	1367.87
Equals: Gross Domestic Product	523.43	2408.81	3267.31	3389.82	3515.40	3561.47	3623.98	3779.83	4051.13	4291.65	4550.24	4757.59

1.3 Cost Components of the Gross Domestic Product

Million Kenyan pounds

	1970	1975	1980	1981	1982	1983	1984	1985	1986	1987	1988	1989
1 Indirect taxes, net	53.72	139.67	397.08	441.35	466.15	509.32	589.53	618.66	759.66	910.90	1079.04	1190.43
A Indirect taxes	54.88	140.48	397.78	442.57	467.73	510.99	591.34	619.65	759.65	911.57	1079.19	1190.50
B Less: Subsidies	1.16	0.81	0.70	1.22	1.58	1.67	1.81	0.99	0.58	0.67	0.15	0.07
2 Consumption of fixed capital	...	...	...	...	...	...	...	...	...	...	...	...
3 Compensation of employees paid by resident producers	236.98	446.19	935.08	1100.85	2366.85	2364.03	1561.65	1806.16	2098.09	2365.77	2685.24	3111.78
4 Operating surplus	282.08	609.17	1297.33	1481.21	3246.09	3246.09	3248.09	2311.28	2612.51	3016.65	3246.72	4218.72
Equals: Gross Domestic Product	572.66	1194.03	2629.49	3023.41	3515.40	3988.02	4448.02	5037.33	5874.17	6523.41	7470.15	8520.94

1.7 External Transactions on Current Account, Summary

Million Kenyan pounds

	1970	1975	1980	1981	1982	1983	1984	1985	1986	1987	1988	1989
	Payments to the Rest of the World											
1 Imports of goods and services	413.00	1052.70	1048.67	1009.39	1014.18	1231.96	1328.40	1506.43	1734.12	2054.30	2492.37	
A Imports of merchandise c.i.f.	314.50	960.60	829.65	801.55	797.30	971.65	1045.61	1180.10	1334.95	1599.20	1899.62	
B Other	98.50	92.10	219.02	207.84	216.88	260.31	282.79	326.33	399.17	455.10	592.75	
2 Factor income to the rest of the world	67.70	104.00	116.33	120.61	151.92	184.99	218.86	239.15	282.24	327.81	375.37	
A Compensation of employees	13.00	12.40	9.93	10.96	12.02	13.24	14.66	16.30	19.44	23.21	27.60	
B Property and entrepreneurial income	54.70	91.60	106.40	109.65	139.90	171.75	204.20	222.85	262.80	304.60	347.77	
3 Current transfers to the rest of the world	16.40	7.20	14.60	16.95	23.30	26.95	23.75	28.34	35.09	35.06	50.75	
4 Surplus of the nation on current transactions	-350.60	-320.69	-213.43	-111.19	-178.85	-188.09	-148.76	-536.45	-608.28	-730.77		
Payments to the Rest of the World and Surplus of the Nation on Current Transactions	813.30	858.40	933.52	1078.21	1265.05	1382.92	1625.16	1515.00	1808.89	2187.72		
	Receipts From The Rest of the World											
1 Exports of goods and services	356.90	753.30	796.91	877.60	996.34	1170.51	1274.84	1516.69	1399.59	1664.85	1997.68	

Kenya

1.7 External Transactions on Current Account, Summary (Continued)

Million Kenyan pounds

	1970	1975	1980	1981	1982	1983	1984	1985	1986	1987	1988	1989
A Exports of merchandise f.o.b.	232.40	...	515.70	489.15	510.90	616.70	745.55	774.95	949.41	757.54	902.84	952.65
B Other	124.50	...	237.60	307.70	366.70	379.64	424.96	499.69	567.28	642.05	762.01	1045.03
2 Factor income from rest of the world	21.40	...	20.00	17.04	20.10	24.71	32.84	35.62	29.99	30.75	7.20	12.32
A Compensation of employees	2.10	...										
B Property and entrepreneurial income	19.30	...										
3 Current transfers from rest of the world	23.20	...	40.00	44.96	35.82	57.16	61.19	72.46	78.48	84.66	136.84	177.72
Receipts from the Rest of the World on Current Transactions	...	...	813.30	858.91	933.52	1078.21	1265.05	1382.92	1625.16	1515.00	1808.89	2187.72

1.10 Gross Domestic Product by Kind of Activity, in Current Prices

Million Kenyan pounds

	1970	1975	1980	1981	1982	1983	1984	1985	1986	1987	1988	1989
1 Agriculture, hunting, forestry and fishing	172.77	361.38	725.37	836.93	1017.30	1188.55	1313.50	1436.69	1690.11	1781.86	2039.09	2271.32
2 Mining and quarrying	2.41	3.42	5.73	5.91	6.61	7.37	8.51	9.97	11.45	13.27	13.69	18.62
3 Manufacturing	62.16	127.00	295.14	328.16	372.32	408.26	460.96	518.40	608.23	652.47	752.96	855.36
4 Electricity, gas and water	11.96	19.98	47.73	58.30	44.27	59.67	68.01	77.63	83.71	91.02	98.36	111.09
5 Construction	26.39	63.65	146.74	167.20	184.78	197.60	195.61	237.83	246.89	287.88	368.30	477.35
6 Wholesale and retail trade, restaurants and hotels a	48.67	114.88	244.66	274.03	306.67	371.03	439.67	520.64	561.01	628.25	712.03	829.07
7 Transport, storage and communication	40.84	60.25	127.81	143.39	185.19	215.89	250.32	296.40	341.08	393.35	433.74	485.79
8 Finance, insurance, real estate and business services b	53.04	132.14	296.88	363.65	462.79	536.59	582.17	654.05	749.26	861.23	1019.74	1160.19
9 Community, social and personal services ab	20.08	23.33	49.41	55.15	82.45	92.21	107.27	129.58	153.27	181.66	197.92	228.00
Total, Industries	438.32	906.03	1939.47	2233.47	2660.72	3082.80	3411.57	3881.19	4445.79	4829.06	5635.83	6436.79
Producers of Government Services	76.48	162.07	332.46	390.92	441.35	475.25	522.22	616.34	756.45	822.72	917.29	1077.84
Other Producers	4.14	8.86	23.34	28.62	32.81	35.63	44.88	51.78	62.96	71.78	83.94	97.49
Subtotal c	518.94	1076.96	2295.27	2653.26	3134.96	3593.21	3978.67	4549.31	5265.20	5723.56	6637.06	7612.12
Less: Imputed bank service charge	...	22.60	58.86	71.21	87.29	114.51	120.18	130.64	150.24	172.98	245.95	281.62
Plus: Import duties	28.58	47.37	141.82	149.41	151.57	188.09	167.45	222.26	246.19	287.48	309.02	
Plus: Value added tax	...	...	...	...	...	...	...	...	...	...	...	...
Plus: Other adjustments d	25.14	92.30	255.26	291.94	309.16	358.22	401.44	451.21	536.95	726.64	791.56	881.41
Equals: Gross Domestic Product	572.66	1194.03	2629.49	3023.41	3515.40	3988.02	4448.02	5037.33	5874.17	6523.41	7470.15	8520.93

a) For the first series, restaurants and hotels are included in item 'Community, social and personal services'.
b) For the first series, business services are included in item 'Community, social and personal services'.
c) Gross domestic product in factor values.
d) Item 'Other adjustments' refers to net indirect taxes other than import duties.

1.11 Gross Domestic Product by Kind of Activity, in Constant Prices

Million Kenyan pounds

	1970	1975	1980	1981	1982	1983	1984	1985	1986	1987	1988	1989

At constant prices of: 1964 / 1982

	1970	1975	1980	1981	1982	1983	1984	1985	1986	1987	1988	1989
1 Agriculture, hunting, forestry and fishing	173.58	708.81	866.26	917.53	1017.26	1038.16	1000.15	1040.29	1091.52	1137.26	1190.72	1237.96
2 Mining and quarrying	2.60	7.08	8.75	5.45	6.61	6.69	7.41	8.11	8.40	9.12	10.15	10.62
3 Manufacturing	52.49	200.68	351.47	364.13	372.32	389.07	405.84	424.07	448.67	474.34	502.80	532.47
4 Electricity, gas and water	9.81	42.51	57.97	54.30	44.27	45.98	47.01	49.69	52.35	55.38	59.03	62.97
5 Construction	18.98	133.64	174.66	184.75	184.78	169.20	163.62	178.67	177.39	184.33	189.92	199.75

1031

Kenya

1.11 Gross Domestic Product by Kind of Activity, in Constant Prices (Continued)

Million Kenyan pounds

At constant prices of: 1964 / 1982

	1970	1975	1980	1981	1982	1983	1984	1985	1986	1987	1988	1989
6 Wholesale and retail trade, restaurants and hotels a	43.81	243.77	318.38	322.52	306.67	315.26	332.60	355.22	389.98	412.53	436.27	455.47
7 Transport, storage and communication	41.18	107.09	148.85	151.71	185.19	201.51	202.29	206.54	215.42	224.90	234.02	241.06
8 Finance, insurance, real estate and business services	45.00 b	261.63	361.36	427.32	462.29	484.07	487.60	517.50	543.62	569.48	596.36	630.15
9 Community, social and personal services	20.33 a,b	41.18	56.99	59.32	82.45	86.26	94.20	99.10	104.05	111.74	119.72	127.86
Total, Industries	407.79	1746.39	2344.69	2497.08	2660.80	2734.20	2740.72	2879.19	3031.40	3179.03	3338.99	3498.31
Producers of Government Services	73.75	403.83	425.20	441.35	459.89	473.13	497.26	528.73	554.13	586.16	618.40	
Other Producers	3.55	13.99	28.33	30.67	32.81	34.94	37.22	39.80	44.00	48.71	55.30	62.36
Subtotal c	485.09	2064.21	2776.86	2953.50	3134.96	3229.03	3251.07	3416.25	3604.13	3781.87	3980.45	4179.07
Less: Imputed bank service charge		43.33	78.41	93.36	87.29	104.10	99.40	102.97	105.94	113.43	121.81	129.12
Plus: Import duties	26.72	187.40	239.67	187.40	158.57	125.27	147.47	136.37	160.16	168.09	188.70	198.22
Plus: Value added tax												
Plus: Other adjustments d	11.62	201.13	329.34	342.28	309.16	312.88	326.48	330.19	393.19	455.56	502.99	509.46
Equals: Gross Domestic Product	523.43	2408.81	3267.46	3389.82	3515.46	3563.08	3625.62	3780.62	4051.54	4292.09	4550.33	4757.63

a) Restaurants and hotels are included in item 'Community, social and personal services'.
b) Business services are included in item 'Community, social and personal services'.
c) Gross domestic product in factor values.
d) Item 'Other adjustments' refers to net indirect taxes other than import duties.

1.12 Relations Among National Accounting Aggregates

Million Kenyan pounds

	1970	1975	1980	1981	1982	1983	1984	1985	1986	1987	1988	1989
Gross Domestic Product	572.66	1194.03	2629.49	3023.41	3515.40	3988.02	4448.02	5037.33	5874.17	6523.41	7470.15	8520.94
Plus: Net factor income from the rest of the world	-20.99	-46.30	-84.00	-99.29	-100.51	-127.21	-152.15	-183.24	-209.16	-251.49	-320.61	-363.05
Factor income from the rest of the world	0.40	21.40	20.00	17.04	24.10	32.84	35.62	29.99	30.75	7.20	12.32	
Less: Factor income to the rest of the world	67.70	104.00	116.33	120.61	151.92	184.99	218.86	239.15	282.24	327.81	375.37	
Equals: Gross National Product	551.67	1147.73	2545.49	2924.11	3414.89	3860.81	4295.87	4854.09	5665.01	6271.92	7149.54	8157.89
Less: Consumption of fixed capital												
Equals: National income a	551.67	1147.73	2545.49	2924.11	3414.89	3860.81	4295.87	4854.09	5665.01	6271.92	7149.54	8157.89
Plus: Net current transfers from the rest of the world	9.13	6.80	32.80	30.36	18.87	33.86	34.75	48.71	50.14	49.57	101.78	126.97
Current transfers from the rest of the world		23.20	40.00	44.96	35.82	57.16	61.70	72.46	78.48	84.66	136.84	177.72
Less: Current transfers to the rest of the world		16.40	7.20	14.60	16.95	23.30	26.95	23.75	28.34	35.09	35.06	50.75
Equals: National Disposable Income b	560.80	1154.53	2578.29	2954.47	3433.76	3894.67	4330.62	4902.80	5715.15	6321.49	7251.32	8284.86
Less: Final consumption	437.79	1033.05	2139.70	2413.70	2879.28	3176.50	3583.73	3804.56	4585.48	5265.39	5966.53	6843.08
Equals: Net Saving c	123.01	121.48	438.59	541.19	554.26	718.13	746.89	1098.24	1129.67	1056.10	1284.79	1441.78
Less: Surplus of the nation on current transactions		-350.60	-320.69	-213.43	-111.19	-178.85	-188.60	-148.76	-536.45	-608.28	-730.77	
Equals: Net Capital Formation	789.19	861.88	767.69	829.32	925.74	1286.33	1278.44	1592.55	1893.07	2172.55		

a) Item 'National income' includes consumption of fixed capital.
b) Item 'National disposable income' includes consumption of fixed capital.
c) Item 'Net saving' includes consumption of fixed capital.

Kenya

2.1 Government Final Consumption Expenditure by Function, in Current Prices

Million Kenyan pounds

	1970	1975	1980	1981	1982	1983	1984	1985	1986	1987	1988	1989
1 General public services	28.54	... 53.12	112.90	136.46	90.87	95.34	103.01	117.96	143.79	165.78	169.20	172.67
2 Defence	8.03	... 23.37	96.62	60.66	17.75	18.28	17.42	16.35	18.17	26.11	15.64	37.59
3 Public order and safety	...	...	...	...	...	...	...	...	...	...	...	...
4 Education	25.81	... 77.68	175.74	201.98	200.04	212.55	240.12	292.78	373.26	399.17	478.48	588.25
5 Health	11.03	... 24.78	61.12	68.96	48.22	52.31	56.56	65.85	77.51	86.45	101.67	114.77
6 Social security and welfare					...	...	...	...	...	...	...	...
7 Housing and community amenities	19.69	... 40.35	87.39	108.36	...	...	...	...	...	...	...	...
8 Recreational, cultural and religious affairs					...	...	...	...	...	...	...	...
9 Economic services	...	...	...	...	...	...	...	...	...	...	...	...
10 Other functions	...	...	...	...	...	...	...	...	...	...	...	...
Total Government Final Consumption Expenditure	93.10	... 219.30	533.77	576.42	647.44	733.11	775.60	880.10	1075.91	1214.46	1287.46	1636.11

2.11 Gross Fixed Capital Formation by Kind of Activity of Owner, ISIC Divisions, in Current Prices

Million Kenyan pounds

	1970	1975	1980	1981	1982	1983	1984	1985	1986	1987	1988	1989
					All Producers							
1 Agriculture, hunting, forestry and fishing	12.58	... 22.69	48.19	55.60	51.88	54.04	58.96	76.30	90.02	106.66	114.98	103.88
2 Mining and quarrying	1.28	... 1.53	5.02	4.85	4.05	5.09	7.12	4.89	7.03	12.74	10.21	9.42
3 Manufacturing	12.95	... 31.23	76.91	90.31	67.03	111.70	95.33	101.76	161.34	171.83	218.74	249.91
4 Electricity, gas and water	3.68	... 17.19	41.26	65.47	75.22	57.19	37.00	43.30	48.55	62.21	81.70	124.51
5 Construction	6.96	... 7.81	33.41	32.90	28.86	59.35	68.25	31.48	50.30	70.19	70.46	65.20
6 Wholesale and retail trade, restaurants and hotels [a]	4.40	... 14.47	28.29	19.68	21.78	26.44	24.76	34.51	24.86	24.88	36.35	33.55
7 Transport, storage and communication	19.86	... 50.39	102.80	113.48	101.50	110.14	149.94	164.19	289.04	306.67	269.28	349.24
8 Finance, insurance, real estate and business services [b]	20.79	... 47.97	116.76	144.32	135.94	130.76	153.18	151.60	186.23	215.66	251.87	280.99
9 Community, social and personal services [ab]	8.30	... 7.16	41.25	53.56	55.29	60.72	59.51	80.02	75.89	85.80	105.98	145.65
Total Industries	90.82	... 200.44	493.89	580.18	541.55	615.44	654.05	688.02	933.27	1056.63	1159.57	1362.35
Producers of Government Services	21.89	... 41.45	128.64	148.31	126.65	102.03	153.11	192.36	219.95	230.11	362.63	349.77
Private Non-Profit Institutions Serving Households	...	...	...	...	...	...	...	...	...	...	...	...
Total	112.70	... 241.89	622.53	728.49	668.20	717.47	807.15	880.38	1153.22	1286.74	1522.20	1712.11

a) For the first series, restaurants and hotels are included in item 'Community, social and personal services'.   b) For the first series, business services are included in item 'Community, social and personal services'.

2.12 Gross Fixed Capital Formation by Kind of Activity of Owner, ISIC Divisions, in Constant Prices

Million Kenyan pounds

	1970	1975	1980	1981	1982	1983	1984	1985	1986	1987	1988	1989
					At constant prices of:							
		1964					**1982**					
					All Producers							
1 Agriculture, hunting, forestry and fishing	11.10	... 60.17	63.08	64.93	51.89	44.02	40.73	51.24	54.02	59.05	60.87	48.21
2 Mining and quarrying	1.24	... 4.80	7.55	6.02	4.05	3.58	4.88	3.11	3.63	6.73	5.44	4.12
3 Manufacturing	12.31	... 92.62	110.08	109.66	67.03	81.01	65.65	65.18	83.87	89.64	112.53	108.59
4 Electricity, gas and water	3.22	... 36.54	49.88	76.01	75.22	49.53	27.01	29.05	29.93	35.68	43.39	60.09

Kenya

2.12 Gross Fixed Capital Formation by Kind of Activity of Owner, ISIC Divisions, in Constant Prices
(Continued)

Million Kenyan pounds

At constant prices of:

	1964						1982					
	1970	1975	1980	1981	1982	1983	1984	1985	1986	1987	1988	1989
5 Construction	6.55	23.31	48.14	40.16	28.86	41.82	46.90	20.29	27.01	37.19	37.06	28.41
6 Wholesale and retail trade, restaurants and hotels	3.84a	43.13	39.51	51.03	27.78	21.44	17.88	24.22	14.23	13.36	18.98	14.80
7 Transport, storage and communication	18.47	115.05	127.84	102.11	83.27	105.30	106.60	144.83	151.08	119.62	145.32	...
8 Finance, insurance, real estate and business services	15.27b	119.16	145.74	165.06	135.94	115.97	126.67	110.23	126.92	131.82	120.61	137.48
9 Community, social and personal services	6.93ab	17.73	55.28	63.57	55.29	47.31	43.87	55.10	45.49	49.55	57.84	69.26
Total Industries	78.92	512.51	647.08	678.93	541.56	487.95	478.89	465.02	529.94	574.10	576.36	616.28
Producers of Government Services	16.60	92.71	160.19	169.24	126.66	88.02	114.66	138.13	133.85	192.93	165.06	...
Private Non-Profit Institutions Serving Households	...	...	...	...	...	...	...	...	...	...	...	...
Total	95.52	605.22	807.28	847.79	668.20	575.97	593.56	597.16	668.08	707.35	769.29	781.34

a) For the first series, restaurants and hotels are included in item 'Community, social and personal services'. b) For the first series, business services are included in item 'Community, social and personal services'.

4.3 Cost Components of Value Added

Million Kenyan pounds

	1980						1981					
	Compensation of Employees	Capital Consumption	Net Operating Surplus	Indirect Taxes	Less: Subsidies Received	Value Added	Compensation of Employees	Capital Consumption	Net Operating Surplus	Indirect Taxes	Less: Subsidies Received	Value Added

All Producers

1 Agriculture, hunting, forestry and fishing	91.10	...	634.27	...	...	725.37	102.82	734.11	...	...	...	836.93
A Agriculture and hunting	78.03	...	610.11	...	...	688.13	86.50	705.24	...	...	...	791.74
B Forestry and logging	11.98	...	20.34	...	...	32.32	14.46	23.35	...	...	...	37.81
C Fishing	1.09	...	3.83	...	...	4.92	1.85	5.53	...	...	...	7.38
2 Mining and quarrying	2.71	...	3.02	...	...	5.73	3.28	2.63	...	...	...	5.91
3 Manufacturing	116.11	...	179.03	...	...	295.14	146.08	182.08	...	...	...	328.16
4 Electricity, gas and water	6.39	...	38.34	...	...	44.73	14.29	44.01	...	...	...	58.30
A Electricity, gas and steam	3.18	...	20.67	...	...	23.85	3.82	26.87	...	...	...	30.69
B Water works and supply	6.21	...	17.67	...	...	23.88	10.47	17.14	...	...	...	27.61
5 Construction	84.53	...	62.21	...	...	146.74	95.87	71.33	...	...	...	167.20
6 Wholesale and retail trade, restaurants and hotels	107.86	...	136.80	...	...	244.66	118.89	155.14	...	...	...	274.03
A Wholesale and retail trade	87.42	...	116.32	...	...	203.74	91.24	128.96	...	...	...	220.20
B Restaurants and hotels	20.44	...	20.48	...	...	40.92	27.65	26.18	...	...	...	53.83
7 Transport, storage and communication	73.54	...	54.27	...	...	127.81	86.59	56.80	...	...	...	143.39
8 Finance, insurance, real estate and business services	62.76	...	234.12	...	...	296.88	74.10	289.55	...	...	...	363.65
9 Community, social and personal services	38.47	...	10.94	...	...	49.41	44.18	11.97	...	...	...	56.15
Total, Industries	586.47	...	1353.00	...	...	1939.47	686.10	1547.62	...	...	...	2233.72
Producers of Government Services	325.27	7.19	...	...	...	332.46	386.13	4.80	...	...	...	390.93
Other Producers	23.34	-	...	...	...	23.34	28.62	-	...	...	...	28.62
Total a	935.08	1360.19	...	...	...	2295.27	1100.85	1552.42	...	...	...	2653.27
Less: Imputed bank service charge	...	62.86	...	...	...	62.86	...	71.21	...	...	...	71.21
Import duties	...	141.82	...	...	...	141.82	...	...	...	149.41	...	149.41
Value added tax	...	...	...	...	...	...	...	...	...	...	...	...
Other adjustments b	...	...	...	255.26	...	255.26	...	...	...	291.94	...	291.94
Total c	935.08	1297.33	397.08	...	2629.49	1100.85	1481.21	441.35	...	3023.41

Kenya

4.3 Cost Components of Value Added

Million Kenyan pounds

	1982						1983					
	Compensation of Employees	Capital Consumption	Net Operating Surplus	Indirect Taxes	Less: Subsidies Received	Value Added	Compensation of Employees	Capital Consumption	Net Operating Surplus	Indirect Taxes	Less: Subsidies Received	Value Added
All Producers												
1 Agriculture, hunting, forestry and fishing	184.20	...	1559.95	...	...	1744.15	155.12	...	1514.14	...	...	1669.26
A Agriculture and hunting	155.12	...	1514.14	...	...	1669.26	...	...	...	...	...	...
B Forestry and logging	23.70	...	32.66	...	...	56.36	...	...	...	...	...	...
C Fishing	5.38	...	13.15	...	...	18.53	...	...	...	...	...	...
2 Mining and quarrying	7.96	...	5.31	...	...	13.27	7.96	...	5.31	...	...	13.27
3 Manufacturing	303.83	...	386.31	...	...	690.14	303.83	...	386.31	...	...	690.14
4 Electricity, gas and water	24.81	...	52.74	...	...	77.55	24.81	...	55.22	...	...	80.03
A Electricity, gas and steam	...	...	...	...	...	...	...	...	...	...	...	...
B Water works and supply	...	...	...	...	...	...	...	...	...	...	...	...
5 Construction	151.75	...	110.13	...	...	261.88	151.94	...	119.98	...	...	271.92
6 Wholesale and retail trade, restaurants and hotels	298.60	...	329.65	...	...	628.25	298.60	...	329.65	...	...	628.25
A Wholesale and retail trade	...	...	...	...	...	...	...	...	...	...	...	...
B Restaurants and hotels	...	...	...	...	...	...	...	...	...	...	...	...
7 Transport, storage and communication	200.33	...	144.77	...	...	345.10	200.33	...	144.77	...	...	345.10
8 Finance, insurance, real estate and business services	177.80	...	618.33	...	...	796.13	177.80	...	634.75	...	...	812.55
9 Community, social and personal services	138.46	...	43.20	...	...	181.66	138.46	...	43.20	...	...	181.60
Total, Industries	1487.74	...	3250.39	...	...	4738.13	1458.85	...	3233.33	...	...	4692.18
Producers of Government Services	840.44	...	5.50	...	...	845.94	840.44	...	5.50	...	...	845.94
Other Producers	32.81	...	-	...	...	32.81	35.63	...	-	...	...	35.63
Total a	2360.99	...	3255.89	...	...	5616.88	2334.92	...	3238.83	...	...	5573.75
Less: Imputed bank service charge	...	...	172.98	...	...	172.98	...	...	172.98	...	...	172.98
Import duties	...	...	...	158.57	...	158.57	...	...	...	125.27	...	125.27
Value added tax	...	...	...	...	...	...	...	...	...	...	...	...
Other adjustments b	...	...	...	309.16	...	309.16	...	...	...	312.88	...	312.88
Total c	2360.99	...	3082.91	467.73	...	5911.63	2334.92	...	3065.85	438.15	...	5638.92

	1984						1985					
	Compensation of Employees	Capital Consumption	Net Operating Surplus	Indirect Taxes	Less: Subsidies Received	Value Added	Compensation of Employees	Capital Consumption	Net Operating Surplus	Indirect Taxes	Less: Subsidies Received	Value Added
All Producers												
1 Agriculture, hunting, forestry and fishing	125.50	...	1188.00	...	...	1313.50	138.57	...	1296.66	...	...	1435.23
A Agriculture and hunting	...	...	...	...	...	...	...	...	...	...	...	...
B Forestry and logging	...	...	...	...	...	...	...	...	...	...	...	...
C Fishing	...	...	...	...	...	...	...	...	...	...	...	...
2 Mining and quarrying	5.08	...	3.43	...	...	8.51	5.96	...	4.01	...	...	9.97
3 Manufacturing	205.54	...	255.42	...	...	460.96	229.76	...	288.64	...	...	518.40
4 Electricity, gas and water	13.64	...	54.36	...	...	68.00	17.31	...	60.32	...	...	77.63
A Electricity, gas and steam	...	...	...	...	...	...	...	...	...	...	...	...
B Water works and supply	...	...	...	...	...	...	...	...	...	...	...	...
5 Construction	97.10	...	98.51	...	...	195.61	127.90	...	109.92	...	...	237.82
6 Wholesale and retail trade, restaurants and hotels	198.86	...	240.81	...	...	439.67	233.96	...	286.68	...	...	520.64
A Wholesale and retail trade	...	...	...	...	...	...	...	...	...	...	...	...
B Restaurants and hotels	...	...	...	...	...	...	...	...	...	...	...	...
7 Transport, storage and communication	138.22	...	112.10	...	...	250.32	149.53	...	146.87	...	...	296.40
8 Finance, insurance, real estate and business services	118.86	...	463.31	...	...	582.17	133.60	...	520.45	...	...	654.05
9 Community, social and personal services	93.33	...	13.94	...	...	107.27	106.81	...	22.77	...	...	129.58
Total, Industries	996.13	...	2429.88	...	...	3426.01	1143.40	...	2736.32	...	...	3879.72
Producers of Government Services	520.64	...	1.58	...	...	522.22	610.98	...	5.36	...	...	616.34

Kenya

4.3 Cost Components of Value Added
(Continued)

Million Kenyan pounds

	1984					1985				
	Compensation of Employees	Capital Consumption	Net Operating Surplus	Indirect Taxes	Less: Subsidies Received	Value Added	Compensation of Employees	Capital Consumption	Net Operating Surplus	Indirect Taxes	Less: Subsidies Received	Value Added

	1984						1985					
Other Producers	44.88	-		51.78							
Total a	1561.65		2431.46	3993.11	1806.16	2741.68	4547.84
Less: Imputed bank service charge			120.18	120.18			130.64	130.64
Import duties			147.47	147.47			136.37	136.37
Value added tax				326.48	326.48				330.97	330.97
Other adjustments b											
Total c	1561.65		2311.28	473.95	4346.88	1806.16	2611.04	467.34	4884.54

All Producers

	1984						1985					
1 Agriculture, hunting, forestry and fishing	164.42		1525.68		185.01	1690.10	1596.85			1781.86
A Agriculture and hunting	...	...	...	...	...	...	...	...
B Forestry and logging	...	...	...	...	...	...	...	...
C Fishing	...	...	...	...	...	...	...	...
2 Mining and quarrying	6.84	4.61		11.45	7.96	5.31		13.27
3 Manufacturing	250.47	357.76	608.23	286.72	365.75	652.47
4 Electricity, gas and water	20.52	63.19		83.71	24.12	66.89		91.01
A Electricity, gas and steam	...	...	...	...	...	...
B Water works and supply	...	...	...	...	...	...
5 Construction	128.30	118.58		246.88	153.30	134.57		287.87
6 Wholesale and retail trade, restaurants and hotels	262.15	298.86	561.01	298.60	329.65	628.25
A Wholesale and retail trade	...	...	...	...
B Restaurants and hotels	...	...	...	...
7 Transport, storage and communication	176.53	164.55	341.08	204.80	188.55	393.35
8 Finance, insurance, real estate and business services	151.90	497.69	649.59	177.80	683.43	861.23
9 Community, social and personal services	123.30	30.42	153.72	138.46	43.20	181.66
Total, Industries	1284.43	3061.36	4345.77	1476.77	3414.20	4890.97
Producers of Government Services	750.91	5.54	756.45	817.22	5.50	822.72
Other Producers	62.96		62.96	71.78			71.78
Total a	2098.30	3066.90	5165.18	2365.77	3419.70	5785.47
Less: Imputed bank service charge		150.24	150.24		172.98	172.98
Import duties		160.16	160.16		168.09	168.09
Value added tax		393.19	393.19		455.56	455.56
Other adjustments b							
Total c	2098.30	2916.66	553.35	5568.29	2365.77	3246.72	623.65	6236.14

	1988						1989					
	Compensation of Employees	Capital Consumption	Net Operating Surplus	Indirect Taxes	Less: Subsidies Received	Value Added	Compensation of Employees	Capital Consumption	Net Operating Surplus	Indirect Taxes	Less: Subsidies Received	Value Added

All Producers

1 Agriculture, hunting, forestry and fishing	219.16		1819.93		245.01	2039.09		2026.30			2271.31
A Agriculture and hunting	...	...	...	...	...	...
B Forestry and logging	...	...	...	...	...	...
C Fishing	...	...	...	...	...	...
2 Mining and quarrying	8.24	5.45		13.69	13.59	5.03		18.62
3 Manufacturing	313.80	439.16	752.96	368.74	486.62	855.36
4 Electricity, gas and water	31.23	67.13		98.36	37.39	73.70		111.09
A Electricity, gas and steam	...	...	...	...
B Water works and supply	...	...	...	...

Kenya

4.3 Cost Components of Value Added
(Continued)

Million Kenyan pounds

	1988						1989					
	Compensation of Employees	Capital Consumption	Net Operating Surplus	Indirect Taxes	Less: Subsidies Received	Value Added	Compensation of Employees	Capital Consumption	Net Operating Surplus	Indirect Taxes	Less: Subsidies Received	Value Added
5 Construction	202.08	...	166.22	...	...	368.30	266.02	...	211.33	...	...	477.35
6 Wholesale and retail trade, restaurants and hotels	341.96	...	370.07	...	...	712.03	368.64	...	460.43	...	...	829.07
A Wholesale and retail trade	...	...	...	...	...	...	...	...	...	...	...	...
B Restaurants and hotels	...	...	...	...	...	...	...	...	...	...	...	...
7 Transport, storage and communication	211.96	...	221.78	...	...	433.74	229.06	...	256.73	...	...	485.79
8 Finance, insurance, real estate and business services	212.22	...	807.52	...	...	1019.74	243.21	...	916.99	...	...	1160.20
9 Community, social and personal services	150.72	...	47.20	...	...	197.92	173.28	...	54.72	...	...	228.00
Total, Industries	1691.37	...	3944.46	...	...	5635.83	1944.94	...	4491.85	...	...	6436.79
Producers of Government Services	909.93	...	7.36	...	...	917.29	1069.35	...	8.50	...	...	1077.84
Other Producers	83.94	...	-	...	...	83.94	97.49	...	...	...	...	97.49
Total ᵃ	2685.24	...	3951.82	...	...	6637.06	3111.78	...	4500.35	...	...	7612.13
Less: Imputed bank service charge	...	...	245.95	...	...	245.95	...	...	281.62	...	...	281.62
Import duties	...	...	...	188.70	...	188.70	...	...	...	198.22	...	198.22
Value added tax	...	...	...	...	...	...	...	...	...	...	...	...
Other adjustments ᵇ	...	...	...	502.99	...	502.99	...	...	...	509.46	...	509.46
Total ᶜ	2685.24	...	3705.87	691.69	...	7082.80	3111.78	...	4218.73	707.68	...	8038.19

a) Gross domestic product in factor values.
b) Item 'Other adjustments' refers to net indirect taxes other than import duties.
c) Column 4 refers to indirect taxes less subsidies received.

Kiribati

Source: Reply to the United Nations National Accounts Questionnaire from the Planning Office, Ministry of Finance, Tarawa.

General note: The estimates shown in the following tables have been prepared in accordance with the United Nations System of National Accounts so far as the existing data would permit. It should be noted that the estimates for 1972-1974 include data for Tuvalu (former Ellice Islands).

1.1 Expenditure on the Gross Domestic Product, in Current Prices

Thousand Australian dollars

	1970	1975	1980	1981	1982	1983	1984	1985	1986	1987	1988	1989
1 Government final consumption expenditure	...	...	7600	...	...	...	...	...	...	...	...	...
2 Private final consumption expenditure	...	...	19400	...	...	...	...	...	...	...	...	...
3 Gross capital formation	...	...	9200	...	...	...	...	...	...	...	...	...
4 Exports of goods and services	...	...	4700	...	...	...	...	...	...	...	...	...
5 Less: Imports of goods and services	...	...	20000	...	...	...	...	...	...	...	...	...
Equals: Gross Domestic Product	...	42077	20900	...	...	...	...	...	...	...	...	...

Korea, Republic of

General note. The preparation of national accounts statistics in the Republic of Korea is undertaken by the Statistics Department of the Bank of Korea, Seoul. The official estimates and methodological notes on sources and methods are published annually by the Bank in *National Income Statistics*. The following presentation is based mainly on information contained in *National Accounts in Developing Countries in Asia*, issued by the Development Centre of the Organization for Economic Co-operation and Development in 1972. The estimates are generally in accordance with the classifications and definitions recommended in the United Nations System of National Accounts (SNA). Input-output tables have been compiled and published by the Bank. The following tables have been prepared from successive replies to the United Nations national accounts questionnaire. When the scope and coverage differ for conceptual or statistical reasons from the definitions and classifications recommended in SNA, a footnote is indicated to the relevant tables.

Sources and methods:

(a) **Gross domestic product.** Gross domestic product is estimated mainly through the production approach.

(b) **Expenditure on the gross domestic product.** All items of GDP by expenditure type are estimated through the expenditure approach except part of private final consumption expenditure which is estimated by the commodity-flow method. The estimates of government consumption expenditure are derived from government fiscal data. Expenditure on all consumer goods, except food grain, is estimated by the commodity-flow method using industry's production data, export and import data, changes in stocks and adjustments are made for net expenditure of goods abroad by residents. For food grain, consumption per household or per head is multiplied by the total number of household or population. Changes in stocks of grain, livestock and total domestic supply, valued at average prices. For mining and manufacturing imported raw materials are estimated by deducting total domestic demand from this ratio is applied to the value of output by subgroups. Investment in the government sector is derived from government accounts. For the private sector, estimates of investment in construction are derived from input data adding incidental costs and excluding repair cost and construction for defence. Estimates for durable equipment are based on production data, import and exports and changes in stocks. Estimates for exports and imports of goods and services are based on balance-of-payments statements. For the constant price estimates, price deflation is used for government consumption expenditure, net expenditure abroad by residents and exports and imports of goods and services. Private expenditure on food grain is extrapolated by the index of consumption while other expenditure is based on constant value of production, imports and exports and increase in stocks. This latter source and method is also used for estimating producers' durable equipment. For increase in stocks of mineral and manufactured goods, the constant output value is multiplied by the rate of inventory change while for agricultural products and imported raw materials, the method is the same as the one used to estimate these items at current market prices.

(c) **Cost-structure of the gross domestic product.** The cost-structure estimates of GDP are compiled by aggregating the value added at factor cost of each industry, making adjustments for net indirect taxes which are obtained from taxation statistics.

(d) **Gross domestic product by kind of economic activity.** The table of GDP by kind of economic activity is prepared at market prices, i.e., producers' values. The income approach is used to estimate the value added in most industries. The communication and part of other services, gas and water, part of transport and data of which are supplied by the National Agricultural Co-operative Federation, obtained by multiplying the quantities produced by the corresponding prices, the financial data consisting of the input-output tables, the Yearbook of Agriculture Statistics are used to obtain the value added of agricultural services. The value added of forestry is obtained by multiplying the value of production by the value-added ratio obtained from the input-output tables. For fisheries, the current value of output is obtained from fishing and marine statistics while the constant price value of intermediate inputs, extrapolated by the index of tonnage of fishing boats, is revalued at current prices by using the appropriate price indexes. Value added of mining and manufacturing sectors is estimated by applying the value-added ratio to current value of output. Value-added ratio is calculated from the current input-output table and the Financial Statement Analysis of Enterprises. For mining, output is estimated by multiplying quantities produced by unit prices collected from wholesale prices, export unit prices and representative producers' prices while quantity data are obtained from the mineral production statistics. For manufacturing, output is obtained by inflating the constant-price value by a weighted price index while quantity data are obtained from industrial production and shipment index statistics. Value added of electricity, gas and water is derived from the financial data by the current input. Value added of the construction sector is obtained by multiplying the construction value of each sector by a corresponding value-added ratio. The construction unit cost and value added ratio are specially calculated by using the base-year composition of input to total construction value. The construction value is estimated by multiplying total floor area by construction unit cost for the private sector and for the public sector, derived from fiscal data. Value added of the trade sector is estimated by volume mark-up by the value-added ratio calculated from the input-output table. For restaurants and hotels, value added in the base-year is extrapolated by volume indicators and re-valued at current prices. Value added of railway and air transportation and communication is derived directly from the respective financial data while for other transportation, the gross earnings in the base-year are extrapolated by a quantity index and then revalued by appropriate price indexes. The value-added of financing and insurance and real-estate is obtained from financial data and taxation data, respectively. For business services, value added is estimated by extrapolating the base-year estimate. The government executed budget is used to estimate the contribution of public administration and defence to GDP. For the private services, estimates are calculated by multiplying the constant price estimates by appropriate price index, using such sources as Statistical Yearbook of Education and Yearbook of Public Health and Social Statistics. For the constant price estimates, double deflation is used for agriculture and fishing. Current price value-added for business services, government services, financial institutions and insurance and government services are deflated by appropriate price indexes. For the remaining sectors of the economic activity, value added in the base-year is extrapolated by quantity indicators.

1.1 Expenditure on the Gross Domestic Product, in Current Prices

Thousand Million Korean won

	1970	1975	1980	1981	1982	1983	1984	1985	1986	1987	1988	1989
1 Government final consumption expenditure	262	1131	4387	5515	6255	6852	7263	8136	8401	10709	12487	14593
2 Private final consumption expenditure	2069	7264	24585	30633	34554	38728	43201	47875	52286	57989	64468	75625
A Households	2049	7203	24343	30343	34210	38259	42594	47131	51497	57113	65410	74415
B Private non-profit institutions serving households	20	61	242	289	344	470	607	744	789	876	1058	1210
3 Gross capital formation	691	2956	12071	13994	15563	18361	21666	23673	26486	31944	39211	49121
A Increase in stocks	-5	215	-154	718	117	-308	669	837	492	813	1857	4342
B Gross fixed capital formation	696	2741	12226	13276	15446	18669	20998	22837	25993	31131	37355	44778
Residential buildings	163	617	2169	1956	2583	3554	3344	3431	3977	4483	5968	7770
Non-residential buildings	150	414	1921	1875	2203	3010	3786	3651	3880	5083	6672	8859
Other construction and land improvement, etc.	169	513	2717	3322	4041	4581	5157	6035	5678	6437	7243	9072
Other	213	1197	5419	6123	6618	7524	8711	9720	12458	15119	17472	19078
4 Exports of goods and services	390	2859	12944	17341	18770	22748	26126	27937	36034	45051	51101	48714
5 Less: Imports of goods and services	659	3728	15774	17719	20174	23049	26039	26919	30365	36355	40567	44791
Statistical discrepancy	16	-180	-171	-281	-525	192	428	145	-415	-906	-738	-995
Equals: Gross Domestic Product	2768	10302	38041	47482	54443	63833	72644	80847	93426	108428	127963	142267

1039

Korea, Republic of

1.2 Expenditure on the Gross Domestic Product, in Constant Prices

Thousand Million Korean won

	1970	1975	1980	1981	1982	1983	1984	1985	1986	1987	1988	1989
	At constant prices of:1985											
1 Government final consumption expenditure	3641	5131	6875	7267	7339	7590	7702	8136	9014	9637	10538	11365
2 Private final consumption expenditure	18180	25467	34366	36000	38337	41831	45006	47875	51712	56020	61520	67537
A Households	18011	25224	33984	35637	37956	41335	44378	47131	50940	55185	60566	66505
B Private non-profit institutions serving households	169	243	382	363	381	497	627	744	772	835	954	1032
3 Gross capital formation	5169	8740	15906	16208	17467	19831	22796	23673	26247	30893	35583	43999
A Increase in stocks	574	1073	136	1082	774	169	984	837	679	1093	1777	4718
B Gross fixed capital formation	4596	7667	15771	15126	16693	19662	21812	22837	25569	29800	33806	39281
Residential buildings	1098	1936	2712	2152	2722	3702	3398	3431	3977	4340	5264	6391
Non-residential buildings	997	1287	2429	2079	2328	3148	3860	3651	3879	4890	5883	7242
Other construction and land improvement etc.	1215	1678	3386	3650	4282	4792	5249	6035	5672	6195	6413	7399
Other	1286	2766	7244	7246	7361	8020	9305	9720	12042	14375	16247	18249
4 Exports of goods and services	2652	8081	17278	19890	20780	24776	26744	27937	35239	42849	48209	46283
5 Less: Imports of goods and services	5149	10161	20662	21871	22528	25233	27090	26919	31714	37871	42732	49698
Statistical discrepancy	320	363	225	120	426	306	449	145	370	277	374	942
Equals: Gross Domestic Product	24813	37621	53989	57615	61821	69101	75606	80847	90868	101804	113492	120429

1.3 Cost Components of the Gross Domestic Product

Thousand Million Korean won

	1970	1975	1980	1981	1982	1983	1984	1985	1986	1987	1988	1989
1 Indirect taxes, net	258	1002	4593	5731	6695	8180	8752	9407	10872	12548	14821	16353
A Indirect taxes	267	1150	4920	6075	7043	8642	9330	9895	11423	13068	15212	16834
B Less: Subsidies	10	148	327	344	348	462	578	488	550	520	391	481
2 Consumption of fixed capital	171	725	2980	3802	4728	5753	6862	7926	9032	11034	13231	14667
3 Compensation of employees paid by resident producers to:	935	3348	15066	18436	21293	25540	28850	31969	36210	43164	52835	61903
A Resident households	935	3348	15063	18431	21288	25535	28838	31956	36197	43143	52817	61889
B Rest of the world	-	-	3	6	5	5	12	13	13	21	18	14
4 Operating surplus	1404	5227	15402	19512	21726	24360	28180	31545	37312	41683	47076	49344
A Corporate and quasi-corporate enterprises	...	842	4961	6503	6648	7922	9020	10378	12011	14556	15854	...
B Private unincorporated enterprises	...	4385	10441	13009	15078	16438	19161	21167	25301	27126	31222	...
C General government	...	...	...	...	...	...	...	...	...	...	...	...
Equals: Gross Domestic Product	2768	10302	38041	47482	54443	63833	72644	80847	93426	108428	127963	142267

1.4 General Government Current Receipts and Disbursements

Thousand Million Korean won

	1970	1975	1980	1981	1982	1983	1984	1985	1986	1987	1988	1989
	Receipts											
1 Operating surplus	...	...	...	...	...	...	...	...	...	...	...	...
2 Property and entrepreneurial income	20	46	242	344	402	468	501	605	646	703	854	1010
3 Taxes, fees and contributions	413	1580	7060	8861	10408	12444	13494	14702	16890	20048	25188	29191
A Indirect taxes	267	1150	4920	6075	7043	8642	9331	9895	11423	13068	15212	16834
B Direct taxes	136	396	1787	2307	2755	3039	3308	3815	4297	5555	7611	9714
C Social security contributions	3	13	223	330	433	538	647	758	944	1171	2039	2321
D Compulsory fees, fines and penalties	7	21	130	148	176	224	209	233	226	253	327	322
4 Other current transfers	32	34	59	55	58	53	63	61	62	80	128	91
Total Current Receipts of General Government	465	1660	7362	9259	10868	12964	14058	15368	17598	20831	26171	30292
	Disbursements											
1 Government final consumption expenditure	262	1131	4387	5515	6255	6852	7263	8136	9401	10709	12487	14593

Korea, Republic of

1.4 General Government Current Receipts and Disbursements
(Continued)

Thousand Million Korean won

	1970	1975	1980	1981	1982	1983	1984	1985	1986	1987	1988	1989
A Compensation of employees	199	620	2745	3407	4094	4565	4911	5508	6176	7086	8285	...
B Consumption of fixed capital	9	37	163	209	251	285	320	337	380	419	486	...
C Purchases of goods and services, net	54	474	1477	1898	1908	1999	2030	2289	2843	3203	3715	...
D Less: Own account fixed capital formation	...	...	...	...	...	...	...	...	...	...	...	...
E Indirect taxes paid, net	-	1	2	2	2	2	2	2	1	2	2	...
2 Property income	9	45	227	295	398	508	585	611	745	778	756	749
A Interest	9	45	226	295	397	507	584	611	745	778	755	...
B Net land rent and royalties	-	-	-	1	-	-	1	-	1	1	1	...
3 Subsidies	10	148	327	344	348	462	578	488	550	520	391	481
4 Other current transfers	24	111	633	816	1028	1108	1283	1468	1562	1882	2576	3576
A Social security benefits	2	11	211	290	438	557	678	806	826	1023	1420	1773
B Social assistance grants	14	66	276	325	352	337	364	400	420	476	639	860
C Other	8	34	146	201	238	213	241	263	315	383	518	944
5 Net saving	160	225	1789	2290	2840	4034	4350	4665	5340	6942	9961	10893
Total Current Disbursements and Net Saving of General Government	465	1660	7362	9259	10868	12964	14058	15368	17598	20831	26171	30292

1.6 Current Income and Outlay of Households and Non-Profit Institutions

Thousand Million Korean won

	1970	1975	1980	1981	1982	1983	1984	1985	1986	1987	1988	1989
Receipts												
1 Compensation of employees	...	3393	15157	18572	21487	25793	29138	32302	36627	43531	53197	...
A From resident producers	...	3348	15063	18431	21288	25535	28838	31956	36197	43143	52817	...
B From rest of the world	...	45	94	141	199	258	300	347	430	389	380	...
2 Operating surplus of private unincorporated enterprises	...	4385	10441	13009	15078	16438	19161	21167	25301	27126	31222	...
3 Property and entrepreneurial income	...	273	2588	3431	3599	3197	3833	4217	4576	5984	6859	...
4 Current transfers	...	456	2775	3923	4642	5619	6481	7704	8602	9804	11887	...
A Social security benefits	...	11	211	290	438	557	678	806	826	1023	1420	...
B Social assistance grants	...	66	276	325	352	337	364	400	420	476	639	...
C Other	...	379	2288	3308	3852	4725	5438	6499	7356	8305	9829	...
Total Current Receipts a	...	8507	30961	38935	44805	51047	58612	65390	75106	86446	103164	...
Disbursements												
1 Private final consumption expenditure	...	7264	24585	30633	34554	38728	43201	47875	52286	57989	66468	...
2 Property income	...	137	1268	1578	1746	1790	2320	2659	2757	3300	3924	...
3 Direct taxes and other current transfers n.e.c. to general government	...	279	1254	1695	2097	2342	2634	2986	3587	4366	6563	...
A Social security contributions	...	13	223	330	433	538	647	758	944	1171	2039	...
B Direct taxes	...	253	948	1265	1547	1661	1852	2071	2486	3014	4271	...
C Fees, fines and penalties	...	14	82	99	117	143	136	156	157	181	254	...
4 Other current transfers	...	242	1062	1423	1630	2134	2831	3654	4204	4868	6289	...
5 Net saving	...	585	2793	3607	4778	6053	7625	8217	12273	15923	19920	...
Total Current Disbursements and Net Saving a	...	8507	30961	38935	44805	51047	58612	65390	75106	86446	103164	...

a) The estimates refer to households only.

1.7 External Transactions on Current Account, Summary

Thousand Million Korean won

	1970	1975	1980	1981	1982	1983	1984	1985	1986	1987	1988	1989
Payments to the Rest of the World												
1 Imports of goods and services	659	3728	15774	19719	20174	23049	26039	26919	30365	36356	40567	44791
A Imports of merchandise c.i.f.	614	3462	14237	17464	17893	20626	23561	24505	27711	33338	37049	40165
B Other	45	266	1537	2255	2281	2422	2478	2415	2654	3018	3517	4626
2 Factor income to the rest of the world	26	235	1725	2583	2960	2823	3443	3799	3987	3432	2860	2753

Korea, Republic of

1.7 External Transactions on Current Account, Summary
(Continued)

Thousand Million Korean won

	1970	1975	1980	1981	1982	1983	1984	1985	1986	1987	1988	1989
A Compensation of employees	-	-	3	6	5	5	12	13	13	21	18	14
B Property and entrepreneurial income	26	235	1721	2577	2955	2818	3431	3786	3974	3411	2841	2740
3 Current transfers to the rest of the world	11	55	227	248	296	303	303	350	288	393	543	973
4 Surplus of the nation on current transactions	-196	-910	-3198	-3085	-1976	-1210	-1098	-781	4021	8009	10210	3234
Payments to the Rest of the World and Surplus of the Nation on Current Transactions	499	3107	14528	19464	21454	24965	28687	30288	38661	48189	54179	51752

Receipts From The Rest of the World

	1970	1975	1980	1981	1982	1983	1984	1985	1986	1987	1988	1989
1 Exports of goods and services	390	2859	12944	17341	18770	22748	26126	27937	36034	45051	51101	48714
A Exports of merchandise f.o.b.	273	2451	10420	13885	14759	18047	21241	23018	29866	37919	43458	41142
B Other	117	409	2524	3455	4010	4702	4885	4919	6168	7131	7644	7573
2 Factor income from rest of the world	43	69	433	629	700	713	883	1040	1160	1028	1127	1553
A Compensation of employees	31	45	94	141	199	258	300	347	430	389	380	404
B Property and entrepreneurial income	12	24	339	488	501	455	583	694	730	639	748	1149
3 Current transfers from rest of the world	67	179	1151	1495	1984	1504	1679	1310	1467	2111	1950	1485
Receipts from the Rest of the World on Current Transactions	499	3107	14528	19464	21454	24965	28687	30288	38661	48189	54179	51752

1.10 Gross Domestic Product by Kind of Activity, in Current Prices

Thousand Million Korean won

	1970	1975	1980	1981	1982	1983	1984	1985	1986	1987	1988	1989
1 Agriculture, hunting, forestry and fishing	739	2571	5677	7431	7989	8678	9392	10352	10729	11353	13494	14546
2 Mining and quarrying	35	144	491	647	637	689	733	791	903	916	928	884
3 Manufacturing	588	2687	11299	14199	15908	19106	22375	24530	29579	34903	41617	44460
4 Electricity, gas and water	42	126	752	1022	1208	1577	2000	2267	2897	3197	3365	3459
5 Construction	139	490	3186	3437	4211	5171	5739	6251	6646	8069	10329	13808
6 Wholesale and retail trade, restaurants and hotels	438	1752	4842	6059	6898	7733	8872	9834	11682	13918	15809	16871
7 Transport, storage and communication	185	606	2897	3874	4626	5166	5789	6155	7118	8126	9240	9936
8 Finance, insurance, real estate and business services	228	684	4173	4592	4804	6313	7532	9509	11041	13173	16689	20022
9 Community, social and personal services	100	325	1254	1553	1950	2415	2854	3332	3836	4250	4905	5808
Total, Industries	2494	9384	34571	42814	48230	56846	65286	73021	84433	97906	116375	129793
Producers of Government Services	208	657	2910	3617	4347	4853	5232	5847	6558	7506	8773	10419
Other Producers	53	202	704	936	1211	1471	1699	2047	2313	2583	3048	3612
Subtotal	2755	10244	38185	47367	53788	63170	72217	80915	93303	107995	128196	143824
Less: Imputed bank service charge	45	176	1279	1324	887	1383	1726	2247	2594	2942	3730	4801
Plus: Import duties	59	234	1135	1439	1542	2045	2153	2180	2717	3376	3497	3244
Plus: Value added tax	...	...	...	...	..	...	...	...	...	...	...	...
Equals: Gross Domestic Product	2768	10302	38041	47482	54443	63833	72644	80847	93426	108428	127963	142267

1.11 Gross Domestic Product by Kind of Activity, in Constant Prices

Thousand Million Korean won

	1970	1975	1980	1981	1982	1983	1984	1985	1986	1987	1988	1989
					At constant prices of:1985							
1 Agriculture, hunting, forestry and fishing	6943	8697	7657	8750	9401	10129	9977	10352	10830	10098	10903	10825
2 Mining and quarrying	499	724	775	781	700	739	762	791	856	845	840	784
3 Manufacturing	3421	7648	14426	15851	16914	19517	22901	24530	29018	34460	39086	40522
4 Electricity, gas and water	211	467	1026	1181	1248	1601	1998	2267	2841	3190	3504	3858
5 Construction	1427	2129	4158	3947	4678	5671	5987	6251	6560	7394	8097	9343
6 Wholesale and retail trade, restaurants and hotels	3144	5362	6637	7147	7701	8413	9084	9834	11466	13177	14634	15114
7 Transport, storage and communication	1125	2119	4318	4534	4800	5223	5872	6155	6757	7633	8530	9368
8 Finance, insurance, real estate and business services	2441	3463	5940	6071	6633	7443	8211	9509	10621	12307	14322	16036
9 Community, social and personal services	892	1302	1956	2025	2242	2589	2946	3332	3700	3991	4364	4890

Korea, Republic of

1.11 Gross Domestic Product by Kind of Activity, in Constant Prices
(Continued)

Thousand Million Korean won

	1970	1975	1980	1981	1982	1983	1984	1985	1986	1987	1988	1989
				At constant prices of:1985								
Total, Industries	20103	31912	46892	50287	54317	61325	67738	73021	82649	93094	104280	110740
Producers of Government Services	3812	4273	5168	5363	5543	5673	5738	5847	6045	6249	6530	6823
Other Producers	690	1032	1292	1378	1501	1651	1820	2047	2232	2382	2635	2880
Subtotal	24605	37216	53352	57029	61361	68649	75297	80915	90926	101725	113445	120443
Less: Imputed bank service charge	234	458	1043	1158	1353	1545	1863	2247	2647	3047	3422	3964
Plus: Import duties	442	863	1680	1745	1813	1997	2173	2180	2589	3125	3469	3950
Plus: Value added tax	...	...	...	...	...	...	...	...	...	...	...	...
Equals: Gross Domestic Product	24813	37621	53989	57615	61821	69101	75606	80847	90868	101804	113492	120429

1.12 Relations Among National Accounting Aggregates

Thousand Million Korean won

	1970	1975	1980	1981	1982	1983	1984	1985	1986	1987	1988	1989
Gross Domestic Product	2768	10302	38041	47482	54443	63833	72644	80847	93426	108428	127963	142267
Plus: Net factor income from the rest of the world	17	-166	-1291	-1954	-2261	-2111	-2560	-2759	-2827	-2404	-1732	-1201
Factor income from the rest of the world	43	69	433	629	700	713	883	1040	1160	1028	1127	1553
Less: Factor income to the rest of the world	26	235	1725	2583	2960	2823	3443	3799	3987	3432	2860	2753
Equals: Gross National Product	2785	10136	36750	45528	52182	61722	70084	78088	90599	106024	126231	141066
Less: Consumption of fixed capital	171	725	2980	3802	4728	5753	6862	7926	9032	11034	13231	14667
Equals: National Income	2614	9411	33770	41726	47454	55970	63222	70162	81567	94990	113000	126399
Plus: Net current transfers from the rest of the world	56	124	924	1247	1689	1201	1376	960	1179	1718	1408	511
Current transfers from the rest of the world	67	179	1151	1495	1984	1504	1679	1310	1467	2111	1950	1485
Less: Current transfers to the rest of the world	11	55	227	248	296	303	303	350	288	393	543	973
Equals: National Disposable Income	2670	9535	34694	42973	49143	57171	64597	71123	82746	96708	114407	126911
Less: Final consumption	2331	8395	28971	36148	40809	45580	50464	56011	61687	68697	78955	90218
Equals: Net Saving	339	1141	5723	6825	8334	11591	14134	15112	21059	28011	35452	36693
Less: Surplus of the nation on current transactions	-196	-910	-3198	-3085	-1976	-1210	-1098	-781	4021	8009	10210	3234
Statistical discrepancy	-16	180	171	281	525	-192	-428	-145	415	908	738	995
Equals: Net Capital Formation	519	2231	9092	10191	10835	12608	14804	15747	17454	20910	25980	34454

2.1 Government Final Consumption Expenditure by Function, in Current Prices

Thousand Million Korean won

	1970	1975	1980	1981	1982	1983	1984	1985	1986	1987	1988	1989
1 General public services	32	140	631	815	940	1027	1112	1203	1376	1675	1852	2191
2 Defence	132	598	2127	2573	2782	2980	2995	3562	4215	4535	5202	5797
3 Public order and safety	22	81	353	491	578	702	724	804	910	1029	1208	1405
4 Education	55	211	831	1018	1258	1405	1578	1793	2036	2419	2763	3426
5 Health	3	16	82	105	101	97	108	92	126	141	182	210
6 Social security and welfare	4	13	66	92	152	190	219	182	222	280	446	512
7 Housing and community amenities	3	17	88	96	111	97	93	106	85	131	157	207
8 Recreational, cultural and religious affairs	2	10	35	49	53	45	58	55	74	95	124	170
9 Economic services	8	36	137	230	231	256	311	271	285	324	450	557
A Fuel and energy	-	2	11	29	34	47	33	37	35	39	31	46
B Agriculture, forestry, fishing and hunting	5	24	95	146	140	150	162	154	168	208	275	324
C Mining, manufacturing and construction, except fuel and energy	1	2	7	21	33	35	67	45	40	25	101	121
D Transportation and communication	2	8	24	34	24	24	49	36	42	53	43	66
E Other economic affairs	...	...	...	...	...	...	...	...	...	...	...	...
10 Other functions	2	8	37	46	49	53	65	68	71	80	102	118
Total Government Final Consumption Expenditure	262	1131	4387	5515	6255	6852	7263	8136	9401	10709	12487	14593

Korea, Republic of

2.2 Government Final Consumption Expenditure by Function, in Constant Prices

Thousand Million Korean won

	1970	1975	1980	1981	1982	1983	1984	1985	1986	1987	1988	1989
					At constant prices of:1985							
1 General public services	503	701	1071	1142	1173	1178	1179	1203	1310	1480	1522	1596
2 Defence	1425	2219	3005	3079	3008	3166	3085	3562	4160	4292	4726	4958
3 Public order and safety	413	481	625	700	727	776	785	804	858	897	966	979
4 Education	979	1245	1453	1506	1604	1647	1738	1793	1862	2024	2094	2434
5 Health	44	74	128	138	118	109	114	92	121	129	157	173
6 Social security and welfare	69	78	122	135	186	190	208	182	204	240	354	385
7 Housing and community amenities	39	79	136	130	128	111	100	106	83	122	138	167
8 Recreational, cultural and religious affairs	22	39	54	63	60	62	65	55	72	89	117	159
9 Economic services	120	177	223	313	273	290	363	271	274	292	379	425
A Fuel and energy	6	9	18	37	40	52	46	37	33	35	27	37
B Agriculture, forestry, fishing and hunting	80	120	144	197	170	170	181	154	161	187	228	240
C Mining, manufacturing and construction, except fuel and energy	7	8	11	26	38	38	75	45	39	23	88	97
D Transportation and communication	27	40	50	53	25	29	62	36	40	47	36	51
E Other economic affairs	...	...	...	...	...	...	...	...	...	...	...	...
10 Other functions	28	38	60	62	62	63	67	68	69	73	86	90
Total Government Final Consumption Expenditure	3641	5131	6875	7267	7339	7590	7702	8136	9014	9637	10538	11365

2.3 Total Government Outlays by Function and Type

Thousand Million Korean won

	Final Consumption Expenditures			Subsidies	Other Current Transfers & Property Income	Total Current Disbursements	Gross Capital Formation	Other Capital Outlays	Total Outlays
	Total	Compensation of Employees	Other						
						1980			
1 General public services	631	422	209	...	...	...	109	...	...
2 Defence	2127	804	1323	...	...	...	15	...	...
3 Public order and safety	353	255	99	...	...	...	70	...	...
4 Education	831	938	-108	...	...	...	252	...	...
5 Health	82	70	11	-	...	...	25	...	...
6 Social security and welfare	66	55	11	-	...	...	25	...	...
7 Housing and community amenities	88	54	34	-	...	...	425	...	...
8 Recreation, culture and religion	35	13	22	...	...	...	50	...	...
9 Economic services	137	115	22	85	...	...	682	...	...
A Fuel and energy	11	10	2	71	...	...	25	...	...
B Agriculture, forestry, fishing and hunting	95	70	26	-	...	...	149	...	...
C Mining (except fuels), manufacturing and construction	7	12	-4	-	...	...	72	...	...
D Transportation and communication	24	24	-1	14	...	...	436	...	...
E Other economic affairs	...	...	...	...	...	...	...	...	...
10 Other functions	37	18	19	241	...	...	57	...	...
Total	4387	2746	1641	327	860	5573	1711	-12	7272
						1981			
1 General public services	815	510	305	...	...	...	127	...	...
2 Defence	2573	974	1599	...	...	...	8	...	...
3 Public order and safety	491	322	169	...	...	...	75	...	...
4 Education	1018	1181	-163	...	...	...	393	...	...
5 Health	105	87	18	-	...	...	37	...	...
6 Social security and welfare	92	75	17	-	...	...	25	...	...
7 Housing and community amenities	96	72	24	-	...	...	352	...	...
8 Recreation, culture and religion	49	19	30	...	...	...	50	...	...
9 Economic services	230	145	85	52	...	...	907	...	...

Korea, Republic of

2.3 Total Government Outlays by Function and Type
(Continued)

Thousand Million Korean won

	Final Consumption Expenditures			Subsidies	Other Current Transfers & Property Income	Total Current Disbursements	Gross Capital Formation	Other Capital Outlays	Total Outlays
	Total	Compensation of Employees	Other						
A Fuel and energy	29	15	14	49	...	...	38	...	...
B Agriculture, forestry, fishing and hunting	146	84	62	-	...	...	287	...	...
C Mining (except fuels), manufacturing and construction	21	14	6	-	...	...	61	...	...
D Transportation and communication	34	31	3	3	...	...	522	...	...
E Other economic affairs	...	...	...	...	...	...	...	...	...
10 Other functions	46	22	24	292	...	...	50	...	...
Total	5515	3407	2109	344	1111	6970	2023	25	9018
1982									
1 General public services	940	626	314	...	...	...	106	...	...
2 Defence	2782	1129	1653	...	...	...	11	...	...
3 Public order and safety	578	383	195	...	...	...	105	...	...
4 Education	1258	1474	-215	...	...	...	442	...	...
5 Health	101	91	11	-	...	...	45	...	...
6 Social security and welfare	152	98	54	-	...	...	23	...	...
7 Housing and community amenities	111	84	28	-	...	...	500	...	...
8 Recreation, culture and religion	53	21	32	...	...	...	60	...	...
9 Economic services	231	166	65	77	...	...	1091	...	...
A Fuel and energy	34	19	15	40	...	...	41	...	...
B Agriculture, forestry, fishing and hunting	140	87	52	-	...	...	214	...	...
C Mining (except fuels), manufacturing and construction	33	16	18	-	...	...	203	...	...
D Transportation and communication	24	44	-20	37	...	...	634	...	...
E Other economic affairs	...	...	...	...	...	...	...	...	...
10 Other functions	49	24	24	271	...	...	52	...	...
Total	6255	4094	2160	348	1425	8028	2433	-19	10442
1983									
1 General public services	1027	687	340	...	...	...	173	...	...
2 Defence	2980	1168	1812	...	...	...	11	...	...
3 Public order and safety	702	466	237	...	...	...	78	...	...
4 Education	1405	1694	-289	...	...	...	438	...	...
5 Health	97	92	5	-	...	...	39	...	...
6 Social security and welfare	190	125	65	-	...	...	39	...	...
7 Housing and community amenities	97	96	1	1	...	...	601	...	...
8 Recreation, culture and religion	45	25	20	...	...	...	109	...	...
9 Economic services	256	186	70	53	...	...	1318	...	...
A Fuel and energy	47	19	29	15	...	...	42	...	...
B Agriculture, forestry, fishing and hunting	150	105	45	-	...	...	307	...	...
C Mining (except fuels), manufacturing and construction	35	14	21	-	...	...	172	...	...
D Transportation and communication	24	49	-25	37	...	...	797	...	...
E Other economic affairs	...	...	...	...	...	...	...	...	...
10 Other functions	53	27	25	409	...	...	57	...	...
Total	6852	4565	2287	462	1615	8930	2863	7	11799
1984									
1 General public services	1112	770	342	...	...	...	165	...	...
2 Defence	2995	1202	1793	...	...	...	14	...	...
3 Public order and safety	724	492	232	...	...	...	109	...	...
4 Education	1578	1849	-271	...	...	...	526	...	...
5 Health	108	97	11	-	...	...	50	...	...
6 Social security and welfare	219	146	73	-	...	...	67	...	...
7 Housing and community amenities	93	97	-4	1	...	...	681	...	...
8 Recreation, culture and religion	58	26	32	...	...	...	114	...	...
9 Economic services	311	202	109	74	...	...	1394	...	...

1045

Korea, Republic of

2.3 Total Government Outlays by Function and Type
(Continued)

Thousand Million Korean won

	Final Consumption Expenditures			Subsidies	Other Current Transfers & Property Income	Total Current Disbursements	Gross Capital Formation	Other Capital Outlays	Total Outlays
	Total	Compensation of Employees	Other						
A Fuel and energy	33	21	13	17	...	...	2	...	...
B Agriculture, forestry, fishing and hunting	162	105	57	-	...	...	249	...	...
C Mining (except fuels), manufacturing and construction	67	23	45	-	...	...	273	...	...
D Transportation and communication	49	54	-5	57	...	...	871	...	...
E Other economic affairs	...	...	...	...	...	...	...	...	...
10 Other functions	65	30	35	503	...	...	122	6	...
Total	7263	4911	2352	578	1868	9708	3241	6	12955
1985									
1 General public services	1203	868	335	...	...	...	176	...	...
2 Defence	3562	1313	2248	...	...	...	21	...	...
3 Public order and safety	804	561	242	...	...	...	114	...	...
4 Education	1793	2094	-301	...	...	...	567	...	...
5 Health	92	108	-16	3	...	...	65	...	...
6 Social security and welfare	182	153	29	-	...	...	40	...	...
7 Housing and community amenities	106	112	-6	1	...	...	782	...	...
8 Recreation, culture and religion	55	35	20	...	...	...	192	...	...
9 Economic services	271	233	38	33	...	...	1553	...	...
A Fuel and energy	37	30	7	18	...	...	43	...	...
B Agriculture, forestry, fishing and hunting	154	117	37	-	...	...	255	...	...
C Mining (except fuels), manufacturing and construction	45	28	17	-	...	...	330	...	...
D Transportation and communication	36	58	-23	15	...	...	924	...	...
E Other economic affairs	...	...	...	...	...	...	...	...	...
10 Other functions	68	31	37	451	...	...	149	...	...
Total	8136	5508	2628	488	2079	10703	3657	-53	14308
1986									
1 General public services	1376	1010	365	...	...	...	166	...	...
2 Defence	4215	1417	2798	...	...	...	20	...	...
3 Public order and safety	910	627	283	...	...	...	117	...	...
4 Education	2036	2342	-305	...	...	...	518	...	...
5 Health	126	126	-1	3	...	...	67	...	...
6 Social security and welfare	222	193	29	-	...	...	25	...	...
7 Housing and community amenities	85	120	-35	3	...	...	907	...	...
8 Recreation, culture and religion	74	46	28	...	...	...	228	...	...
9 Economic services	285	260	25	51	...	...	1470	...	...
A Fuel and energy	35	32	3	18	...	...	47	...	...
B Agriculture, forestry, fishing and hunting	168	132	36	-	...	...	351	...	...
C Mining (except fuels), manufacturing and construction	40	30	10	-	...	...	115	...	...
D Transportation and communication	42	65	-23	33	...	...	956	...	...
E Other economic affairs	...	...	...	...	...	...	...	...	...
10 Other functions	71	35	36	493	...	...	152	...	...
Total	9401	6176	3224	550	2307	12258	3669	-104	15823
1987									
1 General public services	1675	1218	457	...	...	...	223	...	...
2 Defence	4535	1556	2980	...	...	...	33	...	...
3 Public order and safety	1029	720	310	...	...	...	143	...	...
4 Education	2419	2680	-261	...	...	...	526	...	...
5 Health	141	140	1	2	...	...	69	...	...
6 Social security and welfare	280	222	58	-	...	...	30	...	...
7 Housing and community amenities	131	148	-17	4	...	...	1008	...	...
8 Recreation, culture and religion	95	56	39	...	...	...	230	...	...
9 Economic services	324	305	19	48	...	...	1664	...	...

Korea, Republic of

2.3 Total Government Outlays by Function and Type
(Continued)

Thousand Million Korean won

	Final Consumption Expenditures			Subsidies	Other Current Transfers & Property Income	Total Current Disbursements	Gross Capital Formation	Other Capital Outlays	Total Outlays
	Total	Compensation of Employees	Other						
A Fuel and energy	39	39	-	18	...	...	58	...	...
B Agriculture, forestry, fishing and hunting	208	157	51	-	...	...	405	...	...
C Mining (except fuels), manufacturing and construction	25	33	-8	-	...	...	158	...	...
D Transportation and communication	53	76	-23	30	...	...	1043	...	...
E Other economic affairs	...	...	...	...	...	...	...	...	...
10 Other functions	80	42	38	466	...	...	176	...	...
Total	10709	7086	3623	520	2661	13890	4103	-343	17649
1988									
1 General public services	1852	1315	537	...	...	...	294	...	...
2 Defence	5202	1774	3428	...	...	...	52	...	...
3 Public order and safety	1208	885	324	...	...	...	183	...	...
4 Education	2763	3075	-311	...	...	...	606	...	...
5 Health	182	192	-10	-	...	...	62	...	...
6 Social security and welfare	446	330	116	-	...	...	16	...	...
7 Housing and community amenities	157	193	-36	3	...	...	1429	...	...
8 Recreation, culture and religion	124	92	32	...	...	...	75	...	...
9 Economic services	450	374	76	54	...	...	2041	...	...
A Fuel and energy	31	51	-20	16	...	...	20	...	...
B Agriculture, forestry, fishing and hunting	275	193	82	-	...	...	478	...	...
C Mining (except fuels), manufacturing and construction	101	53	48	-	...	...	245	...	...
D Transportation and communication	43	77	-34	39	...	...	1298	...	...
E Other economic affairs	...	...	...	...	...	...	...	...	...
10 Other functions	102	56	46	333	...	...	215	...	...
Total	12487	8285	4202	391	3332	16210	4973	-145	21038
1989									
1 General public services	2191	1567	624	...	...	...	250	...	...
2 Defence	5797	2114	3683	...	...	...	63	...	...
3 Public order and safety	1405	1054	351	...	...	...	249	...	...
4 Education	3426	3664	-238	...	...	...	612	...	...
5 Health	210	229	-19	-	...	...	55	...	...
6 Social security and welfare	512	394	118	-	...	...	71	...	...
7 Housing and community amenities	207	230	-23	...	...	...	1492	...	...
8 Recreation, culture and religion	170	110	61	...	...	...	174	...	...
9 Economic services	557	446	111	71	...	...	2515	...	...
A Fuel and energy	46	61	-14	8	...	...	13	...	...
B Agriculture, forestry, fishing and hunting	324	230	93	-	...	...	457	...	...
C Mining (except fuels), manufacturing and construction	121	63	57	15	...	...	239	...	...
D Transportation and communication	66	92	-26	49	...	...	1805	...	...
E Other economic affairs	...	...	...	...	...	...	...	...	...
10 Other functions	118	67	51	410	...	...	167	...	...
Total	14593	9875	4718	481	4326	19399	5647	-	25046

2.5 Private Final Consumption Expenditure by Type and Purpose, in Current Prices

Thousand Million Korean won

	1970	1975	1980	1981	1982	1983	1984	1985	1986	1987	1988	1989
Final Consumption Expenditure of Resident Households												
1 Food, beverages and tobacco	1127	3898	11765	14756	15635	16512	17481	18851	20362	22296	25140	27862
2 Clothing and footwear	209	726	2113	2369	2329	2496	2612	2432	2665	2957	3326	3622
3 Gross rent, fuel and power	190	601	2507	3142	3583	4143	4753	5323	5805	6232	6869	7563
4 Furniture, furnishings and household equipment and operation	80	313	1165	1272	1456	1754	2201	2434	2905	3426	4092	4598

Korea, Republic of

2.5 Private Final Consumption Expenditure by Type and Purpose, in Current Prices
(Continued)

Thousand Million Korean won

	1970	1975	1980	1981	1982	1983	1984	1985	1986	1987	1988	1989
5 Medical care and health expenses	51	229	962	1264	1642	2095	2509	2968	3372	3964	4676	5412
6 Transport and communication	123	472	2115	2566	3189	3695	4281	4822	5320	6120	6985	7853
7 Recreational, entertainment, education and cultural services	118	452	1797	2544	3224	3895	4524	5152	5883	6712	7791	8837
8 Miscellaneous goods and services	157	574	2036	2545	3220	3816	4399	5383	6047	6757	8035	9718
Total Final Consumption Expenditure in the Domestic Market by Households, of which	2054	7264	24459	30457	34279	38407	42760	47365	52358	58463	66913	75465
A Durable goods	40	177	709	1044	1318	1854	2422	2772	3584	4719	5433	6098
B Semi-durable goods	287	1049	3297	3620	3720	4077	4430	4559	5104	5629	6523	7333
C Non-durable goods	1293	4462	13821	17357	18546	19689	21001	22755	24674	27173	30599	33858
D Services	434	1577	6633	8435	10695	12787	14907	17280	18996	20942	24357	28176
Plus: Direct purchases abroad by resident households	2	7	85	161	250	220	264	323	250	299	556	965
Less: Direct purchases in the domestic market by non-resident households	7	68	201	275	318	368	430	557	1111	1650	2059	2015
Equals: Final Consumption Expenditure of Resident Households	2049	7203	24343	30343	34210	38259	42594	47131	51497	57113	65410	74415
Final Consumption Expenditure of Private Non-profit Institutions Serving Households												
1 Research and science	5	17	76	48	50	128	184	235	261	288	342	399
2 Education												
3 Medical and other health services	3	12	44	64	91	113	145	177	189	210	247	289
4 Welfare services	4	10	33	41	47	55	64	68	75	78	88	97
5 Recreational and related cultural services	...	...	...	...	...	...	...	...	...	...	...	...
6 Religious organisations	...	...	...	...	...	...	...	...	...	...	...	...
7 Professional and labour organisations serving households	...	...	...	...	...	...	...	...	...	...	...	...
8 Miscellaneous	8	22	89	137	155	174	214	264	264	300	381	425
Equals: Final Consumption Expenditure of Private Non-profit Organisations Serving Households	20	61	242	289	344	470	607	744	789	876	1058	1210
Private Final Consumption Expenditure	2069	7264	24585	30633	34554	38728	43201	47875	52286	57989	66468	75625

2.6 Private Final Consumption Expenditure by Type and Purpose, in Constant Prices

Thousand Million Korean won

	1970	1975	1980	1981	1982	1983	1984	1985	1986	1987	1988	1989
At constant prices of:1985												
Final Consumption Expenditure of Resident Households												
1 Food, beverages and tobacco	9475	12437	15847	16214	16769	17847	18237	18851	20493	21775	23193	24774
2 Clothing and footwear	1318	2070	2630	2626	2429	2530	2598	2432	2614	2803	3063	3175
3 Gross rent, fuel and power	2837	3576	4617	4879	4845	5080	5354	5323	5658	5977	6376	6687
4 Furniture, furnishings and household equipment and operation	440	892	1451	1430	1592	1849	2248	2434	2870	3299	3802	4081
5 Medical care and health expenses	332	737	1171	1363	1720	2132	2550	2968	3280	3737	4259	4852
6 Transport and communication	905	1596	2876	3013	3487	3953	4424	4822	5259	6036	6736	7546
7 Recreational, entertainment, education and cultural services	1393	1954	2685	3147	3583	4057	4605	5152	5783	6494	7279	7991
8 Miscellaneous goods and services	1334	2149	2850	3062	3544	4012	4510	5383	5866	6398	7269	8315
Total Final Consumption Expenditure in the Domestic Market by Households, of which	18033	25411	34127	35733	37969	41459	44526	47365	51824	56519	61977	67420
A Durable goods	143	330	784	1063	1311	1803	2374	2772	3537	4628	5438	6179
B Semi-durable goods	1672	2900	3992	3963	3873	4154	4432	4559	5043	5425	6022	6442
C Non-durable goods	10785	14341	18629	19070	19765	21097	21848	22755	24760	26528	28597	30788

Korea, Republic of

2.6 Private Final Consumption Expenditure by Type and Purpose, in Constant Prices
(Continued)

Thousand Million Korean won

	1970	1975	1980	1981	1982	1983	1984	1985	1986	1987	1988	1989
					At constant prices of:1985							
D Services	5432	7839	10721	11637	13020	14405	15871	17280	18484	19938	21921	24012
Plus: Direct purchases abroad by resident households	21	24	140	223	331	261	293	323	197	221	403	764
Less: Direct purchases in the domestic market by non-resident households	44	211	282	319	345	385	441	557	1081	1555	1815	1679
Equals: Final Consumption Expenditure of Resident Households	18011	25224	33984	35637	37956	41335	44378	47131	50940	55185	60566	66505
			Final Consumption Expenditure of Private Non-profit Institutions Serving Households									
1 Research and science	62	93	139	70	63	144	198	235	252	269	295	318
2 Education												
3 Medical and other health services	21	36	60	75	99	118	149	177	186	200	221	248
4 Welfare services	29	34	50	51	53	58	65	68	76	78	84	89
5 Recreational and related cultural services	...	...	...	...	...	...	...	...	...	...	...	...
6 Religious organisations	...	...	...	...	...	...	...	...	...	...	...	...
7 Professional and labour organisations serving households	...	...	...	...	...	...	...	...	...	...	...	...
8 Miscellaneous	58	79	132	167	167	177	215	264	259	288	354	377
Equals: Final Consumption Expenditure of Private Non-profit Organisations Serving Households	169	243	382	363	381	497	627	744	772	835	954	1032
Private Final Consumption Expenditure	18180	25467	34366	36000	38337	41831	45006	47875	51712	56020	61520	67537

2.11 Gross Fixed Capital Formation by Kind of Activity of Owner, ISIC Divisions, in Current Prices

Thousand Million Korean won

	1970	1975	1980	1981	1982	1983	1984	1985	1986	1987	1988	1989
					All Producers							
1 Agriculture, hunting, forestry and fishing	109	281	1005	1045	1131	1400	1591	1632	1957	2536	2702	...
2 Mining and quarrying	3	16	85	113	125	132	154	172	166	155	158	...
3 Manufacturing	104	683	2796	2865	3153	3368	4648	5821	7549	10566	12331	...
4 Electricity, gas and water	35	168	1175	1449	1529	1926	1767	1832	1588	1671	1466	...
5 Construction	7	47	336	383	453	434	554	553	504	715	831	...
6 Wholesale and retail trade, restaurants and hotels	32	121	447	597	893	701	854	946	1360	1549	2110	...
7 Transport, storage and communication	14	238	1493	1934	1884	2877	2799	3069	3080	3076	3535	...
8 Finance, insurance, real estate and business services	231	749	2920	2615	3459	4607	4800	4628	5551	6105	8299	...
9 Community, social and personal services	21	79	261	282	399	403	547	504	622	688	950	...
Total Industries	554	2383	10518	11282	13026	15847	17715	19158	22378	27060	32381	...
Producers of Government Services	141	358	1708	1994	2420	2822	3283	3679	3615	4071	4973	...
Private Non-Profit Institutions Serving Households	...	...	...	...	...	...	...	...	...	...	...	...
Total	696	2741	12226	13276	15446	18669	20998	22837	25993	31131	37355	...

2.12 Gross Fixed Capital Formation by Kind of Activity of Owner, ISIC Divisions, in Constant Prices

Thousand Million Korean won

	1970	1975	1980	1981	1982	1983	1984	1985	1986	1987	1988	1989
					At constant prices of:1985							
					All Producers							
1 Agriculture, hunting, forestry and fishing	798	893	1336	1203	1187	1444	1579	1632	1948	2427	2355	...
2 Mining and quarrying	16	42	110	127	135	139	161	172	163	150	149	...
3 Manufacturing	657	1786	3598	3315	3436	3553	4869	5821	7280	10034	11439	...
4 Electricity, gas and water	217	436	1503	1670	1659	2031	1854	1832	1528	1576	1325	...

1049

Korea, Republic of

2.12 Gross Fixed Capital Formation by Kind of Activity of Owner, ISIC Divisions, in Constant Prices
(Continued)

Thousand Million Korean won

	1970	1975	1980	1981	1982	1983	1984	1985	1986	1987	1988	1989
					At constant prices of:1985							
5 Construction	42	123	427	435	483	449	568	553	501	700	795	...
6 Wholesale and retail trade, restaurants and hotels	204	316	574	679	961	740	956	946	1311	1478	1962	...
7 Transport, storage and communication	92	639	1969	2187	2063	3048	2933	3069	3088	3035	3328	...
8 Finance, insurance, real estate and business services	1506	2224	3714	2943	3725	4849	4948	4628	5520	5824	7126	...
9 Community, social and personal services	130	207	336	326	433	422	571	504	603	657	887	...
Total Industries	3662	6666	13567	12883	14080	16675	18439	19158	21942	25881	29366	...
Producers of Government Services	934	1001	2203	2243	2613	2986	3373	3679	3626	3918	4441	...
Private Non-Profit Institutions Serving Households	...	...	...	...	...	...	...	...	...	...	...	...
Total	4596	7667	15771	15126	16693	19662	21812	22837	25569	29800	33806	...

2.17 Exports and Imports of Goods and Services, Detail

Thousand Million Korean won

	1970	1975	1980	1981	1982	1983	1984	1985	1986	1987	1988	1989
					Exports of Goods and Services							
1 Exports of merchandise, f.o.b.	273	2451	10420	13885	14759	18047	21241	23018	29866	37919	43458	41142
2 Transport and communication	33	233	1584	2214	2583	2779	2971	2769	2903	3280	3533	3523
A In respect of merchandise imports	14	86	601	770	804	862	1020	967	895	972	1096	1116
B Other	19	147	984	1444	1779	1917	1951	1802	2008	2308	2437	2407
3 Insurance service charges	3	17	81	70	73	75	93	75	80	85	124	119
A In respect of merchandise imports	2	8	30	40	41	45	53	48	52	63	66	62
B Other	2	10	51	31	33	31	40	27	29	21	57	57
4 Other commodities	16	57	565	782	892	1310	1199	1313	1763	1771	1621	1607
5 Adjustments of merchandise exports to change-of-ownership basis	...	...	...	...	...	...	...	...	...	...	...	...
6 Direct purchases in the domestic market by non-residential households	7	68	201	275	318	368	430	557	1111	1650	2059	2015
7 Direct purchases in the domestic market by extraterritorial bodies	58	34	93	114	143	170	193	205	311	346	307	309
Total Exports of Goods and Services	390	2859	12944	17341	18770	22748	26126	27937	36034	45051	51101	48714
					Imports of Goods and Services							
1 Imports of merchandise, c.i.f.	614	3462	14237	17464	17893	20626	23561	24505	27711	33338	37049	40165
A Imports of merchandise, f.o.b.	558	3209	13054	16287	16718	19399	22067	23035	26174	31642	35175	38248
B Transport of services on merchandise imports	53	243	1149	1131	1128	1175	1430	1408	1465	1611	1786	1837
By residents	14	86	601	770	804	862	1020	967	895	972	1096	1116
By non-residents	39	158	549	361	324	313	410	441	570	640	690	721
C Insurance service charges on merchandise imports	2	9	34	46	47	52	63	62	72	85	88	80
By residents	2	8	30	40	41	45	53	48	52	63	66	62
By non-residents	-	2	4	6	7	8	11	14	20	21	22	18
2 Adjustments of merchandise imports to change-of-ownership basis	...	...	...	...	...	...	...	...	...	...	...	...
3 Other transport and communication	7	137	846	1115	1131	1122	1071	1177	1378	1618	1581	1760
4 Other insurance service charges	2	24	15	72	91	59	61	84	89	26	64	33
5 Other commodities	25	68	517	805	727	939	1028	765	854	995	1236	1781
6 Direct purchases abroad by government	9	31	74	102	82	83	55	67	84	81	80	88
7 Direct purchases abroad by resident households	2	7	85	161	250	220	264	323	250	299	556	965
Total Imports of Goods and Services	659	3728	15774	19719	20174	23049	26039	26919	30365	36356	40567	44791
Balance of Goods and Services	-269	-868	-2831	-2378	-1404	-300	87	1018	5669	8695	10535	3924
Total Imports and Balance of Goods and Services	390	2859	12944	17341	18770	22748	26126	27937	36034	45051	51101	48714

Korea, Republic of

4.1 Derivation of Value Added by Kind of Activity, in Current Prices

Thousand Million Korean won

	1980			1981			1982			1983		
	Gross Output	Intermediate Consumption	Value Added	Gross Output	Intermediate Consumption	Value Added	Gross Output	Intermediate Consumption	Value Added	Gross Output	Intermediate Consumption	Value Added
						All Producers						
1 Agriculture, hunting, forestry and fishing	7970	2292	5677	10443	3012	7431	11206	3217	7989	12572	3894	8678
A Agriculture and hunting	...	...	4838	...	...	6378	...	...	6918	...	...	7323
B Forestry and logging	...	...	372	...	...	429	...	...	444	...	...	586
C Fishing	...	...	467	...	...	623	...	...	627	...	...	769
2 Mining and quarrying	706	215	491	993	346	647	967	330	637	1060	372	689
A Coal mining	...	...	226	...	...	328	...	...	355	...	...	339
B Crude petroleum and natural gas production	...	...	...	...	...	...	...	...	...	...	...	...
C Metal ore mining	...	...	30	...	...	40	...	...	28	...	...	30
D Other mining	...	...	236	...	...	279	...	...	254	...	...	320
3 Manufacturing	48092	36794	11299	60297	46098	14199	66581	50673	15905	76435	57329	19106
A Manufacture of food, beverages and tobacco	10204	7916	2288	11883	9043	2840	13861	10541	3320	14804	11060	3744
B Textile, wearing apparel and leather industries	8146	6190	1956	10273	7855	2418	10542	8084	2458	11622	8881	2741
C Manufacture of wood and wood products, including furniture	948	795	153	1018	847	170	1093	892	201	1240	978	261
D Manufacture of paper and paper products, printing and publishing	1514	1089	425	1969	1411	558	2221	1597	624	2763	1955	808
E Manufacture of chemicals and chemical petroleum, coal, rubber and plastic products	11490	9073	2417	14507	11615	2892	15545	12253	3292	17446	13554	3891
F Manufacture of non-metallic mineral products, except products of petroleum and coal	1771	1219	552	1944	1340	605	2182	1510	672	2755	1855	900
G Basic metal industries	5411	4582	829	7007	5882	1125	7582	6293	1290	8810	7265	1545
H Manufacture of fabricated metal products, machinery and equipment	7979	5513	2466	10766	7481	3284	12586	8857	3729	15850	11022	4828
I Other manufacturing industries	631	417	214	929	623	306	969	647	322	1145	758	387
4 Electricity, gas and water	1963	1211	752	2678	1656	1022	3140	1932	1208	3486	1909	1577
A Electricity, gas and steam	...	...	703	...	...	949	...	...	1098	...	...	1451
B Water works and supply	...	...	49	...	...	73	...	...	110	...	...	126
5 Construction	7378	4192	3186	8023	4586	3437	9976	5765	4211	12223	7052	5171
6 Wholesale and retail trade, restaurants and hotels	7192	2350	4842	8938	2879	6059	10043	3146	6898	11352	3620	7733
A Wholesale and retail trade	...	...	4254	...	...	5357	...	...	6058	...	...	6776
B Restaurants and hotels	...	...	588	...	...	702	...	...	839	...	...	957
7 Transport, storage and communication	5554	2657	2897	7390	3516	3874	8680	4054	4626	9716	4550	5166
A Transport and storage	...	...	2348	...	...	3160	...	...	3559	...	...	3879
B Communication	...	...	549	...	...	714	...	...	1067	...	...	1287
8 Finance, insurance, real estate and business services	5359	1186	4173	6182	1590	4592	6823	2019	4804	8768	2456	6313
A Financial institutions	...	...	1793	...	...	1666	...	...	1091	...	...	1565
B Insurance	...	...	207	...	...	273	...	...	382	...	...	445
C Real estate and business services	...	...	2173	...	...	2653	...	...	3331	...	...	4303
9 Community, social and personal services	1958	704	1254	2478	925	1553	3089	1140	1950	3789	1374	2415
Total, Industries	86170	51600	34571	107422	64607	42814	120505	72275	48230	139401	82555	56846
Producers of Government Services	4963	2054	2910	6240	2623	3617	7211	2863	4347	8100	3247	4853
Other Producers	1040	335	704	1373	437	936	1737	526	1211	2071	599	1471
Total	92174	53989	38185	115034	67667	47367	129453	75665	53788	149572	86401	63170
Less: Imputed bank service charge	...	-1279	1279	...	-1324	1324	...	-887	887	...	-1383	1383
Import duties	1135	...	1135	1439	...	1439	1542	...	1542	2045	...	2045
Value added tax	...	...	...	...	...	...	...	...	...	...	...	...
Total	93309	55268	38041	116473	68991	47482	130995	76552	54443	151617	87784	63833

1051

Korea, Republic of

4.1 Derivation of Value Added by Kind of Activity, in Current Prices

Thousand Million Korean won

All Producers

	1984			1985			1986			1987		
	Gross Output	Intermediate Consumption	Value Added	Gross Output	Intermediate Consumption	Value Added	Gross Output	Intermediate Consumption	Value Added	Gross Output	Intermediate Consumption	Value Added
1 Agriculture, hunting, forestry and fishing	13655	4263	9392	14848	4496	10352	15605	4877	10729	16361	5008	11353
A Agriculture and hunting	...	...	7972	...	...	8799	...	...	8873	...	...	9324
B Forestry and logging	...	...	616	...	...	579	...	...	579	...	...	591
C Fishing	...	...	804	...	...	973	...	...	1277	...	...	1439
2 Mining and quarrying	1136	404	733	1272	481	791	1453	550	903	1533	617	916
A Coal mining	...	...	352	...	...	372	...	...	432	...	...	482
B Crude petroleum and natural gas production	...	...	...	...	...	...	...	...	...	...	...	...
C Metal ore mining	...	...	31	...	...	31	...	...	...	...	...	37
D Other mining	...	...	350	...	...	388	...	...	439	...	...	398
3 Manufacturing	88860	66185	22375	71067	24530	112256	82679	29679	133296	98393	34903	
A Manufacture of food, beverages and tobacco	16036	12004	4032	17205	12917	4288	19943	14522	4821	20470	15138	5332
B Textile, wearing apparel and leather industries	13450	10221	3230	14435	11028	3407	17421	13198	4223	21443	16081	5363
C Manufacture of wood and wood products, including furniture	1353	1063	290	1358	1055	303	1449	1108	340	1745	1306	439
D Manufacture of paper and paper products, printing and publishing	3216	2277	939	3439	2394	1045	4054	2790	1264	4881	3459	1422
E Manufacture of chemicals and chemical products, coal, rubber and plastic products	19769	15279	4490	21259	16251	5008	22418	16067	6351	24360	17233	7128
F Manufacture of non-metallic mineral products, except products of petroleum and coal	3183	2100	1083	3413	2237	1176	3892	2549	1343	4330	2834	1496
G Basic metal industries	10196	8337	1858	10712	8722	1991	10967	8936	2031	13081	10409	2672
H Manufacture of fabricated metal products, machinery and equipment	19969	13962	6007	22269	15443	6826	30520	21956	8564	40322	30009	10312
I Other manufacturing industries	1389	942	447	1508	1022	486	2195	1552	643	2664	1924	740
4 Electricity, gas and water	3837	1836	2000	4170	1903	2267	4480	1583	2897	5253	2056	3197
A Electricity, gas and steam	1849	...	...	2144	...	...	2736	...	...	3019	...	...
B Water works and supply	152	...	...	123	...	...	161	...	...	178	...	...
5 Construction	13531	7792	5739	14626	8722	6251	15060	8414	6646	17732	9966	8069
6 Wholesale and retail trade, restaurants and hotels	13093	4221	8872	14340	4506	9834	16850	5168	11682	19860	5891	13918
A Wholesale and retail trade	...	...	7855	...	...	8727	...	...	10293	...	...	12428
B Restaurants and hotels	...	...	1018	...	...	1107	...	...	1389	...	...	1491
7 Transport, storage and communication	10721	4932	5789	11445	5290	6155	12545	5427	7118	13948	5822	8126
A Transport and storage	...	...	4236	...	...	4441	...	...	5157	...	...	5711
B Communication	...	...	1553	...	...	1713	...	...	1961	...	...	2415
8 Finance, insurance, real estate and business services	10595	7532	3064	13128	3619	9509	15302	4261	11041	18263	5091	13173
A Financial institutions	...	...	1929	...	...	2608	...	...	2976	...	...	3683
B Insurance	...	...	495	...	...	606	...	...	740	...	...	859
C Real estate and business services	...	...	5108	...	...	6295	...	...	7325	...	...	8631
9 Community, social and personal services	4451	1598	2854	5211	1879	3332	5975	2138	3836	6583	2333	4250
Total, industries	159680	94294	65286	174638	73021	101617	199653	84433	115096	232778	134872	97906
Producers of Government Services	8599	3367	5232	8083	3956	5847	11235	4677	6558	12627	5122	7506
Other Producers	2370	672	1699	2808	761	2047	3109	796	2313	3455	872	2583
Total	170549	98333	72217	187249	106335	80915	213872	120569	93303	248860	140866	107995
Less: imputed bank service charge	-1726	1726	...	-2247	2247	...	-2594	2594	...	-2942	2942	...
Import duties	2153	...	2153	2180	...	2180	2717	...	2717	3376	...	3376
Value added tax	172703	100058	72644	189429	108582	80847	216589	123163	93426	252236	143808	108428

Korea, Republic of

4.1 Derivation of Value Added by Kind of Activity, in Current Prices

Thousand Million Korean won

	1988 Gross Output	Intermediate Consumption	Value Added
	All Producers		
1 Agriculture, hunting, forestry and fishing	18706	5212	13494
A Agriculture and hunting	...	...	11288
B Forestry and logging	...	...	645
C Fishing	...	...	1561
2 Mining and quarrying	1598	670	928
A Coal mining	...	...	529
B Crude petroleum and natural gas production	...	...	...
C Metal ore mining	...	...	29
D Other mining	...	...	370
3 Manufacturing	152229	110611	41617
A Manufacture of food, beverages and tobacco	22745	16515	6231
B Textile, wearing apparel and leather industries	21958	16542	5416
C Manufacture of wood and wood products, including furniture	2096	1533	564
D Manufacture of paper and paper products, printing and publishing	5718	4006	1712
E Manufacture of chemicals and chemical petroleum, coal, rubber and plastic products	28056	19500	8556
F Manufacture of non-metallic mineral products, except products of petroleum and coal	4995	3160	1835
G Basic metal industries	15291	11756	3535
H Manufacture of fabricated metal products, machinery and equipment	48627	35612	13015
I Other manufacturing industries	2742	1988	754
4 Electricity, gas and water	5887	2522	3365
A Electricity, gas and steam	...	...	3163
B Water works and supply	...	...	202
5 Construction	21382	11053	10329
6 Wholesale and retail trade, restaurants and hotels	22243	6434	15809
A Wholesale and retail trade	...	...	14098
B Restaurants and hotels	...	...	1711
7 Transport, storage and communication	15991	6751	9240
A Transport and storage	...	...	6431
B Communication	...	...	2809
8 Finance, insurance, real estate and business services	23079	6390	16689
A Financial institutions	...	...	5004
B Insurance	...	...	1164
C Real estate and business services	...	...	10520
9 Community, social and personal services	7451	2546	4905
Total, Industries	268564	152189	116375
Producers of Government Services	14774	6002	8773
Other Producers	4043	995	3048
Total	287381	159186	128196
Less: Imputed bank service charge	...	3730	-3730
Import duties	3497	...	3497
Value added tax			
Total	290878	162916	127963

Korea, Republic of

4.2 Derivation of Value Added by Kind of Activity, in Constant Prices

Thousand Million Korean won

	1980			1981			1982			1983		
	Gross Output	Intermediate Consumption	Value Added	Gross Output	Intermediate Consumption	Value Added	Gross Output	Intermediate Consumption	Value Added	Gross Output	Intermediate Consumption	Value Added
	At constant prices of:1985											
	All Producers											
1 Agriculture, hunting, forestry and fishing	11013	3356	7657	12249	3499	8750	12841	3440	9401	14218	4090	10129
A Agriculture and hunting	...	...	6262	...	...	7238	...	...	7985	...	...	8615
B Forestry and logging	...	...	601	...	...	608	...	...	503	...	...	620
C Fishing	...	...	794	...	...	904	...	...	913	...	...	894
2 Mining and quarrying	1107	331	775	1129	348	781	1041	341	700	1127	388	739
A Coal mining	...	...	359	...	...	380	...	...	371	...	...	358
B Crude petroleum and natural gas production	...	...	...	...	...	...	...	...	...	...	...	...
C Metal ore mining	...	...	27	...	...	29	...	...	29	...	...	30
D Other mining	...	...	390	...	...	372	...	...	300	...	...	351
3 Manufacturing	61242	46816	14426	65299	49448	15851	69297	52384	16914	79249	59732	19517
A Manufacture of food, beverages and tobacco	...	...	3099	...	...	3149	...	...	3428	...	...	3701
B Textile, wearing apparel and leather industries	...	...	2621	...	...	2839	...	...	2769	...	...	2879
C Manufacture of wood and wood products, including furniture	...	...	188	...	...	193	...	...	223	...	...	256
D Manufacture of paper and paper products, printing and publishing	...	...	526	...	...	603	...	...	678	...	...	843
E Manufacture of chemicals and chemical petroleum, coal, rubber and plastic products	...	...	3201	...	...	3321	...	...	3499	...	...	3947
F Manufacture of non-metallic mineral products, except products of petroleum and coal	...	...	702	...	...	673	...	...	717	...	...	906
G Basic metal industries	...	...	990	...	...	1153	...	...	1281	...	...	1526
H Manufacture of fabricated metal products, machinery and equipment	...	...	2839	...	...	3567	...	...	3971	...	...	5047
I Other manufacturing industries	...	...	260	...	...	354	...	...	348	...	...	413
4 Electricity, gas and water	2649	1623	1026	2862	1681	1181	3060	1812	1248	3548	1947	1601
A Electricity, gas and steam	...	...	925	...	...	1066	...	...	1126	...	...	1458
B Water works and supply	...	...	101	...	...	116	...	...	122	...	...	143
5 Construction	9262	5104	4158	8865	4918	3947	10569	5891	4678	12805	7134	5671
6 Wholesale and retail trade, restaurants and hotels	9863	3226	6637	10541	3393	7147	11216	3515	7701	12344	3931	8413
A Wholesale and retail trade	...	...	5785	...	...	6305	...	...	6779	...	...	7395
B Restaurants and hotels	...	...	852	...	...	842	...	...	922	...	...	1018
7 Transport, storage and communication	7768	3450	4318	8633	4099	4534	9072	4272	4800	9862	4639	5223
A Transport and storage	...	...	3324	...	...	3457	...	...	3764	...	...	3980
B Communication	...	...	994	...	...	1077	...	...	1037	...	...	1244
8 Finance, insurance, real estate and business services	7765	1825	5940	8148	2077	6071	9028	2395	6633	10149	2706	7443
A Financial institutions	...	...	1702	...	...	1523	...	...	1561	...	...	1730
B Insurance	...	...	286	...	...	314	...	...	415	...	...	466
C Real estate and business services	...	...	3952	...	...	4235	...	...	4658	...	...	5247
9 Community, social and personal services	2919	963	1956	3076	1051	2025	3431	1189	2242	3985	1396	2589
Total, Industries	113586	66694	46892	120801	70514	50287	129556	75239	54317	147288	85963	61325
Producers of Government Services	7779	2611	5168	8223	2859	5363	8461	2918	5543	8972	3300	5673
Other Producers	1752	460	1292	1873	495	1378	2038	537	1501	2247	596	1651
Total	123117	69765	53352	130897	73868	57029	140054	78694	61361	158507	89858	68649
Less: Imputed bank service charge	...	-1043	1043	...	-1158	1158	...	-1353	1353	...	-1545	1545
Import duties	1680	...	1680	1745	...	1745	1813	...	1813	1997	...	1997
Value added tax	...	...	...	...	...	...	...	...	...	...	...	...
Total	124797	70808	53989	132641	75026	57615	141868	80047	61821	160504	91403	69101

Korea, Republic of

4.2 Derivation of Value Added by Kind of Activity, in Constant Prices

Thousand Million Korean won

	1984			1985			1986			1987		
	Gross Output	Intermediate Consumption	Value Added	Gross Output	Intermediate Consumption	Value Added	Gross Output	Intermediate Consumption	Value Added	Gross Output	Intermediate Consumption	Value Added

At constant prices of:1985

All Producers

	GO	IC	VA	GO	IC	VA	GO	IC	VA	GO	IC	VA
1 Agriculture, hunting, forestry and fishing	14310	4333	9977	14848	4496	10352	15718	4888	10830	15403	5306	10098
A Agriculture and hunting	...	...	8428	...	...	8799	...	...	9235	...	...	8493
B Forestry and logging	...	...	633	...	...	579	...	...	490	...	...	514
C Fishing	...	...	917	...	...	973	...	...	1105	...	...	1090
2 Mining and quarrying	1189	427	762	1272	481	791	1383	527	856	1364	518	845
A Coal mining	...	...	369	...	...	372	...	...	423	...	...	426
B Crude petroleum and natural gas production	...	...	...	...	...	...	...	...	...	...	...	...
C Metal ore mining	...	...	30	...	...	31	...	...	33	...	...	32
D Other mining	...	...	364	...	...	388	...	...	400	...	...	388
3 Manufacturing	90106	67205	22901	95598	71067	24530	112511	83493	29018	131867	97407	34460
A Manufacture of food, beverages and tobacco	...	...	4086	...	...	4288	...	...	4651	...	...	5024
B Textile, wearing apparel and leather industries	...	...	3201	...	...	3407	...	...	3908	...	...	4538
C Manufacture of wood and wood products, including furniture	...	...	291	...	...	303	...	...	318	...	...	370
D Manufacture of paper and paper products, printing and publishing	...	...	973	...	...	1045	...	...	1194	...	...	1357
E Manufacture of chemicals and chemical petroleum, coal, rubber and plastic products	...	...	4637	...	...	5008	...	...	5798	...	...	6544
F Manufacture of non-metallic mineral products, except products of petroleum and coal	...	...	1085	...	...	1176	...	...	1354	...	...	1515
G Basic metal industries	...	...	1828	...	...	1991	...	...	1900	...	...	2208
H Manufacture of fabricated metal products, machinery and equipment	...	...	6317	...	...	6826	...	...	9185	...	...	12037
I Other manufacturing industries	...	...	484	...	...	486	...	...	709	...	...	866
4 Electricity, gas and water	3863	1865	1998	4170	1903	2267	4625	1784	2841	5661	2471	3190
A Electricity, gas and steam	...	...	1850	...	...	2144	...	...	2699	...	...	3039
B Water works and supply	...	...	148	...	...	123	...	...	142	...	...	151
5 Construction	13780	7793	5987	14626	8376	6251	15051	8491	6560	17104	9710	7394
6 Wholesale and retail trade, restaurants and hotels	13406	4322	9084	14340	4506	9834	16664	5198	11466	19025	5848	13177
A Wholesale and retail trade	...	...	8033	...	...	8727	...	...	10298	...	...	11940
B Restaurants and hotels	...	...	1051	...	...	1107	...	...	1168	...	...	1237
7 Transport, storage and communication	10786	4914	5872	11445	5290	6155	12513	5756	6757	13896	6264	7633
A Transport and storage	...	...	4306	...	...	4441	...	...	4735	...	...	5166
B Communication	...	...	1566	...	...	1713	...	...	2023	...	...	2467
8 Finance, insurance, real estate and business services	11413	3203	8211	13128	3619	9509	14758	4137	10621	17135	4828	12307
A Financial institutions	...	...	2069	...	...	2608	...	...	3034	...	...	3796
B Insurance	...	...	507	...	...	606	...	...	720	...	...	808
C Real estate and business services	...	...	5635	...	...	6295	...	...	6867	...	...	7703
9 Community, social and personal services	4577	1632	2946	5211	1879	3332	5823	2124	3700	6276	2285	3991
Total, Industries	163432	95694	67738	174638	101617	73021	199047	116398	82649	227731	134637	93094
Producers of Government Services	9120	3381	5738	9803	3956	5847	10775	4729	6045	11367	5118	6249
Other Producers	2487	666	1820	2808	761	2047	3024	792	2232	3241	859	2382
Total	175038	99741	75297	187249	106335	80915	212846	121920	90926	242338	140613	101725
Less: Imputed bank service charge		-1863	1863	...	-2247	2247	...	-2647	2647	...	-3047	3047
Import duties	2173	...	2173	2180	...	2180	2589	...	2589	3125	...	3125
Value added tax	...	...	...	...	...	...	...	...	...	...	...	...
Total	177211	101604	75606	189429	108582	80847	215435	124567	90868	245464	143660	101804

Korea, Republic of

4.2 Derivation of Value Added by Kind of Activity, in Constant Prices

Thousand Million Korean won

At constant prices of 1985
All Producers

	1988 Gross Output	1988 Intermediate Consumption	1988 Value Added	1989 Gross Output	1989 Intermediate Consumption	1989 Value Added
1 Agriculture, hunting, forestry and fishing	16335	5433	10903	16463	5638	10825
A Agriculture and hunting	...	...	9342	...	...	9176
B Forestry and logging	...	...	475	...	...	490
C Fishing	...	...	1086	...	...	1159
2 Mining and quarrying	1353	513	840	1258	474	784
A Coal mining	...	...	427	...	...	...
B Crude petroleum and natural gas production	...	...	...	...	...	...
C Metal ore mining	...	...	29	...	...	...
D Other mining	...	...	384	...	...	...
3 Manufacturing	148072	109086	39086	153172	112650	40522
A Manufacture of food, beverages and tobacco	...	...	5575	...	...	5878
B Textile, wearing apparel and leather industries	...	...	4580	...	...	4453
C Manufacture of wood and wood products, including furniture	...	...	419	...	...	436
D Manufacture of paper and paper products, printing and publishing	...	...	1540	...	...	1723
E Manufacture of chemicals and chemical petroleum, coal, rubber and plastic products	...	...	7604	...	...	7726
F Manufacture of non-metallic mineral products, except products of petroleum and coal	...	...	1738	...	...	1804
G Basic metal industries	...	...	2443	...	...	2873
H Manufacture of fabricated metal products, machinery and equipment	...	...	14310	...	...	14843
I Other manufacturing industries	...	...	878	...	...	785
4 Electricity, gas and water	6603	3099	3504	7356	3498	3858
A Electricity, gas and steam	...	...	3341	...	...	3679
B Water works and supply	...	...	164	...	...	179
5 Construction	18871	10774	8097	21909	12566	9343
6 Wholesale and retail trade, restaurants and hotels	20866	6232	14634	21452	6339	15114
A Wholesale and retail trade	...	...	13286	...	...	13657
B Restaurants and hotels	...	...	1348	...	...	1457
7 Transport, storage and communication	15571	7041	8530	16979	7610	9368
A Transport and storage	...	...	5642	...	...	5999
B Communication	...	...	2888	...	...	3370
8 Finance, insurance, real estate and business services	20120	5799	14322	22928	6892	16036
A Financial institutions	...	...	4698	...	...	5333
B Insurance	...	...	1019	...	...	1233
C Real estate and business services	...	...	8645	...	...	9470
9 Community, social and personal services	6849	2485	4364	7648	2757	4890
Total, Industries	254640	150361	104280	269164	158425	110740
Producers of Government Services	12468	5938	6530	13135	6312	6823
Other Producers	3611	976	2635	3649	1069	2580
Total	270719	157274	113445	286248	165805	120443
Less: Imputed bank service charge	...	3422	-3422	...	3964	-3964
Import duties	3469	...	3469	3950	...	3950
Value added tax	...	...	...	...	...	...
Total	274189	160697	113492	290198	169769	120429

Korea, Republic of

4.3 Cost Components of Value Added

Thousand Million Korean won

1980 / 1981

	Compensation of Employees	Capital Consumption	Net Operating Surplus	Indirect Taxes	Less: Subsidies Received	Value Added	Compensation of Employees	Capital Consumption	Net Operating Surplus	Indirect Taxes	Less: Subsidies Received	Value Added
	1980						1981					

All Producers

	Comp.	Cap.Cons.	NOS	Ind.Tax	Subs.	VA	Comp.	Cap.Cons.	NOS	Ind.Tax	Subs.	VA
1 Agriculture, hunting, forestry and fishing	736	147	4771	25	...	5677	895	188	6316	31	...	7431
2 Mining and quarrying	330	58	165	-61	...	491	383	82	222	-40	...	647
3 Manufacturing	4351	1296	3248	2403	...	11299	5488	1644	4142	2924	...	14199
A Manufacture of food, beverages and tobacco	503	134	391	1261	...	2288	619	167	486	1569	...	2840
B Textile, wearing apparel and leather industries	1017	216	622	101	...	1956	1251	270	772	125	...	2418
C Manufacture of wood and wood products, including furniture	122	20	-8	18	...	153	120	20	7	23	...	170
D Manufacture of paper and paper products, printing and publishing	235	35	125	29	...	425	307	47	167	36	...	558
E Manufacture of chemicals and chemical products, petroleum, coal, rubber and plastic products	746	307	883	481	...	2417	877	371	1080	564	...	2892
F Manufacture of non-metallic mineral products, except products of petroleum and coal	246	94	189	24	...	552	271	102	202	29	...	605
G Basic metal industries	291	221	292	25	...	829	395	299	400	31	...	1125
H Manufacture of fabricated metal products, machinery and equipment	1092	258	676	440	...	2466	1504	351	913	517	...	3284
I Other manufacturing industries	99	11	79	25	...	214	144	16	115	31	...	306
4 Electricity, gas and water	156	169	387	40	...	752	174	209	590	49	...	1022
5 Construction	1780	85	908	413	...	3186	1803	115	1064	455	...	3437
6 Wholesale and retail trade, restaurants and hotels	1230	188	3426	-2	...	4842	1520	234	4274	31	...	6059
7 Transport, storage and communication	1289	492	931	185	...	2897	1649	622	1339	265	...	3874
8 Finance, insurance, real estate and business services	1145	286	2410	332	...	4173	1437	373	2356	426	...	4592
9 Community, social and personal services	648	52	435	119	...	1254	809	65	532	146	...	1553
Total, Industries	11665	2772	16681	3454	...	34571	14159	3532	20836	4288	...	42814
Producers of Government Services	2745	163	-	2	...	2910	3407	209	-	2	...	3617
Other Producers	656	46	-	3	...	704	871	62	-	3	...	936
Total	15066	2980	16681	3458	...	38185	18436	3803	20836	4293	...	47367
Less: Imputed bank service charge	...	...	...	1279	...	1279	...	...	...	1324	...	1324
Import duties	...	...	...	1135	...	1135	...	...	...	1439	...	1439
Value added tax	15066	2980	15402	4593	...	38041	18436	3803	19512	5731	...	47482

1982 / 1983

All Producers

	Comp.	Cap.Cons.	NOS	Ind.Tax	Subs.	VA	Comp.	Cap.Cons.	NOS	Ind.Tax	Subs.	VA
1 Agriculture, hunting, forestry and fishing	911	227	6814	37	...	7989	1111	374	7152	41	...	8678
2 Mining and quarrying	368	121	177	-30	...	637	392	131	171	-5	...	689
3 Manufacturing	6160	1881	4596	3271	...	15908	7509	2236	5577	3784	...	19106
A Manufacture of food, beverages and tobacco	776	229	495	1819	...	3320	882	224	579	2058	...	3744

Korea, Republic of

4.3 Cost Components of Value Added
(Continued)

Thousand Million Korean won

	1982						1983					
	Compensation of Employees	Capital Consumption	Net Operating Surplus	Indirect Taxes	Less: Subsidies Received	Value Added	Compensation of Employees	Capital Consumption	Net Operating Surplus	Indirect Taxes	Less: Subsidies Received	Value Added
B Textile, wearing apparel and leather industries	1259	275	785	139	...	2458	1393	305	877	166	...	2741
C Manufacture of wood and wood products, including furniture	128	22	26	26	...	201	172	28	31	30	...	261
D Manufacture of paper and paper products, printing and publishing	348	51	184	41	...	624	451	67	241	49	...	808
E Manufacture of chemicals and chemical petroleum, coal, rubber and plastic products	1008	423	1271	591	...	3292	1204	491	1498	699	...	3891
F Manufacture of non-metallic mineral products, except products of petroleum and coal	300	115	224	33	...	672	400	156	305	40	...	900
G Basic metal industries	457	346	452	35	...	1290	555	411	537	42	...	1545
H Manufacture of fabricated metal products, machinery and equipment	1733	403	1038	554	...	3729	2271	533	1364	661	...	4828
I Other manufacturing industries	151	17	121	33	...	322	182	21	145	39	...	387
4 Electricity, gas and water	188	630	333	57	...	1208	301	407	796	73	...	1577
5 Construction	2134	157	1329	592	...	4211	2594	201	1605	771	...	5171
6 Wholesale and retail trade, restaurants and hotels	1716	262	4787	132	...	6898	1940	297	5411	86	...	7733
7 Transport, storage and communication	1813	848	1641	324	...	4626	2369	960	1441	396	...	5166
8 Finance, insurance, real estate and business services	1762	484	1975	583	...	4804	2125	657	2767	763	...	6313
9 Community, social and personal services	1020	83	665	181	...	1950	1265	106	823	220	...	2415
Total, Industries	16072	4397	22613	5148	...	48230	19606	5370	25743	6127	...	56846
Producers of Government Services	4094	251	-	2	...	4347	4565	285	-	2	...	4853
Other Producers	1127	80	-	4	...	1211	1369	98	-	5	...	1471
Total	21293	4728	22613	5153	...	53788	25540	5753	25743	6134	...	63170
Less: Imputed bank service charge	...	...	...	887	...	887	...	...	...	1383	...	1383
Import duties	...	...	...	1542	...	1542	...	...	...	2045	...	2045
Value added tax	...	...	...	...	...	...	...	...	...	...	...	...
Total a	21293	4728	22613	5695	...	54443	25540	5753	24360	8180	...	63833

	1984						1985					
	Compensation of Employees	Capital Consumption	Net Operating Surplus	Indirect Taxes	Less: Subsidies Received	Value Added	Compensation of Employees	Capital Consumption	Net Operating Surplus	Indirect Taxes	Less: Subsidies Received	Value Added

All Producers

1 Agriculture, hunting, forestry and fishing	1165	404	7777	46	...	9392	1260	443	8598	51	...	10352
2 Mining and quarrying	423	143	172	-6	...	733	530	136	131	-6	...	791
3 Manufacturing	8868	2765	6616	4126	...	22375	9417	3083	7663	4369	...	24530
A Manufacture of food, beverages and tobacco	1007	240	571	2214	...	4032	962	282	710	2334	...	4288
B Textile, wearing apparel and leather industries	1596	415	1041	178	...	3230	1819	358	1043	187	...	3407
C Manufacture of wood and wood products, including furniture	186	29	42	33	...	290	150	31	88	34	...	303
D Manufacture of paper and paper products, printing and publishing	488	84	315	52	...	939	558	106	327	54	...	1045
E Manufacture of chemicals and chemical petroleum, coal, rubber and plastic products	1337	595	1775	782	...	4490	1568	685	1925	831	...	5008
F Manufacture of non-metallic mineral products, except products of petroleum and coal	489	167	384	43	...	1083	470	227	435	45	...	1176
G Basic metal industries	642	552	620	45	...	1858	597	470	875	49	...	1991
H Manufacture of fabricated metal products, machinery and equipment	2914	656	1699	738	...	6007	3048	891	2098	789	...	6826
I Other manufacturing industries	209	27	168	43	...	447	245	33	163	45	...	486
4 Electricity, gas and water	248	469	1201	82	...	2000	399	703	1075	90	...	2267

Korea, Republic of

4.3 Cost Components of Value Added (Continued)

Thousand Million Korean won

1984

	Compensation of Employees	Capital Consumption	Net Operating Surplus	Indirect Taxes	Less: Subsidies Received	Value Added
5 Construction	2916	1734	5739	834	...	6251
6 Wholesale and retail trade, restaurants and hotels	2219	343	6277	33	...	8834
7 Transport, storage and communication	2620	1126	1611	433	...	5155
8 Finance, insurance, real estate and business services	2393	797	3534	808	...	6509
9 Community, social and personal services	1506	129	983	236	...	3332
Total, Industries	22359	6429	29906	6592	...	73021
Producers of Government Services	4911	320	-	2	...	5847
Other Producers	1580	114	-	5	...	2047
Total	28849	6862	29906	6599	...	80915
Less: Imputed bank service charge	...	...	...	1726	...	2247
Import duties	...	...	...	2153	...	2180
Value added tax	...	...	...	...	...	...
Total a	28850	6862	28180	8753	...	80847

1985

	Compensation of Employees	Capital Consumption	Net Operating Surplus	Indirect Taxes	Less: Subsidies Received	Value Added
5 Construction	3203	291	1858	899	...	6251
6 Wholesale and retail trade, restaurants and hotels	2427	376	6882	150	...	9834
7 Transport, storage and communication	2736	1248	1663	508	...	6155
8 Finance, insurance, real estate and business services	2811	1023	4767	909	...	9509
9 Community, social and personal services	1775	150	1156	250	...	3332
Total, Industries	24657	7452	33792	7219	...	73021
Producers of Government Services	5508	337	-	2	...	5847
Other Producers	1904	136	-	7	...	2047
Total	31969	7926	33792	7228	...	80915
Less: Imputed bank service charge	...	...	...	2247	...	2247
Import duties	...	...	...	2180	...	2180
Value added tax	...	...	...	...	...	...
Total a	31969	7926	31545	9407	...	80847

All Producers

1986

	Compensation of Employees	Capital Consumption	Net Operating Surplus	Indirect Taxes	Less: Subsidies Received	Value Added
1 Agriculture, hunting, forestry and fishing	1407	464	8806	52	...	10729
2 Mining and quarrying	570	150	183	-6	...	903
3 Manufacturing	10993	3597	10044	4946	...	29579
A Manufacture of food, beverages and tobacco	1129	347	697	2648	...	4821
B Textile, wearing apparel and leather industries	2003	449	1559	213	...	4223
C Manufacture of wood and wood products, including furniture	168	34	100	39	...	341
D Manufacture of paper and paper products, printing and publishing	681	124	397	62	...	1264
E Manufacture of chemicals and chemical products, petroleum, coal, rubber and plastic products	1796	811	2807	937	...	6351
F Manufacture of non-metallic mineral products, except products of petroleum and coal	533	264	494	52	...	1343
G Basic metal industries	567	424	995	45	...	2031
H Manufacture of fabricated metal products, machinery and equipment	3796	1101	2772	894	...	8564
I Other manufacturing industries	320	44	224	55	...	643
4 Electricity, gas and water	385	712	1699	102	...	2897
5 Construction	3401	317	1910	1019	...	6646
6 Wholesale and retail trade, restaurants and hotels	2815	433	8240	195	...	11682
7 Transport, storage and communication	3043	1437	2071	567	...	7118
8 Finance, insurance, real estate and business services	3217	1224	5609	995	...	11041
9 Community, social and personal services	2048	169	1341	278	...	3836
Total, Industries	27878	8502	39906	8147	...	84433
Producers of Government Services	6176	380	-	1	...	6558
Other Producers	2156	149	8	2313	...	4625 (?)
Total	36210	9032	39906	8156	...	93303
Less: Imputed bank service charge	...	...	...	2594	...	2594
Import duties	...	...	...	2717	...	2717
Value added tax	...	...	...	...	...	...
Total a	36210	9032	37312	10872	...	93426

1987

	Compensation of Employees	Capital Consumption	Net Operating Surplus	Indirect Taxes	Less: Subsidies Received	Value Added
1 Agriculture, hunting, forestry and fishing	1407	464	8806	52	56	11353
2 Mining and quarrying	570	199	153	903	-4	916
3 Manufacturing	10993	45295	13721	...	5339	34903
A Manufacture of food, beverages and tobacco	...	1341	374	833	2785	5332
B Textile, wearing apparel and leather industries	...	2568	608	1947	240	5363
C Manufacture of wood and wood products, including furniture	...	188	37	170	44	439
D Manufacture of paper and paper products, printing and publishing	...	741	151	460	70	1422
E Manufacture of chemicals and chemical products, petroleum, coal, rubber and plastic products	...	2324	884	2894	1026	7128
F Manufacture of non-metallic mineral products, except products of petroleum and coal	...	594	320	523	59	1496
G Basic metal industries	...	743	694	1182	53	2672
H Manufacture of fabricated metal products, machinery and equipment	...	4896	1477	2934	1006	10312
I Other manufacturing industries	...	643	326	50	307	57	740
4 Electricity, gas and water	...	2897	451	826	1810	111	3197
5 Construction	...	9446	4376	383	2165	1146	8008
6 Wholesale and retail trade, restaurants and hotels	...	11682	3494	515	9616	293	13918
7 Transport, storage and communication	...	7118	3467	1792	2202	665	8126
8 Finance, insurance, real estate and business services	...	11041	3809	1475	6641	1247	13173
9 Community, social and personal services	...	3836	2293	188	1460	309	4250
Total, Industries	...	33671	10449	44625	9162	97906
Producers of Government Services	...	7086	419	-	2	7506
Other Producers	...	2407	167	-	9	2583
Total	...	43163	11034	44625	9172	107995
Less: Imputed bank service charge	...	...	2942	...	2942
Import duties	...	...	...	3376	...	3376
Value added tax	...	...	...	...	...	...
Total a	...	43163	11034	41683	12548	108428

Korea, Republic of

4.3 Cost Components of Value Added

Thousand Million Korean won

	1988					
	Compensation of Employees	Capital Consumption	Net Operating Surplus	Indirect Taxes	Less: Subsidies Received	Value Added
	All Producers					
1 Agriculture, hunting, forestry and fishing	1619	573	11240	62	...	13494
2 Mining and quarrying	628	151	148	1	...	928
3 Manufacturing	17299	5702	12291	6325	...	41617
A Manufacture of food, beverages and tobacco	1644	434	798	3354	...	6231
B Textile, wearing apparel and leather industries	2972	670	1497	277	...	5416
C Manufacture of wood and wood products, including furniture	237	56	220	51	...	564
D Manufacture of paper and paper products, printing and publishing	906	184	542	80	...	1712
E Manufacture of chemicals and chemical petroleum, coal, rubber and plastic products	2853	1022	3511	1170	...	8556
F Manufacture of non-metallic mineral products, except products of petroleum and coal	758	362	645	70	...	1835
G Basic metal industries	947	881	1637	70	...	3535
H Manufacture of fabricated metal products, machinery and equipment	6551	2023	3252	1189	...	13015
I Other manufacturing industries	432	69	188	66	...	754
4 Electricity, gas and water	529	974	1738	124	...	3365
5 Construction	5947	444	2620	1318	...	10329
6 Wholesale and retail trade, restaurants and hotels	3923	580	10788	518	...	15809
7 Transport, storage and communication	4229	2094	2147	770	...	9240
8 Finance, insurance, real estate and business services	4846	1817	8201	1825	...	16689
9 Community, social and personal services	2688	216	1633	368	...	4905
Total, Industries	41707	12552	50806	11311	...	116375
Producers of Government Services	8285	486	-	2	...	8773
Other Producers	2843	194	-	12	...	3048
Total	52835	13231	50806	11324	...	128196
Less: Imputed bank service charge	...	...	3730	...	...	3730
Import duties	...	...	...	3497	...	3497
Value added tax	...	...	...	...	...	...
Total a	52835	13231	47076	14821	...	127963

a) Column 4 refers to indirect taxes less subsidies received.

Kuwait

Source. Reply to the United Nations National Accounts Questionnaire from the Central Office of Statistics, Ministry of Planning, Kuwait City. Official estimates are published by the same Office in 'National Accounts Statistics' and 'National Accounts and Input-output Tables of Kuwait', 1976.

General note. The estimates shown in the following tables have been prepared in accordance with the United Nations System of National Accounts so far as the existing data would permit.

1.1 Expenditure on the Gross Domestic Product, in Current Prices

Million Kuwaiti dinars

	1970	1975	1980	1981	1982	1983	1984	1985	1986	1987	1988	1989
1 Government final consumption expenditure	139	386	865	993	1190	1287	1345	1445	1403	1369	1351	1603
2 Private final consumption expenditure	396	756	2325	2630	3344	2649	2735	3084	2683	2823	2988	3162
3 Gross capital formation	124	444	1078	1162	1426	1455	1351	1216	1150	1001	980	1336
A Increase in stocks	-2	26	105	89	129	-18	-8	-61	23	-10	20	44
B Gross fixed capital formation	126	418	973	1073	1297	1473	1359	1277	1127	1011	960	1292
Residential buildings					...	...	...	...	...	...	...	...
Non-residential buildings	63	155	607	636	...	...	...	...	...	...	...	...
Other construction and land improvement etc.					...	...	...	...	...	...	...	...
Other	63	263	366	437	...	...	...	...	...	...	...	...
4 Exports of goods and services	614	2806	6065	4855	3386	3597	3862	3462	2403	3275	2746	3725
5 Less: Imports of goods and services	248	907	2577	2601	3132	2904	2868	2757	2498	2314	2479	3047
Statistical discrepancy	1	-1	...	...	...	...	...	...	...	...	...	...
Equals: Gross Domestic Product a	1026	3485	7755	7039	6214	6083	6425	6450	5141	6154	5586	6779

a) Data in this table have been revised, therefore they are not strictly comparable with the unrevised data in the other tables.

1.2 Expenditure on the Gross Domestic Product, in Constant Prices

Million Kuwaiti dinars

	1970	1975	1980	1981	1982	1983	1984	1985	1986	1987	1988	1989
					At constant prices of:1984							
1 Government final consumption expenditure	461	750	1103	1096	1249	1306	1345	1390	1287	1227	...	...
2 Private final consumption expenditure	970	1286	2849	3006	3543	2681	2735	3041	2620	2738	...	...
3 Gross capital formation	284	637	1150	1160	1363	1411	1351	1216	1015	929	...	...
A Increase in stocks	-5	38	114	91	131	-18	-8	-62	-23	-10	...	...
B Gross fixed capital formation	289	599	1036	1069	1232	1429	1359	1278	1038	939	...	...
4 Exports of goods and services	8898	6497	5667	4171	2968	3516	3862	3520	3953	4164	...	...
5 Less: Imports of goods and services	491	1204	2798	2601	2802	2816	2868	2765	2276	2067	...	...
Statistical discrepancy	-255	-140	-66	-423	-665	7	-	-252	31	-586	...	...
Equals: Gross Domestic Product	9867	7826	7905	6409	5656	6105	6425	6150	6630	6405	...	...

1.3 Cost Components of the Gross Domestic Product

Million Kuwaiti dinars

	1970	1975	1980	1981	1982	1983	1984	1985	1986	1987	1988	1989
1 Indirect taxes, net	...	...	41	56	22	-16	-14	-2	...	...	...	...
A Indirect taxes	...	...	72	92	99	86	74	68	...	...	...	...
B Less: Subsidies	...	...	31	36	77	102	88	70	...	...	...	...
2 Consumption of fixed capital	...	...	263	290	337	346	403	401	...	...	...	...
3 Compensation of employees paid by resident producers to:	...	...	1197	1387	1623	1779	1854	1852	...	...	...	...
4 Operating surplus	...	...	6240	5253	4230	4025	4138	3667	...	...	...	...
Equals: Gross Domestic Product	...	...	7741	6986	6212	6134	6381	5918	...	...	...	...

Kuwait

1.7 External Transactions on Current Account, Summary

Million Kuwaiti dinars

	1970	1975	1980	1981	1982	1983	1984	1985	1986	1987	1988	1989
Payments to the Rest of the World												
1 Imports of goods and services	248	907	2655	2688	3253	3063	3037	2929	2464	...	...	...
2 Factor income to the rest of the world	212	106	173	206	217	197	248	200	175	...	...	...
3 Current transfers to the rest of the world	54	310	427	463	438	452	408	473	368			
4 Surplus of the nation on current transactions	203	1813	4293	3841	1404	1542	1887	1448	1790			
Payments to the Rest of the World and Surplus of the Nation on Current Transactions	717	3136	7548	7198	5312	5254	5580	5050	4797			
Receipts From The Rest of the World												
1 Exports of goods and services	614	2806	6065	4855	3386	3596	3862	3463	2442	...	...	...
2 Factor income from rest of the world	103	330	1483	2343	1926	1658	1718	1587	2355	...	...	...
3 Current transfers from rest of the world	...	...	...	...	...	...	...	...	...	...	...	...
Receipts from the Rest of the World on Current Transactions	717	3136	7548	7198	5312	5254	5580	5050	4797	...	...	...

1.10 Gross Domestic Product by Kind of Activity, in Current Prices

Million Kuwaiti dinars

	1970	1975	1980	1981	1982	1983	1984	1985	1986	1987	1988	1989
1 Agriculture, hunting, forestry and fishing	2	6	14	24	23	18	28	39	42	42	50	46
2 Mining and quarrying	619	2459	5089	4121	2765	3029	3398	3185	1679	2298	1720	2773
3 Manufacturing	43	195	427	415	314	364	309	383	546	825	755	974
4 Electricity, gas and water a	7	13	-74	-167	-231	-216	-180	-152	-70	-31	-42	-43
5 Construction	28	74	278	263	262	273	271	259	181	157	153	155
6 Wholesale and retail trade, restaurants and hotels	85	221	595	664	742	548	564	568	559	535	529	555
7 Transport, storage and communication	29	60	181	215	292	273	267	271	259	253	263	272
8 Finance, insurance, real estate and business services	78	150	523	629	1171	838	729	809	763	854	882	787
9 Community, social and personal services	18	34	660	798	923	1016	1069	1155	1212	1261	1279	1281
Total, Industries	...	...	...	...	...	...	...	...	...	...	...	...
Producers of Government Services	...	...	...	...	...	...	...	...	...	...	...	...
Other Producers	...	...	...	...	...	...	...	...	...	...	...	...
Subtotal	1019	3461	7693	6962	6261	6143	6455	6517	5171	6194	5589	6800
Less: Imputed bank service charge	...	...	...	...	130	134	95	128	92	98	61	80
Plus: Import duties	7	24	61	78	83	74	64	60	60	57	58	59
Plus: Value added tax	...	...	...	...	...	...	...	...	...	...	...	...
Equals: Gross Domestic Product b	1026	3485	7755	7039	6214	6083	6425	6450	5141	6154	5586	6779

a) Beginning 1980, the cost of fuel (natural gas, crude petroleum and gas-oil) consumed in the production of electricity and water has been taken into account as intermediate consumption in estimating the value added of item 'Electricity, gas and water'.   b) Data in this table have been revised, therefore they are not strictly comparable with the unrevised data in the other tables.

1.11 Gross Domestic Product by Kind of Activity, in Constant Prices

Million Kuwaiti dinars

	1970	1975	1980	1981	1982	1983	1984	1985	1986	1987	1988	1989
At constant prices of:1984												
1 Agriculture, hunting, forestry and fishing	12	12	13	21	19	18	28	41	44	61	...	...
2 Mining and quarrying	8735	6096	4861	3295	2404	3115	3398	3099	3763	3497	...	...
3 Manufacturing	132	255	294	285	310	308	300	314	319	346	...	...
4 Electricity, gas and water	-30	-61	-118	-130	-151	-163	-180	-198	-216	-234	...	...
5 Construction	69	125	341	300	278	276	271	255	177	152	...	...
6 Wholesale and retail trade, restaurants and hotels	207	364	714	745	784	556	564	565	553	520	...	...
7 Transport, storage and communication	68	97	225	250	311	276	267	267	240	218	...	...
8 Finance, insurance, real estate and business services	211	274	593	638	674	692	729	749	749	755	...	...
9 Community, social and personal services	55	75	918	930	996	1041	1087	1093	1088	1122	...	...

Kuwait

1.11 Gross Domestic Product by Kind of Activity, in Constant Prices
(Continued)

Million Kuwaiti dinars

	1970	1975	1980	1981	1982	1983	1984	1985	1986	1987	1988	1989
					At constant prices of:1984							
Total, Industries	...	...	...	...	...	...	...	...	...	...	...	...
Producers of Government Services	...	...	...	...	...	...	...	...	...	...	...	...
Other Producers	...	...	...	...	...	...	...	...	...	...	...	...
Subtotal	9852	7795	7841	6334	5625	6119	6455	3185	6717	6437	...	...
Less: Imputed bank service charge	...	...	...	...	44	76	95	91	90	83	...	...
Plus: Import duties	15	32	67	78	75	71	64	60	54	51	...	...
Plus: Value added tax	...	...	...	...	...	...	...	...	...	...	...	...
Equals: Gross Domestic Product a	9867	7827	7905	6409	5656	6105	6425	6150	6630	6403	...	...

a) Data in this table have been revised, therefore they are not strictly comparable with the unrevised data in the other tables.

1.12 Relations Among National Accounting Aggregates

Million Kuwaiti dinars

	1970	1975	1980	1981	1982	1983	1984	1985	1986	1987	1988	1989
Gross Domestic Product	1026	3485	7741	6986	6212	6134	6381	5830	4816	6154	5586	6779
Plus: Net factor income from the rest of the world	-110	224	1310	2137	1709	1461	1470	1388	2182	1504	1978	2375
Factor income from the rest of the world	103	330	1483	2343	1926	1658	1718	...	...	...	...	...
Less: Factor income to the rest of the world	213	106	173	206	217	197	248	...	...	...	...	...
Equals: Gross National Product	916	3709	9051	9123	7921	7595	7851	7218	6998	7658	7564	9154
Less: Consumption of fixed capital	58	93	263	290	337	345	403	431	464	521	532	542
Equals: National Income	858	3616	8788	8833	7584	7250	7448	6787	6534	7136	7033	8612
Plus: Net current transfers from the rest of the world	-54	-310	-427	-463	-438	-452	-408	-473	-368	-351	-368	-440
Current transfers from the rest of the world	...	...	...	...	...	...	...	...	...	...	...	...
Less: Current transfers to the rest of the world	54	310	427	463	438	452	408	473	368	351	...	...
Equals: National Disposable Income	804	3306	8361	8370	7146	6798	7040	6314	6166	6785	6665	8172
Less: Final consumption	535	1142	3253	3657	4514	4094	4235	3814	3844	4192	4339	4765
Equals: Net Saving	269	2164	5108	4713	2632	2703	2805	2500	2322	2593	2326	3407
Less: Surplus of the nation on current transactions	203	1813	4293	3841	1404	1541	1887	1634	1741	2114	1877	2613
Equals: Net Capital Formation a	66	351	815	872	1228	1162	918	866	582	479	449	794

a) Data in this table have been revised, therefore they are not strictly comparable with the unrevised data in the other tables.

2.1 Government Final Consumption Expenditure by Function, in Current Prices

Million Kuwaiti dinars

	1970	1975	1980	1981	1982	1983	1984	1985	1986	1987	1988	1989
1 General public services										...	...	...
2 Defence	60	195	412	467	571	636	673	749	708	...	...	...
3 Public order and safety										...	...	...
4 Education	33	90	197	225	269	283	295	316	332	...	...	...
5 Health	16	39	102	126	159	168	173	182	187	...	...	...
6 Social security and welfare	2	6	22	26	30	29	30	31	34	...	...	...
7 Housing and community amenities	7	18	43	51	60	70	75	65	69	...	...	...
8 Recreational, cultural and religious affairs	6	16	33	36	42	47	51	52	53	...	...	...
9 Economic services	15	22	56	62	66	65	60	62	62	...	...	...
10 Other functions	...	...	...	...	...	...	...	...	...	...	...	...
Total Government Final Consumption Expenditure	139	386	865	993	1197	1298	1356	1457	1445	...	...	...

1063

Kuwait

2.2 Government Final Consumption Expenditure by Function, in Constant Prices

Million Kuwaiti dinars

At constant prices of 1984

	1970	1975	1980	1981	1982	1983	1984	1985	1986	1987	1988	1989
1 General public services												
2 Defence	208	382	517	469	569	638	673	707	623			
3 Public order and safety												
4 Education	113	183	280	287	310	309	295	306	310			
5 Health	49	72	128	146	164	165	173	173	169			
6 Social security and welfare	7	13	25	29	31	27	30	31	34			
7 Housing and community amenities	24	34	54	63	69	74	74	75	75			
8 Recreational, cultural and religious affairs	21	30	43	46	49	49	51	51	51			
9 Economic services	39	36	61	60	63	54	60	58	56			
10 Other functions	...	...	...	...	...	...	...	...	...			
Total Government Final Consumption Expenditure	461	750	1108	1100	1255	1316	1356	1401	1318	...	...	...

4.1 Derivation of Value Added by Kind of Activity, in Current Prices

Million Kuwaiti dinars

	1980 Gross Output	1980 Intermediate Consumption	1980 Value Added	1981 Gross Output	1981 Intermediate Consumption	1981 Value Added	1982 Gross Output	1982 Intermediate Consumption	1982 Value Added	1983 Gross Output	1983 Intermediate Consumption	1983 Value Added
All Producers												
1 Agriculture, hunting, forestry and fishing	27	28		13	13		37	24	13	45	16	29	28
A Agriculture and hunting	24	23		11	12		29	17	12	38	15	23	39	16	23
B Forestry and logging												
C Fishing	3	5	-	2	1		8	7	1	7	5	2	9	1	9	1	5
2 Mining and quarrying	5134	45	5089	4165	44	4121	2819	54	2765	3096	56	3040
A Coal mining												
B Crude petroleum and natural gas production	5125	39	5086	4153	38	4115	2816	53	2763	3093	55	3038
C Metal ore mining	...	...	...	...	...	...	...	...	...	...	...	...
D Other mining	9	6	3	12	6	6	3	2	1	3	1	2
3 Manufacturing	1702	275	1427	1759	415	1344	2084	308	1776	2112	375	1737
A Manufacture of food, beverages and tobacco	78	49	29	79	50	29	90	58	32	96	58	38
B Textile, wearing apparel and leather industries	33	10	23	31	10	21	35	12	23	36	12	24
C Manufacture of wood and wood products, including furniture	43	24	19	45	25	20	35	20	15	32	17	15
D Manufacture of paper and paper products, printing and publishing	25	12	13	31	15	16	34	17	17	34	18	16
E Manufacture of chemicals and chemical products, petroleum, coal, rubber and plastic products	1333	264	1069	1334	232	1102	1627	111	1516	1674	183	1491
F Manufacture of non-metallic mineral products, except products of petroleum and coal	84	54	30	95	63	32	122	82	40	112	69	43
G Basic metal industries	6	3	3	6	2	4	7	3	4	8	4	4
H Manufacture of fabricated metal products, machinery and equipment	94	53	41	136	61	75	132	67	65	118	67	51
I Other manufacturing industries	3	1	2	2	-	2	2	1	1	2	1
4 Electricity, gas and water a	44	118	-74	51	217	-166	52	282	-230	58	279	-221
A Electricity, gas and steam	19	91	-72	24	172	-148	24	224	-200	29	221	-192
B Water works and supply	25	27	-2	27	45	-18	28	58	-30	29	58	-29
5 Construction	627	349	278	594	263	331	592	330	262	665	391	274
6 Wholesale and retail trade, restaurants and hotels	760	165	595	848	184	664	965	197	768	758	212	546
A Wholesale and retail trade	691	137	554	771	153	618	878	163	715	672	174	498
B Restaurants and hotels	69	28	41	77	31	46	87	34	53	86	38	48
7 Transport, storage and communication	323	142	181	376	161	215	457	166	291	435	160	275
A Transport and storage	289	139	150	326	157	169	402	162	240	375	156	219
B Communication	34	3	31	50	4	46	55	4	51	60	4	56
8 Finance, insurance, real estate and business services	580	71	509	659	81	578	1083	61	1022	797	61	736
A Financial institutions	192	25	167	248	32	216	390	23	367	312	21	291

Kuwait

4.1 Derivation of Value Added by Kind of Activity, in Current Prices
(Continued)

Million Kuwaiti dinars

	1980 Gross Output	1980 Intermediate Consumption	1980 Value Added	1981 Gross Output	1981 Intermediate Consumption	1981 Value Added	1982 Gross Output	1982 Intermediate Consumption	1982 Value Added	1983 Gross Output	1983 Intermediate Consumption	1983 Value Added
B Insurance	19	4	15	20	4	16	22	4	18	23	5	18
C Real estate and business services	370	43	327	391	45	346	671	34	637	462	35	427
9 Community, social and personal services	118	38	80	134	43	91	128	30	98	133	33	100
A Sanitary and similar services	5	1	4	7	1	6	11	1	10	12	3	9
B Social and related community services	25	8	17	28	8	18	30	8	22	35	10	25
Educational services	14	4	10	14	4	13	9	16	11
Medical, dental, other health and veterinary services	11	4	7	12	4	8	17	4	13	19	5	14
C Recreational and cultural services	3	1	2	4	2	2	5	1	4	4	2	2
D Personal and household services	85	28	57	97	32	65	82	17	65	82	18	64
Total, Industries	9317	2217	7100	8623	2418	6205	8225	2912	5313	8099	2946	5153
Producers of Government Services	876	319	557	1006	324	682	1214	420	794	1317	434	883
Other Producers	28	6	22	25	5	20	27	5	22	28	5	23
Total	10222	2542	7680	9654	2747	6907	9466	3337	6129	9444	3385	6059
Less: Imputed bank service charge	61	-	61	78	-	78	83	-	83	74	-	74
Import duties	61	-	61	78	-	78	83	-	83	74	-	74
Value added tax												
Total	10282	2542	7740	9732	2747	6985	9549	3337	6212	9518	3385	6133

All Producers

	1984 Gross Output	1984 Intermediate Consumption	1984 Value Added	1985 Gross Output	1985 Intermediate Consumption	1985 Value Added	1986 Gross Output	1986 Intermediate Consumption	1986 Value Added	1987 Value Added
1 Agriculture, hunting, forestry and fishing	55	20	35	62	23	39	52	...	...	42
A Agriculture and hunting	49	19	30	56	22	34	48	...	...	36
B Forestry and logging	...	...	...	...	...	...	...	...	...	...
C Fishing	6	1	5	6	1	5	4	...	...	6
2 Mining and quarrying	3453	50	3403	3037	53	2984	1843	...	...	2299
A Coal mining	...	...	...	...	...	...	...	...	...	...
B Crude petroleum and natural gas production	3444	44	3400	3033	50	2983	1842	...	...	2298
C Metal ore mining	...	...	...	...	...	...	...	...	...	...
D Other mining	9	3	6	4	3	1	1	...	...	1
3 Manufacturing	2030	300	1730	2226	377	1849	555	...	...	825
A Manufacture of food, beverages and tobacco	93	56	37	103	63	40	45	...	...	44
B Textile, wearing apparel and leather industries	39	14	25	38	12	26	26	...	...	36
C Manufacture of wood and wood products, including furniture	34	18	16	32	18	14	12	...	...	13
D Manufacture of paper and paper products, printing and publishing	34	17	17	39	20	19	17	...	...	21
E Manufacture of chemicals and chemical petroleum, coal, rubber and plastic products	1631	118	1513	1810	1615	195	383	...	...	625
F Manufacture of non-metallic mineral products, except products of petroleum and coal	89	49	40	87	53	34	...	...	35
G Basic metal industries	3	1	2	8	4	4	2	...	...	4
H Manufacture of fabricated metal products, machinery and equipment	105	61	44	106	62	44	36	...	...	43
I Other manufacturing industries	2	1	1	3	2	1	1	...	...	3
4 Electricity, gas and water [a]	61	239	-178	62	213	-151	-94	...	...	-31
A Electricity, gas and steam	32	189	-157	33	168	-135	-87	...	...	-40
B Water works and supply	29	50	-21	29	45	-16	-7	...	...	9

1065

Kuwait

4.1 Derivation of Value Added by Kind of Activity, in Current Prices (Continued)

Million Kuwaiti dinars

	1984 Gross Output	1984 Intermediate Consumption	1984 Value Added	1985 Gross Output	1985 Intermediate Consumption	1985 Value Added	1986 Gross Output	1986 Intermediate Consumption	1986 Value Added	1987 Gross Output	1987 Intermediate Consumption	1987 Value Added
5 Construction	767	495	272	623	425	198	...	...	156	...	...	157
6 Wholesale and retail trade, restaurants and hotels	795	221	574	727	178	549	...	...	514	...	...	535
A Wholesale and retail trade	710	181	529	637	137	500	...	...	470	...	...	478
B Restaurants and hotels	85	40	45	90	41	49	...	...	44	...	...	57
7 Transport, storage and communication	446	181	265	379	139	240	...	...	250	...	...	253
A Transport and storage	383	176	207	315	131	184	...	...	191	...	...	184
B Communication	63	5	58	64	8	56	...	...	59	...	...	69
8 Finance, insurance, real estate and business services	650	63	587	554	61	493	...	...	469	...	...	854
A Financial institutions	299	22	277	245	23	222	...	...	217	...	...	146
B Insurance	28	5	23	24	5	19	...	...	16	...	...	13
C Real estate and business services	323	36	287	285	33	252	...	...	236	...	...	695
9 Community, social and personal services	136	33	103	138	34	104	...	...	101	...	...	763
A Sanitary and similar services	17	3	14	13	2	11	...	...	10	...	...	41
B Social and related community services	35	9	26	39	11	28	...	...	26	...	...	539
Educational services	17	5	12	21	7	14	...	...	15	...	...	344
Medical, dental, other health and veterinary services	18	4	14	18	4	14	...	...	11	...	...	161
C Recreational and cultural services	2	1	1	2	1	1	...	...	1	...	...	56
D Personal and household services	82	20	62	84	20	64	...	...	64	...	...	128
Total, Industries	8333	3032	5361	7808	2975	4833	...	...	3846	...	...	5697
Producers of Government Services	1375	451	924	1477	481	996	...	...	1063	...	...	498
Other Producers	39	8	31	32	4	28	...	...	29	...	...	
Total	9807	3491	6316	9317	3460	5857	...	...	4938	...	...	6195
Less: Imputed bank service charge	...	...	...	...	...	...	...	...	...	...	...	98
Import duties	64	-	64	60	-	60	...	...	59	...	...	57
Value added tax	...	...	...	...	...	...	...	...	...	...	...	...
Total	9871	3491	6380	9377	3460	5917	...	...	4997	...	...	6154

All Producers

	1988 Gross Output	1988 Intermediate Consumption	1988 Value Added	1989 Gross Output	1989 Intermediate Consumption	1989 Value Added
1 Agriculture, hunting, forestry and fishing	...	...	50	...	...	46
A Agriculture and hunting	...	...	43	...	...	38
B Forestry and logging	...	...	...	...	...	...
C Fishing	...	...	7	...	...	7
2 Mining and quarrying	...	...	1720	...	...	2773
A Coal mining	...	...	...	...	...	...
B Crude petroleum and natural gas production	...	...	1719	...	...	2772
C Metal ore mining	...	...	...	...	...	...
D Other mining	...	...	1	...	...	1

Kuwait

4.1 Derivation of Value Added by Kind of Activity, in Current Prices
(Continued)

Million Kuwaiti dinars	1988			1989		
	Gross Output	Intermediate Consumption	Value Added	Gross Output	Intermediate Consumption	Value Added
3 Manufacturing	...	755	...	...	...	974
A Manufacture of food, beverages and tobacco	...	45	...	...	...	48
B Textile, wearing apparel and leather industries	...	38	...	...	...	39
C Manufacture of wood and wood products, including furniture	...	14	...	...	...	14
D Manufacture of paper and paper products, printing and publishing	...	24	...	...	...	30
E Manufacture of chemicals and chemical petroleum, coal, rubber and plastic products	...	546	...	...	...	752
F Manufacture of non-metallic mineral products, except products of petroleum and coal	...	36	...	...	...	36
G Basic metal industries	...	5	...	...	...	5
H Manufacture of fabricated metal products, machinery and equipment	...	45	...	...	...	47
I Other manufacturing industries	...	3	...	...	...	3
4 Electricity, gas and water a	...	-42	...	...	...	-43
A Electricity, gas and steam	...	-50	...	...	...	-32
B Water works and supply	...	8	...	...	...	-11
5 Construction	...	153	...	...	...	155
6 Wholesale and retail trade, restaurants and hotels	...	529	...	...	...	555
A Wholesale and retail trade	...	469	...	...	...	492
B Restaurants and hotels	...	60	...	...	...	63
7 Transport, storage and communication	...	263	...	...	...	272
A Transport and storage	...	187	...	...	...	189
B Communication	...	76	...	...	...	83
8 Finance, insurance, real estate and business services	...	882	...	...	...	787
A Financial institutions	...	163	...	...	...	164
B Insurance	...	14	...	...	...	19
C Real estate and business services	...	705	...	...	...	604
9 Community, social and personal services	...	779	...	...	...	807
A Sanitary and similar services	...	41	...	...	...	39
B Social and related community services	...	551	...	...	...	579
Educational services	...	352	...	...	...	366
Medical, dental, other health and veterinary services	...	163	...	...	...	172
C Recreational and cultural services	...	57	...	...	...	56
D Personal and household services	...	130	...	...	...	132
Total, industries	...	5089	...	...	...	6326
Producers of Government Services	...	500	...	...	...	474
Other Producers	...	...	...	...	...	...
Total	...	5589	...	...	...	6800
Less: Imputed bank service charge	...	61	...	...	...	80
Import duties	...	58	...	...	...	59
Value added tax	...	...	...	...	...	...
Total	...	5586	...	...	...	6779

a) Beginning 1980, the cost of fuel (natural gas, crude petroleum and gas-oil) consumed in the production of electricity and water has been taken into account as intermediate consumption in estimating the value added of item 'Electricity, gas and water'.

Kuwait

4.2 Derivation of Value Added by Kind of Activity, in Constant Prices

Million Kuwaiti dinars

	1980			1981			1982			1983		
	Gross Output	Intermediate Consumption	Value Added	Gross Output	Intermediate Consumption	Value Added	Gross Output	Intermediate Consumption	Value Added	Gross Output	Intermediate Consumption	Value Added

At constant prices of:1984

All Producers

	1980 G.O.	1980 I.C.	1980 V.A.	1981 G.O.	1981 I.C.	1981 V.A.	1982 G.O.	1982 I.C.	1982 V.A.	1983 G.O.	1983 I.C.	1983 V.A.
1 Agriculture, hunting, forestry and fishing	...	...	13	...	...	21	...	...	24	...	...	28
A Agriculture and hunting	...	...	10	...	...	15	...	...	14	...	...	23
B Forestry and logging	...	...	...	...	...	...	...	...	...	...	...	...
C Fishing	...	...	3	...	...	6	...	...	5	...	...	5
2 Mining and quarrying	...	...	4865	...	...	3298	...	...	2406	...	...	3117
A Coal mining	...	...	...	...	...	...	...	...	...	...	...	...
B Crude petroleum and natural gas production	...	...	4862	...	...	3293	...	...	2404	...	...	3116
C Metal ore mining	...	...	...	...	...	...	...	...	...	...	...	...
D Other mining	...	...	3	...	...	5	...	...	2	...	...	1
3 Manufacturing	...	...	294	...	...	285	...	...	310	...	...	308
A Manufacture of food, beverages and tobacco	...	...	33	...	...	31	...	...	33	...	...	38
B Textile, wearing apparel and leather industries	...	...	25	...	...	21	...	...	24	...	...	24
C Manufacture of wood and wood products, including furniture	...	...	23	...	...	22	...	...	17	...	...	15
D Manufacture of paper and paper products, printing and publishing	...	...	16	...	...	19	...	...	19	...	...	18
E Manufacture of chemicals and chemical petroleum, coal, rubber and plastic products	...	...	111	...	...	98	...	...	111	...	...	115
F Manufacture of non-metallic mineral products, except products of petroleum and coal	...	...	31	...	...	33	...	...	41	...	...	43
G Basic metal industries	...	...	6	...	...	3	...	...	4	...	...	4
H Manufacture of fabricated metal products, machinery and equipment	...	...	47	...	...	57	...	...	60	...	...	50
I Other manufacturing industries	...	...	2	...	...	1	...	...	1	...	...	1
4 Electricity, gas and water	...	...	-117	...	...	-129	...	...	-150	...	...	-161
A Electricity, gas and steam	...	...	-102	...	...	-113	...	...	-132	...	...	-141
B Water works and supply	...	...	-14	...	...	-15	...	...	-18	...	...	-20
5 Construction	...	...	341	...	...	301	...	...	278	...	...	277
6 Wholesale and retail trade, restaurants and hotels	...	...	714	...	...	745	...	...	810	...	...	555
A Wholesale and retail trade	...	...	645	...	...	673	...	...	743	...	...	501
B Restaurants and hotels	...	...	69	...	...	72	...	...	67	...	...	54
7 Transport, storage and communication	...	...	225	...	...	250	...	...	310	...	...	277
A Transport and storage	...	...	194	...	...	204	...	...	259	...	...	221
B Communication	...	...	31	...	...	46	...	...	51	...	...	56
8 Finance, insurance, real estate and business services	...	...	461	...	...	523	...	...	556	...	...	560
A Financial institutions	...	...	197	...	...	251	...	...	267	...	...	268
B Insurance	...	...	17	...	...	15	...	...	18	...	...	18
C Real estate and business services	...	...	247	...	...	257	...	...	271	...	...	274
9 Community, social and personal services	...	...	116	...	...	120	...	...	111	...	...	103
A Sanitary and similar services	...	...	5	...	...	7	...	...	12	...	...	10
B Social and related community services	...	...	25	...	...	20	...	...	23	...	...	25
Educational services	...	...	14	...	...	12	...	...	10	...	...	11
Medical, dental, other health and veterinary services	...	...	11	...	...	8	...	...	13	...	...	14
C Recreational and cultural services	...	...	2	...	...	3	...	...	1	...	...	2
D Personal and household services	...	...	84	...	...	90	...	...	75	...	...	66

Kuwait

4.2 Derivation of Value Added by Kind of Activity, in Constant Prices
(Continued)

Million Kuwaiti dinars

	1980			1981			1982			1983		
	Gross Output	Intermediate Consumption	Value Added	Gross Output	Intermediate Consumption	Value Added	Gross Output	Intermediate Consumption	Value Added	Gross Output	Intermediate Consumption	Value Added
							At constant prices of:1984					
Total, Industries	...	...	6912	...	...	5414	...	...	4655	...	...	5064
Producers of Government Services	...	...	776	...	...	784	...	...	847	...	...	903
Other Producers	...	...	32	...	...	29	...	...	26	...	...	24
Total	...	...	7720	...	...	6227	...	...	5528	...	...	5991
Less: Imputed bank service charge	...	...	...	...	...	...	...	...	...	...	...	...
Import duties	...	...	67	...	...	78	...	...	75	...	...	71
Value added tax	...	...	...	...	...	...	...	...	...	...	...	...
Total	...	...	7787	...	...	6305	...	...	5603	...	...	6062

	1984			1985			1986		
	Gross Output	Intermediate Consumption	Value Added	Gross Output	Intermediate Consumption	Value Added	Gross Output	Intermediate Consumption	Value Added
				At constant prices of:1984					
				All Producers					
1 Agriculture, hunting, forestry and fishing	...	...	35	...	...	40	...	...	54
A Agriculture and hunting	...	...	30	...	...	35	...	...	51
B Forestry and logging	...	...	...	...	...	...	...	...	...
C Fishing	...	...	5	...	...	5	...	...	3
2 Mining and quarrying	...	...	3403	...	...	3103	...	...	3768
A Coal mining	...	...	...	...	...	...	...	...	...
B Crude petroleum and natural gas production	...	...	3400	...	...	3103	...	...	3768
C Metal ore mining	...	...	...	...	...	...	...	...	...
D Other mining	...	...	3	...	...	1	...	...	1
3 Manufacturing	...	...	300	...	...	314	...	...	318
A Manufacture of food, beverages and tobacco	...	...	37	...	...	40	...	...	44
B Textile, wearing apparel and leather industries	...	...	25	...	...	26	...	...	23
C Manufacture of wood and wood products, including furniture	...	...	16	...	...	15	...	...	13
D Manufacture of paper and paper products, printing and publishing	...	...	17	...	...	20	...	...	17
E Manufacture of chemicals and chemical petroleum, coal, rubber and plastic products	...	...	118	...	...	129	...	...	141
F Manufacture of non-metallic mineral products, except products of petroleum and coal	...	...	40	...	...	33	...	...	33
G Basic metal industries	...	...	2	...	...	3	...	...	2
H Manufacture of fabricated metal products, machinery and equipment	...	...	44	...	...	47	...	...	44
I Other manufacturing industries	...	...	1	...	...	1	...	...	1
4 Electricity, gas and water	...	...	-178	...	...	-196	...	...	-215
A Electricity, gas and steam	...	...	-157	...	...	-174	...	...	-191
B Water works and supply	...	...	-21	...	...	-22	...	...	-23
5 Construction	...	...	272	...	...	195	...	...	152
6 Wholesale and retail trade, restaurants and hotels	...	...	574	...	...	546	...	...	507
A Wholesale and retail trade	...	...	528	...	...	498	...	...	463
B Restaurants and hotels	...	...	46	...	...	48	...	...	44
7 Transport, storage and communication	...	...	265	...	...	236	...	...	232
A Transport and storage	...	...	207	...	...	180	...	...	180
B Communication	...	...	58	...	...	56	...	...	52
8 Finance, insurance, real estate and business services	...	...	587	...	...	587	...	...	580
A Financial institutions	...	...	277	...	...	273	...	...	266

Kuwait

4.2 Derivation of Value Added by Kind of Activity, in Constant Prices
(Continued)

Million Kuwaiti dinars

At constant prices of 1984

	1984			1985			1986		
	Gross Output	Intermediate Consumption	Value Added	Gross Output	Intermediate Consumption	Value Added	Gross Output	Intermediate Consumption	Value Added
B Insurance	...	...	23	...	...	18	...	...	17
C Real estate and business services	...	...	287	...	...	296	...	...	297
9 Community, social and personal services	...	...	103	...	...	104	...	...	100
A Sanitary and similar services	...	...	14	...	...	17	...	...	16
B Social and related community services	...	...	26	...	...	27	...	...	26
Educational services	...	...	12	...	...	15	...	...	15
Medical, dental, other health and veterinary services	...	...	14	...	...	12	...	...	11
C Recreational and cultural services	...	...	1	...	...	1	...	...	1
D Personal and household services	...	...	62	...	...	59	...	...	57
Total, Industries	...	...	5361	...	...	4929	...	...	5496
Producers of Government Services	...	...	924	...	...	934	...	...	936
Other Producers	...	...	31	...	...	26	...	...	26
Total	...	...	6316	...	...	5889	...	...	6458
Less: imputed bank service charge	...	...		...	...		...	...	
Import duties	...	...	64	...	...	61	...	...	54
Value added tax	...	...		...	...		...	...	
Total	...	...	6380	...	...	5950	...	...	6512

كيفية الحصول على منشورات الأمم المتحدة

يمكن الحصول على منشورات الأمم المتحدة من المكتبات ودور التوزيع في جميع أنحاء العالم . استعلم عنها من المكتبة التي تتعامل معها أو اكتب إلى : الأمم المتحدة ، قسم البيع في نيويورك أو في جنيف .

如何购取联合国出版物

联合国出版物在全世界各地的书店和经售处均有发售。请向书店询问或写信到纽约或日内瓦的联合国销售组。

HOW TO OBTAIN UNITED NATIONS PUBLICATIONS

United Nations publications may be obtained from bookstores and distributors throughout the world. Consult your bookstore or write to: United Nations, Sales Section, New York or Geneva.

COMMENT SE PROCURER LES PUBLICATIONS DES NATIONS UNIES

Les publications des Nations Unies sont en vente dans les librairies et les agences dépositaires du monde entier. Informez-vous auprès de votre libraire ou adressez-vous à : Nations Unies, Section des ventes, New York ou Genève.

КАК ПОЛУЧИТЬ ИЗДАНИЯ ОРГАНИЗАЦИИ ОБЪЕДИНЕННЫХ НАЦИЙ

Издания Организации Объединенных Наций можно купить в книжных магазинах и агентствах во всех районах мира. Наводите справки об изданиях в вашем книжном магазине или пишите по адресу: Организация Объединенных Наций, Секция по продаже изданий, Нью-Йорк или Женева.

COMO CONSEGUIR PUBLICACIONES DE LAS NACIONES UNIDAS

Las publicaciones de las Naciones Unidas están en venta en librerías y casas distribuidoras en todas partes del mundo. Consulte a su librero o diríjase a: Naciones Unidas, Sección de Ventas, Nueva York o Ginebra.

Printed in U.S.A.
40982—November 1991—3,580
ISBN 92-1-161339-6

United Nations publication
Sales No. E.91.XVII.16, Part I
ST/ESA/STAT/SER.X/16

WILLIAM F. MAAG LIBRARY
YOUNGSTOWN STATE UNIVERSITY